THE SPORT AMERICANA®

Baseball Card PRICE GUIDE

By

DR. JAMES BECKETT

NUMBER 13

EDGEWATER BOOK COMPANY • CLEVELAND

EDGEWATER BOOK COMPANY
P.O. BOX 40238
CLEVELAND, OHIO 44140

Manufactured in the United States of America.

First Printing

Library of Congress catalog card number: 79-643474

ISBN 0-937424-51-X

Acknowledgements

A great deal of hard work went into this volume, and it could not have been done without help from many people. Our thanks are extended to each and every one of you.

Those who have worked closely with us on this and many other books, have again proven themselves invaluable — Frank and Vivian Barning (*Baseball Hobby News*), Chris Benjamin, Sy Berger (Topps), Card Collectors Co., Peter Brennan, Cartophilium (Andrew Pywowarczuk), Ira Cetron, Barry Colla, Mike Cramer (Pacific Trading Cards), Bill and Diane Dodge, Fleer Corporation (Paul Mullen, Vincent Murray, and Jeff Massien), Steve Freedman, Gervise Ford, Larry and Jeff Fritsch, Tony Galovich (American Card Exchange), Georgia Music and Sports (Dick DeCourcy and Floyd Parr), Dick Gilkeson, Bill Goodwin (St. Louis Baseball Cards), Mike and Howard Gordon, John Greenwald, Wayne Grove, Bill Haber, Bill Henderson, Jay and Mary Kasper, Allan Kaye (*Baseball Card News*), Rick Keplinger, David Kohler (SportsCards Plus), Don Lepore, Paul Lewicki, Neil Lewis (Leaf), Lew Lipset, Norman and Ken Liss (Topps), Mark Macrae, Bill Madden, Major League Marketing (Dan Shedrick, Tom Day, and Julie Haddon), Mid-Atlantic Coin Exchange (Bill Bossert), Dick Millerd, Brian Morris, Ralph Nozaki, Oldies and Goodies (Nigel Spill), Optigraphics (Anne Flavin and Ed Fick), Jack Pollard, Jeff Prillaman (Southern Cards), Paul Reichl, Gavin Riley, Alan Rosen (Mr. Mint), Clifton Rouse, John Rumierz, San Diego Sport Collectibles (Bill Goepner and Nacho Arredondo), Kevin Savage (Sports Gallery), Mike Schechter, Barry Sloate, John Spalding, Phil Spector (Scoreboard, Inc.), Sports Collectors Store, Frank Steele, Murvin Sterling, Lee Temanson, Ed Twombly (New England Bullpen), Gary Walter, Kit Young, and Ted Zanidakis. Finally we owe a special acknowledgment to Dennis W. Eckes, "Mr. Sport Americana." The success of the Beckett Price Guides has always been the result of a team effort.

This Price Guide is our best one yet and you can thank all of the contributors (listed above and below) as well as our staff here for that. Our company now boasts a substantial Technical Services group which has made (and is continuing to make) direct and important contributions to this work. They (Technical Services) capably handled numerous technical details and provided able assistance in pricing for this edition of the annual guide. That effort was directed by Senior Price Guide Analyst B. A. Murry. He was assisted by Theo Chen (general introduction), Rich Klein (new set summaries), as well as price guide analysts Grant Sandground and Mike Hersh. Also contributing to our Technical Service functions were newcomers Wendy Bird and Jason Traub. The price gathering and analytical talents of this fine group of hobbyists has helped to make our Beckett team stronger, while making this guide and its companion monthly price guides even more widely recognized as the hobby's most reliable and relied upon sources of pricing information.

It is very difficult to be "accurate" — one can only do one's best, but this job is especially difficult since we're shooting at a moving target as prices are fluctuating all the time. Having several full-time pricing experts has definitely proven to be better than just one, and I thank all of them for working together to provide you, our readers, the most accurate prices possible.

Many people have provided price input, illustrative material, checklist verifications, errata, and/or background information. We should like to individually thank Aardvark Sports Cards, ABC Stamps (Julio A. Gil), AbD Cards (Dale Wesolewski), David Abrahamson, Jerry Adamic, Ron Adelson, Tony Adkins, A.J.'s Sport Stop, Ali Alamdari, Bob Alexander, All Star Sports Collectibles, Dennis Anderson, Kent Annas, Tom Antonowicz, Ric Apter, Pete Arbogast, Mark Argo (Olde South Cards), Burl Armstrong, Neil Armstrong (World Series Cards), Brian Atkinson, Aarom Atz, Robert August, B&F Sports Cards (William Bryda), Ball Four Cards, Joe Barney, Ed Barry (Ed's Collectibles), Bob Bartosz (Baseball Card Shop), Bay State Cards (Lenny DeAngelico), Burton Beaty, Andrew Beisel, Carl Berg, Bernie's Bullpen, Beulah Sports, Seth Bienstock, Brian Bigelow, Josh Bird, Ralph Black, Ray Blair, Levi Bleam, Ed Bley, Bob Boffa, Tim Bond (Tim's Cards & Comics), Charlie Botello, Chris Brake, Bill Brandt, John Brigandi, Chuck Brooks, Brad Buchta, Gary Bursae, Patrick Buss, Robert Calhoun, California Card Co., Bill Calkins, Jim Carballido, The Card Mart, Danny Cariseo, Joel Carmichael, John Cary, John Castelin, Mark A. Cenicola, Sandy Chan, Dwight Chapin, Ray Cherry, Wayne Christian, Dick Cianciotto, Cincinnati Baseball Cards, Collectibles Unlimited (John Alward and Deb Ingram), Collection de Sport AZ (Ronald Villaneuve), The

Collectory, Andy Collier, Ryan Collins, Alvin Conner, Brian Cook, Steven Cooter, Ron Coscorrosa, Lou Costanzo (Champion Sports), Brian Covington, Josh Coxwell, Taylor Crane, Chad Cripe, James Critzer, Ryan Crosier, George Crowe, John Curtis, Allen Custer.

Dave Dame, Tim Dantes, Don Dart, Paul Davis, Raymond Davis, Kevin Dean, Tim Dellatore, James DeMarco, Gilberto Diaz, Bruce Dickinson, Ken Dinerman (California Cruizers), Richard Dolloff (Dolloff Coin Center), Jonathan Drye, Andy Dubitsky, Richard Duglin (Baseball Cards-n-More), Mike Durfee, Larry Eccles, Ken Edick (Home Plate of Utah), Tim Edmon, Doak Ewing, Bryan Failing, Gail Fairbrother, Richard Faletti, Rob Fannon, Jason Fenwick, Greg Ferguson, Chuck Ferrero, Freddy Ferzo, David Festberg, Jabe Fincher, Jay Finglass, Phillip Flint, Fremont Fong, Perry Fong, Brian Foreman, Craig Frank, Walter Franklin, Mark Friedman, Joshua Frizzell, Michael Funk, Adam Gaines, Robert F. Gallagher, Garland Sports Cards, Robert Garren, Willie George, Matt Gerig, Larry Gevert, Scott Gibson, Dick Goddard, Steve Gold (AU Sports), Greg Goldstein (Dragon's Den), Jeff Goldstein, Stuart Goldstein, Eugene Gomes, Matt Gomes, Jose Gomez, Chris Gordon, Keith Gradwohl, George Grauer, Stephen Grauf, Rosa Green, Jared Grigg, George Griswold, Steven Gudeman.

Hall's Nostalgia, Michael Hamel, Hershell Hanks, Seth Hanson, Zac Hargis, Derek Hayman, Joel Hellman, Mark Hellman, Stacy Henderson, Hill House Baseball Cards, Jason Holcomb, Matt Holmes, Third Hand Shoppe, Dennis Hughes, Paul Hutzler, Tom Imboden, David Ingram, Vern Isenberg, Chris Jackson, John Jamieson, Paul Jastrzembski, Donn Jennings Cards, JJ's Budget Baseball Cards, Kevin Johnson, Richard E. Jones, Stewart W. Jones, Chuck Jungblom, Dave Jurgensmeier, John Just, Steven J. Jvon. Doug Kane, Frank Katen, Jerry Katz, Neil Katz, Randy Kellis, Mike Kelly, Kevin's Kards, Regi King, Ernie Kohlstruk, Koinz and Kards (Tom Zmuda), Neil Krohn, Thomas Kunnecke, John Kyranos, Rick Lafrance, Darren Lai, Jason Lassic, Don and Steve Lassiter, Allan Latawiec, Dan Lavin, Morley Leeking, Glenn Lerch, Irv Lerner, Ramiro Lindado, Michael Linn, David Lloyd, Tom Lobacz, D.J. Loehr, Mike London, David Luftig, Andy Lunt, Glenn MacDonald Jr., Jim Macie, Charles R. Mack, Tom Madigan, Brandon Malcolm, Paul Marchant, Ken Martini, Bill Mastro, Pat McAulay (River City Trading Cards), Dr. William McAvoy, Ras Chaka McCalla, Bill McCalley, Markus McCullough, Jesse & Ben McCune, McDag Productions Inc., Michael McDonald (The Sports Page), Richard McGonigle, Wes McIntosh, Jeffrey McKay, Scott McKevitt, Tony McLaughlin, Mendal Mearkle, Ken Melanson, Eric Melman, Blake Meyer (Lone Star Sportscards), John Meyer, Keith Meyer, J.P. Miceli, Joe Michalowicz, Barry Miller, Cary Miller, David "Otis" Miller, George Miller, Wayne Miller, Mitchell's Baseball Cards, Perry Miyashita, Patrick Montagu, George Moore, Matt Moyer.

Lynn Nance, Stephen Nardiello, Edward Nazzaro (The Collector), Jon Neill, New York Card Company, Jason Newcomb, James Noland, Mark Nordmeyer, Royal Norman, Aaron Oberste, Mike O'Brien, Brian Oehlert, Keith Olbermann, Kevin Oliver, Ron Oser, Ed Paine, Steven Parson, Clay Pasternack, Josh Pelock, Michael Perrotta, Doug and Trevor Perry, Bret Peterson, Tom Pfirrmann, Bob Poet, Gilbert Polasek, Dan Poniatowski, Seth Poppel, Mark Porath, Chip Porter, Michael Poynter, Don Prestia, David Preston, Amy Rankin, Rick Rapa and Barry Sanders (Atlanta Sports Cards), R.W. Ray, William Redmon, Troy C. Redmond, Tom Reid, Billy Richards, Dave Ring, Evan Roberts, Randy Roberts, Randall Robinson, Doug Rodman, Gary Ross, Alan Rubenstein, Jack Rudley, George Rusnak, Rust Coin and Sports Cards.

Terry Sack, P.J. Sahaidachny, Joe Sak, Jennifer Salems, James Samalis, James Sanders, John San Martino, Gary Sawatzki, Jason Scavio, Dan Scheiner, Kurt Schlichting, Bobby Schroeder, Bruce Schwartz, Richard W. Segraves, John Seright, Tom Shanyfelt, Ryan Shapiro, Bill Shaw, John Shaw, Mary Shea, Gerry Shebib, Travis Sheldon, Gabe Shulman, Bob Singer, Daniel Sipp, Robert Skow, Robert Smathers, Adam Smith, Art Smith, Brian W. Smith, Fred J. Smith, Fred Snyder, David Spaudle, Sports Cards Unlimited, Wm. Marr Stein, Bob Stern, Stanley Stinnett, John D. Storms, Brian Stoutenberg, Simon Stoysich, Tim Strandberg (East Texas Sports Cards), Edward Strauss, Richard Strobino, Alan Sugahara, Superior Sport Card, Andy Swartz, Erik Swerdlow, Ian Taylor, Lyle Telfer, Craig Thompson, Jim D. Thompson, Richard Thurman, TJ's Baseball Cards, Al Tom, Bud Tompkins (Minnesota Connection), Karrie Tompkins, John Towe, The Trader (Mike Marshall), Kevin Trexler, Richard Tribby, Dr. Ralph Triplette, Jim Tull, Simeon Vargas, Vintage Wax (David Macaray), Geoff Waidelich, Andrew Waller, Kippie Warden, Luke Weese, Michael

BILL HENDERSON'S CARDS
"King of the Commons"

2320 RUGER AVE. PG13
JANESVILLE, WISCONSIN 53545
1-608-755-0922

"ALWAYS BUYING"
Call or Write
for Quote

"ALWAYS BUYING"
Call or Write
for Quote

	HI # OR SCARCE SERIES	PRICE PER COMMON CARD	COMMONS EACH	EX/MT TO MINT CONDITION		GROUP LOTS FOR SALE 50 Diff.	100 Diff.	300 Asst.	500 Asst.	VG+ to EX Condition 50 Different	100 Different	200 Different
1948 BOWMAN	(37-48)	25.00	18.00									
1949 BOWMAN	(145-240)	80.00	16.00			720.				430.		
50-51 BOWMAN	50 (1-72) 51 (253-324)	60.00	16.00	51 (2-36)	20.00	720.				430.		
1952 TOPPS	(311-407)	P.O.R.	30.00	(2-80)	60.00	1350.				800.		
1952 BOWMAN	(217-252)	30.00	16.00	(2-36)	20.00	720.				430.		
1953 TOPPS	(220-280)	80.00	20.00	(2-165)	30.00	900.				600.		
1953 BOWMAN	(129-160)	40.00	30.00	(113-128)	50.00	1350.				800.		
1954 TOPPS			14.00	(51-75)	30.00	630.				400.		
1954 BOWMAN			8.00	(129-224)	10.00	360.	685.			240.		
1955 TOPPS	(161-210)	20.00	7.00	(151-160)	15.00	360.				210.		
1955 BOWMAN	(225-320) 15.-20. Umps		6.00	(2-96)	8.00	270.	500.			180.	350.	
1956 TOPPS	(261-340)	10.00	8.00	(181-260)	15.00	360.				240.	460.	
1957 TOPPS	(1-80) 7.00 (265-352) 17.50		5.00	(353-407)	5.00	220.	420.			155.	300.	
1958 TOPPS	(111-198)	5.00	3.50	(1-110)	6.00	155.	300.	850.		105.	200.	
1959 TOPPS	(507-572)	12.50	3.00	(1-110)	4.00	135.	260.	750.		90.	175.	385.
1960 TOPPS	(523-572)	12.50	2.00	(441-506)	4.50	90.	175.	500.	800.	60.	115.	220.
1961 TOPPS	(523-589)	30.00	1.50	(371-522)	2.50	65.	125.	360.	700.	45.	80.	155.
1962 TOPPS	(523-590)	12.50	1.50	(371-522)	3.50	65.	125.	360.		45.	80.	155.
1963 TOPPS	(447-522) 10.00 (523-573) 6.00		1.50	(197-446)	2.00	65.	125.			45.	80.	
1964 TOPPS	(523-587)	7.50	1.25	(371-522)	2.50	55.	105.			32.	60.	115.
1965 TOPPS	(447-522) 4.00 (523-598) 6.00		1.00	(284-446)	2.50	45.	90.			32.	60.	115.
1966 TOPPS	(371-446) 2.50 (523-598) 15.00		1.00	(447-522)	5.00	45.	90.			32.	60.	115.
1967 TOPPS	(371-457) 2.00 (534-609) 15.00		1.00	(458-533)	5.00	45.	90.			32.	60.	115.
1968 TOPPS	(534-598)	2.00	1.00	(458-533)	1.50	45.	90.			32.	60.	115.
1969 TOPPS	(589-664)	1.00	.75	(219-327)	1.50	34.	65.	185.		22.	42.	80.
1970 TOPPS	(634-720)	3.50	.45	(547-633)	1.50	22.	42.	120.	190.	14.	26.	50.
1971 TOPPS	(394-523) .75 (644-752) 4.50		.45	(524-643)	1.50	22.	42.	120.	190.	14.	26.	50.
1972 TOPPS	(395-525) .60 (657-787) 4.50		.45	(526-656)	1.50	22.	42.	*120.	190.	14.	26.	50.
1973 TOPPS	(528-660)	2.00	.35	(397-528)	.60	16.	32.	*90.		12.	22.	40.
1974 TOPPS			.35			16.	32.	*90.	*150.		22.	40.
1975 TOPPS		(8-132 .50)	.35			16.	32.	*90.			22.	40.
1976-77			.20				18.	*50.	*85.		10.	18.
1978-1980			.15				13.	*38.	*65.		8.	15.
1981 thru 1991 Topps, Fleer or Donrus			.10				8.	*22.	*35.		5.	10.
Specify Year & Company except below							Per Yr.	Per Yr.	Per Yr.			
1984-86 DONRUS			.15			7.	13.	*38.	*60.			

*These lots are all different.

SPECIAL IN VG+ to EX CONDITION-POSTPAID

250	58-62	300.00
500	58-62	550.00
250	60-69	170.00
500	60-69	320.00
1000	60-69	600.00
250	70-79	50.00
500	70-79	90.00
1000	70-79	160.00
250	80-84	15.00
500	80-84	28.00
1000	80-84	55.00

Special 1 Different from each year 1949-80 EX/MT - $140.00, VG-EX $100.00
Special 100 Different from each year 1956-80 EX/MT - $2900.00, VG-EX $2000.00
Special 10 Different from each year 1956-80 EX/MT - $300.00, VG-EX $210.00

All lot groups are my choice only.

All assorted lots will contain as many different as possible.
Please list alternates whenever possible.
Send your want list and I will fill them at the above price for commons. High numbers, specials, scarce series, and stars extra.
You can use your Master Card or Visa to charge your purchases.
Minimum order $7.50 - Postage and handling .50 per 100 cards (minimum $1.75)

Also interested in purchasing your collection.
Groups include various years of my choice.
ANY CARD NOT LISTED ON PRICE SHEET IS PRICED AT CURRENT BECKETT MONTHLY

SETS AVAILABLE
Topps 1988, 1989, 1990, 1991
20.95 ea. + 2.50 UPS
6 for 20.95 ea. + 9.00 UPS
18 for 20.25 ea. + 20.00 UPS
54 for 19.75 ea. + 60.00 UPS
MIX OR MATCH

Collectory, Andy Collier, Ryan Collins, Alvin Conner, Brian Cook, Steven Cooter, Ron Coscorrosa, Lou Costanzo (Champion Sports), Brian Covington, Josh Coxwell, Taylor Crane, Chad Cripe, James Critzer, Ryan Crosier, George Crowe, John Curtis, Allen Custer.

Dave Dame, Tim Dantes, Don Dart, Paul Davis, Raymond Davis, Kevin Dean, Tim Dellatore, James DeMarco, Gilberto Diaz, Bruce Dickinson, Ken Dinerman (California Cruizers), Richard Dolloff (Dolloff Coin Center), Jonathan Drye, Andy Dubitsky, Richard Duglin (Baseball Cards-n-More), Mike Durfee, Larry Eccles, Ken Edick (Home Plate of Utah), Tim Edmon, Doak Ewing, Bryan Failing, Gail Fairbrother, Richard Faletti, Rob Fannon, Jason Fenwick, Greg Ferguson, Chuck Ferrero, Freddy Ferzo, David Festberg, Jabe Fincher, Jay Finglass, Phillip Flint, Fremont Fong, Perry Fong, Brian Foreman, Craig Frank, Walter Franklin, Mark Friedman, Joshua Frizzell, Michael Funk, Adam Gaines, Robert F. Gallagher, Garland Sports Cards, Robert Garren, Willie George, Matt Gerig, Larry Gevert, Scott Gibson, Dick Goddard, Steve Gold (AU Sports), Greg Goldstein (Dragon's Den), Jeff Goldstein, Stuart Goldstein, Eugene Gomes, Matt Gomes, Jose Gomez, Chris Gordon, Keith Gradwohl, George Grauer, Stephen Grauf, Rosa Green, Jared Grigg, George Griswold, Steven Gudeman.

Hall's Nostalgia, Michael Hamel, Hershell Hanks, Seth Hanson, Zac Hargis, Derek Hayman, Joel Hellman, Mark Hellman, Stacy Henderson, Hill House Baseball Cards, Jason Holcomb, Matt Holmes, Third Hand Shoppe, Dennis Hughes, Paul Hutzler, Tom Imboden, David Ingram, Vern Isenberg, Chris Jackson, John Jamieson, Paul Jastrzembski, Donn Jennings Cards, JJ's Budget Baseball Cards, Kevin Johnson, Richard E. Jones, Stewart W. Jones, Chuck Jungblom, Dave Jurgensmeier, John Just, Steven J. Jvon. Doug Kane, Frank Katen, Jerry Katz, Neil Katz, Randy Kellis, Mike Kelly, Kevin's Kards, Regi King, Ernie Kohlstruk, Koinz and Kards (Tom Zmuda), Neil Krohn, Thomas Kunnecke, John Kyranos, Rick Lafrance, Darren Lai, Jason Lassic, Don and Steve Lassiter, Allan Latawiec, Dan Lavin, Morley Leeking, Glenn Lerch, Irv Lerner, Ramiro Lindado, Michael Linn, David Lloyd, Tom Lobacz, D.J. Loehr, Mike London, David Luftig, Andy Lunt, Glenn MacDonald Jr., Jim Macie, Charles R. Mack, Tom Madigan, Brandon Malcolm, Paul Marchant, Ken Martini, Bill Mastro, Pat McAulay (River City Trading Cards), Dr. William McAvoy, Ras Chaka McCalla, Bill McCalley, Markus McCullough, Jesse & Ben McCune, McDag Productions Inc., Michael McDonald (The Sports Page), Richard McGonigle, Wes McIntosh, Jeffrey McKay, Scott McKevitt, Tony McLaughlin, Mendal Mearkle, Ken Melanson, Eric Melman, Blake Meyer (Lone Star Sportscards), John Meyer, Keith Meyer, J.P. Miceli, Joe Michalowicz, Barry Miller, Cary Miller, David "Otis" Miller, George Miller, Wayne Miller, Mitchell's Baseball Cards, Perry Miyashita, Patrick Montagu, George Moore, Matt Moyer.

Lynn Nance, Stephen Nardiello, Edward Nazzaro (The Collector), Jon Neill, New York Card Company, Jason Newcomb, James Noland, Mark Nordmeyer, Royal Norman, Aaron Oberste, Mike O'Brien, Brian Oehlert, Keith Olbermann, Kevin Oliver, Ron Oser, Ed Paine, Steven Parson, Clay Pasternack, Josh Pelock, Michael Perrotta, Doug and Trevor Perry, Bret Peterson, Tom Pfirrmann, Bob Poet, Gilbert Polasek, Dan Poniatowski, Seth Poppel, Mark Porath, Chip Porter, Michael Poynter, Don Prestia, David Preston, Amy Rankin, Rick Rapa and Barry Sanders (Atlanta Sports Cards), R.W. Ray, William Redmon, Troy C. Redmond, Tom Reid, Billy Richards, Dave Ring, Evan Roberts, Randy Roberts, Randall Robinson, Doug Rodman, Gary Ross, Alan Rubenstein, Jack Rudley, George Rusnak, Rust Coin and Sports Cards.

Terry Sack, P.J. Sahaidachny, Joe Sak, Jennifer Salems, James Samalis, James Sanders, John San Martino, Gary Sawatzki, Jason Scavio, Dan Scheiner, Kurt Schlichting, Bobby Schroeder, Bruce Schwartz, Richard W. Segraves, John Seright, Tom Shanyfelt, Ryan Shapiro, Bill Shaw, John Shaw, Mary Shea, Gerry Shebib, Travis Sheldon, Gabe Shulman, Bob Singer, Daniel Sipp, Robert Skow, Robert Smathers, Adam Smith, Art Smith, Brian W. Smith, Fred J. Smith, Fred Snyder, David Spaudle, Sports Cards Unlimited, Wm. Marr Stein, Bob Stern, Stanley Stinnett, John D. Storms, Brian Stoutenberg, Simon Stoysich, Tim Strandberg (East Texas Sports Cards), Edward Strauss, Richard Strobino, Alan Sugahara, Superior Sport Card, Andy Swartz, Erik Swerdlow, Ian Taylor, Lyle Telfer, Craig Thompson, Jim D. Thompson, Richard Thurman, TJ's Baseball Cards, Al Tom, Bud Tompkins (Minnesota Connection), Karrie Tompkins, John Towe, The Trader (Mike Marshall), Kevin Trexler, Richard Tribby, Dr. Ralph Triplette, Jim Tull, Simeon Vargas, Vintage Wax (David Macaray), Geoff Waidelich, Andrew Waller, Kippie Warden, Luke Weese, Michael

Wehrenberg, Lewis Weinerman, Jason Wells, Bill Wesslund, Richard West, Jud Wildman, Jeff Williams, Matt Williams, Nathan Williams, Nicky and Elena Williams, Ron Williams, Mark Willis, David Wilson, Michael Wilson, Todd Winland, James Winner, Opry Winston, The Wise Guys (Joe and John Weisenburger), Jay Wolt (Cavalcade of Sports), Margaret R. Woodcock, Kevin Woolsey, Pete Wooten, Jeff Wright, Dan Yaw, Yesterday's Heroes, Wes Young, Robert Zanze, Doug Zimmerman, Dean Zindler.

Every year we make active solicitations for input to that year's edition and we are particularly appreciative of help (large and small) provided for this volume. While we receive many inquiries, comments, and questions regarding material within this book — and, in fact, each and every one is read and digested — time constraints prevent us from personally replying. We hope that the letters will continue, and that even though no reply is received, you will feel that you are making significant contributions to the hobby through your interest and comments.

In the years since this guide debuted, Beckett Publications has grown beyond any rational expectation. A great many talented and hard working individuals have been instrumental in this growth and success. Our whole team is to be congratulated for what we together have accomplished. Our Beckett Publications team is led by Associate Publisher Claire Backus and Vice Presidents Joe Galindo and Fred Reed. They are ably assisted by Mat Alancheril, Fernando Albieri, Jeff Amano, Theresa Anderson, Gena Andrews, Barbara Barry, Nancy Bassi, Therese Bellar, Lisa Borden, Louise Bird, Chris Calandro, Mary Campana, Deana Chapman, Lynne Chinn, Belinda Cross, Billy Culbert, Andrew Drago, Louise Ebaugh, Dianne Echols, Susan Elliott, Bruce Felps, George Field, Gean Paul Figari, Jeany Finch, Mark Goeglein, Anita Gonzalez, Mary Gonzalez-Davis, Julie Grove, Joanna Guajardo, Lori Harmeyer, Beth Harwell, Jenny Harwell, Pepper Hastings, Joanna Hayden, Barbara Hinkle, Angela Hogans, E.J. Hradek, Claire Jeanfreau, Gayle Jeffcoat, Sara Jenks, Wendy Jewell, Jay Johnson, Matt Keifer, Fran Keng, Monte King, Debbie Kingsbury, Amy Kirk, Rudy Klancnik, Frances Knight, Lori Lindsey, Chris Longeway, Louis Marroquin, Kaki Matheson, Kirk McKinney, Omar Mediano, Marge Milkie, Glen Morante, Mike Moss, Lynn Nelson, LaQuita Norton, Rich Olivieri, Abraham Pacheco, Suzee Payton, Ronda Pearson, Sally Peck, Sabrina Polley, Reed Poole, Ruth Price, Jill Prince, Roberto Ramirez, Becky Reed, Patrick Richard, Maggie Ryan, Carol Slawson, Steve Slawson, Maggie Seward, Lisa Spaight, Mark Stokes, Cindy Struble, Mark Whitesell, Steve Wilson, and Robert Yearby. In addition, our long-time consultants James and Sandi Beane performed several major system programming jobs for us again this year in order to help us accomplish our work faster and more accurately. The whole Beckett Publications team has my thanks for jobs well done. Thank you, everyone.

I also thank my family, especially my wife, Patti, and daughters, Christina, Rebecca, and Melissa, for putting up with me again.

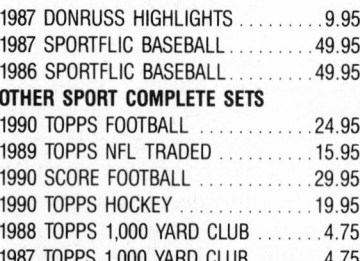

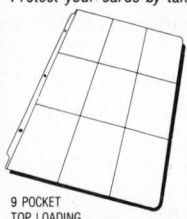

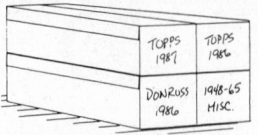

The Sport Americana Baseball Card Price Guide

Table Of Contents

Index to Advertisers

Preface

Isn't it great? Every year this book gets bigger and bigger with all the new sets coming out. But even more exciting is that every year there are more collectors, more shows, more stores, and more interest in the cards we love so much. This edition has been enhanced and expanded from the previous edition. The cards you collect — who they are, what they look like, where they are from, and (most important to many of you) what their current values are — are enumerated within. Many of the features contained in the other Beckett Price Guides have been incorporated into this volume since condition grading, nomenclature, and many other aspects of collecting are common to the card hobby in general. We hope you find the book both interesting and useful in your collecting pursuits.

The Beckett Guide has been successful where other attempts have failed because it is complete, current, and valid. This Price Guide contains not just one, but three, prices by condition for a the baseball cards in the issues listed. These account for almost all the baseball cards in existence. The prices were added to the card lists just prior to printing and reflect not the author's opinions or desires but the going retail prices for each card, based on the marketplace (sports memorabilia conventions and shows, hobby papers, current mail order catalogs, local club meetings, auction results, and other firsthand reportings of actually realized prices).

What is the BEST Price Guide available (on the market) today? Of course card sellers will prefer the Price Guide with the highest prices as the best — while card buyers will naturally prefer the one with the lowest prices. Accuracy, however, is the true test. Use the Price Guide used by more collectors and dealers than all the others combined. Look for the Beckett name. I won't put my name on anything I won't stake my reputation on. Not the lowest and not the highest — but the most accurate, with integrity.

To facilitate your use of this book, read the complete introductory section in the pages following before going to the pricing pages. Every collectible field has its own terminology; we've tried to capture most of these terms and definitions in our glossary. Please read carefully the section on grading and the condition of your cards, as you will not be able to determine which price column is appropriate for a given card without first knowing its condition.

Welcome to the world of baseball cards.

Sincerely, Dr. James Beckett

Introduction

Welcome to the exciting world of baseball card collecting, America's fastest-growing avocation. You have made a good choice in buying this book, since it will open up to you the entire panorama of this field in the simplest, most concise way.

It is estimated that nearly a third of a million different baseball cards have been issued during the past century. And the number of total cards put out by all manufacturers last year has been estimated at several billion, with an initial retail value of more than $300 million. Sales of older cards by dealers may account for a like amount. With all that cardboard available in the marketplace, it should be no surprise that several million sports fans like you collect baseball cards today, and that number is growing by hundreds of thousands each year.

The growth of *Beckett Baseball Card Monthly* is another indication of this rising crescendo of popularity for baseball cards. Founded less than six years ago by Dr. James Beckett, the author of this price guide, *Beckett Baseball Card Monthly* has grown to the pinnacle of the baseball card hobby with more than a million readers anxiously awaiting each enjoyable issue.

So collecting baseball cards — while still pursued as a hobby with youthful exuberance by kids in the neighborhood — has also taken on the trappings of an industry, with thousands of full- and part-time card dealers, as well as vendors of supplies, clubs and conventions. In fact, each year since 1980 thousands of hobbyists have assembled for a National Sports Collectors Convention, at which hundreds of dealers have displayed their wares, seminars have been conducted, autographs penned by sports notables, and millions of cards changed hands. These colossal affairs have been staged in Los Angeles, Detroit, St. Louis, Chicago, New York, Anaheim, Arlington (TX), San Francisco, Atlantic City, Chicago, Arlington (TX), and this year back in Anaheim, California across from Disneyland at the Convention Center. So baseball card collecting really is national in scope!

This increasing interest has been reflected in card values. As more collectors compete for available supplies, card prices (especially for premium-grade cards) rise. A national publication indicated a "very strong advance" in baseball card prices during the past decade, and a quick perusal of prices in this book compared to the figures in earlier editions of this price guide will quickly confirm this. Which brings us back around again to the book you have in your hands. Many prices have literally doubled! It is the best annual guide available to this exciting world of baseball cards. Read it and use it. May your enjoyment and your card collection increase in the coming months and years.

SportsCards Plus

How to Collect

Each collection is personal and reflects the individuality of its owner. There are no set rules on how to collect cards. Since card collecting is a hobby or leisure pastime, what you collect, how much you collect, and how much time and money you spend collecting are entirely up to you. The funds you have available for collecting and your own personal taste should determine how you collect. Information and ideas presented here are intended to help you get the most enjoyment from this hobby.

It is impossible to collect every card ever produced. Therefore, beginners as well as intermediate and advanced collectors usually specialize in some way. One of the reasons this hobby is popular is that individual collectors can define and tailor their collecting methods to match their own tastes. To give you some ideas of the various approaches to collecting, we will list some of the more popular areas of specialization.

Many collectors select complete sets from particular years. For example, they may concentrate on assembling complete sets from all the years since their birth or since they became avid sports fans. They may try to collect a card for every player during that specified period of time. Many others wish to acquire only certain players. Usually such players are the superstars of the sport, but occasionally collectors will specialize in all the cards of players who attended certain colleges or came from certain towns. Some collectors are only interested in the first cards or rookie cards of certain players. A handy guide for collectors interested in pursuing the hobby this way is the *Sport Americana Alphabetical Checklist No. 4*.

Another fun way to collect cards is by team. Most fans have a favorite team, and it is natural for that loyalty to be translated into a desire for cards of the players on that favorite team. For most of the recent years, team sets (all the cards from a given team for that year) are readily available at a reasonable price. *The Sport Americana Team Baseball Card Checklist* will open up this field to the collector.

Obtaining Cards

Several avenues are open to card collectors. Cards can be purchased in the traditional way at the local candy, grocery, or drug stores, with the bubble gum or other products included. For many years it has been possible to purchase complete sets of baseball cards through mail order advertisers found in traditional sports media publications, such as *The Sporting News*, *Baseball Digest*, *Street & Smith* yearbooks, and others. These sets are also advertised in the card collecting periodicals. Many collectors will begin by subscribing to at least one of the hobby periodicals, all with good up-to-date information. In fact, subscription offers can be found in the advertising section of this book. In addition, a great variety of cards (typically from all eras and all sports) can be obtained at the growing number of hobby retail stores dedicated to sports cards and memorabilia around the country.

Most serious card collectors obtain old (and new) cards from one or more of several main sources: (1) trading or buying from other collectors or dealers; (2) responding to sale or auction ads in the hobby publications; (3) buying at a local hobby store; and/or (4) attending sports collectibles shows or conventions. We advise that you try all four methods since each has its own distinct advantages: (1) trading is a great way to make new friends; (2) hobby periodicals help you keep up with what's going on in the hobby (including when and where the conventions are happening); (3) stores provide the opportunity for considering (any day of the week) a great diversity of material in a relaxed sports-oriented atmosphere that most fans love; and (4) shows provide enjoyment and the opportunity to view millions of collectibles under one roof, in addition to meeting some of the hundreds or even thousands of other collectors with similar interests who also attend the shows.

Preserving Your Cards

Cards are fragile. They must be handled properly in order to retain their value. Careless handling can easily result in creased or bent cards. It is, however, not recommended that tweezers or tongs be used to pick up your cards since such utensils might mar or indent card surfaces and thus reduce those cards' conditions and values. In general, your cards should be handled directly as little as possible. This is sometimes easier to say than to do. Although there are still many who use custom boxes, storage trays, or even shoe boxes, plastic sheets are the preferred method of storing cards. A collection stored in plastic pages in a three-ring album allows you to view your collection at any time without the need to touch the card itself. Cards can also be kept in single holders (of various types and thickness) designed for the

enjoyment of each card individually. For a large collection, some collectors may use a combination of the above methods.

When purchasing plastic sheets for your cards, be sure that you find the pocket size that fits the cards snugly. Don't put your 1951 Bowmans in a sheet designed to fit 1981 Topps. Most hobby and collectibles shops and virtually all collectors' conventions will have these plastic pages available in quantity for the various sizes offered or you can purchase them directly from the advertisers in this book. Also remember that pocket size isn't the only factor to consider when looking for plastic sheets. Some collectors concerned with long-term storage of their cards in plastic sheets are cautious to avoid sheets containing PVC and request non-PVC sheets from their dealer.

Damp, sunny and/or hot conditions — no, this is not a weather forecast—are three elements to avoid in extremes if you are interested in preserving your collection. Too much (or too little) humidity can cause gradual deterioration of a card. Direct, bright sun (or fluorescent light) over time will bleach out the color of a card. Extreme heat accelerates the decomposition of the card. On the other hand, many cards have lasted more than 50 years without much scientific intervention. So be cautious, even if the above factors typically present a problem only when present in the extreme. It never hurts to be prudent.

Collecting/Investing

Collecting individual players and collecting complete sets are both popular vehicles for investment and speculation. Most investors and speculators stock up on complete sets or on quantities of players they think have good investment potential. There is obviously no guarantee in this book, or anywhere else for that matter, that cards will outperform the stock market or other investment alternatives in the future. After all, baseball cards do not pay quarterly dividends and cards cannot be sold at their "current values" as easily as stocks or bonds. Nevertheless, investors have noticed a favorable long-term trend in the past performance of baseball and other sports collectibles, and certain cards and sets have outperformed just about any other investment in some years. It has been suggested that the best investment is and always will be the building of a collection, which traditionally has held up better than speculation.

Some of the obvious questions are: Which cards? When to buy? When to sell? The best investment you can make is in your own education. The more you know about your collection and the hobby, the more informed the decisions you will be able to make. We're not selling investment tips. We're selling information about the current value of baseball cards. It's up to you to use that information to your best advantage.

WANTED

Advanced collector seeking singles, lots, accumulations and sets of pre-1948 baseball cards. Of special interest are "E" Cards (Early Gum and Candy), "T" Cards (20th Century Tobacco), "N" Cards (19th Century Tobacco), 1930's Gum Cards, with an extra emphasis on Pacific Coast League items (Zeenuts, Obaks, etc.).

Unlike some dealers who accept only Mint or Excellent cards, I will consider all recognizable grades (Poor-Mint). While I cannot promise "The Absolute Gem Mint Untouchable Top Offer Guaranteed" I will submit a competitive and fair offer on any collection; as I have since 1972. Please feel free to write or call advising me of your holdings.

Thanks.

Mark Macrae
Box 2111
Castro Valley, CA 94546
415-538-6245
Fax: 415-538-4645

Send $1 (check or stamps) for my latest "Old Card" Sales List.

Nomenclature

Each hobby has its own language to describe its area of interest. The nomenclature traditionally used for trading cards is derived from the *American Card Catalog*, published in 1960 by Nostalgia Press. That catalog, written by Jefferson Burdick (who is called the "Father of Card Collecting" for his pioneering work), uses letter and number designations for each separate set of cards.

The letter used in the ACC designation refers to the generic type of card. While both sport and non-sport issues are classified in the ACC, we shall confine ourselves to the sport issues. The following list defines the letters and their meanings as used by the *American Card Catalog*.

(none) or N - 19th Century U.S. Tobacco
B - Blankets
D - Bakery Inserts Including Bread
E - Early Candy and Gum
F - Food Inserts
H - Advertising
M - Periodicals
PC - Postcards
R - Candy and Gum Cards 1930 to Present
T - 20th Century U.S. Tobacco
UO - Gas and Oil Inserts
V - Canadian Candy
W - Exhibits, Strip Cards, Team Issues

Following the letter prefix and an optional hyphen are one-, two-, or three-digit numbers, 1-999. These typically represent the company or entity issuing the cards. In several cases, the ACC number is extended by an additional hyphen and another one- or two-digit numerical suffix. For example, the 1957 Topps regular series baseball card issue carries an ACC designation of R414-11. The "R" indicates a Candy or Gum card produced since 1930. The "414" is the ACC designation for Topps Chewing Gum baseball card issues, and the "11" is the ACC designation for the 1957 regular issue (Topps' eleventh baseball set).

Like other traditional methods of identification, this system provides order to the process of cataloging cards; however, most serious collectors learn the ACC designation of the popular sets by repetition and familiarity, rather than by attempting to "figure out" what they might or should be.

From 1948 forward, collectors and dealers commonly refer to all sets by their year, maker, type of issue, and any other distinguishing characteristic. For example, such a characteristic could be an unusual issue or one of several regular issues put out by a specific maker in a single year. Regional issues are usually referred to by year, maker, and sometimes by title or theme of the set.

Glossary/Legend

Our glossary defines terms frequently used in the card collecting hobby. Many of these terms are also common to other types of sports memorabilia collecting. Some terms may have several meanings depending on use.

AAS - Action All Stars, a postcard-size set issued by the Donruss Company.

ACC - Acronym for *American Card Catalog.*

ALL STAR CARD - A card portraying an All Star Player of the previous year that says "All Star" on its face.

ALPH - Alphabetical.

AS - Abbreviation for All Star (card).

ATG - All Time Great card.

BLANKET - A felt square (normally 5" to 6") portraying a baseball player.

BC - Bonus Card (Used by Donruss for their sets from 1988 through 1991)

BOX - Card issued on a box or a card depicting a Boxer.

BRICK - A group of 50 or more cards having common characteristics that is intended to be bought, sold, or traded as a unit.

CABINETS - Popular and highly valuable photographs on thick card stock produced in the 19th and early 20th century.

CHECKLIST - A list of the cards contained in a particular set. The list is always in numerical order if the cards are numbered. Some unnumbered sets are artificially numbered in alphabetical order, by team and alphabetically within the team, or by uniform number for convenience.

CHECKLIST CARD - A card that lists in order the cards and players in the set or series. Older checklist cards in Mint condition that have not been checked off or marked off are very desirable.

CL - Abbreviation for Checklist.

COA - Abbreviation for Coach.

COIN - A small disc of metal or plastic portraying a player in its center.

COLLECTOR - A person who engages in the hobby of collecting cards primarily for his own enjoyment, with any profit motive being secondary.

COLLECTOR ISSUE - A set produced for the sake of the card itself with no product or service sponsor. It derives its name from the fact

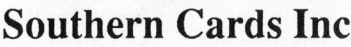

that most of these sets are produced for sale directly to the hobby market.

COMBINATION CARD - A single card depicting two or more players (but not a team card).

COMMON CARD - The typical card of any set; it has no premium value accruing from subject matter, numerical scarcity, popular demand, or anomaly.

COM - Card issued by the Post Cereal Company through their mail-in offer.

CONVENTION - A large weekend gathering of dealers and collectors at a single location for the purpose of buying, selling, and sometimes trading sports memorabilia items. Conventions are open to the public and sometimes feature celebrities, door prizes, films, contests, etc. They are frequently referred to simply as "shows."

CONVENTION ISSUE - A set produced in conjunction with a sports collectibles convention to commemorate or promote the show.

COR - Correct or corrected card.

COUPON - See Tab.

CREASE - A wrinkle on the card, usually caused by bending the card. Creases are a common (and serious) defect from careless handling.

CY - Cy Young Award.

DC - Draft Choice.

DEALER - A person who engages in buying, selling, and trading sports collectibles or supplies. A dealer may also be a collector, but as a dealer, he anticipates a profit.

DIE-CUT - A card with part of its stock partially cut, allowing one or more parts to be folded or removed. After removal or appropriate folding, the remaining part of the card can frequently be made to stand up.

DISC - A circular-shaped card.

DISPLAY CARD - A sheet, usually containing three to nine cards, that is printed and used by the manufacturer to advertise and/or display the packages containing his products and cards. The backs of display cards are blank or contain advertisements.

DK - Diamond King (artwork produced by Perez-Steele for Donruss).

DP - Double Print (a card that was printed in double the quantity compared to the other cards in the same series).

DT - Dream Team (Produced by Score in 1990 and 1991).

ERA - Earned Run Average.

ERR - Error card (see also COR).

ERROR CARD - A card with erroneous information, spelling, or depiction on either side of the card. Most errors are not corrected by the producing card company.

EXHIBIT - The generic name given to thick-stock, postcard-size cards with single color obverse pictures. The name is derived from the Exhibit Supply Co. of Chicago, the principal manufacturer of this type of card. These are also known as Arcade cards since they were found in many arcades.

FDP - First Draft Pick.

FULL SHEET - A complete sheet of cards that has not been cut up into individual cards by the manufacturer. Also called an uncut sheet.

FS - Future Star (Used by Topps from 1987 through 1991)

HALL OF FAMER - (HOF'er) A card that portrays a player who has been inducted into the Hall of Fame.

HIGH NUMBER - The cards in the last series of numbers in a year in which such higher-numbered cards were printed or distributed in significantly lesser amounts than the lower-numbered cards. The high-number designation refers to a scarcity of the high-numbered cards. Not all years have high numbers in terms of this definition.

HL - Highlight card.

HOC - House of Collectibles.

HOF - Hall of Fame.

HOR - Horizontal pose on card as opposed to the standard vertical orientation found on most cards.

HR - Home Run.

IA - In Action (type of card).

IF - Infielder

INSERT - A card of a different type, e.g., a poster, or any other sports collectible contained and sold in the same package along with a card or cards of a major set.

ISSUE - Synonymous with set, but usually used in conjunction with a manufacturer, e.g., a Topps issue.

K - Strikeout.

KP - Kid Picture (a sub-series issued in the Topps Baseball sets of 1972 and 1973).

LAYERING - The separation or peeling of one or more layers of the card stock, usually at the corner of the card.

LEGITIMATE ISSUE - A set produced to promote or boost sales of a product or service, e.g., bubble gum, cereal, cigarettes, etc. Most collector issues are not legitimate issues in this sense.

LHP - Left-Handed Pitcher.

LID - A circular-shaped card (possibly with tab) that forms the top of the container for the

product being promoted.

LL - Living Legends (Donruss 1984) or large letters.

MAJOR SET - A set produced by a national manufacturer of cards containing a large number of cards. Usually 100 or more different cards comprise the set.

MG - Abbreviation for Manager.

MINI - A small card; specifically, a Topps baseball card of identical design but smaller dimensions than the regular Topps issue of 1975.

ML - Major League.

MVP - Most Valuable Player.

NNOF - No Name on Front (see 1949 Bowman).

NOF - Name on Front (see 1949 Bowman).

NON-SPORT CARD - A card from a set whose major theme is a subject other than a sports subject. A card of a sports figure or event that is part of a non-sport set is still a non-sport card, e.g., while the "Look 'N' See" non-sport card set contains a card of Babe Ruth, a sports figure, that card is a non-sport card.

NOTCHING - The grooving of the card, usually caused by fingernails, rubber bands, or bumping card edges against other objects.

NY - New York.

OBVERSE - The front, face, or pictured side of the card.

OF - Outfield or Outfielder.

OLY - Olympics (see 1985 Topps Baseball and 1988 Topps Traded sets; the members of the U.S. Olympic Baseball teams were featured subsets in both of these sets).

OPT - Option.

ORG - Organist.

P - Pitcher or Pitching pose.

P1 - First Printing.

P2 - Second Printing.

P3 - Third Printing.

PANEL - An extended card that is composed of two or more individual cards. Often the panel forms the back part of the container for the product being promoted, e.g., a Hostess panel, a Bazooka panel, an Esskay Meat panel.

PCL - Pacific Coast League.

PG - Price Guide.

PLASTIC SHEET - A clear, plastic page that is punched for insertion into a binder (with standard three-ring spacing) containing pockets for displaying cards. Many different styles of sheets exist with pockets of varying sizes to hold the many differing card formats.

PREMIUM - A card, sometimes on photographic stock, that is purchased or obtained in conjunction with, or redemption for, another card or product. The premium is not packaged in the same unit as the primary item.

PUZZLE CARD - A card whose back contains a part of a picture which, when joined correctly with other puzzle cards, forms the completed picture.

PUZZLE PIECE - A die-cut piece designed to interlock with similar pieces.

PVC - Polyvinyl Chloride, a substance used to make many of the popular card display protective sheets. Non-PVC sheets are considered preferable for long-term storage of cards.

RARE - A card or series of cards of very limited availability. Unfortunately, "rare" is a subjective term sometimes used indiscriminately. "Rare" cards are harder to obtain than "scarce" cards.

RB - Record Breaker card.

REGIONAL - A card or set of cards issued and distributed only in a limited geographical area of the country.

REVERSE - The back or narrative side of the card.

RHP - Right-Handed Pitcher.

ROY - Rookie of the Year.

RP - Relief Pitcher.

RR - Rated Rookies (a subset featured in the Donruss Baseball sets).

SA - Super Action or Sport Americana.

SASE - Self-Addressed, Stamped Envelope.

SB - Stolen Bases.

SCARCE - A card or series of cards of limited availability. This subjective term is sometimes used indiscriminately to promote or hype value. "Scarce" cards are not as difficult to obtain as "rare" cards.

SCR - Script name on back (see 1949 Bowman baseball).

SEMI-HIGH - A card from the next to last series of a sequentially issued set. It has more value than an average card and generally less value than a high number. A card is not called a semi-high unless the next to last series in which it exists has an additional premium attached to it.

SERIES - The entire set of cards issued by a particular producer in a particular year, e.g., the 1971 Topps series. Also, within a particular set, series can refer to a group of (consecutively numbered) cards printed at the same time, e.g., the first series of the 1957 Topps issue (numbers 1 through 88).

SET - One each of the entire run of cards of the same type produced by a particular manufacturer during a single year. In other words, if you have a (complete) set of 1976 Topps then you have every card from number 1 up through

ST. LOUIS BASEBALL CARDS

314-892-4737

— BILL GOODWIN —

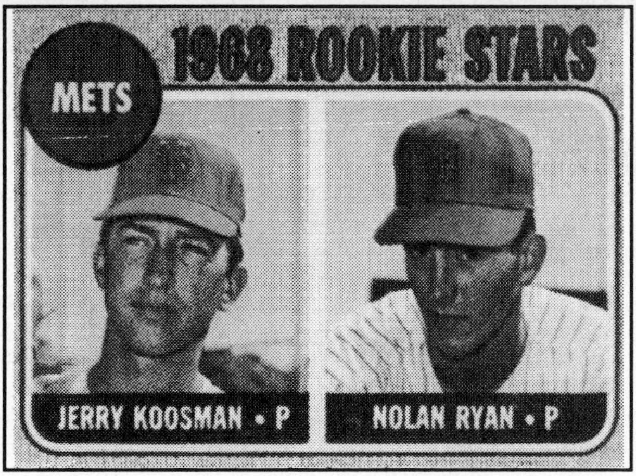

We are paying top prices for

- **!Baseball Cards Star and Commons**
- **!Complete Sets**
- **!Hartland Statues**
- **!Press Pins**
- **!Autographs**
- **!All Sports Memorablilia**

•Over 6000 satisfied customers.

•We have the most competitive buying policy in the industry

•We will travel for large collections, or can suggest the easiest means to ship.

•All transactions are completely confidential.

•We guarantee courtesy and professional transactions.

ST. LOUIS BASEBALL CARDS

Bill Goodwin

"ALWAYS BUYING BASEBALL CARDS & SPORTS MEMORABILIA"
5456 Chatfield, St. Louis, MO 63129 • 314-892-4737

and including number 660, i.e., all the different cards that were produced.

SKIP-NUMBERED - A set that has many unissued card numbers between the lowest number in the set and the highest number in the set, e.g., the 1948 Leaf baseball set contains 98 cards skip-numbered from number 1 to number 168. A major set in which a few numbers were not printed is not considered to be skip-numbered.

SO - Strikeouts.

SP - Single or Short Print (a card which was printed in lesser quantity compared to the other cards in the same series; see also DP and TP).

SPECIAL CARD - A card that portrays something other than a single player or team, for example, a card that portrays the previous year's statistical leaders or the results from the previous year's post-season action.

SS - Shortstop.

STAMP - Adhesive-backed papers depicting a player. The stamp may be individual or in a sheet of many stamps. Moisture must be applied to the adhesive in order for the stamp to be attached to another surface.

STAR CARD - A card that portrays a player of some repute, usually determined by his ability; however, sometimes referring to sheer popularity.

STICKER - A card with a removable layer that can be affixed to (stuck onto) another surface.

STOCK - The cardboard or paper on which the card is printed.

STRIP CARDS - A sheet or strip of cards, particularly popular in the 1920s and 1930s, with the individual cards usually separated by broken or dotted lines.

SUPERSTAR CARD - A card that portrays a superstar, e.g., a Hall of Fame member or one with strong Hall of Fame potential.

SV - Super Veteran (see 1982 Topps).

TAB - A card portion set off from the rest of the card, usually with perforations, that may be removed without damaging the central character or event depicted by the card.

TBC - Turn Back the Clock cards.

TC - Team Checklist cards (see 1989 and 1990 Upper Deck).

TEAM CARD - A card that depicts an entire team.

TEST SET - A set, usually containing a small number of cards, issued by a national card producer and distributed in a limited section or sections of the country. Presumably, the purpose of a test set is to test market appeal for a particular type of card.

TL - Team Leader card.

TP - Triple Print (a card that was printed in triple the quantity compared to the other cards in the same series).

TR - Trade or Traded.

TRIMMED - A card cut down from its original size. Trimmed cards are undesirable to most collectors.

UER - Uncorrected Error.

UMP - Umpire.

VARIATION - One of two or more cards from the same series with the same number (or player with identical pose if the series is unnumbered) differing from one another by some aspect, the different feature stemming from the printing or stock of the card. This can be caused when the manufacturer of the cards notices an error in one (or more) of the cards, makes the changes, and then resumes the print run. In this case there will be two versions or variations of the same card. Sometimes one of the variations is relatively scarce.

VERT - Vertical pose on card.

WAS - Washington National League (Used in 1974 Topps).

WS - World Series card.

YL - Yellow Letters (Used on the front of some 1958 Topps).

YT - Yellow Team (Used on the front of some 1958 Topps).

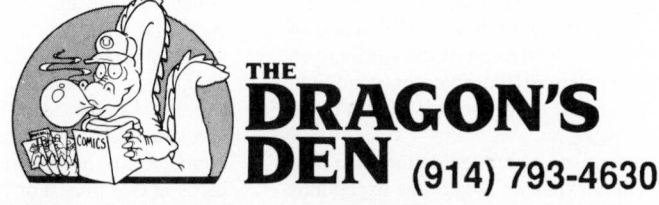

Business of Baseball Card Collecting

Determining Value

Why are some cards more valuable than others? Obviously, the economic laws of supply and demand are applicable to card collecting just as they are to any other field where a commodity is bought, sold, or traded in a free, unregulated market.

Supply (the number of cards available on the market) is less than the total number of cards originally produced since attrition diminishes that original quantity. Each year a percentage of cards is typically thrown away, destroyed, or otherwise lost to collectors. This percentage is much smaller today than it was in the past because more and more people have become increasingly aware of the value of their cards. For those who collect only "Mint" condition cards, the supply of older cards can be quite small indeed. Until recently, collectors were not so conscious of the need to preserve the condition of their cards. For this reason, it is difficult to know exactly how many 1953 Topps are currently available, Mint or otherwise. It is generally accepted that there are fewer 1953 Topps available than 1963, 1973, or 1983 Topps cards. If demand were equal for each of these sets, the law of supply and demand would increase the price for the least available sets. Demand, however, is not equal for all sets, so price correlations can be complicated.

The demand for a card is influenced by many factors. These include: (1) the age of the card; (2) the number of cards printed; (3) the player(s) portrayed on the card; (4) the attractiveness and popularity of the set; and perhaps most important, (5) the physical condition of the card.

In general, (1) the older the card, (2) the fewer the number of the cards printed, (3) the more famous the player, (4) the more attractive and popular the set, or (5) the better the condition of the card, the higher the value of the card will be. There are exceptions to all but one of these factors: the condition of the card. Given two cards similar in all respects except condition, the one in the best condition will ALWAYS be valued higher.

While there are certain guidelines that help to establish the value of a card, the exceptions and peculiarities make any simple, direct mathematical formula to determine card values impossible.

Regional Variation

Two types of price variations exist among the sections of the country where a card is bought or sold. The first is the general price variation on all cards bought and sold in one geographical area as compared to another. Card prices are slightly higher on the East and West coasts, and slightly lower in the middle of the country. Although prices may vary from the East to the West, or from the Southwest to the Midwest, the prices listed in this guide are nonetheless presented as a consensus of all sections of this large and diverse country.

Still, prices for a particular player's cards may well be higher in his home team's area than in other regions. This exhibits the second type of regional price variation in which local players are favored over those from distant areas. For example, an Al Kaline card would be valued higher in Detroit than in Cincinnati because Kaline played in Detroit; therefore, the demand there for Al Kaline cards is higher than it is in Cincinnati. On the other hand, a Johnny Bench card would be priced higher in Cincinnati where he played than in Detroit for similar reasons. Frequently even common player cards command such a premium from hometown collectors.

Set Prices

A somewhat paradoxical situation exists in the price of a complete set versus the combined cost of the individual cards in the set. In nearly every case, the sum of the prices for the individual cards is higher than the cost for the complete set. This is especially prevalent in the cards of the past few years. The reasons for this apparent anomaly stem from the habits of collectors and from the carrying costs to dealers. Today each card in a set is normally produced in the same quantity as all others in its set. However, many collectors pick up only stars, superstars, and particular teams. As a result, the dealer is left with a shortage of certain player cards and an abundance of others. He therefore incurs an expense in simply "carrying" these less desirable cards in stock. On the other hand, if he sells a complete set, he gets rid of large numbers of cards at one time. For this reason, he is often willing to receive less money for a complete set. By doing this, he recovers all of his costs and also receives some profit.

The disparity between the price of the complete set and that for the sum of the individual cards has also been influenced by the fact that the major manufacturers are now pre-collating card sets. Since "pulling" individual cards from the sets of all three manufacturers involves a specific type of labor (and cost), the singles or star card market is not affected significantly by pre-collation.

Set prices also do not include rare card varieties, unless specifically stated. Of course, the prices for sets do include one example of each type for the given set, but this is the least expensive variety.

Scarce Series

Scarce series occur because cards issued before 1974 were made available to the public each year in several series of finite numbers of cards, rather than all cards of the set being available for purchase at one time. At some point during the year, usually toward the end of the baseball season, interest in current year baseball cards waned. Consequently, the manufacturers produced smaller numbers of these later series of cards. Nearly all nationwide issues from post-World War II manufacturers (1948 to 1973) exhibit these series variations. In the past Topps, for example, may have issued series consisting of many different numbers of cards, including 55, 66, 80, 88, and others. Recently Topps has settled on what is now their standard sheet size of 132 cards, six of which comprise its 792-card set.

While the number of cards within a given series is usually the same as the number of cards on one printed sheet, this is not always the case. For example, Bowman used 36 cards on its standard printed sheets, but in 1948 substituted 12 cards during later print runs of that year's baseball cards. Twelve of the cards from the initial sheet of 36 cards were removed and replaced by 12 different cards giving, in effect, a first series of 36 cards and a second series of 12 new cards. This replacement produced a scarcity of 24 cards — the 12 cards removed from the original sheet and the 12 new cards added to the sheet. A full sheet of 1948 Bowman cards (second printing) shows that card numbers 37 through 48 have replaced 12 of the cards on the first printing sheet.

The Topps Gum Company has also created scarcities and/or excesses of certain cards in many of their sets. Topps, however, has most frequently gone the other direction by double printing some of the cards. Double printing causes an abundance of cards of the players who are on the same sheet more than one time. During the years from 1978 to 1981, Topps double printed 66 cards out of their large 726-card set. The Topps' practice of double printing cards in earlier years is the most logical explanation for the known scarcities of particular cards in some of these Topps sets.

Recently Donruss has always been short printing or double printing certain cards in its major sets. Ostensibly this is due to their addition of Bonus MVP cards in their regular issue wax packs.

We are always looking for information or photographs of printing sheets of cards for research. Each year we try to update the hobby's knowledge of distribution anomalies. Please let us know at the address in this book if you have first-hand knowledge that would be helpful in this pursuit.

DEN'S COLLECTORS DEN

PLASTIC CARD PROTECTING PAGES
LARGEST SELECTION IN THE HOBBY

FINEST QUALITY PLASTIC SHEETS

DEN'S COLLECTORS DEN

HOME OF SPORT AMERICANA

DEPT. PG13
P.O. BOX 606, LAUREL, MD 20725

Featuring:

- NON–MIGRATING PLASTIC IN ALL SHEETS
- PLASTIC THAT DOES NOT STICK TOGETHER
- STIFFNESS TO RESIST CARD CURLING
- INTELLIGENT DESIGN
- RESISTANCE TO CRACKING
- FULL COVERAGE OF CARDS, PHOTOS, ENVELOPES

SEND ONLY $ 1.00 for DEN'S BIG CATALOGUE
CATALOGUE sent FREE with each ORDER

NO MIX & MATCH

STYLE	POCKETS / CAPACITY	RECOMMENDED FOR	PRICE EACH (Does not include Post. & Hand.) 1–24	25–99	100–299	300 plus
9	9 / 18	TOPPS (1957 to present), FLEER, DONRUSS SCORE, SPORTFLICS, TCMA, LEAF (1960), All standard 2½" X 3½" cards, SIDE LOAD	.25	.23	.21	.19
9T	9 / 18	SAME AS STYLE 9 ABOVE, TOP LOAD	.25	.23	.21	.19
8	8 / 16	TOPPS (1952–1956, 1988 Big), BOWMAN (1953–1955)	.25	.23	.21	.19
12	12 / 24	BOWMAN (1948–1950), TOPPS (1951), TOPPS (Stickers), FLEER (Minis & Stickers)	.25	.23	.21	.19
1	1 / 2	PHOTOGRAPHS (8" X 10")	.25	.23	.21	.19
2	2 / 4	PHOTOGRAPHS (5" X 7"), TOPPS (1984, 1985 & 1986 Supers)	.25	.23	.21	.19
4	4 / 8	POSTCARDS, EXHIBITS, PEREZ–STEELE (Hall of Fame postcards), DONRUSS (1983–1987 All-Stars), TOPPS (1964,70,71 Supers)	.25	.23	.21	.19
6P	6 / 12	POLICE AND SAFETY CARDS (All sports)	.25	.23	.21	.19
18	18 / 36	T206 and most other T CARDS, BAZOOKA (1963–1967 Individual cards), Many 19th Century cards (N Cards)	.40	.40	35	.35
9G	9 / 18	GOUDEY, DIAMOND STARS, LEAF (1948)	.40	.40	.35	.35
9PB	9 / 18	PLAY BALL, BOWMAN (1951-52), All GUM, INC. Cards, TOPPS (Minis), DOUBLE PLAY	.40	.40	.35	.35
1C	1 / 2	TURKEY RED (T3), PRESS GUIDES, PEREZ–STEELE (Greatest Moments), Many WRAPPERS (Sport & non-sport)	.40	.40	.35	.35
3	3 / 6	3–CARD PANELS (Hostess, Star, Zeller's)	.40	.40	.35	.35
6V	6 / 12	TOPPS (Double Headers, Greatest Moments, 1951 Connie Mack, Current All-Stars, Team, 1965 Football and Hockey, Bucks, 1969–1970 Basketball, T201 (Mecca Double folders), T202 (Hassan Triple folders), DADS (Hockey), DONRUSS (1986–87 Pop–Ups)	.40	.40	.35	.35
6D	6 / 12	RED MAN (With or without tabs), DISCS, KAHN'S (1955–1967)	.40	.40	.35	.35
1Y	1 / 1	YEARBOOKS, PROGRAMS, MAGAZINES, Pocket Size is 9" X 12"	.40	.40	.35	.35
1S	1 / 2	MAGAZINE PAGES and PHOTOS, SMALL PROGRAMS, CRACKER JACK (1982 sheets), Pocket Size is 8½" X 11"	.40	.40	.35	.35
10	10 / 10	MATCHBOOK COVERS (Standard 20 match)	.40	.40	.35	.35
3E	3 / 3	FIRST DAY COVERS, BASEBALL COMMEMORATIVE ENVELOPES	.40	.40	.35	.35
3L	3 / 6	SQUIRT PANELS, PEPSI (1963), FLEER (Stamps in strips)	.40	.40	.35	.35

POSTAGE & HANDLING SCHEDULE
$ .01 to $ 20.00 add $ 2.00
$ 20.01 to $ 29.99 add $ 2.50
$ 30.00 to $ 49.99 add $ 3.00
$ 50.00 or more add $ 4.00

VISA/MASTER CHARGE ACCEPTED

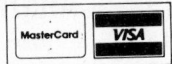

MasterCard VISA

MARYLAND RESIDENTS ADD 5% SALES TAX
CANADIAN ORDERS – BOOKS ONLY
Canadian orders, orders outside the contiguous United States, APO and FPO add 25% additional
U.S. FUNDS ONLY

Grading Your Cards

Each hobby has its own grading terminology — stamps, coins, comic books, beer cans, right down the line. Collectors of sports cards are no exception. The one invariable criterion for determining the value of a card is its condition: the better the condition of the card, the more valuable it is. However, condition grading is very subjective. Individual card dealers and collectors differ in the strictness of their grading, but the stated condition of a card should be determined without regard to whether it is being bought or sold.

The physical defects which lower the condition of a card are usually quite apparent, but each individual places his own estimation (negative value in this case) on these defects. We present the condition guide for use in determining values listed in this price guide in the hopes that excess subjectivity can be minimized.

The defects listed in the condition guide below are those either placed in the card at the time of printing — uneven borders, focus — or those defects that can occur to a card under normal handling — corner sharpness, gloss, edge wear, light creases — and finally, environmental conditions — browning. Other defects to cards are caused by human carelessness and in all cases should be noted separately and in addition to the condition grade. Among the more common alterations are heavy creases, tape, tape stains, rubber band marks, water damage, smoke damage, trimming, paste, tears, writing, pin or tack holes, any back damage, and missing parts (tabs, tops, coupons, backgrounds).

Centering

It is important to define in words and pictures what is meant by certain frequently used hobby terms relating to grading cards. The adjacent pictures portray various stages of centering. Centering can range from well-centered to slightly off-centered to off-centered to badly off-centered to miscut.

Slightly Off-Centered: A slightly off-center card is one which upon close inspection is found to have one border bigger than the opposite border. This degree is only offensive to a purist.

Off-Centered: An off-center card has one border which is noticeably more than twice as wide as the opposite border.

Badly Off-Centered: A badly off-center card has virtually no border on one side of the card.

Miscut: A miscut card actually shows part of the adjacent card in its larger border and consequently a corresponding amount of its card is cut off.

Corner Wear

Degrees of corner wear generate several common terms used and useful to accurate grading. The wear on card corners can be expressed as fuzzy corners, corner wear or slightly rounded corners, rounded corners, badly rounded corners.

Fuzzy Corners: Fuzzy corners still come to a right angle (to a point) but the point has begun to fray slightly.

Corner Wear or Slightly Rounded Corners: The slight fraying of the corners has increased to where there is no longer a point to the corner. Nevertheless the corner is still reasonably sharp. There may be evidence of some slight loss of color in the corner also.

Rounded Corners: The corner is definitely no longer sharp but is not badly rounded.

Badly Rounded Corners: The corner is rounded to an objectionable degree. Excessive wear and rough handling are evident.

Creases

The third, and perhaps most frequent, common defect is the crease; the degree of creasing in a card is very difficult to show in a drawing or picture. On giving the specific condition of an expensive card for sale, the seller should note any creases additionally. Creases can be categorized as to severity according to the following scale.

Light Crease: A light crease is a crease which is barely noticeable on close inspection. In fact when cards are in plastic sheets or holders, a light crease may not be seen (until the card is taken out of the holder). A light crease on the front is much more serious than a light crease on the card back only.

Medium Crease: A medium crease is noticeable when held and studied at arm's length by the naked eye, but does not overly detract from the appearance of the card. It is an obvious crease, but not one that breaks the picture surface of the card.

Heavy Crease: A heavy crease is one which has torn or broken through the card's picture surface, e.g., puts a tear in the photo surface.

Alterations

Deceptive Trimming: Deceptive trimming occurs when someone alters the card in order (1)

Centering

Well-centered

Slightly Off-centered

Off-centered

Badly Off-centered

Miscut

to shave off edge wear, (2) to improve the sharpness of the corners, or (3) to improve centering—obviously their objective is to falsely increase the perceived value of the card to an unsuspecting buyer. The shrinkage is usually only evident if the trimmed card is compared to an adjacent full-sized card or if the trimmed card is itself measured.

Obvious Trimming: Obvious trimming is noticeable and unfortunate. It is usually performed by non-collectors who give no thought to the present or future value of their cards.

Deceptively Retouched Borders: This occurs when the borders (especially on those cards with dark borders) are touched up on the edges and corners with magic marker of appropriate color in order to make the card appear to be mint.

Categorization of Defects

A "Micro Defect" would be fuzzy corners, slight off-centering, printers' lines, printers' spots, slightly out of focus, or slight loss of original gloss. A NrMT card may have one micro defect. An Ex-MT card may have two or more micro defects.

A "Minor Defect" would be corner wear or slight rounding, off-centering, light crease on back, wax or gum stains on reverse, loss of original gloss, writing or tape marks on back, or rubber band marks. An Excellent card may have minor defects.

A "Major Defect" would be rounded corner(s), badly off-centering, crease(s), deceptive trimming, deceptively retouched borders, pin hole, staple hole, incidental writing or tape marks on front, warping, water stains, medium crease(s), or sun fading. A VG card may have one major defect. A Good card may have two or more major defects.

A "Catastrophic Defect" is the worst kind of defect and would include such defects as badly rounded corner(s), miscutting, heavy crease(s), obvious trimming, punch hole, tack hole, tear(s), corner missing or clipped, destructive writing on front. A Fair card may have one catastrophic defect. A Poor card has two or more catastrophic defects.

Corner Wear

The partial cards shown at the right have been photographed at 300%. This was done in order to magnify each card's corner wear to such a degree that differences could be shown on a printed page.

The 1962 Topps Mickey Mantle card definitely has a rounded corner. Some may say that this corner is badly rounded, but that is a judgment call.

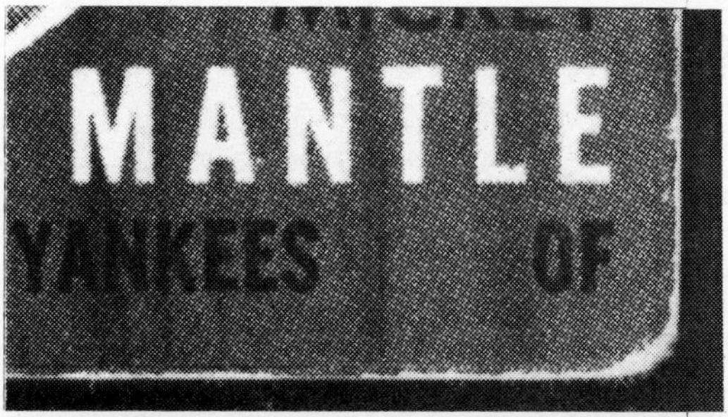

The 1962 Topps Hank Aaron card has a slightly rounded corner. Note that there is definite corner wear evident by the fraying and that there is no longer a sharp point to which the corner converges.

The 1962 Topps Gil Hodges card has corner wear; it is slightly better than the Aaron card above. Nevertheless some collectors might classify this Hodges corner as slightly rounded.

The 1962 Topps Manager's Dream card showing Mantle and Mays has slight corner wear. This is not a fuzzy corner as very slight wear is noticeable on the card's photo surface.

The 1962 Topps Don Mossi card has very slight corner wear such that it might be called a fuzzy corner. A close look at the original card shows that the corner is not perfect, but almost. However, note that corner wear is somewhat academic on this card. As you can plainly see, the heavy crease going across his name breaks through the photo surface.

Condition Guide

MINT (M OR MT) - A card with no defects. The card has sharp corners, even borders, original gloss or shine on the surface, sharp focus of the picture, smooth edges, no signs of wear, and white borders. A Mint card (that is, a card that is worth a "Mint" price) does NOT have printers' lines or other printing defects or other serious quality control problems that should have been discovered by the producing card company before distribution. Note also that there is no allowance made for the age of the card.

NEAR MINT (NrMT) - A card with a micro defect. Any of the following would be sufficient to lower the grade of a card from Mint to the Near Mint category: layering at some of the corners (fuzzy corners), a very small amount of the original gloss lost, very minor wear on the edges, slightly off-center borders, slight wear visible only on close inspection, slight off-whiteness of the borders.

EXCELLENT-MINT (EX-MT) - A card with micro defects, but no minor defects. Two or three of the following would be sufficient to lower the grade of a card from Mint to the Excellent-Mint category: layering at some of the corners (fuzzy corners), a very small amount of the original gloss lost, minor wear on the edges, slightly off-center borders, slight wear visible only on close inspection, slight off-whiteness of the borders.

EXCELLENT (EX OR E) - A card with minor defects. Any of the following would be sufficient to lower the grade of a card from Mint to the Excellent category: slight rounding at some of the corners, a small amount of the original gloss lost, minor wear on the edges, off-center borders, wear visible only on close inspection; off-whiteness of the borders.

VERY GOOD (VG) - A card that has been handled but not abused. Some rounding at all corners, slight layering or scuffing at one or two corners, slight notching on edges, gloss lost from the surface but not scuffed, borders might be somewhat uneven but some white is visible on all borders, noticeable yellowing or browning of borders, light crease(s), pictures may be slightly off focus.

GOOD (G) - A well-handled card, rounding and some layering at the corners, scuffing at the corners and minor scuffing on the face, borders noticeably uneven and browning, loss of gloss on the face, medium crease(s), notching on the edges.

FAIR (F) - Round and layering corners, brown and dirty borders, frayed edges, noticeable scuffing on the face, white not visible on one or more borders, medium to heavy creases, cloudy focus.

POOR (P) - An abused card: The lowest grade of card, frequently some major physical alteration has been performed on the card, collectible only as a filler until a better-condition replacement can be obtained.

Categories between these major condition grades are frequently used, such as Very Good to Excellent (VG-E), Fair to Good (F-G), etc. Such grades indicate a card with all qualities at least in the lower of the two categories, but with several qualities in the higher of the two categories. In the case of EX-MT, it essentially refers to a card which is halfway between Excellent and Mint.

Unopened "Mint" cards and factory-collated sets are considered Mint in their unknown (and presumed perfect) state. However, once opened or broken out, each of these cards is graded (and valued) in its own right by taking into account any quality control defects (such as off-centering, printers' lines, machine creases, or gum stains) that may be present in spite of the fact that the card has never been handled.

Cards before 1980 that are priced in the Price Guide in a top condition of NrMT, are obviously worth an additional premium when offered in strict Mint condition. This additional premium increases relative to the age and scarcity of the card. For example, Mint cards from the late '70s may bring only a 10% premium for Mint (above NrMT), whereas high demand (or condition rarity) cards from early vintage sets can be sold for as much as double (and occasionally even more) the NrMT price when offered in strict Mint condition.

Cards before 1946 which are priced in the Price Guide in a top condition of EX-MT, are obviously worth an additional premium when offered in strict Near Mint or better condition. This additional premium increases relative to the age and scarcity of the card.

Selling Your Cards

Just about every collector sells cards or will sell cards eventually. Someday you may be interested in selling your duplicates or maybe even your whole collection. You may sell to other collectors, friends, or dealers. You may even sell cards you purchased from a certain dealer back to that same dealer. In any event, it helps to know some of the mechanics of the typical transaction between buyer and seller.

Dealers will buy cards in order to resell them to other collectors who are interested in the cards. Dealers will always pay a higher percentage for items which (in their opinion) can be resold quickly, and a much lower percentage for those items which are perceived as having low demand and hence are slow moving. In either case, dealers must buy at a price that allows for the expense of doing business and a fair margin for profit.

If you have cards for sale, the best advice we can give is that you get three offers for your cards and take the best offer, all things considered. Note, the "best" offer may not be the one for the highest amount. And remember, if a dealer really wants your cards, he won't let you get away without making his best competitive offer. Another alternative is to take your cards to a nearby convention and either auction them off in the show auction or offer them for sale to some of the dealers present.

Many people think nothing of going into a department store and paying $15 for an item of clothing for which the store paid $5. But, if you were selling your $15 card to a dealer and he offered you only $5 for it, you might think his mark-up unreasonable. To complete the analogy: most department stores (and card dealers) that pay $10 for $15 items eventually go out of business. An exception to this is when the dealer knows that a willing buyer for the merchandise you are attempting to sell is only a phone call away. Then an offer of 2/3 or maybe 70% of the book value will still allow him to make a reasonable profit due to the short time he will need to hold the merchandise. Nevertheless, most cards and collections will bring offers in the range of 25% to 50% of retail price. Material from the past five to ten years or so is very plentiful. Don't be surprised if your best offer is only 10% to 20% of the book value for these recent years, especially with respect to the more common (very recent) cards.

Interesting Notes

The numerically first card of an issue is the single card most likely to obtain excessive wear. Consequently, you will typically find the price on the number one card (in Mint condition) somewhat higher than might otherwise be the case. Similarly, but to a lesser extent (because normally the less important, reverse side of the card is the one exposed), the numerically last card in an issue is also prone to abnormal wear. This extra wear and tear occurs because the first and last cards are exposed to the elements (human element included) more than any other cards. They are generally end cards in any brick formations, rubber bandings, stackings on wet surfaces, and like activities.

Sports cards have no intrinsic value. The value of a card, like the value of other collectibles, can only be determined by you and your enjoyment in viewing and possessing these cardboard swatches.

Remember, the buyer ultimately determines the price of each baseball card. You are the determining price factor because you have the ability to say "No" to the price of any card by not exchanging your hard-earned money for a given card. When the cost of a trading card exceeds the enjoyment you will receive from it, your answer should be "No." We assess and report the prices. You set them!

We are always interested in receiving the price input of collectors and dealers from around the country. We happily credit major contributors. We welcome your opinions, since your contributions assist us in ensuring a better guide each year. If you would like to join our survey list for the next editions of this book and others authored by Dr. Beckett, please send your name and address to Dr. James Beckett, 4887 Alpha Road, Suite 200, Dallas, Texas 75244.

Advertising

Within this price guide you will find advertisements for sports memorabilia material, mail order, and retail sports collectibles establishments. All advertisements were accepted in good faith based on the reputation of the advertiser; however, neither the author, the publisher, the distributors, nor the other advertisers in the price guide accept any responsibility for any particular advertiser not complying with the terms of his or her ad.

Readers should also be aware that prices in advertisements are subject to change over the annual period before a new edition of this volume is issued each spring. When replying to an advertisement late in the baseball year, the reader should take this into account, and contact the dealer by phone or in writing for up-to-date price information. Should you come into contact with any of the advertisers in this guide as a result of their advertisement herein, please mention to them this source as your contact.

Additional Reading

With the increase in popularity of the hobby in recent years, there has been a corresponding increase in available literature. Below is a list of the books and periodicals which receive our highest recommendation and which we hope will further advance your knowledge and enjoyment of our great hobby.

The Sport Americana Price Guide to Baseball Collectibles by Dr. James Beckett (Second Edition, $12.95, released 1988, published by Edgewater Book Company) — the complete guide/checklist with up-to-date values for box cards, coins, labels, Canadian cards, stamps, stickers, pins, etc.

The Sport Americana Football Card Price Guide by Dr. James Beckett (Seventh Edition, $14.95, released 1990, published by Edgewater Book Company) — the most comprehensive price guide/checklist ever issued on football cards. No serious football card hobbyist should be without it.

The Sport Americana Football, Hockey, Basketball and Boxing Card Price Guide by Dr. James Beckett (Sixth Edition, $14.95, released 1989, published by Edgewater Book Company) — the most comprehensive price guide/checklist ever issued on non-baseball sports cards.

The Official Price Guide to Football Cards by Dr. James Beckett (Ninth Edition, $5.95, released 1989, published by The House of Collectibles) — an abridgement of the Sport Americana Price Guide listed above in a convenient and economical pocket-size format providing Dr. Beckett's pricing of the major football sets since 1948.

The Official Price Guide to Hockey and Basketball Cards by Dr. James Beckett (First Edition, $5.95, released 1989, published by The House of Collectibles) — an abridgement of the Sport Americana Price Guide listed above in a convenient and economical pocket-size format providing Dr. Beckett's pricing of the major hockey and basketball sets since 1948.

The Sport Americana Baseball Memorabilia and Autograph Price Guide by Dr. James Beckett and Dennis W. Eckes (First Edition, $8.95, released 1982, co-published by Den's Collectors Den and Edgewater Book Company) — the most complete book ever produced on baseball memorabilia other than baseball cards. This book presents in an illustrated, logical fashion information on baseball memorabilia and autographs that had been heretofore unavailable to the collector.

The Sport Americana Alphabetical Baseball Card Checklist by Dr. James Beckett (Fourth Edition, $12.95, released 1990, published by Edgewater Book Company) — an alphabetical listing, by the last name of the player portrayed on the card, of virtually all baseball cards (Major League and Minor League) produced up through the 1990 major sets.

The Sport Americana Price Guide to the Non-Sports Cards by Christopher Benjamin and Dennis W. Eckes (Third Edition [Part Two, $12.95, released 1988, published by Edgewater Book Company) — the definitive guide to all popular non-sports American tobacco and bubble gum cards. In addition to cards, illustrations and prices for wrappers are also included. Part Two covers non-sports cards from 1961 through 1987.

The Sport Americana Baseball Address List by Jack Smalling and Dennis W. Eckes (Fifth Edition, $10.95, released 1988, published by Edgewater Book Company) — the definitive guide for autograph hunters, giving addresses and deceased information for virtually all major league baseball players past and present.

The Sport Americana Baseball Card Team Checklist by Jeff Fritsch and Dennis W. Eckes (Fifth Edition, $12.95, released 1990, published by Edgwater Book Company) — includes all Topps, Bowman, Donruss, Fleer, Score, Play Ball, Goudey, and Upper Deck cards, with the players portrayed on the cards listed with the teams for whom they played. The book is invaluable to the collector who specializes in an individual team because it is the most complete baseball card team checklist available.

The Encyclopedia of Baseball Cards, Volume I: 19th Century Cards by Lew Lipset ($11.95, released 1983, published by the author) — everything you ever wanted to know about 19th century cards.

The Encyclopedia of Baseball Cards, Volume II: Early Gum and Candy Cards by Lew Lipset ($10.95, released 1984, published by the author) — everything you ever wanted to know about Early Candy and Gum cards.

The Encyclopedia of Baseball Cards, Volume III: 20th Century Tobacco Cards, 1909-1932 by Lew Lipset ($12.95, released 1986, published by the author) — everything you ever wanted to know about old tobacco cards.

Beckett Baseball Card Monthly authored and edited by Dr. James Beckett — contains the most extensive and accepted monthly price guide, feature articles, "who's hot and who's not" section, convention calendar, and numerous letters to and responses from the editor. Published 12 times annually, it is the hobby's largest paid circulation periodical. *Beckett Football Card Monthly, Beckett Basketball Monthly,* and *Beckett Hockey Monthly* are all very similar to *Beckett Baseball Card Monthly* in style and content.

Errata

There are thousands of names, more than 100,000 prices, and untold other words in this book. There are going to be a few typographical errors, a few misspellings, and possibly, a number or two out of place. If you catch a blooper, drop me a note directly or in care of the publisher, and we will fix it up in the next year's edition.

Prices in this Guide

Prices found in this guide reflect current retail rates just prior to the printing of this book. They do not reflect the FOR SALE prices of the author, the publisher, the distributors, the advertisers, or any card dealers associated with this guide. No one is obligated in any way to buy, sell, or trade his or her cards based on these prices. The price listings were compiled by the author from actual buy/sell transactions at sports conventions, buy/sell advertisements in the hobby papers, for sale prices from dealer catalogs and price lists, and discussions with leading hobbyists in the U.S. and Canada. All prices are in U.S. dollars.

1962 American Tract Society

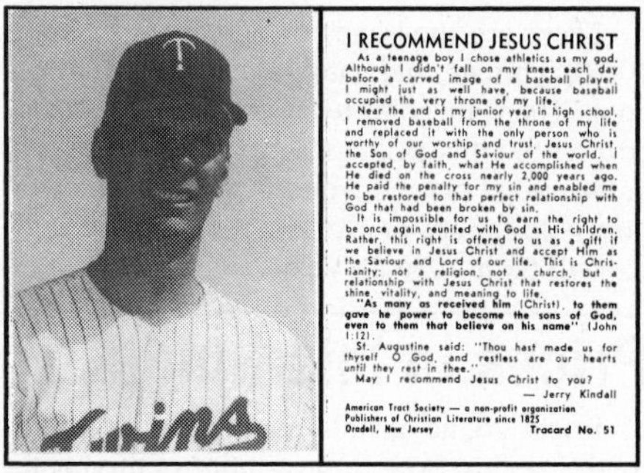

These cards are quite attractive and feature the "pure card" concept that is always popular with collectors, i.e., no borders or anything else on the card front to detract from the color photo. The cards are numbered on the back and are actually part of a much larger set with a Christian theme. The set features Christian ballplayers giving first-person testimonies on the card backs telling how Jesus Christ has changed their lives. These cards are sometimes referred to as "Tracards." The cards measure approximately 2 3/4" by 3 1/2". The set price below refers to only one of each player, not including any variations.

	NRMT	VG-E	GOOD
COMPLETE SET (4)	18.00	8.00	1.60
COMMON PLAYER	4.00	2.00	.40
☐ 43A Bobby Richardson (black print on back)	9.00	4.00	.80
☐ 43B Bobby Richardson (blue print on back)	9.00	4.00	.80
☐ 43C Bobby Richardson (black print on back with Play Ball in red)	9.00	4.00	.80
☐ 43D Bobby Richardson (black print on back with exclamation point after Play Ball)	9.00	4.00	.80
☐ 51A Jerry Kindall (portrait from chest up, black print on back)	4.00	2.00	.40
☐ 51B Jerry Kindall (on one knee with bat, blue print on back)	4.00	2.00	.40
☐ 52A Felipe Alou (on one knee looking up, black print on back)	6.00	2.50	.50
☐ 52B Felipe Alou (on one knee looking up, blue print on back)	6.00	2.50	.50
☐ 52C Felipe Alou (batting pose)	6.00	2.50	.50
☐ 66 Al Worthington (black print on back)	4.00	2.00	.40

1948 Babe Ruth Story

The 1948 Babe Ruth Story set of 28 black and white numbered cards (measuring 2" by 2 1/2") was issued by the Philadelphia Chewing Gum Company to commemorate the 1949 movie of the same name starring William Bendix, Claire Trevor, and Charles Bickford. Babe Ruth himself appears on several cards. The last 12 cards (17 to 28) are more difficult to obtain than other cards in the set and are also more desirable in that most picture actual players as well as actors from the movie. Supposedly these last 12 cards were issued much later after the first 16 cards had already been released and distributed. The catalog designation for this set is R421

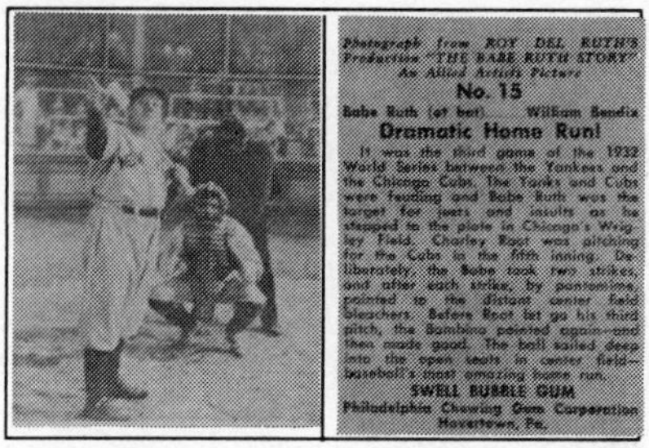

	NRMT	VG-E	GOOD
COMPLETE SET	1000.00	450.00	100.00
COMMON PLAYER (1-16)	12.00	6.00	1.20
COMMON PLAYER (17-24)	40.00	20.00	4.00
COMMON PLAYER (25-28)	125.00	60.00	12.50
☐ 1 The Babe Ruth Story In the Making (Babe Ruth shown with William Bendix)	125.00	25.00	5.00
☐ 2 Bat Boy Becomes the Babe	12.00	6.00	1.20
☐ 3 Claire Hodgson played by Claire Trevor	12.00	6.00	1.20
☐ 4 Babe Ruth played by William Bendix; Claire Hodgson played by Claire Trevor	12.00	6.00	1.20
☐ 5 Brother Matthias played by Charles Bickford	12.00	6.00	1.20
☐ 6 Phil Conrad played by Sam Levene	12.00	6.00	1.20
☐ 7 Night Club Singer played by Gertrude Niesen	12.00	6.00	1.20
☐ 8 Baseball's Famous Deal	12.00	6.00	1.20
☐ 9 Babe Ruth played by William Bendix; Mrs.Babe Ruth played by Claire Trevor	12.00	6.00	1.20
☐ 10 Actors for Babe Ruth, Mrs. Babe Ruth, and Brother Matthias	12.00	6.00	1.20
☐ 11 Babe Ruth played by William Bendix; Miller Huggins played by Fred Lightner	12.00	6.00	1.20
☐ 12 Babe Ruth played by William Bendix; Johnny Sylvester played by George Marshall	12.00	6.00	1.20
☐ 13 Actors for Mr., Mrs. and Johnny Sylvester	12.00	6.00	1.20
☐ 14 When A Feller Needs A Friend	12.00	6.00	1.20
☐ 15 Dramatic Home Run	12.00	6.00	1.20
☐ 16 The Homer That Set the Record	12.00	6.00	1.20
☐ 17 The Slap That Started Baseball's Most Famous Career	40.00	20.00	4.00
☐ 18 The Babe Plays Santa Claus	40.00	20.00	4.00
☐ 19 Actors for Ed Barrow, Jacob Ruppert, and Miller Huggins	40.00	20.00	4.00
☐ 20 Broken Window Paid Off	40.00	20.00	4.00
☐ 21 Regardless of the Generation/ Babe Ruth	40.00	20.00	4.00
☐ 22 Charley Grimm and William Bendix	40.00	20.00	4.00
☐ 23 Ted Lyons and William Bendix	50.00	25.00	5.00

☐ 24 Lefty Gomez, William Bendix, and Bucky Harris	60.00	30.00	6.00
☐ 25 Babe Ruth and William Bendix	125.00	60.00	12.50
☐ 26 Babe Ruth and William Bendix	125.00	60.00	12.50
☐ 27 Babe Ruth and Claire Trevor	125.00	60.00	12.50
☐ 28 William Bendix, Babe Ruth, Claire Trevor	125.00	60.00	12.50

1990 Baseball Wit

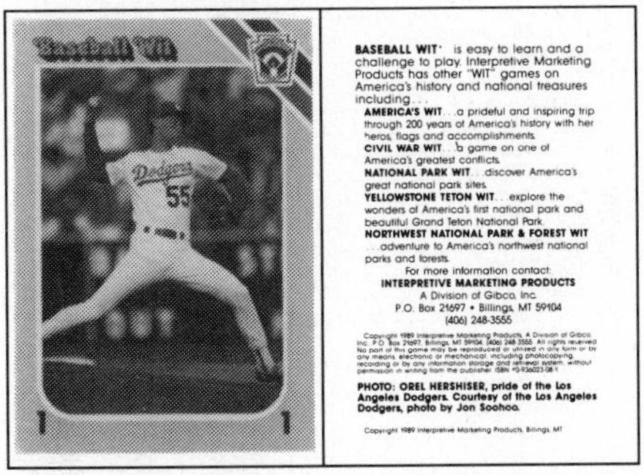

Baseball Wit
Dodgers
55
BASEBALL WIT® is easy to learn and a challenge to play. Interpretive Marketing Products has other "WIT" games on America's history and national treasures including...
AMERICA'S WIT...a prideful and inspiring trip through 200 years of America's history with her heros, flags and accomplishments.
CIVIL WAR WIT...a game on one of America's greatest conflicts.
NATIONAL PARK WIT...discover America's great national park sites.
YELLOWSTONE TETON WIT...explore the wonders of America's first national park and beautiful Grand Teton National Park.
NORTHWEST NATIONAL PARK & FOREST WIT...adventure to America's northwest national parks and forests.
For more information contact:
INTERPRETIVE MARKETING PRODUCTS
A Division of Gibco, Inc.
P.O. Box 21697 • Billings, MT 59104
(406) 248-3555
PHOTO: OREL HERSHISER, pride of the Los Angeles Dodgers. Courtesy of the Los Angeles Dodgers, photo by Jon Soohoo.
Copyright 1989 Interpretive Marketing Products, Billings, MT

The 1990 Baseball Wit set was issued in complete set form only. This set was dedicated to and featured several ex-members of the Little Leagues. This 108-card, standard-size (2 1/2" by 3 1/2") set was available primarily in retail and chain outlets. Most of the older (retired) players in the set are shown in black and white. The card backs typically give three trivia questions with answers following. The cards are not numbered but the set's producer issued a numerically-ordered list which is presented below.

	MINT	VG-E	F-G
COMPLETE SET (108)	10.00	5.00	1.00
COMMON PLAYER (1-108)	.07	.03	.01
☐ 1 Orel Hershiser	.15	.07	.01
☐ 2 Tony Gwynn	.15	.07	.01
☐ 3 Mickey Mantle	.60	.30	.06
☐ 4 Willie Stargell	.15	.07	.01
☐ 5 Don Baylor	.07	.03	.01
☐ 6 Hank Aaron	.25	.12	.02
☐ 7 Don Larsen	.07	.03	.01
☐ 8 Lee Mazzilli	.07	.03	.01
☐ 9 John"Boog" Powell	.07	.03	.01
☐ 10 Little League World Series	.07	.03	.01
☐ 11 Jose Canseco	.50	.25	.05
☐ 12 Mike Scott	.07	.03	.01
☐ 13 Bob Feller	.10	.05	.01
☐ 14 Ron Santo	.07	.03	.01
☐ 15 Mel Stottlemyer UER (sic, Stottlemyre)	.07	.03	.01
☐ 16 Shea Stadium	.07	.03	.01
☐ 17 Brooks Robinson	.10	.05	.01
☐ 18 Willie Mays	.25	.12	.02
☐ 19 Ernie Banks	.15	.07	.01
☐ 20 Keith Hernandez	.07	.03	.01
☐ 21 Bret Saberhagen	.10	.05	.01
☐ 22 Baseball Hall of Fame	.07	.03	.01
☐ 23 Luis Aparicio	.10	.05	.01
☐ 24 Yogi Berra	.15	.07	.01
☐ 25 Manny Mota	.07	.03	.01
☐ 26 Steve Garvey	.10	.05	.01
☐ 27 Bill Shea	.07	.03	.01
☐ 28 Fred Lynn	.07	.03	.01
☐ 29 Todd Worrell	.07	.03	.01
☐ 30 Roy Campanella	.15	.07	.01
☐ 31 Bob Gibson	.10	.05	.01
☐ 32 Gary Carter	.10	.05	.01
☐ 33 Jim Palmer	.15	.07	.01
☐ 34 Carl Yastrzemski	.15	.07	.01
☐ 35 Dwight Gooden	.15	.07	.01
☐ 36 Stan Musial	.25	.12	.02
☐ 37 Rickey Henderson	.35	.17	.03
☐ 38 Dale Murphy	.15	.07	.01
☐ 39 Mike Schmidt	.25	.12	.02
☐ 40 Gaylord Perry	.10	.05	.01
☐ 41 Ozzie Smith	.10	.05	.01
☐ 42 Reggie Jackson	.25	.12	.02
☐ 43 Steve Carlton	.10	.05	.01
☐ 44 Jim Perry	.07	.03	.01
☐ 45 Vince Coleman	.10	.05	.01
☐ 46 Tom Seaver	.20	.10	.02
☐ 47 Marty Marion	.07	.03	.01
☐ 48 Frank Robinson	.10	.05	.01
☐ 49 Joe DiMaggio	.45	.22	.04
☐ 50 Ted Williams	.35	.17	.03
☐ 51 Rollie Fingers	.10	.05	.01
☐ 52 Jackie Robinson	.35	.17	.03
☐ 53 Victor Raschi	.07	.03	.01
☐ 54 Johnny Bench	.20	.10	.02
☐ 55 Nolan Ryan	.45	.22	.04
☐ 56 Ty Cobb	.45	.22	.04
☐ 57 Harry Steinfeldt	.07	.03	.01
☐ 58 James O'Rourke	.07	.03	.01
☐ 59 John McGraw	.10	.05	.01
☐ 60 Candy Cummings	.07	.03	.01
☐ 61 Jimmie Foxx	.10	.05	.01
☐ 62 Walter Johnson	.10	.05	.01
☐ 63 1903 World Series	.07	.03	.01
☐ 64 Satchel Paige	.15	.07	.01
☐ 65 Bobby Wallace	.07	.03	.01
☐ 66 Cap Anson	.10	.05	.01
☐ 67 Hugh Duffy	.07	.03	.01
☐ 68 William(Buck) Ewing	.07	.03	.01
☐ 69 Bobo Holloman	.07	.03	.01
☐ 70 Ed Delahanty	.07	.03	.01
☐ 71 Dizzy Dean	.10	.05	.01
☐ 72 Tris Speaker	.10	.05	.01
☐ 73 Lou Gehrig	.45	.22	.04
☐ 74 Wee Willie Keeler	.07	.03	.01
☐ 75 Cal Hubbard	.07	.03	.01
☐ 76 Eddie Collins	.07	.03	.01
☐ 77 Chris Von Der Ahe	.07	.03	.01
☐ 78 Sam Crawford	.07	.03	.01
☐ 79 Cy Young	.10	.05	.01
☐ 80 Johnny Vander Meer	.07	.03	.01
☐ 81 Joey Jay	.07	.03	.01
☐ 82 Zack Wheat	.07	.03	.01
☐ 83 Jim Bottomley	.07	.03	.01
☐ 84 Honus Wagner	.25	.12	.02
☐ 85 Casey Stengel	.15	.07	.01
☐ 86 Babe Ruth	.60	.30	.06
☐ 87 John Lindemuth/Carl	.07	.03	.01
☐ 88 Max Carey	.07	.03	.01
☐ 89 Mordecai Brown	.07	.03	.01
☐ 90 1869 Cincinnati Red Stockings	.07	.03	.01
☐ 91 Rube Marquard	.07	.03	.01
☐ 92 Charles Radbourne (Horse)	.07	.03	.01
☐ 93 Hack Wilson	.07	.03	.01
☐ 94 Lefty Grove	.10	.05	.01
☐ 95 Carl Hubbell	.07	.03	.01
☐ 96 A.J. Cartwright	.07	.03	.01
☐ 97 Roger Hornsby	.10	.05	.01
☐ 98 Ernest Thayer	.07	.03	.01
☐ 99 Connie Mack	.10	.05	.01
☐ 100 1939 Centennial Celebration	.07	.03	.01
☐ 101 Branch Rickey	.10	.05	.01
☐ 102 Dan Brouthers	.07	.03	.01
☐ 103 First Baseball Uniform	.07	.03	.01
☐ 104 Christy Mathewson	.15	.07	.01
☐ 105 Joe Nuxhall	.07	.03	.01
☐ 106 1939 Centennial Celebration	.07	.03	.01
☐ 107 President Taft	.07	.03	.01
☐ 108 Abner Doubleday	.07	.03	.01

1934-36 Batter-Up

The 1934-36 Batter-Up set issued by National Chicle contains 192 blank-backed die-cut cards. Numbers 1 to 80 are 2 3/8" by 3 1/4" in size while 81 to 192 are 2 3/8" by 3". The latter are more difficult to find than the former. The pictures come in basic black and white or in tints of blue, brown, green, purple, red, or sepia. There are three combination cards (each featuring two players per card) in the high series (98, 111, and 115). The catalog designation for the set is R318. Cards with backs removed are graded fair at best.

	EX-MT	VG-E	GOOD
COMPLETE SET (192)	18000.00	8000.00	2000.00
COMMON PLAYER (1-80)	40.00	20.00	4.00
COMMON PLAYER (81-192)	80.00	40.00	8.00
☐ 1 Wally Berger	80.00	25.00	5.00
☐ 2 Ed Brandt	40.00	20.00	4.00
☐ 3 Al Lopez	100.00	50.00	10.00
☐ 4 Dick Bartell	40.00	20.00	4.00
☐ 5 Carl Hubbell	150.00	75.00	15.00
☐ 6 Bill Terry	150.00	75.00	15.00
☐ 7 Pepper Martin	65.00	32.50	6.50
☐ 8 Jim Bottomley	100.00	50.00	10.00
☐ 9 Tom Bridges	45.00	22.50	4.50
☐ 10 Rick Ferrell	100.00	50.00	10.00
☐ 11 Ray Benge	40.00	20.00	4.00
☐ 12 Wes Ferrell	45.00	22.50	4.50
☐ 13 Chalmer Cissell	40.00	20.00	4.00
☐ 14 Pie Traynor	150.00	75.00	15.00
☐ 15 Leroy Mahaffey	40.00	20.00	4.00
☐ 16 Chick Hafey	100.00	50.00	10.00
☐ 17 Lloyd Waner	100.00	50.00	10.00
☐ 18 Jack Burns	40.00	20.00	4.00
☐ 19 Buddy Myer	40.00	20.00	4.00
☐ 20 Bob Johnson	45.00	22.50	4.50
☐ 21 Arky Vaughan	100.00	50.00	10.00
☐ 22 Red Rolfe	45.00	22.50	4.50
☐ 23 Lefty Gomez	150.00	75.00	15.00
☐ 24 Earl Averill	100.00	50.00	10.00
☐ 25 Mickey Cochrane	150.00	75.00	15.00
☐ 26 Van Lingle Mungo	45.00	22.50	4.50
☐ 27 Mel Ott	175.00	85.00	18.00
☐ 28 Jimmy Foxx	175.00	85.00	18.00
☐ 29 Jimmy Dykes	45.00	22.50	4.50
☐ 30 Bill Dickey	175.00	85.00	18.00
☐ 31 Lefty Grove	175.00	85.00	18.00
☐ 32 Joe Cronin	150.00	75.00	15.00
☐ 33 Frank Frisch	150.00	75.00	15.00
☐ 34 Al Simmons	125.00	60.00	12.50
☐ 35 Rogers Hornsby	175.00	85.00	18.00
☐ 36 Ted Lyons	100.00	50.00	10.00
☐ 37 Rabbit Maranville	100.00	50.00	10.00
☐ 38 Jimmy Wilson	40.00	20.00	4.00
☐ 39 Willie Kamm	40.00	20.00	4.00
☐ 40 Bill Hallahan	40.00	20.00	4.00
☐ 41 Gus Suhr	40.00	20.00	4.00
☐ 42 Charlie Gehringer	125.00	60.00	12.50
☐ 43 Joe Heving	40.00	20.00	4.00
☐ 44 Adam Comorosky	40.00	20.00	4.00
☐ 45 Tony Lazzeri	75.00	37.50	7.50
☐ 46 Sam Leslie	40.00	20.00	4.00
☐ 47 Bob Smith	40.00	20.00	4.00
☐ 48 Willis Hudlin	40.00	20.00	4.00
☐ 49 Carl Reynolds	40.00	20.00	4.00
☐ 50 Fred Schulte	40.00	20.00	4.00
☐ 51 Cookie Lavagetto	45.00	22.50	4.50
☐ 52 Hal Schumacher	40.00	20.00	4.00
☐ 53 Roger Cramer	45.00	22.50	4.50
☐ 54 Sylvester Johnson	40.00	20.00	4.00
☐ 55 Ollie Bejma	40.00	20.00	4.00
☐ 56 Sam Byrd	40.00	20.00	4.00
☐ 57 Hank Greenberg	175.00	85.00	18.00
☐ 58 Bill Knickerbocker	40.00	20.00	4.00
☐ 59 Bill Urbanski	40.00	20.00	4.00
☐ 60 Eddie Morgan	40.00	20.00	4.00
☐ 61 Rabbit McNair	40.00	20.00	4.00
☐ 62 Ben Chapman	45.00	22.50	4.50
☐ 63 Roy Johnson	40.00	20.00	4.00
☐ 64 Dizzy Dean	325.00	160.00	32.00
☐ 65 Zeke Bonura	40.00	20.00	4.00
☐ 66 Fred Marberry	40.00	20.00	4.00
☐ 67 Gus Mancuso	40.00	20.00	4.00
☐ 68 Joe Vosmik	40.00	20.00	4.00
☐ 69 Earl Grace	40.00	20.00	4.00
☐ 70 Tony Piet	40.00	20.00	4.00
☐ 71 Rollie Hemsley	40.00	20.00	4.00
☐ 72 Fred Fitzsimmons	40.00	20.00	4.00
☐ 73 Hack Wilson	150.00	75.00	15.00
☐ 74 Chick Fullis	40.00	20.00	4.00
☐ 75 Fred Frankhouse	40.00	20.00	4.00
☐ 76 Ethan Allen	40.00	20.00	4.00
☐ 77 Heine Manush	100.00	50.00	10.00
☐ 78 Rip Collins	40.00	20.00	4.00
☐ 79 Tony Cuccinello	40.00	20.00	4.00
☐ 80 Joe Kuhel	40.00	20.00	4.00
☐ 81 Tom Bridges	90.00	45.00	9.00
☐ 82 Clint Brown	80.00	40.00	8.00
☐ 83 Albert Blanche	80.00	40.00	8.00
☐ 84 Boze Berger	80.00	40.00	8.00
☐ 85 Goose Goslin	175.00	85.00	18.00
☐ 86 Lefty Gomez	275.00	135.00	27.00
☐ 87 Joe Glenn	80.00	40.00	8.00
☐ 88 Cy Blanton	80.00	40.00	8.00
☐ 89 Tom Carey	80.00	40.00	8.00
☐ 90 Ralph Birkofer	80.00	40.00	8.00
☐ 91 Fred Gabler	80.00	40.00	8.00
☐ 92 Dick Coffman	80.00	40.00	8.00
☐ 93 Ollie Bejma	80.00	40.00	8.00
☐ 94 Leroy Parmelee	80.00	40.00	8.00
☐ 95 Carl Reynolds	80.00	40.00	8.00
☐ 96 Ben Cantwell	80.00	40.00	8.00
☐ 97 Curtis Davis	80.00	40.00	8.00
☐ 98 Webb and Wally Moses	90.00	45.00	9.00
☐ 99 Ray Benge	80.00	40.00	8.00
☐ 100 Pie Traynor	200.00	100.00	20.00
☐ 101 Phil Cavarretta	90.00	45.00	9.00
☐ 102 Pep Young	80.00	40.00	8.00
☐ 103 Willis Hudlin	80.00	40.00	8.00
☐ 104 Mickey Haslin	80.00	40.00	8.00
☐ 105 Oswald Bluege	80.00	40.00	8.00
☐ 106 Paul Andrews	80.00	40.00	8.00
☐ 107 Ed Brandt	80.00	40.00	8.00
☐ 108 Don Taylor	80.00	40.00	8.00
☐ 109 Thornton Lee	80.00	40.00	8.00
☐ 110 Hal Schumacher	80.00	40.00	8.00
☐ 111 Hayes and Ted Lyons	150.00	75.00	15.00
☐ 112 Odell Hale	80.00	40.00	8.00
☐ 113 Earl Averill	175.00	85.00	18.00
☐ 114 Italo Chelini	80.00	40.00	8.00
☐ 115 Andrews and Jim Bottomley	150.00	75.00	15.00
☐ 116 Bill Walker	80.00	40.00	8.00
☐ 117 Bill Dickey	300.00	150.00	30.00
☐ 118 Gerald Walker	80.00	40.00	8.00
☐ 119 Ted Lyons	175.00	85.00	18.00
☐ 120 Eldon Auker	80.00	40.00	8.00
☐ 121 Bill Hallahan	80.00	40.00	8.00
☐ 122 Fred Lindstrom	175.00	85.00	18.00
☐ 123 Oral Hildebrand	80.00	40.00	8.00
☐ 124 Luke Appling	200.00	100.00	20.00
☐ 125 Pepper Martin	110.00	55.00	11.00
☐ 126 Rick Ferrell	175.00	85.00	18.00
☐ 127 Ival Goodman	80.00	40.00	8.00
☐ 128 Joe Kuhel	80.00	40.00	8.00
☐ 129 Ernie Lombardi	175.00	85.00	18.00
☐ 130 Charlie Gehringer	250.00	125.00	25.00
☐ 131 Van Lingle Mungo	90.00	45.00	9.00
☐ 132 Larry French	80.00	40.00	8.00
☐ 133 Buddy Myer	80.00	40.00	8.00
☐ 134 Mel Harder	100.00	50.00	10.00
☐ 135 Augie Galan	80.00	40.00	8.00
☐ 136 Gabby Hartnett	175.00	85.00	18.00
☐ 137 Stan Hack	90.00	45.00	9.00
☐ 138 Billy Herman	175.00	85.00	18.00
☐ 139 Bill Jurges	80.00	40.00	8.00
☐ 140 Bill Lee	80.00	40.00	8.00
☐ 141 Zeke Bonura	80.00	40.00	8.00
☐ 142 Tony Piet	80.00	40.00	8.00
☐ 143 Paul Dean	110.00	55.00	11.00
☐ 144 Jimmy Foxx	375.00	175.00	37.00
☐ 145 Joe Medwick	200.00	100.00	20.00
☐ 146 Rip Collins	80.00	40.00	8.00
☐ 147 Mel Almada	80.00	40.00	8.00
☐ 148 Allan Cooke	80.00	40.00	8.00
☐ 149 Moe Berg	135.00	65.00	13.50
☐ 150 Dolph Camilli	80.00	40.00	8.00
☐ 151 Oscar Melillo	80.00	40.00	8.00
☐ 152 Bruce Campbell	80.00	40.00	8.00

☐ 153 Lefty Grove	300.00	150.00	30.00
☐ 154 Johnny Murphy	90.00	45.00	9.00
☐ 155 Luke Sewell	90.00	45.00	9.00
☐ 156 Leo Durocher	200.00	100.00	20.00
☐ 157 Lloyd Waner	175.00	85.00	18.00
☐ 158 Gus Bush	80.00	40.00	8.00
☐ 159 Jimmy Dykes	90.00	45.00	9.00
☐ 160 Steve O'Neill	80.00	40.00	8.00
☐ 161 General Crowder	80.00	40.00	8.00
☐ 162 Joe Cascarella	80.00	40.00	8.00
☐ 163 Daniel (Bud) Hafey	80.00	40.00	8.00
☐ 164 Gilly Campbell	80.00	40.00	8.00
☐ 165 Ray Hayworth	80.00	40.00	8.00
☐ 166 Frank Demaree	80.00	40.00	8.00
☐ 167 John Babich	80.00	40.00	8.00
☐ 168 Marvin Owen	80.00	40.00	8.00
☐ 169 Ralph Kress	80.00	40.00	8.00
☐ 170 Mule Haas	80.00	40.00	8.00
☐ 171 Frank Higgins	80.00	40.00	8.00
☐ 172 Wally Berger	90.00	45.00	9.00
☐ 173 Frank Frisch	200.00	100.00	20.00
☐ 174 Wes Ferrell	90.00	45.00	9.00
☐ 175 Pete Fox	80.00	40.00	8.00
☐ 176 John Vergez	80.00	40.00	8.00
☐ 177 Billy Rogell	80.00	40.00	8.00
☐ 178 Don Brennan	80.00	40.00	8.00
☐ 179 Jim Bottomley	175.00	85.00	18.00
☐ 180 Travis Jackson	175.00	85.00	18.00
☐ 181 Red Rolfe	100.00	50.00	10.00
☐ 182 Frank Crosetti	125.00	60.00	12.50
☐ 183 Joe Cronin	175.00	85.00	18.00
☐ 184 Schoolboy Rowe	100.00	50.00	10.00
☐ 185 Chuck Klein	200.00	100.00	20.00
☐ 186 Lon Warneke	80.00	40.00	8.00
☐ 187 Gus Suhr	80.00	40.00	8.00
☐ 188 Ben Chapman	90.00	45.00	9.00
☐ 189 Clint Brown	80.00	40.00	8.00
☐ 190 Paul Derringer	110.00	55.00	11.00
☐ 191 John Burns	80.00	40.00	8.00
☐ 192 John Broaca	135.00	65.00	13.50

1988 Bazooka

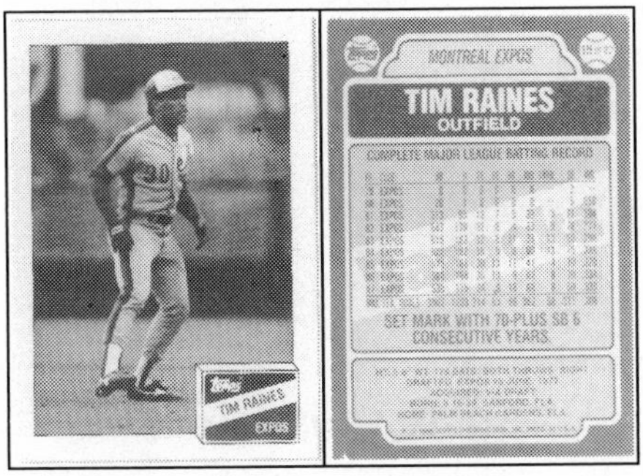

There are 22 cards in the set; cards are standard size, 2 1/2" by 3 1/2". The cards have extra thick white borders. Card backs are printed in blue and red on white card stock. Some sets can also be found with gray backs. Cards are numbered on the back; they were numbered by Topps alphabetically. The word "Bazooka" only appears faintly as background for the statistics on the back of the card. Cards were available inside specially marked boxes of Bazooka gum retailing between 59 cents and 99 cents. The emphasis in the player selection for this set is on the emerging young stars of baseball.

	MINT	EXC	G-VG
COMPLETE SET (22)	9.00	4.50	.90
COMMON PLAYER (1-22)	.30	.15	.03
☐ 1 George Bell	.50	.25	.05
☐ 2 Wade Boggs	1.00	.50	.10
☐ 3 Jose Canseco	1.50	.75	.15
☐ 4 Roger Clemens	1.00	.50	.10
☐ 5 Vince Coleman	.50	.25	.05
☐ 6 Eric Davis	1.00	.50	.10
☐ 7 Tony Fernandez	.30	.15	.03
☐ 8 Dwight Gooden	.80	.40	.08
☐ 9 Tony Gwynn	.60	.30	.06
☐ 10 Wally Joyner	.40	.20	.04
☐ 11 Don Mattingly	1.50	.75	.15
☐ 12 Willie McGee	.30	.15	.03
☐ 13 Mark McGwire	1.00	.50	.10
☐ 14 Kirby Puckett	1.00	.50	.10
☐ 15 Tim Raines	.40	.20	.04
☐ 16 Dave Righetti	.30	.15	.03
☐ 17 Cal Ripken	.60	.30	.06
☐ 18 Juan Samuel	.30	.15	.03
☐ 19 Ryne Sandberg	1.00	.50	.10
☐ 20 Benny Santiago	.40	.20	.04
☐ 21 Darryl Strawberry	1.00	.50	.10
☐ 22 Todd Worrell	.30	.15	.03

1989 Bazooka Shining Stars

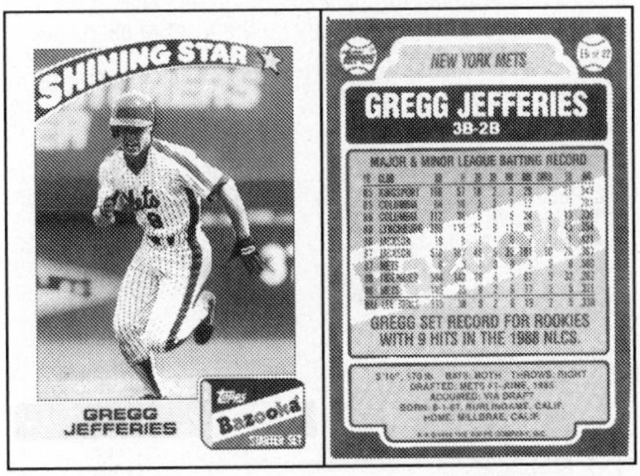

The 1989 Bazooka Shining Stars set contains 22 standard-size (2 1/2 by 3 1/2 inch) cards. The fronts have white borders and a large yellow stripe; the vertically-oriented backs are pink, red and white and have career stats. The cards were inserted one per box of Bazooka Gum.

	MINT	EXC	G-VG
COMPLETE SET (22)	8.00	4.00	.80
COMMON PLAYER (1-22)	.30	.15	.03
☐ 1 Tim Belcher	.30	.15	.03
☐ 2 Damon Berryhill	.30	.15	.03
☐ 3 Wade Boggs	1.00	.50	.10
☐ 4 Jay Buhner	.30	.15	.03
☐ 5 Jose Canseco	1.50	.75	.15
☐ 6 Vince Coleman	.50	.25	.05
☐ 7 Cecil Espy	.30	.15	.03
☐ 8 Dave Gallagher	.30	.15	.03
☐ 9 Ron Gant	.75	.35	.07
☐ 10 Kirk Gibson	.40	.20	.04
☐ 11 Paul Gibson	.30	.15	.03
☐ 12 Mark Grace	1.50	.75	.15
☐ 13 Tony Gwynn	.60	.30	.06
☐ 14 Rickey Henderson	1.00	.50	.10
☐ 15 Orel Hershiser	.60	.30	.06
☐ 16 Gregg Jefferies	.75	.35	.07
☐ 17 Ricky Jordan	.40	.20	.04
☐ 18 Chris Sabo	.60	.30	.06
☐ 19 Gary Sheffield	.60	.30	.06
☐ 20 Darryl Strawberry	1.00	.50	.10
☐ 21 Frank Viola	.40	.20	.04
☐ 22 Walt Weiss	.40	.20	.04

1990 Bazooka Shining Stars

The 1990 Bazooka Shining Stars set contains 22 cards with a mix of award winners, league leaders, and young stars. This standard-size (2 1/2" by 3 1/2") set was issued by Topps using the Bazooka name. Card backs were printed in blue and red on white card stock. Cards are numbered on the back; they were

numbered by Topps alphabetically. The word "Bazooka" appears faintly as background for the statistics on the back of the card as well as appearing prominently on the front of each card.

	MINT	EXC	G-VG
COMPLETE SET (22)	7.00	3.50	.70
COMMON PLAYER (1-22)	.25	.12	.02
☐ 1 Kevin Mitchell	.45	.22	.04
☐ 2 Robin Yount	.45	.22	.04
☐ 3 Mark Davis	.25	.12	.02
☐ 4 Bret Saberhagen	.35	.17	.03
☐ 5 Fred McGriff	.35	.17	.03
☐ 6 Tony Gwynn	.45	.22	.04
☐ 7 Kirby Puckett	.60	.30	.06
☐ 8 Vince Coleman	.35	.17	.03
☐ 9 Rickey Henderson	.75	.35	.07
☐ 10 Ben McDonald	.90	.45	.09
☐ 11 Gregg Olson	.35	.17	.03
☐ 12 Todd Zeile	.45	.22	.04
☐ 13 Carlos Martinez	.25	.12	.02
☐ 14 Gregg Jefferies	.75	.35	.07
☐ 15 Craig Worthington	.25	.12	.02
☐ 16 Gary Sheffield	.45	.22	.04
☐ 17 Greg Briley	.35	.17	.03
☐ 18 Ken Griffey Jr.	1.50	.75	.15
☐ 19 Jerome Walton	.75	.35	.07
☐ 20 Bob Geren	.25	.12	.02
☐ 21 Tom Gordon	.35	.17	.03
☐ 22 Jim Abbott	.60	.30	.06

1958 Bell Brand

The 1958 Bell Brand Potato Chips set of 10 unnumbered cards features members of the Los Angeles Dodgers exclusively. Each card has a 1/4" dark green border, and the Gino Cimoli, Johnny Podres, and Duke Snider cards are more difficult to find; they are marked with an SP (short printed) in the checklist below. The cards measure 3" by 4". This set marks the first year for the Dodgers in Los Angeles and includes a Campanella card despite the fact that he never played for the team in California. The catalog designation is F339-1. Cards found still inside the original cellophane wrapper are valued at 50 percent more than the prices below.

	NRMT	VG-E	GOOD
COMPLETE SET (10)	1150.00	550.00	125.00
COMMON PLAYER (1-10)	40.00	20.00	4.00
☐ 1 Roy Campanella	125.00	60.00	12.50
☐ 2 Gino Cimoli SP	150.00	75.00	15.00
☐ 3 Don Drysdale	100.00	50.00	10.00
☐ 4 Jim Gilliam	40.00	20.00	4.00
☐ 5 Gil Hodges	80.00	40.00	8.00
☐ 6 Sandy Koufax	150.00	75.00	15.00
☐ 7 Johnny Podres SP	150.00	75.00	15.00
☐ 8 Pee Wee Reese	100.00	50.00	10.00
☐ 9 Duke Snider SP	275.00	135.00	27.00
☐ 10 Don Zimmer	40.00	20.00	4.00

1960 Bell Brand

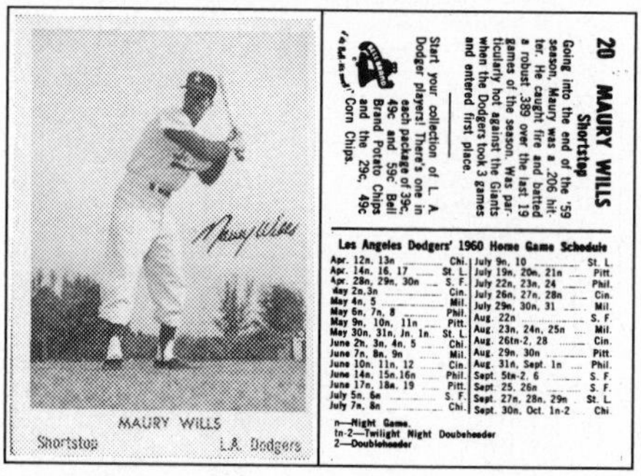

The 1960 Bell Brand Potato Chips set of 20 full color, numbered cards features Los Angeles Dodgers only. Because these cards, measuring approximately 2 1/2" by 3 1/2", were issued in packages of potato chips, many cards suffered from stains. Clem Labine, Johnny Klippstein, and Walter Alston are somewhat more difficult to obtain than other cards in the set; they are marked with SP (short printed) in the checklist below. The catalog designation for this set is F339-2.

	NRMT	VG-E	GOOD
COMPLETE SET (20)	800.00	400.00	80.00
COMMON PLAYER (1-20)	16.00	8.00	1.60
☐ 1 Norm Larker	16.00	8.00	1.60
☐ 2 Duke Snider	75.00	37.50	7.50
☐ 3 Danny McDevitt	16.00	8.00	1.60
☐ 4 Jim Gilliam	20.00	10.00	2.00
☐ 5 Rip Repulski	16.00	8.00	1.60
☐ 6 Clem Labine SP	100.00	50.00	10.00
☐ 7 John Roseboro	16.00	8.00	1.60
☐ 8 Carl Furillo	25.00	12.50	2.50
☐ 9 Sandy Koufax	125.00	60.00	12.50
☐ 10 Joe Pignatano	16.00	8.00	1.60
☐ 11 Chuck Essegian	16.00	8.00	1.60
☐ 12 John Klippstein SP	100.00	50.00	10.00
☐ 13 Ed Roebuck	16.00	8.00	1.60
☐ 14 Don Demeter	16.00	8.00	1.60
☐ 15 Roger Craig	25.00	12.50	2.50
☐ 16 Stan Williams	16.00	8.00	1.60
☐ 17 Don Zimmer	20.00	10.00	2.00
☐ 18 Walt Alston SP	150.00	75.00	15.00
☐ 19 Johnny Podres	25.00	12.50	2.50
☐ 20 Maury Wills	40.00	20.00	4.00

1961 Bell Brand

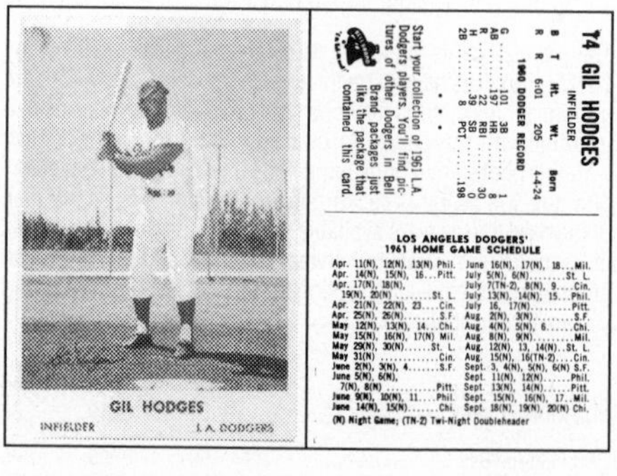

The 1961 Bell Brand Potato Chips set of 20 full color cards features Los Angeles Dodger players only and is numbered by the uniform numbers of the players. The cards are slightly smaller (2 7/16" by 3 1/2") than the 1960 Bell Brand cards and are on thinner paper stock. The catalog designation is F339-3.

	NRMT	VG-E	GOOD
COMPLETE SET (20)	400.00	200.00	40.00
COMMON PLAYER (1-51)	12.00	6.00	1.20
☐ 3 Willie Davis	15.00	7.50	1.50
☐ 4 Duke Snider	60.00	30.00	6.00
☐ 5 Norm Larker	12.00	6.00	1.20
☐ 8 John Roseboro	12.00	6.00	1.20
☐ 9 Wally Moon	12.00	6.00	1.20
☐ 11 Bob Lillis	12.00	6.00	1.20
☐ 12 Tom Davis	15.00	7.50	1.50
☐ 14 Gil Hodges	30.00	15.00	3.00
☐ 16 Don Demeter	12.00	6.00	1.20
☐ 19 Jim Gilliam	15.00	7.50	1.50
☐ 22 John Podres	15.00	7.50	1.50
☐ 24 Walt Alston MG	25.00	12.50	2.50
☐ 30 Maury Wills	25.00	12.50	2.50
☐ 32 Sandy Koufax	100.00	50.00	10.00
☐ 34 Norm Sherry	12.00	6.00	1.20
☐ 37 Ed Roebuck	12.00	6.00	1.20
☐ 38 Roger Craig	18.00	9.00	1.80
☐ 40 Stan Williams	12.00	6.00	1.20
☐ 43 Charlie Neal	12.00	6.00	1.20
☐ 51 Larry Sherry	12.00	6.00	1.20

1962 Bell Brand

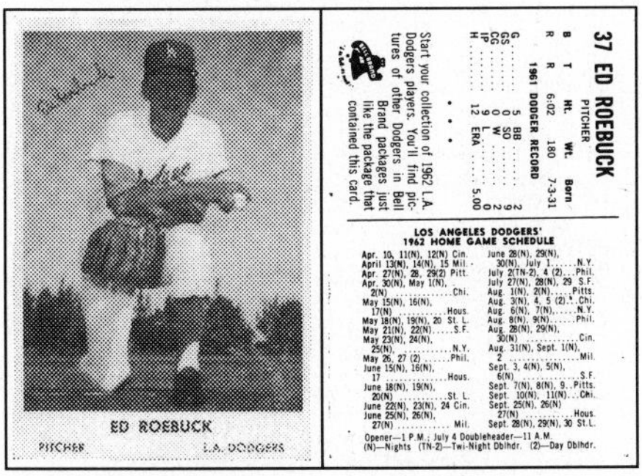

The 1962 Bell Brand Potato Chips set of 20 full color cards features Los Angeles Dodger players only and is numbered by the uniform numbers of the players. These cards were printed on a high quality glossy paper, much better than the previous two years, virtually eliminating the grease stains. This set is distinguished by a 1962 Home schedule on the backs of the cards. The cards measure 2 7/16" by 3 1/2", the same size as the year before. The catalog designation is F339-4.

	NRMT	VG-E	GOOD
COMPLETE SET (20)	400.00	200.00	40.00
COMMON PLAYER (1-56)	12.00	6.00	1.20
☐ 3 Willie Davis	15.00	7.50	1.50
☐ 4 Duke Snider	60.00	30.00	6.00
☐ 6 Ron Fairly	12.00	6.00	1.20
☐ 8 John Roseboro	12.00	6.00	1.20
☐ 9 Wally Moon	12.00	6.00	1.20
☐ 12 Tom Davis	15.00	7.50	1.50
☐ 16 Ron Perranoski	12.00	6.00	1.20
☐ 19 Jim Gilliam	15.00	7.50	1.50
☐ 20 Daryl Spencer	12.00	6.00	1.20
☐ 22 John Podres	15.00	7.50	1.50
☐ 24 Walt Alston MG	25.00	12.50	2.50
☐ 25 Frank Howard	15.00	7.50	1.50
☐ 30 Maury Wills	25.00	12.50	2.50
☐ 32 Sandy Koufax	100.00	50.00	10.00
☐ 34 Norm Sherry	12.00	6.00	1.20
☐ 37 Ed Roebuck	12.00	6.00	1.20
☐ 40 Stan Williams	12.00	6.00	1.20
☐ 51 Larry Sherry	12.00	6.00	1.20
☐ 53 Don Drysdale	40.00	20.00	4.00
☐ 56 Lee Walls	12.00	6.00	1.20

1951 Berk Ross

The 1951 Berk Ross set consists of 72 cards (each measuring 2 1/16" by 2 1/2") with tinted photographs, divided evenly into four series (designated in the checklist as A, B, C and D). The cards were marketed in boxes containing two card panels, without gum, and the set includes stars of other sports as well as baseball players. Intact panels are worth 20 percent more than the sum of the individual cards. The catalog designation is W532-1. In every series the first ten cards are baseball players; the set has a heavy emphasis on Yankees and Phillies players as they were in the World Series the year before.

	NRMT	VG-E	GOOD
COMPLETE SET (72)	750.00	375.00	75.00
COMMON BASEBALL	7.50	3.75	.75
COMMON FOOTBALL	7.50	3.75	.75
COMMON OTHERS	4.50	2.25	.45
☐ A1 Al Rosen	11.00	5.50	1.10
☐ A2 Bob Lemon	16.00	8.00	1.60
☐ A3 Phil Rizzuto	20.00	10.00	2.00
☐ A4 Hank Bauer	11.00	5.50	1.10
☐ A5 Billy Johnson	7.50	3.75	.75
☐ A6 Jerry Coleman	7.50	3.75	.75
☐ A7 Johnny Mize	20.00	10.00	2.00
☐ A8 Dom DiMaggio	11.00	5.50	1.10
☐ A9 Richie Ashburn	15.00	7.50	1.50
☐ A10 Del Ennis	7.50	3.75	.75
☐ A11 Bob Cousy	20.00	10.00	2.00
☐ A12 Dick Schnittker	4.50	2.25	.45
☐ A13 Ezzard Charles	7.50	3.75	.75
☐ A14 Leon Hart	9.00	4.50	.90
☐ A15 James Martin	7.50	3.75	.75
☐ A16 Ben Hogan	7.50	3.75	.75
☐ A17 Bill Durnan	10.00	5.00	1.00
☐ A18 Bill Quackenbush	7.50	3.75	.75
☐ B1 Stan Musial	75.00	37.50	7.50
☐ B2 Warren Spahn	25.00	12.50	2.50
☐ B3 Tom Henrich	11.00	5.50	1.10
☐ B4 Yogi Berra	50.00	25.00	5.00
☐ B5 Joe DiMaggio	125.00	60.00	12.50
☐ B6 Bobby Brown	10.00	5.00	1.00
☐ B7 Granny Hamner	7.50	3.75	.75
☐ B8 Willie Jones	7.50	3.75	.75
☐ B9 Stan Lopata	7.50	3.75	.75
☐ B10 Mike Goliat	7.50	3.75	.75
☐ B11 Sherman White	7.50	3.75	.75
☐ B12 Joe Maxim	6.00	3.00	.60
☐ B13 Ray Robinson	20.00	10.00	2.00
☐ B14 Doak Walker	12.00	6.00	1.20
☐ B15 Emil Sitko	4.50	2.25	.45
☐ B16 Jack Stewart	4.50	2.25	.45
☐ B17 Dick Button	7.50	3.75	.75
☐ B18 Melvin Patton	4.50	2.25	.45
☐ C1 Ralph Kiner	20.00	10.00	2.00
☐ C2 Bill Goodman	7.50	3.75	.75
☐ C3 Allie Reynolds	11.00	5.50	1.10
☐ C4 Vic Raschi	10.00	5.00	1.00
☐ C5 Joe Page	9.00	4.50	.90
☐ C6 Eddie Lopat	11.00	5.50	1.10
☐ C7 Andy Seminick	7.50	3.75	.75
☐ C8 Dick Sisler	7.50	3.75	.75
☐ C9 Eddie Waitkus	7.50	3.75	.75
☐ C10 Ken Heintzelman	7.50	3.75	.75
☐ C11 Paul Unruh	4.50	2.25	.45
☐ C12 Jake LaMotta	15.00	7.50	1.50
☐ C13 Ike Williams	4.50	2.25	.45
☐ C14 Wade Walker	4.50	2.25	.45
☐ C15 Rodney Franz	4.50	2.25	.45

☐ C16 Sid Abel	10.00	5.00	1.00
☐ C17 Claire Sherman	4.50	2.25	.45
☐ C18 Jesse Owens	12.00	6.00	1.20
☐ D1 Gene Woodling	9.00	4.50	.90
☐ D2 Cliff Mapes	7.50	3.75	.75
☐ D3 Fred Sanford	7.50	3.75	.75
☐ D4 Tommy Byrne	7.50	3.75	.75
☐ D5 Whitey Ford	25.00	12.50	2.50
☐ D6 Jim Konstanty	7.50	3.75	.75
☐ D7 Russ Meyer	7.50	3.75	.75
☐ D8 Robin Roberts	20.00	10.00	2.00
☐ D9 Curt Simmons	9.00	4.50	.90
☐ D10 Sam Jethroe	7.50	3.75	.75
☐ D11 Bill Sharman	12.00	6.00	1.20
☐ D12 Sandy Saddler	4.50	2.25	.45
☐ D13 Margaret DuPont	4.50	2.25	.45
☐ D14 Arnold Galiffa	7.50	3.75	.75
☐ D15 Charlie Justice	12.00	6.00	1.20
☐ D16 Glen Cunningham	6.00	3.00	.60
☐ D17 Gregory Rice	4.50	2.25	.45
☐ D18 Harrison Dillard	6.00	3.00	.60

1952 Berk Ross

The 1952 Berk Ross set of 72 unnumbered, tinted photocards, each measuring 2" by 3", seems to have been patterned after the highly successful 1951 Bowman set. The reverses of Ewell Blackwell and Nellie Fox are transposed while Phil Rizzuto comes with two different poses. There is a card of Joe DiMaggio even though he retired after the 1951 season. The catalog designation for this set is W532-2, and the cards have been assigned numbers in the alphabetical checklist below.

	NRMT	VG-E	GOOD
COMPLETE SET (72)	4000.00	1800.00	425.00
COMMON PLAYER (1-71)	12.00	6.00	1.20
☐ 1 Richie Ashburn	40.00	20.00	4.00
☐ 2 Hank Bauer	18.00	9.00	1.80
☐ 3 Yogi Berra	150.00	75.00	15.00
☐ 4 Ewell Blackwell UER (photo actually Nellie Fox)	21.00	10.50	2.10
☐ 5 Bobby Brown	18.00	9.00	1.80
☐ 6 Jim Busby	12.00	6.00	1.20
☐ 7 Roy Campanella	150.00	75.00	15.00
☐ 8 Chico Carrasquel	12.00	6.00	1.20
☐ 9 Jerry Coleman	12.00	6.00	1.20
☐ 10 Joe Collins	12.00	6.00	1.20
☐ 11 Alvin Dark	16.00	8.00	1.60
☐ 12 Dom DiMaggio	18.00	9.00	1.80
☐ 13 Joe DiMaggio	700.00	350.00	70.00
☐ 14 Larry Doby	21.00	10.50	2.10
☐ 15 Bobby Doerr	45.00	22.50	4.50
☐ 16 Bob Elliott	12.00	6.00	1.20
☐ 17 Del Ennis	12.00	6.00	1.20
☐ 18 Ferris Fain	12.00	6.00	1.20
☐ 19 Bob Feller	85.00	42.50	8.50
☐ 20 Nellie Fox (photo actually Ewell Blackwell)	21.00	10.50	2.10
☐ 21 Ned Garver	12.00	6.00	1.20
☐ 22 Clint Hartung	12.00	6.00	1.20
☐ 23 Jim Hearn	12.00	6.00	1.20
☐ 24 Gil Hodges	45.00	22.50	4.50
☐ 25 Monte Irvin	45.00	22.50	4.50
☐ 26 Larry Jansen	12.00	6.00	1.20
☐ 27 Sheldon Jones	12.00	6.00	1.20
☐ 28 George Kell	40.00	20.00	4.00
☐ 29 Monte Kennedy	12.00	6.00	1.20
☐ 30 Ralph Kiner	50.00	25.00	5.00
☐ 31 Dave Koslo	12.00	6.00	1.20
☐ 32 Bob Kuzava	12.00	6.00	1.20
☐ 33 Bob Lemon	40.00	20.00	4.00
☐ 34 Whitey Lockman	12.00	6.00	1.20
☐ 35 Ed Lopat	21.00	10.50	2.10
☐ 36 Sal Maglie	16.00	8.00	1.60
☐ 37 Mickey Mantle	1000.00	400.00	100.00
☐ 38 Billy Martin	50.00	25.00	5.00
☐ 39 Willie Mays	400.00	200.00	40.00
☐ 40 Gil McDougald	18.00	9.00	1.80
☐ 41 Minnie Minoso	18.00	9.00	1.80
☐ 42 Johnny Mize	50.00	25.00	5.00
☐ 43 Tom Morgan	12.00	6.00	1.20
☐ 44 Don Mueller	12.00	6.00	1.20
☐ 45 Stan Musial	225.00	110.00	22.00
☐ 46 Don Newcombe	21.00	10.50	2.10
☐ 47 Ray Noble	12.00	6.00	1.20
☐ 48 Joe Ostrowski	12.00	6.00	1.20
☐ 49 Mel Parnell	16.00	8.00	1.60
☐ 50 Vic Raschi	16.00	8.00	1.60
☐ 51 Pee Wee Reese	75.00	37.50	7.50
☐ 52 Allie Reynolds	21.00	10.50	2.10
☐ 53 Bill Rigney	12.00	6.00	1.20
☐ 54A Phil Rizzuto (bunting)	50.00	25.00	5.00
☐ 54B Phil Rizzuto (swinging)	50.00	25.00	5.00
☐ 55 Robin Roberts	40.00	20.00	4.00
☐ 56 Eddie Robinson	12.00	6.00	1.20
☐ 57 Jackie Robinson	225.00	110.00	22.00
☐ 58 Preacher Roe	16.00	8.00	1.60
☐ 59 Johnny Sain	18.00	9.00	1.80
☐ 60 Red Schoendienst	45.00	22.50	4.50
☐ 61 Duke Snider	150.00	75.00	15.00
☐ 62 George Spencer	12.00	6.00	1.20
☐ 63 Eddie Stanky	16.00	8.00	1.60
☐ 64 Hank Thompson	12.00	6.00	1.20
☐ 65 Bobby Thomson	18.00	9.00	1.80
☐ 66 Vic Wertz	12.00	6.00	1.20
☐ 67 Wally Westlake	12.00	6.00	1.20
☐ 68 Wes Westrum	12.00	6.00	1.20
☐ 69 Ted Williams	325.00	160.00	32.00
☐ 70 Gene Woodling	12.00	6.00	1.20
☐ 71 Gus Zernial	12.00	6.00	1.20

1986 Big League Chew

This 12-card set was produced by Big League Chew and was inserted in with their packages of chewing gum, which were shaped and styled after a pouch of chewing tobacco. The cards were found one per pouch of shredded chewing gum or were available through a mail-in offer of two coupons and 2.00 for a complete set. The players featured are members of the 500 career home run club. The backs are printed in blue ink on white card stock. The cards are standard size, 2 1/2" by 3 1/2" and are subtitled "Home Run Legends." The front of each card shows a year inside a small flag; the year is the year that player passed 500 homers.

	MINT	EXC	G-VG
COMPLETE SET (12)	5.00	2.50	.50
COMMON PLAYER (1-12)	.30	.15	.03
☐ 1 Hank Aaron	.65	.30	.06
☐ 2 Babe Ruth	1.25	.60	.12
☐ 3 Willie Mays	.65	.30	.06
☐ 4 Frank Robinson	.45	.22	.04
☐ 5 Harmon Killebrew	.30	.15	.03
☐ 6 Mickey Mantle	1.25	.60	.12
☐ 7 Jimmie Foxx	.30	.15	.03
☐ 8 Ted Williams	.65	.30	.06
☐ 9 Ernie Banks	.45	.22	.04
☐ 10 Eddie Mathews	.30	.15	.03
☐ 11 Mel Ott	.30	.15	.03
☐ 12 500 HR Members	.30	.15	.03

1987 Boardwalk and Baseball

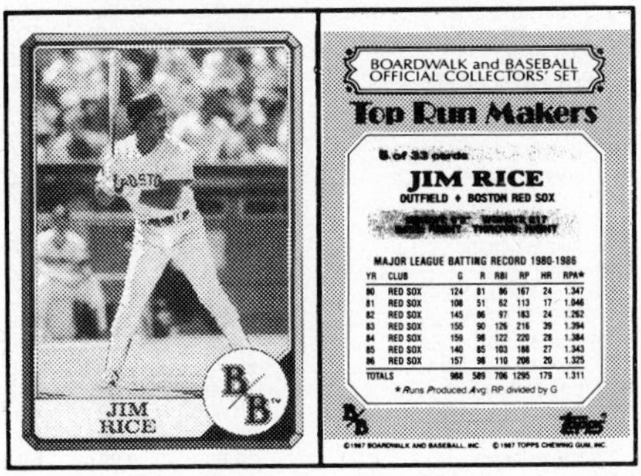

This 33-card set was produced by Topps for distribution by the "Boardwalk and Baseball" Theme Park located near Orlando, Florida. The cards are standard size, 2 1/2" by 3 1/2", and come in a custom blue collector box. The full-color fronts are surrounded by a pink and black frame border. The card backs are printed in pink and black on white card stock. The set is subtitled "Top Run Makers." Hence no pitchers are included in the set. The checklist for the set is given on the back panel of the box.

	MINT	EXC	G-VG
COMPLETE SET (33)	6.00	3.00	.60
COMMON PLAYER (1-33)	.12	.06	.01
☐ 1 Mike Schmidt	.75	.35	.07
☐ 2 Eddie Murray	.40	.20	.04
☐ 3 Dale Murphy	.40	.20	.04
☐ 4 Dave Winfield	.25	.12	.02
☐ 5 Jim Rice	.20	.10	.02
☐ 6 Cecil Cooper	.12	.06	.01
☐ 7 Dwight Evans	.15	.07	.01
☐ 8 Rickey Henderson	.75	.35	.07
☐ 9 Robin Yount	.40	.20	.04
☐ 10 Andre Dawson	.30	.15	.03
☐ 11 Gary Carter	.20	.10	.02
☐ 12 Keith Hernandez	.20	.10	.02
☐ 13 George Brett	.40	.20	.04
☐ 14 Bill Buckner	.12	.06	.01
☐ 15 Tony Armas	.12	.06	.01
☐ 16 Harold Baines	.15	.07	.01
☐ 17 Don Baylor	.12	.06	.01
☐ 18 Steve Garvey	.25	.12	.02
☐ 19 Lance Parrish	.15	.07	.01
☐ 20 Dave Parker	.15	.07	.01
☐ 21 Buddy Bell	.12	.06	.01
☐ 22 Cal Ripken	.40	.20	.04
☐ 23 Bob Horner	.12	.06	.01
☐ 24 Tim Raines	.30	.15	.03
☐ 25 Jack Clark	.20	.10	.02
☐ 26 Leon Durham	.12	.06	.01
☐ 27 Pedro Guerrero	.15	.07	.01
☐ 28 Kent Hrbek	.20	.10	.02
☐ 29 Kirk Gibson	.30	.15	.03
☐ 30 Ryne Sandberg	.75	.35	.07
☐ 31 Wade Boggs	.75	.35	.07
☐ 32 Don Mattingly	1.00	.50	.10
☐ 33 Darryl Strawberry	.60	.30	.06

1987 Bohemian Padres

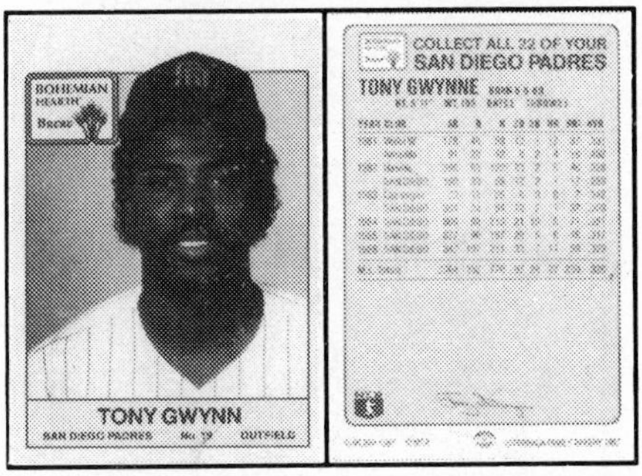

The Bohemian Hearth Bread Company issued this 22-card set of San Diego Padres. The cards measure 2 1/2" by 3 1/2" and feature a distinctive yellow border on the front of the cards. Card backs provide career year-by-year statistics and are numbered.

	MINT	EXC	G-VG
COMPLETE SET (22)	45.00	22.50	4.50
COMMON PLAYER	.75	.35	.07
☐ 1 Garry Templeton	1.00	.50	.10
☐ 4 Joe Cora	.90	.45	.09
☐ 5 Randy Ready	.90	.45	.09
☐ 6 Steve Garvey	6.00	3.00	.60
☐ 7 Kevin Mitchell	7.50	3.75	.75
☐ 8 John Kruk	2.00	1.00	.20
☐ 9 Benito Santiago	6.00	3.00	.60
☐ 10 Larry Bowa MG	1.00	.50	.10
☐ 11 Tim Flannery	.75	.35	.07
☐ 14 Carmelo Martinez	1.00	.50	.10
☐ 16 Marvell Wynne	.75	.35	.07
☐ 19 Tony Gwynn	12.00	6.00	1.20
☐ 21 James Steels	.75	.35	.07
☐ 22 Stan Jefferson	1.00	.50	.10
☐ 30 Eric Show	1.00	.50	.10
☐ 31 Ed Whitson	1.00	.50	.10
☐ 34 Storm Davis	2.00	1.00	.20
☐ 37 Craig Lefferts	1.00	.50	.10
☐ 40 Andy Hawkins	1.00	.50	.10
☐ 41 Lance McCullers	.90	.45	.09
☐ 43 Dave Dravecky	2.00	1.00	.20
☐ 54 Rich Gossage	2.00	1.00	.20

1947 Bond Bread

The 1947 Bond Bread Jackie Robinson set features 13 unnumbered cards of Jackie in different action or portrait poses; each card measures approximately 2 1/4" by 3 1/2". Card number 7, which is the only card in the set to contain a facsimile autograph, was apparently issued in greater quantity than other cards in the set. Several of the cards have a horizontal format; these are marked in the checklist below by HOR. The catalog designation is D302.

	NRMT	VG-E	GOOD
COMPLETE SET (13)	4200.00	2000.00	450.00
COMMON PLAYER (1-13)	350.00	175.00	35.00
☐ 1 Sliding into base, cap, ump in photo, HOR	350.00	175.00	35.00
☐ 2 Running down 3rd base line	350.00	175.00	35.00

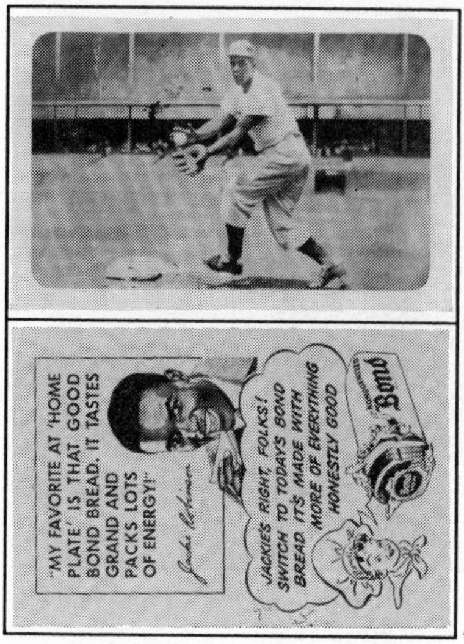

☐ 3 Batting, bat behind head, facing camera	350.00	175.00	35.00
☐ 4 Moving towards second, throw almost to glove, HOR	350.00	175.00	35.00
☐ 5 Taking throw at first, HOR	350.00	175.00	35.00
☐ 6 Jumping high in the air for ball	350.00	175.00	35.00
☐ 7 Profile with glove in front of head; facsimile autograph)	250.00	125.00	25.00
☐ 8 Leaping over second base, ready to throw	350.00	175.00	35.00
☐ 9 Portrait, holding glove over head	350.00	175.00	35.00
☐ 10 Portrait, holding bat perpendicular to body	350.00	175.00	35.00
☐ 11 Reaching for throw, glove near ankle	350.00	175.00	35.00
☐ 12 Leaping for throw, no scoreboard in background	350.00	175.00	35.00
☐ 13 Portrait, holding bat parallel to body	350.00	175.00	35.00

1948 Bowman

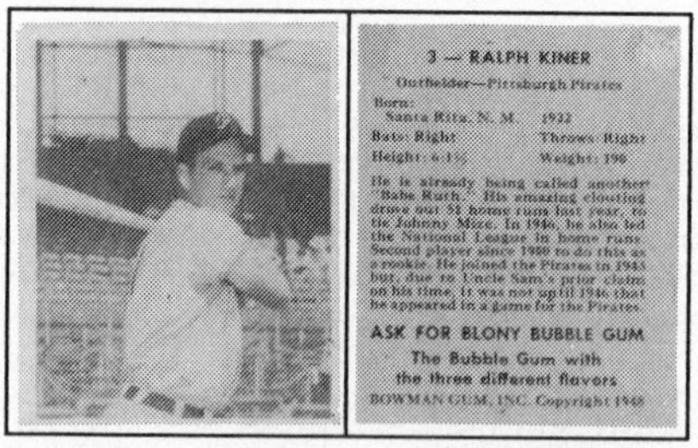

The 48-card Bowman set of 1948 was the first major set of the post-war period. Each 2 1/16" by 2 1/2" card had a black and white photo of a current player, with his biographical information printed in black ink on a gray back. Due to the printing process and the 36-card sheet size upon which Bowman was then printing, the 12 cards marked with an SP in the checklist are scarcer numerically, as they were removed from the printing sheet in order to make room for the 12 high numbers (37-48). Many cards are found with over-printed, transposed, or blank backs. The set features the Rookie Cards of Hall of Famers Yogi Berra, Ralph Kiner, Stan Musial, Red Schoendienst, and Warren Spahn. Half of the cards in the set feature New York players (Yankees or Giants).

	NRMT	VG-E	GOOD
COMPLETE SET	2900.00	1400.00	300.00
COMMON PLAYER (1-36)	16.00	8.00	1.60
COMMON PLAYER (37-48)	25.00	12.50	2.50
COMMON PLAYER SP	33.00	16.00	3.00
☐ 1 Bob Elliott	80.00	10.00	2.00
☐ 2 Ewell Blackwell	33.00	16.00	3.00
☐ 3 Ralph Kiner	135.00	65.00	13.50
☐ 4 Johnny Mize	85.00	42.50	8.50
☐ 5 Bob Feller	175.00	85.00	18.00
☐ 6 Yogi Berra	450.00	225.00	45.00
☐ 7 Pete Reiser SP	42.00	20.00	4.00
☐ 8 Phil Rizzuto SP	225.00	110.00	22.00
☐ 9 Walker Cooper	16.00	8.00	1.60
☐ 10 Buddy Rosar	16.00	8.00	1.60
☐ 11 Johnny Lindell	16.00	8.00	1.60
☐ 12 Johnny Sain	40.00	20.00	4.00
☐ 13 Willard Marshall SP	33.00	16.00	3.00
☐ 14 Allie Reynolds	40.00	20.00	4.00
☐ 15 Eddie Joost	16.00	8.00	1.60
☐ 16 Jack Lohrke SP	33.00	16.00	3.00
☐ 17 Enos Slaughter	85.00	42.50	8.50
☐ 18 Warren Spahn	225.00	110.00	22.00
☐ 19 Tommy Henrich	25.00	12.50	2.50
☐ 20 Buddy Kerr SP	33.00	16.00	3.00
☐ 21 Ferris Fain	20.00	10.00	2.00
☐ 22 Floyd Bevens SP	33.00	16.00	3.00
☐ 23 Larry Jansen	18.00	9.00	1.80
☐ 24 Dutch Leonard SP	33.00	16.00	3.00
☐ 25 Barney McCosky	16.00	8.00	1.60
☐ 26 Frank Shea SP	33.00	16.00	3.00
☐ 27 Sid Gordon	16.00	8.00	1.60
☐ 28 Emil Verban SP	33.00	16.00	3.00
☐ 29 Joe Page SP	40.00	20.00	4.00
☐ 30 Whitey Lockman SP	36.00	18.00	3.60
☐ 31 Bill McCahan	16.00	8.00	1.60
☐ 32 Bill Rigney	18.00	9.00	1.80
☐ 33 Bill Johnson	16.00	8.00	1.60
☐ 34 Sheldon Jones SP	33.00	16.00	3.00
☐ 35 Snuffy Stirnweiss	20.00	10.00	2.00
☐ 36 Stan Musial	700.00	350.00	70.00
☐ 37 Clint Hartung	25.00	12.50	2.50
☐ 38 Red Schoendienst	110.00	55.00	11.00
☐ 39 Augie Galan	25.00	12.50	2.50
☐ 40 Marty Marion	60.00	30.00	6.00
☐ 41 Rex Barney	25.00	12.50	2.50
☐ 42 Ray Poat	25.00	12.50	2.50
☐ 43 Bruce Edwards	25.00	12.50	2.50
☐ 44 Johnny Wyrostek	25.00	12.50	2.50
☐ 45 Hank Sauer	36.00	18.00	3.60
☐ 46 Herman Wehmeier	25.00	12.50	2.50
☐ 47 Bobby Thomson	60.00	30.00	6.00
☐ 48 Dave Koslo	60.00	15.00	3.00

1949 Bowman

The cards in this 240-card set measure 2 1/16" by 2 1/2". In 1949 Bowman took an intermediate step between black and white and full color with this set of tinted photos on colored backgrounds. Collectors should note the series price variations, which reflect some inconsistencies in the printing process. There are four major varieties in name printing, which are noted in the checklist below: NOF: name on front; NNOF: no name on front; PR: printed name on back; and SCR: script name on back. These variations resulted when Bowman used twelve of the lower numbers to fill out the last press sheet of 36 cards, adding to numbers 217-240. Cards 1-3 and 5-73 can be found with either gray or white backs. The set features the Rookie Cards of

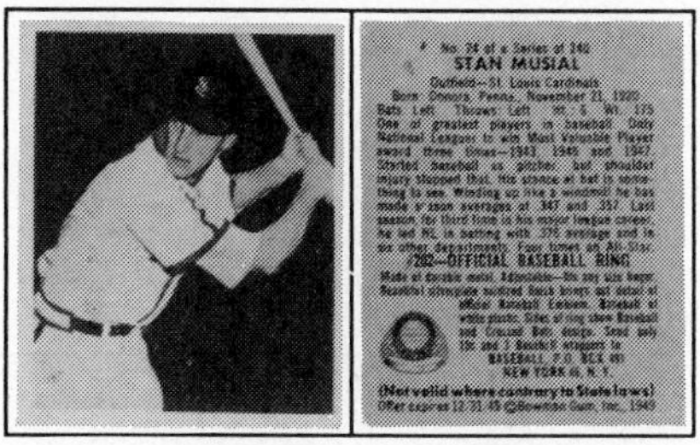

Hall of Famers Roy Campanella, Bob Lemon, Robin Roberts, Duke Snider, and Early Wynn as well as Rookie Cards of Richie Ashburn and Gil Hodges.

	NRMT	VG-E	GOOD
COMPLETE SET	15000.00	6000.00	1500.00
COMMON CARD 1-3/5-36/73	14.00	7.00	1.40
COMMON CARD (37-72)	16.00	8.00	1.60
COMMON CARD (4/74-108)	14.00	7.00	1.40
COMMON CARD (109-144)	12.50	6.25	1.25
COMMON CARD (145-180)	85.00	42.50	8.50
COMMON CARD (181-216)	75.00	37.50	7.50
COMMON CARD (217-240)	75.00	37.50	7.50
☐ 1 Vern Bickford	75.00	10.00	2.00
☐ 2 Whitey Lockman	16.00	8.00	1.60
☐ 3 Bob Porterfield	14.00	7.00	1.40
☐ 4A Jerry Priddy NNOF	14.00	7.00	1.40
☐ 4B Jerry Priddy NOF	40.00	20.00	4.00
☐ 5 Hank Sauer	18.00	9.00	1.80
☐ 6 Phil Cavarretta	18.00	9.00	1.80
☐ 7 Joe Dobson	14.00	7.00	1.40
☐ 8 Murry Dickson	14.00	7.00	1.40
☐ 9 Ferris Fain	18.00	9.00	1.80
☐ 10 Ted Gray	14.00	7.00	1.40
☐ 11 Lou Boudreau MG	55.00	27.50	5.50
☐ 12 Cass Michaels	14.00	7.00	1.40
☐ 13 Bob Chesnes	14.00	7.00	1.40
☐ 14 Curt Simmons	25.00	12.50	2.50
☐ 15 Ned Garver	14.00	7.00	1.40
☐ 16 Al Kozar	14.00	7.00	1.40
☐ 17 Earl Torgeson	14.00	7.00	1.40
☐ 18 Bobby Thomson	24.00	12.00	2.40
☐ 19 Bobby Brown	40.00	18.00	3.75
☐ 20 Gene Hermanski	14.00	7.00	1.40
☐ 21 Frank Baumholtz	14.00	7.00	1.40
☐ 22 Peanuts Lowrey	14.00	7.00	1.40
☐ 23 Bobby Doerr	65.00	32.50	6.50
☐ 24 Stan Musial	450.00	225.00	45.00
☐ 25 Carl Scheib	14.00	7.00	1.40
☐ 26 George Kell	50.00	25.00	5.00
☐ 27 Bob Feller	135.00	65.00	13.50
☐ 28 Don Kolloway	14.00	7.00	1.40
☐ 29 Ralph Kiner	75.00	37.50	7.50
☐ 30 Andy Seminick	14.00	7.00	1.40
☐ 31 Dick Kokos	14.00	7.00	1.40
☐ 32 Eddie Yost	14.00	7.00	1.40
☐ 33 Warren Spahn	150.00	75.00	15.00
☐ 34 Dave Koslo	14.00	7.00	1.40
☐ 35 Vic Raschi	35.00	17.50	3.50
☐ 36 Pee Wee Reese	150.00	75.00	15.00
☐ 37 Johnny Wyrostek	16.00	8.00	1.60
☐ 38 Emil Verban	16.00	8.00	1.60
☐ 39 Billy Goodman	18.00	9.00	1.80
☐ 40 Red Munger	16.00	8.00	1.60
☐ 41 Lou Brissie	16.00	8.00	1.60
☐ 42 Hoot Evers	16.00	8.00	1.60
☐ 43 Dale Mitchell	18.00	9.00	1.80
☐ 44 Dave Philley	16.00	8.00	1.60
☐ 45 Wally Westlake	16.00	8.00	1.60
☐ 46 Robin Roberts	250.00	125.00	25.00
☐ 47 Johnny Sain	27.00	13.50	2.70
☐ 48 Willard Marshall	16.00	8.00	1.60
☐ 49 Frank Shea	16.00	8.00	1.60
☐ 50 Jackie Robinson	650.00	325.00	65.00
☐ 51 Herman Wehmeier	16.00	8.00	1.60
☐ 52 Johnny Schmitz	16.00	8.00	1.60
☐ 53 Jack Kramer	16.00	8.00	1.60
☐ 54 Marty Marion	25.00	12.50	2.50
☐ 55 Eddie Joost	16.00	8.00	1.60
☐ 56 Pat Mullin	16.00	8.00	1.60
☐ 57 Gene Bearden	16.00	8.00	1.60
☐ 58 Bob Elliott	18.00	9.00	1.80
☐ 59 Jack Lohrke	16.00	8.00	1.60
☐ 60 Yogi Berra	300.00	150.00	30.00
☐ 61 Rex Barney	16.00	8.00	1.60
☐ 62 Grady Hatton	16.00	8.00	1.60
☐ 63 Andy Pafko	18.00	9.00	1.80
☐ 64 Dom DiMaggio	25.00	12.50	2.50
☐ 65 Enos Slaughter	75.00	37.50	7.50
☐ 66 Elmer Valo	16.00	8.00	1.60
☐ 67 Alvin Dark	25.00	12.50	2.50
☐ 68 Sheldon Jones	16.00	8.00	1.60
☐ 69 Tommy Henrich	24.00	12.00	2.40
☐ 70 Carl Furillo	45.00	22.50	4.50
☐ 71 Vern Stephens	18.00	9.00	1.80
☐ 72 Tommy Holmes	18.00	9.00	1.80
☐ 73 Billy Cox	24.00	12.00	2.40
☐ 74 Tom McBride	14.00	7.00	1.40
☐ 75 Eddie Mayo	14.00	7.00	1.40
☐ 76 Bill Nicholson	14.00	7.00	1.40
☐ 77 Ernie Bonham	14.00	7.00	1.40
☐ 78A Sam Zoldak NNOF	14.00	7.00	1.40
☐ 78B Sam Zoldak NOF	40.00	20.00	4.00
☐ 79 Ron Northey	14.00	7.00	1.40
☐ 80 Bill McCahan	14.00	7.00	1.40
☐ 81 Virgil Stallcup	14.00	7.00	1.40
☐ 82 Joe Page	21.00	10.50	2.10
☐ 83A Bob Scheffing NNOF	14.00	7.00	1.40
☐ 83B Bob Scheffing NOF	40.00	20.00	4.00
☐ 84 Roy Campanella	600.00	300.00	60.00
☐ 85A Johnny Mize NNOF	70.00	35.00	7.00
☐ 85B Johnny Mize NOF	125.00	60.00	12.50
☐ 86 Johnny Pesky	16.00	8.00	1.60
☐ 87 Randy Gumpert	14.00	7.00	1.40
☐ 88A Bill Salkeld NNOF	14.00	7.00	1.40
☐ 88B Bill Salkeld NOF	40.00	20.00	4.00
☐ 89 Mizell Platt	14.00	7.00	1.40
☐ 90 Gil Coan	14.00	7.00	1.40
☐ 91 Dick Wakefield	14.00	7.00	1.40
☐ 92 Willie Jones	14.00	7.00	1.40
☐ 93 Ed Stevens	14.00	7.00	1.40
☐ 94 Mickey Vernon	27.00	13.50	2.70
☐ 95 Howie Pollet	14.00	7.00	1.40
☐ 96 Taft Wright	14.00	7.00	1.40
☐ 97 Danny Litwhiler	14.00	7.00	1.40
☐ 98A Phil Rizzuto NNOF	90.00	45.00	9.00
☐ 98B Phil Rizzuto NOF	180.00	90.00	18.00
☐ 99 Frank Gustine	14.00	7.00	1.40
☐ 100 Gil Hodges	180.00	90.00	18.00
☐ 101 Sid Gordon	14.00	7.00	1.40
☐ 102 Stan Spence	14.00	7.00	1.40
☐ 103 Joe Tipton	14.00	7.00	1.40
☐ 104 Eddie Stanky	24.00	12.00	2.40
☐ 105 Bill Kennedy	14.00	7.00	1.40
☐ 106 Jake Early	14.00	7.00	1.40
☐ 107 Eddie Lake	14.00	7.00	1.40
☐ 108 Ken Heintzelman	14.00	7.00	1.40
☐ 109A Ed Fitzgerald SCR	12.50	6.25	1.25
☐ 109B Ed Fitzgerald PR	35.00	17.50	3.50
☐ 110 Early Wynn	120.00	60.00	12.00
☐ 111 Red Schoendienst	70.00	35.00	7.00
☐ 112 Sam Chapman	12.50	6.25	1.25
☐ 113 Ray LaManno	12.50	6.25	1.25
☐ 114 Allie Reynolds	27.00	13.50	2.70
☐ 115 Dutch Leonard	12.50	6.25	1.25
☐ 116 Joe Hatton	12.50	6.25	1.25
☐ 117 Walker Cooper	12.50	6.25	1.25
☐ 118 Sam Mele	12.50	6.25	1.25
☐ 119 Floyd Baker	12.50	6.25	1.25
☐ 120 Cliff Fannin	12.50	6.25	1.25
☐ 121 Mark Christman	12.50	6.25	1.25
☐ 122 George Vico	12.50	6.25	1.25
☐ 123 Johnny Blatnick	12.50	6.25	1.25
☐ 124A Danny Murtaugh SCR	12.50	6.25	1.25
☐ 124B Danny Murtaugh PR	35.00	17.50	3.50
☐ 125 Ken Keltner	14.00	7.00	1.40
☐ 126A Al Brazle SCR	12.50	6.25	1.25
☐ 126B Al Brazle PR	35.00	17.50	3.50
☐ 127A Hank Majeski SCR	12.50	6.25	1.25
☐ 127B Hank Majeski PR	35.00	17.50	3.50
☐ 128 Johnny VanderMeer	21.00	10.50	2.10
☐ 129 Bill Johnson	12.50	6.25	1.25
☐ 130 Harry Walker	12.50	6.25	1.25
☐ 131 Paul Lehner	12.50	6.25	1.25
☐ 132A Al Evans SCR	12.50	6.25	1.25
☐ 132B Al Evans PR	35.00	17.50	3.50
☐ 133 Aaron Robinson	12.50	6.25	1.25
☐ 134 Hank Borowy	12.50	6.25	1.25
☐ 135 Stan Rojek	12.50	6.25	1.25
☐ 136 Hank Edwards	12.50	6.25	1.25
☐ 137 Ted Wilks	12.50	6.25	1.25
☐ 138 Buddy Rosar	12.50	6.25	1.25
☐ 139 Hank Arft	12.50	6.25	1.25
☐ 140 Ray Scarborough	12.50	6.25	1.25
☐ 141 Ulysses Lupien	12.50	6.25	1.25
☐ 142 Eddie Waitkus	14.00	7.00	1.40
☐ 143A Bob Dillinger SCR	12.50	6.25	1.25

☐ 143B Bob Dillinger PR	35.00	17.50	3.50
☐ 144 Mickey Haefner	12.50	6.25	1.25
☐ 145 Sylvester Donnelly	85.00	42.50	8.50
☐ 146 Mike McCormick	85.00	42.50	8.50
☐ 147 Bert Singleton	85.00	42.50	8.50
☐ 148 Bob Swift	85.00	42.50	8.50
☐ 149 Roy Partee	85.00	42.50	8.50
☐ 150 Allie Clark	85.00	42.50	8.50
☐ 151 Mickey Harris	85.00	42.50	8.50
☐ 152 Clarence Maddern	85.00	42.50	8.50
☐ 153 Phil Masi	85.00	42.50	8.50
☐ 154 Clint Hartung	85.00	42.50	8.50
☐ 155 Mickey Guerra	85.00	42.50	8.50
☐ 156 Al Zarilla	85.00	42.50	8.50
☐ 157 Walt Masterson	85.00	42.50	8.50
☐ 158 Harry Brecheen	90.00	45.00	9.00
☐ 159 Glen Moulder	85.00	42.50	8.50
☐ 160 Jim Blackburn	85.00	42.50	8.50
☐ 161 Jocko Thompson	85.00	42.50	8.50
☐ 162 Preacher Roe	125.00	60.00	12.50
☐ 163 Clyde McCullough	85.00	42.50	8.50
☐ 164 Vic Wertz	90.00	45.00	9.00
☐ 165 Snuffy Stirnweiss	90.00	45.00	9.00
☐ 166 Mike Tresh	85.00	42.50	8.50
☐ 167 Babe Martin	85.00	42.50	8.50
☐ 168 Doyle Lade	85.00	42.50	8.50
☐ 169 Jeff Heath	85.00	42.50	8.50
☐ 170 Bill Rigney	90.00	45.00	9.00
☐ 171 Dick Fowler	85.00	42.50	8.50
☐ 172 Eddie Pellagrini	85.00	42.50	8.50
☐ 173 Eddie Stewart	85.00	42.50	8.50
☐ 174 Terry Moore	100.00	50.00	10.00
☐ 175 Luke Appling	125.00	60.00	12.50
☐ 176 Ken Raffensberger	85.00	42.50	8.50
☐ 177 Stan Lopata	85.00	42.50	8.50
☐ 178 Tom Brown	85.00	42.50	8.50
☐ 179 Hugh Casey	90.00	45.00	9.00
☐ 180 Connie Berry	85.00	42.50	8.50
☐ 181 Gus Niarhos	75.00	37.50	7.50
☐ 182 Hal Peck	75.00	37.50	7.50
☐ 183 Lou Stringer	75.00	37.50	7.50
☐ 184 Bob Chipman	75.00	37.50	7.50
☐ 185 Pete Reiser	90.00	45.00	9.00
☐ 186 Buddy Kerr	75.00	37.50	7.50
☐ 187 Phil Marchildon	75.00	37.50	7.50
☐ 188 Karl Drews	75.00	37.50	7.50
☐ 189 Earl Wooten	75.00	37.50	7.50
☐ 190 Jim Hearn	75.00	37.50	7.50
☐ 191 Joe Haynes	75.00	37.50	7.50
☐ 192 Harry Gumbert	75.00	37.50	7.50
☐ 193 Ken Trinkle	75.00	37.50	7.50
☐ 194 Ralph Branca	100.00	50.00	10.00
☐ 195 Eddie Bockman	75.00	37.50	7.50
☐ 196 Fred Hutchinson	90.00	45.00	9.00
☐ 197 Johnny Lindell	75.00	37.50	7.50
☐ 198 Steve Gromek	75.00	37.50	7.50
☐ 199 Tex Hughson	75.00	37.50	7.50
☐ 200 Jess Dobernic	75.00	37.50	7.50
☐ 201 Sibby Sisti	75.00	37.50	7.50
☐ 202 Larry Jansen	90.00	45.00	9.00
☐ 203 Barney McCosky	75.00	37.50	7.50
☐ 204 Bob Savage	75.00	37.50	7.50
☐ 205 Dick Sisler	75.00	37.50	7.50
☐ 206 Bruce Edwards	75.00	37.50	7.50
☐ 207 Johnny Hopp	90.00	45.00	9.00
☐ 208 Dizzy Trout	90.00	45.00	9.00
☐ 209 Charlie Keller	100.00	50.00	10.00
☐ 210 Joe Gordon	100.00	50.00	10.00
☐ 211 Boo Ferriss	75.00	37.50	7.50
☐ 212 Ralph Hamner	75.00	37.50	7.50
☐ 213 Red Barrett	75.00	37.50	7.50
☐ 214 Richie Ashburn	500.00	250.00	50.00
☐ 215 Kirby Higbe	75.00	37.50	7.50
☐ 216 Schoolboy Rowe	90.00	45.00	9.00
☐ 217 Marino Pieretti	75.00	37.50	7.50
☐ 218 Dick Kryhoski	75.00	37.50	7.50
☐ 219 Virgil Fire Trucks	90.00	45.00	9.00
☐ 220 Johnny McCarthy	75.00	37.50	7.50
☐ 221 Bob Muncrief	75.00	37.50	7.50
☐ 222 Alex Kellner	75.00	37.50	7.50
☐ 223 Bobby Hofman	75.00	37.50	7.50
☐ 224 Satchell Paige	1200.00	500.00	100.00
☐ 225 Gerry Coleman	90.00	45.00	9.00
☐ 226 Duke Snider	1000.00	400.00	80.00
☐ 227 Fritz Ostermueller	75.00	37.50	7.50
☐ 228 Jackie Mayo	75.00	37.50	7.50
☐ 229 Ed Lopat	135.00	65.00	13.50
☐ 230 Augie Galan	75.00	37.50	7.50
☐ 231 Earl Johnson	75.00	37.50	7.50
☐ 232 George McQuinn	75.00	37.50	7.50
☐ 233 Larry Doby	150.00	75.00	15.00
☐ 234 Rip Sewell	75.00	37.50	7.50
☐ 235 Jim Russell	75.00	37.50	7.50
☐ 236 Fred Sanford	75.00	37.50	7.50
☐ 237 Monte Kennedy	75.00	37.50	7.50
☐ 238 Bob Lemon	250.00	125.00	25.00
☐ 239 Frank McCormick	90.00	45.00	9.00
☐ 240 Babe Young UER (photo actually Bobby Young)	125.00	60.00	12.50

1950 Bowman

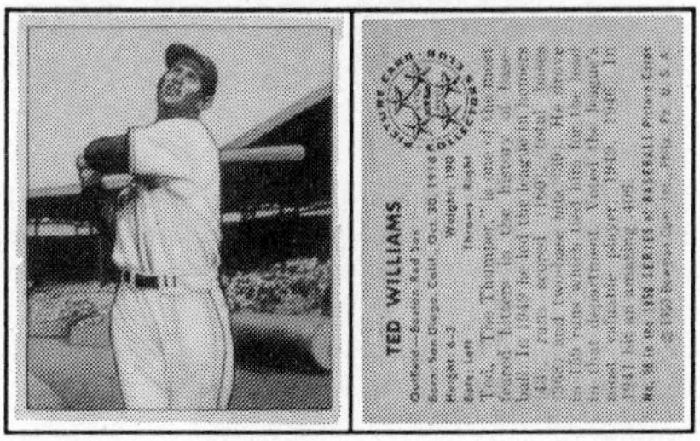

The cards in this 252-card set measure 2 1/16" by 2 1/2". This set, marketed in 1950 by Bowman, represented a major improvement in terms of quality over their previous efforts. Each card was a beautifully colored line drawing developed from a simple photograph. The first 72 cards are the scarcest in the set, while the final 72 cards may be found with or without the copyright line. This was the only Bowman sports set to carry the famous "5-Star" logo. Key rookies in this set are Hank Bauer, Don Newcombe, and Al Rosen.

	NRMT	VG-E	GOOD
COMPLETE SET	8250.00	3750.00	850.00
COMMON PLAYER (1-72)	45.00	22.50	4.50
COMMON PLAYER (73-252)	16.00	8.00	1.60
☐ 1 Mel Parnell	200.00	25.00	5.00
☐ 2 Vern Stephens	50.00	25.00	5.00
☐ 3 Dom DiMaggio	55.00	27.50	5.50
☐ 4 Gus Zernial	50.00	25.00	5.00
☐ 5 Bob Kuzava	45.00	22.50	4.50
☐ 6 Bob Feller	150.00	75.00	15.00
☐ 7 Jim Hegan	50.00	25.00	5.00
☐ 8 George Kell	80.00	40.00	8.00
☐ 9 Vic Wertz	50.00	25.00	5.00
☐ 10 Tommy Henrich	50.00	25.00	5.00
☐ 11 Phil Rizzuto	135.00	65.00	13.50
☐ 12 Joe Page	50.00	25.00	5.00
☐ 13 Ferris Fain	50.00	25.00	5.00
☐ 14 Alex Kellner	45.00	22.50	4.50
☐ 15 Al Kozar	45.00	22.50	4.50
☐ 16 Roy Sievers	50.00	25.00	5.00
☐ 17 Sid Hudson	45.00	22.50	4.50
☐ 18 Eddie Robinson	45.00	22.50	4.50
☐ 19 Warren Spahn	150.00	75.00	15.00
☐ 20 Bob Elliott	50.00	25.00	5.00
☐ 21 Pee Wee Reese	150.00	75.00	15.00
☐ 22 Jackie Robinson	600.00	300.00	60.00
☐ 23 Don Newcombe	100.00	50.00	10.00
☐ 24 Johnny Schmitz	45.00	22.50	4.50
☐ 25 Hank Sauer	50.00	25.00	5.00
☐ 26 Grady Hatton	45.00	22.50	4.50
☐ 27 Herman Wehmeier	45.00	22.50	4.50
☐ 28 Bobby Thomson	55.00	27.50	5.50
☐ 29 Eddie Stanky	50.00	25.00	5.00
☐ 30 Eddie Waitkus	45.00	22.50	4.50
☐ 31 Del Ennis	50.00	25.00	5.00
☐ 32 Robin Roberts	110.00	55.00	11.00
☐ 33 Ralph Kiner	100.00	50.00	10.00
☐ 34 Murry Dickson	45.00	22.50	4.50
☐ 35 Enos Slaughter	100.00	50.00	10.00
☐ 36 Eddie Kazak	45.00	22.50	4.50
☐ 37 Luke Appling	65.00	32.50	6.50
☐ 38 Bill Wight	45.00	22.50	4.50
☐ 39 Larry Doby	60.00	30.00	6.00
☐ 40 Bob Lemon	100.00	50.00	10.00
☐ 41 Hoot Evers	45.00	22.50	4.50
☐ 42 Art Houtteman	45.00	22.50	4.50
☐ 43 Bobby Doerr	90.00	45.00	9.00
☐ 44 Joe Dobson	45.00	22.50	4.50
☐ 45 Al Zarilla	45.00	22.50	4.50

☐	46	Yogi Berra	350.00	175.00	35.00
☐	47	Jerry Coleman	50.00	25.00	5.00
☐	48	Lou Brissie	45.00	22.50	4.50
☐	49	Elmer Valo	45.00	22.50	4.50
☐	50	Dick Kokos	45.00	22.50	4.50
☐	51	Ned Garver	45.00	22.50	4.50
☐	52	Sam Mele	45.00	22.50	4.50
☐	53	Clyde Vollmer	45.00	22.50	4.50
☐	54	Gil Coan	45.00	22.50	4.50
☐	55	Buddy Kerr	45.00	22.50	4.50
☐	56	Del Crandall	50.00	25.00	5.00
☐	57	Vern Bickford	45.00	22.50	4.50
☐	58	Carl Furillo	55.00	27.50	5.50
☐	59	Ralph Branca	55.00	27.50	5.50
☐	60	Andy Pafko	50.00	25.00	5.00
☐	61	Bob Rush	45.00	22.50	4.50
☐	62	Ted Kluszewski	65.00	32.50	6.50
☐	63	Ewell Blackwell	50.00	25.00	5.00
☐	64	Alvin Dark	50.00	25.00	5.00
☐	65	Dave Koslo	45.00	22.50	4.50
☐	66	Larry Jansen	45.00	22.50	4.50
☐	67	Willie Jones	45.00	22.50	4.50
☐	68	Curt Simmons	50.00	25.00	5.00
☐	69	Wally Westlake	45.00	22.50	4.50
☐	70	Bob Chesnes	45.00	22.50	4.50
☐	71	Red Schoendienst	80.00	40.00	8.00
☐	72	Howie Pollet	45.00	22.50	4.50
☐	73	Willard Marshall	16.00	8.00	1.60
☐	74	Johnny Antonelli	24.00	12.00	2.40
☐	75	Roy Campanella	250.00	125.00	25.00
☐	76	Rex Barney	16.00	8.00	1.60
☐	77	Duke Snider	250.00	125.00	25.00
☐	78	Mickey Owen	18.00	9.00	1.80
☐	79	Johnny VanderMeer	21.00	10.50	2.10
☐	80	Howard Fox	16.00	8.00	1.60
☐	81	Ron Northey	16.00	8.00	1.60
☐	82	Whitey Lockman	18.00	9.00	1.80
☐	83	Sheldon Jones	16.00	8.00	1.60
☐	84	Richie Ashburn	65.00	32.50	6.50
☐	85	Ken Heintzelman	16.00	8.00	1.60
☐	86	Stan Rojek	16.00	8.00	1.60
☐	87	Bill Werle	16.00	8.00	1.60
☐	88	Marty Marion	21.00	10.50	2.10
☐	89	Red Munger	16.00	8.00	1.60
☐	90	Harry Brecheen	16.00	8.00	1.60
☐	91	Cass Michaels	16.00	8.00	1.60
☐	92	Hank Majeski	16.00	8.00	1.60
☐	93	Gene Bearden	16.00	8.00	1.60
☐	94	Lou Boudreau	45.00	22.50	4.50
☐	95	Aaron Robinson	16.00	8.00	1.60
☐	96	Virgil Trucks	18.00	9.00	1.80
☐	97	Maurice McDermott	16.00	8.00	1.60
☐	98	Ted Williams	650.00	325.00	65.00
☐	99	Billy Goodman	18.00	9.00	1.80
☐	100	Vic Raschi	24.00	12.00	2.40
☐	101	Bobby Brown	25.00	12.50	2.50
☐	102	Billy Johnson	16.00	8.00	1.60
☐	103	Eddie Joost	16.00	8.00	1.60
☐	104	Sam Chapman	16.00	8.00	1.60
☐	105	Bob Dillinger	16.00	8.00	1.60
☐	106	Cliff Fannin	16.00	8.00	1.60
☐	107	Sam Dente	16.00	8.00	1.60
☐	108	Ray Scarborough	16.00	8.00	1.60
☐	109	Sid Gordon	16.00	8.00	1.60
☐	110	Tommy Holmes	18.00	9.00	1.80
☐	111	Walker Cooper	16.00	8.00	1.60
☐	112	Gil Hodges	80.00	40.00	8.00
☐	113	Gene Hermanski	16.00	8.00	1.60
☐	114	Wayne Terwilliger	16.00	8.00	1.60
☐	115	Roy Smalley	16.00	8.00	1.60
☐	116	Virgil Stallcup	16.00	8.00	1.60
☐	117	Bill Rigney	16.00	8.00	1.60
☐	118	Clint Hartung	16.00	8.00	1.60
☐	119	Dick Sisler	16.00	8.00	1.60
☐	120	John Thompson	16.00	8.00	1.60
☐	121	Andy Seminick	16.00	8.00	1.60
☐	122	Johnny Hopp	18.00	9.00	1.80
☐	123	Dino Restelli	16.00	8.00	1.60
☐	124	Clyde McCullough	16.00	8.00	1.60
☐	125	Del Rice	16.00	8.00	1.60
☐	126	Al Brazle	16.00	8.00	1.60
☐	127	Dave Philley	16.00	8.00	1.60
☐	128	Phil Masi	16.00	8.00	1.60
☐	129	Joe Gordon	20.00	10.00	2.00
☐	130	Dale Mitchell	18.00	9.00	1.80
☐	131	Steve Gromek	16.00	8.00	1.60
☐	132	Mickey Vernon	18.00	9.00	1.80
☐	133	Don Kolloway	16.00	8.00	1.60
☐	134	Paul Trout	16.00	8.00	1.60
☐	135	Pat Mullin	16.00	8.00	1.60
☐	136	Warren Rosar	16.00	8.00	1.60
☐	137	Johnny Pesky	18.00	9.00	1.80
☐	138	Allie Reynolds	25.00	12.50	2.50
☐	139	Johnny Mize	60.00	30.00	6.00
☐	140	Pete Suder	16.00	8.00	1.60
☐	141	Joe Coleman	16.00	8.00	1.60
☐	142	Sherm Lollar	18.00	9.00	1.80
☐	143	Eddie Stewart	16.00	8.00	1.60
☐	144	Al Evans	16.00	8.00	1.60
☐	145	Jack Graham	16.00	8.00	1.60
☐	146	Floyd Baker	16.00	8.00	1.60
☐	147	Mike Garcia	18.00	9.00	1.80
☐	148	Early Wynn	55.00	27.50	5.50
☐	149	Bob Swift	16.00	8.00	1.60
☐	150	George Vico	16.00	8.00	1.60
☐	151	Fred Hutchinson	18.00	9.00	1.80
☐	152	Ellis Kinder	16.00	8.00	1.60
☐	153	Walt Masterson	16.00	8.00	1.60
☐	154	Gus Niarhos	16.00	8.00	1.60
☐	155	Frank Shea	16.00	8.00	1.60
☐	156	Fred Sanford	16.00	8.00	1.60
☐	157	Mike Guerra	16.00	8.00	1.60
☐	158	Paul Lehner	16.00	8.00	1.60
☐	159	Joe Tipton	16.00	8.00	1.60
☐	160	Mickey Harris	16.00	8.00	1.60
☐	161	Sherry Robertson	16.00	8.00	1.60
☐	162	Eddie Yost	16.00	8.00	1.60
☐	163	Earl Torgeson	16.00	8.00	1.60
☐	164	Sibby Sisti	16.00	8.00	1.60
☐	165	Bruce Edwards	16.00	8.00	1.60
☐	166	Joe Hatton	16.00	8.00	1.60
☐	167	Preacher Roe	25.00	12.50	2.50
☐	168	Bob Scheffing	16.00	8.00	1.60
☐	169	Hank Edwards	16.00	8.00	1.60
☐	170	Dutch Leonard	16.00	8.00	1.60
☐	171	Harry Gumbert	16.00	8.00	1.60
☐	172	Peanuts Lowrey	16.00	8.00	1.60
☐	173	Lloyd Merriman	16.00	8.00	1.60
☐	174	Hank Thompson	18.00	9.00	1.80
☐	175	Monte Kennedy	16.00	8.00	1.60
☐	176	Sylvester Donnelly	16.00	8.00	1.60
☐	177	Hank Borowy	16.00	8.00	1.60
☐	178	Ed Fitzgerald	16.00	8.00	1.60
☐	179	Chuck Diering	16.00	8.00	1.60
☐	180	Harry Walker	16.00	8.00	1.60
☐	181	Marino Pieretti	16.00	8.00	1.60
☐	182	Sam Zoldak	16.00	8.00	1.60
☐	183	Mickey Haefner	16.00	8.00	1.60
☐	184	Randy Gumpert	16.00	8.00	1.60
☐	185	Howie Judson	16.00	8.00	1.60
☐	186	Ken Keltner	18.00	9.00	1.80
☐	187	Lou Stringer	16.00	8.00	1.60
☐	188	Earl Johnson	16.00	8.00	1.60
☐	189	Owen Friend	16.00	8.00	1.60
☐	190	Ken Wood	16.00	8.00	1.60
☐	191	Dick Starr	16.00	8.00	1.60
☐	192	Bob Chipman	16.00	8.00	1.60
☐	193	Pete Reiser	18.00	9.00	1.80
☐	194	Billy Cox	18.00	9.00	1.80
☐	195	Phil Cavarretta	18.00	9.00	1.80
☐	196	Doyle Lade	16.00	8.00	1.60
☐	197	Johnny Wyrostek	16.00	8.00	1.60
☐	198	Danny Litwhiler	16.00	8.00	1.60
☐	199	Jack Kramer	16.00	8.00	1.60
☐	200	Kirby Higbe	16.00	8.00	1.60
☐	201	Pete Castiglione	16.00	8.00	1.60
☐	202	Cliff Chambers	16.00	8.00	1.60
☐	203	Danny Murtaugh	16.00	8.00	1.60
☐	204	Granny Hamner	16.00	8.00	1.60
☐	205	Mike Goliat	16.00	8.00	1.60
☐	206	Stan Lopata	16.00	8.00	1.60
☐	207	Max Lanier	16.00	8.00	1.60
☐	208	Jim Hearn	16.00	8.00	1.60
☐	209	Johnny Lindell	16.00	8.00	1.60
☐	210	Ted Gray	16.00	8.00	1.60
☐	211	Charley Keller	18.00	9.00	1.80
☐	212	Jerry Priddy	16.00	8.00	1.60
☐	213	Carl Scheib	16.00	8.00	1.60
☐	214	Dick Fowler	16.00	8.00	1.60
☐	215	Ed Lopat	25.00	12.50	2.50
☐	216	Bob Porterfield	16.00	8.00	1.60
☐	217	Casey Stengel MG	110.00	55.00	11.00
☐	218	Cliff Mapes	18.00	9.00	1.80
☐	219	Hank Bauer	60.00	30.00	6.00
☐	220	Leo Durocher MG	45.00	22.50	4.50
☐	221	Don Mueller	25.00	12.50	2.50
☐	222	Bobby Morgan	16.00	8.00	1.60
☐	223	Jim Russell	16.00	8.00	1.60
☐	224	Jack Banta	16.00	8.00	1.60
☐	225	Eddie Sawyer MG	18.00	9.00	1.80
☐	226	Jim Konstanty	25.00	12.50	2.50
☐	227	Bob Miller	16.00	8.00	1.60
☐	228	Bill Nicholson	16.00	8.00	1.60
☐	229	Frank Frisch	45.00	22.50	4.50
☐	230	Bill Serena	16.00	8.00	1.60
☐	231	Preston Ward	16.00	8.00	1.60
☐	232	Al Rosen	50.00	25.00	5.00
☐	233	Allie Clark	16.00	8.00	1.60

☐ 234 Bobby Shantz	24.00	12.00	2.40
☐ 235 Harold Gilbert	16.00	8.00	1.60
☐ 236 Bob Cain	16.00	8.00	1.60
☐ 237 Bill Salkeld	16.00	8.00	1.60
☐ 238 Vernal Jones	16.00	8.00	1.60
☐ 239 Bill Howerton	16.00	8.00	1.60
☐ 240 Eddie Lake	16.00	8.00	1.60
☐ 241 Neil Berry	16.00	8.00	1.60
☐ 242 Dick Kryhoski	16.00	8.00	1.60
☐ 243 Johnny Groth	16.00	8.00	1.60
☐ 244 Dale Coogan	16.00	8.00	1.60
☐ 245 Al Papai	16.00	8.00	1.60
☐ 246 Walt Dropo	24.00	12.00	2.40
☐ 247 Irv Noren	18.00	9.00	1.80
☐ 248 Sam Jethroe	18.00	9.00	1.80
☐ 249 Snuffy Stirnweiss	18.00	9.00	1.80
☐ 250 Ray Coleman	16.00	8.00	1.60
☐ 251 John Moss	16.00	8.00	1.60
☐ 252 Billy DeMars	100.00	10.00	2.00

1951 Bowman

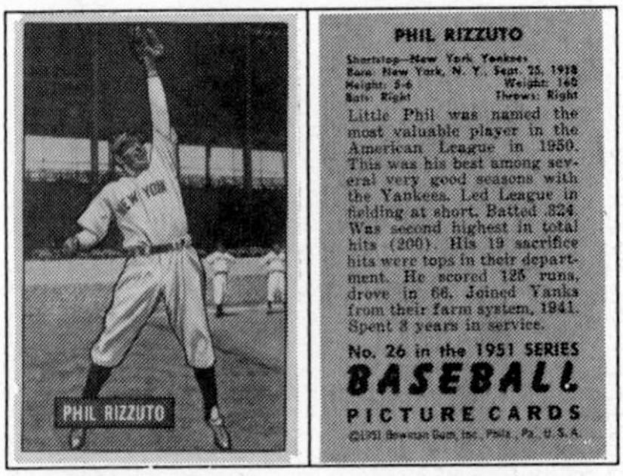

The cards in this 324-card set measure 2 1/16" by 3 1/8". Many of the obverses of the cards appearing in the 1951 Bowman set are enlargements of those appearing in the previous year. The high number series (253-324) is highly valued and contains the true "Rookie" cards of Mickey Mantle and Willie Mays. Card number 195 depicts Paul Richards in caricature. George Kell's card (number 46) incorrectly lists him as being in the "1941" Bowman series. Player names are found printed in a panel on the front of the card. These cards were supposedly also sold in sheets in variety stores in the Philadelphia area.

	NRMT	VG-E	GOOD
COMPLETE SET (324)	16000.00	7000.00	1750.00
COMMON PLAYER (1-36)	21.00	10.50	2.10
COMMON PLAYER (37-72)	16.00	8.00	1.60
COMMON PLAYER (73-252)	12.50	6.25	1.25
COMMON PLAYER (253-324)	60.00	30.00	6.00

☐ 1 Whitey Ford	1250.00	200.00	40.00
☐ 2 Yogi Berra	400.00	200.00	40.00
☐ 3 Robin Roberts	65.00	32.50	6.50
☐ 4 Del Ennis	24.00	12.00	2.40
☐ 5 Dale Mitchell	24.00	12.00	2.40
☐ 6 Don Newcombe	32.00	16.00	3.20
☐ 7 Gil Hodges	75.00	37.50	7.50
☐ 8 Paul Lehner	21.00	10.50	2.10
☐ 9 Sam Chapman	21.00	10.50	2.10
☐ 10 Red Schoendienst	65.00	32.50	6.50
☐ 11 Red Munger	21.00	10.50	2.10
☐ 12 Hank Majeski	21.00	10.50	2.10
☐ 13 Eddie Stanky	24.00	12.00	2.40
☐ 14 Alvin Dark	24.00	12.00	2.40
☐ 15 Johnny Pesky	24.00	12.00	2.40
☐ 16 Maurice McDermott	21.00	10.50	2.10
☐ 17 Pete Castiglione	21.00	10.50	2.10
☐ 18 Gil Coan	21.00	10.50	2.10
☐ 19 Sid Gordon	21.00	10.50	2.10
☐ 20 Del Crandell UER (sic, Crandall)	24.00	12.00	2.40
☐ 21 Snuffy Stirnweiss	24.00	12.00	2.40
☐ 22 Hank Sauer	24.00	12.00	2.40
☐ 23 Hoot Evers	21.00	10.50	2.10
☐ 24 Ewell Blackwell	24.00	12.00	2.40
☐ 25 Vic Raschi	24.00	12.00	2.40
☐ 26 Phil Rizzuto	85.00	42.50	8.50
☐ 27 Jim Konstanty	24.00	12.00	2.40
☐ 28 Eddie Waitkus	21.00	10.50	2.10
☐ 29 Allie Clark	21.00	10.50	2.10
☐ 30 Bob Feller	120.00	60.00	12.00
☐ 31 Roy Campanella	250.00	125.00	25.00
☐ 32 Duke Snider	210.00	100.00	20.00
☐ 33 Bob Hooper	16.00	8.00	1.60
☐ 34 Marty Marion	21.00	10.50	2.10
☐ 35 Al Zarilla	16.00	8.00	1.60
☐ 36 Joe Dobson	16.00	8.00	1.60
☐ 37 Whitey Lockman	18.00	9.00	1.80
☐ 38 Al Evans	16.00	8.00	1.60
☐ 39 Ray Scarborough	16.00	8.00	1.60
☐ 40 Gus Bell	21.00	10.50	2.10
☐ 41 Eddie Yost	16.00	8.00	1.60
☐ 42 Vern Bickford	16.00	8.00	1.60
☐ 43 Billy DeMars	16.00	8.00	1.60
☐ 44 Roy Smalley	16.00	8.00	1.60
☐ 45 Art Houtteman	16.00	8.00	1.60
☐ 46 George Kell 1941	50.00	25.00	5.00
☐ 47 Grady Hatton	16.00	8.00	1.60
☐ 48 Ken Raffensberger	16.00	8.00	1.60
☐ 49 Jerry Coleman	18.00	9.00	1.80
☐ 50 Johnny Mize	50.00	25.00	5.00
☐ 51 Andy Seminick	16.00	8.00	1.60
☐ 52 Dick Sisler	16.00	8.00	1.60
☐ 53 Bob Lemon	50.00	25.00	5.00
☐ 54 Ray Boone	18.00	9.00	1.80
☐ 55 Gene Hermanski	16.00	8.00	1.60
☐ 56 Ralph Branca	22.00	11.00	2.20
☐ 57 Alex Kellner	16.00	8.00	1.60
☐ 58 Enos Slaughter	50.00	25.00	5.00
☐ 59 Randy Gumpert	16.00	8.00	1.60
☐ 60 Chico Carrasquel	16.00	8.00	1.60
☐ 61 Jim Hearn	16.00	8.00	1.60
☐ 62 Lou Boudreau	45.00	22.50	4.50
☐ 63 Bob Dillinger	16.00	8.00	1.60
☐ 64 Bill Werle	16.00	8.00	1.60
☐ 65 Mickey Vernon	18.00	9.00	1.80
☐ 66 Bob Elliott	18.00	9.00	1.80
☐ 67 Roy Sievers	18.00	9.00	1.80
☐ 68 Dick Kokos	16.00	8.00	1.60
☐ 69 Johnny Schmitz	16.00	8.00	1.60
☐ 70 Ron Northey	16.00	8.00	1.60
☐ 71 Jerry Priddy	16.00	8.00	1.60
☐ 72 Lloyd Merriman	16.00	8.00	1.60
☐ 73 Tommy Byrne	15.00	7.50	1.50
☐ 74 Billy Johnson	15.00	7.50	1.50
☐ 75 Russ Meyer	12.50	6.25	1.25
☐ 76 Stan Lopata	12.50	6.25	1.25
☐ 77 Mike Goliat	12.50	6.25	1.25
☐ 78 Early Wynn	45.00	22.50	4.50
☐ 79 Jim Hegan	15.00	7.50	1.50
☐ 80 Pee Wee Reese	110.00	55.00	11.00
☐ 81 Carl Furillo	28.00	14.00	2.80
☐ 82 Joe Tipton	12.50	6.25	1.25
☐ 83 Carl Scheib	12.50	6.25	1.25
☐ 84 Barney McCosky	12.50	6.25	1.25
☐ 85 Eddie Kazak	12.50	6.25	1.25
☐ 86 Harry Brecheen	15.00	7.50	1.50
☐ 87 Floyd Baker	12.50	6.25	1.25
☐ 88 Eddie Robinson	12.50	6.25	1.25
☐ 89 Hank Thompson	15.00	7.50	1.50
☐ 90 Dave Koslo	12.50	6.25	1.25
☐ 91 Clyde Vollmer	12.50	6.25	1.25
☐ 92 Vern Stephens	15.00	7.50	1.50
☐ 93 Danny O'Connell	12.50	6.25	1.25
☐ 94 Clyde McCullough	12.50	6.25	1.25
☐ 95 Sherry Robertson	12.50	6.25	1.25
☐ 96 Sandy Consuegra	12.50	6.25	1.25
☐ 97 Bob Kuzava	12.50	6.25	1.25
☐ 98 Willard Marshall	12.50	6.25	1.25
☐ 99 Earl Torgeson	12.50	6.25	1.25
☐ 100 Sherm Lollar	15.00	7.50	1.50
☐ 101 Owen Friend	12.50	6.25	1.25
☐ 102 Dutch Leonard	12.50	6.25	1.25
☐ 103 Andy Pafko	15.00	7.50	1.50
☐ 104 Virgil Trucks	15.00	7.50	1.50
☐ 105 Don Kolloway	12.50	6.25	1.25
☐ 106 Pat Mullin	12.50	6.25	1.25
☐ 107 Johnny Wyrostek	12.50	6.25	1.25
☐ 108 Virgil Stallcup	12.50	6.25	1.25
☐ 109 Allie Reynolds	25.00	12.50	2.50
☐ 110 Bobby Brown	25.00	12.50	2.50
☐ 111 Curt Simmons	15.00	7.50	1.50
☐ 112 Willie Jones	12.50	6.25	1.25
☐ 113 Bill Nicholson	12.50	6.25	1.25
☐ 114 Sam Zoldak	12.50	6.25	1.25
☐ 115 Steve Gromek	12.50	6.25	1.25
☐ 116 Bruce Edwards	12.50	6.25	1.25
☐ 117 Eddie Miksis	12.50	6.25	1.25
☐ 118 Preacher Roe	25.00	12.50	2.50
☐ 119 Eddie Joost	12.50	6.25	1.25
☐ 120 Joe Coleman	12.50	6.25	1.25
☐ 121 Jerry Staley	12.50	6.25	1.25
☐ 122 Joe Garagiola	125.00	60.00	12.50

☐	123 Howie Judson	12.50	6.25	1.25
☐	124 Gus Niarhos	12.50	6.25	1.25
☐	125 Bill Rigney	12.50	6.25	1.25
☐	126 Bobby Thomson	27.00	13.50	2.70
☐	127 Sal Maglie	36.00	18.00	3.60
☐	128 Ellis Kinder	12.50	6.25	1.25
☐	129 Matt Batts	12.50	6.25	1.25
☐	130 Tom Saffell	12.50	6.25	1.25
☐	131 Cliff Chambers	12.50	6.25	1.25
☐	132 Cass Michaels	12.50	6.25	1.25
☐	133 Sam Dente	12.50	6.25	1.25
☐	134 Warren Spahn	100.00	50.00	10.00
☐	135 Walker Cooper	12.50	6.25	1.25
☐	136 Ray Coleman	12.50	6.25	1.25
☐	137 Dick Starr	12.50	6.25	1.25
☐	138 Phil Cavarretta	15.00	7.50	1.50
☐	139 Doyle Lade	12.50	6.25	1.25
☐	140 Eddie Lake	12.50	6.25	1.25
☐	141 Fred Hutchinson	15.00	7.50	1.50
☐	142 Aaron Robinson	12.50	6.25	1.25
☐	143 Ted Kluszewski	27.00	13.50	2.70
☐	144 Herman Wehmeier	12.50	6.25	1.25
☐	145 Fred Sanford	12.50	6.25	1.25
☐	146 Johnny Hopp	15.00	7.50	1.50
☐	147 Ken Heintzelman	12.50	6.25	1.25
☐	148 Granny Hamner	12.50	6.25	1.25
☐	149 Bubba Church	12.50	6.25	1.25
☐	150 Mike Garcia	15.00	7.50	1.50
☐	151 Larry Doby	22.00	11.00	2.20
☐	152 Cal Abrams	12.50	6.25	1.25
☐	153 Rex Barney	12.50	6.25	1.25
☐	154 Pete Suder	12.50	6.25	1.25
☐	155 Lou Brissie	12.50	6.25	1.25
☐	156 Del Rice	12.50	6.25	1.25
☐	157 Al Brazle	12.50	6.25	1.25
☐	158 Chuck Diering	12.50	6.25	1.25
☐	159 Eddie Stewart	12.50	6.25	1.25
☐	160 Phil Masi	12.50	6.25	1.25
☐	161 Wes Westrum	12.50	6.25	1.25
☐	162 Larry Jansen	12.50	6.25	1.25
☐	163 Monte Kennedy	12.50	6.25	1.25
☐	164 Bill Wight	12.50	6.25	1.25
☐	165 Ted Williams	500.00	250.00	50.00
☐	166 Stan Rojek	12.50	6.25	1.25
☐	167 Murry Dickson	12.50	6.25	1.25
☐	168 Sam Mele	12.50	6.25	1.25
☐	169 Sid Hudson	12.50	6.25	1.25
☐	170 Sibby Sisti	12.50	6.25	1.25
☐	171 Buddy Kerr	12.50	6.25	1.25
☐	172 Ned Garver	12.50	6.25	1.25
☐	173 Hank Arft	12.50	6.25	1.25
☐	174 Mickey Owen	15.00	7.50	1.50
☐	175 Wayne Terwilliger	12.50	6.25	1.25
☐	176 Vic Wertz	15.00	7.50	1.50
☐	177 Charlie Keller	15.00	7.50	1.50
☐	178 Ted Gray	12.50	6.25	1.25
☐	179 Danny Litwhiler	12.50	6.25	1.25
☐	180 Howie Fox	12.50	6.25	1.25
☐	181 Casey Stengel MG	100.00	50.00	10.00
☐	182 Tom Ferrick	12.50	6.25	1.25
☐	183 Hank Bauer	25.00	12.50	2.50
☐	184 Eddie Sawyer MG	15.00	7.50	1.50
☐	185 Jimmy Bloodworth	12.50	6.25	1.25
☐	186 Richie Ashburn	45.00	22.50	4.50
☐	187 Al Rosen	24.00	12.00	2.40
☐	188 Bobby Avila	15.00	7.50	1.50
☐	189 Erv Palica	12.50	6.25	1.25
☐	190 Joe Hatton	12.50	6.25	1.25
☐	191 Billy Hitchcock	12.50	6.25	1.25
☐	192 Hank Wyse	12.50	6.25	1.25
☐	193 Ted Wilks	12.50	6.25	1.25
☐	194 Peanuts Lowrey	12.50	6.25	1.25
☐	195 Paul Richards (caricature)	15.00	7.50	1.50
☐	196 Billy Pierce	25.00	12.50	2.50
☐	197 Bob Cain	12.50	6.25	1.25
☐	198 Monte Irvin	100.00	50.00	10.00
☐	199 Sheldon Jones	12.50	6.25	1.25
☐	200 Jack Kramer	12.50	6.25	1.25
☐	201 Steve O'Neill	12.50	6.25	1.25
☐	202 Mike Guerra	12.50	6.25	1.25
☐	203 Vernon Law	21.00	10.50	2.10
☐	204 Vic Lombardi	12.50	6.25	1.25
☐	205 Mickey Grasso	12.50	6.25	1.25
☐	206 Conrado Marrero	12.50	6.25	1.25
☐	207 Billy Southworth	12.50	6.25	1.25
☐	208 Blix Donnelly	12.50	6.25	1.25
☐	209 Ken Wood	12.50	6.25	1.25
☐	210 Les Moss	12.50	6.25	1.25
☐	211 Hal Jeffcoat	12.50	6.25	1.25
☐	212 Bob Rush	12.50	6.25	1.25
☐	213 Neil Berry	12.50	6.25	1.25
☐	214 Bob Swift	12.50	6.25	1.25
☐	215 Ken Peterson	12.50	6.25	1.25
☐	216 Connie Ryan	12.50	6.25	1.25

☐	217 Joe Page	18.00	9.00	1.80
☐	218 Ed Lopat	25.00	12.50	2.50
☐	219 Gene Woodling	28.00	14.00	2.80
☐	220 Bob Miller	12.50	6.25	1.25
☐	221 Dick Whitman	12.50	6.25	1.25
☐	222 Thurman Tucker	12.50	6.25	1.25
☐	223 Johnny VanderMeer	20.00	10.00	2.00
☐	224 Billy Cox	15.00	7.50	1.50
☐	225 Dan Bankhead	15.00	7.50	1.50
☐	226 Jimmy Dykes	15.00	7.50	1.50
☐	227 Bobby Schantz (sic, Shantz)	18.00	9.00	1.80
☐	228 Cloyd Boyer	15.00	7.50	1.50
☐	229 Bill Howerton	12.50	6.25	1.25
☐	230 Max Lanier	12.50	6.25	1.25
☐	231 Luis Aloma	12.50	6.25	1.25
☐	232 Nelson Fox	100.00	50.00	10.00
☐	233 Leo Durocher MG	40.00	20.00	4.00
☐	234 Clint Hartung	12.50	6.25	1.25
☐	235 Jack Lohrke	12.50	6.25	1.25
☐	236 Warren Rosar	12.50	6.25	1.25
☐	237 Billy Goodman	15.00	7.50	1.50
☐	238 Pete Reiser	18.00	9.00	1.80
☐	239 Bill MacDonald	12.50	6.25	1.25
☐	240 Joe Haynes	12.50	6.25	1.25
☐	241 Irv Noren	12.50	6.25	1.25
☐	242 Sam Jethroe	12.50	6.25	1.25
☐	243 Johnny Antonelli	15.00	7.50	1.50
☐	244 Cliff Fannin	12.50	6.25	1.25
☐	245 John Berardino	15.00	7.50	1.50
☐	246 Bill Serena	12.50	6.25	1.25
☐	247 Bob Ramazotti	12.50	6.25	1.25
☐	248 Johnny Klippstein	12.50	6.25	1.25
☐	249 Johnny Groth	12.50	6.25	1.25
☐	250 Hank Borowy	12.50	6.25	1.25
☐	251 Willard Ramsdell	12.50	6.25	1.25
☐	252 Dixie Howell	12.50	6.25	1.25
☐	253 Mickey Mantle	5000.00	2000.00	400.00
☐	254 Jackie Jensen	110.00	55.00	11.00
☐	255 Milo Candini	60.00	30.00	6.00
☐	256 Ken Sylvestri	60.00	30.00	6.00
☐	257 Birdie Tebbetts	65.00	32.50	6.50
☐	258 Luke Easter	65.00	32.50	6.50
☐	259 Chuck Dressen MG	75.00	37.50	7.50
☐	260 Carl Erskine	110.00	55.00	11.00
☐	261 Wally Moses	65.00	32.50	6.50
☐	262 Gus Zernial	65.00	32.50	6.50
☐	263 Howie Pollet	60.00	30.00	6.00
☐	264 Don Richmond	60.00	30.00	6.00
☐	265 Steve Bilko	60.00	30.00	6.00
☐	266 Harry Dorish	60.00	30.00	6.00
☐	267 Ken Holcombe	60.00	30.00	6.00
☐	268 Don Mueller	65.00	32.50	6.50
☐	269 Ray Noble	60.00	30.00	6.00
☐	270 Willard Nixon	60.00	30.00	6.00
☐	271 Tommy Wright	60.00	30.00	6.00
☐	272 Billy Meyer MG	60.00	30.00	6.00
☐	273 Danny Murtaugh	60.00	30.00	6.00
☐	274 George Metkovich	60.00	30.00	6.00
☐	275 Bucky Harris MG	75.00	37.50	7.50
☐	276 Frank Quinn	60.00	30.00	6.00
☐	277 Roy Hartsfield	60.00	30.00	6.00
☐	278 Norman Roy	60.00	30.00	6.00
☐	279 Jim Delsing	60.00	30.00	6.00
☐	280 Frank Overmire	60.00	30.00	6.00
☐	281 Al Widmar	60.00	30.00	6.00
☐	282 Frank Frisch	100.00	50.00	10.00
☐	283 Walt Dubiel	60.00	30.00	6.00
☐	284 Gene Bearden	65.00	32.50	6.50
☐	285 Johnny Lipon	60.00	30.00	6.00
☐	286 Bob Usher	60.00	30.00	6.00
☐	287 Jim Blackburn	60.00	30.00	6.00
☐	288 Bobby Adams	60.00	30.00	6.00
☐	289 Cliff Mapes	65.00	32.50	6.50
☐	290 Bill Dickey CO	160.00	80.00	16.00
☐	291 Tommy Henrich CO	75.00	37.50	7.50
☐	292 Eddie Pellegrini	60.00	30.00	6.00
☐	293 Ken Johnson	60.00	30.00	6.00
☐	294 Jocko Thompson	60.00	30.00	6.00
☐	295 Al Lopez MG	100.00	50.00	10.00
☐	296 Bob Kennedy	65.00	32.50	6.50
☐	297 Dave Philley	60.00	30.00	6.00
☐	298 Joe Astroth	60.00	30.00	6.00
☐	299 Clyde King	65.00	32.50	6.50
☐	300 Hal Rice	60.00	30.00	6.00
☐	301 Tommy Glaviano	60.00	30.00	6.00
☐	302 Jim Busby	60.00	30.00	6.00
☐	303 Marv Rotblatt	60.00	30.00	6.00
☐	304 Al Gettell	60.00	30.00	6.00
☐	305 Willie Mays	2000.00	800.00	200.00
☐	306 Jim Piersall	100.00	50.00	10.00
☐	307 Walt Masterson	60.00	30.00	6.00
☐	308 Ted Beard	60.00	30.00	6.00
☐	309 Mel Queen	60.00	30.00	6.00
☐	310 Erv Dusak	60.00	30.00	6.00

☐	311 Mickey Harris	60.00	30.00	6.00
☐	312 Gene Mauch	75.00	37.50	7.50
☐	313 Ray Mueller	60.00	30.00	6.00
☐	314 Johnny Sain	75.00	37.50	7.50
☐	315 Zack Taylor	60.00	30.00	6.00
☐	316 Duane Pillette	60.00	30.00	6.00
☐	317 Smokey Burgess	75.00	37.50	7.50
☐	318 Warren Hacker	60.00	30.00	6.00
☐	319 Red Rolfe	65.00	32.50	6.50
☐	320 Hal White	60.00	30.00	6.00
☐	321 Earl Johnson	60.00	30.00	6.00
☐	322 Luke Sewell	65.00	32.50	6.50
☐	323 Joe Adcock	90.00	45.00	9.00
☐	324 Johnny Pramesa	120.00	35.00	7.00

1952 Bowman

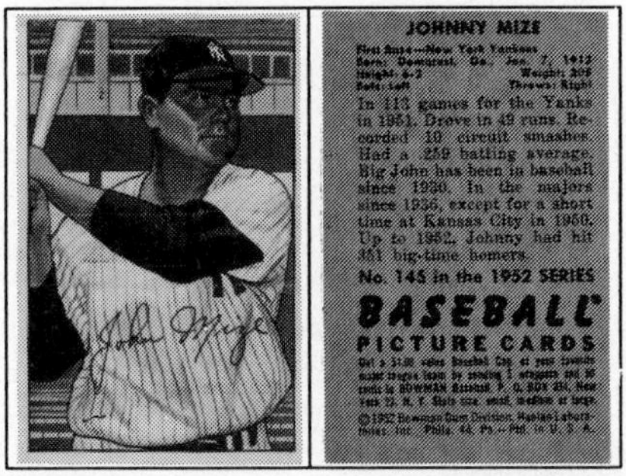

The cards in this 252-card set measure 2 1/16" by 3 1/8". While the Bowman set of 1952 retained the card size introduced in 1951, it employed a modification of color tones from the two preceding years. The cards also appeared with a facsimile autograph on the front and, for the first time since 1949, premium advertising on the back. The 1952 set was sold in sheets as well as in gum packs. Artwork for 15 cards that were never issued was recently discovered. Key rookies in this set are Lew Burdette and Minnie Minoso.

	NRMT	VG-E	GOOD
COMPLETE SET (252)	8200.00	3750.00	800.00
COMMON PLAYER (1-36)	17.00	8.50	1.70
COMMON PLAYER (37-72)	15.00	7.50	1.50
COMMON PLAYER (73-144)	14.00	7.00	1.40
COMMON PLAYER (145-180)	13.00	6.50	1.30
COMMON PLAYER (181-216)	12.00	6.00	1.20
COMMON PLAYER (217-252)	30.00	15.00	3.00

☐	1 Yogi Berra	600.00	150.00	30.00
☐	2 Bobby Thomson	30.00	15.00	3.00
☐	3 Fred Hutchinson	20.00	10.00	2.00
☐	4 Robin Roberts	50.00	25.00	5.00
☐	5 Minnie Minoso	60.00	30.00	6.00
☐	6 Virgil Stallcup	17.00	8.50	1.70
☐	7 Mike Garcia	20.00	10.00	2.00
☐	8 Pee Wee Reese	100.00	50.00	10.00
☐	9 Vern Stephens	20.00	10.00	2.00
☐	10 Bob Hooper	17.00	8.50	1.70
☐	11 Ralph Kiner	50.00	25.00	5.00
☐	12 Max Surkont	17.00	8.50	1.70
☐	13 Cliff Mapes	17.00	8.50	1.70
☐	14 Cliff Chambers	17.00	8.50	1.70
☐	15 Sam Mele	17.00	8.50	1.70
☐	16 Turk Lown	17.00	8.50	1.70
☐	17 Ed Lopat	28.00	14.00	2.80
☐	18 Don Mueller	20.00	10.00	2.00
☐	19 Bob Cain	17.00	8.50	1.70
☐	20 Willie Jones	17.00	8.50	1.70
☐	21 Nellie Fox	35.00	17.50	3.50
☐	22 Willard Ramsdell	17.00	8.50	1.70
☐	23 Bob Lemon	50.00	25.00	5.00
☐	24 Carl Furillo	30.00	15.00	3.00
☐	25 Mickey McDermott	17.00	8.50	1.70
☐	26 Eddie Joost	17.00	8.50	1.70
☐	27 Joe Garagiola	65.00	32.50	6.50
☐	28 Roy Hartsfield	17.00	8.50	1.70
☐	29 Ned Garver	17.00	8.50	1.70
☐	30 Red Schoendienst	65.00	32.50	6.50
☐	31 Eddie Yost	17.00	8.50	1.70
☐	32 Eddie Miksis	17.00	8.50	1.70
☐	33 Gil McDougald	50.00	25.00	5.00
☐	34 Alvin Dark	21.00	10.50	2.10
☐	35 Granny Hamner	17.00	8.50	1.70
☐	36 Cass Michaels	17.00	8.50	1.70
☐	37 Vic Raschi	21.00	10.50	2.10
☐	38 Whitey Lockman	18.00	9.00	1.80
☐	39 Vic Wertz	18.00	9.00	1.80
☐	40 Bubba Church	15.00	7.50	1.50
☐	41 Chico Carrasquel	15.00	7.50	1.50
☐	42 Johnny Wyrostek	15.00	7.50	1.50
☐	43 Bob Feller	100.00	50.00	10.00
☐	44 Roy Campanella	210.00	100.00	20.00
☐	45 Johnny Pesky	18.00	9.00	1.80
☐	46 Carl Scheib	15.00	7.50	1.50
☐	47 Pete Castiglione	15.00	7.50	1.50
☐	48 Vern Bickford	15.00	7.50	1.50
☐	49 Jim Hearn	15.00	7.50	1.50
☐	50 Jerry Staley	15.00	7.50	1.50
☐	51 Gil Coan	15.00	7.50	1.50
☐	52 Phil Rizzuto	65.00	32.50	6.50
☐	53 Richie Ashburn	45.00	22.50	4.50
☐	54 Billy Pierce	21.00	10.50	2.10
☐	55 Ken Raffensberger	15.00	7.50	1.50
☐	56 Clyde King	15.00	7.50	1.50
☐	57 Clyde Vollmer	15.00	7.50	1.50
☐	58 Hank Majeski	15.00	7.50	1.50
☐	59 Murry Dickson	15.00	7.50	1.50
☐	60 Sid Gordon	15.00	7.50	1.50
☐	61 Tommy Byrne	15.00	7.50	1.50
☐	62 Joe Presko	15.00	7.50	1.50
☐	63 Irv Noren	15.00	7.50	1.50
☐	64 Roy Smalley	15.00	7.50	1.50
☐	65 Hank Bauer	24.00	12.00	2.40
☐	66 Sal Maglie	22.00	11.00	2.20
☐	67 Johnny Groth	15.00	7.50	1.50
☐	68 Jim Busby	15.00	7.50	1.50
☐	69 Joe Adcock	20.00	10.00	2.00
☐	70 Carl Erskine	22.00	11.00	2.20
☐	71 Vernon Law	18.00	9.00	1.80
☐	72 Earl Torgeson	15.00	7.50	1.50
☐	73 Gerry Coleman	18.00	9.00	1.80
☐	74 Wes Westrum	14.00	7.00	1.40
☐	75 George Kell	40.00	20.00	4.00
☐	76 Del Ennis	16.00	8.00	1.60
☐	77 Eddie Robinson	14.00	7.00	1.40
☐	78 Lloyd Merriman	14.00	7.00	1.40
☐	79 Lou Brissie	14.00	7.00	1.40
☐	80 Gil Hodges	65.00	32.50	6.50
☐	81 Billy Goodman	16.00	8.00	1.60
☐	82 Gus Zernial	16.00	8.00	1.60
☐	83 Howie Pollet	14.00	7.00	1.40
☐	84 Sam Jethroe	14.00	7.00	1.40
☐	85 Marty Marion CO	20.00	10.00	2.00
☐	86 Cal Abrams	14.00	7.00	1.40
☐	87 Mickey Vernon	18.00	9.00	1.80
☐	88 Bruce Edwards	14.00	7.00	1.40
☐	89 Billy Hitchcock	14.00	7.00	1.40
☐	90 Larry Jansen	14.00	7.00	1.40
☐	91 Don Kolloway	14.00	7.00	1.40
☐	92 Eddie Waitkus	14.00	7.00	1.40
☐	93 Paul Richards	16.00	8.00	1.60
☐	94 Luke Sewell	16.00	8.00	1.60
☐	95 Luke Easter	16.00	8.00	1.60
☐	96 Ralph Branca	20.00	10.00	2.00
☐	97 Willard Marshall	14.00	7.00	1.40
☐	98 Jimmy Dykes	16.00	8.00	1.60
☐	99 Clyde McCullough	14.00	7.00	1.40
☐	100 Sibby Sisti	14.00	7.00	1.40
☐	101 Mickey Mantle	1500.00	600.00	150.00
☐	102 Peanuts Lowrey	14.00	7.00	1.40
☐	103 Joe Haynes	14.00	7.00	1.40
☐	104 Hal Jeffcoat	14.00	7.00	1.40
☐	105 Bobby Brown	22.00	11.00	2.20
☐	106 Randy Gumpert	14.00	7.00	1.40
☐	107 Del Rice	14.00	7.00	1.40
☐	108 George Metkovich	14.00	7.00	1.40
☐	109 Tom Morgan	14.00	7.00	1.40
☐	110 Max Lanier	14.00	7.00	1.40
☐	111 Hoot Evers	14.00	7.00	1.40
☐	112 Smokey Burgess	16.00	8.00	1.60
☐	113 Al Zarilla	14.00	7.00	1.40
☐	114 Frank Hiller	14.00	7.00	1.40
☐	115 Larry Doby	21.00	10.50	2.10
☐	116 Duke Snider	165.00	80.00	15.00
☐	117 Bill Wight	14.00	7.00	1.40
☐	118 Ray Murray	14.00	7.00	1.40
☐	119 Bill Howerton	14.00	7.00	1.40
☐	120 Chet Nichols	14.00	7.00	1.40
☐	121 Al Corwin	14.00	7.00	1.40
☐	122 Billy Johnson	14.00	7.00	1.40
☐	123 Sid Hudson	14.00	7.00	1.40
☐	124 Birdie Tebbetts	16.00	8.00	1.60
☐	125 Howie Fox	14.00	7.00	1.40
☐	126 Phil Cavarretta	16.00	8.00	1.60

☐ 127	Dick Sisler	14.00	7.00	1.40
☐ 128	Don Newcombe	24.00	12.00	2.40
☐ 129	Gus Niarhos	14.00	7.00	1.40
☐ 130	Allie Clark	14.00	7.00	1.40
☐ 131	Bob Swift	14.00	7.00	1.40
☐ 132	Dave Cole	14.00	7.00	1.40
☐ 133	Dick Kryhoski	14.00	7.00	1.40
☐ 134	Al Brazle	14.00	7.00	1.40
☐ 135	Mickey Harris	14.00	7.00	1.40
☐ 136	Gene Hermanski	14.00	7.00	1.40
☐ 137	Stan Rojek	14.00	7.00	1.40
☐ 138	Ted Wilks	14.00	7.00	1.40
☐ 139	Jerry Priddy	14.00	7.00	1.40
☐ 140	Ray Scarborough	14.00	7.00	1.40
☐ 141	Hank Edwards	14.00	7.00	1.40
☐ 142	Early Wynn	40.00	20.00	4.00
☐ 143	Sandy Consuegra	14.00	7.00	1.40
☐ 144	Joe Hatton	14.00	7.00	1.40
☐ 145	Johnny Mize	50.00	25.00	5.00
☐ 146	Leo Durocher MG	36.00	18.00	3.60
☐ 147	Marlin Stuart	13.00	6.50	1.30
☐ 148	Ken Heintzelman	13.00	6.50	1.30
☐ 149	Howie Judson	13.00	6.50	1.30
☐ 150	Herman Wehmeier	13.00	6.50	1.30
☐ 151	Al Rosen	21.00	10.50	2.10
☐ 152	Billy Cox	16.00	8.00	1.60
☐ 153	Fred Hatfield	13.00	6.50	1.30
☐ 154	Ferris Fain	15.00	7.50	1.50
☐ 155	Billy Meyer	13.00	6.50	1.30
☐ 156	Warren Spahn	80.00	40.00	8.00
☐ 157	Jim Delsing	13.00	6.50	1.30
☐ 158	Bucky Harris MG	27.00	13.50	2.70
☐ 159	Dutch Leonard	13.00	6.50	1.30
☐ 160	Eddie Stanky	16.00	8.00	1.60
☐ 161	Jackie Jensen	27.00	13.50	2.70
☐ 162	Monte Irvin	45.00	22.50	4.50
☐ 163	Johnny Lipon	13.00	6.50	1.30
☐ 164	Connie Ryan	13.00	6.50	1.30
☐ 165	Saul Rogovin	13.00	6.50	1.30
☐ 166	Bobby Adams	13.00	6.50	1.30
☐ 167	Bobby Avila	15.00	7.50	1.50
☐ 168	Preacher Roe	24.00	12.00	2.40
☐ 169	Walt Dropo	15.00	7.50	1.50
☐ 170	Joe Astroth	13.00	6.50	1.30
☐ 171	Mel Queen	13.00	6.50	1.30
☐ 172	Ebba St.Claire	13.00	6.50	1.30
☐ 173	Gene Bearden	15.00	7.50	1.50
☐ 174	Mickey Grasso	13.00	6.50	1.30
☐ 175	Randy Jackson	13.00	6.50	1.30
☐ 176	Harry Brecheen	15.00	7.50	1.50
☐ 177	Gene Woodling	18.00	9.00	1.80
☐ 178	Dave Williams	16.00	8.00	1.60
☐ 179	Pete Suder	13.00	6.50	1.30
☐ 180	Ed Fitzgerald	13.00	6.50	1.30
☐ 181	Joe Collins	16.00	8.00	1.60
☐ 182	Dave Koslo	12.00	6.00	1.20
☐ 183	Pat Mullin	12.00	6.00	1.20
☐ 184	Curt Simmons	16.00	8.00	1.60
☐ 185	Eddie Stewart	12.00	6.00	1.20
☐ 186	Frank Smith	12.00	6.00	1.20
☐ 187	Jim Hegan	14.00	7.00	1.40
☐ 188	Charlie Dressen MG	15.00	7.50	1.50
☐ 189	Jim Piersall	18.00	9.00	1.80
☐ 190	Dick Fowler	12.00	6.00	1.20
☐ 191	Bob Friend	22.00	11.00	2.20
☐ 192	John Cusick	12.00	6.00	1.20
☐ 193	Bobby Young	12.00	6.00	1.20
☐ 194	Bob Porterfield	12.00	6.00	1.20
☐ 195	Frank Baumholtz	12.00	6.00	1.20
☐ 196	Stan Musial	425.00	200.00	42.00
☐ 197	Charlie Silvera	12.00	6.00	1.20
☐ 198	Chuck Diering	12.00	6.00	1.20
☐ 199	Ted Gray	12.00	6.00	1.20
☐ 200	Ken Silvestri	12.00	6.00	1.20
☐ 201	Ray Coleman	12.00	6.00	1.20
☐ 202	Harry Perkowski	12.00	6.00	1.20
☐ 203	Steve Gromek	12.00	6.00	1.20
☐ 204	Andy Pafko	14.00	7.00	1.40
☐ 205	Walt Masterson	12.00	6.00	1.20
☐ 206	Elmer Valo	12.00	6.00	1.20
☐ 207	George Strickland	12.00	6.00	1.20
☐ 208	Walker Cooper	12.00	6.00	1.20
☐ 209	Dick Littlefield	12.00	6.00	1.20
☐ 210	Archie Wilson	12.00	6.00	1.20
☐ 211	Paul Minner	12.00	6.00	1.20
☐ 212	Solly Hemus	12.00	6.00	1.20
☐ 213	Monte Kennedy	12.00	6.00	1.20
☐ 214	Ray Boone	14.00	7.00	1.40
☐ 215	Sheldon Jones	12.00	6.00	1.20
☐ 216	Matt Batts	12.00	6.00	1.20
☐ 217	Casey Stengel MG	150.00	75.00	15.00
☐ 218	Willie Mays	825.00	350.00	75.00
☐ 219	Neil Berry	30.00	15.00	3.00
☐ 220	Russ Meyer	30.00	15.00	3.00
☐ 221	Lou Kretlow	30.00	15.00	3.00
☐ 222	Dixie Howell	30.00	15.00	3.00
☐ 223	Harry Simpson	30.00	15.00	3.00
☐ 224	Johnny Schmitz	30.00	15.00	3.00
☐ 225	Del Wilber	30.00	15.00	3.00
☐ 226	Alex Kellner	30.00	15.00	3.00
☐ 227	Clyde Sukeforth	30.00	15.00	3.00
☐ 228	Bob Chipman	30.00	15.00	3.00
☐ 229	Hank Arft	30.00	15.00	3.00
☐ 230	Frank Shea	30.00	15.00	3.00
☐ 231	Dee Fondy	30.00	15.00	3.00
☐ 232	Enos Slaughter	75.00	37.50	7.50
☐ 233	Bob Kuzava	30.00	15.00	3.00
☐ 234	Fred Fitzsimmons	30.00	15.00	3.00
☐ 235	Steve Souchock	30.00	15.00	3.00
☐ 236	Tommy Brown	30.00	15.00	3.00
☐ 237	Sherm Lollar	33.00	16.00	3.00
☐ 238	Roy McMillan	33.00	16.00	3.00
☐ 239	Dale Mitchell	33.00	16.00	3.00
☐ 240	Billy Loes	35.00	17.50	3.50
☐ 241	Mel Parnell	33.00	16.00	3.00
☐ 242	Everett Kell	30.00	15.00	3.00
☐ 243	Red Munger	30.00	15.00	3.00
☐ 244	Lew Burdette	55.00	27.50	5.50
☐ 245	George Schmees	30.00	15.00	3.00
☐ 246	Jerry Snyder	30.00	15.00	3.00
☐ 247	Johnny Pramesa	30.00	15.00	3.00
☐ 248	Bill Werle	30.00	15.00	3.00
☐ 249	Hank Thompson	33.00	16.00	3.00
☐ 250	Ike Delock	30.00	15.00	3.00
☐ 251	Jack Lohrke	30.00	15.00	3.00
☐ 252	Frank Crosetti CO	125.00	25.00	5.00

1953 Bowman Color

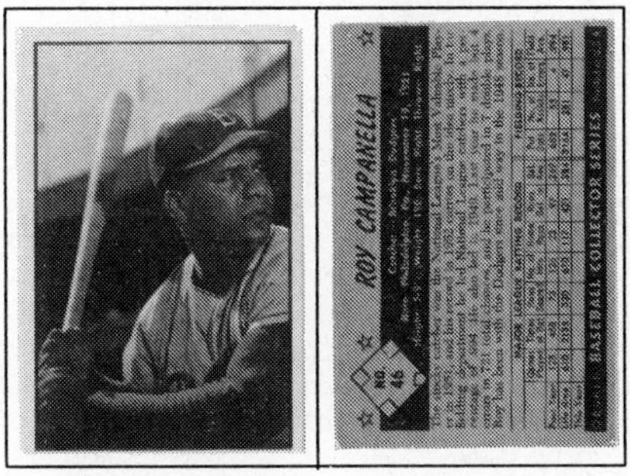

The cards in this 160-card set measure 2 1/2" by 3 3/4". The 1953 Bowman Color set, considered by many to be the best looking set of the modern era, contains Kodachrome photographs with no names or facsimile autographs on the face. Numbers 113 to 160 are somewhat more difficult to obtain. There are two cards of Al Corwin (126 and 149). There are no key rookie cards in this set.

	NRMT	VG-E	GOOD
COMPLETE SET (160)	10000.00	4000.00	1000.00
COMMON PLAYER (1-96)	30.00	15.00	3.00
COMMON PLAYER (97-112)	32.00	16.00	3.20
COMMON PLAYER (113-128)	48.00	22.00	4.50
COMMON PLAYER (129-160)	36.00	18.00	3.60

☐ 1	Dave Williams	100.00	20.00	4.00
☐ 2	Vic Wertz	32.00	16.00	3.20
☐ 3	Sam Jethroe	30.00	15.00	3.00
☐ 4	Art Houtteman	30.00	15.00	3.00
☐ 5	Sid Gordon	30.00	15.00	3.00
☐ 6	Joe Ginsberg	30.00	15.00	3.00
☐ 7	Harry Chiti	30.00	15.00	3.00
☐ 8	Al Rosen	40.00	20.00	4.00
☐ 9	Phil Rizzuto	90.00	45.00	9.00
☐ 10	Richie Ashburn	60.00	30.00	6.00
☐ 11	Bobby Shantz	35.00	17.50	3.50
☐ 12	Carl Erskine	40.00	20.00	4.00
☐ 13	Gus Zernial	32.00	16.00	3.20
☐ 14	Billy Loes	32.00	16.00	3.20
☐ 15	Jim Busby	30.00	15.00	3.00

☐	16 Bob Friend	32.00	16.00	3.20
☐	17 Jerry Staley	30.00	15.00	3.00
☐	18 Nellie Fox	50.00	25.00	5.00
☐	19 Alvin Dark	35.00	17.50	3.50
☐	20 Don Lenhardt	30.00	15.00	3.00
☐	21 Joe Garagiola	60.00	30.00	6.00
☐	22 Bob Porterfield	30.00	15.00	3.00
☐	23 Herman Wehmeier	30.00	15.00	3.00
☐	24 Jackie Jensen	35.00	17.50	3.50
☐	25 Hoot Evers	30.00	15.00	3.00
☐	26 Roy McMillan	30.00	15.00	3.00
☐	27 Vic Raschi	35.00	17.50	3.50
☐	28 Smokey Burgess	32.00	16.00	3.20
☐	29 Bobby Avila	32.00	16.00	3.20
☐	30 Phil Cavarretta	32.00	16.00	3.20
☐	31 Jimmy Dykes	32.00	16.00	3.20
☐	32 Stan Musial	425.00	200.00	42.00
☐	33 Pee Wee Reese HOR	300.00	150.00	30.00
☐	34 Gil Coan	30.00	15.00	3.00
☐	35 Maurice McDermott	30.00	15.00	3.00
☐	36 Minnie Minoso	45.00	22.50	4.50
☐	37 Jim Wilson	30.00	15.00	3.00
☐	38 Harry Byrd	30.00	15.00	3.00
☐	39 Paul Richards MG	32.00	16.00	3.20
☐	40 Larry Doby	40.00	20.00	4.00
☐	41 Sammy White	30.00	15.00	3.00
☐	42 Tommy Brown	30.00	15.00	3.00
☐	43 Mike Garcia	32.00	16.00	3.20
☐	44 Berra/Bauer/Mantle	375.00	175.00	37.00
☐	45 Walt Dropo	32.00	16.00	3.20
☐	46 Roy Campanella	240.00	110.00	22.00
☐	47 Ned Garver	30.00	15.00	3.00
☐	48 Hank Sauer	32.00	16.00	3.20
☐	49 Eddie Stanky	35.00	17.50	3.50
☐	50 Lou Kretlow	30.00	15.00	3.00
☐	51 Monte Irvin	50.00	25.00	5.00
☐	52 Marty Marion	35.00	17.50	3.50
☐	53 Del Rice	30.00	15.00	3.00
☐	54 Chico Carrasquel	30.00	15.00	3.00
☐	55 Leo Durocher MG	50.00	25.00	5.00
☐	56 Bob Cain	30.00	15.00	3.00
☐	57 Lou Boudreau MG	50.00	25.00	5.00
☐	58 Willard Marshall	30.00	15.00	3.00
☐	59 Mickey Mantle	1400.00	600.00	160.00
☐	60 Granny Hamner	30.00	15.00	3.00
☐	61 George Kell	55.00	27.50	5.50
☐	62 Ted Kluszewski	45.00	22.50	4.50
☐	63 Gil McDougald	42.00	20.00	4.00
☐	64 Curt Simmons	35.00	17.50	3.50
☐	65 Robin Roberts	65.00	32.50	6.50
☐	66 Mel Parnell	32.00	16.00	3.20
☐	67 Mel Clark	30.00	15.00	3.00
☐	68 Allie Reynolds	40.00	20.00	4.00
☐	69 Charlie Grimm MG	32.00	16.00	3.20
☐	70 Clint Courtney	30.00	15.00	3.00
☐	71 Paul Minner	30.00	15.00	3.00
☐	72 Ted Gray	30.00	15.00	3.00
☐	73 Billy Pierce	35.00	17.50	3.50
☐	74 Don Mueller	32.00	16.00	3.20
☐	75 Saul Rogovin	30.00	15.00	3.00
☐	76 Jim Hearn	30.00	15.00	3.00
☐	77 Mickey Grasso	30.00	15.00	3.00
☐	78 Carl Furillo	40.00	20.00	4.00
☐	79 Ray Boone	32.00	16.00	3.20
☐	80 Ralph Kiner	70.00	35.00	7.00
☐	81 Enos Slaughter	70.00	35.00	7.00
☐	82 Joe Astroth	30.00	15.00	3.00
☐	83 Jack Daniels	30.00	15.00	3.00
☐	84 Hank Bauer	42.00	20.00	4.00
☐	85 Solly Hemus	30.00	15.00	3.00
☐	86 Harry Simpson	30.00	15.00	3.00
☐	87 Harry Perkowski	30.00	15.00	3.00
☐	88 Joe Dobson	30.00	15.00	3.00
☐	89 Sandy Consuegra	30.00	15.00	3.00
☐	90 Joe Nuxhall	32.00	16.00	3.20
☐	91 Steve Souchock	30.00	15.00	3.00
☐	92 Gil Hodges	100.00	50.00	10.00
☐	93 Phil Rizzuto and Billy Martin	210.00	100.00	20.00
☐	94 Bob Addis	30.00	15.00	3.00
☐	95 Wally Moses	32.00	16.00	3.20
☐	96 Sal Maglie	40.00	20.00	4.00
☐	97 Eddie Mathews	150.00	75.00	15.00
☐	98 Hector Rodriguez	32.00	16.00	3.20
☐	99 Warren Spahn	125.00	60.00	12.50
☐	100 Bill Wight	32.00	16.00	3.20
☐	101 Red Schoendienst	80.00	40.00	8.00
☐	102 Jim Hegan	35.00	17.50	3.50
☐	103 Del Ennis	35.00	17.50	3.50
☐	104 Luke Easter	35.00	17.50	3.50
☐	105 Eddie Joost	32.00	16.00	3.20
☐	106 Ken Raffensberger	32.00	16.00	3.20
☐	107 Alex Kellner	32.00	16.00	3.20
☐	108 Bobby Adams	32.00	16.00	3.20

☐	109 Ken Wood	32.00	16.00	3.20
☐	110 Bob Rush	32.00	16.00	3.20
☐	111 Jim Dyck	32.00	16.00	3.20
☐	112 Toby Atwell	32.00	16.00	3.20
☐	113 Karl Drews	48.00	22.00	4.50
☐	114 Bob Feller	250.00	125.00	25.00
☐	115 Cloyd Boyer	48.00	22.00	4.50
☐	116 Eddie Yost	48.00	22.00	4.50
☐	117 Duke Snider	500.00	250.00	50.00
☐	118 Billy Martin	300.00	150.00	30.00
☐	119 Dale Mitchell	48.00	22.00	4.50
☐	120 Marlin Stuart	48.00	22.00	4.50
☐	121 Yogi Berra	500.00	250.00	50.00
☐	122 Bill Serena	48.00	22.00	4.50
☐	123 Johnny Lipon	48.00	22.00	4.50
☐	124 Charlie Dressen MG	60.00	30.00	6.00
☐	125 Fred Hatfield	48.00	22.00	4.50
☐	126 Al Corwin	48.00	22.00	4.50
☐	127 Dick Kryhoski	48.00	22.00	4.50
☐	128 Whitey Lockman	48.00	22.00	4.50
☐	129 Russ Meyer	36.00	18.00	3.60
☐	130 Cass Michaels	36.00	18.00	3.60
☐	131 Connie Ryan	36.00	18.00	3.60
☐	132 Fred Hutchinson	40.00	20.00	4.00
☐	133 Willie Jones	36.00	18.00	3.60
☐	134 Johnny Pesky	40.00	20.00	4.00
☐	135 Bobby Morgan	36.00	18.00	3.60
☐	136 Jim Brideweser	36.00	18.00	3.60
☐	137 Sam Dente	36.00	18.00	3.60
☐	138 Bubba Church	36.00	18.00	3.60
☐	139 Pete Runnels	40.00	20.00	4.00
☐	140 Al Brazle	36.00	18.00	3.60
☐	141 Frank Shea	36.00	18.00	3.60
☐	142 Larry Miggins	36.00	18.00	3.60
☐	143 Al Lopez MG	65.00	32.50	6.50
☐	144 Warren Hacker	36.00	18.00	3.60
☐	145 George Shuba	40.00	20.00	4.00
☐	146 Early Wynn	120.00	60.00	12.00
☐	147 Clem Koshorek	36.00	18.00	3.60
☐	148 Billy Goodman	40.00	20.00	4.00
☐	149 Al Corwin	36.00	18.00	3.60
☐	150 Carl Scheib	36.00	18.00	3.60
☐	151 Joe Adcock	45.00	22.50	4.50
☐	152 Clyde Vollmer	36.00	18.00	3.60
☐	153 Whitey Ford	400.00	200.00	40.00
☐	154 Turk Lown	36.00	18.00	3.60
☐	155 Allie Clark	36.00	18.00	3.60
☐	156 Max Surkont	36.00	18.00	3.60
☐	157 Sherm Lollar	40.00	20.00	4.00
☐	158 Howard Fox	36.00	18.00	3.60
☐	159 Mickey Vernon UER (photo actually Floyd Baker)	40.00	20.00	4.00
☐	160 Cal Abrams	75.00	20.00	4.00

1953 Bowman BW

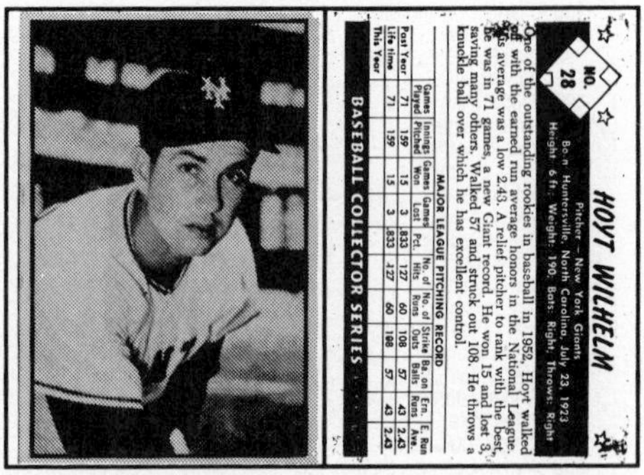

The cards in this 64-card set measure 2 1/2" by 3 3/4". Some collectors believe that the high cost of producing the 1953 color series forced Bowman to issue this set in black and white, since the two sets are identical in design except for the element of color. This set was also produced in fewer numbers than its color counterpart, and is popular among collectors for the challenge involved in completing it. There are no key rookie cards in this set.

	NRMT	VG-E	GOOD
COMPLETE SET (64)	2300.00	1000.00	250.00
COMMON PLAYER (1-64)	30.00	15.00	3.00
☐ 1 Gus Bell	100.00	50.00	10.00
☐ 2 Willard Nixon	30.00	15.00	3.00
☐ 3 Bill Rigney	30.00	15.00	3.00
☐ 4 Pat Mullin	30.00	15.00	3.00
☐ 5 Dee Fondy	30.00	15.00	3.00
☐ 6 Ray Murray	30.00	15.00	3.00
☐ 7 Andy Seminick	30.00	15.00	3.00
☐ 8 Pete Suder	30.00	15.00	3.00
☐ 9 Walt Masterson	30.00	15.00	3.00
☐ 10 Dick Sisler	30.00	15.00	3.00
☐ 11 Dick Gernert	30.00	15.00	3.00
☐ 12 Randy Jackson	30.00	15.00	3.00
☐ 13 Joe Tipton	30.00	15.00	3.00
☐ 14 Bill Nicholson	30.00	15.00	3.00
☐ 15 Johnny Mize	100.00	50.00	10.00
☐ 16 Stu Miller	33.00	16.00	3.00
☐ 17 Virgil Trucks	33.00	16.00	3.00
☐ 18 Billy Hoeft	33.00	16.00	3.00
☐ 19 Paul LaPalme	30.00	15.00	3.00
☐ 20 Eddie Robinson	30.00	15.00	3.00
☐ 21 Clarence Podbielan	30.00	15.00	3.00
☐ 22 Matt Batts	30.00	15.00	3.00
☐ 23 Wilmer Mizell	33.00	16.00	3.00
☐ 24 Del Wilber	30.00	15.00	3.00
☐ 25 Johnny Sain	50.00	25.00	5.00
☐ 26 Preacher Roe	50.00	25.00	5.00
☐ 27 Bob Lemon	100.00	50.00	10.00
☐ 28 Hoyt Wilhelm	100.00	50.00	10.00
☐ 29 Sid Hudson	30.00	15.00	3.00
☐ 30 Walker Cooper	30.00	15.00	3.00
☐ 31 Gene Woodling	40.00	20.00	4.00
☐ 32 Rocky Bridges	30.00	15.00	3.00
☐ 33 Bob Kuzava	30.00	15.00	3.00
☐ 34 Ebba St.Claire	30.00	15.00	3.00
☐ 35 Johnny Wyrostek	30.00	15.00	3.00
☐ 36 Jim Piersall	40.00	20.00	4.00
☐ 37 Hal Jeffcoat	30.00	15.00	3.00
☐ 38 Dave Cole	30.00	15.00	3.00
☐ 39 Casey Stengel MG	300.00	150.00	30.00
☐ 40 Larry Jansen	33.00	16.00	3.00
☐ 41 Bob Ramazotti	30.00	15.00	3.00
☐ 42 Howie Judson	30.00	15.00	3.00
☐ 43 Hal Bevan	30.00	15.00	3.00
☐ 44 Jim Delsing	30.00	15.00	3.00
☐ 45 Irv Noren	33.00	16.00	3.00
☐ 46 Bucky Harris	50.00	25.00	5.00
☐ 47 Jack Lohrke	30.00	15.00	3.00
☐ 48 Steve Ridzik	30.00	15.00	3.00
☐ 49 Floyd Baker	30.00	15.00	3.00
☐ 50 Dutch Leonard	30.00	15.00	3.00
☐ 51 Lou Burdette	42.00	20.00	4.00
☐ 52 Ralph Branca	40.00	20.00	4.00
☐ 53 Morrie Martin	30.00	15.00	3.00
☐ 54 Bill Miller	30.00	15.00	3.00
☐ 55 Don Johnson	30.00	15.00	3.00
☐ 56 Roy Smalley	30.00	15.00	3.00
☐ 57 Andy Pafko	33.00	16.00	3.00
☐ 58 Jim Konstanty	33.00	16.00	3.00
☐ 59 Duane Pillette	30.00	15.00	3.00
☐ 60 Billy Cox	33.00	16.00	3.00
☐ 61 Tom Gorman	30.00	15.00	3.00
☐ 62 Keith Thomas	30.00	15.00	3.00
☐ 63 Steve Gromek	30.00	15.00	3.00
☐ 64 Andy Hansen	45.00	15.00	3.00

1954 Bowman

The cards in this 224-card set measure 2 1/2" by 3 3/4". A contractual problem apparently resulted in the deletion of the number 66 Ted Williams card from this Bowman set, thereby creating a scarcity that is highly valued among collectors. The set price below does NOT include number 66 Williams. Many errors in players' statistics exist (and some were corrected) while a few players' names were printed on the front, instead of appearing as a facsimile autograph. The key rookie cards in this set are Harvey Kuenn and Don Larsen.

	NRMT	VG-E	GOOD
COMPLETE SET (224)	4000.00	1800.00	500.00
COMMON PLAYER (1-128)	8.00	4.00	.80
COMMON PLAYER (129-224)	10.00	5.00	1.00

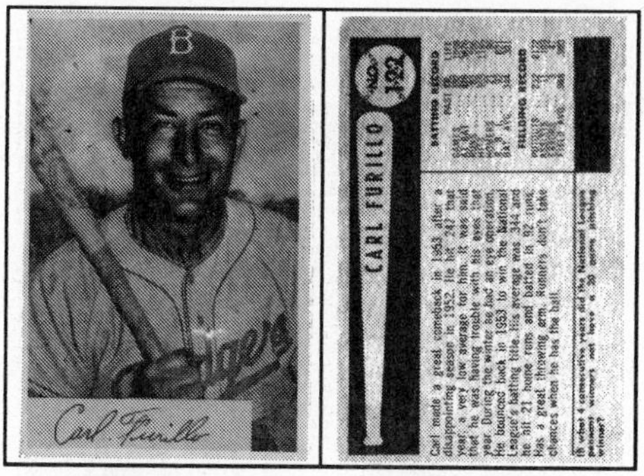

☐ 1 Phil Rizzuto	160.00	30.00	6.00
☐ 2 Jackie Jensen	12.50	6.25	1.25
☐ 3 Marion Fricano	8.00	4.00	.80
☐ 4 Bob Hooper	8.00	4.00	.80
☐ 5 Billy Hunter	8.00	4.00	.80
☐ 6 Nellie Fox	18.00	9.00	1.80
☐ 7 Walt Dropo	9.00	4.50	.90
☐ 8 Jim Busby	8.00	4.00	.80
☐ 9 Davey Williams	9.00	4.50	.90
☐ 10 Carl Erskine	12.50	6.25	1.25
☐ 11 Sid Gordon	8.00	4.00	.80
☐ 12 Roy McMillan	8.00	4.00	.80
☐ 13 Paul Minner	8.00	4.00	.80
☐ 14 Jerry Staley	8.00	4.00	.80
☐ 15 Richie Ashburn	25.00	12.50	2.50
☐ 16 Jim Wilson	8.00	4.00	.80
☐ 17 Tom Gorman	8.00	4.00	.80
☐ 18 Hoot Evers	8.00	4.00	.80
☐ 19 Bobby Shantz	9.00	4.50	.90
☐ 20 Art Houtteman	8.00	4.00	.80
☐ 21 Vic Wertz	9.00	4.50	.90
☐ 22 Sam Mele	8.00	4.00	.80
☐ 23 Harvey Kuenn	25.00	12.50	2.50
☐ 24 Bob Porterfield	8.00	4.00	.80
☐ 25 Wes Westrum	8.00	4.00	.80
☐ 26 Billy Cox	9.00	4.50	.90
☐ 27 Dick Cole	8.00	4.00	.80
☐ 28 Jim Greengrass	8.00	4.00	.80
☐ 29 Johnny Klippstein	8.00	4.00	.80
☐ 30 Del Rice	8.00	4.00	.80
☐ 31 Smoky Burgess	9.00	4.50	.90
☐ 32 Del Crandall	9.00	4.50	.90
☐ 33A Vic Raschi (no mention of trade on back)	14.00	7.00	1.40
☐ 33B Vic Raschi (traded to St.Louis)	25.00	12.50	2.50
☐ 34 Sammy White	8.00	4.00	.80
☐ 35 Eddie Joost	8.00	4.00	.80
☐ 36 George Strickland	8.00	4.00	.80
☐ 37 Dick Kokos	8.00	4.00	.80
☐ 38 Minnie Minoso	14.00	7.00	1.40
☐ 39 Ned Garver	8.00	4.00	.80
☐ 40 Gil Coan	8.00	4.00	.80
☐ 41 Alvin Dark	10.00	5.00	1.00
☐ 42 Billy Loes	8.00	4.00	.80
☐ 43 Bob Friend	9.00	4.50	.90
☐ 44 Harry Perkowski	8.00	4.00	.80
☐ 45 Ralph Kiner	36.00	18.00	3.60
☐ 46 Rip Repulski	8.00	4.00	.80
☐ 47 Granny Hamner	8.00	4.00	.80
☐ 48 Jack Dittmer	8.00	4.00	.80
☐ 49 Harry Byrd	8.00	4.00	.80
☐ 50 George Kell	25.00	12.50	2.50
☐ 51 Alex Kellner	8.00	4.00	.80
☐ 52 Joe Ginsberg	8.00	4.00	.80
☐ 53 Don Lenhardt	8.00	4.00	.80
☐ 54 Chico Carrasquel	8.00	4.00	.80
☐ 55 Jim Delsing	8.00	4.00	.80
☐ 56 Maurice McDermott	8.00	4.00	.80
☐ 57 Hoyt Wilhelm	25.00	12.50	2.50
☐ 58 Pee Wee Reese	55.00	27.50	5.50
☐ 59 Bob Schultz	8.00	4.00	.80
☐ 60 Fred Baczewski	8.00	4.00	.80
☐ 61 Eddie Miksis	8.00	4.00	.80
☐ 62 Enos Slaughter	36.00	18.00	3.60
☐ 63 Earl Torgeson	8.00	4.00	.80
☐ 64 Eddie Mathews	50.00	25.00	5.00
☐ 65 Mickey Mantle	750.00	375.00	75.00
☐ 66A Ted Williams	2800.00	1250.00	300.00
☐ 66B Jim Piersall	100.00	50.00	10.00
☐ 67 Carl Scheib	8.00	4.00	.80

☐ 68	Bobby Avila	8.00	4.00	.80
☐ 69	Clint Courtney	8.00	4.00	.80
☐ 70	Willard Marshall	8.00	4.00	.80
☐ 71	Ted Gray	8.00	4.00	.80
☐ 72	Eddie Yost	8.00	4.00	.80
☐ 73	Don Mueller	9.00	4.50	.90
☐ 74	Jim Gilliam	14.00	7.00	1.40
☐ 75	Max Surkont	8.00	4.00	.80
☐ 76	Joe Nuxhall	9.00	4.50	.90
☐ 77	Bob Rush	8.00	4.00	.80
☐ 78	Sal Yvars	8.00	4.00	.80
☐ 79	Curt Simmons	9.00	4.50	.90
☐ 80	Johnny Logan	9.00	4.50	.90
☐ 81	Jerry Coleman	9.00	4.50	.90
☐ 82	Billy Goodman	9.00	4.50	.90
☐ 83	Ray Murray	8.00	4.00	.80
☐ 84	Larry Doby	12.50	6.25	1.25
☐ 85	Jim Dyck	8.00	4.00	.80
☐ 86	Harry Dorish	8.00	4.00	.80
☐ 87	Don Lund	8.00	4.00	.80
☐ 88	Tom Umphlett	8.00	4.00	.80
☐ 89	Willie Mays	300.00	150.00	30.00
☐ 90	Roy Campanella	125.00	60.00	12.50
☐ 91	Cal Abrams	8.00	4.00	.80
☐ 92	Ken Raffensberger	8.00	4.00	.80
☐ 93	Bill Serena	8.00	4.00	.80
☐ 94	Solly Hemus	8.00	4.00	.80
☐ 95	Robin Roberts	32.00	16.00	3.20
☐ 96	Joe Adcock	9.00	4.50	.90
☐ 97	Gil McDougald	14.00	7.00	1.40
☐ 98	Ellis Kinder	8.00	4.00	.80
☐ 99	Pete Suder	8.00	4.00	.80
☐ 100	Mike Garcia	9.00	4.50	.90
☐ 101	Don Larsen	28.00	14.00	2.80
☐ 102	Billy Pierce	9.00	4.50	.90
☐ 103	Steve Souchock	8.00	4.00	.80
☐ 104	Frank Shea	8.00	4.00	.80
☐ 105	Sal Maglie	12.50	6.25	1.25
☐ 106	Clem Labine	9.00	4.50	.90
☐ 107	Paul LaPalme	8.00	4.00	.80
☐ 108	Bobby Adams	8.00	4.00	.80
☐ 109	Roy Smalley	8.00	4.00	.80
☐ 110	Red Schoendienst	32.00	16.00	3.20
☐ 111	Murry Dickson	8.00	4.00	.80
☐ 112	Andy Pafko	9.00	4.50	.90
☐ 113	Allie Reynolds	13.50	6.00	1.20
☐ 114	Willard Nixon	8.00	4.00	.80
☐ 115	Don Bollweg	8.00	4.00	.80
☐ 116	Luke Easter	8.00	4.00	.80
☐ 117	Dick Kryhoski	8.00	4.00	.80
☐ 118	Bob Boyd	8.00	4.00	.80
☐ 119	Fred Hatfield	8.00	4.00	.80
☐ 120	Mel Hoderlein	8.00	4.00	.80
☐ 121	Ray Katt	8.00	4.00	.80
☐ 122	Carl Furillo	14.00	7.00	1.40
☐ 123	Toby Atwell	8.00	4.00	.80
☐ 124	Gus Bell	9.00	4.50	.90
☐ 125	Warren Hacker	8.00	4.00	.80
☐ 126	Cliff Chambers	8.00	4.00	.80
☐ 127	Del Ennis	9.00	4.50	.90
☐ 128	Ebba St.Claire	8.00	4.00	.80
☐ 129	Hank Bauer	18.00	9.00	1.80
☐ 130	Milt Bolling	10.00	5.00	1.00
☐ 131	Joe Astroth	10.00	5.00	1.00
☐ 132	Bob Feller	75.00	37.50	7.50
☐ 133	Duane Pillette	10.00	5.00	1.00
☐ 134	Luis Aloma	10.00	5.00	1.00
☐ 135	Johnny Pesky	11.00	5.50	1.10
☐ 136	Clyde Vollmer	10.00	5.00	1.00
☐ 137	Al Corwin	10.00	5.00	1.00
☐ 138	Gil Hodges	55.00	27.50	5.50
☐ 139	Preston Ward	10.00	5.00	1.00
☐ 140	Saul Rogovin	10.00	5.00	1.00
☐ 141	Joe Garagiola	40.00	20.00	4.00
☐ 142	Al Brazle	10.00	5.00	1.00
☐ 143	Willie Jones	10.00	5.00	1.00
☐ 144	Ernie Johnson	10.00	5.00	1.00
☐ 145	Billy Martin	60.00	30.00	6.00
☐ 146	Dick Gernert	10.00	5.00	1.00
☐ 147	Joe DeMaestri	10.00	5.00	1.00
☐ 148	Dale Mitchell	11.00	5.50	1.10
☐ 149	Bob Young	10.00	5.00	1.00
☐ 150	Cass Michaels	10.00	5.00	1.00
☐ 151	Pat Mullin	10.00	5.00	1.00
☐ 152	Mickey Vernon	11.00	5.50	1.10
☐ 153	Whitey Lockman	11.00	5.50	1.10
☐ 154	Don Newcombe	16.00	8.00	1.60
☐ 155	Frank Thomas	11.00	5.50	1.10
☐ 156	Rocky Bridges	10.00	5.00	1.00
☐ 157	Turk Lown	10.00	5.00	1.00
☐ 158	Stu Miller	11.00	5.50	1.10
☐ 159	Johnny Lindell	10.00	5.00	1.00
☐ 160	Danny O'Connell	10.00	5.00	1.00
☐ 161	Yogi Berra	150.00	75.00	15.00
☐ 162	Ted Lepcio	10.00	5.00	1.00
☐ 163A	Dave Philley (no mention of trade on back)	11.00	5.50	1.10
☐ 163B	Dave Philley (traded to Cleveland)	20.00	10.00	2.00
☐ 164	Early Wynn	33.00	15.00	3.00
☐ 165	Johnny Groth	10.00	5.00	1.00
☐ 166	Sandy Consuegra	10.00	5.00	1.00
☐ 167	Billy Hoeft	10.00	5.00	1.00
☐ 168	Ed Fitzgerald	10.00	5.00	1.00
☐ 169	Larry Jansen	11.00	5.50	1.10
☐ 170	Duke Snider	125.00	60.00	12.50
☐ 171	Carlos Bernier	10.00	5.00	1.00
☐ 172	Andy Seminick	10.00	5.00	1.00
☐ 173	Dee Fondy	10.00	5.00	1.00
☐ 174	Pete Castiglione	10.00	5.00	1.00
☐ 175	Mel Clark	10.00	5.00	1.00
☐ 176	Vern Bickford	10.00	5.00	1.00
☐ 177	Whitey Ford	80.00	40.00	8.00
☐ 178	Del Wilber	10.00	5.00	1.00
☐ 179	Morrie Martin	10.00	5.00	1.00
☐ 180	Joe Tipton	10.00	5.00	1.00
☐ 181	Les Moss	10.00	5.00	1.00
☐ 182	Sherm Lollar	11.00	5.50	1.10
☐ 183	Matt Batts	10.00	5.00	1.00
☐ 184	Mickey Grasso	10.00	5.00	1.00
☐ 185	Daryl Spencer	10.00	5.00	1.00
☐ 186	Russ Meyer	10.00	5.00	1.00
☐ 187	Vernon Law	11.00	5.50	1.10
☐ 188	Frank Smith	10.00	5.00	1.00
☐ 189	Randy Jackson	10.00	5.00	1.00
☐ 190	Joe Presko	10.00	5.00	1.00
☐ 191	Karl Drews	10.00	5.00	1.00
☐ 192	Lou Burdette	12.50	6.25	1.25
☐ 193	Eddie Robinson	10.00	5.00	1.00
☐ 194	Sid Hudson	10.00	5.00	1.00
☐ 195	Bob Cain	10.00	5.00	1.00
☐ 196	Bob Lemon	33.00	15.00	3.00
☐ 197	Lou Kretlow	10.00	5.00	1.00
☐ 198	Virgil Trucks	11.00	5.50	1.10
☐ 199	Steve Gromek	10.00	5.00	1.00
☐ 200	Conrado Marrero	10.00	5.00	1.00
☐ 201	Bobby Thomson	13.00	6.50	1.30
☐ 202	George Shuba	11.00	5.50	1.10
☐ 203	Vic Janowicz	11.00	5.50	1.10
☐ 204	Jack Collum	10.00	5.00	1.00
☐ 205	Hal Jeffcoat	10.00	5.00	1.00
☐ 206	Steve Bilko	10.00	5.00	1.00
☐ 207	Stan Lopata	10.00	5.00	1.00
☐ 208	Johnny Antonelli	11.00	5.50	1.10
☐ 209	Gene Woodling	12.00	6.00	1.20
☐ 210	Jim Piersall	13.00	6.50	1.30
☐ 211	Al Robertson	10.00	5.00	1.00
☐ 212	Owen Friend	10.00	5.00	1.00
☐ 213	Dick Littlefield	10.00	5.00	1.00
☐ 214	Ferris Fain	11.00	5.50	1.10
☐ 215	Johnny Bucha	10.00	5.00	1.00
☐ 216	Jerry Snyder	10.00	5.00	1.00
☐ 217	Hank Thompson	11.00	5.50	1.10
☐ 218	Preacher Roe	12.50	6.25	1.25
☐ 219	Hal Rice	10.00	5.00	1.00
☐ 220	Hobie Landrith	10.00	5.00	1.00
☐ 221	Frank Baumholtz	10.00	5.00	1.00
☐ 222	Memo Luna	10.00	5.00	1.00
☐ 223	Steve Ridzik	10.00	5.00	1.00
☐ 224	Bill Bruton	24.00	6.00	1.25

1955 Bowman

The cards in this 320-card set measure 2 1/2" by 3 3/4". The Bowman set of 1955 is known as the "TV set" because each player photograph is cleverly shown within a television set design. The set contains umpire cards, some transposed pictures (e.g., Johnsons and Bollings), an incorrect spelling for Harvey Kuenn, and a traded line for Palica (all of which are noted in the checklist below). Some three-card advertising strips exist, the backs of these panels contain advertising for Bowman products. Advertising panels seen include Nellie Fox/Carl Furillo/ Carl Erskine and a panel including Early Wynn and Pee Wee Reese. The key rookie cards in this set are Elston Howard and Don Zimmer.

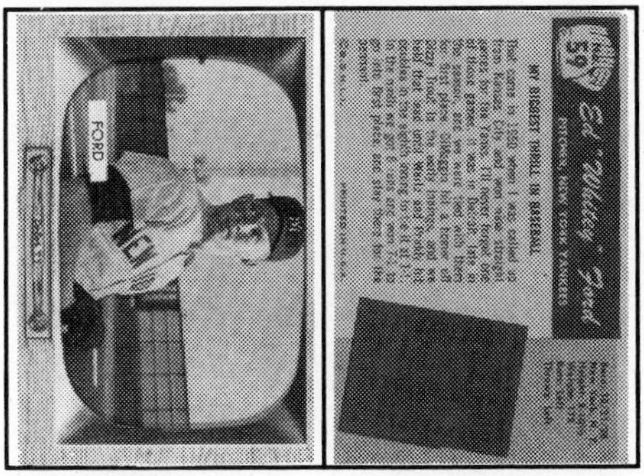

	NRMT	VG-E	GOOD
COMPLETE SET (320)	4500.00	250.00	50.00
COMMON PLAYER (1-96)	6.50	3.25	.65
COMMON PLAYER (97-224)	5.00	2.50	.50
COMMON PLAYER (225-320)	12.50	6.25	1.25
COMMON UMPIRES (225-320)	20.00	10.00	2.00
☐ 1 Hoyt Wilhelm	100.00	15.00	3.00
☐ 2 Alvin Dark	9.00	4.50	.90
☐ 3 Joe Coleman	6.50	3.25	.65
☐ 4 Eddie Waitkus	6.50	3.25	.65
☐ 5 Jim Robertson	6.50	3.25	.65
☐ 6 Pete Suder	6.50	3.25	.65
☐ 7 Gene Baker	6.50	3.25	.65
☐ 8 Warren Hacker	6.50	3.25	.65
☐ 9 Gil McDougald	12.00	6.00	1.20
☐ 10 Phil Rizzuto	50.00	25.00	5.00
☐ 11 Bill Bruton	7.50	3.75	.75
☐ 12 Andy Pafko	7.50	3.75	.75
☐ 13 Clyde Vollmer	6.50	3.25	.65
☐ 14 Gus Keriazakos	6.50	3.25	.65
☐ 15 Frank Sullivan	6.50	3.25	.65
☐ 16 Jim Piersall	9.00	4.50	.90
☐ 17 Del Ennis	7.50	3.75	.75
☐ 18 Stan Lopata	6.50	3.25	.65
☐ 19 Bobby Avila	6.50	3.25	.65
☐ 20 Al Smith	6.50	3.25	.65
☐ 21 Don Hoak	7.50	3.75	.75
☐ 22 Roy Campanella	110.00	55.00	11.00
☐ 23 Al Kaline	130.00	65.00	13.00
☐ 24 Al Aber	6.50	3.25	.65
☐ 25 Minnie Minoso	12.00	6.00	1.20
☐ 26 Virgil Trucks	7.50	3.75	.75
☐ 27 Preston Ward	6.50	3.25	.65
☐ 28 Dick Cole	6.50	3.25	.65
☐ 29 Red Schoendienst	25.00	12.50	2.50
☐ 30 Bill Sarni	6.50	3.25	.65
☐ 31 Johnny Temple	7.50	3.75	.75
☐ 32 Wally Post	7.50	3.75	.75
☐ 33 Nellie Fox	17.00	8.50	1.70
☐ 34 Clint Courtney	6.50	3.25	.65
☐ 35 Bill Tuttle	6.50	3.25	.65
☐ 36 Wayne Belardi	6.50	3.25	.65
☐ 37 Pee Wee Reese	55.00	27.50	5.50
☐ 38 Early Wynn	25.00	12.50	2.50
☐ 39 Bob Darnell	6.50	3.25	.65
☐ 40 Vic Wertz	7.50	3.75	.75
☐ 41 Mel Clark	6.50	3.25	.65
☐ 42 Bob Greenwood	6.50	3.25	.65
☐ 43 Bob Buhl	7.50	3.75	.75
☐ 44 Danny O'Connell	6.50	3.25	.65
☐ 45 Tom Umphlett	6.50	3.25	.65
☐ 46 Mickey Vernon	8.00	4.00	.80
☐ 47 Sammy White	6.50	3.25	.65
☐ 48A Milt Bolling ERR (name on back is Frank Bolling)	10.00	5.00	1.00
☐ 48B Milt Bolling COR	25.00	12.50	2.50
☐ 49 Jim Greengrass	6.50	3.25	.65
☐ 50 Hobie Landrith	6.50	3.25	.65
☐ 51 Elvin Tappe	6.50	3.25	.65
☐ 52 Hal Rice	6.50	3.25	.65
☐ 53 Alex Kellner	6.50	3.25	.65
☐ 54 Don Bollweg	6.50	3.25	.65
☐ 55 Cal Abrams	6.50	3.25	.65
☐ 56 Billy Cox	7.50	3.75	.75
☐ 57 Bob Friend	8.00	4.00	.80
☐ 58 Frank Thomas	7.50	3.75	.75
☐ 59 Whitey Ford	70.00	35.00	7.00
☐ 60 Enos Slaughter	25.00	12.50	2.50
☐ 61 Paul LaPalme	6.50	3.25	.65
☐ 62 Royce Lint	6.50	3.25	.65
☐ 63 Irv Noren	7.50	3.75	.75
☐ 64 Curt Simmons	7.50	3.75	.75
☐ 65 Don Zimmer	20.00	10.00	2.00
☐ 66 George Shuba	7.50	3.75	.75
☐ 67 Don Larsen	14.00	7.00	1.40
☐ 68 Elston Howard	36.00	18.00	3.60
☐ 69 Billy Hunter	6.50	3.25	.65
☐ 70 Lou Burdette	9.00	4.50	.90
☐ 71 Dave Jolly	6.50	3.25	.65
☐ 72 Chet Nichols	6.50	3.25	.65
☐ 73 Eddie Yost	6.50	3.25	.65
☐ 74 Jerry Snyder	6.50	3.25	.65
☐ 75 Brooks Lawrence	6.50	3.25	.65
☐ 76 Tom Poholsky	6.50	3.25	.65
☐ 77 Jim McDonald	6.50	3.25	.65
☐ 78 Gil Coan	6.50	3.25	.65
☐ 79 Willie Miranda	6.50	3.25	.65
☐ 80 Lou Limmer	6.50	3.25	.65
☐ 81 Bobby Morgan	6.50	3.25	.65
☐ 82 Lee Walls	6.50	3.25	.65
☐ 83 Max Surkont	6.50	3.25	.65
☐ 84 George Freese	6.50	3.25	.65
☐ 85 Cass Michaels	6.50	3.25	.65
☐ 86 Ted Gray	6.50	3.25	.65
☐ 87 Randy Jackson	6.50	3.25	.65
☐ 88 Steve Bilko	6.50	3.25	.65
☐ 89 Lou Boudreau MG	20.00	10.00	2.00
☐ 90 Art Ditmar	6.50	3.25	.65
☐ 91 Dick Marlowe	6.50	3.25	.65
☐ 92 George Zuverink	6.50	3.25	.65
☐ 93 Andy Seminick	6.50	3.25	.65
☐ 94 Hank Thompson	7.50	3.75	.75
☐ 95 Sal Maglie	10.00	5.00	1.00
☐ 96 Ray Narleski	6.50	3.25	.65
☐ 97 Johnny Podres	11.00	5.50	1.10
☐ 98 Jim Gilliam	11.00	5.50	1.10
☐ 99 Jerry Coleman	7.50	3.75	.75
☐ 100 Tom Morgan	6.50	3.25	.65
☐ 101A Don Johnson ERR (photo actually Ernie Johnson)	9.00	4.50	.90
☐ 101B Don Johnson COR	20.00	10.00	2.00
☐ 102 Bobby Thomson	10.00	5.00	1.00
☐ 103 Eddie Mathews	45.00	22.50	4.50
☐ 104 Bob Porterfield	5.00	2.50	.50
☐ 105 Johnny Schmitz	5.00	2.50	.50
☐ 106 Del Rice	5.00	2.50	.50
☐ 107 Solly Hemus	5.00	2.50	.50
☐ 108 Lou Kretlow	5.00	2.50	.50
☐ 109 Vern Stephens	6.00	3.00	.60
☐ 110 Bob Miller	5.00	2.50	.50
☐ 111 Steve Ridzik	5.00	2.50	.50
☐ 112 Granny Hamner	5.00	2.50	.50
☐ 113 Bob Hall	5.00	2.50	.50
☐ 114 Vic Janowicz	6.00	3.00	.60
☐ 115 Roger Bowman	5.00	2.50	.50
☐ 116 Sandy Consuegra	5.00	2.50	.50
☐ 117 Johnny Groth	5.00	2.50	.50
☐ 118 Bobby Adams	5.00	2.50	.50
☐ 119 Joe Astroth	5.00	2.50	.50
☐ 120 Ed Burtschy	5.00	2.50	.50
☐ 121 Rufus Crawford	5.00	2.50	.50
☐ 122 Al Corwin	5.00	2.50	.50
☐ 123 Marv Grissom	5.00	2.50	.50
☐ 124 Johnny Antonelli	7.00	3.50	.70
☐ 125 Paul Giel	5.00	2.50	.50
☐ 126 Billy Goodman	6.00	3.00	.60
☐ 127 Hank Majeski	5.00	2.50	.50
☐ 128 Mike Garcia	6.00	3.00	.60
☐ 129 Hal Naragon	5.00	2.50	.50
☐ 130 Richie Ashburn	18.00	9.00	1.80
☐ 131 Willard Marshall	5.00	2.50	.50
☐ 132A Harvey Kueen ERR (sic, Kuenn)	10.00	5.00	1.00
☐ 132B Harvey Kuenn COR	22.00	11.00	2.20
☐ 133 Charles King	5.00	2.50	.50
☐ 134 Bob Feller	55.00	27.50	5.50
☐ 135 Lloyd Merriman	5.00	2.50	.50
☐ 136 Rocky Bridges	5.00	2.50	.50
☐ 137 Bob Talbot	5.00	2.50	.50
☐ 138 Davey Williams	6.00	3.00	.60
☐ 139 Shantz Brothers Wilmer and Bobby	7.00	3.50	.70
☐ 140 Bobby Shantz	6.00	3.00	.60
☐ 141 Wes Westrum	5.00	2.50	.50
☐ 142 Rudy Regalado	5.00	2.50	.50
☐ 143 Don Newcombe	12.00	6.00	1.20
☐ 144 Art Houtteman	5.00	2.50	.50
☐ 145 Bob Nieman	5.00	2.50	.50
☐ 146 Don Liddle	5.00	2.50	.50
☐ 147 Sam Mele	5.00	2.50	.50
☐ 148 Bob Chakales	5.00	2.50	.50
☐ 149 Cloyd Boyer	5.00	2.50	.50
☐ 150 Billy Klaus	5.00	2.50	.50

☐ 151 Jim Brideweser	5.00	2.50	.50
☐ 152 Johnny Klippstein	5.00	2.50	.50
☐ 153 Eddie Robinson	5.00	2.50	.50
☐ 154 Frank Lary	7.00	3.50	.70
☐ 155 Jerry Staley	5.00	2.50	.50
☐ 156 Jim Hughes	5.00	2.50	.50
☐ 157A Ernie Johnson ERR (photo actually Don Johnson)	8.00	4.00	.80
☐ 157B Ernie Johnson COR	20.00	10.00	2.00
☐ 158 Gil Hodges	36.00	18.00	3.60
☐ 159 Harry Byrd	6.00	3.00	.60
☐ 160 Bill Skowron	15.00	7.50	1.50
☐ 161 Matt Batts	5.00	2.50	.50
☐ 162 Charlie Maxwell	6.00	3.00	.60
☐ 163 Sid Gordon	5.00	2.50	.50
☐ 164 Toby Atwell	5.00	2.50	.50
☐ 165 Maurice McDermott	5.00	2.50	.50
☐ 166 Jim Busby	5.00	2.50	.50
☐ 167 Bob Grim	10.00	5.00	1.00
☐ 168 Yogi Berra	90.00	45.00	9.00
☐ 169 Carl Furillo	11.00	5.50	1.10
☐ 170 Carl Erskine	11.00	5.50	1.10
☐ 171 Robin Roberts	24.00	12.00	2.40
☐ 172 Willie Jones	5.00	2.50	.50
☐ 173 Chico Carrasquel	5.00	2.50	.50
☐ 174 Sherm Lollar	6.00	3.00	.60
☐ 175 Wilmer Shantz	5.00	2.50	.50
☐ 176 Joe DeMaestri	5.00	2.50	.50
☐ 177 Willard Nixon	5.00	2.50	.50
☐ 178 Tom Brewer	5.00	2.50	.50
☐ 179 Hank Aaron	210.00	100.00	20.00
☐ 180 Johnny Logan	6.00	3.00	.60
☐ 181 Eddie Miksis	5.00	2.50	.50
☐ 182 Bob Rush	5.00	2.50	.50
☐ 183 Ray Katt	5.00	2.50	.50
☐ 184 Willie Mays	210.00	100.00	20.00
☐ 185 Vic Raschi	8.00	4.00	.80
☐ 186 Alex Grammas	5.00	2.50	.50
☐ 187 Fred Hatfield	5.00	2.50	.50
☐ 188 Ned Garver	5.00	2.50	.50
☐ 189 Jack Collum	5.00	2.50	.50
☐ 190 Fred Baczewski	5.00	2.50	.50
☐ 191 Bob Lemon	24.00	12.00	2.40
☐ 192 George Strickland	5.00	2.50	.50
☐ 193 Howie Judson	5.00	2.50	.50
☐ 194 Joe Nuxhall	6.00	3.00	.60
☐ 195A Erv Palica (without trade)	6.00	3.00	.60
☐ 195B Erv Palica (with trade)	16.00	8.00	1.60
☐ 196 Russ Meyer	5.00	2.50	.50
☐ 197 Ralph Kiner	25.00	12.50	2.50
☐ 198 Dave Pope	5.00	2.50	.50
☐ 199 Vernon Law	7.00	3.50	.70
☐ 200 Dick Littlefield	5.00	2.50	.50
☐ 201 Allie Reynolds	11.00	5.50	1.10
☐ 202 Mickey Mantle	400.00	200.00	40.00
☐ 203 Steve Gromek	5.00	2.50	.50
☐ 204A Frank Bolling ERR (name on back is Milt Bolling)	7.00	3.50	.70
☐ 204B Frank Bolling COR	20.00	10.00	2.00
☐ 205 Rip Repulski	5.00	2.50	.50
☐ 206 Ralph Beard	5.00	2.50	.50
☐ 207 Frank Shea	5.00	2.50	.50
☐ 208 Ed Fitzgerald	5.00	2.50	.50
☐ 209 Smokey Burgess	6.00	3.00	.60
☐ 210 Earl Torgeson	5.00	2.50	.50
☐ 211 Sonny Dixon	5.00	2.50	.50
☐ 212 Jack Dittmer	5.00	2.50	.50
☐ 213 George Kell	20.00	10.00	2.00
☐ 214 Billy Pierce	7.00	3.50	.70
☐ 215 Bob Kuzava	5.00	2.50	.50
☐ 216 Preacher Roe	10.00	5.00	1.00
☐ 217 Del Crandall	6.00	3.00	.60
☐ 218 Joe Adcock	7.00	3.50	.70
☐ 219 Whitey Lockman	6.00	3.00	.60
☐ 220 Jim Hearn	5.00	2.50	.50
☐ 221 Hector Brown	5.00	2.50	.50
☐ 222 Russ Kemmerer	5.00	2.50	.50
☐ 223 Hal Jeffcoat	5.00	2.50	.50
☐ 224 Dee Fondy	5.00	2.50	.50
☐ 225 Paul Richards	15.00	7.50	1.50
☐ 226 W. McKinley UMP	20.00	10.00	2.00
☐ 227 Frank Baumholtz	12.50	6.25	1.25
☐ 228 John Phillips	12.50	6.25	1.25
☐ 229 Jim Brosnan	15.00	7.50	1.50
☐ 230 Al Brazle	12.50	6.25	1.25
☐ 231 Jim Konstanty	15.00	7.50	1.50
☐ 232 Birdie Tebbetts	15.00	7.50	1.50
☐ 233 Bill Serena	12.50	6.25	1.25
☐ 234 Dick Bartell	12.50	6.25	1.25
☐ 235 J. Paparella UMP	20.00	10.00	2.00
☐ 236 Murry Dickson	12.50	6.25	1.25
☐ 237 Johnny Wyrostek	12.50	6.25	1.25
☐ 238 Eddie Stanky	18.00	9.00	1.80
☐ 239 Edwin Rommel UMP	20.00	10.00	2.00
☐ 240 Billy Loes	15.00	7.50	1.50
☐ 241 Johnny Pesky	15.00	7.50	1.50
☐ 242 Ernie Banks	350.00	175.00	35.00
☐ 243 Gus Bell	15.00	7.50	1.50
☐ 244 Duane Pillette	12.50	6.25	1.25
☐ 245 Bill Miller	12.50	6.25	1.25
☐ 246 Hank Bauer	28.00	14.00	2.80
☐ 247 Dutch Leonard	12.50	6.25	1.25
☐ 248 Harry Dorish	12.50	6.25	1.25
☐ 249 Billy Gardner	15.00	7.50	1.50
☐ 250 Larry Napp UMP	20.00	10.00	2.00
☐ 251 Stan Jok	12.50	6.25	1.25
☐ 252 Roy Smalley	12.50	6.25	1.25
☐ 253 Jim Wilson	12.50	6.25	1.25
☐ 254 Bennett Flowers	12.50	6.25	1.25
☐ 255 Pete Runnels	15.00	7.50	1.50
☐ 256 Owen Friend	12.50	6.25	1.25
☐ 257 Tom Alston	12.50	6.25	1.25
☐ 258 John Stevens UMP	20.00	10.00	2.00
☐ 259 Don Mossi	18.00	9.00	1.80
☐ 260 Edwin Hurley UMP	20.00	10.00	2.00
☐ 261 Walt Moryn	12.50	6.25	1.25
☐ 262 Jim Lemon	15.00	7.50	1.50
☐ 263 Eddie Joost	12.50	6.25	1.25
☐ 264 Bill Henry	12.50	6.25	1.25
☐ 265 Albert Barlick UMP	75.00	37.50	7.50
☐ 266 Mike Fornieles	12.50	6.25	1.25
☐ 267 Jim Honochick UMP	65.00	32.50	6.50
☐ 268 Roy Lee Hawes	12.50	6.25	1.25
☐ 269 Joe Amalfitano	12.50	6.25	1.25
☐ 270 Chico Fernandez	12.50	6.25	1.25
☐ 271 Bob Hooper	12.50	6.25	1.25
☐ 272 John Flaherty UMP	20.00	10.00	2.00
☐ 273 Bubba Church	12.50	6.25	1.25
☐ 274 Jim Delsing	12.50	6.25	1.25
☐ 275 William Grieve UMP	20.00	10.00	2.00
☐ 276 Ike Delock	12.50	6.25	1.25
☐ 277 Ed Runge UMP	25.00	12.50	2.50
☐ 278 Charlie Neal	25.00	12.50	2.50
☐ 279 Hank Soar UMP	20.00	10.00	2.00
☐ 280 Clyde McCullough	12.50	6.25	1.25
☐ 281 Charles Berry UMP	20.00	10.00	2.00
☐ 282 Phil Cavarretta	18.00	9.00	1.80
☐ 283 Nestor Chylak UMP	20.00	10.00	2.00
☐ 284 Bill Jackowski UMP	20.00	10.00	2.00
☐ 285 Walt Dropo	15.00	7.50	1.50
☐ 286 Frank Secory UMP	20.00	10.00	2.00
☐ 287 Ron Mrozinski	12.50	6.25	1.25
☐ 288 Dick Smith	12.50	6.25	1.25
☐ 289 Arthur Gore UMP	20.00	10.00	2.00
☐ 290 Hershell Freeman	12.50	6.25	1.25
☐ 291 Frank Dascoli UMP	20.00	10.00	2.00
☐ 292 Marv Blaylock	12.50	6.25	1.25
☐ 293 Thomas Gorman UMP	25.00	12.50	2.50
☐ 294 Wally Moses	15.00	7.50	1.50
☐ 295 Lee Ballanfant UMP	20.00	10.00	2.00
☐ 296 Bill Virdon	30.00	15.00	3.00
☐ 297 Dusty Boggess UMP	20.00	10.00	2.00
☐ 298 Charlie Grimm	15.00	7.50	1.50
☐ 299 Lon Warneke UMP	25.00	12.50	2.50
☐ 300 Tommy Byrne	15.00	7.50	1.50
☐ 301 William Engeln UMP	20.00	10.00	2.00
☐ 302 Frank Malzone	25.00	12.50	2.50
☐ 303 Jocko Conlan UMP	90.00	45.00	9.00
☐ 304 Harry Chiti	12.50	6.25	1.25
☐ 305 Frank Umont UMP	20.00	10.00	2.00
☐ 306 Bob Cerv	22.00	11.00	2.20
☐ 307 Babe Pinelli UMP	25.00	12.50	2.50
☐ 308 Al Lopez MG	42.00	20.00	4.00
☐ 309 Hal Dixon UMP	20.00	10.00	2.00
☐ 310 Ken Lehman	12.50	6.25	1.25
☐ 311 Lawrence Goetz UMP	20.00	10.00	2.00
☐ 312 Bill Wight	12.50	6.25	1.25
☐ 313 Augie Donatelli UMP	30.00	15.00	3.00
☐ 314 Dale Mitchell	15.00	7.50	1.50
☐ 315 Cal Hubbard UMP	75.00	37.50	7.50
☐ 316 Marion Fricano	12.50	6.25	1.25
☐ 317 William Summers UMP	20.00	10.00	2.00
☐ 318 Sid Hudson	12.50	6.25	1.25
☐ 319 Al Schroll	12.50	6.25	1.25
☐ 320 George Susce Jr.	28.00	7.00	1.40

1989 Bowman

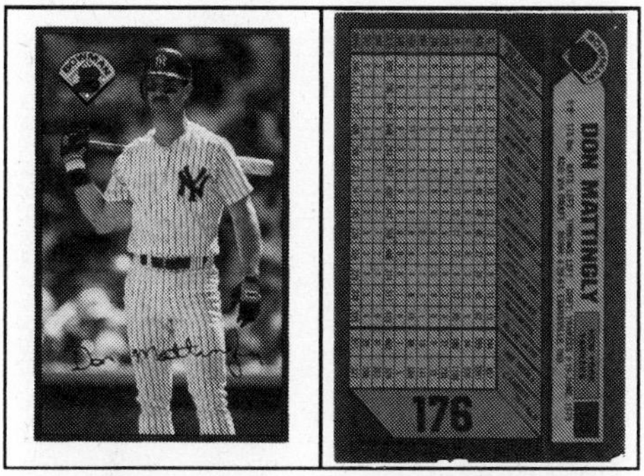

The 1989 Bowman set, which was actually produced by Topps, contains 484 cards measuring 2 1/2" by 3 3/4". The fronts have white-bordered color photos with facsimile autographs and small Bowman logos. The backs are scarlet and feature charts detailing 1988 player performances vs. each team. The set is arranged in alphabetical team order. The player selection is concentrated on prospects and "name" players. The cards were released in midseason 1989 in wax, rack, and cello pack formats. The key rookie cards in this set are Ken Griffey Jr., Tino Martinez, and Jerome Walton. Topps also produced a limited Bowman "Tiffany" set with supposedly only 6,000 sets being produced. This Tiffany version is valued at approximately five times the values listed below.

	MINT	EXC	G-VG
COMPLETE SET (484)	22.00	11.00	2.20
COMMON PLAYER (1-484)	.03	.01	.00
☐ 1 Oswald Peraza	.06	.02	.00
☐ 2 Brian Holton	.06	.03	.00
☐ 3 Jose Bautista	.08	.04	.01
☐ 4 Pete Harnisch	.10	.05	.01
☐ 5 Dave Schmidt	.03	.01	.00
☐ 6 Gregg Olson	.65	.30	.06
☐ 7 Jeff Ballard	.10	.05	.01
☐ 8 Bob Melvin	.03	.01	.00
☐ 9 Cal Ripken	.15	.07	.01
☐ 10 Randy Milligan	.18	.09	.01
☐ 11 Juan Bell	.15	.07	.01
☐ 12 Billy Ripken	.03	.01	.00
☐ 13 Jim Traber	.03	.01	.00
☐ 14 Pete Stanicek	.03	.01	.00
☐ 15 Steve Finley	.25	.12	.02
☐ 16 Larry Sheets	.03	.01	.00
☐ 17 Phil Bradley	.06	.03	.00
☐ 18 Brady Anderson	.20	.10	.02
☐ 19 Lee Smith	.06	.03	.00
☐ 20 Tom Fischer	.08	.04	.01
☐ 21 Mike Boddicker	.06	.03	.00
☐ 22 Rob Murphy	.03	.01	.00
☐ 23 Wes Gardner	.03	.01	.00
☐ 24 John Dopson	.15	.07	.01
☐ 25 Bob Stanley	.03	.01	.00
☐ 26 Roger Clemens	.25	.12	.02
☐ 27 Rich Gedman	.03	.01	.00
☐ 28 Marty Barrett	.03	.01	.00
☐ 29 Luis Rivera	.03	.01	.00
☐ 30 Jody Reed	.08	.04	.01
☐ 31 Nick Esasky	.06	.03	.00
☐ 32 Wade Boggs	.35	.17	.03
☐ 33 Jim Rice	.10	.05	.01
☐ 34 Mike Greenwell	.25	.12	.02
☐ 35 Dwight Evans	.10	.05	.01
☐ 36 Ellis Burks	.25	.12	.02
☐ 37 Mark Clear	.03	.01	.00
☐ 38 Kirk McCaskill	.03	.01	.00
☐ 39 Jim Abbott	.90	.45	.09
☐ 40 Bryan Harvey	.15	.07	.01
☐ 41 Bert Blyleven	.08	.04	.01
☐ 42 Mike Witt	.03	.01	.00
☐ 43 Bob McClure	.03	.01	.00
☐ 44 Bill Schroeder	.03	.01	.00
☐ 45 Lance Parrish	.08	.04	.01
☐ 46 Dick Schofield	.03	.01	.00
☐ 47 Wally Joyner	.12	.06	.01
☐ 48 Jack Howell	.03	.01	.00
☐ 49 Johnny Ray	.03	.01	.00
☐ 50 Chili Davis	.06	.03	.00
☐ 51 Tony Armas	.03	.01	.00
☐ 52 Claudell Washington	.06	.03	.00
☐ 53 Brian Downing	.03	.01	.00
☐ 54 Devon White	.08	.04	.01
☐ 55 Bobby Thigpen	.10	.05	.01
☐ 56 Bill Long	.03	.01	.00
☐ 57 Jerry Reuss	.03	.01	.00
☐ 58 Shawn Hillegas	.03	.01	.00
☐ 59 Melido Perez	.08	.04	.01
☐ 60 Jeff Bittiger	.08	.04	.01
☐ 61 Jack McDowell	.12	.06	.01
☐ 62 Carlton Fisk	.12	.06	.01
☐ 63 Steve Lyons	.03	.01	.00
☐ 64 Ozzie Guillen	.08	.04	.01
☐ 65 Robin Ventura	.60	.30	.06
☐ 66 Fred Manrique	.03	.01	.00
☐ 67 Dan Pasqua	.03	.01	.00
☐ 68 Ivan Calderon	.06	.03	.00
☐ 69 Ron Kittle	.08	.04	.01
☐ 70 Daryl Boston	.06	.03	.00
☐ 71 Dave Gallagher	.10	.05	.01
☐ 72 Harold Baines	.06	.03	.00
☐ 73 Charles Nagy	.18	.09	.01
☐ 74 John Farrell	.03	.01	.00
☐ 75 Kevin Wickander	.08	.04	.01
☐ 76 Greg Swindell	.08	.04	.01
☐ 77 Mike Walker	.10	.05	.01
☐ 78 Doug Jones	.06	.03	.00
☐ 79 Rich Yett	.03	.01	.00
☐ 80 Tom Candiotti	.03	.01	.00
☐ 81 Jesse Orosco	.03	.01	.00
☐ 82 Bud Black	.06	.03	.00
☐ 83 Andy Allanson	.03	.01	.00
☐ 84 Pete O'Brien	.06	.03	.00
☐ 85 Jerry Browne	.03	.01	.00
☐ 86 Brook Jacoby	.06	.03	.00
☐ 87 Mark Lewis	.30	.15	.03
☐ 88 Luis Aguayo	.03	.01	.00
☐ 89 Cory Snyder	.08	.04	.01
☐ 90 Oddibe McDowell	.06	.03	.00
☐ 91 Joe Carter	.10	.05	.01
☐ 92 Frank Tanana	.03	.01	.00
☐ 93 Jack Morris	.06	.03	.00
☐ 94 Doyle Alexander	.03	.01	.00
☐ 95 Steve Searcy	.12	.06	.01
☐ 96 Randy Bockus	.06	.03	.00
☐ 97 Jeff Robinson	.03	.01	.00
☐ 98 Mike Henneman	.03	.01	.00
☐ 99 Paul Gibson	.06	.03	.00
☐ 100 Frank Williams	.03	.01	.00
☐ 101 Matt Nokes	.06	.03	.00
☐ 102 Ricco Brogna	.25	.12	.02
☐ 103 Lou Whitaker	.08	.04	.01
☐ 104 Al Pedrique	.03	.01	.00
☐ 105 Alan Trammell	.10	.05	.01
☐ 106 Chris Brown	.03	.01	.00
☐ 107 Pat Sheridan	.03	.01	.00
☐ 108 Gary Pettis	.03	.01	.00
☐ 109 Keith Moreland	.03	.01	.00
☐ 110 Mel Stottlemyre Jr.	.18	.09	.01
☐ 111 Bret Saberhagen	.12	.06	.01
☐ 112 Floyd Bannister	.03	.01	.00
☐ 113 Jeff Montgomery	.12	.06	.01
☐ 114 Steve Farr	.03	.01	.00
☐ 115 Tom Gordon UER (front shows autograph of Don Gordon)	.50	.25	.05
☐ 116 Charlie Leibrandt	.03	.01	.00
☐ 117 Mark Gubicza	.06	.03	.00
☐ 118 Mike Macfarlane	.12	.06	.01
☐ 119 Bob Boone	.08	.04	.01
☐ 120 Kurt Stillwell	.06	.03	.00
☐ 121 George Brett	.20	.10	.02
☐ 122 Frank White	.06	.03	.00
☐ 123 Kevin Seitzer	.10	.05	.01
☐ 124 Willie Wilson	.08	.04	.01
☐ 125 Pat Tabler	.03	.01	.00
☐ 126 Bo Jackson	.75	.35	.07
☐ 127 Hugh Walker	.10	.05	.01
☐ 128 Danny Tartabull	.08	.04	.01
☐ 129 Teddy Higuera	.06	.03	.00
☐ 130 Don August	.03	.01	.00
☐ 131 Juan Nieves	.03	.01	.00
☐ 132 Mike Birkbeck	.03	.01	.00
☐ 133 Dan Plesac	.03	.01	.00
☐ 134 Chris Bosio	.03	.01	.00
☐ 135 Bill Wegman	.03	.01	.00
☐ 136 Chuck Crim	.03	.01	.00
☐ 137 B.J. Surhoff	.06	.03	.00
☐ 138 Joey Meyer	.06	.03	.00

☐ 139 Dale Sveum	.03	.01	.00
☐ 140 Paul Molitor	.10	.05	.01
☐ 141 Jim Gantner	.03	.01	.00
☐ 142 Gary Sheffield	.90	.45	.09
☐ 143 Greg Brock	.03	.01	.00
☐ 144 Robin Yount	.15	.07	.01
☐ 145 Glenn Braggs	.03	.01	.00
☐ 146 Rob Deer	.06	.03	.00
☐ 147 Fred Toliver	.03	.01	.00
☐ 148 Jeff Reardon	.08	.04	.01
☐ 149 Allan Anderson	.06	.03	.00
☐ 150 Frank Viola	.12	.06	.01
☐ 151 Shane Rawley	.03	.01	.00
☐ 152 Juan Berenguer	.03	.01	.00
☐ 153 Johnny Ard	.18	.09	.01
☐ 154 Tim Laudner	.03	.01	.00
☐ 155 Brian Harper	.06	.03	.00
☐ 156 Al Newman	.03	.01	.00
☐ 157 Kent Hrbek	.10	.05	.01
☐ 158 Gary Gaetti	.08	.04	.01
☐ 159 Wally Backman	.03	.01	.00
☐ 160 Gene Larkin	.03	.01	.00
☐ 161 Greg Gagne	.03	.01	.00
☐ 162 Kirby Puckett	.35	.17	.03
☐ 163 Dan Gladden	.03	.01	.00
☐ 164 Randy Bush	.03	.01	.00
☐ 165 Dave LaPoint	.03	.01	.00
☐ 166 Andy Hawkins	.03	.01	.00
☐ 167 Dave Righetti	.08	.04	.01
☐ 168 Lance McCullers	.03	.01	.00
☐ 169 Jimmy Jones	.03	.01	.00
☐ 170 Al Leiter	.06	.03	.00
☐ 171 John Candelaria	.03	.01	.00
☐ 172 Don Slaught	.03	.01	.00
☐ 173 Jamie Quirk	.03	.01	.00
☐ 174 Rafael Santana	.03	.01	.00
☐ 175 Mike Pagliarulo	.03	.01	.00
☐ 176 Don Mattingly	.65	.30	.06
☐ 177 Ken Phelps	.03	.01	.00
☐ 178 Steve Sax	.08	.04	.01
☐ 179 Dave Winfield	.12	.06	.01
☐ 180 Stan Jefferson	.03	.01	.00
☐ 181 Rickey Henderson	.25	.12	.02
☐ 182 Bob Brower	.03	.01	.00
☐ 183 Roberto Kelly	.25	.12	.02
☐ 184 Curt Young	.03	.01	.00
☐ 185 Gene Nelson	.03	.01	.00
☐ 186 Bob Welch	.10	.05	.01
☐ 187 Rick Honeycutt	.03	.01	.00
☐ 188 Dave Stewart	.12	.06	.01
☐ 189 Mike Moore	.06	.03	.00
☐ 190 Dennis Eckersley	.10	.05	.01
☐ 191 Eric Plunk	.03	.01	.00
☐ 192 Storm Davis	.06	.03	.00
☐ 193 Terry Steinbach	.08	.04	.01
☐ 194 Ron Hassey	.03	.01	.00
☐ 195 Stan Royer	.12	.06	.01
☐ 196 Walt Weiss	.20	.10	.02
☐ 197 Mark McGwire	.50	.25	.05
☐ 198 Carney Lansford	.08	.04	.01
☐ 199 Glenn Hubbard	.03	.01	.00
☐ 200 Dave Henderson	.06	.03	.00
☐ 201 Jose Canseco	.75	.35	.07
☐ 202 Dave Parker	.08	.04	.01
☐ 203 Scott Bankhead	.06	.03	.00
☐ 204 Tom Niedenfuer	.03	.01	.00
☐ 205 Mark Langston	.10	.05	.01
☐ 206 Erik Hanson	.40	.20	.04
☐ 207 Mike Jackson	.03	.01	.00
☐ 208 Dave Valle	.03	.01	.00
☐ 209 Scott Bradley	.03	.01	.00
☐ 210 Harold Reynolds	.06	.03	.00
☐ 211 Tino Martinez	1.00	.50	.10
☐ 212 Rich Renteria	.08	.04	.01
☐ 213 Rey Quinones	.03	.01	.00
☐ 214 Jim Presley	.03	.01	.00
☐ 215 Alvin Davis	.08	.04	.01
☐ 216 Edgar Martinez	.18	.09	.01
☐ 217 Darnell Coles	.03	.01	.00
☐ 218 Jeffrey Leonard	.06	.03	.00
☐ 219 Jay Buhner	.12	.06	.01
☐ 220 Ken Griffey Jr.	5.00	2.50	.50
☐ 221 Drew Hall	.03	.01	.00
☐ 222 Bobby Witt	.10	.05	.01
☐ 223 Jamie Moyer	.03	.01	.00
☐ 224 Charlie Hough	.06	.03	.00
☐ 225 Nolan Ryan	.50	.25	.05
☐ 226 Jeff Russell	.03	.01	.00
☐ 227 Jim Sundberg	.03	.01	.00
☐ 228 Julio Franco	.08	.04	.01
☐ 229 Buddy Bell	.06	.03	.00
☐ 230 Scott Fletcher	.03	.01	.00
☐ 231 Jeff Kunkel	.03	.01	.00
☐ 232 Steve Buechele	.03	.01	.00

☐ 233 Monty Fariss	.15	.07	.01
☐ 234 Rick Leach	.03	.01	.00
☐ 235 Ruben Sierra	.25	.12	.02
☐ 236 Cecil Espy	.08	.04	.01
☐ 237 Rafael Palmeiro	.12	.06	.01
☐ 238 Pete Incaviglia	.08	.04	.01
☐ 239 Dave Stieb	.10	.05	.01
☐ 240 Jeff Musselman	.03	.01	.00
☐ 241 Mike Flanagan	.06	.03	.00
☐ 242 Todd Stottlemyre	.15	.07	.01
☐ 243 Jimmy Key	.06	.03	.00
☐ 244 Tony Castillo	.08	.04	.01
☐ 245 Alex Sanchez	.15	.07	.01
☐ 246 Tom Henke	.06	.03	.00
☐ 247 John Cerutti	.03	.01	.00
☐ 248 Ernie Whitt	.03	.01	.00
☐ 249 Bob Brenly	.03	.01	.00
☐ 250 Rance Mulliniks	.03	.01	.00
☐ 251 Kelly Gruber	.15	.07	.01
☐ 252 Ed Sprague	.20	.10	.02
☐ 253 Fred McGriff	.15	.07	.01
☐ 254 Tony Fernandez	.08	.04	.01
☐ 255 Tom Lawless	.03	.01	.00
☐ 256 George Bell	.10	.05	.01
☐ 257 Jesse Barfield	.08	.04	.01
☐ 258 Roberto Alomar w/Dad	.20	.10	.02
☐ 259 Ken Griffey Jr./Sr.	.85	.40	.08
☐ 260 Cal Ripken Jr./Sr.	.10	.05	.01
☐ 261 M.Stottlemyre Jr./Sr.	.08	.04	.01
☐ 262 Zane Smith	.06	.03	.00
☐ 263 Charlie Puleo	.03	.01	.00
☐ 264 Derek Lilliquist	.12	.06	.01
☐ 265 Paul Assenmacher	.03	.01	.00
☐ 266 John Smoltz	.35	.17	.03
☐ 267 Tom Glavine	.06	.03	.00
☐ 268 Steve Avery	.60	.30	.06
☐ 269 Pete Smith	.08	.04	.01
☐ 270 Jody Davis	.03	.01	.00
☐ 271 Bruce Benedict	.03	.01	.00
☐ 272 Andres Thomas	.03	.01	.00
☐ 273 Gerald Perry	.03	.01	.00
☐ 274 Ron Gant	.25	.12	.02
☐ 275 Darrell Evans	.06	.03	.00
☐ 276 Dale Murphy	.15	.07	.01
☐ 277 Dion James	.03	.01	.00
☐ 278 Lonnie Smith	.06	.03	.00
☐ 279 Geronimo Berroa	.03	.01	.00
☐ 280 Steve Wilson	.12	.06	.01
☐ 281 Rick Sutcliffe	.08	.04	.01
☐ 282 Kevin Coffman	.06	.03	.00
☐ 283 Mitch Williams	.06	.03	.00
☐ 284 Greg Maddux	.10	.05	.01
☐ 285 Paul Kilgus	.03	.01	.00
☐ 286 Mike Harkey	.30	.15	.03
☐ 287 Lloyd McClendon	.06	.03	.00
☐ 288 Damon Berryhill	.15	.07	.01
☐ 289 Ty Griffin	.50	.25	.05
☐ 290 Ryne Sandberg	.25	.12	.02
☐ 291 Mark Grace	1.10	.55	.11
☐ 292 Curt Wilkerson	.03	.01	.00
☐ 293 Vance Law	.03	.01	.00
☐ 294 Shawon Dunston	.10	.05	.01
☐ 295 Jerome Walton	1.50	.75	.15
☐ 296 Mitch Webster	.03	.01	.00
☐ 297 Dwight Smith	.65	.30	.06
☐ 298 Andre Dawson	.15	.07	.01
☐ 299 Jeff Sellers	.03	.01	.00
☐ 300 Jose Rijo	.08	.04	.01
☐ 301 John Franco	.06	.03	.00
☐ 302 Rick Mahler	.03	.01	.00
☐ 303 Ron Robinson	.03	.01	.00
☐ 304 Danny Jackson	.06	.03	.00
☐ 305 Rob Dibble	.30	.15	.03
☐ 306 Tom Browning	.08	.04	.01
☐ 307 Bo Diaz	.03	.01	.00
☐ 308 Manny Trillo	.03	.01	.00
☐ 309 Chris Sabo	.60	.30	.06
☐ 310 Ron Oester	.03	.01	.00
☐ 311 Barry Larkin	.18	.09	.01
☐ 312 Todd Benzinger	.03	.01	.00
☐ 313 Paul O'Neill	.08	.04	.01
☐ 314 Kal Daniels	.08	.04	.01
☐ 315 Joel Youngblood	.03	.01	.00
☐ 316 Eric Davis	.20	.10	.02
☐ 317 Dave Smith	.06	.03	.00
☐ 318 Mark Portugal	.03	.01	.00
☐ 319 Brian Meyer	.10	.05	.01
☐ 320 Jim Deshaies	.03	.01	.00
☐ 321 Juan Agosto	.03	.01	.00
☐ 322 Mike Scott	.10	.05	.01
☐ 323 Rick Rhoden	.03	.01	.00
☐ 324 Jim Clancy	.03	.01	.00
☐ 325 Larry Andersen	.03	.01	.00
☐ 326 Alex Trevino	.03	.01	.00

☐ 327 Alan Ashby	.03	.01	.00
☐ 328 Craig Reynolds	.03	.01	.00
☐ 329 Bill Doran	.06	.03	.00
☐ 330 Rafael Ramirez	.03	.01	.00
☐ 331 Glenn Davis	.15	.07	.01
☐ 332 Willie Ansley	.25	.12	.02
☐ 333 Gerald Young	.03	.01	.00
☐ 334 Cameron Drew	.08	.04	.01
☐ 335 Jay Howell	.03	.01	.00
☐ 336 Tim Belcher	.15	.07	.01
☐ 337 Fernando Valenzuela	.10	.05	.01
☐ 338 Ricky Horton	.03	.01	.00
☐ 339 Tim Leary	.06	.03	.00
☐ 340 Bill Bene	.06	.03	.00
☐ 341 Orel Hershiser	.12	.06	.01
☐ 342 Mike Scioscia	.03	.01	.00
☐ 343 Rick Dempsey	.03	.01	.00
☐ 344 Willie Randolph	.06	.03	.00
☐ 345 Alfredo Griffin	.03	.01	.00
☐ 346 Eddie Murray	.12	.06	.01
☐ 347 Mickey Hatcher	.03	.01	.00
☐ 348 Mike Sharperson	.03	.01	.00
☐ 349 John Shelby	.03	.01	.00
☐ 350 Mike Marshall	.08	.04	.01
☐ 351 Kirk Gibson	.10	.05	.01
☐ 352 Mike Davis	.03	.01	.00
☐ 353 Bryn Smith	.03	.01	.00
☐ 354 Pascual Perez	.06	.03	.00
☐ 355 Kevin Gross	.03	.01	.00
☐ 356 Andy McGaffigan	.03	.01	.00
☐ 357 Brian Holman	.15	.07	.01
☐ 358 Dave Wainhouse	.10	.05	.01
☐ 359 Dennis Martinez	.06	.03	.00
☐ 360 Tim Burke	.06	.03	.00
☐ 361 Nelson Santovenia	.12	.06	.01
☐ 362 Tim Wallach	.08	.04	.01
☐ 363 Spike Owen	.03	.01	.00
☐ 364 Rex Hudler	.06	.03	.00
☐ 365 Andres Galarraga	.08	.04	.01
☐ 366 Otis Nixon	.03	.01	.00
☐ 367 Hubie Brooks	.08	.04	.01
☐ 368 Mike Aldrete	.03	.01	.00
☐ 369 Tim Raines	.10	.05	.01
☐ 370 Dave Martinez	.03	.01	.00
☐ 371 Bob Ojeda	.06	.03	.00
☐ 372 Ron Darling	.08	.04	.01
☐ 373 Wally Whitehurst	.15	.07	.01
☐ 374 Randy Myers	.06	.03	.00
☐ 375 David Cone	.12	.06	.01
☐ 376 Dwight Gooden	.25	.12	.02
☐ 377 Sid Fernandez	.08	.04	.01
☐ 378 Dave Proctor	.10	.05	.01
☐ 379 Gary Carter	.10	.05	.01
☐ 380 Keith Miller	.03	.01	.00
☐ 381 Gregg Jefferies	.75	.35	.07
☐ 382 Tim Teufel	.03	.01	.00
☐ 383 Kevin Elster	.06	.03	.00
☐ 384 Dave Magadan	.12	.06	.01
☐ 385 Keith Hernandez	.10	.05	.01
☐ 386 Mookie Wilson	.06	.03	.00
☐ 387 Darryl Strawberry	.30	.15	.03
☐ 388 Kevin McReynolds	.10	.05	.01
☐ 389 Mark Carreon	.10	.05	.01
☐ 390 Jeff Parrett	.08	.04	.01
☐ 391 Mike Maddux	.03	.01	.00
☐ 392 Don Carman	.03	.01	.00
☐ 393 Bruce Ruffin	.03	.01	.00
☐ 394 Ken Howell	.03	.01	.00
☐ 395 Steve Bedrosian	.08	.04	.01
☐ 396 Floyd Youmans	.03	.01	.00
☐ 397 Larry McWilliams	.03	.01	.00
☐ 398 Pat Combs	.30	.15	.03
☐ 399 Steve Lake	.03	.01	.00
☐ 400 Dickie Thon	.03	.01	.00
☐ 401 Ricky Jordan	.25	.12	.02
☐ 402 Mike Schmidt	.35	.17	.03
☐ 403 Tom Herr	.06	.03	.00
☐ 404 Chris James	.06	.03	.00
☐ 405 Juan Samuel	.08	.04	.01
☐ 406 Von Hayes	.08	.04	.01
☐ 407 Ron Jones	.20	.10	.02
☐ 408 Curt Ford	.03	.01	.00
☐ 409 Bob Walk	.03	.01	.00
☐ 410 Jeff Robinson	.03	.01	.00
☐ 411 Jim Gott	.03	.01	.00
☐ 412 Scott Medvin	.10	.05	.01
☐ 413 John Smiley	.06	.03	.00
☐ 414 Bob Kipper	.03	.01	.00
☐ 415 Brian Fisher	.03	.01	.00
☐ 416 Doug Drabek	.10	.05	.01
☐ 417 Mike LaValliere	.03	.01	.00
☐ 418 Ken Oberkfell	.03	.01	.00
☐ 419 Sid Bream	.03	.01	.00
☐ 420 Austin Manahan	.10	.05	.01
☐ 421 Jose Lind	.03	.01	.00
☐ 422 Bobby Bonilla	.18	.09	.01
☐ 423 Glenn Wilson	.03	.01	.00
☐ 424 Andy Van Slyke	.10	.05	.01
☐ 425 Gary Redus	.03	.01	.00
☐ 426 Barry Bonds	.25	.12	.02
☐ 427 Don Heinkel	.03	.01	.00
☐ 428 Ken Dayley	.03	.01	.00
☐ 429 Todd Worrell	.08	.04	.01
☐ 430 Brad DuVall	.10	.05	.01
☐ 431 Jose DeLeon	.03	.01	.00
☐ 432 Joe Magrane	.08	.04	.01
☐ 433 John Ericks	.20	.10	.02
☐ 434 Frank DiPino	.03	.01	.00
☐ 435 Tony Pena	.06	.03	.00
☐ 436 Ozzie Smith	.12	.06	.01
☐ 437 Terry Pendleton	.06	.03	.00
☐ 438 Jose Oquendo	.03	.01	.00
☐ 439 Tim Jones	.08	.04	.01
☐ 440 Pedro Guerrero	.10	.05	.01
☐ 441 Milt Thompson	.03	.01	.00
☐ 442 Willie McGee	.10	.05	.01
☐ 443 Vince Coleman	.12	.06	.01
☐ 444 Tom Brunansky	.08	.04	.01
☐ 445 Walt Terrell	.03	.01	.00
☐ 446 Eric Show	.03	.01	.00
☐ 447 Mark Davis	.10	.05	.01
☐ 448 Andy Benes	.50	.25	.05
☐ 449 Ed Whitson	.06	.03	.00
☐ 450 Dennis Rasmussen	.03	.01	.00
☐ 451 Bruce Hurst	.08	.04	.01
☐ 452 Pat Clements	.03	.01	.00
☐ 453 Benito Santiago	.15	.07	.01
☐ 454 Sandy Alomar Jr.	.85	.40	.08
☐ 455 Garry Templeton	.06	.03	.00
☐ 456 Jack Clark	.08	.04	.01
☐ 457 Tim Flannery	.03	.01	.00
☐ 458 Roberto Alomar	.45	.22	.04
☐ 459 Carmelo Martinez	.03	.01	.00
☐ 460 John Kruk	.06	.03	.00
☐ 461 Tony Gwynn	.20	.10	.02
☐ 462 Jerald Clark	.18	.09	.01
☐ 463 Don Robinson	.03	.01	.00
☐ 464 Craig Lefferts	.03	.01	.00
☐ 465 Kelly Downs	.03	.01	.00
☐ 466 Rick Reuschel	.06	.03	.00
☐ 467 Scott Garrelts	.06	.03	.00
☐ 468 Wil Tejada	.03	.01	.00
☐ 469 Kirt Manwaring	.06	.03	.00
☐ 470 Terry Kennedy	.03	.01	.00
☐ 471 Jose Uribe	.03	.01	.00
☐ 472 Royce Clayton	.10	.05	.01
☐ 473 Robby Thompson	.03	.01	.00
☐ 474 Kevin Mitchell	.25	.12	.02
☐ 475 Ernie Riles	.03	.01	.00
☐ 476 Will Clark	.65	.30	.06
☐ 477 Donell Nixon	.03	.01	.00
☐ 478 Candy Maldonado	.06	.03	.00
☐ 479 Tracy Jones	.03	.01	.00
☐ 480 Brett Butler	.08	.04	.01
☐ 481 Checklist Card	.06	.01	.00
☐ 482 Checklist Card	.06	.01	.00
☐ 483 Checklist Card	.06	.01	.00
☐ 484 Checklist Card	.06	.01	.00

1989 Bowman Reprint Inserts

The 1989 Bowman Reprint Inserts set contains 11 cards measuring 2 1/2" by 3 3/4". The fronts depict reproduced actual size "classic" Bowman cards, which are noted as reprints. The backs are devoted to a sweepstakes entry form. One of these reprint cards was included in each 1989 Bowman wax pack thus making these "reprints" quite easy to find. Since the cards are unnumbered, they are ordered below in alphabetical order by player's name and year within player.

	MINT	EXC	G-VG
COMPLETE SET (11)	2.00	1.00	.20
COMMON PLAYER (1-11)	.15	.07	.01
☐ 1 Richie Ashburn '49	.15	.07	.01
☐ 2 Yogi Berra '48	.20	.10	.02
☐ 3 Whitey Ford '51	.20	.10	.02
☐ 4 Gil Hodges '49	.20	.10	.02
☐ 5 Mickey Mantle '51	.25	.12	.02
☐ 6 Mickey Mantle '53	.25	.12	.02

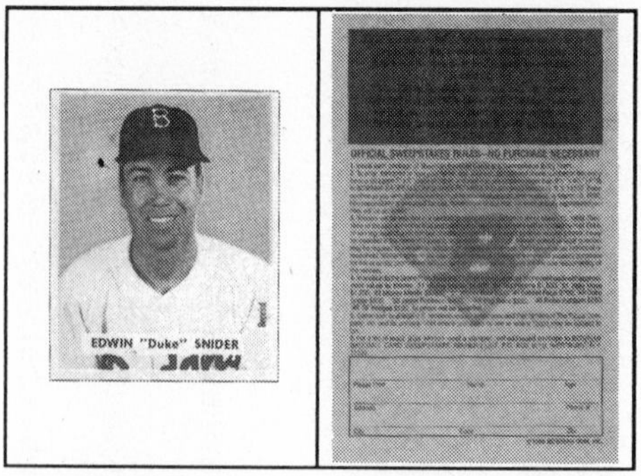

	MINT	EXC	G-VG
☐ 7 Willie Mays '51	.20	.10	.02
☐ 8 Satchel Paige '49	.20	.10	.02
☐ 9 Jackie Robinson '50	.20	.10	.02
☐ 10 Duke Snider '49	.20	.10	.02
☐ 11 Ted Williams '54	.20	.10	.02

1990 Bowman Baseball

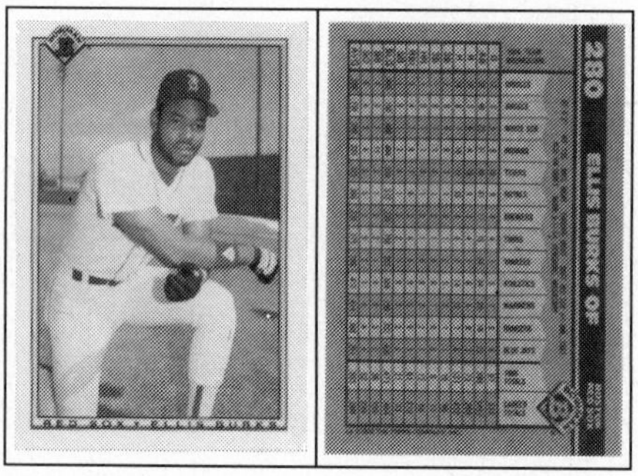

The 1990 Bowman set was issued in the standard card size of 2 1/2" by 3 1/2". This was the second issue by Topps using the Bowman name. The set consists of 528 cards, increased from 1989s edition of 484 cards. The cards feature a white border with the players photo inside and the Bowman logo on top. Again, the Bowman cards were issued with the backs featuring team by team statistics. The card numbering is in team order with the teams themselves being ordered alphabetically within each league. The set numbering is as follows: Atlanta Braves (1-20), Chicago Cubs (21-40), Cincinnati Reds (41-60), Houston Astros (61-81), Los Angeles Dodgers (82-101), Montreal Expos (102-121), New York Mets (122-142), Philadelphia Phillies (143-162), Pittsburgh Pirates (163-182), St. Louis Cardinals (183-202), San Diego Padres (203-222), San Francisco Giants (223-242), Baltimore Orioles (243-262), Boston Red Sox (263-282), California Angels (283-302), Chicago White Sox (303-322), Cleveland Indians (323-342), Detroit Tigers (343-362), Kansas City Royals (363-383), Milwaukee Brewers (384-404), Minnesota Twins (405-424), New York Yankees (425-444), Oakland A's (445-464), Seattle Mariners (465-484), Texas Rangers (485-503), and Toronto Blue Jays (504-524). The key rookie cards in this set are Travis Fryman, Juan Gonzalez, Kevin Maas, Ben McDonald, Jose Offerman, John Olerud, Frank Thomas, and Maurice Vaughn. Topps also produced a Bowman Tiffany glossy set. Production of these Tiffany Bowmans was reported to be approximately 3,000 sets. These Tiffany versions are valued at approximately eight times the values listed below.

	MINT	EXC	G-VG
COMPLETE SET (528)	22.00	11.00	2.20
COMMON PLAYER (1-528)	.03	.01	.00
☐ 1 Tommy Greene	.25	.06	.01
☐ 2 Tom Glavine	.06	.03	.00
☐ 3 Andy Nezelek	.03	.01	.00
☐ 4 Mike Stanton	.10	.05	.01
☐ 5 Rick Luecken	.10	.05	.01
☐ 6 Kent Mercker	.20	.10	.02
☐ 7 Derek Lilliquist	.03	.01	.00
☐ 8 Charlie Leibrandt	.03	.01	.00
☐ 9 Steve Avery	.25	.12	.02
☐ 10 John Smoltz	.08	.04	.01
☐ 11 Mark Lemke	.03	.01	.00
☐ 12 Lonnie Smith	.06	.03	.00
☐ 13 Oddibe McDowell	.06	.03	.00
☐ 14 Tyler Houston	.25	.12	.02
☐ 15 Jeff Blauser	.03	.01	.00
☐ 16 Ernie Whitt	.03	.01	.00
☐ 17 Alexis Infante	.08	.04	.01
☐ 18 Jim Presley	.03	.01	.00
☐ 19 Dale Murphy	.10	.05	.01
☐ 20 Nick Esasky	.06	.03	.00
☐ 21 Rick Sutcliffe	.06	.03	.00
☐ 22 Mike Bielecki	.03	.01	.00
☐ 23 Steve Wilson	.03	.01	.00
☐ 24 Kevin Blankenship	.03	.01	.00
☐ 25 Mitch Williams	.06	.03	.00
☐ 26 Dean Wilkins	.08	.04	.01
☐ 27 Greg Maddux	.08	.04	.01
☐ 28 Mike Harkey	.10	.05	.01
☐ 29 Mark Grace	.20	.10	.02
☐ 30 Ryne Sandberg	.20	.10	.02
☐ 31 Greg Smith	.15	.07	.01
☐ 32 Dwight Smith	.12	.06	.01
☐ 33 Damon Berryhill	.06	.03	.00
☐ 34 Earl Cunningham (errant * by the word "in")	.25	.12	.02
☐ 35 Jerome Walton	.45	.22	.04
☐ 36 Lloyd McClendon	.03	.01	.00
☐ 37 Ty Griffin	.15	.07	.01
☐ 38 Shawon Dunston	.08	.04	.01
☐ 39 Andre Dawson	.10	.05	.01
☐ 40 Luis Salazar	.03	.01	.00
☐ 41 Tim Layana	.20	.10	.02
☐ 42 Rob Dibble	.08	.04	.01
☐ 43 Tom Browning	.06	.03	.00
☐ 44 Danny Jackson	.06	.03	.00
☐ 45 Jose Rijo	.08	.04	.01
☐ 46 Scott Scudder	.15	.07	.01
☐ 47 Randy Myers	.06	.03	.00
☐ 48 Brian Lane	.15	.07	.01
☐ 49 Paul O'Neill	.08	.04	.01
☐ 50 Barry Larkin	.12	.06	.01
☐ 51 Reggie Jefferson	.30	.15	.03
☐ 52 Jeff Branson	.15	.07	.01
☐ 53 Chris Sabo	.12	.06	.01
☐ 54 Joe Oliver	.10	.05	.01
☐ 55 Todd Benzinger	.03	.01	.00
☐ 56 Rolando Roomes	.03	.01	.00
☐ 57 Hal Morris	.25	.12	.02
☐ 58 Eric Davis	.15	.07	.01
☐ 59 Scott Bryant	.20	.10	.02
☐ 60 Ken Griffey	.08	.04	.01
☐ 61 Darryl Kile	.15	.07	.01
☐ 62 Dave Smith	.06	.03	.00
☐ 63 Mark Portugal	.03	.01	.00
☐ 64 Jeff Juden	.30	.15	.03
☐ 65 Bill Gullickson	.03	.01	.00
☐ 66 Danny Darwin	.03	.01	.00
☐ 67 Larry Andersen	.03	.01	.00
☐ 68 Jose Cano	.10	.05	.01
☐ 69 Dan Schatzeder	.03	.01	.00
☐ 70 Jim Deshaies	.03	.01	.00
☐ 71 Mike Scott	.08	.04	.01
☐ 72 Gerald Young	.03	.01	.00
☐ 73 Ken Caminiti	.03	.01	.00
☐ 74 Ken Oberkfell	.03	.01	.00
☐ 75 Dave Rohde	.12	.06	.01
☐ 76 Bill Doran	.06	.03	.00
☐ 77 Andujar Cedeno	.30	.15	.03
☐ 78 Craig Biggio	.08	.04	.01
☐ 79 Karl Rhodes	.15	.07	.01
☐ 80 Glenn Davis	.10	.05	.01
☐ 81 Eric Anthony	.60	.30	.06
☐ 82 John Wetteland	.12	.06	.01
☐ 83 Jay Howell	.03	.01	.00
☐ 84 Orel Hershiser	.10	.05	.01
☐ 85 Tim Belcher	.08	.04	.01
☐ 86 Kiki Jones	.30	.15	.03
☐ 87 Mike Hartley	.10	.05	.01
☐ 88 Ramon Martinez	.40	.20	.04

☐ 89	Mike Scioscia	.03	.01	.00
☐ 90	Willie Randolph	.06	.03	.00
☐ 91	Juan Samuel	.06	.03	.00
☐ 92	Jose Offerman	.80	.40	.08
☐ 93	Dave Hansen	.25	.12	.02
☐ 94	Jeff Hamilton	.03	.01	.00
☐ 95	Alfredo Griffin	.03	.01	.00
☐ 96	Tom Goodwin	.35	.17	.03
☐ 97	Kirk Gibson	.08	.04	.01
☐ 98	Jose Vizcaino	.12	.06	.01
☐ 99	Kal Daniels	.08	.04	.01
☐ 100	Hubie Brooks	.08	.04	.01
☐ 101	Eddie Murray	.10	.05	.01
☐ 102	Dennis Boyd	.06	.03	.00
☐ 103	Tim Burke	.06	.03	.00
☐ 104	Bill Sampen	.20	.10	.02
☐ 105	Brett Gideon	.06	.03	.00
☐ 106	Mark Gardner	.20	.10	.02
☐ 107	Howard Farmer	.15	.07	.01
☐ 108	Mel Rojas	.10	.05	.01
☐ 109	Kevin Gross	.03	.01	.00
☐ 110	Dave Schmidt	.03	.01	.00
☐ 111	Denny Martinez	.03	.01	.00
☐ 112	Jeff Goff	.08	.04	.01
☐ 113	Andres Galarraga	.08	.04	.01
☐ 114	Tim Wallach	.08	.04	.01
☐ 115	Marquis Grissom	.30	.15	.03
☐ 116	Spike Owen	.03	.01	.00
☐ 117	Larry Walker	.25	.12	.02
☐ 118	Rock Raines	.08	.04	.01
☐ 119	Delino DeShields	.50	.25	.05
☐ 120	Tom Foley	.03	.01	.00
☐ 121	Dave Martinez	.03	.01	.00
☐ 122	Frank Viola	.08	.04	.01
☐ 123	Julio Valera	.15	.07	.01
☐ 124	Alejandro Pena	.03	.01	.00
☐ 125	David Cone	.08	.04	.01
☐ 126	Doc Gooden	.15	.07	.01
☐ 127	Kevin D. Brown	.15	.07	.01
☐ 128	John Franco	.06	.03	.00
☐ 129	Terry Bross	.12	.06	.01
☐ 130	Blaine Beatty	.12	.06	.01
☐ 131	Sid Fernandez	.06	.03	.00
☐ 132	Mike Marshall	.06	.03	.00
☐ 133	Howard Johnson	.08	.04	.01
☐ 134	Jaime Roseboro	.25	.12	.02
☐ 135	Alan Zinter	.20	.10	.02
☐ 136	Keith Miller	.03	.01	.00
☐ 137	Kevin Elster	.03	.01	.00
☐ 138	Kevin McReynolds	.08	.04	.01
☐ 139	Barry Lyons	.03	.01	.00
☐ 140	Gregg Jefferies	.25	.12	.02
☐ 141	Darryl Strawberry	.18	.09	.01
☐ 142	Todd Hundley	.20	.10	.02
☐ 143	Scott Service	.06	.03	.00
☐ 144	Chuck Malone	.12	.06	.01
☐ 145	Steve Ontiveros	.03	.01	.00
☐ 146	Roger McDowell	.03	.01	.00
☐ 147	Ken Howell	.03	.01	.00
☐ 148	Pat Combs	.10	.05	.01
☐ 149	Jeff Parrett	.03	.01	.00
☐ 150	Chuck McElroy	.10	.05	.01
☐ 151	Jason Grimsley	.10	.05	.01
☐ 152	Len Dykstra	.08	.04	.01
☐ 153	Mickey Morandini	.15	.07	.01
☐ 154	John Kruk	.03	.01	.00
☐ 155	Dickie Thon	.03	.01	.00
☐ 156	Ricky Jordan	.10	.05	.01
☐ 157	Jeff Jackson	.15	.07	.01
☐ 158	Darren Daulton	.06	.03	.00
☐ 159	Tom Herr	.06	.03	.00
☐ 160	Von Hayes	.06	.03	.00
☐ 161	Dave Hollins	.25	.12	.02
☐ 162	Carmelo Martinez	.03	.01	.00
☐ 163	Bob Walk	.03	.01	.00
☐ 164	Doug Drabek	.08	.04	.01
☐ 165	Walt Terrell	.03	.01	.00
☐ 166	Bill Landrum	.03	.01	.00
☐ 167	Scott Ruskin	.15	.07	.01
☐ 168	Bob Patterson	.03	.01	.00
☐ 169	Bobby Bonilla	.10	.05	.01
☐ 170	Jose Lind	.03	.01	.00
☐ 171	Andy Van Slyke	.08	.04	.01
☐ 172	Mike LaValliere	.03	.01	.00
☐ 173	Willie Greene	.20	.10	.02
☐ 174	Jay Bell	.03	.01	.00
☐ 175	Sid Bream	.03	.01	.00
☐ 176	Tom Prince	.03	.01	.00
☐ 177	Wally Backman	.03	.01	.00
☐ 178	Moises Alou	.25	.12	.02
☐ 179	Steve Carter	.10	.05	.01
☐ 180	Gary Redus	.03	.01	.00
☐ 181	Barry Bonds	.15	.07	.01
☐ 182	Don Slaught	.03	.01	.00
☐ 183	Joe Magrane	.06	.03	.00
☐ 184	Bryn Smith	.03	.01	.00
☐ 185	Todd Worrell	.06	.03	.00
☐ 186	Jose DeLeon	.03	.01	.00
☐ 187	Frank DiPino	.03	.01	.00
☐ 188	John Tudor	.06	.03	.00
☐ 189	Howard Hilton	.12	.06	.01
☐ 190	John Ericks	.06	.03	.00
☐ 191	Ken Dayley	.03	.01	.00
☐ 192	Ray Lankford	.75	.35	.07
☐ 193	Todd Zeile	.60	.30	.06
☐ 194	Willie McGee	.08	.04	.01
☐ 195	Ozzie Smith	.08	.04	.01
☐ 196	Milt Thompson	.03	.01	.00
☐ 197	Terry Pendleton	.03	.01	.00
☐ 198	Vince Coleman	.08	.04	.01
☐ 199	Paul Coleman	.25	.12	.02
☐ 200	Jose Oquendo	.03	.01	.00
☐ 201	Pedro Guerrero	.08	.04	.01
☐ 202	Tom Brunansky	.08	.04	.01
☐ 203	Roger Smithberg	.12	.06	.01
☐ 204	Eddie Whitson	.03	.01	.00
☐ 205	Dennis Rasmussen	.03	.01	.00
☐ 206	Craig Lefferts	.03	.01	.00
☐ 207	Andy Benes	.18	.09	.01
☐ 208	Bruce Hurst	.06	.03	.00
☐ 209	Eric Show	.03	.01	.00
☐ 210	Rafael Valdez	.15	.07	.01
☐ 211	Joey Cora	.03	.01	.00
☐ 212	Thomas Howard	.12	.06	.01
☐ 213	Rob Nelson	.03	.01	.00
☐ 214	Jack Clark	.08	.04	.01
☐ 215	Garry Templeton	.03	.01	.00
☐ 216	Fred Lynn	.08	.04	.01
☐ 217	Tony Gwynn	.10	.05	.01
☐ 218	Benny Santiago	.10	.05	.01
☐ 219	Mike Pagliarulo	.03	.01	.00
☐ 220	Joe Carter	.08	.04	.01
☐ 221	Roberto Alomar	.10	.05	.01
☐ 222	Bip Roberts	.06	.03	.00
☐ 223	Rick Reuschel	.06	.03	.00
☐ 224	Russ Swan	.20	.10	.02
☐ 225	Eric Gunderson	.15	.07	.01
☐ 226	Steve Bedrosian	.06	.03	.00
☐ 227	Mike Remlinger	.15	.07	.01
☐ 228	Scott Garrelts	.06	.03	.00
☐ 229	Ernie Camacho	.03	.01	.00
☐ 230	Andres Santana	.20	.10	.02
☐ 231	Will Clark	.40	.20	.04
☐ 232	Kevin Mitchell	.15	.07	.01
☐ 233	Robby Thompson	.03	.01	.00
☐ 234	Bill Bathe	.03	.01	.00
☐ 235	Tony Perezchica	.03	.01	.00
☐ 236	Gary Carter	.08	.04	.01
☐ 237	Brett Butler	.08	.04	.01
☐ 238	Matt Williams	.15	.07	.01
☐ 239	Earnie Riles	.03	.01	.00
☐ 240	Kevin Bass	.06	.03	.00
☐ 241	Terry Kennedy	.03	.01	.00
☐ 242	Steve Hosey	.25	.12	.02
☐ 243	Ben McDonald	1.25	.60	.12
☐ 244	Jeff Ballard	.03	.01	.00
☐ 245	Joe Price	.03	.01	.00
☐ 246	Curt Schilling	.03	.01	.00
☐ 247	Pete Harnisch	.03	.01	.00
☐ 248	Mark Williamson	.03	.01	.00
☐ 249	Gregg Olson	.20	.10	.02
☐ 250	Chris Myers	.12	.06	.01
☐ 251	David Segui	.35	.17	.03
☐ 252	Joe Orsulak	.03	.01	.00
☐ 253	Craig Worthington	.10	.05	.01
☐ 254	Mickey Tettleton	.06	.03	.00
☐ 255	Cal Ripken	.12	.06	.01
☐ 256	Billy Ripken	.03	.01	.00
☐ 257	Randy Milligan	.08	.04	.01
☐ 258	Brady Anderson	.06	.03	.00
☐ 259	Chris Hoiles	.20	.10	.02
☐ 260	Mike Devereaux	.06	.03	.00
☐ 261	Phil Bradley	.06	.03	.00
☐ 262	Leo Gomez	.45	.22	.04
☐ 263	Lee Smith	.06	.03	.00
☐ 264	Mike Rochford	.03	.01	.00
☐ 265	Jeff Reardon	.06	.03	.00
☐ 266	Wes Gardner	.03	.01	.00
☐ 267	Mike Boddicker	.03	.01	.00
☐ 268	Roger Clemens	.20	.10	.02
☐ 269	Rob Murphy	.03	.01	.00
☐ 270	Mickey Pina	.35	.17	.03
☐ 271	Tony Pena	.06	.03	.00
☐ 272	Jody Reed	.08	.04	.01
☐ 273	Kevin Romine	.03	.01	.00
☐ 274	Mike Greenwell	.15	.07	.01
☐ 275	Maurice Vaughn	.75	.35	.07
☐ 276	Danny Heep	.03	.01	.00

☐ 277	Scott Cooper	.25	.12	.02
☐ 278	Greg Blosser	.30	.15	.03
☐ 279	Dwight Evans (* by "1990 Team Breakdown")	.08	.04	.01
☐ 280	Ellis Burks	.12	.06	.01
☐ 281	Wade Boggs	.18	.09	.01
☐ 282	Marty Barrett	.03	.01	.00
☐ 283	Kirk McCaskill	.03	.01	.00
☐ 284	Mark Langston	.08	.04	.01
☐ 285	Bert Blyleven	.06	.03	.00
☐ 286	Mike Fetters	.12	.06	.01
☐ 287	Kyle Abbott	.20	.10	.02
☐ 288	Jim Abbott	.20	.10	.02
☐ 289	Chuck Finley	.08	.04	.01
☐ 290	Gary DiSarcina	.10	.05	.01
☐ 291	Dick Schofield	.03	.01	.00
☐ 292	Devon White	.08	.04	.01
☐ 293	Bobby Rose	.20	.10	.02
☐ 294	Brian Downing	.03	.01	.00
☐ 295	Lance Parrish	.08	.04	.01
☐ 296	Jack Howell	.03	.01	.00
☐ 297	Claudell Washington	.06	.03	.00
☐ 298	John Orton	.10	.05	.01
☐ 299	Wally Joyner	.08	.04	.01
☐ 300	Lee Stevens	.25	.12	.02
☐ 301	Chili Davis	.06	.03	.00
☐ 302	Johnny Ray	.03	.01	.00
☐ 303	Greg Hibbard	.15	.07	.01
☐ 304	Eric King	.03	.01	.00
☐ 305	Jack McDowell	.08	.04	.01
☐ 306	Bobby Thigpen	.08	.04	.01
☐ 307	Adam Peterson	.03	.01	.00
☐ 308	Scott Radinsky	.15	.07	.01
☐ 309	Wayne Edwards	.15	.07	.01
☐ 310	Melido Perez	.06	.03	.00
☐ 311	Robin Ventura	.20	.10	.02
☐ 312	Sammy Sosa	.40	.20	.04
☐ 313	Dan Pasqua	.03	.01	.00
☐ 314	Carlton Fisk	.10	.05	.01
☐ 315	Ozzie Guillen	.08	.04	.01
☐ 316	Ivan Calderon	.06	.03	.00
☐ 317	Daryl Boston	.06	.03	.00
☐ 318	Craig Grebeck	.10	.05	.01
☐ 319	Scott Fletcher	.03	.01	.00
☐ 320	Frank Thomas	1.75	.85	.17
☐ 321	Steve Lyons	.03	.01	.00
☐ 322	Carlos Martinez	.10	.05	.01
☐ 323	Joe Skalski	.10	.05	.01
☐ 324	Tom Candiotti	.03	.01	.00
☐ 325	Greg Swindell	.08	.04	.01
☐ 326	Steve Olin	.08	.04	.01
☐ 327	Kevin Wickander	.03	.01	.00
☐ 328	Doug Jones	.06	.03	.00
☐ 329	Jeff Shaw	.12	.06	.01
☐ 330	Kevin Bearse	.12	.06	.01
☐ 331	Dion James	.03	.01	.00
☐ 332	Jerry Browne	.03	.01	.00
☐ 333	Joey Belle	.20	.10	.02
☐ 334	Felix Fermin	.03	.01	.00
☐ 335	Candy Maldonado	.06	.03	.00
☐ 336	Cory Snyder	.08	.04	.01
☐ 337	Sandy Alomar Jr.	.25	.12	.02
☐ 338	Mark Lewis	.12	.06	.01
☐ 339	Carlos Baerga	.35	.17	.03
☐ 340	Chris James	.06	.03	.00
☐ 341	Brook Jacoby	.06	.03	.00
☐ 342	Keith Hernandez	.08	.04	.01
☐ 343	Frank Tanana	.06	.03	.00
☐ 344	Scott Aldred	.12	.06	.01
☐ 345	Mike Henneman	.03	.01	.00
☐ 346	Steve Wapnick	.10	.05	.01
☐ 347	Greg Gohr	.15	.07	.01
☐ 348	Eric Stone	.15	.07	.01
☐ 349	Brian DuBois	.10	.05	.01
☐ 350	Kevin Ritz	.10	.05	.01
☐ 351	Rico Brogna	.10	.05	.01
☐ 352	Mike Heath	.03	.01	.00
☐ 353	Alan Trammell	.08	.04	.01
☐ 354	Chet Lemon	.03	.01	.00
☐ 355	Dave Bergman	.03	.01	.00
☐ 356	Lou Whitaker	.06	.03	.00
☐ 357	Cecil Fielder (* by "1990 Team Breakdown")	.50	.25	.05
☐ 358	Milt Cuyler	.25	.12	.02
☐ 359	Tony Phillips	.03	.01	.00
☐ 360	Travis Fryman	.75	.35	.07
☐ 361	Ed Romero	.30	.15	.03
☐ 362	Lloyd Moseby	.06	.03	.00
☐ 363	Mark Gubicza	.06	.03	.00
☐ 364	Bret Saberhagen	.08	.04	.01
☐ 365	Tom Gordon	.15	.07	.01
☐ 366	Steve Farr	.03	.01	.00
☐ 367	Kevin Appier	.25	.12	.02
☐ 368	Storm Davis	.06	.03	.00
☐ 369	Mark Davis	.08	.04	.01
☐ 370	Jeff Montgomery	.06	.03	.00
☐ 371	Frank White	.06	.03	.00
☐ 372	Brent Mayne	.15	.07	.01
☐ 373	Bob Boone	.08	.04	.01
☐ 374	Jim Eisenreich	.03	.01	.00
☐ 375	Danny Tartabull	.08	.04	.01
☐ 376	Kurt Stillwell	.06	.03	.00
☐ 377	Bill Pecota	.03	.01	.00
☐ 378	Bo Jackson	.50	.25	.05
☐ 379	Bob Hamelin	.25	.12	.02
☐ 380	Kevin Seitzer	.08	.04	.01
☐ 381	Rey Palacios	.03	.01	.00
☐ 382	George Brett	.12	.06	.01
☐ 383	Gerald Perry	.03	.01	.00
☐ 384	Teddy Higuera	.06	.03	.00
☐ 385	Tom Filer	.03	.01	.00
☐ 386	Dan Plesac	.03	.01	.00
☐ 387	Cal Eldred	.15	.07	.01
☐ 388	Jaime Navarro	.12	.06	.01
☐ 389	Chris Bosio	.03	.01	.00
☐ 390	Randy Veres	.08	.04	.01
☐ 391	Gary Sheffield	.20	.10	.02
☐ 392	George Canale	.10	.05	.01
☐ 393	B.J. Surhoff	.06	.03	.00
☐ 394	Tim McIntosh	.15	.07	.01
☐ 395	Greg Brock	.03	.01	.00
☐ 396	Greg Vaughn	.50	.25	.05
☐ 397	Darryl Hamilton	.12	.06	.01
☐ 398	Dave Parker	.08	.04	.01
☐ 399	Paul Molitor	.08	.04	.01
☐ 400	Jim Gantner	.03	.01	.00
☐ 401	Rob Deer	.06	.03	.00
☐ 402	Billy Spiers	.12	.06	.01
☐ 403	Glenn Braggs	.03	.01	.00
☐ 404	Robin Yount	.12	.06	.01
☐ 405	Rick Aguilera	.03	.01	.00
☐ 406	Johnny Ard	.06	.03	.00
☐ 407	Kevin Tapani	.25	.12	.02
☐ 408	Park Pittman	.15	.07	.01
☐ 409	Allan Anderson	.06	.03	.00
☐ 410	Juan Berenguer	.03	.01	.00
☐ 411	Willie Banks	.30	.15	.03
☐ 412	Rich Yett	.03	.01	.00
☐ 413	Dave West	.06	.03	.00
☐ 414	Greg Gagne	.03	.01	.00
☐ 415	Chuck Knoblauch	.20	.10	.02
☐ 416	Randy Bush	.03	.01	.00
☐ 417	Gary Gaetti	.06	.03	.00
☐ 418	Kent Hrbek	.08	.04	.01
☐ 419	Al Newman	.03	.01	.00
☐ 420	Danny Gladden	.03	.01	.00
☐ 421	Paul Sorrento	.12	.06	.01
☐ 422	Derek Parks	.20	.10	.02
☐ 423	Scott Leius	.15	.07	.01
☐ 424	Kirby Puckett	.20	.10	.02
☐ 425	Willie Smith	.15	.07	.01
☐ 426	Dave Righetti	.08	.04	.01
☐ 427	Jeff Robinson	.03	.01	.00
☐ 428	Alan Mills	.15	.07	.01
☐ 429	Tim Leary	.06	.03	.00
☐ 430	Pascual Perez	.06	.03	.00
☐ 431	Alvaro Espinoza	.03	.01	.00
☐ 432	Dave Winfield	.10	.05	.01
☐ 433	Jesse Barfield	.08	.04	.01
☐ 434	Randy Velarde	.03	.01	.00
☐ 435	Rick Cerone	.03	.01	.00
☐ 436	Steve Balboni	.03	.01	.00
☐ 437	Mel Hall	.03	.01	.00
☐ 438	Bob Geren	.08	.04	.01
☐ 439	Bernie Williams	.30	.15	.03
☐ 440	Kevin Maas	2.00	1.00	.20
☐ 441	Mike Blowers	.20	.10	.02
☐ 442	Steve Sax	.08	.04	.01
☐ 443	Don Mattingly	.35	.17	.03
☐ 444	Roberto Kelly	.10	.05	.01
☐ 445	Mike Moore	.06	.03	.00
☐ 446	Reggie Harris	.20	.10	.02
☐ 447	Scott Sanderson	.06	.03	.00
☐ 448	Dave Otto	.03	.01	.00
☐ 449	Dave Stewart	.10	.05	.01
☐ 450	Rick Honeycutt	.03	.01	.00
☐ 451	Dennis Eckersley	.10	.05	.01
☐ 452	Carney Lansford	.06	.03	.00
☐ 453	Scott Hemond	.18	.09	.01
☐ 454	Mark McGwire	.20	.10	.02
☐ 455	Felix Jose	.10	.05	.01
☐ 456	Terry Steinbach	.06	.03	.00
☐ 457	Rickey Henderson	.20	.10	.02
☐ 458	Dave Henderson	.06	.03	.00
☐ 459	Mike Gallego	.03	.01	.00
☐ 460	Jose Canseco	.45	.22	.04

☐ 461	Walt Weiss	.08	.04	.01
☐ 462	Ken Phelps	.03	.01	.00
☐ 463	Darren Lewis	.50	.25	.05
☐ 464	Ron Hassey	.03	.01	.00
☐ 465	Roger Salkeld	.20	.10	.02
☐ 466	Scott Bankhead	.03	.01	.00
☐ 467	Keith Comstock	.03	.01	.00
☐ 468	Randy Johnson	.12	.06	.01
☐ 469	Erik Hanson	.15	.07	.01
☐ 470	Mike Schooler	.10	.05	.01
☐ 471	Gary Eave	.10	.05	.01
☐ 472	Jeffrey Leonard	.06	.03	.00
☐ 473	Dave Valle	.03	.01	.00
☐ 474	Omar Vizquel	.08	.04	.01
☐ 475	Pete O'Brien	.06	.03	.00
☐ 476	Henry Cotto	.03	.01	.00
☐ 477	Jay Buhner	.08	.04	.01
☐ 478	Harold Reynolds	.06	.03	.00
☐ 479	Alvin Davis	.08	.04	.01
☐ 480	Darnell Coles	.06	.03	.00
☐ 481	Ken Griffey Jr.	2.00	1.00	.20
☐ 482	Greg Briley	.12	.06	.01
☐ 483	Scott Bradley	.03	.01	.00
☐ 484	Tino Martinez	.40	.20	.04
☐ 485	Jeff Russell	.03	.01	.00
☐ 486	Nolan Ryan	.35	.17	.03
☐ 487	Robb Nen	.20	.10	.02
☐ 488	Kevin Brown	.12	.06	.01
☐ 489	Brian Bohanon	.15	.07	.01
☐ 490	Ruben Sierra	.15	.07	.01
☐ 491	Pete Incaviglia	.06	.03	.00
☐ 492	Juan Gonzalez	1.00	.50	.10
☐ 493	Steve Buechele	.03	.01	.00
☐ 494	Scott Coolbaugh	.12	.06	.01
☐ 495	Geno Petralli	.03	.01	.00
☐ 496	Rafael Palmeiro	.10	.05	.01
☐ 497	Julio Franco	.06	.03	.00
☐ 498	Gary Pettis	.03	.01	.00
☐ 499	Donald Harris	.15	.07	.01
☐ 500	Monty Fariss	.06	.03	.00
☐ 501	Harold Baines	.08	.04	.01
☐ 502	Cecil Espy	.03	.01	.00
☐ 503	Jack Daugherty	.08	.04	.01
☐ 504	Willie Blair	.08	.04	.01
☐ 505	Dave Stieb	.08	.04	.01
☐ 506	Tom Henke	.06	.03	.00
☐ 507	John Cerutti	.03	.01	.00
☐ 508	Paul Kilgus	.03	.01	.00
☐ 509	Jimmy Key	.06	.03	.00
☐ 510	John Olerud	2.00	1.00	.20
☐ 511	Ed Sprague	.08	.04	.01
☐ 512	Manny Lee	.03	.01	.00
☐ 513	Fred McGriff	.10	.05	.01
☐ 514	Glenallen Hill	.10	.05	.01
☐ 515	George Bell	.10	.05	.01
☐ 516	Mookie Wilson	.06	.03	.00
☐ 517	Luis Sojo	.15	.07	.01
☐ 518	Nelson Liriano	.03	.01	.00
☐ 519	Kelly Gruber	.10	.05	.01
☐ 520	Greg Myers	.03	.01	.00
☐ 521	Pat Borders	.03	.01	.00
☐ 522	Junior Felix	.25	.12	.02
☐ 523	Eddie Zosky	.25	.12	.02
☐ 524	Tony Fernandez	.06	.03	.00
☐ 525	Checklist 1-132 (no copyright mark on the back)	.06	.01	.00
☐ 526	Checklist 133-264	.06	.01	.00
☐ 527	Checklist 265-396	.06	.01	.00
☐ 528	Checklist 397-528	.08	.01	.00

1990 Bowman Inserts

These 2 1/2" by 3 1/2" cards were an insert in every 1990 Bowman pack. This set which consists of 11 superstars are drawings by Craig Pursley with the backs being descriptions of the 1990 Bowman sweepstakes. We have checklisted the set alphabetically by player. All the cards in this set can be found with either one asterisk or two on the back.

	MINT	EXC	G-VG
COMPLETE SET (11)	2.00	1.00	.20
COMMON PLAYER (1-11)	.10	.05	.01
☐ 1 Will Clark	.30	.15	.03
☐ 2 Mark Davis	.10	.05	.01

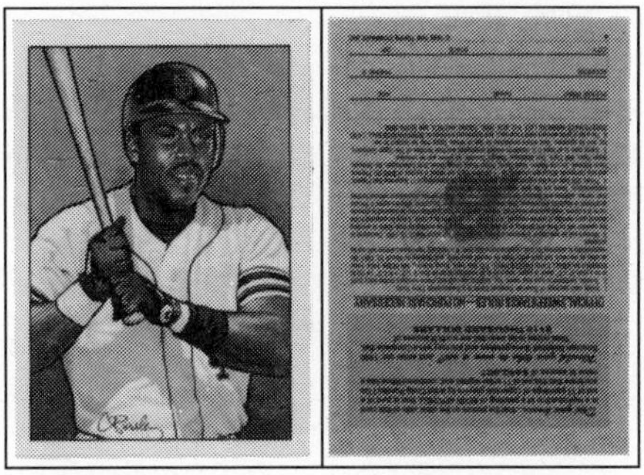

☐ 3 Dwight Gooden	.20	.10	.02
☐ 4 Bo Jackson	.40	.20	.04
☐ 5 Don Mattingly	.30	.15	.03
☐ 6 Kevin Mitchell	.20	.10	.02
☐ 7 Gregg Olson	.20	.10	.02
☐ 8 Nolan Ryan	.40	.20	.04
☐ 9 Bret Saberhagen	.20	.10	.02
☐ 10 Jerome Walton	.20	.10	.02
☐ 11 Robin Yount	.20	.10	.02

1977 Burger King Yankees

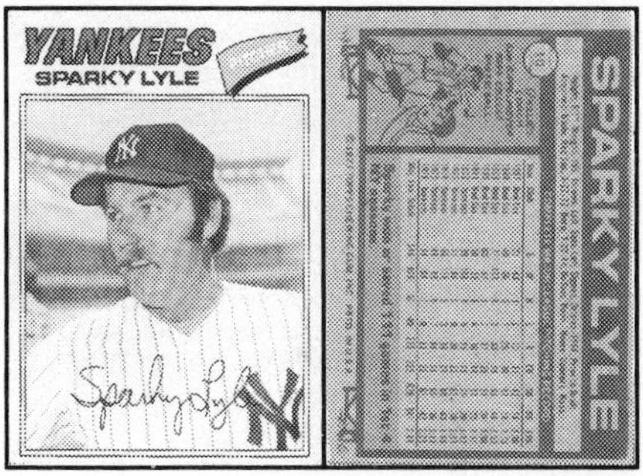

The cards in this 24-card set measure 2 1/2" by 3 1/2". The cards in this set marked with an asterisk have different poses than those cards in the regular 1977 Topps set. The checklist card is unnumbered and the Piniella card was issued subsequent to the original printing. The complete set price below refers to all 24 cards listed, including Piniella.

	NRMT	VG-E	GOOD
COMPLETE SET (24)	35.00	17.50	3.50
COMMON PLAYER (1-23)	.35	.17	.03
☐ 1 Yankees Team Billy Martin MG	1.25	.60	.12
☐ 2 Thurman Munson * (facsimile autograph misspelled)	7.00	3.50	.70
☐ 3 Fran Healy	.35	.17	.03
☐ 4 Jim Hunter	3.00	1.50	.30
☐ 5 Ed Figueroa	.35	.17	.03
☐ 6 Don Gullett * (mouth closed)	.60	.30	.06
☐ 7 Mike Torrez *	.60	.30	.06
☐ 8 Ken Holtzman	.35	.17	.03
☐ 9 Dick Tidrow	.35	.17	.03
☐ 10 Sparky Lyle	.50	.25	.05
☐ 11 Ron Guidry	2.00	1.00	.20
☐ 12 Chris Chambliss	.50	.25	.05
☐ 13 Willie Randolph * (no rookie trophy)	1.25	.60	.12
☐ 14 Bucky Dent * (shown as White Sox in 1977 Topps)	1.25	.60	.12

☐ 15 Graig Nettles * (closer photo than in 1977 Topps)	1.50	.75	.15
☐ 16 Fred Stanley	.35	.17	.03
☐ 17 Reggie Jackson * (looking up with bat)	8.00	4.00	.80
☐ 18 Mickey Rivers	.50	.25	.05
☐ 19 Roy White	.35	.17	.03
☐ 20 Jim Wynn * (shown as Brave in 1977 Topps)	.60	.30	.06
☐ 21 Paul Blair * (shown as Oriole in 1977 Topps)	.60	.30	.06
☐ 22 Carlos May *	.35	.17	.03
☐ 23 Lou Piniella	15.00	7.50	1.50
☐ xx Checklist Card TP (unnumbered)	.15	.02	.00

1978 Burger King Astros

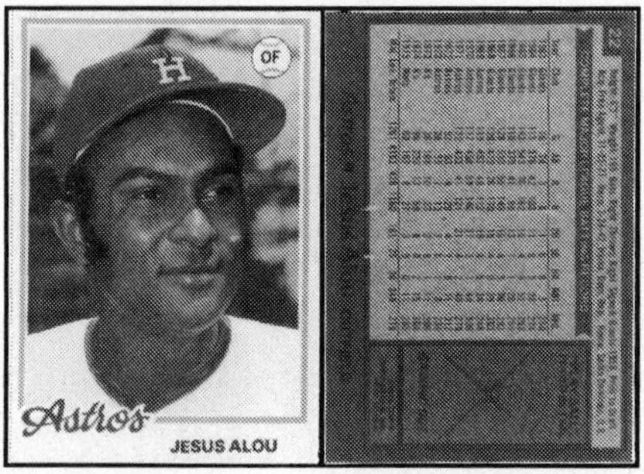

The cards in this 23-card set measure 2 1/2" by 3 1/2". Released in local Houston Burger King outlets during the 1978 season, this Houston Astros series contains the standard 22 numbered player cards and one unnumbered checklist. The player poses found to differ from the regular Topps issue are marked with astericks.

	NRMT	VG-E	GOOD
COMPLETE SET (23)	10.00	5.00	1.00
COMMON PLAYER (1-23)	.35	.17	.03
☐ 1 Bill Virdon MG	.60	.30	.06
☐ 2 Joe Ferguson	.35	.17	.03
☐ 3 Ed Herrmann	.35	.17	.03
☐ 4 J.R. Richard	.90	.45	.09
☐ 5 Joe Niekro	1.00	.50	.10
☐ 6 Floyd Bannister	1.00	.50	.10
☐ 7 Joaquin Andujar	.90	.45	.09
☐ 8 Ken Forsch	.45	.22	.04
☐ 9 Mark Lemongello	.35	.17	.03
☐ 10 Joe Sambito	.45	.22	.04
☐ 11 Gene Pentz	.35	.17	.03
☐ 12 Bob Watson	.60	.30	.06
☐ 13 Julio Gonzales	.35	.17	.03
☐ 14 Enos Cabell	.35	.17	.03
☐ 15 Roger Metzger	.35	.17	.03
☐ 16 Art Howe	.75	.35	.07
☐ 17 Jose Cruz	.90	.45	.09
☐ 18 Cesar Cedeno	.75	.35	.07
☐ 19 Terry Puhl	.60	.30	.06
☐ 20 Wilbur Howard	.35	.17	.03
☐ 21 Dave Bergman *	.45	.22	.04
☐ 22 Jesus Alou *	.45	.22	.04
☐ 23 Checklist Card TP (unnumbered)	.05	.01	.00

1978 Burger King Rangers

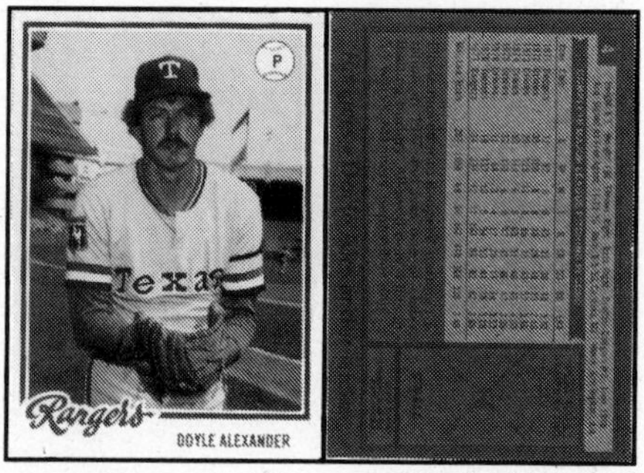

The cards in this 23-card set measure 2 1/2" by 3 1/2". This set of 22 numbered player cards (featuring the Texas Rangers) and one unnumbered checklist was issued regionally by Burger King in 1978. Astericks denote poses different from those found in the regular Topps cards of this year.

	NRMT	VG-E	GOOD
COMPLETE SET (23)	10.00	5.00	1.00
COMMON PLAYER (1-23)	.35	.17	.03
☐ 1 Billy Hunter MG	.35	.17	.03
☐ 2 Jim Sundberg	.60	.30	.06
☐ 3 John Ellis	.35	.17	.03
☐ 4 Doyle Alexander	.60	.30	.06
☐ 5 Jon Matlack *	.60	.30	.06
☐ 6 Dock Ellis	.35	.17	.03
☐ 7 Doc Medich	.45	.22	.04
☐ 8 Fergie Jenkins *	1.50	.75	.15
☐ 9 Len Barker	.35	.17	.03
☐ 10 Reggie Cleveland *	.35	.17	.03
☐ 11 Mike Hargrove	.60	.30	.06
☐ 12 Bump Wills	.35	.17	.03
☐ 13 Toby Harrah	.75	.35	.07
☐ 14 Bert Campaneris	.60	.30	.06
☐ 15 Sandy Alomar	.35	.17	.03
☐ 16 Kurt Bevacqua	.35	.17	.03
☐ 17 Al Oliver *	1.00	.50	.10
☐ 18 Juan Beniquez	.45	.22	.04
☐ 19 Claudell Washington	.75	.35	.07
☐ 20 Richie Zisk	.45	.22	.04
☐ 21 John Lowenstein *	.35	.17	.03
☐ 22 Bobby Thompson *	.35	.17	.03
☐ 23 Checklist Card TP (unnumbered)	.05	.01	.00

1978 Burger King Tigers

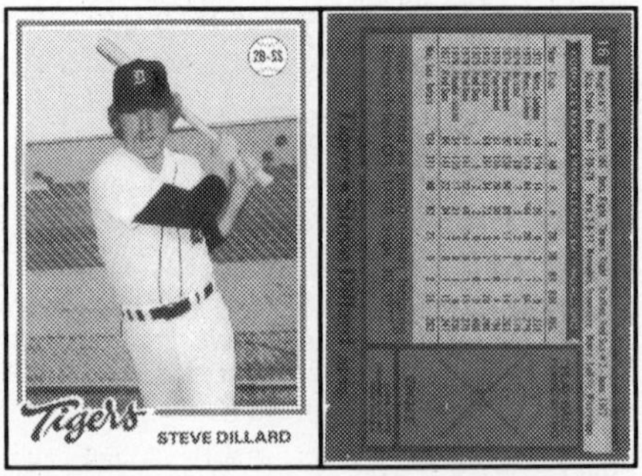

The cards in this 23-card set measure 2 1/2" by 3 1/2". Twenty-three color cards, 22 players and one numbered checklist, comprise the 1978 Burger King Tigers set issued in the Detroit area. The cards marked with an asterisk contain photos different from those appearing on the Topps regular issue cards of that year. For example, Jack Morris, Alan Trammell, and Lou Whitaker (in the 1978 Topps regular issue cards) each appear on rookie prospect cards with three other young players; whereas in this Burger King set, each has his own individual card.

	NRMT	VG-E	GOOD
COMPLETE SET (23)	45.00	20.00	4.00
COMMON PLAYER (1-23)	.35	.17	.03
☐ 1 Ralph Houk MG	.60	.30	.06
☐ 2 Milt May	.35	.17	.03
☐ 3 John Wockenfuss	.35	.17	.03
☐ 4 Mark Fidrych	.75	.35	.07
☐ 5 Dave Rozema	.35	.17	.03
☐ 6 Jack Billingham *	.35	.17	.03
☐ 7 Jim Slaton *	.35	.17	.03
☐ 8 Jack Morris *	9.00	4.50	.90
☐ 9 John Hiller	.60	.30	.06
☐ 10 Steve Foucault	.35	.17	.03
☐ 11 Milt Wilcox	.35	.17	.03
☐ 12 Jason Thompson	.60	.30	.06
☐ 13 Lou Whitaker *	10.00	5.00	1.00
☐ 14 Aurelio Rodriguez	.35	.17	.03
☐ 15 Alan Trammell *	21.00	10.50	2.10
☐ 16 Steve Dillard *	.35	.17	.03
☐ 17 Phil Mankowski	.35	.17	.03
☐ 18 Steve Kemp	.60	.30	.06
☐ 19 Ron LeFlore	.45	.22	.04
☐ 20 Tim Corcoran	.35	.17	.03
☐ 21 Mickey Stanley	.45	.22	.04
☐ 22 Rusty Staub	1.00	.50	.10
☐ 23 Checklist Card TP (unnumbered)	.05	.01	.00

1978 Burger King Yankees

The cards in this 23-card set measure 2 1/2" by 3 1/2". These cards were distributed in packs of three players plus a checklist at Burger King's New York area outlets. Cards with an asterisk have different poses than those in the Topps regular issue.

	NRMT	VG-E	GOOD
COMPLETE SET (23)	12.00	5.00	1.00
COMMON PLAYER (1-23)	.25	.12	.02
☐ 1 Billy Martin MG	.75	.35	.07
☐ 2 Thurman Munson	3.50	1.75	.35
☐ 3 Cliff Johnson	.25	.12	.02
☐ 4 Ron Guidry	1.25	.60	.12
☐ 5 Ed Figueroa	.25	.12	.02
☐ 6 Dick Tidrow	.25	.12	.02
☐ 7 Jim Hunter	1.50	.75	.15
☐ 8 Don Gullett	.35	.17	.03
☐ 9 Sparky Lyle	.50	.25	.05
☐ 10 Rich Gossage *	1.00	.50	.10
☐ 11 Rawly Eastwick *	.25	.12	.02
☐ 12 Chris Chambliss	.35	.17	.03
☐ 13 Willie Randolph	.60	.30	.06
☐ 14 Graig Nettles	.75	.35	.07
☐ 15 Bucky Dent	.60	.30	.06
☐ 16 Jim Spencer *	.25	.12	.02
☐ 17 Fred Stanley	.25	.12	.02
☐ 18 Lou Piniella	.60	.30	.06
☐ 19 Roy White	.35	.17	.03
☐ 20 Mickey Rivers	.35	.17	.03
☐ 21 Reggie Jackson	4.50	2.25	.45
☐ 22 Paul Blair	.25	.12	.02
☐ 23 Checklist Card TP (unnumbered)	.05	.01	.00

1979 Burger King Phillies

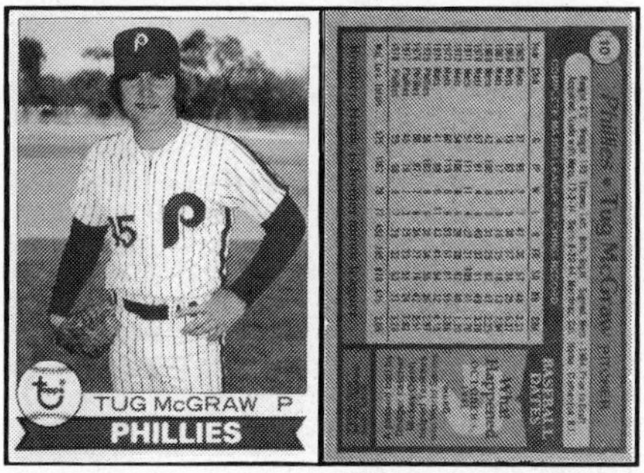

The cards in this 23-card set measure 2 1/2" by 3 1/2". The 1979 Burger King Phillies set follows the regular format of 22 player cards and one unnumbered checklist card. The asterisk indicates where the pose differs from the Topps card of that year.

	NRMT	VG-E	GOOD
COMPLETE SET (23)	8.00	4.00	.80
COMMON PLAYER (1-23)	.15	.07	.01
☐ 1 Danny Ozark MG *	.15	.07	.01
☐ 2 Bob Boone	.50	.25	.05
☐ 3 Tim McCarver	.50	.25	.05
☐ 4 Steve Carlton	2.00	1.00	.20
☐ 5 Larry Christenson	.15	.07	.01
☐ 6 Dick Ruthven	.15	.07	.01
☐ 7 Ron Reed	.15	.07	.01
☐ 8 Randy Lerch	.15	.07	.01
☐ 9 Warren Brusstar	.15	.07	.01
☐ 10 Tug McGraw	.35	.17	.03
☐ 11 Nino Espinosa *	.15	.07	.01
☐ 12 Doug Bird *	.15	.07	.01
☐ 13 Pete Rose *	2.50	1.25	.25
☐ 14 Manny Trillo *	.15	.07	.01
☐ 15 Larry Bowa	.35	.17	.03
☐ 16 Mike Schmidt	3.00	1.50	.30
☐ 17 Pete Mackanin *	.15	.07	.01
☐ 18 Jose Cardenal	.15	.07	.01
☐ 19 Greg Luzinski	.35	.17	.03
☐ 20 Garry Maddox	.15	.07	.01
☐ 21 Bake McBride	.15	.07	.01
☐ 22 Greg Gross *	.15	.07	.01
☐ 23 Checklist Card TP (unnumbered)	.05	.01	.00

1979 Burger King Yankees

The cards in this 23-card set measure 2 1/2" X 3 1/2". There are 22 numbered cards and one unnumbered checklist in the 1979 Burger King Yankee set. The poses of Guidry, Tiant, John and Beniquez, each marked with an asterisk below, are different from their poses appearing in the regular Topps issue. The team card has a picture of Lemon rather than Martin.

	NRMT	VG-E	GOOD
COMPLETE SET (23)	8.00	4.00	.80
COMMON PLAYER (1-23)	.15	.07	.01
☐ 1 Yankees Team: Bob Lemon MG *	.60	.30	.06

☐ 2 Thurman Munson	2.50	1.25	.25
☐ 3 Cliff Johnson	.15	.07	.01
☐ 4 Ron Guidry *	1.25	.60	.12
☐ 5 Jay Johnstone	.35	.17	.03
☐ 6 Jim Hunter	1.25	.60	.12
☐ 7 Jim Beattie	.15	.07	.01
☐ 8 Luis Tiant *	.35	.17	.03
☐ 9 Tommy John *	.90	.45	.09
☐ 10 Rich Gossage	.60	.30	.06
☐ 11 Ed Figueroa	.15	.07	.01
☐ 12 Chris Chambliss	.25	.12	.02
☐ 13 Willie Randolph	.40	.20	.04
☐ 14 Bucky Dent	.40	.20	.04
☐ 15 Graig Nettles	.50	.25	.05
☐ 16 Fred Stanley	.15	.07	.01
☐ 17 Jim Spencer	.15	.07	.01
☐ 18 Lou Piniella	.50	.25	.05
☐ 19 Roy White	.25	.12	.02
☐ 20 Mickey Rivers	.25	.12	.02
☐ 21 Reggie Jackson	3.00	1.50	.30
☐ 22 Juan Beniquez *	.25	.12	.02
☐ 23 Checklist Card TP (unnumbered)	.05	.01	.00

1980 Burger King Phillies

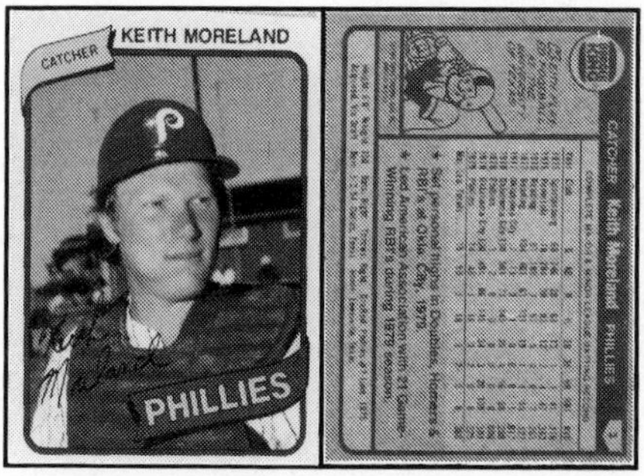

The cards in this 23-card set measure 2 1/2" by 3 1/2". The 1980 edition of Burger King Phillies follows the established pattern of 22 numbered player cards and one unnumbered checklist. Cards marked with astericks contain poses different from those found in the regular 1980 Topps cards. This was the first Burger King set to carry the Burger King logo and hence does not generate the same confusion that the three previous years do for collectors trying to distinguish Burger King cards from the very similar Topps cards of the same years. Keith Moreland's card predates his rookie cards by one year as he did not appear on a regular issue card until 1981.

	MINT	EXC	G-VG
COMPLETE SET (23)	7.00	3.50	.70
COMMON PLAYER (1-23)	.15	.07	.01

☐ 1 Dallas Green MG *	.35	.17	.03
☐ 2 Bob Boone	.40	.20	.04
☐ 3 Keith Moreland *	.60	.30	.06
☐ 4 Pete Rose	2.50	1.25	.25
☐ 5 Manny Trillo	.15	.07	.01
☐ 6 Mike Schmidt	3.00	1.50	.30
☐ 7 Larry Bowa	.35	.17	.03
☐ 8 John Vukovich *	.15	.07	.01
☐ 9 Bake McBride	.15	.07	.01
☐ 10 Garry Maddox	.15	.07	.01
☐ 11 Greg Luzinski	.35	.17	.03
☐ 12 Greg Gross	.15	.07	.01
☐ 13 Del Unser	.15	.07	.01
☐ 14 Lonnie Smith *	.75	.35	.07
☐ 15 Steve Carlton	1.75	.85	.17
☐ 16 Larry Christenson	.15	.07	.01
☐ 17 Nino Espinosa	.15	.07	.01
☐ 18 Randy Lerch	.15	.07	.01
☐ 19 Dick Ruthven	.15	.07	.01
☐ 20 Tug McGraw	.35	.17	.03
☐ 21 Ron Reed	.15	.07	.01
☐ 22 Kevin Saucier *	.15	.07	.01
☐ 23 Checklist Card TP (unnumbered)	.05	.01	.00

1980 Burger King Pitch/Hit/Run

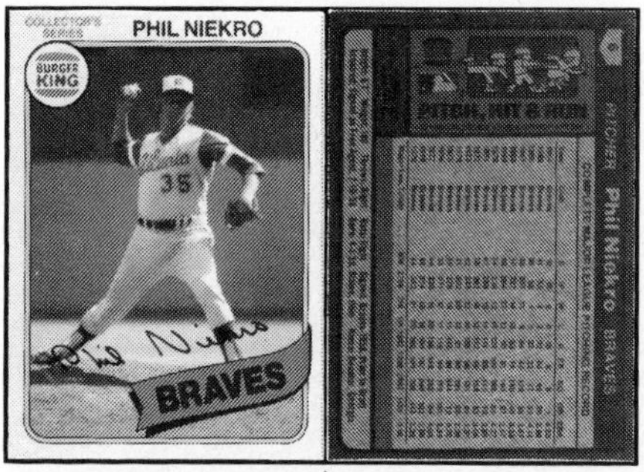

The cards in this 34-card set measure 2 1/2" by 3 1/2". The "Pitch, Hit, and Run" set was a promotion introduced by Burger King in 1980. The cards carry a Burger King logo on the front and those marked by an asterisk in the checklist contain a different photo from that found in the regularly issued Topps series. For example, Nolan Ryan was shown as a California Angel and Joe Morgan was a Cincinnati Red in the 1980 Topps regular set. Cards 1-11 are pitchers, 12-22 are hitters, and 23-33 are speedsters. Within each subgroup, the players are numbered corresponding to the alphabetical order of their names. The unnumbered checklist card was triple printed and is the least valuable card in the set.

	MINT	EXC	G-VG
COMPLETE SET (34)	16.00	8.00	1.60
COMMON PLAYER (1-34)	.15	.07	.01

☐ 1 Vida Blue *	.15	.07	.01
☐ 2 Steve Carlton	1.50	.75	.15
☐ 3 Rollie Fingers	.75	.35	.07
☐ 4 Ron Guidry *	.40	.20	.04
☐ 5 Jerry Koosman *	.25	.12	.02
☐ 6 Phil Niekro	.60	.30	.06
☐ 7 Jim Palmer *	1.25	.60	.12
☐ 8 J.R. Richard	.15	.07	.01
☐ 9 Nolan Ryan * Houston Astros	6.00	3.00	.60
☐ 10 Tom Seaver *	1.75	.85	.17
☐ 11 Bruce Sutter	.15	.07	.01
☐ 12 Don Baylor	.15	.07	.01
☐ 13 George Brett	1.50	.75	.15
☐ 14 Rod Carew	1.00	.50	.10
☐ 15 George Foster	.15	.07	.01
☐ 16 Keith Hernandez *	.60	.30	.06
☐ 17 Reggie Jackson *	2.00	1.00	.20
☐ 18 Fred Lynn *	.20	.10	.02

☐ 19 Dave Parker	.30	.15	.03
☐ 20 Jim Rice	.40	.20	.04
☐ 21 Pete Rose	2.00	1.00	.20
☐ 22 Dave Winfield *	1.25	.60	.12
☐ 23 Bobby Bonds *	.15	.07	.01
☐ 24 Enos Cabell	.15	.07	.01
☐ 25 Cesar Cedeno	.15	.07	.01
☐ 26 Julio Cruz	.15	.07	.01
☐ 27 Ron LeFlore *	.15	.07	.01
☐ 28 Dave Lopes *	.15	.07	.01
☐ 29 Omar Moreno *	.15	.07	.01
☐ 30 Joe Morgan *	1.25	.60	.12
Houston Astros			
☐ 31 Bill North	.15	.07	.01
☐ 32 Frank Taveras	.15	.07	.01
☐ 33 Willie Wilson	.20	.10	.02
☐ 34 Checklist Card TP (unnumbered)	.05	.01	.00

1982 Burger King Indians

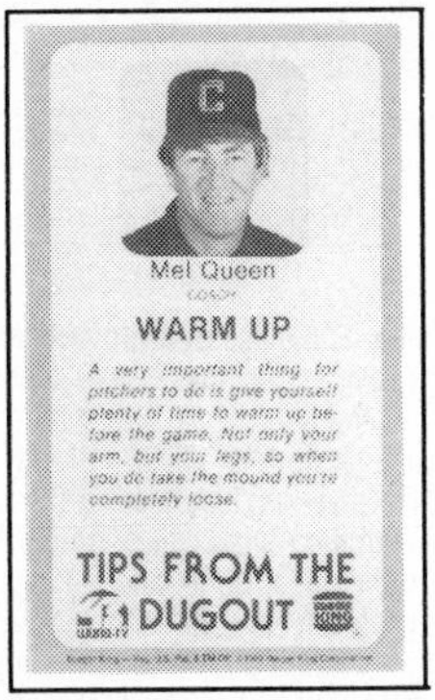

The cards in this 12-card set measure 3" by 5". Tips From The Dugout is the series title of this set issued on a one card per week basis by the Burger King chain in the Cleveland area. Each card contains a black and white photo of manager Dave Garcia or coaches Goryl, McCraw, Queen and Sommers, under whom appears a paragraph explaining some aspect of inside baseball. The photo and "Tip" are set upon a large yellow area surrounded by green borders. The cards are not numbered and are blank-backed. The logos of Burger King and WUAB-TV appear at the base of the card.

	MINT	EXC	G-VG
COMPLETE SET (12)	5.00	2.50	.50
COMMON PLAYER (1-12)	.50	.25	.05
☐ 1 Dave Garcia: Be in the Game	.50	.25	.05
☐ 2 Dave Garcia: Sportsmanship	.50	.25	.05
☐ 3 Johnny Goryl: Rounding Bases	.50	.25	.05
☐ 4 Johnny Goryl: 3B Running	.50	.25	.05
☐ 5 Tom McCraw: Follow Thru	.50	.25	.05
☐ 6 Tom McCraw: Selecting a Bat	.50	.25	.05
☐ 7 Tom McCraw: Watch the Ball	.50	.25	.05
☐ 8 Mel Queen: Master One Pitch	.50	.25	.05
☐ 9 Mel Queen: Warm Up	.50	.25	.05
☐ 10 Dennis Sommers: Protect Fingers	.50	.25	.05
☐ 11 Dennis Sommers: Tagging 1st Base	.50	.25	.05
☐ 12 Dennis Sommers	.50	.25	.05

1986 Burger King All Pro

This 20-card set was distributed in Burger King restaurants across the country. They were produced as panels of three where the middle card was actually a special discount coupon card. The folded panel was given with the purchase of a Whopper. Each individual card measures 2 1/2" by 3 1/2". The team logos have been airbrushed from the pictures. The cards are numbered on the front at the top.

	MINT	EXC	G-VG
COMPLETE SET (20)	6.00	3.00	.60
COMMON PLAYER (1-20)	.20	.10	.02
☐ 1 Tony Pena	.20	.10	.02
☐ 2 Dave Winfield	.40	.20	.04
☐ 3 Fernando Valenzuela	.30	.15	.03
☐ 4 Pete Rose	.80	.40	.08
☐ 5 Mike Schmidt	1.00	.50	.10
☐ 6 Steve Carlton	.50	.25	.05
☐ 7 Glenn Wilson	.20	.10	.02
☐ 8 Jim Rice	.30	.15	.03
☐ 9 Wade Boggs	.80	.40	.08
☐ 10 Juan Samuel	.20	.10	.02
☐ 11 Dale Murphy	.50	.25	.05
☐ 12 Reggie Jackson	.80	.40	.08
☐ 13 Kirk Gibson	.40	.20	.04
☐ 14 Eddie Murray	.50	.25	.05
☐ 15 Cal Ripken	.60	.30	.06
☐ 16 Willie McGee	.30	.15	.03
☐ 17 Dwight Gooden	.60	.30	.06
☐ 18 Steve Garvey	.50	.25	.05
☐ 19 Don Mattingly	1.00	.50	.10
☐ 20 George Brett	.80	.40	.08

1987 Burger King All-Pro

This 20-card set consists of 10 panels of two cards each joined together along with a promotional coupon. Individual cards measure 2 1/2" by 3 1/2" whereas the panels measure approximately 3 1/2" by 7 5/8". MSA (Mike Schechter Associates produced the cards for Burger King; there are no Major League logos on the cards. The cards are numbered on the front. The set card numbering is almost (but not quite) in alphabetical order by player's name.

	MINT	EXC	G-VG
COMPLETE SET (20)	5.00	2.50	.50
COMMON PLAYER (1-20)	.20	.10	.02
☐ 1 Wade Boggs	.80	.40	.08
☐ 2 Gary Carter	.40	.20	.04
☐ 3 Will Clark	1.00	.50	.10
☐ 4 Roger Clemens	.80	.40	.08
☐ 5 Steve Garvey	.40	.20	.04
☐ 6 Ron Darling	.20	.10	.02
☐ 7 Pedro Guerrero	.30	.15	.03
☐ 8 Von Hayes	.20	.10	.02
☐ 9 Rickey Henderson	.80	.40	.08
☐ 10 Keith Hernandez	.30	.15	.03
☐ 11 Wally Joyner	.50	.25	.05
☐ 12 Mike Krukow	.20	.10	.02
☐ 13 Don Mattingly	1.00	.50	.10
☐ 14 Ozzie Smith	.40	.20	.04
☐ 15 Tony Pena	.20	.10	.02
☐ 16 Jim Rice	.30	.15	.03
☐ 17 Mike Schmidt	1.00	.50	.10
☐ 18 Ryne Sandberg	1.00	.50	.10
☐ 19 Darryl Strawberry	.80	.40	.08
☐ 20 Fernando Valenzuela	.30	.15	.03

1956 Carling Black Label Indians

This 10-card, approximately 8 1/2" by 12", set was issued by Carling Beer and celebrated members of the (then) perennial contending Cleveland Indians. These cards feature a black and white photo with the printed name of the player inserted in the photo. Underneath the photo is a joint advertisement for Carling Black Label Beer and The Cleveland Indians. The set looks like it could be easily replicated and may indeed have been reprinted. The checklist for this unnumbered set is ordered alphabetically.

	MINT	EXC	G-VG
COMPLETE SET (10)	75.00	37.50	7.50
COMMON PLAYER (1-10)	5.00	2.50	.50
☐ 1 Bob Feller	25.00	12.50	2.50
☐ 2 Mike Garcia	6.00	3.00	.60
☐ 3 Jim Hegan	5.00	2.50	.50
☐ 4 Art Houtteman	5.00	2.50	.50
☐ 5 Bob Lemon	15.00	7.50	1.50
☐ 6 Al Rosen	10.00	5.00	1.00
☐ 7 Herb Score	10.00	5.00	1.00
☐ 8 Al Smith	5.00	2.50	.50
☐ 9 George Strickland	5.00	2.50	.50
☐ 10 Early Wynn	15.00	7.50	1.50

1987 Champion Phillies

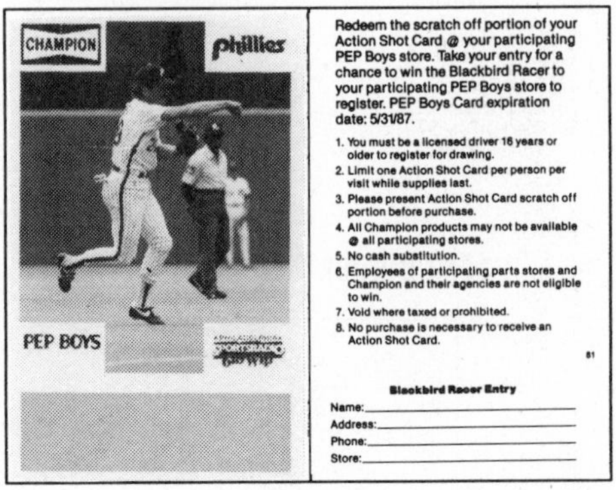

This four-card set which measured approximately 3" by 4 3/4" (with scratch-off tab) is unusual in that there is no way to determine the player's identity other than knowing and recognizing whose photo it is. The top part of the card has a color photo of the player surrounded in the upper left hand corner with a Champion spark plug logo. The Philadelphia Phillies logo is in the upper right hand part of the card. A Pep boys ad is in the lower left hand corner of the photo and the WIP Philadelphia Sports Radio promo is in the lower right hand corner of the photo. The set is checklisted alphabetically by subject since the cards are unnumbered.

	MINT	EXC	G-VG
COMPLETE SET (4)	12.50	6.25	1.25
COMMON PLAYER (1-4)	1.00	.50	.10
☐ 1 Von Hayes	2.00	1.00	.20
☐ 2 Steve Jeltz	1.00	.50	.10
☐ 3 Juan Samuel	2.00	1.00	.20
☐ 4 Mike Schmidt	10.00	5.00	1.00

1988 Chef Boyardee

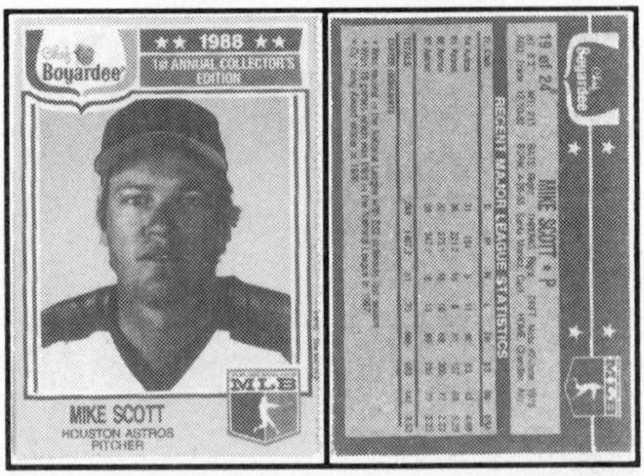

This 24-card set was distributed as a perforated sheet of four rows and six columns of cards in return for ten proofs of purchase of Chef Boyardeee products. The card photos on the fronts are in full color with a light blue border but are not shown with team logos. The card backs are numbered and printed in red and blue on gray card stock. Individual cards measure approximately 2 1/2" by 3 1/2" and show the Chef Boyardee logo in the upper right corner of the obverse. Card backs feature year-by-year season statistics since 1984.

	MINT	EXC	G-VG
COMPLETE SET (24)	12.00	6.00	1.20
COMMON PLAYER (1-24)	.40	.20	.04
☐ 1 Mark McGwire	1.00	.50	.10
☐ 2 Eric Davis	.90	.45	.09
☐ 3 Jack Morris	.40	.20	.04
☐ 4 George Bell	.50	.25	.05
☐ 5 Ozzie Smith	.50	.25	.05
☐ 6 Tony Gwynn	.75	.35	.07
☐ 7 Cal Ripken	.75	.35	.07
☐ 8 Todd Worrell	.40	.20	.04
☐ 9 Larry Parrish	.40	.20	.04
☐ 10 Gary Carter	.50	.25	.05
☐ 11 Ryne Sandberg	1.00	.50	.10
☐ 12 Keith Hernandez	.50	.25	.05
☐ 13 Kirby Puckett	1.00	.50	.10
☐ 14 Mike Schmidt	1.25	.60	.12
☐ 15 Frank Viola	.50	.25	.05
☐ 16 Don Mattingly	1.50	.75	.15
☐ 17 Dale Murphy	.75	.35	.07
☐ 18 Andre Dawson	.60	.30	.06
☐ 19 Mike Scott	.40	.20	.04
☐ 20 Rickey Henderson	1.00	.50	.10
☐ 21 Jim Rice	.50	.25	.05
☐ 22 Wade Boggs	1.00	.50	.10
☐ 23 Roger Clemens	1.00	.50	.10
☐ 24 Fernando Valenzuela	.50	.25	.05

1985 CIGNA Phillies

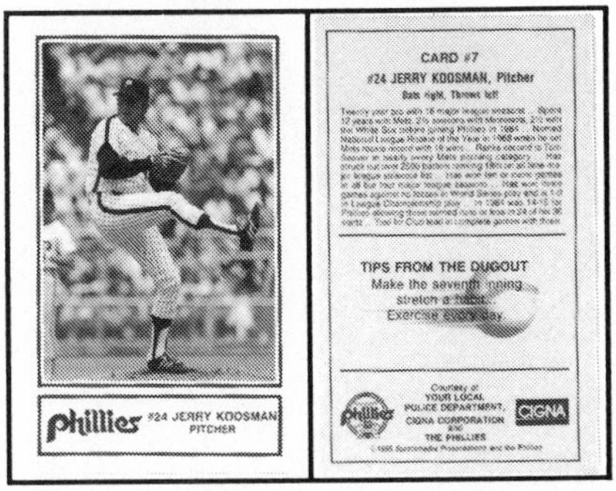

This colorful 16-card set (measuring 2 5/8" by 4 1/8") features the Philadelphia Phillies and was also sponsored by CIGNA Corporation. Cards are numbered on the back and contain a safety tip as such the set is frequently categorized and referenced as a safety set. Cards are also numbered by uniform number on the front.

	MINT	EXC	G-VG
COMPLETE SET (16)	7.00	3.50	.70
COMMON PLAYER (1-16)	.25	.12	.02
☐ 1 Juan Samuel	.50	.25	.05
☐ 2 Von Hayes	.60	.30	.06
☐ 3 Ozzie Virgil	.35	.17	.03
☐ 4 Mike Schmidt	3.00	1.50	.30
☐ 5 Greg Gross	.25	.12	.02
☐ 6 Tim Corcoran	.25	.12	.02
☐ 7 Jerry Koosman	.50	.25	.05
☐ 8 Jeff Stone	.25	.12	.02
☐ 9 Glenn Wilson	.35	.17	.03
☐ 10 Steve Jeltz	.25	.12	.02
☐ 11 Garry Maddox	.35	.17	.03
☐ 12 Steve Carlton	1.50	.75	.15
☐ 13 John Denny	.35	.17	.03
☐ 14 Kevin Gross	.50	.25	.05
☐ 15 Shane Rawley	.35	.17	.03
☐ 16 Charlie Hudson	.25	.12	.02

1986 CIGNA Phillies

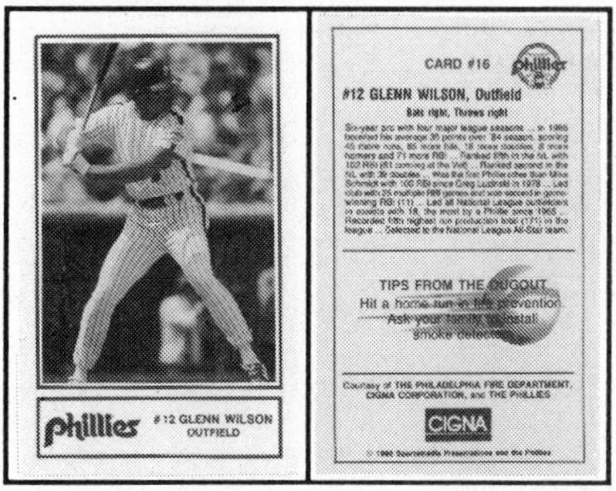

This 16-card set was sponsored by CIGNA Corp. and was given away by the Philadelphia area Fire Departments. Cards measure 2 3/4" by 4 1/8" and feature full color fronts. The card backs are printed in maroon and black on white card stock. Although the uniform numbers are given on the front of the card, the cards are numbered on the back in the order listed below.

	MINT	EXC	G-VG
COMPLETE SET (16)	7.00	3.50	.70
COMMON PLAYER (1-16)	.25	.12	.02
☐ 1 Juan Samuel	.50	.25	.05
☐ 2 Don Carman	.35	.17	.03
☐ 3 Von Hayes	.60	.30	.06
☐ 4 Kent Tekulve	.35	.17	.03
☐ 5 Greg Gross	.25	.12	.02
☐ 6 Shane Rawley	.35	.17	.03
☐ 7 Darren Daulton	.60	.30	.06
☐ 8 Kevin Gross	.35	.17	.03
☐ 9 Steve Jeltz	.25	.12	.02
☐ 10 Mike Schmidt	3.00	1.50	.30
☐ 11 Steve Bedrosian	.75	.35	.07
☐ 12 Gary Redus	.35	.17	.03
☐ 13 Charles Hudson	.25	.12	.02
☐ 14 John Russell	.25	.12	.02
☐ 15 Fred Toliver	.25	.12	.02
☐ 16 Glenn Wilson	.35	.17	.03

1985 Circle K

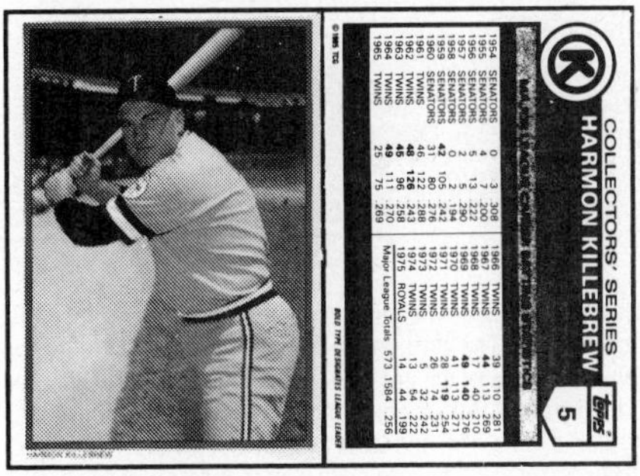

The cards in this 33-card set measure 2 1/2" by 3 1/2" and were issued with accompanying box. In 1985, Topps produced this set for Circle K; cards were printed in Ireland. Cards are numbered on the back according to each player's rank on the all-time career Home Run list. The backs are printed in blue and red on white card stock. The card fronts are glossy and each player is named in the lower left corner. Most of the obverses are in color, although the older vintage players are pictured in black and white. Joe DiMaggio was not included in the set; card number 31 does not exist. It was intended to be DiMaggio but he apparently would not consent to be included in the set.

	MINT	EXC	G-VG
COMPLETE SET (33)	5.00	2.50	.50
COMMON PLAYER (1-34)	.10	.05	.01
☐ 1 Hank Aaron	.60	.30	.06
☐ 2 Babe Ruth	1.00	.50	.10
☐ 3 Willie Mays	.60	.30	.06
☐ 4 Frank Robinson	.20	.10	.02
☐ 5 Harmon Killebrew	.15	.07	.01
☐ 6 Mickey Mantle	1.00	.50	.10
☐ 7 Jimmie Foxx	.15	.07	.01
☐ 8 Willie McCovey	.20	.10	.02
☐ 9 Ted Williams	.50	.25	.05
☐ 10 Ernie Banks	.20	.10	.02
☐ 11 Eddie Mathews	.15	.07	.01
☐ 12 Mel Ott	.15	.07	.01
☐ 13 Reggie Jackson	.50	.25	.05
☐ 14 Lou Gehrig	.60	.30	.06
☐ 15 Stan Musial	.35	.17	.03
☐ 16 Willie Stargell	.20	.10	.02
☐ 17 Carl Yastrzemski	.45	.22	.04
☐ 18 Billy Williams	.15	.07	.01
☐ 19 Mike Schmidt	.60	.30	.06
☐ 20 Duke Snider	.30	.15	.03
☐ 21 Al Kaline	.20	.10	.02
☐ 22 Johnny Bench	.35	.17	.03
☐ 23 Frank Howard	.10	.05	.01
☐ 24 Orlando Cepeda	.10	.05	.01
☐ 25 Norm Cash	.10	.05	.01
☐ 26 Dave Kingman	.10	.05	.01
☐ 27 Rocky Colavito	.10	.05	.01
☐ 28 Tony Perez	.10	.05	.01
☐ 29 Gil Hodges	.10	.05	.01
☐ 30 Ralph Kiner	.10	.05	.01
☐ 31 Joe DiMaggio (not included in set, card does not exist)	.00	.00	.00
☐ 32 Johnny Mize	.15	.07	.01
☐ 33 Yogi Berra	.30	.15	.03
☐ 34 Lee May	.10	.05	.01

1987 Classic Game

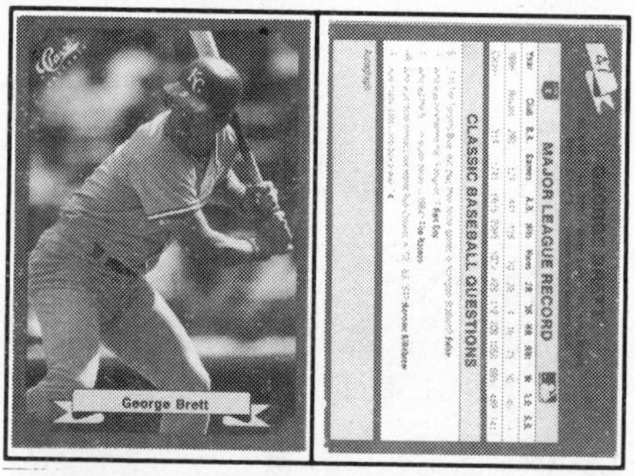

This 100-card set was actually distributed as part of a trivia board game. The card backs contain several trivia questions (and answers) which are used to play the game. A dark green border frames the full color photo. The games were produced by Game Time, Ltd. and were available in toy stores as well as from card dealers. According to the producers of the this game, only 75,000 sets were distributed. The cards are standard size, 2 1/2" by 3 1/2".

	MINT	EXC	G-VG
COMPLETE SET (100)	165.00	70.00	15.00
COMMON PLAYER (1-100)	.25	.12	.02
☐ 1 Pete Rose	2.50	1.25	.25
☐ 2 Len Dykstra	.75	.35	.07
☐ 3 Darryl Strawberry	2.50	1.25	.25
☐ 4 Keith Hernandez	.50	.25	.05
☐ 5 Gary Carter	.60	.30	.06
☐ 6 Wally Joyner	1.50	.75	.15
☐ 7 Andres Thomas	.25	.12	.02
☐ 8 Pat Dodson	.25	.12	.02
☐ 9 Kirk Gibson	.50	.25	.05
☐ 10 Don Mattingly	3.50	1.75	.35
☐ 11 Dave Winfield	.60	.30	.06
☐ 12 Rickey Henderson	3.50	1.75	.35
☐ 13 Dan Pasqua	.25	.12	.02
☐ 14 Don Baylor	.35	.17	.03
☐ 15 Bo Jackson (swinging bat in Auburn FB uniform)	75.00	37.50	7.50
☐ 16 Pete Incaviglia	1.00	.50	.10
☐ 17 Kevin Bass	.25	.12	.02
☐ 18 Barry Larkin	3.50	1.75	.35
☐ 19 Dave Magadan	2.00	1.00	.20
☐ 20 Steve Sax	.50	.25	.05
☐ 21 Eric Davis	2.00	1.00	.20
☐ 22 Mike Pagliarulo	.25	.12	.02
☐ 23 Fred Lynn	.35	.17	.03
☐ 24 Reggie Jackson	1.50	.75	.15
☐ 25 Larry Parrish	.25	.12	.02
☐ 26 Tony Gwynn	1.25	.60	.12
☐ 27 Steve Garvey	1.00	.50	.10
☐ 28 Glenn Davis	.75	.35	.07
☐ 29 Tim Raines	.75	.35	.07
☐ 30 Vince Coleman	.75	.35	.07
☐ 31 Willie McGee	.60	.30	.06
☐ 32 Ozzie Smith	.75	.35	.07
☐ 33 Dave Parker	.60	.30	.06
☐ 34 Tony Pena	.35	.17	.03
☐ 35 Ryne Sandberg	2.00	1.00	.20
☐ 36 Brett Butler	.35	.17	.03
☐ 37 Dale Murphy	1.00	.50	.10
☐ 38 Bob Horner	.35	.17	.03
☐ 39 Pedro Guerrero	.50	.25	.05
☐ 40 Brook Jacoby	.35	.17	.03
☐ 41 Carlton Fisk	.75	.35	.07
☐ 42 Harold Baines	.35	.17	.03
☐ 43 Rob Deer	.35	.17	.03
☐ 44 Robin Yount	1.00	.50	.10
☐ 45 Paul Molitor	.50	.25	.05
☐ 46 Jose Canseco	21.00	10.00	2.00
☐ 47 George Brett	1.50	.75	.15
☐ 48 Jim Presley	.25	.12	.02
☐ 49 Rich Gedman	.25	.12	.02
☐ 50 Lance Parrish	.50	.25	.05
☐ 51 Eddie Murray	1.00	.50	.10
☐ 52 Cal Ripken	1.00	.50	.10
☐ 53 Kent Hrbek	.60	.30	.06
☐ 54 Gary Gaetti	.50	.25	.05
☐ 55 Kirby Puckett	2.00	1.00	.20
☐ 56 George Bell	.50	.25	.05
☐ 57 Tony Fernandez	.35	.17	.03
☐ 58 Jesse Barfield	.35	.17	.03
☐ 59 Jim Rice	.50	.25	.05
☐ 60 Wade Boggs	2.00	1.00	.20
☐ 61 Marty Barrett	.25	.12	.02
☐ 62 Mike Schmidt	3.50	1.75	.35
☐ 63 Von Hayes	.35	.17	.03
☐ 64 Jeff Leonard	.25	.12	.02
☐ 65 Chris Brown	.25	.12	.02
☐ 66 Dave Smith	.25	.12	.02
☐ 67 Mike Krukow	.25	.12	.02
☐ 68 Ron Guidry	.35	.17	.03
☐ 69 Rob Woodward	.25	.12	.02
☐ 70 Rob Murphy	.25	.12	.02
☐ 71 Andres Galarraga	.50	.25	.05
☐ 72 Dwight Gooden	1.25	.60	.12
☐ 73 Bob Ojeda	.35	.17	.03
☐ 74 Sid Fernandez	.35	.17	.03
☐ 75 Jesse Orosco	.25	.12	.02
☐ 76 Roger McDowell	.35	.17	.03
☐ 77 John Tudor (misspelled Tutor)	.35	.17	.03
☐ 78 Tom Browning	.35	.17	.03
☐ 79 Rick Aguilera	.25	.12	.02
☐ 80 Lance McCullers	.25	.12	.02
☐ 81 Mike Scott	.50	.25	.05
☐ 82 Nolan Ryan	5.00	2.50	.50
☐ 83 Bruce Hurst	.35	.17	.03
☐ 84 Roger Clemens	2.00	1.00	.20
☐ 85 Oil Can Boyd	.35	.17	.03
☐ 86 Dave Righetti	.35	.17	.03
☐ 87 Dennis Rasmussen	.25	.12	.02
☐ 88 Bret Saberhagen	.75	.35	.07
☐ 89 Mark Langston	.50	.25	.05
☐ 90 Jack Morris	.50	.25	.05
☐ 91 Fernando Valenzuela	.50	.25	.05
☐ 92 Orel Hershiser	.90	.45	.09
☐ 93 Rick Honeycutt	.25	.12	.02
☐ 94 Jeff Reardon	.35	.17	.03
☐ 95 John Habyan	.25	.12	.02

☐ 96 Goose Gossage	.35	.17	.03
☐ 97 Todd Worrell	.35	.17	.03
☐ 98 Floyd Youmans	.25	.12	.02
☐ 99 Don Aase	.25	.12	.02
☐ 100 John Franco	.35	.17	.03

1987 Classic Update Yellow

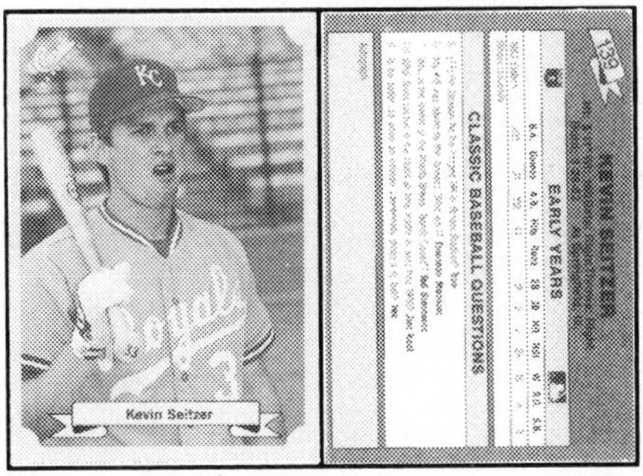

This 50-card set was actually distributed as part of an update to a trivia board game, but (unlike the original Classic game) was sold without the game. The set is sometimes referred to as the "Travel Edition" of the game. The card backs contain several trivia questions (and answers) which are used to play the game. A yellow border frames the full color photo. The games were produced by Game Time, Ltd. and were available in toy stores as well as from card dealers. Cards are numbered beginning with 101, as they are an extension of the original set. According to the set's producers, supposedly about 1/3 of the 150,000 sets printed were error sets in that they had green backs instead of yellow backs. This "green back" variation/error set is valued at approximately 50 percent more than the prices listed below. The cards are standard size, 2 1/2" by 3 1/2".

	MINT	EXC	G-VG
COMPLETE SET (50)	21.00	10.50	2.10
COMMON PLAYER (101-150)	.15	.07	.01
☐ 101 Mike Schmidt	2.00	1.00	.20
☐ 102 Eric Davis	1.25	.60	.12
☐ 103 Pete Rose	1.75	.85	.17
☐ 104 Don Mattingly	2.25	1.10	.22
☐ 105 Wade Boggs	1.50	.75	.15
☐ 106 Dale Murphy	.60	.30	.06
☐ 107 Glenn Davis	.50	.25	.05
☐ 108 Wally Joyner	.60	.30	.06
☐ 109 Bo Jackson	5.00	2.50	.50
☐ 110 Cory Snyder	.35	.17	.03
☐ 111 Jim Lindeman	.15	.07	.01
☐ 112 Kirby Puckett	1.25	.60	.12
☐ 113 Barry Bonds	2.25	1.10	.22
☐ 114 Roger Clemens	1.50	.75	.15
☐ 115 Oddibe McDowell	.20	.10	.02
☐ 116 Bret Saberhagen	.45	.22	.04
☐ 117 Joe Magrane	.25	.12	.02
☐ 118 Scott Fletcher	.15	.07	.01
☐ 119 Mark McLemore	.15	.07	.01
☐ 120 Who Me (Joe Niekro)	.20	.10	.02
☐ 121 Mark McGwire	2.00	1.00	.20
☐ 122 Darryl Strawberry	1.25	.60	.12
☐ 123 Mike Scott	.30	.15	.03
☐ 124 Andre Dawson	.40	.20	.04
☐ 125 Jose Canseco	3.00	1.50	.30
☐ 126 Kevin McReynolds	.40	.20	.04
☐ 127 Joe Carter	.40	.20	.04
☐ 128 Casey Candaele	.15	.07	.01
☐ 129 Matt Nokes	.25	.12	.02
☐ 130 Kal Daniels	.45	.22	.04
☐ 131 Pete Incaviglia	.40	.20	.04
☐ 132 Benito Santiago	1.00	.50	.10
☐ 133 Barry Larkin	.75	.35	.07
☐ 134 Gary Pettis	.20	.10	.02
☐ 135 B.J. Surhoff	.25	.12	.02
☐ 136 Juan Nieves	.15	.07	.01
☐ 137 Jim Deshaies	.15	.07	.01
☐ 138 Pete O'Brien	.15	.07	.01
☐ 139 Kevin Seitzer	.75	.35	.07
☐ 140 Devon White	.35	.17	.03
☐ 141 Rob Deer	.25	.12	.02
☐ 142 Kurt Stillwell	.20	.10	.02
☐ 143 Edwin Correa	.15	.07	.01
☐ 144 Dion James	.15	.07	.01
☐ 145 Danny Tartabull	.35	.17	.03
☐ 146 Jerry Browne	.20	.10	.02
☐ 147 Ted Higuera	.40	.20	.04
☐ 148 Jack Clark	.25	.12	.02
☐ 149 Ruben Sierra	2.00	1.00	.20
☐ 150 McGwire/Eric Davis	.90	.45	.09

1988 Classic Red

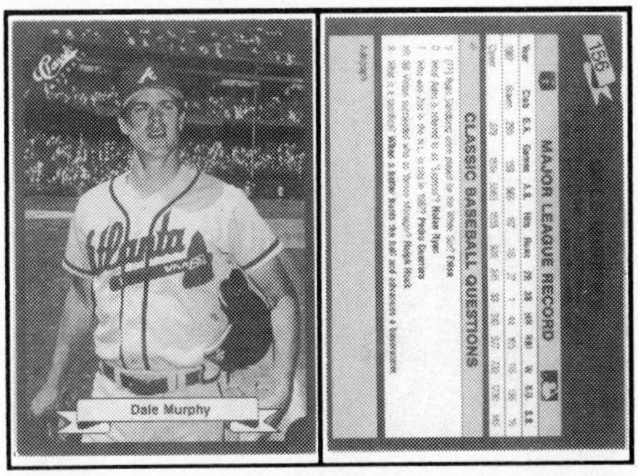

This 50-card red-bordered set was actually distributed as part of an update to a trivia board game, but (unlike the original Classic game) was sold without the game. The card backs contain several trivia questions (and answers) which are used to play the game. A red border frames the full color photo. The games were produced by Game Time, Ltd. and were available in toy stores as well as from card dealers. Cards are numbered beginning with 151 as they are an extension of the original sets. The cards are standard size, 2 1/2" by 3 1/2".

	MINT	EXC	G-VG
COMPLETE SET (50)	12.50	6.25	1.25
COMMON PLAYER (151-200)	.15	.07	.01
☐ 151 Mark McGwire and Don Mattingly	1.50	.75	.15
☐ 152 Don Mattingly	1.50	.75	.15
☐ 153 Mark McGwire	1.00	.50	.10
☐ 154 Eric Davis	.75	.35	.07
☐ 155 Wade Boggs	1.00	.50	.10
☐ 156 Dale Murphy	.50	.25	.05
☐ 157 Andre Dawson	.35	.17	.03
☐ 158 Roger Clemens	1.00	.50	.10
☐ 159 Kevin Seitzer	.50	.25	.05
☐ 160 Benito Santiago	.60	.30	.06
☐ 161 Kal Daniels	.35	.17	.03
☐ 162 John Kruk	.15	.07	.01
☐ 163 Bill Ripken	.25	.12	.02
☐ 164 Kirby Puckett	1.00	.50	.10
☐ 165 Jose Canseco	1.50	.75	.15
☐ 166 Matt Nokes	.25	.12	.02
☐ 167 Mike Schmidt	1.00	.50	.10
☐ 168 Tim Raines	.35	.17	.03
☐ 169 Ryne Sandberg	1.00	.50	.10
☐ 170 Dave Winfield	.50	.25	.05
☐ 171 Dwight Gooden	.60	.30	.06
☐ 172 Bret Saberhagen	.35	.17	.03
☐ 173 Willie McGee	.35	.17	.03
☐ 174 Jack Morris	.25	.12	.02
☐ 175 Jeff Leonard	.15	.07	.01
☐ 176 Cal Ripken	.60	.30	.06
☐ 177 Pete Incaviglia	.35	.17	.03
☐ 178 Devon White	.25	.12	.02
☐ 179 Nolan Ryan	2.00	1.00	.20
☐ 180 Ruben Sierra	.75	.35	.07
☐ 181 Todd Worrell	.25	.12	.02
☐ 182 Glenn Davis	.35	.17	.03
☐ 183 Frank Viola	.35	.17	.03

	MINT	EXC	G-VG
☐ 184 Cory Snyder	.25	.12	.02
☐ 185 Tracy Jones	.15	.07	.01
☐ 186 Terry Steinbach	.25	.12	.02
☐ 187 Julio Franco	.25	.12	.02
☐ 188 Larry Sheets	.15	.07	.01
☐ 189 John Marzano	.15	.07	.01
☐ 190 Kevin Elster	.25	.12	.02
☐ 191 Vincente Palacios	.25	.12	.02
☐ 192 Kent Hrbek	.35	.17	.03
☐ 193 Eric Bell	.15	.07	.01
☐ 194 Kelly Downs	.25	.12	.02
☐ 195 Jose Lind	.25	.12	.02
☐ 196 Dave Stewart	.50	.25	.05
☐ 197 Mark McGwire and Jose Canseco	1.50	.75	.15
☐ 198 Phil Niekro Cleveland Indians	.25	.12	.02
☐ 199 Phil Niekro Toronto Blue Jays	.25	.12	.02
☐ 200 Phil Niekro Atlanta Braves	.25	.12	.02

1988 Classic Blue

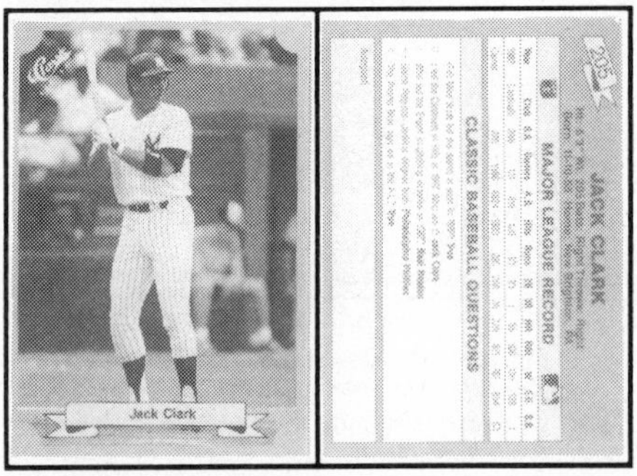

This 50-card blue-bordered set was actually distributed as part of an update to a trivia board game, but (unlike the original Classic game) was sold without the game. The card backs contain several trivia questions (and answers) which are used to play the game. A blue border frames the full color photo. The games were produced by Game Time, Ltd. and were available in toy stores as well as from card dealers. Cards are numbered beginning with 201 as they are an extension of the original sets. The cards are standard size, 2 1/2" by 3 1/2".

	MINT	EXC	G-VG
COMPLETE SET (50)	15.00	7.50	1.50
COMMON PLAYER (201-250)	.15	.07	.01
☐ 201 Eric Davis and Dale Murphy	.75	.35	.07
☐ 202 B.J. Surhoff	.25	.12	.02
☐ 203 John Kruk	.15	.07	.01
☐ 204 Sam Horn	.25	.12	.02
☐ 205 Jack Clark	.25	.12	.02
☐ 206 Wally Joyner	.35	.17	.03
☐ 207 Matt Nokes	.25	.12	.02
☐ 208 Bo Jackson	3.00	1.50	.30
☐ 209 Darryl Strawberry	1.00	.50	.10
☐ 210 Ozzie Smith	.40	.20	.04
☐ 211 Don Mattingly	1.50	.75	.15
☐ 212 Mark McGwire	1.00	.50	.10
☐ 213 Eric Davis	.75	.35	.07
☐ 214 Wade Boggs	1.00	.50	.10
☐ 215 Dale Murphy	.50	.25	.05
☐ 216 Andre Dawson	.35	.17	.03
☐ 217 Roger Clemens	1.00	.50	.10
☐ 218 Kevin Seitzer	.35	.17	.03
☐ 219 Benito Santiago	.50	.25	.05
☐ 220 Tony Gwynn	.60	.30	.06
☐ 221 Mike Scott	.25	.12	.02
☐ 222 Steve Bedrosian	.25	.12	.02
☐ 223 Vince Coleman	.35	.17	.03
☐ 224 Rick Sutcliffe	.25	.12	.02
☐ 225 Will Clark	2.50	1.25	.25
☐ 226 Pete Rose	1.50	.75	.15
☐ 227 Mike Greenwell	1.25	.60	.12
☐ 228 Ken Caminiti	.25	.12	.02
☐ 229 Ellis Burks	1.25	.60	.12
☐ 230 Dave Magadan	.35	.17	.03
☐ 231 Alan Trammell	.35	.17	.03
☐ 232 Paul Molitor	.25	.12	.02
☐ 233 Gary Gaetti	.25	.12	.02
☐ 234 Rickey Henderson	1.50	.75	.15
☐ 235 Danny Tartabull UER (photo actually Hal McRae)	.25	.12	.02
☐ 236 Bobby Bonilla	.75	.35	.07
☐ 237 Mike Dunne	.15	.07	.01
☐ 238 Al Leiter	.15	.07	.01
☐ 239 John Farrell	.15	.07	.01
☐ 240 Joe Magrane	.25	.12	.02
☐ 241 Mike Henneman	.15	.07	.01
☐ 242 George Bell	.35	.17	.03
☐ 243 Gregg Jeffries	2.00	1.00	.20
☐ 244 Jay Buhner	.35	.17	.03
☐ 245 Todd Benzinger	.25	.12	.02
☐ 246 Matt Williams	2.00	1.00	.20
☐ 247 Mark McGwire and Don Mattingly (unnumbered; game instructions on back)	1.50	.75	.15
☐ 248 George Brett	.75	.35	.07
☐ 249 Jimmy Key	.15	.07	.01
☐ 250 Mark Langston	.25	.12	.02

1989 Classic Light Blue

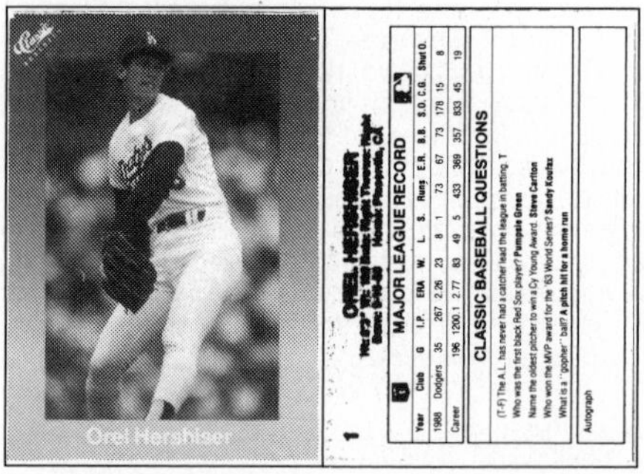

The 1989 Classic set contains 100 standard-size (2 1/2" by 3 1/2") cards. The fronts of these cards have light blue borders. The backs feature 1988 and lifetime stats. The cards were distributed with a baseball boardgame. Supposedly there were 150,000 sets produced.

	MINT	EXC	G-VG
COMPLETE SET (100)	24.00	12.00	2.40
COMMON PLAYER (1-100)	.10	.05	.01
☐ 1 Orel Hershiser	.45	.22	.04
☐ 2 Wade Boggs	.75	.35	.07
☐ 3 Jose Canseco	1.50	.75	.15
☐ 4 Mark McGwire	.75	.35	.07
☐ 5 Don Mattingly	1.50	.75	.15
☐ 6 Gregg Jefferies	1.00	.50	.10
☐ 7 Dwight Gooden	.50	.25	.05
☐ 8 Darryl Strawberry	.75	.35	.07
☐ 9 Eric Davis	.60	.30	.06
☐ 10 Joey Meyer	.10	.05	.01
☐ 11 Joe Carter	.20	.10	.02
☐ 12 Paul Molitor	.20	.10	.02
☐ 13 Mark Grace	2.50	1.25	.25
☐ 14 Kurt Stillwell	.15	.07	.01
☐ 15 Kirby Puckett	.75	.35	.07
☐ 16 Keith Miller	.10	.05	.01
☐ 17 Glenn Davis	.25	.12	.02
☐ 18 Will Clark	1.25	.60	.12
☐ 19 Cory Snyder	.20	.10	.02
☐ 20 Jose Lind	.10	.05	.01
☐ 21 Andres Thomas	.10	.05	.01
☐ 22 Dave Smith	.10	.05	.01
☐ 23 Mike Scott	.25	.12	.02

☐ 24 Kevin McReynolds	.25	.12	.02
☐ 25 B.J. Surhoff	.15	.07	.01
☐ 26 Mackey Sasser	.20	.10	.02
☐ 27 Chad Kreuter	.10	.05	.01
☐ 28 Hal Morris	.50	.25	.05
☐ 29 Wally Joyner	.30	.15	.03
☐ 30 Tony Gwynn	.50	.25	.05
☐ 31 Kevin Mitchell	.75	.35	.07
☐ 32 Dave Winfield	.30	.15	.03
☐ 33 Billy Bean	.10	.05	.01
☐ 34 Steve Bedrosian	.15	.07	.01
☐ 35 Ron Gant	.75	.35	.07
☐ 36 Len Dykstra	.30	.15	.03
☐ 37 Andre Dawson	.30	.15	.03
☐ 38 Brett Butler	.15	.07	.01
☐ 39 Rob Deer	.15	.07	.01
☐ 40 Tommy John	.20	.10	.02
☐ 41 Gary Gaetti	.15	.07	.01
☐ 42 Tim Raines	.25	.12	.02
☐ 43 George Bell	.25	.12	.02
☐ 44 Dwight Evans	.20	.10	.02
☐ 45 Dennis Martinez	.10	.05	.01
☐ 46 Andres Galarraga	.25	.12	.02
☐ 47 George Brett	.75	.35	.07
☐ 48 Mike Schmidt	1.25	.60	.12
☐ 49 Dave Stieb	.20	.10	.02
☐ 50 Rickey Henderson	1.50	.75	.15
☐ 51 Craig Biggio	.30	.15	.03
☐ 52 Mark Lemke	.10	.05	.01
☐ 53 Chris Sabo	1.00	.50	.10
☐ 54 Jeff Treadway	.10	.05	.01
☐ 55 Kent Hrbek	.20	.10	.02
☐ 56 Cal Ripken	.35	.17	.03
☐ 57 Tim Belcher	.20	.10	.02
☐ 58 Ozzie Smith	.25	.12	.02
☐ 59 Keith Hernandez	.20	.10	.02
☐ 60 Pedro Guerrero	.20	.10	.02
☐ 61 Greg Swindell	.15	.07	.01
☐ 62 Bret Saberhagen	.35	.17	.03
☐ 63 John Tudor	.15	.07	.01
☐ 64 Gary Carter	.20	.10	.02
☐ 65 Kevin Seitzer	.20	.10	.02
☐ 66 Jesse Barfield	.15	.07	.01
☐ 67 Luis Medina	.15	.07	.01
☐ 68 Walt Weiss	.25	.12	.02
☐ 69 Terry Steinbach	.20	.10	.02
☐ 70 Barry Larkin	.50	.25	.05
☐ 71 Pete Rose	1.00	.50	.10
☐ 72 Luis Salazar	.10	.05	.01
☐ 73 Benito Santiago	.30	.15	.03
☐ 74 Kal Daniels	.25	.12	.02
☐ 75 Kevin Elster	.15	.07	.01
☐ 76 Rob Dibble	.25	.12	.02
☐ 77 Bobby Witt	.35	.17	.03
☐ 78 Steve Searcy	.15	.07	.01
☐ 79 Sandy Alomar Jr.	1.50	.75	.15
☐ 80 Chili Davis	.15	.07	.01
☐ 81 Alvin Davis	.15	.07	.01
☐ 82 Charlie Leibrandt	.10	.05	.01
☐ 83 Robin Yount	.75	.35	.07
☐ 84 Mark Carreon	.10	.05	.01
☐ 85 Pascual Perez	.15	.07	.01
☐ 86 Dennis Rasmussen	.10	.05	.01
☐ 87 Ernie Riles	.10	.05	.01
☐ 88 Melido Perez	.15	.07	.01
☐ 89 Doug Jones	.15	.07	.01
☐ 90 Dennis Eckersley	.30	.15	.03
☐ 91 Bob Welch	.20	.10	.02
☐ 92 Bob Milacki	.15	.07	.01
☐ 93 Jeff Robinson	.15	.07	.01
☐ 94 Mike Henneman	.10	.05	.01
☐ 95 Randy Johnson	.25	.12	.02
☐ 96 Ron Jones	.15	.07	.01
☐ 97 Jack Armstrong	.30	.15	.03
☐ 98 Willie McGee	.20	.10	.02
☐ 99 Ryne Sandberg	.75	.35	.07
☐ 100 David Cone and Danny Jackson	.25	.12	.02

1989 Classic Travel Orange

The 1989 Classic Travel Orange set contains 50 standard-size (2 1/2" by 3 1/2") cards. The fronts of the cards have orange borders. The backs feature 1988 and lifetime stats. This subset of cards were distributed as a set in blister packs as "Travel Update I" subsets. Supposedly there were 150,000 sets produced.

	MINT	EXC	G-VG
COMPLETE SET (50)	12.00	6.00	1.20
COMMON PLAYER (101-150)	.10	.05	.01
☐ 101 Gary Sheffield	.75	.35	.07
☐ 102 Wade Boggs	.75	.35	.07
☐ 103 Jose Canseco	1.25	.60	.12
☐ 104 Mark McGwire	.75	.35	.07
☐ 105 Orel Hershiser	.30	.15	.03
☐ 106 Don Mattingly	1.00	.50	.10
☐ 107 Dwight Gooden	.40	.20	.04
☐ 108 Darryl Strawberry	.60	.30	.06
☐ 109 Eric Davis	.50	.25	.05
☐ 110 Hensley Meulens (listed on card as Bam Bam Muelens)	.60	.30	.06
☐ 111 Andy Van Slyke	.15	.07	.01
☐ 112 Al Leiter	.10	.05	.01
☐ 113 Matt Nokes	.15	.07	.01
☐ 114 Mike Krukow	.10	.05	.01
☐ 115 Tony Fernandez	.15	.07	.01
☐ 116 Fred McGriff	.50	.25	.05
☐ 117 Barry Bonds	.35	.17	.03
☐ 118 Gerald Perry	.10	.05	.01
☐ 119 Roger Clemens	.75	.35	.07
☐ 120 Kirk Gibson	.20	.10	.02
☐ 121 Greg Maddux	.15	.07	.01
☐ 122 Bo Jackson	1.50	.75	.15
☐ 123 Danny Jackson	.15	.07	.01
☐ 124 Dale Murphy	.35	.17	.03
☐ 125 David Cone	.25	.12	.02
☐ 126 Tom Browning	.15	.07	.01
☐ 127 Roberto Alomar	.45	.22	.04
☐ 128 Alan Trammell	.20	.10	.02
☐ 129 Ricky Jordan UER (misspelled Jordon on card back)	.25	.12	.02
☐ 130 Ramon Martinez	.90	.45	.09
☐ 131 Ken Griffey Jr.	3.50	1.75	.35
☐ 132 Gregg Olson	.50	.25	.05
☐ 133 Carlos Quintana	.35	.17	.03
☐ 134 Dave West	.15	.07	.01
☐ 135 Cameron Drew	.10	.05	.01
☐ 136 Teddy Higuera	.15	.07	.01
☐ 137 Sil Campusano	.15	.07	.01
☐ 138 Mark Gubicza	.15	.07	.01
☐ 139 Mike Boddicker	.10	.05	.01
☐ 140 Paul Gibson	.10	.05	.01
☐ 141 Jose Rijo	.20	.10	.02
☐ 142 John Costello	.10	.05	.01
☐ 143 Cecil Espy	.10	.05	.01
☐ 144 Frank Viola	.20	.10	.02
☐ 145 Erik Hanson	.35	.17	.03
☐ 146 Juan Samuel	.15	.07	.01
☐ 147 Harold Reynolds	.15	.07	.01
☐ 148 Joe Magrane	.15	.07	.01
☐ 149 Mike Greenwell	.40	.20	.04
☐ 150 Darryl Strawberry and Will Clark	.75	.35	.07

1989 Classic Travel Purple

The 1989 Classic "Travel Update II" set contains 50 standard-size (2 1/2" by 3 1/2") cards. The fronts have purple (and gray) borders. The set features "two sport" cards of Bo Jackson and Deion Sanders. The cards were distributed as a set in blister packs.

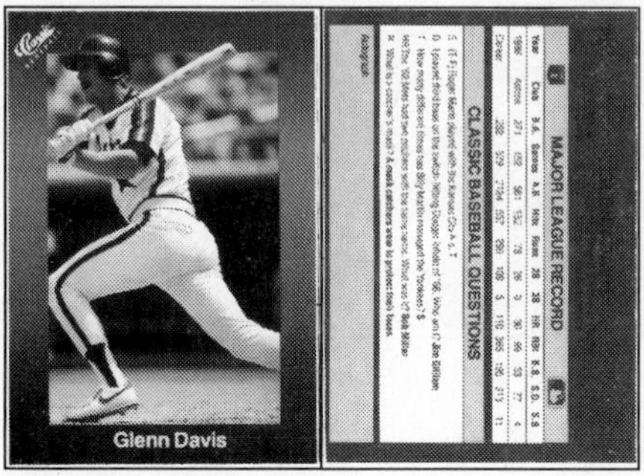

	MINT	EXC	G-VG
COMPLETE SET (50)	10.00	5.00	1.00
COMMON PLAYER (151-200)	.10	.05	.01
☐ 151 Jim Abbott	.50	.25	.05
☐ 152 Ellis Burks	.35	.17	.03
☐ 153 Mike Schmidt	1.00	.50	.10
☐ 154 Gregg Jefferies	.45	.22	.04
☐ 155 Mark Grace	.50	.25	.05
☐ 156 Jerome Walton	.75	.35	.07
☐ 157 Bo Jackson	1.50	.75	.15
☐ 158 Jack Clark	.15	.07	.01
☐ 159 Tom Glavine	.15	.07	.01
☐ 160 Eddie Murray	.25	.12	.02
☐ 161 John Dopson	.15	.07	.01
☐ 162 Ruben Sierra	.40	.20	.04
☐ 163 Rafael Palmeiro	.20	.10	.02
☐ 164 Nolan Ryan	1.25	.60	.12
☐ 165 Barry Larkin	.35	.17	.03
☐ 166 Tommy Herr	.10	.05	.01
☐ 167 Roberto Kelly	.35	.17	.03
☐ 168 Glenn Davis	.20	.10	.02
☐ 169 Glenn Braggs	.15	.07	.01
☐ 170 Juan Bell	.15	.07	.01
☐ 171 Todd Burns	.15	.07	.01
☐ 172 Derek Lilliquist	.10	.05	.01
☐ 173 Orel Hershiser	.25	.12	.02
☐ 174 John Smoltz	.25	.12	.02
☐ 175 Guillen/Burks	.35	.17	.03
☐ 176 Kirby Puckett	.60	.30	.06
☐ 177 Robin Ventura	.45	.22	.04
☐ 178 Allan Anderson	.10	.05	.01
☐ 179 Steve Sax	.15	.07	.01
☐ 180 Will Clark	.75	.35	.07
☐ 181 Mike Devereaux	.15	.07	.01
☐ 182 Tom Gordon	.35	.17	.03
☐ 183 Rob Murphy	.10	.05	.01
☐ 184 Pete O'Brien	.10	.05	.01
☐ 185 Cris Carpenter	.10	.05	.01
☐ 186 Tom Brunansky	.15	.07	.01
☐ 187 Bob Boone	.15	.07	.01
☐ 188 Lou Whitaker	.20	.10	.02
☐ 189 Dwight Gooden	.40	.20	.04
☐ 190 Mark McGwire	.60	.30	.06
☐ 191 John Smiley	.10	.05	.01
☐ 192 Tommy Gregg	.10	.05	.01
☐ 193 Ken Griffey Jr.	2.00	1.00	.20
☐ 194 Bruce Hurst	.10	.05	.01
☐ 195 Greg Swindell	.15	.07	.01
☐ 196 Nelson Liriano	.10	.05	.01
☐ 197 Randy Myers	.15	.07	.01
☐ 198 Kevin Mitchell	.35	.17	.03
☐ 199 Dante Bichette	.10	.05	.01
☐ 200 Deion Sanders	.45	.22	.04

1990 Classic Game

The 1990 Classic Game set contains 150 standard-size (2 1/2" by 3 1/2") cards, the largest Classic set to date in terms of player selection. The front borders are blue with magenta splotches. The backs feature 1989 and career total stats. The cards were distributed as a set in blister packs. According to distributors of the set, supposedly there were 200,000 sets produced. Supposedly the Sanders "correction" was made at Sanders own request; less than 10 percent of the sets contain the first version and hence it has the higher value in the checklist below. The complete set price below does not include any of the more difficult variation cards.

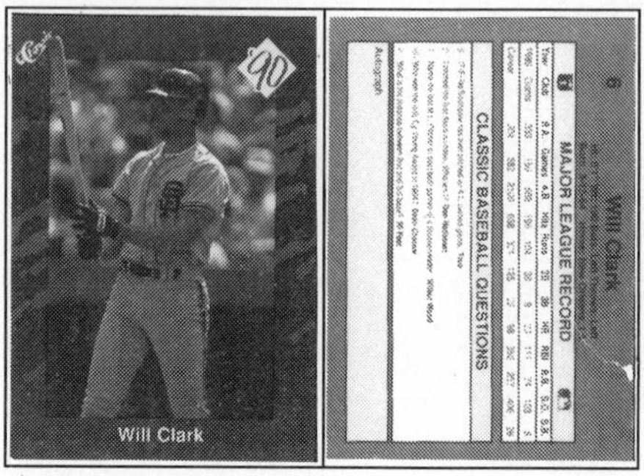

	MINT	EXC	G-VG
COMPLETE SET (150)	18.00	9.00	1.80
COMMON PLAYER (1-150)	.10	.05	.01
☐ 1 Nolan Ryan	1.00	.50	.10
☐ 2 Bo Jackson	1.00	.50	.10
☐ 3 Gregg Olson	.35	.17	.03
☐ 4 Tom Gordon	.25	.12	.02
☐ 5 Robin Ventura	.35	.17	.03
☐ 6 Will Clark	.75	.35	.07
☐ 7 Ruben Sierra	.35	.17	.03
☐ 8 Mark Grace	.45	.22	.04
☐ 9 Luis De Los Santos	.15	.07	.01
☐ 10 Bernie Williams	.35	.17	.03
☐ 11 Eric Davis	.35	.17	.03
☐ 12 Carney Lansford	.15	.07	.01
☐ 13 John Smoltz	.15	.07	.01
☐ 14 Gary Sheffield	.35	.17	.03
☐ 15 Kent Mercker	.20	.10	.02
☐ 16 Don Mattingly	1.00	.50	.10
☐ 17 Tony Gwynn	.35	.17	.03
☐ 18 Ozzie Smith	.20	.10	.02
☐ 19 Fred McGriff	.25	.12	.02
☐ 20 Ken Griffey Jr.	1.25	.60	.12
☐ 21A Deion Sanders (identified only as "Prime Time" on front)	7.50	3.75	.75
☐ 21B Deion Sanders (identified as Deion "Prime Time" Sanders on front of card)	.75	.35	.07
☐ 22 Jose Canseco	1.00	.50	.10
☐ 23 Mitch Williams	.15	.07	.01
☐ 24 Cal Ripken UER (misspelled Ripkin on the card back)	.25	.12	.02
☐ 25 Bob Geren	.15	.07	.01
☐ 26 Wade Boggs	.60	.30	.06
☐ 27 Ryne Sandberg	.60	.30	.06
☐ 28 Kirby Puckett	.45	.22	.04
☐ 29 Mike Scott	.20	.10	.02
☐ 30 Dwight Smith	.25	.12	.02
☐ 31 Craig Worthington	.15	.07	.01
☐ 32A Ricky Jordan ERR (misspelled Jordon on card back)	2.50	1.25	.25
☐ 32B Ricky Jordan COR	.25	.12	.02
☐ 33 Darryl Strawberry	.45	.22	.04
☐ 34 Jerome Walton	.35	.17	.03
☐ 35 John Olerud	1.25	.60	.12
☐ 36 Tom Glavine	.15	.07	.01
☐ 37 Rickey Henderson	.75	.35	.07
☐ 38 Rolando Roomes	.15	.07	.01
☐ 39 Mickey Tettleton	.10	.05	.01
☐ 40 Jim Abbott	.25	.12	.02
☐ 41 Dave Righetti	.15	.07	.01
☐ 42 Mike LaValliere	.10	.05	.01
☐ 43 Rob Dibble	.15	.07	.01
☐ 44 Pete Harnisch	.10	.05	.01

☐ 45 Jose Offerman	.90	.45	.09
☐ 46 Walt Weiss	.15	.07	.01
☐ 47 Mike Greenwell	.35	.17	.03
☐ 48 Barry Larkin	.35	.17	.03
☐ 49 Dave Gallagher	.15	.07	.01
☐ 50 Junior Felix	.30	.15	.03
☐ 51 Roger Clemens	.60	.30	.06
☐ 52 Lonnie Smith	.15	.07	.01
☐ 53 Jerry Browne	.10	.05	.01
☐ 54 Greg Briley	.15	.07	.01
☐ 55 Delino Deshields	.75	.35	.07
☐ 56 Carmelo Martinez	.10	.05	.01
☐ 57 Craig Biggio	.20	.10	.02
☐ 58 Dwight Gooden	.35	.17	.03
☐ 59A Bo/Rubin/Mark Bo Jackson Ruben Sierra Mark McGwire	6.00	3.00	.60
☐ 59B A.L. Fence Busters Bo Jackson Ruben Sierra Mark McGwire	.75	.35	.07
☐ 60 Greg Vaughn	.60	.30	.06
☐ 61 Roberto Alomar	.25	.12	.02
☐ 62 Steve Bedrosian	.15	.07	.01
☐ 63 Devon White	.15	.07	.01
☐ 64 Kevin Mitchell	.30	.15	.03
☐ 65 Marquis Grissom	.30	.15	.03
☐ 66 Brian Holman	.15	.07	.01
☐ 67 Julio Franco	.15	.07	.01
☐ 68 Dave West	.15	.07	.01
☐ 69 Harold Baines	.15	.07	.01
☐ 70 Eric Anthony	.50	.25	.05
☐ 71 Glenn Davis	.20	.10	.02
☐ 72 Mark Langston	.15	.07	.01
☐ 73 Matt Williams	.45	.22	.04
☐ 74 Rafael Palmeiro	.30	.15	.03
☐ 75 Pete Rose Jr.	.50	.25	.05
☐ 76 Ramon Martinez	.30	.15	.03
☐ 77 Dwight Evans	.15	.07	.01
☐ 78 Mackey Sasser	.15	.07	.01
☐ 79 Mike Schooler	.15	.07	.01
☐ 80 Dennis Cook	.10	.05	.01
☐ 81 Orel Hershiser	.25	.12	.02
☐ 82 Barry Bonds	.35	.17	.03
☐ 83 Geronimo Berroa	.10	.05	.01
☐ 84 George Bell	.20	.10	.02
☐ 85 Andre Dawson	.25	.12	.02
☐ 86 John Franco	.15	.07	.01
☐ 87A Clark/Gwynn Will Clark Tony Gwynn	4.00	2.00	.40
☐ 87B N.L. Hit Kings Will Clark Tony Gwynn	.40	.20	.04
☐ 88 Glenallen Hill	.25	.12	.02
☐ 89 Jeff Ballard	.15	.07	.01
☐ 90 Todd Zeile	.75	.35	.07
☐ 91 Frank Viola	.20	.10	.02
☐ 92 Ozzie Guillen	.20	.10	.02
☐ 93 Jeffrey Leonard	.10	.05	.01
☐ 94 Dave Smith	.10	.05	.01
☐ 95 Dave Parker	.20	.10	.02
☐ 96 Jose Gonzalez	.10	.05	.01
☐ 97 Dave Stieb	.20	.10	.02
☐ 98 Charlie Hayes	.15	.07	.01
☐ 99 Jesse Barfield	.15	.07	.01
☐ 100 Joey Belle	.20	.10	.02
☐ 101 Jeff Reardon	.15	.07	.01
☐ 102 Bruce Hurst	.15	.07	.01
☐ 103 Luis Medina	.15	.07	.01
☐ 104 Mike Moore	.15	.07	.01
☐ 105 Vince Coleman	.20	.10	.02
☐ 106 Alan Trammell	.20	.10	.02
☐ 107 Randy Myers	.15	.07	.01
☐ 108 Frank Tanana	.10	.05	.01
☐ 109 Craig Lefferts	.10	.05	.01
☐ 110 John Wetteland	.20	.10	.02
☐ 111 Chris Gwynn	.15	.07	.01
☐ 112 Mark Carreon	.10	.05	.01
☐ 113 Von Hayes	.15	.07	.01
☐ 114 Doug Jones	.15	.07	.01
☐ 115 Andres Galarraga	.20	.10	.02
☐ 116 Carlton Fisk UER (Bellows Falls mis- spelled as Bellow Falls on back)	.25	.12	.02
☐ 117 Paul O'Neill	.20	.10	.02
☐ 118 Tim Raines	.25	.12	.02
☐ 119 Tom Brunansky	.15	.07	.01
☐ 120 Andy Benes	.40	.20	.04
☐ 121 Mark Portugal	.10	.05	.01
☐ 122 Willie Randolph	.15	.07	.01
☐ 123 Jeff Blauser	.10	.05	.01
☐ 124 Don August	.10	.05	.01
☐ 125 Chuck Cary	.10	.05	.01
☐ 126 John Smiley	.10	.05	.01
☐ 127 Terry Mulholland	.10	.05	.01
☐ 128 Harold Reynolds	.15	.07	.01
☐ 129 Hubie Brooks	.15	.07	.01
☐ 130 Ben McDonald	1.00	.50	.10
☐ 131 Kevin Ritz	.15	.07	.01
☐ 132 Luis Quinones	.10	.05	.01
☐ 133A Hensley Meulens ERR (misspelled Muelens on card front)	10.00	5.00	1.00
☐ 133B Hensley Meulens COR	.50	.25	.05
☐ 134 Bill Spiers UER (Orangeburg misspelled as Orangburg on back)	.15	.07	.01
☐ 135 Andy Hawkins	.10	.05	.01
☐ 136 Alvin Davis	.15	.07	.01
☐ 137 Lee Smith	.15	.07	.01
☐ 138 Joe Carter	.20	.10	.02
☐ 139 Bret Saberhagen	.20	.10	.02
☐ 140 Sammy Sosa	.40	.20	.04
☐ 141 Matt Nokes	.15	.07	.01
☐ 142 Bert Blyleven	.15	.07	.01
☐ 143 Bobby Bonilla	.25	.12	.02
☐ 144 Howard Johnson	.20	.10	.02
☐ 145 Joe Magrane	.15	.07	.01
☐ 146 Pedro Guerrero	.20	.10	.02
☐ 147 Robin Yount	.40	.20	.04
☐ 148 Dan Gladden	.10	.05	.01
☐ 149 Steve Sax	.15	.07	.01
☐ 150A Clark/Mitchell Will Clark Kevin Mitchell	4.00	2.00	.40
☐ 150B Bay Bombers Will Clark Kevin Mitchell	.50	.25	.05

1990 Classic Update

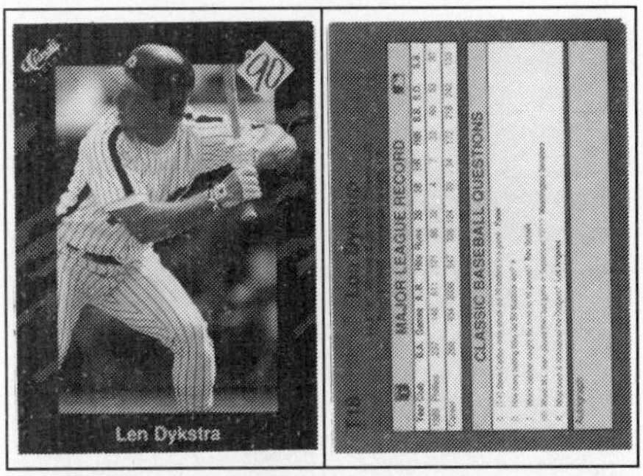

The 1990 Classic Update set was the second set issued by the Classic Game company in 1990. Sometimes referenced as Classic Red, this set included a Kevin Maas card. This 50-card, standard-size (2 1/2" by 3 1/2") set was issued in late June of 1990.

	MINT	EXC	G-VG
COMPLETE SET (50)	9.00	4.50	.90
COMMON PLAYER (T1-T49)	.10	.05	.01
☐ T1 Gregg Jefferies	.30	.15	.03
☐ T2 Steve Adkins	.20	.10	.02
☐ T3 Sandy Alomar Jr.	.30	.15	.03
☐ T4 Steve Avery	.30	.15	.03
☐ T5 Mike Blowers	.20	.10	.02
☐ T6 George Brett	.40	.20	.04
☐ T7 Tom Browning	.10	.05	.01
☐ T8 Ellis Burks	.30	.15	.03
☐ T9 Joe Carter	.20	.10	.02
☐ T10 Jerald Clark	.15	.07	.01
☐ T11 Hot Corners HOR Matt Williams Will Clark	.40	.20	.04
☐ T12 Pat Combs	.20	.10	.02
☐ T13 Scott Cooper	.20	.10	.02
☐ T14 Mark Davis	.15	.07	.01

☐ T15	Storm Davis	.10	.05	.01
☐ T16	Larry Walker	.25	.12	.02
☐ T17	Brian DuBois	.15	.07	.01
☐ T18	Len Dykstra	.20	.10	.02
☐ T19	John Franco	.15	.07	.01
☐ T20	Kirk Gibson	.20	.10	.02
☐ T21	Juan Gonzalez	1.00	.50	.10
☐ T22	Tommy Greene	.15	.07	.01
☐ T23	Kent Hrbek	.15	.07	.01
☐ T24	Mike Huff	.15	.07	.01
☐ T25	Bo Jackson	1.00	.50	.10
☐ T26	Nolan Ryan (Nolan Knows Bo)	2.50	1.25	.25
☐ T27	Roberto Kelly	.25	.12	.02
☐ T28	Mark Langston	.15	.07	.01
☐ T29	Ray Lankford	.50	.25	.05
☐ T30	Kevin Maas	1.25	.60	.12
☐ T31	Julio Machado	.10	.05	.01
☐ T32	Greg Maddux	.15	.07	.01
☐ T33	Mark McGwire	.40	.20	.04
☐ T34	Paul Molitor	.15	.07	.01
☐ T35	Hal Morris	.20	.10	.02
☐ T36	Dale Murphy	.30	.15	.03
☐ T37	Eddie Murray	.25	.12	.02
☐ T38	Jaime Navarro	.15	.07	.01
☐ T39	Dean Palmer	.15	.07	.01
☐ T40	Derek Parks	.15	.07	.01
☐ T41	Bobby Rose	.15	.07	.01
☐ T42	Wally Joyner	.20	.10	.02
☐ T43	Chris Sabo	.25	.12	.02
☐ T44	Benito Santiago	.25	.12	.02
☐ T45	Mike Stanton	.15	.07	.01
☐ T46	Terry Steinbach	.15	.07	.01
☐ T47	Dave Stewart	.20	.10	.02
☐ T48	Greg Swindell	.15	.07	.01
☐ T49	Jose Vizcaino	.15	.07	.01
☐ NNO	Royal Flush Mark Davis Bret Saberhagen (unnnumbered; game instructions on back)	.20	.10	.02

1990 Classic III

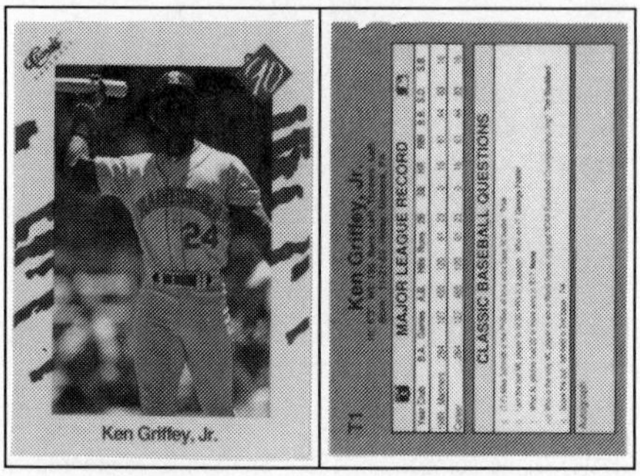

The 1990 Classic III set is also referenced as Classic Yellow. It is numbered as a continuation of the Classic Update set. This set also featured number one draft picks of the current year mixed with the other Classic cards. This 100-card set was issued in standard size (2 1/2" by 3 1/2") and also contained a special Nolan Ryan commemorative card.

	MINT	VG-E	F-G
COMPLETE SET (100)	12.00	6.00	1.20
COMMON PLAYER (T1-T100)	.10	.05	.01

☐ T1	Ken Griffey Jr.	1.00	.50	.10
☐ T2	John Tudor	.15	.07	.01
☐ T3	John Kruk	.10	.05	.01
☐ T4	Mark Gardner	.15	.07	.01
☐ T5	Scott Radinsky	.15	.07	.01
☐ T6	John Burkett	.15	.07	.01
☐ T7	Will Clark	.50	.25	.05
☐ T8	Not issued	.00	.00	.00
☐ T9	Ted Higuera	.15	.07	.01
☐ T10	Dave Parker	.20	.10	.02
☐ T11	Dante Bichette	.15	.07	.01
☐ T12	Don Mattingly	.75	.35	.07
☐ T13	Greg Harris	.10	.05	.01
☐ T14	Dave Hollins	.20	.10	.02
☐ T15	Matt Nokes	.15	.07	.01
☐ T16	Kevin Tapani	.15	.07	.01
☐ T17	Shane Mack	.15	.07	.01
☐ T18	Randy Myers	.10	.05	.01
☐ T19	Greg Olson	.15	.07	.01
☐ T20	Shane Abner	.15	.07	.01
☐ T21	Jim Presley	.10	.05	.01
☐ T22	Randy Johnson	.15	.07	.01
☐ T23	Edgar Martinez	.20	.10	.02
☐ T24	Scott Coolbaugh	.15	.07	.01
☐ T25	Jeff Treadway	.10	.05	.01
☐ T26	Joe Klink	.10	.05	.01
☐ T27	Rickey Henderson	.60	.30	.06
☐ T28	Sam Horn	.15	.07	.01
☐ T29	Kurt Stillwell	.15	.07	.01
☐ T30	Andy Van Slyke	.15	.07	.01
☐ T31	Willie Banks	.20	.10	.02
☐ T32	Jose Canseco	.75	.35	.07
☐ T33	Felix Jose	.15	.07	.01
☐ T34	Candy Maldonado	.10	.05	.01
☐ T35	Carlos Baerga	.20	.10	.02
☐ T36	Keith Hernandez	.15	.07	.01
☐ T37	Frank Viola	.15	.07	.01
☐ T38	Pete O'Brien	.10	.05	.01
☐ T39	Pat Borders	.15	.07	.01
☐ T40	Mike Heath	.10	.05	.01
☐ T41	Kevin Brown	.15	.07	.01
☐ T42	Chris Bosio	.10	.05	.01
☐ T43	Shawn Boskie	.15	.07	.01
☐ T44	Carlos Quintana	.15	.07	.01
☐ T45	Juan Samuel	.15	.07	.01
☐ T46	Tim Layana	.15	.07	.01
☐ T47	Mike Harkey	.20	.10	.02
☐ T48	Gerald Perry	.10	.05	.01
☐ T49	Mike Witt	.10	.05	.01
☐ T50	Joe Orsulak	.10	.05	.01
☐ T51	Not issued	.00	.00	.00
☐ T52	Willie Blair	.10	.05	.01
☐ T53	Gene Larkin	.10	.05	.01
☐ T54	Jody Reed	.15	.07	.01
☐ T55	Jeff Reardon	.15	.07	.01
☐ T56	Kevin McReynolds	.20	.10	.02
☐ T57	Mike Marshall (unnumbered; game instructions on back)	.15	.07	.01
☐ T58	Eric Yelding	.15	.07	.01
☐ T59	Fred Lynn	.15	.07	.01
☐ T60	Jim Leyritz	.15	.07	.01
☐ T61	John Orton	.15	.07	.01
☐ T62	Mike Lieberthal	.20	.10	.02
☐ T63	Mike Hartley	.15	.07	.01
☐ T64	Kal Daniels	.20	.10	.02
☐ T65	Terry Shumpert	.15	.07	.01
☐ T66	Sil Campusano	.15	.07	.01
☐ T67	Tony Pena	.15	.07	.01
☐ T68	Barry Bonds	.30	.15	.03
☐ T69	Roger McDowell	.15	.07	.01
☐ T70	Kelly Gruber	.20	.10	.02
☐ T71	Willie Randolph	.15	.07	.01
☐ T72	Rick Parker	.10	.05	.01
☐ T73	Bobby Bonilla	.25	.12	.02
☐ T74	Jack Armstrong	.15	.07	.01
☐ T75	Hubie Brooks	.15	.07	.01
☐ T76	Sandy Alomar Jr.	.30	.15	.03
☐ T77	Ruben Sierra	.30	.15	.03
☐ T78	Eric Hanson	.20	.10	.02
☐ T79	Tony Phillips	.10	.05	.01
☐ T80	Rondell White	.30	.15	.03
☐ T81	Bobby Thigpen	.20	.10	.02
☐ T82	Ron Walden	.20	.10	.02
☐ T83	Don Peters	.20	.10	.02
☐ T84	Nolan Ryan 6th	1.00	.50	.10
☐ T85	Lance Dickson	.20	.10	.02
☐ T86	Ryne Sandberg	.50	.25	.05
☐ T87	Eric Christopherson	.20	.10	.02
☐ T88	Shane Andrews	.20	.10	.02
☐ T89	Marc Newfield	.20	.10	.02
☐ T90	Adam Hyzdu	.20	.10	.02
☐ T91	Texas Heat Nolan Ryan Reid Ryan	1.25	.60	.12
☐ T92	Chipper Jones	.50	.25	.05
☐ T93	Frank Thomas	1.00	.50	.10
☐ T94	Cecil Fielder	.40	.20	.04
☐ T95	Delino DeShields	.25	.12	.02
☐ T96	John Olerud	.50	.25	.05
☐ T97	Dave Justice	1.25	.60	.12
☐ T98	Joe Oliver	.15	.07	.01
☐ T99	Alex Fernandez	1.00	.50	.10
☐ T100	Todd Hundley	.15	.07	.01

		MINT	EXC	G-VG
☐ NNO	Micro Players Frank Viola Texas Heat Don Mattingly Chipper Jones (blue blank back)	.25	.12	.02

1990 Classic Draft Picks

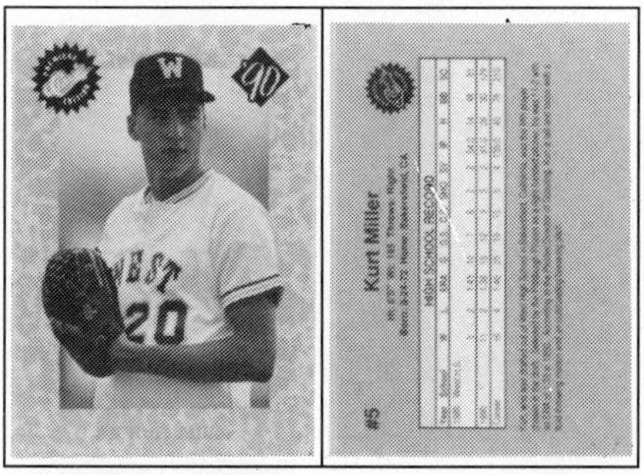

The 1990 Classic Draft Pick set is a standard-size (2 1/2" by 3 1/2"), 26-card set honoring the number one (first round) draft picks of 1990. According to the producer, the printing on this set was limited to 150,000 of each card. This was the first Classic set to not be a game or trivia set. Card numbers 2 and 22 were not issued.

		MINT	EXC	G-VG
	COMPLETE SET (25)	8.00	4.00	.80
	COMMON PLAYER (1-26)	.25	.12	.02
☐ 1	Chipper Jones	.75	.35	.07
☐ 2	Not issued	.00	.00	.00
☐ 3	Mike Lieberthal	.25	.12	.02
☐ 4	Alex Fernandez	.90	.45	.09
☐ 5	Kurt Miller	.25	.12	.02
☐ 6	Marc Newfield	.25	.12	.02
☐ 7	Dan Wilson	.25	.12	.02
☐ 8	Tim Costo	.75	.35	.07
☐ 9	Ron Walden	.25	.12	.02
☐ 10	Carl Everett (misspelled Evertt on card front)	.50	.25	.05
☐ 11	Shane Andrews	.25	.12	.02
☐ 12	Todd Ritchie	.25	.12	.02
☐ 13	Donovan Osborne	.25	.12	.02
☐ 14	Todd Van Poppel	2.00	1.00	.20
☐ 15	Adam Hyzdu	.35	.17	.03
☐ 16	Dan Smith	.25	.12	.02
☐ 17	Jeromy Burnitz	.50	.25	.05
☐ 18	Aaron Holbert	.25	.12	.02
☐ 19	Eric Christopherson	.25	.12	.02
☐ 20	Mike Mussina	.50	.25	.05
☐ 21	Tom Nevers	.25	.12	.02
☐ 22	Not issued	.00	.00	.00
☐ 23	Lance Dickson	.35	.17	.03
☐ 24	Rondell White	.50	.25	.05
☐ 25	Robbie Beckett	.50	.25	.05
☐ 26	Don Peters	.35	.17	.03
☐ NNO	Future Stars HOR Chipper Jones Rondell White (unnumbered; check- list on back)	.35	.17	.03

1991 Classic I

This 100-card set features some of the most popular players in the game of baseball as well as some of the more exciting prospects. The set measures the standard size, 2 1/2" by 3 1/2" and includes trivia questions on the backs of the cards. For the most part the set is arranged alphabetically by team and then alphabetically by players within that team.

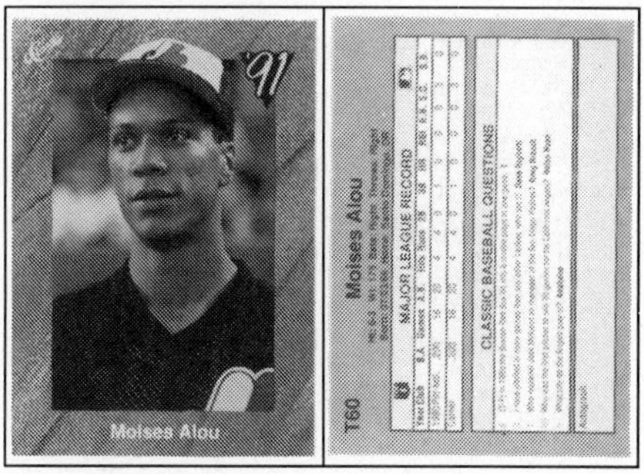

		MINT	EXC	G-VG
	COMPLETE SET (100)	11.00	5.50	1.10
	COMMON PLAYER (1-99)	.10	.05	.01
☐ T1	John Olerud	.35	.17	.03
☐ T2	Tino Martinez	.30	.15	.03
☐ T3	Ken Griffey Jr.	.75	.35	.07
☐ T4	Jeromy Burnitz	.25	.12	.02
☐ T5	Ron Gant	.30	.15	.03
☐ T6	Mike Benjamin	.15	.07	.01
☐ T7	Steve Decker	.25	.12	.02
☐ T8	Matt Williams	.25	.12	.02
☐ T9	Rafael Novoa	.15	.07	.01
☐ T10	Kevin Mitchell	.25	.12	.02
☐ T11	Dave Justice	.50	.25	.05
☐ T12	Leo Gomez	.25	.12	.02
☐ T13	Chris Hoiles	.15	.07	.01
☐ T14	Ben McDonald	.35	.17	.03
☐ T15	David Segui	.20	.10	.02
☐ T16	Anthony Telford	.15	.07	.01
☐ T17	Mike Mussina	.25	.12	.02
☐ T18	Roger Clemens	.40	.20	.04
☐ T19	Wade Boggs	.40	.20	.04
☐ T20	Tim Naehring	.20	.10	.02
☐ T21	Joe Carter	.20	.10	.02
☐ T22	Phil Plantier	.40	.20	.04
☐ T23	Rob Dibble	.15	.07	.01
☐ T24	Maurice Vaughn	.60	.30	.06
☐ T25	Lee Stevens	.20	.10	.02
☐ T26	Chris Sabo	.25	.12	.02
☐ T27	Mark Grace	.30	.15	.03
☐ T28	Derrick May	.30	.15	.03
☐ T29	Ryne Sandberg	.40	.20	.04
☐ T30	Matt Stark	.30	.15	.03
☐ T31	Bobby Thigpen	.15	.07	.01
☐ T32	Frank Thomas	.50	.25	.05
☐ T33	Don Mattingly	.60	.30	.06
☐ T34	Eric Davis	.30	.15	.03
☐ T35	Reggie Jefferson	.25	.12	.02
☐ T36	Alex Cole	.35	.17	.03
☐ T37	Mark Lewis	.25	.12	.02
☐ T38	Tim Costo	.30	.15	.03
☐ T39	Sandy Alomar Jr.	.25	.12	.02
☐ T40	Travis Fryman	.40	.20	.04
☐ T41	Cecil Fielder	.30	.15	.03
☐ T42	Milt Cuyler	.20	.10	.02
☐ T43	Andujar Cedeno	.40	.20	.04
☐ T44	Danny Darwin	.10	.05	.01
☐ T45	Randy Hennis	.15	.07	.01
☐ T46	George Brett	.30	.15	.03
☐ T47	Jeff Conine	.50	.25	.05
☐ T48	Bo Jackson	.75	.35	.07
☐ T49	Brian McRae	.50	.25	.05
☐ T50	Brent Mayne	.20	.10	.02
☐ T51	Eddie Murray	.20	.10	.02
☐ T52	Ramon Martinez	.25	.12	.02
☐ T53	Jim Neidlinger	.15	.07	.01
☐ T54	Jim Poole	.15	.07	.01
☐ T55	Tim McIntosh	.15	.07	.01
☐ T56	Randy Veres	.15	.07	.01
☐ T57	Kirby Puckett	.30	.15	.03
☐ T58	Todd Ritchie	.25	.12	.02
☐ T59	Rich Garces	.20	.10	.02
☐ T60	Moises Alou	.25	.12	.02
☐ T61	Delino DeShields	.20	.10	.02
☐ T62	Oscar Azocar	.25	.12	.02
☐ T63	Kevin Maas	.50	.25	.05
☐ T64	Alan Mills	.20	.10	.02

☐ T65 John Franco	.15	.07	.01
☐ T66 Chris Jelic	.25	.12	.02
☐ T67 Dave Magadan	.15	.07	.01
☐ T68 Darryl Strawberry	.30	.15	.03
☐ T69 Hensley Meulens	.20	.10	.02
☐ T70 Juan Gonzalez	.50	.25	.05
☐ T71 Reggie Harris	.15	.07	.01
☐ T72 Rickey Henderson	.50	.25	.05
☐ T73 Mark McGwire	.40	.20	.04
☐ T74 Willie McGee	.20	.10	.02
☐ T75 Todd Van Poppel	1.00	.50	.10
☐ T76 Bob Welch	.20	.10	.02
☐ T77 Future Aces Todd Van Poppel Don Peters David Zancanaro Kirk Dressendorfer	1.00	.50	.10
☐ T78 Len Dykstra	.20	.10	.02
☐ T79 Mickey Morandini	.20	.10	.02
☐ T80 Wes Chamberlain	.30	.15	.03
☐ T81 Barry Bonds	.25	.12	.02
☐ T82 Doug Drabek	.15	.07	.01
☐ T83 Randy Tomlin	.15	.07	.01
☐ T84 Scott Chiamparino	.25	.12	.02
☐ T85 Rafael Palmiero	.20	.10	.02
☐ T86 Nolan Ryan	.75	.35	.07
☐ T87 Bobby Witt	.15	.07	.01
☐ T88 Fred McGriff	.20	.10	.02
☐ T89 Dave Stieb	.15	.07	.01
☐ T90 Ed Sprague	.20	.10	.02
☐ T91 Vince Coleman	.20	.10	.02
☐ T92 Rod Brewer	.15	.07	.01
☐ T93 Bernard Gilkey	.30	.15	.03
☐ T94 Roberto Alomar	.20	.10	.02
☐ T95 Chuck Finley	.15	.07	.01
☐ T96 Dale Murphy	.25	.12	.02
☐ T97 Jose Rijo	.15	.07	.01
☐ T98 Hal Morris	.20	.10	.02
☐ T99 Friendly Foes Darryl Strawberry Dwight Gooden (instructions on back)	.25	.12	.02
☐ NNO Todd Van Poppel Dave Justice Ryne Sandberg Kevin Maas (blank back)	.75	.35	.07

1988 CMC Don Mattingly

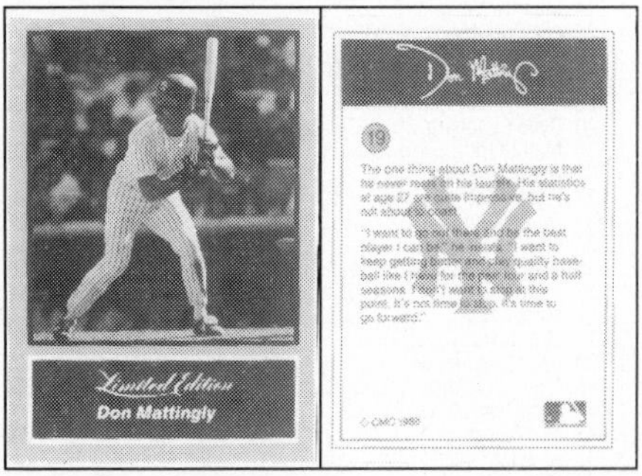

This 20-card set featuring Don Mattingly was distributed as part of a Collecting Kit produced by Collector's Marketing Corp. The cards themselves measure approximately 2 1/2" by 3 1/2" and have a light blue border. The card backs describe some aspect of Mattingly's career. Also in the kit were plastic sheets, a small album, a record, a booklet, and information on how to join Don's Fan Club. The set price below is for the whole kit as well as the cards.

	MINT	EXC	G-VG
COMPLETE SET (20)	9.00	4.50	.90
COMMON PLAYER (1-20)	.60	.30	.06
☐ 1 Game Face	.60	.30	.06
☐ 2 Columbus Clippers	.60	.30	.06
☐ 3 1983 Spring Camp	.60	.30	.06
☐ 4 AL Batting Crown	.60	.30	.06
☐ 5 1981 All-Star Outfielder	.60	.30	.06
☐ 6 The Batting Tee	.60	.30	.06
☐ 7 AL MVP Honors	.60	.30	.06
☐ 8 Gold Glove Winner	.60	.30	.06
☐ 9 Batting Practice	.60	.30	.06
☐ 10 Yankee Records	.60	.30	.06
☐ 11 Baseball On His Mind	.60	.30	.06
☐ 12 Big Home Runs	.60	.30	.06
☐ 13 Hustle and Determination	.60	.30	.06
☐ 14 Delivering In The Clutch	.60	.30	.06
☐ 15 A Slick First Baseman	.60	.30	.06
☐ 16 Keep Playing Hard	.60	.30	.06
☐ 17 Mattingly's Eight-Game Streak	.60	.30	.06
☐ 18 The Textbook Swing	.60	.30	.06
☐ 19 It's Time To Go Forward	.60	.30	.06
☐ 20 Surehanded First Baseman	.60	.30	.06

1989 CMC Jose Canseco

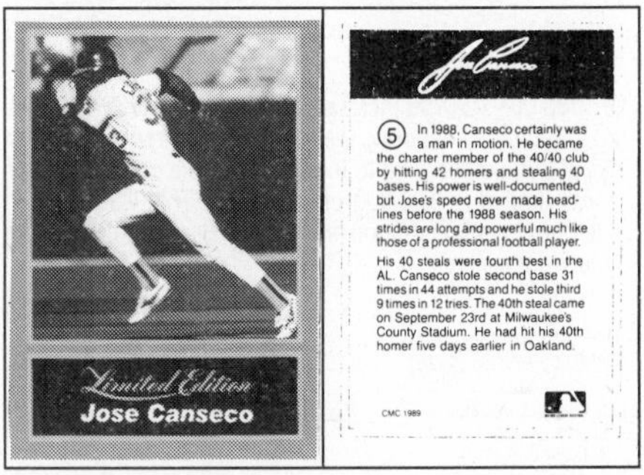

The 1989 CMC Jose Canseco Collector's Kit set contains 20 numbered standard-size (2 1/2 by 3 1/2 inch) cards. The front borders are Oakland A's green and yellow. The backs are green and white, and feature narratives and facsimile signatures. The cards were distributed as a set in a box along with an album and a booklet as well as other elements by CMC, Collectors Marketing Corporation. Since all the cards in the set feature the same player, cards in the checklist below are differentiated by some other characteristic of the particular card.

	MINT	EXC	G-VG
COMPLETE SET (20)	9.00	4.50	.90
COMMON PLAYER (1-20)	.60	.30	.06
☐ 1 Looking up with yellow jersey	.60	.30	.06
☐ 2 Posing with bat from the waist up	.60	.30	.06
☐ 3 Portrait with green cap	.60	.30	.06
☐ 4 Follow-through on swing (catcher visible)	.60	.30	.06
☐ 5 Running the bases	.60	.30	.06
☐ 6 Warming up with bat over head	.60	.30	.06
☐ 7 Sitting in dugout holding bat	.60	.30	.06
☐ 8 Standing in outfield with sunglasses up	.60	.30	.06
☐ 9 Batting stance ready for pitch	.60	.30	.06
☐ 10 Taking a lead off first base	.60	.30	.06
☐ 11 Looking to the side (elephant logo on left shoulder)	.60	.30	.06

☐ 12 Bashing with Mark McGwire after homer	.60	.30	.06
☐ 13 Looking up witrh green batting glove in foreground	.60	.30	.06
☐ 14 Stretching to catch fly ball	.60	.30	.06
☐ 15 Follow through on swing (no catcher visible)	.60	.30	.06
☐ 16 Standing at plate glaring at pitcher	.60	.30	.06
☐ 17 Follow through on swing (stain on pants)	.60	.30	.06
☐ 18 Signing autographs for the fans at the ballpark	.60	.30	.06
☐ 19 Waiting at first base with hands on hips	.60	.30	.06
☐ 20 Admiring his hit at plate with tongue out	.60	.30	.06

1989 CMC Mickey Mantle

The 1989 CMC Mickey Mantle Collector's Kit set contains 20 numbered standard-size (2 1/2 by 3 1/2 inch) cards. The fronts and backs are white, red and navy. The backs feature narratives and facsimile signatures. The cards were distributed as a set in a box along with an album and a booklet as well as other elements by CMC, Collectors Marketing Corporation. Since all the cards in the set feature the same player, cards in the checklist below are differentiated by some other characteristic of the particular card. Some of the cards in this set are sepia-tone photos as the action predates the widespread use of color film.

	MINT	EXC	G-VG
COMPLETE SET (20)	9.00	4.50	.90
COMMON PLAYER (1-20)	.60	.30	.06
☐ 1 Standing with bat on left shoulder	.60	.30	.06
☐ 2 Batting stance lefty (back to camera)	.60	.30	.06
☐ 3 Looking intense in the field (waist up)	.60	.30	.06
☐ 4 Follow through on lefty swing	.60	.30	.06
☐ 5 Half smile (head and shoulders)	.60	.30	.06
☐ 6 Posing with bat alongside Roger Maris	.60	.30	.06
☐ 7 Holding up his 1962 contract (wearing suit and tie)	.60	.30	.06
☐ 8 Receiving 1962 MVP form Joe Cronin	.60	.30	.06
☐ 9 Batting stance lefty (catcher's glove in picture)	.60	.30	.06
☐ 10 Posing with Roger Maris and Yogi Berra	.60	.30	.06
☐ 11 Looking away with eyes closed, holding bat	.60	.30	.06
☐ 12 Swinging righty at pitch	.60	.30	.06
☐ 13 Starting to run to first base	.60	.30	.06
☐ 14 Mickey Mantle Day, September 18, 1965	.60	.30	.06
☐ 15 Shaking hands with Joe DiMaggio at Yankee Stadium	.60	.30	.06
☐ 16 Giving speech at Yankee Stadium	.60	.30	.06
☐ 17 Backing away from plate after pitch	.60	.30	.06
☐ 18 Getting ready at plate with bat in right hand	.60	.30	.06
☐ 19 Holding bat in both hands parallel to ground	.60	.30	.06
☐ 20 Waiting for pitch with bat on shoulder (lefty)	.60	.30	.06

1989 CMC Babe Ruth

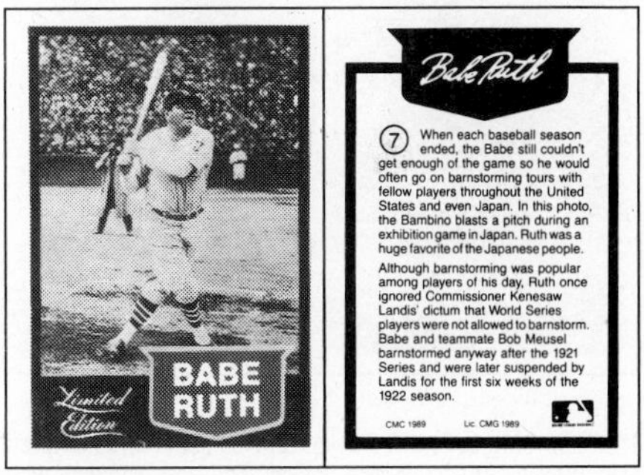

The 1989 CMC Babe Ruth Collector's Kit set contains 20 numbered standard-size (2 1/2" by 3 1/2") cards. The front borders are white, red and navy. The backs are blue and white, and feature narratives and facsimile signatures. The cards were distributed as a set in a box along with an album and a booklet as well as other elements by CMC, Collectors Marketing Corporation. Since all the cards in the set feature the same player, cards in the checklist below are differentiated by some other characteristic of the particular card. All of the cards in this set are sepia-tone photos as the action predates the widespread use of color film.

	MINT	EXC	G-VG
COMPLETE SET (20)	9.00	4.50	.90
COMMON PLAYER (1-20)	.60	.30	.06
☐ 1 Smiling holding three bats	.60	.30	.06
☐ 2 Posing in Red Sox uniform (head and shoulders)	.60	.30	.06
☐ 3 Looking up (waist up)	.60	.30	.06
☐ 4 Holding nine bats in front of him	.60	.30	.06
☐ 5 Golfing swing follow through	.60	.30	.06
☐ 6 Oldtimers' game photo holding two bats	.60	.30	.06
☐ 7 Follow through looking up (in Japan)	.60	.30	.06
☐ 8 Looking dapper in fur coat	.60	.30	.06
☐ 9 Babe Ruth Day, April 27, 1947	.60	.30	.06
☐ 10 Bust photo with no background	.60	.30	.06
☐ 11 Practicing swing (photo from knees up)	.60	.30	.06
☐ 12 Watching his hit after swing (knees up)	.60	.30	.06

		MINT	EXC	G-VG
☐	13 Follow through on swing, starting to first base	.60	.30	.06
☐	14 Practice swing with photographers in background	.60	.30	.06
☐	15 Posing with Jacob Ruppert	.60	.30	.06
☐	16 Follow through from waist up	.60	.30	.06
☐	17 Shaking hands with Miller Huggins	.60	.30	.06
☐	18 Signing autographs for the kids	.60	.30	.06
☐	19 Sitting wearing Braves uniform	.60	.30	.06
☐	20 Hall of Fame Plaque	.60	.30	.06

1990 CMC Collect-A-Books

The 1990 CMC Collect-A-Books were issued in three different sets (boxes) of 12 players apiece. The sets (boxes) were distinguishable by color, red, yellow, or green. The Collect-A-Books were in the style of the 1970 Topps Comic Book inserts but were much more profesionally made. The cards all fit into a 9-pocket sheet (since they are standard size, 2 1/2" by 3 1/2") even though they can be expanded. The set contains an interesting mixture of retired and current players.

	MINT	EXC	G-VG
COMPLETE SET (36)	9.00	4.50	.90
COMMON PLAYER (1-36)	.20	.10	.02

		MINT	EXC	G-VG
☐	1 Bo Jackson	1.00	.50	.10
☐	2 Dwight Gooden	.50	.25	.05
☐	3 Ken Griffey Jr.	1.00	.50	.10
☐	4 Will Clark	.50	.25	.05
☐	5 Ozzie Smith	.25	.12	.02
☐	6 Orel Hershiser	.25	.12	.02
☐	7 Ruben Sierra	.25	.12	.02
☐	8 Rickey Henderson	.50	.25	.05
☐	9 Robin Yount	.25	.12	.02
☐	10 Babe Ruth	.50	.25	.05
☐	11 Ernie Banks	.20	.10	.02
☐	12 Carl Yastrzemski	.35	.17	.03
☐	13 Don Mattingly	1.00	.50	.10
☐	14 Nolan Ryan	1.00	.50	.10
☐	15 Jerome Walton	.25	.12	.02
☐	16 Kevin Mitchell	.25	.12	.02
☐	17 Tony Gwynn	.25	.12	.02
☐	18 Dave Stewart	.20	.10	.02
☐	19 Roger Clemens	.50	.25	.05
☐	20 Darryl Strawberry	.50	.25	.05
☐	21 George Brett	.35	.17	.03
☐	22 Hank Aaron	.40	.20	.04
☐	23 Ted Williams	.40	.20	.04
☐	24 Warren Spahn	.20	.10	.02
☐	25 Jose Canseco	1.00	.50	.10
☐	26 Wade Boggs	.50	.25	.05
☐	27 Jim Abbott	.35	.17	.03
☐	28 Eric Davis	.50	.25	.05
☐	29 Ryne Sandberg	1.00	.50	.10
☐	30 Bret Saberhagen	.20	.10	.02
☐	31 Mark Grace	.50	.25	.05
☐	32 Gregg Olson	.30	.15	.03
☐	33 Kirby Puckett	.50	.25	.05
☐	34 Lou Gehrig	.50	.25	.05
☐	35 Roberto Clemente	.35	.17	.03
☐	36 Bob Feller	.25	.12	.02

1981 Coke

The cards in this 132-card set measure 2 1/2" by 3 1/2". In 1981, Topps produced 11 sets of 12 cards each for the Coca-Cola Company. Each set features 11 star players for a particular team plus an advertising card with the team name on the front. Although the cards are numbered in the upper right corner of the back from 1 to 11, they are re-numbered below within team, i.e., Boston Red Sox (1-12), Chicago Cubs (13-24), Chicago White Sox (25-36), Cincinnati Reds (37-48), Detroit Tigers (49-60), Houston Astros (61-72), Kansas City Royals (73-84), New York Mets (85-96), Philadelphia Phillies (97-108), Pittsburgh Pirates (109-120), and St. Louis Cardinals (121-132). Within each team the player actually numbered number 1 (on the card back) is the first player below and the player numbered number 11 is the last in that team's list. These player cards are quite similar to the 1981 Topps issue but feature a Coca-Cola logo on both the front and the back. The advertising card for each team features, on its back, an offer for obtaining an uncut sheet of 1981 Topps cards. These promotional cards were actually issued by Coke in only a few of the cities, and most of these cards have reached collectors hands through dealers who have purchased the cards through suppliers.

	MINT	EXC	G-VG
COMPLETE SET (132)	28.00	14.00	2.80
COMMON PLAYER (1-132)	.07	.03	.01
COMMON CHECKLIST	.03	.01	.00

		MINT	EXC	G-VG
☐	1 Tom Burgmeier	.07	.03	.01
☐	2 Dennis Eckersley	1.25	.60	.12
☐	3 Dwight Evans	.60	.30	.06
☐	4 Bob Stanley	.10	.05	.01
☐	5 Glenn Hoffman	.07	.03	.01
☐	6 Carney Lansford	.50	.25	.05
☐	7 Frank Tanana	.15	.07	.01
☐	8 Tony Perez	.50	.25	.05
☐	9 Jim Rice	.90	.45	.09
☐	10 Dave Stapleton	.07	.03	.01
☐	11 Carl Yastrzemski	2.50	1.25	.25
☐	12 Red Sox Checklist (unnumbered)	.03	.01	.00
☐	13 Tim Blackwell	.07	.03	.01
☐	14 Bill Buckner	.20	.10	.02
☐	15 Ivan DeJesus	.07	.03	.01
☐	16 Leon Durham	.15	.07	.01
☐	17 Steve Henderson	.07	.03	.01
☐	18 Mike Krukow	.10	.05	.01
☐	19 Ken Reitz	.07	.03	.01
☐	20 Rick Reuschel	.35	.17	.03
☐	21 Scot Thompson	.07	.03	.01
☐	22 Dick Tidrow	.07	.03	.01
☐	23 Mike Tyson	.07	.03	.01
☐	24 Cubs Checklist (unnumbered)	.03	.01	.00

☐ 25 Britt Burns	.10	.05	.01
☐ 26 Todd Cruz	.07	.03	.01
☐ 27 Rich Dotson	.20	.10	.02
☐ 28 Jim Essian	.07	.03	.01
☐ 29 Ed Farmer	.07	.03	.01
☐ 30 Lamar Johnson	.07	.03	.01
☐ 31 Ron LeFlore	.10	.05	.01
☐ 32 Chet Lemon	.10	.05	.01
☐ 33 Bob Molinaro	.07	.03	.01
☐ 34 Jim Morrison	.07	.03	.01
☐ 35 Wayne Nordhagen	.07	.03	.01
☐ 36 White Sox Checklist (unnumbered)	.03	.01	.00
☐ 37 Johnny Bench	2.00	1.00	.20
☐ 38 Dave Collins	.10	.05	.01
☐ 39 Dave Concepcion	.25	.12	.02
☐ 40 Dan Driessen	.07	.03	.01
☐ 41 George Foster	.35	.17	.03
☐ 42 Ken Griffey	.35	.17	.03
☐ 43 Tom Hume	.07	.03	.01
☐ 44 Ray Knight	.20	.10	.02
☐ 45 Ron Oester	.10	.05	.01
☐ 46 Tom Seaver	2.00	1.00	.20
☐ 47 Mario Soto	.10	.05	.01
☐ 48 Reds Checklist (unnumbered)	.03	.01	.00
☐ 49 Champ Summers	.07	.03	.01
☐ 50 Al Cowens	.07	.03	.01
☐ 51 Rich Hebner	.07	.03	.01
☐ 52 Steve Kemp	.10	.05	.01
☐ 53 Aurelio Lopez	.07	.03	.01
☐ 54 Jack Morris	.75	.35	.07
☐ 55 Lance Parrish	1.00	.50	.10
☐ 56 Johnny Wockenfuss	.07	.03	.01
☐ 57 Alan Trammell	1.50	.75	.15
☐ 58 Lou Whitaker	1.00	.50	.10
☐ 59 Kirk Gibson	2.50	1.25	.25
☐ 60 Tigers Checklist (unnumbered)	.03	.01	.00
☐ 61 Alan Ashby	.07	.03	.01
☐ 62 Cesar Cedeno	.10	.05	.01
☐ 63 Jose Cruz	.15	.07	.01
☐ 64 Art Howe	.15	.07	.01
☐ 65 Rafael Landestoy	.07	.03	.01
☐ 66 Joe Niekro	.20	.10	.02
☐ 67 Terry Puhl	.10	.05	.01
☐ 68 J.R. Richard	.15	.07	.01
☐ 69 Nolan Ryan	6.00	3.00	.60
☐ 70 Joe Sambito	.10	.05	.01
☐ 71 Don Sutton	1.00	.50	.10
☐ 72 Astros Checklist (unnumbered)	.03	.01	.00
☐ 73 Willie Aikens	.10	.05	.01
☐ 74 George Brett	2.50	1.25	.25
☐ 75 Larry Gura	.10	.05	.01
☐ 76 Dennis Leonard	.10	.05	.01
☐ 77 Hal McRae	.15	.07	.01
☐ 78 Amos Otis	.15	.07	.01
☐ 79 Dan Quisenberry	.25	.12	.02
☐ 80 U.L. Washington	.07	.03	.01
☐ 81 John Wathan	.15	.07	.01
☐ 82 Frank White	.20	.10	.02
☐ 83 Willie Wilson	.25	.12	.02
☐ 84 Royals Checklist (unnumbered)	.03	.01	.00
☐ 85 Neil Allen	.10	.05	.01
☐ 86 Doug Flynn	.07	.03	.01
☐ 87 Dave Kingman	.25	.12	.02
☐ 88 Randy Jones	.07	.03	.01
☐ 89 Pat Zachry	.07	.03	.01
☐ 90 Lee Mazzilli	.10	.05	.01
☐ 91 Rusty Staub	.20	.10	.02
☐ 92 Craig Swan	.07	.03	.01
☐ 93 Frank Taveras	.07	.03	.01
☐ 94 Alex Trevino	.07	.03	.01
☐ 95 Joel Youngblood	.07	.03	.01
☐ 96 Mets Checklist (unnumbered)	.03	.01	.00
☐ 97 Bob Boone	.30	.15	.03
☐ 98 Larry Bowa	.25	.12	.02
☐ 99 Steve Carlton	1.50	.75	.15
☐ 100 Greg Luzinski	.20	.10	.02
☐ 101 Garry Maddox	.10	.05	.01
☐ 102 Bake McBride	.07	.03	.01
☐ 103 Tug McGraw	.25	.12	.02
☐ 104 Pete Rose	2.00	1.00	.20
☐ 105 Mike Schmidt	3.00	1.50	.30
☐ 106 Lonnie Smith	.25	.12	.02
☐ 107 Manny Trillo	.07	.03	.01
☐ 108 Phillies Checklist (unnumbered)	.03	.01	.00
☐ 109 Jim Bibby	.07	.03	.01
☐ 110 John Candelaria	.10	.05	.01
☐ 111 Mike Easler	.10	.05	.01
☐ 112 Tim Foli	.07	.03	.01
☐ 113 Phil Garner	.10	.05	.01
☐ 114 Bill Madlock	.20	.10	.02
☐ 115 Omar Moreno	.07	.03	.01
☐ 116 Ed Ott	.07	.03	.01
☐ 117 Dave Parker	.90	.45	.09
☐ 118 Willie Stargell	1.00	.50	.10
☐ 119 Kent Tekulve	.10	.05	.01
☐ 120 Pirates Checklist (unnumbered)	.03	.01	.00
☐ 121 Bob Forsch	.10	.05	.01
☐ 122 George Hendrick	.10	.05	.01
☐ 123 Keith Hernandez	.75	.35	.07
☐ 124 Tom Herr	.15	.07	.01
☐ 125 Sixto Lezcano	.07	.03	.01
☐ 126 Ken Oberkfell	.07	.03	.01
☐ 127 Darrell Porter	.10	.05	.01
☐ 128 Tony Scott	.07	.03	.01
☐ 129 Lary Sorensen	.07	.03	.01
☐ 130 Bruce Sutter	.20	.10	.02
☐ 131 Garry Templeton	.10	.05	.01
☐ 132 Cardinals Checklist (unnumbered)	.03	.01	.00

1982 Coke Red Sox

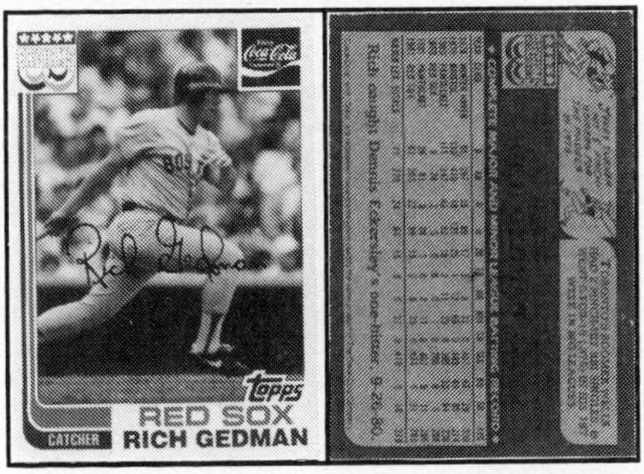

The cards in this 22-card set measure 2 1/2" by 3 1/2". This set of Boston Red Sox ballplayers was issued locally in the Boston area as a joint promotion by Brigham's Ice Cream Stores and Coca-Cola. The pictures are identical to those in the Topps regular 1982 issue, except that the colors are brighter and the Brigham and Coke logos appear inside the frame line. The reverses are done in red, black and gray, in contrast to the Topps set, and the number appears to the right of the position listing. The cards were initally distributed in three-card cello packs with an ice cream or Coca-Cola purchase but later became available as sets within the hobby. The unnumbered title or advertising card carries a premium offer on the reverse.

	MINT	EXC	G-VG
COMPLETE SET (23)	7.00	3.50	.70
COMMON PLAYER (1-23)	.07	.03	.01
☐ 1 Gary Allenson	.07	.03	.01
☐ 2 Tom Burgmeier	.07	.03	.01
☐ 3 Mark Clear	.10	.05	.01
☐ 4 Steve Crawford	.07	.03	.01
☐ 5 Dennis Eckersley	1.25	.60	.12
☐ 6 Dwight Evans	.75	.35	.07
☐ 7 Rich Gedman	.40	.20	.04
☐ 8 Garry Hancock	.07	.03	.01
☐ 9 Glen Hoffman	.07	.03	.01
☐ 10 Carney Lansford	.50	.25	.05
☐ 11 Rick Miller	.07	.03	.01
☐ 12 Reid Nichols	.07	.03	.01
☐ 13 Bob Ojeda	.25	.12	.02
☐ 14 Tony Perez	.50	.25	.05
☐ 15 Chuck Rainey	.07	.03	.01
☐ 16 Jerry Remy	.07	.03	.01
☐ 17 Jim Rice	.90	.45	.09
☐ 18 Bob Stanley	.15	.07	.01
☐ 19 Dave Stapleton	.07	.03	.01
☐ 20 Mike Torrez	.10	.05	.01

	MINT	EXC	G-VG
☐ 21 John Tudor	.40	.20	.04
☐ 22 Carl Yastrzemski	3.00	1.50	.30
☐ 23 Title Card (unnumbered)	.03	.01	.00

1982 Coke Reds

The cards in this 22-card set measure 2 1/2" by 3 1/2". The 1982 Coca-Cola Cincinnati Reds set, issued in conjunction with Topps, contains 22 cards of current Reds players. Although the cards of 15 players feature the exact photo used in the Topps' regular issue, the Coke photos have better coloration and appear sharper than their Topps counterparts. Six players, Cedeno, Harris, Hurdle, Kern, Krenchicki, and Trevino are new to the Redleg uniform via trades, while Paul Householder had formerly appeared on the Reds' 1982 Topps "Future Stars" card. The cards are numbered 1 to 22 on the red and gray reverse, and the Coke logo appears on both sides of the card. There is an unnumbered title card which contains a premium offer on the reverse.

	MINT	EXC	G-VG
COMPLETE SET (23)	7.00	3.50	.70
COMMON PLAYER (1-23)	.07	.03	.01
☐ 1 Johnny Bench	2.50	1.25	.25
☐ 2 Bruce Berenyi	.07	.03	.01
☐ 3 Larry Biittner	.07	.03	.01
☐ 4 Cesar Cedeno	.15	.07	.01
☐ 5 Dave Concepcion	.25	.12	.02
☐ 6 Dan Driessen	.10	.05	.01
☐ 7 Greg Harris	.30	.15	.03
☐ 8 Paul Householder	.07	.03	.01
☐ 9 Tom Hume	.07	.03	.01
☐ 10 Clint Hurdle	.10	.05	.01
☐ 11 Jim Kern	.07	.03	.01
☐ 12 Wayne Krenchicki	.07	.03	.01
☐ 13 Rafael Landestoy	.07	.03	.01
☐ 14 Charlie Leibrandt	.25	.12	.02
☐ 15 Mike O'Berry	.07	.03	.01
☐ 16 Ron Oester	.10	.05	.01
☐ 17 Frank Pastore	.07	.03	.01
☐ 18 Joe Price	.07	.03	.01
☐ 19 Tom Seaver	2.50	1.25	.25
☐ 20 Mario Soto	.15	.07	.01
☐ 21 Alex Trevino	.07	.03	.01
☐ 22 Mike Vail	.07	.03	.01
☐ 23 Title Card (unnumbered)	.03	.01	.00

1985 Coke White Sox

This 30-card set features present and past Chicago White Sox players and personnel. Cards measure 2 5/8" by 4 1/8" and feature a red band at the bottom of the card. Within the red band are the White Sox logo, the player's name, position, uniform number, and a small oval portrait of an all-time White Sox Great at a similar position. the cards were available two at a time at Tuesday night White Sox home games or as a complete set through membership in the Coca-Cola White Sox Fan Club. The cards below are numbered by uniform number; the last three cards are unnumbered.

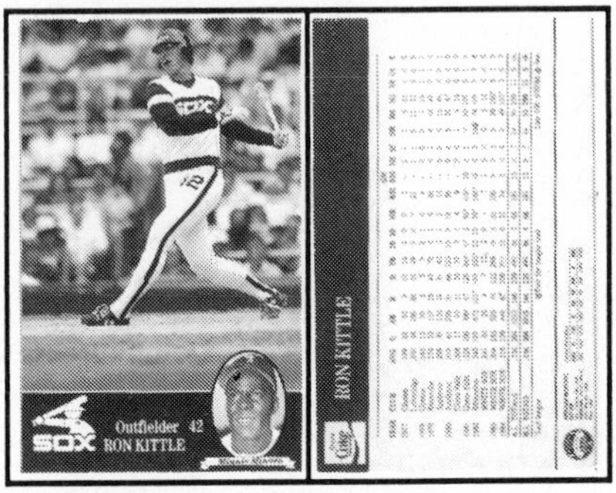

	MINT	EXC	G-VG
COMPLETE SET (30)	11.00	5.50	1.10
COMMON PLAYER	.30	.15	.03
☐ 0 Oscar Gamble / Zeke Bonura	.30	.15	.03
☐ 1 Scott Fletcher / Luke Appling	.60	.30	.06
☐ 3 Harold Baines / Bill Melton	.90	.45	.09
☐ 5 Luis Salazar / Chico Carrasquel	.30	.15	.03
☐ 7 Marc Hill / Sherm Lollar	.30	.15	.03
☐ 8 Daryl Boston / Jim Landis	.40	.20	.04
☐ 10 Tony LaRussa / Al Lopez	.75	.35	.07
☐ 12 Julio Cruz / Nellie Fox	.40	.20	.04
☐ 13 Ozzie Guillen / Luis Aparicio	2.00	1.00	.20
☐ 17 Jerry Hairston / Smoky Burgess	.30	.15	.03
☐ 20 Joe DeSa / Carlos May	.30	.15	.03
☐ 22 Joel Skinner / J.C. Martin	.30	.15	.03
☐ 23 Rudy Law / Bill Skowron	.30	.15	.03
☐ 24 Floyd Bannister / Red Faber	.40	.20	.04
☐ 29 Greg Walker / Dick Allen	.60	.30	.06
☐ 30 Gene Nelson / Early Wynn	.50	.25	.05
☐ 32 Tim Hulett / Pete Ward	.30	.15	.03
☐ 34 Richard Dotson / Ed Walsh	.50	.25	.05
☐ 37 Dan Spillner / Thornton Lee	.30	.15	.03
☐ 40 Britt Burns / Gary Peters	.30	.15	.03
☐ 41 Tom Seaver / Ted Lyons	2.00	1.00	.20
☐ 42 Ron Kittle / Minnie Minoso	.60	.30	.06
☐ 43 Bob James / Hoyt Wilhelm	.40	.20	.04
☐ 44 Tom Paciorek / Eddie Collins	.40	.20	.04
☐ 46 Tim Lollar / Billy Pierce	.30	.15	.03
☐ 50 Juan Agosto / Wilbur Wood	.30	.15	.03
☐ 72 Carlton Fisk / Ray Schalk	1.50	.75	.15
☐ xx Comiskey Park (unnumbered)	.30	.15	.03

		MINT	EXC	G-VG
☐	xx Nancy Faust (park organist) (unnumbered)	.30	.15	.03
☐	xx Ribbie and Roobarb (unnumbered)	.30	.15	.03

1986 Coke White Sox

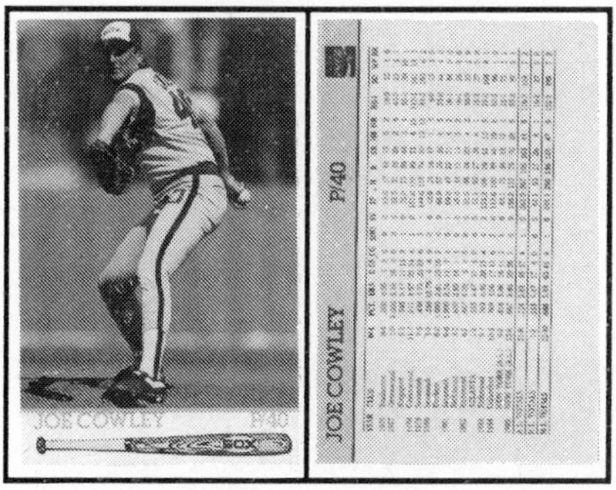

This colorful 30-card set features a borderless photo on top of a blue-on-white name, position, and uniform number. Card backs provide complete major and minor season-by-season career statistical information. Since the cards are unnumbered, they are numbered below according to uniform number. The cards measure approximately 2 5/8" by 4". The five unnumbered non-player cards are listed at the end of the checklist below.

		MINT	EXC	G-VG
	COMPLETE SET (30)	12.00	6.00	1.20
	COMMON PLAYER	.30	.15	.03
☐	1 Wayne Tolleson	.30	.15	.03
☐	3 Harold Baines	1.00	.50	.10
☐	7 Marc Hill	.30	.15	.03
☐	8 Daryl Boston	.40	.20	.04
☐	12 Julio Cruz	.30	.15	.03
☐	13 Ozzie Guillen	1.00	.50	.10
☐	17 Jerry Hairston	.30	.15	.03
☐	19 Floyd Bannister	.40	.20	.04
☐	20 Reid Nichols	.30	.15	.03
☐	22 Joel Skinner	.30	.15	.03
☐	24 Dave Schmidt	.40	.20	.04
☐	26 Bobby Bonilla	3.00	1.50	.30
☐	29 Greg Walker	.50	.25	.05
☐	30 Gene Nelson	.40	.20	.04
☐	32 Tim Hulett	.30	.15	.03
☐	33 Neil Allen	.40	.20	.04
☐	34 Richard Dotson	.40	.20	.04
☐	40 Joe Cowley	.30	.15	.03
☐	41 Tom Seaver	1.50	.75	.15
☐	42 Ron Kittle	.50	.25	.05
☐	43 Bob James	.30	.15	.03
☐	44 John Cangelosi	.30	.15	.03
☐	50 Juan Agosto	.30	.15	.03
☐	52 Joel Davis	.30	.15	.03
☐	72 Carlton Fisk	1.25	.60	.12
☐	xx Nancy Faust ORG (unnumbered)	.30	.15	.03
☐	xx Ken"Hawk" Harrelson (unnumbered)	.40	.20	.04
☐	xx Tony LaRussa MG (unnumbered)	.40	.20	.04
☐	xx Minnie Minoso CO (unnumbered)	.40	.20	.04
☐	xx Ribbie and Roobarb (unnumbered)	.30	.15	.03

1987 Coke Tigers

Coca-Cola in collaboration with S. Abraham and Sons issued a set of 18 cards featuring the Detroit Tigers. The cards are numbered on the back. The cards are distinguished by the bright yellow border framing the full-color picture of the player on the front. The cards were issued in panels of four: three player cards and a team logo card. The cards measure the standard 2 1/2" by 3 1/2" and were produced by MSA, Mike Schechter Associates.

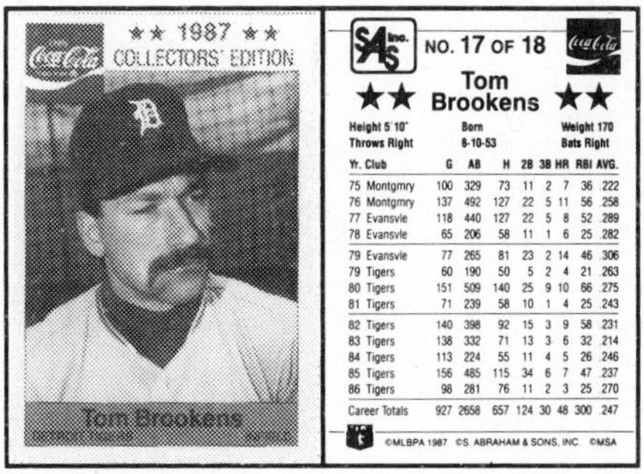

		MINT	EXC	G-VG
	COMPLETE SET (18)	5.00	2.50	.50
	COMMON PLAYER (1-18)	.25	.12	.02
☐	1 Kirk Gibson	.75	.35	.07
☐	2 Larry Herndon	.25	.12	.02
☐	3 Walt Terrell	.35	.17	.03
☐	4 Alan Trammell	.90	.45	.09
☐	5 Frank Tanana	.35	.17	.03
☐	6 Pat Sheridan	.25	.12	.02
☐	7 Jack Morris	.50	.25	.05
☐	8 Mike Heath	.25	.12	.02
☐	9 Dave Bergman	.25	.12	.02
☐	10 Chet Lemon	.35	.17	.03
☐	11 Dwight Lowry	.25	.12	.02
☐	12 Dan Petry	.35	.17	.03
☐	13 Darrell Evans	.35	.17	.03
☐	14 Darnell Coles	.25	.12	.02
☐	15 Willie Hernandez	.35	.17	.03
☐	16 Lou Whitaker	.60	.30	.06
☐	17 Tom Brookens	.25	.12	.02
☐	18 John Grubb	.25	.12	.02

1987 Coke White Sox

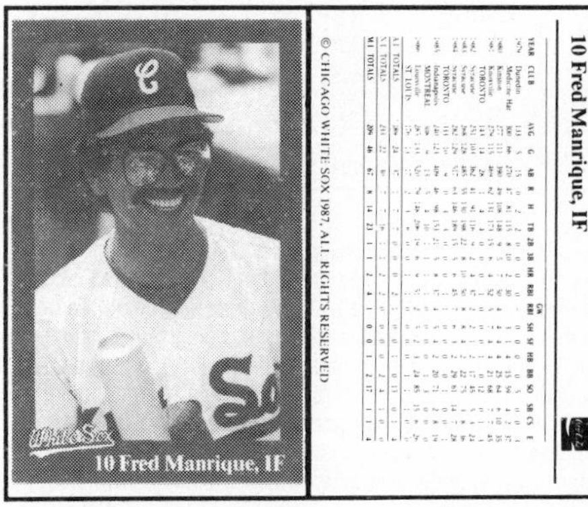

This colorful 30-card set features a card front with a blue-bordered photo and name, position, and uniform number. Card backs provide complete major and minor season-by-season career statistical information. Since the cards are unnumbered, they are numbered below in uniform number order. The cards measure approximately 2 5/8" by 4". The three unnumbered non-player cards are listed at the end. The card set, sponsored by Coca-Cola, is an exclusive for fan club members who join (for 10.00) in 1987.

	MINT	EXC	G-VG
COMPLETE SET (30)	9.00	4.50	.90
COMMON PLAYER (1-30)	.25	.12	.02

☐ 1 Jerry Royster 1	.25	.12	.02
☐ 2 Harold Baines 3	.75	.35	.07
☐ 3 Ron Karkovice 5	.25	.12	.02
☐ 4 Daryl Boston 8	.35	.17	.03
☐ 5 Fred Manrique 10	.25	.12	.02
☐ 6 Steve Lyons 12	.25	.12	.02
☐ 7 Ozzie Guillen 13	.75	.35	.07
☐ 8 Russ Morman 14	.25	.12	.02
☐ 9 Donnie Hill 15	.25	.12	.02
☐ 10 Jim Fregosi MG 16	.35	.17	.03
☐ 11 Jerry Hairston 17	.25	.12	.02
☐ 12 Floyd Bannister 19	.35	.17	.03
☐ 13 Gary Redus 21	.35	.17	.03
☐ 14 Ivan Calderon 22	.60	.30	.06
☐ 15 Ron Hassey 25	.35	.17	.03
☐ 16 Jose DeLeon 26	.35	.17	.03
☐ 17 Greg Walker 29	.50	.25	.05
☐ 18 Tim Hulett 32	.25	.12	.02
☐ 19 Neil Allen 33	.35	.17	.03
☐ 20 Richard Dotson 34	.35	.17	.03
☐ 21 Ray Searage 36	.25	.12	.02
☐ 22 Bobby Thigpen 37	1.00	.50	.10
☐ 23 Jim Winn 40	.25	.12	.02
☐ 24 Bob James 43	.25	.12	.02
☐ 25 Joel McKeon 50	.25	.12	.02
☐ 26 Joel Davis 52	.25	.12	.02
☐ 27 Carlton Fisk 72	1.25	.60	.12
☐ 28 Nancy Faust ORG (unnumbered)	.25	.12	.02
☐ 29 Minnie Minoso (unnumbered)	.35	.17	.03
☐ 30 Robbie and Roobarb (unnumbered)	.25	.12	.02

1988 Coke Padres

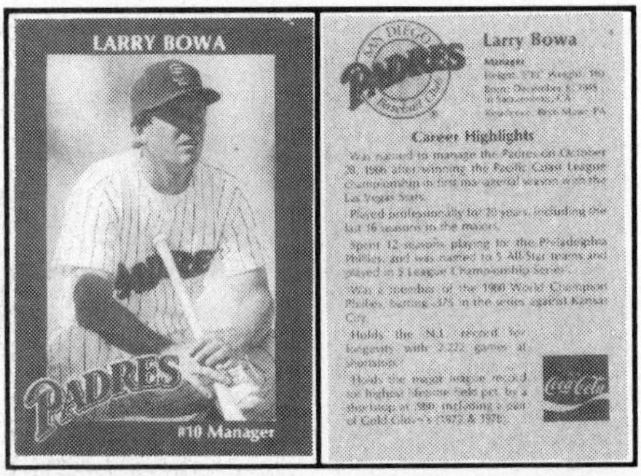

These cards were actually issued as two separate promotions. The first eight cards were issued as a perforated sheet (approximately 7 1/2" by 10 1/2") as a Coca Cola Junior Padres Club promotion. The other 12 cards were issued later on specific game days to members of the Junior Padres Club. All the cards are standard size, 2 1/2" by 3 1/2" and are unnumbered. Cards that were on the perforated panel are indicated by PAN in the checklist below. Since the cards are unnumbered, they are listed below by uniform number, which is featured prominently on the card fronts.

	MINT	EXC	G-VG
COMPLETE SET (21)	30.00	15.00	3.00
COMMON PANEL PLAYER	.50	.25	.05
COMMON NON-PAN PLAYER	1.00	.50	.10

☐ 1 Garry Templeton PAN	.50	.25	.05
☐ 5 Randy Ready PAN	.50	.25	.05
☐ 7 Keith Moreland	1.00	.50	.10
☐ 8 John Kruk	1.50	.75	.15
☐ 9 Benito Santiago	5.00	2.50	.50
☐ 10 Larry Bowa MG PAN	.50	.25	.05
☐ 11 Tim Flannery PAN	.50	.25	.05
☐ 14 Carmelo Martinez	1.00	.50	.10
☐ 15 Jack McKeon MG	1.00	.50	.10
☐ 19 Tony Gwynn	10.00	5.00	1.00
☐ 22 Stan Jefferson	1.25	.60	.12
☐ 27 Mark Parent	1.00	.50	.10
☐ 30 Eric Show	1.25	.60	.12
☐ 31 Eddie Whitson	1.50	.75	.15
☐ 35 Chris Brown PAN	.60	.30	.06
☐ 41 Lance McCullers	1.25	.60	.12
☐ 45 Jimmy Jones PAN	.60	.30	.06
☐ 48 Mark Davis PAN	2.00	1.00	.20
☐ 51 Greg Booker	1.00	.50	.10
☐ 55 Mark Grant PAN	.50	.25	.05
☐ xx Padres Logo PAN (program explanation on reverse)	.50	.25	.05

1988 Coke White Sox

This colorful 30-card set features a card front with a red-bordered photo and name and position. Card backs provide a narrative without any statistical tables. Since the cards are unnumbered, they are numbered below in alphabetical order according to the subject's name or card's title. The cards measure approximately 2 5/8" by 3 1/2". The card set, sponsored by Coca-Cola, was for fan club members who join (for 10.00) in 1988. The cards were also given out at the May 22nd game at Comiskey Park. These cards do not even list the player's uniform number anywhere on the card. Card backs are printed in black and gray on thin white card stock.

	MINT	EXC	G-VG
COMPLETE SET (30)	6.00	3.00	.60
COMMON PLAYER (1-30)	.15	.07	.01

☐ 1 Harold Baines	.50	.25	.05
☐ 2 Daryl Boston	.25	.12	.02
☐ 3 Ivan Calderon	.40	.20	.04
☐ 4 Comiskey Park	.15	.07	.01
☐ 5 John Davis	.25	.12	.02
☐ 6 Nancy Faust (organist)	.15	.07	.01
☐ 7 Jim Fregosi MG	.25	.12	.02
☐ 8 Carlton Fisk	.80	.40	.08
☐ 9 Ozzie Guillen	.60	.30	.06
☐ 10 Donnie Hill	.15	.07	.01
☐ 11 Rick Horton	.25	.12	.02
☐ 12 Lance Johnson	.25	.12	.02
☐ 13 Dave LaPoint	.25	.12	.02
☐ 14 Bill Long	.15	.07	.01
☐ 15 Steve Lyons	.15	.07	.01
☐ 16 Jack McDowell	.35	.17	.03
☐ 17 Fred Manrique	.15	.07	.01
☐ 18 Minnie Minoso	.35	.17	.03
☐ 19 Dan Pasqua	.25	.12	.02
☐ 20 John Pawlowski	.15	.07	.01
☐ 21 Melido Perez	.35	.17	.03
☐ 22 Billy Pierce	.25	.12	.02
☐ 23 Jerry Reuss	.25	.12	.02
☐ 24 Gary Redus	.25	.12	.02

☐ 25 Ribbie and Roobarb	.15	.07	.01
☐ 26 Mark Salas	.15	.07	.01
☐ 27 Jose Segura	.25	.12	.02
☐ 28 Bobby Thigpen	.60	.30	.06
☐ 29 Greg Walker	.35	.17	.03
☐ 30 Kenny Williams	.25	.12	.02

1989 Coke Padres

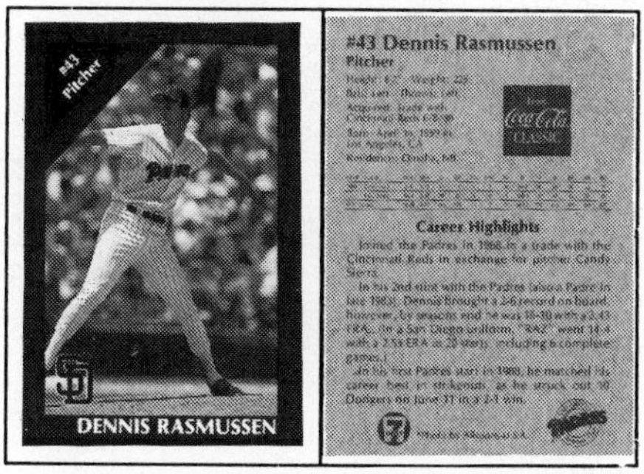

These cards were actually issued as two separate promotions. The first nine cards were issued as a perforated sheet (approximately 7 1/2" by 10 1/2") as a Coca Cola Junior Padres Club promotion. The other 12 cards were issued later on specific game days to members of the Junior Padres Club. All the cards are standard size, 2 1/2" by 3 1/2" and are unnumbered. Cards that were on the perforated panel are indicated by PAN in the checklist below. Since the cards are unnumbered, they are listed below in alphabetical order by subject. Marvell Wynne was planned for the set but was not issued since he was traded before the set was released; Walt Terrell also is tougher to find due to his mid-season trade.

	MINT	EXC	G-VG
COMPLETE SET (21)	25.00	12.50	2.50
COMMON PLAYER (1-21)	1.00	.50	.10
COMMON PLAYER PAN	.50	.25	.05
☐ 1 Roberto Alomar PAN	1.00	.50	.10
☐ 2 Jack Clark	2.50	1.25	.25
☐ 3 Mark Davis	4.00	2.00	.40
☐ 4 Tim Flannery	1.00	.50	.10
☐ 5 Mark Grant	1.00	.50	.10
☐ 6 Tony Gwynn	9.00	4.50	.90
☐ 7 Bruce Hurst	2.00	1.00	.20
☐ 8 Chris James	1.50	.75	.15
☐ 9 Carmelo Martinez PAN	.50	.25	.05
☐ 10 Jack McKeon MG PAN	.50	.25	.05
☐ 11 Mark Parent	1.00	.50	.10
☐ 12 Dennis Rasmussen PAN	.50	.25	.05
☐ 13 Randy Ready PAN	.50	.25	.05
☐ 14 Leon Bip Roberts	1.50	.75	.15
☐ 15 Luis Salazar	1.00	.50	.10
☐ 16 Benito Santiago	3.00	1.50	.30
☐ 17 Eric Show PAN	.60	.30	.06
☐ 18 Gary Templeton PAN	.75	.35	.07
☐ 19 Walt Terrell SP	5.00	2.50	.50
☐ 20 Ed Whitson PAN	.75	.35	.07
☐ xx Padres Logo PAN	.50	.25	.05

1989 Coke White Sox

The 1989 Coke Chicago White Sox set contains 30 cards measuring 2 5/8" by 3 1/2". The players in the set represent the White Sox opening day roster. The fronts are blue. The horizontally-oriented backs are gray and white, and feature biographical information. The set was a promotional give-away August 10, 1989 at the Baseball Card Night game against the Oakland A's to the first 15,000 fans. The set includes a special "New Comiskey Park, 1991" card. The complete set was also available with (10.00) membership in the Chi-Sox Fan Club.

	MINT	EXC	G-VG
COMPLETE SET (30)	6.00	3.00	.60
COMMON PLAYER (1-30)	.15	.07	.01
☐ 1 New Comiskey Park 1991	.15	.07	.01
☐ 2 Comiskey Park	.15	.07	.01
☐ 3 Jeff Torborg MG	.25	.12	.02
☐ 4 Coaching Staff	.15	.07	.01
☐ 5 Harold Baines	.50	.25	.05
☐ 6 Daryl Boston	.25	.12	.02
☐ 7 Ivan Calderon	.40	.20	.04
☐ 8 Carlton Fisk	.80	.40	.08
☐ 9 Dave Gallagher	.25	.12	.02
☐ 10 Ozzie Guillen	.60	.30	.06
☐ 11 Shawn Hillegas	.15	.07	.01
☐ 12 Barry Jones	.25	.12	.02
☐ 13 Ron Karkovice	.15	.07	.01
☐ 14 Eric King	.25	.12	.02
☐ 15 Ron Kittle	.25	.12	.02
☐ 16 Bill Long	.15	.07	.01
☐ 17 Steve Lyons	.15	.07	.01
☐ 18 Donn Pall	.15	.07	.01
☐ 19 Dan Pasqua	.15	.07	.01
☐ 20 Ken Patterson	.15	.07	.01
☐ 21 Melido Perez	.25	.12	.02
☐ 22 Jerry Reuss	.15	.07	.01
☐ 23 Billy Joe Robidoux	.15	.07	.01
☐ 24 Steve Rosenberg	.15	.07	.01
☐ 25 Jeff Schaefer	.15	.07	.01
☐ 26 Bobby Thigpen	.50	.25	.05
☐ 27 Greg Walker	.25	.12	.02
☐ 28 Eddie Williams	.15	.07	.01
☐ 29 Nancy Faust (organist)	.15	.07	.01
☐ 30 Minnie Minoso	.25	.12	.02

1990 Coke/Kroger Tigers

The 1990 Coke/Kroger Detroit Tigers set contains 28 cards, measuring approximately 2 7/8" by 4 1/4", which was used as a giveaway at the July 14th Detroit Tigers home game. The player photo is surrounded by green borders with complete career statistical information printed on the back of each card. This set is checklisted alphabetically in the listings below.

	MINT	EXC	G-VG
COMPLETE SET (28)	7.00	3.50	.70
COMMON PLAYER (1-28)	.20	.10	.02
☐ 1 Sparky Anderson MG	.30	.15	.03
☐ 2 Dave Bergman	.20	.10	.02
☐ 3 Brian DuBois	.30	.15	.03
☐ 4 Cecil Fielder	1.00	.50	.10
☐ 5 Paul Gibson	.20	.10	.02
☐ 6 Jerry Don Gleaton	.20	.10	.02
☐ 7 Mike Heath	.20	.10	.02

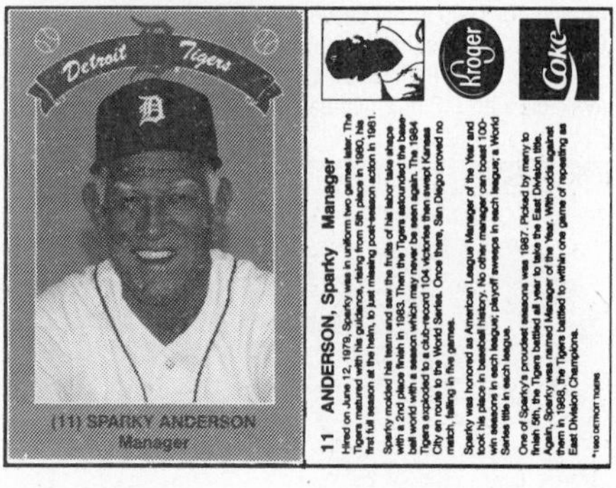

☐ 8 Mike Henneman	.30	.15	.03
☐ 9 Tracy Jones	.20	.10	.02
☐ 10 Chet Lemon	.30	.15	.03
☐ 11 Urbano Lugo	.20	.10	.02
☐ 12 Jack Morris	.50	.25	.05
☐ 13 Lloyd Moseby	.30	.15	.03
☐ 14 Matt Nokes	.30	.15	.03
☐ 15 Edwin Nunez	.20	.10	.02
☐ 16 Dan Petry	.30	.15	.03
☐ 17 Tony Phillips	.20	.10	.02
☐ 18 Kevin Ritz	.30	.15	.03
☐ 19 Jeff Robinson	.30	.15	.03
☐ 20 Ed Romero	.20	.10	.02
☐ 21 Mark Salas	.20	.10	.02
☐ 22 Larry Sheets	.20	.10	.02
☐ 23 Frank Tanana	.30	.15	.03
☐ 24 Alan Trammell	.90	.45	.09
☐ 25 Gary Ward	.20	.10	.02
☐ 26 Lou Whitaker	.50	.25	.05
☐ 27 Ken Williams	.20	.10	.02
☐ 28 Tigers Coaches Billy Consolo Alex Grammas Billy Muffet (sic, Muffett) Vada Pinson Dick Tracewski	.20	.10	.02

1990 Coke White Sox

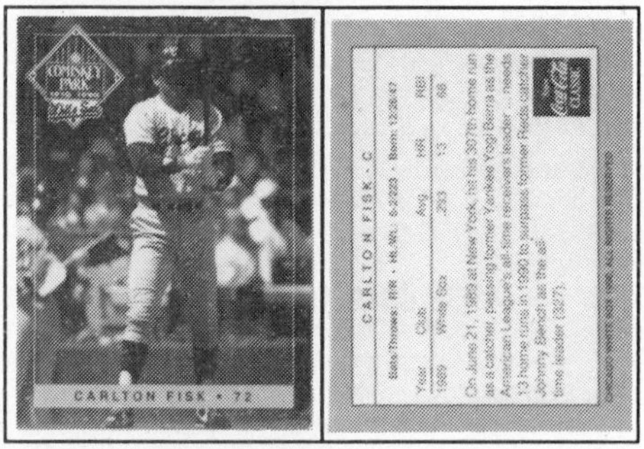

The 1990 Coca Cola White Sox set contains 30 cards. The set is a beautiful full-color set commemorating the 1990 White Sox who were celebrating the eightieth and last season played in old Comiskey Park. This (approximately) 2 5/8" by 3 1/2" set has a Comiskey Park logo on the front with 1989 statistics and a brief biography on the back. The set is checklisted alphabetically and notated by the uniform number on the front of the card.

	MINT	EXC	G-VG
COMPLETE SET (30)	6.00	3.00	.60
COMMON PLAYER (1-30)	.20	.10	.02
☐ 1 Ivan Calderon 22	.50	.25	.05
☐ 2 Wayne Edwards 45	.30	.15	.03
☐ 3 Carlton Fisk 72	.75	.35	.07
☐ 4 Scott Fletcher 7	.20	.10	.02
☐ 5 Dave Gallagher 17	.20	.10	.02
☐ 6 Craig Grebeck 14	.30	.15	.03
☐ 7 Ozzie Guillen 13	.60	.30	.06
☐ 8 Greg Hibbard 27	.30	.15	.03
☐ 9 Lance Johnson 1	.30	.15	.03
☐ 10 Barry Jones 50	.30	.15	.03
☐ 11 Ron Karkovice 20	.20	.10	.02
☐ 12 Eric King 36	.30	.15	.03
☐ 13 Ron Kittle 42	.30	.15	.03
☐ 14 Jerry Kutzler 52	.20	.10	.02
☐ 15 Steve Lyons 12	.20	.10	.02
☐ 16 Carlos Martinez 24	.30	.15	.03
☐ 17 Jack McDowell 29	.30	.15	.03
☐ 18 Donn Pall 30	.20	.10	.02
☐ 19 Dan Pasqua 44	.30	.15	.03
☐ 20 Ken Patterson 34	.20	.10	.02
☐ 21 Melido Perez 33	.30	.15	.03
☐ 22 Scott Radinsky 31	.30	.15	.03
☐ 23 Sammy Sosa 25	.60	.30	.06
☐ 24 Bobby Thigpen 37	.50	.25	.05
☐ 25 Frank Thomas	1.50	.75	.15
☐ 26 Jeff Torborg MG 10	.30	.15	.03
☐ 27 Robin Ventura 23	.50	.25	.05
☐ 28 Rookies: Jerry Kutzler Wayne Edwards Craig Grebeck Scott Radinsky Robin Ventura	.30	.15	.03
☐ 29 Captains: Ozzie Guillen and Carlton Fisk	.50	.25	.05
☐ 30 Coaches: Barry Foote Sammy Ellis Walt Hriniak Terry Bevington Dave LaRoche Joe Nossek Ron Clark	.20	.10	.02

1990 Colla Canseco

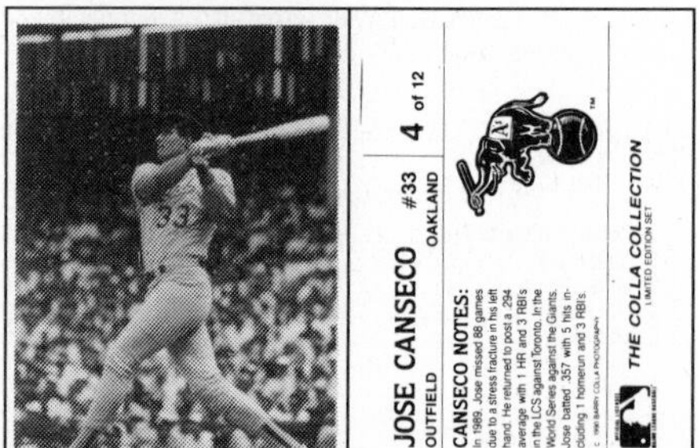

This 12-card set, issued by noted photographer Barry Colla, measures the standard size 2 1/2" by 3 1/2" and features Jose Canseco in various poses. The fronts are beautiful full-color photos while the backs contain notes about Canseco. According to the back of card 1, 20,000 numbered sets were issued.

	MINT	EXC	G-VG
COMPLETE SET (12)	10.00	5.00	1.00
COMMON PLAYER (1-12)	1.00	.50	.10
☐ 1 Jose Canseco (Portrait)	1.00	.50	.10
☐ 2 Jose Canseco (Follow-Through, Bat at Waist)	1.00	.50	.10
☐ 3 Jose Canseco (Follow-Through, Bat at Shoulders)	1.00	.50	.10
☐ 4 Jose Canseco (Follow-Through, Helmetless)	1.00	.50	.10

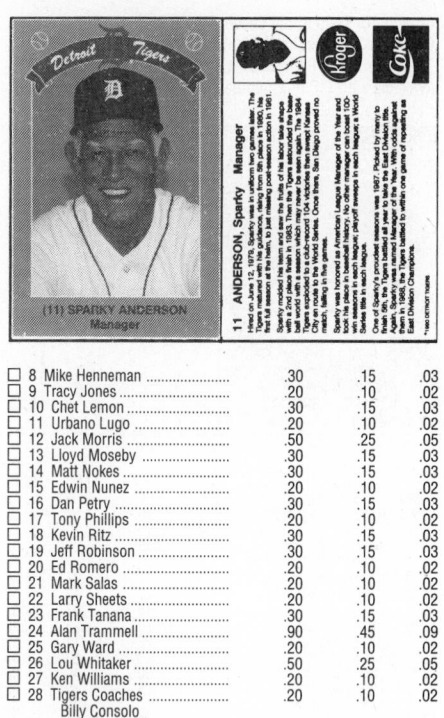

☐ 5 Jose Canseco (Dugout Portrait)	1.00	.50	.10
☐ 6 Jose Canseco (Profile, Bat on Shoulder)	1.00	.50	.10
☐ 7 Jose Canseco (Batting Cage Pose)	1.00	.50	.10
☐ 8 Jose Canseco (Follow-Through, ready to run)	1.00	.50	.10
☐ 9 Jose Canseco (Portrait, Kneeling)	1.00	.50	.10
☐ 10 Jose Canseco (Portrait, bat under shoulder)	1.00	.50	.10
☐ 11 Jose Canseco (At Bat-rack)	1.00	.50	.10
☐ 12 Jose Canseco (Running Bases)	1.00	.50	.10

1990 Colla Will Clark

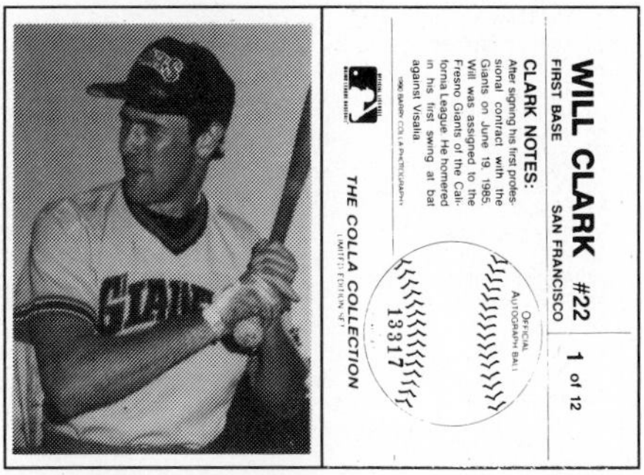

This 12-card set again features the beautiful photography of Barry Colla; this time Will Clark is the featured player. Each card in the set measures the standard size, 2 1/2" by 3 1/2". Again the fronts are borderless photos while the back contains notes about Will Clark. According to card number one, 15,000 numbered sets were produced.

	MINT	EXC	G-VG
COMPLETE SET (12)	10.00	5.00	1.00
COMMON PLAYER (1-12)	1.00	.50	.10
☐ 1 Will Clark (Batting Pose, Gray Shirt)	1.00	.50	.10
☐ 2 Will Clark (Bat at Shoulder, Short Sleeves)	1.00	.50	.10
☐ 3 Will Clark (Smiling)	1.00	.50	.10
☐ 4 Will Clark (Ball in Glove)	1.00	.50	.10
☐ 5 Will Clark (Batting Pose, Long Sleeves)	1.00	.50	.10
☐ 6 Will Clark (Follow-Through, bat over head)	1.00	.50	.10
☐ 7 Will Clark (Follow-Through, hand released)	1.00	.50	.10
☐ 8 Will Clark (Standing, bat on ground)	1.00	.50	.10
☐ 9 Will Clark (Pose with bat at waist)	1.00	.50	.10
☐ 10 Will Clark (Portrait with Bat)	1.00	.50	.10
☐ 11 Will Clark (Kneeling with Glove)	1.00	.50	.10
☐ 12 Will Clark (Preparing to Field)	1.00	.50	.10

1991 Colla Kevin Maas

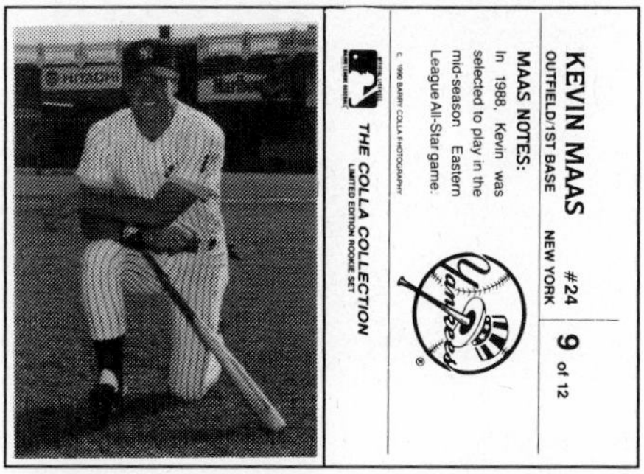

This extremely attractive 12-card standard size 2 1/2" by 3 1/2" card set was produced by photographer Barry Colla. The set was limited to 7,500 made and each card has some facts relevant to Maas' career on the back of the card. The set was produced to be sold in its own special box and the boxes were issued 24 sets to each bigger box. All of the boxes were produced in the team's colors.

	MINT	EXC	G-VG
COMPLETE SET (12)	10.00	5.00	1.00
COMMON PLAYER (1-12)	1.00	.50	.10
☐ 1 Kevin Maas (Batting Pose)	1.00	.50	.10
☐ 2 Kevin Maas (Sitting on Dugout Steps)	1.00	.50	.10
☐ 3 Kevin Maas (Taking a lead on basepaths)	1.00	.50	.10
☐ 4 Kevin Maas (Close-Up)	1.00	.50	.10
☐ 5 Kevin Maas (Standing in Dugout)	1.00	.50	.10
☐ 6 Kevin Maas (Kneeling with bat)	1.00	.50	.10
☐ 7 Kevin Maas (Fielding Pose)	1.00	.50	.10
☐ 8 Kevin Maas (Follow Through 24 showing)	1.00	.50	.10
☐ 9 Kevin Maas (Portrait with Bat)	1.00	.50	.10
☐ 10 Kevin Maas (Follow Through)	1.00	.50	.10
☐ 11 Kevin Maas (Side Portrait)	1.00	.50	.10
☐ 12 Kevin Maas (Taking Batting Practice)	1.00	.50	.10

1990 Colla Mattingly

This 13-card set features the photography of Barry Colla as he features Don Mattingly in various poses. Each card in the set measures the standard size, 2 1/2" by 3 1/2". The set was limited to 15,000 numbered sets and feature full-color photographs on the borderless fronts along with notes about Mattingly on the back.

	MINT	EXC	G-VG
COMPLETE SET (13)	10.00	5.00	1.00
COMMON PLAYER (1-13)	1.00	.50	.10
☐ 1 Don Mattingly (Head-On Portrait)	1.00	.50	.10
☐ 2 Don Mattingly (Preparing to Swing)	1.00	.50	.10

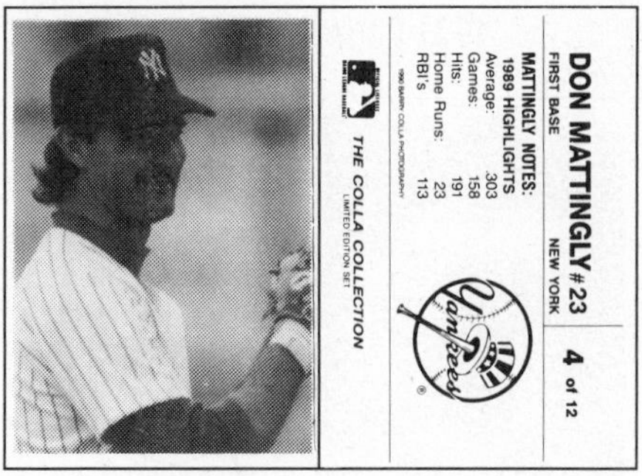

☐ 3 Don Mattingly (Running Bases)	1.00	.50	.10
☐ 4 Don Mattingly (Portrait with glove in hand)	1.00	.50	.10
☐ 5 Don Mattingly (Backhanding a Ball)	1.00	.50	.10
☐ 6 Don Mattingly (Follow-Through, Bat Pointing Up)	1.00	.50	.10
☐ 7 Don Mattingly (Follow-Through, bat to be released)	1.00	.50	.10
☐ 8 Don Mattingly (Facing left, bat on shoulder)	1.00	.50	.10
☐ 9 Don Mattingly (Portrait, facing right)	1.00	.50	.10
☐ 10 Don Mattingly (Practice Swing, bat at waist)	1.00	.50	.10
☐ 11 Don Mattingly (Preparing to field ball)	1.00	.50	.10
☐ 12 Don Mattingly (Kneeling)	1.00	.50	.10
☐ 13 Promo Card	1.00	.50	.10

1983 Conlon Marketcom

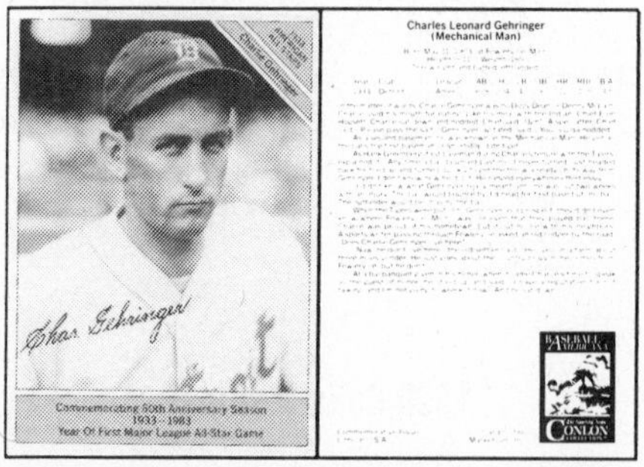

This set of 60 Charles Martin Conlon photo cards was produced by Marketcom in conjunction with The Sporting News. The cards are large size, approximately 4 1/2" by 6 1/8" and are in a sepia tone. The players selected for the set are members of the 1933 American and National League All-Star teams as well as Negro League All-Stars. These cards are numbered at the bootom of each reverse. The set numbering is American League (1-24), National League (25-48), and Negro League (49-60). In the upper right corner of each card's obverse is printed "1933 American (National or Negro League as appropriate) All Stars." Each obverse also features a facsimile autograph of the player pictured.

	MINT	EXC	G-VG
COMPLETE SET (60)	18.00	8.00	1.60
COMMON PLAYER (1-24)	.20	.10	.02
COMMON PLAYER (25-48)	.20	.10	.02
COMMON PLAYER (49-60)	.30	.15	.03
☐ 1 James Emory Foxx	.45	.15	.03
☐ 2 Heinie Manush	.20	.10	.02
☐ 3 Lou Gehrig	.80	.40	.08
☐ 4 Al Simmons	.20	.10	.02
☐ 5 Charlie Gehringer	.30	.15	.03
☐ 6 Luke Appling	.30	.15	.03
☐ 7 Mickey Cochrane	.35	.17	.03
☐ 8 Joe Kuhel	.20	.10	.02
☐ 9 Bill Dickey	.35	.17	.03
☐ 10 Pinky Higgins	.20	.10	.02
☐ 11 Roy Johnson	.20	.10	.02
☐ 12 Ben Chapman	.20	.10	.02
☐ 13 Urban Hodapp	.20	.10	.02
☐ 14 Joe Cronin	.30	.15	.03
☐ 15 Evar Swanson	.20	.10	.02
☐ 16 Earl Averill	.20	.10	.02
☐ 17 Babe Ruth	1.25	.60	.12
☐ 18 Tony Lazzeri	.25	.12	.02
☐ 19 Alvin Crowder	.20	.10	.02
☐ 20 Lefty Grove	.35	.17	.03
☐ 21 Earl Whitehill	.20	.10	.02
☐ 22 Lefty Gomez	.30	.15	.03
☐ 23 Mel Harder	.20	.10	.02
☐ 24 Tommy Bridges	.20	.10	.02
☐ 25 Chuck Klein	.30	.15	.03
☐ 26 Spud Davis	.20	.10	.02
☐ 27 Riggs Stephenson	.20	.10	.02
☐ 28 Tony Piet	.20	.10	.02
☐ 29 Bill Terry	.30	.15	.03
☐ 30 Wes Schulmerich	.20	.10	.02
☐ 31 Pepper Martin	.20	.10	.02
☐ 32 Arky Vaughan	.25	.12	.02
☐ 33 Wally Berger	.20	.10	.02
☐ 34 Ripper Collins	.20	.10	.02
☐ 35 Fred Lindstrom	.20	.10	.02
☐ 36 Chick Fullis	.20	.10	.02
☐ 37 Paul Waner	.25	.12	.02
☐ 38 Johnny Frederick	.20	.10	.02
☐ 39 Joe Medwick	.25	.12	.02
☐ 40 Pie Traynor	.25	.12	.02
☐ 41 Frankie Frisch	.25	.12	.02
☐ 42 Chick Hafey	.20	.10	.02
☐ 43 Carl Hubbell	.30	.15	.03
☐ 44 Guy Bush	.20	.10	.02
☐ 45 Dizzy Dean	.40	.20	.04
☐ 46 Hal Schumacher	.20	.10	.02
☐ 47 Larry French	.20	.10	.02
☐ 48 Lon Warneke	.20	.10	.02
☐ 49 Cool Papa Bell	.50	.25	.05
☐ 50 Oscar Charleston	.50	.25	.05
☐ 51 Josh Gibson	.60	.30	.06
☐ 52 Satch Paige	.60	.30	.06
☐ 53 Dave Malarcher	.30	.15	.03
☐ 54 John Henry Lloyd	.50	.25	.05
☐ 55 Rube Foster	.50	.25	.05
☐ 56 Buck Leonard	.50	.25	.05
☐ 57 Smoky Joe Williams	.30	.15	.03
☐ 58 Willie Wells	.30	.15	.03
☐ 59 Judy Johnson	.50	.25	.05
☐ 60 Martin DiHigo	.50	.25	.05

1986 Conlon Series 1

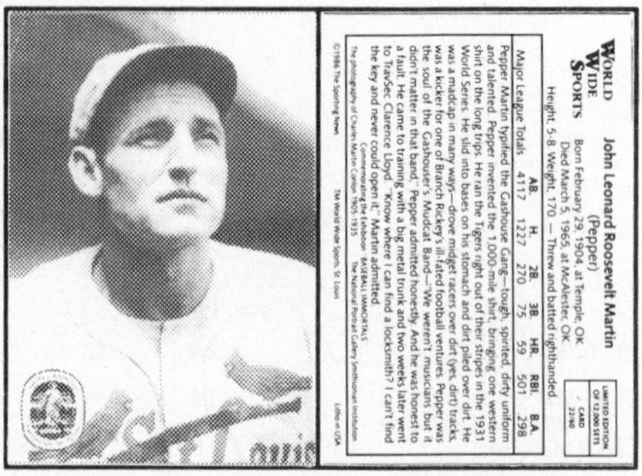

This 60-card set was produced from the black and white photos in the Charles Martin Conlon collection. Each set comes with a special card which contains the number of that set out of the 12,000 sets which were produced. The cards measure 2 1/2" by 3 1/2" and are printed in sepia tones. The cards are individually numbered on the back.

	MINT	EXC	G-VG
COMPLETE SET (60)	12.00	6.00	1.20
COMMON PLAYER (1-60)	.20	.10	.02
□ 1 Henry Louis Gehrig	1.00	.40	.08
□ 2 Tyrus Raymond Cobb	.80	.40	.08
□ 3 Grover C. Alexander	.30	.15	.03
□ 4 Walter Perry Johnson	.50	.25	.05
□ 5 William Joseph Klem	.40	.20	.04
□ 6 Tyrus Raymond Cobb	.80	.40	.08
□ 7 Gordon S. Cochrane	.30	.15	.03
□ 8 Paul Glee Waner	.20	.10	.02
□ 9 Joseph Edward Cronin	.20	.10	.02
□ 10 Jay Hanna Dean	.50	.25	.05
□ 11 Leo Ernest Durocher	.30	.15	.03
□ 12 James Emory Foxx	.30	.15	.03
□ 13 George Herman Ruth	1.25	.60	.12
□ 14 Miguel Angel Gonzalez Frank Francis Frisch Clyde Ellsworth Wares	.20	.10	.02
□ 15 Carl Owen Hubbell	.30	.15	.03
□ 16 Miller James Huggins	.20	.10	.02
□ 17 Henry Louis Gehrig	.80	.40	.08
□ 18 Connie McGillicuddy	.30	.15	.03
□ 19 Henry Emmett Manush	.20	.10	.02
□ 20 George Herman Ruth	1.25	.60	.12
□ 22 John L.R. Martin	.20	.10	.02
□ 23 Christopher Mathewson	.50	.25	.05
□ 24 Tyrus Raymond Cobb	.80	.40	.08
□ 25 Stanley R. Harris	.20	.10	.02
□ 26 Waite Charles Hoyt	.20	.10	.02
□ 27 Richard W. Marquard	.20	.10	.02
□ 28 Joseph V. McCarthy	.20	.10	.02
□ 29 John Joseph McGraw	.20	.10	.02
□ 30 Tristram Speaker	.30	.15	.03
□ 31 William Harold Terry	.30	.15	.03
□ 32 Christopher Mathewson	.50	.25	.05
□ 33 Charles D. Stengel	.50	.25	.05
□ 34 Robert William Meusel	.20	.10	.02
□ 35 George Edward Waddell	.20	.10	.02
□ 36 Melvin Thomas Ott	.30	.15	.03
□ 37 Roger T. Peckinpaugh	.20	.10	.02
□ 38 Harold Joseph Traynor	.20	.10	.02
□ 39 Charles Albert Bender	.20	.10	.02
□ 40 John Wesley Coombs	.20	.10	.02
□ 41 Tyrus Raymond Cobb	.80	.40	.08
□ 42 Harry Edwin Heilmann	.20	.10	.02
□ 43 Charles L. Gehringer	.30	.15	.03
□ 44 Rogers Hornsby	.50	.25	.05
□ 45 Vernon Gomez	.40	.20	.04
□ 46 Christopher Mathewson	.50	.25	.05
□ 47 Robert Moses Grove	.45	.22	.04
□ 48 George Herman Ruth	1.25	.60	.12
□ 49 Frederick C. Merkle	.20	.10	.02
□ 50 George Herman Ruth	1.25	.60	.12
□ 51 Herbert J. Pennock	.20	.10	.02
□ 52 Henry Louis Gehrig	.80	.40	.08
□ 53 Fred Clifford Clarke	.20	.10	.02
□ 54 George Herman Ruth	1.25	.60	.12
□ 55 John Peter Wagner	.50	.25	.05
□ 56 Lewis Robert Wilson	.30	.15	.03
□ 57 Henry Louis Gehrig	.80	.40	.08
□ 58 Lloyd James Waner	.20	.10	.02
□ 59 Charles Martin Conlon	.20	.10	.02
□ 60 Conlon and Margie	.20	.10	.02
□ xx Set Number Card (unnumbered)	.20	.10	.02

1987 Conlon Series 2

The second series of 60 Charles Martin Conlon photo cards was produced by World Wide Sports in conjunction with The Sporting News. The cards are standard size, 2 1/2" by 3 1/2" and are in a sepia tone. Supposedly 12,000 sets were produced. The photos were selected and background information written by Paul MacFarlane of The Sporting News. The cards are individually numbered on the back.

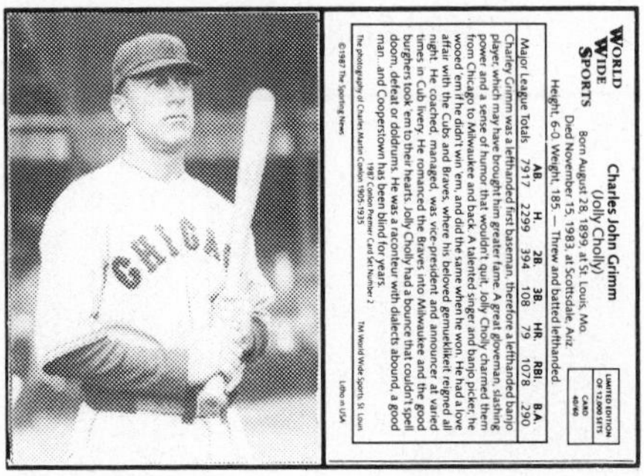

	MINT	EXC	G-VG
COMPLETE SET (60)	10.00	5.00	1.00
COMMON PLAYER (1-60)	.20	.10	.02
□ 1 Henry Gehrig	1.00	.40	.08
□ 2 Vernon Gomez	.40	.20	.04
□ 3 Christopher Mathewson	.50	.25	.05
□ 4 Grover Alexander	.30	.15	.03
□ 5 Tyrus Cobb	.80	.40	.08
□ 6 Walter Johnson	.50	.25	.05
□ 7 Charles Adams	.20	.10	.02
□ 8 Nicholas Altrock	.20	.10	.02
□ 9 Al Schacht	.20	.10	.02
□ 10 Hugh Critz	.20	.10	.02
□ 11 Henry Cullop	.20	.10	.02
□ 12 Jacob Daubert	.20	.10	.02
□ 13 William Donovan	.20	.10	.02
□ 14 Charles Hafey	.20	.10	.02
□ 15 William Hallahan	.20	.10	.02
□ 16 Fred Haney	.20	.10	.02
□ 17 Charles Hartnett	.20	.10	.02
□ 18 Walter Henline	.20	.10	.02
□ 19 Edwin Rommel	.20	.10	.02
□ 20 Ralph Pinelli	.20	.10	.02
□ 21 Robert Meusel	.20	.10	.02
□ 22 Emil Meusel	.20	.10	.02
□ 23 Smead Jolley	.20	.10	.02
□ 24 Isaac Boone	.20	.10	.02
□ 25 Earl Webb	.20	.10	.02
□ 26 Charles Comiskey	.30	.15	.03
□ 27 Edward Collins	.30	.15	.03
□ 28 George Weaver	.30	.15	.03
□ 29 Edward Cicotte	.30	.15	.03
□ 30 Samuel Crawford	.20	.10	.02
□ 31 Charles Dressen	.20	.10	.02
□ 32 Arthur Fletcher	.20	.10	.02
□ 33 Hugh Duffy	.30	.15	.03
□ 34 Ira Flagstead	.20	.10	.02
□ 35 Harry Hooper	.20	.10	.02
□ 36 George Lewis	.20	.10	.02
□ 37 James Dykes	.20	.10	.02
□ 38 Leon Goslin	.20	.10	.02
□ 39 Henry Gowdy	.20	.10	.02
□ 40 Charles Grimm	.20	.10	.02
□ 41 Mark Koenig	.20	.10	.02
□ 42 James Hogan	.20	.10	.02
□ 43 William Jacobson	.20	.10	.02
□ 44 Fielder Jones	.20	.10	.02
□ 45 George Kelly	.20	.10	.02
□ 46 Adolpho Luque	.20	.10	.02
□ 47 Walter Maranville	.20	.10	.02
□ 48 Carl Mays	.20	.10	.02
□ 49 Edward Plank	.30	.15	.03
□ 50 Hubert Pruett	.20	.10	.02
□ 51 John Quinn	.20	.10	.02
□ 52 Charles Rhem	.20	.10	.02
□ 53 Amos Rusie	.30	.15	.03
□ 54 Edd Roush	.20	.10	.02
□ 55 Raymond Schalk	.30	.15	.03
□ 56 Ernest Shore	.20	.10	.02
□ 57 Joe Wood	.20	.10	.02
□ 58 George Sisler	.30	.15	.03
□ 59 James Thorpe	1.25	.60	.12
□ 60 Earl Whitehill	.20	.10	.02

1988 Conlon Series 3

This third series of 30 Charles Martin Conlon photo cards was produced by World Wide Sports in conjunction with The Sporting News. The cards are standard size, 2 1/2" by 3 1/2" and are in a sepia tone. The photos were selected and background information written by Paul MacFarlane of The Sporting News. These cards are unnumbered and hence are listed below in alphabetical order. Series 3 is indicated in the lower right corner of each card's reverse. A black and white logo for the "Baseball Immortals" and The Conlon Collection is over-printed in the lower left corner of each obverse.

	MINT	EXC	G-VG
COMPLETE SET (30)	5.00	2.50	.50
COMMON PLAYER (1-30)	.20	.10	.02
☐ 1 Ace Adams	.20	.10	.02
☐ 2 Grover C. Alexander	.25	.12	.02
☐ 3 Elden Auker	.20	.10	.02
☐ 4 Jack Barry	.20	.10	.02
☐ 5 Wally Berger	.20	.10	.02
☐ 6 Ben Chapman	.20	.10	.02
☐ 7 Mickey Cochrane	.25	.12	.02
☐ 8 Frankie Crosetti	.20	.10	.02
☐ 9 Paul Dean	.20	.10	.02
☐ 10 Leo Durocher	.25	.12	.02
☐ 11 Wes Ferrell	.20	.10	.02
☐ 12 Hank Gowdy	.20	.10	.02
☐ 13 Andy High	.20	.10	.02
☐ 14 Rogers Hornsby	.30	.15	.03
☐ 15 Carl Hubbell	.25	.12	.02
☐ 16 Joe Judge	.20	.10	.02
☐ 17 Tony Lazzeri	.20	.10	.02
☐ 18 Pepper Martin	.20	.10	.02
☐ 19 Lee Meadows	.20	.10	.02
☐ 20 Johnny Murphy	.20	.10	.02
☐ 21 Steve O'Neil	.20	.10	.02
☐ 22 Ed Plank	.25	.12	.02
☐ 23 Jack"Picus" Quinn	.20	.10	.02
☐ 24 Charley Root	.20	.10	.02
☐ 25 Babe Ruth	1.25	.60	.12
☐ 26 Fred Snodgrass	.20	.10	.02
☐ 27 Tris Speaker	.30	.15	.03
☐ 28 Bill Terry	.25	.12	.02
☐ 29 Jeff Tesreau	.20	.10	.02
☐ 30 George Toporcer	.20	.10	.02

1988 Conlon Series 4

This fourth series of 30 Charles Martin Conlon photo cards was produced by World Wide Sports in conjunction with The Sporting News. The cards are standard size, 2 1/2" by 3 1/2" and are in a sepia tone. The photos were selected and background information written by Paul MacFarlane of The Sporting News. These cards are unnumbered and hence are listed below in alphabetical order. Series 4 is indicated in the lower right corner of each card's reverse. A black and white logo for the "Baseball Immortals" and The Conlon Collection is over-printed in the lower left corner of each obverse.

	MINT	EXC	G-VG
COMPLETE SET (30)	5.00	2.50	.50
COMMON PLAYER (1-30)	.20	.10	.02
☐ 1 Dale Alexander	.20	.10	.02
☐ 2 Morris Badgro	.20	.10	.02
☐ 3 Dick Bartell	.20	.10	.02
☐ 4 Max Bishop	.20	.10	.02
☐ 5 Hal Chase	.20	.10	.02
☐ 6 Ty Cobb	.75	.35	.07
☐ 7 Nick Cullop	.20	.10	.02
☐ 8 Dizzy Dean	.40	.20	.04
☐ 9 Charlie Dressen	.20	.10	.02
☐ 10 Jimmy Dykes	.20	.10	.02
☐ 11 Art Fletcher	.20	.10	.02
☐ 12 Charlie Grimm	.20	.10	.02
☐ 13 Lefty Grove	.30	.15	.03
☐ 14 Baby Doll Jacobson	.20	.10	.02
☐ 15 Bill Klem	.40	.20	.04
☐ 16 Mark Koenig	.20	.10	.02
☐ 17 Duffy Lewis	.20	.10	.02
☐ 18 Carl Mays	.20	.10	.02
☐ 19 Fred Merkle	.20	.10	.02
☐ 20 Greasy Neale	.20	.10	.02
☐ 21 Mel Ott	.30	.15	.03
☐ 22 Babe Pinelli	.20	.10	.02
☐ 23 Flint Rhem	.20	.10	.02
☐ 24 Slim Sallee (misspelled Salee on card back)	.20	.10	.02
☐ 25 Al Simmons	.20	.10	.02
☐ 26 George Sisler	.25	.12	.02
☐ 27 Riggs Stephenson	.20	.10	.02
☐ 28 Jim Thorpe	1.00	.50	.10
☐ 29 Bill Wambsganss	.20	.10	.02
☐ 30 Cy Young	.35	.17	.03

1988 Conlon Series 5

This fifth series of 30 Charles Martin Conlon photo cards was produced by World Wide Sports in conjunction with The

Sporting News. The cards are standard size, 2 1/2" by 3 1/2" and are in a sepia tone. The photos were selected and background information written by Paul MacFarlane of The Sporting News. These cards are unnumbered and hence are listed below in alphabetical order. Series 5 is indicated in the lower right corner of each card's reverse. A black and white logo for the "Baseball Immortals" and The Conlon Collection is over-printed in the lower left corner of each obverse.

	MINT	EXC	G-VG
COMPLETE SET (30)	5.00	2.50	.50
COMMON PLAYER (1-30)	.20	.10	.02
☐ 1 Nick Altrock	.20	.10	.02
☐ 2 Del Baker	.20	.10	.02
☐ 3 Moe Berg	.25	.12	.02
☐ 4 Zeke Bonura	.20	.10	.02
☐ 5 Eddie Collins	.25	.12	.02
☐ 6 Hughie Critz	.20	.10	.02
☐ 7 George Dauss	.20	.10	.02
☐ 8 Joe Dugan	.20	.10	.02
☐ 9 Howard Ehmke	.20	.10	.02
☐ 10 James Emory Foxx	.35	.17	.03
☐ 11 Frankie Frisch	.25	.12	.02
☐ 12 Lou Gehrig	.75	.35	.07
☐ 13 Charlie Gehringer	.25	.12	.02
☐ 14 Kid Gleason	.20	.10	.02
☐ 15 Lefty Gomez	.25	.12	.02
☐ 16 Babe Herman	.20	.10	.02
☐ 17 Bill James	.20	.10	.02
☐ 18 Joe Kuhel	.20	.10	.02
☐ 19 Dolf Luque	.20	.10	.02
☐ 20 John McGraw	.25	.12	.02
☐ 21 Stuffy McInnis	.20	.10	.02
☐ 22 Bob Meusel	.20	.10	.02
☐ 23 Lefty O'Doul	.20	.10	.02
☐ 24 Hub Pruett	.20	.10	.02
☐ 25 Paul Richards	.20	.10	.02
☐ 26 Bob Shawkey	.20	.10	.02
☐ 27 Gabby Street	.20	.10	.02
☐ 28 Johnny Tobin	.20	.10	.02
☐ 29 Rube Waddell	.25	.12	.02
☐ 30 Billy Werber	.20	.10	.02

1988 Conlon American All-Stars

This set of 24 Charles Martin Conlon photo cards was produced by World Wide Sports in conjunction with The Sporting News. The cards are standard size, 2 1/2" by 3 1/2" and are in a sepia tone. The photos (members of the 1933 American League All-Star team) were selected and background information written by Paul MacFarlane of The Sporting News. These cards are unnumbered and hence are listed below in alphabetical order. American League is indicated in the lower right corner of each card's reverse. In the upper right corner of each card's obverse is printed "1933 American All Stars."

	MINT	EXC	G-VG
COMPLETE SET (24)	4.50	2.25	.45
COMMON PLAYER (1-24)	.20	.10	.02
☐ 1 Luke Appling	.30	.15	.03
☐ 2 Earl Averill	.20	.10	.02
☐ 3 Tommy Bridges	.20	.10	.02
☐ 4 Ben Chapman	.20	.10	.02
☐ 5 Mickey Cochrane	.30	.15	.03
☐ 6 Joe Cronin	.25	.12	.02
☐ 7 Alvin Crowder	.20	.10	.02
☐ 8 Bill Dickey	.30	.15	.03
☐ 9 James Emory Foxx	.30	.15	.03
☐ 10 Lou Gehrig	.75	.35	.07
☐ 11 Charlie Gehringer	.25	.12	.02
☐ 12 Lefty Gomez	.25	.12	.02
☐ 13 Lefty Grove	.30	.15	.03
☐ 14 Mel Harder	.20	.10	.02
☐ 15 Pinky Higgins	.20	.10	.02
☐ 16 Urban Hodapp	.20	.10	.02
☐ 17 Roy Johnson	.20	.10	.02
☐ 18 Joe Kuhel	.20	.10	.02
☐ 19 Tony Lazzeri	.25	.12	.02
☐ 20 Heinie Manush	.20	.10	.02
☐ 21 Babe Ruth	1.00	.50	.10
☐ 22 Al Simmons	.20	.10	.02
☐ 23 Evar Swanson	.20	.10	.02
☐ 24 Earl Whitehill	.20	.10	.02

1988 Conlon National All-Stars

This set of 24 Charles Martin Conlon photo cards was produced by World Wide Sports in conjunction with The Sporting News. The cards are standard size, 2 1/2" by 3 1/2" and are in a sepia tone. The photos (members of the 1933 National League All-Star team) were selected and background information written by Paul MacFarlane of The Sporting News. These cards are unnumbered and hence are listed below in alphabetical order. American League is indicated in the lower right corner of each card's reverse. In the upper right corner of each card's obverse is printed "1933 National All Stars."

	MINT	EXC	G-VG
COMPLETE SET (24)	4.50	2.25	.45
COMMON PLAYER (1-24)	.20	.10	.02
☐ 1 Wally Berger	.20	.10	.02
☐ 2 Guy Bush	.20	.10	.02
☐ 3 Ripper Collins	.20	.10	.02
☐ 4 Spud Davis	.20	.10	.02
☐ 5 Dizzy Dean	.40	.20	.04
☐ 6 Johnny Frederick	.20	.10	.02
☐ 7 Larry French	.20	.10	.02
☐ 8 Frankie Frisch	.25	.12	.02
☐ 9 Chick Fullis	.20	.10	.02
☐ 10 Chick Hafey	.20	.10	.02
☐ 11 Carl Hubbell	.30	.15	.03
☐ 12 Chuck Klein	.25	.12	.02
☐ 13 Fred Lindstrom	.20	.10	.02
☐ 14 Pepper Martin	.20	.10	.02
☐ 15 Joe Medwick	.25	.12	.02
☐ 16 Tony Piet	.20	.10	.02
☐ 17 Wes Schulmerich	.20	.10	.02
☐ 18 Hal Schumacher	.20	.10	.02
☐ 19 Riggs Stephenson	.20	.10	.02
☐ 20 Bill Terry	.30	.15	.03
☐ 21 Pie Traynor	.25	.12	.02
☐ 22 Arky Vaughan	.25	.12	.02
☐ 23 Paul Waner	.25	.12	.02
☐ 24 Lon Warneke	.20	.10	.02

1988 Conlon Negro All-Stars

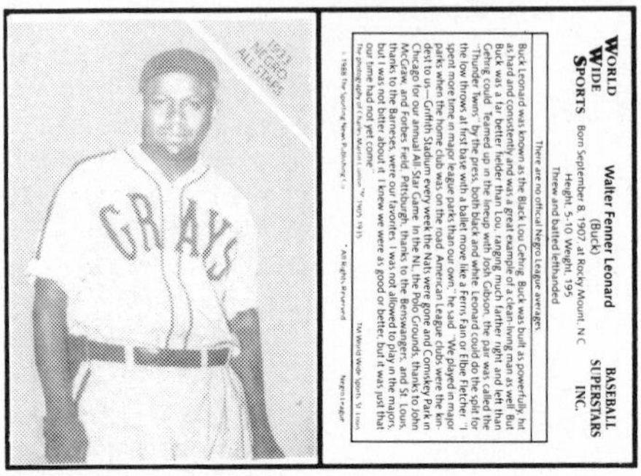

This set of 12 Charles Martin Conlon photo cards was produced by World Wide Sports in conjunction with The Sporting News. The cards are standard size, 2 1/2" by 3 1/2" and are in a sepia tone. The photos (Negro League All Stars from 1933) were selected and background information written by Paul MacFarlane of The Sporting News. These cards are unnumbered and hence are listed below in alphabetical order. Negro League is indicated in the lower right corner of each card's reverse. In the upper right corner of each card's obverse is printed "1933 Negro All Stars." The photo quality on some of the cards is very poor suggesting that the original photo or negative may have been enlarged to an excessive degree.

	MINT	EXC	G-VG
COMPLETE SET (12)	3.50	1.75	.35
COMMON PLAYER (1-12)	.30	.15	.03
☐ 1 Cool Papa Bell	.50	.25	.05
☐ 2 Oscar Charleston	.50	.25	.05
☐ 3 Martin DiHigo	.50	.25	.05
☐ 4 Rube Foster	.50	.25	.05
☐ 5 Josh Gibson	.60	.30	.06
☐ 6 Judy Johnson	.50	.25	.05
☐ 7 Buck Leonard	.50	.25	.05
☐ 8 John Henry Lloyd	.50	.25	.05
☐ 9 Dave Malarcher	.30	.15	.03
☐ 10 Satch Paige	.60	.30	.06
☐ 11 Willie Wells	.30	.15	.03
☐ 12 Smoky Joe Williams	.30	.15	.03

1988 Conlon Hardee's/Coke

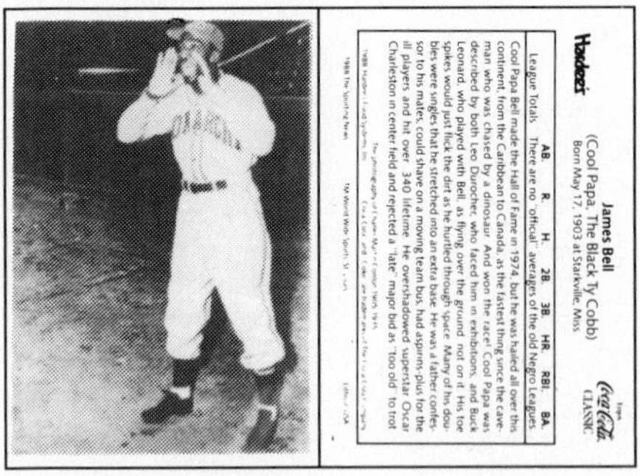

This six-card set was issued in 18 central Indiana Hardee's restaurants over a six-week period, a different card per purchase per week. The set features the vintage photography of Charles Conlon. The cards are sepia tone and are standard size, 2 1/2" by 3 1/2". The card backs contain biographical information, Hardee's logo, and a Coca Cola Classic logo. The cards are also copyrighted by The Sporting News.

	MINT	EXC	G-VG
COMPLETE SET (6)	4.00	2.00	.40
COMMON PLAYER (1-6)	.50	.25	.05
☐ 1 James Bell (Cool Papa)	.50	.25	.05
☐ 2 Tyrus Raymond Cobb (Georgia Peach)	1.50	.75	.15
☐ 3 Henry Louis Gehrig (Iron Horse)	1.50	.75	.15
☐ 4 Cornelius McGillicuddy (Connie Mack)	.50	.25	.05
☐ 5 Charles Dillon Stengel (Casey)	.75	.35	.07
☐ 6 George Edward Waddell (Rube)	.50	.25	.05

1991 Conlon Sporting News

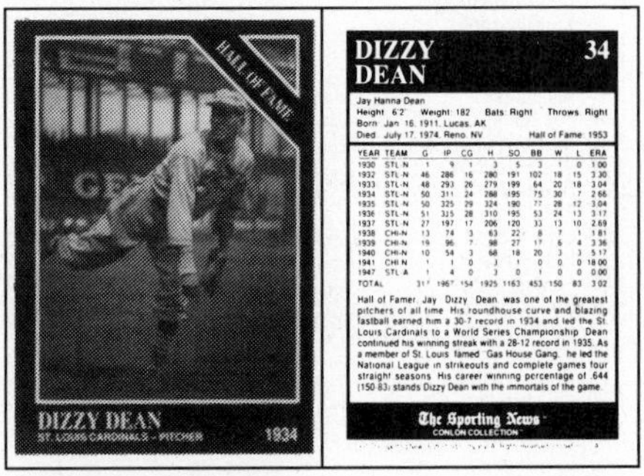

This 330-card set issued in black and white again featured the photography of Charles Conlon. The set was produced by MegaCards in conjunction with The Sporting News. The set features standard size, 2 1/2" by 3 1/2", cards with black and white borders surrounded by black borders. While the back contains pertinent information relevant to the front of the cards whether it is career statistics or all-time leaders format or the special cards commemorating the great teams of the first part of the twentieth century.

	MINT	EXC	G-VG
COMPLETE SET (330)	30.00	15.00	3.00
COMMON PLAYER (1-330)	.10	.05	.01
☐ 1 HOF: Hornsby	.30	.15	.03
☐ 2 HOF: Foxx	.30	.15	.03
☐ 3 HOF: Dean	.30	.15	.03
☐ 4 HOF: Maranville	.20	.10	.02
☐ 5 HOF: P.Waner	.20	.10	.02
☐ 6 HOF: L.Waner	.20	.10	.02
☐ 7 HOF: Ott	.20	.10	.02
☐ 8 HOF: Wagner	.30	.15	.03
☐ 9 HOF: Johnson	.30	.15	.03
☐ 10 HOF: Hubbell	.20	.10	.02
☐ 11 HOF: Frisch	.20	.10	.02
☐ 12 HOF: Cuyler	.20	.10	.02
☐ 13 HOF: Ruffing	.20	.10	.02
☐ 14 HOF: Greenberg	.30	.15	.03
☐ 15 HOF: Evers	.20	.10	.02
☐ 16 HOF: Jennings	.20	.10	.02
☐ 17 HOF: Bancroft	.20	.10	.02
☐ 18 HOF: Medwick	.20	.10	.02
☐ 19 HOF: Lyons	.20	.10	.02
☐ 20 HOF: Bender	.20	.10	.02
☐ 21 HOF: Collins	.20	.10	.02
☐ 22 HOF: Bottomley	.20	.10	.02
☐ 23 HOF: Grove	.30	.15	.03
☐ 24 HOF: Carey	.20	.10	.02
☐ 25 HOF: Grimes	.20	.10	.02
☐ 26 HOF: Youngs	.20	.10	.02

☐ 27 HOF: Lombardi	.20	.10	.02
☐ 28 HOF: McCarthy	.20	.10	.02
☐ 29 HOF: Wilson	.30	.15	.03
☐ 30 HOF: Klein	.20	.10	.02
☐ 31 HOF: Averill	.20	.10	.02
☐ 32 HOF: Alexander	.20	.10	.02
☐ 33 HOF: Hafey	.20	.10	.02
☐ 34 HOF: McKechnie	.20	.10	.02
☐ 35 HOF: Feller	.30	.15	.03
☐ 36 HOF: Traynor	.20	.10	.02
☐ 37 HOF: Stengel	.30	.15	.03
☐ 38 HOF: Vaughan	.20	.10	.02
☐ 39 HOF: Rixey	.20	.10	.02
☐ 40 HOF: Sewell	.20	.10	.02
☐ 41 HOF: Faber	.20	.10	.02
☐ 42 HOF: Jackson	.20	.10	.02
☐ 43 HOF: Haines	.20	.10	.02
☐ 44 HOF: Speaker	.20	.10	.02
☐ 45 HOF: Mack	.20	.10	.02
☐ 46 HOF: Mack	.20	.10	.02
☐ 47 HOF: Mack	.20	.10	.02
☐ 48 HOF: Schalk	.20	.10	.02
☐ 49 HOF: Simmons	.20	.10	.02
☐ 50 HOF: Cronin	.20	.10	.02
☐ 51 HOF: Cochrane	.20	.10	.02
☐ 52 HOF: Heilmann	.20	.10	.02
☐ 53 HOF: Mize	.20	.10	.02
☐ 54 HOF: Rice	.20	.10	.02
☐ 55 HOF: Roush	.20	.10	.02
☐ 56 HOF: Slaughter	.20	.10	.02
☐ 57 HOF: Mathewson	.30	.15	.03
☐ 58 HOF: Lindstrom	.20	.10	.02
☐ 59 HOF: Hartnett	.20	.10	.02
☐ 60 HOF: Kelly	.20	.10	.02
☐ 61 HOF: Harris	.20	.10	.02
☐ 62 HOF: Goslin	.20	.10	.02
☐ 63 HOF: Manush	.20	.10	.02
☐ 64 HOF: Terry	.20	.10	.02
☐ 65 HOF: McGraw	.20	.10	.02
☐ 66 HOF: Sisler	.20	.10	.02
☐ 67 HOF: Gomez	.20	.10	.02
☐ 68 Joe Judge	.10	.05	.01
☐ 69 Tommy Thevenow	.10	.05	.01
☐ 70 Charlie Gelbert	.10	.05	.01
☐ 71 Jackie Hayes	.10	.05	.01
☐ 72 Bob Fothergill	.10	.05	.01
☐ 73 Adam Comorosky	.10	.05	.01
☐ 74 Earl Smith	.10	.05	.01
☐ 75 Sam Gray	.10	.05	.01
☐ 76 Pete Appleton	.10	.05	.01
☐ 77 Gene Moore	.10	.05	.01
☐ 78 Art Jorgens	.10	.05	.01
☐ 79 Bill Knickerbocker	.10	.05	.01
☐ 80 Carl Reynolds	.10	.05	.01
☐ 81 Ski Melillo	.10	.05	.01
☐ 82 Johnny Burnett	.10	.05	.01
☐ 83 Jake Powell	.10	.05	.01
☐ 84 Johnny Murphy	.10	.05	.01
☐ 85 Roy Parmelee	.10	.05	.01
☐ 86 Jimmy Ripple	.10	.05	.01
☐ 87 Gee Walker	.10	.05	.01
☐ 88 George Earnshaw	.10	.05	.01
☐ 89 Billy Southworth	.10	.05	.01
☐ 90 Wally Moses	.10	.05	.01
☐ 91 Rube Walberg	.10	.05	.01
☐ 92 Jimmy Dykes	.10	.05	.01
☐ 93 Charlie Root	.10	.05	.01
☐ 94 Johnny Cooney	.10	.05	.01
☐ 95 Charlie Grimm	.10	.05	.01
☐ 96 Bob Johnson	.10	.05	.01
☐ 97 Jack Scott	.10	.05	.01
☐ 98 Rip Radcliff	.10	.05	.01
☐ 99 Fritz Ostermueller	.10	.05	.01
☐ 100 '27NY: Wera	.10	.05	.01
☐ 101 '27NY: Huggins	.20	.10	.02
☐ 102 '27NY: Morehart	.10	.05	.01
☐ 103 '27NY: Bengough	.10	.05	.01
☐ 104 '27NY: Ruether	.10	.05	.01
☐ 105 '27NY: Combs	.20	.10	.02
☐ 106 '27NY: Thomas	.10	.05	.01
☐ 107 '27NY: Paschal	.10	.05	.01
☐ 108 '27NY: Durst	.10	.05	.01
☐ 109 '27NY: Moore	.10	.05	.01
☐ 110 '27NY: Ruth	.50	.25	.05
☐ 111 '27NY: Gehrig	.40	.20	.04
☐ 112 '27NY: Dugan	.10	.05	.01
☐ 113 '27NY: Lazzeri	.20	.10	.02
☐ 114 '27NY: Shocker	.10	.05	.01
☐ 115 '27NY: Hoyt	.20	.10	.02
☐ 116 '27NY: O'Leary	.10	.05	.01
☐ 117 '27NY: Fletcher	.10	.05	.01
☐ 118 '27NY: Collins	.10	.05	.01
☐ 119 '27NY: Giard	.10	.05	.01
☐ 120 '27NY: Pennock	.20	.10	.02
☐ 121 '27NY: Gazella	.10	.05	.01
☐ 122 '27NY: Meusel	.10	.05	.01
☐ 123 '27NY: Pipgras	.10	.05	.01
☐ 124 '27NY: Grabowski	.10	.05	.01
☐ 125 '27NY: Koenig	.10	.05	.01
☐ 126 Stan Hack	.10	.05	.01
☐ 127 Earl Whitehill	.10	.05	.01
☐ 128 Bill Lee	.10	.05	.01
☐ 129 Gus Mancuso	.10	.05	.01
☐ 130 Ray Blades	.10	.05	.01
☐ 131 Jack Burns	.10	.05	.01
☐ 132 Clint Brown	.10	.05	.01
☐ 133 Bill Dietrich	.10	.05	.01
☐ 134 Cy Blanton	.10	.05	.01
☐ 135 '16Champs: Hooper	.20	.10	.02
☐ 136 '16Champs: Shorten	.10	.05	.01
☐ 137 '16Champs: Walker	.10	.05	.01
☐ 138 '16Champs: Foster	.10	.05	.01
☐ 139 '16Champs: Barry	.10	.05	.01
☐ 140 '16Champs: Jones	.10	.05	.01
☐ 141 '16Champs: Shore	.10	.05	.01
☐ 142 '16Champs: Leonard	.10	.05	.01
☐ 143 '16Champs: Pennock	.20	.10	.02
☐ 144 '16Champs: Janvrin	.10	.05	.01
☐ 145 '16Champs: Ruth	.60	.30	.06
☐ 146 '16Champs: Lewis	.10	.05	.01
☐ 147 '16Champs: Gardner	.10	.05	.01
☐ 148 '16Champs: Hoblitzel	.10	.05	.01
☐ 149 '16Champs: Scott	.10	.05	.01
☐ 150 '16Champs: Mays	.10	.05	.01
☐ 151 '16LL: Niehoff	.10	.05	.01
☐ 152 '16LL: Shotton	.10	.05	.01
☐ 153 '16LL: Ames	.10	.05	.01
☐ 154 '16LL: Williams	.10	.05	.01
☐ 155 '16LL: Hinchman	.10	.05	.01
☐ 156 '16LL: Shawkey	.10	.05	.01
☐ 157 '16LL: Pipp	.10	.05	.01
☐ 158 '16LL: Geo.J.Burns	.10	.05	.01
☐ 159 '16LL: Veach	.10	.05	.01
☐ 160 '16LL: Chase	.10	.05	.01
☐ 161 '16LL: Hughes	.10	.05	.01
☐ 162 '16LL: Pratt	.10	.05	.01
☐ 163 '16LL: Groh	.10	.05	.01
☐ 164 '16LL: Wheat	.20	.10	.02
☐ 165 Story: O'Doul	.10	.05	.01
☐ 166 Story: Kamm	.10	.05	.01
☐ 167 Story: P.Waner	.20	.10	.02
☐ 168 Story: Snodgrass	.10	.05	.01
☐ 169 Story: Herman	.20	.10	.02
☐ 170 Story: Bridwell	.10	.05	.01
☐ 171 Story: Meyers	.10	.05	.01
☐ 172 Story: Lobert	.10	.05	.01
☐ 173 Story: Bressler	.10	.05	.01
☐ 174 Story: Jones	.10	.05	.01
☐ 175 Story: O'Farrell	.10	.05	.01
☐ 176 Story: Toporcer	.10	.05	.01
☐ 177 Story: Earl McNeely	.10	.05	.01
☐ 178 Story: Jack Knott	.10	.05	.01
☐ 179 Heinie Mueller	.10	.05	.01
☐ 180 Tommy Bridges	.10	.05	.01
☐ 181 Lloyd Brown	.10	.05	.01
☐ 182 Larry Benton	.10	.05	.01
☐ 183 Max Bishop	.10	.05	.01
☐ 184 Moe Berg	.20	.10	.02
☐ 185 Cy Perkins	.10	.05	.01
☐ 186 Steve O'Neill	.10	.05	.01
☐ 187 Glenn Myatt	.10	.05	.01
☐ 188 Joe Kuhel	.10	.05	.01
☐ 189 Marty McManus	.10	.05	.01
☐ 190 Red Lucas	.10	.05	.01
☐ 191 Stuffy McInnis	.10	.05	.01
☐ 192 Bing Miller	.10	.05	.01
☐ 193 Luke Sewell	.10	.05	.01
☐ 194 Bill Sherdel	.10	.05	.01
☐ 195 Hal Rhyne	.10	.05	.01
☐ 196 Guy Bush	.10	.05	.01
☐ 197 Pete Fox	.10	.05	.01
☐ 198 Wes Ferrell	.10	.05	.01
☐ 199 Roy Johnson	.10	.05	.01
☐ 200 Tr.Play: Wambsganss	.10	.05	.01
☐ 201 Tr.Play: G.H.Burns	.10	.05	.01
☐ 202 Tr.Play: Mitchell	.10	.05	.01
☐ 203 Tr.Play: Ball	.10	.05	.01
☐ 204 Tr.Play: Neun	.10	.05	.01
☐ 205 Tr.Play: Summa	.10	.05	.01
☐ 206 Tr.Play: Padgett	.10	.05	.01
☐ 207 Tr.Play: Holke	.10	.05	.01
☐ 208 Tr.Play: Wright	.10	.05	.01
☐ 209 Hank Gowdy	.10	.05	.01
☐ 210 Zack Taylor	.10	.05	.01
☐ 211 Ben Cantwell	.10	.05	.01
☐ 212 Frank Demaree	.10	.05	.01
☐ 213 Paul Derringer	.10	.05	.01
☐ 214 Bill Hallahan	.10	.05	.01

☐ 215	Danny MacFayden	.10	.05	.01
☐ 216	Harry Rice	.10	.05	.01
☐ 217	Bob Smith	.10	.05	.01
☐ 218	Riggs Stephenson	.10	.05	.01
☐ 219	Pat Malone	.10	.05	.01
☐ 220	Bennie Tate	.10	.05	.01
☐ 221	Joe Vosmik	.10	.05	.01
☐ 222	George Watkins	.10	.05	.01
☐ 223	Jimmie Wilson	.10	.05	.01
☐ 224	George Uhle	.10	.05	.01
☐ 225	Trivia: Ott	.20	.10	.02
☐ 226	Trivia: Altrock	.10	.05	.01
☐ 227	Trivia: Ruffing	.20	.10	.02
☐ 228	Trivia: Krakauskas	.10	.05	.01
☐ 229	Trivia: Berger	.10	.05	.01
☐ 230	Bobo Newsom	.10	.05	.01
☐ 231	Lon Warneke	.10	.05	.01
☐ 232	Frank Snyder	.10	.05	.01
☐ 233	Myril Hoag	.10	.05	.01
☐ 234	Mel Almada	.10	.05	.01
☐ 235	Ivey Wingo	.10	.05	.01
☐ 236	Jimmy Austin	.10	.05	.01
☐ 237	Zeke Bonura	.10	.05	.01
☐ 238	Russ Wrightstone	.10	.05	.01
☐ 239	Al Todd	.10	.05	.01
☐ 240	Rabbit Warstler	.10	.05	.01
☐ 241	Sammy West	.10	.05	.01
☐ 242	Art Reinhart	.10	.05	.01
☐ 243	Lefty Stewart	.10	.05	.01
☐ 244	Johnny Gooch	.10	.05	.01
☐ 245	Bubbles Hargrave	.10	.05	.01
☐ 246	George Harper	.10	.05	.01
☐ 247	Sarge Connally	.10	.05	.01
☐ 248	Garland Braxton	.10	.05	.01
☐ 249	Wally Schang	.10	.05	.01
☐ 250	ATL: Cobb	.40	.20	.04
☐ 251	ATL: Hornsby	.30	.15	.03
☐ 252	ATL: Marquard	.20	.10	.02
☐ 253	ATL: Hubbell	.20	.10	.02
☐ 254	ATL: Wood	.20	.10	.02
☐ 255	ATL: Grove	.30	.15	.03
☐ 256	ATL: Rowe	.10	.05	.01
☐ 257	ATL: Crowder	.10	.05	.01
☐ 258	ATL: Johnson	.10	.05	.01
☐ 259	ATL: Hafey	.20	.10	.02
☐ 260	ATL: Fitzsimmons	.10	.05	.01
☐ 261	ATL: Webb	.10	.05	.01
☐ 262	ATL: Combs	.20	.10	.02
☐ 263	ATL: Konetchy	.10	.05	.01
☐ 264	ATL: Douthit	.10	.05	.01
☐ 265	ATL: L.Waner	.20	.10	.02
☐ 266	ATL: Cochrane	.20	.10	.02
☐ 267	ATL: Wilson	.20	.10	.02
☐ 268	ATL: Traynor	.20	.10	.02
☐ 269	ATL: Davis	.10	.05	.01
☐ 270	ATL: Manush	.20	.10	.02
☐ 271	ATL: Higgins	.10	.05	.01
☐ 272	ATL: Joss	.20	.10	.02
☐ 273	ATL: Walsh	.20	.10	.02
☐ 274	ATL: Martin	.20	.10	.02
☐ 275	ATL: Sewell	.20	.10	.02
☐ 276	ATL: Leonard	.10	.05	.01
☐ 277	ATL: Cravath	.10	.05	.01
☐ 278	Oral Hildebrand	.10	.05	.01
☐ 279	Ray Kremer	.10	.05	.01
☐ 280	Frankie Pytlak	.10	.05	.01
☐ 281	Sammy Byrd	.10	.05	.01
☐ 282	Curt Davis	.10	.05	.01
☐ 283	Lew Fonseca	.10	.05	.01
☐ 284	Muddy Ruel	.10	.05	.01
☐ 285	Moose Solters	.10	.05	.01
☐ 286	Fred Schulte	.10	.05	.01
☐ 287	Jack Quinn	.10	.05	.01
☐ 288	Pinky Whitney	.10	.05	.01
☐ 289	John Stone	.10	.05	.01
☐ 290	Hughie Critz	.10	.05	.01
☐ 291	Ira Flagstead	.10	.05	.01
☐ 292	George Grantham	.10	.05	.01
☐ 293	Sammy Hale	.10	.05	.01
☐ 294	Shanty Hogan	.10	.05	.01
☐ 295	Ossie Bluege	.10	.05	.01
☐ 296	Debs Garms	.10	.05	.01
☐ 297	Barney Friberg	.10	.05	.01
☐ 298	Ed Brandt	.10	.05	.01
☐ 299	Rollie Hemsley	.10	.05	.01
☐ 300	MVP: Klein	.20	.10	.02
☐ 301	MVP: Cooper	.10	.05	.01
☐ 302	MVP: Bottomley	.20	.10	.02
☐ 303	MVP: Foxx	.30	.15	.03
☐ 304	MVP: Schulte	.10	.05	.01
☐ 305	MVP: Frisch	.20	.10	.02
☐ 306	MVP: McCormick	.10	.05	.01
☐ 307	MVP: Daubert	.10	.05	.01
☐ 308	MVP: Peckinpaugh	.10	.05	.01
☐ 309	MVP: Geo.H.Burns	.10	.05	.01
☐ 310	MVP: Gehrig	.40	.20	.04
☐ 311	MVP: Simmons	.20	.10	.02
☐ 312	MVP: Collins	.20	.10	.02
☐ 313	MVP: Hartnett	.20	.10	.02
☐ 314	MVP: Cronin	.20	.10	.02
☐ 315	MVP: P.Waner	.20	.10	.02
☐ 316	MVP: O'Farrell	.10	.05	.01
☐ 317	MVP: Doyle	.10	.05	.01
☐ 318	Lyn Lary	.10	.05	.01
☐ 319	Jakie May	.10	.05	.01
☐ 320	Roy Spencer	.10	.05	.01
☐ 321	Dick Coffman	.10	.05	.01
☐ 322	Pete Donohue	.10	.05	.01
☐ 323	Mule Haas	.10	.05	.01
☐ 324	Doc Farrell	.10	.05	.01
☐ 325	Flint Rhem	.10	.05	.01
☐ 326	Firpo Marberry	.10	.05	.01
☐ 327	Charles Conlon	.10	.05	.01
☐ 328	Checklist 1-110	.10	.05	.01
☐ 329	Checklist 111-220	.10	.05	.01
☐ 330	Checklist 221-330	.10	.05	.01

1914 Cracker Jack

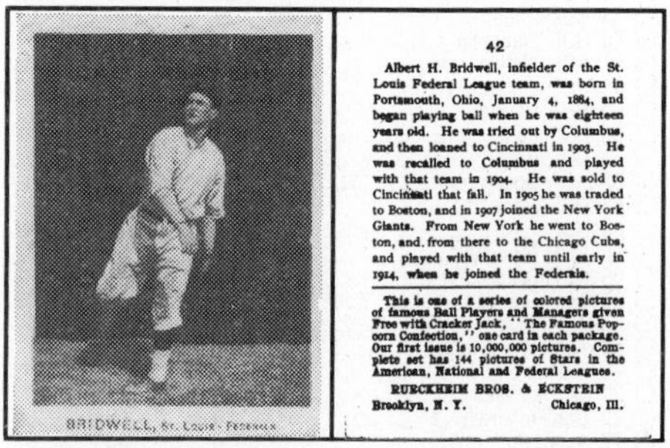

The cards in this 144-card set measure approximately 2 1/4" by 3". This "Series of colored pictures of Famous Ball Players and Managers" was issued in packages of Cracker Jack in 1914. The cards have tinted photos set against red backgrounds and many are found with caramel stains. The set also contains Federal League players. The company claims to have printed 15 million cards. The 1914 series can be distinguished from the 1915 issue by the advertising found on the back of the cards. The catalog number for this set is E145-1.

	EX-MT	VG-E	GOOD
COMPLETE SET (144)	29000.	13000.	3200.
COMMON PLAYER (1-144)	110.00	55.00	11.00
☐ 1 Otto Knabe	110.00	55.00	11.00
☐ 2 Frank Baker	300.00	150.00	30.00
☐ 3 Joe Tinker	225.00	110.00	22.00
☐ 4 Larry Doyle	110.00	55.00	11.00
☐ 5 Ward Miller	110.00	55.00	11.00
☐ 6 Eddie Plank (Phila. AL)	325.00	160.00	32.00
☐ 7 Eddie Collins (Phila. AL)	325.00	160.00	32.00
☐ 8 Rube Oldring	110.00	55.00	11.00
☐ 9 Artie Hoffman	110.00	55.00	11.00
☐ 10 John McInnis	125.00	60.00	12.50
☐ 11 George Stovall	110.00	55.00	11.00
☐ 12 Connie Mack	350.00	175.00	35.00
☐ 13 Art Wilson	110.00	55.00	11.00
☐ 14 Sam Crawford	225.00	110.00	22.00
☐ 15 Reb Russell	110.00	55.00	11.00
☐ 16 Howie Camnitz	110.00	55.00	11.00
☐ 17 Roger Bresnahan (Catcher)	250.00	125.00	25.00
☐ 18 Johnny Evers	225.00	110.00	22.00
☐ 19 Chief Bender (Phila. AL)	325.00	160.00	32.00
☐ 20 Cy Falkenberg	110.00	55.00	11.00
☐ 21 Heine Zimmerman	110.00	55.00	11.00
☐ 22 Joe Wood	160.00	80.00	16.00
☐ 23 Charles Comiskey	250.00	125.00	25.00
☐ 24 George Mullen	110.00	55.00	11.00
☐ 25 Michael Simon	110.00	55.00	11.00

☐ 26 James Scott	110.00	55.00	11.00
☐ 27 Bill Carrigan	110.00	55.00	11.00
☐ 28 Jack Barry	110.00	55.00	11.00
☐ 29 Vean Gregg (Cleveland)	135.00	65.00	13.50
☐ 30 Ty Cobb	3500.00	1400.00	350.00
☐ 31 Heine Wagner	110.00	55.00	11.00
☐ 32 Mordecai Brown	225.00	110.00	22.00
☐ 33 Amos Strunk	110.00	55.00	11.00
☐ 34 Ira Thomas	110.00	55.00	11.00
☐ 35 Harry Hooper	225.00	110.00	22.00
☐ 36 Ed Walsh	225.00	110.00	22.00
☐ 37 Grover Alexander	450.00	225.00	45.00
☐ 38 Red Dooin (Phila. NL)	135.00	65.00	13.50
☐ 39 Chick Gandil	160.00	80.00	16.00
☐ 40 Jimmy Austin (St.L. AL)	135.00	65.00	13.50
☐ 41 Tommy Leach	110.00	55.00	11.00
☐ 42 Al Bridwell	110.00	55.00	11.00
☐ 43 Rube Marquard (NY NL)	275.00	135.00	27.00
☐ 44 Charles Tesreau	110.00	55.00	11.00
☐ 45 Fred Luderus	110.00	55.00	11.00
☐ 46 Bob Groom	110.00	55.00	11.00
☐ 47 Josh Devore (Phila. NL)	135.00	65.00	13.50
☐ 48 Harry Lord	200.00	100.00	20.00
☐ 49 John Miller	110.00	55.00	11.00
☐ 50 John Hummell	110.00	55.00	11.00
☐ 51 Nap Rucker	110.00	55.00	11.00
☐ 52 Zach Wheat	225.00	110.00	22.00
☐ 53 Otto Miller	110.00	55.00	11.00
☐ 54 Marty O'Toole	110.00	55.00	11.00
☐ 55 Dick Hoblitzel (Cinc.)	135.00	65.00	13.50
☐ 56 Clyde Milan	110.00	55.00	11.00
☐ 57 Walter Johnson	1000.00	400.00	100.00
☐ 58 Wally Schang	110.00	55.00	11.00
☐ 59 Harry Gessler	110.00	55.00	11.00
☐ 60 Rollie Zeider	180.00	90.00	18.00
☐ 61 Ray Schalk	250.00	125.00	25.00
☐ 62 Jay Cashion	200.00	100.00	20.00
☐ 63 Babe Adams	110.00	55.00	11.00
☐ 64 Jimmy Archer	110.00	55.00	11.00
☐ 65 Tris Speaker	500.00	250.00	50.00
☐ 66 Napoleon Lajoie (Cleve.)	650.00	325.00	65.00
☐ 67 Otis Crandall	110.00	55.00	11.00
☐ 68 Honus Wagner	1000.00	400.00	100.00
☐ 69 John McGraw	300.00	150.00	30.00
☐ 70 Fred Clarke	225.00	110.00	22.00
☐ 71 Chief Meyers	110.00	55.00	11.00
☐ 72 John Boehling	110.00	55.00	11.00
☐ 73 Max Carey	225.00	110.00	22.00
☐ 74 Frank Owens	110.00	55.00	11.00
☐ 75 Miller Huggins	225.00	110.00	22.00
☐ 76 Claude Hendrix	110.00	55.00	11.00
☐ 77 Hugh Jennings	225.00	110.00	22.00
☐ 78 Fred Merkle	135.00	65.00	13.50
☐ 79 Ping Bodie	110.00	55.00	11.00
☐ 80 Ed Ruelbach	110.00	55.00	11.00
☐ 81 J.C. Delehanty	110.00	55.00	11.00
☐ 82 Gavvy Cravath	135.00	65.00	13.50
☐ 83 Russ Ford	110.00	55.00	11.00
☐ 84 E.E. Knetzer	110.00	55.00	11.00
☐ 85 Buck Herzog	110.00	55.00	11.00
☐ 86 Burt Shotten	110.00	55.00	11.00
☐ 87 Forrest Cady	110.00	55.00	11.00
☐ 88 Christy Mathewson (Pitching)	1250.00	500.00	125.00
☐ 89 Lawrence Cheney	110.00	55.00	11.00
☐ 90 Frank Smith	110.00	55.00	11.00
☐ 91 Roger Peckinpaugh	110.00	55.00	11.00
☐ 92 Al Demaree (N.Y. NL)	110.00	55.00	11.00
☐ 93 Derrill Pratt (Throwing)	200.00	100.00	20.00
☐ 94 Eddie Cicotte	160.00	80.00	16.00
☐ 95 Ray Keating	110.00	55.00	11.00
☐ 96 Beals Becker	110.00	55.00	11.00
☐ 97 John (Rube) Benton	110.00	55.00	11.00
☐ 98 Frank LaPorte	110.00	55.00	11.00
☐ 99 Frank Chance	800.00	400.00	80.00
☐ 100 Thomas Seaton	110.00	55.00	11.00
☐ 101 Frank Schulte	110.00	55.00	11.00
☐ 102 Ray Fisher	110.00	55.00	11.00
☐ 103 Joe Jackson	3500.00	1400.00	350.00
☐ 104 Vic Saier	110.00	55.00	11.00
☐ 105 James Lavender	110.00	55.00	11.00
☐ 106 Joe Birmingham	110.00	55.00	11.00
☐ 107 Tom Downey	110.00	55.00	11.00
☐ 108 Sherwood Magee (Phila. NL)	135.00	65.00	13.50
☐ 109 Fred Blanding	110.00	55.00	11.00
☐ 110 Bob Bescher	110.00	55.00	11.00
☐ 111 Jim Callahan	200.00	100.00	20.00
☐ 112 Ed Sweeney	110.00	55.00	11.00
☐ 113 George Suggs	110.00	55.00	11.00
☐ 114 Geo. J. Moriarty	110.00	55.00	11.00
☐ 115 Addison Brennan	110.00	55.00	11.00
☐ 116 Rollie Zeider	110.00	55.00	11.00
☐ 117 Ted Easterly	110.00	55.00	11.00
☐ 118 Ed Konetchy (Pittsburgh)	135.00	65.00	13.50
☐ 119 George Perring	110.00	55.00	11.00
☐ 120 Mike Doolan	110.00	55.00	11.00
☐ 121 Perdue (Boston NL)	135.00	65.00	13.50
☐ 122 Owen Bush	110.00	55.00	11.00
☐ 123 Slim Sallee	110.00	55.00	11.00
☐ 124 Earl Moore	110.00	55.00	11.00
☐ 125 Bert Niehoff	110.00	55.00	11.00
☐ 126 Walter Blair	110.00	55.00	11.00
☐ 127 Butch Schmidt	110.00	55.00	11.00
☐ 128 Steve Evans	110.00	55.00	11.00
☐ 129 Ray Caldwell	110.00	55.00	11.00
☐ 130 Ivy Wingo	110.00	55.00	11.00
☐ 131 George Baumgardner	110.00	55.00	11.00
☐ 132 Les Nunamaker	110.00	55.00	11.00
☐ 133 Branch Rickey	325.00	160.00	32.00
☐ 134 Armando Marsans (Cincinnati)	135.00	65.00	13.50
☐ 135 Bill Killefer	110.00	55.00	11.00
☐ 136 Rabbit Maranville	225.00	110.00	22.00
☐ 137 William Rariden	110.00	55.00	11.00
☐ 138 Hank Gowdy	110.00	55.00	11.00
☐ 139 Rebel Oakes	110.00	55.00	11.00
☐ 140 Danny Murphy	110.00	55.00	11.00
☐ 141 Cy Barger	110.00	55.00	11.00
☐ 142 Eugene Packard	110.00	55.00	11.00
☐ 143 Jake Daubert	135.00	65.00	13.50
☐ 144 James C. Walsh	135.00	65.00	13.50

1915 Cracker Jack

106

Joseph Birmingham, manager of the Cleveland American League team, was born in Elmira, N. Y., August 6, 1884. He played on local nines in 1901 and with the Mercersburg, Pa., Preparatory School team during 1902 and 1903. In 1906 he played baseball professionally with the A. J. G. Club of the New York State League, and was secured by Cleveland in August of the same year.

This is one of a series of pictures of famous Ball Players and Managers in the American, National and Federal Leagues, given Free with Cracker Jack, "The Famous Popcorn Confection," one card in each package. Send 100 Cracker Jack Coupons, or 1 Coupon and 25c. to CHICAGO OFFICE for complete set of 176 Pictures. Handsome Album to hold full set of pictures sent postpaid for 50 Coupons, or 1 Coupon and 10c. in coin or stamps.

RUECKHEIM BROS. & ECKSTEIN
Brooklyn, N. Y. Chicago, Ill.

The cards in this 176-card set measure approximately 2 1/4" by 3". When turned over in a lateral motion, a 1915 "series of 176" Cracker Jack card shows the back printing upside-down. Cards were available in boxes of Cracker Jack or from the company for "100 Cracker Jack coupons, or one coupon and 25 cents." An album was available for "50 coupons or one coupon and 10 cents." Because of this send-in offer, the 1915 Cracker Jack cards are noticeably easier to find than the 1914 Cracker Jack cards, although obviously neither set is plentiful. The set essentially duplicates E145-1 (1914 Cracker Jack) except for some additional cards and new poses. Players in the Federal League are indicated by FED in the checklist below. The catalog designation for the set is E145-2.

	EX-MT	VG-E	GOOD
COMPLETE SET (176)	22000.	10000.	2350.
COMMON PLAYER (1-144)	75.00	37.50	7.50
COMMON PLAYER (145-176)	100.00	50.00	10.00
☐ 1 Otto Knabe	75.00	37.50	7.50
☐ 2 Frank Baker	225.00	110.00	22.00
☐ 3 Joe Tinker	175.00	85.00	18.00
☐ 4 Larry Doyle	75.00	37.50	7.50
☐ 5 Ward Miller	75.00	37.50	7.50
☐ 6 Eddie Plank (St.L. FED)	250.00	125.00	25.00

☐ 7 Eddie Collins (Chicago AL)	250.00	125.00	25.00
☐ 8 Rube Oldring	75.00	37.50	7.50
☐ 9 Artie Hoffman	75.00	37.50	7.50
☐ 10 John McInnis	90.00	45.00	9.00
☐ 11 George Stovall	75.00	37.50	7.50
☐ 12 Connie Mack	300.00	150.00	30.00
☐ 13 Art Wilson	75.00	37.50	7.50
☐ 14 Sam Crawford	175.00	85.00	18.00
☐ 15 Reb Russell	75.00	37.50	7.50
☐ 16 Howie Camnitz	75.00	37.50	7.50
☐ 17 Roger Bresnahan	175.00	85.00	18.00
☐ 18 Johnny Evers	175.00	85.00	18.00
☐ 19 Chief Bender (Baltimore FED)	250.00	125.00	25.00
☐ 20 Cy Falkenberg	75.00	37.50	7.50
☐ 21 Heine Zimmerman	75.00	37.50	7.50
☐ 22 Joe Wood	135.00	65.00	13.50
☐ 23 Charles Comiskey	200.00	100.00	20.00
☐ 24 George Mullen	75.00	37.50	7.50
☐ 25 Michael Simon	75.00	37.50	7.50
☐ 26 James Scott	75.00	37.50	7.50
☐ 27 Bill Carrigan	75.00	37.50	7.50
☐ 28 Jack Barry	75.00	37.50	7.50
☐ 29 Vean Gregg (Boston AL)	90.00	45.00	9.00
☐ 30 Ty Cobb	3000.00	1200.00	300.00
☐ 31 Heine Wagner	75.00	37.50	7.50
☐ 32 Mordecai Brown	175.00	85.00	18.00
☐ 33 Amos Strunk	75.00	37.50	7.50
☐ 34 Ira Thomas	75.00	37.50	7.50
☐ 35 Harry Hooper	175.00	85.00	18.00
☐ 36 Ed Walsh	175.00	85.00	18.00
☐ 37 Grover C. Alexander	350.00	175.00	35.00
☐ 38 Red Dooin (Cincinnati)	90.00	45.00	9.00
☐ 39 Chick Gandil	135.00	65.00	13.50
☐ 40 Jimmy Austin (Pitts. FED)	90.00	45.00	9.00
☐ 41 Tommy Leach	75.00	37.50	7.50
☐ 42 Al Bridwell	75.00	37.50	7.50
☐ 43 Rube Marquard (Brooklyn FED)	225.00	110.00	22.00
☐ 44 Charles Tesreau	75.00	37.50	7.50
☐ 45 Fred Luderus	75.00	37.50	7.50
☐ 46 Bob Groom	75.00	37.50	7.50
☐ 47 Josh Devore (Boston NL)	90.00	45.00	9.00
☐ 48 Steve O'Neill	75.00	37.50	7.50
☐ 49 John Miller	75.00	37.50	7.50
☐ 50 John Hummell	75.00	37.50	7.50
☐ 51 Nap Rucker	75.00	37.50	7.50
☐ 52 Zach Wheat	175.00	85.00	18.00
☐ 53 Otto Miller	75.00	37.50	7.50
☐ 54 Marty O'Toole	75.00	37.50	7.50
☐ 55 Dick Hoblitzel (Boston AL)	90.00	45.00	9.00
☐ 56 Clyde Milan	75.00	37.50	7.50
☐ 57 Walter Johnson	800.00	400.00	80.00
☐ 58 Wally Schang	75.00	37.50	7.50
☐ 59 Harry Gessler	75.00	37.50	7.50
☐ 60 Oscar Dugey	75.00	37.50	7.50
☐ 61 Ray Schalk	175.00	85.00	18.00
☐ 62 Willie Mitchell	75.00	37.50	7.50
☐ 63 Babe Adams	75.00	37.50	7.50
☐ 64 Jimmy Archer	75.00	37.50	7.50
☐ 65 Tris Speaker	400.00	200.00	40.00
☐ 66 Napoleon Lajoie (Phila. AL)	500.00	250.00	50.00
☐ 67 Otis Crandall	75.00	37.50	7.50
☐ 68 Honus Wagner	800.00	400.00	80.00
☐ 69 John McGraw	225.00	110.00	22.00
☐ 70 Fred Clarke	175.00	85.00	18.00
☐ 71 Chief Meyers	75.00	37.50	7.50
☐ 72 John Boehling	75.00	37.50	7.50
☐ 73 Max Carey	175.00	85.00	18.00
☐ 74 Frank Owens	75.00	37.50	7.50
☐ 75 Miller Huggins	175.00	85.00	18.00
☐ 76 Claude Hendrix	75.00	37.50	7.50
☐ 77 Hugh Jennings	175.00	85.00	18.00
☐ 78 Fred Merkle	90.00	45.00	9.00
☐ 79 Ping Bodie	75.00	37.50	7.50
☐ 80 Ed Ruelbach	75.00	37.50	7.50
☐ 81 J.C. Delehanty	75.00	37.50	7.50
☐ 82 Gavvy Cravath	90.00	45.00	9.00
☐ 83 Russ Ford	75.00	37.50	7.50
☐ 84 E.E. Knetzer	75.00	37.50	7.50
☐ 85 Buck Herzog	75.00	37.50	7.50
☐ 86 Burt Shotten	75.00	37.50	7.50
☐ 87 Forrest Cady	75.00	37.50	7.50
☐ 88 Christy Mathewson (Portrait)	900.00	450.00	90.00
☐ 89 Lawrence Cheney	75.00	37.50	7.50
☐ 90 Frank Smith	75.00	37.50	7.50
☐ 91 Roger Peckinpaugh	90.00	45.00	9.00
☐ 92 Al Demaree (Phila. NL)	90.00	45.00	9.00
☐ 93 Derrill Pratt (Portrait)	100.00	50.00	10.00
☐ 94 Eddie Cicotte	135.00	65.00	13.50
☐ 95 Ray Keating	75.00	37.50	7.50
☐ 96 Beals Becker	75.00	37.50	7.50
☐ 97 John (Rube) Benton	75.00	37.50	7.50
☐ 98 Frank LaPorte	75.00	37.50	7.50
☐ 99 Hal Chase	200.00	100.00	20.00
☐ 100 Thomas Seaton	75.00	37.50	7.50
☐ 101 Frank Schulte	75.00	37.50	7.50
☐ 102 Ray Fisher	75.00	37.50	7.50
☐ 103 Joe Jackson	3000.00	1200.00	300.00
☐ 104 Vic Saier	75.00	37.50	7.50
☐ 105 James Lavender	75.00	37.50	7.50
☐ 106 Joe Birmingham	75.00	37.50	7.50
☐ 107 Thomas Downey	75.00	37.50	7.50
☐ 108 Sherwood Magee (Boston NL)	90.00	45.00	9.00
☐ 109 Fred Blanding	75.00	37.50	7.50
☐ 110 Bob Bescher	75.00	37.50	7.50
☐ 111 Herbie Moran	75.00	37.50	7.50
☐ 112 Ed Sweeney	75.00	37.50	7.50
☐ 113 George Suggs	75.00	37.50	7.50
☐ 114 Geo. J. Moriarty	75.00	37.50	7.50
☐ 115 Addison Brennan	75.00	37.50	7.50
☐ 116 Rollie Zeider	75.00	37.50	7.50
☐ 117 Ted Easterly	75.00	37.50	7.50
☐ 118 Ed Konetchy (Pitts. FED)	90.00	45.00	9.00
☐ 119 George Perring	75.00	37.50	7.50
☐ 120 Mike Doolan	75.00	37.50	7.50
☐ 121 Perdue (St.L. NL)	90.00	45.00	9.00
☐ 122 Owen Bush	75.00	37.50	7.50
☐ 123 Slim Sallee	75.00	37.50	7.50
☐ 124 Earl Moore	75.00	37.50	7.50
☐ 125 Bert Niehoff (Phila. NL)	90.00	45.00	9.00
☐ 126 Walter Blair	75.00	37.50	7.50
☐ 127 Butch Schmidt	75.00	37.50	7.50
☐ 128 Steve Evans	75.00	37.50	7.50
☐ 129 Ray Caldwell	75.00	37.50	7.50
☐ 130 Ivy Wingo	75.00	37.50	7.50
☐ 131 Geo. Baumgardner	75.00	37.50	7.50
☐ 132 Les Nunamaker	75.00	37.50	7.50
☐ 133 Branch Rickey	250.00	125.00	25.00
☐ 134 Armando Marsans (St.L. FED)	90.00	45.00	9.00
☐ 135 William Killefer	75.00	37.50	7.50
☐ 136 Rabbit Maranville	175.00	85.00	18.00
☐ 137 William Rariden	75.00	37.50	7.50
☐ 138 Hank Gowdy	75.00	37.50	7.50
☐ 139 Rebel Oakes	75.00	37.50	7.50
☐ 140 Danny Murphy	75.00	37.50	7.50
☐ 141 Cy Barger	75.00	37.50	7.50
☐ 142 Eugene Packard	75.00	37.50	7.50
☐ 143 Jake Daubert	90.00	45.00	9.00
☐ 144 James C. Walsh	75.00	37.50	7.50
☐ 145 Ted Cather	100.00	50.00	10.00
☐ 146 George Tyler	100.00	50.00	10.00
☐ 147 Lee Magee	100.00	50.00	10.00
☐ 148 Owen Wilson	100.00	50.00	10.00
☐ 149 Hal Janvrin	100.00	50.00	10.00
☐ 150 Doc Johnston	100.00	50.00	10.00
☐ 151 George Whitted	100.00	50.00	10.00
☐ 152 George McQuillen	100.00	50.00	10.00
☐ 153 Bill James	100.00	50.00	10.00
☐ 154 Dick Rudolph	100.00	50.00	10.00
☐ 155 Joe Connolly	100.00	50.00	10.00
☐ 156 Jean Dubuc	100.00	50.00	10.00
☐ 157 George Kaiserling	100.00	50.00	10.00
☐ 158 Fritz Maisel	100.00	50.00	10.00
☐ 159 Heine Groh	100.00	50.00	10.00
☐ 160 Benny Kauff	100.00	50.00	10.00
☐ 161 Ed Rousch	250.00	125.00	25.00
☐ 162 George Stallings	100.00	50.00	10.00
☐ 163 Bert Whaling	100.00	50.00	10.00
☐ 164 Bob Shawkey	125.00	60.00	12.50
☐ 165 Eddie Murphy	100.00	50.00	10.00
☐ 166 Joe Bush	125.00	60.00	12.50
☐ 167 Clark Griffith	225.00	110.00	22.00
☐ 168 Vin Campbell	100.00	50.00	10.00
☐ 169 Raymond Collins	100.00	50.00	10.00
☐ 170 Hans Lobert	100.00	50.00	10.00
☐ 171 Earl Hamilton	100.00	50.00	10.00
☐ 172 Erskine Mayer	100.00	50.00	10.00
☐ 173 Tilly Walker	100.00	50.00	10.00
☐ 174 Robert Veach	100.00	50.00	10.00
☐ 175 Joseph Benz	100.00	50.00	10.00
☐ 176 Jim Vaughn	125.00	60.00	12.50

1982 Cracker Jack

The cards in this 16-card set measure 2 1/2" by 3 1/2"; cards came in two sheets of 8 cards, plus an advertising card with a title in the center, which measured approximately 7 1/2" by 10 1/2". Cracker Jack reentered the baseball card market for the first time since 1915 to promote the first "Old Timers Baseball Classic" held July 19, 1982. The color player photos have a Cracker Jack border and have either green (NL) or red (AL) frame lines and name panels. The Cracker Jack logo appears on both sides of each card, with AL players numbered 1-8 and NL players numbered 9-16. Of the 16 ballplayers pictured, five did not appear at the game. At first, the two sheets were available only through the mail but are now commonly found in hobby circles. The set was prepared for Cracker Jack by Topps. The prices below reflect individual card prices; the price for complete panels would be about the same as the sum of the card prices for those players on the panel due to the easy availability of uncut sheets.

	MINT	EXC	G-VG
COMPLETE SET (16)	7.50	3.75	.75
COMMON PLAYER (1-16)	.15	.07	.01
☐ 1 Larry Doby	.15	.07	.01
☐ 2 Bob Feller	.75	.35	.07
☐ 3 Whitey Ford	.75	.35	.07
☐ 4 Al Kaline	.75	.35	.07
☐ 5 Harmon Killebrew	.45	.22	.04
☐ 6 Mickey Mantle	2.00	1.00	.20
☐ 7 Tony Oliva	.15	.07	.01
☐ 8 Brooks Robinson	.75	.35	.07
☐ 9 Hank Aaron	1.00	.50	.10
☐ 10 Ernie Banks	.75	.35	.07
☐ 11 Ralph Kiner	.45	.22	.04
☐ 12 Ed Mathews	.35	.17	.03
☐ 13 Willie Mays	1.00	.50	.10
☐ 14 Robin Roberts	.35	.17	.03
☐ 15 Duke Snider	.75	.35	.07
☐ 16 Warren Spahn	.50	.25	.05

1982 Cubs Red Lobster

The cards in this 28-card set measure 2 1/4" by 3 1/2". This set of Chicago Cubs players was co-produced by the Cubs and Chicago-area Red Lobster restaurants and was introduced as a promotional giveaway on August 20, 1982, at Wrigley Field. The cards contain borderless color photos of 25 players, manager Lee Elia, the coaching staff, and a team picture. A facsimile autograph appears on the front, and the cards run in sequence by uniform number. While the coaches have a short biographical sketch on back, the player cards simply list the individual's professional record.

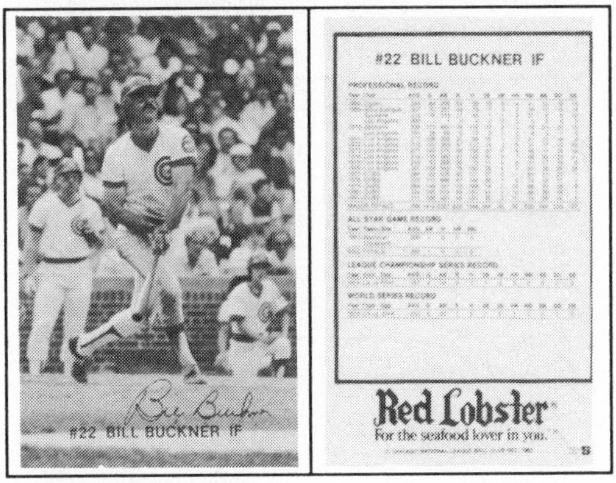

	MINT	EXC	G-VG
COMPLETE SET (28)	35.00	17.50	3.50
COMMON PLAYER	.35	.17	.03
☐ 1 Larry Bowa	.60	.30	.06
☐ 4 Lee Elia MG	.35	.17	.03
☐ 6 Keith Moreland	.45	.22	.04
☐ 7 Jody Davis	.60	.30	.06
☐ 10 Leon Durham	.45	.22	.04
☐ 15 Junior Kennedy	.35	.17	.03
☐ 17 Bump Wills	.35	.17	.03
☐ 18 Scot Thompson	.35	.17	.03
☐ 21 Jay Johnstone	.45	.22	.04
☐ 22 Bill Buckner	.60	.30	.06
☐ 23 Ryne Sandberg	25.00	12.50	2.50
☐ 24 Jerry Morales	.35	.17	.03
☐ 25 Gary Woods	.35	.17	.03
☐ 28 Steve Henderson	.35	.17	.03
☐ 29 Bob Molinaro	.35	.17	.03
☐ 31 Fergie Jenkins	1.50	.60	.12
☐ 33 Al Ripley	.35	.17	.03
☐ 34 Randy Martz	.35	.17	.03
☐ 36 Mike Proly	.35	.17	.03
☐ 37 Ken Kravec	.35	.17	.03
☐ 38 Willie Hernandez	.45	.22	.04
☐ 39 Bill Campbell	.35	.17	.03
☐ 41 Dick Tidrow	.35	.17	.03
☐ 46 Lee Smith	1.00	.50	.10
☐ 47 Doug Bird	.35	.17	.03
☐ 48 Dickie Noles	.35	.17	.03
☐ xx Team Picture (unnumbered)	.45	.22	.04
☐ xx Coaches Card (unnumbered)	.35	.17	.03

1983 Cubs Thorn Apple Valley

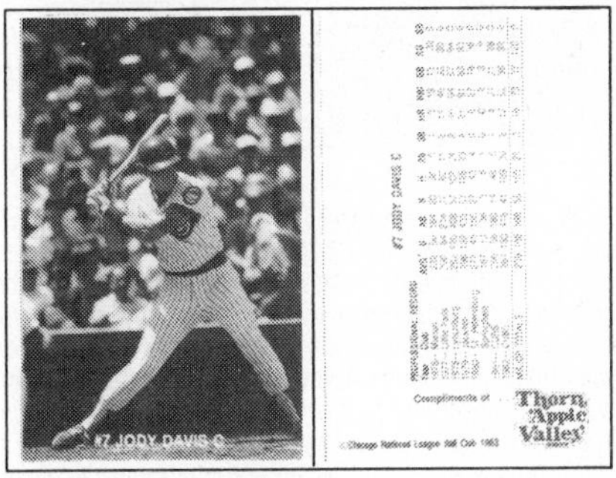

This set of 28 Chicago Cubs features full-color action photos on the front and was sponsored by Thorn Apple Valley. The cards measure 2 1/4" by 3 1/2". The backs provide year-by-year statistics. The cards are unnumbered except for uniform number; they are listed below by uniform with the special cards listed at the end.

	MINT	EXC	G-VG
COMPLETE SET (28)	13.50	6.00	1.20
COMMON PLAYER	.35	.17	.03
☐ 1 Larry Bowa	.60	.30	.06
☐ 6 Keith Moreland	.45	.22	.04
☐ 7 Jody Davis	.45	.22	.04
☐ 10 Leon Durham	.45	.22	.04
☐ 11 Ron Cey	.60	.30	.06
☐ 16 Steve Lake	.35	.17	.03
☐ 20 Thad Bosley	.35	.17	.03
☐ 21 Jay Johnstone	.45	.22	.04
☐ 22 Bill Buckner	.60	.30	.06
☐ 23 Ryne Sandberg	6.00	3.00	.60
☐ 24 Jerry Morales	.35	.17	.03
☐ 25 Gary Woods	.35	.17	.03
☐ 27 Mel Hall	.60	.30	.06
☐ 29 Tom Veryzer	.35	.17	.03
☐ 30 Chuck Rainey	.35	.17	.03
☐ 31 Fergie Jenkins	1.00	.40	.08
☐ 32 Craig Lefferts	.45	.22	.04
☐ 33 Joe Carter	3.50	1.75	.35
☐ 34 Steve Trout	.35	.17	.03
☐ 36 Mike Proly	.35	.17	.03
☐ 39 Bill Campbell	.35	.17	.03
☐ 41 Warren Brusstar	.35	.17	.03
☐ 44 Dick Ruthven	.35	.17	.03
☐ 46 Lee Smith	.60	.30	.06
☐ 48 Dickie Noles	.35	.17	.03
☐ xx Manager/Coaches Lee Elia MG Ruben Amaro Billy Connors Duffy Dyer Fred Koenig John Vukovich (unnumbered)	.35	.17	.03
☐ xx Team Photo (unnumbered)	.35	.17	.03

1984 Cubs Seven-Up

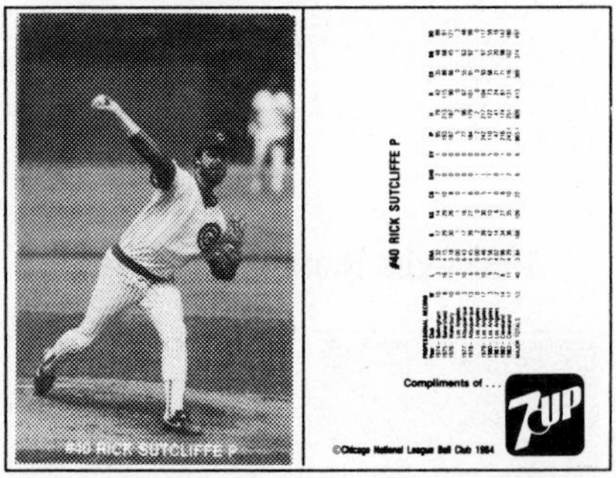

This 28-card set was sponsored by 7-Up. The cards are in full color and measure 2 1/4" by 3 1/2". The card backs are printed in black on white card stock. This set is tougher to find than the other similar Cubs sets since the Cubs were more successful (on the field) in 1984 winning their division, that is, virtually all of the cards printed were distributed during the "Baseball Card Day" promotion (August 12th) which was much better attended that year. There actually were two additional cards produced (in limited quantities) later which some collectors consider part of this set; these late issue cards show four Cubs rookies on each card.

	MINT	EXC	G-VG
COMPLETE SET (28)	18.00	9.00	1.80
COMMON PLAYER	.50	.25	.05
☐ 1 Larry Bowa	.75	.35	.07
☐ 6 Keith Moreland	.60	.30	.06
☐ 7 Jody Davis	.60	.30	.06
☐ 10 Leon Durham	.60	.30	.06
☐ 11 Ron Cey	.75	.35	.07
☐ 15 Ron Hassey	.50	.25	.05
☐ 18 Richie Hebner	.50	.25	.05
☐ 19 Dave Owen	.50	.25	.05
☐ 20 Bob Dernier	.50	.25	.05
☐ 21 Jay Johnstone	.60	.30	.06
☐ 23 Ryne Sandberg	5.00	2.50	.50
☐ 24 Scott Sanderson	.75	.35	.07
☐ 25 Gary Woods	.50	.25	.05
☐ 27 Thad Bosley	.50	.25	.05
☐ 28 Henry Cotto	.50	.25	.05
☐ 34 Steve Trout	.50	.25	.05
☐ 36 Gary Matthews	.60	.30	.06
☐ 39 George Frazier	.50	.25	.05
☐ 40 Rick Sutcliffe	1.00	.50	.10
☐ 41 Warren Brusstar	.50	.25	.05
☐ 42 Rich Bordi	.50	.25	.05
☐ 43 Dennis Eckersley	1.50	.75	.15
☐ 44 Dick Ruthven	.50	.25	.05
☐ 46 Lee Smith	.75	.35	.07
☐ 47 Rick Reuschel	.90	.45	.09
☐ 49 Tim Stoddard	.50	.25	.05
☐ xx Coaches (unnumbered)	.50	.25	.05
☐ xx Jim Frey MG (unnumbered)	.50	.25	.05

1985 Cubs Seven-Up

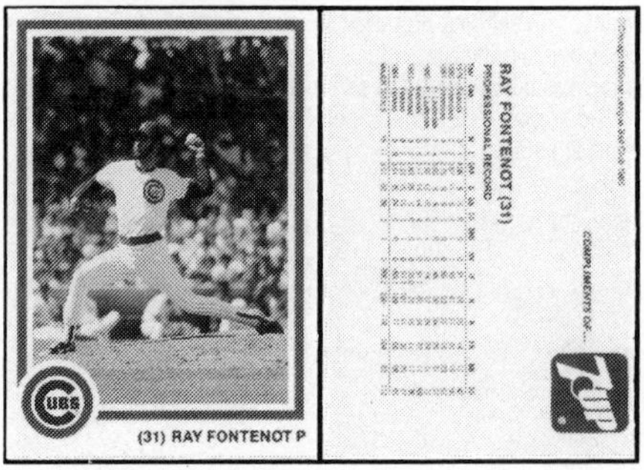

This 28-card set was distributed on August 14th at Wrigley Field for the game against the Expos. The cards measure 2 1/2" by 3 1/2" and were distributed wrapped in cellophane. The cards are unnumbered except for uniform number. The card backs are printed in black on white with a 7-Up logo in the upper right hand corner.

	MINT	EXC	G-VG
COMPLETE SET (28)	8.00	4.00	.80
COMMON PLAYER	.15	.07	.01
☐ 1 Larry Bowa	.35	.17	.03
☐ 6 Keith Moreland	.25	.12	.02
☐ 7 Jody Davis	.25	.12	.02
☐ 10 Leon Durham	.25	.12	.02
☐ 11 Ron Cey	.25	.12	.02
☐ 15 Davey Lopes	.25	.12	.02
☐ 16 Steve Lake	.15	.07	.01
☐ 18 Rich Hebner	.15	.07	.01
☐ 20 Bob Dernier	.15	.07	.01
☐ 21 Scott Sanderson	.25	.12	.02
☐ 22 Billy Hatcher	.35	.17	.03
☐ 23 Ryne Sandberg	3.00	1.50	.30
☐ 24 Brian Dayett	.15	.07	.01
☐ 25 Gary Woods	.15	.07	.01
☐ 27 Thad Bosley	.15	.07	.01
☐ 28 Chris Speier	.15	.07	.01
☐ 31 Ray Fontenot	.15	.07	.01

☐ 34 Steve Trout	.15	.07	.01
☐ 36 Gary Matthews	.25	.12	.02
☐ 39 George Frazier	.15	.07	.01
☐ 40 Rick Sutcliffe	.60	.30	.06
☐ 41 Warren Brusstar	.15	.07	.01
☐ 42 Lary Sorensen	.15	.07	.01
☐ 43 Dennis Eckersley	.75	.35	.07
☐ 44 Dick Ruthven	.15	.07	.01
☐ 46 Lee Smith	.35	.17	.03
☐ xx Jim Frey MG (unnumbered)	.15	.07	.01
☐ xx Cubs Coaching Staff: Ruben Amaro, Billy Connors, Johnny Oates, John Vukovich, Don Zimmer (unnumbered)	.15	.07	.01

1986 Cubs Gatorade

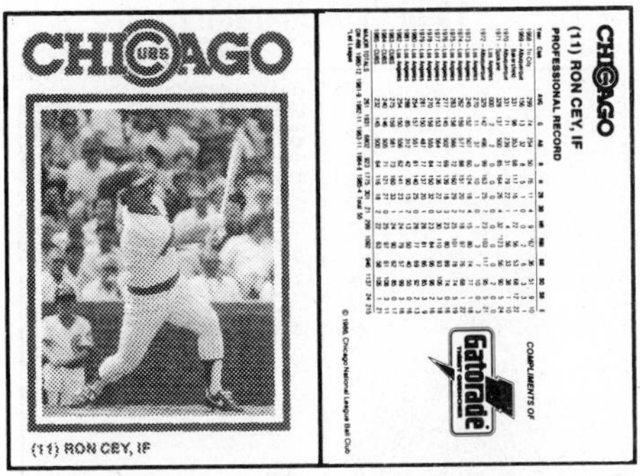

This 28-card set was given out at Wrigley Field on the Cubs' special "baseball card" promotion held July 17th for the game against the Giants. The set was sponsored by Gatorade. The cards are unnumbered except for uniform number. Card backs feature blue print on white card stock. The cards measure 2 7/8" by 4 1/4" and are in full color.

	MINT	EXC	G-VG
COMPLETE SET (28)	8.00	4.00	.80
COMMON PLAYER	.15	.07	.01
☐ 4 Gene Michael MG	.25	.12	.02
☐ 6 Keith Moreland	.25	.12	.02
☐ 7 Jody Davis	.25	.12	.02
☐ 10 Leon Durham	.25	.12	.02
☐ 11 Ron Cey	.25	.12	.02
☐ 12 Shawon Dunston	1.00	.50	.10
☐ 15 Davey Lopes	.25	.12	.02
☐ 16 Terry Francona	.15	.07	.01
☐ 18 Steve Christmas	.15	.07	.01
☐ 19 Manny Trillo	.15	.07	.01
☐ 20 Bob Dernier	.15	.07	.01
☐ 21 Scott Sanderson	.25	.12	.02
☐ 22 Jerry Mumphrey	.15	.07	.01
☐ 23 Ryne Sandberg	2.50	1.25	.25
☐ 27 Thad Bosley	.15	.07	.01
☐ 28 Chris Speier	.15	.07	.01
☐ 29 Steve Lake	.15	.07	.01
☐ 31 Ray Fontenot	.15	.07	.01
☐ 34 Steve Trout	.15	.07	.01
☐ 36 Gary Matthews	.25	.12	.02
☐ 39 George Frazier	.15	.07	.01
☐ 40 Rick Sutcliffe	.50	.25	.05
☐ 43 Dennis Eckersley	.75	.35	.07
☐ 46 Lee Smith	.25	.12	.02
☐ 48 Jay Baller	.15	.07	.01
☐ 49 Jamie Moyer	.15	.07	.01
☐ 50 Guy Hoffman	.15	.07	.01
☐ xx Coaches Card (unnumbered)	.15	.07	.01

1987 Cubs David Berg

This 28-card set was given out at Wrigley Field on the Cubs' special "baseball card" promotion held July 29th. The set was sponsored by David Berg Pure Beef Hot Dogs. The cards are unnumbered except for uniform number. Card backs feature red and blue print on white card stock. The cards measure 2 7/8" by 4 1/4" and are in full color.

	MINT	EXC	G-VG
COMPLETE SET (28)	8.00	4.00	.80
COMMON PLAYER	.15	.07	.01
☐ 1 Dave Martinez	.25	.12	.02
☐ 4 Gene Michael MG	.25	.12	.02
☐ 6 Keith Moreland	.25	.12	.02
☐ 7 Jody Davis	.25	.12	.02
☐ 8 Andre Dawson	1.50	.75	.15
☐ 10 Leon Durham	.25	.12	.02
☐ 11 Jim Sundberg	.15	.07	.01
☐ 12 Shawon Dunston	.75	.35	.07
☐ 19 Manny Trillo	.15	.07	.01
☐ 20 Bob Dernier	.15	.07	.01
☐ 21 Scott Sanderson	.25	.12	.02
☐ 22 Jerry Mumphrey	.15	.07	.01
☐ 23 Ryne Sandberg	2.00	1.00	.20
☐ 24 Brian Dayett	.15	.07	.01
☐ 29 Chico Walker	.25	.12	.02
☐ 31 Greg Maddux	.75	.35	.07
☐ 33 Frank DiPino	.15	.07	.01
☐ 34 Steve Trout	.15	.07	.01
☐ 36 Gary Matthews	.25	.12	.02
☐ 37 Ed Lynch	.15	.07	.01
☐ 39 Ron Davis	.15	.07	.01
☐ 40 Rick Sutcliffe	.35	.17	.03
☐ 46 Lee Smith	.25	.12	.02
☐ 47 Dickie Noles	.15	.07	.01
☐ 49 Jamie Moyer	.15	.07	.01
☐ xx Coaching Staff	.15	.07	.01

1988 Cubs David Berg

This 27-card set was given out at Wrigley Field with every paid admission on the Cubs' special "baseball card" promotion held August 24th. The set was sponsored by David Berg Pure Beef Hot Dogs and the Venture store chain. The cards are unnumbered except for uniform number. Card backs feature primarily black print on white card stock. The cards measure approximately 2 7/8" by 4 1/4" and are in full color.

	MINT	EXC	G-VG
COMPLETE SET (27)	8.00	4.00	.80
COMMON PLAYER	.15	.07	.01
☐ 2 Vance Law	.25	.12	.02
☐ 4 Don Zimmer MG	.35	.17	.03
☐ 7 Jody Davis	.25	.12	.02
☐ 8 Andre Dawson	1.00	.50	.10
☐ 9 Damon Berryhill	.50	.25	.05
☐ 12 Shawon Dunston	.50	.25	.05
☐ 17 Mark Grace	1.50	.75	.15
☐ 18 Angel Salazar	.15	.07	.01
☐ 19 Manny Trillo	.15	.07	.01
☐ 21 Scott Sanderson	.25	.12	.02
☐ 22 Jerry Mumphrey	.15	.07	.01
☐ 23 Ryne Sandberg	1.00	.50	.10
☐ 24 Gary Varsho	.25	.12	.02
☐ 25 Rafael Palmiero	1.00	.50	.10
☐ 28 Mitch Webster	.15	.07	.01
☐ 30 Darrin Jackson	.25	.12	.02
☐ 31 Greg Maddux	.50	.25	.05
☐ 32 Calvin Schiraldi	.15	.07	.01
☐ 33 Frank DiPino	.15	.07	.01
☐ 37 Pat Perry	.15	.07	.01
☐ 40 Rick Sutcliffe	.35	.17	.03
☐ 41 Jeff Pico	.15	.07	.01
☐ 45 Al Nipper	.15	.07	.01
☐ 49 Jamie Moyer	.15	.07	.01
☐ 50 Les Lancaster	.15	.07	.01
☐ 54 Rich Gossage	.25	.12	.02
☐ xx Cubs Coaching Staff Joe Altobelli CO Chuck Cottier CO Larry Cox CO Jose Martinez CO Dick Pole CO	.15	.07	.01

1989 Cubs Marathon

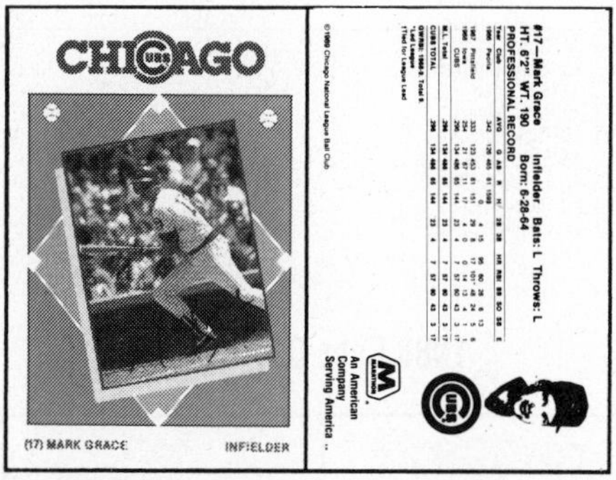

The 1989 Marathon Cubs set features 25 cards measuring 2 3/4" by 4 1/4". The fronts are green and white, and feature facsimile autographs. The backs show black and white mug shots and career stats. The set was given away at the August 10, 1989 Cubs home game. The cards are numbered by the players' uniform numbers.

	MINT	EXC	G-VG
COMPLETE SET (25)	13.50	6.00	1.00
COMMON PLAYER	.30	.15	.03
☐ 2 Vance Law	.40	.20	.04
☐ 4 Don Zimmer MG	.40	.20	.04
☐ 7 Joe Girardi	.40	.20	.04
☐ 8 Andre Dawson	1.00	.50	.10
☐ 9 Damon Berryhill	.50	.25	.05
☐ 10 Lloyd McClendon	.30	.15	.03
☐ 12 Shawon Dunston	.90	.45	.09
☐ 15 Domingo Ramos	.30	.15	.03
☐ 17 Mark Grace	1.50	.75	.15
☐ 18 Dwight Smith	.75	.35	.07
☐ 19 Curt Wilkerson	.30	.15	.03
☐ 20 Jerome Walton	1.25	.60	.12
☐ 21 Scott Sanderson	.40	.20	.04
☐ 23 Ryne Sandberg	2.00	1.00	.20
☐ 28 Mitch Williams	.50	.25	.05
☐ 31 Greg Maddux	.60	.30	.06
☐ 32 Calvin Schiraldi	.30	.15	.03
☐ 33 Mitch Webster	.30	.15	.03
☐ 36 Mike Bielecki	.40	.20	.04
☐ 39 Paul Kilgus	.30	.15	.03
☐ 40 Rick Sutcliffe	.50	.25	.05
☐ 41 Jeff Pico	.30	.15	.03
☐ 44 Steve Wilson	.40	.20	.04
☐ 50 Les Lancaster	.40	.20	.04
☐ xx Cubs Coaches	.30	.15	.03

1990 Cubs Marathon

The Marathon Oil Chicago Cubs set contains 28 cards measuring 2 7/8" by 4 1/4" which was given away at the August 17th Cub game. This set is checklisted alphabetically below with the uniform number next to the players name.

	MINT	EXC	G-VG
COMPLETE SET (28)	9.00	4.50	.90
COMMON PLAYER (1-28)	.25	.12	.02
☐ 1 Paul Assenmacher 45	.25	.12	.02
☐ 2 Mike Bielecki 36	.25	.12	.02
☐ 3 Shawn Boskie 47	.35	.17	.03
☐ 4 Dave Clark 30	.25	.12	.02
☐ 5 Doug Dascenzo 29	.25	.12	.02
☐ 6 Andre Dawson 8	.75	.35	.07
☐ 7 Shawon Dunston 12	.60	.30	.06
☐ 8 Joe Girardi 7	.35	.17	.03
☐ 9 Mark Grace 17	1.00	.50	.10
☐ 10 Mike Harkey 22	.75	.35	.07
☐ 11 Les Lancaster 50	.25	.12	.02
☐ 12 Bill Long 37	.25	.12	.02
☐ 13 Greg Maddux 31	.50	.25	.05
☐ 14 Lloyd McClendon 10	.25	.12	.02
☐ 15 Jeff Pico 41	.25	.12	.02
☐ 16 Domingo Ramos 15	.25	.12	.02
☐ 17 Luis Salazar 11	.25	.12	.02
☐ 18 Ryne Sandberg 23	1.50	.75	.15
☐ 19 Dwight Smith 18	.35	.17	.03
☐ 20 Rick Sutcliffe 40	.35	.17	.03
☐ 21 Hector Villanueva 32	.35	.17	.03
☐ 22 Jerome Walton 20	.75	.35	.07
☐ 23 Curtis Wilkerson 19	.25	.12	.02
☐ 24 Mitch Williams 28	.35	.17	.03
☐ 25 Steve Wilson 44	.25	.12	.02
☐ 26 Marvell Wynne 25	.25	.12	.02
☐ 27 Don Zimmer 4 MG	.35	.17	.03
☐ 28 Cubs Coaches Joe Altobelli Jose Martinez Phil Roof Chuck Cottier Dick Pole	.25	.12	.02

1954 Dan Dee

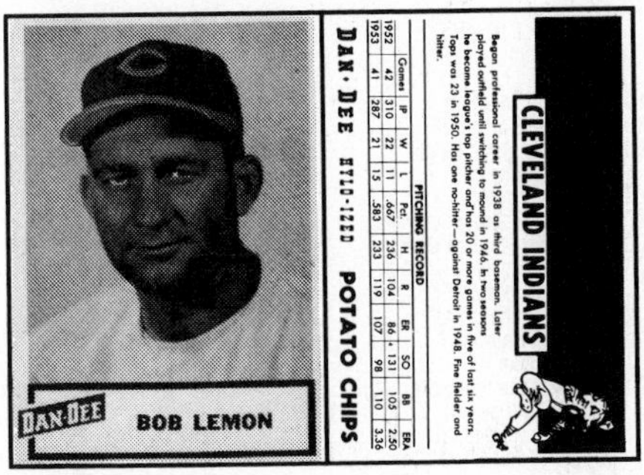

The cards in this 29-card set measure 2 1/2" by 3 5/8". Most of the cards marketed by Dan Dee in bags of potato chips in 1954 depict players from the Indians or Pirates. The Pirate players in the set are much tougher to find than the Cleveland Indians players. The pictures used for Yankee players were also employed in the Briggs and Stahl-Meyer sets. Dan Dee cards have a waxed surface, but are commonly found with product stains. Paul Smith and Walker Cooper are considered the known scarcities. The catalog designation for this set is F342.

	NRMT	VG-E	GOOD
COMPLETE SET (29)	3500.00	1500.00	350.00
COMMON PLAYER (1-29)	45.00	22.50	4.50
COMMON PIRATE PLAYER	65.00	32.50	6.50
☐ 1 Bobby Avila	45.00	22.50	4.50
☐ 2 Hank Bauer	65.00	32.50	6.50
☐ 3 Walker Cooper Pittsburgh Pirates	300.00	150.00	30.00
☐ 4 Larry Doby	55.00	27.50	5.50
☐ 5 Luke Easter	45.00	22.50	4.50
☐ 6 Bob Feller	200.00	100.00	20.00
☐ 7 Bob Friend Pittsburgh Pirates	90.00	45.00	9.00
☐ 8 Mike Garcia	45.00	22.50	4.50
☐ 9 Sid Gordon Pittsburgh Pirates	65.00	32.50	6.50
☐ 10 Jim Hegan	45.00	22.50	4.50
☐ 11 Gil Hodges	150.00	75.00	15.00
☐ 12 Art Houtteman	45.00	22.50	4.50
☐ 13 Monte Irvin	100.00	50.00	10.00
☐ 14 Paul LaPalme Pittsburgh Pirates	65.00	32.50	6.50
☐ 15 Bob Lemon	100.00	50.00	10.00
☐ 16 Al Lopez	100.00	50.00	10.00
☐ 17 Mickey Mantle	900.00	450.00	90.00
☐ 18 Dale Mitchell	45.00	22.50	4.50
☐ 19 Phil Rizzuto	150.00	75.00	15.00
☐ 20 Curt Roberts Pittsburgh Pirates	65.00	32.50	6.50
☐ 21 Al Rosen	65.00	32.50	6.50
☐ 22 Red Schoendienst	125.00	60.00	12.50
☐ 23 Paul Smith Pittsburgh Pirates	450.00	225.00	45.00
☐ 24 Duke Snider	200.00	100.00	20.00
☐ 25 George Strickland	45.00	22.50	4.50
☐ 26 Max Surkont Pittsburgh Pirates	65.00	32.50	6.50
☐ 27 Frank Thomas Pittsburgh Pirates	100.00	50.00	10.00
☐ 28 Wally Westlake	45.00	22.50	4.50
☐ 29 Early Wynn	100.00	50.00	10.00

1933 Delong

The cards in this 24-card set measures 2" by 3". The 1933 Delong Gum set of 24 multi-colored cards was, along with the 1933 Goudey Big League series, one of the first baseball card sets issued with chewing gum. It was the only card set issued by this company. The reverse text was written by Austen Lake, who also wrote the sports tips found on the Diamond Stars series which began in 1934, leading to speculation that Delong was bought out by National Chicle. The catalog designation for this set is R333.

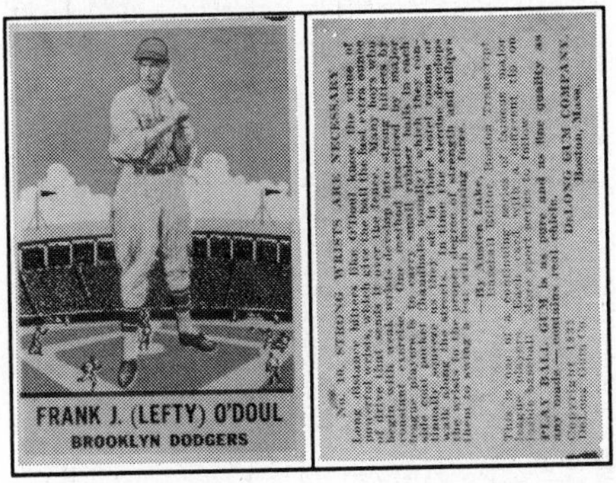

	EX-MT	VG-E	GOOD
COMPLETE SET (24)	9250.00	4500.00	950.00
COMMON PLAYER (1-24)	180.00	90.00	18.00
☐ 1 Marty McManus	180.00	90.00	18.00
☐ 2 Al Simmons	300.00	150.00	30.00
☐ 3 Oscar Melillo	180.00	90.00	18.00
☐ 4 William Terry	350.00	175.00	35.00
☐ 5 Charlie Gehringer	350.00	175.00	35.00
☐ 6 Mickey Cochrane	350.00	175.00	35.00
☐ 7 Lou Gehrig	3000.00	1200.00	300.00
☐ 8 Kiki Cuyler	300.00	150.00	30.00
☐ 9 Bill Urbanski	180.00	90.00	18.00
☐ 10 Lefty O'Doul	200.00	100.00	20.00
☐ 11 Fred Lindstrom	300.00	150.00	30.00
☐ 12 Pie Traynor	350.00	175.00	35.00
☐ 13 Rabbit Maranville	300.00	150.00	30.00
☐ 14 Lefty Gomez	350.00	175.00	35.00
☐ 15 Riggs Stephenson	200.00	100.00	20.00
☐ 16 Lon Warneke	180.00	90.00	18.00
☐ 17 Pepper Martin	200.00	100.00	20.00
☐ 18 Jim Dykes	180.00	90.00	18.00
☐ 19 Chick Hafey	300.00	150.00	30.00
☐ 20 Joe Vosmik	180.00	90.00	18.00
☐ 21 Jimmie Foxx	600.00	300.00	60.00
☐ 22 Chuck Klein	350.00	175.00	35.00
☐ 23 Lefty Grove	450.00	225.00	45.00
☐ 24 Goose Goslin	300.00	150.00	30.00

1981 Detroit News

This 135-card, standard-size, 2 1/2" by 3 1/2" set was issued in 1981 to celebrate the centennial of professional baseball in Detroit. This set features black and white photos surrounded by solid red borders, while the back provides information about either the player or event featured on the front of the card. This set was issued by the Detroit newspaper, the Detroit News and covered players from the nineteenth century right up to players and other personnel active at the time of issue.

	MINT	EXC	G-VG
COMPLETE SET (135)	12.00	6.00	1.20
COMMON PLAYER (1-135)	.09	.04	.01
□ 1 Detroit's Boys of Summer 100th Anniversary	.15	.07	.01
□ 2 Charles W. Bennett C	.09	.04	.01
□ 3 Mickey Cochrane C	.30	.15	.03
□ 4 Harry Heilmann, OF	.30	.15	.03
□ 5 Walter O. Briggs, Owner	.09	.04	.01
□ 6 Mark Fidrych P	.15	.07	.01
□ 7 1887 Tigers	.15	.07	.01
□ 8 Tiger Stadium	.09	.04	.01
□ 9 Rudy York 1B	.09	.04	.01
□ 10 George Kell 3B	.15	.07	.01
□ 11 Steve O'Neill Mgr.	.09	.04	.01
□ 12 John Hiller P	.09	.04	.01
□ 13 1934 Tigers	.15	.07	.01
□ 14 Charlie Gehringer 2B	.30	.15	.03
□ 15 Denny McLain P	.15	.07	.01
□ 16 Billy Rogell SS	.09	.04	.01
□ 17 Ty Cobb OF	.75	.35	.07
□ 18 Sparky Anderson Mgr.	.15	.07	.01
□ 19 Davy Jones OF	.09	.04	.01
□ 20 Kirk Gibson OF	.15	.07	.01
□ 21 Pat Mullin OF	.09	.04	.01
□ 22 1972 Tigers	.15	.07	.01
□ 23 What A Night	.09	.04	.01
□ 24 Doc Cramer OF	.09	.04	.01
□ 25 Mickey Stanley OF	.09	.04	.01
□ 26 John Lipon SS	.09	.04	.01
□ 27 Jo Jo White OF	.09	.04	.01
□ 28 Recreation Park	.09	.04	.01
□ 29 Wild Bill Donovan P	.09	.04	.01
□ 30 Ray Oyler SS	.09	.04	.01
□ 31 Earl Whitehill P	.09	.04	.01
□ 32 Billy Hoeft P	.09	.04	.01
□ 33 Johnny Groth OF	.09	.04	.01
□ 34 Hughie Jennings SS/Mgr.	.30	.15	.03
□ 35 Mayo Smith Mgr.	.09	.04	.01
□ 36 Bennett Park	.09	.04	.01
□ 37 Tigers Win	.09	.04	.01
□ 38 Donie Bush SS/Mgr.	.09	.04	.01
□ 39 Harry Coveleski P	.09	.04	.01
□ 40 Paul Richards C	.09	.04	.01
□ 41 Jonathon Stone OF	.09	.04	.01
□ 42 Bob Swift C	.09	.04	.01
□ 43 Roy Cullenbine OF	.09	.04	.01
□ 44 Hoot Evers OF	.09	.04	.01
□ 45 Tigers Win Series	.15	.07	.01
□ 46 Art Houtteman P	.09	.04	.01
□ 47 Aurelio Rodriguez 3B	.09	.04	.01
□ 48 Fred Hutchinson P/Mgr.	.15	.07	.01
□ 49 Don Mossi P	.09	.04	.01
□ 50 Lou Gehrig Streak Ends in Detroit At 2130 Games	.15	.07	.01
□ 51 Earl Wilson P	.09	.04	.01
□ 52 Jim Northrup OF	.09	.04	.01
□ 53 1907 Tigers	.09	.04	.01
□ 54 Hank Hits 2 Homers to Draw Even with Ruth	.30	.15	.03
□ 55 Mickey Lolich P	.15	.07	.01
□ 56 Tommy Bridges P	.09	.04	.01
□ 57 Al Benton P	.09	.04	.01
□ 58 Del Baker Mgr.	.09	.04	.01
□ 59 Lou Whitaker 2B	.09	.04	.01
□ 60 Navin Field	.09	.04	.01
□ 61 1945 Tigers	.15	.07	.01
□ 62 Ernie Harwell, Announcer	.15	.07	.01
□ 63 Tigers League Champs	.15	.07	.01
□ 64 Bobo Newsom P	.09	.04	.01
□ 65 Don Wert 3B	.09	.04	.01
□ 66 Ed Summers P	.09	.04	.01
□ 67 Billy Martin Mgr.	.30	.15	.03
□ 68 Alan Trammell SS	.09	.04	.01
□ 69 Dale Alexander 1B	.09	.04	.01
□ 70 Ed Brinkman SS	.09	.04	.01
□ 71 Right Man in Right Place in Right Park Wins Game	.09	.04	.01
□ 72 Bill Freehan C	.15	.07	.01
□ 73 Norm Cash 1B	.15	.07	.01
□ 74 George Dauss P	.09	.04	.01
□ 75 Aurelio Lopez P	.09	.04	.01
□ 76 Charlie Maxwell OF	.09	.04	.01
□ 77 Ed Barrow Mgr.	.15	.07	.01
□ 78 Willie Horton OF	.15	.07	.01
□ 79 Denny Sets Record 31 Wins	.15	.07	.01
□ 80 Dan Brouthers 1B	.30	.15	.03
□ 81 John E. Fetzer, Owner	.09	.04	.01
□ 82 Heinie Manush OF	.15	.07	.01
□ 83 1935 Tigers	.15	.07	.01
□ 84 Ray Boone INF	.09	.04	.01
□ 85 Bob Fothergill OF	.09	.04	.01
□ 86 Steve Kemp OF	.15	.07	.01
□ 87 Ed Killian P	.09	.04	.01
□ 88 Giebell Is Ineligible for Series But ...	.09	.04	.01
□ 89 Pinky Higgins 3B	.09	.04	.01
□ 90 Lance Parrish C	.15	.07	.01
□ 91 Eldon Auker P	.09	.04	.01
□ 92 Birdie Tebbetts C	.09	.04	.01
□ 93 Schoolboy Rowe P	.09	.04	.01
□ 94 Tiger rally gives McLain 30	.15	.07	.01
□ 95 1909 Tigers	.15	.07	.01
□ 96 Harvey Kuenn SS/OF	.15	.07	.01
□ 97 Jim Bunning P	.15	.07	.01
□ 98 1940 Tigers	.15	.07	.01
□ 99 Rocky Colavito OF	.15	.07	.01
□ 100 Kaline Enters Hall Of Fame	.30	.15	.03
□ 101 Billy Bruton OF	.09	.04	.01
□ 102 Germany Schaefer 2B	.09	.04	.01
□ 103 Frank Bolling 2B	.09	.04	.01
□ 104 Briggs Stadium	.09	.04	.01
□ 105 Bucky Harris 2B/Mgr.	.15	.07	.01
□ 106 Gates Brown OF	.09	.04	.01
□ 107 Billy Martin made the difference	.15	.07	.01
□ 108 1908 Tigers	.15	.07	.01
□ 109 Gee Walker OF	.09	.04	.01
□ 110 Pete Fox OF	.09	.04	.01
□ 111 Virgil Trucks P	.09	.04	.01
□ 112 1968 Tigers	.15	.07	.01
□ 113 Dizzy Trout P	.09	.04	.01
□ 114 Barney McCosky OF	.09	.04	.01
□ 115 Lu Blue 1B	.09	.04	.01
□ 116 Hal Newhouser P	.15	.07	.01
□ 117 Tigers Are Home To Prepare For World's Championship Series	.09	.04	.01
□ 118 Bobby Veach OF	.09	.04	.01
□ 119 George Mullin P	.09	.04	.01
□ 120 Reggie's super homer ignites A.L.	.15	.07	.01
□ 121 Sam Crawford OF	.15	.07	.01
□ 122 Hank Aguirre P	.09	.04	.01
□ 123 Vic Wertz 1B	.09	.04	.01
□ 124 Goose Goslin OF	.15	.07	.01
□ 125 Frank Lary P	.09	.04	.01
□ 126 Joe Coleman P	.09	.04	.01
□ 127 Ed Katalinas Scout	.09	.04	.01
□ 128 Jack Morris P	.15	.07	.01
□ 129 Tigers Picked As Winners Of Pirate Battle	.09	.04	.01
□ 130 James A. Campbell GM	.09	.04	.01
□ 131 Ted Gray P	.09	.04	.01
□ 132 Al Kaline OF	.60	.30	.06
□ 133 Hank Greenberg 1B	.30	.15	.03
□ 134 Dick McAuliffe INF	.09	.04	.01
□ 135 Ozzie Virgil INF	.09	.04	.01

1968 Dexter Press

This 77-card set, which measures approximately 3 1/2" by 5 1/2", has beautiful full-color photos on the front of the card with biographical and career information on the back of the card. There are no year by year statistical lines on the back of the card. Dexter Press is another name for cards which the Coca-Cola

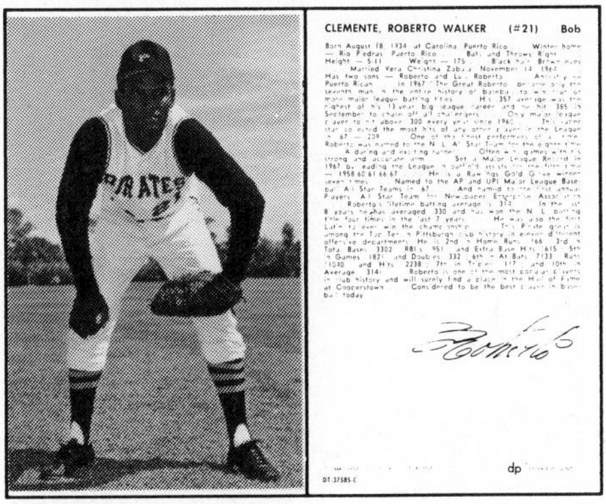

Company helped to distribute during the mid sixties. The backs of the cards have a facsimile autograph. Dexter Press was located in West Nyack, New York.

	NRMT	VG-E	GOOD
COMPLETE SET (77)	350.00	175.00	35.00
COMMON PLAYER (1-77)	2.00	1.00	.20
☐ 1 Hank Aaron	30.00	15.00	3.00
☐ 2 Jerry Adair	2.00	1.00	.20
☐ 3 Richie Allen	3.50	1.75	.35
☐ 4 Bob Allison	2.00	1.00	.20
☐ 5 Felipe Alou	2.50	1.25	.25
☐ 6 Jesus Alou	2.00	1.00	.20
☐ 7 Mike Andrews	2.00	1.00	.20
☐ 8 Bob Aspromonte	2.00	1.00	.20
☐ 9 Johnny Bateman	2.00	1.00	.20
☐ 10 Mark Belanger	2.00	1.00	.20
☐ 11 Gary Bell	2.00	1.00	.20
☐ 12 Paul Blair	2.00	1.00	.20
☐ 13 Curt Blefary	2.00	1.00	.20
☐ 14 Bobby Bolin	2.00	1.00	.20
☐ 15 Ken Boswell	2.00	1.00	.20
☐ 16 Clete Boyer	2.50	1.25	.25
☐ 17 Ron Brand	2.00	1.00	.20
☐ 18 Darrell Brandon	2.00	1.00	.20
☐ 19 Don Buford	2.00	1.00	.20
☐ 20 Rod Carew	25.00	12.50	2.50
☐ 21 Clay Carroll	2.00	1.00	.20
☐ 22 Rico Carty	2.50	1.25	.25
☐ 23 Dean Chance	2.00	1.00	.20
☐ 24 Roberto Clemente	30.00	15.00	3.00
☐ 25 Tony Cloninger	2.00	1.00	.20
☐ 26 Mike Cuellar	2.50	1.25	.25
☐ 27 Jim Davenport	2.00	1.00	.20
☐ 28 Ron Davis	2.00	1.00	.20
☐ 29 Moe Drabowsky	2.00	1.00	.20
☐ 30 Dick Ellsworth	2.50	1.25	.25
☐ 31 Andy Etchebarren	2.00	1.00	.20
☐ 32 Joe Foy	2.00	1.00	.20
☐ 33 Bill Freehan	2.50	1.25	.25
☐ 34 Jim Fregosi	2.50	1.25	.25
☐ 35 Julio Gotay	2.00	1.00	.20
☐ 36 Dave Giusti	2.00	1.00	.20
☐ 37 Jim Ray Hart	2.00	1.00	.20
☐ 38 Jack Hiatt	2.00	1.00	.20
☐ 39 Ron Hunt	2.00	1.00	.20
☐ 40 Sonny Jackson	2.00	1.00	.20
☐ 41 Pat Jarvis	2.00	1.00	.20
☐ 42 Dave Johnson	2.50	1.25	.25
☐ 43 Ken Johnson	2.00	1.00	.20
☐ 44 Dalton Jones	2.00	1.00	.20
☐ 45 Jim Kaat	5.00	2.50	.50
☐ 46 Harmon Killebrew	16.00	8.00	1.60
☐ 47 Denny Lemaster	2.00	1.00	.20
☐ 48 Frank Linzy	2.00	1.00	.20
☐ 49 Jim Lonborg	2.50	1.25	.25
☐ 50 Juan Marichal	12.00	6.00	1.20
☐ 51 Willie Mays	30.00	15.00	3.00
☐ 52 Bill Mazeroski	3.50	1.75	.35
☐ 53 Mike McCormick	2.50	1.25	.25
☐ 54 Dave McNally	2.50	1.25	.25
☐ 55 Denis Menke	2.00	1.00	.20
☐ 56 Joe Morgan	16.00	8.00	1.60
☐ 57 Dave Morehead	2.00	1.00	.20
☐ 58 Phil Niekro	10.00	5.00	1.00
☐ 59 Russ Nixon	2.00	1.00	.20
☐ 60 Tony Oliva	5.00	2.50	.50
☐ 61 Gaylord Perry	12.00	6.00	1.20
☐ 62 Rico Petrocelli	2.50	1.25	.25
☐ 63 Tom Phoebus	2.00	1.00	.20
☐ 64 Boog Powell	3.50	1.75	.35
☐ 65 Brooks Robinson	16.00	8.00	1.60
☐ 66 Frank Robinson	16.00	8.00	1.60
☐ 67 Rich Rollins	2.00	1.00	.20
☐ 68 John Roseboro	2.00	1.00	.20
☐ 69 Ray Sadecki	2.00	1.00	.20
☐ 70 George Scott	2.50	1.25	.25
☐ 71 Rusty Staub	5.00	2.50	.50
☐ 72 Cesar Tovar	2.00	1.00	.20
☐ 73 Joe Torre	5.00	2.50	.50
☐ 74 Ted Uhlaender	2.00	1.00	.20
☐ 75 Woody Woodward	2.00	1.00	.20
☐ 76 John Wyatt	2.00	1.00	.20
☐ 77 Jimmy Wynn	2.50	1.25	.25

1934-36 Diamond Stars

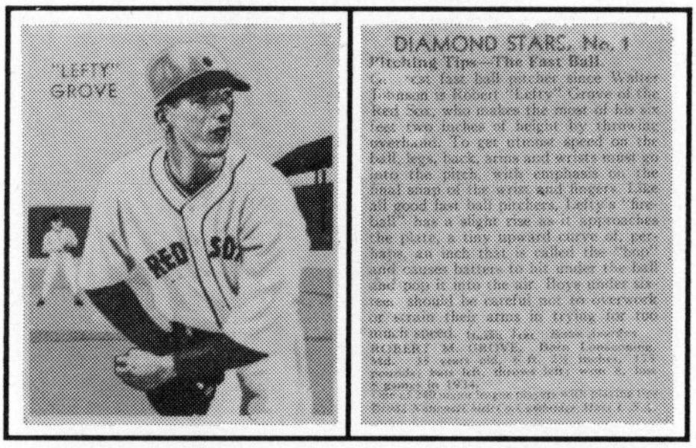

The cards in this 108-card set measure approximately 2 3/8" by 2 7/8". The Diamond Stars set produced by National Chicle from 1934-36 is also commonly known by its catalog designation, R327. The year of production can be determined by the statistics contained on the back of the card. There are at least 168 possible front/back combinations counting blue (B) and green (G) backs over all three years. The last twelve cards are repeat players and are quite scarce. The checklist below lists the year(s) and back color(s) for the cards. Cards 32 through 72 were issued only in 1935 with green ink on back. Cards 73 through 84 were issued three ways: 35B, 35G, and 36B. Card numbers 85 through 108 were issued only in 1936 with blue ink on back. The complete set price below refers to the set of all variations listed explicitly below. A blank backed proof sheet of 12 additional (never-issued) cards was discovered in 1980.

	EX-MT	VG-E	GOOD
COMPLETE SET (114)	14250.00	6750.00	1500.00
COMMON PLAYER (1-31)	45.00	22.50	4.50
COMMON PLAYER (32-72)	50.00	25.00	5.00
COMMON PLAYER (73-84)	60.00	30.00	6.00
COMMON PLAYER (85-96)	100.00	50.00	10.00
COMMON PLAYER (97-108)	300.00	150.00	30.00
☐ 1 Lefty Grove (34G, 35G)	800.00	125.00	25.00
☐ 2A Al Simmons (34G, 35G) (Sox on uniform)	125.00	60.00	12.50
☐ 2B Al Simmons (36B) (No name on uniform)	175.00	85.00	18.00
☐ 3 Rabbit Maranville (34G, 35G)	100.00	50.00	10.00
☐ 4 Buddy Myer (34G, 35G, 36B)	45.00	22.50	4.50
☐ 5 Tommy Bridges (34G, 35G, 36B)	45.00	22.50	4.50
☐ 6 Max Bishop (34G, 35G)	45.00	22.50	4.50
☐ 7 Lew Fonseca (34G, 35G)	45.00	22.50	4.50
☐ 8 Joe Vosmik (34G, 35G, 36B)	45.00	22.50	4.50

☐ 9 Mickey Cochrane (34G, 35G, 36B)	125.00	60.00	12.50
☐ 10A Leroy Mahaffey (34G, 35G) (A's on uniform)	45.00	22.50	4.50
☐ 10B Leroy Mahaffey (36B) (No name on uniform)	75.00	37.50	7.50
☐ 11 Bill Dickey (34G, 35G)	200.00	100.00	20.00
☐ 12A F. Walker (34G) (Ruth retires mentioned on back)	45.00	22.50	4.50
☐ 12B F. Walker (35G) (Ruth to Boston mentioned on back)	45.00	22.50	4.50
☐ 12C F. Walker (36B)	45.00	22.50	4.50
☐ 13 George Blaeholder (34G, 35G)	45.00	22.50	4.50
☐ 14 Bill Terry (34G, 35G)	125.00	60.00	12.50
☐ 15A Dick Bartell (34G) (Philadelphia Phillies on card back)	45.00	22.50	4.50
☐ 15B Dick Bartell (35G) (New York Giants on card back)	45.00	22.50	4.50
☐ 16 Lloyd Waner (34G, 35G, 36B)	100.00	50.00	10.00
☐ 17 Frank Frisch (34G, 35G)	125.00	60.00	12.50
☐ 18 Chick Hafey (34G, 35G)	100.00	50.00	10.00
☐ 19 Van Lingle Mungo (34G, 35G)	45.00	22.50	4.50
☐ 20 Frank Hogan (34G, 35G)	45.00	22.50	4.50
☐ 21A Johnny Vergez (34G) (New York Giants on card back)	45.00	22.50	4.50
☐ 21B Johnny Vergez (35G) (Philadelphia Phillies on card back)	45.00	22.50	4.50
☐ 22 Jimmy Wilson (34G, 35G, 36B)	45.00	22.50	4.50
☐ 23 Bill Hallahan (34G, 35G)	45.00	22.50	4.50
☐ 24 Earl Adams (34G, 35G)	45.00	22.50	4.50
☐ 25 Wally Berger (35G)	60.00	30.00	6.00
☐ 26 Pepper Martin 35G, 36B)	75.00	37.50	7.50
☐ 27 Pie Traynor (35G)	150.00	75.00	15.00
☐ 28 Al Lopez (35G)	125.00	60.00	12.50
☐ 29 Red Rolfe (35G)	60.00	30.00	6.00
☐ 30A Heine Manush (35G) (W on sleeve)	125.00	60.00	12.50
☐ 30B Heine Manush (36B) (No W on sleeve)	175.00	85.00	18.00
☐ 31A Kiki Cuyler (35G) (Chicago Cubs)	100.00	50.00	10.00
☐ 31B Kiki Cuyler (36B) (Cincinnati Reds)	100.00	50.00	10.00
☐ 32 Sam Rice	100.00	50.00	10.00
☐ 33 Schoolboy Rowe	50.00	25.00	5.00
☐ 34 Stan Hack	50.00	25.00	5.00
☐ 35 Earl Averill	100.00	50.00	10.00
☐ 36A "Earnie" Lombardi (sic, Ernie)	250.00	125.00	25.00
☐ 36B "Ernie" Lombardi	100.00	50.00	10.00
☐ 37 Billy Urbanski	50.00	25.00	5.00
☐ 38 Ben Chapman	60.00	30.00	6.00
☐ 39 Carl Hubbell	125.00	60.00	12.50
☐ 40 Blondy Ryan	50.00	25.00	5.00
☐ 41 Harvey Hendrick	50.00	25.00	5.00
☐ 42 Jimmy Dykes	60.00	30.00	6.00
☐ 43 Ted Lyons	100.00	50.00	10.00
☐ 44 Rogers Hornsby	300.00	150.00	30.00
☐ 45 Jo Jo White	50.00	25.00	5.00
☐ 46 Red Lucas	50.00	25.00	5.00
☐ 47 Bob Bolton	50.00	25.00	5.00
☐ 48 Rick Ferrell	100.00	50.00	10.00
☐ 49 Buck Jordan	50.00	25.00	5.00
☐ 50 Mel Ott	200.00	100.00	20.00
☐ 51 Burgess Whitehead	50.00	25.00	5.00
☐ 52 Tuck Stainback	50.00	25.00	5.00
☐ 53 Oscar Melillo	50.00	25.00	5.00
☐ 54A "Hank" Greenburg (sic, Greenberg)	400.00	200.00	40.00
☐ 54B "Hank" Greenberg	200.00	100.00	20.00
☐ 55 Tony Cuccinello	50.00	25.00	5.00
☐ 56 Gus Suhr	50.00	25.00	5.00
☐ 57 Cy Blanton	50.00	25.00	5.00
☐ 58 Glenn Myatt	50.00	25.00	5.00
☐ 59 Jim Bottomley	100.00	50.00	10.00
☐ 60 Red Ruffing	125.00	60.00	12.50
☐ 61 Bill Werber	50.00	25.00	5.00
☐ 62 Fred Frankhouse	50.00	25.00	5.00
☐ 63 Travis Jackson	100.00	50.00	10.00
☐ 64 Jimmy Foxx	300.00	150.00	30.00
☐ 65 Zeke Bonura	50.00	25.00	5.00
☐ 66 Ducky Medwick	125.00	60.00	12.50
☐ 67 Marvin Owen	50.00	25.00	5.00
☐ 68 Sam Leslie	50.00	25.00	5.00
☐ 69 Earl Grace	50.00	25.00	5.00
☐ 70 Hal Trosky	60.00	30.00	6.00
☐ 71 Ossie Bluege	50.00	25.00	5.00
☐ 72 Tony Piet	50.00	25.00	5.00
☐ 73 Fritz Ostermueller	60.00	30.00	6.00
☐ 74 Tony Lazzeri	90.00	45.00	9.00
☐ 75 Jack Burns	60.00	30.00	6.00
☐ 76 Billy Rogell	60.00	30.00	6.00
☐ 77 Charlie Gehringer	150.00	75.00	15.00
☐ 78 Joe Kuhel	60.00	30.00	6.00
☐ 79 Willis Hudlin	60.00	30.00	6.00
☐ 80 Lou Chiozza	60.00	30.00	6.00
☐ 81 Bill Delancey	60.00	30.00	6.00
☐ 82A Johnny Babich (Dodgers on uniform; 35G, 35B)	60.00	30.00	6.00
☐ 82B Johnny Babich (No name on uniform; 36B)	100.00	50.00	10.00
☐ 83 Paul Waner	150.00	75.00	15.00
☐ 84 Sam Byrd	60.00	30.00	6.00
☐ 85 Moose Solters	100.00	50.00	10.00
☐ 86 Frank Crosetti	125.00	60.00	12.50
☐ 87 Steve O'Neill	100.00	50.00	10.00
☐ 88 George Selkirk	125.00	60.00	12.50
☐ 89 Joe Stripp	100.00	50.00	10.00
☐ 90 Ray Hayworth	100.00	50.00	10.00
☐ 91 Bucky Harris	175.00	85.00	18.00
☐ 92 Ethan Allen	100.00	50.00	10.00
☐ 93 General Crowder	100.00	50.00	10.00
☐ 94 Wes Ferrell	125.00	60.00	12.50
☐ 95 Luke Appling	200.00	100.00	20.00
☐ 96 Lew Riggs	100.00	50.00	10.00
☐ 97 Al Lopez	500.00	250.00	50.00
☐ 98 Schoolboy Rowe	350.00	175.00	35.00
☐ 99 Pie Traynor	600.00	300.00	60.00
☐ 100 Earl Averill	500.00	250.00	50.00
☐ 101 Dick Bartell	300.00	150.00	30.00
☐ 102 Van Lingle Mungo	300.00	150.00	30.00
☐ 103 Bill Dickey	800.00	400.00	80.00
☐ 104 Red Rolfe	300.00	150.00	30.00
☐ 105 Ernie Lombardi	500.00	250.00	50.00
☐ 106 Red Lucas	300.00	150.00	30.00
☐ 107 Stan Hack	300.00	150.00	30.00
☐ 108 Wally Berger	350.00	175.00	35.00

1988 Domino's Tigers

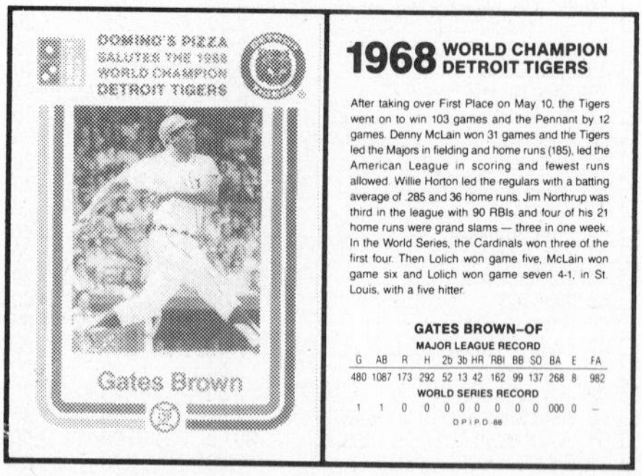

This rather unattractive set commemorates the 20th anniversary of the Detroit Tigers' World Championship season in 1968. The card stock used is rather thin. The cards measure approximately 2 1/2" by 3 1/2". There are a number of errors in the set including biographical errors, misspellings, and photo misidentifications.

Players are pictured in black and white inside a red and blue horseshoe. The numerous factual errors in the set detract from the set's collectibility in the eyes of many collectors.

	MINT	EXC	G-VG
COMPLETE SET (28)	6.00	3.00	.60
COMMON PLAYER (1-28)	.15	.07	.01
☐ 1 Gates Brown	.15	.07	.01
☐ 2 Norm Cash	.35	.17	.03
☐ 3 Wayne Comer	.15	.07	.01
☐ 4 Pat Dobson	.15	.07	.01
☐ 5 Bill Freehan	.35	.17	.03
☐ 6 Ernie Harwell	.25	.12	.02
(announcer)			
☐ 7 John Hiller	.25	.12	.02
☐ 8 Willie Horton	.25	.12	.02
☐ 9 Al Kaline	1.00	.50	.10
☐ 10 Fred Lasher	.15	.07	.01
☐ 11 Mickey Lolich	.35	.17	.03
☐ 12 Tom Matchick	.15	.07	.01
☐ 13 Ed Mathews	.75	.35	.07
☐ 14 Dick McAuliffe	.25	.12	.02
☐ 15 Denny McLain	.35	.17	.03
☐ 16 Don McMahon	.15	.07	.01
☐ 17 Jim Northrup	.15	.07	.01
☐ 18 Ray Oyler	.15	.07	.01
☐ 19 Daryl Patterson	.15	.07	.01
☐ 20 Jim Price	.15	.07	.01
☐ 21 Joe Sparma	.15	.07	.01
☐ 22 Mickey Stanley	.25	.12	.02
☐ 23 Dick Tracewski	.15	.07	.01
☐ 24 Jon Warden	.15	.07	.01
☐ 25 Don Wert	.15	.07	.01
☐ 26 Earl Wilson	.15	.07	.01
☐ 27 Pizza Buck Coupon	.15	.07	.01
☐ 28 Title Card	.15	.07	.01
Old Timers Game 1988			

1981 Donruss

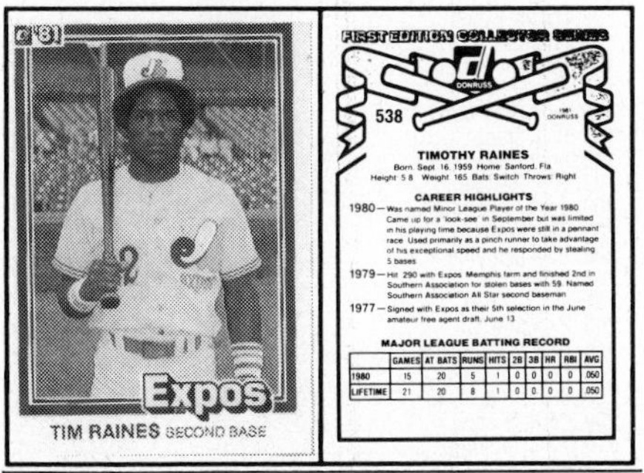

The cards in this 605-card set measure 2 1/2" by 3 1/2". In 1981 Donruss launched itself into the baseball card market with a set containing 600 numbered cards and five unnumbered checklists. Even though the five checklist cards are unnumbered, they are numbered below (601-605) for convenience in reference. The cards are printed on thin stock and more than one pose exists for several popular players. The numerous errors of the first print run were later corrected by the company. These are marked P1 and P2 in the checklist below. The key rookie card in this set is Tim Raines.

	MINT	EXC	G-VG
COMPLETE SET (605)	50.00	25.00	5.00
COMMON PLAYER (1-605)	.04	.02	.00
☐ 1 Ozzie Smith	1.20	.30	.06
☐ 2 Rollie Fingers	.45	.22	.04
☐ 3 Rick Wise	.04	.02	.00
☐ 4 Gene Richards	.04	.02	.00
☐ 5 Alan Trammell	.50	.25	.05
☐ 6 Tom Brookens	.04	.02	.00
☐ 7A Duffy Dyer P1	.10	.05	.01
1980 batting average			
has decimal point			
☐ 7B Duffy Dyer P2	.07	.03	.01
1980 batting average			
has no decimal point			
☐ 8 Mark Fidrych	.10	.05	.01
☐ 9 Dave Rozema	.04	.02	.00
☐ 10 Ricky Peters	.04	.02	.00
☐ 11 Mike Schmidt	2.25	1.10	.22
☐ 12 Willie Stargell	.40	.20	.04
☐ 13 Tim Foli	.04	.02	.00
☐ 14 Manny Sanguillen	.07	.03	.01
☐ 15 Grant Jackson	.04	.02	.00
☐ 16 Eddie Solomon	.04	.02	.00
☐ 17 Omar Moreno	.04	.02	.00
☐ 18 Joe Morgan	.50	.25	.05
☐ 19 Rafael Landestoy	.04	.02	.00
☐ 20 Bruce Bochy	.04	.02	.00
☐ 21 Joe Sambito	.04	.02	.00
☐ 22 Manny Trillo	.04	.02	.00
☐ 23A Dave Smith P1	.45	.22	.04
Line box around stats			
is not complete			
☐ 23B Dave Smith P2	.45	.22	.04
Box totally encloses			
stats at top			
☐ 24 Terry Puhl	.07	.03	.01
☐ 25 Bump Wills	.04	.02	.00
☐ 26A John Ellis P1 ERR	.60	.30	.06
Photo on front			
shows Danny Walton			
☐ 26B John Ellis P2 COR	.10	.05	.01
☐ 27 Jim Kern	.04	.02	.00
☐ 28 Richie Zisk	.07	.03	.01
☐ 29 John Mayberry	.07	.03	.01
☐ 30 Bob Davis	.04	.02	.00
☐ 31 Jackson Todd	.04	.02	.00
☐ 32 Alvis Woods	.04	.02	.00
☐ 33 Steve Carlton	1.00	.50	.10
☐ 34 Lee Mazzilli	.04	.02	.00
☐ 35 John Stearns	.04	.02	.00
☐ 36 Roy Lee Jackson	.04	.02	.00
☐ 37 Mike Scott	.90	.45	.09
☐ 38 Lamar Johnson	.04	.02	.00
☐ 39 Kevin Bell	.04	.02	.00
☐ 40 Ed Farmer	.04	.02	.00
☐ 41 Ross Baumgarten	.04	.02	.00
☐ 42 Leo Sutherland	.04	.02	.00
☐ 43 Dan Meyer	.04	.02	.00
☐ 44 Ron Reed	.04	.02	.00
☐ 45 Mario Mendoza	.04	.02	.00
☐ 46 Rick Honeycutt	.04	.02	.00
☐ 47 Glenn Abbott	.04	.02	.00
☐ 48 Leon Roberts	.04	.02	.00
☐ 49 Rod Carew	1.00	.50	.10
☐ 50 Bert Campaneris	.07	.03	.01
☐ 51A Tom Donahue P1 ERR	.15	.07	.01
Name on front			
misspelled Donahue			
☐ 51B Tom Donohue	.10	.05	.01
P2 COR			
☐ 52 Dave Frost	.04	.02	.00
☐ 53 Ed Halicki	.04	.02	.00
☐ 54 Dan Ford	.04	.02	.00
☐ 55 Garry Maddox	.07	.03	.01
☐ 56A Steve Garvey P1	1.25	.60	.12
"Surpassed 25 HR"			
☐ 56B Steve Garvey P2	.75	.35	.07
"Surpassed 21 HR"			
☐ 57 Bill Russell	.07	.03	.01
☐ 58 Don Sutton	.35	.17	.03
☐ 59 Reggie Smith	.10	.05	.01
☐ 60 Rick Monday	.07	.03	.01
☐ 61 Ray Knight	.10	.05	.01
☐ 62 Johnny Bench	1.10	.55	.11
☐ 63 Mario Soto	.10	.05	.01
☐ 64 Doug Bair	.04	.02	.00
☐ 65 George Foster	.18	.09	.01
☐ 66 Jeff Burroughs	.07	.03	.01
☐ 67 Keith Hernandez	.35	.17	.03
☐ 68 Tom Herr	.15	.07	.01
☐ 69 Bob Forsch	.07	.03	.01
☐ 70 John Fulgham	.04	.02	.00
☐ 71A Bobby Bonds P1 ERR	.40	.20	.04
986 lifetime HR			
☐ 71B Bobby Bonds P2 COR	.15	.07	.01
326 lifetime HR			
☐ 72A Rennie Stennett P1	.10	.05	.01
"breaking broke leg"			
☐ 72B Rennie Stennett P2	.07	.03	.01
Word "broke" deleted			
☐ 73 Joe Strain	.04	.02	.00
☐ 74 Ed Whitson	.10	.05	.01

☐ 75 Tom Griffin	.04	.02	.00
☐ 76 Billy North	.04	.02	.00
☐ 77 Gene Garber	.04	.02	.00
☐ 78 Mike Hargrove	.07	.03	.01
☐ 79 Dave Rosello	.04	.02	.00
☐ 80 Ron Hassey	.07	.03	.01
☐ 81 Sid Monge	.04	.02	.00
☐ 82A Joe Charboneau P1 '78 highlights, "For some reason"	.15	.07	.01
☐ 82B Joe Charboneau P2 phrase "For some reason" deleted	.10	.05	.01
☐ 83 Cecil Cooper	.15	.07	.01
☐ 84 Sal Bando	.07	.03	.01
☐ 85 Moose Haas	.07	.03	.01
☐ 86 Mike Caldwell	.04	.02	.00
☐ 87A Larry Hisle P1 '77 highlights, line ends with "28 RBI"	.15	.07	.01
☐ 87B Larry Hisle P2 correct line "28 HR"	.10	.05	.01
☐ 88 Luis Gomez	.04	.02	.00
☐ 89 Larry Parrish	.07	.03	.01
☐ 90 Gary Carter	.50	.25	.05
☐ 91 Bill Gullickson	.25	.12	.02
☐ 92 Fred Norman	.04	.02	.00
☐ 93 Tommy Hutton	.04	.02	.00
☐ 94 Carl Yastrzemski	1.10	.55	.11
☐ 95 Glenn Hoffman	.04	.02	.00
☐ 96 Dennis Eckersley	.40	.20	.04
☐ 97A Tom Burgmeier P1 ERR Throws: Right	.10	.05	.01
☐ 97B Tom Burgmeier P2 COR Throws: Left	.07	.03	.01
☐ 98 Win Remmerswaal	.04	.02	.00
☐ 99 Bob Horner	.12	.06	.01
☐ 100 George Brett	1.75	.85	.17
☐ 101 Dave Chalk	.04	.02	.00
☐ 102 Dennis Leonard	.07	.03	.01
☐ 103 Renie Martin	.04	.02	.00
☐ 104 Amos Otis	.10	.05	.01
☐ 105 Graig Nettles	.15	.07	.01
☐ 106 Eric Soderholm	.04	.02	.00
☐ 107 Tommy John	.20	.10	.02
☐ 108 Tom Underwood	.04	.02	.00
☐ 109 Lou Piniella	.12	.06	.01
☐ 110 Mickey Klutts	.04	.02	.00
☐ 111 Bobby Murcer	.10	.05	.01
☐ 112 Eddie Murray	1.00	.50	.10
☐ 113 Rick Dempsey	.04	.02	.00
☐ 114 Scott McGregor	.07	.03	.01
☐ 115 Ken Singleton	.10	.05	.01
☐ 116 Gary Roenicke	.04	.02	.00
☐ 117 Dave Revering	.04	.02	.00
☐ 118 Mike Norris	.04	.02	.00
☐ 119 Rickey Henderson	22.00	11.00	2.20
☐ 120 Mike Heath	.04	.02	.00
☐ 121 Dave Cash	.04	.02	.00
☐ 122 Randy Jones	.04	.02	.00
☐ 123 Eric Rasmussen	.04	.02	.00
☐ 124 Jerry Mumphrey	.04	.02	.00
☐ 125 Richie Hebner	.04	.02	.00
☐ 126 Mark Wagner	.04	.02	.00
☐ 127 Jack Morris	.30	.15	.03
☐ 128 Dan Petry	.10	.05	.01
☐ 129 Bruce Robbins	.04	.02	.00
☐ 130 Champ Summers	.04	.02	.00
☐ 131A Pete Rose P1 last line ends with "see card 251"	2.00	1.00	.20
☐ 131B Pete Rose P2 last line corrected "see card 371"	1.25	.60	.12
☐ 132 Willie Stargell	.40	.20	.04
☐ 133 Ed Ott	.04	.02	.00
☐ 134 Jim Bibby	.04	.02	.00
☐ 135 Bert Blyleven	.25	.12	.02
☐ 136 Dave Parker	.40	.20	.04
☐ 137 Bill Robinson	.07	.03	.01
☐ 138 Enos Cabell	.04	.02	.00
☐ 139 Dave Bergman	.04	.02	.00
☐ 140 J.R. Richard	.07	.03	.01
☐ 141 Ken Forsch	.04	.02	.00
☐ 142 Larry Bowa UER (shortshop on front)	.15	.07	.01
☐ 143 Frank LaCorte UER (photo actually Randy Niemann)	.04	.02	.00
☐ 144 Denny Walling	.04	.02	.00
☐ 145 Buddy Bell	.12	.06	.01
☐ 146 Ferguson Jenkins	.20	.10	.02
☐ 147 Dannny Darwin	.10	.05	.01
☐ 148 John Grubb	.04	.02	.00
☐ 149 Alfredo Griffin	.10	.05	.01
☐ 150 Jerry Garvin	.04	.02	.00
☐ 151 Paul Mirabella	.04	.02	.00
☐ 152 Rick Bosetti	.04	.02	.00
☐ 153 Dick Ruthven	.04	.02	.00
☐ 154 Frank Taveras	.04	.02	.00
☐ 155 Craig Swan	.04	.02	.00
☐ 156 Jeff Reardon	1.00	.50	.10
☐ 157 Steve Henderson	.04	.02	.00
☐ 158 Jim Morrison	.04	.02	.00
☐ 159 Glenn Borgmann	.04	.02	.00
☐ 160 LaMarr Hoyt	.20	.10	.02
☐ 161 Rich Wortham	.04	.02	.00
☐ 162 Thad Bosley	.04	.02	.00
☐ 163 Julio Cruz	.04	.02	.00
☐ 164A Del Unser P1 no "3B" heading	.10	.05	.01
☐ 164B Del Unser P2 Batting record on back corrected ("3B")	.07	.03	.01
☐ 165 Jim Anderson	.04	.02	.00
☐ 166 Jim Beattie	.04	.02	.00
☐ 167 Shane Rawley	.04	.02	.00
☐ 168 Joe Simpson	.04	.02	.00
☐ 169 Rod Carew	1.00	.50	.10
☐ 170 Fred Patek	.04	.02	.00
☐ 171 Frank Tanana	.07	.03	.01
☐ 172 Alfredo Martinez	.04	.02	.00
☐ 173 Chris Knapp	.04	.02	.00
☐ 174 Joe Rudi	.07	.03	.01
☐ 175 Greg Luzinski	.12	.06	.01
☐ 176 Steve Garvey	.75	.35	.07
☐ 177 Joe Ferguson	.04	.02	.00
☐ 178 Bob Welch	.45	.22	.04
☐ 179 Dusty Baker	.07	.03	.01
☐ 180 Rudy Law	.04	.02	.00
☐ 181 Dave Concepcion	.15	.07	.01
☐ 182 Johnny Bench	1.10	.55	.11
☐ 183 Mike LaCoss	.04	.02	.00
☐ 184 Ken Griffey	.20	.10	.02
☐ 185 Dave Collins	.04	.02	.00
☐ 186 Brian Asselstine	.04	.02	.00
☐ 187 Garry Templeton	.07	.03	.01
☐ 188 Mike Phillips	.04	.02	.00
☐ 189 Pete Vuckovich	.07	.03	.01
☐ 190 John Urrea	.04	.02	.00
☐ 191 Tony Scott	.04	.02	.00
☐ 192 Darrell Evans	.15	.07	.01
☐ 193 Milt May	.04	.02	.00
☐ 194 Bob Knepper	.07	.03	.01
☐ 195 Randy Moffitt	.04	.02	.00
☐ 196 Larry Herndon	.04	.02	.00
☐ 197 Rick Camp	.04	.02	.00
☐ 198 Andre Thornton	.07	.03	.01
☐ 199 Tom Veryzer	.04	.02	.00
☐ 200 Gary Alexander	.04	.02	.00
☐ 201 Rick Waits	.04	.02	.00
☐ 202 Rick Manning	.04	.02	.00
☐ 203 Paul Molitor	.35	.17	.03
☐ 204 Jim Gantner	.07	.03	.01
☐ 205 Paul Mitchell	.04	.02	.00
☐ 206 Reggie Cleveland	.04	.02	.00
☐ 207 Sixto Lezcano	.04	.02	.00
☐ 208 Bruce Benedict	.04	.02	.00
☐ 209 Rodney Scott	.04	.02	.00
☐ 210 John Tamargo	.04	.02	.00
☐ 211 Bill Lee	.07	.03	.01
☐ 212 Andre Dawson	1.00	.50	.10
☐ 213 Rowland Office	.04	.02	.00
☐ 214 Carl Yastrzemski	1.10	.55	.11
☐ 215 Jerry Remy	.04	.02	.00
☐ 216 Mike Torrez	.04	.02	.00
☐ 217 Skip Lockwood	.04	.02	.00
☐ 218 Fred Lynn	.20	.10	.02
☐ 219 Chris Chambliss	.07	.03	.01
☐ 220 Willie Aikens	.04	.02	.00
☐ 221 John Wathan	.07	.03	.01
☐ 222 Dan Quisenberry	.15	.07	.01
☐ 223 Willie Wilson	.15	.07	.01
☐ 224 Clint Hurdle	.04	.02	.00
☐ 225 Bob Watson	.07	.03	.01
☐ 226 Jim Spencer	.04	.02	.00
☐ 227 Ron Guidry	.20	.10	.02
☐ 228 Reggie Jackson	1.35	.65	.13
☐ 229 Oscar Gamble	.07	.03	.01
☐ 230 Jeff Cox	.04	.02	.00
☐ 231 Luis Tiant	.10	.05	.01
☐ 232 Rich Dauer	.04	.02	.00
☐ 233 Dan Graham	.04	.02	.00
☐ 234 Mike Flanagan	.10	.05	.01
☐ 235 John Lowenstein	.04	.02	.00
☐ 236 Benny Ayala	.04	.02	.00
☐ 237 Wayne Gross	.04	.02	.00
☐ 238 Rick Langford	.04	.02	.00

☐ 239 Tony Armas	.07	.03	.01
☐ 240A Bob Lacy P1 ERR	.30	.15	.03
Name misspelled			
Bob "Lacy"			
☐ 240B Bob Lacey P2 COR	.10	.05	.01
☐ 241 Gene Tenace	.07	.03	.01
☐ 242 Bob Shirley	.04	.02	.00
☐ 243 Gary Lucas	.04	.02	.00
☐ 244 Jerry Turner	.04	.02	.00
☐ 245 John Wockenfuss	.04	.02	.00
☐ 246 Stan Papi	.04	.02	.00
☐ 247 Milt Wilcox	.04	.02	.00
☐ 248 Dan Schatzeder	.04	.02	.00
☐ 249 Steve Kemp	.07	.03	.01
☐ 250 Jim Lentine	.04	.02	.00
☐ 251 Pete Rose	1.25	.60	.12
☐ 252 Bill Madlock	.15	.07	.01
☐ 253 Dale Berra	.04	.02	.00
☐ 254 Kent Tekulve	.07	.03	.01
☐ 255 Enrique Romo	.04	.02	.00
☐ 256 Mike Easler	.07	.03	.01
☐ 257 Chuck Tanner MG	.07	.03	.01
☐ 258 Art Howe	.10	.05	.01
☐ 259 Alan Ashby	.04	.02	.00
☐ 260 Nolan Ryan	3.75	1.85	.37
☐ 261A Vern Ruhle P1 ERR	.60	.30	.06
Photo on front			
actually Ken Forsch			
☐ 261B Vern Ruhle P2 COR	.10	.05	.01
☐ 262 Bob Boone	.15	.07	.01
☐ 263 Cesar Cedeno	.10	.05	.01
☐ 264 Jeff Leonard	.15	.07	.01
☐ 265 Pat Putnam	.04	.02	.00
☐ 266 Jon Matlack	.07	.03	.01
☐ 267 Dave Rajsich	.04	.02	.00
☐ 268 Billy Sample	.04	.02	.00
☐ 269 Damaso Garcia	.07	.03	.01
☐ 270 Tom Buskey	.04	.02	.00
☐ 271 Joey McLaughlin	.04	.02	.00
☐ 272 Barry Bonnell	.04	.02	.00
☐ 273 Tug McGraw	.10	.05	.01
☐ 274 Mike Jorgensen	.04	.02	.00
☐ 275 Pat Zachry	.04	.02	.00
☐ 276 Neil Allen	.07	.03	.01
☐ 277 Joel Youngblood	.04	.02	.00
☐ 278 Greg Pryor	.04	.02	.00
☐ 279 Britt Burns	.12	.06	.01
☐ 280 Rich Dotson	.25	.12	.02
☐ 281 Chet Lemon	.04	.02	.00
☐ 282 Rusty Kuntz	.04	.02	.00
☐ 283 Ted Cox	.04	.02	.00
☐ 284 Sparky Lyle	.10	.05	.01
☐ 285 Larry Cox	.04	.02	.00
☐ 286 Floyd Bannister	.04	.02	.00
☐ 287 Byron McLaughlin	.04	.02	.00
☐ 288 Rodney Craig	.04	.02	.00
☐ 289 Bobby Grich	.07	.03	.01
☐ 290 Dickie Thon	.10	.05	.01
☐ 291 Mark Clear	.07	.03	.01
☐ 292 Dave Lemanczyk	.04	.02	.00
☐ 293 Jason Thompson	.04	.02	.00
☐ 294 Rick Miller	.04	.02	.00
☐ 295 Lonnie Smith	.15	.07	.01
☐ 296 Ron Cey	.10	.05	.01
☐ 297 Steve Yeager	.04	.02	.00
☐ 298 Bobby Castillo	.04	.02	.00
☐ 299 Manny Mota	.07	.03	.01
☐ 300 Jay Johnstone	.07	.03	.01
☐ 301 Dan Driessen	.04	.02	.00
☐ 302 Joe Nolan	.04	.02	.00
☐ 303 Paul Householder	.04	.02	.00
☐ 304 Harry Spilman	.04	.02	.00
☐ 305 Cesar Geronimo	.04	.02	.00
☐ 306A Gary Mathews P1 ERR	.30	.15	.03
Name misspelled			
☐ 306B Gary Matthews P2	.10	.05	.01
COR			
☐ 307 Ken Reitz	.04	.02	.00
☐ 308 Ted Simmons	.15	.07	.01
☐ 309 John Littlefield	.04	.02	.00
☐ 310 George Frazier	.04	.02	.00
☐ 311 Dane Iorg	.04	.02	.00
☐ 312 Mike Ivie	.04	.02	.00
☐ 313 Dennis Littlejohn	.04	.02	.00
☐ 314 Gary Lavelle	.04	.02	.00
☐ 315 Jack Clark	.30	.15	.03
☐ 316 Jim Wohlford	.04	.02	.00
☐ 317 Rick Matula	.04	.02	.00
☐ 318 Toby Harrah	.07	.03	.01
☐ 319A Dwane Kuiper P1 ERR	.15	.07	.01
Name misspelled			
☐ 319B Duane Kuiper P2 COR	.10	.05	.01
☐ 320 Len Barker	.04	.02	.00
☐ 321 Victor Cruz	.04	.02	.00

☐ 322 Dell Alston	.04	.02	.00
☐ 323 Robin Yount	1.25	.60	.12
☐ 324 Charlie Moore	.04	.02	.00
☐ 325 Lary Sorensen	.04	.02	.00
☐ 326A Gorman Thomas P1	.30	.15	.03
2nd line on back:			
"30 HR mark 4th"			
☐ 326B Gorman Thomas P2	.10	.05	.01
"30 HR mark 3rd"			
☐ 327 Bob Rodgers MG	.04	.02	.00
☐ 328 Phil Niekro	.30	.15	.03
☐ 329 Chris Speier	.04	.02	.00
☐ 330A Steve Rodgers P1	.30	.15	.03
ERR Name misspelled			
☐ 330B Steve Rogers P2 COR	.10	.05	.01
☐ 331 Woodie Fryman	.04	.02	.00
☐ 332 Warren Cromartie	.04	.02	.00
☐ 333 Jerry White	.04	.02	.00
☐ 334 Tony Perez	.20	.10	.02
☐ 335 Carlton Fisk	.65	.30	.06
☐ 336 Dick Drago	.04	.02	.00
☐ 337 Steve Renko	.04	.02	.00
☐ 338 Jim Rice	.30	.15	.03
☐ 339 Jerry Royster	.04	.02	.00
☐ 340 Frank White	.10	.05	.01
☐ 341 Jamie Quirk	.04	.02	.00
☐ 342A Paul Spittorff P1 ERR	.15	.07	.01
Name misspelled			
☐ 342B Paul Splittorff	.10	.05	.01
P2 COR			
☐ 343 Marty Pattin	.04	.02	.00
☐ 344 Pete LaCock	.04	.02	.00
☐ 345 Willie Randolph	.10	.05	.01
☐ 346 Rick Cerone	.04	.02	.00
☐ 347 Rich Gossage	.20	.10	.02
☐ 348 Reggie Jackson	1.35	.65	.13
☐ 349 Ruppert Jones	.04	.02	.00
☐ 350 Dave McKay	.04	.02	.00
☐ 351 Yogi Berra CO	.20	.10	.02
☐ 352 Doug DeCinces	.07	.03	.01
☐ 353 Jim Palmer	.75	.35	.07
☐ 354 Tippy Martinez	.04	.02	.00
☐ 355 Al Bumbry	.04	.02	.00
☐ 356 Earl Weaver MG	.10	.05	.01
☐ 357A Bob Picciolo P1 ERR	.15	.07	.01
Name misspelled			
☐ 357B Rob Picciolo P2 COR	.06	.03	.00
☐ 358 Matt Keough	.04	.02	.00
☐ 359 Dwayne Murphy	.04	.02	.00
☐ 360 Brian Kingman	.04	.02	.00
☐ 361 Bill Fahey	.04	.02	.00
☐ 362 Steve Mura	.04	.02	.00
☐ 363 Dennis Kinney	.04	.02	.00
☐ 364 Dave Winfield	.65	.30	.06
☐ 365 Lou Whitaker	.30	.15	.03
☐ 366 Lance Parrish	.35	.17	.03
☐ 367 Tim Corcoran	.04	.02	.00
☐ 368 Pat Underwood	.04	.02	.00
☐ 369 Al Cowens	.07	.03	.01
☐ 370 Sparky Anderson MG	.10	.05	.01
☐ 371 Pete Rose	1.25	.60	.12
☐ 372 Phil Garner	.04	.02	.00
☐ 373 Steve Nicosia	.04	.02	.00
☐ 374 John Candelaria	.07	.03	.01
☐ 375 Don Robinson	.07	.03	.01
☐ 376 Lee Lacy	.04	.02	.00
☐ 377 John Milner	.04	.02	.00
☐ 378 Craig Reynolds	.04	.02	.00
☐ 379A Luis Pujois P1 ERR	.15	.07	.01
Name misspelled			
☐ 379B Luis Pujols P2 COR	.07	.03	.01
☐ 380 Joe Niekro	.10	.05	.01
☐ 381 Joaquin Andujar	.10	.05	.01
☐ 382 Keith Moreland	.25	.12	.02
☐ 383 Jose Cruz	.07	.03	.01
☐ 384 Bill Virdon MG	.07	.03	.01
☐ 385 Jim Sundberg	.04	.02	.00
☐ 386 Doc Medich	.04	.02	.00
☐ 387 Al Oliver	.10	.05	.01
☐ 388 Jim Norris	.04	.02	.00
☐ 389 Bob Bailor	.04	.02	.00
☐ 390 Ernie Whitt	.07	.03	.01
☐ 391 Otto Velez	.04	.02	.00
☐ 392 Roy Howell	.04	.02	.00
☐ 393 Bob Walk	.30	.15	.03
☐ 394 Doug Flynn	.04	.02	.00
☐ 395 Pete Falcone	.04	.02	.00
☐ 396 Tom Hausman	.04	.02	.00
☐ 397 Elliott Maddox	.04	.02	.00
☐ 398 Mike Squires	.04	.02	.00
☐ 399 Marvis Foley	.04	.02	.00
☐ 400 Steve Trout	.04	.02	.00
☐ 401 Wayne Nordhagen	.04	.02	.00
☐ 402 Tony LaRussa MG	.07	.03	.01

☐ 403 Bruce Bochte	.04	.02	.00
☐ 404 Bake McBride	.04	.02	.00
☐ 405 Jerry Narron	.04	.02	.00
☐ 406 Rob Dressler	.04	.02	.00
☐ 407 Dave Heaverlo	.04	.02	.00
☐ 408 Tom Paciorek	.04	.02	.00
☐ 409 Carney Lansford	.25	.12	.02
☐ 410 Brian Downing	.07	.03	.01
☐ 411 Don Aase	.04	.02	.00
☐ 412 Jim Barr	.04	.02	.00
☐ 413 Don Baylor	.15	.07	.01
☐ 414 Jim Fregosi	.06	.03	.00
☐ 415 Dallas Green MG	.10	.05	.01
☐ 416 Dave Lopes	.10	.05	.01
☐ 417 Jerry Reuss	.07	.03	.01
☐ 418 Rick Sutcliffe	.30	.15	.03
☐ 419 Derrel Thomas	.04	.02	.00
☐ 420 Tom Lasorda MG	.10	.05	.01
☐ 421 Charles Leibrandt	.30	.15	.03
☐ 422 Tom Seaver	1.00	.50	.10
☐ 423 Ron Oester	.07	.03	.01
☐ 424 Junior Kennedy	.04	.02	.00
☐ 425 Tom Seaver	1.00	.50	.10
☐ 426 Bobby Cox MG	.04	.02	.00
☐ 427 Leon Durham	.25	.12	.02
☐ 428 Terry Kennedy	.07	.03	.01
☐ 429 Silvio Martinez	.04	.02	.00
☐ 430 George Hendrick	.07	.03	.01
☐ 431 Red Schoendienst MG	.15	.07	.01
☐ 432 Johnnie LeMaster	.04	.02	.00
☐ 433 Vida Blue	.10	.05	.01
☐ 434 John Montefusco	.07	.03	.01
☐ 435 Terry Whitfield	.04	.02	.00
☐ 436 Dave Bristol MG	.04	.02	.00
☐ 437 Dale Murphy	1.25	.60	.12
☐ 438 Jerry Dybzinski	.04	.02	.00
☐ 439 Jorge Orta	.04	.02	.00
☐ 440 Wayne Garland	.04	.02	.00
☐ 441 Miguel Dilone	.04	.02	.00
☐ 442 Dave Garcia MG	.04	.02	.00
☐ 443 Don Money	.04	.02	.00
☐ 444A Buck Martinez P1 ERR (reverse negative)	.15	.07	.01
☐ 444B Buck Martinez P2 COR	.07	.03	.01
☐ 445 Jerry Augustine	.04	.02	.00
☐ 446 Ben Oglivie	.07	.03	.01
☐ 447 Jim Slaton	.04	.02	.00
☐ 448 Doyle Alexander	.07	.03	.01
☐ 449 Tony Bernazard	.07	.03	.01
☐ 450 Scott Sanderson	.07	.03	.01
☐ 451 David Palmer	.07	.03	.01
☐ 452 Stan Bahnsen	.04	.02	.00
☐ 453 Dick Williams MG	.07	.03	.01
☐ 454 Rick Burleson	.07	.03	.01
☐ 455 Gary Allenson	.04	.02	.00
☐ 456 Bob Stanley	.04	.02	.00
☐ 457A John Tudor P1 ERR lifetime W-L "9.7"	1.50	.75	.15
☐ 457B John Tudor P2 COR corrected "9-7"	1.25	.60	.12
☐ 458 Dwight Evans	.35	.17	.03
☐ 459 Glenn Hubbard	.04	.02	.00
☐ 460 U.L. Washington	.04	.02	.00
☐ 461 Larry Gura	.04	.02	.00
☐ 462 Rich Gale	.04	.02	.00
☐ 463 Hal McRae	.07	.03	.01
☐ 464 Jim Frey MG	.04	.02	.00
☐ 465 Bucky Dent	.10	.05	.01
☐ 466 Dennis Werth	.04	.02	.00
☐ 467 Ron Davis	.04	.02	.00
☐ 468 Reggie Jackson	1.35	.65	.13
☐ 469 Bobby Brown	.04	.02	.00
☐ 470 Mike Davis	.18	.09	.01
☐ 471 Gaylord Perry	.30	.15	.03
☐ 472 Mark Belanger	.07	.03	.01
☐ 473 Jim Palmer	.75	.35	.07
☐ 474 Sammy Stewart	.04	.02	.00
☐ 475 Tim Stoddard	.04	.02	.00
☐ 476 Steve Stone	.07	.03	.01
☐ 477 Jeff Newman	.04	.02	.00
☐ 478 Steve McCatty	.04	.02	.00
☐ 479 Billy Martin MG	.20	.10	.02
☐ 480 Mitchell Page	.04	.02	.00
☐ 481 Cy Young Winner 1980 Steve Carlton	.40	.20	.04
☐ 482 Bill Buckner	.12	.06	.01
☐ 483A Ivan DeJesus P1 ERR lifetime hits "702"	.10	.05	.01
☐ 483B Ivan DeJesus P2 COR lifetime hits "642"	.07	.03	.01
☐ 484 Cliff Johnson	.04	.02	.00
☐ 485 Lenny Randle	.04	.02	.00
☐ 486 Larry Milbourne	.04	.02	.00

☐ 487 Roy Smalley	.04	.02	.00
☐ 488 John Castino	.04	.02	.00
☐ 489 Ron Jackson	.04	.02	.00
☐ 490A Dave Roberts P1 Career Highlights: "Showed pop in"	.10	.05	.01
☐ 490B Dave Roberts P2 "Declared himself"	.07	.03	.01
☐ 491 MVP: George Brett	1.00	.50	.10
☐ 492 Mike Cubbage	.04	.02	.00
☐ 493 Rob Wilfong	.04	.02	.00
☐ 494 Danny Goodwin	.04	.02	.00
☐ 495 Jose Morales	.04	.02	.00
☐ 496 Mickey Rivers	.07	.03	.01
☐ 497 Mike Edwards	.04	.02	.00
☐ 498 Mike Sadek	.04	.02	.00
☐ 499 Lenn Sakata	.04	.02	.00
☐ 500 Gene Michael MG	.04	.02	.00
☐ 501 Dave Roberts	.04	.02	.00
☐ 502 Steve Dillard	.04	.02	.00
☐ 503 Jim Essian	.04	.02	.00
☐ 504 Rance Mulliniks	.04	.02	.00
☐ 505 Darrell Porter	.04	.02	.00
☐ 506 Joe Torre MG	.10	.05	.01
☐ 507 Terry Crowley	.04	.02	.00
☐ 508 Bill Travers	.04	.02	.00
☐ 509 Nelson Norman	.04	.02	.00
☐ 510 Bob McClure	.04	.02	.00
☐ 511 Steve Howe	.10	.05	.01
☐ 512 Dave Rader	.04	.02	.00
☐ 513 Mick Kelleher	.04	.02	.00
☐ 514 Kiko Garcia	.04	.02	.00
☐ 515 Larry Biittner	.04	.02	.00
☐ 516A Willie Norwood P1 Career Highlights "Spent most of"	.10	.05	.01
☐ 516B Willie Norwood P2 "Traded to Seattle"	.07	.03	.01
☐ 517 Bo Diaz	.04	.02	.00
☐ 518 Juan Beniquez	.04	.02	.00
☐ 519 Scot Thompson	.04	.02	.00
☐ 520 Jim Tracy	.04	.02	.00
☐ 521 Carlos Lezcano	.04	.02	.00
☐ 522 Joe Amalfitano MG	.04	.02	.00
☐ 523 Preston Hanna	.04	.02	.00
☐ 524A Ray Burris P1 Career Highlights: "Went on ..."	.10	.05	.01
☐ 524B Ray Burris P2 "Drafted by ..."	.07	.03	.01
☐ 525 Broderick Perkins	.04	.02	.00
☐ 526 Mickey Hatcher	.10	.05	.01
☐ 527 John Goryl MG	.04	.02	.00
☐ 528 Dick Davis	.04	.02	.00
☐ 529 Butch Wynegar	.04	.02	.00
☐ 530 Sal Butera	.04	.02	.00
☐ 531 Jerry Koosman	.10	.05	.01
☐ 532A Geoff Zahn P1 Career Highlights: "Was 2nd in"	.10	.05	.01
☐ 532B Geoff Zahn P2 "Signed a 3 year"	.07	.03	.01
☐ 533 Dennis Martinez	.10	.05	.01
☐ 534 Gary Thomasson	.04	.02	.00
☐ 535 Steve Macko	.04	.02	.00
☐ 536 Jim Kaat	.20	.10	.02
☐ 537 Best Hitters George Brett Rod Carew	1.75	.85	.17
☐ 538 Tim Raines	5.00	2.50	.50
☐ 539 Keith Smith	.04	.02	.00
☐ 540 Ken Macha	.04	.02	.00
☐ 541 Burt Hooton	.04	.02	.00
☐ 542 Butch Hobson	.04	.02	.00
☐ 543 Bill Stein	.04	.02	.00
☐ 544 Dave Stapleton	.04	.02	.00
☐ 545 Bob Pate	.04	.02	.00
☐ 546 Doug Corbett	.04	.02	.00
☐ 547 Darrell Jackson	.04	.02	.00
☐ 548 Pete Redfern	.04	.02	.00
☐ 549 Roger Erickson	.04	.02	.00
☐ 550 Al Hrabosky	.07	.03	.01
☐ 551 Dick Tidrow	.04	.02	.00
☐ 552 Dave Ford	.04	.02	.00
☐ 553 Dave Kingman	.15	.07	.01
☐ 554A Mike Vail P1 Career Highlights: "After two ..."	.10	.05	.01
☐ 554B Mike Vail P2 "Traded to ..."	.07	.03	.01
☐ 555A Jerry Martin P1 Career Highlights: "Overcame a ..."	.10	.05	.01

☐ 555B Jerry Martin P2 "Traded to ..."	.07	.03	.01
☐ 556A Jesus Figueroa P1 Career Highlights: "Had an ..."	.10	.05	.01
☐ 556B Jesus Figueroa P2 "Traded to ..."	.07	.03	.01
☐ 557 Don Stanhouse	.04	.02	.00
☐ 558 Barry Foote	.04	.02	.00
☐ 559 Tim Blackwell	.04	.02	.00
☐ 560 Bruce Sutter	.20	.10	.02
☐ 561 Rick Reuschel	.20	.10	.02
☐ 562 Lynn McGlothen	.04	.02	.00
☐ 563A Bob Owchinko P1 Career Highlights: "Traded to ..."	.10	.05	.01
☐ 563B Bob Owchinko P2 "Involved in a ..."	.07	.03	.01
☐ 564 John Verhoeven	.04	.02	.00
☐ 565 Ken Landreaux	.04	.02	.00
☐ 566A Glen Adams P1 ERR Name misspelled	.15	.07	.01
☐ 566B Glenn Adams P2 COR	.07	.03	.01
☐ 567 Hosken Powell	.04	.02	.00
☐ 568 Dick Noles	.04	.02	.00
☐ 569 Danny Ainge	.45	.22	.04
☐ 570 Bobby Mattick MG	.04	.02	.00
☐ 571 Joe Lefebvre	.07	.03	.01
☐ 572 Bobby Clark	.04	.02	.00
☐ 573 Dennis Lamp	.04	.02	.00
☐ 574 Randy Lerch	.04	.02	.00
☐ 575 Mookie Wilson	.60	.30	.06
☐ 576 Ron LeFlore	.07	.03	.01
☐ 577 Jim Dwyer	.04	.02	.00
☐ 578 Bill Castro	.04	.02	.00
☐ 579 Greg Minton	.04	.02	.00
☐ 580 Mark Littell	.04	.02	.00
☐ 581 Andy Hassler	.04	.02	.00
☐ 582 Dave Stieb	.60	.30	.06
☐ 583 Ken Oberkfell	.04	.02	.00
☐ 584 Larry Bradford	.04	.02	.00
☐ 585 Fred Stanley	.04	.02	.00
☐ 586 Bill Caudill	.04	.02	.00
☐ 587 Doug Capilla	.04	.02	.00
☐ 588 George Riley	.04	.02	.00
☐ 589 Willie Hernandez	.15	.07	.01
☐ 590 MVP: Mike Schmidt	1.10	.55	.11
☐ 591 Cy Young Winner 1980: Steve Stone	.07	.03	.01
☐ 592 Rick Sofield	.04	.02	.00
☐ 593 Bombo Rivera	.04	.02	.00
☐ 594 Gary Ward	.07	.03	.01
☐ 595A Dave Edwards P1 Career Highlights: "Sidelined the"	.10	.05	.01
☐ 595B Dave Edwards P2 "Traded to ..."	.07	.03	.01
☐ 596 Mike Proly	.04	.02	.00
☐ 597 Tommy Boggs	.04	.02	.00
☐ 598 Greg Gross	.04	.02	.00
☐ 599 Elias Sosa	.04	.02	.00
☐ 600 Pat Kelly	.04	.02	.00
☐ 601A Checklist 1 P1 ERR unnumbered (51 Donahue)	.10	.01	.00
☐ 601B Checklist 1 P2 COR unnumbered (51 Donohue)	.75	.07	.01
☐ 602 Checklist 2 unnumbered	.10	.01	.00
☐ 603A Checklist 3 P1 ERR unnumbered (306 Mathews)	.10	.01	.00
☐ 603B Checklist 3 P2 COR unnumbered (306 Matthews)	.10	.01	.00
☐ 604A Checklist 4 P1 ERR unnumbered (379 Pujois)	.10	.01	.00
☐ 604B Checklist 4 P2 COR unnumbered (379 Pujols)	.10	.01	.00
☐ 605A Checklist 5 P1 ERR unnumbered (566 Glen Adams)	.10	.01	.00
☐ 605B Checklist 5 P2 COR unnumbered (566 Glenn Adams)	.10	.01	.00

1982 Donruss

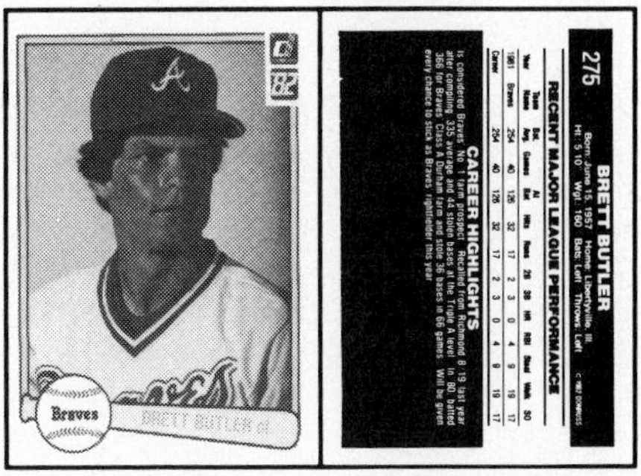

The 1982 Donruss set contains 653 numbered cards and the seven unnumbered checklists; each card measures 2 1/2" by 3 1/2". The first 26 cards of this set are entitled Donruss Diamond Kings (DK) and feature the artwork of Dick Perez of Perez-Steele Galleries. The set was marketed with puzzle pieces rather than with bubble gum. There are 63 pieces to the puzzle, which, when put together, make a collage of Babe Ruth entitled "Hall of Fame Diamond King." The card stock in this year's Donruss cards is considerably thicker than that of the 1981 cards. The seven unnumbered checklist cards are arbitrarily assigned numbers 654 through 660 and are listed at the end of the list below. The key rookie cards in this set are George Bell, Cal Ripken Jr., and Dave Stewart.

	MINT	EXC	G-VG
COMPLETE SET (660)	52.00	24.00	4.00
COMMON PLAYER (1-660)	.04	.02	.00
☐ 1 Pete Rose DK	1.75	.85	.17
☐ 2 Gary Carter DK	.40	.20	.04
☐ 3 Steve Garvey DK	.45	.22	.04
☐ 4 Vida Blue DK	.07	.03	.01
☐ 5A Alan Trammel DK ERR (name misspelled)	1.50	.75	.15
☐ 5B Alan Trammell DK COR	.40	.20	.04
☐ 6 Len Barker DK	.07	.03	.01
☐ 7 Dwight Evans DK	.20	.10	.02
☐ 8 Rod Carew DK	.50	.25	.05
☐ 9 George Hendrick DK	.07	.03	.01
☐ 10 Phil Niekro DK	.25	.12	.02
☐ 11 Richie Zisk DK	.07	.03	.01
☐ 12 Dave Parker DK	.20	.10	.02
☐ 13 Nolan Ryan DK	1.75	.85	.17
☐ 14 Ivan DeJesus DK	.07	.03	.01
☐ 15 George Brett DK	.80	.40	.08
☐ 16 Tom Seaver DK	.50	.25	.05
☐ 17 Dave Kingman DK	.10	.05	.01
☐ 18 Dave Winfield DK	.45	.22	.04
☐ 19 Mike Norris DK	.07	.03	.01
☐ 20 Carlton Fisk DK	.35	.17	.03
☐ 21 Ozzie Smith DK	.40	.20	.04
☐ 22 Roy Smalley DK	.07	.03	.01
☐ 23 Buddy Bell DK	.07	.03	.01
☐ 24 Ken Singleton DK	.07	.03	.01
☐ 25 John Mayberry DK	.07	.03	.01
☐ 26 Gorman Thomas DK	.07	.03	.01
☐ 27 Earl Weaver MG	.07	.03	.01
☐ 28 Rollie Fingers	.25	.12	.02
☐ 29 Sparky Anderson MG	.07	.03	.01
☐ 30 Dennis Eckersley	.30	.15	.03
☐ 31 Dave Winfield	.50	.25	.05
☐ 32 Burt Hooton	.04	.02	.00
☐ 33 Rick Waits	.04	.02	.00
☐ 34 George Brett	1.25	.60	.12
☐ 35 Steve McCatty	.04	.02	.00
☐ 36 Steve Rogers	.04	.02	.00
☐ 37 Bill Stein	.04	.02	.00
☐ 38 Steve Renko	.04	.02	.00
☐ 39 Mike Squires	.04	.02	.00
☐ 40 George Hendrick	.07	.03	.01
☐ 41 Bob Knepper	.07	.03	.01
☐ 42 Steve Carlton	.80	.40	.08
☐ 43 Larry Biittner	.04	.02	.00

☐ 44	Chris Welsh	.04	.02	.00
☐ 45	Steve Nicosia	.04	.02	.00
☐ 46	Jack Clark	.25	.12	.02
☐ 47	Chris Chambliss	.07	.03	.01
☐ 48	Ivan DeJesus	.04	.02	.00
☐ 49	Lee Mazzilli	.04	.02	.00
☐ 50	Julio Cruz	.04	.02	.00
☐ 51	Pete Redfern	.04	.02	.00
☐ 52	Dave Stieb	.40	.20	.04
☐ 53	Doug Corbett	.04	.02	.00
☐ 54	Jorge Bell	7.50	3.75	.75
☐ 55	Joe Simpson	.04	.02	.00
☐ 56	Rusty Staub	.12	.06	.01
☐ 57	Hector Cruz	.04	.02	.00
☐ 58	Claudell Washington	.07	.03	.01
☐ 59	Enrique Romo	.04	.02	.00
☐ 60	Gary Lavelle	.04	.02	.00
☐ 61	Tim Flannery	.04	.02	.00
☐ 62	Joe Nolan	.04	.02	.00
☐ 63	Larry Bowa	.15	.07	.01
☐ 64	Sixto Lezcano	.04	.02	.00
☐ 65	Joe Sambito	.04	.02	.00
☐ 66	Bruce Kison	.04	.02	.00
☐ 67	Wayne Nordhagen	.04	.02	.00
☐ 68	Woodie Fryman	.04	.02	.00
☐ 69	Billy Sample	.04	.02	.00
☐ 70	Amos Otis	.07	.03	.01
☐ 71	Matt Keough	.04	.02	.00
☐ 72	Toby Harrah	.07	.03	.01
☐ 73	Dave Righetti	1.50	.75	.15
☐ 74	Carl Yastrzemski	1.10	.55	.11
☐ 75	Bob Welch	.40	.20	.04
☐ 76A	Alan Trammel ERR (name misspelled)	1.50	.75	.15
☐ 76B	Alan Trammell COR	.50	.25	.05
☐ 77	Rick Dempsey	.04	.02	.00
☐ 78	Paul Molitor	.25	.12	.02
☐ 79	Dennis Martinez	.07	.03	.01
☐ 80	Jim Slaton	.04	.02	.00
☐ 81	Champ Summers	.04	.02	.00
☐ 82	Carney Lansford	.25	.12	.02
☐ 83	Barry Foote	.04	.02	.00
☐ 84	Steve Garvey	.50	.25	.05
☐ 85	Rick Manning	.04	.02	.00
☐ 86	John Wathan	.07	.03	.01
☐ 87	Brian Kingman	.04	.02	.00
☐ 88	Andre Dawson	.75	.35	.07
☐ 89	Jim Kern	.04	.02	.00
☐ 90	Bobby Grich	.07	.03	.01
☐ 91	Bob Forsch	.04	.02	.00
☐ 92	Art Howe	.07	.03	.01
☐ 93	Marty Bystrom	.04	.02	.00
☐ 94	Ozzie Smith	.60	.30	.06
☐ 95	Dave Parker	.30	.15	.03
☐ 96	Doyle Alexander	.07	.03	.01
☐ 97	Al Hrabosky	.07	.03	.01
☐ 98	Frank Taveras	.04	.02	.00
☐ 99	Tim Blackwell	.04	.02	.00
☐ 100	Floyd Bannister	.04	.02	.00
☐ 101	Alfredo Griffin	.07	.03	.01
☐ 102	Dave Engle	.04	.02	.00
☐ 103	Mario Soto	.07	.03	.01
☐ 104	Ross Baumgarten	.04	.02	.00
☐ 105	Ken Singleton	.07	.03	.01
☐ 106	Ted Simmons	.15	.07	.01
☐ 107	Jack Morris	.20	.10	.02
☐ 108	Bob Watson	.07	.03	.01
☐ 109	Dwight Evans	.25	.12	.02
☐ 110	Tom Lasorda MG	.07	.03	.01
☐ 111	Bert Blyleven	.25	.12	.02
☐ 112	Dan Quisenberry	.12	.06	.01
☐ 113	Rickey Henderson	5.00	2.50	.50
☐ 114	Gary Carter	.50	.25	.05
☐ 115	Brian Downing	.07	.03	.01
☐ 116	Al Oliver	.10	.05	.01
☐ 117	LaMarr Hoyt	.07	.03	.01
☐ 118	Cesar Cedeno	.07	.03	.01
☐ 119	Keith Moreland	.04	.02	.00
☐ 120	Bob Shirley	.04	.02	.00
☐ 121	Terry Kennedy	.04	.02	.00
☐ 122	Frank Pastore	.04	.02	.00
☐ 123	Gene Garber	.04	.02	.00
☐ 124	Tony Pena	.65	.30	.06
☐ 125	Allen Ripley	.04	.02	.00
☐ 126	Randy Martz	.04	.02	.00
☐ 127	Richie Zisk	.04	.02	.00
☐ 128	Mike Scott	.40	.20	.04
☐ 129	Lloyd Moseby	.35	.17	.03
☐ 130	Rob Wilfong	.04	.02	.00
☐ 131	Tim Stoddard	.04	.02	.00
☐ 132	Gorman Thomas	.10	.05	.01
☐ 133	Dan Petry	.07	.03	.01
☐ 134	Bob Stanley	.04	.02	.00
☐ 135	Lou Piniella	.12	.06	.01
☐ 136	Pedro Guerrero	.75	.35	.07
☐ 137	Len Barker	.04	.02	.00
☐ 138	Rich Gale	.04	.02	.00
☐ 139	Wayne Gross	.04	.02	.00
☐ 140	Tim Wallach	1.75	.85	.17
☐ 141	Gene Mauch MG	.04	.02	.00
☐ 142	Doc Medich	.04	.02	.00
☐ 143	Tony Bernazard	.07	.03	.01
☐ 144	Bill Virdon MG	.04	.02	.00
☐ 145	John Littlefield	.04	.02	.00
☐ 146	Dave Bergman	.04	.02	.00
☐ 147	Dick Davis	.04	.02	.00
☐ 148	Tom Seaver	.90	.45	.09
☐ 149	Matt Sinatro	.04	.02	.00
☐ 150	Chuck Tanner MG	.04	.02	.00
☐ 151	Leon Durham	.07	.03	.01
☐ 152	Gene Tenace	.04	.02	.00
☐ 153	Al Bumbry	.04	.02	.00
☐ 154	Mark Brouhard	.04	.02	.00
☐ 155	Rick Peters	.04	.02	.00
☐ 156	Jerry Remy	.04	.02	.00
☐ 157	Rick Reuschel	.15	.07	.01
☐ 158	Steve Howe	.04	.02	.00
☐ 159	Alan Bannister	.04	.02	.00
☐ 160	U.L. Washington	.04	.02	.00
☐ 161	Rick Langford	.04	.02	.00
☐ 162	Bill Gullickson	.07	.03	.01
☐ 163	Mark Wagner	.04	.02	.00
☐ 164	Geoff Zahn	.04	.02	.00
☐ 165	Ron LeFlore	.07	.03	.01
☐ 166	Dane Iorg	.04	.02	.00
☐ 167	Joe Niekro	.10	.05	.01
☐ 168	Pete Rose	1.25	.60	.12
☐ 169	Dave Collins	.04	.02	.00
☐ 170	Rick Wise	.04	.02	.00
☐ 171	Jim Bibby	.04	.02	.00
☐ 172	Larry Herndon	.04	.02	.00
☐ 173	Bob Horner	.12	.06	.01
☐ 174	Steve Dillard	.04	.02	.00
☐ 175	Mookie Wilson	.12	.06	.01
☐ 176	Dan Meyer	.04	.02	.00
☐ 177	Fernando Arroyo	.04	.02	.00
☐ 178	Jackson Todd	.04	.02	.00
☐ 179	Darrell Jackson	.04	.02	.00
☐ 180	Alvis Woods	.04	.02	.00
☐ 181	Jim Anderson	.04	.02	.00
☐ 182	Dave Kingman	.15	.07	.01
☐ 183	Steve Henderson	.04	.02	.00
☐ 184	Brian Asselstine	.04	.02	.00
☐ 185	Rod Scurry	.04	.02	.00
☐ 186	Fred Breining	.04	.02	.00
☐ 187	Danny Boone	.04	.02	.00
☐ 188	Junior Kennedy	.04	.02	.00
☐ 189	Sparky Lyle	.10	.05	.01
☐ 190	Whitey Herzog MG	.07	.03	.01
☐ 191	Dave Smith	.10	.05	.01
☐ 192	Ed Ott	.04	.02	.00
☐ 193	Greg Luzinski	.12	.06	.01
☐ 194	Bill Lee	.07	.03	.01
☐ 195	Don Zimmer MG	.04	.02	.00
☐ 196	Hal McRae	.07	.03	.01
☐ 197	Mike Norris	.04	.02	.00
☐ 198	Duane Kuiper	.04	.02	.00
☐ 199	Rick Cerone	.04	.02	.00
☐ 200	Jim Rice	.25	.12	.02
☐ 201	Steve Yeager	.04	.02	.00
☐ 202	Tom Brookens	.04	.02	.00
☐ 203	Jose Morales	.04	.02	.00
☐ 204	Roy Howell	.04	.02	.00
☐ 205	Tippy Martinez	.04	.02	.00
☐ 206	Moose Haas	.04	.02	.00
☐ 207	Al Cowens	.04	.02	.00
☐ 208	Dave Stapleton	.04	.02	.00
☐ 209	Bucky Dent	.10	.05	.01
☐ 210	Ron Cey	.10	.05	.01
☐ 211	Jorge Orta	.04	.02	.00
☐ 212	Jamie Quirk	.04	.02	.00
☐ 213	Jeff Jones	.04	.02	.00
☐ 214	Tim Raines	1.25	.60	.12
☐ 215	Jon Matlack	.04	.02	.00
☐ 216	Rod Carew	.80	.40	.08
☐ 217	Jim Kaat	.15	.07	.01
☐ 218	Joe Pittman	.04	.02	.00
☐ 219	Larry Christenson	.04	.02	.00
☐ 220	Juan Bonilla	.04	.02	.00
☐ 221	Mike Easler	.04	.02	.00
☐ 222	Vida Blue	.07	.03	.01
☐ 223	Rick Camp	.04	.02	.00
☐ 224	Mike Jorgensen	.04	.02	.00
☐ 225	Jody Davis	.35	.17	.03
☐ 226	Mike Parrott	.04	.02	.00
☐ 227	Jim Clancy	.04	.02	.00
☐ 228	Hosken Powell	.04	.02	.00
☐ 229	Tom Hume	.04	.02	.00

☐ 230	Britt Burns	.04	.02	.00
☐ 231	Jim Palmer	.65	.30	.06
☐ 232	Bob Rodgers MG	.04	.02	.00
☐ 233	Milt Wilcox	.04	.02	.00
☐ 234	Dave Revering	.04	.02	.00
☐ 235	Mike Torrez	.04	.02	.00
☐ 236	Robert Castillo	.04	.02	.00
☐ 237	Von Hayes	1.25	.60	.12
☐ 238	Renie Martin	.04	.02	.00
☐ 239	Dwayne Murphy	.04	.02	.00
☐ 240	Rodney Scott	.04	.02	.00
☐ 241	Fred Patek	.04	.02	.00
☐ 242	Mickey Rivers	.07	.03	.01
☐ 243	Steve Trout	.04	.02	.00
☐ 244	Jose Cruz	.07	.03	.01
☐ 245	Manny Trillo	.04	.02	.00
☐ 246	Lary Sorensen	.04	.02	.00
☐ 247	Dave Edwards	.04	.02	.00
☐ 248	Dan Driessen	.04	.02	.00
☐ 249	Tommy Boggs	.04	.02	.00
☐ 250	Dale Berra	.04	.02	.00
☐ 251	Ed Whitson	.07	.03	.01
☐ 252	Lee Smith	.75	.35	.07
☐ 253	Tom Paciorek	.04	.02	.00
☐ 254	Pat Zachry	.04	.02	.00
☐ 255	Luis Leal	.04	.02	.00
☐ 256	John Castino	.04	.02	.00
☐ 257	Rich Dauer	.04	.02	.00
☐ 258	Cecil Cooper	.15	.07	.01
☐ 259	Dave Rozema	.04	.02	.00
☐ 260	John Tudor	.30	.15	.03
☐ 261	Jerry Mumphrey	.04	.02	.00
☐ 262	Jay Johnstone	.07	.03	.01
☐ 263	Bo Diaz	.04	.02	.00
☐ 264	Dennis Leonard	.07	.03	.01
☐ 265	Jim Spencer	.04	.02	.00
☐ 266	John Milner	.04	.02	.00
☐ 267	Don Aase	.04	.02	.00
☐ 268	Jim Sundberg	.04	.02	.00
☐ 269	Lamar Johnson	.04	.02	.00
☐ 270	Frank LaCorte	.04	.02	.00
☐ 271	Barry Evans	.04	.02	.00
☐ 272	Enos Cabell	.04	.02	.00
☐ 273	Del Unser	.04	.02	.00
☐ 274	George Foster	.12	.06	.01
☐ 275	Brett Butler	1.25	.60	.12
☐ 276	Lee Lacy	.04	.02	.00
☐ 277	Ken Reitz	.04	.02	.00
☐ 278	Keith Hernandez	.35	.17	.03
☐ 279	Doug DeCinces	.07	.03	.01
☐ 280	Charlie Moore	.04	.02	.00
☐ 281	Lance Parrish	.25	.12	.02
☐ 282	Ralph Houk MG	.04	.02	.00
☐ 283	Rich Gossage	.20	.10	.02
☐ 284	Jerry Reuss	.07	.03	.01
☐ 285	Mike Stanton	.04	.02	.00
☐ 286	Frank White	.07	.03	.01
☐ 287	Bob Owchinko	.04	.02	.00
☐ 288	Scott Sanderson	.07	.03	.01
☐ 289	Bump Wills	.04	.02	.00
☐ 290	Dave Frost	.04	.02	.00
☐ 291	Chet Lemon	.04	.02	.00
☐ 292	Tito Landrum	.04	.02	.00
☐ 293	Vern Ruhle	.04	.02	.00
☐ 294	Mike Schmidt	2.00	1.00	.20
☐ 295	Sam Mejias	.04	.02	.00
☐ 296	Gary Lucas	.04	.02	.00
☐ 297	John Candelaria	.07	.03	.01
☐ 298	Jerry Martin	.04	.02	.00
☐ 299	Dale Murphy	1.10	.55	.11
☐ 300	Mike Lum	.04	.02	.00
☐ 301	Tom Hausman	.04	.02	.00
☐ 302	Glenn Abbott	.04	.02	.00
☐ 303	Roger Erickson	.04	.02	.00
☐ 304	Otto Velez	.04	.02	.00
☐ 305	Danny Goodwin	.04	.02	.00
☐ 306	John Mayberry	.07	.03	.01
☐ 307	Lenny Randle	.04	.02	.00
☐ 308	Bob Bailor	.04	.02	.00
☐ 309	Jerry Morales	.04	.02	.00
☐ 310	Rufino Linares	.04	.02	.00
☐ 311	Kent Tekulve	.07	.03	.01
☐ 312	Joe Morgan	.35	.17	.03
☐ 313	John Urrea	.04	.02	.00
☐ 314	Paul Householder	.04	.02	.00
☐ 315	Garry Maddox	.07	.03	.01
☐ 316	Mike Ramsey	.04	.02	.00
☐ 317	Alan Ashby	.04	.02	.00
☐ 318	Bob Clark	.04	.02	.00
☐ 319	Tony LaRussa MG	.07	.03	.01
☐ 320	Charlie Lea	.04	.02	.00
☐ 321	Danny Darwin	.07	.03	.01
☐ 322	Cesar Geronimo	.04	.02	.00
☐ 323	Tom Underwood	.04	.02	.00
☐ 324	Andre Thornton	.07	.03	.01
☐ 325	Rudy May	.04	.02	.00
☐ 326	Frank Tanana	.07	.03	.01
☐ 327	Dave Lopes	.07	.03	.01
☐ 328	Richie Hebner	.04	.02	.00
☐ 329	Mike Flanagan	.07	.03	.01
☐ 330	Mike Caldwell	.04	.02	.00
☐ 331	Scott McGregor	.07	.03	.01
☐ 332	Jerry Augustine	.04	.02	.00
☐ 333	Stan Papi	.04	.02	.00
☐ 334	Rick Miller	.04	.02	.00
☐ 335	Graig Nettles	.12	.06	.01
☐ 336	Dusty Baker	.07	.03	.01
☐ 337	Dave Garcia MG	.04	.02	.00
☐ 338	Larry Gura	.04	.02	.00
☐ 339	Cliff Johnson	.04	.02	.00
☐ 340	Warren Cromartie	.04	.02	.00
☐ 341	Steve Comer	.04	.02	.00
☐ 342	Rick Burleson	.07	.03	.01
☐ 343	John Martin	.04	.02	.00
☐ 344	Craig Reynolds	.04	.02	.00
☐ 345	Mike Proly	.04	.02	.00
☐ 346	Ruppert Jones	.04	.02	.00
☐ 347	Omar Moreno	.04	.02	.00
☐ 348	Greg Minton	.04	.02	.00
☐ 349	Rick Mahler	.25	.12	.02
☐ 350	Alex Trevino	.04	.02	.00
☐ 351	Mike Krukow	.07	.03	.01
☐ 352A	Shane Rawley ERR (photo actually Jim Anderson)	.75	.35	.07
☐ 352B	Shane Rawley COR	.10	.05	.01
☐ 353	Garth Iorg	.04	.02	.00
☐ 354	Pete Mackanin	.04	.02	.00
☐ 355	Paul Moskau	.04	.02	.00
☐ 356	Richard Dotson	.07	.03	.01
☐ 357	Steve Stone	.07	.03	.01
☐ 358	Larry Hisle	.04	.02	.00
☐ 359	Aurelio Lopez	.04	.02	.00
☐ 360	Oscar Gamble	.04	.02	.00
☐ 361	Tom Burgmeier	.04	.02	.00
☐ 362	Terry Forster	.07	.03	.01
☐ 363	Joe Charboneau	.07	.03	.01
☐ 364	Ken Brett	.04	.02	.00
☐ 365	Tony Armas	.07	.03	.01
☐ 366	Chris Speier	.04	.02	.00
☐ 367	Fred Lynn	.20	.10	.02
☐ 368	Buddy Bell	.12	.06	.01
☐ 369	Jim Essian	.04	.02	.00
☐ 370	Terry Puhl	.04	.02	.00
☐ 371	Greg Gross	.04	.02	.00
☐ 372	Bruce Sutter	.15	.07	.01
☐ 373	Joe Lefebvre	.04	.02	.00
☐ 374	Ray Knight	.10	.05	.01
☐ 375	Bruce Benedict	.04	.02	.00
☐ 376	Tim Foli	.04	.02	.00
☐ 377	Al Holland	.04	.02	.00
☐ 378	Ken Kravec	.04	.02	.00
☐ 379	Jeff Burroughs	.04	.02	.00
☐ 380	Pete Falcone	.04	.02	.00
☐ 381	Ernie Whitt	.04	.02	.00
☐ 382	Brad Havens	.04	.02	.00
☐ 383	Terry Crowley	.04	.02	.00
☐ 384	Don Money	.04	.02	.00
☐ 385	Dan Schatzeder	.04	.02	.00
☐ 386	Gary Allenson	.04	.02	.00
☐ 387	Yogi Berra CO	.20	.10	.02
☐ 388	Ken Landreaux	.04	.02	.00
☐ 389	Mike Hargrove	.07	.03	.01
☐ 390	Darryl Motley	.04	.02	.00
☐ 391	Dave McKay	.04	.02	.00
☐ 392	Stan Bahnsen	.04	.02	.00
☐ 393	Ken Forsch	.04	.02	.00
☐ 394	Mario Mendoza	.04	.02	.00
☐ 395	Jim Morrison	.04	.02	.00
☐ 396	Mike Ivie	.04	.02	.00
☐ 397	Broderick Perkins	.04	.02	.00
☐ 398	Darrell Evans	.12	.06	.01
☐ 399	Ron Reed	.04	.02	.00
☐ 400	Johnny Bench	.80	.40	.08
☐ 401	Steve Bedrosian	1.00	.50	.10
☐ 402	Bill Robinson	.07	.03	.01
☐ 403	Bill Buckner	.12	.06	.01
☐ 404	Ken Oberkfell	.04	.02	.00
☐ 405	Cal Ripken Jr.	18.00	9.00	1.80
☐ 406	Jim Gantner	.04	.02	.00
☐ 407	Kirk Gibson	1.50	.75	.15
☐ 408	Tony Perez	.18	.09	.01
☐ 409	Tommy John	.18	.09	.01
☐ 410	Dave Stewart	7.50	3.75	.75
☐ 411	Dan Spillner	.04	.02	.00
☐ 412	Willie Aikens	.04	.02	.00
☐ 413	Mike Heath	.04	.02	.00
☐ 414	Ray Burris	.04	.02	.00

☐ 415	Leon Roberts	.04	.02	.00
☐ 416	Mike Witt	.60	.30	.06
☐ 417	Bob Molinaro	.04	.02	.00
☐ 418	Steve Braun	.04	.02	.00
☐ 419	Nolan Ryan	3.75	1.85	.37
☐ 420	Tug McGraw	.10	.05	.01
☐ 421	Dave Concepcion	.12	.06	.01
☐ 422A	Juan Eichelberger ERR (photo actually Gary Lucas)	.65	.30	.06
☐ 422B	Juan Eichelberger COR	.08	.04	.01
☐ 423	Rick Rhoden	.07	.03	.01
☐ 424	Frank Robinson MG	.15	.07	.01
☐ 425	Eddie Miller	.04	.02	.00
☐ 426	Bill Caudill	.04	.02	.00
☐ 427	Doug Flynn	.04	.02	.00
☐ 428	Larry Andersen UER (misspelled Anderson on card front)	.07	.03	.01
☐ 429	Al Williams	.04	.02	.00
☐ 430	Jerry Garvin	.04	.02	.00
☐ 431	Glenn Adams	.04	.02	.00
☐ 432	Barry Bonnell	.04	.02	.00
☐ 433	Jerry Narron	.04	.02	.00
☐ 434	John Stearns	.04	.02	.00
☐ 435	Mike Tyson	.04	.02	.00
☐ 436	Glenn Hubbard	.04	.02	.00
☐ 437	Eddie Solomon	.04	.02	.00
☐ 438	Jeff Leonard	.07	.03	.01
☐ 439	Randy Bass	.07	.03	.01
☐ 440	Mike LaCoss	.04	.02	.00
☐ 441	Gary Matthews	.07	.03	.01
☐ 442	Mark Littell	.04	.02	.00
☐ 443	Don Sutton	.30	.15	.03
☐ 444	John Harris	.04	.02	.00
☐ 445	Vada Pinson CO	.07	.03	.01
☐ 446	Elias Sosa	.04	.02	.00
☐ 447	Charlie Hough	.07	.03	.01
☐ 448	Willie Wilson	.12	.06	.01
☐ 449	Fred Stanley	.04	.02	.00
☐ 450	Tom Veryzer	.04	.02	.00
☐ 451	Ron Davis	.04	.02	.00
☐ 452	Mark Clear	.04	.02	.00
☐ 453	Bill Russell	.07	.03	.01
☐ 454	Lou Whitaker	.25	.12	.02
☐ 455	Dan Graham	.04	.02	.00
☐ 456	Reggie Cleveland	.04	.02	.00
☐ 457	Sammy Stewart	.04	.02	.00
☐ 458	Pete Vuckovich	.07	.03	.01
☐ 459	John Wockenfuss	.04	.02	.00
☐ 460	Glenn Hoffman	.04	.02	.00
☐ 461	Willie Randolph	.10	.05	.01
☐ 462	Fernando Valenzuela	1.25	.60	.12
☐ 463	Ron Hassey	.04	.02	.00
☐ 464	Paul Splittorff	.04	.02	.00
☐ 465	Rob Picciolo	.04	.02	.00
☐ 466	Larry Parrish	.07	.03	.01
☐ 467	Johnny Grubb	.04	.02	.00
☐ 468	Dan Ford	.04	.02	.00
☐ 469	Silvio Martinez	.04	.02	.00
☐ 470	Kiko Garcia	.04	.02	.00
☐ 471	Bob Boone	.12	.06	.01
☐ 472	Luis Salazar	.10	.05	.01
☐ 473	Randy Niemann	.04	.02	.00
☐ 474	Tom Griffin	.04	.02	.00
☐ 475	Phil Niekro	.30	.15	.03
☐ 476	Hubie Brooks	.75	.35	.07
☐ 477	Dick Tidrow	.04	.02	.00
☐ 478	Jim Beattie	.04	.02	.00
☐ 479	Damaso Garcia	.07	.03	.01
☐ 480	Mickey Hatcher	.07	.03	.01
☐ 481	Joe Price	.04	.02	.00
☐ 482	Ed Farmer	.04	.02	.00
☐ 483	Eddie Murray	.75	.35	.07
☐ 484	Ben Oglivie	.07	.03	.01
☐ 485	Kevin Saucier	.04	.02	.00
☐ 486	Bobby Murcer	.10	.05	.01
☐ 487	Bill Campbell	.04	.02	.00
☐ 488	Reggie Smith	.07	.03	.01
☐ 489	Wayne Garland	.04	.02	.00
☐ 490	Jim Wright	.04	.02	.00
☐ 491	Billy Martin MG	.20	.10	.02
☐ 492	Jim Fanning MG	.04	.02	.00
☐ 493	Don Baylor	.15	.07	.01
☐ 494	Rick Honeycutt	.04	.02	.00
☐ 495	Carlton Fisk	.60	.30	.06
☐ 496	Denny Walling	.04	.02	.00
☐ 497	Bake McBride	.04	.02	.00
☐ 498	Darrell Porter	.04	.02	.00
☐ 499	Gene Richards	.04	.02	.00
☐ 500	Ron Oester	.04	.02	.00
☐ 501	Ken Dayley	.18	.09	.01
☐ 502	Jason Thompson	.04	.02	.00

☐ 503	Milt May	.04	.02	.00
☐ 504	Doug Bird	.04	.02	.00
☐ 505	Bruce Bochte	.04	.02	.00
☐ 506	Neil Allen	.04	.02	.00
☐ 507	Joey McLaughlin	.04	.02	.00
☐ 508	Butch Wynegar	.04	.02	.00
☐ 509	Gary Roenicke	.04	.02	.00
☐ 510	Robin Yount	1.25	.60	.12
☐ 511	Dave Tobik	.04	.02	.00
☐ 512	Rich Gedman	.30	.15	.03
☐ 513	Gene Nelson	.07	.03	.01
☐ 514	Rick Monday	.07	.03	.01
☐ 515	Miguel Dilone	.04	.02	.00
☐ 516	Clint Hurdle	.04	.02	.00
☐ 517	Jeff Newman	.04	.02	.00
☐ 518	Grant Jackson	.04	.02	.00
☐ 519	Andy Hassler	.04	.02	.00
☐ 520	Pat Putnam	.04	.02	.00
☐ 521	Greg Pryor	.04	.02	.00
☐ 522	Tony Scott	.04	.02	.00
☐ 523	Steve Mura	.04	.02	.00
☐ 524	Johnnie LeMaster	.04	.02	.00
☐ 525	Dick Ruthven	.04	.02	.00
☐ 526	John McNamara MG	.07	.03	.01
☐ 527	Larry McWilliams	.04	.02	.00
☐ 528	Johnny Ray	.75	.35	.07
☐ 529	Pat Tabler	.50	.25	.05
☐ 530	Tom Herr	.10	.05	.01
☐ 531A	San Diego Chicken (with TM)	.90	.45	.09
☐ 531B	San Diego Chicken (without TM)	.75	.35	.07
☐ 532	Sal Butera	.04	.02	.00
☐ 533	Mike Griffin	.04	.02	.00
☐ 534	Kelvin Moore	.04	.02	.00
☐ 535	Reggie Jackson	1.00	.50	.10
☐ 536	Ed Romero	.04	.02	.00
☐ 537	Derrel Thomas	.04	.02	.00
☐ 538	Mike O'Berry	.04	.02	.00
☐ 539	Jack O'Connor	.04	.02	.00
☐ 540	Bob Ojeda	.65	.30	.06
☐ 541	Roy Lee Jackson	.04	.02	.00
☐ 542	Lynn Jones	.04	.02	.00
☐ 543	Gaylord Perry	.30	.15	.03
☐ 544A	Phil Garner ERR (reverse negative)	.75	.35	.07
☐ 544B	Phil Garner COR	.10	.05	.01
☐ 545	Garry Templeton	.07	.03	.01
☐ 546	Rafael Ramirez	.04	.02	.00
☐ 547	Jeff Reardon	.25	.12	.02
☐ 548	Ron Guidry	.25	.12	.02
☐ 549	Tim Laudner	.15	.07	.01
☐ 550	John Henry Johnson	.04	.02	.00
☐ 551	Chris Bando	.04	.02	.00
☐ 552	Bobby Brown	.04	.02	.00
☐ 553	Larry Bradford	.04	.02	.00
☐ 554	Scott Fletcher	.40	.20	.04
☐ 555	Jerry Royster	.04	.02	.00
☐ 556	Shooty Babitt (spelled Babbitt on front)	.04	.02	.00
☐ 557	Kent Hrbek	3.50	1.75	.35
☐ 558	Yankee Winners Ron Guidry Tommy John	.12	.06	.01
☐ 559	Mark Bomback	.04	.02	.00
☐ 560	Julio Valdez	.04	.02	.00
☐ 561	Buck Martinez	.04	.02	.00
☐ 562	Mike Marshall (Dodger hitter)	1.25	.60	.12
☐ 563	Rennie Stennett	.04	.02	.00
☐ 564	Steve Crawford	.04	.02	.00
☐ 565	Bob Babcock	.04	.02	.00
☐ 566	Johnny Podres CO	.07	.03	.01
☐ 567	Paul Serna	.04	.02	.00
☐ 568	Harold Baines	1.50	.75	.15
☐ 569	Dave LaRoche	.04	.02	.00
☐ 570	Lee May	.04	.02	.00
☐ 571	Gary Ward	.07	.03	.01
☐ 572	John Denny	.07	.03	.01
☐ 573	Roy Smalley	.04	.02	.00
☐ 574	Bob Brenly	.15	.07	.01
☐ 575	Bronx Bombers Reggie Jackson Dave Winfield	.50	.25	.05
☐ 576	Luis Pujols	.04	.02	.00
☐ 577	Butch Hobson	.04	.02	.00
☐ 578	Harvey Kuenn MG	.07	.03	.01
☐ 579	Cal Ripken Sr. CO	.07	.03	.01
☐ 580	Juan Berenguer	.04	.02	.00
☐ 581	Benny Ayala	.04	.02	.00
☐ 582	Vance Law	.18	.09	.01
☐ 583	Rick Leach	.04	.02	.00
☐ 584	George Frazier	.04	.02	.00

☐ 585 Phillies Finest Pete Rose Mike Schmidt	1.00	.50	.10
☐ 586 Joe Rudi	.07	.03	.01
☐ 587 Juan Beniquez	.04	.02	.00
☐ 588 Luis DeLeon	.04	.02	.00
☐ 589 Craig Swan	.04	.02	.00
☐ 590 Dave Chalk	.04	.02	.00
☐ 591 Billy Gardner MG	.04	.02	.00
☐ 592 Sal Bando	.07	.03	.01
☐ 593 Bert Campaneris	.07	.03	.01
☐ 594 Steve Kemp	.07	.03	.01
☐ 595A Randy Lerch ERR (Braves)	.65	.30	.06
☐ 595B Randy Lerch COR (Brewers)	.07	.03	.01
☐ 596 Bryan Clark	.04	.02	.00
☐ 597 Dave Ford	.04	.02	.00
☐ 598 Mike Scioscia	.30	.15	.03
☐ 599 John Lowenstein	.04	.02	.00
☐ 600 Rene Lachemann MG	.07	.03	.01
☐ 601 Mick Kelleher	.04	.02	.00
☐ 602 Ron Jackson	.04	.02	.00
☐ 603 Jerry Koosman	.07	.03	.01
☐ 604 Dave Goltz	.04	.02	.00
☐ 605 Ellis Valentine	.04	.02	.00
☐ 606 Lonnie Smith	.10	.05	.01
☐ 607 Joaquin Andujar	.10	.05	.01
☐ 608 Garry Hancock	.04	.02	.00
☐ 609 Jerry Turner	.04	.02	.00
☐ 610 Bob Bonner	.04	.02	.00
☐ 611 Jim Dwyer	.04	.02	.00
☐ 612 Terry Bulling	.04	.02	.00
☐ 613 Joel Youngblood	.04	.02	.00
☐ 614 Larry Milbourne	.04	.02	.00
☐ 615 Gene Roof (name on front is Phil Roof)	.07	.03	.01
☐ 616 Keith Drumwright	.04	.02	.00
☐ 617 Dave Rosello	.04	.02	.00
☐ 618 Rickey Keeton	.04	.02	.00
☐ 619 Dennis Lamp	.04	.02	.00
☐ 620 Sid Monge	.04	.02	.00
☐ 621 Jerry White	.04	.02	.00
☐ 622 Luis Aguayo	.04	.02	.00
☐ 623 Jamie Easterly	.04	.02	.00
☐ 624 Steve Sax	3.50	1.75	.35
☐ 625 Dave Roberts	.04	.02	.00
☐ 626 Rick Bosetti	.04	.02	.00
☐ 627 Terry Francona	.07	.03	.01
☐ 628 Pride of Reds Tom Seaver Johnny Bench	.65	.30	.06
☐ 629 Paul Mirabella	.04	.02	.00
☐ 630 Rance Mulliniks	.04	.02	.00
☐ 631 Kevin Hickey	.04	.02	.00
☐ 632 Reid Nichols	.04	.02	.00
☐ 633 Dave Geisel	.04	.02	.00
☐ 634 Ken Griffey	.20	.10	.02
☐ 635 Bob Lemon MG	.10	.05	.01
☐ 636 Orlando Sanchez	.04	.02	.00
☐ 637 Bill Almon	.04	.02	.00
☐ 638 Danny Ainge	.15	.07	.01
☐ 639 Willie Stargell	.40	.20	.04
☐ 640 Bob Sykes	.04	.02	.00
☐ 641 Ed Lynch	.04	.02	.00
☐ 642 John Ellis	.04	.02	.00
☐ 643 Ferguson Jenkins	.15	.07	.01
☐ 644 Lenn Sakata	.04	.02	.00
☐ 645 Julio Gonzalez	.04	.02	.00
☐ 646 Jesse Orosco	.07	.03	.01
☐ 647 Jerry Dybzinski	.04	.02	.00
☐ 648 Tommy Davis CO	.07	.03	.01
☐ 649 Ron Gardenhire	.07	.03	.01
☐ 650 Felipe Alou CO	.07	.03	.01
☐ 651 Harvey Haddix CO	.04	.02	.00
☐ 652 Willie Upshaw	.07	.03	.01
☐ 653 Bill Madlock	.10	.05	.01
☐ 654A DK Checklist (unnumbered) (with Trammel)	.25	.02	.00
☐ 654B DK Checklist (unnumbered) (with Trammell)	.12	.01	.00
☐ 655 Checklist 1 (unnumbered)	.08	.01	.00
☐ 656 Checklist 2 (unnumbered)	.08	.01	.00
☐ 657 Checklist 3 (unnumbered)	.08	.01	.00
☐ 658 Checklist 4 (unnumbered)	.08	.01	.00
☐ 659 Checklist 5 (unnumbered)	.08	.01	.00
☐ 660 Checklist 6 (unnumbered)	.08	.01	.00

1983 Donruss

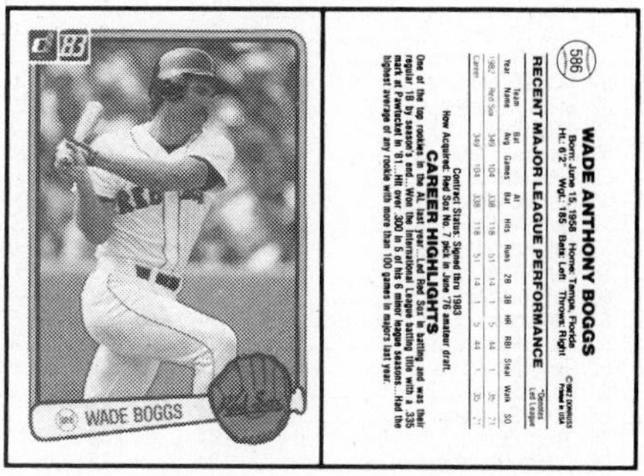

The cards in this 660-card set measure 2 1/2" by 3 1/2". The 1983 Donruss baseball set, issued with a 63-piece Diamond King puzzle, again leads off with a 26-card Diamond Kings (DK) series. Of the remaining 634 cards, two are combination cards, one portrays the San Diego Chicken, one shows the completed Ty Cobb puzzle, and seven are unnumbered checklist cards. The seven unnumbered checklist cards are arbitrarily assigned numbers 654 through 660 and are listed at the end of the list below. The Donruss logo and the year of issue are shown in the upper left corner of the obverse. The card backs have black print on yellow and white and are numbered on a small ball design. The complete set price below includes only the more common of each variation pair. The key rookie cards in this set are Wade Boggs, Julio Franco, Tony Gwynn, Howard Johnson, Ryne Sandberg, and Frank Viola.

	MINT	EXC	G-VG
COMPLETE SET (660)	105.00	45.00	9.00
COMMON PLAYER (1-660)	.04	.02	.00
☐ 1 Fernando Valenzuela DK	.50	.25	.05
☐ 2 Rollie Fingers DK	.15	.07	.01
☐ 3 Reggie Jackson DK	.50	.25	.05
☐ 4 Jim Palmer DK	.35	.17	.03
☐ 5 Jack Morris DK	.15	.07	.01
☐ 6 George Foster DK	.10	.05	.01
☐ 7 Jim Sundberg DK	.07	.03	.01
☐ 8 Willie Stargell DK	.35	.17	.03
☐ 9 Dave Stieb DK	.15	.07	.01
☐ 10 Joe Niekro DK	.07	.03	.01
☐ 11 Rickey Henderson DK	1.75	.85	.17
☐ 12 Dale Murphy DK	.60	.30	.06
☐ 13 Toby Harrah DK	.07	.03	.01
☐ 14 Bill Buckner DK	.07	.03	.01
☐ 15 Willie Wilson DK	.10	.05	.01
☐ 16 Steve Carlton DK	.40	.20	.04
☐ 17 Ron Guidry DK	.20	.10	.02
☐ 18 Steve Rogers DK	.07	.03	.01
☐ 19 Kent Hrbek DK	.40	.20	.04
☐ 20 Keith Hernandez DK	.25	.12	.02
☐ 21 Floyd Bannister DK	.07	.03	.01
☐ 22 Johnny Bench DK	.60	.30	.06
☐ 23 Britt Burns DK	.07	.03	.01
☐ 24 Joe Morgan DK	.25	.12	.02
☐ 25 Carl Yastrzemski DK	.80	.40	.08
☐ 26 Terry Kennedy DK	.07	.03	.01
☐ 27 Gary Roenicke	.04	.02	.00
☐ 28 Dwight Bernard	.04	.02	.00
☐ 29 Pat Underwood	.04	.02	.00
☐ 30 Gary Allenson	.04	.02	.00
☐ 31 Ron Guidry	.18	.09	.01
☐ 32 Burt Hooton	.04	.02	.00
☐ 33 Chris Bando	.04	.02	.00
☐ 34 Vida Blue	.07	.03	.01
☐ 35 Rickey Henderson	4.00	2.00	.40
☐ 36 Ray Burris	.04	.02	.00
☐ 37 John Butcher	.04	.02	.00
☐ 38 Don Aase	.04	.02	.00

☐ 39 Jerry Koosman	.07	.03	.01
☐ 40 Bruce Sutter	.15	.07	.01
☐ 41 Jose Cruz	.07	.03	.01
☐ 42 Pete Rose	1.00	.50	.10
☐ 43 Cesar Cedeno	.07	.03	.01
☐ 44 Floyd Chiffer	.04	.02	.00
☐ 45 Larry McWilliams	.04	.02	.00
☐ 46 Alan Fowlkes	.04	.02	.00
☐ 47 Dale Murphy	1.00	.50	.10
☐ 48 Doug Bird	.04	.02	.00
☐ 49 Hubie Brooks	.25	.12	.02
☐ 50 Floyd Bannister	.04	.02	.00
☐ 51 Jack O'Connor	.04	.02	.00
☐ 52 Steve Senteney	.04	.02	.00
☐ 53 Gary Gaetti	3.00	1.50	.30
☐ 54 Damaso Garcia	.04	.02	.00
☐ 55 Gene Nelson	.04	.02	.00
☐ 56 Mookie Wilson	.10	05	.01
☐ 57 Allen Ripley	.04	.02	.00
☐ 58 Bob Horner	.12	.06	.01
☐ 59 Tony Pena	.20	.10	.02
☐ 60 Gary Lavelle	.04	.02	.00
☐ 61 Tim Lollar	.04	.02	.00
☐ 62 Frank Pastore	.04	.02	.00
☐ 63 Garry Maddox	.07	.03	.01
☐ 64 Bob Forsch	.04	.02	.00
☐ 65 Harry Spilman	.04	.02	.00
☐ 66 Geoff Zahn	.04	.02	.00
☐ 67 Salome Barojas	.04	.02	.00
☐ 68 David Palmer	.04	.02	.00
☐ 69 Charlie Hough	.07	.03	.01
☐ 70 Dan Quisenberry	.12	.06	.01
☐ 71 Tony Armas	.07	.03	.01
☐ 72 Rick Sutcliffe	.15	.07	.01
☐ 73 Steve Balboni	.07	.03	.01
☐ 74 Jerry Remy	.04	.02	.00
☐ 75 Mike Scioscia	.07	.03	.01
☐ 76 John Wockenfuss	.04	.02	.00
☐ 77 Jim Palmer	.50	.25	.05
☐ 78 Rollie Fingers	.25	.12	.02
☐ 79 Joe Nolan	.04	.02	.00
☐ 80 Pete Vuckovich	.07	.03	.01
☐ 81 Rick Leach	.04	.02	.00
☐ 82 Rick Miller	.04	.02	.00
☐ 83 Graig Nettles	.12	.06	.01
☐ 84 Ron Cey	.10	.05	.01
☐ 85 Miguel Dilone	.04	.02	.00
☐ 86 John Wathan	.07	.03	.01
☐ 87 Kelvin Moore	.04	.02	.00
☐ 88A Byrn Smith ERR (sic, Bryn)	.50	.25	.05
☐ 88B Bryn Smith COR	1.00	.50	.10
☐ 89 Dave Hostetler	.04	.02	.00
☐ 90 Rod Carew	.60	.30	.06
☐ 91 Lonnie Smith	.12	.06	.01
☐ 92 Bob Knepper	.07	.03	.01
☐ 93 Marty Bystrom	.04	.02	.00
☐ 94 Chris Welsh	.04	.02	.00
☐ 95 Jason Thompson	.04	.02	.00
☐ 96 Tom O'Malley	.04	.02	.00
☐ 97 Phil Niekro	.25	.12	.02
☐ 98 Neil Allen	.04	.02	.00
☐ 99 Bill Buckner	.10	.05	.01
☐ 100 Ed VandeBerg	.04	.02	.00
☐ 101 Jim Clancy	.04	.02	.00
☐ 102 Robert Castillo	.04	.02	.00
☐ 103 Bruce Berenyi	.04	.02	.00
☐ 104 Carlton Fisk	.50	.25	.05
☐ 105 Mike Flanagan	.07	.03	.01
☐ 106 Cecil Cooper	.12	.06	.01
☐ 107 Jack Morris	.20	.10	.02
☐ 108 Mike Morgan	.07	.03	.01
☐ 109 Luis Aponte	.04	.02	.00
☐ 110 Pedro Guerrero	.35	.17	.03
☐ 111 Len Barker	.04	.02	.00
☐ 112 Willie Wilson	.12	.06	.01
☐ 113 Dave Beard	.04	.02	.00
☐ 114 Mike Gates	.04	.02	.00
☐ 115 Reggie Jackson	.70	.35	.07
☐ 116 George Wright	.04	.02	.00
☐ 117 Vance Law	.07	.03	.01
☐ 118 Nolan Ryan	3.25	1.60	.32
☐ 119 Mike Krukow	.07	.03	.01
☐ 120 Ozzie Smith	.50	.25	.05
☐ 121 Broderick Perkins	.04	.02	.00
☐ 122 Tom Seaver	.70	.35	.07
☐ 123 Chris Chambliss	.07	.03	.01
☐ 124 Chuck Tanner MG	.04	.02	.00
☐ 125 Johnnie LeMaster	.04	.02	.00
☐ 126 Mel Hall	.70	.35	.07
☐ 127 Bruce Bochte	.04	.02	.00
☐ 128 Charlie Puleo	.04	.02	.00
☐ 129 Luis Leal	.04	.02	.00
☐ 130 John Pacella	.04	.02	.00
☐ 131 Glenn Gulliver	.04	.02	.00
☐ 132 Don Money	.04	.02	.00
☐ 133 Dave Rozema	.04	.02	.00
☐ 134 Bruce Hurst	.45	.22	.04
☐ 135 Rudy May	.04	.02	.00
☐ 136 Tom Lasorda MG	.07	.03	.01
☐ 137 Dan Spillner UER (photo actually Ed Whitson)	.07	.03	.01
☐ 138 Jerry Martin	.04	.02	.00
☐ 139 Mike Norris	.04	.02	.00
☐ 140 Al Oliver	.07	.03	.01
☐ 141 Daryl Sconiers	.04	.02	.00
☐ 142 Lamar Johnson	.04	.02	.00
☐ 143 Harold Baines	.25	.12	.02
☐ 144 Alan Ashby	.04	.02	.00
☐ 145 Garry Templeton	.07	.03	.01
☐ 146 Al Holland	.04	.02	.00
☐ 147 Bo Diaz	.04	.02	.00
☐ 148 Dave Concepcion	.10	.05	.01
☐ 149 Rick Camp	.04	.02	.00
☐ 150 Jim Morrison	.04	.02	.00
☐ 151 Randy Martz	.04	.02	.00
☐ 152 Keith Hernandez	.35	.17	.03
☐ 153 John Lowenstein	.04	.02	.00
☐ 154 Mike Caldwell	.04	.02	.00
☐ 155 Milt Wilcox	.04	.02	.00
☐ 156 Rich Gedman	.07	.03	.01
☐ 157 Rich Gossage	.15	.07	.01
☐ 158 Jerry Reuss	.07	.03	.01
☐ 159 Ron Hassey	.04	.02	.00
☐ 160 Larry Gura	.04	.02	.00
☐ 161 Dwayne Murphy	.04	.02	.00
☐ 162 Woodie Fryman	.04	.02	.00
☐ 163 Steve Comer	.04	.02	.00
☐ 164 Ken Forsch	.04	.02	.00
☐ 165 Dennis Lamp	.04	.02	.00
☐ 166 David Green	.04	.02	.00
☐ 167 Terry Puhl	.04	.02	.00
☐ 168 Mike Schmidt (wearing 37 rather than 20)	2.00	1.00	.20
☐ 169 Eddie Milner	.07	.03	.01
☐ 170 John Curtis	.04	.02	.00
☐ 171 Don Robinson	.04	.02	.00
☐ 172 Rich Gale	.04	.02	.00
☐ 173 Steve Bedrosian	.25	.12	.02
☐ 174 Willie Hernandez	.07	.03	.01
☐ 175 Ron Gardenhire	.04	.02	.00
☐ 176 Jim Beattie	.04	.02	.00
☐ 177 Tim Laudner	.04	.02	.00
☐ 178 Buck Martinez	.04	.02	.00
☐ 179 Kent Hrbek	.60	.30	.06
☐ 180 Alfredo Griffin	.07	.03	.01
☐ 181 Larry Andersen	.04	.02	.00
☐ 182 Pete Falcone	.04	.02	.00
☐ 183 Jody Davis	.07	.03	.01
☐ 184 Glenn Hubbard	.04	.02	.00
☐ 185 Dale Berra	.04	.02	.00
☐ 186 Greg Minton	.04	.02	.00
☐ 187 Gary Lucas	.04	.02	.00
☐ 188 Dave Van Gorder	.04	.02	.00
☐ 189 Bob Dernier	.04	.02	.00
☐ 190 Willie McGee	3.00	1.50	.30
☐ 191 Dickie Thon	.04	.02	.00
☐ 192 Bob Boone	.12	.06	.01
☐ 193 Britt Burns	.04	.02	.00
☐ 194 Jeff Reardon	.15	.07	.01
☐ 195 Jon Matlack	.04	.02	.00
☐ 196 Don Slaught	.35	.17	.03
☐ 197 Fred Stanley	.04	.02	.00
☐ 198 Rick Manning	.04	.02	.00
☐ 199 Dave Righetti	.25	.12	.02
☐ 200 Dave Stapleton	.04	.02	.00
☐ 201 Steve Yeager	.04	.02	.00
☐ 202 Enos Cabell	.04	.02	.00
☐ 203 Sammy Stewart	.04	.02	.00
☐ 204 Moose Haas	.04	.02	.00
☐ 205 Lenn Sakata	.04	.02	.00
☐ 206 Charlie Moore	.04	.02	.00
☐ 207 Alan Trammell	.30	.15	.03
☐ 208 Jim Rice	.25	.12	.02
☐ 209 Roy Smalley	.04	.02	.00
☐ 210 Bill Russell	.07	.03	.01
☐ 211 Andre Thornton	.07	.03	.01
☐ 212 Willie Aikens	.04	.02	.00
☐ 213 Dave McKay	.04	.02	.00
☐ 214 Tim Blackwell	.04	.02	.00
☐ 215 Buddy Bell	.07	.03	.01
☐ 216 Doug DeCinces	.07	.03	.01
☐ 217 Tom Herr	.07	.03	.01
☐ 218 Frank LaCorte	.04	.02	.00
☐ 219 Steve Carlton	.50	.25	.05
☐ 220 Terry Kennedy	.04	.02	.00

☐ 221	Mike Easler	.04	.02	.00
☐ 222	Jack Clark	.25	.12	.02
☐ 223	Gene Garber	.04	.02	.00
☐ 224	Scott Holman	.04	.02	.00
☐ 225	Mike Proly	.04	.02	.00
☐ 226	Terry Bulling	.04	.02	.00
☐ 227	Jerry Garvin	.04	.02	.00
☐ 228	Ron Davis	.04	.02	.00
☐ 229	Tom Hume	.04	.02	.00
☐ 230	Marc Hill	.04	.02	.00
☐ 231	Dennis Martinez	.07	.03	.01
☐ 232	Jim Gantner	.04	.02	.00
☐ 233	Larry Pashnick	.04	.02	.00
☐ 234	Dave Collins	.04	.02	.00
☐ 235	Tom Burgmeier	.04	.02	.00
☐ 236	Ken Landreaux	.04	.02	.00
☐ 237	John Denny	.07	.03	.01
☐ 238	Hal McRae	.07	.03	.01
☐ 239	Matt Keough	.04	.02	.00
☐ 240	Doug Flynn	.04	.02	.00
☐ 241	Fred Lynn	.18	.09	.01
☐ 242	Billy Sample	.04	.02	.00
☐ 243	Tom Paciorek	.04	.02	.00
☐ 244	Joe Sambito	.04	.02	.00
☐ 245	Sid Monge	.04	.02	.00
☐ 246	Ken Oberkfell	.04	.02	.00
☐ 247	Joe Pittman UER (photo actually Juan Eichelberger)	.07	.03	.01
☐ 248	Mario Soto	.07	.03	.01
☐ 249	Claudell Washington	.07	.03	.01
☐ 250	Rick Rhoden	.07	.03	.01
☐ 251	Darrell Evans	.10	.05	.01
☐ 252	Steve Henderson	.04	.02	.00
☐ 253	Manny Castillo	.04	.02	.00
☐ 254	Craig Swan	.04	.02	.00
☐ 255	Joey McLaughlin	.04	.02	.00
☐ 256	Pete Redfern	.04	.02	.00
☐ 257	Ken Singleton	.07	.03	.01
☐ 258	Robin Yount	.80	.40	.08
☐ 259	Elias Sosa	.04	.02	.00
☐ 260	Bob Ojeda	.10	.05	.01
☐ 261	Bobby Murcer	.10	.05	.01
☐ 262	Candy Maldonado	1.00	.50	.10
☐ 263	Rick Waits	.04	.02	.00
☐ 264	Greg Pryor	.04	.02	.00
☐ 265	Bob Owchinko	.04	.02	.00
☐ 266	Chris Speier	.04	.02	.00
☐ 267	Bruce Kison	.04	.02	.00
☐ 268	Mark Wagner	.04	.02	.00
☐ 269	Steve Kemp	.04	.02	.00
☐ 270	Phil Garner	.04	.02	.00
☐ 271	Gene Richards	.04	.02	.00
☐ 272	Renie Martin	.04	.02	.00
☐ 273	Dave Roberts	.04	.02	.00
☐ 274	Dan Driessen	.04	.02	.00
☐ 275	Rufino Linares	.04	.02	.00
☐ 276	Lee Lacy	.04	.02	.00
☐ 277	Ryne Sandberg	28.00	14.00	2.80
☐ 278	Darrell Porter	.04	.02	.00
☐ 279	Cal Ripken	4.00	2.00	.40
☐ 280	Jamie Easterly	.04	.02	.00
☐ 281	Bill Fahey	.04	.02	.00
☐ 282	Glenn Hoffman	.04	.02	.00
☐ 283	Willie Randolph	.07	.03	.01
☐ 284	Fernando Valenzuela	.35	.17	.03
☐ 285	Alan Bannister	.04	.02	.00
☐ 286	Paul Splittorff	.04	.02	.00
☐ 287	Joe Rudi	.07	.03	.01
☐ 288	Bill Gullickson	.04	.02	.00
☐ 289	Danny Darwin	.07	.03	.01
☐ 290	Andy Hassler	.04	.02	.00
☐ 291	Ernesto Escarrega	.04	.02	.00
☐ 292	Steve Mura	.04	.02	.00
☐ 293	Tony Scott	.04	.02	.00
☐ 294	Manny Trillo	.04	.02	.00
☐ 295	Greg Harris	.04	.02	.00
☐ 296	Luis DeLeon	.04	.02	.00
☐ 297	Kent Tekulve	.07	.03	.01
☐ 298	Atlee Hammaker	.07	.03	.01
☐ 299	Bruce Benedict	.04	.02	.00
☐ 300	Fergie Jenkins	.15	.07	.01
☐ 301	Dave Kingman	.10	.05	.01
☐ 302	Bill Caudill	.04	.02	.00
☐ 303	John Castino	.04	.02	.00
☐ 304	Ernie Whitt	.04	.02	.00
☐ 305	Randy Johnson	.04	.02	.00
☐ 306	Garth Iorg	.04	.02	.00
☐ 307	Gaylord Perry	.25	.12	.02
☐ 308	Ed Lynch	.04	.02	.00
☐ 309	Keith Moreland	.04	.02	.00
☐ 310	Rafael Ramirez	.04	.02	.00
☐ 311	Bill Madlock	.07	.03	.01
☐ 312	Milt May	.04	.02	.00
☐ 313	John Montefusco	.07	.03	.01
☐ 314	Wayne Krenchicki	.04	.02	.00
☐ 315	George Vukovich	.04	.02	.00
☐ 316	Joaquin Andujar	.07	.03	.01
☐ 317	Craig Reynolds	.04	.02	.00
☐ 318	Rick Burleson	.07	.03	.01
☐ 319	Richard Dotson	.07	.03	.01
☐ 320	Steve Rogers	.04	.02	.00
☐ 321	Dave Schmidt	.12	.06	.01
☐ 322	Bud Black	.50	.25	.05
☐ 323	Jeff Burroughs	.07	.03	.01
☐ 324	Von Hayes	.30	.15	.03
☐ 325	Butch Wynegar	.04	.02	.00
☐ 326	Carl Yastrzemski	1.00	.50	.10
☐ 327	Ron Roenicke	.04	.02	.00
☐ 328	Howard Johnson	9.00	4.50	.90
☐ 329	Rick Dempsey (posing as a left-handed batter)	.04	.02	.00
☐ 330A	Jim Slaton (bio printed black on white)	.07	.03	.01
☐ 330B	Jim Slaton (bio printed black on yellow)	.15	.07	.01
☐ 331	Benny Ayala	.04	.02	.00
☐ 332	Ted Simmons	.12	.06	.01
☐ 333	Lou Whitaker	.25	.12	.02
☐ 334	Chuck Rainey	.04	.02	.00
☐ 335	Lou Piniella	.12	.06	.01
☐ 336	Steve Sax	.60	.30	.06
☐ 337	Toby Harrah	.07	.03	.01
☐ 338	George Brett	1.00	.50	.10
☐ 339	Dave Lopes	.07	.03	.01
☐ 340	Gary Carter	.35	.17	.03
☐ 341	John Grubb	.04	.02	.00
☐ 342	Tim Foli	.04	.02	.00
☐ 343	Jim Kaat	.12	.06	.01
☐ 344	Mike LaCoss	.04	.02	.00
☐ 345	Larry Christenson	.04	.02	.00
☐ 346	Juan Bonilla	.04	.02	.00
☐ 347	Omar Moreno	.04	.02	.00
☐ 348	Chili Davis	.30	.15	.03
☐ 349	Tommy Boggs	.04	.02	.00
☐ 350	Rusty Staub	.10	.05	.01
☐ 351	Bump Wills	.04	.02	.00
☐ 352	Rick Sweet	.04	.02	.00
☐ 353	Jim Gott	.30	.15	.03
☐ 354	Terry Felton	.04	.02	.00
☐ 355	Jim Kern	.04	.02	.00
☐ 356	Bill Almon (Expos/Mets in 1983, not Padres/Mets)	.04	.02	.00
☐ 357	Tippy Martinez	.04	.02	.00
☐ 358	Roy Howell	.04	.02	.00
☐ 359	Dan Petry	.04	.02	.00
☐ 360	Jerry Mumphrey	.04	.02	.00
☐ 361	Mark Clear	.04	.02	.00
☐ 362	Mike Marshall	.25	.12	.02
☐ 363	Lary Sorensen	.04	.02	.00
☐ 364	Amos Otis	.07	.03	.01
☐ 365	Rick Langford	.04	.02	.00
☐ 366	Brad Mills	.04	.02	.00
☐ 367	Brian Downing	.07	.03	.01
☐ 368	Mike Richardt	.04	.02	.00
☐ 369	Aurelio Rodriguez	.04	.02	.00
☐ 370	Dave Smith	.07	.03	.01
☐ 371	Tug McGraw	.10	.05	.01
☐ 372	Doug Bair	.04	.02	.00
☐ 373	Ruppert Jones	.04	.02	.00
☐ 374	Alex Trevino	.04	.02	.00
☐ 375	Ken Dayley	.07	.03	.01
☐ 376	Rod Scurry	.04	.02	.00
☐ 377	Bob Brenly	.04	.02	.00
☐ 378	Scot Thompson	.04	.02	.00
☐ 379	Julio Cruz	.04	.02	.00
☐ 380	John Stearns	.04	.02	.00
☐ 381	Dale Murray	.04	.02	.00
☐ 382	Frank Viola	7.00	3.50	.70
☐ 383	Al Bumbry	.04	.02	.00
☐ 384	Ben Oglivie	.07	.03	.01
☐ 385	Dave Tobik	.04	.02	.00
☐ 386	Bob Stanley	.04	.02	.00
☐ 387	Andre Robertson	.04	.02	.00
☐ 388	Jorge Orta	.04	.02	.00
☐ 389	Ed Whitson	.07	.03	.01
☐ 390	Don Hood	.04	.02	.00
☐ 391	Tom Underwood	.04	.02	.00
☐ 392	Tim Wallach	.30	.15	.03
☐ 393	Steve Renko	.04	.02	.00
☐ 394	Mickey Rivers	.07	.03	.01
☐ 395	Greg Luzinski	.10	.05	.01
☐ 396	Art Howe	.07	.03	.01
☐ 397	Alan Wiggins	.10	.05	.01

☐ 398	Jim Barr	.04	.02	.00
☐ 399	Ivan DeJesus	.04	.02	.00
☐ 400	Tom Lawless	.07	.03	.01
☐ 401	Bob Walk	.04	.02	.00
☐ 402	Jimmy Smith	.04	.02	.00
☐ 403	Lee Smith	.10	.05	.01
☐ 404	George Hendrick	.07	.03	.01
☐ 405	Eddie Murray	.65	.30	.06
☐ 406	Marshall Edwards	.04	.02	.00
☐ 407	Lance Parrish	.20	.10	.02
☐ 408	Carney Lansford	.20	.10	.02
☐ 409	Dave Winfield	.40	.20	.04
☐ 410	Bob Welch	.25	.12	.02
☐ 411	Larry Milbourne	.04	.02	.00
☐ 412	Dennis Leonard	.07	.03	.01
☐ 413	Dan Meyer	.04	.02	.00
☐ 414	Charlie Lea	.04	.02	.00
☐ 415	Rick Honeycutt	.04	.02	.00
☐ 416	Mike Witt	.12	.06	.01
☐ 417	Steve Trout	.04	.02	.00
☐ 418	Glenn Brummer	.04	.02	.00
☐ 419	Denny Walling	.04	.02	.00
☐ 420	Gary Matthews	.07	.03	.01
☐ 421	Charlie Leibrandt UER (Liebrandt on front of card)	.07	.03	.01
☐ 422	Juan Eichelberger UER (photo actually Joe Pittman)	.07	.03	.01
☐ 423	Matt Guante	.04	.02	.00
☐ 424	Bill Laskey	.04	.02	.00
☐ 425	Jerry Royster	.04	.02	.00
☐ 426	Dickie Noles	.04	.02	.00
☐ 427	George Foster	.15	.07	.01
☐ 428	Mike Moore	1.00	.50	.10
☐ 429	Gary Ward	.07	.03	.01
☐ 430	Barry Bonnell	.04	.02	.00
☐ 431	Ron Washington	.04	.02	.00
☐ 432	Rance Mulliniks	.04	.02	.00
☐ 433	Mike Stanton	.04	.02	.00
☐ 434	Jesse Orosco	.04	.02	.00
☐ 435	Larry Bowa	.10	.05	.01
☐ 436	Biff Pocoroba	.04	.02	.00
☐ 437	Johnny Ray	.10	.05	.01
☐ 438	Joe Morgan	.35	.17	.03
☐ 439	Eric Show	.30	.15	.03
☐ 440	Larry Biittner	.04	.02	.00
☐ 441	Greg Gross	.04	.02	.00
☐ 442	Gene Tenace	.04	.02	.00
☐ 443	Danny Heep	.04	.02	.00
☐ 444	Bobby Clark	.04	.02	.00
☐ 445	Kevin Hickey	.04	.02	.00
☐ 446	Scott Sanderson	.07	.03	.01
☐ 447	Frank Tanana	.07	.03	.01
☐ 448	Cesar Geronimo	.04	.02	.00
☐ 449	Jimmy Sexton	.04	.02	.00
☐ 450	Mike Hargrove	.04	.02	.00
☐ 451	Doyle Alexander	.07	.03	.01
☐ 452	Dwight Evans	.25	.12	.02
☐ 453	Terry Forster	.07	.03	.01
☐ 454	Tom Brookens	.04	.02	.00
☐ 455	Rich Dauer	.04	.02	.00
☐ 456	Rob Picciolo	.04	.02	.00
☐ 457	Terry Crowley	.04	.02	.00
☐ 458	Ned Yost	.04	.02	.00
☐ 459	Kirk Gibson	.35	.17	.03
☐ 460	Reid Nichols	.04	.02	.00
☐ 461	Oscar Gamble	.04	.02	.00
☐ 462	Dusty Baker	.07	.03	.01
☐ 463	Jack Perconte	.04	.02	.00
☐ 464	Frank White	.07	.03	.01
☐ 465	Mickey Klutts	.04	.02	.00
☐ 466	Warren Cromartie	.04	.02	.00
☐ 467	Larry Parrish	.07	.03	.01
☐ 468	Bobby Grich	.07	.03	.01
☐ 469	Dane Iorg	.04	.02	.00
☐ 470	Joe Niekro	.07	.03	.01
☐ 471	Ed Farmer	.04	.02	.00
☐ 472	Tim Flannery	.04	.02	.00
☐ 473	Dave Parker	.25	.12	.02
☐ 474	Jeff Leonard	.07	.03	.01
☐ 475	Al Hrabosky	.07	.03	.01
☐ 476	Ron Hodges	.04	.02	.00
☐ 477	Leon Durham	.04	.02	.00
☐ 478	Jim Essian	.04	.02	.00
☐ 479	Roy Lee Jackson	.04	.02	.00
☐ 480	Brad Havens	.04	.02	.00
☐ 481	Joe Price	.04	.02	.00
☐ 482	Tony Bernazard	.07	.03	.01
☐ 483	Scott McGregor	.07	.03	.01
☐ 484	Paul Molitor	.20	.10	.02
☐ 485	Mike Ivie	.04	.02	.00
☐ 486	Ken Griffey	.15	.07	.01
☐ 487	Dennis Eckersley	.30	.15	.03
☐ 488	Steve Garvey	.45	.22	.04
☐ 489	Mike Fischlin	.04	.02	.00
☐ 490	U.L. Washington	.04	.02	.00
☐ 491	Steve McCatty	.04	.02	.00
☐ 492	Roy Johnson	.04	.02	.00
☐ 493	Don Baylor	.12	.06	.01
☐ 494	Bobby Johnson	.04	.02	.00
☐ 495	Mike Squires	.04	.02	.00
☐ 496	Bert Roberge	.04	.02	.00
☐ 497	Dick Ruthven	.04	.02	.00
☐ 498	Tito Landrum	.04	.02	.00
☐ 499	Sixto Lezcano	.04	.02	.00
☐ 500	Johnny Bench	.70	.35	.07
☐ 501	Larry Whisenton	.04	.02	.00
☐ 502	Manny Sarmiento	.04	.02	.00
☐ 503	Fred Breining	.04	.02	.00
☐ 504	Bill Campbell	.04	.02	.00
☐ 505	Todd Cruz	.04	.02	.00
☐ 506	Bob Bailor	.04	.02	.00
☐ 507	Dave Stieb	.30	.15	.03
☐ 508	Al Williams	.04	.02	.00
☐ 509	Dan Ford	.04	.02	.00
☐ 510	Gorman Thomas	.07	.03	.01
☐ 511	Chet Lemon	.04	.02	.00
☐ 512	Mike Torrez	.04	.02	.00
☐ 513	Shane Rawley	.04	.02	.00
☐ 514	Mark Belanger	.07	.03	.01
☐ 515	Rodney Craig	.04	.02	.00
☐ 516	Onix Concepcion	.04	.02	.00
☐ 517	Mike Heath	.04	.02	.00
☐ 518	Andre Dawson	.60	.30	.06
☐ 519	Luis Sanchez	.04	.02	.00
☐ 520	Terry Bogener	.04	.02	.00
☐ 521	Rudy Law	.04	.02	.00
☐ 522	Ray Knight	.07	.03	.01
☐ 523	Joe Lefebvre	.04	.02	.00
☐ 524	Jim Wohlford	.04	.02	.00
☐ 525	Julio Franco	6.00	3.00	.60
☐ 526	Ron Oester	.04	.02	.00
☐ 527	Rick Mahler	.04	.02	.00
☐ 528	Steve Nicosia	.04	.02	.00
☐ 529	Junior Kennedy	.04	.02	.00
☐ 530A	Whitey Herzog MG (bio printed black on white)	.10	.05	.01
☐ 530B	Whitey Herzog MG (bio printed black on yellow)	.10	.05	.01
☐ 531A	Don Sutton (blue border on photo)	.40	.20	.04
☐ 531B	Don Sutton (green border on photo)	.40	.20	.04
☐ 532	Mark Brouhard	.04	.02	.00
☐ 533A	Sparky Anderson MG (bio printed black on white)	.10	.05	.01
☐ 533B	Sparky Anderson MG (bio printed black on yellow)	.10	.05	.01
☐ 534	Roger LaFrancois	.04	.02	.00
☐ 535	George Frazier	.04	.02	.00
☐ 536	Tom Niedenfuer	.07	.03	.01
☐ 537	Ed Glynn	.04	.02	.00
☐ 538	Lee May	.07	.03	.01
☐ 539	Bob Kearney	.04	.02	.00
☐ 540	Tim Raines	.60	.30	.06
☐ 541	Paul Mirabella	.04	.02	.00
☐ 542	Luis Tiant	.07	.03	.01
☐ 543	Ron LeFlore	.07	.03	.01
☐ 544	Dave LaPoint	.35	.17	.03
☐ 545	Randy Moffitt	.04	.02	.00
☐ 546	Luis Aguayo	.04	.02	.00
☐ 547	Brad Lesley	.04	.02	.00
☐ 548	Luis Salazar	.04	.02	.00
☐ 549	John Candelaria	.07	.03	.01
☐ 550	Dave Bergman	.04	.02	.00
☐ 551	Bob Watson	.07	.03	.01
☐ 552	Pat Tabler	.10	.05	.01
☐ 553	Brent Gaff	.04	.02	.00
☐ 554	Al Cowens	.04	.02	.00
☐ 555	Tom Brunansky	.90	.45	.09
☐ 556	Lloyd Moseby	.10	.05	.01
☐ 557A	Pascual Perez ERR (Twins in glove)	2.00	1.00	.20
☐ 557B	Pascual Perez COR (Braves in glove)	.25	.12	.02
☐ 558	Willie Upshaw	.04	.02	.00
☐ 559	Richie Zisk	.04	.02	.00
☐ 560	Pat Zachry	.04	.02	.00
☐ 561	Jay Johnstone	.07	.03	.01
☐ 562	Carlos Diaz	.04	.02	.00
☐ 563	John Tudor	.20	.10	.02

☐ 564 Frank Robinson MG	.15	.07	.01
☐ 565 Dave Edwards	.04	.02	.00
☐ 566 Paul Householder	.04	.02	.00
☐ 567 Ron Reed	.04	.02	.00
☐ 568 Mike Ramsey	.04	.02	.00
☐ 569 Kiko Garcia	.04	.02	.00
☐ 570 Tommy John	.15	.07	.01
☐ 571 Tony LaRussa MG	.07	.03	.01
☐ 572 Joel Youngblood	.04	.02	.00
☐ 573 Wayne Tolleson	.12	.06	.01
☐ 574 Keith Creel	.04	.02	.00
☐ 575 Billy Martin MG	.15	.07	.01
☐ 576 Jerry Dybzinski	.04	.02	.00
☐ 577 Rick Cerone	.04	.02	.00
☐ 578 Tony Perez	.15	.07	.01
☐ 579 Greg Brock	.25	.12	.02
☐ 580 Glenn Wilson	.35	.17	.03
☐ 581 Tim Stoddard	.04	.02	.00
☐ 582 Bob McClure	.04	.02	.00
☐ 583 Jim Dwyer	.04	.02	.00
☐ 584 Ed Romero	.04	.02	.00
☐ 585 Larry Herndon	.04	.02	.00
☐ 586 Wade Boggs	20.00	10.00	2.00
☐ 587 Jay Howell	.06	.03	.00
☐ 588 Dave Stewart	1.50	.75	.15
☐ 589 Bert Blyleven	.20	.10	.02
☐ 590 Dick Howser MG	.07	.03	.01
☐ 591 Wayne Gross	.04	.02	.00
☐ 592 Terry Francona	.04	.02	.00
☐ 593 Don Werner	.04	.02	.00
☐ 594 Bill Stein	.04	.02	.00
☐ 595 Jesse Barfield	.75	.35	.07
☐ 596 Bob Molinaro	.04	.02	.00
☐ 597 Mike Vail	.04	.02	.00
☐ 598 Tony Gwynn	16.00	8.00	1.60
☐ 599 Gary Rajsich	.04	.02	.00
☐ 600 Jerry Ujdur	.04	.02	.00
☐ 601 Cliff Johnson	.04	.02	.00
☐ 602 Jerry White	.04	.02	.00
☐ 603 Bryan Clark	.04	.02	.00
☐ 604 Joe Ferguson	.04	.02	.00
☐ 605 Guy Sularz	.04	.02	.00
☐ 606A Ozzie Virgil (green border on photo)	.10	.05	.01
☐ 606B Ozzie Virgil (orange border on photo)	.10	.05	.01
☐ 607 Terry Harper	.04	.02	.00
☐ 608 Harvey Kuenn MG	.07	.03	.01
☐ 609 Jim Sundberg	.04	.02	.00
☐ 610 Willie Stargell	.35	.17	.03
☐ 611 Reggie Smith	.07	.03	.01
☐ 612 Rob Wilfong	.04	.02	.00
☐ 613 The Niekro Brothers Joe Niekro Phil Niekro	.12	.06	.01
☐ 614 Lee Elia MG	.04	.02	.00
☐ 615 Mickey Hatcher	.04	.02	.00
☐ 616 Jerry Hairston	.04	.02	.00
☐ 617 John Martin	.04	.02	.00
☐ 618 Wally Backman	.30	.15	.03
☐ 619 Storm Davis	.60	.30	.06
☐ 620 Alan Knicely	.04	.02	.00
☐ 621 John Stuper	.04	.02	.00
☐ 622 Matt Sinatro	.04	.02	.00
☐ 623 Geno Petralli	.15	.07	.01
☐ 624 Duane Walker	.04	.02	.00
☐ 625 Dick Williams MG	.04	.02	.00
☐ 626 Pat Corrales MG	.04	.02	.00
☐ 627 Vern Ruhle	.04	.02	.00
☐ 628 Joe Torre MG	.07	.03	.01
☐ 629 Anthony Johnson	.04	.02	.00
☐ 630 Steve Howe	.04	.02	.00
☐ 631 Gary Woods	.04	.02	.00
☐ 632 LaMarr Hoyt	.07	.03	.01
☐ 633 Steve Swisher	.04	.02	.00
☐ 634 Terry Leach	.15	.07	.01
☐ 635 Jeff Newman	.04	.02	.00
☐ 636 Brett Butler	.20	.10	.02
☐ 637 Gary Gray	.04	.02	.00
☐ 638 Lee Mazzilli	.04	.02	.00
☐ 639A Ron Jackson ERR (A's in glove)	12.00	6.00	1.20
☐ 639B Ron Jackson COR (Angels in glove, red border on photo)	.15	.07	.01
☐ 639C Ron Jackson COR (Angels in glove, green border on photo)	.50	.25	.05
☐ 640 Juan Beniquez	.04	.02	.00
☐ 641 Dave Rucker	.04	.02	.00
☐ 642 Luis Pujols	.04	.02	.00
☐ 643 Rick Monday	.07	.03	.01
☐ 644 Hosken Powell	.04	.02	.00
☐ 645 The Chicken	.20	.10	.02
☐ 646 Dave Engle	.04	.02	.00
☐ 647 Dick Davis	.04	.02	.00
☐ 648 Frank Robinson Vida Blue Joe Morgan	.20	.10	.02
☐ 649 Al Chambers	.04	.02	.00
☐ 650 Jesus Vega	.04	.02	.00
☐ 651 Jeff Jones	.04	.02	.00
☐ 652 Marvis Foley	.04	.02	.00
☐ 653 Ty Cobb Puzzle Card	.04	.02	.00
☐ 654A Dick Perez/Diamond King Checklist (unnumbered) (word "checklist" omitted from back)	.15	.02	.00
☐ 654B Dick Perez/Diamond King Checklist (unnumbered) (word "checklist" is on back)	.15	.02	.00
☐ 655 Checklist 1 (unnumbered)	.07	.01	.00
☐ 656 Checklist 2 (unnumbered)	.07	.01	.00
☐ 657 Checklist 3 (unnumbered)	.07	.01	.00
☐ 658 Checklist 4 (unnumbered)	.07	.01	.00
☐ 659 Checklist 5 (unnumbered)	.07	.01	.00
☐ 660 Checklist 6 (unnumbered)	.07	.01	.00

1983 Donruss Action All-Stars

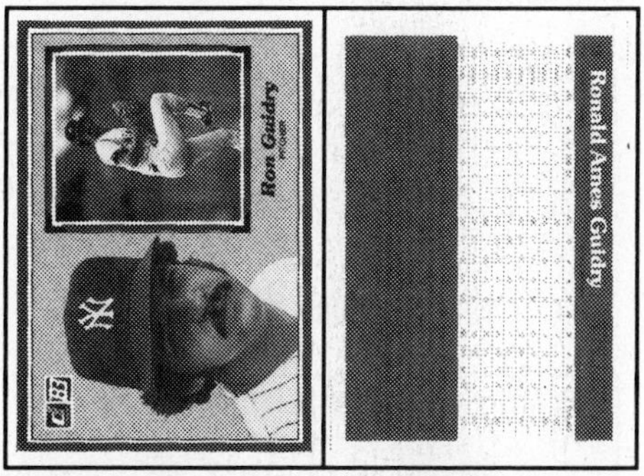

The cards in this 60-card set measure approximately 3 1/2" by 5". The 1983 Action All-Stars series depicts 60 major leagers in a distinctive new style. Each card contains a large close-up on the left and an action photo on the right. Team affiliations appear as part of the background design, and the cards have cranberry color borders. The backs contain the card number, the player's major league line record, and biographical material. A 63-piece Mickey Mantle puzzle (three pieces on one card per pack) was marketed as an insert premium.

	MINT	EXC	G-VG
COMPLETE SET (60)	7.00	3.50	.70
COMMON PLAYER (1-60)	.07	.03	.01
☐ 1 Eddie Murray	.35	.17	.03
☐ 2 Dwight Evans	.15	.07	.01
☐ 3A Reggie Jackson ERR (red screen on back covers some stats)	1.00	.50	.10
☐ 3B Reggie Jackson COR	.75	.35	.07
☐ 4 Greg Luzinski	.10	.05	.01
☐ 5 Larry Herndon	.07	.03	.01
☐ 6 Al Oliver	.10	.05	.01
☐ 7 Bill Buckner	.10	.05	.01
☐ 8 Jason Thompson	.07	.03	.01

☐	9 Andre Dawson	.35	.17	.03
☐	10 Greg Minton	.07	.03	.01
☐	11 Terry Kennedy	.07	.03	.01
☐	12 Phil Niekro	.20	.10	.02
☐	13 Willie Wilson	.10	.05	.01
☐	14 Johnny Bench	.40	.20	.04
☐	15 Ron Guidry	.10	.05	.01
☐	16 Hal McRae	.07	.03	.01
☐	17 Damaso Garcia	.07	.03	.01
☐	18 Gary Ward	.07	.03	.01
☐	19 Cecil Cooper	.10	.05	.01
☐	20 Keith Hernandez	.15	.07	.01
☐	21 Ron Cey	.07	.03	.01
☐	22 Rickey Henderson	1.00	.50	.10
☐	23 Nolan Ryan	1.25	.60	.12
☐	24 Steve Carlton	.35	.17	.03
☐	25 John Stearns	.07	.03	.01
☐	26 Jim Sundberg	.07	.03	.01
☐	27 Joaquin Andujar	.07	.03	.01
☐	28 Gaylord Perry	.20	.10	.02
☐	29 Jack Clark	.20	.10	.02
☐	30 Bill Madlock	.07	.03	.01
☐	31 Pete Rose	.75	.35	.07
☐	32 Mookie Wilson	.07	.03	.01
☐	33 Rollie Fingers	.15	.07	.01
☐	34 Lonnie Smith	.10	.05	.01
☐	35 Tony Pena	.07	.03	.01
☐	36 Dave Winfield	.20	.10	.02
☐	37 Tim Lollar	.07	.03	.01
☐	38 Rod Carew	.35	.17	.03
☐	39 Toby Harrah	.07	.03	.01
☐	40 Buddy Bell	.07	.03	.01
☐	41 Bruce Sutter	.10	.05	.01
☐	42 George Brett	.50	.25	.05
☐	43 Carlton Fisk	.35	.17	.03
☐	44 Carl Yastrzemski	.75	.35	.07
☐	45 Dale Murphy	.40	.20	.04
☐	46 Bob Horner	.10	.05	.01
☐	47 Dave Concepcion	.07	.03	.01
☐	48 Dave Stieb	.15	.07	.01
☐	49 Kent Hrbek	.20	.10	.02
☐	50 Lance Parrish	.15	.07	.01
☐	51 Joe Niekro	.10	.05	.01
☐	52 Cal Ripken	.35	.17	.03
☐	53 Fernando Valenzuela	.25	.12	.02
☐	54 Richie Zisk	.07	.03	.01
☐	55 Leon Durham	.07	.03	.01
☐	56 Robin Yount	.50	.25	.05
☐	57 Mike Schmidt	1.00	.50	.10
☐	58 Gary Carter	.30	.15	.03
☐	59 Fred Lynn	.10	.05	.01
☐	60 Checklist Card	.07	.01	.00

1983 Donruss HOF Heroes

The cards in this 44-card set measure 2 1/2" by 3 1/2". Although it was issued with the same Mantle puzzle as the Action All Stars set, the Donruss Hall of Fame Heroes set is completely different in content and design. Of the 44 cards in the set, 42 are Dick Perez artwork portraying Hall of Fame members, while one card depicts the completed Mantle puzzle and the last card is a checklist. The red, white, and blue backs contain the card number and a short player biography. The cards were packaged 8 cards plus one puzzle card (3 pieces) for 30 cents in the summer of 1983.

		MINT	EXC	G-VG
	COMPLETE SET (44)	5.00	2.50	.50
	COMMON PLAYER (1-44)	.05	.02	.00
☐	1 Ty Cobb	.60	.30	.06
☐	2 Walter Johnson	.20	.10	.02
☐	3 Christy Mathewson	.20	.10	.02
☐	4 Josh Gibson	.20	.10	.02
☐	5 Honus Wagner	.20	.10	.02
☐	6 Jackie Robinson	.25	.12	.02
☐	7 Mickey Mantle	1.00	.50	.10
☐	8 Luke Appling	.05	.02	.00
☐	9 Ted Williams	.25	.12	.02
☐	10 Johnny Mize	.05	.02	.00
☐	11 Satchel Paige	.15	.07	.01
☐	12 Lou Boudreau	.05	.02	.00
☐	13 Jimmie Foxx	.10	.05	.01
☐	14 Duke Snider	.20	.10	.02
☐	15 Monte Irvin	.05	.02	.00
☐	16 Hank Greenberg	.05	.02	.00
☐	17 Roberto Clemente	.20	.10	.02
☐	18 Al Kaline	.15	.07	.01
☐	19 Frank Robinson	.15	.07	.01
☐	20 Joe Cronin	.05	.02	.00
☐	21 Burleigh Grimes	.05	.02	.00
☐	22 The Waner Brothers Paul Waner Lloyd Waner	.05	.02	.00
☐	23 Grover Alexander	.05	.02	.00
☐	24 Yogi Berra	.20	.10	.02
☐	25 Cool Papa Bell	.05	.02	.00
☐	26 Bill Dickey	.10	.05	.01
☐	27 Cy Young	.10	.05	.01
☐	28 Charlie Gehringer	.05	.02	.00
☐	29 Dizzy Dean	.15	.07	.01
☐	30 Bob Lemon	.05	.02	.00
☐	31 Red Ruffing	.05	.02	.00
☐	32 Stan Musial	.20	.10	.02
☐	33 Carl Hubbell	.10	.05	.01
☐	34 Hank Aaron	.30	.15	.03
☐	35 John McGraw	.05	.02	.00
☐	36 Bob Feller	.15	.07	.01
☐	37 Casey Stengel	.10	.05	.01
☐	38 Ralph Kiner	.10	.05	.01
☐	39 Roy Campanella	.20	.10	.02
☐	40 Mel Ott	.10	.05	.01
☐	41 Robin Roberts	.10	.05	.01
☐	42 Early Wynn	.05	.02	.00
☐	43 Mantle Puzzle Card	.05	.02	.00
☐	44 Checklist Card	.05	.01	.00

1984 Donruss

The 1984 Donruss set contains a total of 660 cards, each measuring 2 1/2" by 3 1/2"; however, only 658 are numbered. The first 26 cards in the set are again Diamond Kings (DK), although the drawings this year were styled differently and are easily differentiated from other DK issues. A new feature, Rated Rookies (RR), was introduced with this set with Bill Madden's 20 selections comprising numbers 27 through 46. Two "Living Legend" cards designated A (featuring Gaylord Perry and Rollie Fingers) and B (featuring Johnny Bench and Carl Yastrzemski) were issued as bonus cards in wax packs, but were not issued in the vending sets sold to hobby dealers. The seven unnumbered checklist cards are arbitrarily assigned numbers 652 through 658 and are listed at the end of the list below. The designs on the fronts of the Donruss cards changed considerably from the past two years. The backs contain statistics and are printed in green and black ink. The cards were distributed with a 63-piece puzzle of Duke Snider. There are no extra variation cards included in the complete set price below. The variation cards apparently resulted from a different printing for the factory sets as the Darling and Stenhouse no number variations as well as the Perez-Steel errors were corrected in the factory sets which were released later in the year. The key rookie cards in this set are Joe Carter, Sid Fernandez, Tony Fernandez, Don Mattingly, Kevin McReynolds, Darryl Strawberry, and Andy Van Slyke.

	MINT	EXC	G-VG
COMPLETE SET (658)	350.00	175.00	35.00
COMMON PLAYER (1-658)	.10	.05	.01
□ 1A Robin Yount DK ERR (Perez Steel)	1.25	.60	.12
□ 1B Robin Yount DK COR	2.00	1.00	.20
□ 2A Dave Concepcion DK ERR (Perez Steel)	.15	.07	.01
□ 2B Dave Concepcion DK COR	.25	.12	.02
□ 3A Dwayne Murphy DK ERR (Perez Steel)	.15	.07	.01
□ 3B Dwayne Murphy DK COR	.25	.12	.02
□ 4A John Castino DK ERR (Perez Steel)	.15	.07	.01
□ 4B John Castino DK COR	.25	.12	.02
□ 5A Leon Durham DK ERR (Perez Steel)	.15	.07	.01
□ 5B Leon Durham DK COR	.25	.12	.02
□ 6A Rusty Staub DK ERR (Perez Steel)	.15	.07	.01
□ 6B Rusty Staub DK COR	.25	.12	.02
□ 7A Jack Clark DK ERR (Perez Steel)	.30	.15	.03
□ 7B Jack Clark DK COR	.50	.25	.05
□ 8A Dave Dravecky DK ERR (Perez Steel)	.15	.07	.01
□ 8B Dave Dravecky DK COR	.25	.12	.02
□ 9A Al Oliver DK ERR (Perez Steel)	.15	.07	.01
□ 9B Al Oliver DK COR	.25	.12	.02
□ 10A Dave Righetti DK ERR (Perez Steel)	.20	.10	.02
□ 10B Dave Righetti DK COR	.30	.15	.03
□ 11A Hal McRae DK ERR (Perez Steel)	.15	.07	.01
□ 11B Hal McRae DK COR	.25	.12	.02
□ 12A Ray Knight DK ERR (Perez Steel)	.15	.07	.01
□ 12B Ray Knight DK COR	.25	.12	.02
□ 13A Bruce Sutter DK ERR (Perez Steel)	.15	.07	.01
□ 13B Bruce Sutter DK COR	.25	.12	.02
□ 14A Bob Horner DK ERR (Perez Steel)	.15	.07	.01
□ 14B Bob Horner DK COR	.25	.12	.02
□ 15A Lance Parrish DK ERR (Perez Steel)	.30	.15	.03
□ 15B Lance Parrish DK COR	.50	.25	.05
□ 16A Matt Young DK ERR (Perez Steel)	.15	.07	.01
□ 16B Matt Young DK COR	.25	.12	.02
□ 17A Fred Lynn DK ERR (Perez Steel) (A's logo on back)	.20	.10	.02
□ 17B Fred Lynn DK COR	.30	.15	.03
□ 18A Ron Kittle DK ERR (Perez Steel)	.20	.10	.02
□ 18B Ron Kittle DK COR	.30	.15	.03
□ 19A Jim Clancy DK ERR (Perez Steel)	.15	.07	.01
□ 19B Jim Clancy DK COR	.25	.12	.02
□ 20A Bill Madlock DK ERR (Perez Steel)	.15	.07	.01
□ 20B Bill Madlock DK COR	.25	.12	.02
□ 21A Larry Parrish DK ERR (Perez Steel)	.15	.07	.01
□ 21B Larry Parrish DK COR	.25	.12	.02
□ 22A Eddie Murray DK ERR (Perez Steel)	1.00	.50	.10
□ 22B Eddie Murray DK COR	2.00	1.00	.20
□ 23A Mike Schmidt DK ERR (Perez Steel)	2.50	1.25	.25
□ 23B Mike Schmidt DK COR	4.00	2.00	.40
□ 24A Pedro Guerrero DK ERR (Perez Steel)	.40	.20	.04
□ 24B Pedro Guerrero DK COR	.60	.30	.06
□ 25A Andre Thornton DK ERR (Perez Steel)	.15	.07	.01
□ 25B Andre Thornton DK COR	.25	.12	.02
□ 26A Wade Boggs DK ERR (Perez Steel)	3.50	1.75	.35
□ 26B Wade Boggs DK COR	5.50	2.75	.55
□ 27 Joel Skinner RR	.25	.12	.02
□ 28 Tommy Dunbar RR	.15	.07	.01
□ 29A Mike Stenhouse RR ERR (no back number)	.25	.12	.02
□ 29B Mike Stenhouse RR COR (number on back)	3.00	1.50	.30
□ 30A Ron Darling RR ERR (no number on back)	4.50	2.25	.45
□ 30B Ron Darling RR COR	14.00	7.00	1.40
□ 31 Dion James RR	.50	.25	.05
□ 32 Tony Fernandez RR	7.50	3.75	.75
□ 33 Angel Salazar RR	.15	.07	.01
□ 34 Kevin McReynolds RR	11.00	5.50	1.10
□ 35 Dick Schofield RR	.65	.30	.06
□ 36 Brad Komminsk RR	.20	.10	.02
□ 37 Tim Teufel RR	.50	.25	.05
□ 38 Doug Frobel RR	.15	.07	.01
□ 39 Greg Gagne RR	.50	.25	.05
□ 40 Mike Fuentes RR	.15	.07	.01
□ 41 Joe Carter RR	16.00	8.00	1.60
□ 42 Mike Brown RR (Angels OF)	.15	.07	.01
□ 43 Mike Jeffcoat RR	.15	.07	.01
□ 44 Sid Fernandez RR	6.50	3.25	.65
□ 45 Brian Dayett RR	.15	.07	.01
□ 46 Chris Smith RR	.15	.07	.01
□ 47 Eddie Murray	1.75	.85	.17
□ 48 Robin Yount	2.25	1.10	.22
□ 49 Lance Parrish	.50	.25	.05
□ 50 Jim Rice	.50	.25	.05
□ 51 Dave Winfield	1.25	.60	.12
□ 52 Fernando Valenzuela	.65	.30	.06
□ 53 George Brett	3.50	1.75	.35
□ 54 Rickey Henderson	12.50	6.25	1.25
□ 55 Gary Carter	.75	.35	.07
□ 56 Buddy Bell	.15	.07	.01
□ 57 Reggie Jackson	2.00	1.00	.20
□ 58 Harold Baines	.40	.20	.04
□ 59 Ozzie Smith	1.00	.50	.10
□ 60 Nolan Ryan	8.50	4.25	.85
□ 61 Pete Rose	3.00	1.50	.30
□ 62 Ron Oester	.10	.05	.01
□ 63 Steve Garvey	1.00	.50	.10
□ 64 Jason Thompson	.10	.05	.01
□ 65 Jack Clark	.40	.20	.04
□ 66 Dale Murphy	2.00	1.00	.20
□ 67 Leon Durham	.10	.05	.01
□ 68 Darryl Strawberry	45.00	22.50	4.50
□ 69 Richie Zisk	.10	.05	.01
□ 70 Kent Hrbek	.75	.35	.07
□ 71 Dave Stieb	.45	.22	.04
□ 72 Ken Schrom	.10	.05	.01
□ 73 George Bell	2.25	1.10	.22
□ 74 John Moses	.15	.07	.01
□ 75 Ed Lynch	.10	.05	.01
□ 76 Chuck Rainey	.10	.05	.01
□ 77 Biff Pocoroba	.10	.05	.01
□ 78 Cecilio Guante	.10	.05	.01
□ 79 Jim Barr	.10	.05	.01
□ 80 Kurt Bevacqua	.10	.05	.01
□ 81 Tom Foley	.10	.05	.01
□ 82 Joe Lefebvre	.10	.05	.01
□ 83 Andy Van Slyke	7.00	3.50	.70
□ 84 Bob Lillis MG	.10	.05	.01
□ 85 Ricky Adams	.10	.05	.01
□ 86 Jerry Hairston	.10	.05	.01
□ 87 Bob James	.15	.07	.01
□ 88 Joe Altobelli MG	.10	.05	.01
□ 89 Ed Romero	.10	.05	.01
□ 90 John Grubb	.10	.05	.01
□ 91 John Henry Johnson	.10	.05	.01
□ 92 Juan Espino	.10	.05	.01
□ 93 Candy Maldonado	.40	.20	.04
□ 94 Andre Thornton	.15	.07	.01
□ 95 Onix Concepcion	.10	.05	.01
□ 96 Donnie Hill (listed as P, should be 2B)	.15	.07	.01

☐ 97 Andre Dawson UER (wrong middle name, should be Nolan)	1.50	.75	.15
☐ 98 Frank Tanana	.15	.07	.01
☐ 99 Curt Wilkerson	.15	.07	.01
☐ 100 Larry Gura	.10	.05	.01
☐ 101 Dwayne Murphy	.10	.05	.01
☐ 102 Tom Brennan	.10	.05	.01
☐ 103 Dave Righetti	.30	.15	.03
☐ 104 Steve Sax	.60	.30	.06
☐ 105 Dan Petry	.10	.05	.01
☐ 106 Cal Ripken	5.50	2.75	.55
☐ 107 Paul Molitor	.35	.17	.03
☐ 108 Fred Lynn	.25	.12	.02
☐ 109 Neil Allen	.10	.05	.01
☐ 110 Joe Niekro	.15	.07	.01
☐ 111 Steve Carlton	1.75	.85	.17
☐ 112 Terry Kennedy	.10	.05	.01
☐ 113 Bill Madlock	.20	.10	.02
☐ 114 Chili Davis	.20	.10	.02
☐ 115 Jim Gantner	.10	.05	.01
☐ 116 Tom Seaver	3.00	1.50	.30
☐ 117 Bill Buckner	.20	.10	.02
☐ 118 Bill Caudill	.10	.05	.01
☐ 119 Jim Clancy	.10	.05	.01
☐ 120 John Castino	.10	.05	.01
☐ 121 Dave Concepcion	.20	.10	.02
☐ 122 Greg Luzinski	.20	.10	.02
☐ 123 Mike Boddicker	.20	.10	.02
☐ 124 Pete Ladd	.10	.05	.01
☐ 125 Juan Berenguer	.10	.05	.01
☐ 126 John Montefusco	.10	.05	.01
☐ 127 Ed Jurak	.10	.05	.01
☐ 128 Tom Niedenfuer	.10	.05	.01
☐ 129 Bert Blyleven	.35	.17	.03
☐ 130 Bud Black	.25	.12	.02
☐ 131 Gorman Heimueller	.10	.05	.01
☐ 132 Dan Schatzeder	.10	.05	.01
☐ 133 Ron Jackson	.10	.05	.01
☐ 134 Tom Henke	1.00	.50	.10
☐ 135 Kevin Hickey	.10	.05	.01
☐ 136 Mike Scott	.55	.27	.05
☐ 137 Bo Diaz	.10	.05	.01
☐ 138 Glenn Brummer	.10	.05	.01
☐ 139 Sid Monge	.10	.05	.01
☐ 140 Rich Gale	.10	.05	.01
☐ 141 Brett Butler	.30	.15	.03
☐ 142 Brian Harper	1.00	.50	.10
☐ 143 John Rabb	.10	.05	.01
☐ 144 Gary Woods	.10	.05	.01
☐ 145 Pat Putnam	.10	.05	.01
☐ 146 Jim Acker	.15	.07	.01
☐ 147 Mickey Hatcher	.10	.05	.01
☐ 148 Todd Cruz	.10	.05	.01
☐ 149 Tom Tellmann	.10	.05	.01
☐ 150 John Wockenfuss	.10	.05	.01
☐ 151 Wade Boggs	10.00	5.00	1.00
☐ 152 Don Baylor	.20	.10	.02
☐ 153 Bob Welch	.40	.20	.04
☐ 154 Alan Bannister	.10	.05	.01
☐ 155 Willie Aikens	.10	.05	.01
☐ 156 Jeff Burroughs	.10	.05	.01
☐ 157 Bryan Little	.10	.05	.01
☐ 158 Bob Boone	.25	.12	.02
☐ 159 Dave Hostetler	.10	.05	.01
☐ 160 Jerry Dybzinski	.10	.05	.01
☐ 161 Mike Madden	.10	.05	.01
☐ 162 Luis DeLeon	.10	.05	.01
☐ 163 Willie Hernandez	.25	.12	.02
☐ 164 Frank Pastore	.10	.05	.01
☐ 165 Rick Camp	.10	.05	.01
☐ 166 Lee Mazzilli	.10	.05	.01
☐ 167 Scot Thompson	.10	.05	.01
☐ 168 Bob Forsch	.10	.05	.01
☐ 169 Mike Flanagan	.15	.07	.01
☐ 170 Rick Manning	.10	.05	.01
☐ 171 Chet Lemon	.10	.05	.01
☐ 172 Jerry Remy	.10	.05	.01
☐ 173 Ron Guidry	.35	.17	.03
☐ 174 Pedro Guerrero	.60	.30	.06
☐ 175 Willie Wilson	.20	.10	.02
☐ 176 Carney Lansford	.25	.12	.02
☐ 177 Al Oliver	.20	.10	.02
☐ 178 Jim Sundberg	.10	.05	.01
☐ 179 Bobby Grich	.15	.07	.01
☐ 180 Rich Dotson	.15	.07	.01
☐ 181 Joaquin Andujar	.15	.07	.01
☐ 182 Jose Cruz	.15	.07	.01
☐ 183 Mike Schmidt	10.00	5.00	1.00
☐ 184 Gary Redus	.40	.20	.04
☐ 185 Garry Templeton	.15	.07	.01
☐ 186 Tony Pena	.30	.15	.03
☐ 187 Greg Minton	.10	.05	.01
☐ 188 Phil Niekro	.40	.20	.04
☐ 189 Ferguson Jenkins	.25	.12	.02
☐ 190 Mookie Wilson	.20	.10	.02
☐ 191 Jim Beattie	.10	.05	.01
☐ 192 Gary Ward	.10	.05	.01
☐ 193 Jesse Barfield	.40	.20	.04
☐ 194 Pete Filson	.10	.05	.01
☐ 195 Roy Lee Jackson	.10	.05	.01
☐ 196 Rick Sweet	.10	.05	.01
☐ 197 Jesse Orosco	.10	.05	.01
☐ 198 Steve Lake	.10	.05	.01
☐ 199 Ken Dayley	.10	.05	.01
☐ 200 Manny Sarmiento	.10	.05	.01
☐ 201 Mark Davis	.90	.45	.09
☐ 202 Tim Flannery	.10	.05	.01
☐ 203 Bill Scherrer	.10	.05	.01
☐ 204 Al Holland	.10	.05	.01
☐ 205 Dave Von Ohlen	.10	.05	.01
☐ 206 Mike LaCoss	.10	.05	.01
☐ 207 Juan Beniquez	.10	.05	.01
☐ 208 Juan Agosto	.15	.07	.01
☐ 209 Bobby Ramos	.10	.05	.01
☐ 210 Al Bumbry	.10	.05	.01
☐ 211 Mark Brouhard	.10	.05	.01
☐ 212 Howard Bailey	.10	.05	.01
☐ 213 Bruce Hurst	.30	.15	.03
☐ 214 Bob Shirley	.10	.05	.01
☐ 215 Pat Zachry	.10	.05	.01
☐ 216 Julio Franco	1.50	.75	.15
☐ 217 Mike Armstrong	.10	.05	.01
☐ 218 Dave Beard	.10	.05	.01
☐ 219 Steve Rogers	.10	.05	.01
☐ 220 John Butcher	.10	.05	.01
☐ 221 Mike Smithson	.15	.07	.01
☐ 222 Frank White	.15	.07	.01
☐ 223 Mike Heath	.10	.05	.01
☐ 224 Chris Bando	.10	.05	.01
☐ 225 Roy Smalley	.10	.05	.01
☐ 226 Dusty Baker	.15	.07	.01
☐ 227 Lou Whitaker	.45	.22	.04
☐ 228 John Lowenstein	.10	.05	.01
☐ 229 Ben Oglivie	.15	.07	.01
☐ 230 Doug DeCinces	.15	.07	.01
☐ 231 Lonnie Smith	.20	.10	.02
☐ 232 Ray Knight	.15	.07	.01
☐ 233 Gary Matthews	.15	.07	.01
☐ 234 Juan Bonilla	.10	.05	.01
☐ 235 Rod Scurry	.10	.05	.01
☐ 236 Atlee Hammaker	.10	.05	.01
☐ 237 Mike Caldwell	.10	.05	.01
☐ 238 Keith Hernandez	.50	.25	.05
☐ 239 Larry Bowa	.15	.07	.01
☐ 240 Tony Bernazard	.10	.05	.01
☐ 241 Damaso Garcia	.10	.05	.01
☐ 242 Tom Brunansky	.40	.20	.04
☐ 243 Dan Driessen	.10	.05	.01
☐ 244 Ron Kittle	.40	.20	.04
☐ 245 Tim Stoddard	.10	.05	.01
☐ 246 Bob L. Gibson (Brewers Pitcher)	.15	.07	.01
☐ 247 Marty Castillo	.10	.05	.01
☐ 248 Don Mattingly UER ("traiing" on back)	90.00	45.00	9.00
☐ 249 Jeff Newman	.10	.05	.01
☐ 250 Alejandro Pena	.45	.22	.04
☐ 251 Toby Harrah	.15	.07	.01
☐ 252 Cesar Geronimo	.10	.05	.01
☐ 253 Tom Underwood	.10	.05	.01
☐ 254 Doug Flynn	.10	.05	.01
☐ 255 Andy Hassler	.10	.05	.01
☐ 256 Odell Jones	.10	.05	.01
☐ 257 Rudy Law	.10	.05	.01
☐ 258 Harry Spilman	.10	.05	.01
☐ 259 Marty Bystrom	.10	.05	.01
☐ 260 Dave Rucker	.10	.05	.01
☐ 261 Ruppert Jones	.10	.05	.01
☐ 262 Jeff R. Jones (Reds OF)	.10	.05	.01
☐ 263 Gerald Perry	1.00	.50	.10
☐ 264 Gene Tenace	.10	.05	.01
☐ 265 Brad Wellman	.10	.05	.01
☐ 266 Dickie Noles	.10	.05	.01
☐ 267 Jamie Allen	.10	.05	.01
☐ 268 Jim Gott	.15	.07	.01
☐ 269 Ron Davis	.10	.05	.01
☐ 270 Benny Ayala	.10	.05	.01
☐ 271 Ned Yost	.10	.05	.01
☐ 272 Dave Rozema	.10	.05	.01
☐ 273 Dave Stapleton	.10	.05	.01
☐ 274 Lou Piniella	.20	.10	.02
☐ 275 Jose Morales	.10	.05	.01
☐ 276 Broderick Perkins	.10	.05	.01
☐ 277 Butch Davis	.10	.05	.01
☐ 278 Tony Phillips	.35	.17	.03
☐ 279 Jeff Reardon	.20	.10	.02

☐ 280	Ken Forsch	.10	.05	.01
☐ 281	Pete O'Brien	1.00	.50	.10
☐ 282	Tom Paciorek	.10	.05	.01
☐ 283	Frank LaCorte	.10	.05	.01
☐ 284	Tim Lollar	.10	.05	.01
☐ 285	Greg Gross	.10	.05	.01
☐ 286	Alex Trevino	.10	.05	.01
☐ 287	Gene Garber	.10	.05	.01
☐ 288	Dave Parker	.75	.35	.07
☐ 289	Lee Smith	.20	.10	.02
☐ 290	Dave LaPoint	.15	.07	.01
☐ 291	John Shelby	.40	.20	.04
☐ 292	Charlie Moore	.10	.05	.01
☐ 293	Alan Trammell	1.00	.50	.10
☐ 294	Tony Armas	.15	.07	.01
☐ 295	Shane Rawley	.10	.05	.01
☐ 296	Greg Brock	.15	.07	.01
☐ 297	Hal McRae	.15	.07	.01
☐ 298	Mike Davis	.10	.05	.01
☐ 299	Tim Raines	.90	.45	.09
☐ 300	Bucky Dent	.20	.10	.02
☐ 301	Tommy John	.30	.15	.03
☐ 302	Carlton Fisk	1.25	.60	.12
☐ 303	Darrell Porter	.10	.05	.01
☐ 304	Dickie Thon	.15	.07	.01
☐ 305	Garry Maddox	.10	.05	.01
☐ 306	Cesar Cedeno	.15	.07	.01
☐ 307	Gary Lucas	.10	.05	.01
☐ 308	Johnny Ray	.15	.07	.01
☐ 309	Andy McGaffigan	.10	.05	.01
☐ 310	Claudell Washington	.15	.07	.01
☐ 311	Ryne Sandberg	16.00	8.00	1.60
☐ 312	George Foster	.25	.12	.02
☐ 313	Spike Owen	.40	.20	.04
☐ 314	Gary Gaetti	1.00	.50	.10
☐ 315	Willie Upshaw	.10	.05	.01
☐ 316	Al Williams	.10	.05	.01
☐ 317	Jorge Orta	.10	.05	.01
☐ 318	Orlando Mercado	.10	.05	.01
☐ 319	Junior Ortiz	.10	.05	.01
☐ 320	Mike Proly	.10	.05	.01
☐ 321	Randy Johnson UER ('72-'82 stats are from one Randy Johnson (Twins), '83 stats are from the other (Braves)	.10	.05	.01
☐ 322	Jim Morrison	.10	.05	.01
☐ 323	Max Venable	.10	.05	.01
☐ 324	Tony Gwynn	7.50	3.75	.75
☐ 325	Duane Walker	.10	.05	.01
☐ 326	Ozzie Virgil	.10	.05	.01
☐ 327	Jeff Lahti	.10	.05	.01
☐ 328	Bill Dawley	.10	.05	.01
☐ 329	Rob Wilfong	.10	.05	.01
☐ 330	Marc Hill	.10	.05	.01
☐ 331	Ray Burris	.10	.05	.01
☐ 332	Allan Ramirez	.10	.05	.01
☐ 333	Chuck Porter	.10	.05	.01
☐ 334	Wayne Krenchicki	.10	.05	.01
☐ 335	Gary Allenson	.10	.05	.01
☐ 336	Bobby Meacham	.10	.05	.01
☐ 337	Joe Beckwith	.10	.05	.01
☐ 338	Rick Sutcliffe	.35	.17	.03
☐ 339	Mark Huismann	.15	.07	.01
☐ 340	Tim Conroy	.10	.05	.01
☐ 341	Scott Sanderson	.10	.05	.01
☐ 342	Larry Biittner	.10	.05	.01
☐ 343	Dave Stewart	2.00	1.00	.20
☐ 344	Darryl Motley	.10	.05	.01
☐ 345	Chris Codiroli	.15	.07	.01
☐ 346	Rich Behenna	.10	.05	.01
☐ 347	Andre Robertson	.10	.05	.01
☐ 348	Mike Marshall	.35	.17	.03
☐ 349	Larry Herndon	.10	.05	.01
☐ 350	Rich Dauer	.10	.05	.01
☐ 351	Cecil Cooper	.15	.07	.01
☐ 352	Rod Carew	1.75	.85	.17
☐ 353	Willie McGee	.80	.40	.08
☐ 354	Phil Garner	.10	.05	.01
☐ 355	Joe Morgan	.75	.35	.07
☐ 356	Luis Salazar	.15	.07	.01
☐ 357	John Candelaria	.15	.07	.01
☐ 358	Bill Laskey	.10	.05	.01
☐ 359	Bob McClure	.10	.05	.01
☐ 360	Dave Kingman	.20	.10	.02
☐ 361	Ron Cey	.15	.07	.01
☐ 362	Matt Young	.15	.07	.01
☐ 363	Lloyd Moseby	.20	.10	.02
☐ 364	Frank Viola	2.50	1.25	.25
☐ 365	Eddie Milner	.10	.05	.01
☐ 366	Floyd Bannister	.10	.05	.01
☐ 367	Dan Ford	.10	.05	.01
☐ 368	Moose Haas	.10	.05	.01
☐ 369	Doug Bair	.10	.05	.01
☐ 370	Ray Fontenot	.10	.05	.01
☐ 371	Luis Aponte	.10	.05	.01
☐ 372	Jack Fimple	.10	.05	.01
☐ 373	Neal Heaton	.50	.25	.05
☐ 374	Greg Pryor	.10	.05	.01
☐ 375	Wayne Gross	.10	.05	.01
☐ 376	Charlie Lea	.10	.05	.01
☐ 377	Steve Lubratich	.10	.05	.01
☐ 378	Jon Matlack	.10	.05	.01
☐ 379	Julio Cruz	.10	.05	.01
☐ 380	John Mizerock	.10	.05	.01
☐ 381	Kevin Gross	.60	.30	.06
☐ 382	Mike Ramsey	.10	.05	.01
☐ 383	Doug Gwosdz	.10	.05	.01
☐ 384	Kelly Paris	.10	.05	.01
☐ 385	Pete Falcone	.10	.05	.01
☐ 386	Milt May	.10	.05	.01
☐ 387	Fred Breining	.10	.05	.01
☐ 388	Craig Lefferts	.60	.30	.06
☐ 389	Steve Henderson	.10	.05	.01
☐ 390	Randy Moffitt	.10	.05	.01
☐ 391	Ron Washington	.10	.05	.01
☐ 392	Gary Roenicke	.10	.05	.01
☐ 393	Tom Candiotti	.85	.40	.08
☐ 394	Larry Pashnick	.10	.05	.01
☐ 395	Dwight Evans	.50	.25	.05
☐ 396	Goose Gossage	.30	.15	.03
☐ 397	Derrel Thomas	.10	.05	.01
☐ 398	Juan Eichelberger	.10	.05	.01
☐ 399	Leon Roberts	.10	.05	.01
☐ 400	Dave Lopes	.15	.07	.01
☐ 401	Bill Gullickson	.10	.05	.01
☐ 402	Geoff Zahn	.10	.05	.01
☐ 403	Billy Sample	.10	.05	.01
☐ 404	Mike Squires	.10	.05	.01
☐ 405	Craig Reynolds	.10	.05	.01
☐ 406	Eric Show	.15	.07	.01
☐ 407	John Denny	.15	.07	.01
☐ 408	Dann Bilardello	.10	.05	.01
☐ 409	Bruce Benedict	.10	.05	.01
☐ 410	Kent Tekulve	.15	.07	.01
☐ 411	Mel Hall	.20	.10	.02
☐ 412	John Stuper	.10	.05	.01
☐ 413	Rick Dempsey	.10	.05	.01
☐ 414	Don Sutton	.40	.20	.04
☐ 415	Jack Morris	.30	.15	.03
☐ 416	John Tudor	.30	.15	.03
☐ 417	Willie Randolph	.20	.10	.02
☐ 418	Jerry Reuss	.15	.07	.01
☐ 419	Don Slaught	.15	.07	.01
☐ 420	Steve McCatty	.10	.05	.01
☐ 421	Tim Wallach	.40	.20	.04
☐ 422	Larry Parrish	.15	.07	.01
☐ 423	Brian Downing	.15	.07	.01
☐ 424	Britt Burns	.10	.05	.01
☐ 425	David Green	.10	.05	.01
☐ 426	Jerry Mumphrey	.10	.05	.01
☐ 427	Ivan DeJesus	.10	.05	.01
☐ 428	Mario Soto	.10	.05	.01
☐ 429	Gene Richards	.10	.05	.01
☐ 430	Dale Berra	.10	.05	.01
☐ 431	Darrell Evans	.20	.10	.02
☐ 432	Glenn Hubbard	.10	.05	.01
☐ 433	Jody Davis	.15	.07	.01
☐ 434	Danny Heep	.10	.05	.01
☐ 435	Ed Nunez	.20	.10	.02
☐ 436	Bobby Castillo	.10	.05	.01
☐ 437	Ernie Whitt	.10	.05	.01
☐ 438	Scott Ullger	.10	.05	.01
☐ 439	Doyle Alexander	.15	.07	.01
☐ 440	Domingo Ramos	.10	.05	.01
☐ 441	Craig Swan	.10	.05	.01
☐ 442	Warren Brusstar	.10	.05	.01
☐ 443	Len Barker	.10	.05	.01
☐ 444	Mike Easler	.10	.05	.01
☐ 445	Renie Martin	.10	.05	.01
☐ 446	Dennis Rasmussen	.85	.40	.08
☐ 447	Ted Power	.20	.10	.02
☐ 448	Charles Hudson	.20	.10	.02
☐ 449	Danny Cox	.45	.22	.04
☐ 450	Kevin Bass	.20	.10	.02
☐ 451	Daryl Sconiers	.10	.05	.01
☐ 452	Scott Fletcher	.20	.10	.02
☐ 453	Bryn Smith	.20	.10	.02
☐ 454	Jim Dwyer	.10	.05	.01
☐ 455	Rob Picciolo	.10	.05	.01
☐ 456	Enos Cabell	.10	.05	.01
☐ 457	Dennis Boyd	1.25	.60	.12
☐ 458	Butch Wynegar	.10	.05	.01
☐ 459	Burt Hooton	.10	.05	.01
☐ 460	Ron Hassey	.10	.05	.01
☐ 461	Danny Jackson	2.00	1.00	.20
☐ 462	Bob Kearney	.10	.05	.01
☐ 463	Terry Francona	.10	.05	.01

□ 464 Wayne Tolleson	.10	.05	.01
□ 465 Mickey Rivers	.10	.05	.01
□ 466 John Wathan	.10	.05	.01
□ 467 Bill Almon	.10	.05	.01
□ 468 George Vukovich	.10	.05	.01
□ 469 Steve Kemp	.10	.05	.01
□ 470 Ken Landreaux	.10	.05	.01
□ 471 Milt Wilcox	.10	.05	.01
□ 472 Tippy Martinez	.10	.05	.01
□ 473 Ted Simmons	.20	.10	.02
□ 474 Tim Foli	.10	.05	.01
□ 475 George Hendrick	.15	.07	.01
□ 476 Terry Puhl	.10	.05	.01
□ 477 Von Hayes	.40	.20	.04
□ 478 Bobby Brown	.10	.05	.01
□ 479 Lee Lacy	.10	.05	.01
□ 480 Joel Youngblood	.10	.05	.01
□ 481 Jim Slaton	.10	.05	.01
□ 482 Mike Fitzgerald	.10	.05	.01
□ 483 Keith Moreland	.10	.05	.01
□ 484 Ron Roenicke	.10	.05	.01
□ 485 Luis Leal	.10	.05	.01
□ 486 Bryan Oelkers	.10	.05	.01
□ 487 Bruce Berenyi	.10	.05	.01
□ 488 LaMarr Hoyt	.15	.07	.01
□ 489 Joe Nolan	.10	.05	.01
□ 490 Marshall Edwards	.10	.05	.01
□ 491 Mike Laga	.10	.05	.01
□ 492 Rick Cerone	.10	.05	.01
□ 493 Rick Miller UER (listed as Mike on card front)	.10	.05	.01
□ 494 Rick Honeycutt	.10	.05	.01
□ 495 Mike Hargrove	.15	.07	.01
□ 496 Joe Simpson	.10	.05	.01
□ 497 Keith Atherton	.10	.05	.01
□ 498 Chris Welsh	.10	.05	.01
□ 499 Bruce Kison	.10	.05	.01
□ 500 Bobby Johnson	.10	.05	.01
□ 501 Jerry Koosman	.20	.10	.02
□ 502 Frank DiPino	.10	.05	.01
□ 503 Tony Perez	.40	.20	.04
□ 504 Ken Oberkfell	.10	.05	.01
□ 505 Mark Thurmond	.15	.07	.01
□ 506 Joe Price	.10	.05	.01
□ 507 Pascual Perez	.30	.15	.03
□ 508 Marvell Wynne	.15	.07	.01
□ 509 Mike Krukow	.15	.07	.01
□ 510 Dick Ruthven	.10	.05	.01
□ 511 Al Cowens	.10	.05	.01
□ 512 Cliff Johnson	.10	.05	.01
□ 513 Randy Bush	.25	.12	.02
□ 514 Sammy Stewart	.10	.05	.01
□ 515 Bill Schroeder	.15	.07	.01
□ 516 Aurelio Lopez	.10	.05	.01
□ 517 Mike Brown (Red Sox pitcher)	.15	.07	.01
□ 518 Graig Nettles	.20	.10	.02
□ 519 Dave Sax	.10	.05	.01
□ 520 Jerry Willard	.10	.05	.01
□ 521 Paul Splittorff	.10	.05	.01
□ 522 Tom Burgmeier	.10	.05	.01
□ 523 Chris Speier	.10	.05	.01
□ 524 Bobby Clark	.10	.05	.01
□ 525 George Wright	.10	.05	.01
□ 526 Dennis Lamp	.10	.05	.01
□ 527 Tony Scott	.10	.05	.01
□ 528 Ed Whitson	.15	.07	.01
□ 529 Ron Reed	.10	.05	.01
□ 530 Charlie Puleo	.10	.05	.01
□ 531 Jerry Royster	.10	.05	.01
□ 532 Don Robinson	.10	.05	.01
□ 533 Steve Trout	.10	.05	.01
□ 534 Bruce Sutter	.20	.10	.02
□ 535 Bob Horner	.20	.10	.02
□ 536 Pat Tabler	.20	.10	.02
□ 537 Chris Chambliss	.15	.07	.01
□ 538 Bob Ojeda	.20	.10	.02
□ 539 Alan Ashby	.10	.05	.01
□ 540 Jay Johnstone	.15	.07	.01
□ 541 Bob Dernier	.10	.05	.01
□ 542 Brook Jacoby	3.00	1.50	.30
□ 543 U.L. Washington	.10	.05	.01
□ 544 Danny Darwin	.15	.07	.01
□ 545 Kiko Garcia	.10	.05	.01
□ 546 Vance Law UER (listed as P on card front)	.15	.07	.01
□ 547 Tug McGraw	.20	.10	.02
□ 548 Dave Smith	.15	.07	.01
□ 549 Len Matuszek	.10	.05	.01
□ 550 Tom Hume	.10	.05	.01
□ 551 Dave Dravecky	.55	.27	.05
□ 552 Rick Rhoden	.15	.07	.01
□ 553 Duane Kuiper	.10	.05	.01
□ 554 Rusty Staub	.20	.10	.02
□ 555 Bill Campbell	.10	.05	.01
□ 556 Mike Torrez	.10	.05	.01
□ 557 Dave Henderson	.75	.35	.07
□ 558 Len Whitehouse	.10	.05	.01
□ 559 Barry Bonnell	.10	.05	.01
□ 560 Rick Lysander	.10	.05	.01
□ 561 Garth Iorg	.10	.05	.01
□ 562 Bryan Clark	.10	.05	.01
□ 563 Brian Giles	.10	.05	.01
□ 564 Vern Ruhle	.10	.05	.01
□ 565 Steve Bedrosian	.30	.15	.03
□ 566 Larry McWilliams	.10	.05	.01
□ 567 Jeff Leonard UER (listed as P on card front)	.20	.10	.02
□ 568 Alan Wiggins	.10	.05	.01
□ 569 Jeff Russell	.65	.30	.06
□ 570 Salome Barojas	.10	.05	.01
□ 571 Dane Iorg	.10	.05	.01
□ 572 Bob Knepper	.15	.07	.01
□ 573 Gary Lavelle	.10	.05	.01
□ 574 Gorman Thomas	.15	.07	.01
□ 575 Manny Trillo	.10	.05	.01
□ 576 Jim Palmer	1.75	.85	.17
□ 577 Dale Murray	.10	.05	.01
□ 578 Tom Brookens	.10	.05	.01
□ 579 Rich Gedman	.15	.07	.01
□ 580 Bill Doran	1.75	.85	.17
□ 581 Steve Yeager	.10	.05	.01
□ 582 Dan Spillner	.10	.05	.01
□ 583 Dan Quisenberry	.20	.10	.02
□ 584 Rance Mulliniks	.10	.05	.01
□ 585 Storm Davis	.20	.10	.02
□ 586 Dave Schmidt	.15	.07	.01
□ 587 Bill Russell	.15	.07	.01
□ 588 Pat Sheridan	.20	.10	.02
□ 589 Rafael Ramirez UER (A's on front)	.15	.07	.01
□ 590 Bud Anderson	.10	.05	.01
□ 591 George Frazier	.10	.05	.01
□ 592 Lee Tunnell	.15	.07	.01
□ 593 Kirk Gibson	.75	.35	.07
□ 594 Scott McGregor	.15	.07	.01
□ 595 Bob Bailor	.10	.05	.01
□ 596 Tommy Herr	.15	.07	.01
□ 597 Luis Sanchez	.10	.05	.01
□ 598 Dave Engle	.10	.05	.01
□ 599 Craig McMurtry	.15	.07	.01
□ 600 Carlos Diaz	.10	.05	.01
□ 601 Tom O'Malley	.10	.05	.01
□ 602 Nick Esasky	1.50	.75	.15
□ 603 Ron Hodges	.10	.05	.01
□ 604 Ed VandeBerg	.10	.05	.01
□ 605 Alfredo Griffin	.10	.05	.01
□ 606 Glenn Hoffman	.10	.05	.01
□ 607 Hubie Brooks	.35	.17	.03
□ 608 Richard Barnes UER (photo actually Neal Heaton)	.10	.05	.01
□ 609 Greg Walker	.40	.20	.04
□ 610 Ken Singleton	.15	.07	.01
□ 611 Mark Clear	.10	.05	.01
□ 612 Buck Martinez	.10	.05	.01
□ 613 Ken Griffey	.25	.12	.02
□ 614 Reid Nichols	.10	.05	.01
□ 615 Doug Sisk	.10	.05	.01
□ 616 Bob Brenly	.10	.05	.01
□ 617 Joey McLaughlin	.10	.05	.01
□ 618 Glenn Wilson	.15	.07	.01
□ 619 Bob Stoddard	.10	.05	.01
□ 620 Lenn Sakata UER (listed as Len on card front)	.10	.05	.01
□ 621 Mike Young	.20	.10	.02
□ 622 John Stefero	.15	.07	.01
□ 623 Carmelo Martinez	.45	.22	.04
□ 624 Dave Bergman	.10	.05	.01
□ 625 Runnin' Reds UER (sic, Redbirds) David Green Willie McGee Lonnie Smith Ozzie Smith	.20	.10	.02
□ 626 Rudy May	.10	.05	.01
□ 627 Matt Keough	.10	.05	.01
□ 628 Jose DeLeon	.50	.25	.05
□ 629 Jim Essian	.10	.05	.01
□ 630 Darnell Coles	.40	.20	.04
□ 631 Mike Warren	.15	.07	.01
□ 632 Del Crandall MG	.10	.05	.01
□ 633 Dennis Martinez	.15	.07	.01
□ 634 Mike Moore	.25	.12	.02

☐ 635 Lary Sorensen	.10	.05	.01
☐ 636 Ricky Nelson	.10	.05	.01
☐ 637 Omar Moreno	.10	.05	.01
☐ 638 Charlie Hough	.15	.07	.01
☐ 639 Dennis Eckersley	.75	.35	.07
☐ 640 Walt Terrell	.45	.22	.04
☐ 641 Denny Walling	.10	.05	.01
☐ 642 Dave Anderson	.20	.10	.02
☐ 643 Jose Oquendo	.85	.40	.08
☐ 644 Bob Stanley	.10	.05	.01
☐ 645 Dave Geisel	.10	.05	.01
☐ 646 Scott Garrelts	.90	.45	.09
☐ 647 Gary Pettis	.50	.25	.05
☐ 648 Duke Snider Puzzle Card	.10	.05	.01
☐ 649 Johnnie LeMaster	.10	.05	.01
☐ 650 Dave Collins	.10	.05	.01
☐ 651 The Chicken	.25	.12	.02
☐ 652 DK Checklist (unnumbered)	.10	.01	.00
☐ 653 Checklist 1-130 (unnumbered)	.10	.05	.01
☐ 654 Checklist 131-234 (unnumbered)	.10	.05	.01
☐ 655 Checklist 235-338 (unnumbered)	.10	.05	.01
☐ 656 Checklist 339-442 (unnumbered)	.10	.05	.01
☐ 657 Checklist 443-546 (unnumbered)	.10	.05	.01
☐ 658 Checklist 547-651 (unnumbered)	.10	.05	.01
☐ A Living Legends A Gaylord Perry Rollie Fingers	3.75	1.85	.37
☐ B Living Legends B Carl Yastrzemski Johnny Bench	8.00	4.00	.80

1984 Donruss Action All-Stars

The cards in this 60-card set measure approximately 3 1/2" by 5". For the second year in a row, Donruss issued a postcard-size card set. The set was distributed with a 63-piece Ted Williams puzzle. Unlike last year, when the fronts of the cards contained both an action and a portrait shot of the player, the fronts of this year's cards contain only an action photo. On the backs, the top section contains the card number and a full-color portrait of the player pictured on the front. The bottom half features the player's career statistics.

	MINT	EXC	G-VG
COMPLETE SET (60)	7.00	3.50	.70
COMMON PLAYER (1-60)	.07	.03	.01
☐ 1 Gary Lavelle	.07	.03	.01
☐ 2 Willie McGee	.20	.10	.02
☐ 3 Tony Pena	.07	.03	.01
☐ 4 Lou Whitaker	.15	.07	.01
☐ 5 Robin Yount	.45	.22	.04
☐ 6 Doug DeCinces	.07	.03	.01
☐ 7 John Castino	.07	.03	.01
☐ 8 Terry Kennedy	.07	.03	.01
☐ 9 Rickey Henderson	1.00	.50	.10
☐ 10 Bob Horner	.15	.07	.01
☐ 11 Harold Baines	.15	.07	.01
☐ 12 Buddy Bell	.07	.03	.01
☐ 13 Fernando Valenzuela	.20	.10	.02
☐ 14 Nolan Ryan	1.25	.60	.12
☐ 15 Andre Thornton	.07	.03	.01
☐ 16 Gary Redus	.07	.03	.01
☐ 17 Pedro Guerrero	.20	.10	.02
☐ 18 Andre Dawson	.30	.15	.03
☐ 19 Dave Stieb	.10	.05	.01
☐ 20 Cal Ripken	.35	.17	.03
☐ 21 Ken Griffey	.15	.07	.01
☐ 22 Wade Boggs	1.00	.50	.10
☐ 23 Keith Hernandez	.15	.07	.01
☐ 24 Steve Carlton	.35	.17	.03
☐ 25 Hal McRae	.07	.03	.01
☐ 26 John Lowenstein	.07	.03	.01
☐ 27 Fred Lynn	.10	.05	.01
☐ 28 Bill Buckner	.10	.05	.01
☐ 29 Chris Chambliss	.07	.03	.01
☐ 30 Richie Zisk	.07	.03	.01
☐ 31 Jack Clark	.20	.10	.02
☐ 32 George Hendrick	.07	.03	.01
☐ 33 Bill Madlock	.07	.03	.01
☐ 34 Lance Parrish	.15	.07	.01
☐ 35 Paul Molitor	.20	.10	.02
☐ 36 Reggie Jackson	.75	.35	.07
☐ 37 Kent Hrbek	.20	.10	.02
☐ 38 Steve Garvey	.40	.20	.04
☐ 39 Carney Lansford	.15	.07	.01
☐ 40 Dale Murphy	.45	.22	.04
☐ 41 Greg Luzinski	.10	.05	.01
☐ 42 Larry Parrish	.07	.03	.01
☐ 43 Ryne Sandberg	1.00	.50	.10
☐ 44 Dickie Thon	.07	.03	.01
☐ 45 Bert Blyleven	.15	.07	.01
☐ 46 Ron Oester	.07	.03	.01
☐ 47 Dusty Baker	.07	.03	.01
☐ 48 Steve Rogers	.07	.03	.01
☐ 49 Jim Clancy	.07	.03	.01
☐ 50 Eddie Murray	.35	.17	.03
☐ 51 Ron Guidry	.20	.10	.02
☐ 52 Jim Rice	.20	.10	.02
☐ 53 Tom Seaver	.45	.22	.04
☐ 54 Pete Rose	.75	.35	.07
☐ 55 George Brett	.50	.25	.05
☐ 56 Dan Quisenberry	.10	.05	.01
☐ 57 Mike Schmidt	1.00	.50	.10
☐ 58 Ted Simmons	.10	.05	.01
☐ 59 Dave Righetti	.15	.07	.01
☐ 60 Checklist Card	.07	.01	.00

1984 Donruss Champions

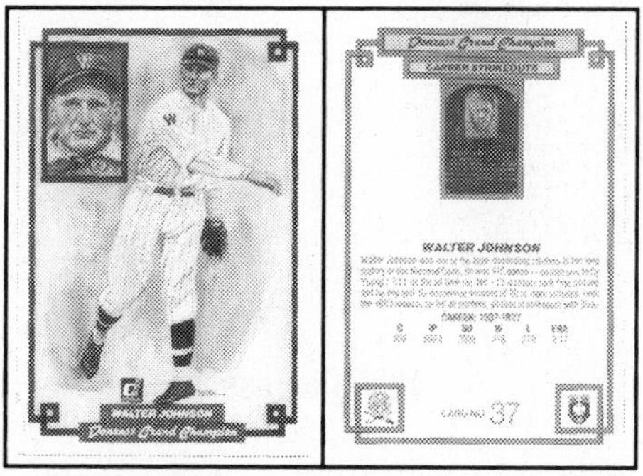

The cards in this 60-card set measure approximately 3 1/2" by 5". The 1984 Donruss Champions set is a hybrid photo/artwork issue. Grand Champions, listed GC in the checklist below, feature the artwork of Dick Perez of Perez-Steele Galleries. Current players in the set feature photographs. The theme of this postcard-size set features a Grand Champion and those current players that are directly behind him in a baseball statistical category, for example, Season Home Runs (1-7), Career Home Runs (8-13), Season Batting Average (14-19), Career Batting Average (20-25), Career Hits (26-30), Career

Victories (31-36), Career Strikeouts (37-42), Most Valuable Players (43-49), World Series stars (50-54), and All-Star heroes (55-59). The cards were issued in cello packs with pieces of the Duke Snider puzzle.

	MINT	EXC	G-VG
COMPLETE SET (60)	7.00	3.50	.70
COMMON PLAYER (1-60)	.07	.03	.01
☐ 1 Babe Ruth GC	1.00	.50	.10
☐ 2 George Foster	.10	.05	.01
☐ 3 Dave Kingman	.10	.05	.01
☐ 4 Jim Rice	.20	.10	.02
☐ 5 Gorman Thomas	.07	.03	.01
☐ 6 Ben Oglivie	.07	.03	.01
☐ 7 Jeff Burroughs	.07	.03	.01
☐ 8 Hank Aaron GC	.35	.17	.03
☐ 9 Reggie Jackson	.60	.30	.06
☐ 10 Carl Yastrzemski	.60	.30	.06
☐ 11 Mike Schmidt	1.00	.50	.10
☐ 12 Graig Nettles	.10	.05	.01
☐ 13 Greg Luzinski	.07	.03	.01
☐ 14 Ted Williams GC	.40	.20	.04
☐ 15 George Brett	.45	.22	.04
☐ 16 Wade Boggs	.75	.35	.07
☐ 17 Hal McRae	.07	.03	.01
☐ 18 Bill Buckner	.10	.05	.01
☐ 19 Eddie Murray	.35	.17	.03
☐ 20 Rogers Hornsby GC	.10	.05	.01
☐ 21 Rod Carew	.30	.15	.03
☐ 22 Bill Madlock	.07	.03	.01
☐ 23 Lonnie Smith	.10	.05	.01
☐ 24 Cecil Cooper	.10	.05	.01
☐ 25 Ken Griffey	.10	.05	.01
☐ 26 Ty Cobb GC	.50	.25	.05
☐ 27 Pete Rose	.60	.30	.06
☐ 28 Rusty Staub	.07	.03	.01
☐ 29 Tony Perez	.15	.07	.01
☐ 30 Al Oliver	.10	.05	.01
☐ 31 Cy Young GC	.10	.05	.01
☐ 32 Gaylord Perry	.15	.07	.01
☐ 33 Ferguson Jenkins	.10	.05	.01
☐ 34 Phil Niekro	.20	.10	.02
☐ 35 Jim Palmer	.30	.15	.03
☐ 36 Tommy John	.10	.05	.01
☐ 37 Walter Johnson GC	.15	.07	.01
☐ 38 Steve Carlton	.30	.15	.03
☐ 39 Nolan Ryan	1.00	.50	.10
☐ 40 Tom Seaver	.40	.20	.04
☐ 41 Don Sutton	.15	.07	.01
☐ 42 Bert Blyleven	.15	.07	.01
☐ 43 Frank Robinson GC	.15	.07	.01
☐ 44 Joe Morgan	.25	.12	.02
☐ 45 Rollie Fingers	.15	.07	.01
☐ 46 Keith Hernandez	.15	.07	.01
☐ 47 Robin Yount	.35	.17	.03
☐ 48 Cal Ripken	.35	.17	.03
☐ 49 Dale Murphy	.35	.17	.03
☐ 50 Mickey Mantle GC	1.00	.50	.10
☐ 51 Johnny Bench	.45	.22	.04
☐ 52 Carlton Fisk	.30	.15	.03
☐ 53 Tug McGraw	.07	.03	.01
☐ 54 Paul Molitor	.15	.07	.01
☐ 55 Carl Hubbell GC	.10	.05	.01
☐ 56 Steve Garvey	.30	.15	.03
☐ 57 Dave Parker	.20	.10	.02
☐ 58 Gary Carter	.20	.10	.02
☐ 59 Fred Lynn	.10	.05	.01
☐ 60 Checklist Card	.07	.01	.00

1985 Donruss

The cards in this 660-card set measure 2 1/2" by 3 1/2". The 1985 Donruss regular issue cards have fronts that feature jet black borders on which orange lines have been placed. The fronts contain the standard team logo, player's name, position, and Donruss logo. The cards were distributed with puzzle pieces from a Dick Perez rendition of Lou Gehrig. The first 26 cards of the set feature Diamond Kings (DK), for the fourth year in a row; the artwork on the Diamond Kings was again produced by the Perez-Steele Galleries. Cards 27-46 feature Rated Rookies (RR). The unnumbered checklist cards are arbitrarily numbered below as numbers 654 through 660. This set is noted for containing the Rookie Cards of Roger Clemens, Alvin Davis, Eric Davis, Shawon Dunston, Dwight Gooden, Orel Hershiser, Mark Langston, Kirby Puckett, Jose Rijo, Bret Saberhagen, and Danny Tartabull.

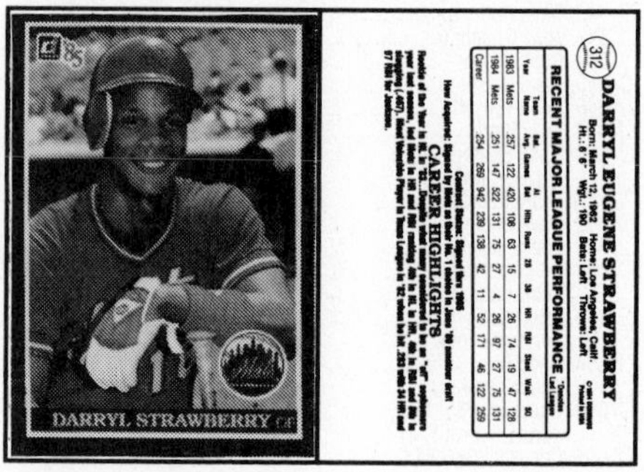

	MINT	EXC	G-VG
COMPLETE SET (660)	165.00	75.00	14.00
COMMON PLAYER (1-660)	.07	.03	.01
☐ 1 Ryne Sandberg DK	2.50	.50	.10
☐ 2 Doug DeCinces DK	.10	.05	.01
☐ 3 Richard Dotson DK	.10	.05	.01
☐ 4 Bert Blyleven DK	.15	.07	.01
☐ 5 Lou Whitaker DK	.20	.10	.02
☐ 6 Dan Quisenberry DK	.15	.07	.01
☐ 7 Don Mattingly DK	6.00	3.00	.60
☐ 8 Carney Lansford DK	.15	.07	.01
☐ 9 Frank Tanana DK	.10	.05	.01
☐ 10 Willie Upshaw DK	.10	.05	.01
☐ 11 Claudell Washington DK	.10	.05	.01
☐ 12 Mike Marshall DK	.15	.07	.01
☐ 13 Joaquin Andujar DK	.10	.05	.01
☐ 14 Cal Ripken DK	.85	.40	.08
☐ 15 Jim Rice DK	.25	.12	.02
☐ 16 Don Sutton DK	.25	.12	.02
☐ 17 Frank Viola DK	.45	.22	.04
☐ 18 Alvin Davis DK	.40	.20	.04
☐ 19 Mario Soto DK	.10	.05	.01
☐ 20 Jose Cruz DK	.10	.05	.01
☐ 21 Charlie Lea DK	.10	.05	.01
☐ 22 Jesse Orosco DK	.10	.05	.01
☐ 23 Juan Samuel DK	.25	.12	.02
☐ 24 Tony Pena DK	.15	.07	.01
☐ 25 Tony Gwynn DK	.75	.35	.07
☐ 26 Bob Brenly DK	.10	.05	.01
☐ 27 Danny Tartabull RR	4.50	2.25	.45
☐ 28 Mike Bielecki RR	.45	.22	.04
☐ 29 Steve Lyons RR	.25	.12	.02
☐ 30 Jeff Reed RR	.10	.05	.01
☐ 31 Tony Brewer RR	.10	.05	.01
☐ 32 John Morris RR	.15	.07	.01
☐ 33 Daryl Boston RR	.75	.35	.07
☐ 34 Al Pulido RR	.10	.05	.01
☐ 35 Steve Kiefer RR	.15	.07	.01
☐ 36 Larry Sheets RR	.35	.17	.03
☐ 37 Scott Bradley RR	.30	.15	.03
☐ 38 Calvin Schiraldi RR	.25	.12	.02
☐ 39 Shawon Dunston RR	5.50	2.75	.55
☐ 40 Charlie Mitchell RR	.10	.05	.01
☐ 41 Billy Hatcher RR	1.50	.75	.15
☐ 42 Russ Stephans RR	.10	.05	.01
☐ 43 Alejandro Sanchez RR	.10	.05	.01
☐ 44 Steve Jeltz RR	.10	.05	.01
☐ 45 Jim Traber RR	.25	.12	.02
☐ 46 Doug Loman RR	.15	.07	.01
☐ 47 Eddie Murray	.65	.30	.06
☐ 48 Robin Yount	.80	.40	.08
☐ 49 Lance Parrish	.25	.12	.02
☐ 50 Jim Rice	.25	.12	.02
☐ 51 Dave Winfield	.45	.22	.04
☐ 52 Fernando Valenzuela	.30	.15	.03
☐ 53 George Brett	1.00	.50	.10
☐ 54 Dave Kingman	.12	.06	.01
☐ 55 Gary Carter	.35	.17	.03
☐ 56 Buddy Bell	.10	.05	.01
☐ 57 Reggie Jackson	.90	.45	.09
☐ 58 Harold Baines	.25	.12	.02
☐ 59 Ozzie Smith	.45	.22	.04
☐ 60 Nolan Ryan	3.75	1.85	.37
☐ 61 Mike Schmidt	2.50	1.25	.25

☐	62 Dave Parker	.25	.12	.02
☐	63 Tony Gwynn	2.25	1.10	.22
☐	64 Tony Pena	.12	.06	.01
☐	65 Jack Clark	.25	.12	.02
☐	66 Dale Murphy	.75	.35	.07
☐	67 Ryne Sandberg	5.00	2.50	.50
☐	68 Keith Hernandez	.35	.17	.03
☐	69 Alvin Davis	4.00	2.00	.40
☐	70 Kent Hrbek	.35	.17	.03
☐	71 Willie Upshaw	.07	.03	.01
☐	72 Dave Engle	.07	.03	.01
☐	73 Alfredo Griffin	.07	.03	.01
☐	74A Jack Perconte (Career Highlights takes four lines)	.15	.07	.01
☐	74B Jack Perconte (Career Highlights takes three lines)	.15	.07	.01
☐	75 Jesse Orosco	.07	.03	.01
☐	76 Jody Davis	.07	.03	.01
☐	77 Bob Horner	.10	.05	.01
☐	78 Larry McWilliams	.07	.03	.01
☐	79 Joel Youngblood	.07	.03	.01
☐	80 Alan Wiggins	.07	.03	.01
☐	81 Ron Oester	.07	.03	.01
☐	82 Ozzie Virgil	.07	.03	.01
☐	83 Ricky Horton	.20	.10	.02
☐	84 Bill Doran	.15	.07	.01
☐	85 Rod Carew	.65	.30	.06
☐	86 LaMarr Hoyt	.10	.05	.01
☐	87 Tim Wallach	.15	.07	.01
☐	88 Mike Flanagan	.10	.05	.01
☐	89 Jim Sundberg	.07	.03	.01
☐	90 Chet Lemon	.07	.03	.01
☐	91 Bob Stanley	.07	.03	.01
☐	92 Willie Randolph	.10	.05	.01
☐	93 Bill Russell	.10	.05	.01
☐	94 Julio Franco	.50	.25	.05
☐	95 Dan Quisenberry	.15	.07	.01
☐	96 Bill Caudill	.07	.03	.01
☐	97 Bill Gullickson	.07	.03	.01
☐	98 Danny Darwin	.10	.05	.01
☐	99 Curtis Wilkerson	.07	.03	.01
☐	100 Bud Black	.10	.05	.01
☐	101 Tony Phillips	.07	.03	.01
☐	102 Tony Bernazard	.07	.03	.01
☐	103 Jay Howell	.07	.03	.01
☐	104 Burt Hooton	.07	.03	.01
☐	105 Milt Wilcox	.07	.03	.01
☐	106 Rich Dauer	.07	.03	.01
☐	107 Don Sutton	.25	.12	.02
☐	108 Mike Witt	.10	.05	.01
☐	109 Bruce Sutter	.12	.06	.01
☐	110 Enos Cabell	.07	.03	.01
☐	111 John Denny	.07	.03	.01
☐	112 Dave Dravecky	.15	.07	.01
☐	113 Marvell Wynne	.07	.03	.01
☐	114 Johnnie LeMaster	.07	.03	.01
☐	115 Chuck Porter	.07	.03	.01
☐	116 John Gibbons	.07	.03	.01
☐	117 Keith Moreland	.07	.03	.01
☐	118 Darnell Coles	.10	.05	.01
☐	119 Dennis Lamp	.07	.03	.01
☐	120 Ron Davis	.07	.03	.01
☐	121 Nick Esasky	.20	.10	.02
☐	122 Vance Law	.07	.03	.01
☐	123 Gary Roenicke	.07	.03	.01
☐	124 Bill Schroeder	.07	.03	.01
☐	125 Dave Rozema	.07	.03	.01
☐	126 Bobby Meacham	.07	.03	.01
☐	127 Marty Barrett	.20	.10	.02
☐	128 R.J. Reynolds	.35	.17	.03
☐	129 Ernie Camacho UER (photo actually Rich Thompson)	.07	.03	.01
☐	130 Jorge Orta	.07	.03	.01
☐	131 Lary Sorensen	.07	.03	.01
☐	132 Terry Francona	.07	.03	.01
☐	133 Fred Lynn	.15	.07	.01
☐	134 Bob Jones	.07	.03	.01
☐	135 Jerry Hairston	.07	.03	.01
☐	136 Kevin Bass	.12	.06	.01
☐	137 Garry Maddox	.07	.03	.01
☐	138 Dave LaPoint	.07	.03	.01
☐	139 Kevin McReynolds	1.25	.60	.12
☐	140 Wayne Krenchicki	.07	.03	.01
☐	141 Rafael Ramirez	.07	.03	.01
☐	142 Rod Scurry	.07	.03	.01
☐	143 Greg Minton	.07	.03	.01
☐	144 Tim Stoddard	.07	.03	.01
☐	145 Steve Henderson	.07	.03	.01
☐	146 George Bell	.75	.35	.07
☐	147 Dave Meier	.07	.03	.01
☐	148 Sammy Stewart	.07	.03	.01

☐	149 Mark Brouhard	.07	.03	.01
☐	150 Larry Herndon	.07	.03	.01
☐	151 Oil Can Boyd	.15	.07	.01
☐	152 Brian Dayett	.07	.03	.01
☐	153 Tom Niedenfuer	.07	.03	.01
☐	154 Brook Jacoby	.20	.10	.02
☐	155 Onix Concepcion	.07	.03	.01
☐	156 Tim Conroy	.07	.03	.01
☐	157 Joe Hesketh	.12	.06	.01
☐	158 Brian Downing	.10	.05	.01
☐	159 Tommy Dunbar	.07	.03	.01
☐	160 Marc Hill	.07	.03	.01
☐	161 Phil Garner	.07	.03	.01
☐	162 Jerry Davis	.07	.03	.01
☐	163 Bill Campbell	.07	.03	.01
☐	164 John Franco	2.50	1.25	.25
☐	165 Len Barker	.07	.03	.01
☐	166 Benny Distefano	.10	.05	.01
☐	167 George Frazier	.07	.03	.01
☐	168 Tito Landrum	.07	.03	.01
☐	169 Cal Ripken	1.50	.75	.15
☐	170 Cecil Cooper	.12	.06	.01
☐	171 Alan Trammell	.40	.20	.04
☐	172 Wade Boggs	4.50	2.25	.45
☐	173 Don Baylor	.15	.07	.01
☐	174 Pedro Guerrero	.30	.15	.03
☐	175 Frank White	.10	.05	.01
☐	176 Rickey Henderson	3.75	1.85	.37
☐	177 Charlie Lea	.07	.03	.01
☐	178 Pete O'Brien	.12	.06	.01
☐	179 Doug DeCinces	.10	.05	.01
☐	180 Ron Kittle	.18	.09	.01
☐	181 George Hendrick	.10	.05	.01
☐	182 Joe Niekro	.10	.05	.01
☐	183 Juan Samuel	.80	.40	.08
☐	184 Mario Soto	.07	.03	.01
☐	185 Goose Gossage	.15	.07	.01
☐	186 Johnny Ray	.10	.05	.01
☐	187 Bob Brenly	.07	.03	.01
☐	188 Craig McMurtry	.07	.03	.01
☐	189 Leon Durham	.07	.03	.01
☐	190 Dwight Gooden	13.50	6.00	1.00
☐	191 Barry Bonnell	.07	.03	.01
☐	192 Tim Teufel	.10	.05	.01
☐	193 Dave Stieb	.18	.09	.01
☐	194 Mickey Hatcher	.07	.03	.01
☐	195 Jesse Barfield	.20	.10	.02
☐	196 Al Cowens	.07	.03	.01
☐	197 Hubie Brooks	.15	.07	.01
☐	198 Steve Trout	.07	.03	.01
☐	199 Glenn Hubbard	.07	.03	.01
☐	200 Bill Madlock	.10	.05	.01
☐	201 Jeff Robinson (Giants pitcher)	.30	.15	.03
☐	202 Eric Show	.07	.03	.01
☐	203 Dave Concepcion	.10	.05	.01
☐	204 Ivan DeJesus	.07	.03	.01
☐	205 Neil Allen	.07	.03	.01
☐	206 Jerry Mumphrey	.07	.03	.01
☐	207 Mike Brown (Angels OF)	.07	.03	.01
☐	208 Carlton Fisk	.45	.22	.04
☐	209 Bryn Smith	.10	.05	.01
☐	210 Tippy Martinez	.07	.03	.01
☐	211 Dion James	.10	.05	.01
☐	212 Willie Hernandez	.10	.05	.01
☐	213 Mike Easler	.07	.03	.01
☐	214 Ron Guidry	.20	.10	.02
☐	215 Rick Honeycutt	.07	.03	.01
☐	216 Brett Butler	.15	.07	.01
☐	217 Larry Gura	.07	.03	.01
☐	218 Ray Burris	.07	.03	.01
☐	219 Steve Rogers	.07	.03	.01
☐	220 Frank Tanana UER (Bats Left listed twice on card back)	.10	.05	.01
☐	221 Ned Yost	.07	.03	.01
☐	222 Bret Saberhagen UER (18 career IP on back)	8.00	4.00	.80
☐	223 Mike Davis	.07	.03	.01
☐	224 Bert Blyleven	.20	.10	.02
☐	225 Steve Kemp	.07	.03	.01
☐	226 Jerry Reuss	.07	.03	.01
☐	227 Darrell Evans UER (80 homers in 1980)	.15	.07	.01
☐	228 Wayne Gross	.07	.03	.01
☐	229 Jim Gantner	.07	.03	.01
☐	230 Bob Boone	.12	.06	.01
☐	231 Lonnie Smith	.12	.06	.01
☐	232 Frank DiPino	.07	.03	.01
☐	233 Jerry Koosman	.10	.05	.01
☐	234 Graig Nettles	.15	.07	.01
☐	235 John Tudor	.15	.07	.01
☐	236 John Rabb	.07	.03	.01

□ 237 Rick Manning	.07	.03	.01
□ 238 Mike Fitzgerald	.07	.03	.01
□ 239 Gary Matthews	.10	.05	.01
□ 240 Jim Presley	.90	.45	.09
□ 241 Dave Collins	.07	.03	.01
□ 242 Gary Gaetti	.40	.20	.04
□ 243 Dann Bilardello	.07	.03	.01
□ 244 Rudy Law	.07	.03	.01
□ 245 John Lowenstein	.07	.03	.01
□ 246 Tom Tellmann	.07	.03	.01
□ 247 Howard Johnson	1.75	.85	.17
□ 248 Ray Fontenot	.07	.03	.01
□ 249 Tony Armas	.07	.03	.01
□ 250 Candy Maldonado	.25	.12	.02
□ 251 Mike Jeffcoat	.10	.05	.01
□ 252 Dane Iorg	.07	.03	.01
□ 253 Bruce Bochte	.07	.03	.01
□ 254 Pete Rose	1.50	.75	.15
□ 255 Don Aase	.07	.03	.01
□ 256 George Wright	.07	.03	.01
□ 257 Britt Burns	.07	.03	.01
□ 258 Mike Scott	.40	.20	.04
□ 259 Len Matuszek	.07	.03	.01
□ 260 Dave Rucker	.07	.03	.01
□ 261 Craig Lefferts	.10	.05	.01
□ 262 Jay Tibbs	.10	.05	.01
□ 263 Bruce Benedict	.07	.03	.01
□ 264 Don Robinson	.07	.03	.01
□ 265 Gary Lavelle	.07	.03	.01
□ 266 Scott Sanderson	.10	.05	.01
□ 267 Matt Young	.07	.03	.01
□ 268 Ernie Whitt	.07	.03	.01
□ 269 Houston Jimenez	.07	.03	.01
□ 270 Ken Dixon	.07	.03	.01
□ 271 Pete Ladd	.07	.03	.01
□ 272 Juan Berenguer	.07	.03	.01
□ 273 Roger Clemens	24.00	12.00	2.40
□ 274 Rick Cerone	.07	.03	.01
□ 275 Dave Anderson	.07	.03	.01
□ 276 George Vukovich	.07	.03	.01
□ 277 Greg Pryor	.07	.03	.01
□ 278 Mike Warren	.07	.03	.01
□ 279 Bob James	.07	.03	.01
□ 280 Bobby Grich	.10	.05	.01
□ 281 Mike Mason	.07	.03	.01
□ 282 Ron Reed	.07	.03	.01
□ 283 Alan Ashby	.07	.03	.01
□ 284 Mark Thurmond	.07	.03	.01
□ 285 Joe Lefebvre	.07	.03	.01
□ 286 Ted Power	.07	.03	.01
□ 287 Chris Chambliss	.10	.05	.01
□ 288 Lee Tunnell	.07	.03	.01
□ 289 Rich Bordi	.07	.03	.01
□ 290 Glenn Brummer	.07	.03	.01
□ 291 Mike Boddicker	.10	.05	.01
□ 292 Rollie Fingers	.20	.10	.02
□ 293 Lou Whitaker	.25	.12	.02
□ 294 Dwight Evans	.20	.10	.02
□ 295 Don Mattingly	16.00	8.00	1.60
□ 296 Mike Marshall	.15	.07	.01
□ 297 Willie Wilson	.12	.06	.01
□ 298 Mike Heath	.07	.03	.01
□ 299 Tim Raines	.50	.25	.05
□ 300 Larry Parrish	.10	.05	.01
□ 301 Geoff Zahn	.07	.03	.01
□ 302 Rich Dotson	.07	.03	.01
□ 303 David Green	.07	.03	.01
□ 304 Jose Cruz	.10	.05	.01
□ 305 Steve Carlton	.50	.25	.05
□ 306 Gary Redus	.07	.03	.01
□ 307 Steve Garvey	.50	.25	.05
□ 308 Jose DeLeon	.10	.05	.01
□ 309 Randy Lerch	.07	.03	.01
□ 310 Claudell Washington	.10	.05	.01
□ 311 Lee Smith	.10	.05	.01
□ 312 Darryl Strawberry	7.00	3.50	.70
□ 313 Jim Beattie	.07	.03	.01
□ 314 John Butcher	.07	.03	.01
□ 315 Damaso Garcia	.07	.03	.01
□ 316 Mike Smithson	.07	.03	.01
□ 317 Luis Leal	.07	.03	.01
□ 318 Ken Phelps	.30	.15	.03
□ 319 Wally Backman	.10	.05	.01
□ 320 Ron Cey	.10	.05	.01
□ 321 Brad Komminsk	.07	.03	.01
□ 322 Jason Thompson	.07	.03	.01
□ 323 Frank Williams	.10	.05	.01
□ 324 Tim Lollar	.07	.03	.01
□ 325 Eric Davis	20.00	10.00	2.00
□ 326 Von Hayes	.18	.09	.01
□ 327 Andy Van Slyke	.90	.45	.09
□ 328 Craig Reynolds	.07	.03	.01
□ 329 Dick Schofield	.10	.05	.01
□ 330 Scott Fletcher	.10	.05	.01
□ 331 Jeff Reardon	.12	.06	.01
□ 332 Rick Dempsey	.07	.03	.01
□ 333 Ben Oglivie	.10	.05	.01
□ 334 Dan Petry	.07	.03	.01
□ 335 Jackie Gutierrez	.07	.03	.01
□ 336 Dave Righetti	.15	.07	.01
□ 337 Alejandro Pena	.10	.05	.01
□ 338 Mel Hall	.12	.06	.01
□ 339 Pat Sheridan	.07	.03	.01
□ 340 Keith Atherton	.07	.03	.01
□ 341 David Palmer	.07	.03	.01
□ 342 Gary Ward	.07	.03	.01
□ 343 Dave Stewart	.65	.30	.06
□ 344 Mark Gubicza	1.75	.85	.17
□ 345 Carney Lansford	.15	.07	.01
□ 346 Jerry Willard	.07	.03	.01
□ 347 Ken Griffey	.15	.07	.01
□ 348 Franklin Stubbs	.75	.35	.07
□ 349 Aurelio Lopez	.07	.03	.01
□ 350 Al Bumbry	.07	.03	.01
□ 351 Charlie Moore	.07	.03	.01
□ 352 Luis Sanchez	.07	.03	.01
□ 353 Darrell Porter	.07	.03	.01
□ 354 Bill Dawley	.07	.03	.01
□ 355 Charles Hudson	.07	.03	.01
□ 356 Garry Templeton	.10	.05	.01
□ 357 Cecilio Guante	.07	.03	.01
□ 358 Jeff Leonard	.10	.05	.01
□ 359 Paul Molitor	.20	.10	.02
□ 360 Ron Gardenhire	.07	.03	.01
□ 361 Larry Bowa	.10	.05	.01
□ 362 Bob Kearney	.07	.03	.01
□ 363 Garth Iorg	.07	.03	.01
□ 364 Tom Brunansky	.25	.12	.02
□ 365 Brad Gulden	.07	.03	.01
□ 366 Greg Walker	.10	.05	.01
□ 367 Mike Young	.10	.05	.01
□ 368 Rick Waits	.07	.03	.01
□ 369 Doug Bair	.07	.03	.01
□ 370 Bob Shirley	.07	.03	.01
□ 371 Bob Ojeda	.10	.05	.01
□ 372 Bob Welch	.20	.10	.02
□ 373 Neal Heaton	.07	.03	.01
□ 374 Danny Jackson UER (photo actually Frank Wills)	.40	.20	.04
□ 375 Donnie Hill	.07	.03	.01
□ 376 Mike Stenhouse	.07	.03	.01
□ 377 Bruce Kison	.07	.03	.01
□ 378 Wayne Tolleson	.07	.03	.01
□ 379 Floyd Bannister	.07	.03	.01
□ 380 Vern Ruhle	.07	.03	.01
□ 381 Tim Corcoran	.07	.03	.01
□ 382 Kurt Kepshire	.07	.03	.01
□ 383 Bobby Brown	.07	.03	.01
□ 384 Dave Van Gorder	.07	.03	.01
□ 385 Rick Mahler	.07	.03	.01
□ 386 Lee Mazzilli	.07	.03	.01
□ 387 Bill Laskey	.07	.03	.01
□ 388 Thad Bosley	.07	.03	.01
□ 389 Al Chambers	.07	.03	.01
□ 390 Tony Fernandez	.75	.35	.07
□ 391 Ron Washington	.07	.03	.01
□ 392 Bill Swaggerty	.07	.03	.01
□ 393 Bob L. Gibson	.07	.03	.01
□ 394 Marty Castillo	.07	.03	.01
□ 395 Steve Crawford	.07	.03	.01
□ 396 Clay Christiansen	.07	.03	.01
□ 397 Bob Bailor	.07	.03	.01
□ 398 Mike Hargrove	.07	.03	.01
□ 399 Charlie Leibrandt	.07	.03	.01
□ 400 Tom Burgmeier	.07	.03	.01
□ 401 Razor Shines	.07	.03	.01
□ 402 Rob Wilfong	.07	.03	.01
□ 403 Tom Henke	.15	.07	.01
□ 404 Al Jones	.07	.03	.01
□ 405 Mike LaCoss	.07	.03	.01
□ 406 Luis DeLeon	.07	.03	.01
□ 407 Greg Gross	.07	.03	.01
□ 408 Tom Hume	.07	.03	.01
□ 409 Rick Camp	.07	.03	.01
□ 410 Milt May	.07	.03	.01
□ 411 Henry Cotto	.15	.07	.01
□ 412 David Von Ohlen	.07	.03	.01
□ 413 Scott McGregor	.10	.05	.01
□ 414 Ted Simmons	.12	.06	.01
□ 415 Jack Morris	.18	.09	.01
□ 416 Bill Buckner	.10	.05	.01
□ 417 Butch Wynegar	.07	.03	.01
□ 418 Steve Sax	.35	.17	.03
□ 419 Steve Balboni	.07	.03	.01
□ 420 Dwayne Murphy	.07	.03	.01
□ 421 Andre Dawson	.50	.25	.05
□ 422 Charlie Hough	.10	.05	.01

☐ 423 Tommy John	.15	.07	.01
☐ 424A Tom Seaver ERR (photo actually Floyd Bannister)	1.25	.60	.12
☐ 424B Tom Seaver COR	16.00	8.00	1.60
☐ 425 Tommy Herr	.10	.05	.01
☐ 426 Terry Puhl	.07	.03	.01
☐ 427 Al Holland	.07	.03	.01
☐ 428 Eddie Milner	.07	.03	.01
☐ 429 Terry Kennedy	.07	.03	.01
☐ 430 John Candelaria	.10	.05	.01
☐ 431 Manny Trillo	.07	.03	.01
☐ 432 Ken Oberkfell	.07	.03	.01
☐ 433 Rick Sutcliffe	.18	.09	.01
☐ 434 Ron Darling	.75	.35	.07
☐ 435 Spike Owen	.07	.03	.01
☐ 436 Frank Viola	.75	.35	.07
☐ 437 Lloyd Moseby	.10	.05	.01
☐ 438 Kirby Puckett	24.00	12.00	2.40
☐ 439 Jim Clancy	.07	.03	.01
☐ 440 Mike Moore	.10	.05	.01
☐ 441 Doug Sisk	.07	.03	.01
☐ 442 Dennis Eckersley	.25	.12	.02
☐ 443 Gerald Perry	.15	.07	.01
☐ 444 Dale Berra	.07	.03	.01
☐ 445 Dusty Baker	.10	.05	.01
☐ 446 Ed Whitson	.10	.05	.01
☐ 447 Cesar Cedeno	.10	.05	.01
☐ 448 Rick Schu	.15	.07	.01
☐ 449 Joaquin Andujar	.10	.05	.01
☐ 450 Mark Bailey	.07	.03	.01
☐ 451 Ron Romanick	.07	.03	.01
☐ 452 Julio Cruz	.07	.03	.01
☐ 453 Miguel Dilone	.07	.03	.01
☐ 454 Storm Davis	.10	.05	.01
☐ 455 Jaime Cocanower	.07	.03	.01
☐ 456 Barbaro Garbey	.07	.03	.01
☐ 457 Rich Gedman	.07	.03	.01
☐ 458 Phil Niekro	.25	.12	.02
☐ 459 Mike Scioscia	.07	.03	.01
☐ 460 Pat Tabler	.10	.05	.01
☐ 461 Darryl Motley	.07	.03	.01
☐ 462 Chris Codiroli	.07	.03	.01
☐ 463 Doug Flynn	.07	.03	.01
☐ 464 Billy Sample	.07	.03	.01
☐ 465 Mickey Rivers	.07	.03	.01
☐ 466 John Wathan	.07	.03	.01
☐ 467 Bill Krueger	.07	.03	.01
☐ 468 Andre Thornton	.10	.05	.01
☐ 469 Rex Hudler	.30	.15	.03
☐ 470 Sid Bream	.45	.22	.04
☐ 471 Kirk Gibson	.35	.17	.03
☐ 472 John Shelby	.07	.03	.01
☐ 473 Moose Haas	.07	.03	.01
☐ 474 Doug Corbett	.07	.03	.01
☐ 475 Willie McGee	.60	.30	.06
☐ 476 Bob Knepper	.10	.05	.01
☐ 477 Kevin Gross	.07	.03	.01
☐ 478 Carmelo Martinez	.07	.03	.01
☐ 479 Kent Tekulve	.07	.03	.01
☐ 480 Chili Davis	.10	.05	.01
☐ 481 Bobby Clark	.07	.03	.01
☐ 482 Mookie Wilson	.10	.05	.01
☐ 483 Dave Owen	.07	.03	.01
☐ 484 Ed Nunez	.07	.03	.01
☐ 485 Rance Mulliniks	.07	.03	.01
☐ 486 Ken Schrom	.07	.03	.01
☐ 487 Jeff Russell	.07	.03	.01
☐ 488 Tom Paciorek	.07	.03	.01
☐ 489 Dan Ford	.07	.03	.01
☐ 490 Mike Caldwell	.07	.03	.01
☐ 491 Scottie Earl	.07	.03	.01
☐ 492 Jose Rijo	2.00	1.00	.20
☐ 493 Bruce Hurst	.15	.07	.01
☐ 494 Ken Landreaux	.07	.03	.01
☐ 495 Mike Fischlin	.07	.03	.01
☐ 496 Don Slaught	.07	.03	.01
☐ 497 Steve McCatty	.07	.03	.01
☐ 498 Gary Lucas	.07	.03	.01
☐ 499 Gary Pettis	.10	.05	.01
☐ 500 Marvis Foley	.07	.03	.01
☐ 501 Mike Squires	.07	.03	.01
☐ 502 Jim Pankovits	.07	.03	.01
☐ 503 Luis Aguayo	.07	.03	.01
☐ 504 Ralph Citarella	.07	.03	.01
☐ 505 Bruce Bochy	.07	.03	.01
☐ 506 Bob Owchinko	.07	.03	.01
☐ 507 Pascual Perez	.12	.06	.01
☐ 508 Lee Lacy	.07	.03	.01
☐ 509 Atlee Hammaker	.07	.03	.01
☐ 510 Bob Dernier	.07	.03	.01
☐ 511 Ed VandeBerg	.07	.03	.01
☐ 512 Cliff Johnson	.07	.03	.01
☐ 513 Len Whitehouse	.07	.03	.01
☐ 514 Dennis Martinez	.10	.05	.01
☐ 515 Ed Romero	.07	.03	.01
☐ 516 Rusty Kuntz	.07	.03	.01
☐ 517 Rick Miller	.07	.03	.01
☐ 518 Dennis Rasmussen	.12	.06	.01
☐ 519 Steve Yeager	.07	.03	.01
☐ 520 Chris Bando	.07	.03	.01
☐ 521 U.L. Washington	.07	.03	.01
☐ 522 Curt Young	.25	.12	.02
☐ 523 Angel Salazar	.07	.03	.01
☐ 524 Curt Kaufman	.07	.03	.01
☐ 525 Odell Jones	.07	.03	.01
☐ 526 Juan Agosto	.07	.03	.01
☐ 527 Denny Walling	.07	.03	.01
☐ 528 Andy Hawkins	.25	.12	.02
☐ 529 Sixto Lezcano	.07	.03	.01
☐ 530 Skeeter Barnes	.07	.03	.01
☐ 531 Randy Johnson	.07	.03	.01
☐ 532 Jim Morrison	.07	.03	.01
☐ 533 Warren Brusstar	.07	.03	.01
☐ 534A Jeff Pendleton ERR (wrong first name)	.75	.35	.07
☐ 534B Terry Pendleton COR	3.50	1.75	.35
☐ 535 Vic Rodriguez	.10	.05	.01
☐ 536 Bob McClure	.07	.03	.01
☐ 537 Dave Bergman	.07	.03	.01
☐ 538 Mark Clear	.07	.03	.01
☐ 539 Mike Pagliarulo	.90	.45	.09
☐ 540 Terry Whitfield	.07	.03	.01
☐ 541 Joe Beckwith	.07	.03	.01
☐ 542 Jeff Burroughs	.07	.03	.01
☐ 543 Dan Schatzeder	.07	.03	.01
☐ 544 Donnie Scott	.07	.03	.01
☐ 545 Jim Slaton	.07	.03	.01
☐ 546 Greg Luzinski	.12	.06	.01
☐ 547 Mark Salas	.10	.05	.01
☐ 548 Dave Smith	.10	.05	.01
☐ 549 John Wockenfuss	.07	.03	.01
☐ 550 Frank Pastore	.07	.03	.01
☐ 551 Tim Flannery	.07	.03	.01
☐ 552 Rick Rhoden	.10	.05	.01
☐ 553 Mark Davis	.20	.10	.02
☐ 554 Jeff Dedmon	.07	.03	.01
☐ 555 Gary Woods	.07	.03	.01
☐ 556 Danny Heep	.07	.03	.01
☐ 557 Mark Langston	5.50	2.75	.55
☐ 558 Darrell Brown	.07	.03	.01
☐ 559 Jimmy Key	1.25	.60	.12
☐ 560 Rick Lysander	.07	.03	.01
☐ 561 Doyle Alexander	.07	.03	.01
☐ 562 Mike Stanton	.07	.03	.01
☐ 563 Sid Fernandez	.65	.30	.06
☐ 564 Richie Hebner	.07	.03	.01
☐ 565 Alex Trevino	.07	.03	.01
☐ 566 Brian Harper	.18	.09	.01
☐ 567 Dan Gladden	.65	.30	.06
☐ 568 Luis Salazar	.07	.03	.01
☐ 569 Tom Foley	.07	.03	.01
☐ 570 Larry Andersen	.07	.03	.01
☐ 571 Danny Cox	.07	.03	.01
☐ 572 Joe Sambito	.07	.03	.01
☐ 573 Juan Beniquez	.07	.03	.01
☐ 574 Joel Skinner	.07	.03	.01
☐ 575 Randy St.Claire	.07	.03	.01
☐ 576 Floyd Rayford	.07	.03	.01
☐ 577 Roy Howell	.07	.03	.01
☐ 578 John Grubb	.07	.03	.01
☐ 579 Ed Jurak	.07	.03	.01
☐ 580 John Montefusco	.07	.03	.01
☐ 581 Orel Hershiser	7.50	3.75	.75
☐ 582 Tom Waddell	.07	.03	.01
☐ 583 Mark Huismann	.07	.03	.01
☐ 584 Joe Morgan	.35	.17	.03
☐ 585 Jim Wohlford	.07	.03	.01
☐ 586 Dave Schmidt	.07	.03	.01
☐ 587 Jeff Kunkel	.10	.05	.01
☐ 588 Hal McRae	.10	.05	.01
☐ 589 Bill Almon	.07	.03	.01
☐ 590 Carmen Castillo	.07	.03	.01
☐ 591 Omar Moreno	.07	.03	.01
☐ 592 Ken Howell	.20	.10	.02
☐ 593 Tom Brookens	.07	.03	.01
☐ 594 Joe Nolan	.07	.03	.01
☐ 595 Willie Lozado	.07	.03	.01
☐ 596 Tom Nieto	.07	.03	.01
☐ 597 Walt Terrell	.07	.03	.01
☐ 598 Al Oliver	.10	.05	.01
☐ 599 Shane Rawley	.07	.03	.01
☐ 600 Denny Gonzalez	.10	.05	.01
☐ 601 Mark Grant	.10	.05	.01
☐ 602 Mike Armstrong	.07	.03	.01
☐ 603 George Foster	.12	.06	.01
☐ 604 Dave Lopes	.10	.05	.01
☐ 605 Salome Barojas	.07	.03	.01

☐ 606 Roy Lee Jackson	.07	.03	.01
☐ 607 Pete Filson	.07	.03	.01
☐ 608 Duane Walker	.07	.03	.01
☐ 609 Glenn Wilson	.10	.05	.01
☐ 610 Rafael Santana	.20	.10	.02
☐ 611 Roy Smith	.10	.05	.01
☐ 612 Ruppert Jones	.07	.03	.01
☐ 613 Joe Cowley	.07	.03	.01
☐ 614 Al Nipper UER (photo actually Mike Brown)	.20	.10	.02
☐ 615 Gene Nelson	.07	.03	.01
☐ 616 Joe Carter	2.75	1.35	.27
☐ 617 Ray Knight	.10	.05	.01
☐ 618 Chuck Rainey	.07	.03	.01
☐ 619 Dan Driessen	.07	.03	.01
☐ 620 Daryl Sconiers	.07	.03	.01
☐ 621 Bill Stein	.07	.03	.01
☐ 622 Roy Smalley	.07	.03	.01
☐ 623 Ed Lynch	.07	.03	.01
☐ 624 Jeff Stone	.10	.05	.01
☐ 625 Bruce Berenyi	.07	.03	.01
☐ 626 Kelvin Chapman	.07	.03	.01
☐ 627 Joe Price	.07	.03	.01
☐ 628 Steve Bedrosian	.15	.07	.01
☐ 629 Vic Mata	.07	.03	.01
☐ 630 Mike Krukow	.07	.03	.01
☐ 631 Phil Bradley	.90	.45	.09
☐ 632 Jim Gott	.10	.05	.01
☐ 633 Randy Bush	.10	.05	.01
☐ 634 Tom Browning	2.00	1.00	.20
☐ 635 Lou Gehrig Puzzle Card	.07	.03	.01
☐ 636 Reid Nichols	.07	.03	.01
☐ 637 Dan Pasqua	.75	.35	.07
☐ 638 German Rivera	.07	.03	.01
☐ 639 Don Schulze	.07	.03	.01
☐ 640A Mike Jones (Career Highlights, takes five lines)	.10	.05	.01
☐ 640B Mike Jones (Career Highlights, takes four lines)	.10	.05	.01
☐ 641 Pete Rose	1.00	.50	.10
☐ 642 Wade Rowdon	.07	.03	.01
☐ 643 Jerry Narron	.07	.03	.01
☐ 644 Darrell Miller	.10	.05	.01
☐ 645 Tim Hulett	.10	.05	.01
☐ 646 Andy McGaffigan	.07	.03	.01
☐ 647 Kurt Bevacqua	.07	.03	.01
☐ 648 John Russell	.10	.05	.01
☐ 649 Ron Robinson	.50	.25	.05
☐ 650 Donnie Moore	.07	.03	.01
☐ 651A Two for the Title Dave Winfield Don Mattingly (yellow letters)	5.00	2.50	.50
☐ 651B Two for the Title Dave Winfield Don Mattingly (white letters)	9.00	4.50	.90
☐ 652 Tim Laudner	.07	.03	.01
☐ 653 Steve Farr	.40	.20	.04
☐ 654 DK Checklist 1-26 (unnumbered)	.09	.01	.00
☐ 655 Checklist 27-130 (unnumbered)	.07	.01	.00
☐ 656 Checklist 131-234 (unnumbered)	.07	.01	.00
☐ 657 Checklist 235-338 (unnumbered)	.07	.01	.00
☐ 658 Checklist 339-442 (unnumbered)	.07	.01	.00
☐ 659 Checklist 443-546 (unnumbered)	.07	.01	.00
☐ 660 Checklist 547-653 (unnumbered)	.07	.01	.00

1985 Donruss Wax Box Cards

The boxes in which the wax packs (of the 1985 Donruss regular issue baseball cards) were contained feature four baseball cards, with backs. The complete set price of the regular issue set does not include these cards; they are considered a separate set. The cards measure the standard 2 1/2" by 3 1/2" and are styled the same as the regular Donruss cards. The cards are numbered but with the prefix PC before the number. The value of the panel uncut is slightly greater, perhaps by 25 percent greater, than the value of the individual cards cut up carefully.

	MINT	EXC	G-VG
COMPLETE SET (4)	6.00	3.00	.60
COMMON PLAYER	.05	.02	.00
☐ PC1 Dwight Gooden	4.50	2.25	.45
☐ PC2 Ryne Sandberg	2.00	1.00	.20
☐ PC3 Ron Kittle	.15	.07	.01
☐ PUZ Lou Gehrig Puzzle Card	.05	.02	.00

1985 Donruss Super DK's

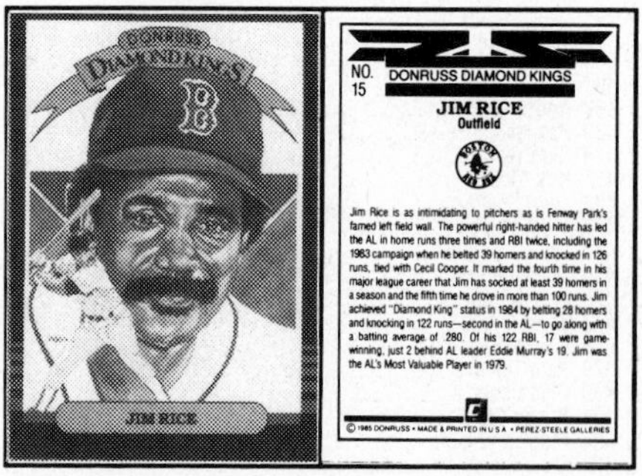

The cards in this 28-card set measure 4 15/16 by 6 3/4". The 1985 Donruss Diamond Kings Supers set contains enlarged cards of the first 26 cards of the Donruss regular set of this year. In addition, the Diamond Kings checklist card, a card of artist Dick Perez, and a Lou Gehrig puzzle card are included in the set. The set was the brain-child of the Perez-Steele Galleries and could be obtained via a write-in offer on the wrappers of the Donruss regular cards of this year. The Gehrig puzzle card is actually a 12-piece jigsaw puzzle. The back of the checklist card is blank; however, the Dick Perez card back gives a short history of Dick Perez and the Perez-Steele Galleries. The offer for obtaining this set was detailed on the wax pack wrappers; three wrappers plus 9.00 was required for this mail-in offer.

	MINT	EXC	G-VG
COMPLETE SET (28)	12.00	6.00	1.20
COMMON PLAYER (1-26)	.25	.12	.02
☐ 1 Ryne Sandberg	2.00	1.00	.20
☐ 2 Doug DeCinces	.25	.12	.02
☐ 3 Richard Dotson	.25	.12	.02
☐ 4 Bert Blyleven	.35	.17	.03
☐ 5 Lou Whitaker	.45	.22	.04
☐ 6 Dan Quisenberry	.35	.17	.03

☐ 7 Don Mattingly	5.00	2.50	.50
☐ 8 Carney Lansford	.45	.22	.04
☐ 9 Frank Tanana	.25	.12	.02
☐ 10 Willie Upshaw	.25	.12	.02
☐ 11 Claudell Washington	.25	.12	.02
☐ 12 Mike Marshall	.35	.17	.03
☐ 13 Joaquin Andujar	.25	.12	.02
☐ 14 Cal Ripken	1.50	.75	.15
☐ 15 Jim Rice	.45	.22	.04
☐ 16 Don Sutton	.45	.22	.04
☐ 17 Frank Viola	.75	.35	.07
☐ 18 Alvin Davis	.60	.30	.06
☐ 19 Mario Soto	.25	.12	.02
☐ 20 Jose Cruz	.25	.12	.02
☐ 21 Charlie Lea	.25	.12	.02
☐ 22 Jesse Orosco	.25	.12	.02
☐ 23 Juan Samuel	.35	.17	.03
☐ 24 Tony Pena	.25	.12	.02
☐ 25 Tony Gwynn	1.50	.75	.15
☐ 26 Bob Brenly	.25	.12	.02
☐ 27 Checklist Card (unnumbered)	.25	.02	.00
☐ 28 Dick Perez (unnumbered) (History of DK's)	.25	.12	.02

1985 Donruss Action All-Stars

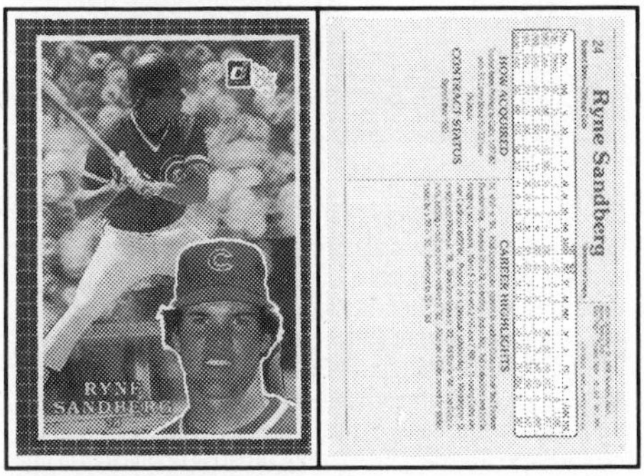

The cards in this 60-card set measure approximately 3 1/2" by 5". For the third year in a row, Donruss issued a set of Action All-Stars. This set features action photos on the obverse which also contains a portrait inset of the player. The backs, unlike the year before, do not contain a full color picture of the player but list, if space is available, full statistical data, biographical data, career highlights, and acquisition and contract status. The cards were issued with a Lou Gehrig puzzle card.

	MINT	EXC	G-VG
COMPLETE SET (60)	7.00	3.50	.70
COMMON PLAYER (1-60)	.07	.03	.01
☐ 1 Tim Raines	.35	.17	.03
☐ 2 Jim Gantner	.07	.03	.01
☐ 3 Mario Soto	.07	.03	.01
☐ 4 Spike Owen	.07	.03	.01
☐ 5 Lloyd Moseby	.10	.05	.01
☐ 6 Damaso Garcia	.07	.03	.01
☐ 7 Cal Ripken	.35	.17	.03
☐ 8 Dan Quisenberry	.10	.05	.01
☐ 9 Eddie Murray	.30	.15	.03
☐ 10 Tony Pena	.10	.05	.01
☐ 11 Buddy Bell	.10	.05	.01
☐ 12 Dave Winfield	.20	.10	.02
☐ 13 Ron Kittle	.10	.05	.01
☐ 14 Rich Gossage	.10	.05	.01
☐ 15 Dwight Evans	.15	.07	.01
☐ 16 Alvin Davis	.15	.07	.01
☐ 17 Mike Schmidt	.90	.45	.09
☐ 18 Pascual Perez	.10	.05	.01
☐ 19 Tony Gwynn	.50	.25	.05
☐ 20 Nolan Ryan	1.25	.60	.12
☐ 21 Robin Yount	.35	.17	.03
☐ 22 Mike Marshall	.15	.07	.01
☐ 23 Brett Butler	.15	.07	.01
☐ 24 Ryne Sandberg	.90	.45	.09
☐ 25 Dale Murphy	.50	.25	.05
☐ 26 George Brett	.50	.25	.05
☐ 27 Jim Rice	.20	.10	.02
☐ 28 Ozzie Smith	.25	.12	.02
☐ 29 Larry Parrish	.07	.03	.01
☐ 30 Jack Clark	.15	.07	.01
☐ 31 Manny Trillo	.07	.03	.01
☐ 32 Dave Kingman	.10	.05	.01
☐ 33 Geoff Zahn	.07	.03	.01
☐ 34 Pedro Guerrero	.15	.07	.01
☐ 35 Dave Parker	.15	.07	.01
☐ 36 Rollie Fingers	.15	.07	.01
☐ 37 Fernando Valenzuela	.20	.10	.02
☐ 38 Wade Boggs	.75	.35	.07
☐ 39 Reggie Jackson	.60	.30	.06
☐ 40 Kent Hrbek	.25	.12	.02
☐ 41 Keith Hernandez	.15	.07	.01
☐ 42 Lou Whitaker	.15	.07	.01
☐ 43 Tom Herr	.07	.03	.01
☐ 44 Alan Trammell	.20	.10	.02
☐ 45 Butch Wynegar	.07	.03	.01
☐ 46 Leon Durham	.07	.03	.01
☐ 47 Dwight Gooden	1.25	.60	.12
☐ 48 Don Mattingly	1.50	.75	.15
☐ 49 Phil Niekro	.20	.10	.02
☐ 50 Johnny Ray	.07	.03	.01
☐ 51 Doug DeCinces	.07	.03	.01
☐ 52 Willie Upshaw	.07	.03	.01
☐ 53 Lance Parrish	.10	.05	.01
☐ 54 Jody Davis	.07	.03	.01
☐ 55 Steve Carlton	.35	.17	.03
☐ 56 Juan Samuel	.10	.05	.01
☐ 57 Gary Carter	.20	.10	.02
☐ 58 Harold Baines	.10	.05	.01
☐ 59 Eric Show	.07	.03	.01
☐ 60 Checklist Card	.07	.01	.00

1985 Donruss Highlights

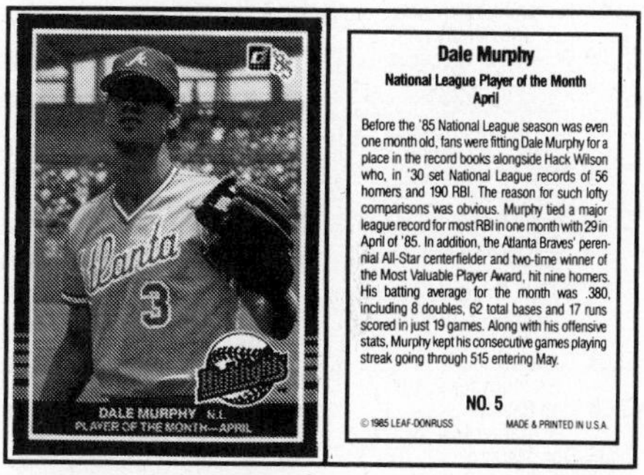

This 56-card set features the players and pitchers of the month for each league as well as a number of highlight cards commemorating the 1985 season. The Donruss Company dedicated the last two cards to their own selections for Rookies of the Year (ROY). This set proved to be more popular than the Donruss Company had predicted, as their first and only print run was exhausted before card dealers' initial orders were filled.

	MINT	EXC	G-VG
COMPLETE SET (56)	27.00	13.50	2.70
COMMON PLAYER (1-56)	.10	.05	.01
☐ 1 Tom Seaver: Sets Opening Day Record	.60	.30	.06
☐ 2 Rollie Fingers: Sets AL Save Mark	.25	.12	.02
☐ 3 Mike Davis: AL Player April	.10	.05	.01
☐ 4 Charlie Leibrandt: AL Pitcher April	.10	.05	.01
☐ 5 Dale Murphy: NL Player April	.75	.35	.07
☐ 6 Fernando Valenzuela: NL Pitcher April	.25	.12	.02
☐ 7 Larry Bowa: NL Shortstop Record	.10	.05	.01

☐ 8 Dave Concepcion: Joins Reds' 2000 Hit Club	.10	.05	.01
☐ 9 Tony Perez: Eldest Grand Slammer	.15	.07	.01
☐ 10 Pete Rose: NL Career Run Leader	1.25	.60	.12
☐ 11 George Brett: AL Player May	.80	.40	.08
☐ 12 Dave Stieb: AL Pitcher May	.20	.10	.02
☐ 13 Dave Parker: NL Player May	.20	.10	.02
☐ 14 Andy Hawkins: NL Pitcher May	.10	.05	.01
☐ 15 Andy Hawkins: Records 11th Straight Win	.10	.05	.01
☐ 16 Von Hayes: Two Homers in First Inning	.15	.07	.01
☐ 17 Rickey Henderson: AL Player June	1.00	.50	.10
☐ 18 Jay Howell: AL Pitcher June	.10	.05	.01
☐ 19 Pedro Guerrero: NL Player June	.20	.10	.02
☐ 20 John Tudor: NL Pitcher June	.15	.07	.01
☐ 21 Hernandez/Carter: Marathon Game Iron Men	.20	.10	.02
☐ 22 Nolan Ryan: Records 4000th K	1.50	.75	.15
☐ 23 LaMarr Hoyt: All-Star Game MVP	.10	.05	.01
☐ 24 Oddibe McDowell: 1st Ranger to Hit for Cycle	.25	.12	.02
☐ 25 George Brett: AL Player July	.80	.40	.08
☐ 26 Bret Saberhagen: AL Pitcher July	.75	.35	.07
☐ 27 Keith Hernandez: NL Player July	.20	.10	.02
☐ 28 Fernando Valenzuela: NL Pitcher July	.20	.10	.02
☐ 29 W.McGee/V.Coleman: Record Setting Base Stealers	.80	.40	.08
☐ 30 Tom Seaver: Notches 300th Career Win	.35	.17	.03
☐ 31 Rod Carew: Strokes 3000th Hit	.35	.17	.03
☐ 32 Dwight Gooden: Establishes Met Record	1.25	.60	.12
☐ 33 Dwight Gooden: Achieves Strikeout Milestone	1.25	.60	.12
☐ 34 Eddie Murray: Explodes for 9 RBI	.40	.20	.04
☐ 35 Don Baylor: AL Career HBP Leader	.15	.07	.01
☐ 36 Don Mattingly: AL Player August	2.50	1.25	.25
☐ 37 Dave Righetti: AL Pitcher August	.15	.07	.01
☐ 38 Willie McGee: NL Player August	.25	.12	.02
☐ 39 Shane Rawley: NL Pitcher August	.10	.05	.01
☐ 40 Pete Rose: Ty-Breaking Hit	1.25	.60	.12
☐ 41 Andre Dawson: Hits 3 HR's Drives in 8 Runs	.30	.15	.03
☐ 42 Rickey Henderson: Sets Yankee Theft Mark	1.25	.60	.12
☐ 43 Tom Browning: 20 Wins in Rookie Season	.20	.10	.02
☐ 44 Don Mattingly: Yankee Milestone for Hits	2.50	1.25	.25
☐ 45 Don Mattingly: AL Player September	2.50	1.25	.25
☐ 46 Charlie Leibrandt: AL Pitcher September	.10	.05	.01
☐ 47 Gary Carter: NL Player September	.25	.12	.02
☐ 48 Dwight Gooden: NL Pitcher September	1.25	.60	.12
☐ 49 Wade Boggs: Major League Record Setter	1.75	.85	.17
☐ 50 Phil Niekro: Hurls Shutout for 300th Win	.20	.10	.02
☐ 51 Darrell Evans: Venerable HR King	.10	.05	.01
☐ 52 Willie McGee: NL Switch-Hitting Record	.20	.10	.02
☐ 53 Dave Winfield: Equals DiMaggio Feat	.30	.15	.03
☐ 54 Vince Coleman: Donruss NL ROY	2.00	1.00	.20
☐ 55 Ozzie Guillen: Donruss AL ROY	.75	.35	.07
☐ 56 Checklist Card	.10	.01	.00

1986 Donruss

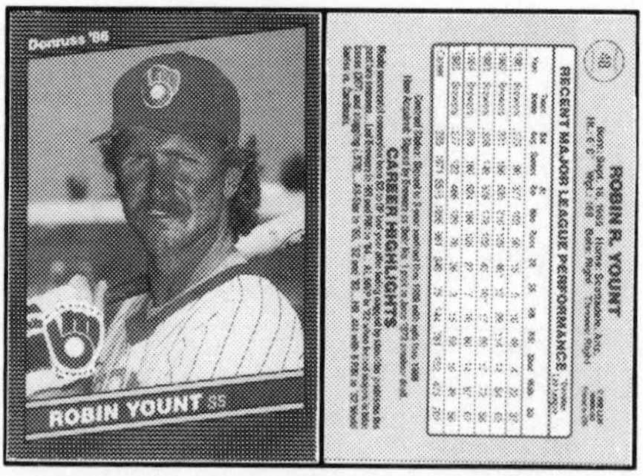

The cards in this 660-card set measure 2 1/2" by 3 1/2". The 1986 Donruss regular issue cards have fronts that feature blue borders. The fronts contain the standard team logo, player's name, position, and Donruss logo. The cards were distributed with puzzle pieces from a Dick Perez rendition of Hank Aaron. The first 26 cards of the set are Diamond Kings (DK), for the fifth year in a row; the artwork on the Diamond Kings was again produced by the Perez-Steele Galleries. Cards 27-46 again feature Rated Rookies (RR); Danny Tartabull is included in this subset for the second year in a row. The unnumbered checklist cards are arbitrarily numbered below as numbers 654 through 660. The key rookie cards in this set are Jose Canseco, Vince Coleman, Kal Daniels, Cecil Fielder, and Fred McGriff.

	MINT	EXC	G-VG
COMPLETE SET (660)	190.00	95.00	19.00
COMMON PLAYER (1-660)	.06	.03	.00
☐ 1 Kirk Gibson DK	.35	.17	.03
☐ 2 Goose Gossage DK	.12	.06	.01
☐ 3 Willie McGee DK	.15	.07	.01
☐ 4 George Bell DK	.18	.09	.01
☐ 5 Tony Armas DK	.10	.05	.01
☐ 6 Chili Davis DK	.10	.05	.01
☐ 7 Cecil Cooper DK	.10	.05	.01
☐ 8 Mike Boddicker DK	.10	.05	.01
☐ 9 Dave Lopes DK	.10	.05	.01
☐ 10 Bill Doran DK	.10	.05	.01
☐ 11 Bret Saberhagen DK	.50	.25	.05
☐ 12 Brett Butler DK	.12	.06	.01
☐ 13 Harold Baines DK	.12	.06	.01
☐ 14 Mike Davis DK	.10	.05	.01
☐ 15 Tony Perez DK	.12	.06	.01
☐ 16 Willie Randolph DK	.10	.05	.01
☐ 17 Bob Boone DK	.10	.05	.01
☐ 18 Orel Hershiser DK	.65	.30	.06
☐ 19 Johnny Ray DK	.10	.05	.01
☐ 20 Gary Ward DK	.10	.05	.01
☐ 21 Rick Mahler DK	.10	.05	.01
☐ 22 Phil Bradley DK	.10	.05	.01
☐ 23 Jerry Koosman DK	.10	.05	.01
☐ 24 Tom Brunansky DK	.12	.06	.01
☐ 25 Andre Dawson DK	.35	.17	.03
☐ 26 Dwight Gooden DK	1.00	.50	.10
☐ 27 Kal Daniels RR	4.00	2.00	.40
☐ 28 Fred McGriff RR	16.00	8.00	1.60
☐ 29 Cory Snyder RR	2.50	1.25	.25
☐ 30 Jose Guzman RR	.25	.12	.02
☐ 31 Ty Gainey RR	.10	.05	.01

☐ 32 Johnny Abrego RR	.10	.05	.01
☐ 33A Andres Galarraga RR (no accent)	2.50	1.25	.25
☐ 33B Andrés Galarraga RR (accent over e)	3.50	1.75	.35
☐ 34 Dave Shipanoff RR	.10	.05	.01
☐ 35 Mark McLemore RR	.10	.05	.01
☐ 36 Marty Clary RR	.10	.05	.01
☐ 37 Paul O'Neill RR	2.75	1.35	.27
☐ 38 Danny Tartabull RR	1.00	.50	.10
☐ 39 Jose Canseco RR	110.00	55.00	11.00
☐ 40 Juan Nieves RR	.15	.07	.01
☐ 41 Lance McCullers RR	.25	.12	.02
☐ 42 Rick Surhoff RR	.10	.05	.01
☐ 43 Todd Worrell RR	.70	.35	.07
☐ 44 Bob Kipper RR	.15	.07	.01
☐ 45 John Habyan RR	.10	.05	.01
☐ 46 Mike Woodard RR	.10	.05	.01
☐ 47 Mike Boddicker	.10	.05	.01
☐ 48 Robin Yount	.65	.30	.06
☐ 49 Lou Whitaker	.15	.07	.01
☐ 50 Oil Can Boyd	.10	.05	.01
☐ 51 Rickey Henderson	2.00	1.00	.20
☐ 52 Mike Marshall	.12	.06	.01
☐ 53 George Brett	.75	.35	.07
☐ 54 Dave Kingman	.10	.05	.01
☐ 55 Hubie Brooks	.12	.06	.01
☐ 56 Oddibe McDowell	.25	.12	.02
☐ 57 Doug DeCinces	.10	.05	.01
☐ 58 Britt Burns	.06	.03	.00
☐ 59 Ozzie Smith	.30	.15	.03
☐ 60 Jose Cruz	.10	.05	.01
☐ 61 Mike Schmidt	2.00	1.00	.20
☐ 62 Pete Rose	.80	.40	.08
☐ 63 Steve Garvey	.40	.20	.04
☐ 64 Tony Pena	.10	.05	.01
☐ 65 Chili Davis	.10	.05	.01
☐ 66 Dale Murphy	.50	.25	.05
☐ 67 Ryne Sandberg	2.50	1.25	.25
☐ 68 Gary Carter	.30	.15	.03
☐ 69 Alvin Davis	.30	.15	.03
☐ 70 Kent Hrbek	.25	.12	.02
☐ 71 George Bell	.30	.15	.03
☐ 72 Kirby Puckett	5.00	2.50	.50
☐ 73 Lloyd Moseby	.10	.05	.01
☐ 74 Bob Kearney	.06	.03	.00
☐ 75 Dwight Gooden	3.00	1.50	.30
☐ 76 Gary Matthews	.06	.03	.00
☐ 77 Rick Mahler	.06	.03	.00
☐ 78 Benny Distefano	.06	.03	.00
☐ 79 Jeff Leonard	.10	.05	.01
☐ 80 Kevin McReynolds	.45	.22	.04
☐ 81 Ron Oester	.06	.03	.00
☐ 82 John Russell	.06	.03	.00
☐ 83 Tommy Herr	.10	.05	.01
☐ 84 Jerry Mumphrey	.06	.03	.00
☐ 85 Ron Romanick	.06	.03	.00
☐ 86 Daryl Boston	.12	.06	.01
☐ 87 Andre Dawson	.40	.20	.04
☐ 88 Eddie Murray	.40	.20	.04
☐ 89 Dion James	.06	.03	.00
☐ 90 Chet Lemon	.06	.03	.00
☐ 91 Bob Stanley	.06	.03	.00
☐ 92 Willie Randolph	.10	.05	.01
☐ 93 Mike Scioscia	.06	.03	.00
☐ 94 Tom Waddell	.06	.03	.00
☐ 95 Danny Jackson	.20	.10	.02
☐ 96 Mike Davis	.06	.03	.00
☐ 97 Mike Fitzgerald	.06	.03	.00
☐ 98 Gary Ward	.06	.03	.00
☐ 99 Pete O'Brien	.10	.05	.01
☐ 100 Bret Saberhagen	1.00	.50	.10
☐ 101 Alfredo Griffin	.06	.03	.00
☐ 102 Brett Butler	.12	.06	.01
☐ 103 Ron Guidry	.15	.07	.01
☐ 104 Jerry Reuss	.06	.03	.00
☐ 105 Jack Morris	.15	.07	.01
☐ 106 Rick Dempsey	.06	.03	.00
☐ 107 Ray Burris	.06	.03	.00
☐ 108 Brian Downing	.06	.03	.00
☐ 109 Willie McGee	.25	.12	.02
☐ 110 Bill Doran	.10	.05	.01
☐ 111 Kent Tekulve	.06	.03	.00
☐ 112 Tony Gwynn	1.25	.60	.12
☐ 113 Marvell Wynne	.06	.03	.00
☐ 114 David Green	.06	.03	.00
☐ 115 Jim Gantner	.06	.03	.00
☐ 116 George Foster	.12	.06	.01
☐ 117 Steve Trout	.06	.03	.00
☐ 118 Mark Langston	.60	.30	.06
☐ 119 Tony Fernandez	.25	.12	.02
☐ 120 John Butcher	.06	.03	.00
☐ 121 Ron Robinson	.06	.03	.00
☐ 122 Dan Spillner	.06	.03	.00
☐ 123 Mike Young	.06	.03	.00
☐ 124 Paul Molitor	.15	.07	.01
☐ 125 Kirk Gibson	.25	.12	.02
☐ 126 Ken Griffey	.12	.06	.01
☐ 127 Tony Armas	.06	.03	.00
☐ 128 Mariano Duncan	.45	.22	.04
☐ 129 Pat Tabler	.10	.05	.01
☐ 130 Frank White	.10	.05	.01
☐ 131 Carney Lansford	.12	.06	.01
☐ 132 Vance Law	.06	.03	.00
☐ 133 Dick Schofield	.10	.05	.01
☐ 134 Wayne Tolleson	.06	.03	.00
☐ 135 Greg Walker	.06	.03	.00
☐ 136 Denny Walling	.06	.03	.00
☐ 137 Ozzie Virgil	.06	.03	.00
☐ 138 Ricky Horton	.06	.03	.00
☐ 139 LaMarr Hoyt	.06	.03	.00
☐ 140 Wayne Krenchicki	.06	.03	.00
☐ 141 Glenn Hubbard	.06	.03	.00
☐ 142 Cecilio Guante	.06	.03	.00
☐ 143 Mike Krukow	.06	.03	.00
☐ 144 Lee Smith	.10	.05	.01
☐ 145 Edwin Nunez	.06	.03	.00
☐ 146 Dave Stieb	.12	.06	.01
☐ 147 Mike Smithson	.06	.03	.00
☐ 148 Ken Dixon	.06	.03	.00
☐ 149 Danny Darwin	.10	.05	.01
☐ 150 Chris Pittaro	.06	.03	.00
☐ 151 Bill Buckner	.10	.05	.01
☐ 152 Mike Pagliarulo	.10	.05	.01
☐ 153 Bill Russell	.06	.03	.00
☐ 154 Brook Jacoby	.10	.05	.01
☐ 155 Pat Sheridan	.06	.03	.00
☐ 156 Mike Gallego	.06	.03	.00
☐ 157 Jim Wohlford	.06	.03	.00
☐ 158 Gary Pettis	.06	.03	.00
☐ 159 Toby Harrah	.06	.03	.00
☐ 160 Richard Dotson	.06	.03	.00
☐ 161 Bob Knepper	.06	.03	.00
☐ 162 Dave Dravecky	.10	.05	.01
☐ 163 Greg Gross	.06	.03	.00
☐ 164 Eric Davis	3.50	1.75	.35
☐ 165 Gerald Perry	.12	.06	.01
☐ 166 Rick Rhoden	.06	.03	.00
☐ 167 Keith Moreland	.06	.03	.00
☐ 168 Jack Clark	.25	.12	.02
☐ 169 Storm Davis	.10	.05	.01
☐ 170 Cecil Cooper	.10	.05	.01
☐ 171 Alan Trammell	.25	.12	.02
☐ 172 Roger Clemens	5.50	2.75	.55
☐ 173 Don Mattingly	5.00	2.50	.50
☐ 174 Pedro Guerrero	.25	.12	.02
☐ 175 Willie Wilson	.10	.05	.01
☐ 176 Dwayne Murphy	.06	.03	.00
☐ 177 Tim Raines	.30	.15	.03
☐ 178 Larry Parrish	.06	.03	.00
☐ 179 Mike Witt	.06	.03	.00
☐ 180 Harold Baines	.15	.07	.01
☐ 181 Vince Coleman (BA 2.67 on back)	4.50	2.25	.45
☐ 182 Jeff Heathcock	.06	.03	.00
☐ 183 Steve Carlton	.40	.20	.04
☐ 184 Mario Soto	.06	.03	.00
☐ 185 Goose Gossage	.12	.06	.01
☐ 186 Johnny Ray	.10	.05	.01
☐ 187 Dan Gladden	.10	.05	.01
☐ 188 Bob Horner	.12	.06	.01
☐ 189 Rick Sutcliffe	.12	.06	.01
☐ 190 Keith Hernandez	.25	.12	.02
☐ 191 Phil Bradley	.12	.06	.01
☐ 192 Tom Brunansky	.15	.07	.01
☐ 193 Jesse Barfield	.15	.07	.01
☐ 194 Frank Viola	.35	.17	.03
☐ 195 Willie Upshaw	.06	.03	.00
☐ 196 Jim Beattie	.06	.03	.00
☐ 197 Darryl Strawberry	3.75	1.85	.37
☐ 198 Ron Cey	.10	.05	.01
☐ 199 Steve Bedrosian	.12	.06	.01
☐ 200 Steve Kemp	.06	.03	.00
☐ 201 Manny Trillo	.06	.03	.00
☐ 202 Garry Templeton	.10	.05	.01
☐ 203 Dave Parker	.18	.09	.01
☐ 204 John Denny	.06	.03	.00
☐ 205 Terry Pendleton	.10	.05	.01
☐ 206 Terry Puhl	.06	.03	.00
☐ 207 Bobby Grich	.10	.05	.01
☐ 208 Ozzie Guillen	1.50	.75	.15
☐ 209 Jeff Reardon	.10	.05	.01
☐ 210 Cal Ripken	.90	.45	.09
☐ 211 Bill Schroeder	.06	.03	.00
☐ 212 Dan Petry	.06	.03	.00
☐ 213 Jim Rice	.20	.10	.02
☐ 214 Dave Righetti	.12	.06	.01
☐ 215 Fernando Valenzuela	.25	.12	.02

☐ 216	Julio Franco	.25	.12	.02
☐ 217	Darryl Motley	.06	.03	.00
☐ 218	Dave Collins	.06	.03	.00
☐ 219	Tim Wallach	.10	.05	.01
☐ 220	George Wright	.06	.03	.00
☐ 221	Tommy Dunbar	.06	.03	.00
☐ 222	Steve Balboni	.06	.03	.00
☐ 223	Jay Howell	.06	.03	.00
☐ 224	Joe Carter	.60	.30	.06
☐ 225	Ed Whitson	.10	.05	.01
☐ 226	Orel Hershiser	1.50	.75	.15
☐ 227	Willie Hernandez	.10	.05	.01
☐ 228	Lee Lacy	.06	.03	.00
☐ 229	Rollie Fingers	.18	.09	.01
☐ 230	Bob Boone	.12	.06	.01
☐ 231	Joaquin Andujar	.10	.05	.01
☐ 232	Craig Reynolds	.06	.03	.00
☐ 233	Shane Rawley	.06	.03	.00
☐ 234	Eric Show	.06	.03	.00
☐ 235	Jose DeLeon	.06	.03	.00
☐ 236	Jose Uribe	.25	.12	.02
☐ 237	Moose Haas	.06	.03	.00
☐ 238	Wally Backman	.06	.03	.00
☐ 239	Dennis Eckersley	.20	.10	.02
☐ 240	Mike Moore	.10	.05	.01
☐ 241	Damaso Garcia	.06	.03	.00
☐ 242	Tim Teufel	.06	.03	.00
☐ 243	Dave Concepcion	.10	.05	.01
☐ 244	Floyd Bannister	.06	.03	.00
☐ 245	Fred Lynn	.15	.07	.01
☐ 246	Charlie Moore	.06	.03	.00
☐ 247	Walt Terrell	.06	.03	.00
☐ 248	Dave Winfield	.35	.17	.03
☐ 249	Dwight Evans	.15	.07	.01
☐ 250	Dennis Powell	.06	.03	.00
☐ 251	Andre Thornton	.06	.03	.00
☐ 252	Onix Concepcion	.06	.03	.00
☐ 253	Mike Heath	.06	.03	.00
☐ 254A	David Palmer ERR (position 2B)	.10	.05	.01
☐ 254B	David Palmer COR (position P)	.60	.30	.06
☐ 255	Donnie Moore	.06	.03	.00
☐ 256	Curtis Wilkerson	.06	.03	.00
☐ 257	Julio Cruz	.06	.03	.00
☐ 258	Nolan Ryan	2.25	1.10	.22
☐ 259	Jeff Stone	.06	.03	.00
☐ 260	John Tudor	.12	.06	.01
☐ 261	Mark Thurmond	.06	.03	.00
☐ 262	Jay Tibbs	.06	.03	.00
☐ 263	Rafael Ramirez	.06	.03	.00
☐ 264	Larry McWilliams	.06	.03	.00
☐ 265	Mark Davis	.12	.06	.01
☐ 266	Bob Dernier	.06	.03	.00
☐ 267	Matt Young	.06	.03	.00
☐ 268	Jim Clancy	.06	.03	.00
☐ 269	Mickey Hatcher	.06	.03	.00
☐ 270	Sammy Stewart	.06	.03	.00
☐ 271	Bob L. Gibson	.06	.03	.00
☐ 272	Nelson Simmons	.06	.03	.00
☐ 273	Rich Gedman	.06	.03	.00
☐ 274	Butch Wynegar	.06	.03	.00
☐ 275	Ken Howell	.06	.03	.00
☐ 276	Mel Hall	.10	.05	.01
☐ 277	Jim Sundberg	.06	.03	.00
☐ 278	Chris Codiroli	.06	.03	.00
☐ 279	Herm Winningham	.10	.05	.01
☐ 280	Rod Carew	.45	.22	.04
☐ 281	Don Slaught	.06	.03	.00
☐ 282	Scott Fletcher	.06	.03	.00
☐ 283	Bill Dawley	.06	.03	.00
☐ 284	Andy Hawkins	.06	.03	.00
☐ 285	Glenn Wilson	.06	.03	.00
☐ 286	Nick Esasky	.10	.05	.01
☐ 287	Claudell Washington	.10	.05	.01
☐ 288	Lee Mazzilli	.06	.03	.00
☐ 289	Jody Davis	.06	.03	.00
☐ 290	Darrell Porter	.06	.03	.00
☐ 291	Scott McGregor	.06	.03	.00
☐ 292	Ted Simmons	.10	.05	.01
☐ 293	Aurelio Lopez	.06	.03	.00
☐ 294	Marty Barrett	.10	.05	.01
☐ 295	Dale Berra	.06	.03	.00
☐ 296	Greg Brock	.06	.03	.00
☐ 297	Charlie Leibrandt	.06	.03	.00
☐ 298	Bill Krueger	.06	.03	.00
☐ 299	Bryn Smith	.10	.05	.01
☐ 300	Burt Hooton	.06	.03	.00
☐ 301	Stu Cliburn	.06	.03	.00
☐ 302	Luis Salazar	.06	.03	.00
☐ 303	Ken Dayley	.06	.03	.00
☐ 304	Frank DiPino	.06	.03	.00
☐ 305	Von Hayes	.12	.06	.01
☐ 306	Gary Redus	.06	.03	.00
☐ 307	Craig Lefferts	.06	.03	.00
☐ 308	Sammy Khalifa	.06	.03	.00
☐ 309	Scott Garrelts	.10	.05	.01
☐ 310	Rick Cerone	.06	.03	.00
☐ 311	Shawon Dunston	1.00	.50	.10
☐ 312	Howard Johnson	.50	.25	.05
☐ 313	Jim Presley	.12	.06	.01
☐ 314	Gary Gaetti	.25	.12	.02
☐ 315	Luis Leal	.06	.03	.00
☐ 316	Mark Salas	.06	.03	.00
☐ 317	Bill Caudill	.06	.03	.00
☐ 318	Dave Henderson	.10	.05	.01
☐ 319	Rafael Santana	.06	.03	.00
☐ 320	Leon Durham	.06	.03	.00
☐ 321	Bruce Sutter	.12	.06	.01
☐ 322	Jason Thompson	.06	.03	.00
☐ 323	Bob Brenly	.06	.03	.00
☐ 324	Carmelo Martinez	.06	.03	.00
☐ 325	Eddie Milner	.06	.03	.00
☐ 326	Juan Samuel	.15	.07	.01
☐ 327	Tom Nieto	.06	.03	.00
☐ 328	Dave Smith	.06	.03	.00
☐ 329	Urbano Lugo	.06	.03	.00
☐ 330	Joel Skinner	.06	.03	.00
☐ 331	Bill Gullickson	.06	.03	.00
☐ 332	Floyd Rayford	.06	.03	.00
☐ 333	Ben Oglivie	.06	.03	.00
☐ 334	Lance Parrish	.15	.07	.01
☐ 335	Jackie Gutierrez	.06	.03	.00
☐ 336	Dennis Rasmussen	.10	.05	.01
☐ 337	Terry Whitfield	.06	.03	.00
☐ 338	Neal Heaton	.06	.03	.00
☐ 339	Jorge Orta	.06	.03	.00
☐ 340	Donnie Hill	.06	.03	.00
☐ 341	Joe Hesketh	.06	.03	.00
☐ 342	Charlie Hough	.06	.03	.00
☐ 343	Dave Rozema	.06	.03	.00
☐ 344	Greg Pryor	.06	.03	.00
☐ 345	Mickey Tettleton	.65	.30	.06
☐ 346	George Vukovich	.06	.03	.00
☐ 347	Don Baylor	.10	.05	.01
☐ 348	Carlos Diaz	.06	.03	.00
☐ 349	Barbaro Garbey	.06	.03	.00
☐ 350	Larry Sheets	.06	.03	.00
☐ 351	Ted Higuera	1.50	.75	.15
☐ 352	Juan Beniquez	.06	.03	.00
☐ 353	Bob Forsch	.06	.03	.00
☐ 354	Mark Bailey	.06	.03	.00
☐ 355	Larry Andersen	.06	.03	.00
☐ 356	Terry Kennedy	.06	.03	.00
☐ 357	Don Robinson	.06	.03	.00
☐ 358	Jim Gott	.06	.03	.00
☐ 359	Earnie Riles	.20	.10	.02
☐ 360	John Christensen	.06	.03	.00
☐ 361	Ray Fontenot	.06	.03	.00
☐ 362	Spike Owen	.06	.03	.00
☐ 363	Jim Acker	.06	.03	.00
☐ 364	Ron Davis	.06	.03	.00
☐ 365	Tom Hume	.06	.03	.00
☐ 366	Carlton Fisk	.40	.20	.04
☐ 367	Nate Snell	.06	.03	.00
☐ 368	Rick Manning	.06	.03	.00
☐ 369	Darrell Evans	.10	.05	.01
☐ 370	Ron Hassey	.06	.03	.00
☐ 371	Wade Boggs	2.50	1.25	.25
☐ 372	Rick Honeycutt	.06	.03	.00
☐ 373	Chris Bando	.06	.03	.00
☐ 374	Bud Black	.10	.05	.01
☐ 375	Steve Henderson	.06	.03	.00
☐ 376	Charlie Lea	.06	.03	.00
☐ 377	Reggie Jackson	.60	.30	.06
☐ 378	Dave Schmidt	.06	.03	.00
☐ 379	Bob James	.06	.03	.00
☐ 380	Glenn Davis	4.50	2.25	.45
☐ 381	Tim Corcoran	.06	.03	.00
☐ 382	Danny Cox	.06	.03	.00
☐ 383	Tim Flannery	.06	.03	.00
☐ 384	Tom Browning	.20	.10	.02
☐ 385	Rick Camp	.06	.03	.00
☐ 386	Jim Morrison	.06	.03	.00
☐ 387	Dave LaPoint	.06	.03	.00
☐ 388	Dave Lopes	.10	.05	.01
☐ 389	Al Cowens	.06	.03	.00
☐ 390	Doyle Alexander	.06	.03	.00
☐ 391	Tim Laudner	.06	.03	.00
☐ 392	Don Aase	.06	.03	.00
☐ 393	Jaime Cocanower	.06	.03	.00
☐ 394	Randy O'Neal	.06	.03	.00
☐ 395	Mike Easler	.06	.03	.00
☐ 396	Scott Bradley	.06	.03	.00
☐ 397	Tom Niedenfuer	.06	.03	.00
☐ 398	Jerry Willard	.06	.03	.00
☐ 399	Lonnie Smith	.10	.05	.01
☐ 400	Bruce Bochte	.06	.03	.00

☐ 401 Terry Francona	.06	.03	.00
☐ 402 Jim Slaton	.06	.03	.00
☐ 403 Bill Stein	.06	.03	.00
☐ 404 Tim Hulett	.06	.03	.00
☐ 405 Alan Ashby	.06	.03	.00
☐ 406 Tim Stoddard	.06	.03	.00
☐ 407 Garry Maddox	.06	.03	.00
☐ 408 Ted Power	.06	.03	.00
☐ 409 Len Barker	.06	.03	.00
☐ 410 Denny Gonzalez	.06	.03	.00
☐ 411 George Frazier	.06	.03	.00
☐ 412 Andy Van Slyke	.30	.15	.03
☐ 413 Jim Dwyer	.06	.03	.00
☐ 414 Paul Householder	.06	.03	.00
☐ 415 Alejandro Sanchez	.06	.03	.00
☐ 416 Steve Crawford	.06	.03	.00
☐ 417 Dan Pasqua	.15	.07	.01
☐ 418 Enos Cabell	.06	.03	.00
☐ 419 Mike Jones	.06	.03	.00
☐ 420 Steve Kiefer	.06	.03	.00
☐ 421 Tim Burke	.40	.20	.04
☐ 422 Mike Mason	.06	.03	.00
☐ 423 Ruppert Jones	.06	.03	.00
☐ 424 Jerry Hairston	.06	.03	.00
☐ 425 Tito Landrum	.06	.03	.00
☐ 426 Jeff Calhoun	.06	.03	.00
☐ 427 Don Carman	.25	.12	.02
☐ 428 Tony Perez	.12	.06	.01
☐ 429 Jerry Davis	.06	.03	.00
☐ 430 Bob Walk	.06	.03	.00
☐ 431 Brad Wellman	.06	.03	.00
☐ 432 Terry Forster	.06	.03	.00
☐ 433 Billy Hatcher	.25	.12	.02
☐ 434 Clint Hurdle	.06	.03	.00
☐ 435 Ivan Calderon	1.25	.60	.12
☐ 436 Pete Filson	.06	.03	.00
☐ 437 Tom Henke	.10	.05	.01
☐ 438 Dave Engle	.06	.03	.00
☐ 439 Tom Filer	.06	.03	.00
☐ 440 Gorman Thomas	.10	.05	.01
☐ 441 Rick Aguilera	.50	.25	.05
☐ 442 Scott Sanderson	.10	.05	.01
☐ 443 Jeff Dedmon	.06	.03	.00
☐ 444 Joe Orsulak	.30	.15	.03
☐ 445 Atlee Hammaker	.06	.03	.00
☐ 446 Jerry Royster	.06	.03	.00
☐ 447 Buddy Bell	.10	.05	.01
☐ 448 Dave Rucker	.06	.03	.00
☐ 449 Ivan DeJesus	.06	.03	.00
☐ 450 Jim Pankovits	.06	.03	.00
☐ 451 Jerry Narron	.06	.03	.00
☐ 452 Bryan Little	.06	.03	.00
☐ 453 Gary Lucas	.06	.03	.00
☐ 454 Dennis Martinez	.10	.05	.01
☐ 455 Ed Romero	.06	.03	.00
☐ 456 Bob Melvin	.10	.05	.01
☐ 457 Glenn Hoffman	.06	.03	.00
☐ 458 Bob Shirley	.06	.03	.00
☐ 459 Bob Welch	.15	.07	.01
☐ 460 Carmen Castillo	.06	.03	.00
☐ 461 Dave Leeper (outfielder)	.06	.03	.00
☐ 462 Tim Birtsas	.10	.05	.01
☐ 463 Randy St.Claire	.06	.03	.00
☐ 464 Chris Welsh	.06	.03	.00
☐ 465 Greg Harris	.06	.03	.00
☐ 466 Lynn Jones	.06	.03	.00
☐ 467 Dusty Baker	.10	.05	.01
☐ 468 Roy Smith	.06	.03	.00
☐ 469 Andre Robertson	.06	.03	.00
☐ 470 Ken Landreaux	.06	.03	.00
☐ 471 Dave Bergman	.06	.03	.00
☐ 472 Gary Roenicke	.06	.03	.00
☐ 473 Pete Vuckovich	.06	.03	.00
☐ 474 Kirk McCaskill	.50	.25	.05
☐ 475 Jeff Lahti	.06	.03	.00
☐ 476 Mike Scott	.35	.17	.03
☐ 477 Darren Daulton	.50	.25	.05
☐ 478 Graig Nettles	.10	.05	.01
☐ 479 Bill Almon	.06	.03	.00
☐ 480 Greg Minton	.06	.03	.00
☐ 481 Randy Ready	.06	.03	.00
☐ 482 Len Dykstra	4.00	2.00	.40
☐ 483 Thad Bosley	.06	.03	.00
☐ 484 Harold Reynolds	.75	.35	.07
☐ 485 Al Oliver	.10	.05	.01
☐ 486 Roy Smalley	.06	.03	.00
☐ 487 John Franco	.30	.15	.03
☐ 488 Juan Agosto	.06	.03	.00
☐ 489 Al Pardo	.06	.03	.00
☐ 490 Bill Wegman	.10	.05	.01
☐ 491 Frank Tanana	.10	.05	.01
☐ 492 Brian Fisher	.15	.07	.01
☐ 493 Mark Clear	.06	.03	.00
☐ 494 Len Matuszek	.06	.03	.00
☐ 495 Ramon Romero	.06	.03	.00
☐ 496 John Wathan	.06	.03	.00
☐ 497 Rob Picciolo	.06	.03	.00
☐ 498 U.L. Washington	.06	.03	.00
☐ 499 John Candelaria	.06	.03	.00
☐ 500 Duane Walker	.06	.03	.00
☐ 501 Gene Nelson	.06	.03	.00
☐ 502 John Mizerock	.06	.03	.00
☐ 503 Luis Aguayo	.06	.03	.00
☐ 504 Kurt Kepshire	.06	.03	.00
☐ 505 Ed Wojna	.10	.05	.01
☐ 506 Joe Price	.06	.03	.00
☐ 507 Milt Thompson	.30	.15	.03
☐ 508 Junior Ortiz	.06	.03	.00
☐ 509 Vida Blue	.10	.05	.01
☐ 510 Steve Engel	.06	.03	.00
☐ 511 Karl Best	.06	.03	.00
☐ 512 Cecil Fielder	16.00	8.00	1.60
☐ 513 Frank Eufemia	.06	.03	.00
☐ 514 Tippy Martinez	.06	.03	.00
☐ 515 Billy Jo Robidoux	.10	.05	.01
☐ 516 Bill Scherrer	.06	.03	.00
☐ 517 Bruce Hurst	.12	.06	.01
☐ 518 Rich Bordi	.06	.03	.00
☐ 519 Steve Yeager	.06	.03	.00
☐ 520 Tony Bernazard	.06	.03	.00
☐ 521 Hal McRae	.06	.03	.00
☐ 522 Jose Rijo	.25	.12	.02
☐ 523 Mitch Webster	.25	.12	.02
☐ 524 Jack Howell	.35	.17	.03
☐ 525 Alan Bannister	.06	.03	.00
☐ 526 Ron Kittle	.10	.05	.01
☐ 527 Phil Garner	.06	.03	.00
☐ 528 Kurt Bevacqua	.06	.03	.00
☐ 529 Kevin Gross	.06	.03	.00
☐ 530 Bo Diaz	.06	.03	.00
☐ 531 Ken Oberkfell	.06	.03	.00
☐ 532 Rick Reuschel	.12	.06	.01
☐ 533 Ron Meridith	.06	.03	.00
☐ 534 Steve Braun	.06	.03	.00
☐ 535 Wayne Gross	.06	.03	.00
☐ 536 Ray Searage	.06	.03	.00
☐ 537 Tom Brookens	.06	.03	.00
☐ 538 Al Nipper	.06	.03	.00
☐ 539 Billy Sample	.06	.03	.00
☐ 540 Steve Sax	.25	.12	.02
☐ 541 Dan Quisenberry	.10	.05	.01
☐ 542 Tony Phillips	.06	.03	.00
☐ 543 Floyd Youmans	.20	.10	.02
☐ 544 Steve Buechele	.25	.12	.02
☐ 545 Craig Gerber	.06	.03	.00
☐ 546 Joe DeSa	.06	.03	.00
☐ 547 Brian Harper	.12	.06	.01
☐ 548 Kevin Bass	.10	.05	.01
☐ 549 Tom Foley	.06	.03	.00
☐ 550 Dave Van Gorder	.06	.03	.00
☐ 551 Bruce Bochy	.06	.03	.00
☐ 552 R.J. Reynolds	.06	.03	.00
☐ 553 Chris Brown	.12	.06	.01
☐ 554 Bruce Benedict	.06	.03	.00
☐ 555 Warren Brusstar	.06	.03	.00
☐ 556 Danny Heep	.06	.03	.00
☐ 557 Darnell Coles	.06	.03	.00
☐ 558 Greg Gagne	.10	.05	.01
☐ 559 Ernie Whitt	.06	.03	.00
☐ 560 Ron Washington	.06	.03	.00
☐ 561 Jimmy Key	.15	.07	.01
☐ 562 Billy Swift	.10	.05	.01
☐ 563 Ron Darling	.20	.10	.02
☐ 564 Dick Ruthven	.06	.03	.00
☐ 565 Zane Smith	.45	.22	.04
☐ 566 Sid Bream	.06	.03	.00
☐ 567A Joel Youngblood ERR (position P)	.10	.05	.01
☐ 567B Joel Youngblood COR (position IF)	.60	.30	.06
☐ 568 Mario Ramirez	.06	.03	.00
☐ 569 Tom Runnels	.06	.03	.00
☐ 570 Rick Schu	.06	.03	.00
☐ 571 Bill Campbell	.06	.03	.00
☐ 572 Dickie Thon	.06	.03	.00
☐ 573 Al Holland	.06	.03	.00
☐ 574 Reid Nichols	.06	.03	.00
☐ 575 Bert Roberge	.06	.03	.00
☐ 576 Mike Flanagan	.10	.05	.01
☐ 577 Tim Leary	.35	.17	.03
☐ 578 Mike Laga	.06	.03	.00
☐ 579 Steve Lyons	.06	.03	.00
☐ 580 Phil Niekro	.20	.10	.02
☐ 581 Gilberto Reyes	.06	.03	.00
☐ 582 Jamie Easterly	.06	.03	.00
☐ 583 Mark Gubicza	.20	.10	.02
☐ 584 Stan Javier	.45	.22	.04

☐ 585 Bill Laskey	.06	.03	.00
☐ 586 Jeff Russell	.10	.05	.01
☐ 587 Dickie Noles	.06	.03	.00
☐ 588 Steve Farr	.10	.05	.01
☐ 589 Steve Ontiveros	.10	.05	.01
☐ 590 Mike Hargrove	.06	.03	.00
☐ 591 Marty Bystrom	.06	.03	.00
☐ 592 Franklin Stubbs	.10	.05	.01
☐ 593 Larry Herndon	.06	.03	.00
☐ 594 Bill Swaggerty	.06	.03	.00
☐ 595 Carlos Ponce	.06	.03	.00
☐ 596 Pat Perry	.10	.05	.01
☐ 597 Ray Knight	.10	.05	.01
☐ 598 Steve Lombardozzi	.10	.05	.01
☐ 599 Brad Havens	.06	.03	.00
☐ 600 Pat Clements	.10	.05	.01
☐ 601 Joe Niekro	.10	.05	.01
☐ 602 Hank Aaron Puzzle Card	.06	.03	.00
☐ 603 Dwayne Henry	.10	.05	.01
☐ 604 Mookie Wilson	.10	.05	.01
☐ 605 Buddy Biancalana	.06	.03	.00
☐ 606 Rance Mulliniks	.06	.03	.00
☐ 607 Alan Wiggins	.06	.03	.00
☐ 608 Joe Cowley	.06	.03	.00
☐ 609A Tom Seaver (green borders on name)	.50	.25	.05
☐ 609B Tom Seaver (yellow borders on name)	1.50	.75	.15
☐ 610 Neil Allen	.06	.03	.00
☐ 611 Don Sutton	.25	.12	.02
☐ 612 Fred Toliver	.10	.05	.01
☐ 613 Jay Baller	.06	.03	.00
☐ 614 Marc Sullivan	.06	.03	.00
☐ 615 John Grubb	.06	.03	.00
☐ 616 Bruce Kison	.06	.03	.00
☐ 617 Bill Madlock	.10	.05	.01
☐ 618 Chris Chambliss	.10	.05	.01
☐ 619 Dave Stewart	.50	.25	.05
☐ 620 Tim Lollar	.06	.03	.00
☐ 621 Gary Lavelle	.06	.03	.00
☐ 622 Charles Hudson	.06	.03	.00
☐ 623 Joel Davis	.10	.05	.01
☐ 624 Joe Johnson	.10	.05	.01
☐ 625 Sid Fernandez	.25	.12	.02
☐ 626 Dennis Lamp	.06	.03	.00
☐ 627 Terry Harper	.06	.03	.00
☐ 628 Jack Lazorko	.06	.03	.00
☐ 629 Roger McDowell	.60	.30	.06
☐ 630 Mark Funderburk	.10	.05	.01
☐ 631 Ed Lynch	.06	.03	.00
☐ 632 Rudy Law	.06	.03	.00
☐ 633 Roger Mason	.10	.05	.01
☐ 634 Mike Felder	.12	.06	.01
☐ 635 Ken Schrom	.06	.03	.00
☐ 636 Bob Ojeda	.10	.05	.01
☐ 637 Ed VandeBerg	.06	.03	.00
☐ 638 Bobby Meacham	.06	.03	.00
☐ 639 Cliff Johnson	.06	.03	.00
☐ 640 Garth Iorg	.06	.03	.00
☐ 641 Dan Driessen	.06	.03	.00
☐ 642 Mike Brown OF	.06	.03	.00
☐ 643 John Shelby	.06	.03	.00
☐ 644 Pete Rose (Ty-Breaking)	.35	.17	.03
☐ 645 The Knuckle Brothers Phil Niekro Joe Niekro	.10	.05	.01
☐ 646 Jesse Orosco	.06	.03	.00
☐ 647 Billy Beane	.10	.05	.01
☐ 648 Cesar Cedeno	.10	.05	.01
☐ 649 Bert Blyleven	.12	.06	.01
☐ 650 Max Venable	.06	.03	.00
☐ 651 Fleet Feet Vince Coleman Willie McGee	.35	.17	.03
☐ 652 Calvin Schiraldi	.06	.03	.00
☐ 653 King of Kings (Pete Rose)	.75	.35	.07
☐ 654 CL: Diamond Kings (unnumbered)	.08	.01	.00
☐ 655A CL 1: 27-130 (unnumbered) (45 Beane ERR)	.10	.01	.00
☐ 655B CL 1: 27-130 (unnumbered) (45 Habyan COR)	.50	.10	.02
☐ 656 CL 2: 131-234 (unnumbered)	.06	.01	.00
☐ 657 CL 3: 235-338 (unnumbered)	.06	.01	.00
☐ 658 CL 4: 339-442 (unnumbered)	.06	.01	.00
☐ 659 CL 5: 443-546 (unnumbered)	.06	.01	.00
☐ 660 CL 6: 547-653 (unnumbered)	.06	.01	.00

1986 Donruss Wax Box Cards

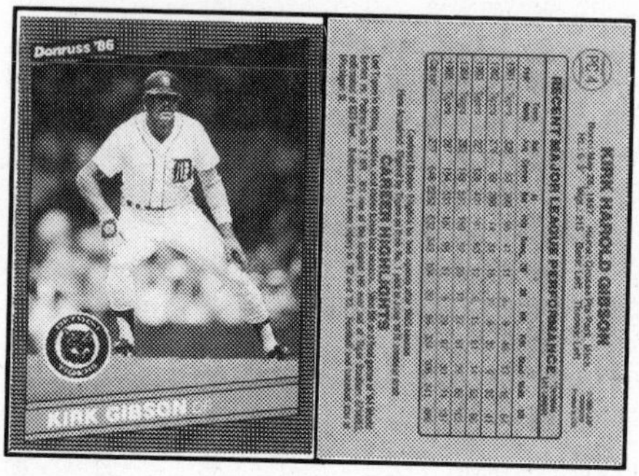

The cards in this 4-card set measure the standard 2 1/2" by 3 1/2". Cards have essentially the same design as the 1986 Donruss regular issue set. The cards were printed on the bottoms of the regular issue wax pack boxes. The four cards (PC4 to PC6 plus a Hank Aaron puzzle card) are considered a separate set in their own right and are not typically included in a complete set of the regular issue 1986 Donruss cards. The value of the panel uncut is slightly greater, perhaps by 25 percent greater, than the value of the individual cards cut up carefully.

	MINT	EXC	G-VG
COMPLETE SET (4)	.60	.30	.06
COMMON PLAYERS	.05	.02	.00
☐ PC4 Kirk Gibson	.50	.25	.05
☐ PC5 Willie Hernandez	.10	.05	.01
☐ PC6 Doug DeCinces	.10	.05	.01
☐ PUZ Hank Aaron Puzzle Card	.05	.02	.00

1986 Donruss All-Stars

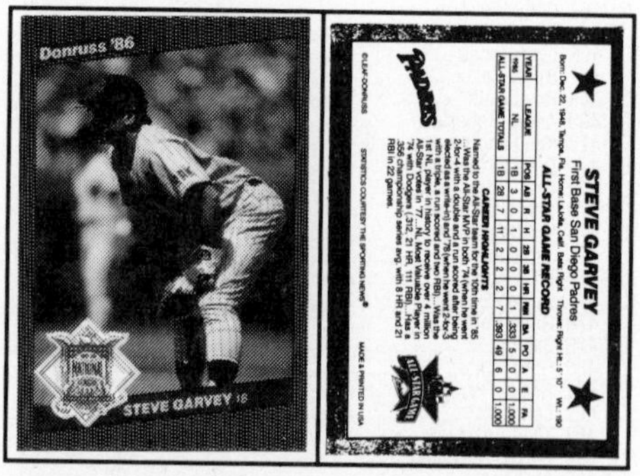

The cards in this 60-card set measure approximately 3 1/2" by 5". Players featured were involved in the 1985 All-Star game played in Minnesota. Cards are very similar in design to the 1986 Donruss regular issue set. The backs give each player's All-Star game statistics and have an orange-yellow border.

	MINT	EXC	G-VG
COMPLETE SET (60)	7.00	3.50	.70
COMMON PLAYERS (1-60)	.07	.03	.01
☐ 1 Tony Gwynn	.35	.17	.03
☐ 2 Tommy Herr	.07	.03	.01
☐ 3 Steve Garvey	.30	.15	.03
☐ 4 Dale Murphy	.45	.22	.04
☐ 5 Darryl Strawberry	.75	.35	.07
☐ 6 Graig Nettles	.10	.05	.01
☐ 7 Terry Kennedy	.07	.03	.01
☐ 8 Ozzie Smith	.20	.10	.02
☐ 9 LaMarr Hoyt	.07	.03	.01
☐ 10 Rickey Henderson	1.00	.50	.10
☐ 11 Lou Whitaker	.15	.07	.01
☐ 12 George Brett	.45	.22	.04
☐ 13 Eddie Murray	.35	.17	.03
☐ 14 Cal Ripken	.35	.17	.03
☐ 15 Dave Winfield	.20	.10	.02
☐ 16 Jim Rice	.20	.10	.02
☐ 17 Carlton Fisk	.30	.15	.03
☐ 18 Jack Morris	.10	.05	.01
☐ 19 Jose Cruz	.07	.03	.01
☐ 20 Tim Raines	.20	.10	.02
☐ 21 Nolan Ryan	1.25	.60	.12
☐ 22 Tony Pena	.07	.03	.01
☐ 23 Jack Clark	.15	.07	.01
☐ 24 Dave Parker	.15	.07	.01
☐ 25 Tim Wallach	.07	.03	.01
☐ 26 Ozzie Virgil	.07	.03	.01
☐ 27 Fernando Valenzuela	.20	.10	.02
☐ 28 Dwight Gooden	.75	.35	.07
☐ 29 Glenn Wilson	.07	.03	.01
☐ 30 Garry Templeton	.07	.03	.01
☐ 31 Goose Gossage	.10	.05	.01
☐ 32 Ryne Sandberg	1.00	.50	.10
☐ 33 Jeff Reardon	.10	.05	.01
☐ 34 Pete Rose	.90	.45	.09
☐ 35 Scott Garrelts	.07	.03	.01
☐ 36 Willie McGee	.15	.07	.01
☐ 37 Ron Darling	.10	.05	.01
☐ 38 Dick Williams MG	.07	.03	.01
☐ 39 Paul Molitor	.20	.10	.02
☐ 40 Damaso Garcia	.07	.03	.01
☐ 41 Phil Bradley	.10	.05	.01
☐ 42 Dan Petry	.07	.03	.01
☐ 43 Willie Hernandez	.10	.05	.01
☐ 44 Tom Brunansky	.10	.05	.01
☐ 45 Alan Trammell	.20	.10	.02
☐ 46 Donnie Moore	.07	.03	.01
☐ 47 Wade Boggs	.90	.45	.09
☐ 48 Ernie Whitt	.07	.03	.01
☐ 49 Harold Baines	.10	.05	.01
☐ 50 Don Mattingly	1.25	.60	.12
☐ 51 Gary Ward	.07	.03	.01
☐ 52 Bert Blyleven	.15	.07	.01
☐ 53 Jimmy Key	.10	.05	.01
☐ 54 Cecil Cooper	.10	.05	.01
☐ 55 Dave Stieb	.10	.05	.01
☐ 56 Rich Gedman	.07	.03	.01
☐ 57 Jay Howell	.07	.03	.01
☐ 58 Sparky Anderson MG	.07	.03	.01
☐ 59 Minneapolis Metrodome	.07	.03	.01
☐ 60 Checklist Card (unnumbered)	.07	.01	.00

1986 Donruss All-Star Box

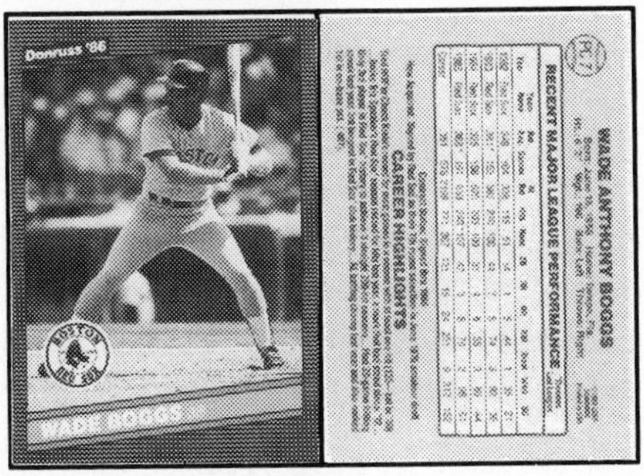

The cards in this 4-card set measure the standard 2 1/2" by 3 1/2" in spite of the fact that they form the bottom of the wax pack box for the larger Donruss All-Star cards. These box cards have essentially the same design as the 1986 Donruss regular issue set. The cards were printed on the bottoms of the Donruss All-Star (3 1/2" by 5") wax pack boxes. The four cards (PC7 to PC9 plus a Hank Aaron puzzle card) are considered a separate set in their own right and are not typically included in a complete set of the regular issue 1986 Donruss All-Star (or regular) cards. The value of the panel uncut is slightly greater, perhaps by 25 percent greater, than the value of the individual cards cut up carefully.

	MINT	EXC	G-VG
COMPLETE SET (4)	1.00	.50	.10
COMMON PLAYERS	.05	.02	.00
☐ PC7 Wade Boggs	.90	.45	.09
☐ PC8 Lee Smith	.15	.07	.01
☐ PC9 Cecil Cooper	.10	.05	.01
☐ PUZ Hank Aaron Puzzle Card	.05	.02	.00

1986 Donruss Pop-Ups

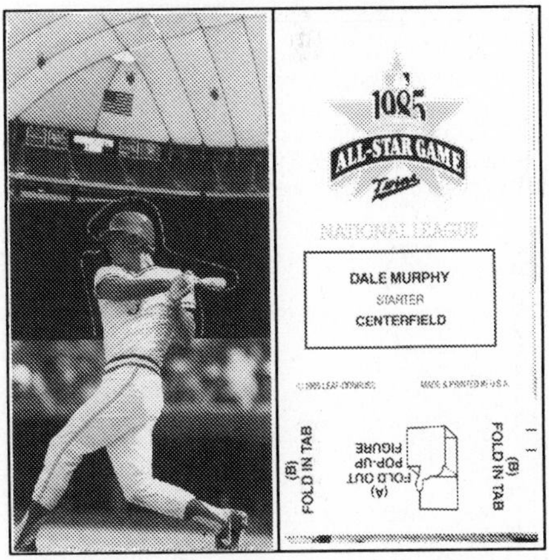

This set is the companion of the 1986 Donruss All-Star (60) set; as such it features the first 18 cards of that set (the All-Star starting line-ups) in a pop-up, die-cut type of card. These cards (measuring (2 1/2" by 5") can be "popped up" to feature a standing card showing the player in action in front of the Metrodome ballpark background. Although this set is unnumbered it is numbered in the same order as its companion set, presumably according to the respective batting orders of the starting line-ups. The first nine numbers below are National Leaguers and the last nine are American Leaguers. See also the Donruss All-Star checklist card which contains a checklist for the Pop-Ups as well.

	MINT	EXC	G-VG
COMPLETE SET (18)	4.00	2.00	.40
COMMON PLAYERS (1-18)	.10	.05	.01
☐ 1 Tony Gwynn	.40	.20	.04
☐ 2 Tommy Herr	.10	.05	.01
☐ 3 Steve Garvey	.40	.20	.04
☐ 4 Dale Murphy	.40	.20	.04
☐ 5 Darryl Strawberry	.75	.35	.07
☐ 6 Graig Nettles	.10	.05	.01
☐ 7 Terry Kennedy	.10	.05	.01
☐ 8 Ozzie Smith	.20	.10	.02
☐ 9 LaMarr Hoyt	.10	.05	.01
☐ 10 Rickey Henderson	1.00	.50	.10
☐ 11 Lou Whitaker	.20	.10	.02

☐ 12 George Brett	.60	.30	.06
☐ 13 Eddie Murray	.35	.17	.03
☐ 14 Cal Ripken	.40	.20	.04
☐ 15 Dave Winfield	.20	.10	.02
☐ 16 Jim Rice	.20	.10	.02
☐ 17 Carlton Fisk	.25	.12	.02
☐ 18 Jack Morris	.10	.05	.01

1986 Donruss Super DK's

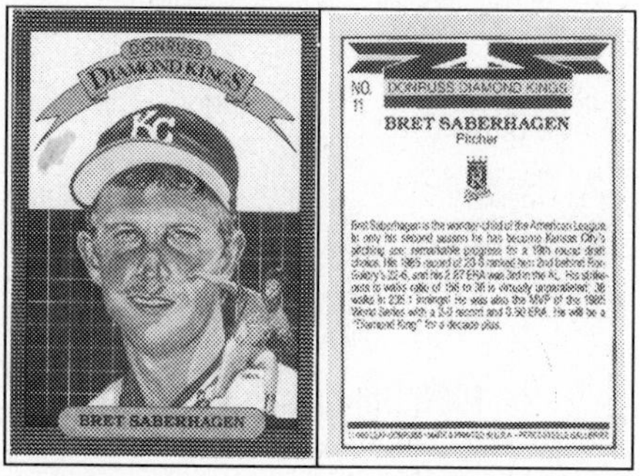

This 29-card set of large Diamond Kings features the full-color artwork of Dick Perez. The set could be obtained from Perez-Steele Galleries by sending three Donruss wrappers and 9.00. The cards measure 4 7/8" by 6 13/16" and are identical in design to the Diamond King cards in the Donruss regular issue.

	MINT	EXC	G-VG
COMPLETE SET (29)	10.00	5.00	1.00
COMMON PLAYER (1-27)	.20	.10	.02
☐ 1 Kirk Gibson	.50	.25	.05
☐ 2 Goose Gossage	.30	.15	.03
☐ 3 Willie McGee	.30	.15	.03
☐ 4 George Bell	.40	.20	.04
☐ 5 Tony Armas	.20	.10	.02
☐ 6 Chili Davis	.20	.10	.02
☐ 7 Cecil Cooper	.20	.10	.02
☐ 8 Mike Boddicker	.20	.10	.02
☐ 9 Dave Lopes	.20	.10	.02
☐ 10 Bill Doran	.20	.10	.02
☐ 11 Bret Saberhagen	.60	.30	.06
☐ 12 Brett Butler	.30	.15	.03
☐ 13 Harold Baines	.30	.15	.03
☐ 14 Mike Davis	.20	.10	.02
☐ 15 Tony Perez	.30	.15	.03
☐ 16 Willie Randolph	.30	.15	.03
☐ 17 Bob Boone	.30	.15	.03
☐ 18 Orel Hershiser	.90	.45	.09
☐ 19 Johnny Ray	.20	.10	.02
☐ 20 Gary Ward	.20	.10	.02
☐ 21 Rick Mahler	.20	.10	.02
☐ 22 Phil Bradley	.30	.15	.03
☐ 23 Jerry Koosman	.30	.15	.03
☐ 24 Tom Brunansky	.30	.15	.03
☐ 25 Andre Dawson	.60	.30	.06
☐ 26 Dwight Gooden	1.25	.60	.12
☐ 27 Pete Rose King of Kings	1.25	.60	.12
☐ 28 Checklist Card (unnumbered)	.20	.02	.00
☐ 29 Aaron Large Puzzle (unnumbered)	.20	.10	.02

1986 Donruss Rookies

The 1986 Donruss "The Rookies" set features 56 cards plus a 15-piece puzzle of Hank Aaron. Cards are in full color and are standard size, 2 1/2" by 3 1/2". The set was distributed in a small green box with gold lettering. Although the set was wrapped in cellophane, the top card was number 1 Joyner, resulting in a percentage of the Joyner cards arriving in less than perfect condition. Donruss fixed the problem after it was called to their attention and even went so far as to include a customer service phone number in their second printing. Card fronts are similar in design to the 1986 Donruss regular issue except for the presence of "The Rookies" logo in the lower left corner and a bluish green border instead of a blue border. The key (extended) rookie cards in this set are Barry Bonds, Bobby Bonilla, Will Clark, Bo Jackson, Kevin Mitchell, and Ruben Sierra.

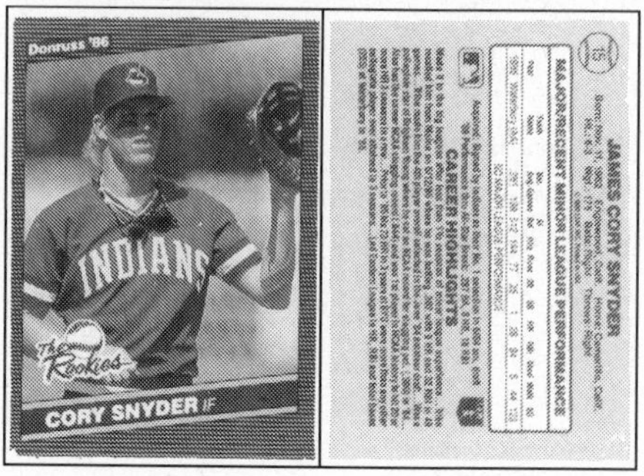

	MINT	EXC	G-VG
COMPLETE SET (56)	55.00	27.50	5.50
COMMON PLAYER (1-56)	.10	.05	.01
☐ 1 Wally Joyner	3.00	1.00	.20
☐ 2 Tracy Jones	.20	.10	.02
☐ 3 Allan Anderson	.40	.20	.04
☐ 4 Ed Correa	.15	.07	.01
☐ 5 Reggie Williams	.10	.05	.01
☐ 6 Charlie Kerfeld	.15	.07	.01
☐ 7 Andres Galarraga	.80	.40	.08
☐ 8 Bob Tewksbury	.15	.07	.01
☐ 9 Al Newman	.15	.07	.01
☐ 10 Andres Thomas	.15	.07	.01
☐ 11 Barry Bonds	6.50	3.25	.65
☐ 12 Juan Nieves	.10	.05	.01
☐ 13 Mark Eichhorn	.10	.05	.01
☐ 14 Dan Plesac	.20	.10	.02
☐ 15 Cory Snyder	.80	.40	.08
☐ 16 Kelly Gruber	2.50	1.25	.25
☐ 17 Kevin Mitchell	6.50	3.25	.65
☐ 18 Steve Lombardozzi	.10	.05	.01
☐ 19 Mitch Williams	.40	.20	.04
☐ 20 John Cerutti	.20	.10	.02
☐ 21 Todd Worrell	.35	.17	.03
☐ 22 Jose Canseco	12.00	6.00	1.20
☐ 23 Pete Incaviglia	1.25	.60	.12
☐ 24 Jose Guzman	.15	.07	.01
☐ 25 Scott Bailes	.15	.07	.01
☐ 26 Greg Mathews	.15	.07	.01
☐ 27 Eric King	.30	.15	.03
☐ 28 Paul Assenmacher	.15	.07	.01
☐ 29 Jeff Sellers	.15	.07	.01
☐ 30 Bobby Bonilla	4.00	2.00	.40
☐ 31 Doug Drabek	1.50	.75	.15
☐ 32 Will Clark	10.00	5.00	1.00
☐ 33 Bip Roberts	.60	.30	.06
☐ 34 Jim Deshaies	.25	.12	.02
☐ 35 Mike LaValliere	.25	.12	.02
☐ 36 Scott Bankhead	.30	.15	.03
☐ 37 Dale Sveum	.15	.07	.01
☐ 38 Bo Jackson	12.00	6.00	1.20
☐ 39 Rob Thompson	.35	.17	.03
☐ 40 Eric Plunk	.15	.07	.01
☐ 41 Bill Bathe	.15	.07	.01
☐ 42 John Kruk	.45	.22	.04
☐ 43 Andy Allanson	.15	.07	.01
☐ 44 Mark Portugal	.15	.07	.01
☐ 45 Danny Tartabull	.65	.30	.06
☐ 46 Bob Kipper	.10	.05	.01
☐ 47 Gene Walter	.15	.07	.01
☐ 48 Rey Quinones	.10	.05	.01
☐ 49 Bobby Witt	1.00	.50	.10
☐ 50 Bill Mooneyham	.10	.05	.01
☐ 51 John Cangelosi	.10	.05	.01
☐ 52 Ruben Sierra	8.00	4.00	.80
☐ 53 Rob Woodward	.10	.05	.01

	MINT	EXC	G-VG
☐ 54 Ed Hearn	.10	.05	.01
☐ 55 Joel McKeon	.10	.05	.01
☐ 56 Checklist Card	.10	.01	.00

1986 Donruss Highlights

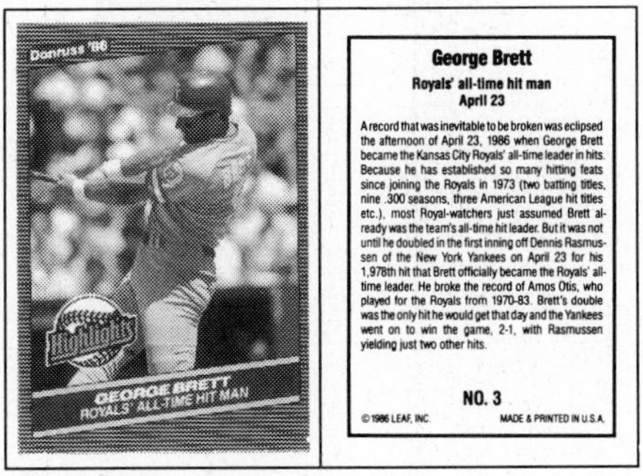

Donruss' second edition of Highlights was released late in 1986. These glossy-coated cards are standard size, measuring 2 1/2" by 3 1/2". Cards commemorate events during the 1986 season, as well as players and pitchers of the month from each league. The set was distributed in its own red, white, blue, and gold box along with a small Hank Aaron puzzle. Card fronts are similar to the regular 1986 Donruss issue except that the Highlights logo is positioned in the lower left-hand corner and the borders are in gold instead of blue. The backs are printed in black and gold on white card stock.

	MINT	EXC	G-VG
COMPLETE SET (56)	10.00	5.00	1.00
COMMON PLAYER (1-56)	.06	.03	.00
☐ 1 Will Clark Homers in First At-Bat	1.00	.50	.10
☐ 2 Jose Rijo Oakland Milestone for Strikeouts	.25	.12	.02
☐ 3 George Brett Royals' All-Time Hit Man	.30	.15	.03
☐ 4 Mike Schmidt Phillies RBI Leader	.75	.35	.07
☐ 5 Roger Clemens KKKKKKKKKK KKKKKKKKKK	.50	.25	.05
☐ 6 Roger Clemens AL Pitcher April	.50	.25	.05
☐ 7 Kirby Puckett AL Player April	.50	.25	.05
☐ 8 Dwight Gooden NL Pitcher April	.40	.20	.04
☐ 9 Johnny Ray NL Player April	.06	.03	.00
☐ 10 Reggie Jackson Eclipses Mantle HR Record	.40	.20	.04
☐ 11 Wade Boggs First Five Hit Game of Career	.65	.30	.06
☐ 12 Don Aase AL Pitcher May	.06	.03	.00
☐ 13 Wade Boggs AL Player May	.65	.30	.06
☐ 14 Jeff Reardon NL Pitcher May	.06	.03	.00
☐ 15 Hubie Brooks NL Player May	.06	.03	.00
☐ 16 Don Sutton Notches 300th	.10	.05	.01
☐ 17 Roger Clemens Starts 14-0	.50	.25	.05
☐ 18 Roger Clemens AL Pitcher June	.50	.25	.05
☐ 19 Kent Hrbek AL Player June	.15	.07	.01
☐ 20 Rick Rhoden NL Pitcher June	.06	.03	.00
☐ 21 Kevin Bass NL Player June	.06	.03	.00
☐ 22 Bob Horner Blasts four HRs in one Game	.10	.05	.01
☐ 23 Wally Joyner Starting All-Star Rookie	.50	.25	.05
☐ 24 Darryl Strawberry Starts Third Straight All-Star Game	.60	.30	.06
☐ 25 Fernando Valenzuela Ties All-Star Game Record	.15	.07	.01
☐ 26 Roger Clemens All-Star Game MVP	.50	.25	.05
☐ 27 Jack Morris AL Pitcher July	.10	.05	.01
☐ 28 Scott Fletcher AL Player July	.06	.03	.00
☐ 29 Todd Worrell NL Pitcher July	.10	.05	.01
☐ 30 Eric Davis NL Player July	.65	.30	.06
☐ 31 Bert Blyleven Records 3000th Strikeout	.15	.07	.01
☐ 32 Bobby Doerr '86 HOF Inductee	.15	.07	.01
☐ 33 Ernie Lombardi '86 HOF Inductee	.15	.07	.01
☐ 34 Willie McCovey '86 HOF Inductee	.25	.12	.02
☐ 35 Steve Carlton Notches 4000th K	.25	.12	.02
☐ 36 Mike Schmidt Surpasses DiMaggio Record	.75	.35	.07
☐ 37 Juan Samuel Records 3rd "Quadruple Double"	.10	.05	.01
☐ 38 Mike Witt AL Pitcher August	.06	.03	.00
☐ 39 Doug DeCinces AL Player August	.06	.03	.00
☐ 40 Bill Gullickson NL Pitcher August	.06	.03	.00
☐ 41 Dale Murphy NL Player August	.30	.15	.03
☐ 42 Joe Carter Sets Tribe Offensive Record	.15	.07	.01
☐ 43 Bo Jackson Longest HR in Royals Stadium	2.50	1.25	.25
☐ 44 Joe Cowley Majors 1st No- Hitter in 2 Years	.06	.03	.00
☐ 45 Jim Deshaies Sets ML Strikeout Record	.06	.03	.00
☐ 46 Mike Scott No Hitter Clinches Division	.15	.07	.01
☐ 47 Bruce Hurst AL Pitcher September	.10	.05	.01
☐ 48 Don Mattingly AL Player September	1.00	.50	.10
☐ 49 Mike Krukow NL Pitcher September	.06	.03	.00
☐ 50 Steve Sax NL Player September	.15	.07	.01
☐ 51 John Cangelosi AL Rookie Steals Record	.10	.05	.01
☐ 52 Dave Righetti ML Save Mark	.10	.05	.01
☐ 53 Don Mattingly Yankee Record for Hits and Doubles	1.25	.60	.12
☐ 54 Todd Worrell Donruss NL ROY	.15	.07	.01
☐ 55 Jose Canseco Donruss AL ROY	2.00	1.00	.20
☐ 56 Checklist Card	.06	.01	.00

1987 Donruss

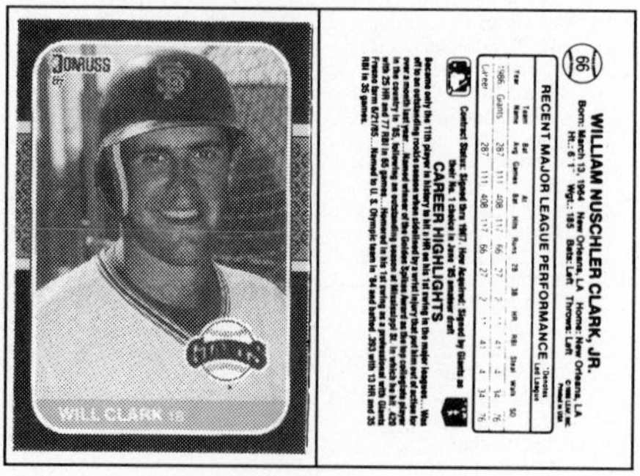

This 660-card set was distributed along with a puzzle of Roberto Clemente. The checklist cards are numbered throughout the set as multiples of 100. The wax pack boxes again contain four separate cards printed on the bottom of the box. Cards measure 2 1/2" by 3 1/2" and feature a black and gold border on the front; the backs are also done in black and gold on white card stock. The popular Diamond King subset returns for the sixth consecutive year. Some of the Diamond King (1-26) selections are repeats from prior years; Perez-Steele Galleries has indicated that a five-year rotation will be maintained in order to avoid depleting the pool of available worthy "kings" on some of the teams. Three of the Diamond Kings have a variation (on the reverse) where the yellow strip behind the words "Donruss Diamond Kings" is not printed and, hence, the background is white. The key rookie cards in this set are Barry Bonds, Bobby Bonilla, Will Clark, David Cone, Mike Greenwell, Bo Jackson, Barry Larkin, Dave Magadan, Kevin Mitchell, Rafael Palmiero, and Ruben Sierra. The backs of the cards in the factory sets are oriented differently than cards taken from wax packs, giving the appearance that one version or the other is upside down when sorting from the card backs.

	MINT	EXC	G-VG
COMPLETE SET (660)	80.00	40.00	8.00
COMMON PLAYER (1-660)	.04	.02	.00
☐ 1 Wally Joyner DK	.60	.15	.03
☐ 2 Roger Clemens DK	.65	.30	.06
☐ 3 Dale Murphy DK	.35	.17	.03
☐ 4 Darryl Strawberry DK	.50	.25	.05
☐ 5 Ozzie Smith DK	.15	.07	.01
☐ 6 Jose Canseco DK	1.50	.75	.15
☐ 7 Charlie Hough DK	.07	.03	.01
☐ 8 Brook Jacoby DK	.07	.03	.01
☐ 9 Fred Lynn DK	.12	.06	.01
☐ 10 Rick Rhoden DK	.07	.03	.01
☐ 11 Chris Brown DK	.07	.03	.01
☐ 12 Von Hayes DK	.10	.05	.01
☐ 13 Jack Morris DK	.12	.06	.01
☐ 14A Kevin McReynolds DK (yellow strip missing on back)	1.00	.50	.10
☐ 14B Kevin McReynolds DK	.25	.12	.02
☐ 15 George Brett DK	.40	.20	.04
☐ 16 Ted Higuera DK	.12	.06	.01
☐ 17 Hubie Brooks DK	.07	.03	.01
☐ 18 Mike Scott DK	.12	.06	.01
☐ 19 Kirby Puckett DK	.50	.25	.05
☐ 20 Dave Winfield DK	.25	.12	.02
☐ 21 Lloyd Moseby DK	.07	.03	.01
☐ 22A Eric Davis DK (yellow strip missing on back)	3.00	1.50	.30
☐ 22B Eric Davis DK	1.00	.50	.10
☐ 23 Jim Presley DK	.07	.03	.01
☐ 24 Keith Moreland DK	.07	.03	.01
☐ 25A Greg Walker DK (yellow strip missing on back)	.75	.35	.07
☐ 25B Greg Walker DK	.10	.05	.01
☐ 26 Steve Sax DK	.12	.06	.01
☐ 27 DK Checklist 1-26	.07	.01	.00
☐ 28 B.J. Surhoff RR	.45	.22	.04
☐ 29 Randy Myers RR	.75	.35	.07
☐ 30 Ken Gerhart RR	.07	.03	.01
☐ 31 Benito Santiago RR	2.50	1.25	.25
☐ 32 Greg Swindell RR	1.10	.55	.11
☐ 33 Mike Birkbeck RR	.10	.05	.01
☐ 34 Terry Steinbach RR	.75	.35	.07
☐ 35 Bo Jackson RR	12.00	6.00	1.20
☐ 36 Greg Maddux RR	1.50	.75	.15
☐ 37 Jim Lindeman RR	.07	.03	.01
☐ 38 Devon White RR	.75	.35	.07
☐ 39 Eric Bell RR	.07	.03	.01
☐ 40 Willie Fraser RR	.07	.03	.01
☐ 41 Jerry Browne RR	.35	.17	.03
☐ 42 Chris James RR	1.00	.50	.10
☐ 43 Rafael Palmeiro RR	3.25	1.60	.32
☐ 44 Pat Dodson RR	.07	.03	.01
☐ 45 Duane Ward RR	.18	.09	.01
☐ 46 Mark McGwire RR	8.00	4.00	.80
☐ 47 Bruce Fields RR (photo actually Darnell Coles)	.07	.03	.01
☐ 48 Eddie Murray	.30	.15	.03
☐ 49 Ted Higuera	.15	.07	.01
☐ 50 Kirk Gibson	.20	.10	.02
☐ 51 Oil Can Boyd	.07	.03	.01
☐ 52 Don Mattingly	2.00	1.00	.20
☐ 53 Pedro Guerrero	.15	.07	.01
☐ 54 George Brett	.50	.25	.05
☐ 55 Jose Rijo	.12	.06	.01
☐ 56 Tim Raines	.25	.12	.02
☐ 57 Ed Correa	.10	.05	.01
☐ 58 Mike Witt	.07	.03	.01
☐ 59 Greg Walker	.07	.03	.01
☐ 60 Ozzie Smith	.25	.12	.02
☐ 61 Glenn Davis	.35	.17	.03
☐ 62 Glenn Wilson	.04	.02	.00
☐ 63 Tom Browning	.10	.05	.01
☐ 64 Tony Gwynn	.50	.25	.05
☐ 65 R.J. Reynolds	.04	.02	.00
☐ 66 Will Clark	10.00	5.00	1.00
☐ 67 Ozzie Virgil	.04	.02	.00
☐ 68 Rick Sutcliffe	.10	.05	.01
☐ 69 Gary Carter	.20	.10	.02
☐ 70 Mike Moore	.07	.03	.01
☐ 71 Bert Blyleven	.12	.06	.01
☐ 72 Tony Fernandez	.15	.07	.01
☐ 73 Kent Hrbek	.15	.07	.01
☐ 74 Lloyd Moseby	.07	.03	.01
☐ 75 Alvin Davis	.12	.06	.01
☐ 76 Keith Hernandez	.20	.10	.02
☐ 77 Ryne Sandberg	.80	.40	.08
☐ 78 Dale Murphy	.35	.17	.03
☐ 79 Sid Bream	.04	.02	.00
☐ 80 Chris Brown	.04	.02	.00
☐ 81 Steve Garvey	.25	.12	.02
☐ 82 Mario Soto	.04	.02	.00
☐ 83 Shane Rawley	.04	.02	.00
☐ 84 Willie McGee	.15	.07	.01
☐ 85 Jose Cruz	.07	.03	.01
☐ 86 Brian Downing	.07	.03	.01
☐ 87 Ozzie Guillen	.25	.12	.02
☐ 88 Hubie Brooks	.10	.05	.01
☐ 89 Cal Ripken	.40	.20	.04
☐ 90 Juan Nieves	.04	.02	.00
☐ 91 Lance Parrish	.10	.05	.01
☐ 92 Jim Rice	.15	.07	.01
☐ 93 Ron Guidry	.12	.06	.01
☐ 94 Fernando Valenzuela	.18	.09	.01
☐ 95 Andy Allanson	.07	.03	.01
☐ 96 Willie Wilson	.10	.05	.01
☐ 97 Jose Canseco	10.00	5.00	1.00
☐ 98 Jeff Reardon	.10	.05	.01
☐ 99 Bobby Witt	.90	.45	.09
☐ 100 Checklist Card	.07	.01	.00
☐ 101 Jose Guzman	.04	.02	.00
☐ 102 Steve Balboni	.04	.02	.00
☐ 103 Tony Phillips	.04	.02	.00
☐ 104 Brook Jacoby	.07	.03	.01
☐ 105 Dave Winfield	.30	.15	.03
☐ 106 Orel Hershiser	.35	.17	.03
☐ 107 Lou Whitaker	.12	.06	.01
☐ 108 Fred Lynn	.12	.06	.01
☐ 109 Bill Wegman	.04	.02	.00
☐ 110 Donnie Moore	.04	.02	.00
☐ 111 Jack Clark	.18	.09	.01
☐ 112 Bob Knepper	.04	.02	.00
☐ 113 Von Hayes	.10	.05	.01
☐ 114 Bip Roberts	.40	.20	.04
☐ 115 Tony Pena	.10	.05	.01
☐ 116 Scott Garrelts	.07	.03	.01
☐ 117 Paul Molitor	.12	.06	.01
☐ 118 Darryl Strawberry	.90	.45	.09

☐ 119 Shawon Dunston	.35	.17	.03
☐ 120 Jim Presley	.07	.03	.01
☐ 121 Jesse Barfield	.12	.06	.01
☐ 122 Gary Gaetti	.15	.07	.01
☐ 123 Kurt Stillwell	.45	.22	.04
☐ 124 Joel Davis	.04	.02	.00
☐ 125 Mike Boddicker	.07	.03	.01
☐ 126 Robin Yount	.40	.20	.04
☐ 127 Alan Trammell	.20	.10	.02
☐ 128 Dave Righetti	.10	.05	.01
☐ 129 Dwight Evans	.15	.07	.01
☐ 130 Mike Scioscia	.04	.02	.00
☐ 131 Julio Franco	.15	.07	.01
☐ 132 Bret Saberhagen	.30	.15	.03
☐ 133 Mike Davis	.04	.02	.00
☐ 134 Joe Hesketh	.04	.02	.00
☐ 135 Wally Joyner	1.25	.60	.12
☐ 136 Don Slaught	.04	.02	.00
☐ 137 Daryl Boston	.07	.03	.01
☐ 138 Nolan Ryan	1.25	.60	.12
☐ 139 Mike Schmidt	.80	.40	.08
☐ 140 Tommy Herr	.07	.03	.01
☐ 141 Garry Templeton	.07	.03	.01
☐ 142 Kal Daniels	.75	.35	.07
☐ 143 Billy Sample	.04	.02	.00
☐ 144 Johnny Ray	.07	.03	.01
☐ 145 Rob Thompson	.30	.15	.03
☐ 146 Bob Dernier	.04	.02	.00
☐ 147 Danny Tartabull	.15	.07	.01
☐ 148 Ernie Whitt	.04	.02	.00
☐ 149 Kirby Puckett	1.75	.85	.17
☐ 150 Mike Young	.04	.02	.00
☐ 151 Ernest Riles	.04	.02	.00
☐ 152 Frank Tanana	.07	.03	.01
☐ 153 Rich Gedman	.04	.02	.00
☐ 154 Willie Randolph	.07	.03	.01
☐ 155 Bill Madlock	.07	.03	.01
☐ 156 Joe Carter	.30	.15	.03
☐ 157 Danny Jackson	.07	.03	.01
☐ 158 Carney Lansford	.10	.05	.01
☐ 159 Bryn Smith	.07	.03	.01
☐ 160 Gary Pettis	.04	.02	.00
☐ 161 Oddibe McDowell	.10	.05	.01
☐ 162 John Cangelosi	.07	.03	.01
☐ 163 Mike Scott	.18	.09	.01
☐ 164 Eric Show	.04	.02	.00
☐ 165 Juan Samuel	.12	.06	.01
☐ 166 Nick Esasky	.10	.05	.01
☐ 167 Zane Smith	.10	.05	.01
☐ 168 Mike Brown	.04	.02	.00
(Pirates OF)			
☐ 169 Keith Moreland	.04	.02	.00
☐ 170 John Tudor	.10	.05	.01
☐ 171 Ken Dixon	.04	.02	.00
☐ 172 Jim Gantner	.04	.02	.00
☐ 173 Jack Morris	.12	.06	.01
☐ 174 Bruce Hurst	.12	.06	.01
☐ 175 Dennis Rasmussen	.07	.03	.01
☐ 176 Mike Marshall	.10	.05	.01
☐ 177 Dan Quisenberry	.10	.05	.01
☐ 178 Eric Plunk	.07	.03	.01
☐ 179 Tim Wallach	.10	.05	.01
☐ 180 Steve Buechele	.04	.02	.00
☐ 181 Don Sutton	.15	.07	.01
☐ 182 Dave Schmidt	.04	.02	.00
☐ 183 Terry Pendleton	.07	.03	.01
☐ 184 Jim Deshaies	.25	.12	.02
☐ 185 Steve Bedrosian	.12	.06	.01
☐ 186 Pete Rose	.60	.30	.06
☐ 187 Dave Dravecky	.10	.05	.01
☐ 188 Rick Reuschel	.10	.05	.01
☐ 189 Dan Gladden	.07	.03	.01
☐ 190 Rick Mahler	.04	.02	.00
☐ 191 Thad Bosley	.04	.02	.00
☐ 192 Ron Darling	.15	.07	.01
☐ 193 Matt Young	.04	.02	.00
☐ 194 Tom Brunansky	.12	.06	.01
☐ 195 Dave Stieb	.12	.06	.01
☐ 196 Frank Viola	.30	.15	.03
☐ 197 Tom Henke	.07	.03	.01
☐ 198 Karl Best	.04	.02	.00
☐ 199 Dwight Gooden	.85	.40	.08
☐ 200 Checklist Card	.07	.01	.00
☐ 201 Steve Trout	.04	.02	.00
☐ 202 Rafael Ramirez	.04	.02	.00
☐ 203 Bob Walk	.04	.02	.00
☐ 204 Roger Mason	.04	.02	.00
☐ 205 Terry Kennedy	.04	.02	.00
☐ 206 Ron Oester	.04	.02	.00
☐ 207 John Russell	.04	.02	.00
☐ 208 Greg Mathews	.10	.05	.01
☐ 209 Charlie Kerfeld	.04	.02	.00
☐ 210 Reggie Jackson	.50	.25	.05
☐ 211 Floyd Bannister	.04	.02	.00
☐ 212 Vance Law	.04	.02	.00
☐ 213 Rich Bordi	.04	.02	.00
☐ 214 Dan Plesac	.25	.12	.02
☐ 215 Dave Collins	.04	.02	.00
☐ 216 Bob Stanley	.04	.02	.00
☐ 217 Joe Niekro	.07	.03	.01
☐ 218 Tom Niedenfuer	.04	.02	.00
☐ 219 Brett Butler	.10	.05	.01
☐ 220 Charlie Leibrandt	.04	.02	.00
☐ 221 Steve Ontiveros	.04	.02	.00
☐ 222 Tim Burke	.07	.03	.01
☐ 223 Curtis Wilkerson	.04	.02	.00
☐ 224 Pete Incaviglia	.90	.45	.09
☐ 225 Lonnie Smith	.07	.03	.01
☐ 226 Chris Codiroli	.04	.02	.00
☐ 227 Scott Bailes	.10	.05	.01
☐ 228 Rickey Henderson	.80	.40	.08
☐ 229 Ken Howell	.04	.02	.00
☐ 230 Darnell Coles	.04	.02	.00
☐ 231 Don Aase	.04	.02	.00
☐ 232 Tim Leary	.10	.05	.01
☐ 233 Bob Boone	.10	.05	.01
☐ 234 Ricky Horton	.04	.02	.00
☐ 235 Mark Bailey	.04	.02	.00
☐ 236 Kevin Gross	.04	.02	.00
☐ 237 Lance McCullers	.04	.02	.00
☐ 238 Cecilio Guante	.04	.02	.00
☐ 239 Bob Melvin	.04	.02	.00
☐ 240 Billy Jo Robidoux	.04	.02	.00
☐ 241 Roger McDowell	.07	.03	.01
☐ 242 Leon Durham	.04	.02	.00
☐ 243 Ed Nunez	.04	.02	.00
☐ 244 Jimmy Key	.10	.05	.01
☐ 245 Mike Smithson	.04	.02	.00
☐ 246 Bo Diaz	.04	.02	.00
☐ 247 Carlton Fisk	.25	.12	.02
☐ 248 Larry Sheets	.07	.03	.01
☐ 249 Juan Castillo	.04	.02	.00
☐ 250 Eric King	.25	.12	.02
☐ 251 Doug Drabek	1.25	.60	.12
☐ 252 Wade Boggs	1.00	.50	.10
☐ 253 Mariano Duncan	.04	.02	.00
☐ 254 Pat Tabler	.07	.03	.01
☐ 255 Frank White	.07	.03	.01
☐ 256 Alfredo Griffin	.04	.02	.00
☐ 257 Floyd Youmans	.04	.02	.00
☐ 258 Rob Wilfong	.04	.02	.00
☐ 259 Pete O'Brien	.07	.03	.01
☐ 260 Tim Hulett	.04	.02	.00
☐ 261 Dickie Thon	.04	.02	.00
☐ 262 Darren Daulton	.10	.05	.01
☐ 263 Vince Coleman	.40	.20	.04
☐ 264 Andy Hawkins	.04	.02	.00
☐ 265 Eric Davis	1.25	.60	.12
☐ 266 Andres Thomas	.15	.07	.01
☐ 267 Mike Diaz	.07	.03	.01
☐ 268 Chili Davis	.07	.03	.01
☐ 269 Jody Davis	.04	.02	.00
☐ 270 Phil Bradley	.07	.03	.01
☐ 271 George Bell	.30	.15	.03
☐ 272 Keith Atherton	.04	.02	.00
☐ 273 Storm Davis	.07	.03	.01
☐ 274 Rob Deer	.20	.10	.02
☐ 275 Walt Terrell	.04	.02	.00
☐ 276 Roger Clemens	1.75	.85	.17
☐ 277 Mike Easler	.04	.02	.00
☐ 278 Steve Sax	.15	.07	.01
☐ 279 Andre Thornton	.07	.03	.01
☐ 280 Jim Sundberg	.04	.02	.00
☐ 281 Bill Bathe	.04	.02	.00
☐ 282 Jay Tibbs	.04	.02	.00
☐ 283 Dick Schofield	.04	.02	.00
☐ 284 Mike Mason	.04	.02	.00
☐ 285 Jerry Hairston	.04	.02	.00
☐ 286 Bill Doran	.07	.03	.01
☐ 287 Tim Flannery	.04	.02	.00
☐ 288 Gary Redus	.04	.02	.00
☐ 289 John Franco	.10	.05	.01
☐ 290 Paul Assenmacher	.04	.02	.00
☐ 291 Joe Orsulak	.04	.02	.00
☐ 292 Lee Smith	.07	.03	.01
☐ 293 Mike Laga	.04	.02	.00
☐ 294 Rick Dempsey	.04	.02	.00
☐ 295 Mike Felder	.07	.03	.01
☐ 296 Tom Brookens	.04	.02	.00
☐ 297 Al Nipper	.04	.02	.00
☐ 298 Mike Pagliarulo	.07	.03	.01
☐ 299 Franklin Stubbs	.10	.05	.01
☐ 300 Checklist Card	.07	.01	.00
☐ 301 Steve Farr	.07	.03	.01
☐ 302 Bill Mooneyham	.07	.03	.01
☐ 303 Andres Galarraga	.25	.12	.02
☐ 304 Scott Fletcher	.04	.02	.00
☐ 305 Jack Howell	.04	.02	.00

☐ 306	Russ Morman	.07	.03	.01
☐ 307	Todd Worrell	.12	.06	.01
☐ 308	Dave Smith	.07	.03	.01
☐ 309	Jeff Stone	.04	.02	.00
☐ 310	Ron Robinson	.04	.02	.00
☐ 311	Bruce Bochy	.04	.02	.00
☐ 312	Jim Winn	.04	.02	.00
☐ 313	Mark Davis	.10	.05	.01
☐ 314	Jeff Dedmon	.04	.02	.00
☐ 315	Jamie Moyer	.10	.05	.01
☐ 316	Wally Backman	.04	.02	.00
☐ 317	Ken Phelps	.07	.03	.01
☐ 318	Steve Lombardozzi	.04	.02	.00
☐ 319	Rance Mulliniks	.04	.02	.00
☐ 320	Tim Laudner	.04	.02	.00
☐ 321	Mark Eichhorn	.07	.03	.01
☐ 322	Lee Guetterman	.12	.06	.01
☐ 323	Sid Fernandez	.12	.06	.01
☐ 324	Jerry Mumphrey	.04	.02	.00
☐ 325	David Palmer	.04	.02	.00
☐ 326	Bill Almon	.04	.02	.00
☐ 327	Candy Maldonado	.10	.05	.01
☐ 328	John Kruk	.35	.17	.03
☐ 329	John Denny	.04	.02	.00
☐ 330	Milt Thompson	.07	.03	.01
☐ 331	Mike LaValliere	.20	.10	.02
☐ 332	Alan Ashby	.04	.02	.00
☐ 333	Doug Corbett	.04	.02	.00
☐ 334	Ron Karkovice	.07	.03	.01
☐ 335	Mitch Webster	.04	.02	.00
☐ 336	Lee Lacy	.04	.02	.00
☐ 337	Glenn Braggs	.60	.30	.06
☐ 338	Dwight Lowry	.07	.03	.01
☐ 339	Don Baylor	.07	.03	.01
☐ 340	Brian Fisher	.04	.02	.00
☐ 341	Reggie Williams	.07	.03	.01
☐ 342	Tom Candiotti	.07	.03	.01
☐ 343	Rudy Law	.04	.02	.00
☐ 344	Curt Young	.04	.02	.00
☐ 345	Mike Fitzgerald	.04	.02	.00
☐ 346	Ruben Sierra	7.00	3.50	.70
☐ 347	Mitch Williams	.35	.17	.03
☐ 348	Jorge Orta	.04	.02	.00
☐ 349	Mickey Tettleton	.12	.06	.01
☐ 350	Ernie Camacho	.04	.02	.00
☐ 351	Ron Kittle	.10	.05	.01
☐ 352	Ken Landreaux	.04	.02	.00
☐ 353	Chet Lemon	.04	.02	.00
☐ 354	John Shelby	.04	.02	.00
☐ 355	Mark Clear	.04	.02	.00
☐ 356	Doug DeCinces	.07	.03	.01
☐ 357	Ken Dayley	.04	.02	.00
☐ 358	Phil Garner	.04	.02	.00
☐ 359	Steve Jeltz	.04	.02	.00
☐ 360	Ed Whitson	.07	.03	.01
☐ 361	Barry Bonds	7.00	3.50	.70
☐ 362	Vida Blue	.07	.03	.01
☐ 363	Cecil Cooper	.07	.03	.01
☐ 364	Bob Ojeda	.07	.03	.01
☐ 365	Dennis Eckersley	.15	.07	.01
☐ 366	Mike Morgan	.07	.03	.01
☐ 367	Willie Upshaw	.04	.02	.00
☐ 368	Allan Anderson	.30	.15	.03
☐ 369	Bill Gullickson	.04	.02	.00
☐ 370	Bobby Thigpen	1.00	.50	.10
☐ 371	Juan Beniquez	.04	.02	.00
☐ 372	Charlie Moore	.04	.02	.00
☐ 373	Dan Petry	.04	.02	.00
☐ 374	Rod Scurry	.04	.02	.00
☐ 375	Tom Seaver	.35	.17	.03
☐ 376	Ed VandeBerg	.04	.02	.00
☐ 377	Tony Bernazard	.04	.02	.00
☐ 378	Greg Pryor	.04	.02	.00
☐ 379	Dwayne Murphy	.04	.02	.00
☐ 380	Andy McGaffigan	.04	.02	.00
☐ 381	Kirk McCaskill	.04	.02	.00
☐ 382	Greg Harris	.04	.02	.00
☐ 383	Rich Dotson	.04	.02	.00
☐ 384	Craig Reynolds	.04	.02	.00
☐ 385	Greg Gross	.04	.02	.00
☐ 386	Tito Landrum	.04	.02	.00
☐ 387	Craig Lefferts	.04	.02	.00
☐ 388	Dave Parker	.15	.07	.01
☐ 389	Bob Horner	.10	.05	.01
☐ 390	Pat Clements	.04	.02	.00
☐ 391	Jeff Leonard	.07	.03	.01
☐ 392	Chris Speier	.04	.02	.00
☐ 393	John Moses	.04	.02	.00
☐ 394	Garth Iorg	.04	.02	.00
☐ 395	Greg Gagne	.04	.02	.00
☐ 396	Nate Snell	.04	.02	.00
☐ 397	Bryan Clutterbuck	.04	.02	.00
☐ 398	Darrell Evans	.07	.03	.01
☐ 399	Steve Crawford	.04	.02	.00
☐ 400	Checklist Card	.07	.01	.00
☐ 401	Phil Lombardi	.10	.05	.01
☐ 402	Rick Honeycutt	.04	.02	.00
☐ 403	Ken Schrom	.04	.02	.00
☐ 404	Bud Black	.07	.03	.01
☐ 405	Donnie Hill	.04	.02	.00
☐ 406	Wayne Krenchicki	.04	.02	.00
☐ 407	Chuck Finley	1.50	.75	.15
☐ 408	Toby Harrah	.04	.02	.00
☐ 409	Steve Lyons	.04	.02	.00
☐ 410	Kevin Bass	.07	.03	.01
☐ 411	Marvell Wynne	.04	.02	.00
☐ 412	Ron Roenicke	.04	.02	.00
☐ 413	Tracy Jones	.15	.07	.01
☐ 414	Gene Garber	.04	.02	.00
☐ 415	Mike Bielecki	.10	.05	.01
☐ 416	Frank DiPino	.04	.02	.00
☐ 417	Andy Van Slyke	.20	.10	.02
☐ 418	Jim Dwyer	.04	.02	.00
☐ 419	Ben Oglivie	.07	.03	.01
☐ 420	Dave Bergman	.04	.02	.00
☐ 421	Joe Sambito	.04	.02	.00
☐ 422	Bob Tewksbury	.10	.05	.01
☐ 423	Len Matuszek	.04	.02	.00
☐ 424	Mike Kingery	.10	.05	.01
☐ 425	Dave Kingman	.10	.05	.01
☐ 426	Al Newman	.07	.03	.01
☐ 427	Gary Ward	.04	.02	.00
☐ 428	Ruppert Jones	.04	.02	.00
☐ 429	Harold Baines	.10	.05	.01
☐ 430	Pat Perry	.04	.02	.00
☐ 431	Terry Puhl	.04	.02	.00
☐ 432	Don Carman	.04	.02	.00
☐ 433	Eddie Milner	.04	.02	.00
☐ 434	LaMarr Hoyt	.07	.03	.01
☐ 435	Rick Rhoden	.04	.02	.00
☐ 436	Jose Uribe	.04	.02	.00
☐ 437	Ken Oberkfell	.04	.02	.00
☐ 438	Ron Davis	.04	.02	.00
☐ 439	Jesse Orosco	.04	.02	.00
☐ 440	Scott Bradley	.04	.02	.00
☐ 441	Randy Bush	.04	.02	.00
☐ 442	John Cerutti	.15	.07	.01
☐ 443	Roy Smalley	.04	.02	.00
☐ 444	Kelly Gruber	2.25	1.10	.22
☐ 445	Bob Kearney	.04	.02	.00
☐ 446	Ed Hearn	.04	.02	.00
☐ 447	Scott Sanderson	.07	.03	.01
☐ 448	Bruce Benedict	.04	.02	.00
☐ 449	Junior Ortiz	.04	.02	.00
☐ 450	Mike Aldrete	.10	.05	.01
☐ 451	Kevin McReynolds	.25	.12	.02
☐ 452	Rob Murphy	.15	.07	.01
☐ 453	Kent Tekulve	.04	.02	.00
☐ 454	Curt Ford	.04	.02	.00
☐ 455	Dave Lopes	.07	.03	.01
☐ 456	Bob Grich	.07	.03	.01
☐ 457	Jose DeLeon	.04	.02	.00
☐ 458	Andre Dawson	.40	.20	.04
☐ 459	Mike Flanagan	.07	.03	.01
☐ 460	Joey Meyer	.18	.09	.01
☐ 461	Chuck Cary	.12	.06	.01
☐ 462	Bill Buckner	.07	.03	.01
☐ 463	Bob Shirley	.04	.02	.00
☐ 464	Jeff Hamilton	.18	.09	.01
☐ 465	Phil Niekro	.15	.07	.01
☐ 466	Mark Gubicza	.10	.05	.01
☐ 467	Jerry Willard	.04	.02	.00
☐ 468	Bob Sebra	.07	.03	.01
☐ 469	Larry Parrish	.04	.02	.00
☐ 470	Charlie Hough	.04	.02	.00
☐ 471	Hal McRae	.07	.03	.01
☐ 472	Dave Leiper	.07	.03	.01
☐ 473	Mel Hall	.10	.05	.01
☐ 474	Dan Pasqua	.07	.03	.01
☐ 475	Bob Welch	.12	.06	.01
☐ 476	Johnny Grubb	.04	.02	.00
☐ 477	Jim Traber	.04	.02	.00
☐ 478	Chris Bosio	.30	.15	.03
☐ 479	Mark McLemore	.04	.02	.00
☐ 480	John Morris	.04	.02	.00
☐ 481	Billy Hatcher	.10	.05	.01
☐ 482	Dan Schatzeder	.04	.02	.00
☐ 483	Rich Gossage	.10	.05	.01
☐ 484	Jim Morrison	.04	.02	.00
☐ 485	Bob Brenly	.04	.02	.00
☐ 486	Bill Schroeder	.04	.02	.00
☐ 487	Mookie Wilson	.07	.03	.01
☐ 488	Dave Martinez	.20	.10	.02
☐ 489	Harold Reynolds	.07	.03	.01
☐ 490	Jeff Hearron	.04	.02	.00
☐ 491	Mickey Hatcher	.04	.02	.00
☐ 492	Barry Larkin	4.50	2.25	.45
☐ 493	Bob James	.04	.02	.00

☐ 494	John Habyan	.04	.02	.00
☐ 495	Jim Adduci	.07	.03	.01
☐ 496	Mike Heath	.04	.02	.00
☐ 497	Tim Stoddard	.04	.02	.00
☐ 498	Tony Armas	.07	.03	.01
☐ 499	Dennis Powell	.04	.02	.00
☐ 500	Checklist Card	.07	.01	.00
☐ 501	Chris Bando	.04	.02	.00
☐ 502	David Cone	3.00	1.50	.30
☐ 503	Jay Howell	.04	.02	.00
☐ 504	Tom Foley	.04	.02	.00
☐ 505	Ray Chadwick	.04	.02	.00
☐ 506	Mike Loynd	.04	.02	.00
☐ 507	Neil Allen	.04	.02	.00
☐ 508	Danny Darwin	.07	.03	.01
☐ 509	Rick Schu	.04	.02	.00
☐ 510	Jose Oquendo	.04	.02	.00
☐ 511	Gene Walter	.04	.02	.00
☐ 512	Terry McGriff	.10	.05	.01
☐ 513	Ken Griffey	.12	.06	.01
☐ 514	Benny Distefano	.04	.02	.00
☐ 515	Terry Mulholland	.25	.12	.02
☐ 516	Ed Lynch	.04	.02	.00
☐ 517	Bill Swift	.07	.03	.01
☐ 518	Manny Lee	.07	.03	.01
☐ 519	Andre David	.04	.02	.00
☐ 520	Scott McGregor	.07	.03	.01
☐ 521	Rick Manning	.04	.02	.00
☐ 522	Willie Hernandez	.07	.03	.01
☐ 523	Marty Barrett	.07	.03	.01
☐ 524	Wayne Tolleson	.04	.02	.00
☐ 525	Jose Gonzalez	.18	.09	.01
☐ 526	Cory Snyder	.40	.20	.04
☐ 527	Buddy Biancalana	.04	.02	.00
☐ 528	Moose Haas	.04	.02	.00
☐ 529	Wilfredo Tejada	.04	.02	.00
☐ 530	Stu Cliburn	.04	.02	.00
☐ 531	Dale Mohorcic	.10	.05	.01
☐ 532	Ron Hassey	.04	.02	.00
☐ 533	Ty Gainey	.04	.02	.00
☐ 534	Jerry Royster	.04	.02	.00
☐ 535	Mike Maddux	.10	.05	.01
☐ 536	Ted Power	.04	.02	.00
☐ 537	Ted Simmons	.10	.05	.01
☐ 538	Rafael Belliard	.07	.03	.01
☐ 539	Chico Walker	.04	.02	.00
☐ 540	Bob Forsch	.04	.02	.00
☐ 541	John Stefero	.04	.02	.00
☐ 542	Dale Sveum	.12	.06	.01
☐ 543	Mark Thurmond	.04	.02	.00
☐ 544	Jeff Sellers	.10	.05	.01
☐ 545	Joel Skinner	.04	.02	.00
☐ 546	Alex Trevino	.04	.02	.00
☐ 547	Randy Kutcher	.04	.02	.00
☐ 548	Joaquin Andujar	.04	.02	.00
☐ 549	Casey Candaele	.07	.03	.01
☐ 550	Jeff Russell	.07	.03	.01
☐ 551	John Candelaria	.07	.03	.01
☐ 552	Joe Cowley	.04	.02	.00
☐ 553	Danny Cox	.07	.03	.01
☐ 554	Denny Walling	.04	.02	.00
☐ 555	Bruce Ruffin	.12	.06	.01
☐ 556	Buddy Bell	.07	.03	.01
☐ 557	Jimmy Jones	.12	.06	.01
☐ 558	Bobby Bonilla	5.00	2.50	.50
☐ 559	Jeff Robinson (Giants pitcher)	.07	.03	.01
☐ 560	Ed Olwine	.04	.02	.00
☐ 561	Glenallen Hill	1.00	.50	.10
☐ 562	Lee Mazzilli	.04	.02	.00
☐ 563	Mike Brown (pitcher)	.04	.02	.00
☐ 564	George Frazier	.04	.02	.00
☐ 565	Mike Sharperson	.07	.03	.01
☐ 566	Mark Portugal	.15	.07	.01
☐ 567	Rick Leach	.04	.02	.00
☐ 568	Mark Langston	.20	.10	.02
☐ 569	Rafael Santana	.04	.02	.00
☐ 570	Manny Trillo	.04	.02	.00
☐ 571	Cliff Speck	.04	.02	.00
☐ 572	Bob Kipper	.04	.02	.00
☐ 573	Kelly Downs	.20	.10	.02
☐ 574	Randy Asadoor	.04	.02	.00
☐ 575	Dave Magadan	2.25	1.10	.22
☐ 576	Marvin Freeman	.10	.05	.01
☐ 577	Jeff Lahti	.04	.02	.00
☐ 578	Jeff Calhoun	.04	.02	.00
☐ 579	Gus Polidor	.04	.02	.00
☐ 580	Gene Nelson	.04	.02	.00
☐ 581	Tim Teufel	.04	.02	.00
☐ 582	Odell Jones	.04	.02	.00
☐ 583	Mark Ryal	.04	.02	.00
☐ 584	Randy O'Neal	.04	.02	.00
☐ 585	Mike Greenwell	7.00	3.50	.70
☐ 586	Ray Knight	.07	.03	.01
☐ 587	Ralph Bryant	.10	.05	.01
☐ 588	Carmen Castillo	.04	.02	.00
☐ 589	Ed Wojna	.04	.02	.00
☐ 590	Stan Javier	.07	.03	.01
☐ 591	Jeff Musselman	.10	.05	.01
☐ 592	Mike Stanley	.12	.06	.01
☐ 593	Darrell Porter	.04	.02	.00
☐ 594	Drew Hall	.07	.03	.01
☐ 595	Rob Nelson	.15	.07	.01
☐ 596	Bryan Oelkers	.04	.02	.00
☐ 597	Scott Nielsen	.15	.07	.01
☐ 598	Brian Holton	.12	.06	.01
☐ 599	Kevin Mitchell	4.50	2.25	.45
☐ 600	Checklist Card	.07	.01	.00
☐ 601	Jackie Gutierrez	.04	.02	.00
☐ 602	Barry Jones	.35	.17	.03
☐ 603	Jerry Narron	.04	.02	.00
☐ 604	Steve Lake	.04	.02	.00
☐ 605	Jim Pankovits	.04	.02	.00
☐ 606	Ed Romero	.04	.02	.00
☐ 607	Dave LaPoint	.04	.02	.00
☐ 608	Don Robinson	.04	.02	.00
☐ 609	Mike Krukow	.04	.02	.00
☐ 610	Dave Valle	.04	.02	.00
☐ 611	Len Dykstra	.50	.25	.05
☐ 612	Roberto Clemente Puzzle Card	.07	.03	.01
☐ 613	Mike Trujillo	.04	.02	.00
☐ 614	Damaso Garcia	.04	.02	.00
☐ 615	Neal Heaton	.04	.02	.00
☐ 616	Juan Berenguer	.04	.02	.00
☐ 617	Steve Carlton	.25	.12	.02
☐ 618	Gary Lucas	.04	.02	.00
☐ 619	Geno Petralli	.04	.02	.00
☐ 620	Rick Aguilera	.04	.02	.00
☐ 621	Fred McGriff	3.50	1.75	.35
☐ 622	Dave Henderson	.07	.03	.01
☐ 623	Dave Clark	.35	.17	.03
☐ 624	Angel Salazar	.04	.02	.00
☐ 625	Randy Hunt	.04	.02	.00
☐ 626	John Gibbons	.04	.02	.00
☐ 627	Kevin Brown	1.50	.75	.15
☐ 628	Bill Dawley	.04	.02	.00
☐ 629	Aurelio Lopez	.04	.02	.00
☐ 630	Charles Hudson	.04	.02	.00
☐ 631	Ray Soff	.04	.02	.00
☐ 632	Ray Hayward	.04	.02	.00
☐ 633	Spike Owen	.04	.02	.00
☐ 634	Glenn Hubbard	.04	.02	.00
☐ 635	Kevin Elster	.45	.22	.04
☐ 636	Mike LaCoss	.04	.02	.00
☐ 637	Dwayne Henry	.04	.02	.00
☐ 638	Rey Quinones	.07	.03	.01
☐ 639	Jim Clancy	.04	.02	.00
☐ 640	Larry Andersen	.04	.02	.00
☐ 641	Calvin Schiraldi	.07	.03	.01
☐ 642	Stan Jefferson	.12	.06	.01
☐ 643	Marc Sullivan	.04	.02	.00
☐ 644	Mark Grant	.04	.02	.00
☐ 645	Cliff Johnson	.04	.02	.00
☐ 646	Howard Johnson	.30	.15	.03
☐ 647	Dave Sax	.04	.02	.00
☐ 648	Dave Stewart	.30	.15	.03
☐ 649	Danny Heep	.04	.02	.00
☐ 650	Joe Johnson	.04	.02	.00
☐ 651	Bob Brower	.10	.05	.01
☐ 652	Rob Woodward	.04	.02	.00
☐ 653	John Mizerock	.04	.02	.00
☐ 654	Tim Pyznarski	.07	.03	.01
☐ 655	Luis Aquino	.04	.02	.00
☐ 656	Mickey Brantley	.12	.06	.01
☐ 657	Doyle Alexander	.04	.02	.00
☐ 658	Sammy Stewart	.04	.02	.00
☐ 659	Jim Acker	.04	.02	.00
☐ 660	Pete Ladd	.07	.03	.01

1987 Donruss Wax Box Cards

The cards in this 4-card set measure the standard 2 1/2" by 3 1/2". Cards have essentially the same design as the 1987 Donruss regular issue set. The cards were printed on the bottoms of the regular issue wax pack boxes. The four cards (PC10 to PC12 plus a Roberto Clemente puzzle card) are considered a separate set in their own right and are not typically included in a complete set of the regular issue 1987 Donruss cards. The value of the panel uncut is slightly greater, perhaps by 25 percent greater, than the value of the individual cards cut up carefully.

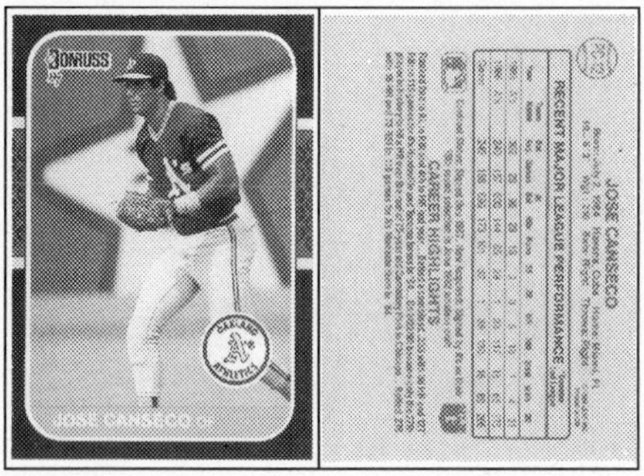

	MINT	EXC	G-VG
COMPLETE SET (4)	2.25	1.10	.22
COMMON PLAYER	.05	.02	.00
☐ PC10 Dale Murphy	.35	.17	.03
☐ PC11 Jeff Reardon	.15	.07	.01
☐ PC12 Jose Canseco	2.00	1.00	.20
☐ PUZ Roberto Clemente (Puzzle Card)	.05	.02	.00

1987 Donruss Super DK's

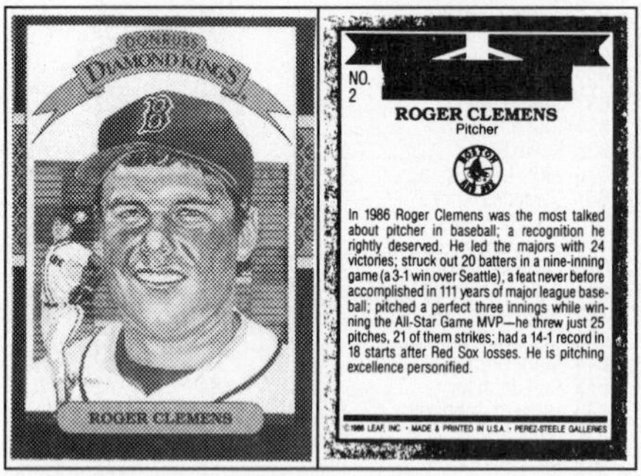

This 28-card set was available through a mail-in offer detailed on the wax packs. The set was sent in return for 8.00 and three wrappers plus 1.50 postage and handling. The set features the popular Diamond King subseries in large (approximately 4 7/8" by 6 13/16") form. Dick Perez of Perez-Steele Galleries did another outstanding job on the artwork. The cards are essentially a large version of the Donruss regular issue Diamond Kings.

	MINT	EXC	G-VG
COMPLETE SET (28)	12.00	6.00	1.20
COMMON PLAYER (1-26)	.20	.10	.02
☐ 1 Wally Joyner	.75	.35	.07
☐ 2 Roger Clemens	1.00	.50	.10
☐ 3 Dale Murphy	.50	.25	.05
☐ 4 Darryl Strawberry	.75	.35	.07
☐ 5 Ozzie Smith	.40	.20	.04
☐ 6 Jose Canseco	2.50	1.25	.25
☐ 7 Charlie Hough	.20	.10	.02
☐ 8 Brook Jacoby	.20	.10	.02
☐ 9 Fred Lynn	.20	.10	.02
☐ 10 Rick Rhoden	.20	.10	.02
☐ 11 Chris Brown	.20	.10	.02
☐ 12 Von Hayes	.30	.15	.03
☐ 13 Jack Morris	.30	.15	.03
☐ 14 Kevin McReynolds	.50	.25	.05
☐ 15 George Brett	.75	.35	.07
☐ 16 Ted Higuera	.30	.15	.03
☐ 17 Hubie Brooks	.30	.15	.03
☐ 18 Mike Scott	.40	.20	.04
☐ 19 Kirby Puckett	1.00	.50	.10
☐ 20 Dave Winfield	.40	.20	.04
☐ 21 Lloyd Moseby	.20	.10	.02
☐ 22 Eric Davis	1.00	.50	.10
☐ 23 Jim Presley	.20	.10	.02
☐ 24 Keith Moreland	.20	.10	.02
☐ 25 Greg Walker	.20	.10	.02
☐ 26 Steve Sax	.30	.15	.03
☐ 27 DK Checklist 1-26	.20	.02	.00
☐ 28 Roberto Clemente Large Puzzle (unnumbered)	.20	.10	.02

1987 Donruss All-Stars

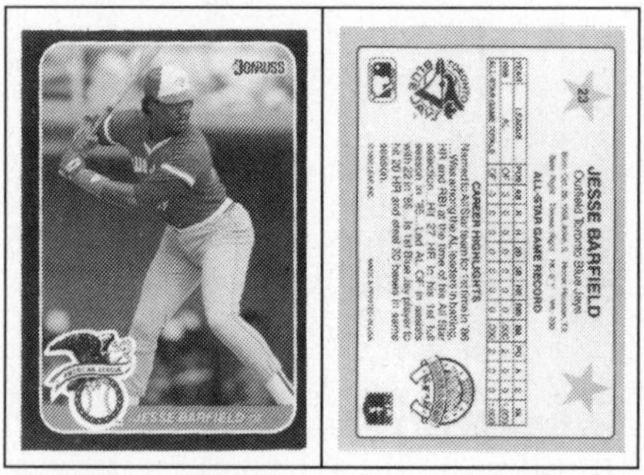

This 60-card set features cards measuring approximately 3 1/2" by 5". Card fronts are in full color with a black border. The card backs are printed in black and blue on white card stock. Cards are numbered on the back. Card backs feature statistical information about the player's performance in past All-Star games. The set was distributed in packs which also contained a Pop-Up.

	MINT	EXC	G-VG
COMPLETE SET (60)	7.00	3.50	.70
COMMON PLAYER (1-60)	.07	.03	.01
☐ 1 Wally Joyner	.45	.22	.04
☐ 2 Dave Winfield	.25	.12	.02
☐ 3 Lou Whitaker	.15	.07	.01
☐ 4 Kirby Puckett	.60	.30	.06
☐ 5 Cal Ripken	.35	.17	.03
☐ 6 Rickey Henderson	.75	.35	.07
☐ 7 Wade Boggs	.75	.35	.07
☐ 8 Roger Clemens	.60	.30	.06
☐ 9 Lance Parrish	.10	.05	.01
☐ 10 Dick Howser MG	.07	.03	.01
☐ 11 Keith Hernandez	.15	.07	.01
☐ 12 Darryl Strawberry	.60	.30	.06
☐ 13 Ryne Sandberg	.75	.35	.07
☐ 14 Dale Murphy	.35	.17	.03
☐ 15 Ozzie Smith	.25	.12	.02
☐ 16 Tony Gwynn	.40	.20	.04
☐ 17 Mike Schmidt	.75	.35	.07
☐ 18 Dwight Gooden	.60	.30	.06
☐ 19 Gary Carter	.25	.12	.02
☐ 20 Whitey Herzog MG	.07	.03	.01
☐ 21 Jose Canseco	1.00	.50	.10
☐ 22 John Franco	.10	.05	.01
☐ 23 Jesse Barfield	.10	.05	.01
☐ 24 Rick Rhoden	.07	.03	.01
☐ 25 Harold Baines	.10	.05	.01
☐ 26 Sid Fernandez	.10	.05	.01
☐ 27 George Brett	.45	.22	.04
☐ 28 Steve Sax	.15	.07	.01
☐ 29 Jim Presley	.10	.05	.01
☐ 30 Dave Smith	.07	.03	.01
☐ 31 Eddie Murray	.25	.12	.02
☐ 32 Mike Scott	.15	.07	.01
☐ 33 Don Mattingly	1.00	.50	.10
☐ 34 Dave Parker	.20	.10	.02

☐ 35 Tony Fernandez	.15	.07	.01
☐ 36 Tim Raines	.30	.15	.03
☐ 37 Brook Jacoby	.10	.05	.01
☐ 38 Chili Davis	.10	.05	.01
☐ 39 Rich Gedman	.07	.03	.01
☐ 40 Kevin Bass	.07	.03	.01
☐ 41 Frank White	.07	.03	.01
☐ 42 Glenn Davis	.20	.10	.02
☐ 43 Willie Hernandez	.10	.05	.01
☐ 44 Chris Brown	.07	.03	.01
☐ 45 Jim Rice	.20	.10	.02
☐ 46 Tony Pena	.07	.03	.01
☐ 47 Don Aase	.07	.03	.01
☐ 48 Hubie Brooks	.07	.03	.01
☐ 49 Charlie Hough	.07	.03	.01
☐ 50 Jody Davis	.07	.03	.01
☐ 51 Mike Witt	.07	.03	.01
☐ 52 Jeff Reardon	.10	.05	.01
☐ 53 Ken Schrom	.07	.03	.01
☐ 54 Fernando Valenzuela	.20	.10	.02
☐ 55 Dave Righetti	.15	.07	.01
☐ 56 Shane Rawley	.07	.03	.01
☐ 57 Ted Higuera	.15	.07	.01
☐ 58 Mike Krukow	.07	.03	.01
☐ 59 Lloyd Moseby	.10	.05	.01
☐ 60 Checklist Card	.07	.01	.00

1987 Donruss All-Star Box

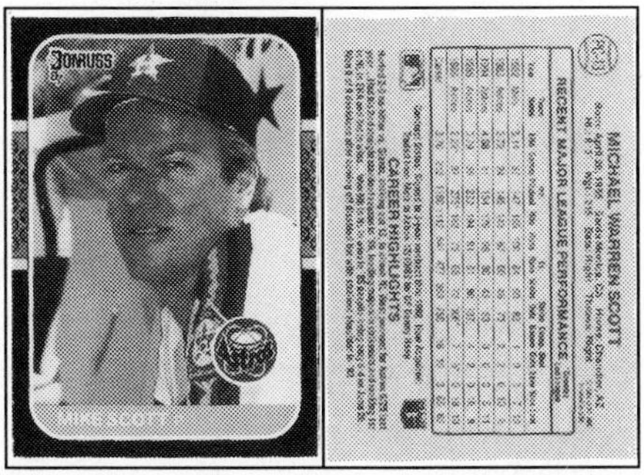

The cards in this 4-card set measure the standard 2 1/2" by 3 1/2" in spite of the fact that they form the bottom of the wax pack box for the larger Donruss All-Star cards. These box cards have essentially the same design as the 1987 Donruss regular issue set. The cards were printed on the bottoms of the Donruss All-Star (3 1/2" by 5") wax pack boxes. The four cards (PC13 to PC15 plus a Roberto Clemente puzzle card) are considered a separate set in their own right and are not typically included in a complete set of the 1987 Donruss All-Star (or regular) cards. The value of the panel uncut is slightly greater, perhaps by 25 percent greater, than the value of the individual cards cut up carefully.

	MINT	EXC	G-VG
COMPLETE SET (4)	1.00	.50	.10
COMMON PLAYERS	.05	.02	.00
☐ PC13 Mike Scott	.25	.12	.02
☐ PC14 Roger Clemens	.90	.45	.09
☐ PC15 Mike Krukow	.05	.02	.00
☐ PUZ Roberto Clemente Puzzle Card	.05	.02	.00

1987 Donruss Pop-Ups

This 20-card set features "fold-out" cards measuring 2 1/2" by 5". Card fronts are in full color. Cards are unnumbered but are listed in the same order as the Donruss All-Stars on the All-Star checklist card. Card backs present essentially no information about the player. The set was distributed in packs which also contained All-Star cards (3 1/2" by 5").

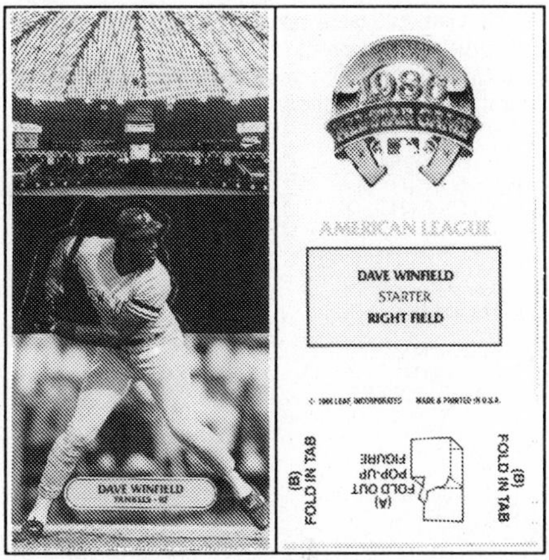

	MINT	EXC	G-VG
COMPLETE SET (20)	4.00	2.00	.40
COMMON PLAYER (1-20)	.10	.05	.01
☐ 1 Wally Joyner	.40	.20	.04
☐ 2 Dave Winfield	.25	.12	.02
☐ 3 Lou Whitaker	.15	.07	.01
☐ 4 Kirby Puckett	.60	.30	.06
☐ 5 Cal Ripken	.35	.17	.03
☐ 6 Rickey Henderson	.75	.35	.07
☐ 7 Wade Boggs	.75	.35	.07
☐ 8 Roger Clemens	.60	.30	.06
☐ 9 Lance Parrish	.10	.05	.01
☐ 10 Dick Howser MG	.10	.05	.01
☐ 11 Keith Hernandez	.15	.07	.01
☐ 12 Darryl Strawberry	.60	.30	.06
☐ 13 Ryne Sandberg	.75	.35	.07
☐ 14 Dale Murphy	.35	.17	.03
☐ 15 Ozzie Smith	.25	.12	.02
☐ 16 Tony Gwynn	.40	.20	.04
☐ 17 Mike Schmidt	.75	.35	.07
☐ 18 Dwight Gooden	.60	.30	.06
☐ 19 Gary Carter	.25	.12	.02
☐ 20 Whitey Herzog MG	.10	.05	.01

1987 Donruss Opening Day

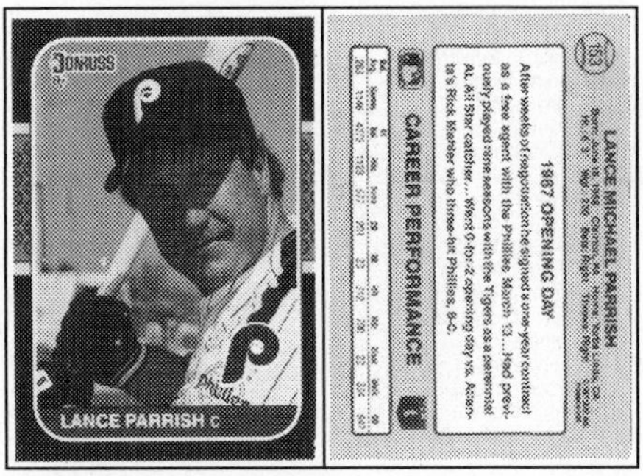

This innovative set of 272 cards features a card for each of the players in the starting line-ups of all the teams on Opening Day 1987. Cards are the standard size, 2 1/2" by 3 1/2", and are packaged as a complete set in a specially designed box. Cards are very similar in design to the 1987 regular Donruss issue except that these "OD" cards have a maroon border instead of a black border. The set features the first card in a Major League uniform of Joey Cora, Mark Davidson, Donnell Nixon, Bob Patterson, and Alonzo Powell. Teams in the same city share a checklist card. A 15-piece puzzle of Roberto Clemente is also included with every complete set. The error on Barry Bonds was corrected very early in the press run; supposedly less than one percent of the sets have the error.

	MINT	EXC	G-VG
COMPLETE SET (272)	20.00	10.00	2.00
COMMON PLAYER (1-248)	.05	.02	.00
COMMON LOGO (249-272)	.03	.01	.00
☐ 1 Doug DeCinces	.05	.02	.00
☐ 2 Mike Witt	.05	.02	.00
☐ 3 George Hendrick	.05	.02	.00
☐ 4 Dick Schofield	.05	.02	.00
☐ 5 Devon White	.35	.17	.03
☐ 6 Butch Wynegar	.05	.02	.00
☐ 7 Wally Joyner	.90	.45	.09
☐ 8 Mark McLemore	.05	.02	.00
☐ 9 Brian Downing	.05	.02	.00
☐ 10 Gary Pettis	.05	.02	.00
☐ 11 Bill Doran	.10	.05	.01
☐ 12 Phil Garner	.05	.02	.00
☐ 13 Jose Cruz	.10	.05	.01
☐ 14 Kevin Bass	.10	.05	.01
☐ 15 Mike Scott	.20	.10	.02
☐ 16 Glenn Davis	.30	.15	.03
☐ 17 Alan Ashby	.05	.02	.00
☐ 18 Billy Hatcher	.15	.07	.01
☐ 19 Craig Reynolds	.05	.02	.00
☐ 20 Carney Lansford	.15	.07	.01
☐ 21 Mike Davis	.05	.02	.00
☐ 22 Reggie Jackson	.60	.30	.06
☐ 23 Mickey Tettleton	.15	.07	.01
☐ 24 Jose Canseco	3.00	1.50	.30
☐ 25 Rob Nelson	.05	.02	.00
☐ 26 Tony Phillips	.05	.02	.00
☐ 27 Dwayne Murphy	.05	.02	.00
☐ 28 Alfredo Griffin	.05	.02	.00
☐ 29 Curt Young	.05	.02	.00
☐ 30 Willie Upshaw	.05	.02	.00
☐ 31 Mike Sharperson	.05	.02	.00
☐ 32 Rance Mulliniks	.05	.02	.00
☐ 33 Ernie Whitt	.05	.02	.00
☐ 34 Jesse Barfield	.15	.07	.01
☐ 35 Tony Fernandez	.15	.07	.01
☐ 36 Lloyd Moseby	.10	.05	.01
☐ 37 Jimmy Key	.10	.05	.01
☐ 38 Fred McGriff	1.00	.50	.10
☐ 39 George Bell	.25	.12	.02
☐ 40 Dale Murphy	.35	.17	.03
☐ 41 Rick Mahler	.05	.02	.00
☐ 42 Ken Griffey	.10	.05	.01
☐ 43 Andres Thomas	.05	.02	.00
☐ 44 Dion James	.05	.02	.00
☐ 45 Ozzie Virgil	.05	.02	.00
☐ 46 Ken Oberkfell	.05	.02	.00
☐ 47 Gary Roenicke	.05	.02	.00
☐ 48 Glenn Hubbard	.05	.02	.00
☐ 49 Bill Schroeder	.05	.02	.00
☐ 50 Greg Brock	.05	.02	.00
☐ 51 Billy Jo Robidoux	.05	.02	.00
☐ 52 Glenn Braggs	.25	.12	.02
☐ 53 Jim Gantner	.05	.02	.00
☐ 54 Paul Molitor	.15	.07	.01
☐ 55 Dale Sveum	.10	.05	.01
☐ 56 Ted Higuera	.15	.07	.01
☐ 57 Rob Deer	.10	.05	.01
☐ 58 Robin Yount	.45	.22	.04
☐ 59 Jim Lindeman	.10	.05	.01
☐ 60 Vince Coleman	.35	.17	.03
☐ 61 Tommy Herr	.05	.02	.00
☐ 62 Terry Pendleton	.05	.02	.00
☐ 63 John Tudor	.15	.07	.01
☐ 64 Tony Pena	.10	.05	.01
☐ 65 Ozzie Smith	.25	.12	.02
☐ 66 Tito Landrum	.05	.02	.00
☐ 67 Jack Clark	.20	.10	.02
☐ 68 Bob Dernier	.05	.02	.00
☐ 69 Rick Sutcliffe	.15	.07	.01
☐ 70 Andre Dawson	.30	.15	.03
☐ 71 Keith Moreland	.05	.02	.00
☐ 72 Jody Davis	.05	.02	.00
☐ 73 Brian Dayett	.05	.02	.00
☐ 74 Leon Durham	.05	.02	.00
☐ 75 Ryne Sandberg	1.00	.50	.10
☐ 76 Shawon Dunston	.35	.17	.03
☐ 77 Mike Marshall	.15	.07	.01
☐ 78 Bill Madlock	.05	.02	.00
☐ 79 Orel Hershiser	.50	.25	.05
☐ 80 Mike Ramsey	.10	.05	.01
☐ 81 Ken Landreaux	.05	.02	.00
☐ 82 Mike Scioscia	.05	.02	.00
☐ 83 Franklin Stubbs	.10	.05	.01
☐ 84 Mariano Duncan	.10	.05	.01
☐ 85 Steve Sax	.15	.07	.01
☐ 86 Mitch Webster	.05	.02	.00
☐ 87 Reid Nichols	.05	.02	.00
☐ 88 Tim Wallach	.15	.07	.01
☐ 89 Floyd Youmans	.05	.02	.00
☐ 90 Andres Galarraga	.25	.12	.02
☐ 91 Hubie Brooks	.10	.05	.01
☐ 92 Jeff Reed	.05	.02	.00
☐ 93 Alonzo Powell	.10	.05	.01
☐ 94 Vance Law	.05	.02	.00
☐ 95 Bob Brenly	.05	.02	.00
☐ 96 Will Clark	3.00	1.50	.30
☐ 97 Chili Davis	.10	.05	.01
☐ 98 Mike Krukow	.05	.02	.00
☐ 99 Jose Uribe	.05	.02	.00
☐ 100 Chris Brown	.05	.02	.00
☐ 101 Rob Thompson	.10	.05	.01
☐ 102 Candy Maldonado	.15	.07	.01
☐ 103 Jeff Leonard	.10	.05	.01
☐ 104 Tom Candiotti	.05	.02	.00
☐ 105 Chris Bando	.05	.02	.00
☐ 106 Cory Snyder	.35	.17	.03
☐ 107 Pat Tabler	.05	.02	.00
☐ 108 Andre Thornton	.05	.02	.00
☐ 109 Joe Carter	.25	.12	.02
☐ 110 Tony Bernazard	.05	.02	.00
☐ 111 Julio Franco	.15	.07	.01
☐ 112 Brook Jacoby	.10	.05	.01
☐ 113 Brett Butler	.15	.07	.01
☐ 114 Donnell Nixon	.10	.05	.01
☐ 115 Alvin Davis	.20	.10	.02
☐ 116 Mark Langston	.25	.12	.02
☐ 117 Harold Reynolds	.10	.05	.01
☐ 118 Ken Phelps	.05	.02	.00
☐ 119 Mike Kingery	.05	.02	.00
☐ 120 Dave Valle	.05	.02	.00
☐ 121 Rey Quinones	.05	.02	.00
☐ 122 Phil Bradley	.10	.05	.01
☐ 123 Jim Presley	.10	.05	.01
☐ 124 Keith Hernandez	.20	.10	.02
☐ 125 Kevin McReynolds	.25	.12	.02
☐ 126 Rafael Santana	.05	.02	.00
☐ 127 Bob Ojeda	.10	.05	.01
☐ 128 Darryl Strawberry	1.00	.50	.10
☐ 129 Mookie Wilson	.05	.02	.00
☐ 130 Gary Carter	.20	.10	.02
☐ 131 Tim Teufel	.05	.02	.00
☐ 132 Howard Johnson	.25	.12	.02
☐ 133 Cal Ripken	.40	.20	.04
☐ 134 Rick Burleson	.05	.02	.00
☐ 135 Fred Lynn	.10	.05	.01
☐ 136 Eddie Murray	.25	.12	.02
☐ 137 Ray Knight	.10	.05	.01
☐ 138 Alan Wiggins	.05	.02	.00
☐ 139 John Shelby	.05	.02	.00
☐ 140 Mike Boddicker	.05	.02	.00
☐ 141 Ken Gerhart	.10	.05	.01
☐ 142 Terry Kennedy	.05	.02	.00
☐ 143 Steve Garvey	.30	.15	.03
☐ 144 Marvell Wynne	.05	.02	.00
☐ 145 Kevin Mitchell	1.25	.60	.12
☐ 146 Tony Gwynn	.75	.35	.07
☐ 147 Joey Cora	.10	.05	.01
☐ 148 Benito Santiago	1.00	.50	.10
☐ 149 Eric Show	.05	.02	.00
☐ 150 Garry Templeton	.10	.05	.01
☐ 151 Carmelo Martinez	.05	.02	.00
☐ 152 Von Hayes	.10	.05	.01
☐ 153 Lance Parrish	.15	.07	.01
☐ 154 Milt Thompson	.05	.02	.00
☐ 155 Mike Easler	.05	.02	.00
☐ 156 Juan Samuel	.15	.07	.01
☐ 157 Steve Jeltz	.05	.02	.00
☐ 158 Glenn Wilson	.05	.02	.00
☐ 159 Shane Rawley	.05	.02	.00
☐ 160 Mike Schmidt	1.00	.50	.10
☐ 161 Andy Van Slyke	.25	.12	.02
☐ 162 Johnny Ray	.10	.05	.01
☐ 163A Barry Bonds ERR (photo actually Johnny Ray)	250.00	100.00	20.00
☐ 163B Barry Bonds COR	.75	.35	.07
☐ 164 Junior Ortiz	.05	.02	.00
☐ 165 Rafael Belliard	.05	.02	.00
☐ 166 Bob Patterson	.10	.05	.01

☐ 167 Bobby Bonilla	.45	.22	.04
☐ 168 Sid Bream	.05	.02	.00
☐ 169 Jim Morrison	.05	.02	.00
☐ 170 Jerry Browne	.10	.05	.01
☐ 171 Scott Fletcher	.05	.02	.00
☐ 172 Ruben Sierra	2.00	1.00	.20
☐ 173 Larry Parrish	.05	.02	.00
☐ 174 Pete O'Brien	.10	.05	.01
☐ 175 Pete Incaviglia	.35	.17	.03
☐ 176 Don Slaught	.05	.02	.00
☐ 177 Oddibe McDowell	.10	.05	.01
☐ 178 Charlie Hough	.05	.02	.00
☐ 179 Steve Buechele	.05	.02	.00
☐ 180 Bob Stanley	.05	.02	.00
☐ 181 Wade Boggs	1.00	.50	.10
☐ 182 Jim Rice	.20	.10	.02
☐ 183 Bill Buckner	.10	.05	.01
☐ 184 Dwight Evans	.15	.07	.01
☐ 185 Spike Owen	.05	.02	.00
☐ 186 Don Baylor	.10	.05	.01
☐ 187 Marc Sullivan	.05	.02	.00
☐ 188 Marty Barrett	.05	.02	.00
☐ 189 Dave Henderson	.10	.05	.01
☐ 190 Bo Diaz	.05	.02	.00
☐ 191 Barry Larkin	1.25	.60	.12
☐ 192 Kal Daniels	.60	.30	.06
☐ 193 Terry Francona	.05	.02	.00
☐ 194 Tom Browning	.15	.07	.01
☐ 195 Ron Oester	.05	.02	.00
☐ 196 Buddy Bell	.10	.05	.01
☐ 197 Eric Davis	1.00	.50	.10
☐ 198 Dave Parker	.20	.10	.02
☐ 199 Steve Balboni	.05	.02	.00
☐ 200 Danny Tartabull	.25	.12	.02
☐ 201 Ed Hearn	.05	.02	.00
☐ 202 Buddy Biancalana	.05	.02	.00
☐ 203 Danny Jackson	.15	.07	.01
☐ 204 Frank White	.10	.05	.01
☐ 205 Bo Jackson	3.00	1.50	.30
☐ 206 George Brett	.45	.22	.04
☐ 207 Kevin Seitzer	1.00	.50	.10
☐ 208 Willie Wilson	.10	.05	.01
☐ 209 Orlando Mercado	.05	.02	.00
☐ 210 Darrell Evans	.10	.05	.01
☐ 211 Larry Herndon	.05	.02	.00
☐ 212 Jack Morris	.15	.07	.01
☐ 213 Chet Lemon	.05	.02	.00
☐ 214 Mike Heath	.05	.02	.00
☐ 215 Darnell Coles	.05	.02	.00
☐ 216 Alan Trammell	.25	.12	.02
☐ 217 Terry Harper	.05	.02	.00
☐ 218 Lou Whitaker	.15	.07	.01
☐ 219 Gary Gaetti	.15	.07	.01
☐ 220 Tom Nieto	.05	.02	.00
☐ 221 Kirby Puckett	.75	.35	.07
☐ 222 Tom Brunansky	.15	.07	.01
☐ 223 Greg Gagne	.05	.02	.00
☐ 224 Dan Gladden	.05	.02	.00
☐ 225 Mark Davidson	.10	.05	.01
☐ 226 Bert Blyleven	.15	.07	.01
☐ 227 Steve Lombardozzi	.05	.02	.00
☐ 228 Kent Hrbek	.25	.12	.02
☐ 229 Gary Redus	.05	.02	.00
☐ 230 Ivan Calderon	.15	.07	.01
☐ 231 Tim Hulett	.05	.02	.00
☐ 232 Carlton Fisk	.35	.17	.03
☐ 233 Greg Walker	.10	.05	.01
☐ 234 Ron Karkovice	.05	.02	.00
☐ 235 Ozzie Guillen	.25	.12	.02
☐ 236 Harold Baines	.15	.07	.01
☐ 237 Donnie Hill	.05	.02	.00
☐ 238 Rich Dotson	.05	.02	.00
☐ 239 Mike Pagliarulo	.10	.05	.01
☐ 240 Joel Skinner	.05	.02	.00
☐ 241 Don Mattingly	1.50	.75	.15
☐ 242 Gary Ward	.05	.02	.00
☐ 243 Dave Winfield	.25	.12	.02
☐ 244 Dan Pasqua	.10	.05	.01
☐ 245 Wayne Tolleson	.05	.02	.00
☐ 246 Willie Randolph	.10	.05	.01
☐ 247 Dennis Rasmussen	.10	.05	.01
☐ 248 Rickey Henderson	1.00	.50	.10
☐ 249 Angels Logo	.03	.01	.00
☐ 250 Astros Logo	.03	.01	.00
☐ 251 A's Logo	.03	.01	.00
☐ 252 Blue Jays Logo	.03	.01	.00
☐ 253 Braves Logo	.03	.01	.00
☐ 254 Brewers Logo	.03	.01	.00
☐ 255 Cardinals Logo	.03	.01	.00
☐ 256 Dodgers Logo	.03	.01	.00
☐ 257 Expos Logo	.03	.01	.00
☐ 258 Giants Logo	.03	.01	.00
☐ 259 Indians Logo	.03	.01	.00
☐ 260 Mariners Logo	.03	.01	.00
☐ 261 Orioles Logo	.03	.01	.00
☐ 262 Padres Logo	.03	.01	.00
☐ 263 Phillies Logo	.03	.01	.00
☐ 264 Pirates Logo	.03	.01	.00
☐ 265 Rangers Logo	.03	.01	.00
☐ 266 Red Sox Logo	.03	.01	.00
☐ 267 Reds Logo	.03	.01	.00
☐ 268 Royals Logo	.03	.01	.00
☐ 269 Tigers Logo	.03	.01	.00
☐ 270 Twins Logo	.03	.01	.00
☐ 271 Chicago Logos	.03	.01	.00
☐ 272 New York Logos	.03	.01	.00

1987 Donruss Rookies

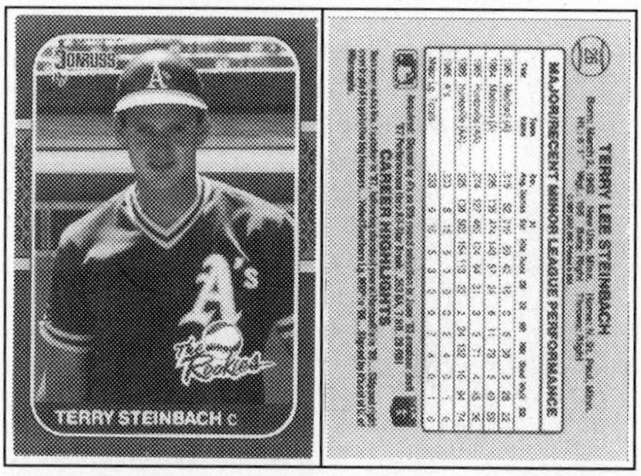

The 1987 Donruss "The Rookies" set features 56 cards plus a 15-piece puzzle of Roberto Clemente. Cards are in full color and are standard size, 2 1/2" by 3 1/2". The set was distributed in a small green and black box with gold lettering. Card fronts are similar in design to the 1987 Donruss regular issue except for the presence of "The Rookies" logo in the lower left corner and a green border instead of a black border. The key (extended) rookie cards in this set are Ellis Burks and Matt Williams.

	MINT	EXC	G-VG
COMPLETE SET (56)	20.00	10.00	2.00
COMMON PLAYER (1-56)	.07	.03	.01
☐ 1 Mark McGwire	3.50	1.75	.35
☐ 2 Eric Bell	.07	.03	.01
☐ 3 Mark Williamson	.20	.10	.02
☐ 4 Mike Greenwell	2.50	1.25	.25
☐ 5 Ellis Burks	3.75	1.85	.37
☐ 6 DeWayne Buice	.10	.05	.01
☐ 7 Mark McLemore	.07	.03	.01
☐ 8 Devon White	.25	.12	.02
☐ 9 Willie Fraser	.07	.03	.01
☐ 10 Les Lancaster	.10	.05	.01
☐ 11 Ken Williams	.25	.12	.02
☐ 12 Matt Nokes	.45	.22	.04
☐ 13 Jeff Robinson (Tigers pitcher)	.25	.12	.02
☐ 14 Bo Jackson	4.50	2.25	.45
☐ 15 Kevin Seitzer	1.00	.50	.10
☐ 16 Billy Ripken	.25	.12	.02
☐ 17 B.J. Surhoff	.12	.06	.01
☐ 18 Chuck Crim	.10	.05	.01
☐ 19 Mike Birkbeck	.07	.03	.01
☐ 20 Chris Bosio	.10	.05	.01
☐ 21 Les Straker	.10	.05	.01
☐ 22 Mark Davidson	.10	.05	.01
☐ 23 Gene Larkin	.35	.17	.03
☐ 24 Ken Gerhart	.10	.05	.01
☐ 25 Luis Polonia	.25	.12	.02
☐ 26 Terry Steinbach	.25	.12	.02
☐ 27 Mickey Brantley	.12	.06	.01
☐ 28 Mike Stanley	.10	.05	.01
☐ 29 Jerry Browne	.10	.05	.01
☐ 30 Todd Benzinger	.35	.17	.03
☐ 31 Fred McGriff	2.00	1.00	.20
☐ 32 Mike Henneman	.30	.15	.03
☐ 33 Casey Candaele	.10	.05	.01
☐ 34 Dave Magadan	.75	.35	.07
☐ 35 David Cone	.90	.45	.09
☐ 36 Mike Jackson	.15	.07	.01

☐ 37 John Mitchell	.10	.05	.01
☐ 38 Mike Dunne	.12	.06	.01
☐ 39 John Smiley	.35	.17	.03
☐ 40 Joe Magrane	.90	.45	.09
☐ 41 Jim Lindeman	.10	.05	.01
☐ 42 Shane Mack	.20	.10	.02
☐ 43 Stan Jefferson	.10	.05	.01
☐ 44 Benito Santiago	.75	.35	.07
☐ 45 Matt Williams	6.50	3.25	.65
☐ 46 Dave Meads	.10	.05	.01
☐ 47 Rafael Palmeiro	1.25	.60	.12
☐ 48 Bill Long	.10	.05	.01
☐ 49 Bob Brower	.10	.05	.01
☐ 50 James Steels	.10	.05	.01
☐ 51 Paul Noce	.10	.05	.01
☐ 52 Greg Maddux	.50	.25	.05
☐ 53 Jeff Musselman	.10	.05	.01
☐ 54 Brian Holton	.10	.05	.01
☐ 55 Chuck Jackson	.10	.05	.01
☐ 56 Checklist Card	.07	.01	.00

1987 Donruss Highlights

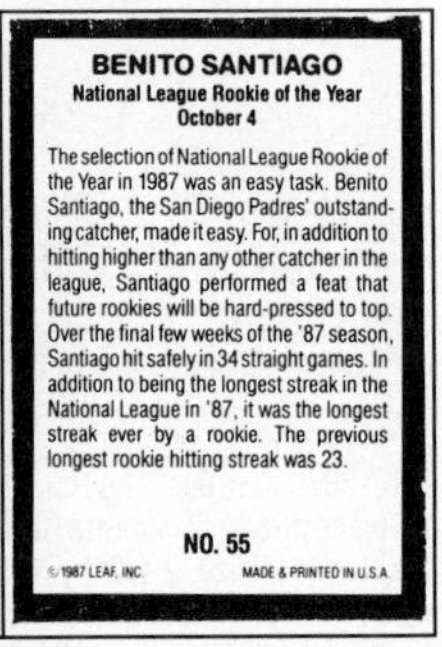

BENITO SANTIAGO
National League Rookie of the Year
October 4

The selection of National League Rookie of the Year in 1987 was an easy task. Benito Santiago, the San Diego Padres' outstanding catcher, made it easy. For, in addition to hitting higher than any other catcher in the league, Santiago performed a feat that future rookies will be hard-pressed to top. Over the final few weeks of the '87 season, Santiago hit safely in 34 straight games. In addition to being the longest streak in the National League in '87, it was the longest streak ever by a rookie. The previous longest rookie hitting streak was 23.

NO. 55

© 1987 LEAF, INC. MADE & PRINTED IN U.S.A.

Donruss' third (and last) edition of Highlights was released late in 1987. The cards are standard size, measuring 2 1/2" by 3 1/2", and are glossy in appearance. Cards commemorate events during the 1987 season, as well as players and pitchers of the month from each league. The set was distributed in its own red, black, blue, and gold box along with a small Roberto Clemente puzzle. Card fronts are similar to the regular 1987 Donruss issue except that the Highlights logo is positioned in the lower right-hand corner and the borders are in blue instead of black. The backs are printed in black and gold on white card stock.

	MINT	EXC	G-VG
COMPLETE SET (56)	7.00	3.50	.70
COMMON PLAYER (1-56)	.06	.03	.00
☐ 1 Juan Nieves First No-Hitter	.06	.03	.00
☐ 2 Mike Schmidt Hits 500th Homer	.45	.22	.04
☐ 3 Eric Davis NL Player April	.35	.17	.03
☐ 4 Sid Fernandez NL Pitcher April	.10	.05	.01
☐ 5 Brian Downing AL Player April	.06	.03	.00
☐ 6 Bret Saberhagen AL Pitcher April	.20	.10	.02
☐ 7 Tim Raines Free Agent Returns	.15	.07	.01
☐ 8 Eric Davis NL Player May	.30	.15	.03
☐ 9 Steve Bedrosian NL Pitcher May	.10	.05	.01
☐ 10 Larry Parrish AL Player May	.06	.03	.00
☐ 11 Jim Clancy AL Pitcher May	.06	.03	.00
☐ 12 Tony Gwynn NL Player June ERR (over "20" hits)	.25	.12	.02
☐ 13 Orel Hershiser NL Pitcher June	.30	.15	.03
☐ 14 Wade Boggs AL Player June	.50	.25	.05
☐ 15 Steve Ontiveros AL Pitcher June	.06	.03	.00
☐ 16 Tim Raines All Star Game Hero	.15	.07	.01
☐ 17 Don Mattingly Consecutive Game Homerun Streak	.75	.35	.07
☐ 18 Ray Dandridge 1987 HOF Inductee	.15	.07	.01
☐ 19 Jim "Catfish" Hunter 1987 HOF Inductee	.15	.07	.01
☐ 20 Billy Williams 1987 HOF Inductee	.15	.07	.01
☐ 21 Bo Diaz NL Player July	.06	.03	.00
☐ 22 Floyd Youmans NL Pitcher July	.06	.03	.00
☐ 23 Don Mattingly AL Player July	.75	.35	.07
☐ 24 Frank Viola AL Pitcher July	.15	.07	.01
☐ 25 Bobby Witt Strikes Out Four Batters in One Inning	.25	.12	.02
☐ 26 Kevin Seitzer Ties AL 9-Inning Game Hit Mark	.40	.20	.04
☐ 27 Mark McGwire Sets Rookie HR Record	.90	.45	.09
☐ 28 Andre Dawson Sets Cubs' 1st Year Homer Mark	.25	.12	.02
☐ 29 Paul Molitor Hits in 39 Straight Games	.15	.07	.01
☐ 30 Kirby Puckett Record Weekend	.50	.25	.05
☐ 31 Andre Dawson NL Player August	.25	.12	.02
☐ 32 Doug Drabek NL Pitcher August	.35	.17	.03
☐ 33 Dwight Evans AL Player August	.10	.05	.01
☐ 34 Mark Langston AL Pitcher August	.15	.07	.01
☐ 35 Wally Joyner 100 RBI in 1st Two Major League Seasons	.20	.10	.02
☐ 36 Vince Coleman 100 SB in 1st Three Major League Seasons	.25	.12	.02
☐ 37 Eddie Murray Orioles' All Time Homer King	.25	.12	.02
☐ 38 Cal Ripken Ends Consecutive Innings Streak	.25	.12	.02
☐ 39 Blue Jays Hit Record 10 Homers In One Game (McGriff/Ducey/Whitt)	.06	.03	.00
☐ 40 McGwire/Canseco Equal A's RBI Marks	1.00	.50	.10
☐ 41 Bob Boone Sets All-Time Catching Record	.10	.05	.01
☐ 42 Darryl Strawberry Sets Mets' One-Season Home Run Mark	.35	.17	.03
☐ 43 Howard Johnson NL's All-Time Switchhit HR King	.20	.10	.02
☐ 44 Wade Boggs Five Straight 200 Hit Seasons	.50	.25	.05
☐ 45 Benito Santiago Eclipses Rookie Game Hitting Streak	.35	.17	.03
☐ 46 Mark McGwire Eclipses Jackson's A's HR Record	.90	.45	.09
☐ 47 Kevin Seitzer 13th Rookie to Collect 200 Hits	.40	.20	.04
☐ 48 Don Mattingly Sets Slam Record	1.00	.50	.10
☐ 49 Darryl Strawberry NL Player September	.40	.20	.04
☐ 50 Pascual Perez NL Pitcher September	.10	.05	.01
☐ 51 Alan Trammell AL Player September	.15	.07	.01

		MINT	EXC	G-VG
☐ 52	Doyle Alexander AL Pitcher September	.06	.03	.00
☐ 53	Nolan Ryan Strikeout King Again	1.25	.60	.12
☐ 54	Mark McGwire Donruss AL ROY	1.00	.50	.10
☐ 55	Benito Santiago Donruss NL ROY	.50	.25	.05
☐ 56	Checklist Card	.06	.01	.00

1988 Donruss

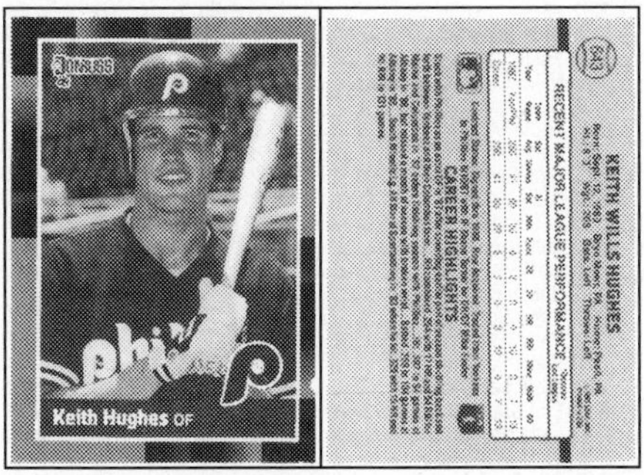

This 660-card set was distributed along with a puzzle of Stan Musial. The six regular checklist cards are numbered throughout the set as multiples of 100. Cards measure 2 1/2" by 3 1/2" and feature a distinctive black and blue border on the front. The popular Diamond King subset returns for the seventh consecutive year. Rated Rookies are featured again as cards 28-47. Cards marked as SP (short printed) from 648-660 are more difficult to find than the other 13 SP's in the lower 600s. These 26 cards listed as SP were apparently pulled from the printing sheet to make room for the 26 Bonus MVP cards. Six of the checklist cards were done two different ways to reflect the inclusion or exclusion of the Bonus MVP cards in the wax packs. In the checklist below, the A variations (for the checklist cards) are from the wax packs and the B variations are from the factory-collated sets. The key rookie cards in this set are Roberto Alomar, Ellis Burks, Ron Gant, Mark Grace, Gregg Jefferies, Roberto Kelly, and Matt Williams. There was also a Kirby Puckett card issued as the package back of Donruss blister packs; it uses a different photo from both of Kirby's regular and Bonus MVP cards and is unnumbered on the back.

	MINT	EXC	G-VG
COMPLETE SET (660)	25.00	12.50	2.50
COMMON PLAYER (1-647)	.03	.01	.00
COMMON PLAYER (648-660)	.10	.05	.01

		MINT	EXC	G-VG
☐ 1	Mark McGwire DK	.45	.15	.03
☐ 2	Tim Raines DK	.10	.05	.01
☐ 3	Benito Santiago DK	.12	.06	.01
☐ 4	Alan Trammell DK	.12	.06	.01
☐ 5	Danny Tartabull DK	.10	.05	.01
☐ 6	Ron Darling DK	.08	.04	.01
☐ 7	Paul Molitor DK	.10	.05	.01
☐ 8	Devon White DK	.10	.05	.01
☐ 9	Andre Dawson DK	.12	.06	.01
☐ 10	Julio Franco DK	.08	.04	.01
☐ 11	Scott Fletcher DK	.06	.03	.00
☐ 12	Tony Fernandez DK	.08	.04	.01
☐ 13	Shane Rawley DK	.06	.03	.00
☐ 14	Kal Daniels DK	.10	.05	.01
☐ 15	Jack Clark DK	.10	.05	.01
☐ 16	Dwight Evans DK	.10	.05	.01
☐ 17	Tommy John DK	.10	.05	.01
☐ 18	Andy Van Slyke DK	.10	.05	.01
☐ 19	Gary Gaetti DK	.08	.04	.01
☐ 20	Mark Langston DK	.10	.05	.01
☐ 21	Will Clark DK	.45	.22	.04
☐ 22	Glenn Hubbard DK	.06	.03	.00
☐ 23	Billy Hatcher DK	.08	.04	.01
☐ 24	Bob Welch DK	.10	.05	.01
☐ 25	Ivan Calderon DK	.08	.04	.01
☐ 26	Cal Ripken Jr. DK	.20	.10	.02
☐ 27	DK Checklist 1-26	.06	.01	.00
☐ 28	Mackey Sasser RR	.40	.20	.04
☐ 29	Jeff Treadway RR	.20	.10	.02
☐ 30	Mike Campbell RR	.12	.06	.01
☐ 31	Lance Johnson RR	.25	.12	.02
☐ 32	Nelson Liriano RR	.15	.07	.01
☐ 33	Shawn Abner RR	.20	.10	.02
☐ 34	Roberto Alomar RR	2.00	1.00	.20
☐ 35	Shawn Hillegas RR	.12	.06	.01
☐ 36	Joey Meyer RR	.10	.05	.01
☐ 37	Kevin Elster RR	.12	.06	.01
☐ 38	Jose Lind RR	.30	.15	.03
☐ 39	Kirt Manwaring RR	.10	.05	.01
☐ 40	Mark Grace RR	3.00	1.50	.30
☐ 41	Jody Reed RR	.45	.22	.04
☐ 42	John Farrell RR	.18	.09	.01
☐ 43	Al Leiter RR	.18	.09	.01
☐ 44	Gary Thurman RR	.15	.07	.01
☐ 45	Vicente Palacios RR	.10	.05	.01
☐ 46	Eddie Williams RR	.12	.06	.01
☐ 47	Jack McDowell RR	.35	.17	.03
☐ 48	Ken Dixon	.03	.01	.00
☐ 49	Mike Birkbeck	.03	.01	.00
☐ 50	Eric King	.03	.01	.00
☐ 51	Roger Clemens	.45	.22	.04
☐ 52	Pat Clements	.03	.01	.00
☐ 53	Fernando Valenzuela	.12	.06	.01
☐ 54	Mark Gubicza	.08	.04	.01
☐ 55	Jay Howell	.03	.01	.00
☐ 56	Floyd Youmans	.03	.01	.00
☐ 57	Ed Correa	.03	.01	.00
☐ 58	DeWayne Buice	.06	.03	.00
☐ 59	Jose DeLeon	.03	.01	.00
☐ 60	Danny Cox	.03	.01	.00
☐ 61	Nolan Ryan	.50	.25	.05
☐ 62	Steve Bedrosian	.08	.04	.01
☐ 63	Tom Browning	.08	.04	.01
☐ 64	Mark Davis	.10	.05	.01
☐ 65	R.J. Reynolds	.03	.01	.00
☐ 66	Kevin Mitchell	.40	.20	.04
☐ 67	Ken Oberkfell	.03	.01	.00
☐ 68	Rick Sutcliffe	.08	.04	.01
☐ 69	Dwight Gooden	.40	.20	.04
☐ 70	Scott Bankhead	.10	.05	.01
☐ 71	Bert Blyleven	.10	.05	.01
☐ 72	Jimmy Key	.06	.03	.00
☐ 73	Les Straker	.06	.03	.00
☐ 74	Jim Clancy	.03	.01	.00
☐ 75	Mike Moore	.06	.03	.00
☐ 76	Ron Darling	.08	.04	.01
☐ 77	Ed Lynch	.03	.01	.00
☐ 78	Dale Murphy	.20	.10	.02
☐ 79	Doug Drabek	.18	.09	.01
☐ 80	Scott Garrelts	.06	.03	.00
☐ 81	Ed Whitson	.06	.03	.00
☐ 82	Rob Murphy	.03	.01	.00
☐ 83	Shane Rawley	.03	.01	.00
☐ 84	Greg Mathews	.03	.01	.00
☐ 85	Jim Deshaies	.03	.01	.00
☐ 86	Mike Witt	.03	.01	.00
☐ 87	Donnie Hill	.03	.01	.00
☐ 88	Jeff Reed	.03	.01	.00
☐ 89	Mike Boddicker	.06	.03	.00
☐ 90	Ted Higuera	.06	.03	.00
☐ 91	Walt Terrell	.03	.01	.00
☐ 92	Bob Stanley	.03	.01	.00
☐ 93	Dave Righetti	.08	.04	.01
☐ 94	Orel Hershiser	.18	.09	.01
☐ 95	Chris Bando	.03	.01	.00
☐ 96	Bret Saberhagen	.15	.07	.01
☐ 97	Curt Young	.03	.01	.00
☐ 98	Tim Burke	.06	.03	.00
☐ 99	Charlie Hough	.03	.01	.00
☐ 100A	Checklist 28-137	.06	.01	.00
☐ 100B	Checklist 28-133	.06	.01	.00
☐ 101	Bobby Witt	.18	.09	.01
☐ 102	George Brett	.25	.12	.02
☐ 103	Mickey Tettleton	.06	.03	.00
☐ 104	Scott Bailes	.03	.01	.00
☐ 105	Mike Pagliarulo	.03	.01	.00
☐ 106	Mike Scioscia	.03	.01	.00
☐ 107	Tom Brookens	.03	.01	.00
☐ 108	Ray Knight	.06	.03	.00
☐ 109	Dan Plesac	.03	.01	.00
☐ 110	Wally Joyner	.20	.10	.02
☐ 111	Bob Forsch	.03	.01	.00
☐ 112	Mike Scott	.10	.05	.01
☐ 113	Kevin Gross	.03	.01	.00
☐ 114	Benito Santiago	.30	.15	.03
☐ 115	Bob Kipper	.03	.01	.00
☐ 116	Mike Krukow	.03	.01	.00

☐ 117 Chris Bosio	.06	.03	.00
☐ 118 Sid Fernandez	.08	.04	.01
☐ 119 Jody Davis	.03	.01	.00
☐ 120 Mike Morgan	.03	.01	.00
☐ 121 Mark Eichhorn	.03	.01	.00
☐ 122 Jeff Reardon	.08	.04	.01
☐ 123 John Franco	.08	.04	.01
☐ 124 Richard Dotson	.03	.01	.00
☐ 125 Eric Bell	.03	.01	.00
☐ 126 Juan Nieves	.03	.01	.00
☐ 127 Jack Morris	.10	.05	.01
☐ 128 Rick Rhoden	.03	.01	.00
☐ 129 Rich Gedman	.03	.01	.00
☐ 130 Ken Howell	.03	.01	.00
☐ 131 Brook Jacoby	.06	.03	.00
☐ 132 Danny Jackson	.06	.03	.00
☐ 133 Gene Nelson	.03	.01	.00
☐ 134 Neal Heaton	.03	.01	.00
☐ 135 Willie Fraser	.03	.01	.00
☐ 136 Jose Guzman	.03	.01	.00
☐ 137 Ozzie Guillen	.10	.05	.01
☐ 138 Bob Knepper	.03	.01	.00
☐ 139 Mike Jackson	.10	.05	.01
☐ 140 Joe Magrane	.35	.17	.03
☐ 141 Jimmy Jones	.06	.03	.00
☐ 142 Ted Power	.03	.01	.00
☐ 143 Ozzie Virgil	.03	.01	.00
☐ 144 Felix Fermin	.06	.03	.00
☐ 145 Kelly Downs	.06	.03	.00
☐ 146 Shawon Dunston	.12	.06	.01
☐ 147 Scott Bradley	.03	.01	.00
☐ 148 Dave Stieb	.10	.05	.01
☐ 149 Frank Viola	.15	.07	.01
☐ 150 Terry Kennedy	.03	.01	.00
☐ 151 Bill Wegman	.03	.01	.00
☐ 152 Matt Nokes	.25	.12	.02
☐ 153 Wade Boggs	.45	.22	.04
☐ 154 Wayne Tolleson	.03	.01	.00
☐ 155 Mariano Duncan	.06	.03	.00
☐ 156 Julio Franco	.10	.05	.01
☐ 157 Charlie Leibrandt	.03	.01	.00
☐ 158 Terry Steinbach	.12	.06	.01
☐ 159 Mike Fitzgerald	.03	.01	.00
☐ 160 Jack Lazorko	.03	.01	.00
☐ 161 Mitch Williams	.06	.03	.00
☐ 162 Greg Walker	.03	.01	.00
☐ 163 Alan Ashby	.03	.01	.00
☐ 164 Tony Gwynn	.25	.12	.02
☐ 165 Bruce Ruffin	.03	.01	.00
☐ 166 Ron Robinson	.03	.01	.00
☐ 167 Zane Smith	.08	.04	.01
☐ 168 Junior Ortiz	.03	.01	.00
☐ 169 Jamie Moyer	.03	.01	.00
☐ 170 Tony Pena	.08	.04	.01
☐ 171 Cal Ripken	.25	.12	.02
☐ 172 B.J. Surhoff	.10	.05	.01
☐ 173 Lou Whitaker	.10	.05	.01
☐ 174 Ellis Burks	1.25	.60	.12
☐ 175 Ron Guidry	.10	.05	.01
☐ 176 Steve Sax	.12	.06	.01
☐ 177 Danny Tartabull	.15	.07	.01
☐ 178 Carney Lansford	.08	.04	.01
☐ 179 Casey Candaele	.03	.01	.00
☐ 180 Scott Fletcher	.03	.01	.00
☐ 181 Mark McLemore	.03	.01	.00
☐ 182 Ivan Calderon	.06	.03	.00
☐ 183 Jack Clark	.10	.05	.01
☐ 184 Glenn Davis	.18	.09	.01
☐ 185 Luis Aguayo	.03	.01	.00
☐ 186 Bo Diaz	.03	.01	.00
☐ 187 Stan Jefferson	.03	.01	.00
☐ 188 Sid Bream	.03	.01	.00
☐ 189 Bob Brenly	.03	.01	.00
☐ 190 Dion James	.03	.01	.00
☐ 191 Leon Durham	.03	.01	.00
☐ 192 Jesse Orosco	.03	.01	.00
☐ 193 Alvin Davis	.10	.05	.01
☐ 194 Gary Gaetti	.10	.05	.01
☐ 195 Fred McGriff	.40	.20	.04
☐ 196 Steve Lombardozzi	.03	.01	.00
☐ 197 Rance Mulliniks	.03	.01	.00
☐ 198 Rey Quinones	.03	.01	.00
☐ 199 Gary Carter	.15	.07	.01
☐ 200A Checklist 138-247	.06	.01	.00
☐ 200B Checklist 134-239	.06	.01	.00
☐ 201 Keith Moreland	.03	.01	.00
☐ 202 Ken Griffey	.10	.05	.01
☐ 203 Tommy Gregg	.18	.09	.01
☐ 204 Will Clark	1.10	.55	.11
☐ 205 John Kruk	.06	.03	.00
☐ 206 Buddy Bell	.06	.03	.00
☐ 207 Von Hayes	.08	.04	.01
☐ 208 Tommy Herr	.06	.03	.00
☐ 209 Craig Reynolds	.03	.01	.00
☐ 210 Gary Pettis	.03	.01	.00
☐ 211 Harold Baines	.08	.04	.01
☐ 212 Vance Law	.03	.01	.00
☐ 213 Ken Gerhart	.03	.01	.00
☐ 214 Jim Gantner	.03	.01	.00
☐ 215 Chet Lemon	.03	.01	.00
☐ 216 Dwight Evans	.10	.05	.01
☐ 217 Don Mattingly	1.00	.50	.10
☐ 218 Franklin Stubbs	.03	.01	.00
☐ 219 Pat Tabler	.06	.03	.00
☐ 220 Bo Jackson	1.25	.60	.12
☐ 221 Tony Phillips	.03	.01	.00
☐ 222 Tim Wallach	.08	.04	.01
☐ 223 Ruben Sierra	.50	.25	.05
☐ 224 Steve Buechele	.03	.01	.00
☐ 225 Frank White	.06	.03	.00
☐ 226 Alfredo Griffin	.03	.01	.00
☐ 227 Greg Swindell	.12	.06	.01
☐ 228 Willie Randolph	.06	.03	.00
☐ 229 Mike Marshall	.10	.05	.01
☐ 230 Alan Trammell	.12	.06	.01
☐ 231 Eddie Murray	.15	.07	.01
☐ 232 Dale Sveum	.03	.01	.00
☐ 233 Dick Schofield	.03	.01	.00
☐ 234 Jose Oquendo	.03	.01	.00
☐ 235 Bill Doran	.06	.03	.00
☐ 236 Milt Thompson	.03	.01	.00
☐ 237 Marvell Wynne	.03	.01	.00
☐ 238 Bobby Bonilla	.35	.17	.03
☐ 239 Chris Speier	.03	.01	.00
☐ 240 Glenn Braggs	.06	.03	.00
☐ 241 Wally Backman	.03	.01	.00
☐ 242 Ryne Sandberg	.50	.25	.05
☐ 243 Phil Bradley	.06	.03	.00
☐ 244 Kelly Gruber	.35	.17	.03
☐ 245 Tom Brunansky	.10	.05	.01
☐ 246 Ron Oester	.03	.01	.00
☐ 247 Bobby Thigpen	.15	.07	.01
☐ 248 Fred Lynn	.10	.05	.01
☐ 249 Paul Molitor	.10	.05	.01
☐ 250 Darrell Evans	.08	.04	.01
☐ 251 Gary Ward	.03	.01	.00
☐ 252 Bruce Hurst	.08	.04	.01
☐ 253 Bob Welch	.10	.05	.01
☐ 254 Joe Carter	.15	.07	.01
☐ 255 Willie Wilson	.06	.03	.00
☐ 256 Mark McGwire	.65	.30	.06
☐ 257 Mitch Webster	.03	.01	.00
☐ 258 Brian Downing	.03	.01	.00
☐ 259 Mike Stanley	.03	.01	.00
☐ 260 Carlton Fisk	.15	.07	.01
☐ 261 Billy Hatcher	.08	.04	.01
☐ 262 Glenn Wilson	.03	.01	.00
☐ 263 Ozzie Smith	.15	.07	.01
☐ 264 Randy Ready	.03	.01	.00
☐ 265 Kurt Stillwell	.10	.05	.01
☐ 266 David Palmer	.03	.01	.00
☐ 267 Mike Diaz	.03	.01	.00
☐ 268 Robby Thompson	.03	.01	.00
☐ 269 Andre Dawson	.15	.07	.01
☐ 270 Lee Guetterman	.03	.01	.00
☐ 271 Willie Upshaw	.03	.01	.00
☐ 272 Randy Bush	.03	.01	.00
☐ 273 Larry Sheets	.03	.01	.00
☐ 274 Rob Deer	.08	.04	.01
☐ 275 Kirk Gibson	.12	.06	.01
☐ 276 Marty Barrett	.06	.03	.00
☐ 277 Rickey Henderson	.35	.17	.03
☐ 278 Pedro Guerrero	.10	.05	.01
☐ 279 Brett Butler	.08	.04	.01
☐ 280 Kevin Seitzer	.45	.22	.04
☐ 281 Mike Davis	.03	.01	.00
☐ 282 Andres Galarraga	.12	.06	.01
☐ 283 Devon White	.12	.06	.01
☐ 284 Pete O'Brien	.06	.03	.00
☐ 285 Jerry Hairston	.03	.01	.00
☐ 286 Kevin Bass	.06	.03	.00
☐ 287 Carmelo Martinez	.03	.01	.00
☐ 288 Juan Samuel	.08	.04	.01
☐ 289 Kal Daniels	.15	.07	.01
☐ 290 Albert Hall	.03	.01	.00
☐ 291 Andy Van Slyke	.12	.06	.01
☐ 292 Lee Smith	.06	.03	.00
☐ 293 Vince Coleman	.15	.07	.01
☐ 294 Tom Niedenfuer	.03	.01	.00
☐ 295 Robin Yount	.20	.10	.02
☐ 296 Jeff Robinson (Tigers pitcher)	.20	.10	.02
☐ 297 Todd Benzinger	.20	.10	.02
☐ 298 Dave Winfield	.15	.07	.01
☐ 299 Mickey Hatcher	.03	.01	.00
☐ 300A Checklist 248-357	.06	.01	.00
☐ 300B Checklist 240-345	.06	.01	.00
☐ 301 Bud Black	.03	.01	.00

☐ 302	Jose Canseco	1.25	.60	.12
☐ 303	Tom Foley	.03	.01	.00
☐ 304	Pete Incaviglia	.15	.07	.01
☐ 305	Bob Boone	.08	.04	.01
☐ 306	Bill Long	.06	.03	.00
☐ 307	Willie McGee	.10	.05	.01
☐ 308	Ken Caminiti	.15	.07	.01
☐ 309	Darren Daulton	.06	.03	.00
☐ 310	Tracy Jones	.06	.03	.00
☐ 311	Greg Booker	.03	.01	.00
☐ 312	Mike LaValliere	.03	.01	.00
☐ 313	Chili Davis	.06	.03	.00
☐ 314	Glenn Hubbard	.03	.01	.00
☐ 315	Paul Noce	.06	.03	.00
☐ 316	Keith Hernandez	.10	.05	.01
☐ 317	Mark Langston	.10	.05	.01
☐ 318	Keith Atherton	.03	.01	.00
☐ 319	Tony Fernandez	.10	.05	.01
☐ 320	Kent Hrbek	.12	.06	.01
☐ 321	John Cerutti	.03	.01	.00
☐ 322	Mike Kingery	.03	.01	.00
☐ 323	Dave Magadan	.20	.10	.02
☐ 324	Rafael Palmeiro	.35	.17	.03
☐ 325	Jeff Dedmon	.03	.01	.00
☐ 326	Barry Bonds	.50	.25	.05
☐ 327	Jeffrey Leonard	.06	.03	.00
☐ 328	Tim Flannery	.03	.01	.00
☐ 329	Dave Concepcion	.06	.03	.00
☐ 330	Mike Schmidt	.40	.20	.04
☐ 331	Bill Dawley	.03	.01	.00
☐ 332	Larry Andersen	.03	.01	.00
☐ 333	Jack Howell	.03	.01	.00
☐ 334	Ken Williams	.12	.06	.01
☐ 335	Bryn Smith	.03	.01	.00
☐ 336	Billy Ripken	.15	.07	.01
☐ 337	Greg Brock	.03	.01	.00
☐ 338	Mike Heath	.03	.01	.00
☐ 339	Mike Greenwell	.65	.30	.06
☐ 340	Claudell Washington	.06	.03	.00
☐ 341	Jose Gonzalez	.03	.01	.00
☐ 342	Mel Hall	.06	.03	.00
☐ 343	Jim Eisenreich	.06	.03	.00
☐ 344	Tony Bernazard	.03	.01	.00
☐ 345	Tim Raines	.18	.09	.01
☐ 346	Bob Brower	.03	.01	.00
☐ 347	Larry Parrish	.03	.01	.00
☐ 348	Thad Bosley	.03	.01	.00
☐ 349	Dennis Eckersley	.12	.06	.01
☐ 350	Cory Snyder	.12	.06	.01
☐ 351	Rick Cerone	.03	.01	.00
☐ 352	John Shelby	.03	.01	.00
☐ 353	Larry Herndon	.03	.01	.00
☐ 354	John Habyan	.03	.01	.00
☐ 355	Chuck Crim	.03	.01	.00
☐ 356	Gus Polidor	.03	.01	.00
☐ 357	Ken Dayley	.03	.01	.00
☐ 358	Danny Darwin	.06	.03	.00
☐ 359	Lance Parrish	.10	.05	.01
☐ 360	James Steels	.06	.03	.00
☐ 361	Al Pedrique	.06	.03	.00
☐ 362	Mike Aldrete	.03	.01	.00
☐ 363	Juan Castillo	.03	.01	.00
☐ 364	Len Dykstra	.25	.12	.02
☐ 365	Luis Quinones	.03	.01	.00
☐ 366	Jim Presley	.06	.03	.00
☐ 367	Lloyd Moseby	.06	.03	.00
☐ 368	Kirby Puckett	.45	.22	.04
☐ 369	Eric Davis	.35	.17	.03
☐ 370	Gary Redus	.03	.01	.00
☐ 371	Dave Schmidt	.03	.01	.00
☐ 372	Mark Clear	.03	.01	.00
☐ 373	Dave Bergman	.03	.01	.00
☐ 374	Charles Hudson	.03	.01	.00
☐ 375	Calvin Schiraldi	.03	.01	.00
☐ 376	Alex Trevino	.03	.01	.00
☐ 377	Tom Candiotti	.06	.03	.00
☐ 378	Steve Farr	.06	.03	.00
☐ 379	Mike Gallego	.03	.01	.00
☐ 380	Andy McGaffigan	.03	.01	.00
☐ 381	Kirk McCaskill	.03	.01	.00
☐ 382	Oddibe McDowell	.06	.03	.00
☐ 383	Floyd Bannister	.03	.01	.00
☐ 384	Denny Walling	.03	.01	.00
☐ 385	Don Carman	.03	.01	.00
☐ 386	Todd Worrell	.08	.04	.01
☐ 387	Eric Show	.03	.01	.00
☐ 388	Dave Parker	.10	.05	.01
☐ 389	Rick Mahler	.03	.01	.00
☐ 390	Mike Dunne	.06	.03	.00
☐ 391	Candy Maldonado	.08	.04	.01
☐ 392	Bob Dernier	.03	.01	.00
☐ 393	Dave Valle	.03	.01	.00
☐ 394	Ernie Whitt	.03	.01	.00
☐ 395	Juan Berenguer	.03	.01	.00
☐ 396	Mike Young	.03	.01	.00
☐ 397	Mike Felder	.03	.01	.00
☐ 398	Willie Hernandez	.06	.03	.00
☐ 399	Jim Rice	.10	.05	.01
☐ 400A	Checklist 358-467	.06	.01	.00
☐ 400B	Checklist 346-451	.06	.01	.00
☐ 401	Tommy John	.10	.05	.01
☐ 402	Brian Holton	.03	.01	.00
☐ 403	Carmen Castillo	.03	.01	.00
☐ 404	Jamie Quirk	.03	.01	.00
☐ 405	Dwayne Murphy	.03	.01	.00
☐ 406	Jeff Parrett	.15	.07	.01
☐ 407	Don Sutton	.12	.06	.01
☐ 408	Jerry Browne	.06	.03	.00
☐ 409	Jim Winn	.03	.01	.00
☐ 410	Dave Smith	.03	.01	.00
☐ 411	Shane Mack	.10	.05	.01
☐ 412	Greg Gross	.03	.01	.00
☐ 413	Nick Esasky	.08	.04	.01
☐ 414	Damaso Garcia	.03	.01	.00
☐ 415	Brian Fisher	.03	.01	.00
☐ 416	Brian Dayett	.03	.01	.00
☐ 417	Curt Ford	.03	.01	.00
☐ 418	Mark Williamson	.08	.04	.01
☐ 419	Bill Schroeder	.03	.01	.00
☐ 420	Mike Henneman	.20	.10	.02
☐ 421	John Marzano	.06	.03	.00
☐ 422	Ron Kittle	.08	.04	.01
☐ 423	Matt Young	.03	.01	.00
☐ 424	Steve Balboni	.03	.01	.00
☐ 425	Luis Polonia	.18	.09	.01
☐ 426	Randy St.Claire	.03	.01	.00
☐ 427	Greg Harris	.03	.01	.00
☐ 428	Johnny Ray	.06	.03	.00
☐ 429	Ray Searage	.03	.01	.00
☐ 430	Ricky Horton	.03	.01	.00
☐ 431	Gerald Young	.15	.07	.01
☐ 432	Rick Schu	.03	.01	.00
☐ 433	Paul O'Neill	.12	.06	.01
☐ 434	Rich Gossage	.08	.04	.01
☐ 435	John Cangelosi	.03	.01	.00
☐ 436	Mike LaCoss	.03	.01	.00
☐ 437	Gerald Perry	.06	.03	.00
☐ 438	Dave Martinez	.06	.03	.00
☐ 439	Darryl Strawberry	.40	.20	.04
☐ 440	John Moses	.03	.01	.00
☐ 441	Greg Gagne	.03	.01	.00
☐ 442	Jesse Barfield	.10	.05	.01
☐ 443	George Frazier	.03	.01	.00
☐ 444	Garth Iorg	.03	.01	.00
☐ 445	Ed Nunez	.03	.01	.00
☐ 446	Rick Aguilera	.03	.01	.00
☐ 447	Jerry Mumphrey	.03	.01	.00
☐ 448	Rafael Ramirez	.03	.01	.00
☐ 449	John Smiley	.25	.12	.02
☐ 450	Atlee Hammaker	.03	.01	.00
☐ 451	Lance McCullers	.03	.01	.00
☐ 452	Guy Hoffman	.03	.01	.00
☐ 453	Chris James	.12	.06	.01
☐ 454	Terry Pendleton	.03	.01	.00
☐ 455	Dave Meads	.06	.03	.00
☐ 456	Bill Buckner	.06	.03	.00
☐ 457	John Pawlowski	.06	.03	.00
☐ 458	Bob Sebra	.03	.01	.00
☐ 459	Jim Dwyer	.03	.01	.00
☐ 460	Jay Aldrich	.03	.01	.00
☐ 461	Frank Tanana	.03	.01	.00
☐ 462	Oil Can Boyd	.06	.03	.00
☐ 463	Dan Pasqua	.06	.03	.00
☐ 464	Tim Crews	.06	.03	.00
☐ 465	Andy Allanson	.03	.01	.00
☐ 466	Bill Pecota	.06	.03	.00
☐ 467	Steve Ontiveros	.03	.01	.00
☐ 468	Hubie Brooks	.08	.04	.01
☐ 469	Paul Kilgus	.08	.04	.01
☐ 470	Dale Mohorcic	.03	.01	.00
☐ 471	Dan Quisenberry	.08	.04	.01
☐ 472	Dave Stewart	.15	.07	.01
☐ 473	Dave Clark	.06	.03	.00
☐ 474	Joel Skinner	.03	.01	.00
☐ 475	Dave Anderson	.03	.01	.00
☐ 476	Dan Petry	.03	.01	.00
☐ 477	Carl Nichols	.03	.01	.00
☐ 478	Ernest Riles	.03	.01	.00
☐ 479	George Hendrick	.03	.01	.00
☐ 480	John Morris	.03	.01	.00
☐ 481	Manny Hernandez	.03	.01	.00
☐ 482	Jeff Stone	.03	.01	.00
☐ 483	Chris Brown	.03	.01	.00
☐ 484	Mike Bielecki	.06	.03	.00
☐ 485	Dave Dravecky	.08	.04	.01
☐ 486	Rick Manning	.03	.01	.00
☐ 487	Bill Almon	.03	.01	.00
☐ 488	Jim Sundberg	.03	.01	.00

□ 489 Ken Phelps	.06	.03	.00
□ 490 Tom Henke	.06	.03	.00
□ 491 Dan Gladden	.06	.03	.00
□ 492 Barry Larkin	.35	.17	.03
□ 493 Fred Manrique	.08	.04	.01
□ 494 Mike Griffin	.03	.01	.00
□ 495 Mark Knudson	.10	.05	.01
□ 496 Bill Madlock	.06	.03	.00
□ 497 Tim Stoddard	.03	.01	.00
□ 498 Sam Horn	.15	.07	.01
□ 499 Tracy Woodson	.12	.06	.01
□ 500A Checklist 468-577	.06	.01	.00
□ 500B Checklist 452-557	.06	.01	.00
□ 501 Ken Schrom	.03	.01	.00
□ 502 Angel Salazar	.03	.01	.00
□ 503 Eric Plunk	.03	.01	.00
□ 504 Joe Hesketh	.03	.01	.00
□ 505 Greg Minton	.03	.01	.00
□ 506 Geno Petralli	.03	.01	.00
□ 507 Bob James	.03	.01	.00
□ 508 Robbie Wine	.03	.01	.00
□ 509 Jeff Calhoun	.03	.01	.00
□ 510 Steve Lake	.03	.01	.00
□ 511 Mark Grant	.03	.01	.00
□ 512 Frank Williams	.03	.01	.00
□ 513 Jeff Blauser	.15	.07	.01
□ 514 Bob Walk	.03	.01	.00
□ 515 Craig Lefferts	.03	.01	.00
□ 516 Manny Trillo	.03	.01	.00
□ 517 Jerry Reed	.03	.01	.00
□ 518 Rick Leach	.03	.01	.00
□ 519 Mark Davidson	.10	.05	.01
□ 520 Jeff Ballard	.25	.12	.02
□ 521 Dave Stapleton	.03	.01	.00
□ 522 Pat Sheridan	.03	.01	.00
□ 523 Al Nipper	.03	.01	.00
□ 524 Steve Trout	.03	.01	.00
□ 525 Jeff Hamilton	.06	.03	.00
□ 526 Tommy Hinzo	.03	.01	.00
□ 527 Lonnie Smith	.06	.03	.00
□ 528 Greg Cadaret	.12	.06	.01
□ 529 Bob McClure UER ("Rob" on front)	.03	.01	.00
□ 530 Chuck Finley	.18	.09	.01
□ 531 Jeff Russell	.03	.01	.00
□ 532 Steve Lyons	.03	.01	.00
□ 533 Terry Puhl	.03	.01	.00
□ 534 Eric Nolte	.08	.04	.01
□ 535 Kent Tekulve	.03	.01	.00
□ 536 Pat Pacillo	.08	.04	.01
□ 537 Charlie Puleo	.03	.01	.00
□ 538 Tom Prince	.08	.04	.01
□ 539 Greg Maddux	.18	.09	.01
□ 540 Jim Lindeman	.03	.01	.00
□ 541 Pete Stanicek	.06	.03	.00
□ 542 Steve Kiefer	.03	.01	.00
□ 543A Jim Morrison ERR (no decimal before lifetime average)	.25	.12	.02
□ 543B Jim Morrison COR	.06	.03	.00
□ 544 Spike Owen	.03	.01	.00
□ 545 Jay Buhner	.25	.12	.02
□ 546 Mike Devereaux	.20	.10	.02
□ 547 Jerry Don Gleaton	.03	.01	.00
□ 548 Jose Rijo	.08	.04	.01
□ 549 Dennis Martinez	.03	.01	.00
□ 550 Mike Loynd	.03	.01	.00
□ 551 Darrell Miller	.03	.01	.00
□ 552 Dave LaPoint	.03	.01	.00
□ 553 John Tudor	.08	.04	.01
□ 554 Rocky Childress	.03	.01	.00
□ 555 Wally Ritchie	.03	.01	.00
□ 556 Terry McGriff	.06	.03	.00
□ 557 Dave Leiper	.03	.01	.00
□ 558 Jeff Robinson (Pirates pitcher)	.06	.03	.00
□ 559 Jose Uribe	.03	.01	.00
□ 560 Ted Simmons	.08	.04	.01
□ 561 Les Lancaster	.10	.05	.01
□ 562 Keith Miller (New York Mets)	.15	.07	.01
□ 563 Harold Reynolds	.06	.03	.00
□ 564 Gene Larkin	.20	.10	.02
□ 565 Cecil Fielder	.50	.25	.05
□ 566 Roy Smalley	.03	.01	.00
□ 567 Duane Ward	.03	.01	.00
□ 568 Bill Wilkinson	.06	.03	.00
□ 569 Howard Johnson	.15	.07	.01
□ 570 Frank DiPino	.03	.01	.00
□ 571 Pete Smith	.15	.07	.01
□ 572 Darnell Coles	.03	.01	.00
□ 573 Don Robinson	.03	.01	.00
□ 574 Rob Nelson	.03	.01	.00
□ 575 Dennis Rasmussen	.06	.03	.00
□ 576 Steve Jeltz	.03	.01	.00
□ 577 Tom Pagnozzi	.08	.04	.01
□ 578 Ty Gainey	.03	.01	.00
□ 579 Gary Lucas	.03	.01	.00
□ 580 Ron Hassey	.03	.01	.00
□ 581 Herm Winningham	.03	.01	.00
□ 582 Rene Gonzales	.08	.04	.01
□ 583 Brad Komminsk	.03	.01	.00
□ 584 Doyle Alexander	.03	.01	.00
□ 585 Jeff Sellers	.03	.01	.00
□ 586 Bill Gullickson	.03	.01	.00
□ 587 Tim Belcher	.35	.17	.03
□ 588 Doug Jones	.30	.15	.03
□ 589 Melido Perez	.20	.10	.02
□ 590 Rick Honeycutt	.03	.01	.00
□ 591 Pascual Perez	.06	.03	.00
□ 592 Curt Wilkerson	.03	.01	.00
□ 593 Steve Howe	.03	.01	.00
□ 594 John Davis	.08	.04	.01
□ 595 Storm Davis	.06	.03	.00
□ 596 Sammy Stewart	.03	.01	.00
□ 597 Neil Allen	.03	.01	.00
□ 598 Alejandro Pena	.03	.01	.00
□ 599 Mark Thurmond	.03	.01	.00
□ 600A Checklist 578-BC26	.06	.01	.00
□ 600B Checklist 558-660	.06	.01	.00
□ 601 Jose Mesa	.08	.04	.01
□ 602 Don August	.08	.04	.01
□ 603 Terry Leach SP	.10	.05	.01
□ 604 Tom Newell	.08	.04	.01
□ 605 Randall Byers SP	.20	.10	.02
□ 606 Jim Gott	.03	.01	.00
□ 607 Harry Spilman	.03	.01	.00
□ 608 John Candelaria	.03	.01	.00
□ 609 Mike Brumley	.10	.05	.01
□ 610 Mickey Brantley	.06	.03	.00
□ 611 Jose Nunez SP	.12	.06	.01
□ 612 Tom Nieto	.03	.01	.00
□ 613 Rick Reuschel	.06	.03	.00
□ 614 Lee Mazzilli SP	.10	.05	.01
□ 615 Scott Lusader	.08	.04	.01
□ 616 Bobby Meacham	.03	.01	.00
□ 617 Kevin McReynolds SP	.15	.07	.01
□ 618 Gene Garber	.03	.01	.00
□ 619 Barry Lyons SP	.18	.09	.01
□ 620 Randy Myers	.08	.04	.01
□ 621 Donnie Moore	.03	.01	.00
□ 622 Domingo Ramos	.03	.01	.00
□ 623 Ed Romero	.03	.01	.00
□ 624 Greg Myers	.10	.05	.01
□ 625 Ripken Family	.08	.04	.01
□ 626 Pat Perry	.03	.01	.00
□ 627 Andres Thomas SP	.10	.05	.01
□ 628 Matt Williams SP	3.25	1.60	.32
□ 629 Dave Hengel	.10	.05	.01
□ 630 Jeff Musselman SP	.10	.05	.01
□ 631 Tim Laudner	.03	.01	.00
□ 632 Bob Ojeda SP	.10	.05	.01
□ 633 Rafael Santana	.03	.01	.00
□ 634 Wes Gardner	.12	.06	.01
□ 635 Roberto Kelly SP	1.25	.60	.12
□ 636 Mike Flanagan SP	.10	.05	.01
□ 637 Jay Bell	.20	.10	.02
□ 638 Bob Melvin	.03	.01	.00
□ 639 Damon Berryhill	.25	.12	.02
□ 640 David Wells SP	.35	.17	.03
□ 641 Puzzle Card (Stan Musial)	.03	.01	.00
□ 642 Doug Sisk	.03	.01	.00
□ 643 Keith Hughes	.08	.04	.01
□ 644 Tom Glavine	.25	.12	.02
□ 645 Al Newman	.03	.01	.00
□ 646 Scott Sanderson	.06	.03	.00
□ 647 Scott Terry	.08	.04	.01
□ 648 Tim Teufel SP	.10	.05	.01
□ 649 Garry Templeton SP	.10	.05	.01
□ 650 Manny Lee SP	.10	.05	.01
□ 651 Roger McDowell SP	.10	.05	.01
□ 652 Mookie Wilson SP	.10	.05	.01
□ 653 David Cone SP	.50	.25	.05
□ 654 Ron Gant SP	1.75	.85	.17
□ 655 Joe Price SP	.10	.05	.01
□ 656 George Bell SP	.25	.12	.02
□ 657 Gregg Jefferies SP	4.00	2.00	.40
□ 658 Todd Stottlemyre SP	.40	.20	.04
□ 659 Geronimo Berroa SP	.30	.15	.03
□ 660 Jerry Royster SP	.10	.05	.01

1988 Donruss Bonus MVP's

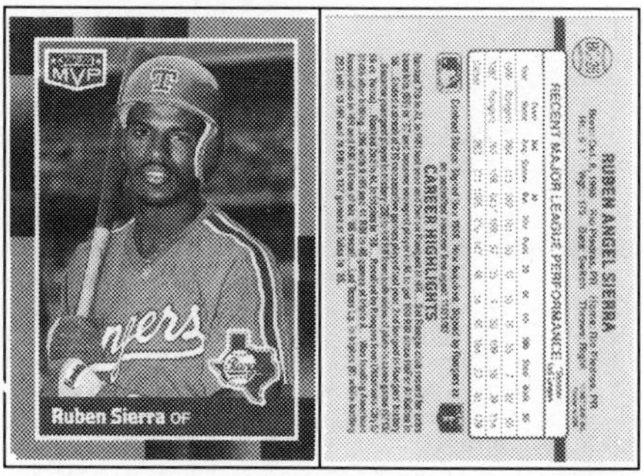

This 26-card set was distributed along with the regular 1988 Donruss issue as random inserts with the rack and wax packs. These bonus cards are numbered with the prefix BC for bonus cards and were supposedly produced in the same quantities as the other 660 regular issue cards. The "most valuable" player was selected from each of the 26 teams. Cards measure 2 1/2" by 3 1/2" and feature the same distinctive black and blue border on the front as the regular issue. The cards are distinguished by the MVP logo in the upper left corner of the obverse. The last 13 cards numerically are considered to be somewhat tougher to find than the first 13 cards.

	MINT	EXC	G-VG
COMPLETE SET (26)	6.00	3.00	.60
COMMON CARD (BC1-BC13)	.05	.02	.00
COMMON CARD (BC14-BC26)	.10	.05	.01
☐ BC1 Cal Ripken	.20	.10	.02
☐ BC2 Eric Davis	.20	.10	.02
☐ BC3 Paul Molitor	.10	.05	.01
☐ BC4 Mike Schmidt	.30	.15	.03
☐ BC5 Ivan Calderon	.05	.02	.00
☐ BC6 Tony Gwynn	.20	.10	.02
☐ BC7 Wade Boggs	.30	.15	.03
☐ BC8 Andy Van Slyke	.10	.05	.01
☐ BC9 Joe Carter	.10	.05	.01
☐ BC10 Andre Dawson	.15	.07	.01
☐ BC11 Alan Trammell	.10	.05	.01
☐ BC12 Mike Scott	.10	.05	.01
☐ BC13 Wally Joyner	.15	.07	.01
☐ BC14 Dale Murphy	.30	.15	.03
☐ BC15 Kirby Puckett	.40	.20	.04
☐ BC16 Pedro Guerrero	.10	.05	.01
☐ BC17 Kevin Seitzer	.20	.10	.02
☐ BC18 Tim Raines	.20	.10	.02
☐ BC19 George Bell	.20	.10	.02
☐ BC20 Darryl Strawberry	.40	.20	.04
☐ BC21 Don Mattingly	.65	.30	.06
☐ BC22 Ozzie Smith	.20	.10	.02
☐ BC23 Mark McGwire	.50	.25	.05
☐ BC24 Will Clark	.75	.35	.07
☐ BC25 Alvin Davis	.10	.05	.01
☐ BC26 Ruben Sierra	.30	.15	.03

1988 Donruss Super DK's

This 26-player card set was available through a mail-in offer detailed on the wax packs. The set was sent in return for 8.00 and three wrappers plus 1.50 postage and handling. The set features the popular Diamond King subseries in large (approximately 4 7/8" by 6 13/16") form. Dick Perez of Perez-Steele Galleries did another outstanding job on the artwork. The cards are essentially a large version of the Donruss regular issue Diamond Kings.

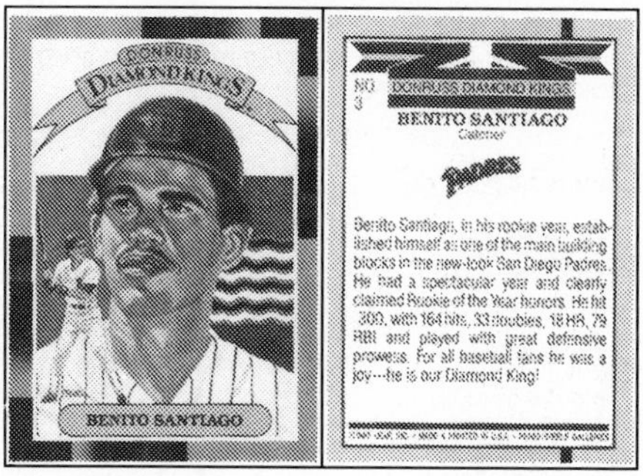

	MINT	EXC	G-VG
COMPLETE SET (26)	10.00	5.00	1.00
COMMON PLAYER (1-26)	.20	.10	.02
☐ 1 Mark McGwire DK	1.50	.75	.15
☐ 2 Tim Raines DK	.40	.20	.04
☐ 3 Benito Santiago DK	.75	.35	.07
☐ 4 Alan Trammell DK	.30	.15	.03
☐ 5 Danny Tartabull DK	.40	.20	.04
☐ 6 Ron Darling DK	.25	.12	.02
☐ 7 Paul Molitor DK	.25	.12	.02
☐ 8 Devon White DK	.30	.15	.03
☐ 9 Andre Dawson DK	.35	.17	.03
☐ 10 Julio Franco DK	.25	.12	.02
☐ 11 Scott Fletcher DK	.20	.10	.02
☐ 12 Tony Fernandez DK	.25	.12	.02
☐ 13 Shane Rawley DK	.20	.10	.02
☐ 14 Kal Daniels DK	.35	.17	.03
☐ 15 Jack Clark DK	.35	.17	.03
☐ 16 Dwight Evans DK	.25	.12	.02
☐ 17 Tommy John DK	.25	.12	.02
☐ 18 Andy Van Slyke DK	.25	.12	.02
☐ 19 Gary Gaetti DK	.25	.12	.02
☐ 20 Mark Langston DK	.30	.15	.03
☐ 21 Will Clark DK	1.50	.75	.15
☐ 22 Glenn Hubbard DK	.20	.10	.02
☐ 23 Billy Hatcher DK	.25	.12	.02
☐ 24 Bob Welch DK	.35	.17	.03
☐ 25 Ivan Calderon DK	.25	.12	.02
☐ 26 Cal Ripken Jr. DK	.75	.35	.07

1988 Donruss All-Stars

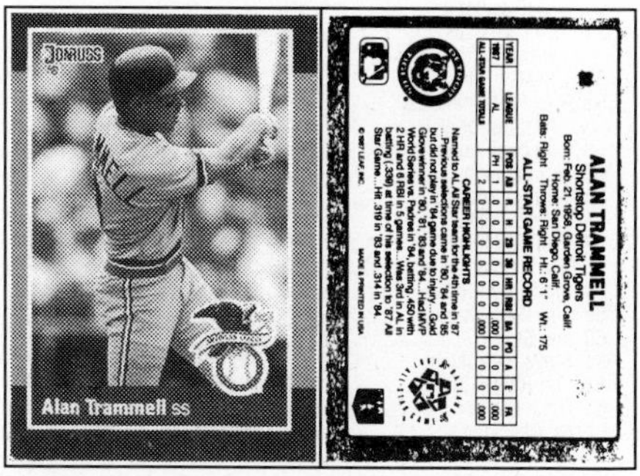

This 64-card set features cards measuring standard size, 2 1/2" by 3 1/2". Card fronts are in full color with a solid blue and black border. The card backs are printed in black and blue on white card stock. Cards are numbered on the back inside a blue star in the upper right hand corner. Card backs feature statistical information about the player's performance in past All-Star games. The set was distributed in packs which also contained a Pop-Up. The AL Checklist card number 32 has two uncorrected errors on it, Wade Boggs is erroneously listed as the AL Leftfielder and Dan Plesac is erroneously listed as being the Tigers Pitcher.

	MINT	EXC	G-VG
COMPLETE SET (64)	8.00	4.00	.80
COMMON PLAYER (1-64)	.10	.05	.01
☐ 1 Don Mattingly	.80	.40	.08
☐ 2 Dave Winfield	.25	.12	.02
☐ 3 Willie Randolph	.15	.07	.01
☐ 4 Rickey Henderson	.75	.35	.07
☐ 5 Cal Ripken	.35	.17	.03
☐ 6 George Bell	.20	.10	.02
☐ 7 Wade Boggs	.75	.35	.07
☐ 8 Bret Saberhagen	.25	.12	.02
☐ 9 Terry Kennedy	.10	.05	.01
☐ 10 John McNamara MG	.10	.05	.01
☐ 11 Jay Howell	.10	.05	.01
☐ 12 Harold Baines	.15	.07	.01
☐ 13 Harold Reynolds	.10	.05	.01
☐ 14 Bruce Hurst	.15	.07	.01
☐ 15 Kirby Puckett	.40	.20	.04
☐ 16 Matt Nokes	.15	.07	.01
☐ 17 Pat Tabler	.10	.05	.01
☐ 18 Dan Plesac	.10	.05	.01
☐ 19 Mark McGwire	.75	.35	.07
☐ 20 Mike Witt	.10	.05	.01
☐ 21 Larry Parrish	.10	.05	.01
☐ 22 Alan Trammell	.20	.10	.02
☐ 23 Dwight Evans	.15	.07	.01
☐ 24 Jack Morris	.15	.07	.01
☐ 25 Tony Fernandez	.15	.07	.01
☐ 26 Mark Langston	.20	.10	.02
☐ 27 Kevin Seitzer	.40	.20	.04
☐ 28 Tom Henke	.10	.05	.01
☐ 29 Dave Righetti	.15	.07	.01
☐ 30 Oakland Stadium	.10	.05	.01
☐ 31 Wade Boggs	.75	.35	.07
☐ 32 AL Checklist UER	.10	.01	.00
☐ 33 Jack Clark	.20	.10	.02
☐ 34 Darryl Strawberry	.40	.20	.04
☐ 35 Ryne Sandberg	.75	.35	.07
☐ 36 Andre Dawson	.30	.15	.03
☐ 37 Ozzie Smith	.25	.12	.02
☐ 38 Eric Davis	.50	.25	.05
☐ 39 Mike Schmidt	.75	.35	.07
☐ 40 Mike Scott	.20	.10	.02
☐ 41 Gary Carter	.20	.10	.02
☐ 42 Davey Johnson MG	.10	.05	.01
☐ 43 Rick Sutcliffe	.10	.05	.01
☐ 44 Willie McGee	.15	.07	.01
☐ 45 Hubie Brooks	.10	.05	.01
☐ 46 Dale Murphy	.30	.15	.03
☐ 47 Bo Diaz	.10	.05	.01
☐ 48 Pedro Guerrero	.20	.10	.02
☐ 49 Keith Hernandez	.20	.10	.02
☐ 50 Ozzie Virgil UER (Phillies logo on card back, wrong birth year)	.10	.05	.01
☐ 51 Tony Gwynn	.35	.17	.03
☐ 52 Rick Reuschel UER (Pirates logo on card back)	.10	.05	.01
☐ 53 John Franco	.15	.07	.01
☐ 54 Jeffrey Leonard	.10	.05	.01
☐ 55 Juan Samuel	.15	.07	.01
☐ 56 Orel Hershiser	.40	.20	.04
☐ 57 Tim Raines	.25	.12	.02
☐ 58 Sid Fernandez	.15	.07	.01
☐ 59 Tim Wallach	.10	.05	.01
☐ 60 Lee Smith	.10	.05	.01
☐ 61 Steve Bedrosian	.10	.05	.01
☐ 62 Tim Raines	.25	.12	.02
☐ 63 Ozzie Smith	.20	.10	.02
☐ 64 NL Checklist	.10	.01	.00

1988 Donruss Pop-Ups

This 20-card set features "fold-out" cards measuring standard size, 2 1/2" by 3 1/2". Card fronts are in full color. Cards are unnumbered but are listed in the same order as the Donruss All-Stars on the All-Star checklist card. Card backs present essentially no information about the player. The set was distributed in packs which also contained All-Star cards. In order to remain in mint condition, the cards should not be popped up.

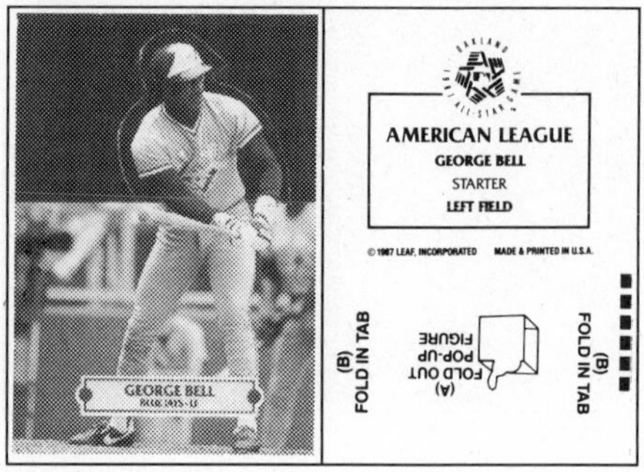

	MINT	EXC	G-VG
COMPLETE SET (20)	4.00	2.00	.40
COMMON PLAYER (1-20)	.10	.05	.01
☐ 1 Don Mattingly	.75	.35	.07
☐ 2 Dave Winfield	.25	.12	.02
☐ 3 Willie Randolph	.15	.07	.01
☐ 4 Rickey Henderson	.75	.35	.07
☐ 5 Cal Ripken	.35	.17	.03
☐ 6 George Bell	.20	.10	.02
☐ 7 Wade Boggs	.75	.35	.07
☐ 8 Bret Saberhagen	.25	.12	.02
☐ 9 Terry Kennedy	.10	.05	.01
☐ 10 John McNamara MG	.10	.05	.01
☐ 11 Jack Clark	.20	.10	.02
☐ 12 Darryl Strawberry	.50	.25	.05
☐ 13 Ryne Sandberg	.75	.35	.07
☐ 14 Andre Dawson	.30	.15	.03
☐ 15 Ozzie Smith	.25	.12	.02
☐ 16 Eric Davis	.50	.25	.05
☐ 17 Mike Schmidt	.75	.35	.07
☐ 18 Mike Scott	.20	.10	.02
☐ 19 Gary Carter	.20	.10	.02
☐ 20 Davey Johnson MG	.10	.05	.01

1988 Donruss Rookies

The 1988 Donruss "The Rookies" set features 56 cards plus a 15-piece puzzle of Stan Musial. Cards are in full color and are standard size, 2 1/2" by 3 1/2". The set was distributed in a small green and black box with gold lettering. Card fronts are similar in design to the 1988 Donruss regular issue except for the presence of "The Rookies" logo in the lower right corner and a green and black border instead of a blue and black border on the fronts. The key rookies in this set are ROY's, Chris Sabo and Walt Weiss.

	MINT	EXC	G-VG
COMPLETE SET (56)	12.50	6.25	1.25
COMMON PLAYER (1-56)	.07	.03	.01
☐ 1 Mark Grace	4.00	1.00	.20
☐ 2 Mike Campbell	.10	.05	.01
☐ 3 Todd Frohwirth	.10	.05	.01
☐ 4 Dave Stapleton	.07	.03	.01
☐ 5 Shawn Abner	.12	.06	.01
☐ 6 Jose Cecena	.07	.03	.01
☐ 7 Dave Gallagher	.20	.10	.02
☐ 8 Mark Parent	.15	.07	.01
☐ 9 Cecil Espy	.12	.06	.01
☐ 10 Pete Smith	.10	.05	.01
☐ 11 Jay Buhner	.20	.10	.02
☐ 12 Pat Borders	.35	.17	.03
☐ 13 Doug Jennings	.25	.12	.02
☐ 14 Brady Anderson	.35	.17	.03
☐ 15 Pete Stanicek	.10	.05	.01
☐ 16 Roberto Kelly	.50	.25	.05
☐ 17 Jeff Treadway	.10	.05	.01
☐ 18 Walt Weiss	1.00	.50	.10
☐ 19 Paul Gibson	.10	.05	.01
☐ 20 Tim Crews	.07	.03	.01
☐ 21 Melido Perez	.12	.06	.01
☐ 22 Steve Peters	.12	.06	.01
☐ 23 Craig Worthington	.40	.20	.04
☐ 24 John Trautwein	.10	.05	.01
☐ 25 DeWayne Vaughn	.07	.03	.01
☐ 26 David Wells	.10	.05	.01
☐ 27 Al Leiter	.12	.06	.01
☐ 28 Tim Belcher	.25	.12	.02
☐ 29 Johnny Paredes	.10	.05	.01
☐ 30 Chris Sabo	2.50	1.25	.25
☐ 31 Damon Berryhill	.20	.10	.02
☐ 32 Randy Milligan	.50	.25	.05
☐ 33 Gary Thurman	.12	.06	.01
☐ 34 Kevin Elster	.15	.07	.01
☐ 35 Roberto Alomar	.60	.30	.06
☐ 36 Edgar Martinez UER (photo actually Edwin Nunez)	.50	.25	.05
☐ 37 Todd Stottlemyre	.15	.07	.01
☐ 38 Joey Meyer	.10	.05	.01
☐ 39 Carl Nichols	.07	.03	.01
☐ 40 Jack McDowell	.18	.09	.01
☐ 41 Jose Bautista	.12	.06	.01
☐ 42 Sil Campusano	.20	.10	.02
☐ 43 John Dopson	.20	.10	.02
☐ 44 Jody Reed	.20	.10	.02
☐ 45 Darrin Jackson	.12	.06	.01
☐ 46 Mike Capel	.10	.05	.01
☐ 47 Ron Gant	.75	.35	.07
☐ 48 John Davis	.07	.03	.01
☐ 49 Kevin Coffman	.07	.03	.01
☐ 50 Cris Carpenter	.15	.07	.01
☐ 51 Mackey Sasser	.15	.07	.01
☐ 52 Luis Alicea	.10	.05	.01
☐ 53 Bryan Harvey	.20	.10	.02
☐ 54 Steve Ellsworth	.10	.05	.01
☐ 55 Mike Macfarlane	.20	.10	.02
☐ 56 Checklist Card	.07	.01	.00

1988 Donruss Athletics Book

The 1988 Donruss Athletics Team Book set features 27 cards (three pages with nine cards on each page) plus a large full-page puzzle of Stan Musial. Cards are in full color and are standard size, 2 1/2" by 3 1/2". The set was distributed as a four-page book; although the puzzle page was perforated, the card pages were not. The cover of the "Team Collection" book is primarily bright red. Card fronts are very similar in design to the 1988 Donruss regular issue. The card numbers on the backs are the same for those players that are the same as in the regular Donruss set; the new players pictured are numbered on the back as "NEW." In fact 1988 A.L. Rookie of the Year Walt Weiss makes his first Donruss appearance in this set as a "NEW" card. The book is usually sold intact. When cut from the book into individual cards, these cards are distinguishable from the regular 1988 Donruss cards since these have a 1988 copyright on the back whereas the regular issue has a 1987 copyright on the back.

	MINT	EXC	G-VG
COMPLETE SET (27)	5.00	2.50	.50
COMMON PLAYER	.10	.05	.01
☐ 97 Curt Young	.10	.05	.01
☐ 133 Gene Nelson	.10	.05	.01
☐ 158 Terry Steinbach	.25	.12	.02
☐ 178 Carney Lansford	.20	.10	.02
☐ 221 Tony Phillips	.10	.05	.01
☐ 256 Mark McGwire	1.00	.50	.10
☐ 302 Jose Canseco	1.50	.75	.15
☐ 349 Dennis Eckersley	.40	.20	.04
☐ 379 Mike Gallego	.10	.05	.01
☐ 425 Luis Polonia	.10	.05	.01
☐ 467 Steve Ontiveros	.10	.05	.01
☐ 472 Dave Stewart	.50	.25	.05
☐ 503 Eric Plunk	.10	.05	.01
☐ 528 Greg Cadaret	.10	.05	.01
☐ 590 Rick Honeycutt	.10	.05	.01
☐ 595 Storm Davis	.20	.10	.02
☐ NEW Don Baylor UER (career stats are incorrect)	.20	.10	.02
☐ NEW Ron Hassey	.10	.05	.01
☐ NEW Dave Henderson	.20	.10	.02
☐ NEW Glenn Hubbard	.10	.05	.01
☐ NEW Stan Javier	.10	.05	.01
☐ NEW Doug Jennings	.25	.12	.02
☐ NEW Edward Jurak	.10	.05	.01
☐ NEW Dave Parker	.25	.12	.02
☐ NEW Walt Weiss	1.00	.50	.10
☐ NEW Bob Welch	.30	.15	.03
☐ NEW Matt Young	.10	.05	.01

1988 Donruss Cubs Team Book

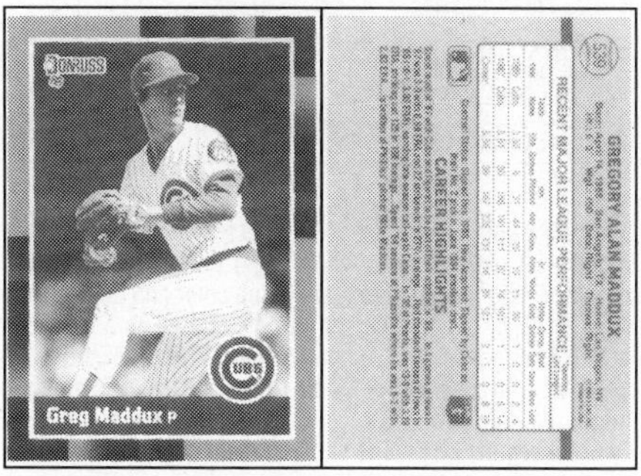

The 1988 Donruss Cubs Team Book set features 27 cards (three pages with nine cards on each page) plus a large full-page puzzle of Stan Musial. Cards are in full color and are standard size, 2 1/2" by 3 1/2". The set was distributed as a four-page book; although the puzzle page was perforated, the card pages were not. The cover of the "Team Collection" book is primarily bright red. Card fronts are very similar in design to the 1988 Donruss regular issue. The card numbers on the backs are the same for those players that are the same as in the regular Donruss set; the new players pictured are numbered on the back as "NEW." The book is usually sold intact. When cut from the book into individual cards, these cards are distinguishable from the regular 1988 Donruss cards since these have a 1988 copyright on the back whereas the regular issue has a 1987 copyright on the back.

	MINT	EXC	G-VG
COMPLETE SET (27)	5.00	2.50	.50
COMMON PLAYER	.10	.05	.01
☐ 40 Mark Grace	2.00	1.00	.20
☐ 68 Rick Sutcliffe	.20	.10	.02
☐ 119 Jody Davis	.15	.07	.01
☐ 146 Shawon Dunston	.30	.15	.03
☐ 169 Jamie Moyer	.10	.05	.01
☐ 191 Leon Durham	.10	.05	.01
☐ 242 Ryne Sandberg	.75	.35	.07
☐ 269 Andre Dawson	.45	.22	.04
☐ 315 Paul Noce	.15	.07	.01
☐ 324 Rafael Palmeiro	.75	.35	.07
☐ 438 Dave Martinez	.15	.07	.01
☐ 447 Jerry Mumphrey	.10	.05	.01
☐ 488 Jim Sundberg	.10	.05	.01
☐ 516 Manny Trillo	.10	.05	.01
☐ 539 Greg Maddux	.35	.17	.03
☐ 561 Les Lancaster	.10	.05	.01
☐ 570 Frank DiPino	.10	.05	.01
☐ 639 Damon Berryhill	.35	.17	.03
☐ 646 Scott Sanderson	.15	.07	.01
☐ NEW Mike Bielecki	.20	.10	.02
☐ NEW Rich Gossage	.20	.10	.02
☐ NEW Drew Hall	.15	.07	.01
☐ NEW Darrin Jackson	.20	.10	.02
☐ NEW Vance Law	.10	.05	.01
☐ NEW Al Nipper	.10	.05	.01
☐ NEW Angel Salazar	.10	.05	.01
☐ NEW Calvin Schiraldi	.10	.05	.01

1988 Donruss Mets Team Book

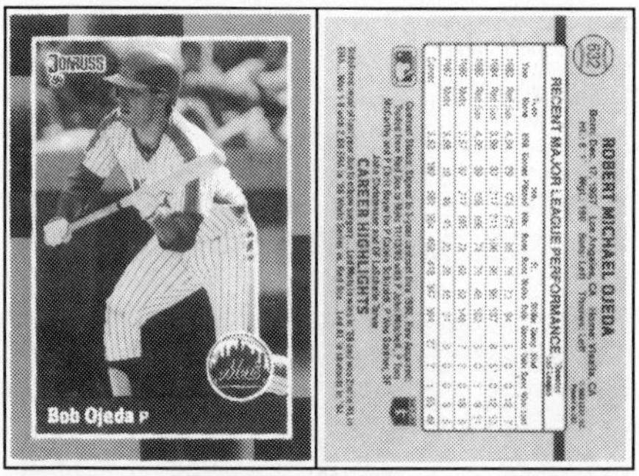

The 1988 Donruss Mets Team Book set features 27 cards (three pages with nine cards on each page) plus a large full-page puzzle of Stan Musial. Cards are in full color and are standard size, 2 1/2" by 3 1/2". The set was distributed as a four-page book; although the puzzle page was perforated, the card pages were not. The cover of the "Team Collection" book is primarily bright red. Card fronts are very similar in design to the 1988 Donruss regular issue. The card numbers on the backs are the same for those players that are the same as in the regular Donruss set; the new players pictured are numbered on the back as "NEW." The book is usually sold intact. When cut from the book into individual cards, these cards are distinguishable from the regular 1988 Donruss cards since these have a 1988 copyright on the back whereas the regular issue has a 1987 copyright on the back.

	MINT	EXC	G-VG
COMPLETE SET (27)	5.00	2.50	.50
COMMON PLAYER	.10	.05	.01
☐ 37 Kevin Elster	.15	.07	.01
☐ 69 Dwight Gooden	.50	.25	.05
☐ 76 Ron Darling	.20	.10	.02
☐ 118 Sid Fernandez	.20	.10	.02
☐ 199 Gary Carter	.25	.12	.02
☐ 241 Wally Backman	.10	.05	.01
☐ 316 Keith Hernandez	.25	.12	.02
☐ 323 Dave Magadan	.40	.20	.04
☐ 364 Lee Dykstra	.35	.17	.03
☐ 439 Darryl Strawberry	.75	.35	.07
☐ 446 Rick Aguilera	.15	.07	.01
☐ 562 Keith Miller	.15	.07	.01
☐ 569 Howard Johnson	.30	.15	.03
☐ 603 Terry Leach	.15	.07	.01
☐ 614 Lee Mazzilli	.10	.05	.01
☐ 617 Kevin McReynolds	.25	.12	.02
☐ 619 Barry Lyons	.10	.05	.01
☐ 620 Randy Myers	.20	.10	.02
☐ 632 Bob Ojeda	.15	.07	.01
☐ 648 Tim Teufel	.10	.05	.01
☐ 651 Roger McDowell	.15	.07	.01
☐ 652 Mookie Wilson	.15	.07	.01
☐ 653 David Cone	.40	.20	.04
☐ 657 Gregg Jefferies	1.50	.75	.15
☐ NEW Jeff Innis	.20	.10	.02
☐ NEW Mackey Sasser	.25	.12	.02
☐ NEW Gene Walter	.10	.05	.01

1988 Donruss Red Sox Team Book

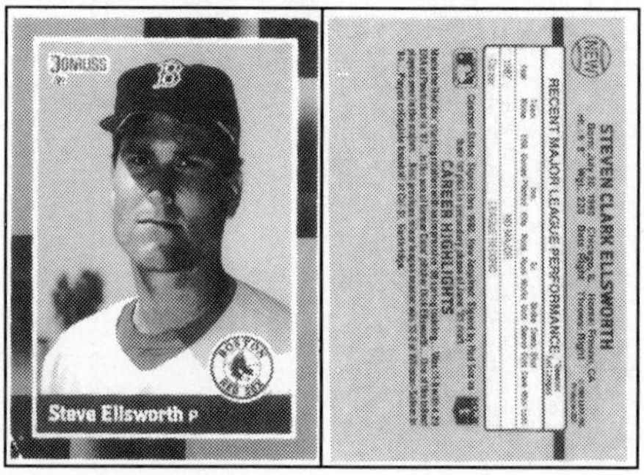

The 1988 Donruss Red Sox Team Book set features 27 cards (three pages with nine cards on each page) plus a large full-page puzzle of Stan Musial. Cards are in full color and are standard size, 2 1/2" by 3 1/2". The set was distributed as a four-page book; although the puzzle page was perforated, the card pages were not. The cover of the "Team Collection" book is primarily bright red. Card fronts are very similar in design to the 1988 Donruss regular issue. The card numbers on the backs are the same for those players that are the same as in the regular Donruss set; the new players pictured are numbered on the back as "NEW." The book is usually sold intact. When cut from the book into individual cards, these cards are distinguishable from the regular 1988 Donruss cards since these have a 1988 copyright on the back whereas the regular issue has a 1987 copyright on the back.

	MINT	EXC	G-VG
COMPLETE SET (27)	5.00	2.50	.50
COMMON PLAYER	.10	.05	.01
☐ 41 Jody Reed	.25	.12	.02
☐ 51 Roger Clemens	.60	.30	.06
☐ 92 Bob Stanley	.10	.05	.01
☐ 129 Rich Gedman	.10	.05	.01
☐ 153 Wade Boggs	.90	.45	.09
☐ 174 Ellis Burks	1.25	.60	.12
☐ 216 Dwight Evans	.20	.10	.02
☐ 252 Bruce Hurst	.20	.10	.02
☐ 276 Marty Barrett	.15	.07	.01
☐ 297 Todd Benzinger	.20	.10	.02
☐ 339 Mike Greenwell	1.25	.60	.12
☐ 399 Jim Rice	.25	.12	.02

☐ 421 John Marzano	.10	.05	.01
☐ 462 Oil Can Boyd	.15	.07	.01
☐ 498 Sam Horn	.15	.07	.01
☐ 544 Spike Owen	.10	.05	.01
☐ 585 Jeff Sellers	.10	.05	.01
☐ 623 Ed Romero	.10	.05	.01
☐ 634 Wes Gardner	.15	.07	.01
☐ NEW Brady Anderson	.30	.15	.03
☐ NEW Rick Cerone	.10	.05	.01
☐ NEW Steve Ellsworth	.15	.07	.01
☐ NEW Dennis Lamp	.10	.05	.01
☐ NEW Kevin Romine	.10	.05	.01
☐ NEW Lee Smith	.20	.10	.02
☐ NEW Mike Smithson	.10	.05	.01
☐ NEW John Trautwein	.15	.07	.01

1988 Donruss Yankees Team Book

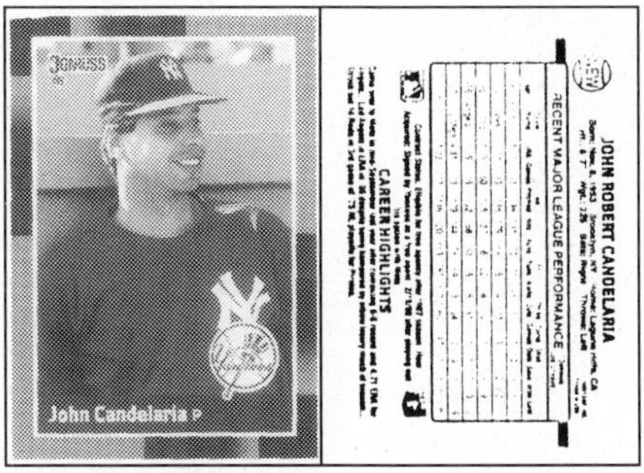

The 1988 Donruss Yankees Team Book set features 27 cards (three pages with nine cards on each page) plus a large full-page puzzle of Stan Musial. Cards are in full color and are standard size, 2 1/2" by 3 1/2". The set was distributed as a four-page book; although the puzzle page was perforated, the card pages were not. The cover of the "Team Collection" book is primarily bright red. Card fronts are very similar in design to the 1988 Donruss regular issue. The card numbers on the backs are the same for those players that are the same as in the regular Donruss set; the new players pictured are numbered on the back as "NEW." The book is usually sold intact. When cut from the book into individual cards, these cards are distinguishable from the regular 1988 Donruss cards since these have a 1988 copyright on the back whereas the regular issue has a 1987 copyright on the back.

	MINT	EXC	G-VG
COMPLETE SET (27)	5.00	2.50	.50
COMMON PLAYER	.10	.05	.01
☐ 43 Al Leiter	.15	.07	.01
☐ 93 Dave Righetti	.20	.10	.02
☐ 105 Mike Pagliarulo	.15	.07	.01
☐ 128 Rick Rhoden	.10	.05	.01
☐ 175 Ron Guidry	.25	.12	.02
☐ 217 Don Mattingly	1.50	.75	.15
☐ 228 Willie Randolph	.20	.10	.02
☐ 251 Gary Ward	.10	.05	.01
☐ 277 Rickey Henderson	1.00	.50	.10
☐ 278 Dave Winfield	.35	.17	.03
☐ 340 Claudell Washington	.15	.07	.01
☐ 374 Charles Hudson	.10	.05	.01
☐ 401 Tommy John	.20	.10	.02
☐ 474 Joel Skinner	.10	.05	.01
☐ 497 Tim Stoddard	.10	.05	.01
☐ 545 Jay Buhner	.35	.17	.03
☐ 616 Bobby Meacham	.10	.05	.01
☐ 635 Roberto Kelly	1.00	.50	.10
☐ NEW John Candelaria	.20	.10	.02
☐ NEW Jack Clark	.35	.17	.03
☐ NEW Jose Cruz	.15	.07	.01
☐ NEW Richard Dotson	.15	.07	.01
☐ NEW Cecilo Guante	.10	.05	.01
☐ NEW Lee Guetterman	.15	.07	.01

☐ NEW Rafael Santana	.10	.05	.01
☐ NEW Steve Shields	.10	.05	.01
☐ NEW Don Slaught	.10	.05	.01

1988 Donruss Baseball's Best

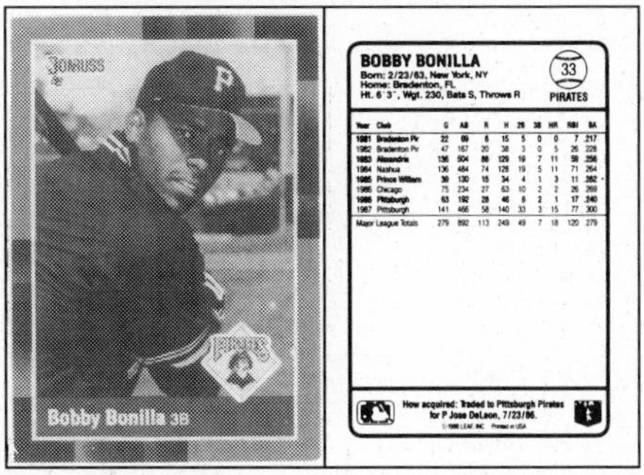

This innovative set of 336 cards was released by Donruss very late in the 1988 season to be sold in large national retail chains as a complete packaged set. Cards are the standard size, 2 1/2" by 3 1/2", and are packaged as a complete set in a specially designed box. Cards are very similar in design to the 1988 regular Donruss issue except that these cards have orange and black borders instead of blue and black borders. The set is also sometimes referred to as the Halloween set because of the orange box and design of the cards. Six (2 1/2" by 3 1/2") 15-piece puzzles of Stan Musial are also included with every complete set.

	MINT	EXC	G-VG
COMPLETE SET (336)	20.00	10.00	2.00
COMMON PLAYER (1-336)	.04	.02	.00
☐ 1 Don Mattingly	1.00	.50	.10
☐ 2 Ron Gant	1.00	.50	.10
☐ 3 Bob Boone	.10	.05	.01
☐ 4 Mark Grace	1.25	.60	.12
☐ 5 Andy Allanson	.04	.02	.00
☐ 6 Kal Daniels	.10	.05	.01
☐ 7 Floyd Bannister	.04	.02	.00
☐ 8 Alan Ashby	.04	.02	.00
☐ 9 Marty Barrett	.07	.03	.01
☐ 10 Tim Belcher	.15	.07	.01
☐ 11 Harold Baines	.10	.05	.01
☐ 12 Hubie Brooks	.07	.03	.01
☐ 13 Doyle Alexander	.04	.02	.00
☐ 14 Gary Carter	.20	.10	.02
☐ 15 Glenn Braggs	.10	.05	.01
☐ 16 Steve Bedrosian	.10	.05	.01
☐ 17 Barry Bonds	.60	.30	.06
☐ 18 Bert Blyleven	.10	.05	.01
☐ 19 Tom Brunansky	.10	.05	.01
☐ 20 John Candelaria	.04	.02	.00
☐ 21 Shawn Abner	.10	.05	.01
☐ 22 Jose Canseco	1.25	.60	.12
☐ 23 Brett Butler	.10	.05	.01
☐ 24 Scott Bradley	.04	.02	.00
☐ 25 Ivan Calderon	.07	.03	.01
☐ 26 Rich Gossage	.10	.05	.01
☐ 27 Brian Downing	.04	.02	.00
☐ 28 Jim Rice	.15	.07	.01
☐ 29 Dion James	.04	.02	.00
☐ 30 Terry Kennedy	.04	.02	.00
☐ 31 George Bell	.15	.07	.01
☐ 32 Scott Fletcher	.04	.02	.00
☐ 33 Bobby Bonilla	.35	.17	.03
☐ 34 Tim Burke	.04	.02	.00
☐ 35 Darrell Evans	.07	.03	.01
☐ 36 Mike Davis	.04	.02	.00
☐ 37 Shawon Dunston	.20	.10	.02
☐ 38 Kevin Bass	.07	.03	.01
☐ 39 George Brett	.30	.15	.03
☐ 40 David Cone	.30	.15	.03
☐ 41 Ron Darling	.10	.05	.01
☐ 42 Roberto Alomar	1.00	.50	.10

☐ 43 Dennis Eckersley	.20	.10	.02
☐ 44 Vince Coleman	.20	.10	.02
☐ 45 Sid Bream	.04	.02	.00
☐ 46 Gary Gaetti	.15	.07	.01
☐ 47 Phil Bradley	.07	.03	.01
☐ 48 Jim Clancy	.04	.02	.00
☐ 49 Jack Clark	.15	.07	.01
☐ 50 Mike Krukow	.04	.02	.00
☐ 51 Henry Cotto	.04	.02	.00
☐ 52 Rich Dotson	.04	.02	.00
☐ 53 Jim Gantner	.04	.02	.00
☐ 54 John Franco	.07	.03	.01
☐ 55 Pete Incaviglia	.15	.07	.01
☐ 56 Joe Carter	.15	.07	.01
☐ 57 Roger Clemens	.50	.25	.05
☐ 58 Gerald Perry	.04	.02	.00
☐ 59 Jack Howell	.04	.02	.00
☐ 60 Vance Law	.04	.02	.00
☐ 61 Jay Bell	.04	.02	.00
☐ 62 Eric Davis	.50	.25	.05
☐ 63 Gene Garber	.04	.02	.00
☐ 64 Glenn Davis	.15	.07	.01
☐ 65 Wade Boggs	.75	.35	.07
☐ 66 Kirk Gibson	.20	.10	.02
☐ 67 Carlton Fisk	.25	.12	.02
☐ 68 Casey Candaele	.04	.02	.00
☐ 69 Mike Heath	.04	.02	.00
☐ 70 Kevin Elster	.10	.05	.01
☐ 71 Greg Brock	.04	.02	.00
☐ 72 Don Carman	.04	.02	.00
☐ 73 Doug Drabek	.20	.10	.02
☐ 74 Greg Gagne	.04	.02	.00
☐ 75 Danny Cox	.07	.03	.01
☐ 76 Rickey Henderson	.75	.35	.07
☐ 77 Chris Brown	.04	.02	.00
☐ 78 Terry Steinbach	.10	.05	.01
☐ 79 Will Clark	1.25	.60	.12
☐ 80 Mickey Brantley	.07	.03	.01
☐ 81 Ozzie Guillen	.10	.05	.01
☐ 82 Greg Maddux	.15	.07	.01
☐ 83 Kirk McCaskill	.04	.02	.00
☐ 84 Dwight Evans	.15	.07	.01
☐ 85 Ozzie Virgil	.04	.02	.00
☐ 86 Mike Morgan	.04	.02	.00
☐ 87 Tony Fernandez	.10	.05	.01
☐ 88 Jose Guzman	.04	.02	.00
☐ 89 Mike Dunne	.07	.03	.01
☐ 90 Andres Galarraga	.20	.10	.02
☐ 91 Mike Henneman	.07	.03	.01
☐ 92 Alfredo Griffin	.04	.02	.00
☐ 93 Rafael Palmeiro	.30	.15	.03
☐ 94 Jim Deshaies	.04	.02	.00
☐ 95 Mark Gubicza	.10	.05	.01
☐ 96 Dwight Gooden	.50	.25	.05
☐ 97 Howard Johnson	.20	.10	.02
☐ 98 Mark Davis	.20	.10	.02
☐ 99 Dave Stewart	.30	.15	.03
☐ 100 Joe Magrane	.15	.07	.01
☐ 101 Brian Fisher	.04	.02	.00
☐ 102 Kent Hrbek	.15	.07	.01
☐ 103 Kevin Gross	.04	.02	.00
☐ 104 Tom Henke	.07	.03	.01
☐ 105 Mike Pagliarulo	.07	.03	.01
☐ 106 Kelly Downs	.04	.02	.00
☐ 107 Alvin Davis	.10	.05	.01
☐ 108 Willie Randolph	.10	.05	.01
☐ 109 Rob Deer	.10	.05	.01
☐ 110 Bo Diaz	.04	.02	.00
☐ 111 Paul Kilgus	.04	.02	.00
☐ 112 Tom Candiotti	.04	.02	.00
☐ 113 Dale Murphy	.30	.15	.03
☐ 114 Rick Mahler	.04	.02	.00
☐ 115 Wally Joyner	.35	.17	.03
☐ 116 Ryne Sandberg	.75	.35	.07
☐ 117 John Farrell	.10	.05	.01
☐ 118 Nick Esasky	.07	.03	.01
☐ 119 Bo Jackson	1.50	.75	.15
☐ 120 Bill Doran	.07	.03	.01
☐ 121 Ellis Burks	1.00	.50	.10
☐ 122 Pedro Guerrero	.15	.07	.01
☐ 123 Dave LaPoint	.07	.03	.01
☐ 124 Neal Heaton	.04	.02	.00
☐ 125 Willie Hernandez	.07	.03	.01
☐ 126 Roger McDowell	.07	.03	.01
☐ 127 Ted Higuera	.07	.03	.01
☐ 128 Von Hayes	.10	.05	.01
☐ 129 Mike LaValliere	.04	.02	.00
☐ 130 Dan Gladden	.04	.02	.00
☐ 131 Willie McGee	.10	.05	.01
☐ 132 Al Leiter	.10	.05	.01
☐ 133 Mark Grant	.04	.02	.00
☐ 134 Bob Welch	.15	.07	.01
☐ 135 Dave Dravecky	.10	.05	.01
☐ 136 Mark Langston	.15	.07	.01
☐ 137 Dan Pasqua	.07	.03	.01
☐ 138 Rick Sutcliffe	.10	.05	.01
☐ 139 Dan Petry	.04	.02	.00
☐ 140 Rich Gedman	.07	.03	.01
☐ 141 Ken Griffey Sr.	.10	.05	.01
☐ 142 Eddie Murray	.20	.10	.02
☐ 143 Jimmy Key	.07	.03	.01
☐ 144 Dale Mohorcic	.04	.02	.00
☐ 145 Jose Lind	.07	.03	.01
☐ 146 Dennis Martinez	.07	.03	.01
☐ 147 Chet Lemon	.04	.02	.00
☐ 148 Orel Hershiser	.30	.15	.03
☐ 149 Dave Martinez	.04	.02	.00
☐ 150 Billy Hatcher	.10	.05	.01
☐ 151 Charlie Leibrandt	.04	.02	.00
☐ 152 Keith Hernandez	.15	.07	.01
☐ 153 Kevin McReynolds	.20	.10	.02
☐ 154 Tony Gwynn	.35	.17	.03
☐ 155 Stan Javier	.04	.02	.00
☐ 156 Tony Pena	.04	.02	.00
☐ 157 Andy Van Slyke	.15	.07	.01
☐ 158 Gene Larkin	.07	.03	.01
☐ 159 Chris James	.07	.03	.01
☐ 160 Fred McGriff	.50	.25	.05
☐ 161 Rick Rhoden	.07	.03	.01
☐ 162 Scott Garrelts	.07	.03	.01
☐ 163 Mike Campbell	.07	.03	.01
☐ 164 Dave Righetti	.10	.05	.01
☐ 165 Paul Molitor	.15	.07	.01
☐ 166 Danny Jackson	.10	.05	.01
☐ 167 Pete O'Brien	.10	.05	.01
☐ 168 Julio Franco	.15	.07	.01
☐ 169 Mark McGwire	1.00	.50	.10
☐ 170 Zane Smith	.10	.05	.01
☐ 171 Johnny Ray	.07	.03	.01
☐ 172 Lester Lancaster	.07	.03	.01
☐ 173 Mel Hall	.10	.05	.01
☐ 174 Tracy Jones	.07	.03	.01
☐ 175 Kevin Seitzer	.30	.15	.03
☐ 176 Bob Knepper	.04	.02	.00
☐ 177 Mike Greenwell	.90	.45	.09
☐ 178 Mike Marshall	.10	.05	.01
☐ 179 Melido Perez	.15	.07	.01
☐ 180 Tim Raines	.20	.10	.02
☐ 181 Jack Morris	.10	.05	.01
☐ 182 Darryl Strawberry	.50	.25	.05
☐ 183 Robin Yount	.35	.17	.03
☐ 184 Lance Parrish	.10	.05	.01
☐ 185 Darnell Coles	.04	.02	.00
☐ 186 Kirby Puckett	.50	.25	.05
☐ 187 Terry Pendleton	.04	.02	.00
☐ 188 Don Slaught	.04	.02	.00
☐ 189 Jimmy Jones	.07	.03	.01
☐ 190 Dave Parker	.15	.07	.01
☐ 191 Mike Aldrete	.04	.02	.00
☐ 192 Mike Moore	.07	.03	.01
☐ 193 Greg Walker	.07	.03	.01
☐ 194 Calvin Schiraldi	.04	.02	.00
☐ 195 Dick Schofield	.04	.02	.00
☐ 196 Jody Reed	.15	.07	.01
☐ 197 Pete Smith	.07	.03	.01
☐ 198 Cal Ripken	.30	.15	.03
☐ 199 Lloyd Moseby	.10	.05	.01
☐ 200 Ruben Sierra	.50	.25	.05
☐ 201 R.J. Reynolds	.04	.02	.00
☐ 202 Bryn Smith	.04	.02	.00
☐ 203 Gary Pettis	.04	.02	.00
☐ 204 Steve Sax	.15	.07	.01
☐ 205 Frank DiPino	.04	.02	.00
☐ 206 Mike Scott	.15	.07	.01
☐ 207 Kurt Stillwell	.07	.03	.01
☐ 208 Mookie Wilson	.07	.03	.01
☐ 209 Lee Mazzilli	.04	.02	.00
☐ 210 Lance McCullers	.04	.02	.00
☐ 211 Rick Honeycutt	.04	.02	.00
☐ 212 John Tudor	.10	.05	.01
☐ 213 Jim Gott	.04	.02	.00
☐ 214 Frank Viola	.15	.07	.01
☐ 215 Juan Samuel	.10	.05	.01
☐ 216 Jesse Barfield	.15	.07	.01
☐ 217 Claudell Washington	.07	.03	.01
☐ 218 Rick Reuschel	.10	.05	.01
☐ 219 Jim Presley	.07	.03	.01
☐ 220 Tommy John	.15	.07	.01
☐ 221 Dan Plesac	.07	.03	.01
☐ 222 Barry Larkin	.35	.17	.03
☐ 223 Mike Stanley	.04	.02	.00
☐ 224 Cory Snyder	.15	.07	.01
☐ 225 Andre Dawson	.25	.12	.02
☐ 226 Ken Oberkfell	.04	.02	.00
☐ 227 Devon White	.15	.07	.01
☐ 228 Jamie Moyer	.04	.02	.00
☐ 229 Brook Jacoby	.07	.03	.01
☐ 230 Rob Murphy	.04	.02	.00

☐ 231 Bret Saberhagen	.20	.10	.02
☐ 232 Nolan Ryan	1.25	.60	.12
☐ 233 Bruce Hurst	.10	.05	.01
☐ 234 Jesse Orosco	.04	.02	.00
☐ 235 Bobby Thigpen	.25	.12	.02
☐ 236 Pascual Perez	.07	.03	.01
☐ 237 Matt Nokes	.10	.05	.01
☐ 238 Bob Ojeda	.07	.03	.01
☐ 239 Joey Meyer	.07	.03	.01
☐ 240 Shane Rawley	.04	.02	.00
☐ 241 Jeff Robinson	.07	.03	.01
☐ 242 Jeff Reardon	.10	.05	.01
☐ 243 Ozzie Smith	.15	.07	.01
☐ 244 Dave Winfield	.20	.10	.02
☐ 245 John Kruk	.10	.05	.01
☐ 246 Carney Lansford	.15	.07	.01
☐ 247 Candy Maldonado	.10	.05	.01
☐ 248 Ken Phelps	.07	.03	.01
☐ 249 Ken Williams	.07	.03	.01
☐ 250 Al Nipper	.04	.02	.00
☐ 251 Mark McLemore	.04	.02	.00
☐ 252 Lee Smith	.07	.03	.01
☐ 253 Albert Hall	.04	.02	.00
☐ 254 Billy Ripken	.07	.03	.01
☐ 255 Kelly Gruber	.25	.12	.02
☐ 256 Charlie Hough	.04	.02	.00
☐ 257 John Smiley	.07	.03	.01
☐ 258 Tim Wallach	.10	.05	.01
☐ 259 Frank Tanana	.07	.03	.01
☐ 260 Mike Scioscia	.04	.02	.00
☐ 261 Damon Berryhill	.15	.07	.01
☐ 262 Dave Smith	.04	.02	.00
☐ 263 Willie Wilson	.07	.03	.01
☐ 264 Len Dykstra	.15	.07	.01
☐ 265 Randy Myers	.07	.03	.01
☐ 266 Keith Moreland	.04	.02	.00
☐ 267 Eric Plunk	.04	.02	.00
☐ 268 Todd Worrell	.10	.05	.01
☐ 269 Bob Walk	.04	.02	.00
☐ 270 Keith Atherton	.04	.02	.00
☐ 271 Mike Schmidt	.60	.30	.06
☐ 272 Mike Flanagan	.04	.02	.00
☐ 273 Rafael Santana	.04	.02	.00
☐ 274 Robby Thompson	.07	.03	.01
☐ 275 Rey Quinones	.04	.02	.00
☐ 276 Cecilio Guante	.04	.02	.00
☐ 277 B.J. Surhoff	.10	.05	.01
☐ 278 Chris Sabo	.75	.35	.07
☐ 279 Mitch Williams	.07	.03	.01
☐ 280 Greg Swindell	.10	.05	.01
☐ 281 Alan Trammell	.15	.07	.01
☐ 282 Storm Davis	.07	.03	.01
☐ 283 Chuck Finley	.15	.07	.01
☐ 284 Dave Stieb	.10	.05	.01
☐ 285 Scott Bailes	.04	.02	.00
☐ 286 Larry Sheets	.07	.03	.01
☐ 287 Danny Tartabull	.15	.07	.01
☐ 288 Checklist Card	.04	.02	.00
☐ 289 Todd Benzinger	.10	.05	.01
☐ 290 John Shelby	.04	.02	.00
☐ 291 Steve Lyons	.04	.02	.00
☐ 292 Mitch Webster	.04	.02	.00
☐ 293 Walt Terrell	.04	.02	.00
☐ 294 Pete Stanicek	.04	.02	.00
☐ 295 Chris Bosio	.04	.02	.00
☐ 296 Milt Thompson	.04	.02	.00
☐ 297 Fred Lynn	.10	.05	.01
☐ 298 Juan Berenguer	.04	.02	.00
☐ 299 Ken Dayley	.04	.02	.00
☐ 300 Joel Skinner	.04	.02	.00
☐ 301 Benito Santiago	.35	.17	.03
☐ 302 Ron Hassey	.04	.02	.00
☐ 303 Jose Uribe	.04	.02	.00
☐ 304 Harold Reynolds	.07	.03	.01
☐ 305 Dale Sveum	.04	.02	.00
☐ 306 Glenn Wilson	.04	.02	.00
☐ 307 Mike Witt	.04	.02	.00
☐ 308 Ron Robinson	.04	.02	.00
☐ 309 Denny Walling	.04	.02	.00
☐ 310 Joe Orsulak	.04	.02	.00
☐ 311 David Wells	.04	.02	.00
☐ 312 Steve Buechele	.04	.02	.00
☐ 313 Jose Oquendo	.04	.02	.00
☐ 314 Floyd Youmans	.04	.02	.00
☐ 315 Lou Whitaker	.10	.05	.01
☐ 316 Fernando Valenzuela	.15	.07	.01
☐ 317 Mike Boddicker	.07	.03	.01
☐ 318 Gerald Young	.07	.03	.01
☐ 319 Frank White	.07	.03	.01
☐ 320 Bill Wegman	.04	.02	.00
☐ 321 Tom Niedenfuer	.04	.02	.00
☐ 322 Ed Whitson	.07	.03	.01
☐ 323 Curt Young	.04	.02	.00
☐ 324 Greg Mathews	.04	.02	.00
☐ 325 Doug Jones	.10	.05	.01
☐ 326 Tommy Herr	.07	.03	.01
☐ 327 Kent Tekulve	.04	.02	.00
☐ 328 Rance Mulliniks	.04	.02	.00
☐ 329 Checklist Card	.04	.02	.00
☐ 330 Craig Lefferts	.07	.03	.01
☐ 331 Franklin Stubbs	.07	.03	.01
☐ 332 Rick Cerone	.04	.02	.00
☐ 333 Dave Schmidt	.04	.02	.00
☐ 334 Larry Parrish	.04	.02	.00
☐ 335 Tom Browning	.10	.05	.01
☐ 336 Checklist Card	.04	.02	.00

1989 Donruss

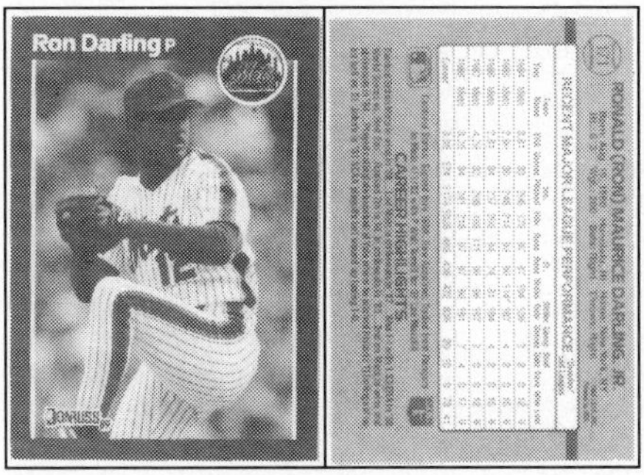

This 660-card set was distributed along with a puzzle of Warren Spahn. The six regular checklist cards are numbered throughout the set as multiples of 100. Cards measure 2 1/2" by 3 1/2" and feature a distinctive black side border with an alternating coating. The popular Diamond King subset returns for the eighth consecutive year. Rated Rookies are featured again as cards 28-47. The Donruss '89 logo appears in the lower left corner of every obverse. There are two variations that occur throughout most of the set. On the card backs "Denotes Led League" can be found with one asterisk to the left or with an asterisk on each side. On the card fronts the horizontal lines on the left and right borders can be glossy or non-glossy. Since both of these variation types are relatively minor and seem equally common, there is no premium value for either type. Rather than short-printing 26 cards in order to make room for printing the Bonus MVP's this year, Donruss apparently chose to double print 106 cards. These double prints are listed below by DP. The key rookie cards in this set are Sandy Alomar Jr., Ken Griffey Jr., Ramon Martinez, and Gary Sheffield.

	MINT	EXC	G-VG
COMPLETE SET (660)	25.00	12.50	2.50
COMMON PLAYER (1-660)	.03	.01	.00
☐ 1 Mike Greenwell DK	.25	.06	.01
☐ 2 Bobby Bonilla DK DP	.10	.05	.01
☐ 3 Pete Incaviglia DK	.08	.04	.01
☐ 4 Chris Sabo DK DP	.12	.06	.01
☐ 5 Robin Yount DK	.15	.07	.01
☐ 6 Tony Gwynn DK DP	.12	.06	.01
☐ 7 Carlton Fisk DK (OF on back)	.12	.06	.01
☐ 8 Cory Snyder DK	.08	.04	.01
☐ 9 David Cone DK UER (sic, "hurdlers")	.12	.06	.01
☐ 10 Kevin Seitzer DK	.10	.05	.01
☐ 11 Rick Reuschel DK	.08	.04	.01
☐ 12 Johnny Ray DK	.06	.03	.00
☐ 13 Dave Schmidt DK	.06	.03	.00
☐ 14 Andres Galarraga DK	.08	.04	.01
☐ 15 Kirk Gibson DK	.12	.06	.01
☐ 16 Fred McGriff DK	.15	.07	.01
☐ 17 Mark Grace DK	.35	.17	.03
☐ 18 Jeff Robinson DT DK	.06	.03	.00
☐ 19 Vince Coleman DK DP	.10	.05	.01
☐ 20 Dave Henderson DK	.06	.03	.00

☐ 21 Harold Reynolds DK	.06	.03	.00
☐ 22 Gerald Perry DK	.06	.03	.00
☐ 23 Frank Viola DK	.12	.06	.01
☐ 24 Steve Bedrosian DK	.08	.04	.01
☐ 25 Glenn Davis DK	.12	.06	.01
☐ 26 Don Mattingly DK UER (doesn't mention Don's previous DK in 1985)	.40	.20	.04
☐ 27 DK Checklist DP	.06	.01	.00
☐ 28 Sandy Alomar Jr. RR	1.75	.85	.17
☐ 29 Steve Searcy RR	.15	.07	.01
☐ 30 Cameron Drew RR	.10	.05	.01
☐ 31 Gary Sheffield RR	1.50	.75	.15
☐ 32 Erik Hanson RR	.75	.35	.07
☐ 33 Ken Griffey Jr. RR	6.50	3.25	.65
☐ 34 Greg Harris RR San Diego Padres	.20	.10	.02
☐ 35 Gregg Jefferies RR	1.00	.50	.10
☐ 36 Luis Medina RR	.20	.10	.02
☐ 37 Carlos Quintana RR	.45	.22	.04
☐ 38 Felix Jose RR	.35	.17	.03
☐ 39 Cris Carpenter RR	.18	.09	.01
☐ 40 Ron Jones RR	.18	.09	.01
☐ 41 Dave West RR	.18	.09	.01
☐ 42 Randy Johnson RR	.35	.17	.03
☐ 43 Mike Harkey RR	.45	.22	.04
☐ 44 Pete Harnisch RR DP	.10	.05	.01
☐ 45 Tom Gordon RR DP	.50	.25	.05
☐ 46 Gregg Olson RR DP	.75	.35	.07
☐ 47 Alex Sanchez RR DP	.18	.09	.01
☐ 48 Ruben Sierra	.25	.12	.02
☐ 49 Rafael Palmeiro	.15	.07	.01
☐ 50 Ron Gant	.25	.12	.02
☐ 51 Cal Ripken	.15	.07	.01
☐ 52 Wally Joyner	.12	.06	.01
☐ 53 Gary Carter	.12	.06	.01
☐ 54 Andy Van Slyke	.10	.05	.01
☐ 55 Robin Yount	.18	.09	.01
☐ 56 Pete Incaviglia	.10	.05	.01
☐ 57 Greg Brock	.03	.01	.00
☐ 58 Melido Perez	.06	.03	.00
☐ 59 Craig Lefferts	.03	.01	.00
☐ 60 Gary Pettis	.03	.01	.00
☐ 61 Danny Tartabull	.08	.04	.01
☐ 62 Guillermo Hernandez	.03	.01	.00
☐ 63 Ozzie Smith	.12	.06	.01
☐ 64 Gary Gaetti	.08	.04	.01
☐ 65 Mark Davis	.10	.05	.01
☐ 66 Lee Smith	.06	.03	.00
☐ 67 Dennis Eckersley	.12	.06	.01
☐ 68 Wade Boggs	.30	.15	.03
☐ 69 Mike Scott	.10	.05	.01
☐ 70 Fred McGriff	.18	.09	.01
☐ 71 Tom Browning	.08	.04	.01
☐ 72 Claudell Washington	.06	.03	.00
☐ 73 Mel Hall	.06	.03	.00
☐ 74 Don Mattingly	.50	.25	.05
☐ 75 Steve Bedrosian	.08	.04	.01
☐ 76 Juan Samuel	.08	.04	.01
☐ 77 Mike Scioscia	.03	.01	.00
☐ 78 Dave Righetti	.08	.04	.01
☐ 79 Alfredo Griffin	.03	.01	.00
☐ 80 Eric Davis UER (165 games in 1988, should be 135)	.25	.12	.02
☐ 81 Juan Berenguer	.03	.01	.00
☐ 82 Todd Worrell	.08	.04	.01
☐ 83 Joe Carter	.12	.06	.01
☐ 84 Steve Sax	.10	.05	.01
☐ 85 Frank White	.06	.03	.00
☐ 86 John Kruk	.03	.01	.00
☐ 87 Rance Mulliniks	.03	.01	.00
☐ 88 Alan Ashby	.03	.01	.00
☐ 89 Charlie Leibrandt	.03	.01	.00
☐ 90 Frank Tanana	.06	.03	.00
☐ 91 Jose Canseco	.90	.45	.09
☐ 92 Barry Bonds	.30	.15	.03
☐ 93 Harold Reynolds	.06	.03	.00
☐ 94 Mark McLemore	.03	.01	.00
☐ 95 Mark McGwire	.40	.20	.04
☐ 96 Eddie Murray	.15	.07	.01
☐ 97 Tim Raines	.12	.06	.01
☐ 98 Robby Thompson	.03	.01	.00
☐ 99 Kevin McReynolds	.10	.05	.01
☐ 100 Checklist Card	.06	.01	.00
☐ 101 Carlton Fisk	.15	.07	.01
☐ 102 Dave Martinez	.03	.01	.00
☐ 103 Glenn Braggs	.03	.01	.00
☐ 104 Dale Murphy	.15	.07	.01
☐ 105 Ryne Sandberg	.30	.15	.03
☐ 106 Dennis Martinez	.06	.03	.00
☐ 107 Pete O'Brien	.06	.03	.00
☐ 108 Dick Schofield	.03	.01	.00
☐ 109 Henry Cotto	.03	.01	.00
☐ 110 Mike Marshall	.08	.04	.01
☐ 111 Keith Moreland	.03	.01	.00
☐ 112 Tom Brunansky	.08	.04	.01
☐ 113 Kelly Gruber UER (wrong birthdate)	.20	.10	.02
☐ 114 Brook Jacoby	.06	.03	.00
☐ 115 Keith Brown	.10	.05	.01
☐ 116 Matt Nokes	.06	.03	.00
☐ 117 Keith Hernandez	.10	.05	.01
☐ 118 Bob Forsch	.03	.01	.00
☐ 119 Bert Blyleven UER (... 3000 strikeouts in 1987, should be 1986)	.08	.04	.01
☐ 120 Willie Wilson	.08	.04	.01
☐ 121 Tommy Gregg	.03	.01	.00
☐ 122 Jim Rice	.12	.06	.01
☐ 123 Bob Knepper	.03	.01	.00
☐ 124 Danny Jackson	.06	.03	.00
☐ 125 Eric Plunk	.03	.01	.00
☐ 126 Brian Fisher	.03	.01	.00
☐ 127 Mike Pagliarulo	.03	.01	.00
☐ 128 Tony Gwynn	.15	.07	.01
☐ 129 Lance McCullers	.03	.01	.00
☐ 130 Andres Galarraga	.08	.04	.01
☐ 131 Jose Uribe	.03	.01	.00
☐ 132 Kirk Gibson UER (wrong birthdate)	.12	.06	.01
☐ 133 David Palmer	.03	.01	.00
☐ 134 R.J. Reynolds	.03	.01	.00
☐ 135 Greg Walker	.06	.03	.00
☐ 136 Kirk McCaskill UER (wrong birthdate)	.03	.01	.00
☐ 137 Shawon Dunston	.12	.06	.01
☐ 138 Andy Allanson	.03	.01	.00
☐ 139 Rob Murphy	.03	.01	.00
☐ 140 Mike Aldrete	.03	.01	.00
☐ 141 Terry Kennedy	.03	.01	.00
☐ 142 Scott Fletcher	.03	.01	.00
☐ 143 Steve Balboni	.03	.01	.00
☐ 144 Bret Saberhagen	.15	.07	.01
☐ 145 Ozzie Virgil	.03	.01	.00
☐ 146 Dale Sveum	.03	.01	.00
☐ 147 Darryl Strawberry	.40	.20	.04
☐ 148 Harold Baines	.08	.04	.01
☐ 149 George Bell	.12	.06	.01
☐ 150 Dave Parker	.08	.04	.01
☐ 151 Bobby Bonilla	.20	.10	.02
☐ 152 Mookie Wilson	.06	.03	.00
☐ 153 Ted Power	.03	.01	.00
☐ 154 Nolan Ryan	.45	.22	.04
☐ 155 Jeff Reardon	.06	.03	.00
☐ 156 Tim Wallach	.06	.03	.00
☐ 157 Jamie Moyer	.03	.01	.00
☐ 158 Rich Gossage	.08	.04	.01
☐ 159 Dave Winfield	.12	.06	.01
☐ 160 Von Hayes	.08	.04	.01
☐ 161 Willie McGee	.10	.05	.01
☐ 162 Rich Gedman	.03	.01	.00
☐ 163 Tony Pena	.06	.03	.00
☐ 164 Mike Morgan	.03	.01	.00
☐ 165 Charlie Hough	.03	.01	.00
☐ 166 Mike Stanley	.03	.01	.00
☐ 167 Andre Dawson	.12	.06	.01
☐ 168 Joe Boever	.08	.04	.01
☐ 169 Pete Stanicek	.03	.01	.00
☐ 170 Bob Boone	.06	.03	.00
☐ 171 Ron Darling	.08	.04	.01
☐ 172 Bob Walk	.03	.01	.00
☐ 173 Rob Deer	.06	.03	.00
☐ 174 Steve Buechele	.03	.01	.00
☐ 175 Ted Higuera	.06	.03	.00
☐ 176 Ozzie Guillen	.08	.04	.01
☐ 177 Candy Maldonado	.06	.03	.00
☐ 178 Doyle Alexander	.03	.01	.00
☐ 179 Mark Gubicza	.06	.03	.00
☐ 180 Alan Trammell	.12	.06	.01
☐ 181 Vince Coleman	.12	.06	.01
☐ 182 Kirby Puckett	.30	.15	.03
☐ 183 Chris Brown	.03	.01	.00
☐ 184 Marty Barrett	.03	.01	.00
☐ 185 Stan Javier	.03	.01	.00
☐ 186 Mike Greenwell	.30	.15	.03
☐ 187 Billy Hatcher	.03	.01	.00
☐ 188 Jimmy Key	.06	.03	.00
☐ 189 Nick Esasky	.06	.03	.00
☐ 190 Don Slaught	.03	.01	.00
☐ 191 Cory Snyder	.08	.04	.01
☐ 192 John Candelaria	.03	.01	.00
☐ 193 Mike Schmidt	.30	.15	.03
☐ 194 Kevin Gross	.03	.01	.00
☐ 195 John Tudor	.06	.03	.00
☐ 196 Neil Allen	.03	.01	.00
☐ 197 Orel Hershiser	.12	.06	.01
☐ 198 Kal Daniels	.10	.05	.01

☐ 199 Kent Hrbek	.10	.05	.01
☐ 200 Checklist Card	.06	.01	.00
☐ 201 Joe Magrane	.08	.04	.01
☐ 202 Scott Bailes	.03	.01	.00
☐ 203 Tim Belcher	.08	.04	.01
☐ 204 George Brett	.20	.10	.02
☐ 205 Benito Santiago	.15	.07	.01
☐ 206 Tony Fernandez	.08	.04	.01
☐ 207 Gerald Young	.03	.01	.00
☐ 208 Bo Jackson	.75	.35	.07
☐ 209 Chet Lemon	.03	.01	.00
☐ 210 Storm Davis	.06	.03	.00
☐ 211 Doug Drabek	.10	.05	.01
☐ 212 Mickey Brantley UER (photo actually Nelson Simmons)	.06	.03	.00
☐ 213 Devon White	.08	.04	.01
☐ 214 Dave Stewart	.12	.06	.01
☐ 215 Dave Schmidt	.03	.01	.00
☐ 216 Bryn Smith	.03	.01	.00
☐ 217 Brett Butler	.08	.04	.01
☐ 218 Bob Ojeda	.06	.03	.00
☐ 219 Steve Rosenberg	.08	.04	.01
☐ 220 Hubie Brooks	.06	.03	.00
☐ 221 B.J. Surhoff	.06	.03	.00
☐ 222 Rick Mahler	.03	.01	.00
☐ 223 Rick Sutcliffe	.08	.04	.01
☐ 224 Neal Heaton	.03	.01	.00
☐ 225 Mitch Williams	.06	.03	.00
☐ 226 Chuck Finley	.08	.04	.01
☐ 227 Mark Langston	.10	.05	.01
☐ 228 Jesse Orosco	.03	.01	.00
☐ 229 Ed Whitson	.06	.03	.00
☐ 230 Terry Pendleton	.06	.03	.00
☐ 231 Lloyd Moseby	.06	.03	.00
☐ 232 Greg Swindell	.08	.04	.01
☐ 233 John Franco	.08	.04	.01
☐ 234 Jack Morris	.08	.04	.01
☐ 235 Howard Johnson	.12	.06	.01
☐ 236 Glenn Davis	.12	.06	.01
☐ 237 Frank Viola	.12	.06	.01
☐ 238 Kevin Seitzer	.10	.05	.01
☐ 239 Gerald Perry	.03	.01	.00
☐ 240 Dwight Evans	.08	.04	.01
☐ 241 Jim Deshaies	.03	.01	.00
☐ 242 Bo Diaz	.03	.01	.00
☐ 243 Carney Lansford	.08	.04	.01
☐ 244 Mike LaValliere	.03	.01	.00
☐ 245 Rickey Henderson	.30	.15	.03
☐ 246 Roberto Alomar	.30	.15	.03
☐ 247 Jimmy Jones	.03	.01	.00
☐ 248 Pascual Perez	.06	.03	.00
☐ 249 Will Clark	.60	.30	.06
☐ 250 Fernando Valenzuela	.10	.05	.01
☐ 251 Shane Rawley	.03	.01	.00
☐ 252 Sid Bream	.03	.01	.00
☐ 253 Steve Lyons	.03	.01	.00
☐ 254 Brian Downing	.03	.01	.00
☐ 255 Mark Grace	.75	.35	.07
☐ 256 Tom Candiotti	.03	.01	.00
☐ 257 Barry Larkin	.18	.09	.01
☐ 258 Mike Krukow	.03	.01	.00
☐ 259 Billy Ripken	.03	.01	.00
☐ 260 Cecilio Guante	.03	.01	.00
☐ 261 Scott Bradley	.03	.01	.00
☐ 262 Floyd Bannister	.03	.01	.00
☐ 263 Pete Smith	.03	.01	.00
☐ 264 Jim Gantner UER (wrong birtdate)	.03	.01	.00
☐ 265 Roger McDowell	.06	.03	.00
☐ 266 Bobby Thigpen	.10	.05	.01
☐ 267 Jim Clancy	.03	.01	.00
☐ 268 Terry Steinbach	.08	.04	.01
☐ 269 Mike Dunne	.06	.03	.00
☐ 270 Dwight Gooden	.25	.12	.02
☐ 271 Mike Heath	.03	.01	.00
☐ 272 Dave Smith	.06	.03	.00
☐ 273 Keith Atherton	.03	.01	.00
☐ 274 Tim Burke	.06	.03	.00
☐ 275 Damon Berryhill	.10	.05	.01
☐ 276 Vance Law	.03	.01	.00
☐ 277 Rich Dotson	.03	.01	.00
☐ 278 Lance Parrish	.08	.04	.01
☐ 279 Denny Walling	.03	.01	.00
☐ 280 Roger Clemens	.20	.10	.02
☐ 281 Greg Mathews	.03	.01	.00
☐ 282 Tom Niedenfuer	.03	.01	.00
☐ 283 Paul Kilgus	.03	.01	.00
☐ 284 Jose Guzman	.03	.01	.00
☐ 285 Calvin Schiraldi	.03	.01	.00
☐ 286 Charlie Puleo UER (career ERA 4.24, should be 4.23)	.03	.01	.00
☐ 287 Joe Orsulak	.03	.01	.00

☐ 288 Jack Howell	.03	.01	.00
☐ 289 Kevin Elster	.06	.03	.00
☐ 290 Jose Lind	.03	.01	.00
☐ 291 Paul Molitor	.10	.05	.01
☐ 292 Cecil Espy	.10	.05	.01
☐ 293 Bill Wegman	.03	.01	.00
☐ 294 Dan Pasqua	.03	.01	.00
☐ 295 Scott Garrelts UER (wrong birthdate)	.06	.03	.00
☐ 296 Walt Terrell	.03	.01	.00
☐ 297 Ed Hearn	.03	.01	.00
☐ 298 Lou Whitaker	.08	.04	.01
☐ 299 Ken Dayley	.03	.01	.00
☐ 300 Checklist Card	.06	.01	.00
☐ 301 Tommy Herr	.06	.03	.00
☐ 302 Mike Brumley	.03	.01	.00
☐ 303 Ellis Burks	.25	.12	.02
☐ 304 Curt Young UER (wrong birthdate)	.03	.01	.00
☐ 305 Jody Reed	.10	.05	.01
☐ 306 Bill Doran	.06	.03	.00
☐ 307 David Wells	.03	.01	.00
☐ 308 Ron Robinson	.03	.01	.00
☐ 309 Rafael Santana	.03	.01	.00
☐ 310 Julio Franco	.08	.04	.01
☐ 311 Jack Clark	.10	.05	.01
☐ 312 Chris James	.06	.03	.00
☐ 313 Milt Thompson	.03	.01	.00
☐ 314 John Shelby	.03	.01	.00
☐ 315 Al Leiter	.06	.03	.00
☐ 316 Mike Davis	.03	.01	.00
☐ 317 Chris Sabo	.75	.35	.07
☐ 318 Greg Gagne	.03	.01	.00
☐ 319 Jose Oquendo	.03	.01	.00
☐ 320 John Farrell	.03	.01	.00
☐ 321 Franklin Stubbs	.06	.03	.00
☐ 322 Kurt Stillwell	.06	.03	.00
☐ 323 Shawn Abner	.06	.03	.00
☐ 324 Mike Flanagan	.06	.03	.00
☐ 325 Kevin Bass	.06	.03	.00
☐ 326 Pat Tabler	.03	.01	.00
☐ 327 Mike Henneman	.03	.01	.00
☐ 328 Rick Honeycutt	.03	.01	.00
☐ 329 John Smiley	.03	.01	.00
☐ 330 Rey Quinones	.03	.01	.00
☐ 331 Johnny Ray	.03	.01	.00
☐ 332 Bob Welch	.10	.05	.01
☐ 333 Larry Sheets	.03	.01	.00
☐ 334 Jeff Parrett	.03	.01	.00
☐ 335 Rick Reuschel UER (for Don Robinson, should be Jeff)	.08	.04	.01
☐ 336 Randy Myers	.08	.04	.01
☐ 337 Ken Williams	.03	.01	.00
☐ 338 Andy McGaffigan	.03	.01	.00
☐ 339 Joey Meyer	.06	.03	.00
☐ 340 Dion James	.03	.01	.00
☐ 341 Les Lancaster	.03	.01	.00
☐ 342 Tom Foley	.03	.01	.00
☐ 343 Geno Petralli	.03	.01	.00
☐ 344 Dan Petry	.03	.01	.00
☐ 345 Alvin Davis	.08	.04	.01
☐ 346 Mickey Hatcher	.03	.01	.00
☐ 347 Marvell Wynne	.03	.01	.00
☐ 348 Danny Cox	.03	.01	.00
☐ 349 Dave Stieb	.08	.04	.01
☐ 350 Jay Bell	.03	.01	.00
☐ 351 Jeff Treadway	.06	.03	.00
☐ 352 Luis Salazar	.03	.01	.00
☐ 353 Len Dykstra	.12	.06	.01
☐ 354 Juan Agosto	.03	.01	.00
☐ 355 Gene Larkin	.06	.03	.00
☐ 356 Steve Farr	.03	.01	.00
☐ 357 Paul Assenmacher	.03	.01	.00
☐ 358 Todd Benzinger	.03	.01	.00
☐ 359 Larry Andersen	.03	.01	.00
☐ 360 Paul O'Neill	.10	.05	.01
☐ 361 Ron Hassey	.03	.01	.00
☐ 362 Jim Gott	.03	.01	.00
☐ 363 Ken Phelps	.06	.03	.00
☐ 364 Tim Flannery	.03	.01	.00
☐ 365 Randy Ready	.03	.01	.00
☐ 366 Nelson Santovenia	.12	.06	.01
☐ 367 Kelly Downs	.03	.01	.00
☐ 368 Danny Heep	.03	.01	.00
☐ 369 Phil Bradley	.06	.03	.00
☐ 370 Jeff Robinson Pittsburgh Pirates	.03	.01	.00
☐ 371 Ivan Calderon	.06	.03	.00
☐ 372 Mike Witt	.03	.01	.00
☐ 373 Greg Maddux	.10	.05	.01
☐ 374 Carmen Castillo	.03	.01	.00
☐ 375 Jose Rijo	.08	.04	.01
☐ 376 Joe Price	.03	.01	.00

☐ 377 Rene C. Gonzales	.03	.01	.00
☐ 378 Oddibe McDowell	.06	.03	.00
☐ 379 Jim Presley	.03	.01	.00
☐ 380 Brad Wellman	.03	.01	.00
☐ 381 Tom Glavine	.06	.03	.00
☐ 382 Dan Plesac	.03	.01	.00
☐ 383 Wally Backman	.03	.01	.00
☐ 384 Dave Gallagher	.10	.05	.01
☐ 385 Tom Henke	.06	.03	.00
☐ 386 Luis Polonia	.06	.03	.00
☐ 387 Junior Ortiz	.03	.01	.00
☐ 388 David Cone	.10	.05	.01
☐ 389 Dave Bergman	.03	.01	.00
☐ 390 Danny Darwin	.06	.03	.00
☐ 391 Dan Gladden	.03	.01	.00
☐ 392 John Dopson	.12	.06	.01
☐ 393 Frank DiPino	.03	.01	.00
☐ 394 Al Nipper	.03	.01	.00
☐ 395 Willie Randolph	.06	.03	.00
☐ 396 Don Carman	.03	.01	.00
☐ 397 Scott Terry	.03	.01	.00
☐ 398 Rick Cerone	.03	.01	.00
☐ 399 Tom Pagnozzi	.03	.01	.00
☐ 400 Checklist Card	.06	.01	.00
☐ 401 Mickey Tettleton	.06	.03	.00
☐ 402 Curtis Wilkerson	.03	.01	.00
☐ 403 Jeff Russell	.03	.01	.00
☐ 404 Pat Perry	.03	.01	.00
☐ 405 Jose Alvarez	.06	.03	.00
☐ 406 Rick Schu	.03	.01	.00
☐ 407 Sherman Corbett	.06	.03	.00
☐ 408 Dave Magadan	.10	.05	.01
☐ 409 Bob Kipper	.03	.01	.00
☐ 410 Don August	.03	.01	.00
☐ 411 Bob Brower	.03	.01	.00
☐ 412 Chris Bosio	.03	.01	.00
☐ 413 Jerry Reuss	.03	.01	.00
☐ 414 Atlee Hammaker	.03	.01	.00
☐ 415 Jim Walewander	.06	.03	.00
☐ 416 Mike Macfarlane	.12	.06	.01
☐ 417 Pat Sheridan	.03	.01	.00
☐ 418 Pedro Guerrero	.10	.05	.01
☐ 419 Allan Anderson	.06	.03	.00
☐ 420 Mark Parent	.10	.05	.01
☐ 421 Bob Stanley	.03	.01	.00
☐ 422 Mike Gallego	.03	.01	.00
☐ 423 Bruce Hurst	.08	.04	.01
☐ 424 Dave Meads	.03	.01	.00
☐ 425 Jesse Barfield	.08	.04	.01
☐ 426 Rob Dibble	.35	.17	.03
☐ 427 Joel Skinner	.03	.01	.00
☐ 428 Ron Kittle	.08	.04	.01
☐ 429 Rick Rhoden	.03	.01	.00
☐ 430 Bob Dernier	.03	.01	.00
☐ 431 Steve Jeltz	.03	.01	.00
☐ 432 Rick Dempsey	.03	.01	.00
☐ 433 Roberto Kelly	.15	.07	.01
☐ 434 Dave Anderson	.03	.01	.00
☐ 435 Herm Winningham	.03	.01	.00
☐ 436 Al Newman	.03	.01	.00
☐ 437 Jose DeLeon	.06	.03	.00
☐ 438 Doug Jones	.06	.03	.00
☐ 439 Brian Holton	.03	.01	.00
☐ 440 Jeff Montgomery	.15	.07	.01
☐ 441 Dickie Thon	.03	.01	.00
☐ 442 Cecil Fielder	.30	.15	.03
☐ 443 John Fishel	.06	.03	.00
☐ 444 Jerry Don Gleaton	.03	.01	.00
☐ 445 Paul Gibson	.06	.03	.00
☐ 446 Walt Weiss	.25	.12	.02
☐ 447 Glenn Wilson	.03	.01	.00
☐ 448 Mike Moore	.06	.03	.00
☐ 449 Chili Davis	.06	.03	.00
☐ 450 Dave Henderson	.06	.03	.00
☐ 451 Jose Bautista	.08	.04	.01
☐ 452 Rex Hudler	.06	.03	.00
☐ 453 Bob Brenly	.03	.01	.00
☐ 454 Mackey Sasser	.08	.04	.01
☐ 455 Daryl Boston	.06	.03	.00
☐ 456 Mike Fitzgerald	.03	.01	.00
Montreal Expos			
☐ 457 Jeffrey Leonard	.06	.03	.00
☐ 458 Bruce Sutter	.08	.04	.01
☐ 459 Mitch Webster	.03	.01	.00
☐ 460 Joe Hesketh	.03	.01	.00
☐ 461 Bobby Witt	.10	.05	.01
☐ 462 Stew Cliburn	.03	.01	.00
☐ 463 Scott Bankhead	.06	.03	.00
☐ 464 Ramon Martinez	1.25	.60	.12
☐ 465 Dave Leiper	.03	.01	.00
☐ 466 Luis Alicea	.06	.03	.00
☐ 467 John Cerutti	.03	.01	.00
☐ 468 Ron Washington	.03	.01	.00
☐ 469 Jeff Reed	.03	.01	.00
☐ 470 Jeff Robinson	.06	.03	.00
Detroit Tigers			
☐ 471 Sid Fernandez	.08	.04	.01
☐ 472 Terry Puhl	.03	.01	.00
☐ 473 Charlie Lea	.03	.01	.00
☐ 474 Israel Sanchez	.08	.04	.01
☐ 475 Bruce Benedict	.03	.01	.00
☐ 476 Oil Can Boyd	.06	.03	.00
☐ 477 Craig Reynolds	.03	.01	.00
☐ 478 Frank Williams	.03	.01	.00
☐ 479 Greg Cadaret	.03	.01	.00
☐ 480 Randy Kramer	.10	.05	.01
☐ 481 Dave Eiland	.12	.06	.01
☐ 482 Eric Show	.03	.01	.00
☐ 483 Garry Templeton	.06	.03	.00
☐ 484 Wallace Johnson	.03	.01	.00
☐ 485 Kevin Mitchell	.25	.12	.02
☐ 486 Tim Crews	.03	.01	.00
☐ 487 Mike Maddux	.03	.01	.00
☐ 488 Dave LaPoint	.03	.01	.00
☐ 489 Fred Manrique	.03	.01	.00
☐ 490 Greg Minton	.03	.01	.00
☐ 491 Doug Dascenzo UER	.12	.06	.01
(photo actually			
Damon Berryhill)			
☐ 492 Willie Upshaw	.03	.01	.00
☐ 493 Jack Armstrong	.25	.12	.02
☐ 494 Kirt Manwaring	.03	.01	.00
☐ 495 Jeff Ballard	.06	.03	.00
☐ 496 Jeff Kunkel	.03	.01	.00
☐ 497 Mike Campbell	.03	.01	.00
☐ 498 Gary Thurman	.03	.01	.00
☐ 499 Zane Smith	.06	.03	.00
☐ 500 Checklist Card DP	.06	.01	.00
☐ 501 Mike Birkbeck	.03	.01	.00
☐ 502 Terry Leach	.06	.03	.00
☐ 503 Shawn Hillegas	.03	.01	.00
☐ 504 Manny Lee	.06	.03	.00
☐ 505 Doug Jennings	.15	.07	.01
☐ 506 Ken Oberkfell	.03	.01	.00
☐ 507 Tim Teufel	.03	.01	.00
☐ 508 Tom Brookens	.03	.01	.00
☐ 509 Rafael Ramirez	.03	.01	.00
☐ 510 Fred Toliver	.03	.01	.00
☐ 511 Brian Holman	.15	.07	.01
☐ 512 Mike Bielecki	.06	.03	.00
☐ 513 Jeff Pico	.08	.04	.01
☐ 514 Charles Hudson	.03	.01	.00
☐ 515 Bruce Ruffin	.03	.01	.00
☐ 516 Larry McWilliams UER	.03	.01	.00
(New Richland, should			
be North Richland)			
☐ 517 Jeff Sellers	.03	.01	.00
☐ 518 John Costello	.08	.04	.01
☐ 519 Brady Anderson	.20	.10	.02
☐ 520 Craig McMurtry	.03	.01	.00
☐ 521 Ray Hayward DP	.03	.01	.00
☐ 522 Drew Hall DP	.03	.01	.00
☐ 523 Mark Lemke DP	.10	.05	.01
☐ 524 Oswald Peraza DP	.08	.04	.01
☐ 525 Bryan Harvey DP	.12	.06	.01
☐ 526 Rick Aguilera DP	.03	.01	.00
☐ 527 Tom Prince DP	.03	.01	.00
☐ 528 Mark Clear DP	.03	.01	.00
☐ 529 Jerry Browne DP	.03	.01	.00
☐ 530 Juan Castillo DP	.03	.01	.00
☐ 531 Jack McDowell DP	.08	.04	.01
☐ 532 Chris Speier DP	.03	.01	.00
☐ 533 Darrell Evans DP	.06	.03	.00
☐ 534 Luis Aquino DP	.03	.01	.00
☐ 535 Eric King DP	.03	.01	.00
☐ 536 Ken Hill DP	.18	.09	.01
☐ 537 Randy Bush DP	.03	.01	.00
☐ 538 Shane Mack DP	.06	.03	.00
☐ 539 Tom Bolton DP	.06	.03	.00
☐ 540 Gene Nelson DP	.03	.01	.00
☐ 541 Wes Gardner DP	.03	.01	.00
☐ 542 Ken Caminiti DP	.03	.01	.00
☐ 543 Duane Ward DP	.03	.01	.00
☐ 544 Norm Charlton DP	.20	.10	.02
☐ 545 Hal Morris DP	.75	.35	.07
☐ 546 Rich Yett DP	.03	.01	.00
☐ 547 Hensley Meulens DP	.65	.30	.06
☐ 548 Greg Harris DP	.03	.01	.00
Philadelphia Phillies			
☐ 549 Darren Daulton DP	.06	.03	.00
(posing as right-			
handed hitter)			
☐ 550 Jeff Hamilton DP	.03	.01	.00
☐ 551 Luis Aguayo DP	.03	.01	.00
☐ 552 Tim Leary DP	.06	.03	.00
(resembles M.Marshall)			
☐ 553 Ron Oester DP	.03	.01	.00
☐ 554 Steve Lombardozzi DP	.03	.01	.00

☐ 555	Tim Jones DP	.08	.04	.01
☐ 556	Bud Black DP	.06	.03	.00
☐ 557	Alejandro Pena DP	.03	.01	.00
☐ 558	Jose DeJesus DP	.10	.05	.01
☐ 559	Dennis Rasmussen DP	.03	.01	.00
☐ 560	Pat Borders DP	.12	.06	.01
☐ 561	Craig Biggio DP	.30	.15	.03
☐ 562	Luis De Los Santos DP	.12	.06	.01
☐ 563	Fred Lynn DP	.06	.03	.00
☐ 564	Todd Burns DP	.18	.09	.01
☐ 565	Felix Fermin DP	.03	.01	.00
☐ 566	Darnell Coles DP	.03	.01	.00
☐ 567	Willie Fraser DP	.03	.01	.00
☐ 568	Glenn Hubbard DP	.03	.01	.00
☐ 569	Craig Worthington DP	.20	.10	.02
☐ 570	Johnny Paredes DP	.08	.04	.01
☐ 571	Don Robinson DP	.03	.01	.00
☐ 572	Barry Lyons DP	.03	.01	.00
☐ 573	Bill Long DP	.03	.01	.00
☐ 574	Tracy Jones DP	.03	.01	.00
☐ 575	Juan Nieves DP	.03	.01	.00
☐ 576	Andres Thomas DP	.03	.01	.00
☐ 577	Rolando Roomes DP	.15	.07	.01
☐ 578	Luis Rivera UER DP (wrong birthdate)	.03	.01	.00
☐ 579	Chad Kreuter DP	.10	.05	.01
☐ 580	Tony Armas DP	.03	.01	.00
☐ 581	Jay Buhner	.10	.05	.01
☐ 582	Ricky Horton DP	.03	.01	.00
☐ 583	Andy Hawkins DP	.03	.01	.00
☐ 584	Sil Campusano	.18	.09	.01
☐ 585	Dave Clark	.06	.03	.00
☐ 586	Van Snider DP	.15	.07	.01
☐ 587	Todd Frohwirth DP	.03	.01	.00
☐ 588	Puzzle Card DP Warren Spahn	.03	.01	.00
☐ 589	William Brennan	.08	.04	.01
☐ 590	German Gonzalez	.08	.04	.01
☐ 591	Ernie Whitt DP	.03	.01	.00
☐ 592	Jeff Blauser	.03	.01	.00
☐ 593	Spike Owen DP	.03	.01	.00
☐ 594	Matt Williams	.35	.17	.03
☐ 595	Lloyd McClendon DP	.06	.03	.00
☐ 596	Steve Ontiveros	.03	.01	.00
☐ 597	Scott Medvin	.10	.05	.01
☐ 598	Hipolito Pena DP	.08	.04	.01
☐ 599	Jerald Clark DP	.18	.09	.01
☐ 600A	Checklist Card DP 635 Kurt Schilling	.25	.03	.01
☐ 600B	Checklist Card DP 635 Curt Schilling (MVP's not listed on checklist card)	.06	.01	.00
☐ 600C	Checklist Card DP 635 Curt Schilling (MVP's listed following 660)	.06	.01	.00
☐ 601	Carmelo Martinez DP	.03	.01	.00
☐ 602	Mike LaCoss	.03	.01	.00
☐ 603	Mike Devereaux	.06	.03	.00
☐ 604	Alex Madrid DP	.08	.04	.01
☐ 605	Gary Redus DP	.03	.01	.00
☐ 606	Lance Johnson	.03	.01	.00
☐ 607	Terry Clark DP	.08	.04	.01
☐ 608	Manny Trillo DP	.03	.01	.00
☐ 609	Scott Jordan	.10	.05	.01
☐ 610	Jay Howell DP	.03	.01	.00
☐ 611	Francisco Melendez	.15	.07	.01
☐ 612	Mike Boddicker	.06	.03	.00
☐ 613	Kevin Brown DP	.15	.07	.01
☐ 614	Dave Valle	.03	.01	.00
☐ 615	Tim Laudner DP	.03	.01	.00
☐ 616	Andy Nezelek UER (wrong birthdate)	.12	.06	.01
☐ 617	Chuck Crim	.03	.01	.00
☐ 618	Jack Savage DP	.08	.04	.01
☐ 619	Adam Peterson	.06	.03	.00
☐ 620	Todd Stottlemyre	.08	.04	.01
☐ 621	Lance Blankenship	.10	.05	.01
☐ 622	Miguel Garcia DP	.08	.04	.01
☐ 623	Keith Miller DP New York Mets	.03	.01	.00
☐ 624	Ricky Jordan DP	.30	.15	.03
☐ 625	Ernest Riles DP	.03	.01	.00
☐ 626	John Moses DP	.03	.01	.00
☐ 627	Nelson Liriano DP	.03	.01	.00
☐ 628	Mike Smithson DP	.03	.01	.00
☐ 629	Scott Sanderson	.06	.03	.00
☐ 630	Dale Mohorcic	.03	.01	.00
☐ 631	Marvin Freeman DP	.03	.01	.00
☐ 632	Mike Young DP	.03	.01	.00
☐ 633	Dennis Lamp	.03	.01	.00
☐ 634	Dante Bichette DP	.25	.12	.02
☐ 635	Curt Schilling DP	.10	.05	.01
☐ 636	Scott May DP	.08	.04	.01
☐ 637	Mike Schooler	.30	.15	.03
☐ 638	Rick Leach	.03	.01	.00
☐ 639	Tom Lampkin UER (Throws Left, should be Throws Right)	.08	.04	.01
☐ 640	Brian Meyer	.10	.05	.01
☐ 641	Brian Harper	.06	.03	.00
☐ 642	John Smoltz	.40	.20	.04
☐ 643	Jose: 40/40 Club (Jose Canseco)	.50	.25	.05
☐ 644	Bill Schroeder	.03	.01	.00
☐ 645	Edgar Martinez	.25	.12	.02
☐ 646	Dennis Cook	.20	.10	.02
☐ 647	Barry Jones	.06	.03	.00
☐ 648	Orel: 59 and Counting (Orel Hershiser)	.12	.06	.01
☐ 649	Rod Nichols	.08	.04	.01
☐ 650	Jody Davis	.03	.01	.00
☐ 651	Bob Milacki	.20	.10	.02
☐ 652	Mike Jackson	.03	.01	.00
☐ 653	Derek Lilliquist	.15	.07	.01
☐ 654	Paul Mirabella	.03	.01	.00
☐ 655	Mike Diaz	.03	.01	.00
☐ 656	Jeff Musselman	.03	.01	.00
☐ 657	Jerry Reed	.03	.01	.00
☐ 658	Kevin Blankenship	.10	.05	.01
☐ 659	Wayne Tolleson	.03	.01	.00
☐ 660	Eric Hetzel	.10	.05	.01

1989 Donruss Bonus MVP's

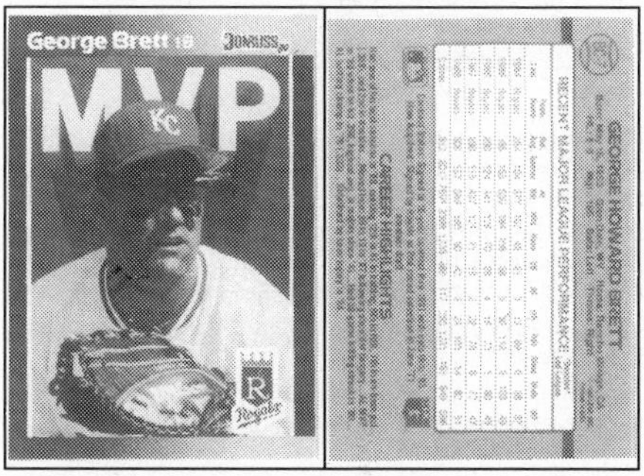

This 26-card set was distributed along with the regular 1989 Donruss issue as random inserts with the rack and wax packs. These bonus cards are numbered with the prefix BC for bonus cards and were supposedly produced in the same quantities as the other 660 regular issue cards. The %most valuable" player was selected from each of the 26 teams. Cards measure 2 1/2" by 3 1/2" and feature the same distinctive side border as the regular issue. The cards are distinguished by the bold MVP logo in the upper background of the obverse. Four of these cards were double printed with respect to the other cards in the set; these four are denoted by DP in the checklist below.

	MINT	EXC	G-VG
COMPLETE SET (26)	5.00	2.50	.50
COMMON CARD (BC1-BC26)	.05	.02	.00

☐ BC1	Kirby Puckett	.20	.10	.02
☐ BC2	Mike Scott	.08	.04	.01
☐ BC3	Joe Carter	.10	.05	.01
☐ BC4	Orel Hershiser	.12	.06	.01
☐ BC5	Jose Canseco	.40	.20	.04
☐ BC6	Darryl Strawberry	.30	.15	.03
☐ BC7	George Brett	.20	.10	.02
☐ BC8	Andre Dawson	.12	.06	.01
☐ BC9	Paul Molitor UER (Brewers logo missing the word Milwaukee)	.10	.05	.01
☐ BC10	Andy Van Slyke	.08	.04	.01
☐ BC11	Dave Winfield	.10	.05	.01
☐ BC12	Kevin Gross	.05	.02	.00
☐ BC13	Mike Greenwell	.15	.07	.01
☐ BC14	Ozzie Smith	.10	.05	.01

☐ BC15 Cal Ripken	.15	.07	.01
☐ BC16 Andres Galarraga	.08	.04	.01
☐ BC17 Alan Trammell	.10	.05	.01
☐ BC18 Kal Daniels	.08	.04	.01
☐ BC19 Fred McGriff	.12	.06	.01
☐ BC20 Tony Gwynn	.15	.07	.01
☐ BC21 Wally Joyner DP	.08	.04	.01
☐ BC22 Will Clark DP	.25	.12	.02
☐ BC23 Ozzie Guillen	.08	.04	.01
☐ BC24 Gerald Perry DP	.05	.02	.00
☐ BC25 Alvin Davis DP	.05	.02	.00
☐ BC26 Ruben Sierra	.20	.10	.02

1989 Donruss Super DK's

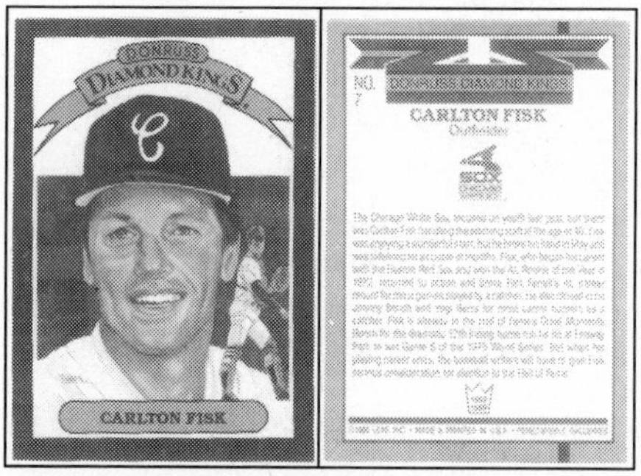

This 26-player card set was available through a mail-in offer detailed on the wax packs. The set was sent in return for 8.00 and three wrappers plus 2.00 postage and handling. The set features the popular Diamond King subseries in large (approximately 4 7/8" by 6 13/16") form. Dick Perez of Perez-Steele Galleries did another outstanding job on the artwork. The cards are essentially a large version of the Donruss regular issue Diamond Kings.

	MINT	EXC	G-VG
COMPLETE SET (26)	10.00	5.00	1.00
COMMON PLAYER (1-26)	.20	.10	.02
☐ 1 Mike Greenwell DK	.75	.35	.07
☐ 2 Bobby Bonilla DK	.40	.20	.04
☐ 3 Pete Incaviglia DK	.30	.15	.03
☐ 4 Chris Sabo DK	.75	.35	.07
☐ 5 Robin Yount DK	.60	.30	.06
☐ 6 Tony Gwynn DK	.60	.30	.06
☐ 7 Carlton Fisk DK	.40	.20	.04
☐ 8 Cory Snyder DK	.30	.15	.03
☐ 9 David Cone DK	.40	.20	.04
☐ 10 Kevin Seitzer DK	.40	.20	.04
☐ 11 Rick Reuschel DK	.30	.15	.03
☐ 12 Johnny Ray DK	.20	.10	.02
☐ 13 Dave Schmidt DK	.20	.10	.02
☐ 14 Andres Galarraga DK	.30	.15	.03
☐ 15 Kirk Gibson DK	.45	.22	.04
☐ 16 Fred McGriff DK	.50	.25	.05
☐ 17 Mark Grace DK	1.25	.60	.12
☐ 18 Jeff Robinson DT DK	.20	.10	.02
☐ 19 Vince Coleman DK	.35	.17	.03
☐ 20 Dave Henderson DK	.20	.10	.02
☐ 21 Harold Reynolds DK	.20	.10	.02
☐ 22 Gerald Perry DK	.20	.10	.02
☐ 23 Frank Viola DK	.35	.17	.03
☐ 24 Steve Bedrosian DK	.25	.12	.02
☐ 25 Glenn Davis DK	.40	.20	.04
☐ 26 Don Mattingly DK	1.50	.75	.15

1989 Donruss All-Stars

These All-Stars are standard size, 2 1/2" by 3 1/2" and very similar in design to the regular issue of 1989 Donruss. The set is distinguished by the presence of the respective League logos in the lower right corner of each obverse. The cards are numbered on the backs. The players chosen for the set are essentially the participants at the previous year's All-Star Game. Individual wax packs of All Stars (suggested retail price of 35 cents) contained one Pop-Up, five All-Star cards, and a Warren Spahn puzzle card.

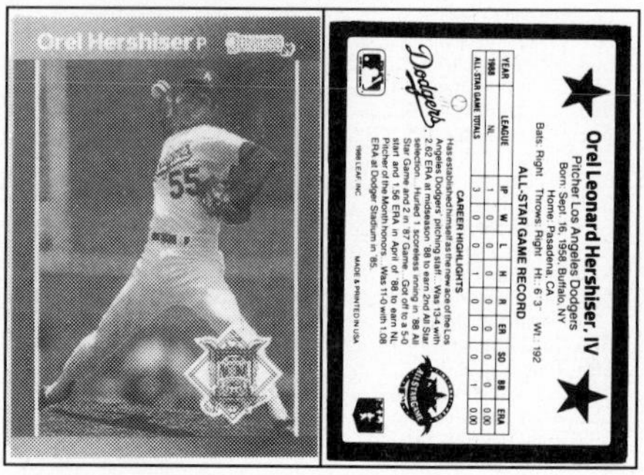

	MINT	EXC	G-VG
COMPLETE SET (64)	8.00	4.00	.80
COMMON PLAYER (1-64)	.07	.03	.01
☐ 1 Mark McGwire	.75	.35	.07
☐ 2 Jose Canseco	1.00	.50	.10
☐ 3 Paul Molitor	.15	.07	.01
☐ 4 Rickey Henderson	.75	.35	.07
☐ 5 Cal Ripken Jr.	.30	.15	.03
☐ 6 Dave Winfield	.20	.10	.02
☐ 7 Wade Boggs	.75	.35	.07
☐ 8 Frank Viola	.15	.07	.01
☐ 9 Terry Steinbach	.10	.05	.01
☐ 10 Tom Kelly MG	.07	.03	.01
☐ 11 George Brett	.40	.20	.04
☐ 12 Doyle Alexander	.07	.03	.01
☐ 13 Gary Gaetti	.15	.07	.01
☐ 14 Roger Clemens	.60	.30	.06
☐ 15 Mike Greenwell	.90	.45	.09
☐ 16 Dennis Eckersley	.25	.12	.02
☐ 17 Carney Lansford	.15	.07	.01
☐ 18 Mark Gubicza	.15	.07	.01
☐ 19 Tim Laudner	.07	.03	.01
☐ 20 Doug Jones	.10	.05	.01
☐ 21 Don Mattingly	1.00	.50	.10
☐ 22 Dan Plesac	.10	.05	.01
☐ 23 Kirby Puckett	.60	.30	.06
☐ 24 Jeff Reardon	.10	.05	.01
☐ 25 Johnny Ray	.07	.03	.01
☐ 26 Jeff Russell	.07	.03	.01
☐ 27 Harold Reynolds	.07	.03	.01
☐ 28 Dave Stieb	.15	.07	.01
☐ 29 Kurt Stillwell	.10	.05	.01
☐ 30 Jose Canseco	1.25	.60	.12
☐ 31 Terry Steinbach	.10	.05	.01
☐ 32 AL Checklist	.07	.01	.00
☐ 33 Will Clark	1.25	.60	.12
☐ 34 Darryl Strawberry	.75	.35	.07
☐ 35 Ryne Sandberg	.75	.35	.07
☐ 36 Andre Dawson	.30	.15	.03
☐ 37 Ozzie Smith	.25	.12	.02
☐ 38 Vince Coleman	.20	.10	.02
☐ 39 Bobby Bonilla	.35	.17	.03
☐ 40 Dwight Gooden	.50	.25	.05
☐ 41 Gary Carter	.25	.12	.02
☐ 42 Whitey Herzog MG	.07	.03	.01
☐ 43 Shawon Dunston	.25	.12	.02
☐ 44 David Cone	.35	.17	.03
☐ 45 Andres Galarraga	.25	.12	.02
☐ 46 Mark Davis	.07	.03	.01
☐ 47 Barry Larkin	.35	.17	.03
☐ 48 Kevin Gross	.07	.03	.01
☐ 49 Vance Law	.07	.03	.01
☐ 50 Orel Hershiser	.40	.20	.04
☐ 51 Willie McGee	.15	.07	.01
☐ 52 Danny Jackson	.10	.05	.01
☐ 53 Rafael Palmeiro	.30	.15	.03
☐ 54 Bob Knepper	.07	.03	.01
☐ 55 Lance Parrish	.10	.05	.01
☐ 56 Greg Maddux	.15	.07	.01

☐ 57 Gerald Perry	.07	.03	.01
☐ 58 Bob Walk	.07	.03	.01
☐ 59 Chris Sabo	.45	.22	.04
☐ 60 Todd Worrell	.15	.07	.01
☐ 61 Andy Van Slyke	.15	.07	.01
☐ 62 Ozzie Smith	.25	.12	.02
☐ 63 Riverfront Stadium	.07	.03	.01
☐ 64 NL Checklist	.07	.01	.00

1989 Donruss Pop-Ups

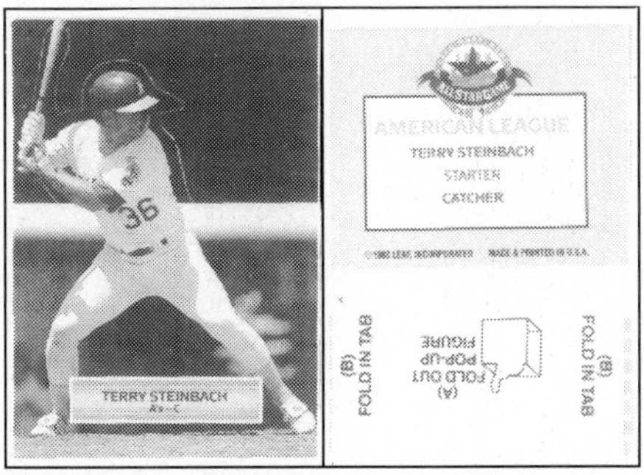

These Pop-Ups are borderless and standard size, 2 1/2" by 3 1/2". The cards are unnumbered; however the All Star checklist card lists the same numbers as the All Star cards. Those numbers are used below for reference. The players chosen for the set are essentially the starting lineups for the previous year's All-Star Game. Individual wax packs of All Stars (suggested retail price of 35 cents) contained one Pop-Up, five All-Star cards, and a puzzle card.

	MINT	EXC	G-VG
COMPLETE SET (20)	4.00	2.00	.40
COMMON PLAYER	.10	.05	.01
☐ 1 Mark McGwire	.75	.35	.07
☐ 2 Jose Canseco	1.00	.50	.10
☐ 3 Paul Molitor	.15	.07	.01
☐ 4 Rickey Henderson	.75	.35	.07
☐ 5 Cal Ripken Jr.	.30	.15	.03
☐ 6 Dave Winfield	.20	.10	.02
☐ 7 Wade Boggs	.75	.35	.07
☐ 8 Frank Viola	.20	.10	.02
☐ 9 Terry Steinbach	.10	.05	.01
☐ 10 Tom Kelly MG	.10	.05	.01
☐ 33 Will Clark	1.25	.60	.12
☐ 34 Darryl Strawberry	.75	.35	.07
☐ 35 Ryne Sandberg	.75	.35	.07
☐ 36 Andre Dawson	.30	.15	.03
☐ 37 Ozzie Smith	.25	.12	.02
☐ 38 Vince Coleman	.20	.10	.02
☐ 39 Bobby Bonilla	.35	.17	.03
☐ 40 Dwight Gooden	.50	.25	.05
☐ 41 Gary Carter	.25	.12	.02
☐ 42 Whitey Herzog MG	.10	.05	.01

1989 Donruss Traded

The 1989 Donruss Traded set contains 56 standard-size (2 1/2" by 3 1/2") cards. The fronts have yellowish-orange borders; the backs are yellow and feature recent statistics. The cards were distributed as a boxed set. The set was never very popular with collectors since it included (as the name implies) only traded players rather than rookies.

	MINT	EXC	G-VG
COMPLETE SET (56)	4.50	2.25	.45
COMMON PLAYER (1-55)	.05	.02	.00

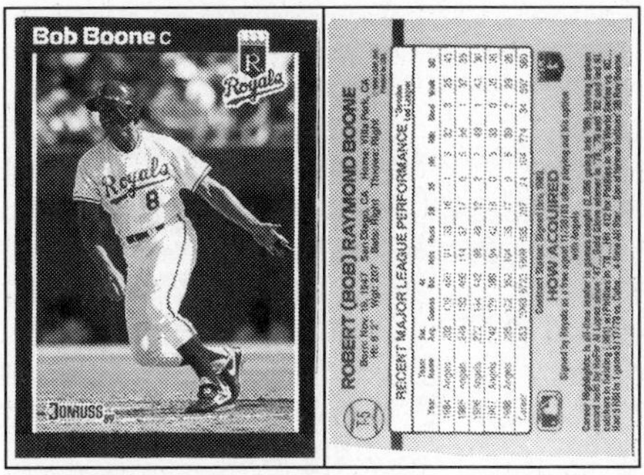

☐ 1 Jeffrey Leonard	.10	.05	.01
☐ 2 Jack Clark	.20	.10	.02
☐ 3 Kevin Gross	.05	.02	.00
☐ 4 Tommy Herr	.10	.05	.01
☐ 5 Bob Boone	.15	.07	.01
☐ 6 Rafael Palmeiro	.30	.15	.03
☐ 7 John Dopson	.05	.02	.00
☐ 8 Willie Randolph	.10	.05	.01
☐ 9 Chris Brown	.05	.02	.00
☐ 10 Wally Backman	.05	.02	.00
☐ 11 Steve Ontiveros	.05	.02	.00
☐ 12 Eddie Murray	.20	.10	.02
☐ 13 Lance McCullers	.05	.02	.00
☐ 14 Spike Owen	.05	.02	.00
☐ 15 Rob Murphy	.05	.02	.00
☐ 16 Pete O'Brien	.10	.05	.01
☐ 17 Ken Williams	.05	.02	.00
☐ 18 Nick Esasky	.10	.05	.01
☐ 19 Nolan Ryan	1.75	.85	.17
☐ 20 Brian Holton	.05	.02	.00
☐ 21 Mike Moore	.10	.05	.01
☐ 22 Joel Skinner	.05	.02	.00
☐ 23 Steve Sax	.15	.07	.01
☐ 24 Rick Mahler	.05	.02	.00
☐ 25 Mike Aldrete	.05	.02	.00
☐ 26 Jesse Orosco	.05	.02	.00
☐ 27 Dave LaPoint	.05	.02	.00
☐ 28 Walt Terrell	.05	.02	.00
☐ 29 Eddie Williams	.05	.02	.00
☐ 30 Mike Devereaux	.05	.02	.00
☐ 31 Julio Franco	.15	.07	.01
☐ 32 Jim Clancy	.05	.02	.00
☐ 33 Felix Fermin	.05	.02	.00
☐ 34 Curt Wilkerson	.05	.02	.00
☐ 35 Bert Blyleven	.15	.07	.01
☐ 36 Mel Hall	.10	.05	.01
☐ 37 Eric King	.10	.05	.01
☐ 38 Mitch Williams	.10	.05	.01
☐ 39 Jamie Moyer	.05	.02	.00
☐ 40 Rick Rhoden	.05	.02	.00
☐ 41 Phil Bradley	.10	.05	.01
☐ 42 Paul Kilgus	.05	.02	.00
☐ 43 Milt Thompson	.05	.02	.00
☐ 44 Jerry Browne	.10	.05	.01
☐ 45 Bruce Hurst	.10	.05	.01
☐ 46 Claudell Washington	.10	.05	.01
☐ 47 Todd Benzinger	.10	.05	.01
☐ 48 Steve Balboni	.05	.02	.00
☐ 49 Oddibe McDowell	.10	.05	.01
☐ 50 Charles Hudson	.05	.02	.00
☐ 51 Ron Kittle	.10	.05	.01
☐ 52 Andy Hawkins	.05	.02	.00
☐ 53 Tom Brookens	.05	.02	.00
☐ 54 Tom Niedenfuer	.05	.02	.00
☐ 55 Jeff Parrett	.05	.02	.00
☐ 56 Checklist Card	.05	.01	.00

1989 Donruss Grand Slammers

The 1989 Donruss Grand Slammers set contains 12 standard-size (2 1/2" by 3 1/2") cards. Each card in the set can be found with five different colored border combinations, but no color combination of borders appears to be scarcer than any other. The set includes cards for each player who hit one or more grand slams in 1988. The backs detail the players' grand slams. The cards were distributed one per cello pack as well as an insert (complete) set in each factory set.

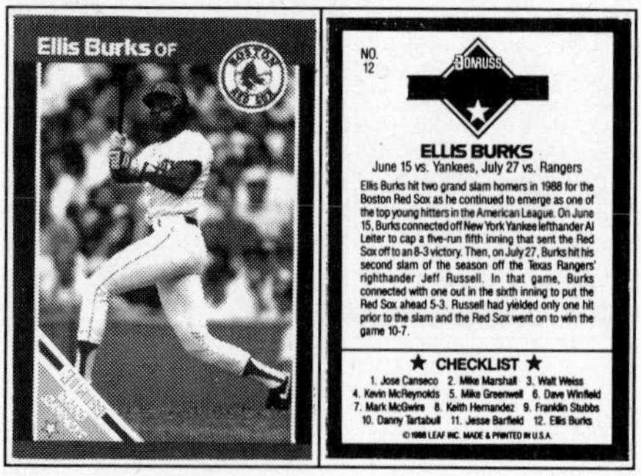

	MINT	EXC	G-VG
COMPLETE SET (12)	3.00	1.50	.30
COMMON PLAYER (1-12)	.10	.05	.01
☐ 1 Jose Canseco	1.00	.50	.10
☐ 2 Mike Marshall	.15	.07	.01
☐ 3 Walt Weiss	.20	.10	.02
☐ 4 Kevin McReynolds	.20	.10	.02
☐ 5 Mike Greenwell	.40	.20	.04
☐ 6 Dave Winfield	.25	.12	.02
☐ 7 Mark McGwire	.60	.30	.06
☐ 8 Keith Hernandez	.15	.07	.01
☐ 9 Franklin Stubbs	.10	.05	.01
☐ 10 Danny Tartabull	.20	.10	.02
☐ 11 Jesse Barfield	.20	.10	.02
☐ 12 Ellis Burks	.30	.15	.03

1989 Donruss Baseball's Best

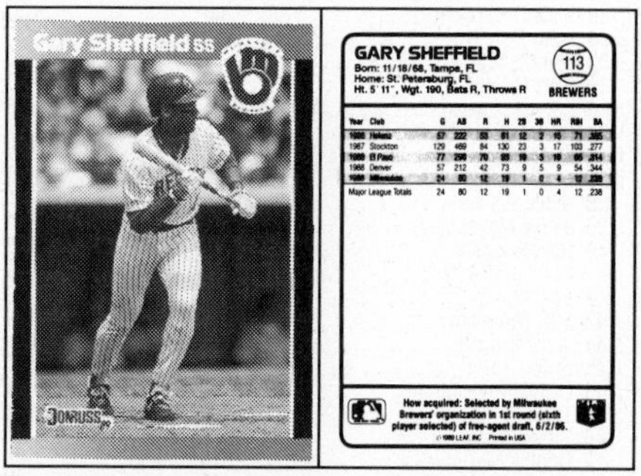

The 1989 Donruss Baseball's Best set contains 336 standard-size (2 1/2" by 3 1/2") glossy cards. The fronts are green and yellow, and the backs feature career highlight information. The backs are green, and feature vertically-oriented career stats. The cards were distributed as a set in a blister pack through various retail and department store chains.

	MINT	EXC	G-VG
COMPLETE SET (336)	20.00	10.00	2.00
COMMON PLAYER (1-336)	.04	.02	.00
☐ 1 Don Mattingly	1.00	.50	.10
☐ 2 Tom Glavine	.15	.07	.01
☐ 3 Bert Blyleven	.10	.05	.01
☐ 4 Andre Dawson	.20	.10	.02
☐ 5 Pete O'Brien	.07	.03	.01
☐ 6 Eric Davis	.45	.22	.04
☐ 7 George Brett	.40	.20	.04
☐ 8 Glenn Davis	.25	.12	.02
☐ 9 Ellis Burks	.35	.17	.03
☐ 10 Kirk Gibson	.20	.10	.02
☐ 11 Carlton Fisk	.25	.12	.02
☐ 12 Andres Galarraga	.20	.10	.02
☐ 13 Alan Trammell	.15	.07	.01
☐ 14 Dwight Gooden	.40	.20	.04
☐ 15 Paul Molitor	.15	.07	.01
☐ 16 Roger McDowell	.07	.03	.01
☐ 17 Doug Drabek	.15	.07	.01
☐ 18 Kent Hrbek	.15	.07	.01
☐ 19 Vince Coleman	.20	.10	.02
☐ 20 Steve Sax	.15	.07	.01
☐ 21 Roberto Alomar	.25	.12	.02
☐ 22 Carney Lansford	.15	.07	.01
☐ 23 Will Clark	1.00	.50	.10
☐ 24 Alvin Davis	.10	.05	.01
☐ 25 Bobby Thigpen	.15	.07	.01
☐ 26 Ryne Sandberg	.75	.35	.07
☐ 27 Devon White	.10	.05	.01
☐ 28 Mike Greenwell	.35	.17	.03
☐ 29 Dale Murphy	.35	.17	.03
☐ 30 Jeff Ballard	.10	.05	.01
☐ 31 Kelly Gruber	.07	.03	.01
☐ 32 Julio Franco	.10	.05	.01
☐ 33 Bobby Bonilla	.20	.10	.02
☐ 34 Tim Wallach	.07	.03	.01
☐ 35 Lou Whitaker	.10	.05	.01
☐ 36 Jay Howell	.07	.03	.01
☐ 37 Greg Maddux	.10	.05	.01
☐ 38 Bill Doran	.07	.03	.01
☐ 39 Danny Tartabull	.15	.07	.01
☐ 40 Darryl Strawberry	.40	.20	.04
☐ 41 Ron Darling	.10	.05	.01
☐ 42 Tony Gwynn	.30	.15	.03
☐ 43 Mark McGwire	.60	.30	.06
☐ 44 Ozzie Smith	.20	.10	.02
☐ 45 Andy Van Slyke	.10	.05	.01
☐ 46 Juan Berenguer	.04	.02	.00
☐ 47 Von Hayes	.10	.05	.01
☐ 48 Tony Fernandez	.10	.05	.01
☐ 49 Eric Plunk	.04	.02	.00
☐ 50 Ernest Riles	.04	.02	.00
☐ 51 Harold Reynolds	.07	.03	.01
☐ 52 Andy Hawkins	.04	.02	.00
☐ 53 Robin Yount	.35	.17	.03
☐ 54 Danny Jackson	.10	.05	.01
☐ 55 Nolan Ryan	1.25	.60	.12
☐ 56 Joe Carter	.15	.07	.01
☐ 57 Jose Canseco	1.00	.50	.10
☐ 58 Jody Davis	.04	.02	.00
☐ 59 Lance Parrish	.07	.03	.01
☐ 60 Mitch Williams	.07	.03	.01
☐ 61 Brook Jacoby	.07	.03	.01
☐ 62 Tom Browning	.07	.03	.01
☐ 63 Kurt Stillwell	.07	.03	.01
☐ 64 Rafael Ramirez	.04	.02	.00
☐ 65 Roger Clemens	.50	.25	.05
☐ 66 Mike Scioscia	.04	.02	.00
☐ 67 Dave Gallagher	.04	.02	.00
☐ 68 Mark Langston	.15	.07	.01
☐ 69 Chet Lemon	.04	.02	.00
☐ 70 Kevin McReynolds	.10	.05	.01
☐ 71 Rob Deer	.07	.03	.01
☐ 72 Tommy Herr	.07	.03	.01
☐ 73 Barry Bonds	.40	.20	.04
☐ 74 Frank Viola	.15	.07	.01
☐ 75 Pedro Guerrero	.15	.07	.01
☐ 76 Dave Righetti	.10	.05	.01
☐ 77 Bruce Hurst	.07	.03	.01
☐ 78 Rickey Henderson	.75	.35	.07
☐ 79 Robby Thompson	.04	.02	.00
☐ 80 Randy Johnson	.07	.03	.01
☐ 81 Harold Baines	.10	.05	.01
☐ 82 Calvin Schiraldi	.04	.02	.00
☐ 83 Kirk McCaskill	.04	.02	.00
☐ 84 Lee Smith	.07	.03	.01
☐ 85 John Smoltz	.10	.05	.01
☐ 86 Mickey Tettleton	.10	.05	.01
☐ 87 Jimmy Key	.07	.03	.01
☐ 88 Rafael Palmeiro	.20	.10	.02
☐ 89 Sid Bream	.04	.02	.00
☐ 90 Dennis Martinez	.07	.03	.01
☐ 91 Frank Tanana	.04	.02	.00
☐ 92 Eddie Murray	.25	.12	.02
☐ 93 Shawon Dunston	.20	.10	.02
☐ 94 Mike Scott	.15	.07	.01
☐ 95 Bret Saberhagen	.20	.10	.02
☐ 96 David Cone	.20	.10	.02
☐ 97 Kevin Elster	.07	.03	.01
☐ 98 Jack Clark	.15	.07	.01
☐ 99 Dave Stewart	.25	.12	.02
☐ 100 Jose Oquendo	.04	.02	.00
☐ 101 Jose Lind	.04	.02	.00
☐ 102 Gary Gaetti	.10	.05	.01

☐ 103	Ricky Jordan	.15	.07	.01
☐ 104	Fred McGriff	.35	.17	.03
☐ 105	Don Slaught	.04	.02	.00
☐ 106	Jose Uribe	.04	.02	.00
☐ 107	Jeffrey Leonard	.07	.03	.01
☐ 108	Lee Guetterman	.04	.02	.00
☐ 109	Chris Bosio	.04	.02	.00
☐ 110	Barry Larkin	.25	.12	.02
☐ 111	Ruben Sierra	.40	.20	.04
☐ 112	Greg Swindell	.10	.05	.01
☐ 113	Gary Sheffield	.50	.25	.05
☐ 114	Lonnie Smith	.07	.03	.01
☐ 115	Chili Davis	.04	.02	.00
☐ 116	Damon Berryhill	.10	.05	.01
☐ 117	Tom Candiotti	.04	.02	.00
☐ 118	Kal Daniels	.10	.05	.01
☐ 119	Mark Gubicza	.10	.05	.01
☐ 120	Jim Deshaies	.04	.02	.00
☐ 121	Dwight Evans	.10	.05	.01
☐ 122	Mike Morgan	.07	.03	.01
☐ 123	Dan Pasqua	.04	.02	.00
☐ 124	Bryn Smith	.04	.02	.00
☐ 125	Doyle Alexander	.04	.02	.00
☐ 126	Howard Johnson	.15	.07	.01
☐ 127	Chuck Crim	.04	.02	.00
☐ 128	Darren Daulton	.10	.05	.01
☐ 129	Jeff Robinson	.07	.03	.01
☐ 130	Kirby Puckett	.40	.20	.04
☐ 131	Joe Magrane	.10	.05	.01
☐ 132	Jesse Barfield	.10	.05	.01
☐ 133	Mark Davis UER (photo actually Dave Leiper)	.20	.10	.02
☐ 134	Dennis Eckersley	.20	.10	.02
☐ 135	Mike Krukow	.04	.02	.00
☐ 136	Jay Buhner	.15	.07	.01
☐ 137	Ozzie Guillen	.10	.05	.01
☐ 138	Rick Sutcliffe	.07	.03	.01
☐ 139	Wally Joyner	.15	.07	.01
☐ 140	Wade Boggs	.45	.22	.04
☐ 141	Jeff Treadway	.04	.02	.00
☐ 142	Cal Ripken	.25	.12	.02
☐ 143	Dave Stieb	.10	.05	.01
☐ 144	Pete Incaviglia	.10	.05	.01
☐ 145	Bob Walk	.04	.02	.00
☐ 146	Nelson Santovenia	.07	.03	.01
☐ 147	Mike Heath	.04	.02	.00
☐ 148	Willie Randolph	.07	.03	.01
☐ 149	Paul Kilgus	.04	.02	.00
☐ 150	Billy Hatcher	.07	.03	.01
☐ 151	Steve Farr	.04	.02	.00
☐ 152	Gregg Jefferies	.75	.35	.07
☐ 153	Randy Myers	.07	.03	.01
☐ 154	Garry Templeton	.07	.03	.01
☐ 155	Walt Weiss	.15	.07	.01
☐ 156	Terry Pendleton	.04	.02	.00
☐ 157	John Smiley	.07	.03	.01
☐ 158	Greg Gagne	.04	.02	.00
☐ 159	Len Dykstra	.15	.07	.01
☐ 160	Nelson Liriano	.04	.02	.00
☐ 161	Alvaro Espinoza	.04	.02	.00
☐ 162	Rick Reuschel	.10	.05	.01
☐ 163	Omar Vizquel UER (photo actually Darnell Coles)	.15	.07	.01
☐ 164	Clay Parker	.07	.03	.01
☐ 165	Dan Plesac	.07	.03	.01
☐ 166	John Franco	.10	.05	.01
☐ 167	Scott Fletcher	.04	.02	.00
☐ 168	Cory Snyder	.10	.05	.01
☐ 169	Bo Jackson	1.50	.75	.15
☐ 170	Tommy Gregg	.07	.03	.01
☐ 171	Jim Abbott	.75	.35	.07
☐ 172	Jerome Walton	.90	.45	.09
☐ 173	Doug Jones	.07	.03	.01
☐ 174	Todd Benzinger	.07	.03	.01
☐ 175	Frank White	.07	.03	.01
☐ 176	Craig Biggio	.20	.10	.02
☐ 177	John Dopson	.04	.02	.00
☐ 178	Alfredo Griffin	.04	.02	.00
☐ 179	Melido Perez	.07	.03	.01
☐ 180	Tim Burke	.07	.03	.01
☐ 181	Matt Nokes	.10	.05	.01
☐ 182	Gary Carter	.20	.10	.02
☐ 183	Ted Higuera	.10	.05	.01
☐ 184	Ken Howell	.04	.02	.00
☐ 185	Rey Quinones	.04	.02	.00
☐ 186	Wally Backman	.04	.02	.00
☐ 187	Tom Brunansky	.10	.05	.01
☐ 188	Steve Balboni	.04	.02	.00
☐ 189	Marvell Wynne	.04	.02	.00
☐ 190	Dave Henderson	.04	.02	.00
☐ 191	Don Robinson	.04	.02	.00
☐ 192	Ken Griffey Jr.	3.00	1.50	.30
☐ 193	Ivan Calderon	.07	.03	.01
☐ 194	Mike Bielecki	.04	.02	.00
☐ 195	Johnny Ray	.04	.02	.00
☐ 196	Rob Murphy	.04	.02	.00
☐ 197	Andres Thomas	.04	.02	.00
☐ 198	Phil Bradley	.07	.03	.01
☐ 199	Junior Felix	.35	.17	.03
☐ 200	Jeff Russell	.04	.02	.00
☐ 201	Mike LaValliere	.04	.02	.00
☐ 202	Kevin Gross	.04	.02	.00
☐ 203	Keith Moreland	.04	.02	.00
☐ 204	Mike Marshall	.10	.05	.01
☐ 205	Dwight Smith	.35	.17	.03
☐ 206	Jim Clancy	.04	.02	.00
☐ 207	Kevin Seitzer	.15	.07	.01
☐ 208	Keith Hernandez	.15	.07	.01
☐ 209	Bob Ojeda	.07	.03	.01
☐ 210	Ed Whitson	.07	.03	.01
☐ 211	Tony Phillips	.04	.02	.00
☐ 212	Milt Thompson	.04	.02	.00
☐ 213	Randy Kramer	.04	.02	.00
☐ 214	Randy Bush	.04	.02	.00
☐ 215	Randy Ready	.04	.02	.00
☐ 216	Duane Ward	.04	.02	.00
☐ 217	Jimmy Jones	.07	.03	.01
☐ 218	Scott Garrelts	.07	.03	.01
☐ 219	Scott Bankhead	.07	.03	.01
☐ 220	Lance McCullers	.04	.02	.00
☐ 221	B.J. Surhoff	.07	.03	.01
☐ 222	Chris Sabo	.20	.10	.02
☐ 223	Steve Buechele	.04	.02	.00
☐ 224	Joel Skinner	.04	.02	.00
☐ 225	Orel Hershiser	.25	.12	.02
☐ 226	Derek Lilliquist	.10	.05	.01
☐ 227	Claudell Washington	.07	.03	.01
☐ 228	Lloyd McClendon	.04	.02	.00
☐ 229	Felix Fermin	.04	.02	.00
☐ 230	Paul O'Neill	.15	.07	.01
☐ 231	Charlie Leibrandt	.04	.02	.00
☐ 232	Dave Smith	.04	.02	.00
☐ 233	Bob Stanley	.04	.02	.00
☐ 234	Tim Belcher	.10	.05	.01
☐ 235	Eric King	.07	.03	.01
☐ 236	Spike Owen	.04	.02	.00
☐ 237	Mike Henneman	.07	.03	.01
☐ 238	Juan Samuel	.10	.05	.01
☐ 239	Greg Brock	.04	.02	.00
☐ 240	John Kruk	.10	.05	.01
☐ 241	Glenn Wilson	.04	.02	.00
☐ 242	Jeff Reardon	.07	.03	.01
☐ 243	Todd Worrell	.10	.05	.01
☐ 244	Dave LaPoint	.04	.02	.00
☐ 245	Walt Terrell	.04	.02	.00
☐ 246	Mike Moore	.07	.03	.01
☐ 247	Kelly Downs	.04	.02	.00
☐ 248	Dave Valle	.04	.02	.00
☐ 249	Ron Kittle	.10	.05	.01
☐ 250	Steve Wilson	.07	.03	.01
☐ 251	Dick Schofield	.04	.02	.00
☐ 252	Marty Barrett	.04	.02	.00
☐ 253	Dion James	.04	.02	.00
☐ 254	Bob Milacki	.10	.05	.01
☐ 255	Ernie Whitt	.04	.02	.00
☐ 256	Kevin Brown	.15	.07	.01
☐ 257	R.J. Reynolds	.04	.02	.00
☐ 258	Tim Raines	.20	.10	.02
☐ 259	Frank Williams	.04	.02	.00
☐ 260	Jose Gonzalez	.04	.02	.00
☐ 261	Mitch Webster	.04	.02	.00
☐ 262	Ken Caminiti	.04	.02	.00
☐ 263	Bob Boone	.10	.05	.01
☐ 264	Dave Magadan	.15	.07	.01
☐ 265	Rick Aguilera	.04	.02	.00
☐ 266	Chris James	.10	.05	.01
☐ 267	Bob Welch	.15	.07	.01
☐ 268	Ken Dayley	.04	.02	.00
☐ 269	Junior Ortiz	.04	.02	.00
☐ 270	Allan Anderson	.07	.03	.01
☐ 271	Steve Jeltz	.04	.02	.00
☐ 272	George Bell	.15	.07	.01
☐ 273	Roberto Kelly	.30	.15	.03
☐ 274	Brett Butler	.10	.05	.01
☐ 275	Mike Schooler	.15	.07	.01
☐ 276	Ken Phelps	.07	.03	.01
☐ 277	Glenn Braggs	.10	.05	.01
☐ 278	Jose Rijo	.15	.07	.01
☐ 279	Bobby Witt	.15	.07	.01
☐ 280	Jerry Browne	.07	.03	.01
☐ 281	Kevin Mitchell	.45	.22	.04
☐ 282	Craig Worthington	.20	.10	.02
☐ 283	Greg Minton	.04	.02	.00
☐ 284	Nick Esasky	.07	.03	.01
☐ 285	John Farrell	.07	.03	.01
☐ 286	Rick Mahler	.04	.02	.00

☐ 287 Tom Gordon	.40	.20	.04
☐ 288 Gerald Young	.10	.05	.01
☐ 289 Jody Reed	.10	.05	.01
☐ 290 Jeff Hamilton	.04	.02	.00
☐ 291 Gerald Perry	.04	.02	.00
☐ 292 Hubie Brooks	.07	.03	.01
☐ 293 Bo Diaz	.04	.02	.00
☐ 294 Terry Puhl	.04	.02	.00
☐ 295 Jim Gantner	.04	.02	.00
☐ 296 Jeff Parrett	.04	.02	.00
☐ 297 Mike Boddicker	.04	.02	.00
☐ 298 Dan Gladden	.04	.02	.00
☐ 299 Tony Pena	.07	.03	.01
☐ 300 Checklist Card	.04	.02	.00
☐ 301 Tom Henke	.07	.03	.01
☐ 302 Pascual Perez	.07	.03	.01
☐ 303 Steve Bedrosian	.07	.03	.01
☐ 304 Ken Hill	.07	.03	.01
☐ 305 Jerry Reuss	.04	.02	.00
☐ 306 Jim Eisenreich	.07	.03	.01
☐ 307 Jack Howell	.04	.02	.00
☐ 308 Rick Cerone	.04	.02	.00
☐ 309 Tim Leary	.07	.03	.01
☐ 310 Joe Orsulak	.04	.02	.00
☐ 311 Jim Dwyer	.04	.02	.00
☐ 312 Geno Petralli	.04	.02	.00
☐ 313 Rick Honeycutt	.04	.02	.00
☐ 314 Tom Foley	.04	.02	.00
☐ 315 Kenny Rogers	.04	.02	.00
☐ 316 Mike Flanagan	.04	.02	.00
☐ 317 Bryan Harvey	.10	.05	.01
☐ 318 Billy Ripken	.04	.02	.00
☐ 319 Jeff Montgomery	.10	.05	.01
☐ 320 Erik Hanson	.07	.03	.01
☐ 321 Brian Downing	.04	.02	.00
☐ 322 Gregg Olson	.50	.25	.05
☐ 323 Terry Steinbach	.10	.05	.01
☐ 324 Sammy Sosa	.50	.25	.05
☐ 325 Gene Harris	.15	.07	.01
☐ 326 Mike Devereaux	.07	.03	.01
☐ 327 Dennis Cook	.07	.03	.01
☐ 328 David Wells	.04	.02	.00
☐ 329 Checklist Card	.04	.02	.00
☐ 330 Kirt Manwaring	.07	.03	.01
☐ 331 Jim Presley	.04	.02	.00
☐ 332 Checklist Card	.04	.02	.00
☐ 333 Chuck Finley	.15	.07	.01
☐ 334 Rob Dibble	.15	.07	.01
☐ 335 Cecil Espy	.07	.03	.01
☐ 336 Dave Parker	.15	.07	.01

1989 Donruss Rookies

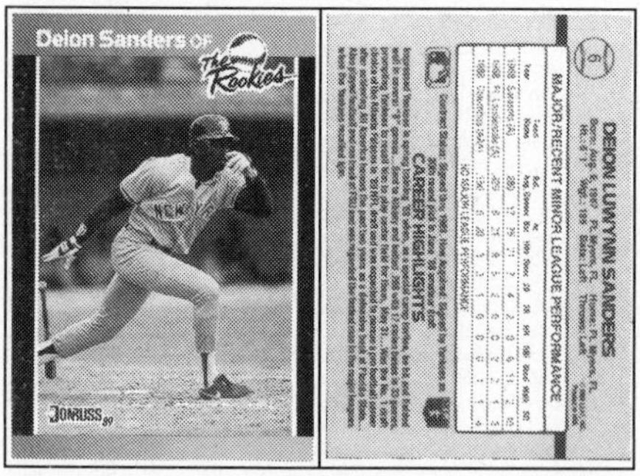

The 1989 Donruss Rookies set contains 56 standard-size (2 1/2" by 3 1/2") cards. The fronts have green and black borders; the backs are green and feature career highlights. The cards were distributed as a boxed set. The key rookie cards in this set are Jim Abbott, Junior Felix, Deion Sanders, and Jerome Walton.

	MINT	EXC	G-VG
COMPLETE SET (56)	20.00	10.00	2.00
COMMON PLAYER (1-56)	.08	.04	.01
☐ 1 Gary Sheffield	1.25	.40	.08
☐ 2 Gregg Jefferies	1.00	.50	.10
☐ 3 Ken Griffey Jr.	6.50	3.25	.65
☐ 4 Tom Gordon	.60	.30	.06
☐ 5 Billy Spiers	.20	.10	.02
☐ 6 Deion Sanders	1.00	.50	.10
☐ 7 Donn Pall	.12	.06	.01
☐ 8 Steve Carter	.20	.10	.02
☐ 9 Francisco Oliveras	.12	.06	.01
☐ 10 Steve Wilson	.12	.06	.01
☐ 11 Bob Geren	.20	.10	.02
☐ 12 Tony Castillo	.12	.06	.01
☐ 13 Kenny Rogers	.20	.10	.02
☐ 14 Carlos Martinez	.25	.12	.02
☐ 15 Edgar Martinez	.30	.15	.03
☐ 16 Jim Abbott	1.25	.60	.12
☐ 17 Torey Lovullo	.15	.07	.01
☐ 18 Mark Carreon	.12	.06	.01
☐ 19 Geronimo Berroa	.08	.04	.01
☐ 20 Luis Medina	.15	.07	.01
☐ 21 Sandy Alomar Jr.	.85	.40	.08
☐ 22 Bob Milacki	.12	.06	.01
☐ 23 Joe Girardi	.25	.12	.02
☐ 24 German Gonzalez	.08	.04	.01
☐ 25 Craig Worthington	.12	.06	.01
☐ 26 Jerome Walton	2.00	1.00	.20
☐ 27 Gary Wayne	.12	.06	.01
☐ 28 Tim Jones	.12	.06	.01
☐ 29 Dante Bichette	.12	.06	.01
☐ 30 Alexis Infante	.15	.07	.01
☐ 31 Ken Hill	.12	.06	.01
☐ 32 Dwight Smith	.65	.30	.06
☐ 33 Luis de los Santos	.12	.06	.01
☐ 34 Eric Yelding	.35	.17	.03
☐ 35 Gregg Olson	1.00	.50	.10
☐ 36 Phil Stephenson	.12	.06	.01
☐ 37 Ken Patterson	.12	.06	.01
☐ 38 Rick Wrona	.15	.07	.01
☐ 39 Mike Brumley	.12	.06	.01
☐ 40 Cris Carpenter	.12	.06	.01
☐ 41 Jeff Brantley	.30	.15	.03
☐ 42 Ron Jones	.15	.07	.01
☐ 43 Randy Johnson	.12	.06	.01
☐ 44 Kevin Brown	.20	.10	.02
☐ 45 Ramon Martinez	1.00	.50	.10
☐ 46 Greg W.Harris	.15	.07	.01
☐ 47 Steve Finley	.30	.15	.03
☐ 48 Randy Kramer	.12	.06	.01
☐ 49 Erik Hanson	.35	.17	.03
☐ 50 Matt Merullo	.12	.06	.01
☐ 51 Mike Devereaux	.12	.06	.01
☐ 52 Clay Parker	.12	.06	.01
☐ 53 Omar Vizquel	.15	.07	.01
☐ 54 Derek Lilliquist	.12	.06	.01
☐ 55 Junior Felix	1.25	.60	.12
☐ 56 Checklist Card	.08	.01	.00

1990 Donruss Preview

The 1990 Donruss Preview set contains 12 standard-size (2 1/2" by 3 1/2") cards. The bright red borders are exactly like the regular 1990 Donruss cards, but many of the photos are different. The horizontally-oriented backs are plain white with career highlights in black lettering. Two cards were sent to each dealer in the Donruss dealer network thus making it quite difficult to put together a set.

	MINT	EXC	G-VG
COMPLETE SET (12)	300.00	150.00	30.00
COMMON PLAYER (1-12)	20.00	10.00	2.00
☐ 1 Todd Zeile (not shown as Rated Rookie on front)	35.00	17.50	3.50
☐ 2 Ben McDonald	45.00	22.50	4.50
☐ 3 Bo Jackson	75.00	37.50	7.50
☐ 4 Will Clark	60.00	30.00	6.00
☐ 5 Dave Stewart	20.00	10.00	2.00
☐ 6 Kevin Mitchell	25.00	12.50	2.50
☐ 7 Nolan Ryan	75.00	37.50	7.50
☐ 8 Howard Johnson	20.00	10.00	2.00
☐ 9 Tony Gwynn	25.00	12.50	2.50
☐ 10 Jerome Walton (shown ready to bunt)	35.00	17.50	3.50
☐ 11 Wade Boggs	45.00	22.50	4.50
☐ 12 Kirby Puckett	35.00	17.50	3.50

1990 Donruss

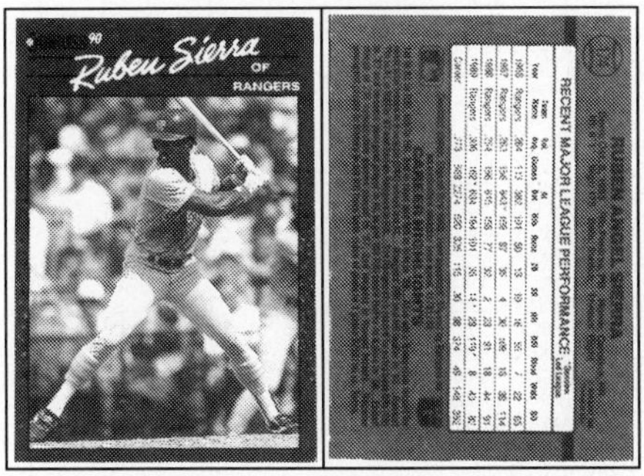

The 1990 Donruss set contains 716 standard-size (2 1/2" by 3 1/2") cards. The front borders are bright red. The horizontally-oriented backs are amber. Cards numbered 1-26 are Diamond Kings; cards numbered 28-47 are Rated Rookies. Card number 716 was added to the set shortly after the set's initial production, necessitating the checklist variation on card number 700. The set was the largest ever produced by Donruss, unfortunately it also had a large number of errors which were corrected after the cards were released. Every All-Star selection in the set has two versions, the statistical heading on the back is either "Recent Major League Performance" or "All-Star Game Performance." There are a number of cards that have been discovered to have minor printing flaws, which are insignificant variations, that collectors have found unworthy of price differentials. These very minor variations include numbers 1, 18, 154, 168, 206, 270, 321, 347, 405, 408, 425, 583, 585, 619, 637, 639, 699, 701, and 716. The factory sets were distributed without the Bonus Cards; thus there were again new checklist cards printed to reflect the exclusion of the Bonus Cards. These factory set checklist cards are the B variations below (except for 700C). The key rookie cards in this set are Delino DeShields, Juan Gonzalez, Dave Justice, Ben McDonald, and John Olerud. The unusual number of cards in the set (716 plus 26 BC's, i.e., not divisible by 132) apparently led to 50 double-printed numbers, which are indicated in the checklists below (1990 Donruss and 1990 Donruss Bonus MVP's) by DP.

	MINT	EXC	G-VG
COMPLETE SET (716)	23.00	11.50	2.30
COMMON PLAYER (1-716)	.03	.01	.00
☐ 1 Bo Jackson DK	.60	.15	.03
☐ 2 Steve Sax DK	.08	.04	.01
☐ 3A Ruben Sierra DK ERR (no small line on top border on card back)	1.25	.60	.12
☐ 3B Ruben Sierra DK COR	.15	.07	.01
☐ 4 Ken Griffey Jr. DK	.75	.35	.07
☐ 5 Mickey Tettleton DK	.06	.03	.00
☐ 6 Dave Stewart DK	.10	.05	.01
☐ 7 Jim Deshaies DK DP	.06	.03	.00
☐ 8 John Smoltz DK	.08	.04	.01
☐ 9 Mike Bielecki DK	.06	.03	.00
☐ 10A Brian Downing DK ERR (reverse negative on card front)	1.25	.60	.12
☐ 10B Brian Downing DK COR	.10	.05	.01
☐ 11 Kevin Mitchell DK	.12	.06	.01
☐ 12 Kelly Gruber DK	.10	.05	.01
☐ 13 Joe Magrane DK	.06	.03	.00
☐ 14 John Franco DK	.06	.03	.00
☐ 15 Ozzie Guillen DK	.08	.04	.01
☐ 16 Lou Whitaker DK	.08	.04	.01
☐ 17 John Smiley DK	.06	.03	.00
☐ 18 Howard Johnson DK	.08	.04	.01
☐ 19 Willie Randolph DK	.06	.03	.00
☐ 20 Chris Bosio DK	.06	.03	.00
☐ 21 Tommy Herr DK DP	.06	.03	.00
☐ 22 Dan Gladden DK	.06	.03	.00
☐ 23 Ellis Burks DK	.12	.06	.01
☐ 24 Pete O'Brien DK	.06	.03	.00
☐ 25 Bryn Smith DK	.06	.03	.00
☐ 26 Ed Whitson DK DP	.06	.03	.00
☐ 27 DK Checklist DP	.06	.01	.00
☐ 28 Robin Ventura	.30	.15	.03
☐ 29 Todd Zeile	.75	.35	.07
☐ 30 Sandy Alomar Jr.	.30	.15	.03
☐ 31 Kent Mercker	.20	.10	.02
☐ 32 Ben McDonald	1.75	.85	.17
☐ 33A Juan Gonzalez ERR (reverse negative)	3.00	1.50	.30
☐ 33B Juan Gonzalez COR	2.25	1.10	.22
☐ 34 Eric Anthony	.75	.35	.07
☐ 35 Mike Fetters	.12	.06	.01
☐ 36 Marquis Grissom	.40	.20	.04
☐ 37 Greg Vaughn	.60	.30	.06
☐ 38 Brian Dubois	.10	.05	.01
☐ 39 Steve Avery UER (born in MI not NJ)	.50	.25	.05
☐ 40 Mark Gardner	.18	.09	.01
☐ 41 Andy Benes	.30	.15	.03
☐ 42 Delino DeShields	.60	.30	.06
☐ 43 Scott Coolbaugh	.15	.07	.01
☐ 44 Pat Combs DP	.10	.05	.01
☐ 45 Alex Sanchez DP	.10	.05	.01
☐ 46 Kelly Mann DP	.10	.05	.01
☐ 47 Julio Machado DP	.10	.05	.01
☐ 48 Pete Incaviglia	.08	.04	.01
☐ 49 Shawon Dunston	.10	.05	.01
☐ 50 Jeff Treadway	.03	.01	.00
☐ 51 Jeff Ballard	.06	.03	.00
☐ 52 Claudell Washington	.06	.03	.00
☐ 53 Juan Samuel	.08	.04	.01
☐ 54 John Smiley	.03	.01	.00
☐ 55 Rob Deer	.06	.03	.00
☐ 56 Geno Petralli	.03	.01	.00
☐ 57 Chris Bosio	.03	.01	.00
☐ 58 Carlton Fisk	.12	.06	.01
☐ 59 Kirt Manwaring	.03	.01	.00
☐ 60 Chet Lemon	.03	.01	.00
☐ 61 Bo Jackson	.75	.35	.07
☐ 62 Doyle Alexander	.03	.01	.00
☐ 63 Pedro Guerrero	.08	.04	.01
☐ 64 Allan Anderson	.06	.03	.00
☐ 65 Greg Harris	.03	.01	.00
☐ 66 Mike Greenwell	.15	.07	.01
☐ 67 Walt Weiss	.08	.04	.01
☐ 68 Wade Boggs	.20	.10	.02
☐ 69 Jim Clancy	.03	.01	.00
☐ 70 Junior Felix	.30	.15	.03
☐ 71 Barry Larkin	.15	.07	.01
☐ 72 Dave LaPoint	.03	.01	.00
☐ 73 Joel Skinner	.03	.01	.00
☐ 74 Jesse Barfield	.08	.04	.01
☐ 75 Tommy Herr	.06	.03	.00
☐ 76 Ricky Jordan	.12	.06	.01
☐ 77 Eddie Murray	.12	.06	.01
☐ 78 Steve Sax	.08	.04	.01
☐ 79 Tim Belcher	.06	.03	.00
☐ 80 Danny Jackson	.06	.03	.00
☐ 81 Kent Hrbek	.08	.04	.01
☐ 82 Milt Thompson	.03	.01	.00
☐ 83 Brook Jacoby	.06	.03	.00
☐ 84 Mike Marshall	.08	.04	.01
☐ 85 Kevin Seitzer	.08	.04	.01
☐ 86 Tony Gwynn	.15	.07	.01
☐ 87 Dave Stieb	.08	.04	.01
☐ 88 Dave Smith	.03	.01	.00
☐ 89 Bret Saberhagen	.10	.05	.01
☐ 90 Alan Trammell	.08	.04	.01

☐ 91 Tony Phillips	.03	.01	.00
☐ 92 Doug Drabek	.08	.04	.01
☐ 93 Jeffrey Leonard	.06	.03	.00
☐ 94 Wally Joyner	.08	.04	.01
☐ 95 Carney Lansford	.08	.04	.01
☐ 96 Cal Ripken	.15	.07	.01
☐ 97 Andres Galarraga	.08	.04	.01
☐ 98 Kevin Mitchell	.20	.10	.02
☐ 99 Howard Johnson	.08	.04	.01
☐ 100A Checklist Card	.06	.01	.00
☐ 100B Checklist Card (28-125)	.06	.01	.00
☐ 101 Melido Perez	.03	.01	.00
☐ 102 Spike Owen	.03	.01	.00
☐ 103 Paul Molitor	.08	.04	.01
☐ 104 Geronimo Berroa	.03	.01	.00
☐ 105 Ryne Sandberg	.20	.10	.02
☐ 106 Bryn Smith	.03	.01	.00
☐ 107 Steve Buechele	.03	.01	.00
☐ 108 Jim Abbott	.25	.12	.02
☐ 109 Alvin Davis	.08	.04	.01
☐ 110 Lee Smith	.06	.03	.00
☐ 111 Roberto Alomar	.12	.06	.01
☐ 112 Rick Reuschel	.06	.03	.00
☐ 113A Kelly Gruber ERR (born 2/22)	.12	.06	.01
☐ 113B Kelly Gruber COR (born 2/26; corrected in factory sets)	.12	.06	.01
☐ 114 Joe Carter	.10	.05	.01
☐ 115 Jose Rijo	.08	.04	.01
☐ 116 Greg Minton	.03	.01	.00
☐ 117 Bob Ojeda	.06	.03	.00
☐ 118 Glenn Davis	.10	.05	.01
☐ 119 Jeff Reardon	.06	.03	.00
☐ 120 Kurt Stillwell	.06	.03	.00
☐ 121 John Smoltz	.10	.05	.01
☐ 122 Dwight Evans	.08	.04	.01
☐ 123 Eric Yelding	.15	.07	.01
☐ 124 John Franco	.08	.04	.01
☐ 125 Jose Canseco	.60	.30	.06
☐ 126 Barry Bonds	.20	.10	.02
☐ 127 Lee Guetterman	.03	.01	.00
☐ 128 Jack Clark	.08	.04	.01
☐ 129 Dave Valle	.03	.01	.00
☐ 130 Hubie Brooks	.06	.03	.00
☐ 131 Ernest Riles	.03	.01	.00
☐ 132 Mike Morgan	.03	.01	.00
☐ 133 Steve Jeltz	.03	.01	.00
☐ 134 Jeff Robinson	.03	.01	.00
☐ 135 Ozzie Guillen	.08	.04	.01
☐ 136 Chili Davis	.06	.03	.00
☐ 137 Mitch Webster	.03	.01	.00
☐ 138 Jerry Browne	.03	.01	.00
☐ 139 Bo Diaz	.03	.01	.00
☐ 140 Robby Thompson	.03	.01	.00
☐ 141 Craig Worthington	.08	.04	.01
☐ 142 Julio Franco	.08	.04	.01
☐ 143 Brian Holman	.03	.01	.00
☐ 144 George Brett	.15	.07	.01
☐ 145 Tom Glavine	.06	.03	.00
☐ 146 Robin Yount	.15	.07	.01
☐ 147 Gary Carter	.08	.04	.01
☐ 148 Ron Kittle	.06	.03	.00
☐ 149 Tony Fernandez	.08	.04	.01
☐ 150 Dave Stewart	.10	.05	.01
☐ 151 Gary Gaetti	.08	.04	.01
☐ 152 Kevin Elster	.06	.03	.00
☐ 153 Gerald Perry	.03	.01	.00
☐ 154 Jesse Orosco	.03	.01	.00
☐ 155 Wally Backman	.03	.01	.00
☐ 156 Dennis Martinez	.03	.01	.00
☐ 157 Rick Sutcliffe	.06	.03	.00
☐ 158 Greg Maddux	.08	.04	.01
☐ 159 Andy Hawkins	.03	.01	.00
☐ 160 John Kruk	.03	.01	.00
☐ 161 Jose Oquendo	.03	.01	.00
☐ 162 John Dopson	.06	.03	.00
☐ 163 Joe Magrane	.06	.03	.00
☐ 164 Bill Ripken	.03	.01	.00
☐ 165 Fred Manrique	.03	.01	.00
☐ 166 Nolan Ryan UER (Did not lead NL in K's in '89 as he was in AL in '89)	.40	.20	.04
☐ 167 Damon Berryhill	.08	.04	.01
☐ 168 Dale Murphy	.12	.06	.01
☐ 169 Mickey Tettleton	.06	.03	.00
☐ 170A Kirk McCaskill ERR (born 4/19)	.03	.01	.00
☐ 170B Kirk McCaskill COR (born 4/9; corrected in factory sets)	.03	.01	.00
☐ 171 Dwight Gooden	.18	.09	.01
☐ 172 Jose Lind	.03	.01	.00
☐ 173 B.J. Surhoff	.06	.03	.00
☐ 174 Ruben Sierra	.15	.07	.01
☐ 175 Dan Plesac	.06	.03	.00
☐ 176 Dan Pasqua	.03	.01	.00
☐ 177 Kelly Downs	.03	.01	.00
☐ 178 Matt Nokes	.06	.03	.00
☐ 179 Luis Aquino	.03	.01	.00
☐ 180 Frank Tanana	.06	.03	.00
☐ 181 Tony Pena	.06	.03	.00
☐ 182 Dan Gladden	.03	.01	.00
☐ 183 Bruce Hurst	.06	.03	.00
☐ 184 Roger Clemens	.20	.10	.02
☐ 185 Mark McGwire	.20	.10	.02
☐ 186 Rob Murphy	.03	.01	.00
☐ 187 Jim Deshaies	.03	.01	.00
☐ 188 Fred McGriff	.12	.06	.01
☐ 189 Rob Dibble	.06	.03	.00
☐ 190 Don Mattingly	.40	.20	.04
☐ 191 Felix Fermin	.03	.01	.00
☐ 192 Roberto Kelly	.12	.06	.01
☐ 193 Dennis Cook	.08	.04	.01
☐ 194 Darren Daulton	.06	.03	.00
☐ 195 Alfredo Griffin	.03	.01	.00
☐ 196 Eric Plunk	.03	.01	.00
☐ 197 Orel Hershiser	.10	.05	.01
☐ 198 Paul O'Neill	.08	.04	.01
☐ 199 Randy Bush	.03	.01	.00
☐ 200A Checklist Card	.06	.01	.00
☐ 200B Checklist Card (126-223)	.06	.01	.00
☐ 201 Ozzie Smith	.10	.05	.01
☐ 202 Pete O'Brien	.06	.03	.00
☐ 203 Jay Howell	.03	.01	.00
☐ 204 Mark Gubicza	.06	.03	.00
☐ 205 Ed Whitson	.03	.01	.00
☐ 206 George Bell	.08	.04	.01
☐ 207 Mike Scott	.08	.04	.01
☐ 208 Charlie Leibrandt	.03	.01	.00
☐ 209 Mike Heath	.03	.01	.00
☐ 210 Dennis Eckersley	.10	.05	.01
☐ 211 Mike LaValliere	.03	.01	.00
☐ 212 Darnell Coles	.03	.01	.00
☐ 213 Lance Parrish	.08	.04	.01
☐ 214 Mike Moore	.06	.03	.00
☐ 215 Steve Finley	.12	.06	.01
☐ 216 Tim Raines	.10	.05	.01
☐ 217A Scott Garrelts ERR (born 10/20)	.06	.03	.00
☐ 217B Scott Garrelts COR (born 10/30; corrected in factory sets)	.06	.03	.00
☐ 218 Kevin McReynolds	.08	.04	.01
☐ 219 Dave Gallagher	.03	.01	.00
☐ 220 Tim Wallach	.08	.04	.01
☐ 221 Chuck Crim	.03	.01	.00
☐ 222 Lonnie Smith	.06	.03	.00
☐ 223 Andre Dawson	.10	.05	.01
☐ 224 Nelson Santovenia	.06	.03	.00
☐ 225 Rafael Palmeiro	.12	.06	.01
☐ 226 Devon White	.08	.04	.01
☐ 227 Harold Reynolds	.06	.03	.00
☐ 228 Ellis Burks	.12	.06	.01
☐ 229 Mark Parent	.03	.01	.00
☐ 230 Will Clark	.45	.22	.04
☐ 231 Jimmy Key	.06	.03	.00
☐ 232 John Farrell	.03	.01	.00
☐ 233 Eric Davis	.18	.09	.01
☐ 234 Johnny Ray	.03	.01	.00
☐ 235 Darryl Strawberry	.20	.10	.02
☐ 236 Bill Doran	.06	.03	.00
☐ 237 Greg Gagne	.03	.01	.00
☐ 238 Jim Eisenreich	.03	.01	.00
☐ 239 Tommy Gregg	.03	.01	.00
☐ 240 Marty Barrett	.03	.01	.00
☐ 241 Rafael Ramirez	.03	.01	.00
☐ 242 Chris Sabo	.15	.07	.01
☐ 243 Dave Henderson	.03	.01	.00
☐ 244 Andy Van Slyke	.08	.04	.01
☐ 245 Alvaro Espinoza	.03	.01	.00
☐ 246 Garry Templeton	.06	.03	.00
☐ 247 Gene Harris	.12	.06	.01
☐ 248 Kevin Gross	.03	.01	.00
☐ 249 Brett Butler	.08	.04	.01
☐ 250 Willie Randolph	.06	.03	.00
☐ 251 Roger McDowell	.06	.03	.00
☐ 252 Rafael Belliard	.03	.01	.00
☐ 253 Steve Rosenberg	.03	.01	.00
☐ 254 Jack Howell	.03	.01	.00
☐ 255 Marvell Wynne	.03	.01	.00
☐ 256 Tom Candiotti	.03	.01	.00
☐ 257 Todd Benzinger	.03	.01	.00
☐ 258 Don Robinson	.03	.01	.00
☐ 259 Phil Bradley	.06	.03	.00

☐ 260 Cecil Espy	.03	.01	.00
☐ 261 Scott Bankhead	.06	.03	.00
☐ 262 Frank White	.06	.03	.00
☐ 263 Andres Thomas	.03	.01	.00
☐ 264 Glenn Braggs	.03	.01	.00
☐ 265 David Cone	.08	.04	.01
☐ 266 Bobby Thigpen	.10	.05	.01
☐ 267 Nelson Liriano	.03	.01	.00
☐ 268 Terry Steinbach	.08	.04	.01
☐ 269 Kirby Puckett UER (back doesn't consider Joe Torre's .363 in '71)	.25	.12	.02
☐ 270 Gregg Jefferies	.30	.15	.03
☐ 271 Jeff Blauser	.03	.01	.00
☐ 272 Cory Snyder	.08	.04	.01
☐ 273 Roy Smith	.03	.01	.00
☐ 274 Tom Foley	.03	.01	.00
☐ 275 Mitch Williams	.03	.01	.00
☐ 276 Paul Kilgus	.03	.01	.00
☐ 277 Don Slaught	.03	.01	.00
☐ 278 Von Hayes	.08	.04	.01
☐ 279 Vince Coleman	.08	.04	.01
☐ 280 Mike Boddicker	.03	.01	.00
☐ 281 Ken Dayley	.03	.01	.00
☐ 282 Mike Devereaux	.03	.01	.00
☐ 283 Kenny Rogers	.10	.05	.01
☐ 284 Jeff Russell	.03	.01	.00
☐ 285 Jerome Walton	.50	.25	.05
☐ 286 Derek Lilliquist	.03	.01	.00
☐ 287 Joe Orsulak	.03	.01	.00
☐ 288 Dick Schofield	.03	.01	.00
☐ 289 Ron Darling	.08	.04	.01
☐ 290 Bobby Bonilla	.15	.07	.01
☐ 291 Jim Gantner	.03	.01	.00
☐ 292 Bobby Witt	.08	.04	.01
☐ 293 Greg Brock	.03	.01	.00
☐ 294 Ivan Calderon	.06	.03	.00
☐ 295 Steve Bedrosian	.06	.03	.00
☐ 296 Mike Henneman	.03	.01	.00
☐ 297 Tom Gordon	.15	.07	.01
☐ 298 Lou Whitaker	.08	.04	.01
☐ 299 Terry Pendleton	.03	.01	.00
☐ 300A Checklist Card	.06	.01	.00
☐ 300B Checklist Card (224-321)	.06	.01	.00
☐ 301 Juan Berenguer	.03	.01	.00
☐ 302 Mark Davis	.08	.04	.01
☐ 303 Nick Esasky	.06	.03	.00
☐ 304 Rickey Henderson	.25	.12	.02
☐ 305 Rick Cerone	.03	.01	.00
☐ 306 Craig Biggio	.08	.04	.01
☐ 307 Duane Ward	.03	.01	.00
☐ 308 Tom Browning	.06	.03	.00
☐ 309 Walt Terrell	.03	.01	.00
☐ 310 Greg Swindell	.08	.04	.01
☐ 311 Dave Righetti	.08	.04	.01
☐ 312 Mike Maddux	.03	.01	.00
☐ 313 Len Dykstra	.10	.05	.01
☐ 314 Jose Gonzalez	.03	.01	.00
☐ 315 Steve Balboni	.03	.01	.00
☐ 316 Mike Scioscia	.03	.01	.00
☐ 317 Ron Oester	.03	.01	.00
☐ 318 Gary Wayne	.08	.04	.01
☐ 319 Todd Worrell	.08	.04	.01
☐ 320 Doug Jones	.06	.03	.00
☐ 321 Jeff Hamilton	.06	.03	.00
☐ 322 Danny Tartabull	.08	.04	.01
☐ 323 Chris James	.06	.03	.00
☐ 324 Mike Flanagan	.03	.01	.00
☐ 325 Gerald Young	.03	.01	.00
☐ 326 Bob Boone	.06	.03	.00
☐ 327 Frank Williams	.03	.01	.00
☐ 328 Dave Parker	.08	.04	.01
☐ 329 Sid Bream	.03	.01	.00
☐ 330 Mike Schooler	.06	.03	.00
☐ 331 Bert Blyleven	.08	.04	.01
☐ 332 Bob Welch	.08	.04	.01
☐ 333 Bob Milacki	.06	.03	.00
☐ 334 Tim Burke	.06	.03	.00
☐ 335 Jose Uribe	.03	.01	.00
☐ 336 Randy Myers	.03	.01	.00
☐ 337 Eric King	.03	.01	.00
☐ 338 Mark Langston	.08	.04	.01
☐ 339 Teddy Higuera	.06	.03	.00
☐ 340 Oddibe McDowell	.06	.03	.00
☐ 341 Lloyd McClendon	.03	.01	.00
☐ 342 Pascual Perez	.06	.03	.00
☐ 343 Kevin Brown (signed is misspelled as signeed on back)	.10	.05	.01
☐ 344 Chuck Finley	.08	.04	.01
☐ 345 Erik Hanson	.08	.04	.01
☐ 346 Rich Gedman	.03	.01	.00
☐ 347 Bip Roberts	.06	.03	.00

☐ 348 Matt Williams	.20	.10	.02
☐ 349 Tom Henke	.06	.03	.00
☐ 350 Brad Komminsk	.03	.01	.00
☐ 351 Jeff Reed	.03	.01	.00
☐ 352 Brian Downing	.03	.01	.00
☐ 353 Frank Viola	.10	.05	.01
☐ 354 Terry Puhl	.03	.01	.00
☐ 355 Brian Harper	.06	.03	.00
☐ 356 Steve Farr	.03	.01	.00
☐ 357 Joe Boever	.03	.01	.00
☐ 358 Danny Heep	.03	.01	.00
☐ 359 Larry Andersen	.03	.01	.00
☐ 360 Rolando Roomes	.06	.03	.00
☐ 361 Mike Gallego	.03	.01	.00
☐ 362 Bob Kipper	.03	.01	.00
☐ 363 Clay Parker	.08	.04	.01
☐ 364 Mike Pagliarulo	.03	.01	.00
☐ 365 Ken Griffey Jr. UER (signed through 1990, should be 1991)	2.25	1.10	.22
☐ 366 Rex Hudler	.03	.01	.00
☐ 367 Pat Sheridan	.03	.01	.00
☐ 368 Kirk Gibson	.08	.04	.01
☐ 369 Jeff Parrett	.03	.01	.00
☐ 370 Bob Walk	.03	.01	.00
☐ 371 Ken Patterson	.06	.03	.00
☐ 372 Bryan Harvey	.03	.01	.00
☐ 373 Mike Bielecki	.06	.03	.00
☐ 374 Tom Magrann	.10	.05	.01
☐ 375 Rick Mahler	.03	.01	.00
☐ 376 Craig Lefferts	.03	.01	.00
☐ 377 Gregg Olson	.25	.12	.02
☐ 378 Jamie Moyer	.03	.01	.00
☐ 379 Randy Johnson	.03	.01	.00
☐ 380 Jeff Montgomery	.06	.03	.00
☐ 381 Marty Clary	.03	.01	.00
☐ 382 Bill Spiers	.10	.05	.01
☐ 383 Dave Magadan	.08	.04	.01
☐ 384 Greg Hibbard	.20	.10	.02
☐ 385 Ernie Whitt	.03	.01	.00
☐ 386 Rick Honeycutt	.03	.01	.00
☐ 387 Dave West	.06	.03	.00
☐ 388 Keith Hernandez	.08	.04	.01
☐ 389 Jose Alvarez	.03	.01	.00
☐ 390 Joey Belle	.20	.10	.02
☐ 391 Rick Aguilera	.03	.01	.00
☐ 392 Mike Fitzgerald	.03	.01	.00
☐ 393 Dwight Smith	.12	.06	.01
☐ 394 Steve Wilson	.08	.04	.01
☐ 395 Bob Geren	.08	.04	.01
☐ 396 Randy Ready	.03	.01	.00
☐ 397 Ken Hill	.06	.03	.00
☐ 398 Jody Reed	.08	.04	.01
☐ 399 Tom Brunansky	.08	.04	.01
☐ 400A Checklist Card	.06	.01	.00
☐ 400B Checklist Card (322-419)	.06	.01	.00
☐ 401 Rene Gonzales	.03	.01	.00
☐ 402 Harold Baines	.08	.04	.01
☐ 403 Cecilio Guante	.03	.01	.00
☐ 404 Joe Girardi	.10	.05	.01
☐ 405A Sergio Valdez ERR	.45	.22	.04
☐ 405B Sergio Valdez COR	.12	.06	.01
☐ 406 Mark Williamson	.03	.01	.00
☐ 407 Glenn Hoffman	.03	.01	.00
☐ 408 Jeff Innis	.08	.04	.01
☐ 409 Randy Kramer	.03	.01	.00
☐ 410 Charlie O'Brien	.03	.01	.00
☐ 411 Charlie Hough	.03	.01	.00
☐ 412 Gus Polidor	.03	.01	.00
☐ 413 Ron Karkovice	.03	.01	.00
☐ 414 Trevor Wilson	.12	.06	.01
☐ 415 Kevin Ritz	.10	.05	.01
☐ 416 Gary Thurman	.03	.01	.00
☐ 417 Jeff Robinson	.03	.01	.00
☐ 418 Scott Terry	.03	.01	.00
☐ 419 Tim Laudner	.03	.01	.00
☐ 420 Dennis Rasmussen	.03	.01	.00
☐ 421 Luis Rivera	.03	.01	.00
☐ 422 Jim Corsi	.06	.03	.00
☐ 423 Dennis Lamp	.03	.01	.00
☐ 424 Ken Caminiti	.03	.01	.00
☐ 425 David Wells	.03	.01	.00
☐ 426 Norm Charlton	.06	.03	.00
☐ 427 Deion Sanders	.30	.15	.03
☐ 428 Dion James	.03	.01	.00
☐ 429 Chuck Cary	.03	.01	.00
☐ 430 Ken Howell	.03	.01	.00
☐ 431 Steve Lake	.03	.01	.00
☐ 432 Kal Daniels	.08	.04	.01
☐ 433 Lance McCullers	.03	.01	.00
☐ 434 Lenny Harris	.10	.05	.01
☐ 435 Scott Scudder	.15	.07	.01
☐ 436 Gene Larkin	.03	.01	.00

☐ 437	Dan Quisenberry	.06	.03	.00
☐ 438	Steve Olin	.08	.04	.01
☐ 439	Mickey Hatcher	.03	.01	.00
☐ 440	Willie Wilson	.06	.03	.00
☐ 441	Mark Grant	.03	.01	.00
☐ 442	Mookie Wilson	.06	.03	.00
☐ 443	Alex Trevino	.03	.01	.00
☐ 444	Pat Tabler	.03	.01	.00
☐ 445	Dave Bergman	.03	.01	.00
☐ 446	Todd Burns	.06	.03	.00
☐ 447	R.J. Reynolds	.03	.01	.00
☐ 448	Jay Buhner	.08	.04	.01
☐ 449	Lee Stevens	.35	.17	.03
☐ 450	Ron Hassey	.03	.01	.00
☐ 451	Bob Melvin	.03	.01	.00
☐ 452	Dave Martinez	.03	.01	.00
☐ 453	Greg Litton	.15	.07	.01
☐ 454	Mark Carreon	.06	.03	.00
☐ 455	Scott Fletcher	.03	.01	.00
☐ 456	Otis Nixon	.03	.01	.00
☐ 457	Tony Fossas	.08	.04	.01
☐ 458	John Russell	.03	.01	.00
☐ 459	Paul Assenmacher	.03	.01	.00
☐ 460	Zane Smith	.06	.03	.00
☐ 461	Jack Daugherty	.10	.05	.01
☐ 462	Rich Monteleone	.10	.05	.01
☐ 463	Greg Briley	.15	.07	.01
☐ 464	Mike Smithson	.03	.01	.00
☐ 465	Benito Santiago	.12	.06	.01
☐ 466	Jeff Brantley	.15	.07	.01
☐ 467	Jose Nunez	.03	.01	.00
☐ 468	Scott Bailes	.03	.01	.00
☐ 469	Ken Griffey Sr.	.08	.04	.01
☐ 470	Bob McClure	.03	.01	.00
☐ 471	Mackey Sasser	.06	.03	.00
☐ 472	Glenn Wilson	.03	.01	.00
☐ 473	Kevin Tapani	.30	.15	.03
☐ 474	Bill Buckner	.06	.03	.00
☐ 475	Ron Gant	.06	.03	.00
☐ 476	Kevin Romine	.03	.01	.00
☐ 477	Juan Agosto	.03	.01	.00
☐ 478	Herm Winningham	.03	.01	.00
☐ 479	Storm Davis	.06	.03	.00
☐ 480	Jeff King	.10	.05	.01
☐ 481	Kevin Mmahat	.12	.06	.01
☐ 482	Carmelo Martinez	.03	.01	.00
☐ 483	Omar Vizquel	.08	.04	.01
☐ 484	Jim Dwyer	.03	.01	.00
☐ 485	Bob Knepper	.03	.01	.00
☐ 486	Dave Anderson	.03	.01	.00
☐ 487	Ron Jones	.06	.03	.00
☐ 488	Jay Bell	.03	.01	.00
☐ 489	Sammy Sosa	.45	.22	.04
☐ 490	Kent Anderson	.08	.04	.01
☐ 491	Domingo Ramos	.03	.01	.00
☐ 492	Dave Clark	.06	.03	.00
☐ 493	Tim Birtsas	.03	.01	.00
☐ 494	Ken Oberkfell	.03	.01	.00
☐ 495	Larry Sheets	.03	.01	.00
☐ 496	Jeff Kunkel	.03	.01	.00
☐ 497	Jim Presley	.03	.01	.00
☐ 498	Mike Macfarlane	.03	.01	.00
☐ 499	Pete Smith	.03	.01	.00
☐ 500A	Checklist Card DP	.06	.01	.00
☐ 500B	Checklist Card (420-517)	.06	.01	.00
☐ 501	Gary Sheffield	.25	.12	.02
☐ 502	Terry Bross	.12	.06	.01
☐ 503	Jerry Kutzler	.12	.06	.01
☐ 504	Lloyd Moseby	.06	.03	.00
☐ 505	Curt Young	.03	.01	.00
☐ 506	Al Newman	.03	.01	.00
☐ 507	Keith Miller	.03	.01	.00
☐ 508	Mike Stanton	.12	.06	.01
☐ 509	Rich Yett	.03	.01	.00
☐ 510	Tim Drummond	.12	.06	.01
☐ 511	Joe Hesketh	.03	.01	.00
☐ 512	Rick Wrona	.08	.04	.01
☐ 513	Luis Salazar	.03	.01	.00
☐ 514	Hal Morris	.25	.12	.02
☐ 515	Terry Mulholland	.03	.01	.00
☐ 516	John Morris	.03	.01	.00
☐ 517	Carlos Quintana	.15	.07	.01
☐ 518	Frank DiPino	.03	.01	.00
☐ 519	Randy Milligan	.15	.07	.01
☐ 520	Chad Kreuter	.03	.01	.00
☐ 521	Mike Jeffcoat	.03	.01	.00
☐ 522	Mike Harkey	.10	.05	.01
☐ 523A	Andy Nezelek ERR (wrong birth year)	.03	.01	.00
☐ 523B	Andy Nezelek COR (finally corrected in factory sets)	.03	.01	.00
☐ 524	Dave Schmidt	.03	.01	.00
☐ 525	Tony Armas	.03	.01	.00
☐ 526	Barry Lyons	.03	.01	.00
☐ 527	Rick Reed	.10	.05	.01
☐ 528	Jerry Reuss	.03	.01	.00
☐ 529	Dean Palmer	.20	.10	.02
☐ 530	Jeff Peterek	.12	.06	.01
☐ 531	Carlos Martinez	.12	.06	.01
☐ 532	Atlee Hammaker	.03	.01	.00
☐ 533	Mike Brumley	.03	.01	.00
☐ 534	Terry Leach	.03	.01	.00
☐ 535	Doug Strange	.10	.05	.01
☐ 536	Jose DeLeon	.03	.01	.00
☐ 537	Shane Rawley	.03	.01	.00
☐ 538	Joey Cora	.03	.01	.00
☐ 539	Eric Hetzel	.03	.01	.00
☐ 540	Gene Nelson	.03	.01	.00
☐ 541	Wes Gardner	.03	.01	.00
☐ 542	Mark Portugal	.03	.01	.00
☐ 543	Al Leiter	.06	.03	.00
☐ 544	Jack Armstrong	.08	.04	.01
☐ 545	Greg Cadaret	.03	.01	.00
☐ 546	Rod Nichols	.03	.01	.00
☐ 547	Luis Polonia	.03	.01	.00
☐ 548	Charlie Hayes	.08	.04	.01
☐ 549	Dickie Thon	.03	.01	.00
☐ 550	Tim Crews	.03	.01	.00
☐ 551	Dave Winfield	.10	.05	.01
☐ 552	Mike Davis	.03	.01	.00
☐ 553	Ron Robinson	.03	.01	.00
☐ 554	Carmen Castillo	.03	.01	.00
☐ 555	John Costello	.03	.01	.00
☐ 556	Bud Black	.03	.01	.00
☐ 557	Rick Dempsey	.03	.01	.00
☐ 558	Jim Acker	.03	.01	.00
☐ 559	Eric Show	.03	.01	.00
☐ 560	Pat Borders	.03	.01	.00
☐ 561	Danny Darwin	.03	.01	.00
☐ 562	Rick Luecken	.08	.04	.01
☐ 563	Edwin Nunez	.03	.01	.00
☐ 564	Felix Jose	.10	.05	.01
☐ 565	John Cangelosi	.03	.01	.00
☐ 566	Bill Swift	.03	.01	.00
☐ 567	Bill Schroeder	.03	.01	.00
☐ 568	Stan Javier	.03	.01	.00
☐ 569	Jim Traber	.03	.01	.00
☐ 570	Wallace Johnson	.03	.01	.00
☐ 571	Donell Nixon	.03	.01	.00
☐ 572	Sid Fernandez	.08	.04	.01
☐ 573	Lance Johnson	.06	.03	.00
☐ 574	Andy McGaffigan	.03	.01	.00
☐ 575	Mark Knudson	.03	.01	.00
☐ 576	Tommy Greene	.20	.10	.02
☐ 577	Mark Grace	.25	.12	.02
☐ 578	Larry Walker	.35	.17	.03
☐ 579	Mike Stanley	.03	.01	.00
☐ 580	Mike Witt DP	.03	.01	.00
☐ 581	Scott Bradley	.03	.01	.00
☐ 582	Greg Harris	.03	.01	.00
☐ 583A	Kevin Hickey ERR	.50	.25	.05
☐ 583B	Kevin Hickey COR	.06	.03	.00
☐ 584	Lee Mazzilli	.03	.01	.00
☐ 585	Jeff Pico	.03	.01	.00
☐ 586	Joe Oliver	.12	.06	.01
☐ 587	Willie Fraser DP	.03	.01	.00
☐ 588	Carl Yastrzemski PUZ Puzzle Card DP	.06	.03	.00
☐ 589	Kevin Bass DP	.03	.01	.00
☐ 590	John Moses DP	.03	.01	.00
☐ 591	Tom Pagnozzi DP	.03	.01	.00
☐ 592	Tony Castillo DP	.06	.03	.00
☐ 593	Jerald Clark DP	.03	.01	.00
☐ 594	Dan Schatzeder	.03	.01	.00
☐ 595	Luis Quinones DP	.03	.01	.00
☐ 596	Pete Harnisch DP	.03	.01	.00
☐ 597	Gary Redus	.03	.01	.00
☐ 598	Mel Hall	.06	.03	.00
☐ 599	Rick Schu	.03	.01	.00
☐ 600A	Checklist Card	.06	.01	.00
☐ 600B	Checklist Card (518-617)	.06	.01	.00
☐ 601	Mike Kingery DP	.03	.01	.00
☐ 602	Terry Kennedy DP	.03	.01	.00
☐ 603	Mike Sharperson DP	.03	.01	.00
☐ 604	Don Carman DP	.03	.01	.00
☐ 605	Jim Gott	.03	.01	.00
☐ 606	Donn Pall DP	.06	.03	.00
☐ 607	Rance Mulliniks	.03	.01	.00
☐ 608	Curt Wilkerson DP	.03	.01	.00
☐ 609	Mike Felder DP	.03	.01	.00
☐ 610	Guillermo Hernandez DP	.03	.01	.00
☐ 611	Candy Maldonado DP	.03	.01	.00
☐ 612	Mark Thurmond DP	.03	.01	.00
☐ 613	Rick Leach DP	.03	.01	.00
☐ 614	Jerry Reed DP	.03	.01	.00

☐ 615 Franklin Stubbs	.06	.03	.00
☐ 616 Billy Hatcher DP	.03	.01	.00
☐ 617 Don August DP	.03	.01	.00
☐ 618 Tim Teufel	.03	.01	.00
☐ 619 Shawn Hillegas DP	.03	.01	.00
☐ 620 Manny Lee	.03	.01	.00
☐ 621 Gary Ward DP	.03	.01	.00
☐ 622 Mark Guthrie DP	.08	.04	.01
☐ 623 Jeff Musselman DP	.03	.01	.00
☐ 624 Mark Lemke DP	.03	.01	.00
☐ 625 Fernando Valenzuela	.08	.04	.01
☐ 626 Paul Sorrento DP	.10	.05	.01
☐ 627 Glenallen Hill DP	.10	.05	.01
☐ 628 Les Lancaster DP	.03	.01	.00
☐ 629 Vance Law DP	.03	.01	.00
☐ 630 Randy Velarde DP	.03	.01	.00
☐ 631 Todd Frohwirth DP	.03	.01	.00
☐ 632 Willie McGee	.08	.04	.01
☐ 633 Dennis Boyd DP	.03	.01	.00
☐ 634 Cris Carpenter DP	.03	.01	.00
☐ 635 Brian Holton	.03	.01	.00
☐ 636 Tracy Jones DP	.03	.01	.00
☐ 637A Terry Steinbach AS (Recent Major League Performance)	.15	.07	.01
☐ 637B Terry Steinbach AS (All-Star Game Performance)	.08	.04	.01
☐ 638 Brady Anderson	.06	.03	.00
☐ 639A Jack Morris ERR	.50	.25	.05
☐ 639B Jack Morris COR	.08	.04	.01
☐ 640 Jaime Navarro	.15	.07	.01
☐ 641 Darrin Jackson	.03	.01	.00
☐ 642 Mike Dyer	.12	.06	.01
☐ 643 Mike Schmidt	.25	.12	.02
☐ 644 Henry Cotto	.03	.01	.00
☐ 645 John Cerutti	.03	.01	.00
☐ 646 Francisco Cabrera	.20	.10	.02
☐ 647 Scott Sanderson	.03	.01	.00
☐ 648 Brian Meyer	.03	.01	.00
☐ 649 Ray Searage	.03	.01	.00
☐ 650A Bo Jackson AS (Recent Major League Performance)	.70	.35	.07
☐ 650B Bo Jackson AS (All-Star Game Performance)	.35	.17	.03
☐ 651 Steve Lyons	.03	.01	.00
☐ 652 Mike LaCoss	.03	.01	.00
☐ 653 Ted Power	.03	.01	.00
☐ 654A Howard Johnson AS (Recent Major League Performance)	.15	.07	.01
☐ 654B Howard Johnson AS (All-Star Game Performance)	.08	.04	.01
☐ 655 Mauro Gozzo	.12	.06	.01
☐ 656 Mike Blowers	.20	.10	.02
☐ 657 Paul Gibson	.03	.01	.00
☐ 658 Neal Heaton	.03	.01	.00
☐ 659A Nolan Ryan 5000K (665 King of Kings back) ERR	8.00	4.00	.80
☐ 659B Nolan Ryan 5000K COR (still an error as Ryan did not lead AL in K's in '75)	1.00	.50	.10
☐ 660A Harold Baines AS (black line through star on front; Recent Major League Performance)	6.00	3.00	.60
☐ 660B Harold Baines AS (black line through star on front; All-Star Game Performance)	8.00	4.00	.80
☐ 660C Harold Baines AS (black line behind star on front; Recent Major League Performance)	7.00	3.50	.70
☐ 660D Harold Baines AS (black line behind star on front; All-Star Game Performance)	.12	.06	.01
☐ 661 Gary Pettis	.03	.01	.00
☐ 662 Clint Zavaras	.10	.05	.01
☐ 663A Rick Reuschel AS (Recent Major League Performance)	.15	.07	.01

☐ 663B Rick Reuschel AS (All-Star Game Performance)	.08	.04	.01
☐ 664 Alejandro Pena	.03	.01	.00
☐ 665A Nolan Ryan KING (659 5000 K back) ERR	8.00	4.00	.80
☐ 665B Nolan Ryan KING COR	1.00	.50	.10
☐ 665C Nolan Ryan KING ERR (no number on back; in factory sets)	4.00	2.00	.40
☐ 666 Ricky Horton	.03	.01	.00
☐ 667 Curt Schilling	.03	.01	.00
☐ 668 Bill Landrum	.03	.01	.00
☐ 669 Todd Stottlemyre	.06	.03	.00
☐ 670 Tim Leary	.06	.03	.00
☐ 671 John Wetteland	.15	.07	.01
☐ 672 Calvin Schiraldi	.03	.01	.00
☐ 673A Ruben Sierra AS (Recent Major League Performance)	.40	.20	.04
☐ 673B Ruben Sierra AS (All-Star Game Performance)	.20	.10	.02
☐ 674A Pedro Guerrero AS (Recent Major League Performance)	.15	.07	.01
☐ 674B Pedro Guerrero AS (All-Star Game Performance)	.08	.04	.01
☐ 675 Ken Phelps	.03	.01	.00
☐ 676A Cal Ripken AS (Recent Major League Performance)	.30	.15	.03
☐ 676B Cal Ripken AS (All-Star Game Performance)	.15	.07	.01
☐ 677 Denny Walling	.03	.01	.00
☐ 678 Goose Gossage	.06	.03	.00
☐ 679 Gary Mielke	.10	.05	.01
☐ 680 Bill Bathe	.03	.01	.00
☐ 681 Tom Lawless	.03	.01	.00
☐ 682 Xavier Hernandez	.10	.05	.01
☐ 683A Kirby Puckett AS (Recent Major League Performance)	.40	.20	.04
☐ 683B Kirby Puckett AS (All-Star Game Performance)	.20	.10	.02
☐ 684 Mariano Duncan	.03	.01	.00
☐ 685 Ramon Martinez	.40	.20	.04
☐ 686 Tim Jones	.03	.01	.00
☐ 687 Tom Filer	.03	.01	.00
☐ 688 Steve Lombardozzi	.03	.01	.00
☐ 689 Bernie Williams	.35	.17	.03
☐ 690 Chip Hale	.10	.05	.01
☐ 691 Beau Allred	.12	.06	.01
☐ 692A Ryne Sandberg AS (Recent Major League Performance)	.40	.20	.04
☐ 692B Ryne Sandberg AS (All-Star Game Performance)	.20	.10	.02
☐ 693 Jeff Huson	.15	.07	.01
☐ 694 Curt Ford	.03	.01	.00
☐ 695A Eric Davis AS (Recent Major League Performance)	.30	.15	.03
☐ 695B Eric Davis AS (All-Star Game Performance)	.15	.07	.01
☐ 696 Scott Lusader	.03	.01	.00
☐ 697A Mark McGwire AS (Recent Major League Performance)	.40	.20	.04
☐ 697B Mark McGwire AS (All-Star Game Performance)	.20	.10	.02
☐ 698 Steve Cummings	.12	.06	.01
☐ 699 George Canale	.12	.06	.01
☐ 700A Checklist Card (716 not listed)	1.00	.10	.02
☐ 700B Checklist Card (716 listed)	.10	.01	.00
☐ 700C Checklist Card (618-716)	.10	.01	.00
☐ 701A Julio Franco AS (Recent Major League Performance)	.15	.07	.01
☐ 701B Julio Franco AS (All-Star Game Performance)	.08	.04	.01
☐ 702 Dave Johnson (P)	.12	.06	.01

☐ 703A Dave Stewart AS (Recent Major League Performance)	.15	.07	.01
☐ 703B Dave Stewart AS (All-Star Game Performance)	.08	.04	.01
☐ 704 Dave Justice	3.00	1.50	.30
☐ 705A Tony Gwynn AS (Recent Major League Performance)	.30	.15	.03
☐ 705B Tony Gwynn AS (All-Star Game Performance)	.15	.07	.01
☐ 706 Greg Myers	.03	.01	.00
☐ 707A Will Clark AS (Recent Major League Performance)	.50	.25	.05
☐ 707B Will Clark AS (All-Star Game Performance)	.25	.12	.02
☐ 708A Benito Santiago AS (Recent Major League Performance)	.15	.07	.01
☐ 708B Benito Santiago AS (All-Star Game Performance)	.08	.04	.01
☐ 709 Larry McWilliams	.03	.01	.00
☐ 710A Ozzie Smith AS (Recent Major League Performance)	.15	.07	.01
☐ 710B Ozzie Smith AS (All-Star Game Performance)	.08	.04	.01
☐ 711 John Olerud	2.50	1.25	.25
☐ 712A Wade Boggs AS (Recent Major League Performance)	.30	.15	.03
☐ 712B Wade Boggs AS (All-Star Game Performance)	.15	.07	.01
☐ 713 Gary Eave	.12	.06	.01
☐ 714 Bob Tewksbury	.03	.01	.00
☐ 715A Kevin Mitchell AS (Recent Major League Performance)	.30	.15	.03
☐ 715B Kevin Mitchell AS (All-Star Game Performance)	.15	.07	.01
☐ 716 Bart Giamatti	1.25	.60	.12

1990 Donruss Bonus MVP's

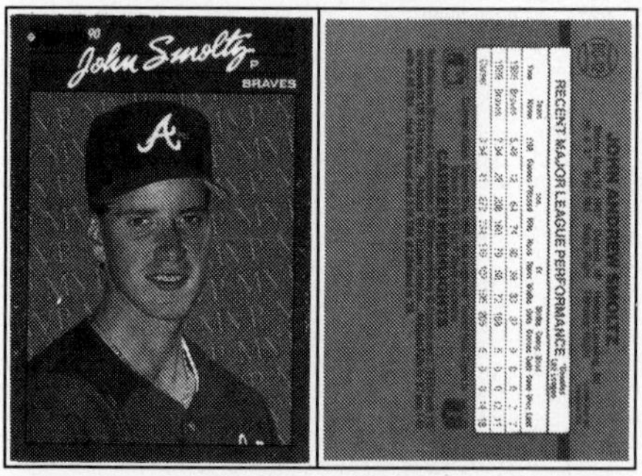

The 1990 Donruss Bonus MVP's set contains 26 standard-size (2 1/2" by 3 1/2") cards. The front borders are bright red. The horizontally-oriented backs are amber. These cards were randomly distributed in all 1990 Donruss unopened pack formats. The selection of players in the set is Donruss' opinion of each team's MVP. The complete set price below does not include any variation cards. These Bonus MVP cards were printed with and distributed with the Donruss regular issue cards.

	MINT	EXC	G-VG
COMPLETE SET (26)	4.00	2.00	.40
COMMON CARD (BC1-BC26)	.05	.02	.00

☐ BC1 Bo Jackson	.50	.25	.05
☐ BC2 Howard Johnson	.08	.04	.01
☐ BC3 Dave Stewart	.08	.04	.01
☐ BC4 Tony Gwynn	.12	.06	.01
☐ BC5 Orel Hershiser	.10	.05	.01
☐ BC6 Pedro Guerrero	.08	.04	.01
☐ BC7 Tim Raines	.10	.05	.01
☐ BC8 Kirby Puckett	.18	.09	.01
☐ BC9 Alvin Davis	.08	.04	.01
☐ BC10 Ryne Sandberg	.15	.07	.01
☐ BC11 Kevin Mitchell	.12	.06	.01
☐ BC12A John Smoltz ERR (photo actually Tom Glavine)	.40	.20	.04
☐ BC12B John Smoltz COR	.65	.30	.06
☐ BC13 George Bell	.08	.04	.01
☐ BC14 Julio Franco	.08	.04	.01
☐ BC15 Paul Molitor	.08	.04	.01
☐ BC16 Bobby Bonilla	.10	.05	.01
☐ BC17 Mike Greenwell	.12	.06	.01
☐ BC18 Cal Ripken	.12	.06	.01
☐ BC19 Carlton Fisk	.10	.05	.01
☐ BC20 Chili Davis	.05	.02	.00
☐ BC21 Glenn Davis	.08	.04	.01
☐ BC22 Steve Sax	.08	.04	.01
☐ BC23 Eric Davis DP	.10	.05	.01
☐ BC24 Greg Swindell DP	.05	.02	.00
☐ BC25 Von Hayes DP	.05	.02	.00
☐ BC26 Alan Trammell	.08	.04	.01

1990 Donruss Grand Slammers

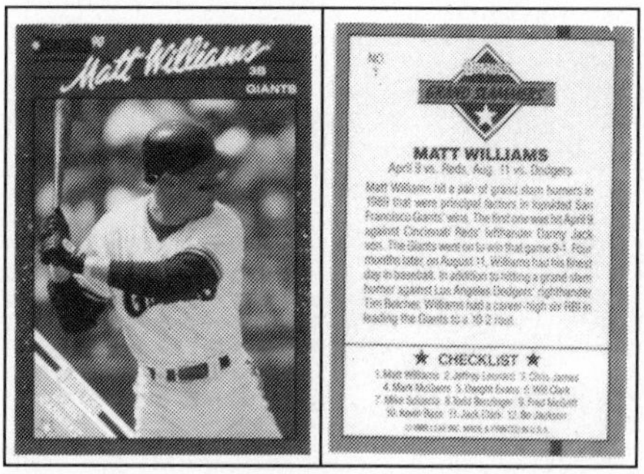

This 12-card standard size 2 1/2" by 3 1/2" set was in the 1990 Donruss set as a special card deliniating each 55-card section of the 1990 Factory Set. This set honors those players who connected for grand slam homers during the 1989 season. The cards are in the 1990 Donruss design and the back describes the grand slam homer hit by each player.

	MINT	EXC	G-VG
COMPLETE SET (12)	3.00	1.50	.30
COMMON PLAYER (1-12)	.10	.05	.01
☐ 1 Matt Williams	.30	.15	.03
☐ 2 Jeffrey Leonard	.10	.05	.01
☐ 3 Chris James	.10	.05	.01
☐ 4 Mark McGwire	.60	.30	.06
☐ 5 Dwight Evans	.15	.07	.01
☐ 6 Will Clark	.75	.35	.07
☐ 7 Mike Scioscia	.10	.05	.01
☐ 8 Todd Benzinger	.10	.05	.01
☐ 9 Fred McGriff	.20	.10	.02
☐ 10 Kevin Bass	.10	.05	.01
☐ 11 Jack Clark	.20	.10	.02
☐ 12 Bo Jackson	1.00	.50	.10

1990 Donruss Super DK's

This 26-player card set was available through a mail-in offer detailed on the wax packs. The set was sent in return for 10.00

and three wrappers plus 2.00 postage and handling. The set features the popular Diamond King subseries in large (approximately 4 7/8" by 6 13/16") form. Dick Perez of Perez-Steele Galleries did another outstanding job on the artwork. The cards are essentially a large version of the Donruss regular issue Diamond Kings.

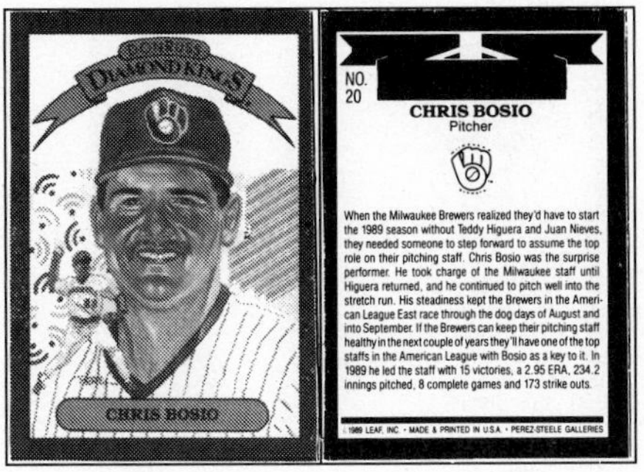

	MINT	EXC	G-VG
COMPLETE SET (26)	10.00	5.00	1.00
COMMON PLAYER (1-26)	.20	.10	.02
☐ 1 Bo Jackson DK	1.50	.75	.15
☐ 2 Steve Sax DK	.30	.15	.03
☐ 3 Ruben Sierra DK	.40	.20	.04
☐ 4 Ken Griffey Jr. DK	1.50	.75	.15
☐ 5 Mickey Tettleton DK	.20	.10	.02
☐ 6 Dave Stewart DK	.30	.15	.03
☐ 7 Jim Deshaies DK	.20	.10	.02
☐ 8 John Smoltz DK	.25	.12	.02
☐ 9 Mike Bielecki DK	.20	.10	.02
☐ 10 Brian Downing DK	.20	.10	.02
☐ 11 Kevin Mitchell DK	.40	.20	.04
☐ 12 Kelly Gruber DK	.35	.17	.03
☐ 13 Joe Magrane DK	.25	.12	.02
☐ 14 John Franco DK	.25	.12	.02
☐ 15 Ozzie Guillen DK	.30	.15	.03
☐ 16 Lou Whitaker DK	.30	.15	.03
☐ 17 John Smiley DK	.20	.10	.02
☐ 18 Howard Johnson DK	.30	.15	.03
☐ 19 Willie Randolph DK	.20	.10	.02
☐ 20 Chris Bosio DK	.20	.10	.02
☐ 21 Tommy Herr DK	.20	.10	.02
☐ 22 Dan Gladden DK	.20	.10	.02
☐ 23 Ellis Burks DK	.35	.17	.03
☐ 24 Pete O'Brien DK	.20	.10	.02
☐ 25 Bryn Smith DK	.20	.10	.02
☐ 26 Ed Whitson DK	.20	.10	.02

1990 Donruss Rookies

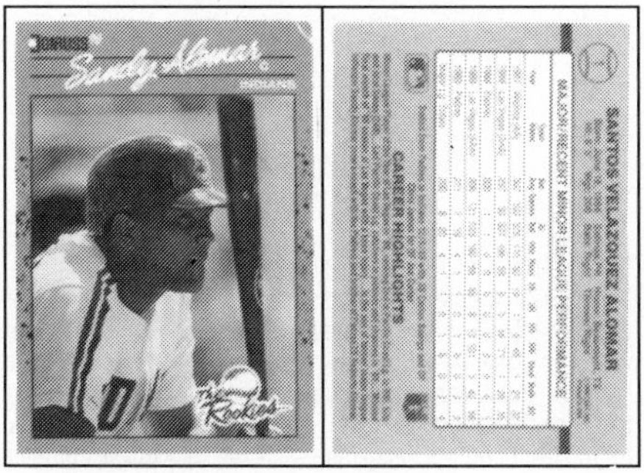

The 1990 Donruss Rookies set marked the fifth consecutive year that Donruss issued a boxed set honoring the best rookies of the season. This set, which used the 1990 Donruss design but featured a green border, was issued exclusively through the Donruss dealer network to hobby dealers. This 56-card standard size 2 1/2" by 3 1/2" set came in its own box and the words "The Rookies" are featured prominently on the front of the cards.

	MINT	EXC	G-VG
COMPLETE SET (56)	10.00	5.00	1.00
COMMON PLAYER (1-56)	.07	.03	.01
☐ 1 Sandy Alomar Jr.	.30	.15	.03
☐ 2 John Olerud	1.50	.75	.15
☐ 3 Pat Combs	.10	.05	.01
☐ 4 Brian Dubois	.10	.05	.01
☐ 5 Felix Jose	.10	.05	.01
☐ 6 Delino DeShields	.60	.30	.06
☐ 7 Mike Stanton	.10	.05	.01
☐ 8 Mike Munoz	.10	.05	.01
☐ 9 Craig Grebeck	.12	.06	.01
☐ 10 Joe Kraemer	.12	.06	.01
☐ 11 Jeff Huson	.07	.03	.01
☐ 12 Bill Sampen	.20	.10	.02
☐ 13 Brian Bohanon	.15	.07	.01
☐ 14 Dave Justice	2.50	1.25	.25
☐ 15 Robin Ventura	.20	.10	.02
☐ 16 Greg Vaughn	.45	.22	.04
☐ 17 Wayne Edwards	.18	.09	.01
☐ 18 Shawn Boskie	.20	.10	.02
☐ 19 Carlos Baerga	.35	.17	.03
☐ 20 Mark Gardner	.10	.05	.01
☐ 21 Kevin Appier	.25	.12	.02
☐ 22 Mike Harkey	.20	.10	.02
☐ 23 Tim Layana	.20	.10	.02
☐ 24 Glenallen Hill	.10	.05	.01
☐ 25 Jerry Kutzler	.10	.05	.01
☐ 26 Mike Blowers	.12	.06	.01
☐ 27 Scott Ruskin	.20	.10	.02
☐ 28 Dana Kiecker	.20	.10	.02
☐ 29 Willie Blair	.10	.05	.01
☐ 30 Ben McDonald	1.00	.50	.10
☐ 31 Todd Zeile	.50	.25	.05
☐ 32 Scott Coolbaugh	.12	.06	.01
☐ 33 Xavier Hernandez	.07	.03	.01
☐ 34 Mike Hartley	.15	.07	.01
☐ 35 Kevin Tapani	.20	.10	.02
☐ 36 Kevin Wickander	.10	.05	.01
☐ 37 Carlos Hernandez	.12	.06	.01
☐ 38 Brian Traxler	.15	.07	.01
☐ 39 Marty Brown	.10	.05	.01
☐ 40 Scott Radinsky	.20	.10	.02
☐ 41 Julio Machado	.10	.05	.01
☐ 42 Steve Avery	.25	.12	.02
☐ 43 Mark Lemke	.07	.03	.01
☐ 44 Alan Mills	.15	.07	.01
☐ 45 Marquis Grissom	.25	.12	.02
☐ 46 Greg Olson	.25	.12	.02
☐ 47 Dave Hollins	.25	.12	.02
☐ 48 Jerald Clark	.07	.03	.01
☐ 49 Eric Anthony	.45	.22	.04
☐ 50 Tim Drummond	.10	.05	.01
☐ 51 John Burkett	.25	.12	.02
☐ 52 Brent Knackert	.20	.10	.02
☐ 53 Jeff Shaw	.12	.06	.01
☐ 54 John Orton	.10	.05	.01
☐ 55 Terry Shumpert	.15	.07	.01
☐ 56 Checklist Card	.07	.01	.00

1990 Donruss Best AL

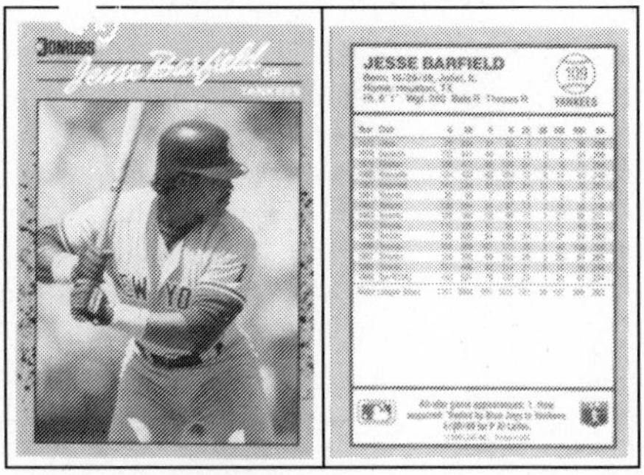

The 1990 Donruss Best of the American League set consists of 144 cards in the standard card size of 2 1/2" by 3 1/2". This was Donruss latest version of what had been titled the previous two years as Baseball's Best. In 1990, the sets were split into National and American League and marketed separately. The front design was similar to the regular issue Donruss set except for the front borders being blue while the backs have complete major and minor league statistics as compared to the regular Donruss cards which only cover the past five major-league seasons.

	MINT	EXC	G-VG
COMPLETE SET (144)	10.00	5.00	1.00
COMMON PLAYER (1-144)	.04	.02	.00
☐ 1 Ken Griffey Jr.	1.00	.50	.10
☐ 2 Bob Milacki	.04	.02	.00
☐ 3 Mike Boddicker	.04	.02	.00
☐ 4 Bert Blyleven	.10	.05	.01
☐ 5 Carlton Fisk	.15	.07	.01
☐ 6 Greg Swindell	.07	.03	.01
☐ 7 Alan Trammell	.15	.07	.01
☐ 8 Mark Davis	.07	.03	.01
☐ 9 Chris Bosio	.04	.02	.00
☐ 10 Gary Gaetti	.10	.05	.01
☐ 11 Matt Nokes	.07	.03	.01
☐ 12 Dennis Eckersley	.15	.07	.01
☐ 13 Kevin Brown	.10	.05	.01
☐ 14 Tom Henke	.07	.03	.01
☐ 15 Mickey Tettleton	.07	.03	.01
☐ 16 Jody Reed	.10	.05	.01
☐ 17 Mark Langston	.10	.05	.01
☐ 18 Melido Perez UER (listed as an Expo rather than White Sox)	.07	.03	.01
☐ 19 John Farrell	.04	.02	.00
☐ 20 Tony Phillips	.04	.02	.00
☐ 21 Bret Saberhagen	.15	.07	.01
☐ 22 Robin Yount	.20	.10	.02
☐ 23 Kirby Puckett	.25	.12	.02
☐ 24 Steve Sax	.10	.05	.01
☐ 25 Dave Stewart	.15	.07	.01
☐ 26 Alvin Davis	.07	.03	.01
☐ 27 Geno Petralli	.04	.02	.00
☐ 28 Mookie Wilson	.07	.03	.01
☐ 29 Jeff Ballard	.04	.02	.00
☐ 30 Ellis Burks	.15	.07	.01
☐ 31 Wally Joyner	.15	.07	.01
☐ 32 Bobby Thigpen	.15	.07	.01
☐ 33 Keith Hernandez	.15	.07	.01
☐ 34 Jack Morris	.10	.05	.01
☐ 35 George Brett	.25	.12	.02
☐ 36 Dan Plesac	.04	.02	.00
☐ 37 Brian Harper	.04	.02	.00
☐ 38 Don Mattingly	.75	.35	.07
☐ 39 Dave Henderson	.07	.03	.01
☐ 40 Scott Bankhead	.07	.03	.01
☐ 41 Rafael Palmeiro	.15	.07	.01
☐ 42 Jimmy Key	.07	.03	.01
☐ 43 Gregg Olson	.20	.10	.02
☐ 44 Tony Pena	.07	.03	.01
☐ 45 Jack Howell	.04	.02	.00
☐ 46 Eric King	.04	.02	.00
☐ 47 Cory Snyder	.10	.05	.01
☐ 48 Frank Tanana	.07	.03	.01
☐ 49 Nolan Ryan	.75	.35	.07
☐ 50 Bob Boone	.07	.03	.01
☐ 51 Dave Parker	.15	.07	.01
☐ 52 Allan Anderson	.07	.03	.01
☐ 53 Tim Leary	.07	.03	.01
☐ 54 Mark McGwire	.50	.25	.05
☐ 55 Dave Valle	.04	.02	.00
☐ 56 Fred McGriff	.20	.10	.02
☐ 57 Cal Ripken	.25	.12	.02
☐ 58 Roger Clemens	.30	.15	.03
☐ 59 Lance Parrish	.10	.05	.01
☐ 60 Robin Ventura	.30	.15	.03
☐ 61 Doug Jones	.07	.03	.01
☐ 62 Lloyd Moseby	.07	.03	.01
☐ 63 Bo Jackson	1.00	.50	.10
☐ 64 Paul Molitor	.10	.05	.01
☐ 65 Kent Hrbek	.10	.05	.01
☐ 66 Mel Hall	.04	.02	.00
☐ 67 Bob Welch	.15	.07	.01
☐ 68 Erik Hanson	.20	.10	.02
☐ 69 Harold Baines	.10	.05	.01
☐ 70 Junior Felix	.30	.15	.03
☐ 71 Craig Worthington	.10	.05	.01
☐ 72 Jeff Reardon	.07	.03	.01
☐ 73 Johnny Ray	.04	.02	.00
☐ 74 Ozzie Guillen	.10	.05	.01
☐ 75 Brook Jacoby	.07	.03	.01
☐ 76 Chet Lemon	.04	.02	.00
☐ 77 Mark Gubicza	.10	.05	.01
☐ 78 B.J. Surhoff	.07	.03	.01
☐ 79 Rick Aguilera	.04	.02	.00
☐ 80 Pascual Perez	.07	.03	.01
☐ 81 Jose Canseco	.75	.35	.07
☐ 82 Mike Schooler	.07	.03	.01
☐ 83 Jeff Huson	.04	.02	.00
☐ 84 Kelly Gruber	.15	.07	.01
☐ 85 Randy Milligan	.10	.05	.01
☐ 86 Wade Boggs	.40	.20	.04
☐ 87 Dave Winfield	.20	.10	.02
☐ 88 Scott Fletcher	.04	.02	.00
☐ 89 Tom Candiotti	.04	.02	.00
☐ 90 Mike Heath	.04	.02	.00
☐ 91 Kevin Seitzer	.10	.05	.01
☐ 92 Ted Higuera	.07	.03	.01
☐ 93 Kevin Tapani	.20	.10	.02
☐ 94 Roberto Kelly	.20	.10	.02
☐ 95 Walt Weiss	.10	.05	.01
☐ 96 Checklist Card	.04	.02	.00
☐ 97 Sandy Alomar Jr.	.40	.20	.04
☐ 98 Pete O'Brien	.04	.02	.00
☐ 99 Jeff Russell	.04	.02	.00
☐ 100 John Olerud	1.00	.50	.10
☐ 101 Pete Harnisch	.04	.02	.00
☐ 102 Dwight Evans	.10	.05	.01
☐ 103 Chuck Finley	.10	.05	.01
☐ 104 Sammy Sosa	.30	.15	.03
☐ 105 Mike Henneman	.04	.02	.00
☐ 106 Kurt Stillwell	.07	.03	.01
☐ 107 Greg Vaughn	.40	.20	.04
☐ 108 Dan Gladden	.04	.02	.00
☐ 109 Jesse Barfield	.10	.05	.01
☐ 110 Willie Randolph	.07	.03	.01
☐ 111 Randy Johnson	.10	.05	.01
☐ 112 Julio Franco	.10	.05	.01
☐ 113 Tony Fernandez	.10	.05	.01
☐ 114 Ben McDonald	1.00	.50	.10
☐ 115 Mike Greenwell	.25	.12	.02
☐ 116 Luis Polonia	.04	.02	.00
☐ 117 Carney Lansford	.07	.03	.01
☐ 118 Bud Black	.04	.02	.00
☐ 119 Lou Whitaker	.10	.05	.01
☐ 120 Jim Eisenreich	.04	.02	.00
☐ 121 Gary Sheffield	.30	.15	.03
☐ 122 Shane Mack	.07	.03	.01
☐ 123 Alvaro Espinoza	.04	.02	.00
☐ 124 Rickey Henderson	.45	.22	.04
☐ 125 Jeffrey Leonard	.07	.03	.01
☐ 126 Gary Pettis	.04	.02	.00
☐ 127 Dave Stieb	.10	.05	.01
☐ 128 Danny Tartabull	.10	.05	.01
☐ 129 Joe Orsulak	.04	.02	.00
☐ 130 Tom Brunansky	.10	.05	.01
☐ 131 Dick Schofield	.04	.02	.00
☐ 132 Candy Maldonado	.07	.03	.01
☐ 133 Cecil Fielder	.40	.20	.04
☐ 134 Terry Shumpert	.10	.05	.01
☐ 135 Greg Gagne	.04	.02	.00
☐ 136 Dave Righetti	.10	.05	.01
☐ 137 Terry Steinbach	.07	.03	.01
☐ 138 Harold Reynolds	.07	.03	.01
☐ 139 George Bell	.15	.07	.01
☐ 140 Carlos Quintana	.10	.05	.01
☐ 141 Ivan Calderon	.07	.03	.01
☐ 142 Greg Brock	.04	.02	.00
☐ 143 Ruben Sierra	.20	.10	.02
☐ 144 Checklist Card	.04	.02	.00

1990 Donruss Best NL

The 1990 Donruss Best of the National League set consists of 144 cards in the standard card size of 2 1/2" by 3 1/2". This was Donruss latest version of what had been titled the previous two years as Baseball's Best. In 1990, the sets were split into National and American League and marketed separately. The front design was similar to the regular issue Donruss set except for the front borders being blue while the backs have complete major and minor league statistics as compared to the regular Donruss cards which only cover the past five major-league seasons.

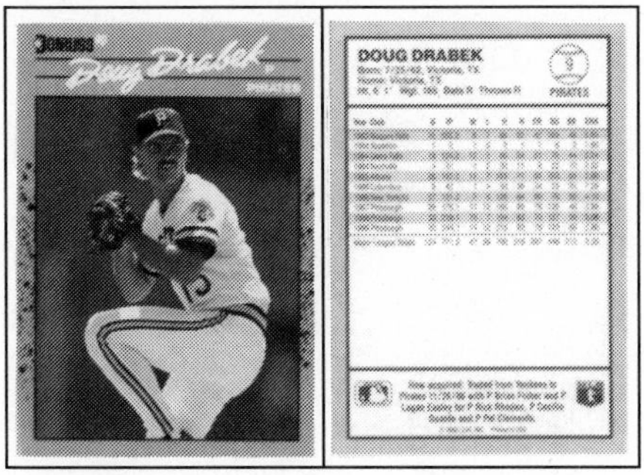

		MINT	EXC	G-VG
	COMPLETE SET (144)	10.00	5.00	1.00
	COMMON PLAYER (1-144)	.04	.02	.00
☐ 1	Eric Davis	.25	.12	.02
☐ 2	Tom Glavine	.07	.03	.01
☐ 3	Mike Bielecki	.04	.02	.00
☐ 4	Jim Deshaies	.04	.02	.00
☐ 5	Mike Scioscia	.04	.02	.00
☐ 6	Spike Owen	.04	.02	.00
☐ 7	Dwight Gooden	.20	.10	.02
☐ 8	Ricky Jordan	.10	.05	.01
☐ 9	Doug Drabek	.10	.05	.01
☐ 10	Bryn Smith	.04	.02	.00
☐ 11	Tony Gwynn	.20	.10	.02
☐ 12	John Burkett	.20	.10	.02
☐ 13	Nick Esasky	.07	.03	.01
☐ 14	Greg Maddux	.10	.05	.01
☐ 15	Joe Oliver	.10	.05	.01
☐ 16	Mike Scott	.10	.05	.01
☐ 17	Tim Belcher	.10	.05	.01
☐ 18	Kevin Gross	.04	.02	.00
☐ 19	Howard Johnson	.10	.05	.01
☐ 20	Darren Daulton	.07	.03	.01
☐ 21	John Smiley	.04	.02	.00
☐ 22	Ken Dayley	.04	.02	.00
☐ 23	Craig Lefferts	.07	.03	.01
☐ 24	Will Clark	.50	.25	.05
☐ 25	Greg Olson	.25	.12	.02
☐ 26	Ryne Sandberg	.40	.20	.04
☐ 27	Tom Browning	.07	.03	.01
☐ 28	Eric Anthony	.40	.20	.04
☐ 29	Juan Samuel	.07	.03	.01
☐ 30	Dennis Martinez	.04	.02	.00
☐ 31	Kevin Elster	.04	.02	.00
☐ 32	Tom Herr	.04	.02	.00
☐ 33	Sid Bream	.04	.02	.00
☐ 34	Terry Pendleton	.04	.02	.00
☐ 35	Roberto Alomar	.15	.07	.01
☐ 36	Kevin Bass	.07	.03	.01
☐ 37	Jim Presley	.07	.03	.01
☐ 38	Les Lancaster	.04	.02	.00
☐ 39	Paul O'Neill	.10	.05	.01
☐ 40	Dave Smith	.07	.03	.01
☐ 41	Kirk Gibson	.10	.05	.01
☐ 42	Tim Burke	.07	.03	.01
☐ 43	David Cone	.10	.05	.01
☐ 44	Ken Howell	.04	.02	.00
☐ 45	Barry Bonds	.25	.12	.02
☐ 46	Joe Magrane	.07	.03	.01
☐ 47	Andy Benes	.15	.07	.01
☐ 48	Gary Carter	.10	.05	.01
☐ 49	Pat Combs	.10	.05	.01
☐ 50	John Smoltz	.10	.05	.01
☐ 51	Mark Grace	.40	.20	.04
☐ 52	Barry Larkin	.15	.07	.01
☐ 53	Danny Darwin	.07	.03	.01
☐ 54	Orel Hershiser	.15	.07	.01
☐ 55	Tim Wallach	.10	.05	.01
☐ 56	Dave Magadan	.10	.05	.01
☐ 57	Roger McDowell	.07	.03	.01
☐ 58	Bill Landrum	.04	.02	.00
☐ 59	Jose DeLeon	.04	.02	.00
☐ 60	Bip Roberts	.07	.03	.01
☐ 61	Matt Williams	.20	.10	.02
☐ 62	Dale Murphy	.20	.10	.02
☐ 63	Dwight Smith	.15	.07	.01
☐ 64	Chris Sabo	.15	.07	.01
☐ 65	Glenn Davis	.15	.07	.01
☐ 66	Jay Howell	.04	.02	.00
☐ 67	Andres Galarraga	.10	.05	.01
☐ 68	Frank Viola	.15	.07	.01
☐ 69	John Kruk	.04	.02	.00
☐ 70	Bobby Bonilla	.15	.07	.01
☐ 71	Todd Zeile	.40	.20	.04
☐ 72	Joe Carter	.15	.07	.01
☐ 73	Robby Thompson	.04	.02	.00
☐ 74	Jeff Blauser	.04	.02	.00
☐ 75	Mitch Williams	.04	.02	.00
☐ 76	Rob Dibble	.10	.05	.01
☐ 77	Rafael Ramirez	.04	.02	.00
☐ 78	Eddie Murray	.15	.07	.01
☐ 79	Dave Martinez	.04	.02	.00
☐ 80	Darryl Strawberry	.25	.12	.02
☐ 81	Dickie Thon	.04	.02	.00
☐ 82	Jose Lind	.04	.02	.00
☐ 83	Ozzie Smith	.10	.05	.01
☐ 84	Bruce Hurst	.07	.03	.01
☐ 85	Kevin Mitchell	.20	.10	.02
☐ 86	Lonnie Smith	.07	.03	.01
☐ 87	Joe Girardi	.07	.03	.01
☐ 88	Randy Myers	.07	.03	.01
☐ 89	Craig Biggio	.07	.03	.01
☐ 90	Fernando Valenzuela	.10	.05	.01
☐ 91	Larry Walker	.20	.10	.02
☐ 92	John Franco	.07	.03	.01
☐ 93	Dennis Cook	.07	.03	.01
☐ 94	Bob Walk	.04	.02	.00
☐ 95	Pedro Guerrero	.10	.05	.01
☐ 96	Checklist Card	.04	.02	.00
☐ 97	Andre Dawson	.15	.07	.01
☐ 98	Ed Whitson	.07	.03	.01
☐ 99	Steve Bedrosian	.07	.03	.01
☐ 100	Oddibe McDowell	.07	.03	.01
☐ 101	Todd Benzinger	.04	.02	.00
☐ 102	Bill Doran	.07	.03	.01
☐ 103	Alfredo Griffin	.04	.02	.00
☐ 104	Tim Raines	.15	.07	.01
☐ 105	Sid Fernandez	.07	.03	.01
☐ 106	Charlie Hayes	.07	.03	.01
☐ 107	Mike Lavalliere	.04	.02	.00
☐ 108	Jose Oquendo	.04	.02	.00
☐ 109	Jack Clark	.15	.07	.01
☐ 110	Scott Garrelts	.07	.03	.01
☐ 111	Ron Gant	.20	.10	.02
☐ 112	Shawon Dunston	.15	.07	.01
☐ 113	Mariano Duncan	.07	.03	.01
☐ 114	Eric Yelding	.07	.03	.01
☐ 115	Hubie Brooks	.07	.03	.01
☐ 116	Delino DeShields	.40	.20	.04
☐ 117	Gregg Jefferies	.25	.12	.02
☐ 118	Len Dykstra	.10	.05	.01
☐ 119	Andy Van Slyke	.10	.05	.01
☐ 120	Lee Smith	.07	.03	.01
☐ 121	Benito Santiago	.15	.07	.01
☐ 122	Jose Uribe	.04	.02	.00
☐ 123	Jeff Treadway	.04	.02	.00
☐ 124	Jerome Walton	.20	.10	.02
☐ 125	Billy Hatcher	.07	.03	.01
☐ 126	Ken Caminiti	.04	.02	.00
☐ 127	Kal Daniels	.10	.05	.01
☐ 128	Marquis Grissom	.30	.15	.03
☐ 129	Kevin McReynolds	.10	.05	.01
☐ 130	Wally Backman	.04	.02	.00
☐ 131	Willie McGee	.10	.05	.01
☐ 132	Terry Kennedy	.04	.02	.00
☐ 133	Garry Templeton	.07	.03	.01
☐ 134	Lloyd McClendon	.04	.02	.00
☐ 135	Daryl Boston	.07	.03	.01
☐ 136	Jay Bell	.04	.02	.00
☐ 137	Mike Pagliarulo	.04	.02	.00
☐ 138	Vince Coleman	.15	.07	.01
☐ 139	Brett Butler	.07	.03	.01
☐ 140	Von Hayes	.10	.05	.01
☐ 141	Ramon Martinez	.30	.15	.03
☐ 142	Jack Armstrong	.15	.07	.01
☐ 143	Franklin Stubbs	.07	.03	.01
☐ 144	Checklist Card	.04	.02	.00

1991 Donruss Preview

This 12-card set was issued by Donruss for hobby dealers as examples of what the 1991 Donruss cards would look like. This standard size, 2 1/2" by 3 1/2", set had the 1991 Donruss design on the front; the back merely says 1991 Preview card and identifies the player and the team.

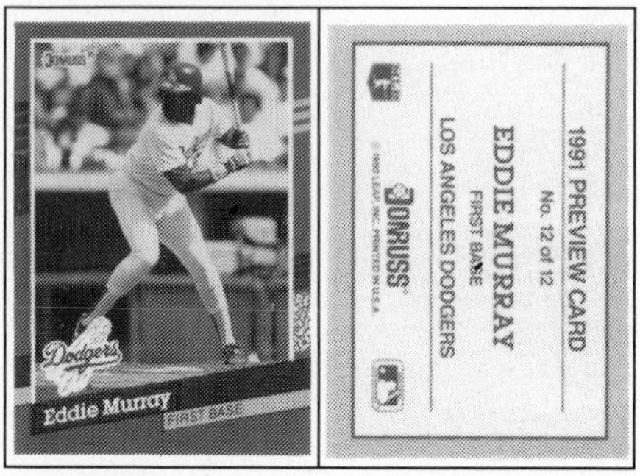

	MINT	EXC	G-VG
COMPLETE SET (12)	300.00	150.00	30.00
COMMON PLAYER (1-12)	20.00	10.00	2.00
☐ 1 Dave Justice	65.00	30.00	6.00
☐ 2 Doug Drabek	30.00	15.00	3.00
☐ 3 Scott Chiamparino	20.00	10.00	2.00
☐ 4 Ken Griffey Jr.	65.00	30.00	6.00
☐ 5 Bob Welch	20.00	10.00	2.00
☐ 6 Tino Martinez	30.00	15.00	3.00
☐ 7 Nolan Ryan	65.00	30.00	6.00
☐ 8 Dwight Gooden	40.00	20.00	4.00
☐ 9 Ryne Sandberg	50.00	25.00	5.00
☐ 10 Barry Bonds	40.00	20.00	4.00
☐ 11 Jose Canseco	65.00	30.00	6.00
☐ 12 Eddie Murray	30.00	15.00	3.00

1991 Donruss Series 1

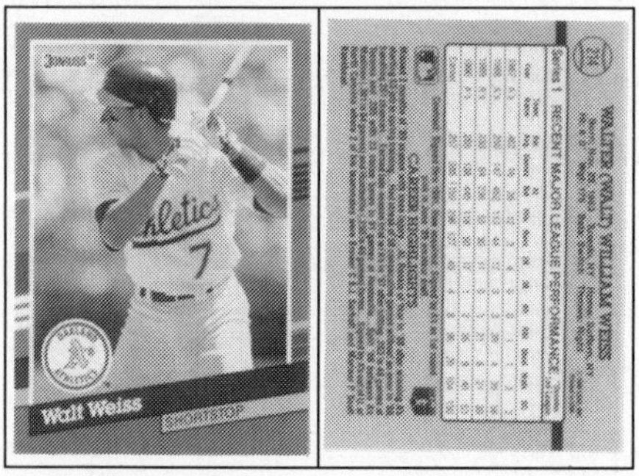

The 1991 Donruss Series 1 contains 396 cards, 386 are numbered 1-386 and the other 10 are numbered BC1-BC10. The cards measure the standard size of 2 1/2" by 3 1/2". This set marks the first time Donruss has issued their cards in series. The cards again feature the artwork of Dick Perez drawing each team's Diamond King, which comprise the first 26 cards of the set. There are also 20 Rated Rookie (RR) cards and nine All-Star cards (the AS cards are all American Leaguers in this first series). The cards feature a blue border with some stripes and the players name in white against a red background.

	MINT	EXC	G-VG
COMPLETE SET (396)	15.00	7.50	1.50
COMMON PLAYER (1-386)	.03	.01	.00
COMMON BONUS (BC1-BC10)	.05	.02	.00
☐ 1 Dave Stieb DK	.10	.05	.01
☐ 2 Craig Biggio DK	.06	.03	.00
☐ 3 Cecil Fielder DK	.12	.06	.01
☐ 4 Barry Bonds DK	.10	.05	.01
☐ 5 Barry Larkin DK	.08	.04	.01
☐ 6 Dave Parker DK	.08	.04	.01
☐ 7 Len Dykstra DK	.08	.04	.01
☐ 8 Bobby Thigpen DK	.08	.04	.01
☐ 9 Roger Clemens DK	.10	.05	.01
☐ 10 Ron Gant DK (no trademark on team logo on back)	.10	.05	.01
☐ 11 Delino DeShields DK	.15	.07	.01
☐ 12 Roberto Alomar DK (no trademark on team logo on back)	.10	.05	.01
☐ 13 Sandy Alomar Jr. DK	.10	.05	.01
☐ 14 Ryne Sandberg DK (was DK in '85, not '83 as shown)	.12	.06	.01
☐ 15 Ramon Martinez DK	.10	.05	.01
☐ 16 Edgar Martinez DK	.06	.03	.00
☐ 17 Dave Magadan DK	.08	.04	.01
☐ 18 Matt Williams DK	.10	.05	.01
☐ 19 Rafael Palmeiro DK (no trademark on team logo on back)	.10	.05	.01
☐ 20 Bob Welch DK	.08	.04	.01
☐ 21 Dave Righetti DK	.08	.04	.01
☐ 22 Brian Harper DK	.06	.03	.00
☐ 23 Gregg Olson DK	.08	.04	.01
☐ 24 Kurt Stillwell DK	.06	.03	.00
☐ 25 Pedro Guerrero DK (no trademark on team logo on back)	.06	.03	.00
☐ 26 Chuck Finley DK (no trademark on team logo on back)	.06	.03	.00
☐ 27 DK Checklist	.06	.01	.00
☐ 28 Tino Martinez RR	.35	.17	.03
☐ 29 Mark Lewis RR	.20	.10	.02
☐ 30 Bernard Gilkey RR	.25	.12	.02
☐ 31 Hensley Meulens RR	.15	.07	.01
☐ 32 Derek Bell RR	.30	.15	.03
☐ 33 Jose Offerman RR	.35	.17	.03
☐ 34 Terry Bross RR	.08	.04	.01
☐ 35 Leo Gomez RR	.40	.20	.04
☐ 36 Derrick May RR	.35	.17	.03
☐ 37 Kevin Morton RR	.15	.07	.01
☐ 38 Moises Alou RR	.20	.10	.02
☐ 39 Julio Valera RR	.10	.05	.01
☐ 40 Milt Cuyler RR	.15	.07	.01
☐ 41 Phil Plantier RR	.50	.25	.05
☐ 42 Scott Chiamparino RR	.25	.12	.02
☐ 43 Ray Lankford RR	.40	.20	.04
☐ 44 Mickey Morandini RR	.15	.07	.01
☐ 45 Dave Hansen RR	.20	.10	.02
☐ 46 Kevin Belcher RR	.15	.07	.01
☐ 47 Darrin Fletcher RR	.12	.06	.01
☐ 48 Steve Sax AS	.06	.03	.00
☐ 49 Ken Griffey Jr. AS	.35	.17	.03
☐ 50 Jose Canseco AS UER (team in stat box should be AL not A's)	.25	.12	.02
☐ 51 Sandy Alomar AS	.10	.05	.01
☐ 52 Cal Ripken AS	.10	.05	.01
☐ 53 Rickey Henderson AS	.12	.06	.01
☐ 54 Bob Welch AS	.06	.03	.00
☐ 55 Wade Boggs AS	.10	.05	.01
☐ 56 Mark McGwire AS	.12	.06	.01
☐ 57 Jack McDowell UER (career stats do not include 1990)	.06	.03	.00
☐ 58 Jose Lind	.03	.01	.00
☐ 59 Alex Fernandez	1.00	.50	.10
☐ 60 Pat Combs	.06	.03	.00
☐ 61 Mike Walker	.08	.04	.01
☐ 62 Juan Samuel	.06	.03	.00
☐ 63 Mike Blowers	.06	.03	.00
☐ 64 Mark Guthrie	.03	.01	.00
☐ 65 Mark Salas	.03	.01	.00
☐ 66 Tim Jones	.03	.01	.00
☐ 67 Tim Leary	.06	.03	.00
☐ 68 Andres Galarraga	.08	.04	.01
☐ 69 Bob Milacki	.03	.01	.00
☐ 70 Tim Belcher	.06	.03	.00
☐ 71 Todd Zeile	.15	.07	.01
☐ 72 Jerome Walton	.20	.10	.02
☐ 73 Kevin Seitzer	.08	.04	.01
☐ 74 Jerald Clark	.03	.01	.00
☐ 75 John Smoltz	.06	.03	.00
☐ 76 Mike Henneman	.03	.01	.00
☐ 77 Ken Griffey Jr.	.75	.35	.07
☐ 78 Jim Abbott	.12	.06	.01
☐ 79 Gregg Jefferies	.15	.07	.01
☐ 80 Kevin Reimer	.08	.04	.01
☐ 81 Roger Clemens	.15	.07	.01
☐ 82 Mike Fitzgerald	.03	.01	.00
☐ 83 Bruce Hurst	.06	.03	.00
☐ 84 Eric Davis	.12	.06	.01
☐ 85 Paul Molitor	.08	.04	.01

☐ 86 Will Clark	.25	.12	.02
☐ 87 Mike Bielecki	.03	.01	.00
☐ 88 Bret Saberhagen	.08	.04	.01
☐ 89 Nolan Ryan	.25	.12	.02
☐ 90 Bobby Thigpen	.08	.04	.01
☐ 91 Dickie Thon	.03	.01	.00
☐ 92 Duane Ward	.03	.01	.00
☐ 93 Luis Polonia	.03	.01	.00
☐ 94 Terry Kennedy	.03	.01	.00
☐ 95 Kent Hrbek	.08	.04	.01
☐ 96 Danny Jackson	.06	.03	.00
☐ 97 Sid Fernandez	.06	.03	.00
☐ 98 Jimmy Key	.06	.03	.00
☐ 99 Franklin Stubbs	.06	.03	.00
☐ 100 Checklist Card	.06	.01	.00
☐ 101 R.J. Reynolds	.03	.01	.00
☐ 102 Dave Stewart	.08	.04	.01
☐ 103 Dan Pasqua	.03	.01	.00
☐ 104 Dan Plesac	.03	.01	.00
☐ 105 Mark McGwire	.20	.10	.02
☐ 106 John Farrell	.03	.01	.00
☐ 107 Don Mattingly	.25	.12	.02
☐ 108 Carlton Fisk	.10	.05	.01
☐ 109 Ken Oberkfell	.03	.01	.00
☐ 110 Darrel Akerfelds	.03	.01	.00
☐ 111 Gregg Olson	.10	.05	.01
☐ 112 Mike Scioscia	.03	.01	.00
☐ 113 Bryn Smith	.03	.01	.00
☐ 114 Bob Geren	.03	.01	.00
☐ 115 Tom Candiotti	.03	.01	.00
☐ 116 Kevin Tapani	.08	.04	.01
☐ 117 Jeff Treadway	.03	.01	.00
☐ 118 Alan Trammell	.08	.04	.01
☐ 119 Pete O'Brien	.06	.03	.00
☐ 120 Joel Skinner	.03	.01	.00
☐ 121 Mike LaValliere	.03	.01	.00
☐ 122 Dwight Evans	.08	.04	.01
☐ 123 Jody Reed	.08	.04	.01
☐ 124 Lee Guetterman	.03	.01	.00
☐ 125 Tim Burke	.06	.03	.00
☐ 126 Dave Johnson	.03	.01	.00
☐ 127 Fernando Valenzuela	.08	.04	.01
☐ 128 Jose DeLeon	.03	.01	.00
☐ 129 Andre Dawson	.10	.05	.01
☐ 130 Gerald Perry	.03	.01	.00
☐ 131 Greg Harris	.03	.01	.00
☐ 132 Tom Glavine	.03	.01	.00
☐ 133 Lance McCullers	.03	.01	.00
☐ 134 Randy Johnson	.03	.01	.00
☐ 135 Lance Parrish	.08	.04	.01
☐ 136 Mackey Sasser	.06	.03	.00
☐ 137 Geno Petralli	.03	.01	.00
☐ 138 Dennis Lamp	.03	.01	.00
☐ 139 Dennis Martinez	.03	.01	.00
☐ 140 Mike Pagliarulo	.03	.01	.00
☐ 141 Hal Morris	.15	.07	.01
☐ 142 Dave Parker	.08	.04	.01
☐ 143 Brett Butler	.06	.03	.00
☐ 144 Paul Assenmacher	.03	.01	.00
☐ 145 Mark Gubicza	.06	.03	.00
☐ 146 Charlie Hough	.03	.01	.00
☐ 147 Sammy Sosa	.15	.07	.01
☐ 148 Randy Ready	.03	.01	.00
☐ 149 Kelly Gruber	.10	.05	.01
☐ 150 Devon White	.06	.03	.00
☐ 151 Gary Carter	.08	.04	.01
☐ 152 Gene Larkin	.03	.01	.00
☐ 153 Chris Sabo	.10	.05	.01
☐ 154 David Cone	.08	.04	.01
☐ 155 Todd Stottlemyre	.06	.03	.00
☐ 156 Glenn Wilson	.03	.01	.00
☐ 157 Bob Walk	.03	.01	.00
☐ 158 Mike Gallego	.03	.01	.00
☐ 159 Greg Hibbard	.03	.01	.00
☐ 160 Chris Bosio	.03	.01	.00
☐ 161 Mike Moore	.06	.03	.00
☐ 162 Jerry Browne	.03	.01	.00
☐ 163 Steve Sax	.08	.04	.01
☐ 164 Melido Perez	.06	.03	.00
☐ 165 Danny Darwin	.03	.01	.00
☐ 166 Roger McDowell	.06	.03	.00
☐ 167 Bill Ripken	.03	.01	.00
☐ 168 Mike Sharperson	.03	.01	.00
☐ 169 Lee Smith	.06	.03	.00
☐ 170 Matt Nokes	.06	.03	.00
☐ 171 Jesse Orosco	.03	.01	.00
☐ 172 Rick Aguilera	.03	.01	.00
☐ 173 Jim Presley	.03	.01	.00
☐ 174 Lou Whitaker	.06	.03	.00
☐ 175 Harold Reynolds	.06	.03	.00
☐ 176 Brook Jacoby	.06	.03	.00
☐ 177 Wally Backman	.03	.01	.00
☐ 178 Wade Boggs	.15	.07	.01
☐ 179 Chuck Cary	.03	.01	.00
☐ 180 Tom Foley	.03	.01	.00
☐ 181 Pete Harnisch	.03	.01	.00
☐ 182 Mike Morgan	.03	.01	.00
☐ 183 Bob Tewksbury	.03	.01	.00
☐ 184 Joe Girardi	.03	.01	.00
☐ 185 Storm Davis	.06	.03	.00
☐ 186 Ed Whitson	.03	.01	.00
☐ 187 Steve Avery	.15	.07	.01
☐ 188 Lloyd Moseby	.06	.03	.00
☐ 189 Scott Bankhead	.03	.01	.00
☐ 190 Mark Langston	.08	.04	.01
☐ 191 Kevin McReynolds	.08	.04	.01
☐ 192 Julio Franco	.06	.03	.00
☐ 193 John Dopson	.03	.01	.00
☐ 194 Oil Can Boyd	.03	.01	.00
☐ 195 Bip Roberts	.06	.03	.00
☐ 196 Billy Hatcher	.06	.03	.00
☐ 197 Edgar Diaz	.08	.04	.01
☐ 198 Greg Litton	.06	.03	.00
☐ 199 Mark Grace	.15	.07	.01
☐ 200 Checklist Card	.06	.01	.00
☐ 201 George Brett	.12	.06	.01
☐ 202 Jeff Russell	.03	.01	.00
☐ 203 Ivan Calderon	.06	.03	.00
☐ 204 Ken Howell	.03	.01	.00
☐ 205 Tom Henke	.06	.03	.00
☐ 206 Bryan Harvey	.03	.01	.00
☐ 207 Steve Bedrosian	.06	.03	.00
☐ 208 Al Newman	.03	.01	.00
☐ 209 Randy Myers	.06	.03	.00
☐ 210 Daryl Boston	.06	.03	.00
☐ 211 Manny Lee	.03	.01	.00
☐ 212 Dave Smith	.03	.01	.00
☐ 213 Don Slaught	.03	.01	.00
☐ 214 Walt Weiss	.06	.03	.00
☐ 215 Donn Pall	.03	.01	.00
☐ 216 Jaime Navarro	.06	.03	.00
☐ 217 Willie Randolph	.06	.03	.00
☐ 218 Rudy Seanez	.08	.04	.01
☐ 219 Jim Leyritz	.10	.05	.01
☐ 220 Ron Karkovice	.03	.01	.00
☐ 221 Ken Caminiti	.03	.01	.00
☐ 222 Von Hayes	.08	.04	.01
☐ 223 Cal Ripken	.12	.06	.01
☐ 224 Lenny Harris	.06	.03	.00
☐ 225 Milt Thompson	.03	.01	.00
☐ 226 Alvaro Espinoza	.03	.01	.00
☐ 227 Chris James	.06	.03	.00
☐ 228 Dan Gladden	.03	.01	.00
☐ 229 Jeff Blauser	.03	.01	.00
☐ 230 Mike Heath	.03	.01	.00
☐ 231 Omar Vizquel	.03	.01	.00
☐ 232 Doug Jones	.06	.03	.00
☐ 233 Jeff King	.03	.01	.00
☐ 234 Luis Rivera	.03	.01	.00
☐ 235 Ellis Burks	.10	.05	.01
☐ 236 Greg Cadaret	.03	.01	.00
☐ 237 Dave Martinez	.03	.01	.00
☐ 238 Mark Williamson	.03	.01	.00
☐ 239 Stan Javier	.03	.01	.00
☐ 240 Ozzie Smith	.08	.04	.01
☐ 241 Shawn Boskie	.06	.03	.00
☐ 242 Tom Gordon	.10	.05	.01
☐ 243 Tony Gwynn	.12	.06	.01
☐ 244 Tommy Gregg	.03	.01	.00
☐ 245 Jeff Robinson	.03	.01	.00
☐ 246 Keith Comstock	.03	.01	.00
☐ 247 Jack Howell	.03	.01	.00
☐ 248 Keith Miller	.03	.01	.00
☐ 249 Bobby Witt	.06	.03	.00
☐ 250 Rob Murphy UER (shown as on Reds in '89 in stats)	.03	.01	.00
☐ 251 Spike Owen	.03	.01	.00
☐ 252 Garry Templeton	.03	.01	.00
☐ 253 Glenn Braggs	.03	.01	.00
☐ 254 Ron Robinson	.03	.01	.00
☐ 255 Kevin Mitchell	.15	.07	.01
☐ 256 Les Lancaster	.03	.01	.00
☐ 257 Mel Stottlemyre Jr.	.08	.04	.01
☐ 258 Kenny Rogers	.03	.01	.00
☐ 259 Lance Johnson	.03	.01	.00
☐ 260 John Kruk	.03	.01	.00
☐ 261 Fred McGriff	.10	.05	.01
☐ 262 Dick Schofield	.03	.01	.00
☐ 263 Trevor Wilson	.06	.03	.00
☐ 264 David West	.03	.01	.00
☐ 265 Scott Scudder	.06	.03	.00
☐ 266 Dwight Gooden	.12	.06	.01
☐ 267 Willie Blair	.03	.01	.00
☐ 268 Mark Portugal	.03	.01	.00
☐ 269 Doug Drabek	.08	.04	.01
☐ 270 Dennis Eckersley	.08	.04	.01
☐ 271 Eric King	.03	.01	.00

☐ 272	Robin Yount	.12	.06	.01
☐ 273	Carney Lansford	.06	.03	.00
☐ 274	Carlos Baerga	.15	.07	.01
☐ 275	Dave Righetti	.06	.03	.00
☐ 276	Scott Fletcher	.03	.01	.00
☐ 277	Eric Yelding	.06	.03	.00
☐ 278	Charlie Hayes	.03	.01	.00
☐ 279	Jeff Ballard	.03	.01	.00
☐ 280	Orel Hershiser	.08	.04	.01
☐ 281	Jose Oquendo	.03	.01	.00
☐ 282	Mike Witt	.03	.01	.00
☐ 283	Mitch Webster	.03	.01	.00
☐ 284	Greg Gagne	.03	.01	.00
☐ 285	Greg Olson	.08	.04	.01
☐ 286	Tony Phillips	.03	.01	.00
☐ 287	Scott Bradley	.03	.01	.00
☐ 288	Cory Snyder	.08	.04	.01
☐ 289	Jay Bell	.03	.01	.00
☐ 290	Kevin Romine	.03	.01	.00
☐ 291	Jeff Robinson	.03	.01	.00
☐ 292	Steve Frey	.08	.04	.01
☐ 293	Craig Worthington	.06	.03	.00
☐ 294	Tim Crews	.03	.01	.00
☐ 295	Joe Magrane	.06	.03	.00
☐ 296	Hector Villanueva	.12	.06	.01
☐ 297	Terry Shumpert	.06	.03	.00
☐ 298	Joe Carter	.08	.04	.01
☐ 299	Kent Mercker	.08	.04	.01
☐ 300	Checklist Card	.06	.01	.00
☐ 301	Chet Lemon	.03	.01	.00
☐ 302	Mike Schooler	.03	.01	.00
☐ 303	Dante Bichette	.06	.03	.00
☐ 304	Kevin Elster	.03	.01	.00
☐ 305	Jeff Huson	.03	.01	.00
☐ 306	Greg Harris	.03	.01	.00
☐ 307	Marquis Grissom	.12	.06	.01
☐ 308	Calvin Schiraldi	.03	.01	.00
☐ 309	Mariano Duncan	.06	.03	.00
☐ 310	Bill Spiers	.03	.01	.00
☐ 311	Scott Garrelts	.03	.01	.00
☐ 312	Mitch Williams	.03	.01	.00
☐ 313	Mike Macfarlane	.03	.01	.00
☐ 314	Kevin Brown	.06	.03	.00
☐ 315	Robin Ventura	.15	.07	.01
☐ 316	Darren Daulton	.06	.03	.00
☐ 317	Pat Borders	.06	.03	.00
☐ 318	Mark Eichhorn	.03	.01	.00
☐ 319	Jeff Brantley	.06	.03	.00
☐ 320	Shane Mack	.06	.03	.00
☐ 321	Rob Dibble	.06	.03	.00
☐ 322	John Franco	.06	.03	.00
☐ 323	Junior Felix	.10	.05	.01
☐ 324	Casey Candaele	.03	.01	.00
☐ 325	Bobby Bonilla	.12	.06	.01
☐ 326	Dave Henderson	.06	.03	.00
☐ 327	Wayne Edwards	.06	.03	.00
☐ 328	Mark Knudson	.03	.01	.00
☐ 329	Terry Steinbach	.06	.03	.00
☐ 330	Colby Ward	.10	.05	.01
☐ 331	Oscar Azocar	.20	.10	.02
☐ 332	Scott Radinsky	.08	.04	.01
☐ 333	Eric Anthony	.15	.07	.01
☐ 334	Steve Lake	.03	.01	.00
☐ 335	Bob Melvin	.03	.01	.00
☐ 336	Kal Daniels	.08	.04	.01
☐ 337	Tom Pagnozzi	.03	.01	.00
☐ 338	Alan Mills	.06	.03	.00
☐ 339	Steve Olin	.03	.01	.00
☐ 340	Juan Berenguer	.03	.01	.00
☐ 341	Francisco Cabrera	.06	.03	.00
☐ 342	Dave Bergman	.03	.01	.00
☐ 343	Henry Cotto	.03	.01	.00
☐ 344	Sergio Valdez	.06	.03	.00
☐ 345	Bob Patterson	.03	.01	.00
☐ 346	John Marzano	.03	.01	.00
☐ 347	Dana Kiecker	.06	.03	.00
☐ 348	Dion James	.03	.01	.00
☐ 349	Hubie Brooks	.06	.03	.00
☐ 350	Bill Landrum	.03	.01	.00
☐ 351	Bill Sampen	.06	.03	.00
☐ 352	Greg Briley	.08	.04	.01
☐ 353	Paul Gibson	.03	.01	.00
☐ 354	Dave Eiland	.03	.01	.00
☐ 355	Steve Finley	.06	.03	.00
☐ 356	Bob Boone	.06	.03	.00
☐ 357	Steve Buechele	.03	.01	.00
☐ 358	Chris Hoiles	.15	.07	.01
☐ 359	Larry Walker	.10	.05	.01
☐ 360	Frank DiPino	.03	.01	.00
☐ 361	Mark Grant	.03	.01	.00
☐ 362	Dave Magadan	.08	.04	.01
☐ 363	Robby Thompson	.03	.01	.00
☐ 364	Lonnie Smith	.06	.03	.00
☐ 365	Steve Farr	.03	.01	.00
☐ 366	Dave Valle	.03	.01	.00
☐ 367	Tim Naehring	.20	.10	.02
☐ 368	Jim Acker	.03	.01	.00
☐ 369	Jeff Reardon	.06	.03	.00
☐ 370	Tim Teufel	.03	.01	.00
☐ 371	Juan Gonzalez	.25	.12	.02
☐ 372	Luis Salazar	.03	.01	.00
☐ 373	Rick Honeycutt	.03	.01	.00
☐ 374	Greg Maddux	.06	.03	.00
☐ 375	Jose Uribe	.03	.01	.00
☐ 376	Donnie Hill	.03	.01	.00
☐ 377	Don Carman	.03	.01	.00
☐ 378	Craig Grebeck	.03	.01	.00
☐ 379	Willie Fraser	.03	.01	.00
☐ 380	Glenallen Hill	.06	.03	.00
☐ 381	Joe Oliver	.06	.03	.00
☐ 382	Randy Bush	.03	.01	.00
☐ 383	Alex Cole	:30	.15	.03
☐ 384	Norm Charlton	.06	.03	.00
☐ 385	Gene Nelson	.03	.01	.00
☐ 386	Checklist Card	.06	.01	.00
☐ BC1	Langston/Witt No-Hits Mariners	.05	.02	.00
☐ BC2	Randy Johnson No-Hits Tigers	.05	.02	.00
☐ BC3	Nolan Ryan No-Hits A's	.20	.10	.02
☐ BC4	Dave Stewart No-Hits Blue Jays	.08	.04	.01
☐ BC5	Cecil Fielder 50 Homer Club	.12	.06	.01
☐ BC6	Carlton Fisk Record Home Run	.08	.04	.01
☐ BC7	Ryne Sandberg Sets Fielding Records	.12	.06	.01
☐ BC8	Gary Carter Breaks Catching Mark	.08	.04	.01
☐ BC9	Mark McGwire Home Run Milestone	.12	.06	.01
☐ BC10	Bo Jackson Four Consecutive HR's	.20	.10	.02

1991 Donruss II

This 396-card series was the second series released by Donruss in 1991. These standard size, 2 1/2" by 3 1/2" cards were issued approximately three months after the first 1991 series was issued. This series features the 26 MVP cards which Donruss had issued for the three previous years as their Bonus Cards, twenty more rated rookie cards and nine All-Star Cards (National Leaguers in this series). There were also special cards to honor the award winners and the heroes of the World Series. The 11 Bonus Cards pick up in time beginning with Valenzuela's no-hitter through the end of the season. This set marks the first time Donruss has issued their cards in two different series.

		MINT	EXC	G-VG
COMPLETE SET (396)		15.00	7.50	1.50
COMMON PLAYER (387-770)		.03	.01	.00
COMMON PLAYER (BC11-BC22)		.06	.03	.00
☐ 387	Rickey Henderson MVP	.12	.06	.01
☐ 388	Lance Parrish MVP	.06	.03	.00
☐ 389	Fred McGriff MVP	.08	.04	.01

☐ 390	Dave Parker MVP	.08	.04	.01
☐ 391	Candy Maldonado MVP	.06	.03	.00
☐ 392	Ken Griffey Jr. MVP	.35	.17	.03
☐ 393	Gregg Olson MVP	.08	.04	.01
☐ 394	Rafael Palmeiro MVP	.08	.04	.01
☐ 395	Roger Clemens MVP	.10	.05	.01
☐ 396	George Brett MVP	.10	.05	.01
☐ 397	Cecil Fielder MVP	.12	.06	.01
☐ 398	Brian Harper MVP	.03	.01	.00
☐ 399	Bobby Thigpen MVP	.06	.03	.00
☐ 400	Roberto Kelly MVP	.08	.04	.01
☐ 401	Danny Darwin MVP	.03	.01	.00
☐ 402	Dave Justice MVP	.30	.15	.03
☐ 403	Lee Smith MVP	.03	.01	.00
☐ 404	Ryne Sandberg MVP	.12	.06	.01
☐ 405	Eddie Murray MVP	.08	.04	.01
☐ 406	Tim Wallach MVP	.06	.03	.00
☐ 407	Kevin Mitchell MVP	.10	.05	.01
☐ 408	Darryl Strawberry MVP	.12	.06	.01
☐ 409	Joe Carter MVP	.08	.04	.01
☐ 410	Len Dykstra MVP	.08	.04	.01
☐ 411	Doug Drabek MVP	.08	.04	.01
☐ 412	Chris Sabo MVP	.08	.04	.01
☐ 413	Paul Marak RR	.10	.05	.01
☐ 414	Tim McIntosh RR	.08	.04	.01
☐ 415	Brian Barnes RR	.10	.05	.01
☐ 416	Eric Gunderson RR	.15	.07	.01
☐ 417	Mike Gardiner RR	.12	.06	.01
☐ 418	Steve Carter RR	.03	.01	.00
☐ 419	Gerald Alexander RR	.10	.05	.01
☐ 420	Rich Garces RR	.12	.06	.01
☐ 421	Chuck Knoblauch RR	.10	.05	.01
☐ 422	Scott Aldred RR	.10	.05	.01
☐ 423	Wes Chamberlain RR	.30	.15	.03
☐ 424	Lance Dickson RR	.25	.12	.02
☐ 425	Greg Colbrunn RR	.20	.10	.02
☐ 426	Rich Delucia RR	.10	.05	.01
☐ 427	Jeff Conine RR	.50	.25	.05
☐ 428	Steve Decker RR	.30	.15	.03
☐ 429	Turner Ward RR	.20	.10	.02
☐ 430	Mo Vaughn RR	.60	.30	.06
☐ 431	Steve Chitren RR	.10	.05	.01
☐ 432	Mike Benjamin RR	.10	.05	.01
☐ 433	Ryne Sandberg AS	.12	.06	.01
☐ 434	Len Dykstra AS	.08	.04	.01
☐ 435	Andre Dawson AS	.08	.04	.01
☐ 436	Mike Scioscia AS	.03	.01	.00
☐ 437	Ozzie Smith AS	.08	.04	.01
☐ 438	Kevin Mitchell AS	.10	.05	.01
☐ 439	Jack Armstrong AS	.06	.03	.00
☐ 440	Chris Sabo AS	.08	.04	.01
☐ 441	Will Clark AS	.15	.07	.01
☐ 442	Mel Hall	.03	.01	.00
☐ 443	Mark Gardner	.03	.01	.00
☐ 444	Mike Devereaux	.03	.01	.00
☐ 445	Kirk Gibson	.08	.04	.01
☐ 446	Terry Pendleton	.03	.01	.00
☐ 447	Mike Harkey	.06	.03	.00
☐ 448	Jim Eisenreich	.04	.02	.00
☐ 449	Benito Santiago	.08	.04	.01
☐ 450	Oddibe McDowell	.03	.01	.00
☐ 451	Cecil Fielder	.20	.10	.02
☐ 452	Ken Griffey Sr.	.06	.03	.00
☐ 453	Bert Blyleven	.06	.03	.00
☐ 454	Howard Johnson	.08	.04	.01
☐ 455	Monty Farris	.12	.06	.01
☐ 456	Tony Pena	.06	.03	.00
☐ 457	Tim Raines	.08	.04	.01
☐ 458	Dennis Rasmussen	.03	.01	.00
☐ 459	Luis Quinones	.03	.01	.00
☐ 460	B.J. Surhoff	.06	.03	.00
☐ 461	Ernest Riles	.03	.01	.00
☐ 462	Rick Sutcliffe	.06	.03	.00
☐ 463	Danny Tartabull	.06	.03	.00
☐ 464	Pete Incaviglia	.06	.03	.00
☐ 465	Carlos Martinez	.03	.01	.00
☐ 466	Ricky Jordan	.06	.03	.00
☐ 467	John Cerutti	.03	.01	.00
☐ 468	Dave Winfield	.10	.05	.01
☐ 469	Francisco Oliveras	.03	.01	.00
☐ 470	Roy Smith	.03	.01	.00
☐ 471	Barry Larkin	.10	.05	.01
☐ 472	Ron Darling	.06	.03	.00
☐ 473	David Wells	.03	.01	.00
☐ 474	Glenn Davis	.08	.04	.01
☐ 475	Neal Heaton	.03	.01	.00
☐ 476	Ron Hassey	.03	.01	.00
☐ 477	Frank Thomas	.90	.45	.09
☐ 478	Greg Vaughn	.12	.06	.01
☐ 479	Todd Burns	.03	.01	.00
☐ 480	Candy Maldonado	.06	.03	.00
☐ 481	Dave LaPoint	.03	.01	.00
☐ 482	Alvin Davis	.06	.03	.00
☐ 483	Mike Scott	.06	.03	.00
☐ 484	Dale Murphy	.10	.05	.01
☐ 485	Ben McDonald	.25	.12	.02
☐ 486	Jay Howell	.03	.01	.00
☐ 487	Vince Coleman	.08	.04	.01
☐ 488	Alfredo Griffin	.03	.01	.00
☐ 489	Sandy Alomar Jr.	.15	.07	.01
☐ 490	Kirby Puckett	.15	.07	.01
☐ 491	Andres Thomas	.03	.01	.00
☐ 492	Jack Morris	.06	.03	.00
☐ 493	Matt Young	.03	.01	.00
☐ 494	Greg Myers	.03	.01	.00
☐ 495	Barry Bonds	.15	.07	.01
☐ 496	Scott Cooper	.15	.07	.01
☐ 497	Dan Schatzeder	.03	.01	.00
☐ 498	Jesse Barfield	.06	.03	.00
☐ 499	Jerry Goff	.08	.04	.01
☐ 500	Checklist Card	.06	.03	.00
☐ 501	Anthony Telford	.10	.05	.01
☐ 502	Eddie Murray	.10	.05	.01
☐ 503	Omar Olivares	.10	.05	.01
☐ 504	Ryne Sandberg	.15	.07	.01
☐ 505	Jeff Montgomery	.03	.01	.00
☐ 506	Mark Parent	.03	.01	.00
☐ 507	Ron Gant	.10	.05	.01
☐ 508	Frank Tanana	.06	.03	.00
☐ 509	Jay Buhner	.06	.03	.00
☐ 510	Max Venable	.03	.01	.00
☐ 511	Wally Whitehurst	.08	.04	.01
☐ 512	Gary Pettis	.03	.01	.00
☐ 513	Tom Brunansky	.06	.03	.00
☐ 514	Tim Wallach	.06	.03	.00
☐ 515	Craig Lefferts	.03	.01	.00
☐ 516	Tim Layana	.03	.01	.00
☐ 517	Darryl Hamilton	.08	.04	.01
☐ 518	Rick Reuschel	.06	.03	.00
☐ 519	Steve Wilson	.03	.01	.00
☐ 520	Kurt Stillwell	.06	.03	.00
☐ 521	Rafael Palmeiro	.10	.05	.01
☐ 522	Ken Patterson	.03	.01	.00
☐ 523	Len Dykstra	.08	.04	.01
☐ 524	Tony Fernandez	.06	.03	.00
☐ 525	Kent Anderson	.03	.01	.00
☐ 526	Mark Leonard	.20	.10	.02
☐ 527	Allan Anderson	.03	.01	.00
☐ 528	Tom Browning	.06	.03	.00
☐ 529	Frank Viola	.08	.04	.01
☐ 530	John Olerud	.35	.17	.03
☐ 531	Juan Agosto	.03	.01	.00
☐ 532	Zane Smith	.06	.03	.00
☐ 533	Scott Sanderson	.03	.01	.00
☐ 534	Barry Jones	.03	.01	.00
☐ 535	Mike Felder	.03	.01	.00
☐ 536	Jose Canseco	.30	.15	.03
☐ 537	Felix Fermin	.03	.01	.00
☐ 538	Roberto Kelly	.08	.04	.01
☐ 539	Brian Holman	.03	.01	.00
☐ 540	Mark Davidson	.03	.01	.00
☐ 541	Terry Mulholland	.03	.01	.00
☐ 542	Randy Milligan	.06	.03	.00
☐ 543	Jose Gonzalez	.03	.01	.00
☐ 544	Craig Wilson	.10	.05	.01
☐ 545	Mike Hartley	.06	.03	.00
☐ 546	Greg Swindell	.06	.03	.00
☐ 547	Gary Gaetti	.06	.03	.00
☐ 548	Dave Justice	.65	.30	.06
☐ 549	Steve Searcy	.03	.01	.00
☐ 550	Erik Hansen	.06	.03	.00
☐ 551	Dave Stieb	.06	.03	.00
☐ 552	Andy Van Slyke	.08	.04	.01
☐ 553	Mike Greenwell	.12	.06	.01
☐ 554	Kevin Maas	.40	.20	.04
☐ 555	Delino DeShields	.20	.10	.02
☐ 556	Curt Schilling	.03	.01	.00
☐ 557	Ramon Martinez	.15	.07	.01
☐ 558	Pedro Guerrero	.08	.04	.01
☐ 559	Dwight Smith	.06	.03	.00
☐ 560	Mark Davis	.06	.03	.00
☐ 561	Shawn Abner	.06	.03	.00
☐ 562	Charlie Leibrandt	.03	.01	.00
☐ 563	John Shelby	.03	.01	.00
☐ 564	Bill Swift	.03	.01	.00
☐ 565	Mike Fetters	.03	.01	.00
☐ 566	Alejandro Pena	.03	.01	.00
☐ 567	Ruben Sierra	.12	.06	.01
☐ 568	Carlos Quintana	.08	.04	.01
☐ 569	Kevin Gross	.03	.01	.00
☐ 570	Derek Lilliquist	.03	.01	.00
☐ 571	Jack Armstrong	.06	.03	.00
☐ 572	Greg Brock	.03	.01	.00
☐ 573	Mike Kingery	.03	.01	.00
☐ 574	Greg Smith	.08	.04	.01
☐ 575	Brian McRae	.60	.30	.06
☐ 576	Jack Daugherty	.03	.01	.00
☐ 577	Ozzie Guillen	.06	.03	.00

☐ 578	Joe Boever	.03	.01	.00
☐ 579	Luis Sojo	.08	.04	.01
☐ 580	Chili Davis	.06	.03	.00
☐ 581	Don Robinson	.03	.01	.00
☐ 582	Brian Harper	.03	.01	.00
☐ 583	Paul O'Neill	.06	.03	.00
☐ 584	Bob Ojeda	.06	.03	.00
☐ 585	Mookie Wilson	.06	.03	.00
☐ 586	Rafael Ramirez	.03	.01	.00
☐ 587	Gary Redus	.03	.01	.00
☐ 588	Jamie Quirk	.03	.01	.00
☐ 589	Shawn Hillegas	.03	.01	.00
☐ 590	Tom Edens	.10	.05	.01
☐ 591	Joe Klink	.08	.04	.01
☐ 592	Charles Nagy	.12	.06	.01
☐ 593	Eric Plunk	.03	.01	.00
☐ 594	Tracy Jones	.03	.01	.00
☐ 595	Craig Biggio	.06	.03	.00
☐ 596	Jose DeJesus	.06	.03	.00
☐ 597	Mickey Tettleton	.06	.03	.00
☐ 598	Chris Gwynn	.08	.04	.01
☐ 599	Rex Hudler	.03	.01	.00
☐ 600	Checklist Card	.06	.03	.00
☐ 601	Jim Gott	.03	.01	.00
☐ 602	Jeff Manto	.10	.05	.01
☐ 603	Nelson Liriano	.03	.01	.00
☐ 604	Mark Lemke	.03	.01	.00
☐ 605	Clay Parker	.03	.01	.00
☐ 606	Edgar Martinez	.06	.03	.00
☐ 607	Mark Whiten	.30	.15	.03
☐ 608	Ted Power	.03	.01	.00
☐ 609	Tom Bolton	.03	.01	.00
☐ 610	Tom Herr	.06	.03	.00
☐ 611	Andy Hawkins	.03	.01	.00
☐ 612	Scott Ruskin	.03	.01	.00
☐ 613	Ron Kittle	.06	.03	.00
☐ 614	John Wetteland	.06	.03	.00
☐ 615	Mike Perez	.10	.05	.01
☐ 616	Dave Clark	.03	.01	.00
☐ 617	Brent Mayne	.08	.04	.01
☐ 618	Jack Clark	.08	.04	.01
☐ 619	Marvin Freeman	.03	.01	.00
☐ 620	Edwin Nunez	.03	.01	.00
☐ 621	Russ Swan	.08	.04	.01
☐ 622	Johnny Ray	.03	.01	.00
☐ 623	Charlie O'Brien	.03	.01	.00
☐ 624	Joe Bitker	.10	.05	.01
☐ 625	Mike Marshall	.06	.03	.00
☐ 626	Otis Nixon	.03	.01	.00
☐ 627	Andy Benes	.10	.05	.01
☐ 628	Ron Oester	.03	.01	.00
☐ 629	Ted Higuera	.06	.03	.00
☐ 630	Kevin Bass	.06	.03	.00
☐ 631	Damon Berryhill	.06	.03	.00
☐ 632	Bo Jackson	.30	.15	.03
☐ 633	Brad Arnsberg	.08	.04	.01
☐ 634	Jerry Willard	.03	.01	.00
☐ 635	Tommy Greene	.03	.01	.00
☐ 636	Bob MacDonald	.10	.05	.01
☐ 637	Kirk McCaskill	.03	.01	.00
☐ 638	John Burkett	.06	.03	.00
☐ 639	Paul Abbott	.15	.07	.01
☐ 640	Todd Benzinger	.03	.01	.00
☐ 641	Todd Hundley	.12	.06	.01
☐ 642	George Bell	.08	.04	.01
☐ 643	Javier Ortiz	.08	.04	.01
☐ 644	Sid Bream	.03	.01	.00
☐ 645	Bob Welch	.08	.04	.01
☐ 646	Phil Bradley	.06	.03	.00
☐ 647	Bill Krueger	.03	.01	.00
☐ 648	Rickey Henderson	.20	.10	.02
☐ 649	Kevin Wickander	.03	.01	.00
☐ 650	Steve Balboni	.03	.01	.00
☐ 651	Gene Harris	.03	.01	.00
☐ 652	Jim Deshaies	.03	.01	.00
☐ 653	Jason Grimsley	.10	.05	.01
☐ 654	Joe Orsulak	.03	.01	.00
☐ 655	Jimmy Poole	.10	.05	.01
☐ 656	Felix Jose	.06	.03	.00
☐ 657	Denis Cook	.03	.01	.00
☐ 658	Tom Brookens	.03	.01	.00
☐ 659	Junior Ortiz	.03	.01	.00
☐ 660	Jeff Parrett	.03	.01	.00
☐ 661	Jerry Don Gleaton	.03	.01	.00
☐ 662	Brent Knackert	.08	.04	.01
☐ 663	Rance Mulliniks	.03	.01	.00
☐ 664	John Smiley	.03	.01	.00
☐ 665	Larry Andersen	.03	.01	.00
☐ 666	Willie McGee	.08	.04	.01
☐ 667	Chris Nabholz	.15	.07	.01
☐ 668	Brady Anderson	.03	.01	.00
☐ 669	Darren Holmes	.10	.05	.01
☐ 670	Ken Hill	.03	.01	.00
☐ 671	Gary Varsho	.08	.04	.01
☐ 672	Bill Pecota	.03	.01	.00
☐ 673	Fred Lynn	.06	.03	.00
☐ 674	Kevin Brown	.06	.03	.00
☐ 675	Dan Petry	.03	.01	.00
☐ 676	Mike Jackson	.06	.03	.00
☐ 677	Wally Joyner	.08	.04	.01
☐ 678	Danny Jackson	.06	.03	.00
☐ 679	Bill Haselman	.10	.05	.01
☐ 680	Mike Boddicker	.06	.03	.00
☐ 681	Mel Rojas	.08	.04	.01
☐ 682	Roberto Alomar	.08	.04	.01
☐ 683	Dave Justice ROY	.30	.15	.03
☐ 684	Chuck Crim	.03	.01	.00
☐ 685	Matt Williams	.12	.06	.01
☐ 686	Shawon Dunston	.08	.04	.01
☐ 687	Jeff Schulz	.10	.05	.01
☐ 688	John Barfield	.10	.05	.01
☐ 689	Gerald Young	.03	.01	.00
☐ 690	Luis Gonzalez	.10	.05	.01
☐ 691	Frank Wills	.08	.04	.01
☐ 692	Chuck Finley	.06	.03	.00
☐ 693	Sandy Alomar Jr. ROY	.10	.05	.01
☐ 694	Tim Drummond	.03	.01	.00
☐ 695	Herm Winningham	.03	.01	.00
☐ 696	Darryl Strawberry	.15	.07	.01
☐ 697	Al Leiter	.03	.01	.00
☐ 698	Karl Rhodes	.10	.05	.01
☐ 699	Stan Belinda	.08	.04	.01
☐ 700	Checklist Card	.06	.03	.00
☐ 701	Lance Blankenship	.03	.01	.00
☐ 702	Puzzle Card Willie Stargell	.06	.03	.00
☐ 703	Jim Gantner	.03	.01	.00
☐ 704	Reggie Harris	.12	.06	.01
☐ 705	Rob Ducey	.08	.04	.01
☐ 706	Tim Hulett	.03	.01	.00
☐ 707	Atlee Hammaker	.03	.01	.00
☐ 708	Xavier Hernandez	.03	.01	.00
☐ 709	Chuck McElroy	.08	.04	.01
☐ 710	John Mitchell	.03	.01	.00
☐ 711	Carlos Hernandez	.03	.01	.00
☐ 712	Geronimo Pena	.12	.06	.01
☐ 713	Jim Neidlinger	.15	.07	.01
☐ 714	John Orton	.06	.03	.00
☐ 715	Terry Leach	.03	.01	.00
☐ 716	Mike Stanton	.03	.01	.00
☐ 717	Walt Terrell	.03	.01	.00
☐ 718	Luis Aquino	.03	.01	.00
☐ 719	Bud Black	.03	.01	.00
☐ 720	Bob Kipper	.03	.01	.00
☐ 721	Jeff Gray	.10	.05	.01
☐ 722	Jose Rijo	.06	.03	.00
☐ 723	Curt Young	.03	.01	.00
☐ 724	Jose Vizcaino	.08	.04	.01
☐ 725	Randy Tomlin	.10	.05	.01
☐ 726	Junior Noboa	.08	.04	.01
☐ 727	Bob Welch CY	.06	.03	.00
☐ 728	Gary Ward	.03	.01	.00
☐ 729	Rob Deer	.06	.03	.00
☐ 730	David Segui	.25	.12	.02
☐ 731	Mark Carreon	.03	.01	.00
☐ 732	Vicente Palacios	.03	.01	.00
☐ 733	Sam Horn	.06	.03	.00
☐ 734	Howard Farmer	.12	.06	.01
☐ 735	Ken Dayley	.03	.01	.00
☐ 736	Kelly Mann	.03	.01	.00
☐ 737	Joe Grahe	.10	.05	.01
☐ 738	Kelly Downs	.03	.01	.00
☐ 739	Jimmy Kremers	.10	.05	.01
☐ 740	Kevin Appier	.06	.03	.00
☐ 741	Jeff Reed	.03	.01	.00
☐ 742	Jose Rijo WS	.06	.03	.00
☐ 743	Dave Rohde	.08	.04	.01
☐ 744	Dr.Dirt/Mr.Clean	.15	.07	.01
☐ 745	Paul Sorrento	.03	.01	.00
☐ 746	Thomas Howard	.15	.07	.01
☐ 747	Matt Stark	.20	.10	.02
☐ 748	Harold Baines	.06	.03	.00
☐ 749	Doug Dascenzo	.03	.01	.00
☐ 750	Doug Drabek CY	.06	.03	.00
☐ 751	Gary Sheffield	.12	.06	.01
☐ 752	Terry Lee	.15	.07	.01
☐ 753	Jim Vatcher	.15	.07	.01
☐ 754	Lee Stevens	.15	.07	.01
☐ 755	Randy Veres	.08	.04	.01
☐ 756	Bill Doran	.06	.03	.00
☐ 757	Gary Wayne	.03	.01	.00
☐ 758	Pedro Munoz	.15	.07	.01
☐ 759	Chris Hammond	.10	.05	.01
☐ 760	Checklist Card	.06	.03	.00
☐ 761	Rickey Henderson MVP	.12	.06	.01
☐ 762	Barry Bonds MVP	.10	.05	.01
☐ 763	Billy Hatcher WS	.06	.03	.00
☐ 764	Julio Machado	.03	.01	.00

☐ 765 Jose Mesa	.03	.01	.00
☐ 766 Willie Randolph WS	.03	.01	.00
☐ 767 Scott Erickson	.15	.07	.01
☐ 768 Travis Fryman	.40	.20	.04
☐ 769 Rich Rodriguez	.10	.05	.01
☐ 770 Checklist Card	.06	.03	.00
☐ BC11 Fernando Valenzuela No Hits Cardinals	.08	.04	.01
☐ BC12 Andy Hawkins No Hits White Sox	.06	.03	.00
☐ BC13 Melido Perez No Hits Yankees	.06	.03	.00
☐ BC14 Terry Mulholland No Hits Giants	.06	.03	.00
☐ BC15 Nolan Ryan 300th Win	.20	.10	.02
☐ BC16 Delino DeShields 4 Hits in Debut	.15	.07	.01
☐ BC17 Cal Ripken Errorless Games	.10	.05	.01
☐ BC18 Eddie Murray Switch Hit Homers	.08	.04	.01
☐ BC19 George Brett 3 Decade Champ	.10	.05	.01
☐ BC20 Bobby Thigpen Shatters Save Mark	.08	.04	.01
☐ BC21 Dave Stieb No Hits Indians	.08	.04	.01
☐ BC22 Willie McGee NL Batting Champ	.10	.05	.01

1991 Donruss Elite

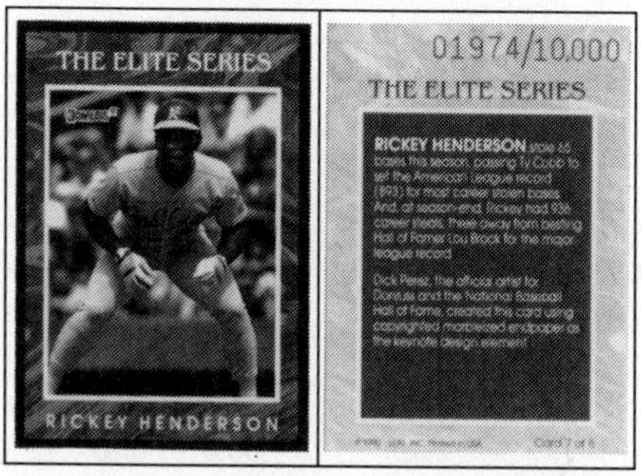

These special cards were inserted in the 1991 Donruss first series wax packs. Production was limited to a maximum of 10,000 cards for each card in the Elite series, and lesser production for the Sandberg Signature (5,000) and Ryan Legend (7,500) cards. The regular Elite cards are photos enclosed in a bronze marble borders which surround an evenly squared photo of the players. The Sandberg Signature card has a green marble border and is signed in a blue sharpie. The Nolan Ryan Legend card is a Dick Perez drawing with silver borders. The cards are all numbered on the back, 1 out of 10,000, etc. All of these special cards measure the standard, 2 1/2" by 3 1/2".

	MINT	EXC	G-VG
COMPLETE SET (10)	1350.00	450.00	90.00
COMMON PLAYER (1-8)	90.00	37.50	7.50
☐ E1 Barry Bonds	120.00	50.00	10.00
☐ E2 George Brett	120.00	50.00	10.00
☐ E3 Jose Canseco	225.00	100.00	20.00
☐ E4 Andre Dawson	100.00	45.00	9.00
☐ E5 Doug Drabek	90.00	37.50	7.50
☐ E6 Cecil Fielder	120.00	50.00	10.00
☐ E7 Rickey Henderson	150.00	60.00	12.50
☐ E8 Matt Williams	120.00	50.00	10.00
☐ L1 Nolan Ryan (Legend)	300.00	125.00	25.00
☐ S1 Ryne Sandberg (Signature Series)	250.00	110.00	22.00

1991 Donruss Super DK's

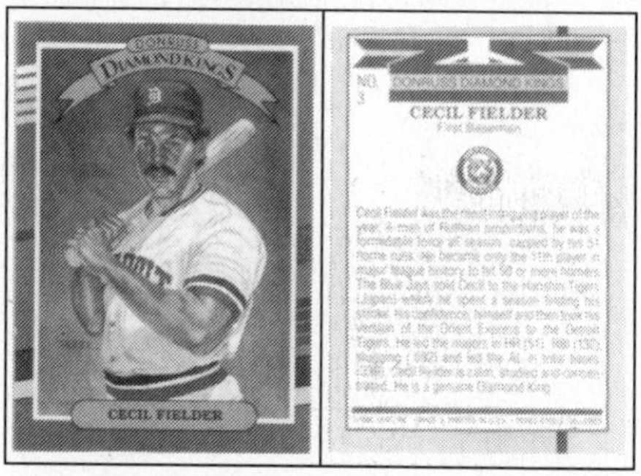

For the seventh consecutive year Donruss has issued a card set featuring the players used in the current year's Diamond King subset in a larger size, approximately 5" by 7". The set again features the art work of famed sports artist Dick Perez and is available through a postpaid mail-in offer detailed on the 1991 Donruss wax packs involving 14.00 and three wax wrappers.

	MINT	EXC	G-VG
COMPLETE SET (26)	12.00	6.00	1.20
COMMON PLAYER (1-26)	.40	.20	.04
☐ 1 Dave Stieb DK	.50	.25	.05
☐ 2 Craig Biggio DK	.40	.20	.04
☐ 3 Cecil Fielder DK	.80	.40	.08
☐ 4 Barry Bonds DK	.70	.35	.07
☐ 5 Barry Larkin DK	.60	.30	.06
☐ 6 Dave Parker DK	.50	.25	.05
☐ 7 Len Dykstra DK	.50	.25	.05
☐ 8 Bobby Thigpen DK	.50	.25	.05
☐ 9 Roger Clemens DK	.60	.30	.06
☐ 10 Ron Gant DK	.60	.30	.06
☐ 11 Delino DeShields DK	.80	.40	.08
☐ 12 Roberto Alomar DK	.60	.30	.06
☐ 13 Sandy Alomar Jr. DK	.60	.30	.06
☐ 14 Ryne Sandberg DK	.80	.40	.08
☐ 15 Ramon Martinez DK	.70	.35	.07
☐ 16 Edgar Martinez DK	.50	.25	.05
☐ 17 Dave Magadan DK	.50	.25	.05
☐ 18 Matt Williams DK	.70	.35	.07
☐ 19 Rafael Palmeiro DK	.70	.35	.07
☐ 20 Bob Welch DK	.60	.30	.06
☐ 21 Dave Righetti DK	.50	.25	.05
☐ 22 Brian Harper DK	.40	.20	.04
☐ 23 Gregg Olson DK	.50	.25	.05
☐ 24 Kurt Stillwell DK	.40	.20	.04
☐ 25 Pedro Guerrero DK	.50	.25	.05
☐ 26 Chuck Finley DK	.50	.25	.05

1986 Dorman's Cheese

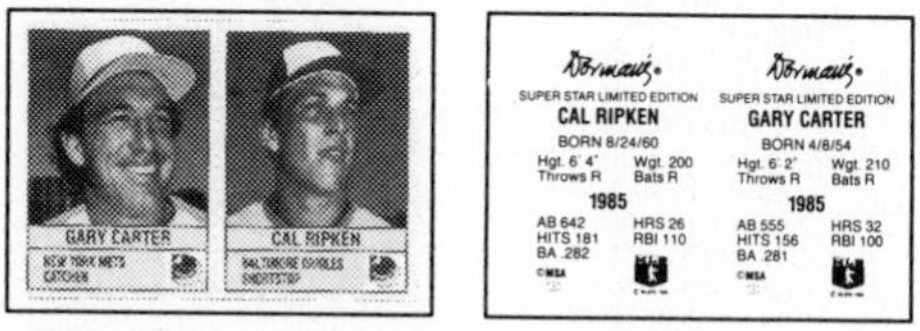

This 20-card set was issued in panels of two cards. The individual cards measure 1 1/2" by 2" whereas the panels measure 3" by 2". Team logos have been removed from the photos as these cards were not licensed by Major League Baseball (team owners). The backs contain a minimum of information.

	MINT	EXC	G-VG
COMPLETE SET (20)	20.00	10.00	2.00
COMMON PLAYER (1-20)	.75	.35	.07
☐ 1 George Brett	1.25	.60	.12
☐ 2 Jack Morris	.75	.35	.07
☐ 3 Gary Carter	.90	.45	.09
☐ 4 Cal Ripken	1.00	.50	.10
☐ 5 Dwight Gooden	1.25	.60	.12
☐ 6 Kent Hrbek	.90	.45	.09
☐ 7 Rickey Henderson	1.50	.75	.15
☐ 8 Mike Schmidt	1.50	.75	.15
☐ 9 Keith Hernandez	.90	.45	.09
☐ 10 Dale Murphy	1.00	.50	.10
☐ 11 Reggie Jackson	1.00	.50	.10
☐ 12 Eddie Murray	1.00	.50	.10
☐ 13 Don Mattingly	2.50	1.25	.25
☐ 14 Ryne Sandberg	1.50	.75	.15
☐ 15 Willie McGee	.90	.45	.09
☐ 16 Robin Yount	1.25	.60	.12
☐ 17 Rick Sutcliffe	.75	.35	.07
☐ 18 Wade Boggs	1.75	.85	.17
☐ 19 Dave Winfield	1.00	.50	.10
☐ 20 Jim Rice	.90	.45	.09

1941 Double Play

The cards in this 75-card set measure 2 1/2" by 3 1/8". The 1941 Double Play set, listed as R330 in the American Card Catalog, was a blank-backed issue distributed by Gum Products. It consists of 75 numbered cards (two consecutive numbers per card), each depicting two players in sepia tone photographs. Cards 81-100 contain action poses, and the last 50 numbers of the set are slightly harder to find. Cards that have been cut in half to form "singles" have a greatly reduced value.

	EX-MT	VG-E	GOOD
COMPLETE SET (150)	4200.00	2000.00	450.00
COMMON PAIRS (1-100)	25.00	12.50	2.50
COMMON PAIRS (101-150)	32.00	16.00	3.20
☐ 1 Larry French and 2 Vance Page	25.00	12.50	2.50
☐ 3 Billy Herman and 4 Stan Hack	32.00	16.00	3.20
☐ 5 Lonnie Frey and 6 Johnny VanderMeer	32.00	16.00	3.20
☐ 7 Paul Derringer and 8 Bucky Walters	32.00	16.00	3.20
☐ 9 Frank McCormick and 10 Bill Werber	25.00	12.50	2.50
☐ 11 Jimmy Ripple and 12 Ernie Lombardi	32.00	16.00	3.20
☐ 13 Alex Kampouris and 14 Whitlow Wyatt	25.00	12.50	2.50
☐ 15 Mickey Owen and 16 Paul Waner	36.00	18.00	3.60
☐ 17 Cookie Lavagetto and 18 Pete Reiser	25.00	12.50	2.50
☐ 19 James Wasdell and 20 Dolf Camilli	25.00	12.50	2.50
☐ 21 Dixie Walker and 22 Joe Medwick	32.00	16.00	3.20
☐ 23 Pee Wee Reese and 24 Kirby Higbe	135.00	65.00	13.50
☐ 25 Harry Danning and 26 Cliff Melton	25.00	12.50	2.50
☐ 27 Harry Gumbert and 28 Burgess Whitehead	25.00	12.50	2.50
☐ 29 Joe Orengo and 30 Joe Moore	25.00	12.50	2.50
☐ 31 Mel Ott and 32 Norman Young	80.00	40.00	8.00
☐ 33 Lee Handley and 34 Arky Vaughan	36.00	18.00	3.60
☐ 35 Bob Klinger and 36 Stanley Brown	25.00	12.50	2.50
☐ 37 Terry Moore and 38 Gus Mancuso	25.00	12.50	2.50
☐ 39 Johnny Mize and 40 Enos Slaughter	135.00	65.00	13.50
☐ 41 Johnny Cooney and 42 Sibby Sisti	25.00	12.50	2.50
☐ 43 Max West and 44 Carvel Rowell	25.00	12.50	2.50
☐ 45 Danny Litwhiler and 46 Merrill May	25.00	12.50	2.50
☐ 47 Frank Hayes and 48 Al Brancato	25.00	12.50	2.50
☐ 49 Bob Johnson and 50 Bill Nagel	25.00	12.50	2.50
☐ 51 Buck Newsom and 52 Hank Greenberg	55.00	27.50	5.50
☐ 53 Barney McCosky and 54 Charlie Gehringer	55.00	27.50	5.50
☐ 55 Mike Higgins and 56 Dick Bartell	25.00	12.50	2.50
☐ 57 Ted Williams and 58 Jim Tabor	350.00	175.00	35.00
☐ 59 Joe Cronin and 60 Jimmie Foxx	175.00	85.00	18.00
☐ 61 Lefty Gomez and 62 Phil Rizzuto	225.00	110.00	22.00
☐ 63 Joe DiMaggio and 64 Charlie Keller	600.00	300.00	60.00
☐ 65 Red Rolfe and 66 Bill Dickey	120.00	60.00	12.00
☐ 67 Joe Gordon and 68 Red Ruffing	80.00	40.00	8.00
☐ 69 Mike Tresh and 70 Luke Appling	40.00	20.00	4.00
☐ 71 Moose Solters and 72 Johnny Rigney	25.00	12.50	2.50
☐ 73 Buddy Myer and 74 Ben Chapman	25.00	12.50	2.50
☐ 75 Cecil Travis and 76 George Case	25.00	12.50	2.50
☐ 77 Joe Krakauskas and 78 Bob Feller	120.00	60.00	12.00
☐ 79 Ken Keltner and 80 Hal Trosky	25.00	12.50	2.50
☐ 81 Ted Williams and 82 Joe Cronin	400.00	200.00	40.00
☐ 83 Joe Gordon and 84 Charlie Keller	36.00	18.00	3.60
☐ 85 Hank Greenberg and 86 Red Ruffing	175.00	85.00	18.00
☐ 87 Hal Trosky and 88 George Case	25.00	12.50	2.50
☐ 89 Mel Ott and 90 Burgess Whitehead	80.00	40.00	8.00
☐ 91 Harry Danning and 92 Harry Gumbert	25.00	12.50	2.50
☐ 93 Norman Young and 94 Cliff Melton	25.00	12.50	2.50
☐ 95 Jimmy Ripple and 96 Bucky Walters	25.00	12.50	2.50
☐ 97 Stanley Jack and 98 Bob Klinger	25.00	12.50	2.50
☐ 99 Johnny Mize and 100 Dan Litwhiler	50.00	25.00	5.00
☐ 101 Dom Dallesandro and 102 Augie Galan	32.00	16.00	3.20
☐ 103 Bill Lee and 104 Phil Cavarretta	32.00	16.00	3.20
☐ 105 Lefty Grove and 106 Bobby Doerr	175.00	85.00	18.00
☐ 107 Frank Pytlak and 108 Dom DiMaggio	40.00	20.00	4.00
☐ 109 Jerry Priddy and 110 Johnny Murphy	32.00	16.00	3.20
☐ 111 Tommy Henrich and 112 Marius Russo	40.00	20.00	4.00
☐ 113 Frank Crosetti and 114 John Sturm	40.00	20.00	4.00

☐ 115 Ival Goodman and 116 Myron McCormick	32.00	16.00	3.20
☐ 117 Eddie Joost and 118 Ernie Koy	32.00	16.00	3.20
☐ 119 Lloyd Waner and 120 Hank Majeski	50.00	25.00	5.00
☐ 121 Buddy Hassett and 122 Eugene Moore	32.00	16.00	3.20
☐ 123 Nick Etten and 124 John Rizzo	32.00	16.00	3.20
☐ 125 Sam Chapman and 126 Wally Moses	32.00	16.00	3.20
☐ 127 Johnny Babich and 128 Dick Siebert	32.00	16.00	3.20
☐ 129 Nelson Potter and 130 Benny McCoy	32.00	16.00	3.20
☐ 131 Clarence Campbell and 132 Lou Boudreau	50.00	25.00	5.00
☐ 133 Rollie Hemsley and 134 Mel Harder	40.00	20.00	4.00
☐ 135 Gerald Walker and 136 Joe Heving	32.00	16.00	3.20
☐ 137 Johnny Rucker and 138 Ace Adams	32.00	16.00	3.20
☐ 139 Morris Arnovich and 140 Carl Hubbell	80.00	40.00	8.00
☐ 141 Lew Riggs and 142 Leo Durocher	50.00	25.00	5.00
☐ 143 Fred Fitzsimmons and 144 Joe Vosmik	32.00	16.00	3.20
☐ 145 Frank Crespi and 146 Jim Brown	32.00	16.00	3.20
☐ 147 Don Heffner and 148 Harland Clift	32.00	16.00	3.20
☐ 149 Debs Garms and 150 Elbert Fletcher	32.00	16.00	3.20

1950 Drake's

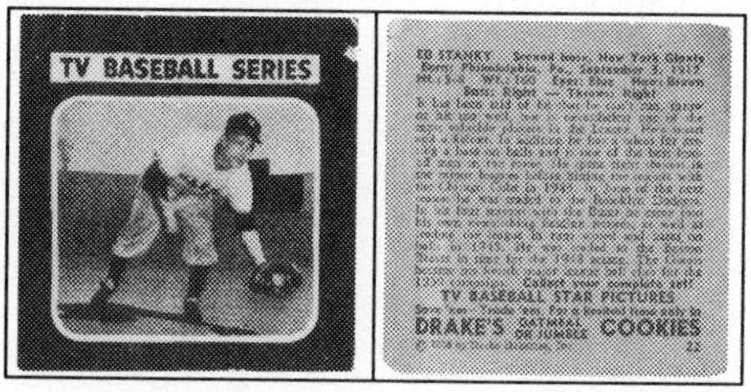

The cards in this 36-card set measure approximately 2 1/2" by 2 1/2". The 1950 Drake's Cookies set contains numbered black and white cards. The players are pictured inside a simulated television screen and the caption "TV Baseball Series" appears on the cards. The players selected for this set show a heavy representation of players from New York teams. The catalog designation for this set is D358.

	NRMT	VG-E	GOOD
COMPLETE SET (36)	3200.00	1500.00	350.00
COMMON PLAYER (1-36)	50.00	25.00	5.00
☐ 1 Preacher Roe	65.00	32.50	6.50
☐ 2 Clint Hartung	50.00	25.00	5.00
☐ 3 Earl Torgeson	50.00	25.00	5.00
☐ 4 Lou Brissie	50.00	25.00	5.00
☐ 5 Duke Snider	275.00	135.00	27.00
☐ 6 Roy Campanella	325.00	160.00	32.00
☐ 7 Sheldon Jones	50.00	25.00	5.00
☐ 8 Whitey Lockman	50.00	25.00	5.00
☐ 9 Bobby Thomson	65.00	32.50	6.50
☐ 10 Dick Sisler	50.00	25.00	5.00
☐ 11 Gil Hodges	150.00	75.00	15.00
☐ 12 Eddie Waitkus	50.00	25.00	5.00
☐ 13 Bobby Doerr	50.00	25.00	5.00
☐ 14 Warren Spahn	210.00	100.00	20.00
☐ 15 Buddy Kerr	50.00	25.00	5.00
☐ 16 Sid Gordon	50.00	25.00	5.00
☐ 17 Willard Marshall	50.00	25.00	5.00
☐ 18 Carl Furillo	75.00	37.50	7.50
☐ 19 Pee Wee Reese	210.00	100.00	20.00
☐ 20 Alvin Dark	65.00	32.50	6.50
☐ 21 Del Ennis	50.00	25.00	5.00
☐ 22 Ed Stanky	55.00	27.50	5.50
☐ 23 Tom Henrich	65.00	32.50	6.50
☐ 24 Yogi Berra	325.00	160.00	32.00
☐ 25 Phil Rizzuto	180.00	90.00	18.00
☐ 26 Jerry Coleman	55.00	27.50	5.50
☐ 27 Joe Page	55.00	27.50	5.50
☐ 28 Allie Reynolds	65.00	32.50	6.50
☐ 29 Ray Scarborough	50.00	25.00	5.00
☐ 30 Birdie Tebbetts	50.00	25.00	5.00
☐ 31 Maurice McDermott	50.00	25.00	5.00
☐ 32 Johnny Pesky	50.00	25.00	5.00
☐ 33 Dom DiMaggio	75.00	37.50	7.50
☐ 34 Vern Stephens	55.00	27.50	5.50
☐ 35 Bob Elliott	50.00	25.00	5.00
☐ 36 Enos Slaughter	180.00	90.00	18.00

1981 Drake's

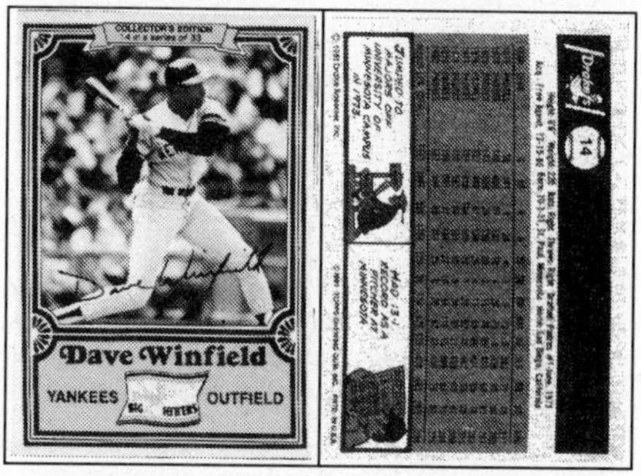

The cards in this 33-card set measure 2 1/2" by 3 1/2". The 1981 Drake's Bakeries set contains National and American League stars. Produced in conjunction with Topps and released to the public in Drake's Cakes, this set features red frames for American League players and blue frames for National League players. A Drake's Cakes logo with the words "Big Hitters" appears on the lower front of each card. The backs are quite similar to the 1981 Topps backs but contain the Drake's logo, a different card number, and a short paragraph entitled "What Makes a Big Hitter?" at the top of the card.

	MINT	EXC	G-VG
COMPLETE SET (33)	7.50	3.75	.75
COMMON PLAYER (1-33)	.05	.02	.00
☐ 1 Carl Yastrzemski	1.00	.50	.10
☐ 2 Rod Carew	.50	.25	.05
☐ 3 Pete Rose	1.00	.50	.10
☐ 4 Dave Parker	.25	.12	.02
☐ 5 George Brett	.75	.35	.07
☐ 6 Eddie Murray	.60	.30	.06
☐ 7 Mike Schmidt	1.00	.50	.10
☐ 8 Jim Rice	.25	.12	.02
☐ 9 Fred Lynn	.15	.07	.01
☐ 10 Reggie Jackson	.75	.35	.07
☐ 11 Steve Garvey	.45	.22	.04
☐ 12 Ken Singleton	.05	.02	.00
☐ 13 Bill Buckner	.05	.02	.00
☐ 14 Dave Winfield	.30	.15	.03
☐ 15 Jack Clark	.20	.10	.02
☐ 16 Cecil Cooper	.10	.05	.01
☐ 17 Bob Horner	.10	.05	.01
☐ 18 George Foster	.10	.05	.01
☐ 19 Dave Kingman	.10	.05	.01
☐ 20 Cesar Cedeno	.05	.02	.00
☐ 21 Joe Charboneau	.05	.02	.00
☐ 22 George Hendrick	.05	.02	.00
☐ 23 Gary Carter	.25	.12	.02
☐ 24 Al Oliver	.10	.05	.01
☐ 25 Bruce Bochte	.05	.02	.00
☐ 26 Jerry Mumphrey	.05	.02	.00
☐ 27 Steve Kemp	.05	.02	.00

	MINT	EXC	G-VG
☐ 28 Bob Watson	.05	.02	.00
☐ 29 John Castino	.05	.02	.00
☐ 30 Tony Armas	.05	.02	.00
☐ 31 John Mayberry	.05	.02	.00
☐ 32 Carlton Fisk	.30	.15	.03
☐ 33 Lee Mazzilli	.05	.02	.00

1982 Drake's

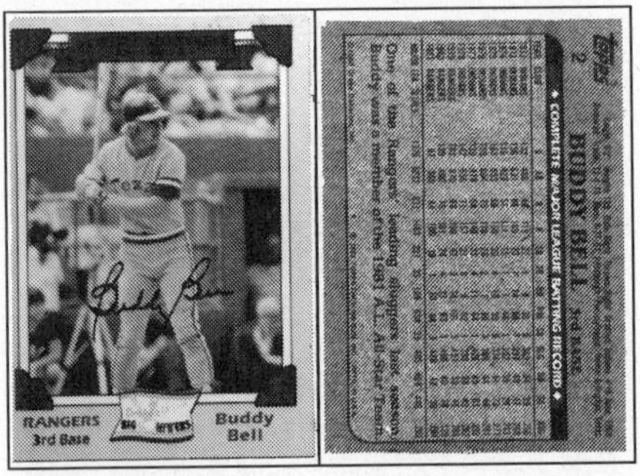

The cards in this 33-card set measure 2 1/2" by 3 1/2". The 1982 Drake's Big Hitters series cards each has the title "2nd Annual Collectors' Edition" in a ribbon design at the top of the picture area. Each color player photo has "photo mount" designs in the corners, red for the AL and green for the NL. The reverses are green and blue, the same as the regular 1982 Topps format, and the photos are larger than those of the previous year. Of the 33 hitters featured, 19 represent the National League. There are 21 returnees from the 1981 set and only one photo, that of Kennedy, is the same as that appearing in the regular Topps issue. The Drake's logo appears centered in the bottom border on the obverse.

	MINT	EXC	G-VG
COMPLETE SET (33)	8.00	4.00	.80
COMMON PLAYER (1-33)	.05	.02	.00
☐ 1 Tony Armas	.05	.02	.00
☐ 2 Buddy Bell	.10	.05	.01
☐ 3 Johnny Bench	.75	.35	.07
☐ 4 George Brett	.75	.35	.07
☐ 5 Bill Buckner	.05	.02	.00
☐ 6 Rod Carew	.50	.25	.05
☐ 7 Gary Carter	.30	.15	.03
☐ 8 Jack Clark	.20	.10	.02
☐ 9 Cecil Cooper	.10	.05	.01
☐ 10 Jose Cruz	.05	.02	.00
☐ 11 Dwight Evans	.15	.07	.01
☐ 12 Carlton Fisk	.30	.15	.03
☐ 13 George Foster	.10	.05	.01
☐ 14 Steve Garvey	.45	.22	.04
☐ 15 Kirk Gibson	.40	.20	.04
☐ 16 Mike Hargrove	.10	.05	.01
☐ 17 George Hendrick	.05	.02	.00
☐ 18 Bob Horner	.15	.07	.01
☐ 19 Reggie Jackson	.75	.35	.07
☐ 20 Terry Kennedy	.05	.02	.00
☐ 21 Dave Kingman	.10	.05	.01
☐ 22 Greg Luzinski	.10	.05	.01
☐ 23 Bill Madlock	.05	.02	.00
☐ 24 John Mayberry	.05	.02	.00
☐ 25 Eddie Murray	.50	.25	.05
☐ 26 Graig Nettles	.10	.05	.01
☐ 27 Jim Rice	.25	.12	.02
☐ 28 Pete Rose	.80	.40	.08
☐ 29 Mike Schmidt	1.00	.50	.10
☐ 30 Ken Singleton	.05	.02	.00
☐ 31 Dave Winfield	.30	.15	.03
☐ 32 Butch Wynegar	.05	.02	.00
☐ 33 Richie Zisk	.05	.02	.00

1983 Drake's

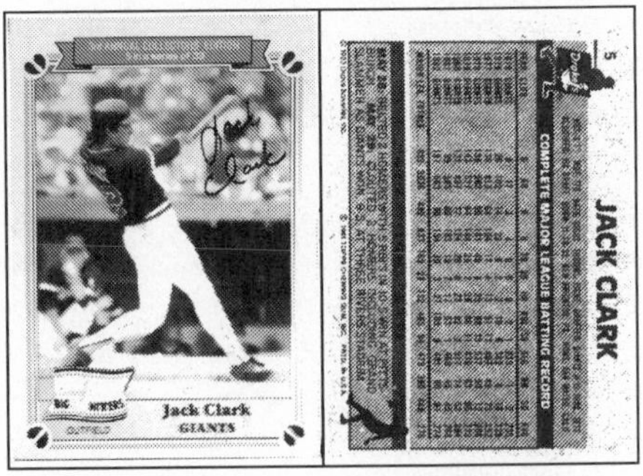

The cards in this 33-card series measure 2 1/2" by 3 1/2". For the third year in a row, Drake's Cakes, in conjunction with Topps, issued a set entitled Big Hitters. The fronts appear very similar to those of the previous two years with slight variations on the framelines and player identification sections. The backs are the same as the Topps backs of this year except for the card number and the Drake's logo.

	MINT	EXC	G-VG
COMPLETE SET (33)	6.00	3.00	.60
COMMON PLAYER (1-33)	.05	.02	.00
☐ 1 Don Baylor	.10	.05	.01
☐ 2 Bill Buckner	.10	.05	.01
☐ 3 Rod Carew	.40	.20	.04
☐ 4 Gary Carter	.30	.15	.03
☐ 5 Jack Clark	.20	.10	.02
☐ 6 Cecil Cooper	.10	.05	.01
☐ 7 Dwight Evans	.15	.07	.01
☐ 8 George Foster	.10	.05	.01
☐ 9 Pedro Guerrero	.20	.10	.02
☐ 10 George Hendrick	.05	.02	.00
☐ 11 Bob Horner	.15	.07	.01
☐ 12 Reggie Jackson	.65	.30	.06
☐ 13 Steve Kemp	.05	.02	.00
☐ 14 Dave Kingman	.10	.05	.01
☐ 15 Bill Madlock	.05	.02	.00
☐ 16 Gary Matthews	.05	.02	.00
☐ 17 Hal McRae	.05	.02	.00
☐ 18 Dale Murphy	.50	.25	.05
☐ 19 Eddie Murray	.50	.25	.05
☐ 20 Ben Oglivie	.05	.02	.00
☐ 21 Al Oliver	.10	.05	.01
☐ 22 Jim Rice	.25	.12	.02
☐ 23 Cal Ripken	.40	.20	.04
☐ 24 Pete Rose	.90	.45	.09
☐ 25 Mike Schmidt	1.00	.50	.10
☐ 26 Ken Singleton	.05	.02	.00
☐ 27 Gorman Thomas	.05	.02	.00
☐ 28 Jason Thompson	.05	.02	.00
☐ 29 Mookie Wilson	.10	.05	.01
☐ 30 Willie Wilson	.10	.05	.01
☐ 31 Dave Winfield	.35	.17	.03
☐ 32 Carl Yastrzemski	.90	.45	.09
☐ 33 Robin Yount	.60	.30	.06

1984 Drake's

The cards in this 33-card set measure 2 1/2" by 3 1/2". The Fourth Annual Collectors Edition of baseball cards produced by Drake's Cakes in conjunction with Topps continued this now annual set entitled Big Hitters. As in previous years, the front contains a frameline in which the title of the set, the Drake's logo, and the player's name, his team, and position appear. The cards all feature the player in a batting action pose. While the cards fronts are different from the Topps fronts of this year, the backs differ only in the card number and the use of the Drake's logo instead of the Topps logo.

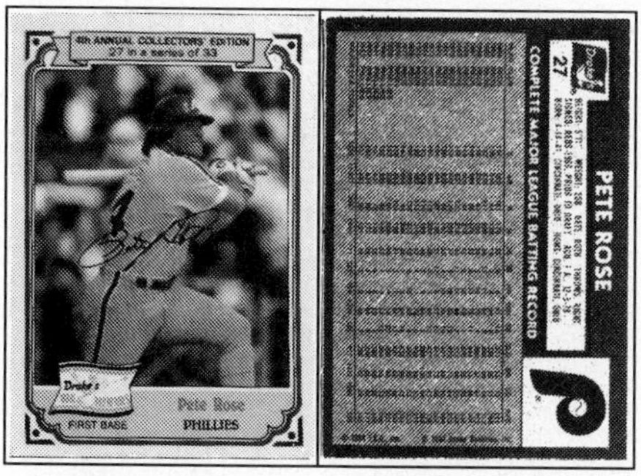

	MINT	EXC	G-VG
COMPLETE SET (33)	7.50	3.75	.75
COMMON PLAYER (1-33)	.05	.02	.00
☐ 1 Don Baylor	.10	.05	.01
☐ 2 Wade Boggs	1.00	.50	.10
☐ 3 George Brett	.75	.35	.07
☐ 4 Bill Buckner	.05	.02	.00
☐ 5 Rod Carew	.40	.20	.04
☐ 6 Gary Carter	.30	.15	.03
☐ 7 Ron Cey	.05	.02	.00
☐ 8 Cecil Cooper	.10	.05	.01
☐ 9 Andre Dawson	.30	.15	.03
☐ 10 Steve Garvey	.40	.20	.04
☐ 11 Pedro Guerrero	.20	.10	.02
☐ 12 George Hendrick	.05	.02	.00
☐ 13 Keith Hernandez	.20	.10	.02
☐ 14 Bob Horner	.15	.07	.01
☐ 15 Reggie Jackson	.60	.30	.06
☐ 16 Steve Kemp	.05	.02	.00
☐ 17 Ron Kittle	.10	.05	.01
☐ 18 Greg Luzinski	.10	.05	.01
☐ 19 Fred Lynn	.10	.05	.01
☐ 20 Bill Madlock	.05	.02	.00
☐ 21 Gary Matthews	.05	.02	.00
☐ 22 Dale Murphy	.50	.25	.05
☐ 23 Eddie Murray	.45	.22	.04
☐ 24 Al Oliver	.10	.05	.01
☐ 25 Jim Rice	.20	.10	.02
☐ 26 Cal Ripken	.40	.20	.04
☐ 27 Pete Rose	.90	.45	.09
☐ 28 Mike Schmidt	1.00	.50	.10
☐ 29 Darryl Strawberry	1.50	.75	.15
☐ 30 Alan Trammell	.20	.10	.02
☐ 31 Mookie Wilson	.05	.02	.00
☐ 32 Dave Winfield	.30	.15	.03
☐ 33 Robin Yount	.60	.30	.06

1985 Drake's

The cards in this 44-card set measure 2 1/2" by 3 1/2". The Fifth Annual Collectors Edition of baseball cards produced by Drake's Cakes in conjunction with Topps continued this apparently annual set with a new twist, for the first time, 11 pitchers were included. The "Big Hitters" are numbered 1-33 and the pitchers are numbered 34-44; each subgroup is ordered alphabetically. The cards are numbered in the upper right corner of the backs of the cards. The complete set could be obtained directly from the company by sending 2.95 with four proofs of purchase.

	MINT	EXC	G-VG
COMPLETE SET (44)	12.50	6.25	1.25
COMMON PLAYER (1-33)	.05	.02	.00
COMMON PLAYER (34-44)	.10	.05	.01
☐ 1 Tony Armas	.05	.02	.00
☐ 2 Harold Baines	.10	.05	.01
☐ 3 Don Baylor	.10	.05	.01
☐ 4 George Brett	.75	.35	.07
☐ 5 Gary Carter	.30	.15	.03
☐ 6 Ron Cey	.05	.02	.00
☐ 7 Jose Cruz	.05	.02	.00
☐ 8 Alvin Davis	.15	.07	.01
☐ 9 Chili Davis	.05	.02	.00
☐ 10 Dwight Evans	.15	.07	.01
☐ 11 Steve Garvey	.40	.20	.04
☐ 12 Kirk Gibson	.35	.17	.03
☐ 13 Pedro Guerrero	.20	.10	.02
☐ 14 Tony Gwynn	.45	.22	.04
☐ 15 Keith Hernandez	.20	.10	.02
☐ 16 Kent Hrbek	.20	.10	.02
☐ 17 Reggie Jackson	.65	.30	.06
☐ 18 Gary Matthews	.05	.02	.00
☐ 19 Don Mattingly	1.25	.60	.12
☐ 20 Dale Murphy	.50	.25	.05
☐ 21 Eddie Murray	.45	.22	.04
☐ 22 Dave Parker	.20	.10	.02
☐ 23 Lance Parrish	.10	.05	.01
☐ 24 Tim Raines	.25	.12	.02
☐ 25 Jim Rice	.20	.10	.02
☐ 26 Cal Ripken	.45	.22	.04
☐ 27 Juan Samuel	.15	.07	.01
☐ 28 Ryne Sandberg	1.00	.50	.10
☐ 29 Mike Schmidt	1.00	.50	.10
☐ 30 Darryl Strawberry	1.00	.50	.10
☐ 31 Alan Trammell	.25	.12	.02
☐ 32 Dave Winfield	.30	.15	.03
☐ 33 Robin Yount	.50	.25	.05
☐ 34 Mike Boddicker	.10	.05	.01
☐ 35 Steve Carlton	.35	.17	.03
☐ 36 Dwight Gooden	1.00	.50	.10
☐ 37 Willie Hernandez	.10	.05	.01
☐ 38 Mark Langston	.25	.12	.02
☐ 39 Dan Quisenberry	.10	.05	.01
☐ 40 Dave Righetti	.15	.07	.01
☐ 41 Tom Seaver	.40	.20	.04
☐ 42 Bob Stanley	.10	.05	.01
☐ 43 Rick Sutcliffe	.10	.05	.01
☐ 44 Bruce Sutter	.15	.07	.01

1986 Drake's

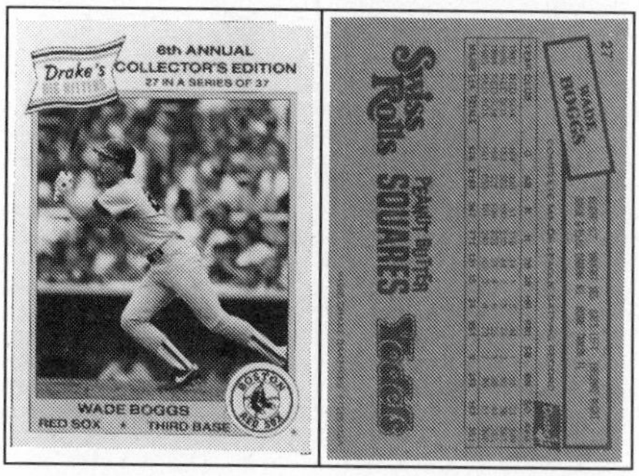

This set of 37 cards was distributed as back panels of various Drake's snack products. Each individual card measures 2 1/2" by 3 1/2". Each specially marked package features two, three, or four cards on the back. The set is easily recognized by the Drake's logo and "6th Annual Collector's Edition" at the top of the obverse. Cards are numbered on the front and the back. Cards below are coded based on the product upon which they appeared, for example, Apple Pies (AP), Cherry Pies (CP), Chocolate Donut Delites (CDD), Coffee Cake Jr. (CCJ), Creme Shortcakes (CS), Devil Dogs (DD), Fudge Brownies (FUD), Funny Bones (FB), Peanut Butter Squares (PBS), Powdered Sugar Donut Delites (PSDD), Ring Ding Jr. (RDJ), Sunny Doodles (SD), Swiss Rolls (SR), Yankee Doodles (YD), and Yodels (Y). The last nine cards are pitchers. Complete panels would be valued approximately 25 percent higher than the individual card prices listed below.

	MINT	EXC	G-VG
COMPLETE SET (37)	33.00	15.00	3.00
COMMON PLAYER (1-37)	.30	.15	.03
☐ 1 Gary Carter Y	.50	.25	.05
☐ 2 Dwight Evans Y	.40	.20	.04
☐ 3 Reggie Jackson SR	1.00	.50	.10
☐ 4 Dave Parker SR	.50	.25	.05
☐ 5 Rickey Henderson FB	1.50	.75	.15
☐ 6 Pedro Guerrero FB	.40	.20	.04
☐ 7 Don Mattingly YD	3.00	1.50	.30
☐ 8 Mike Marshall YD	.40	.20	.04
☐ 9 Keith Moreland YD	.30	.15	.03
☐ 10 Keith Hernandez CS	.50	.25	.05
☐ 11 Cal Ripken CS	.90	.45	.09
☐ 12 Dale Murphy RDJ	.90	.45	.09
☐ 13 Jim Rice RDJ	.40	.20	.04
☐ 14 George Brett CCJ	1.00	.50	.10
☐ 15 Tim Raines CCJ	.60	.30	.06
☐ 16 Darryl Strawberry DD	1.25	.60	.12
☐ 17 Bill Buckner DD	.30	.15	.03
☐ 18 Dave Winfield AP	.50	.25	.05
☐ 19 Ryne Sandberg AP	1.25	.60	.12
☐ 20 Steve Balboni AP	.30	.15	.03
☐ 21 Tommy Herr AP	.30	.15	.03
☐ 22 Pete Rose CP	1.25	.60	.12
☐ 23 Willie McGee CP	.40	.20	.04
☐ 24 Harold Baines CP	.40	.20	.04
☐ 25 Eddie Murray CP	.75	.35	.07
☐ 26 Mike Schmidt SD/FUD	1.50	.75	.15
☐ 27 Wade Boggs SD/FUD	2.00	1.00	.20
☐ 28 Kirk Gibson SD/FUD	.60	.30	.06
☐ 29 Bret Saberhagen PBS	.75	.35	.07
☐ 30 John Tudor PBS	.40	.20	.04
☐ 31 Orel Hershiser PBS	.75	.35	.07
☐ 32 Ron Guidry CDD	.40	.20	.04
☐ 33 Nolan Ryan CDD	3.00	1.50	.30
☐ 34 Dave Stieb CDD	.40	.20	.04
☐ 35 Dwight Gooden SDD	1.00	.50	.10
☐ 36 Fern.Valenzuela SDD	.50	.25	.05
☐ 37 Tom Browning SDD	.40	.20	.04

1987 Drake's

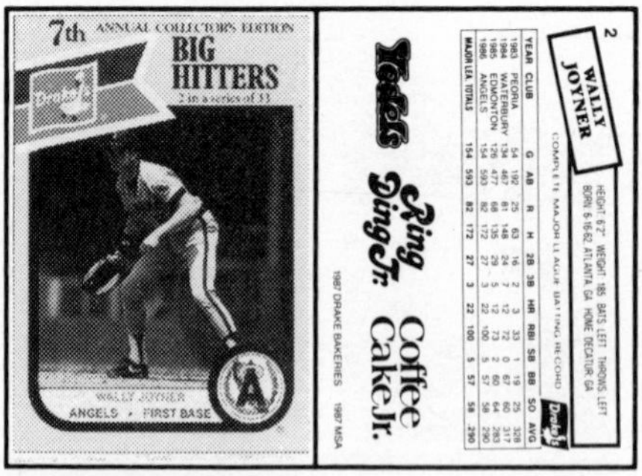

This 33-card set features 25 top hitters and eight top pitchers. Cards were printed in groups of two, three, or four on the backs of Drake's bakery products. Individual cards measure 2 1/2" by 3 1/2" and tout the 7th annual edition. Card backs feature year-by-year season statistics. The cards are numbered such that the pitchers are listed numerically last. Complete panels would be valued approximately 25 percent higher than the individual card prices listed below.

	MINT	EXC	G-VG
COMPLETE SET (33)	30.00	15.00	3.00
COMMON PLAYER (1-33)	.30	.15	.03
☐ 1 Darryl Strawberry	1.25	.60	.12
☐ 2 Wally Joyner	.90	.45	.09
☐ 3 Von Hayes	.40	.20	.04
☐ 4 Jose Canseco	2.50	1.25	.25
☐ 5 Dave Winfield	.60	.30	.06
☐ 6 Cal Ripken	.90	.45	.09
☐ 7 Keith Moreland	.30	.15	.03
☐ 8 Don Mattingly	2.50	1.25	.25
☐ 9 Willie McGee	.50	.25	.05
☐ 10 Keith Hernandez	.50	.25	.05
☐ 11 Tony Gwynn	.90	.45	.09
☐ 12 Rickey Henderson	1.50	.75	.15
☐ 13 Dale Murphy	1.00	.50	.10
☐ 14 George Brett	1.00	.50	.10
☐ 15 Jim Rice	.50	.25	.05
☐ 16 Wade Boggs	2.00	1.00	.20
☐ 17 Kevin Bass	.30	.15	.03
☐ 18 Dave Parker	.50	.25	.05
☐ 19 Kirby Puckett	1.00	.50	.10
☐ 20 Gary Carter	.50	.25	.05
☐ 21 Ryne Sandberg	1.25	.60	.12
☐ 22 Harold Baines	.40	.20	.04
☐ 23 Mike Schmidt	2.00	1.00	.20
☐ 24 Eddie Murray	.75	.35	.07
☐ 25 Steve Sax	.40	.20	.04
☐ 26 Dwight Gooden	.75	.35	.07
☐ 27 Jack Morris	.40	.20	.04
☐ 28 Ron Darling	.40	.20	.04
☐ 29 Fernando Valenzuela	.50	.25	.05
☐ 30 John Tudor	.40	.20	.04
☐ 31 Roger Clemens	1.00	.50	.10
☐ 32 Nolan Ryan	2.50	1.25	.25
☐ 33 Mike Scott	.50	.25	.05

1988 Drake's

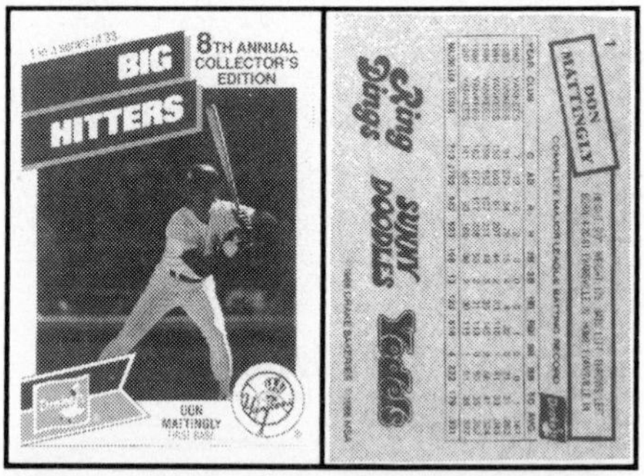

This 33-card set features 27 top hitters and six top pitchers. Cards were printed in groups of two, three, or four on the backs of Drake's bakery products. Individual cards measure approximately 2 1/2" by 3 1/2" and tout the 8th annual edition. Card backs feature year-by-year season statistics. The cards are numbered such that the pitchers are listed numerically last. The product affiliations are as follows, 1-2 Ring Dings, 3-4 Devil Dogs, 5-6 Coffee Cakes, 7-9 Yankee Doodles, 10-11 Funny Bones, 12-14 Fudge Brownies, 15-18 Cherry Pies, 19-21 Sunny Doodles, 22-24 Powdered Sugar Donuts, 25-27 Chocolate Donuts, 28-29 Yodels, and 30-33 Apple Pies. Complete panels would be valued approximately 25 percent higher than the individual card prices listed below.

	MINT	EXC	G-VG
COMPLETE SET (33)	30.00	15.00	3.00
COMMON PLAYER (1-33)	.30	.15	.03
☐ 1 Don Mattingly	2.50	1.25	.25

☐ 2 Tim Raines	.50	.25	.05
☐ 3 Darryl Strawberry	1.25	.60	.12
☐ 4 Wade Boggs	2.00	1.00	.20
☐ 5 Keith Hernandez	.50	.25	.05
☐ 6 Mark McGwire	1.00	.50	.10
☐ 7 Rickey Henderson	1.25	.60	.12
☐ 8 Mike Schmidt	2.00	1.00	.20
☐ 9 Dwight Evans	.40	.20	.04
☐ 10 Gary Carter	.50	.25	.05
☐ 11 Paul Molitor	.40	.20	.04
☐ 12 Dave Winfield	.60	.30	.06
☐ 13 Alan Trammell	.50	.25	.05
☐ 14 Tony Gwynn	.75	.35	.07
☐ 15 Dale Murphy	.90	.45	.09
☐ 16 Andre Dawson	.50	.25	.05
☐ 17 Von Hayes	.40	.20	.04
☐ 18 Willie Randolph	.30	.15	.03
☐ 19 Kirby Puckett	1.00	.50	.10
☐ 20 Juan Samuel	.30	.15	.03
☐ 21 Eddie Murray	.90	.45	.09
☐ 22 George Bell	.40	.20	.04
☐ 23 Larry Sheets	.30	.15	.03
☐ 24 Eric Davis	.90	.45	.09
☐ 25 Cal Ripken	.75	.35	.07
☐ 26 Pedro Guerrero	.40	.20	.04
☐ 27 Will Clark	2.00	1.00	.20
☐ 28 Dwight Gooden	.90	.45	.09
☐ 29 Frank Viola	.50	.25	.05
☐ 30 Roger Clemens	.90	.45	.09
☐ 31 Rick Sutcliffe	.40	.20	.04
☐ 32 Jack Morris	.40	.20	.04
☐ 33 John Tudor	.40	.20	.04

1966 East Hills Pirates

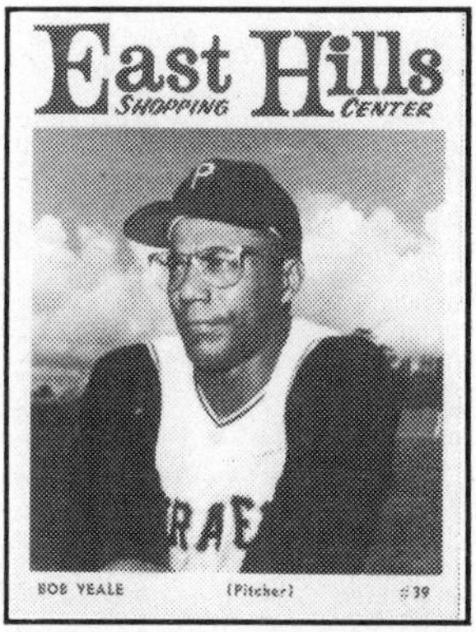

The 1966 East Hills Pirates set consists of 25 large (approximately 3 1/4" by 4 1/4"), full color photos of Pittsburgh Pirate ballplayers. These blank-backed cards are numbered in the lower right corner according to the uniform number of the individual depicted. The set was distributed by various stores located in the East Hills Shopping Center. The catalog number for this set is F405.

	NRMT	VG-E	GOOD
COMPLETE SET (25)	32.00	16.00	3.20
COMMON PLAYER (1-45)	.40	.20	.04
☐ 3 Harry Walker MG	.50	.25	.05
☐ 7 Bob Bailey	.40	.20	.04
☐ 8 Willie Stargell	8.00	4.00	.80
☐ 9 Bill Mazeroski	2.50	1.25	.25
☐ 10 Jim Pagliaroni	.40	.20	.04
☐ 11 Jose Pagan	.40	.20	.04
☐ 12 Jerry May	.40	.20	.04
☐ 14 Gene Alley	.75	.35	.07
☐ 15 Manny Mota	.75	.35	.07
☐ 16 Andy Rodgers	.40	.20	.04
☐ 17 Donn Clendenon	.75	.35	.07
☐ 18 Matty Alou	1.00	.50	.10
☐ 19 Pete Mikkelsen	.40	.20	.04
☐ 20 Jesse Gonder	.40	.20	.04

☐ 21 Bob Clemente	16.00	8.00	1.60
☐ 22 Woody Fryman	.40	.20	.04
☐ 24 Jerry Lynch	.40	.20	.04
☐ 25 Tommie Sisk	.40	.20	.04
☐ 26 Roy Face	1.25	.60	.12
☐ 28 Steve Blass	.75	.35	.07
☐ 32 Vernon Law	1.00	.50	.10
☐ 34 Al McBean	.40	.20	.04
☐ 39 Bob Veale	.75	.35	.07
☐ 43 Don Cardwell	.40	.20	.04
☐ 45 Gene Michael	.60	.30	.06

1990 Elite Senior League

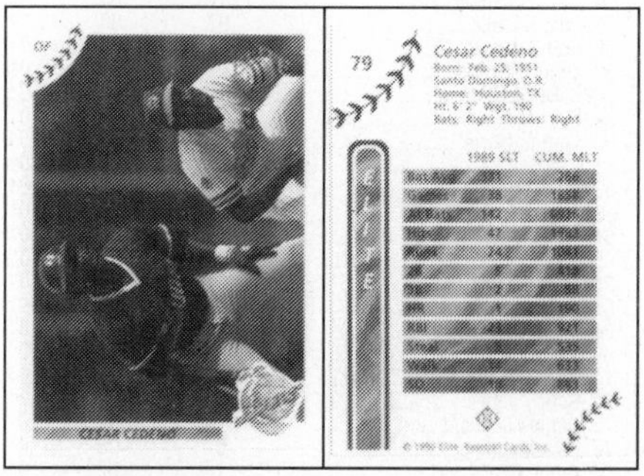

The 1990 Elite Senior Pro League Set was a 126-card set issued after the conclusion of the first Senior League season. The card stock was essentially the same type of card stock used by Upper Deck. The set featured full-color fronts and had complete Senior League stats on the back. This set is standard size, 2 1/2" by 3 1/2". It has been reported that there were 5,000 cases of these cards produced. Prior to the debut of the set, Elite also passed out (to prospective dealers) two promo cards for the set, Earl Weaver (numbered 120 rather than 91) and Mike Easler (numbered 1 rather than 19).

	MINT	EXC	G-VG
COMPLETE SET (126)	9.00	4.50	.90
COMMON PLAYER (1-126)	.07	.03	.01
☐ 1 Curt Flood	.35	.17	.03
☐ 2 Bob Tolan	.10	.05	.01
☐ 3 Dick Bosman	.07	.03	.01
☐ 4 Ivan DeJesus	.07	.03	.01
☐ 5 Dock Ellis	.07	.03	.01
☐ 6 Roy Howell	.07	.03	.01
☐ 7 Lamar Johnson	.07	.03	.01
☐ 8 Steve Kemp	.10	.05	.01
☐ 9 Ken Landreaux	.10	.05	.01
☐ 10 Randy Lerch	.07	.03	.01
☐ 11 Jon Matlack	.10	.05	.01
☐ 12 Gary Rajsich	.07	.03	.01
☐ 13 Lenny Randle	.07	.03	.01
☐ 14 Elias Sosa	.07	.03	.01
☐ 15 Ozzie Virgil	.07	.03	.01
☐ 16 Milt Wilcox	.07	.03	.01
☐ 17 Steve Henderson 3X	.10	.05	.01
☐ 18 Ray Burris	.10	.05	.01
☐ 19 Mike Easler	.07	.03	.01
☐ 20 Juan Eichelberger	.07	.03	.01
☐ 21 Rollie Fingers	.75	.35	.07
☐ 22 Toby Harrah	.10	.05	.01
☐ 23 Randy Johnson	.07	.03	.01
☐ 24 Dave Kingman	.35	.17	.03
☐ 25 Lee Lacy	.07	.03	.01
☐ 26 Tito Landrum	.10	.05	.01
☐ 27 Paul Mirabella	.07	.03	.01
☐ 28 Mickey Rivers	.15	.07	.01
☐ 29 Rodney Scott	.07	.03	.01
☐ 30 Tim Stoddard	.07	.03	.01
☐ 31 Ron Washington	.07	.03	.01
☐ 32 Jerry White	.07	.03	.01
☐ 33 Dick Williams	.10	.05	.01
☐ 34 Clete Boyer	.10	.05	.01
☐ 35 Steve Dillard	.07	.03	.01

☐ 36 Garth Iorg	.07	.03	.01
☐ 37 Bruce Kison	.07	.03	.01
☐ 38 Wayne Krenchicki	.07	.03	.01
☐ 39 Ron LeFlore	.10	.05	.01
☐ 40 Tippy Martinez	.07	.03	.01
☐ 41 Omar Moreno	.07	.03	.01
☐ 42 Jim Morrison	.07	.03	.01
☐ 43 Graig Nettles	.20	.10	.02
☐ 44 Jim Nettles	.07	.03	.01
☐ 45 Wayne Nordhagen	.07	.03	.01
☐ 46 Al Oliver	.20	.10	.02
☐ 47 Jerry Royster	.07	.03	.01
☐ 48 Sammy Stewart	.07	.03	.01
☐ 49 Randy Bass	.10	.05	.01
☐ 50 Vida Blue	.15	.07	.01
☐ 51 Bruce Bochy	.07	.03	.01
☐ 52 Doug Corbett	.07	.03	.01
☐ 53 Jose Cruz	.15	.07	.01
☐ 54 Jamie Easterly	.07	.03	.01
☐ 55 Pete Falcone	.07	.03	.01
☐ 56 Bob Galasso	.07	.03	.01
☐ 57 Johnny Grubb	.07	.03	.01
☐ 58 Bake McBride	.07	.03	.01
☐ 59 Dyar Miller	.07	.03	.01
☐ 60 Tom Paciorek	.07	.03	.01
☐ 61 Ken Reitz	.07	.03	.01
☐ 62 U.L. Washington	.07	.03	.01
☐ 63 Alan Ashby	.07	.03	.01
☐ 64 Pat Dobson	.10	.05	.01
☐ 65 Doug Bird	.07	.03	.01
☐ 66 Marty Castillo	.07	.03	.01
☐ 67 Dan Driessen	.10	.05	.01
☐ 68 Wayne Garland	.07	.03	.01
☐ 69 Tim Ireland	.07	.03	.01
☐ 70 Ron Jackson	.07	.03	.01
☐ 71 Bobby Jones	.07	.03	.01
☐ 72 Dennis Leonard	.10	.05	.01
☐ 73 Rick Manning	.07	.03	.01
☐ 74 Amos Otis	.15	.07	.01
☐ 75 Pat Putnam	.07	.03	.01
☐ 76 Eric Rasmussen	.07	.03	.01
☐ 77 Paul Blair	.10	.05	.01
☐ 78 Bert Campaneris	.10	.05	.01
☐ 79 Cesar Cedeno	.15	.07	.01
☐ 80 Ed Figueroa	.07	.03	.01
☐ 81 Ross Grimsley	.07	.03	.01
☐ 82 George Hendrick	.10	.05	.01
☐ 83 Cliff Johnson	.07	.03	.01
☐ 84 Mike Kekich	.07	.03	.01
☐ 85 Rafael Landestoy	.07	.03	.01
☐ 86 Larry Milbourne	.07	.03	.01
☐ 87 Bobby Molinaro	.07	.03	.01
☐ 88 Sid Monge	.07	.03	.01
☐ 89 Rennie Stennett	.07	.03	.01
☐ 90 Derrell Thomas	.07	.03	.01
☐ 91 Earl Weaver	.25	.12	.02
☐ 92 Gary Allenson	.07	.03	.01
☐ 93 Pedro Borbon	.07	.03	.01
☐ 94 Al Bumbry	.10	.05	.01
☐ 95 Bill Campbell	.07	.03	.01
☐ 96 Bernie Carbo	.07	.03	.01
☐ 97 Fergie Jenkins	.50	.25	.05
☐ 98 Pete LaCock	.07	.03	.01
☐ 99 Bill Lee	.10	.05	.01
☐ 100 Tommy McMillan	.07	.03	.01
☐ 101 Joe Pittman	.07	.03	.01
☐ 102 Gene Richards	.07	.03	.01
☐ 103 Leon Roberts	.07	.03	.01
☐ 104 Tony Scott	.07	.03	.01
☐ 105 Doug Simunic	.07	.03	.01
☐ 106 Rick Wise	.10	.05	.01
☐ 107 Willie Aikens	.10	.05	.01
☐ 108 Juan Beniquez	.10	.05	.01
☐ 109 Bobby Bonds	.25	.12	.02
☐ 110 Sergio Ferrer	.07	.03	.01
☐ 111 Chuck Ficks	.07	.03	.01
☐ 112 George Foster	.20	.10	.02
☐ 113 Dave Hilton	.07	.03	.01
☐ 114 Al Holland	.07	.03	.01
☐ 115 Clint Hurdle	.10	.05	.01
☐ 116 Bill Madlock	.15	.07	.01
☐ 117 Steve Ontiveros	.07	.03	.01
☐ 118 Roy Thomas	.07	.03	.01
☐ 119 Luis Tiant	.15	.07	.01
☐ 120 Walt Williams	.10	.05	.01
☐ 121 Vida Blue	.15	.07	.01
☐ 122 Bobby Bonds	.25	.12	.02
☐ 123 Rollie Fingers	.75	.35	.07
☐ 124 George Foster	.40	.20	.04
☐ 125 Fergie Jenkins	.50	.25	.05
☐ 126 Dave Kingman	.40	.20	.04

1959 Fleer

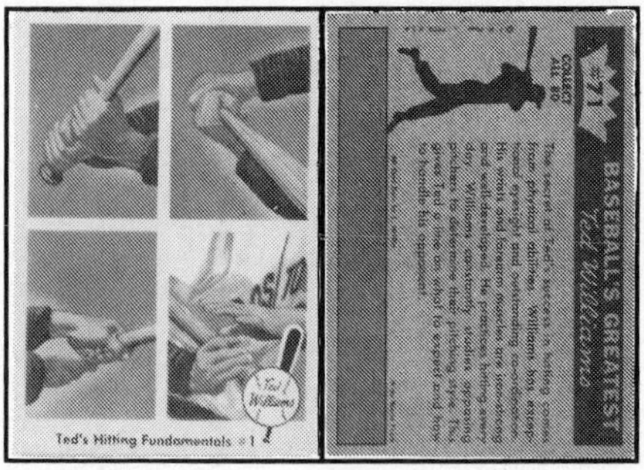

The cards in this 80-card set measure 2 1/2" by 3 1/2". The 1959 Fleer set, with a catalog designation of R418-1, portrays the life of Ted Williams. The wording of the wrapper, "Baseball's Greatest Series," has led to speculation that Fleer contemplated similar sets honoring other baseball immortals, but chose to develop instead the format of the 1960 and 1961 issues. Card number 68, which was withdrawn early in production, is considered scarce and has even been counterfeited; the fake has a rosy coloration and a cross-hatch pattern visible over the picture area.

	NRMT	VG-E	GOOD
COMPLETE SET (80)	900.00	450.00	90.00
COMMON CARDS (1-80)	5.00	2.50	.50
☐ 1 The Early Years	25.00	3.00	.60
☐ 2 Ted's Idol Babe Ruth	20.00	10.00	2.00
☐ 3 Practice Makes Perfect	5.00	2.50	.50
☐ 4 Learns Fine Points	5.00	2.50	.50
☐ 5 Ted's Fame Spreads	5.00	2.50	.50
☐ 6 Ted Turns Pro	5.00	2.50	.50
☐ 7 From Mound to Plate	5.00	2.50	.50
☐ 8 1937 First Full Season	5.00	2.50	.50
☐ 9 First Step to Majors	5.00	2.50	.50
☐ 10 Gunning as Pastime	5.00	2.50	.50
☐ 11 First Spring Training (with Jimmie Foxx)	10.00	5.00	1.00
☐ 12 Burning Up Minors	5.00	2.50	.50
☐ 13 1939 Shows Will Stay	5.00	2.50	.50
☐ 14 Outstanding Rookie '39	5.00	2.50	.50
☐ 15 Licks Sophomore Jinx	5.00	2.50	.50
☐ 16 1941 Greatest Year	5.00	2.50	.50
☐ 17 How Ted Hit .400	5.00	2.50	.50
☐ 18 1941 All Star Hero	5.00	2.50	.50
☐ 19 Ted Wins Triple Crown	5.00	2.50	.50
☐ 20 On to Naval Training	5.00	2.50	.50
☐ 21 Honors for Williams	5.00	2.50	.50
☐ 22 1944 Ted Solos	5.00	2.50	.50
☐ 23 Williams Wins Wings	5.00	2.50	.50
☐ 24 1945 Sharpshooter	5.00	2.50	.50
☐ 25 1945 Ted Discharged	5.00	2.50	.50
☐ 26 Off to Flying Start	5.00	2.50	.50
☐ 27 7/9/46 One Man Show	5.00	2.50	.50
☐ 28 The Williams Shift	5.00	2.50	.50
☐ 29 Ted Hits for Cycle	5.00	2.50	.50
☐ 30 Beating Williams Shift	5.00	2.50	.50
☐ 31 Sox Lose Series	5.00	2.50	.50
☐ 32 Most Valuable Player	5.00	2.50	.50
☐ 33 Another Triple Crown	5.00	2.50	.50
☐ 34 Runs Scored Record	5.00	2.50	.50
☐ 35 Sox Miss Pennant	5.00	2.50	.50
☐ 36 Banner Year for Ted	5.00	2.50	.50
☐ 37 1949 Sox Miss Again	5.00	2.50	.50
☐ 38 1949 Power Rampage	5.00	2.50	.50
☐ 39 1950 Great Start	5.00	2.50	.50
☐ 40 Ted Crashes into Wall	5.00	2.50	.50
☐ 41 1950 Ted Recovers	5.00	2.50	.50
☐ 42 Slowed by Injury	5.00	2.50	.50
☐ 43 Double Play Lead	5.00	2.50	.50
☐ 44 Back to Marines	5.00	2.50	.50
☐ 45 Farewell to Baseball	5.00	2.50	.50
☐ 46 Ready for Combat	5.00	2.50	.50

☐ 47 Ted Crash Lands Jet	5.00	2.50	.50
☐ 48 1953 Ted Returns	5.00	2.50	.50
☐ 49 Smash Return	5.00	2.50	.50
☐ 50 1954 Spring Injury	5.00	2.50	.50
☐ 51 Ted is Patched Up	5.00	2.50	.50
☐ 52 1954 Ted's Comeback	5.00	2.50	.50
☐ 53 Comeback is Success	5.00	2.50	.50
☐ 54 Ted Hooks Big One	5.00	2.50	.50
☐ 55 Retirement "No Go"	5.00	2.50	.50
☐ 56 2000th Hit	5.00	2.50	.50
☐ 57 400th Homer	5.00	2.50	.50
☐ 58 Williams Hits .388	5.00	2.50	.50
☐ 59 Hot September for Ted	5.00	2.50	.50
☐ 60 More Records for Ted	5.00	2.50	.50
☐ 61 1957 Outfielder Ted	5.00	2.50	.50
☐ 62 1958 Sixth Batting Title	5.00	2.50	.50
☐ 63 Ted's All-Star Record	5.00	2.50	.50
☐ 64 Daughter and Daddy	5.00	2.50	.50
☐ 65 1958 August 30	5.00	2.50	.50
☐ 66 1958 Powerhouse	5.00	2.50	.50
☐ 67 Two Famous Fishermen	10.00	5.00	1.00
☐ 68 Ted Signs for 1959	500.00	250.00	50.00
☐ 69 A Future Ted Williams	5.00	2.50	.50
☐ 70 Williams and Thorpe	10.00	5.00	1.00
☐ 71 Hitting Fund. 1	5.00	2.50	.50
☐ 72 Hitting Fund. 2	5.00	2.50	.50
☐ 73 Hitting Fund. 3	5.00	2.50	.50
☐ 74 Here's How	5.00	2.50	.50
☐ 75 Williams' Value to Sox	5.00	2.50	.50
☐ 76 On Base Record	5.00	2.50	.50
☐ 77 Ted Relaxes	5.00	2.50	.50
☐ 78 Honors for Williams	5.00	2.50	.50
☐ 79 Where Ted Stands	5.00	2.50	.50
☐ 80 Ted's Goals for 1959	10.00	5.00	1.00

1960 Fleer

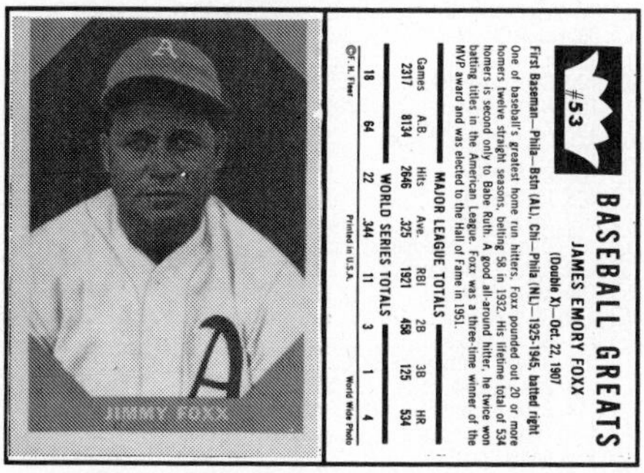

The cards in this 79-card set measure 2 1/2" by 3 1/2". The cards from the 1960 Fleer series of Baseball Greats are sometimes mistaken for 1930s cards by collectors not familiar with this set. The cards each contain a tinted photo of a baseball immortal, and were issued in one series. There are no known scarcities, although a number 80 card (Pepper Martin reverse with either Eddie Collins or Lefty Grove obverse) exists (this is not considered part of the set). The catalog designation for 1960 Fleer is R418-2. The cards were printed on a 96-card sheet with 17 double prints. These are noted in the checklist below by DP. On the sheet the second Eddie Collins card is typically found in the number 80 position.

	NRMT	VG-E	GOOD
COMPLETE SET (79)	350.00	175.00	35.00
COMMON PLAYER (1-79)	2.50	1.25	.25
COMMON PLAYER DP	1.75	.85	.17

☐ 1 Napoleon Lajoie DP	12.00	2.00	.40
☐ 2 Christy Mathewson	8.00	4.00	.80
☐ 3 George H. Ruth	65.00	32.50	6.50
☐ 4 Carl Hubbell	4.00	2.00	.40
☐ 5 Grover Alexander	4.00	2.00	.40
☐ 6 Walter Johnson DP	6.00	3.00	.60
☐ 7 Charles A. Bender	2.50	1.25	.25
☐ 8 Roger P. Bresnahan	2.50	1.25	.25
☐ 9 Mordecai P. Brown	2.50	1.25	.25
☐ 10 Tristram Speaker	4.00	2.00	.40
☐ 11 Arky Vaughan DP	1.75	.85	.17
☐ 12 Zachariah Wheat	2.50	1.25	.25
☐ 13 George Sisler	2.50	1.25	.25
☐ 14 Connie Mack	4.00	2.00	.40
☐ 15 Clark C. Griffith	2.50	1.25	.25
☐ 16 Louis Boudreau DP	3.50	1.75	.35
☐ 17 Ernest Lombardi	2.50	1.25	.25
☐ 18 Henry Manush	2.50	1.25	.25
☐ 19 Martin Marion	2.50	1.25	.25
☐ 20 Edward Collins DP	1.75	.85	.17
☐ 21 James Maranville DP	1.75	.85	.17
☐ 22 Joseph Medwick	2.50	1.25	.25
☐ 23 Edward Barrow	2.50	1.25	.25
☐ 24 Gordon Cochrane	3.50	1.75	.35
☐ 25 James J. Collins	2.50	1.25	.25
☐ 26 Robert Feller DP	9.00	4.50	.90
☐ 27 Lucius Appling	4.00	2.00	.40
☐ 28 Lou Gehrig	33.00	15.00	3.00
☐ 29 Charles Hartnett	2.50	1.25	.25
☐ 30 Charles Klein	2.50	1.25	.25
☐ 31 Anthony Lazzeri DP	1.75	.85	.17
☐ 32 Aloysius Simmons	2.50	1.25	.25
☐ 33 Wilbert Robinson	2.50	1.25	.25
☐ 34 Edgar Rice	2.50	1.25	.25
☐ 35 Herbert Pennock	2.50	1.25	.25
☐ 36 Melvin Ott DP	3.00	1.50	.30
☐ 37 Frank O'Doul	2.50	1.25	.25
☐ 38 John Mize	5.00	2.50	.50
☐ 39 Edmund Miller	2.50	1.25	.25
☐ 40 Joseph Tinker	2.50	1.25	.25
☐ 41 John Baker DP	1.75	.85	.17
☐ 42 Tyrus Cobb	33.00	15.00	3.00
☐ 43 Paul Derringer	2.50	1.25	.25
☐ 44 Adrian Anson	2.50	1.25	.25
☐ 45 James Bottomley	2.50	1.25	.25
☐ 46 Edward S. Plank DP	1.75	.85	.17
☐ 47 Denton (Cy) Young	6.00	3.00	.60
☐ 48 Hack Wilson	4.00	2.00	.40
☐ 49 Edward Walsh UER (photo actually Ed Walsh Jr.)	2.50	1.25	.25
☐ 50 Frank Chance	2.50	1.25	.25
☐ 51 Arthur Vance DP	1.75	.85	.17
☐ 52 William Terry	4.00	2.00	.40
☐ 53 James Foxx	6.00	3.00	.60
☐ 54 Vernon Gomez	4.00	2.00	.40
☐ 55 Branch Rickey	2.50	1.25	.25
☐ 56 Raymond Schalk DP	1.75	.85	.17
☐ 57 John Evers	2.50	1.25	.25
☐ 58 Charles Gehringer	4.00	2.00	.40
☐ 59 Burleigh Grimes	2.50	1.25	.25
☐ 60 Robert (Lefty) Grove	5.00	2.50	.50
☐ 61 George Waddell DP	1.75	.85	.17
☐ 62 John (Honus) Wagner	8.00	4.00	.80
☐ 63 Charles(Red) Ruffing	2.50	1.25	.25
☐ 64 Kenesaw M. Landis	2.50	1.25	.25
☐ 65 Harry Heilmann	2.50	1.25	.25
☐ 66 John McGraw DP	2.50	1.25	.25
☐ 67 Hugh Jennings	2.50	1.25	.25
☐ 68 Harold Newhouser	2.50	1.25	.25
☐ 69 Waite Hoyt	2.50	1.25	.25
☐ 70 Louis(Bobo) Newsom	2.50	1.25	.25
☐ 71 Earl Averill DP	1.75	.85	.17
☐ 72 Theodore Williams	50.00	25.00	5.00
☐ 73 Warren Giles	2.50	1.25	.25
☐ 74 Ford Frick	2.50	1.25	.25
☐ 75 Hazen (Kiki) Cuyler	2.50	1.25	.25
☐ 76 Paul Waner DP	1.75	.85	.17
☐ 77 Harold(Pie) Traynor	2.50	1.25	.25
☐ 78 Lloyd Waner	2.50	1.25	.25
☐ 79 Ralph Kiner	6.00	3.00	.60
☐ 80A Pepper Martin SP (Eddie Collins pictured on obverse)	750.00	300.00	60.00
☐ 80B Pepper Martin SP (Lefty Grove pictured on obverse)	750.00	300.00	60.00

1961 Fleer

The cards in this 154-card set measure 2 1/2" by 3 1/2". In 1961, Fleer continued its Baseball Greats format by issuing this series of cards. The set was released in two distinct series, 1-88 and

89-154 (of which the latter is more difficult to obtain). The players within each series are conveniently numbered in alphabetical order. It appears that this set continued to be issued the following year by Fleer. The catalog number for this set is F418-3. In each first series pack Fleer inserted a Major League team decal and a pennant sticker honoring past World Series winners.

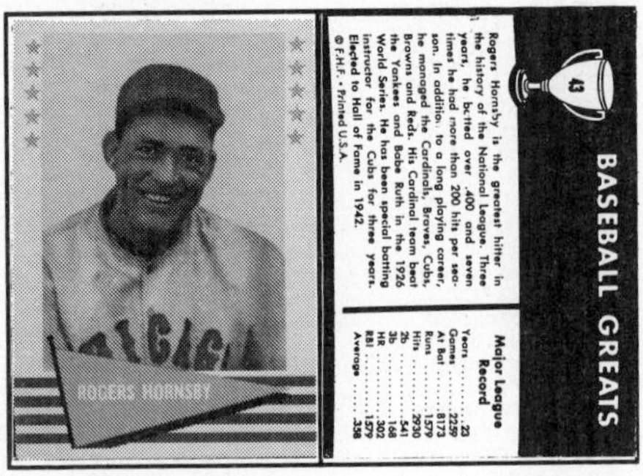

	NRMT	VG-E	GOOD
COMPLETE SET (154)	700.00	350.00	70.00
COMMON PLAYER (1-88)	2.00	1.00	.20
COMMON PLAYER (89-154)	4.00	2.00	.40
☐ 1 Baker/Cobb/Wheat (checklist back)	20.00	3.00	.60
☐ 2 Grover C. Alexander	4.00	2.00	.40
☐ 3 Nick Altrock	2.00	1.00	.20
☐ 4 Cap Anson	2.00	1.00	.20
☐ 5 Earl Averill	2.00	1.00	.20
☐ 6 Frank Baker	2.00	1.00	.20
☐ 7 Dave Bancroft	2.00	1.00	.20
☐ 8 Chief Bender	2.00	1.00	.20
☐ 9 Jim Bottomley	2.00	1.00	.20
☐ 10 Roger Bresnahan	2.00	1.00	.20
☐ 11 Mordecai Brown	2.00	1.00	.20
☐ 12 Max Carey	2.00	1.00	.20
☐ 13 Jack Chesbro	2.00	1.00	.20
☐ 14 Ty Cobb	30.00	15.00	3.00
☐ 15 Mickey Cochrane	3.50	1.75	.35
☐ 16 Eddie Collins	2.00	1.00	.20
☐ 17 Earle Combs	2.00	1.00	.20
☐ 18 Charles Comiskey	2.00	1.00	.20
☐ 19 Kiki Cuyler	2.00	1.00	.20
☐ 20 Paul Derringer	2.00	1.00	.20
☐ 21 Howard Ehmke	2.00	1.00	.20
☐ 22 W. Evans	2.00	1.00	.20
☐ 23 Johnny Evers	2.00	1.00	.20
☐ 24 Urban Faber	2.00	1.00	.20
☐ 25 Bob Feller	8.00	4.00	.80
☐ 26 Wes Ferrell	2.00	1.00	.20
☐ 27 Lew Fonseca	2.00	1.00	.20
☐ 28 Jimmy Foxx	5.00	2.50	.50
☐ 29 Ford Frick	2.00	1.00	.20
☐ 30 Frank Frisch	3.50	1.75	.35
☐ 31 Lou Gehrig	30.00	15.00	3.00
☐ 32 Charlie Gehringer	3.50	1.75	.35
☐ 33 Warren Giles	2.00	1.00	.20
☐ 34 Lefty Gomez	3.50	1.75	.35
☐ 35 Goose Goslin	2.00	1.00	.20
☐ 36 Clark Griffith	2.00	1.00	.20
☐ 37 Burleigh Grimes	2.00	1.00	.20
☐ 38 Lefty Grove	4.00	2.00	.40
☐ 39 Chick Hafey	2.00	1.00	.20
☐ 40 Jesse Haines	2.00	1.00	.20
☐ 41 Gabby Hartnett	2.00	1.00	.20
☐ 42 Harry Heilmann	2.00	1.00	.20
☐ 43 Rogers Hornsby	5.00	2.50	.50
☐ 44 Waite Hoyt	2.00	1.00	.20
☐ 45 Carl Hubbell	3.50	1.75	.35
☐ 46 Miller Huggins	2.00	1.00	.20
☐ 47 Hugh Jennings	2.00	1.00	.20
☐ 48 Ban Johnson	2.00	1.00	.20
☐ 49 Walter Johnson	8.00	4.00	.80
☐ 50 Ralph Kiner	5.00	2.50	.50
☐ 51 Chuck Klein	2.00	1.00	.20
☐ 52 Johnny Kling	2.00	1.00	.20
☐ 53 K.M. Landis	2.00	1.00	.20
☐ 54 Tony Lazzeri	2.00	1.00	.20
☐ 55 Ernie Lombardi	2.00	1.00	.20
☐ 56 Dolf Luque	2.00	1.00	.20
☐ 57 Heinie Manush	2.00	1.00	.20
☐ 58 Marty Marion	2.00	1.00	.20
☐ 59 Christy Mathewson	8.00	4.00	.80
☐ 60 John McGraw	3.50	1.75	.35
☐ 61 Joe Medwick	2.00	1.00	.20
☐ 62 E. (Bing) Miller	2.00	1.00	.20
☐ 63 Johnny Mize	4.50	2.25	.45
☐ 64 John Mostil	2.00	1.00	.20
☐ 65 Art Nehf	2.00	1.00	.20
☐ 66 Hal Newhouser	2.00	1.00	.20
☐ 67 D. (Bobo) Newsom	2.00	1.00	.20
☐ 68 Mel Ott	3.50	1.75	.35
☐ 69 Allie Reynolds	2.00	1.00	.20
☐ 70 Sam Rice	2.00	1.00	.20
☐ 71 Eppa Rixey	2.00	1.00	.20
☐ 72 Edd Roush	2.00	1.00	.20
☐ 73 Schoolboy Rowe	2.00	1.00	.20
☐ 74 Red Ruffing	2.00	1.00	.20
☐ 75 Babe Ruth	60.00	30.00	6.00
☐ 76 Joe Sewell	2.00	1.00	.20
☐ 77 Al Simmons	2.00	1.00	.20
☐ 78 George Sisler	2.00	1.00	.20
☐ 79 Tris Speaker	4.00	2.00	.40
☐ 80 Fred Toney	2.00	1.00	.20
☐ 81 Dazzy Vance	2.00	1.00	.20
☐ 82 Jim Vaughn	2.00	1.00	.20
☐ 83 Ed Walsh	2.00	1.00	.20
☐ 84 Lloyd Waner	2.00	1.00	.20
☐ 85 Paul Waner	2.00	1.00	.20
☐ 86 Zack Wheat	2.00	1.00	.20
☐ 87 Hack Wilson	3.50	1.75	.35
☐ 88 Jimmy Wilson	2.00	1.00	.20
☐ 89 Sisler and Traynor (checklist back)	15.00	3.00	.60
☐ 90 Babe Adams	4.00	2.00	.40
☐ 91 Dale Alexander	4.00	2.00	.40
☐ 92 Jim Bagby	4.00	2.00	.40
☐ 93 Ossie Bluege	4.00	2.00	.40
☐ 94 Lou Boudreau	8.00	4.00	.80
☐ 95 Tom Bridges	4.00	2.00	.40
☐ 96 Donie Bush	4.00	2.00	.40
☐ 97 Dolph Camilli	4.00	2.00	.40
☐ 98 Frank Chance	6.00	3.00	.60
☐ 99 Jimmy Collins	6.00	3.00	.60
☐ 100 Stan Coveleskie	6.00	3.00	.60
☐ 101 Hugh Critz	4.00	2.00	.40
☐ 102 Alvin Crowder	4.00	2.00	.40
☐ 103 Joe Dugan	4.00	2.00	.40
☐ 104 Bibb Falk	4.00	2.00	.40
☐ 105 Rick Ferrell	6.00	3.00	.60
☐ 106 Art Fletcher	4.00	2.00	.40
☐ 107 Dennis Galehouse	4.00	2.00	.40
☐ 108 Chick Galloway	4.00	2.00	.40
☐ 109 Mule Haas	4.00	2.00	.40
☐ 110 Stan Hack	4.00	2.00	.40
☐ 111 Bump Hadley	4.00	2.00	.40
☐ 112 Billy B. Hamilton	6.00	3.00	.60
☐ 113 Joe Hauser	4.00	2.00	.40
☐ 114 Babe Herman	4.00	2.00	.40
☐ 115 Travis Jackson	8.00	4.00	.80
☐ 116 Eddie Joost	4.00	2.00	.40
☐ 117 Addie Joss	8.00	4.00	.80
☐ 118 Joe Judge	4.00	2.00	.40
☐ 119 Joe Kuhel	4.00	2.00	.40
☐ 120 Napoleon Lajoie	10.00	5.00	1.00
☐ 121 Dutch Leonard	4.00	2.00	.40
☐ 122 Ted Lyons	6.00	3.00	.60
☐ 123 Connie Mack	10.00	5.00	1.00
☐ 124 Rabbit Maranville	6.00	3.00	.60
☐ 125 Fred Marberry	4.00	2.00	.40
☐ 126 Joe McGinnity	8.00	4.00	.80
☐ 127 Oscar Melillo	4.00	2.00	.40
☐ 128 Ray Mueller	4.00	2.00	.40
☐ 129 Kid Nichols	6.00	3.00	.60
☐ 130 Lefty O'Doul	4.00	2.00	.40
☐ 131 Bob O'Farrell	4.00	2.00	.40
☐ 132 Roger Peckinpaugh	4.00	2.00	.40
☐ 133 Herb Pennock	6.00	3.00	.60
☐ 134 George Pipgras	4.00	2.00	.40
☐ 135 Eddie Plank	8.00	4.00	.80
☐ 136 Ray Schalk	6.00	3.00	.60
☐ 137 Hal Schumacher	4.00	2.00	.40
☐ 138 Luke Sewell	4.00	2.00	.40
☐ 139 Bob Shawkey	4.00	2.00	.40
☐ 140 Riggs Stephenson	4.00	2.00	.40
☐ 141 Billy Sullivan	4.00	2.00	.40
☐ 142 Bill Terry	9.00	4.50	.90
☐ 143 Joe Tinker	6.00	3.00	.60
☐ 144 Pie Traynor	8.00	4.00	.80
☐ 145 Hal Trosky	4.00	2.00	.40
☐ 146 George Uhle	4.00	2.00	.40
☐ 147 Johnny VanderMeer	6.00	3.00	.60

☐ 148 Arky Vaughan	6.00	3.00	.60
☐ 149 Rube Waddell	6.00	3.00	.60
☐ 150 Honus Wagner	30.00	15.00	3.00
☐ 151 Dixie Walker	4.00	2.00	.40
☐ 152 Ted Williams	60.00	30.00	6.00
☐ 153 Cy Young	16.00	8.00	1.60
☐ 154 Ross Young	12.00	6.00	1.20

1963 Fleer

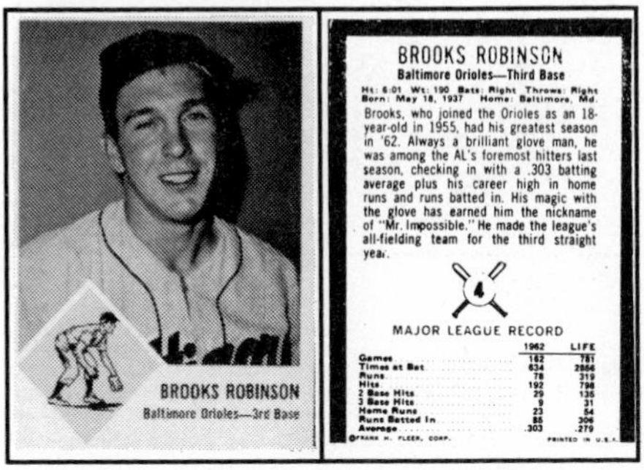

The cards in this 66-card set measure 2 1/2" by 3 1/2". The Fleer set of current baseball players was marketed in 1963 in a gum card-style waxed wrapper package which contained a cherry cookie instead of gum. The cards were printed in sheets of 66 with the scarce card of Adcock apparently being replaced by the unnumbered checklist card for the final press run. The complete set price includes the checklist card. The catalog designation for this set is R418-4. The key rookie card in this set is Maury Wills.

	NRMT	VG-E	GOOD
COMPLETE SET (67)	900.00	450.00	90.00
COMMON PLAYER (1-66)	5.00	2.50	.50
☐ 1 Steve Barber	7.50	2.50	.50
☐ 2 Ron Hansen	5.00	2.50	.50
☐ 3 Milt Pappas	6.00	3.00	.60
☐ 4 Brooks Robinson	33.00	15.00	3.00
☐ 5 Willie Mays	75.00	37.50	7.50
☐ 6 Lou Clinton	5.00	2.50	.50
☐ 7 Bill Monbouquette	5.00	2.50	.50
☐ 8 Carl Yastrzemski	65.00	32.50	6.50
☐ 9 Ray Herbert	5.00	2.50	.50
☐ 10 Jim Landis	5.00	2.50	.50
☐ 11 Dick Donovan	5.00	2.50	.50
☐ 12 Tito Francona	5.00	2.50	.50
☐ 13 Jerry Kindall	5.00	2.50	.50
☐ 14 Frank Lary	6.00	3.00	.60
☐ 15 Dick Howser	6.00	3.00	.60
☐ 16 Jerry Lumpe	5.00	2.50	.50
☐ 17 Norm Siebern	5.00	2.50	.50
☐ 18 Don Lee	5.00	2.50	.50
☐ 19 Albie Pearson	5.00	2.50	.50
☐ 20 Bob Rodgers	6.00	3.00	.60
☐ 21 Leon Wagner	5.00	2.50	.50
☐ 22 Jim Kaat	8.00	4.00	.80
☐ 23 Vic Power	5.00	2.50	.50
☐ 24 Rich Rollins	5.00	2.50	.50
☐ 25 Bobby Richardson	8.00	4.00	.80
☐ 26 Ralph Terry	6.00	3.00	.60
☐ 27 Tom Cheney	5.00	2.50	.50
☐ 28 Chuck Cottier	5.00	2.50	.50
☐ 29 Jim Piersall	6.00	3.00	.60
☐ 30 Dave Stenhouse	5.00	2.50	.50
☐ 31 Glen Hobbie	5.00	2.50	.50
☐ 32 Ron Santo	7.50	3.75	.75
☐ 33 Gene Freese	5.00	2.50	.50
☐ 34 Vada Pinson	7.50	3.75	.75
☐ 35 Bob Purkey	5.00	2.50	.50
☐ 36 Joe Amalfitano	5.00	2.50	.50
☐ 37 Bob Aspromonte	5.00	2.50	.50
☐ 38 Dick Farrell	5.00	2.50	.50
☐ 39 Al Spangler	5.00	2.50	.50
☐ 40 Tommy Davis	7.00	3.50	.70
☐ 41 Don Drysdale	25.00	12.50	2.50
☐ 42 Sandy Koufax	75.00	37.50	7.50
☐ 43 Maury Wills	45.00	22.50	4.50
☐ 44 Frank Bolling	5.00	2.50	.50
☐ 45 Warren Spahn	25.00	12.50	2.50
☐ 46 Joe Adcock SP	110.00	55.00	11.00
☐ 47 Roger Craig	7.50	3.75	.75
☐ 48 Al Jackson	5.00	2.50	.50
☐ 49 Rod Kanehl	5.00	2.50	.50
☐ 50 Ruben Amaro	5.00	2.50	.50
☐ 51 Johnny Callison	6.00	3.00	.60
☐ 52 Clay Dalrymple	5.00	2.50	.50
☐ 53 Don Demeter	5.00	2.50	.50
☐ 54 Art Mahaffey	5.00	2.50	.50
☐ 55 Smokey Burgess	6.00	3.00	.60
☐ 56 Roberto Clemente	65.00	32.50	6.50
☐ 57 Roy Face	7.00	3.50	.70
☐ 58 Vern Law	6.00	3.00	.60
☐ 59 Bill Mazeroski	7.50	3.75	.75
☐ 60 Ken Boyer	8.00	4.00	.80
☐ 61 Bob Gibson	25.00	12.50	2.50
☐ 62 Gene Oliver	5.00	2.50	.50
☐ 63 Bill White	8.00	4.00	.80
☐ 64 Orlando Cepeda	9.00	4.50	.90
☐ 65 Jim Davenport	5.00	2.50	.50
☐ 66 Billy O'Dell	6.00	3.00	.60
☐ 67 Checklist card (unnumbered)	300.00	75.00	15.00

1970 Fleer World Series

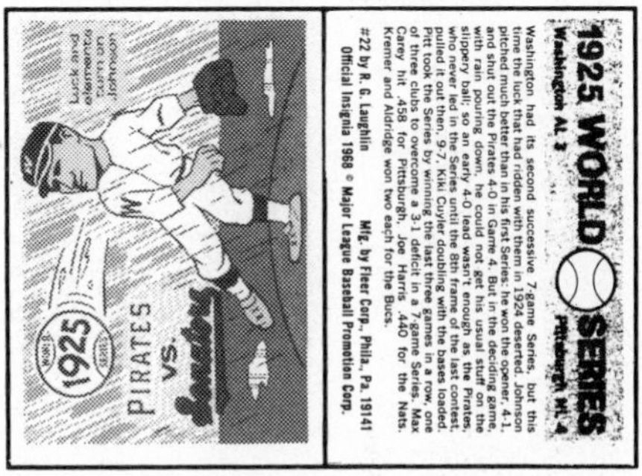

This set of 66 cards was distributed by Fleer. The cards are standard size, 2 1/2" by 3 1/2" and are in crude color on the front with light blue printing on white card stock on the back. All the years are represented except for 1904 when no World Series was played. In the list below, the winning series team is listed first. The year of the Series on the obverse is inside a white baseball.

	NRMT	VG-E	GOOD
COMPLETE SET (66)	33.00	15.00	3.00
COMMON PLAYER (1-66)	.45	.22	.04
☐ 1 1903 Red Sox/Pirates	.45	.22	.04
☐ 2 1905 Giants/A's (Christy Mathewson)	.60	.30	.06
☐ 3 1906 White Sox/Cubs	.45	.22	.04
☐ 4 1907 Cubs/Tigers	.45	.22	.04
☐ 5 1908 Cubs/Tigers (Tinker/Evers/Chance)	.60	.30	.06
☐ 6 1909 Pirates/Tigers (Wagner/Cobb)	.75	.35	.07
☐ 7 1910 A's/Cubs (Bender/Coombs)	.45	.22	.04
☐ 8 1911 A's/Giants (John McGraw)	.60	.30	.06
☐ 9 1912 Red Sox/Giants	.45	.22	.04
☐ 10 1913 A's/Giants	.45	.22	.04
☐ 11 1914 Braves/A's	.45	.22	.04
☐ 12 1915 Red Sox/Phillies (Babe Ruth)	1.00	.50	.10
☐ 13 1916 Red Sox/Dodgers (Babe Ruth)	1.00	.50	.10
☐ 14 1917 White Sox/Giants	.45	.22	.04
☐ 15 1918 Red Sox/Cubs	.45	.22	.04

□ 16	1919 Reds/White Sox	.45	.22	.04
□ 17	1920 Indians/Dodgers (Stan Coveleski)	.45	.22	.04
□ 18	1921 Giants/Yankees (Commissioner Landis)	.45	.22	.04
□ 19	1922 Giants/Yankees	.45	.22	.04
□ 20	1923 Yankees/Giants (Babe Ruth)	1.00	.50	.10
□ 21	1924 Senators/Giants (John McGraw)	.60	.30	.06
□ 22	1925 Pirates/Senators (Walter Johnson)	.75	.35	.07
□ 23	1926 Cardinals/Yankees (Alexander/Lazzeri)	.60	.30	.06
□ 24	1927 Yankees/Pirates	.45	.22	.04
□ 25	1928 Yankees/Cardinals (Ruth/Gehrig)	1.00	.50	.10
□ 26	1929 A's/Cubs	.45	.22	.04
□ 27	1930 A's/Cardinals	.45	.22	.04
□ 28	1931 Cardinals/A's (Pepper Martin)	.45	.22	.04
□ 29	1932 Yankees/Cubs (Ruth/Gehrig)	1.00	.50	.10
□ 30	1933 Giants/Senators (Mel Ott)	.60	.30	.06
□ 31	1934 Cardinals/Tigers	.45	.22	.04
□ 32	1935 Tigers/Cubs (Gehringer/Bridges)	.60	.30	.06
□ 33	1936 Yankees/Giants	.45	.22	.04
□ 34	1937 Yankees/Giants (Carl Hubbell)	.45	.22	.04
□ 35	1938 Yankees/Cubs (Lou Gehrig)	.80	.40	.08
□ 36	1939 Yankees/Reds	.45	.22	.04
□ 37	1940 Reds/Tigers	.45	.22	.04
□ 38	1941 Yankees/Dodgers	.45	.22	.04
□ 39	1942 Cardinals/Yankees	.45	.22	.04
□ 40	1943 Yankees/Cardinals	.45	.22	.04
□ 41	1944 Cardinals/Browns	.45	.22	.04
□ 42	1945 Tigers/Cubs (Hank Greenberg)	.60	.30	.06
□ 43	1946 Cardinals/Red Sox (Enos Slaughter)	.60	.30	.06
□ 44	1947 Yankees/Dodgers (Al Gionfriddo)	.45	.22	.04
□ 45	1948 Indians/Braves	.45	.22	.04
□ 46	1949 Yankees/Dodgers (Reynolds/Roe)	.45	.22	.04
□ 47	1950 Yankees/Phillies	.45	.22	.04
□ 48	1951 Yankees/Giants	.45	.22	.04
□ 49	1952 Yankees/Dodgers (Mize/Snider)	.80	.40	.08
□ 50	1953 Yankees/Dodgers (Carl Erskine)	.45	.22	.04
□ 51	1954 Giants/Indians (Johnny Antonelli)	.45	.22	.04
□ 52	1955 Dodgers/Yankees (Johnny Podres)	.45	.22	.04
□ 53	1956 Yankees/Dodgers	.45	.22	.04
□ 54	1957 Braves/Yankees (Lew Burdette)	.45	.22	.04
□ 55	1958 Yankees/Braves (Bob Turley)	.45	.22	.04
□ 56	1959 Dodgers/Wh.Sox (Chuck Essegian)	.45	.22	.04
□ 57	1960 Pirates/Yankees	.45	.22	.04
□ 58	1961 Yankees/Reds (Whitey Ford)	.60	.30	.06
□ 59	1962 Yankees/Giants	.45	.22	.04
□ 60	1963 Dodgers/Yankees (Moose Skowron)	.45	.22	.04
□ 61	1964 Cardinals/Yankees (Bobby Richardson)	.60	.30	.06
□ 62	1965 Dodgers/Twins	.45	.22	.04
□ 63	1966 Orioles/Dodgers	.45	.22	.04
□ 64	1967 Cardinals/Red Sox	.45	.22	.04
□ 65	1968 Tigers/Cardinals	.45	.22	.04
□ 66	1969 Mets/Orioles	.60	.30	.06

1971 Fleer World Series

This set of 68 cards was distributed by Fleer. The cards are standard size, 2 1/2" by 3 1/2" and are in crude color on the front with brown printing on white card stock on the back. All the years since 1903 are represented in this set including 1904 when no World Series was played as a card was printed explaining why there was no World Series that year. In the list below, the winning series team is listed first. The year of the Series on the obverse is inside a white square over the official World Series logo.

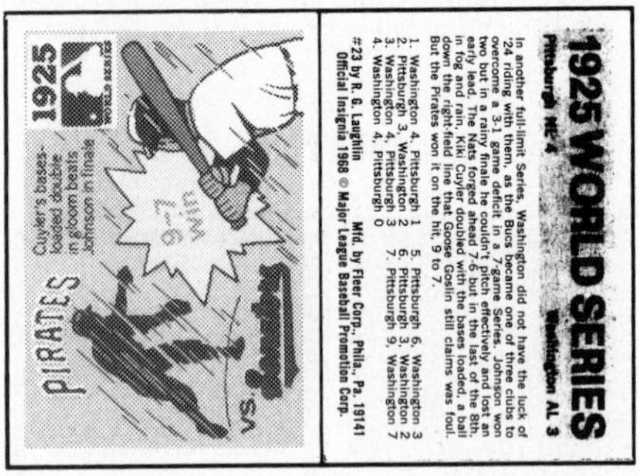

		NRMT	VG-E	GOOD
	COMPLETE SET (68)	33.00	15.00	3.00
	COMMON PLAYER (1-68)	.45	.22	.04
□ 1	1903 Red Sox/Pirates (Cy Young)	.60	.30	.06
□ 2	1904 NO Series (John McGraw)	.60	.30	.06
□ 3	1905 Giants/A's (Mathewson, Bender, and McGinnity)	.60	.30	.06
□ 4	1906 White Sox/Cubs	.45	.22	.04
□ 5	1907 Cubs/Tigers	.45	.22	.04
□ 6	1908 Cubs/Tigers (Ty Cobb)	.80	.40	.08
□ 7	1909 Pirates/Tigers	.45	.22	.04
□ 8	1910 A's/Cubs (Eddie Collins)	.45	.22	.04
□ 9	1911 A's/Giants (Home Run Baker)	.45	.22	.04
□ 10	1912 Red Sox/Giants	.45	.22	.04
□ 11	1913 A's/Giants (Christy Mathewson)	.60	.30	.06
□ 12	1914 Braves/A's	.45	.22	.04
□ 13	1915 Red Sox/Phillies (Grover Alexander)	.60	.30	.06
□ 14	1916 Red Sox/Dodgers	.45	.22	.04
□ 15	1917 White Sox/Giants (Red Faber)	.45	.22	.04
□ 16	1918 Red Sox/Cubs (Babe Ruth)	1.00	.50	.10
□ 17	1919 Reds/White Sox	.45	.22	.04
□ 18	1920 Indians/Dodgers	.45	.22	.04
□ 19	1921 Giants/Yankees (Waite Hoyt)	.45	.22	.04
□ 20	1922 Giants/Yankees	.45	.22	.04
□ 21	1923 Yankees/Giants (Herb Pennock)	.45	.22	.04
□ 22	1924 Senators/Giants (Walter Johnson)	.60	.30	.06
□ 23	1925 Pirates/Senators (Cuyler/W.Johnson)	.60	.30	.06
□ 24	1926 Cardinals/Yankees (Rogers Hornsby)	.60	.30	.06
□ 25	1927 Yankees/Pirates	.45	.22	.04
□ 26	1928 Yankees/Cardinals (Lou Gehrig)	.80	.40	.08
□ 27	1929 A's/Cubs	.45	.22	.04
□ 28	1930 A's/Cardinals (Jimmie Foxx)	.60	.30	.06
□ 29	1931 Cardinals/A's (Pepper Martin)	.45	.22	.04
□ 30	1932 Yankees/Cubs (Babe Ruth)	1.00	.50	.10
□ 31	1933 Giants/Senators (Carl Hubbell)	.45	.22	.04
□ 32	1934 Cardinals/Tigers	.45	.22	.04
□ 33	1935 Tigers/Cubs (Mickey Cochrane)	.60	.30	.06
□ 34	1936 Yankees/Giants (Red Rolfe)	.45	.22	.04
□ 35	1937 Yankees/Giants (Tony Lazzeri)	.45	.22	.04
□ 36	1938 Yankees/Cubs	.45	.22	.04
□ 37	1939 Yankees/Reds	.45	.22	.04

☐ 38 1940 Reds/Tigers	.45	.22	.04
☐ 39 1941 Yankees/Dodgers	.45	.22	.04
☐ 40 1942 Cardinals/Yankees	.45	.22	.04
☐ 41 1943 Yankees/Cardinals	.45	.22	.04
☐ 42 1944 Cardinals/Browns	.45	.22	.04
☐ 43 1945 Tigers/Cubs (Hank Greenberg)	.60	.30	.06
☐ 44 1946 Cardinals/Red Sox (Enos Slaughter)	.60	.30	.06
☐ 45 1947 Yankees/Dodgers	.45	.22	.04
☐ 46 1948 Indians/Braves	.45	.22	.04
☐ 47 1949 Yankees/Dodgers (Preacher Roe)	.45	.22	.04
☐ 48 1950 Yankees/Phillies (Allie Reynolds)	.45	.22	.04
☐ 49 1951 Yankees/Giants (Ed Lopat)	.45	.22	.04
☐ 50 1952 Yankees/Dodgers (Johnny Mize)	.60	.30	.06
☐ 51 1953 Yankees/Dodgers	.45	.22	.04
☐ 52 1954 Giants/Indians	.45	.22	.04
☐ 53 1955 Dodgers/Yankees (Duke Snider)	.60	.30	.06
☐ 54 1956 Yankees/Dodgers	.45	.22	.04
☐ 55 1957 Braves/Yankees	.45	.22	.04
☐ 56 1958 Yankees/Braves (Hank Bauer)	.45	.22	.04
☐ 57 1959 Dodgers/Wh.Sox (Duke Snider)	.60	.30	.06
☐ 58 1960 Pirates/Yankees	.45	.22	.04
☐ 59 1961 Yankees/Reds (Whitey Ford)	.60	.30	.06
☐ 60 1962 Yankees/Giants	.45	.22	.04
☐ 61 1963 Dodgers/Yankees	.45	.22	.04
☐ 62 1964 Cardinals/Yankees	.45	.22	.04
☐ 63 1965 Dodgers/Twins	.45	.22	.04
☐ 64 1966 Orioles/Dodgers	.45	.22	.04
☐ 65 1967 Cardinals/Red Sox	.45	.22	.04
☐ 66 1968 Tigers/Cardinals	.45	.22	.04
☐ 67 1969 Mets/Orioles	.45	.22	.04
☐ 68 1970 Orioles/Reds	.45	.22	.04

1972 Fleer Famous Feats

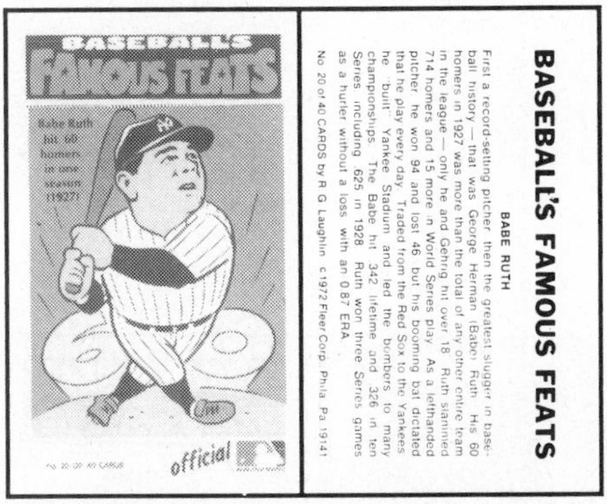

This Fleer set of 40 cards features the artwork of sports artist R.G. Laughlin. The set is titled "Baseball's Famous Feats." The cards are numbered both on the front and back. The backs are printed in light blue on white card stock. The cards measure approximately 2 1/2" by 4". This set was licensed by Major League Baseball.

	NRMT	VG-E	GOOD
COMPLETE SET (40)	15.00	7.50	1.50
COMMON PLAYER (1-40)	.45	.22	.04
☐ 1 Joe McGinnity	.45	.22	.04
☐ 2 Rogers Hornsby	.75	.35	.07
☐ 3 Christy Mathewson	.75	.35	.07
☐ 4 Dazzy Vance	.45	.22	.04
☐ 5 Lou Gehrig	1.00	.50	.10
☐ 6 Jim Bottomley	.45	.22	.04
☐ 7 Johnny Evers	.45	.22	.04
☐ 8 Walter Johnson	.75	.35	.07
☐ 9 Hack Wilson	.60	.30	.06
☐ 10 Wilbert Robinson	.45	.22	.04
☐ 11 Cy Young	.60	.30	.06
☐ 12 Rudy York	.45	.22	.04
☐ 13 Grover C. Alexander	.45	.22	.04
☐ 14 Fred Toney and Hippo Vaughan	.45	.22	.04
☐ 15 Ty Cobb	1.00	.50	.10
☐ 16 Jimmie Foxx	.75	.35	.07
☐ 17 Hub Leonard	.45	.22	.04
☐ 18 Eddie Collins	.45	.22	.04
☐ 19 Joe Oeschger and Leon Cadore	.45	.22	.04
☐ 20 Babe Ruth	1.50	.75	.15
☐ 21 Honus Wagner	.75	.35	.07
☐ 22 Red Rolfe	.45	.22	.04
☐ 23 Ed Walsh	.45	.22	.04
☐ 24 Paul Waner	.45	.22	.04
☐ 25 Mel Ott	.60	.30	.06
☐ 26 Eddie Plank	.45	.22	.04
☐ 27 Sam Crawford	.45	.22	.04
☐ 28 Napoleon Lajoie	.60	.30	.06
☐ 29 Ed Reulbach	.45	.22	.04
☐ 30 Pinky Higgins	.45	.22	.04
☐ 31 Bill Klem	.60	.30	.06
☐ 32 Tris Speaker	.60	.30	.06
☐ 33 Hank Gowdy	.45	.22	.04
☐ 34 Lefty O'Doul	.45	.22	.04
☐ 35 Lloyd Waner	.45	.22	.04
☐ 36 Chuck Klein	.45	.22	.04
☐ 37 Deacon Phillippe	.45	.22	.04
☐ 38 Ed Delahanty	.45	.22	.04
☐ 39 Jack Chesbro	.45	.22	.04
☐ 40 Willie Keeler	.45	.22	.04

1973 Fleer Wildest Days

Baseball's WILDEST DAYS AND PLAYS
Baseball's WILDEST DAYS AND PLAYS
The Star Who Sat Out The World Series!
It's often the unhappy lot of a star player to miss the World Series due to an injury —but in 1927 a healthy star sat out the fall classic. Kiki Cuyler, a future Hall-of-Famer, had broken up the '25 Series with a bases-clearing double off Walter Johnson in the final game. While missing much of the '27 season with an injury, he still hit over .300. But he had quarreled with his new manager, Donie Bush, over being moved from third to second in the batting order—where Kiki didn't want to hit. He was fined once for not sliding. Both were stubborn, and Bush traded Cuyler before the next season. Despite Pittsburgh chants of "We want Cuyler!" he never appeared in the '27 Series.
No. 14 of 42 CARDS by R. G. Laughlin
©1973 Fleer Corp., Phila., Pa. 19141

This Fleer set of 42 cards is titled "Baseball's Wildest Days and Plays" and features the artwork of sports artist R.G. Laughlin. The cards are numbered on the back. The backs are printed in dark red on white card stock. The cards measure approximately 2 1/2" by 4". This set was not licensed by Major League Baseball.

	NRMT	VG-E	GOOD
COMPLETE SET (42)	15.00	7.50	1.50
COMMON PLAYER (1-42)	.45	.22	.04
☐ 1 Cubs and Phillies Score 49 Runs in Game	.45	.22	.04
☐ 2 Frank Chance Five HBP's in One Day	.45	.22	.04
☐ 3 Jim Thorpe Homered into 3 States	1.00	.50	.10
☐ 4 Eddie Gaedel Midget in Majors	.60	.30	.06
☐ 5 Most Tied Game Ever	.45	.22	.04
☐ 6 Seven Errors in One Inning	.45	.22	.04
☐ 7 Four 20-Game Winners But No Pennant	.45	.22	.04
☐ 8 Dummy Hoy Umpires Signal Strikes	.60	.30	.06
☐ 9 Fourteeen Hits in One Inning	.45	.22	.04

☐ 10	Yankees Not Shut Out For Two Years	.45	.22	.04
☐ 11	Buck Weaver 17 Straight Fouls	.60	.30	.06
☐ 12	George Sisler Greatest Thrill Was as a Pitcher	.45	.22	.04
☐ 13	Wrong-Way Baserunner	.45	.22	.04
☐ 14	Kiki Cuyler Sits Out Series	.45	.22	.04
☐ 15	Grounder Climbed Wall	.45	.22	.04
☐ 16	Gabby Street Washington Monument	.45	.22	.04
☐ 17	Mel Ott Ejected Twice	.60	.30	.06
☐ 18	Shortest Pitching Career	.45	.22	.04
☐ 19	Three Homers in One Inning	.45	.22	.04
☐ 20	Bill Byron Singing Umpire	.45	.22	.04
☐ 21	Fred Clarke Walking Steal of Home	.45	.22	.04
☐ 22	Christy Mathewson 373rd Win Discovered	.60	.30	.06
☐ 23	Hitting Through the Unglaub Arc	.45	.22	.04
☐ 24	Jim O'Rourke Catching at 52	.45	.22	.04
☐ 25	Fired for Striking Out in Series	.45	.22	.04
☐ 26	Eleven Run Inning on One Hit	.45	.22	.04
☐ 27	58 Innings in 3 Days	.45	.22	.04
☐ 28	Homer on Warm-Up Pitch	.45	.22	.04
☐ 29	Giants Win 26 Straight But Finish Fourth	.45	.22	.04
☐ 30	Player Who Stole First Base	.45	.22	.04
☐ 31	Ernie Shore Perfect Game in Relief	.45	.22	.04
☐ 32	Greatest Comeback	.45	.22	.04
☐ 33	All-Time Flash-In-The-Pan	.45	.22	.04
☐ 34	Pruett Fanned Ruth 19 out of 31	.75	.35	.07
☐ 35	Fixed Batting Race Cobb/Lajoie	.75	.35	.07
☐ 36	Wild-Pitch Rebound Play	.45	.22	.04
☐ 37	17 Straight Scoring Innings	.45	.22	.04
☐ 38	Wildest Opening Day	.45	.22	.04
☐ 39	Baseball's Strike One	.45	.22	.04
☐ 40	Opening Day No Hitter That Didn't Count	.45	.22	.04
☐ 41	Jimmie Foxx Six Straight Walks in One Game	.60	.30	.06
☐ 42	Entire Team Hit and Scored in Inning	.45	.22	.04

1974 Fleer Baseball Firsts

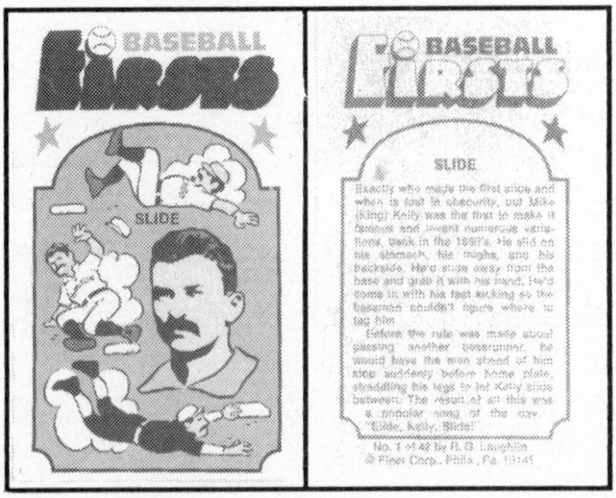

This Fleer set of 42 cards is titled "Baseball Firsts" and features the artwork of sports artist R.G. Laughlin. The cards are numbered on the back. The backs are printed in black on gray card stock. The cards measure approximately 2 1/2" by 4". This set was not licensed by Major League Baseball.

		NRMT	VG-E	GOOD
	COMPLETE SET (42)	9.00	4.50	.90
	COMMON PLAYER (1-42)	.25	.12	.02
☐ 1	Slide	.25	.12	.02
☐ 2	Spring Training	.25	.12	.02
☐ 3	Bunt	.25	.12	.02
☐ 4	Catcher's Mask	.25	.12	.02
☐ 5	Four Straight Homers (Lou Gehrig)	1.00	.50	.10
☐ 6	Radio Broadcast	.25	.12	.02
☐ 7	Numbered Uniforms	.25	.12	.02
☐ 8	Shin Guards	.25	.12	.02
☐ 9	Players Association	.25	.12	.02
☐ 10	Knuckleball	.25	.12	.02
☐ 11	Player With Glasses	.25	.12	.02
☐ 12	Baseball Cards	1.00	.50	.10
☐ 13	Standardized Rules	.25	.12	.02
☐ 14	Grand Slam	.25	.12	.02
☐ 15	Player Fined	.25	.12	.02
☐ 16	Presidential Opener	.25	.12	.02
☐ 17	Player Transaction	.25	.12	.02
☐ 18	All-Star Game	.25	.12	.02
☐ 19	Scoreboard	.25	.12	.02
☐ 20	Cork Center Ball	.25	.12	.02
☐ 21	Scorekeeping	.25	.12	.02
☐ 22	Domed Stadium	.25	.12	.02
☐ 23	Batting Helmet	.25	.12	.02
☐ 24	Fatality	.25	.12	.02
☐ 25	Unassisted Triple Play	.25	.12	.02
☐ 26	Home Run At Night	.20	.10	.02
☐ 27	Black Major Leaguer	.40	.20	.04
☐ 28	Pinch Hitter	.25	.12	.02
☐ 29	Million-Dollar World Series	.25	.12	.02
☐ 30	Tarpaulin	.25	.12	.02
☐ 31	Team Initials	.25	.12	.02
☐ 32	Pennant Playoff	.25	.12	.02
☐ 33	Glove	.25	.12	.02
☐ 34	Curve Ball	.25	.12	.02
☐ 35	Night Game	.25	.12	.02
☐ 36	Admission Charge	.25	.12	.02
☐ 37	Farm System	.25	.12	.02
☐ 38	Telecast	.25	.12	.02
☐ 39	Commissioner	.25	.12	.02
☐ 40	.400 Hitter	.25	.12	.02
☐ 41	World Series	.25	.12	.02
☐ 42	Player Into Service	.25	.12	.02

1975 Fleer Pioneers

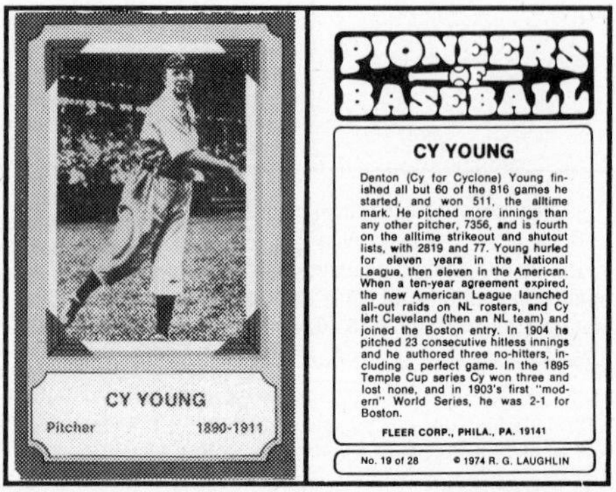

This 28-card set of brown and white sepia-toned photos of old timers is subtitled "Pioneers of Baseball. The graphics artwork was done by R.G. Laughlin. The cards measure 2 1/2" by 4". The card backs are a narrative about the particular player. The cards are numbered on the back at the bottom.

	NRMT	VG-E	GOOD
COMPLETE SET (28)	12.00	6.00	1.20
COMMON PLAYER (1-28)	.45	.22	.04
□ 1 Cap Anson	.75	.35	.07
□ 2 Harry Wright	.60	.30	.06
□ 3 Buck Ewing	.60	.30	.06
□ 4 A.G. Spalding	.60	.30	.06
□ 5 Old Hoss Radbourn	.60	.30	.06
□ 6 Dan Brouthers	.60	.30	.06
□ 7 Roger Bresnahan	.45	.22	.04
□ 8 Mike Kelly	.60	.30	.06
□ 9 Ned Hanlon	.45	.22	.04
□ 10 Ed Delahanty	.60	.30	.06
□ 11 Pud Galvin	.60	.30	.06
□ 12 Amos Rusie	.60	.30	.06
□ 13 Tommy McCarthy	.60	.30	.06
□ 14 Ty Cobb	1.25	.60	.12
□ 15 John McGraw	.60	.30	.06
□ 16 Home Run Baker	.60	.30	.06
□ 17 Johnny Evers	.45	.22	.04
□ 18 Nap Lajoie	.60	.30	.06
□ 19 Cy Young	.75	.35	.07
□ 20 Eddie Collins	.60	.30	.06
□ 21 John Glasscock	.45	.22	.04
□ 22 Hal Chase	.45	.22	.04
□ 23 Mordecai Brown	.45	.22	.04
□ 24 Jake Daubert	.45	.22	.04
□ 25 Mike Donlin	.45	.22	.04
□ 26 John Clarkson	.60	.30	.06
□ 27 Buck Herzog	.45	.22	.04
□ 28 Art Nehf	.45	.22	.04

1981 Fleer

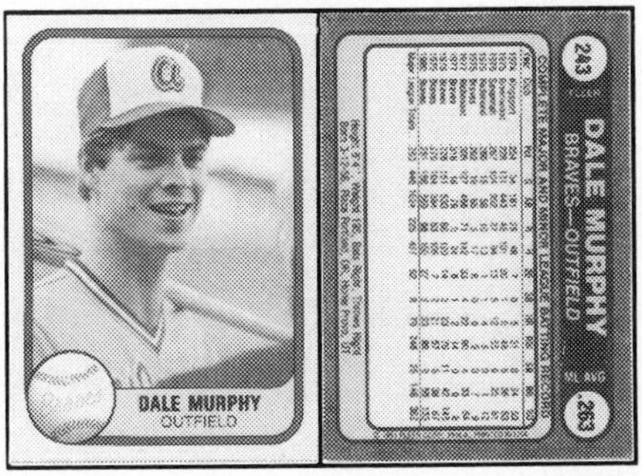

The cards in this 660-card set measure 2 1/2" by 3 1/2". This issue of cards marks Fleer's first entry into the current player baseball card market since 1963. Players from the same team are conveniently grouped together by number in the set. The teams are ordered (by 1980 standings) as follows: Philadelphia (1-27), Kansas City (28-50), Houston (51-78), New York Yankees (79-109), Los Angeles (110-141), Montreal (142-168), Baltimore (169-195), Cincinnati (196-220), Boston (221-241), Atlanta (242-267), California (268-290), Chicago Cubs (291-315), New York Mets (316-338), Chicago White Sox (339-350 and 352-359), Pittsburgh (360-386), Cleveland (387-408), Toronto (409-431), San Francisco (432-458), Detroit (459-483), San Diego (484-506), Milwaukee (507-527), St. Louis (528-550), Minnesota (551-571), Oakland (351 and 572-594), Seattle (595-616), and Texas (617-637). Cards 638-660 feature specials and checklists. The cards of pitchers in this set erroneously show a heading (on the card backs) of "Batting Record" over their career pitching statistics. There were three distinct printings: the two following the primary run were designed to correct numerous errors. The variations caused by these multiple printings are noted in the checklist below (P1, P2, or P3). The C. Nettles variation was corrected before the end of the first printing. The key rookie card in this set is Fernando Valenzuela, whose first name was erroneously spelled Fernand on the card front.

	MINT	EXC	G-VG
COMPLETE SET (660)	50.00	25.00	5.00
COMMON PLAYER (1-660)	.04	.02	.00
□ 1 Pete Rose	2.00	.50	.10
□ 2 Larry Bowa	.15	.07	.01
□ 3 Manny Trillo	.04	.02	.00
□ 4 Bob Boone	.15	.07	.01
□ 5 Mike Schmidt	2.25	1.10	.22
See also 640A			
□ 6A Steve Carlton P1	1.25	.60	.12
Pitcher of Year			
See also 660A			
Back "1066 Cardinals"			
□ 6B Steve Carlton P2	1.25	.60	.12
Pitcher of Year			
Back "1066 Cardinals"			
□ 6C Steve Carlton P3	2.00	1.00	.20
"1966 Cardinals"			
□ 7 Tug McGraw	.10	.05	.01
See 657A			
□ 8 Larry Christenson	.04	.02	.00
□ 9 Bake McBride	.04	.02	.00
□ 10 Greg Luzinski	.12	.06	.01
□ 11 Ron Reed	.04	.02	.00
□ 12 Dickie Noles	.04	.02	.00
□ 13 Keith Moreland	.25	.12	.02
□ 14 Bob Walk	.30	.15	.03
□ 15 Lonnie Smith	.15	.07	.01
□ 16 Dick Ruthven	.04	.02	.00
□ 17 Sparky Lyle	.10	.05	.01
□ 18 Greg Gross	.04	.02	.00
□ 19 Garry Maddox	.07	.03	.01
□ 20 Nino Espinosa	.04	.02	.00
□ 21 George Vukovich	.04	.02	.00
□ 22 John Vukovich	.04	.02	.00
□ 23 Ramon Aviles	.04	.02	.00
□ 24A Ken Saucier P1	.07	.03	.01
Name on front "Ken"			
□ 24B Ken Saucier P2	.07	.03	.01
Name on front "Ken"			
□ 24C Kevin Saucier P3	.35	.17	.03
Name on front "Kevin"			
□ 25 Randy Lerch	.04	.02	.00
□ 26 Del Unser	.04	.02	.00
□ 27 Tim McCarver	.15	.07	.01
□ 28 George Brett	1.75	.85	.17
See also 655A			
□ 29 Willie Wilson	.15	.07	.01
See also 653A			
□ 30 Paul Splittorff	.04	.02	.00
□ 31 Dan Quisenberry	.15	.07	.01
□ 32A Amos Otis P1	.10	.05	.01
Batting Pose			
"Outfield"			
(32 on back)			
□ 32B Amos Otis P2	.10	.05	.01
"Series Starter"			
(483 on back)			
□ 33 Steve Busby	.04	.02	.00
□ 34 U.L. Washington	.04	.02	.00
□ 35 Dave Chalk	.04	.02	.00
□ 36 Darrell Porter	.04	.02	.00
□ 37 Marty Pattin	.04	.02	.00
□ 38 Larry Gura	.04	.02	.00
□ 39 Renie Martin	.04	.02	.00
□ 40 Rich Gale	.04	.02	.00
□ 41A Hal McRae P1	.50	.25	.05
"Royals" on front			
in black letters			
□ 41B Hal McRae P2	.10	.05	.01
"Royals" on front			
in blue letters			
□ 42 Dennis Leonard	.07	.03	.01
□ 43 Willie Aikens	.07	.03	.01
□ 44 Frank White	.10	.05	.01
□ 45 Clint Hurdle	.04	.02	.00
□ 46 John Wathan	.07	.03	.01
□ 47 Pete LaCock	.04	.02	.00
□ 48 Rance Mulliniks	.04	.02	.00
□ 49 Jeff Twitty	.04	.02	.00
□ 50 Jamie Quirk	.04	.02	.00
□ 51 Art Howe	.10	.05	.01
□ 52 Ken Forsch	.04	.02	.00
□ 53 Vern Ruhle	.04	.02	.00
□ 54 Joe Niekro	.10	.05	.01
□ 55 Frank LaCorte	.04	.02	.00
□ 56 J.R. Richard	.10	.05	.01
□ 57 Nolan Ryan	3.75	1.85	.37
□ 58 Enos Cabell	.04	.02	.00
□ 59 Cesar Cedeno	.10	.05	.01
□ 60 Jose Cruz	.07	.03	.01

☐ 61 Bill Virdon MG	.07	.03	.01
☐ 62 Terry Puhl	.07	.03	.01
☐ 63 Joaquin Andujar	.10	.05	.01
☐ 64 Alan Ashby	.04	.02	.00
☐ 65 Joe Sambito	.04	.02	.00
☐ 66 Denny Walling	.04	.02	.00
☐ 67 Jeff Leonard	.15	.07	.01
☐ 68 Luis Pujols	.04	.02	.00
☐ 69 Bruce Bochy	.04	.02	.00
☐ 70 Rafael Landestoy	.04	.02	.00
☐ 71 Dave Smith	.45	.22	.04
☐ 72 Danny Heep	.20	.10	.02
☐ 73 Julio Gonzalez	.04	.02	.00
☐ 74 Craig Reynolds	.04	.02	.00
☐ 75 Gary Woods	.04	.02	.00
☐ 76 Dave Bergman	.04	.02	.00
☐ 77 Randy Niemann	.04	.02	.00
☐ 78 Joe Morgan	.50	.25	.05
☐ 79 Reggie Jackson See 650A	1.50	.75	.15
☐ 80 Bucky Dent	.12	.06	.01
☐ 81 Tommy John	.20	.10	.02
☐ 82 Luis Tiant	.10	.05	.01
☐ 83 Rick Cerone	.04	.02	.00
☐ 84 Dick Howser MG	.07	.03	.01
☐ 85 Lou Piniella	.12	.06	.01
☐ 86 Ron Davis	.04	.02	.00
☐ 87A Craig Nettles P1 ERR (Name on back misspelled "Craig")	10.00	5.00	1.00
☐ 87B Graig Nettles P2 COR "Graig"	.30	.15	.03
☐ 88 Ron Guidry	.20	.10	.02
☐ 89 Rich Gossage	.20	.10	.02
☐ 90 Rudy May	.04	.02	.00
☐ 91 Gaylord Perry	.30	.15	.03
☐ 92 Eric Soderholm	.04	.02	.00
☐ 93 Bob Watson	.07	.03	.01
☐ 94 Bobby Murcer	.10	.05	.01
☐ 95 Bobby Brown	.04	.02	.00
☐ 96 Jim Spencer	.04	.02	.00
☐ 97 Tom Underwood	.04	.02	.00
☐ 98 Oscar Gamble	.04	.02	.00
☐ 99 Johnny Oates	.04	.02	.00
☐ 100 Fred Stanley	.04	.02	.00
☐ 101 Ruppert Jones	.04	.02	.00
☐ 102 Dennis Werth	.04	.02	.00
☐ 103 Joe Lefebvre	.07	.03	.01
☐ 104 Brian Doyle	.04	.02	.00
☐ 105 Aurelio Rodriguez	.04	.02	.00
☐ 106 Doug Bird	.04	.02	.00
☐ 107 Mike Griffin	.04	.02	.00
☐ 108 Tim Lollar	.04	.02	.00
☐ 109 Willie Randolph	.10	.05	.01
☐ 110 Steve Garvey	.65	.30	.06
☐ 111 Reggie Smith	.10	.05	.01
☐ 112 Don Sutton	.35	.17	.03
☐ 113 Burt Hooton	.04	.02	.00
☐ 114A Dave Lopes P1 Small hand on back	.50	.25	.05
☐ 114B Dave Lopes P2 No hand	.10	.05	.01
☐ 115 Dusty Baker	.07	.03	.01
☐ 116 Tom Lasorda MG	.10	.05	.01
☐ 117 Bill Russell	.07	.03	.01
☐ 118 Jerry Reuss	.07	.03	.01
☐ 119 Terry Forster	.07	.03	.01
☐ 120A Bob Welch P1 Name on back is "Bob"	.45	.22	.04
☐ 120B Bob Welch P2 Name on back is "Robert"	.45	.22	.04
☐ 121 Don Stanhouse	.04	.02	.00
☐ 122 Rick Monday	.04	.02	.00
☐ 123 Derrel Thomas	.04	.02	.00
☐ 124 Joe Ferguson	.04	.02	.00
☐ 125 Rick Sutcliffe	.30	.15	.03
☐ 126A Ron Cey P1 Small hand on back	.50	.25	.05
☐ 126B Ron Cey P2 No hand	.10	.05	.01
☐ 127 Dave Goltz	.04	.02	.00
☐ 128 Jay Johnstone	.07	.03	.01
☐ 129 Steve Yeager	.04	.02	.00
☐ 130 Gary Weiss	.04	.02	.00
☐ 131 Mike Scioscia	.60	.30	.06
☐ 132 Vic Davalillo	.04	.02	.00
☐ 133 Doug Rau	.04	.02	.00
☐ 134 Pepe Frias	.04	.02	.00
☐ 135 Mickey Hatcher	.07	.03	.01
☐ 136 Steve Howe	.10	.05	.01
☐ 137 Robert Castillo	.04	.02	.00
☐ 138 Gary Thomasson	.04	.02	.00
☐ 139 Rudy Law	.04	.02	.00
☐ 140 Fernand Valenzuela UER (sic, Fernando)	5.00	2.50	.50
☐ 141 Manny Mota	.07	.03	.01
☐ 142 Gary Carter	.50	.25	.05
☐ 143 Steve Rogers	.07	.03	.01
☐ 144 Warren Cromartie	.04	.02	.00
☐ 145 Andre Dawson	1.00	.50	.10
☐ 146 Larry Parrish	.07	.03	.01
☐ 147 Rowland Office	.04	.02	.00
☐ 148 Ellis Valentine	.04	.02	.00
☐ 149 Dick Williams MG	.04	.02	.00
☐ 150 Bill Gullickson	.25	.12	.02
☐ 151 Elias Sosa	.04	.02	.00
☐ 152 John Tamargo	.04	.02	.00
☐ 153 Chris Speier	.04	.02	.00
☐ 154 Ron LeFlore	.07	.03	.01
☐ 155 Rodney Scott	.04	.02	.00
☐ 156 Stan Bahnsen	.04	.02	.00
☐ 157 Bill Lee	.07	.03	.01
☐ 158 Fred Norman	.04	.02	.00
☐ 159 Woodie Fryman	.04	.02	.00
☐ 160 David Palmer	.07	.03	.01
☐ 161 Jerry White	.04	.02	.00
☐ 162 Roberto Ramos	.04	.02	.00
☐ 163 John D'Acquisto	.04	.02	.00
☐ 164 Tommy Hutton	.04	.02	.00
☐ 165 Charlie Lea	.20	.10	.02
☐ 166 Scott Sanderson	.07	.03	.01
☐ 167 Ken Macha	.04	.02	.00
☐ 168 Tony Bernazard	.07	.03	.01
☐ 169 Jim Palmer	.75	.35	.07
☐ 170 Steve Stone	.07	.03	.01
☐ 171 Mike Flanagan	.10	.05	.01
☐ 172 Al Bumbry	.04	.02	.00
☐ 173 Doug DeCinces	.07	.03	.01
☐ 174 Scott McGregor	.07	.03	.01
☐ 175 Mark Belanger	.07	.03	.01
☐ 176 Tim Stoddard	.04	.02	.00
☐ 177A Rick Dempsey P1 Small hand on front	.50	.25	.05
☐ 177B Rick Dempsey P2 No hand	.10	.05	.01
☐ 178 Earl Weaver MG	.07	.03	.01
☐ 179 Tippy Martinez	.04	.02	.00
☐ 180 Dennis Martinez	.10	.05	.01
☐ 181 Sammy Stewart	.04	.02	.00
☐ 182 Rich Dauer	.04	.02	.00
☐ 183 Lee May	.07	.03	.01
☐ 184 Eddie Murray	1.00	.50	.10
☐ 185 Benny Ayala	.04	.02	.00
☐ 186 John Lowenstein	.04	.02	.00
☐ 187 Gary Roenicke	.04	.02	.00
☐ 188 Ken Singleton	.07	.03	.01
☐ 189 Dan Graham	.04	.02	.00
☐ 190 Terry Crowley	.04	.02	.00
☐ 191 Kiko Garcia	.04	.02	.00
☐ 192 Dave Ford	.04	.02	.00
☐ 193 Mark Corey	.04	.02	.00
☐ 194 Lenn Sakata	.04	.02	.00
☐ 195 Doug DeCinces	.07	.03	.01
☐ 196 Johnny Bench	1.10	.55	.11
☐ 197 Dave Concepcion	.15	.07	.01
☐ 198 Ray Knight	.10	.05	.01
☐ 199 Ken Griffey	.20	.10	.02
☐ 200 Tom Seaver	1.00	.50	.10
☐ 201 Dave Collins	.04	.02	.00
☐ 202A George Foster P1 Slugger Number on back 216	.15	.07	.01
☐ 202B George Foster P2 Slugger Number on back 202	.15	.07	.01
☐ 203 Junior Kennedy	.04	.02	.00
☐ 204 Frank Pastore	.04	.02	.00
☐ 205 Dan Driessen	.04	.02	.00
☐ 206 Hector Cruz	.04	.02	.00
☐ 207 Paul Moskau	.04	.02	.00
☐ 208 Charlie Leibrandt	.30	.15	.03
☐ 209 Harry Spilman	.04	.02	.00
☐ 210 Joe Price	.07	.03	.01
☐ 211 Tom Hume	.04	.02	.00
☐ 212 Joe Nolan	.04	.02	.00
☐ 213 Doug Bair	.04	.02	.00
☐ 214 Mario Soto	.10	.05	.01
☐ 215A Bill Bonham P1 Small hand on back	.50	.25	.05
☐ 215B Bill Bonham P2 No hand	.07	.03	.01
☐ 216 George Foster (See 202)	.15	.07	.01
☐ 217 Paul Householder	.04	.02	.00

☐ 218	Ron Oester	.07	.03	.01
☐ 219	Sam Mejias	.04	.02	.00
☐ 220	Sheldon Burnside	.04	.02	.00
☐ 221	Carl Yastrzemski	1.10	.55	.11
☐ 222	Jim Rice	.30	.15	.03
☐ 223	Fred Lynn	.20	.10	.02
☐ 224	Carlton Fisk	.65	.30	.06
☐ 225	Rick Burleson	.07	.03	.01
☐ 226	Dennis Eckersley	.40	.20	.04
☐ 227	Butch Hobson	.04	.02	.00
☐ 228	Tom Burgmeier	.04	.02	.00
☐ 229	Garry Hancock	.04	.02	.00
☐ 230	Don Zimmer MG	.07	.03	.01
☐ 231	Steve Renko	.04	.02	.00
☐ 232	Dwight Evans	.35	.17	.03
☐ 233	Mike Torrez	.04	.02	.00
☐ 234	Bob Stanley	.04	.02	.00
☐ 235	Jim Dwyer	.04	.02	.00
☐ 236	Dave Stapleton	.04	.02	.00
☐ 237	Glen Hoffman	.04	.02	.00
☐ 238	Jerry Remy	.04	.02	.00
☐ 239	Dick Drago	.04	.02	.00
☐ 240	Bill Campbell	.04	.02	.00
☐ 241	Tony Perez	.20	.10	.02
☐ 242	Phil Niekro	.30	.15	.03
☐ 243	Dale Murphy	1.25	.60	.12
☐ 244	Bob Horner	.12	.06	.01
☐ 245	Jeff Burroughs	.04	.02	.00
☐ 246	Rick Camp	.04	.02	.00
☐ 247	Bobby Cox MG	.04	.02	.00
☐ 248	Bruce Benedict	.04	.02	.00
☐ 249	Gene Garber	.04	.02	.00
☐ 250	Jerry Royster	.04	.02	.00
☐ 251A	Gary Matthews P1	.50	.25	.05
	Small hand on back			
☐ 251B	Gary Matthews P2	.10	.05	.01
	No hand			
☐ 252	Chris Chambliss	.07	.03	.01
☐ 253	Luis Gomez	.04	.02	.00
☐ 254	Bill Nahorodny	.04	.02	.00
☐ 255	Doyle Alexander	.07	.03	.01
☐ 256	Brian Asselstine	.04	.02	.00
☐ 257	Biff Pocoroba	.04	.02	.00
☐ 258	Mike Lum	.04	.02	.00
☐ 259	Charlie Spikes	.04	.02	.00
☐ 260	Glenn Hubbard	.04	.02	.00
☐ 261	Tommy Boggs	.04	.02	.00
☐ 262	Al Hrabosky	.07	.03	.01
☐ 263	Rick Matula	.04	.02	.00
☐ 264	Preston Hanna	.04	.02	.00
☐ 265	Larry Bradford	.04	.02	.00
☐ 266	Rafael Ramirez	.25	.12	.02
☐ 267	Larry McWilliams	.04	.02	.00
☐ 268	Rod Carew	1.00	.50	.10
☐ 269	Bobby Grich	.10	.05	.01
☐ 270	Carney Lansford	.25	.12	.02
☐ 271	Don Baylor	.15	.07	.01
☐ 272	Joe Rudi	.07	.03	.01
☐ 273	Dan Ford	.04	.02	.00
☐ 274	Jim Fregosi	.07	.03	.01
☐ 275	Dave Frost	.04	.02	.00
☐ 276	Frank Tanana	.07	.03	.01
☐ 277	Dickie Thon	.10	.05	.01
☐ 278	Jason Thompson	.04	.02	.00
☐ 279	Rick Miller	.04	.02	.00
☐ 280	Bert Campaneris	.07	.03	.01
☐ 281	Tom Donohue	.04	.02	.00
☐ 282	Brian Downing	.07	.03	.01
☐ 283	Fred Patek	.04	.02	.00
☐ 284	Bruce Kison	.04	.02	.00
☐ 285	Dave LaRoche	.04	.02	.00
☐ 286	Don Aase	.04	.02	.00
☐ 287	Jim Barr	.04	.02	.00
☐ 288	Alfredo Martinez	.04	.02	.00
☐ 289	Larry Harlow	.04	.02	.00
☐ 290	Andy Hassler	.04	.02	.00
☐ 291	Dave Kingman	.15	.07	.01
☐ 292	Bill Buckner	.10	.05	.01
☐ 293	Rick Reuschel	.20	.10	.02
☐ 294	Bruce Sutter	.20	.10	.02
☐ 295	Jerry Martin	.04	.02	.00
☐ 296	Scot Thompson	.04	.02	.00
☐ 297	Ivan DeJesus	.04	.02	.00
☐ 298	Steve Dillard	.04	.02	.00
☐ 299	Dick Tidrow	.04	.02	.00
☐ 300	Randy Martz	.04	.02	.00
☐ 301	Lenny Randle	.04	.02	.00
☐ 302	Lynn McGlothen	.04	.02	.00
☐ 303	Cliff Johnson	.04	.02	.00
☐ 304	Tim Blackwell	.04	.02	.00
☐ 305	Dennis Lamp	.04	.02	.00
☐ 306	Bill Caudill	.04	.02	.00
☐ 307	Carlos Lezcano	.04	.02	.00
☐ 308	Jim Tracy	.04	.02	.00

☐ 309	Doug Capilla UER	.04	.02	.00
	(Cubs on front but			
	Braves on back)			
☐ 310	Willie Hernandez	.12	.06	.01
☐ 311	Mike Vail	.04	.02	.00
☐ 312	Mike Krukow	.07	.03	.01
☐ 313	Barry Foote	.04	.02	.00
☐ 314	Larry Biittner	.04	.02	.00
☐ 315	Mike Tyson	.04	.02	.00
☐ 316	Lee Mazzilli	.04	.02	.00
☐ 317	John Stearns	.04	.02	.00
☐ 318	Alex Trevino	.04	.02	.00
☐ 319	Craig Swan	.04	.02	.00
☐ 320	Frank Taveras	.04	.02	.00
☐ 321	Steve Henderson	.04	.02	.00
☐ 322	Neil Allen	.07	.03	.01
☐ 323	Mark Bomback	.04	.02	.00
☐ 324	Mike Jorgensen	.04	.02	.00
☐ 325	Joe Torre MG	.10	.05	.01
☐ 326	Elliott Maddox	.04	.02	.00
☐ 327	Pete Falcone	.04	.02	.00
☐ 328	Ray Burris	.04	.02	.00
☐ 329	Claudell Washington	.07	.03	.01
☐ 330	Doug Flynn	.04	.02	.00
☐ 331	Joel Youngblood	.04	.02	.00
☐ 332	Bill Almon	.04	.02	.00
☐ 333	Tom Hausman	.04	.02	.00
☐ 334	Pat Zachry	.04	.02	.00
☐ 335	Jeff Reardon	1.00	.50	.10
☐ 336	Wally Backman	.45	.22	.04
☐ 337	Dan Norman	.04	.02	.00
☐ 338	Jerry Morales	.04	.02	.00
☐ 339	Ed Farmer	.04	.02	.00
☐ 340	Bob Molinaro	.04	.02	.00
☐ 341	Todd Cruz	.04	.02	.00
☐ 342A	Britt Burns P1	.60	.30	.06
	Small hand on front			
☐ 342B	Britt Burns P2	.25	.12	.02
	No hand			
☐ 343	Kevin Bell	.04	.02	.00
☐ 344	Tony LaRussa MG	.07	.03	.01
☐ 345	Steve Trout	.04	.02	.00
☐ 346	Harold Baines	2.50	1.25	.25
☐ 347	Richard Wortham	.04	.02	.00
☐ 348	Wayne Nordhagen	.04	.02	.00
☐ 349	Mike Squires	.04	.02	.00
☐ 350	Lamar Johnson	.04	.02	.00
☐ 351	Rickey Henderson	12.50	6.25	1.25
	(Most Stolen Bases AL)			
☐ 352	Francisco Barrios	.04	.02	.00
☐ 353	Thad Bosley	.04	.02	.00
☐ 354	Chet Lemon	.07	.03	.01
☐ 355	Bruce Kimm	.04	.02	.00
☐ 356	Richard Dotson	.25	.12	.02
☐ 357	Jim Morrison	.04	.02	.00
☐ 358	Mike Proly	.04	.02	.00
☐ 359	Greg Pryor	.04	.02	.00
☐ 360	Dave Parker	.40	.20	.04
☐ 361	Omar Moreno	.04	.02	.00
☐ 362A	Kent Tekulve P1	.15	.07	.01
	Back "1071 Waterbury"			
	and "1078 Pirates"			
☐ 362B	Kent Tekulve P2	.10	.05	.01
	"1971 Waterbury" and			
	"1978 Pirates"			
☐ 363	Willie Stargell	.40	.20	.04
☐ 364	Phil Garner	.04	.02	.00
☐ 365	Ed Ott	.04	.02	.00
☐ 366	Don Robinson	.07	.03	.01
☐ 367	Chuck Tanner MG	.07	.03	.01
☐ 368	Jim Rooker	.04	.02	.00
☐ 369	Dale Berra	.04	.02	.00
☐ 370	Jim Bibby	.04	.02	.00
☐ 371	Steve Nicosia	.04	.02	.00
☐ 372	Mike Easler	.07	.03	.01
☐ 373	Bill Robinson	.07	.03	.01
☐ 374	Lee Lacy	.04	.02	.00
☐ 375	John Candelaria	.07	.03	.01
☐ 376	Manny Sanguillen	.07	.03	.01
☐ 377	Rick Rhoden	.07	.03	.01
☐ 378	Grant Jackson	.04	.02	.00
☐ 379	Tim Foli	.04	.02	.00
☐ 380	Rod Scurry	.04	.02	.00
☐ 381	Bill Madlock	.10	.05	.01
☐ 382A	Kurt Bevacqua	.20	.10	.02
	P1 ERR			
	(P on cap backwards)			
☐ 382B	Kurt Bevacqua P2	.07	.03	.01
	COR			
☐ 383	Bert Blyleven	.25	.12	.02
☐ 384	Eddie Solomon	.04	.02	.00
☐ 385	Enrique Romo	.04	.02	.00
☐ 386	John Milner	.04	.02	.00
☐ 387	Mike Hargrove	.07	.03	.01

☐ 388 Jorge Orta	.04	.02	.00
☐ 389 Toby Harrah	.07	.03	.01
☐ 390 Tom Veryzer	.04	.02	.00
☐ 391 Miguel Dilone	.04	.02	.00
☐ 392 Dan Spillner	.04	.02	.00
☐ 393 Jack Brohamer	.04	.02	.00
☐ 394 Wayne Garland	.04	.02	.00
☐ 395 Sid Monge	.04	.02	.00
☐ 396 Rick Waits	.04	.02	.00
☐ 397 Joe Charboneau	.10	.05	.01
☐ 398 Gary Alexander	.04	.02	.00
☐ 399 Jerry Dybzinski	.04	.02	.00
☐ 400 Mike Stanton	.04	.02	.00
☐ 401 Mike Paxton	.04	.02	.00
☐ 402 Gary Gray	.04	.02	.00
☐ 403 Rick Manning	.04	.02	.00
☐ 404 Bo Diaz	.04	.02	.00
☐ 405 Ron Hassey	.04	.02	.00
☐ 406 Ross Grimsley	.04	.02	.00
☐ 407 Victor Cruz	.04	.02	.00
☐ 408 Len Barker	.04	.02	.00
☐ 409 Bob Bailor	.04	.02	.00
☐ 410 Otto Velez	.04	.02	.00
☐ 411 Ernie Whitt	.07	.03	.01
☐ 412 Jim Clancy	.07	.03	.01
☐ 413 Barry Bonnell	.04	.02	.00
☐ 414 Dave Stieb	.60	.30	.06
☐ 415 Damaso Garcia	.10	.05	.01
☐ 416 John Mayberry	.07	.03	.01
☐ 417 Roy Howell	.04	.02	.00
☐ 418 Danny Ainge	.45	.22	.04
☐ 419A Jesse Jefferson P1	.07	.03	.01
Back says Pirates			
☐ 419B Jesse Jefferson P2	.07	.03	.01
Back says Pirates			
☐ 419C Jesse Jefferson P3	.35	.17	.03
Back says Blue Jays			
☐ 420 Joey McLaughlin	.04	.02	.00
☐ 421 Lloyd Moseby	.75	.35	.07
☐ 422 Alvis Woods	.04	.02	.00
☐ 423 Garth Iorg	.04	.02	.00
☐ 424 Doug Ault	.04	.02	.00
☐ 425 Ken Schrom	.04	.02	.00
☐ 426 Mike Willis	.04	.02	.00
☐ 427 Steve Braun	.04	.02	.00
☐ 428 Bob Davis	.04	.02	.00
☐ 429 Jerry Garvin	.04	.02	.00
☐ 430 Alfredo Griffin	.10	.05	.01
☐ 431 Bob Mattick MG	.04	.02	.00
☐ 432 Vida Blue	.10	.05	.01
☐ 433 Jack Clark	.30	.15	.03
☐ 434 Willie McCovey	.40	.20	.04
☐ 435 Mike Ivie	.04	.02	.00
☐ 436A Darrel Evans P1 ERR	.40	.20	.04
Name on front "Darrel"			
☐ 436B Darrell Evans P2	.15	.07	.01
Name on front "Darrell"			
☐ 437 Terry Whitfield	.04	.02	.00
☐ 438 Rennie Stennett	.04	.02	.00
☐ 439 John Montefusco	.07	.03	.01
☐ 440 Jim Wohlford	.04	.02	.00
☐ 441 Bill North	.04	.02	.00
☐ 442 Milt May	.04	.02	.00
☐ 443 Max Venable	.04	.02	.00
☐ 444 Ed Whitson	.07	.03	.01
☐ 445 Al Holland	.07	.03	.01
☐ 446 Randy Moffitt	.04	.02	.00
☐ 447 Bob Knepper	.07	.03	.01
☐ 448 Gary Lavelle	.04	.02	.00
☐ 449 Greg Minton	.04	.02	.00
☐ 450 Johnnie LeMaster	.04	.02	.00
☐ 451 Larry Herndon	.04	.02	.00
☐ 452 Rich Murray	.04	.02	.00
☐ 453 Joe Pettini	.04	.02	.00
☐ 454 Allen Ripley	.04	.02	.00
☐ 455 Dennis Littlejohn	.04	.02	.00
☐ 456 Tom Griffin	.04	.02	.00
☐ 457 Alan Hargesheimer	.04	.02	.00
☐ 458 Joe Strain	.04	.02	.00
☐ 459 Steve Kemp	.07	.03	.01
☐ 460 Sparky Anderson MG	.10	.05	.01
☐ 461 Alan Trammell	.50	.25	.05
☐ 462 Mark Fidrych	.10	.05	.01
☐ 463 Lou Whitaker	.30	.15	.03
☐ 464 Dave Rozema	.04	.02	.00
☐ 465 Milt Wilcox	.04	.02	.00
☐ 466 Champ Summers	.04	.02	.00
☐ 467 Lance Parrish	.35	.17	.03
☐ 468 Dan Petry	.10	.05	.01
☐ 469 Pat Underwood	.04	.02	.00
☐ 470 Rick Peters	.04	.02	.00
☐ 471 Al Cowens	.04	.02	.00
☐ 472 John Wockenfuss	.04	.02	.00
☐ 473 Tom Brookens	.04	.02	.00
☐ 474 Richie Hebner	.04	.02	.00
☐ 475 Jack Morris	.30	.15	.03
☐ 476 Jim Lentine	.04	.02	.00
☐ 477 Bruce Robbins	.04	.02	.00
☐ 478 Mark Wagner	.04	.02	.00
☐ 479 Tim Corcoran	.04	.02	.00
☐ 480A Stan Papi P1	.15	.07	.01
Front as Pitcher			
☐ 480B Stan Papi P2	.10	.05	.01
Front as Shortstop			
☐ 481 Kirk Gibson	3.50	1.75	.35
☐ 482 Dan Schatzeder	.04	.02	.00
☐ 483A Amos Otis P1	.10	.05	.01
See card 32			
☐ 483B Amos Otis P2	.10	.05	.01
See card 32			
☐ 484 Dave Winfield	.65	.30	.06
☐ 485 Rollie Fingers	.45	.22	.04
☐ 486 Gene Richards	.04	.02	.00
☐ 487 Randy Jones	.04	.02	.00
☐ 488 Ozzie Smith	.80	.40	.08
☐ 489 Gene Tenace	.04	.02	.00
☐ 490 Bill Fahey	.04	.02	.00
☐ 491 John Curtis	.04	.02	.00
☐ 492 Dave Cash	.04	.02	.00
☐ 493A Tim Flannery P1	.15	.07	.01
Batting right			
☐ 493B Tim Flannery P2	.07	.03	.01
Batting left			
☐ 494 Jerry Mumphrey	.04	.02	.00
☐ 495 Bob Shirley	.04	.02	.00
☐ 496 Steve Mura	.04	.02	.00
☐ 497 Eric Rasmussen	.04	.02	.00
☐ 498 Broderick Perkins	.04	.02	.00
☐ 499 Barry Evans	.04	.02	.00
☐ 500 Chuck Baker	.04	.02	.00
☐ 501 Luis Salazar	.15	.07	.01
☐ 502 Gary Lucas	.04	.02	.00
☐ 503 Mike Armstrong	.04	.02	.00
☐ 504 Jerry Turner	.04	.02	.00
☐ 505 Dennis Kinney	.04	.02	.00
☐ 506 Willie Montanez	.04	.02	.00
☐ 507 Gorman Thomas	.10	.05	.01
☐ 508 Ben Oglivie	.07	.03	.01
☐ 509 Larry Hisle	.04	.02	.00
☐ 510 Sal Bando	.07	.03	.01
☐ 511 Robin Yount	1.25	.60	.12
☐ 512 Mike Caldwell	.04	.02	.00
☐ 513 Sixto Lezcano	.04	.02	.00
☐ 514A Bill Travers P1 ERR	.20	.10	.02
"Jerry Augustine" with Augustine back			
☐ 514B Bill Travers P2 COR	.10	.05	.01
☐ 515 Paul Molitor	.35	.17	.03
☐ 516 Moose Haas	.04	.02	.00
☐ 517 Bill Castro	.04	.02	.00
☐ 518 Jim Slaton	.04	.02	.00
☐ 519 Lary Sorensen	.04	.02	.00
☐ 520 Bob McClure	.04	.02	.00
☐ 521 Charlie Moore	.04	.02	.00
☐ 522 Jim Gantner	.07	.03	.01
☐ 523 Reggie Cleveland	.04	.02	.00
☐ 524 Don Money	.04	.02	.00
☐ 525 Bill Travers	.04	.02	.00
☐ 526 Buck Martinez	.04	.02	.00
☐ 527 Dick Davis	.04	.02	.00
☐ 528 Ted Simmons	.12	.06	.01
☐ 529 Garry Templeton	.10	.05	.01
☐ 530 Ken Reitz	.04	.02	.00
☐ 531 Tony Scott	.04	.02	.00
☐ 532 Ken Oberkfell	.04	.02	.00
☐ 533 Bob Sykes	.04	.02	.00
☐ 534 Keith Smith	.04	.02	.00
☐ 535 John Littlefield	.04	.02	.00
☐ 536 Jim Kaat	.20	.10	.02
☐ 537 Bob Forsch	.04	.02	.00
☐ 538 Mike Phillips	.04	.02	.00
☐ 539 Terry Landrum	.07	.03	.01
☐ 540 Leon Durham	.25	.12	.02
☐ 541 Terry Kennedy	.07	.03	.01
☐ 542 George Hendrick	.07	.03	.01
☐ 543 Dane Iorg	.04	.02	.00
☐ 544 Mark Littell	.04	.02	.00
☐ 545 Keith Hernandez	.35	.17	.03
☐ 546 Silvio Martinez	.04	.02	.00
☐ 547A Don Hood P1 ERR	.20	.10	.02
"Pete Vuckovich" with Vuckovich back			
☐ 547B Don Hood P2 COR	.10	.05	.01
☐ 548 Bobby Bonds	.12	.06	.01
☐ 549 Mike Ramsey	.04	.02	.00
☐ 550 Tom Herr	.12	.06	.01
☐ 551 Roy Smalley	.04	.02	.00

☐ 552	Jerry Koosman	.10	.05	.01
☐ 553	Ken Landreaux	.04	.02	.00
☐ 554	John Castino	.04	.02	.00
☐ 555	Doug Corbett	.04	.02	.00
☐ 556	Bombo Rivera	.04	.02	.00
☐ 557	Ron Jackson	.04	.02	.00
☐ 558	Butch Wynegar	.04	.02	.00
☐ 559	Hosken Powell	.04	.02	.00
☐ 560	Pete Redfern	.04	.02	.00
☐ 561	Roger Erickson	.04	.02	.00
☐ 562	Glenn Adams	.04	.02	.00
☐ 563	Rick Sofield	.04	.02	.00
☐ 564	Geoff Zahn	.04	.02	.00
☐ 565	Pete Mackanin	.04	.02	.00
☐ 566	Mike Cubbage	.04	.02	.00
☐ 567	Darrell Jackson	.04	.02	.00
☐ 568	Dave Edwards	.04	.02	.00
☐ 569	Rob Wilfong	.04	.02	.00
☐ 570	Sal Butera	.04	.02	.00
☐ 571	Jose Morales	.04	.02	.00
☐ 572	Rick Langford	.04	.02	.00
☐ 573	Mike Norris	.04	.02	.00
☐ 574	Rickey Henderson	16.50	7.50	1.50
☐ 575	Tony Armas	.07	.03	.01
☐ 576	Dave Revering	.04	.02	.00
☐ 577	Jeff Newman	.04	.02	.00
☐ 578	Bob Lacey	.04	.02	.00
☐ 579	Brian Kingman	.04	.02	.00
☐ 580	Mitchell Page	.04	.02	.00
☐ 581	Billy Martin MG	.20	.10	.02
☐ 582	Rob Picciolo	.04	.02	.00
☐ 583	Mike Heath	.04	.02	.00
☐ 584	Mickey Klutts	.04	.02	.00
☐ 585	Orlando Gonzalez	.04	.02	.00
☐ 586	Mike Davis	.18	.09	.01
☐ 587	Wayne Gross	.04	.02	.00
☐ 588	Matt Keough	.04	.02	.00
☐ 589	Steve McCatty	.04	.02	.00
☐ 590	Dwayne Murphy	.04	.02	.00
☐ 591	Mario Guerrero	.04	.02	.00
☐ 592	Dave McKay	.04	.02	.00
☐ 593	Jim Essian	.04	.02	.00
☐ 594	Dave Heaverlo	.04	.02	.00
☐ 595	Maury Wills MG	.10	.05	.01
☐ 596	Juan Beniquez	.04	.02	.00
☐ 597	Rodney Craig	.04	.02	.00
☐ 598	Jim Anderson	.04	.02	.00
☐ 599	Floyd Bannister	.07	.03	.01
☐ 600	Bruce Bochte	.04	.02	.00
☐ 601	Julio Cruz	.04	.02	.00
☐ 602	Ted Cox	.04	.02	.00
☐ 603	Dan Meyer	.04	.02	.00
☐ 604	Larry Cox	.04	.02	.00
☐ 605	Bill Stein	.04	.02	.00
☐ 606	Steve Garvey	.65	.30	.06
☐ 607	Dave Roberts	.04	.02	.00
☐ 608	Leon Roberts	.04	.02	.00
☐ 609	Reggie Walton	.04	.02	.00
☐ 610	Dave Edler	.04	.02	.00
☐ 611	Larry Milbourne	.04	.02	.00
☐ 612	Kim Allen	.04	.02	.00
☐ 613	Mario Mendoza	.04	.02	.00
☐ 614	Tom Paciorek	.04	.02	.00
☐ 615	Glenn Abbott	.04	.02	.00
☐ 616	Joe Simpson	.04	.02	.00
☐ 617	Mickey Rivers	.07	.03	.01
☐ 618	Jim Kern	.04	.02	.00
☐ 619	Jim Sundberg	.04	.02	.00
☐ 620	Richie Zisk	.04	.02	.00
☐ 621	Jon Matlack	.04	.02	.00
☐ 622	Ferguson Jenkins	.15	.07	.01
☐ 623	Pat Corrales MG	.04	.02	.00
☐ 624	Ed Figueroa	.04	.02	.00
☐ 625	Buddy Bell	.12	.06	.01
☐ 626	Al Oliver	.12	.06	.01
☐ 627	Doc Medich	.04	.02	.00
☐ 628	Bump Wills	.04	.02	.00
☐ 629	Rusty Staub	.12	.06	.01
☐ 630	Pat Putnam	.04	.02	.00
☐ 631	John Grubb	.04	.02	.00
☐ 632	Danny Darwin	.10	.05	.01
☐ 633	Ken Clay	.04	.02	.00
☐ 634	Jim Norris	.04	.02	.00
☐ 635	John Butcher	.04	.02	.00
☐ 636	Dave Roberts	.04	.02	.00
☐ 637	Billy Sample	.04	.02	.00
☐ 638	Carl Yastrzemski	1.10	.55	.11
☐ 639	Cecil Cooper	.15	.07	.01
☐ 640A	Mike Schmidt P1	1.75	.85	.17
	(Portrait)			
	"Third Base"			
	(number on back 5)			
☐ 640B	Mike Schmidt P2	1.50	.75	.15
	"1980 Home Run King"			
	(640 on back)			
☐ 641A	CL: Phils/Royals P1	.10	.01	.00
	41 is Hal McRae			
☐ 641B	CL: Phils/Royals P2	.10	.01	.00
	41 is Hal McRae,			
	Double Threat			
☐ 642	CL: Astros/Yankees	.08	.01	.00
☐ 643	CL: Expos/Dodgers	.08	.01	.00
☐ 644A	CL: Reds/Orioles P1	.10	.01	.00
	202 is George Foster			
☐ 644B	CL: Reds/Orioles P2	.10	.01	.00
	202 is Foster Slugger			
☐ 645A	Rose/Bowa/Schmidt	2.00	1.00	.20
	Triple Threat P1			
	(No number on back)			
☐ 645B	Rose/Bowa/Schmidt	1.00	.50	.10
	Triple Threat P2			
	(Back numbered 645)			
☐ 646	CL: Braves/Red Sox	.08	.01	.00
☐ 647	CL: Cubs/Angels	.08	.01	.00
☐ 648	CL: Mets/White Sox	.08	.01	.00
☐ 649	CL: Indians/Pirates	.08	.01	.00
☐ 650A	Reggie Jackson	1.50	.75	.15
	Mr. Baseball P1			
	Number on back 79			
☐ 650B	Reggie Jackson	1.25	.60	.12
	Mr. Baseball P2			
	Number on back 650			
☐ 651	CL: Giants/Blue Jays	.08	.01	.00
☐ 652A	CL: Tigers/Padres P1	.10	.01	.00
	483 is listed			
☐ 652B	CL: Tigers/Padres P2	.10	.01	.00
	483 is deleted			
☐ 653A	Willie Wilson P1	.15	.07	.01
	Most Hits Most Runs			
	Number on back 29			
☐ 653B	Willie Wilson P2	.15	.07	.01
	Most Hits Most Runs			
	Number on back 653			
☐ 654A	CL:Brewers/Cards P1	.10	.01	.00
	514 Jerry Augustine			
	547 Pete Vuckovich			
☐ 654B	CL:Brewers/Cards P2	.10	.01	.00
	514 Billy Travers			
	547 Don Hood			
☐ 655A	George Brett P1	1.50	.75	.15
	.390 Average			
	Number on back 28			
☐ 655B	George Brett P2	1.25	.60	.12
	.390 Average			
	Number on back 655			
☐ 656	CL: Twins/Oakland A's	.08	.01	.00
☐ 657A	Tug McGraw P1	.10	.05	.01
	Game Saver			
	Number on back 7			
☐ 657B	Tug McGraw P2	.10	.05	.01
	Game Saver			
	Number on back 657			
☐ 658	CL: Rangers/Mariners	.08	.01	.00
☐ 659A	Checklist P1	.10	.01	.00
	of Special Cards			
	Last lines on front			
	Wilson Most Hits			
☐ 659B	Checklist P2	.10	.01	.00
	of Special Cards			
	Last lines on front			
	Otis Series Starter			
☐ 660A	Steve Carlton P1	1.25	.60	.12
	Golden Arm			
	Back "1066 Cardinals"			
	Number on back 6			
☐ 660B	Steve Carlton P2	1.00	.50	.10
	Golden Arm			
	Number on back 660			
	Back "1066 Cardinals"			
☐ 660C	Steve Carlton P3	2.00	1.00	.20
	Golden Arm			
	"1966 Cardinals"			

1981 Fleer Sticker Cards

The stickers in this 128-sticker set measure 2 1/2" by 3 1/2". The 1981 Fleer Baseball Star Stickers consist of numbered cards with peelable, full-color sticker fronts and three unnumbered checklists. The backs of the numbered player cards are the same as the 1981 Fleer regular issue cards except for the numbers, while the checklist cards (cards 126-128 below) have sticker fronts of Jackson (1-42), Brett (43-83), and Schmidt (84-125).

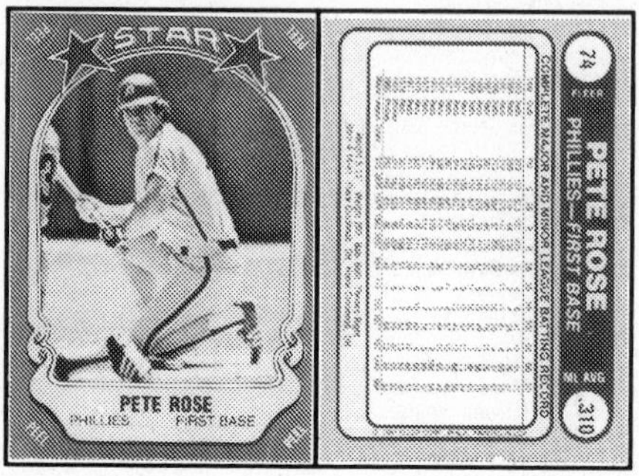

	MINT	EXC	G-VG
COMPLETE SET (128)	50.00	25.00	5.00
COMMON PLAYER (1-128)	.15	.07	.01
☐ 1 Steve Garvey	2.00	1.00	.20
☐ 2 Ron LeFlore	.15	.07	.01
☐ 3 Ron Cey	.20	.10	.02
☐ 4 Dave Revering	.15	.07	.01
☐ 5 Tony Armas	.15	.07	.01
☐ 6 Mike Norris	.15	.07	.01
☐ 7 Steve Kemp	.20	.10	.02
☐ 8 Bruce Bochte	.15	.07	.01
☐ 9 Mike Schmidt	4.50	2.25	.45
☐ 10 Scott McGregor	.20	.10	.02
☐ 11 Buddy Bell	.25	.12	.02
☐ 12 Carney Lansford	.35	.17	.03
☐ 13 Carl Yastrzemski	3.00	1.50	.30
☐ 14 Ben Oglivie	.15	.07	.01
☐ 15 Willie Stargell	1.25	.60	.12
☐ 16 Cecil Cooper	.20	.10	.02
☐ 17 Gene Richards	.15	.07	.01
☐ 18 Jim Kern	.15	.07	.01
☐ 19 Jerry Koosman	.20	.10	.02
☐ 20 Larry Bowa	.25	.12	.02
☐ 21 Kent Tekulve	.15	.07	.01
☐ 22 Dan Driessen	.15	.07	.01
☐ 23 Phil Niekro	.90	.45	.09
☐ 24 Dan Quisenberry	.25	.12	.02
☐ 25 Dave Winfield	1.50	.75	.15
☐ 26 Dave Parker	.90	.45	.09
☐ 27 Rick Langford	.15	.07	.01
☐ 28 Amos Otis	.20	.10	.02
☐ 29 Bill Buckner	.20	.10	.02
☐ 30 Al Bumbry	.15	.07	.01
☐ 31 Bake McBride	.15	.07	.01
☐ 32 Mickey Rivers	.15	.07	.01
☐ 33 Rick Burleson	.20	.10	.02
☐ 34 Dennis Eckersley	.75	.35	.07
☐ 35 Cesar Cedeno	.20	.10	.02
☐ 36 Enos Cabell	.15	.07	.01
☐ 37 Johnny Bench	3.00	1.50	.30
☐ 38 Robin Yount	3.00	1.50	.30
☐ 39 Mark Belanger	.15	.07	.01
☐ 40 Rod Carew	2.50	1.25	.25
☐ 41 George Foster	.60	.30	.06
☐ 42 Lee Mazzilli	.15	.07	.01
☐ 43 Triple Threat: Pete Rose, Larry Bowa, Mike Schmidt	3.00	1.50	.30
☐ 44 J.R. Richard	.20	.10	.02
☐ 45 Lou Piniella	.30	.15	.03
☐ 46 Ken Landreaux	.15	.07	.01
☐ 47 Rollie Fingers	.60	.30	.06
☐ 48 Joaquin Andujar	.20	.10	.02
☐ 49 Tom Seaver	2.50	1.25	.25
☐ 50 Bobby Grich	.20	.10	.02
☐ 51 Jon Matlack	.15	.07	.01
☐ 52 Jack Clark	.60	.30	.06
☐ 53 Jim Rice	.90	.45	.09
☐ 54 Rickey Henderson	6.00	3.00	.60
☐ 55 Roy Smalley	.15	.07	.01
☐ 56 Mike Flanagan	.20	.10	.02
☐ 57 Steve Rogers	.15	.07	.01
☐ 58 Carlton Fisk	1.00	.50	.10
☐ 59 Don Sutton	.75	.35	.07
☐ 60 Ken Griffey	.30	.15	.03
☐ 61 Burt Hooton	.15	.07	.01
☐ 62 Dusty Baker	.20	.10	.02
☐ 63 Vida Blue	.20	.10	.02
☐ 64 Al Oliver	.20	.10	.02
☐ 65 Jim Bibby	.15	.07	.01
☐ 66 Tony Perez	.50	.25	.05
☐ 67 Davy Lopes	.20	.10	.02
☐ 68 Bill Russell	.15	.07	.01
☐ 69 Larry Parrish	.15	.07	.01
☐ 70 Garry Maddox	.15	.07	.01
☐ 71 Phil Garner	.15	.07	.01
☐ 72 Graig Nettles	.35	.17	.03
☐ 73 Gary Carter	1.50	.75	.15
☐ 74 Pete Rose	4.50	2.25	.45
☐ 75 Greg Luzinski	.25	.12	.02
☐ 76 Ron Guidry	.50	.25	.05
☐ 77 Gorman Thomas	.20	.10	.02
☐ 78 Jose Cruz	.20	.10	.02
☐ 79 Bob Boone	.40	.20	.04
☐ 80 Bruce Sutter	.25	.12	.02
☐ 81 Chris Chambliss	.20	.10	.02
☐ 82 Paul Molitor	.60	.30	.06
☐ 83 Tug McGraw	.25	.12	.02
☐ 84 Ferguson Jenkins	.90	.45	.09
☐ 85 Steve Carlton	2.00	1.00	.20
☐ 86 Miguel Dilone	.15	.07	.01
☐ 87 Reggie Smith	.25	.12	.02
☐ 88 Rick Cerone	.15	.07	.01
☐ 89 Alan Trammell	1.25	.60	.12
☐ 90 Doug DeCinces	.20	.10	.02
☐ 91 Sparky Lyle	.25	.12	.02
☐ 92 Warren Cromartie	.15	.07	.01
☐ 93 Rick Reuschel	.35	.17	.03
☐ 94 Larry Hisle	.15	.07	.01
☐ 95 Paul Splittorff	.20	.10	.02
☐ 96 Manny Trillo	.15	.07	.01
☐ 97 Frank White	.20	.10	.02
☐ 98 Fred Lynn	.50	.25	.05
☐ 99 Bob Horner	.40	.20	.04
☐ 100 Omar Moreno	.15	.07	.01
☐ 101 Dave Concepcion	.20	.10	.02
☐ 102 Larry Gura	.15	.07	.01
☐ 103 Ken Singleton	.20	.10	.02
☐ 104 Steve Stone	.15	.07	.01
☐ 105 Richie Zisk	.15	.07	.01
☐ 106 Willie Wilson	.25	.12	.02
☐ 107 Willie Randolph	.20	.10	.02
☐ 108 Nolan Ryan	6.00	3.00	.60
☐ 109 Joe Morgan	1.50	.75	.15
☐ 110 Bucky Dent	.40	.20	.04
☐ 111 Dave Kingman	.35	.17	.03
☐ 112 John Castino	.15	.07	.01
☐ 113 Joe Rudi	.15	.07	.01
☐ 114 Ed Farmer	.15	.07	.01
☐ 115 Reggie Jackson	3.00	1.50	.30
☐ 116 George Brett	3.00	1.50	.30
☐ 117 Eddie Murray	2.00	1.00	.20
☐ 118 Rich Gossage	.40	.20	.04
☐ 119 Dale Murphy	2.00	1.00	.20
☐ 120 Ted Simmons	.25	.12	.02
☐ 121 Tommy John	.50	.25	.05
☐ 122 Don Baylor	.40	.20	.04
☐ 123 Andre Dawson	2.00	1.00	.20
☐ 124 Jim Palmer	1.50	.75	.15
☐ 125 Garry Templeton	.20	.10	.02
☐ 126 CL 1: Reggie Jackson	2.00	1.00	.20
☐ 127 CL 2: George Brett	2.00	1.00	.20
☐ 128 CL 3: Mike Schmidt	3.00	1.50	.30

1982 Fleer

The cards in this 660-card set measure 2 1/2" by 3 1/2". The 1982 Fleer set is again ordered by teams; in fact, the players within each team are listed in alphabetical order. The teams are ordered (by 1981 standings) as follows: Los Angeles (1-29), New York Yankees (30-56), Cincinnati (57-84), Oakland (85-109), St. Louis (110-132), Milwaukee (133-156), Baltimore (157-182), Montreal (183-211), Houston (212-237), Philadelphia (238-262), Detroit (263-286), Boston (287-312), Texas (313-334), Chicago White Sox (335-358), Cleveland (359-382), San Francisco (383-403), Kansas City (404-427), Atlanta (428-449), California (450-474), Pittsburgh (475-501), Seattle (502-519), New York Mets (520-544), Minnesota (545-

565), San Diego (566-585), Chicago Cubs (586-607), and Toronto (608-627). Cards numbered 628 through 646 are special cards highlighting some of the stars and leaders of the 1981 season. The last 14 cards in the set (647-660) are checklist cards. The backs feature player statistics and a full-color team logo in the upper right-hand corner of each card. The complete set price below does not include any of the more valuable variation cards listed. The key rookie cards in this set are George Bell, Cal Ripken Jr., and Dave Stewart.

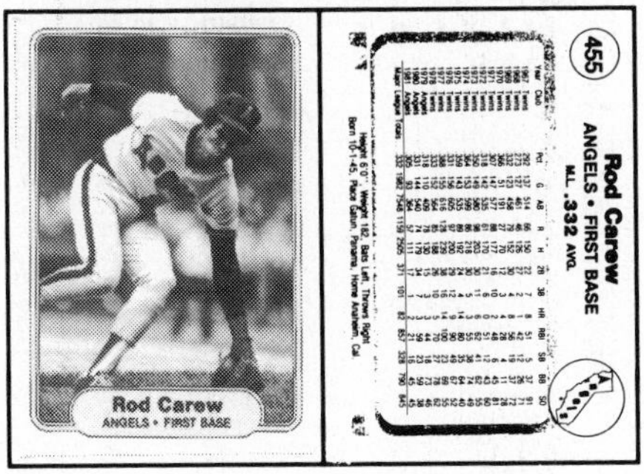

	MINT	EXC	G-VG
COMPLETE SET (660)	52.00	24.00	4.00
COMMON PLAYER (1-660)	.04	.02	.00
☐ 1 Dusty Baker	.12	.06	.01
☐ 2 Robert Castillo	.04	.02	.00
☐ 3 Ron Cey	.10	.05	.01
☐ 4 Terry Forster	.07	.03	.01
☐ 5 Steve Garvey	.50	.25	.05
☐ 6 Dave Goltz	.04	.02	.00
☐ 7 Pedro Guerrero	.75	.35	.07
☐ 8 Burt Hooton	.04	.02	.00
☐ 9 Steve Howe	.04	.02	.00
☐ 10 Jay Johnstone	.07	.03	.01
☐ 11 Ken Landreaux	.04	.02	.00
☐ 12 Dave Lopes	.07	.03	.01
☐ 13 Mike Marshall (outfielder)	1.25	.60	.12
☐ 14 Bobby Mitchell	.04	.02	.00
☐ 15 Rick Monday	.07	.03	.01
☐ 16 Tom Niedenfuer	.25	.12	.02
☐ 17 Ted Power	.30	.15	.03
☐ 18 Jerry Reuss	.07	.03	.01
☐ 19 Ron Roenicke	.04	.02	.00
☐ 20 Bill Russell	.07	.03	.01
☐ 21 Steve Sax	3.50	1.75	.35
☐ 22 Mike Scioscia	.10	.05	.01
☐ 23 Reggie Smith	.07	.03	.01
☐ 24 Dave Stewart	7.50	3.75	.75
☐ 25 Rick Sutcliffe	.20	.10	.02
☐ 26 Derrel Thomas	.04	.02	.00
☐ 27 Fernando Valenzuela	.75	.35	.07
☐ 28 Bob Welch	.40	.20	.04
☐ 29 Steve Yeager	.04	.02	.00
☐ 30 Bobby Brown	.04	.02	.00
☐ 31 Rick Cerone	.04	.02	.00
☐ 32 Ron Davis	.04	.02	.00
☐ 33 Bucky Dent	.10	.05	.01
☐ 34 Barry Foote	.04	.02	.00
☐ 35 George Frazier	.04	.02	.00
☐ 36 Oscar Gamble	.04	.02	.00
☐ 37 Rich Gossage	.20	.10	.02
☐ 38 Ron Guidry	.20	.10	.02
☐ 39 Reggie Jackson	1.00	.50	.10
☐ 40 Tommy John	.18	.09	.01
☐ 41 Rudy May	.04	.02	.00
☐ 42 Larry Milbourne	.04	.02	.00
☐ 43 Jerry Mumphrey	.04	.02	.00
☐ 44 Bobby Murcer	.07	.03	.01
☐ 45 Gene Nelson	.10	.05	.01
☐ 46 Graig Nettles	.12	.06	.01
☐ 47 Johnny Oates	.04	.02	.00
☐ 48 Lou Piniella	.10	.05	.01
☐ 49 Willie Randolph	.07	.03	.01
☐ 50 Rick Reuschel	.15	.07	.01
☐ 51 Dave Revering	.04	.02	.00
☐ 52 Dave Righetti	1.50	.75	.15
☐ 53 Aurelio Rodriguez	.04	.02	.00
☐ 54 Bob Watson	.07	.03	.01
☐ 55 Dennis Werth	.04	.02	.00
☐ 56 Dave Winfield	.50	.25	.05
☐ 57 Johnny Bench	.80	.40	.08
☐ 58 Bruce Berenyi	.04	.02	.00
☐ 59 Larry Biittner	.04	.02	.00
☐ 60 Scott Brown	.04	.02	.00
☐ 61 Dave Collins	.04	.02	.00
☐ 62 Geoff Combe	.04	.02	.00
☐ 63 Dave Concepcion	.10	.05	.01
☐ 64 Dan Driessen	.04	.02	.00
☐ 65 Joe Edelen	.04	.02	.00
☐ 66 George Foster	.15	.07	.01
☐ 67 Ken Griffey	.20	.10	.02
☐ 68 Paul Householder	.04	.02	.00
☐ 69 Tom Hume	.04	.02	.00
☐ 70 Junior Kennedy	.04	.02	.00
☐ 71 Ray Knight	.10	.05	.01
☐ 72 Mike LaCoss	.04	.02	.00
☐ 73 Rafael Landestoy	.04	.02	.00
☐ 74 Charlie Leibrandt	.07	.03	.01
☐ 75 Sam Mejias	.04	.02	.00
☐ 76 Paul Moskau	.04	.02	.00
☐ 77 Joe Nolan	.04	.02	.00
☐ 78 Mike O'Berry	.04	.02	.00
☐ 79 Ron Oester	.04	.02	.00
☐ 80 Frank Pastore	.04	.02	.00
☐ 81 Joe Price	.04	.02	.00
☐ 82 Tom Seaver	.80	.40	.08
☐ 83 Mario Soto	.07	.03	.01
☐ 84 Mike Vail	.04	.02	.00
☐ 85 Tony Armas	.07	.03	.01
☐ 86 Shooty Babitt	.04	.02	.00
☐ 87 Dave Beard	.04	.02	.00
☐ 88 Rick Bosetti	.04	.02	.00
☐ 89 Keith Drumwright	.04	.02	.00
☐ 90 Wayne Gross	.04	.02	.00
☐ 91 Mike Heath	.04	.02	.00
☐ 92 Rickey Henderson	5.00	2.50	.50
☐ 93 Cliff Johnson	.04	.02	.00
☐ 94 Jeff Jones	.04	.02	.00
☐ 95 Matt Keough	.04	.02	.00
☐ 96 Brian Kingman	.04	.02	.00
☐ 97 Mickey Klutts	.04	.02	.00
☐ 98 Rick Langford	.04	.02	.00
☐ 99 Steve McCatty	.04	.02	.00
☐ 100 Dave McKay	.04	.02	.00
☐ 101 Dwayne Murphy	.04	.02	.00
☐ 102 Jeff Newman	.04	.02	.00
☐ 103 Mike Norris	.04	.02	.00
☐ 104 Bob Owchinko	.04	.02	.00
☐ 105 Mitchell Page	.04	.02	.00
☐ 106 Rob Picciolo	.04	.02	.00
☐ 107 Jim Spencer	.04	.02	.00
☐ 108 Fred Stanley	.04	.02	.00
☐ 109 Tom Underwood	.04	.02	.00
☐ 110 Joaquin Andujar	.07	.03	.01
☐ 111 Steve Braun	.04	.02	.00
☐ 112 Bob Forsch	.04	.02	.00
☐ 113 George Hendrick	.07	.03	.01
☐ 114 Keith Hernandez	.35	.17	.03
☐ 115 Tom Herr	.07	.03	.01
☐ 116 Dane Iorg	.04	.02	.00
☐ 117 Jim Kaat	.15	.07	.01
☐ 118 Tito Landrum	.04	.02	.00
☐ 119 Sixto Lezcano	.04	.02	.00
☐ 120 Mark Littell	.04	.02	.00
☐ 121 John Martin	.04	.02	.00
☐ 122 Silvio Martinez	.04	.02	.00
☐ 123 Ken Oberkfell	.04	.02	.00
☐ 124 Darrell Porter	.04	.02	.00
☐ 125 Mike Ramsey	.04	.02	.00
☐ 126 Orlando Sanchez	.04	.02	.00
☐ 127 Bob Shirley	.04	.02	.00
☐ 128 Lary Sorensen	.04	.02	.00
☐ 129 Bruce Sutter	.15	.07	.01
☐ 130 Bob Sykes	.04	.02	.00
☐ 131 Garry Templeton	.07	.03	.01
☐ 132 Gene Tenace	.04	.02	.00
☐ 133 Jerry Augustine	.04	.02	.00
☐ 134 Sal Bando	.07	.03	.01
☐ 135 Mark Brouhard	.04	.02	.00
☐ 136 Mike Caldwell	.04	.02	.00
☐ 137 Reggie Cleveland	.04	.02	.00
☐ 138 Cecil Cooper	.15	.07	.01
☐ 139 Jamie Easterly	.04	.02	.00
☐ 140 Marshall Edwards	.04	.02	.00
☐ 141 Rollie Fingers	.25	.12	.02
☐ 142 Jim Gantner	.04	.02	.00
☐ 143 Moose Haas	.04	.02	.00
☐ 144 Larry Hisle	.04	.02	.00
☐ 145 Roy Howell	.04	.02	.00

☐	146 Rickey Keeton	.04	.02	.00
☐	147 Randy Lerch	.04	.02	.00
☐	148 Paul Molitor	.25	.12	.02
☐	149 Don Money	.04	.02	.00
☐	150 Charlie Moore	.04	.02	.00
☐	151 Ben Oglivie	.07	.03	.01
☐	152 Ted Simmons	.12	.06	.01
☐	153 Jim Slaton	.04	.02	.00
☐	154 Gorman Thomas	.07	.03	.01
☐	155 Robin Yount	1.25	.60	.12
☐	156 Pete Vuckovich	.07	.03	.01
☐	157 Benny Ayala	.04	.02	.00
☐	158 Mark Belanger	.07	.03	.01
☐	159 Al Bumbry	.04	.02	.00
☐	160 Terry Crowley	.04	.02	.00
☐	161 Rich Dauer	.04	.02	.00
☐	162 Doug DeCinces	.07	.03	.01
☐	163 Rick Dempsey	.04	.02	.00
☐	164 Jim Dwyer	.04	.02	.00
☐	165 Mike Flanagan	.07	.03	.01
☐	166 Dave Ford	.04	.02	.00
☐	167 Dan Graham	.04	.02	.00
☐	168 Wayne Krenchicki	.04	.02	.00
☐	169 John Lowenstein	.04	.02	.00
☐	170 Dennis Martinez	.07	.03	.01
☐	171 Tippy Martinez	.04	.02	.00
☐	172 Scott McGregor	.07	.03	.01
☐	173 Jose Morales	.04	.02	.00
☐	174 Eddie Murray	.75	.35	.07
☐	175 Jim Palmer	.65	.30	.06
☐	176 Cal Ripken	18.00	9.00	1.80
☐	177 Gary Roenicke	.04	.02	.00
☐	178 Lenn Sakata	.04	.02	.00
☐	179 Ken Singleton	.07	.03	.01
☐	180 Sammy Stewart	.04	.02	.00
☐	181 Tim Stoddard	.04	.02	.00
☐	182 Steve Stone	.07	.03	.01
☐	183 Stan Bahnsen	.04	.02	.00
☐	184 Ray Burris	.04	.02	.00
☐	185 Gary Carter	.50	.25	.05
☐	186 Warren Cromartie	.04	.02	.00
☐	187 Andre Dawson	.75	.35	.07
☐	188 Terry Francona	.07	.03	.01
☐	189 Woodie Fryman	.04	.02	.00
☐	190 Bill Gullickson	.07	.03	.01
☐	191 Grant Jackson	.04	.02	.00
☐	192 Wallace Johnson	.07	.03	.01
☐	193 Charlie Lea	.07	.03	.01
☐	194 Bill Lee	.07	.03	.01
☐	195 Jerry Manuel	.04	.02	.00
☐	196 Brad Mills	.04	.02	.00
☐	197 John Milner	.04	.02	.00
☐	198 Rowland Office	.04	.02	.00
☐	199 David Palmer	.04	.02	.00
☐	200 Larry Parrish	.07	.03	.01
☐	201 Mike Phillips	.04	.02	.00
☐	202 Tim Raines	2.25	1.10	.22
☐	203 Bobby Ramos	.04	.02	.00
☐	204 Jeff Reardon	.25	.12	.02
☐	205 Steve Rogers	.07	.03	.01
☐	206 Scott Sanderson	.04	.02	.00
☐	207 Rodney Scott UER (photo actually Tim Raines)	.20	.10	.02
☐	208 Elias Sosa	.04	.02	.00
☐	209 Chris Speier	.04	.02	.00
☐	210 Tim Wallach	1.75	.85	.17
☐	211 Jerry White	.04	.02	.00
☐	212 Alan Ashby	.04	.02	.00
☐	213 Cesar Cedeno	.07	.03	.01
☐	214 Jose Cruz	.07	.03	.01
☐	215 Kiko Garcia	.04	.02	.00
☐	216 Phil Garner	.04	.02	.00
☐	217 Danny Heep	.04	.02	.00
☐	218 Art Howe	.07	.03	.01
☐	219 Bob Knepper	.07	.03	.01
☐	220 Frank LaCorte	.04	.02	.00
☐	221 Joe Niekro	.10	.05	.01
☐	222 Joe Pittman	.04	.02	.00
☐	223 Terry Puhl	.07	.03	.01
☐	224 Luis Pujols	.04	.02	.00
☐	225 Craig Reynolds	.04	.02	.00
☐	226 J.R. Richard	.07	.03	.01
☐	227 Dave Roberts	.04	.02	.00
☐	228 Vern Ruhle	.04	.02	.00
☐	229 Nolan Ryan	3.75	1.85	.37
☐	230 Joe Sambito	.04	.02	.00
☐	231 Tony Scott	.04	.02	.00
☐	232 Dave Smith	.10	.05	.01
☐	233 Harry Spilman	.04	.02	.00
☐	234 Don Sutton	.30	.15	.03
☐	235 Dickie Thon	.07	.03	.01
☐	236 Denny Walling	.04	.02	.00
☐	237 Gary Woods	.04	.02	.00
☐	238 Luis Aguayo	.04	.02	.00
☐	239 Ramon Aviles	.04	.02	.00
☐	240 Bob Boone	.12	.06	.01
☐	241 Larry Bowa	.12	.06	.01
☐	242 Warren Brusstar	.04	.02	.00
☐	243 Steve Carlton	.80	.40	.08
☐	244 Larry Christenson	.04	.02	.00
☐	245 Dick Davis	.04	.02	.00
☐	246 Greg Gross	.04	.02	.00
☐	247 Sparky Lyle	.10	.05	.01
☐	248 Garry Maddox	.07	.03	.01
☐	249 Gary Matthews	.07	.03	.01
☐	250 Bake McBride	.04	.02	.00
☐	251 Tug McGraw	.10	.05	.01
☐	252 Keith Moreland	.04	.02	.00
☐	253 Dickie Noles	.04	.02	.00
☐	254 Mike Proly	.04	.02	.00
☐	255 Ron Reed	.04	.02	.00
☐	256 Pete Rose	1.25	.60	.12
☐	257 Dick Ruthven	.04	.02	.00
☐	258 Mike Schmidt	2.00	1.00	.20
☐	259 Lonnie Smith	.12	.06	.01
☐	260 Manny Trillo	.04	.02	.00
☐	261 Del Unser	.04	.02	.00
☐	262 George Vukovich	.04	.02	.00
☐	263 Tom Brookens	.04	.02	.00
☐	264 George Cappuzzello	.04	.02	.00
☐	265 Marty Castillo	.04	.02	.00
☐	266 Al Cowens	.04	.02	.00
☐	267 Kirk Gibson	.75	.35	.07
☐	268 Richie Hebner	.04	.02	.00
☐	269 Ron Jackson	.04	.02	.00
☐	270 Lynn Jones	.04	.02	.00
☐	271 Steve Kemp	.07	.03	.01
☐	272 Rick Leach	.04	.02	.00
☐	273 Aurelio Lopez	.04	.02	.00
☐	274 Jack Morris	.20	.10	.02
☐	275 Kevin Saucier	.04	.02	.00
☐	276 Lance Parrish	.25	.12	.02
☐	277 Rick Peters	.04	.02	.00
☐	278 Dan Petry	.04	.02	.00
☐	279 Dave Rozema	.04	.02	.00
☐	280 Stan Papi	.04	.02	.00
☐	281 Dan Schatzeder	.04	.02	.00
☐	282 Champ Summers	.04	.02	.00
☐	283 Alan Trammell	.35	.17	.03
☐	284 Lou Whitaker	.25	.12	.02
☐	285 Milt Wilcox	.04	.02	.00
☐	286 John Wockenfuss	.04	.02	.00
☐	287 Gary Allenson	.04	.02	.00
☐	288 Tom Burgmeier	.04	.02	.00
☐	289 Bill Campbell	.04	.02	.00
☐	290 Mark Clear	.04	.02	.00
☐	291 Steve Crawford	.04	.02	.00
☐	292 Dennis Eckersley	.30	.15	.03
☐	293 Dwight Evans	.25	.12	.02
☐	294 Rich Gedman	.30	.15	.03
☐	295 Garry Hancock	.04	.02	.00
☐	296 Glenn Hoffman	.04	.02	.00
☐	297 Bruce Hurst	.65	.30	.06
☐	298 Carney Lansford	.25	.12	.02
☐	299 Rick Miller	.04	.02	.00
☐	300 Reid Nichols	.04	.02	.00
☐	301 Bob Ojeda	.65	.30	.06
☐	302 Tony Perez	.18	.09	.01
☐	303 Chuck Rainey	.04	.02	.00
☐	304 Jerry Remy	.04	.02	.00
☐	305 Jim Rice	.25	.12	.02
☐	306 Joe Rudi	.07	.03	.01
☐	307 Bob Stanley	.04	.02	.00
☐	308 Dave Stapleton	.04	.02	.00
☐	309 Frank Tanana	.07	.03	.01
☐	310 Mike Torrez	.04	.02	.00
☐	311 John Tudor	.50	.25	.05
☐	312 Carl Yastrzemski	1.10	.55	.11
☐	313 Buddy Bell	.10	.05	.01
☐	314 Steve Comer	.04	.02	.00
☐	315 Danny Darwin	.07	.03	.01
☐	316 John Ellis	.04	.02	.00
☐	317 John Grubb	.04	.02	.00
☐	318 Rick Honeycutt	.04	.02	.00
☐	319 Charlie Hough	.07	.03	.01
☐	320 Ferguson Jenkins	.15	.07	.01
☐	321 John Henry Johnson	.04	.02	.00
☐	322 Jim Kern	.04	.02	.00
☐	323 Jon Matlack	.04	.02	.00
☐	324 Doc Medich	.04	.02	.00
☐	325 Mario Mendoza	.04	.02	.00
☐	326 Al Oliver	.10	.05	.01
☐	327 Pat Putnam	.04	.02	.00
☐	328 Mickey Rivers	.07	.03	.01
☐	329 Leon Roberts	.04	.02	.00
☐	330 Billy Sample	.04	.02	.00
☐	331 Bill Stein	.04	.02	.00

☐ 332	Jim Sundberg	.04	.02	.00
☐ 333	Mark Wagner	.04	.02	.00
☐ 334	Bump Wills	.04	.02	.00
☐ 335	Bill Almon	.04	.02	.00
☐ 336	Harold Baines	.35	.17	.03
☐ 337	Ross Baumgarten	.04	.02	.00
☐ 338	Tony Bernazard	.04	.02	.00
☐ 339	Britt Burns	.07	.03	.01
☐ 340	Richard Dotson	.04	.02	.00
☐ 341	Jim Essian	.04	.02	.00
☐ 342	Ed Farmer	.04	.02	.00
☐ 343	Carlton Fisk	.60	.30	.06
☐ 344	Kevin Hickey	.04	.02	.00
☐ 345	LaMarr Hoyt	.07	.03	.01
☐ 346	Lamar Johnson	.04	.02	.00
☐ 347	Jerry Koosman	.07	.03	.01
☐ 348	Rusty Kuntz	.04	.02	.00
☐ 349	Dennis Lamp	.04	.02	.00
☐ 350	Ron LeFlore	.07	.03	.01
☐ 351	Chet Lemon	.04	.02	.00
☐ 352	Greg Luzinski	.10	.05	.01
☐ 353	Bob Molinaro	.04	.02	.00
☐ 354	Jim Morrison	.04	.02	.00
☐ 355	Wayne Nordhagen	.04	.02	.00
☐ 356	Greg Pryor	.04	.02	.00
☐ 357	Mike Squires	.04	.02	.00
☐ 358	Steve Trout	.04	.02	.00
☐ 359	Alan Bannister	.04	.02	.00
☐ 360	Len Barker	.04	.02	.00
☐ 361	Bert Blyleven	.25	.12	.02
☐ 362	Joe Charboneau	.07	.03	.01
☐ 363	John Denny	.07	.03	.01
☐ 364	Bo Diaz	.04	.02	.00
☐ 365	Miguel Dilone	.04	.02	.00
☐ 366	Jerry Dybzinski	.04	.02	.00
☐ 367	Wayne Garland	.04	.02	.00
☐ 368	Mike Hargrove	.07	.03	.01
☐ 369	Toby Harrah	.07	.03	.01
☐ 370	Ron Hassey	.04	.02	.00
☐ 371	Von Hayes	1.25	.60	.12
☐ 372	Pat Kelly	.04	.02	.00
☐ 373	Duane Kuiper	.04	.02	.00
☐ 374	Rick Manning	.04	.02	.00
☐ 375	Sid Monge	.04	.02	.00
☐ 376	Jorge Orta	.04	.02	.00
☐ 377	Dave Rosello	.04	.02	.00
☐ 378	Dan Spillner	.04	.02	.00
☐ 379	Mike Stanton	.04	.02	.00
☐ 380	Andre Thornton	.07	.03	.01
☐ 381	Tom Veryzer	.04	.02	.00
☐ 382	Rick Waits	.04	.02	.00
☐ 383	Doyle Alexander	.07	.03	.01
☐ 384	Vida Blue	.07	.03	.01
☐ 385	Fred Breining	.04	.02	.00
☐ 386	Enos Cabell	.04	.02	.00
☐ 387	Jack Clark	.25	.12	.02
☐ 388	Darrell Evans	.12	.06	.01
☐ 389	Tom Griffin	.04	.02	.00
☐ 390	Larry Herndon	.04	.02	.00
☐ 391	Al Holland	.04	.02	.00
☐ 392	Gary Lavelle	.04	.02	.00
☐ 393	Johnnie LeMaster	.04	.02	.00
☐ 394	Jerry Martin	.04	.02	.00
☐ 395	Milt May	.04	.02	.00
☐ 396	Greg Minton	.04	.02	.00
☐ 397	Joe Morgan	.35	.17	.03
☐ 398	Joe Pettini	.04	.02	.00
☐ 399	Allen Ripley	.04	.02	.00
☐ 400	Billy Smith	.04	.02	.00
☐ 401	Rennie Stennett	.04	.02	.00
☐ 402	Ed Whitson	.07	.03	.01
☐ 403	Jim Wohlford	.04	.02	.00
☐ 404	Willie Aikens	.04	.02	.00
☐ 405	George Brett	1.25	.60	.12
☐ 406	Ken Brett	.04	.02	.00
☐ 407	Dave Chalk	.04	.02	.00
☐ 408	Rich Gale	.04	.02	.00
☐ 409	Cesar Geronimo	.04	.02	.00
☐ 410	Larry Gura	.04	.02	.00
☐ 411	Clint Hurdle	.04	.02	.00
☐ 412	Mike Jones	.04	.02	.00
☐ 413	Dennis Leonard	.07	.03	.01
☐ 414	Renie Martin	.04	.02	.00
☐ 415	Lee May	.07	.03	.01
☐ 416	Hal McRae	.07	.03	.01
☐ 417	Darryl Motley	.04	.02	.00
☐ 418	Rance Mulliniks	.04	.02	.00
☐ 419	Amos Otis	.07	.03	.01
☐ 420	Ken Phelps	.50	.25	.05
☐ 421	Jamie Quirk	.04	.02	.00
☐ 422	Dan Quisenberry	.15	.07	.01
☐ 423	Paul Splittorff	.04	.02	.00
☐ 424	U.L. Washington	.04	.02	.00
☐ 425	John Wathan	.04	.02	.00

☐ 426	Frank White	.07	.03	.01
☐ 427	Willie Wilson	.12	.06	.01
☐ 428	Brian Asselstine	.04	.02	.00
☐ 429	Bruce Benedict	.04	.02	.00
☐ 430	Tommy Boggs	.04	.02	.00
☐ 431	Larry Bradford	.04	.02	.00
☐ 432	Rick Camp	.04	.02	.00
☐ 433	Chris Chambliss	.07	.03	.01
☐ 434	Gene Garber	.04	.02	.00
☐ 435	Preston Hanna	.04	.02	.00
☐ 436	Bob Horner	.12	.06	.01
☐ 437	Glenn Hubbard	.04	.02	.00
☐ 438A	All Hrabosky ERR (height 5'1", All on reverse)	20.00	10.00	2.00
☐ 438B	Al Hrabosky ERR (height 5'1")	1.25	.60	.12
☐ 438C	Al Hrabosky (height 5'10")	.10	.05	.01
☐ 439	Rufino Linares	.04	.02	.00
☐ 440	Rick Mahler	.25	.12	.02
☐ 441	Ed Miller	.04	.02	.00
☐ 442	John Montefusco	.07	.03	.01
☐ 443	Dale Murphy	1.10	.55	.11
☐ 444	Phil Niekro	.30	.15	.03
☐ 445	Gaylord Perry	.30	.15	.03
☐ 446	Biff Pocoroba	.04	.02	.00
☐ 447	Rafael Ramirez	.04	.02	.00
☐ 448	Jerry Royster	.04	.02	.00
☐ 449	Claudell Washington	.07	.03	.01
☐ 450	Don Aase	.04	.02	.00
☐ 451	Don Baylor	.15	.07	.01
☐ 452	Juan Beniquez	.04	.02	.00
☐ 453	Rick Burleson	.07	.03	.01
☐ 454	Bert Campaneris	.07	.03	.01
☐ 455	Rod Carew	.75	.35	.07
☐ 456	Bob Clark	.04	.02	.00
☐ 457	Brian Downing	.07	.03	.01
☐ 458	Dan Ford	.04	.02	.00
☐ 459	Ken Forsch	.04	.02	.00
☐ 460A	Dave Frost (5 mm space before ERA)	.40	.20	.04
☐ 460B	Dave Frost (1 mm space)	.07	.03	.01
☐ 461	Bobby Grich	.07	.03	.01
☐ 462	Larry Harlow	.04	.02	.00
☐ 463	John Harris	.04	.02	.00
☐ 464	Andy Hassler	.04	.02	.00
☐ 465	Butch Hobson	.04	.02	.00
☐ 466	Jesse Jefferson	.04	.02	.00
☐ 467	Bruce Kison	.04	.02	.00
☐ 468	Fred Lynn	.20	.10	.02
☐ 469	Angel Moreno	.04	.02	.00
☐ 470	Ed Ott	.04	.02	.00
☐ 471	Fred Patek	.04	.02	.00
☐ 472	Steve Renko	.04	.02	.00
☐ 473	Mike Witt	.60	.30	.06
☐ 474	Geoff Zahn	.04	.02	.00
☐ 475	Gary Alexander	.04	.02	.00
☐ 476	Dale Berra	.04	.02	.00
☐ 477	Kurt Bevacqua	.04	.02	.00
☐ 478	Jim Bibby	.04	.02	.00
☐ 479	John Candelaria	.07	.03	.01
☐ 480	Victor Cruz	.04	.02	.00
☐ 481	Mike Easler	.07	.03	.01
☐ 482	Tim Foli	.04	.02	.00
☐ 483	Lee Lacy	.04	.02	.00
☐ 484	Vance Law	.20	.10	.02
☐ 485	Bill Madlock	.12	.06	.01
☐ 486	Willie Montanez	.04	.02	.00
☐ 487	Omar Moreno	.04	.02	.00
☐ 488	Steve Nicosia	.04	.02	.00
☐ 489	Dave Parker	.30	.15	.03
☐ 490	Tony Pena	.65	.30	.06
☐ 491	Pascual Perez	.35	.17	.03
☐ 492	Johnny Ray	.75	.35	.07
☐ 493	Rick Rhoden	.07	.03	.01
☐ 494	Bill Robinson	.07	.03	.01
☐ 495	Don Robinson	.07	.03	.01
☐ 496	Enrique Romo	.04	.02	.00
☐ 497	Rod Scurry	.04	.02	.00
☐ 498	Eddie Solomon	.04	.02	.00
☐ 499	Willie Stargell	.40	.20	.04
☐ 500	Kent Tekulve	.07	.03	.01
☐ 501	Jason Thompson	.04	.02	.00
☐ 502	Glenn Abbott	.04	.02	.00
☐ 503	Jim Anderson	.04	.02	.00
☐ 504	Floyd Bannister	.04	.02	.00
☐ 505	Bruce Bochte	.04	.02	.00
☐ 506	Jeff Burroughs	.07	.03	.01
☐ 507	Bryan Clark	.04	.02	.00
☐ 508	Ken Clay	.04	.02	.00
☐ 509	Julio Cruz	.04	.02	.00
☐ 510	Dick Drago	.04	.02	.00

☐ 511 Gary Gray	.04	.02	.00
☐ 512 Dan Meyer	.04	.02	.00
☐ 513 Jerry Narron	.04	.02	.00
☐ 514 Tom Paciorek	.04	.02	.00
☐ 515 Casey Parsons	.04	.02	.00
☐ 516 Lenny Randle	.04	.02	.00
☐ 517 Shane Rawley	.04	.02	.00
☐ 518 Joe Simpson	.04	.02	.00
☐ 519 Richie Zisk	.04	.02	.00
☐ 520 Neil Allen	.04	.02	.00
☐ 521 Bob Bailor	.04	.02	.00
☐ 522 Hubie Brooks	.75	.35	.07
☐ 523 Mike Cubbage	.04	.02	.00
☐ 524 Pete Falcone	.04	.02	.00
☐ 525 Doug Flynn	.04	.02	.00
☐ 526 Tom Hausman	.04	.02	.00
☐ 527 Ron Hodges	.04	.02	.00
☐ 528 Randy Jones	.04	.02	.00
☐ 529 Mike Jorgensen	.04	.02	.00
☐ 530 Dave Kingman	.12	.06	.01
☐ 531 Ed Lynch	.04	.02	.00
☐ 532 Mike Marshall	.07	.03	.01
(screwball pitcher)			
☐ 533 Lee Mazzilli	.04	.02	.00
☐ 534 Dyar Miller	.04	.02	.00
☐ 535 Mike Scott	.40	.20	.04
☐ 536 Rusty Staub	.10	.05	.01
☐ 537 John Stearns	.04	.02	.00
☐ 538 Craig Swan	.04	.02	.00
☐ 539 Frank Taveras	.04	.02	.00
☐ 540 Alex Trevino	.04	.02	.00
☐ 541 Ellis Valentine	.04	.02	.00
☐ 542 Mookie Wilson	.10	.05	.01
☐ 543 Joel Youngblood	.04	.02	.00
☐ 544 Pat Zachry	.04	.02	.00
☐ 545 Glenn Adams	.04	.02	.00
☐ 546 Fernando Arroyo	.04	.02	.00
☐ 547 John Verhoeven	.04	.02	.00
☐ 548 Sal Butera	.04	.02	.00
☐ 549 John Castino	.04	.02	.00
☐ 550 Don Cooper	.04	.02	.00
☐ 551 Doug Corbett	.04	.02	.00
☐ 552 Dave Engle	.04	.02	.00
☐ 553 Roger Erickson	.04	.02	.00
☐ 554 Danny Goodwin	.04	.02	.00
☐ 555A Darrell Jackson	1.00	.50	.10
(black cap)			
☐ 555B Darrell Jackson	.10	.05	.01
(red cap with T)			
☐ 555C Darrell Jackson	5.00	2.50	.50
(red cap, no emblem)			
☐ 556 Pete Mackanin	.04	.02	.00
☐ 557 Jack O'Connor	.04	.02	.00
☐ 558 Hosken Powell	.04	.02	.00
☐ 559 Pete Redfern	.04	.02	.00
☐ 560 Roy Smalley	.04	.02	.00
☐ 561 Chuck Baker UER	.04	.02	.00
(shortshop on front)			
☐ 562 Gary Ward	.07	.03	.01
☐ 563 Rob Wilfong	.04	.02	.00
☐ 564 Al Williams	.04	.02	.00
☐ 565 Butch Wynegar	.04	.02	.00
☐ 566 Randy Bass	.07	.03	.01
☐ 567 Juan Bonilla	.04	.02	.00
☐ 568 Danny Boone	.04	.02	.00
☐ 569 John Curtis	.04	.02	.00
☐ 570 Juan Eichelberger	.04	.02	.00
☐ 571 Barry Evans	.04	.02	.00
☐ 572 Tim Flannery	.04	.02	.00
☐ 573 Ruppert Jones	.04	.02	.00
☐ 574 Terry Kennedy	.04	.02	.00
☐ 575 Joe Lefebvre	.04	.02	.00
☐ 576A John Littlefield ERR	200.00	80.00	16.00
(left handed)			
☐ 576B John Littlefield COR	.07	.03	.01
(right handed)			
☐ 577 Gary Lucas	.04	.02	.00
☐ 578 Steve Mura	.04	.02	.00
☐ 579 Broderick Perkins	.04	.02	.00
☐ 580 Gene Richards	.04	.02	.00
☐ 581 Luis Salazar	.07	.03	.01
☐ 582 Ozzie Smith	.60	.30	.06
☐ 583 John Urrea	.04	.02	.00
☐ 584 Chris Welsh	.04	.02	.00
☐ 585 Rick Wise	.04	.02	.00
☐ 586 Doug Bird	.04	.02	.00
☐ 587 Tim Blackwell	.04	.02	.00
☐ 588 Bobby Bonds	.10	.05	.01
☐ 589 Bill Buckner	.10	.05	.01
☐ 590 Bill Caudill	.04	.02	.00
☐ 591 Hector Cruz	.04	.02	.00
☐ 592 Jody Davis	.35	.17	.03
☐ 593 Ivan DeJesus	.04	.02	.00
☐ 594 Steve Dillard	.04	.02	.00

☐ 595 Leon Durham	.07	.03	.01
☐ 596 Rawly Eastwick	.04	.02	.00
☐ 597 Steve Henderson	.04	.02	.00
☐ 598 Mike Krukow	.07	.03	.01
☐ 599 Mike Lum	.04	.02	.00
☐ 600 Randy Martz	.04	.02	.00
☐ 601 Jerry Morales	.04	.02	.00
☐ 602 Ken Reitz	.04	.02	.00
☐ 603A Lee Smith ERR	1.25	.60	.12
(Cubs logo reversed)			
☐ 603B Lee Smith COR	.75	.35	.07
☐ 604 Dick Tidrow	.04	.02	.00
☐ 605 Jim Tracy	.04	.02	.00
☐ 606 Mike Tyson	.04	.02	.00
☐ 607 Ty Waller	.04	.02	.00
☐ 608 Danny Ainge	.15	.07	.01
☐ 609 Jorge Bell	7.50	3.75	.75
☐ 610 Mark Bomback	.04	.02	.00
☐ 611 Barry Bonnell	.04	.02	.00
☐ 612 Jim Clancy	.04	.02	.00
☐ 613 Damaso Garcia	.04	.02	.00
☐ 614 Jerry Garvin	.04	.02	.00
☐ 615 Alfredo Griffin	.07	.03	.01
☐ 616 Garth Iorg	.04	.02	.00
☐ 617 Luis Leal	.04	.02	.00
☐ 618 Ken Macha	.04	.02	.00
☐ 619 John Mayberry	.07	.03	.01
☐ 620 Joey McLaughlin	.04	.02	.00
☐ 621 Lloyd Moseby	.15	.07	.01
☐ 622 Dave Stieb	.40	.20	.04
☐ 623 Jackson Todd	.04	.02	.00
☐ 624 Willie Upshaw	.04	.02	.00
☐ 625 Otto Velez	.04	.02	.00
☐ 626 Ernie Whitt	.04	.02	.00
☐ 627 Alvis Woods	.04	.02	.00
☐ 628 All Star Game	.04	.02	.00
Cleveland, Ohio			
☐ 629 All Star Infielders	.07	.03	.01
Frank White and			
Bucky Dent			
☐ 630 Big Red Machine	.07	.03	.01
Dan Driessen			
Dave Concepcion			
George Foster			
☐ 631 Bruce Sutter	.07	.03	.01
Top NL Relief Pitcher			
☐ 632 "Steve and Carlton"	.20	.10	.02
Steve Carlton and			
Carlton Fisk			
☐ 633 Carl Yastrzemski	.35	.17	.03
3000th Game			
☐ 634 Dynamic Duo	.40	.20	.04
Johnny Bench and			
Tom Seaver			
☐ 635 West Meets East	.18	.09	.01
Fernando Valenzuela			
and Gary Carter			
☐ 636A Fernando Valenzuela:	.60	.30	.06
NL SO King ("he" NL)			
☐ 636B Fernando Valenzuela:	.30	.15	.03
NL SO King ("the" NL)			
☐ 637 Mike Schmidt	.75	.35	.07
Home Run King			
☐ 638 NL All Stars	.15	.07	.01
Gary Carter and			
Dave Parker			
☐ 639 Perfect Game UER	.07	.03	.01
Len Barker and			
Bo Diaz			
(catcher actually			
Ron Hassey)			
☐ 640 Pete and Re-Pete	2.50	1.25	.25
Pete Rose and Son			
☐ 641 Phillies Finest	.35	.17	.03
Lonnie Smith			
Mike Schmidt			
Steve Carlton			
☐ 642 Red Sox Reunion	.07	.03	.01
Fred Lynn and			
Dwight Evans			
☐ 643 Rickey Henderson	2.00	1.00	.20
Most Hits and Runs			
☐ 644 Rollie Fingers	.10	.05	.01
Most Saves AL			
☐ 645 Tom Seaver	.25	.12	.02
Most 1981 Wins			
☐ 646A Yankee Powerhouse	.80	.40	.08
Reggie Jackson and			
Dave Winfield			
(comma on back			
after outfielder)			

	MINT	EXC	G-VG
☐ 646B Yankee Powerhouse .... Reggie Jackson and Dave Winfield (no comma)	.40	.20	.04
☐ 647 CL: Yankees/Dodgers	.08	.01	.00
☐ 648 CL: A's/Reds	.07	.01	.00
☐ 649 CL: Cards/Brewers	.07	.01	.00
☐ 650 CL: Expos/Orioles	.07	.01	.00
☐ 651 CL: Astros/Phillies	.07	.01	.00
☐ 652 CL: Tigers/Red Sox	.07	.01	.00
☐ 653 CL: Rangers/White Sox	.07	.01	.00
☐ 654 CL: Giants/Indians	.07	.01	.00
☐ 655 CL: Royals/Braves	.07	.01	.00
☐ 656 CL: Angels/Pirates	.07	.01	.00
☐ 657 CL: Mariners/Mets	.07	.01	.00
☐ 658 CL: Padres/Twins	.07	.01	.00
☐ 659 CL: Blue Jays/Cubs	.07	.01	.00
☐ 660 Specials Checklist	.10	.01	.00

1983 Fleer

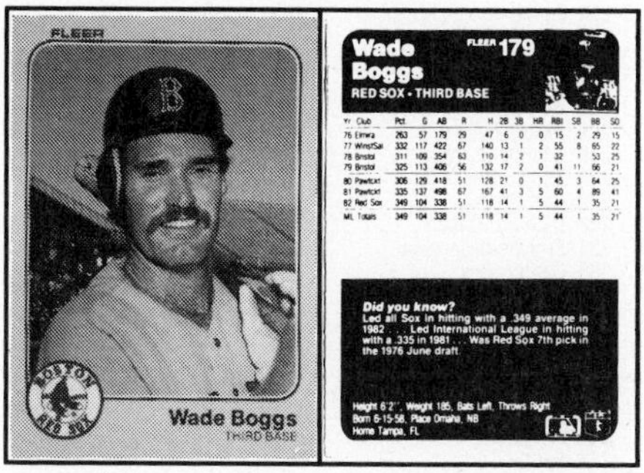

The cards in this 660-card set measure 2 1/2" by 3 1/2". In 1983, for the third straight year, Fleer has produced a baseball series numbering 660 cards. Of these, 1-628 are player cards, 629-646 are special cards, and 647-660 are checklist cards. The player cards are again ordered alphabetically within team. The team order relates back to each team's on-field performance during the previous year, i.e., World Champion Cardinals (1-25), AL Champion Brewers (26-51), Baltimore (52-75), California (76-103), Kansas City (104-128), Atlanta (129-152), Philadelphia (153-176), Boston (177-200), Los Angeles (201-227), Chicago White Sox (228-251), San Francisco (252-276), Montreal (277-301), Pittsburgh (302-326), Detroit (327-351), San Diego (352-375), New York Yankees (376-399), Cleveland (400-423), Toronto (424-444), Houston (445-469), Seattle (470-489), Chicago Cubs (490-512), Oakland (513-535), New York Mets (536-561), Texas (562-583), Cincinnati (584-606), and Minnesota (607-628). The front of each card has a colorful team logo at bottom left and the player's name and position at lower right. The reverses are done in shades of brown on white. The cards are numbered on the back next to a small black and white photo of the player. The key rookie cards in this set are Wade Boggs, Tony Gwynn, Howard Johnson, Ryne Sandberg, and Frank Viola.

	MINT	EXC	G-VG
COMPLETE SET (660)	105.00	45.00	9.00
COMMON PLAYER (1-660)	.04	.02	.00
☐ 1 Joaquin Andujar	.10	.05	.01
☐ 2 Doug Bair	.04	.02	.00
☐ 3 Steve Braun	.04	.02	.00
☐ 4 Glenn Brummer	.04	.02	.00
☐ 5 Bob Forsch	.04	.02	.00
☐ 6 David Green	.04	.02	.00
☐ 7 George Hendrick	.07	.03	.01
☐ 8 Keith Hernandez	.35	.17	.03
☐ 9 Tom Herr	.07	.03	.01
☐ 10 Dane Iorg	.04	.02	.00
☐ 11 Jim Kaat	.12	.06	.01
☐ 12 Jeff Lahti	.04	.02	.00
☐ 13 Tito Landrum	.04	.02	.00
☐ 14 Dave LaPoint	.35	.17	.03
☐ 15 Willie McGee	3.00	1.50	.30
☐ 16 Steve Mura	.04	.02	.00
☐ 17 Ken Oberkfell	.04	.02	.00
☐ 18 Darrell Porter	.04	.02	.00
☐ 19 Mike Ramsey	.04	.02	.00
☐ 20 Gene Roof	.04	.02	.00
☐ 21 Lonnie Smith	.10	.05	.01
☐ 22 Ozzie Smith	.50	.25	.05
☐ 23 John Stuper	.04	.02	.00
☐ 24 Bruce Sutter	.15	.07	.01
☐ 25 Gene Tenace	.04	.02	.00
☐ 26 Jerry Augustine	.04	.02	.00
☐ 27 Dwight Bernard	.04	.02	.00
☐ 28 Mark Brouhard	.04	.02	.00
☐ 29 Mike Caldwell	.04	.02	.00
☐ 30 Cecil Cooper	.10	.05	.01
☐ 31 Jamie Easterly	.04	.02	.00
☐ 32 Marshall Edwards	.04	.02	.00
☐ 33 Rollie Fingers	.25	.12	.02
☐ 34 Jim Gantner	.04	.02	.00
☐ 35 Moose Haas	.04	.02	.00
☐ 36 Roy Howell	.04	.02	.00
☐ 37 Pete Ladd	.04	.02	.00
☐ 38 Bob McClure	.04	.02	.00
☐ 39 Doc Medich	.04	.02	.00
☐ 40 Paul Molitor	.20	.10	.02
☐ 41 Don Money	.04	.02	.00
☐ 42 Charlie Moore	.04	.02	.00
☐ 43 Ben Oglivie	.07	.03	.01
☐ 44 Ed Romero	.04	.02	.00
☐ 45 Ted Simmons	.12	.06	.01
☐ 46 Jim Slaton	.04	.02	.00
☐ 47 Don Sutton	.30	.15	.03
☐ 48 Gorman Thomas	.07	.03	.01
☐ 49 Pete Vuckovich	.07	.03	.01
☐ 50 Ned Yost	.04	.02	.00
☐ 51 Robin Yount	.80	.40	.08
☐ 52 Benny Ayala	.04	.02	.00
☐ 53 Bob Bonner	.04	.02	.00
☐ 54 Al Bumbry	.04	.02	.00
☐ 55 Terry Crowley	.04	.02	.00
☐ 56 Storm Davis	.60	.30	.06
☐ 57 Rich Dauer	.04	.02	.00
☐ 58 Rick Dempsey UER .... (posing batting lefty)	.07	.03	.01
☐ 59 Jim Dwyer	.04	.02	.00
☐ 60 Mike Flanagan	.07	.03	.01
☐ 61 Dan Ford	.04	.02	.00
☐ 62 Glenn Gulliver	.04	.02	.00
☐ 63 John Lowenstein	.04	.02	.00
☐ 64 Dennis Martinez	.07	.03	.01
☐ 65 Tippy Martinez	.04	.02	.00
☐ 66 Scott McGregor	.07	.03	.01
☐ 67 Eddie Murray	.65	.30	.06
☐ 68 Joe Nolan	.04	.02	.00
☐ 69 Jim Palmer	.50	.25	.05
☐ 70 Cal Ripken Jr.	3.75	1.85	.37
☐ 71 Gary Roenicke	.04	.02	.00
☐ 72 Lenn Sakata	.04	.02	.00
☐ 73 Ken Singleton	.07	.03	.01
☐ 74 Sammy Stewart	.04	.02	.00
☐ 75 Tim Stoddard	.04	.02	.00
☐ 76 Don Aase	.04	.02	.00
☐ 77 Don Baylor	.12	.06	.01
☐ 78 Juan Beniquez	.04	.02	.00
☐ 79 Bob Boone	.12	.06	.01
☐ 80 Rick Burleson	.07	.03	.01
☐ 81 Rod Carew	.60	.30	.06
☐ 82 Bobby Clark	.04	.02	.00
☐ 83 Doug Corbett	.04	.02	.00
☐ 84 John Curtis	.04	.02	.00
☐ 85 Doug DeCinces	.07	.03	.01
☐ 86 Brian Downing	.07	.03	.01
☐ 87 Joe Ferguson	.04	.02	.00
☐ 88 Tim Foli	.04	.02	.00
☐ 89 Ken Forsch	.04	.02	.00
☐ 90 Dave Goltz	.04	.02	.00
☐ 91 Bobby Grich	.07	.03	.01
☐ 92 Andy Hassler	.04	.02	.00
☐ 93 Reggie Jackson	.70	.35	.07
☐ 94 Ron Jackson	.04	.02	.00
☐ 95 Tommy John	.15	.07	.01
☐ 96 Bruce Kison	.04	.02	.00
☐ 97 Fred Lynn	.15	.07	.01
☐ 98 Ed Ott	.04	.02	.00
☐ 99 Steve Renko	.04	.02	.00
☐ 100 Luis Sanchez	.04	.02	.00
☐ 101 Rob Wilfong	.04	.02	.00
☐ 102 Mike Witt	.12	.06	.01
☐ 103 Geoff Zahn	.04	.02	.00
☐ 104 Willie Aikens	.04	.02	.00

☐ 105	Mike Armstrong	.04	.02	.00
☐ 106	Vida Blue	.07	.03	.01
☐ 107	Bud Black	.50	.25	.05
☐ 108	George Brett	1.00	.50	.10
☐ 109	Bill Castro	.04	.02	.00
☐ 110	Onix Concepcion	.04	.02	.00
☐ 111	Dave Frost	.04	.02	.00
☐ 112	Cesar Geronimo	.04	.02	.00
☐ 113	Larry Gura	.04	.02	.00
☐ 114	Steve Hammond	.04	.02	.00
☐ 115	Don Hood	.04	.02	.00
☐ 116	Dennis Leonard	.07	.03	.01
☐ 117	Jerry Martin	.04	.02	.00
☐ 118	Lee May	.07	.03	.01
☐ 119	Hal McRae	.07	.03	.01
☐ 120	Amos Otis	.07	.03	.01
☐ 121	Greg Pryor	.04	.02	.00
☐ 122	Dan Quisenberry	.12	.06	.01
☐ 123	Don Slaught	.35	.17	.03
☐ 124	Paul Splittorff	.04	.02	.00
☐ 125	U.L. Washington	.04	.02	.00
☐ 126	John Wathan	.07	.03	.01
☐ 127	Frank White	.07	.03	.01
☐ 128	Willie Wilson	.12	.06	.01
☐ 129	Steve Bedrosian	.40	.20	.04
☐ 130	Bruce Benedict	.04	.02	.00
☐ 131	Tommy Boggs	.04	.02	.00
☐ 132	Brett Butler	.40	.20	.04
☐ 133	Rick Camp	.04	.02	.00
☐ 134	Chris Chambliss	.07	.03	.01
☐ 135	Ken Dayley	.07	.03	.01
☐ 136	Gene Garber	.04	.02	.00
☐ 137	Terry Harper	.04	.02	.00
☐ 138	Bob Horner	.12	.06	.01
☐ 139	Glenn Hubbard	.04	.02	.00
☐ 140	Rufino Linares	.04	.02	.00
☐ 141	Rick Mahler	.04	.02	.00
☐ 142	Dale Murphy	1.00	.50	.10
☐ 143	Phil Niekro	.25	.12	.02
☐ 144	Pascual Perez	.10	.05	.01
☐ 145	Biff Pocoroba	.04	.02	.00
☐ 146	Rafael Ramirez	.04	.02	.00
☐ 147	Jerry Royster	.04	.02	.00
☐ 148	Ken Smith	.04	.02	.00
☐ 149	Bob Walk	.04	.02	.00
☐ 150	Claudell Washington	.07	.03	.01
☐ 151	Bob Watson	.07	.03	.01
☐ 152	Larry Whisenton	.04	.02	.00
☐ 153	Porfirio Altamirano	.04	.02	.00
☐ 154	Marty Bystrom	.04	.02	.00
☐ 155	Steve Carlton	.50	.25	.05
☐ 156	Larry Christenson	.04	.02	.00
☐ 157	Ivan DeJesus	.04	.02	.00
☐ 158	John Denny	.07	.03	.01
☐ 159	Bob Dernier	.04	.02	.00
☐ 160	Bo Diaz	.04	.02	.00
☐ 161	Ed Farmer	.04	.02	.00
☐ 162	Greg Gross	.04	.02	.00
☐ 163	Mike Krukow	.07	.03	.01
☐ 164	Garry Maddox	.04	.02	.00
☐ 165	Gary Matthews	.07	.03	.01
☐ 166	Tug McGraw	.10	.05	.01
☐ 167	Bob Molinaro	.04	.02	.00
☐ 168	Sid Monge	.04	.02	.00
☐ 169	Ron Reed	.04	.02	.00
☐ 170	Bill Robinson	.07	.03	.01
☐ 171	Pete Rose	1.00	.50	.10
☐ 172	Dick Ruthven	.04	.02	.00
☐ 173	Mike Schmidt	2.00	1.00	.20
☐ 174	Manny Trillo	.04	.02	.00
☐ 175	Ozzie Virgil	.04	.02	.00
☐ 176	George Vukovich	.04	.02	.00
☐ 177	Gary Allenson	.04	.02	.00
☐ 178	Luis Aponte	.04	.02	.00
☐ 179	Wade Boggs	20.00	10.00	2.00
☐ 180	Tom Burgmeier	.04	.02	.00
☐ 181	Mark Clear	.04	.02	.00
☐ 182	Dennis Eckersley	.30	.15	.03
☐ 183	Dwight Evans	.25	.12	.02
☐ 184	Rich Gedman	.07	.03	.01
☐ 185	Glenn Hoffman	.04	.02	.00
☐ 186	Bruce Hurst	.15	.07	.01
☐ 187	Carney Lansford	.20	.10	.02
☐ 188	Rick Miller	.04	.02	.00
☐ 189	Reid Nichols	.04	.02	.00
☐ 190	Bob Ojeda	.10	.05	.01
☐ 191	Tony Perez	.15	.07	.01
☐ 192	Chuck Rainey	.04	.02	.00
☐ 193	Jerry Remy	.04	.02	.00
☐ 194	Jim Rice	.25	.12	.02
☐ 195	Bob Stanley	.04	.02	.00
☐ 196	Dave Stapleton	.04	.02	.00
☐ 197	Mike Torrez	.04	.02	.00
☐ 198	John Tudor	.20	.10	.02
☐ 199	Julio Valdez	.04	.02	.00
☐ 200	Carl Yastrzemski	1.00	.50	.10
☐ 201	Dusty Baker	.07	.03	.01
☐ 202	Joe Beckwith	.04	.02	.00
☐ 203	Greg Brock	.25	.12	.02
☐ 204	Ron Cey	.10	.05	.01
☐ 205	Terry Forster	.07	.03	.01
☐ 206	Steve Garvey	.45	.22	.04
☐ 207	Pedro Guerrero	.35	.17	.03
☐ 208	Burt Hooton	.04	.02	.00
☐ 209	Steve Howe	.04	.02	.00
☐ 210	Ken Landreaux	.04	.02	.00
☐ 211	Mike Marshall	.25	.12	.02
☐ 212	Candy Maldonado	1.00	.50	.10
☐ 213	Rick Monday	.07	.03	.01
☐ 214	Tom Niedenfuer	.04	.02	.00
☐ 215	Jorge Orta	.04	.02	.00
☐ 216	Jerry Reuss	.07	.03	.01
☐ 217	Ron Roenicke	.04	.02	.00
☐ 218	Vicente Romo	.04	.02	.00
☐ 219	Bill Russell	.07	.03	.01
☐ 220	Steve Sax	.60	.30	.06
☐ 221	Mike Scioscia	.07	.03	.01
☐ 222	Dave Stewart	1.50	.75	.15
☐ 223	Derrel Thomas	.04	.02	.00
☐ 224	Fernando Valenzuela	.35	.17	.03
☐ 225	Bob Welch	.30	.15	.03
☐ 226	Ricky Wright	.04	.02	.00
☐ 227	Steve Yeager	.04	.02	.00
☐ 228	Bill Almon	.04	.02	.00
☐ 229	Harold Baines	.25	.12	.02
☐ 230	Salome Barojas	.04	.02	.00
☐ 231	Tony Bernazard	.07	.03	.01
☐ 232	Britt Burns	.04	.02	.00
☐ 233	Richard Dotson	.07	.03	.01
☐ 234	Ernesto Escarrega	.04	.02	.00
☐ 235	Carlton Fisk	.50	.25	.05
☐ 236	Jerry Hairston	.04	.02	.00
☐ 237	Kevin Hickey	.04	.02	.00
☐ 238	LaMarr Hoyt	.07	.03	.01
☐ 239	Steve Kemp	.04	.02	.00
☐ 240	Jim Kern	.04	.02	.00
☐ 241	Ron Kittle	1.00	.50	.10
☐ 242	Jerry Koosman	.07	.03	.01
☐ 243	Dennis Lamp	.04	.02	.00
☐ 244	Rudy Law	.04	.02	.00
☐ 245	Vance Law	.07	.03	.01
☐ 246	Ron LeFlore	.07	.03	.01
☐ 247	Greg Luzinski	.10	.05	.01
☐ 248	Tom Paciorek	.04	.02	.00
☐ 249	Aurelio Rodriguez	.04	.02	.00
☐ 250	Mike Squires	.04	.02	.00
☐ 251	Steve Trout	.04	.02	.00
☐ 252	Jim Barr	.04	.02	.00
☐ 253	Dave Bergman	.04	.02	.00
☐ 254	Fred Breining	.04	.02	.00
☐ 255	Bob Brenly	.04	.02	.00
☐ 256	Jack Clark	.25	.12	.02
☐ 257	Chili Davis	.25	.12	.02
☐ 258	Darrell Evans	.10	.05	.01
☐ 259	Alan Fowlkes	.04	.02	.00
☐ 260	Rich Gale	.04	.02	.00
☐ 261	Atlee Hammaker	.04	.02	.00
☐ 262	Al Holland	.04	.02	.00
☐ 263	Duane Kuiper	.04	.02	.00
☐ 264	Bill Laskey	.04	.02	.00
☐ 265	Gary Lavelle	.04	.02	.00
☐ 266	Johnnie LeMaster	.04	.02	.00
☐ 267	Renie Martin	.04	.02	.00
☐ 268	Milt May	.04	.02	.00
☐ 269	Greg Minton	.04	.02	.00
☐ 270	Joe Morgan	.35	.17	.03
☐ 271	Tom O'Malley	.07	.03	.01
☐ 272	Reggie Smith	.07	.03	.01
☐ 273	Guy Sularz	.04	.02	.00
☐ 274	Champ Summers	.04	.02	.00
☐ 275	Max Venable	.04	.02	.00
☐ 276	Jim Wohlford	.04	.02	.00
☐ 277	Ray Burris	.04	.02	.00
☐ 278	Gary Carter	.35	.17	.03
☐ 279	Warren Cromartie	.04	.02	.00
☐ 280	Andre Dawson	.60	.30	.06
☐ 281	Terry Francona	.04	.02	.00
☐ 282	Doug Flynn	.04	.02	.00
☐ 283	Woodie Fryman	.04	.02	.00
☐ 284	Bill Gullickson	.04	.02	.00
☐ 285	Wallace Johnson	.07	.03	.01
☐ 286	Charlie Lea	.04	.02	.00
☐ 287	Randy Lerch	.04	.02	.00
☐ 288	Brad Mills	.04	.02	.00
☐ 289	Dan Norman	.04	.02	.00
☐ 290	Al Oliver	.07	.03	.01
☐ 291	David Palmer	.04	.02	.00
☐ 292	Tim Raines	.60	.30	.06

☐	293	Jeff Reardon	.12	.06	.01
☐	294	Steve Rogers	.04	.02	.00
☐	295	Scott Sanderson	.04	.02	.00
☐	296	Dan Schatzeder	.04	.02	.00
☐	297	Bryn Smith	.50	.25	.05
☐	298	Chris Speier	.04	.02	.00
☐	299	Tim Wallach	.25	.12	.02
☐	300	Jerry White	.04	.02	.00
☐	301	Joel Youngblood	.04	.02	.00
☐	302	Ross Baumgarten	.04	.02	.00
☐	303	Dale Berra	.04	.02	.00
☐	304	John Candelaria	.07	.03	.01
☐	305	Dick Davis	.04	.02	.00
☐	306	Mike Easler	.04	.02	.00
☐	307	Richie Hebner	.04	.02	.00
☐	308	Lee Lacy	.04	.02	.00
☐	309	Bill Madlock	.07	.03	.01
☐	310	Larry McWilliams	.04	.02	.00
☐	311	John Milner	.04	.02	.00
☐	312	Omar Moreno	.04	.02	.00
☐	313	Jim Morrison	.04	.02	.00
☐	314	Steve Nicosia	.04	.02	.00
☐	315	Dave Parker	.25	.12	.02
☐	316	Tony Pena	.20	.10	.02
☐	317	Johnny Ray	.12	.06	.01
☐	318	Rick Rhoden	.07	.03	.01
☐	319	Don Robinson	.04	.02	.00
☐	320	Enrique Romo	.04	.02	.00
☐	321	Manny Sarmiento	.04	.02	.00
☐	322	Rod Scurry	.04	.02	.00
☐	323	Jimmy Smith	.04	.02	.00
☐	324	Willie Stargell	.35	.17	.03
☐	325	Jason Thompson	.04	.02	.00
☐	326	Kent Tekulve	.07	.03	.01
☐	327	Tom Brookens	.04	.02	.00
☐	328	Enos Cabell	.04	.02	.00
☐	329	Kirk Gibson	.35	.17	.03
☐	330	Larry Herndon	.04	.02	.00
☐	331	Mike Ivie	.04	.02	.00
☐	332	Howard Johnson	9.00	4.50	.90
☐	333	Lynn Jones	.04	.02	.00
☐	334	Rick Leach	.04	.02	.00
☐	335	Chet Lemon	.04	.02	.00
☐	336	Jack Morris	.18	.09	.01
☐	337	Lance Parrish	.20	.10	.02
☐	338	Larry Pashnick	.04	.02	.00
☐	339	Dan Petry	.04	.02	.00
☐	340	Dave Rozema	.04	.02	.00
☐	341	Dave Rucker	.04	.02	.00
☐	342	Elias Sosa	.04	.02	.00
☐	343	Dave Tobik	.04	.02	.00
☐	344	Alan Trammell	.30	.15	.03
☐	345	Jerry Turner	.04	.02	.00
☐	346	Jerry Ujdur	.04	.02	.00
☐	347	Pat Underwood	.04	.02	.00
☐	348	Lou Whitaker	.25	.12	.02
☐	349	Milt Wilcox	.04	.02	.00
☐	350	Glenn Wilson	.35	.17	.03
☐	351	John Wockenfuss	.04	.02	.00
☐	352	Kurt Bevacqua	.04	.02	.00
☐	353	Juan Bonilla	.04	.02	.00
☐	354	Floyd Chiffer	.04	.02	.00
☐	355	Luis DeLeon	.04	.02	.00
☐	356	Dave Dravecky	.70	.35	.07
☐	357	Dave Edwards	.04	.02	.00
☐	358	Juan Eichelberger	.04	.02	.00
☐	359	Tim Flannery	.04	.02	.00
☐	360	Tony Gwynn	16.00	8.00	1.60
☐	361	Ruppert Jones	.04	.02	.00
☐	362	Terry Kennedy	.04	.02	.00
☐	363	Joe Lefebvre	.04	.02	.00
☐	364	Sixto Lezcano	.04	.02	.00
☐	365	Tim Lollar	.04	.02	.00
☐	366	Gary Lucas	.04	.02	.00
☐	367	John Montefusco	.04	.02	.00
☐	368	Broderick Perkins	.04	.02	.00
☐	369	Joe Pittman	.04	.02	.00
☐	370	Gene Richards	.04	.02	.00
☐	371	Luis Salazar	.04	.02	.00
☐	372	Eric Show	.30	.15	.03
☐	373	Garry Templeton	.07	.03	.01
☐	374	Chris Welsh	.04	.02	.00
☐	375	Alan Wiggins	.07	.03	.01
☐	376	Rick Cerone	.04	.02	.00
☐	377	Dave Collins	.04	.02	.00
☐	378	Roger Erickson	.04	.02	.00
☐	379	George Frazier	.04	.02	.00
☐	380	Oscar Gamble	.04	.02	.00
☐	381	Goose Gossage	.15	.07	.01
☐	382	Ken Griffey	.15	.07	.01
☐	383	Ron Guidry	.18	.09	.01
☐	384	Dave LaRoche	.04	.02	.00
☐	385	Rudy May	.04	.02	.00
☐	386	John Mayberry	.07	.03	.01

☐	387	Lee Mazzilli	.04	.02	.00
☐	388	Mike Morgan	.07	.03	.01
☐	389	Jerry Mumphrey	.04	.02	.00
☐	390	Bobby Murcer	.10	.05	.01
☐	391	Graig Nettles	.12	.06	.01
☐	392	Lou Piniella	.10	.05	.01
☐	393	Willie Randolph	.07	.03	.01
☐	394	Shane Rawley	.04	.02	.00
☐	395	Dave Righetti	.25	.12	.02
☐	396	Andre Robertson	.04	.02	.00
☐	397	Roy Smalley	.04	.02	.00
☐	398	Dave Winfield	.40	.20	.04
☐	399	Butch Wynegar	.04	.02	.00
☐	400	Chris Bando	.04	.02	.00
☐	401	Alan Bannister	.04	.02	.00
☐	402	Len Barker	.04	.02	.00
☐	403	Tom Brennan	.04	.02	.00
☐	404	Carmelo Castillo	.07	.03	.01
☐	405	Miguel Dilone	.04	.02	.00
☐	406	Jerry Dybzinski	.04	.02	.00
☐	407	Mike Fischlin	.04	.02	.00
☐	408	Ed Glynn UER (photo actually Bud Anderson)	.04	.02	.00
☐	409	Mike Hargrove	.07	.03	.01
☐	410	Toby Harrah	.07	.03	.01
☐	411	Ron Hassey	.04	.02	.00
☐	412	Von Hayes	.30	.15	.03
☐	413	Rick Manning	.04	.02	.00
☐	414	Bake McBride	.04	.02	.00
☐	415	Larry Milbourne	.04	.02	.00
☐	416	Bill Nahorodny	.04	.02	.00
☐	417	Jack Perconte	.04	.02	.00
☐	418	Lary Sorensen	.04	.02	.00
☐	419	Dan Spillner	.04	.02	.00
☐	420	Rick Sutcliffe	.15	.07	.01
☐	421	Andre Thornton	.07	.03	.01
☐	422	Rick Waits	.04	.02	.00
☐	423	Eddie Whitson	.07	.03	.01
☐	424	Jesse Barfield	.75	.35	.07
☐	425	Barry Bonnell	.04	.02	.00
☐	426	Jim Clancy	.04	.02	.00
☐	427	Damaso Garcia	.04	.02	.00
☐	428	Jerry Garvin	.04	.02	.00
☐	429	Alfredo Griffin	.07	.03	.01
☐	430	Garth Iorg	.04	.02	.00
☐	431	Roy Lee Jackson	.04	.02	.00
☐	432	Luis Leal	.04	.02	.00
☐	433	Buck Martinez	.04	.02	.00
☐	434	Joey McLaughlin	.04	.02	.00
☐	435	Lloyd Moseby	.10	.05	.01
☐	436	Rance Mulliniks	.04	.02	.00
☐	437	Dale Murray	.04	.02	.00
☐	438	Wayne Nordhagen	.04	.02	.00
☐	439	Geno Petralli	.15	.07	.01
☐	440	Hosken Powell	.04	.02	.00
☐	441	Dave Stieb	.25	.12	.02
☐	442	Willie Upshaw	.04	.02	.00
☐	443	Ernie Whitt	.04	.02	.00
☐	444	Alvis Woods	.04	.02	.00
☐	445	Alan Ashby	.04	.02	.00
☐	446	Jose Cruz	.07	.03	.01
☐	447	Kiko Garcia	.04	.02	.00
☐	448	Phil Garner	.04	.02	.00
☐	449	Danny Heep	.04	.02	.00
☐	450	Art Howe	.07	.03	.01
☐	451	Bob Knepper	.07	.03	.01
☐	452	Alan Knicely	.04	.02	.00
☐	453	Ray Knight	.07	.03	.01
☐	454	Frank LaCorte	.04	.02	.00
☐	455	Mike LaCoss	.04	.02	.00
☐	456	Randy Moffitt	.04	.02	.00
☐	457	Joe Niekro	.07	.03	.01
☐	458	Terry Puhl	.04	.02	.00
☐	459	Luis Pujols	.04	.02	.00
☐	460	Craig Reynolds	.04	.02	.00
☐	461	Bert Roberge	.04	.02	.00
☐	462	Vern Ruhle	.04	.02	.00
☐	463	Nolan Ryan	3.25	1.60	.32
☐	464	Joe Sambito	.04	.02	.00
☐	465	Tony Scott	.04	.02	.00
☐	466	Dave Smith	.07	.03	.01
☐	467	Harry Spilman	.04	.02	.00
☐	468	Dickie Thon	.04	.02	.00
☐	469	Denny Walling	.04	.02	.00
☐	470	Larry Andersen	.04	.02	.00
☐	471	Floyd Bannister	.04	.02	.00
☐	472	Jim Beattie	.04	.02	.00
☐	473	Bruce Bochte	.04	.02	.00
☐	474	Manny Castillo	.04	.02	.00
☐	475	Bill Caudill	.04	.02	.00
☐	476	Bryan Clark	.04	.02	.00
☐	477	Al Cowens	.04	.02	.00
☐	478	Julio Cruz	.04	.02	.00

☐	479	Todd Cruz	.04	.02	.00
☐	480	Gary Gray	.04	.02	.00
☐	481	Dave Henderson	.75	.35	.07
☐	482	Mike Moore	1.00	.50	.10
☐	483	Gaylord Perry	.25	.12	.02
☐	484	Dave Revering	.04	.02	.00
☐	485	Joe Simpson	.04	.02	.00
☐	486	Mike Stanton	.04	.02	.00
☐	487	Rick Sweet	.04	.02	.00
☐	488	Ed VandeBerg	.04	.02	.00
☐	489	Richie Zisk	.04	.02	.00
☐	490	Doug Bird	.04	.02	.00
☐	491	Larry Bowa	.10	.05	.01
☐	492	Bill Buckner	.10	.05	.01
☐	493	Bill Campbell	.04	.02	.00
☐	494	Jody Davis	.07	.03	.01
☐	495	Leon Durham	.04	.02	.00
☐	496	Steve Henderson	.04	.02	.00
☐	497	Willie Hernandez	.07	.03	.01
☐	498	Ferguson Jenkins	.15	.07	.01
☐	499	Jay Johnstone	.07	.03	.01
☐	500	Junior Kennedy	.04	.02	.00
☐	501	Randy Martz	.04	.02	.00
☐	502	Jerry Morales	.04	.02	.00
☐	503	Keith Moreland	.04	.02	.00
☐	504	Dickie Noles	.04	.02	.00
☐	505	Mike Proly	.04	.02	.00
☐	506	Allen Ripley	.04	.02	.00
☐	507	Ryne Sandberg	28.00	14.00	2.80
☐	508	Lee Smith	.10	.05	.01
☐	509	Pat Tabler	.30	.15	.03
☐	510	Dick Tidrow	.04	.02	.00
☐	511	Bump Wills	.04	.02	.00
☐	512	Gary Woods	.04	.02	.00
☐	513	Tony Armas	.07	.03	.01
☐	514	Dave Beard	.04	.02	.00
☐	515	Jeff Burroughs	.07	.03	.01
☐	516	John D'Acquisto	.04	.02	.00
☐	517	Wayne Gross	.04	.02	.00
☐	518	Mike Heath	.04	.02	.00
☐	519	Rickey Henderson UER (Brock record listed as 120 steals)	4.00	2.00	.40
☐	520	Cliff Johnson	.04	.02	.00
☐	521	Matt Keough	.04	.02	.00
☐	522	Brian Kingman	.04	.02	.00
☐	523	Rick Langford	.04	.02	.00
☐	524	Dave Lopes	.07	.03	.01
☐	525	Steve McCatty	.04	.02	.00
☐	526	Dave McKay	.04	.02	.00
☐	527	Dan Meyer	.04	.02	.00
☐	528	Dwayne Murphy	.04	.02	.00
☐	529	Jeff Newman	.04	.02	.00
☐	530	Mike Norris	.04	.02	.00
☐	531	Bob Owchinko	.04	.02	.00
☐	532	Joe Rudi	.07	.03	.01
☐	533	Jimmy Sexton	.04	.02	.00
☐	534	Fred Stanley	.04	.02	.00
☐	535	Tom Underwood	.04	.02	.00
☐	536	Neil Allen	.04	.02	.00
☐	537	Wally Backman	.07	.03	.01
☐	538	Bob Bailor	.04	.02	.00
☐	539	Hubie Brooks	.25	.12	.02
☐	540	Carlos Diaz	.04	.02	.00
☐	541	Pete Falcone	.04	.02	.00
☐	542	George Foster	.15	.07	.01
☐	543	Ron Gardenhire	.04	.02	.00
☐	544	Brian Giles	.04	.02	.00
☐	545	Ron Hodges	.04	.02	.00
☐	546	Randy Jones	.04	.02	.00
☐	547	Mike Jorgensen	.04	.02	.00
☐	548	Dave Kingman	.12	.06	.01
☐	549	Ed Lynch	.04	.02	.00
☐	550	Jesse Orosco	.04	.02	.00
☐	551	Rick Ownbey	.04	.02	.00
☐	552	Charlie Puleo	.04	.02	.00
☐	553	Gary Rajsich	.04	.02	.00
☐	554	Mike Scott	.25	.12	.02
☐	555	Rusty Staub	.10	.05	.01
☐	556	John Stearns	.04	.02	.00
☐	557	Craig Swan	.04	.02	.00
☐	558	Ellis Valentine	.04	.02	.00
☐	559	Tom Veryzer	.04	.02	.00
☐	560	Mookie Wilson	.10	.05	.01
☐	561	Pat Zachry	.04	.02	.00
☐	562	Buddy Bell	.10	.05	.01
☐	563	John Butcher	.04	.02	.00
☐	564	Steve Comer	.04	.02	.00
☐	565	Danny Darwin	.07	.03	.01
☐	566	Bucky Dent	.10	.05	.01
☐	567	John Grubb	.04	.02	.00
☐	568	Rick Honeycutt	.04	.02	.00
☐	569	Dave Hostetler	.04	.02	.00
☐	570	Charlie Hough	.07	.03	.01
☐	571	Lamar Johnson	.04	.02	.00
☐	572	Jon Matlack	.04	.02	.00
☐	573	Paul Mirabella	.04	.02	.00
☐	574	Larry Parrish	.07	.03	.01
☐	575	Mike Richardt	.04	.02	.00
☐	576	Mickey Rivers	.07	.03	.01
☐	577	Billy Sample	.04	.02	.00
☐	578	Dave Schmidt	.15	.07	.01
☐	579	Bill Stein	.04	.02	.00
☐	580	Jim Sundberg	.04	.02	.00
☐	581	Frank Tanana	.07	.03	.01
☐	582	Mark Wagner	.04	.02	.00
☐	583	George Wright	.04	.02	.00
☐	584	Johnny Bench	.70	.35	.07
☐	585	Bruce Berenyi	.04	.02	.00
☐	586	Larry Biittner	.04	.02	.00
☐	587	Cesar Cedeno	.07	.03	.01
☐	588	Dave Concepcion	.10	.05	.01
☐	589	Dan Driessen	.04	.02	.00
☐	590	Greg Harris	.04	.02	.00
☐	591	Ben Hayes	.04	.02	.00
☐	592	Paul Householder	.04	.02	.00
☐	593	Tom Hume	.04	.02	.00
☐	594	Wayne Krenchicki	.04	.02	.00
☐	595	Rafael Landestoy	.04	.02	.00
☐	596	Charlie Leibrandt	.04	.02	.00
☐	597	Eddie Milner	.07	.03	.01
☐	598	Ron Oester	.04	.02	.00
☐	599	Frank Pastore	.04	.02	.00
☐	600	Joe Price	.04	.02	.00
☐	601	Tom Seaver	.70	.35	.07
☐	602	Bob Shirley	.04	.02	.00
☐	603	Mario Soto	.07	.03	.01
☐	604	Alex Trevino	.04	.02	.00
☐	605	Mike Vail	.04	.02	.00
☐	606	Duane Walker	.04	.02	.00
☐	607	Tom Brunansky	.90	.45	.09
☐	608	Bobby Castillo	.04	.02	.00
☐	609	John Castino	.04	.02	.00
☐	610	Ron Davis	.04	.02	.00
☐	611	Lenny Faedo	.04	.02	.00
☐	612	Terry Felton	.04	.02	.00
☐	613	Gary Gaetti	3.00	1.50	.30
☐	614	Mickey Hatcher	.04	.02	.00
☐	615	Brad Havens	.04	.02	.00
☐	616	Kent Hrbek	1.75	.85	.17
☐	617	Randy Johnson	.04	.02	.00
☐	618	Tim Laudner	.04	.02	.00
☐	619	Jeff Little	.04	.02	.00
☐	620	Bobby Mitchell	.04	.02	.00
☐	621	Jack O'Connor	.04	.02	.00
☐	622	John Pacella	.04	.02	.00
☐	623	Pete Redfern	.04	.02	.00
☐	624	Jesus Vega	.04	.02	.00
☐	625	Frank Viola	7.00	3.50	.70
☐	626	Ron Washington	.04	.02	.00
☐	627	Gary Ward	.04	.02	.00
☐	628	Al Williams	.04	.02	.00
☐	629	Red Sox All-Stars Carl Yastrzemski Dennis Eckersley Mark Clear	.25	.12	.02
☐	630	"300 Career Wins" Gaylord Perry and Terry Bulling 5/6/82	.10	.05	.01
☐	631	Pride of Venezuela Dave Concepcion and Manny Trillo	.07	.03	.01
☐	632	All-Star Infielders Robin Yount and Buddy Bell	.12	.06	.01
☐	633	Mr.Vet and Mr.Rookie Dave Winfield and Kent Hrbek	.20	.10	.02
☐	634	Fountain of Youth Willie Stargell and Pete Rose	.60	.30	.06
☐	635	Big Chiefs Toby Harrah and Andre Thornton	.07	.03	.01
☐	636	Smith Brothers Ozzie and Lonnie	.07	.03	.01
☐	637	Base Stealers' Threat Bo Diaz and Gary Carter	.07	.03	.01
☐	638	All-Star Catchers Carlton Fisk and Gary Carter	.12	.06	.01
☐	639	The Silver Shoe Rickey Henderson	1.00	.50	.10
☐	640	Home Run Threats Ben Oglivie and Reggie Jackson	.18	.09	.01

☐ 641 Two Teams Same Day Joel Youngblood August 4, 1982	.07	.03	.01
☐ 642 Last Perfect Game Ron Hassey and Len Barker	.07	.03	.01
☐ 643 Black and Blue Bud Black	.07	.03	.01
☐ 644 Black and Blue Vida Blue	.07	.03	.01
☐ 645 Speed and Power Reggie Jackson	.25	.12	.02
☐ 646 Speed and Power Rickey Henderson	.60	.30	.06
☐ 647 CL: Cards/Brewers	.07	.01	.00
☐ 648 CL: Orioles/Angels	.07	.01	.00
☐ 649 CL: Royals/Braves	.07	.01	.00
☐ 650 CL: Phillies/Red Sox	.07	.01	.00
☐ 651 CL: Dodgers/White Sox	.07	.01	.00
☐ 652 CL: Giants/Expos	.07	.01	.00
☐ 653 CL: Pirates/Tigers	.07	.01	.00
☐ 654 CL: Padres/Yankees	.07	.01	.00
☐ 655 CL: Indians/Blue Jays	.07	.01	.00
☐ 656 CL: Astros/Mariners	.07	.01	.00
☐ 657 CL: Cubs/A's	.07	.01	.00
☐ 658 CL: Mets/Rangers	.07	.01	.00
☐ 659 CL: Reds/Twins	.07	.01	.00
☐ 660 CL: Specials/Teams	.09	.01	.00

1984 Fleer

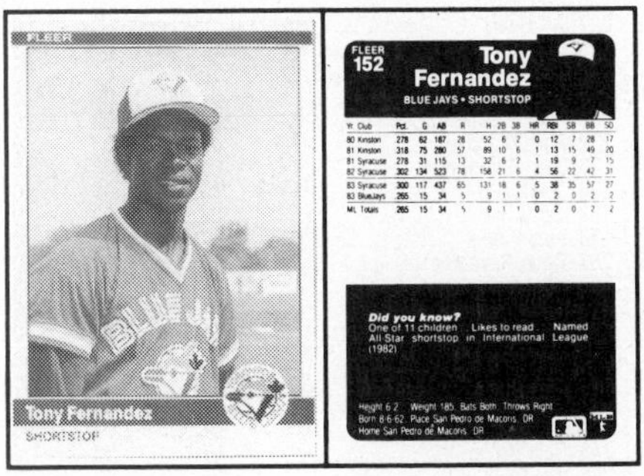

The cards in this 660-card set measure 2 1/2" by 3 1/2". The 1984 Fleer card set featured fronts with full-color team logos along with the player's name and position and the Fleer identification. The set features many imaginative photos, several multi-player cards, and many more action shots than the 1983 card set. The backs are quite similar to the 1983 backs except that blue rather than brown ink is used. The player cards are alphabetized within team and the teams are ordered by their 1983 season finish and won-lost record, e.g., Baltimore (1-23), Philadelphia (24-49), Chicago White Sox (50-73), Detroit (74-95), Los Angeles (96-118), New York Yankees (119-144), Toronto (145-169), Atlanta (170-193), Milwaukee (194-219), Houston (220-244), Pittsburgh (245-269), Montreal (270-293), San Diego (294-317), St. Louis (318-340), Kansas City (341-364), San Francisco (365-387), Boston (388-412), Texas (413-435), Oakland (436-461), Cincinnati (462-485), Chicago (486-507), California (508-532), Cleveland (533-555), Minnesota (556-579), New York Mets (580-603), and Seattle (604-625). Specials (626-646) and checklist cards (647-660) make up the end of the set. The key rookie cards in this set are Tony Fernandez, Don Mattingly, Kevin McReynolds, Darryl Strawberry, and Andy Van Slyke.

	MINT	EXC	G-VG
COMPLETE SET (660)	180.00	90.00	18.00
COMMON PLAYER (1-660)	.07	.03	.01

☐ 1 Mike Boddicker	.20	.10	.02
☐ 2 Al Bumbry	.07	.03	.01
☐ 3 Todd Cruz	.07	.03	.01
☐ 4 Rich Dauer	.07	.03	.01
☐ 5 Storm Davis	.15	.07	.01
☐ 6 Rick Dempsey	.07	.03	.01
☐ 7 Jim Dwyer	.07	.03	.01
☐ 8 Mike Flanagan	.10	.05	.01
☐ 9 Dan Ford	.07	.03	.01
☐ 10 John Lowenstein	.07	.03	.01
☐ 11 Dennis Martinez	.10	.05	.01
☐ 12 Tippy Martinez	.07	.03	.01
☐ 13 Scott McGregor	.10	.05	.01
☐ 14 Eddie Murray	1.00	.50	.10
☐ 15 Joe Nolan	.07	.03	.01
☐ 16 Jim Palmer	1.00	.50	.10
☐ 17 Cal Ripken	4.00	2.00	.40
☐ 18 Gary Roenicke	.07	.03	.01
☐ 19 Lenn Sakata	.07	.03	.01
☐ 20 John Shelby	.30	.15	.03
☐ 21 Ken Singleton	.10	.05	.01
☐ 22 Sammy Stewart	.07	.03	.01
☐ 23 Tim Stoddard	.07	.03	.01
☐ 24 Marty Bystrom	.07	.03	.01
☐ 25 Steve Carlton	.85	.40	.08
☐ 26 Ivan DeJesus	.07	.03	.01
☐ 27 John Denny	.10	.05	.01
☐ 28 Bob Dernier	.07	.03	.01
☐ 29 Bo Diaz	.07	.03	.01
☐ 30 Kiko Garcia	.07	.03	.01
☐ 31 Greg Gross	.07	.03	.01
☐ 32 Kevin Gross	.50	.25	.05
☐ 33 Von Hayes	.30	.15	.03
☐ 34 Willie Hernandez	.15	.07	.01
☐ 35 Al Holland	.07	.03	.01
☐ 36 Charles Hudson	.15	.07	.01
☐ 37 Joe Lefebvre	.07	.03	.01
☐ 38 Sixto Lezcano	.07	.03	.01
☐ 39 Garry Maddox	.07	.03	.01
☐ 40 Gary Matthews	.10	.05	.01
☐ 41 Len Matuszek	.07	.03	.01
☐ 42 Tug McGraw	.10	.05	.01
☐ 43 Joe Morgan	.50	.25	.05
☐ 44 Tony Perez	.25	.12	.02
☐ 45 Ron Reed	.07	.03	.01
☐ 46 Pete Rose	1.50	.75	.15
☐ 47 Juan Samuel	3.00	1.50	.30
☐ 48 Mike Schmidt	6.50	3.25	.65
☐ 49 Ozzie Virgil	.07	.03	.01
☐ 50 Juan Agosto	.12	.06	.01
☐ 51 Harold Baines	.35	.17	.03
☐ 52 Floyd Bannister	.07	.03	.01
☐ 53 Salome Barojas	.07	.03	.01
☐ 54 Britt Burns	.07	.03	.01
☐ 55 Julio Cruz	.07	.03	.01
☐ 56 Richard Dotson	.07	.03	.01
☐ 57 Jerry Dybzinski	.07	.03	.01
☐ 58 Carlton Fisk	.85	.40	.08
☐ 59 Scott Fletcher	.25	.12	.02
☐ 60 Jerry Hairston	.07	.03	.01
☐ 61 Kevin Hickey	.07	.03	.01
☐ 62 Marc Hill	.07	.03	.01
☐ 63 LaMarr Hoyt	.10	.05	.01
☐ 64 Ron Kittle	.20	.10	.02
☐ 65 Jerry Koosman	.10	.05	.01
☐ 66 Dennis Lamp	.07	.03	.01
☐ 67 Rudy Law	.07	.03	.01
☐ 68 Vance Law	.10	.05	.01
☐ 69 Greg Luzinski	.12	.06	.01
☐ 70 Tom Paciorek	.07	.03	.01
☐ 71 Mike Squires	.07	.03	.01
☐ 72 Dick Tidrow	.07	.03	.01
☐ 73 Greg Walker	.35	.17	.03
☐ 74 Glenn Abbott	.07	.03	.01
☐ 75 Howard Bailey	.07	.03	.01
☐ 76 Doug Bair	.07	.03	.01
☐ 77 Juan Berenguer	.07	.03	.01
☐ 78 Tom Brookens	.07	.03	.01
☐ 79 Enos Cabell	.07	.03	.01
☐ 80 Kirk Gibson	.50	.25	.05
☐ 81 John Grubb	.07	.03	.01
☐ 82 Larry Herndon	.07	.03	.01
☐ 83 Wayne Krenchicki	.07	.03	.01
☐ 84 Rick Leach	.07	.03	.01
☐ 85 Chet Lemon	.07	.03	.01
☐ 86 Aurelio Lopez	.07	.03	.01
☐ 87 Jack Morris	.25	.12	.02
☐ 88 Lance Parrish	.35	.17	.03
☐ 89 Dan Petry	.07	.03	.01
☐ 90 Dave Rozema	.07	.03	.01
☐ 91 Alan Trammell	.60	.30	.06
☐ 92 Lou Whitaker	.35	.17	.03
☐ 93 Milt Wilcox	.07	.03	.01
☐ 94 Glenn Wilson	.10	.05	.01
☐ 95 John Wockenfuss	.07	.03	.01
☐ 96 Dusty Baker	.10	.05	.01

☐ 97 Joe Beckwith	.07	.03	.01
☐ 98 Greg Brock	.10	.05	.01
☐ 99 Jack Fimple	.07	.03	.01
☐ 100 Pedro Guerrero	.45	.22	.04
☐ 101 Rick Honeycutt	.07	.03	.01
☐ 102 Burt Hooton	.07	.03	.01
☐ 103 Steve Howe	.07	.03	.01
☐ 104 Ken Landreaux	.07	.03	.01
☐ 105 Mike Marshall	.25	.12	.02
☐ 106 Rick Monday	.10	.05	.01
☐ 107 Jose Morales	.07	.03	.01
☐ 108 Tom Niedenfuer	.07	.03	.01
☐ 109 Alejandro Pena	.35	.17	.03
☐ 110 Jerry Reuss	.10	.05	.01
☐ 111 Bill Russell	.10	.05	.01
☐ 112 Steve Sax	.45	.22	.04
☐ 113 Mike Scioscia	.10	.05	.01
☐ 114 Derrel Thomas	.07	.03	.01
☐ 115 Fernando Valenzuela	.45	.22	.04
☐ 116 Bob Welch	.35	.17	.03
☐ 117 Steve Yeager	.07	.03	.01
☐ 118 Pat Zachry	.07	.03	.01
☐ 119 Don Baylor	.15	.07	.01
☐ 120 Bert Campaneris	.10	.05	.01
☐ 121 Rick Cerone	.07	.03	.01
☐ 122 Ray Fontenot	.07	.03	.01
☐ 123 George Frazier	.07	.03	.01
☐ 124 Oscar Gamble	.07	.03	.01
☐ 125 Goose Gossage	.25	.12	.02
☐ 126 Ken Griffey	.20	.10	.02
☐ 127 Ron Guidry	.30	.15	.03
☐ 128 Jay Howell	.35	.17	.03
☐ 129 Steve Kemp	.07	.03	.01
☐ 130 Matt Keough	.07	.03	.01
☐ 131 Don Mattingly	48.00	22.00	4.00
☐ 132 John Montefusco	.07	.03	.01
☐ 133 Omar Moreno	.07	.03	.01
☐ 134 Dale Murray	.07	.03	.01
☐ 135 Graig Nettles	.15	.07	.01
☐ 136 Lou Piniella	.10	.05	.01
☐ 137 Willie Randolph	.15	.07	.01
☐ 138 Shane Rawley	.07	.03	.01
☐ 139 Dave Righetti	.25	.12	.02
☐ 140 Andre Robertson	.07	.03	.01
☐ 141 Bob Shirley	.07	.03	.01
☐ 142 Roy Smalley	.07	.03	.01
☐ 143 Dave Winfield	.60	.30	.06
☐ 144 Butch Wynegar	.07	.03	.01
☐ 145 Jim Acker	.10	.05	.01
☐ 146 Doyle Alexander	.10	.05	.01
☐ 147 Jesse Barfield	.25	.12	.02
☐ 148 Jorge Bell	1.50	.75	.15
☐ 149 Barry Bonnell	.07	.03	.01
☐ 150 Jim Clancy	.07	.03	.01
☐ 151 Dave Collins	.07	.03	.01
☐ 152 Tony Fernandez	5.00	2.50	.50
☐ 153 Damaso Garcia	.07	.03	.01
☐ 154 Dave Geisel	.07	.03	.01
☐ 155 Jim Gott	.18	.09	.01
☐ 156 Alfredo Griffin	.07	.03	.01
☐ 157 Garth Iorg	.07	.03	.01
☐ 158 Roy Lee Jackson	.07	.03	.01
☐ 159 Cliff Johnson	.07	.03	.01
☐ 160 Luis Leal	.07	.03	.01
☐ 161 Buck Martinez	.07	.03	.01
☐ 162 Joey McLaughlin	.07	.03	.01
☐ 163 Randy Moffitt	.07	.03	.01
☐ 164 Lloyd Moseby	.15	.07	.01
☐ 165 Rance Mulliniks	.07	.03	.01
☐ 166 Jorge Orta	.07	.03	.01
☐ 167 Dave Stieb	.40	.20	.04
☐ 168 Willie Upshaw	.07	.03	.01
☐ 169 Ernie Whitt	.07	.03	.01
☐ 170 Len Barker	.07	.03	.01
☐ 171 Steve Bedrosian	.20	.10	.02
☐ 172 Bruce Benedict	.07	.03	.01
☐ 173 Brett Butler	.20	.10	.02
☐ 174 Rick Camp	.07	.03	.01
☐ 175 Chris Chambliss	.10	.05	.01
☐ 176 Ken Dayley	.07	.03	.01
☐ 177 Pete Falcone	.07	.03	.01
☐ 178 Terry Forster	.10	.05	.01
☐ 179 Gene Garber	.07	.03	.01
☐ 180 Terry Harper	.07	.03	.01
☐ 181 Bob Horner	.15	.07	.01
☐ 182 Glenn Hubbard	.07	.03	.01
☐ 183 Randy Johnson	.07	.03	.01
☐ 184 Craig McMurtry	.07	.03	.01
☐ 185 Donnie Moore	.07	.03	.01
☐ 186 Dale Murphy	1.50	.75	.15
☐ 187 Phil Niekro	.30	.15	.03
☐ 188 Pascual Perez	.20	.10	.02
☐ 189 Biff Pocoroba	.07	.03	.01
☐ 190 Rafael Ramirez	.07	.03	.01
☐ 191 Jerry Royster	.07	.03	.01
☐ 192 Claudell Washington	.10	.05	.01
☐ 193 Bob Watson	.10	.05	.01
☐ 194 Jerry Augustine	.07	.03	.01
☐ 195 Mark Brouhard	.07	.03	.01
☐ 196 Mike Caldwell	.07	.03	.01
☐ 197 Tom Candiotti	.65	.30	.06
☐ 198 Cecil Cooper	.15	.07	.01
☐ 199 Rollie Fingers	.30	.15	.03
☐ 200 Jim Gantner	.07	.03	.01
☐ 201 Bob L. Gibson	.10	.05	.01
☐ 202 Moose Haas	.07	.03	.01
☐ 203 Roy Howell	.07	.03	.01
☐ 204 Pete Ladd	.07	.03	.01
☐ 205 Rick Manning	.07	.03	.01
☐ 206 Bob McClure	.07	.03	.01
☐ 207 Paul Molitor	.25	.12	.02
☐ 208 Don Money	.07	.03	.01
☐ 209 Charlie Moore	.07	.03	.01
☐ 210 Ben Oglivie	.10	.05	.01
☐ 211 Chuck Porter	.07	.03	.01
☐ 212 Ed Romero	.07	.03	.01
☐ 213 Ted Simmons	.15	.07	.01
☐ 214 Jim Slaton	.07	.03	.01
☐ 215 Don Sutton	.30	.15	.03
☐ 216 Tom Tellmann	.07	.03	.01
☐ 217 Pete Vuckovich	.10	.05	.01
☐ 218 Ned Yost	.07	.03	.01
☐ 219 Robin Yount	1.75	.85	.17
☐ 220 Alan Ashby	.07	.03	.01
☐ 221 Kevin Bass	.15	.07	.01
☐ 222 Jose Cruz	.10	.05	.01
☐ 223 Bill Dawley	.07	.03	.01
☐ 224 Frank DiPino	.07	.03	.01
☐ 225 Bill Doran	1.25	.60	.12
☐ 226 Phil Garner	.07	.03	.01
☐ 227 Art Howe	.10	.05	.01
☐ 228 Bob Knepper	.10	.05	.01
☐ 229 Ray Knight	.10	.05	.01
☐ 230 Frank LaCorte	.07	.03	.01
☐ 231 Mike LaCoss	.07	.03	.01
☐ 232 Mike Madden	.07	.03	.01
☐ 233 Jerry Mumphrey	.07	.03	.01
☐ 234 Joe Niekro	.10	.05	.01
☐ 235 Terry Puhl	.07	.03	.01
☐ 236 Luis Pujols	.07	.03	.01
☐ 237 Craig Reynolds	.07	.03	.01
☐ 238 Vern Ruhle	.07	.03	.01
☐ 239 Nolan Ryan	5.00	2.50	.50
☐ 240 Mike Scott	.35	.17	.03
☐ 241 Tony Scott	.07	.03	.01
☐ 242 Dave Smith	.10	.05	.01
☐ 243 Dickie Thon	.07	.03	.01
☐ 244 Denny Walling	.07	.03	.01
☐ 245 Dale Berra	.07	.03	.01
☐ 246 Jim Bibby	.07	.03	.01
☐ 247 John Candelaria	.10	.05	.01
☐ 248 Jose DeLeon	.35	.17	.03
☐ 249 Mike Easler	.07	.03	.01
☐ 250 Cecilio Guante	.07	.03	.01
☐ 251 Richie Hebner	.07	.03	.01
☐ 252 Lee Lacy	.07	.03	.01
☐ 253 Bill Madlock	.15	.07	.01
☐ 254 Milt May	.07	.03	.01
☐ 255 Lee Mazzilli	.07	.03	.01
☐ 256 Larry McWilliams	.07	.03	.01
☐ 257 Jim Morrison	.07	.03	.01
☐ 258 Dave Parker	.40	.20	.04
☐ 259 Tony Pena	.25	.12	.02
☐ 260 Johnny Ray	.12	.06	.01
☐ 261 Rick Rhoden	.10	.05	.01
☐ 262 Don Robinson	.07	.03	.01
☐ 263 Manny Sarmiento	.07	.03	.01
☐ 264 Rod Scurry	.07	.03	.01
☐ 265 Kent Tekulve	.10	.05	.01
☐ 266 Gene Tenace	.07	.03	.01
☐ 267 Jason Thompson	.07	.03	.01
☐ 268 Lee Tunnell	.10	.05	.01
☐ 269 Marvell Wynne	.10	.05	.01
☐ 270 Ray Burris	.07	.03	.01
☐ 271 Gary Carter	.45	.22	.04
☐ 272 Warren Cromartie	.07	.03	.01
☐ 273 Andre Dawson	.90	.45	.09
☐ 274 Doug Flynn	.07	.03	.01
☐ 275 Terry Francona	.07	.03	.01
☐ 276 Bill Gullickson	.07	.03	.01
☐ 277 Bob James	.10	.05	.01
☐ 278 Charlie Lea	.07	.03	.01
☐ 279 Bryan Little	.07	.03	.01
☐ 280 Al Oliver	.10	.05	.01
☐ 281 Tim Raines	.65	.30	.06
☐ 282 Bobby Ramos	.07	.03	.01
☐ 283 Jeff Reardon	.15	.07	.01
☐ 284 Steve Rogers	.07	.03	.01

☐ 285 Scott Sanderson	.10	.05	.01
☐ 286 Dan Schatzeder	.07	.03	.01
☐ 287 Bryn Smith	.15	.07	.01
☐ 288 Chris Speier	.07	.03	.01
☐ 289 Manny Trillo	.07	.03	.01
☐ 290 Mike Vail	.07	.03	.01
☐ 291 Tim Wallach	.30	.15	.03
☐ 292 Chris Welsh	.07	.03	.01
☐ 293 Jim Wohlford	.07	.03	.01
☐ 294 Kurt Bevacqua	.07	.03	.01
☐ 295 Juan Bonilla	.07	.03	.01
☐ 296 Bobby Brown	.07	.03	.01
☐ 297 Luis DeLeon	.07	.03	.01
☐ 298 Dave Dravecky	.18	.09	.01
☐ 299 Tim Flannery	.07	.03	.01
☐ 300 Steve Garvey	.60	.30	.06
☐ 301 Tony Gwynn	4.50	2.25	.45
☐ 302 Andy Hawkins	.60	.30	.06
☐ 303 Ruppert Jones	.07	.03	.01
☐ 304 Terry Kennedy	.10	.05	.01
☐ 305 Tim Lollar	.07	.03	.01
☐ 306 Gary Lucas	.07	.03	.01
☐ 307 Kevin McReynolds	6.50	3.25	.65
☐ 308 Sid Monge	.07	.03	.01
☐ 309 Mario Ramirez	.07	.03	.01
☐ 310 Gene Richards	.07	.03	.01
☐ 311 Luis Salazar	.07	.03	.01
☐ 312 Eric Show	.10	.05	.01
☐ 313 Elias Sosa	.07	.03	.01
☐ 314 Garry Templeton	.10	.05	.01
☐ 315 Mark Thurmond	.10	.05	.01
☐ 316 Ed Whitson	.10	.05	.01
☐ 317 Alan Wiggins	.07	.03	.01
☐ 318 Neil Allen	.07	.03	.01
☐ 319 Joaquin Andujar	.10	.05	.01
☐ 320 Steve Braun	.07	.03	.01
☐ 321 Glenn Brummer	.07	.03	.01
☐ 322 Bob Forsch	.07	.03	.01
☐ 323 David Green	.07	.03	.01
☐ 324 George Hendrick	.10	.05	.01
☐ 325 Tom Herr	.10	.05	.01
☐ 326 Dane Iorg	.07	.03	.01
☐ 327 Jeff Lahti	.07	.03	.01
☐ 328 Dave LaPoint	.10	.05	.01
☐ 329 Willie McGee	.65	.30	.06
☐ 330 Ken Oberkfell	.07	.03	.01
☐ 331 Darrell Porter	.07	.03	.01
☐ 332 Jamie Quirk	.07	.03	.01
☐ 333 Mike Ramsey	.07	.03	.01
☐ 334 Floyd Rayford	.07	.03	.01
☐ 335 Lonnie Smith	.15	.07	.01
☐ 336 Ozzie Smith	.65	.30	.06
☐ 337 John Stuper	.07	.03	.01
☐ 338 Bruce Sutter	.15	.07	.01
☐ 339 Andy Van Slyke	4.00	2.00	.40
☐ 340 Dave Von Ohlen	.07	.03	.01
☐ 341 Willie Aikens	.07	.03	.01
☐ 342 Mike Armstrong	.07	.03	.01
☐ 343 Bud Black	.15	.07	.01
☐ 344 George Brett	2.00	1.00	.20
☐ 345 Onix Concepcion	.07	.03	.01
☐ 346 Keith Creel	.07	.03	.01
☐ 347 Larry Gura	.07	.03	.01
☐ 348 Don Hood	.07	.03	.01
☐ 349 Dennis Leonard	.10	.05	.01
☐ 350 Hal McRae	.10	.05	.01
☐ 351 Amos Otis	.10	.05	.01
☐ 352 Gaylord Perry	.25	.12	.02
☐ 353 Greg Pryor	.07	.03	.01
☐ 354 Dan Quisenberry	.15	.07	.01
☐ 355 Steve Renko	.07	.03	.01
☐ 356 Leon Roberts	.07	.03	.01
☐ 357 Pat Sheridan	.20	.10	.02
☐ 358 Joe Simpson	.07	.03	.01
☐ 359 Don Slaught	.10	.05	.01
☐ 360 Paul Splittorff	.07	.03	.01
☐ 361 U.L. Washington	.07	.03	.01
☐ 362 John Wathan	.07	.03	.01
☐ 363 Frank White	.10	.05	.01
☐ 364 Willie Wilson	.15	.07	.01
☐ 365 Jim Barr	.07	.03	.01
☐ 366 Dave Bergman	.07	.03	.01
☐ 367 Fred Breining	.07	.03	.01
☐ 368 Bob Brenly	.07	.03	.01
☐ 369 Jack Clark	.30	.15	.03
☐ 370 Chili Davis	.20	.10	.02
☐ 371 Mark Davis	.45	.22	.04
☐ 372 Darrell Evans	.15	.07	.01
☐ 373 Atlee Hammaker	.07	.03	.01
☐ 374 Mike Krukow	.10	.05	.01
☐ 375 Duane Kuiper	.07	.03	.01
☐ 376 Bill Laskey	.07	.03	.01
☐ 377 Gary Lavelle	.07	.03	.01
☐ 378 Johnnie LeMaster	.07	.03	.01
☐ 379 Jeff Leonard	.10	.05	.01
☐ 380 Randy Lerch	.07	.03	.01
☐ 381 Renie Martin	.07	.03	.01
☐ 382 Andy McGaffigan	.07	.03	.01
☐ 383 Greg Minton	.07	.03	.01
☐ 384 Tom O'Malley	.07	.03	.01
☐ 385 Max Venable	.07	.03	.01
☐ 386 Brad Wellman	.07	.03	.01
☐ 387 Joel Youngblood	.07	.03	.01
☐ 388 Gary Allenson	.07	.03	.01
☐ 389 Luis Aponte	.07	.03	.01
☐ 390 Tony Armas	.10	.05	.01
☐ 391 Doug Bird	.07	.03	.01
☐ 392 Wade Boggs	7.50	3.75	.75
☐ 393 Dennis Boyd	.75	.35	.07
☐ 394 Mike Brown UER (Red Sox pitcher, shown with record of 31-104)	.10	.05	.01
☐ 395 Mark Clear	.07	.03	.01
☐ 396 Dennis Eckersley	.40	.20	.04
☐ 397 Dwight Evans	.35	.17	.03
☐ 398 Rich Gedman	.07	.03	.01
☐ 399 Glenn Hoffman	.07	.03	.01
☐ 400 Bruce Hurst	.20	.10	.02
☐ 401 John Henry Johnson	.07	.03	.01
☐ 402 Ed Jurak	.07	.03	.01
☐ 403 Rick Miller	.07	.03	.01
☐ 404 Jeff Newman	.07	.03	.01
☐ 405 Reid Nichols	.07	.03	.01
☐ 406 Bob Ojeda	.10	.05	.01
☐ 407 Jerry Remy	.07	.03	.01
☐ 408 Jim Rice	.30	.15	.03
☐ 409 Bob Stanley	.07	.03	.01
☐ 410 Dave Stapleton	.07	.03	.01
☐ 411 John Tudor	.20	.10	.02
☐ 412 Carl Yastrzemski	1.25	.60	.12
☐ 413 Buddy Bell	.15	.07	.01
☐ 414 Larry Biittner	.07	.03	.01
☐ 415 John Butcher	.07	.03	.01
☐ 416 Danny Darwin	.10	.05	.01
☐ 417 Bucky Dent	.15	.07	.01
☐ 418 Dave Hostetler	.07	.03	.01
☐ 419 Charlie Hough	.10	.05	.01
☐ 420 Bobby Johnson	.07	.03	.01
☐ 421 Odell Jones	.07	.03	.01
☐ 422 Jon Matlack	.07	.03	.01
☐ 423 Pete O'Brien	.80	.40	.08
☐ 424 Larry Parrish	.10	.05	.01
☐ 425 Mickey Rivers	.10	.05	.01
☐ 426 Billy Sample	.07	.03	.01
☐ 427 Dave Schmidt	.10	.05	.01
☐ 428 Mike Smithson	.10	.05	.01
☐ 429 Bill Stein	.07	.03	.01
☐ 430 Dave Stewart	1.25	.60	.12
☐ 431 Jim Sundberg	.07	.03	.01
☐ 432 Frank Tanana	.10	.05	.01
☐ 433 Dave Tobik	.07	.03	.01
☐ 434 Wayne Tolleson	.10	.05	.01
☐ 435 George Wright	.07	.03	.01
☐ 436 Bill Almon	.07	.03	.01
☐ 437 Keith Atherton	.07	.03	.01
☐ 438 Dave Beard	.07	.03	.01
☐ 439 Tom Burgmeier	.07	.03	.01
☐ 440 Jeff Burroughs	.10	.05	.01
☐ 441 Chris Codiroli	.10	.05	.01
☐ 442 Tim Conroy	.07	.03	.01
☐ 443 Mike Davis	.07	.03	.01
☐ 444 Wayne Gross	.07	.03	.01
☐ 445 Garry Hancock	.07	.03	.01
☐ 446 Mike Heath	.07	.03	.01
☐ 447 Rickey Henderson	7.00	3.50	.70
☐ 448 Donnie Hill	.07	.03	.01
☐ 449 Bob Kearney	.07	.03	.01
☐ 450 Bill Krueger	.07	.03	.01
☐ 451 Rick Langford	.07	.03	.01
☐ 452 Carney Lansford	.20	.10	.02
☐ 453 Dave Lopes	.10	.05	.01
☐ 454 Steve McCatty	.07	.03	.01
☐ 455 Dan Meyer	.07	.03	.01
☐ 456 Dwayne Murphy	.07	.03	.01
☐ 457 Mike Norris	.07	.03	.01
☐ 458 Ricky Peters	.07	.03	.01
☐ 459 Tony Phillips	.30	.15	.03
☐ 460 Tom Underwood	.07	.03	.01
☐ 461 Mike Warren	.10	.05	.01
☐ 462 Johnny Bench	1.25	.60	.12
☐ 463 Bruce Berenyi	.07	.03	.01
☐ 464 Dann Bilardello	.07	.03	.01
☐ 465 Cesar Cedeno	.10	.05	.01
☐ 466 Dave Concepcion	.15	.07	.01
☐ 467 Dan Driessen	.07	.03	.01
☐ 468 Nick Esasky	1.00	.50	.10
☐ 469 Rich Gale	.07	.03	.01

☐ 470	Ben Hayes	.07	.03	.01
☐ 471	Paul Householder	.07	.03	.01
☐ 472	Tom Hume	.07	.03	.01
☐ 473	Alan Knicely	.07	.03	.01
☐ 474	Eddie Milner	.07	.03	.01
☐ 475	Ron Oester	.07	.03	.01
☐ 476	Kelly Paris	.07	.03	.01
☐ 477	Frank Pastore	.07	.03	.01
☐ 478	Ted Power	.10	.05	.01
☐ 479	Joe Price	.07	.03	.01
☐ 480	Charlie Puleo	.07	.03	.01
☐ 481	Gary Redus	.25	.12	.02
☐ 482	Bill Scherrer	.07	.03	.01
☐ 483	Mario Soto	.07	.03	.01
☐ 484	Alex Trevino	.07	.03	.01
☐ 485	Duane Walker	.07	.03	.01
☐ 486	Larry Bowa	.10	.05	.01
☐ 487	Warren Brusstar	.07	.03	.01
☐ 488	Bill Buckner	.10	.05	.01
☐ 489	Bill Campbell	.07	.03	.01
☐ 490	Ron Cey	.10	.05	.01
☐ 491	Jody Davis	.10	.05	.01
☐ 492	Leon Durham	.07	.03	.01
☐ 493	Mel Hall	.45	.22	.04
☐ 494	Ferguson Jenkins	.20	.10	.02
☐ 495	Jay Johnstone	.10	.05	.01
☐ 496	Craig Lefferts	.40	.20	.04
☐ 497	Carmelo Martinez	.40	.20	.04
☐ 498	Jerry Morales	.07	.03	.01
☐ 499	Keith Moreland	.07	.03	.01
☐ 500	Dickie Noles	.07	.03	.01
☐ 501	Mike Proly	.07	.03	.01
☐ 502	Chuck Rainey	.07	.03	.01
☐ 503	Dick Ruthven	.07	.03	.01
☐ 504	Ryne Sandberg	12.00	6.00	1.20
☐ 505	Lee Smith	.15	.07	.01
☐ 506	Steve Trout	.07	.03	.01
☐ 507	Gary Woods	.07	.03	.01
☐ 508	Juan Beniquez	.07	.03	.01
☐ 509	Bob Boone	.18	.09	.01
☐ 510	Rick Burleson	.10	.05	.01
☐ 511	Rod Carew	1.00	.50	.10
☐ 512	Bobby Clark	.07	.03	.01
☐ 513	John Curtis	.07	.03	.01
☐ 514	Doug DeCinces	.10	.05	.01
☐ 515	Brian Downing	.10	.05	.01
☐ 516	Tim Foli	.07	.03	.01
☐ 517	Ken Forsch	.07	.03	.01
☐ 518	Bobby Grich	.10	.05	.01
☐ 519	Andy Hassler	.07	.03	.01
☐ 520	Reggie Jackson	1.25	.60	.12
☐ 521	Ron Jackson	.07	.03	.01
☐ 522	Tommy John	.18	.09	.01
☐ 523	Bruce Kison	.07	.03	.01
☐ 524	Steve Lubratich	.07	.03	.01
☐ 525	Fred Lynn	.20	.10	.02
☐ 526	Gary Pettis	.35	.17	.03
☐ 527	Luis Sanchez	.07	.03	.01
☐ 528	Daryl Sconiers	.07	.03	.01
☐ 529	Ellis Valentine	.07	.03	.01
☐ 530	Rob Wilfong	.07	.03	.01
☐ 531	Mike Witt	.10	.05	.01
☐ 532	Geoff Zahn	.07	.03	.01
☐ 533	Bud Anderson	.07	.03	.01
☐ 534	Chris Bando	.07	.03	.01
☐ 535	Alan Bannister	.07	.03	.01
☐ 536	Bert Blyleven	.30	.15	.03
☐ 537	Tom Brennan	.07	.03	.01
☐ 538	Jamie Easterly	.07	.03	.01
☐ 539	Juan Eichelberger	.07	.03	.01
☐ 540	Jim Essian	.07	.03	.01
☐ 541	Mike Fischlin	.07	.03	.01
☐ 542	Julio Franco	2.50	1.25	.25
☐ 543	Mike Hargrove	.10	.05	.01
☐ 544	Toby Harrah	.10	.05	.01
☐ 545	Ron Hassey	.07	.03	.01
☐ 546	Neal Heaton	.45	.22	.04
☐ 547	Bake McBride	.07	.03	.01
☐ 548	Broderick Perkins	.07	.03	.01
☐ 549	Lary Sorensen	.07	.03	.01
☐ 550	Dan Spillner	.07	.03	.01
☐ 551	Rick Sutcliffe	.25	.12	.02
☐ 552	Pat Tabler	.15	.07	.01
☐ 553	Gorman Thomas	.10	.05	.01
☐ 554	Andre Thornton	.10	.05	.01
☐ 555	George Vukovich	.07	.03	.01
☐ 556	Darrell Brown	.07	.03	.01
☐ 557	Tom Brunansky	.30	.15	.03
☐ 558	Randy Bush	.25	.12	.02
☐ 559	Bobby Castillo	.07	.03	.01
☐ 560	John Castino	.07	.03	.01
☐ 561	Ron Davis	.07	.03	.01
☐ 562	Dave Engle	.07	.03	.01
☐ 563	Lenny Faedo	.07	.03	.01
☐ 564	Pete Filson	.07	.03	.01
☐ 565	Gary Gaetti	.90	.45	.09
☐ 566	Mickey Hatcher	.07	.03	.01
☐ 567	Kent Hrbek	.60	.30	.06
☐ 568	Rusty Kuntz	.07	.03	.01
☐ 569	Tim Laudner	.07	.03	.01
☐ 570	Rick Lysander	.07	.03	.01
☐ 571	Bobby Mitchell	.07	.03	.01
☐ 572	Ken Schrom	.07	.03	.01
☐ 573	Ray Smith	.07	.03	.01
☐ 574	Tim Teufel	.30	.15	.03
☐ 575	Frank Viola	2.00	1.00	.20
☐ 576	Gary Ward	.07	.03	.01
☐ 577	Ron Washington	.07	.03	.01
☐ 578	Len Whitehouse	.07	.03	.01
☐ 579	Al Williams	.07	.03	.01
☐ 580	Bob Bailor	.07	.03	.01
☐ 581	Mark Bradley	.07	.03	.01
☐ 582	Hubie Brooks	.25	.12	.02
☐ 583	Carlos Diaz	.07	.03	.01
☐ 584	George Foster	.15	.07	.01
☐ 585	Brian Giles	.07	.03	.01
☐ 586	Danny Heep	.07	.03	.01
☐ 587	Keith Hernandez	.40	.20	.04
☐ 588	Ron Hodges	.07	.03	.01
☐ 589	Scott Holman	.07	.03	.01
☐ 590	Dave Kingman	.15	.07	.01
☐ 591	Ed Lynch	.07	.03	.01
☐ 592	Jose Oquendo	.65	.30	.06
☐ 593	Jesse Orosco	.07	.03	.01
☐ 594	Junior Ortiz	.07	.03	.01
☐ 595	Tom Seaver	1.75	.85	.17
☐ 596	Doug Sisk	.07	.03	.01
☐ 597	Rusty Staub	.15	.07	.01
☐ 598	John Stearns	.07	.03	.01
☐ 599	Darryl Strawberry	33.00	14.00	3.00
☐ 600	Craig Swan	.07	.03	.01
☐ 601	Walt Terrell	.35	.17	.03
☐ 602	Mike Torrez	.07	.03	.01
☐ 603	Mookie Wilson	.15	.07	.01
☐ 604	Jamie Allen	.07	.03	.01
☐ 605	Jim Beattie	.07	.03	.01
☐ 606	Tony Bernazard	.10	.05	.01
☐ 607	Manny Castillo	.07	.03	.01
☐ 608	Bill Caudill	.07	.03	.01
☐ 609	Bryan Clark	.07	.03	.01
☐ 610	Al Cowens	.07	.03	.01
☐ 611	Dave Henderson	.35	.17	.03
☐ 612	Steve Henderson	.07	.03	.01
☐ 613	Orlando Mercado	.07	.03	.01
☐ 614	Mike Moore	.30	.15	.03
☐ 615	Ricky Nelson UER (Jamie Nelson's stats on back)	.10	.05	.01
☐ 616	Spike Owen	.35	.17	.03
☐ 617	Pat Putnam	.07	.03	.01
☐ 618	Ron Roenicke	.07	.03	.01
☐ 619	Mike Stanton	.07	.03	.01
☐ 620	Bob Stoddard	.07	.03	.01
☐ 621	Rick Sweet	.07	.03	.01
☐ 622	Roy Thomas	.07	.03	.01
☐ 623	Ed VandeBerg	.07	.03	.01
☐ 624	Matt Young	.10	.05	.01
☐ 625	Richie Zisk	.07	.03	.01
☐ 626	Fred Lynn 1982 AS Game RB	.10	.05	.01
☐ 627	Manny Trillo 1983 AS Game RB	.10	.05	.01
☐ 628	Steve Garvey NL Iron Man	.25	.12	.02
☐ 629	Rod Carew AL Batting Runner-Up	.35	.17	.03
☐ 630	Wade Boggs AL Batting Champion	.75	.35	.07
☐ 631	Tim Raines: Letting Go of the Raines	.20	.10	.02
☐ 632	Al Oliver Double Trouble	.10	.05	.01
☐ 633	Steve Sax AS Second Base	.15	.07	.01
☐ 634	Dickie Thon AS Shortstop	.10	.05	.01
☐ 635	Ace Firemen Dan Quisenberry and Tippy Martinez	.10	.05	.01
☐ 636	Reds Reunited Joe Morgan Pete Rose Tony Perez	.40	.20	.04
☐ 637	Backstop Stars Lance Parrish Bob Boone	.10	.05	.01
☐ 638	Geo.Brett and G.Perry Pine Tar 7/24/83	.35	.17	.03

☐	639 1983 No Hitters	.10	.05	.01
	Dave Righetti			
	Mike Warren			
	Bob Forsch			
☐	640 Bench and Yaz	1.75	.85	.17
	Retiring Superstars			
☐	641 Gaylord Perry	.15	.07	.01
	Going Out In Style			
☐	642 Steve Carlton	.25	.12	.02
	300 Club and			
	Strikeout Record			
☐	643 Altobelli and Owens	.10	.05	.01
	WS Managers			
☐	644 Rick Dempsey	.10	.05	.01
	World Series MVP			
☐	645 Mike Boddicker	.10	.05	.01
	WS Rookie Winner			
☐	646 Scott McGregor	.10	.05	.01
	WS Clincher			
☐	647 CL: Orioles/Royals	.08	.01	.00
☐	648 CL: Phillies/Giants	.07	.01	.00
☐	649 CL: White Sox/Red Sox	.07	.01	.00
☐	650 CL: Tigers/Rangers	.07	.01	.00
☐	651 CL: Dodgers/A's	.07	.01	.00
☐	652 CL: Yankees/Reds	.07	.01	.00
☐	653 CL: Blue Jays/Cubs	.07	.01	.00
☐	654 CL: Braves/Angels	.07	.01	.00
☐	655 CL: Brewers/Indians	.07	.01	.00
☐	656 CL: Astros/Twins	.07	.01	.00
☐	657 CL: Pirates/Mets	.07	.01	.00
☐	658 CL: Expos/Mariners	.07	.01	.00
☐	659 CL: Padres/Specials	.07	.01	.00
☐	660 CL: Cardinals/Teams	.08	.01	.00

1984 Fleer Update

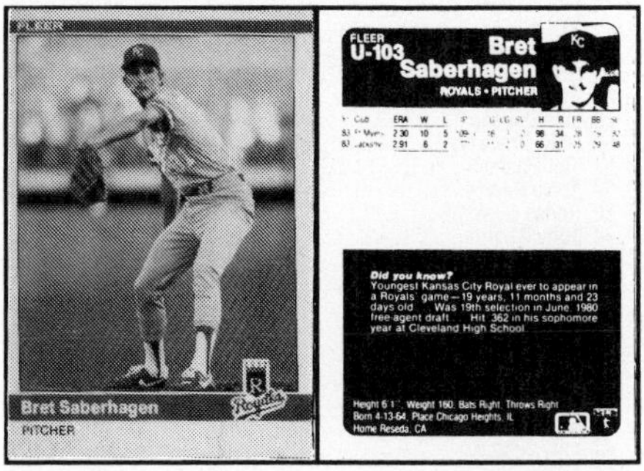

The cards in this 132-card set measure 2 1/2" by 3 1/2". For the first time, the Fleer Gum Company issued a traded, extended, or update set. The purpose of the set was the same as the traded sets issued by Topps over the past four years, i.e., to portray players with their proper team for the current year and to portray rookies who were not in their regular issue. Like the Topps Traded sets of the past four years, the Fleer Update sets were distributed through hobby dealers only. The set was quite popular with collectors, and, apparently, the print run was relatively short, as the set was quickly in short supply and exhibited a rapid and dramatic price increase. The cards are numbered on the back with a U prefix; the order corresponds to the alphabetical order of the subjects' names. The key (extended) rookie cards in this set are Roger Clemens, Alvin Davis, John Franco, Dwight Gooden, Mark Langston, Kirby Puckett, Jose Rijo, and Bret Saberhagen. Collectors are urged to be careful if purchasing single cards of Clemens, Darling, Gooden, Puckett, Rose, or Saberhagen as these specific cards have been illegally reprinted. These fakes are blurry when compared to the real thing.

	MINT	EXC	G-VG
COMPLETE SET (132)	525.00	250.00	50.00
COMMON PLAYER (1-132)	.25	.12	.02

☐	U1 Willie Aikens	.35	.17	.03
☐	U2 Luis Aponte	.25	.12	.02
☐	U3 Mark Bailey	.35	.17	.03
☐	U4 Bob Bailor	.25	.12	.02
☐	U5 Dusty Baker	.35	.17	.03
☐	U6 Steve Balboni	.35	.17	.03
☐	U7 Alan Bannister	.25	.12	.02
☐	U8 Marty Barrett	2.25	1.10	.22
☐	U9 Dave Beard	.25	.12	.02
☐	U10 Joe Beckwith	.25	.12	.02
☐	U11 Dave Bergman	.25	.12	.02
☐	U12 Tony Bernazard	.35	.17	.03
☐	U13 Bruce Bochte	.25	.12	.02
☐	U14 Barry Bonnell	.25	.12	.02
☐	U15 Phil Bradley	4.50	2.25	.45
☐	U16 Fred Breining	.25	.12	.02
☐	U17 Mike Brown	.25	.12	.02
	(Angels OF)			
☐	U18 Bill Buckner	.35	.17	.03
☐	U19 Ray Burris	.25	.12	.02
☐	U20 John Butcher	.25	.12	.02
☐	U21 Brett Butler	.50	.25	.05
☐	U22 Enos Cabell	.25	.12	.02
☐	U23 Bill Campbell	.25	.12	.02
☐	U24 Bill Caudill	.25	.12	.02
☐	U25 Bobby Clark	.25	.12	.02
☐	U26 Bryan Clark	.25	.12	.02
☐	U27 Roger Clemens	160.00	80.00	16.00
☐	U28 Jaime Cocanower	.25	.12	.02
☐	U29 Ron Darling	7.50	3.75	.75
☐	U30 Alvin Davis	16.00	8.00	1.60
☐	U31 Bob Dernier	.25	.12	.02
☐	U32 Carlos Diaz	.25	.12	.02
☐	U33 Mike Easler	.25	.12	.02
☐	U34 Dennis Eckersley	2.25	1.10	.22
☐	U35 Jim Essian	.25	.12	.02
☐	U36 Darrell Evans	.50	.25	.05
☐	U37 Mike Fitzgerald	.35	.17	.03
☐	U38 Tim Foli	.25	.12	.02
☐	U39 John Franco	10.00	5.00	1.00
☐	U40 George Frazier	.25	.12	.02
☐	U41 Rich Gale	.25	.12	.02
☐	U42 Barbaro Garbey	.25	.12	.02
☐	U43 Dwight Gooden	110.00	55.00	11.00
☐	U44 Goose Gossage	.75	.35	.07
☐	U45 Wayne Gross	.25	.12	.02
☐	U46 Mark Gubicza	6.00	3.00	.60
☐	U47 Jackie Gutierrez	.25	.12	.02
☐	U48 Toby Harrah	.35	.17	.03
☐	U49 Ron Hassey	.25	.12	.02
☐	U50 Richie Hebner	.25	.12	.02
☐	U51 Willie Hernandez	.45	.22	.04
☐	U52 Ed Hodge	.25	.12	.02
☐	U53 Ricky Horton	.45	.22	.04
☐	U54 Art Howe	.35	.17	.03
☐	U55 Dane Iorg	.25	.12	.02
☐	U56 Brook Jacoby	3.50	1.75	.35
☐	U57 Dion James	.45	.22	.04
☐	U58 Mike Jeffcoat	.35	.17	.03
☐	U59 Ruppert Jones	.25	.12	.02
☐	U60 Bob Kearney	.25	.12	.02
☐	U61 Jimmy Key	4.50	2.25	.45
☐	U62 Dave Kingman	.50	.25	.05
☐	U63 Brad Komminsk	.35	.17	.03
☐	U64 Jerry Koosman	.35	.17	.03
☐	U65 Wayne Krenchicki	.25	.12	.02
☐	U66 Rusty Kuntz	.25	.12	.02
☐	U67 Frank LaCorte	.25	.12	.02
☐	U68 Dennis Lamp	.25	.12	.02
☐	U69 Tito Landrum	.35	.17	.03
☐	U70 Mark Langston	17.00	8.50	1.70
☐	U71 Rick Leach	.25	.12	.02
☐	U72 Craig Lefferts	.50	.25	.05
☐	U73 Gary Lucas	.25	.12	.02
☐	U74 Jerry Martin	.25	.12	.02
☐	U75 Carmelo Martinez	.50	.25	.05
☐	U76 Mike Mason	.25	.12	.02
☐	U77 Gary Matthews	.35	.17	.03
☐	U78 Andy McGaffigan	.35	.17	.03
☐	U79 Joey McLaughlin	.25	.12	.02
☐	U80 Joe Morgan	4.50	2.25	.45
☐	U81 Darryl Motley	.35	.17	.03
☐	U82 Graig Nettles	.75	.35	.07
☐	U83 Phil Niekro	3.00	1.50	.30
☐	U84 Ken Oberkfell	.25	.12	.02
☐	U85 Al Oliver	.40	.20	.04
☐	U86 Jorge Orta	.25	.12	.02
☐	U87 Amos Otis	.35	.17	.03
☐	U88 Bob Owchinko	.25	.12	.02
☐	U89 Dave Parker	2.50	1.25	.25
☐	U90 Jack Perconte	.25	.12	.02
☐	U91 Tony Perez	2.00	1.00	.20
☐	U92 Gerald Perry	1.50	.75	.15
☐	U93 Kirby Puckett	180.00	90.00	18.00

☐ U94 Shane Rawley	.25	.12	.02
☐ U95 Floyd Rayford	.25	.12	.02
☐ U96 Ron Reed	.25	.12	.02
☐ U97 R.J. Reynolds	1.25	.60	.12
☐ U98 Gene Richards	.25	.12	.02
☐ U99 Jose Rijo	10.00	5.00	1.00
☐ U100 Jeff Robinson (Giants pitcher)	.50	.25	.05
☐ U101 Ron Romanick	.25	.12	.02
☐ U102 Pete Rose	15.00	7.50	1.50
☐ U103 Bret Saberhagen	35.00	17.50	3.50
☐ U104 Scott Sanderson	.50	.25	.05
☐ U105 Dick Schofield	.50	.25	.05
☐ U106 Tom Seaver	15.00	7.50	1.50
☐ U107 Jim Slaton	.25	.12	.02
☐ U108 Mike Smithson	.25	.12	.02
☐ U109 Lary Sorensen	.25	.12	.02
☐ U110 Tim Stoddard	.25	.12	.02
☐ U111 Jeff Stone	.35	.17	.03
☐ U112 Champ Summers	.25	.12	.02
☐ U113 Jim Sundberg	.35	.17	.03
☐ U114 Rick Sutcliffe	.75	.35	.07
☐ U115 Craig Swan	.30	.15	.03
☐ U116 Derrel Thomas	.25	.12	.02
☐ U117 Gorman Thomas	.40	.20	.04
☐ U118 Alex Trevino	.25	.12	.02
☐ U119 Manny Trillo	.25	.12	.02
☐ U120 John Tudor	.50	.25	.05
☐ U121 Tom Underwood	.25	.12	.02
☐ U122 Mike Vail	.25	.12	.02
☐ U123 Tom Waddell	.25	.12	.02
☐ U124 Gary Ward	.25	.12	.02
☐ U125 Terry Whitfield	.25	.12	.02
☐ U126 Curtis Wilkerson	.35	.17	.03
☐ U127 Frank Williams	.35	.17	.03
☐ U128 Glenn Wilson	.35	.17	.03
☐ U129 John Wockenfuss	.25	.12	.02
☐ U130 Ned Yost	.25	.12	.02
☐ U131 Mike Young	.40	.20	.04
☐ U132 Checklist: 1-132	.25	.05	.01

1985 Fleer

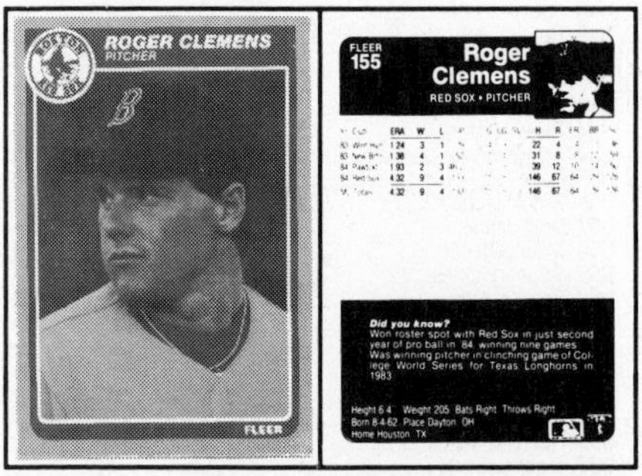

The cards in this 660-card set measure 2 1/2" by 3 1/2". The 1985 Fleer set features fronts that contain the team logo along with the player's name and position. The borders enclosing the photo are color-coded to correspond to the player's team. In each case, the color is one of the standard colors of that team, e.g., orange for Baltimore, red for St. Louis, etc. The backs feature the same name, number, and statistics format that Fleer has been using over the past few years. The cards are ordered alphabetically within team. The teams are ordered based on their respective performance during the prior year, e.g., World Champion Detroit Tigers (1-25), NL Champion San Diego (26-48), Chicago Cubs (49-71), New York Mets (72-95), Toronto (96-119), New York Yankees (120-147), Boston (148-169), Baltimore (170-195), Kansas City (196-218), St. Louis (219-243), Philadelphia (244-269), Minnesota (270-292), California (293-317), Atlanta (318-342), Houston (343-365), Los Angeles (366-391), Montreal (392-413), Oakland (414-436), Cleveland (437-460), Pittsburgh (461-481), Seattle (482-505), Chicago White Sox (506-530), Cincinnati (531-554), Texas (555-575), Milwaukee (576-601), and San Francisco (602-625). Specials (626-643), Major League Prospects (644-653), and checklist cards (654-660) complete the set. The black and white photo on the reverse is included for the third straight year. This set is noted for containing the Rookie Cards of Roger Clemens, Alvin Davis, Eric Davis, Glenn Davis, Shawon Dunston, Dwight Gooden, Kelly Gruber, Orel Hershiser, Mark Langston, Kirby Puckett, Jose Rijo, Bret Saberhagen, and Danny Tartabull.

	MINT	EXC	G-VG
COMPLETE SET (660)	150.00	75.00	15.00
COMMON PLAYER (1-660)	.06	.03	.00
☐ 1 Doug Bair	.10	.05	.01
☐ 2 Juan Berenguer	.06	.03	.00
☐ 3 Dave Bergman	.06	.03	.00
☐ 4 Tom Brookens	.06	.03	.00
☐ 5 Marty Castillo	.06	.03	.00
☐ 6 Darrell Evans	.12	.06	.01
☐ 7 Barbaro Garbey	.06	.03	.00
☐ 8 Kirk Gibson	.30	.15	.03
☐ 9 John Grubb	.06	.03	.00
☐ 10 Willie Hernandez	.10	.05	.01
☐ 11 Larry Herndon	.06	.03	.00
☐ 12 Howard Johnson	1.75	.85	.17
☐ 13 Ruppert Jones	.06	.03	.00
☐ 14 Rusty Kuntz	.06	.03	.00
☐ 15 Chet Lemon	.06	.03	.00
☐ 16 Aurelio Lopez	.06	.03	.00
☐ 17 Sid Monge	.06	.03	.00
☐ 18 Jack Morris	.18	.09	.01
☐ 19 Lance Parrish	.25	.12	.02
☐ 20 Dan Petry	.06	.03	.00
☐ 21 Dave Rozema	.06	.03	.00
☐ 22 Bill Scherrer	.06	.03	.00
☐ 23 Alan Trammell	.40	.20	.04
☐ 24 Lou Whitaker	.25	.12	.02
☐ 25 Milt Wilcox	.06	.03	.00
☐ 26 Kurt Bevacqua	.06	.03	.00
☐ 27 Greg Booker	.06	.03	.00
☐ 28 Bobby Brown	.06	.03	.00
☐ 29 Luis DeLeon	.06	.03	.00
☐ 30 Dave Dravecky	.15	.07	.01
☐ 31 Tim Flannery	.06	.03	.00
☐ 32 Steve Garvey	.45	.22	.04
☐ 33 Goose Gossage	.15	.07	.01
☐ 34 Tony Gwynn	2.25	1.10	.22
☐ 35 Greg Harris	.06	.03	.00
☐ 36 Andy Hawkins	.10	.05	.01
☐ 37 Terry Kennedy	.06	.03	.00
☐ 38 Craig Lefferts	.10	.05	.01
☐ 39 Tim Lollar	.06	.03	.00
☐ 40 Carmelo Martinez	.06	.03	.00
☐ 41 Kevin McReynolds	1.00	.50	.10
☐ 42 Graig Nettles	.12	.06	.01
☐ 43 Luis Salazar	.06	.03	.00
☐ 44 Eric Show	.06	.03	.00
☐ 45 Garry Templeton	.10	.05	.01
☐ 46 Mark Thurmond	.06	.03	.00
☐ 47 Ed Whitson	.10	.05	.01
☐ 48 Alan Wiggins	.06	.03	.00
☐ 49 Rich Bordi	.06	.03	.00
☐ 50 Larry Bowa	.10	.05	.01
☐ 51 Warren Brusstar	.06	.03	.00
☐ 52 Ron Cey	.10	.05	.01
☐ 53 Henry Cotto	.15	.07	.01
☐ 54 Jody Davis	.06	.03	.00
☐ 55 Bob Dernier	.06	.03	.00
☐ 56 Leon Durham	.06	.03	.00
☐ 57 Dennis Eckersley	.25	.12	.02
☐ 58 George Frazier	.06	.03	.00
☐ 59 Richie Hebner	.06	.03	.00
☐ 60 Dave Lopes	.10	.05	.01
☐ 61 Gary Matthews	.06	.03	.00
☐ 62 Keith Moreland	.06	.03	.00
☐ 63 Rick Reuschel	.12	.06	.01
☐ 64 Dick Ruthven	.06	.03	.00
☐ 65 Ryne Sandberg	4.50	2.25	.45
☐ 66 Scott Sanderson	.06	.03	.00
☐ 67 Lee Smith	.10	.05	.01
☐ 68 Tim Stoddard	.06	.03	.00
☐ 69 Rick Sutcliffe	.15	.07	.01
☐ 70 Steve Trout	.06	.03	.00
☐ 71 Gary Woods	.06	.03	.00
☐ 72 Wally Backman	.06	.03	.00
☐ 73 Bruce Berenyi	.06	.03	.00
☐ 74 Hubie Brooks UER (Kelvin Chapman's stats on card back)	.15	.07	.01
☐ 75 Kelvin Chapman	.06	.03	.00

☐ 76	Ron Darling	.75	.35	.07
☐ 77	Sid Fernandez	1.00	.50	.10
☐ 78	Mike Fitzgerald	.06	.03	.00
☐ 79	George Foster	.12	.06	.01
☐ 80	Brent Gaff	.06	.03	.00
☐ 81	Ron Gardenhire	.06	.03	.00
☐ 82	Dwight Gooden	12.00	6.00	1.20
☐ 83	Tom Gorman	.06	.03	.00
☐ 84	Danny Heep	.06	.03	.00
☐ 85	Keith Hernandez	.30	.15	.03
☐ 86	Ray Knight	.10	.05	.01
☐ 87	Ed Lynch	.06	.03	.00
☐ 88	Jose Oquendo	.10	.05	.01
☐ 89	Jesse Orosco	.06	.03	.00
☐ 90	Rafael Santana	.15	.07	.01
☐ 91	Doug Sisk	.06	.03	.00
☐ 92	Rusty Staub	.12	.06	.01
☐ 93	Darryl Strawberry	6.50	3.25	.65
☐ 94	Walt Terrell	.06	.03	.00
☐ 95	Mookie Wilson	.10	.05	.01
☐ 96	Jim Acker	.06	.03	.00
☐ 97	Willie Aikens	.06	.03	.00
☐ 98	Doyle Alexander	.06	.03	.00
☐ 99	Jesse Barfield	.20	.10	.02
☐ 100	George Bell	.60	.30	.06
☐ 101	Jim Clancy	.06	.03	.00
☐ 102	Dave Collins	.06	.03	.00
☐ 103	Tony Fernandez	.60	.30	.06
☐ 104	Damaso Garcia	.06	.03	.00
☐ 105	Jim Gott	.06	.03	.00
☐ 106	Alfredo Griffin	.06	.03	.00
☐ 107	Garth Iorg	.06	.03	.00
☐ 108	Roy Lee Jackson	.06	.03	.00
☐ 109	Cliff Johnson	.06	.03	.00
☐ 110	Jimmy Key	1.00	.50	.10
☐ 111	Dennis Lamp	.06	.03	.00
☐ 112	Rick Leach	.06	.03	.00
☐ 113	Luis Leal	.06	.03	.00
☐ 114	Buck Martinez	.06	.03	.00
☐ 115	Lloyd Moseby	.10	.05	.01
☐ 116	Rance Mulliniks	.06	.03	.00
☐ 117	Dave Stieb	.15	.07	.01
☐ 118	Willie Upshaw	.06	.03	.00
☐ 119	Ernie Whitt	.06	.03	.00
☐ 120	Mike Armstrong	.06	.03	.00
☐ 121	Don Baylor	.12	.06	.01
☐ 122	Marty Bystrom	.06	.03	.00
☐ 123	Rick Cerone	.06	.03	.00
☐ 124	Joe Cowley	.06	.03	.00
☐ 125	Brian Dayett	.06	.03	.00
☐ 126	Tim Foli	.06	.03	.00
☐ 127	Ray Fontenot	.06	.03	.00
☐ 128	Ken Griffey	.15	.07	.01
☐ 129	Ron Guidry	.15	.07	.01
☐ 130	Toby Harrah	.06	.03	.00
☐ 131	Jay Howell	.06	.03	.00
☐ 132	Steve Kemp	.06	.03	.00
☐ 133	Don Mattingly	12.50	6.25	1.25
☐ 134	Bobby Meacham	.06	.03	.00
☐ 135	John Montefusco	.06	.03	.00
☐ 136	Omar Moreno	.06	.03	.00
☐ 137	Dale Murray	.06	.03	.00
☐ 138	Phil Niekro	.25	.12	.02
☐ 139	Mike Pagliarulo	.75	.35	.07
☐ 140	Willie Randolph	.10	.05	.01
☐ 141	Dennis Rasmussen	.25	.12	.02
☐ 142	Dave Righetti	.18	.09	.01
☐ 143	Jose Rijo	2.00	1.00	.20
☐ 144	Andre Robertson	.06	.03	.00
☐ 145	Bob Shirley	.06	.03	.00
☐ 146	Dave Winfield	.40	.20	.04
☐ 147	Butch Wynegar	.06	.03	.00
☐ 148	Gary Allenson	.06	.03	.00
☐ 149	Tony Armas	.06	.03	.00
☐ 150	Marty Barrett	.20	.10	.02
☐ 151	Wade Boggs	4.00	2.00	.40
☐ 152	Dennis Boyd	.15	.07	.01
☐ 153	Bill Buckner	.10	.05	.01
☐ 154	Mark Clear	.06	.03	.00
☐ 155	Roger Clemens	18.00	9.00	1.80
☐ 156	Steve Crawford	.06	.03	.00
☐ 157	Mike Easler	.06	.03	.00
☐ 158	Dwight Evans	.20	.10	.02
☐ 159	Rich Gedman	.06	.03	.00
☐ 160	Jackie Gutierrez (W.Boggs on deck)	.15	.07	.01
☐ 161	Bruce Hurst	.12	.06	.01
☐ 162	John Henry Johnson	.06	.03	.00
☐ 163	Rick Miller	.06	.03	.00
☐ 164	Reid Nichols	.06	.03	.00
☐ 165	Al Nipper	.10	.05	.01
☐ 166	Bob Ojeda	.10	.05	.01
☐ 167	Jerry Remy	.06	.03	.00
☐ 168	Jim Rice	.25	.12	.02
☐ 169	Bob Stanley	.06	.03	.00
☐ 170	Mike Boddicker	.10	.05	.01
☐ 171	Al Bumbry	.06	.03	.00
☐ 172	Todd Cruz	.06	.03	.00
☐ 173	Rich Dauer	.06	.03	.00
☐ 174	Storm Davis	.10	.05	.01
☐ 175	Rick Dempsey	.06	.03	.00
☐ 176	Jim Dwyer	.06	.03	.00
☐ 177	Mike Flanagan	.10	.05	.01
☐ 178	Dan Ford	.06	.03	.00
☐ 179	Wayne Gross	.06	.03	.00
☐ 180	John Lowenstein	.06	.03	.00
☐ 181	Dennis Martinez	.10	.05	.01
☐ 182	Tippy Martinez	.06	.03	.00
☐ 183	Scott McGregor	.10	.05	.01
☐ 184	Eddie Murray	.50	.25	.05
☐ 185	Joe Nolan	.06	.03	.00
☐ 186	Floyd Rayford	.06	.03	.00
☐ 187	Cal Ripken	1.50	.75	.15
☐ 188	Gary Roenicke	.06	.03	.00
☐ 189	Lenn Sakata	.06	.03	.00
☐ 190	John Shelby	.06	.03	.00
☐ 191	Ken Singleton	.10	.05	.01
☐ 192	Sammy Stewart	.06	.03	.00
☐ 193	Bill Swaggerty	.06	.03	.00
☐ 194	Tom Underwood	.06	.03	.00
☐ 195	Mike Young	.10	.05	.01
☐ 196	Steve Balboni	.06	.03	.00
☐ 197	Joe Beckwith	.06	.03	.00
☐ 198	Bud Black	.10	.05	.01
☐ 199	George Brett	.90	.45	.09
☐ 200	Onix Concepcion	.06	.03	.00
☐ 201	Mark Gubicza	1.50	.75	.15
☐ 202	Larry Gura	.06	.03	.00
☐ 203	Mark Huismann	.06	.03	.00
☐ 204	Dane Iorg	.06	.03	.00
☐ 205	Danny Jackson	.75	.35	.07
☐ 206	Charlie Leibrandt	.06	.03	.00
☐ 207	Hal McRae	.06	.03	.00
☐ 208	Darryl Motley	.06	.03	.00
☐ 209	Jorge Orta	.06	.03	.00
☐ 210	Greg Pryor	.06	.03	.00
☐ 211	Dan Quisenberry	.10	.05	.01
☐ 212	Bret Saberhagen	7.00	3.50	.70
☐ 213	Pat Sheridan	.06	.03	.00
☐ 214	Don Slaught	.06	.03	.00
☐ 215	U.L. Washington	.06	.03	.00
☐ 216	John Wathan	.06	.03	.00
☐ 217	Frank White	.10	.05	.01
☐ 218	Willie Wilson	.12	.06	.01
☐ 219	Neil Allen	.06	.03	.00
☐ 220	Joaquin Andujar	.06	.03	.00
☐ 221	Steve Braun	.06	.03	.00
☐ 222	Danny Cox	.06	.03	.00
☐ 223	Bob Forsch	.06	.03	.00
☐ 224	David Green	.06	.03	.00
☐ 225	George Hendrick	.06	.03	.00
☐ 226	Tom Herr	.10	.05	.01
☐ 227	Ricky Horton	.25	.12	.02
☐ 228	Art Howe	.10	.05	.01
☐ 229	Mike Jorgensen	.06	.03	.00
☐ 230	Kurt Kepshire	.06	.03	.00
☐ 231	Jeff Lahti	.06	.03	.00
☐ 232	Tito Landrum	.06	.03	.00
☐ 233	Dave LaPoint	.06	.03	.00
☐ 234	Willie McGee	.45	.22	.04
☐ 235	Tom Nieto	.06	.03	.00
☐ 236	Terry Pendleton	.60	.30	.06
☐ 237	Darrell Porter	.06	.03	.00
☐ 238	Dave Rucker	.06	.03	.00
☐ 239	Lonnie Smith	.12	.06	.01
☐ 240	Ozzie Smith	.45	.22	.04
☐ 241	Bruce Sutter	.12	.06	.01
☐ 242	Andy Van Slyke UER (Bats Right, Throws Left)	.70	.35	.07
☐ 243	Dave Von Ohlen	.06	.03	.00
☐ 244	Larry Andersen	.06	.03	.00
☐ 245	Bill Campbell	.06	.03	.00
☐ 246	Steve Carlton	.45	.22	.04
☐ 247	Tim Corcoran	.06	.03	.00
☐ 248	Ivan DeJesus	.06	.03	.00
☐ 249	John Denny	.06	.03	.00
☐ 250	Bo Diaz	.06	.03	.00
☐ 251	Greg Gross	.06	.03	.00
☐ 252	Kevin Gross	.10	.05	.01
☐ 253	Von Hayes	.20	.10	.02
☐ 254	Al Holland	.06	.03	.00
☐ 255	Charles Hudson	.06	.03	.00
☐ 256	Jerry Koosman	.10	.05	.01
☐ 257	Joe Lefebvre	.06	.03	.00
☐ 258	Sixto Lezcano	.06	.03	.00
☐ 259	Garry Maddox	.06	.03	.00
☐ 260	Len Matuszek	.06	.03	.00

☐ 261	Tug McGraw	.10	.05	.01
☐ 262	Al Oliver	.10	.05	.01
☐ 263	Shane Rawley	.06	.03	.00
☐ 264	Juan Samuel	.30	.15	.03
☐ 265	Mike Schmidt	2.25	1.10	.22
☐ 266	Jeff Stone	.10	.05	.01
☐ 267	Ozzie Virgil	.06	.03	.00
☐ 268	Glenn Wilson	.06	.03	.00
☐ 269	John Wockenfuss	.06	.03	.00
☐ 270	Darrell Brown	.06	.03	.00
☐ 271	Tom Brunansky	.20	.10	.02
☐ 272	Randy Bush	.06	.03	.00
☐ 273	John Butcher	.06	.03	.00
☐ 274	Bobby Castillo	.06	.03	.00
☐ 275	Ron Davis	.06	.03	.00
☐ 276	Dave Engle	.06	.03	.00
☐ 277	Pete Filson	.06	.03	.00
☐ 278	Gary Gaetti	.35	.17	.03
☐ 279	Mickey Hatcher	.06	.03	.00
☐ 280	Ed Hodge	.06	.03	.00
☐ 281	Kent Hrbek	.35	.17	.03
☐ 282	Houston Jimenez	.06	.03	.00
☐ 283	Tim Laudner	.06	.03	.00
☐ 284	Rick Lysander	.06	.03	.00
☐ 285	Dave Meier	.06	.03	.00
☐ 286	Kirby Puckett	21.00	10.50	2.10
☐ 287	Pat Putnam	.06	.03	.00
☐ 288	Ken Schrom	.06	.03	.00
☐ 289	Mike Smithson	.06	.03	.00
☐ 290	Tim Teufel	.06	.03	.00
☐ 291	Frank Viola	.65	.30	.06
☐ 292	Ron Washington	.06	.03	.00
☐ 293	Don Aase	.06	.03	.00
☐ 294	Juan Beniquez	.06	.03	.00
☐ 295	Bob Boone	.12	.06	.01
☐ 296	Mike Brown (Angels OF)	.06	.03	.00
☐ 297	Rod Carew	.60	.30	.06
☐ 298	Doug Corbett	.06	.03	.00
☐ 299	Doug DeCinces	.10	.05	.01
☐ 300	Brian Downing	.10	.05	.01
☐ 301	Ken Forsch	.06	.03	.00
☐ 302	Bobby Grich	.10	.05	.01
☐ 303	Reggie Jackson	.75	.35	.07
☐ 304	Tommy John	.15	.07	.01
☐ 305	Curt Kaufman	.06	.03	.00
☐ 306	Bruce Kison	.06	.03	.00
☐ 307	Fred Lynn	.15	.07	.01
☐ 308	Gary Pettis	.10	.05	.01
☐ 309	Ron Romanick	.06	.03	.00
☐ 310	Luis Sanchez	.06	.03	.00
☐ 311	Dick Schofield	.15	.07	.01
☐ 312	Daryl Sconiers	.06	.03	.00
☐ 313	Jim Slaton	.06	.03	.00
☐ 314	Derrel Thomas	.06	.03	.00
☐ 315	Rob Wilfong	.06	.03	.00
☐ 316	Mike Witt	.10	.05	.01
☐ 317	Geoff Zahn	.06	.03	.00
☐ 318	Len Barker	.06	.03	.00
☐ 319	Steve Bedrosian	.15	.07	.01
☐ 320	Bruce Benedict	.06	.03	.00
☐ 321	Rick Camp	.06	.03	.00
☐ 322	Chris Chambliss	.10	.05	.01
☐ 323	Jeff Dedmon	.06	.03	.00
☐ 324	Terry Forster	.06	.03	.00
☐ 325	Gene Garber	.06	.03	.00
☐ 326	Albert Hall	.06	.03	.00
☐ 327	Terry Harper	.06	.03	.00
☐ 328	Bob Horner	.10	.05	.01
☐ 329	Glenn Hubbard	.06	.03	.00
☐ 330	Randy Johnson	.06	.03	.00
☐ 331	Brad Komminsk	.06	.03	.00
☐ 332	Rick Mahler	.06	.03	.00
☐ 333	Craig McMurtry	.06	.03	.00
☐ 334	Donnie Moore	.06	.03	.00
☐ 335	Dale Murphy	.75	.35	.07
☐ 336	Ken Oberkfell	.06	.03	.00
☐ 337	Pascual Perez	.12	.06	.01
☐ 338	Gerald Perry	.35	.17	.03
☐ 339	Rafael Ramirez	.06	.03	.00
☐ 340	Jerry Royster	.06	.03	.00
☐ 341	Alex Trevino	.06	.03	.00
☐ 342	Claudell Washington	.10	.05	.01
☐ 343	Alan Ashby	.06	.03	.00
☐ 344	Mark Bailey	.06	.03	.00
☐ 345	Kevin Bass	.10	.05	.01
☐ 346	Enos Cabell	.06	.03	.00
☐ 347	Jose Cruz	.10	.05	.01
☐ 348	Bill Dawley	.06	.03	.00
☐ 349	Frank DiPino	.06	.03	.00
☐ 350	Bill Doran	.15	.07	.01
☐ 351	Phil Garner	.06	.03	.00
☐ 352	Bob Knepper	.06	.03	.00
☐ 353	Mike LaCoss	.06	.03	.00

☐ 354	Jerry Mumphrey	.06	.03	.00
☐ 355	Joe Niekro	.10	.05	.01
☐ 356	Terry Puhl	.06	.03	.00
☐ 357	Craig Reynolds	.06	.03	.00
☐ 358	Vern Ruhle	.06	.03	.00
☐ 359	Nolan Ryan	3.50	1.75	.35
☐ 360	Joe Sambito	.06	.03	.00
☐ 361	Mike Scott	.35	.17	.03
☐ 362	Dave Smith	.10	.05	.01
☐ 363	Julio Solano	.06	.03	.00
☐ 364	Dickie Thon	.06	.03	.00
☐ 365	Denny Walling	.06	.03	.00
☐ 366	Dave Anderson	.06	.03	.00
☐ 367	Bob Bailor	.06	.03	.00
☐ 368	Greg Brock	.06	.03	.00
☐ 369	Carlos Diaz	.06	.03	.00
☐ 370	Pedro Guerrero	.30	.15	.03
☐ 371	Orel Hershiser	7.00	3.50	.70
☐ 372	Rick Honeycutt	.06	.03	.00
☐ 373	Burt Hooton	.06	.03	.00
☐ 374	Ken Howell	.25	.12	.02
☐ 375	Ken Landreaux	.06	.03	.00
☐ 376	Candy Maldonado	.25	.12	.02
☐ 377	Mike Marshall	.15	.07	.01
☐ 378	Tom Niedenfuer	.06	.03	.00
☐ 379	Alejandro Pena	.06	.03	.00
☐ 380	Jerry Reuss	.06	.03	.00
☐ 381	R.J. Reynolds	.35	.17	.03
☐ 382	German Rivera	.06	.03	.00
☐ 383	Bill Russell	.06	.03	.00
☐ 384	Steve Sax	.30	.15	.03
☐ 385	Mike Scioscia	.06	.03	.00
☐ 386	Franklin Stubbs	.70	.35	.07
☐ 387	Fernando Valenzuela	.30	.15	.03
☐ 388	Bob Welch	.15	.07	.01
☐ 389	Terry Whitfield	.06	.03	.00
☐ 390	Steve Yeager	.06	.03	.00
☐ 391	Pat Zachry	.06	.03	.00
☐ 392	Fred Breining	.06	.03	.00
☐ 393	Gary Carter	.35	.17	.03
☐ 394	Andre Dawson	.50	.25	.05
☐ 395	Miguel Dilone	.06	.03	.00
☐ 396	Dan Driessen	.06	.03	.00
☐ 397	Doug Flynn	.06	.03	.00
☐ 398	Terry Francona	.06	.03	.00
☐ 399	Bill Gullickson	.06	.03	.00
☐ 400	Bob James	.06	.03	.00
☐ 401	Charlie Lea	.06	.03	.00
☐ 402	Bryan Little	.06	.03	.00
☐ 403	Gary Lucas	.06	.03	.00
☐ 404	David Palmer	.06	.03	.00
☐ 405	Tim Raines	.40	.20	.04
☐ 406	Mike Ramsey	.06	.03	.00
☐ 407	Jeff Reardon	.12	.06	.01
☐ 408	Steve Rogers	.06	.03	.00
☐ 409	Dan Schatzeder	.06	.03	.00
☐ 410	Bryn Smith	.10	.05	.01
☐ 411	Mike Stenhouse	.06	.03	.00
☐ 412	Tim Wallach	.15	.07	.01
☐ 413	Jim Wohlford	.06	.03	.00
☐ 414	Bill Almon	.06	.03	.00
☐ 415	Keith Atherton	.06	.03	.00
☐ 416	Bruce Bochte	.06	.03	.00
☐ 417	Tom Burgmeier	.06	.03	.00
☐ 418	Ray Burris	.06	.03	.00
☐ 419	Bill Caudill	.06	.03	.00
☐ 420	Chris Codiroli	.06	.03	.00
☐ 421	Tim Conroy	.06	.03	.00
☐ 422	Mike Davis	.06	.03	.00
☐ 423	Jim Essian	.06	.03	.00
☐ 424	Mike Heath	.06	.03	.00
☐ 425	Rickey Henderson	3.50	1.75	.35
☐ 426	Donnie Hill	.06	.03	.00
☐ 427	Dave Kingman	.12	.06	.01
☐ 428	Bill Krueger	.06	.03	.00
☐ 429	Carney Lansford	.12	.06	.01
☐ 430	Steve McCatty	.06	.03	.00
☐ 431	Joe Morgan	.30	.15	.03
☐ 432	Dwayne Murphy	.06	.03	.00
☐ 433	Tony Phillips	.06	.03	.00
☐ 434	Lary Sorensen	.06	.03	.00
☐ 435	Mike Warren	.06	.03	.00
☐ 436	Curt Young	.25	.12	.02
☐ 437	Luis Aponte	.06	.03	.00
☐ 438	Chris Bando	.06	.03	.00
☐ 439	Tony Bernazard	.06	.03	.00
☐ 440	Bert Blyleven	.18	.09	.01
☐ 441	Brett Butler	.15	.07	.01
☐ 442	Ernie Camacho	.06	.03	.00
☐ 443	Joe Carter	4.00	2.00	.40
☐ 444	Carmelo Castillo	.06	.03	.00
☐ 445	Jamie Easterly	.06	.03	.00
☐ 446	Steve Farr	.30	.15	.03
☐ 447	Mike Fischlin	.06	.03	.00

☐ 448	Julio Franco	.50	.25	.05
☐ 449	Mel Hall	.10	.05	.01
☐ 450	Mike Hargrove	.06	.03	.00
☐ 451	Neal Heaton	.10	.05	.01
☐ 452	Brook Jacoby	.40	.20	.04
☐ 453	Mike Jeffcoat	.06	.03	.00
☐ 454	Don Schulze	.10	.05	.01
☐ 455	Roy Smith	.06	.03	.00
☐ 456	Pat Tabler	.10	.05	.01
☐ 457	Andre Thornton	.10	.05	.01
☐ 458	George Vukovich	.06	.03	.00
☐ 459	Tom Waddell	.06	.03	.00
☐ 460	Jerry Willard	.06	.03	.00
☐ 461	Dale Berra	.06	.03	.00
☐ 462	John Candelaria	.10	.05	.01
☐ 463	Jose DeLeon	.10	.05	.01
☐ 464	Doug Frobel	.06	.03	.00
☐ 465	Cecilio Guante	.06	.03	.00
☐ 466	Brian Harper	.30	.15	.03
☐ 467	Lee Lacy	.06	.03	.00
☐ 468	Bill Madlock	.10	.05	.01
☐ 469	Lee Mazzilli	.06	.03	.00
☐ 470	Larry McWilliams	.06	.03	.00
☐ 471	Jim Morrison	.06	.03	.00
☐ 472	Tony Pena	.12	.06	.01
☐ 473	Johnny Ray	.10	.05	.01
☐ 474	Rick Rhoden	.10	.05	.01
☐ 475	Don Robinson	.06	.03	.00
☐ 476	Rod Scurry	.06	.03	.00
☐ 477	Kent Tekulve	.06	.03	.00
☐ 478	Jason Thompson	.06	.03	.00
☐ 479	John Tudor	.15	.07	.01
☐ 480	Lee Tunnell	.06	.03	.00
☐ 481	Marvell Wynne	.06	.03	.00
☐ 482	Salome Barojas	.06	.03	.00
☐ 483	Dave Beard	.06	.03	.00
☐ 484	Jim Beattie	.06	.03	.00
☐ 485	Barry Bonnell	.06	.03	.00
☐ 486	Phil Bradley	.90	.45	.09
☐ 487	Al Cowens	.06	.03	.00
☐ 488	Alvin Davis	3.50	1.75	.35
☐ 489	Dave Henderson	.18	.09	.01
☐ 490	Steve Henderson	.06	.03	.00
☐ 491	Bob Kearney	.06	.03	.00
☐ 492	Mark Langston	4.00	2.00	.40
☐ 493	Larry Milbourne	.06	.03	.00
☐ 494	Paul Mirabella	.06	.03	.00
☐ 495	Mike Moore	.12	.06	.01
☐ 496	Edwin Nunez	.06	.03	.00
☐ 497	Spike Owen	.06	.03	.00
☐ 498	Jack Perconte	.06	.03	.00
☐ 499	Ken Phelps	.10	.05	.01
☐ 500	Jim Presley	.85	.40	.08
☐ 501	Mike Stanton	.06	.03	.00
☐ 502	Bob Stoddard	.06	.03	.00
☐ 503	Gorman Thomas	.10	.05	.01
☐ 504	Ed VandeBerg	.06	.03	.00
☐ 505	Matt Young	.06	.03	.00
☐ 506	Juan Agosto	.06	.03	.00
☐ 507	Harold Baines	.25	.12	.02
☐ 508	Floyd Bannister	.06	.03	.00
☐ 509	Britt Burns	.06	.03	.00
☐ 510	Julio Cruz	.06	.03	.00
☐ 511	Richard Dotson	.06	.03	.00
☐ 512	Jerry Dybzinski	.06	.03	.00
☐ 513	Carlton Fisk	.40	.20	.04
☐ 514	Scott Fletcher	.06	.03	.00
☐ 515	Jerry Hairston	.06	.03	.00
☐ 516	Marc Hill	.06	.03	.00
☐ 517	LaMarr Hoyt	.06	.03	.00
☐ 518	Ron Kittle	.15	.07	.01
☐ 519	Rudy Law	.06	.03	.00
☐ 520	Vance Law	.06	.03	.00
☐ 521	Greg Luzinski	.10	.05	.01
☐ 522	Gene Nelson	.06	.03	.00
☐ 523	Tom Paciorek	.06	.03	.00
☐ 524	Ron Reed	.06	.03	.00
☐ 525	Bert Roberge	.06	.03	.00
☐ 526	Tom Seaver	.60	.30	.06
☐ 527	Roy Smalley	.06	.03	.00
☐ 528	Dan Spillner	.06	.03	.00
☐ 529	Mike Squires	.06	.03	.00
☐ 530	Greg Walker	.10	.05	.01
☐ 531	Cesar Cedeno	.10	.05	.01
☐ 532	Dave Concepcion	.10	.05	.01
☐ 533	Eric Davis	18.00	9.00	1.80
☐ 534	Nick Esasky	.18	.09	.01
☐ 535	Tom Foley	.06	.03	.00
☐ 536	John Franco	2.00	1.00	.20
☐ 537	Brad Gulden	.06	.03	.00
☐ 538	Tom Hume	.06	.03	.00
☐ 539	Wayne Krenchicki	.06	.03	.00
☐ 540	Andy McGaffigan	.06	.03	.00
☐ 541	Eddie Milner	.06	.03	.00
☐ 542	Ron Oester	.06	.03	.00
☐ 543	Bob Owchinko	.06	.03	.00
☐ 544	Dave Parker	.25	.12	.02
☐ 545	Frank Pastore	.06	.03	.00
☐ 546	Tony Perez	.18	.09	.01
☐ 547	Ted Power	.06	.03	.00
☐ 548	Joe Price	.06	.03	.00
☐ 549	Gary Redus	.06	.03	.00
☐ 550	Pete Rose	1.00	.50	.10
☐ 551	Jeff Russell	.30	.15	.03
☐ 552	Mario Soto	.06	.03	.00
☐ 553	Jay Tibbs	.10	.05	.01
☐ 554	Duane Walker	.06	.03	.00
☐ 555	Alan Bannister	.06	.03	.00
☐ 556	Buddy Bell	.10	.05	.01
☐ 557	Danny Darwin	.10	.05	.01
☐ 558	Charlie Hough	.10	.05	.01
☐ 559	Bobby Jones	.06	.03	.00
☐ 560	Odell Jones	.06	.03	.00
☐ 561	Jeff Kunkel	.10	.05	.01
☐ 562	Mike Mason	.06	.03	.00
☐ 563	Pete O'Brien	.10	.05	.01
☐ 564	Larry Parrish	.10	.05	.01
☐ 565	Mickey Rivers	.06	.03	.00
☐ 566	Billy Sample	.06	.03	.00
☐ 567	Dave Schmidt	.06	.03	.00
☐ 568	Donnie Scott	.06	.03	.00
☐ 569	Dave Stewart	.60	.30	.06
☐ 570	Frank Tanana	.10	.05	.01
☐ 571	Wayne Tolleson	.06	.03	.00
☐ 572	Gary Ward	.06	.03	.00
☐ 573	Curtis Wilkerson	.06	.03	.00
☐ 574	George Wright	.06	.03	.00
☐ 575	Ned Yost	.06	.03	.00
☐ 576	Mark Brouhard	.06	.03	.00
☐ 577	Mike Caldwell	.06	.03	.00
☐ 578	Bobby Clark	.06	.03	.00
☐ 579	Jaime Cocanower	.06	.03	.00
☐ 580	Cecil Cooper	.12	.06	.01
☐ 581	Rollie Fingers	.18	.09	.01
☐ 582	Jim Gantner	.06	.03	.00
☐ 583	Moose Haas	.06	.03	.00
☐ 584	Dion James	.10	.05	.01
☐ 585	Pete Ladd	.06	.03	.00
☐ 586	Rick Manning	.06	.03	.00
☐ 587	Bob McClure	.06	.03	.00
☐ 588	Paul Molitor	.20	.10	.02
☐ 589	Charlie Moore	.06	.03	.00
☐ 590	Ben Oglivie	.10	.05	.01
☐ 591	Chuck Porter	.06	.03	.00
☐ 592	Randy Ready	.20	.10	.02
☐ 593	Ed Romero	.06	.03	.00
☐ 594	Bill Schroeder	.06	.03	.00
☐ 595	Ray Searage	.06	.03	.00
☐ 596	Ted Simmons	.12	.06	.01
☐ 597	Jim Sundberg	.06	.03	.00
☐ 598	Don Sutton	.25	.12	.02
☐ 599	Tom Tellmann	.06	.03	.00
☐ 600	Rick Waits	.06	.03	.00
☐ 601	Robin Yount	.75	.35	.07
☐ 602	Dusty Baker	.10	.05	.01
☐ 603	Bob Brenly	.06	.03	.00
☐ 604	Jack Clark	.25	.12	.02
☐ 605	Chili Davis	.10	.05	.01
☐ 606	Mark Davis	.15	.07	.01
☐ 607	Dan Gladden	.60	.30	.06
☐ 608	Atlee Hammaker	.06	.03	.00
☐ 609	Mike Krukow	.06	.03	.00
☐ 610	Duane Kuiper	.06	.03	.00
☐ 611	Bob Lacey	.06	.03	.00
☐ 612	Bill Laskey	.06	.03	.00
☐ 613	Gary Lavelle	.06	.03	.00
☐ 614	Johnnie LeMaster	.06	.03	.00
☐ 615	Jeff Leonard	.10	.05	.01
☐ 616	Randy Lerch	.06	.03	.00
☐ 617	Greg Minton	.06	.03	.00
☐ 618	Steve Nicosia	.06	.03	.00
☐ 619	Gene Richards	.06	.03	.00
☐ 620	Jeff Robinson (Giants pitcher)	.25	.12	.02
☐ 621	Scot Thompson	.06	.03	.00
☐ 622	Manny Trillo	.06	.03	.00
☐ 623	Brad Wellman	.06	.03	.00
☐ 624	Frank Williams	.10	.05	.01
☐ 625	Joel Youngblood	.06	.03	.00
☐ 626	Cal Ripken IA	.45	.22	.04
☐ 627	Mike Schmidt IA	.65	.30	.06
☐ 628	Giving The Signs Sparky Anderson	.06	.03	.00
☐ 629	AL Pitcher's Nightmare Dave Winfield Rickey Henderson	.40	.20	.04

☐ 630 NL Pitcher's Nightmare Mike Schmidt Ryne Sandberg	.90	.45	.09
☐ 631 NL All-Stars Darryl Strawberry Gary Carter Steve Garvey Ozzie Smith	.30	.15	.03
☐ 632 A-S Winning Battery Gary Carter Charlie Lea	.10	.05	.01
☐ 633 NL Pennant Clinchers Steve Garvey Goose Gossage	.12	.06	.01
☐ 634 NL Rookie Phenoms Dwight Gooden Juan Samuel	1.00	.50	.10
☐ 635 Toronto's Big Guns Willie Upshaw	.06	.03	.00
☐ 636 Toronto's Big Guns Lloyd Moseby	.06	.03	.00
☐ 637 HOLLAND: Al Holland	.06	.03	.00
☐ 638 TUNNELL: Lee Tunnell	.06	.03	.00
☐ 639 500th Homer Reggie Jackson	.30	.15	.03
☐ 640 4000th Hit Pete Rose	.45	.22	.04
☐ 641 Father and Son Cal Ripken Jr. and Sr.	.25	.12	.02
☐ 642 Cubs: Division Champs	.06	.03	.00
☐ 643 Two Perfect Games and One No-Hitter: Mike Witt David Palmer Jack Morris	.10	.05	.01
☐ 644 Willie Lozado and Vic Mata	.10	.05	.01
☐ 645 Kelly Gruber and Randy O'Neal	7.50	3.75	.75
☐ 646 Jose Roman and Joel Skinner	.10	.05	.01
☐ 647 Steve Kiefer and Danny Tartabull	4.00	2.00	.40
☐ 648 Rob Deer and Alejandro Sanchez	1.50	.75	.15
☐ 649 Billy Hatcher and Shawon Dunston	6.50	3.25	.65
☐ 650 Ron Robinson and Mike Bielecki	.75	.35	.07
☐ 651 Zane Smith and Paul Zuvella	.85	.40	.08
☐ 652 Joe Hesketh and Glenn Davis	12.50	6.25	1.25
☐ 653 John Russell and Steve Jeltz	.15	.07	.01
☐ 654 CL: Tigers/Padres and Cubs/Mets	.07	.01	.00
☐ 655 CL: Blue Jays/Yankees and Red Sox/Orioles	.07	.01	.00
☐ 656 CL: Royals/Cardinals and Phillies/Twins	.07	.01	.00
☐ 657 CL: Angels/Braves and Astros/Dodgers	.07	.01	.00
☐ 658 CL: Expos/A's and Indians/Pirates	.07	.01	.00
☐ 659 CL: Mariners/Wh.Sox and Reds/Rangers	.07	.01	.00
☐ 660 CL: Brewers/Giants and Special Cards	.10	.01	.00

1985 Fleer Limited Edition

This 44-card set features standard size cards (2 1/2" by 3 1/2") which were distributed in a colorful box as a complete set. The back of the box gives a complete checklist of the cards in the set. The cards are ordered alphabetically by the player's name. Backs of the cards are yellow and white whereas the fronts show a picture of the player inside a red banner-type border.

	MINT	EXC	G-VG
COMPLETE SET (44)	5.00	2.50	.50
COMMON PLAYER (1-44)	.10	.05	.01

☐ 1 Buddy Bell	.10	.05	.01
☐ 2 Bert Blyleven	.15	.07	.01
☐ 3 Wade Boggs	1.00	.50	.10

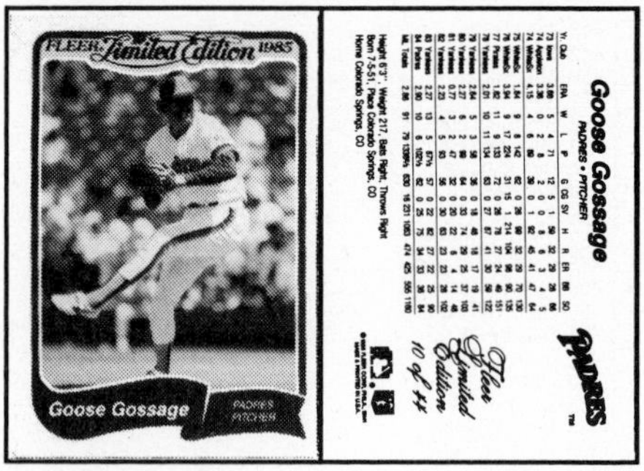

☐ 4 George Brett	.75	.35	.07
☐ 5 Rod Carew	.60	.30	.06
☐ 6 Steve Carlton	.40	.20	.04
☐ 7 Alvin Davis	.15	.07	.01
☐ 8 Andre Dawson	.30	.15	.03
☐ 9 Steve Garvey	.30	.15	.03
☐ 10 Goose Gossage	.10	.05	.01
☐ 11 Tony Gwynn	.40	.20	.04
☐ 12 Keith Hernandez	.15	.07	.01
☐ 13 Kent Hrbek	.15	.07	.01
☐ 14 Reggie Jackson	.60	.30	.06
☐ 15 Dave Kingman	.10	.05	.01
☐ 16 Ron Kittle	.10	.05	.01
☐ 17 Mark Langston	.20	.10	.02
☐ 18 Jeff Leonard	.10	.05	.01
☐ 19 Bill Madlock	.10	.05	.01
☐ 20 Don Mattingly	1.25	.60	.12
☐ 21 Jack Morris	.15	.07	.01
☐ 22 Dale Murphy	.45	.22	.04
☐ 23 Eddie Murray	.45	.22	.04
☐ 24 Tony Pena	.10	.05	.01
☐ 25 Dan Quisenberry	.10	.05	.01
☐ 26 Tim Raines	.20	.10	.02
☐ 27 Jim Rice	.20	.10	.02
☐ 28 Cal Ripken	.40	.20	.04
☐ 29 Pete Rose	.75	.35	.07
☐ 30 Nolan Ryan	1.50	.75	.15
☐ 31 Ryne Sandberg	.90	.45	.09
☐ 32 Steve Sax	.15	.07	.01
☐ 33 Mike Schmidt	1.00	.50	.10
☐ 34 Tom Seaver	.40	.20	.04
☐ 35 Ozzie Smith	.25	.12	.02
☐ 36 Mario Soto	.10	.05	.01
☐ 37 Dave Stieb	.10	.05	.01
☐ 38 Darryl Strawberry	.75	.35	.07
☐ 39 Rick Sutcliffe	.10	.05	.01
☐ 40 Alan Trammell	.20	.10	.02
☐ 41 Willie Upshaw	.10	.05	.01
☐ 42 Fernando Valenzuela	.20	.10	.02
☐ 43 Dave Winfield	.25	.12	.02
☐ 44 Robin Yount	.50	.25	.05

1985 Fleer Update

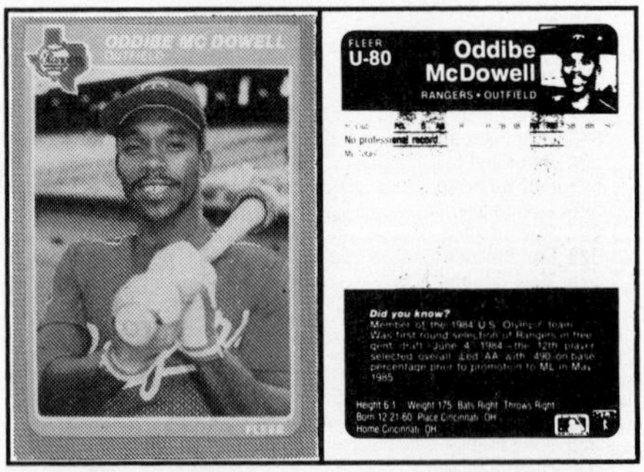

This 132-card set was issued late in the collecting year and features new players and players on new teams compared to the 1985 Fleer regular issue cards. Cards measure 2 1/2" by 3 1/2" and were distributed together as a complete set in a special box. The cards are numbered with a U prefix and are ordered alphabetically by the player's name. This set features the Extended Rookie Cards of Vince Coleman, Ozzie Guillen, Teddy Higuera, and Mickey Tettleton.

	MINT	EXC	G-VG
COMPLETE SET (132)	20.00	10.00	2.00
COMMON PLAYER (1-132)	.07	.03	.01
☐ U1 Don Aase	.15	.07	.01
☐ U2 Bill Almon	.07	.03	.01
☐ U3 Dusty Baker	.10	.05	.01
☐ U4 Dale Berra	.07	.03	.01
☐ U5 Karl Best	.10	.05	.01
☐ U6 Tim Birtsas	.12	.06	.01
☐ U7 Vida Blue	.10	.05	.01
☐ U8 Rich Bordi	.07	.03	.01
☐ U9 Daryl Boston	.35	.17	.03
☐ U10 Hubie Brooks	.30	.15	.03
☐ U11 Chris Brown	.15	.07	.01
☐ U12 Tom Browning	1.25	.60	.12
☐ U13 Al Bumbry	.07	.03	.01
☐ U14 Tim Burke	.60	.30	.06
☐ U15 Ray Burris	.07	.03	.01
☐ U16 Jeff Burroughs	.07	.03	.01
☐ U17 Ivan Calderon	1.75	.85	.17
☐ U18 Jeff Calhoun	.07	.03	.01
☐ U19 Bill Campbell	.07	.03	.01
☐ U20 Don Carman	.25	.12	.02
☐ U21 Gary Carter	.90	.45	.09
☐ U22 Bobby Castillo	.07	.03	.01
☐ U23 Bill Caudill	.07	.03	.01
☐ U24 Rick Cerone	.07	.03	.01
☐ U25 Jack Clark	.45	.22	.04
☐ U26 Pat Clements	.10	.05	.01
☐ U27 Stewart Cliburn	.10	.05	.01
☐ U28 Vince Coleman	8.00	4.00	.80
☐ U29 Dave Collins	.07	.03	.01
☐ U30 Fritz Connally	.07	.03	.01
☐ U31 Henry Cotto	.07	.03	.01
☐ U32 Danny Darwin	.10	.05	.01
☐ U33 Darren Daulton	.65	.30	.06
☐ U34 Jerry Davis	.07	.03	.01
☐ U35 Brian Dayett	.10	.05	.01
☐ U36 Ken Dixon	.07	.03	.01
☐ U37 Tommy Dunbar	.07	.03	.01
☐ U38 Mariano Duncan	.85	.40	.08
☐ U39 Bob Fallon	.07	.03	.01
☐ U40 Brian Fisher	.20	.10	.02
☐ U41 Mike Fitzgerald	.07	.03	.01
☐ U42 Ray Fontenot	.07	.03	.01
☐ U43 Greg Gagne	.30	.15	.03
☐ U44 Oscar Gamble	.07	.03	.01
☐ U45 Jim Gott	.10	.05	.01
☐ U46 David Green	.07	.03	.01
☐ U47 Alfredo Griffin	.07	.03	.01
☐ U48 Ozzie Guillen	2.50	1.25	.25
☐ U49 Toby Harrah	.10	.05	.01
☐ U50 Ron Hassey	.07	.03	.01
☐ U51 Rickey Henderson	3.75	1.85	.37
☐ U52 Steve Henderson	.07	.03	.01
☐ U53 George Hendrick	.10	.05	.01
☐ U54 Teddy Higuera	2.00	1.00	.20
☐ U55 Al Holland	.07	.03	.01
☐ U56 Burt Hooton	.07	.03	.01
☐ U57 Jay Howell	.10	.05	.01
☐ U58 LaMarr Hoyt	.10	.05	.01
☐ U59 Tim Hulett	.10	.05	.01
☐ U60 Bob James	.10	.05	.01
☐ U61 Cliff Johnson	.07	.03	.01
☐ U62 Howard Johnson	2.25	1.10	.22
☐ U63 Ruppert Jones	.07	.03	.01
☐ U64 Steve Kemp	.10	.05	.01
☐ U65 Bruce Kison	.07	.03	.01
☐ U66 Mike LaCoss	.07	.03	.01
☐ U67 Lee Lacy	.07	.03	.01
☐ U68 Dave LaPoint	.10	.05	.01
☐ U69 Gary Lavelle	.07	.03	.01
☐ U70 Vance Law	.10	.05	.01
☐ U71 Manny Lee	.25	.12	.02
☐ U72 Sixto Lezcano	.07	.03	.01
☐ U73 Tim Lollar	.07	.03	.01
☐ U74 Urbano Lugo	.07	.03	.01
☐ U75 Fred Lynn	.25	.12	.02
☐ U76 Steve Lyons	.15	.07	.01
☐ U77 Mickey Mahler	.07	.03	.01
☐ U78 Ron Mathis	.07	.03	.01
☐ U79 Len Matuszek	.07	.03	.01
☐ U80 Oddibe McDowell UER (part of bio actually Roger's)	.65	.30	.06
☐ U81 Roger McDowell UER (part of bio actually Oddibe's)	.85	.40	.08
☐ U82 Donnie Moore	.07	.03	.01
☐ U83 Ron Musselman	.07	.03	.01
☐ U84 Al Oliver	.15	.07	.01
☐ U85 Joe Orsulak	.40	.20	.04
☐ U86 Dan Pasqua	.50	.25	.05
☐ U87 Chris Pittaro	.10	.05	.01
☐ U88 Rick Reuschel	.25	.12	.02
☐ U89 Earnie Riles	.20	.10	.02
☐ U90 Jerry Royster	.07	.03	.01
☐ U91 Dave Rozema	.07	.03	.01
☐ U92 Dave Rucker	.07	.03	.01
☐ U93 Vern Ruhle	.07	.03	.01
☐ U94 Mark Salas	.10	.05	.01
☐ U95 Luis Salazar	.10	.05	.01
☐ U96 Joe Sambito	.07	.03	.01
☐ U97 Billy Sample	.07	.03	.01
☐ U98 Alejandro Sanchez	.10	.05	.01
☐ U99 Calvin Schiraldi	.20	.10	.02
☐ U100 Rick Schu	.15	.07	.01
☐ U101 Larry Sheets	.30	.15	.03
☐ U102 Ron Shephard	.07	.03	.01
☐ U103 Nelson Simmons	.10	.05	.01
☐ U104 Don Slaught	.07	.03	.01
☐ U105 Roy Smalley	.07	.03	.01
☐ U106 Lonnie Smith	.20	.10	.02
☐ U107 Nate Snell	.07	.03	.01
☐ U108 Lary Sorensen	.07	.03	.01
☐ U109 Chris Speier	.07	.03	.01
☐ U110 Mike Stenhouse	.10	.05	.01
☐ U111 Tim Stoddard	.07	.03	.01
☐ U112 John Stuper	.07	.03	.01
☐ U113 Jim Sundberg	.10	.05	.01
☐ U114 Bruce Sutter	.20	.10	.02
☐ U115 Don Sutton	.50	.25	.05
☐ U116 Bruce Tanner	.10	.05	.01
☐ U117 Kent Tekulve	.10	.05	.01
☐ U118 Walt Terrell	.12	.06	.01
☐ U119 Mickey Tettleton	1.00	.50	.10
☐ U120 Rich Thompson	.10	.05	.01
☐ U121 Louis Thornton	.10	.05	.01
☐ U122 Alex Trevino	.07	.03	.01
☐ U123 John Tudor	.20	.10	.02
☐ U124 Jose Uribe	.25	.12	.02
☐ U125 Dave Valle	.10	.05	.01
☐ U126 Dave Von Ohlen	.07	.03	.01
☐ U127 Curt Wardle	.07	.03	.01
☐ U128 U.L. Washington	.07	.03	.01
☐ U129 Ed Whitson	.12	.06	.01
☐ U130 Herm Winningham	.15	.07	.01
☐ U131 Rich Yett	.10	.05	.01

1986 Fleer

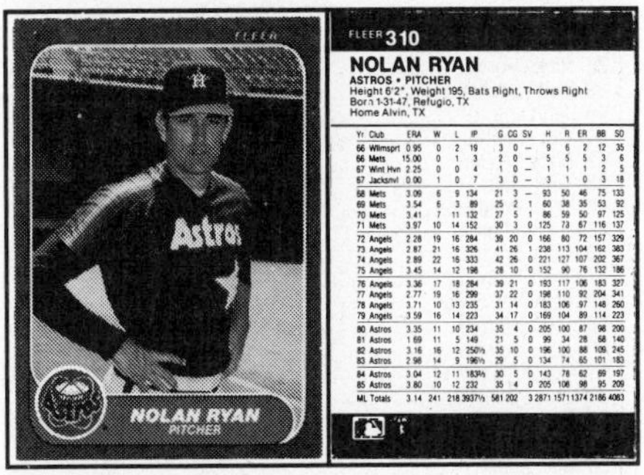

The cards in this 660-card set measure 2 1/2" by 3 1/2". The 1986 Fleer set features fronts that contain the team logo along with the player's name and position. The player cards are alphabetized within team and the teams are ordered by their 1985 season finish and won-lost record, e.g., Kansas City (1-25), St. Louis (26-49), Toronto (50-73), New York Mets (74-

97), New York Yankees (98-122), Los Angeles (123-147), California (148-171), Cincinnati (172-196), Chicago White Sox (197-220), Detroit (221-243), Montreal (244-267), Baltimore (268-291), Houston (292-314), San Diego (315-338), Boston (339-360), Chicago Cubs (361-385), Minnesota (386-409), Oakland (410-432), Philadelphia (433-457), Seattle (458-481), Milwaukee (482-506), Atlanta (507-532), San Francisco (533-555), Texas (556-578), Cleveland (579-601), and Pittsburgh (602-625). Specials (626-643), Major League Prospects (644-653), and checklist cards (654-660) complete the set. The border enclosing the photo is dark blue. The backs feature the same name, number, and statistics format that Fleer has been using over the past few years. The Dennis and Tippy Martinez cards were apparently switched in the set numbering, as their adjacent numbers (279 and 280) were reversed on the Orioles checklist card. The set includes the rookie cards of Jose Canseco, Vince Coleman, Kal Daniels, Len Dykstra, Cecil Fielder, and Benito Santiago.

	MINT	EXC	G-VG
COMPLETE SET (660)	135.00	65.00	13.50
COMMON PLAYER (1-660)	.06	.03	.00
☐ 1 Steve Balboni	.10	.05	.01
☐ 2 Joe Beckwith	.06	.03	.00
☐ 3 Buddy Biancalana	.06	.03	.00
☐ 4 Bud Black	.10	.05	.01
☐ 5 George Brett	.75	.35	.07
☐ 6 Onix Concepcion	.06	.03	.00
☐ 7 Steve Farr	.10	.05	.01
☐ 8 Mark Gubicza	.20	.10	.02
☐ 9 Dane Iorg	.06	.03	.00
☐ 10 Danny Jackson	.18	.09	.01
☐ 11 Lynn Jones	.06	.03	.00
☐ 12 Mike Jones	.06	.03	.00
☐ 13 Charlie Leibrandt	.06	.03	.00
☐ 14 Hal McRae	.10	.05	.01
☐ 15 Omar Moreno	.06	.03	.00
☐ 16 Darryl Motley	.06	.03	.00
☐ 17 Jorge Orta	.06	.03	.00
☐ 18 Dan Quisenberry	.12	.06	.01
☐ 19 Bret Saberhagen	1.00	.50	.10
☐ 20 Pat Sheridan	.06	.03	.00
☐ 21 Lonnie Smith	.10	.05	.01
☐ 22 Jim Sundberg	.06	.03	.00
☐ 23 John Wathan	.06	.03	.00
☐ 24 Frank White	.10	.05	.01
☐ 25 Willie Wilson	.10	.05	.01
☐ 26 Joaquin Andujar	.06	.03	.00
☐ 27 Steve Braun	.06	.03	.00
☐ 28 Bill Campbell	.06	.03	.00
☐ 29 Cesar Cedeno	.10	.05	.01
☐ 30 Jack Clark	.25	.12	.02
☐ 31 Vince Coleman	4.00	2.00	.40
☐ 32 Danny Cox	.06	.03	.00
☐ 33 Ken Dayley	.06	.03	.00
☐ 34 Ivan DeJesus	.06	.03	.00
☐ 35 Bob Forsch	.06	.03	.00
☐ 36 Brian Harper	.12	.06	.01
☐ 37 Tom Herr	.10	.05	.01
☐ 38 Ricky Horton	.06	.03	.00
☐ 39 Kurt Kepshire	.06	.03	.00
☐ 40 Jeff Lahti	.06	.03	.00
☐ 41 Tito Landrum	.06	.03	.00
☐ 42 Willie McGee	.25	.12	.02
☐ 43 Tom Nieto	.06	.03	.00
☐ 44 Terry Pendleton	.10	.05	.01
☐ 45 Darrell Porter	.06	.03	.00
☐ 46 Ozzie Smith	.30	.15	.03
☐ 47 John Tudor	.12	.06	.01
☐ 48 Andy Van Slyke	.25	.12	.02
☐ 49 Todd Worrell	.70	.35	.07
☐ 50 Jim Acker	.06	.03	.00
☐ 51 Doyle Alexander	.06	.03	.00
☐ 52 Jesse Barfield	.15	.07	.01
☐ 53 George Bell	.30	.15	.03
☐ 54 Jeff Burroughs	.06	.03	.00
☐ 55 Bill Caudill	.06	.03	.00
☐ 56 Jim Clancy	.06	.03	.00
☐ 57 Tony Fernandez	.25	.12	.02
☐ 58 Tom Filer	.06	.03	.00
☐ 59 Damaso Garcia	.06	.03	.00
☐ 60 Tom Henke	.30	.15	.03
☐ 61 Garth Iorg	.06	.03	.00
☐ 62 Cliff Johnson	.06	.03	.00
☐ 63 Jimmy Key	.12	.06	.01
☐ 64 Dennis Lamp	.06	.03	.00
☐ 65 Gary Lavelle	.06	.03	.00
☐ 66 Buck Martinez	.06	.03	.00
☐ 67 Lloyd Moseby	.10	.05	.01
☐ 68 Rance Mulliniks	.06	.03	.00
☐ 69 Al Oliver	.10	.05	.01
☐ 70 Dave Stieb	.15	.07	.01
☐ 71 Louis Thornton	.10	.05	.01
☐ 72 Willie Upshaw	.06	.03	.00
☐ 73 Ernie Whitt	.06	.03	.00
☐ 74 Rick Aguilera	.50	.25	.05
☐ 75 Wally Backman	.06	.03	.00
☐ 76 Gary Carter	.30	.15	.03
☐ 77 Ron Darling	.20	.10	.02
☐ 78 Len Dykstra	4.00	2.00	.40
☐ 79 Sid Fernandez	.15	.07	.01
☐ 80 George Foster	.12	.06	.01
☐ 81 Dwight Gooden	2.75	1.35	.27
☐ 82 Tom Gorman	.06	.03	.00
☐ 83 Danny Heep	.06	.03	.00
☐ 84 Keith Hernandez	.25	.12	.02
☐ 85 Howard Johnson	.60	.30	.06
☐ 86 Ray Knight	.10	.05	.01
☐ 87 Terry Leach	.12	.06	.01
☐ 88 Ed Lynch	.06	.03	.00
☐ 89 Roger McDowell	.60	.30	.06
☐ 90 Jesse Orosco	.06	.03	.00
☐ 91 Tom Paciorek	.06	.03	.00
☐ 92 Ronn Reynolds	.06	.03	.00
☐ 93 Rafael Santana	.06	.03	.00
☐ 94 Doug Sisk	.06	.03	.00
☐ 95 Rusty Staub	.10	.05	.01
☐ 96 Darryl Strawberry	3.50	1.75	.35
☐ 97 Mookie Wilson	.10	.05	.01
☐ 98 Neil Allen	.06	.03	.00
☐ 99 Don Baylor	.10	.05	.01
☐ 100 Dale Berra	.06	.03	.00
☐ 101 Rich Bordi	.06	.03	.00
☐ 102 Marty Bystrom	.06	.03	.00
☐ 103 Joe Cowley	.06	.03	.00
☐ 104 Brian Fisher	.15	.07	.01
☐ 105 Ken Griffey	.15	.07	.01
☐ 106 Ron Guidry	.15	.07	.01
☐ 107 Ron Hassey	.06	.03	.00
☐ 108 Rickey Henderson	2.00	1.00	.20
☐ 109 Don Mattingly	4.50	2.25	.45
☐ 110 Bobby Meacham	.06	.03	.00
☐ 111 John Montefusco	.06	.03	.00
☐ 112 Phil Niekro	.18	.09	.01
☐ 113 Mike Pagliarulo	.10	.05	.01
☐ 114 Dan Pasqua	.25	.12	.02
☐ 115 Willie Randolph	.10	.05	.01
☐ 116 Dave Righetti	.12	.06	.01
☐ 117 Andre Robertson	.06	.03	.00
☐ 118 Billy Sample	.06	.03	.00
☐ 119 Bob Shirley	.06	.03	.00
☐ 120 Ed Whitson	.10	.05	.01
☐ 121 Dave Winfield	.30	.15	.03
☐ 122 Butch Wynegar	.06	.03	.00
☐ 123 Dave Anderson	.06	.03	.00
☐ 124 Bob Bailor	.06	.03	.00
☐ 125 Greg Brock	.06	.03	.00
☐ 126 Enos Cabell	.06	.03	.00
☐ 127 Bobby Castillo	.06	.03	.00
☐ 128 Carlos Diaz	.06	.03	.00
☐ 129 Mariano Duncan	.50	.25	.05
☐ 130 Pedro Guerrero	.25	.12	.02
☐ 131 Orel Hershiser	1.25	.60	.12
☐ 132 Rick Honeycutt	.06	.03	.00
☐ 133 Ken Howell	.06	.03	.00
☐ 134 Ken Landreaux	.06	.03	.00
☐ 135 Bill Madlock	.10	.05	.01
☐ 136 Candy Maldonado	.12	.06	.01
☐ 137 Mike Marshall	.12	.06	.01
☐ 138 Len Matuszek	.06	.03	.00
☐ 139 Tom Niedenfuer	.06	.03	.00
☐ 140 Alejandro Pena	.06	.03	.00
☐ 141 Jerry Reuss	.06	.03	.00
☐ 142 Bill Russell	.06	.03	.00
☐ 143 Steve Sax	.18	.09	.01
☐ 144 Mike Scioscia	.06	.03	.00
☐ 145 Fernando Valenzuela	.25	.12	.02
☐ 146 Bob Welch	.15	.07	.01
☐ 147 Terry Whitfield	.06	.03	.00
☐ 148 Juan Beniquez	.06	.03	.00
☐ 149 Bob Boone	.12	.06	.01
☐ 150 John Candelaria	.06	.03	.00
☐ 151 Rod Carew	.40	.20	.04
☐ 152 Stewart Cliburn	.06	.03	.00
☐ 153 Doug DeCinces	.10	.05	.01
☐ 154 Brian Downing	.10	.05	.01
☐ 155 Ken Forsch	.06	.03	.00
☐ 156 Craig Gerber	.06	.03	.00
☐ 157 Bobby Grich	.10	.05	.01
☐ 158 George Hendrick	.06	.03	.00
☐ 159 Al Holland	.06	.03	.00

☐ 160	Reggie Jackson	.60	.30	.06
☐ 161	Ruppert Jones	.06	.03	.00
☐ 162	Urbano Lugo	.06	.03	.00
☐ 163	Kirk McCaskill	.50	.25	.05
☐ 164	Donnie Moore	.06	.03	.00
☐ 165	Gary Pettis	.06	.03	.00
☐ 166	Ron Romanick	.06	.03	.00
☐ 167	Dick Schofield	.06	.03	.00
☐ 168	Daryl Sconiers	.06	.03	.00
☐ 169	Jim Slaton	.06	.03	.00
☐ 170	Don Sutton	.18	.09	.01
☐ 171	Mike Witt	.10	.05	.01
☐ 172	Buddy Bell	.10	.05	.01
☐ 173	Tom Browning	.35	.17	.03
☐ 174	Dave Concepcion	.10	.05	.01
☐ 175	Eric Davis	3.25	1.60	.32
☐ 176	Bo Diaz	.06	.03	.00
☐ 177	Nick Esasky	.10	.05	.01
☐ 178	John Franco	.20	.10	.02
☐ 179	Tom Hume	.06	.03	.00
☐ 180	Wayne Krenchicki	.06	.03	.00
☐ 181	Andy McGaffigan	.06	.03	.00
☐ 182	Eddie Milner	.06	.03	.00
☐ 183	Ron Oester	.06	.03	.00
☐ 184	Dave Parker	.15	.07	.01
☐ 185	Frank Pastore	.06	.03	.00
☐ 186	Tony Perez	.15	.07	.01
☐ 187	Ted Power	.06	.03	.00
☐ 188	Joe Price	.06	.03	.00
☐ 189	Gary Redus	.06	.03	.00
☐ 190	Ron Robinson	.06	.03	.00
☐ 191	Pete Rose	.75	.35	.07
☐ 192	Mario Soto	.06	.03	.00
☐ 193	John Stuper	.06	.03	.00
☐ 194	Jay Tibbs	.06	.03	.00
☐ 195	Dave Van Gorder	.06	.03	.00
☐ 196	Max Venable	.06	.03	.00
☐ 197	Juan Agosto	.06	.03	.00
☐ 198	Harold Baines	.12	.06	.01
☐ 199	Floyd Bannister	.06	.03	.00
☐ 200	Britt Burns	.06	.03	.00
☐ 201	Julio Cruz	.06	.03	.00
☐ 202	Joel Davis	.10	.05	.01
☐ 203	Richard Dotson	.06	.03	.00
☐ 204	Carlton Fisk	.40	.20	.04
☐ 205	Scott Fletcher	.06	.03	.00
☐ 206	Ozzie Guillen	1.50	.75	.15
☐ 207	Jerry Hairston	.06	.03	.00
☐ 208	Tim Hulett	.06	.03	.00
☐ 209	Bob James	.06	.03	.00
☐ 210	Ron Kittle	.10	.05	.01
☐ 211	Rudy Law	.06	.03	.00
☐ 212	Bryan Little	.06	.03	.00
☐ 213	Gene Nelson	.06	.03	.00
☐ 214	Reid Nichols	.06	.03	.00
☐ 215	Luis Salazar	.06	.03	.00
☐ 216	Tom Seaver	.50	.25	.05
☐ 217	Dan Spillner	.06	.03	.00
☐ 218	Bruce Tanner	.10	.05	.01
☐ 219	Greg Walker	.06	.03	.00
☐ 220	Dave Wehrmeister	.06	.03	.00
☐ 221	Juan Berenguer	.06	.03	.00
☐ 222	Dave Bergman	.06	.03	.00
☐ 223	Tom Brookens	.06	.03	.00
☐ 224	Darrell Evans	.10	.05	.01
☐ 225	Barbaro Garbey	.06	.03	.00
☐ 226	Kirk Gibson	.25	.12	.02
☐ 227	John Grubb	.06	.03	.00
☐ 228	Willie Hernandez	.10	.05	.01
☐ 229	Larry Herndon	.06	.03	.00
☐ 230	Chet Lemon	.06	.03	.00
☐ 231	Aurelio Lopez	.06	.03	.00
☐ 232	Jack Morris	.15	.07	.01
☐ 233	Randy O'Neal	.06	.03	.00
☐ 234	Lance Parrish	.15	.07	.01
☐ 235	Dan Petry	.06	.03	.00
☐ 236	Alejandro Sanchez	.06	.03	.00
☐ 237	Bill Scherrer	.06	.03	.00
☐ 238	Nelson Simmons	.06	.03	.00
☐ 239	Frank Tanana	.10	.05	.01
☐ 240	Walt Terrell	.06	.03	.00
☐ 241	Alan Trammell	.25	.12	.02
☐ 242	Lou Whitaker	.15	.07	.01
☐ 243	Milt Wilcox	.06	.03	.00
☐ 244	Hubie Brooks	.12	.06	.01
☐ 245	Tim Burke	.40	.20	.04
☐ 246	Andre Dawson	.40	.20	.04
☐ 247	Mike Fitzgerald	.06	.03	.00
☐ 248	Terry Francona	.06	.03	.00
☐ 249	Bill Gullickson	.06	.03	.00
☐ 250	Joe Hesketh	.06	.03	.00
☐ 251	Bill Laskey	.06	.03	.00
☐ 252	Vance Law	.06	.03	.00
☐ 253	Charlie Lea	.06	.03	.00

☐ 254	Gary Lucas	.06	.03	.00
☐ 255	David Palmer	.06	.03	.00
☐ 256	Tim Raines	.30	.15	.03
☐ 257	Jeff Reardon	.10	.05	.01
☐ 258	Bert Roberge	.06	.03	.00
☐ 259	Dan Schatzeder	.06	.03	.00
☐ 260	Bryn Smith	.10	.05	.01
☐ 261	Randy St.Claire	.06	.03	.00
☐ 262	Scot Thompson	.06	.03	.00
☐ 263	Tim Wallach	.12	.06	.01
☐ 264	U.L. Washington	.06	.03	.00
☐ 265	Mitch Webster	.30	.15	.03
☐ 266	Herm Winningham	.10	.05	.01
☐ 267	Floyd Youmans	.20	.10	.02
☐ 268	Don Aase	.06	.03	.00
☐ 269	Mike Boddicker	.10	.05	.01
☐ 270	Rich Dauer	.06	.03	.00
☐ 271	Storm Davis	.10	.05	.01
☐ 272	Rick Dempsey	.06	.03	.00
☐ 273	Ken Dixon	.06	.03	.00
☐ 274	Jim Dwyer	.06	.03	.00
☐ 275	Mike Flanagan	.10	.05	.01
☐ 276	Wayne Gross	.06	.03	.00
☐ 277	Lee Lacy	.06	.03	.00
☐ 278	Fred Lynn	.15	.07	.01
☐ 279	Tippy Martinez	.06	.03	.00
☐ 280	Dennis Martinez	.10	.05	.01
☐ 281	Scott McGregor	.06	.03	.00
☐ 282	Eddie Murray	.40	.20	.04
☐ 283	Floyd Rayford	.06	.03	.00
☐ 284	Cal Ripken	.90	.45	.09
☐ 285	Gary Roenicke	.06	.03	.00
☐ 286	Larry Sheets	.15	.07	.01
☐ 287	John Shelby	.06	.03	.00
☐ 288	Nate Snell	.06	.03	.00
☐ 289	Sammy Stewart	.06	.03	.00
☐ 290	Alan Wiggins	.06	.03	.00
☐ 291	Mike Young	.06	.03	.00
☐ 292	Alan Ashby	.06	.03	.00
☐ 293	Mark Bailey	.06	.03	.00
☐ 294	Kevin Bass	.10	.05	.01
☐ 295	Jeff Calhoun	.06	.03	.00
☐ 296	Jose Cruz	.10	.05	.01
☐ 297	Glenn Davis	2.00	1.00	.20
☐ 298	Bill Dawley	.06	.03	.00
☐ 299	Frank DiPino	.06	.03	.00
☐ 300	Bill Doran	.10	.05	.01
☐ 301	Phil Garner	.06	.03	.00
☐ 302	Jeff Heathcock	.06	.03	.00
☐ 303	Charlie Kerfeld	.10	.05	.01
☐ 304	Bob Knepper	.06	.03	.00
☐ 305	Ron Mathis	.06	.03	.00
☐ 306	Jerry Mumphrey	.06	.03	.00
☐ 307	Jim Pankovits	.06	.03	.00
☐ 308	Terry Puhl	.06	.03	.00
☐ 309	Craig Reynolds	.06	.03	.00
☐ 310	Nolan Ryan	2.25	1.10	.22
☐ 311	Mike Scott	.30	.15	.03
☐ 312	Dave Smith	.06	.03	.00
☐ 313	Dickie Thon	.06	.03	.00
☐ 314	Denny Walling	.06	.03	.00
☐ 315	Kurt Bevacqua	.06	.03	.00
☐ 316	Al Bumbry	.06	.03	.00
☐ 317	Jerry Davis	.06	.03	.00
☐ 318	Luis DeLeon	.06	.03	.00
☐ 319	Dave Dravecky	.12	.06	.01
☐ 320	Tim Flannery	.06	.03	.00
☐ 321	Steve Garvey	.35	.17	.03
☐ 322	Goose Gossage	.12	.06	.01
☐ 323	Tony Gwynn	.90	.45	.09
☐ 324	Andy Hawkins	.06	.03	.00
☐ 325	LaMarr Hoyt	.06	.03	.00
☐ 326	Roy Lee Jackson	.06	.03	.00
☐ 327	Terry Kennedy	.06	.03	.00
☐ 328	Craig Lefferts	.06	.03	.00
☐ 329	Carmelo Martinez	.06	.03	.00
☐ 330	Lance McCullers	.25	.12	.02
☐ 331	Kevin McReynolds	.35	.17	.03
☐ 332	Graig Nettles	.10	.05	.01
☐ 333	Jerry Royster	.06	.03	.00
☐ 334	Eric Show	.06	.03	.00
☐ 335	Tim Stoddard	.06	.03	.00
☐ 336	Garry Templeton	.10	.05	.01
☐ 337	Mark Thurmond	.06	.03	.00
☐ 338	Ed Wojna	.06	.03	.00
☐ 339	Tony Armas	.06	.03	.00
☐ 340	Marty Barrett	.10	.05	.01
☐ 341	Wade Boggs	2.25	1.10	.22
☐ 342	Dennis Boyd	.10	.05	.01
☐ 343	Bill Buckner	.10	.05	.01
☐ 344	Mark Clear	.06	.03	.00
☐ 345	Roger Clemens	4.50	2.25	.45
☐ 346	Steve Crawford	.06	.03	.00
☐ 347	Mike Easler	.06	.03	.00

☐ 348	Dwight Evans	.15	.07	.01
☐ 349	Rich Gedman	.06	.03	.00
☐ 350	Jackie Gutierrez	.06	.03	.00
☐ 351	Glenn Hoffman	.06	.03	.00
☐ 352	Bruce Hurst	.12	.06	.01
☐ 353	Bruce Kison	.06	.03	.00
☐ 354	Tim Lollar	.06	.03	.00
☐ 355	Steve Lyons	.10	.05	.01
☐ 356	Al Nipper	.06	.03	.00
☐ 357	Bob Ojeda	.10	.05	.01
☐ 358	Jim Rice	.20	.10	.02
☐ 359	Bob Stanley	.06	.03	.00
☐ 360	Mike Trujillo	.06	.03	.00
☐ 361	Thad Bosley	.06	.03	.00
☐ 362	Warren Brusstar	.06	.03	.00
☐ 363	Ron Cey	.10	.05	.01
☐ 364	Jody Davis	.06	.03	.00
☐ 365	Bob Dernier	.06	.03	.00
☐ 366	Shawon Dunston	1.00	.50	.10
☐ 367	Leon Durham	.06	.03	.00
☐ 368	Dennis Eckersley	.20	.10	.02
☐ 369	Ray Fontenot	.06	.03	.00
☐ 370	George Frazier	.06	.03	.00
☐ 371	Billy Hatcher	.25	.12	.02
☐ 372	Dave Lopes	.10	.05	.01
☐ 373	Gary Matthews	.06	.03	.00
☐ 374	Ron Meredith	.06	.03	.00
☐ 375	Keith Moreland	.06	.03	.00
☐ 376	Reggie Patterson	.06	.03	.00
☐ 377	Dick Ruthven	.06	.03	.00
☐ 378	Ryne Sandberg	2.50	1.25	.25
☐ 379	Scott Sanderson	.10	.05	.01
☐ 380	Lee Smith	.10	.05	.01
☐ 381	Lary Sorensen	.06	.03	.00
☐ 382	Chris Speier	.06	.03	.00
☐ 383	Rick Sutcliffe	.12	.06	.01
☐ 384	Steve Trout	.06	.03	.00
☐ 385	Gary Woods	.06	.03	.00
☐ 386	Bert Blyleven	.15	.07	.01
☐ 387	Tom Brunansky	.15	.07	.01
☐ 388	Randy Bush	.06	.03	.00
☐ 389	John Butcher	.06	.03	.00
☐ 390	Ron Davis	.06	.03	.00
☐ 391	Dave Engle	.06	.03	.00
☐ 392	Frank Eufemia	.06	.03	.00
☐ 393	Pete Filson	.06	.03	.00
☐ 394	Gary Gaetti	.20	.10	.02
☐ 395	Greg Gagne	.10	.05	.01
☐ 396	Mickey Hatcher	.06	.03	.00
☐ 397	Kent Hrbek	.25	.12	.02
☐ 398	Tim Laudner	.06	.03	.00
☐ 399	Rick Lysander	.06	.03	.00
☐ 400	Dave Meier	.06	.03	.00
☐ 401	Kirby Puckett	4.50	2.25	.45
☐ 402	Mark Salas	.06	.03	.00
☐ 403	Ken Schrom	.06	.03	.00
☐ 404	Roy Smalley	.06	.03	.00
☐ 405	Mike Smithson	.06	.03	.00
☐ 406	Mike Stenhouse	.06	.03	.00
☐ 407	Tim Teufel	.10	.05	.01
☐ 408	Frank Viola	.40	.20	.04
☐ 409	Ron Washington	.06	.03	.00
☐ 410	Keith Atherton	.06	.03	.00
☐ 411	Dusty Baker	.10	.05	.01
☐ 412	Tim Birtsas	.10	.05	.01
☐ 413	Bruce Bochte	.06	.03	.00
☐ 414	Chris Codiroli	.06	.03	.00
☐ 415	Dave Collins	.06	.03	.00
☐ 416	Mike Davis	.06	.03	.00
☐ 417	Alfredo Griffin	.06	.03	.00
☐ 418	Mike Heath	.06	.03	.00
☐ 419	Steve Henderson	.06	.03	.00
☐ 420	Donnie Hill	.06	.03	.00
☐ 421	Jay Howell	.06	.03	.00
☐ 422	Tommy John	.15	.07	.01
☐ 423	Dave Kingman	.12	.06	.01
☐ 424	Bill Krueger	.06	.03	.00
☐ 425	Rick Langford	.06	.03	.00
☐ 426	Carney Lansford	.12	.06	.01
☐ 427	Steve McCatty	.06	.03	.00
☐ 428	Dwayne Murphy	.06	.03	.00
☐ 429	Steve Ontiveros	.10	.05	.01
☐ 430	Tony Phillips	.06	.03	.00
☐ 431	Jose Rijo	.25	.12	.02
☐ 432	Mickey Tettleton	.65	.30	.06
☐ 433	Luis Aguayo	.06	.03	.00
☐ 434	Larry Andersen	.06	.03	.00
☐ 435	Steve Carlton	.35	.17	.03
☐ 436	Don Carman	.25	.12	.02
☐ 437	Tim Corcoran	.06	.03	.00
☐ 438	Darren Daulton	.45	.22	.04
☐ 439	John Denny	.06	.03	.00
☐ 440	Tom Foley	.06	.03	.00
☐ 441	Greg Gross	.06	.03	.00
☐ 442	Kevin Gross	.06	.03	.00
☐ 443	Von Hayes	.12	.06	.01
☐ 444	Charles Hudson	.06	.03	.00
☐ 445	Garry Maddox	.06	.03	.00
☐ 446	Shane Rawley	.06	.03	.00
☐ 447	Dave Rucker	.06	.03	.00
☐ 448	John Russell	.06	.03	.00
☐ 449	Juan Samuel	.15	.07	.01
☐ 450	Mike Schmidt	1.75	.85	.17
☐ 451	Rick Schu	.06	.03	.00
☐ 452	Dave Shipanoff	.06	.03	.00
☐ 453	Dave Stewart	.50	.25	.05
☐ 454	Jeff Stone	.06	.03	.00
☐ 455	Kent Tekulve	.06	.03	.00
☐ 456	Ozzie Virgil	.06	.03	.00
☐ 457	Glenn Wilson	.06	.03	.00
☐ 458	Jim Beattie	.06	.03	.00
☐ 459	Karl Best	.06	.03	.00
☐ 460	Barry Bonnell	.06	.03	.00
☐ 461	Phil Bradley	.12	.06	.01
☐ 462	Ivan Calderon	1.25	.60	.12
☐ 463	Al Cowens	.06	.03	.00
☐ 464	Alvin Davis	.25	.12	.02
☐ 465	Dave Henderson	.12	.06	.01
☐ 466	Bob Kearney	.06	.03	.00
☐ 467	Mark Langston	.40	.20	.04
☐ 468	Bob Long	.06	.03	.00
☐ 469	Mike Moore	.10	.05	.01
☐ 470	Edwin Nunez	.06	.03	.00
☐ 471	Spike Owen	.06	.03	.00
☐ 472	Jack Perconte	.06	.03	.00
☐ 473	Jim Presley	.12	.06	.01
☐ 474	Donnie Scott	.06	.03	.00
☐ 475	Bill Swift	.10	.05	.01
☐ 476	Danny Tartabull	.60	.30	.06
☐ 477	Gorman Thomas	.10	.05	.01
☐ 478	Roy Thomas	.06	.03	.00
☐ 479	Ed VandeBerg	.06	.03	.00
☐ 480	Frank Wills	.10	.05	.01
☐ 481	Matt Young	.06	.03	.00
☐ 482	Ray Burris	.06	.03	.00
☐ 483	Jaime Cocanower	.06	.03	.00
☐ 484	Cecil Cooper	.10	.05	.01
☐ 485	Danny Darwin	.10	.05	.01
☐ 486	Rollie Fingers	.18	.09	.01
☐ 487	Jim Gantner	.06	.03	.00
☐ 488	Bob L. Gibson	.06	.03	.00
☐ 489	Moose Haas	.06	.03	.00
☐ 490	Teddy Higuera	1.25	.60	.12
☐ 491	Paul Householder	.06	.03	.00
☐ 492	Pete Ladd	.06	.03	.00
☐ 493	Rick Manning	.06	.03	.00
☐ 494	Bob McClure	.06	.03	.00
☐ 495	Paul Molitor	.18	.09	.01
☐ 496	Charlie Moore	.06	.03	.00
☐ 497	Ben Oglivie	.06	.03	.00
☐ 498	Randy Ready	.06	.03	.00
☐ 499	Earnie Riles	.20	.10	.02
☐ 500	Ed Romero	.06	.03	.00
☐ 501	Bill Schroeder	.06	.03	.00
☐ 502	Ray Searage	.06	.03	.00
☐ 503	Ted Simmons	.10	.05	.01
☐ 504	Pete Vuckovich	.06	.03	.00
☐ 505	Rick Waits	.06	.03	.00
☐ 506	Robin Yount	.50	.25	.05
☐ 507	Len Barker	.06	.03	.00
☐ 508	Steve Bedrosian	.12	.06	.01
☐ 509	Bruce Benedict	.06	.03	.00
☐ 510	Rick Camp	.06	.03	.00
☐ 511	Rick Cerone	.06	.03	.00
☐ 512	Chris Chambliss	.10	.05	.01
☐ 513	Jeff Dedmon	.06	.03	.00
☐ 514	Terry Forster	.06	.03	.00
☐ 515	Gene Garber	.06	.03	.00
☐ 516	Terry Harper	.06	.03	.00
☐ 517	Bob Horner	.10	.05	.01
☐ 518	Glenn Hubbard	.06	.03	.00
☐ 519	Joe Johnson	.10	.05	.01
☐ 520	Brad Komminsk	.06	.03	.00
☐ 521	Rick Mahler	.06	.03	.00
☐ 522	Dale Murphy	.45	.22	.04
☐ 523	Ken Oberkfell	.06	.03	.00
☐ 524	Pascual Perez	.12	.06	.01
☐ 525	Gerald Perry	.10	.05	.01
☐ 526	Rafael Ramirez	.06	.03	.00
☐ 527	Steve Shields	.06	.03	.00
☐ 528	Zane Smith	.15	.07	.01
☐ 529	Bruce Sutter	.12	.06	.01
☐ 530	Milt Thompson	.35	.17	.03
☐ 531	Claudell Washington	.10	.05	.01
☐ 532	Paul Zuvella	.06	.03	.00
☐ 533	Vida Blue	.10	.05	.01
☐ 534	Bob Brenly	.06	.03	.00
☐ 535	Chris Brown	.15	.07	.01

☐ 536	Chili Davis	.10	.05	.01
☐ 537	Mark Davis	.12	.06	.01
☐ 538	Rob Deer	.35	.17	.03
☐ 539	Dan Driessen	.06	.03	.00
☐ 540	Scott Garrelts	.35	.17	.03
☐ 541	Dan Gladden	.10	.05	.01
☐ 542	Jim Gott	.06	.03	.00
☐ 543	David Green	.06	.03	.00
☐ 544	Atlee Hammaker	.06	.03	.00
☐ 545	Mike Jeffcoat	.06	.03	.00
☐ 546	Mike Krukow	.06	.03	.00
☐ 547	Dave LaPoint	.06	.03	.00
☐ 548	Jeff Leonard	.10	.05	.01
☐ 549	Greg Minton	.06	.03	.00
☐ 550	Alex Trevino	.06	.03	.00
☐ 551	Manny Trillo	.06	.03	.00
☐ 552	Jose Uribe	.30	.15	.03
☐ 553	Brad Wellman	.06	.03	.00
☐ 554	Frank Williams	.06	.03	.00
☐ 555	Joel Youngblood	.06	.03	.00
☐ 556	Alan Bannister	.06	.03	.00
☐ 557	Glenn Brummer	.06	.03	.00
☐ 558	Steve Buechele	.25	.12	.02
☐ 559	Jose Guzman	.25	.12	.02
☐ 560	Toby Harrah	.06	.03	.00
☐ 561	Greg Harris	.06	.03	.00
☐ 562	Dwayne Henry	.10	.05	.01
☐ 563	Burt Hooton	.06	.03	.00
☐ 564	Charlie Hough	.06	.03	.00
☐ 565	Mike Mason	.06	.03	.00
☐ 566	Oddibe McDowell	.18	.09	.01
☐ 567	Dickie Noles	.06	.03	.00
☐ 568	Pete O'Brien	.10	.05	.01
☐ 569	Larry Parrish	.06	.03	.00
☐ 570	Dave Rozema	.06	.03	.00
☐ 571	Dave Schmidt	.06	.03	.00
☐ 572	Don Slaught	.06	.03	.00
☐ 573	Wayne Tolleson	.06	.03	.00
☐ 574	Duane Walker	.06	.03	.00
☐ 575	Gary Ward	.06	.03	.00
☐ 576	Chris Welsh	.06	.03	.00
☐ 577	Curtis Wilkerson	.06	.03	.00
☐ 578	George Wright	.06	.03	.00
☐ 579	Chris Bando	.06	.03	.00
☐ 580	Tony Bernazard	.06	.03	.00
☐ 581	Brett Butler	.12	.06	.01
☐ 582	Ernie Camacho	.06	.03	.00
☐ 583	Joe Carter	.60	.30	.06
☐ 584	Carmen Castillo	.06	.03	.00
☐ 585	Jamie Easterly	.06	.03	.00
☐ 586	Julio Franco	.25	.12	.02
☐ 587	Mel Hall	.10	.05	.01
☐ 588	Mike Hargrove	.06	.03	.00
☐ 589	Neal Heaton	.06	.03	.00
☐ 590	Brook Jacoby	.12	.06	.01
☐ 591	Otis Nixon	.12	.06	.01
☐ 592	Jerry Reed	.06	.03	.00
☐ 593	Vern Ruhle	.06	.03	.00
☐ 594	Pat Tabler	.10	.05	.01
☐ 595	Rich Thompson	.06	.03	.00
☐ 596	Andre Thornton	.10	.05	.01
☐ 597	Dave Von Ohlen	.06	.03	.00
☐ 598	George Vukovich	.06	.03	.00
☐ 599	Tom Waddell	.06	.03	.00
☐ 600	Curt Wardle	.06	.03	.00
☐ 601	Jerry Willard	.06	.03	.00
☐ 602	Bill Almon	.06	.03	.00
☐ 603	Mike Bielecki	.10	.05	.01
☐ 604	Sid Bream	.10	.05	.01
☐ 605	Mike Brown OF	.06	.03	.00
☐ 606	Pat Clements	.10	.05	.01
☐ 607	Jose DeLeon	.10	.05	.01
☐ 608	Denny Gonzalez	.06	.03	.00
☐ 609	Cecilio Guante	.06	.03	.00
☐ 610	Steve Kemp	.06	.03	.00
☐ 611	Sammy Khalifa	.06	.03	.00
☐ 612	Lee Mazzilli	.06	.03	.00
☐ 613	Larry McWilliams	.06	.03	.00
☐ 614	Jim Morrison	.06	.03	.00
☐ 615	Joe Orsulak	.30	.15	.03
☐ 616	Tony Pena	.10	.05	.01
☐ 617	Johnny Ray	.10	.05	.01
☐ 618	Rick Reuschel	.10	.05	.01
☐ 619	R.J. Reynolds	.06	.03	.00
☐ 620	Rick Rhoden	.06	.03	.00
☐ 621	Don Robinson	.06	.03	.00
☐ 622	Jason Thompson	.06	.03	.00
☐ 623	Lee Tunnell	.06	.03	.00
☐ 624	Jim Winn	.06	.03	.00
☐ 625	Marvell Wynne	.06	.03	.00
☐ 626	Dwight Gooden IA	.50	.25	.05
☐ 627	Don Mattingly IA	1.50	.75	.15
☐ 628	4192 (Pete Rose)	.40	.20	.04
☐ 629	3000 Career Hits Rod Carew	.30	.15	.03
☐ 630	300 Career Wins Tom Seaver Phil Niekro	.15	.07	.01
☐ 631	Ouch (Don Baylor)	.10	.05	.01
☐ 632	Instant Offense Darryl Strawberry Tim Raines	.30	.15	.03
☐ 633	Shortstops Supreme Cal Ripken Alan Trammell	.15	.07	.01
☐ 634	Boggs and "Hero" Wade Boggs George Brett	.60	.30	.06
☐ 635	Braves Dynamic Duo Bob Horner Dale Murphy	.15	.07	.01
☐ 636	Cardinal Ignitors Willie McGee Vince Coleman	.30	.15	.03
☐ 637	Terror on Basepaths Vince Coleman	.35	.17	.03
☐ 638	Charlie Hustle / Dr.K Pete Rose Dwight Gooden	.75	.35	.07
☐ 639	1984 and 1985 AL Batting Champs Wade Boggs Don Mattingly	1.75	.85	.17
☐ 640	NL West Sluggers Dale Murphy Steve Garvey Dave Parker	.15	.07	.01
☐ 641	Staff Aces Fernando Valenzuela Dwight Gooden	.30	.15	.03
☐ 642	Blue Jay Stoppers Jimmy Key Dave Stieb	.10	.05	.01
☐ 643	AL All-Star Backstops Carlton Fisk Rich Gedman	.10	.05	.01
☐ 644	Gene Walter and Benito Santiago	6.50	3.25	.65
☐ 645	Mike Woodard and Collin Ward	.10	.05	.01
☐ 646	Kal Daniels and Paul O'Neill	5.50	2.75	.55
☐ 647	Andres Galarraga and Fred Toliver	2.50	1.25	.25
☐ 648	Bob Kipper and Curt Ford	.10	.05	.01
☐ 649	Jose Canseco and Eric Plunk	55.00	27.50	5.50
☐ 650	Mark McLemore and Gus Polidor	.10	.05	.01
☐ 651	Rob Woodward and Mickey Brantley	.25	.12	.02
☐ 652	Billy Jo Robidoux and Mark Funderburk	.10	.05	.01
☐ 653	Cecil Fielder and Cory Snyder	18.00	9.00	1.80
☐ 654	CL: Royals/Cardinals Blue Jays/Mets	.08	.01	.00
☐ 655	CL: Yankees/Dodgers Angels/Reds	.08	.01	.00
☐ 656	CL: White Sox/Tigers Expos/Orioles (279 Dennis, 280 Tippy)	.08	.01	.00
☐ 657	CL: Astros/Padres Red Sox/Cubs	.08	.01	.00
☐ 658	CL: Twins/A's Phillies/Mariners	.08	.01	.00
☐ 659	CL: Brewers/Braves Giants/Rangers	.08	.01	.00
☐ 660	CL: Indians/Pirates Special Cards	.08	.01	.00

1986 Fleer Wax Box Cards

The cards in this 8-card set measure the standard 2 1/2" by 3 1/2" and were found on the bottom of the Fleer regular issue wax pack and cello pack boxes as four-card panel. Cards have essentially the same design as the 1986 Fleer regular issue set. These 8 cards (C1 to C8) are considered a separate set in their own right and are not typically included in a complete set of the regular issue 1986 Fleer cards. The value of the panel uncut is slightly greater, perhaps by 25 percent greater, than the value of the individual cards cut up carefully.

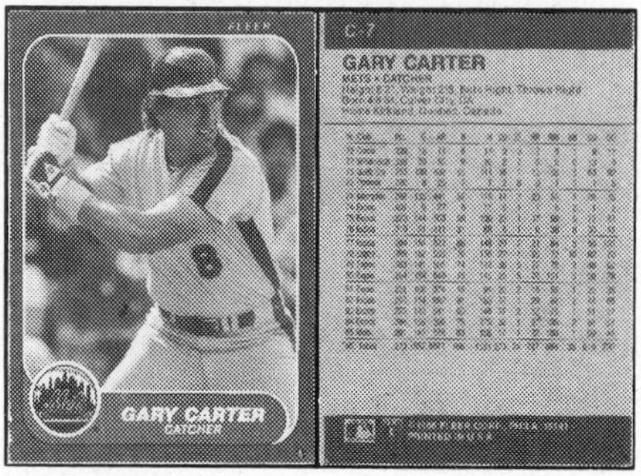

	MINT	EXC	G-VG
COMPLETE SET (8)	2.00	1.00	.20
COMMON PLAYERS	.10	.05	.01
☐ C1 Royals Logo	.10	.05	.01
☐ C2 George Brett	.50	.25	.05
☐ C3 Ozzie Guillen	.50	.25	.05
☐ C4 Dale Murphy	.50	.25	.05
☐ C5 Cardinals Logo	.10	.05	.01
☐ C6 Tom Browning	.15	.07	.01
☐ C7 Gary Carter	.20	.10	.02
☐ C8 Carlton Fisk	.35	.17	.03

1986 Fleer All-Star Inserts

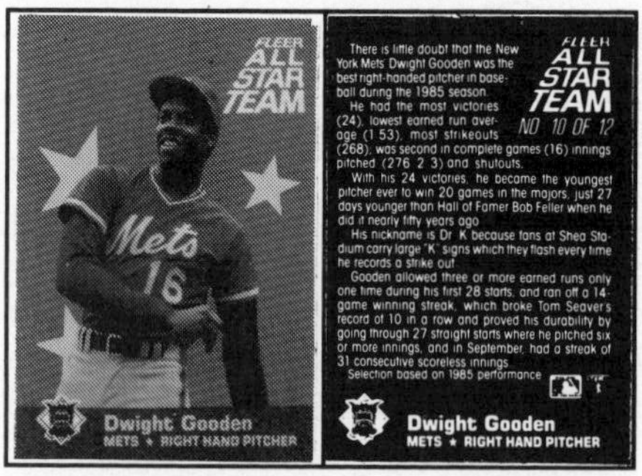

Fleer selected a 12-card (Major League) All-Star team to be included as inserts in their 39 cent wax packs and 59 cent cello packs. However they were randomly inserted in such a way that not all wax packs contain the insert. Cards measure 2 1/2" by 3 1/2" and feature attractive red backgrounds (American Leaguers) and blue backgrounds (National Leaguers). The 12 selections cover each position, left and right-handed starting pitchers, a reliever, and a designated hitter.

	MINT	EXC	G-VG
COMPLETE SET (12)	18.00	9.00	1.80
COMMON PLAYER (1-12)	.30	.15	.03
☐ 1 Don Mattingly First Base	8.00	4.00	.80
☐ 2 Tom Herr Second Base	.30	.15	.03
☐ 3 George Brett Third Base	1.50	.75	.15
☐ 4 Gary Carter Catcher	.75	.35	.07
☐ 5 Cal Ripken Shortstop	1.50	.75	.15
☐ 6 Dave Parker Outfield	.60	.30	.06
☐ 7 Rickey Henderson Outfield	4.00	2.00	.40
☐ 8 Pedro Guerrero Outfield	.40	.20	.04
☐ 9 Dan Quisenberry Relief Pitcher	.30	.15	.03
☐ 10 Dwight Gooden Right-Hand Pitcher	3.00	1.50	.30
☐ 11 Gorman Thomas Designated Hitter	.30	.15	.03
☐ 12 John Tudor Left-Hand Pitcher	.30	.15	.03

1986 Fleer Future HOF

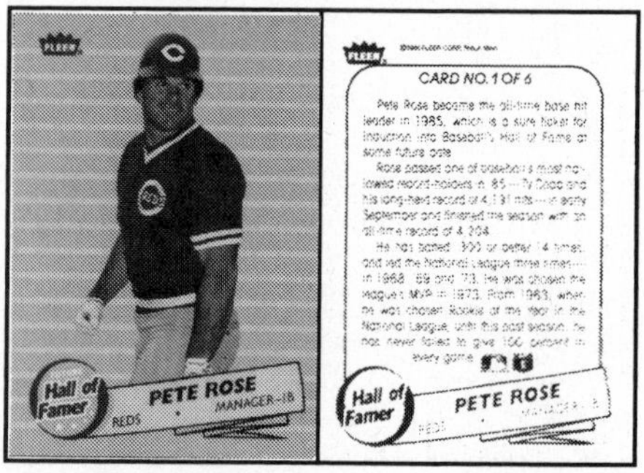

These attractive cards were issued as inserts with the Fleer three-packs. They are the same size as the regular issue (2 1/2" by 3 1/2") and feature players that Fleer predicts will be "Future Hall of Famers." The card backs describe career highlights, records, and honors won by the player. The cards are numbered on the back; Pete Rose is given the honor of being card number 1.

	MINT	EXC	G-VG
COMPLETE SET (6)	9.00	4.50	.90
COMMON PLAYER (1-6)	1.25	.60	.12
☐ 1 Pete Rose Cincinnati Reds	2.00	1.00	.20
☐ 2 Steve Carlton Philadelphia Phillies	1.25	.60	.12
☐ 3 Tom Seaver Chicago White Sox	1.25	.60	.12
☐ 4 Rod Carew California Angels	1.50	.75	.15
☐ 5 Nolan Ryan Houston Astros	3.50	1.75	.35
☐ 6 Reggie Jackson California Angels	1.50	.75	.15

1986 Fleer League Leaders

This 44-card set is also sometimes referred to as the Walgreen's set. Although the set was distributed through Walgreen's, there is no mention on the cards or box of that fact. The cards are easily recognizable by the fact that they contain the phrase "Fleer League Leaders" at the top of the obverse. Both sides of the cards are designed with a blue stripe on white pattern. The checklist for the set is given on the outside of the red, white, blue, and gold box in which the set was packaged. Cards are numbered on the back and measure the standard 2 1/2" by 3 1/2".

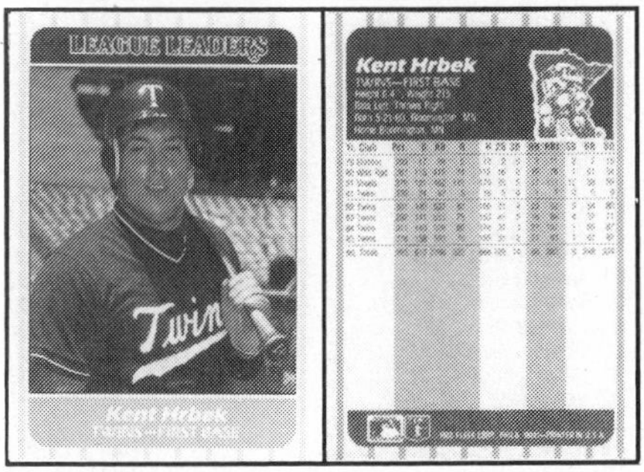

	MINT	EXC	G-VG
COMPLETE SET (44)	5.00	2.50	.50
COMMON PLAYER (1-44)	.10	.05	.01
☐ 1 Wade Boggs	.75	.35	.07
☐ 2 George Brett	.50	.25	.05
☐ 3 Jose Canseco	1.25	.60	.12
☐ 4 Rod Carew	.40	.20	.04
☐ 5 Gary Carter	.20	.10	.02
☐ 6 Jack Clark	.20	.10	.02
☐ 7 Vince Coleman	.40	.20	.04
☐ 8 Jose Cruz	.10	.05	.01
☐ 9 Alvin Davis	.15	.07	.01
☐ 10 Mariano Duncan	.10	.05	.01
☐ 11 Leon Durham	.10	.05	.01
☐ 12 Carlton Fisk	.30	.15	.03
☐ 13 Julio Franco	.10	.05	.01
☐ 14 Scott Garrelts	.10	.05	.01
☐ 15 Steve Garvey	.30	.15	.03
☐ 16 Dwight Gooden	.50	.25	.05
☐ 17 Ozzie Guillen	.25	.12	.02
☐ 18 Willie Hernandez	.10	.05	.01
☐ 19 Bob Horner	.15	.07	.01
☐ 20 Kent Hrbek	.20	.10	.02
☐ 21 Charlie Leibrandt	.10	.05	.01
☐ 22 Don Mattingly	1.00	.50	.10
☐ 23 Oddibe McDowell	.15	.07	.01
☐ 24 Willie McGee	.20	.10	.02
☐ 25 Keith Moreland	.10	.05	.01
☐ 26 Lloyd Moseby	.10	.05	.01
☐ 27 Dale Murphy	.35	.17	.03
☐ 28 Phil Niekro	.20	.10	.02
☐ 29 Joe Orsulak	.10	.05	.01
☐ 30 Dave Parker	.25	.12	.02
☐ 31 Lance Parrish	.15	.07	.01
☐ 32 Kirby Puckett	.60	.30	.06
☐ 33 Tim Raines	.25	.12	.02
☐ 34 Earnie Riles	.10	.05	.01
☐ 35 Cal Ripken	.35	.17	.03
☐ 36 Pete Rose	.60	.30	.06
☐ 37 Bret Saberhagen	.30	.15	.03
☐ 38 Juan Samuel	.15	.07	.01
☐ 39 Ryne Sandberg	.75	.35	.07
☐ 40 Tom Seaver	.35	.17	.03
☐ 41 Lee Smith	.10	.05	.01
☐ 42 Ozzie Smith	.20	.10	.02
☐ 43 Dave Stieb	.15	.07	.01
☐ 44 Robin Yount	.35	.17	.03

1986 Fleer Limited Edition

The 44-card boxed set was produced by Fleer for McCrory's. The cards are standard size 2 1/2" by 3 1/2" and have green and yellow borders. Card backs are printed in red and black on white card stock. Cards are numbered on the back; the back of the original box gives a complete checklist of the players in the set. The set box also contains six logo stickers.

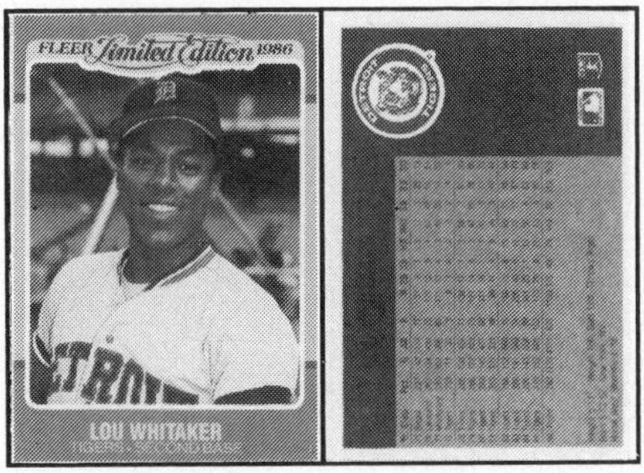

	MINT	EXC	G-VG
COMPLETE SET (44)	5.00	2.50	.50
COMMON PLAYER (1-44)	.10	.05	.01
☐ 1 Doyle Alexander	.10	.05	.01
☐ 2 Joaquin Andujar	.10	.05	.01
☐ 3 Harold Baines	.15	.07	.01
☐ 4 Wade Boggs	.75	.35	.07
☐ 5 Phil Bradley	.15	.07	.01
☐ 6 George Brett	.45	.22	.04
☐ 7 Hubie Brooks	.10	.05	.01
☐ 8 Chris Brown	.10	.05	.01
☐ 9 Tom Brunansky	.15	.07	.01
☐ 10 Gary Carter	.25	.12	.02
☐ 11 Vince Coleman	.40	.20	.04
☐ 12 Cecil Cooper	.15	.07	.01
☐ 13 Jose Cruz	.10	.05	.01
☐ 14 Mike Davis	.10	.05	.01
☐ 15 Carlton Fisk	.30	.15	.03
☐ 16 Julio Franco	.15	.07	.01
☐ 17 Damaso Garcia	.10	.05	.01
☐ 18 Rich Gedman	.10	.05	.01
☐ 19 Kirk Gibson	.35	.17	.03
☐ 20 Dwight Gooden	.50	.25	.05
☐ 21 Pedro Guerrero	.20	.10	.02
☐ 22 Tony Gwynn	.40	.20	.04
☐ 23 Rickey Henderson	.75	.35	.07
☐ 24 Orel Hershiser	.50	.25	.05
☐ 25 LaMarr Hoyt	.10	.05	.01
☐ 26 Reggie Jackson	.60	.30	.06
☐ 27 Don Mattingly	1.00	.50	.10
☐ 28 Oddibe McDowell	.15	.07	.01
☐ 29 Willie McGee	.20	.10	.02
☐ 30 Paul Molitor	.20	.10	.02
☐ 31 Dale Murphy	.35	.17	.03
☐ 32 Eddie Murray	.35	.17	.03
☐ 33 Dave Parker	.25	.12	.02
☐ 34 Tony Pena	.10	.05	.01
☐ 35 Jeff Reardon	.15	.07	.01
☐ 36 Cal Ripken	.35	.17	.03
☐ 37 Pete Rose	.60	.30	.06
☐ 38 Bret Saberhagen	.30	.15	.03
☐ 39 Juan Samuel	.15	.07	.01
☐ 40 Ryne Sandberg	.75	.35	.07
☐ 41 Mike Schmidt	.75	.35	.07
☐ 42 Lee Smith	.10	.05	.01
☐ 43 Don Sutton	.20	.10	.02
☐ 44 Lou Whitaker	.20	.10	.02

1986 Fleer Mini

The Fleer "Classic Miniatures" set consists of 120 small cards with all new pictures of the players as compared to the 1986 Fleer regular issue. The cards are only 1 13/16" by 2 9/16", making them one of the smallest (in size) produced in recent memory. Card backs provide career year-by-year statistics. The complete set was distributed in a red, white, and silver box along with 18 logo stickers. The card numbering is done in team order as is the usual Fleer style.

	MINT	EXC	G-VG
COMPLETE SET (120)	15.00	7.50	1.50
COMMON PLAYER (1-120)	.05	.02	.00

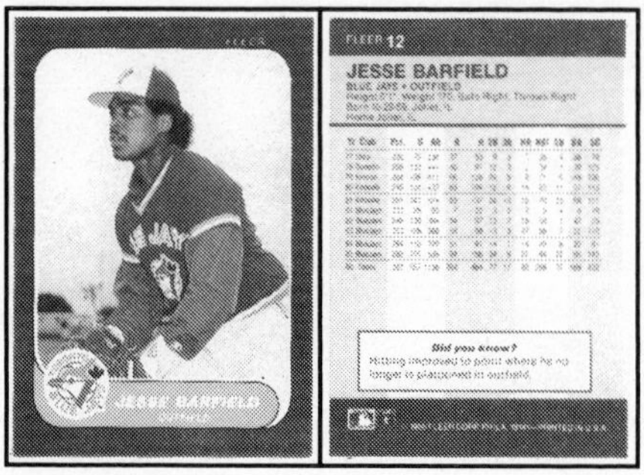

☐ 1 George Brett	.50	.25	.05
☐ 2 Dan Quisenberry	.10	.05	.01
☐ 3 Bret Saberhagen	.30	.15	.03
☐ 4 Lonnie Smith	.10	.05	.01
☐ 5 Willie Wilson	.10	.05	.01
☐ 6 Jack Clark	.20	.10	.02
☐ 7 Vince Coleman	.40	.20	.04
☐ 8 Tom Herr	.05	.02	.00
☐ 9 Willie McGee	.15	.07	.01
☐ 10 Ozzie Smith	.20	.10	.02
☐ 11 John Tudor	.10	.05	.01
☐ 12 Jesse Barfield	.15	.07	.01
☐ 13 George Bell	.25	.12	.02
☐ 14 Tony Fernandez	.15	.07	.01
☐ 15 Damaso Garcia	.05	.02	.00
☐ 16 Dave Stieb	.15	.07	.01
☐ 17 Gary Carter	.20	.10	.02
☐ 18 Ron Darling	.10	.05	.01
☐ 19A Dwight Gooden (R on Mets logo)	1.50	.75	.15
☐ 19B Dwight Gooden (no R on Mets logo)	1.50	.75	.15
☐ 20 Keith Hernandez	.20	.10	.02
☐ 21 Darryl Strawberry	.75	.35	.07
☐ 22 Ron Guidry	.15	.07	.01
☐ 23 Rickey Henderson	1.00	.50	.10
☐ 24 Don Mattingly	1.50	.75	.15
☐ 25 Dave Righetti	.15	.07	.01
☐ 26 Dave Winfield	.20	.10	.02
☐ 27 Mariano Duncan	.05	.02	.00
☐ 28 Pedro Guerrero	.15	.07	.01
☐ 29 Bill Madlock	.05	.02	.00
☐ 30 Mike Marshall	.10	.05	.01
☐ 31 Fernando Valenzuela	.15	.07	.01
☐ 32 Reggie Jackson	.40	.20	.04
☐ 33 Gary Pettis	.05	.02	.00
☐ 34 Ron Romanick	.05	.02	.00
☐ 35 Don Sutton	.15	.07	.01
☐ 36 Mike Witt	.05	.02	.00
☐ 37 Buddy Bell	.10	.05	.01
☐ 38 Tom Browning	.10	.05	.01
☐ 39 Dave Parker	.20	.10	.02
☐ 40 Pete Rose	.75	.35	.07
☐ 41 Mario Soto	.05	.02	.00
☐ 42 Harold Baines	.10	.05	.01
☐ 43 Carlton Fisk	.30	.15	.03
☐ 44 Ozzie Guillen	.20	.10	.02
☐ 45 Ron Kittle	.10	.05	.01
☐ 46 Tom Seaver	.25	.12	.02
☐ 47 Kirk Gibson	.25	.12	.02
☐ 48 Jack Morris	.10	.05	.01
☐ 49 Lance Parrish	.10	.05	.01
☐ 50 Alan Trammell	.15	.07	.01
☐ 51 Lou Whitaker	.15	.07	.01
☐ 52 Hubie Brooks	.10	.05	.01
☐ 53 Andre Dawson	.25	.12	.02
☐ 54 Tim Raines	.20	.10	.02
☐ 55 Bryn Smith	.05	.02	.00
☐ 56 Tim Wallach	.10	.05	.01
☐ 57 Mike Boddicker	.05	.02	.00
☐ 58 Eddie Murray	.30	.15	.03
☐ 59 Cal Ripken	.35	.17	.03
☐ 60 John Shelby	.05	.02	.00
☐ 61 Mike Young	.05	.02	.00
☐ 62 Jose Cruz	.05	.02	.00
☐ 63 Glenn Davis	.35	.17	.03
☐ 64 Phil Garner	.05	.02	.00
☐ 65 Nolan Ryan	1.50	.75	.15
☐ 66 Mike Scott	.15	.07	.01
☐ 67 Steve Garvey	.20	.10	.02
☐ 68 Goose Gossage	.10	.05	.01
☐ 69 Tony Gwynn	.30	.15	.03
☐ 70 Andy Hawkins	.05	.02	.00
☐ 71 Garry Templeton	.05	.02	.00
☐ 72 Wade Boggs	.90	.45	.09
☐ 73 Roger Clemens	.90	.45	.09
☐ 74 Dwight Evans	.15	.07	.01
☐ 75 Rich Gedman	.05	.02	.00
☐ 76 Jim Rice	.20	.10	.02
☐ 77 Shawon Dunston	.25	.12	.02
☐ 78 Leon Durham	.05	.02	.00
☐ 79 Keith Moreland	.05	.02	.00
☐ 80 Ryne Sandberg	.75	.35	.07
☐ 81 Rick Sutcliffe	.10	.05	.01
☐ 82 Bert Blyleven	.15	.07	.01
☐ 83 Tom Brunansky	.10	.05	.01
☐ 84 Kent Hrbek	.15	.07	.01
☐ 85 Kirby Puckett	.50	.25	.05
☐ 86 Bruce Bochte	.05	.02	.00
☐ 87 Jose Canseco	3.00	1.50	.30
☐ 88 Mike Davis	.05	.02	.00
☐ 89 Jay Howell	.05	.02	.00
☐ 90 Dwayne Murphy	.05	.02	.00
☐ 91 Steve Carlton	.25	.12	.02
☐ 92 Von Hayes	.10	.05	.01
☐ 93 Juan Samuel	.10	.05	.01
☐ 94 Mike Schmidt	.75	.35	.07
☐ 95 Glenn Wilson	.05	.02	.00
☐ 96 Phil Bradley	.10	.05	.01
☐ 97 Alvin Davis	.10	.05	.01
☐ 98 Jim Presley	.05	.02	.00
☐ 99 Danny Tartabull	.20	.10	.02
☐ 100 Cecil Cooper	.10	.05	.01
☐ 101 Paul Molitor	.15	.07	.01
☐ 102 Ernie Riles	.05	.02	.00
☐ 103 Robin Yount	.50	.25	.05
☐ 104 Bob Horner	.10	.05	.01
☐ 105 Dale Murphy	.30	.15	.03
☐ 106 Bruce Sutter	.10	.05	.01
☐ 107 Claudell Washington	.05	.02	.00
☐ 108 Chris Brown	.05	.02	.00
☐ 109 Chili Davis	.05	.02	.00
☐ 110 Scott Garrelts	.05	.02	.00
☐ 111 Oddibe McDowell	.10	.05	.01
☐ 112 Pete O'Brien	.10	.05	.01
☐ 113 Gary Ward	.05	.02	.00
☐ 114 Brett Butler	.15	.07	.01
☐ 115 Julio Franco	.10	.05	.01
☐ 116 Brook Jacoby	.10	.05	.01
☐ 117 Mike Brown OF	.05	.02	.00
☐ 118 Joe Orsulak	.05	.02	.00
☐ 119 Tony Pena	.10	.05	.01
☐ 120 R.J. Reynolds	.05	.02	.00

1986 Fleer Sluggers/Pitchers

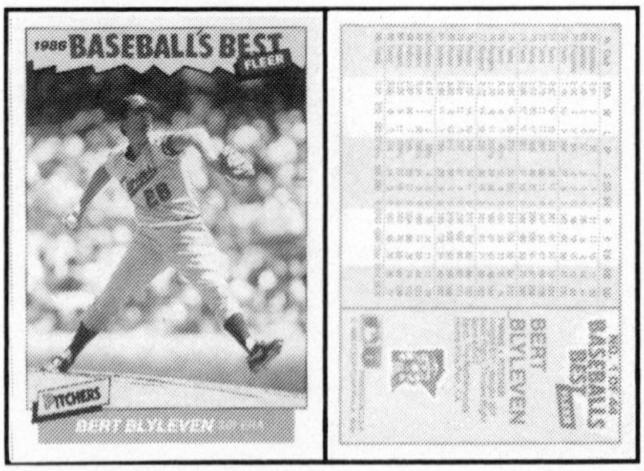

Fleer produced this 44-card boxed set although it was primarily distributed by Kress, McCrory, Newberry, T.G.Y., and other similar stores. The set features 22 sluggers and 22 pitchers and is subtitled "Baseball's Best". Cards are standard-size, 2 1/2" by 3 1/2", and were packaged in a red, white, blue, and yellow custom box along with six logo stickers. The set checklist is given on the back of the box.

	MINT	EXC	G-VG
COMPLETE SET (44)	7.50	3.75	.75
COMMON PLAYER (1-44)	.10	.05	.01

☐ 1 Bert Blyleven	.15	.07	.01
☐ 2 Wade Boggs	.75	.35	.07
☐ 3 George Brett	.45	.22	.04
☐ 4 Tom Browning	.10	.05	.01
☐ 5 Jose Canseco	2.50	1.25	.25
☐ 6 Will Clark	2.00	1.00	.20
☐ 7 Roger Clemens	.75	.35	.07
☐ 8 Alvin Davis	.15	.07	.01
☐ 9 Julio Franco	.15	.07	.01
☐ 10 Kirk Gibson	.30	.15	.03
☐ 11 Dwight Gooden	.50	.25	.05
☐ 12 Goose Gossage	.15	.07	.01
☐ 13 Pedro Guerrero	.20	.10	.02
☐ 14 Ron Guidry	.15	.07	.01
☐ 15 Tony Gwynn	.35	.17	.03
☐ 16 Orel Hershiser	.45	.22	.04
☐ 17 Kent Hrbek	.20	.10	.02
☐ 18 Reggie Jackson	.40	.20	.04
☐ 19 Wally Joyner	.90	.45	.09
☐ 20 Charlie Leibrandt	.10	.05	.01
☐ 21 Don Mattingly	.90	.45	.09
☐ 22 Willie McGee	.20	.10	.02
☐ 23 Jack Morris	.15	.07	.01
☐ 24 Dale Murphy	.35	.17	.03
☐ 25 Eddie Murray	.35	.17	.03
☐ 26 Jeff Reardon	.10	.05	.01
☐ 27 Rick Reuschel	.15	.07	.01
☐ 28 Cal Ripken	.30	.15	.03
☐ 29 Pete Rose	.60	.30	.06
☐ 30 Nolan Ryan	1.25	.60	.12
☐ 31 Bret Saberhagen	.30	.15	.03
☐ 32 Ryne Sandberg	.25	.12	.02
☐ 33 Mike Schmidt	.75	.35	.07
☐ 34 Tom Seaver	.35	.17	.03
☐ 35 Bryn Smith	.10	.05	.01
☐ 36 Mario Soto	.10	.05	.01
☐ 37 Dave Stieb	.15	.07	.01
☐ 38 Darryl Strawberry	.60	.30	.06
☐ 39 Rick Sutcliffe	.15	.07	.01
☐ 40 John Tudor	.15	.07	.01
☐ 41 Fernando Valenzuela	.20	.10	.02
☐ 42 Bobby Witt	.30	.15	.03
☐ 43 Mike Witt	.10	.05	.01
☐ 44 Robin Yount	.35	.17	.03

1986 Fleer Slug/Pitch Box Cards

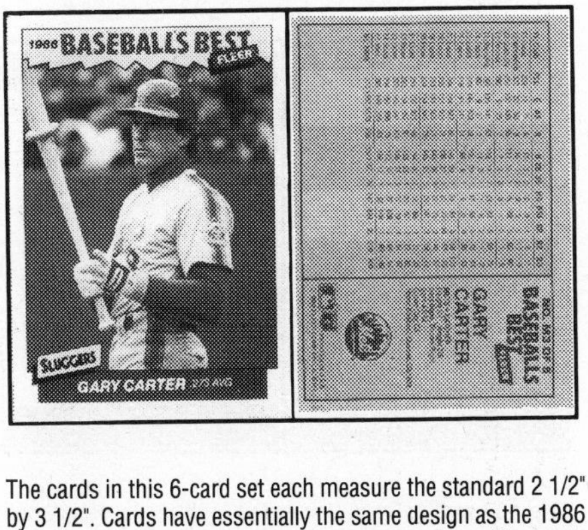

The cards in this 6-card set each measure the standard 2 1/2" by 3 1/2". Cards have essentially the same design as the 1986 Fleer Sluggers vs. Pitchers set of Baseball's Best. The cards were printed on the bottom of the counter display box which held 24 small boxed sets; hence theoretically these box cards are 1/24 as plentiful as the regular boxed set cards. These 6 cards, numbered M1 to M5 with one blank-back (unnumbered) card, are considered a separate set in their own right and are not typically included in a complete set of the 1986 Fleer Sluggers vs. Pitchers set of 44. The value of the panels uncut is slightly greater, perhaps by 25 percent greater, than the value of the individual cards cut up carefully.

	MINT	EXC	G-VG
COMPLETE SET	3.00	1.50	.30
COMMON PLAYERS	.10	.05	.01

☐ M1 Harold Baines	.20	.10	.02
☐ M2 Steve Carlton	.80	.40	.08
☐ M3 Gary Carter	.50	.25	.05
☐ M4 Vince Coleman	1.00	.50	.10
☐ M5 Kirby Puckett	1.25	.60	.12
☐ xx Team Logo (unnumbered, blank back)	.10	.05	.01

1986 Fleer Sticker Cards

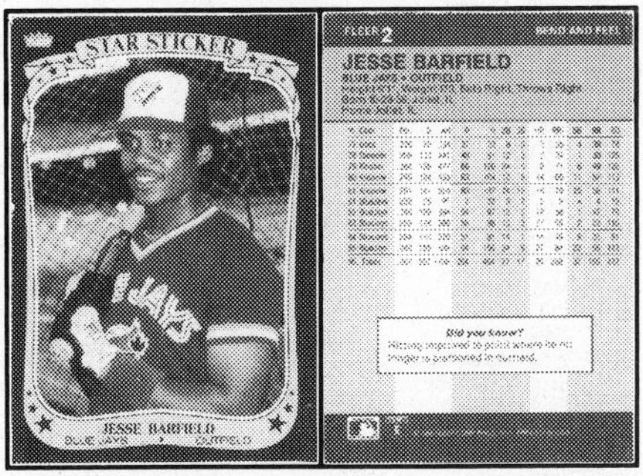

The stickers in this 132-sticker card set are standard card size, 2 1/2" by 3 1/2". The card photo on the front is surrounded by a yellow border and a cranberry frame. The backs are printed in blue and black on white card stock. The backs contain year-by-year statistical information. They are numbered on the back in the upper left-hand corner.

	MINT	EXC	G-VG
COMPLETE SET (132)	30.00	15.00	3.00
COMMON PLAYER (1-132)	.05	.02	.00

☐ 1 Harold Baines	.15	.07	.01
☐ 2 Jesse Barfield	.15	.07	.01
☐ 3 Don Baylor	.10	.05	.01
☐ 4 Juan Beniquez	.05	.02	.00
☐ 5 Tim Birtsas	.05	.02	.00
☐ 6 Bert Blyleven	.15	.07	.01
☐ 7 Bruce Bochte	.05	.02	.00
☐ 8 Wade Boggs	1.25	.60	.12
☐ 9 Dennis Boyd	.10	.05	.01
☐ 10 Phil Bradley	.10	.05	.01
☐ 11 George Brett	.90	.45	.09
☐ 12 Hubie Brooks	.10	.05	.01
☐ 13 Chris Brown	.05	.02	.00
☐ 14 Tom Browning	.15	.07	.01
☐ 15 Tom Brunansky	.15	.07	.01
☐ 16 Bill Buckner	.10	.05	.01
☐ 17 Britt Burns	.05	.02	.00
☐ 18 Brett Butler	.15	.07	.01
☐ 19 Jose Canseco	3.50	1.75	.35
☐ 20 Rod Carew	.50	.25	.05
☐ 21 Steve Carlton	.40	.20	.04
☐ 22 Don Carman	.10	.05	.01
☐ 23 Gary Carter	.30	.15	.03
☐ 24 Jack Clark	.20	.10	.02
☐ 25 Vince Coleman	1.50	.75	.15
☐ 26 Cecil Cooper	.10	.05	.01
☐ 27 Jose Cruz	.05	.02	.00
☐ 28 Ron Darling	.15	.07	.01
☐ 29 Alvin Davis	.20	.10	.02
☐ 30 Jody Davis	.05	.02	.00
☐ 31 Mike Davis	.05	.02	.00
☐ 32 Andre Dawson	.30	.15	.03
☐ 33 Mariano Duncan	.10	.05	.01
☐ 34 Shawon Dunston	.25	.12	.02
☐ 35 Leon Durham	.05	.02	.00
☐ 36 Darrell Evans	.10	.05	.01
☐ 37 Tony Fernandez	.15	.07	.01
☐ 38 Carlton Fisk	.35	.17	.03
☐ 39 John Franco	.10	.05	.01
☐ 40 Julio Franco	.10	.05	.01
☐ 41 Damaso Garcia	.05	.02	.00
☐ 42 Scott Garrelts	.10	.05	.01
☐ 43 Steve Garvey	.40	.20	.04

☐ 44 Rich Gedman	.05	.02	.00
☐ 45 Kirk Gibson	.35	.17	.03
☐ 46 Dwight Gooden	1.00	.50	.10
☐ 47 Pedro Guerrero	.20	.10	.02
☐ 48 Ron Guidry	.15	.07	.01
☐ 49 Ozzie Guillen	.35	.17	.03
☐ 50 Tony Gwynn	.45	.22	.04
☐ 51 Andy Hawkins	.05	.02	.00
☐ 52 Von Hayes	.10	.05	.01
☐ 53 Rickey Henderson	1.50	.75	.15
☐ 54 Tom Henke	.10	.05	.01
☐ 55 Keith Hernandez	.25	.12	.02
☐ 56 Willie Hernandez	.05	.02	.00
☐ 57 Tommy Herr	.05	.02	.00
☐ 58 Orel Hershiser	.50	.25	.05
☐ 59 Teddy Higuera	.40	.20	.04
☐ 60 Bob Horner	.10	.05	.01
☐ 61 Charlie Hough	.05	.02	.00
☐ 62 Jay Howell	.05	.02	.00
☐ 63 LaMarr Hoyt	.05	.02	.00
☐ 64 Kent Hrbek	.20	.10	.02
☐ 65 Reggie Jackson	.50	.25	.05
☐ 66 Bob James	.05	.02	.00
☐ 67 Dave Kingman	.10	.05	.01
☐ 68 Ron Kittle	.10	.05	.01
☐ 69 Charlie Leibrandt	.05	.02	.00
☐ 70 Fred Lynn	.15	.07	.01
☐ 71 Mike Marshall	.15	.07	.01
☐ 72 Don Mattingly	2.00	1.00	.20
☐ 73 Oddibe McDowell	.10	.05	.01
☐ 74 Willie McGee	.20	.10	.02
☐ 75 Scott McGregor	.05	.02	.00
☐ 76 Paul Molitor	.20	.10	.02
☐ 77 Charlie Moore	.05	.02	.00
☐ 78 Keith Moreland	.05	.02	.00
☐ 79 Jack Morris	.15	.07	.01
☐ 80 Dale Murphy	.50	.25	.05
☐ 81 Eddie Murray	.50	.25	.05
☐ 82 Phil Niekro	.25	.12	.02
☐ 83 Joe Orsulak	.05	.02	.00
☐ 84 Dave Parker	.20	.10	.02
☐ 85 Lance Parrish	.15	.07	.01
☐ 86 Larry Parrish	.05	.02	.00
☐ 87 Tony Pena	.10	.05	.01
☐ 88 Gary Pettis	.10	.05	.01
☐ 89 Jim Presley	.10	.05	.01
☐ 90 Kirby Puckett	1.00	.50	.10
☐ 91 Dan Quisenberry	.10	.05	.01
☐ 92 Tim Raines	.20	.10	.02
☐ 93 Johnny Ray	.10	.05	.01
☐ 94 Jeff Reardon	.10	.05	.01
☐ 95 Rick Reuschel	.15	.07	.01
☐ 96 Jim Rice	.20	.10	.02
☐ 97 Dave Righetti	.15	.07	.01
☐ 98 Earnie Riles	.05	.02	.00
☐ 99 Cal Ripken	.50	.25	.05
☐ 100 Ron Romanick	.05	.02	.00
☐ 101 Pete Rose	1.00	.50	.10
☐ 102 Nolan Ryan	2.00	1.00	.20
☐ 103 Bret Saberhagen	.50	.25	.05
☐ 104 Mark Salas	.05	.02	.00
☐ 105 Juan Samuel	.15	.07	.01
☐ 106 Ryne Sandberg	1.00	.50	.10
☐ 107 Mike Schmidt	1.25	.60	.12
☐ 108 Mike Scott	.20	.10	.02
☐ 109 Tom Seaver	.40	.20	.04
☐ 110 Bryn Smith	.05	.02	.00
☐ 111 Dave Smith	.05	.02	.00
☐ 112 Lonnie Smith	.10	.05	.01
☐ 113 Ozzie Smith	.30	.15	.03
☐ 114 Mario Soto	.05	.02	.00
☐ 115 Dave Stieb	.15	.07	.01
☐ 116 Darryl Strawberry	.90	.45	.09
☐ 117 Bruce Sutter	.10	.05	.01
☐ 118 Garry Templeton	.05	.02	.00
☐ 119 Gorman Thomas	.10	.05	.01
☐ 120 Andre Thornton	.05	.02	.00
☐ 121 Alan Trammell	.25	.12	.02
☐ 122 John Tudor	.15	.07	.01
☐ 123 Fernando Valenzuela	.20	.10	.02
☐ 124 Frank Viola	.25	.12	.02
☐ 125 Gary Ward	.05	.02	.00
☐ 126 Lou Whitaker	.15	.07	.01
☐ 127 Frank White	.05	.02	.00
☐ 128 Glenn Wilson	.05	.02	.00
☐ 129 Willie Wilson	.15	.07	.01
☐ 130 Dave Winfield	.30	.15	.03
☐ 131 Robin Yount	.50	.25	.05
☐ 132 Checklist Card Dwight Gooden Dale Murphy	1.25	.60	.12

1986 Fleer Sticker Wax Box

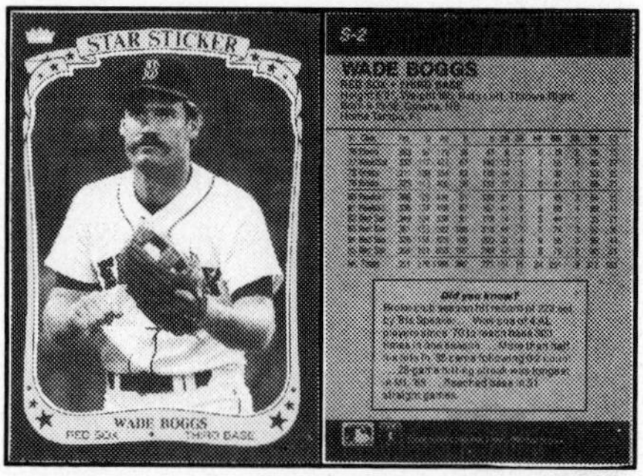

The bottoms of the Star Sticker wax boxes contained a set of four cards done in a similar format to the stickers; these cards (they are not stickers but truly cards) are numbered with the prefix S and are considered a separate set. Each individual card measures 2 1/2" by 3 1/2". The value of the panel uncut is slightly greater, perhaps by 25 percent greater, than the value of the individual cards cut up carefully.

	MINT	EXC	G-VG
COMPLETE SET (4)	2.00	1.00	.20
COMMON PLAYER (S1-S4)	.10	.05	.01
☐ S1 Team Logo (checklist back)	.10	.05	.01
☐ S2 Wade Boggs	1.25	.60	.12
☐ S3 Steve Garvey	.40	.20	.04
☐ S4 Dave Winfield	.40	.20	.04

1986 Fleer Update

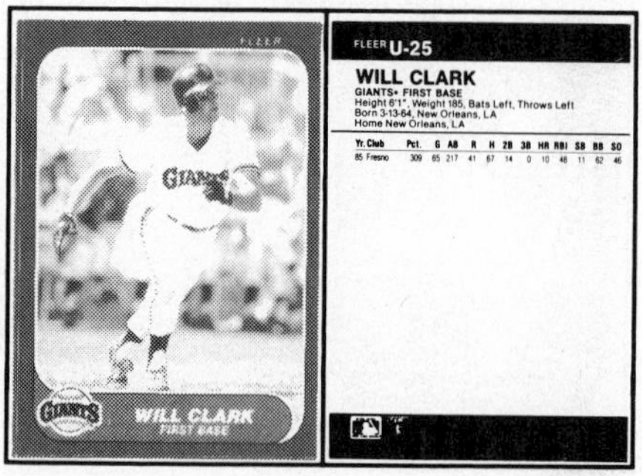

This 132-card set was distributed by Fleer to dealers as a complete set in a custom box. In addition to the complete set of 132 cards, the box also contains 25 Team Logo Stickers. The card fronts look very similar to the 1986 Fleer regular issue. The cards are numbered (with a U prefix) alphabetically according to player's last name. Cards measure the standard size, 2 1/2" by 3 1/2". The key (extended) rookie cards in this set are Barry Bonds, Bobby Bonilla, Will Clark, Kevin Mitchell, and Ruben Sierra.

	MINT	EXC	G-VG
COMPLETE SET (132)	35.00	17.50	3.50
COMMON PLAYER (1-132)	.07	.03	.01
☐ U1 Mike Aldrete	.15	.07	.01
☐ U2 Andy Allanson	.10	.05	.01
☐ U3 Neil Allen	.07	.03	.01

☐ U4 Joaquin Andujar	.10	.05	.01
☐ U5 Paul Assenmacher	.12	.06	.01
☐ U6 Scott Bailes	.12	.06	.01
☐ U7 Jay Baller	.10	.05	.01
☐ U8 Scott Bankhead	.30	.15	.03
☐ U9 Bill Bathe	.10	.05	.01
☐ U10 Don Baylor	.10	.05	.01
☐ U11 Billy Beane	.10	.05	.01
☐ U12 Steve Bedrosian	.12	.06	.01
☐ U13 Juan Beniquez	.07	.03	.01
☐ U14 Barry Bonds	6.00	3.00	.60
☐ U15 Bobby Bonilla UER (wrong birthday)	4.00	2.00	.40
☐ U16 Rich Bordi	.07	.03	.01
☐ U17 Bill Campbell	.07	.03	.01
☐ U18 Tom Candiotti	.10	.05	.01
☐ U19 John Cangelosi	.10	.05	.01
☐ U20 Jose Canseco UER (headings on back for a pitcher)	12.00	6.00	1.20
☐ U21 Chuck Cary	.15	.07	.01
☐ U22 Juan Castillo	.10	.05	.01
☐ U23 Rick Cerone	.07	.03	.01
☐ U24 John Cerutti	.15	.07	.01
☐ U25 Will Clark	11.00	5.50	1.10
☐ U26 Mark Clear	.07	.03	.01
☐ U27 Darnell Coles	.10	.05	.01
☐ U28 Dave Collins	.07	.03	.01
☐ U29 Tim Conroy	.07	.03	.01
☐ U30 Ed Correa	.12	.06	.01
☐ U31 Joe Cowley	.07	.03	.01
☐ U32 Bill Dawley	.07	.03	.01
☐ U33 Rob Deer	.18	.09	.01
☐ U34 John Denny	.07	.03	.01
☐ U35 Jim Deshaies	.25	.12	.02
☐ U36 Doug Drabek	1.25	.60	.12
☐ U37 Mike Easler	.07	.03	.01
☐ U38 Mark Eichhorn	.07	.03	.01
☐ U39 Dave Engle	.07	.03	.01
☐ U40 Mike Fischlin	.07	.03	.01
☐ U41 Scott Fletcher	.07	.03	.01
☐ U42 Terry Forster	.10	.05	.01
☐ U43 Terry Francona	.07	.03	.01
☐ U44 Andres Galarraga	.65	.30	.06
☐ U45 Lee Guetterman	.15	.07	.01
☐ U46 Bill Gullickson	.07	.03	.01
☐ U47 Jackie Gutierrez	.07	.03	.01
☐ U48 Moose Haas	.07	.03	.01
☐ U49 Billy Hatcher	.25	.12	.02
☐ U50 Mike Heath	.07	.03	.01
☐ U51 Guy Hoffman	.07	.03	.01
☐ U52 Tom Hume	.07	.03	.01
☐ U53 Pete Incaviglia	1.00	.50	.10
☐ U54 Dane Iorg	.07	.03	.01
☐ U55 Chris James	1.25	.60	.12
☐ U56 Stan Javier	.40	.20	.04
☐ U57 Tommy John	.15	.07	.01
☐ U58 Tracy Jones	.20	.10	.02
☐ U59 Wally Joyner	2.00	1.00	.20
☐ U60 Wayne Krenchicki	.07	.03	.01
☐ U61 John Kruk	.45	.22	.04
☐ U62 Mike LaCoss	.07	.03	.01
☐ U63 Pete Ladd	.07	.03	.01
☐ U64 Dave LaPoint	.07	.03	.01
☐ U65 Mike LaValliere	.25	.12	.02
☐ U66 Rudy Law	.07	.03	.01
☐ U67 Dennis Leonard	.10	.05	.01
☐ U68 Steve Lombardozzi	.10	.05	.01
☐ U69 Aurelio Lopez	.07	.03	.01
☐ U70 Mickey Mahler	.07	.03	.01
☐ U71 Candy Maldonado	.15	.07	.01
☐ U72 Roger Mason	.10	.05	.01
☐ U73 Greg Mathews	.15	.07	.01
☐ U74 Andy McGaffigan	.07	.03	.01
☐ U75 Joel McKeon	.10	.05	.01
☐ U76 Kevin Mitchell	6.00	3.00	.60
☐ U77 Bill Mooneyham	.07	.03	.01
☐ U78 Omar Moreno	.07	.03	.01
☐ U79 Jerry Mumphrey	.07	.03	.01
☐ U80 Al Newman	.10	.05	.01
☐ U81 Phil Niekro	.35	.17	.03
☐ U82 Randy Niemann	.07	.03	.01
☐ U83 Juan Nieves	.10	.05	.01
☐ U84 Bob Ojeda	.10	.05	.01
☐ U85 Rick Ownbey	.07	.03	.01
☐ U86 Tom Paciorek	.07	.03	.01
☐ U87 David Palmer	.07	.03	.01
☐ U88 Jeff Parrett	.20	.10	.02
☐ U89 Pat Perry	.10	.05	.01
☐ U90 Dan Plesac	.20	.10	.02
☐ U91 Darrell Porter	.07	.03	.01
☐ U92 Luis Quinones	.12	.06	.01
☐ U93 Rey Quinones	.10	.05	.01
☐ U94 Gary Redus	.07	.03	.01
☐ U95 Jeff Reed	.07	.03	.01
☐ U96 Bip Roberts	.60	.30	.06
☐ U97 Billy Jo Robidoux	.10	.05	.01
☐ U98 Gary Roenicke	.07	.03	.01
☐ U99 Ron Roenicke	.07	.03	.01
☐ U100 Angel Salazar	.07	.03	.01
☐ U101 Joe Sambito	.07	.03	.01
☐ U102 Billy Sample	.07	.03	.01
☐ U103 Dave Schmidt	.10	.05	.01
☐ U104 Ken Schrom	.07	.03	.01
☐ U105 Ruben Sierra	7.50	3.75	.75
☐ U106 Ted Simmons	.20	.10	.02
☐ U107 Sammy Stewart	.07	.03	.01
☐ U108 Kurt Stillwell	.45	.22	.04
☐ U109 Dale Sveum	.15	.07	.01
☐ U110 Tim Teufel	.10	.05	.01
☐ U111 Bob Tewksbury	.12	.06	.01
☐ U112 Andres Thomas	.15	.07	.01
☐ U113 Jason Thompson	.07	.03	.01
☐ U114 Milt Thompson	.10	.05	.01
☐ U115 Robby Thompson	.30	.15	.03
☐ U116 Jay Tibbs	.07	.03	.01
☐ U117 Fred Toliver	.10	.05	.01
☐ U118 Wayne Tolleson	.07	.03	.01
☐ U119 Alex Trevino	.07	.03	.01
☐ U120 Manny Trillo	.07	.03	.01
☐ U121 Ed VandeBerg	.07	.03	.01
☐ U122 Ozzie Virgil	.07	.03	.01
☐ U123 Tony Walker	.10	.05	.01
☐ U124 Gene Walter	.10	.05	.01
☐ U125 Duane Ward	.15	.07	.01
☐ U126 Jerry Willard	.07	.03	.01
☐ U127 Mitch Williams	.35	.17	.03
☐ U128 Reggie Williams	.10	.05	.01
☐ U129 Bobby Witt	.90	.45	.09
☐ U130 Marvell Wynne	.07	.03	.01
☐ U131 Steve Yeager	.07	.03	.01
☐ U132 Checklist 1-132	.07	.01	.00

1987 Fleer

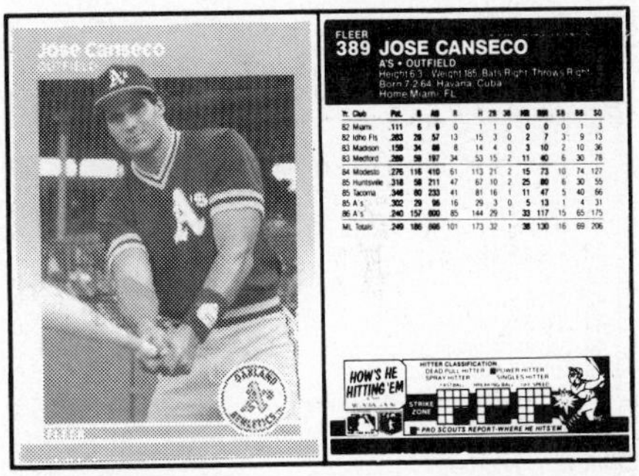

This 660-card set features a distinctive blue border, which fades to white on the card fronts. The backs are printed in blue, red, and pink on white card stock. The bottom of the card back shows an innovative graph of the player's ability, e.g., "He's got the stuff" for pitchers and "How he's hitting 'em," for hitters. Cards are numbered on the back and are again the standard 2 1/2" by 3 1/2". Cards are again organized numerically by teams, i.e., World Champion Mets (1-25), Boston Red Sox (26-48), Houston Astros (49-72), California Angels (73-95), New York Yankees (96-120), Texas Rangers (121-143), Detroit Tigers (144-168), Philadelphia Phillies (169-192), Cincinnati Reds (193-218), Toronto Blue Jays (219-240), Cleveland Indians (241-263), San Francisco Giants (264-288), St. Louis Cardinals (289-312), Montreal Expos (313-337), Milwaukee Brewers (338-361), Kansas City Royals (362-384), Oakland A's (385-410), San Diego Padres (411-435), Los Angeles Dodgers (436-460), Baltimore Orioles (461-483), Chicago White Sox (484-508), Atlanta Braves (509-532), Minnesota Twins (533-554), Chicago Cubs (555-578), Seattle Mariners (579-600), and Pittsburgh Pirates (601-624). The last 36 cards in the set consist of Specials (625-643), Rookie Pairs (644-653), and checklists (654-660). The key rookie cards in this set are Barry Bonds, Bobby Bonilla, Will Clark, Bo Jackson, Barry Larkin, Dave Magadan, Kevin Mitchell, Kevin Seitzer, and Ruben Sierra. Fleer also produced a "limited" edition version of this set with glossy coating and packaged in a "tin." However, this tin set was apparently not limited enough (estimated between 75,000 and 100,000 1987 tin sets produced by Fleer), since the price of the "tin" glossy cards is now the same as the regular set.

	MINT	EXC	G-VG
COMPLETE SET (660)	110.00	55.00	11.00
COMMON PLAYER (1-660)	.06	.03	.00
☐ 1 Rick Aguilera	.10	.05	.01
☐ 2 Richard Anderson	.06	.03	.00
☐ 3 Wally Backman	.06	.03	.00
☐ 4 Gary Carter	.25	.12	.02
☐ 5 Ron Darling	.18	.09	.01
☐ 6 Len Dykstra	.75	.35	.07
☐ 7 Kevin Elster	.60	.30	.06
☐ 8 Sid Fernandez	.15	.07	.01
☐ 9 Dwight Gooden	1.00	.50	.10
☐ 10 Ed Hearn	.06	.03	.00
☐ 11 Danny Heep	.06	.03	.00
☐ 12 Keith Hernandez	.25	.12	.02
☐ 13 Howard Johnson	.35	.17	.03
☐ 14 Ray Knight	.10	.05	.01
☐ 15 Lee Mazzilli	.06	.03	.00
☐ 16 Roger McDowell	.10	.05	.01
☐ 17 Kevin Mitchell	9.00	4.50	.90
☐ 18 Randy Niemann	.06	.03	.00
☐ 19 Bob Ojeda	.10	.05	.01
☐ 20 Jesse Orosco	.06	.03	.00
☐ 21 Rafael Santana	.06	.03	.00
☐ 22 Doug Sisk	.06	.03	.00
☐ 23 Darryl Strawberry	1.25	.60	.12
☐ 24 Tim Teufel	.06	.03	.00
☐ 25 Mookie Wilson	.10	.05	.01
☐ 26 Tony Armas	.06	.03	.00
☐ 27 Marty Barrett	.10	.05	.01
☐ 28 Don Baylor	.10	.05	.01
☐ 29 Wade Boggs	1.50	.75	.15
☐ 30 Oil Can Boyd	.10	.05	.01
☐ 31 Bill Buckner	.10	.05	.01
☐ 32 Roger Clemens	2.50	1.25	.25
☐ 33 Steve Crawford	.06	.03	.00
☐ 34 Dwight Evans	.18	.09	.01
☐ 35 Rich Gedman	.06	.03	.00
☐ 36 Dave Henderson	.10	.05	.01
☐ 37 Bruce Hurst	.12	.06	.01
☐ 38 Tim Lollar	.06	.03	.00
☐ 39 Al Nipper	.06	.03	.00
☐ 40 Spike Owen	.06	.03	.00
☐ 41 Jim Rice	.15	.07	.01
☐ 42 Ed Romero	.06	.03	.00
☐ 43 Joe Sambito	.06	.03	.00
☐ 44 Calvin Schiraldi	.06	.03	.00
☐ 45 Tom Seaver	.40	.20	.04
☐ 46 Jeff Sellers	.10	.05	.01
☐ 47 Bob Stanley	.06	.03	.00
☐ 48 Sammy Stewart	.06	.03	.00
☐ 49 Larry Andersen	.06	.03	.00
☐ 50 Alan Ashby	.06	.03	.00
☐ 51 Kevin Bass	.10	.05	.01
☐ 52 Jeff Calhoun	.06	.03	.00
☐ 53 Jose Cruz	.10	.05	.01
☐ 54 Danny Darwin	.10	.05	.01
☐ 55 Glenn Davis	.45	.22	.04
☐ 56 Jim Deshaies	.25	.12	.02
☐ 57 Bill Doran	.10	.05	.01
☐ 58 Phil Garner	.06	.03	.00
☐ 59 Billy Hatcher	.12	.06	.01
☐ 60 Charlie Kerfeld	.06	.03	.00
☐ 61 Bob Knepper	.06	.03	.00
☐ 62 Dave Lopes	.10	.05	.01
☐ 63 Aurelio Lopez	.06	.03	.00
☐ 64 Jim Pankovits	.06	.03	.00
☐ 65 Terry Puhl	.06	.03	.00
☐ 66 Craig Reynolds	.06	.03	.00
☐ 67 Nolan Ryan	1.75	.85	.17
☐ 68 Mike Scott	.20	.10	.02
☐ 69 Dave Smith	.06	.03	.00
☐ 70 Dickie Thon	.06	.03	.00
☐ 71 Tony Walker	.06	.03	.00
☐ 72 Denny Walling	.06	.03	.00
☐ 73 Bob Boone	.12	.06	.01
☐ 74 Rick Burleson	.10	.05	.01
☐ 75 John Candelaria	.06	.03	.00
☐ 76 Doug Corbett	.06	.03	.00
☐ 77 Doug DeCinces	.10	.05	.01
☐ 78 Brian Downing	.10	.05	.01
☐ 79 Chuck Finley	2.25	1.10	.22
☐ 80 Terry Forster	.10	.05	.01
☐ 81 Bob Grich	.10	.05	.01
☐ 82 George Hendrick	.06	.03	.00
☐ 83 Jack Howell	.10	.05	.01
☐ 84 Reggie Jackson	.50	.25	.05
☐ 85 Ruppert Jones	.06	.03	.00
☐ 86 Wally Joyner	2.00	1.00	.20
☐ 87 Gary Lucas	.06	.03	.00
☐ 88 Kirk McCaskill	.10	.05	.01
☐ 89 Donnie Moore	.06	.03	.00
☐ 90 Gary Pettis	.06	.03	.00
☐ 91 Vern Ruhle	.06	.03	.00
☐ 92 Dick Schofield	.06	.03	.00
☐ 93 Don Sutton	.15	.07	.01
☐ 94 Rob Wilfong	.06	.03	.00
☐ 95 Mike Witt	.10	.05	.01
☐ 96 Doug Drabek	3.00	1.50	.30
☐ 97 Mike Easler	.06	.03	.00
☐ 98 Mike Fischlin	.06	.03	.00
☐ 99 Brian Fisher	.06	.03	.00
☐ 100 Ron Guidry	.12	.06	.01
☐ 101 Rickey Henderson	1.50	.75	.15
☐ 102 Tommy John	.15	.07	.01
☐ 103 Ron Kittle	.10	.05	.01
☐ 104 Don Mattingly	3.00	1.50	.30
☐ 105 Bobby Meacham	.06	.03	.00
☐ 106 Joe Niekro	.10	.05	.01
☐ 107 Mike Pagliarulo	.10	.05	.01
☐ 108 Dan Pasqua	.10	.05	.01
☐ 109 Willie Randolph	.10	.05	.01
☐ 110 Dennis Rasmussen	.10	.05	.01
☐ 111 Dave Righetti	.12	.06	.01
☐ 112 Gary Roenicke	.06	.03	.00
☐ 113 Rod Scurry	.06	.03	.00
☐ 114 Bob Shirley	.06	.03	.00
☐ 115 Joel Skinner	.06	.03	.00
☐ 116 Tim Stoddard	.06	.03	.00
☐ 117 Bob Tewksbury	.10	.05	.01
☐ 118 Wayne Tolleson	.06	.03	.00
☐ 119 Claudell Washington	.10	.05	.01
☐ 120 Dave Winfield	.30	.15	.03
☐ 121 Steve Buechele	.06	.03	.00
☐ 122 Ed Correa	.10	.05	.01
☐ 123 Scott Fletcher	.06	.03	.00
☐ 124 Jose Guzman	.06	.03	.00
☐ 125 Toby Harrah	.06	.03	.00
☐ 126 Greg Harris	.06	.03	.00
☐ 127 Charlie Hough	.06	.03	.00
☐ 128 Pete Incaviglia	1.00	.50	.10
☐ 129 Mike Mason	.06	.03	.00
☐ 130 Oddibe McDowell	.10	.05	.01
☐ 131 Dale Mohorcic	.10	.05	.01
☐ 132 Pete O'Brien	.10	.05	.01
☐ 133 Tom Paciorek	.06	.03	.00
☐ 134 Larry Parrish	.06	.03	.00
☐ 135 Geno Petralli	.06	.03	.00
☐ 136 Darrell Porter	.06	.03	.00
☐ 137 Jeff Russell	.06	.03	.00
☐ 138 Ruben Sierra	11.00	5.50	1.10
☐ 139 Don Slaught	.06	.03	.00
☐ 140 Gary Ward	.06	.03	.00
☐ 141 Curtis Wilkerson	.06	.03	.00
☐ 142 Mitch Williams	.50	.25	.05
☐ 143 Bobby Witt	1.35	.65	.13
☐ 144 Dave Bergman	.06	.03	.00
☐ 145 Tom Brookens	.06	.03	.00
☐ 146 Bill Campbell	.06	.03	.00
☐ 147 Chuck Cary	.18	.09	.01
☐ 148 Darnell Coles	.10	.05	.01
☐ 149 Dave Collins	.06	.03	.00
☐ 150 Darrell Evans	.12	.06	.01
☐ 151 Kirk Gibson	.25	.12	.02
☐ 152 John Grubb	.06	.03	.00
☐ 153 Willie Hernandez	.10	.05	.01
☐ 154 Larry Herndon	.06	.03	.00
☐ 155 Eric King	.45	.22	.04
☐ 156 Chet Lemon	.06	.03	.00
☐ 157 Dwight Lowry	.06	.03	.00
☐ 158 Jack Morris	.15	.07	.01
☐ 159 Randy O'Neal	.06	.03	.00
☐ 160 Lance Parrish	.12	.06	.01
☐ 161 Dan Petry	.06	.03	.00
☐ 162 Pat Sheridan	.06	.03	.00
☐ 163 Jim Slaton	.06	.03	.00
☐ 164 Frank Tanana	.10	.05	.01
☐ 165 Walt Terrell	.06	.03	.00
☐ 166 Mark Thurmond	.06	.03	.00
☐ 167 Alan Trammell	.25	.12	.02
☐ 168 Lou Whitaker	.12	.06	.01
☐ 169 Luis Aguayo	.06	.03	.00
☐ 170 Steve Bedrosian	.12	.06	.01
☐ 171 Don Carman	.06	.03	.00

☐ 172 Darren Daulton	.12	.06	.01
☐ 173 Greg Gross	.06	.03	.00
☐ 174 Kevin Gross	.06	.03	.00
☐ 175 Von Hayes	.12	.06	.01
☐ 176 Charles Hudson	.06	.03	.00
☐ 177 Tom Hume	.06	.03	.00
☐ 178 Steve Jeltz	.06	.03	.00
☐ 179 Mike Maddux	.12	.06	.01
☐ 180 Shane Rawley	.06	.03	.00
☐ 181 Gary Redus	.06	.03	.00
☐ 182 Ron Roenicke	.06	.03	.00
☐ 183 Bruce Ruffin	.12	.06	.01
☐ 184 John Russell	.06	.03	.00
☐ 185 Juan Samuel	.12	.06	.01
☐ 186 Dan Schatzeder	.06	.03	.00
☐ 187 Mike Schmidt	1.25	.60	.12
☐ 188 Rick Schu	.06	.03	.00
☐ 189 Jeff Stone	.06	.03	.00
☐ 190 Kent Tekulve	.06	.03	.00
☐ 191 Milt Thompson	.10	.05	.01
☐ 192 Glenn Wilson	.06	.03	.00
☐ 193 Buddy Bell	.10	.05	.01
☐ 194 Tom Browning	.12	.06	.01
☐ 195 Sal Butera	.06	.03	.00
☐ 196 Dave Concepcion	.10	.05	.01
☐ 197 Kal Daniels	1.00	.50	.10
☐ 198 Eric Davis	1.50	.75	.15
☐ 199 John Denny	.06	.03	.00
☐ 200 Bo Diaz	.06	.03	.00
☐ 201 Nick Esasky	.10	.05	.01
☐ 202 John Franco	.10	.05	.01
☐ 203 Bill Gullickson	.06	.03	.00
☐ 204 Barry Larkin	7.00	3.50	.70
☐ 205 Eddie Milner	.06	.03	.00
☐ 206 Rob Murphy	.20	.10	.02
☐ 207 Ron Oester	.06	.03	.00
☐ 208 Dave Parker	.18	.09	.01
☐ 209 Tony Perez	.15	.07	.01
☐ 210 Ted Power	.06	.03	.00
☐ 211 Joe Price	.06	.03	.00
☐ 212 Ron Robinson	.06	.03	.00
☐ 213 Pete Rose	.75	.35	.07
☐ 214 Mario Soto	.06	.03	.00
☐ 215 Kurt Stillwell	.75	.35	.07
☐ 216 Max Venable	.06	.03	.00
☐ 217 Chris Welsh	.06	.03	.00
☐ 218 Carl Willis	.06	.03	.00
☐ 219 Jesse Barfield	.15	.07	.01
☐ 220 George Bell	.40	.20	.04
☐ 221 Bill Caudill	.06	.03	.00
☐ 222 John Cerutti	.30	.15	.03
☐ 223 Jim Clancy	.06	.03	.00
☐ 224 Mark Eichhorn	.10	.05	.01
☐ 225 Tony Fernandez	.20	.10	.02
☐ 226 Damaso Garcia	.06	.03	.00
☐ 227 Kelly Gruber ERR (wrong birth year)	1.00	.50	.10
☐ 228 Tom Henke	.10	.05	.01
☐ 229 Garth Iorg	.06	.03	.00
☐ 230 Joe Johnson	.06	.03	.00
☐ 231 Cliff Johnson	.06	.03	.00
☐ 232 Jimmy Key	.10	.05	.01
☐ 233 Dennis Lamp	.06	.03	.00
☐ 234 Rick Leach	.06	.03	.00
☐ 235 Buck Martinez	.06	.03	.00
☐ 236 Lloyd Moseby	.10	.05	.01
☐ 237 Rance Mulliniks	.06	.03	.00
☐ 238 Dave Stieb	.15	.07	.01
☐ 239 Willie Upshaw	.06	.03	.00
☐ 240 Ernie Whitt	.06	.03	.00
☐ 241 Andy Allanson	.06	.03	.00
☐ 242 Scott Bailes	.10	.05	.01
☐ 243 Chris Bando	.06	.03	.00
☐ 244 Tony Bernazard	.06	.03	.00
☐ 245 John Butcher	.06	.03	.00
☐ 246 Brett Butler	.12	.06	.01
☐ 247 Ernie Camacho	.06	.03	.00
☐ 248 Tom Candiotti	.10	.05	.01
☐ 249 Joe Carter	.40	.20	.04
☐ 250 Carmen Castillo	.06	.03	.00
☐ 251 Julio Franco	.18	.09	.01
☐ 252 Mel Hall	.10	.05	.01
☐ 253 Brook Jacoby	.10	.05	.01
☐ 254 Phil Niekro	.18	.09	.01
☐ 255 Otis Nixon	.10	.05	.01
☐ 256 Dickie Noles	.06	.03	.00
☐ 257 Bryan Oelkers	.06	.03	.00
☐ 258 Ken Schrom	.06	.03	.00
☐ 259 Don Schulze	.06	.03	.00
☐ 260 Cory Snyder	.50	.25	.05
☐ 261 Pat Tabler	.10	.05	.01
☐ 262 Andre Thornton	.10	.05	.01
☐ 263 Rich Yett	.06	.03	.00
☐ 264 Mike Aldrete	.10	.05	.01

☐ 265 Juan Berenguer	.06	.03	.00
☐ 266 Vida Blue	.10	.05	.01
☐ 267 Bob Brenly	.06	.03	.00
☐ 268 Chris Brown	.06	.03	.00
☐ 269 Will Clark	27.00	13.50	2.70
☐ 270 Chili Davis	.10	.05	.01
☐ 271 Mark Davis	.12	.06	.01
☐ 272 Kelly Downs	.30	.15	.03
☐ 273 Scott Garrelts	.10	.05	.01
☐ 274 Dan Gladden	.10	.05	.01
☐ 275 Mike Krukow	.06	.03	.00
☐ 276 Randy Kutcher	.06	.03	.00
☐ 277 Mike LaCoss	.06	.03	.00
☐ 278 Jeff Leonard	.10	.05	.01
☐ 279 Candy Maldonado	.12	.06	.01
☐ 280 Roger Mason	.06	.03	.00
☐ 281 Bob Melvin	.06	.03	.00
☐ 282 Greg Minton	.06	.03	.00
☐ 283 Jeff Robinson (Giants pitcher)	.10	.05	.01
☐ 284 Harry Spilman	.06	.03	.00
☐ 285 Robby Thompson	.35	.17	.03
☐ 286 Jose Uribe	.06	.03	.00
☐ 287 Frank Williams	.06	.03	.00
☐ 288 Joel Youngblood	.06	.03	.00
☐ 289 Jack Clark	.18	.09	.01
☐ 290 Vince Coleman	.50	.25	.05
☐ 291 Tim Conroy	.06	.03	.00
☐ 292 Danny Cox	.06	.03	.00
☐ 293 Ken Dayley	.06	.03	.00
☐ 294 Curt Ford	.06	.03	.00
☐ 295 Bob Forsch	.06	.03	.00
☐ 296 Tom Herr	.10	.05	.01
☐ 297 Ricky Horton	.06	.03	.00
☐ 298 Clint Hurdle	.06	.03	.00
☐ 299 Jeff Lahti	.06	.03	.00
☐ 300 Steve Lake	.06	.03	.00
☐ 301 Tito Landrum	.06	.03	.00
☐ 302 Mike LaValliere	.25	.12	.02
☐ 303 Greg Mathews	.12	.06	.01
☐ 304 Willie McGee	.18	.09	.01
☐ 305 Jose Oquendo	.06	.03	.00
☐ 306 Terry Pendleton	.10	.05	.01
☐ 307 Pat Perry	.06	.03	.00
☐ 308 Ozzie Smith	.25	.12	.02
☐ 309 Ray Soff	.06	.03	.00
☐ 310 John Tudor	.12	.06	.01
☐ 311 Andy Van Slyke ERR (Bats R, Throws L)	.25	.12	.02
☐ 312 Todd Worrell	.15	.07	.01
☐ 313 Dann Bilardello	.06	.03	.00
☐ 314 Hubie Brooks	.12	.06	.01
☐ 315 Tim Burke	.10	.05	.01
☐ 316 Andre Dawson	.45	.22	.04
☐ 317 Mike Fitzgerald	.06	.03	.00
☐ 318 Tom Foley	.06	.03	.00
☐ 319 Andres Galarraga	.25	.12	.02
☐ 320 Joe Hesketh	.06	.03	.00
☐ 321 Wallace Johnson	.06	.03	.00
☐ 322 Wayne Krenchicki	.06	.03	.00
☐ 323 Vance Law	.06	.03	.00
☐ 324 Dennis Martinez	.10	.05	.01
☐ 325 Bob McClure	.06	.03	.00
☐ 326 Andy McGaffigan	.06	.03	.00
☐ 327 Al Newman	.10	.05	.01
☐ 328 Tim Raines	.25	.12	.02
☐ 329 Jeff Reardon	.10	.05	.01
☐ 330 Luis Rivera	.06	.03	.00
☐ 331 Bob Sebra	.06	.03	.00
☐ 332 Bryn Smith	.06	.03	.00
☐ 333 Jay Tibbs	.06	.03	.00
☐ 334 Tim Wallach	.12	.06	.01
☐ 335 Mitch Webster	.06	.03	.00
☐ 336 Jim Wohlford	.06	.03	.00
☐ 337 Floyd Youmans	.06	.03	.00
☐ 338 Chris Bosio	.45	.22	.04
☐ 339 Glenn Braggs	.75	.35	.07
☐ 340 Rick Cerone	.06	.03	.00
☐ 341 Mark Clear	.06	.03	.00
☐ 342 Bryan Clutterbuck	.06	.03	.00
☐ 343 Cecil Cooper	.10	.05	.01
☐ 344 Rob Deer	.25	.12	.02
☐ 345 Jim Gantner	.06	.03	.00
☐ 346 Ted Higuera	.25	.12	.02
☐ 347 John Henry Johnson	.06	.03	.00
☐ 348 Tim Leary	.25	.12	.02
☐ 349 Rick Manning	.06	.03	.00
☐ 350 Paul Molitor	.12	.06	.01
☐ 351 Charlie Moore	.06	.03	.00
☐ 352 Juan Nieves	.10	.05	.01
☐ 353 Ben Oglivie	.10	.05	.01
☐ 354 Dan Plesac	.25	.12	.02
☐ 355 Ernest Riles	.06	.03	.00
☐ 356 Billy Jo Robidoux	.06	.03	.00

☐ 357	Bill Schroeder	.06	.03	.00
☐ 358	Dale Sveum	.12	.06	.01
☐ 359	Gorman Thomas	.10	.05	.01
☐ 360	Bill Wegman	.10	.05	.01
☐ 361	Robin Yount	.60	.30	.06
☐ 362	Steve Balboni	.06	.03	.00
☐ 363	Scott Bankhead	.15	.07	.01
☐ 364	Buddy Biancalana	.06	.03	.00
☐ 365	Bud Black	.10	.05	.01
☐ 366	George Brett	.75	.35	.07
☐ 367	Steve Farr	.10	.05	.01
☐ 368	Mark Gubicza	.12	.06	.01
☐ 369	Bo Jackson	21.00	10.50	2.10
☐ 370	Danny Jackson	.10	.05	.01
☐ 371	Mike Kingery	.10	.05	.01
☐ 372	Rudy Law	.06	.03	.00
☐ 373	Charlie Leibrandt	.06	.03	.00
☐ 374	Dennis Leonard	.06	.03	.00
☐ 375	Hal McRae	.10	.05	.01
☐ 376	Jorge Orta	.06	.03	.00
☐ 377	Jamie Quirk	.06	.03	.00
☐ 378	Dan Quisenberry	.10	.05	.01
☐ 379	Bret Saberhagen	.40	.20	.04
☐ 380	Angel Salazar	.06	.03	.00
☐ 381	Lonnie Smith	.10	.05	.01
☐ 382	Jim Sundberg	.06	.03	.00
☐ 383	Frank White	.10	.05	.01
☐ 384	Willie Wilson	.10	.05	.01
☐ 385	Joaquin Andujar	.06	.03	.00
☐ 386	Doug Bair	.06	.03	.00
☐ 387	Dusty Baker	.10	.05	.01
☐ 388	Bruce Bochte	.06	.03	.00
☐ 389	Jose Canseco	12.00	6.00	1.20
☐ 390	Chris Codiroli	.06	.03	.00
☐ 391	Mike Davis	.06	.03	.00
☐ 392	Alfredo Griffin	.06	.03	.00
☐ 393	Moose Haas	.06	.03	.00
☐ 394	Donnie Hill	.06	.03	.00
☐ 395	Jay Howell	.06	.03	.00
☐ 396	Dave Kingman	.10	.05	.01
☐ 397	Carney Lansford	.12	.06	.01
☐ 398	Dave Leiper	.06	.03	.00
☐ 399	Bill Mooneyham	.06	.03	.00
☐ 400	Dwayne Murphy	.06	.03	.00
☐ 401	Steve Ontiveros	.06	.03	.00
☐ 402	Tony Phillips	.06	.03	.00
☐ 403	Eric Plunk	.06	.03	.00
☐ 404	Jose Rijo	.18	.09	.01
☐ 405	Terry Steinbach	1.25	.60	.12
☐ 406	Dave Stewart	.50	.25	.05
☐ 407	Mickey Tettleton	.15	.07	.01
☐ 408	Dave Von Ohlen	.06	.03	.00
☐ 409	Jerry Willard	.06	.03	.00
☐ 410	Curt Young	.06	.03	.00
☐ 411	Bruce Bochy	.06	.03	.00
☐ 412	Dave Dravecky	.10	.05	.01
☐ 413	Tim Flannery	.06	.03	.00
☐ 414	Steve Garvey	.30	.15	.03
☐ 415	Goose Gossage	.10	.05	.01
☐ 416	Tony Gwynn	.75	.35	.07
☐ 417	Andy Hawkins	.06	.03	.00
☐ 418	LaMarr Hoyt	.06	.03	.00
☐ 419	Terry Kennedy	.06	.03	.00
☐ 420	John Kruk	.45	.22	.04
☐ 421	Dave LaPoint	.06	.03	.00
☐ 422	Craig Lefferts	.06	.03	.00
☐ 423	Carmelo Martinez	.06	.03	.00
☐ 424	Lance McCullers	.06	.03	.00
☐ 425	Kevin McReynolds	.30	.15	.03
☐ 426	Graig Nettles	.10	.05	.01
☐ 427	Bip Roberts	.60	.30	.06
☐ 428	Jerry Royster	.06	.03	.00
☐ 429	Benito Santiago	1.25	.60	.12
☐ 430	Eric Show	.06	.03	.00
☐ 431	Bob Stoddard	.06	.03	.00
☐ 432	Garry Templeton	.10	.05	.01
☐ 433	Gene Walter	.06	.03	.00
☐ 434	Ed Whitson	.10	.05	.01
☐ 435	Marvell Wynne	.06	.03	.00
☐ 436	Dave Anderson	.06	.03	.00
☐ 437	Greg Brock	.06	.03	.00
☐ 438	Enos Cabell	.06	.03	.00
☐ 439	Mariano Duncan	.12	.06	.01
☐ 440	Pedro Guerrero	.18	.09	.01
☐ 441	Orel Hershiser	.35	.17	.03
☐ 442	Rick Honeycutt	.06	.03	.00
☐ 443	Ken Howell	.06	.03	.00
☐ 444	Ken Landreaux	.06	.03	.00
☐ 445	Bill Madlock	.10	.05	.01
☐ 446	Mike Marshall	.10	.05	.01
☐ 447	Len Matuszek	.06	.03	.00
☐ 448	Tom Niedenfuer	.06	.03	.00
☐ 449	Alejandro Pena	.06	.03	.00
☐ 450	Dennis Powell	.06	.03	.00
☐ 451	Jerry Reuss	.06	.03	.00
☐ 452	Bill Russell	.06	.03	.00
☐ 453	Steve Sax	.18	.09	.01
☐ 454	Mike Scioscia	.06	.03	.00
☐ 455	Franklin Stubbs	.06	.03	.00
☐ 456	Alex Trevino	.06	.03	.00
☐ 457	Fernando Valenzuela	.25	.12	.02
☐ 458	Ed VandeBerg	.06	.03	.00
☐ 459	Bob Welch	.15	.07	.01
☐ 460	Reggie Williams	.06	.03	.00
☐ 461	Don Aase	.06	.03	.00
☐ 462	Juan Beniquez	.06	.03	.00
☐ 463	Mike Boddicker	.10	.05	.01
☐ 464	Juan Bonilla	.06	.03	.00
☐ 465	Rich Bordi	.06	.03	.00
☐ 466	Storm Davis	.10	.05	.01
☐ 467	Rick Dempsey	.06	.03	.00
☐ 468	Ken Dixon	.06	.03	.00
☐ 469	Jim Dwyer	.06	.03	.00
☐ 470	Mike Flanagan	.10	.05	.01
☐ 471	Jackie Gutierrez	.06	.03	.00
☐ 472	Brad Havens	.06	.03	.00
☐ 473	Lee Lacy	.06	.03	.00
☐ 474	Fred Lynn	.12	.06	.01
☐ 475	Scott McGregor	.10	.05	.01
☐ 476	Eddie Murray	.40	.20	.04
☐ 477	Tom O'Malley	.06	.03	.00
☐ 478	Cal Ripken Jr.	.50	.25	.05
☐ 479	Larry Sheets	.10	.05	.01
☐ 480	John Shelby	.06	.03	.00
☐ 481	Nate Snell	.06	.03	.00
☐ 482	Jim Traber	.06	.03	.00
☐ 483	Mike Young	.06	.03	.00
☐ 484	Neil Allen	.06	.03	.00
☐ 485	Harold Baines	.12	.06	.01
☐ 486	Floyd Bannister	.06	.03	.00
☐ 487	Daryl Boston	.06	.03	.00
☐ 488	Ivan Calderon	.12	.06	.01
☐ 489	John Cangelosi	.06	.03	.00
☐ 490	Steve Carlton	.35	.17	.03
☐ 491	Joe Cowley	.06	.03	.00
☐ 492	Julio Cruz	.06	.03	.00
☐ 493	Bill Dawley	.06	.03	.00
☐ 494	Jose DeLeon	.06	.03	.00
☐ 495	Richard Dotson	.06	.03	.00
☐ 496	Carlton Fisk	.35	.17	.03
☐ 497	Ozzie Guillen	.30	.15	.03
☐ 498	Jerry Hairston	.06	.03	.00
☐ 499	Ron Hassey	.06	.03	.00
☐ 500	Tim Hulett	.06	.03	.00
☐ 501	Bob James	.06	.03	.00
☐ 502	Steve Lyons	.06	.03	.00
☐ 503	Joel McKeon	.06	.03	.00
☐ 504	Gene Nelson	.06	.03	.00
☐ 505	Dave Schmidt	.06	.03	.00
☐ 506	Ray Searage	.06	.03	.00
☐ 507	Bobby Thigpen	2.50	1.25	.25
☐ 508	Greg Walker	.06	.03	.00
☐ 509	Jim Acker	.06	.03	.00
☐ 510	Doyle Alexander	.06	.03	.00
☐ 511	Paul Assenmacher	.06	.03	.00
☐ 512	Bruce Benedict	.06	.03	.00
☐ 513	Chris Chambliss	.10	.05	.01
☐ 514	Jeff Dedmon	.06	.03	.00
☐ 515	Gene Garber	.06	.03	.00
☐ 516	Ken Griffey	.15	.07	.01
☐ 517	Terry Harper	.06	.03	.00
☐ 518	Bob Horner	.12	.06	.01
☐ 519	Glenn Hubbard	.06	.03	.00
☐ 520	Rick Mahler	.06	.03	.00
☐ 521	Omar Moreno	.06	.03	.00
☐ 522	Dale Murphy	.50	.25	.05
☐ 523	Ken Oberkfell	.06	.03	.00
☐ 524	Ed Olwine	.06	.03	.00
☐ 525	David Palmer	.06	.03	.00
☐ 526	Rafael Ramirez	.06	.03	.00
☐ 527	Billy Sample	.06	.03	.00
☐ 528	Ted Simmons	.10	.05	.01
☐ 529	Zane Smith	.12	.06	.01
☐ 530	Bruce Sutter	.10	.05	.01
☐ 531	Andres Thomas	.18	.09	.01
☐ 532	Ozzie Virgil	.06	.03	.00
☐ 533	Allan Anderson	.40	.20	.04
☐ 534	Keith Atherton	.06	.03	.00
☐ 535	Billy Beane	.06	.03	.00
☐ 536	Bert Blyleven	.12	.06	.01
☐ 537	Tom Brunansky	.12	.06	.01
☐ 538	Randy Bush	.06	.03	.00
☐ 539	George Frazier	.06	.03	.00
☐ 540	Gary Gaetti	.15	.07	.01
☐ 541	Greg Gagne	.06	.03	.00
☐ 542	Mickey Hatcher	.06	.03	.00
☐ 543	Neal Heaton	.06	.03	.00
☐ 544	Kent Hrbek	.15	.07	.01

☐ 545 Roy Lee Jackson	.06	.03	.00
☐ 546 Tim Laudner	.06	.03	.00
☐ 547 Steve Lombardozzi	.06	.03	.00
☐ 548 Mark Portugal	.18	.09	.01
☐ 549 Kirby Puckett	2.50	1.25	.25
☐ 550 Jeff Reed	.06	.03	.00
☐ 551 Mark Salas	.06	.03	.00
☐ 552 Roy Smalley	.06	.03	.00
☐ 553 Mike Smithson	.06	.03	.00
☐ 554 Frank Viola	.35	.17	.03
☐ 555 Thad Bosley	.06	.03	.00
☐ 556 Ron Cey	.10	.05	.01
☐ 557 Jody Davis	.06	.03	.00
☐ 558 Ron Davis	.06	.03	.00
☐ 559 Bob Dernier	.06	.03	.00
☐ 560 Frank DiPino	.06	.03	.00
☐ 561 Shawon Dunston UER (wrong birth year listed on card back)	.35	.17	.03
☐ 562 Leon Durham	.06	.03	.00
☐ 563 Dennis Eckersley	.15	.07	.01
☐ 564 Terry Francona	.06	.03	.00
☐ 565 Dave Gumpert	.06	.03	.00
☐ 566 Guy Hoffman	.06	.03	.00
☐ 567 Ed Lynch	.06	.03	.00
☐ 568 Gary Matthews	.06	.03	.00
☐ 569 Keith Moreland	.06	.03	.00
☐ 570 Jamie Moyer	.10	.05	.01
☐ 571 Jerry Mumphrey	.06	.03	.00
☐ 572 Ryne Sandberg	1.25	.60	.12
☐ 573 Scott Sanderson	.10	.05	.01
☐ 574 Lee Smith	.10	.05	.01
☐ 575 Chris Speier	.06	.03	.00
☐ 576 Rick Sutcliffe	.10	.05	.01
☐ 577 Manny Trillo	.06	.03	.00
☐ 578 Steve Trout	.06	.03	.00
☐ 579 Karl Best	.06	.03	.00
☐ 580 Scott Bradley	.06	.03	.00
☐ 581 Phil Bradley	.10	.05	.01
☐ 582 Mickey Brantley	.06	.03	.00
☐ 583 Mike Brown (Mariners pitcher)	.06	.03	.00
☐ 584 Alvin Davis	.18	.09	.01
☐ 585 Lee Guetterman	.20	.10	.02
☐ 586 Mark Huismann	.06	.03	.00
☐ 587 Bob Kearney	.06	.03	.00
☐ 588 Pete Ladd	.06	.03	.00
☐ 589 Mark Langston	.25	.12	.02
☐ 590 Mike Moore	.10	.05	.01
☐ 591 Mike Morgan	.06	.03	.00
☐ 592 John Moses	.06	.03	.00
☐ 593 Ken Phelps	.06	.03	.00
☐ 594 Jim Presley	.10	.05	.01
☐ 595 Rey Quinones UER (Quinonez on front)	.10	.05	.01
☐ 596 Harold Reynolds	.25	.12	.02
☐ 597 Billy Swift	.06	.03	.00
☐ 598 Danny Tartabull	.25	.12	.02
☐ 599 Steve Yeager	.06	.03	.00
☐ 600 Matt Young	.06	.03	.00
☐ 601 Bill Almon	.06	.03	.00
☐ 602 Rafael Belliard	.10	.05	.01
☐ 603 Mike Bielecki	.10	.05	.01
☐ 604 Barry Bonds	11.00	5.50	1.10
☐ 605 Bobby Bonilla	7.50	3.75	.75
☐ 606 Sid Bream	.06	.03	.00
☐ 607 Mike Brown (Pirates OF)	.06	.03	.00
☐ 608 Pat Clements	.06	.03	.00
☐ 609 Mike Diaz	.10	.05	.01
☐ 610 Cecilio Guante	.06	.03	.00
☐ 611 Barry Jones	.35	.17	.03
☐ 612 Bob Kipper	.06	.03	.00
☐ 613 Larry McWilliams	.06	.03	.00
☐ 614 Jim Morrison	.06	.03	.00
☐ 615 Joe Orsulak	.06	.03	.00
☐ 616 Junior Ortiz	.06	.03	.00
☐ 617 Tony Pena	.10	.05	.01
☐ 618 Johnny Ray	.10	.05	.01
☐ 619 Rick Reuschel	.10	.05	.01
☐ 620 R.J. Reynolds	.06	.03	.00
☐ 621 Rick Rhoden	.06	.03	.00
☐ 622 Don Robinson	.06	.03	.00
☐ 623 Bob Walk	.06	.03	.00
☐ 624 Jim Winn	.06	.03	.00
☐ 625 Youthful Power Pete Incaviglia Jose Canseco	.75	.35	.07
☐ 626 300 Game Winners Don Sutton Phil Niekro	.10	.05	.01
☐ 627 AL Firemen Dave Righetti Don Aase	.06	.03	.00
☐ 628 Rookie All-Stars Wally Joyner Jose Canseco	1.50	.75	.15
☐ 629 Magic Mets Gary Carter Sid Fernandez Dwight Gooden Keith Hernandez Darryl Strawberry	.50	.25	.05
☐ 630 NL Best Righties Mike Scott Mike Krukow	.10	.05	.01
☐ 631 Sensational Southpaws Fernando Valenzuela John Franco	.10	.05	.01
☐ 632 Count'Em Bob Horner	.06	.03	.00
☐ 633 AL Pitcher's Nightmare Jose Canseco Jim Rice Kirby Puckett	.75	.35	.07
☐ 634 All-Star Battery Gary Carter Roger Clemens	.20	.10	.02
☐ 635 4000 Strikeouts Steve Carlton	.20	.10	.02
☐ 636 Big Bats at First Glenn Davis Eddie Murray	.20	.10	.02
☐ 637 On Base Wade Boggs Keith Hernandez	.25	.12	.02
☐ 638 Sluggers Left Side Don Mattingly Darryl Strawberry	1.00	.50	.10
☐ 639 Former MVP's Dave Parker Ryne Sandberg	.20	.10	.02
☐ 640 Dr. K , Super K Dwight Gooden Roger Clemens	.65	.30	.06
☐ 641 AL West Stoppers Mike Witt Charlie Hough	.06	.03	.00
☐ 642 Doubles and Triples Juan Samuel Tim Raines	.10	.05	.01
☐ 643 Outfielders with Punch Harold Baines Jesse Barfield	.10	.05	.01
☐ 644 Dave Clark and Greg Swindell	1.50	.75	.15
☐ 645 Ron Karkovice and Russ Morman	.10	.05	.01
☐ 646 Devon White and Willie Fraser	1.00	.50	.10
☐ 647 Mike Stanley and Jerry Browne	.35	.17	.03
☐ 648 Dave Magadan and Phil Lombardi	4.00	2.00	.40
☐ 649 Jose Gonzalez and Ralph Bryant	.12	.06	.01
☐ 650 Jimmy Jones and Randy Asadoor	.18	.09	.01
☐ 651 Tracy Jones and Marvin Freeman	.18	.09	.01
☐ 652 John Stefero and Kevin Seitzer	5.00	2.50	.50
☐ 653 Rob Nelson and Steve Fireovid	.15	.07	.01
☐ 654 CL: Mets/Red Sox Astros/Angels	.08	.01	.00
☐ 655 CL: Yankees/Rangers Tigers/Phillies	.08	.01	.00
☐ 656 CL: Reds/Blue Jays Indians/Giants ERR (230/231 wrong)	.08	.01	.00
☐ 657 CL: Cardinals/Expos Brewers/Royals	.08	.01	.00
☐ 658 CL: A's/Padres Dodgers/Orioles	.08	.01	.00
☐ 659 CL: White Sox/Braves Twins/Cubs	.08	.01	.00
☐ 660 CL: Mariners/Pirates Special Cards ERR (580/581 wrong)	.08	.01	.00

1987 Fleer Wax Box Cards

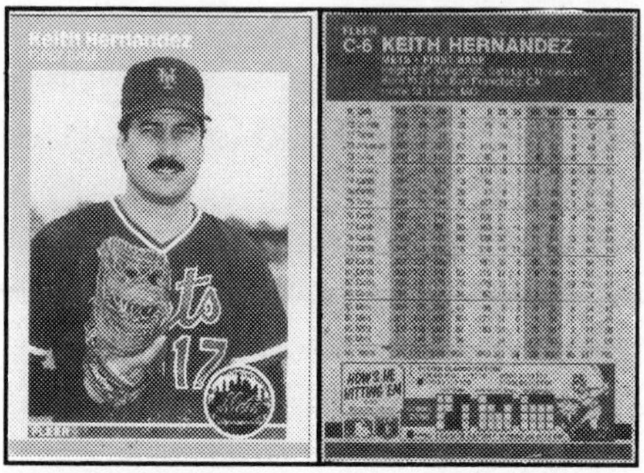

The cards in this 16-card set measure the standard 2 1/2" by 3 1/2". Cards have essentially the same design as the 1987 Fleer regular issue set. The cards were printed on the bottoms of the regular issue wax pack boxes. These 16 cards (C1 to C16) are considered a separate set in their own right and are not typically included in a complete set of the regular issue 1987 Fleer cards. The value of the panel uncut is slightly greater, perhaps by 25 percent greater, than the value of the individual cards cut up carefully.

	MINT	EXC	G-VG
COMPLETE SET (16)	5.00	2.50	.50
COMMON CARDS (C1-C16)	.10	.05	.01
☐ C1 Mets Logo	.10	.05	.01
☐ C2 Jesse Barfield	.15	.07	.01
☐ C3 George Brett	.50	.25	.05
☐ C4 Dwight Gooden	.60	.30	.06
☐ C5 Boston Logo	.10	.05	.01
☐ C6 Keith Hernandez	.20	.10	.02
☐ C7 Wally Joyner	.90	.45	.09
☐ C8 Dale Murphy	.50	.25	.05
☐ C9 Astros Logo	.10	.05	.01
☐ C10 Dave Parker	.25	.12	.02
☐ C11 Kirby Puckett	.60	.30	.06
☐ C12 Dave Righetti	.15	.07	.01
☐ C13 Angels Logo	.10	.05	.01
☐ C14 Ryne Sandberg	.60	.30	.06
☐ C15 Mike Schmidt	.75	.35	.07
☐ C16 Robin Yount	.50	.25	.05

1987 Fleer All-Star Inserts

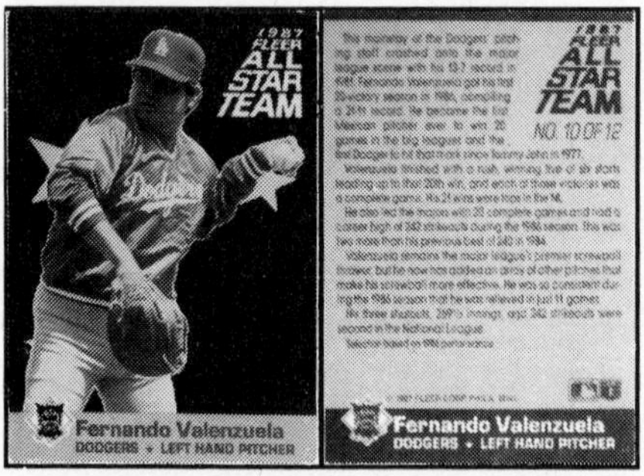

This 12-card set was distributed as an insert in packs of the Fleer regular issue. The cards are 2 1/2" by 3 1/2" and designed with a color player photo superimposed on a gray or black background with yellow stars. The player's name, team, and position are printed in orange on black or gray at the bottom of the obverse. The card backs are done predominantly in gray, red, and black. Cards are numbered on the back in the upper right hand corner.

	MINT	EXC	G-VG
COMPLETE SET (12)	15.00	7.50	1.50
COMMON PLAYER (1-12)	.35	.17	.03
☐ 1 Don Mattingly First Base	5.00	2.50	.50
☐ 2 Gary Carter Catcher	.90	.45	.09
☐ 3 Tony Fernandez Shortstop	.50	.25	.05
☐ 4 Steve Sax Second Base	.50	.25	.05
☐ 5 Kirby Puckett Outfield	2.00	1.00	.20
☐ 6 Mike Schmidt Third Base	2.00	1.00	.20
☐ 7 Mike Easler Designated Hitter	.35	.17	.03
☐ 8 Todd Worrell Relief Pitcher	.50	.25	.05
☐ 9 George Bell Outfield	.60	.30	.06
☐ 10 Fernando Valenzuela Left Hand Starter	.60	.30	.06
☐ 11 Roger Clemens Right Hand Starter	2.50	1.25	.25
☐ 12 Tim Raines Outfield	1.00	.50	.10

1987 Fleer Headliners

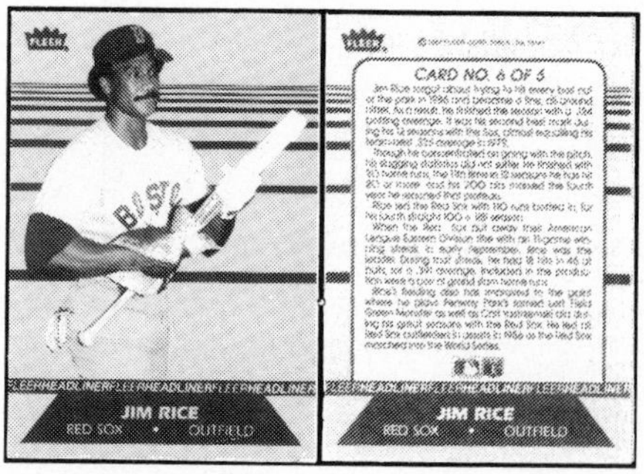

This six-card set was distributed as a special insert in rack packs as well as with three-pack wax pack rack packs. The obverse features the player photo against a beige background with irregular red stripes. Cards are 2 1/2" by 3 1/2". The cards are numbered on the back. The checklist below also lists each player's team affiliation.

	MINT	EXC	G-VG
COMPLETE SET (6)	8.00	4.00	.80
COMMON PLAYER (1-6)	.65	.30	.06
☐ 1 Wade Boggs Boston Red Sox	2.00	1.00	.20
☐ 2 Jose Canseco Oakland Athletics	3.00	1.50	.30
☐ 3 Dwight Gooden New York Mets	1.00	.50	.10
☐ 4 Rickey Henderson New York Yankees	2.00	1.00	.20
☐ 5 Keith Hernandez New York Mets	.65	.30	.06
☐ 6 Jim Rice Boston Red Sox	.65	.30	.06

1987 Fleer Sticker Cards

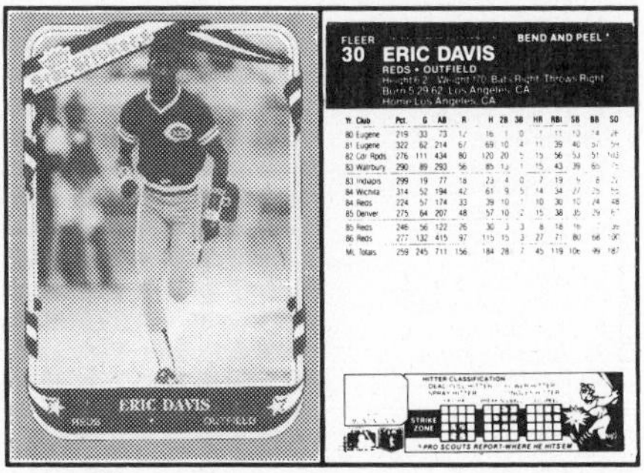

These Star Stickers were distributed as a separate issue by Fleer with five star stickers and a logo sticker in each wax pack. The 132-card (sticker) set features 2 1/2" by 3 1/2" full-color fronts and even statistics on the sticker back, which is an indication that the Fleer Company understands that these stickers are rarely used as stickers but more like traditional cards. The card fronts are surrounded by a green border and the backs are printed in green and yellow on white card stock.

	MINT	EXC	G-VG
COMPLETE SET (132)	27.00	13.50	2.70
COMMON PLAYER (1-132)	.05	.02	.00
☐ 1 Don Aase	.05	.02	.00
☐ 2 Harold Baines	.10	.05	.01
☐ 3 Floyd Bannister	.05	.02	.00
☐ 4 Jesse Barfield	.15	.07	.01
☐ 5 Marty Barrett	.05	.02	.00
☐ 6 Kevin Bass	.05	.02	.00
☐ 7 Don Baylor	.10	.05	.01
☐ 8 Steve Bedrosian	.10	.05	.01
☐ 9 George Bell	.25	.12	.02
☐ 10 Bert Blyleven	.15	.07	.01
☐ 11 Mike Boddicker	.10	.05	.01
☐ 12 Wade Boggs	1.25	.60	.12
☐ 13 Phil Bradley	.10	.05	.01
☐ 14 Sid Bream	.05	.02	.00
☐ 15 George Brett	.60	.30	.06
☐ 16 Hubie Brooks	.10	.05	.01
☐ 17 Tom Brunansky	.15	.07	.01
☐ 18 Tom Candiotti	.05	.02	.00
☐ 19 Jose Canseco	2.50	1.25	.25
☐ 20 Gary Carter	.30	.15	.03
☐ 21 Joe Carter	.25	.12	.02
☐ 22 Will Clark	2.00	1.00	.20
☐ 23 Mark Clear	.05	.02	.00
☐ 24 Roger Clemens	1.25	.60	.12
☐ 25 Vince Coleman	.40	.20	.04
☐ 26 Jose Cruz	.10	.05	.01
☐ 27 Ron Darling	.10	.05	.01
☐ 28 Alvin Davis	.10	.05	.01
☐ 29 Chili Davis	.10	.05	.01
☐ 30 Eric Davis	1.00	.50	.10
☐ 31 Glenn Davis	.35	.17	.03
☐ 32 Mike Davis	.05	.02	.00
☐ 33 Andre Dawson	.35	.17	.03
☐ 34 Doug DeCinces	.05	.02	.00
☐ 35 Brian Downing	.05	.02	.00
☐ 36 Shawon Dunston	.25	.12	.02
☐ 37 Mark Eichhorn	.05	.02	.00
☐ 38 Dwight Evans	.20	.10	.02
☐ 39 Tony Fernandez	.15	.07	.01
☐ 40 Bob Forsch	.05	.02	.00
☐ 41 John Franco	.10	.05	.01
☐ 42 Julio Franco	.10	.05	.01
☐ 43 Gary Gaetti	.15	.07	.01
☐ 44 Gene Garber	.05	.02	.00
☐ 45 Scott Garrelts	.10	.05	.01
☐ 46 Steve Garvey	.45	.22	.04
☐ 47 Kirk Gibson	.35	.17	.03
☐ 48 Dwight Gooden	.75	.35	.07
☐ 49 Ken Griffey Sr.	.15	.07	.01
☐ 50 Ozzie Guillen	.20	.10	.02
☐ 51 Bill Gullickson	.05	.02	.00
☐ 52 Tony Gwynn	.50	.25	.05
☐ 53 Mel Hall	.10	.05	.01
☐ 54 Greg Harris	.05	.02	.00
☐ 55 Von Hayes	.10	.05	.01
☐ 56 Rickey Henderson	1.50	.75	.15
☐ 57 Tom Henke	.10	.05	.01
☐ 58 Keith Hernandez	.20	.10	.02
☐ 59 Willie Hernandez	.05	.02	.00
☐ 60 Ted Higuera	.10	.05	.01
☐ 61 Bob Horner	.10	.05	.01
☐ 62 Charlie Hough	.05	.02	.00
☐ 63 Jay Howell	.05	.02	.00
☐ 64 Kent Hrbek	.15	.07	.01
☐ 65 Bruce Hurst	.10	.05	.01
☐ 66 Pete Incaviglia	.25	.12	.02
☐ 67 Bob James	.05	.02	.00
☐ 68 Wally Joyner	.90	.45	.09
☐ 69 Mike Krukow	.05	.02	.00
☐ 70 Mark Langston	.20	.10	.02
☐ 71 Carney Lansford	.15	.07	.01
☐ 72 Fred Lynn	.15	.07	.01
☐ 73 Bill Madlock	.05	.02	.00
☐ 74 Don Mattingly	2.00	1.00	.20
☐ 75 Kirk McCaskill	.05	.02	.00
☐ 76 Lance McCullers	.05	.02	.00
☐ 77 Oddibe McDowell	.10	.05	.01
☐ 78 Paul Molitor	.20	.10	.02
☐ 79 Keith Moreland	.05	.02	.00
☐ 80 Jack Morris	.15	.07	.01
☐ 81 Jim Morrison	.05	.02	.00
☐ 82 Jerry Mumphrey	.05	.02	.00
☐ 83 Dale Murphy	.40	.20	.04
☐ 84 Eddie Murray	.45	.22	.04
☐ 85 Ben Oglivie	.05	.02	.00
☐ 86 Bob Ojeda	.10	.05	.01
☐ 87 Jesse Orosco	.05	.02	.00
☐ 88 Dave Parker	.20	.10	.02
☐ 89 Larry Parrish	.05	.02	.00
☐ 90 Tony Pena	.05	.02	.00
☐ 91 Jim Presley	.10	.05	.01
☐ 92 Kirby Puckett	1.00	.50	.10
☐ 93 Dan Quisenberry	.10	.05	.01
☐ 94 Tim Raines	.25	.12	.02
☐ 95 Dennis Rasmussen	.05	.02	.00
☐ 96 Shane Rawley	.05	.02	.00
☐ 97 Johnny Ray	.05	.02	.00
☐ 98 Jeff Reardon	.10	.05	.01
☐ 99 Jim Rice	.20	.10	.02
☐ 100 Dave Righetti	.15	.07	.01
☐ 101 Cal Ripken Jr.	.45	.22	.04
☐ 102 Pete Rose	.75	.35	.07
☐ 103 Nolan Ryan	2.00	1.00	.20
☐ 104 Juan Samuel	.15	.07	.01
☐ 105 Ryne Sandberg	1.00	.50	.10
☐ 106 Steve Sax	.15	.07	.01
☐ 107 Mike Schmidt	1.25	.60	.12
☐ 108 Mike Scott	.20	.10	.02
☐ 109 Dave Smith	.05	.02	.00
☐ 110 Lee Smith	.10	.05	.01
☐ 111 Lonnie Smith	.10	.05	.01
☐ 112 Ozzie Smith	.25	.12	.02
☐ 113 Cory Snyder	.20	.10	.02
☐ 114 Darryl Strawberry	.75	.35	.07
☐ 115 Don Sutton	.20	.10	.02
☐ 116 Kent Tekulve	.05	.02	.00
☐ 117 Andres Thomas	.05	.02	.00
☐ 118 Alan Trammell	.25	.12	.02
☐ 119 John Tudor	.15	.07	.01
☐ 120 Fernando Valenzuela	.20	.10	.02
☐ 121 Bob Welch	.25	.12	.02
☐ 122 Lou Whitaker	.15	.07	.01
☐ 123 Frank White	.10	.05	.01
☐ 124 Reggie Williams	.05	.02	.00
☐ 125 Willie Wilson	.10	.05	.01
☐ 126 Dave Winfield	.25	.12	.02
☐ 127 Mike Witt	.05	.02	.00
☐ 128 Todd Worrell	.15	.07	.01
☐ 129 Curt Young	.05	.02	.00
☐ 130 Robin Yount	.75	.35	.07
☐ 131 Checklist Jose Canseco Don Mattingly	2.50	1.25	.25
☐ 132 Checklist Bo Jackson Eric Davis	2.50	1.25	.25

1987 Fleer Sticker Wax Box

The bottoms of the Star Sticker wax boxes contained two different sets of four cards done in a similar format to the stickers; these cards (they are not stickers but truly cards) are numbered with the prefix S and are considered a separate set. The value of the panels uncut is slightly greater, perhaps by 25 percent greater, than the value of the individual cards cut up carefully.

	MINT	EXC	G-VG
COMPLETE SET (8)	2.25	1.10	.22
COMMON PLAYER (S1-S8)	.10	.05	.01
☐ S1 Detroit Logo	.10	.05	.01
☐ S2 Wade Boggs	.75	.35	.07
☐ S3 Bert Blyleven	.15	.07	.01
☐ S4 Jose Cruz	.10	.05	.01
☐ S5 Glenn Davis	.25	.12	.02
☐ S6 Phillies Logo	.10	.05	.01
☐ S7 Bob Horner	.15	.07	.01
☐ S8 Don Mattingly	1.25	.60	.12

1987 Fleer Award Winners

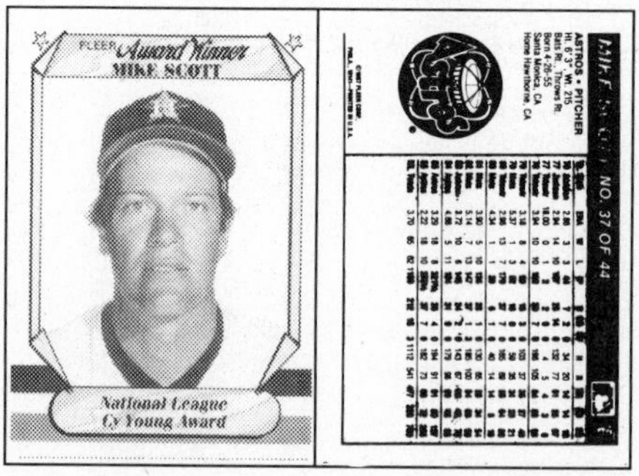

This small set of 44 cards was (mass)-produced for 7-Eleven stores by Fleer. The cards measure the standard 2 1/2" by 3 1/2" and feature full color fronts and yellow, white, and black backs. The card fronts are distinguished by their yellow frame around the player's full-color photo. The box for the cards describes the set as the "1987 Limited Edition Baseball's Award Winners." The checklist for the set is given on the back of the set box.

	MINT	EXC	G-VG
COMPLETE SET (44)	4.00	2.00	.40
COMMON PLAYER (1-44)	.10	.05	.01
☐ 1 Marty Barrett	.10	.05	.01
☐ 2 George Bell	.15	.07	.01
☐ 3 Bert Blyleven	.15	.07	.01
☐ 4 Bob Boone	.15	.07	.01
☐ 5 John Candelaria	.10	.05	.01
☐ 6 Jose Canseco	1.00	.50	.10
☐ 7 Gary Carter	.25	.12	.02
☐ 8 Joe Carter	.15	.07	.01
☐ 9 Roger Clemens	.75	.35	.07
☐ 10 Cecil Cooper	.10	.05	.01
☐ 11 Eric Davis	.60	.30	.06
☐ 12 Tony Fernandez	.15	.07	.01
☐ 13 Scott Fletcher	.10	.05	.01
☐ 14 Bob Forsch	.10	.05	.01
☐ 15 Dwight Gooden	.40	.20	.04
☐ 16 Ron Guidry	.15	.07	.01
☐ 17 Ozzie Guillen	.20	.10	.02
☐ 18 Bill Gullickson	.10	.05	.01
☐ 19 Tony Gwynn	.40	.20	.04
☐ 20 Bob Knepper	.10	.05	.01
☐ 21 Ray Knight	.15	.07	.01
☐ 22 Mark Langston	.15	.07	.01
☐ 23 Candy Maldonado	.10	.05	.01
☐ 24 Don Mattingly	1.00	.50	.10
☐ 25 Roger McDowell	.10	.05	.01
☐ 26 Dale Murphy	.35	.17	.03
☐ 27 Dave Parker	.20	.10	.02
☐ 28 Lance Parrish	.15	.07	.01
☐ 29 Gary Pettis	.10	.05	.01
☐ 30 Kirby Puckett	.60	.30	.06
☐ 31 Johnny Ray	.10	.05	.01
☐ 32 Dave Righetti	.15	.07	.01
☐ 33 Cal Ripken	.35	.17	.03
☐ 34 Bret Saberhagen	.20	.10	.02
☐ 35 Ryne Sandberg	.75	.35	.07
☐ 36 Mike Schmidt	.75	.35	.07
☐ 37 Mike Scott	.20	.10	.02
☐ 38 Ozzie Smith	.25	.12	.02
☐ 39 Robby Thompson	.10	.05	.01
☐ 40 Fernando Valenzuela	.20	.10	.02
☐ 41 Mitch Webster UER (Mike on front)	.10	.05	.01
☐ 42 Frank White	.10	.05	.01
☐ 43 Mike Witt	.10	.05	.01
☐ 44 Todd Worrell	.15	.07	.01

1987 Fleer Exciting Stars

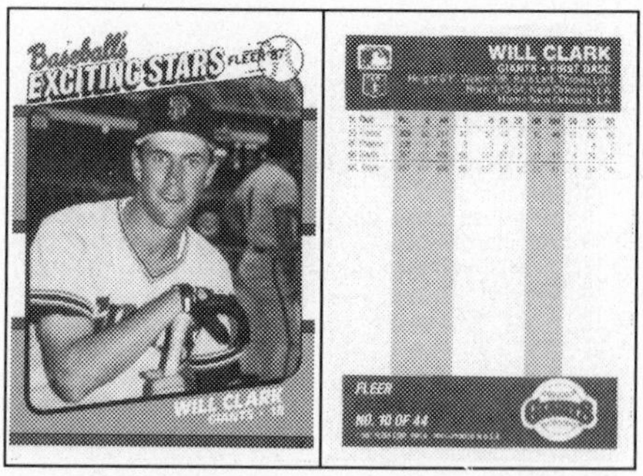

This small 44-card boxed set was produced by Fleer for distribution by the Cumberland Farm stores. The cards measure the standard 2 1/2" by 3 1/2" and feature full color fronts. The set is titled "Baseball's Exciting Stars." Each individual boxed set includes the 44 cards and 6 logo stickers. The checklist for the set is found on the back panel of the box.

	MINT	EXC	G-VG
COMPLETE SET (44)	5.00	2.50	.50
COMMON PLAYER (1-44)	.10	.05	.01
☐ 1 Don Aase	.10	.05	.01
☐ 2 Rick Aguilera	.10	.05	.01
☐ 3 Jesse Barfield	.15	.07	.01
☐ 4 Wade Boggs	.75	.35	.07
☐ 5 Oil Can Boyd	.15	.07	.01
☐ 6 Sid Bream	.10	.05	.01
☐ 7 Jose Canseco	1.25	.60	.12
☐ 8 Steve Carlton	.30	.15	.03
☐ 9 Gary Carter	.25	.12	.02
☐ 10 Will Clark	1.00	.50	.10
☐ 11 Roger Clemens	.75	.35	.07
☐ 12 Danny Cox	.10	.05	.01

☐ 13 Alvin Davis	.15	.07	.01
☐ 14 Eric Davis	.60	.30	.06
☐ 15 Rob Deer	.15	.07	.01
☐ 16 Brian Downing	.10	.05	.01
☐ 17 Gene Garber	.10	.05	.01
☐ 18 Steve Garvey	.30	.15	.03
☐ 19 Dwight Gooden	.45	.22	.04
☐ 20 Mark Gubicza	.15	.07	.01
☐ 21 Mel Hall	.10	.05	.01
☐ 22 Terry Harper	.10	.05	.01
☐ 23 Von Hayes	.15	.07	.01
☐ 24 Rickey Henderson	.75	.35	.07
☐ 25 Tom Henke	.15	.07	.01
☐ 26 Willie Hernandez	.10	.05	.01
☐ 27 Ted Higuera	.15	.07	.01
☐ 28 Rick Honeycutt	.10	.05	.01
☐ 29 Kent Hrbek	.20	.10	.02
☐ 30 Wally Joyner	.40	.20	.04
☐ 31 Charlie Kerfeld	.10	.05	.01
☐ 32 Fred Lynn	.15	.07	.01
☐ 33 Don Mattingly	1.00	.50	.10
☐ 34 Tim Raines	.25	.12	.02
☐ 35 Dennis Rasmussen	.10	.05	.01
☐ 36 Johnny Ray	.15	.07	.01
☐ 37 Jim Rice	.20	.10	.02
☐ 38 Pete Rose	.65	.30	.06
☐ 39 Lee Smith	.10	.05	.01
☐ 40 Cory Snyder	.20	.10	.02
☐ 41 Darryl Strawberry	.65	.30	.06
☐ 42 Kent Tekulve	.10	.05	.01
☐ 43 Willie Wilson	.15	.07	.01
☐ 44 Bobby Witt	.20	.10	.02

1987 Fleer Game Winners

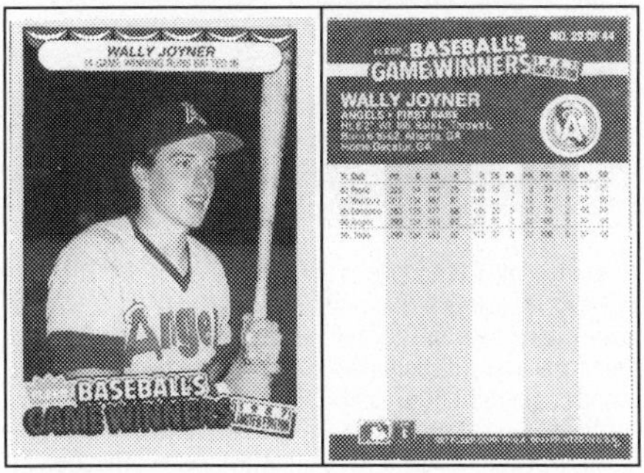

This small 44-card boxed set was produced by Fleer for distribution by several store chains, including Bi-Mart, Pay'n'Save, Mott's, M.E.Moses, and Winn's. The cards measure the standard 2 1/2" by 3 1/2" and feature full color fronts. The set is titled "Baseball's Game Winners." Each individual boxed set includes the 44 cards and 6 logo stickers. The checklist for the set is found on the back panel of the box.

	MINT	EXC	G-VG
COMPLETE SET (44)	4.00	2.00	.40
COMMON PLAYER (1-44)	.10	.05	.01
☐ 1 Harold Baines	.15	.07	.01
☐ 2 Don Baylor	.15	.07	.01
☐ 3 George Bell	.15	.07	.01
☐ 4 Tony Bernazard	.10	.05	.01
☐ 5 Wade Boggs	.75	.35	.07
☐ 6 George Brett	.45	.22	.04
☐ 7 Hubie Brooks	.15	.07	.01
☐ 8 Jose Canseco	1.00	.50	.10
☐ 9 Gary Carter	.25	.12	.02
☐ 10 Roger Clemens	.75	.35	.07
☐ 11 Eric Davis	.60	.30	.06
☐ 12 Glenn Davis	.25	.12	.02
☐ 13 Shawon Dunston	.25	.12	.02
☐ 14 Mark Eichhorn	.10	.05	.01
☐ 15 Gary Gaetti	.15	.07	.01
☐ 16 Steve Garvey	.30	.15	.03
☐ 17 Kirk Gibson	.30	.15	.03
☐ 18 Dwight Gooden	.40	.20	.04

☐ 19 Von Hayes	.15	.07	.01
☐ 20 Willie Hernandez	.10	.05	.01
☐ 21 Ted Higuera	.15	.07	.01
☐ 22 Wally Joyner	.40	.20	.04
☐ 23 Bob Knepper	.10	.05	.01
☐ 24 Mike Krukow	.10	.05	.01
☐ 25 Jeff Leonard	.10	.05	.01
☐ 26 Don Mattingly	1.00	.50	.10
☐ 27 Kirk McCaskill	.10	.05	.01
☐ 28 Kevin McReynolds	.20	.10	.02
☐ 29 Jim Morrison	.10	.05	.01
☐ 30 Dale Murphy	.35	.17	.03
☐ 31 Pete O'Brien	.10	.05	.01
☐ 32 Bob Ojeda	.15	.07	.01
☐ 33 Larry Parrish	.10	.05	.01
☐ 34 Ken Phelps	.10	.05	.01
☐ 35 Dennis Rasmussen	.10	.05	.01
☐ 36 Ernest Riles	.10	.05	.01
☐ 37 Cal Ripken	.40	.20	.04
☐ 38 Ron Robinson	.10	.05	.01
☐ 39 Steve Sax	.15	.07	.01
☐ 40 Mike Schmidt	.75	.35	.07
☐ 41 John Tudor	.10	.05	.01
☐ 42 Fernando Valenzuela	.20	.10	.02
☐ 43 Mike Witt	.10	.05	.01
☐ 44 Curt Young	.10	.05	.01

1987 Fleer Hottest Stars

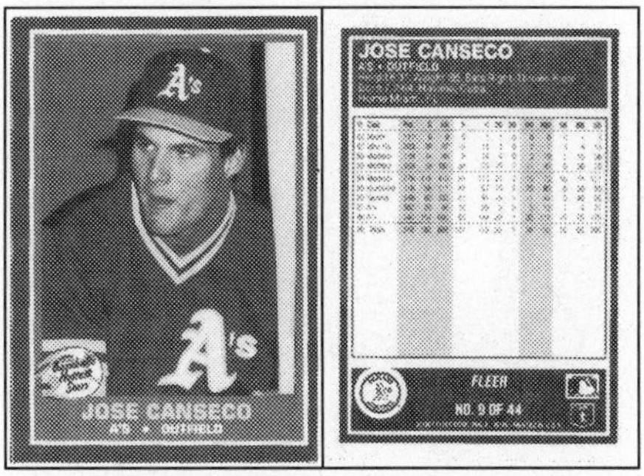

This 44-card boxed set was produced by Fleer for distribution by Revco stores all over the country. The cards measure the standard 2 1/2" by 3 1/2" and feature full color fronts and red, white, and black backs. The card fronts are easily distinguished by their solid red outside borders and and white and blue inner borders framing the player's picture. The box for the cards proclaims "1987 Limited Edition Baseball's Hottest Stars" and is styled in the same manner and color scheme as the cards themselves. The checklist for the set is given on the back of the set box.

	MINT	EXC	G-VG
COMPLETE SET (44)	5.00	2.50	.50
COMMON PLAYER (1-44)	.10	.05	.01
☐ 1 Joaquin Andujar	.10	.05	.01
☐ 2 Harold Baines	.15	.07	.01
☐ 3 Kevin Bass	.10	.05	.01
☐ 4 Don Baylor	.15	.07	.01
☐ 5 Barry Bonds	.75	.35	.07
☐ 6 George Brett	.45	.22	.04
☐ 7 Tom Brunansky	.15	.07	.01
☐ 8 Brett Butler	.15	.07	.01
☐ 9 Jose Canseco	1.25	.60	.12
☐ 10 Roger Clemens	.75	.35	.07
☐ 11 Ron Darling	.20	.10	.02
☐ 12 Eric Davis	.60	.30	.06
☐ 13 Andre Dawson	.25	.12	.02
☐ 14 Doug DeCinces	.10	.05	.01
☐ 15 Leon Durham	.10	.05	.01
☐ 16 Mark Eichhorn	.10	.05	.01
☐ 17 Scott Garrelts	.15	.07	.01
☐ 18 Dwight Gooden	.50	.25	.05
☐ 19 Dave Henderson	.10	.05	.01
☐ 20 Rickey Henderson	.75	.35	.07

☐ 21 Keith Hernandez	.20	.10	.02
☐ 22 Ted Higuera	.15	.07	.01
☐ 23 Bob Horner	.15	.07	.01
☐ 24 Pete Incaviglia	.20	.10	.02
☐ 25 Wally Joyner	.40	.20	.04
☐ 26 Mark Langston	.20	.10	.02
☐ 27 Don Mattingly UER (Pirates logo on back)	1.25	.60	.12
☐ 28 Dale Murphy	.35	.17	.03
☐ 29 Kirk McCaskill	.10	.05	.01
☐ 30 Willie McGee	.15	.07	.01
☐ 31 Dave Righetti	.15	.07	.01
☐ 32 Pete Rose	.65	.30	.06
☐ 33 Bruce Ruffin	.10	.05	.01
☐ 34 Steve Sax	.20	.10	.02
☐ 35 Mike Schmidt	.75	.35	.07
☐ 36 Larry Sheets	.10	.05	.01
☐ 37 Eric Show	.10	.05	.01
☐ 38 Dave Smith	.10	.05	.01
☐ 39 Cory Snyder	.20	.10	.02
☐ 40 Frank Tanana	.10	.05	.01
☐ 41 Alan Trammell	.25	.12	.02
☐ 42 Reggie Williams	.10	.05	.01
☐ 43 Mookie Wilson	.10	.05	.01
☐ 44 Todd Worrell	.15	.07	.01

1987 Fleer League Leaders

This small set of 44 cards was produced for Walgreens by Fleer. The cards measure the standard 2 1/2" by 3 1/2" and feature full color fronts and red, white, and blue backs. The card fronts are easily distinguished by their light blue vertical stripes over a white background. The box for the cards proclaims a "Walgreens Exclusive" and is styled in the same manner and color scheme as the cards themselves. The checklist for the set is given on the back of the set box.

	MINT	EXC	G-VG
COMPLETE SET (44)	5.00	2.50	.50
COMMON PLAYER (1-44)	.10	.05	.01
☐ 1 Jesse Barfield	.15	.07	.01
☐ 2 Mike Boddicker	.10	.05	.01
☐ 3 Wade Boggs	.75	.35	.07
☐ 4 Phil Bradley	.15	.07	.01
☐ 5 George Brett	.45	.22	.04
☐ 6 Hubie Brooks	.15	.07	.01
☐ 7 Chris Brown	.10	.05	.01
☐ 8 Jose Canseco	1.00	.50	.10
☐ 9 Joe Carter	.25	.12	.02
☐ 10 Roger Clemens	.75	.35	.07
☐ 11 Vince Coleman	.40	.20	.04
☐ 12 Joe Cowley	.10	.05	.01
☐ 13 Kal Daniels	.25	.12	.02
☐ 14 Glenn Davis	.25	.12	.02
☐ 15 Jody Davis	.10	.05	.01
☐ 16 Darrell Evans	.15	.07	.01
☐ 17 Dwight Evans	.20	.10	.02
☐ 18 John Franco	.15	.07	.01
☐ 19 Julio Franco	.15	.07	.01
☐ 20 Dwight Gooden	.45	.22	.04
☐ 21 Goose Gossage	.15	.07	.01
☐ 22 Tom Herr	.10	.05	.01
☐ 23 Ted Higuera	.15	.07	.01
☐ 24 Bob Horner	.15	.07	.01
☐ 25 Pete Incaviglia	.20	.10	.02
☐ 26 Wally Joyner	.40	.20	.04
☐ 27 Dave Kingman	.15	.07	.01
☐ 28 Don Mattingly	1.00	.50	.10
☐ 29 Willie McGee	.20	.10	.02
☐ 30 Donnie Moore	.10	.05	.01
☐ 31 Keith Moreland	.10	.05	.01
☐ 32 Eddie Murray	.35	.17	.03
☐ 33 Mike Pagliarulo	.15	.07	.01
☐ 34 Larry Parrish	.10	.05	.01
☐ 35 Tony Pena	.10	.05	.01
☐ 36 Kirby Puckett	.50	.25	.05
☐ 37 Pete Rose	.65	.30	.06
☐ 38 Juan Samuel	.20	.10	.02
☐ 39 Ryne Sandberg	.75	.35	.07
☐ 40 Mike Schmidt	.75	.35	.07
☐ 41 Darryl Strawberry	.60	.30	.06
☐ 42 Greg Walker	.15	.07	.01
☐ 43 Bob Welch	.25	.12	.02
☐ 44 Todd Worrell	.20	.10	.02

1987 Fleer Baseball All-Stars

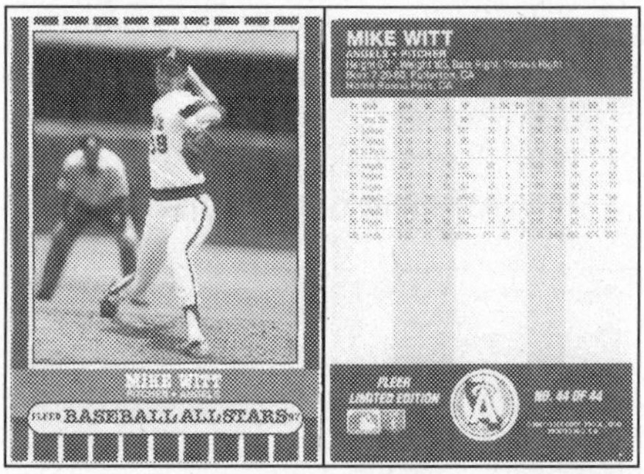

This small set of 44 cards was produced for Ben Franklin stores by Fleer. The cards measure the standard 2 1/2" by 3 1/2" and feature full color fronts and red, white, and blue backs. The card fronts are easily distinguished by their white vertical stripes over a bright red background. The box for the cards proclaims "Limited Edition Baseball All-Stars" and is styled in the same manner and color scheme as the cards themselves. The checklist for the set is given on the back of the set box.

	MINT	EXC	G-VG
COMPLETE SET (44)	5.00	2.50	.50
COMMON PLAYER (1-44)	.10	.05	.01
☐ 1 Harold Baines	.15	.07	.01
☐ 2 Jesse Barfield	.15	.07	.01
☐ 3 Wade Boggs	.75	.35	.07
☐ 4 Oil Can Boyd	.15	.07	.01
☐ 5 Scott Bradley	.10	.05	.01
☐ 6 Jose Canseco	1.00	.50	.10
☐ 7 Gary Carter	.25	.12	.02
☐ 8 Joe Carter	.25	.12	.02
☐ 9 Mark Clear	.10	.05	.01
☐ 10 Roger Clemens	.75	.35	.07
☐ 11 Jose Cruz	.10	.05	.01
☐ 12 Chili Davis	.10	.05	.01
☐ 13 Jody Davis	.10	.05	.01
☐ 14 Rob Deer	.15	.07	.01
☐ 15 Brian Downing	.10	.05	.01
☐ 16 Sid Fernandez	.15	.07	.01
☐ 17 John Franco	.15	.07	.01
☐ 18 Andres Galarraga	.25	.12	.02
☐ 19 Dwight Gooden	.45	.22	.04
☐ 20 Tony Gwynn	.45	.22	.04
☐ 21 Charlie Hough	.10	.05	.01
☐ 22 Bruce Hurst	.15	.07	.01
☐ 23 Wally Joyner	.40	.20	.04
☐ 24 Carney Lansford	.20	.10	.02
☐ 25 Fred Lynn	.15	.07	.01
☐ 26 Don Mattingly	1.00	.50	.10
☐ 27 Willie McGee	.20	.10	.02
☐ 28 Jack Morris	.15	.07	.01

	MINT	EXC	G-VG
☐ 29 Dale Murphy	.35	.17	.03
☐ 30 Bob Ojeda	.15	.07	.01
☐ 31 Tony Pena	.10	.05	.01
☐ 32 Kirby Puckett	.50	.25	.05
☐ 33 Dan Quisenberry	.15	.07	.01
☐ 34 Tim Raines	.25	.12	.02
☐ 35 Willie Randolph	.15	.07	.01
☐ 36 Cal Ripken	.40	.20	.04
☐ 37 Pete Rose	.60	.30	.06
☐ 38 Nolan Ryan	1.25	.60	.12
☐ 39 Juan Samuel	.15	.07	.01
☐ 40 Mike Schmidt	.75	.35	.07
☐ 41 Ozzie Smith	.25	.12	.02
☐ 42 Andres Thomas	.10	.05	.01
☐ 43 Fernando Valenzuela	.20	.10	.02
☐ 44 Mike Witt	.10	.05	.01

1987 Fleer Limited Edition

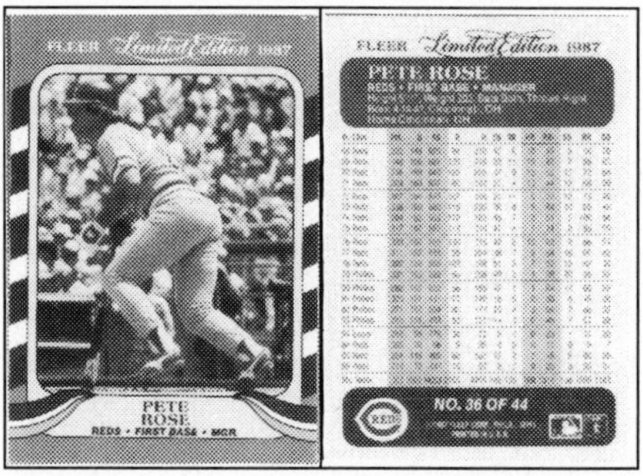

This 44-card boxed set was (mass) produced by Fleer for distribution by McCrory's and is sometimes referred to as the McCrory's set. The numerical checklist on the back of the box shows that the set is numbered alphabetically. The cards measure 2 1/2" by 3 1/2".

	MINT	EXC	G-VG
COMPLETE SET (44)	4.00	2.00	.40
COMMON PLAYER (1-44)	.10	.05	.01
☐ 1 Floyd Bannister	.10	.05	.01
☐ 2 Marty Barrett	.10	.05	.01
☐ 3 Steve Bedrosian	.10	.05	.01
☐ 4 George Bell	.20	.10	.02
☐ 5 George Brett	.40	.20	.04
☐ 6 Jose Canseco	1.00	.50	.10
☐ 7 Joe Carter	.20	.10	.02
☐ 8 Will Clark	.90	.45	.09
☐ 9 Roger Clemens	.75	.35	.07
☐ 10 Vince Coleman	.30	.15	.03
☐ 11 Glenn Davis	.20	.10	.02
☐ 12 Mike Davis	.10	.05	.01
☐ 13 Len Dykstra	.20	.10	.02
☐ 14 John Franco	.15	.07	.01
☐ 15 Julio Franco	.15	.07	.01
☐ 16 Steve Garvey	.30	.15	.03
☐ 17 Kirk Gibson	.30	.15	.03
☐ 18 Dwight Gooden	.50	.25	.05
☐ 19 Tony Gwynn	.40	.20	.04
☐ 20 Keith Hernandez	.15	.07	.01
☐ 21 Teddy Higuera	.10	.05	.01
☐ 22 Kent Hrbek	.15	.07	.01
☐ 23 Wally Joyner	.35	.17	.03
☐ 24 Mike Krukow	.10	.05	.01
☐ 25 Mike Marshall	.15	.07	.01
☐ 26 Don Mattingly	1.00	.50	.10
☐ 27 Oddibe McDowell	.10	.05	.01
☐ 28 Jack Morris	.15	.07	.01
☐ 29 Lloyd Moseby	.10	.05	.01
☐ 30 Dale Murphy	.35	.17	.03
☐ 31 Eddie Murray	.35	.17	.03
☐ 32 Tony Pena	.10	.05	.01
☐ 33 Jim Presley	.10	.05	.01
☐ 34 Jeff Reardon	.15	.07	.01
☐ 35 Jim Rice	.20	.10	.02
☐ 36 Pete Rose	.60	.30	.06
☐ 37 Mike Schmidt	.75	.35	.07
☐ 38 Mike Scott	.15	.07	.01
☐ 39 Lee Smith	.10	.05	.01
☐ 40 Lonnie Smith	.10	.05	.01
☐ 41 Gary Ward	.10	.05	.01
☐ 42 Dave Winfield	.25	.12	.02
☐ 43 Todd Worrell	.15	.07	.01
☐ 44 Robin Yount	.45	.22	.04

1987 Fleer Limited Box Cards

The cards in this 6-card set each measure the standard 2 1/2" by 3 1/2". Cards have essentially the same design as the 1987 Fleer Limited Edition cards which were distributed by McCrory's. The cards were printed on the bottom of the counter display box which held 24 small boxed sets; hence theoretically these box cards are 1/24 as plentiful as the regular boxed set cards. These 6 cards, numbered C1 to C6, are considered a separate set in their own right and are not typically included in a complete set of the 1987 Fleer Limited Edition set of 44. The value of the panels uncut is slightly greater, perhaps by 25 percent greater, than the value of the individual cards cut up carefully.

	MINT	EXC	G-VG
COMPLETE SET (6)	1.25	.60	.12
COMMON PLAYERS (C1-C6)	.10	.05	.01
☐ C1 Ron Darling (box bottom card)	.25	.12	.02
☐ C2 Bill Buckner (box bottom card)	.15	.07	.01
☐ C3 John Candelaria (box bottom card)	.15	.07	.01
☐ C4 Jack Clark (box bottom card)	.35	.17	.03
☐ C5 Bret Saberhagen (box bottom card)	.50	.25	.05
☐ C6 Team Logo (box bottom card; checklist back)	.10	.05	.01

1987 Fleer Mini

The 1987 Fleer "Classic Miniatures" set consists of 120 small cards with all new pictures of the players as compared to the 1987 Fleer regular issue. The cards are only 1 13/16" by 2 9/16", making them one of the smallest cards available. Card backs provide career year-by-year statistics. The complete set was distributed in a blue, red, white, and silver box along with 18 logo stickers. The card numbering is by alphabetical order.

	MINT	EXC	G-VG
COMPLETE SET (120)	8.00	4.00	.80
COMMON PLAYER (1-120)	.05	.02	.00
☐ 1 Don Aase	.05	.02	.00
☐ 2 Joaquin Andujar	.05	.02	.00

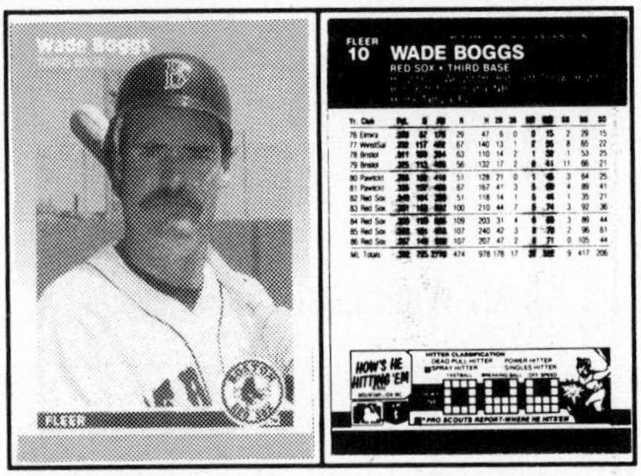

☐ 3 Harold Baines	.10	.05	.01
☐ 4 Jesse Barfield	.15	.07	.01
☐ 5 Kevin Bass	.05	.02	.00
☐ 6 Don Baylor	.10	.05	.01
☐ 7 George Bell	.15	.07	.01
☐ 8 Tony Bernazard	.05	.02	.00
☐ 9 Bert Blyleven	.10	.05	.01
☐ 10 Wade Boggs	.75	.35	.07
☐ 11 Phil Bradley	.10	.05	.01
☐ 12 Sid Bream	.05	.02	.00
☐ 13 George Brett	.45	.22	.04
☐ 14 Hubie Brooks	.05	.02	.00
☐ 15 Chris Brown	.05	.02	.00
☐ 16 Tom Candiotti	.05	.02	.00
☐ 17 Jose Canseco	1.00	.50	.10
☐ 18 Gary Carter	.20	.10	.02
☐ 19 Joe Carter	.15	.07	.01
☐ 20 Roger Clemens	.75	.35	.07
☐ 21 Vince Coleman	.25	.12	.02
☐ 22 Cecil Cooper	.10	.05	.01
☐ 23 Ron Darling	.10	.05	.01
☐ 24 Alvin Davis	.10	.05	.01
☐ 25 Chili Davis	.05	.02	.00
☐ 26 Eric Davis	.60	.30	.06
☐ 27 Glenn Davis	.20	.10	.02
☐ 28 Mike Davis	.05	.02	.00
☐ 29 Doug DeCinces	.05	.02	.00
☐ 30 Rob Deer	.10	.05	.01
☐ 31 Jim Deshaies	.05	.02	.00
☐ 32 Bo Diaz	.05	.02	.00
☐ 33 Richard Dotson	.05	.02	.00
☐ 34 Brian Downing	.05	.02	.00
☐ 35 Shawon Dunston	.15	.07	.01
☐ 36 Mark Eichhorn	.05	.02	.00
☐ 37 Dwight Evans	.10	.05	.01
☐ 38 Tony Fernandez	.10	.05	.01
☐ 39 Julio Franco	.10	.05	.01
☐ 40 Gary Gaetti	.10	.05	.01
☐ 41 Andres Galarraga	.20	.10	.02
☐ 42 Scott Garrelts	.05	.02	.00
☐ 43 Steve Garvey	.25	.12	.02
☐ 44 Kirk Gibson	.25	.12	.02
☐ 45 Dwight Gooden	.45	.22	.04
☐ 46 Ken Griffey Sr.	.10	.05	.01
☐ 47 Mark Gubicza	.10	.05	.01
☐ 48 Ozzie Guillen	.15	.07	.01
☐ 49 Bill Gullickson	.05	.02	.00
☐ 50 Tony Gwynn	.35	.17	.03
☐ 51 Von Hayes	.10	.05	.01
☐ 52 Rickey Henderson	.75	.35	.07
☐ 53 Keith Hernandez	.15	.07	.01
☐ 54 Willie Hernandez	.05	.02	.00
☐ 55 Ted Higuera	.10	.05	.01
☐ 56 Charlie Hough	.05	.02	.00
☐ 57 Kent Hrbek	.15	.07	.01
☐ 58 Pete Incaviglia	.15	.07	.01
☐ 59 Wally Joyner	.35	.17	.03
☐ 60 Bob Knepper	.05	.02	.00
☐ 61 Mike Krukow	.05	.02	.00
☐ 62 Mark Langston	.15	.07	.01
☐ 63 Carney Lansford	.10	.05	.01
☐ 64 Jim Lindeman	.05	.02	.00
☐ 65 Bill Madlock	.05	.02	.00
☐ 66 Don Mattingly	1.00	.50	.10
☐ 67 Kirk McCaskill	.05	.02	.00
☐ 68 Lance McCullers	.05	.02	.00
☐ 69 Keith Moreland	.05	.02	.00
☐ 70 Jack Morris	.10	.05	.01
☐ 71 Jim Morrison	.05	.02	.00
☐ 72 Lloyd Moseby	.05	.02	.00
☐ 73 Jerry Mumphrey	.05	.02	.00
☐ 74 Dale Murphy	.35	.17	.03
☐ 75 Eddie Murray	.35	.17	.03
☐ 76 Pete O'Brien	.10	.05	.01
☐ 77 Bob Ojeda	.10	.05	.01
☐ 78 Jesse Orosco	.05	.02	.00
☐ 79 Dan Pasqua	.05	.02	.00
☐ 80 Dave Parker	.15	.07	.01
☐ 81 Larry Parrish	.05	.02	.00
☐ 82 Jim Presley	.05	.02	.00
☐ 83 Kirby Puckett	.50	.25	.05
☐ 84 Dan Quisenberry	.10	.05	.01
☐ 85 Tim Raines	.25	.12	.02
☐ 86 Dennis Rasmussen	.05	.02	.00
☐ 87 Johnny Ray	.05	.02	.00
☐ 88 Jeff Reardon	.10	.05	.01
☐ 89 Jim Rice	.20	.10	.02
☐ 90 Dave Righetti	.10	.05	.01
☐ 91 Earnest Riles	.05	.02	.00
☐ 92 Cal Ripken	.35	.17	.03
☐ 93 Ron Robinson	.05	.02	.00
☐ 94 Juan Samuel	.10	.05	.01
☐ 95 Ryne Sandberg	.75	.35	.07
☐ 96 Steve Sax	.15	.07	.01
☐ 97 Mike Schmidt	.75	.35	.07
☐ 98 Ken Schrom	.05	.02	.00
☐ 99 Mike Scott	.20	.10	.02
☐ 100 Ruben Sierra	.60	.30	.06
☐ 101 Lee Smith	.10	.05	.01
☐ 102 Ozzie Smith	.15	.07	.01
☐ 103 Cory Snyder	.15	.07	.01
☐ 104 Kent Tekulve	.05	.02	.00
☐ 105 Andres Thomas	.05	.02	.00
☐ 106 Robby Thompson	.05	.02	.00
☐ 107 Alan Trammell	.20	.10	.02
☐ 108 John Tudor	.10	.05	.01
☐ 109 Fernando Valenzuela	.15	.07	.01
☐ 110 Greg Walker	.10	.05	.01
☐ 111 Mitch Webster	.05	.02	.00
☐ 112 Lou Whitaker	.10	.05	.01
☐ 113 Frank White	.05	.02	.00
☐ 114 Reggie Williams	.05	.02	.00
☐ 115 Glenn Wilson	.05	.02	.00
☐ 116 Willie Wilson	.10	.05	.01
☐ 117 Dave Winfield	.25	.12	.02
☐ 118 Mike Witt	.05	.02	.00
☐ 119 Todd Worrell	.15	.07	.01
☐ 120 Floyd Youmans	.05	.02	.00

1987 Fleer Record Setters

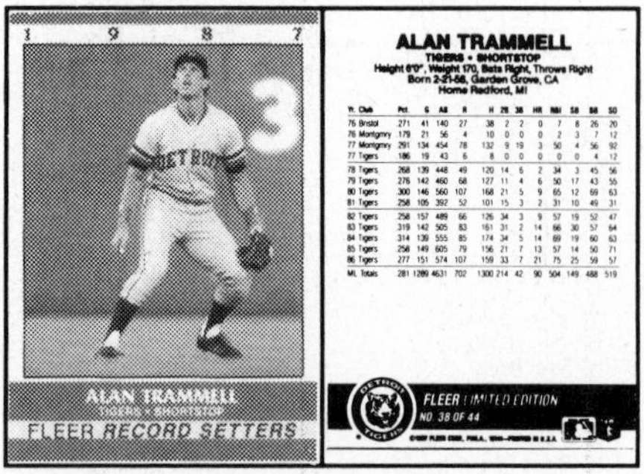

This 44-card boxed set was produced by Fleer for distribution by Eckerd's Drug Stores and is sometimes referred to as the Eckerd's set. Six team logo stickers are included in the box with the complete set. The numerical checklist on the back of the box shows that the set is numbered alphabetically. The cards measure 2 1/2" by 3 1/2".

	MINT	EXC	G-VG
COMPLETE SET (44)	5.00	2.50	.50
COMMON PLAYER (1-44)	.10	.05	.01
☐ 1 George Brett	.40	.20	.04
☐ 2 Chris Brown	.10	.05	.01
☐ 3 Jose Canseco UER (3 of 444 on back)	1.25	.60	.12
☐ 4 Roger Clemens	.75	.35	.07

☐ 5 Alvin Davis UER (5 of 441 on back, upside down one)	.15	.07	.01
☐ 6 Shawon Dunston	.20	.10	.02
☐ 7 Tony Fernandez	.15	.07	.01
☐ 8 Carlton Fisk UER (8 of 44' on back)	.30	.15	.03
☐ 9 Gary Gaetti UER (9 of 444 on back)	.15	.07	.01
☐ 10 Gene Garber	.10	.05	.01
☐ 11 Rich Gedman	.10	.05	.01
☐ 12 Dwight Gooden	.50	.25	.05
☐ 13 Ozzie Guillen	.15	.07	.01
☐ 14 Bill Gullickson	.10	.05	.01
☐ 15 Billy Hatcher	.15	.07	.01
☐ 16 Orel Hershiser	.40	.20	.04
☐ 17 Wally Joyner	.35	.17	.03
☐ 18 Ray Knight	.15	.07	.01
☐ 19 Craig Lefferts	.10	.05	.01
☐ 20 Don Mattingly	1.00	.50	.10
☐ 21 Kevin Mitchell	.60	.30	.06
☐ 22 Lloyd Moseby	.10	.05	.01
☐ 23 Dale Murphy	.35	.17	.03
☐ 24 Eddie Murray	.35	.17	.03
☐ 25 Phil Niekro	.20	.10	.02
☐ 26 Ben Oglivie	.10	.05	.01
☐ 27 Jesse Orosco	.10	.05	.01
☐ 28 Joe Orsulak	.10	.05	.01
☐ 29 Larry Parrish	.10	.05	.01
☐ 30 Tim Raines	.20	.10	.02
☐ 31 Shane Rawley	.10	.05	.01
☐ 32 Dave Righetti	.15	.07	.01
☐ 33 Pete Rose	.60	.30	.06
☐ 34 Steve Sax	.15	.07	.01
☐ 35 Mike Schmidt	.75	.35	.07
☐ 36 Mike Scott	.20	.10	.02
☐ 37 Don Sutton	.20	.10	.02
☐ 38 Alan Trammell	.20	.10	.02
☐ 39 John Tudor	.10	.05	.01
☐ 40 Gary Ward	.10	.05	.01
☐ 41 Lou Whitaker	.15	.07	.01
☐ 42 Willie Wilson	.15	.07	.01
☐ 43 Todd Worrell	.15	.07	.01
☐ 44 Floyd Youmans	.10	.05	.01

1987 Fleer Sluggers/Pitchers

Fleer produced this 44-card boxed set although it was primarily distributed by McCrory, McLellan, Newberry, H.L.Green, T.G.Y., and other similar stores. The set features 28 sluggers and 16 pitchers and is subtitled "Baseball's Best". Cards are standard-size, 2 1/2" by 3 1/2", and were packaged in a red, white, blue, and yellow custom box along with six logo stickers. The set checklist is given on the back of the box. The checklist on the back of the set box misspells McGwire as McGuire.

	MINT	EXC	G-VG
COMPLETE SET (44)	5.00	2.50	.50
COMMON PLAYER (1-44)	.10	.05	.01
☐ 1 Kevin Bass	.10	.05	.01
☐ 2 Jesse Barfield	.15	.07	.01
☐ 3 George Bell	.20	.10	.02
☐ 4 Wade Boggs	.75	.35	.07
☐ 5 Sid Bream	.10	.05	.01
☐ 6 George Brett	.45	.22	.04
☐ 7 Ivan Calderon	.15	.07	.01
☐ 8 Jose Canseco	1.00	.50	.10
☐ 9 Jack Clark	.20	.10	.02
☐ 10 Roger Clemens	.75	.35	.07
☐ 11 Eric Davis	.60	.30	.06
☐ 12 Andre Dawson	.30	.15	.03
☐ 13 Sid Fernandez	.15	.07	.01
☐ 14 John Franco	.15	.07	.01
☐ 15 Dwight Gooden	.40	.20	.04
☐ 16 Pedro Guerrero	.20	.10	.02
☐ 17 Tony Gwynn	.35	.17	.03
☐ 18 Rickey Henderson	.75	.35	.07
☐ 19 Tom Henke	.10	.05	.01
☐ 20 Ted Higuera	.15	.07	.01
☐ 21 Pete Incaviglia	.20	.10	.02
☐ 22 Wally Joyner	.35	.17	.03
☐ 23 Jeff Leonard	.10	.05	.01
☐ 24 Joe Magrane	.15	.07	.01
☐ 25 Don Mattingly	1.00	.50	.10
☐ 26 Mark McGwire	1.00	.50	.10
☐ 27 Jack Morris	.15	.07	.01
☐ 28 Dale Murphy	.35	.17	.03
☐ 29 Dave Parker	.20	.10	.02
☐ 30 Ken Phelps	.10	.05	.01
☐ 31 Kirby Puckett	.40	.20	.04
☐ 32 Tim Raines	.25	.12	.02
☐ 33 Jeff Reardon	.10	.05	.01
☐ 34 Dave Righetti	.15	.07	.01
☐ 35 Cal Ripken	.35	.17	.03
☐ 36 Bret Saberhagen	.30	.15	.03
☐ 37 Mike Schmidt	.75	.35	.07
☐ 38 Mike Scott	.20	.10	.02
☐ 39 Kevin Seitzer	.50	.25	.05
☐ 40 Darryl Strawberry	.60	.30	.06
☐ 41 Rick Sutcliffe	.15	.07	.01
☐ 42 Pat Tabler	.10	.05	.01
☐ 43 Fernando Valenzuela	.20	.10	.02
☐ 44 Mike Witt	.10	.05	.01

1987 Fleer Slug/Pitch Box Cards

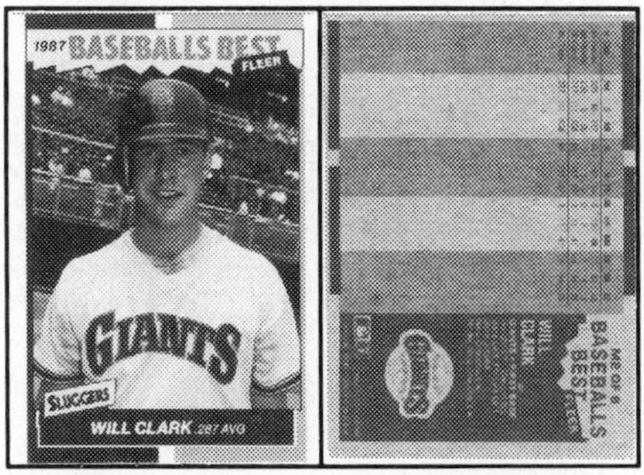

The cards in this 6-card set each measure the standard 2 1/2" by 3 1/2". Cards have essentially the same design as the 1987 Fleer Sluggers vs. Pitchers set of Baseball's Best. The cards were printed on the bottom of the counter display box which held 24 small boxed sets; hence theoretically these box cards are 1/24 as plentiful as the regular boxed set cards. These 6 cards, numbered M1 to M5 with one blank-back (unnumbered) card, are considered a separate set in their own right and are not typically included in a complete set of the 1987 Fleer Sluggers vs. Pitchers set of 44. The value of the panels uncut is slightly greater, perhaps by 25 percent greater, than the value of the individual cards cut up carefully.

	MINT	EXC	G-VG
COMPLETE SET (6)	4.00	2.00	.40
COMMON PLAYERS (M1-M5)	.10	.05	.01
☐ M1 Steve Bedrosian (box bottom card)	.15	.07	.01
☐ M2 Will Clark (box bottom card)	1.25	.60	.12

☐ M3 Vince Coleman (box bottom card)	.45	.22	.04
☐ M4 Bo Jackson (box bottom card)	2.50	1.25	.25
☐ M5 Cory Snyder (box bottom card)	.35	.17	.03
☐ xx Team Logo (box bottom card, unnumbered, blank back)	.10	.05	.01

1987 Fleer Update

This 132-card set was distributed by Fleer to dealers as a complete set in a custom box. In addition to the complete set of 132 cards, the box also contains 25 Team Logo stickers. The card fronts look very similar to the 1987 Fleer regular issue. The cards are numbered (with a U prefix) alphabetically according to player's last name. Cards measure the standard size, 2 1/2" by 3 1/2". Fleer misalphabetized Jim Winn in their set numbering by putting him ahead of the next four players listed. The key (extended) rookie cards in this set are Ellis Burks, Mike Greenwell, Fred McGriff, Mark McGwire and Matt Williams. Fleer also produced a "limited" edition version of this set with glossy coating and packaged in a "tin." However, this tin set was apparently not limited enough (estimated between 75,000 and 100,000 1987 Update tin sets produced by Fleer), since the price of the "tin" glossy cards is now the same as the regular set.

	MINT	EXC	G-VG
COMPLETE SET (132)	17.00	8.50	1.70
COMMON PLAYER (1-132)	.07	.03	.01
☐ U1 Scott Bankhead	.15	.07	.01
☐ U2 Eric Bell	.10	.05	.01
☐ U3 Juan Beniquez	.07	.03	.01
☐ U4 Juan Berenguer	.07	.03	.01
☐ U5 Mike Birkbeck	.12	.06	.01
☐ U6 Randy Bockus	.10	.05	.01
☐ U7 Rod Booker	.07	.03	.01
☐ U8 Thad Bosley	.07	.03	.01
☐ U9 Greg Brock	.07	.03	.01
☐ U10 Bob Brower	.10	.05	.01
☐ U11 Chris Brown	.10	.05	.01
☐ U12 Jerry Browne	.12	.06	.01
☐ U13 Ralph Bryant	.10	.05	.01
☐ U14 DeWayne Buice	.10	.05	.01
☐ U15 Ellis Burks	3.25	1.60	.32
☐ U16 Casey Candaele	.10	.05	.01
☐ U17 Steve Carlton	.35	.17	.03
☐ U18 Juan Castillo	.07	.03	.01
☐ U19 Chuck Crim	.10	.05	.01
☐ U20 Mark Davidson	.10	.05	.01
☐ U21 Mark Davis	.15	.07	.01
☐ U22 Storm Davis	.12	.06	.01
☐ U23 Bill Dawley	.07	.03	.01
☐ U24 Andre Dawson	.40	.20	.04
☐ U25 Brian Dayett	.07	.03	.01
☐ U26 Rick Dempsey	.07	.03	.01
☐ U27 Ken Dowell	.10	.05	.01
☐ U28 Dave Dravecky	.15	.07	.01
☐ U29 Mike Dunne	.12	.06	.01
☐ U30 Dennis Eckersley	.30	.15	.03
☐ U31 Cecil Fielder	2.25	1.10	.22
☐ U32 Brian Fisher	.10	.05	.01
☐ U33 Willie Fraser	.10	.05	.01
☐ U34 Ken Gerhart	.10	.05	.01
☐ U35 Jim Gott	.10	.05	.01
☐ U36 Dan Gladden	.10	.05	.01
☐ U37 Mike Greenwell	2.75	1.35	.27
☐ U38 Cecilio Guante	.07	.03	.01
☐ U39 Albert Hall	.07	.03	.01
☐ U40 Atlee Hammaker	.07	.03	.01
☐ U41 Mickey Hatcher	.07	.03	.01
☐ U42 Mike Heath	.07	.03	.01
☐ U43 Neal Heaton	.07	.03	.01
☐ U44 Mike Henneman	.30	.15	.03
☐ U45 Guy Hoffman	.10	.05	.01
☐ U46 Charles Hudson	.07	.03	.01
☐ U47 Chuck Jackson	.10	.05	.01
☐ U48 Mike Jackson	.15	.07	.01
☐ U49 Reggie Jackson	.50	.25	.05
☐ U50 Chris James	.30	.15	.03
☐ U51 Dion James	.10	.05	.01
☐ U52 Stan Javier	.10	.05	.01
☐ U53 Stan Jefferson	.12	.06	.01
☐ U54 Jimmy Jones	.10	.05	.01
☐ U55 Tracy Jones	.12	.06	.01
☐ U56 Terry Kennedy	.07	.03	.01
☐ U57 Mike Kingery	.10	.05	.01
☐ U58 Ray Knight	.10	.05	.01
☐ U59 Gene Larkin	.35	.17	.03
☐ U60 Mike LaValliere	.10	.05	.01
☐ U61 Jack Lazorko	.07	.03	.01
☐ U62 Terry Leach	.10	.05	.01
☐ U63 Rick Leach	.07	.03	.01
☐ U64 Craig Lefferts	.07	.03	.01
☐ U65 Jim Lindeman	.10	.05	.01
☐ U66 Bill Long	.10	.05	.01
☐ U67 Mike Loynd	.07	.03	.01
☐ U68 Greg Maddux	1.00	.50	.10
☐ U69 Bill Madlock	.12	.06	.01
☐ U70 Dave Magadan	.75	.35	.07
☐ U71 Joe Magrane	.90	.45	.09
☐ U72 Fred Manrique	.10	.05	.01
☐ U73 Mike Mason	.07	.03	.01
☐ U74 Lloyd McClendon	.15	.07	.01
☐ U75 Fred McGriff	2.75	1.35	.27
☐ U76 Mark McGwire	2.75	1.35	.27
☐ U77 Mark McLemore	.07	.03	.01
☐ U78 Kevin McReynolds	.30	.15	.03
☐ U79 Dave Meads	.07	.03	.01
☐ U80 Greg Minton	.07	.03	.01
☐ U81 John Mitchell	.12	.06	.01
☐ U82 Kevin Mitchell	1.75	.85	.17
☐ U83 John Morris	.07	.03	.01
☐ U84 Jeff Musselman	.12	.06	.01
☐ U85 Randy Myers	.60	.30	.06
☐ U86 Gene Nelson	.07	.03	.01
☐ U87 Joe Niekro	.12	.06	.01
☐ U88 Tom Nieto	.07	.03	.01
☐ U89 Reid Nichols	.07	.03	.01
☐ U90 Matt Nokes	.45	.22	.04
☐ U91 Dickie Noles	.07	.03	.01
☐ U92 Edwin Nunez	.07	.03	.01
☐ U93 Jose Nunez	.12	.06	.01
☐ U94 Paul O'Neill	.40	.20	.04
☐ U95 Jim Paciorek	.10	.05	.01
☐ U96 Lance Parrish	.12	.06	.01
☐ U97 Bill Pecota	.10	.05	.01
☐ U98 Tony Pena	.12	.06	.01
☐ U99 Luis Polonia	.30	.15	.03
☐ U100 Randy Ready	.10	.05	.01
☐ U101 Jeff Reardon	.15	.07	.01
☐ U102 Gary Redus	.07	.03	.01
☐ U103 Rick Rhoden	.10	.05	.01
☐ U104 Wally Ritchie	.10	.05	.01
☐ U105 Jeff Robinson UER (wrong Jeff's stats on back)	.25	.12	.02
☐ U106 Mark Salas	.07	.03	.01
☐ U107 Dave Schmidt	.10	.05	.01
☐ U108 Kevin Seitzer UER (wrong birth year)	.90	.45	.09
☐ U109 John Shelby	.07	.03	.01
☐ U110 John Smiley	.40	.20	.04
☐ U111 Lary Sorensen	.07	.03	.01
☐ U112 Chris Speier	.07	.03	.01
☐ U113 Randy St.Claire	.07	.03	.01
☐ U114 Jim Sundberg	.07	.03	.01
☐ U115 B.J. Surhoff	.30	.15	.03
☐ U116 Greg Swindell	.45	.22	.04
☐ U117 Danny Tartabull	.25	.12	.02
☐ U118 Dorn Taylor	.12	.06	.01
☐ U119 Lee Tunnell	.07	.03	.01

☐ U120 Ed VandeBerg	.07	.03	.01
☐ U121 Andy Van Slyke	.20	.10	.02
☐ U122 Gary Ward	.07	.03	.01
☐ U123 Devon White	.30	.15	.03
☐ U124 Alan Wiggins	.07	.03	.01
☐ U125 Bill Wilkinson	.07	.03	.01
☐ U126 Jim Winn	.07	.03	.01
☐ U127 Frank Williams	.07	.03	.01
☐ U128 Ken Williams	.12	.06	.01
☐ U129 Matt Williams	6.00	3.00	.60
☐ U130 Herm Willingham	.10	.05	.01
☐ U131 Matt Young	.07	.03	.01
☐ U132 Checklist	.07	.01	.00

1987 Fleer World Series

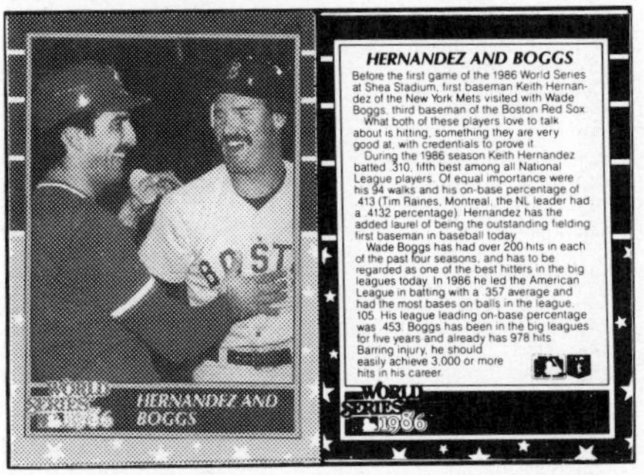

This 12-card set of 2 1/2" by 3 1/2" cards features highlights of the previous year's World Series between the Mets and the Red Sox. The sets were packaged as a complete set insert with the collated sets (of the 1987 Fleer regular issue) which were sold by Fleer directly to hobby card dealers; they were not available in the general retail candy store outlets.

	MINT	EXC	G-VG
COMPLETE SET (12)	4.00	2.00	.40
COMMON PLAYER (1-12)	.25	.12	.02
☐ 1 Bruce Hurst Left Hand Finesse Beats Mets	.35	.17	.03
☐ 2 Keith Hernandez and Wade Boggs	.60	.30	.06
☐ 3 Roger Clemens HOR	1.00	.50	.10
☐ 4 Clutch Hitting (Gary Carter)	.35	.17	.03
☐ 5 Ron Darling Picks Up Slack	.35	.17	.03
☐ 6 Marty Barrett .433 Series BA	.25	.12	.02
☐ 7 Dwight Gooden	.60	.30	.06
☐ 8 Strategy at Work (Mets Conference)	.25	.12	.02
☐ 9 Dewey Evans (Congratulated by Rich Gedman)	.35	.17	.03
☐ 10 One Strike From Boston Victory (Dave Henderson)	.25	.12	.02
☐ 11 Series Home Run Duo (Ray Knight and Darryl Strawberry)	.50	.25	.05
☐ 12 Ray Knight (Series MVP)	.35	.17	.03

1988 Fleer

This 660-card set features a distinctive white background with red and blue diagonal stripes across the card. The backs are printed in gray and red on white card stock. The bottom of the card back shows an innovative breakdown of the player's demonstrated ability with respect to day, night, home, and road games. Cards are numbered on the back and are again the standard 2 1/2" by 3 1/2". Cards are again organized numerically by teams, i.e., World Champion Twins (1-25), St. Louis Cardinals (26-50), Detroit Tigers (51-75), San Francisco Giants (76-101), Toronto Blue Jays (102-126), New York Mets (127-154), Milwaukee Brewers (155-178), Montreal Expos (179-201), New York Yankees (202-226), Cincinnati Reds (227-250), Kansas City Royals (251-274), Oakland A's (275-296), Philadelphia Phillies (297-320), Pittsburgh Pirates (321-342), Boston Red Sox (343-367), Seattle Mariners (368-390), Chicago White Sox (391-413), Chicago Cubs (414-436), Houston Astros (437-460), Texas Rangers (461-483), California Angels (484-507), Los Angeles Dodgers (508-530), Atlanta Braves (531-552), Baltimore Orioles (553-575), San Diego Padres (576-599), and Cleveland Indians (600-621). The last 39 cards in the set consist of Specials (622-640), Rookie Pairs (641-653), and checklists (654-660). Cards 90 and 91 are incorrectly numbered on the checklist card number 654. The key rookie cards in this set are Ellis Burks, Ron Gant, Mark Grace, Gregg Jefferies, Roberto Kelly, and Matt Williams. Fleer also produced a "limited" edition version of this set with glossy coating and packaged in a "tin." However, this tin set was apparently not limited enough (estimated between 40,000 and 60,000 1988 tin sets produced by Fleer), since the price of the "tin" glossy cards is now only double the price of the regular set.

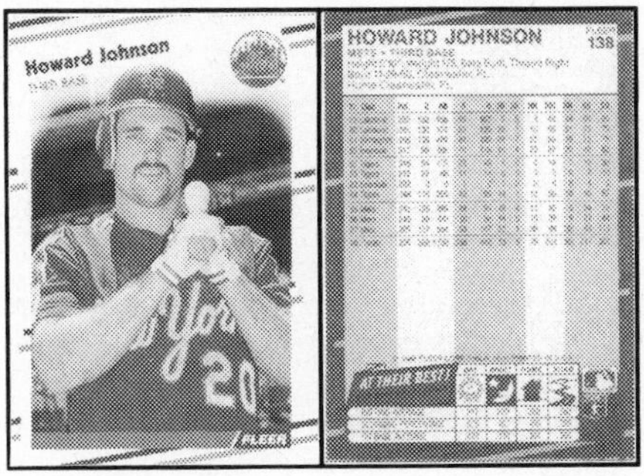

	MINT	EXC	G-VG
COMPLETE SET (660)	42.00	18.00	4.00
COMMON PLAYER (1-660)	.04	.02	.00
☐ 1 Keith Atherton	.08	.02	.01
☐ 2 Don Baylor	.07	.03	.01
☐ 3 Juan Berenguer	.04	.02	.00
☐ 4 Bert Blyleven	.10	.05	.01
☐ 5 Tom Brunansky	.10	.05	.01
☐ 6 Randy Bush	.04	.02	.00
☐ 7 Steve Carlton	.18	.09	.01
☐ 8 Mark Davidson	.10	.05	.01
☐ 9 George Frazier	.04	.02	.00
☐ 10 Gary Gaetti	.10	.05	.01
☐ 11 Greg Gagne	.04	.02	.00
☐ 12 Dan Gladden	.07	.03	.01
☐ 13 Kent Hrbek	.12	.06	.01
☐ 14 Gene Larkin	.25	.12	.02
☐ 15 Tim Laudner	.04	.02	.00
☐ 16 Steve Lombardozzi	.04	.02	.00
☐ 17 Al Newman	.04	.02	.00
☐ 18 Joe Niekro	.07	.03	.01
☐ 19 Kirby Puckett	.65	.30	.06
☐ 20 Jeff Reardon	.07	.03	.01
☐ 21A Dan Schatzeder ERR (misspelled Schatzader on card front)	.20	.10	.02
☐ 21B Dan Schatzeder COR	.07	.03	.01
☐ 22 Roy Smalley	.04	.02	.00
☐ 23 Mike Smithson	.04	.02	.00
☐ 24 Les Straker	.07	.03	.01
☐ 25 Frank Viola	.25	.12	.02
☐ 26 Jack Clark	.15	.07	.01
☐ 27 Vince Coleman	.20	.10	.02

☐ 28	Danny Cox	.04	.02	.00
☐ 29	Bill Dawley	.04	.02	.00
☐ 30	Ken Dayley	.04	.02	.00
☐ 31	Doug DeCinces	.07	.03	.01
☐ 32	Curt Ford	.04	.02	.00
☐ 33	Bob Forsch	.04	.02	.00
☐ 34	David Green	.04	.02	.00
☐ 35	Tom Herr	.07	.03	.01
☐ 36	Ricky Horton	.04	.02	.00
☐ 37	Lance Johnson	.35	.17	.03
☐ 38	Steve Lake	.04	.02	.00
☐ 39	Jim Lindeman	.04	.02	.00
☐ 40	Joe Magrane	.60	.30	.06
☐ 41	Greg Mathews	.04	.02	.00
☐ 42	Willie McGee	.15	.07	.01
☐ 43	John Morris	.04	.02	.00
☐ 44	Jose Oquendo	.04	.02	.00
☐ 45	Tony Pena	.07	.03	.01
☐ 46	Terry Pendleton	.04	.02	.00
☐ 47	Ozzie Smith	.18	.09	.01
☐ 48	John Tudor	.10	.05	.01
☐ 49	Lee Tunnell	.04	.02	.00
☐ 50	Todd Worrell	.10	.05	.01
☐ 51	Doyle Alexander	.04	.02	.00
☐ 52	Dave Bergman	.04	.02	.00
☐ 53	Tom Brookens	.04	.02	.00
☐ 54	Darrell Evans	.07	.03	.01
☐ 55	Kirk Gibson	.20	.10	.02
☐ 56	Mike Heath	.04	.02	.00
☐ 57	Mike Henneman	.25	.12	.02
☐ 58	Willie Hernandez	.07	.03	.01
☐ 59	Larry Herndon	.04	.02	.00
☐ 60	Eric King	.07	.03	.01
☐ 61	Chet Lemon	.04	.02	.00
☐ 62	Scott Lusader	.15	.07	.01
☐ 63	Bill Madlock	.07	.03	.01
☐ 64	Jack Morris	.10	.05	.01
☐ 65	Jim Morrison	.04	.02	.00
☐ 66	Matt Nokes	.35	.17	.03
☐ 67	Dan Petry	.04	.02	.00
☐ 68A	Jeff Robinson ERR Detroit Tigers (stats for other Jeff Robinson on card back)	.75	.35	.07
☐ 68B	Jeff Robinson COR Detroit Tigers	.30	.15	.03
☐ 69	Pat Sheridan	.04	.02	.00
☐ 70	Nate Snell	.04	.02	.00
☐ 71	Frank Tanana	.07	.03	.01
☐ 72	Walt Terrell	.04	.02	.00
☐ 73	Mark Thurmond	.04	.02	.00
☐ 74	Alan Trammell	.15	.07	.01
☐ 75	Lou Whitaker	.12	.06	.01
☐ 76	Mike Aldrete	.04	.02	.00
☐ 77	Bob Brenly	.04	.02	.00
☐ 78	Will Clark	4.00	2.00	.40
☐ 79	Chili Davis	.07	.03	.01
☐ 80	Kelly Downs	.07	.03	.01
☐ 81	Dave Dravecky	.07	.03	.01
☐ 82	Scott Garrelts	.07	.03	.01
☐ 83	Atlee Hammaker	.04	.02	.00
☐ 84	Dave Henderson	.07	.03	.01
☐ 85	Mike Krukow	.04	.02	.00
☐ 86	Mike LaCoss	.04	.02	.00
☐ 87	Craig Lefferts	.04	.02	.00
☐ 88	Jeff Leonard	.07	.03	.01
☐ 89	Candy Maldonado	.07	.03	.01
☐ 90	Eddie Milner	.04	.02	.00
☐ 91	Bob Melvin	.04	.02	.00
☐ 92	Kevin Mitchell	.90	.45	.09
☐ 93	Jon Perlman	.04	.02	.00
☐ 94	Rick Reuschel	.07	.03	.01
☐ 95	Don Robinson	.04	.02	.00
☐ 96	Chris Speier	.04	.02	.00
☐ 97	Harry Spilman	.04	.02	.00
☐ 98	Robby Thompson	.04	.02	.00
☐ 99	Jose Uribe	.04	.02	.00
☐ 100	Mark Wasinger	.07	.03	.01
☐ 101	Matt Williams	6.00	3.00	.60
☐ 102	Jesse Barfield	.10	.05	.01
☐ 103	George Bell	.18	.09	.01
☐ 104	Juan Beniquez	.04	.02	.00
☐ 105	John Cerutti	.04	.02	.00
☐ 106	Jim Clancy	.04	.02	.00
☐ 107	Rob Ducey	.18	.09	.01
☐ 108	Mark Eichhorn	.04	.02	.00
☐ 109	Tony Fernandez	.10	.05	.01
☐ 110	Cecil Fielder	1.50	.75	.15
☐ 111	Kelly Gruber	.60	.30	.06
☐ 112	Tom Henke	.07	.03	.01
☐ 113A	Garth Iorg ERR (misspelled Iorq on card front)	.20	.10	.02
☐ 113B	Garth Iorg COR	.07	.03	.01
☐ 114	Jimmy Key	.07	.03	.01
☐ 115	Rick Leach	.04	.02	.00
☐ 116	Manny Lee	.07	.03	.01
☐ 117	Nelson Liriano	.25	.12	.02
☐ 118	Fred McGriff	2.25	1.10	.22
☐ 119	Lloyd Moseby	.07	.03	.01
☐ 120	Rance Mulliniks	.04	.02	.00
☐ 121	Jeff Musselman	.07	.03	.01
☐ 122	Jose Nunez	.10	.05	.01
☐ 123	Dave Stieb	.10	.05	.01
☐ 124	Willie Upshaw	.04	.02	.00
☐ 125	Duane Ward	.07	.03	.01
☐ 126	Ernie Whitt	.04	.02	.00
☐ 127	Rick Aguilera	.04	.02	.00
☐ 128	Wally Backman	.04	.02	.00
☐ 129	Mark Carreon	.45	.22	.04
☐ 130	Gary Carter	.18	.09	.01
☐ 131	David Cone	1.00	.50	.10
☐ 132	Ron Darling	.10	.05	.01
☐ 133	Len Dykstra	.40	.20	.04
☐ 134	Sid Fernandez	.10	.05	.01
☐ 135	Dwight Gooden	.60	.30	.06
☐ 136	Keith Hernandez	.18	.09	.01
☐ 137	Gregg Jefferies	7.00	3.50	.70
☐ 138	Howard Johnson	.30	.15	.03
☐ 139	Terry Leach	.07	.03	.01
☐ 140	Barry Lyons	.20	.10	.02
☐ 141	Dave Magadan	.40	.20	.04
☐ 142	Roger McDowell	.07	.03	.01
☐ 143	Kevin McReynolds	.15	.07	.01
☐ 144	Keith Miller (New York Mets)	.20	.10	.02
☐ 145	John Mitchell	.12	.06	.01
☐ 146	Randy Myers	.30	.15	.03
☐ 147	Bob Ojeda	.07	.03	.01
☐ 148	Jesse Orosco	.04	.02	.00
☐ 149	Rafael Santana	.04	.02	.00
☐ 150	Doug Sisk	.04	.02	.00
☐ 151	Darryl Strawberry	.50	.25	.05
☐ 152	Tim Teufel	.04	.02	.00
☐ 153	Gene Walter	.04	.02	.00
☐ 154	Mookie Wilson	.07	.03	.01
☐ 155	Jay Aldrich	.04	.02	.00
☐ 156	Chris Bosio	.04	.02	.00
☐ 157	Glenn Braggs	.07	.03	.01
☐ 158	Greg Brock	.04	.02	.00
☐ 159	Juan Castillo	.04	.02	.00
☐ 160	Mark Clear	.04	.02	.00
☐ 161	Cecil Cooper	.07	.03	.01
☐ 162	Chuck Crim	.10	.05	.01
☐ 163	Rob Deer	.07	.03	.01
☐ 164	Mike Felder	.04	.02	.00
☐ 165	Jim Gantner	.04	.02	.00
☐ 166	Ted Higuera	.10	.05	.01
☐ 167	Steve Kiefer	.04	.02	.00
☐ 168	Rick Manning	.04	.02	.00
☐ 169	Paul Molitor	.12	.06	.01
☐ 170	Juan Nieves	.04	.02	.00
☐ 171	Dan Plesac	.04	.02	.00
☐ 172	Earnest Riles	.04	.02	.00
☐ 173	Bill Schroeder	.04	.02	.00
☐ 174	Steve Stanicek	.07	.03	.01
☐ 175	B.J. Surhoff	.15	.07	.01
☐ 176	Dale Sveum	.04	.02	.00
☐ 177	Bill Wegman	.04	.02	.00
☐ 178	Robin Yount	.30	.15	.03
☐ 179	Hubie Brooks	.10	.05	.01
☐ 180	Tim Burke	.07	.03	.01
☐ 181	Casey Candaele	.04	.02	.00
☐ 182	Mike Fitzgerald	.04	.02	.00
☐ 183	Tom Foley	.04	.02	.00
☐ 184	Andres Galarraga	.18	.09	.01
☐ 185	Neal Heaton	.04	.02	.00
☐ 186	Wallace Johnson	.04	.02	.00
☐ 187	Vance Law	.04	.02	.00
☐ 188	Dennis Martinez	.07	.03	.01
☐ 189	Bob McClure	.04	.02	.00
☐ 190	Andy McGaffigan	.04	.02	.00
☐ 191	Reid Nichols	.04	.02	.00
☐ 192	Pascual Perez	.07	.03	.01
☐ 193	Tim Raines	.18	.09	.01
☐ 194	Jeff Reed	.04	.02	.00
☐ 195	Bob Sebra	.04	.02	.00
☐ 196	Bryn Smith	.04	.02	.00
☐ 197	Randy St.Claire	.04	.02	.00
☐ 198	Tim Wallach	.10	.05	.01
☐ 199	Mitch Webster	.04	.02	.00
☐ 200	Herm Winningham	.04	.02	.00
☐ 201	Floyd Youmans	.04	.02	.00
☐ 202	Brad Arnsberg	.30	.15	.03
☐ 203	Rick Cerone	.04	.02	.00
☐ 204	Pat Clements	.04	.02	.00
☐ 205	Henry Cotto	.04	.02	.00
☐ 206	Mike Easler	.04	.02	.00

☐ 207 Ron Guidry	.10	.05	.01
☐ 208 Bill Gullickson	.04	.02	.00
☐ 209 Rickey Henderson	.50	.25	.05
☐ 210 Charles Hudson	.04	.02	.00
☐ 211 Tommy John	.10	.05	.01
☐ 212 Roberto Kelly	1.75	.85	.17
☐ 213 Ron Kittle	.10	.05	.01
☐ 214 Don Mattingly	1.50	.75	.15
☐ 215 Bobby Meacham	.04	.02	.00
☐ 216 Mike Pagliarulo	.04	.02	.00
☐ 217 Dan Pasqua	.04	.02	.00
☐ 218 Willie Randolph	.07	.03	.01
☐ 219 Rick Rhoden	.04	.02	.00
☐ 220 Dave Righetti	.10	.05	.01
☐ 221 Jerry Royster	.04	.02	.00
☐ 222 Tim Stoddard	.04	.02	.00
☐ 223 Wayne Tolleson	.04	.02	.00
☐ 224 Gary Ward	.04	.02	.00
☐ 225 Claudell Washington	.07	.03	.01
☐ 226 Dave Winfield	.25	.12	.02
☐ 227 Buddy Bell	.07	.03	.01
☐ 228 Tom Browning	.07	.03	.01
☐ 229 Dave Concepcion	.07	.03	.01
☐ 230 Kal Daniels	.30	.15	.03
☐ 231 Eric Davis	.75	.35	.07
☐ 232 Bo Diaz	.04	.02	.00
☐ 233 Nick Esasky (has a dollar sign before '87 SB totals)	.07	.03	.01
☐ 234 John Franco	.07	.03	.01
☐ 235 Guy Hoffman	.04	.02	.00
☐ 236 Tom Hume	.04	.02	.00
☐ 237 Tracy Jones	.04	.02	.00
☐ 238 Bill Landrum	.25	.12	.02
☐ 239 Barry Larkin	1.25	.60	.12
☐ 240 Terry McGriff	.10	.05	.01
☐ 241 Rob Murphy	.04	.02	.00
☐ 242 Ron Oester	.04	.02	.00
☐ 243 Dave Parker	.12	.06	.01
☐ 244 Pat Perry	.04	.02	.00
☐ 245 Ted Power	.04	.02	.00
☐ 246 Dennis Rasmussen	.04	.02	.00
☐ 247 Ron Robinson	.04	.02	.00
☐ 248 Kurt Stillwell	.10	.05	.01
☐ 249 Jeff Treadway	.30	.15	.03
☐ 250 Frank Williams	.04	.02	.00
☐ 251 Steve Balboni	.04	.02	.00
☐ 252 Bud Black	.07	.03	.01
☐ 253 Thad Bosley	.04	.02	.00
☐ 254 George Brett	.35	.17	.03
☐ 255 John Davis	.12	.06	.01
☐ 256 Steve Farr	.07	.03	.01
☐ 257 Gene Garber	.04	.02	.00
☐ 258 Jerry Don Gleaton	.04	.02	.00
☐ 259 Mark Gubicza	.10	.05	.01
☐ 260 Bo Jackson	4.00	2.00	.40
☐ 261 Danny Jackson	.07	.03	.01
☐ 262 Ross Jones	.04	.02	.00
☐ 263 Charlie Leibrandt	.04	.02	.00
☐ 264 Bill Pecota	.07	.03	.01
☐ 265 Melido Perez	.30	.15	.03
☐ 266 Jamie Quirk	.04	.02	.00
☐ 267 Dan Quisenberry	.07	.03	.01
☐ 268 Bret Saberhagen	.30	.15	.03
☐ 269 Angel Salazar	.04	.02	.00
☐ 270 Kevin Seitzer UER (wrong birth year)	.30	.15	.03
☐ 271 Danny Tartabull	.20	.10	.02
☐ 272 Gary Thurman	.20	.10	.02
☐ 273 Frank White	.07	.03	.01
☐ 274 Willie Wilson	.07	.03	.01
☐ 275 Tony Bernazard	.04	.02	.00
☐ 276 Jose Canseco	3.25	1.60	.32
☐ 277 Mike Davis	.04	.02	.00
☐ 278 Storm Davis	.07	.03	.01
☐ 279 Dennis Eckersley	.15	.07	.01
☐ 280 Alfredo Griffin	.04	.02	.00
☐ 281 Rick Honeycutt	.04	.02	.00
☐ 282 Jay Howell	.04	.02	.00
☐ 283 Reggie Jackson	.30	.15	.03
☐ 284 Dennis Lamp	.04	.02	.00
☐ 285 Carney Lansford	.10	.05	.01
☐ 286 Mark McGwire	3.25	1.60	.32
☐ 287 Dwayne Murphy	.04	.02	.00
☐ 288 Gene Nelson	.04	.02	.00
☐ 289 Steve Ontiveros	.04	.02	.00
☐ 290 Tony Phillips	.04	.02	.00
☐ 291 Eric Plunk	.04	.02	.00
☐ 292 Luis Polonia	.30	.15	.03
☐ 293 Rick Rodriguez	.07	.03	.01
☐ 294 Terry Steinbach	.12	.06	.01
☐ 295 Dave Stewart	.20	.10	.02
☐ 296 Curt Young	.04	.02	.00
☐ 297 Luis Aguayo	.04	.02	.00

☐ 298 Steve Bedrosian	.07	.03	.01
☐ 299 Jeff Calhoun	.04	.02	.00
☐ 300 Don Carman	.04	.02	.00
☐ 301 Todd Frohwirth	.10	.05	.01
☐ 302 Greg Gross	.04	.02	.00
☐ 303 Kevin Gross	.04	.02	.00
☐ 304 Von Hayes	.10	.05	.01
☐ 305 Keith Hughes	.10	.05	.01
☐ 306 Mike Jackson	.15	.07	.01
☐ 307 Chris James	.25	.12	.02
☐ 308 Steve Jeltz	.04	.02	.00
☐ 309 Mike Maddux	.04	.02	.00
☐ 310 Lance Parrish	.10	.05	.01
☐ 311 Shane Rawley	.04	.02	.00
☐ 312 Wally Ritchie	.04	.02	.00
☐ 313 Bruce Ruffin	.04	.02	.00
☐ 314 Juan Samuel	.07	.03	.01
☐ 315 Mike Schmidt	.50	.25	.05
☐ 316 Rick Schu	.04	.02	.00
☐ 317 Jeff Stone	.04	.02	.00
☐ 318 Kent Tekulve	.04	.02	.00
☐ 319 Milt Thompson	.04	.02	.00
☐ 320 Glenn Wilson	.04	.02	.00
☐ 321 Rafael Belliard	.04	.02	.00
☐ 322 Barry Bonds	1.50	.75	.15
☐ 323 Bobby Bonilla UER (wrong birth year)	1.00	.50	.10
☐ 324 Sid Bream	.04	.02	.00
☐ 325 John Cangelosi	.04	.02	.00
☐ 326 Mike Diaz	.04	.02	.00
☐ 327 Doug Drabek	.25	.12	.02
☐ 328 Mike Dunne	.12	.06	.01
☐ 329 Brian Fisher	.04	.02	.00
☐ 330 Brett Gideon	.07	.03	.01
☐ 331 Terry Harper	.04	.02	.00
☐ 332 Bob Kipper	.04	.02	.00
☐ 333 Mike LaValliere	.04	.02	.00
☐ 334 Jose Lind	.60	.30	.06
☐ 335 Junior Ortiz	.04	.02	.00
☐ 336 Vicente Palacios	.15	.07	.01
☐ 337 Bob Patterson	.07	.03	.01
☐ 338 Al Pedrique	.07	.03	.01
☐ 339 R.J. Reynolds	.04	.02	.00
☐ 340 John Smiley	.35	.17	.03
☐ 341 Andy Van Slyke UER (wrong batting and throwing listed)	.15	.07	.01
☐ 342 Bob Walk	.04	.02	.00
☐ 343 Marty Barrett	.07	.03	.01
☐ 344 Todd Benzinger	.30	.15	.03
☐ 345 Wade Boggs	.75	.35	.07
☐ 346 Tom Bolton	.35	.17	.03
☐ 347 Oil Can Boyd	.07	.03	.01
☐ 348 Ellis Burks	3.00	1.50	.30
☐ 349 Roger Clemens	1.00	.50	.10
☐ 350 Steve Crawford	.07	.03	.01
☐ 351 Dwight Evans	.12	.06	.01
☐ 352 Wes Gardner	.15	.07	.01
☐ 353 Rich Gedman	.04	.02	.00
☐ 354 Mike Greenwell	2.00	1.00	.20
☐ 355 Sam Horn	.25	.12	.02
☐ 356 Bruce Hurst	.10	.05	.01
☐ 357 John Marzano	.10	.05	.01
☐ 358 Al Nipper	.04	.02	.00
☐ 359 Spike Owen	.04	.02	.00
☐ 360 Jody Reed	1.00	.50	.10
☐ 361 Jim Rice	.15	.07	.01
☐ 362 Ed Romero	.04	.02	.00
☐ 363 Kevin Romine	.07	.03	.01
☐ 364 Joe Sambito	.04	.02	.00
☐ 365 Calvin Schiraldi	.04	.02	.00
☐ 366 Jeff Sellers	.04	.02	.00
☐ 367 Bob Stanley	.04	.02	.00
☐ 368 Scott Bankhead	.07	.03	.01
☐ 369 Phil Bradley	.07	.03	.01
☐ 370 Scott Bradley	.04	.02	.00
☐ 371 Mickey Brantley	.07	.03	.01
☐ 372 Mike Campbell	.10	.05	.01
☐ 373 Alvin Davis	.10	.05	.01
☐ 374 Lee Guetterman	.04	.02	.00
☐ 375 Dave Hengel	.10	.05	.01
☐ 376 Mike Kingery	.04	.02	.00
☐ 377 Mark Langston	.15	.07	.01
☐ 378 Edgar Martinez	.90	.45	.09
☐ 379 Mike Moore	.07	.03	.01
☐ 380 Mike Morgan	.04	.02	.00
☐ 381 John Moses	.04	.02	.00
☐ 382 Donnell Nixon	.10	.05	.01
☐ 383 Edwin Nunez	.04	.02	.00
☐ 384 Ken Phelps	.07	.03	.01
☐ 385 Jim Presley	.07	.03	.01
☐ 386 Rey Quinones	.04	.02	.00
☐ 387 Jerry Reed	.04	.02	.00
☐ 388 Harold Reynolds	.07	.03	.01

☐ 389	Dave Valle	.04	.02	.00
☐ 390	Bill Wilkinson	.07	.03	.01
☐ 391	Harold Baines	.10	.05	.01
☐ 392	Floyd Bannister	.04	.02	.00
☐ 393	Daryl Boston	.07	.03	.01
☐ 394	Ivan Calderon	.07	.03	.01
☐ 395	Jose DeLeon	.04	.02	.00
☐ 396	Richard Dotson	.04	.02	.00
☐ 397	Carlton Fisk	.15	.07	.01
☐ 398	Ozzie Guillen	.10	.05	.01
☐ 399	Ron Hassey	.04	.02	.00
☐ 400	Donnie Hill	.04	.02	.00
☐ 401	Bob James	.04	.02	.00
☐ 402	Dave LaPoint	.04	.02	.00
☐ 403	Bill Lindsey	.04	.02	.00
☐ 404	Bill Long	.07	.03	.01
☐ 405	Steve Lyons	.04	.02	.00
☐ 406	Fred Manrique	.07	.03	.01
☐ 407	Jack McDowell	.50	.25	.05
☐ 408	Gary Redus	.04	.02	.00
☐ 409	Ray Searage	.04	.02	.00
☐ 410	Bobby Thigpen	.20	.10	.02
☐ 411	Greg Walker	.04	.02	.00
☐ 412	Ken Williams	.15	.07	.01
☐ 413	Jim Winn	.04	.02	.00
☐ 414	Jody Davis	.04	.02	.00
☐ 415	Andre Dawson	.30	.15	.03
☐ 416	Brian Dayett	.04	.02	.00
☐ 417	Bob Dernier	.04	.02	.00
☐ 418	Frank DiPino	.04	.02	.00
☐ 419	Shawon Dunston	.30	.15	.03
☐ 420	Leon Durham	.04	.02	.00
☐ 421	Les Lancaster	.15	.07	.01
☐ 422	Ed Lynch	.04	.02	.00
☐ 423	Greg Maddux	.65	.30	.06
☐ 424	Dave Martinez	.12	.06	.01
☐ 425A	Keith Moreland ERR (photo actually Jody Davis)	4.00	2.00	.40
☐ 425B	Keith Moreland COR (bat on shoulder)	.15	.07	.01
☐ 426	Jamie Moyer	.04	.02	.00
☐ 427	Jerry Mumphrey	.04	.02	.00
☐ 428	Paul Noce	.07	.03	.01
☐ 429	Rafael Palmeiro	1.50	.75	.15
☐ 430	Wade Rowdon	.07	.03	.01
☐ 431	Ryne Sandberg	.75	.35	.07
☐ 432	Scott Sanderson	.07	.03	.01
☐ 433	Lee Smith	.07	.03	.01
☐ 434	Jim Sundberg	.04	.02	.00
☐ 435	Rick Sutcliffe	.07	.03	.01
☐ 436	Manny Trillo	.04	.02	.00
☐ 437	Juan Agosto	.04	.02	.00
☐ 438	Larry Andersen	.04	.02	.00
☐ 439	Alan Ashby	.04	.02	.00
☐ 440	Kevin Bass	.07	.03	.01
☐ 441	Ken Caminiti	.25	.12	.02
☐ 442	Rocky Childress	.04	.02	.00
☐ 443	Jose Cruz	.07	.03	.01
☐ 444	Danny Darwin	.07	.03	.01
☐ 445	Glenn Davis	.18	.09	.01
☐ 446	Jim Deshaies	.04	.02	.00
☐ 447	Bill Doran	.07	.03	.01
☐ 448	Ty Gainey	.04	.02	.00
☐ 449	Billy Hatcher	.10	.05	.01
☐ 450	Jeff Heathcock	.04	.02	.00
☐ 451	Bob Knepper	.04	.02	.00
☐ 452	Rob Mallicoat	.04	.02	.00
☐ 453	Dave Meads	.04	.02	.00
☐ 454	Craig Reynolds	.04	.02	.00
☐ 455	Nolan Ryan	.90	.45	.09
☐ 456	Mike Scott	.15	.07	.01
☐ 457	Dave Smith	.04	.02	.00
☐ 458	Denny Walling	.04	.02	.00
☐ 459	Robbie Wine	.04	.02	.00
☐ 460	Gerald Young	.25	.12	.02
☐ 461	Bob Brower	.07	.03	.01
☐ 462A	Jerry Browne ERR (photo actually Bob Brower, white player)	4.00	2.00	.40
☐ 462B	Jerry Browne COR (black player)	.15	.07	.01
☐ 463	Steve Buechele	.04	.02	.00
☐ 464	Edwin Correa	.04	.02	.00
☐ 465	Cecil Espy	.15	.07	.01
☐ 466	Scott Fletcher	.04	.02	.00
☐ 467	Jose Guzman	.04	.02	.00
☐ 468	Greg Harris	.04	.02	.00
☐ 469	Charlie Hough	.04	.02	.00
☐ 470	Pete Incaviglia	.15	.07	.01
☐ 471	Paul Kilgus	.10	.05	.01
☐ 472	Mike Loynd	.04	.02	.00
☐ 473	Oddibe McDowell	.07	.03	.01
☐ 474	Dale Mohorcic	.04	.02	.00
☐ 475	Pete O'Brien	.07	.03	.01
☐ 476	Larry Parrish	.04	.02	.00
☐ 477	Geno Petralli	.04	.02	.00
☐ 478	Jeff Russell	.04	.02	.00
☐ 479	Ruben Sierra	1.50	.75	.15
☐ 480	Mike Stanley	.04	.02	.00
☐ 481	Curtis Wilkerson	.04	.02	.00
☐ 482	Mitch Williams	.07	.03	.01
☐ 483	Bobby Witt	.20	.10	.02
☐ 484	Tony Armas	.04	.02	.00
☐ 485	Bob Boone	.07	.03	.01
☐ 486	Bill Buckner	.07	.03	.01
☐ 487	DeWayne Buice	.07	.03	.01
☐ 488	Brian Downing	.04	.02	.00
☐ 489	Chuck Finley	.30	.15	.03
☐ 490	Willie Fraser UER (wrong bio stats, for George Hendrick)	.04	.02	.00
☐ 491	Jack Howell	.04	.02	.00
☐ 492	Ruppert Jones	.04	.02	.00
☐ 493	Wally Joyner	.30	.15	.03
☐ 494	Jack Lazorko	.04	.02	.00
☐ 495	Gary Lucas	.04	.02	.00
☐ 496	Kirk McCaskill	.04	.02	.00
☐ 497	Mark McLemore	.04	.02	.00
☐ 498	Darrell Miller	.04	.02	.00
☐ 499	Greg Minton	.04	.02	.00
☐ 500	Donnie Moore	.04	.02	.00
☐ 501	Gus Polidor	.04	.02	.00
☐ 502	Johnny Ray	.07	.03	.01
☐ 503	Mark Ryal	.07	.03	.01
☐ 504	Dick Schofield	.04	.02	.00
☐ 505	Don Sutton	.15	.07	.01
☐ 506	Devon White	.15	.07	.01
☐ 507	Mike Witt	.04	.02	.00
☐ 508	Dave Anderson	.04	.02	.00
☐ 509	Tim Belcher	.50	.25	.05
☐ 510	Ralph Bryant	.04	.02	.00
☐ 511	Tim Crews	.07	.03	.01
☐ 512	Mike Devereaux	.25	.12	.02
☐ 513	Mariano Duncan	.07	.03	.01
☐ 514	Pedro Guerrero	.15	.07	.01
☐ 515	Jeff Hamilton	.12	.06	.01
☐ 516	Mickey Hatcher	.04	.02	.00
☐ 517	Brad Havens	.04	.02	.00
☐ 518	Orel Hershiser	.25	.12	.02
☐ 519	Shawn Hillegas	.15	.07	.01
☐ 520	Ken Howell	.04	.02	.00
☐ 521	Tim Leary	.07	.03	.01
☐ 522	Mike Marshall	.10	.05	.01
☐ 523	Steve Sax	.15	.07	.01
☐ 524	Mike Scioscia	.04	.02	.00
☐ 525	Mike Sharperson	.07	.03	.01
☐ 526	John Shelby	.04	.02	.00
☐ 527	Franklin Stubbs	.07	.03	.01
☐ 528	Fernando Valenzuela	.12	.06	.01
☐ 529	Bob Welch	.12	.06	.01
☐ 530	Matt Young	.04	.02	.00
☐ 531	Jim Acker	.04	.02	.00
☐ 532	Paul Assenmacher	.04	.02	.00
☐ 533	Jeff Blauser	.30	.15	.03
☐ 534	Joe Boever	.10	.05	.01
☐ 535	Martin Clary	.04	.02	.00
☐ 536	Kevin Coffman	.07	.03	.01
☐ 537	Jeff Dedmon	.04	.02	.00
☐ 538	Ron Gant	3.00	1.50	.30
☐ 539	Tom Glavine	.35	.17	.03
☐ 540	Ken Griffey	.10	.05	.01
☐ 541	Albert Hall	.04	.02	.00
☐ 542	Glenn Hubbard	.04	.02	.00
☐ 543	Dion James	.04	.02	.00
☐ 544	Dale Murphy	.30	.15	.03
☐ 545	Ken Oberkfell	.04	.02	.00
☐ 546	David Palmer	.04	.02	.00
☐ 547	Gerald Perry	.04	.02	.00
☐ 548	Charlie Puleo	.04	.02	.00
☐ 549	Ted Simmons	.07	.03	.01
☐ 550	Zane Smith	.07	.03	.01
☐ 551	Andres Thomas	.04	.02	.00
☐ 552	Ozzie Virgil	.04	.02	.00
☐ 553	Don Aase	.04	.02	.00
☐ 554	Jeff Ballard	.35	.17	.03
☐ 555	Eric Bell	.04	.02	.00
☐ 556	Mike Boddicker	.07	.03	.01
☐ 557	Ken Dixon	.04	.02	.00
☐ 558	Jim Dwyer	.04	.02	.00
☐ 559	Ken Gerhart	.04	.02	.00
☐ 560	Rene Gonzales	.07	.03	.01
☐ 561	Mike Griffin	.04	.02	.00
☐ 562	John Habyan UER (misspelled Hayban on both sides of card)	.07	.03	.01
☐ 563	Terry Kennedy	.04	.02	.00

☐ 564 Ray Knight	.07	.03	.01
☐ 565 Lee Lacy	.04	.02	.00
☐ 566 Fred Lynn	.10	.05	.01
☐ 567 Eddie Murray	.25	.12	.02
☐ 568 Tom Niedenfuer	.04	.02	.00
☐ 569 Bill Ripken	.25	.12	.02
☐ 570 Cal Ripken Jr.	.30	.15	.03
☐ 571 Dave Schmidt	.04	.02	.00
☐ 572 Larry Sheets	.04	.02	.00
☐ 573 Pete Stanicek	.07	.03	.01
☐ 574 Mark Williamson	.12	.06	.01
☐ 575 Mike Young	.04	.02	.00
☐ 576 Shawn Abner	.18	.09	.01
☐ 577 Greg Booker	.04	.02	.00
☐ 578 Chris Brown	.04	.02	.00
☐ 579 Keith Comstock	.07	.03	.01
☐ 580 Joey Cora	.07	.03	.01
☐ 581 Mark Davis	.10	.05	.01
☐ 582 Tim Flannery (with surfboard)	.04	.02	.00
☐ 583 Goose Gossage	.07	.03	.01
☐ 584 Mark Grant	.04	.02	.00
☐ 585 Tony Gwynn	.35	.17	.03
☐ 586 Andy Hawkins	.04	.02	.00
☐ 587 Stan Jefferson	.10	.05	.01
☐ 588 Jimmy Jones	.07	.03	.01
☐ 589 John Kruk	.07	.03	.01
☐ 590 Shane Mack	.20	.10	.02
☐ 591 Carmelo Martinez	.04	.02	.00
☐ 592 Lance McCullers UER (6'11" tall)	.04	.02	.00
☐ 593 Eric Nolte	.07	.03	.01
☐ 594 Randy Ready	.04	.02	.00
☐ 595 Luis Salazar	.04	.02	.00
☐ 596 Benito Santiago	.50	.25	.05
☐ 597 Eric Show	.04	.02	.00
☐ 598 Garry Templeton	.07	.03	.01
☐ 599 Ed Whitson	.07	.03	.01
☐ 600 Scott Bailes	.04	.02	.00
☐ 601 Chris Bando	.04	.02	.00
☐ 602 Jay Bell	.30	.15	.03
☐ 603 Brett Butler	.07	.03	.01
☐ 604 Tom Candiotti	.04	.02	.00
☐ 605 Joe Carter	.25	.12	.02
☐ 606 Carmen Castillo	.04	.02	.00
☐ 607 Brian Dorsett	.07	.03	.01
☐ 608 John Farrell	.25	.12	.02
☐ 609 Julio Franco	.12	.06	.01
☐ 610 Mel Hall	.07	.03	.01
☐ 611 Tommy Hinzo	.07	.03	.01
☐ 612 Brook Jacoby	.07	.03	.01
☐ 613 Doug Jones	.45	.22	.04
☐ 614 Ken Schrom	.04	.02	.00
☐ 615 Cory Snyder	.15	.07	.01
☐ 616 Sammy Stewart	.04	.02	.00
☐ 617 Greg Swindell	.18	.09	.01
☐ 618 Pat Tabler	.07	.03	.01
☐ 619 Ed VandeBerg	.04	.02	.00
☐ 620 Eddie Williams	.15	.07	.01
☐ 621 Rich Yett	.04	.02	.00
☐ 622 Slugging Sophomores Wally Joyner Cory Snyder	.10	.05	.01
☐ 623 Dominican Dynamite George Bell Pedro Guerrero	.10	.05	.01
☐ 624 Oakland's Power Team Mark McGwire Jose Canseco	.75	.35	.07
☐ 625 Classic Relief Dave Righetti Dan Plesac	.10	.05	.01
☐ 626 All Star Righties Bret Saberhagen Mike Witt Jack Morris	.10	.05	.01
☐ 627 Game Closers John Franco Steve Bedrosian	.08	.04	.01
☐ 628 Masters/Double Play Ozzie Smith Ryne Sandberg	.15	.07	.01
☐ 629 Rookie Record Setter Mark McGwire	.40	.20	.04
☐ 630 Changing the Guard Mike Greenwell Ellis Burks Todd Benzinger	.65	.30	.06
☐ 631 NL Batting Champs Tony Gwynn Tim Raines	.12	.06	.01
☐ 632 Pitching Magic Mike Scott Orel Hershiser	.10	.05	.01
☐ 633 Big Bats at First Pat Tabler Mark McGwire	.20	.10	.02
☐ 634 Hitting King/Thief Tony Gwynn Vince Coleman	.12	.06	.01
☐ 635 Slugging Shortstops Tony Fernandez Cal Ripken Alan Trammell	.12	.06	.01
☐ 636 Tried/True Sluggers Mike Schmidt Gary Carter	.15	.07	.01
☐ 637 Crunch Time Darryl Strawberry Eric Davis	.30	.15	.03
☐ 638 AL All-Stars Matt Nokes Kirby Puckett	.15	.07	.01
☐ 639 NL All-Stars Keith Hernandez Dale Murphy	.10	.05	.01
☐ 640 The O's Brothers Billy Ripken Cal Ripken	.10	.05	.01
☐ 641 Mark Grace and Darrin Jackson	8.00	4.00	.80
☐ 642 Damon Berryhill and Jeff Montgomery	.75	.35	.07
☐ 643 Felix Fermin and Jesse Reid	.10	.05	.01
☐ 644 Greg Myers and Greg Tabor	.10	.05	.01
☐ 645 Joey Meyer and Jim Eppard	.10	.05	.01
☐ 646 Adam Peterson and Randy Velarde	.10	.05	.01
☐ 647 Peter Smith and Chris Gwynn	.35	.17	.03
☐ 648 Tom Newell and Greg Jelks	.10	.05	.01
☐ 649 Mario Diaz and Clay Parker	.25	.12	.02
☐ 650 Jack Savage and Todd Simmons	.15	.07	.01
☐ 651 John Burkett and Kirt Manwaring	1.25	.60	.12
☐ 652 Dave Otto and Walt Weiss	1.25	.60	.12
☐ 653 Jeff King and Randell Byers	.35	.17	.03
☐ 654 CL: Twins/Cards Tigers/Giants UER (90 Bob Melvin, 91 Eddie Milner)	.06	.01	.00
☐ 655 CL: Blue Jays/Mets Brewers/Expos UER (Mets listed before Blue Jays on card)	.06	.01	.00
☐ 656 CL: Yankees/Reds Royals/A's	.06	.01	.00
☐ 657 CL: Phillies/Pirates Red Sox/Mariners	.06	.01	.00
☐ 658 CL: White Sox/Cubs Astros/Rangers	.06	.01	.00
☐ 659 CL: Angels/Dodgers Braves/Orioles	.06	.01	.00
☐ 660 CL: Padres/Indians Rookies/Specials	.06	.01	.00

1988 Fleer Wax Box Cards

The cards in this 16-card set measure the standard 2 1/2" by 3 1/2". Cards have essentially the same design as the 1988 Fleer regular issue set. The cards were printed on the bottoms of the regular issue wax pack boxes. These 16 cards (C1 to C16) are considered a separate set in their own right and are not typically included in a complete set of the regular issue 1988 Fleer cards. The value of the panel uncut is slightly greater, perhaps by 25 percent greater, than the value of the individual cards cut up carefully.

	MINT	EXC	G-VG
COMPLETE SET (16)	4.00	2.00	.40
COMMON PLAYER (C1-C16)	.10	.05	.01

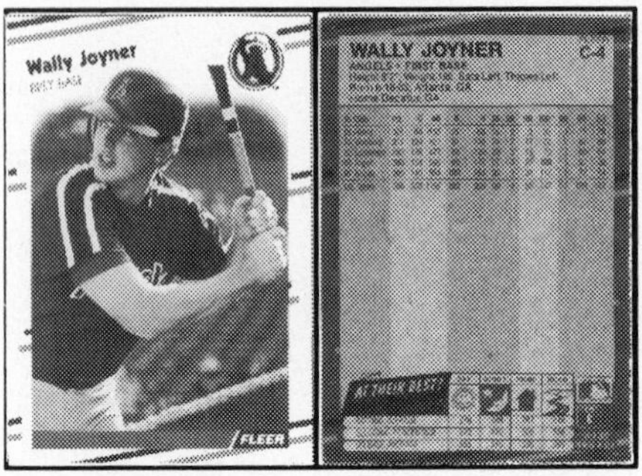

☐ C1 Cardinals Logo	.10	.05	.01
☐ C2 Dwight Evans	.10	.05	.01
☐ C3 Andres Galarraga	.20	.10	.02
☐ C4 Wally Joyner	.40	.20	.04
☐ C5 Twins Logo	.10	.05	.01
☐ C6 Dale Murphy	.35	.17	.03
☐ C7 Kirby Puckett	.60	.30	.06
☐ C8 Shane Rawley	.10	.05	.01
☐ C9 Giants Logo	.10	.05	.01
☐ C10 Ryne Sandberg	.75	.35	.07
☐ C11 Mike Schmidt	.75	.35	.07
☐ C12 Kevin Seitzer	.50	.25	.05
☐ C13 Tigers Logo	.10	.05	.01
☐ C14 Dave Stewart	.25	.12	.02
☐ C15 Tim Wallach	.15	.07	.01
☐ C16 Todd Worrell	.15	.07	.01

1988 Fleer All-Star Inserts

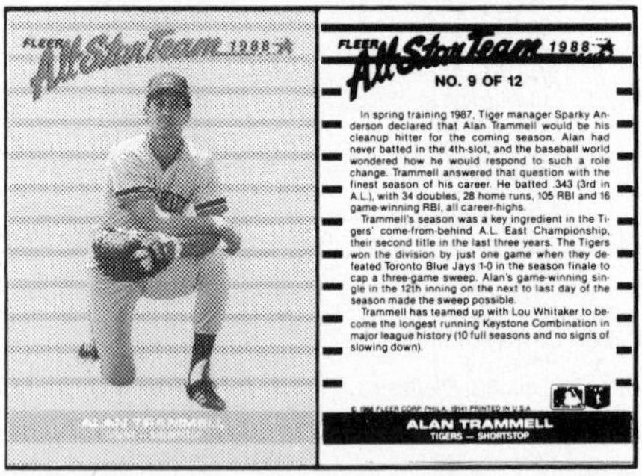

The cards in this 12-card set measure the standard 2 1/2" by 3 1/2". These cards were inserted (randomly) in wax and cello packs of the 1988 Fleer regular issue set. The cards show the player silhouetted against a light green background with dark green stripes. The player's name, team, and position are printed in yellow at the bottom of the obverse. The card backs are done predominantly in green, white, and black. Cards are numbered on the back. These 12 cards are considered a separate set in their own right and are not typically included in a complete set of the regular issue 1988 Fleer cards. The players are the "best" at each position, three pitchers, eight position players, and a designated hitter.

	MINT	EXC	G-VG
COMPLETE SET (12)	12.00	6.00	1.20
COMMON PLAYERS (1-12)	.25	.12	.02
☐ 1 Matt Nokes Catcher	.50	.25	.05
☐ 2 Tom Henke Relief Pitcher	.25	.12	.02
☐ 3 Ted Higuera Left Hand Pitcher	.35	.17	.03
☐ 4 Roger Clemens Right Hand Pitcher	2.50	1.25	.25
☐ 5 George Bell Outfielder	.60	.30	.06
☐ 6 Andre Dawson Outfielder	.60	.30	.06
☐ 7 Eric Davis Outfielder	2.00	1.00	.20
☐ 8 Wade Boggs Third Baseman	2.50	1.25	.25
☐ 9 Alan Trammell Shortstop	.75	.35	.07
☐ 10 Juan Samuel Second Baseman	.35	.17	.03
☐ 11 Jack Clark First Baseman	.50	.25	.05
☐ 12 Paul Molitor Designated Hitter	.50	.25	.05

1988 Fleer Headliners

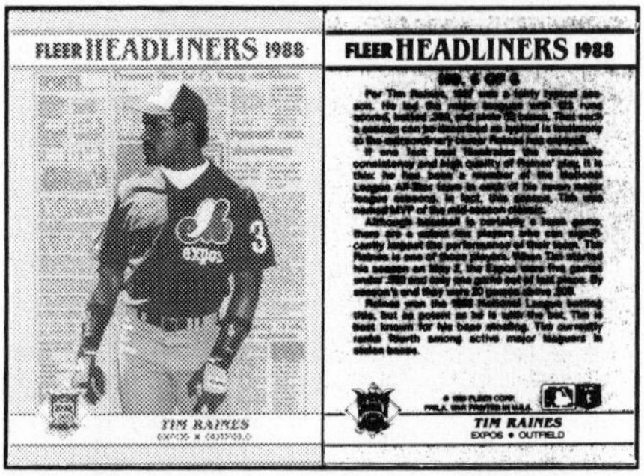

This six-card set was distributed as a special insert in rack packs. The obverse features the player photo superimposed on a gray newsprint background. Cards are 2 1/2" by 3 1/2". The cards are printed in red, black, and white on the back describing why that particular player made headlines the previous season. The cards are numbered on the back.

	MINT	EXC	G-VG
COMPLETE SET (6)	8.00	4.00	.80
COMMON PLAYER (1-6)	.65	.30	.06
☐ 1 Don Mattingly New York Yankees	2.50	1.25	.25
☐ 2 Mark McGwire Oakland Athletics	2.00	1.00	.20
☐ 3 Jack Morris Detroit Tigers	.65	.30	.06
☐ 4 Darryl Strawberry New York Mets	1.50	.75	.15
☐ 5 Dwight Gooden New York Mets	1.00	.50	.10
☐ 6 Tim Raines Montreal Expos	.80	.40	.08

1988 Fleer Update

This 132-card set was distributed by Fleer to dealers as a complete set in a custom box. In addition to the complete set of 132 cards, the box also contains 25 Team Logo stickers.The card fronts look very similar to the 1987 Fleer regular issue. The cards are numbered (with a U prefix) alphabetically according to player's last name. Cards measure the standard size, 2 1/2" by 3 1/2". This was the first Fleer Update set to adopt the Fleer "alphabetical within team" numbering system. The key (extended) rookie cards in this set are Roberto Alomar, Craig

Biggio, and Chris Sabo. Fleer also produced a "limited" edition version of this set with glossy coating and packaged in a "tin." However, this tin set was apparently not limited enough (estimated between 40,000 and 60,000 1988 Update tin sets produced by Fleer), since the price of the "tin" glossy cards is now only double the price of the regular set.

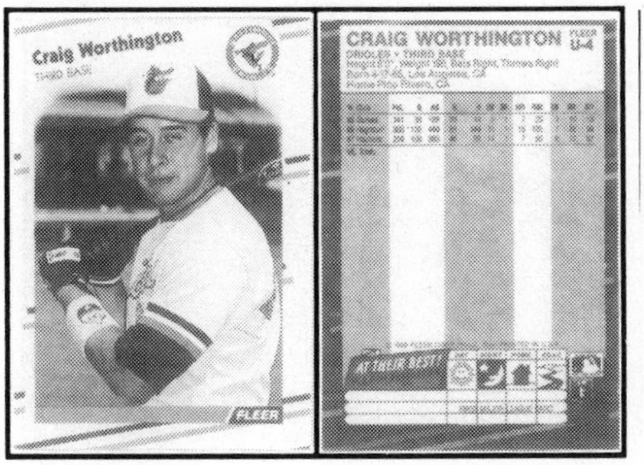

	MINT	EXC	G-VG
COMPLETE SET (132)	13.50	6.00	1.20
COMMON PLAYER (1-132)	.06	.03	.00

	MINT	EXC	G-VG
☐ U1 Jose Bautista	.12	.06	.01
☐ U2 Joe Orsulak	.10	.05	.01
☐ U3 Doug Sisk	.06	.03	.00
☐ U4 Craig Worthington	.40	.20	.04
☐ U5 Mike Boddicker	.10	.05	.01
☐ U6 Rick Cerone	.06	.03	.00
☐ U7 Larry Parrish	.06	.03	.00
☐ U8 Lee Smith	.10	.05	.01
☐ U9 Mike Smithson	.06	.03	.00
☐ U10 John Trautwein	.10	.05	.01
☐ U11 Sherman Corbett	.10	.05	.01
☐ U12 Chili Davis	.10	.05	.01
☐ U13 Jim Eppard	.06	.03	.00
☐ U14 Bryan Harvey	.20	.10	.02
☐ U15 John Davis	.06	.03	.00
☐ U16 Dave Gallagher	.20	.10	.02
☐ U17 Ricky Horton	.06	.03	.00
☐ U18 Dan Pasqua	.06	.03	.00
☐ U19 Melido Perez	.10	.05	.01
☐ U20 Jose Segura	.10	.05	.01
☐ U21 Andy Allanson	.06	.03	.00
☐ U22 Jon Perlman	.06	.03	.00
☐ U23 Domingo Ramos	.06	.03	.00
☐ U24 Rick Rodriguez	.06	.03	.00
☐ U25 Willie Upshaw	.06	.03	.00
☐ U26 Paul Gibson	.10	.05	.01
☐ U27 Don Heinkel	.10	.05	.01
☐ U28 Ray Knight	.10	.05	.01
☐ U29 Gary Pettis	.10	.05	.01
☐ U30 Luis Salazar	.06	.03	.00
☐ U31 Mike MacFarlane	.20	.10	.02
☐ U32 Jeff Montgomery	.15	.07	.01
☐ U33 Ted Power	.06	.03	.00
☐ U34 Israel Sanchez	.10	.05	.01
☐ U35 Kurt Stillwell	.15	.07	.01
☐ U36 Pat Tabler	.10	.05	.01
☐ U37 Don August	.15	.07	.01
☐ U38 Darryl Hamilton	.20	.10	.02
☐ U39 Jeff Leonard	.10	.05	.01
☐ U40 Joey Meyer	.10	.05	.01
☐ U41 Allan Anderson	.15	.07	.01
☐ U42 Brian Harper	.15	.07	.01
☐ U43 Tom Herr	.10	.05	.01
☐ U44 Charlie Lea	.06	.03	.00
☐ U45 John Moses (listed as Hohn on checklist card)	.06	.03	.00
☐ U46 John Candelaria	.06	.03	.00
☐ U47 Jack Clark	.15	.07	.01
☐ U48 Richard Dotson	.06	.03	.00
☐ U49 Al Leiter	.15	.07	.01
☐ U50 Rafael Santana	.06	.03	.00
☐ U51 Don Slaught	.06	.03	.00
☐ U52 Todd Burns	.25	.12	.02
☐ U53 Dave Henderson	.10	.05	.01
☐ U54 Doug Jennings	.25	.12	.02
☐ U55 Dave Parker	.15	.07	.01
☐ U56 Walt Weiss	.50	.25	.05
☐ U57 Bob Welch	.20	.10	.02
☐ U58 Henry Cotto	.06	.03	.00
☐ U59 Mario Diaz UER (listed as Marion on card front)	.10	.05	.01
☐ U60 Mike Jackson	.10	.05	.01
☐ U61 Bill Swift	.10	.05	.01
☐ U62 Jose Cecena	.10	.05	.01
☐ U63 Ray Hayward	.10	.05	.01
☐ U64 Jim Steels UER (listed as Jim Steele on card back)	.10	.05	.01
☐ U65 Pat Borders	.40	.20	.04
☐ U66 Sil Campusano	.20	.10	.02
☐ U67 Mike Flanagan	.10	.05	.01
☐ U68 Todd Stottlemyre	.25	.12	.02
☐ U69 David Wells	.15	.07	.01
☐ U70 Jose Alvarez	.10	.05	.01
☐ U71 Paul Runge	.06	.03	.00
☐ U72 Cesar Jimenez (card was intended for German Jiminez, it's his photo)	.10	.05	.01
☐ U73 Pete Smith	.10	.05	.01
☐ U74 John Smoltz	1.25	.60	.12
☐ U75 Damon Berryhill	.20	.10	.02
☐ U76 Goose Gossage	.12	.06	.01
☐ U77 Mark Grace	3.50	1.75	.35
☐ U78 Darrin Jackson	.10	.05	.01
☐ U79 Vance Law	.06	.03	.00
☐ U80 Jeff Pico	.10	.05	.01
☐ U81 Gary Varsho	.15	.07	.01
☐ U82 Tim Birtsas	.06	.03	.00
☐ U83 Rob Dibble	.80	.40	.08
☐ U84 Danny Jackson	.10	.05	.01
☐ U85 Paul O'Neill	.15	.07	.01
☐ U86 Jose Rijo	.20	.10	.02
☐ U87 Chris Sabo	3.00	1.50	.30
☐ U88 John Fishel	.10	.05	.01
☐ U89 Craig Biggio	.90	.45	.09
☐ U90 Terry Puhl	.06	.03	.00
☐ U91 Rafael Ramirez	.06	.03	.00
☐ U92 Louie Meadows	.10	.05	.01
☐ U93 Kirk Gibson	.25	.12	.02
☐ U94 Alfredo Griffin	.06	.03	.00
☐ U95 Jay Howell	.06	.03	.00
☐ U96 Jesse Orosco	.06	.03	.00
☐ U97 Alejandro Pena	.06	.03	.00
☐ U98 Tracy Woodson	.15	.07	.01
☐ U99 John Dopson	.20	.10	.02
☐ U100 Brian Holman	.35	.17	.03
☐ U101 Rex Hudler	.15	.07	.01
☐ U102 Jeff Parrett	.10	.05	.01
☐ U103 Nelson Santovenia	.25	.12	.02
☐ U104 Kevin Elster	.15	.07	.01
☐ U105 Jeff Innis	.15	.07	.01
☐ U106 Mackey Sasser	.35	.17	.03
☐ U107 Phil Bradley	.10	.05	.01
☐ U108 Danny Clay	.10	.05	.01
☐ U109 Greg Harris	.06	.03	.00
☐ U110 Ricky Jordan	.90	.45	.09
☐ U111 David Palmer	.06	.03	.00
☐ U112 Jim Gott	.06	.03	.00
☐ U113 Tommy Gregg UER (photo actually Randy Milligan)	.20	.10	.02
☐ U114 Barry Jones	.06	.03	.00
☐ U115 Randy Milligan	.45	.22	.04
☐ U116 Luis Alicea	.10	.05	.01
☐ U117 Tom Brunansky	.10	.05	.01
☐ U118 John Costello	.10	.05	.01
☐ U119 Jose DeLeon	.06	.03	.00
☐ U120 Bob Horner	.10	.05	.01
☐ U121 Scott Terry	.10	.05	.01
☐ U122 Roberto Alomar	2.00	1.00	.20
☐ U123 Dave Leiper	.06	.03	.00
☐ U124 Keith Moreland	.06	.03	.00
☐ U125 Mark Parent	.15	.07	.01
☐ U126 Dennis Rasmussen	.10	.05	.01
☐ U127 Randy Bockus	.06	.03	.00
☐ U128 Brett Butler	.15	.07	.01
☐ U129 Donell Nixon	.10	.05	.01
☐ U130 Earnest Riles	.06	.03	.00
☐ U131 Roger Samuels	.10	.05	.01
☐ U132 Checklist U1-U132	.06	.01	.00

1988 Fleer Award Winners

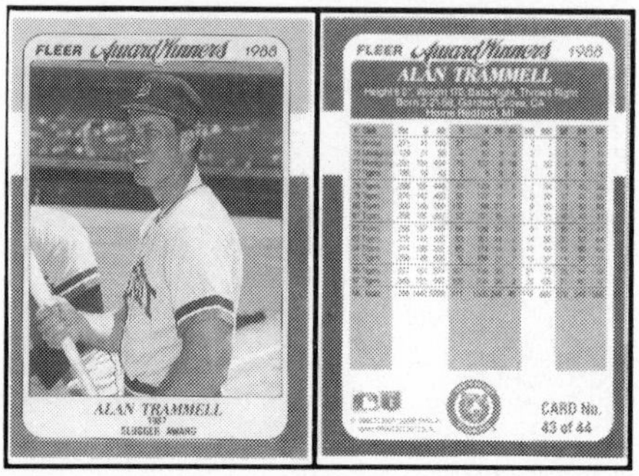

This small set of 44 cards was produced for 7-Eleven stores by Fleer. The cards measure the standard 2 1/2" by 3 1/2" and feature full color fronts and red, white, and blue backs. The card fronts are distinguished by the red, white, and blue frame around the player's full-color photo. The box for the cards describes the set as the "1988 Limited Edition Baseball Award Winners." The checklist for the set is given on the back of the set box.

	MINT	EXC	G-VG
COMPLETE SET (44)	4.00	2.00	.40
COMMON PLAYER (1-44)	.10	.05	.01
☐ 1 Steve Bedrosian	.10	.05	.01
☐ 2 George Bell	.20	.10	.02
☐ 3 Wade Boggs	.65	.30	.06
☐ 4 Jose Canseco	1.00	.50	.10
☐ 5 Will Clark	.90	.45	.09
☐ 6 Roger Clemens	.65	.30	.06
☐ 7 Kal Daniels	.20	.10	.02
☐ 8 Eric Davis	.50	.25	.05
☐ 9 Andre Dawson	.25	.12	.02
☐ 10 Mike Dunne	.10	.05	.01
☐ 11 Dwight Evans	.15	.07	.01
☐ 12 Carlton Fisk	.25	.12	.02
☐ 13 Julio Franco	.15	.07	.01
☐ 14 Dwight Gooden	.35	.17	.03
☐ 15 Pedro Guerrero	.15	.07	.01
☐ 16 Tony Gwynn	.30	.15	.03
☐ 17 Orel Hershiser	.25	.12	.02
☐ 18 Tom Henke	.10	.05	.01
☐ 19 Ted Higuera	.15	.07	.01
☐ 20 Charlie Hough	.10	.05	.01
☐ 21 Wally Joyner	.20	.10	.02
☐ 22 Jimmy Key	.10	.05	.01
☐ 23 Don Mattingly	1.00	.50	.10
☐ 24 Mark McGwire	.65	.30	.06
☐ 25 Paul Molitor	.15	.07	.01
☐ 26 Jack Morris	.15	.07	.01
☐ 27 Dale Murphy	.30	.15	.03
☐ 28 Terry Pendleton	.10	.05	.01
☐ 29 Kirby Puckett	.40	.20	.04
☐ 30 Tim Raines	.20	.10	.02
☐ 31 Jeff Reardon	.15	.07	.01
☐ 32 Harold Reynolds	.10	.05	.01
☐ 33 Dave Righetti	.15	.07	.01
☐ 34 Benito Santiago	.25	.12	.02
☐ 35 Mike Schmidt	.65	.30	.06
☐ 36 Mike Scott	.15	.07	.01
☐ 37 Kevin Seitzer	.20	.10	.02
☐ 38 Larry Sheets	.10	.05	.01
☐ 39 Ozzie Smith	.20	.10	.02
☐ 40 Darryl Strawberry	.50	.25	.05
☐ 41 Rick Sutcliffe	.10	.05	.01
☐ 42 Danny Tartabull	.20	.10	.02
☐ 43 Alan Trammell	.15	.07	.01
☐ 44 Tim Wallach	.15	.07	.01

1988 Fleer Baseball All-Stars

This small boxed set of 44 cards was produced exclusively for Ben Franklin Stores. The cards measure the standard 2 1/2" by 3 1/2" and feature full color fronts and white and blue backs. The card fronts are distinguished by the yellow and blue striped background behind the player's full-color photo. The box for the cards describes the set as the "1988 Fleer Baseball All-Stars." The checklist for the set is given on the back of the set box.

	MINT	EXC	G-VG
COMPLETE SET (44)	5.00	2.50	.50
COMMON PLAYER (1-44)	.10	.05	.01
☐ 1 George Bell	.20	.10	.02
☐ 2 Wade Boggs	.65	.30	.06
☐ 3 Bobby Bonilla	.35	.17	.03
☐ 4 George Brett	.40	.20	.04
☐ 5 Jose Canseco	1.00	.50	.10
☐ 6 Jack Clark	.20	.10	.02
☐ 7 Will Clark	.90	.45	.09
☐ 8 Roger Clemens	.65	.30	.06
☐ 9 Eric Davis	.60	.30	.06
☐ 10 Andre Dawson	.25	.12	.02
☐ 11 Julio Franco	.15	.07	.01
☐ 12 Dwight Gooden	.50	.25	.05
☐ 13 Tony Gwynn	.45	.22	.04
☐ 14 Orel Hershiser	.35	.17	.03
☐ 15 Teddy Higuera	.15	.07	.01
☐ 16 Charlie Hough	.10	.05	.01
☐ 17 Kent Hrbek	.20	.10	.02
☐ 18 Bruce Hurst	.15	.07	.01
☐ 19 Wally Joyner	.30	.15	.03
☐ 20 Mark Langston	.20	.10	.02
☐ 21 Dave LaPoint	.10	.05	.01
☐ 22 Candy Maldonado	.10	.05	.01
☐ 23 Don Mattingly	1.00	.50	.10
☐ 24 Roger McDowell	.10	.05	.01
☐ 25 Mark McGwire	.75	.35	.07
☐ 26 Jack Morris	.15	.07	.01
☐ 27 Dale Murphy	.35	.17	.03
☐ 28 Eddie Murray	.35	.17	.03
☐ 29 Matt Nokes	.20	.10	.02
☐ 30 Kirby Puckett	.40	.20	.04
☐ 31 Tim Raines	.20	.10	.02
☐ 32 Willie Randolph	.15	.07	.01
☐ 33 Jeff Reardon	.15	.07	.01
☐ 34 Nolan Ryan	1.25	.60	.12
☐ 35 Juan Samuel	.15	.07	.01
☐ 36 Mike Schmidt	.75	.35	.07
☐ 37 Mike Scott	.20	.10	.02
☐ 38 Kevin Seitzer	.25	.12	.02
☐ 39 Ozzie Smith	.20	.10	.02
☐ 40 Darryl Strawberry	.60	.30	.06
☐ 41 Rick Sutcliffe	.15	.07	.01
☐ 42 Alan Trammell	.20	.10	.02
☐ 43 Tim Wallach	.15	.07	.01
☐ 44 Dave Winfield	.25	.12	.02

1988 Fleer Baseball MVP

This small 44-card boxed set was produced by Fleer for distribution by the Toys'r'Us stores. The cards measure the standard 2 1/2" by 3 1/2" and feature full color fronts. The set is titled "Baseball MVP." Each individual boxed set includes the

44 cards and 6 logo stickers. The checklist for the set is found on the back panel of the box. The card fronts have a vanilla-yellow and blue border. The box refers to Toys'r'Us but there is no mention of Toys'r'Us anywhere on the cards themselves.

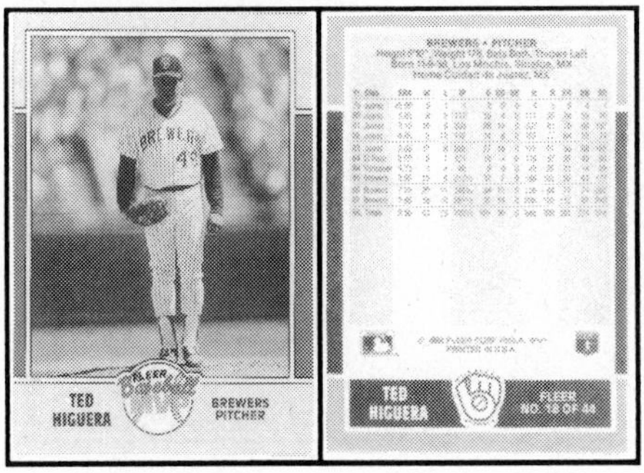

	MINT	EXC	G-VG
COMPLETE SET (44)	5.00	2.50	.50
COMMON PLAYER (1-44)	.10	.05	.01
□ 1 George Bell	.20	.10	.02
□ 2 Wade Boggs	.65	.30	.06
□ 3 Jose Canseco	1.00	.50	.10
□ 4 Ivan Calderon	.15	.07	.01
□ 5 Will Clark	.90	.45	.09
□ 6 Roger Clemens	.65	.30	.06
□ 7 Vince Coleman	.25	.12	.02
□ 8 Eric Davis	.60	.30	.06
□ 9 Andre Dawson	.25	.12	.02
□ 10 Dave Dravecky	.15	.07	.01
□ 11 Mike Dunne	.10	.05	.01
□ 12 Dwight Evans	.15	.07	.01
□ 13 Sid Fernandez	.15	.07	.01
□ 14 Tony Fernandez	.15	.07	.01
□ 15 Julio Franco	.15	.07	.01
□ 16 Dwight Gooden	.40	.20	.04
□ 17 Tony Gwynn	.35	.17	.03
□ 18 Ted Higuera	.15	.07	.01
□ 19 Charlie Hough	.10	.05	.01
□ 20 Wally Joyner	.25	.12	.02
□ 21 Mark Langston	.20	.10	.02
□ 22 Don Mattingly	1.00	.50	.10
□ 23 Mark McGwire	.75	.35	.07
□ 24 Jack Morris	.15	.07	.01
□ 25 Dale Murphy	.35	.17	.03
□ 26 Kirby Puckett	.45	.22	.04
□ 27 Tim Raines	.20	.10	.02
□ 28 Willie Randolph	.15	.07	.01
□ 29 Ryne Sandberg	.75	.35	.07
□ 30 Benito Santiago	.30	.15	.03
□ 31 Mike Schmidt	.75	.35	.07
□ 32 Mike Scott	.20	.10	.02
□ 33 Kevin Seitzer	.25	.12	.02
□ 34 Larry Sheets	.10	.05	.01
□ 35 Ozzie Smith	.20	.10	.02
□ 36 Dave Stewart	.25	.12	.02
□ 37 Darryl Strawberry	.60	.30	.06
□ 38 Rick Sutcliffe	.15	.07	.01
□ 39 Alan Trammell	.20	.10	.02
□ 40 Fernando Valenzuela	.20	.10	.02
□ 41 Frank Viola	.20	.10	.02
□ 42 Tim Wallach	.15	.07	.01
□ 43 Dave Winfield	.25	.12	.02
□ 44 Robin Yount	.50	.25	.05

1988 Fleer Exciting Stars

This small boxed set of 44 cards was produced exclusively for Cumberland Farm Stores. The cards measure the standard 2 1/2" by 3 1/2" and feature full color fronts and red, white, and blue backs. The card fronts are distinguished by the framing of the player's full-color photo with a blue border with a red and white bar stripe across the middle. The box for the cards describes the set as the "1988 Fleer Baseball's Exciting Stars." The checklist for the set is given on the back of the set box.

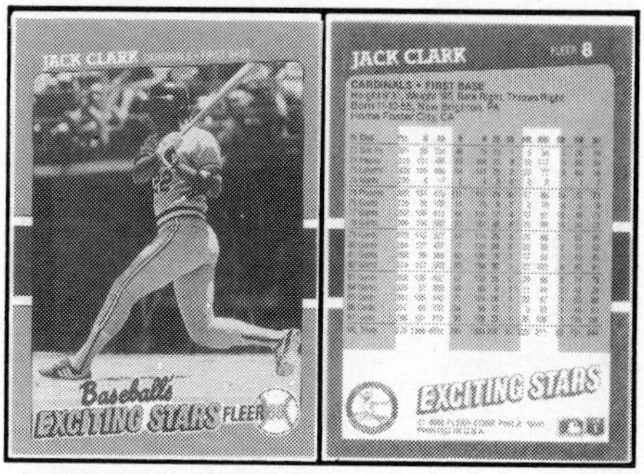

	MINT	EXC	G-VG
COMPLETE SET (44)	5.00	2.50	.50
COMMON PLAYER (1-44)	.10	.05	.01
□ 1 Harold Baines	.15	.07	.01
□ 2 Kevin Bass	.10	.05	.01
□ 3 George Bell	.20	.10	.02
□ 4 Wade Boggs	.65	.30	.06
□ 5 Mickey Brantley	.10	.05	.01
□ 6 Sid Bream	.10	.05	.01
□ 7 Jose Canseco	1.00	.50	.10
□ 8 Jack Clark	.20	.10	.02
□ 9 Will Clark	.90	.45	.09
□ 10 Roger Clemens	.65	.30	.06
□ 11 Vince Coleman	.25	.12	.02
□ 12 Eric Davis	.60	.30	.06
□ 13 Andre Dawson	.25	.12	.02
□ 14 Julio Franco	.15	.07	.01
□ 15 Dwight Gooden	.50	.25	.05
□ 16 Mike Greenwell	.65	.30	.06
□ 17 Tony Gwynn	.35	.17	.03
□ 18 Von Hayes	.15	.07	.01
□ 19 Tom Henke	.10	.05	.01
□ 20 Orel Hershiser	.35	.17	.03
□ 21 Teddy Higuera	.15	.07	.01
□ 22 Brook Jacoby	.15	.07	.01
□ 23 Wally Joyner	.30	.15	.03
□ 24 Jimmy Key	.15	.07	.01
□ 25 Don Mattingly	1.00	.50	.10
□ 26 Mark McGwire	.75	.35	.07
□ 27 Jack Morris	.15	.07	.01
□ 28 Dale Murphy	.30	.15	.03
□ 29 Matt Nokes	.20	.10	.02
□ 30 Kirby Puckett	.40	.20	.04
□ 31 Tim Raines	.20	.10	.02
□ 32 Ryne Sandberg	.75	.35	.07
□ 33 Benito Santiago	.30	.15	.03
□ 34 Mike Schmidt	.75	.35	.07
□ 35 Mike Scott	.20	.10	.02
□ 36 Kevin Seitzer	.25	.12	.02
□ 37 Larry Sheets	.10	.05	.01
□ 38 Ruben Sierra	.60	.30	.06
□ 39 Darryl Strawberry	.60	.30	.06
□ 40 Rick Sutcliffe	.15	.07	.01
□ 41 Danny Tartabull	.20	.10	.02
□ 42 Alan Trammell	.20	.10	.02
□ 43 Fernando Valenzuela	.15	.07	.01
□ 44 Devon White	.20	.10	.02

1988 Fleer Hottest Stars

This 44-card boxed set was produced by Fleer for exclusive distribution by Revco Discount Drug stores all over the country. The cards measure the standard 2 1/2" by 3 1/2" and feature full color fronts and red, white, and blue backs. The card fronts are easily distinguished by the flaming baseball in the lower right corner which says "Fleer Baseball's Hottest Stars." The player's picture is framed in red fading from orange down to yellow. The box for the cards proclaims "1988 Limited Edition Baseball's

Hottest Stars" and is styled in blue, red, and yellow. The checklist for the set is given on the back of the set box. The box refers to Revco but there is no mention of Revco anywhere on the cards themselves.

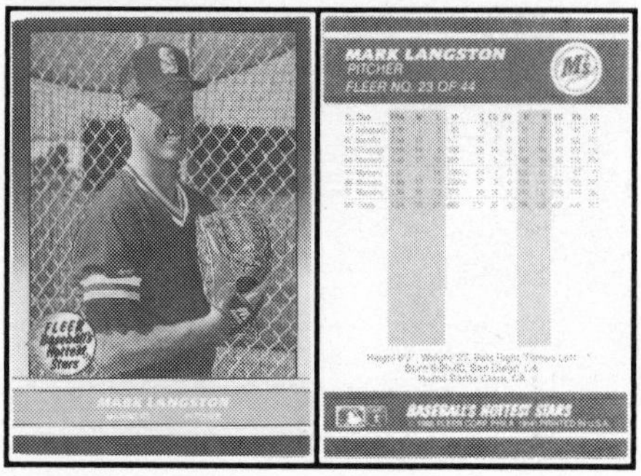

	MINT	EXC	G-VG
COMPLETE SET (44)	5.00	2.50	.50
COMMON PLAYER (1-44)	.10	.05	.01
☐ 1 George Bell	.20	.10	.02
☐ 2 Wade Boggs	.65	.30	.06
☐ 3 Bobby Bonilla	.35	.17	.03
☐ 4 George Brett	.40	.20	.04
☐ 5 Jose Canseco	1.00	.50	.10
☐ 6 Will Clark	.90	.45	.09
☐ 7 Roger Clemens	.65	.30	.06
☐ 8 Eric Davis	.60	.30	.06
☐ 9 Andre Dawson	.25	.12	.02
☐ 10 Tony Fernandez	.15	.07	.01
☐ 11 Julio Franco	.10	.05	.01
☐ 12 Gary Gaetti	.15	.07	.01
☐ 13 Dwight Gooden	.40	.20	.04
☐ 14 Mike Greenwell	.65	.30	.06
☐ 15 Tony Gwynn	.35	.17	.03
☐ 16 Rickey Henderson	.75	.35	.07
☐ 17 Keith Hernandez	.20	.10	.02
☐ 18 Tom Herr	.10	.05	.01
☐ 19 Orel Hershiser	.35	.17	.03
☐ 20 Ted Higuera	.15	.07	.01
☐ 21 Wally Joyner	.30	.15	.03
☐ 22 Jimmy Key	.10	.05	.01
☐ 23 Mark Langston	.20	.10	.02
☐ 24 Don Mattingly	1.00	.50	.10
☐ 25 Jack McDowell	.25	.12	.02
☐ 26 Mark McGwire	.75	.35	.07
☐ 27 Kevin Mitchell	.50	.25	.05
☐ 28 Jack Morris	.15	.07	.01
☐ 29 Dale Murphy	.35	.17	.03
☐ 30 Kirby Puckett	.40	.20	.04
☐ 31 Tim Raines	.20	.10	.02
☐ 32 Shane Rawley	.10	.05	.01
☐ 33 Benito Santiago	.35	.17	.03
☐ 34 Mike Schmidt	.75	.35	.07
☐ 35 Mike Scott	.20	.10	.02
☐ 36 Kevin Seitzer	.25	.12	.02
☐ 37 Larry Sheets	.10	.05	.01
☐ 38 Ruben Sierra	.60	.30	.06
☐ 39 Dave Smith	.10	.05	.01
☐ 40 Ozzie Smith	.25	.12	.02
☐ 41 Darryl Strawberry	.60	.30	.06
☐ 42 Rick Sutcliffe	.15	.07	.01
☐ 43 Pat Tabler	.10	.05	.01
☐ 44 Alan Trammell	.20	.10	.02

1988 Fleer League Leaders

This small boxed set of 44 cards was produced exclusively for Walgreen Drug Stores. The cards measure the standard 2 1/2" by 3 1/2" and feature full color fronts and pink, white, and blue backs. The card fronts are distinguished by the blue solid and striped background behind the player's full-color photo. The box for the cards describes the set as the "1988 Fleer Baseball's League Leaders." The checklist for the set is given on the back of the set box.

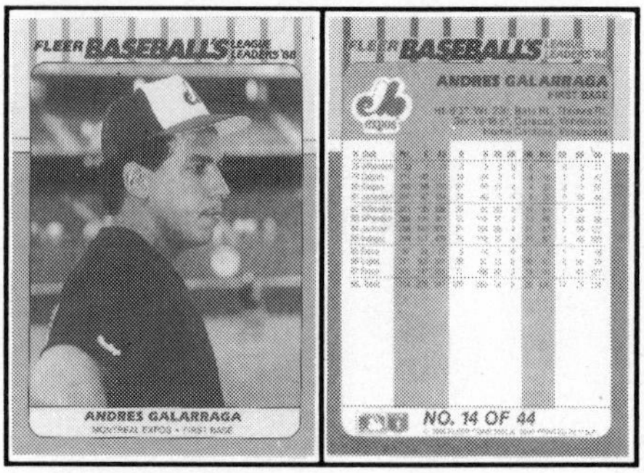

	MINT	EXC	G-VG
COMPLETE SET (44)	5.00	2.50	.50
COMMON PLAYER (1-44)	.10	.05	.01
☐ 1 George Bell	.20	.10	.02
☐ 2 Wade Boggs	.65	.30	.06
☐ 3 Ivan Calderon	.15	.07	.01
☐ 4 Jose Canseco	1.00	.50	.10
☐ 5 Will Clark	.90	.45	.09
☐ 6 Roger Clemens	.65	.30	.06
☐ 7 Vince Coleman	.30	.15	.03
☐ 8 Eric Davis	.60	.30	.06
☐ 9 Andre Dawson	.25	.12	.02
☐ 10 Bill Doran	.15	.07	.01
☐ 11 Dwight Evans	.15	.07	.01
☐ 12 Julio Franco	.15	.07	.01
☐ 13 Gary Gaetti	.15	.07	.01
☐ 14 Andres Galarraga	.20	.10	.02
☐ 15 Dwight Gooden	.50	.25	.05
☐ 16 Tony Gwynn	.40	.20	.04
☐ 17 Tom Henke	.10	.05	.01
☐ 18 Keith Hernandez	.20	.10	.02
☐ 19 Orel Hershiser	.35	.17	.03
☐ 20 Ted Higuera	.15	.07	.01
☐ 21 Kent Hrbek	.20	.10	.02
☐ 22 Wally Joyner	.30	.15	.03
☐ 23 Jimmy Key	.10	.05	.01
☐ 24 Mark Langston	.20	.10	.02
☐ 25 Don Mattingly	1.00	.50	.10
☐ 26 Mark McGwire	.75	.35	.07
☐ 27 Paul Molitor	.20	.10	.02
☐ 28 Jack Morris	.15	.07	.01
☐ 29 Dale Murphy	.35	.17	.03
☐ 30 Kirby Puckett	.40	.20	.04
☐ 31 Tim Raines	.20	.10	.02
☐ 32 Rick Reuschel	.15	.07	.01
☐ 33 Bret Saberhagen	.25	.12	.02
☐ 34 Benito Santiago	.30	.15	.03
☐ 35 Mike Schmidt	.75	.35	.07
☐ 36 Mike Scott	.20	.10	.02
☐ 37 Kevin Seitzer	.25	.12	.02
☐ 38 Larry Sheets	.10	.05	.01
☐ 39 Ruben Sierra	.60	.30	.06
☐ 40 Darryl Strawberry	.60	.30	.06
☐ 41 Rick Sutcliffe	.15	.07	.01
☐ 42 Alan Trammell	.20	.10	.02
☐ 43 Andy Van Slyke	.20	.10	.02
☐ 44 Todd Worrell	.15	.07	.01

1988 Fleer Mini

The 1988 Fleer "Classic Miniatures" set consists of 120 small cards with all new pictures of the players as compared to the 1988 Fleer regular issue. The cards are only 1 13/16" by 2 9/16", making them one of the smallest cards available. Card backs provide career year-by-year statistics. The complete set was distributed in a green, red, white, and silver box along with 18 logo stickers. The card numbering is by team order.

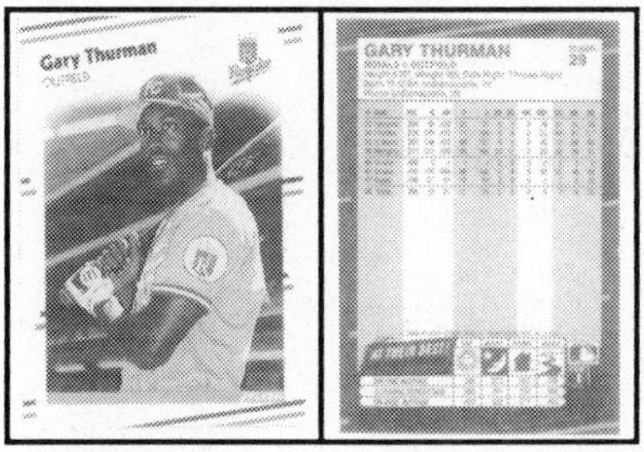

	MINT	EXC	G-VG
COMPLETE SET (120)	11.00	5.50	1.10
COMMON PLAYER (1-120)	.05	.02	.00
☐ 1 Eddie Murray	.25	.12	.02
☐ 2 Dave Schmidt	.05	.02	.00
☐ 3 Larry Sheets	.05	.02	.00
☐ 4 Wade Boggs	.75	.35	.07
☐ 5 Roger Clemens	.75	.35	.07
☐ 6 Dwight Evans	.10	.05	.01
☐ 7 Mike Greenwell	.60	.30	.06
☐ 8 Sam Horn	.10	.05	.01
☐ 9 Lee Smith	.05	.02	.00
☐ 10 Brian Downing	.05	.02	.00
☐ 11 Wally Joyner	.25	.12	.02
☐ 12 Devon White	.15	.07	.01
☐ 13 Mike Witt	.05	.02	.00
☐ 14 Ivan Calderon	.10	.05	.01
☐ 15 Ozzie Guillen	.15	.07	.01
☐ 16 Jack McDowell	.15	.07	.01
☐ 17 Kenny Williams	.10	.05	.01
☐ 18 Joe Carter	.15	.07	.01
☐ 19 Julio Franco	.10	.05	.01
☐ 20 Pat Tabler	.05	.02	.00
☐ 21 Doyle Alexander	.05	.02	.00
☐ 22 Jack Morris	.10	.05	.01
☐ 23 Matt Nokes	.15	.07	.01
☐ 24 Walt Terrell	.05	.02	.00
☐ 25 Alan Trammell	.15	.07	.01
☐ 26 Bret Saberhagen	.25	.12	.02
☐ 27 Kevin Seitzer	.25	.12	.02
☐ 28 Danny Tartabull	.20	.10	.02
☐ 29 Gary Thurman	.10	.05	.01
☐ 30 Ted Higuera	.10	.05	.01
☐ 31 Paul Molitor	.15	.07	.01
☐ 32 Dan Plesac	.10	.05	.01
☐ 33 Robin Yount	.40	.20	.04
☐ 34 Gary Gaetti	.15	.07	.01
☐ 35 Kent Hrbek	.15	.07	.01
☐ 36 Kirby Puckett	.40	.20	.04
☐ 37 Jeff Reardon	.10	.05	.01
☐ 38 Frank Viola	.15	.07	.01
☐ 39 Jack Clark	.15	.07	.01
☐ 40 Rickey Henderson	.75	.35	.07
☐ 41 Don Mattingly	1.00	.50	.10
☐ 42 Willie Randolph	.10	.05	.01
☐ 43 Dave Righetti	.10	.05	.01
☐ 44 Dave Winfield	.25	.12	.02
☐ 45 Jose Canseco	1.25	.60	.12
☐ 46 Mark McGwire	.75	.35	.07
☐ 47 Dave Parker	.20	.10	.02
☐ 48 Dave Stewart	.20	.10	.02
☐ 49 Walt Weiss	.35	.17	.03
☐ 50 Bob Welch	.15	.07	.01
☐ 51 Mickey Brantley	.05	.02	.00
☐ 52 Mark Langston	.15	.07	.01
☐ 53 Harold Reynolds	.05	.02	.00
☐ 54 Scott Fletcher	.05	.02	.00
☐ 55 Charlie Hough	.05	.02	.00
☐ 56 Pete Incaviglia	.15	.07	.01
☐ 57 Larry Parrish	.05	.02	.00
☐ 58 Ruben Sierra	.50	.25	.05
☐ 59 George Bell	.20	.10	.02
☐ 60 Mark Eichhorn	.05	.02	.00
☐ 61 Tony Fernandez	.10	.05	.01
☐ 62 Tom Henke	.05	.02	.00
☐ 63 Jimmy Key	.10	.05	.01
☐ 64 Dion James	.05	.02	.00
☐ 65 Dale Murphy	.30	.15	.03
☐ 66 Zane Smith	.10	.05	.01
☐ 67 Andre Dawson	.20	.10	.02
☐ 68 Mark Grace	2.00	1.00	.20
☐ 69 Jerry Mumphrey	.05	.02	.00
☐ 70 Ryne Sandberg	.75	.35	.07
☐ 71 Rick Sutcliffe	.10	.05	.01
☐ 72 Kal Daniels	.15	.07	.01
☐ 73 Eric Davis	.60	.30	.06
☐ 74 John Franco	.05	.02	.00
☐ 75 Ron Robinson	.05	.02	.00
☐ 76 Jeff Treadway	.10	.05	.01
☐ 77 Kevin Bass	.05	.02	.00
☐ 78 Glenn Davis	.20	.10	.02
☐ 79 Nolan Ryan	1.25	.60	.12
☐ 80 Mike Scott	.15	.07	.01
☐ 81 Dave Smith	.05	.02	.00
☐ 82 Kirk Gibson	.25	.12	.02
☐ 83 Pedro Guerrero	.15	.07	.01
☐ 84 Orel Hershiser	.35	.17	.03
☐ 85 Steve Sax	.15	.07	.01
☐ 86 Fernando Valenzuela	.15	.07	.01
☐ 87 Tim Burke	.10	.05	.01
☐ 88 Andres Galarraga	.20	.10	.02
☐ 89 Neal Heaton	.05	.02	.00
☐ 90 Tim Raines	.25	.12	.02
☐ 91 Tim Wallach	.10	.05	.01
☐ 92 Dwight Gooden	.45	.22	.04
☐ 93 Keith Hernandez	.15	.07	.01
☐ 94 Gregg Jefferies	1.50	.75	.15
☐ 95 Howard Johnson	.20	.10	.02
☐ 96 Roger McDowell	.05	.02	.00
☐ 97 Darryl Strawberry	.50	.25	.05
☐ 98 Steve Bedrosian	.10	.05	.01
☐ 99 Von Hayes	.10	.05	.01
☐ 100 Shane Rawley	.05	.02	.00
☐ 101 Juan Samuel	.10	.05	.01
☐ 102 Mike Schmidt	.75	.35	.07
☐ 103 Bobby Bonilla	.35	.17	.03
☐ 104 Mike Dunne	.05	.02	.00
☐ 105 Andy Van Slyke	.15	.07	.01
☐ 106 Vince Coleman	.20	.10	.02
☐ 107 Bob Horner	.10	.05	.01
☐ 108 Willie McGee	.15	.07	.01
☐ 109 Ozzie Smith	.15	.07	.01
☐ 110 John Tudor	.10	.05	.01
☐ 111 Todd Worrell	.15	.07	.01
☐ 112 Tony Gwynn	.35	.17	.03
☐ 113 John Kruk	.10	.05	.01
☐ 114 Lance McCullers	.05	.02	.00
☐ 115 Benito Santiago	.35	.17	.03
☐ 116 Will Clark	1.00	.50	.10
☐ 117 Jeff Leonard	.05	.02	.00
☐ 118 Candy Maldonado	.05	.02	.00
☐ 119 Kirt Manwaring	.05	.02	.00
☐ 120 Don Robinson	.05	.02	.00

1988 Fleer Record Setters

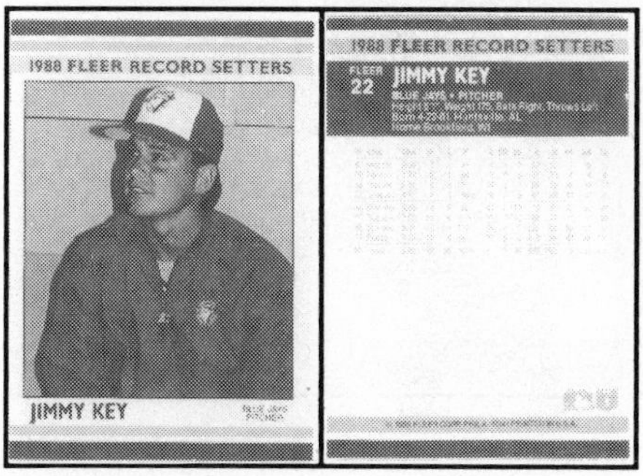

This small boxed set of 44 cards was produced exclusively for Eckerd's Drug Stores. The cards measure the standard 2 1/2" by 3 1/2" and feature full color fronts and red, white, and blue backs. The card fronts are distinguished by the red and blue frame around the player's full-color photo. The box for the cards describes the set as the "1988 Baseball Record Setters." The checklist for the set is given on the back of the set box.

	MINT	EXC	G-VG
COMPLETE SET (44)	5.00	2.50	.50
COMMON PLAYER (1-44)	.10	.05	.01
☐ 1 Jesse Barfield	.20	.10	.02
☐ 2 George Bell	.20	.10	.02
☐ 3 Wade Boggs	.65	.30	.06
☐ 4 Jose Canseco	1.00	.50	.10

	MINT	EXC	G-VG
☐ 5 Jack Clark	.20	.10	.02
☐ 6 Will Clark	.90	.45	.09
☐ 7 Roger Clemens	.65	.30	.06
☐ 8 Alvin Davis	.15	.07	.01
☐ 9 Eric Davis	.60	.30	.06
☐ 10 Andre Dawson	.25	.12	.02
☐ 11 Mike Dunne	.10	.05	.01
☐ 12 John Franco	.15	.07	.01
☐ 13 Julio Franco	.15	.07	.01
☐ 14 Dwight Gooden	.50	.25	.05
☐ 15 Mark Gubicza (listed as Gubiczo on box checklist)	.15	.07	.01
☐ 16 Ozzie Guillen	.20	.10	.02
☐ 17 Tony Gwynn	.40	.20	.04
☐ 18 Orel Hershiser	.35	.17	.03
☐ 19 Teddy Higuera	.15	.07	.01
☐ 20 Howard Johnson UER (missing '87 stats on card back)	.20	.10	.02
☐ 21 Wally Joyner	.30	.15	.03
☐ 22 Jimmy Key	.15	.07	.01
☐ 23 Jeff Leonard	.10	.05	.01
☐ 24 Don Mattingly	1.00	.50	.10
☐ 25 Mark McGwire	.75	.35	.07
☐ 26 Jack Morris	.15	.07	.01
☐ 27 Dale Murphy	.35	.17	.03
☐ 28 Larry Parrish	.10	.05	.01
☐ 29 Kirby Puckett	.45	.22	.04
☐ 30 Tim Raines	.20	.10	.02
☐ 31 Harold Reynolds	.10	.05	.01
☐ 32 Dave Righetti	.15	.07	.01
☐ 33 Cal Ripken	.30	.15	.03
☐ 34 Benito Santiago	.30	.15	.03
☐ 35 Mike Schmidt	.75	.35	.07
☐ 36 Mike Scott	.20	.10	.02
☐ 37 Kevin Seitzer	.25	.12	.02
☐ 38 Ozzie Smith	.20	.10	.02
☐ 39 Darryl Strawberry	.60	.30	.06
☐ 40 Rick Sutcliffe	.15	.07	.01
☐ 41 Alan Trammell	.20	.10	.02
☐ 42 Frank Viola	.20	.10	.02
☐ 43 Mitch Williams	.15	.07	.01
☐ 44 Todd Worrell	.15	.07	.01

1988 Fleer Sluggers/Pitchers

Fleer produced this 44-card boxed set although it was primarily distributed by McCrory, McLellan, J.J Newberry, H.L.Green, T.G.Y., and other similar stores. The set is subtitled "Baseball's Best". Cards are standard-size, 2 1/2" by 3 1/2", and were packaged in a green custom box along with six logo stickers. The set checklist is given on the back of the box. The bottoms of the boxes which held the individual set boxes also contained a panel of six cards; these box bottom cards were numbered C1 through C6.

	MINT	EXC	G-VG
COMPLETE SET (44)	5.00	2.50	.50
COMMON PLAYER (1-44)	.10	.05	.01
☐ 1 George Bell	.20	.10	.02
☐ 2 Wade Boggs	.65	.30	.06
☐ 3 Bobby Bonilla	.35	.17	.03
☐ 4 Tom Brunansky	.15	.07	.01
☐ 5 Ellis Burks	.75	.35	.07
☐ 6 Jose Canseco	1.00	.50	.10
☐ 7 Joe Carter	.20	.10	.02
☐ 8 Will Clark	.90	.45	.09
☐ 9 Roger Clemens	.65	.30	.06
☐ 10 Eric Davis	.60	.30	.06
☐ 11 Glenn Davis	.20	.10	.02
☐ 12 Andre Dawson	.25	.12	.02
☐ 13 Dennis Eckersley	.30	.15	.03
☐ 14 Andres Galarraga	.25	.12	.02
☐ 15 Dwight Gooden	.50	.25	.05
☐ 16 Pedro Guerrero	.20	.10	.02
☐ 17 Tony Gwynn	.35	.17	.03
☐ 18 Orel Hershiser	.30	.15	.03
☐ 19 Ted Higuera	.15	.07	.01
☐ 20 Pete Incaviglia	.15	.07	.01
☐ 21 Danny Jackson	.10	.05	.01
☐ 22 Doug Jennings	.15	.07	.01
☐ 23 Mark Langston	.20	.10	.02
☐ 24 Dave LaPoint	.10	.05	.01
☐ 25 Mike LaValliere	.10	.05	.01
☐ 26 Don Mattingly	1.00	.50	.10
☐ 27 Mark McGwire	.75	.35	.07
☐ 28 Dale Murphy	.35	.17	.03
☐ 29 Ken Phelps	.10	.05	.01
☐ 30 Kirby Puckett	.40	.20	.04
☐ 31 Johnny Ray	.10	.05	.01
☐ 32 Jeff Reardon	.15	.07	.01
☐ 33 Dave Righetti	.15	.07	.01
☐ 34 Cal Ripken UER (misspelled Ripkin on card front)	.35	.17	.03
☐ 35 Chris Sabo	.60	.30	.06
☐ 36 Mike Schmidt	.75	.35	.07
☐ 37 Mike Scott	.20	.10	.02
☐ 38 Kevin Seitzer	.25	.12	.02
☐ 39 Dave Stewart	.25	.12	.02
☐ 40 Darryl Strawberry	.60	.30	.06
☐ 41 Greg Swindell	.15	.07	.01
☐ 42 Frank Tanana	.10	.05	.01
☐ 43 Dave Winfield	.25	.12	.02
☐ 44 Todd Worrell	.15	.07	.01

1988 Fleer Slug/Pitch Box Cards

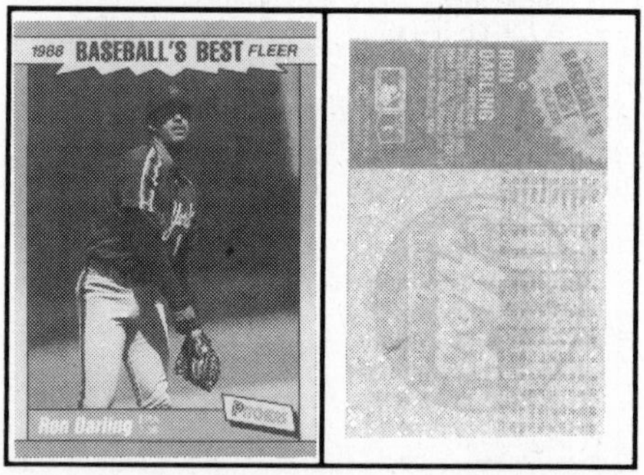

The cards in this 6-card set each measure the standard 2 1/2" by 3 1/2". Cards have essentially the same design as the 1988 Fleer Sluggers vs. Pitchers set of Baseball's Best. The cards were printed on the bottom of the counter display box which held 24 small boxed sets; hence theoretically these box cards are 1/24 as plentiful as the regular boxed set cards. These 6 cards, numbered C1 to C6 are considered a separate set in their own right and are not typically included in a complete set of the 1988 Fleer Sluggers vs. Pitchers set of 44. The value of the panels uncut is slightly greater, perhaps by 25 percent greater, than the value of the individual cards cut up carefully.

	MINT	EXC	G-VG
COMPLETE SET (6)	2.50	1.25	.25
COMMON PLAYERS (C1-C6)	.10	.05	.01
☐ C1 Ron Darling (box bottom card)	.20	.10	.02

☐ C2 Rickey Henderson (box bottom card)	1.50	.75	.15
☐ C3 Carney Lansford (box bottom card)	.25	.12	.02
☐ C4 Rafael Palmeiro (box bottom card)	.50	.25	.05
☐ C5 Frank Viola (box bottom card)	.30	.15	.03
☐ C6 Twins Logo (checklist back) (box bottom card)	.10	.05	.01

1988 Fleer Sticker Cards

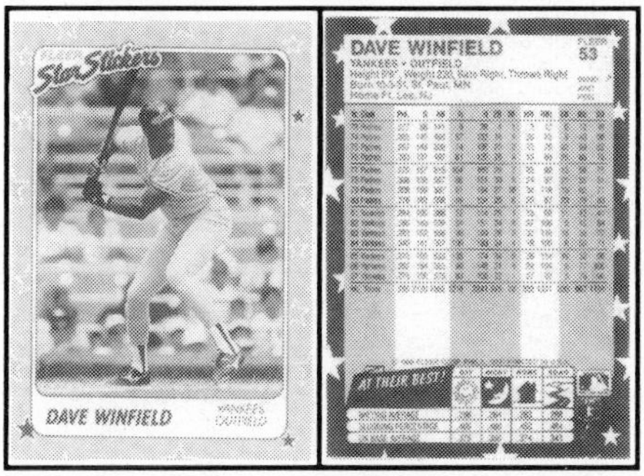

These Star Stickers were distributed as a separate issue by Fleer, with five star stickers and a logo sticker in each wax pack. The 132-card (sticker) set features 2 1/2" by 3 1/2" full-color fronts and even statistics on the sticker back, which is an indication that the Fleer Company understands that these stickers are rarely used as stickers but more like traditional cards. The card fronts are surrounded by a silver-gray border and the backs are printed in red and black on white card stock.

	MINT	EXC	G-VG
COMPLETE SET (132)	21.00	10.50	2.10
COMMON PLAYER (1-132)	.05	.02	.00

☐ 1 Mike Boddicker	.10	.05	.01
☐ 2 Eddie Murray	.25	.12	.02
☐ 3 Cal Ripken	.25	.12	.02
☐ 4 Larry Sheets	.05	.02	.00
☐ 5 Wade Boggs	1.00	.50	.10
☐ 6 Ellis Burks	1.00	.50	.10
☐ 7 Roger Clemens	1.00	.50	.10
☐ 8 Dwight Evans	.15	.07	.01
☐ 9 Mike Greenwell	.75	.35	.07
☐ 10 Bruce Hurst	.10	.05	.01
☐ 11 Brian Downing	.05	.02	.00
☐ 12 Wally Joyner	.40	.20	.04
☐ 13 Mike Witt	.05	.02	.00
☐ 14 Ivan Calderon	.10	.05	.01
☐ 15 Jose DeLeon	.05	.02	.00
☐ 16 Ozzie Guillen	.15	.07	.01
☐ 17 Bobby Thigpen	.25	.12	.02
☐ 18 Joe Carter	.15	.07	.01
☐ 19 Julio Franco	.15	.07	.01
☐ 20 Brook Jacoby	.10	.05	.01
☐ 21 Cory Snyder	.20	.10	.02
☐ 22 Pat Tabler	.05	.02	.00
☐ 23 Doyle Alexander	.05	.02	.00
☐ 24 Kirk Gibson	.25	.12	.02
☐ 25 Mike Henneman	.10	.05	.01
☐ 26 Jack Morris	.15	.07	.01
☐ 27 Matt Nokes	.15	.07	.01
☐ 28 Walt Terrell	.05	.02	.00
☐ 29 Alan Trammell	.25	.12	.02
☐ 30 George Brett	.50	.25	.05
☐ 31 Charlie Leibrandt	.05	.02	.00
☐ 32 Bret Saberhagen	.30	.15	.03
☐ 33 Kevin Seitzer	.30	.15	.03
☐ 34 Danny Tartabull	.25	.12	.02
☐ 35 Frank White	.10	.05	.01
☐ 36 Rob Deer	.10	.05	.01
☐ 37 Ted Higuera	.10	.05	.01
☐ 38 Paul Molitor	.15	.07	.01
☐ 39 Dan Plesac	.10	.05	.01
☐ 40 Robin Yount	.45	.22	.04
☐ 41 Bert Blyleven	.15	.07	.01
☐ 42 Tom Brunansky	.15	.07	.01
☐ 43 Gary Gaetti	.15	.07	.01
☐ 44 Kent Hrbek	.20	.10	.02
☐ 45 Kirby Puckett	.60	.30	.06
☐ 46 Jeff Reardon	.10	.05	.01
☐ 47 Frank Viola	.15	.07	.01
☐ 48 Don Mattingly	2.00	1.00	.20
☐ 49 Mike Pagliarulo	.05	.02	.00
☐ 50 Willie Randolph	.10	.05	.01
☐ 51 Rick Rhoden	.05	.02	.00
☐ 52 Dave Righetti	.15	.07	.01
☐ 53 Dave Winfield	.25	.12	.02
☐ 54 Jose Canseco	2.00	1.00	.20
☐ 55 Carney Lansford	.15	.07	.01
☐ 56 Mark McGwire	1.00	.50	.10
☐ 57 Dave Stewart	.25	.12	.02
☐ 58 Curt Young	.05	.02	.00
☐ 59 Alvin Davis	.10	.05	.01
☐ 60 Mark Langston	.15	.07	.01
☐ 61 Ken Phelps	.05	.02	.00
☐ 62 Harold Reynolds	.05	.02	.00
☐ 63 Scott Fletcher	.05	.02	.00
☐ 64 Charlie Hough	.05	.02	.00
☐ 65 Pete Incaviglia	.20	.10	.02
☐ 66 Oddibe McDowell	.10	.05	.01
☐ 67 Pete O'Brien	.10	.05	.01
☐ 68 Larry Parrish	.05	.02	.00
☐ 69 Ruben Sierra	.75	.35	.07
☐ 70 Jesse Barfield	.15	.07	.01
☐ 71 George Bell	.20	.10	.02
☐ 72 Tony Fernandez	.15	.07	.01
☐ 73 Tom Henke	.05	.02	.00
☐ 74 Jimmy Key	.10	.05	.01
☐ 75 Lloyd Moseby	.10	.05	.01
☐ 76 Dion James	.05	.02	.00
☐ 77 Dale Murphy	.40	.20	.04
☐ 78 Zane Smith	.10	.05	.01
☐ 79 Andre Dawson	.25	.12	.02
☐ 80 Ryne Sandberg	1.00	.50	.10
☐ 81 Rick Sutcliffe	.10	.05	.01
☐ 82 Kal Daniels	.20	.10	.02
☐ 83 Eric Davis	.90	.45	.09
☐ 84 John Franco	.10	.05	.01
☐ 85 Kevin Bass	.05	.02	.00
☐ 86 Glenn Davis	.15	.07	.01
☐ 87 Bill Doran	.10	.05	.01
☐ 88 Nolan Ryan	2.00	1.00	.20
☐ 89 Mike Scott	.20	.10	.02
☐ 90 Dave Smith	.05	.02	.00
☐ 91 Pedro Guerrero	.20	.10	.02
☐ 92 Orel Hershiser	.40	.20	.04
☐ 93 Steve Sax	.15	.07	.01
☐ 94 Fernando Valenzuela	.15	.07	.01
☐ 95 Tim Burke	.10	.05	.01
☐ 96 Andres Galarraga	.25	.12	.02
☐ 97 Tim Raines	.25	.12	.02
☐ 98 Tim Wallach	.10	.05	.01
☐ 99 Mitch Webster	.05	.02	.00
☐ 100 Ron Darling	.10	.05	.01
☐ 101 Sid Fernandez	.10	.05	.01
☐ 102 Dwight Gooden	.50	.25	.05
☐ 103 Keith Hernandez	.15	.07	.01
☐ 104 Howard Johnson	.20	.10	.02
☐ 105 Roger McDowell	.05	.02	.00
☐ 106 Darryl Strawberry	.75	.35	.07
☐ 107 Steve Bedrosian	.10	.05	.01
☐ 108 Von Hayes	.10	.05	.01
☐ 109 Shane Rawley	.05	.02	.00
☐ 110 Juan Samuel	.15	.07	.01
☐ 111 Mike Schmidt	.75	.35	.07
☐ 112 Milt Thompson	.05	.02	.00
☐ 113 Sid Bream	.05	.02	.00
☐ 114 Bobby Bonilla	.35	.17	.03
☐ 115 Mike Dunne	.05	.02	.00
☐ 116 Any Van Slyke	.15	.07	.01
☐ 117 Vince Coleman	.25	.12	.02
☐ 118 Willie McGee	.15	.07	.01
☐ 119 Terry Pendleton	.05	.02	.00
☐ 120 Ozzie Smith	.20	.10	.02
☐ 121 John Tudor	.10	.05	.01
☐ 122 Todd Worrell	.15	.07	.01
☐ 123 Tony Gwynn	.45	.22	.04
☐ 124 John Kruk	.10	.05	.01
☐ 125 Benito Santiago	.45	.22	.04
☐ 126 Will Clark	1.50	.75	.15
☐ 127 Dave Dravecky	.15	.07	.01
☐ 128 Jeff Leonard	.05	.02	.00
☐ 129 Candy Maldonado	.05	.02	.00
☐ 130 Rick Reuschel	.10	.05	.01
☐ 131 Don Robinson	.05	.02	.00
☐ 132 Checklist Card	.05	.02	.00

1988 Fleer Sticker Box Cards

The bottoms of the Star Sticker wax boxes contained two different sets of four cards done in a similar format to the stickers; these cards (they are not stickers but truly cards) are numbered with the prefix S and are considered a separate set. The value of the panels uncut is slightly greater, perhaps by 25 percent greater, than the value of the individual cards cut up carefully.

	MINT	EXC	G-VG
COMPLETE SET (8)	3.50	1.75	.35
COMMON PLAYER	.10	.05	.01
☐ S1 Don Baylor (wax box card)	.15	.07	.01
☐ S2 Gary Carter (wax box card)	.35	.17	.03
☐ S3 Ron Guidry (wax box card)	.20	.10	.02
☐ S4 Rickey Henderson (wax box card)	1.50	.75	.15
☐ S5 Kevin Mitchell (wax box card)	.60	.30	.06
☐ S6 Mark McGwire and Eric Davis (wax box card)	1.50	.75	.15
☐ S7 Giants Logo (wax box card)	.10	.05	.01
☐ S8 Detroit Logo (wax box card)	.10	.05	.01

1988 Fleer Superstars

Fleer produced this 44-card boxed set although it was primarily distributed by McCrory, McLellan, J.J Newberry, H.L.Green, T.G.Y., and other similar stores. The set is subtitled "Fleer Superstars." Cards are standard-size, 2 1/2" by 3 1/2", and were packaged in a red, white, blue, and yellow custom box along with six logo stickers. The set checklist is given on the back of the box. The bottoms of the boxes which held the individual set boxes also contained a panel of six cards; these box bottom cards were numbered C1 through C6.

	MINT	EXC	G-VG
COMPLETE SET (44)	4.00	2.00	.40
COMMON PLAYER (1-44)	.10	.05	.01
☐ 1 Steve Bedrosian	.15	.07	.01
☐ 2 George Bell	.20	.10	.02
☐ 3 Wade Boggs	.65	.30	.06
☐ 4 Barry Bonds	.65	.30	.06
☐ 5 Jose Canseco	1.00	.50	.10
☐ 6 Joe Carter	.20	.10	.02
☐ 7 Jack Clark	.15	.07	.01
☐ 8 Will Clark	.90	.45	.09
☐ 9 Roger Clemens	.65	.30	.06
☐ 10 Alvin Davis	.10	.05	.01
☐ 11 Eric Davis	.50	.25	.05
☐ 12 Glenn Davis	.15	.07	.01
☐ 13 Andre Dawson	.25	.12	.02
☐ 14 Dwight Gooden	.35	.17	.03
☐ 15 Orel Hershiser	.30	.15	.03
☐ 16 Teddy Higuera	.15	.07	.01
☐ 17 Kent Hrbek	.15	.07	.01
☐ 18 Wally Joyner	.25	.12	.02
☐ 19 Jimmy Key	.10	.05	.01
☐ 20 John Kruk	.10	.05	.01
☐ 21 Jeff Leonard	.10	.05	.01
☐ 22 Don Mattingly	1.00	.50	.10
☐ 23 Mark McGwire	.65	.30	.06
☐ 24 Kevin McReynolds	.15	.07	.01
☐ 25 Dale Murphy	.30	.15	.03
☐ 26 Matt Nokes	.15	.07	.01
☐ 27 Terry Pendleton	.10	.05	.01
☐ 28 Kirby Puckett	.40	.20	.04
☐ 29 Tim Raines	.20	.10	.02
☐ 30 Rick Rhoden	.10	.05	.01
☐ 31 Cal Ripken Jr.	.30	.15	.03
☐ 32 Benito Santiago	.30	.15	.03
☐ 33 Mike Schmidt	.75	.35	.07
☐ 34 Mike Scott	.15	.07	.01
☐ 35 Kevin Seitzer	.25	.12	.02
☐ 36 Ruben Sierra	.50	.25	.05
☐ 37 Cory Snyder	.20	.10	.02
☐ 38 Darryl Strawberry	.50	.25	.05
☐ 39 Rick Sutcliffe	.10	.05	.01
☐ 40 Danny Tartabull	.20	.10	.02
☐ 41 Alan Trammell	.15	.07	.01
☐ 42 Kenny Williams	.10	.05	.01
☐ 43 Mike Witt	.10	.05	.01
☐ 44 Robin Yount	.35	.17	.03

1988 Fleer Superstars Box Cards

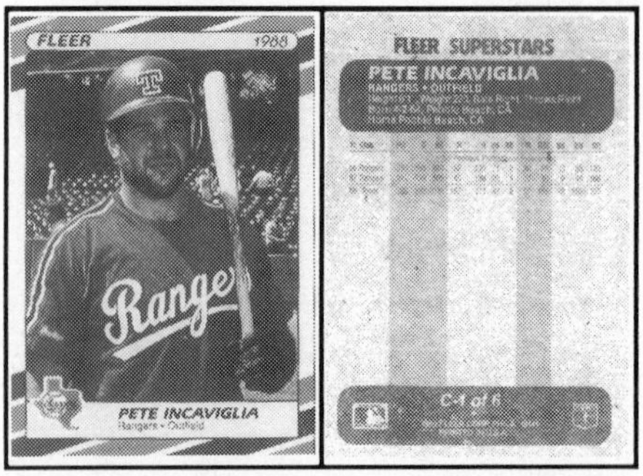

The cards in this 6-card set each measure the standard 2 1/2" by 3 1/2". Cards have essentially the same design as the 1988 Fleer Superstars set. The cards were printed on the bottom of the counter display box which held 24 small boxed sets; hence theoretically these box cards are 1/24 as plentiful as the regular boxed set cards. These 6 cards, numbered C1 to C6 are considered a separate set in their own right and are not typically included in a complete set of the 1988 Fleer Superstars set of

44. The value of the panels uncut is slightly greater, perhaps by 25 percent greater, than the value of the individual cards cut up carefully.

	MINT	EXC	G-VG
COMPLETE SET (6)	3.00	1.50	.30
COMMON PLAYER (C1-C6)	.10	.05	.01
☐ C1 Pete Incaviglia (box bottom card)	.30	.15	.03
☐ C2 Rickey Henderson (box bottom card)	1.50	.75	.15
☐ C3 Tony Fernandez (box bottom card)	.25	.12	.02
☐ C4 Shane Rawley (box bottom card)	.10	.05	.01
☐ C5 Ryne Sandberg (box bottom card)	1.00	.50	.10
☐ C6 Cardinals Logo (checklist back) (box bottom card)	.10	.05	.01

1988 Fleer Team Leaders

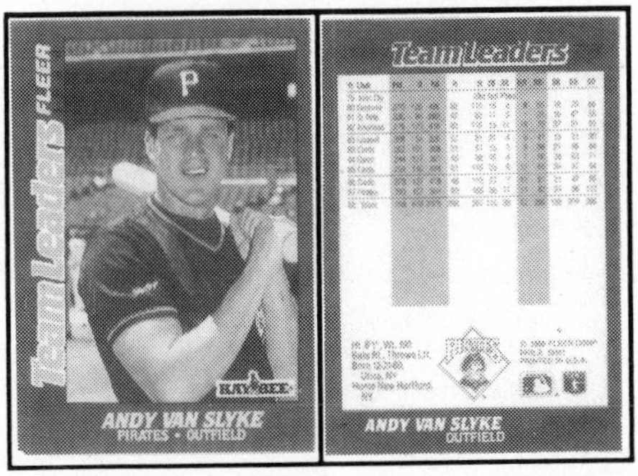

This 44-card boxed set was produced by Fleer for exclusive distribution by Kay Bee Toys and is sometimes referred to as the Fleer Kay Bee set. Six team logo stickers are included in the box with the complete set. The numerical checklist on the back of the box shows that the set is numbered alphabetically. The cards measure 2 1/2" by 3 1/2" and have a distinctive red border on the fronts. The Kay Bee logo is printed in the lower right corner of the obverse of each card.

	MINT	EXC	G-VG
COMPLETE SET (44)	5.00	2.50	.50
COMMON PLAYER (1-44)	.10	.05	.01
☐ 1 George Bell	.20	.10	.02
☐ 2 Wade Boggs	.65	.30	.06
☐ 3 Jose Canseco	1.00	.50	.10
☐ 4 Will Clark	.90	.45	.09
☐ 5 Roger Clemens	.65	.30	.06
☐ 6 Eric Davis	.60	.30	.06
☐ 7 Andre Dawson	.25	.12	.02
☐ 8 Julio Franco	.15	.07	.01
☐ 9 Andres Galarraga	.20	.10	.02
☐ 10 Dwight Gooden	.50	.25	.05
☐ 11 Tony Gwynn	.40	.20	.04
☐ 12 Tom Henke	.10	.05	.01
☐ 13 Orel Hershiser	.35	.17	.03
☐ 14 Kent Hrbek	.15	.07	.01
☐ 15 Ted Higuera	.15	.07	.01
☐ 16 Wally Joyner	.25	.12	.02
☐ 17 Jimmy Key	.10	.05	.01
☐ 18 Mark Langston	.20	.10	.02
☐ 19 Don Mattingly	1.00	.50	.10
☐ 20 Willie McGee	.20	.10	.02
☐ 21 Mark McGwire	.75	.35	.07
☐ 22 Paul Molitor	.15	.07	.01
☐ 23 Jack Morris	.15	.07	.01
☐ 24 Dale Murphy	.30	.15	.03
☐ 25 Larry Parrish	.10	.05	.01
☐ 26 Kirby Puckett	.45	.22	.04
☐ 27 Tim Raines	.20	.10	.02
☐ 28 Jeff Reardon	.15	.07	.01
☐ 29 Dave Righetti	.15	.07	.01
☐ 30 Cal Ripken	.30	.15	.03
☐ 31 Don Robinson	.10	.05	.01
☐ 32 Bret Saberhagen	.30	.15	.03
☐ 33 Juan Samuel	.15	.07	.01
☐ 34 Mike Schmidt	.75	.35	.07
☐ 35 Mike Scott	.20	.10	.02
☐ 36 Kevin Seitzer	.25	.12	.02
☐ 37 Dave Smith	.10	.05	.01
☐ 38 Ozzie Smith	.20	.10	.02
☐ 39 Zane Smith	.15	.07	.01
☐ 40 Darryl Strawberry	.60	.30	.06
☐ 41 Rick Sutcliffe	.15	.07	.01
☐ 42 Bobby Thigpen	.25	.12	.02
☐ 43 Alan Trammell	.20	.10	.02
☐ 44 Andy Van Slyke	.15	.07	.01

1988 Fleer World Series

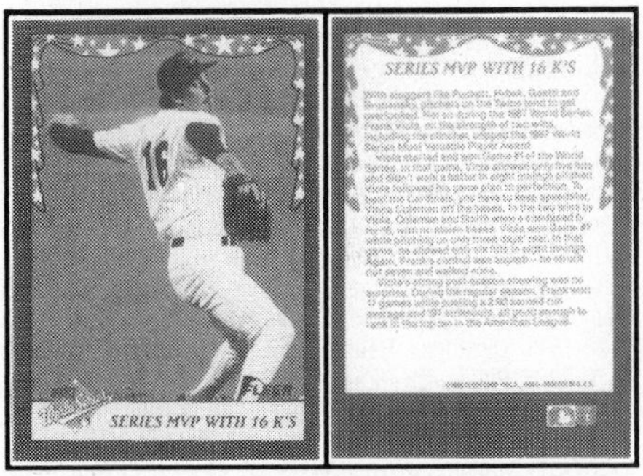

This 12-card set of 2 1/2" by 3 1/2" cards features highlights of the previous year's World Series between the Minnesota Twins and the St. Louis Cardinals. The sets were packaged as a complete set insert with the collated sets (of the 1988 Fleer regular issue) which were sold by Fleer directly to hobby card dealers; they were not available in the general retail candy store outlets.

	MINT	EXC	G-VG
COMPLETE SET (12)	4.00	2.00	.40
COMMON PLAYER (1-12)	.25	.12	.02
☐ 1 Dan Gladden Grand Hero Game 1	.25	.12	.02
☐ 2 Randy Bush Cardinals "Bush" Wacked	.25	.12	.02
☐ 3 John Tudor Masterful Perfor- mance in Game 3	.35	.17	.03
☐ 4 Ozzie Smith The Wizard	.75	.35	.07
☐ 5 Todd Worrell and Tony Pena Throw Smoke	.35	.17	.03
☐ 6 Vince Coleman Cardinal Attack	.50	.25	.05
☐ 7 Tom Herr/Dan Driessen Herr's Wallop	.25	.12	.02
☐ 8 Kirby Puckett Kirby's Bat Comes Alive	1.00	.50	.10
☐ 9 Kent Hrbek Hrbek's Slam Forces Game 7	.50	.25	.05
☐ 10 Tom Herr Out at First	.25	.12	.02
☐ 11 Don Baylor Game 7's Play At The Plate	.25	.12	.02
☐ 12 Frank Viola Series MVP, 16 K's	.75	.35	.07

1989 Fleer

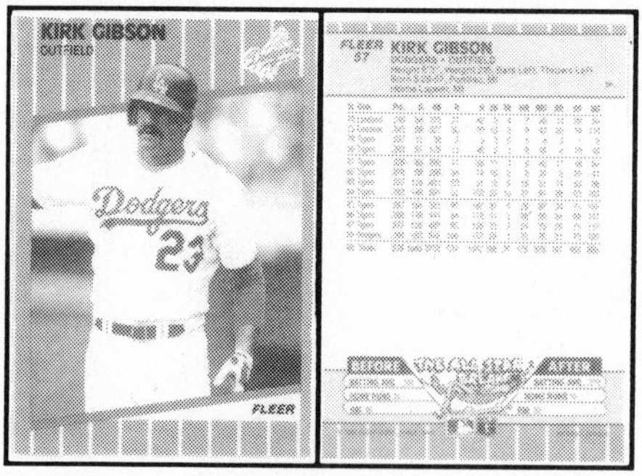

This 660-card set features a distinctive gray border background with white and yellow trim. The backs are printed in gray, black, and yellow on white card stock. The bottom of the card back shows an innovative breakdown of the player's demonstrated ability with respect to his performance before and after the All-Star break. Cards are numbered on the back and are again the standard 2 1/2" by 3 1/2". Cards are again organized numerically by teams and alphabetically within teams: Oakland A's (1-26), New York Mets (27-52), Los Angeles Dodgers (53-77), Boston Red Sox (78-101), Minnesota Twins (102-127), Detroit Tigers (128-151), Cincinnati Reds (152-175), Milwaukee Brewers (176-200), Pittsburgh Pirates (201-224), Toronto Blue Jays (225-248), New York Yankees (249-274), Kansas City Royals (275-298), San Diego Padres (299-322), San Francisco Giants (323-347), Houston Astros (348-370), Montreal Expos (371-395), Cleveland Indians (396-417), Chicago Cubs (418-442), St. Louis Cardinals (443-466), California Angels (467-490), Chicago White Sox (491-513), Texas Rangers (514-537), Seattle Mariners (538-561), Philadelphia Phillies (562-584), Atlanta Braves (585-605), and Baltimore Orioles (606-627). However, pairs 148/149, 153/154, 272/273, 283/284, and 367/368 were apparently mis-alphabetized by Fleer. The last 33 cards in the set consist of Specials (628-639), Rookie Pairs (640-653), and checklists (654-660). Due to the early beginning of production of this set, it seems Fleer "presumed" that the A's would win the World Series, since they are listed as the first team in the numerical order; in fact, Fleer had the Mets over the underdog (but eventual World Champion) Dodgers as well. Approximately half of the California Angels players have white rather than yellow halos. Certain Oakland A's player cards have red instead of green lines for front photo borders. Checklist cards are available either with or without positions listed for each player. The key rookies in this set are Sandy Alomar Jr., Ken Griffey Jr., Ramon Martinez, and Gary Sheffield. Fleer also produced the last of their three-year run of "limited" edition glossy, tin sets. This tin set was limited, but only compared to the previous year, as collector and dealer interest in the tin sets was apparently waning. It has been estimated that approximately 30,000 1989 tin sets were produced by Fleer; as a result, the price of the "tin" glossy cards is now about double the price of the regular set cards.

	MINT	EXC	G-VG
COMPLETE SET (660)	30.00	15.00	3.00
COMMON PLAYER (1-660)	.04	.02	.00
□ 1 Don Baylor	.10	.05	.01
□ 2 Lance Blankenship	.15	.07	.01
□ 3 Todd Burns UER (wrong birthdate; before/after All-Star stats missing)	.25	.12	.02
□ 4 Greg Cadaret UER (All-Star Break stats show 3 losses, should be 2)	.10	.05	.01
□ 5 Jose Canseco	1.25	.60	.12
□ 6 Storm Davis	.06	.03	.00
□ 7 Dennis Eckersley	.12	.06	.01
□ 8 Mike Gallego	.04	.02	.00
□ 9 Ron Hassey	.04	.02	.00
□ 10 Dave Henderson	.07	.03	.01
□ 11 Rick Honeycutt	.04	.02	.00
□ 12 Glenn Hubbard	.04	.02	.00
□ 13 Stan Javier	.04	.02	.00
□ 14 Doug Jennings	.20	.10	.02
□ 15 Felix Jose	.45	.22	.04
□ 16 Carney Lansford	.07	.03	.01
□ 17 Mark McGwire	.60	.30	.06
□ 18 Gene Nelson	.04	.02	.00
□ 19 Dave Parker	.10	.05	.01
□ 20 Eric Plunk	.04	.02	.00
□ 21 Luis Polonia	.04	.02	.00
□ 22 Terry Steinbach	.07	.03	.01
□ 23 Dave Stewart	.15	.07	.01
□ 24 Walt Weiss	.20	.10	.02
□ 25 Bob Welch	.10	.05	.01
□ 26 Curt Young	.04	.02	.00
□ 27 Rick Aguilera	.04	.02	.00
□ 28 Wally Backman	.04	.02	.00
□ 29 Mark Carreon UER (after All-Star Break batting 7.14)	.07	.03	.01
□ 30 Gary Carter	.15	.07	.01
□ 31 David Cone	.20	.10	.02
□ 32 Ron Darling	.08	.04	.01
□ 33 Len Dykstra	.15	.07	.01
□ 34 Kevin Elster	.07	.03	.01
□ 35 Sid Fernandez	.07	.03	.01
□ 36 Dwight Gooden	.30	.15	.03
□ 37 Keith Hernandez	.12	.06	.01
□ 38 Gregg Jefferies	1.25	.60	.12
□ 39 Howard Johnson	.15	.07	.01
□ 40 Terry Leach	.06	.03	.00
□ 41 Dave Magadan UER (bio says 15 doubles, should be 13)	.12	.06	.01
□ 42 Bob McClure	.04	.02	.00
□ 43 Roger McDowell UER (led Mets with 58, should be 62)	.07	.03	.01
□ 44 Kevin McReynolds	.12	.06	.01
□ 45 Keith Miller New York Mets	.04	.02	.00
□ 46 Randy Myers	.07	.03	.01
□ 47 Bob Ojeda	.07	.03	.01
□ 48 Mackey Sasser	.15	.07	.01
□ 49 Darryl Strawberry	.40	.20	.04
□ 50 Tim Teufel	.04	.02	.00
□ 51 Dave West	.25	.12	.02
□ 52 Mookie Wilson	.07	.03	.01
□ 53 Dave Anderson	.04	.02	.00
□ 54 Tim Belcher	.12	.06	.01
□ 55 Mike Davis	.04	.02	.00
□ 56 Mike Devereaux	.07	.03	.01
□ 57 Kirk Gibson	.15	.07	.01
□ 58 Alfredo Griffin	.04	.02	.00
□ 59 Chris Gwynn	.07	.03	.01
□ 60 Jeff Hamilton	.04	.02	.00
□ 61A Danny Heep (Home: Lake Hills)	.75	.35	.07
□ 61B Danny Heep (Home: San Antonio)	.12	.06	.01
□ 62 Orel Hershiser	.20	.10	.02
□ 63 Brian Holton	.04	.02	.00
□ 64 Jay Howell	.04	.02	.00
□ 65 Tim Leary	.07	.03	.01
□ 66 Mike Marshall	.07	.03	.01
□ 67 Ramon Martinez	2.00	1.00	.20
□ 68 Jesse Orosco	.04	.02	.00
□ 69 Alejandro Pena	.04	.02	.00
□ 70 Steve Sax	.10	.05	.01
□ 71 Mike Scioscia	.04	.02	.00
□ 72 Mike Sharperson	.04	.02	.00
□ 73 John Shelby	.04	.02	.00
□ 74 Franklin Stubbs	.07	.03	.01
□ 75 John Tudor	.07	.03	.01
□ 76 Fernando Valenzuela	.12	.06	.01
□ 77 Tracy Woodson	.10	.05	.01
□ 78 Marty Barrett	.04	.02	.00
□ 79 Todd Benzinger	.04	.02	.00
□ 80 Mike Boddicker UER (Rochester in '76, should be '78)	.07	.03	.01
□ 81 Wade Boggs	.40	.20	.04
□ 82 Oil Can Boyd	.07	.03	.01

☐ 83 Ellis Burks	.35	.17	.03
☐ 84 Rick Cerone	.04	.02	.00
☐ 85 Roger Clemens	.30	.15	.03
☐ 86 Steve Curry	.10	.05	.01
☐ 87 Dwight Evans	.10	.05	.01
☐ 88 Wes Gardner	.04	.02	.00
☐ 89 Rich Gedman	.04	.02	.00
☐ 90 Mike Greenwell	.35	.17	.03
☐ 91 Bruce Hurst	.10	.05	.01
☐ 92 Dennis Lamp	.04	.02	.00
☐ 93 Spike Owen	.04	.02	.00
☐ 94 Larry Parrish UER (before All-Star Break batting 1.90)	.04	.02	.00
☐ 95 Carlos Quintana	.55	.27	.05
☐ 96 Jody Reed	.12	.06	.01
☐ 97 Jim Rice	.12	.06	.01
☐ 98A Kevin Romine ERR (photo actually Randy Kutcher batting)	.50	.25	.05
☐ 98B Kevin Romine COR (arms folded)	.25	.12	.02
☐ 99 Lee Smith	.07	.03	.01
☐ 100 Mike Smithson	.04	.02	.00
☐ 101 Bob Stanley	.04	.02	.00
☐ 102 Allan Anderson	.07	.03	.01
☐ 103 Keith Atherton	.04	.02	.00
☐ 104 Juan Berenguer	.04	.02	.00
☐ 105 Bert Blyleven	.10	.05	.01
☐ 106 Eric Bullock UER (Bats/Throws Right, should be Left)	.10	.05	.01
☐ 107 Randy Bush	.04	.02	.00
☐ 108 John Christensen	.04	.02	.00
☐ 109 Mark Davidson	.04	.02	.00
☐ 110 Gary Gaetti	.10	.05	.01
☐ 111 Greg Gagne	.04	.02	.00
☐ 112 Dan Gladden	.04	.02	.00
☐ 113 German Gonzalez	.10	.05	.01
☐ 114 Brian Harper	.07	.03	.01
☐ 115 Tom Herr	.07	.03	.01
☐ 116 Kent Hrbek	.12	.06	.01
☐ 117 Gene Larkin	.07	.03	.01
☐ 118 Tim Laudner	.04	.02	.00
☐ 119 Charlie Lea	.04	.02	.00
☐ 120 Steve Lombardozzi	.04	.02	.00
☐ 121A John Moses (Home: Tempe)	.75	.35	.07
☐ 121B John Moses (Home: Phoenix)	.12	.06	.01
☐ 122 Al Newman	.04	.02	.00
☐ 123 Mark Portugal	.04	.02	.00
☐ 124 Kirby Puckett	.35	.17	.03
☐ 125 Jeff Reardon	.07	.03	.01
☐ 126 Fred Toliver	.04	.02	.00
☐ 127 Frank Viola	.15	.07	.01
☐ 128 Doyle Alexander	.04	.02	.00
☐ 129 Dave Bergman	.04	.02	.00
☐ 130A Tom Brookens ERR (Mike Heath back)	1.25	.60	.12
☐ 130B Tom Brookens COR	.12	.06	.01
☐ 131 Paul Gibson	.10	.05	.01
☐ 132A Mike Heath ERR (Tom Brookens back)	1.25	.60	.12
☐ 132B Mike Heath COR	.12	.06	.01
☐ 133 Don Heinkel	.07	.03	.01
☐ 134 Mike Henneman	.04	.02	.00
☐ 135 Guillermo Hernandez	.04	.02	.00
☐ 136 Eric King	.04	.02	.00
☐ 137 Chet Lemon	.04	.02	.00
☐ 138 Fred Lynn UER ('74, '75 stats missing)	.10	.05	.01
☐ 139 Jack Morris	.10	.05	.01
☐ 140 Matt Nokes	.10	.05	.01
☐ 141 Gary Pettis	.04	.02	.00
☐ 142 Ted Power	.04	.02	.00
☐ 143 Jeff M. Robinson Detroit Tigers	.07	.03	.01
☐ 144 Luis Salazar	.04	.02	.00
☐ 145 Steve Searcy	.18	.09	.01
☐ 146 Pat Sheridan	.04	.02	.00
☐ 147 Frank Tanana	.07	.03	.01
☐ 148 Alan Trammell	.15	.07	.01
☐ 149 Walt Terrell	.04	.02	.00
☐ 150 Jim Walewander	.07	.03	.01
☐ 151 Lou Whitaker	.07	.03	.01
☐ 152 Tim Birtsas	.04	.02	.00
☐ 153 Tom Browning	.07	.03	.01
☐ 154 Keith Brown	.10	.05	.01
☐ 155 Norm Charlton	.30	.15	.03
☐ 156 Dave Concepcion	.07	.03	.01
☐ 157 Kal Daniels	.15	.07	.01
☐ 158 Eric Davis	.35	.17	.03
☐ 159 Bo Diaz	.04	.02	.00
☐ 160 Rob Dibble	.60	.30	.06
☐ 161 Nick Esasky	.07	.03	.01
☐ 162 John Franco	.07	.03	.01
☐ 163 Danny Jackson	.07	.03	.01
☐ 164 Barry Larkin	.25	.12	.02
☐ 165 Rob Murphy	.04	.02	.00
☐ 166 Paul O'Neill	.12	.06	.01
☐ 167 Jeff Reed	.04	.02	.00
☐ 168 Jose Rijo	.10	.05	.01
☐ 169 Ron Robinson	.04	.02	.00
☐ 170 Chris Sabo	1.50	.75	.15
☐ 171 Candy Sierra	.07	.03	.01
☐ 172 Van Snider	.20	.10	.02
☐ 173A Jeff Treadway (target registration mark above head on front in light blue)	15.00	7.50	1.50
☐ 173B Jeff Treadway (no target on front)	.07	.03	.01
☐ 174 Frank Williams (after All-Star Break stats are jumbled)	.04	.02	.00
☐ 175 Herm Winningham	.04	.02	.00
☐ 176 Jim Adduci	.04	.02	.00
☐ 177 Don August	.04	.02	.00
☐ 178 Mike Birkbeck	.04	.02	.00
☐ 179 Chris Bosio	.04	.02	.00
☐ 180 Glenn Braggs	.04	.02	.00
☐ 181 Greg Brock	.04	.02	.00
☐ 182 Mark Clear	.04	.02	.00
☐ 183 Chuck Crim	.04	.02	.00
☐ 184 Rob Deer	.07	.03	.01
☐ 185 Tom Filer	.04	.02	.00
☐ 186 Jim Gantner	.04	.02	.00
☐ 187 Darryl Hamilton	.20	.10	.02
☐ 188 Ted Higuera	.07	.03	.01
☐ 189 Odell Jones	.04	.02	.00
☐ 190 Jeffrey Leonard	.07	.03	.01
☐ 191 Joey Meyer	.07	.03	.01
☐ 192 Paul Mirabella	.04	.02	.00
☐ 193 Paul Molitor	.10	.05	.01
☐ 194 Charlie O'Brien	.10	.05	.01
☐ 195 Dan Plesac	.04	.02	.00
☐ 196 Gary Sheffield	2.00	1.00	.20
☐ 197 B.J. Surhoff	.07	.03	.01
☐ 198 Dale Sveum	.04	.02	.00
☐ 199 Bill Wegman	.04	.02	.00
☐ 200 Robin Yount	.20	.10	.02
☐ 201 Rafael Belliard	.04	.02	.00
☐ 202 Barry Bonds	.35	.17	.03
☐ 203 Bobby Bonilla	.25	.12	.02
☐ 204 Sid Bream	.04	.02	.00
☐ 205 Benny Distefano	.04	.02	.00
☐ 206 Doug Drabek	.12	.06	.01
☐ 207 Mike Dunne	.04	.02	.00
☐ 208 Felix Fermin	.04	.02	.00
☐ 209 Brian Fisher	.04	.02	.00
☐ 210 Jim Gott	.04	.02	.00
☐ 211 Bob Kipper	.04	.02	.00
☐ 212 Dave LaPoint	.04	.02	.00
☐ 213 Mike LaValliere	.04	.02	.00
☐ 214 Jose Lind	.07	.03	.01
☐ 215 Junior Ortiz	.04	.02	.00
☐ 216 Vicente Palacios	.07	.03	.01
☐ 217 Tom Prince	.07	.03	.01
☐ 218 Gary Redus	.04	.02	.00
☐ 219 R.J. Reynolds	.04	.02	.00
☐ 220 Jeff Robinson Pittsburgh Pirates	.04	.02	.00
☐ 221 John Smiley	.04	.02	.00
☐ 222 Andy Van Slyke	.12	.06	.01
☐ 223 Bob Walk	.04	.02	.00
☐ 224 Glenn Wilson	.04	.02	.00
☐ 225 Jesse Barfield	.10	.05	.01
☐ 226 George Bell	.12	.06	.01
☐ 227 Pat Borders	.30	.15	.03
☐ 228 John Cerutti	.04	.02	.00
☐ 229 Jim Clancy	.04	.02	.00
☐ 230 Mark Eichhorn	.04	.02	.00
☐ 231 Tony Fernandez	.10	.05	.01
☐ 232 Cecil Fielder	.45	.22	.04
☐ 233 Mike Flanagan	.07	.03	.01
☐ 234 Kelly Gruber	.25	.12	.02
☐ 235 Tom Henke	.07	.03	.01
☐ 236 Jimmy Key	.07	.03	.01
☐ 237 Rick Leach	.04	.02	.00
☐ 238 Manny Lee UER (bio says regular shortstop, sic, Tony Fernandez)	.07	.03	.01
☐ 239 Nelson Liriano	.04	.02	.00
☐ 240 Fred McGriff	.25	.12	.02

☐ 241	Lloyd Moseby	.07	.03	.01
☐ 242	Rance Mulliniks	.04	.02	.00
☐ 243	Jeff Musselman	.04	.02	.00
☐ 244	Dave Stieb	.10	.05	.01
☐ 245	Todd Stottlemyre	.25	.12	.02
☐ 246	Duane Ward	.04	.02	.00
☐ 247	David Wells	.12	.06	.01
☐ 248	Ernie Whitt UER (HR total 21, should be 121)	.04	.02	.00
☐ 249	Luis Aguayo	.04	.02	.00
☐ 250A	Neil Allen (Home: Sarasota, FL)	1.25	.60	.12
☐ 250B	Neil Allen (Home: Syosset, NY)	.15	.07	.01
☐ 251	John Candelaria	.04	.02	.00
☐ 252	Jack Clark	.10	.05	.01
☐ 253	Richard Dotson	.04	.02	.00
☐ 254	Rickey Henderson	.35	.17	.03
☐ 255	Tommy John	.10	.05	.01
☐ 256	Roberto Kelly	.20	.10	.02
☐ 257	Al Leiter	.10	.05	.01
☐ 258	Don Mattingly	.90	.45	.09
☐ 259	Dale Mohorcic	.04	.02	.00
☐ 260	Hal Morris	1.75	.85	.17
☐ 261	Scott Nielsen	.04	.02	.00
☐ 262	Mike Pagliarulo UER (wrong birthdate)	.04	.02	.00
☐ 263	Hipolito Pena	.10	.05	.01
☐ 264	Ken Phelps	.07	.03	.01
☐ 265	Willie Randolph	.07	.03	.01
☐ 266	Rick Rhoden	.04	.02	.00
☐ 267	Dave Righetti	.07	.03	.01
☐ 268	Rafael Santana	.04	.02	.00
☐ 269	Steve Shields	.04	.02	.00
☐ 270	Joel Skinner	.04	.02	.00
☐ 271	Don Slaught	.04	.02	.00
☐ 272	Claudell Washington	.07	.03	.01
☐ 273	Gary Ward	.04	.02	.00
☐ 274	Dave Winfield	.15	.07	.01
☐ 275	Luis Aquino	.04	.02	.00
☐ 276	Floyd Bannister	.04	.02	.00
☐ 277	George Brett	.25	.12	.02
☐ 278	Bill Buckner	.07	.03	.01
☐ 279	Nick Capra	.07	.03	.01
☐ 280	Jose DeJesus	.25	.12	.02
☐ 281	Steve Farr	.04	.02	.00
☐ 282	Jerry Don Gleaton	.04	.02	.00
☐ 283	Mark Gubicza	.07	.03	.01
☐ 284	Tom Gordon UER (16.2 innings in '88, should be 15.2)	.75	.35	.07
☐ 285	Bo Jackson	1.00	.50	.10
☐ 286	Charlie Leibrandt	.04	.02	.00
☐ 287	Mike Macfarlane	.15	.07	.01
☐ 288	Jeff Montgomery	.07	.03	.01
☐ 289	Bill Pecota UER (photo actually Brad Wellman)	.04	.02	.00
☐ 290	Jamie Quirk	.04	.02	.00
☐ 291	Bret Saberhagen	.15	.07	.01
☐ 292	Kevin Seitzer	.12	.06	.01
☐ 293	Kurt Stillwell	.07	.03	.01
☐ 294	Pat Tabler	.04	.02	.00
☐ 295	Danny Tartabull	.10	.05	.01
☐ 296	Gary Thurman	.04	.02	.00
☐ 297	Frank White	.07	.03	.01
☐ 298	Willie Wilson	.07	.03	.01
☐ 299	Roberto Alomar	1.00	.50	.10
☐ 300	Sandy Alomar Jr. UER (wrong birthdate)	2.00	1.00	.20
☐ 301	Chris Brown	.04	.02	.00
☐ 302	Mike Brumley UER (133 hits in '88, should be 134)	.07	.03	.01
☐ 303	Mark Davis	.12	.06	.01
☐ 304	Mark Grant	.04	.02	.00
☐ 305	Tony Gwynn	.25	.12	.02
☐ 306	Greg W. Harris San Diego Padres	.25	.12	.02
☐ 307	Andy Hawkins	.04	.02	.00
☐ 308	Jimmy Jones	.07	.03	.01
☐ 309	John Kruk	.07	.03	.01
☐ 310	Dave Leiper	.04	.02	.00
☐ 311	Carmelo Martinez	.04	.02	.00
☐ 312	Lance McCullers	.04	.02	.00
☐ 313	Keith Moreland	.04	.02	.00
☐ 314	Dennis Rasmussen	.04	.02	.00
☐ 315	Randy Ready UER (1214 games in '88, should be 114)	.04	.02	.00
☐ 316	Benito Santiago	.25	.12	.02
☐ 317	Eric Show	.04	.02	.00
☐ 318	Todd Simmons	.07	.03	.01

☐ 319	Garry Templeton	.07	.03	.01
☐ 320	Dickie Thon	.04	.02	.00
☐ 321	Ed Whitson	.07	.03	.01
☐ 322	Marvell Wynne	.04	.02	.00
☐ 323	Mike Aldrete	.04	.02	.00
☐ 324	Brett Butler	.10	.05	.01
☐ 325	Will Clark UER (three consecutive 100 RBI seasons)	.90	.45	.09
☐ 326	Kelly Downs UER ('88 stats missing)	.07	.03	.01
☐ 327	Dave Dravecky	.07	.03	.01
☐ 328	Scott Garrelts	.07	.03	.01
☐ 329	Atlee Hammaker	.04	.02	.00
☐ 330	Charlie Hayes	.30	.15	.03
☐ 331	Mike Krukow	.04	.02	.00
☐ 332	Craig Lefferts	.04	.02	.00
☐ 333	Candy Maldonado	.07	.03	.01
☐ 334	Kirt Manwaring UER (Bats Rights)	.04	.02	.00
☐ 335	Bob Melvin	.04	.02	.00
☐ 336	Kevin Mitchell	.35	.17	.03
☐ 337	Donell Nixon	.04	.02	.00
☐ 338	Tony Perezchica	.10	.05	.01
☐ 339	Joe Price	.04	.02	.00
☐ 340	Rick Reuschel	.07	.03	.01
☐ 341	Earnest Riles	.04	.02	.00
☐ 342	Don Robinson	.04	.02	.00
☐ 343	Chris Speier	.04	.02	.00
☐ 344	Robby Thompson UER (West Plam Beach)	.04	.02	.00
☐ 345	Jose Uribe	.04	.02	.00
☐ 346	Matt Williams	.50	.25	.05
☐ 347	Trevor Wilson	.35	.17	.03
☐ 348	Juan Agosto	.04	.02	.00
☐ 349	Larry Andersen	.04	.02	.00
☐ 350A	Alan Ashby ERR (Throws Rig)	3.00	1.50	.30
☐ 350B	Alan Ashby COR	.07	.03	.01
☐ 351	Kevin Bass	.07	.03	.01
☐ 352	Buddy Bell	.07	.03	.01
☐ 353	Craig Biggio	.45	.22	.04
☐ 354	Danny Darwin	.07	.03	.01
☐ 355	Glenn Davis	.15	.07	.01
☐ 356	Jim Deshaies	.04	.02	.00
☐ 357	Bill Doran	.07	.03	.01
☐ 358	John Fishel	.07	.03	.01
☐ 359	Billy Hatcher	.07	.03	.01
☐ 360	Bob Knepper	.04	.02	.00
☐ 361	Louie Meadows UER (bio says 10 EBH's and 6 SB's in '88, should be 3 and 4)	.07	.03	.01
☐ 362	Dave Meads	.04	.02	.00
☐ 363	Jim Pankovits	.04	.02	.00
☐ 364	Terry Puhl	.04	.02	.00
☐ 365	Rafael Ramirez	.04	.02	.00
☐ 366	Craig Reynolds	.04	.02	.00
☐ 367	Mike Scott (card number listed as 368 on Astros CL)	.10	.05	.01
☐ 368	Nolan Ryan (card number listed as 367 on Astros CL)	.60	.30	.06
☐ 369	Dave Smith	.07	.03	.01
☐ 370	Gerald Young	.04	.02	.00
☐ 371	Hubie Brooks	.07	.03	.01
☐ 372	Tim Burke	.07	.03	.01
☐ 373	John Dopson	.15	.07	.01
☐ 374	Mike Fitzgerald Montreal Expos	.04	.02	.00
☐ 375	Tom Foley	.04	.02	.00
☐ 376	Andres Galarraga UER (Home: Caracus)	.10	.05	.01
☐ 377	Neal Heaton	.04	.02	.00
☐ 378	Joe Hesketh	.04	.02	.00
☐ 379	Brian Holman	.25	.12	.02
☐ 380	Rex Hudler	.07	.03	.01
☐ 381	Randy Johnson UER (innings for '85 and '86 shown as 27 and 120, should be 27.1 and 119.2)	.40	.20	.04
☐ 382	Wallace Johnson	.04	.02	.00
☐ 383	Tracy Jones	.04	.02	.00
☐ 384	Dave Martinez	.04	.02	.00
☐ 385	Dennis Martinez	.07	.03	.01
☐ 386	Andy McGaffigan	.04	.02	.00
☐ 387	Otis Nixon	.04	.02	.00
☐ 388	Johnny Paredes	.07	.03	.01
☐ 389	Jeff Parrett	.07	.03	.01
☐ 390	Pascual Perez	.07	.03	.01
☐ 391	Tim Raines	.15	.07	.01
☐ 392	Luis Rivera	.04	.02	.00

☐ 393	Nelson Santovenia	.15	.07	.01
☐ 394	Bryn Smith	.04	.02	.00
☐ 395	Tim Wallach	.07	.03	.01
☐ 396	Andy Allanson UER (1214 hits in '88, should be 114)	.04	.02	.00
☐ 397	Rod Allen	.10	.05	.01
☐ 398	Scott Bailes	.04	.02	.00
☐ 399	Tom Candiotti	.04	.02	.00
☐ 400	Joe Carter	.12	.06	.01
☐ 401	Carmen Castillo UER (after All-Star Break batting 2.50)	.04	.02	.00
☐ 402	Dave Clark UER (card front shows position as Rookie; after All-Star Break batting 3.14)	.07	.03	.01
☐ 403	John Farrell UER (typo in runs allowed in '88)	.04	.02	.00
☐ 404	Julio Franco	.07	.03	.01
☐ 405	Don Gordon	.07	.03	.01
☐ 406	Mel Hall	.07	.03	.01
☐ 407	Brad Havens	.04	.02	.00
☐ 408	Brook Jacoby	.07	.03	.01
☐ 409	Doug Jones	.07	.03	.01
☐ 410	Jeff Kaiser	.10	.05	.01
☐ 411	Luis Medina	.20	.10	.02
☐ 412	Cory Snyder	.10	.05	.01
☐ 413	Greg Swindell	.10	.05	.01
☐ 414	Ron Tingley UER (hit HR in first ML at-bat, should be first AL at-bat)	.07	.03	.01
☐ 415	Willie Upshaw	.04	.02	.00
☐ 416	Ron Washington	.04	.02	.00
☐ 417	Rich Yett	.04	.02	.00
☐ 418	Damon Berryhill	.10	.05	.01
☐ 419	Mike Bielecki	.07	.03	.01
☐ 420	Doug Dascenzo	.12	.06	.01
☐ 421	Jody Davis UER (Braves stats for '88 missing)	.04	.02	.00
☐ 422	Andre Dawson	.15	.07	.01
☐ 423	Frank DiPino	.04	.02	.00
☐ 424	Shawon Dunston	.18	.09	.01
☐ 425	Goose Gossage	.08	.04	.01
☐ 426	Mark Grace UER (Minor League stats for '88 missing)	1.50	.75	.15
☐ 427	Mike Harkey	.50	.25	.05
☐ 428	Darrin Jackson	.07	.03	.01
☐ 429	Les Lancaster	.04	.02	.00
☐ 430	Vance Law	.04	.02	.00
☐ 431	Greg Maddux	.12	.06	.01
☐ 432	Jamie Moyer	.04	.02	.00
☐ 433	Al Nipper	.04	.02	.00
☐ 434	Rafael Palmeiro UER (170 hits in '88, should be 178)	.18	.09	.01
☐ 435	Pat Perry	.04	.02	.00
☐ 436	Jeff Pico	.07	.03	.01
☐ 437	Ryne Sandberg	.35	.17	.03
☐ 438	Calvin Schiraldi	.04	.02	.00
☐ 439	Rick Sutcliffe	.07	.03	.01
☐ 440A	Manny Trillo ERR (Throws Rig)	3.00	1.50	.30
☐ 440B	Manny Trillo COR	.07	.03	.01
☐ 441	Gary Varsho UER (wrong birthdate; .303 should be .302; 11/28 should be 9/19)	.12	.06	.01
☐ 442	Mitch Webster	.04	.02	.00
☐ 443	Luis Alicea	.07	.03	.01
☐ 444	Tom Brunansky	.07	.03	.01
☐ 445	Vince Coleman UER (third straight with 83, should be fourth straight with 81)	.15	.07	.01
☐ 446	John Costello	.07	.03	.01
☐ 447	Danny Cox	.04	.02	.00
☐ 448	Ken Dayley	.04	.02	.00
☐ 449	Jose DeLeon	.04	.02	.00
☐ 450	Curt Ford	.04	.02	.00
☐ 451	Pedro Guerrero	.10	.05	.01
☐ 452	Bob Horner	.07	.03	.01
☐ 453	Tim Jones	.10	.05	.01
☐ 454	Steve Lake	.04	.02	.00
☐ 455	Joe Magrane UER (Des Moines, IO)	.07	.03	.01
☐ 456	Greg Mathews	.04	.02	.00
☐ 457	Willie McGee	.10	.05	.01
☐ 458	Larry McWilliams	.04	.02	.00
☐ 459	Jose Oquendo	.04	.02	.00
☐ 460	Tony Pena	.07	.03	.01
☐ 461	Terry Pendleton	.04	.02	.00
☐ 462	Steve Peters	.10	.05	.01
☐ 463	Ozzie Smith	.15	.07	.01
☐ 464	Scott Terry	.04	.02	.00
☐ 465	Denny Walling	.04	.02	.00
☐ 466	Todd Worrell	.07	.03	.01
☐ 467	Tony Armas UER (before All-Star Break batting 2.39)	.07	.03	.01
☐ 468	Dante Bichette	.30	.15	.03
☐ 469	Bob Boone	.07	.03	.01
☐ 470	Terry Clark	.10	.05	.01
☐ 471	Stew Cliburn	.04	.02	.00
☐ 472	Mike Cook UER (TM near Angels logo missing from front)	.10	.05	.01
☐ 473	Sherman Corbett	.07	.03	.01
☐ 474	Chili Davis	.07	.03	.01
☐ 475	Brian Downing	.04	.02	.00
☐ 476	Jim Eppard	.04	.02	.00
☐ 477	Chuck Finley	.07	.03	.01
☐ 478	Willie Fraser	.04	.02	.00
☐ 479	Bryan Harvey UER (ML record shows 0-0, should be 7-5)	.18	.09	.01
☐ 480	Jack Howell	.04	.02	.00
☐ 481	Wally Joyner UER (Yorba Linda, GA)	.15	.07	.01
☐ 482	Jack Lazorko	.04	.02	.00
☐ 483	Kirk McCaskill	.04	.02	.00
☐ 484	Mark McLemore	.04	.02	.00
☐ 485	Greg Minton	.04	.02	.00
☐ 486	Dan Petry	.04	.02	.00
☐ 487	Johnny Ray	.04	.02	.00
☐ 488	Dick Schofield	.04	.02	.00
☐ 489	Devon White	.10	.05	.01
☐ 490	Mike Witt	.04	.02	.00
☐ 491	Harold Baines	.07	.03	.01
☐ 492	Daryl Boston	.07	.03	.01
☐ 493	Ivan Calderon UER ('80 stats shifted)	.07	.03	.01
☐ 494	Mike Diaz	.04	.02	.00
☐ 495	Carlton Fisk	.15	.07	.01
☐ 496	Dave Gallagher	.15	.07	.01
☐ 497	Ozzie Guillen	.10	.05	.01
☐ 498	Shawn Hillegas	.04	.02	.00
☐ 499	Lance Johnson	.04	.02	.00
☐ 500	Barry Jones	.07	.03	.01
☐ 501	Bill Long	.04	.02	.00
☐ 502	Steve Lyons	.04	.02	.00
☐ 503	Fred Manrique	.04	.02	.00
☐ 504	Jack McDowell	.12	.06	.01
☐ 505	Donn Pall	.10	.05	.01
☐ 506	Kelly Paris	.04	.02	.00
☐ 507	Dan Pasqua	.04	.02	.00
☐ 508	Ken Patterson	.10	.05	.01
☐ 509	Melido Perez	.07	.03	.01
☐ 510	Jerry Reuss	.04	.02	.00
☐ 511	Mark Salas	.04	.02	.00
☐ 512	Bobby Thigpen UER ('86 ERA 4.69, should be 4.68)	.12	.06	.01
☐ 513	Mike Woodard	.04	.02	.00
☐ 514	Bob Brower	.04	.02	.00
☐ 515	Steve Buechele	.04	.02	.00
☐ 516	Jose Cecena	.07	.03	.01
☐ 517	Cecil Espy	.07	.03	.01
☐ 518	Scott Fletcher	.04	.02	.00
☐ 519	Cecilio Guante ('87 Yankee stats are off-centered)	.04	.02	.00
☐ 520	Jose Guzman	.04	.02	.00
☐ 521	Ray Hayward	.07	.03	.01
☐ 522	Charlie Hough	.04	.02	.00
☐ 523	Pete Incaviglia	.10	.05	.01
☐ 524	Mike Jeffcoat	.04	.02	.00
☐ 525	Paul Kilgus	.04	.02	.00
☐ 526	Chad Kreuter	.12	.06	.01
☐ 527	Jeff Kunkel	.04	.02	.00
☐ 528	Oddibe McDowell	.07	.03	.01
☐ 529	Pete O'Brien	.07	.03	.01
☐ 530	Geno Petralli	.04	.02	.00
☐ 531	Jeff Russell	.04	.02	.00
☐ 532	Ruben Sierra	.30	.15	.03
☐ 533	Mike Stanley	.04	.02	.00
☐ 534A	Ed VandeBerg ERR (Throws Lef)	3.00	1.50	.30
☐ 534B	Ed VandeBerg COR	.07	.03	.01
☐ 535	Curtis Wilkerson ERR (pitcher headings at bottom)	.04	.02	.00
☐ 536	Mitch Williams	.07	.03	.01

☐ 537 Bobby Witt UER ('85 ERA .643, should be 6.43)	.12	.06	.01
☐ 538 Steve Balboni	.04	.02	.00
☐ 539 Scott Bankhead	.07	.03	.01
☐ 540 Scott Bradley	.04	.02	.00
☐ 541 Mickey Brantley	.07	.03	.01
☐ 542 Jay Buhner	.15	.07	.01
☐ 543 Mike Campbell	.04	.02	.00
☐ 544 Darnell Coles	.04	.02	.00
☐ 545 Henry Cotto	.04	.02	.00
☐ 546 Alvin Davis	.10	.05	.01
☐ 547 Mario Diaz	.04	.02	.00
☐ 548 Ken Griffey Jr.	10.00	5.00	1.00
☐ 549 Erik Hanson	.90	.45	.09
☐ 550 Mike Jackson UER (Lifetime ERA 3.345, should be 3.45)	.04	.02	.00
☐ 551 Mark Langston	.12	.06	.01
☐ 552 Edgar Martinez	.15	.07	.01
☐ 553 Bill McGuire	.07	.03	.01
☐ 554 Mike Moore	.07	.03	.01
☐ 555 Jim Presley	.04	.02	.00
☐ 556 Rey Quinones	.04	.02	.00
☐ 557 Jerry Reed	.04	.02	.00
☐ 558 Harold Reynolds	.07	.03	.01
☐ 559 Mike Schooler	.35	.17	.03
☐ 560 Bill Swift	.04	.02	.00
☐ 561 Dave Valle	.04	.02	.00
☐ 562 Steve Bedrosian	.07	.03	.01
☐ 563 Phil Bradley	.07	.03	.01
☐ 564 Don Carman	.04	.02	.00
☐ 565 Bob Dernier	.04	.02	.00
☐ 566 Marvin Freeman	.04	.02	.00
☐ 567 Todd Frohwirth	.04	.02	.00
☐ 568 Greg Gross	.04	.02	.00
☐ 569 Kevin Gross	.04	.02	.00
☐ 570 Greg Harris Philadelphia Phillies	.04	.02	.00
☐ 571 Von Hayes	.07	.03	.01
☐ 572 Chris James	.07	.03	.01
☐ 573 Steve Jeltz	.04	.02	.00
☐ 574 Ron Jones UER (Led IL in '88 with 85, should be 75)	.20	.10	.02
☐ 575 Ricky Jordan	.50	.25	.05
☐ 576 Mike Maddux	.04	.02	.00
☐ 577 David Palmer	.04	.02	.00
☐ 578 Lance Parrish	.07	.03	.01
☐ 579 Shane Rawley	.04	.02	.00
☐ 580 Bruce Ruffin	.04	.02	.00
☐ 581 Juan Samuel	.07	.03	.01
☐ 582 Mike Schmidt	.40	.20	.04
☐ 583 Kent Tekulve	.04	.02	.00
☐ 584 Milt Thompson UER (19 hits in '88, should be 109)	.04	.02	.00
☐ 585 Jose Alvarez	.07	.03	.01
☐ 586 Paul Assenmacher	.04	.02	.00
☐ 587 Bruce Benedict	.04	.02	.00
☐ 588 Jeff Blauser	.04	.02	.00
☐ 589 Terry Blocker	.10	.05	.01
☐ 590 Ron Gant	.30	.15	.03
☐ 591 Tom Glavine	.07	.03	.01
☐ 592 Tommy Gregg	.12	.06	.01
☐ 593 Albert Hall	.04	.02	.00
☐ 594 Dion James	.04	.02	.00
☐ 595 Rick Mahler	.04	.02	.00
☐ 596 Dale Murphy	.20	.10	.02
☐ 597 Gerald Perry	.04	.02	.00
☐ 598 Charlie Puleo	.04	.02	.00
☐ 599 Ted Simmons	.07	.03	.01
☐ 600 Pete Smith	.07	.03	.01
☐ 601 Zane Smith	.07	.03	.01
☐ 602 John Smoltz	.50	.25	.05
☐ 603 Bruce Sutter	.07	.03	.01
☐ 604 Andres Thomas	.04	.02	.00
☐ 605 Ozzie Virgil	.04	.02	.00
☐ 606 Brady Anderson	.25	.12	.02
☐ 607 Jeff Ballard	.07	.03	.01
☐ 608 Jose Bautista	.10	.05	.01
☐ 609 Ken Gerhart	.04	.02	.00
☐ 610 Terry Kennedy	.04	.02	.00
☐ 611 Eddie Murray	.15	.07	.01
☐ 612 Carl Nichols UER (before All-Star Break batting 1.88)	.07	.03	.01
☐ 613 Tom Niedenfuer	.04	.02	.00
☐ 614 Joe Orsulak	.04	.02	.00
☐ 615 Oswald Peraza UER (shown as Oswaldo)	.10	.05	.01
☐ 616A Bill Ripken ERR (Rick Face written on knob of bat)	12.00	6.00	1.20
☐ 616B Bill Ripken (bat knob whited out)	40.00	20.00	4.00
☐ 616C Bill Ripken (words on bat knob scribbled out)	12.00	6.00	1.20
☐ 616D Bill Ripken DP (black box covering bat knob	.25	.12	.02
☐ 617 Cal Ripken Jr.	.15	.07	.01
☐ 618 Dave Schmidt	.04	.02	.00
☐ 619 Rick Schu	.04	.02	.00
☐ 620 Larry Sheets	.04	.02	.00
☐ 621 Doug Sisk	.04	.02	.00
☐ 622 Pete Stanicek	.04	.02	.00
☐ 623 Mickey Tettleton	.07	.03	.01
☐ 624 Jay Tibbs	.04	.02	.00
☐ 625 Jim Traber	.04	.02	.00
☐ 626 Mark Williamson	.04	.02	.00
☐ 627 Craig Worthington	.30	.15	.03
☐ 628 Speed/Power Jose Canseco	.60	.30	.06
☐ 629 Pitcher Perfect Tom Browning	.07	.03	.01
☐ 630 Like Father/Like Sons Roberto Alomar Sandy Alomar Jr. (names on card listed in wrong order) UER	.30	.15	.03
☐ 631 NL All Stars UER Will Clark Rafael Palmeiro (Gallaraga, sic; Clark 3 consecutive 100 RBI seasons; third with 102 RBI's)	.20	.10	.02
☐ 632 Homeruns - Coast to Coast UER Darryl Strawberry Will Clark (Homeruns should be two words)	.30	.15	.03
☐ 633 Hot Corners - Hot Hitters UER Wade Boggs Carney Lansford (Boggs hit .366 in '86, should be '88)	.15	.07	.01
☐ 634 Triple A's Jose Canseco Terry Steinbach Mark McGwire	.35	.17	.03
☐ 635 Dual Heat Mark Davis Dwight Gooden	.15	.07	.01
☐ 636 NL Pitching Power UER Danny Jackson David Cone (Hersheiser, sic)	.07	.03	.01
☐ 637 Cannon Arms UER Chris Sabo Bobby Bonilla (Bobby Bonds, sic)	.15	.07	.01
☐ 638 Double Trouble UER Andres Galarraga (misspelled Gallaraga on card back) Gerald Perry	.07	.03	.01
☐ 639 Power Center Kirby Puckett Eric Davis	.15	.07	.01
☐ 640 Steve Wilson and Cameron Drew	.15	.07	.01
☐ 641 Kevin Brown and Kevin Reimer	.40	.20	.04
☐ 642 Brad Pounders and Jerald Clark	.25	.12	.02
☐ 643 Mike Capel and Drew Hall	.15	.07	.01
☐ 644 Joe Girardi and Rolando Roomes	.30	.15	.03
☐ 645 Lenny Harris and Marty Brown	.45	.22	.04
☐ 646 Luis De Los Santos and Jim Campbell	.15	.07	.01
☐ 647 Randy Kramer and Miguel Garcia	.15	.07	.01
☐ 648 Torey Lovullo and Robert Palacios	.15	.07	.01
☐ 649 Jim Corsi and Bob Milacki	.20	.10	.02
☐ 650 Grady Hall and Mike Rochford	.15	.07	.01
☐ 651 Terry Taylor and Vance Lovelace	.15	.07	.01

☐ 652 Ken Hill and Dennis Cook	.50	.25	.05
☐ 653 Scott Service and Shane Turner	.15	.07	.01
☐ 654 CL: Oakland/Mets Dodgers/Red Sox (10 Hendersor; 68 Jess Orosco)	.07	.01	.00
☐ 655 CL: Twins/Tigers Reds/Brewers (179 Boslo)	.07	.01	.00
☐ 656 CL: Pirates/Blue Jays Yankees/Royals (225 Jess Barfield)	.07	.01	.00
☐ 657 CL: Padres/Giants Astros/Expos (367/368 wrong)	.07	.01	.00
☐ 658 CL: Indians/Cubs Cardinals/Angels (449 Deleon)	.07	.01	.00
☐ 659 CL: White Sox/Rangers Mariners/Phillies	.07	.01	.00
☐ 660 CL: Braves/Orioles Specials/Checklists (632 hyphenated differently and 650 Hali; 595 Rich Mahler; 619 Rich Schu)	.07	.01	.00

1989 Fleer Wax Box Cards

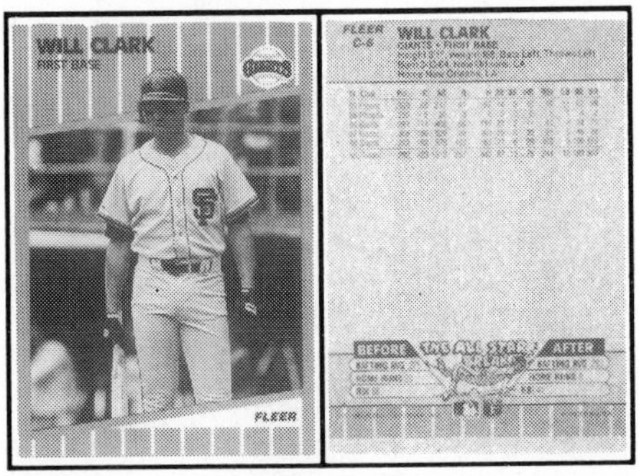

The cards in this 28-card set measure the standard 2 1/2" by 3 1/2". Cards have essentially the same design as the 1989 Fleer regular issue set. The cards were printed on the bottoms of the regular issue wax pack boxes. These 28 cards (C1 to C28) are considered a separate set in their own right and are not typically included in a complete set of the regular issue 1989 Fleer cards. The value of the panel uncut is slightly greater, perhaps by 25 percent greater, than the value of the individual cards cut up carefully. The wax box cards are further distinguished by the gray card stock used.

	MINT	EXC	G-VG
COMPLETE SET (28)	5.00	2.50	.50
COMMON PLAYER (C1-C28)	.10	.05	.01
☐ C1 Mets Logo	.10	.05	.01
☐ C2 Wade Boggs	.50	.25	.05
☐ C3 George Brett	.40	.20	.04
☐ C4 Jose Canseco UER ('88 strikeouts 121 and career strikeouts 49, should be 128 and 491)	1.00	.50	.10
☐ C5 A's Logo	.10	.05	.01
☐ C6 Will Clark	.90	.45	.09
☐ C7 David Cone	.25	.12	.02
☐ C8 Andres Galarraga UER (career average .289 should be .269)	.20	.10	.02
☐ C9 Dodgers Logo	.10	.05	.01
☐ C10 Kirk Gibson	.25	.12	.02
☐ C11 Mike Greenwell	.40	.20	.04
☐ C12 Tony Gwynn	.30	.15	.03
☐ C13 Tigers Logo	.10	.05	.01
☐ C14 Orel Hershiser	.25	.12	.02
☐ C15 Danny Jackson	.10	.05	.01
☐ C16 Wally Joyner	.25	.12	.02
☐ C17 Red Sox Logo	.10	.05	.01
☐ C18 Yankees Logo	.10	.05	.01
☐ C19 Fred McGriff UER career BA of .289 should be .269)	.25	.12	.02
☐ C20 Kirby Puckett	.50	.25	.05
☐ C21 Chris Sabo	.40	.20	.04
☐ C22 Kevin Seitzer	.20	.10	.02
☐ C23 Pirates Logo	.10	.05	.01
☐ C24 Astros Logo	.10	.05	.01
☐ C25 Darryl Strawberry	.50	.25	.05
☐ C26 Alan Trammell	.20	.10	.02
☐ C27 Andy Van Slyke	.15	.07	.01
☐ C28 Frank Viola	.20	.10	.02

1989 Fleer All Star Inserts

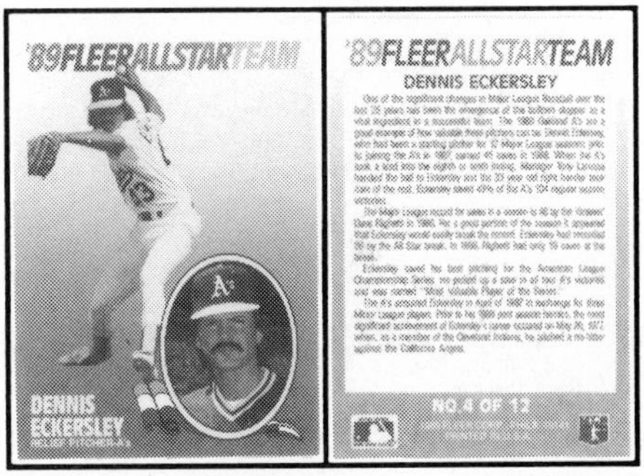

This twelve-card subset was randomly inserted in Fleer wax packs (15 regular cards) and Fleer value packs (36 regular cards). The players selected are the 1989 Fleer Major League All-Star team. One player has been selected for each position along with a DH and three pitchers. The cards are attractively designed and are standard size, 2 1/2" by 3 1/2". The cards are numbered on the backs and feature a distinctive green background on the card fronts.

	MINT	EXC	G-VG
COMPLETE SET (12)	12.00	6.00	1.20
COMMON PLAYER (1-12)	.30	.15	.03
☐ 1 Bobby Bonilla Third Baseman	1.00	.50	.10
☐ 2 Jose Canseco Outfielder	3.00	1.50	.30
☐ 3 Will Clark First Baseman	2.50	1.25	.25
☐ 4 Dennis Eckersley Relief Pitcher	.75	.35	.07
☐ 5 Julio Franco Second Baseman	.50	.25	.05
☐ 6 Mike Greenwell Outfielder	1.50	.75	.15
☐ 7 Orel Hershiser Righthand Pitcher	1.00	.50	.10
☐ 8 Paul Molitor Designated Hitter	.50	.25	.05
☐ 9 Mike Scioscia Catcher	.30	.15	.03
☐ 10 Darryl Strawberry Outfielder	1.25	.60	.12
☐ 11 Alan Trammell Shortstop	.60	.30	.06
☐ 12 Frank Viola Lefthand Pitcher	.60	.30	.06

1989 Fleer For The Record

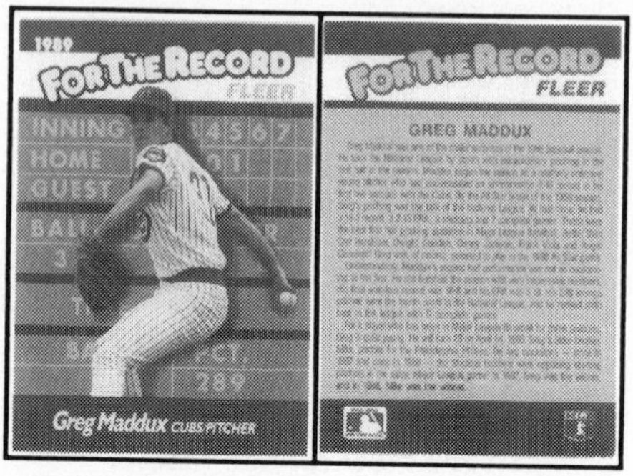

This six-card subset was distributed randomly (as an insert) in Fleer rack packs. These cards are standard size, 2 1/2" by 3 1/2" and are quite attractive. The set is subtitled "For The Record" and commemorates record-breaking events for those players from the previous season. The cards are numbered on the backs. The card backs are printed in red, black, and gray on white card stock.

	MINT	EXC	G-VG
COMPLETE SET (6)	6.00	3.00	.60
COMMON PLAYER (1-6)	.65	.30	.06
☐ 1 Wade Boggs Boston Red Sox	1.50	.75	.15
☐ 2 Roger Clemens Boston Red Sox	1.50	.75	.15
☐ 3 Andres Galarraga Montreal Expos	.65	.30	.06
☐ 4 Kirk Gibson Los Angeles Dodgers	1.00	.50	.10
☐ 5 Greg Maddux Chicago Cubs	.65	.30	.06
☐ 6 Don Mattingly UER New York Yankees (won batting title '83, should say '84)	2.00	1.00	.20

1989 Fleer Baseball All-Stars

The 1989 Fleer Baseball All-Stars set contains 44 standard-size (2 1/2" by 3 1/2") cards. The fronts are yellowish beige with salmon pinstripes; the vertically-oriented backs are red, white and pink and feature career stats. The cards were distributed through Ben Franklin stores as a boxed set.

	MINT	EXC	G-VG
COMPLETE SET (44)	5.00	2.50	.50
COMMON PLAYER (1-44)	.10	.05	.01

☐ 1 Doyle Alexander	.10	.05	.01
☐ 2 George Bell	.15	.07	.01
☐ 3 Wade Boggs	.60	.30	.06
☐ 4 Bobby Bonilla	.10	.05	.01
☐ 5 Jose Canseco	1.00	.50	.10
☐ 6 Will Clark	.90	.45	.09
☐ 7 Roger Clemens	.60	.30	.06
☐ 8 Vince Coleman	.25	.12	.02
☐ 9 David Cone	.20	.10	.02
☐ 10 Mark Davis	.15	.07	.01
☐ 11 Andre Dawson	.20	.10	.02
☐ 12 Dennis Eckersley	.20	.10	.02
☐ 13 Andres Galarraga	.20	.10	.02
☐ 14 Kirk Gibson	.20	.10	.02
☐ 15 Dwight Gooden	.40	.20	.04
☐ 16 Mike Greenwell	.40	.20	.04
☐ 17 Mark Gubicza	.15	.07	.01
☐ 18 Ozzie Guillen	.15	.07	.01
☐ 19 Tony Gwynn	.35	.17	.03
☐ 20 Rickey Henderson	.75	.35	.07
☐ 21 Orel Hershiser	.25	.12	.02
☐ 22 Danny Jackson	.10	.05	.01
☐ 23 Doug Jones	.10	.05	.01
☐ 24 Ricky Jordan	.15	.07	.01
☐ 25 Bob Knepper	.10	.05	.01
☐ 26 Barry Larkin	.20	.10	.02
☐ 27 Vance Law	.10	.05	.01
☐ 28 Don Mattingly	1.00	.50	.10
☐ 29 Mark McGwire	.75	.35	.07
☐ 30 Paul Molitor	.15	.07	.01
☐ 31 Gerald Perry	.10	.05	.01
☐ 32 Kirby Puckett	.45	.22	.04
☐ 33 Johnny Ray	.10	.05	.01
☐ 34 Harold Reynolds	.10	.05	.01
☐ 35 Cal Ripken	.35	.17	.03
☐ 36 Don Robinson	.10	.05	.01
☐ 37 Ruben Sierra	.50	.25	.05
☐ 38 Dave Smith	.10	.05	.01
☐ 39 Darryl Strawberry	.50	.25	.05
☐ 40 Dave Stieb	.15	.07	.01
☐ 41 Alan Trammell	.20	.10	.02
☐ 42 Andy Van Slyke	.15	.07	.01
☐ 43 Frank Viola	.20	.10	.02
☐ 44 Dave Winfield	.20	.10	.02

1989 Fleer Baseball MVP's

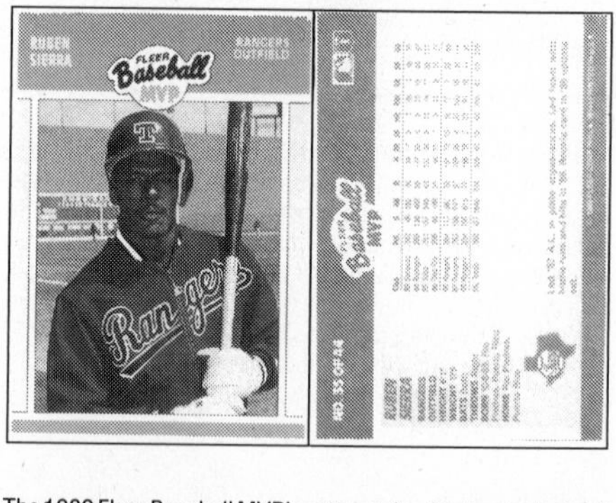

The 1989 Fleer Baseball MVP's set contains 44 standard-size (2 1/2" by 3 1/2") cards. The fronts and backs are green and yellow. The horizontally-oriented backs feature career stats. The cards were distributed through Toys 'R' Us stores as a boxed set.

	MINT	EXC	G-VG
COMPLETE SET (44)	5.00	2.50	.50
COMMON PLAYER (1-44)	.10	.05	.01
☐ 1 Steve Bedrosian	.15	.07	.01
☐ 2 George Bell	.20	.10	.02
☐ 3 Wade Boggs	.60	.30	.06
☐ 4 George Brett	.40	.20	.04
☐ 5 Hubie Brooks	.15	.07	.01
☐ 6 Jose Canseco	1.00	.50	.10
☐ 7 Will Clark	.90	.45	.09
☐ 8 Roger Clemens	.60	.30	.06
☐ 9 Eric Davis	.50	.25	.05
☐ 10 Glenn Davis	.20	.10	.02

☐ 11 Andre Dawson	.20	.10	.02
☐ 12 Andres Galarraga	.20	.10	.02
☐ 13 Kirk Gibson	.20	.10	.02
☐ 14 Dwight Gooden	.40	.20	.04
☐ 15 Mark Grace	1.00	.50	.10
☐ 16 Mike Greenwell	.40	.20	.04
☐ 17 Tony Gwynn	.35	.17	.03
☐ 18 Bryan Harvey	.15	.07	.01
☐ 19 Orel Hershiser	.25	.12	.02
☐ 20 Ted Higuera	.15	.07	.01
☐ 21 Danny Jackson	.10	.05	.01
☐ 22 Mike Jackson	.10	.05	.01
☐ 23 Doug Jones	.10	.05	.01
☐ 24 Greg Maddux	.15	.07	.01
☐ 25 Mike Marshall	.10	.05	.01
☐ 26 Don Mattingly	1.00	.50	.10
☐ 27 Fred McGriff	.25	.12	.02
☐ 28 Mark McGwire	.75	.35	.07
☐ 29 Kevin McReynolds	.15	.07	.01
☐ 30 Jack Morris	.15	.07	.01
☐ 31 Gerald Perry	.10	.05	.01
☐ 32 Kirby Puckett	.45	.22	.04
☐ 33 Chris Sabo	.45	.22	.04
☐ 34 Mike Scott	.20	.10	.02
☐ 35 Ruben Sierra	.50	.25	.05
☐ 36 Darryl Strawberry	.50	.25	.05
☐ 37 Danny Tartabull	.15	.07	.01
☐ 38 Bobby Thigpen	.20	.10	.02
☐ 39 Alan Trammell	.20	.10	.02
☐ 40 Andy Van Slyke	.15	.07	.01
☐ 41 Frank Viola	.20	.10	.02
☐ 42 Walt Weiss	.15	.07	.01
☐ 43 Dave Winfield	.20	.10	.02
☐ 44 Todd Worrell	.10	.05	.01

1989 Fleer Exciting Stars

The 1989 Fleer Exciting Stars set contains 44 standard-size (2 1/2" by 3 1/2") cards. The fronts have baby blue borders; the backs are pink and blue. The vertically-oriented backs feature career stats. The cards were distributed as a boxed set.

	MINT	EXC	G-VG
COMPLETE SET (44)	5.00	2.50	.50
COMMON PLAYER (1-44)	.10	.05	.01
☐ 1 Harold Baines	.15	.07	.01
☐ 2 Wade Boggs	.60	.30	.06
☐ 3 Jose Canseco	1.00	.50	.10
☐ 4 Joe Carter	.20	.10	.02
☐ 5 Will Clark	.90	.45	.09
☐ 6 Roger Clemens	.60	.30	.06
☐ 7 Vince Coleman	.25	.12	.02
☐ 8 David Cone	.20	.10	.02
☐ 9 Eric Davis	.50	.25	.05
☐ 10 Glenn Davis	.20	.10	.02
☐ 11 Andre Dawson	.20	.10	.02
☐ 12 Dwight Evans	.15	.07	.01
☐ 13 Andres Galarraga	.20	.10	.02
☐ 14 Kirk Gibson	.20	.10	.02
☐ 15 Dwight Gooden	.40	.20	.04
☐ 16 Jim Gott	.10	.05	.01
☐ 17 Mark Grace	1.00	.50	.10
☐ 18 Mike Greenwell	.40	.20	.04
☐ 19 Mark Gubicza	.15	.07	.01
☐ 20 Tony Gwynn	.35	.17	.03
☐ 21 Rickey Henderson	.75	.35	.07
☐ 22 Tom Henke	.10	.05	.01
☐ 23 Mike Henneman	.10	.05	.01
☐ 24 Orel Hershiser	.25	.12	.02
☐ 25 Danny Jackson	.10	.05	.01
☐ 26 Gregg Jefferies	.75	.35	.07
☐ 27 Ricky Jordan	.15	.07	.01
☐ 28 Wally Joyner	.20	.10	.02
☐ 29 Mark Langston	.15	.07	.01
☐ 30 Tim Leary	.10	.05	.01
☐ 31 Don Mattingly	1.00	.50	.10
☐ 32 Mark McGwire	.75	.35	.07
☐ 33 Dale Murphy	.35	.17	.03
☐ 34 Kirby Puckett	.45	.22	.04
☐ 35 Chris Sabo	.45	.22	.04
☐ 36 Kevin Seitzer	.20	.10	.02
☐ 37 Ruben Sierra	.50	.25	.05
☐ 38 Ozzie Smith	.15	.07	.01
☐ 39 Dave Stewart	.20	.10	.02
☐ 40 Darryl Strawberry	.50	.25	.05
☐ 41 Alan Trammell	.20	.10	.02
☐ 42 Frank Viola	.20	.10	.02
☐ 43 Dave Winfield	.20	.10	.02
☐ 44 Robin Yount	.35	.17	.03

1989 Fleer Heroes of Baseball

The 1989 Fleer Heroes of Baseball set contains 44 standard-size (2 1/2" by 3 1/2") cards. The fronts and backs are red, white and blue. The vertically-oriented backs feature career stats. The cards were distributed through Woolworth stores as a boxed set.

	MINT	EXC	G-VG
COMPLETE SET (44)	5.00	2.50	.50
COMMON PLAYER (1-44)	.10	.05	.01
☐ 1 George Bell	.20	.10	.02
☐ 2 Wade Boggs	.60	.30	.06
☐ 3 Barry Bonds	.50	.25	.05
☐ 4 Tom Brunansky	.15	.07	.01
☐ 5 Jose Canseco	1.00	.50	.10
☐ 6 Joe Carter	.20	.10	.02
☐ 7 Will Clark	.90	.45	.09
☐ 8 Roger Clemens	.60	.30	.06
☐ 9 David Cone	.20	.10	.02
☐ 10 Eric Davis	.50	.25	.05
☐ 11 Glenn Davis	.20	.10	.02
☐ 12 Andre Dawson	.20	.10	.02
☐ 13 Dennis Eckersley	.20	.10	.02
☐ 14 John Franco	.15	.07	.01
☐ 15 Gary Gaetti	.15	.07	.01
☐ 16 Andres Galarraga	.20	.10	.02
☐ 17 Kirk Gibson	.20	.10	.02
☐ 18 Dwight Gooden	.40	.20	.04
☐ 19 Mike Greenwell	.40	.20	.04
☐ 20 Tony Gwynn	.35	.17	.03
☐ 21 Bryan Harvey	.15	.07	.01
☐ 22 Orel Hershiser	.25	.12	.02
☐ 23 Ted Higuera	.15	.07	.01
☐ 24 Danny Jackson	.10	.05	.01
☐ 25 Ricky Jordan	.15	.07	.01
☐ 26 Don Mattingly	1.00	.50	.10
☐ 27 Fred McGriff	.25	.12	.02
☐ 28 Mark McGwire	.75	.35	.07
☐ 29 Kevin McReynolds	.15	.07	.01

☐ 30 Gerald Perry	.10	.05	.01
☐ 31 Kirby Puckett	.45	.22	.04
☐ 32 Johnny Ray	.10	.05	.01
☐ 33 Harold Reynolds	.10	.05	.01
☐ 34 Cal Ripken Jr.	.30	.15	.03
☐ 35 Ryne Sandberg	.75	.35	.07
☐ 36 Kevin Seitzer	.20	.10	.02
☐ 37 Ruben Sierra	.50	.25	.05
☐ 38 Darryl Strawberry	.50	.25	.05
☐ 39 Bobby Thigpen	.20	.10	.02
☐ 40 Alan Trammell	.20	.10	.02
☐ 41 Andy Van Slyke	.15	.07	.01
☐ 42 Frank Viola	.20	.10	.02
☐ 43 Dave Winfield	.20	.10	.02
☐ 44 Robin Yount	.40	.20	.04

1989 Fleer League Leaders

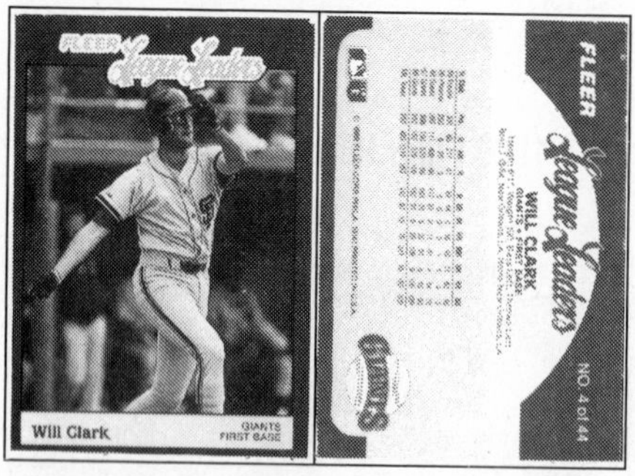

The 1989 Fleer League Leaders set contains 44 standard-size (2 1/2" by 3 1/2") cards. The fronts are red and yellow; the horizontally-oriented backs are light blue and red, and feature career stats. The cards were distributed through Woolworth stores as a boxed set.

	MINT	EXC	G-VG
COMPLETE SET (44)	5.00	2.50	.50
COMMON PLAYER (1-44)	.10	.05	.01
☐ 1 Allan Anderson	.10	.05	.01
☐ 2 Wade Boggs	.60	.30	.06
☐ 3 Jose Canseco	1.00	.50	.10
☐ 4 Will Clark	.90	.45	.09
☐ 5 Roger Clemens	.60	.30	.06
☐ 6 Vince Coleman	.25	.12	.02
☐ 7 David Cone	.20	.10	.02
☐ 8 Kal Daniels	.15	.07	.01
☐ 9 Chili Davis	.10	.05	.01
☐ 10 Eric Davis	.50	.25	.05
☐ 11 Glenn Davis	.20	.10	.02
☐ 12 Andre Dawson	.20	.10	.02
☐ 13 John Franco	.15	.07	.01
☐ 14 Andres Galarraga	.20	.10	.02
☐ 15 Kirk Gibson	.20	.10	.02
☐ 16 Dwight Gooden	.40	.20	.04
☐ 17 Mark Grace	1.00	.50	.10
☐ 18 Mike Greenwell	.40	.20	.04
☐ 19 Tony Gwynn	.35	.17	.03
☐ 20 Orel Hershiser	.25	.12	.02
☐ 21 Pete Incaviglia	.15	.07	.01
☐ 22 Danny Jackson	.10	.05	.01
☐ 23 Gregg Jefferies	.75	.35	.07
☐ 24 Joe Magrane	.15	.07	.01
☐ 25 Don Mattingly	1.00	.50	.10
☐ 26 Fred McGriff	.30	.15	.03
☐ 27 Mark McGwire	.75	.35	.07
☐ 28 Dale Murphy	.35	.17	.03
☐ 29 Dan Plesac	.10	.05	.01
☐ 30 Kirby Puckett	.45	.22	.04
☐ 31 Harold Reynolds	.10	.05	.01
☐ 32 Cal Ripken Jr.	.30	.15	.03
☐ 33 Jeff Robinson	.10	.05	.01
☐ 34 Mike Scott	.20	.10	.02
☐ 35 Ozzie Smith	.20	.10	.02
☐ 36 Dave Stewart	.20	.10	.02
☐ 37 Darryl Strawberry	.50	.25	.05
☐ 38 Greg Swindell	.15	.07	.01
☐ 39 Bobby Thigpen	.20	.10	.02
☐ 40 Alan Trammell	.20	.10	.02
☐ 41 Andy Van Slyke	.15	.07	.01
☐ 42 Frank Viola	.20	.10	.02
☐ 43 Dave Winfield	.20	.10	.02
☐ 44 Robin Yount	.40	.20	.04

1989 Fleer Super Stars

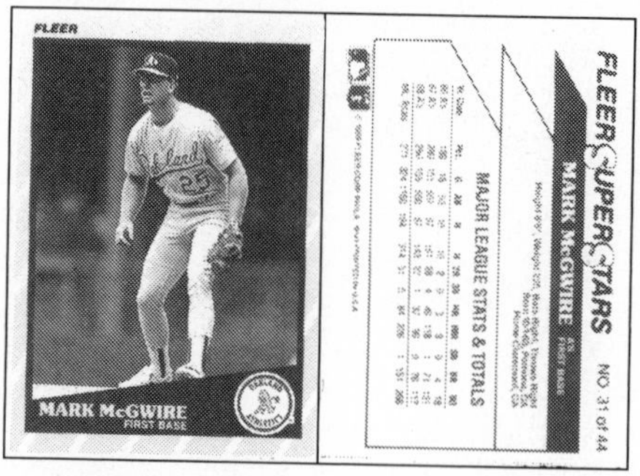

The 1989 Fleer Super Stars set contains 44 standard-size (2 1/2" by 3 1/2") cards. The fronts are red and beige; the horizontally-oriented backs are yellow, and feature career stats. The cards were distributed as a boxed set. The back panel of the box contains the complete set checklist.

	MINT	EXC	G-VG
COMPLETE SET (44)	5.00	2.50	.50
COMMON PLAYER (1-44)	.10	.05	.01
☐ 1 Roberto Alomar	.25	.12	.02
☐ 2 Harold Baines	.15	.07	.01
☐ 3 Tim Belcher	.15	.07	.01
☐ 4 Wade Boggs	.60	.30	.06
☐ 5 George Brett	.40	.20	.04
☐ 6 Jose Canseco	1.00	.50	.10
☐ 7 Gary Carter	.20	.10	.02
☐ 8 Will Clark	.90	.45	.09
☐ 9 Roger Clemens	.60	.30	.06
☐ 10 Kal Daniels UER (reverse negative photo on front)	.15	.07	.01
☐ 11 Eric Davis	.50	.25	.05
☐ 12 Andre Dawson	.20	.10	.02
☐ 13 Tony Fernandez	.15	.07	.01
☐ 14 Scott Fletcher	.10	.05	.01
☐ 15 Andres Galarraga	.20	.10	.02
☐ 16 Kirk Gibson	.20	.10	.02
☐ 17 Dwight Gooden	.40	.20	.04
☐ 18 Jim Gott	.10	.05	.01
☐ 19 Mark Grace	1.00	.50	.10
☐ 20 Mike Greenwell	.40	.20	.04
☐ 21 Tony Gwynn	.35	.17	.03
☐ 22 Rickey Henderson	.75	.35	.07
☐ 23 Orel Hershiser	.25	.12	.02
☐ 24 Ted Higuera	.15	.07	.01
☐ 25 Gregg Jefferies	.75	.35	.07
☐ 26 Wally Joyner	.20	.10	.02
☐ 27 Mark Langston	.15	.07	.01
☐ 28 Greg Maddux	.15	.07	.01
☐ 29 Don Mattingly	1.00	.50	.10
☐ 30 Fred McGriff	.30	.15	.03
☐ 31 Mark McGwire	.75	.35	.07
☐ 32 Dan Plesac	.10	.05	.01
☐ 33 Kirby Puckett	.45	.22	.04
☐ 34 Jeff Reardon	.10	.05	.01
☐ 35 Chris Sabo	.45	.22	.04
☐ 36 Mike Schmidt	.75	.35	.07
☐ 37 Mike Scott	.20	.10	.02
☐ 38 Cory Snyder	.15	.07	.01
☐ 39 Darryl Strawberry	.50	.25	.05
☐ 40 Alan Trammell	.20	.10	.02
☐ 41 Frank Viola	.20	.10	.02
☐ 42 Walt Weiss	.15	.07	.01
☐ 43 Dave Winfield	.20	.10	.02
☐ 44 Todd Worrell UER (statistical headings on back for hitter)	.10	.05	.01

1989 Fleer World Series

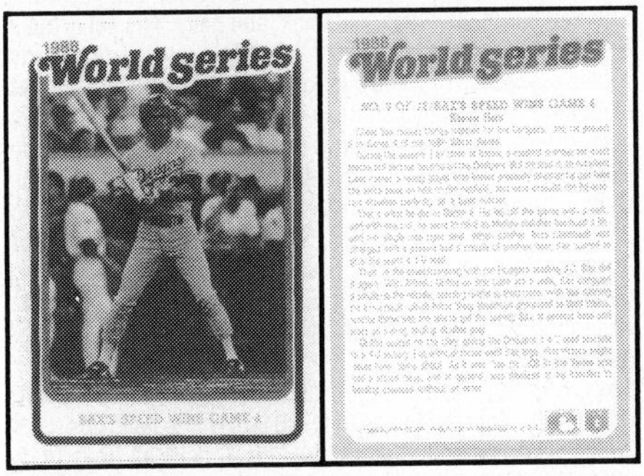

This 12-card set of 2 1/2" by 3 1/2" cards features highlights of the previous year's World Series between the Dodgers and the Athletics. The sets were packaged as a complete set insert with the collated sets (of the 1989 Fleer regular issue) which were sold by Fleer directly to hobby card dealers; they were not available in the general retail candy store outlets.

	MINT	EXC	G-VG
COMPLETE SET (12)	3.00	1.50	.30
COMMON PLAYER (1-12)	.25	.12	.02
☐ 1 Mickey Hatcher Dodgers' Secret Weapon	.25	.12	.02
☐ 2 Tim Belcher Rookie Starts Series	.35	.17	.03
☐ 3 Jose Canseco Canseco Slams L.A.	1.00	.50	.10
☐ 4 Mike Scioscia Dramatic Comeback	.25	.12	.02
☐ 5 Kirk Gibson Gibson Steals The Show	.60	.30	.06
☐ 6 Orel Hershiser Bulldog	.50	.25	.05
☐ 7 Mike Marshall One Swing, Three RBI's	.25	.12	.02
☐ 8 Mark McGwire Game-Winning Homer	.75	.35	.07
☐ 9 Steve Sax UER Sax's Speed Wins Game 4 (actually stole 42 bases in '88)	.35	.17	.03
☐ 10 Walt Weiss Series Caps Award- Winning Year	.35	.17	.03
☐ 11 Orel Hershiser Series MVP Uses Shutout Magic	.50	.25	.05
☐ 12 Dodger Blue, World Champs	.25	.12	.02

1989 Fleer Update

The 1989 Fleer Update set contains 132 standard-size (2 1/2" by 3 1/2") cards. The fronts are gray with white pinstripes. The vertically-oriented backs show lifetime stats and performance "Before and After the All-Star Break." The set does not include a card of 1989 AL Rookie of the Year Gregg Olson, but contains the first major card of Greg Vaughn and special cards for Nolan Ryan's 5,000th strikeout and Mike Schmidt's retirement. Other key rookies in this set are Junior Felix, Jerome Walton and Todd Zeile. Fleer did NOT produce a limited (tin) edition version of this set with glossy coating.

	MINT	EXC	G-VG
COMPLETE SET (132)	16.00	8.00	1.60
COMMON PLAYER (1-132)	.07	.03	.01
☐ U1 Phil Bradley	.15	.07	.01
☐ U2 Mike Devereaux	.10	.05	.01
☐ U3 Steve Finley	.30	.15	.03
☐ U4 Kevin Hickey	.07	.03	.01
☐ U5 Brian Holton	.10	.05	.01
☐ U6 Bob Milacki	.12	.06	.01
☐ U7 Randy Milligan	.18	.09	.01
☐ U8 John Dopson	.10	.05	.01
☐ U9 Nick Esasky	.12	.06	.01
☐ U10 Rob Murphy	.07	.03	.01
☐ U11 Jim Abbott	.90	.45	.09
☐ U12 Bert Blyleven	.15	.07	.01
☐ U13 Jeff Manto	.30	.15	.03
☐ U14 Bob McClure	.07	.03	.01
☐ U15 Lance Parrish	.12	.06	.01
☐ U16 Lee Stevens	.75	.35	.07
☐ U17 Claudell Washington	.10	.05	.01
☐ U18 Mark Davis	.15	.07	.01
☐ U19 Eric King	.12	.06	.01
☐ U20 Ron Kittle	.12	.06	.01
☐ U21 Matt Merullo	.12	.06	.01
☐ U22 Steve Rosenberg	.10	.05	.01
☐ U23 Robin Ventura	.90	.45	.09
☐ U24 Keith Atherton	.07	.03	.01
☐ U25 Joey Belle	.50	.25	.05
☐ U26 Jerry Browne	.10	.05	.01
☐ U27 Felix Fermin	.07	.03	.01
☐ U28 Brad Komminsk	.07	.03	.01
☐ U29 Pete O'Brien	.10	.05	.01
☐ U30 Mike Brumley	.10	.05	.01
☐ U31 Tracy Jones	.07	.03	.01
☐ U32 Mike Schwabe	.15	.07	.01
☐ U33 Gary Ward	.07	.03	.01
☐ U34 Frank Williams	.07	.03	.01
☐ U35 Kevin Appier	.50	.25	.05
☐ U36 Bob Boone	.15	.07	.01
☐ U37 Luis de los Santos	.15	.07	.01
☐ U38 Jim Eisenreich	.10	.05	.01
☐ U39 Jaime Navarro	.30	.15	.03
☐ U40 Bill Spiers	.20	.10	.02
☐ U41 Greg Vaughn	1.75	.85	.17
☐ U42 Randy Veres	.12	.06	.01
☐ U43 Wally Backman	.07	.03	.01
☐ U44 Shane Rawley	.07	.03	.01
☐ U45 Steve Balboni	.07	.03	.01
☐ U46 Jesse Barfield	.15	.07	.01
☐ U47 Alvaro Espinoza	.10	.05	.01
☐ U48 Bob Geren	.20	.10	.02
☐ U49 Mel Hall	.10	.05	.01
☐ U50 Andy Hawkins	.07	.03	.01
☐ U51 Hensley Meulens	.60	.30	.06
☐ U52 Steve Sax	.15	.07	.01
☐ U53 Deion Sanders	.90	.45	.09
☐ U54 Rickey Henderson	.50	.25	.05
☐ U55 Mike Moore	.15	.07	.01
☐ U56 Tony Phillips	.07	.03	.01
☐ U57 Greg Briley	.40	.20	.04
☐ U58 Gene Harris	.25	.12	.02
☐ U59 Randy Johnson	.15	.07	.01
☐ U60 Jeffrey Leonard	.10	.05	.01
☐ U61 Dennis Powell	.07	.03	.01
☐ U62 Omar Vizquel	.15	.07	.01
☐ U63 Kevin Brown	.25	.12	.02
☐ U64 Julio Franco	.15	.07	.01
☐ U65 Jamie Moyer	.07	.03	.01
☐ U66 Rafael Palmeiro	.25	.12	.02
☐ U67 Nolan Ryan	1.50	.75	.15
☐ U68 Francisco Cabrera	.50	.25	.05

☐	U69 Junior Felix	1.25	.60	.12
☐	U70 Al Leiter	.10	.05	.01
☐	U71 Alex Sanchez	.20	.10	.02
☐	U72 Geronimo Berroa	.07	.03	.01
☐	U73 Derek Lilliquist	.15	.07	.01
☐	U74 Lonnie Smith	.15	.07	.01
☐	U75 Jeff Treadway	.10	.05	.01
☐	U76 Paul Kilgus	.07	.03	.01
☐	U77 Lloyd McClendon	.10	.05	.01
☐	U78 Scott Sanderson	.10	.05	.01
☐	U79 Dwight Smith	.75	.35	.07
☐	U80 Jerome Walton	1.50	.75	.15
☐	U81 Mitch Williams	.12	.06	.01
☐	U82 Steve Wilson	.10	.05	.01
☐	U83 Todd Benzinger	.10	.05	.01
☐	U84 Ken Griffey Sr.	.15	.07	.01
☐	U85 Rick Mahler	.07	.03	.01
☐	U86 Rolando Roomes	.12	.06	.01
☐	U87 Scott Scudder	.30	.15	.03
☐	U88 Jim Clancy	.07	.03	.01
☐	U89 Rick Rhoden	.07	.03	.01
☐	U90 Dan Schatzeder	.07	.03	.01
☐	U91 Mike Morgan	.07	.03	.01
☐	U92 Eddie Murray	.15	.07	.01
☐	U93 Willie Randolph	.10	.05	.01
☐	U94 Ray Searage	.07	.03	.01
☐	U95 Mike Aldrete	.07	.03	.01
☐	U96 Kevin Gross	.10	.05	.01
☐	U97 Mark Langston	.15	.07	.01
☐	U98 Spike Owen	.07	.03	.01
☐	U99 Zane Smith	.12	.06	.01
☐	U100 Don Aase	.07	.03	.01
☐	U101 Barry Lyons	.07	.03	.01
☐	U102 Juan Samuel	.12	.06	.01
☐	U103 Wally Whitehurst	.20	.10	.02
☐	U104 Dennis Cook	.12	.06	.01
☐	U105 Len Dykstra	.15	.07	.01
☐	U106 Charlie Hayes	.12	.06	.01
☐	U107 Tommy Herr	.10	.05	.01
☐	U108 Ken Howell	.07	.03	.01
☐	U109 John Kruk	.10	.05	.01
☐	U110 Roger McDowell	.10	.05	.01
☐	U111 Terry Mulholland	.07	.03	.01
☐	U112 Jeff Parrett	.10	.05	.01
☐	U113 Neal Heaton	.07	.03	.01
☐	U114 Jeff King	.12	.06	.01
☐	U115 Randy Kramer	.10	.05	.01
☐	U116 Bill Landrum	.10	.05	.01
☐	U117 Cris Carpenter	.10	.05	.01
☐	U118 Frank DiPino	.07	.03	.01
☐	U119 Ken Hill	.12	.06	.01
☐	U120 Dan Quisenberry	.12	.06	.01
☐	U121 Milt Thompson	.07	.03	.01
☐	U122 Todd Zeile	1.50	.75	.15
☐	U123 Jack Clark	.12	.06	.01
☐	U124 Bruce Hurst	.10	.05	.01
☐	U125 Mark Parent	.07	.03	.01
☐	U126 Bip Roberts	.12	.06	.01
☐	U127 Jeff Brantley UER (photo actually Joe Kmak)	.30	.15	.03
☐	U128 Terry Kennedy	.07	.03	.01
☐	U129 Mike LaCoss	.07	.03	.01
☐	U130 Greg Litton	.20	.10	.02
☐	U131 Mike Schmidt	2.00	1.00	.20
☐	U132 Checklist 1-132	.07	.01	.00

1990 Fleer

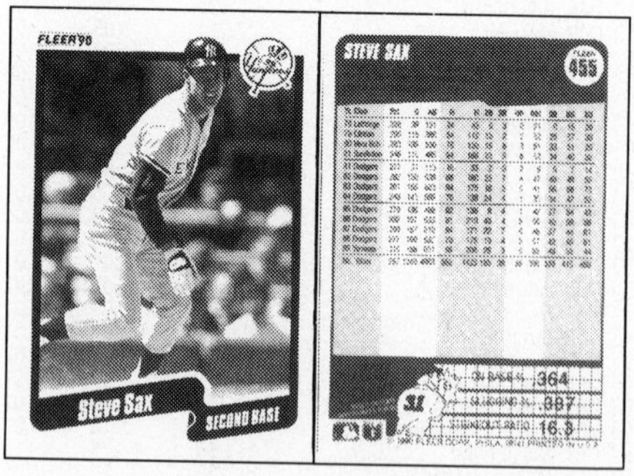

The 1990 Fleer set contains 660 standard-size (2 1/2" by 3 1/2") cards. The outer front borders are white; the inner, ribbon-like borders are different depending on the team. The vertically-oriented backs are white, red, pink, and navy. The set is again ordered numerically by teams, followed by combination cards, rookie prospect pairs, and checklists. Just as with the 1989 set, Fleer incorrectly anticipated the outcome of the 1989 Playoffs according to the team ordering. The A's, listed first, did win the World Series, but their opponents were the Giants, not the Cubs. The complete team ordering is as follows: Oakland A's (1-24), Chicago Cubs (25-49), San Francisco Giants (50-75), Toronto Blue Jays (76-99), Kansas City Royals (100-124), California Angels (125-148), San Diego Padres (149-171), Baltimore Orioles (172-195), New York Mets (196-219), Houston Astros (220-241), St. Louis Cardinals (242-265), Boston Red Sox (266-289), Texas Rangers (290-315), Milwaukee Brewers (316-340), Montreal Expos (341-364), Minnesota Twins (365-388), Los Angeles Dodgers (389-411), Cincinnati Reds (412-435), New York Yankees (436-458), Pittsburgh Pirates (459-482), Cleveland Indians (483-504), Seattle Mariners (505-528), Chicago White Sox (529-551), Philadelphia Phillies (552-573), Atlanta Braves (574-598), and Detroit Tigers (599-620). The key rookie cards in this set are Alex Cole, Delino DeShields, Juan Gonzalez, Dave Justice, Kevin Maas, and Ben McDonald. The following five cards have minor printing differences, 6, 162, 260, 469, and 550; these differences are so minor that collectors have deemed them not significant enough to effect a price differential. Fleer also produced a separate set for Canada. The Canadian set only differs from the regular set in that it shows copyright "FLEER LTD./LTEE PTD. IN CANADA" on the card backs. Although these Canadian cards were undoubtedly produced in much lesser quantities compared to the U.S. issue, the fact that the versions are so similar has kept the demand (and the price differential) for the Canadian cards down.

		MINT	EXC	G-VG
	COMPLETE SET (660)	23.00	11.50	2.30
	COMMON PLAYER (1-660)	.03	.01	.00
☐	1 Lance Blankenship	.08	.04	.01
☐	2 Todd Burns	.06	.03	.00
☐	3 Jose Canseco	.60	.30	.06
☐	4 Jim Corsi	.03	.01	.00
☐	5 Storm Davis	.06	.03	.00
☐	6 Dennis Eckersley	.10	.05	.01
☐	7 Mike Gallego	.03	.01	.00
☐	8 Ron Hassey	.03	.01	.00
☐	9 Dave Henderson	.03	.01	.00
☐	10 Rickey Henderson	.25	.12	.02
☐	11 Rick Honeycutt	.03	.01	.00
☐	12 Stan Javier	.03	.01	.00
☐	13 Felix Jose	.10	.05	.01
☐	14 Carney Lansford	.08	.04	.01
☐	15 Mark McGwire	.25	.12	.02
☐	16 Mike Moore	.06	.03	.00
☐	17 Gene Nelson	.03	.01	.00
☐	18 Dave Parker	.08	.04	.01
☐	19 Tony Phillips	.03	.01	.00
☐	20 Terry Steinbach	.06	.03	.00
☐	21 Dave Stewart	.10	.05	.01
☐	22 Walt Weiss	.08	.04	.01
☐	23 Bob Welch	.08	.04	.01
☐	24 Curt Young	.03	.01	.00
☐	25 Paul Assenmacher	.03	.01	.00
☐	26 Damon Berryhill	.08	.04	.01
☐	27 Mike Bielecki	.03	.01	.00
☐	28 Kevin Blankenship	.08	.04	.01
☐	29 Andre Dawson	.10	.05	.01
☐	30 Shawon Dunston	.10	.05	.01
☐	31 Joe Girardi	.06	.03	.00
☐	32 Mark Grace	.25	.12	.02
☐	33 Mike Harkey	.10	.05	.01
☐	34 Paul Kilgus	.03	.01	.00
☐	35 Les Lancaster	.03	.01	.00
☐	36 Vance Law	.03	.01	.00
☐	37 Greg Maddux	.06	.03	.00
☐	38 Lloyd McClendon	.03	.01	.00
☐	39 Jeff Pico	.03	.01	.00
☐	40 Ryne Sandberg	.20	.10	.02
☐	41 Scott Sanderson	.03	.01	.00
☐	42 Dwight Smith	.12	.06	.01
☐	43 Rick Sutcliffe	.06	.03	.00
☐	44 Jerome Walton	.50	.25	.05

☐ 45	Mitch Webster	.03	.01	.00
☐ 46	Curt Wilkerson	.03	.01	.00
☐ 47	Dean Wilkins	.15	.07	.01
☐ 48	Mitch Williams	.03	.01	.00
☐ 49	Steve Wilson	.03	.01	.00
☐ 50	Steve Bedrosian	.06	.03	.00
☐ 51	Mike Benjamin	.20	.10	.02
☐ 52	Jeff Brantley	.12	.06	.01
☐ 53	Brett Butler	.06	.03	.00
☐ 54	Will Clark UER ("Did You Know" says first in runs, should say tied for first)	.50	.25	.05
☐ 55	Kelly Downs	.03	.01	.00
☐ 56	Scott Garrelts	.06	.03	.00
☐ 57	Atlee Hammaker	.03	.01	.00
☐ 58	Terry Kennedy	.03	.01	.00
☐ 59	Mike LaCoss	.03	.01	.00
☐ 60	Craig Lefferts	.03	.01	.00
☐ 61	Greg Litton	.10	.05	.01
☐ 62	Candy Maldonado	.06	.03	.00
☐ 63	Kirt Manwaring UER (no '88 Phoenix stats as noted in box)	.06	.03	.00
☐ 64	Randy McCament	.10	.05	.01
☐ 65	Kevin Mitchell	.20	.10	.02
☐ 66	Donell Nixon	.03	.01	.00
☐ 67	Ken Oberkfell	.03	.01	.00
☐ 68	Rick Reuschel	.06	.03	.00
☐ 69	Ernest Riles	.03	.01	.00
☐ 70	Don Robinson	.03	.01	.00
☐ 71	Pat Sheridan	.03	.01	.00
☐ 72	Chris Speier	.03	.01	.00
☐ 73	Robby Thompson	.03	.01	.00
☐ 74	Jose Uribe	.03	.01	.00
☐ 75	Matt Williams	.20	.10	.02
☐ 76	George Bell	.08	.04	.01
☐ 77	Pat Borders	.03	.01	.00
☐ 78	John Cerutti	.03	.01	.00
☐ 79	Junior Felix	.35	.17	.03
☐ 80	Tony Fernandez	.08	.04	.01
☐ 81	Mike Flanagan	.03	.01	.00
☐ 82	Mauro Gozzo	.12	.06	.01
☐ 83	Kelly Gruber	.12	.06	.01
☐ 84	Tom Henke	.06	.03	.00
☐ 85	Jimmy Key	.03	.01	.00
☐ 86	Manny Lee	.03	.01	.00
☐ 87	Nelson Liriano UER (should say "led the IL" instead of "led the TL")	.03	.01	.00
☐ 88	Lee Mazzilli	.03	.01	.00
☐ 89	Fred McGriff	.12	.06	.01
☐ 90	Lloyd Moseby	.06	.03	.00
☐ 91	Rance Mulliniks	.03	.01	.00
☐ 92	Alex Sanchez	.10	.05	.01
☐ 93	Dave Stieb	.08	.04	.01
☐ 94	Todd Stottlemyre	.06	.03	.00
☐ 95	Duane Ward UER (double line of '87 Syracuse stats)	.03	.01	.00
☐ 96	David Wells	.03	.01	.00
☐ 97	Ernie Whitt	.03	.01	.00
☐ 98	Frank Wills	.03	.01	.00
☐ 99	Mookie Wilson	.06	.03	.00
☐ 100	Kevin Appier	.25	.12	.02
☐ 101	Luis Aquino	.03	.01	.00
☐ 102	Bob Boone	.06	.03	.00
☐ 103	George Brett	.15	.07	.01
☐ 104	Jose DeJesus	.03	.01	.00
☐ 105	Luis De Los Santos	.03	.01	.00
☐ 106	Jim Eisenreich	.03	.01	.00
☐ 107	Steve Farr	.03	.01	.00
☐ 108	Tom Gordon	.15	.07	.01
☐ 109	Mark Gubicza	.06	.03	.00
☐ 110	Bo Jackson	.75	.35	.07
☐ 111	Terry Leach	.03	.01	.00
☐ 112	Charlie Leibrandt	.03	.01	.00
☐ 113	Rick Luecken	.10	.05	.01
☐ 114	Mike Macfarlane	.03	.01	.00
☐ 115	Jeff Montgomery	.06	.03	.00
☐ 116	Bret Saberhagen	.10	.05	.01
☐ 117	Kevin Seitzer	.08	.04	.01
☐ 118	Kurt Stillwell	.06	.03	.00
☐ 119	Pat Tabler	.03	.01	.00
☐ 120	Danny Tartabull	.08	.04	.01
☐ 121	Gary Thurman	.03	.01	.00
☐ 122	Frank White	.06	.03	.00
☐ 123	Willie Wilson	.06	.03	.00
☐ 124	Matt Winters	.12	.06	.01
☐ 125	Jim Abbott	.25	.12	.02
☐ 126	Tony Armas	.03	.01	.00
☐ 127	Dante Bichette	.08	.04	.01
☐ 128	Bert Blyleven	.08	.04	.01
☐ 129	Chili Davis	.06	.03	.00
☐ 130	Brian Downing	.03	.01	.00
☐ 131	Mike Fetters	.12	.06	.01
☐ 132	Chuck Finley	.08	.04	.01
☐ 133	Willie Fraser	.03	.01	.00
☐ 134	Bryan Harvey	.03	.01	.00
☐ 135	Jack Howell	.03	.01	.00
☐ 136	Wally Joyner	.08	.04	.01
☐ 137	Jeff Manto	.10	.05	.01
☐ 138	Kirk McCaskill	.03	.01	.00
☐ 139	Bob McClure	.03	.01	.00
☐ 140	Greg Minton	.03	.01	.00
☐ 141	Lance Parrish	.08	.04	.01
☐ 142	Dan Petry	.03	.01	.00
☐ 143	Johnny Ray	.03	.01	.00
☐ 144	Dick Schofield	.03	.01	.00
☐ 145	Lee Stevens	.25	.12	.02
☐ 146	Claudell Washington	.06	.03	.00
☐ 147	Devon White	.06	.03	.00
☐ 148	Mike Witt	.03	.01	.00
☐ 149	Roberto Alomar	.12	.06	.01
☐ 150	Sandy Alomar Jr.	.30	.15	.03
☐ 151	Andy Benes	.25	.12	.02
☐ 152	Jack Clark	.08	.04	.01
☐ 153	Pat Clements	.03	.01	.00
☐ 154	Joey Cora	.03	.01	.00
☐ 155	Mark Davis	.08	.04	.01
☐ 156	Mark Grant	.03	.01	.00
☐ 157	Tony Gwynn	.15	.07	.01
☐ 158	Greg W. Harris	.06	.03	.00
☐ 159	Bruce Hurst	.06	.03	.00
☐ 160	Darrin Jackson	.03	.01	.00
☐ 161	Chris James	.06	.03	.00
☐ 162	Carmelo Martinez	.03	.01	.00
☐ 163	Mike Pagliarulo	.03	.01	.00
☐ 164	Mark Parent	.06	.03	.00
☐ 165	Dennis Rasmussen	.03	.01	.00
☐ 166	Bip Roberts	.06	.03	.00
☐ 167	Benito Santiago	.12	.06	.01
☐ 168	Calvin Schiraldi	.03	.01	.00
☐ 169	Eric Show	.03	.01	.00
☐ 170	Garry Templeton	.03	.01	.00
☐ 171	Ed Whitson	.03	.01	.00
☐ 172	Brady Anderson	.06	.03	.00
☐ 173	Jeff Ballard	.03	.01	.00
☐ 174	Phil Bradley	.06	.03	.00
☐ 175	Mike Devereaux	.06	.03	.00
☐ 176	Steve Finley	.12	.06	.01
☐ 177	Pete Harnisch	.06	.03	.00
☐ 178	Kevin Hickey	.03	.01	.00
☐ 179	Brian Holton	.03	.01	.00
☐ 180	Ben McDonald	1.75	.85	.17
☐ 181	Bob Melvin	.03	.01	.00
☐ 182	Bob Milacki	.08	.04	.01
☐ 183	Randy Milligan UER (double line of '87 stats)	.12	.06	.01
☐ 184	Gregg Olson	.25	.12	.02
☐ 185	Joe Orsulak	.03	.01	.00
☐ 186	Bill Ripken	.03	.01	.00
☐ 187	Cal Ripken	.15	.07	.01
☐ 188	Dave Schmidt	.03	.01	.00
☐ 189	Larry Sheets	.03	.01	.00
☐ 190	Mickey Tettleton	.06	.03	.00
☐ 191	Mark Thurmond	.03	.01	.00
☐ 192	Jay Tibbs	.03	.01	.00
☐ 193	Jim Traber	.03	.01	.00
☐ 194	Mark Williamson	.03	.01	.00
☐ 195	Craig Worthington	.08	.04	.01
☐ 196	Don Aase	.03	.01	.00
☐ 197	Blaine Beatty	.12	.06	.01
☐ 198	Mark Carreon	.03	.01	.00
☐ 199	Gary Carter	.08	.04	.01
☐ 200	David Cone	.08	.04	.01
☐ 201	Ron Darling	.08	.04	.01
☐ 202	Kevin Elster	.06	.03	.00
☐ 203	Sid Fernandez	.06	.03	.00
☐ 204	Dwight Gooden	.18	.09	.01
☐ 205	Keith Hernandez	.08	.04	.01
☐ 206	Jeff Innis	.08	.04	.01
☐ 207	Gregg Jefferies	.30	.15	.03
☐ 208	Howard Johnson	.08	.04	.01
☐ 209	Barry Lyons UER (double line of '87 stats)	.03	.01	.00
☐ 210	Dave Magadan	.08	.04	.01
☐ 211	Kevin McReynolds	.08	.04	.01
☐ 212	Jeff Musselman	.03	.01	.00
☐ 213	Randy Myers	.06	.03	.00
☐ 214	Bob Ojeda	.06	.03	.00
☐ 215	Juan Samuel	.06	.03	.00
☐ 216	Mackey Sasser	.06	.03	.00
☐ 217	Darryl Strawberry	.20	.10	.02
☐ 218	Tim Teufel	.03	.01	.00

☐ 219 Frank Viola	.08	.04	.01
☐ 220 Juan Agosto	.03	.01	.00
☐ 221 Larry Andersen	.03	.01	.00
☐ 222 Eric Anthony	.75	.35	.07
☐ 223 Kevin Bass	.03	.01	.00
☐ 224 Craig Biggio	.08	.04	.01
☐ 225 Ken Caminiti	.03	.01	.00
☐ 226 Jim Clancy	.03	.01	.00
☐ 227 Danny Darwin	.03	.01	.00
☐ 228 Glenn Davis	.10	.05	.01
☐ 229 Jim Deshaies	.03	.01	.00
☐ 230 Bill Doran	.06	.03	.00
☐ 231 Bob Forsch	.03	.01	.00
☐ 232 Brian Meyer	.08	.04	.01
☐ 233 Terry Puhl	.03	.01	.00
☐ 234 Rafael Ramirez	.03	.01	.00
☐ 235 Rick Rhoden	.03	.01	.00
☐ 236 Dan Schatzeder	.03	.01	.00
☐ 237 Mike Scott	.08	.04	.01
☐ 238 Dave Smith	.03	.01	.00
☐ 239 Alex Trevino	.03	.01	.00
☐ 240 Glenn Wilson	.03	.01	.00
☐ 241 Gerald Young	.03	.01	.00
☐ 242 Tom Brunansky	.08	.04	.01
☐ 243 Cris Carpenter	.03	.01	.00
☐ 244 Alex Cole	.90	.45	.09
☐ 245 Vince Coleman	.08	.04	.01
☐ 246 John Costello	.03	.01	.00
☐ 247 Ken Dayley	.03	.01	.00
☐ 248 Jose DeLeon	.03	.01	.00
☐ 249 Frank DiPino	.03	.01	.00
☐ 250 Pedro Guerrero	.08	.04	.01
☐ 251 Ken Hill	.03	.01	.00
☐ 252 Joe Magrane	.06	.03	.00
☐ 253 Willie McGee UER (no decimal point before 353)	.08	.04	.01
☐ 254 John Morris	.03	.01	.00
☐ 255 Jose Oquendo	.03	.01	.00
☐ 256 Tony Pena	.06	.03	.00
☐ 257 Terry Pendleton	.03	.01	.00
☐ 258 Ted Power	.03	.01	.00
☐ 259 Dan Quisenberry	.06	.03	.00
☐ 260 Ozzie Smith	.10	.05	.01
☐ 261 Scott Terry	.03	.01	.00
☐ 262 Milt Thompson	.03	.01	.00
☐ 263 Denny Walling	.03	.01	.00
☐ 264 Todd Worrell	.08	.04	.01
☐ 265 Todd Zeile	.75	.35	.07
☐ 266 Marty Barrett	.03	.01	.00
☐ 267 Mike Boddicker	.03	.01	.00
☐ 268 Wade Boggs	.20	.10	.02
☐ 269 Ellis Burks	.15	.07	.01
☐ 270 Rick Cerone	.03	.01	.00
☐ 271 Roger Clemens	.20	.10	.02
☐ 272 John Dopson	.03	.01	.00
☐ 273 Nick Esasky	.06	.03	.00
☐ 274 Dwight Evans	.08	.04	.01
☐ 275 Wes Gardner	.03	.01	.00
☐ 276 Rich Gedman	.03	.01	.00
☐ 277 Mike Greenwell	.15	.07	.01
☐ 278 Danny Heep	.03	.01	.00
☐ 279 Eric Hetzel	.06	.03	.00
☐ 280 Dennis Lamp	.03	.01	.00
☐ 281 Rob Murphy UER ('89 stats say Reds, should say Red Sox)	.03	.01	.00
☐ 282 Joe Price	.03	.01	.00
☐ 283 Carlos Quintana	.15	.07	.01
☐ 284 Jody Reed	.08	.04	.01
☐ 285 Luis Rivera	.03	.01	.00
☐ 286 Kevin Romine	.03	.01	.00
☐ 287 Lee Smith	.06	.03	.00
☐ 288 Mike Smithson	.03	.01	.00
☐ 289 Bob Stanley	.03	.01	.00
☐ 290 Harold Baines	.08	.04	.01
☐ 291 Kevin Brown	.08	.04	.01
☐ 292 Steve Buechele	.03	.01	.00
☐ 293 Scott Coolbaugh	.15	.07	.01
☐ 294 Jack Daugherty	.10	.05	.01
☐ 295 Cecil Espy	.03	.01	.00
☐ 296 Julio Franco	.08	.04	.01
☐ 297 Juan Gonzalez	1.75	.85	.17
☐ 298 Cecilio Guante	.03	.01	.00
☐ 299 Drew Hall	.03	.01	.00
☐ 300 Charlie Hough	.03	.01	.00
☐ 301 Pete Incaviglia	.08	.04	.01
☐ 302 Mike Jeffcoat	.03	.01	.00
☐ 303 Chad Kreuter	.03	.01	.00
☐ 304 Jeff Kunkel	.03	.01	.00
☐ 305 Rick Leach	.03	.01	.00
☐ 306 Fred Manrique	.03	.01	.00
☐ 307 Jamie Moyer	.03	.01	.00
☐ 308 Rafael Palmeiro	.12	.06	.01
☐ 309 Geno Petralli	.03	.01	.00
☐ 310 Kevin Reimer	.03	.01	.00
☐ 311 Kenny Rogers	.10	.05	.01
☐ 312 Jeff Russell	.03	.01	.00
☐ 313 Nolan Ryan	.40	.20	.04
☐ 314 Ruben Sierra	.15	.07	.01
☐ 315 Bobby Witt	.08	.04	.01
☐ 316 Chris Bosio	.03	.01	.00
☐ 317 Glenn Braggs UER (stats say 111 K's, but bio says 117 K's)	.03	.01	.00
☐ 318 Greg Brock	.03	.01	.00
☐ 319 Chuck Crim	.03	.01	.00
☐ 320 Rob Deer	.06	.03	.00
☐ 321 Mike Felder	.03	.01	.00
☐ 322 Tom Filer	.03	.01	.00
☐ 323 Tony Fossas	.08	.04	.01
☐ 324 Jim Gantner	.03	.01	.00
☐ 325 Darryl Hamilton	.06	.03	.00
☐ 326 Teddy Higuera	.06	.03	.00
☐ 327 Mark Knudson	.06	.03	.00
☐ 328 Bill Krueger UER ('86 stats missing)	.03	.01	.00
☐ 329 Tim McIntosh	.15	.07	.01
☐ 330 Paul Molitor	.08	.04	.01
☐ 331 Jaime Navarro	.12	.06	.01
☐ 332 Charlie O'Brien	.03	.01	.00
☐ 333 Jeff Peterek	.12	.06	.01
☐ 334 Dan Plesac	.03	.01	.00
☐ 335 Jerry Reuss	.03	.01	.00
☐ 336 Gary Sheffield UER (bio says played for 3 teams in '87, but stats say in '88)	.25	.12	.02
☐ 337 Bill Spiers	.10	.05	.01
☐ 338 B.J. Surhoff	.06	.03	.00
☐ 339 Greg Vaughn	.60	.30	.06
☐ 340 Robin Yount	.15	.07	.01
☐ 341 Hubie Brooks	.06	.03	.00
☐ 342 Tim Burke	.06	.03	.00
☐ 343 Mike Fitzgerald	.03	.01	.00
☐ 344 Tom Foley	.03	.01	.00
☐ 345 Andres Galarraga	.08	.04	.01
☐ 346 Damaso Garcia	.03	.01	.00
☐ 347 Marquis Grissom	.40	.20	.04
☐ 348 Kevin Gross	.03	.01	.00
☐ 349 Joe Hesketh	.03	.01	.00
☐ 350 Jeff Huson	.12	.06	.01
☐ 351 Wallace Johnson	.03	.01	.00
☐ 352 Mark Langston	.08	.04	.01
☐ 353A Dave Martinez (yellow on front)	3.00	1.50	.30
☐ 353B Dave Martinez (red on front)	.06	.03	.00
☐ 354 Dennis Martinez UER ('87 ERA is 616, should be 6.16)	.03	.01	.00
☐ 355 Andy McGaffigan	.03	.01	.00
☐ 356 Otis Nixon	.03	.01	.00
☐ 357 Spike Owen	.03	.01	.00
☐ 358 Pascual Perez	.06	.03	.00
☐ 359 Tim Raines	.10	.05	.01
☐ 360 Nelson Santovenia	.03	.01	.00
☐ 361 Bryn Smith	.03	.01	.00
☐ 362 Zane Smith	.06	.03	.00
☐ 363 Larry Walker	.35	.17	.03
☐ 364 Tim Wallach	.08	.04	.01
☐ 365 Rick Aguilera	.03	.01	.00
☐ 366 Allan Anderson	.06	.03	.00
☐ 367 Wally Backman	.03	.01	.00
☐ 368 Doug Baker	.03	.01	.00
☐ 369 Juan Berenguer	.03	.01	.00
☐ 370 Randy Bush	.03	.01	.00
☐ 371 Carmen Castillo	.03	.01	.00
☐ 372 Mike Dyer	.12	.06	.01
☐ 373 Gary Gaetti	.08	.04	.01
☐ 374 Greg Gagne	.03	.01	.00
☐ 375 Dan Gladden	.03	.01	.00
☐ 376 German Gonzalez UER (bio says 31 saves in '88, but stats say 30)	.06	.03	.00
☐ 377 Brian Harper	.03	.01	.00
☐ 378 Kent Hrbek	.08	.04	.01
☐ 379 Gene Larkin	.03	.01	.00
☐ 380 Tim Laudner UER (no decimal point before '85 BA of 238)	.03	.01	.00
☐ 381 John Moses	.03	.01	.00
☐ 382 Al Newman	.03	.01	.00
☐ 383 Kirby Puckett	.25	.12	.02
☐ 384 Shane Rawley	.03	.01	.00
☐ 385 Jeff Reardon	.06	.03	.00
☐ 386 Roy Smith	.03	.01	.00
☐ 387 Gary Wayne	.10	.05	.01

☐ 388	Dave West	.06	.03	.00
☐ 389	Tim Belcher	.06	.03	.00
☐ 390	Tim Crews UER	.03	.01	.00
	(stats say 163 IP for			
	'83, but bio says 136)			
☐ 391	Mike Davis	.03	.01	.00
☐ 392	Rick Dempsey	.03	.01	.00
☐ 393	Kirk Gibson	.08	.04	.01
☐ 394	Jose Gonzalez	.03	.01	.00
☐ 395	Alfredo Griffin	.03	.01	.00
☐ 396	Jeff Hamilton	.03	.01	.00
☐ 397	Lenny Harris	.03	.01	.00
☐ 398	Mickey Hatcher	.03	.01	.00
☐ 399	Orel Hershiser	.08	.04	.01
☐ 400	Jay Howell	.03	.01	.00
☐ 401	Mike Marshall	.08	.04	.01
☐ 402	Ramon Martinez	.40	.20	.04
☐ 403	Mike Morgan	.03	.01	.00
☐ 404	Eddie Murray	.12	.06	.01
☐ 405	Alejandro Pena	.03	.01	.00
☐ 406	Willie Randolph	.06	.03	.00
☐ 407	Mike Scioscia	.03	.01	.00
☐ 408	Ray Searage	.03	.01	.00
☐ 409	Fernando Valenzuela	.08	.04	.01
☐ 410	Jose Vizcaino	.15	.07	.01
☐ 411	John Wetteland	.12	.06	.01
☐ 412	Jack Armstrong	.15	.07	.01
☐ 413	Todd Benzinger UER	.03	.01	.00
	(bio says .323 at			
	Pawtucket, but			
	stats say .321)			
☐ 414	Tim Birtsas	.03	.01	.00
☐ 415	Tom Browning	.06	.03	.00
☐ 416	Norm Charlton	.06	.03	.00
☐ 417	Eric Davis	.18	.09	.01
☐ 418	Rob Dibble	.06	.03	.00
☐ 419	John Franco	.06	.03	.00
☐ 420	Ken Griffey Sr.	.06	.03	.00
☐ 421	Chris Hammond	.20	.10	.02
	(no 1989 used for			
	"Did Not Play" stat)			
☐ 422	Danny Jackson	.06	.03	.00
☐ 423	Barry Larkin	.15	.07	.01
☐ 424	Tim Leary	.06	.03	.00
☐ 425	Rick Mahler	.03	.01	.00
☐ 426	Joe Oliver	.12	.06	.01
☐ 427	Paul O'Neill	.08	.04	.01
☐ 428	Luis Quinones	.03	.01	.00
☐ 429	Jeff Reed	.03	.01	.00
☐ 430	Jose Rijo	.08	.04	.01
☐ 431	Ron Robinson	.03	.01	.00
☐ 432	Rolando Roomes	.06	.03	.00
☐ 433	Chris Sabo	.15	.07	.01
☐ 434	Scott Scudder	.18	.09	.01
☐ 435	Herm Winningham	.03	.01	.00
☐ 436	Steve Balboni	.03	.01	.00
☐ 437	Jesse Barfield	.08	.04	.01
☐ 438	Mike Blowers	.20	.10	.02
☐ 439	Tom Brookens	.03	.01	.00
☐ 440	Greg Cadaret	.03	.01	.00
☐ 441	Alvaro Espinoza UER	.03	.01	.00
	(career games say			
	218, should be 219)			
☐ 442	Bob Geren	.08	.04	.01
☐ 443	Lee Guetterman	.03	.01	.00
☐ 444	Mel Hall	.06	.03	.00
☐ 445	Andy Hawkins	.03	.01	.00
☐ 446	Roberto Kelly	.10	.05	.01
☐ 447	Don Mattingly	.40	.20	.04
☐ 448	Lance McCullers	.03	.01	.00
☐ 449	Hensley Meulens	.30	.15	.03
☐ 450	Dale Mohorcic	.03	.01	.00
☐ 451	Clay Parker	.03	.01	.00
☐ 452	Eric Plunk	.03	.01	.00
☐ 453	Dave Righetti	.08	.04	.01
☐ 454	Deion Sanders	.30	.15	.03
☐ 455	Steve Sax	.08	.04	.01
☐ 456	Don Slaught	.03	.01	.00
☐ 457	Walt Terrell	.03	.01	.00
☐ 458	Dave Winfield	.10	.05	.01
☐ 459	Jay Bell	.03	.01	.00
☐ 460	Rafael Belliard	.03	.01	.00
☐ 461	Barry Bonds	.20	.10	.02
☐ 462	Bobby Bonilla	.15	.07	.01
☐ 463	Sid Bream	.03	.01	.00
☐ 464	Benny Distefano	.03	.01	.00
☐ 465	Doug Drabek	.08	.04	.01
☐ 466	Jim Gott	.03	.01	.00
☐ 467	Billy Hatcher UER	.06	.03	.00
	(.1 hits for Cubs			
	in 1984)			
☐ 468	Neal Heaton	.03	.01	.00
☐ 469	Jeff King	.06	.03	.00
☐ 470	Bob Kipper	.03	.01	.00
☐ 471	Randy Kramer	.03	.01	.00
☐ 472	Bill Landrum	.03	.01	.00
☐ 473	Mike LaValliere	.03	.01	.00
☐ 474	Jose Lind	.03	.01	.00
☐ 475	Junior Ortiz	.03	.01	.00
☐ 476	Gary Redus	.03	.01	.00
☐ 477	Rick Reed	.12	.06	.01
☐ 478	R.J. Reynolds	.03	.01	.00
☐ 479	Jeff Robinson	.03	.01	.00
☐ 480	John Smiley	.03	.01	.00
☐ 481	Andy Van Slyke	.08	.04	.01
☐ 482	Bob Walk	.03	.01	.00
☐ 483	Andy Allanson	.03	.01	.00
☐ 484	Scott Bailes	.03	.01	.00
☐ 485	Joey Belle UER	.20	.10	.02
	(has Jay Bell			
	"Did You Know")			
☐ 486	Bud Black	.03	.01	.00
☐ 487	Jerry Browne	.03	.01	.00
☐ 488	Tom Candiotti	.03	.01	.00
☐ 489	Joe Carter	.10	.05	.01
☐ 490	Dave Clark	.03	.01	.00
	(no '84 stats)			
☐ 491	John Farrell	.03	.01	.00
☐ 492	Felix Fermin	.03	.01	.00
☐ 493	Brook Jacoby	.06	.03	.00
☐ 494	Dion James	.03	.01	.00
☐ 495	Doug Jones	.06	.03	.00
☐ 496	Brad Komminsk	.03	.01	.00
☐ 497	Rod Nichols	.06	.03	.00
☐ 498	Pete O'Brien	.06	.03	.00
☐ 499	Steve Olin	.10	.05	.01
☐ 500	Jesse Orosco	.03	.01	.00
☐ 501	Joel Skinner	.03	.01	.00
☐ 502	Cory Snyder	.08	.04	.01
☐ 503	Greg Swindell	.08	.04	.01
☐ 504	Rich Yett	.03	.01	.00
☐ 505	Scott Bankhead	.06	.03	.00
☐ 506	Scott Bradley	.03	.01	.00
☐ 507	Greg Briley UER	.12	.06	.01
	(28 SB's in bio,			
	but 27 in stats)			
☐ 508	Jay Buhner	.06	.03	.00
☐ 509	Darnell Coles	.03	.01	.00
☐ 510	Keith Comstock	.03	.01	.00
☐ 511	Henry Cotto	.03	.01	.00
☐ 512	Alvin Davis	.08	.04	.01
☐ 513	Ken Griffey Jr.	2.25	1.10	.22
☐ 514	Erik Hanson	.08	.04	.01
☐ 515	Gene Harris	.10	.05	.01
☐ 516	Brian Holman	.03	.01	.00
☐ 517	Mike Jackson	.03	.01	.00
☐ 518	Randy Johnson	.06	.03	.00
☐ 519	Jeffrey Leonard	.03	.01	.00
☐ 520	Edgar Martinez	.10	.05	.01
☐ 521	Dennis Powell	.03	.01	.00
☐ 522	Jim Presley	.03	.01	.00
☐ 523	Jerry Reed	.03	.01	.00
☐ 524	Harold Reynolds	.06	.03	.00
☐ 525	Mike Schooler	.06	.03	.00
☐ 526	Bill Swift	.03	.01	.00
☐ 527	Dave Valle	.03	.01	.00
☐ 528	Omar Vizquel	.08	.04	.01
☐ 529	Ivan Calderon	.06	.03	.00
☐ 530	Carlton Fisk UER	.10	.05	.01
	(Bellow Falls, should			
	be Bellows Falls)			
☐ 531	Scott Fletcher	.03	.01	.00
☐ 532	Dave Gallagher	.06	.03	.00
☐ 533	Ozzie Guillen	.06	.03	.00
☐ 534	Greg Hibbard	.18	.09	.01
☐ 535	Shawn Hillegas	.03	.01	.00
☐ 536	Lance Johnson	.03	.01	.00
☐ 537	Eric King	.03	.01	.00
☐ 538	Ron Kittle	.06	.03	.00
☐ 539	Steve Lyons	.03	.01	.00
☐ 540	Carlos Martinez	.12	.06	.01
☐ 541	Tom McCarthy	.10	.05	.01
☐ 542	Matt Merullo	.12	.06	.01
	(had 5 ML runs scored			
	entering '90, not 6)			
☐ 543	Donn Pall UER	.03	.01	.00
	(stats say pro career			
	began in '85,			
	bio says '88)			
☐ 544	Dan Pasqua	.03	.01	.00
☐ 545	Ken Patterson	.03	.01	.00
☐ 546	Melido Perez	.06	.03	.00
☐ 547	Steve Rosenberg	.08	.04	.01
☐ 548	Sammy Sosa	.50	.25	.05
☐ 549	Bobby Thigpen	.08	.04	.01
☐ 550	Robin Ventura	.30	.15	.03
☐ 551	Greg Walker	.03	.01	.00
☐ 552	Don Carman	.03	.01	.00

☐ 553 Pat Combs	.12	.06	.01
☐ 554 Dennis Cook	.06	.03	.00
☐ 555 Darren Daulton	.06	.03	.00
☐ 556 Len Dykstra	.10	.05	.01
☐ 557 Curt Ford	.03	.01	.00
☐ 558 Charlie Hayes	.06	.03	.00
☐ 559 Von Hayes	.08	.04	.01
☐ 560 Tommy Herr	.06	.03	.00
☐ 561 Ken Howell	.03	.01	.00
☐ 562 Steve Jeltz	.03	.01	.00
☐ 563 Ron Jones	.06	.03	.00
☐ 564 Ricky Jordan UER (duplicate line of statistics on back)	.12	.06	.01
☐ 565 John Kruk	.03	.01	.00
☐ 566 Steve Lake	.03	.01	.00
☐ 567 Roger McDowell	.06	.03	.00
☐ 568 Terry Mulholland UER ("Did You Know" refers to Dave Magadan)	.03	.01	.00
☐ 569 Dwayne Murphy	.03	.01	.00
☐ 570 Jeff Parrett	.03	.01	.00
☐ 571 Randy Ready	.03	.01	.00
☐ 572 Bruce Ruffin	.03	.01	.00
☐ 573 Dickie Thon	.03	.01	.00
☐ 574 Jose Alvarez UER ('78 and '79 stats are reversed)	.03	.01	.00
☐ 575 Geronimo Berroa	.06	.03	.00
☐ 576 Jeff Blauser	.03	.01	.00
☐ 577 Joe Boever	.03	.01	.00
☐ 578 Marty Clary UER (no comma between city and state)	.03	.01	.00
☐ 579 Jody Davis	.03	.01	.00
☐ 580 Mark Eichhorn	.03	.01	.00
☐ 581 Darrell Evans	.06	.03	.00
☐ 582 Ron Gant	.20	.10	.02
☐ 583 Tom Glavine	.06	.03	.00
☐ 584 Tommy Greene	.25	.12	.02
☐ 585 Tommy Gregg	.03	.01	.00
☐ 586 Dave Justice	3.00	1.50	.30
☐ 587 Mark Lemke	.08	.04	.01
☐ 588 Derek Lilliquist	.06	.03	.00
☐ 589 Oddibe McDowell	.06	.03	.00
☐ 590 Kent Mercker ERA (bio says 2.75 ERA, stats say 2.68 ERA)	.20	.10	.02
☐ 591 Dale Murphy	.12	.06	.01
☐ 592 Gerald Perry	.03	.01	.00
☐ 593 Lonnie Smith	.06	.03	.00
☐ 594 Pete Smith	.03	.01	.00
☐ 595 John Smoltz	.08	.04	.01
☐ 596 Mike Stanton UER (no comma between city and state)	.12	.06	.01
☐ 597 Andres Thomas	.03	.01	.00
☐ 598 Jeff Treadway	.03	.01	.00
☐ 599 Doyle Alexander	.03	.01	.00
☐ 600 Dave Bergman	.03	.01	.00
☐ 601 Brian Dubois	.10	.05	.01
☐ 602 Paul Gibson	.03	.01	.00
☐ 603 Mike Heath	.03	.01	.00
☐ 604 Mike Henneman	.03	.01	.00
☐ 605 Guillermo Hernandez	.03	.01	.00
☐ 606 Shawn Holman	.12	.06	.01
☐ 607 Tracy Jones	.03	.01	.00
☐ 608 Chet Lemon	.03	.01	.00
☐ 609 Fred Lynn	.08	.04	.01
☐ 610 Jack Morris	.08	.04	.01
☐ 611 Matt Nokes	.03	.01	.00
☐ 612 Gary Pettis	.03	.01	.00
☐ 613 Kevin Ritz	.10	.05	.01
☐ 614 Jeff Robinson ('88 stats are not in line)	.03	.01	.00
☐ 615 Steve Searcy	.03	.01	.00
☐ 616 Frank Tanana	.06	.03	.00
☐ 617 Alan Trammell	.08	.04	.01
☐ 618 Gary Ward	.03	.01	.00
☐ 619 Lou Whitaker	.08	.04	.01
☐ 620 Frank Williams	.03	.01	.00
☐ 621A George Brett '80 ERR (had 10 .390 hitting seasons)	2.50	1.25	.25
☐ 621A George Brett '80 COR	.18	.09	.01
☐ 622 Fern.Valenzuela '81	.08	.04	.01
☐ 623 Dale Murphy '82	.10	.05	.01
☐ 624A Cal Ripken '83 ERR (misspelled Ripkin on card back)	2.50	1.25	.25
☐ 624B Cal Ripken '83 COR	.18	.09	.01
☐ 625 Ryne Sandberg '84	.15	.07	.01

☐ 626 Don Mattingly '85	.30	.15	.03
☐ 627 Roger Clemens '86	.15	.07	.01
☐ 628 George Bell '87	.08	.04	.01
☐ 629 Jose Canseco '88 UER (Reggie won MVP in '83, should say '73)	.50	.25	.05
☐ 630A Will Clark '89 ERR (32 total bases on card back)	2.50	1.25	.25
☐ 630B Will Clark '89 COR (321 total bases; technically still an error, listing only 24 runs)	.30	.15	.03
☐ 631 Game Savers Mark Davis Mitch Williams	.06	.03	.00
☐ 632 Boston Igniters Wade Boggs Mike Greenwell	.15	.07	.01
☐ 633 Starter and Stopper Mark Gubicza Jeff Russell	.06	.03	.00
☐ 634 League's Best Shortstops Tony Fernandez Cal Ripken	.08	.04	.01
☐ 635 Human Dynamos Kirby Puckett Bo Jackson	.25	.12	.02
☐ 636 300 Strikeout Club Nolan Ryan Mike Scott	.15	.07	.01
☐ 637 The Dynamic Duo Will Clark Kevin Mitchell	.20	.10	.02
☐ 638 AL All-Stars Don Mattingly Mark McGwire	.20	.10	.02
☐ 639 NL East Rivals Howard Johnson Ryne Sandberg	.12	.06	.01
☐ 640 Rudy Seanez Colin Charland	.15	.07	.01
☐ 641 George Canale Kevin Maas	3.00	1.50	.30
☐ 642 Kelly Mann Dave Hansen	.25	.12	.02
☐ 643 Greg Smith Stu Tate	.20	.10	.02
☐ 644 Tom Drees Dan Howitt	.20	.10	.02
☐ 645 Mike Roesler Derrick May	.75	.35	.07
☐ 646 Scott Hemond Mark Gardner	.30	.15	.03
☐ 647 John Orton Scott Leius	.15	.07	.01
☐ 648 Rich Monteleone Dana Williams	.15	.07	.01
☐ 649 Mike Huff Steve Frey	.20	.10	.02
☐ 650 Chuck McElroy Moises Alou	.35	.17	.03
☐ 651 Bobby Rose Mike Hartley	.20	.10	.02
☐ 652 Matt Kinzer Wayne Edwards	.20	.10	.02
☐ 653 Delino DeShields Jason Grimsley	.75	.35	.07
☐ 654 CL: A's/Cubs Giants/Blue Jays	.06	.01	.00
☐ 655 CL: Royals/Angels Padres/Orioles	.06	.01	.00
☐ 656 CL: Mets/Astros Cards/Red Sox	.06	.01	.00
☐ 657 CL: Rangers/Brewers Expos/Twins	.06	.01	.00
☐ 658 CL: Dodgers/Reds Yankees/Pirates	.06	.01	.00
☐ 659 CL: Indians/Mariners White Sox/Phillies	.06	.01	.00
☐ 660 CL: Braves/Tigers Specials/Checklists	.06	.01	.00

1990 Fleer Wax Box Cards

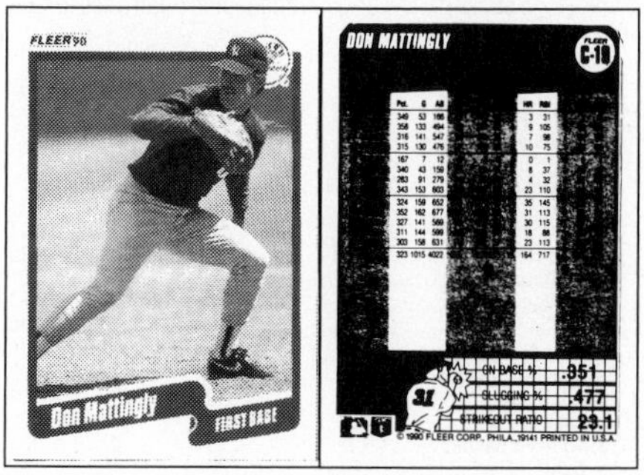

The 1990 Fleer wax box cards comprise seven different box bottoms with four cards each, for a total of 28 standard-size (2 1/2" by 3 1/2") cards. The outer front borders are white; the inner, ribbon-like borders are different depending on the team. The vertically-oriented backs are gray. The cards are numbered with a C prefix.

	MINT	EXC	G-VG
COMPLETE SET (28)	6.00	3.00	.60
COMMON PLAYER (C1-C28)	.10	.05	.01
☐ C1 Giants Logo	.10	.05	.01
☐ C2 Tim Belcher	.10	.05	.01
☐ C3 Roger Clemens	.60	.30	.06
☐ C4 Eric Davis	.50	.25	.05
☐ C5 Glenn Davis	.25	.12	.02
☐ C6 Cubs Logo	.10	.05	.01
☐ C7 John Franco	.15	.07	.01
☐ C8 Mike Greenwell	.40	.20	.04
☐ C9 A's Logo	.10	.05	.01
☐ C10 Ken Griffey Jr.	1.50	.75	.15
☐ C11 Pedro Guerrero	.15	.07	.01
☐ C12 Tony Gwynn	.35	.17	.03
☐ C13 Blue Jays Logo	.10	.05	.01
☐ C14 Orel Hershiser	.25	.12	.02
☐ C15 Bo Jackson	1.25	.60	.12
☐ C16 Howard Johnson	.20	.10	.02
☐ C17 Mets Logo	.10	.05	.01
☐ C18 Cardinals Logo	.10	.05	.01
☐ C19 Don Mattingly	1.00	.50	.10
☐ C20 Mark McGwire	.75	.35	.07
☐ C21 Kevin Mitchell	.40	.20	.04
☐ C22 Kirby Puckett	.40	.20	.04
☐ C23 Royals Logo	.10	.05	.01
☐ C24 Orioles Logo	.10	.05	.01
☐ C25 Ruben Sierra	.50	.25	.05
☐ C26 Dave Stewart	.20	.10	.02
☐ C27 Jerome Walton	.75	.35	.07
☐ C28 Robin Yount	.40	.20	.04

1990 Fleer All-Star Inserts

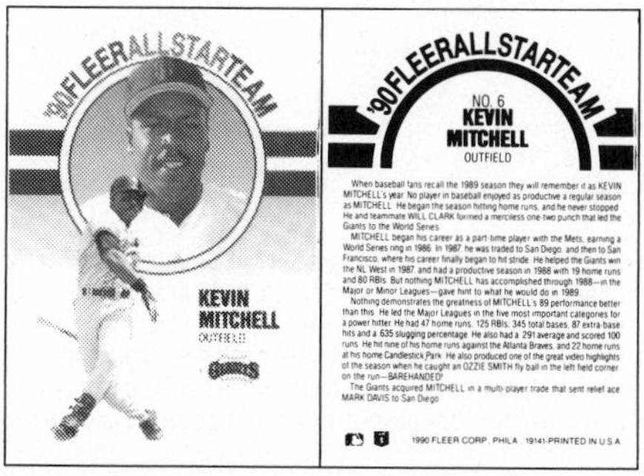

The 1990 Fleer All-Star insert set includes 12 standard-size (2 1/2" by 3 1/2") cards. The fronts are white with a light gray screen and bright red stripes. The vertically-oriented backs are red, pink and white. The player selection for the set is Fleer's opinion of the best Major Leaguer at each position. Cards were individually distributed as an insert in 33-card cellos and random wax packs.

	MINT	EXC	G-VG
COMPLETE SET (12)	9.00	4.50	.90
COMMON PLAYER (1-12)	.25	.12	.02
☐ 1 Harold Baines Designated Hitter	.35	.17	.03
☐ 2 Will Clark First Base	2.00	1.00	.20
☐ 3 Mark Davis Relief Pitcher	.50	.25	.05
☐ 4 Howard Johnson UER Third Base (in middle of 5th line, the is misspelled th)	.50	.25	.05
☐ 5 Joe Magrane Left Handed Pitcher	.35	.17	.03
☐ 6 Kevin Mitchell Outfielder	.90	.45	.09
☐ 7 Kirby Puckett Outfielder	1.00	.50	.10
☐ 8 Cal Ripken Shortstop	.90	.45	.09
☐ 9 Ryne Sandberg Second Base	1.25	.60	.12
☐ 10 Mike Scott Right Handed Pitcher	.50	.25	.05
☐ 11 Ruben Sierra Outfielder	1.00	.50	.10
☐ 12 Mickey Tettleton Catcher	.35	.17	.03

1990 Fleer League Standouts

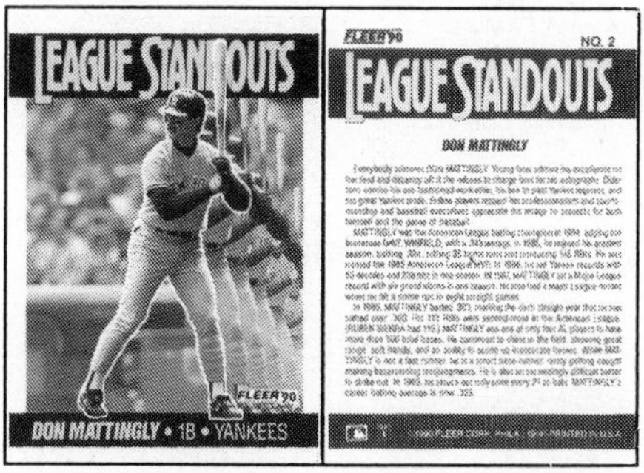

This six-card subset was distributed randomly (as an insert) in Fleer's 45-card rack packs. These cards are standard size, 2 1/2" by 3 1/2" and are quite attractive. The set is subtitled "Standouts" and commemorates outstanding events for those players from the previous season. The cards are numbered on the backs. The card backs are printed on white card stock.

	MINT	EXC	G-VG
COMPLETE SET (6)	5.00	2.50	.50
COMMON PLAYER (1-6)	.65	.30	.06
☐ 1 Barry Larkin Cincinnati Reds	.65	.30	.06
☐ 2 Don Mattingly New York Yankees	1.25	.60	.12
☐ 3 Darryl Strawberry New York Mets	1.00	.50	.10
☐ 4 Jose Canseco Oakland A's	1.50	.75	.15
☐ 5 Wade Boggs Boston Red Sox	1.00	.50	.10

☐ 6 Mark Grace Chicago Cubs	1.25	.60	.12

1990 Fleer Soaring Stars

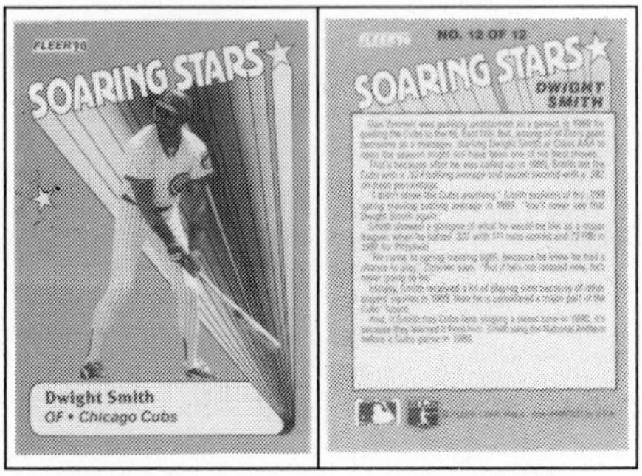

The 1990 Fleer Soaring Stars set was issued by Fleer in their jumbo cello packs. This 12-card, standard-size (2 1/2" by 3 1/2") set featured 12 of the most popular young players entering the 1990 season. The set gives the visual impression of rockets exploding in the air to honor these young players.

	MINT	EXC	G-VG
COMPLETE SET (12)	6.00	3.00	.60
COMMON PLAYER (1-12)	.30	.15	.03
☐ 1 Todd Zeile	.75	.35	.07
☐ 2 Mike Stanton	.30	.15	.03
☐ 3 Larry Walker	.50	.25	.05
☐ 4 Robin Ventura	.75	.35	.07
☐ 5 Scott Coolbaugh	.30	.15	.03
☐ 6 Ken Griffey Jr.	2.00	1.00	.20
☐ 7 Tom Gordon	.50	.25	.05
☐ 8 Jerome Walton	.75	.35	.07
☐ 9 Junior Felix	.75	.35	.07
☐ 10 Jim Abbott	.75	.35	.07
☐ 11 Ricky Jordan	.50	.25	.05
☐ 12 Dwight Smith	.50	.25	.05

1990 Fleer Award Winners

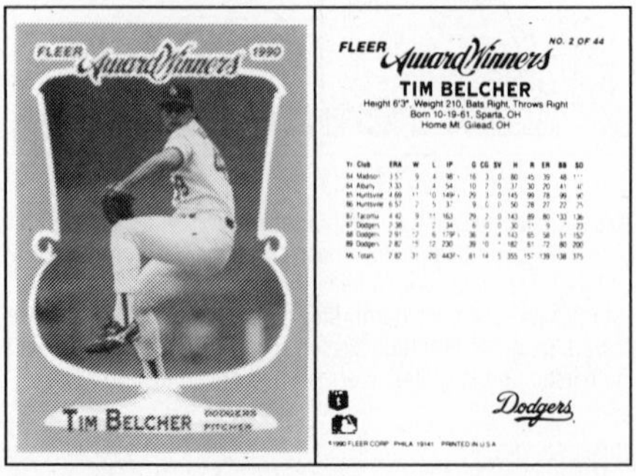

The 1990 Fleer Award Winners set was printed by Fleer for Hills stores (as well as for some 7/Eleven's) and released early in the summer of 1990. The set features an unattractive design of a face inside solid blue borders with the players photo within the face caricature. This 44-card, standard-size (2 1/2" by 3 1/2") set is numbered in alphabetical order. Card number 10 is listed on the box checklist as being Ron Darling, but Darling is not in the set. Consequently the numbers on the box checklist between 10 and 37 are off by one. Darryl Strawberry (38) is not listed on the box, but is included in the set. The box also includes six peel-off team logo stickers. The original suggested retail price for the set at Hills was 2.49.

	MINT	EXC	G-VG
COMPLETE SET (44)	4.00	2.00	.40
COMMON PLAYER (1-44)	.10	.05	.01
☐ 1 Jeff Ballard	.10	.05	.01
☐ 2 Tim Belcher	.10	.05	.01
☐ 3 Bert Blyleven	.15	.07	.01
☐ 4 Wade Boggs	.50	.25	.05
☐ 5 Bob Boone	.15	.07	.01
☐ 6 Jose Canseco	1.00	.50	.10
☐ 7 Will Clark	.80	.40	.08
☐ 8 Jack Clark	.15	.07	.01
☐ 9 Vince Coleman	.20	.10	.02
☐ 10 Eric Davis	.40	.20	.04
☐ 11 Jóse DeLeon	.10	.05	.01
☐ 12 Tony Fernandez	.15	.07	.01
☐ 13 Carlton Fisk	.20	.10	.02
☐ 14 Scott Garrelts	.10	.05	.01
☐ 15 Tom Gordon	.20	.10	.02
☐ 16 Ken Griffey Jr.	1.25	.60	.12
☐ 17 Von Hayes	.15	.07	.01
☐ 18 Rickey Henderson	.75	.35	.07
☐ 19 Bo Jackson	1.00	.50	.10
☐ 20 Howard Johnson	.15	.07	.01
☐ 21 Don Mattingly	1.00	.50	.10
☐ 22 Fred McGriff	.20	.10	.02
☐ 23 Kevin Mitchell	.30	.15	.03
☐ 24 Greg Olson	.20	.10	.02
☐ 25 Gary Pettis	.10	.05	.01
☐ 26 Kirby Puckett	.40	.20	.04
☐ 27 Harold Reynolds	.10	.05	.01
☐ 28 Jeff Russell	.10	.05	.01
☐ 29 Nolan Ryan	1.00	.50	.10
☐ 30 Bret Saberhagen	.25	.12	.02
☐ 31 Ryne Sandberg	.75	.35	.07
☐ 32 Benito Santiago	.20	.10	.02
☐ 33 Mike Scott	.15	.07	.01
☐ 34 Ruben Sierra	.40	.20	.04
☐ 35 Lonnie Smith	.10	.05	.01
☐ 36 Ozzie Smith	.20	.10	.02
☐ 37 Dave Stewart	.20	.10	.02
☐ 38 Darryl Strawberry	.50	.25	.05
☐ 39 Greg Swindell	.15	.07	.01
☐ 40 Andy Van Slyke	.15	.07	.01
☐ 41 Tim Wallach	.15	.07	.01
☐ 42 Jerome Walton	.30	.15	.03
☐ 43 Mitch Williams	.10	.05	.01
☐ 44 Robin Yount	.35	.17	.03

1990 Fleer Baseball All-Stars

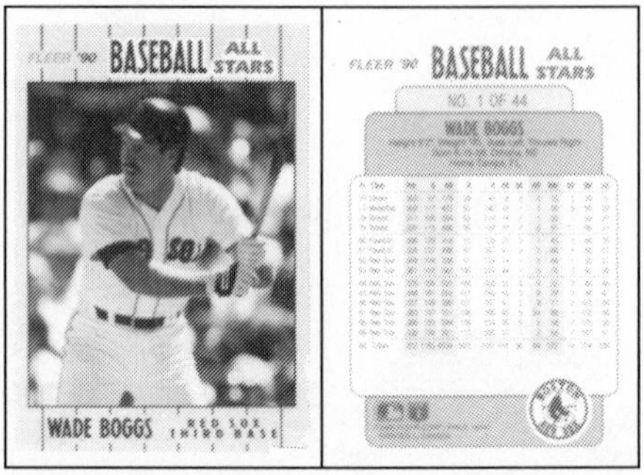

The 1990 Fleer Baseball All-Stars Set was produced by Fleer for the Ben Franklin chain and released early in the summer of 1990. This standard-size (2 1/2" by 3 1/2"), 44-card set features some of the best of today's players in alphabetical order. The design of the cards has vertical stripes on the front of the card. The set's custom box gives the set checklist on the back panel.

The box also includes six peel-off team logo stickers each with a trivia quiz on back.

	MINT	EXC	G-VG
COMPLETE SET (44)	4.00	2.00	.40
COMMON PLAYER (1-44)	.10	.05	.01

☐ 1 Wade Boggs	.50	.25	.05
☐ 2 Bobby Bonilla	.30	.15	.03
☐ 3 Tim Burke	.10	.05	.01
☐ 4 Jose Canseco	1.00	.50	.10
☐ 5 Will Clark	.80	.40	.08
☐ 6 Eric Davis	.40	.20	.04
☐ 7 Glenn Davis	.20	.10	.02
☐ 8 Julio Franco	.15	.07	.01
☐ 9 Tony Fernandez	.15	.07	.01
☐ 10 Gary Gaetti	.15	.07	.01
☐ 11 Scott Garrelts	.10	.05	.01
☐ 12 Mark Grace	.50	.25	.05
☐ 13 Mike Greenwell	.35	.17	.03
☐ 14 Ken Griffey Jr.	1.25	.60	.12
☐ 15 Mark Gubicza	.10	.05	.01
☐ 16 Pedro Guerrero	.15	.07	.01
☐ 17 Von Hayes	.15	.07	.01
☐ 18 Orel Hershiser	.20	.10	.02
☐ 19 Bruce Hurst	.10	.05	.01
☐ 20 Bo Jackson	1.00	.50	.10
☐ 21 Howard Johnson	.15	.07	.01
☐ 22 Doug Jones	.10	.05	.01
☐ 23 Barry Larkin	.20	.10	.02
☐ 24 Don Mattingly	1.00	.50	.10
☐ 25 Mark McGwire	.60	.30	.06
☐ 26 Kevin McReynolds	.15	.07	.01
☐ 27 Kevin Mitchell	.25	.12	.02
☐ 28 Dan Plesac	.10	.05	.01
☐ 29 Kirby Puckett	.35	.17	.03
☐ 30 Cal Ripken Jr.	.30	.15	.03
☐ 31 Bret Saberhagen	.20	.10	.02
☐ 32 Ryne Sandberg	.75	.35	.07
☐ 33 Steve Sax	.15	.07	.01
☐ 34 Ruben Sierra	.35	.17	.03
☐ 35 Ozzie Smith	.20	.10	.02
☐ 36 John Smoltz	.15	.07	.01
☐ 37 Daryl Strawberry	.40	.20	.04
☐ 38 Terry Steinbach	.15	.07	.01
☐ 39 Dave Stewart	.20	.10	.02
☐ 40 Bobby Thigpen	.20	.10	.02
☐ 41 Alan Trammell	.20	.10	.02
☐ 42 Devon White	.15	.07	.01
☐ 43 Mitch Williams	.10	.05	.01
☐ 44 Robin Yount	.35	.17	.03

1990 Fleer Baseball MVP's

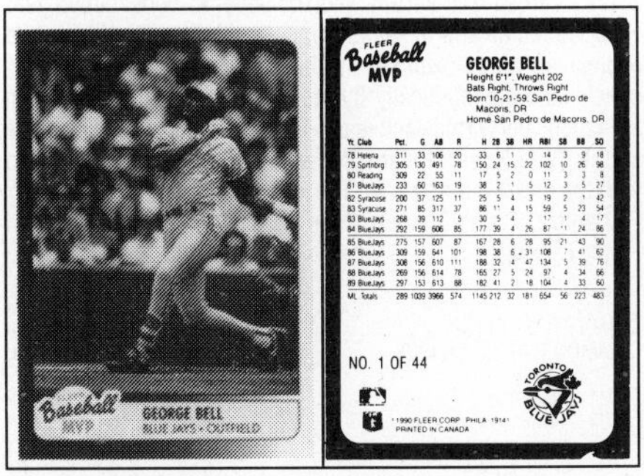

The 1990 Fleer Baseball MVP's were produced by Fleer exclusively for the Toys'R'Us chain and released early in the summer of 1990. This set has a multi-colored border, is standard size, 2 1/2" by 3 1/2", and has 44 players arranged in alphabetical order. The set's custom box gives the set checklist on the back panel. The box also includes six peel-off team logo stickers.

	MINT	EXC	G-VG
COMPLETE SET (44)	4.00	2.00	.40
COMMON PLAYER (1-44)	.10	.05	.01

☐ 1 George Bell	.20	.10	.02
☐ 2 Bert Blyleven	.15	.07	.01
☐ 3 Wade Boggs	.50	.25	.05
☐ 4 Bobby Bonilla	.30	.15	.03
☐ 5 George Brett	.35	.17	.03
☐ 6 Jose Canseco	1.00	.50	.10
☐ 7 Will Clark	.80	.40	.08
☐ 8 Roger Clemens	.60	.30	.06
☐ 9 Eric Davis	.40	.20	.04
☐ 10 Glenn Davis	.20	.10	.02
☐ 11 Tony Fernandez	.15	.07	.01
☐ 12 Dwight Gooden	.30	.15	.03
☐ 13 Mike Greenwell	.30	.15	.03
☐ 14 Ken Griffey Jr.	1.25	.60	.12
☐ 15 Pedro Guerrero	.15	.07	.01
☐ 16 Tony Gwynn	.30	.15	.03
☐ 17 Rickey Henderson	.75	.35	.07
☐ 18 Tom Herr	.10	.05	.01
☐ 19 Orel Hershiser	.20	.10	.02
☐ 20 Kent Hrbek	.15	.07	.01
☐ 21 Bo Jackson	1.00	.50	.10
☐ 22 Howard Johnson	.15	.07	.01
☐ 23 Don Mattingly	1.00	.50	.10
☐ 24 Fred McGriff	.25	.12	.02
☐ 25 Mark McGwire	.60	.30	.06
☐ 26 Kevin Mitchell	.40	.20	.04
☐ 27 Paul Molitor	.15	.07	.01
☐ 28 Dale Murphy	.30	.15	.03
☐ 29 Kirby Purkett	.35	.17	.03
☐ 30 Tim Raines	.20	.10	.02
☐ 31 Cal Ripken Jr.	.30	.15	.03
☐ 32 Bret Saberhagen	.20	.10	.02
☐ 33 Ryne Sandberg	.75	.35	.07
☐ 34 Ruben Sierra	.30	.15	.03
☐ 35 Dwight Smith	.20	.10	.02
☐ 36 Ozzie Smith	.20	.10	.02
☐ 37 Darryl Strawberry	.40	.20	.04
☐ 38 Dave Stewart	.20	.10	.02
☐ 39 Greg Swindell	.15	.07	.01
☐ 40 Bobby Thigpen	.20	.10	.02
☐ 41 Alan Trammell	.20	.10	.02
☐ 42 Jerome Walton	.30	.15	.03
☐ 43 Mitch Williams	.10	.05	.01
☐ 44 Robin Yount	.30	.15	.03

1990 Fleer League Leaders

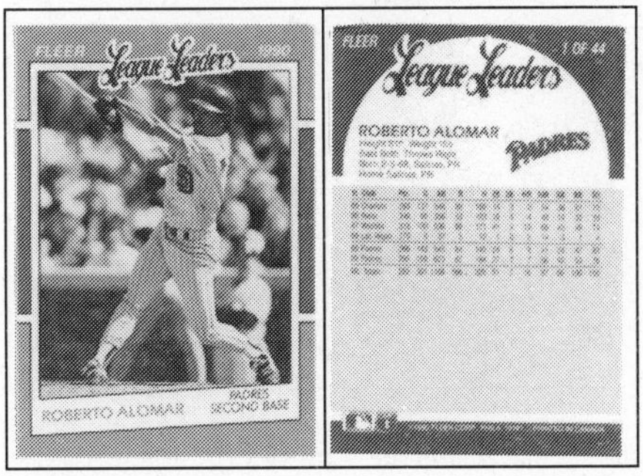

The 1990 Fleer League Leader set was issued by Fleer for Walgreen stores. This set design features solid blue borders with the players photo inset within the middle of the card. This 44-card, standard-size (2 1/2" by 3 1/2") set is numbered in alphabetical order. The set's custom box gives the set checklist on the back panel. The box also includes six peel-off team logo stickers. The original suggested retail price for the set at Walgreen's was 2.49.

	MINT	EXC	G-VG
COMPLETE SET (44)	4.00	2.00	.40
COMMON PLAYER (1-44)	.10	.05	.01

☐ 1 Roberto Alomar	.25	.12	.02
☐ 2 Tim Belcher	.15	.07	.01
☐ 3 George Bell	.15	.07	.01
☐ 4 Wade Boggs	.50	.25	.05
☐ 5 Jose Canseco	1.00	.50	.10

	MINT	EXC	G-VG
☐ 6 Will Clark	.80	.40	.08
☐ 7 David Cone	.20	.10	.02
☐ 8 Eric Davis	.40	.20	.04
☐ 9 Glenn Davis	.20	.10	.02
☐ 10 Nick Esasky	.10	.05	.01
☐ 11 Dennis Eckersley	.20	.10	.02
☐ 12 Mark Grace	.60	.30	.06
☐ 13 Mike Greenwell	.30	.15	.03
☐ 14 Ken Griffey Jr.	1.25	.60	.12
☐ 15 Mark Gubicza	.10	.05	.01
☐ 16 Pedro Guerrero	.15	.07	.01
☐ 17 Tony Gwynn	.30	.15	.03
☐ 18 Rickey Henderson	.75	.35	.07
☐ 19 Bo Jackson	1.00	.50	.10
☐ 20 Doug Jones	.10	.05	.01
☐ 21 Ricky Jordan	.15	.07	.01
☐ 22 Barry Larkin	.20	.10	.02
☐ 23 Don Mattingly	1.00	.50	.10
☐ 24 Fred McGriff	.25	.12	.02
☐ 25 Mark McGwire	.60	.30	.06
☐ 26 Kevin Mitchell	.30	.15	.03
☐ 27 Jack Morris	.15	.07	.01
☐ 28 Greg Olson	.20	.10	.02
☐ 29 Dan Plesac	.10	.05	.01
☐ 30 Kirby Puckett	.30	.15	.03
☐ 31 Nolan Ryan	1.00	.50	.10
☐ 32 Bret Saberhagen	.20	.10	.02
☐ 33 Ryne Sandberg	.75	.35	.07
☐ 34 Steve Sax	.15	.07	.01
☐ 35 Mike Scott	.15	.07	.01
☐ 36 Ruben Sierra	.30	.15	.03
☐ 37 Lonnie Smith	.10	.05	.01
☐ 38 Darryl Strawberry	.40	.20	.04
☐ 39 Bobby Thigpen	.20	.10	.02
☐ 40 Andy Van Slyke	.15	.07	.01
☐ 41 Tim Wallach	.15	.07	.01
☐ 42 Jerome Walton UER (photo actually Doug Dascenzo)	.30	.15	.03
☐ 43 Devon White	.15	.07	.01
☐ 44 Robin Yount	.30	.15	.03

1990 Fleer World Series

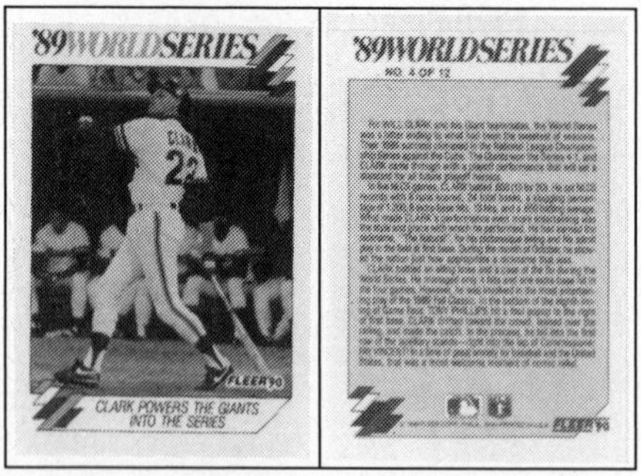

This 12-card standard size, 2 1/2" by 3 1/2" set was issued as an insert in with the Fleer factory sets, celebrating the 1989 World Series. This set marked the fourth year that Fleer issued a special World Series set in their factory (or vend) set. The design of these cards are different from the regular Fleer issue as the photo is framed by a white border with red and blue World Series cards and the player description in black.

	MINT	EXC	G-VG
COMPLETE SET (12)	3.00	1.50	.30
COMMON PLAYER (1-12)	.25	.12	.02
☐ 1 Mike Moore The final piece of the puzzle	.25	.12	.02
☐ 2 Kevin Mitchell N.L. MVP	.50	.25	.05
☐ 3 Terry Steinbach Game Two's Crushing Blow	.25	.12	.02
☐ 4 Will Clark Clark Powers Giants into the Series	.75	.35	.07
☐ 5 Jose Canseco Canseco Crushed World Series Slump	1.00	.50	.10
☐ 6 Walt Weiss Great Leather in the field	.25	.12	.02
☐ 7 Terry Steinbach Game One and A's Break Out on Top	.25	.12	.02
☐ 8 Dave Stewart Oakland's MVP	.35	.17	.03
☐ 9 Dave Parker Parker's Bat Produces Power	.35	.17	.03
☐ 10 Dave Parker, Jose Canseco, and Will Clark: World Series Record Book Game 3	.50	.25	.05
☐ 11 Rickey Henderson Henderson Swipes Championship Series Records	.75	.35	.07
☐ 12 Oakland A's Celebrate Oakland A's: Baseball's Best in 89	.25	.12	.02

1990 Fleer Update

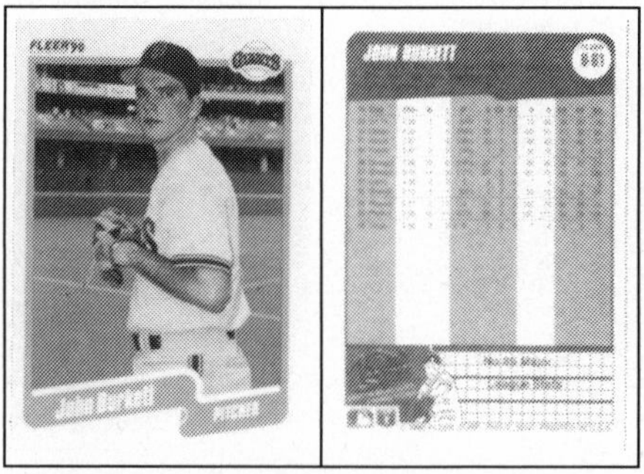

The 1990 Fleer Update set contains 132 standard-size (2 1/2" by 3 1/2") cards. This set marked the seventh consecutive year Fleer issued an end of season Update set. The set was issued exclusively as a boxed set through hobby dealers. The set is checklisted alphabetically by team for each league and then alphabetically within each team. The fronts are styled the same as the 1990 Fleer regular issue set. The backs are numbered with the prefix U for Update. The key rookies in this set are Alex Fernandez, Travis Fryman, Jose Offerman, John Olerud, and Frank Thomas.

	MINT	EXC	G-VG
COMPLETE SET (132)	11.00	5.50	1.10
COMMON PLAYER (1-132)	.06	.03	.00
☐ U1 Steve Avery	.30	.10	.02
☐ U2 Francisco Cabrera	.15	.07	.01
☐ U3 Nick Esasky	.10	.05	.01
☐ U4 Jim Kremers	.15	.07	.01
☐ U5 Greg Olson	.25	.12	.02
☐ U6 Jim Presley	.06	.03	.00
☐ U7 Shawn Boskie	.20	.10	.02
☐ U8 Joe Kraemer	.12	.06	.01
☐ U9 Luis Salazar	.06	.03	.00
☐ U10 Hector Villanueve	.25	.12	.02
☐ U11 Glenn Braggs	.10	.05	.01
☐ U12 Mariano Duncan	.10	.05	.01
☐ U13 Billy Hatcher	.10	.05	.01
☐ U14 Tim Layana	.20	.10	.02
☐ U15 Hal Morris	.25	.12	.02
☐ U16 Javier Ortiz	.12	.06	.01
☐ U17 Dave Rohde	.15	.07	.01
☐ U18 Eric Yelding	.20	.10	.02

☐ U19 Hubie Brooks	.10	.05	.01
☐ U20 Kal Daniels	.10	.05	.01
☐ U21 Dave Hansen	.20	.10	.02
☐ U22 Mike Hartley	.10	.05	.01
☐ U23 Stan Javier	.06	.03	.00
☐ U24 Jose Offerman	1.00	.50	.10
☐ U25 Juan Samuel	.10	.05	.01
☐ U26 Dennis Boyd	.10	.05	.01
☐ U27 Delino DeShields	.60	.30	.06
☐ U28 Steve Frey	.10	.05	.01
☐ U29 Mark Gardner	.10	.05	.01
☐ U30 Chris Nabholz	.25	.12	.02
☐ U31 Bill Sampen	.20	.10	.02
☐ U32 Dave Schmidt	.06	.03	.00
☐ U33 Daryl Boston	.10	.05	.01
☐ U34 Chuck Carr	.15	.07	.01
☐ U35 John Franco	.10	.05	.01
☐ U36 Todd Hundley	.20	.10	.02
☐ U37 Julio Machado	.12	.06	.01
☐ U38 Alejandro Pena	.06	.03	.00
☐ U39 Darren Reed	.15	.07	.01
☐ U40 Kelvin Torve	.10	.05	.01
☐ U41 Darrel Akerfelds	.06	.03	.00
☐ U42 Jose DeJesus	.10	.05	.01
☐ U43 Dave Hollins (misspelled Dane on card back)	.25	.12	.02
☐ U44 Carmelo Martinez	.06	.03	.00
☐ U45 Brad Moore	.10	.05	.01
☐ U46 Dale Murphy	.15	.07	.01
☐ U47 Wally Backman	.06	.03	.00
☐ U48 Stan Belinda	.15	.07	.01
☐ U49 Bob Patterson	.06	.03	.00
☐ U50 Ted Power	.06	.03	.00
☐ U51 Don Slaught	.06	.03	.00
☐ U52 Geronimo Pena	.15	.07	.01
☐ U53 Lee Smith	.10	.05	.01
☐ U54 John Tudor	.10	.05	.01
☐ U55 Joe Carter	.12	.06	.01
☐ U56 Tom Howard	.15	.07	.01
☐ U57 Craig Lefferts	.06	.03	.00
☐ U58 Rafael Valdez	.15	.07	.01
☐ U59 Dave Anderson	.06	.03	.00
☐ U60 Kevin Bass	.10	.05	.01
☐ U61 John Burkett	.15	.07	.01
☐ U62 Gary Carter	.10	.05	.01
☐ U63 Rick Parker	.12	.06	.01
☐ U64 Trevor Wilson	.12	.06	.01
☐ U65 Chris Hoiles	.25	.12	.02
☐ U66 Tim Hulett	.06	.03	.00
☐ U67 Dave Johnson	.12	.06	.01
☐ U68 Curt Schilling	.10	.05	.01
☐ U69 David Segui	.35	.17	.03
☐ U70 Tom Brunansky	.10	.05	.01
☐ U71 Greg Harris	.06	.03	.00
☐ U72 Dana Kiecker	.20	.10	.02
☐ U73 Tim Naehring	.25	.12	.02
☐ U74 Tony Pena	.10	.05	.01
☐ U75 Jeff Reardon	.10	.05	.01
☐ U76 Jerry Reed	.06	.03	.00
☐ U77 Mark Eichhorn	.06	.03	.00
☐ U78 Mark Langston	.10	.05	.01
☐ U79 John Orton	.06	.03	.00
☐ U80 Luis Polonia	.06	.03	.00
☐ U81 Dave Winfield	.12	.06	.01
☐ U82 Cliff Young	.15	.07	.01
☐ U83 Wayne Edwards	.10	.05	.01
☐ U84 Alex Fernandez	1.75	.85	.17
☐ U85 Craig Grebeck	.15	.07	.01
☐ U86 Scott Radinsky	.20	.10	.02
☐ U87 Frank Thomas	1.75	.85	.17
☐ U88 Beau Allred	.15	.07	.01
☐ U89 Sandy Alomar Jr.	.30	.15	.03
☐ U90 Carlos Baerga	.35	.17	.03
☐ U91 Kevin Bearse	.15	.07	.01
☐ U92 Chris James	.10	.05	.01
☐ U93 Candy Maldonado	.10	.05	.01
☐ U94 Jeff Manto	.10	.05	.01
☐ U95 Cecil Fielder	.50	.25	.05
☐ U96 Travis Fryman	.80	.40	.08
☐ U97 Lloyd Moseby	.10	.05	.01
☐ U98 Edwin Nunez	.06	.03	.00
☐ U99 Tony Phillips	.06	.03	.00
☐ U100 Larry Sheets	.06	.03	.00
☐ U101 Mark Davis	.12	.06	.01
☐ U102 Storm Davis	.10	.05	.01
☐ U103 Gerald Perry	.06	.03	.00
☐ U104 Terry Shumpert	.15	.07	.01
☐ U105 Edgar Diaz	.12	.06	.01
☐ U106 Dave Parker	.10	.05	.01
☐ U107 Tim Drummond	.12	.06	.01
☐ U108 Junior Ortiz	.06	.03	.00
☐ U109 Park Pittman	.15	.07	.01
☐ U110 Kevin Tapani	.20	.10	.02
☐ U111 Oscar Azocar	.35	.17	.03
☐ U112 Jim Leyritz	.25	.12	.02
☐ U113 Kevin Maas	2.00	1.00	.20
☐ U114 Alan Mills	.15	.07	.01
☐ U115 Matt Nokes	.10	.05	.01
☐ U116 Pascual Perez	.10	.05	.01
☐ U117 Ozzie Canseco	.45	.22	.04
☐ U118 Scott Sanderson	.10	.05	.01
☐ U119 Tino Martinez	.75	.35	.07
☐ U120 Jeff Schneider	.12	.06	.01
☐ U121 Matt Young	.06	.03	.00
☐ U122 Brian Bohanon	.15	.07	.01
☐ U123 Jeff Huson	.10	.05	.01
☐ U124 Ramon Manon	.15	.07	.01
☐ U125 Gary Mielke UER (shown as Blue Jay on front)	.10	.05	.01
☐ U126 Willie Blair	.10	.05	.01
☐ U127 Glenallen Hill	.12	.06	.01
☐ U128 John Olerud	1.75	.85	.17
☐ U129 Luis Sojo	.15	.07	.01
☐ U130 Mark Whiten	.50	.25	.05
☐ U131 Nolan Ryan	1.00	.50	.10
☐ U132 Checklist Card	.06	.01	.00

1991 Fleer

The 1991 Fleer Set consists of 720 cards which measure the now standard size of 2 1/2" by 3 1/2". This set marks Fleer's eleventh consecutive year of issuing sets of current players. This set does not have what has been a Fleer tradition in recent years, the two-player rookie cards and there are less two-player special cards than in prior years. Apparently this was an attempt by Fleer to increase the number of single player cards in the set. The design features solid yellow borders with the information in black indicating name, position, and team. The backs feature beautiful full-color photos along with the career statistics and a biography for those players where there is room. The set is again ordered numerically by teams, followed by combination cards, rookie prospect pairs, and checklists. Again Fleer incorrectly anticipated the outcome of the 1990 Playoffs according to the team ordering. The A's, listed first, did not win the World Series and their opponents (and Series winners) were the Reds, not the Pirates. The complete team ordering is as follows: Oakland A's (1-28), Pittsburgh Pirates (29-54), Cincinnati Reds (55-82), Boston Red Sox (83-113), Chicago White Sox (114-139), New York Mets (140-166), Toronto Blue Jays (167-192), Los Angeles Dodgers (193-223), Montreal Expos (224-251), San Francisco Giants (252-277), Texas Rangers (278-304), California Angels (305-330), Detroit Tigers (331-357), Cleveland Indians (358-385), Philadelphia Phillies (386-412), Chicago Cubs (413-441), Seattle Mariners (442-465), Baltimore Orioles (466-496), Houston Astros (497-522) San Diego Padres (523-548), Kansas City Royals (549-575), Milwaukee Brewers (576-601), Minnesota Twins (602-627), St. Louis Cardinals (628-654), New York Yankees (655-680), and Atlanta Braves (681-708).

	MINT	EXC	G-VG
COMPLETE SET (720)	24.00	12.00	2.40
COMMON PLAYER (1-720)	.03	.01	.00
☐ 1 Troy Afenir	.10	.03	.01
☐ 2 Harold Baines	.08	.04	.01
☐ 3 Lance Blankenship	.03	.01	.00
☐ 4 Todd Burns	.03	.01	.00
☐ 5 Jose Canseco	.30	.15	.03
☐ 6 Dennis Eckersley	.08	.04	.01
☐ 7 Mike Gallego	.03	.01	.00
☐ 8 Ron Hassey	.03	.01	.00
☐ 9 Dave Henderson	.06	.03	.00
☐ 10 Rickey Henderson	.20	.10	.02
☐ 11 Rick Honeycutt	.03	.01	.00
☐ 12 Doug Jennings	.03	.01	.00
☐ 13 Joe Klink	.08	.04	.01
☐ 14 Carney Lansford	.06	.03	.00
☐ 15 Darren Lewis	.30	.15	.03
☐ 16 Willie McGee	.08	.04	.01
☐ 17 Mark McGwire	.20	.10	.02
☐ 18 Mike Moore	.06	.03	.00
☐ 19 Gene Nelson	.03	.01	.00
☐ 20 Dave Otto	.03	.01	.00
☐ 21 Jamie Quirk	.03	.01	.00
☐ 22 Willie Randolph	.06	.03	.00
☐ 23 Scott Sanderson	.03	.01	.00
☐ 24 Terry Steinbach	.06	.03	.00
☐ 25 Dave Stewart	.10	.05	.01
☐ 26 Walt Weiss	.06	.03	.00
☐ 27 Bob Welch	.08	.04	.01
☐ 28 Curt Young	.03	.01	.00
☐ 29 Wally Backman	.03	.01	.00
☐ 30 Stan Belinda	.06	.03	.00
☐ 31 Jay Bell	.03	.01	.00
☐ 32 Rafael Belliard	.03	.01	.00
☐ 33 Barry Bonds	.15	.07	.01
☐ 34 Bobby Bonilla	.12	.06	.01
☐ 35 Sid Bream	.03	.01	.00
☐ 36 Doug Drabek	.08	.04	.01
☐ 37 Carlos Garcia	.10	.05	.01
☐ 38 Neal Heaton	.03	.01	.00
☐ 39 Jeff King	.06	.03	.00
☐ 40 Bob Kipper	.03	.01	.00
☐ 41 Bill Landrum	.03	.01	.00
☐ 42 Mike LaValliere	.03	.01	.00
☐ 43 Jose Lind	.03	.01	.00
☐ 44 Carmelo Martinez	.03	.01	.00
☐ 45 Bob Patterson	.03	.01	.00
☐ 46 Ted Power	.03	.01	.00
☐ 47 Gary Redus	.03	.01	.00
☐ 48 R.J. Reynolds	.03	.01	.00
☐ 49 Don Slaught	.03	.01	.00
☐ 50 John Smiley	.03	.01	.00
☐ 51 Zane Smith	.06	.03	.00
☐ 52 Randy Tomlin	.10	.05	.01
☐ 53 Andy Van Slyke	.08	.04	.01
☐ 54 Bob Walk	.03	.01	.00
☐ 55 Jack Armstrong	.08	.04	.01
☐ 56 Todd Benzinger	.03	.01	.00
☐ 57 Glenn Braggs	.03	.01	.00
☐ 58 Keith Brown	.03	.01	.00
☐ 59 Tom Browning	.06	.03	.00
☐ 60 Norm Charlton	.06	.03	.00
☐ 61 Eric Davis	.12	.06	.01
☐ 62 Rob Dibble	.06	.03	.00
☐ 63 Bill Doran	.06	.03	.00
☐ 64 Mariano Duncan	.06	.03	.00
☐ 65 Chris Hammond	.06	.03	.00
☐ 66 Billy Hatcher	.06	.03	.00
☐ 67 Danny Jackson	.06	.03	.00
☐ 68 Barry Larkin	.10	.05	.01
☐ 69 Tim Layana	.06	.03	.00
☐ 70 Terry Lee	.15	.07	.01
☐ 71 Rick Mahler	.03	.01	.00
☐ 72 Hal Morris	.15	.07	.01
☐ 73 Randy Myers	.06	.03	.00
☐ 74 Ron Oester	.03	.01	.00
☐ 75 Joe Oliver	.06	.03	.00
☐ 76 Paul O'Neill	.08	.04	.01
☐ 77 Luis Quinones	.03	.01	.00
☐ 78 Jeff Reed	.03	.01	.00
☐ 79 Jose Rijo	.06	.03	.00
☐ 80 Chris Sabo	.10	.05	.01
☐ 81 Scott Scudder	.06	.03	.00
☐ 82 Herm Winningham	.03	.01	.00
☐ 83 Larry Anderson	.03	.01	.00
☐ 84 Marty Barrett	.03	.01	.00
☐ 85 Mike Boddicker	.03	.01	.00
☐ 86 Wade Boggs	.15	.07	.01
☐ 87 Tom Bolton	.03	.01	.00
☐ 88 Tom Brunansky	.08	.04	.01
☐ 89 Ellis Burks	.10	.05	.01
☐ 90 Roger Clemens	.15	.07	.01
☐ 91 Scott Cooper	.15	.07	.01
☐ 92 John Dopson	.03	.01	.00
☐ 93 Dwight Evans	.08	.04	.01
☐ 94 Wes Gardner	.03	.01	.00
☐ 95 Jeff Gray	.10	.05	.01
☐ 96 Mike Greenwell	.12	.06	.01
☐ 97 Greg Harris	.03	.01	.00
☐ 98 Daryl Irvine	.10	.05	.01
☐ 99 Dana Kiecker	.06	.03	.00
☐ 100 Randy Kutcher	.03	.01	.00
☐ 101 Dennis Lamp	.03	.01	.00
☐ 102 Mike Marshall	.06	.03	.00
☐ 103 John Marzano	.03	.01	.00
☐ 104 Rob Murphy	.03	.01	.00
☐ 105 Tim Naehring	.20	.10	.02
☐ 106 Tony Pena	.06	.03	.00
☐ 107 Phil Plantier	.50	.25	.05
☐ 108 Carlos Quintana	.08	.04	.01
☐ 109 Jeff Reardon	.06	.03	.00
☐ 110 Jerry Reed	.03	.01	.00
☐ 111 Jody Reed	.08	.04	.01
☐ 112 Luis Rivera	.03	.01	.00
☐ 113 Kevin Romine	.03	.01	.00
☐ 114 Phil Bradley	.06	.03	.00
☐ 115 Ivan Calderon	.06	.03	.00
☐ 116 Wayne Edwards	.06	.03	.00
☐ 117 Alex Fernandez	.90	.45	.09
☐ 118 Carlton Fisk	.10	.05	.01
☐ 119 Scott Fletcher	.03	.01	.00
☐ 120 Craig Grebeck	.03	.01	.00
☐ 121 Ozzie Guillen	.06	.03	.00
☐ 122 Greg Hibbard	.03	.01	.00
☐ 123 Lance Johnson	.03	.01	.00
☐ 124 Barry Jones	.03	.01	.00
☐ 125 Ron Karkovice	.03	.01	.00
☐ 126 Eric King	.03	.01	.00
☐ 127 Steve Lyons	.03	.01	.00
☐ 128 Carlos Martinez	.03	.01	.00
☐ 129 Jack McDowell	.06	.03	.00
☐ 130 Donn Pall	.03	.01	.00
☐ 131 Dan Pasqua	.03	.01	.00
☐ 132 Ken Patterson	.03	.01	.00
☐ 133 Melido Perez	.06	.03	.00
☐ 134 Adam Peterson	.03	.01	.00
☐ 135 Scott Radinsky	.06	.03	.00
☐ 136 Sammy Sosa	.15	.07	.01
☐ 137 Bobby Thigpen	.08	.04	.01
☐ 138 Frank Thomas	.75	.35	.07
☐ 139 Robin Ventura	.15	.07	.01
☐ 140 Daryl Boston	.06	.03	.00
☐ 141 Chuck Carr	.06	.03	.00
☐ 142 Mark Carreon	.03	.01	.00
☐ 143 David Cone	.08	.04	.01
☐ 144 Ron Darling	.06	.03	.00
☐ 145 Kevin Elster	.03	.01	.00
☐ 146 Sid Fernandez	.06	.03	.00
☐ 147 John Franco	.06	.03	.00
☐ 148 Dwight Gooden	.12	.06	.01
☐ 149 Tom Herr	.06	.03	.00
☐ 150 Todd Hundley	.12	.06	.01
☐ 151 Gregg Jefferies	.15	.07	.01
☐ 152 Howard Johnson	.08	.04	.01
☐ 153 Dave Magadan	.08	.04	.01
☐ 154 Kevin McReynolds	.08	.04	.01
☐ 155 Keith Miller	.03	.01	.00
☐ 156 Bob Ojeda	.06	.03	.00
☐ 157 Tom O'Malley	.03	.01	.00
☐ 158 Alejandro Pena	.03	.01	.00
☐ 159 Darren Reed	.06	.03	.00
☐ 160 Mackey Sasser	.06	.03	.00
☐ 161 Darryl Strawberry	.15	.07	.01
☐ 162 Tim Teufel	.03	.01	.00
☐ 163 Kelvin Torve	.03	.01	.00
☐ 164 Julio Valera	.10	.05	.01
☐ 165 Frank Viola	.08	.04	.01
☐ 166 Wally Whitehurst	.03	.01	.00
☐ 167 Jim Acker	.03	.01	.00
☐ 168 Derek Bell	.30	.15	.03
☐ 169 George Bell	.08	.04	.01
☐ 170 Willie Blair	.03	.01	.00
☐ 171 Pat Borders	.06	.03	.00
☐ 172 John Cerutti	.03	.01	.00
☐ 173 Junior Felix	.10	.05	.01
☐ 174 Tony Fernandez	.08	.04	.01
☐ 175 Kelly Gruber	.10	.05	.01
☐ 176 Tom Henke	.06	.03	.00
☐ 177 Glenallen Hill	.06	.03	.00
☐ 178 Jimmy Key	.06	.03	.00
☐ 179 Manny Lee	.03	.01	.00
☐ 180 Fred McGriff	.10	.05	.01
☐ 181 Rance Mulliniks	.03	.01	.00
☐ 182 Greg Myers	.03	.01	.00
☐ 183 John Olerud	.35	.17	.03
☐ 184 Luis Sojo	.06	.03	.00

☐ 185 Dave Stieb	.08	.04	.01
☐ 186 Todd Stottlemyre	.06	.03	.00
☐ 187 Duane Ward	.03	.01	.00
☐ 188 David Wells	.03	.01	.00
☐ 189 Mark Whiten	.25	.12	.02
☐ 190 Ken Williams	.03	.01	.00
☐ 191 Frank Wills	.03	.01	.00
☐ 192 Mookie Wilson	.06	.03	.00
☐ 193 Don Aase	.03	.01	.00
☐ 194 Tim Belcher	.06	.03	.00
☐ 195 Hubie Brooks	.06	.03	.00
☐ 196 Dennis Cook	.03	.01	.00
☐ 197 Tim Crews	.03	.01	.00
☐ 198 Kal Daniels	.08	.04	.01
☐ 199 Kirk Gibson	.08	.04	.01
☐ 200 Jim Gott	.03	.01	.00
☐ 201 Alfredo Griffin	.03	.01	.00
☐ 202 Chris Gwynn	.03	.01	.00
☐ 203 Dave Hansen	.12	.06	.01
☐ 204 Lenny Harris	.06	.03	.00
☐ 205 Mike Hartley	.03	.01	.00
☐ 206 Mickey Hatcher	.03	.01	.00
☐ 207 Carlos Hernandez	.08	.04	.01
☐ 208 Orel Hershiser	.08	.04	.01
☐ 209 Jay Howell	.03	.01	.00
☐ 210 Mike Huff	.08	.04	.01
☐ 211 Stan Javier	.03	.01	.00
☐ 212 Ramon Martinez	.15	.07	.01
☐ 213 Mike Morgan	.03	.01	.00
☐ 214 Eddie Murray	.10	.05	.01
☐ 215 Jim Neidlinger	.15	.07	.01
☐ 216 Jose Offerman	.35	.17	.03
☐ 217 Jim Poole	.10	.05	.01
☐ 218 Juan Samuel	.06	.03	.00
☐ 219 Mike Scioscia	.03	.01	.00
☐ 220 Ray Searage	.03	.01	.00
☐ 221 Mike Sharperson	.03	.01	.00
☐ 222 Fernando Valenzuela	.08	.04	.01
☐ 223 Jose Vizcaino	.06	.03	.00
☐ 224 Mike Aldrete	.03	.01	.00
☐ 225 Scott Anderson	.10	.05	.01
☐ 226 Dennis Boyd	.06	.03	.00
☐ 227 Tim Burke	.06	.03	.00
☐ 228 Delino DeShields	.20	.10	.02
☐ 229 Mike Fitzgerald	.03	.01	.00
☐ 230 Tom Foley	.03	.01	.00
☐ 231 Steve Frey	.03	.01	.00
☐ 232 Andres Galarraga	.08	.04	.01
☐ 233 Mark Gardner	.06	.03	.00
☐ 234 Marquis Grissom	.12	.06	.01
☐ 235 Kevin Gross	.03	.01	.00
☐ 236 Drew Hall	.03	.01	.00
☐ 237 Dave Martinez	.03	.01	.00
☐ 238 Dennis Martinez	.03	.01	.00
☐ 239 Dale Mohorcic	.03	.01	.00
☐ 240 Chris Nabholz	.08	.04	.01
☐ 241 Otis Nixon	.03	.01	.00
☐ 242 Junior Noboa	.03	.01	.00
☐ 243 Spike Owen	.03	.01	.00
☐ 244 Tim Raines	.08	.04	.01
☐ 245 Mel Rojas	.08	.04	.01
☐ 246 Scott Ruskin	.10	.05	.01
☐ 247 Bill Sampen	.06	.03	.00
☐ 248 Nelson Santovenia	.03	.01	.00
☐ 249 Dave Schmidt	.03	.01	.00
☐ 250 Larry Walker	.10	.05	.01
☐ 251 Tim Wallach	.08	.04	.01
☐ 252 Dave Anderson	.03	.01	.00
☐ 253 Kevin Bass	.06	.03	.00
☐ 254 Steve Bedrosian	.06	.03	.00
☐ 255 Jeff Brantley	.06	.03	.00
☐ 256 John Burkett	.06	.03	.00
☐ 257 Brett Butler	.06	.03	.00
☐ 258 Gary Carter	.08	.04	.01
☐ 259 Will Clark	.25	.12	.02
☐ 260 Steve Decker	.30	.15	.03
☐ 261 Kelly Downs	.03	.01	.00
☐ 262 Scott Garrelts	.03	.01	.00
☐ 263 Terry Kennedy	.03	.01	.00
☐ 264 Mike LaCoss	.03	.01	.00
☐ 265 Mark Leonard	.20	.10	.02
☐ 266 Greg Litton	.06	.03	.00
☐ 267 Kevin Mitchell	.15	.07	.01
☐ 268 Randy O'Neal	.03	.01	.00
☐ 269 Rick Parker	.03	.01	.00
☐ 270 Rick Reuschel	.06	.03	.00
☐ 271 Ernest Riles	.03	.01	.00
☐ 272 Don Robinson	.03	.01	.00
☐ 273 Robby Thompson	.03	.01	.00
☐ 274 Mark Thurmond	.03	.01	.00
☐ 275 Jose Uribe	.03	.01	.00
☐ 276 Matt Williams	.12	.06	.01
☐ 277 Trevor Wilson	.06	.03	.00
☐ 278 Gerald Alexander	.10	.05	.01

☐ 279 Brad Arnsberg	.06	.03	.00
☐ 280 Kevin Belcher	.15	.07	.01
☐ 281 Joe Bitker	.10	.05	.01
☐ 282 Kevin Brown	.08	.04	.01
☐ 283 Steve Buechele	.03	.01	.00
☐ 284 Jack Daugherty	.03	.01	.00
☐ 285 Julio Franco	.06	.03	.00
☐ 286 Juan Gonzalez	.25	.12	.02
☐ 287 Bill Haselman	.10	.05	.01
☐ 288 Charlie Hough	.03	.01	.00
☐ 289 Jeff Huson	.03	.01	.00
☐ 290 Pete Incaviglia	.08	.04	.01
☐ 291 Mike Jeffcoat	.03	.01	.00
☐ 292 Jeff Kunkel	.03	.01	.00
☐ 293 Gary Mielke	.03	.01	.00
☐ 294 Jamie Moyer	.03	.01	.00
☐ 295 Rafael Palmeiro	.08	.04	.01
☐ 296 Geno Petralli	.03	.01	.00
☐ 297 Gary Pettis	.03	.01	.00
☐ 298 Kevin Reimer	.08	.04	.01
☐ 299 Kenny Rogers	.03	.01	.00
☐ 300 Jeff Russell	.03	.01	.00
☐ 301 John Russell	.03	.01	.00
☐ 302 Nolan Ryan	.25	.12	.02
☐ 303 Ruben Sierra	.12	.06	.01
☐ 304 Bobby Witt	.08	.04	.01
☐ 305 Jim Abbott	.12	.06	.01
☐ 306 Kent Anderson	.03	.01	.00
☐ 307 Dante Bichette	.06	.03	.00
☐ 308 Bert Blyleven	.06	.03	.00
☐ 309 Chili Davis	.06	.03	.00
☐ 310 Brian Downing	.03	.01	.00
☐ 311 Mark Eichhorn	.03	.01	.00
☐ 312 Mike Fetters	.03	.01	.00
☐ 313 Chuck Finley	.08	.04	.01
☐ 314 Willie Fraser	.03	.01	.00
☐ 315 Bryan Harvey	.03	.01	.00
☐ 316 Donnie Hill	.03	.01	.00
☐ 317 Wally Joyner	.08	.04	.01
☐ 318 Mark Langston	.08	.04	.01
☐ 319 Kirk McCaskill	.03	.01	.00
☐ 320 John Orton	.03	.01	.00
☐ 321 Lance Parrish	.08	.04	.01
☐ 322 Luis Polonia	.03	.01	.00
☐ 323 Johnny Ray	.03	.01	.00
☐ 324 Bobby Rose	.06	.03	.00
☐ 325 Dick Schofield	.03	.01	.00
☐ 326 Rick Schu	.03	.01	.00
☐ 327 Lee Stevens	.15	.07	.01
☐ 328 Devon White	.06	.03	.00
☐ 329 Dave Winfield	.10	.05	.01
☐ 330 Cliff Young	.03	.01	.00
☐ 331 Dave Bergman	.03	.01	.00
☐ 332 Phil Clark	.20	.10	.02
☐ 333 Darnell Coles	.03	.01	.00
☐ 334 Milt Cuyler	.15	.07	.01
☐ 335 Cecil Fielder	.20	.10	.02
☐ 336 Travis Fryman	.40	.20	.04
☐ 337 Paul Gibson	.03	.01	.00
☐ 338 Jerry Don Gleaton	.03	.01	.00
☐ 339 Mike Heath	.03	.01	.00
☐ 340 Mike Henneman	.03	.01	.00
☐ 341 Chet Lemon	.03	.01	.00
☐ 342 Lance McCullers	.03	.01	.00
☐ 343 Jack Morris	.06	.03	.00
☐ 344 Lloyd Moseby	.06	.03	.00
☐ 345 Edwin Nunez	.03	.01	.00
☐ 346 Clay Parker	.03	.01	.00
☐ 347 Dan Petry	.03	.01	.00
☐ 348 Tony Phillips	.03	.01	.00
☐ 349 Jeff Robinson	.03	.01	.00
☐ 350 Mark Salas	.03	.01	.00
☐ 351 Mike Schwabe	.03	.01	.00
☐ 352 Larry Sheets	.03	.01	.00
☐ 353 John Shelby	.03	.01	.00
☐ 354 Frank Tanana	.03	.01	.00
☐ 355 Alan Trammell	.08	.04	.01
☐ 356 Gary Ward	.03	.01	.00
☐ 357 Lou Whitaker	.06	.03	.00
☐ 358 Beau Allred	.06	.03	.00
☐ 359 Sandy Alomar Jr.	.15	.07	.01
☐ 360 Carlos Baerga	.15	.07	.01
☐ 361 Kevin Bearse	.03	.01	.00
☐ 362 Tom Brookens	.03	.01	.00
☐ 363 Jerry Browne	.03	.01	.00
☐ 364 Tom Candiotti	.03	.01	.00
☐ 365 Alex Cole	.20	.10	.02
☐ 366 John Farrell	.03	.01	.00
☐ 367 Felix Fermin	.03	.01	.00
☐ 368 Keith Hernandez	.08	.04	.01
☐ 369 Brook Jacoby	.06	.03	.00
☐ 370 Chris James	.06	.03	.00
☐ 371 Dion James	.03	.01	.00
☐ 372 Doug Jones	.06	.03	.00

☐ 373 Candy Maldonado	.06	.03	.00
☐ 374 Steve Olin	.03	.01	.00
☐ 375 Jesse Orosco	.03	.01	.00
☐ 376 Rudy Seanez	.03	.01	.00
☐ 377 Joel Skinner	.03	.01	.00
☐ 378 Cory Snyder	.08	.04	.01
☐ 379 Greg Swindell	.06	.03	.00
☐ 380 Sergio Valdez	.08	.04	.01
☐ 381 Mike Walker	.08	.04	.01
☐ 382 Colby Ward	.10	.05	.01
☐ 383 Turner Ward	.20	.10	.02
☐ 384 Mitch Webster	.03	.01	.00
☐ 385 Kevin Wickander	.03	.01	.00
☐ 386 Darrel Akerfelds	.03	.01	.00
☐ 387 Joe Boever	.03	.01	.00
☐ 388 Rod Booker	.03	.01	.00
☐ 389 Sil Campusano	.03	.01	.00
☐ 390 Don Carman	.03	.01	.00
☐ 391 Wes Chamberlain	.30	.15	.03
☐ 392 Pat Combs	.06	.03	.00
☐ 393 Darren Daulton	.06	.03	.00
☐ 394 Jose DeJesus	.03	.01	.00
☐ 395 Len Dykstra	.08	.04	.01
☐ 396 Jason Grimsley	.03	.01	.00
☐ 397 Charlie Hayes	.06	.03	.00
☐ 398 Von Hayes	.08	.04	.01
☐ 399 David Hollins	.10	.05	.01
☐ 400 Ken Howell	.03	.01	.00
☐ 401 Ricky Jordan	.06	.03	.00
☐ 402 John Kruk	.03	.01	.00
☐ 403 Steve Lake	.03	.01	.00
☐ 404 Chuck Malone	.08	.04	.01
☐ 405 Roger McDowell	.03	.01	.00
☐ 406 Chuck McElroy	.03	.01	.00
☐ 407 Mickey Morandini	.15	.07	.01
☐ 408 Terry Mulholland	.03	.01	.00
☐ 409 Dale Murphy	.10	.05	.01
☐ 410 Randy Ready	.03	.01	.00
☐ 411 Bruce Ruffin	.03	.01	.00
☐ 412 Dickie Thon	.03	.01	.00
☐ 413 Paul Assenmacher	.03	.01	.00
☐ 414 Damon Berryhill	.03	.01	.00
☐ 415 Mike Bielecki	.03	.01	.00
☐ 416 Shawn Boskie	.06	.03	.00
☐ 417 Dave Clark	.03	.01	.00
☐ 418 Doug Dascenzo	.03	.01	.00
☐ 419 Andre Dawson	.10	.05	.01
☐ 420 Shawon Dunston	.08	.04	.01
☐ 421 Joe Girardi	.03	.01	.00
☐ 422 Mark Grace	.15	.07	.01
☐ 423 Mike Harkey	.08	.04	.01
☐ 424 Les Lancaster	.03	.01	.00
☐ 425 Bill Long	.03	.01	.00
☐ 426 Greg Maddux	.06	.03	.00
☐ 427 Derrick May	.30	.15	.03
☐ 428 Jeff Pico	.03	.01	.00
☐ 429 Domingo Ramos	.03	.01	.00
☐ 430 Luis Salazar	.03	.01	.00
☐ 431 Ryne Sandberg	.15	.07	.01
☐ 432 Dwight Smith	.06	.03	.00
☐ 433 Greg Smith	.06	.03	.00
☐ 434 Rick Sutcliffe	.06	.03	.00
☐ 435 Gary Varsho	.03	.01	.00
☐ 436 Hector Villanueva	.10	.05	.01
☐ 437 Jerome Walton	.20	.10	.02
☐ 438 Curtis Wilkerson	.03	.01	.00
☐ 439 Mitch Williams	.03	.01	.00
☐ 440 Steve Wilson	.03	.01	.00
☐ 441 Marvell Wynne	.03	.01	.00
☐ 442 Scott Bankhead	.03	.01	.00
☐ 443 Scott Bradley	.03	.01	.00
☐ 444 Greg Briley	.06	.03	.00
☐ 445 Mike Brumley	.03	.01	.00
☐ 446 Jay Buhner	.06	.03	.00
☐ 447 Dave Burba	.10	.05	.01
☐ 448 Henry Cotto	.03	.01	.00
☐ 449 Alvin Davis	.08	.04	.01
☐ 450 Ken Griffey Jr.	.75	.35	.07
☐ 451 Erik Hanson	.10	.05	.01
☐ 452 Gene Harris	.03	.01	.00
☐ 453 Brian Holman	.06	.03	.00
☐ 454 Mike Jackson	.03	.01	.00
☐ 455 Randy Johnson	.06	.03	.00
☐ 456 Jeffrey Leonard	.06	.03	.00
☐ 457 Edgar Martinez	.06	.03	.00
☐ 458 Tino Martinez	.30	.15	.03
☐ 459 Pete O'Brien	.06	.03	.00
☐ 460 Harold Reynolds	.06	.03	.00
☐ 461 Mike Schooler	.03	.01	.00
☐ 462 Bill Swift	.03	.01	.00
☐ 463 David Valle	.03	.01	.00
☐ 464 Omar Vizquel	.03	.01	.00
☐ 465 Matt Young	.03	.01	.00
☐ 466 Brady Anderson	.03	.01	.00
☐ 467 Jeff Ballard	.03	.01	.00
☐ 468 Juan Bell	.08	.04	.01
☐ 469 Mike Devereaux	.03	.01	.00
☐ 470 Steve Finley	.06	.03	.00
☐ 471 Dave Gallagher	.03	.01	.00
☐ 472 Leo Gomez	.40	.20	.04
☐ 473 Rene Gonzales	.03	.01	.00
☐ 474 Pete Harnisch	.03	.01	.00
☐ 475 Kevin Hickey	.03	.01	.00
☐ 476 Chris Hoiles	.12	.06	.01
☐ 477 Sam Horn	.06	.03	.00
☐ 478 Tim Hulett	.03	.01	.00
☐ 479 Dave Johnson	.03	.01	.00
☐ 480 Ron Kittle	.06	.03	.00
☐ 481 Ben McDonald	.25	.12	.02
☐ 482 Bob Melvin	.03	.01	.00
☐ 483 Bob Milacki	.03	.01	.00
☐ 484 Randy Milligan	.08	.04	.01
☐ 485 John Mitchell	.03	.01	.00
☐ 486 Gregg Olson	.10	.05	.01
☐ 487 Joe Orsulak	.03	.01	.00
☐ 488 Joe Price	.03	.01	.00
☐ 489 Bill Ripken	.03	.01	.00
☐ 490 Cal Ripken Jr.	.12	.06	.01
☐ 491 Curt Schilling	.03	.01	.00
☐ 492 David Segui	.25	.12	.02
☐ 493 Anthony Telford	.10	.05	.01
☐ 494 Mickey Tettleton	.06	.03	.00
☐ 495 Mark Williamson	.03	.01	.00
☐ 496 Craig Worthington	.06	.03	.00
☐ 497 Juan Agosto	.03	.01	.00
☐ 498 Eric Anthony	.15	.07	.01
☐ 499 Craig Biggio	.06	.03	.00
☐ 500 Ken Caminiti	.03	.01	.00
☐ 501 Casey Candaele	.03	.01	.00
☐ 502 Andujar Cedeno	.50	.25	.05
☐ 503 Danny Darwin	.03	.01	.00
☐ 504 Mark Davidson	.03	.01	.00
☐ 505 Glenn Davis	.08	.04	.01
☐ 506 Jim Deshaies	.03	.01	.00
☐ 507 Luis Gonzalez	.10	.05	.01
☐ 508 Bill Gullickson	.03	.01	.00
☐ 509 Xavier Hernandez	.08	.04	.01
☐ 510 Brian Meyer	.03	.01	.00
☐ 511 Ken Oberkfell	.03	.01	.00
☐ 512 Mark Portugal	.03	.01	.00
☐ 513 Rafael Ramirez	.03	.01	.00
☐ 514 Karl Rhodes	.10	.05	.01
☐ 515 Mike Scott	.08	.04	.01
☐ 516 Mike Simms	.10	.05	.01
☐ 517 Dave Smith	.03	.01	.00
☐ 518 Franklin Stubbs	.06	.03	.00
☐ 519 Glenn Wilson	.03	.01	.00
☐ 520 Eric Yelding	.06	.03	.00
☐ 521 Gerald Young	.03	.01	.00
☐ 522 Shawn Abner	.06	.03	.00
☐ 523 Roberto Alomar	.08	.04	.01
☐ 524 Andy Benes	.10	.05	.01
☐ 525 Joe Carter	.08	.04	.01
☐ 526 Jack Clark	.08	.04	.01
☐ 527 Joey Cora	.03	.01	.00
☐ 528 Paul Faries	.10	.05	.01
☐ 529 Tony Gwynn	.12	.06	.01
☐ 530 Atlee Hammaker	.03	.01	.00
☐ 531 Greg Harris	.06	.03	.00
☐ 532 Thomas Howard	.06	.03	.00
☐ 533 Bruce Hurst	.06	.03	.00
☐ 534 Craig Lefferts	.03	.01	.00
☐ 535 Derek Lilliquist	.03	.01	.00
☐ 536 Fred Lynn	.06	.03	.00
☐ 537 Mike Pagliarulo	.03	.01	.00
☐ 538 Mark Parent	.03	.01	.00
☐ 539 Dennis Rasmussen	.03	.01	.00
☐ 540 Bip Roberts	.06	.03	.00
☐ 541 Richard Rodriguez	.06	.03	.00
☐ 542 Benito Santiago	.08	.04	.01
☐ 543 Calvin Schiraldi	.03	.01	.00
☐ 544 Eric Show	.03	.01	.00
☐ 545 Phil Stephenson	.03	.01	.00
☐ 546 Garry Templeton	.03	.01	.00
☐ 547 Ed Whitson	.03	.01	.00
☐ 548 Eddie Williams	.03	.01	.00
☐ 549 Kevin Appier	.08	.04	.01
☐ 550 Luis Aquino	.03	.01	.00
☐ 551 Bob Boone	.06	.03	.00
☐ 552 George Brett	.12	.06	.01
☐ 553 Jeff Conine	.50	.25	.05
☐ 554 Steve Crawford	.03	.01	.00
☐ 555 Mark Davis	.08	.04	.01
☐ 556 Storm Davis	.06	.03	.00
☐ 557 Jim Eisenreich	.03	.01	.00
☐ 558 Steve Farr	.03	.01	.00
☐ 559 Tom Gordon	.10	.05	.01
☐ 560 Mark Gubicza	.06	.03	.00

☐ 561	Bo Jackson	.30	.15	.03
☐ 562	Mike Macfarlane	.03	.01	.00
☐ 563	Brian McRae	.60	.30	.06
☐ 564	Jeff Montgomery	.06	.03	.00
☐ 565	Bill Pecota	.03	.01	.00
☐ 566	Gerald Perry	.03	.01	.00
☐ 567	Bret Saberhagen	.08	.04	.01
☐ 568	Jeff Schulz	.10	.05	.01
☐ 569	Kevin Seitzer	.08	.04	.01
☐ 570	Terry Shumpert	.06	.03	.00
☐ 571	Kurt Stillwell	.06	.03	.00
☐ 572	Danny Tartabull	.08	.04	.01
☐ 573	Gary Thurman	.03	.01	.00
☐ 574	Frank White	.06	.03	.00
☐ 575	Willie Wilson	.06	.03	.00
☐ 576	Chris Bosio	.03	.01	.00
☐ 577	Greg Brock	.03	.01	.00
☐ 578	George Canale	.03	.01	.00
☐ 579	Chuck Crim	.03	.01	.00
☐ 580	Rob Deer	.06	.03	.00
☐ 581	Edgar Diaz	.06	.03	.00
☐ 582	Tom Edens	.10	.05	.01
☐ 583	Mike Felder	.03	.01	.00
☐ 584	Jim Gantner	.03	.01	.00
☐ 585	Darryl Hamilton	.03	.01	.00
☐ 586	Ted Higuera	.06	.03	.00
☐ 587	Mark Knudson	.03	.01	.00
☐ 588	Bill Krueger	.03	.01	.00
☐ 589	Tim McIntosh	.08	.04	.01
☐ 590	Paul Mirabella	.03	.01	.00
☐ 591	Paul Molitor	.08	.04	.01
☐ 592	Jaime Navarro	.06	.03	.00
☐ 593	Dave Parker	.08	.04	.01
☐ 594	Dan Plesac	.03	.01	.00
☐ 595	Ron Robinson	.03	.01	.00
☐ 596	Gary Sheffield	.12	.06	.01
☐ 597	Bill Spiers	.03	.01	.00
☐ 598	B.J. Surhoff	.06	.03	.00
☐ 599	Greg Vaughn	.12	.06	.01
☐ 600	Randy Veres	.03	.01	.00
☐ 601	Robin Yount	.12	.06	.01
☐ 602	Rick Aguilera	.03	.01	.00
☐ 603	Allan Anderson	.03	.01	.00
☐ 604	Juan Berenguer	.03	.01	.00
☐ 605	Randy Bush	.03	.01	.00
☐ 606	Carmen Castillo	.03	.01	.00
☐ 607	Tim Drummond	.03	.01	.00
☐ 608	Scott Erickson	.15	.07	.01
☐ 609	Gary Gaetti	.08	.04	.01
☐ 610	Greg Gagne	.03	.01	.00
☐ 611	Dan Gladden	.03	.01	.00
☐ 612	Mark Guthrie	.08	.04	.01
☐ 613	Brian Harper	.03	.01	.00
☐ 614	Kent Hrbek	.08	.04	.01
☐ 615	Gene Larkin	.03	.01	.00
☐ 616	Terry Leach	.03	.01	.00
☐ 617	Nelson Liriano	.03	.01	.00
☐ 618	Shane Mack	.06	.03	.00
☐ 619	John Moses	.03	.01	.00
☐ 620	Pedro Munoz	.15	.07	.01
☐ 621	Al Newman	.03	.01	.00
☐ 622	Junior Ortiz	.03	.01	.00
☐ 623	Kirby Puckett	.15	.07	.01
☐ 624	Roy Smith	.03	.01	.00
☐ 625	Kevin Tapani	.08	.04	.01
☐ 626	Gary Wayne	.03	.01	.00
☐ 627	David West	.03	.01	.00
☐ 628	Cris Carpenter	.03	.01	.00
☐ 629	Vince Coleman	.08	.04	.01
☐ 630	Ken Dayley	.03	.01	.00
☐ 631	Jose DeLeon	.03	.01	.00
☐ 632	Frank DiPino	.03	.01	.00
☐ 633	Bernard Gilkey	.25	.12	.02
☐ 634	Pedro Guerrero	.08	.04	.01
☐ 635	Ken Hill	.06	.03	.00
☐ 636	Felix Jose	.06	.03	.00
☐ 637	Ray Lankford	.40	.20	.04
☐ 638	Joe Magrane	.06	.03	.00
☐ 639	Tom Niedenfuer	.03	.01	.00
☐ 640	Jose Oquendo	.03	.01	.00
☐ 641	Tom Pagnozzi	.03	.01	.00
☐ 642	Terry Pendleton	.03	.01	.00
☐ 643	Mike Perez	.10	.05	.01
☐ 644	Bryn Smith	.03	.01	.00
☐ 645	Lee Smith	.06	.03	.00
☐ 646	Ozzie Smith	.08	.04	.01
☐ 647	Scott Terry	.03	.01	.00
☐ 648	Bob Tewksbury	.03	.01	.00
☐ 649	Milt Thompson	.03	.01	.00
☐ 650	John Tudor	.06	.03	.00
☐ 651	Denny Walling	.03	.01	.00
☐ 652	Craig Wilson	.10	.05	.01
☐ 653	Todd Worrell	.06	.03	.00
☐ 654	Todd Zeile	.15	.07	.01
☐ 655	Oscar Azocar	.20	.10	.02
☐ 656	Steve Balboni	.03	.01	.00
☐ 657	Jesse Barfield	.08	.04	.01
☐ 658	Greg Cadaret	.03	.01	.00
☐ 659	Chuck Cary	.03	.01	.00
☐ 660	Rick Cerone	.03	.01	.00
☐ 661	David Eiland	.03	.01	.00
☐ 662	Alvaro Espinoza	.03	.01	.00
☐ 663	Bob Geren	.03	.01	.00
☐ 664	Lee Guetterman	.03	.01	.00
☐ 665	Mel Hall	.03	.01	.00
☐ 666	Andy Hawkins	.03	.01	.00
☐ 667	Jimmy Jones	.03	.01	.00
☐ 668	Roberto Kelly	.08	.04	.01
☐ 669	Dave LaPoint	.03	.01	.00
☐ 670	Tim Leary	.06	.03	.00
☐ 671	Jim Leyritz	.10	.05	.01
☐ 672	Kevin Maas	.40	.20	.04
☐ 673	Don Mattingly	.25	.12	.02
☐ 674	Matt Nokes	.06	.03	.00
☐ 675	Pascual Perez	.06	.03	.00
☐ 676	Eric Plunk	.03	.01	.00
☐ 677	Dave Righetti	.08	.04	.01
☐ 678	Jeff Robinson	.03	.01	.00
☐ 679	Steve Sax	.08	.04	.01
☐ 680	Mike Witt	.03	.01	.00
☐ 681	Steve Avery	.15	.07	.01
☐ 682	Mike Bell	.10	.05	.01
☐ 683	Jeff Blauser	.03	.01	.00
☐ 684	Francisco Cabrera	.06	.03	.00
☐ 685	Tony Castillo	.03	.01	.00
☐ 686	Marty Clary	.03	.01	.00
☐ 687	Nick Esasky	.06	.03	.00
☐ 688	Ron Gant	.10	.05	.01
☐ 689	Tom Glavine	.03	.01	.00
☐ 690	Mark Grant	.03	.01	.00
☐ 691	Tommy Gregg	.03	.01	.00
☐ 692	Dwayne Henry	.03	.01	.00
☐ 693	Dave Justice	.65	.30	.06
☐ 694	Jimmy Kremers	.06	.03	.00
☐ 695	Charlie Leibrandt	.03	.01	.00
☐ 696	Mark Lemke	.03	.01	.00
☐ 697	Oddibe McDowell	.06	.03	.00
☐ 698	Greg Olson	.10	.05	.01
☐ 699	Jeff Parrett	.03	.01	.00
☐ 700	Jim Presley	.03	.01	.00
☐ 701	Victor Rosario	.08	.04	.01
☐ 702	Lonnie Smith	.06	.03	.00
☐ 703	Pete Smith	.03	.01	.00
☐ 704	John Smoltz	.08	.04	.01
☐ 705	Mike Stanton	.03	.01	.00
☐ 706	Andres Thomas	.03	.01	.00
☐ 707	Jeff Treadway	.03	.01	.00
☐ 708	Jim Vatcher	.15	.07	.01
☐ 709	Home Run Kings Ryne Sandberg Cecil Fielder	.15	.07	.01
☐ 710	2nd Generation Stars Barry Bonds Ken Griffey Jr.	.25	.12	.02
☐ 711	NLCS Team Leaders Bobby Bonilla Barry Larkin	.08	.04	.01
☐ 712	Top Game Savers Bobby Thigpen John Franco	.06	.03	.00
☐ 713	Chicago's 100 Club Andre Dawson Ryne Sandberg	.10	.05	.01
☐ 714	CL:A's/Pirates Reds/Red Sox	.06	.01	.00
☐ 715	CL:White Sox/Mets Blue Jays/Dodgers	.06	.01	.00
☐ 716	CL:Expos/Giants Rangers/Angels	.06	.01	.00
☐ 717	CL:Tigers/Indians Phillies/Cubs	.06	.01	.00
☐ 718	CL:Mariners/Orioles Astros/Padres	.06	.01	.00
☐ 719	CL:Royals/Brewers Twins/Cardinals	.06	.01	.00
☐ 720	CL:Yankees/Braves Superstars/Specials	.06	.01	.00

1991 Fleer Box Bottoms

These cards were issued on the bottom of 1991 Fleer wax boxes. This set celebrated the spate of no-hitters in 1990 and were printed on three different boxes. These standard size cards, 2 1/2" by 3 1/2", come four to a box, three about the no-hitters and one team logo card on each box. The cards are blank backed and are numbered on the front in a subtle way. They are ordered below as they are numbered, which is by chronological order of their no-hitters. Only the player cards are listed below since there was a different team logo card on each box.

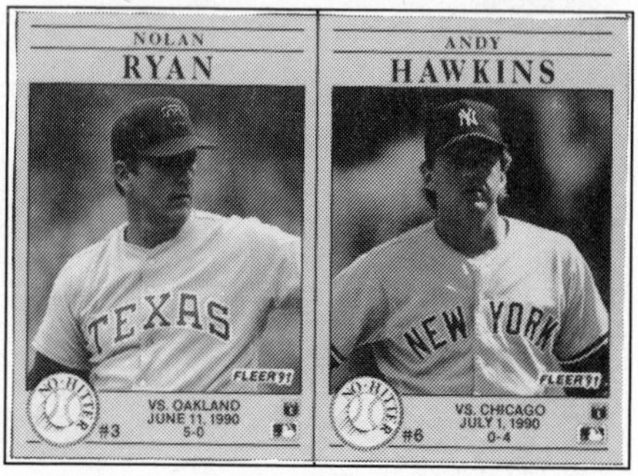

	MINT	EXC	G-VG
COMPLETE SET (9)	1.50	.75	.15
COMMON PLAYER (1-9)	.10	.05	.01
☐ 1 Mark Langston and Mike Witt	.10	.05	.01
☐ 2 Randy Johnson	.15	.07	.01
☐ 3 Nolan Ryan	.60	.30	.06
☐ 4 Dave Stewart	.25	.12	.02
☐ 5 Fernando Valenzuela	.20	.10	.02
☐ 6 Andy Hawkins	.10	.05	.01
☐ 7 Melido Perez	.10	.05	.01
☐ 8 Terry Mulholland	.10	.05	.01
☐ 9 Dave Stieb	.15	.07	.01

1991 Fleer All-Stars

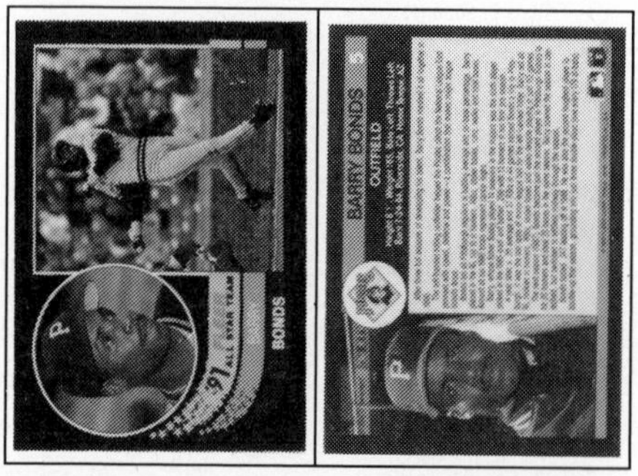

For the sixth consecutive year Fleer issued an All-Star insert set. This year the cards were only available in Fleer cello packs. This 10-card set measures the standard size of 2 1/2" by 3 1/2" and is reminiscent of the 1971 Topps Greatest Moments set with the two pictures on the front with a photo on the back as well.

	MINT	EXC	G-VG
COMPLETE SET (10)	10.00	5.00	1.00
COMMON PLAYER (1-10)	.75	.35	.07
☐ 1 Ryne Sandberg	1.25	.60	.12
☐ 2 Barry Larkin	.75	.35	.07
☐ 3 Matt Williams	.75	.35	.07
☐ 4 Cecil Fielder	.75	.35	.07
☐ 5 Barry Bonds	.75	.35	.07
☐ 6 Rickey Henderson	1.25	.60	.12
☐ 7 Ken Griffey Jr.	2.00	1.00	.20
☐ 8 Jose Canseco	1.50	.75	.15
☐ 9 Benito Santiago	.75	.35	.07
☐ 10 Roger Clemens	1.25	.60	.12

1991 Fleer Pro-Visions

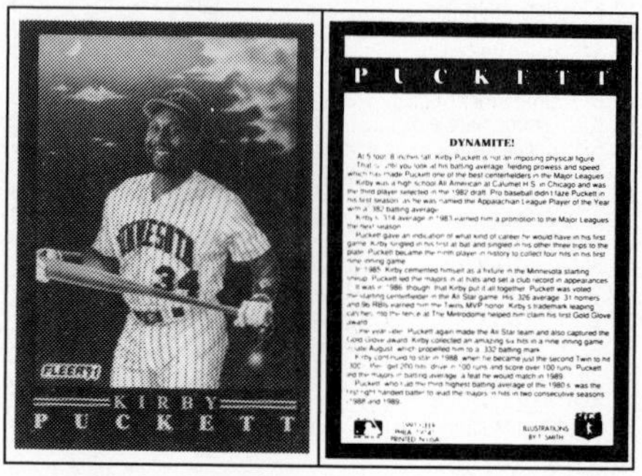

This 12-card subset is in the standard size of 2 1/2" by 3 1/2" and features drawings by talented artist Terry Smith on the front of the card with a description on the back explaining why the card is painted in that way. These cards were only available in Fleer wax and Rak packs. The formal description of this set is the 1991 Fleer Pro-Visions TM Sports Art Cards. The cards have distinctive black borders.

	MINT	EXC	G-VG
COMPLETE SET (12)	9.00	4.50	.90
COMMON PLAYER (1-12)	.60	.30	.06
☐ 1 Jose Canseco	1.25	.60	.12
☐ 2 Will Clark	1.00	.50	.10
☐ 3 Roger Clemens	1.00	.50	.10
☐ 4 Eric Davis	.90	.45	.09
☐ 5 Dwight Gooden	.90	.45	.09
☐ 6 Mike Greenwell	.90	.45	.09
☐ 7 Bo Jackson	1.25	.60	.12
☐ 8 Don Mattingly	1.25	.60	.12
☐ 9 Mark McGwire	1.00	.50	.10
☐ 10 Kirby Puckett	.90	.45	.09
☐ 11 Ruben Sierra	.60	.30	.06
☐ 12 Darryl Strawberry	.90	.45	.09

1987 French Bray Orioles

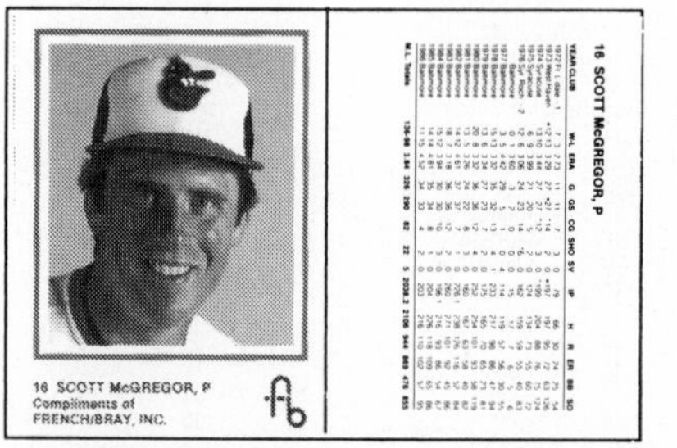

The 1987 French Bray set contains 30 cards (featuring members of the Baltimore Orioles) measuring 2 1/4 by 3 inches. The fronts have facial photos with white and orange borders; the horizontally-oriented backs are white and feature career stats. The cards were given away in perforated sheet form on Photo

Card Day at the Orioles home game on July 26, 1987. A large team photo was also included as one of the three panels in this perforated card set. The cards are unnumbered except for uniform number.

	MINT	EXC	G-VG
COMPLETE SET (30)	10.00	5.00	1.00
COMMON PLAYER	.25	.12	.02
☐ 2 Alan Wiggins	.25	.12	.02
☐ 3 Bill Ripken	.35	.17	.03
☐ 6 Floyd Rayford	.25	.12	.02
☐ 7 Cal Ripken Sr. MG	.35	.17	.03
☐ 8 Cal Ripken Jr.	1.50	.75	.15
☐ 9 Jim Dwyer	.25	.12	.02
☐ 10 Terry Crowley CO	.25	.12	.02
☐ 15 Terry Kennedy	.25	.12	.02
☐ 16 Scott McGregor	.35	.17	.03
☐ 18 Larry Sheets	.35	.17	.03
☐ 19 Fred Lynn	.50	.25	.05
☐ 20 Frank Robinson CO	1.00	.50	.10
☐ 24 Dave Schmidt	.35	.17	.03
☐ 25 Ray Knight	.35	.17	.03
☐ 27 Lee Lacy	.25	.12	.02
☐ 31 Mark Wiley CO	.25	.12	.02
☐ 32 Mark Williamson	.25	.12	.02
☐ 33 Eddie Murray	1.00	.50	.10
☐ 38 Ken Gerhart	.35	.17	.03
☐ 39 Ken Dixon	.25	.12	.02
☐ 40 Jimmy Williams CO	.25	.12	.02
☐ 42 Mike Griffin	.25	.12	.02
☐ 43 Mike Young	.25	.12	.02
☐ 44 Elrod Hendricks CO	.25	.12	.02
☐ 45 Eric Bell	.25	.12	.02
☐ 46 Mike Flanagan	.35	.17	.03
☐ 49 Tom Niedenfuer	.25	.12	.02
☐ 52 Mike Boddicker	.35	.17	.03
☐ 54 John Habyan	.25	.12	.02
☐ 57 Tony Arnold	.25	.12	.02

1988 French Bray Orioles

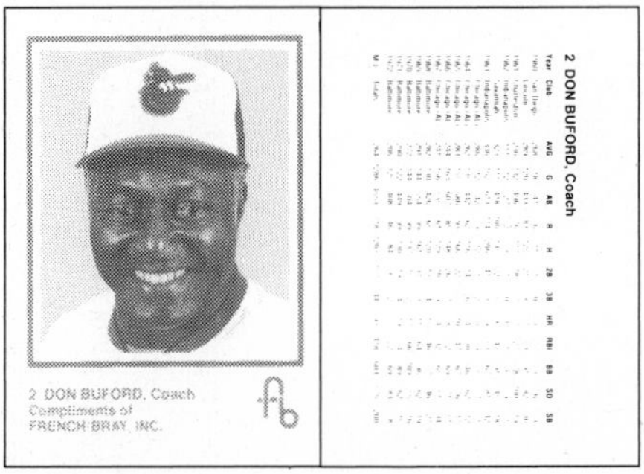

This set was distributed as a perforated set of 30 full-color cards attached to a large team photo on July 31, 1988, the Baltimore Orioles' Photo Card Day. The cards measure approximately 2 1/4" by 3 1/16". Card backs are simply done in black and white with statistics but no narrative or any personal information. Cards are unnumbered except for uniform number. Card front have a thin orange inner border and have the French Bray (Printing and Graphic Communication) logo in the lower right corner.

	MINT	EXC	G-VG
COMPLETE SET (30)	8.00	4.00	.80
COMMON PLAYER	.25	.12	.02
☐ 2 Don Buford CO	.25	.12	.02
☐ 6 Joe Orsulak	.35	.17	.03
☐ 7 Bill Ripken	.35	.17	.03
☐ 8 Cal Ripken	1.25	.60	.12
☐ 9 Jim Dwyer	.25	.12	.02
☐ 10 Terry Crowley CO	.25	.12	.02
☐ 12 Mike Morgan	.35	.17	.03
☐ 14 Mickey Tettleton	.50	.25	.05
☐ 15 Terry Kennedy	.25	.12	.02
☐ 17 Pete Stanicek	.25	.12	.02
☐ 18 Larry Sheets	.35	.17	.03
☐ 19 Fred Lynn	.50	.25	.05
☐ 20 Frank Robinson MG	.90	.45	.09
☐ 23 Ozzie Peraza	.35	.17	.03
☐ 24 Dave Schmidt	.35	.17	.03
☐ 25 Rick Schu	.25	.12	.02
☐ 28 Jim Traber	.25	.12	.02
☐ 31 Herm Starrette CO	.25	.12	.02
☐ 33 Eddie Murray	.90	.45	.09
☐ 34 Jeff Ballard	.50	.25	.05
☐ 38 Ken Gerhart	.35	.17	.03
☐ 40 Minnie Mendoza CO	.25	.12	.02
☐ 41 Don Aase	.25	.12	.02
☐ 44 Elrod Hendricks CO	.25	.12	.02
☐ 47 John Hart CO	.25	.12	.02
☐ 48 Jose Bautista	.25	.12	.02
☐ 49 Tom Niedenfuer	.25	.12	.02
☐ 52 Mike Boddicker	.35	.17	.03
☐ 53 Jay Tibbs	.25	.12	.02
☐ 88 Rene Gonzales	.25	.12	.02

1989 French Bray Orioles

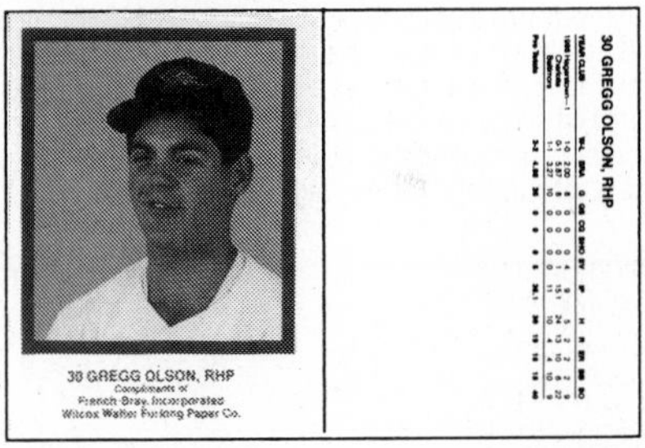

The 1989 French Bray Orioles set contains 31 cards measuring 2 1/4" by 3". The fronts have facial photos with orange and white borders; the backs are white and feature career stats. The set was given away at a Baltimore home game. The cards are numbered by the players' uniform numbers.

	MINT	EXC	G-VG
COMPLETE SET (31)	8.00	4.00	.80
COMMON PLAYER	.25	.12	.02
☐ 3 Bill Ripken	.35	.17	.03
☐ 6 Joe Orsulak	.35	.17	.03
☐ 7 Cal Ripken Sr. CO	.35	.17	.03
☐ 8 Cal Ripken Jr.	1.25	.60	.12
☐ 9 Brady Anderson	.50	.25	.05
☐ 10 Steve Finley	.50	.25	.05
☐ 11 Craig Worthington	.50	.25	.05
☐ 12 Mike Devereaux	.35	.17	.03
☐ 14 Mickey Tettleton	.50	.25	.05
☐ 15 Randy Milligan	.60	.30	.06
☐ 16 Phil Bradley	.50	.25	.05
☐ 18 Bob Milacki	.50	.25	.05
☐ 19 Larry Sheets	.35	.17	.03
☐ 20 Frank Robinson MG	.90	.45	.09
☐ 21 Mark Thurmond	.25	.12	.02
☐ 23 Kevin Hickey	.25	.12	.02
☐ 24 Dave Schmidt	.35	.17	.03
☐ 28 Jim Traber	.25	.12	.02
☐ 29 Jeff Ballard	.35	.17	.03
☐ 30 Gregg Olson	1.00	.50	.10
☐ 31 Al Jackson	.25	.12	.02
☐ 32 Mark Williamson	.25	.12	.02
☐ 36 Bob Melvin	.25	.12	.02
☐ 37 Brian Holton	.25	.12	.02
☐ 40 Tom McCraw CO	.25	.12	.02
☐ 42 Pete Harnisch	.25	.12	.02
☐ 43 Francisco Melendez	.35	.17	.03
☐ 44 Elrod Hendricks CO	.25	.12	.02
☐ 46 Johnny Oates CO	.25	.12	.02
☐ 48 Jose Bautista	.25	.12	.02
☐ 88 Rene Gonzales	.25	.12	.02

1986 Fritsch Negro League

This 119-card set of Negro League stars was issued in the standard size of 2 1/2" by 3 1/2". The set features black and white photos framed by the title "Negro League Baseball Stars" in red above the player's name and the player's name in red below the photo. Each card back features a brief biography of the player pictured on the front of the card. The set was produced by long time Wisconsin card hobbyist Larry Fritsch and featured most of the great players of the old Negro Leagues.

	MINT	VG-E	F-G
COMPLETE SET (119)	12.00	6.00	1.20
COMMON PLAYER (1-119)	.10	.05	.01
☐ 1 Buck Leonard	.50	.25	.05
☐ 2 Ted Page	.30	.15	.03
☐ 3 Cool Papa Bell	.50	.25	.05
☐ 4 Charleston/Gibson/ Page/Johnson	.50	.25	.05
☐ 5 Judy Johnson	.50	.25	.05
☐ 6 Monte Irvin	.50	.25	.05
☐ 7 Ray Dandridge	.50	.25	.05
☐ 8 Oscar Charleston	.50	.25	.05
☐ 9 Josh Gibson	.75	.35	.07
☐ 10 Satchel Paige	.75	.35	.07
☐ 11 Jackie Robinson	.75	.35	.07
☐ 12 Lorenzo Piper Davis	.20	.10	.02
☐ 13 Josh Johnson	.10	.05	.01
☐ 14 Lou Dials	.30	.15	.03
☐ 15 Andy Porter	.10	.05	.01
☐ 16 John Henry Lloyd	.50	.25	.05
☐ 17 Andy Watts	.10	.05	.01
☐ 18 Rube Foster	.50	.25	.05
☐ 19 Martin Dihigo	.50	.25	.05
☐ 20 Lou Dials	.30	.15	.03
☐ 21 Satchel Paige	.75	.35	.07
☐ 22 Crush Holloway	.10	.05	.01
☐ 23 Josh Gibson	.75	.35	.07
☐ 24 Oscar Charleston	.50	.25	.05
☐ 25 Jackie Robinson	.75	.35	.07
☐ 26 Larry Brown	.10	.05	.01
☐ 27 Hilton Smith	.10	.05	.01
☐ 28 Moses F. Walker	.10	.05	.01
☐ 29 Jimmie Crutchfield	.10	.05	.01
☐ 30 Josh Gibson	.75	.35	.07
☐ 31 Josh Gibson	.75	.35	.07
☐ 32 Bullet Rogan	.20	.10	.02
☐ 33 Clint Thomas	.10	.05	.01
☐ 34 Rats Henderson	.10	.05	.01
☐ 35 Pat Scantlebury	.10	.05	.01
☐ 36 Sydney Sy Morton	.10	.05	.01
☐ 37 Larry Kimbrough	.10	.05	.01
☐ 38 Sam Jethroe	.20	.10	.02
☐ 39 Normal (Tweed) Webb	.10	.05	.01
☐ 40 Mahlon Duckett	.10	.05	.01
☐ 41 Andy Anderson	.10	.05	.01
☐ 42 Buster Haywood	.10	.05	.01
☐ 43 Bob Trice	.10	.05	.01
☐ 44 Buster Clarkson	.10	.05	.01
☐ 45 Buck O'Neil	.10	.05	.01
☐ 46 Jim Zapp	.10	.05	.01
☐ 47 Lorenzo Piper Davis	.10	.05	.01
☐ 48 Ed Steel	.10	.05	.01
☐ 49 Bob Boyd	.10	.05	.01
☐ 50 Marlin Carter	.10	.05	.01
☐ 51 George Giles	.10	.05	.01
☐ 52 Bill Byrd	.10	.05	.01
☐ 53 Art Pennington	.10	.05	.01
☐ 54 Max Manning	.10	.05	.01
☐ 55 Ronald Teasley	.10	.05	.01
☐ 56 Ziggy Marcell	.10	.05	.01
☐ 57 Bill Cash	.10	.05	.01
☐ 58 Joe Scott	.10	.05	.01
☐ 59 Joe Fillmore	.10	.05	.01
☐ 60 Bob Thurman	.10	.05	.01
☐ 61 Larry Kimbrough	.10	.05	.01
☐ 62 Verdell Mathis	.10	.05	.01
☐ 63 Josh Johnson	.20	.10	.02
☐ 64 Ted Radcliffe	.20	.10	.02
☐ 65 William Bobby Robinson	.10	.05	.01
☐ 66 Bingo DeMoss	.20	.10	.02
☐ 67 John Beckwith	.10	.05	.01
☐ 68 Bill Jackman	.10	.05	.01
☐ 69 Bill Drake	.10	.05	.01
☐ 70 Charlie Grant	.10	.05	.01
☐ 71 Willie Wells	.20	.10	.02
☐ 72 Jose Fernandez	.10	.05	.01
☐ 73 Isidro Fabri	.10	.05	.01
☐ 74 Frank Austin	.10	.05	.01
☐ 75 Dick Lundy	.10	.05	.01
☐ 76 Junior Gilliam	.30	.15	.03
☐ 77 John Donaldson	.10	.05	.01
☐ 78 Rap Dixon	.10	.05	.01
☐ 79 Slim Jones	.10	.05	.01
☐ 80 Sam Jones	.10	.05	.01
☐ 81 Dave Hoskins	.10	.05	.01
☐ 82 Jerry Benjamin	.10	.05	.01
☐ 83 Luke Easter	.20	.10	.02
☐ 84 Ramon Herrera	.10	.05	.01
☐ 85 Matthew Carlisle	.10	.05	.01
☐ 86 Smokey Joe Williams	.30	.15	.03
☐ 87 Marvin Williams	.10	.05	.01
☐ 88 William Yancey	.10	.05	.01
☐ 89 Monte Irvin	.50	.25	.05
☐ 90 Cool Papa Bell	.50	.25	.05
☐ 91 Biz Mackey	.40	.20	.04
☐ 92 Harry Simpson	.20	.10	.02
☐ 93 Lazerio Salazar	.10	.05	.01
☐ 94 Bill Perkins	.10	.05	.01
☐ 95 Johnny Davis	.10	.05	.01
☐ 96 Jelly Jackson	.20	.10	.02
☐ 97 Sam Bankhead	.10	.05	.01
☐ 98 Hank Thompson	.20	.10	.02
☐ 99 William Bell	.10	.05	.01
☐ 100 Cliff Bell	.10	.05	.01
☐ 101 Dave Barnhill	.10	.05	.01
☐ 102 Dan Bankhead	.10	.05	.01
☐ 103 Pepper Bassett	.10	.05	.01
☐ 104 Newt Allen	.10	.05	.01
☐ 105 George Jefferson	.10	.05	.01
☐ 106 Pat Paterson	.10	.05	.01
☐ 107 Goose Tatum	.30	.15	.03
☐ 108 Dave Malarcher	.20	.10	.02
☐ 109 Home Run Johnson	.20	.10	.02
☐ 110 Bill Monroe	.10	.05	.01
☐ 111 Sammy Hughes	.10	.05	.01
☐ 112 Dick Redding	.20	.10	.02
☐ 113 Fats Jenkins	.10	.05	.01
☐ 114 Jimmie Lyons	.10	.05	.01
☐ 115 Mule Suttles	.10	.05	.01
☐ 116 Ted Trent	.10	.05	.01
☐ 117 George Sweatt	.10	.05	.01
☐ 118 Frank Duncan	.10	.05	.01
☐ 119 Checklist Card	.10	.05	.01

1928 Fro Joy

The cards in this 6-card set measure 2 1/16" by 4". The Fro Joy set of 1928 was designed to exploit the advertising potential of the mighty Babe Ruth. Six black and white cards explained specific baseball techniques while the reverse advertising extolled the virtues of Fro Joy ice cream and ice cream cones. Unfortunately this small set has been illegally reprinted (several times) and many of these virtually-worthless fakes have been introduced into the hobby. The easiest fakes to spot are those cards (or uncut sheets) that are slightly over-sized and blue tinted; however some of the other fakes are more cleverly faithful to the original. Be very careful before purchasing Fro-Joys; obtain a qualified opinion on authenticity from an experienced dealer (preferably one who is unrelated to the dealer trying to sell you his cards). You might also show the cards (before you commit to purchase them) to an experienced printer who can advise you on the true age of the paper stock. One dealer has been quoted as saying that 99 percent of the Fro Joys he sees are fakes.

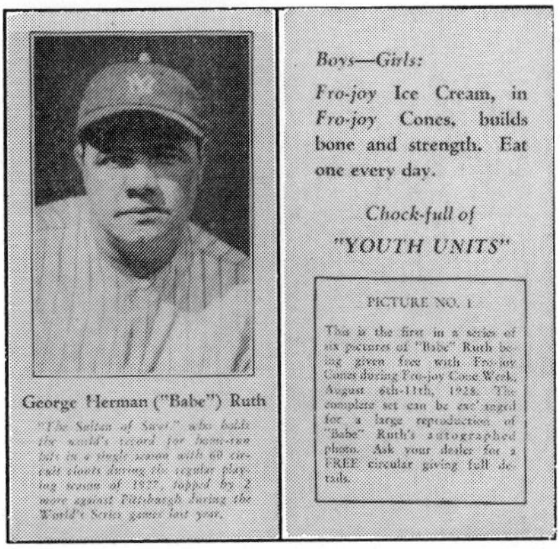

	EX-MT	VG-E	GOOD
COMPLETE SET (6)	600.00	300.00	60.00
COMMON PLAYER (1-6)	100.00	50.00	10.00
☐ 1 George Herman (Babe) Ruth	150.00	75.00	15.00
☐ 2 Look Out, Mr. Pitcher	100.00	50.00	10.00
☐ 3 Bang; The Babe Lines one out	100.00	50.00	10.00
☐ 4 When the Babe Comes Out	100.00	50.00	10.00
☐ 5 Babe Ruth's Grip	100.00	50.00	10.00
☐ 6 Ruth is a Crack Fielder	100.00	50.00	10.00

1983 Gardner's Brewers

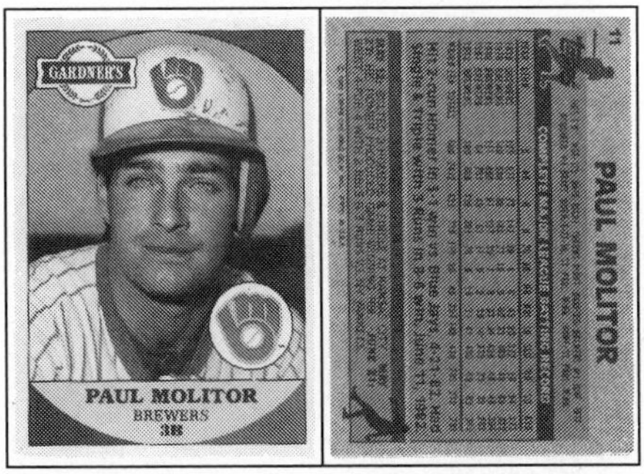

The cards in this 22-card set measure 2 1/2" by 3 1/2". The 1983 Gardner's Brewers set features Milwaukee Brewer players and manager Harvey Kuenn. Topps printed the set for the Madison (Wisconsin) bakery, hence, the backs are identical to the 1983 Topps backs except for the card number. The fronts of the cards, however, feature all new photos and include the Gardner's logo and the Brewers' logo. Many of the cards are grease laden, as they were issued with packages of bread and hamburger and hot-dog buns.

	MINT	EXC	G-VG
COMPLETE SET (22)	25.00	12.50	2.50
COMMON PLAYER (1-22)	.50	.25	.05
☐ 1 Harvey Kuenn MG	1.00	.50	.10
☐ 2 Dwight Bernard	.50	.25	.05
☐ 3 Mark Brouhard	.50	.25	.05
☐ 4 Mike Caldwell	.75	.35	.07
☐ 5 Cecil Cooper	1.50	.75	.15
☐ 6 Marshall Edwards	.50	.25	.05
☐ 7 Rollie Fingers	5.00	2.50	.50
☐ 8 Jim Gantner	.75	.35	.07
☐ 9 Moose Haas	.75	.35	.07
☐ 10 Bob McClure	.50	.25	.05
☐ 11 Paul Molitor	4.00	2.00	.40
☐ 12 Don Money	.75	.35	.07
☐ 13 Charlie Moore	.75	.35	.07
☐ 14 Ben Oglivie	.75	.35	.07
☐ 15 Ed Romero	.50	.25	.05
☐ 16 Ted Simmons	1.50	.75	.15
☐ 17 Jim Slaton	.75	.35	.07
☐ 18 Don Sutton	3.00	1.50	.30
☐ 19 Gorman Thomas	1.00	.50	.10
☐ 20 Pete Vuckovich	.75	.35	.07
☐ 21 Ned Yost	.50	.25	.05
☐ 22 Robin Yount	9.00	4.50	.90

1984 Gardner's Brewers

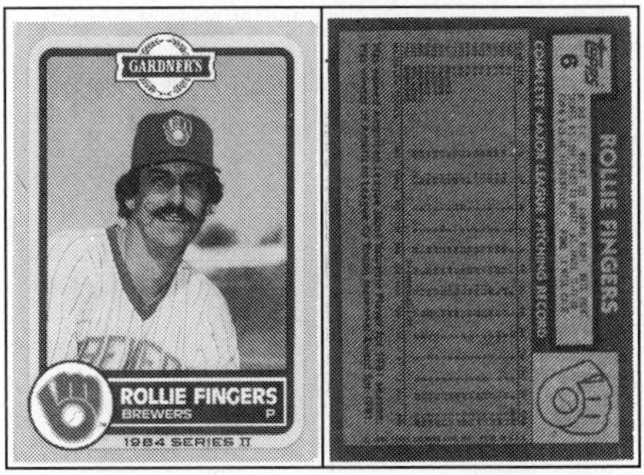

The cards in this 22-card set measure 2 1/2" by 3 1/2". For the second year in a row, the Gardner Bakery Company issued a set of cards available in packages of Gardner Bakery products. The set was manufactured by Topps, and the backs of the cards are identical to the Topps cards of this year except for the numbers. The Gardner logo appears on the fronts of the cards with the player's name, position abbreviation, the name Brewers, and the words 1984 Series II.

	MINT	EXC	G-VG
COMPLETE SET (22)	9.00	4.50	.90
COMMON PLAYER (1-22)	.35	.17	.03
☐ 1 Rene Lachemann MG	.45	.22	.04
☐ 2 Mark Brouhard	.35	.17	.03
☐ 3 Mike Caldwell	.45	.22	.04
☐ 4 Bobby Clark	.35	.17	.03
☐ 5 Cecil Cooper	.75	.35	.07
☐ 6 Rollie Fingers	2.00	1.00	.20
☐ 7 Jim Gantner	.60	.30	.06
☐ 8 Moose Haas	.45	.22	.04
☐ 9 Roy Howell	.35	.17	.03
☐ 10 Pete Ladd	.35	.17	.03
☐ 11 Rick Manning	.35	.17	.03
☐ 12 Bob McClure	.35	.17	.03
☐ 13 Paul Molitor	2.00	1.00	.20
☐ 14 Charlie Moore	.45	.22	.04
☐ 15 Ben Oglivie	.60	.30	.06
☐ 16 Ed Romero	.35	.17	.03
☐ 17 Ted Simmons	1.00	.50	.10
☐ 18 Jim Sundberg	.45	.22	.04
☐ 19 Don Sutton	1.75	.85	.17
☐ 20 Tom Tellman	.35	.17	.03
☐ 21 Pete Vuckovich	.60	.30	.06
☐ 22 Robin Yount	4.00	2.00	.40

1985 Gardner's Brewers

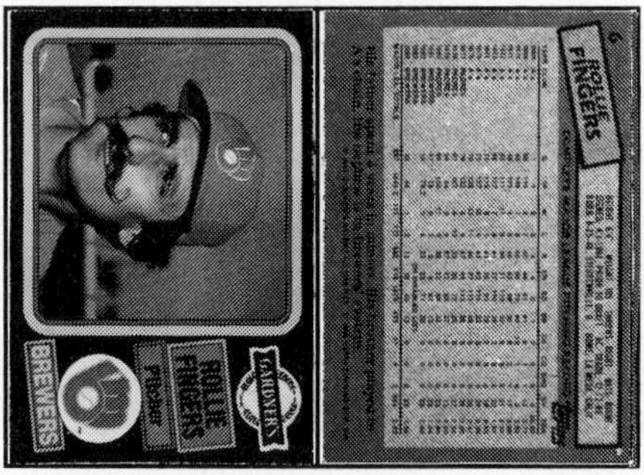

The cards in this 22-card set measure 2 1/2" by 3 1/2". For the third year in a row, the Gardner Bakery Company issued a set of cards available in packages of Gardner Bakery products. The set was manufactured by Topps, and the backs of the cards are identical to the Topps cards of this year except for the card numbers and copyright information. The Gardner logo appears on the fronts of the cards with the player's name, position abbreviation, and the name Brewers.

	MINT	EXC	G-VG
COMPLETE SET (22)	9.00	4.50	.90
COMMON PLAYER (1-22)	.35	.17	.03
☐ 1 George Bamberger MG	.45	.22	.04
☐ 2 Mark Brouhard	.35	.17	.03
☐ 3 Bobby Clark	.35	.17	.03
☐ 4 Jaime Cocanower	.35	.17	.03
☐ 5 Cecil Cooper	.90	.45	.09
☐ 6 Rollie Fingers	2.00	1.00	.20
☐ 7 Jim Gantner	.45	.22	.04
☐ 8 Moose Haas	.45	.22	.04
☐ 9 Dion James	.35	.17	.03
☐ 10 Pete Ladd	.35	.17	.03
☐ 11 Rick Manning	.35	.17	.03
☐ 12 Bob McClure	.35	.17	.03
☐ 13 Paul Molitor	2.00	1.00	.20
☐ 14 Charlie Moore	.45	.22	.04
☐ 15 Ben Oglivie	.45	.22	.04
☐ 16 Chuck Porter	.35	.17	.03
☐ 17 Ed Romero	.35	.17	.03
☐ 18 Bill Schroeder	.45	.22	.04
☐ 19 Ted Simmons	1.00	.50	.10
☐ 20 Tom Tellman	.35	.17	.03
☐ 21 Pete Vuckovich	.60	.30	.06
☐ 22 Robin Yount	4.00	2.00	.40

1989 Gardner's Brewers

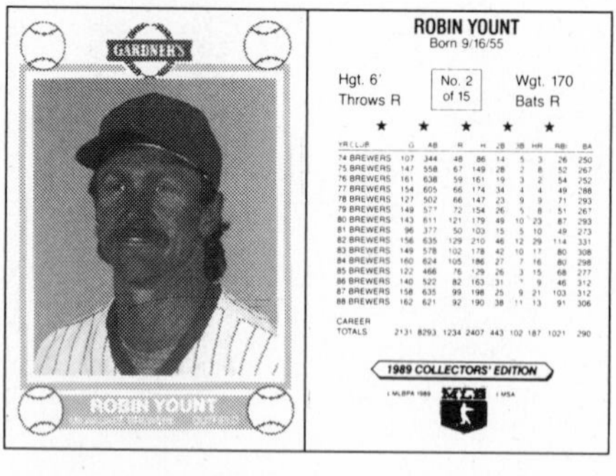

The 1989 Gardner's Brewers set contains 15 standard-size (2 1/2" by 3 1/2") cards. The fronts feature airbrushed mugshots with sky blue backgrounds and white borders. The backs are white and feature career stats. One card was distributed in each specially marked Gardner's bakery product. Cards were issued during the middle of the season. For some reason Riles is included in the set even though he had been traded by the Brewers during the 1988 season.

	MINT	EXC	G-VG
COMPLETE SET (15)	5.00	2.50	.50
COMMON PLAYER (1-15)	.25	.12	.02
☐ 1 Paul Molitor	1.25	.60	.12
☐ 2 Robin Yount	2.50	1.25	.25
☐ 3 Jim Gantner	.35	.17	.03
☐ 4 Rob Deer	.50	.25	.05
☐ 5 B.J. Surhoff	.50	.25	.05
☐ 6 Dale Sveum	.25	.12	.02
☐ 7 Ted Higuera	.50	.25	.05
☐ 8 Dan Plesac	.35	.17	.03
☐ 9 Bill Wegman	.25	.12	.02
☐ 10 Juan Nieves	.25	.12	.02
☐ 11 Greg Brock	.25	.12	.02
☐ 12 Glenn Braggs	.35	.17	.03
☐ 13 Joey Meyer	.25	.12	.02
☐ 14 Earnest Riles	.25	.12	.02
☐ 15 Don August	.25	.12	.02

1987 Gatorade Indians

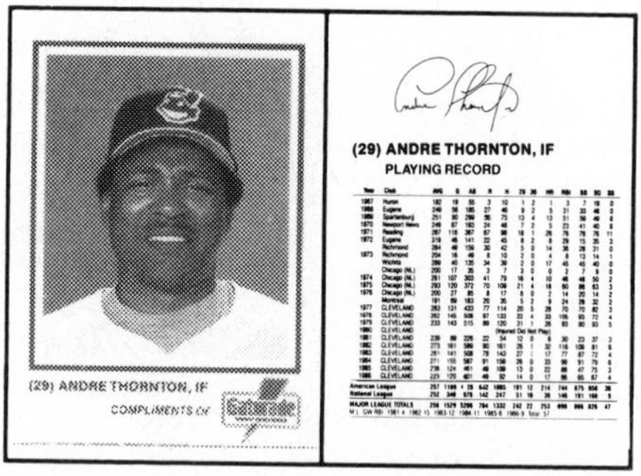

Gatorade sponsored this perforated set of 30 full-color cards of the Cleveland Indians. The cards measure 2 1/8" by 3" (or 3 1/8") and feature the Gatorade logo prominently on the fronts of the cards. The cards were distributed as a tri-folded sheet (each part approximately 9 5/8" by 11 3/16") on April 25th at the stadium during the game against the Yankees. The large team photo is approximately 11 3/16" by 9 5/8". Card backs for the individual players contain year-by-year stats for that player.

	MINT	EXC	G-VG
COMPLETE SET (30)	9.00	4.50	.90
COMMON PLAYER	.25	.12	.02
☐ 2 Brett Butler	.60	.30	.06
☐ 4 Tony Bernazard	.35	.17	.03
☐ 6 Andy Allanson	.35	.17	.03
☐ 7 Pat Corrales MG	.25	.12	.02
☐ 8 Carmen Castillo	.25	.12	.02
☐ 10 Pat Tabler	.35	.17	.03
☐ 11 Jamie Easterly	.25	.12	.02
☐ 12 Dave Clark	.35	.17	.03
☐ 13 Ernie Camacho	.25	.12	.02
☐ 14 Julio Franco	.75	.35	.07
☐ 17 Junior Noboa	.35	.17	.03
☐ 18 Ken Schrom	.25	.12	.02
☐ 20 Otis Nixon	.25	.12	.02
☐ 21 Greg Swindell	.75	.35	.07
☐ 22 Frank Wills	.25	.12	.02
☐ 23 Chris Bando	.25	.12	.02
☐ 24 Rick Dempsey	.25	.12	.02
☐ 26 Brook Jacoby	.50	.25	.05
☐ 27 Mel Hall	.50	.25	.05
☐ 28 Cory Snyder	.75	.35	.07
☐ 29 Andre Thornton	.35	.17	.03

☐ 30 Joe Carter	1.00	.50	.10
☐ 35 Phil Niekro	1.00	.50	.10
☐ 36 Ed VandeBerg	.25	.12	.02
☐ 42 Rich Yett	.25	.12	.02
☐ 43 Scott Bailes	.25	.12	.02
☐ 46 Doug Jones	.50	.25	.05
☐ 49 Tom Candiotti	.25	.12	.02
☐ 54 Tom Waddell	.25	.12	.02
☐ xx Indians MG/Coaches Bobby Bonds 25 Johnny Goryl 45 Pat Corrales MG 7 Doc Edwards 32 Jack Aker 1	.35	.17	.03
☐ xx Team Photo (large size)	1.00	.50	.10

1988 Gatorade Indians

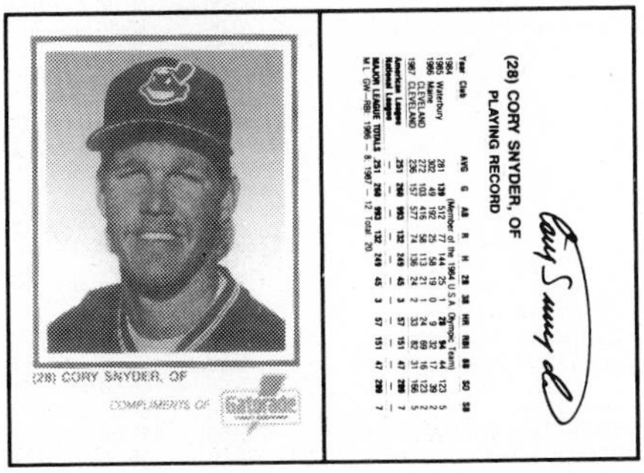

This set was distributed as 30 perforated player cards attached to a large team photo of the Cleveland Indians. The cards measure approximately 2 1/4" by 3". Card backs are oriented either horizontally or vertically. Card backs are printed in red, blue, and black on white card stock. Card backs contain a facsimile autograph of the player. Cards are not arranged on the sheet in any order. The cards are unnumbered except for uniform number, which is given on the front and back of each card. The Gatorade logo is on the front of every card in the lower right corner.

	MINT	EXC	G-VG
COMPLETE SET (30)	8.00	4.00	.80
COMMON PLAYER	.20	.10	.02
☐ 2 Tom Spencer CO	.20	.10	.02
☐ 6 Andy Allanson	.20	.10	.02
☐ 7 Luis Isaac CO	.20	.10	.02
☐ 8 Carmen Castillo	.20	.10	.02
☐ 9 Charlie Manuel CO	.20	.10	.02
☐ 10 Pat Tabler	.30	.15	.03
☐ 11 Doug Jones	.40	.20	.04
☐ 14 Julio Franco	.50	.25	.05
☐ 15 Ron Washington	.20	.10	.02
☐ 16 Jay Bell	.40	.20	.04
☐ 17 Bill Laskey	.20	.10	.02
☐ 20 Willie Upshaw	.20	.10	.02
☐ 21 Greg Swindell	.50	.25	.05
☐ 23 Chris Bando	.20	.10	.02
☐ 25 Dave Clark	.30	.15	.03
☐ 26 Brook Jacoby	.40	.20	.04
☐ 27 Mel Hall	.40	.20	.04
☐ 28 Cory Snyder	.60	.30	.06
☐ 30 Joe Carter	.80	.40	.08
☐ 31 Dan Schatzeder	.20	.10	.02
☐ 32 Doc Edwards MG	.20	.10	.02
☐ 33 Ron Kittle	.40	.20	.04
☐ 35 Mark Wiley CO	.20	.10	.02
☐ 42 Rich Yett	.20	.10	.02
☐ 43 Scott Bailes	.30	.15	.03
☐ 45 John Goryl CO	.20	.10	.02
☐ 47 Jeff Kaiser	.20	.10	.02
☐ 49 Tom Candiotti	.30	.15	.03
☐ 50 Jeff Dedmon	.20	.10	.02
☐ 52 John Farrell	.40	.20	.04

1953 Glendale

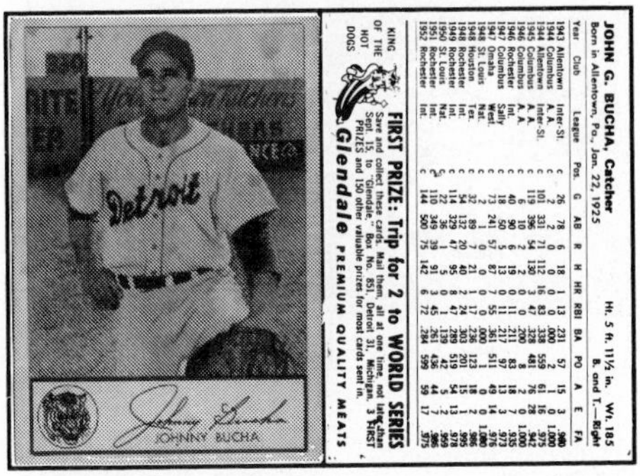

The cards in this 28-card set measure 2 5/8" by 3 3/4". The 1953 Glendale Meats set of full-color, unnumbered cards features Detroit Tiger ballplayers exclusively and was distributed one per package of Glendale Meats in the Detroit area. The back contains the complete major and minor league record through the 1952 season. The scarcer cards of the set command higher prices, with the Houtteman card being the most difficult to find. There is an album associated with the set (which also is quite scarce now). The catalog designation for this scarce regional set is F151. Since the cards are unnumbered, they are ordered below alphabetically.

	NRMT	VG-E	GOOD
COMPLETE SET (28)	5000.00	2350.00	600.00
COMMON PLAYER (1-28)	125.00	60.00	12.50
☐ 1 Matt Batts	125.00	60.00	12.50
☐ 2 Johnny Bucha	125.00	60.00	12.50
☐ 3 Frank Carswell	125.00	60.00	12.50
☐ 4 Jim Delsing	125.00	60.00	12.50
☐ 5 Walt Dropo	150.00	75.00	15.00
☐ 6 Hal Erickson	125.00	60.00	12.50
☐ 7 Paul Foytack	125.00	60.00	12.50
☐ 8 Owen Friend	125.00	60.00	12.50
☐ 9 Ned Garver	125.00	60.00	12.50
☐ 10 Joe Ginsberg	300.00	150.00	30.00
☐ 11 Ted Gray	125.00	60.00	12.50
☐ 12 Fred Hatfield	125.00	60.00	12.50
☐ 13 Ray Herbert	125.00	60.00	12.50
☐ 14 Bill Hitchcock	125.00	60.00	12.50
☐ 15 Bill Hoeft	200.00	100.00	20.00
☐ 16 Art Houtteman	2100.00	900.00	250.00
☐ 17 Milt Jordan	150.00	75.00	15.00
☐ 18 Harvey Kuenn	350.00	175.00	35.00
☐ 19 Don Lund	125.00	60.00	12.50
☐ 20 Dave Madison	125.00	60.00	12.50
☐ 21 Dick Marlowe	125.00	60.00	12.50
☐ 22 Pat Mullin	125.00	60.00	12.50
☐ 23 Bob Nieman	125.00	60.00	12.50
☐ 24 Johnny Pesky	150.00	75.00	15.00
☐ 25 Jerry Priddy	125.00	60.00	12.50
☐ 26 Steve Souchock	125.00	60.00	12.50
☐ 27 Russ Sullivan	125.00	60.00	12.50
☐ 28 Bill Wight	150.00	75.00	15.00

1961 Golden Press

The cards in this 33-card set measure 2 1/2" by 3 1/2". The 1961 Golden Press set of full color cards features members of Baseball's Hall of Fame. The cards came in a booklet with perforations for punching the cards out of the book. The catalog designation is W524. The price for the full book intact is 25 percent higher than the complete set price listed.

	NRMT	VG-E	GOOD
COMPLETE SET (33)	65.00	32.50	6.50
COMMON PLAYER (1-33)	.75	.35	.07

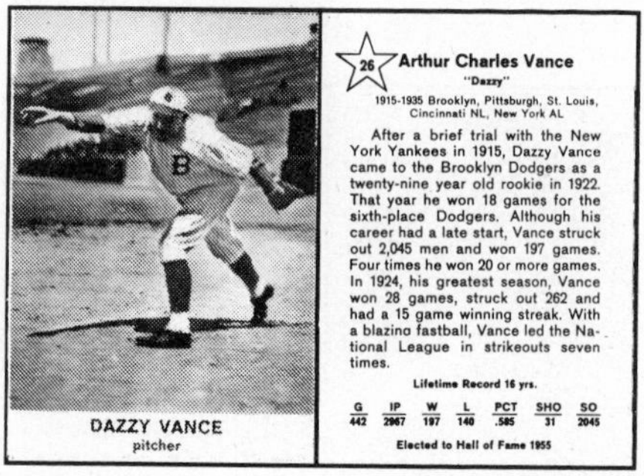
DAZZY VANCE
pitcher
26
Arthur Charles Vance
"Dazzy"
1915-1935 Brooklyn, Pittsburgh, St. Louis, Cincinnati NL, New York AL
After a brief trial with the New York Yankees in 1915, Dazzy Vance came to the Brooklyn Dodgers as a twenty-nine year old rookie in 1922. That year he won 18 games for the sixth-place Dodgers. Although his career had a late start, Vance struck out 2,045 men and won 197 games. Four times he won 20 or more games. In 1924, his greatest season, Vance won 28 games, struck out 262 and had a 15 game winning streak. With a blazing fastball, Vance led the National League in strikeouts seven times.
Lifetime Record 16 yrs.
G IP W L PCT SHO SO
442 2967 197 140 .585 31 2045
Elected to Hall of Fame 1955

☐ 1 Mel Ott	2.00	1.00	.20
☐ 2 Grover C. Alexander	1.50	.75	.15
☐ 3 Babe Ruth	20.00	10.00	2.00
☐ 4 Hank Greenberg	1.50	.75	.15
☐ 5 Bill Terry	1.00	.50	.10
☐ 6 Carl Hubbell	1.00	.50	.10
☐ 7 Rogers Hornsby	2.50	1.25	.25
☐ 8 Dizzy Dean	5.00	2.50	.50
☐ 9 Joe DiMaggio	15.00	7.50	1.50
☐ 10 Charlie Gehringer	1.00	.50	.10
☐ 11 Gabby Hartnett	.75	.35	.07
☐ 12 Mickey Cochrane	1.00	.50	.10
☐ 13 George Sisler	1.00	.50	.10
☐ 14 Joe Cronin	.75	.35	.07
☐ 15 Pie Traynor	.75	.35	.07
☐ 16 Lou Gehrig	15.00	7.50	1.50
☐ 17 Lefty Grove	2.00	1.00	.20
☐ 18 Chief Bender	.75	.35	.07
☐ 19 Frankie Frisch	.75	.35	.07
☐ 20 Al Simmons	.75	.35	.07
☐ 21 Home Run Baker	.75	.35	.07
☐ 22 Jimmy Foxx	2.50	1.25	.25
☐ 23 John McGraw	1.00	.50	.10
☐ 24 Christy Mathewson	4.00	2.00	.40
☐ 25 Ty Cobb	15.00	7.50	1.50
☐ 26 Dazzy Vance	.75	.35	.07
☐ 27 Bill Dickey	1.50	.75	.15
☐ 28 Eddie Collins	.75	.35	.07
☐ 29 Walter Johnson	4.00	2.00	.40
☐ 30 Tris Speaker	2.50	1.25	.25
☐ 31 Nap Lajoie	2.50	1.25	.25
☐ 32 Honus Wagner	4.00	2.00	.40
☐ 33 Cy Young	2.50	1.25	.25

1933 Goudey

The cards in this 240-card set measure 2 3/8" by 2 7/8". The 1933 Goudey set, designated R319 by the ACC, was that company's first baseball issue. The four Babe Ruth and two Lou Gehrig cards in the set are extremely popular with collectors. Card number 106, Napoleon Lajoie, was not printed in 1933, and was circulated to a limited number of collectors in 1934 upon request (it was printed along with the 1934 Goudey cards). An album was offered to house the 1933 set. Several minor leaguers are depicted. Card number 1 (Bengough) is very rarely found in mint condition; in fact, as a general rule all the first series cards are more difficult to find in Mint condition. Players with more than one card are also sometimes differentiated below by their pose: BAT (Batting), FIELD (Fielding), PIT (Pitching), THROW (Throwing). One of the Babe Ruth cards was double printed (DP) apparently in place of the Lajoie and hence is easier to obtain than the others. Due to the scarcity of the Lajoie card, the set is considered complete at 239 cards and is priced as such below.

	EX-MT	VG-E	GOOD
COMPLETE SET (239)	34000.	15000.	3750.
COMMON PLAYER (1-40)	70.00	35.00	7.00
COMMON PLAYER (41-44)	55.00	27.50	5.50
COMMON PLAYER (45-52)	70.00	35.00	7.00
COMMON PLAYER (53-240)	55.00	27.50	5.50
☐ 1 Benny Bengough	1200.00	60.00	12.00
☐ 2 Dazzy Vance	160.00	80.00	16.00
☐ 3 Hugh Critz	70.00	35.00	7.00
☐ 4 Heine Schuble	70.00	35.00	7.00
☐ 5 Babe Herman	100.00	50.00	10.00
☐ 6 Jimmy Dykes	90.00	45.00	9.00
☐ 7 Ted Lyons	160.00	80.00	16.00
☐ 8 Roy Johnson	70.00	35.00	7.00
☐ 9 Dave Harris	70.00	35.00	7.00
☐ 10 Glenn Myatt	70.00	35.00	7.00
☐ 11 Billy Rogell	70.00	35.00	7.00
☐ 12 George Pipgras	70.00	35.00	7.00
☐ 13 Lafayette Thompson	70.00	35.00	7.00
☐ 14 Henry Johnson	70.00	35.00	7.00
☐ 15 Victor Sorrell	70.00	35.00	7.00
☐ 16 George Blaeholder	70.00	35.00	7.00
☐ 17 Watson Clark	70.00	35.00	7.00
☐ 18 Muddy Ruel	70.00	35.00	7.00
☐ 19 Bill Dickey	325.00	160.00	32.00
☐ 20 Bill Terry THROW	225.00	110.00	22.00
☐ 21 Phil Collins	70.00	35.00	7.00
☐ 22 Pie Traynor	200.00	100.00	20.00
☐ 23 Kiki Cuyler	160.00	80.00	16.00
☐ 24 Horace Ford	70.00	35.00	7.00
☐ 25 Paul Waner	160.00	80.00	16.00
☐ 26 Chalmer Cissell	70.00	35.00	7.00
☐ 27 George Connally	70.00	35.00	7.00
☐ 28 Dick Bartell	70.00	35.00	7.00
☐ 29 Jimmy Foxx	350.00	175.00	35.00
☐ 30 Frank Hogan	70.00	35.00	7.00
☐ 31 Tony Lazzeri	125.00	60.00	12.50
☐ 32 Bud Clancy	70.00	35.00	7.00
☐ 33 Ralph Kress	70.00	35.00	7.00
☐ 34 Bob O'Farrell	70.00	35.00	7.00
☐ 35 Al Simmons	225.00	110.00	22.00
☐ 36 Tommy Thevenow	70.00	35.00	7.00
☐ 37 Jimmy Wilson	70.00	35.00	7.00
☐ 38 Fred Brickell	70.00	35.00	7.00
☐ 39 Mark Koenig	70.00	35.00	7.00
☐ 40 Taylor Douthit	70.00	35.00	7.00
☐ 41 Gus Mancuso	55.00	27.50	5.50
☐ 42 Eddie Collins	100.00	50.00	10.00
☐ 43 Lew Fonseca	55.00	27.50	5.50
☐ 44 Jim Bottomley	100.00	50.00	10.00
☐ 45 Larry Benton	70.00	35.00	7.00
☐ 46 Ethan Allen	70.00	35.00	7.00
☐ 47 Heinie Manush BAT	150.00	75.00	15.00
☐ 48 Marty McManus	70.00	35.00	7.00
☐ 49 Frank Frisch	225.00	110.00	22.00
☐ 50 Ed Brandt	70.00	35.00	7.00
☐ 51 Charlie Grimm	90.00	45.00	9.00
☐ 52 Andy Cohen	70.00	35.00	7.00
☐ 53 Babe Ruth	3500.00	1500.00	400.00
☐ 54 Ray Kremer	55.00	27.50	5.50
☐ 55 Pat Malone	55.00	27.50	5.50
☐ 56 Charlie Ruffing	125.00	60.00	12.50
☐ 57 Earl Clark	55.00	27.50	5.50
☐ 58 Lefty O'Doul	70.00	35.00	7.00
☐ 59 Bing Miller	55.00	27.50	5.50
☐ 60 Waite Hoyt	100.00	50.00	10.00
☐ 61 Max Bishop	55.00	27.50	5.50
☐ 62 Pepper Martin	75.00	37.50	7.50
☐ 63 Joe Cronin BAT	125.00	60.00	12.50
☐ 64 Burleigh Grimes	100.00	50.00	10.00
☐ 65 Milt Gaston	55.00	27.50	5.50
☐ 66 George Grantham	55.00	27.50	5.50
☐ 67 Guy Bush	55.00	27.50	5.50
☐ 68 Horace Lisenbee	55.00	27.50	5.50
☐ 69 Randy Moore	55.00	27.50	5.50
☐ 70 Floyd (Pete) Scott	55.00	27.50	5.50
☐ 71 Robert J. Burke	55.00	27.50	5.50
☐ 72 Owen Carroll	55.00	27.50	5.50
☐ 73 Jess Haines	100.00	50.00	10.00
☐ 74 Eppa Rixey	100.00	50.00	10.00

☐ 75 Willie Kamm	55.00	27.50	5.50
☐ 76 Mickey Cochrane	150.00	75.00	15.00
☐ 77 Adam Comorosky	55.00	27.50	5.50
☐ 78 Jack Quinn	55.00	27.50	5.50
☐ 79 Red Faber	100.00	50.00	10.00
☐ 80 Clyde Manion	55.00	27.50	5.50
☐ 81 Sam Jones	55.00	27.50	5.50
☐ 82 Dibrell Williams	55.00	27.50	5.50
☐ 83 Pete Jablonowski	55.00	27.50	5.50
☐ 84 Glenn Spencer	55.00	27.50	5.50
☐ 85 Heine Sand	55.00	27.50	5.50
☐ 86 Phil Todt	55.00	27.50	5.50
☐ 87 Frank O'Rourke	55.00	27.50	5.50
☐ 88 Russell Rollings	55.00	27.50	5.50
☐ 89 Tris Speaker	300.00	150.00	30.00
☐ 90 Jess Petty	55.00	27.50	5.50
☐ 91 Tom Zachary	55.00	27.50	5.50
☐ 92 Lou Gehrig	1800.00	750.00	200.00
☐ 93 John Welch	55.00	27.50	5.50
☐ 94 Bill Walker	55.00	27.50	5.50
☐ 95 Alvin Crowder	55.00	27.50	5.50
☐ 96 Willis Hudlin	55.00	27.50	5.50
☐ 97 Joe Morrissey	55.00	27.50	5.50
☐ 98 Walter Berger	65.00	32.50	6.50
☐ 99 Tony Cuccinello	65.00	32.50	6.50
☐ 100 George Uhle	55.00	27.50	5.50
☐ 101 Richard Coffman	55.00	27.50	5.50
☐ 102 Travis Jackson	100.00	50.00	10.00
☐ 103 Earl Combs	100.00	50.00	10.00
☐ 104 Fred Marberry	55.00	27.50	5.50
☐ 105 Bernie Friberg	55.00	27.50	5.50
☐ 106 Napoleon Lajoie (not issued until 1934)	17500.	7500.00	2000.00
☐ 107 Heinie Manush	100.00	50.00	10.00
☐ 108 Joe Kuhel	55.00	27.50	5.50
☐ 109 Joe Cronin	125.00	60.00	12.50
☐ 110 Goose Goslin	100.00	50.00	10.00
☐ 111 Monte Weaver	55.00	27.50	5.50
☐ 112 Fred Schulte	55.00	27.50	5.50
☐ 113 Oswald Bluege	55.00	27.50	5.50
☐ 114 Luke Sewell	65.00	32.50	6.50
☐ 115 Cliff Heathcote	55.00	27.50	5.50
☐ 116 Eddie Morgan	55.00	27.50	5.50
☐ 117 Rabbit Maranville	100.00	50.00	10.00
☐ 118 Val Picinich	55.00	27.50	5.50
☐ 119 Rogers Hornsby FIELD	300.00	150.00	30.00
☐ 120 Carl Reynolds	55.00	27.50	5.50
☐ 121 Walter Stewart	55.00	27.50	5.50
☐ 122 Alvin Crowder	55.00	27.50	5.50
☐ 123 Jack Russell	55.00	27.50	5.50
☐ 124 Earl Whitehill	55.00	27.50	5.50
☐ 125 Bill Terry	200.00	100.00	20.00
☐ 126 Joe Moore	55.00	27.50	5.50
☐ 127 Mel Ott	225.00	110.00	22.00
☐ 128 Chuck Klein	150.00	75.00	15.00
☐ 129 Hal Schumacher PIT	55.00	27.50	5.50
☐ 130 Fred Fitzsimmons	55.00	27.50	5.50
☐ 131 Fred Frankhouse	55.00	27.50	5.50
☐ 132 Jim Elliott	55.00	27.50	5.50
☐ 133 Fred Lindstrom	100.00	50.00	10.00
☐ 134 Sam Rice	100.00	50.00	10.00
☐ 135 Woody English	55.00	27.50	5.50
☐ 136 Flint Rhem	55.00	27.50	5.50
☐ 137 Fred (Red) Lucas	55.00	27.50	5.50
☐ 138 Herb Pennock	100.00	50.00	10.00
☐ 139 Ben Cantwell	55.00	27.50	5.50
☐ 140 Bump Hadley	55.00	27.50	5.50
☐ 141 Ray Benge	55.00	27.50	5.50
☐ 142 Paul Richards	65.00	32.50	6.50
☐ 143 Glenn Wright	55.00	27.50	5.50
☐ 144 Babe Ruth BAT DP	3000.00	1350.00	350.00
☐ 145 George Walberg	55.00	27.50	5.50
☐ 146 Walter Stewart PIT	55.00	27.50	5.50
☐ 147 Leo Durocher	100.00	50.00	10.00
☐ 148 Eddie Farrell	55.00	27.50	5.50
☐ 149 Babe Ruth	3500.00	1500.00	400.00
☐ 150 Ray Kolp	55.00	27.50	5.50
☐ 151 Jake Flowers	55.00	27.50	5.50
☐ 152 Zack Taylor	55.00	27.50	5.50
☐ 153 Buddy Myer	55.00	27.50	5.50
☐ 154 Jimmy Foxx	300.00	150.00	30.00
☐ 155 Joe Judge	55.00	27.50	5.50
☐ 156 Danny MacFayden	55.00	27.50	5.50
☐ 157 Sam Byrd	55.00	27.50	5.50
☐ 158 Moe Berg	100.00	50.00	10.00
☐ 159 Oswald Bluege	55.00	27.50	5.50
☐ 160 Lou Gehrig	1800.00	750.00	200.00
☐ 161 Al Spohrer	55.00	27.50	5.50
☐ 162 Leo Mangum	55.00	27.50	5.50
☐ 163 Luke Sewell	65.00	32.50	6.50
☐ 164 Lloyd Waner	100.00	50.00	10.00
☐ 165 Joe Sewell	100.00	50.00	10.00
☐ 166 Sam West	55.00	27.50	5.50
☐ 167 Jack Russell	55.00	27.50	5.50
☐ 168 Goose Goslin	100.00	50.00	10.00
☐ 169 Al Thomas	55.00	27.50	5.50
☐ 170 Harry McCurdy	55.00	27.50	5.50
☐ 171 Charlie Jamieson	55.00	27.50	5.50
☐ 172 Billy Hargrave	55.00	27.50	5.50
☐ 173 Roscoe Holm	55.00	27.50	5.50
☐ 174 Warren(Curly) Ogden	55.00	27.50	5.50
☐ 175 Dan Howley	55.00	27.50	5.50
☐ 176 John Ogden	55.00	27.50	5.50
☐ 177 Walter French	55.00	27.50	5.50
☐ 178 Jackie Warner	55.00	27.50	5.50
☐ 179 Fred Leach	55.00	27.50	5.50
☐ 180 Eddie Moore	55.00	27.50	5.50
☐ 181 Babe Ruth	3500.00	1500.00	400.00
☐ 182 Andy High	55.00	27.50	5.50
☐ 183 George Walberg	55.00	27.50	5.50
☐ 184 Charley Berry	55.00	27.50	5.50
☐ 185 Bob Smith	55.00	27.50	5.50
☐ 186 John Schulte	55.00	27.50	5.50
☐ 187 Heinie Manush	100.00	50.00	10.00
☐ 188 Rogers Hornsby	300.00	150.00	30.00
☐ 189 Joe Cronin	125.00	60.00	12.50
☐ 190 Fred Schulte	55.00	27.50	5.50
☐ 191 Ben Chapman	65.00	32.50	6.50
☐ 192 Walter Brown	55.00	27.50	5.50
☐ 193 Lynford Lary	55.00	27.50	5.50
☐ 194 Earl Averill	100.00	50.00	10.00
☐ 195 Evar Swanson	55.00	27.50	5.50
☐ 196 Leroy Mahaffey	55.00	27.50	5.50
☐ 197 Rick Ferrell	100.00	50.00	10.00
☐ 198 Jack Burns	55.00	27.50	5.50
☐ 199 Tom Bridges	65.00	32.50	6.50
☐ 200 Bill Hallahan	55.00	27.50	5.50
☐ 201 Ernie Orsatti	55.00	27.50	5.50
☐ 202 Gabby Hartnett	100.00	50.00	10.00
☐ 203 Lon Warneke	55.00	27.50	5.50
☐ 204 Riggs Stephenson	65.00	32.50	6.50
☐ 205 Heinie Meine	55.00	27.50	5.50
☐ 206 Gus Suhr	55.00	27.50	5.50
☐ 207 Mel Ott BAT	225.00	110.00	22.00
☐ 208 Bernie James	55.00	27.50	5.50
☐ 209 Adolfo Luque	55.00	27.50	5.50
☐ 210 Virgil Davis	55.00	27.50	5.50
☐ 211 Hack Wilson	200.00	100.00	20.00
☐ 212 Billy Urbanski	55.00	27.50	5.50
☐ 213 Earl Adams	55.00	27.50	5.50
☐ 214 John Kerr	55.00	27.50	5.50
☐ 215 Russ Van Atta	55.00	27.50	5.50
☐ 216 Vernon Gomez	300.00	150.00	30.00
☐ 217 Frank Crosetti	90.00	45.00	9.00
☐ 218 Wes Ferrell	65.00	32.50	6.50
☐ 219 Mule Haas	55.00	27.50	5.50
☐ 220 Lefty Grove	350.00	175.00	35.00
☐ 221 Dale Alexander	55.00	27.50	5.50
☐ 222 Charley Gehringer	200.00	100.00	20.00
☐ 223 Dizzy Dean	600.00	300.00	60.00
☐ 224 Frank Demaree	55.00	27.50	5.50
☐ 225 Bill Jurges	55.00	27.50	5.50
☐ 226 Charley Root	55.00	27.50	5.50
☐ 227 Billy Herman	100.00	50.00	10.00
☐ 228 Tony Piet	55.00	27.50	5.50
☐ 229 Floyd(Arky) Vaughan	100.00	50.00	10.00
☐ 230 Carl Hubbell PIT	175.00	85.00	18.00
☐ 231 Joe Moore FIELD	55.00	27.50	5.50
☐ 232 Lefty O'Doul	65.00	32.50	6.50
☐ 233 Johnny Vergez	55.00	27.50	5.50
☐ 234 Carl Hubbell	175.00	85.00	18.00
☐ 235 Fred Fitzsimmons	65.00	32.50	6.50
☐ 236 George Davis	55.00	27.50	5.50
☐ 237 Gus Mancuso	55.00	27.50	5.50
☐ 238 Hugh Critz	55.00	27.50	5.50
☐ 239 Leroy Parmelee	55.00	27.50	5.50
☐ 240 Hal Schumacher	100.00	50.00	10.00

1934 Goudey

The cards in this 96-card set measure 2 3/8" by 2 7/8". The 1934 Goudey set of color cards carries the catalog number R320. Cards 1-48 are considered to be the easiest to find (although card number 1, Foxx, is very scarce in mint condition) while 73-96 are much more difficult to find. Cards of this 1934 Goudey series are slightly less abundant than cards of the 1933 Goudey set. Of the 96 cards, 84 contain a "Lou Gehrig Says" line on the front in a blue design, while 12 of the high series contain a

"Chuck Klein Says" line in a red design. These Chuck Klein cards are indicated in the checklist below by CK and are in fact the 12 National Leaguers in the high series.

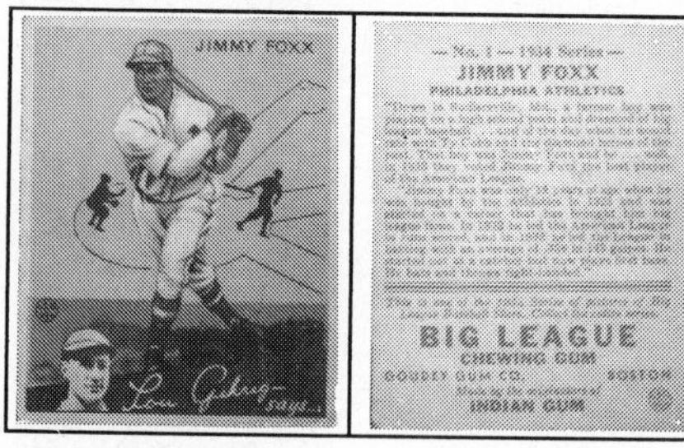

	EX-MT	VG-E	GOOD
COMPLETE SET (96)	15000.00	6000.00	1000.00
COMMON PLAYER (1-48)	55.00	27.50	5.50
COMMON PLAYER (49-72)	75.00	37.50	7.50
COMMON PLAYER (73-96)	200.00	100.00	20.00

☐ 1 Jimmy Foxx	650.00	100.00	20.00
☐ 2 Mickey Cochrane	150.00	75.00	15.00
☐ 3 Charlie Grimm	65.00	32.50	6.50
☐ 4 Woody English	55.00	27.50	5.50
☐ 5 Ed Brandt	55.00	27.50	5.50
☐ 6 Dizzy Dean	500.00	250.00	50.00
☐ 7 Leo Durocher	75.00	37.50	7.50
☐ 8 Tony Piet	55.00	27.50	5.50
☐ 9 Ben Chapman	65.00	32.50	6.50
☐ 10 Chuck Klein	100.00	50.00	10.00
☐ 11 Paul Waner	100.00	50.00	10.00
☐ 12 Carl Hubbell	150.00	75.00	15.00
☐ 13 Frank Frisch	150.00	75.00	15.00
☐ 14 Willie Kamm	55.00	27.50	5.50
☐ 15 Alvin Crowder	55.00	27.50	5.50
☐ 16 Joe Kuhel	55.00	27.50	5.50
☐ 17 Hugh Critz	55.00	27.50	5.50
☐ 18 Heinie Manush	100.00	50.00	10.00
☐ 19 Lefty Grove	200.00	100.00	20.00
☐ 20 Frank Hogan	55.00	27.50	5.50
☐ 21 Bill Terry	150.00	75.00	15.00
☐ 22 Arky Vaughan	100.00	50.00	10.00
☐ 23 Charlie Gehringer	150.00	75.00	15.00
☐ 24 Ray Benge	55.00	27.50	5.50
☐ 25 Roger Cramer	65.00	32.50	6.50
☐ 26 Gerald Walker	55.00	27.50	5.50
☐ 27 Luke Appling	100.00	50.00	10.00
☐ 28 Ed Coleman	55.00	27.50	5.50
☐ 29 Larry French	55.00	27.50	5.50
☐ 30 Julius Solters	55.00	27.50	5.50
☐ 31 Buck Jordan	55.00	27.50	5.50
☐ 32 Blondy Ryan	55.00	27.50	5.50
☐ 33 Frank Hurst	55.00	27.50	5.50
☐ 34 Chick Hafey	100.00	50.00	10.00
☐ 35 Ernie Lombardi	100.00	50.00	10.00
☐ 36 Walter Betts	55.00	27.50	5.50
☐ 37 Lou Gehrig	2000.00	800.00	225.00
☐ 38 Oral Hildebrand	55.00	27.50	5.50
☐ 39 Fred Walker	55.00	27.50	5.50
☐ 40 John Stone	55.00	27.50	5.50
☐ 41 George Earnshaw	55.00	27.50	5.50
☐ 42 John Allen	55.00	27.50	5.50
☐ 43 Dick Porter	55.00	27.50	5.50
☐ 44 Tom Bridges	65.00	32.50	6.50
☐ 45 Oscar Melillo	55.00	27.50	5.50
☐ 46 Joe Stripp	55.00	27.50	5.50
☐ 47 John Frederick	55.00	27.50	5.50
☐ 48 Tex Carleton	55.00	27.50	5.50
☐ 49 Sam Leslie	75.00	37.50	7.50
☐ 50 Walter Beck	75.00	37.50	7.50
☐ 51 Rip Collins	75.00	37.50	7.50
☐ 52 Herman Bell	75.00	37.50	7.50
☐ 53 George Watkins	75.00	37.50	7.50
☐ 54 Wesley Schulmerich	75.00	37.50	7.50
☐ 55 Ed Holley	75.00	37.50	7.50
☐ 56 Mark Koenig	75.00	37.50	7.50
☐ 57 Bill Swift	75.00	37.50	7.50
☐ 58 Earl Grace	75.00	37.50	7.50
☐ 59 Joe Mowry	75.00	37.50	7.50
☐ 60 Lynn Nelson	75.00	37.50	7.50
☐ 61 Lou Gehrig	2250.00	900.00	250.00
☐ 62 Hank Greenberg	250.00	125.00	25.00
☐ 63 Minter Hayes	75.00	37.50	7.50
☐ 64 Frank Grube	75.00	37.50	7.50
☐ 65 Cliff Bolton	75.00	37.50	7.50
☐ 66 Mel Harder	90.00	45.00	9.00
☐ 67 Bob Weiland	75.00	37.50	7.50
☐ 68 Bob Johnson	90.00	45.00	9.00
☐ 69 John Marcum	75.00	37.50	7.50
☐ 70 Pete Fox	75.00	37.50	7.50
☐ 71 Lyle Tinning	75.00	37.50	7.50
☐ 72 Arndt Jorgens	75.00	37.50	7.50
☐ 73 Ed Wells	200.00	100.00	20.00
☐ 74 Bob Boken	200.00	100.00	20.00
☐ 75 Bill Werber	200.00	100.00	20.00
☐ 76 Hal Trosky	225.00	110.00	22.00
☐ 77 Joe Vosmik	200.00	100.00	20.00
☐ 78 Pinky Higgins	225.00	110.00	22.00
☐ 79 Ed Durham	200.00	100.00	20.00
☐ 80 Marty McManus CK	200.00	100.00	20.00
☐ 81 Bob Brown CK	200.00	100.00	20.00
☐ 82 Bill Hallahan CK	200.00	100.00	20.00
☐ 83 Jim Mooney CK	200.00	100.00	20.00
☐ 84 Paul Derringer CK	225.00	110.00	22.00
☐ 85 Adam Comorosky CK	200.00	100.00	20.00
☐ 86 Lloyd Johnson CK	200.00	100.00	20.00
☐ 87 George Darrow CK	200.00	100.00	20.00
☐ 88 Homer Peel CK	200.00	100.00	20.00
☐ 89 Linus Frey CK	200.00	100.00	20.00
☐ 90 Ki-Ki Cuyler CK	400.00	200.00	40.00
☐ 91 Dolph Camilli CK	225.00	110.00	22.00
☐ 92 Steve Larkin	200.00	100.00	20.00
☐ 93 Fred Ostermueller	200.00	100.00	20.00
☐ 94 Red Rolfe	225.00	110.00	22.00
☐ 95 Myril Hoag	200.00	100.00	20.00
☐ 96 James DeShong	300.00	120.00	25.00

1935 Goudey

The cards in this 36-card set (the number of different front pictures) measure 2 3/8" by 2 7/8". The 1935 Goudey set is sometimes called the Goudey Puzzle Set, the Goudey 4-in-1's, or R321 (ACC). There are 36 different card fronts but 114 different front/back combinations. The card number in the checklist refers to the back puzzle number, as the backs can be arranged to form a puzzle picturing a player or team. To avoid the confusion caused by two different fronts having the same back number, the rarer cards have been arbitrarily given a "1" prefix. The scarcer puzzle cards are hence all listed at the numerical end of the list below, i.e. rare puzzle 1 is listed as number 11, rare puzzle 2 is listed as 12, etc. The BLUE in the checklist refers to a card with a blue border, as most cards have a red border. The set price below includes all the cards listed. The following is the list of the puzzle back pictures: 1) Detroit Tigers; 2) Chuck Klein; 3) Frankie Frisch; 4) Mickey Cochrane; 5) Joe Cronin; 6) Jimmy Foxx; 7) Al Simmons; 8) Cleveland Indians; and 9) Washington Senators.

	EX-MT	VG-E	GOOD
COMPLETE SET (114)	15000.00	6500.00	1250.00
COMMON CARDS (1-9)	50.00	25.00	5.00
COMMON CARDS (11-17)	100.00	50.00	10.00
☐ 1A F.Frisch/Dizzy Dean Orsatti/Carleton	160.00	80.00	16.00
☐ 1B Mahaffey/Jimmie Foxx Williams/Higgins	110.00	55.00	11.00

☐ 1C	Heinie Manush/Lary Weaver/Hadley	65.00	32.50	6.50
☐ 1D	Cochrane/C.Gehringer Bridges/Rogell	110.00	55.00	11.00
☐ 1E	Paul Waner/Bush W.Hoyt/Lloyd Waner	110.00	55.00	11.00
☐ 1F	B.Grimes/Chuck Klein K.Cuyler/English	110.00	55.00	11.00
☐ 1G	Leslie/Frey Joe Stripp/Clark	50.00	25.00	5.00
☐ 1H	Piet/Comorosky Bottomley/Adams	65.00	32.50	6.50
☐ 1I	Earnshaw/Dykes Luke Sewell/Appling	65.00	32.50	6.50
☐ 1J	Babe Ruth/McManus Brandt/Maranville	1000.00	400.00	100.00
☐ 1K	Bill Terry/Schumacher Mancuso/T.Jackson	110.00	55.00	11.00
☐ 1L	Kamm/Hildebrand Averill/Trosky	65.00	32.50	6.50
☐ 2A	F.Frisch/Dizzy Dean Orsatti/Carleton	160.00	80.00	16.00
☐ 2B	Mahaffey/Jimmie Foxx Williams/Higgins	110.00	55.00	11.00
☐ 2C	Heinie Manush/Lary Weaver/Hadley	65.00	32.50	6.50
☐ 2D	Cochrane/C.Gehringer Bridges/Rogell	110.00	55.00	11.00
☐ 2E	Kamm/Hildebrand Earl Averill/Trosky	65.00	32.50	6.50
☐ 2F	Earnshaw/Dykes Luke Sewell/Appling	65.00	32.50	6.50
☐ 3A	Babe Ruth/McManus Brandt/Maranville	1000.00	400.00	100.00
☐ 3B	Bill Terry/Schumacher Mancuso/T.Jackson	110.00	55.00	11.00
☐ 3C	Paul Waner/Bush W.Hoyt/Lloyd Waner	110.00	55.00	11.00
☐ 3D	B.Grimes/Chuck Klein K.Cuyler/English	110.00	55.00	11.00
☐ 3E	Leslie/Frey Joe Stripp/Clark	50.00	25.00	5.00
☐ 3F	Piet/Comorosky Jim Bottomley/Adams	65.00	32.50	6.50
☐ 4A	Critz/D.Bartell BLUE Mel Ott/Mancuso	100.00	50.00	10.00
☐ 4B	Pie Traynor/Lucas BLUE Tom Thevenow/Wright	65.00	32.50	6.50
☐ 4C	Berry/Burke BLUE Kress/Dazzy Vance	65.00	32.50	6.50
☐ 4D	R.Ruffing/Malone BLUE Lazzeri/Bill Dickey	160.00	80.00	16.00
☐ 4E	Moore/Hogan BLUE Frankhouse/Brandt	50.00	25.00	5.00
☐ 4F	Martin/O'Farrell BLUE Byrd/MacFayden	50.00	25.00	5.00
☐ 5A	Ruel/Al Simmons Kamm/M.Cochrane	110.00	55.00	11.00
☐ 5B	Willis Hudlin/Myatt Comorosky/Bottomley	65.00	32.50	6.50
☐ 5C	Paul Waner/Bush W.Hoyt/Lloyd Waner	110.00	55.00	11.00
☐ 5D	West/Oscar Melillo Blaeholder/Coffman	50.00	25.00	5.00
☐ 5E	Leslie/Frey Joe Stripp/Clark	50.00	25.00	5.00
☐ 5F	Schuble/Marberry Goose Goslin/Crowder	65.00	32.50	6.50
☐ 6A	Ruel/Al Simmons Kamm/M.Cochrane	110.00	55.00	11.00
☐ 6B	Willis Hudlin/Myatt Comorosky/Bottomley	65.00	32.50	6.50
☐ 6C	Wilson/Allen Jonnard/Brickell	50.00	25.00	5.00
☐ 6D	West/Oscar Melillo Blaeholder/Coffman	50.00	25.00	5.00
☐ 6E	Joe Cronin/Reynolds Bishop/Cissell	65.00	32.50	6.50
☐ 6F	Schuble/Marberry Goose Goslin/Crowder	65.00	32.50	6.50
☐ 7A	Critz/Bartell BLUE Mel Ott/Mancuso	100.00	50.00	10.00
☐ 7B	Pie Traynor/Lucas BLUE Tom Thevenow/Wright	65.00	32.50	6.50
☐ 7C	Berry/Burke BLUE Kress/Dazzy Vance	65.00	32.50	6.50
☐ 7D	R.Ruffing/Malone BLUE Lazzeri/Bill Dickey	160.00	80.00	16.00
☐ 7E	Moore/Hogan BLUE Frankhouse/Brandt	50.00	25.00	5.00
☐ 7F	Martin/O'Farrell BLUE Byrd/MacFayden	50.00	25.00	5.00
☐ 8A	M.Koenig/Fitzsimmons Benge/Zachary	50.00	25.00	5.00

☐ 8B	Hayes/Ted Lyons Haas/Zeke Bonura	65.00	32.50	6.50
☐ 8C	Burns/Rollie Hemsley Grube/Weiland	50.00	25.00	5.00
☐ 8D	Campbell/Meyers Goodman/Kampouris	50.00	25.00	5.00
☐ 8E	DeShong/Allen Red Rolfe/Walker	50.00	25.00	5.00
☐ 8F	P.Fox/Hank Greenberg Walker/Rowe	90.00	45.00	9.00
☐ 8G	Werber/Rick Ferrell W.Ferrell/Ostermueller	65.00	32.50	6.50
☐ 8H	Joe Kuhel/Whitehill Meyer/Stone	50.00	25.00	5.00
☐ 8I	J.Vosmik/Knickerbocker Mel Harder/Stewart	50.00	25.00	5.00
☐ 8J	Johnson/Coleman Marcum/Cramer	50.00	25.00	5.00
☐ 8K	Herman/Suhr Padden/Blanton	50.00	25.00	5.00
☐ 8L	Spohrer/Rhem Cantwell/Benton	50.00	25.00	5.00
☐ 8M	M.Koenig/Fitzsimmons Benge/Zachary	50.00	25.00	5.00
☐ 9B	Hayes/Ted Lyons Haas/Zeke Bonura	65.00	32.50	6.50
☐ 9C	Burns/Rollie Hemsley Grube/Weiland	50.00	25.00	5.00
☐ 9D	Campbell/Meyers Goodman/Kampouris	50.00	25.00	5.00
☐ 9E	DeShong/Allen Red Rolfe/Walker	50.00	25.00	5.00
☐ 9F	P.Fox/Hank Greenberg Walker/Rowe	90.00	45.00	9.00
☐ 9G	Werber/Rick Ferrell W.Ferrell/Ostermueller	65.00	32.50	6.50
☐ 9H	Joe Kuhel/Whitehill Meyer/Stone	50.00	25.00	5.00
☐ 9I	J.Vosmik/Knickerbocker Mel Harder/Stewart	50.00	25.00	5.00
☐ 9J	Johnson/Coleman Marcum/Cramer	50.00	25.00	5.00
☐ 9K	Herman/Suhr Padden/Blanton	50.00	25.00	5.00
☐ 9L	Spohrer/Rhem Cantwell/Benton	50.00	25.00	5.00
☐ 11E	Wilson/Allen Jonnard/Brickell	100.00	50.00	10.00
☐ 11F	West/Melillo Blaeholder/Coffman	100.00	50.00	10.00
☐ 11G	Joe Cronin/Reynolds Bishop/Cissel	150.00	75.00	15.00
☐ 11H	Schuble/Marberry Goose Goslin/Crowder	125.00	60.00	12.50
☐ 11J	Ruel/Al Simmons Kamm/M.Cochrane	180.00	90.00	18.00
☐ 11K	Hudlin/Myatt Comorosky/Bottomley	125.00	60.00	12.50
☐ 12A	Critz/Bartell BLUE Mel Ott/Mancuso	150.00	75.00	15.00
☐ 12B	P.Traynor/Lucas BLUE Thevenow/Wright	125.00	60.00	12.50
☐ 12C	Berry/Burke BLUE Kress/D.Vance	125.00	60.00	12.50
☐ 12D	Ruffing/Malone BLUE Lazzeri/Bill Dickey	250.00	125.00	25.00
☐ 12E	Moore/Hogan BLUE Frankhouse/Brandt	100.00	50.00	10.00
☐ 12F	Martin/O'Farrell BLUE Byrd/MacFayden	100.00	50.00	10.00
☐ 13A	Ruel/Al Simmons Kamm/M.Cochrane	180.00	90.00	18.00
☐ 13B	Hudlin/Myatt Comorosky/Bottomley	125.00	60.00	12.50
☐ 13C	Wilson/Allen Jonnard/Brickell	100.00	50.00	10.00
☐ 13D	West/Oscar Melillo Blaeholder/Coffman	100.00	50.00	10.00
☐ 13E	Joe Cronin/Reynolds Bishop/Cissell	125.00	60.00	12.50
☐ 13F	Schuble/Marberry Goose Goslin/Crowder	125.00	60.00	12.50
☐ 14A	Babe Ruth/McManus Brandt/Maranville	2000.00	800.00	200.00
☐ 14B	Bill Terry/Schumacher Mancuso/T.Jackson	160.00	80.00	16.00
☐ 14C	Paul Waner/Bush W.Hoyt/Lloyd Waner	160.00	80.00	16.00
☐ 14D	B.Grimes/Chuck Klein K.Cuyler/English	160.00	80.00	16.00
☐ 14E	Leslie/Frey Joe Stripp/Clark	100.00	50.00	10.00
☐ 14F	Piet/Comorosky Jim Bottomley/Adams	125.00	60.00	12.50

☐	15A Babe Ruth/McManus Brandt/Maranville	2000.00	800.00	200.00
☐	15B Bill Terry/Schumacher Mancuso/T.Jackson	160.00	80.00	16.00
☐	15C Wilson/Allen Jonnard/Brickell	100.00	50.00	10.00
☐	15D B.Grimes/Chuck Klein K.Cuyler/English	160.00	80.00	16.00
☐	15E Joe Cronin/Reynolds Bishop/Cissell	125.00	60.00	12.50
☐	15F Piet/Comorosky Jim Bottomley/Adams	125.00	60.00	12.50
☐	16A F.Frisch/Dizzy Dean E.Orsatti/Carleton	250.00	125.00	25.00
☐	16B Mahaffey/Jimmie Foxx Williams/Higgins	160.00	80.00	16.00
☐	16C Heinie Manush/Lary Weaver/Hadley	125.00	60.00	12.50
☐	16D Cochrane/C.Gehringer Tom Bridges/Rogell	180.00	90.00	18.00
☐	16E Kamm/Hildebrand Earl Averill/Trosky	125.00	60.00	12.50
☐	16F G.Earnshaw/Dykes Luke Sewell/Appling	125.00	60.00	12.50
☐	17A F.Frisch/Dizzy Dean E.Orsatti/Carleton	250.00	125.00	25.00
☐	17B Mahaffey/Jimmie Foxx Williams/Higgins	160.00	80.00	16.00
☐	17C Heinie Manush/Lary Weaver/Hadley	125.00	60.00	12.50
☐	17D Cochrane/C.Gehringer Tom Bridges/Rogell	180.00	90.00	18.00
☐	17E Kamm/Hildebrand Earl Averill/Trosky	125.00	60.00	12.50
☐	17F G.Earnshaw/Dykes Luke Sewell/Appling	125.00	60.00	12.50

1936 Goudey

THREE BAGGER
What a smash down 1st base line!—Too fast for the 1st sacker to even get near it.
Louis (Buck) Newsom — came up with St. Louis in 1934 from the Pacific Coast League. With Los Angeles in 1933 he had won 31 and lost 10. First he was an underhand pitcher; but now he flings overhand. A very colorful player — doing fine work with the Senators.
A line drive to center. The fielder had to move fast to spear this one.
OUT

The cards in this 25-card black and white set measure 2 3/8" by 2 7/8". In contrast to the color artwork of its previous sets, the 1936 Goudey set contained a simple black and white player photograph. A facsimile autograph appeared within the picture area. Each card was issued with a number of different "game situation" backs, and there may be as many as 200 different front/back combinations. The catalog designation for this set is R322.

	EX-MT	VG-E	GOOD
COMPLETE SET (25)	1500.00	650.00	150.00
COMMON PLAYER (1-25)	35.00	17.50	3.50
☐ 1 Wally Berger	40.00	20.00	4.00
☐ 2 Zeke Bonura	35.00	17.50	3.50
☐ 3 Stan Bordagaray	35.00	17.50	3.50
☐ 4 Bill Brubaker	35.00	17.50	3.50
☐ 5 Dolph Camilli	35.00	17.50	3.50
☐ 6 Clyde Castleman	35.00	17.50	3.50
☐ 7 Mickey Cochrane	150.00	75.00	15.00
☐ 8 Joe Coscarart	35.00	17.50	3.50
☐ 9 Frank Crosetti	60.00	30.00	6.00
☐ 10 Kiki Cuyler	85.00	42.50	8.50
☐ 11 Paul Derringer	45.00	22.50	4.50
☐ 12 Jimmy Dykes	45.00	22.50	4.50
☐ 13 Rick Ferrell	85.00	42.50	8.50
☐ 14 Lefty Gomez	150.00	75.00	15.00
☐ 15 Hank Greenberg	175.00	85.00	18.00
☐ 16 Bucky Harris	85.00	42.50	8.50
☐ 17 Rollie Hemsley	35.00	17.50	3.50
☐ 18 Pinky Higgins	35.00	17.50	3.50
☐ 19 Oral Hildebrand	35.00	17.50	3.50
☐ 20 Chuck Klein	100.00	50.00	10.00
☐ 21 Pepper Martin	50.00	25.00	5.00
☐ 22 Bobo Newsom	40.00	20.00	4.00
☐ 23 Joe Vosmik	35.00	17.50	3.50
☐ 24 Paul Waner	85.00	42.50	8.50
☐ 25 Bill Werber	35.00	17.50	3.50

1938 Goudey Heads Up

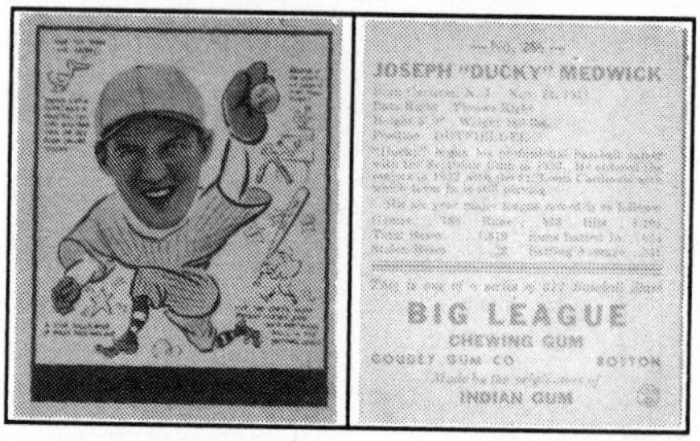

The cards in this 48-card set measure 2 3/8" by 2 7/8". The 1938 Goudey set is commonly referred to as the Heads-Up set, or R323 (ACC). These very popular but difficult to obtain cards came in two series of the same 24 players. The first series, numbers 241-264, is distinguished from the second series, numbers 265-288, in that the second contains etched cartoons and comments surrounding the player picture. Although the set starts with number 241, it is not a continuation of the 1933 Goudey set, but a separate set in its own right.

	EX-MT	VG-E	GOOD
COMPLETE SET (48)	13500.00	6000.00	1500.00
COMMON PLAYER (241-264)	80.00	40.00	8.00
COMMON PLAYER (265-288)	100.00	50.00	10.00
☐ 241 Charlie Gehringer	300.00	150.00	30.00
☐ 242 Pete Fox	80.00	40.00	8.00
☐ 243 Joe Kuhel	80.00	40.00	8.00
☐ 244 Frank Demaree	80.00	40.00	8.00
☐ 245 Frank Pytlak	80.00	40.00	8.00
☐ 246 Ernie Lombardi	175.00	85.00	18.00
☐ 247 Joe Vosmik	80.00	40.00	8.00
☐ 248 Dick Bartell	80.00	40.00	8.00
☐ 249 Jimmie Foxx	400.00	200.00	40.00
☐ 250 Joe DiMaggio	3000.00	1200.00	300.00
☐ 251 Bump Hadley	80.00	40.00	8.00
☐ 252 Zeke Bonura	80.00	40.00	8.00
☐ 253 Hank Greenberg	350.00	175.00	35.00
☐ 254 Van Lingle Mungo	80.00	40.00	8.00
☐ 255 Moose Solters	80.00	40.00	8.00
☐ 256 Vernon Kennedy	80.00	40.00	8.00
☐ 257 Al Lopez	175.00	85.00	18.00
☐ 258 Bobby Doerr	300.00	150.00	30.00
☐ 259 Billy Werber	80.00	40.00	8.00
☐ 260 Rudy York	80.00	40.00	8.00
☐ 261 Rip Radcliff	80.00	40.00	8.00
☐ 262 Joe Medwick	250.00	125.00	25.00
☐ 263 Marvin Owen	80.00	40.00	8.00
☐ 264 Bob Feller	600.00	300.00	60.00
☐ 265 Charlie Gehringer	350.00	175.00	35.00
☐ 266 Pete Fox	100.00	50.00	10.00
☐ 267 Joe Kuhel	100.00	50.00	10.00
☐ 268 Frank Demaree	100.00	50.00	10.00
☐ 269 Frank Pytlak	100.00	50.00	10.00
☐ 270 Ernie Lombardi	225.00	110.00	22.00
☐ 271 Joe Vosmik	100.00	50.00	10.00
☐ 272 Dick Bartell	100.00	50.00	10.00
☐ 273 Jimmie Foxx	450.00	225.00	45.00
☐ 274 Joe DiMaggio	3250.00	1350.00	325.00
☐ 275 Bump Hadley	100.00	50.00	10.00
☐ 276 Zeke Bonura	100.00	50.00	10.00
☐ 277 Hank Greenberg	400.00	200.00	40.00
☐ 278 Van Lingle Mungo	100.00	50.00	10.00
☐ 279 Moose Solters	100.00	50.00	10.00
☐ 280 Vernon Kennedy	100.00	50.00	10.00

☐ 281 Al Lopez	225.00	110.00	22.00
☐ 282 Bobby Doerr	350.00	175.00	35.00
☐ 283 Billy Werber	100.00	50.00	10.00
☐ 284 Rudy York	100.00	50.00	10.00
☐ 285 Rip Radcliff	100.00	50.00	10.00
☐ 286 Joe Medwick	300.00	150.00	30.00
☐ 287 Marvin Owen	100.00	50.00	10.00
☐ 288 Bob Feller	700.00	350.00	70.00

1981 Granny Goose

RICKEY HENDERSON
35 OUTFIELD
Rickey Henley Henderson
35 Outfield
Height: 5'10"
Weight: 198
Bats: Right
Throws: Left
In 1980 Rickey became the first American Leaguer and the 3rd in baseball history to steal 100 bases in a season. Rickey was 2nd in the league in walks with 117, and led the A's with 179 hits.
©1981 East West Promotions, Inc

This set is the hardest to obtain of the three years Granny Goose issued cards of the Oakland A's. The Revering card was supposedly destroyed by the printer soon after he was traded away and hence is in shorter supply than the other 14 cards in the set. Wayne Gross is also supposedly available in lesser quantity compared to the other players. Cards are standard size (2 1/2" by 3 1/2") and were issued in bags of potato chips. Cards are numbered on the front and back by the player's uniform number.

	MINT	EXC	G-VG
COMPLETE SET (15)	80.00	40.00	8.00
COMMON PLAYER	1.25	.60	.12
☐ 1 Billy Martin MG	8.00	4.00	.80
☐ 2 Mike Heath	1.25	.60	.12
☐ 5 Jeff Newman	1.25	.60	.12
☐ 6 Mitchell Page	1.25	.60	.12
☐ 8 Rob Picciolo	1.25	.60	.12
☐ 10 Wayne Gross	6.00	3.00	.60
☐ 13 Dave Revering SP	30.00	15.00	3.00
☐ 17 Mike Norris	1.25	.60	.12
☐ 20 Tony Armas	2.00	1.00	.20
☐ 21 Dwayne Murphy	2.00	1.00	.20
☐ 22 Rick Langford	1.50	.75	.15
☐ 27 Matt Keough	1.25	.60	.12
☐ 35 Rickey Henderson	35.00	17.50	3.50
☐ 39 Dave McKay	1.25	.60	.12
☐ 54 Steve McCatty	1.25	.60	.12

1982 Granny Goose

The cards in this 15-card set measure 2 1/2" by 3 1/2". Granny Goose Foods, Inc., a California based company, repeated its successful promotional idea of 1981 by issuing a new set of Oakland A's baseball cards for 1982. Each color player picture is surrounded by white borders and has trim and lettering done in Oakland's green and yellow colors. The cards are numbered according to the uniform number of the player, and the backs carry vital statistics done in black print on a white background. The cards were distributed in packages of potato chips and were also handed out on Fan Appreciation Day at the stadium. Although Picciolo was traded, his card was not withdrawn (as was Revering last year) and, therefore, its value is no greater than other cards in the set.

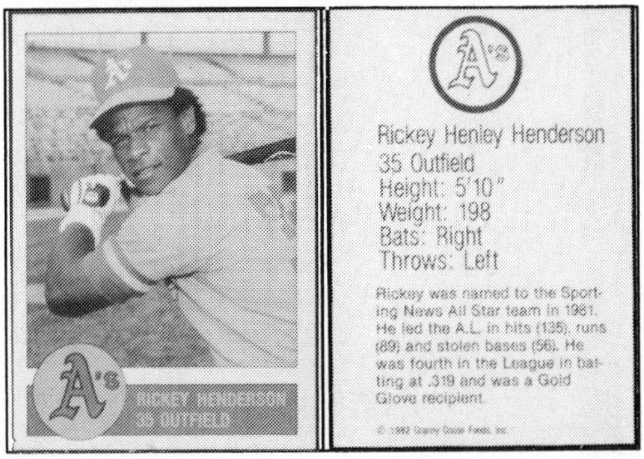
RICKEY HENDERSON
35 OUTFIELD
Rickey Henley Henderson
35 Outfield
Height: 5'10"
Weight: 198
Bats: Right
Throws: Left
Rickey was named to the Sporting News All Star team in 1981. He led the A.L. in hits (135), runs (89), and stolen bases (56). He was fourth in the League in batting at .319 and was a Gold Glove recipient.

	MINT	EXC	G-VG
COMPLETE SET (15)	18.00	9.00	1.80
COMMON PLAYER (1-15)	.50	.25	.05
☐ 1 Tony Armas	.75	.35	.07
☐ 2 Wayne Gross	.50	.25	.05
☐ 3 Mike Heath	.50	.25	.05
☐ 4 Rickey Henderson	12.00	6.00	1.20
☐ 5 Cliff Johnson	.50	.25	.05
☐ 6 Matt Keough	.50	.25	.05
☐ 7 Rick Langford	.50	.25	.05
☐ 8 Davey Lopes	.75	.35	.07
☐ 9 Billy Martin MG	2.50	1.25	.25
☐ 10 Steve McCatty	.50	.25	.05
☐ 11 Dwayne Murphy	.75	.35	.07
☐ 12 Jeff Newman	.50	.25	.05
☐ 13 Mike Norris	.50	.25	.05
☐ 14 Rob Picciolo	.50	.25	.05
☐ 15 Fred Stanley	.50	.25	.05

1983 Granny Goose

1983
Granny Goose GRAND SLAM Instant Winner Game
Mike Davis
16 Outfield
Height: 6'3"
Weight: 185
Bats: Left
Throws: Left
Granny Goose

The cards in this 15-card set measure 2 1/2" by 4 1/4". The 1983 Granny Goose Potato Chips set again features Oakland A's players. The cards that were issued in bags of potato chips have a tear off coupon on the bottom with a scratch off section featuring prizes. In addition to their release in bags of potato chips, the Granny Goose cards were also given away to fans attending the Oakland game of July 3, 1983. These give away cards did not contain the coupon on the bottom. Prices listed below are for cards without the detachable tabs that came on the bottom of the cards; cards with tabs intact are valued 50 percent higher than the prices below.

	MINT	EXC	G-VG
COMPLETE SET (15)	12.50	6.25	1.25
COMMON PLAYER	.50	.25	.05
☐ 2 Mike Heath	.50	.25	.05
☐ 4 Carney Lansford	2.00	1.00	.20
☐ 10 Wayne Gross	.50	.25	.05
☐ 14 Steve Boros MG	.50	.25	.05
☐ 15 Davey Lopes	.75	.35	.07
☐ 16 Mike Davis	.75	.35	.07
☐ 17 Mike Norris	.50	.25	.05
☐ 21 Dwayne Murphy	.75	.35	.07
☐ 22 Rick Langford	.50	.25	.05
☐ 27 Matt Keough	.50	.25	.05
☐ 31 Tom Underwood	.50	.25	.05
☐ 33 Dave Beard	.50	.25	.05
☐ 35 Rickey Henderson	8.00	4.00	.80
☐ 39 Tom Burgmeier	.50	.25	.05
☐ 54 Steve McCatty	.50	.25	.05

1958 Hires

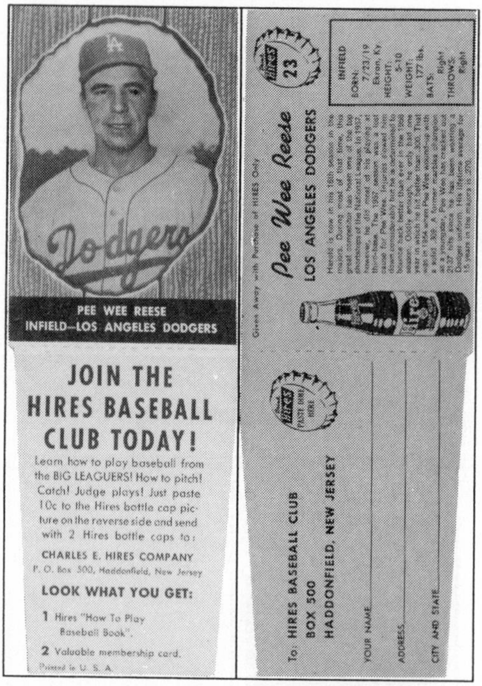

The cards in this 66-card set measure approximately 2 5/16" by 3 1/2" or 2 5/16" by 7" with tabs. The 1958 Hires Root Beer set of numbered, colored cards was issued with detachable coupons as inserts with Hires Root Beer cartons. Cards with the coupon still intact are worth double the prices listed below. The card front picture is surrounded by a wood grain effect which makes it look like the player is seen through a knot hole. The numbering of this set is rather strange in that it begins with 10 and skips 69.

	NRMT	VG-E	GOOD
COMPLETE SET (66)	1250.00	600.00	125.00
COMMON PLAYER (10-76)	10.00	5.00	1.00
☐ 10 Richie Ashburn	35.00	17.50	3.50
☐ 11 Chico Carrasquel	10.00	5.00	1.00
☐ 12 Dave Philley	10.00	5.00	1.00
☐ 13 Don Newcombe	15.00	7.50	1.50
☐ 14 Wally Post	10.00	5.00	1.00
☐ 15 Rip Repulski	10.00	5.00	1.00
☐ 16 Chico Fernandez	10.00	5.00	1.00
☐ 17 Larry Doby	15.00	7.50	1.50
☐ 18 Hector Brown	10.00	5.00	1.00
☐ 19 Danny O'Connell	10.00	5.00	1.00
☐ 20 Granny Hamner	10.00	5.00	1.00
☐ 21 Dick Groat	13.50	6.00	1.20
☐ 22 Ray Narleski	10.00	5.00	1.00
☐ 23 Pee Wee Reese	60.00	30.00	6.00
☐ 24 Bob Friend	12.00	6.00	1.20
☐ 25 Willie Mays	225.00	110.00	22.00
☐ 26 Bob Nieman	10.00	5.00	1.00
☐ 27 Frank Thomas	10.00	5.00	1.00
☐ 28 Curt Simmons	12.00	6.00	1.20
☐ 29 Stan Lopata	10.00	5.00	1.00
☐ 30 Bob Skinner	10.00	5.00	1.00
☐ 31 Ron Kline	10.00	5.00	1.00
☐ 32 Willie Miranda	10.00	5.00	1.00
☐ 33 Bobby Avila	10.00	5.00	1.00
☐ 34 Clem Labine	12.00	6.00	1.20
☐ 35 Ray Jablonski	10.00	5.00	1.00
☐ 36 Bill Mazeroski	16.00	8.00	1.60
☐ 37 Billy Gardner	10.00	5.00	1.00
☐ 38 Pete Runnels	12.00	6.00	1.20
☐ 39 Jack Sanford	10.00	5.00	1.00
☐ 40 Dave Sisler	10.00	5.00	1.00
☐ 41 Don Zimmer	15.00	7.50	1.50
☐ 42 Johnny Podres	15.00	7.50	1.50
☐ 43 Dick Farrell	10.00	5.00	1.00
☐ 44 Hank Aaron	225.00	110.00	22.00
☐ 45 Bill Virdon	15.00	7.50	1.50
☐ 46 Bobby Thomson	15.00	7.50	1.50
☐ 47 Willard Nixon	10.00	5.00	1.00
☐ 48 Billy Loes	10.00	5.00	1.00
☐ 49 Hank Sauer	12.00	6.00	1.20
☐ 50 Johnny Antonelli	12.00	6.00	1.20
☐ 51 Daryl Spencer	10.00	5.00	1.00
☐ 52 Ken Lehman	10.00	5.00	1.00
☐ 53 Sammy White	10.00	5.00	1.00
☐ 54 Charley Neal	12.00	6.00	1.20
☐ 55 Don Drysdale	45.00	22.50	4.50
☐ 56 Jackie Jensen	16.00	8.00	1.60
☐ 57 Ray Katt	10.00	5.00	1.00
☐ 58 Frank Sullivan	10.00	5.00	1.00
☐ 59 Roy Face	13.50	6.00	1.20
☐ 60 Willie Jones	10.00	5.00	1.00
☐ 61 Duke Snider	100.00	50.00	10.00
☐ 62 Whitey Lockman	10.00	5.00	1.00
☐ 63 Gino Cimoli	10.00	5.00	1.00
☐ 64 Marv Grissom	10.00	5.00	1.00
☐ 65 Gene Baker	10.00	5.00	1.00
☐ 66 George Zuverink	10.00	5.00	1.00
☐ 67 Ted Kluszewski	18.00	9.00	1.80
☐ 68 Jim Busby	10.00	5.00	1.00
☐ 69 Not Issued	00.00	0.00	0.00
☐ 70 Curt Barclay	10.00	5.00	1.00
☐ 71 Hank Foiles	10.00	5.00	1.00
☐ 72 Gene Stephens	10.00	5.00	1.00
☐ 73 Al Worthington	10.00	5.00	1.00
☐ 74 Al Walker	10.00	5.00	1.00
☐ 75 Bob Boyd	10.00	5.00	1.00
☐ 76 Al Pilarcik	10.00	5.00	1.00

1958 Hires Test

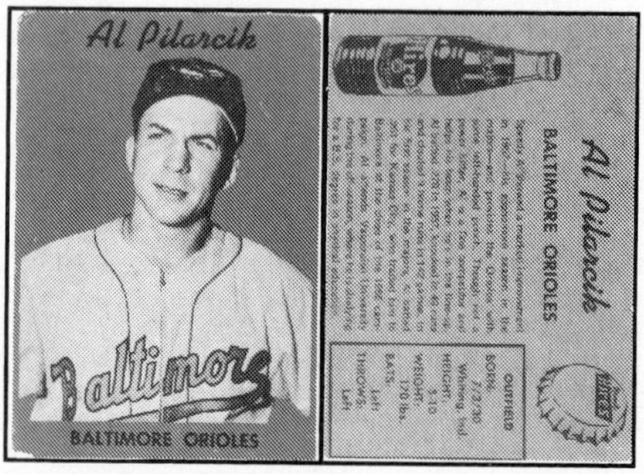

The cards in this 8-card test set measure approximately 2 5/16" by 3 1/2" or 2 5/16" by 7" with tabs. The 1958 Hires Root Beer test set features unnumbered, color cards. The card front photos are shown on a yellow or orange back ground instead of the wood grain background used in the Hires regular set. The cards contain a detachable coupon just as the regular Hires issue does. Cards were test marketed on a very limited basis in a few cities. Cards with the coupon still intact are worth double the prices in the checklist below. The checklist below is ordered alphabetically.

	NRMT	VG-E	GOOD
COMPLETE SET (8)	1000.00	400.00	100.00
COMMON PLAYER (1-8)	100.00	50.00	10.00
☐ 1 Johnny Antonelli	120.00	60.00	12.00
☐ 2 Jim Busby	100.00	50.00	10.00
☐ 3 Chico Fernandez	100.00	50.00	10.00
☐ 4 Bob Friend	120.00	60.00	12.00
☐ 5 Vern Law	120.00	60.00	12.00
☐ 6 Stan Lopata	100.00	50.00	10.00
☐ 7 Willie Mays	400.00	200.00	40.00
☐ 8 Al Pilarcik	100.00	50.00	10.00

1959 Home Run Derby

This 20-card set was produced in 1959 by American Motors to publicize a TV program. The cards are black and white and blank backed. The cards measure approximately 3 1/8" by 5 1/4". The cards are unnumbered and are ordered alphabetically below for convenience. During 1988, the 19 player cards in this set were publicly reprinted.

	NRMT	VG-E	GOOD
COMPLETE SET (20)	2500.00	1000.00	250.00
COMMON PLAYER (1-20)	40.00	20.00	4.00
☐ 1 Hank Aaron	300.00	150.00	30.00
☐ 2 Bob Allison	40.00	20.00	4.00
☐ 3 Ernie Banks	125.00	60.00	12.50
☐ 4 Ken Boyer	60.00	30.00	6.00
☐ 5 Bob Cerv	40.00	20.00	4.00
☐ 6 Rocky Colavito	60.00	30.00	6.00
☐ 7 Gil Hodges	100.00	50.00	10.00
☐ 8 Jackie Jensen	60.00	30.00	6.00
☐ 9 Al Kaline	150.00	75.00	15.00
☐ 10 Harmon Killebrew	125.00	60.00	12.50
☐ 11 Jim Lemon	40.00	20.00	4.00
☐ 12 Mickey Mantle	800.00	400.00	80.00
☐ 13 Ed Mathews	125.00	60.00	12.50
☐ 14 Willie Mays	300.00	150.00	30.00
☐ 15 Wally Post	40.00	20.00	4.00
☐ 16 Frank Robinson	125.00	60.00	12.50
☐ 17 Mark Scott (TV show host)	40.00	20.00	4.00
☐ 18 Duke Snider	200.00	100.00	20.00
☐ 19 Dick Stuart	40.00	20.00	4.00
☐ 20 Gus Triandos	40.00	20.00	4.00

1990 Homers Cookies Pirates

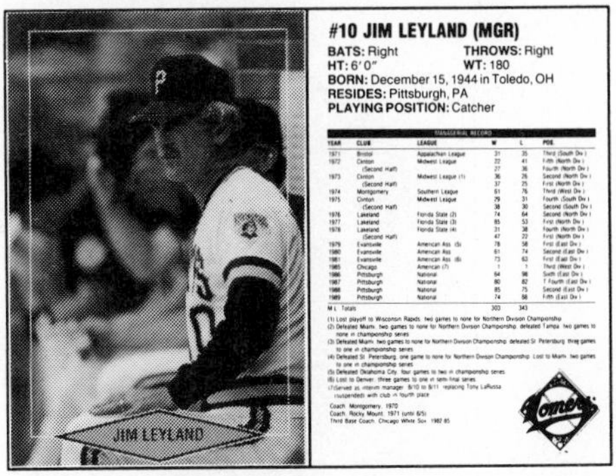

The 1990 Homers Cookies Pittsburgh Pirates set is an attractive 31-card set measuring approximately 4" by 6", used as a giveaway at a Pirates home game. It has been reported that 25,000 of these sets were produced. Four Homers Baseball trivia question cards were also included with the complete set. The fronts are full-color action photos with the back containing complete statistical information on the back. The set has been checklisted alphabetically below.

	MINT	EXC	G-VG
COMPLETE SET (31)	10.00	5.00	1.00
COMMON PLAYER (1-31)	.30	.15	.03
☐ 1 Wally Backman	.30	.15	.03
☐ 2 Doug Bair	.30	.15	.03
☐ 3 Rafael Belliard	.30	.15	.03
☐ 4 Jay Bell	.30	.15	.03
☐ 5 Barry Bonds	1.00	.50	.10
☐ 6 Bobby Bonilla	.90	.45	.09
☐ 7 Sid Bream	.30	.15	.03
☐ 8 John Cangelosi	.30	.15	.03
☐ 9 Rich Donnelly CO	.30	.15	.03
☐ 10 Doug Drabek	.60	.30	.06
☐ 11 Billy Hatcher	.40	.20	.04
☐ 12 Neal Heaton	.30	.15	.03
☐ 13 Jeff King	.40	.20	.04
☐ 14 Bob Kipper	.30	.15	.03
☐ 15 Randy Kramer	.30	.15	.03
☐ 16 Gene Lamont CO	.30	.15	.03
☐ 17 Bill Landrum	.30	.15	.03
☐ 18 Mike LaValliere	.30	.15	.03
☐ 19 Jim Leyland MG	.40	.20	.04
☐ 20 Jose Lind	.40	.20	.04
☐ 21 Milt May	.30	.15	.03
☐ 22 Ray Miller CO	.30	.15	.03
☐ 23 Ted Power	.30	.15	.03
☐ 24 Gary Redus	.30	.15	.03
☐ 25 R.J. Reynolds	.30	.15	.03
☐ 26 Tommy Sandt CO	.30	.15	.03
☐ 27 Don Slaught	.30	.15	.03
☐ 28 Walt Terrell	.30	.15	.03
☐ 29 Andy Van Slyke	.60	.30	.06
☐ 30 John Smiley	.40	.20	.04
☐ 31 Bob Walk	.30	.15	.03

1947 Homogenized Bond

The cards in this 48-card set measure 2 1/4" by 3 1/2". The 1947 W571/D305 Homogenized Bread are sets of unnumbered cards containing 44 baseball players and four boxers. The W571 set exists in two styles. Style one is identical to the D305 set except for the back printing while style two has perforated edges and movie stars depicted on the backs. The second style of W571 cards contains only 13 cards. The four boxers in the checklist below are indicated by BOX. The checklist below is ordered alphabetically. There are 24 cards in the set which were definitely produced in greater supply. These 24 (marked by DP below) are quite a bit more common than the other 24 cards in the set.

	NRMT	VG-E	GOOD
COMPLETE SET	550.00	275.00	55.00
COMMON PLAYER (1-48)	7.50	3.75	.75
COMMON BOXER	3.00	1.50	.30
COMMON DP BASEBALL	2.50	1.25	.25
COMMON DP BOXER	1.50	.75	.15

	NRMT	VG-E	GOOD
□ 1 Rex Barney	7.50	3.75	.75
□ 2 Larry Berra	50.00	25.00	5.00
□ 3 Ewell Blackwell DP	2.50	1.25	.25
□ 4 Lou Boudreau DP	6.00	3.00	.60
□ 5 Ralph Branca	9.00	4.50	.90
□ 6 Harry Brecheen DP	2.50	1.25	.25
□ 7 Primo Carnera BOX DP	1.50	.75	.15
□ 8 Marcel Cerdan BOX	3.00	1.50	.30
□ 9 Dom DiMaggio	10.00	5.00	1.00
□ 10 Joe DiMaggio	125.00	60.00	12.50
□ 11 Bobby Doerr DP	6.00	3.00	.60
□ 12 Bruce Edwards	7.50	3.75	.75
□ 13 Bob Elliott DP	2.50	1.25	.25
□ 14 Del Ennis DP	2.50	1.25	.25
□ 15 Bob Feller DP	12.50	6.25	1.25
□ 16 Carl Furillo	12.00	6.00	1.20
□ 17 Joe Gordon DP	2.50	1.25	.25
□ 18 Sid Gordon	7.50	3.75	.75
□ 19 Joe Hatten	7.50	3.75	.75
□ 20 Gil Hodges	30.00	15.00	3.00
□ 21 Tommy Holmes DP	2.50	1.25	.25
□ 22 Larry Jansen	7.50	3.75	.75
□ 23 Sheldon Jones	7.50	3.75	.75
□ 24 Edwin Joost	7.50	3.75	.75
□ 25 Charlie Keller	9.00	4.50	.90
□ 26 Ken Keltner DP	2.50	1.25	.25
□ 27 Buddy Kerr	7.50	3.75	.75
□ 28 Ralph Kiner DP	9.00	4.50	.90
□ 29 Jake LaMotta BOX	6.00	3.00	.60
□ 30 John Lindell	7.50	3.75	.75
□ 31 Whitey Lockman	7.50	3.75	.75
□ 32 Joe Louis BOX DP	7.50	3.75	.75
□ 33 Willard Marshall	7.50	3.75	.75
□ 34 Johnny Mize DP	9.00	4.50	.90
□ 35 Stan Musial DP	40.00	20.00	4.00
□ 36 Andy Pafko DP	2.50	1.25	.25
□ 37 Johnny Pesky DP	2.50	1.25	.25
□ 38 Pee Wee Reese	35.00	17.50	3.50
□ 39 Phil Rizzuto DP	12.00	6.00	1.20
□ 40 Aaron Robinson DP	2.50	1.25	.25
□ 41 Jackie Robinson DP	50.00	25.00	5.00
□ 42 John Sain DP	6.00	3.00	.60
□ 43 Enos Slaughter DP	9.00	4.50	.90
□ 44 Vern Stephens DP	2.50	1.25	.25
□ 45 George Tebbetts	7.50	3.75	.75
□ 46 Bobby Thomson	9.00	4.50	.90
□ 47 Johnny VanderMeer	9.00	4.50	.90
□ 48 Ted Williams DP	45.00	22.50	4.50

1975 Hostess

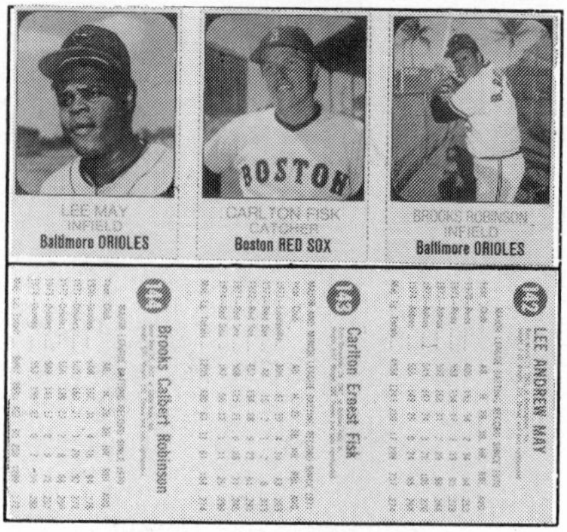

The cards in this 150-card set measure 2 1/4" by 3 1/4" individually or 3 1/4" by 7 1/4" as panels of three. The 1975 Hostess set was issued in panels of three cards each on the backs of family-size packages of Hostess cakes. Card number 125, Bill Madlock, was listed correctly as an infielder and incorrectly as a pitcher. Number 11, Burt Hooton, and number 89, Doug Rader, are spelled two different ways. Some panels are more difficult to find than others as they were issued only on the backs of less popular Hostess products. These scarcer panels are shown with asterisks in the checklist. Although complete panel prices are not explicitly listed, they would generally have a value 25 percent greater than the sum of the values of the individual players on that panel. One of the more interesting cards in the set is that of Robin Yount; Hostess had one of the few Yount cards available in 1975, his rookie year for cards.

	NRMT	VG-E	GOOD
COMPLETE INDIV.SET	200.00	100.00	20.00
COMMON PLAYER (1-150)	.50	.25	.05

	NRMT	VG-E	GOOD
□ 1 Bob Tolan	.50	.25	.05
□ 2 Cookie Rojas	.50	.25	.05
□ 3 Darrell Evans	.75	.35	.07
□ 4 Sal Bando	.60	.30	.06
□ 5 Joe Morgan	4.00	2.00	.40
□ 6 Mickey Lolich	.75	.35	.07
□ 7 Don Sutton	2.50	1.25	.25
□ 8 Bill Melton	.50	.25	.05
□ 9 Tim Foli	.50	.25	.05
□ 10 Joe LaHoud	.50	.25	.05
□ 11A Bert Hooten (sic)	1.00	.50	.10
□ 11B Burt Hooton	1.00	.50	.10
□ 12 Paul Blair	.50	.25	.05
□ 13 Jim Barr	.50	.25	.05
□ 14 Toby Harrah	.60	.30	.06
□ 15 John Milner	.50	.25	.05
□ 16 Ken Holtzman	.60	.30	.06
□ 17 Cesar Cedeno	.60	.30	.06
□ 18 Dwight Evans	1.50	.75	.15
□ 19 Willie McCovey	3.00	1.50	.30
□ 20 Tony Oliva	1.00	.50	.10
□ 21 Manny Sanguillen	.60	.30	.06
□ 22 Mickey Rivers	.50	.25	.05
□ 23 Lou Brock	3.50	1.75	.35
□ 24 Graig Nettles (Craig on front)	1.50	.75	.15
□ 25 Jim Wynn	.60	.30	.06
□ 26 George Scott	.50	.25	.05
□ 27 Greg Luzinski	.60	.30	.06
□ 28 Bert Campaneris	.60	.30	.06
□ 29 Pete Rose	10.00	5.00	1.00
□ 30 Buddy Bell	.75	.35	.07
□ 31 Gary Matthews	.60	.30	.06
□ 32 Freddie Patek	.50	.25	.05
□ 33 Mike Lum	.50	.25	.05
□ 34 Ellie Rodriguez	.50	.25	.05

☐ 35	Milt May UER (photo actually Lee May)	.60	.30	.06
☐ 36	Willie Horton	.60	.30	.06
☐ 37	Dave Winfield	4.50	2.25	.45
☐ 38	Tom Grieve	.60	.30	.06
☐ 39	Barry Foote	.50	.25	.05
☐ 40	Joe Rudi	.60	.30	.06
☐ 41	Bake McBride	.50	.25	.05
☐ 42	Mike Cuellar	.60	.30	.06
☐ 43	Garry Maddox	.60	.30	.06
☐ 44	Carlos May	.50	.25	.05
☐ 45	Bud Harrelson	.60	.30	.06
☐ 46	Dave Chalk	.50	.25	.05
☐ 47	Dave Concepcion	.75	.35	.07
☐ 48	Carl Yastrzemski	8.00	4.00	.80
☐ 49	Steve Garvey	4.50	2.25	.45
☐ 50	Amos Otis	.60	.30	.06
☐ 51	Rick Reuschel	.75	.35	.07
☐ 52	Rollie Fingers	1.50	.75	.15
☐ 53	Bob Watson	.60	.30	.06
☐ 54	John Ellis	.50	.25	.05
☐ 55	Bob Bailey	.50	.25	.05
☐ 56	Rod Carew	5.00	2.50	.50
☐ 57	Rich Hebner	.50	.25	.05
☐ 58	Nolan Ryan	10.00	5.00	1.00
☐ 59	Reggie Smith	.60	.30	.06
☐ 60	Joe Coleman	.50	.25	.05
☐ 61	Ron Cey	.60	.30	.06
☐ 62	Darrell Porter	.50	.25	.05
☐ 63	Steve Carlton	4.50	2.25	.45
☐ 64	Gene Tenace	.50	.25	.05
☐ 65	Jose Cardenal	.50	.25	.05
☐ 66	Bill Lee	.50	.25	.05
☐ 67	Dave Lopes	.60	.30	.06
☐ 68	Wilbur Wood	.60	.30	.06
☐ 69	Steve Renko	.50	.25	.05
☐ 70	Joe Torre	.80	.40	.08
☐ 71	Ted Sizemore	.50	.25	.05
☐ 72	Bobby Grich	.60	.30	.06
☐ 73	Chris Speier	.50	.25	.05
☐ 74	Bert Blyleven	1.00	.50	.10
☐ 75	Tom Seaver	4.50	2.25	.45
☐ 76	Nate Colbert	.50	.25	.05
☐ 77	Don Kessinger	.60	.30	.06
☐ 78	George Medich	.50	.25	.05
☐ 79	Andy Messersmith *	.60	.30	.06
☐ 80	Robin Yount *	20.00	10.00	2.00
☐ 81	Al Oliver *	.90	.45	.09
☐ 82	Bill Singer *	.60	.30	.06
☐ 83	Johnny Bench *	8.00	4.00	.80
☐ 84	Gaylord Perry *	3.50	1.75	.35
☐ 85	Dave Kingman *	.90	.45	.09
☐ 86	Ed Herrmann *	.60	.30	.06
☐ 87	Ralph Garr *	.60	.30	.06
☐ 88	Reggie Jackson *	8.00	4.00	.80
☐ 89A	Doug Radar ERR * (sic, Rader)	1.00	.50	.10
☐ 89B	Doug Rader COR *	2.00	1.00	.20
☐ 90	Elliott Maddox *	.60	.30	.06
☐ 91	Bill Russell *	.75	.35	.07
☐ 92	John Mayberry *	.60	.30	.06
☐ 93	Dave Cash *	.60	.30	.06
☐ 94	Jeff Burroughs *	.60	.30	.06
☐ 95	Ted Simmons *	1.00	.50	.10
☐ 96	Joe Decker *	.60	.30	.06
☐ 97	Bill Buckner *	.90	.45	.09
☐ 98	Bobby Darwin *	.60	.30	.06
☐ 99	Phil Niekro *	3.00	1.50	.30
☐ 100	Jim Sundberg	.60	.30	.06
☐ 101	Greg Gross	.50	.25	.05
☐ 102	Luis Tiant	.75	.35	.07
☐ 103	Glenn Beckert	.50	.25	.05
☐ 104	Hal McRae	.60	.30	.06
☐ 105	Mike Jorgensen	.50	.25	.05
☐ 106	Mike Hargrove	.60	.30	.06
☐ 107	Don Gullett	.60	.30	.06
☐ 108	Tito Fuentes	.50	.25	.05
☐ 109	John Grubb	.50	.25	.05
☐ 110	Jim Kaat	1.00	.50	.10
☐ 111	Felix Millan	.50	.25	.05
☐ 112	Don Money	.50	.25	.05
☐ 113	Rick Monday	.60	.30	.06
☐ 114	Dick Bosman	.50	.25	.05
☐ 115	Roger Metzger	.50	.25	.05
☐ 116	Fergie Jenkins	2.50	1.25	.25
☐ 117	Dusty Baker	.60	.30	.06
☐ 118	Billy Champion *	.60	.30	.06
☐ 119	Bob Gibson *	3.50	1.75	.35
☐ 120	Bill Freehan *	.75	.35	.07
☐ 121	Cesar Geronimo	.50	.25	.05
☐ 122	Jorge Orta	.50	.25	.05
☐ 123	Cleon Jones	.50	.25	.05
☐ 124	Steve Busby	.60	.30	.06
☐ 125A	Bill Madlock ERR (pitcher)	1.50	.75	.15
☐ 125B	Bill Madlock COR (infielder)	1.50	.75	.15
☐ 126	Jim Palmer	3.50	1.75	.35
☐ 127	Tony Perez	1.00	.50	.10
☐ 128	Larry Hisle	.60	.30	.06
☐ 129	Rusty Staub	.60	.30	.06
☐ 130	Hank Aaron *	10.00	5.00	1.00
☐ 131	Rennie Stennett *	.60	.30	.06
☐ 132	Rico Petrocelli *	.60	.30	.06
☐ 133	Mike Schmidt	10.00	5.00	1.00
☐ 134	Sparky Lyle	.75	.35	.07
☐ 135	Willie Stargell	3.50	1.75	.35
☐ 136	Ken Henderson	.50	.25	.05
☐ 137	Willie Montanez	.50	.25	.05
☐ 138	Thurman Munson	5.00	2.50	.50
☐ 139	Richie Zisk	.60	.30	.06
☐ 140	George Hendrick	.60	.30	.06
☐ 141	Bobby Murcer	.75	.35	.07
☐ 142	Lee May	.60	.30	.06
☐ 143	Carlton Fisk	2.50	1.25	.25
☐ 144	Brooks Robinson	3.50	1.75	.35
☐ 145	Bobby Bonds	.80	.40	.08
☐ 146	Gary Sutherland	.50	.25	.05
☐ 147	Oscar Gamble	.60	.30	.06
☐ 148	Jim Hunter	2.50	1.25	.25
☐ 149	Tug McGraw	.75	.35	.07
☐ 150	Dave McNally	.60	.30	.06

1975 Hostess Twinkie

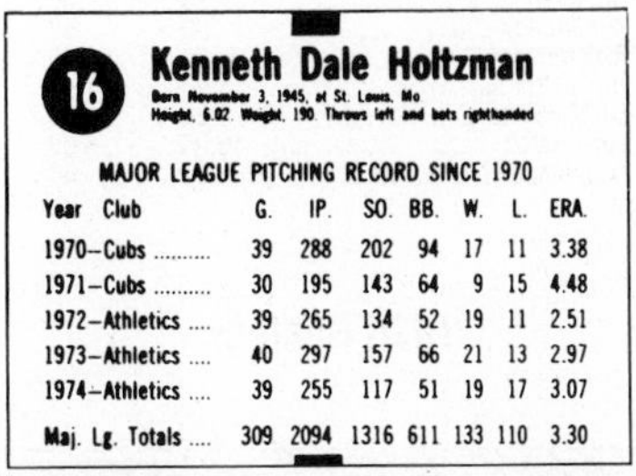

16 Kenneth Dale Holtzman
Born November 3, 1945, at St. Louis, Mo
Height, 6.02 Weight, 190 Throws left and bats righthanded

MAJOR LEAGUE PITCHING RECORD SINCE 1970

Year Club	G.	IP.	SO.	BB.	W.	L.	ERA.
1970–Cubs	39	288	202	94	17	11	3.38
1971–Cubs	30	195	143	64	9	15	4.48
1972–Athletics	39	265	134	52	19	11	2.51
1973–Athletics	40	297	157	66	21	13	2.97
1974–Athletics	39	255	117	51	19	17	3.07
Maj. Lg. Totals	309	2094	1316	611	133	110	3.30

The cards in this 60-card set measure 2 1/4" by 3 1/4". The 1975 Hostess Twinkie set was issued on a limited basis in the far western part of the country. The set contains the same numbers as the regular set to number 36; however, the set is skip numbered after number 36. The cards were issued as the backs for 25-cent Twinkies packs. The fronts are indistinguishable from the regular Hostess cards; however the card backs are different in that the Twinkie cards have a thick black bar in the middle of the reverse. One of the more interesting cards in the set is that of Robin Yount; Hostess had one of the few Yount cards available in 1975, his rookie year for cards.

		NRMT	VG-E	GOOD
COMPLETE SET (60)		100.00	50.00	10.00
COMMON PLAYER		.90	.45	.09
☐ 1	Bob Tolan	.90	.45	.09
☐ 2	Cookie Rojas	.90	.45	.09
☐ 3	Darrell Evans	1.00	.50	.10
☐ 4	Sal Bando	.90	.45	.09
☐ 5	Joe Morgan	4.00	2.00	.40
☐ 6	Mickey Lolich	1.00	.50	.10
☐ 7	Don Sutton	2.50	1.25	.25
☐ 8	Bill Melton	.90	.45	.09
☐ 9	Tim Foli	.90	.45	.09
☐ 10	Joe LaHoud	.90	.45	.09
☐ 11	Bert Hooten (sic)	1.00	.50	.10
☐ 12	Paul Blair	.90	.45	.09
☐ 13	Jim Barr	.90	.45	.09
☐ 14	Toby Harrah	.90	.45	.09
☐ 15	John Milner	.90	.45	.09
☐ 16	Ken Holtzman	.90	.45	.09
☐ 17	Cesar Cedeno	1.00	.50	.10
☐ 18	Dwight Evans	1.50	.75	.15
☐ 19	Willie McCovey	3.00	1.50	.30

☐ 20 Tony Oliva	1.25	.60	.12
☐ 21 Manny Sanguillen	.90	.45	.09
☐ 22 Mickey Rivers	1.00	.50	.10
☐ 23 Lou Brock	3.50	1.75	.35
☐ 24 Graig Nettles (Craig on front)	1.50	.75	.15
☐ 25 Jim Wynn	.90	.45	.09
☐ 26 George Scott	.90	.45	.09
☐ 27 Greg Luzinski	1.00	.50	.10
☐ 28 Bert Campaneris	.90	.45	.09
☐ 29 Pete Rose	10.00	5.00	1.00
☐ 30 Buddy Bell	1.00	.50	.10
☐ 31 Gary Matthews	.90	.45	.09
☐ 32 Freddie Patek	.90	.45	.09
☐ 33 Mike Lum	.90	.45	.09
☐ 34 Ellie Rodriguez	.90	.45	.09
☐ 35 Milt May UER (Lee May picture)	.90	.45	.09
☐ 36 Willie Horton	1.00	.50	.10
☐ 40 Joe Rudi	1.00	.50	.10
☐ 43 Garry Maddox	.90	.45	.09
☐ 46 Dave Chalk	.90	.45	.09
☐ 49 Steve Garvey	4.50	2.25	.45
☐ 52 Rollie Fingers	1.50	.75	.15
☐ 58 Nolan Ryan	10.00	5.00	1.00
☐ 61 Ron Cey	1.00	.50	.10
☐ 64 Gene Tenace	.90	.45	.09
☐ 65 Jose Cardenal	.90	.45	.09
☐ 67 Dave Lopes	1.00	.50	.10
☐ 68 Wilbur Wood	.90	.45	.09
☐ 73 Chris Speier	.90	.45	.09
☐ 77 Don Kessinger	1.00	.50	.10
☐ 79 Andy Messersmith	.90	.45	.09
☐ 80 Robin Yount	20.00	10.00	2.00
☐ 82 Bill Singer	.90	.45	.09
☐ 103 Glenn Beckert	.90	.45	.09
☐ 110 Jim Kaat	1.25	.60	.12
☐ 112 Don Money	.90	.45	.09
☐ 113 Rick Monday	.90	.45	.09
☐ 122 Jorge Orta	.90	.45	.09
☐ 125 Bill Madlock	1.00	.50	.10
☐ 130 Hank Aaron	10.00	5.00	1.00
☐ 136 Ken Henderson	.90	.45	.09

1976 Hostess

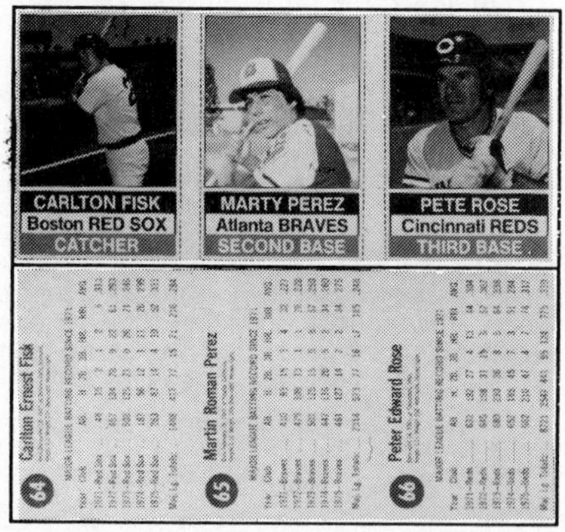

The cards in this 150-card set measure 2 1/4" by 3 1/4" individually or 3 1/4" by 7 1/4" as panels of three. The 1976 Hostess set contains full-color, numbered cards issued in panels of three cards each on family-size packages of Hostess cakes. Scarcer panels (those only found on less popular Hostess products) are listed in the checklist below with asterisks. Complete panels of three have a value 25 percent more than the sum of the individual cards on the panel. Nine additional numbers (151-159) were apparently planned but never actually issued. These exist as proof cards and are quite scarce, e.g., 151 Ferguson Jenkins, 152 Mike Cuellar, 153 Tom Murphy, 154 Al Cowens, 155 Barry Foote, 156 Steve Carlton, 157 Richie Zisk, 158 Ken Holtzman, and 159 Cliff Johnson. One of the more interesting cards in the set is that of Dennis Eckersley; Hostess had one of the few Eckersley cards available in 1976, his rookie year for cards.

	NRMT	VG-E	GOOD
COMPLETE INDIV.SET(150)	200.00	100.00	20.00
COMMON PLAYER (1-150)	.50	.25	.05
☐ 1 Fred Lynn	1.25	.60	.12
☐ 2 Joe Morgan	3.50	1.75	.35
☐ 3 Phil Niekro	3.00	1.50	.30
☐ 4 Gaylord Perry	3.00	1.50	.30
☐ 5 Bob Watson	.60	.30	.06
☐ 6 Bill Freehan	.75	.35	.07
☐ 7 Lou Brock	3.50	1.75	.35
☐ 8 Al Fitzmorris	.50	.25	.05
☐ 9 Rennie Stennett	.50	.25	.05
☐ 10 Tony Oliva	1.00	.50	.10
☐ 11 Robin Yount	10.00	5.00	1.00
☐ 12 Rick Manning	.50	.25	.05
☐ 13 Bobby Grich	.60	.30	.06
☐ 14 Terry Forster	.60	.30	.06
☐ 15 Dave Kingman	.75	.35	.07
☐ 16 Thurman Munson	5.00	2.50	.50
☐ 17 Rick Reuschel	.75	.35	.07
☐ 18 Bobby Bonds	.80	.40	.08
☐ 19 Steve Garvey	4.00	2.00	.40
☐ 20 Vida Blue	.60	.30	.06
☐ 21 Dave Rader	.50	.25	.05
☐ 22 Johnny Bench	6.00	3.00	.60
☐ 23 Luis Tiant	.75	.35	.07
☐ 24 Darrell Evans	.75	.35	.07
☐ 25 Larry Dierker	.50	.25	.05
☐ 26 Willie Horton	.60	.30	.06
☐ 27 John Ellis	.50	.25	.05
☐ 28 Al Cowens	.50	.25	.05
☐ 29 Jerry Reuss	.50	.25	.05
☐ 30 Reggie Smith	.60	.30	.06
☐ 31 Bobby Darwin *	.60	.30	.06
☐ 32 Fritz Peterson *	.60	.30	.06
☐ 33 Rod Carew *	5.00	2.50	.50
☐ 34 Carlos May *	.60	.30	.06
☐ 35 Tom Seaver *	5.00	2.50	.50
☐ 36 Brooks Robinson *	4.50	2.25	.45
☐ 37 Jose Cardenal	.50	.25	.05
☐ 38 Ron Blomberg	.50	.25	.05
☐ 39 Leroy Stanton	.50	.25	.05
☐ 40 Dave Cash	.50	.25	.05
☐ 41 John Montefusco	.60	.30	.06
☐ 42 Bob Tolan	.50	.25	.05
☐ 43 Carl Morton	.50	.25	.05
☐ 44 Rick Burleson	.60	.30	.06
☐ 45 Don Gullett	.60	.30	.06
☐ 46 Vern Ruhle	.50	.25	.05
☐ 47 Cesar Cedeno	.60	.30	.06
☐ 48 Toby Harrah	.60	.30	.06
☐ 49 Willie Stargell	3.50	1.75	.35
☐ 50 Al Hrabosky	.60	.30	.06
☐ 51 Amos Otis	.60	.30	.06
☐ 52 Bud Harrelson	.60	.30	.06
☐ 53 Jim Hughes	.50	.25	.05
☐ 54 George Scott	.50	.25	.05
☐ 55 Mike Vail *	.60	.30	.06
☐ 56 Jim Palmer *	4.50	2.25	.45
☐ 57 Jorge Orta *	.60	.30	.06
☐ 58 Chris Chambliss *	.75	.35	.07
☐ 59 Dave Chalk *	.60	.30	.06
☐ 60 Ray Burris *	.60	.30	.06
☐ 61 Bert Campaneris *	.75	.35	.07
☐ 62 Gary Carter *	6.00	3.00	.60
☐ 63 Ron Cey *	.75	.35	.07
☐ 64 Carlton Fisk *	2.50	1.25	.25
☐ 65 Marty Perez *	.60	.30	.06
☐ 66 Pete Rose *	10.00	5.00	1.00
☐ 67 Roger Metzger *	.60	.30	.06
☐ 68 Jim Sundberg *	.60	.30	.06
☐ 69 Ron LeFlore *	.60	.30	.06
☐ 70 Ted Sizemore *	.60	.30	.06
☐ 71 Steve Busby *	.75	.35	.07
☐ 72 Manny Sanguillen *	.75	.35	.07
☐ 73 Larry Hisle *	.60	.30	.06
☐ 74 Pete Broberg *	.60	.30	.06
☐ 75 Boog Powell *	1.00	.50	.10
☐ 76 Ken Singleton *	.75	.35	.07
☐ 77 Rich Gossage *	1.25	.60	.12
☐ 78 Jerry Grote *	.60	.30	.06
☐ 79 Nolan Ryan *	10.00	5.00	1.00
☐ 80 Rick Monday *	.75	.35	.07
☐ 81 Graig Nettles *	1.00	.50	.10
☐ 82 Chris Speier	.50	.25	.05
☐ 83 Dave Winfield	3.50	1.75	.35
☐ 84 Mike Schmidt	9.00	4.50	.90

☐ 85 Buzz Capra	.50	.25	.05
☐ 86 Tony Perez	1.00	.50	.10
☐ 87 Dwight Evans	1.00	.50	.10
☐ 88 Mike Hargrove	.60	.30	.06
☐ 89 Joe Coleman	.50	.25	.05
☐ 90 Greg Gross	.50	.25	.05
☐ 91 John Mayberry	.60	.30	.06
☐ 92 John Candelaria	.75	.35	.07
☐ 93 Bake McBride	.50	.25	.05
☐ 94 Hank Aaron	8.00	4.00	.80
☐ 95 Buddy Bell	.60	.30	.06
☐ 96 Steve Braun	.50	.25	.05
☐ 97 Jon Matlack	.60	.30	.06
☐ 98 Lee May	.60	.30	.06
☐ 99 Wilbur Wood	.60	.30	.06
☐ 100 Bill Madlock	.75	.35	.07
☐ 101 Frank Tanana	.60	.30	.06
☐ 102 Mickey Rivers	.50	.25	.05
☐ 103 Mike Ivie	.50	.25	.05
☐ 104 Rollie Fingers	1.25	.60	.12
☐ 105 Dave Lopes	.60	.30	.06
☐ 106 George Foster	1.00	.50	.10
☐ 107 Denny Doyle	.50	.25	.05
☐ 108 Earl Williams	.50	.25	.05
☐ 109 Tom Veryzer	.50	.25	.05
☐ 110 J.R. Richard	.60	.30	.06
☐ 111 Jeff Burroughs	.50	.25	.05
☐ 112 Al Oliver	.75	.35	.07
☐ 113 Ted Simmons	.75	.35	.07
☐ 114 George Brett	10.00	5.00	1.00
☐ 115 Frank Duffy	.50	.25	.05
☐ 116 Bert Blyleven	.90	.45	.09
☐ 117 Darrell Porter	.50	.25	.05
☐ 118 Don Baylor	.75	.35	.07
☐ 119 Bucky Dent	.75	.35	.07
☐ 120 Felix Millan	.50	.25	.05
☐ 121 Mike Cuellar	.60	.30	.06
☐ 122 Gene Tenace	.50	.25	.05
☐ 123 Bobby Murcer	.60	.30	.06
☐ 124 Willie McCovey	2.50	1.25	.25
☐ 125 Greg Luzinski	.75	.35	.07
☐ 126 Larry Parrish	.50	.25	.05
☐ 127 Jim Rice	3.50	1.75	.35
☐ 128 Dave Concepcion	.75	.35	.07
☐ 129 Jim Wynn	.60	.30	.06
☐ 130 Tom Grieve	.60	.30	.06
☐ 131 Mike Cosgrove	.50	.25	.05
☐ 132 Dan Meyer	.50	.25	.05
☐ 133 Dave Parker	2.00	1.00	.20
☐ 134 Don Kessinger	.60	.30	.06
☐ 135 Hal McRae	.60	.30	.06
☐ 136 Don Money	.50	.25	.05
☐ 137 Dennis Eckersley	5.00	2.50	.50
☐ 138 Fergie Jenkins	2.50	1.25	.25
☐ 139 Mike Torrez	.60	.30	.06
☐ 140 Jerry Morales	.50	.25	.05
☐ 141 Jim Hunter	2.50	1.25	.25
☐ 142 Gary Matthews	.60	.30	.06
☐ 143 Randy Jones	.60	.30	.06
☐ 144 Mike Jorgensen	.50	.25	.05
☐ 145 Larry Bowa	.75	.35	.07
☐ 146 Reggie Jackson	6.00	3.00	.60
☐ 147 Steve Yeager	.50	.25	.05
☐ 148 Dave May	.50	.25	.05
☐ 149 Carl Yastrzemski	7.00	3.50	.70
☐ 150 Cesar Geronimo	.50	.25	.05

1976 Hostess Twinkie

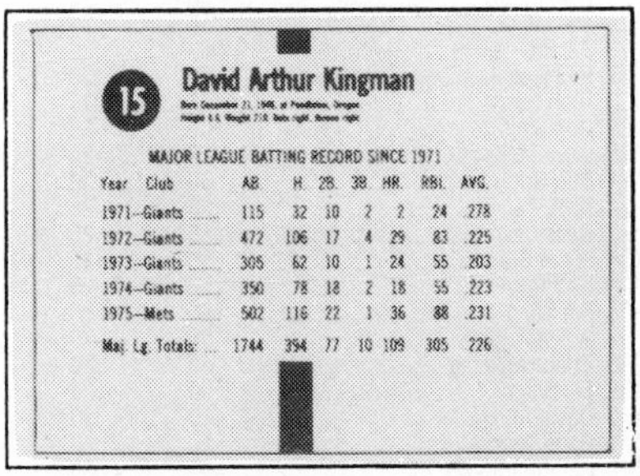

The cards in this 60-card set measure 2 1/4" by 3 1/4". The 1976 Hostess Twinkies set contains the first 60 cards of the 1976 Hostess set. These cards were issued as backs on 25-cent Twinkie packages as in the 1975 Twinkies set. The fronts are indistinguishable from the regular Hostess cards; however the card backs are different in that the Twinkie cards have a thick black bar in the middle of the reverse.

	NRMT	VG-E	GOOD
COMPLETE SET (60)	100.00	50.00	10.00
COMMON PLAYER (1-60)	.90	.45	.09
☐ 1 Fred Lynn	1.25	.60	.12
☐ 2 Joe Morgan	3.50	1.75	.35
☐ 3 Phil Niekro	3.00	1.50	.30
☐ 4 Gaylord Perry	3.00	1.50	.30
☐ 5 Bob Watson	.90	.45	.09
☐ 6 Bill Freehan	1.00	.50	.10
☐ 7 Lou Brock	3.50	1.75	.35
☐ 8 Al Fitzmorris	.90	.45	.09
☐ 9 Rennie Stennett	.90	.45	.09
☐ 10 Tony Oliva	1.25	.60	.12
☐ 11 Robin Yount	10.00	5.00	1.00
☐ 12 Rick Manning	.90	.45	.09
☐ 13 Bobby Grich	1.00	.50	.10
☐ 14 Terry Forster	.90	.45	.09
☐ 15 Dave Kingman	1.25	.60	.12
☐ 16 Thurman Munson	5.00	2.50	.50
☐ 17 Rick Reuschel	1.00	.50	.10
☐ 18 Bobby Bonds	1.25	.60	.12
☐ 19 Steve Garvey	4.00	2.00	.40
☐ 20 Vida Blue	1.00	.50	.10
☐ 21 Dave Rader	.90	.45	.09
☐ 22 Johnny Bench	6.00	3.00	.60
☐ 23 Luis Tiant	1.00	.50	.10
☐ 24 Darrell Evans	1.00	.50	.10
☐ 25 Larry Dierker	.90	.45	.09
☐ 26 Willie Horton	1.00	.50	.10
☐ 27 John Ellis	.90	.45	.09
☐ 28 Al Cowens	.90	.45	.09
☐ 29 Jerry Reuss	.90	.45	.09
☐ 30 Reggie Smith	1.00	.50	.10
☐ 31 Bobby Darwin	.90	.45	.09
☐ 32 Fritz Peterson	.90	.45	.09
☐ 33 Rod Carew	5.00	2.50	.50
☐ 34 Carlos May	.90	.45	.09
☐ 35 Tom Seaver	5.00	2.50	.50
☐ 36 Brooks Robinson	4.50	2.25	.45
☐ 37 Jose Cardenal	.90	.45	.09
☐ 38 Ron Blomberg	.90	.45	.09
☐ 39 Leroy Stanton	.90	.45	.09
☐ 40 Dave Cash	.90	.45	.09
☐ 41 John Montefusco	.90	.45	.09
☐ 42 Bob Tolan	.90	.45	.09
☐ 43 Carl Morton	.90	.45	.09
☐ 44 Rick Burleson	.90	.45	.09
☐ 45 Don Gullett	.90	.45	.09
☐ 46 Vern Ruhle	.90	.45	.09
☐ 47 Cesar Cedeno	1.00	.50	.10
☐ 48 Toby Harrah	.90	.45	.09
☐ 49 Willie Stargell	3.50	1.75	.35
☐ 50 Al Hrabosky	.90	.45	.09
☐ 51 Amos Otis	1.00	.50	.10
☐ 52 Bud Harrelson	1.00	.50	.10
☐ 53 Jim Hughes	.90	.45	.09
☐ 54 George Scott	.90	.45	.09
☐ 55 Mike Vail	.90	.45	.09
☐ 56 Jim Palmer	4.00	2.00	.40
☐ 57 Jorge Orta	.90	.45	.09
☐ 58 Chris Chambliss	1.00	.50	.10
☐ 59 Dave Chalk	.90	.45	.09
☐ 60 Ray Burris	.90	.45	.09

1977 Hostess

The cards in this 150-card set measure 2 1/4" by 3 1/4" individually or 3 1/4" by 7 1/4" as panels of three. The 1977 Hostess set contains full-color, numbered cards issued in panels of three cards each with Hostess family-size cake products. Scarcer panels are listed in the checklist below with asterisks. Although complete panel prices are not explicitly listed below, they would generally have a value 25 percent greater than the sum of the individual players on the panel. There were 10 additional cards proofed, but not produced or distributed; they are 151 Ed Kranepool, 152 Ross Grimsley, 153 Ken Brett, 154 Rowland Office, 155 Rick Wise, 156 Paul

Splittorff, 157 Gerald Augustine, 158 Ken Forsch, 159 Jerry Reuss (Reuss is also number 119 in the set), and 160 Nelson Briles. There is also a complete variation set that was available one card per Twinkie package. Common cards in this Twinkie set are worth double the prices listed below, although the stars are only worth about 20 percent more. The Twinkie cards are distinguished by the thick printing bar or band printed on the card backs just below the statistics.

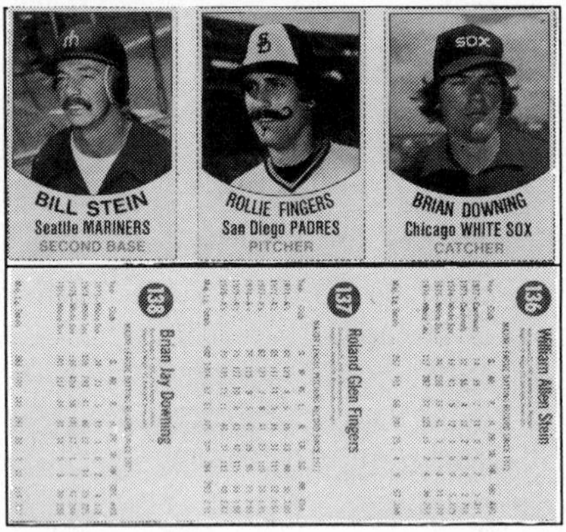

	NRMT	VG-E	GOOD
COMPLETE IND.SET (150)	200.00	100.00	20.00
COMMON PLAYER (1-150)	.50	.25	.05
☐ 1 Jim Palmer	3.50	1.75	.35
☐ 2 Joe Morgan	3.50	1.75	.35
☐ 3 Reggie Jackson	6.00	3.00	.60
☐ 4 Carl Yastrzemski	7.00	3.50	.70
☐ 5 Thurman Munson	5.00	2.50	.50
☐ 6 Johnny Bench	6.00	3.00	.60
☐ 7 Tom Seaver	4.50	2.25	.45
☐ 8 Pete Rose	9.00	4.50	.90
☐ 9 Rod Carew	5.00	2.50	.50
☐ 10 Luis Tiant	.75	.35	.07
☐ 11 Phil Garner	.50	.25	.05
☐ 12 Sixto Lezcano	.50	.25	.05
☐ 13 Mike Torrez	.50	.25	.05
☐ 14 Dave Lopes	.60	.30	.06
☐ 15 Doug DeCinces	.60	.30	.06
☐ 16 Jim Spencer	.50	.25	.05
☐ 17 Hal McRae	.60	.30	.06
☐ 18 Mike Hargrove	.60	.30	.06
☐ 19 Willie Montanez *	.60	.30	.06
☐ 20 Roger Metzger *	.60	.30	.06
☐ 21 Dwight Evans *	1.50	.75	.15
☐ 22 Steve Rogers *	.75	.35	.07
☐ 23 Jim Rice *	3.50	1.75	.35
☐ 24 Pete Falcone *	.60	.30	.06
☐ 25 Greg Luzinski *	.90	.45	.09
☐ 26 Randy Jones *	.60	.30	.06
☐ 27 Willie Stargell *	3.50	1.75	.35
☐ 28 John Hiller *	.60	.30	.06
☐ 29 Bobby Murcer *	.75	.35	.07
☐ 30 Rick Monday *	.60	.30	.06
☐ 31 John Montefusco *	.60	.30	.06
☐ 32 Lou Brock *	3.50	1.75	.35
☐ 33 Bill North *	.60	.30	.06
☐ 34 Robin Yount *	7.50	3.75	.75
☐ 35 Steve Garvey *	5.00	2.50	.50
☐ 36 George Brett *	9.00	4.50	.90
☐ 37 Toby Harrah *	.60	.30	.06
☐ 38 Jerry Royster *	.60	.30	.06
☐ 39 Bob Watson *	.60	.30	.06
☐ 40 George Foster	.90	.45	.09
☐ 41 Gary Carter	3.50	1.75	.35
☐ 42 John Denny	.60	.30	.06
☐ 43 Mike Schmidt	8.00	4.00	.80
☐ 44 Dave Winfield	3.00	1.50	.30
☐ 45 Al Oliver	.75	.35	.07
☐ 46 Mark Fidrych	.60	.30	.06
☐ 47 Larry Herndon	.50	.25	.05
☐ 48 Dave Goltz	.50	.25	.05
☐ 49 Jerry Morales	.50	.25	.05
☐ 50 Ron LeFlore	.60	.30	.06
☐ 51 Fred Lynn	1.00	.50	.10
☐ 52 Vida Blue	.60	.30	.06
☐ 53 Rick Manning	.50	.25	.05
☐ 54 Bill Buckner	.75	.35	.07
☐ 55 Lee May	.60	.30	.06
☐ 56 John Mayberry	.60	.30	.06
☐ 57 Darrell Chaney	.50	.25	.05
☐ 58 Cesar Cedeno	.60	.30	.06
☐ 59 Ken Griffey	.90	.45	.09
☐ 60 Dave Kingman	.75	.35	.07
☐ 61 Ted Simmons	.90	.45	.09
☐ 62 Larry Bowa	.60	.30	.06
☐ 63 Frank Tanana	.60	.30	.06
☐ 64 Jason Thompson	.60	.30	.06
☐ 65 Ken Brett	.50	.25	.05
☐ 66 Roy Smalley	.60	.30	.06
☐ 67 Ray Burris	.50	.25	.05
☐ 68 Rick Burleson	.60	.30	.06
☐ 69 Buddy Bell	.75	.35	.07
☐ 70 Don Sutton	2.00	1.00	.20
☐ 71 Mark Belanger	.60	.30	.06
☐ 72 Dennis Leonard	.60	.30	.06
☐ 73 Gaylord Perry	2.50	1.25	.25
☐ 74 Dick Ruthven	.50	.25	.05
☐ 75 Jose Cruz	.60	.30	.06
☐ 76 Cesar Geronimo	.50	.25	.05
☐ 77 Jerry Koosman	.75	.35	.07
☐ 78 Garry Templeton	.75	.35	.07
☐ 79 Jim Hunter	2.50	1.25	.25
☐ 80 John Candelaria	.60	.30	.06
☐ 81 Nolan Ryan	10.00	5.00	1.00
☐ 82 Rusty Staub	.75	.35	.07
☐ 83 Jim Barr	.50	.25	.05
☐ 84 Butch Wynegar	.50	.25	.05
☐ 85 Jose Cardenal	.50	.25	.05
☐ 86 Claudell Washington	.60	.30	.06
☐ 87 Bill Travers	.50	.25	.05
☐ 88 Rick Waits	.50	.25	.05
☐ 89 Ron Cey	.75	.35	.07
☐ 90 Al Bumbry	.50	.25	.05
☐ 91 Bucky Dent	.75	.35	.07
☐ 92 Amos Otis	.60	.30	.06
☐ 93 Tom Grieve	.60	.30	.06
☐ 94 Enos Cabell	.50	.25	.05
☐ 95 Dave Concepcion	.75	.35	.07
☐ 96 Felix Millan	.50	.25	.05
☐ 97 Bake McBride	.50	.25	.05
☐ 98 Chris Chambliss	.60	.30	.06
☐ 99 Butch Metzger	.50	.25	.05
☐ 100 Rennie Stennett	.50	.25	.05
☐ 101 Dave Roberts	.50	.25	.05
☐ 102 Lyman Bostock	.60	.30	.06
☐ 103 Rick Reuschel	.75	.35	.07
☐ 104 Carlton Fisk	2.00	1.00	.20
☐ 105 Jim Slaton	.50	.25	.05
☐ 106 Dennis Eckersley	2.00	1.00	.20
☐ 107 Ken Singleton	.60	.30	.06
☐ 108 Ralph Garr	.50	.25	.05
☐ 109 Freddie Patek *	.60	.30	.06
☐ 110 Jim Sundberg *	.60	.30	.06
☐ 111 Phil Niekro *	2.00	1.00	.20
☐ 112 J.R. Richard *	.60	.30	.06
☐ 113 Gary Nolan *	.60	.30	.06
☐ 114 Jon Matlack *	.60	.30	.06
☐ 115 Keith Hernandez *	4.00	2.00	.40
☐ 116 Graig Nettles *	1.00	.50	.10
☐ 117 Steve Carlton *	4.00	2.00	.40
☐ 118 Bill Madlock *	1.25	.60	.12
☐ 119 Jerry Reuss *	.60	.30	.06
☐ 120 Aurelio Rodriguez *	.60	.30	.06
☐ 121 Dan Ford *	.60	.30	.06
☐ 122 Ray Fosse *	.60	.30	.06
☐ 123 George Hendrick *	.60	.30	.06
☐ 124 Alan Ashby	.50	.25	.05
☐ 125 Joe Lis	.50	.25	.05
☐ 126 Sal Bando	.60	.30	.06
☐ 127 Richie Zisk	.60	.30	.06
☐ 128 Rich Gossage	.75	.35	.07
☐ 129 Don Baylor	.60	.30	.06
☐ 130 Dave McKay	.50	.25	.05
☐ 131 Bob Grich	.60	.30	.06
☐ 132 Dave Pagan	.50	.25	.05
☐ 133 Dave Cash	.50	.25	.05
☐ 134 Steve Braun	.50	.25	.05
☐ 135 Dan Meyer	.50	.25	.05
☐ 136 Bill Stein	.50	.25	.05
☐ 137 Rollie Fingers	1.50	.75	.15
☐ 138 Brian Downing	.60	.30	.06
☐ 139 Bill Singer	.50	.25	.05
☐ 140 Doyle Alexander	.60	.30	.06
☐ 141 Gene Tenace	.50	.25	.05
☐ 142 Gary Matthews	.60	.30	.06
☐ 143 Don Gullett	.60	.30	.06
☐ 144 Wayne Garland	.50	.25	.05

☐ 145 Pete Broberg	.50	.25	.05
☐ 146 Joe Rudi	.60	.30	.06
☐ 147 Glenn Abbott	.50	.25	.05
☐ 148 George Scott	.50	.25	.05
☐ 149 Bert Campaneris	.60	.30	.06
☐ 150 Andy Messersmith	.60	.30	.06

1978 Hostess

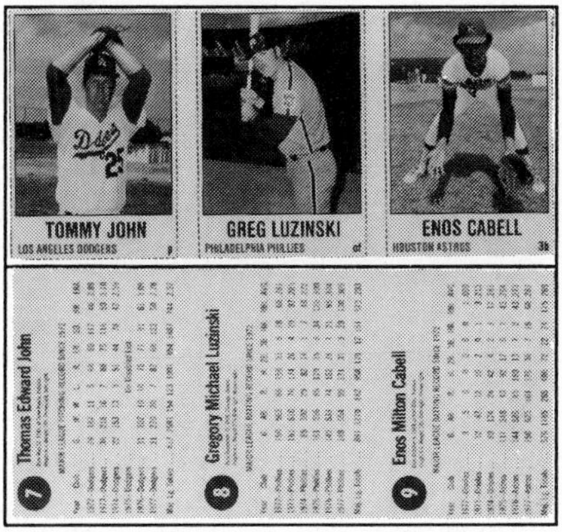

The cards in this 150-card set measure 2 1/4" by 3 1/4" individually or 3 1/4" by 7 1/4" as panels of three. The 1978 Hostess set contains full-color, numbered cards issued in panels of three cards each on family packages of Hostess cake products. Scarcer panels are listed in the checklist with asterisks. The 1978 Hostess panels are considered by some collectors to be somewhat more difficult to obtain than Hostess panels of other years. Although complete panel prices are not explicitly listed below, they would generally have a value 25 percent greater than the sum of the individual players on the panel. There is additional interest in Eddie Murray number 31, since this card corresponds to his "rookie" year in cards.

	NRMT	VG-E	GOOD
COMPLETE IND.SET (150)	200.00	100.00	20.00
COMMON PLAYER (1-150)	.50	.25	.05
☐ 1 Butch Hobson	.50	.25	.05
☐ 2 George Foster	.90	.45	.09
☐ 3 Bob Forsch	.60	.30	.06
☐ 4 Tony Perez	.90	.45	.09
☐ 5 Bruce Sutter	.90	.45	.09
☐ 6 Hal McRae	.40	.20	.04
☐ 7 Tommy John	1.00	.50	.10
☐ 8 Greg Luzinski	.60	.30	.06
☐ 9 Enos Cabell	.50	.25	.05
☐ 10 Doug DeCinces	.60	.30	.06
☐ 11 Willie Stargell	2.50	1.25	.25
☐ 12 Ed Halicki	.50	.25	.05
☐ 13 Larry Hisle	.50	.25	.05
☐ 14 Jim Slaton	.50	.25	.05
☐ 15 Buddy Bell	.75	.35	.07
☐ 16 Earl Williams	.50	.25	.05
☐ 17 Glenn Abbott	.50	.25	.05
☐ 18 Dan Ford	.50	.25	.05
☐ 19 Gary Matthews	.60	.30	.06
☐ 20 Eric Soderholm	.50	.25	.05
☐ 21 Bump Wills	.50	.25	.05
☐ 22 Keith Hernandez	2.50	1.25	.25
☐ 23 Dave Cash	.50	.25	.05
☐ 24 George Scott	.50	.25	.05
☐ 25 Ron Guidry	1.50	.75	.15
☐ 26 Dave Kingman	.75	.35	.07
☐ 27 George Brett	7.50	3.75	.75
☐ 28 Bob Watson *	.60	.30	.06
☐ 29 Bob Boone *	1.00	.50	.10
☐ 30 Reggie Smith *	.75	.35	.07
☐ 31 Eddie Murray *	15.00	7.50	1.50
☐ 32 Gary Lavelle *	.60	.30	.06
☐ 33 Rennie Stennett *	.60	.30	.06
☐ 34 Duane Kuiper *	.60	.30	.06
☐ 35 Sixto Lezcano *	.60	.30	.06
☐ 36 Dave Rozema *	.60	.30	.06
☐ 37 Butch Wynegar *	.60	.30	.06
☐ 38 Mitchell Page *	.60	.30	.06
☐ 39 Bill Stein *	.60	.30	.06
☐ 40 Elliott Maddox	.50	.25	.05
☐ 41 Mike Hargrove	.60	.30	.06
☐ 42 Bobby Bonds	.80	.40	.08
☐ 43 Garry Templeton	.60	.30	.06
☐ 44 Johnny Bench	5.00	2.50	.50
☐ 45 Jim Rice	3.00	1.50	.30
☐ 46 Bill Buckner	.60	.30	.06
☐ 47 Reggie Jackson	5.00	2.50	.50
☐ 48 Freddie Patek	.50	.25	.05
☐ 49 Steve Carlton	3.50	1.75	.35
☐ 50 Cesar Cedeno	.60	.30	.06
☐ 51 Steve Yeager	.50	.25	.05
☐ 52 Phil Garner	.50	.25	.05
☐ 53 Lee May	.60	.30	.06
☐ 54 Darrell Evans	.75	.35	.07
☐ 55 Steve Kemp	.60	.30	.06
☐ 56 Dusty Baker	.60	.30	.06
☐ 57 Ray Fosse	.50	.25	.05
☐ 58 Manny Sanguillen	.60	.30	.06
☐ 59 Tom Johnson	.50	.25	.05
☐ 60 Lee Stanton	.50	.25	.05
☐ 61 Jeff Burroughs	.60	.30	.06
☐ 62 Bobby Grich	.60	.30	.06
☐ 63 Dave Winfield	3.00	1.50	.30
☐ 64 Dan Driessen	.60	.30	.06
☐ 65 Ted Simmons	.75	.35	.07
☐ 66 Jerry Remy	.50	.25	.05
☐ 67 Al Cowens	.60	.30	.06
☐ 68 Sparky Lyle	.75	.35	.07
☐ 69 Manny Trillo	.60	.30	.06
☐ 70 Don Sutton	2.00	1.00	.20
☐ 71 Larry Bowa	.60	.30	.06
☐ 72 Jose Cruz	.60	.30	.06
☐ 73 Willie McCovey	2.00	1.00	.20
☐ 74 Bert Blyleven	.90	.45	.09
☐ 75 Ken Singleton	.60	.30	.06
☐ 76 Bill North	.50	.25	.05
☐ 77 Jason Thompson	.60	.30	.06
☐ 78 Dennis Eckersley	1.50	.75	.15
☐ 79 Jim Sundberg	.60	.30	.06
☐ 80 Jerry Koosman	.60	.30	.06
☐ 81 Bruce Bochte	.50	.25	.05
☐ 82 George Hendrick	.50	.25	.05
☐ 83 Nolan Ryan	9.00	4.50	.90
☐ 84 Roy Howell	.50	.25	.05
☐ 85 Roger Metzger	.50	.25	.05
☐ 86 Doc Medich	.50	.25	.05
☐ 87 Joe Morgan	3.00	1.50	.30
☐ 88 Dennis Leonard	.60	.30	.06
☐ 89 Willie Randolph	.75	.35	.07
☐ 90 Bobby Murcer	.60	.30	.06
☐ 91 Rick Manning	.50	.25	.05
☐ 92 J.R. Richard	.60	.30	.06
☐ 93 Ron Cey	.60	.30	.06
☐ 94 Sal Bando	.60	.30	.06
☐ 95 Ron LeFlore	.60	.30	.06
☐ 96 Dave Goltz	.50	.25	.05
☐ 97 Dan Meyer	.50	.25	.05
☐ 98 Chris Chambliss	.60	.30	.06
☐ 99 Biff Pocoroba	.50	.25	.05
☐ 100 Oscar Gamble	.60	.30	.06
☐ 101 Frank Tanana	.60	.30	.06
☐ 102 Len Randle	.50	.25	.05
☐ 103 Tommy Hutton	.50	.25	.05
☐ 104 John Candelaria	.60	.30	.06
☐ 105 Jorge Orta	.50	.25	.05
☐ 106 Ken Reitz	.50	.25	.05
☐ 107 Bill Campbell	.50	.25	.05
☐ 108 Dave Concepcion	.75	.35	.07
☐ 109 Joe Ferguson	.50	.25	.05
☐ 110 Mickey Rivers	.60	.30	.06
☐ 111 Paul Splittorff	.60	.30	.06
☐ 112 Dave Lopes	.60	.30	.06
☐ 113 Mike Schmidt	7.50	3.75	.75
☐ 114 Joe Rudi	.60	.30	.06
☐ 115 Milt May	.50	.25	.05
☐ 116 Jim Palmer	3.00	1.50	.30
☐ 117 Bill Madlock	.90	.45	.09
☐ 118 Roy Smalley	.60	.30	.06
☐ 119 Cecil Cooper	.90	.45	.09
☐ 120 Rick Langford	.50	.25	.05
☐ 121 Ruppert Jones	.60	.30	.06
☐ 122 Phil Niekro	1.50	.75	.15
☐ 123 Toby Harrah	.60	.30	.06
☐ 124 Chet Lemon	.60	.30	.06
☐ 125 Gene Tenace	.50	.25	.05
☐ 126 Steve Henderson	.50	.25	.05

☐ 127 Mike Torrez	.50	.25	.05
☐ 128 Pete Rose	9.00	4.50	.90
☐ 129 John Denny	.60	.30	.06
☐ 130 Darrell Porter	.60	.30	.06
☐ 131 Rick Reuschel	.75	.35	.07
☐ 132 Graig Nettles	.75	.35	.07
☐ 133 Garry Maddox	.50	.25	.05
☐ 134 Mike Flanagan	.60	.30	.06
☐ 135 Dave Parker	2.00	1.00	.20
☐ 136 Terry Whitfield	.50	.25	.05
☐ 137 Wayne Garland	.50	.25	.05
☐ 138 Robin Yount	7.50	3.75	.75
☐ 139 Gaylord Perry	2.00	1.00	.20
☐ 140 Rod Carew	4.50	2.25	.45
☐ 141 Wayne Gross	.50	.25	.05
☐ 142 Barry Bonnell	.50	.25	.05
☐ 143 Willie Montanez	.50	.25	.05
☐ 144 Rollie Fingers	1.50	.75	.15
☐ 145 Lyman Bostock	.60	.30	.06
☐ 146 Gary Carter	3.50	1.75	.35
☐ 147 Ron Blomberg	.50	.25	.05
☐ 148 Bob Bailor	.50	.25	.05
☐ 149 Tom Seaver	4.00	2.00	.40
☐ 150 Thurman Munson	4.00	2.00	.40

1979 Hostess

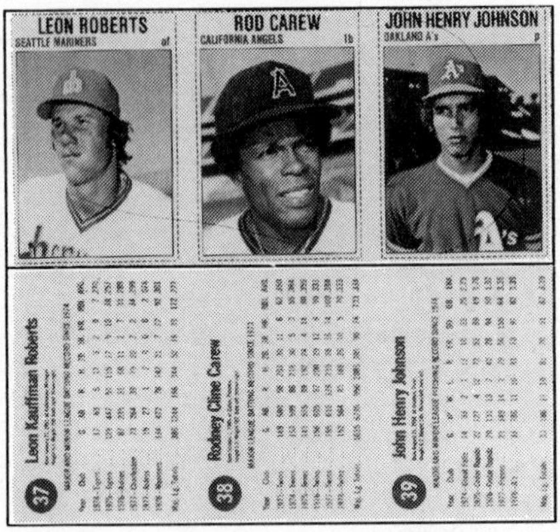

The cards in this 150-card set measure 2 1/4" by 3 1/4" individually or 3 1/4" by 7 1/4" as panels of three. The 1979 Hostess set contains full color, numbered cards issued in panels of three cards each on the backs of family sized Hostess cake products. Scarcer panels are listed in the checklist below with asterisks. Although complete panel prices are not explicitly listed below they would generally have a value 25 percent greater than the sum of the individual players on the panel. There is additional interest in Ozzie Smith number 102 since this card corresponds to his rookie year in cards.

	NRMT	VG-E	GOOD
COMPLETE INDIV. SET	200.00	100.00	20.00
COMMON PLAYER (1-150)	.50	.25	.05

☐ 1 John Denny	.60	.30	.06
☐ 2 Jim Rice	3.00	1.50	.30
☐ 3 Doug Bair	.50	.25	.05
☐ 4 Darrell Porter	.50	.25	.05
☐ 5 Ross Grimsley	.50	.25	.05
☐ 6 Bobby Murcer	.60	.30	.06
☐ 7 Lee Mazzilli	.50	.25	.05
☐ 8 Steve Garvey	3.50	1.75	.35
☐ 9 Mike Schmidt	7.50	3.75	.75
☐ 10 Terry Whitfield	.50	.25	.05
☐ 11 Jim Palmer	3.00	1.50	.30
☐ 12 Omar Moreno	.50	.25	.05
☐ 13 Duane Kuiper	.50	.25	.05
☐ 14 Mike Caldwell	.50	.25	.05
☐ 15 Steve Kemp	.50	.25	.05
☐ 16 Dave Goltz	.50	.25	.05
☐ 17 Mitchell Page	.50	.25	.05
☐ 18 Bill Stein	.50	.25	.05
☐ 19 Gene Tenace	.50	.25	.05
☐ 20 Jeff Burroughs	.50	.25	.05
☐ 21 Francisco Barrios	.50	.25	.05
☐ 22 Mike Torrez	.50	.25	.05
☐ 23 Ken Reitz	.50	.25	.05
☐ 24 Gary Carter	3.00	1.50	.30
☐ 25 Al Hrabosky	.60	.30	.06
☐ 26 Thurman Munson	4.00	2.00	.40
☐ 27 Bill Buckner	.60	.30	.06
☐ 28 Ron Cey *	.75	.35	.07
☐ 29 J.R. Richard *	.60	.30	.06
☐ 30 Greg Luzinski *	.90	.45	.09
☐ 31 Ed Ott *	.60	.30	.06
☐ 32 Dennis Martinez *	.75	.35	.07
☐ 33 Darrell Evans *	.75	.35	.07
☐ 34 Ron LeFlore	.50	.25	.05
☐ 35 Rick Waits	.50	.25	.05
☐ 36 Cecil Cooper	.75	.35	.07
☐ 37 Leon Roberts	.50	.25	.05
☐ 38 Rod Carew	4.50	2.25	.45
☐ 39 John Henry Johnson	.50	.25	.05
☐ 40 Chet Lemon	.50	.25	.05
☐ 41 Craig Swan	.50	.25	.05
☐ 42 Gary Matthews	.50	.25	.05
☐ 43 Lamar Johnson	.50	.25	.05
☐ 44 Ted Simmons	.90	.45	.09
☐ 45 Ken Griffey	.90	.45	.09
☐ 46 Fred Patek	.50	.25	.05
☐ 47 Frank Tanana	.60	.30	.06
☐ 48 Goose Gossage	.90	.45	.09
☐ 49 Burt Hooton	.50	.25	.05
☐ 50 Ellis Valentine	.50	.25	.05
☐ 51 Ken Forsch	.50	.25	.05
☐ 52 Bob Knepper	.50	.25	.05
☐ 53 Dave Parker	2.00	1.00	.20
☐ 54 Doug DeCinces	.60	.30	.06
☐ 55 Robin Yount	6.00	3.00	.60
☐ 56 Rusty Staub	.60	.30	.06
☐ 57 Gary Alexander	.50	.25	.05
☐ 58 Julio Cruz	.50	.25	.05
☐ 59 Matt Keough	.50	.25	.05
☐ 60 Roy Smalley	.50	.25	.05
☐ 61 Joe Morgan	3.00	1.50	.30
☐ 62 Phil Niekro	2.00	1.00	.20
☐ 63 Don Baylor	.60	.30	.06
☐ 64 Dwight Evans	1.00	.50	.10
☐ 65 Tom Seaver	4.00	2.00	.40
☐ 66 George Hendrick	.50	.25	.05
☐ 67 Rick Reuschel	.60	.30	.06
☐ 68 George Brett	6.00	3.00	.60
☐ 69 Lou Piniella	.90	.45	.09
☐ 70 Enos Cabell	.50	.25	.05
☐ 71 Steve Carlton	3.50	1.75	.35
☐ 72 Reggie Smith	.60	.30	.06
☐ 73 Rick Dempsey *	.60	.30	.06
☐ 74 Vida Blue *	.60	.30	.06
☐ 75 Phil Garner *	.60	.30	.06
☐ 76 Rick Manning *	.60	.30	.06
☐ 77 Mark Fidrych *	.75	.35	.07
☐ 78 Mario Guerrero *	.60	.30	.06
☐ 79 Bob Stinson *	.60	.30	.06
☐ 80 Al Oliver *	.90	.45	.09
☐ 81 Doug Flynn *	.60	.30	.06
☐ 82 John Mayberry	.60	.30	.06
☐ 83 Gaylord Perry	2.00	1.00	.20
☐ 84 Joe Rudi	.60	.30	.06
☐ 85 Dave Concepcion	.75	.35	.07
☐ 86 John Candelaria	.60	.30	.06
☐ 87 Pete Vuckovich	.60	.30	.06
☐ 88 Ivan DeJesus	.50	.25	.05
☐ 89 Ron Guidry	1.50	.75	.15
☐ 90 Hal McRae	.60	.30	.06
☐ 91 Cesar Cedeno	.60	.30	.06
☐ 92 Don Sutton	2.00	1.00	.20
☐ 93 Andre Thornton	.60	.30	.06
☐ 94 Roger Erickson	.50	.25	.05
☐ 95 Larry Hisle	.60	.30	.06
☐ 96 Jason Thompson	.60	.30	.06
☐ 97 Jim Sundberg	.60	.30	.06
☐ 98 Bob Horner	1.50	.75	.15
☐ 99 Ruppert Jones	.50	.25	.05
☐ 100 Willie Montanez	.50	.25	.05
☐ 101 Nolan Ryan	9.00	4.50	.90
☐ 102 Ozzie Smith	15.00	7.50	1.50
☐ 103 Eric Soderholm	.50	.25	.05
☐ 104 Willie Stargell	2.50	1.25	.25
☐ 105A Bob Bailor ERR (reverse negative)	.60	.30	.06
☐ 105B Bob Bailor COR	1.00	.50	.10
☐ 106 Carlton Fisk	2.00	1.00	.20
☐ 107 George Foster	1.00	.50	.10
☐ 108 Keith Hernandez	2.50	1.25	.25
☐ 109 Dennis Leonard	.60	.30	.06

□ 110 Graig Nettles	.75	.35	.07
□ 111 Jose Cruz	.60	.30	.06
□ 112 Bobby Grich	.60	.30	.06
□ 113 Bob Boone	.90	.45	.09
□ 114 Dave Lopes	.60	.30	.06
□ 115 Eddie Murray	7.50	3.75	.75
□ 116 Jack Clark	2.50	1.25	.25
□ 117 Lou Whitaker	1.50	.75	.15
□ 118 Miguel Dilone	.50	.25	.05
□ 119 Sal Bando	.60	.30	.06
□ 120 Reggie Jackson	5.00	2.50	.50
□ 121 Dale Murphy	9.00	4.50	.90
□ 122 Jon Matlack	.50	.25	.05
□ 123 Bruce Bochte	.50	.25	.05
□ 124 John Stearns	.50	.25	.05
□ 125 Dave Winfield	3.00	1.50	.30
□ 126 Jorge Orta	.50	.25	.05
□ 127 Garry Templeton	.50	.25	.05
□ 128 Johnny Bench	4.00	2.00	.40
□ 129 Butch Hobson	.50	.25	.05
□ 130 Bruce Sutter	.90	.45	.09
□ 131 Bucky Dent	.75	.35	.07
□ 132 Amos Otis	.60	.30	.06
□ 133 Bert Blyleven	.90	.45	.09
□ 134 Larry Bowa	.60	.30	.06
□ 135 Ken Singleton	.60	.30	.06
□ 136 Sixto Lezcano	.50	.25	.05
□ 137 Roy Howell	.50	.25	.05
□ 138 Bill Madlock	.90	.45	.09
□ 139 Dave Revering	.50	.25	.05
□ 140 Richie Zisk	.60	.30	.06
□ 141 Butch Wynegar	.50	.25	.05
□ 142 Alan Ashby	.50	.25	.05
□ 143 Sparky Lyle	.75	.35	.07
□ 144 Pete Rose	9.00	4.50	.90
□ 145 Dennis Eckersley	1.25	.60	.12
□ 146 Dave Kingman	.75	.35	.07
□ 147 Buddy Bell	.60	.30	.06
□ 148 Mike Hargrove	.60	.30	.06
□ 149 Jerry Koosman	.60	.30	.06
□ 150 Toby Harrah	.60	.30	.06

1985 Hostess Braves

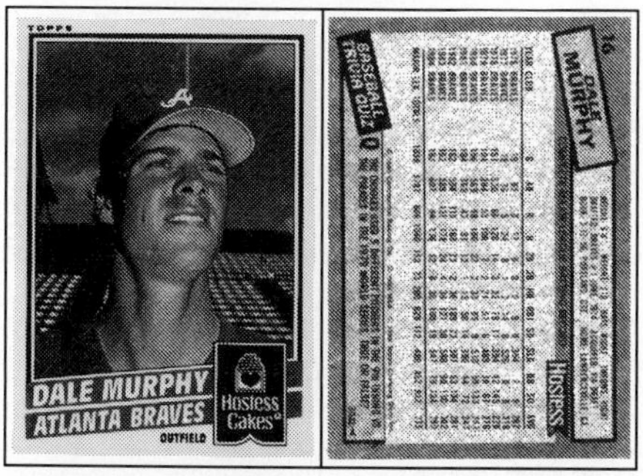

The cards in this 22-card set measure 2 1/2" by 3 1/2" and feature players of the Atlanta Braves. Cards were produced by Topps for Hostess (Continental Baking Co.) and are quite attractive. The card backs are similar in design to the 1985 Topps regular issue; however all photos are different from those that Topps used as these were apparently taken during Spring Training. Cards were available in boxes of Hostess products in packs of four (three players and a contest card).

	MINT	EXC	G-VG
COMPLETE SET (22)	8.00	4.00	.80
COMMON PLAYER (1-22)	.30	.15	.03
□ 1 Eddie Haas MG	.30	.15	.03
□ 2 Len Barker	.30	.15	.03
□ 3 Steve Bedrosian	.75	.35	.07
□ 4 Bruce Benedict	.30	.15	.03
□ 5 Rick Camp	.30	.15	.03
□ 6 Rick Cerone	.30	.15	.03
□ 7 Chris Chambliss	.40	.20	.04
□ 8 Terry Forster	.40	.20	.04
□ 9 Gene Garber	.30	.15	.03
□ 10 Albert Hall	.30	.15	.03
□ 11 Bob Horner	.75	.35	.07
□ 12 Glenn Hubbard	.30	.15	.03
□ 13 Brad Komminsk	.40	.20	.04
□ 14 Rick Mahler	.30	.15	.03
□ 15 Craig McMurtry	.30	.15	.03
□ 16 Dale Murphy	4.00	2.00	.40
□ 17 Ken Oberkfell	.30	.15	.03
□ 18 Pascual Perez	.50	.25	.05
□ 19 Gerald Perry	.40	.20	.04
□ 20 Rafael Ramirez	.30	.15	.03
□ 21 Bruce Sutter	.75	.35	.07
□ 22 Claudell Washington	.40	.20	.04

1963 IDL Pirates

This 25-card set measures approximately 4" by 5" and is blank backed. The fronts have black and white photos on the top of the card along with the IDL Drug Store logo in the lower left corner of the card and the players name printed in block letters underneath the picture. The only card which has any designation as to position is the manager card of Danny Murtaugh. These cards are unnumbered and feature members of the Pittsburgh Pirates. The catalog designation for the set is H801-13 although it is infrequently referenced. The Stargell card is one of his few cards from 1963, his rookie year for cards.

	NRMT	VG-E	GOOD
COMPLETE SET (25)	60.00	30.00	6.00
COMMON PLAYER (1-25)	1.50	.75	.15
□ 1 Bob Bailey	1.50	.75	.15
□ 2 Smokey Burgess	2.50	1.25	.25
□ 3 Don Cardwell	1.50	.75	.15
□ 4 Roberto Clemente	25.00	12.50	2.50
□ 5 Donn Clendenon	2.50	1.25	.25
□ 6 Roy Face	2.50	1.25	.25
□ 7 Earl Francis	1.50	.75	.15
□ 8 Bob Friend	2.00	1.00	.20
□ 9 Joe Gibbon	1.50	.75	.15
□ 10 Julio Gotay	1.50	.75	.15
□ 11 Harvey Haddix	2.00	1.00	.20
□ 12 Bill Mazeroski	5.00	2.50	.50
□ 13 Al McBean	1.50	.75	.15
□ 14 Danny Murtaugh MG	2.00	1.00	.20
□ 15 Sam Narron CO	1.50	.75	.15
□ 16 Ron Northey CO	1.50	.75	.15
□ 17 Frank Oceak CO	1.50	.75	.15
□ 18 Jim Pagliaroni	1.50	.75	.15
□ 19 Ted Savage	1.50	.75	.15
□ 20 Dick Schofield	1.50	.75	.15
□ 21 Willie Stargell	20.00	10.00	2.00
□ 22 Tom Sturdivant	1.50	.75	.15
□ 23 Virgil Fire Trucks CO	1.50	.75	.15
□ 24 Bob Veale	2.50	1.25	.25
□ 25 Bill Virdon	2.50	1.25	.25

1973 Johnny Pro Orioles

This 25-card set measures approximately 4 1/4" by 7 1/4" and features members of the 1973 Baltimore Orioles. The cards were designed to be pushed-out in a style similar to the 1964 Topps Stand Ups. The sides of the cards have a small advertisement for Johnny Pro Enterprises and even gives a phone number where they could have been reached. Oddly, the Orlando Pena card was not available in a die-cut version. The cards have the player's photo against a distinctive solid green background. The cards are blank backed. There are several variations within the set; the complete set price below does not include the any of the variation cards. The set is checklisted in order by uniform number. According to informed sources, there were 15,000 sets produced.

	NRMT	VG-E	GOOD
COMPLETE SET (25)	125.00	60.00	12.50
COMMON PLAYER	3.00	1.50	.40
☐ 1 Al Bumbry OF	3.00	1.50	.40
☐ 2 Rich Coggins OF	3.00	1.50	.40
☐ 3A Bobby Grich 2B (fielding)	6.00	3.00	.60
☐ 3B Bobby Grich 2B (batting)	12.00	6.00	1.20
☐ 4 Earl Weaver	6.00	3.00	.60
☐ 5A Brooks Robinson 3B (fielding)	15.00	7.50	1.50
☐ 5B Brooks Robinson 3B (batting)	25.00	12.50	2.50
☐ 6 Paul Blair OF	5.00	2.50	.50
☐ 7 Mark Belanger SS	5.00	2.50	.50
☐ 8 Andy Etchebarren C	3.00	1.50	.40
☐ 10 Elrod Hendricks C	3.00	1.50	.40
☐ 11 Terry Crowley OF	3.00	1.50	.40
☐ 12 Tommy Davis OF	5.00	2.50	.50
☐ 13 Doyle Alexander P	5.00	2.50	.50
☐ 14 Merv Rettenmund OF	3.00	1.50	.40
☐ 15 Frank Baker IF	3.00	1.50	.40
☐ 19 Dave McNally P	5.00	2.50	.50
☐ 21 Larry Brown IF	3.00	1.50	.40
☐ 22A Jim Palmer P	15.00	7.50	1.50
☐ 22B Jim Palmer P (pitching)	25.00	12.50	2.50
☐ 23 Grant Jackson P	3.00	1.50	.40
☐ 25 Don Baylor OF	8.00	3.00	.80
☐ 26 John Boog Powell 1B	10.00	5.00	1.00
☐ 27 Orlando Pena NOT die-cut	10.00	5.00	1.00
☐ 32 Earl Williams C	3.00	1.50	.40
☐ 34 Bob Reynolds P	3.00	1.50	.40
☐ 35 Mike Cuellar P	5.00	2.50	.50
☐ 39 Eddie Watt P	3.00	1.50	.40

1974 Johnny Pro Phillies

This 11-card set measures approximately 3 3/4" by 7 1/8" and features members of the 1974 Philadelphia Phillies. The most significant player in this series is an early card of Mike Schmidt. The cards are designed to be pushed out and have the players photo against a solid white background. The backs are blank and marked the second straight year that Johnny Pro issued cards of a major league team. The set is checklisted by uniform number. According to informed sources, there were between less than 15,000 sets produced.

	NRMT	VG-E	GOOD
COMPLETE SET (11)	125.00	60.00	12.50
COMMON PLAYER	3.00	1.50	.40
☐ 8 Bob Boone	10.00	5.00	1.00
☐ 10 Larry Bowa IF	6.00	3.00	.60
☐ 16 Dave Cash IF	3.00	1.50	.40
☐ 19 Greg Luzinski OF	8.00	3.00	.80
☐ 20 Mike Schmidt	90.00	45.00	9.00
☐ 22 Mike Anderson OF	3.00	1.50	.40
☐ 24 Bill Robinson OF	6.00	3.00	.60
☐ 27 Willie Montanez IF	3.00	1.50	.40
☐ 32 Steve Carlton P	20.00	10.00	1.50
☐ 37 Ron Schueler P	3.00	1.50	.40
☐ 41 Jim Lonborg P	5.00	2.50	.50

1953 Johnston Cookies

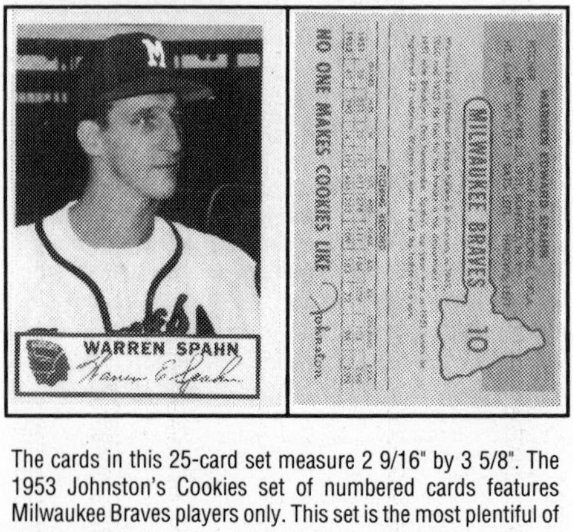

The cards in this 25-card set measure 2 9/16" by 3 5/8". The 1953 Johnston's Cookies set of numbered cards features Milwaukee Braves players only. This set is the most plentiful of the three Johnston's Cookies sets and no known scarcities exist. The catalog designation for this set is D356-1.

	NRMT	VG-E	GOOD
COMPLETE SET (25)	250.00	125.00	25.00
COMMON PLAYER (1-25)	8.00	4.00	.80
☐ 1 Charlie Grimm MG	10.00	5.00	1.00
☐ 2 John Antonelli	10.00	5.00	1.00
☐ 3 Vern Bickford	8.00	4.00	.80
☐ 4 Bob Buhl	8.00	4.00	.80
☐ 5 Lew Burdette	12.50	6.25	1.25
☐ 6 Dave Cole	8.00	4.00	.80
☐ 7 Ernie Johnson	10.00	5.00	1.00
☐ 8 Dave Jolly	8.00	4.00	.80
☐ 9 Don Liddle	8.00	4.00	.80
☐ 10 Warren Spahn	50.00	25.00	5.00
☐ 11 Max Surkont	8.00	4.00	.80
☐ 12 Jim Wilson	8.00	4.00	.80
☐ 13 Sibbi Sisti	8.00	4.00	.80
☐ 14 Walker Cooper	8.00	4.00	.80
☐ 15 Del Crandall	10.00	5.00	1.00
☐ 16 Ebba St.Claire	8.00	4.00	.80
☐ 17 Joe Adcock	12.00	6.00	1.20
☐ 18 George Crowe	8.00	4.00	.80
☐ 19 Jack Dittmer	8.00	4.00	.80
☐ 20 Johnny Logan	10.00	5.00	1.00
☐ 21 Ed Mathews	50.00	25.00	5.00
☐ 22 Bill Bruton	10.00	5.00	1.00
☐ 23 Sid Gordon	8.00	4.00	.80
☐ 24 Andy Pafko	10.00	5.00	1.00
☐ 25 Jim Pendleton	8.00	4.00	.80

1954 Johnston Cookies

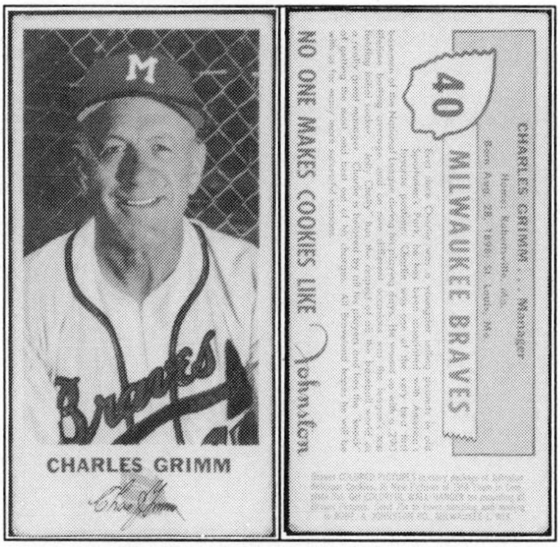

The cards in this 35-card set measure 2" by 3 7/8". The 1954 Johnston's Cookies set of color cards of Milwaukee Braves are numbered according to the player's uniform number, except for the non-players, Lacks and Taylor, who are found at the end of the set. The Bobby Thomson card was withdrawn early in the year after his injury and is scarce. The catalog number for this set is D356-2.

	NRMT	VG-E	GOOD
COMPLETE SET (35)	1000.00	450.00	100.00
COMMON PLAYER (1-50)	10.00	5.00	1.00
☐ 1 Del Crandall	12.00	6.00	1.20
☐ 3 Jim Pendleton	10.00	5.00	1.00
☐ 4 Danny O'Connell	10.00	5.00	1.00
☐ 5 Hank Aaron	500.00	200.00	50.00
☐ 6 Jack Dittmer	10.00	5.00	1.00
☐ 9 Joe Adcock	13.50	6.00	1.20
☐ 10 Bob Buhl	10.00	5.00	1.00
☐ 11 Phil Paine	10.00	5.00	1.00
☐ 12 Ben Johnson	10.00	5.00	1.00
☐ 13 Sibbi Sisti	10.00	5.00	1.00
☐ 15 Charles Gorin	10.00	5.00	1.00
☐ 16 Chet Nichols	10.00	5.00	1.00
☐ 17 Dave Jolly	10.00	5.00	1.00
☐ 19 Jim Wilson	10.00	5.00	1.00
☐ 20 Ray Crone	10.00	5.00	1.00
☐ 21 Warren Spahn	60.00	30.00	6.00
☐ 22 Gene Conley	10.00	5.00	1.00
☐ 23 Johnny Logan	12.00	6.00	1.20
☐ 24 Charlie White	10.00	5.00	1.00
☐ 27 George Metkovich	10.00	5.00	1.00
☐ 28 Johnny Cooney	10.00	5.00	1.00
☐ 29 Paul Burris	10.00	5.00	1.00
☐ 31 Bucky Walters	12.00	6.00	1.20
☐ 32 Ernie Johnson	12.00	6.00	1.20
☐ 33 Lou Burdette	20.00	10.00	2.00
☐ 34 Bob Thomson	225.00	110.00	22.00
☐ 35 Bob Keely	10.00	5.00	1.00
☐ 38 Bill Bruton	12.00	6.00	1.20
☐ 40 Charlie Grimm MG	12.00	6.00	1.20
☐ 41 Eddie Mathews	60.00	30.00	6.00
☐ 42 Sam Calderone	10.00	5.00	1.00
☐ 47 Joey Jay	10.00	5.00	1.00
☐ 48 Andy Pafko	10.00	5.00	1.00
☐ 49 Dr. Charles Lacks (unnumbered)	10.00	5.00	1.00
☐ 50 Joseph F. Taylor (unnumbered)	10.00	5.00	1.00

1955 Johnston Cookies

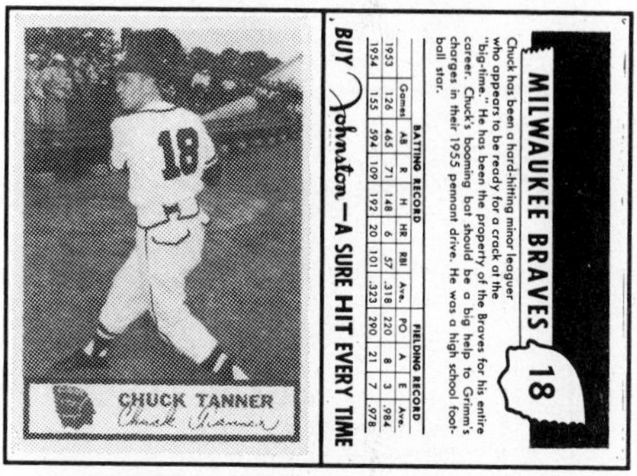

The cards in this 35-card set measure 2 3/4" by 4". This set of Milwaukee Braves issued in 1955 by Johnston Cookies are numbered by the uniform number of the player depicted, except for non-players Lacks, Lewis and Taylor. The cards were issued in strips of six which accounts for the rouletted edges found on single cards. They are larger in size than the two previous sets but are printed on thinner cardboard. Each player in the checklist has been marked to show on which panel or strip he appeared (Pafko appears twice). A complete panel of six cards is worth 25 percent more than the sum of the individual players. The catalog designation for this set is D356-3.

	NRMT	VG-E	GOOD
COMPLETE SET (35)	1000.00	450.00	100.00
COMMON PLAYER (1-51)	18.00	9.00	1.80
☐ 1 Del Crandall P1	21.00	10.50	2.10
☐ 3 Jim Pendleton P3	18.00	9.00	1.80
☐ 4 Danny O'Connell P1	18.00	9.00	1.80
☐ 6 Jack Dittmer P6	18.00	9.00	1.80
☐ 9 Joe Adcock P2	24.00	12.00	2.40
☐ 10 Bob Buhl P6	18.00	9.00	1.80
☐ 11 Phil Paine P5	18.00	9.00	1.80
☐ 12 Ray Crone P5	18.00	9.00	1.80
☐ 15 Charlie Gorin P1	18.00	9.00	1.80
☐ 16 Dave Jolly P4	18.00	9.00	1.80
☐ 17 Chet Nichols P2	18.00	9.00	1.80
☐ 18 Chuck Tanner P5	24.00	12.00	2.40
☐ 19 Jim Wilson P6	18.00	9.00	1.80
☐ 20 Dave Koslo P4	18.00	9.00	1.80
☐ 21 Warren Spahn P3	80.00	40.00	8.00
☐ 22 Gene Conley P3	18.00	9.00	1.80
☐ 23 Johnny Logan P4	21.00	10.50	2.10
☐ 24 Charlie White P2	18.00	9.00	1.80
☐ 28 Johnny Cooney P4	18.00	9.00	1.80

☐ 30 Roy Smalley P3	18.00	9.00	1.80
☐ 31 Bucky Walters P6	21.00	10.50	2.10
☐ 32 Ernie Johnson P5	21.00	10.50	2.10
☐ 33 Lew Burdette P1	30.00	15.00	3.00
☐ 34 Bobby Thomson P6	24.00	12.00	2.40
☐ 35 Bob Keely P1	18.00	9.00	1.80
☐ 38 Bill Bruton P4	21.00	10.50	2.10
☐ 39 George Crowe P3	18.00	9.00	1.80
☐ 40 Charlie Grimm MG P6	21.00	10.50	2.10
☐ 41 Eddie Mathews P5	80.00	40.00	8.00
☐ 44 Hank Aaron P1	300.00	150.00	30.00
☐ 47 Joey Jay P2	18.00	9.00	1.80
☐ 48 Andy Pafko P2 P4	18.00	9.00	1.80
☐ 49 Dr. Charles Leaks P2 (unnumbered)	18.00	9.00	1.80
☐ 50 Duffy Lewis P5 (unnumbered)	18.00	9.00	1.80
☐ 51 Joe Taylor P3 (unnumbered)	18.00	9.00	1.80

1955 Kahn's

The cards in this 6-card set measure 3 1/4" by 4". The 1955 Kahn's Wieners set received very limited distribution. The cards were supposedly given away at an amusement park. The set portrays the players in street clothes rather than in uniform and hence are sometimes referred to as "street clothes" Kahn's. All Kahn's sets from 1955 through 1963 are black and white and contain a 1/2" tab. Cards with the tab still intact are worth approximately 50 percent more than cards without the tab. Cards feature a facsimile autograph of the player on the front. Cards are blank-backed. Cincinnati Redlegs players only are featured.

	NRMT	VG-E	GOOD
COMPLETE SET (6)	3000.00	1400.00	325.00
COMMON PLAYER (1-6)	450.00	225.00	45.00
☐ 1 Gus Bell (street clothes)	750.00	375.00	75.00
☐ 2 Ted Kluszewski (street clothes)	750.00	375.00	75.00
☐ 3 Roy McMillan (street clothes)	450.00	225.00	45.00
☐ 4 Joe Nuxhall (street clothes)	500.00	250.00	50.00
☐ 5 Wally Post (street clothes)	450.00	225.00	45.00
☐ 6 Johnny Temple (street clothes)	450.00	225.00	45.00

1956 Kahn's

The cards in this 15-card set measure 3 1/4" by 4". The 1956 Kahn's set was the first set to be issued with Kahn's meat products. The cards are blank backed. The set is distinguished by the old style, short sleeve shirts on the players and the existence of backgounds (Kahn's cards of later years utilize a blank background). Cards which have the tab still intact are worth approximately 50 percent more than cards without the tab. Cincinnati Redlegs players only are featured.

	NRMT	VG-E	GOOD
COMPLETE SET (15)	1500.00	700.00	175.00
COMMON PLAYER (1-15)	80.00	40.00	8.00
☐ 1 Ed Bailey	80.00	40.00	8.00
☐ 2 Gus Bell	90.00	45.00	9.00
☐ 3 Joe Black	90.00	45.00	9.00
☐ 4 Smoky Burgess	90.00	45.00	9.00
☐ 5 Art Fowler	80.00	40.00	8.00
☐ 6 Hershel Freeman	80.00	40.00	8.00
☐ 7 Ray Jablonski	80.00	40.00	8.00
☐ 8 John Klippstein	80.00	40.00	8.00
☐ 9 Ted Kluszewski	150.00	75.00	15.00
☐ 10 Brooks Lawrence	80.00	40.00	8.00
☐ 11 Roy McMillan	80.00	40.00	8.00
☐ 12 Joe Nuxhall	90.00	45.00	9.00
☐ 13 Wally Post	80.00	40.00	8.00
☐ 14 Frank Robinson	350.00	175.00	35.00
☐ 15 Johnny Temple	90.00	45.00	9.00

1957 Kahn's

The cards in this 29-card set measure 3 1/4" by 4". The 1957 Kahn's Wieners set contains black and white, blank backed, unnumbered cards. The set features the Cincinnati Redlegs and Pittsburgh Pirates only. The cards feature a light background. Each card features a facsimile autograph of the player on the front. The Groat card exists with a "Richard Groat" autograph and also exists with the printed name "Dick Groat" on the card. The catalog designation is F155-3.

	NRMT	VG-E	GOOD
COMPLETE SET (29)	2500.00	1200.00	275.00
COMMON PLAYER (1-29)	60.00	30.00	6.00
☐ 1 Tom Acker	60.00	30.00	6.00
☐ 2 Ed Bailey	60.00	30.00	6.00
☐ 3 Gus Bell	75.00	37.50	7.50
☐ 4 Smoky Burgess	75.00	37.50	7.50
☐ 5 Robert Clemente	625.00	250.00	50.00
☐ 6 George Crowe	60.00	30.00	6.00
☐ 7 Elroy Face	90.00	45.00	9.00
☐ 8 Hershel Freeman	60.00	30.00	6.00
☐ 9 Bob Friend	75.00	37.50	7.50
☐ 10 Dick Groat	90.00	45.00	9.00
☐ 11 Richard Groat	175.00	85.00	18.00
☐ 12 Don Gross	60.00	30.00	6.00
☐ 13 Warren Hacker	60.00	30.00	6.00
☐ 14 Don Hoak	60.00	30.00	6.00
☐ 15 Hal Jeffcoat	60.00	30.00	6.00
☐ 16 Ron Kline	60.00	30.00	6.00
☐ 17 John Klippstein	60.00	30.00	6.00
☐ 18 Ted Kluszewski	125.00	60.00	12.50
☐ 19 Brooks Lawrence	60.00	30.00	6.00
☐ 20 Dale Long	75.00	37.50	7.50
☐ 21 Bill Mazeroski	135.00	65.00	13.50
☐ 22 Roy McMillan	60.00	30.00	6.00
☐ 23 Joe Nuxhall	75.00	37.50	7.50
☐ 24 Wally Post	60.00	30.00	6.00
☐ 25 Frank Robinson	250.00	125.00	25.00
☐ 26 John Temple	75.00	37.50	7.50
☐ 27 Frank Thomas	75.00	37.50	7.50
☐ 28 Bob Thurman	60.00	30.00	6.00
☐ 29 Lee Walls	60.00	30.00	6.00

1958 Kahn's

Compliments of Kahn's Wieners
"THE WIENER THE WORLD AWAITED"
MY GREATEST THRILL IN BASEBALL
By FRANK ROBINSON
In 1956, my rookie year in the big leagues, I was named by Birdie Tebbetts to start the season in left field for the Cincinnati Redlegs. Everybody had told me that Opening Day in Cincinnati was almost a national holiday, and it was really the truth.
When I came out on the field the park was overflowing with fans. They were even sitting out on the terrace in back of my left field position.
My first time at bat in the major leagues came that day, and I doubled off the center-field wall. That was my big moment in baseball, the one I'll always remember .

The cards in this 29-card set measure 3 1/4" by 4". The 1958 Kahn's Wieners set of unnumbered, black and white cards features Cincinnati Redlegs, Philadelphia Phillies, and Pittsburgh Pirates. The backs present a story for each player entitled "My Greatest Thrill in Baseball". A method of distinguishing 1958 Kahn's from 1959 Kahn's is that the word Wieners is found on the front of the 1958 but not on the front of the 1959 cards. Cards of Wally Post, Charlie Rabe, and Frank Thomas are somewhat more difficult to find and are marked with an asterisk in the checklist below.

	NRMT	VG-E	GOOD
COMPLETE SET (29)	2800.00	1350.00	300.00
COMMON PLAYER (1-29)	50.00	25.00	5.00
☐ 1 Ed Bailey	50.00	25.00	5.00
☐ 2 Gene Baker	50.00	25.00	5.00
☐ 3 Gus Bell	60.00	30.00	6.00
☐ 4 Smoky Burgess	60.00	30.00	6.00
☐ 5 Roberto Clemente	525.00	250.00	50.00
☐ 6 George Crowe	50.00	25.00	5.00
☐ 7 Elroy Face	75.00	37.50	7.50
☐ 8 Hank Foiles	50.00	25.00	5.00
☐ 9 Dee Fondy	50.00	25.00	5.00
☐ 10 Bob Friend	60.00	30.00	6.00
☐ 11 Dick Groat	75.00	37.50	7.50
☐ 12 Harvey Haddix	60.00	30.00	6.00
☐ 13 Don Hoak	50.00	25.00	5.00
☐ 14 Hal Jeffcoat	50.00	25.00	5.00
☐ 15 Ron Kline	50.00	25.00	5.00
☐ 16 Ted Kluszewski	100.00	50.00	10.00
☐ 17 Vernon Law	60.00	30.00	6.00
☐ 18 Brooks Lawrence	50.00	25.00	5.00
☐ 19 Bill Mazeroski	90.00	45.00	9.00
☐ 20 Roy McMillan	50.00	25.00	5.00
☐ 21 Joe Nuxhall	60.00	30.00	6.00
☐ 22 Wally Post *	300.00	150.00	30.00
☐ 23 John Powers	50.00	25.00	5.00
☐ 24 Bob Purkey	50.00	25.00	5.00
☐ 25 Charlie Rabe *	300.00	150.00	30.00
☐ 26 Frank Robinson	200.00	100.00	20.00
☐ 27 Bob Skinner	50.00	25.00	5.00
☐ 28 Johnny Temple	60.00	30.00	6.00
☐ 29 Frank Thomas *	300.00	150.00	30.00

1959 Kahn's

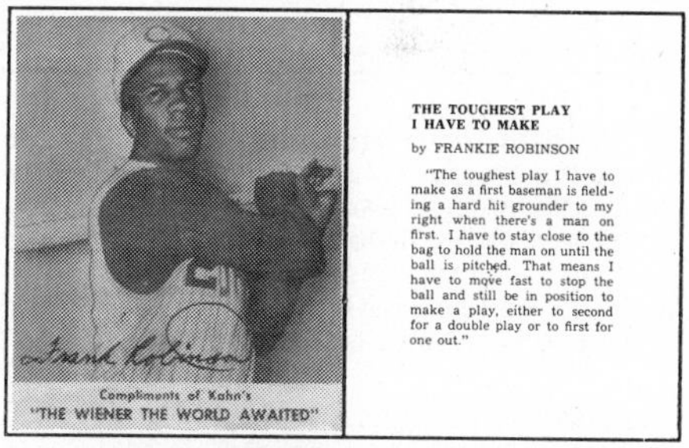
Compliments of Kahn's
"THE WIENER THE WORLD AWAITED"
THE TOUGHEST PLAY
I HAVE TO MAKE
by FRANKIE ROBINSON
"The toughest play I have to make as a first baseman is fielding a hard hit grounder to my right when there's a man on first. I have to stay close to the bag to hold the man on until the ball is pitched. That means I have to move fast to stop the ball and still be in position to make a play, either to second for a double play or to first for one out."

The cards in this 38-card set measure 3 1/4" by 4". The 1959 Kahn's set features Cincinnati, Cleveland, and Pittsburgh players. The backs feature stories entitled "The Toughest Play I have to Make," or "The Toughest Batter I Have To Face." The Brodowski card is very scarce while Haddix, Held and McLish are considered quite difficult to obtain; these scarcities are the asterisked cards in the checklist below.

	NRMT	VG-E	GOOD
COMPLETE SET (38)	4000.00	1800.00	350.00
COMMON PLAYER (1-38)	50.00	25.00	5.00
☐ 1 Ed Bailey	50.00	25.00	5.00
☐ 2 Gary Bell	50.00	25.00	5.00
☐ 3 Gus Bell	60.00	30.00	6.00
☐ 4 Dick Brodowski *	500.00	250.00	50.00
☐ 5 Smoky Burgess	60.00	30.00	6.00
☐ 6 Roberto Clemente	475.00	225.00	47.00
☐ 7 Rocky Colavito	100.00	50.00	10.00
☐ 8 Elroy Face	75.00	37.50	7.50
☐ 9 Bob Friend	60.00	30.00	6.00
☐ 10 Joe Gordon	60.00	30.00	6.00
☐ 11 Jim Grant	50.00	25.00	5.00
☐ 12 Dick Groat	75.00	37.50	7.50
☐ 13 Harvey Haddix * (blank back)	350.00	175.00	35.00
☐ 14 Woodie Held *	350.00	175.00	35.00
☐ 15 Don Hoak	50.00	25.00	5.00
☐ 16 Ron Kline	50.00	25.00	5.00
☐ 17 Ted Kluszewski	90.00	45.00	9.00
☐ 18 Vernon Law	60.00	30.00	6.00
☐ 19 Jerry Lynch	50.00	25.00	5.00
☐ 20 Billy Martin	125.00	60.00	12.50
☐ 21 Bill Mazeroski	90.00	45.00	9.00
☐ 22 Cal McLish *	350.00	175.00	35.00
☐ 23 Roy McMillan	50.00	25.00	5.00
☐ 24 Minnie Minoso	90.00	45.00	9.00
☐ 25 Russ Nixon	60.00	30.00	6.00
☐ 26 Joe Nuxhall	60.00	30.00	6.00
☐ 27 Jim Perry	75.00	37.50	7.50

		NRMT	VG-E	GOOD
☐ 28	Vada Pinson	75.00	37.50	7.50
☐ 29	Vic Power	50.00	25.00	5.00
☐ 30	Bob Purkey	50.00	25.00	5.00
☐ 31	Frank Robinson	200.00	100.00	20.00
☐ 32	Herb Score	75.00	37.50	7.50
☐ 33	Bob Skinner	50.00	25.00	5.00
☐ 34	George Strickland	50.00	25.00	5.00
☐ 35	Dick Stuart	60.00	30.00	6.00
☐ 36	Johnny Temple	50.00	25.00	5.00
☐ 37	Frank Thomas	60.00	30.00	6.00
☐ 38	George Witt	50.00	25.00	5.00
☐ 39	Dick Stuart	30.00	15.00	3.00
☐ 40	Johnny Temple	30.00	15.00	3.00
☐ 41	Frank Thomas	30.00	15.00	3.00
☐ 42	Lee Walls	25.00	12.50	2.50

1960 Kahn's

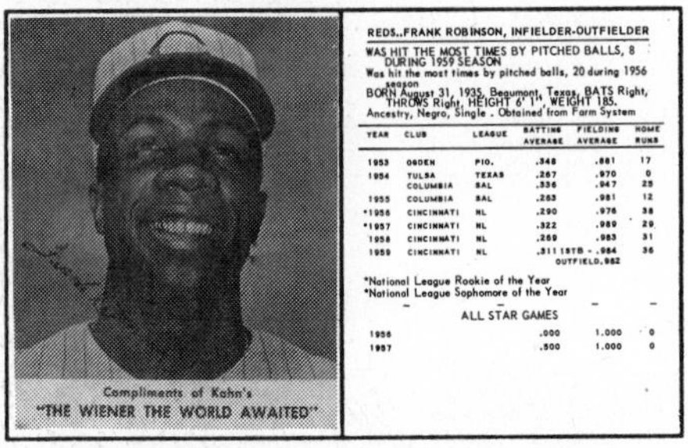

The cards in this 42-card set measure 3 1/4" by 4". The 1960 Kahn's set features players of the Chicago Cubs, Chicago White Sox, Cincinnati Redlegs, Cleveland Indians, Pittsburgh Pirates, and St. Louis Cardinals. The backs give vital player information and records through the 1959 season. Kline appears with either St. Louis or Pittsburgh. The Harvey Kuenn card (asterisked below) appears with a blank back, and is scarce.

		NRMT	VG-E	GOOD
COMPLETE SET (43)		1800.00	800.00	200.00
COMMON PLAYER (1-42)		25.00	12.50	2.50
☐ 1	Ed Bailey	25.00	12.50	2.50
☐ 2	Gary Bell	25.00	12.50	2.50
☐ 3	Gus Bell	30.00	15.00	3.00
☐ 4	Smoky Burgess	30.00	15.00	3.00
☐ 5	Gino Cimoli	25.00	12.50	2.50
☐ 6	Roberto Clemente	325.00	160.00	32.00
☐ 7	Roy Face	35.00	17.50	3.50
☐ 8	Tito Francona	25.00	12.50	2.50
☐ 9	Bob Friend	30.00	15.00	3.00
☐ 10	Jim Grant	25.00	12.50	2.50
☐ 11	Dick Groat	35.00	17.50	3.50
☐ 12	Harvey Haddix	30.00	15.00	3.00
☐ 13	Woodie Held	25.00	12.50	2.50
☐ 14	Bill Henry	25.00	12.50	2.50
☐ 15	Don Hoak	25.00	12.50	2.50
☐ 16	Jay Hook	25.00	12.50	2.50
☐ 17	Eddie Kasko	25.00	12.50	2.50
☐ 18A	Ron Kline (Pittsburgh)	45.00	22.50	4.50
☐ 18B	Ron Kline (St. Louis)	45.00	22.50	4.50
☐ 19	Ted Kluszewski	50.00	25.00	5.00
☐ 20	Harvey Kuenn (blank back)	300.00	150.00	30.00
☐ 21	Vernon Law	30.00	15.00	3.00
☐ 22	Brooks Lawrence	25.00	12.50	2.50
☐ 23	Jerry Lynch	25.00	12.50	2.50
☐ 24	Billy Martin	60.00	30.00	6.00
☐ 25	Bill Mazeroski	40.00	20.00	4.00
☐ 26	Cal McLish	25.00	12.50	2.50
☐ 27	Roy McMillan	25.00	12.50	2.50
☐ 28	Don Newcombe	35.00	17.50	3.50
☐ 29	Russ Nixon	30.00	15.00	3.00
☐ 30	Joe Nuxhall	30.00	15.00	3.00
☐ 31	Jim O'Toole	25.00	12.50	2.50
☐ 32	Jim Perry	30.00	15.00	3.00
☐ 33	Vada Pinson	35.00	17.50	3.50
☐ 34	Vic Power	25.00	12.50	2.50
☐ 35	Bob Purkey	25.00	12.50	2.50
☐ 36	Frank Robinson	150.00	75.00	15.00
☐ 37	Herb Score	35.00	17.50	3.50
☐ 38	Bob Skinner	25.00	12.50	2.50

1961 Kahn's

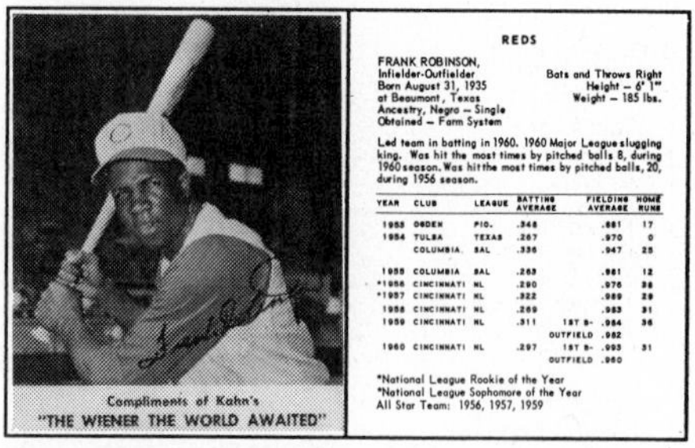

The cards in this 43-card set measure approximately 3 1/4" by 4". The 1961 Kahn's Wieners set of black and white, unnumbered cards features players from Cincinnati, Cleveland, and Pittsburgh. This year was the first year Kahn's made complete sets available to the public; hence they are more available, especially in the better condition grades, than the Kahn's of the previous years. The backs give vital player information and year by year career statistics through 1960. The catalog designation is F155-7.

		NRMT	VG-E	GOOD
COMPLETE SET (43)		675.00	300.00	50.00
COMMON PLAYER (1-43)		12.00	6.00	1.20
☐ 1	John Antonelli	13.50	6.25	1.25
☐ 2	Ed Bailey	12.00	6.00	1.20
☐ 3	Gary Bell	12.00	6.00	1.20
☐ 4	Gus Bell	13.50	6.25	1.25
☐ 5	Jim Brosnan	12.00	6.00	1.20
☐ 6	Smoky Burgess	15.00	7.50	1.50
☐ 7	Gino Cimoli	12.00	6.00	1.20
☐ 8	Roberto Clemente	225.00	110.00	22.00
☐ 9	Gordie Coleman	12.00	6.00	1.20
☐ 10	Jimmy Dykes	13.50	6.25	1.25
☐ 11	Roy Face	15.00	7.50	1.50
☐ 12	Tito Francona	12.00	6.00	1.20
☐ 13	Gene Freese	12.00	6.00	1.20
☐ 14	Bob Friend	13.50	6.25	1.25
☐ 15	Jim Grant	12.00	6.00	1.20
☐ 16	Dick Groat	18.00	9.00	1.80
☐ 17	Harvey Haddix	13.50	6.25	1.25
☐ 18	Woodie Held	12.00	6.00	1.20
☐ 19	Don Hoak	12.00	6.00	1.20
☐ 20	Jay Hook	12.00	6.00	1.20
☐ 21	Joey Jay	12.00	6.00	1.20
☐ 22	Eddie Kasko	12.00	6.00	1.20
☐ 23	Willie Kirkland	12.00	6.00	1.20
☐ 24	Vernon Law	13.50	6.25	1.25
☐ 25	Jerry Lynch	12.00	6.00	1.20
☐ 26	Jim Maloney	15.00	7.50	1.50
☐ 27	Bill Mazeroski	20.00	10.00	2.00
☐ 28	Wilmer Mizell	12.00	6.00	1.20
☐ 29	Rocky Nelson	12.00	6.00	1.20
☐ 30	Jim O'Toole	12.00	6.00	1.20
☐ 31	Jim Perry	15.00	7.50	1.50
☐ 32	Bubba Phillips	12.00	6.00	1.20
☐ 33	Vada Pinson	18.00	9.00	1.80
☐ 34	Wally Post	12.00	6.00	1.20
☐ 35	Vic Power	12.00	6.00	1.20
☐ 36	Bob Purkey	12.00	6.00	1.20
☐ 37	Frank Robinson	90.00	45.00	9.00
☐ 38	John Romano	12.00	6.00	1.20
☐ 39	Dick Schofield	12.00	6.00	1.20
☐ 40	Bob Skinner	12.00	6.00	1.20
☐ 41	Hal Smith	12.00	6.00	1.20
☐ 42	Dick Stuart	15.00	7.50	1.50
☐ 43	Johnny Temple	12.00	6.00	1.20

1962 Kahn's

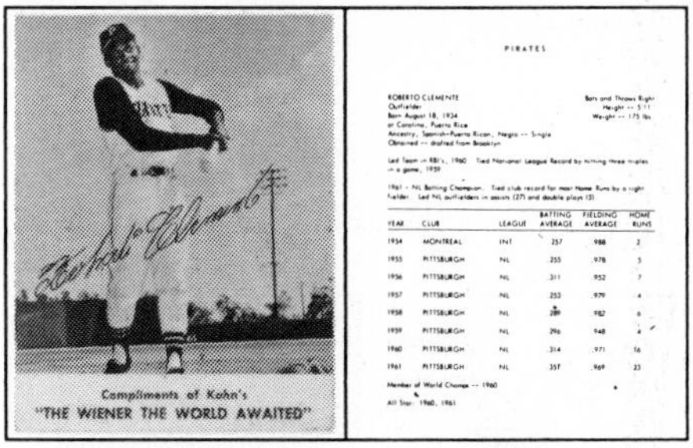

The cards in this 38-card set measure approximately 3 1/4" by 4". The 1962 Kahn's Wieners set of black and white, unnumbered cards features Cincinnati, Cleveland, Minnesota, and Pittsburgh players. Card numbers 1 Bell, 33 Power, and 34 Purkey exist in two different forms; these variations are listed in the checklist below. The backs of the cards contain career information. The catalog designation is F155-8. The set price below includes the set with all variation cards.

	NRMT	VG-E	GOOD
COMPLETE SET (41)	1000.00	450.00	100.00
COMMON PLAYER (1-38)	10.00	5.00	1.00
☐ 1A Gary Bell (with fat man)	100.00	50.00	10.00
☐ 1B Gary Bell (no fat man)	35.00	17.50	3.50
☐ 2 Jim Brosnan	10.00	5.00	1.00
☐ 3 Smoky Burgess	12.00	6.00	1.20
☐ 4 Chico Cardenas	10.00	5.00	1.00
☐ 5 Roberto Clemente	175.00	85.00	18.00
☐ 6 Ty Cline	10.00	5.00	1.00
☐ 7 Gordon Coleman	10.00	5.00	1.00
☐ 8 Dick Donovan	10.00	5.00	1.00
☐ 9 John Edwards	10.00	5.00	1.00
☐ 10 Tito Francona	10.00	5.00	1.00
☐ 11 Gene Freese	10.00	5.00	1.00
☐ 12 Bob Friend	12.00	6.00	1.20
☐ 13 Joe Gibbon	100.00	50.00	10.00
☐ 14 Jim Grant	10.00	5.00	1.00
☐ 15 Dick Groat	15.00	7.50	1.50
☐ 16 Harvey Haddix	12.00	6.00	1.20
☐ 17 Woodie Held	10.00	5.00	1.00
☐ 18 Bill Henry	10.00	5.00	1.00
☐ 19 Don Hoak	10.00	5.00	1.00
☐ 20 Ken Hunt	10.00	5.00	1.00
☐ 21 Joey Jay	10.00	5.00	1.00
☐ 22 Eddie Kasko	10.00	5.00	1.00
☐ 23 Willie Kirkland	10.00	5.00	1.00
☐ 24 Barry Latman	10.00	5.00	1.00
☐ 25 Jerry Lynch	10.00	5.00	1.00
☐ 26 Jim Maloney	12.00	6.00	1.20
☐ 27 Bill Mazeroski	16.00	8.00	1.60
☐ 28 Jim O'Toole	10.00	5.00	1.00
☐ 29 Jim Perry	12.00	6.00	1.20
☐ 30 Bubba Phillips	10.00	5.00	1.00
☐ 31 Vada Pinson	15.00	7.50	1.50
☐ 32 Wally Post	10.00	5.00	1.00
☐ 33A Vic Power (Indians)	35.00	17.50	3.50
☐ 33B Vic Power (Twins)	100.00	50.00	10.00
☐ 34A Bob Purkey (with autograph)	35.00	17.50	3.50
☐ 34B Bob Purkey (no autograph)	100.00	50.00	10.00
☐ 35 Frank Robinson	80.00	40.00	8.00
☐ 36 John Romano	10.00	5.00	1.00
☐ 37 Dick Stuart	12.00	6.00	1.20
☐ 38 Bill Virdon	15.00	7.50	1.50

1962 Kahn's Atlanta

The cards in this 24-card set measure 3 1/4" by 4". The 1962 Kahn's Wieners Atlanta set features unnumbered, black and white cards of the Atlanta Crackers of the International League. The backs contain player statistical information as well as instructions on how to obtain free tickets. The catalog designation is F155-9.

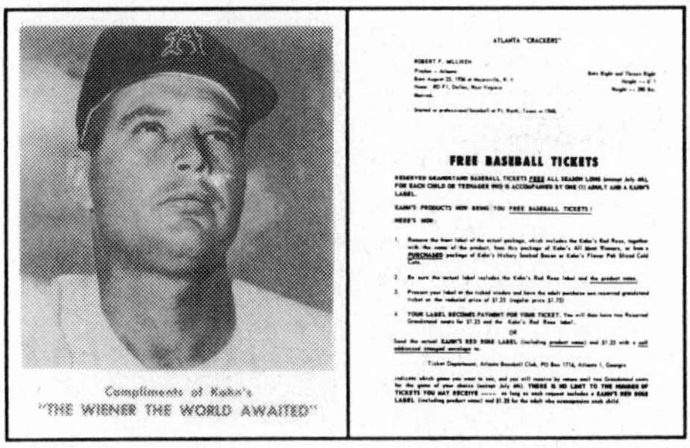

	NRMT	VG-E	GOOD
COMPLETE SET (24)	350.00	175.00	35.00
COMMON PLAYER (1-24)	12.00	6.00	1.20
☐ 1 Jim Beauchamp	15.00	7.50	1.50
☐ 2 Gerry Buchek	12.00	6.00	1.20
☐ 3 Bob Burda	12.00	6.00	1.20
☐ 4 Dick Dietz	15.00	7.50	1.50
☐ 5 Bob Duliba	12.00	6.00	1.20
☐ 6 Harry Fanok	12.00	6.00	1.20
☐ 7 Phil Gagliano	15.00	7.50	1.50
☐ 8 John Glenn	12.00	6.00	1.20
☐ 9 Leroy Gregory	12.00	6.00	1.20
☐ 10 Dick Hughes	12.00	6.00	1.20
☐ 11 Johnny Kucks	15.00	7.50	1.50
☐ 12 Johnny Lewis	12.00	6.00	1.20
☐ 13 Tim McCarver	75.00	37.50	7.50
☐ 14 Bob Milliken	12.00	6.00	1.20
☐ 15 Joe M. Morgan	30.00	15.00	3.00
☐ 16 Ron Plaza	12.00	6.00	1.20
☐ 17 Bob Sadowski	12.00	6.00	1.20
☐ 18 Jim Saul	12.00	6.00	1.20
☐ 19 Willard Schmidt	12.00	6.00	1.20
☐ 20 Joe Schultz	12.00	6.00	1.20
☐ 21 Mike Shannon	30.00	15.00	3.00
☐ 22 Paul Toth	12.00	6.00	1.20
☐ 23 Lou Vickery	12.00	6.00	1.20
☐ 24 Fred Whitfield	15.00	7.50	1.50

1963 Kahn's

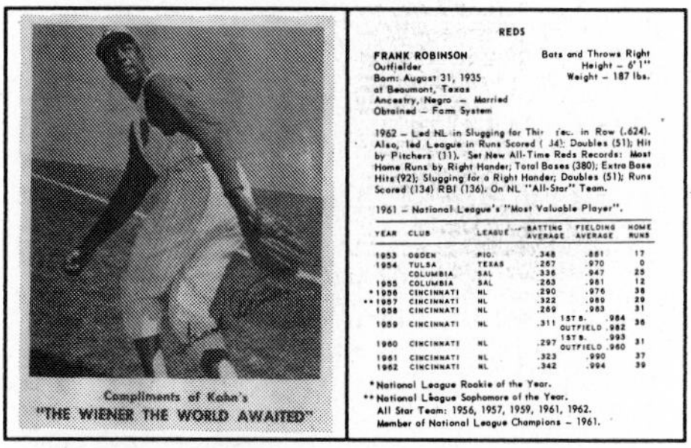

The cards in this 30-card set measure 3 1/4" by 4". The 1963 Kahn's Wieners set of black and white, unnumbered cards features players from Cincinnati, Cleveland, St. Louis, Pittsburgh and the New York Yankees. The cards feature a white border around the picture of the players. The backs contain career information. The catalog designation is F155-10.

	NRMT	VG-E	GOOD
COMPLETE SET (30)	500.00	250.00	50.00
COMMON PLAYER (1-30)	10.00	5.00	1.00

☐ 1 Bob Bailey	10.00	5.00	1.00
☐ 2 Don Blasingame	10.00	5.00	1.00
☐ 3 Clete Boyer	13.50	6.25	1.25
☐ 4 Smoky Burgess	10.00	5.00	1.00
☐ 5 Chico Cardenas	10.00	5.00	1.00
☐ 6 Roberto Clemente	175.00	85.00	18.00
☐ 7 Donn Clendenon	12.00	6.00	1.20
☐ 8 Gordon Coleman	10.00	5.00	1.00
☐ 9 John Edwards	10.00	5.00	1.00
☐ 10 Gene Freese	10.00	5.00	1.00
☐ 11 Bob Friend	12.00	6.00	1.20
☐ 12 Joe Gibbon	10.00	5.00	1.00
☐ 13 Dick Groat	15.00	7.50	1.50
☐ 14 Harvey Haddix	12.00	6.00	1.20
☐ 15 Elston Howard	18.00	9.00	1.80
☐ 16 Joey Jay	10.00	5.00	1.00
☐ 17 Eddie Kasko	10.00	5.00	1.00
☐ 18 Tony Kubek	24.00	12.00	2.40
☐ 19 Jerry Lynch	10.00	5.00	1.00
☐ 20 Jim Maloney	12.00	6.00	1.20
☐ 21 Bill Mazeroski	16.00	8.00	1.60
☐ 22 Joe Nuxhall	12.00	6.00	1.20
☐ 23 Jim O'Toole	10.00	5.00	1.00
☐ 24 Vada Pinson	15.00	7.50	1.50
☐ 25 Bob Purkey	10.00	5.00	1.00
☐ 26 Bobby Richardson	24.00	12.00	2.40
☐ 27 Frank Robinson	80.00	40.00	8.00
☐ 28 Bill Stafford	10.00	5.00	1.00
☐ 29 Ralph Terry	12.00	6.00	1.20
☐ 30 Bill Virdon	12.00	6.00	1.20

1964 Kahn's

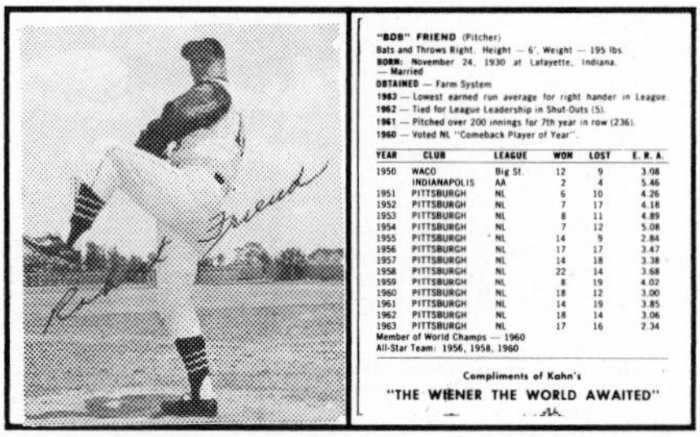

The cards in this 31-card set measure 3" by 3 1/2". The 1964 Kahn's set marks the beginning of the full color cards and the elimination of the tabs which existed on previous Kahn's cards. The set of unnumbered cards contains player information through the 1963 season on the backs. The set features Cincinnati, Cleveland and Pittsburgh players.

	NRMT	VG-E	GOOD
COMPLETE SET (31)	750.00	375.00	75.00
COMMON PLAYER (1-31)	10.00	5.00	1.00
☐ 1 Max Alvis	10.00	5.00	1.00
☐ 2 Bob Bailey	10.00	5.00	1.00
☐ 3 Chico Cardenas	10.00	5.00	1.00
☐ 4 Roberto Clemente	175.00	85.00	18.00
☐ 5 Donn Clendenon	12.00	6.00	1.20
☐ 6 Vic Davalillo	10.00	5.00	1.00
☐ 7 Dick Donovan	10.00	5.00	1.00
☐ 8 John Edwards	10.00	5.00	1.00
☐ 9 Bob Friend	12.00	6.00	1.20
☐ 10 Jim Grant	10.00	5.00	1.00
☐ 11 Tommy Harper	10.00	5.00	1.00
☐ 12 Woodie Held	10.00	5.00	1.00
☐ 13 Joey Jay	10.00	5.00	1.00
☐ 14 Jack Kralick	10.00	5.00	1.00
☐ 15 Jerry Lynch	10.00	5.00	1.00
☐ 16 Jim Maloney	12.00	6.00	1.20
☐ 17 Bill Mazeroski	16.00	8.00	1.60
☐ 18 Alvin McBean	10.00	5.00	1.00
☐ 19 Joe Nuxhall	12.00	6.00	1.20
☐ 20 Jim Pagliaroni	10.00	5.00	1.00
☐ 21 Vada Pinson	15.00	7.50	1.50
☐ 22 Bob Purkey	10.00	5.00	1.00
☐ 23 Pedro Ramos	10.00	5.00	1.00
☐ 24 Frank Robinson	80.00	40.00	8.00
☐ 25 John Romano	10.00	5.00	1.00
☐ 26 Pete Rose	350.00	175.00	35.00
☐ 27 John Tsitouris	10.00	5.00	1.00
☐ 28 Bob Veale	10.00	5.00	1.00
☐ 29 Bill Virdon	12.00	6.00	1.20
☐ 30 Leon Wagner	10.00	5.00	1.00
☐ 31 Fred Whitfield	10.00	5.00	1.00

1965 Kahn's

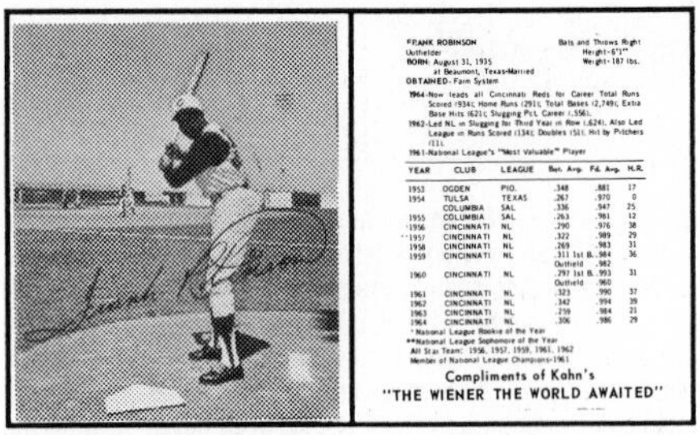

The cards in this 45-card set measure 3" by 3 1/2". The 1965 Kahn's set contains full color, unnumbered cards. The set features Cincinnati, Cleveland, Pittsburgh, and Milwaukee players. Backs contain statistical information through the 1964 season.

	NRMT	VG-E	GOOD
COMPLETE SET (45)	900.00	450.00	90.00
COMMON PLAYER (1-45)	10.00	5.00	1.00
☐ 1 Henry Aaron	150.00	75.00	15.00
☐ 2 Max Alvis	10.00	5.00	1.00
☐ 3 Joe Azcue	10.00	5.00	1.00
☐ 4 Bob Bailey	10.00	5.00	1.00
☐ 5 Frank Bolling	10.00	5.00	1.00
☐ 6 Chico Cardenas	10.00	5.00	1.00
☐ 7 Rico Carty	15.00	7.50	1.50
☐ 8 Donn Clendenon	12.00	6.00	1.20
☐ 9 Tony Cloninger	10.00	5.00	1.00
☐ 10 Gordon Coleman	10.00	5.00	1.00
☐ 11 Vic Davalillo	10.00	5.00	1.00
☐ 12 John Edwards	10.00	5.00	1.00
☐ 13 Sammy Ellis	10.00	5.00	1.00
☐ 14 Bob Friend	12.00	6.00	1.20
☐ 15 Tommy Harper	10.00	5.00	1.00
☐ 16 Chuck Hinton	10.00	5.00	1.00
☐ 17 Dick Howser	15.00	7.50	1.50
☐ 18 Joey Jay	10.00	5.00	1.00
☐ 19 Deron Johnson	10.00	5.00	1.00
☐ 20 Jack Kralick	10.00	5.00	1.00
☐ 21 Denver LeMaster	10.00	5.00	1.00
☐ 22 Jerry Lynch	10.00	5.00	1.00
☐ 23 Jim Maloney	12.00	6.00	1.20
☐ 24 Lee Maye	10.00	5.00	1.00
☐ 25 Bill Mazeroski	16.00	8.00	1.60
☐ 26 Alvin McBean	10.00	5.00	1.00
☐ 27 Bill McCool	10.00	5.00	1.00
☐ 28 Sam McDowell	13.50	6.25	1.20
☐ 29 Don McMahon	10.00	5.00	1.00
☐ 30 Denis Menke	10.00	5.00	1.00
☐ 31 Joe Nuxhall	12.00	6.00	1.20
☐ 32 Gene Oliver	10.00	5.00	1.00
☐ 33 Jim O'Toole	10.00	5.00	1.00
☐ 34 Jim Pagliaroni	10.00	5.00	1.00
☐ 35 Vada Pinson	15.00	7.50	1.50
☐ 36 Frank Robinson	80.00	40.00	8.00
☐ 37 Pete Rose	225.00	110.00	22.00
☐ 38 Willie Stargell	100.00	50.00	10.00
☐ 39 Ralph Terry	12.00	6.00	1.20
☐ 40 Luis Tiant	15.00	7.50	1.50
☐ 41 Joe Torre	18.00	9.00	1.80
☐ 42 John Tsitouris	10.00	5.00	1.00
☐ 43 Bob Veale	12.00	6.00	1.20
☐ 44 Bill Virdon	12.00	6.00	1.20
☐ 45 Leon Wagner	10.00	5.00	1.00

1966 Kahn's

The cards in this 32-card set measure 2 13/16" by 4". 1966 Kahn's full color, unnumbered set features players from Atlanta, Cincinnati, Cleveland, and Pittsburgh. The set is identified by yellow and white vertical stripes and the name Kahn's written in red across a red rose at the top. The cards contain a 1 5/16" ad in the form of a tab. Cards with the ad (tab) are worth twice as much as cards without the ad, i.e., double the prices below.

	NRMT	VG-E	GOOD
COMPLETE SET (32)	550.00	275.00	55.00
COMMON PLAYER (1-32)	8.00	4.00	.80
☐ 1 Henry Aaron (portrait, no wind-breaker under jersey	80.00	40.00	8.00
☐ 2 Felipe Alou: Braves (full pose, batting screen in background)	10.00	5.00	1.00
☐ 3 Max Alvis: Indians (kneeling, full pose, with bat, no patch on jersey)	8.00	4.00	.80
☐ 4 Bob Bailey	8.00	4.00	.80
☐ 5 Wade Blasingame	8.00	4.00	.80
☐ 6 Frank Bolling	8.00	4.00	.80
☐ 7 Chico Cardenas: Reds (fielding, feet at base)	8.00	4.00	.80
☐ 8 Roberto Clemente	90.00	45.00	9.00
☐ 9 Tony Cloninger: Braves (pitching, foulpole in background)	8.00	4.00	.80
☐ 10 Vic Davalillo	8.00	4.00	.80
☐ 11 John Edwards: Reds (catching)	8.00	4.00	.80
☐ 12 Sam Ellis: Reds (white hat)	8.00	4.00	.80
☐ 13 Pedro Gonzalez	8.00	4.00	.80
☐ 14 Tommy Harper: Reds (arm cocked)	8.00	4.00	.80
☐ 15 Deron Johnson: Reds (batting with batting cage in background)	8.00	4.00	.80
☐ 16 Mack Jones	8.00	4.00	.80
☐ 17 Denver Lemaster	8.00	4.00	.80
☐ 18 Jim Maloney: Reds (pitching, white hat)	10.00	5.00	1.00
☐ 19 Bill Mazeroski: PIrates (throwing)	12.00	6.00	1.20
☐ 20 Bill McCool: Reds (white hat)	8.00	4.00	.80
☐ 21 Sam McDowell: Indians (kneeling)	10.00	5.00	1.00
☐ 22 Denis Menke: Braves (white windbreaker under jersey)	8.00	4.00	.80
☐ 23 Joe Nuxhall	10.00	5.00	1.00
☐ 24 Jim Pagliaroni: Pirates (catching)	8.00	4.00	.80
☐ 25 Milt Pappas	10.00	5.00	1.00
☐ 26 Vada Pinson: Reds (fielding, ball on ground)	12.00	6.00	1.20
☐ 27 Pete Rose: Reds (with glove)	125.00	60.00	12.50
☐ 28 Sonny Siebert: Indians (pitching, signature at feet)	8.00	4.00	.80
☐ 29 Willie Stargell: Pirates (batting, clouds in sky)	40.00	20.00	4.00
☐ 30 Joe Torre: Braves (catching with hand on mask)	12.00	6.00	1.20
☐ 31 Bob Veale: Pirates (hands at knee with glasses)	8.00	4.00	.80
☐ 32 Fred Whitfield	8.00	4.00	.80

1967 Kahn's

The cards in this 41-player set measure 2 13/16" by 4". The 1967 Kahn's set of full color, unnumbered cards is almost identical in style to the 1966 issue. Different meat products had different background colors (yellow and white stripes, red and white stripes, etc.). The set features players from Atlanta, Cincinnati, Cleveland, New York Mets and Pittsburgh. Cards with the ads (see 1966 set) are worth twice as much as cards without the ad, i.e., double the prices below. The complete set price below includes all variations.

	NRMT	VG-E	GOOD
COMPLETE SET (51)	750.00	375.00	75.00
COMMON PLAYER (1-41)	8.00	4.00	.80
☐ 1A Henry Aaron: Braves (swinging pose, batting glove, ball, and hat on ground)	80.00	40.00	8.00
☐ 1B Henry Aaron: Braves (swinging pose, batting glove, ball, and hat on ground; Cut Along Dotted Lines printed on lower tab)	125.00	60.00	12.50
☐ 2 Gene Alley: Pirates (portrait)	8.00	4.00	.80
☐ 3 Felipe Alou: Braves (full pose, bat on shoulder)	10.00	5.00	1.00
☐ 4A Matty Alou: Pirates (portrait with bat, "Matio Rojas Alou"; yellow stripes)	10.00	5.00	1.00
☐ 4B Matty Alou: Pirates (portrait with bat, "Matio Rojas Alou"; red stripes)	12.00	6.00	1.20
☐ 5 Max Alvis: Indians (fielding, hands on knees)	8.00	4.00	.80

☐ 6A Ken Boyer (batting righthanded; autograph at waist)	12.00	6.00	1.20
☐ 6B Ken Boyer (batting righthanded; autograph at shoulders; Cut Along Dotted Lines printed on lower tab)	16.00	8.00	1.60
☐ 7 Chico Cardenas: Reds (fielding, hand on knee)	8.00	4.00	.80
☐ 8 Rico Carty	10.00	5.00	1.00
☐ 9 Tony Cloninger: Braves (pitching, no foul-pole in background)	8.00	4.00	.80
☐ 10 Tommy Davis	10.00	5.00	1.00
☐ 11 John Edwards: Reds (kneeling with bat)	8.00	4.00	.80
☐ 12A Sam Ellis: Reds (all red hat)	8.00	4.00	.80
☐ 12B Sam Ellis: Reds (all red hat) Cut Along Dotted Lines printed on lower tab)	10.00	5.00	1.00
☐ 13 Jack Fisher	8.00	4.00	.80
☐ 14 Steve Hargan: Indians (pitching, no clouds, blue sky)	8.00	4.00	.80
☐ 15 Tommy Harper: Reds (fielding, glove on ground)	8.00	4.00	.80
☐ 16A Tommy Helms (batting righthanded; top of bat visible)	8.00	4.00	.80
☐ 16B Tommy Helms (batting righthanded; bat chopped above hat; Cut Along Dotted Lines printed on lower tab)	10.00	5.00	1.00
☐ 17 Deron Johnson: Reds (batting, blue sky)	8.00	4.00	.80
☐ 18 Ken Johnson	8.00	4.00	.80
☐ 19 Cleon Jones	8.00	4.00	.80
☐ 20A Ed Kranepool (ready for throw; yellow stripes)	10.00	5.00	1.00
☐ 20B Ed Kranepool (ready for throw; red stripes)	12.00	6.00	1.20
☐ 21A Jim Maloney: Reds (pitching, red hat, follow thru delivery; yellow stripes)	10.00	5.00	1.00
☐ 21B Jim Maloney: Reds (pitching, red hat, follow thru delivery; red stripes)	12.00	6.00	1.20
☐ 22 Lee May: Reds (hands on knee)	10.00	5.00	1.00
☐ 23A Bill Mazeroski: Pirates (portrait; autograph below waist)	12.00	6.00	1.20
☐ 23B Bill Mazeroski: Pirates (portrait; autograph above waist; Cut Along Dotted Lines printed on lower tab)	16.00	8.00	1.60
☐ 24 Bill McCool: Reds (red hat, left hand out)	8.00	4.00	.80
☐ 25 Sam McDowell: Indians (pitching, left hand under glove)	10.00	5.00	1.00
☐ 26 Denis Menke: Braves (blue sleeves)	8.00	4.00	.80
☐ 27 Jim Pagliaroni: Pirates (catching, no chest protector)	8.00	4.00	.80
☐ 28 Don Pavletich	8.00	4.00	.80
☐ 29 Tony Perez: Reds (throwing)	20.00	10.00	2.00
☐ 30 Vada Pinson: Reds (ready to throw)	12.00	6.00	1.20
☐ 31 Dennis Ribant	8.00	4.00	.80
☐ 32 Pete Rose: Reds (batting)	125.00	60.00	12.50
☐ 33 Art Shamsky: Reds	8.00	4.00	.80
☐ 34 Bob Shaw	8.00	4.00	.80
☐ 35 Sonny Siebert: Indians (pitching, signature at knees)	8.00	4.00	.80
☐ 36 Willie Stargell: Pirates (batting, no clouds)	40.00	20.00	4.00
☐ 37A Joe Torre: Braves (catching, mask on ground)	12.00	6.00	1.20
☐ 37B Joe Torre: Braves (catching, mask on ground; Cut Along Dotted Lines printed on lower tab)	16.00	8.00	1.60
☐ 38 Bob Veale: Pirates (portrait, hands not shown)	8.00	4.00	.80
☐ 39 Leon Wagner: Indians (fielding)	8.00	4.00	.80
☐ 40A Fred Whitfield (batting lefthanded)	8.00	4.00	.80
☐ 40B Fred Whitfield (batting lefthanded; Cut Along Dotted Lines printed on lower tab)	10.00	5.00	1.00
☐ 41 Woody Woodward	10.00	5.00	1.00

1968 Kahn's

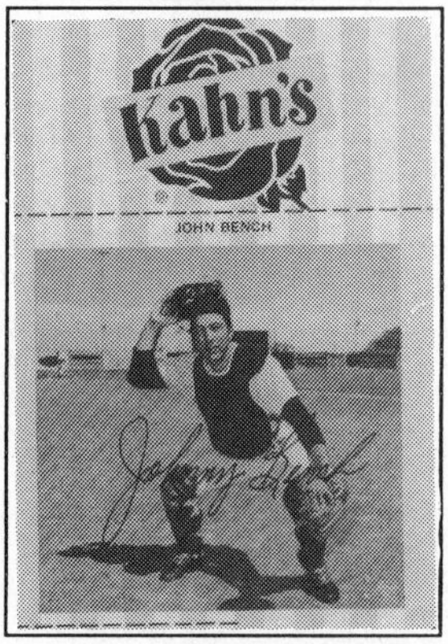

The cards in this 50-card set contain two different sizes. The smaller of the two sizes, which contains 12 cards, is 2 13/16" by 3 1/4" with the ad tab and 2 13/16" by 1 7/8" without the ad tab. The larger size, which contains 38 cards, measures 2 13/16" by 3 7/8" with the ad tab and 2 13/16" by 2 11/16" without the ad tab. The 1968 Kahn's set of full color, blank backed, unnumbered cards features players from Atlanta, Chicago Cubs, Chicago White Sox, Cincinnati, Cleveland, Detroit, New York Mets, and Pittsburgh. In the set of 12, listed with the letter A in the checklist, Maloney exists with either yellow or yellow and green stripes at the top of the card. The large set of 38, listed with a letter B in the checklist, contains five cards which exist in two variations. The variations in this large set have either yellow or red stripes at the top of the cards, with Maloney being an exception. Maloney has either a yellow stripe or a Blue Mountain ad at the top. Cards with the ad tabs (see other Kahn's sets) are worth twice as much as cards without the ad, i.e., double the prices below.

	NRMT	VG-E	GOOD
COMPLETE SET (50)	800.00	400.00	80.00
COMMON PLAYER	8.00	4.00	.80
☐ A1 Hank Aaron	80.00	40.00	8.00
☐ A2 Gene Alley	8.00	4.00	.80
☐ A3 Max Alvis	8.00	4.00	.80
☐ A4 Clete Boyer	10.00	5.00	1.00
☐ A5 Chico Cardenas	8.00	4.00	.80
☐ A6 Bill Freehan	12.00	6.00	1.20
☐ A7 Jim Maloney (2)	10.00	5.00	1.00
☐ A8 Lee May	8.00	4.00	.80
☐ A9 Bill Mazeroski	12.00	6.00	1.20
☐ A10 Vada Pinson	12.00	6.00	1.20
☐ A11 Joe Torre	12.00	6.00	1.20
☐ A12 Bob Veale	8.00	4.00	.80

☐ B1 Hank Aaron: Braves (full pose, batting bat cocked)	80.00	40.00	8.00
☐ B2 Tommy Agee	8.00	4.00	.80
☐ B3 Gene Alley: Pirates (fielding, full pose)	8.00	4.00	.80
☐ B4 Felipe Alou (full pose, batting, swinging, player in background)	10.00	5.00	1.00
☐ B5 Matty Alou: Pirates (portrait with bat, "Matio Alou" (2)	10.00	5.00	1.00
☐ B6 Max Alvis (fielding, glove on ground)	8.00	4.00	.80
☐ B7 Gerry Arrigo: Reds (pitching, follow thru delivery)	8.00	4.00	.80
☐ B8 John Bench	300.00	150.00	30.00
☐ B9 Clete Boyer	10.00	5.00	1.00
☐ B10 Larry Brown	8.00	4.00	.80
☐ B11 Leo Cardenas: Reds (leaping in the air)	8.00	4.00	.80
☐ B12 Bill Freehan	10.00	5.00	1.00
☐ B13 Steve Hargan: Indians (pitching, clouds in background)	8.00	4.00	.80
☐ B14 Joel Horlen: White Sox (portrait)	8.00	4.00	.80
☐ B15 Tony Horton: Indians (portrait, signed Anthony)	8.00	4.00	.80
☐ B16 Willie Horton	10.00	5.00	1.00
☐ B17 Ferguson Jenkins	35.00	17.50	3.50
☐ B18 Deron Johnson: Braves	8.00	4.00	.80
☐ B19 Mack Jones: Reds	8.00	4.00	.80
☐ B20 Bob Lee	8.00	4.00	.80
☐ B21 Jim Maloney: Reds (red hat, pitching hands up) (2)	10.00	5.00	1.00
☐ B22 Lee May: Reds (batting)	10.00	5.00	1.00
☐ B23 Bill Mazeroski: Pirates (fielding, hands in front of body)	12.00	6.00	1.20
☐ B24 Dick McAuliffe	10.00	5.00	1.00
☐ B25 Bill McCool (red hat, left hand down)	8.00	4.00	.80
☐ B26 Sam McDowell: Indians (pitching, left hand over glove (2)	10.00	5.00	1.00
☐ B27 Tony Perez (fielding ball in glove (2)	20.00	10.00	2.00
☐ B28 Gary Peters: White Sox (portrait)	8.00	4.00	.80
☐ B29 Vada Pinson: Reds (batting)	12.00	6.00	1.20
☐ B30 Chico Ruiz	8.00	4.00	.80
☐ B31 Ron Santo: Cubs (batting, follow thru (2)	12.00	6.00	1.20
☐ B32 Art Shamsky: Mets	8.00	4.00	.80
☐ B33 Luis Tiant: Indians (hands over head)	10.00	5.00	1.00
☐ B34 Joe Torre: Braves (batting)	12.00	6.00	1.20
☐ B35 Bob Veale: Pirates (hands chest high)	8.00	4.00	.80
☐ B36 Leon Wagner: Indians (batting)	8.00	4.00	.80
☐ B37 Billy Williams: Cubs (bat behind back)	35.00	17.50	3.50
☐ B38 Earl Wilson	8.00	4.00	.80

1969 Kahn's

The cards in this 25-card set contain two different sizes. The three small cards (see 1968 description) measure 2 13/16" by 3 1/4" and the 22 large cards (see 1968 description) measure 2 13/16" by 3 15/16". The 1969 Kahn's Wieners set of full color, unnumbered cards features players from Atlanta, Chicago Cubs, Chicago White Sox, Cincinnati, Cleveland, Pittsburgh, and St. Louis. The small cards have the letter A in the checklist while the large cards have the letter B in the checklist. Four of the larger cards exist in two variations (red or yellow color stripes at the top of the card). These variations are identified in the checklist below. Cards with the ad tabs (see other Kahn's sets) are worth twice as much as cards without the ad, i.e., double the prices below.

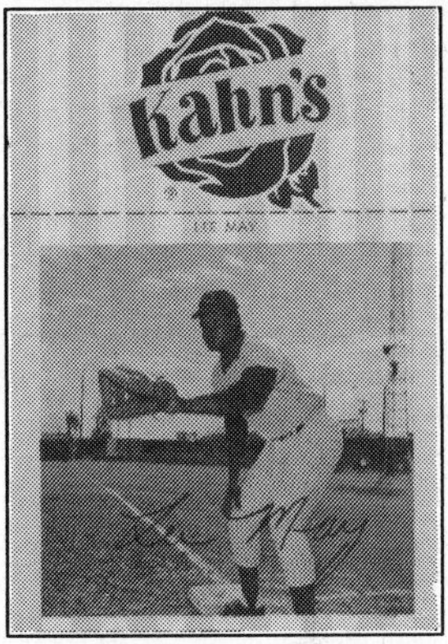

	NRMT	VG-E	GOOD
COMPLETE SET (25)	400.00	200.00	40.00
COMMON PLAYER	8.00	4.00	.80
☐ A1 Hank Aaron (portrait)	80.00	40.00	8.00
☐ A2 Jim Maloney (pitching, hands at side)	10.00	5.00	1.00
☐ A3 Tony Perez (glove on)	20.00	10.00	2.00
☐ B1 Hank Aaron	80.00	40.00	8.00
☐ B2 Matty Alou (batting)	10.00	5.00	1.00
☐ B3 Max Alvis ('69 patch)	8.00	4.00	.80
☐ B4 Gerry Arrigo (leg up)	8.00	4.00	.80
☐ B5 Steve Blass	10.00	5.00	1.00
☐ B6 Clay Carroll	8.00	4.00	.80
☐ B7 Tony Cloninger: Reds	8.00	4.00	.80
☐ B8 George Culver	8.00	4.00	.80
☐ B9 Joel Horlen (pitching)	8.00	4.00	.80
☐ B10 Tony Horton (batting)	8.00	4.00	.80
☐ B11 Alex Johnson	8.00	4.00	.80
☐ B12 Jim Maloney	10.00	5.00	1.00
☐ B13 Lee May (foot on bag) (2)	10.00	5.00	1.00
☐ B14 Bill Mazeroski (hands on knees) (2)	12.00	6.00	1.20
☐ B15 Sam McDowell (leg up) (2)	10.00	5.00	1.00
☐ B16 Tony Perez	20.00	10.00	2.00
☐ B17 Gary Peters (pitching)	8.00	4.00	.80
☐ B18 Ron Santo (emblem) (2)	12.00	6.00	1.20
☐ B19 Luis Tiant (glove at knee)	10.00	5.00	1.00
☐ B20 Joe Torre: Cardinals	12.00	6.00	1.20
☐ B21 Bob Veale (hands at knees, no glasses)	8.00	4.00	.80
☐ B22 Billy Williams (bat behind head)	35.00	17.50	3.50

1987 Kahn's Weiners Reds

This 30-card set was issued to the first 20,000 fans at the August 2nd game between the Reds and the San Francisco Giants at Riverfront Stadium. Cards are standard size, 2 1/2" by

3 1/2". The cards are unnumbered except for uniform number and feature full-color photos bordered in red and white on the front. The Kahn's logo is printed in red in the corner of the reverse.

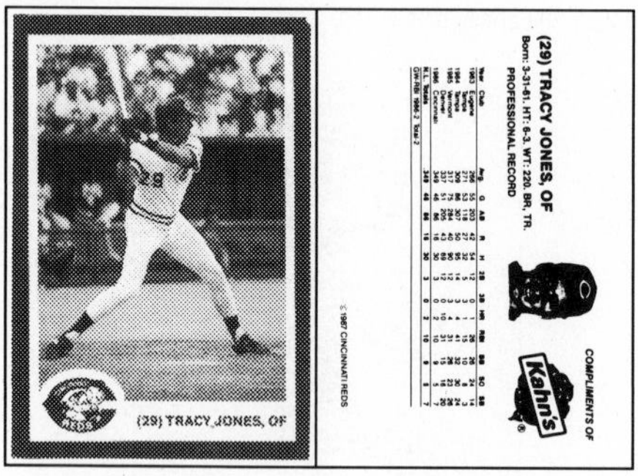

	MINT	EXC	G-VG
COMPLETE SET (30)	20.00	10.00	2.00
COMMON PLAYER	.50	.25	.05
☐ 6 Bo Diaz	.50	.25	.05
☐ 10 Terry Francona	.50	.25	.05
☐ 11 Kurt Stillwell	.75	.35	.07
☐ 12 Nick Esasky	.75	.35	.07
☐ 13 Dave Concepcion	.90	.45	.09
☐ 15 Barry Larkin	3.50	1.75	.35
☐ 16 Ron Oester	.50	.25	.05
☐ 21 Paul O'Neill	1.50	.75	.15
☐ 23 Lloyd McClendon	.50	.25	.05
☐ 25 Buddy Bell	.75	.35	.07
☐ 28 Kal Daniels	2.50	1.25	.25
☐ 29 Tracy Jones	.60	.30	.06
☐ 30 Guy Hoffman	.50	.25	.05
☐ 31 John Franco	1.00	.50	.10
☐ 32 Tom Browning	1.25	.60	.12
☐ 33 Ron Robinson	.60	.30	.06
☐ 34 Bill Gullickson	.50	.25	.05
☐ 35 Pat Pacillo	.60	.30	.06
☐ 39 Dave Parker	1.25	.60	.12
☐ 43 Bill Landrum	.50	.25	.05
☐ 44 Eric Davis	5.00	2.50	.50
☐ 46 Rob Murphy	.60	.30	.06
☐ 47 Frank Williams	.50	.25	.05
☐ 48 Ted Power	.50	.25	.05
☐ xx Pete Rose MG	1.50	.75	.15
☐ xx Coaches Card Scott Breeden Billy DeMars Tommy Helms Bruce Kimm Jim Lett Tony Perez	.50	.25	.05
☐ xx Ad Card Save 25 cents on Corn Dogs	.50	.25	.05
☐ xx Ad Card Save 30 cents on Smokeys	.50	.25	.05

1988 Kahn's Mets

These 32-card sets were issued to the first 48,000 fans at the June 30th game between the Mets and the Houston Astros at Shea Stadium. The set includes 30 players, a team card, and a discount coupon card (to be redeemed at the grocery store). Cards are standard size, 2 1/2" by 3 1/2". The cards are unnumbered except for uniform number and feature full-color photos bordered in blue and orange on the front. The Kahn's logo is printed in red in the corner of the reverse.

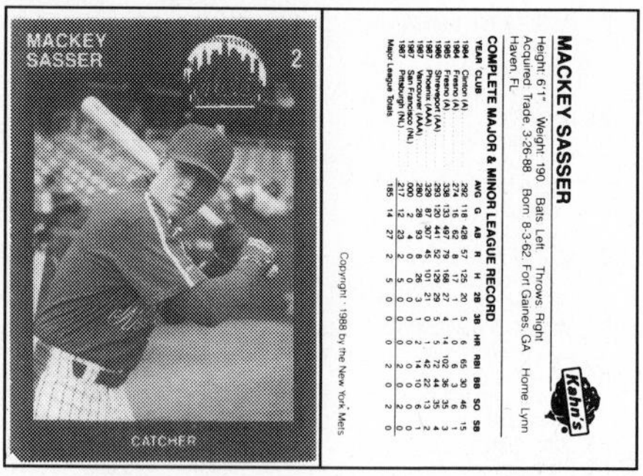

	MINT	EXC	G-VG
COMPLETE SET (32)	14.00	7.00	1.40
COMMON PLAYER	.40	.20	.04
☐ 1 Mookie Wilson	.50	.25	.05
☐ 2 Mackey Sasser	.50	.25	.05
☐ 3 Bud Harrelson CO	.50	.25	.05
☐ 4 Lenny Dykstra	.75	.35	.07
☐ 5 Davey Johnson MG	.50	.25	.05
☐ 6 Wally Backman	.40	.20	.04
☐ 8 Gary Carter	.75	.35	.07
☐ 11 Tim Teufel	.40	.20	.04
☐ 12 Ron Darling	.60	.30	.06
☐ 13 Lee Mazzilli	.40	.20	.04
☐ 15 Rick Aguilera	.50	.25	.05
☐ 16 Dwight Gooden	1.00	.50	.10
☐ 17 Keith Hernandez	.75	.35	:07
☐ 18 Darryl Strawberry	1.50	.75	.15
☐ 19 Bob Ojeda	.50	.25	.05
☐ 20 Howard Johnson	.75	.35	.07
☐ 21 Kevin Elster	.50	.25	.05
☐ 22 Kevin McReynolds	1.00	.50	.10
☐ 26 Terry Leach	.40	.20	.04
☐ 28 Bill Robinson CO	.50	.25	.05
☐ 29 Dave Magadan	.60	.30	.06
☐ 30 Mel Stottlemyre CO	.50	.25	.05
☐ 31 Gene Walter	.40	.20	.04
☐ 33 Barry Lyons	.40	.20	.04
☐ 34 Sam Perlozzo CO	.40	.20	.04
☐ 42 Roger McDowell	.50	.25	.05
☐ 44 David Cone	1.00	.50	.10
☐ 48 Randy Myers	.60	.30	.06
☐ 50 Sid Fernandez	.50	.25	.05
☐ 52 Greg Pavlick	.40	.20	.04
☐ x Team Photo Card (unnumbered)	.40	.20	.04
☐ x Discount Coupon (unnumbered)	.40	.20	.04

1988 Kahn's Reds

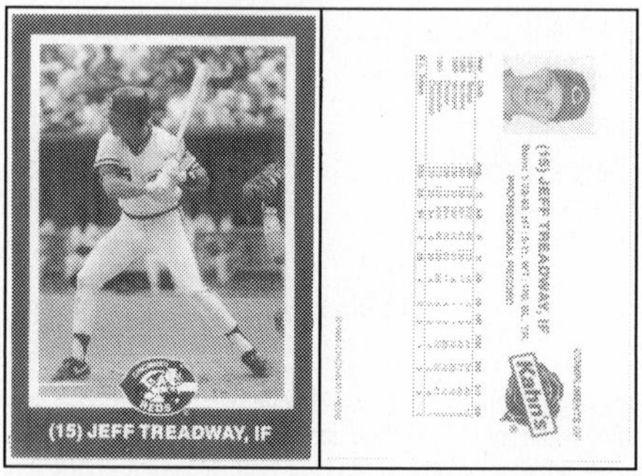

These 26-card sets were issued to fans at the August 14th game between the Reds and the Atlanta Braves at Riverfront Stadium. Cards are standard size, 2 1/2" by 3 1/2". The cards are unnumbered except for uniform number and feature full-color photos bordered in red and white on the front. The Kahn's logo is printed in red in the corner of the reverse. The cards are numbered below by uniform number which is listed parenthetically on the front of the cards.

	MINT	EXC	G-VG
COMPLETE SET (26)	14.00	7.00	1.40
COMMON PLAYER	.40	.20	.04
☐ 6 Bo Diaz	.40	.20	.04
☐ 8 Terry McGriff	.40	.20	.04
☐ 9 Eddie Milner	.40	.20	.04
☐ 10 Leon Durham	.40	.20	.04
☐ 11 Barry Larkin	1.50	.75	.15
☐ 12 Nick Esasky	.60	.30	.06
☐ 13 Dave Concepcion	.60	.30	.06
☐ 14 Pete Rose MG	1.00	.50	.10
☐ 15 Jeff Treadway	.50	.25	.05
☐ 17 Chris Sabo	2.50	1.25	.25
☐ 20 Danny Jackson	.60	.30	.06
☐ 21 Paul O'Neill	.90	.45	.09
☐ 22 Dave Collins	.40	.20	.04
☐ 27 Jose Rijo	.75	.35	.07
☐ 28 Kal Daniels	1.00	.50	.10
☐ 29 Tracy Jones	.40	.20	.04
☐ 30 Lloyd McClendon	.40	.20	.04
☐ 31 John Franco	.60	.30	.06
☐ 32 Tom Browning	.60	.30	.06
☐ 33 Ron Robinson	.50	.25	.05
☐ 40 Jack Armstrong	.75	.35	.07
☐ 44 Eric Davis	1.50	.75	.15
☐ 46 Rob Murphy	.50	.25	.05
☐ 47 Frank Williams	.40	.20	.04
☐ 48 Tim Birtsas	.40	.20	.04
☐ xx Reds Coaches Lee May CO Tony Perez CO Bruce Kimm CO Tommy Helms CO Jim Lett CO Scott Breeden CO	.40	.20	.04

1989 Kahn's Cooperstown

The 1989 Kahn's Cooperstown set contains 11 standard-size (2 1/2 by 3 1/2 inch) cards. This set is sometimes referenced as Hillshire Farms or Kahn's Cooperstown Collection. All players included in the set are members (for the most part they are recent inductees) of the Hall of Fame. The pictures are actually paintings and are surrounded by gold borders. The fronts resemble plaques and also have facsimile autographs. The cards were available from the company via a send-in offer. A set of cards was available in return for three proofs of purchase (and 1.00 postage and handling) from Hillshire Farms. The last card in the set is actually a coupon card for Kahn's products; this card is not even considered part of the set by some collectors. A related promotion offered two coin cards (coins laminated on cards) featuring Johnny Bench and Carl Yastrzemski. These coin cards are approximately 5 1/2" by 3 3/4" and are blank backed.

	MINT	EXC	G-VG
COMPLETE SET (12)	6.00	3.00	.60
COMMON PLAYER (1-11)	.50	.25	.05
☐ 1 Cool Papa Bell	.50	.25	.05
☐ 2 Johnny Bench	1.00	.50	.10
☐ 3 Lou Brock	.75	.35	.07
☐ 4 Whitey Ford	.75	.35	.07
☐ 5 Bob Gibson	.75	.35	.07
☐ 6 Billy Herman	.60	.30	.06
☐ 7 Harmon Killebrew	.75	.35	.07
☐ 8 Eddie Mathews	1.00	.50	.10
☐ 9 Brooks Robinson	1.00	.50	.10
☐ 10 Willie Stargell	1.00	.50	.10
☐ 11 Carl Yastrzemski	1.25	.60	.12
☐ 12 Coupon Card	.50	.25	.05

1989 Kahn's Mets

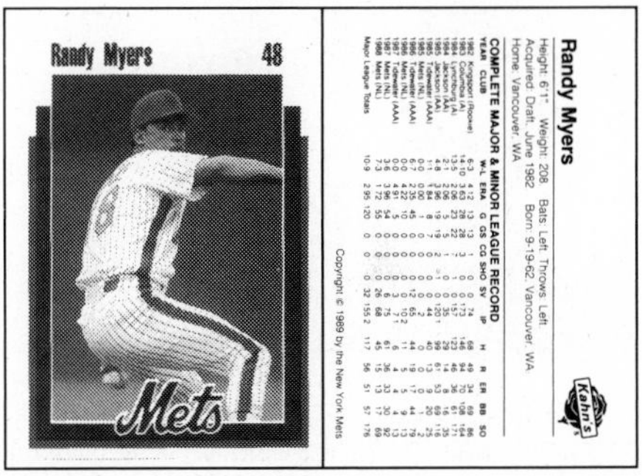

The 1989 Kahn's Mets set contains 36 (32 original and 4 update) standard-size (2 1/2" by 3 1/2") cards. The fronts have color photos with Mets' colored borders (blue, orange and white). The horizontally-oriented backs have career stats. The cards were available from Kahn's by sending three UPC symbols from Kahn's products and a coupon appearing in certain local newspapers. There was also a small late-season update set of Kahn's Mets showing new Mets players arriving in mid-season trades, e.g., Jeff Innis, Keith Miller, Jeff Musselman, and Frank Viola. This "Update" subset was distributed at a different Mets Baseball Card Night game than the main set. These update cards are given the prefix U in the checklist below.

	MINT	EXC	G-VG
COMPLETE SET (32)	9.00	4.50	.90
COMPLETE UPDATE SET (4)	2.50	1.25	.25
COMMON PLAYER	.25	.12	.02
COMMON UPDATE PLAYER	.60	.30	.06
☐ 1 Mookie Wilson	.35	.17	.03
☐ 2 Mackey Sasser	.35	.17	.03
☐ 3 Bud Harrelson CO	.35	.17	.03
☐ 5 Dave Johnson MG	.35	.17	.03
☐ 7 Juan Samuel	.45	.22	.04
☐ 8 Gary Carter	.75	.35	.07
☐ 9 Gregg Jefferies	1.00	.50	.10
☐ 11 Tim Teufel	.25	.12	.02
☐ 12 Ron Darling	.35	.17	.03
☐ 13 Lee Mazzilli	.25	.12	.02
☐ 16 Dwight Gooden	1.00	.50	.10
☐ 17 Keith Hernandez	.45	.22	.04
☐ 18 Darryl Strawberry	1.00	.50	.10
☐ 19 Bob Ojeda	.35	.17	.03
☐ 20 Howard Johnson	.75	.35	.07
☐ 21 Kevin Elster	.35	.17	.03
☐ 22 Kevin McReynolds	.45	.22	.04
☐ 28 Bill Robinson CO	.35	.17	.03
☐ 29 Dave Magadan	.45	.22	.04
☐ 30 Mel Stottlemyre CO	.35	.17	.03
☐ 32 Mark Carreon	.25	.12	.02
☐ 33 Barry Lyons	.25	.12	.02
☐ 34 Sam Perlozzo CO	.25	.12	.02
☐ 38 Rick Aguilera	.25	.12	.02
☐ 44 David Cone	.45	.22	.04

☐ 46 Dave West	.35	.17	.03
☐ 48 Randy Myers	.35	.17	.03
☐ 49 Don Aase	.25	.12	.02
☐ 50 Sid Fernandez	.45	.22	.04
☐ 52 Greg Pavlick CO	.25	.12	.02
☐ xx Mets Team Photo	.25	.12	.02
☐ xx Sponsors Card	.25	.12	.02
☐ U1 Jeff Innis	.60	.30	.06
☐ U2 Keith Miller	.60	.30	.06
☐ U3 Jeff Musselman	.60	.30	.06
☐ U4 Frank Viola	1.25	.60	.12

1989 Kahn's Reds

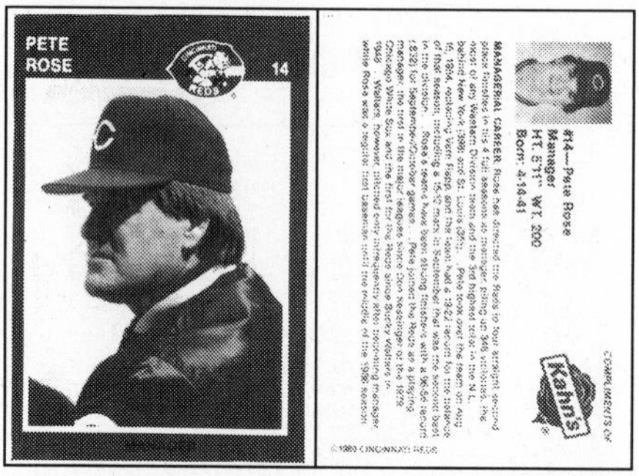

The 1989 Kahn's Reds set contains 28 standard-size (2 1/2" by 3 1/2") cards; each card features a member of the Cincinnati Reds. The fronts have color photos with red borders. The horizontally-oriented backs have career stats.

	MINT	EXC	G-VG
COMPLETE SET (28)	12.00	6.00	1.20
COMMON PLAYER	.35	.17	.03

☐ 6 Bo Diaz	.35	.17	.03
☐ 7 Lenny Harris	.50	.25	.05
☐ 11 Barry Larkin	1.25	.60	.12
☐ 12 Joel Youngblood	.35	.17	.03
☐ 14 Pete Rose MG	1.00	.50	.10
☐ 16 Ron Oester	.35	.17	.03
☐ 17 Chris Sabo	.75	.35	.07
☐ 20 Danny Jackson	.50	.25	.05
☐ 21 Paul O'Neill	.75	.35	.07
☐ 25 Todd Benzinger	.50	.25	.05
☐ 27 Jose Rijo	.60	.30	.06
☐ 28 Kal Daniels	.75	.35	.07
☐ 29 Herm Winningham	.35	.17	.03
☐ 30 Ken Griffey Sr.	.60	.30	.06
☐ 31 John Franco	.50	.25	.05
☐ 32 Tom Browning	.60	.30	.06
☐ 33 Ron Robinson	.50	.25	.05
☐ 34 Jeff Reed	.35	.17	.03
☐ 36 Rolando Roomes	.50	.25	.05
☐ 37 Norm Charlton	.50	.25	.05
☐ 42 Rick Mahler	.35	.17	.03
☐ 43 Kent Tekulve	.35	.17	.03
☐ 44 Eric Davis	1.25	.60	.12
☐ 48 Tim Birtsas	.35	.17	.03
☐ 49 Rob Dibble	.60	.30	.06
☐ xx Coaches Card	.35	.17	.03
☐ xx Sponsors Card	.35	.17	.03
☐ xx Sponsors Card	.35	.17	.03

1990 Kahn's Mets

The 1990 Kahn's Met Set was given away as a New York Mets stadium promotion. This standard-size (2 1/2" by 3 1/2") set is skip-numbered by uniform number within the set and features 34 cards and two Kahn's coupon cards. Three players, Thornton, Magadan, and Mercado are wearing different uniform numbers than listed on the front of their cards.

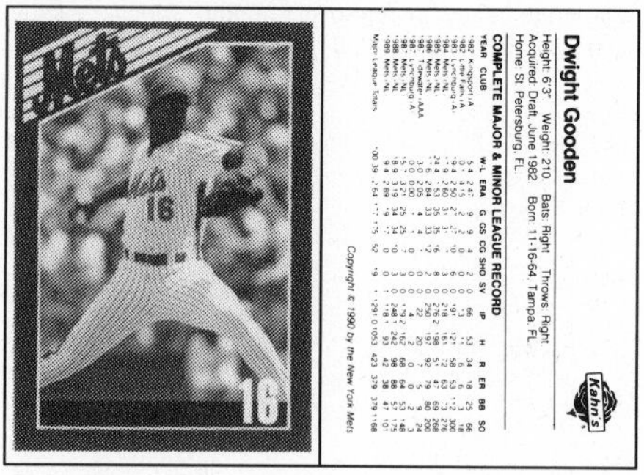

	MINT	EXC	G-VG
COMPLETE SET (34)	8.00	4.00	.80
COMMON PLAYER	.20	.10	.02

☐ 1 Lou Thornton	.20	.10	.02
☐ 2 Mackey Sasser	.30	.15	.03
☐ 3 Bud Harrelson	.30	.15	.03
☐ 4 Mike Cubbage	.20	.10	.02
☐ 5 Davey Johnson MG	.30	.15	.03
☐ 6 Mike Marshall	.30	.15	.03
☐ 9 Gregg Jefferies	.75	.35	.07
☐ 10 Dave Magadan	.50	.25	.05
☐ 11 Tim Teufel	.20	.10	.02
☐ 13 Jeff Musselman	.20	.10	.02
☐ 15 Ron Darling	.30	.15	.03
☐ 16 Dwight Gooden	.75	.35	.07
☐ 18 Darryl Strawberry	.75	.35	.07
☐ 19 Bob Ojeda	.30	.15	.03
☐ 20 Howard Johnson	.50	.25	.05
☐ 21 Kevin Elster	.20	.10	.02
☐ 22 Kevin McReynolds	.40	.20	.04
☐ 25 Keith Miller	.20	.10	.02
☐ 26 Alejandro Pena	.20	.10	.02
☐ 27 Tom O'Malley	.20	.10	.02
☐ 29 Frank Viola	.40	.20	.04
☐ 30 Mel Stottlemyre CO	.30	.15	.03
☐ 31 John Franco	.30	.15	.03
☐ 32 Doc Edwards CO	.20	.10	.02
☐ 33 Barry Lyons	.20	.10	.02
☐ 35 Orlando Mercado	.20	.10	.02
☐ 40 Jeff Innis	.20	.10	.02
☐ 44 David Cone	.40	.20	.04
☐ 45 Mark Carreon	.30	.15	.03
☐ 47 Wally Whitehurst	.30	.15	.03
☐ 48 Julio Machado	.30	.15	.03
☐ 50 Sid Fernandez	.30	.15	.03
☐ 52 Greg Pavlick	.20	.10	.02
☐ xx Team Photo	.30	.15	.03

1990 Kahn's Reds

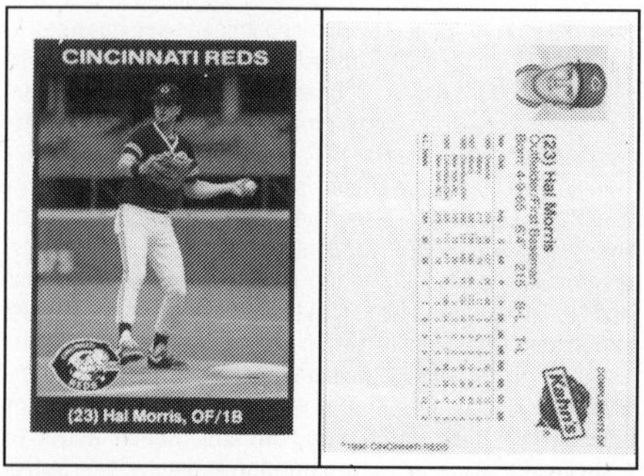

This 27-card, standard size, 2 1/2" by 3 1/2", set was issued by Kahn's Meats. This set which continued a more than 30-year tradition of Kahn's issuing Cincinnati Reds cards had the player's photos framed by red and white borders. The front have full-color photos while the back have a small black and white photo in the upper left hand corner and complete career statistics on the back of the card. The set is checklisted alphabetically since the cards are unnumbered except for uniform numbers. The number next to the player represents his uniform number.

	MINT	EXC	G-VG
COMPLETE SET (27)	12.00	6.00	1.20
COMMON PLAYER (1-27)	.40	.20	.04
☐ 1 Jack Armstrong 40	.75	.35	.07
☐ 2 Todd Benzinger 25	.50	.25	.05
☐ 3 Tim Birtsas 48	.40	.20	.04
☐ 4 Glenn Braggs 15	.50	.25	.05
☐ 5 Tom Browning 32	.60	.30	.06
☐ 6 Norm Charlton 37	.60	.30	.06
☐ 7 Eric Davis 44	2.00	1.00	.20
☐ 8 Rob Dibble 49	.60	.30	.06
☐ 9 Mariano Duncan 7	.50	.25	.05
☐ 10 Ken Griffey 30	.60	.30	.06
☐ 11 Billy Hatcher 22	.60	.30	.06
☐ 12 Barry Larkin 11	1.00	.50	.10
☐ 13 Danny Jackson 20	.50	.25	.05
☐ 14 Tim Layana 43	.50	.25	.05
☐ 15 Rick Mahler 42	.40	.20	.04
☐ 16 Hal Morris 23	1.00	.50	.10
☐ 17 Randy Myers 28	.60	.30	.06
☐ 18 Ron Oester 16	.40	.20	.04
☐ 19 Joe Oliver 9	.50	.25	.05
☐ 20 Paul O'Neill 21	.60	.30	.06
☐ 21 Lou Piniella MG 41	.60	.30	.06
☐ 22 Luis Quinones 10	.40	.20	.04
☐ 23 Jeff Reed 34	.40	.20	.04
☐ 24 Jose Rijo 27	.60	.30	.06
☐ 25 Chris Sabo 17	1.00	.50	.10
☐ 26 Herm Winningham 29	.40	.20	.04
☐ 27 Red Coaches Jackie Moore Tony Perez Sam Perlozzo Larry Rothschild Stan Williams	.40	.20	.04

1983 Kaline Story

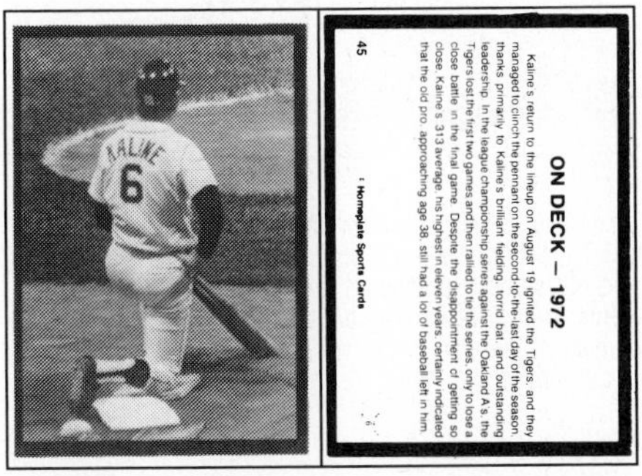

This 72-card set was issued in 1983 to celebrate Al Kaline's thirtieth year of association with the Detroit Tigers. The set was issued in its own orange box and most of the cards in the series have orange borders. There are some cards which have black borders and those cards are the cards in the set which feature color photos. The set is basically in chronological order and covers events crucial to Kaline's career and the backs of the cards give further details about the picture on the front. The set was produced by Homeplate Sports Cards.

	MINT	EXC	G-VG
COMPLETE SET (73)	10.00	5.00	1.00
COMMON PLAYER (1-72)	.20	.10	.02
☐ 1A Autographed Title Card (color)	1.00	.50	.10
☐ 1B I'd play for nothing (color)	.40	.20	.04
☐ 2 Sandlot Days	.20	.10	.02
☐ 3 Prep MVP	.20	.10	.02
☐ 4 Learning the Ropes	.20	.10	.02
☐ 5 Working for a Living	.20	.10	.02
☐ 6 Pleasing a Young Fan	.20	.10	.02
☐ 7 The Newlyweds Al and Louise Kaline	.20	.10	.02
☐ 8 Al and Pat Mullin	.20	.10	.02
☐ 9 How Al Does It, 1	.20	.10	.02
☐ 10 How Al Does It, 2	.20	.10	.02
☐ 11 Silver Bat 1955	.20	.10	.02
☐ 12 Al and George Stark	.20	.10	.02
☐ 13 Al watching Gordie Howe (Howe taking batting practice)	.50	.25	.05
☐ 14 Kaline and Mantle	.50	.25	.05
☐ 15 1958 Group Photo (Jim Hegan, Billy Martin, Ray Boone, Harvey Kuenn, Jim Bunning, Al Kaline)	.20	.10	.02
☐ 16 AL All-Stars Billy Martin, Al Kaline, Harvey Kuenn, Mickey Mantle, Whitey Ford (color)	.50	.25	.05
☐ 17 Crossing the Plate	.20	.10	.02
☐ 18 1959 All-Star Game (Bill Skowron and Al Kaline)	.20	.10	.02
☐ 19 1960 Tigers Stars (Norm Cash, Rocky Colavito, Al Kaline)	.30	.15	.03
☐ 20 Kaline Slides Under Fox (Al Kaline and Nellie Fox)	.30	.15	.03
☐ 21 1961 Gold Glove	.20	.10	.02
☐ 22 1962 Tigers Al Kaline, Jim Campbell GM, Norm Cash	.30	.15	.03
☐ 23 Costly Catch	.20	.10	.02
☐ 24 Japanese Tour 1962 (Jim Bunning, Al Kaline, Norm Cash, and others)	.20	.10	.02
☐ 25 Perfect Form	.20	.10	.02
☐ 26 Receiving Awards (Ernie Harwell ANN, Al Kaline, George Kell ANN)	.30	.15	.03
☐ 27 Life Isn't Always Easy	.20	.10	.02
☐ 28 Family Game 1964 (Al, Michael, and Mark Kaline)	.20	.10	.02
☐ 29 Al and Charlie Dressen	.20	.10	.02
☐ 30 George Kell and Al	.30	.15	.03
☐ 31 Al and Hal Newhouser	.30	.15	.03
☐ 32 The Kaline Family (Michael, Louise, Al, and Mark Kaline)	.20	.10	.02
☐ 33 Receiving Gold Glove (Al Kaline, Charlie Gehringer, and Bill Freehan)	.30	.15	.03
☐ 34 Rapping a Hit, 1967 (color)	.30	.15	.03
☐ 35 Veteran Rivals (Mickey Mantle and Al)	.50	.25	.05
☐ 36 Al Homers vs. Boston	.20	.10	.02
☐ 37 1968 World Series Homer	.20	.10	.02
☐ 38 Premier Fielder	.20	.10	.02
☐ 39 1969 All-Time Tigers (Hank Greenberg, Hal Newhouser, Billy Rogell, Al Kaline, John Fetzer OWN, Dennis McLain, George Kell, Charlie Gehringer)	.20	.10	.02
☐ 40 Part of the Game	.20	.10	.02
☐ 41 Family Portrait (color)	.30	.15	.03
☐ 42 Spring Training Tribute	.20	.10	.02
☐ 43 Billy Martin and Al	.20	.10	.02
☐ 44 First 100,000 Tiger (with John Fetzer OWN and Jim Campbell GM)	.20	.10	.02

☐ 45 On Deck, 1972 (color)	.30	.15	.03
☐ 46 A Close Call	.20	.10	.02
☐ 47 On Deck in Baltimore	.20	.10	.02
☐ 48 Hit Number 3,000	.30	.15	.03
☐ 49 April 17, 1955, Three Homers	.20	.10	.02
☐ 50 All-Star Game Record	.20	.10	.02
☐ 51 1968 World Series (Al Kaline and Orlando Cepeda)	.30	.15	.03
☐ 52 1968 World Series Celebration (Al Kaline, John Hiller, Jim Northrup)	.30	.15	.03
☐ 53 Al Kaline Day (color)	.40	.20	.04
☐ 54 3,000 Hit Day (Al Kaline, Father and Mother, Lee McPhail PRES, Jim Campbell GM	.20	.10	.02
☐ 55 September 29, 1974, Thank You	.20	.10	.02
☐ 56 Silver Salute	.20	.10	.02
☐ 57 Al and George Kell (color)	.30	.15	.03
☐ 58 Voices of the Tigers Al and George Kell	.30	.15	.03
☐ 59 Tiger Record Setter (color)	.30	.15	.03
☐ 60 Al's Last All-Star Team (color)	.30	.15	.03
☐ 61 Pat Mullin and Al	.20	.10	.02
☐ 62 Al and Mickey Lolich (color)	.40	.20	.04
☐ 63 Hall of Fame Plaque	.20	.10	.02
☐ 64 Al and Bowie Kuhn (color)	.30	.15	.03
☐ 65 Al and Parents (color)	.30	.15	.03
☐ 66 Kaline Family at Hall (color)	.30	.15	.03
☐ 67 The Man and the Boy (Stan Musial and Al)	.40	.20	.04
☐ 68 Two Kids (Ted Williams and Al)	.40	.20	.04
☐ 69 Master Glovemen (Al and Brooks Robinson) (color)	.40	.20	.04
☐ 70 Coach and Pupil (Al and Pat Underwood)	.20	.10	.02
☐ 71 Al at Batting Cage	.20	.10	.02
☐ 72 A Tiger Forever (color)	.40	.20	.04

1986 Kay-Bee

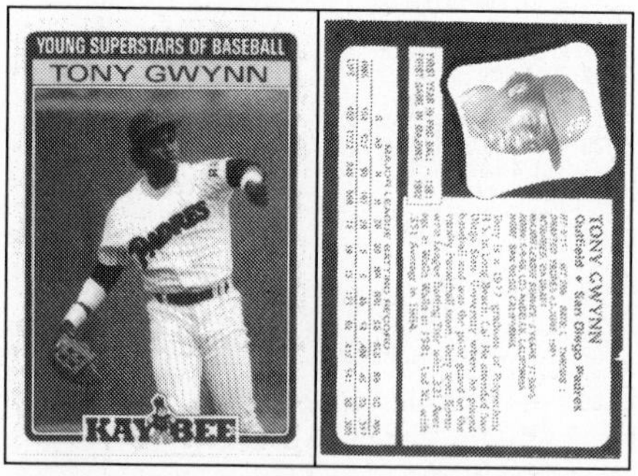

This 33-card, standard-sized (2 1/2" by 3 1/2") set was produced by Topps, although manufactured in Northern Ireland. This boxed set retailed in Kay-Bee stores for 1.99; the checklist was listed on the back of the box. The set is subtitled "Young Superstars of Baseball" and does indeed feature many young players. The cards are numbered on the back; the set card numbering is alphabetical by player's name.

	MINT	EXC	G-VG
COMPLETE SET (33)	5.00	2.50	.50
COMMON PLAYER (1-33)	.10	.05	.01
☐ 1 Rick Aguilera	.15	.07	.01
☐ 2 Chris Brown	.10	.05	.01
☐ 3 Tom Browning	.15	.07	.01
☐ 4 Tom Brunansky	.15	.07	.01
☐ 5 Vince Coleman	.30	.15	.03
☐ 6 Ron Darling	.15	.07	.01
☐ 7 Alvin Davis	.15	.07	.01
☐ 8 Mariano Duncan	.15	.07	.01
☐ 9 Shawon Dunston	.25	.12	.02
☐ 10 Sid Fernandez	.15	.07	.01
☐ 11 Tony Fernandez	.20	.10	.02
☐ 12 Brian Fisher	.10	.05	.01
☐ 13 John Franco	.15	.07	.01
☐ 14 Julio Franco	.20	.10	.02
☐ 15 Dwight Gooden	.75	.35	.07
☐ 16 Ozzie Guillen	.25	.12	.02
☐ 17 Tony Gwynn	.45	.22	.04
☐ 18 Jimmy Key	.15	.07	.01
☐ 19 Don Mattingly	1.00	.50	.10
☐ 20 Oddibe McDowell	.15	.07	.01
☐ 21 Roger McDowell	.10	.05	.01
☐ 22 Dan Pasqua	.10	.05	.01
☐ 23 Terry Pendleton	.10	.05	.01
☐ 24 Jim Presley	.10	.05	.01
☐ 25 Kirby Puckett	.75	.35	.07
☐ 26 Earnie Riles	.10	.05	.01
☐ 27 Bret Saberhagen	.30	.15	.03
☐ 28 Mark Salas	.10	.05	.01
☐ 29 Juan Samuel	.15	.07	.01
☐ 30 Jeff Stone	.10	.05	.01
☐ 31 Darryl Strawberry	.75	.35	.07
☐ 32 Andy Van Slyke	.20	.10	.02
☐ 33 Frank Viola	.20	.10	.02

1987 Kay-Bee

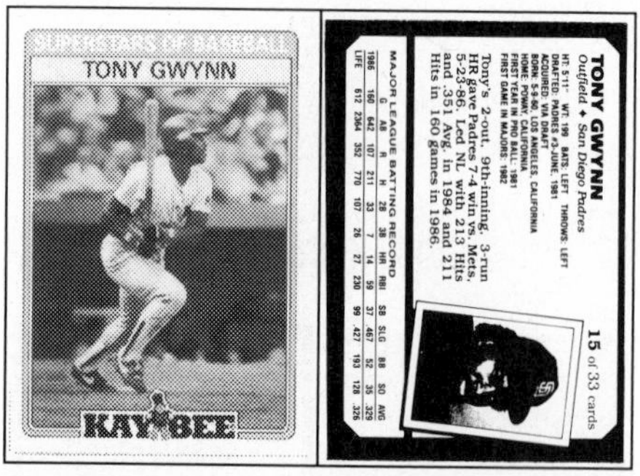

This small 33-card boxed set was produced by Topps for Kay-Bee Toy Stores. The set is subtitled "Super Stars of Baseball" and measures the standard 2 1/2" by 3 1/2" with full-color fronts. The card backs are printed in blue and black on white card stock. The checklist for the set is printed on the back panel of the yellow box.

	MINT	EXC	G-VG
COMPLETE SET (33)	5.00	2.50	.50
COMMON PLAYER (1-33)	.10	.05	.01
☐ 1 Harold Baines	.15	.07	.01
☐ 2 Jesse Barfield	.15	.07	.01
☐ 3 Don Baylor	.10	.05	.01
☐ 4 Wade Boggs	.60	.30	.06
☐ 5 George Brett	.45	.22	.04
☐ 6 Hubie Brooks	.15	.07	.01
☐ 7 Jose Canseco	1.00	.50	.10
☐ 8 Gary Carter	.20	.10	.02
☐ 9 Joe Carter	.20	.10	.02
☐ 10 Roger Clemens	.60	.30	.06
☐ 11 Vince Coleman	.25	.12	.02
☐ 12 Glenn Davis	.20	.10	.02
☐ 13 Dwight Gooden	.45	.22	.04
☐ 14 Pedro Guerrero	.20	.10	.02

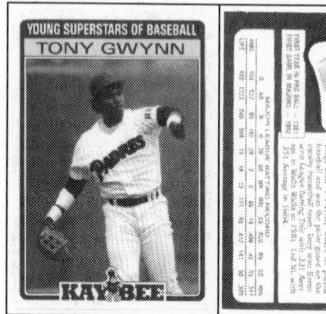

☐ 15 Tony Gwynn	.40	.20	.04
☐ 16 Rickey Henderson	.75	.35	.07
☐ 17 Keith Hernandez	.20	.10	.02
☐ 18 Wally Joyner	.35	.17	.03
☐ 19 Don Mattingly	1.00	.50	.10
☐ 20 Jack Morris	.20	.10	.02
☐ 21 Dale Murphy	.35	.17	.03
☐ 22 Eddie Murray	.35	.17	.03
☐ 23 Dave Parker	.20	.10	.02
☐ 24 Kirby Puckett	.50	.25	.05
☐ 25 Tim Raines	.20	.10	.02
☐ 26 Jim Rice	.20	.10	.02
☐ 27 Dave Righetti	.15	.07	.01
☐ 28 Ryne Sandberg	.75	.35	.07
☐ 29 Mike Schmidt	.75	.35	.07
☐ 30 Mike Scott	.20	.10	.02
☐ 31 Darryl Strawberry	.50	.25	.05
☐ 32 Fernando Valenzuela	.20	.10	.02
☐ 33 Dave Winfield	.25	.12	.02

1988 Kay-Bee

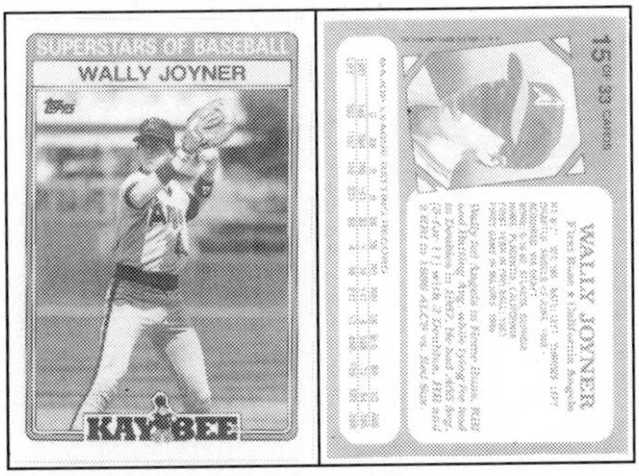

This small 33-card boxed set was produced by Topps for Kay-Bee Toy Stores. The set is subtitled "Superstars of Baseball" and measures the standard 2 1/2" by 3 1/2" with full-color fronts. The card backs are printed in blue and green on white card stock. The checklist for the set is printed on the back panel of the box. These cards are numbered on the back.

	MINT	EXC	G-VG
COMPLETE SET (33)	4.00	2.00	.40
COMMON PLAYER (1-33)	.10	.05	.01

☐ 1 George Bell	.20	.10	.02
☐ 2 Wade Boggs	.50	.25	.05
☐ 3 Jose Canseco	1.00	.50	.10
☐ 4 Joe Carter	.20	.10	.02
☐ 5 Jack Clark	.20	.10	.02
☐ 6 Alvin Davis	.15	.07	.01
☐ 7 Eric Davis	.40	.20	.04
☐ 8 Andre Dawson	.20	.10	.02
☐ 9 Darrell Evans	.10	.05	.01
☐ 10 Dwight Evans	.15	.07	.01
☐ 11 Gary Gaetti	.15	.07	.01
☐ 12 Pedro Guerrero	.15	.07	.01
☐ 13 Tony Gwynn	.35	.17	.03
☐ 14 Howard Johnson	.20	.10	.02
☐ 15 Wally Joyner	.25	.12	.02
☐ 16 Don Mattingly	1.00	.50	.10
☐ 17 Willie McGee	.20	.10	.02
☐ 18 Mark McGwire	.75	.35	.07
☐ 19 Paul Molitor	.20	.10	.02
☐ 20 Dale Murphy	.30	.15	.03
☐ 21 Dave Parker	.20	.10	.02
☐ 22 Lance Parrish	.15	.07	.01
☐ 23 Kirby Puckett	.50	.25	.05
☐ 24 Tim Raines	.20	.10	.02
☐ 25 Cal Ripken	.30	.15	.03
☐ 26 Juan Samuel	.15	.07	.01
☐ 27 Mike Schmidt	.60	.30	.06
☐ 28 Ruben Sierra	.50	.25	.05
☐ 29 Darryl Strawberry	.60	.30	.06
☐ 30 Danny Tartabull	.25	.12	.02
☐ 31 Alan Trammell	.20	.10	.02
☐ 32 Tim Wallach	.15	.07	.01
☐ 33 Dave Winfield	.25	.12	.02

1989 Kay-Bee

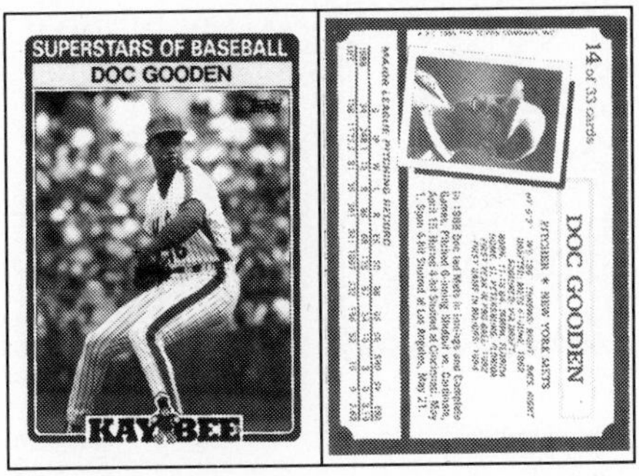

The 1989 Kay-Bee set contains 33 standard-size (2 1/2" by 3 1/2") glossy cards. The fronts have magenta and yellow borders. The horizontally oriented backs are brown and yellow. The cards were distributed as boxed sets through Kay-Bee toy stores.

	MINT	EXC	G-VG
COMPLETE SET (33)	4.00	2.00	.40
COMMON PLAYER (1-33)	.10	.05	.01

☐ 1 Wade Boggs	.50	.25	.05
☐ 2 George Brett	.35	.17	.03
☐ 3 Jose Canseco	1.00	.50	.10
☐ 4 Gary Carter	.20	.10	.02
☐ 5 Jack Clark	.20	.10	.02
☐ 6 Will Clark	.90	.45	.09
☐ 7 Roger Clemens	.50	.25	.05
☐ 8 Eric Davis	.40	.20	.04
☐ 9 Andre Dawson	.20	.10	.02
☐ 10 Dwight Evans	.15	.07	.01
☐ 11 Carlton Fisk	.25	.12	.02
☐ 12 Andres Galarraga	.20	.10	.02
☐ 13 Kirk Gibson	.20	.10	.02
☐ 14 Dwight Gooden	.40	.20	.04
☐ 15 Mike Greenwell	.35	.17	.03
☐ 16 Pedro Guerrero	.15	.07	.01
☐ 17 Tony Gwynn	.35	.17	.03
☐ 18 Rickey Henderson	.75	.35	.07
☐ 19 Orel Hershiser	.25	.12	.02
☐ 20 Don Mattingly	1.00	.50	.10
☐ 21 Mark McGwire	.60	.30	.06
☐ 22 Dale Murphy	.30	.15	.03
☐ 23 Eddie Murray	.30	.15	.03
☐ 24 Kirby Puckett	.45	.22	.04
☐ 25 Tim Raines	.20	.10	.02
☐ 26 Ryne Sandberg	.60	.30	.06
☐ 27 Mike Schmidt	.60	.30	.06
☐ 28 Ozzie Smith	.20	.10	.02
☐ 29 Darryl Strawberry	.50	.25	.05
☐ 30 Alan Trammell	.20	.10	.02
☐ 31 Frank Viola	.15	.07	.01
☐ 32 Dave Winfield	.20	.10	.02
☐ 33 Robin Yount	.45	.22	.04

1990 Kay-Bee

The 1990 Kay-Bee Kings of Baseball set is a standard-size (2 1/2" by 3 1/2"), 33-card set sequenced alphabetically that Topps produced for the Kay-Bee toy store chain. A solid red border inside a purple white striped box is the major design feature of this set.

	MINT	EXC	G-VG
COMPLETE SET (33)	4.00	2.00	.40
COMMON PLAYER (1-33)	.10	.05	.01

☐ 1 Doyle Alexander	.10	.05	.01
☐ 2 Bert Blyleven	.15	.07	.01
☐ 3 Wade Boggs	.50	.25	.05

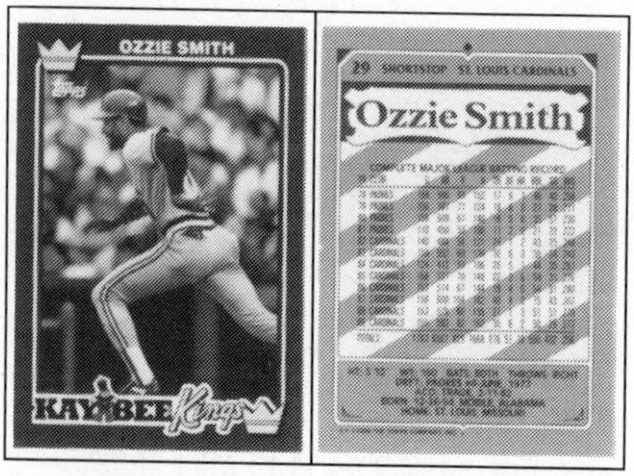

☐ 4 George Brett	.35	.17	.03
☐ 5 John Candelaria	.10	.05	.01
☐ 6 Gary Carter	.20	.10	.02
☐ 7 Vince Coleman	.20	.10	.02
☐ 8 Andre Dawson	.20	.10	.02
☐ 9 Dennis Eckersley	.20	.10	.02
☐ 10 Darrell Evans	.10	.05	.01
☐ 11 Dwight Evans	.15	.07	.01
☐ 12 Carlton Fisk	.20	.10	.02
☐ 13 Ken Griffey Sr.	.15	.07	.01
☐ 14 Tony Gwynn	.30	.15	.03
☐ 15 Rickey Henderson	.60	.30	.06
☐ 16 Keith Hernandez	.15	.07	.01
☐ 17 Charlie Hough	.10	.05	.01
☐ 18 Don Mattingly	.90	.45	.09
☐ 19 Jack Morris	.15	.07	.01
☐ 20 Dale Murphy	.30	.15	.03
☐ 21 Eddie Murray	.30	.15	.03
☐ 22 Dave Parker	.20	.10	.02
☐ 23 Kirby Puckett	.30	.15	.03
☐ 24 Rock Raines	.20	.10	.02
☐ 25 Rick Reuschel	.10	.05	.01
☐ 26 Jerry Reuss	.10	.05	.01
☐ 27 Jim Rice	.20	.10	.02
☐ 28 Nolan Ryan	.90	.45	.09
☐ 29 Ozzie Smith	.20	.10	.02
☐ 30 Frank Tanana	.10	.05	.01
☐ 31 Willie Wilson	.15	.07	.01
☐ 32 Dave Winfield	.20	.10	.02
☐ 33 Robin Yount	.30	.15	.03

1968 KDKA Pirates

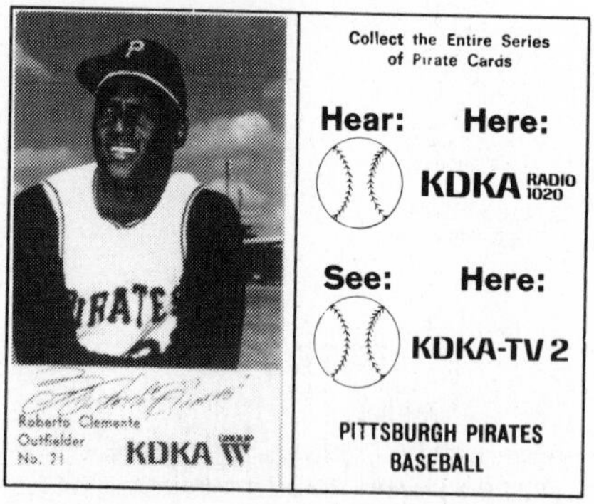

This 23-card set measures approximately 2 3/8" by 4" and was issued by radio and television station KDKA to promote the Pittsburgh Pirates, whom they were covering at the time. The fronts have the players' photo on the top 2/3 of the card and a facsimile autograph, the players name and position and uniform number on the lower left hand corner and an ad for KDKA on the lower right corner of the card. The back has an advertisment for both KDKA radio and television. The set is checklisted below by uniform number.

	NRMT	VG-E	GOOD
COMPLETE SET (23)	60.00	30.00	6.00
COMMON PLAYER	1.50	.75	.15
☐ 7 Larry Shepard MG	1.50	.75	.15
☐ 8 Willie Stargell	15.00	7.50	1.50
☐ 9 Bill Mazeroski	5.00	2.50	.50
☐ 10 Gary Kolb	1.50	.75	.15
☐ 11 Jose Pagan	1.50	.75	.15
☐ 12 Jerry May	1.50	.75	.15
☐ 14 Jim Bunning	5.00	2.50	.50
☐ 15 Manny Mota	2.50	1.25	.25
☐ 17 Donn Clendenon	2.50	1.25	.25
☐ 18 Matty Alou	2.50	1.25	.25
☐ 21 Bob Clemente	25.00	12.50	2.50
☐ 22 Gene Alley	2.50	1.25	.25
☐ 25 Tommy Sisk	1.50	.75	.15
☐ 26 Roy Face	2.50	1.25	.25
☐ 27 Ron Kline	1.50	.75	.15
☐ 28 Steve Blass	2.00	1.00	.20
☐ 29 Juan Pizzaro	1.50	.75	.15
☐ 30 Maury Wills	5.00	2.50	.50
☐ 34 Al McBean	1.50	.75	.15
☐ 35 Manny Sanguillen	2.50	1.25	.25
☐ 38 Bob Moose	1.50	.75	.15
☐ 39 Bob Veale	2.00	1.00	.20
☐ 40 Dave Wickersham	1.50	.75	.15

1970 Kellogg's

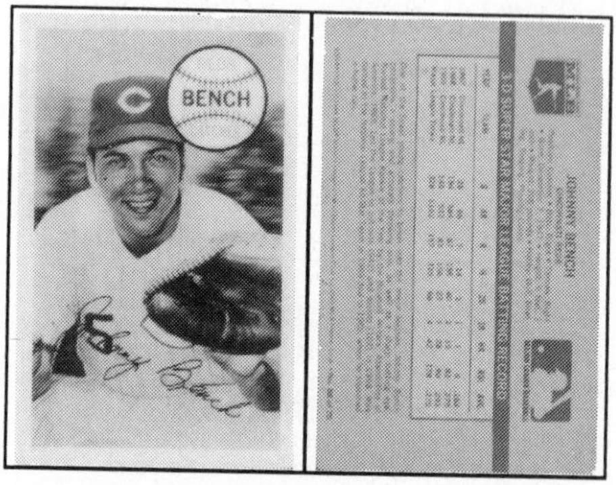

The cards in this 75-card set measure 2 1/4" by 3 1/2". The 1970 Kellogg's set was Kellogg's first venture into the baseball card producing field. The design incorporates a brilliant color photo of the player set against an indistinct background, which is then covered with a layer of plastic to simulate a 3-D look. Cards 16-30 seem to be in shorter supply than the other cards in the set.

	NRMT	VG-E	GOOD
COMPLETE SET (75)	150.00	75.00	15.00
COMMON PLAYER (1-75)	1.00	.50	.10
☐ 1 Ed Kranepool	1.00	.50	.10
☐ 2 Pete Rose	16.00	8.00	1.60
☐ 3 Cleon Jones	1.00	.50	.10
☐ 4 Willie McCovey	5.00	2.50	.50
☐ 5 Mel Stottlemyre	1.50	.75	.15
☐ 6 Frank Howard	1.50	.75	.15
☐ 7 Tom Seaver	10.00	5.00	1.00
☐ 8 Don Sutton	3.00	1.50	.30
☐ 9 Jim Wynn	1.50	.75	.15
☐ 10 Jim Maloney	1.50	.75	.15
☐ 11 Tommie Agee	1.00	.50	.10
☐ 12 Willie Mays	12.00	6.00	1.20
☐ 13 Juan Marichal	4.00	2.00	.40
☐ 14 Dave McNally	1.50	.75	.15
☐ 15 Frank Robinson	4.00	2.00	.40
☐ 16 Carlos May	1.00	.50	.10
☐ 17 Bill Singer	1.00	.50	.10
☐ 18 Rick Reichardt	1.00	.50	.10
☐ 19 Boog Powell	1.50	.75	.15
☐ 20 Gaylord Perry	4.00	2.00	.40
☐ 21 Brooks Robinson	6.00	3.00	.60
☐ 22 Luis Aparicio	4.00	2.00	.40
☐ 23 Joel Horlen	1.00	.50	.10

☐ 24 Mike Epstein	1.00	.50	.10
☐ 25 Tom Haller	1.00	.50	.10
☐ 26 Willie Crawford	1.00	.50	.10
☐ 27 Roberto Clemente	12.00	6.00	1.20
☐ 28 Matty Alou	1.00	.50	.10
☐ 29 Willie Stargell	5.00	2.50	.50
☐ 30 Tim Cullen	1.00	.50	.10
☐ 31 Randy Hundley	1.00	.50	.10
☐ 32 Reggie Jackson	13.50	6.25	1.20
☐ 33 Rich Allen	1.00	.50	.10
☐ 34 Tim McCarver	1.50	.75	.15
☐ 35 Ray Culp	1.00	.50	.10
☐ 36 Jim Fregosi	1.50	.75	.15
☐ 37 Billy Williams	4.00	2.00	.40
☐ 38 Johnny Odom	1.00	.50	.10
☐ 39 Bert Campaneris	1.50	.75	.15
☐ 40 Ernie Banks	6.00	3.00	.60
☐ 41 Chris Short	1.00	.50	.10
☐ 42 Ron Santo	1.50	.75	.15
☐ 43 Glenn Beckert	1.00	.50	.10
☐ 44 Lou Brock	4.00	2.00	.40
☐ 45 Larry Hisle	1.00	.50	.10
☐ 46 Reggie Smith	1.50	.75	.15
☐ 47 Rod Carew	6.00	3.00	.60
☐ 48 Curt Flood	1.50	.75	.15
☐ 49 Jim Lonborg	1.50	.75	.15
☐ 50 Sam McDowell	1.50	.75	.15
☐ 51 Sal Bando	1.50	.75	.15
☐ 52 Al Kaline	6.00	3.00	.60
☐ 53 Gary Nolan	1.00	.50	.10
☐ 54 Rico Petrocelli	1.00	.50	.10
☐ 55 Ollie Brown	1.00	.50	.10
☐ 56 Luis Tiant	1.50	.75	.15
☐ 57 Bill Freehan	1.50	.75	.15
☐ 58 Johnny Bench	12.00	6.00	1.20
☐ 59 Joe Pepitone	1.50	.75	.15
☐ 60 Bobby Murcer	1.50	.75	.15
☐ 61 Harmon Killebrew	4.00	2.00	.40
☐ 62 Don Wilson	1.00	.50	.10
☐ 63 Tony Oliva	2.00	1.00	.20
☐ 64 Jim Perry	1.50	.75	.15
☐ 65 Mickey Lolich	1.50	.75	.15
☐ 66 Jose Laboy	1.00	.50	.10
☐ 67 Dean Chance	1.00	.50	.10
☐ 68 Ken Harrelson	1.50	.75	.15
☐ 69 Willie Horton	1.00	.50	.10
☐ 70 Wally Bunker	1.00	.50	.10
☐ 71A Bob Gibson ERR (1959 innings pitched is blank)	5.00	2.50	.50
☐ 71B Bob Gibson COR (1959 innings is 76)	5.00	2.50	.50
☐ 72 Joe Morgan	4.00	2.00	.40
☐ 73 Denny McLain	1.50	.75	.15
☐ 74 Tommy Harper	1.00	.50	.10
☐ 75 Don Mincher	1.00	.50	.10

1971 Kellogg's

The cards in this 75-card set measure 2 1/4" by 3 1/2". The 1971 set of 3-D cards marketed by the Kellogg Company is the scarcest of all that company's issues. It was distributed as single cards, one in each package of cereal, without the usual complete set mail-in offer. In addition, card dealers were unable to obtain this set in quantity, as they have in other years. All the cards are available with and without the year 1970 before XOGRAPH on the back in the lower left corner; the version without carries a slight premium for most numbers. Prices listed below are for the more common variety with the year 1970.

	NRMT	VG-E	GOOD
COMPLETE SET (75)	750.00	375.00	75.00
COMMON PLAYER (1-75)	6.50	3.25	.65
☐ 1 Wayne Simpson	6.50	3.25	.65
☐ 2 Tom Seaver	27.00	13.50	2.70
☐ 3 Jim Perry	7.50	3.75	.75
☐ 4 Bob Robertson	6.50	3.25	.65
☐ 5 Roberto Clemente	32.00	16.00	3.20
☐ 6 Gaylord Perry	20.00	10.00	2.00
☐ 7 Felipe Alou	7.50	3.75	.75
☐ 8 Denis Menke	6.50	3.25	.65
☐ 9A Don Kessinger (no 1970 date)	8.50	4.25	.85
☐ 9B Don Kessinger ERR (dated, 1970 hits 167, avg. .265)	8.50	4.25	.85
☐ 9C Don Kessinger COR (dated, 1970 hits 168, avg. .266)	8.50	4.25	.85
☐ 10 Willie Mays	36.00	18.00	3.60
☐ 11 Jim Hickman	6.50	3.25	.65
☐ 12 Tony Oliva	10.00	5.00	1.00
☐ 13 Manny Sanguillen	7.50	3.75	.75
☐ 14 Frank Howard	7.50	3.75	.75
☐ 15 Frank Robinson	20.00	10.00	2.00
☐ 16 Willie Davis	7.50	3.75	.75
☐ 17 Lou Brock	20.00	10.00	2.00
☐ 18 Cesar Tovar	6.50	3.25	.65
☐ 19 Luis Aparicio	15.00	7.50	1.50
☐ 20 Boog Powell	10.00	5.00	1.00
☐ 21 Dick Selma	6.50	3.25	.65
☐ 22 Danny Walton	6.50	3.25	.65
☐ 23 Carl Morton	6.50	3.25	.65
☐ 24 Sonny Siebert	6.50	3.25	.65
☐ 25 Jim Merritt	6.50	3.25	.65
☐ 26 Jose Cardenal	6.50	3.25	.65
☐ 27 Don Mincher	6.50	3.25	.65
☐ 28A Clyde Wright (no 1970 date, team logo is Angels crest)	10.00	5.00	1.00
☐ 28B Clyde Wright (no 1970 date, team logo is California outline with Angels written inside)	10.00	5.00	1.00
☐ 28C Clyde Wright (dated 1970, team logo is California state outline)	7.50	3.75	.75
☐ 29 Les Cain	6.50	3.25	.65
☐ 30 Danny Cater	6.50	3.25	.65
☐ 31 Don Sutton	16.00	8.00	1.60
☐ 32 Chuck Dobson	6.50	3.25	.65
☐ 33 Willie McCovey	20.00	10.00	2.00
☐ 34 Mike Epstein	6.50	3.25	.65
☐ 35 Paul Blair	6.50	3.25	.65
☐ 36A Gary Nolan (no 1970 date)	7.50	3.75	.75
☐ 36B Gary Nolan (dated 1970, 1970 BB 95, SO 177)	7.50	3.75	.75
☐ 36C Gary Nolan (dated 1970, 1970 BB 96, SO 181)	7.50	3.75	.75
☐ 37 Sam McDowell	7.50	3.75	.75
☐ 38 Amos Otis	7.50	3.75	.75
☐ 39 Ray Fosse	6.50	3.25	.65
☐ 40 Mel Stottlemyre	7.50	3.75	.75
☐ 41 Clarence Gaston	7.50	3.75	.75
☐ 42 Dick Dietz	6.50	3.25	.65
☐ 43 Roy White	7.50	3.75	.75
☐ 44 Al Kaline	25.00	12.50	2.50
☐ 45 Carlos May	6.50	3.25	.65
☐ 46 Tommie Agee	6.50	3.25	.65
☐ 47 Tommy Harper	6.50	3.25	.65
☐ 48 Larry Dierker	6.50	3.25	.65
☐ 49 Mike Cuellar	6.50	3.25	.65
☐ 50 Ernie Banks	25.00	12.50	2.50
☐ 51 Bob Gibson	20.00	10.00	2.00
☐ 52 Reggie Smith	7.50	3.75	.75
☐ 53 Matty Alou	7.50	3.75	.75
☐ 54A Alex Johnson (no 1970 date, team logo is Angels crest)	10.00	5.00	1.00

☐ 54B Alex Johnson (no 1970 date, team logo is California state outline)	10.00	5.00	1.00
☐ 54C Alex Johnson (dated 1970, team logo is California state outline)	7.50	3.75	.75
☐ 55 Harmon Killebrew	20.00	10.00	2.00
☐ 56 Bill Grabarkewitz	6.50	3.25	.65
☐ 57 Richie Allen	10.00	5.00	1.00
☐ 58 Tony Perez	12.00	6.00	1.20
☐ 59 Dave McNally	7.50	3.75	.75
☐ 60 Jim Palmer	25.00	12.50	2.50
☐ 61 Billy Williams	20.00	10.00	2.00
☐ 62 Joe Torre	10.00	5.00	1.00
☐ 63 Jim Northrup	7.50	3.75	.75
☐ 64A Jim Fregosi (no 1970 date, team logo is Angels crest)	10.00	5.00	1.00
☐ 64B Jim Fregosi (no 1970 date, team logo is California state outline	10.00	5.00	1.00
☐ 64C Jim Fregosi (dated1970, 1970 Hits 166, avg. .276)	8.50	4.25	.85
☐ 64D Jim Fregosi (dated1970, 1970 Hits 167, avg. .278)	8.50	4.25	.85
☐ 65 Pete Rose	60.00	30.00	6.00
☐ 66A Bud Harrelson (no 1970 date)	8.50	4.25	.85
☐ 66B Bud Harrelson ERR (dated 1970, 1970 RBI 43)	8.50	4.25	.85
☐ 66C Bud Harrelson COR (dated 1970, 1970 RBI 42)	8.50	4.25	.85
☐ 67 Tony Taylor	6.50	3.25	.65
☐ 68 Willie Stargell	20.00	10.00	2.00
☐ 69 Tony Horton	7.50	3.75	.75
☐ 70A Claude Osteen ERR (no 1970 date, card number missing)	10.00	5.00	1.00
☐ 70B Claude Osteen COR (no 1970 date, card number present)	10.00	5.00	1.00
☐ 70C Claude Osteen COR (dated 1970)	7.50	3.75	.75
☐ 71 Glenn Beckert	6.50	3.25	.65
☐ 72 Nate Colbert	6.50	3.25	.65
☐ 73A Rick Monday (no 1970 date)	8.50	4.25	.85
☐ 73B Rick Monday ERR (dated 1970, 1970 AB 377, avg. .289)	8.50	4.25	.85
☐ 73C Rick Monday COR (dated 1970, 1970 AB 376, avg. .290)	8.50	4.25	.85
☐ 74 Tommy John	12.00	6.00	1.20
☐ 75 Chris Short	6.50	3.25	.65

1972 Kellogg's

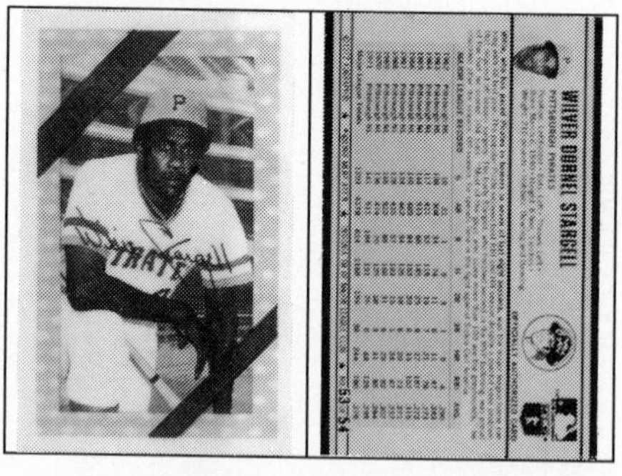

The cards in this 54-card set measure 2 1/8" by 3 1/4". The dimensions of the cards in the 1972 Kellogg's set were reduced in comparison to those of the 1971 series. In addition, the length of the set was set at 54 cards rather than the 75 of the previous year. The cards of this Kellogg's set are characterized by the diagonal bands found on the obverse.

	NRMT	VG-E	GOOD
COMPLETE SET (54)	65.00	32.50	6.50
COMMON PLAYER (1-54)	.60	.30	.06
☐ 1A Tom Seaver ERR (1970 ERA 2.85)	8.00	4.00	.80
☐ 1B Tom Seaver COR (1970 ERA 2.81)	16.00	8.00	1.60
☐ 2 Amos Otis	.75	.35	.07
☐ 3A Willie Davis ERR (lifetime runs 842)	1.50	.75	.15
☐ 3B Willie Davis COR (lifetime runs 841)	.75	.35	.07
☐ 4 Wilbur Wood	.60	.30	.06
☐ 5 Bill Parsons	.60	.30	.06
☐ 6 Pete Rose	15.00	7.50	1.50
☐ 7A Willie McCovey ERR (lifetime HR 360)	3.50	1.75	.35
☐ 7B Willie McCovey COR (lifetime HR 370)	7.00	3.50	.70
☐ 8 Ferguson Jenkins	2.50	1.25	.25
☐ 9A Vida Blue ERR (lifetime ERA 2.35)	1.50	.75	.15
☐ 9B Vida Blue COR (lifetime ERA 2.31)	.75	.35	.07
☐ 10 Joe Torre	1.00	.50	.10
☐ 11 Merv Rettenmund	.60	.30	.06
☐ 12 Bill Melton	.60	.30	.06
☐ 13A Jim Palmer ERR (lifetime games 170)	4.00	2.00	.40
☐ 13B Jim Palmer COR (lifetime games 168)	8.00	4.00	.80
☐ 14 Doug Rader	.75	.35	.07
☐ 15A Dave Roberts ERR ("NL" missing in bio)	.60	.30	.06
☐ 15B Dave Roberts COR ("NL" in bio, line 2)	1.25	.60	.12
☐ 16 Bobby Murcer	.75	.35	.07
☐ 17 Wes Parker	.75	.35	.07
☐ 18A Joe Coleman ERR (lifetime BB 294)	1.25	.60	.12
☐ 18B Joe Coleman COR (lifetime BB 393)	.60	.30	.06
☐ 19 Manny Sanguillen	.75	.35	.07
☐ 20 Reggie Jackson	10.00	5.00	1.00
☐ 21 Ralph Garr	.60	.30	.06
☐ 22 Jim Hunter	2.50	1.25	.25
☐ 23 Rick Wise	.60	.30	.06
☐ 24 Glenn Beckert	.60	.30	.06
☐ 25 Tony Oliva	1.50	.75	.15
☐ 26A Bob Gibson ERR (lifetime SO 2577)	7.00	3.50	.70
☐ 26B Bob Gibson COR (lifetime SO 2578)	3.50	1.75	.35
☐ 27A Mike Cuellar ERR (1971 ERA 3.80)	1.25	.60	.12
☐ 27B Mike Cuellar COR (1971 ERA 3.08)	.60	.30	.06
☐ 28 Chris Speier	.60	.30	.06
☐ 29A Dave McNally ERR (lifetime ERA 3.18)	1.50	.75	.15
☐ 29B Dave McNally COR (lifetime ERA 3.15)	.75	.35	.07
☐ 30 Leo Cardenas	.60	.30	.06
☐ 31A Bill Freehan ERR (lifetime runs 497)	.75	.35	.07
☐ 31B Bill Freehan COR (lifetime runs 500)	1.50	.75	.15
☐ 32A Bud Harrelson ERR (lifetime hits 634)	1.50	.75	.15
☐ 32B Bud Harrelson COR (lifetime hits 624)	.75	.35	.07
☐ 33A Sam McDowell ERR (bio line 3 has "less than 200")	.75	.35	.07
☐ 33B Sam McDowell COR (bio line 3 has "less than 225")	1.50	.75	.15
☐ 34A Claude Osteen ERR (1971 ERA 3.25)	.60	.30	.06
☐ 34B Claude Osteen COR (1971 ERA 3.51)	1.25	.60	.12
☐ 35 Reggie Smith	.75	.35	.07
☐ 36 Sonny Siebert	.60	.30	.06
☐ 37 Lee May	.75	.35	.07
☐ 38 Mickey Lolich	1.00	.50	.10

☐ 39A Cookie Rojas ERR (lifetime 2B 149)	1.25	.60	.12
☐ 39B Cookie Rojas COR (lifetime 2B 150)	.60	.30	.06
☐ 40A Dick Drago ERR (bio line 3 has Poyals)	1.25	.60	.12
☐ 40B Dick Drago COR (bio line 3 has Royals)	.60	.30	.06
☐ 41 Nate Colbert	.60	.30	.06
☐ 42 Andy Messersmith	.75	.35	.07
☐ 43A Dave Johnson ERR (lifetime AB 3110, avg. .262)	2.00	1.00	.20
☐ 43B Dave Johnson COR (lifetime AB 3113, avg. .264)	1.00	.50	.10
☐ 44 Steve Blass	.75	.35	.07
☐ 45 Bob Robertson	.60	.30	.06
☐ 46A Billy Williams ERR (bio has "missed only one game")	3.50	1.75	.35
☐ 46B Billy Williams COR (bio has that line eliminated)	7.00	3.50	.70
☐ 47 Juan Marichal	3.50	1.75	.35
☐ 48 Lou Brock	4.00	2.00	.40
☐ 49 Roberto Clemente	9.00	4.50	.90
☐ 50 Mel Stottlemyre	.75	.35	.07
☐ 51 Don Wilson	.60	.30	.06
☐ 52A Sal Bando ERR (lifetime RBI 355)	.75	.35	.07
☐ 52B Sal Bando COR (lifetime RBI 356)	1.50	.75	.15
☐ 53A Willie Stargell ERR (lifetime 2B 197)	8.00	4.00	.80
☐ 53B Willie Stargell COR (lifetime 2B 196)	4.00	2.00	.40
☐ 54A Willie Mays ERR (lifetime RBI 1855)	20.00	10.00	2.00
☐ 54B Willie Mays COR (lifetime RBI 1856)	10.00	5.00	1.00

1972 Kellogg's ATG

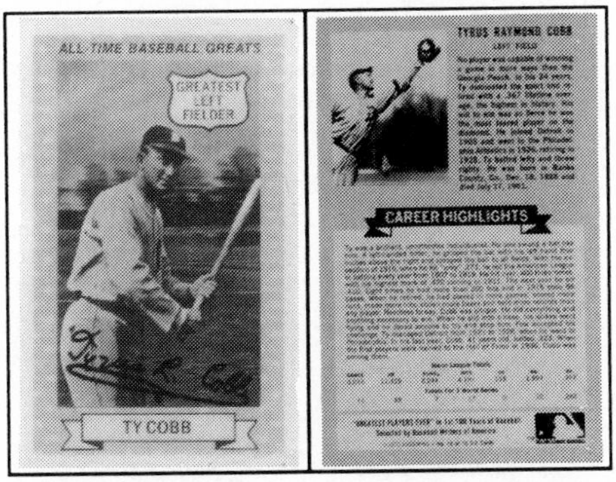

The cards in this 15-card set measure 2 1/4" by 3 1/2". The 1972 All-Time Greats 3-D set was issued with Kellogg's Danish Go Rounds. The set contains two different cards of Babe Ruth. The set is a reissue of a 1970 set issued by Rold Gold Pretzels to commemorate baseball's first 100 years. The Rold Gold cards are copyrighted 1970 on the reverse and are valued at approximately double the prices listed below.

	NRMT	VG-E	GOOD
COMPLETE SET (15)	15.00	7.50	1.50
COMMON PLAYER (1-15)	.50	.25	.05
☐ 1 Walter Johnson	1.25	.60	.12
☐ 2 Rogers Hornsby	.75	.35	.07
☐ 3 John McGraw	.50	.25	.05
☐ 4 Mickey Cochrane	.60	.30	.06
☐ 5 George Sisler	.60	.30	.06
☐ 6 Babe Ruth	4.00	2.00	.40
☐ 7 Lefty Grove	.75	.35	.07
☐ 8 Pie Traynor	.50	.25	.05
☐ 9 Honus Wagner	1.25	.60	.12
☐ 10 Eddie Collins	.50	.25	.05
☐ 11 Tris Speaker	.75	.35	.07
☐ 12 Cy Young	.90	.45	.09
☐ 13 Lou Gehrig	2.25	1.10	.22
☐ 14 Babe Ruth	4.00	2.00	.40
☐ 15 Ty Cobb	2.25	1.10	.22

1973 Kellogg's 2D

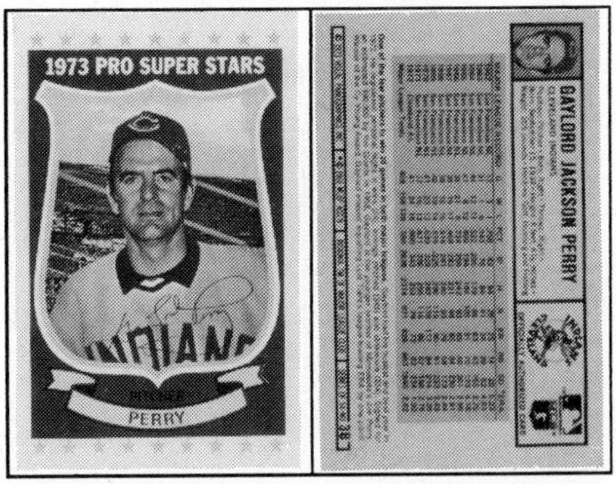

The cards in this 54-card set measure 2 1/4" by 3 1/2". The 1973 Kellogg's set is the only non-3D set produced by the Kellogg Company. Apparently Kellogg's decided to have the cards produced through Visual Panographics rather than by Xograph, as in the other years. The complete set could be obtained from the company through a box-top redemption procedure. The card size is slightly larger than the previous year.

	NRMT	VG-E	GOOD
COMPLETE SET (54)	70.00	35.00	7.00
COMMON PLAYER (1-54)	.60	.30	.06
☐ 1 Amos Otis	.75	.35	.07
☐ 2 Ellie Rodriguez	.60	.30	.06
☐ 3 Mickey Lolich	1.00	.50	.10
☐ 4 Tony Oliva	1.25	.60	.12
☐ 5 Don Sutton	2.50	1.25	.25
☐ 6 Pete Rose	15.00	7.50	1.50
☐ 7 Steve Carlton	5.00	2.50	.50
☐ 8 Bobby Bonds	1.00	.50	.10
☐ 9 Wilbur Wood	.60	.30	.06
☐ 10 Billy Williams	3.00	1.50	.30
☐ 11 Steve Blass	.75	.35	.07
☐ 12 Jon Matlack	.75	.35	.07
☐ 13 Cesar Cedeno	.75	.35	.07
☐ 14 Bob Gibson	3.00	1.50	.30
☐ 15 Sparky Lyle	1.00	.50	.10
☐ 16 Nolan Ryan	15.00	7.50	1.50
☐ 17 Jim Palmer	4.00	2.00	.40
☐ 18 Ray Fosse	.60	.30	.06
☐ 19 Bobby Murcer	.75	.35	.07
☐ 20 Jim Hunter	2.50	1.25	.25
☐ 21 Tom McCraw	.60	.30	.06
☐ 22 Reggie Jackson	8.00	4.00	.80
☐ 23 Bill Stoneman	.60	.30	.06
☐ 24 Lou Piniella	.90	.45	.09
☐ 25 Willie Stargell	3.50	1.75	.35
☐ 26 Dick Allen	.90	.45	.09
☐ 27 Carlton Fisk	4.00	2.00	.40
☐ 28 Ferguson Jenkins	2.50	1.25	.25
☐ 29 Phil Niekro	2.50	1.25	.25
☐ 30 Gary Nolan	.60	.30	.06
☐ 31 Joe Torre	.90	.45	.09
☐ 32 Bobby Tolan	.60	.30	.06
☐ 33 Nate Colbert	.60	.30	.06
☐ 34 Joe Morgan	3.50	1.75	.35
☐ 35 Bert Blyleven	1.00	.50	.10
☐ 36 Joe Rudi	.75	.35	.07
☐ 37 Ralph Garr	.60	.30	.06
☐ 38 Gaylord Perry	2.50	1.25	.25

	NRMT	VG-E	GOOD
☐ 39 Bobby Grich	.75	.35	.07
☐ 40 Lou Brock	3.00	1.50	.30
☐ 41 Pete Broberg	.60	.30	.06
☐ 42 Manny Sanguillen	.75	.35	.07
☐ 43 Willie Davis	.75	.35	.07
☐ 44 Dave Kingman	.90	.45	.09
☐ 45 Carlos May	.60	.30	.06
☐ 46 Tom Seaver	5.00	2.50	.50
☐ 47 Mike Cuellar	.60	.30	.06
☐ 48 Joe Coleman	.60	.30	.06
☐ 49 Claude Osteen	.60	.30	.06
☐ 50 Steve Kline	.60	.30	.06
☐ 51 Rod Carew	5.00	2.50	.50
☐ 52 Al Kaline	5.00	2.50	.50
☐ 53 Larry Dierker	.60	.30	.06
☐ 54 Ron Santo	1.00	.50	.10

1974 Kellogg's

The cards in this 54-card set measure 2 1/8" by 3 1/4". In 1974 the Kellogg's set returned to its 3-D format; it also returned to the smaller-size card. Complete sets could be obtained from the company through a box-top offer. The cards are numbered on the back.

	NRMT	VG-E	GOOD
COMPLETE SET (54)	55.00	27.50	5.50
COMMON PLAYER (1-54)	.40	.20	.04
☐ 1 Bob Gibson	3.00	1.50	.30
☐ 2 Rick Monday	.50	.25	.05
☐ 3 Joe Coleman	.40	.20	.04
☐ 4 Bert Campaneris	.50	.25	.05
☐ 5 Carlton Fisk	2.00	1.00	.20
☐ 6 Jim Palmer	3.00	1.50	.30
☐ 7A Ron Santo ERR Chicago White Sox	.75	.35	.07
☐ 7B Ron Santo COR Chicago Cubs	5.00	2.50	.50
☐ 8 Nolan Ryan	12.00	6.00	1.20
☐ 9 Greg Luzinski	.60	.30	.06
☐ 10 Buddy Bell	.60	.30	.06
☐ 11 Bob Watson	.50	.25	.05
☐ 12 Bill Singer	.40	.20	.04
☐ 13 Dave May	.40	.20	.04
☐ 14 Jim Brewer	.40	.20	.04
☐ 15 Manny Sanguillen	.50	.25	.05
☐ 16 Jeff Burroughs	.50	.25	.05
☐ 17 Amos Otis	.50	.25	.05
☐ 18 Ed Goodson	.40	.20	.04
☐ 19 Nate Colbert	.40	.20	.04
☐ 20 Reggie Jackson	8.00	4.00	.80
☐ 21 Ted Simmons	.75	.35	.07
☐ 22 Bobby Murcer	.60	.30	.06
☐ 23 Willie Horton	.50	.25	.05
☐ 24 Orlando Cepeda	1.00	.50	.10
☐ 25 Ron Hunt	.40	.20	.04
☐ 26 Wayne Twitchell	.40	.20	.04
☐ 27 Ron Fairly	.40	.20	.04
☐ 28 Johnny Bench	6.00	3.00	.60
☐ 29 John Mayberry	.40	.20	.04
☐ 30 Rod Carew	5.00	2.50	.50
☐ 31 Ken Holtzman	.50	.25	.05
☐ 32 Billy Williams	2.00	1.00	.20
☐ 33 Dick Allen	.75	.35	.07
☐ 34A Wilbur Wood ERR (1973 K 198)	3.00	1.50	.30
☐ 34B Wilbur Wood COR (1973 K 199)	.50	.25	.05
☐ 35 Danny Thompson	.40	.20	.04
☐ 36 Joe Morgan	3.00	1.50	.30
☐ 37 Willie Stargell	3.00	1.50	.30
☐ 38 Pete Rose	12.00	6.00	1.20
☐ 39 Bobby Bonds	.60	.30	.06
☐ 40 Chris Speier	.40	.20	.04
☐ 41 Sparky Lyle	.75	.35	.07
☐ 42 Cookie Rojas	.40	.20	.04
☐ 43 Tommy Davis	.50	.25	.05
☐ 44 Jim Hunter	2.00	1.00	.20
☐ 45 Willie Davis	.60	.30	.06
☐ 46 Bert Blyleven	.90	.45	.09
☐ 47 Pat Kelly	.40	.20	.04
☐ 48 Ken Singleton	.60	.30	.06
☐ 49 Manny Mota	.50	.25	.05
☐ 50 Dave Johnson	.75	.35	.07
☐ 51 Sal Bando	.50	.25	.05
☐ 52 Tom Seaver	5.00	2.50	.50
☐ 53 Felix Millan	.40	.20	.04
☐ 54 Ron Blomberg	.40	.20	.04

1975 Kellogg's

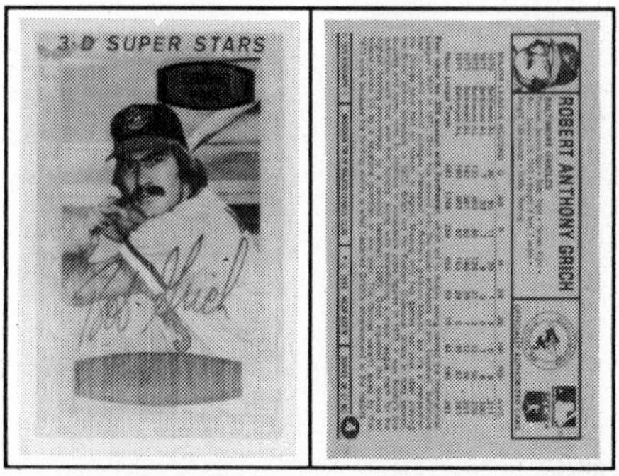

The cards in this 57-card set measure 2 1/8" by 3 1/4". The 1975 Kellogg's 3-D set could be obtained card by card in cereal boxes or as a set from a box-top offer from the company. Card number 44, Jim Hunter, exists with the A's emblem or the Yankees emblem on the back of the card.

	NRMT	VG-E	GOOD
COMPLETE SET (57)	150.00	75.00	15.00
COMMON PLAYER (1-57)	.75	.35	.07
☐ 1 Roy White	.75	.35	.07
☐ 2 Ross Grimsley	.75	.35	.07
☐ 3 Reggie Smith	1.00	.50	.10
☐ 4A Bob Grich ERR (bio last line begins "1973 work")	1.00	.50	.10
☐ 4B Bob Grich COR (bio last line begins "because his fielding")	2.00	1.00	.20
☐ 5 Greg Gross	.75	.35	.07
☐ 6 Bob Watson	.90	.45	.09
☐ 7 Johnny Bench	10.00	5.00	1.00
☐ 8 Jeff Burroughs	.75	.35	.07
☐ 9 Elliott Maddox	.75	.35	.07
☐ 10 Jon Matlack	.75	.35	.07
☐ 11 Pete Rose	18.00	9.00	1.80
☐ 12 Lee Stanton	.75	.35	.07
☐ 13 Bake McBride	.75	.35	.07
☐ 14 Jorge Orta	.75	.35	.07
☐ 15 Al Oliver	1.00	.50	.10
☐ 16 John Briggs	.75	.35	.07
☐ 17 Steve Garvey	6.50	3.25	.65
☐ 18 Brooks Robinson	5.00	2.50	.50
☐ 19 John Hiller	.75	.35	.07
☐ 20 Lynn McGlothen	.75	.35	.07
☐ 21 Cleon Jones	.75	.35	.07
☐ 22 Fergie Jenkins	2.50	1.25	.25
☐ 23 Bill North	.75	.35	.07

☐ 24 Steve Busby	.75	.35	.07
☐ 25 Richie Zisk	.90	.45	.09
☐ 26 Nolan Ryan	18.00	9.00	1.80
☐ 27 Joe Morgan	4.00	2.00	.40
☐ 28 Joe Rudi	.90	.45	.09
☐ 29 Jose Cardenal	.75	.35	.07
☐ 30 Andy Messersmith	.75	.35	.07
☐ 31 Willie Montanez	.75	.35	.07
☐ 32 Bill Buckner	1.00	.50	.10
☐ 33 Rod Carew	6.00	3.00	.60
☐ 34 Lou Piniella	1.25	.60	.12
☐ 35 Ralph Garr	.75	.35	.07
☐ 36 Mike Marshall	.75	.35	.07
☐ 37 Garry Maddox	.75	.35	.07
☐ 38 Dwight Evans	1.50	.75	.15
☐ 39 Lou Brock	5.00	2.50	.50
☐ 40 Ken Singleton	.90	.45	.09
☐ 41 Steve Braun	.75	.35	.07
☐ 42 Rich Allen	1.00	.50	.10
☐ 43 John Grubb	.75	.35	.07
☐ 44A Jim Hunter (Oakland A's team logo on back)	4.00	2.00	.40
☐ 44B Jim Hunter (New York Yankees team logo on back)	10.00	5.00	1.00
☐ 45 Gaylord Perry	3.00	1.50	.30
☐ 46 George Hendrick	.90	.45	.09
☐ 47 Sparky Lyle	.90	.45	.09
☐ 48 Dave Cash	.75	.35	.07
☐ 49 Luis Tiant	.90	.45	.09
☐ 50 Cesar Geronimo	.75	.35	.07
☐ 51 Carl Yastrzemski	15.00	7.50	1.50
☐ 52 Ken Brett	.75	.35	.07
☐ 53 Hal McRae	.90	.45	.09
☐ 54 Reggie Jackson	15.00	7.50	1.50
☐ 55 Rollie Fingers	3.00	1.50	.30
☐ 56 Mike Schmidt	15.00	7.50	1.50
☐ 57 Richie Hebner	.75	.35	.07

1976 Kellogg's

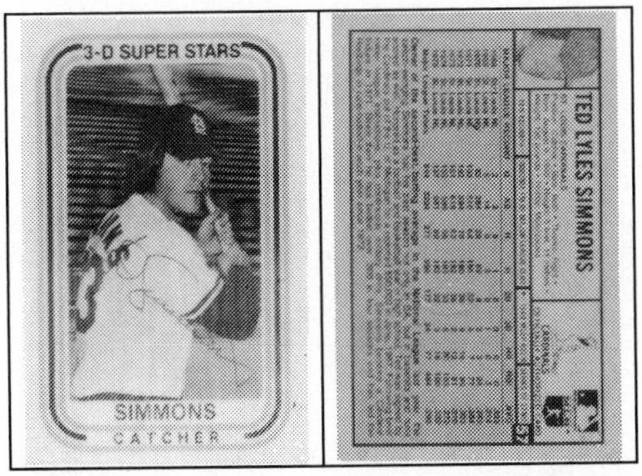

The cards in this 57-card set measure 2 1/8" by 3 1/4". The 1976 Kellogg's 3-D set could be obtained card by card in cereal boxes or as a set from the company for box-tops. Card number 6, that of Clay Carroll, exists with both a Reds or White Sox emblem on the back. Cards 1-3 (marked in the checklist below with SP) were apparently printed apart from the other 54 and are in shorter supply.

	NRMT	VG-E	GOOD
COMPLETE SET	75.00	37.50	7.50
COMMON PLAYER (1-3) SP	9.00	4.50	.90
COMMON PLAYER (4-57)	.40	.20	.04
☐ 1 Steve Hargan SP	9.00	4.50	.90
☐ 2 Claudell Washington SP	9.00	4.50	.90
☐ 3 Don Gullett SP	9.00	4.50	.90
☐ 4 Randy Jones	.50	.25	.05
☐ 5 Jim Hunter	2.00	1.00	.20
☐ 6A Clay Carroll (team logo Chicago White Sox on back)	1.00	.50	.10
☐ 6B Clay Carroll (team logo Cincinnati Reds on back)	1.00	.50	.10
☐ 7 Joe Rudi	.50	.25	.05
☐ 8 Reggie Jackson	6.00	3.00	.60
☐ 9 Felix Millan	.40	.20	.04
☐ 10 Jim Rice	3.00	1.50	.30
☐ 11 Bert Blyleven	.75	.35	.07
☐ 12 Ken Singleton	.50	.25	.05
☐ 13 Don Sutton	1.50	.75	.15
☐ 14 Joe Morgan	3.50	1.75	.35
☐ 15 Dave Parker	1.50	.75	.15
☐ 16 Dave Cash	.40	.20	.04
☐ 17 Ron LeFlore	.40	.20	.04
☐ 18 Greg Luzinski	1.50	.75	.15
☐ 19 Dennis Eckersley	2.50	1.25	.25
☐ 20 Bill Madlock	.80	.40	.08
☐ 21 George Scott	.40	.20	.04
☐ 22 Willie Stargell	2.50	1.25	.25
☐ 23 Al Hrabosky	.50	.25	.05
☐ 24 Carl Yastrzemski	7.00	3.50	.70
☐ 25A Jim Kaat (team logo Philadelphia Phillies on back)	1.25	.60	.12
☐ 25B Jim Kaat (team logo Chicago White Sox on back)	1.25	.60	.12
☐ 26 Marty Perez	.40	.20	.04
☐ 27 Bob Watson	.50	.25	.05
☐ 28 Eric Soderholm	.40	.20	.04
☐ 29 Bill Lee	.50	.25	.05
☐ 30A Frank Tanana ERR (1975 ERA 2.63)	.60	.30	.06
☐ 30B Frank Tanana COR (1975 ERA 2.62)	.60	.30	.06
☐ 31 Fred Lynn	1.50	.75	.15
☐ 32A Tom Seaver ERR (1967 Pct. 552 with no decimal point)	5.00	2.50	.50
☐ 32B Tom Seaver COR (1967 Pct. .552)	5.00	2.50	.50
☐ 33 Steve Busby	.50	.25	.05
☐ 34 Gary Carter	3.50	1.75	.35
☐ 35 Rick Wise	.40	.20	.04
☐ 36 Johnny Bench	5.00	2.50	.50
☐ 37 Jim Palmer	2.50	1.25	.25
☐ 38 Bobby Murcer	.60	.30	.06
☐ 39 Von Joshua	.40	.20	.04
☐ 40 Lou Brock	3.00	1.50	.30
☐ 41A Mickey Rivers (missing line in bio about Yankees)	.60	.30	.06
☐ 41B Mickey Rivers (bio has "Yankees obtained ...")	.60	.30	.06
☐ 42 Manny Sanguillen	.50	.25	.05
☐ 43 Jerry Reuss	.40	.20	.04
☐ 44 Ken Griffey	.60	.30	.06
☐ 45A Jorge Orta ERR (lifetime AB 1615)	.50	.25	.05
☐ 45B Jorge Orta COR (lifetime AB 1616)	.50	.25	.05
☐ 46 John Mayberry	.40	.20	.04
☐ 47A Vida Blue (bio "struck out more batters")	.60	.30	.06
☐ 47B Vida Blue (bio "pitched more innings")	.60	.30	.06
☐ 48 Rod Carew	4.00	2.00	.40
☐ 49A Jon Matlack ERR (1975 ER 87)	.60	.30	.06
☐ 49B Jon Matlack COR (1975 ER 86)	.60	.30	.06
☐ 50 Boog Powell	.75	.35	.07
☐ 51A Mike Hargrove ERR (lifetime AB 935)	.60	.30	.06
☐ 51B Mike Hargrove COR (lifetime AB 934)	.60	.30	.06
☐ 52A Paul Lindblad ERR (1975 ERA 2.43)	.50	.25	.05
☐ 52B Paul Lindblad COR (1975 ERA 2.72)	.50	.25	.05
☐ 53 Thurman Munson	4.00	2.00	.40
☐ 54 Steve Garvey	3.50	1.75	.35
☐ 55 Pete Rose	12.00	6.00	1.20
☐ 56A Greg Gross ERR (lifetime games 334)	.50	.25	.05
☐ 56B Greg Gross COR (lifetime games 302)	.50	.25	.05
☐ 57 Ted Simmons	.75	.35	.07

1977 Kellogg's

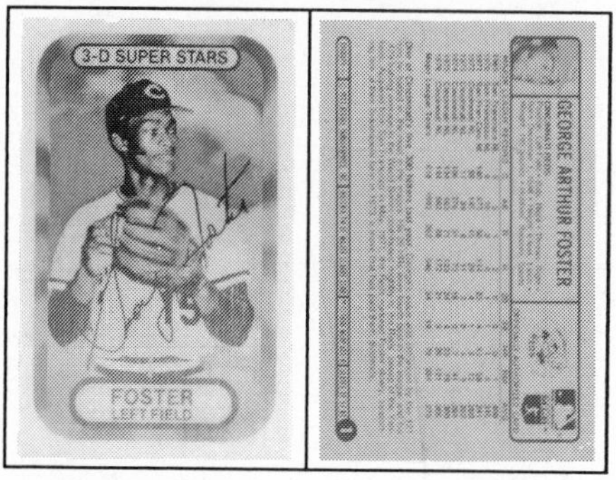

The cards in this 57-card set measure 2 1/8" by 3 1/4". The 1977 Kellogg's series of 3-D baseball player cards could be obtained card by card from cereal boxes or by sending in box-tops and money. Each player's picture appears in miniature form on the reverse, an idea begun in 1971 and replaced in subsequent years by the use of a picture of the Kellogg's mascot.

	NRMT	VG-E	GOOD
COMPLETE SET (57)	55.00	27.50	5.50
COMMON PLAYER (1-57)	.35	.17	.03
☐ 1 George Foster	.80	.40	.08
☐ 2 Bert Campaneris	.45	.22	.04
☐ 3 Fergie Jenkins	1.75	.85	.17
☐ 4 Dock Ellis	.35	.17	.03
☐ 5 John Montefusco	.35	.17	.03
☐ 6 George Brett	7.50	3.75	.75
☐ 7 John Candelaria	.45	.22	.04
☐ 8 Fred Norman	.35	.17	.03
☐ 9 Bill Travers	.35	.17	.03
☐ 10 Hal McRae	.45	.22	.04
☐ 11 Doug Rau	.35	.17	.03
☐ 12 Greg Luzinski	.45	.22	.04
☐ 13 Ralph Garr	.35	.17	.03
☐ 14 Steve Garvey	3.50	1.75	.35
☐ 15 Rick Manning	.35	.17	.03
☐ 16A Lyman Bostock ERR (Dock Ellis photo on back)	2.00	1.00	.20
☐ 16B Lyman Bostock COR	.45	.22	.04
☐ 17 Randy Jones	.35	.17	.03
☐ 18 Ron Cey	.45	.22	.04
☐ 19 Dave Parker	1.25	.60	.12
☐ 20 Pete Rose	9.00	4.50	.90
☐ 21A Wayne Garland (no trade to Cleveland is mentioned)	.35	.17	.03
☐ 21B Wayne Garland (trade mentioned, bio ends "now flip for Cleveland)	1.50	.75	.15
☐ 22 Bill North	.35	.17	.03
☐ 23 Thurman Munson	3.50	1.75	.35
☐ 24 Tom Poquette	.35	.17	.03
☐ 25 Ron LeFlore	.45	.22	.04
☐ 26 Mark Fidrych	.45	.22	.04
☐ 27 Sixto Lezcano	.35	.17	.03
☐ 28 Dave Winfield	2.50	1.25	.25
☐ 29 Jerry Koosman	.45	.22	.04
☐ 30 Mike Hargrove	.35	.17	.03
☐ 31 Willie Montanez	.35	.17	.03
☐ 32 Don Stanhouse	.35	.17	.03
☐ 33 Jay Johnstone	.45	.22	.04
☐ 34 Bake McBride	.35	.17	.03
☐ 35 Dave Kingman	.60	.30	.06
☐ 36 Fred Patek	.35	.17	.03
☐ 37 Garry Maddox	.35	.17	.03
☐ 38A Ken Reitz (no trade mentioned)	.35	.17	.03
☐ 38B Ken Reitz (trade mentioned)	1.50	.75	.15
☐ 39 Bobby Grich	.45	.22	.04
☐ 40 Cesar Geronimo	.35	.17	.03
☐ 41 Jim Lonborg	.45	.22	.04
☐ 42 Ed Figueroa	.35	.17	.03
☐ 43 Bill Madlock	.75	.35	.07
☐ 44 Jerry Remy	.35	.17	.03
☐ 45 Frank Tanana	.45	.22	.04
☐ 46 Al Oliver	.75	.35	.07
☐ 47 Charlie Hough	.45	.22	.04
☐ 48 Lou Piniella	.75	.35	.07
☐ 49 Ken Griffey	.75	.35	.07
☐ 50 Jose Cruz	.45	.22	.04
☐ 51 Rollie Fingers	1.50	.75	.15
☐ 52 Chris Chambliss	.45	.22	.04
☐ 53 Rod Carew	4.00	2.00	.40
☐ 54 Andy Messersmith	.45	.22	.04
☐ 55 Mickey Rivers	.45	.22	.04
☐ 56 Butch Wynegar	.45	.22	.04
☐ 57 Steve Carlton	4.00	2.00	.40

1978 Kellogg's

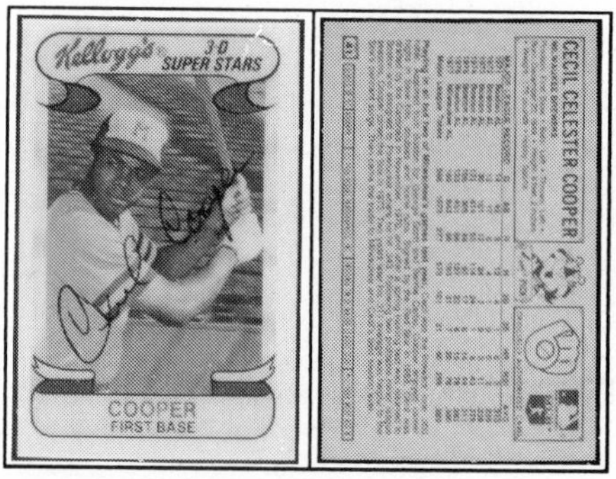

The cards in this 57-card set measure 2 1/8" by 3 1/4". This 1978 3-D Kellogg's series marks the first year in which Tony the Tiger appears on the reverse of each card next to the team and MLB logos. Once again the set could be obtained as individually wrapped cards in cereal boxes or as a set via a mail-in offer.

	NRMT	VG-E	GOOD
COMPLETE SET (57)	50.00	25.00	5.00
COMMON PLAYER (1-57)	.35	.17	.03
☐ 1 Steve Carlton	3.50	1.75	.35
☐ 2 Bucky Dent	.60	.30	.06
☐ 3 Mike Schmidt	6.50	3.25	.65
☐ 4 Ken Griffey	.60	.30	.06
☐ 5 Al Cowens	.35	.17	.03
☐ 6 George Brett	6.00	3.00	.60
☐ 7 Lou Brock	2.50	1.25	.25
☐ 8 Rich Gossage	.75	.35	.07
☐ 9 Tom Johnson	.35	.17	.03
☐ 10 George Foster	.75	.35	.07
☐ 11 Dave Winfield	2.50	1.25	.25
☐ 12 Dan Meyer	.35	.17	.03
☐ 13 Chris Chambliss	.45	.22	.04
☐ 14 Paul Dade	.35	.17	.03
☐ 15 Jeff Burroughs	.35	.17	.03
☐ 16 Jose Cruz	.45	.22	.04
☐ 17 Mickey Rivers	.45	.22	.04
☐ 18 John Candelaria	.45	.22	.04
☐ 19 Ellis Valentine	.35	.17	.03
☐ 20 Hal McRae	.45	.22	.04
☐ 21 Dave Rozema	.35	.17	.03
☐ 22 Lenny Randle	.35	.17	.03
☐ 23 Willie McCovey	2.00	1.00	.20
☐ 24 Ron Cey	.45	.22	.04
☐ 25 Eddie Murray	15.00	7.50	1.50
☐ 26 Larry Bowa	.45	.22	.04
☐ 27 Tom Seaver	4.00	2.00	.40
☐ 28 Garry Maddox	.35	.17	.03
☐ 29 Rod Carew	4.00	2.00	.40
☐ 30 Thurman Munson	4.00	2.00	.40
☐ 31 Gary Templeton	.45	.22	.04
☐ 32 Eric Soderholm	.35	.17	.03
☐ 33 Greg Luzinski	.45	.22	.04
☐ 34 Reggie Smith	.45	.22	.04
☐ 35 Dave Goltz	.35	.17	.03
☐ 36 Tommy John	.75	.35	.07
☐ 37 Ralph Garr	.35	.17	.03
☐ 38 Alan Bannister	.35	.17	.03
☐ 39 Bob Bailor	.35	.17	.03

☐ 40 Reggie Jackson	5.00	2.50	.50
☐ 41 Cecil Cooper	.45	.22	.04
☐ 42 Burt Hooton	.35	.17	.03
☐ 43 Sparky Lyle	.45	.22	.04
☐ 44 Steve Ontiveros	.35	.17	.03
☐ 45 Rick Reuschel	.60	.30	.06
☐ 46 Lyman Bostock	.45	.22	.04
☐ 47 Mitchell Page	.35	.17	.03
☐ 48 Bruce Sutter	.60	.30	.06
☐ 49 Jim Rice	2.00	1.00	.20
☐ 50 Ken Forsch	.35	.17	.03
☐ 51 Nolan Ryan	8.00	4.00	.80
☐ 52 Dave Parker	1.50	.75	.15
☐ 53 Bert Blyleven	.60	.30	.06
☐ 54 Frank Tanana	.45	.22	.04
☐ 55 Ken Singleton	.45	.22	.04
☐ 56 Mike Hargrove	.45	.22	.04
☐ 57 Don Sutton	1.50	.75	.15

1979 Kellogg's

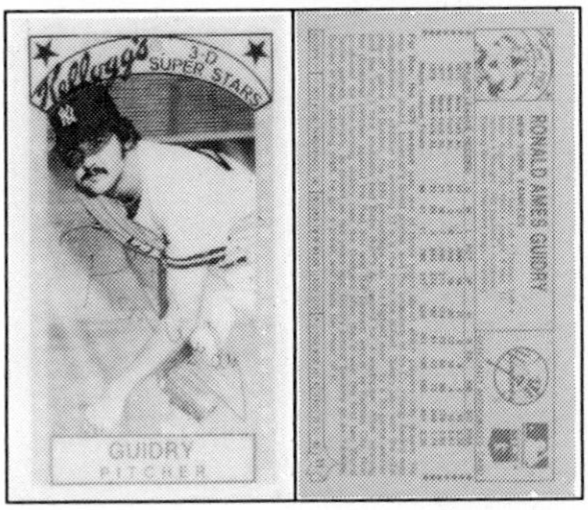

The cards in this 60-card set measure 1 15/16" by 3 1/4". The 1979 edition of Kellogg's 3-D baseball cards have a 3/16" reduced width from the previous year; a nicely designed curved panel above the picture gives this set a distinctive appearance. The set contains the largest number of cards issued in a Kellogg's set since the 1971 series.

	NRMT	VG-E	GOOD
COMPLETE SET (60)	33.00	14.00	3.00
COMMON PLAYER (1-60)	.25	.12	.02
☐ 1 Bruce Sutter	.50	.25	.05
☐ 2 Ted Simmons	.50	.25	.05
☐ 3 Ross Grimsley	.25	.12	.02
☐ 4 Wayne Nordhagen	.25	.12	.02
☐ 5 Jim Palmer	2.00	1.00	.20
☐ 6 John Henry Johnson	.25	.12	.02
☐ 7 Jason Thompson	.25	.12	.02
☐ 8 Pat Zachry	.25	.12	.02
☐ 9 Dennis Eckersley	1.25	.60	.12
☐ 10 Paul Splittorff	.25	.12	.02
☐ 11 Ron Guidry	1.25	.60	.12
☐ 12 Jeff Burroughs	.25	.12	.02
☐ 13 Rod Carew	3.00	1.50	.30
☐ 14A Buddy Bell (no trade mentioned)	1.50	.75	.15
☐ 14B Buddy Bell (traded to Rangers)	.35	.17	.03
☐ 15 Jim Rice	2.00	1.00	.20
☐ 16 Garry Maddox	.25	.12	.02
☐ 17 Willie McCovey	1.50	.75	.15
☐ 18 Steve Carlton	2.50	1.25	.25
☐ 19 J.R. Richard	.35	.17	.03
☐ 20 Paul Molitor	1.25	.60	.12
☐ 21 Dave Parker	1.50	.75	.15
☐ 22 Pete Rose	7.00	3.50	.70
☐ 23 Vida Blue	.35	.17	.03
☐ 24 Richie Zisk	.25	.12	.02
☐ 25 Darrell Porter	.25	.12	.02
☐ 26 Dan Driessen	.25	.12	.02
☐ 27 Geoff Zahn	.25	.12	.02
☐ 28 Phil Niekro	1.25	.60	.12
☐ 29 Tom Seaver	3.50	1.75	.35
☐ 30 Fred Lynn	.75	.35	.07
☐ 31 Bill Bonham	.25	.12	.02
☐ 32 George Foster	.50	.25	.05
☐ 33 Terry Puhl	.25	.12	.02
☐ 34 John Candelaria	.35	.17	.03
☐ 35 Bob Knepper	.25	.12	.02
☐ 36 Fred Patek	.25	.12	.02
☐ 37 Chris Chambliss	.35	.17	.03
☐ 38 Bob Forsch	.25	.12	.02
☐ 39 Ken Griffey	.50	.25	.05
☐ 40 Jack Clark	1.50	.75	.15
☐ 41 Dwight Evans	1.00	.50	.10
☐ 42 Lee Mazzilli	.25	.12	.02
☐ 43 Mario Guerrero	.25	.12	.02
☐ 44 Larry Bowa	.35	.17	.03
☐ 45 Carl Yastrzemski	5.00	2.50	.50
☐ 46 Reggie Jackson	5.00	2.50	.50
☐ 47 Rick Reuschel	.50	.25	.05
☐ 48 Mike Flanagan	.35	.17	.03
☐ 49 Gaylord Perry	2.00	1.00	.20
☐ 50 George Brett	5.00	2.50	.50
☐ 51 Craig Reynolds	.25	.12	.02
☐ 52 Dave Lopes	.35	.17	.03
☐ 53 Bill Almon	.25	.12	.02
☐ 54 Roy Howell	.25	.12	.02
☐ 55 Frank Tanana	.35	.17	.03
☐ 56 Doug Rau	.25	.12	.02
☐ 57 Rick Monday	.35	.17	.03
☐ 58 Jon Matlack	.25	.12	.02
☐ 59 Ron Jackson	.25	.12	.02
☐ 60 Jim Sundberg	.25	.12	.02

1980 Kellogg's

The cards in this 60-card set measure 1 7/8" by 3 1/4". The 1980 Kellogg's 3-D set is quite similar to, but smaller (narrower) than, the other recent Kellogg's issues. Sets could be obtained card by card from cereal boxes or as a set from a box-top offer from the company.

	MINT	EXC	G-VG
COMPLETE SET (60)	27.00	13.50	2.70
COMMON PLAYER (1-60)	.25	.12	.02
☐ 1 Ross Grimsley	.25	.12	.02
☐ 2 Mike Schmidt	5.00	2.50	.50
☐ 3 Mike Flanagan	.35	.17	.03
☐ 4 Ron Guidry	.75	.35	.07
☐ 5 Bert Blyleven	.60	.30	.06
☐ 6 Dave Kingman	.50	.25	.05
☐ 7 Jeff Newman	.25	.12	.02
☐ 8 Steve Rogers	.35	.17	.03
☐ 9 George Brett	4.00	2.00	.40
☐ 10 Bruce Sutter	.50	.25	.05
☐ 11 Gorman Thomas	.35	.17	.03
☐ 12 Darrell Porter	.25	.12	.02
☐ 13 Roy Smalley	.25	.12	.02
☐ 14 Steve Carlton	2.50	1.25	.25
☐ 15 Jim Palmer	2.50	1.25	.25
☐ 16 Bob Bailor	.25	.12	.02
☐ 17 Jason Thompson	.25	.12	.02
☐ 18 Graig Nettles	.35	.17	.03
☐ 19 Ron Cey	.35	.17	.03
☐ 20 Nolan Ryan	6.00	3.00	.60
☐ 21 Ellis Valentine	.25	.12	.02
☐ 22 Larry Hisle	.25	.12	.02
☐ 23 Dave Parker	1.00	.50	.10

☐ 24 Eddie Murray	3.00	1.50	.30
☐ 25 Willie Stargell	1.50	.75	.15
☐ 26 Reggie Jackson	3.50	1.75	.35
☐ 27 Carl Yastrzemski	3.50	1.75	.35
☐ 28 Andre Thornton	.25	.12	.02
☐ 29 Dave Lopes	.35	.17	.03
☐ 30 Ken Singleton	.35	.17	.03
☐ 31 Steve Garvey	2.00	1.00	.20
☐ 32 Dave Winfield	2.00	1.00	.20
☐ 33 Steve Kemp	.35	.17	.03
☐ 34 Claudell Washington	.35	.17	.03
☐ 35 Pete Rose	6.00	3.00	.60
☐ 36 Cesar Cedeno	.35	.17	.03
☐ 37 John Stearns	.25	.12	.02
☐ 38 Lee Mazzilli	.25	.12	.02
☐ 39 Larry Bowa	.35	.17	.03
☐ 40 Fred Lynn	.60	.30	.06
☐ 41 Carlton Fisk	1.50	.75	.15
☐ 42 Vida Blue	.35	.17	.03
☐ 43 Keith Hernandez	1.25	.60	.12
☐ 44 Jim Rice	1.50	.75	.15
☐ 45 Ted Simmons	.50	.25	.05
☐ 46 Chet Lemon	.35	.17	.03
☐ 47 Ferguson Jenkins	1.50	.75	.15
☐ 48 Gary Matthews	.35	.17	.03
☐ 49 Tom Seaver	2.50	1.25	.25
☐ 50 George Foster	.60	.30	.06
☐ 51 Phil Niekro	1.25	.60	.12
☐ 52 Johnny Bench	3.00	1.50	.30
☐ 53 Buddy Bell	.45	.22	.04
☐ 54 Lance Parrish	1.00	.50	.10
☐ 55 Joaquin Andujar	.35	.17	.03
☐ 56 Don Baylor	.35	.17	.03
☐ 57 Jack Clark	1.00	.50	.10
☐ 58 J.R. Richard	.35	.17	.03
☐ 59 Bruce Bochte	.25	.12	.02
☐ 60 Rod Carew	3.00	1.50	.30

1981 Kellogg's

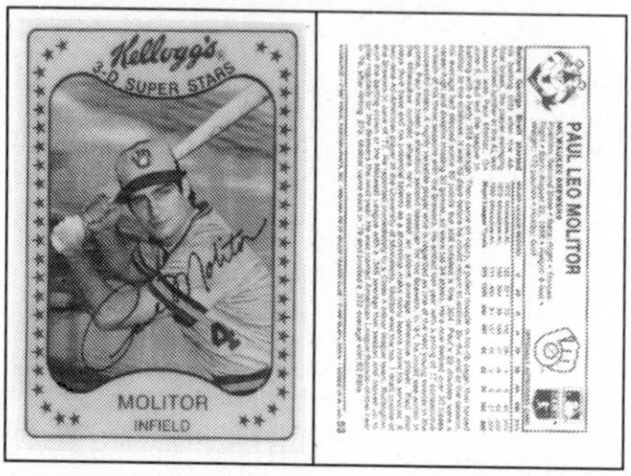

The cards in this 66-card set measure 2 1/2" by 3 1/2". The 1981 Kellogg's set witnessed an increase in both the size of the card and the size of the set. For the first time, cards were not packed in cereal sizes but available only by mail-in procedure. The offer for the card set was advertised on boxes of Kellogg's Corn Flakes. The cards were printed on a different stock than in previous years, presumably to prevent the cracking problem which has plagued all Kellogg's 3-D issues. At the end of the promotion, the remainder of the sets not distributed (to cereal-eaters), were "sold" into the organized hobby, thus creating a situation where the set is relatively plentiful compared to other years of Kellogg's.

	MINT	EXC	G-VG
COMPLETE SET (66)	10.00	5.00	1.00
COMMON PLAYER (1-66)	.10	.05	.01
☐ 1 George Foster	.15	.07	.01
☐ 2 Jim Palmer	.50	.25	.05
☐ 3 Reggie Jackson	1.25	.60	.12
☐ 4 Al Oliver	.10	.05	.01
☐ 5 Mike Schmidt	1.50	.75	.15
☐ 6 Nolan Ryan	2.00	1.00	.20
☐ 7 Bucky Dent	.15	.07	.01
☐ 8 George Brett	1.50	.75	.15
☐ 9 Jim Rice	.30	.15	.03
☐ 10 Steve Garvey	.50	.25	.05
☐ 11 Willie Stargell	.40	.20	.04
☐ 12 Phil Niekro	.30	.15	.03
☐ 13 Dave Parker	.30	.15	.03
☐ 14 Cesar Cedeno	.10	.05	.01
☐ 15 Don Baylor	.15	.07	.01
☐ 16 J.R. Richard	.10	.05	.01
☐ 17 Tony Perez	.20	.10	.02
☐ 18 Eddie Murray	1.00	.50	.10
☐ 19 Chet Lemon	.10	.05	.01
☐ 20 Ben Oglivie	.10	.05	.01
☐ 21 Dave Winfield	.50	.25	.05
☐ 22 Joe Morgan	.50	.25	.05
☐ 23 Vida Blue	.10	.05	.01
☐ 24 Willie Wilson	.15	.07	.01
☐ 25 Steve Henderson	.10	.05	.01
☐ 26 Rod Carew	1.00	.50	.10
☐ 27 Garry Templeton	.10	.05	.01
☐ 28 Dave Concepcion	.10	.05	.01
☐ 29 Dave Lopes	.10	.05	.01
☐ 30 Ken Landreaux	.10	.05	.01
☐ 31 Keith Hernandez	.30	.15	.03
☐ 32 Cecil Cooper	.10	.05	.01
☐ 33 Rickey Henderson	1.50	.75	.15
☐ 34 Frank White	.10	.05	.01
☐ 35 George Hendrick	.10	.05	.01
☐ 36 Reggie Smith	.10	.05	.01
☐ 37 Tug McGraw	.10	.05	.01
☐ 38 Tom Seaver	.75	.35	.07
☐ 39 Ken Singleton	.10	.05	.01
☐ 40 Fred Lynn	.15	.07	.01
☐ 41 Rich Gossage	.10	.05	.01
☐ 42 Terry Puhl	.10	.05	.01
☐ 43 Larry Bowa	.10	.05	.01
☐ 44 Phil Garner	.10	.05	.01
☐ 45 Ron Guidry	.20	.10	.02
☐ 46 Lee Mazzilli	.10	.05	.01
☐ 47 Dave Kingman	.10	.05	.01
☐ 48 Carl Yastrzemski	1.00	.50	.10
☐ 49 Rick Burleson	.10	.05	.01
☐ 50 Steve Carlton	.60	.30	.06
☐ 51 Alan Trammell	.30	.15	.03
☐ 52 Tommy John	.15	.07	.01
☐ 53 Paul Molitor	.25	.12	.02
☐ 54 Joe Charbonneau	.10	.05	.01
☐ 55 Rick Langford	.10	.05	.01
☐ 56 Bruce Sutter	.10	.05	.01
☐ 57 Robin Yount	.90	.45	.09
☐ 58 Steve Stone	.10	.05	.01
☐ 59 Larry Gura	.10	.05	.01
☐ 60 Mike Flanagan	.10	.05	.01
☐ 61 Bob Horner	.15	.07	.01
☐ 62 Bruce Bochte	.10	.05	.01
☐ 63 Pete Rose	1.00	.50	.10
☐ 64 Buddy Bell	.10	.05	.01
☐ 65 Johnny Bench	.90	.45	.09
☐ 66 Mike Hargrove	.10	.05	.01

1982 Kellogg's

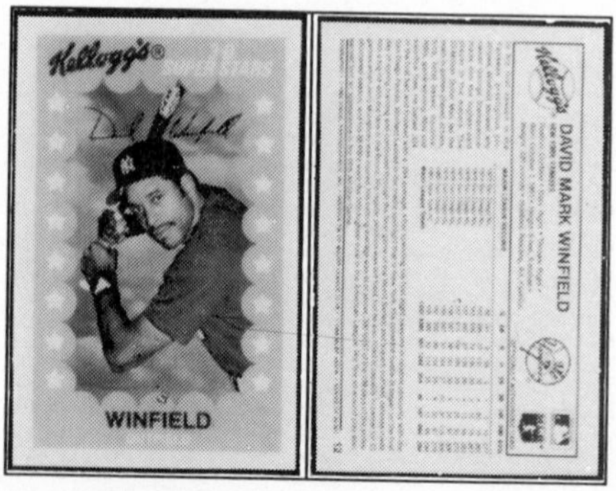

The cards in this 64-card set measure 2 1/8" by 3 1/4". The 1982 version of 3-D cards prepared for the Kellogg Company by Visual Panographics, Inc., is not only smaller in physical dimensions from the 1981 series (which was standard card size at 2 1/2" by 3 1/2") but is also two cards shorter in length (64 in '82 and 66 in '81). In addition, while retaining the policy of not inserting single cards into cereal packages and offering the sets through box-top mail-ins only, the Kellogg Company accepted box tops from four types of cereals, as opposed to only one type the previous year. Each card features a color 3-D ballplayer picture with a vertical line of white stars on each side set upon a blue background. The player's name and the word Kellogg's are printed in red on the obverse, and the card number is found on the bottom right of the reverse. Every card in the set has a statistical procedural error that was never corrected. All seasonal averages were added up and then divided by the number of seasons played

	MINT	EXC	G-VG
COMPLETE SET (64)	16.00	8.00	1.60
COMMON PLAYER (1-64)	.10	.05	.01

	MINT	EXC	G-VG
☐ 1 Richie Zisk	.10	.05	.01
☐ 2 Bill Buckner	.15	.07	.01
☐ 3 George Brett	1.25	.60	.12
☐ 4 Rickey Henderson	1.50	.75	.15
☐ 5 Jack Morris	.15	.07	.01
☐ 6 Ozzie Smith	.50	.25	.05
☐ 7 Rollie Fingers	.15	.07	.01
☐ 8 Tom Seaver	.75	.35	.07
☐ 9 Fernando Valuenzuela	.40	.20	.04
☐ 10 Hubie Brooks	.15	.07	.01
☐ 11 Nolan Ryan	1.50	.75	.15
☐ 12 Dave Winfield	.35	.17	.03
☐ 13 Bob Horner	.20	.10	.02
☐ 14 Reggie Jackson	1.00	.50	.10
☐ 15 Burt Hooton	.10	.05	.01
☐ 16 Mike Schmidt	1.25	.60	.12
☐ 17 Bruce Sutter	.15	.07	.01
☐ 18 Pete Rose	1.00	.50	.10
☐ 19 Dave Kingman	.15	.07	.01
☐ 20 Neil Allen	.10	.05	.01
☐ 21 Don Sutton	.30	.15	.03
☐ 22 Dave Concepcion	.15	.07	.01
☐ 23 Keith Hernandez	.25	.12	.02
☐ 24 Gary Carter	.35	.17	.03
☐ 25 Carlton Fisk	.40	.20	.04
☐ 26 Ron Guidry	.20	.10	.02
☐ 27 Steve Carlton	.40	.20	.04
☐ 28 Robin Yount	.75	.35	.07
☐ 29 John Castino	.10	.05	.01
☐ 30 Johnny Bench	.75	.35	.07
☐ 31 Bob Knepper	.10	.05	.01
☐ 32 Rich Gossage	.15	.07	.01
☐ 33 Buddy Bell	.15	.07	.01
☐ 34 Art Howe	.15	.07	.01
☐ 35 Tony Armas	.15	.07	.01
☐ 36 Phil Niekro	.25	.12	.02
☐ 37 Len Barker	.10	.05	.01
☐ 38 Bob Grich	.15	.07	.01
☐ 39 Steve Kemp	.10	.05	.01
☐ 40 Kirk Gibson	.40	.20	.04
☐ 41 Carney Lansford	.25	.12	.02
☐ 42 Jim Palmer	.45	.22	.04
☐ 43 Carl Yastrzemski	1.00	.50	.10
☐ 44 Rick Burleson	.10	.05	.01
☐ 45 Dwight Evans	.20	.10	.02
☐ 46 Ron Cey	.15	.07	.01
☐ 47 Steve Garvey	.45	.22	.04
☐ 48 Dave Parker	.25	.12	.02
☐ 49 Mike Easler	.10	.05	.01
☐ 50 Dusty Baker	.10	.05	.01
☐ 51 Rod Carew	.75	.35	.07
☐ 52 Chris Chambliss	.15	.07	.01
☐ 53 Tim Raines	.40	.20	.04
☐ 54 Chet Lemon	.10	.05	.01
☐ 55 Bill Madlock	.15	.07	.01
☐ 56 George Foster	.15	.07	.01
☐ 57 Dwayne Murphy	.10	.05	.01
☐ 58 Ken Singleton	.15	.07	.01
☐ 59 Mike Norris	.10	.05	.01
☐ 60 Cecil Cooper	.15	.07	.01
☐ 61 Al Oliver	.15	.07	.01
☐ 62 Willie Wilson	.15	.07	.01
☐ 63 Vida Blue	.15	.07	.01
☐ 64 Eddie Murray	.75	.35	.07

1983 Kellogg's

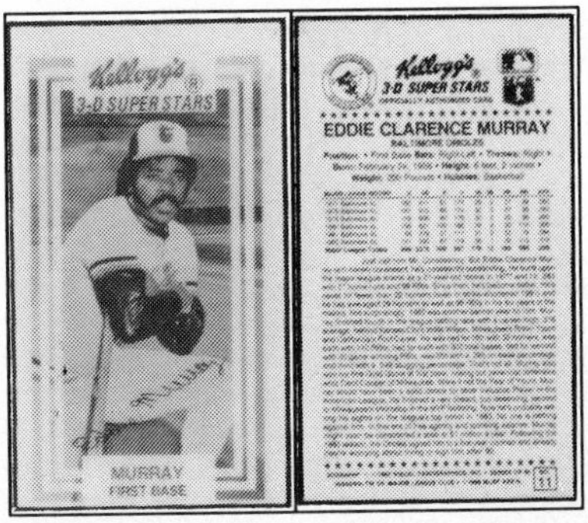

The cards in this 60-card set measure 1 7/8" by 3 1/4". For the 14th year in a row, the Kellogg Company issued a card set of Major League players. The set of 3-D cards contains the photo, player's autograph, Kellogg's logo, and name and position of the player on the front of the card. The backs feature the player's team logo, career statistics, player biography, and a narrative on the player's career.

	MINT	EXC	G-VG
COMPLETE SET (60)	16.00	8.00	1.60
COMMON PLAYER (1-60)	.10	.05	.01

	MINT	EXC	G-VG
☐ 1 Rod Carew	.75	.35	.07
☐ 2 Rollie Fingers	.35	.17	.03
☐ 3 Reggie Jackson	1.00	.50	.10
☐ 4 George Brett	1.25	.60	.12
☐ 5 Hal McRae	.15	.07	.01
☐ 6 Pete Rose	1.00	.50	.10
☐ 7 Fernando Valenzuela	.35	.17	.03
☐ 8 Rickey Henderson	1.50	.75	.15
☐ 9 Carl Yastrzemski	1.00	.50	.10
☐ 10 Rich Gossage	.15	.07	.01
☐ 11 Eddie Murray	.75	.35	.07
☐ 12 Buddy Bell	.15	.07	.01
☐ 13 Jim Rice	.30	.15	.03
☐ 14 Robin Yount	.75	.35	.07
☐ 15 Dave Winfield	.35	.17	.03
☐ 16 Harold Baines	.20	.10	.02
☐ 17 Garry Templeton	.10	.05	.01
☐ 18 Bill Madlock	.15	.07	.01
☐ 19 Pete Vuckovich	.10	.05	.01
☐ 20 Pedro Guerrero	.20	.10	.02
☐ 21 Ozzie Smith	.35	.17	.03
☐ 22 George Foster	.15	.07	.01
☐ 23 Willie Wilson	.15	.07	.01
☐ 24 Johnny Ray	.10	.05	.01
☐ 25 George Hendrick	.10	.05	.01
☐ 26 Andre Thornton	.10	.05	.01
☐ 27 Leon Durham	.10	.05	.01
☐ 28 Cecil Cooper	.15	.07	.01
☐ 29 Don Baylor	.15	.07	.01
☐ 30 Lonnie Smith	.15	.07	.01
☐ 31 Nolan Ryan	1.50	.75	.15
☐ 32 Dan Quisenberry	.15	.07	.01
☐ 33 Len Barker	.10	.05	.01
☐ 34 Neil Allen	.10	.05	.01
☐ 35 Jack Morris	.20	.10	.02
☐ 36 Dave Stieb	.20	.10	.02
☐ 37 Bruce Sutter	.15	.07	.01
☐ 38 Jim Sundberg	.10	.05	.01
☐ 39 Jim Palmer	.60	.30	.06
☐ 40 Lance Parrish	.25	.12	.02
☐ 41 Floyd Bannister	.10	.05	.01
☐ 42 Larry Gura	.10	.05	.01
☐ 43 Britt Burns	.10	.05	.01
☐ 44 Toby Harrah	.10	.05	.01
☐ 45 Steve Carlton	.50	.25	.05
☐ 46 Greg Minton	.10	.05	.01
☐ 47 Gorman Thomas	.15	.07	.01
☐ 48 Jack Clark	.25	.12	.02
☐ 49 Keith Hernandez	.25	.12	.02
☐ 50 Greg Luzinski	.15	.07	.01
☐ 51 Fred Lynn	.15	.07	.01
☐ 52 Dale Murphy	.75	.35	.07
☐ 53 Kent Hrbek	.35	.17	.03
☐ 54 Bob Horner	.20	.10	.02

□ 55 Gary Carter	.35	.17	.03
□ 56 Carlton Fisk	.40	.20	.04
□ 57 Dave Concepcion	.15	.07	.01
□ 58 Mike Schmidt	1.50	.75	.15
□ 59 Bill Buckner	.15	.07	.01
□ 60 Bob Grich	.15	.07	.01

1982 K-Mart

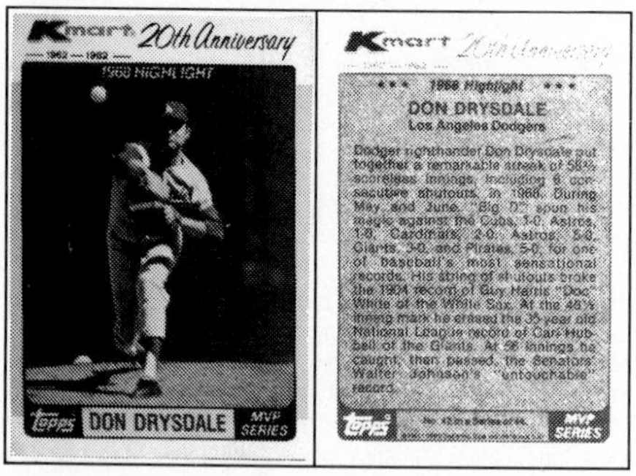

The cards in this 44-card set measure 2 1/2" by 3 1/2". This set was produced by Topps for K Mart's 20th Anniversary Celebration. The set features Topps cards of National and American League MVP's from 1962 through 1981. The backs highlight individual MVP winning performances. The dual National League MVP winners of 1979 and special cards commemorating the accomplishments of Drysdale (scoreless consecutive innings pitched streak), Aaron (home run record), and Rose (National League most hits lifetime record) round out the set. The 1975 Fred Lynn card is an original construction from the multi-player "Rookie Outfielders" card of Lynn of 1975. The Maury Wills card number 2, similarly, was created after the fact as Maury was not originally included in the 1962 Topps set. The set was "Mass" produced for K-Mart distribution as a complete set in a box. Some collectors consider this to be one of the most plentiful sets ever produced.

	MINT	EXC	G-VG
COMPLETE SET (44)	1.25	.60	.12
COMMON PLAYER (1-44)	.02	.01	.00
□ 1 Mickey Mantle: 62AL	.25	.12	.02
□ 2 Maury Wills: 62NL	.02	.01	.00
□ 3 Elston Howard: 63AL	.02	.01	.00
□ 4 Sandy Koufax: 63NL	.07	.03	.01
□ 5 Brooks Robinson: 64AL	.05	.02	.00
□ 6 Ken Boyer: 64NL	.02	.01	.00
□ 7 Zoilo Versalles: 65AL	.02	.01	.00
□ 8 Willie Mays: 65NL	.10	.05	.01
□ 9 Frank Robinson: 66AL	.04	.02	.00
□ 10 Bob Clemente: 66NL	.08	.04	.01
□ 11 Carl Yastrzemski: 67AL	.10	.05	.01
□ 12 Orlando Cepeda: 67NL	.02	.01	.00
□ 13 Denny McLain: 68AL	.02	.01	.00
□ 14 Bob Gibson: 68NL	.04	.02	.00
□ 15 Harmon Killebrew: 69AL	.03	.01	.00
□ 16 Willie McCovey: 69NL	.04	.02	.00
□ 17 Boog Powell: 70AL	.02	.01	.00
□ 18 Johnny Bench: 70NL	.07	.03	.01
□ 19 Vida Blue: 71AL	.02	.01	.00
□ 20 Joe Torre: 71NL	.02	.01	.00
□ 21 Rich Allen: 72AL	.02	.01	.00
□ 22 Johnny Bench: 72NL	.07	.03	.01
□ 23 Reggie Jackson: 73AL	.07	.03	.01
□ 24 Pete Rose: 73NL	.08	.04	.01
□ 25 Jeff Burroughs: 74AL	.02	.01	.00
□ 26 Steve Garvey: 74NL	.04	.02	.00
□ 27 Fred Lynn: 75AL	.02	.01	.00
□ 28 Joe Morgan: 75NL	.03	.01	.00
□ 29 Thurman Munson: 76AL	.05	.02	.00
□ 30 Joe Morgan: 76NL	.03	.01	.00
□ 31 Rod Carew: 77AL	.05	.02	.00
□ 32 George Foster: 77NL	.02	.01	.00
□ 33 Jim Rice: 78AL	.02	.01	.00
□ 34 Dave Parker: 78NL	.02	.01	.00
□ 35 Don Baylor: 79AL	.02	.01	.00
□ 36 Keith Hernandez: 79NL	.02	.01	.00
□ 37 Willie Stargell: 79NL	.04	.02	.00
□ 38 George Brett: 80AL	.06	.03	.00
□ 39 Mike Schmidt: 80NL	.08	.04	.01
□ 40 Rollie Fingers: 81AL	.02	.01	.00
□ 41 Mike Schmidt: 81NL	.08	.04	.01
□ 42 '68 HL: Don Drysdale (scoreless innings)	.03	.01	.00
□ 43 '74 HL: Hank Aaron (home run record)	.10	.05	.01
□ 44 '81 HL: Pete Rose (NL most hits)	.10	.05	.01

1987 K-Mart

Topps produced this 33-card boxed set for K-Mart. The set celebrates K-Mart's 25th anniversary and is subtitled, "Stars of the Decades." Card fronts feature a color photo of the player oriented diagonally. Cards measure 2 1/2" by 3 1/2" and are numbered on the back. Card backs provide statistics for the player's best decade.

	MINT	EXC	G-VG
COMPLETE SET (33)	4.50	2.25	.45
COMMON PLAYER (1-33)	.10	.05	.01
□ 1 Hank Aaron	.40	.20	.04
□ 2 Roberto Clemente	.35	.17	.03
□ 3 Bob Gibson	.15	.07	.01
□ 4 Harmon Killebrew	.15	.07	.01
□ 5 Mickey Mantle	1.00	.50	.10
□ 6 Juan Marichal	.15	.07	.01
□ 7 Roger Maris	.30	.15	.03
□ 8 Willie Mays	.40	.20	.04
□ 9 Brooks Robinson	.20	.10	.02
□ 10 Frank Robinson	.15	.07	.01
□ 11 Carl Yastrzemski	.35	.17	.03
□ 12 Johnny Bench	.25	.12	.02
□ 13 Lou Brock	.20	.10	.02
□ 14 Rod Carew	.25	.12	.02
□ 15 Steve Carlton	.25	.12	.02
□ 16 Reggie Jackson	.35	.17	.03
□ 17 Jim Palmer	.20	.10	.02
□ 18 Jim Rice	.10	.05	.01
□ 19 Pete Rose	.50	.25	.05
□ 20 Nolan Ryan	1.00	.50	.10
□ 21 Tom Seaver	.30	.15	.03
□ 22 Willie Stargell	.15	.07	.01
□ 23 Wade Boggs	.40	.20	.04
□ 24 George Brett	.35	.17	.03
□ 25 Gary Carter	.15	.07	.01
□ 26 Dwight Gooden	.35	.17	.03
□ 27 Rickey Henderson	.50	.25	.05
□ 28 Don Mattingly	.75	.35	.07
□ 29 Dale Murphy	.25	.12	.02
□ 30 Eddie Murray	.25	.12	.02
□ 31 Mike Schmidt	.50	.25	.05
□ 32 Darryl Strawberry	.35	.17	.03
□ 33 Fernando Valenzuela	.15	.07	.01

1988 K-Mart Moments

Topps produced this 33-card boxed set exclusively for K-Mart. The set is subtitled, "Memorable Moments." Card fronts feature a color photo of the player with the K-Mart logo in lower right corner. Cards measure 2 1/2" by 3 1/2" and are numbered on the back. Card backs provide details for that player's "memorable moment." The set is packaged in a bright yellow and green box with a checklist on the back panel of the box.

	MINT	EXC	G-VG
COMPLETE SET (33)	4.50	2.25	.45
COMMON PLAYER (1-33)	.10	.05	.01
☐ 1 George Bell	.15	.07	.01
☐ 2 Wade Boggs	.50	.25	.05
☐ 3 George Brett	.40	.20	.04
☐ 4 Jose Canseco	1.00	.50	.10
☐ 5 Jack Clark	.15	.07	.01
☐ 6 Will Clark	.90	.45	.09
☐ 7 Roger Clemens	.40	.20	.04
☐ 8 Vince Coleman	.25	.12	.02
☐ 9 Andre Dawson	.25	.12	.02
☐ 10 Dwight Gooden	.30	.15	.03
☐ 11 Pedro Guerrero	.15	.07	.01
☐ 12 Tony Gywnn	.30	.15	.03
☐ 13 Rickey Henderson	.75	.35	.07
☐ 14 Keith Hernandez	.20	.10	.02
☐ 15 Don Mattingly	1.00	.50	.10
☐ 16 Mark McGwire	.60	.30	.06
☐ 17 Paul Molitor	.15	.07	.01
☐ 18 Dale Murphy	.30	.15	.03
☐ 19 Tim Raines	.20	.10	.02
☐ 20 Dave Righetti	.15	.07	.01
☐ 21 Cal Ripken	.30	.15	.03
☐ 22 Pete Rose	.60	.30	.06
☐ 23 Nolan Ryan	1.00	.50	.10
☐ 24 Benny Santiago	.25	.12	.02
☐ 25 Mike Schmidt	.75	.35	.07
☐ 26 Mike Scott	.15	.07	.01
☐ 27 Kevin Seitzer	.20	.10	.02
☐ 28 Ozzie Smith	.20	.10	.02
☐ 29 Darryl Strawberry	.45	.22	.04
☐ 30 Rick Sutcliffe	.10	.05	.01
☐ 31 Fernando Valenzuela	.15	.07	.01
☐ 32 Todd Worrell	.10	.05	.01
☐ 33 Robin Yount	.45	.22	.04

1989 K-Mart Batting Leaders

The 1989 K-Mart Career Batting Leaders set contains 22 standard-size (2 1/2 by 3 1/2 inch) glossy cards. The fronts are bright red. The set depicts the 22 veterans with the highest lifetime batting averages. The cards were distributed one per Topps blister pack. These blister packs were sold exclusively through K-Mart stores.

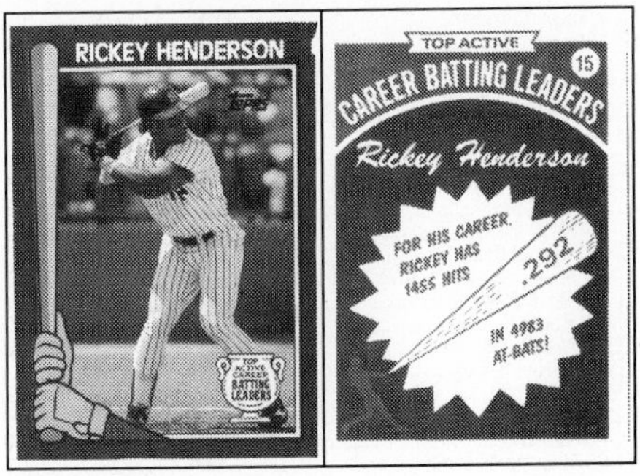

	MINT	EXC	G-VG
COMPLETE SET (22)	6.00	3.00	.60
COMMON PLAYER (1-22)	.20	.10	.02
☐ 1 Wade Boggs	.60	.30	.06
☐ 2 Tony Gwynn	.35	.17	.03
☐ 3 Don Mattingly	1.00	.50	.10
☐ 4 Kirby Puckett	.50	.25	.05
☐ 5 George Brett	.40	.20	.04
☐ 6 Pedro Guerrero	.30	.15	.03
☐ 7 Tim Raines	.30	.15	.03
☐ 8 Keith Hernandez	.25	.12	.02
☐ 9 Jim Rice	.30	.15	.03
☐ 10 Paul Molitor	.25	.12	.02
☐ 11 Eddie Murray	.35	.17	.03
☐ 12 Willie McGee	.25	.12	.02
☐ 13 Dave Parker	.25	.12	.02
☐ 14 Julio Franco	.20	.10	.02
☐ 15 Rickey Henderson	.75	.35	.07
☐ 16 Kent Hrbek	.25	.12	.02
☐ 17 Willie Wilson	.20	.10	.02
☐ 18 Johnny Ray	.20	.10	.02
☐ 19 Pat Tabler	.20	.10	.02
☐ 20 Carney Lansford	.25	.12	.02
☐ 21 Robin Yount	.50	.25	.05
☐ 22 Alan Trammell	.25	.12	.02

1989 K-Mart Dream Team

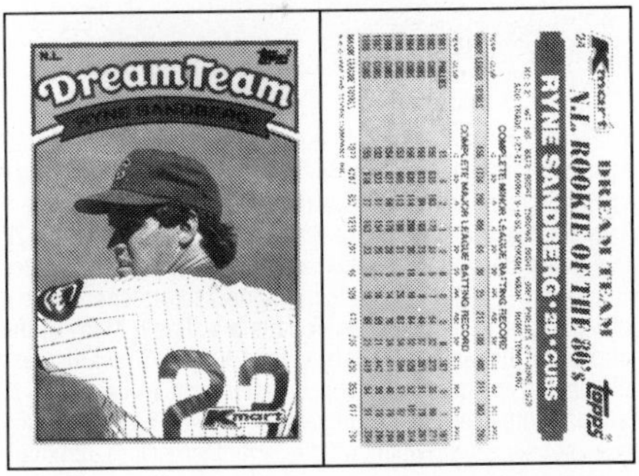

The 1989 K-Mart Dream Team set contains 33 standard-size (2 1/2" by 3 1/2") glossy cards. The fronts are blue. The cards were distributed as a boxed set through K-Mart stores. The set features 11 major league rookies of 1988 plus 11 "American League Rookies of the '80s" and 11 "National League Rookies of the '80s". The complete subject list for the set is provided on the back panel of the custom box.

	MINT	EXC	G-VG
COMPLETE SET (33)	4.00	2.00	.40
COMMON PLAYER (1-33)	.10	.05	.01
☐ 1 Mark Grace	.75	.35	.07
☐ 2 Ron Gant	.50	.25	.05
☐ 3 Chris Sabo	.50	.25	.05
☐ 4 Walt Weiss	.20	.10	.02
☐ 5 Jay Buhner	.20	.10	.02
☐ 6 Cecil Espy	.10	.05	.01

☐ 7 Dave Gallagher	.10	.05	.01
☐ 8 Damon Berryhill	.20	.10	.02
☐ 9 Tim Belcher	.15	.07	.01
☐ 10 Paul Gibson	.10	.05	.01
☐ 11 Gregg Jefferies	.75	.35	.07
☐ 12 Don Mattingly	1.00	.50	.10
☐ 13 Harold Reynolds	.10	.05	.01
☐ 14 Wade Boggs	.50	.25	.05
☐ 15 Cal Ripken	.35	.17	.03
☐ 16 Kirby Puckett	.45	.22	.04
☐ 17 George Bell	.20	.10	.02
☐ 18 Jose Canseco	1.00	.50	.10
☐ 19 Terry Steinbach	.15	.07	.01
☐ 20 Roger Clemens	.50	.25	.05
☐ 21 Mark Langston	.20	.10	.02
☐ 22 Harold Baines	.15	.07	.01
☐ 23 Will Clark	.75	.35	.07
☐ 24 Ryne Sandberg	.65	.30	.06
☐ 25 Tim Wallach	.15	.07	.01
☐ 26 Shawon Dunston	.15	.07	.01
☐ 27 Tim Raines	.20	.10	.02
☐ 28 Darryl Strawberry	.40	.20	.04
☐ 29 Tony Gwynn	.30	.15	.03
☐ 30 Tony Pena	.10	.05	.01
☐ 31 Dwight Gooden	.30	.15	.03
☐ 32 Fernando Valenzuela	.20	.10	.02
☐ 33 Pedro Guerrero	.15	.07	.01

1990 K-Mart Batting Leaders

The 1990 K-Mart Career Batting Leaders set contains 22 standard-size (2 1/2 by 3 1/2 inch) cards. The front borders are emerald green, and the backs are white, blue and evergreen. This set, like the 1989 set of the same name, depicts the 22 major leaguers with the highest lifetime batting averages (minimum 765 games). The card numbers correspond to the player's rank in terms of career batting average. Many of the photos are the same as those from the 1989 set. The cards were distributed one per special Topps blister pack available only at K-Mart stores and were produced by Topps. The K-Mart logo does not appear anywhere on the cards themselves, although there is a Topps logo on the front and back of each card.

	MINT	EXC	G-VG
COMPLETE SET (22)	6.00	3.00	.60
COMMON PLAYER (1-22)	.20	.10	.02
☐ 1 Wade Boggs	.60	.30	.06
☐ 2 Tony Gwynn	.35	.17	.03
☐ 3 Kirby Puckett	.50	.25	.05
☐ 4 Don Mattingly	1.00	.50	.10
☐ 5 George Brett	.40	.20	.04
☐ 6 Pedro Guerrero	.25	.12	.02
☐ 7 Tim Raines	.25	.12	.02
☐ 8 Paul Molitor	.25	.12	.02
☐ 9 Jim Rice	.25	.12	.02
☐ 10 Keith Hernandez	.25	.12	.02
☐ 11 Julio Franco	.20	.10	.02
☐ 12 Carney Lansford	.25	.12	.02
☐ 13 Dave Parker	.25	.12	.02
☐ 14 Willie McGee	.25	.12	.02
☐ 15 Robin Yount	.50	.25	.05
☐ 16 Tony Fernandez	.20	.10	.02
☐ 17 Eddie Murray	.30	.15	.03
☐ 18 Johnny Ray	.20	.10	.02
☐ 19 Lonnie Smith	.20	.10	.02
☐ 20 Phil Bradley	.20	.10	.02
☐ 21 Rickey Henderson	.75	.35	.07
☐ 22 Kent Hrbek	.25	.12	.02

1990 K-Mart Superstars

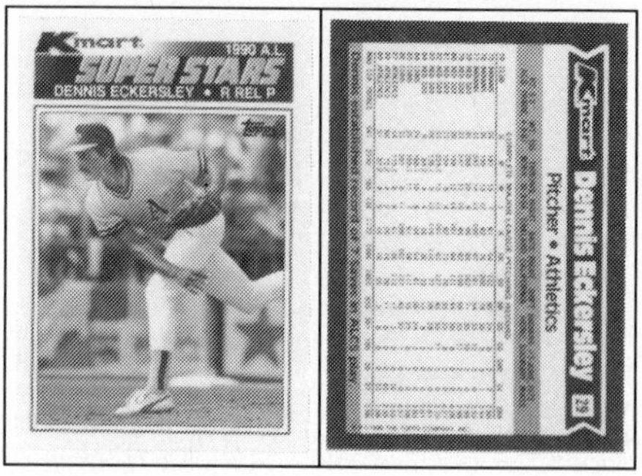

The 1990 K-Mart Superstars set is a 33-card, standard-size (2 1/2" by 3 1/2") set issued for the K-Mart chain by the Topps Company. This set was issued with a piece of gum in the custom set box.

	MINT	EXC	G-VG
COMPLETE SET (33)	4.00	2.00	.40
COMMON PLAYER (1-33)	.10	.05	.01
☐ 1 Will Clark	.75	.35	.07
☐ 2 Ryne Sandberg	.75	.35	.07
☐ 3 Howard Johnson	.20	.10	.02
☐ 4 Ozzie Smith	.20	.10	.02
☐ 5 Tony Gwynn	.30	.15	.03
☐ 6 Kevin Mitchell	.30	.15	.03
☐ 7 Jerome Walton	.30	.15	.03
☐ 8 Craig Biggio	.15	.07	.01
☐ 9 Mike Scott	.15	.07	.01
☐ 10 Doc Gooden	.30	.15	.03
☐ 11 Sid Fernandez	.15	.07	.01
☐ 12 Joe Magrane	.10	.05	.01
☐ 13 Jay Howell	.10	.05	.01
☐ 14 Mark Davis	.15	.07	.01
☐ 15 Pedro Guerrero	.15	.07	.01
☐ 16 Glenn Davis	.15	.07	.01
☐ 17 Don Mattingly	1.00	.50	.10
☐ 18 Julio Franco	.15	.07	.01
☐ 19 Wade Boggs	.50	.25	.05
☐ 20 Cal Ripken	.30	.15	.03
☐ 21 Jose Canseco	1.00	.50	.10
☐ 22 Kirby Puckett	.40	.20	.04
☐ 23 Rickey Henderson	.75	.35	.07
☐ 24 Mickey Tettleton	.10	.05	.01
☐ 25 Nolan Ryan	1.00	.50	.10
☐ 26 Bret Saberhagen	.20	.10	.02
☐ 27 Jeff Ballard	.10	.05	.01
☐ 28 Chuck Finley	.15	.07	.01
☐ 29 Dennis Eckersley	.20	.10	.02
☐ 30 Dan Plesac	.10	.05	.01
☐ 31 Fred McGriff	.20	.10	.02
☐ 32 Mark McGwire	.60	.30	.06
☐ 33 Tony LaRussa MG and Roger Craig MG	.10	.05	.01

1988 Kodak White Sox

This five-card, approximately 8" by 11 1/2" set was issued by Kodak including members of the 1988 Chicago White Sox. The cards are borderless and say "1988 Kodak Collectible Series" on top with the player's photo dominating the middle of the photo. Underneath the photo is a facsimile autograph and on the bottom left of the photo is an advertisment for Kodak and the bottom right of the card the White Sox logo is featured. The backs are blank.

	MINT	EXC	G-VG
COMPLETE SET (5)	7.50	3.75	.75
COMMON PLAYER (1-5)	1.00	.50	.10
☐ 1 Ozzie Guillen	2.00	1.00	.20
☐ 2 Carlton Fisk	3.00	1.50	.30
☐ 3 Rick Horton	1.00	.50	.10
☐ 4 Ivan Calderon	1.50	.75	.15
☐ 5 Harold Baines	2.00	1.00	.20

1989 Kodak White Sox

For the second consecutive year Kodak in conjunction with the Chicago White Sox isued a set about the White Sox. The 1989 set was marked by a color photo of the active star dominating the upper right half of the card and the bottom half of the card was another famous player at the same position that the current star played. This six-card approximately 8" by 11 1/2" set was given away at various games at Comiskey Park.

	MINT	EXC	G-VG
COMPLETE SET (6)	7.50	3.75	.75
COMMON PLAYER (1-6)	1.00	.50	.10
☐ 1 Greg Walker Dick Allen Ted Kluszewski	1.50	.75	.15
☐ 2 Steve Lyons Eddie Collins Nellie Fox	1.50	.75	.15
☐ 3 Carlton Fisk Sherm Lollar Ray Schalk	3.00	1.50	.30
☐ 4 Harold Baines Minnie Minoso Jim Landis	1.50	.75	.15
☐ 5 Bobby Thigpen Gerry Staley Hoyt Wilhelm	1.00	.50	.10
☐ 6 Ozzie Guillen Luke Appling Luis Aparicio	2.00	1.00	.20

1990 Kodak White Sox

In 1990 Kodak again in conjunction with the Chicago White Sox issued a beautiful six-card set about some key members of the 1990 White Sox. This was slightly reduced in size (from the previous two years) to be approximately 7" by 11" and featured a full-color picture with an advertisement for Kodak on the lower left corner of the front of the card and the White Sox logo in the lower right hand corner. The cards were again borderless and blank-backed.

	MINT	EXC	G-VG
COMPLETE SET (6)	6.00	3.00	.60
COMMON PLAYER (1-6)	1.00	.50	.10
☐ 1 Carlton Fisk	2.50	1.25	.25
☐ 2 Melido Perez	1.25	.60	.12
☐ 3 Ozzie Guillen	1.75	.85	.17
☐ 4 Ron Kittle	1.25	.60	.12
☐ 5 Scott Fletcher	1.00	.50	.10
☐ 6 Comiskey Park	1.00	.50	.10

1960 Lake to Lake

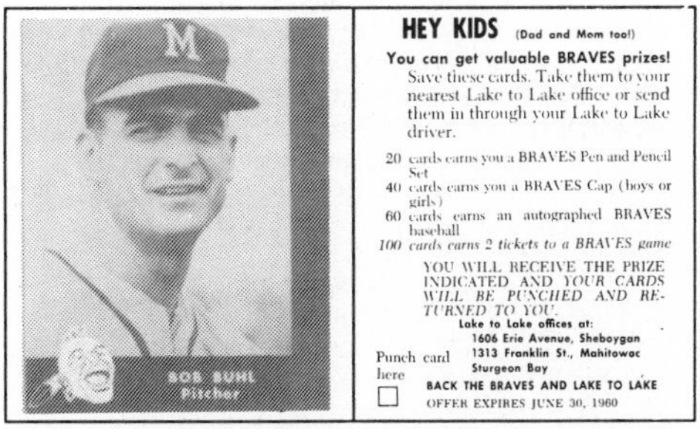

The cards in this 28-card set measure 2 1/2" by 3 1/4". The 1960 Lake to Lake set of unnumbered, blue tinted cards features Milwaukee Braves players only. For some reason, this set of Braves does not include Eddie Mathews. The cards were issued on milk cartons by Lake to Lake Dairy. Most cards have staple holes in the upper right corner. The backs are in red and give details and prizes associated with the card promotion. Cards with staple holes can be considered very good to excellent at best. The catalog designation for this set is F102-1.

	NRMT	VG-E	GOOD
COMPLETE SET (28)	1050.00	500.00	120.00
COMMON PLAYER (1-28)	12.50	6.25	1.25
☐ 1 Hank Aaron	300.00	150.00	30.00
☐ 2 Joe Adcock	16.00	8.00	1.60

☐ 3 Ray Boone	125.00	60.00	12.50
☐ 4 Bill Bruton	250.00	125.00	25.00
☐ 5 Bob Buhl	12.50	6.25	1.25
☐ 6 Lew Burdette	18.00	9.00	1.80
☐ 7 Chuck Cottier	12.50	6.25	1.25
☐ 8 Wes Covington	12.50	6.25	1.25
☐ 9 Del Crandall	14.00	7.00	1.40
☐ 10 Chuck Dressen	12.50	6.25	1.25
☐ 11 Bob Giggie	12.50	6.25	1.25
☐ 12 Joey Jay	12.50	6.25	1.25
☐ 13 Johnny Logan	14.00	7.00	1.40
☐ 14 Felix Mantilla	12.50	6.25	1.25
☐ 15 Lee Maye	12.50	6.25	1.25
☐ 16 Don McMahon	12.50	6.25	1.25
☐ 17 George Myatt CO	12.50	6.25	1.25
☐ 18 Andy Pafko	12.50	6.25	1.25
☐ 19 Juan Pizarro	12.50	6.25	1.25
☐ 20 Mel Roach	12.50	6.25	1.25
☐ 21 Bob Rush	12.50	6.25	1.25
☐ 22 Bob Scheffing	12.50	6.25	1.25
☐ 23 Red Schoendienst	45.00	22.50	4.50
☐ 24 Warren Spahn	60.00	30.00	6.00
☐ 25 Al Spangler	12.50	6.25	1.25
☐ 26 Frank Torre	12.50	6.25	1.25
☐ 27 Carlton Willey	12.50	6.25	1.25
☐ 28 Whit Wyatt CO	12.50	6.25	1.25

1968 Laughlin World Series

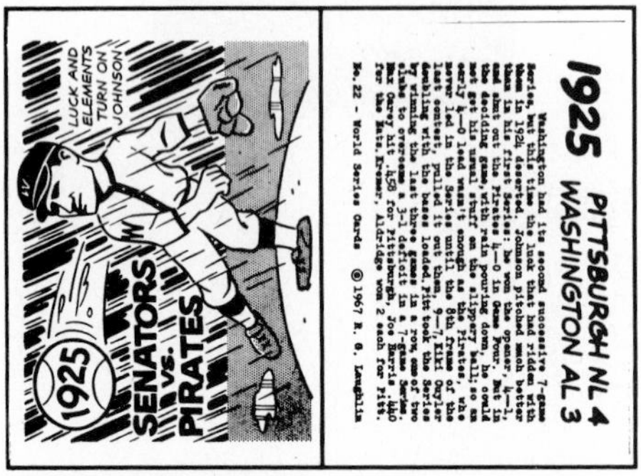

This set of 64 cards was apparently a limited test issue by sports artist R.G. Laughlin for the World Series set concept that was mass marketed by Fleer two and three years later. The cards are slightly oversized, 2 3/4" by 3 1/2" and are black and white on the front and red and white on the back. All the years are represented except for 1904 when no World Series was played. In the list below, the winning series team is listed first.

	NRMT	VG-E	GOOD
COMPLETE SET (64)	65.00	30.00	6.00
COMMON PLAYER (1-64)	1.00	.50	.10
☐ 1 1903 Red Sox/Pirates	1.00	.50	.10
☐ 2 1905 Giants/A's (Christy Mathewson)	1.25	.60	.12
☐ 3 1906 White Sox/Cubs	1.00	.50	.10
☐ 4 1907 Cubs/Tigers	1.00	.50	.10
☐ 5 1908 Cubs/Tigers (Tinker/Evers/Chance)	1.25	.60	.12
☐ 6 1909 Pirates/Tigers (Wagner/Cobb)	2.00	1.00	.20
☐ 7 1910 A's/Cubs	1.00	.50	.10
☐ 8 1911 A's/Giants (John McGraw)	1.25	.60	.12
☐ 9 1912 Red Sox/Giants	1.00	.50	.10
☐ 10 1913 A's/Giants	1.00	.50	.10
☐ 11 1914 Braves/A's	1.00	.50	.10
☐ 12 1915 Red Sox/Phillies (Babe Ruth)	2.50	1.25	.25
☐ 13 1916 Red Sox/Dodgers (Babe Ruth)	2.50	1.25	.25
☐ 14 1917 White Sox/Giants	1.00	.50	.10
☐ 15 1918 Red Sox/Cubs	1.00	.50	.10
☐ 16 1919 Reds/White Sox	1.00	.50	.10
☐ 17 1920 Indians/Dodgers	1.00	.50	.10
☐ 18 1921 Giants/Yankees (Waite Hoyt)	1.00	.50	.10
☐ 19 1922 Giants/Yankees (Frisch/Groh)	1.00	.50	.10
☐ 20 1923 Yankees/Giants (Babe Ruth)	2.50	1.25	.25
☐ 21 1924 Senators/Giants	1.00	.50	.10
☐ 22 1925 Pirates/Senators (Walter Johnson)	1.50	.75	.15
☐ 23 1926 Cardinals/Yankees (Alexander/Lazzeri)	1.25	.60	.12
☐ 24 1927 Yankees/Pirates	1.00	.50	.10
☐ 25 1928 Yankees/Cardinals (Ruth/Gehrig)	2.50	1.25	.25
☐ 26 1929 A's/Cubs	1.00	.50	.10
☐ 27 1930 A's/Cardinals	1.00	.50	.10
☐ 28 1931 Cardinals/A's (Pepper Martin)	1.00	.50	.10
☐ 29 1932 Yankees/Cubs (Babe Ruth)	2.50	1.25	.25
☐ 30 1933 Giants/Senators (Mel Ott)	1.50	.75	.15
☐ 31 1934 Cardinals/Tigers (Dizzy/Paul Dean)	1.50	.75	.15
☐ 32 1935 Tigers/Cubs	1.00	.50	.10
☐ 33 1936 Yankees/Giants	1.00	.50	.10
☐ 34 1937 Yankees/Giants (Carl Hubbell)	1.25	.60	.12
☐ 35 1938 Yankees/Cubs	1.00	.50	.10
☐ 36 1939 Yankees/Reds (Joe DiMaggio)	2.00	1.00	.20
☐ 37 1940 Reds/Tigers	1.00	.50	.10
☐ 38 1941 Yankees/Dodgers (Mickey Owen)	1.00	.50	.10
☐ 39 1942 Cardinals/Yankees	1.00	.50	.10
☐ 40 1943 Yankees/Cardinals (Joe McCarthy)	1.00	.50	.10
☐ 41 1944 Cardinals/Browns	1.00	.50	.10
☐ 42 1945 Tigers/Cubs (Hank Greenberg)	1.50	.75	.15
☐ 43 1946 Cardinals/Red Sox (Enos Slaughter)	1.25	.60	.12
☐ 44 1947 Yankees/Dodgers (Al Gionfriddo)	1.00	.50	.10
☐ 45 1948 Indians/Braves (Bob Feller)	1.50	.75	.15
☐ 46 1949 Yankees/Dodgers (Reynolds/Roe)	1.00	.50	.10
☐ 47 1950 Yankees/Phillies	1.00	.50	.10
☐ 48 1951 Yankees/Giants	1.00	.50	.10
☐ 49 1952 Yankees/Dodgers (Mize/Snider)	1.50	.75	.15
☐ 50 1953 Yankees/Dodgers (Casey Stengel)	1.50	.75	.15
☐ 51 1954 Giants/Indians (Dusty Rhodes)	1.00	.50	.10
☐ 52 1955 Dodgers/Yankees (Johnny Podres)	1.00	.50	.10
☐ 53 1956 Yankees/Dodgers (Don Larsen)	1.25	.60	.12
☐ 54 1957 Braves/Yankees (Lew Burdette)	1.00	.50	.10
☐ 55 1958 Yankees/Braves (Hank Bauer)	1.00	.50	.10
☐ 56 1959 Dodgers/Wh.Sox (Larry Sherry)	1.00	.50	.10
☐ 57 1960 Pirates/Yankees	1.00	.50	.10
☐ 58 1961 Yankees/Reds (Whitey Ford)	1.50	.75	.15
☐ 59 1962 Yankees/Giants	1.00	.50	.10
☐ 60 1963 Dodgers/Yankees (Sandy Koufax)	1.50	.75	.15
☐ 61 1964 Cardinals/Yankees (Mickey Mantle)	2.50	1.25	.25
☐ 62 1965 Dodgers/Twins	1.00	.50	.10
☐ 63 1966 Orioles/Dodgers	1.00	.50	.10
☐ 64 1967 Cardinals/Red Sox (Bob Gibson)	1.50	.75	.15

1972 Laughlin Great Feats

This set of 51 cards is printed on white card stock. Sports artist R.G. Laughlin 1972 is copyrighted only on the unnumbered title card but not on each card. The obverses are line drawings in black and white inside a red border. The cards measure approximately 2 9/16" by 3 9/16". The set features "Great Feats" from baseball's past. The cards are blank backed and hence are numbered and captioned on the front. There is a variation set with a blue border and colored in flesh tones in the players pictured; this variation is a little more attractive and hence is valued a little higher. The blue-bordered variation set has larger type in the captions; in fact, the type has been reset and there are some minor wording differences. The blue-bordered set is also 1/16" wider.

	NRMT	VG-E	GOOD
COMPLETE SET (51)	16.00	8.00	1.60
COMMON PLAYER (1-51)	.35	.17	.03
☐ 1 Joe DiMaggio	1.50	.75	.15
☐ 2 Walter Johnson	.60	.30	.06
☐ 3 Rudy York	.35	.17	.03
☐ 4 Sandy Koufax	.75	.35	.07
☐ 5 George Sisler	.35	.17	.03
☐ 6 Iron Man McGinnity	.35	.17	.03
☐ 7 Johnny VanderMeer	.35	.17	.03
☐ 8 Lou Gehrig	1.00	.50	.10
☐ 9 Max Carey	.35	.17	.03
☐ 10 Ed Delahanty	.35	.17	.03
☐ 11 Pinky Higgins	.35	.17	.03
☐ 12 Jack Chesbro	.35	.17	.03
☐ 13 Jim Bottomley	.35	.17	.03
☐ 14 Rube Marquard	.35	.17	.03
☐ 15 Rogers Hornsby	.50	.25	.05
☐ 16 Lefty Grove	.35	.17	.03
☐ 17 Johnny Mize	.50	.25	.05
☐ 18 Lefty Gomez	.35	.17	.03
☐ 19 Jimmie Foxx	.50	.25	.05
☐ 20 Casey Stengel	.60	.30	.06
☐ 21 Dazzy Vance	.35	.17	.03
☐ 22 Jerry Lynch	.35	.17	.03
☐ 23 Hughie Jennings	.35	.17	.03
☐ 24 Stan Musial	.60	.30	.06
☐ 25 Christy Mathewson	.60	.30	.06
☐ 26 Elroy Face	.35	.17	.03
☐ 27 Hack Wilson	.35	.17	.03
☐ 28 Smoky Burgess	.35	.17	.03
☐ 29 Cy Young	.50	.25	.05
☐ 30 Wilbert Robinson	.35	.17	.03
☐ 31 Wee Willie Keeler	.35	.17	.03
☐ 32 Babe Ruth	1.50	.75	.15
☐ 33 Mickey Mantle	1.50	.75	.15
☐ 34 Hub Leonard	.35	.17	.03
☐ 35 Ty Cobb	1.00	.50	.10
☐ 36 Carl Hubbell	.35	.17	.03
☐ 37 Joe Oeschger and Leon Cadore	.35	.17	.03
☐ 38 Don Drysdale	.50	.25	.05
☐ 39 Fred Toney and Hippo Vaughn	.35	.17	.03
☐ 40 Joe Sewell	.35	.17	.03
☐ 41 Grover C. Alexander	.35	.17	.03
☐ 42 Joe Adcock	.35	.17	.03
☐ 43 Eddie Collins	.35	.17	.03
☐ 44 Bob Feller	.60	.30	.06
☐ 45 Don Larsen	.35	.17	.03
☐ 46 Dave Philley	.35	.17	.03
☐ 47 Bill Fischer	.35	.17	.03
☐ 48 Dale Long	.35	.17	.03
☐ 49 Bill Wambsganss	.35	.17	.03
☐ 50 Roger Maris	.60	.30	.06
☐ x Title Card	.35	.17	.03

1974 Laughlin All-Star Games

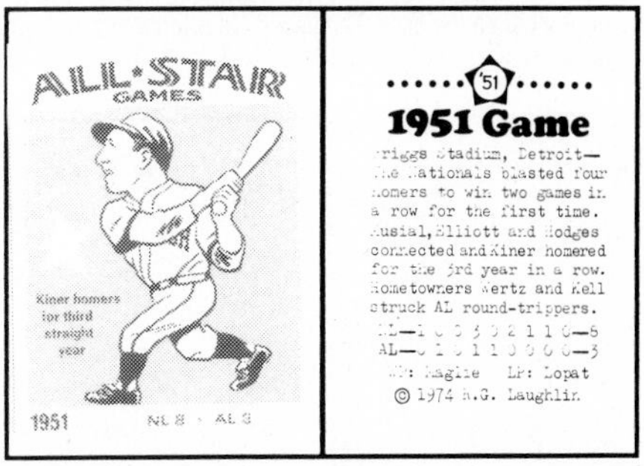

This set of 40 cards is printed on white card stock. Sports artist R.G. Laughlin 1974 is copyrighted at the bottom of the reverse of each card. The obverses are line drawings primarily in red, light blue, black, and white inside a white border. The cards measure approximately 2 11/16" by 3 3/8". The set features memorable moments from each year's All-Star Game(s). The cards are numbered on the back according to the last two digits of the year and captioned on the front. The backs are printed in blue on white stock.

	NRMT	VG-E	GOOD
COMPLETE SET (40)	12.00	6.00	1.20
COMMON PLAYER (33-73)	.30	.15	.03
☐ 33 Babe's Homer	1.25	.60	.12
☐ 34 Hubbell Fans Five	.40	.20	.04
☐ 35 Foxx Smashes Homer	.40	.20	.04
☐ 36 Ol' Diz Fogs 'Em	.50	.25	.05
☐ 37 Four Hits for Ducky	.30	.15	.03
☐ 38 No-Hit Vandy	.30	.15	.03
☐ 39 DiMaggio Homers	.90	.45	.09
☐ 40 West's 3-Run Shot	.30	.15	.03
☐ 41 Vaughan Busts Two	.30	.15	.03
☐ 42 York's 2-Run Smash	.30	.15	.03
☐ 43 Doerr 3-Run Blast	.40	.20	.04
☐ 44 Cavarretta Reaches	.30	.15	.03
☐ 46 Field Day for Ted	.60	.30	.06
☐ 47 Big Cat Plants One	.40	.20	.04
☐ 48 Raschi Pitches	.30	.15	.03
☐ 49 Jackie Scores	.40	.20	.04
☐ 50 Schoendienst Breaks	.40	.20	.04
☐ 51 Kiner Homers	.40	.20	.04
☐ 52 Sauer's Shot	.30	.15	.03
☐ 53 Slaughter Hustles	.40	.20	.04
☐ 54 Rosen Hits	.30	.15	.03
☐ 55 Stan the Man's Homer	.50	.25	.05
☐ 56 Ken Boyer Super	.30	.15	.03
☐ 57 Kaline Hits	.40	.20	.04
☐ 58 Only Nellie Gets Two	.30	.15	.03
☐ 59 F.Robbie Perfect	.40	.20	.04
☐ 60 Willie 3-for-4	.60	.30	.06
☐ 61 Bunning Hitless	.30	.15	.03
☐ 62 Roberto Perfect	.50	.25	.05
☐ 63 Monster Strikeouts	.30	.15	.03
☐ 64 Callison's Homer	.30	.15	.03
☐ 65 Stargell Big Day	.40	.20	.04
☐ 66 Brooks Hits	.40	.20	.04
☐ 67 Fergie Fans Six	.30	.15	.03
☐ 68 Tom Terrific	.50	.25	.05
☐ 69 Stretch Belts Two	.40	.20	.04
☐ 70 Yaz Four Hits	.50	.25	.05
☐ 71 Reggie Unloads	.60	.30	.06
☐ 72 Henry Hammers	.50	.25	.05
☐ 73 Bonds Perfect	.30	.15	.03

1974 Laughlin Old Time Black Stars

This set of 36 cards is printed on flat (non-glossy) white card stock. Sports artist R.G. Laughlin's work is evident but there are no copyright notices or any mention of him anywhere on any of the cards in this set. The obverses are line drawings in tan and brown. The cards measure approximately 2 5/8" by 3 1/2". The set features outstanding black players form the past. The cards are numbered on the back. The backs are printed in brown on white stock.

26 RAYMOND (HOOKS) DANDRIDGE 3b

After a lifetime in Negro ball, Dandridge came close to major league stardom. Signed by Minneapolis of the American Association in 1949, he hit .362 his first year in the AA and the next season was the league MVP. But he was already past 40; had he been younger he surely would have come to the majors. On the Millers Ray roomed with Willie Mays. Most of his career was spent as a top third baseman with the Newark Dodgers (later the Eagles). He also could handle shortstop and second.

	NRMT	VG-E	GOOD
COMPLETE SET (36)	21.00	10.50	2.10
COMMON PLAYER (1-36)	.50	.25	.05

	NRMT	VG-E	GOOD
☐ 1 Smokey Joe Williams	1.00	.50	.10
☐ 2 Rap Dixon	.50	.25	.05
☐ 3 Oliver Marcelle	.50	.25	.05
☐ 4 Bingo DeMoss	.60	.30	.06
☐ 5 Willie Foster	.60	.30	.06
☐ 6 John Beckwith	.50	.25	.05
☐ 7 Floyd(Jelly) Gardner	.50	.25	.05
☐ 8 Josh Gibson	1.50	.75	.15
☐ 9 Jose Mendez	.50	.25	.05
☐ 10 Pete Hill	.50	.25	.05
☐ 11 Buck Leonard	1.00	.50	.10
☐ 12 Jud Wilson	.50	.25	.05
☐ 13 Willie Wells	.75	.35	.07
☐ 14 Jimmie Lyons	.50	.25	.05
☐ 15 Satchel Paige	1.50	.75	.15
☐ 16 Louis Santop	.50	.25	.05
☐ 17 Frank Grant	.50	.25	.05
☐ 18 Christobel Torrienti	.50	.25	.05
☐ 19 Bullet Rogon	.50	.25	.05
☐ 20 Dave Malarcher	.60	.30	.06
☐ 21 Spot Poles	.50	.25	.05
☐ 22 Home Run Johnson	.60	.30	.06
☐ 23 Charlie Grant	.50	.25	.05
☐ 24 Cool Papa Bell	1.00	.50	.10
☐ 25 Cannonball Dick Redding	.50	.25	.05
☐ 26 Ray Dandridge	1.00	.50	.10
☐ 27 Biz Mackey	.75	.35	.07
☐ 28 Fats Jenkins	.50	.25	.05
☐ 29 Martin Dihigo	1.00	.50	.10
☐ 30 Mule Suttles	.50	.25	.05
☐ 31 Bill Monroe	.50	.25	.05
☐ 32 Dan McClellan	.50	.25	.05
☐ 33 John Henry Lloyd	1.00	.50	.10
☐ 34 Oscar Charleston	1.00	.50	.10
☐ 35 Andrew(Rube) Foster	1.00	.50	.10
☐ 36 William(Judy) Johnson	1.00	.50	.10

1974 Laughlin Sportslang

This set of 41 cards is printed on white card stock. Sports artist R.G. Laughlin 1974 is copyrighted at the bottom of every reverse. The obverses are drawings in red and blue on a white enamel card stock. The cards measure approximately 2 3/4" by 3 3/8". The set actually features the slang of several sports, not just baseball. The cards are numbered on the back and captioned on the front. The card back also provides an explanation of the slang term pictured on the card front.

	NRMT	VG-E	GOOD
COMPLETE SET (41)	8.00	4.00	.80
COMMON PLAYER (1-41)	.25	.12	.02

SPORTSlang

19 — "The Upper Hand"

Getting the upper hand is a goal in a sports contest. Kids still do the same thing—throw a bat to another kid, who catches it one-handed, somewhere about the middle. Then they alternate hands to the end to see who gets first pick or who's last at bat. Gamblers in the fifteenth century started it all. They tossed a stick to each other and used the same system to decide first play.

© 1974 R.G. Laughlin

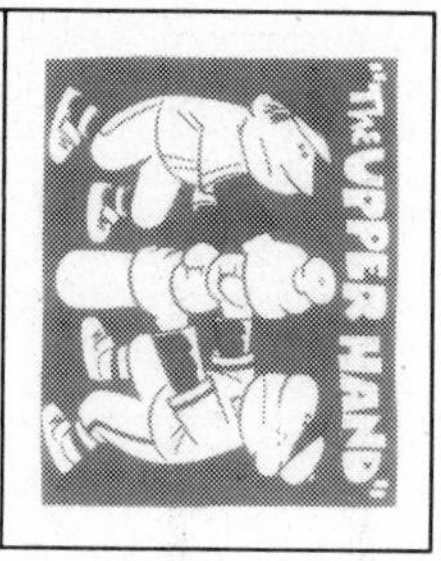

☐ 1 Bull Pen	.25	.12	.02
☐ 2 Charley Horse	.25	.12	.02
☐ 3 Derby	.25	.12	.02
☐ 4 Anchor Man	.25	.12	.02
☐ 5 Mascot	.25	.12	.02
☐ 6 Annie Oakley	.25	.12	.02
☐ 7 Taxi Squad	.25	.12	.02
☐ 8 Dukes	.25	.12	.02
☐ 9 Rookie	.25	.12	.02
☐ 10 Jinx	.25	.12	.02
☐ 11 Dark Horse	.25	.12	.02
☐ 12 Hat Trick	.25	.12	.02
☐ 13 Bell Wether	.25	.12	.02
☐ 14 Love	.25	.12	.02
☐ 15 Red Dog	.25	.12	.02
☐ 16 Barnstorm	.25	.12	.02
☐ 17 Bull's Eye	.25	.12	.02
☐ 18 Rabbit Punch	.25	.12	.02
☐ 19 The Upper Hand	.25	.12	.02
☐ 20 Handi Cap	.25	.12	.02
☐ 21 Marathon	.25	.12	.02
☐ 22 Southpaw	.25	.12	.02
☐ 23 Boner	.25	.12	.02
☐ 24 Gridiron	.25	.12	.02
☐ 25 Fan	.25	.12	.02
☐ 26 Moxie	.25	.12	.02
☐ 27 Birdie	.25	.12	.02
☐ 28 Sulky	.25	.12	.02
☐ 29 Dribble	.25	.12	.02
☐ 30 Donnybrook	.25	.12	.02
☐ 31 The Real McCoy	.25	.12	.02
☐ 32 Even Stephen	.25	.12	.02
☐ 33 Chinese Homer	.25	.12	.02
☐ 34 English	.25	.12	.02
☐ 35 Garrison Finish	.25	.12	.02
☐ 36 Foot in the Bucket	.25	.12	.02
☐ 37 Steeple Chase	.25	.12	.02
☐ 38 Long Shot	.25	.12	.02
☐ 39 Nip and Tuck	.25	.12	.02
☐ 40 Battery	.25	.12	.02
☐ xx Title Card (unnumbered)	.25	.12	.02

1975 Laughlin Batty Baseball

This set of 25 cards is printed on white card stock. Sports artist R.G. Laughlin 1975 is copyrighted on the title card. The obverses are line drawings primarily in orange, black, and white. The cards measure approximately 2 9/16" by 3 7/16". The set features a card for each team with a depiction of a fractured nickname for the team. The cards are numbered on the front. The backs are blank, but on white stock.

	NRMT	VG-E	GOOD
COMPLETE SET (25)	5.00	2.50	.50
COMMON PLAYER (1-24)	.25	.12	.02
☐ 1 Oakland Daze	.25	.12	.02
☐ 2 Boston Wet Sox	.25	.12	.02
☐ 3 Cincinnati Dreads	.25	.12	.02
☐ 4 Chicago Wide Sox	.25	.12	.02
☐ 5 Milwaukee Boozers	.25	.12	.02
☐ 6 Philadelphia Fillies	.25	.12	.02
☐ 7 Cleveland Engines	.25	.12	.02
☐ 8 New York Mitts	.25	.12	.02
☐ 9 Texas Ranchers	.25	.12	.02
☐ 10 San Francisco Gents	.25	.12	.02
☐ 11 Houston Disastros	.25	.12	.02
☐ 12 Chicago Clubs	.25	.12	.02
☐ 13 Minnesota Wins	.25	.12	.02
☐ 14 St. Louis Gardeners	.25	.12	.02
☐ 15 New York Yankers	.25	.12	.02
☐ 16 California Angles	.25	.12	.02
☐ 17 Pittsburgh Irates	.25	.12	.02
☐ 18 Los Angeles Smoggers	.25	.12	.02
☐ 19 Baltimore Oreos	.25	.12	.02
☐ 20 Montreal Expose	.25	.12	.02
☐ 21 San Diego Parties	.25	.12	.02
☐ 22 Detroit Taggers	.25	.12	.02
☐ 23 Kansas City Broils	.25	.12	.02
☐ 24 Atlanta Briefs	.25	.12	.02
☐ xx Title Card (unnumbered)	.25	.12	.02

1976 Laughlin Diamond Jubilee

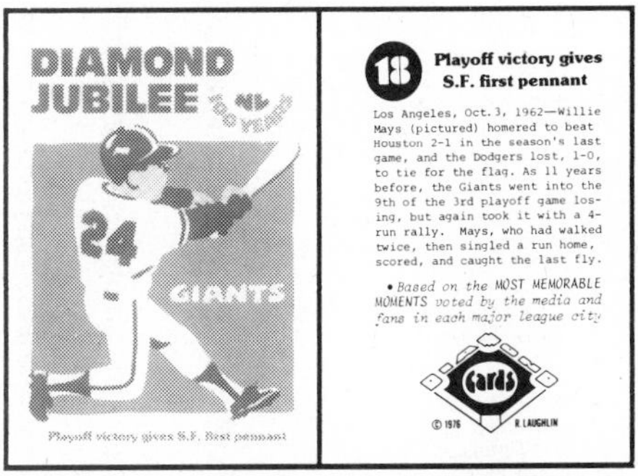

This set of 32 cards is printed on flat (non-glossy) white card stock. Sports artist R.Laughlin 1976 is copyrighted at the bottom of the reverse of each card. The obverses are line drawings primarily in red, blue, black, and white inside a red border. The cards measure approximately 2 13/16" by 3 15/16". The set features memorable moments voted by the media and fans in each major league city. The cards are numbered on the back and captioned on the front and the back. The backs are printed in dark blue on white stock.

	NRMT	VG-E	GOOD
COMPLETE SET (32)	12.00	6.00	1.20
COMMON PLAYER (1-32)	.35	.17	.03
☐ 1 Nolan Ryan	1.50	.75	.15
☐ 2 Ernie Banks	.50	.25	.05
☐ 3 Mickey Lolich	.35	.17	.03
☐ 4 Sandy Koufax	.75	.35	.07
☐ 5 Frank Robinson	.50	.25	.05
☐ 6 Bill Mazeroski	.35	.17	.03
☐ 7 Jim Hunter	.50	.25	.05
☐ 8 Hank Aaron	.90	.45	.09
☐ 9 Carl Yastrzemski	.90	.45	.09
☐ 10 Jim Bunning	.35	.17	.03
☐ 11 Brooks Robinson	.50	.25	.05
☐ 12 John Vander Meer	.35	.17	.03
☐ 13 Harmon Killebrew	.50	.25	.05
☐ 14 Lou Brock	.50	.25	.05
☐ 15 Steve Busby	.35	.17	.03
☐ 16 Nate Colbert	.35	.17	.03
☐ 17 Don Larsen	.35	.17	.03
☐ 18 Willie Mays	.90	.45	.09
☐ 19 David Clyde	.35	.17	.03
☐ 20 Mack Jones	.35	.17	.03
☐ 21 Mike Hegan	.35	.17	.03
☐ 22 Jerry Koosman	.35	.17	.03
☐ 23 Early Wynn	.50	.25	.05
☐ 24 Nellie Fox	.35	.17	.03
☐ 25 Joe DiMaggio	1.00	.50	.10
☐ 26 Jackie Robinson	.90	.45	.09
☐ 27 Ted Williams	.90	.45	.09
☐ 28 Lou Gehrig	1.00	.50	.10
☐ 29 Bobby Thomson	.35	.17	.03
☐ 30 Roger Maris	.60	.30	.06
☐ 31 Harvey Haddix	.35	.17	.03
☐ 32 Babe Ruth	1.50	.75	.15

1978 Laughlin Long Ago Black Stars

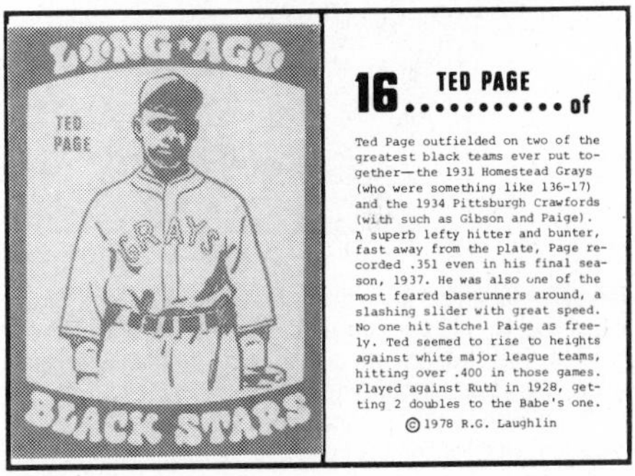

This set of 36 cards is printed on flat (non-glossy) white card stock. Sports artist R.G. Laughlin's work is evident and the reverse of each card indicates copyright by R.G. Laughlin 1978. The obverses are line drawings in light and dark green. The cards measure approximately 2 5/8" by 3 1/2". The set features outstanding black players form the past. The cards are numbered on the back. The backs are printed in black on white stock. This is not a reissue of the similar Laughlin set from 1974 Old Time Black Stars but is actually in effect a second series with all new players.

	NRMT	VG-E	GOOD
COMPLETE SET (36)	15.00	7.50	1.50
COMMON PLAYER (1-36)	.50	.25	.05
☐ 1 Ted Trent	.50	.25	.05
☐ 2 Larry Brown	.50	.25	.05
☐ 3 Newt Allen	.50	.25	.05
☐ 4 Norman Stearns	.50	.25	.05
☐ 5 Leon Day	.60	.30	.06
☐ 6 Dick Lundy	.50	.25	.05
☐ 7 Bruce Petway	.60	.30	.06
☐ 8 Bill Drake	.50	.25	.05
☐ 9 Chaney White	.50	.25	.05
☐ 10 Webster McDonald	.50	.25	.05
☐ 11 Tommy Butts	.50	.25	.05
☐ 12 Ben Taylor	.50	.25	.05
☐ 13 James (Joe) Greene	.50	.25	.05
☐ 14 Dick Seay	.50	.25	.05
☐ 15 Sammy Hughes	.50	.25	.05
☐ 16 Ted Page	.75	.35	.07
☐ 17 Willie Cornelius	.50	.25	.05
☐ 18 Pat Patterson	.50	.25	.05
☐ 19 Frank Wickware	.50	.25	.05
☐ 20 Albert Haywood	.50	.25	.05
☐ 21 Bill Holland	.50	.25	.05
☐ 22 Sol White	.50	.25	.05
☐ 23 Chet Brewer	.75	.35	.07
☐ 24 Crush Holloway	.50	.25	.05
☐ 25 George Johnson	.50	.25	.05
☐ 26 George Scales	.50	.25	.05
☐ 27 Dave Brown	.50	.25	.05
☐ 28 John Donaldson	.50	.25	.05

☐ 29 William Johnson	.50	.25	.05
☐ 30 Bill Yancey	.50	.25	.05
☐ 31 Sam Bankhead	.60	.30	.06
☐ 32 Leroy Matlock	.50	.25	.05
☐ 33 Quincy Troupe	.50	.25	.05
☐ 34 Hilton Smith	.50	.25	.05
☐ 35 Jim Crutchfield	.50	.25	.05
☐ 36 Ted Radcliffe	.60	.30	.06

1980 Laughlin Famous Feats

This set of 40 cards is printed on white card stock. Sports artist R.G. Laughlin 1980 is copyrighted at the bottom of every obverse. The obverses are line drawings primarily in many colors. The cards measure approximately 2 1/2" by 3 1/2". The set is subtitled as the "Second Series" of Famous Feats. The cards are numbered on the front. The backs are blank, but on white stock.

	MINT	EXC	G-VG
COMPLETE SET (40)	8.00	4.00	.80
COMMON PLAYER (1-40)	.20	.10	.02
☐ 1 Honus Wagner	.40	.20	.04
☐ 2 Herb Pennock	.20	.10	.02
☐ 3 Al Simmons	.20	.10	.02
☐ 4 Hack Wilson	.20	.10	.02
☐ 5 Dizzy Dean	.30	.15	.03
☐ 6 Chuck Klein	.20	.10	.02
☐ 7 Nellie Fox	.20	.10	.02
☐ 8 Lefty Grove	.30	.15	.03
☐ 9 George Sisler	.20	.10	.02
☐ 10 Lou Gehrig	.60	.30	.06
☐ 11 Rube Waddell	.20	.10	.02
☐ 12 Max Carey	.20	.10	.02
☐ 13 Thurman Munson	.30	.15	.03
☐ 14 Mel Ott	.30	.15	.03
☐ 15 Doc White	.20	.10	.02
☐ 16 Babe Ruth	.75	.35	.07
☐ 17 Schoolboy Rowe	.20	.10	.02
☐ 18 Jackie Robinson	.40	.20	.04
☐ 19 Joe Medwick	.20	.10	.02
☐ 20 Casey Stengel	.30	.15	.03
☐ 21 Roberto Clemente	.30	.15	.03
☐ 22 Christy Mathewson	.30	.15	.03
☐ 23 Jimmie Foxx	.30	.15	.03
☐ 24 Joe Jackson	.60	.30	.06
☐ 25 Walter Johnson	.30	.15	.03
☐ 26 Tony Lazzeri	.20	.10	.02
☐ 27 Hugh Casey	.20	.10	.02
☐ 28 Ty Cobb	.60	.30	.06
☐ 29 Stuffy McInnis	.20	.10	.02
☐ 30 Cy Young	.30	.15	.03
☐ 31 Lefty O'Doul	.20	.10	.02
☐ 32 Eddie Collins	.20	.10	.02
☐ 33 Joe McCarthy	.20	.10	.02
☐ 34 Ed Walsh	.20	.10	.02
☐ 35 George Burns	.20	.10	.02
☐ 36 Walt Dropo	.20	.10	.02
☐ 37 Connie Mack	.30	.15	.03
☐ 38 Babe Adams	.20	.10	.02
☐ 39 Roger Hornsby	.30	.15	.03
☐ 40 Grover C. Alexander	.30	.15	.03

1980 Laughlin 300/400/500

This square (approximately 3 1/4" square) set of 30 players features members of the 300/400/500 club, namely, 300 pitching wins, batting .400 or better, or hitting 500 homers since 1900. Cards are blank backed but are numbered on the front. The cards feature the artwork of R.G. Laughlin for the player's body connected to an out of proportion head shot stock photo. This creates an effect faintly reminiscent of the Goudey Heads Up cards.

	NRMT	VG-E	GOOD
COMPLETE SET (30)	12.00	6.00	1.20
COMMON PLAYER (1-30)	.40	.20	.04
☐ 1 Title Card	.40	.20	.04
☐ 2 Babe Ruth	1.25	.60	.12
☐ 3 Walter Johnson	.60	.30	.06
☐ 4 Ty Cobb	.75	.35	.07
☐ 5 Christy Mathewson	.60	.30	.06
☐ 6 Ted Williams	.75	.35	.07
☐ 7 Bill Terry	.50	.25	.05
☐ 8 Grover C. Alexander	.40	.20	.04
☐ 9 Napoleon Lajoie	.50	.25	.05
☐ 10 Willie Mays	.75	.35	.07
☐ 11 Cy Young	.60	.30	.06
☐ 12 Mel Ott	.50	.25	.05
☐ 13 Joe Jackson	.90	.45	.09
☐ 14 Harmon Killebrew	.50	.25	.05
☐ 15 Warren Spahn	.50	.25	.05
☐ 16 Hank Aaron	.75	.35	.07
☐ 17 Rogers Hornsby	.50	.25	.05
☐ 18 Mickey Mantle	1.25	.60	.12
☐ 19 Lefty Grove	.50	.25	.05
☐ 20 Ted Williams	.75	.35	.07
☐ 21 Jimmie Foxx	.50	.25	.05
☐ 22 Eddie Plank	.40	.20	.04
☐ 23 Frank Robinson	.50	.25	.05
☐ 24 George Sisler	.40	.20	.04
☐ 25 Eddie Mathews	.40	.20	.04
☐ 26 Early Wynn	.40	.20	.04
☐ 27 Ernie Banks	.50	.25	.05
☐ 28 Harry Heilmann	.40	.20	.04
☐ 29 Lou Gehrig	.90	.45	.09
☐ 30 Willie McCovey	.50	.25	.05

1948-49 Leaf

The cards in this 98-card set measure 2 3/8" by 2 7/8". The 1948-49 Leaf set was the first post-war baseball series issued in color. This effort was not entirely successful due to a lack of refinement which resulted in many color variations and cards out of register. In addition, the set was skip numbered from 1-168, with 49 of the 98 cards printed in limited quantities (marked with an asterisk in the checklist). Cards 102 and 136 have variations, and cards are sometimes found with overprinted or incorrect backs.

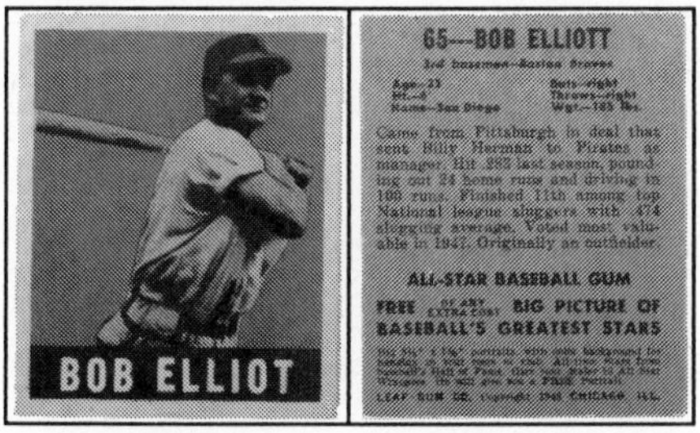

	NRMT	VG-E	GOOD
COMPLETE SET (98)	26000.	12500.	3300.
COMMON NUMBERS	22.00	11.00	2.20
COMMON * NUMBERS	400.00	200.00	40.00

	NRMT	VG-E	GOOD
☐ 1 Joe DiMaggio	1600.00	500.00	80.00
☐ 3 Babe Ruth	1750.00	750.00	150.00
☐ 4 Stan Musial	500.00	250.00	50.00
☐ 5 Virgil Trucks *	400.00	200.00	40.00
☐ 8 Satchel Paige *	2000.00	800.00	200.00
☐ 10 Dizzy Trout	22.00	11.00	2.20
☐ 11 Phil Rizzuto	120.00	60.00	12.00
☐ 13 Cass Michaels *	400.00	200.00	40.00
☐ 14 Billy Johnson	22.00	11.00	2.20
☐ 17 Frank Overmire	22.00	11.00	2.20
☐ 19 Johnny Wyrostek *	400.00	200.00	40.00
☐ 20 Hank Sauer *	400.00	200.00	40.00
☐ 22 Al Evans	22.00	11.00	2.20
☐ 26 Sam Chapman	22.00	11.00	2.20
☐ 27 Mickey Harris	22.00	11.00	2.20
☐ 28 Jim Hegan	22.00	11.00	2.20
☐ 29 Elmer Valo	22.00	11.00	2.20
☐ 30 Billy Goodman *	400.00	200.00	40.00
☐ 31 Lou Brissie	22.00	11.00	2.20
☐ 32 Warren Spahn	200.00	100.00	20.00
☐ 33 Peanuts Lowrey *	400.00	200.00	40.00
☐ 36 Al Zarilla *	400.00	200.00	40.00
☐ 38 Ted Kluszewski	45.00	22.50	4.50
☐ 39 Ewell Blackwell	35.00	17.50	3.50
☐ 42 Kent Peterson	22.00	11.00	2.20
☐ 43 Ed Stevens *	400.00	200.00	40.00
☐ 45 Ken Keltner *	400.00	200.00	40.00
☐ 46 Johnny Mize	110.00	55.00	11.00
☐ 47 George Vico	22.00	11.00	2.20
☐ 48 Johnny Schmitz *	400.00	200.00	40.00
☐ 49 Del Ennis	22.00	11.00	2.20
☐ 50 Dick Wakefield	22.00	11.00	2.20
☐ 51 Al Dark *	450.00	225.00	45.00
☐ 53 Johnny VanderMeer	30.00	15.00	3.00
☐ 54 Bobby Adams *	400.00	200.00	40.00
☐ 55 Tommy Henrich *	450.00	225.00	45.00
☐ 56 Larry Jansen	22.00	11.00	2.20
☐ 57 Bob McCall	22.00	11.00	2.20
☐ 59 Luke Appling	60.00	30.00	6.00
☐ 61 Jake Early	22.00	11.00	2.20
☐ 62 Eddie Joost *	400.00	200.00	40.00
☐ 63 Barney McCosky *	400.00	200.00	40.00
☐ 65 Robert Elliott (misspelled Elliot on card front)	22.00	11.00	2.20
☐ 66 Orval Grove *	400.00	200.00	40.00
☐ 68 Eddie Miller *	400.00	200.00	40.00
☐ 70 Honus Wagner	225.00	110.00	22.00
☐ 72 Hank Edwards	22.00	11.00	2.20
☐ 73 Pat Seerey	22.00	11.00	2.20
☐ 75 Dom DiMaggio *	500.00	250.00	50.00
☐ 76 Ted Williams	450.00	225.00	45.00
☐ 77 Roy Smalley	22.00	11.00	2.20
☐ 78 Hoot Evers *	400.00	200.00	40.00
☐ 79 Jackie Robinson	500.00	250.00	50.00
☐ 81 Whitey Kurowski *	400.00	200.00	40.00
☐ 82 Johnny Lindell	22.00	11.00	2.20
☐ 83 Bobby Doerr	100.00	50.00	10.00
☐ 84 Sid Hudson	22.00	11.00	2.20
☐ 85 Dave Philley *	400.00	200.00	40.00
☐ 86 Ralph Weigel	22.00	11.00	2.20
☐ 88 Frank Gustine *	400.00	200.00	40.00
☐ 91 Ralph Kiner	120.00	60.00	12.00
☐ 93 Bob Feller *	1250.00	500.00	125.00
☐ 95 George Stirnweiss	22.00	11.00	2.20
☐ 97 Marty Marion	30.00	15.00	3.00
☐ 98 Hal Newhouser *	500.00	250.00	50.00
☐ 102A Gene Hermansk (sic)	250.00	125.00	25.00
☐ 102B Gene Hermanski	22.00	11.00	2.20
☐ 104 Eddie Stewart *	400.00	200.00	40.00
☐ 106 Lou Boudreau	100.00	50.00	10.00
☐ 108 Matt Batts *	400.00	200.00	40.00
☐ 111 Jerry Priddy	22.00	11.00	2.20
☐ 113 Dutch Leonard *	400.00	200.00	40.00
☐ 117 Joe Gordon	27.00	13.50	2.70
☐ 120 George Kell *	650.00	325.00	65.00
☐ 121 Johnny Pesky *	400.00	200.00	40.00
☐ 123 Cliff Fannin *	400.00	200.00	40.00
☐ 125 Andy Pafko	22.00	11.00	2.20
☐ 127 Enos Slaughter *	750.00	375.00	75.00
☐ 128 Buddy Rosar	22.00	11.00	2.20
☐ 129 Kirby Higbe *	400.00	200.00	40.00
☐ 131 Sid Gordon *	400.00	200.00	40.00
☐ 133 Tommy Holmes *	400.00	200.00	40.00
☐ 136A Cliff Aberson (full sleeve)	22.00	11.00	2.20
☐ 136B Cliff Aberson (short sleeve)	250.00	125.00	25.00
☐ 137 Harry Walker *	400.00	200.00	40.00
☐ 138 Larry Doby *	500.00	250.00	50.00
☐ 139 Johnny Hopp	22.00	11.00	2.20
☐ 142 Danny Murtaugh *	400.00	200.00	40.00
☐ 143 Dick Sisler *	400.00	200.00	40.00
☐ 144 Bob Dillinger *	400.00	200.00	40.00
☐ 146 Pete Reiser *	450.00	225.00	45.00
☐ 149 Hank Majeski *	400.00	200.00	40.00
☐ 153 Floyd Baker *	400.00	200.00	40.00
☐ 158 Harry Brecheen *	400.00	200.00	40.00
☐ 159 Mizell Platt	22.00	11.00	2.20
☐ 160 Bob Scheffing *	400.00	200.00	40.00
☐ 161 Vern Stephens *	400.00	200.00	40.00
☐ 163 Fred Hutchinson *	450.00	225.00	45.00
☐ 165 Dale Mitchell *	400.00	200.00	40.00
☐ 168 Phil Cavarretta *	450.00	225.00	45.00

1960 Leaf

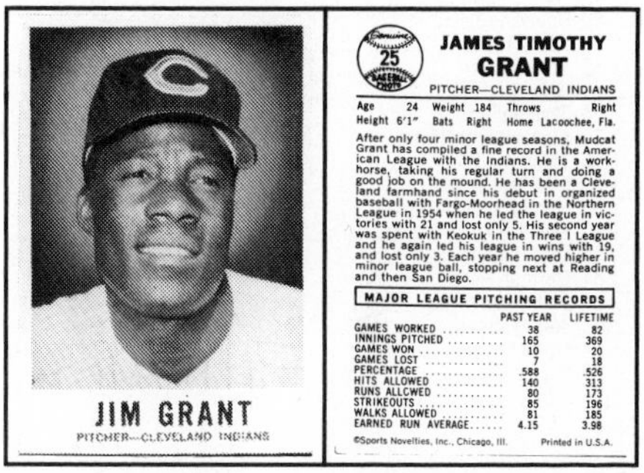

The cards in this 144-card set measure 2 1/2" by 3 1/2". The 1960 Leaf set was issued in a regular gum package style but with a marble instead of gum. The series was a joint production by Sports Novelties, Inc., and Leaf, two Chicago-based companies. Cards 73-144 are more difficult to find than the lower numbers. Photo variations exist (probably proof cards) for the seven cards listed with an asterisk and there is a well-known error card, number 25 showing Brooks Lawrence (in a Reds uniform) with Jim Grant's name on front, and Grant's biography and record on back. The corrected version with Grant's photo is the more difficult variety.

	NRMT	VG-E	GOOD
COMPLETE SET (145)	1100.00	500.00	125.00
COMMON PLAYER (1-72)	1.75	.85	.17
COMMON PLAYER (73-144)	12.00	6.00	1.20

	NRMT	VG-E	GOOD
☐ 1 Luis Aparicio *	20.00	4.00	.80
☐ 2 Woodson Held	1.75	.85	.17
☐ 3 Frank Lary	2.25	1.10	.22
☐ 4 Camilo Pascual	2.25	1.10	.22
☐ 5 Juan Herrera	1.75	.85	.17
☐ 6 Felipe Alou	3.00	1.50	.30
☐ 7 Benjamin Daniels	1.75	.85	.17
☐ 8 Roger Craig	4.00	2.00	.40
☐ 9 Edward Kasko	1.75	.85	.17
☐ 10 Robert Anton Grim	2.25	1.10	.22

☐ 11 James Busby	1.75	.85	.17
☐ 12 Ken Boyer	4.00	2.00	.40
☐ 13 Robert Boyd	1.75	.85	.17
☐ 14 Samuel Jones	2.25	1.10	.22
☐ 15 Lawrence Jackson	1.75	.85	.17
☐ 16 Elroy Face	3.00	1.50	.30
☐ 17 Walt Moryn *	1.75	.85	.17
☐ 18 James Gilliam	4.00	2.00	.40
☐ 19 Don Newcombe	3.00	1.50	.30
☐ 20 Glen Hobbie	1.75	.85	.17
☐ 21 Pedro Ramos	1.75	.85	.17
☐ 22 Rinold Duren	3.00	1.50	.30
☐ 23 Joseph Jay *	1.75	.85	.17
☐ 24 Lou Berberet	1.75	.85	.17
☐ 25A Jim Grant ERR (photo actually Brooks Lawrence)	12.00	6.00	1.20
☐ 25B Jim Grant COR	18.00	9.00	1.80
☐ 26 Thomas Borland	1.75	.85	.17
☐ 27 Brooks Robinson	25.00	12.50	2.50
☐ 28 Jerry Adair	1.75	.85	.17
☐ 29 Ronald Jackson	1.75	.85	.17
☐ 30 George Strickland	1.75	.85	.17
☐ 31 Everett Rocky Bridges	1.75	.85	.17
☐ 32 William Tuttle	1.75	.85	.17
☐ 33 Kenneth Hunt	1.75	.85	.17
☐ 34 Harold Griggs	1.75	.85	.17
☐ 35 James Coates *	1.75	.85	.17
☐ 36 Brooks Lawrence	1.75	.85	.17
☐ 37 Edwin (Duke) Snider	33.00	15.00	3.00
☐ 38 Albert Spangler	1.75	.85	.17
☐ 39 James Owens	1.75	.85	.17
☐ 40 William Virdon	3.00	1.50	.30
☐ 41 Ernest Broglio	1.75	.85	.17
☐ 42 Andre Rodgers	1.75	.85	.17
☐ 43 Julio Becquer	1.75	.85	.17
☐ 44 Antonio(Tony) Taylor	1.75	.85	.17
☐ 45 Gerald Lynch	1.75	.85	.17
☐ 46 Cletis Boyer	3.00	1.50	.30
☐ 47 Jerry Lumpe	1.75	.85	.17
☐ 48 Charles Maxwell	1.75	.85	.17
☐ 49 James Perry	3.00	1.50	.30
☐ 50 Daniel McDevitt	1.75	.85	.17
☐ 51 Juan Pizarro	1.75	.85	.17
☐ 52 Dallas Green	4.00	2.00	.40
☐ 53 Robert Friend	2.25	1.10	.22
☐ 54 Jack Sanford	2.25	1.10	.22
☐ 55 Manuel(Jim) Rivera	1.75	.85	.17
☐ 56 Theodore Wills	1.75	.85	.17
☐ 57 Milt Pappas	2.25	1.10	.22
☐ 58 Harold Smith *	1.75	.85	.17
☐ 59 Roberto Avila	2.25	1.10	.22
☐ 60 Clem Labine	2.25	1.10	.22
☐ 61 Norman Rehm *	1.75	.85	.17
☐ 62 John Gabler	1.75	.85	.17
☐ 63 John Tsitouris	1.75	.85	.17
☐ 64 David Sisler	1.75	.85	.17
☐ 65 Vic Power	1.75	.85	.17
☐ 66 Earl Battey	1.75	.85	.17
☐ 67 Robert Purkey	1.75	.85	.17
☐ 68 Myron(Moe) Drabowsky	1.75	.85	.17
☐ 69 James(Hoyt) Wilhelm	13.50	6.25	1.20
☐ 70 Humberto Robinson	1.75	.85	.17
☐ 71 Dorrel(Whitey) Herzog	4.00	2.00	.40
☐ 72 Richard Donovan *	1.75	.85	.17
☐ 73 Gordon Jones	12.00	6.00	1.20
☐ 74 Joe Hicks	12.00	6.00	1.20
☐ 75 Ray Culp	12.00	6.00	1.20
☐ 76 Dick Drott	12.00	6.00	1.20
☐ 77 Bob Duliba	12.00	6.00	1.20
☐ 78 Art Ditmar	12.00	6.00	1.20
☐ 79 Steve Korcheck	12.00	6.00	1.20
☐ 80 Henry Mason	12.00	6.00	1.20
☐ 81 Harry Simpson	12.00	6.00	1.20
☐ 82 Gene Green	12.00	6.00	1.20
☐ 83 Bob Shaw	12.00	6.00	1.20
☐ 84 Howard Reed	12.00	6.00	1.20
☐ 85 Dick Stigman	12.00	6.00	1.20
☐ 86 Rip Repulski	12.00	6.00	1.20
☐ 87 Seth Morehead	12.00	6.00	1.20
☐ 88 Camilo Carreon	12.00	6.00	1.20
☐ 89 John Blanchard	13.50	6.25	1.25
☐ 90 Billy Hoeft	12.00	6.00	1.20
☐ 91 Fred Hopke	12.00	6.00	1.20
☐ 92 Joe Martin	12.00	6.00	1.20
☐ 93 Wally Shannon	12.00	6.00	1.20
☐ 94 Two Hal Smith's Hal R. Smith Hal W. Smith	15.00	7.50	1.50
☐ 95 Al Schroll	12.00	6.00	1.20
☐ 96 John Kucks	12.00	6.00	1.20
☐ 97 Tom Morgan	12.00	6.00	1.20
☐ 98 Willie Jones	12.00	6.00	1.20
☐ 99 Marshall Renfroe	12.00	6.00	1.20
☐ 100 Willie Tasby	12.00	6.00	1.20
☐ 101 Irv Noren	12.00	6.00	1.20
☐ 102 Russ Snyder	12.00	6.00	1.20
☐ 103 Bob Turley	13.50	6.25	1.25
☐ 104 Jim Woods	12.00	6.00	1.20
☐ 105 Ronnie Kline	12.00	6.00	1.20
☐ 106 Steve Bilko	12.00	6.00	1.20
☐ 107 Elmer Valo	12.00	6.00	1.20
☐ 108 Tom McAvoy	12.00	6.00	1.20
☐ 109 Stan Williams	12.00	6.00	1.20
☐ 110 Earl Averill Jr.	12.00	6.00	1.20
☐ 111 Lee Walls	12.00	6.00	1.20
☐ 112 Paul Richards MG	13.50	6.25	1.25
☐ 113 Ed Sadowski	12.00	6.00	1.20
☐ 114 Stover McIlwain	12.00	6.00	1.20
☐ 115 Chuck Tanner (photo actually Ken Kuhn)	15.00	7.50	1.50
☐ 116 Lou Klimchock	12.00	6.00	1.20
☐ 117 Neil Chrisley	12.00	6.00	1.20
☐ 118 John Callison	15.00	7.50	1.50
☐ 119 Hal Smith	12.00	6.00	1.20
☐ 120 Carl Sawatski	12.00	6.00	1.20
☐ 121 Frank Leja	12.00	6.00	1.20
☐ 122 Earl Torgeson	12.00	6.00	1.20
☐ 123 Art Schult	12.00	6.00	1.20
☐ 124 Jim Brosnan	13.50	6.25	1.25
☐ 125 George Anderson	27.00	13.50	2.70
☐ 126 Joe Pignatano	12.00	6.00	1.20
☐ 127 Rocky Nelson	12.00	6.00	1.20
☐ 128 Orlando Cepeda	40.00	20.00	4.00
☐ 129 Daryl Spencer	12.00	6.00	1.20
☐ 130 Ralph Lumenti	12.00	6.00	1.20
☐ 131 Sam Taylor	12.00	6.00	1.20
☐ 132 Harry Brecheen	12.00	6.00	1.20
☐ 133 Johnny Groth	12.00	6.00	1.20
☐ 134 Wayne Terwilliger	12.00	6.00	1.20
☐ 135 Kent Hadley	12.00	6.00	1.20
☐ 136 Faye Throneberry	12.00	6.00	1.20
☐ 137 Jack Meyer	12.00	6.00	1.20
☐ 138 Chuck Cottier	12.00	6.00	1.20
☐ 139 Joe DeMaestri	12.00	6.00	1.20
☐ 140 Gene Freese	12.00	6.00	1.20
☐ 141 Curt Flood	20.00	10.00	2.00
☐ 142 Gino Cimoli	12.00	6.00	1.20
☐ 143 Clay Dalrymple	12.00	6.00	1.20
☐ 144 Jim Bunning	40.00	20.00	4.00

1987 Leaf Special Olympics

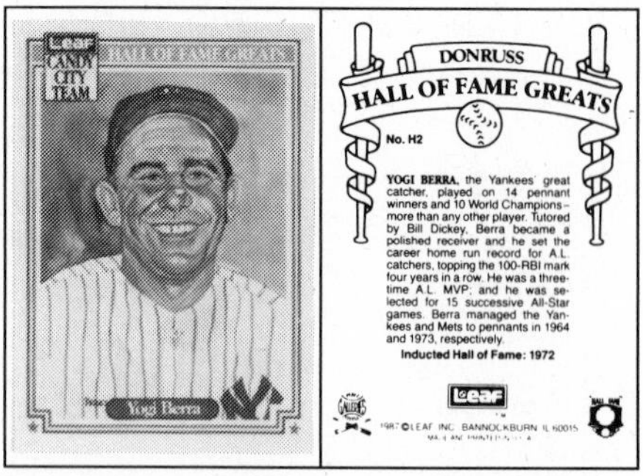

This set is also known as the Candy City team as that is the logo which appears on the front of the card. This set was issued for the proceeds of the set to go to the Special Olympics. The set was in the style of the 1983 Donruss Hall of Fame Heroes set and the only additions were generic cards about various sports. The cards are standard size, 2 1/2" by 3 1/2".

	MINT	VG-E	F-G
COMPLETE SET (18)	4.00	2.00	.40
COMMON PLAYER (H1-H12)	.20	.10	.02
COMMON PLAYER (S1-S6)	.10	.05	.01
☐ H1 Mickey Mantle	1.00	.50	.10
☐ H2 Yogi Berra	.40	.20	.04
☐ H3 Roy Campanella	.40	.20	.04

		MINT	EXC	G-VG
☐ H4	Stan Musial	.40	.20	.04
☐ H5	Ted Williams	.40	.20	.04
☐ H6	Duke Snider	.30	.15	.03
☐ H7	Hank Aaron	.40	.20	.04
☐ H8	Pee Wee Reese	.30	.15	.03
☐ H9	Brooks Robinson	.30	.15	.03
☐ H10	Al Kaline	.30	.15	.03
☐ H11	Willie McCovey	.30	.15	.03
☐ H12	Cool Papa Bell	.20	.10	.02
☐ S1	Basketball	.20	.10	.02
☐ S2	Softball	.10	.05	.01
☐ S3	Track And Field	.10	.05	.01
☐ S4	Soccer	.20	.10	.02
☐ S5	Gymnastics	.10	.05	.01
☐ S6	VII International Summer Games	.10	.05	.01

1990 Leaf Promo

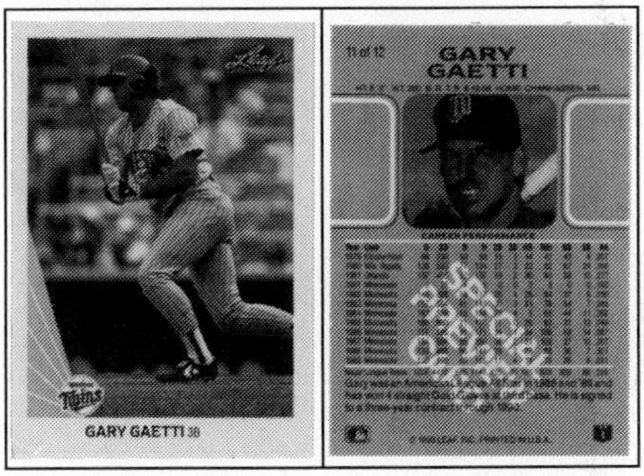

The 1990 Leaf Promo set contains standard-size (2 1/2" by 3 1/2") cards which were mailed to dealers to announce the 1990 version of Donruss' second major set of the year marketed as an upscale alternative under their Leaf name. This 12-card set was presented in the same style as the other Leaf cards were done in except that "Special Preview" was imprinted in white on the back. The cards were released in two series of 264 and the first series was not released until mid-season.

		MINT	EXC	G-VG
COMPLETE SET (12)		300.00	150.00	30.00
COMMON PLAYER (1-12)		20.00	10.00	2.00
☐ 1	Steve Sax	20.00	10.00	2.00
☐ 2	Joe Carter	30.00	15.00	3.00
☐ 3	Dennis Eckersley	30.00	15.00	3.00
☐ 4	Ken Griffey Jr.	90.00	45.00	9.00
☐ 5	Barry Larkin	35.00	17.50	3.50
☐ 6	Mark Langston	25.00	12.50	2.50
☐ 7	Eric Anthony	50.00	25.00	5.00
☐ 8	Robin Ventura	50.00	25.00	5.00
☐ 9	Greg Vaughn	50.00	25.00	5.00
☐ 10	Bobby Bonilla	40.00	20.00	4.00
☐ 11	Gary Gaetti	20.00	10.00	2.00
☐ 12	Ozzie Smith	35.00	17.50	3.50

1990 Leaf I

The 1990 Leaf set was another major, premium set introduced by Donruss in 1990. This set, which was produced on high quality paper stock, was issued in two separate series of 264 cards each. The cards are in the standard size of 2 1/2" by 3 1/2" and have full-color photos on both the front and the back of the cards. The first card of the set includes a brief history of the Leaf company and the checklists feature player photos in a style very reminiscent to the Topps checklists of the late 1960s. The card style is very similar to Upper Deck, but the Leaf sets were only distributed through hobby channels. The key rookie cards in this series are Delino DeShields, Ben McDonald, John Olerud, Sammy Sosa, and Todd Zeile.

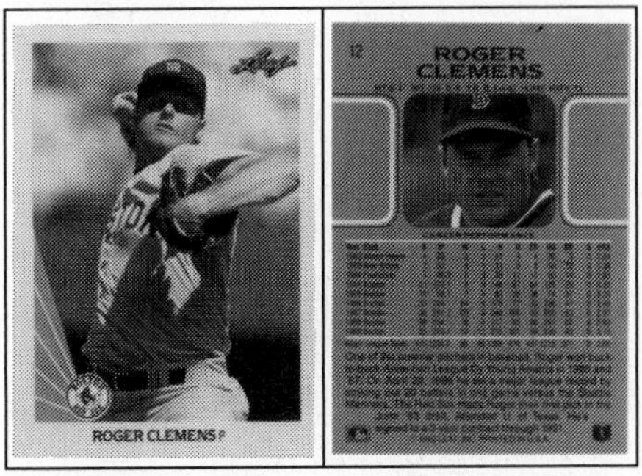

		MINT	EXC	G-VG
COMPLETE SET (264)		40.00	20.00	4.00
COMMON PLAYER (1-264)		.07	.03	.01
☐ 1	Introductory Card	.10	.05	.01
☐ 2	Mike Henneman	.07	.03	.01
☐ 3	Steve Bedrosian	.10	.05	.01
☐ 4	Mike Scott	.12	.06	.01
☐ 5	Allan Anderson	.10	.05	.01
☐ 6	Rick Sutcliffe	.10	.05	.01
☐ 7	Gregg Olson	.40	.20	.04
☐ 8	Kevin Elster	.10	.05	.01
☐ 9	Pete O'Brien	.10	.05	.01
☐ 10	Carlton Fisk	.20	.10	.02
☐ 11	Joe Magrane	.10	.05	.01
☐ 12	Roger Clemens	.40	.20	.04
☐ 13	Tom Glavine	.10	.05	.01
☐ 14	Tom Gordon	.30	.15	.03
☐ 15	Todd Benzinger	.07	.03	.01
☐ 16	Hubie Brooks	.10	.05	.01
☐ 17	Roberto Kelly	.20	.10	.02
☐ 18	Barry Larkin	.25	.12	.02
☐ 19	Mike Boddicker	.07	.03	.01
☐ 20	Roger McDowell	.10	.05	.01
☐ 21	Nolan Ryan	1.50	.75	.15
☐ 22	John Farrell	.07	.03	.01
☐ 23	Bruce Hurst	.10	.05	.01
☐ 24	Wally Joyner	.15	.07	.01
☐ 25	Greg Maddux	.12	.06	.01
☐ 26	Chris Bosio	.07	.03	.01
☐ 27	John Cerutti	.07	.03	.01
☐ 28	Tim Burke	.10	.05	.01
☐ 29	Dennis Eckersley	.15	.07	.01
☐ 30	Glenn Davis	.15	.07	.01
☐ 31	Jim Abbott	.50	.25	.05
☐ 32	Mike LaValliere	.07	.03	.01
☐ 33	Andres Thomas	.07	.03	.01
☐ 34	Lou Whitaker	.12	.06	.01
☐ 35	Alvin Davis	.12	.06	.01
☐ 36	Melido Perez	.10	.05	.01
☐ 37	Craig Biggio	.15	.07	.01
☐ 38	Rick Aguilera	.07	.03	.01
☐ 39	Pete Harnisch	.12	.06	.01
☐ 40	David Cone	.15	.07	.01
☐ 41	Scott Garrelts	.10	.05	.01
☐ 42	Jay Howell	.07	.03	.01
☐ 43	Eric King	.07	.03	.01
☐ 44	Pedro Guerrero	.15	.07	.01
☐ 45	Mike Bielecki	.07	.03	.01
☐ 46	Bob Boone	.10	.05	.01
☐ 47	Kevin Brown	.15	.07	.01
☐ 48	Jerry Browne	.07	.03	.01
☐ 49	Mike Scioscia	.07	.03	.01
☐ 50	Chuck Cary	.07	.03	.01
☐ 51	Wade Boggs	.35	.17	.03
☐ 52	Von Hayes	.12	.06	.01
☐ 53	Tony Fernandez	.10	.05	.01
☐ 54	Dennis Martinez	.07	.03	.01
☐ 55	Tom Candiotti	.07	.03	.01
☐ 56	Andy Benes	.35	.17	.03
☐ 57	Rob Dibble	.12	.06	.01
☐ 58	Chuck Crim	.07	.03	.01
☐ 59	John Smoltz	.15	.07	.01
☐ 60	Mike Heath	.07	.03	.01
☐ 61	Kevin Gross	.07	.03	.01

☐ 62 Mark McGwire	.40	.20	.04
☐ 63 Bert Blyleven	.12	.06	.01
☐ 64 Bob Walk	.07	.03	.01
☐ 65 Mickey Tettleton	.10	.05	.01
☐ 66 Sid Fernandez	.10	.05	.01
☐ 67 Terry Kennedy	.07	.03	.01
☐ 68 Fernando Valenzuela	.15	.07	.01
☐ 69 Don Mattingly	.75	.35	.07
☐ 70 Paul O'Neill	.15	.07	.01
☐ 71 Robin Yount	.25	.12	.02
☐ 72 Bret Saberhagen	.15	.07	.01
☐ 73 Geno Petralli	.07	.03	.01
☐ 74 Brook Jacoby	.10	.05	.01
☐ 75 Roberto Alomar	.20	.10	.02
☐ 76 Devon White	.12	.06	.01
☐ 77 Jose Lind	.07	.03	.01
☐ 78 Pat Combs	.15	.07	.01
☐ 79 Dave Stieb	.12	.06	.01
☐ 80 Tim Wallach	.12	.06	.01
☐ 81 Dave Stewart	.15	.07	.01
☐ 82 Eric Anthony	1.00	.50	.10
☐ 83 Randy Bush	.07	.03	.01
☐ 84 Checklist Card (Rickey Henderson)	.25	.12	.02
☐ 85 Jaime Navarro	.25	.12	.02
☐ 86 Tommy Gregg	.07	.03	.01
☐ 87 Frank Tanana	.10	.05	.01
☐ 88 Omar Vizquel	.15	.07	.01
☐ 89 Ivan Calderon	.10	.05	.01
☐ 90 Vince Coleman	.15	.07	.01
☐ 91 Barry Bonds	.40	.20	.04
☐ 92 Randy Milligan	.15	.07	.01
☐ 93 Frank Viola	.15	.07	.01
☐ 94 Matt Williams	.35	.17	.03
☐ 95 Alfredo Griffin	.07	.03	.01
☐ 96 Steve Sax	.12	.06	.01
☐ 97 Gary Gaetti	.12	.06	.01
☐ 98 Ryne Sandberg	.50	.25	.05
☐ 99 Danny Tartabull	.12	.06	.01
☐ 100 Rafael Palmeiro	.20	.10	.02
☐ 101 Jesse Orosco	.07	.03	.01
☐ 102 Garry Templeton	.10	.05	.01
☐ 103 Frank DiPino	.07	.03	.01
☐ 104 Tony Pena	.10	.05	.01
☐ 105 Dickie Thon	.07	.03	.01
☐ 106 Kelly Gruber	.20	.10	.02
☐ 107 Marquis Grissom	.60	.30	.06
☐ 108 Jose Canseco	1.00	.50	.10
☐ 109 Mike Blowers	.30	.15	.03
☐ 110 Tom Browning	.07	.03	.01
☐ 111 Greg Vaughn	.75	.35	.07
☐ 112 Oddibe McDowell	.10	.05	.01
☐ 113 Gary Ward	.07	.03	.01
☐ 114 Jay Buhner	.10	.05	.01
☐ 115 Eric Show	.07	.03	.01
☐ 116 Bryan Harvey	.10	.05	.01
☐ 117 Andy Van Slyke	.15	.07	.01
☐ 118 Jeff Ballard	.07	.03	.01
☐ 119 Barry Lyons	.07	.03	.01
☐ 120 Kevin Mitchell	.30	.15	.03
☐ 121 Mike Gallego	.07	.03	.01
☐ 122 Dave Smith	.07	.03	.01
☐ 123 Kirby Puckett	.35	.17	.03
☐ 124 Jerome Walton	.75	.35	.07
☐ 125 Bo Jackson	1.50	.75	.15
☐ 126 Harold Baines	.12	.06	.01
☐ 127 Scott Bankhead	.07	.03	.01
☐ 128 Ozzie Guillen	.12	.06	.01
☐ 129 Jose Oquendo	.07	.03	.01
☐ 130 John Dopson	.07	.03	.01
☐ 131 Charlie Hayes	.15	.07	.01
☐ 132 Fred McGriff	.20	.10	.02
☐ 133 Chet Lemon	.07	.03	.01
☐ 134 Gary Carter	.15	.07	.01
☐ 135 Rafael Ramirez	.07	.03	.01
☐ 136 Shane Mack	.10	.05	.01
☐ 137 Mark Grace	.50	.25	.05
☐ 138 Phil Bradley	.10	.05	.01
☐ 139 Dwight Gooden	.30	.15	.03
☐ 140 Harold Reynolds	.10	.05	.01
☐ 141 Scott Fletcher	.07	.03	.01
☐ 142 Ozzie Smith	.15	.07	.01
☐ 143 Mike Greenwell	.25	.12	.02
☐ 144 Pete Smith	.07	.03	.01
☐ 145 Mark Gubicza	.10	.05	.01
☐ 146 Chris Sabo	.25	.12	.02
☐ 147 Ramon Martinez	1.50	.75	.15
☐ 148 Tim Leary	.10	.05	.01
☐ 149 Randy Myers	.10	.05	.01
☐ 150 Jody Reed	.12	.06	.01
☐ 151 Bruce Ruffin	.07	.03	.01
☐ 152 Jeff Russell	.07	.03	.01
☐ 153 Doug Jones	.10	.05	.01
☐ 154 Tony Gwynn	.25	.12	.02
☐ 155 Mark Langston	.15	.07	.01
☐ 156 Mitch Williams	.07	.03	.01
☐ 157 Gary Sheffield	.40	.20	.04
☐ 158 Tom Henke	.10	.05	.01
☐ 159 Oil Can Boyd	.10	.05	.01
☐ 160 Rickey Henderson	.50	.25	.05
☐ 161 Bill Doran	.10	.05	.01
☐ 162 Chuck Finley	.12	.06	.01
☐ 163 Jeff King	.10	.05	.01
☐ 164 Nick Esasky	.10	.05	.01
☐ 165 Cecil Fielder	1.00	.50	.10
☐ 166 Dave Valle	.07	.03	.01
☐ 167 Robin Ventura	.50	.25	.05
☐ 168 Jim Deshaies	.07	.03	.01
☐ 169 Juan Berenguer	.07	.03	.01
☐ 170 Craig Worthington	.15	.07	.01
☐ 171 Gregg Jeffries	.45	.22	.04
☐ 172 Will Clark	.75	.35	.07
☐ 173 Kirk Gibson	.15	.07	.01
☐ 174 Checklist Card (Carlton Fisk)	.15	.07	.01
☐ 175 Bobby Thigpen	.15	.07	.01
☐ 176 John Tudor	.10	.05	.01
☐ 177 Andre Dawson	.20	.10	.02
☐ 178 George Brett	.35	.17	.03
☐ 179 Steve Buechele	.07	.03	.01
☐ 180 Joey Belle	.25	.12	.02
☐ 181 Eddie Murray	.15	.07	.01
☐ 182 Bob Geren	.12	.06	.01
☐ 183 Rob Murphy	.07	.03	.01
☐ 184 Tom Herr	.10	.05	.01
☐ 185 George Bell	.15	.07	.01
☐ 186 Spike Owen	.07	.03	.01
☐ 187 Cory Snyder	.12	.06	.01
☐ 188 Fred Lynn	.12	.06	.01
☐ 189 Eric Davis	.25	.12	.02
☐ 190 Dave Parker	.15	.07	.01
☐ 191 Jeff Blauser	.07	.03	.01
☐ 192 Matt Nokes	.10	.05	.01
☐ 193 Delino DeShields	1.50	.75	.15
☐ 194 Scott Sanderson	.10	.05	.01
☐ 195 Lance Parrish	.12	.06	.01
☐ 196 Bobby Bonilla	.30	.15	.03
☐ 197 Cal Ripken	.25	.12	.02
☐ 198 Kevin McReynolds	.15	.07	.01
☐ 199 Robby Thompson	.07	.03	.01
☐ 200 Tim Belcher	.12	.06	.01
☐ 201 Jesse Barfield	.12	.06	.01
☐ 202 Mariano Duncan	.10	.05	.01
☐ 203 Bill Spiers	.20	.10	.02
☐ 204 Frank White	.10	.05	.01
☐ 205 Julio Franco	.12	.06	.01
☐ 206 Greg Swindell	.12	.06	.01
☐ 207 Benito Santiago	.20	.10	.02
☐ 208 Johnny Ray	.07	.03	.01
☐ 209 Gary Redus	.07	.03	.01
☐ 210 Jeff Parrett	.07	.03	.01
☐ 211 Jimmy Key	.10	.05	.01
☐ 212 Tim Raines	.15	.07	.01
☐ 213 Carney Lansford	.12	.06	.01
☐ 214 Gerald Young	.07	.03	.01
☐ 215 Gene Larkin	.07	.03	.01
☐ 216 Dan Plesac	.07	.03	.01
☐ 217 Lonnie Smith	.10	.05	.01
☐ 218 Alan Trammell	.15	.07	.01
☐ 219 Jeffrey Leonard	.10	.05	.01
☐ 220 Sammy Sosa	1.00	.50	.10
☐ 221 Todd Zeile	1.00	.50	.10
☐ 222 Bill Landrum	.07	.03	.01
☐ 223 Mike Devereaux	.10	.05	.01
☐ 224 Mike Marshall	.12	.06	.01
☐ 225 Jose Uribe	.07	.03	.01
☐ 226 Juan Samuel	.10	.05	.01
☐ 227 Mel Hall	.10	.05	.01
☐ 228 Kent Hrbek	.15	.07	.01
☐ 229 Shawon Dunston	.15	.07	.01
☐ 230 Kevin Seitzer	.12	.06	.01
☐ 231 Pete Incaviglia	.12	.06	.01
☐ 232 Sandy Alomar Jr.	.60	.30	.06
☐ 233 Bip Roberts	.12	.06	.01
☐ 234 Scott Terry	.07	.03	.01
☐ 235 Dwight Evans	.12	.06	.01
☐ 236 Ricky Jordan	.15	.07	.01
☐ 237 John Olerud	4.00	2.00	.40
☐ 238 Zane Smith	.10	.05	.01
☐ 239 Walt Weiss	.12	.06	.01
☐ 240 Alvaro Espinoza	.07	.03	.01
☐ 241 Billy Hatcher	.10	.05	.01
☐ 242 Paul Molitor	.15	.07	.01
☐ 243 Dale Murphy	.20	.10	.02
☐ 244 Dave Bergman	.07	.03	.01
☐ 245 Ken Griffey Jr.	6.00	3.00	.60
☐ 246 Ed Whitson	.07	.03	.01
☐ 247 Kirk McCaskill	.07	.03	.01

☐ 248 Jay Bell	.07	.03	.01
☐ 249 Ben McDonald	4.00	2.00	.40
☐ 250 Darryl Strawberry	.45	.22	.04
☐ 251 Brett Butler	.10	.05	.01
☐ 252 Terry Steinbach	.10	.05	.01
☐ 253 Ken Caminiti	.07	.03	.01
☐ 254 Dan Gladden	.07	.03	.01
☐ 255 Dwight Smith	.20	.10	.02
☐ 256 Kurt Stillwell	.10	.05	.01
☐ 257 Ruben Sierra	.25	.12	.02
☐ 258 Mike Schooler	.15	.07	.01
☐ 259 Lance Johnson	.07	.03	.01
☐ 260 Terry Pendleton	.07	.03	.01
☐ 261 Ellis Burks	.25	.12	.02
☐ 262 Len Dykstra	.15	.07	.01
☐ 263 Mookie Wilson	.10	.05	.01
☐ 264 Checklist Card (Nolan Ryan)	.25	.12	.02

1990 Leaf II

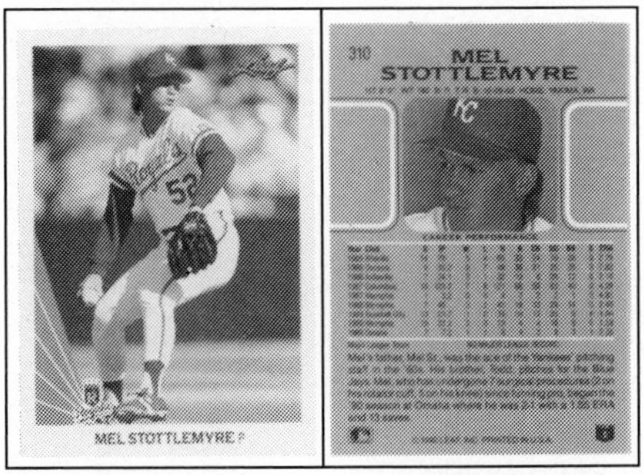

This 264-card, standard size, 2 1/2" by 3 1/2" set was issued approximately six weeks after the release of the first series. The cards, which were in the same style as series one, were issued as more expensive Donruss cards and were not available in factory sets. The key rookies in the set are Dave Justice, Kevin Maas, Jose Offerman, and Frank Thomas.

	MINT	EXC	G-VG
COMPLETE SET (264)	38.00	16.00	3.00
COMMON PLAYER (265-528)	.07	.03	.01
☐ 265 No Hit King (Nolan Ryan)	2.00	1.00	.20
☐ 266 Brian DuBois	.15	.07	.01
☐ 267 Don Robinson	.07	.03	.01
☐ 268 Glenn Wilson	.07	.03	.01
☐ 269 Kevin Tapani	.60	.30	.06
☐ 270 Marvell Wynne	.07	.03	.01
☐ 271 Billy Ripken	.07	.03	.01
☐ 272 Howard Johnson	.15	.07	.01
☐ 273 Brian Holman	.15	.07	.01
☐ 274 Dan Pasqua	.07	.03	.01
☐ 275 Ken Dayley	.07	.03	.01
☐ 276 Jeff Reardon	.10	.05	.01
☐ 277 Jim Presley	.07	.03	.01
☐ 278 Jim Eisenreich	.07	.03	.01
☐ 279 Danny Jackson	.10	.05	.01
☐ 280 Orel Hershiser	.15	.07	.01
☐ 281 Andy Hawkins	.07	.03	.01
☐ 282 Jose Rijo	.10	.05	.01
☐ 283 Luis Rivera	.07	.03	.01
☐ 284 John Kruk	.07	.03	.01
☐ 285 Jeff Huson	.20	.10	.02
☐ 286 Joel Skinner	.07	.03	.01
☐ 287 Jack Clark	.15	.07	.01
☐ 288 Chili Davis	.10	.05	.01
☐ 289 Joe Girardi	.15	.07	.01
☐ 290 B.J. Surhoff	.10	.05	.01
☐ 291 Luis Sojo	.25	.12	.02
☐ 292 Tom Foley	.07	.03	.01
☐ 293 Mike Moore	.10	.05	.01
☐ 294 Ken Oberkfell	.07	.03	.01
☐ 295 Luis Polonia	.07	.03	.01
☐ 296 Doug Drabek	.15	.07	.01
☐ 297 Dave Justice	7.00	3.50	.70
☐ 298 Paul Gibson	.07	.03	.01
☐ 299 Edgar Martinez	.15	.07	.01
☐ 300 Frank Thomas	6.00	3.00	.60
☐ 301 Eric Yelding	.30	.15	.03
☐ 302 Greg Gagne	.07	.03	.01
☐ 303 Brad Komminsk	.07	.03	.01
☐ 304 Ron Darling	.10	.05	.01
☐ 305 Kevin Bass	.10	.05	.01
☐ 306 Jeff Hamilton	.07	.03	.01
☐ 307 Ron Karkovice	.07	.03	.01
☐ 308 Milt Thompson	.07	.03	.01
☐ 309 Mike Harkey	.35	.17	.03
☐ 310 Mel Stottlemyre Jr.	.15	.07	.01
☐ 311 Kenny Rogers	.15	.07	.01
☐ 312 Mitch Webster	.07	.03	.01
☐ 313 Kal Daniels	.15	.07	.01
☐ 314 Matt Nokes	.10	.05	.01
☐ 315 Dennis Lamp	.07	.03	.01
☐ 316 Ken Howell	.07	.03	.01
☐ 317 Glenallen Hill	.20	.10	.02
☐ 318 Dave Martinez	.07	.03	.01
☐ 319 Chris James	.10	.05	.01
☐ 320 Mike Pagliarulo	.07	.03	.01
☐ 321 Hal Morris	1.00	.50	.10
☐ 322 Rob Deer	.10	.05	.01
☐ 323 Greg Olson	.30	.15	.03
☐ 324 Tony Phillips	.07	.03	.01
☐ 325 Larry Walker	.75	.35	.07
☐ 326 Ron Hassey	.07	.03	.01
☐ 327 Jack Howell	.07	.03	.01
☐ 328 John Smiley	.07	.03	.01
☐ 329 Steve Finley	.20	.10	.02
☐ 330 Dave Magadan	.12	.06	.01
☐ 331 Greg Litton	.20	.10	.02
☐ 332 Mickey Hatcher	.07	.03	.01
☐ 333 Lee Guetterman	.07	.03	.01
☐ 334 Norm Charlton	.30	.15	.03
☐ 335 Edgar Diaz	.15	.07	.01
☐ 336 Willie Wilson	.12	.06	.01
☐ 337 Bobby Witt	.12	.06	.01
☐ 338 Candy Maldonado	.10	.05	.01
☐ 339 Craig Lefferts	.07	.03	.01
☐ 340 Dante Bichette	.20	.10	.02
☐ 341 Wally Backman	.07	.03	.01
☐ 342 Dennis Cook	.15	.07	.01
☐ 343 Pat Borders	.25	.12	.02
☐ 344 Wallace Johnson	.07	.03	.01
☐ 345 Willie Randolph	.10	.05	.01
☐ 346 Danny Darwin	.07	.03	.01
☐ 347 Al Newman	.07	.03	.01
☐ 348 Mark Knudson	.07	.03	.01
☐ 349 Joe Boever	.07	.03	.01
☐ 350 Larry Sheets	.07	.03	.01
☐ 351 Mike Jackson	.07	.03	.01
☐ 352 Wayne Edwards	.25	.12	.02
☐ 353 Bernard Gilkey	.60	.30	.06
☐ 354 Don Slaught	.07	.03	.01
☐ 355 Joe Orsulak	.07	.03	.01
☐ 356 John Franco	.10	.05	.01
☐ 357 Jeff Brantley	.30	.15	.03
☐ 358 Mike Morgan	.07	.03	.01
☐ 359 Deion Sanders	.50	.25	.05
☐ 360 Terry Leach	.10	.05	.01
☐ 361 Les Lancaster	.07	.03	.01
☐ 362 Storm Davis	.10	.05	.01
☐ 363 Scott Coolbaugh	.30	.15	.03
☐ 364 Checklist Card (Ozzie Smith)	.15	.07	.01
☐ 365 Cecilio Guante	.07	.03	.01
☐ 366 Joey Cora	.07	.03	.01
☐ 367 Willie McGee	.15	.07	.01
☐ 368 Jerry Reed	.07	.03	.01
☐ 369 Darren Daulton	.10	.05	.01
☐ 370 Manny Lee	.07	.03	.01
☐ 371 Mark Gardner	.30	.15	.03
☐ 372 Rick Honeycutt	.07	.03	.01
☐ 373 Steve Balboni	.07	.03	.01
☐ 374 Jack Armstrong	.25	.12	.02
☐ 375 Charlie O'Brien	.07	.03	.01
☐ 376 Ron Gant	.50	.25	.05
☐ 377 Lloyd Moseby	.10	.05	.01
☐ 378 Gene Harris	.15	.07	.01
☐ 379 Joe Carter	.15	.07	.01
☐ 380 Scott Bailes	.07	.03	.01
☐ 381 R.J. Reynolds	.07	.03	.01
☐ 382 Bob Melvin	.07	.03	.01
☐ 383 Tim Teufel	.07	.03	.01
☐ 384 John Burkett	.35	.17	.03
☐ 385 Felix Jose	.18	.09	.01
☐ 386 Larry Andersen	.07	.03	.01
☐ 387 David West	.10	.05	.01
☐ 388 Luis Salazar	.07	.03	.01
☐ 389 Mike MacFarlane	.07	.03	.01

☐ 390 Charlie Hough	.07	.03	.01
☐ 391 Greg Briley	.20	.10	.02
☐ 392 Donn Pall	.07	.03	.01
☐ 393 Bryn Smith	.07	.03	.01
☐ 394 Carlos Quintana	.20	.10	.02
☐ 395 Steve Lake	.07	.03	.01
☐ 396 Mark Whiten	.90	.45	.09
☐ 397 Edwin Nunez	.07	.03	.01
☐ 398 Rick Parker	.15	.07	.01
☐ 399 Mark Portugal	.07	.03	.01
☐ 400 Roy Smith	.07	.03	.01
☐ 401 Hector Villanueva	.30	.15	.03
☐ 402 Bob Milacki	.15	.07	.01
☐ 403 Alejandro Pena	.07	.03	.01
☐ 404 Scott Bradley	.07	.03	.01
☐ 405 Ron Kittle	.10	.05	.01
☐ 406 Bob Tewksbury	.07	.03	.01
☐ 407 Wes Gardner	.07	.03	.01
☐ 408 Ernie Whitt	.07	.03	.01
☐ 409 Terry Shumpert	.25	.12	.02
☐ 410 Tim Layana	.30	.15	.03
☐ 411 Chris Gwynn	.07	.03	.01
☐ 412 Jeff Robinson	.07	.03	.01
☐ 413 Scott Scudder	.25	.12	.02
☐ 414 Kevin Romine	.07	.03	.01
☐ 415 Jose DeJesus	.20	.10	.02
☐ 416 Mike Jeffcoat	.07	.03	.01
☐ 417 Rudy Seanez	.15	.07	.01
☐ 418 Mike Dunne	.07	.03	.01
☐ 419 Dick Schofield	.07	.03	.01
☐ 420 Steve Wilson	.15	.07	.01
☐ 421 Bill Krueger	.07	.03	.01
☐ 422 Junior Felix	.60	.30	.06
☐ 423 Drew Hall	.07	.03	.01
☐ 424 Curt Young	.07	.03	.01
☐ 425 Franklin Stubbs	.10	.05	.01
☐ 426 Dave Winfield	.15	.07	.01
☐ 427 Rick Reed	.15	.07	.01
☐ 428 Charlie Leibrandt	.07	.03	.01
☐ 429 Jeff Robinson	.07	.03	.01
☐ 430 Erik Hanson	.45	.22	.04
☐ 431 Barry Jones	.10	.05	.01
☐ 432 Alex Trevino	.07	.03	.01
☐ 433 John Moses	.07	.03	.01
☐ 434 Dave Johnson	.20	.10	.02
☐ 435 Mackey Sasser	.07	.03	.01
☐ 436 Rick Leach	.07	.03	.01
☐ 437 Lenny Harris	.20	.10	.02
☐ 438 Carlos Martinez	.10	.05	.01
☐ 439 Rex Hudler	.07	.03	.01
☐ 440 Domingo Ramos	.07	.03	.01
☐ 441 Gerald Perry	.07	.03	.01
☐ 442 Jeff Russell	.07	.03	.01
☐ 443 Carlos Baerga	.75	.35	.07
☐ 444 Checklist Card (Will Clark)	.15	.07	.01
☐ 445 Stan Javier	.07	.03	.01
☐ 446 Kevin Maas	4.50	2.25	.45
☐ 447 Tom Brunansky	.12	.06	.01
☐ 448 Carmelo Martinez	.07	.03	.01
☐ 449 Willie Blair	.15	.07	.01
☐ 450 Andres Galarraga	.15	.07	.01
☐ 451 Bud Black	.07	.03	.01
☐ 452 Greg Harris	.15	.07	.01
☐ 453 Joe Oliver	.25	.12	.02
☐ 454 Greg Brock	.07	.03	.01
☐ 455 Jeff Treadway	.07	.03	.01
☐ 456 Lance McCullers	.07	.03	.01
☐ 457 Dave Schmidt	.07	.03	.01
☐ 458 Todd Burns	.07	.03	.01
☐ 459 Max Venable	.07	.03	.01
☐ 460 Neal Heaton	.07	.03	.01
☐ 461 Mark Williamson	.07	.03	.01
☐ 462 Keith Miller	.07	.03	.01
☐ 463 Mike LaCoss	.07	.03	.01
☐ 464 Jose Offerman	1.75	.85	.17
☐ 465 Jim Leyritz	.35	.17	.03
☐ 466 Glenn Braggs	.07	.03	.01
☐ 467 Ron Robinson	.07	.03	.01
☐ 468 Mark Davis	.12	.06	.01
☐ 469 Gary Pettis	.07	.03	.01
☐ 470 Keith Hernandez	.12	.06	.01
☐ 471 Dennis Rasmussen	.07	.03	.01
☐ 472 Mark Eichhorn	.07	.03	.01
☐ 473 Ted Power	.07	.03	.01
☐ 474 Terry Mulholland	.07	.03	.01
☐ 475 Todd Stottlemyre	.12	.06	.01
☐ 476 Jerry Goff	.15	.07	.01
☐ 477 Gene Nelson	.07	.03	.01
☐ 478 Rich Gedman	.07	.03	.01
☐ 479 Brian Harper	.07	.03	.01
☐ 480 Mike Felder	.07	.03	.01
☐ 481 Steve Avery	.60	.30	.06
☐ 482 Jack Morris	.12	.06	.01
☐ 483 Randy Johnson	.20	.10	.02
☐ 484 Scott Radinsky	.30	.15	.03
☐ 485 Jose DeLeon	.07	.03	.01
☐ 486 Stan Belinda	.25	.12	.02
☐ 487 Brian Holton	.07	.03	.01
☐ 488 Mark Carreon	.07	.03	.01
☐ 489 Trevor Wilson	.25	.12	.02
☐ 490 Mike Sharperson	.07	.03	.01
☐ 491 Alan Mills	.25	.12	.02
☐ 492 John Candelaria	.07	.03	.01
☐ 493 Paul Assenmacher	.07	.03	.01
☐ 494 Steve Crawford	.07	.03	.01
☐ 495 Brad Arnsberg	.07	.03	.01
☐ 496 Sergio Valdez	.15	.07	.01
☐ 497 Mark Parent	.07	.03	.01
☐ 498 Tom Pagnozzi	.07	.03	.01
☐ 499 Greg Harris	.07	.03	.01
☐ 500 Randy Ready	.07	.03	.01
☐ 501 Duane Ward	.07	.03	.01
☐ 502 Nelson Santovenia	.07	.03	.01
☐ 503 Joe Klink	.15	.07	.01
☐ 504 Eric Plunk	.07	.03	.01
☐ 505 Jeff Reed	.07	.03	.01
☐ 506 Ted Higuera	.10	.05	.01
☐ 507 Joe Hesketh	.07	.03	.01
☐ 508 Dan Petry	.07	.03	.01
☐ 509 Matt Young	.07	.03	.01
☐ 510 Jerald Clark	.15	.07	.01
☐ 511 John Orton	.20	.10	.02
☐ 512 Scott Ruskin	.35	.17	.03
☐ 513 Chris Hoiles	.35	.17	.03
☐ 514 Daryl Boston	.10	.05	.01
☐ 515 Francisco Oliveras	.15	.07	.01
☐ 516 Ozzie Canseco	.75	.35	.07
☐ 517 Xavier Hernandez	.15	.07	.01
☐ 518 Fred Manrique	.07	.03	.01
☐ 519 Shawn Boskie	.30	.15	.03
☐ 520 Jeff Montgomery	.10	.05	.01
☐ 521 Jack Daugherty	.20	.10	.02
☐ 522 Keith Comstock	.07	.03	.01
☐ 523 Greg Hibbard	.30	.15	.03
☐ 524 Lee Smith	.10	.05	.01
☐ 525 Dana Kiecker	.30	.15	.03
☐ 526 Darrel Akerfelds	.07	.03	.01
☐ 527 Greg Myers	.07	.03	.01
☐ 528 Checklist Card (Ryne Sandberg)	.15	.07	.01

1989 Lennox HSE Astros

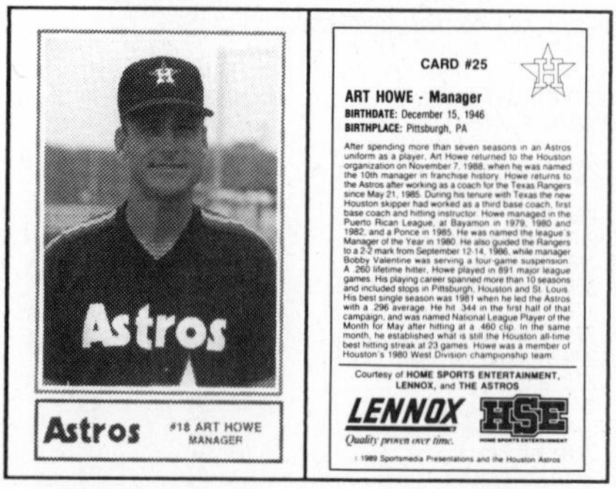

The 1989 Lennox HSE Astros set contains 26 cards measuring approximately 2 5/8" by 4 1/8". The fronts have color photos with burnt orange and white borders; the backs feature biographical information and career highlights. The set looks very much like the Police Astros sets of the previous years but is not since it was not sponsored by any Police Department and does not have a safety tip anywhere on the card.

	MINT	EXC	G-VG
COMPLETE SET (26)	6.00	3.00	.60
COMMON PLAYER (1-26)	.25	.12	.02
☐ 1 Billy Hatcher	.35	.17	.03
☐ 2 Greg Gross	.25	.12	.02
☐ 3 Rick Rhoden	.25	.12	.02

☐ 4 Mike Scott	.60	.30	.06
☐ 5 Kevin Bass	.35	.17	.03
☐ 6 Alex Trevino	.25	.12	.02
☐ 7 Jim Clancy	.25	.12	.02
☐ 8 Bill Doran	.35	.17	.03
☐ 9 Dan Schatzeder	.25	.12	.02
☐ 10 Bob Knepper	.25	.12	.02
☐ 11 Jim Deshaies	.35	.17	.03
☐ 12 Eric Yelding	.35	.17	.03
☐ 13 Danny Darwin	.35	.17	.03
☐ 14 Astros Coaches	.25	.12	.02
☐ 15 Craig Reynolds	.25	.12	.02
☐ 16 Rafael Ramirez	.25	.12	.02
☐ 17 Juan Agosto	.25	.12	.02
☐ 18 Larry Andersen	.25	.12	.02
☐ 19 Dave Smith	.35	.17	.03
☐ 20 Gerald Young	.35	.17	.03
☐ 21 Ken Caminiti	.25	.12	.02
☐ 22 Terry Puhl	.35	.17	.03
☐ 23 Bob Forsch	.35	.17	.03
☐ 24 Craig Biggio	.50	.25	.05
☐ 25 Art Howe MG	.35	.17	.03
☐ 26 Glenn Davis	.75	.35	.07

1990 Lennox HSE Astros

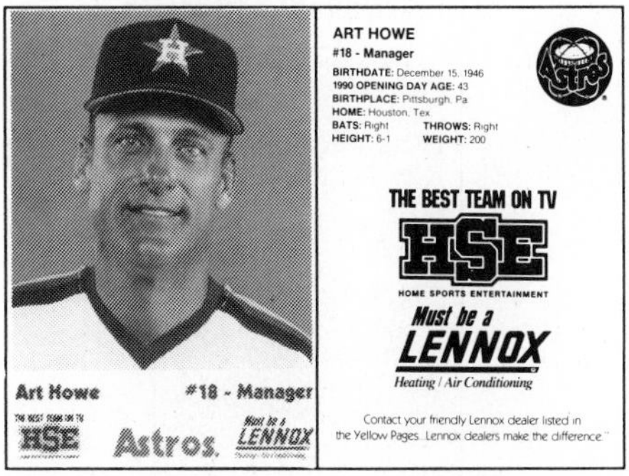

This 28-card, approximately 3 1/2" by 5", set (of 1990 Houston Astros) was issued in conjunction with HSE Cable Network and Lennox Heating and Air Conditioning as indicated on both the front and back of the cards. The front of the cards have full color portraits of the player while the back gives brief information about the player. The set has been checklisted below in alphabetical order with the player's uniform number noted next to his name.

	MINT	EXC	G-VG
COMPLETE SET (28)	10.00	5.00	1.00
COMMON PLAYER (1-28)	.40	.20	.04
☐ 1 Juan Agosto 49	.40	.20	.04
☐ 2 Larry Andersen 47	.40	.20	.04
☐ 3 Eric Anthony 23	.80	.40	.08
☐ 4 Craig Biggio 7	.60	.30	.06
☐ 5 Ken Caminiti 11	.50	.25	.05
☐ 6 Casey Candaele 1	.40	.20	.04
☐ 7 Jose Cano 39	.40	.20	.04
☐ 8 Jim Clancy 38	.40	.20	.04
☐ 9 Danny Darwin 44	.50	.25	.05
☐ 10 Mark Davidson 22	.40	.20	.04
☐ 11 Glenn Davis 27	1.00	.50	.10
☐ 12 Jim Deshaies 43	.40	.20	.04
☐ 13 Bill Doran 19	.50	.25	.05
☐ 14 Bill Gullickson 36	.50	.25	.05
☐ 15 Xavier Hernandez 31	.40	.20	.04
☐ 16 Art Howe MG 18	.50	.25	.05
☐ 17 Mark Portugal 51	.40	.20	.04
☐ 18 Terry Puhl 21	.50	.25	.05
☐ 19 Rafael Ramirez 16	.40	.20	.04
☐ 20 David Rohde 6	.50	.25	.05
☐ 21 Dan Schatzeder 20	.40	.20	.04
☐ 22 Mike Scott 33	.60	.30	.06
☐ 23 Dave Smith 45	.50	.25	.05
☐ 24 Franklin Stubbs 24	.50	.25	.05
☐ 25 Alex Trevino 9	.40	.20	.04
☐ 26 Glenn Wilson 12	.40	.20	.04
☐ 27 Eric Yelding 15	.50	.25	.05
☐ 28 Gerald Young 13	.40	.20	.04

1960 MacGregor Staff

This 25-card set represents members of the MacGregor Sporting Goods Advisory Staff. Since the cards are unnumbered they ordered below in alphabetical order. The cards are blank backed and measure approximately 3 3/4" by 5". The photos are in black and white. The catalog designation for the set is H825-1. Cards have a facsimile autograph in white lettering on the front.

	NRMT	VG-E	GOOD
COMPLETE SET (25)	500.00	250.00	50.00
COMMON PLAYER (1-25)	8.00	4.00	.80
☐ 1 Hank Aaron	100.00	50.00	10.00
☐ 2 Richie Ashburn	18.00	9.00	1.80
☐ 3 Gus Bell	8.00	4.00	.80
☐ 4 Lou Berberet	8.00	4.00	.80
☐ 5 Jerry Casale	8.00	4.00	.80
☐ 6 Del Crandall	8.00	4.00	.80
☐ 7 Art Ditmar	8.00	4.00	.80
☐ 8 Gene Freese	8.00	4.00	.80
☐ 9 James Gilliam	12.00	6.00	1.20
☐ 10 Ted Kluszewski	15.00	7.50	1.50
☐ 11 Jim Landis	8.00	4.00	.80
☐ 12 Al Lopez	12.00	6.00	1.20
☐ 13 Willie Mays	100.00	50.00	10.00
☐ 14 Bill Mazeroski	12.00	6.00	1.20
☐ 15 Mike McCormick	8.00	4.00	.80
☐ 16 Gil McDougald	12.00	6.00	1.20
☐ 17 Russ Nixon	8.00	4.00	.80
☐ 18 Bill Rigney	8.00	4.00	.80
☐ 19 Robin Roberts	21.00	10.50	2.10
☐ 20 Frank Robinson	36.00	18.00	3.60
☐ 21 John Roseboro	8.00	4.00	.80
☐ 22 Red Schoendienst	21.00	10.50	2.10
☐ 23 Bill Skowron	12.00	6.00	1.20
☐ 24 Daryl Spencer	8.00	4.00	.80
☐ 25 Johnny Temple	8.00	4.00	.80

1965 MacGregor Staff

This 10-card set represents members of the MacGregor Sporting Goods Advisory Staff. Since the cards are unnumbered they ordered below in alphabetical order. The cards are blank backed and measure approximately 3 9/16" by 5 1/8". The photos are in black and white. The catalog designation for the set is H825-2.

	NRMT	VG-E	GOOD
COMPLETE SET (10)	225.00	110.00	22.00
COMMON PLAYER (1-10)	7.00	3.50	.70
☐ 1 Roberto Clemente	90.00	45.00	9.00
☐ 2 Al Downing	7.00	3.50	.70
☐ 3 Johnny Edwards	7.00	3.50	.70
☐ 4 Ron Hansen	7.00	3.50	.70
☐ 5 Deron Johnson	7.00	3.50	.70
☐ 6 Willie Mays	100.00	50.00	10.00
☐ 7 Tony Oliva	15.00	7.50	1.50
☐ 8 Claude Osteen	7.00	3.50	.70
☐ 9 Bobby Richardson	15.00	7.50	1.50
☐ 10 Zoilo Versalles	7.00	3.50	.70

1989 Marathon Tigers

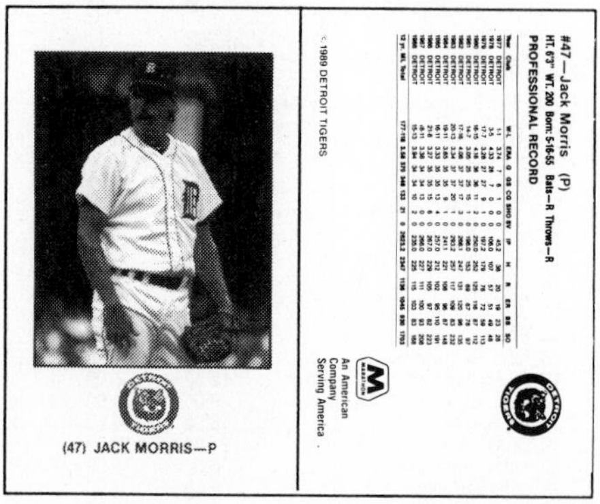

The 1989 Marathon Tigers set features 28 cards measuring 2 3/4" by 4 1/2". The set features color photos surrounded by blue borders and a white background. The Tigers logo is featured prominently under the photo and then the players uniform number name and position is underneath the Tiger logo. The horizontally-oriented backs show career stats. The set was given away at the July 15, 1989 Tigers home game against the Seattle Mariners. The cards are numbered by the players' uniform numbers.

	MINT	EXC	G-VG
COMPLETE SET (28)	7.00	3.50	.70
COMMON PLAYER	.25	.12	.02
☐ 1 Lou Whitaker	.50	.25	.05
☐ 3 Alan Trammell	.75	.35	.07
☐ 8 Mike Heath	.25	.12	.02
☐ 9 Fred Lynn	.35	.17	.03
☐ 10 Keith Moreland	.25	.12	.02
☐ 11 Sparky Anderson MG	.50	.25	.05
☐ 12 Mike Brumley	.25	.12	.02
☐ 14 Dave Bergman	.25	.12	.02
☐ 15 Pat Sheridan	.25	.12	.02
☐ 17 Al Pedrique	.25	.12	.02
☐ 18 Ramon Pena	.25	.12	.02
☐ 19 Doyle Alexander	.25	.12	.02
☐ 21 Guillermo Hernandez	.25	.12	.02
☐ 23 Torey Lovullo	.25	.12	.02
☐ 24 Gary Pettis	.25	.12	.02
☐ 25 Ken Williams	.25	.12	.02
☐ 26 Frank Tanana	.35	.17	.03
☐ 27 Charles Hudson	.25	.12	.02
☐ 32 Gary Ward	.25	.12	.02
☐ 33 Matt Nokes	.35	.17	.03
☐ 34 Chet Lemon	.35	.17	.03
☐ 35 Rick Schu	.25	.12	.02
☐ 36 Frank Williams	.25	.12	.02
☐ 39 Mike Henneman	.35	.17	.03
☐ 44 Jeff Robinson	.35	.17	.03
☐ 47 Jack Morris	.50	.25	.05
☐ 48 Paul Gibson	.25	.12	.02
☐ xx Tiger Coaches Billy Consolo Alex Grammas Billy Muffet Vada Pinson Dick Tracewski	.25	.12	.02

1970 McDonald's Brewers

BREWERS
No. 38 BOB MEYER, Pitcher
Bats R, Throws L, Ht. 6'2", 195 lbs., 30 yrs.
Born: Toledo, Ohio. 1969: Seattle
W 0, L 3, ERA 3.27

This 31-card set features cards measuring approximately 2 15/16" by 4 3/8" and was issued during the Brewers' first year in Milwaukee after moving from Seattle. The cards are drawings of the members of the 1970 Milwaukee Brewers and underneath the drawings there is information about the players. These cards are still often found in uncut sheet form and hence have no extra value in that form. The backs are blank. The set is checklisted alphabetically with the number of the sheet being listed next to the players name. There were six different sheets of six cards each although only one sheet contained six players; the other sheets depicted five players and a Brewers' logo.

	NRMT	VG-E	GOOD
COMPLETE SET (31)	6.00	3.00	.60
COMMON PLAYER (1-31)	.25	.12	.02
☐ 1 Max Alvis 6	.25	.12	.02
☐ 2 Bob Bolin 1	.25	.12	.02
☐ 3 Gene Brabender 3	.25	.12	.02
☐ 4 Dave Bristol 5	.35	.17	.03
☐ 5 Wayne Comer 2	.25	.12	.02
☐ 6 Cal Ermer 3	.25	.12	.02
☐ 7 John Gelner 4	.25	.12	.02
☐ 8 Greg Goossen 5	.25	.12	.02
☐ 9 Tommy Harper 5	.35	.17	.03
☐ 10 Mike Hegan 3	.35	.17	.03
☐ 11 Mike Hershberger 3	.25	.12	.02
☐ 12 Steve Hovley 2	.25	.12	.02
☐ 13 John Kennedy 2	.25	.12	.02
☐ 14 Lew Krausse 4	.25	.12	.02
☐ 15 Ted Kubiak 1	.25	.12	.02
☐ 16 George Lauzerique 6	.25	.12	.02
☐ 17 Bob Locker 5	.25	.12	.02
☐ 18 Roy McMillan 4	.35	.17	.03
☐ 19 Jerry McNertney 4	.25	.12	.02

☐ 20 Bob Meyer 2	.25	.12	.02
☐ 21 Jackie Moore 6	.35	.17	.03
☐ 22 John Morris 1	.25	.12	.02
☐ 23 John O'Donoghue 1	.25	.12	.02
☐ 24 Marty Pattin 6	.25	.12	.02
☐ 25 Rich Rollins 4	.35	.17	.03
☐ 26 Phil Roof 5	.25	.12	.02
☐ 27 Ted Savage 1	.25	.12	.02
☐ 28 Russ Snyder 6	.25	.12	.02
☐ 29 Wes Stock 2	.35	.17	.03
☐ 30 Sandy Valdespino 2	.25	.12	.02
☐ 31 Danny Walton 3	.25	.12	.02

1984 Mets Fan Club

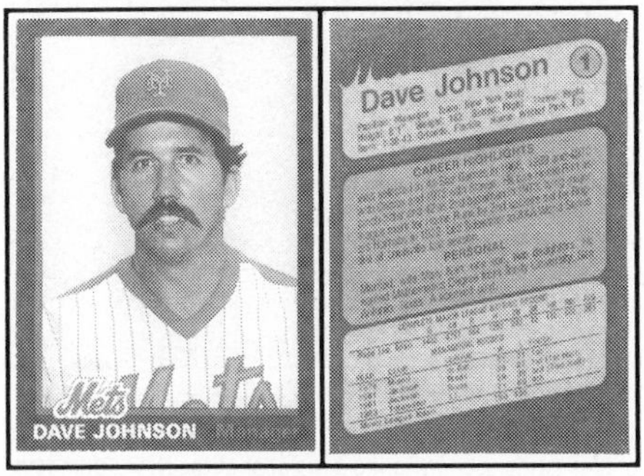

The cards in this 8-player set measure 2 1/2" by 3 1/2". The sheets were produced by Topps for the New York Mets and feature only Mets. The full sheet measures 7 1/2" by 10 1/2". Cards are together on the sheet but are perforated for those collectors who want to separate the individual player cards. The middle (ninth) card is a Mets Fan club membership card which details various promotional days at Shea Stadium on the back. The cards are numbered on the back and printed in orange and blue.

	MINT	EXC	G-VG
COMPLETE SET (8)	12.00	6.00	1.20
COMMON PLAYER	.50	.25	.05
☐ 1 Dave Johnson MG	.60	.30	.06
☐ 2 Ron Darling	1.50	.75	.15
☐ 3 George Foster	1.00	.50	.10
☐ 4 Keith Hernandez	1.75	.85	.17
☐ 5 Jesse Orosco	.50	.25	.05
☐ 6 Rusty Staub	1.00	.50	.10
☐ 7 Darryl Strawberry	9.00	4.50	.90
☐ 8 Mookie Wilson	.75	.35	.07

1985 Mets Fan Club

The cards in this 8-player set measure 2 1/2" by 3 1/2". The sheets were produced by Topps for the New York Mets and feature only Mets players. The full sheet measures approximately 7 1/2" by 10 1/2". Cards are together on the sheet but are perforated for those collectors who want to separate the individual player cards. The middle (ninth) card is a Mets Fan club membership card. The set was available as a membership premium for joining the Junior Mets Fan Club for 4.00.

	MINT	EXC	G-VG
COMPLETE SET (8)	20.00	10.00	2.00
COMMON PLAYER	.50	.25	.05
☐ 1 Wally Backman	.50	.25	.05
☐ 2 Bruce Berenyi	.50	.25	.05
☐ 3 Gary Carter	2.00	1.00	.20
☐ 4 George Foster	1.25	.60	.12
☐ 5 Dwight Gooden	12.00	6.00	1.20
☐ 6 Keith Hernandez	1.75	.85	.17
☐ 7 Doug Sisk	.50	.25	.05
☐ 8 Darryl Strawberry	6.00	3.00	.60

1986 Mets Fan Club

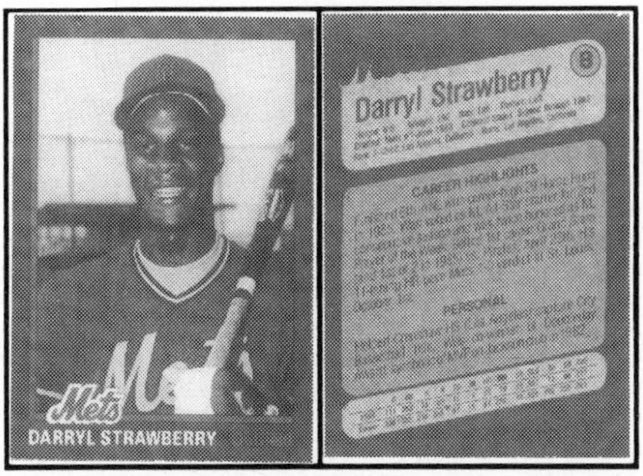

The cards in this 8-player set measure 2 1/2" by 3 1/2". The sheets were produced by Topps for the New York Mets and feature only Mets. The full sheet measures approximately 7 1/2" by 10 1/2". Cards are together on the sheet but are perforated for those collectors who want to separate the individual player cards. The middle (ninth) card is a Mets Fan club membership card. The set was available as a membership premium for joining the Junior Mets Fan Club for 5.00.

	MINT	EXC	G-VG
COMPLETE SET (8)	15.00	7.50	1.50
COMMON PLAYER	.50	.25	.05
☐ 1 Wally Backman	.60	.30	.06
☐ 2 Gary Carter	2.00	1.00	.20
☐ 3 Ron Darling	1.00	.50	.10
☐ 4 Dwight Gooden	5.00	2.50	.50
☐ 5 Keith Hernandez	1.75	.85	.17
☐ 6 Howard Johnson	1.50	.75	.15
☐ 7 Roger McDowell	.75	.35	.07
☐ 8 Darryl Strawberry	5.00	2.50	.50

1987 Mets Fan Club

The cards in this 8-player set measure 2 1/2" by 3 1/2". The sheets were produced by Topps for the New York Mets and feature only Mets. The full sheet measures approximately 7 1/2" by 10 1/2". Cards are together on the sheet but are perforated for those collectors who want to separate the individual player cards. The cards have an outer orange border. The set was available as a membership premium for joining the Junior Mets Fan Club for 6.00. The set and club were also sponsored by Farmland Dairies Milk. The cards are unnumbered on the back although they do contain the player's uniform number on the front.

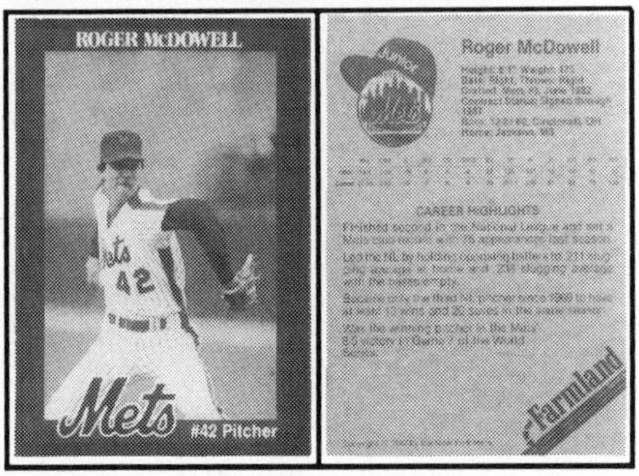

	MINT	EXC	G-VG
COMPLETE SET (9)	10.00	5.00	1.00
COMMON PLAYER	.50	.25	.05
□ 1 Gary Carter 8	1.50	.75	.15
□ 2 Ron Darling 12	1.00	.50	.10
□ 3 Lenny Dykstra 4	1.25	.60	.12
□ 4 Roger McDowell 42	.60	.30	.06
□ 5 Kevin McReynolds 22	2.00	1.00	.20
□ 6 Bob Ojeda 19	.75	.35	.07
□ 7 Darryl Strawberry 18	5.00	2.50	.50
□ 8 Mookie Wilson 1	.60	.30	.06
□ 9 Mets Team Card (1986 World Champs)	.50	.25	.05

1988 Mets Fan Club

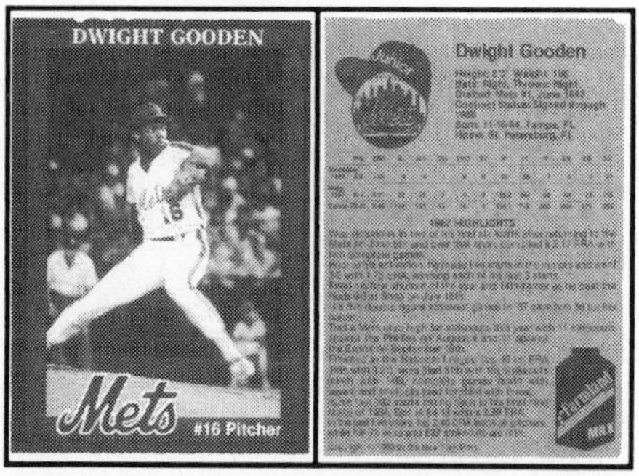

The cards in this 9-player set measure 2 1/2" by 3 1/2". The sheets were produced by Topps for the New York Mets and feature only Mets. The full sheet measures 7 1/2" by 10 1/2". Cards are together on the sheet but are perforated for those collectors who want to separate the individual player cards. The cards have an outer orange border and an inner dark blue border. The set was available as a membership premium for joining the Junior Mets Fan Club for 6.00. The set and club were also sponsored by Farmland Dairies Milk. The cards are unnumbered on the back although they do contain the player's uniform number on the front.

	MINT	EXC	G-VG
COMPLETE SET (9)	6.00	3.00	.60
COMMON PLAYER	.40	.20	.04
□ 8 Gary Carter	.90	.45	.09
□ 16 Dwight Gooden	1.00	.50	.10
□ 17 Keith Hernandez	.75	.35	.07
□ 18 Darryl Strawberry	2.00	1.00	.20
□ 20 Howard Johnson	.90	.45	.09
□ 21 Kevin Elster	.60	.30	.06
□ 42 Roger McDowell	.40	.20	.04
□ 48 Randy Myers	.60	.30	.06
□ 50 Sid Fernandez	.60	.30	.06

1989 Mets Fan Club

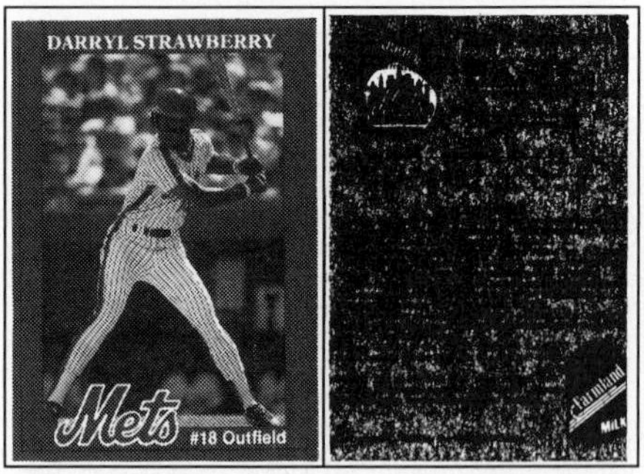

This set was produced by Topps for the Mets Fan Club as a sheet of nine cards each featuring a member of the New York Mets. The individual cards are standard size, 2 1/2" by 3 1/2"; however the set is typically traded as a sheet rather than as individual cards.

	MINT	EXC	G-VG
COMPLETE SET (9)	6.00	3.00	.60
COMMON PLAYER	.40	.20	.04
□ 8 Gary Carter	.90	.45	.09
□ 9 Gregg Jefferies	1.25	.60	.12
□ 16 Dwight Gooden	1.00	.50	.10
□ 18 Darryl Strawberry	1.50	.75	.15
□ 22 Kevin McReynolds	.75	.35	.07
□ 25 Keith Miller	.50	.25	.05
□ 42 Roger McDowell	.60	.30	.06
□ 44 David Cone	.90	.45	.09
□ xx Mets Team Card Eastern Div. Champs	.50	.25	.05

1990 Mets Fan Club

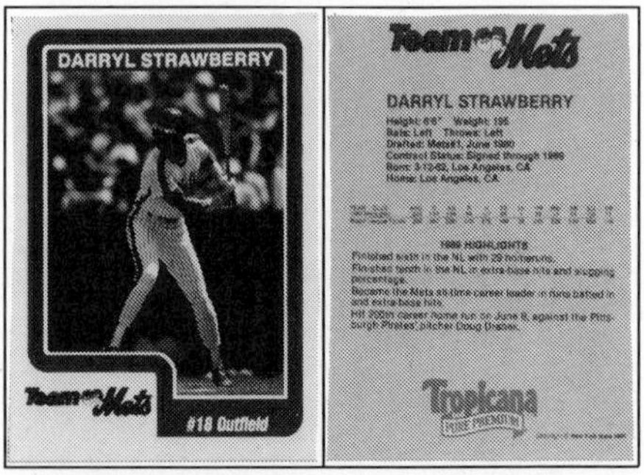

The 1990 Mets Fan Club Tropicana set was issued by the New York Mets fan club in association with the Tropicana Juice Company. For the seventh year, the Mets issued a perforated card sheet in conjunction with their fan clubs. This 9-card, standard-size (2 1/2" by 3 1/2") set is skip-numbered and arranged by uniform numbers.

	MINT	EXC	G-VG
COMPLETE SET (9)	6.00	3.00	.60
COMMON PLAYER	.40	.20	.04
☐ 9 Gregg Jefferies	1.00	.50	.10
☐ 16 Dwight Gooden	1.00	.50	.10
☐ 18 Darryl Strawberry	1.00	.50	.10
☐ 20 Howard Johnson	.75	.35	.07
☐ 21 Kevin Elster	.50	.25	.05
☐ 25 Keith Miller	.40	.20	.04
☐ 29 Frank Viola	.75	.35	.07
☐ 44 David Cone	.75	.35	.07
☐ 50 Sid Fernandez	.50	.25	.05

1984 Milton Bradley

The cards in this 30-card set measure 2 1/2" by 3 1/2". This set of full color cards was produced by Topps for the Milton Bradley Co. The set was included in a board game entitled Championship Baseball. The fronts feature portraits of the players and the name, Championship Baseball, by Milton Bradley. The backs feature the Topps logo, statistics for the past year (pitchers' cards have career statistics), and dice rolls which are part of the board game. Pitcher cards have no dice roll charts. There are 15 players from each league. These unnumbered cards are listed below in alphabetical order. The cap logos and uniforms have been air-brushed to remove all team references.

	MINT	EXC	G-VG
COMPLETE SET (30)	10.00	5.00	1.00
COMMON PLAYER (1-30)	.15	.07	.01
☐ 1 Wade Boggs	1.00	.50	.10
☐ 2 George Brett	.80	.40	.08
☐ 3 Rod Carew	.60	.30	.06
☐ 4 Steve Carlton	.50	.25	.05
☐ 5 Gary Carter	.35	.17	.03
☐ 6 Dave Concepcion	.15	.07	.01
☐ 7 Cecil Cooper	.15	.07	.01
☐ 8 Andre Dawson	.40	.20	.04
☐ 9 Carlton Fisk	.40	.20	.04
☐ 10 Steve Garvey	.40	.20	.04
☐ 11 Pedro Guerrero	.25	.12	.02
☐ 12 Ron Guidry	.25	.12	.02
☐ 13 Rickey Henderson	1.00	.50	.10
☐ 14 Reggie Jackson	.75	.35	.07
☐ 15 Ron Kittle	.15	.07	.01
☐ 16 Bill Madlock	.15	.07	.01
☐ 17 Dale Murphy	.65	.30	.06
☐ 18 Al Oliver	.15	.07	.01
☐ 19 Darrell Porter	.15	.07	.01
☐ 20 Cal Ripken	.65	.30	.06
☐ 21 Pete Rose	1.00	.50	.10
☐ 22 Steve Sax	.30	.15	.03
☐ 23 Mike Schmidt	1.00	.50	.10
☐ 24 Ted Simmons	.15	.07	.01
☐ 25 Ozzie Smith	.35	.17	.03
☐ 26 Dave Stieb	.20	.10	.02
☐ 27 Fernando Valenzuela	.25	.12	.02
☐ 28 Lou Whitaker	.25	.12	.02
☐ 29 Dave Winfield	.35	.17	.03
☐ 30 Robin Yount	.75	.35	.07

1987 MnM's Star Lineup

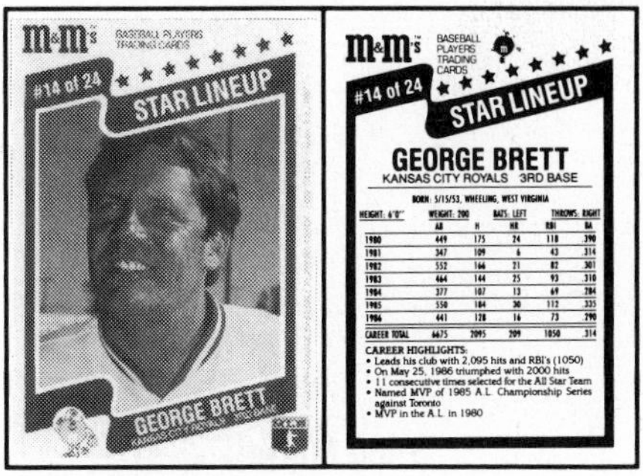

The Mars Candy Company is the sponsor of this 24-card set of cards. The cards were printed in perforated pairs. The pairs measure 5" by 3 1/2" whereas the individual cards measure the standard 2 1/2" by 3 1/2". The players are shown without team logos. The cards were designed and produced by MSA, Mike Schechter Associates. The cards are numbered on the front and back. The backs show statistics for every year since 1980 even if the player was not even playing during those earlier years. The values below are for individual players; panels intact would be valued at 25 percent more than the sum of the two individual players.

	MINT	EXC	G-VG
COMPLETE SET (24)	12.00	6.00	1.20
COMMON PLAYER (1-24)	.30	.15	.03
☐ 1 Wally Joyner	.90	.45	.09
☐ 2 Tony Pena	.30	.15	.03
☐ 3 Mike Schmidt	1.25	.60	.12
☐ 4 Ryne Sandberg	1.25	.60	.12
☐ 5 Wade Boggs	1.25	.60	.12
☐ 6 Jack Morris	.50	.25	.05
☐ 7 Roger Clemens	1.25	.60	.12
☐ 8 Harold Baines	.40	.20	.04
☐ 9 Dale Murphy	.75	.35	.07
☐ 10 Jose Canseco	2.00	1.00	.20
☐ 11 Don Mattingly	2.00	1.00	.20
☐ 12 Gary Carter	.75	.35	.07
☐ 13 Cal Ripken Jr.	.75	.35	.07
☐ 14 George Brett	1.00	.50	.10
☐ 15 Kirby Puckett	1.00	.50	.10
☐ 16 Joe Carter	.50	.25	.05
☐ 17 Mike Witt	.30	.15	.03
☐ 18 Mike Scott	.50	.25	.05
☐ 19 Fernando Valenzuela	.50	.25	.05
☐ 20 Steve Garvey	.75	.35	.07
☐ 21 Steve Sax	.50	.25	.05
☐ 22 Nolan Ryan	2.00	1.00	.20
☐ 23 Tony Gwynn	.75	.35	.07
☐ 24 Ozzie Smith	.50	.25	.05

1959 Morrell

The cards in this 12-card set measure 2 1/2" by 3 1/2". The 1959 Morrell Meats set of full color, unnumbered cards features Los Angeles Dodger players only. The photos used are the same as those selected for the Dodger team issue postcards in 1959. The Morrell Meats logo is on the backs of the cards. The Clem Labine card actually features a picture of Stan Williams and the Norm Larker card actually features a picture of Joe Pignatano as indicated in the checklist below. The catalog designation is F172-1.

	NRMT	VG-E	GOOD
COMPLETE SET (12)	1100.00	500.00	100.00
COMMON PLAYER (1-12)	60.00	30.00	6.00
☐ 1 Don Drysdale	125.00	60.00	12.50
☐ 2 Carl Furillo	75.00	37.50	7.50
☐ 3 Jim Gilliam	75.00	37.50	7.50
☐ 4 Gil Hodges	125.00	60.00	12.50
☐ 5 Sandy Koufax	250.00	125.00	25.00
☐ 6 Clem Labine UER (photo actually Stan Williams)	60.00	30.00	6.00
☐ 7 Norm Larker UER (photo actually Joe Pignatano)	60.00	30.00	6.00
☐ 8 Charlie Neal	60.00	30.00	6.00
☐ 9 Johnny Podres	75.00	37.50	7.50
☐ 10 John Roseboro	60.00	30.00	6.00
☐ 11 Duke Snider	250.00	125.00	25.00
☐ 12 Don Zimmer	75.00	37.50	7.50

1960 Morrell

The cards in this 12-card set measure 2 1/2" by 3 1/2". The 1960 Morrell Meats set of full color, unnumbered cards is similar in format to the 1959 Morrell set but can be distinguished from the 1959 set by a red heart which appears in the Morrell logo on the back. The photos used are the same as those selected for the Dodger team issue postcards in 1960. The Furillo, Hodges, and Snider cards received limited distribution and are hence more scarce. The catalog designation is F172-2. The cards were printed in Japan.

	NRMT	VG-E	GOOD
COMPLETE SET (12)	750.00	375.00	75.00
COMMON PLAYER (1-12)	20.00	10.00	2.00
☐ 1 Walt Alston MG	40.00	20.00	4.00
☐ 2 Roger Craig	30.00	15.00	3.00
☐ 3 Don Drysdale	50.00	25.00	5.00
☐ 4 Carl Furillo SP	100.00	50.00	10.00
☐ 5 Gil Hodges SP	150.00	75.00	15.00
☐ 6 Sandy Koufax	125.00	60.00	12.50
☐ 7 Wally Moon	20.00	10.00	2.00
☐ 8 Charlie Neal	20.00	10.00	2.00
☐ 9 Johnny Podres	25.00	12.50	2.50
☐ 10 John Roseboro	20.00	10.00	2.00
☐ 11 Larry Sherry	20.00	10.00	2.00
☐ 12 Duke Snider SP	250.00	125.00	25.00

1961 Morrell

The cards in this 6-card set measure 2 1/2" by 3 1/2". The 1961 Morrell Meats set of full color, unnumbered cards features Los Angeles Dodger players only and contains statistical information on the backs of the cards in brown print. The catalog designation is F172-3.

	NRMT	VG-E	GOOD
COMPLETE SET (6)	225.00	110.00	22.00
COMMON PLAYER (1-6)	16.00	8.00	1.60
☐ 1 Tommy Davis	20.00	10.00	2.00
☐ 2 Don Drysdale	50.00	25.00	5.00
☐ 3 Frank Howard	20.00	10.00	2.00
☐ 4 Sandy Koufax	125.00	60.00	12.50
☐ 5 Norm Larker	16.00	8.00	1.60
☐ 6 Maury Wills	35.00	17.50	3.50

1983 Mother's Giants

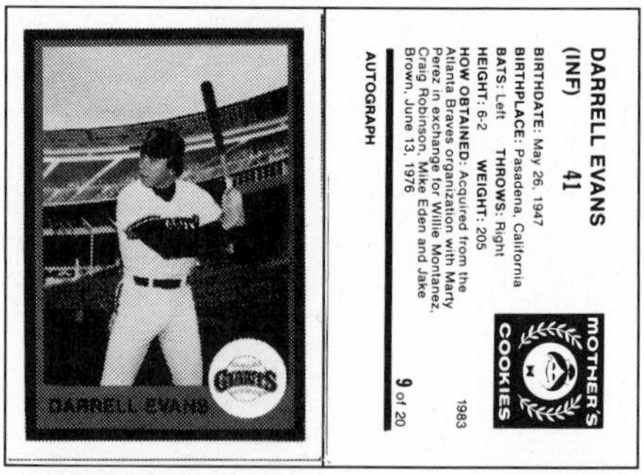

The cards in this 20-card set measure 2 1/2" by 3 1/2". For the first time in 30 years, Mother's Cookies issued a baseball card set. The full color set, produced by hobbyist Barry Colla, features San Francisco Giants players only. Fifteen cards were issued at the Astros vs. Giants game of August 7, 1983. Five of the cards were redeemable by sending in a coupon. The five additional cards received from redemption of the coupon were not guaranteed to be the five needed to complete the set. The fronts feature the player's photo, his name, and the Giants' logo, while the backs feature player biographies and the Mother's Cookies logo. The backs also contain a space in which to obtain the player's autograph.

	MINT	EXC	G-VG
COMPLETE SET (20)	18.00	9.00	1.80
COMMON PLAYER (1-20)	.60	.30	.06
☐ 1 Frank Robinson MG	2.50	1.25	.25
☐ 2 Jack Clark	2.50	1.25	.25
☐ 3 Chili Davis	1.50	.75	.15
☐ 4 Johnnie LeMaster	.60	.30	.06
☐ 5 Greg Minton	.75	.35	.07
☐ 6 Bob Brenly	.60	.30	.06
☐ 7 Fred Breining	.60	.30	.06
☐ 8 Jeff Leonard	.90	.45	.09
☐ 9 Darrell Evans	1.25	.60	.12
☐ 10 Tom O'Malley	.60	.30	.06
☐ 11 Duane Kuiper	.60	.30	.06
☐ 12 Mike Krukow	.75	.35	.07
☐ 13 Atlee Hammaker	.75	.35	.07
☐ 14 Gary Lavelle	.60	.30	.06
☐ 15 Bill Laskey	.60	.30	.06
☐ 16 Max Venable	.60	.30	.06
☐ 17 Joel Youngblood	.60	.30	.06
☐ 18 Dave Bergman	.60	.30	.06
☐ 19 Mike Vail	.60	.30	.06
☐ 20 Andy McGaffigan	.60	.30	.06

1984 Mother's A's

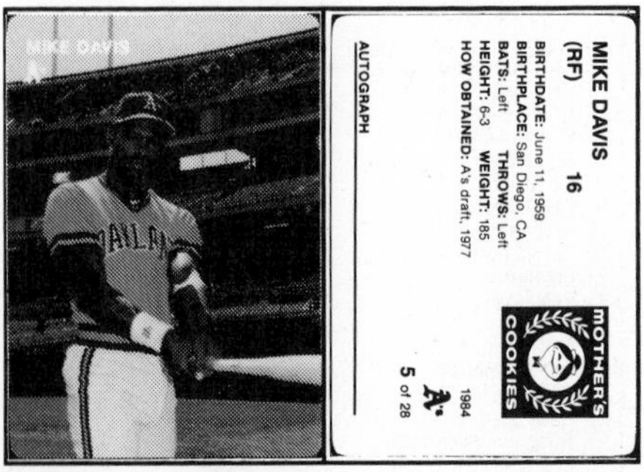

The cards in this 28-card set measure 2 1/2" by 3 1/2". In 1984, the Los Angeles based Mother's Cookies Co. issued five sets of cards featuring players from major league teams. The Oakland A's set features current players depicted by photos. Similar to their 1952 and 1953 issues, the cards have rounded corners. The backs of the cards contain the Mother's Cookies logo. The cards were distributed in partial sets to fans at the respective stadiums of the teams involved. Whereas 20 cards were given to each patron, a redemption card, redeemable for eight more cards was included. Unfortunately, the eight cards received by redeeming the coupon were not necessarily the eight needed to complete a set. Hobbyist Barry Colla was involved in the production of these sets.

	MINT	EXC	G-VG
COMPLETE SET (28)	16.00	8.00	1.60
COMMON PLAYER (1-28)	.40	.20	.04
☐ 1 Steve Boros MG	.40	.20	.04
☐ 2 Rickey Henderson	6.00	3.00	.60
☐ 3 Joe Morgan	2.00	1.00	.20
☐ 4 Dwayne Murphy	.60	.30	.06
☐ 5 Mike Davis	.60	.30	.06
☐ 6 Bruce Bochte	.40	.20	.04
☐ 7 Carney Lansford	1.00	.50	.10
☐ 8 Steve McCatty	.40	.20	.04
☐ 9 Mike Heath	.40	.20	.04
☐ 10 Chris Codiroli	.40	.20	.04
☐ 11 Bill Almon	.40	.20	.04
☐ 12 Bill Caudill	.50	.25	.05
☐ 13 Donnie Hill	.40	.20	.04
☐ 14 Lary Sorensen	.40	.20	.04
☐ 15 Dave Kingman	.80	.40	.08
☐ 16 Garry Hancock	.40	.20	.04
☐ 17 Jeff Burroughs	.50	.25	.05
☐ 18 Tom Burgmeier	.40	.20	.04
☐ 19 Jim Essian	.40	.20	.04
☐ 20 Mike Warren	.40	.20	.04
☐ 21 Davey Lopes	.50	.25	.05
☐ 22 Ray Burris	.50	.25	.05
☐ 23 Tony Phillips	.50	.25	.05
☐ 24 Tim Conroy	.40	.20	.04
☐ 25 Jeff Bettendorf	.40	.20	.04
☐ 26 Keith Atherton	.40	.20	.04
☐ 27 A's Coaches	.40	.20	.04
☐ 28 A's Checklist	.40	.20	.04

1984 Mother's Astros

The cards in this 28-card set measure 2 1/2" by 3 1/2". In 1984, the Los Angeles based Mother's Cookies Co. issued five sets of cards featuring players from major league teams. The Houston Astros set features current players depicted by photos. Similar to their 1952 and 1953 issues, the cards have rounded corners. The backs of the cards contain the Mother's Cookies logo. The cards were distributed in partial sets to fans at the respective stadiums of the teams involved. Whereas 20 cards were given to each patron, a redemption card, redeemable for eight more cards was included. Unfortunately, the eight cards received by redeeming the coupon were not necessarily the eight needed to complete a set. Hobbyist Barry Colla was involved in the production of these sets.

	MINT	EXC	G-VG
COMPLETE SET (28)	14.00	7.00	1.40
COMMON PLAYER (1-28)	.35	.17	.03
☐ 1 Nolan Ryan	5.00	2.50	.50
☐ 2 Joe Niekro	.75	.35	.07
☐ 3 Alan Ashby	.45	.22	.04
☐ 4 Bill Doran	1.00	.50	.10
☐ 5 Phil Garner	.45	.22	.04
☐ 6 Ray Knight	.60	.30	.06
☐ 7 Dickie Thon	.45	.22	.04
☐ 8 Jose Cruz	.60	.30	.06
☐ 9 Jerry Mumphrey	.35	.17	.03
☐ 10 Terry Puhl	.45	.22	.04
☐ 11 Enos Cabell	.35	.17	.03
☐ 12 Harry Spilman	.35	.17	.03
☐ 13 Dave Smith	.60	.30	.06
☐ 14 Mike Scott	1.50	.75	.15
☐ 15 Bob Lillis MG	.35	.17	.03
☐ 16 Bob Knepper	.45	.22	.04
☐ 17 Frank DiPino	.35	.17	.03
☐ 18 Tom Wieghaus	.35	.17	.03
☐ 19 Denny Walling	.35	.17	.03
☐ 20 Tony Scott	.35	.17	.03
☐ 21 Alan Bannister	.35	.17	.03
☐ 22 Bill Dawley	.35	.17	.03
☐ 23 Vern Ruhle	.35	.17	.03
☐ 24 Mike LaCoss	.35	.17	.03
☐ 25 Mike Madden	.35	.17	.03
☐ 26 Craig Reynolds	.45	.22	.04
☐ 27 Astros' Coaches	.35	.17	.03
☐ 28 Astros' Checklist	.35	.17	.03

1984 Mother's Giants

The cards in this 28-card set measure 2 1/2" by 3 1/2". In 1984, the Los Angeles based Mother's Cookies Co. issued five sets of cards featuring players from major league teams. The San Francisco Giants set features previous Giant All-Star selections depicted by drawings. Similar to their 1952 and 1953 issues, the cards have rounded corners. The backs of the cards contain the Mother's Cookies logo. The cards were distributed in partial sets to fans at the respective stadiums of the teams involved. Whereas 20 cards were given to each patron, a redemption card, redeemable for eight more cards was included. Unfortunately, the eight cards received by redeeming the coupon were not necessarily the eight needed to complete a set. Hobbyist Barry Colla was involved in the production of these sets.

	MINT	EXC	G-VG
COMPLETE SET (28)	15.00	7.50	1.50
COMMON PLAYER (1-28)	.40	.20	.04
☐ 1 Willie Mays	3.50	1.75	.35
☐ 2 Willie McCovey	2.50	1.25	.25
☐ 3 Juan Marichal	2.00	1.00	.20
☐ 4 Gaylord Perry	2.00	1.00	.20

☐ 5 Tom Haller	.40	.20	.04
☐ 6 Jim Davenport	.40	.20	.04
☐ 7 Jack Clark	1.25	.60	.12
☐ 8 Greg Minton	.40	.20	.04
☐ 9 Atlee Hammaker	.40	.20	.04
☐ 10 Gary Lavelle	.40	.20	.04
☐ 11 Orlando Cepeda	1.00	.50	.10
☐ 12 Bobby Bonds	.75	.35	.07
☐ 13 John Antonelli	.40	.20	.04
☐ 14 Bob Schmidt (photo actually Wes Westrum)	.40	.20	.04
☐ 15 Sam Jones	.40	.20	.04
☐ 16 Mike McCormick	.40	.20	.04
☐ 17 Ed Bailey	.40	.20	.04
☐ 18 Stu Miller	.40	.20	.04
☐ 19 Felipe Alou	.60	.30	.06
☐ 20 Jim Ray Hart	.40	.20	.04
☐ 21 Dick Dietz	.40	.20	.04
☐ 22 Chris Speier	.40	.20	.04
☐ 23 Bobby Murcer	.60	.30	.06
☐ 24 John Montefusco	.40	.20	.04
☐ 25 Vida Blue	.50	.25	.05
☐ 26 Ed Whitson	.50	.25	.05
☐ 27 Darrell Evans	.75	.35	.07
☐ 28 Checklist Card	.40	.20	.04

1984 Mother's Mariners

The cards in this 28-card set measure 2 1/2" by 3 1/2". In 1984, The Los Angeles-based Mother's Cookies Co. issued five sets of cards featuring players from major league teams. The Seattle Mariners set features current players depicted by photos. Similar to their 1952 and 1953 issues, the cards have rounded corners. The backs of the cards contain the Mother's Cookies logo. The cards were distributed in partial sets to fans at the respective stadiums of the teams involved. Whereas 20 cards were given to each patron, a redemption card, redeemable for eight more cards was included. Unfortunately, the eight cards received by redeeming the coupon were not necessarily the eight needed to complete a set. Hobbyist Barry Colla was involved in the production of these sets.

	MINT	EXC	G-VG
COMPLETE SET (28)	14.00	7.00	1.40
COMMON PLAYER (1-28)	.40	.20	.04
☐ 1 Del Crandall MG	.50	.25	.05
☐ 2 Barry Bonnell	.40	.20	.04
☐ 3 Dave Henderson	.75	.35	.07
☐ 4 Bob Kearney	.40	.20	.04
☐ 5 Mike Moore	1.00	.50	.10
☐ 6 Spike Owen	.50	.25	.05
☐ 7 Gorman Thomas	.60	.30	.06
☐ 8 Ed VandeBerg	.40	.20	.04
☐ 9 Matt Young	.40	.20	.04
☐ 10 Larry Milbourne	.40	.20	.04
☐ 11 Dave Beard	.40	.20	.04
☐ 12 Jim Beattie	.40	.20	.04
☐ 13 Mark Langston	2.50	1.25	.25
☐ 14 Orlando Mercado	.40	.20	.04
☐ 15 Jack Perconte	.40	.20	.04
☐ 16 Pat Putnam	.40	.20	.04
☐ 17 Paul Mirabella	.40	.20	.04
☐ 18 Domingo Ramos	.40	.20	.04
☐ 19 Al Cowens	.40	.20	.04
☐ 20 Mike Stanton	.40	.20	.04
☐ 21 Steve Henderson	.40	.20	.04
☐ 22 Bob Stoddard	.40	.20	.04
☐ 23 Alvin Davis	2.50	1.25	.25
☐ 24 Phil Bradley	1.00	.50	.10
☐ 25 Roy Thomas	.40	.20	.04
☐ 26 Darnell Coles	.60	.30	.06
☐ 27 Mariners' Coaches	.40	.20	.04
☐ 28 Mariners' Checklist	.40	.20	.04

1984 Mother's Padres

The cards in this 28-card set measure 2 1/2" by 3 1/2". In 1984, the Los Angeles based Mother's Cookies Co. issued five sets of cards featuring players from major league teams. The San Diego Padres set features current players depicted by photos. Similar to their 1952 and 1953 issues, the cards have rounded corners. The backs of the cards contain the Mother's Cookies logo. The cards were distributed in partial sets to fans at the respective stadiums of the teams involved. Whereas 20 cards were given to each patron, a redemption card, redeemable for eight more cards was included. Unfortunately, the eight cards received by redeeming the coupon were not necessarily the eight needed to complete a set. Hobbyist Barry Colla was involved in the production of these sets.

	MINT	EXC	G-VG
COMPLETE SET (28)	18.00	9.00	1.80
COMMON PLAYER (1-28)	.50	.25	.05
☐ 1 Dick Williams MG	.60	.30	.06
☐ 2 Rich Gossage	.90	.45	.09
☐ 3 Tim Lollar	.50	.25	.05
☐ 4 Eric Show	.75	.35	.07
☐ 5 Terry Kennedy	.60	.30	.06
☐ 6 Kurt Bevacqua	.50	.25	.05
☐ 7 Steve Garvey	2.00	1.00	.20
☐ 8 Garry Templeton	.60	.30	.06
☐ 9 Tony Gwynn	4.00	2.00	.40
☐ 10 Alan Wiggins	.50	.25	.05
☐ 11 Dave Dravecky	1.00	.50	.10
☐ 12 Tim Flannery	.50	.25	.05
☐ 13 Kevin McReynolds	3.00	1.50	.30
☐ 14 Bobby Brown	.50	.25	.05
☐ 15 Ed Whitson	.75	.35	.07
☐ 16 Doug Gwosdz	.50	.25	.05
☐ 17 Luis DeLeon	.50	.25	.05
☐ 18 Andy Hawkins	.75	.35	.07
☐ 19 Craig Lefferts	.60	.30	.06
☐ 20 Carmelo Martinez	.60	.30	.06
☐ 21 Sid Monge	.50	.25	.05
☐ 22 Graig Nettles	.75	.35	.07
☐ 23 Mario Ramirez	.50	.25	.05
☐ 24 Luis Salazar	.60	.30	.06
☐ 25 Champ Summers	.50	.25	.05
☐ 26 Mark Thurmond	.50	.25	.05
☐ 27 Padres' Coaches	.50	.25	.05
☐ 28 Padres' Checklist	.50	.25	.05

1985 Mother's A's

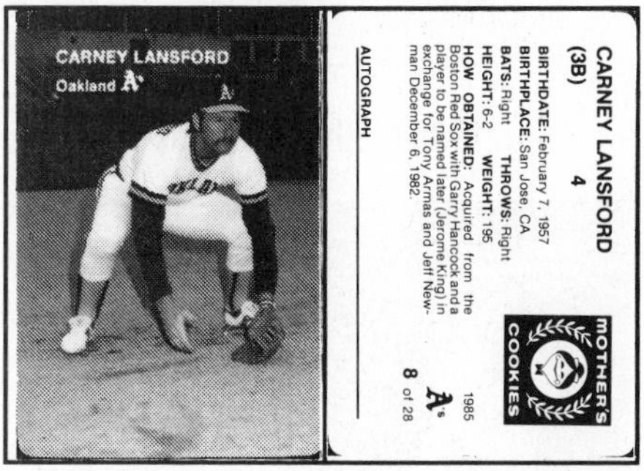

The cards in this 28-card set measure 2 1/2" by 3 1/2". In 1985, the Los Angeles based Mother's Cookies Co. again issued five sets of cards featuring players from major league teams. The Oakland A's set features current players depicted by photos on cards with rounded corners. The backs of the cards contain the Mother's Cookies logo. Cards were passed out at the stadium on July 6.

	MINT	EXC	G-VG
COMPLETE SET (28)	12.00	6.00	1.20
COMMON PLAYER (1-28)	.35	.17	.03
☐ 1 Jackie Moore MG	.35	.17	.03
☐ 2 Dave Kingman	.65	.30	.06
☐ 3 Don Sutton	1.25	.60	.12
☐ 4 Mike Heath	.35	.17	.03
☐ 5 Alfredo Griffin	.50	.25	.05
☐ 6 Dwayne Murphy	.50	.25	.05
☐ 7 Mike Davis	.50	.25	.05
☐ 8 Carney Lansford	.75	.35	.07
☐ 9 Chris Codiroli	.35	.17	.03
☐ 10 Bruce Bochte	.35	.17	.03
☐ 11 Mickey Tettleton	.75	.35	.07
☐ 12 Donnie Hill	.35	.17	.03
☐ 13 Rob Picciolo	.35	.17	.03
☐ 14 Dave Collins	.35	.17	.03
☐ 15 Dusty Baker	.50	.25	.05
☐ 16 Tim Conroy	.35	.17	.03
☐ 17 Keith Atherton	.35	.17	.03
☐ 18 Jay Howell	.50	.25	.05
☐ 19 Mike Warren	.35	.17	.03
☐ 20 Steve McCatty	.35	.17	.03
☐ 21 Bill Krueger	.35	.17	.03
☐ 22 Curt Young	.50	.25	.05
☐ 23 Dan Meyer	.35	.17	.03
☐ 24 Mike Gallego	.35	.17	.03
☐ 25 Jeff Kaiser	.35	.17	.03
☐ 26 Steve Henderson	.35	.17	.03
☐ 27 A's Coaches	.35	.17	.03
☐ 28 A's Checklist	.35	.17	.03

1985 Mother's Astros

The cards in this 28-card set measure 2 1/2" by 3 1/2". In 1985, the Los Angeles-based Mother's Cookies Co. again issued five sets of cards featuring players from major league teams. The Houston Astros set features current players depicted by photos on cards with rounded corners. The backs of the cards contain the Mother's Cookies logo. Cards were passed out at the stadium on July 13. The checklist card features the Astros logo on the obverse.

	MINT	EXC	G-VG
COMPLETE SET (28)	13.00	6.50	1.30
COMMON PLAYER (1-28)	.35	.17	.03
☐ 1 Bob Lillis MG	.35	.17	.03
☐ 2 Nolan Ryan	4.00	2.00	.40
☐ 3 Phil Garner	.45	.22	.04
☐ 4 Jose Cruz	.60	.30	.06
☐ 5 Denny Walling	.35	.17	.03
☐ 6 Joe Niekro	.75	.35	.07
☐ 7 Terry Puhl	.45	.22	.04
☐ 8 Bill Doran	.75	.35	.07
☐ 9 Dickie Thon	.45	.22	.04
☐ 10 Enos Cabell	.35	.17	.03
☐ 11 Frank DiPino	.35	.17	.03
☐ 12 Julio Solano	.35	.17	.03
☐ 13 Alan Ashby	.45	.22	.04
☐ 14 Craig Reynolds	.35	.17	.03
☐ 15 Jerry Mumphrey	.35	.17	.03
☐ 16 Bill Dawley	.35	.17	.03
☐ 17 Mark Bailey	.35	.17	.03
☐ 18 Mike Scott	1.25	.60	.12
☐ 19 Harry Spilman	.35	.17	.03
☐ 20 Bob Knepper	.45	.22	.04
☐ 21 Dave Smith	.60	.30	.06
☐ 22 Kevin Bass	.60	.30	.06
☐ 23 Tim Tolman	.35	.17	.03
☐ 24 Jeff Calhoun	.35	.17	.03
☐ 25 Jim Pankovits	.35	.17	.03
☐ 26 Ron Mathis	.35	.17	.03
☐ 27 Astros' Coaches	.35	.17	.03
☐ 28 Astros' Checklist	.35	.17	.03

1985 Mother's Giants

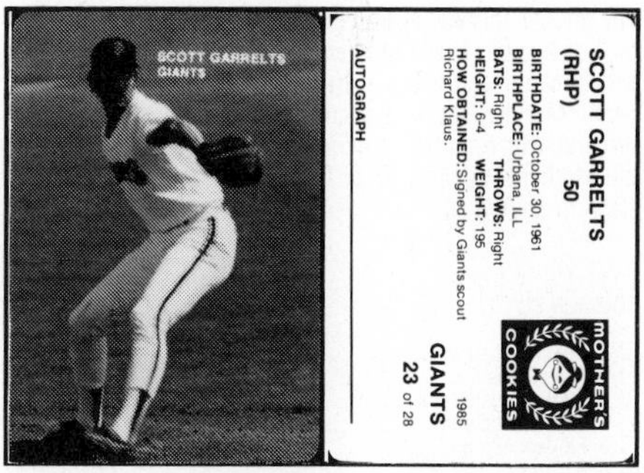

The cards in this 28-card set measure 2 1/2" by 3 1/2". In 1985, the Los Angeles based Mother's Cookies Co. again issued five sets of cards featuring players from major league teams. The San Francisco Giants set features current players depicted by photos on cards with rounded corners. The backs of the cards contain the Mother's Cookies logo. Cards were passed out at the stadium on June 30.

	MINT	EXC	G-VG
COMPLETE SET (28)	11.00	5.50	1.10
COMMON PLAYER (1-28)	.35	.17	.03
☐ 1 Jim Davenport MG	.35	.17	.03
☐ 2 Chili Davis	.75	.35	.07

☐ 3 Dan Gladden	.60	.30	.06
☐ 4 Jeff Leonard	.60	.30	.06
☐ 5 Manny Trillo	.35	.17	.03
☐ 6 Atlee Hammaker	.35	.17	.03
☐ 7 Bob Brenly	.35	.17	.03
☐ 8 Greg Minton	.35	.17	.03
☐ 9 Bill Laskey	.35	.17	.03
☐ 10 Vida Blue	.50	.25	.05
☐ 11 Mike Krukow	.50	.25	.05
☐ 12 Frank Williams	.35	.17	.03
☐ 13 Jose Uribe	.50	.25	.05
☐ 14 Johnnie LeMaster	.35	.17	.03
☐ 15 Scot Thompson	.35	.17	.03
☐ 16 Dave LaPoint	.35	.17	.03
☐ 17 David Green	.35	.17	.03
☐ 18 Chris Brown	.35	.17	.03
☐ 19 Joel Youngblood	.35	.17	.03
☐ 20 Mark Davis	1.25	.60	.12
☐ 21 Jim Gott	.50	.25	.05
☐ 22 Doug Gwosdz	.35	.17	.03
☐ 23 Scott Garrelts	.75	.35	.07
☐ 24 Gary Rajsich	.35	.17	.03
☐ 25 Rob Deer	1.00	.50	.10
☐ 26 Brad Wellman	.35	.17	.03
☐ 27 Giants' Coaches	.35	.17	.03
☐ 28 Giants' Checklist	.35	.17	.03

1985 Mother's Mariners

The cards in this 28-card set measure 2 1/2" by 3 1/2". In 1985, the Los Angeles based Mother's Cookies Co. again issued five sets of cards featuring players from major league teams. The Seattle Mariners set features current players depicted by photos on cards with rounded corners. The backs of the cards contain the Mother's Cookies logo. Cards were passed out at the stadium on August 10.

	MINT	EXC	G-VG
COMPLETE SET (28)	12.00	6.00	1.20
COMMON PLAYER (1-28)	.35	.17	.03
☐ 1 Chuck Cottier MG	.35	.17	.03
☐ 2 Alvin Davis	1.50	.75	.15
☐ 3 Mark Langston	1.50	.75	.15
☐ 4 Dave Henderson	.50	.25	.05
☐ 5 Ed VandeBerg	.35	.17	.03
☐ 6 Al Cowens	.35	.17	.03
☐ 7 Spike Owen	.35	.17	.03
☐ 8 Mike Moore	.75	.35	.07
☐ 9 Gorman Thomas	.50	.25	.05
☐ 10 Barry Bonnell	.35	.17	.03
☐ 11 Jack Perconte	.35	.17	.03
☐ 12 Domingo Ramos	.35	.17	.03
☐ 13 Bob Kearney	.35	.17	.03
☐ 14 Matt Young	.35	.17	.03
☐ 15 Jim Beattie	.35	.17	.03
☐ 16 Mike Stanton	.35	.17	.03
☐ 17 David Valle	.35	.17	.03
☐ 18 Ken Phelps	.50	.25	.05
☐ 19 Salome Barojas	.35	.17	.03
☐ 20 Jim Presley	.90	.45	.09
☐ 21 Phil Bradley	.90	.45	.09
☐ 22 Dave Geisel	.35	.17	.03
☐ 23 Harold Reynolds	.90	.45	.09
☐ 24 Ed Nunez	.50	.25	.05
☐ 25 Mike Morgan	.50	.25	.05
☐ 26 Ivan Calderon	.90	.45	.09
☐ 27 Mariners Coaches	.35	.17	.03
☐ 28 Checklist Card	.35	.17	.03

1985 Mother's Padres

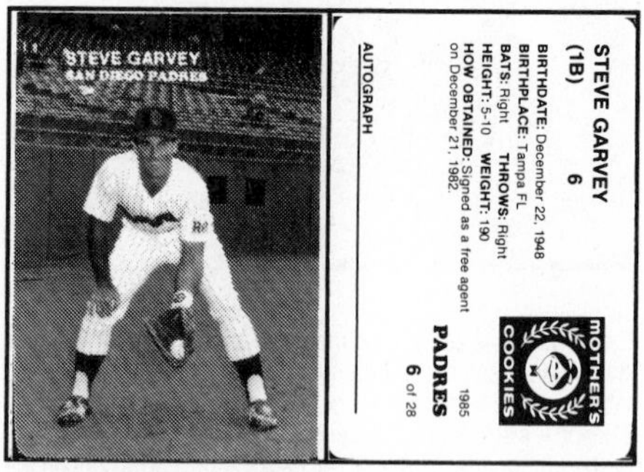

The cards in this 28-card set measure 2 1/2" by 3 1/2". In 1985, the Los Angeles based Mother's Cookies Co. again issued five sets of cards featuring players from major league teams. The San Diego Padres set features current players depicted by photos on cards with rounded corners. The backs of the cards contain the Mother's Cookies logo. Cards were passed out at the stadium on August 11.

	MINT	EXC	G-VG
COMPLETE SET (28)	12.00	6.00	1.20
COMMON PLAYER (1-28)	.35	.17	.03
☐ 1 Dick Williams MG	.35	.17	.03
☐ 2 Tony Gwynn	2.50	1.25	.25
☐ 3 Kevin McReynolds	1.50	.75	.15
☐ 4 Graig Nettles	.75	.35	.07
☐ 5 Rich Gossage	.75	.35	.07
☐ 6 Steve Garvey	1.50	.75	.15
☐ 7 Garry Templeton	.50	.25	.05
☐ 8 Dave Dravecky	.75	.35	.07
☐ 9 Eric Show	.50	.25	.05
☐ 10 Terry Kennedy	.35	.17	.03
☐ 11 Luis DeLeon	.35	.17	.03
☐ 12 Bruce Bochy	.35	.17	.03
☐ 13 Andy Hawkins	.50	.25	.05
☐ 14 Kurt Bevacqua	.35	.17	.03
☐ 15 Craig Lefferts	.50	.25	.05
☐ 16 Mario Ramirez	.35	.17	.03
☐ 17 LaMarr Hoyt	.35	.17	.03
☐ 18 Jerry Royster	.35	.17	.03
☐ 19 Tim Stoddard	.35	.17	.03
☐ 20 Tim Flannery	.35	.17	.03
☐ 21 Mark Thurmond	.35	.17	.03
☐ 22 Greg Booker	.35	.17	.03
☐ 23 Bobby Brown	.35	.17	.03
☐ 24 Carmelo Martinez	.50	.25	.05
☐ 25 Al Bumbry	.35	.17	.03
☐ 26 Jerry Davis	.35	.17	.03
☐ 27 Padres' Coaches	.35	.17	.03
☐ 28 Padres' Checklist	.35	.17	.03

1986 Mother's A's

This set consists of 28 full-color, rounded-corner cards each measuring 2 1/2" by 3 1/2". Starter sets (only 20 cards but also including a certificate for eight more cards) were given out at the ballpark and collectors were encouraged to trade to fill in the rest of their set. The cards were originally given away on July 20th at Oakland Coliseum.

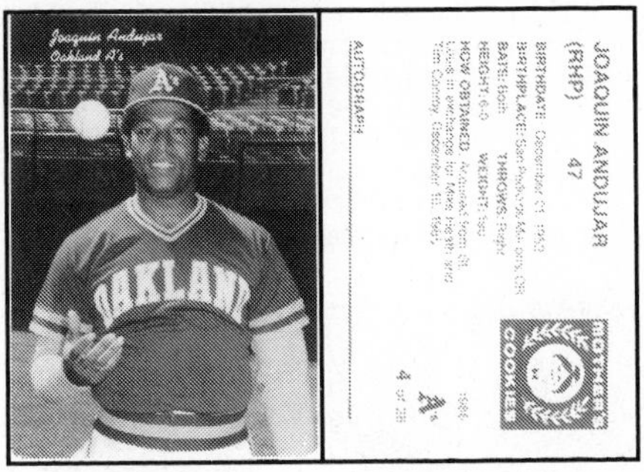

	MINT	EXC	G-VG
COMPLETE SET (28)	30.00	15.00	3.00
COMMON PLAYER (1-28)	.35	.17	.03
☐ 1 Jackie Moore MG	.35	.17	.03
☐ 2 Dave Kingman	.60	.30	.06
☐ 3 Dusty Baker	.50	.25	.05
☐ 4 Joaquin Andujar	.50	.25	.05
☐ 5 Alfredo Griffin	.50	.25	.05
☐ 6 Dwayne Murphy	.50	.25	.05
☐ 7 Mike Davis	.50	.25	.05
☐ 8 Carney Lansford	.75	.35	.07
☐ 9 Jose Canseco	20.00	10.00	2.00
☐ 10 Bruce Bochte	.35	.17	.03
☐ 11 Mickey Tettleton	.50	.25	.05
☐ 12 Donnie Hill	.35	.17	.03
☐ 13 Jose Rijo	1.00	.50	.10
☐ 14 Rick Langford	.35	.17	.03
☐ 15 Chris Codiroli	.35	.17	.03
☐ 16 Moose Haas	.35	.17	.03
☐ 17 Keith Atherton	.35	.17	.03
☐ 18 Jay Howell	.50	.25	.05
☐ 19 Tony Phillips	.35	.17	.03
☐ 20 Steve Henderson	.35	.17	.03
☐ 21 Bill Krueger	.35	.17	.03
☐ 22 Steve Ontiveros	.35	.17	.03
☐ 23 Bill Bathe	.35	.17	.03
☐ 24 Ricky Peters	.35	.17	.03
☐ 25 Tim Birtsas	.35	.17	.03
☐ 26 A's Trainers and Equipment Managers	.35	.17	.03
☐ 27 A's Coaches	.35	.17	.03
☐ 28 Checklist Card	.35	.17	.03

1986 Mother's Astros

This set consists of 28 full-color, rounded-corner cards each measuring 2 1/2" by 3 1/2". Starter sets (only 20 cards but also including a certificate for eight more cards) were given out at the ballpark and collectors were encouraged to trade to fill in the rest of their set. Cards were originally given out at the Astrodome on July 10th. Since the 1986 All-Star Game was held in Houston, the set features Astro All-Stars since 1962 as painted by artist Richard Wallich.

	MINT	EXC	G-VG
COMPLETE SET (28)	10.00	5.00	1.00
COMMON PLAYER (1-28)	.35	.17	.03
☐ 1 Dick Farrell	.35	.17	.03
☐ 2 Hal Woodeshick	.35	.17	.03
☐ 3 Joe Morgan	1.50	.75	.15
☐ 4 Claude Raymond	.35	.17	.03
☐ 5 Mike Cuellar	.50	.25	.05
☐ 6 Rusty Staub	.75	.35	.07
☐ 7 Jimmy Wynn	.50	.25	.05
☐ 8 Larry Dierker	.50	.25	.05
☐ 9 Denis Menke	.35	.17	.03
☐ 10 Don Wilson	.35	.17	.03
☐ 11 Cesar Cedeno	.50	.25	.05
☐ 12 Lee May	.50	.25	.05
☐ 13 Bob Watson	.50	.25	.05
☐ 14 Ken Forsch	.35	.17	.03
☐ 15 Joaquin Andujar	.50	.25	.05
☐ 16 Terry Puhl	.50	.25	.05
☐ 17 Joe Niekro	.50	.25	.05
☐ 18 Craig Reynolds	.35	.17	.03
☐ 19 Joe Sambito	.35	.17	.03
☐ 20 Jose Cruz	.50	.25	.05
☐ 21 J.R. Richard	.50	.25	.05
☐ 22 Bob Knepper	.35	.17	.03
☐ 23 Nolan Ryan	3.00	1.50	.30
☐ 24 Ray Knight	.50	.25	.05
☐ 25 Bill Dawley	.35	.17	.03
☐ 26 Dickie Thon	.35	.17	.03
☐ 27 Jerry Mumphrey	.35	.17	.03
☐ 28 Checklist Card	.35	.17	.03

1986 Mother's Giants

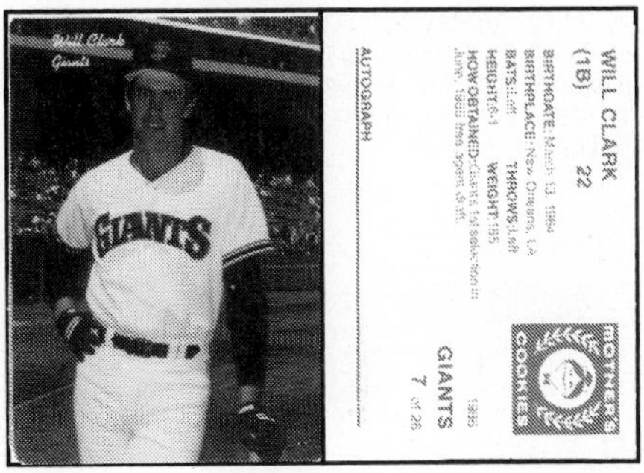

This set consists of 28 full-color, rounded-corner cards each measuring 2 1/2" by 3 1/2". Starter sets (only 20 cards but also including a certificate for eight more cards) were given out at the ballpark and collectors were encouraged to trade to fill in the rest of their set. Cards were originally given out at Candlestick Park on July 13th.

	MINT	EXC	G-VG
COMPLETE SET (28)	20.00	10.00	2.00
COMMON PLAYER (1-28)	.35	.17	.03
☐ 1 Roger Craig MG	.60	.30	.06
☐ 2 Chili Davis	.50	.25	.05
☐ 3 Dan Gladden	.50	.25	.05
☐ 4 Jeff Leonard	.50	.25	.05
☐ 5 Bob Brenly	.35	.17	.03
☐ 6 Atlee Hammaker	.50	.25	.05
☐ 7 Will Clark	13.50	6.00	1.00
☐ 8 Greg Minton	.35	.17	.03
☐ 9 Candy Maldonado	.60	.30	.06
☐ 10 Vida Blue	.50	.25	.05
☐ 11 Mike Krukow	.50	.25	.05
☐ 12 Bob Melvin	.35	.17	.03
☐ 13 Jose Uribe	.50	.25	.05
☐ 14 Dan Driessen	.35	.17	.03
☐ 15 Jeff Robinson	.50	.25	.05
☐ 16 Robby Thompson	.50	.25	.05
☐ 17 Mike LaCoss	.35	.17	.03
☐ 18 Chris Brown	.35	.17	.03
☐ 19 Scott Garrelts	.50	.25	.05

	MINT	EXC	G-VG
☐ 20 Mark Davis	.90	.45	.09
☐ 21 Jim Gott	.50	.25	.05
☐ 22 Brad Wellman	.35	.17	.03
☐ 23 Roger Mason	.35	.17	.03
☐ 24 Bill Laskey	.35	.17	.03
☐ 25 Brad Gulden	.35	.17	.03
☐ 26 Joel Youngblood	.35	.17	.03
☐ 27 Juan Berenguer	.35	.17	.03
☐ 28 Checklist Card	.35	.17	.03

1986 Mother's Mariners

This set consists of 28 full-color, rounded-corner cards each measuring 2 1/2" by 3 1/2". Starter sets (only 20 cards but also including a certificate for eight more cards) were given out at the ballpark and collectors were encouraged to trade to fill in the rest of their set. Cards were originally given out on July 27th at the Seattle Kingdome.

	MINT	EXC	G-VG
COMPLETE SET (28)	10.00	5.00	1.00
COMMON PLAYER (1-28)	.35	.17	.03
☐ 1 Dick Williams MG	.35	.17	.03
☐ 2 Alvin Davis	.75	.35	.07
☐ 3 Mark Langston	1.00	.50	.10
☐ 4 Dave Henderson	.50	.25	.05
☐ 5 Steve Yeager	.35	.17	.03
☐ 6 Al Cowens	.35	.17	.03
☐ 7 Jim Presley	.50	.25	.05
☐ 8 Phil Bradley	.60	.30	.06
☐ 9 Gorman Thomas	.50	.25	.05
☐ 10 Barry Bonnell	.35	.17	.03
☐ 11 Milt Wilcox	.35	.17	.03
☐ 12 Domingo Ramos	.35	.17	.03
☐ 13 Paul Mirabella	.35	.17	.03
☐ 14 Matt Young	.50	.25	.05
☐ 15 Ivan Calderon	.60	.30	.06
☐ 16 Bill Swift	.50	.25	.05
☐ 17 Pete Ladd	.35	.17	.03
☐ 18 Ken Phelps	.50	.25	.05
☐ 19 Karl Best	.35	.17	.03
☐ 20 Spike Owen	.50	.25	.05
☐ 21 Mike Moore	.60	.30	.06
☐ 22 Danny Tartabull	1.25	.60	.12
☐ 23 Bob Kearney	.35	.17	.03
☐ 24 Edwin Nunez	.35	.17	.03
☐ 25 Mike Morgan	.50	.25	.05
☐ 26 Roy Thomas	.35	.17	.03
☐ 27 Jim Beattie	.35	.17	.03
☐ 28 Checklist Card	.35	.17	.03

1987 Mother's Cookies A's

This set consists of 28 full-color, rounded-corner cards each measuring 2 1/2" by 3 1/2". Starter sets (only 20 cards but also including a certificate for eight more cards) were given out at the ballpark and collectors were encouraged to trade to fill in the rest of their set. The cards were originally given away on July 5th at Oakland Coliseum during a game against the Boston Red Sox. This set is actually an All-Time All-Star set including every A's All-Star player since 1968 (when the franchise moved to Oakland). The vintage photos (each shot during the year of All-Star appearance) were taken from the collection of Doug McWilliams. The sets were supposedly given out free to the first 25,000 paid admissions at the game.

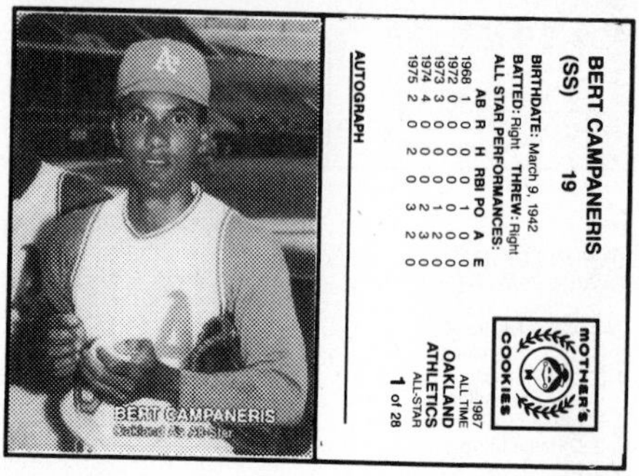

	MINT	EXC	G-VG
COMPLETE SET (28)	18.00	9.00	1.80
COMMON PLAYER (1-28)	.35	.17	.03
☐ 1 Bert Campaneris	.35	.17	.03
☐ 2 Rick Monday	.35	.17	.03
☐ 3 John Odom	.35	.17	.03
☐ 4 Sal Bando	.50	.25	.05
☐ 5 Reggie Jackson	2.00	1.00	.20
☐ 6 Jim Hunter	1.25	.60	.12
☐ 7 Vida Blue	.50	.25	.05
☐ 8 Dave Duncan	.35	.17	.03
☐ 9 Joe Rudi	.50	.25	.05
☐ 10 Rollie Fingers	1.00	.50	.10
☐ 11 Ken Holtzman	.35	.17	.03
☐ 12 Dick Williams	.35	.17	.03
☐ 13 Alvin Dark	.35	.17	.03
☐ 14 Gene Tenace	.35	.17	.03
☐ 15 Claudell Washington	.35	.17	.03
☐ 16 Phil Garner	.35	.17	.03
☐ 17 Wayne Gross	.35	.17	.03
☐ 18 Matt Keough	.35	.17	.03
☐ 19 Jeff Newman	.35	.17	.03
☐ 20 Rickey Henderson	3.50	1.75	.35
☐ 21 Tony Armas	.50	.25	.05
☐ 22 Mike Norris	.35	.17	.03
☐ 23 Billy Martin	1.00	.50	.10
☐ 24 Bill Caudill	.35	.17	.03
☐ 25 Jay Howell	.50	.25	.05
☐ 26 Jose Canseco	5.00	2.50	.50
☐ 27 Jose and Reggie	3.50	1.75	.35
☐ 28 Checklist Card	.35	.17	.03

1987 Mother's Cookies Astros

This set consists of 28 full-color, rounded-corner cards each measuring 2 1/2" by 3 1/2". Starter sets (only 20 cards but also including a certificate for eight more cards) were given out at the ballpark and collectors were encouraged to trade to fill in the rest of their set. Cards were originally given out at the Astrodome on July 17th during a game against the Phillies. Photos were taken by Barry Colla. The sets were supposedly given out free to the first 25,000 paid admissions at the game.

	MINT	EXC	G-VG
COMPLETE SET (28)	11.00	5.50	1.10
COMMON PLAYER (1-28)	.35	.17	.03
☐ 1 Hal Lanier MG	.50	.25	.05
☐ 2 Mike Scott	1.00	.50	.10
☐ 3 Jose Cruz	.50	.25	.05
☐ 4 Bill Doran	.75	.35	.07
☐ 5 Bob Knepper	.35	.17	.03
☐ 6 Phil Garner	.50	.25	.05
☐ 7 Terry Puhl	.50	.25	.05
☐ 8 Nolan Ryan	4.50	2.25	.45
☐ 9 Kevin Bass	.50	.25	.05
☐ 10 Glenn Davis	1.00	.50	.10
☐ 11 Alan Ashby	.35	.17	.03
☐ 12 Charlie Kerfeld	.35	.17	.03
☐ 13 Denny Walling	.35	.17	.03
☐ 14 Danny Darwin	.50	.25	.05
☐ 15 Mark Bailey	.35	.17	.03
☐ 16 Davey Lopes	.50	.25	.05
☐ 17 Dave Meads	.35	.17	.03
☐ 18 Aurelio Lopez	.35	.17	.03
☐ 19 Craig Reynolds	.35	.17	.03
☐ 20 Dave Smith	.50	.25	.05
☐ 21 Larry Andersen	.35	.17	.03
☐ 22 Jim Pankovits	.35	.17	.03
☐ 23 Jim Deshaies	.50	.25	.05
☐ 24 Bert Pena	.35	.17	.03
☐ 25 Dickie Thon	.50	.25	.05
☐ 26 Billy Hatcher	.60	.30	.06
☐ 27 Astros' Coaches	.35	.17	.03
☐ 28 Checklist Card	.35	.17	.03

1987 Mother's Cookies Dodgers

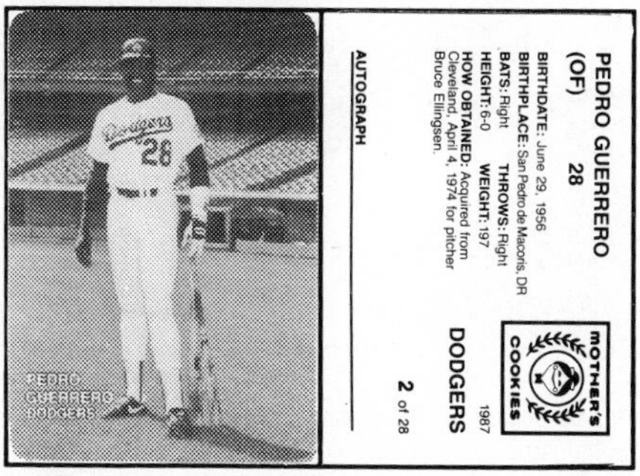

This set consists of 28 full-color, rounded-corner cards each measuring 2 1/2" by 3 1/2". Starter sets (only 20 cards but also including a certificate for eight more cards) were given out at the ballpark and collectors were encouraged to trade to fill in the rest of their set. Cards were originally given out at Dodger Stadium on August 9th. Photos were taken by Barry Colla. The sets were supposedly given out free to all game attendees 14 years of age and under.

	MINT	EXC	G-VG
COMPLETE SET (28)	11.00	5.50	1.10
COMMON PLAYER (1-28)	.35	.17	.03
☐ 1 Tom Lasorda MG	.75	.35	.07
☐ 2 Pedro Guerrero	1.00	.50	.10
☐ 3 Steve Sax	.75	.35	.07
☐ 4 Fernando Valenzuela	1.00	.50	.10
☐ 5 Mike Marshall	.60	.30	.06
☐ 6 Orel Hershiser	1.75	.85	.17
☐ 7 Mariano Duncan	.50	.25	.05
☐ 8 Bill Madlock	.50	.25	.05
☐ 9 Bob Welch	1.00	.50	.10
☐ 10 Mike Scioscia	.50	.25	.05
☐ 11 Mike Ramsey	.50	.25	.05
☐ 12 Matt Young	.50	.25	.05
☐ 13 Franklin Stubbs	.60	.30	.06
☐ 14 Tom Niedenfuer	.35	.17	.03
☐ 15 Reggie Williams	.35	.17	.03
☐ 16 Rick Honeycutt	.35	.17	.03
☐ 17 Dave Anderson	.35	.17	.03
☐ 18 Alejandro Pena	.50	.25	.05
☐ 19 Ken Howell	.35	.17	.03
☐ 20 Len Matuszek	.35	.17	.03
☐ 21 Tim Leary	.60	.30	.06
☐ 22 Tracy Woodson	.50	.25	.05
☐ 23 Alex Trevino	.35	.17	.03
☐ 24 Ken Landreaux	.35	.17	.03
☐ 25 Mickey Hatcher	.35	.17	.03
☐ 26 Brian Holton	.35	.17	.03
☐ 27 Dodgers' Coaches	.35	.17	.03
☐ 28 Checklist Card	.35	.17	.03

1987 Mother's Cookies Giants

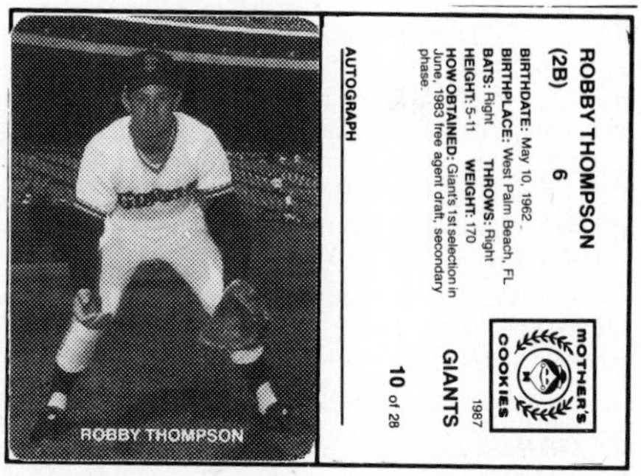

This set consists of 28 full-color, rounded-corner cards each measuring 2 1/2" by 3 1/2". Starter sets (only 20 cards but also including a certificate for eight more cards) were given out at the ballpark and collectors were encouraged to trade to fill in the rest of their set. Cards were originally given out at Candlestick Park on June 27th during a game against the Astros. Photos were taken by Dennis Desprois. The sets were supposedly given out free to the first 25,000 paid admissions at the game.

	MINT	EXC	G-VG
COMPLETE SET (28)	15.00	7.50	1.50
COMMON PLAYER (1-28)	.35	.17	.03
☐ 1 Roger Craig MG	.60	.30	.06
☐ 2 Will Clark	5.00	2.50	.50
☐ 3 Chili Davis	.50	.25	.05
☐ 4 Bob Brenly	.35	.17	.03
☐ 5 Chris Brown	.35	.17	.03
☐ 6 Mike Krukow	.35	.17	.03
☐ 7 Candy Maldonado	.50	.25	.05
☐ 8 Jeffrey Leonard	.50	.25	.05
☐ 9 Greg Minton	.35	.17	.03
☐ 10 Robby Thompson	.50	.25	.05
☐ 11 Scott Garrelts	.50	.25	.05
☐ 12 Bob Melvin	.35	.17	.03
☐ 13 Jose Uribe	.50	.25	.05
☐ 14 Mark Davis	.90	.45	.09
☐ 15 Eddie Milner	.35	.17	.03
☐ 16 Harry Spilman	.35	.17	.03
☐ 17 Kelly Downs	.50	.25	.05
☐ 18 Chris Speier	.35	.17	.03
☐ 19 Jim Gott	.50	.25	.05
☐ 20 Joel Youngblood	.35	.17	.03
☐ 21 Mike LaCoss	.35	.17	.03
☐ 22 Matt Williams	3.50	1.75	.35
☐ 23 Roger Mason	.35	.17	.03
☐ 24 Mike Aldrete	.35	.17	.03
☐ 25 Jeff Robinson	.50	.25	.05
☐ 26 Mark Grant	.35	.17	.03

☐ 27 Giants' Coaches	.35	.17	.03
☐ 28 Checklist Card	.35	.17	.03

1987 Mother's Cookies Mariners

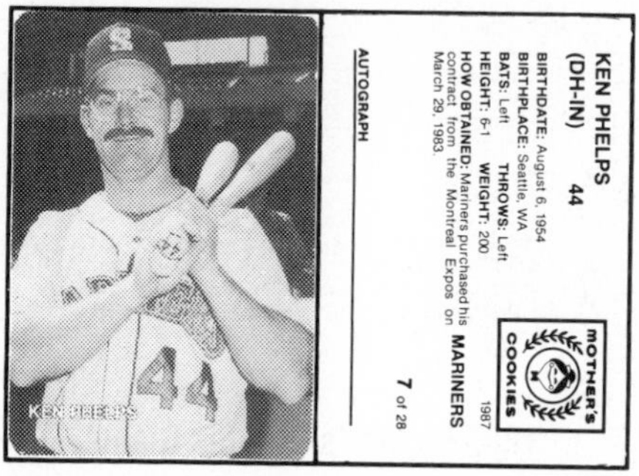

This set consists of 28 full-color, rounded-corner cards each measuring 2 1/2" by 3 1/2". Starter sets (only 20 cards but also including a certificate for eight more cards) were given out at the ballpark and collectors were encouraged to trade to fill in the rest of their set. Cards were originally given out on August 9th at the Seattle Kingdome. Photos were taken by Barry Colla. The sets were supposedly given out free to the first 20,000 paid admissions at the game.

	MINT	EXC	G-VG
COMPLETE SET (28)	10.00	5.00	1.00
COMMON PLAYER (1-28)	.35	.17	.03
☐ 1 Dick Williams MG	.35	.17	.03
☐ 2 Alvin Davis	.75	.35	.07
☐ 3 Mike Moore	.50	.25	.05
☐ 4 Jim Presley	.50	.25	.05
☐ 5 Mark Langston	.90	.45	.09
☐ 6 Phil Bradley	.50	.25	.05
☐ 7 Ken Phelps	.50	.25	.05
☐ 8 Mike Morgan	.50	.25	.05
☐ 9 David Valle	.35	.17	.03
☐ 10 Harold Reynolds	.75	.35	.07
☐ 11 Edwin Nunez	.35	.17	.03
☐ 12 Bob Kearney	.35	.17	.03
☐ 13 Scott Bankhead	.50	.25	.05
☐ 14 Scott Bradley	.35	.17	.03
☐ 15 Mickey Brantley	.50	.25	.05
☐ 16 Mark Huismann	.35	.17	.03
☐ 17 Mike Kingery	.35	.17	.03
☐ 18 John Moses	.35	.17	.03
☐ 19 Donell Nixon	.35	.17	.03
☐ 20 Rey Quinones	.35	.17	.03
☐ 21 Domingo Ramos	.35	.17	.03
☐ 22 Jerry Reed	.35	.17	.03
☐ 23 Rich Renteria	.50	.25	.05
☐ 24 Rich Monteleone	.35	.17	.03
☐ 25 Mike Trujillo	.35	.17	.03
☐ 26 Bill Wilkinson	.35	.17	.03
☐ 27 John Christensen	.35	.17	.03
☐ 28 Checklist Card	.35	.17	.03

1987 Mother's Cookies McGwire

This set consists of 4 full-color, rounded-corner cards each measuring 2 1/2" by 3 1/2" and showing a different pose of A's slugging rookie Mark McGwire. Cards were originally given out at the national Card Collectors Convention in San Francisco. Later they were available through a mail-in offer involving collectors sending in two proofs-of-purchase from any Mother's Cookies products to get one free card. Photos were taken by Doug McWilliams. The cards are numbered on the back.

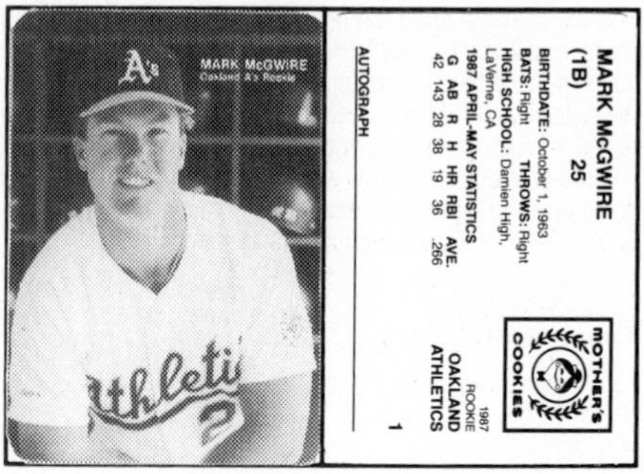

	MINT	EXC	G-VG
COMPLETE SET (4)	16.00	8.00	1.60
COMMON PLAYER (1-4)	4.00	2.00	.40
☐ 1 Mark McGwire close-up shot, head and shoulders	4.00	2.00	.40
☐ 2 Mark McGwire waist up, holding bat	4.50	2.25	.45
☐ 3 Mark McGwire batting stance, ready to swing	4.50	2.25	.45
☐ 4 Mark McGwire home run swing, follow through	5.00	2.50	.50

1987 Mother's Cookies Rangers

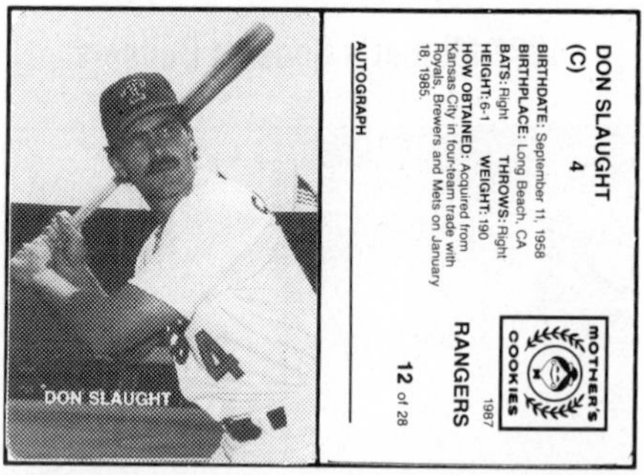

This set consists of 28 full-color, rounded-corner cards each measuring 2 1/2" by 3 1/2". Starter sets (only 20 cards but also including a certificate for eight more cards) were given out at the ballpark and collectors were encouraged to trade to fill in the rest of their set. Cards were originally given out on July 17th during the game against the Yankees. Photos were taken by Barry Colla. The sets were supposedly given out free to the first 25,000 paid admissions at the game.

	MINT	EXC	G-VG
COMPLETE SET (28)	11.00	5.50	1.10
COMMON PLAYER (1-28)	.35	.17	.03
☐ 1 Bobby Valentine MG	.50	.25	.05
☐ 2 Pete Incaviglia	.90	.45	.09
☐ 3 Charlie Hough	.50	.25	.05
☐ 4 Oddibe McDowell	.50	.25	.05
☐ 5 Larry Parrish	.35	.17	.03
☐ 6 Scott Fletcher	.35	.17	.03
☐ 7 Steve Buechele	.50	.25	.05
☐ 8 Tom Paciorek	.35	.17	.03
☐ 9 Pete O'Brien	.60	.30	.06
☐ 10 Darrell Porter	.35	.17	.03

☐ 11 Greg Harris	.35	.17	.03
☐ 12 Don Slaught	.35	.17	.03
☐ 13 Ruben Sierra	4.00	2.00	.40
☐ 14 Curtis Wilkerson	.35	.17	.03
☐ 15 Dale Mohorcic	.35	.17	.03
☐ 16 Ron Meredith	.35	.17	.03
☐ 17 Mitch Williams	.50	.25	.05
☐ 18 Bob Brower	.35	.17	.03
☐ 19 Edwin Correa	.35	.17	.03
☐ 20 Geno Petralli	.35	.17	.03
☐ 21 Mike Loynd	.35	.17	.03
☐ 22 Jerry Browne	.50	.25	.05
☐ 23 Jose Guzman	.50	.25	.05
☐ 24 Jeff Kunkel	.50	.25	.05
☐ 25 Bobby Witt	1.50	.75	.15
☐ 26 Jeff Russell	.60	.30	.06
☐ 27 Ranger's Trainers	.35	.17	.03
☐ 28 Checklist Card	.35	.17	.03

1988 Mother's Cookies A's

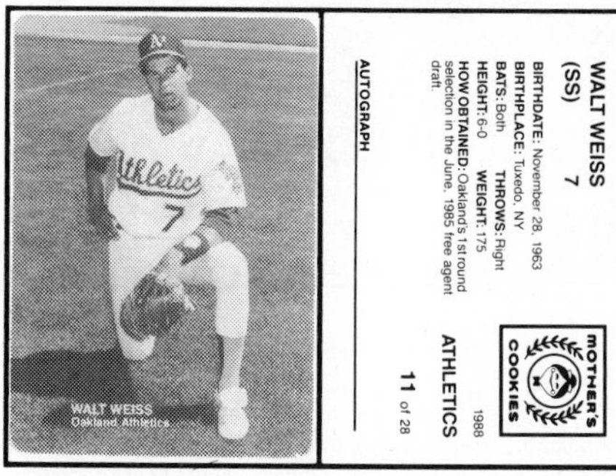

This set consists of 28 full-color, rounded-corner cards each measuring 2 1/2" by 3 1/2". Starter sets (only 20 cards but also including a certificate for eight more cards) were given out at the ballpark and collectors were encouraged to trade to fill in the rest of their set. The cards were originally given away on July 23rd at Oakland Coliseum during a game. Short sets (20 cards plus certificate) were supposedly given out free to the first 35,000 paid admissions at the game.

	MINT	EXC	G-VG
COMPLETE SET (28)	16.00	8.00	1.60
COMMON PLAYER (1-28)	.35	.17	.03
☐ 1 Tony LaRussa MG	.60	.30	.06
☐ 2 Mark McGwire	2.50	1.25	.25
☐ 3 Dave Stewart	1.25	.60	.12
☐ 4 Terry Steinbach	.75	.35	.07
☐ 5 Dave Parker	.75	.35	.07
☐ 6 Carney Lansford	.75	.35	.07
☐ 7 Jose Canseco	3.50	1.75	.35
☐ 8 Don Baylor	.50	.25	.05
☐ 9 Bob Welch	.75	.35	.07
☐ 10 Dennis Eckersley	1.25	.60	.12
☐ 11 Walt Weiss	1.25	.60	.12
☐ 12 Tony Phillips	.35	.17	.03
☐ 13 Steve Ontiveros	.35	.17	.03
☐ 14 Dave Henderson	.50	.25	.05
☐ 15 Stan Javier	.50	.25	.05
☐ 16 Ron Hassey	.35	.17	.03
☐ 17 Curt Young	.35	.17	.03
☐ 18 Glenn Hubbard	.35	.17	.03
☐ 19 Storm Davis	.75	.35	.07
☐ 20 Eric Plunk	.35	.17	.03
☐ 21 Matt Young	.35	.17	.03
☐ 22 Mike Gallego	.35	.17	.03
☐ 23 Rick Honeycutt	.35	.17	.03
☐ 24 Doug Jennings	.50	.25	.05
☐ 25 Gene Nelson	.35	.17	.03
☐ 26 Greg Cadaret	.35	.17	.03
☐ 27 Athletics Coaches	.35	.17	.03
☐ 28 Checklist Card	.35	.17	.03

1988 Mother's Cookies Astros

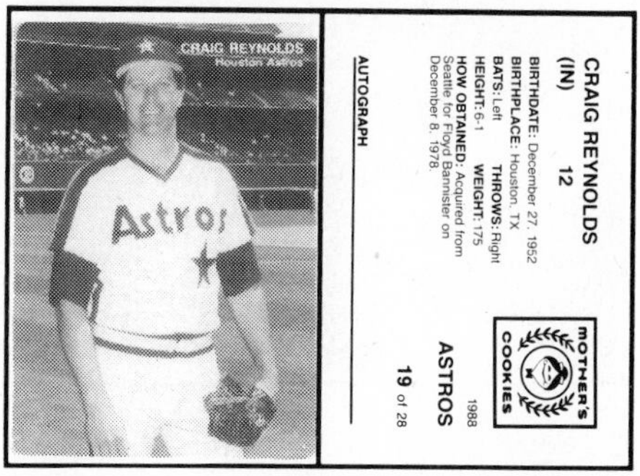

This set consists of 28 full-color, rounded-corner cards each measuring 2 1/2" by 3 1/2". Starter sets (only 20 cards but also including a certificate for eight more cards) were given out at the ballpark and collectors were encouraged to trade to fill in the rest of their set. Cards were originally given out at the Astrodome on August 26th during a game. The sets were supposedly given out free to the first 25,000 paid admissions at the game.

	MINT	EXC	G-VG
COMPLETE SET (28)	10.00	5.00	1.00
COMMON PLAYER (1-28)	.35	.17	.03
☐ 1 Hal Lanier MG	.35	.17	.03
☐ 2 Mike Scott	1.00	.50	.10
☐ 3 Gerald Young	.50	.25	.05
☐ 4 Bill Doran	.50	.25	.05
☐ 5 Bob Knepper	.35	.17	.03
☐ 6 Billy Hatcher	.50	.25	.05
☐ 7 Terry Puhl	.50	.25	.05
☐ 8 Nolan Ryan	3.00	1.50	.30
☐ 9 Kevin Bass	.50	.25	.05
☐ 10 Glenn Davis	1.00	.50	.10
☐ 11 Alan Ashby	.35	.17	.03
☐ 12 Steve Henderson	.35	.17	.03
☐ 13 Denny Walling	.35	.17	.03
☐ 14 Danny Darwin	.50	.25	.05
☐ 15 Mark Bailey	.35	.17	.03
☐ 16 Ernie Camacho	.35	.17	.03
☐ 17 Rafael Ramirez	.35	.17	.03
☐ 18 Jeff Heathcock	.35	.17	.03
☐ 19 Craig Reynolds	.35	.17	.03
☐ 20 Dave Smith	.50	.25	.05
☐ 21 Larry Andersen	.35	.17	.03
☐ 22 Jim Pankovits	.35	.17	.03
☐ 23 Jim Deshaies	.35	.17	.03
☐ 24 Juan Agosto	.35	.17	.03
☐ 25 Chuck Jackson	.35	.17	.03
☐ 26 Joaquin Andujar	.50	.25	.05
☐ 27 Astros' Coaches	.35	.17	.03
☐ 28 Checklist Card	.35	.17	.03

1988 Mother's Cookies Will Clark

This regional set consists of 4 full-color, rounded-corner cards each measuring 2 1/2" by 3 1/2" and showing a different pose of Giants' slugging first baseman Will Clark. Cards were originally found in 18 oz. packages of "Big Bags" of Mother's Cookies at stores in the Northern California area in February and March of 1988. The cards are numbered on the back. Card backs are done in red and purple on white card stock.

	MINT	EXC	G-VG
COMPLETE SET (4)	15.00	7.50	1.50
COMMON PLAYER (1-4)	4.00	2.00	.40
☐ 1 Will Clark Batting Pose, Waist Up	4.00	2.00	.40

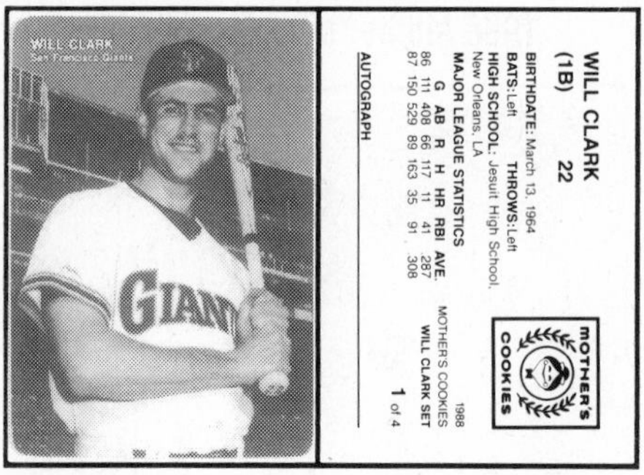

☐ 2 Will Clark Kneeling In On Deck Circle	4.00	2.00	.40
☐ 3 Will Clark Follow Through Swing	4.00	2.00	.40
☐ 4 Will Clark Starting Toward First Base	4.00	2.00	.40

1988 Mother's Cookies Dodgers

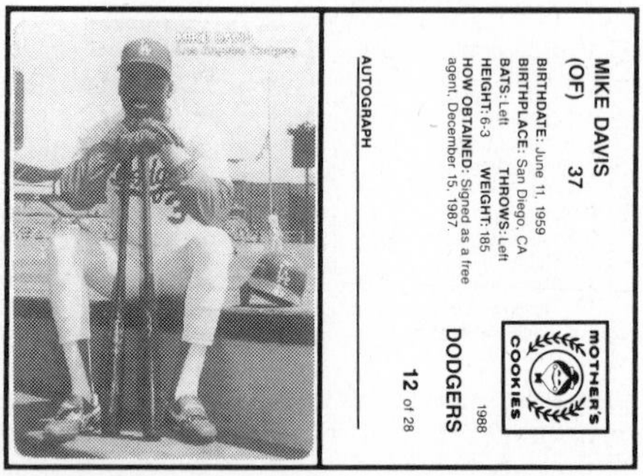

This set consists of 28 full-color, rounded-corner cards each measuring 2 1/2" by 3 1/2". Starter sets (only 20 cards but also including a certificate for eight more cards) were given out at the ballpark and collectors were encouraged to trade to fill in the rest of their set. Cards were originally given out at Dodger Stadium on July 31st. Photos were taken by Barry Colla. The sets were supposedly given out free to the first 25,000 game attendees 14 years of age and under.

	MINT	EXC	G-VG
COMPLETE SET (28)	12.00	6.00	1.20
COMMON PLAYER (1-28)	.35	.17	.03
☐ 1 Tom Lasorda MG	.50	.25	.05
☐ 2 Pedro Guerrero	.75	.35	.07
☐ 3 Steve Sax	.75	.35	.07
☐ 4 Fernando Valenzuela	.75	.35	.07
☐ 5 Mike Marshall	.50	.25	.05
☐ 6 Orel Hershiser	1.25	.60	.12
☐ 7 Alfredo Griffin	.35	.17	.03
☐ 8 Kirk Gibson	1.00	.50	.10
☐ 9 Don Sutton	.75	.35	.07
☐ 10 Mike Scioscia	.35	.17	.03
☐ 11 Franklin Stubbs	.50	.25	.05
☐ 12 Mike Davis	.35	.17	.03
☐ 13 Jesse Orosco	.35	.17	.03
☐ 14 John Shelby	.35	.17	.03
☐ 15 Rick Dempsey	.35	.17	.03
☐ 16 Jay Howell	.50	.25	.05
☐ 17 Dave Anderson	.35	.17	.03
☐ 18 Alejandro Pena	.35	.17	.03
☐ 19 Jeff Hamilton	.35	.17	.03
☐ 20 Danny Heep	.35	.17	.03
☐ 21 Tim Leary	.50	.25	.05
☐ 22 Brad Havens	.35	.17	.03
☐ 23 Tim Belcher	.75	.35	.07
☐ 24 Ken Howell	.35	.17	.03
☐ 25 Mickey Hatcher	.35	.17	.03
☐ 26 Brian Holton	.35	.17	.03
☐ 27 Mike Devereaux	.50	.25	.05
☐ 28 Checklist Card	.35	.17	.03

1988 Mother's Cookies Giants

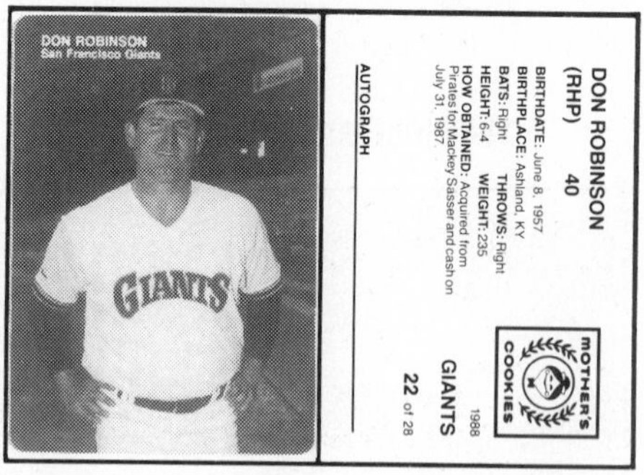

This set consists of 28 full-color, rounded-corner cards each measuring 2 1/2" by 3 1/2". Starter sets (only 20 cards but also including a certificate for eight more cards) were given out at the ballpark and collectors were encouraged to trade to fill in the rest of their set. Cards were originally given out at Candlestick Park on July 30th during a game. Photos were taken by Dennis Desprois. The sets were supposedly given out free to the first 35,000 paid admissions at the game.

	MINT	EXC	G-VG
COMPLETE SET (28)	12.00	6.00	1.20
COMMON PLAYER (1-28)	.35	.17	.03
☐ 1 Roger Craig MG	.50	.25	.05
☐ 2 Will Clark	3.50	1.75	.35
☐ 3 Kevin Mitchell	1.25	.60	.12
☐ 4 Bob Brenly	.35	.17	.03
☐ 5 Mike Aldrete	.35	.17	.03
☐ 6 Mike Krukow	.35	.17	.03
☐ 7 Candy Maldonado	.50	.25	.05
☐ 8 Jeffrey Leonard	.50	.25	.05
☐ 9 Dave Dravecky	.60	.30	.06
☐ 10 Robby Thompson	.50	.25	.05
☐ 11 Scott Garrelts	.50	.25	.05
☐ 12 Bob Melvin	.35	.17	.03
☐ 13 Jose Uribe	.50	.25	.05
☐ 14 Brett Butler	.75	.35	.07
☐ 15 Rick Reuschel	.60	.30	.06
☐ 16 Harry Spilman	.35	.17	.03
☐ 17 Kelly Downs	.50	.25	.05
☐ 18 Chris Speier	.35	.17	.03
☐ 19 Atlee Hammaker	.35	.17	.03
☐ 20 Joel Youngblood	.35	.17	.03
☐ 21 Mike LaCoss	.35	.17	.03
☐ 22 Don Robinson	.35	.17	.03
☐ 23 Mark Wasinger	.50	.25	.05
☐ 24 Craig Lefferts	.50	.25	.05
☐ 25 Phil Garner	.50	.25	.05
☐ 26 Joe Price	.35	.17	.03
☐ 27 Giants' Coaches	.35	.17	.03
☐ 28 Checklist Card	.35	.17	.03

1988 Mother's Cookies Mariners

This set consists of 28 full-color, rounded-corner cards each measuring 2 1/2" by 3 1/2". Starter sets (only 20 cards but also including a certificate for eight more cards) were given out at the ballpark and collectors were encouraged to trade to fill in the rest of their set. Cards were originally given out on August 14th at the Seattle Kingdome. Photos were taken by Barry Colla. The sets were supposedly given out free to the first 20,000 paid admissions at the game.

	MINT	EXC	G-VG
COMPLETE SET (28)	9.00	4.50	.90
COMMON PLAYER (1-28)	.35	.17	.03
☐ 1 Dick Williams MG	.35	.17	.03
☐ 2 Alvin Davis	.75	.35	.07
☐ 3 Mike Moore	.50	.25	.05
☐ 4 Jim Presley	.50	.25	.05
☐ 5 Mark Langston	.90	.45	.09
☐ 6 Henry Cotto	.35	.17	.03
☐ 7 Ken Phelps	.35	.17	.03
☐ 8 Steve Trout	.35	.17	.03
☐ 9 David Valle	.35	.17	.03
☐ 10 Harold Reynolds	.60	.30	.06
☐ 11 Edwin Nunez	.35	.17	.03
☐ 12 Glenn Wilson	.35	.17	.03
☐ 13 Scott Bankhead	.50	.25	.05
☐ 14 Scott Bradley	.35	.17	.03
☐ 15 Mickey Brantley	.50	.25	.05
☐ 16 Bruce Fields	.35	.17	.03
☐ 17 Mike Kingery	.35	.17	.03
☐ 18 Mike Campbell	.35	.17	.03
☐ 19 Mike Jackson	.35	.17	.03
☐ 20 Rey Quinones	.35	.17	.03
☐ 21 Mario Diaz	.35	.17	.03
☐ 22 Jerry Reed	.35	.17	.03
☐ 23 Rich Renteria	.35	.17	.03
☐ 24 Julio Solano	.35	.17	.03
☐ 25 Bill Swift	.50	.25	.05
☐ 26 Bill Wilkinson	.35	.17	.03
☐ 27 Mariners Coaches	.35	.17	.03
☐ 28 Checklist Card	.35	.17	.03

1988 Mother's Cookies McGwire

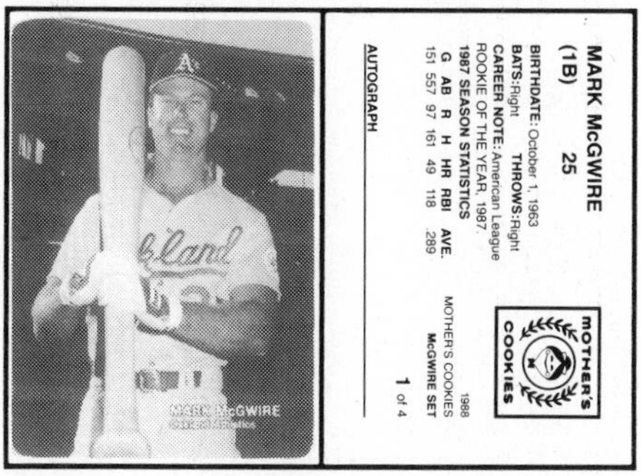

This regional set consists of 4 full-color, rounded-corner cards each measuring 2 1/2" by 3 1/2" and showing a different pose of Athletics' slugging first baseman Mark McGwire. Cards were originally found in 18 oz. packages of "Big Bags" of Mother's Cookies at stores in the Northern California area in February and March of 1988. The cards are numbered on the back. Card backs are done in red and purple on white card stock.

	MINT	EXC	G-VG
COMPLETE SET (4)	15.00	7.50	1.50
COMMON PLAYER (1-4)	4.00	2.00	.40
☐ 1 Mark McGwire Holding Big Bat	4.00	2.00	.40
☐ 2 Mark McGwire Fielding at First Base	4.00	2.00	.40
☐ 3 Mark McGwire Kneeling In On Deck Circle	4.00	2.00	.40
☐ 4 Mark McGwire Batting Pose, Waist Up	4.00	2.00	.40

1988 Mother's Cookies Rangers

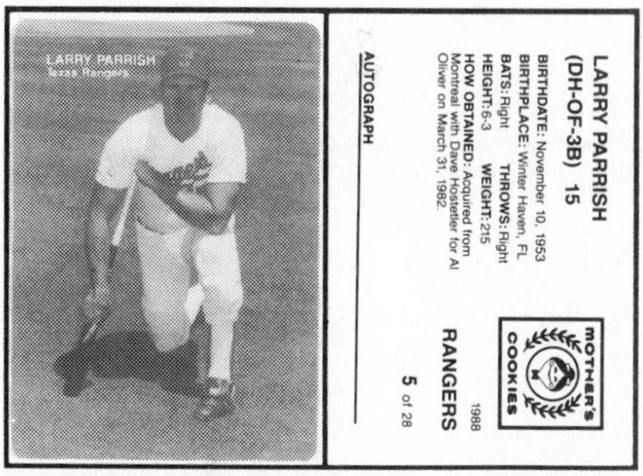

This set consists of 28 full-color, rounded-corner cards each measuring 2 1/2" by 3 1/2". Starter sets (only 20 cards but also including a certificate for eight more cards) were given out at the ballpark and collectors were encouraged to trade to fill in the rest of their set. Cards were originally given out on August 7th. Photos were taken by Barry Colla. The sets were supposedly given out free to the first 25,000 paid admissions at the game.

	MINT	EXC	G-VG
COMPLETE SET (28)	9.00	4.50	.90
COMMON PLAYER (1-28)	.35	.17	.03
☐ 1 Bobby Valentine MG	.50	.25	.05
☐ 2 Pete Incaviglia	.60	.30	.06
☐ 3 Charlie Hough	.50	.25	.05
☐ 4 Oddibe McDowell	.50	.25	.05
☐ 5 Larry Parrish	.35	.17	.03
☐ 6 Scott Fletcher	.35	.17	.03
☐ 7 Steve Buechele	.35	.17	.03
☐ 8 Steve Kemp	.35	.17	.03
☐ 9 Pete O'Brien	.50	.25	.05
☐ 10 Ruben Sierra	1.50	.75	.15
☐ 11 Mike Stanley	.35	.17	.03
☐ 12 Jose Cecena	.35	.17	.03
☐ 13 Cecil Espy	.35	.17	.03
☐ 14 Curtis Wilkerson	.35	.17	.03
☐ 15 Dale Mohorcic	.35	.17	.03
☐ 16 Ray Hayward	.35	.17	.03
☐ 17 Mitch Williams	.50	.25	.05
☐ 18 Bob Brower	.35	.17	.03
☐ 19 Paul Kilgus	.35	.17	.03
☐ 20 Geno Petralli	.35	.17	.03
☐ 21 James Steels	.35	.17	.03
☐ 22 Jerry Browne	.50	.25	.05
☐ 23 Jose Guzman	.35	.17	.03
☐ 24 DeWayne Vaughn	.35	.17	.03
☐ 25 Bobby Witt	.75	.35	.07

☐ 26 Jeff Russell	.50	.25	.05
☐ 27 Rangers Coaches	.35	.17	.03
☐ 28 Checklist Card	.35	.17	.03

1989 Mother's Cookies A's

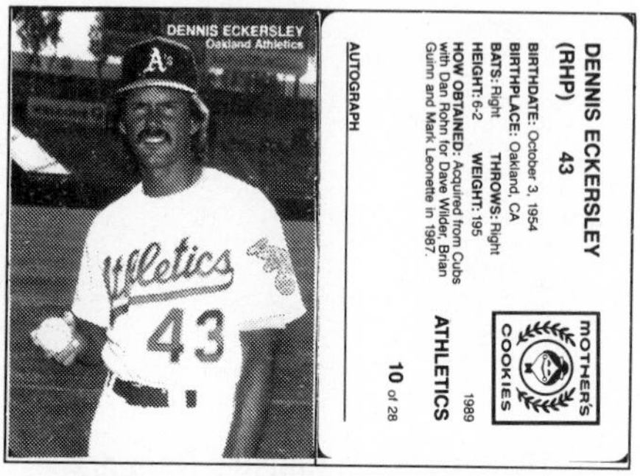

The 1989 Mother's Cookies Oakland A's set contains 28 standard-size (2 1/2" by 3 1/2") cards with rounded corners. The fronts have borderless color photos, and the horizontally-oriented backs have biographical information. Starter sets containing 20 of these cards were given away at an A's home game during the 1989 season.

	MINT	EXC	G-VG
COMPLETE SET (28)	14.00	7.00	1.40
COMMON PLAYER (1-28)	.35	.17	.03
☐ 1 Tony LaRussa MG	.50	.25	.05
☐ 2 Mark McGwire	1.50	.75	.15
☐ 3 Terry Steinbach	.60	.30	.06
☐ 4 Dave Parker	.75	.35	.07
☐ 5 Carney Lansford	.75	.35	.07
☐ 6 Dave Stewart	.90	.45	.09
☐ 7 Jose Canseco	2.50	1.25	.25
☐ 8 Walt Weiss	.60	.30	.06
☐ 9 Bob Welch	.75	.35	.07
☐ 10 Dennis Eckersley	.90	.45	.09
☐ 11 Tony Phillips	.35	.17	.03
☐ 12 Mike Moore	.50	.25	.05
☐ 13 Dave Henderson	.50	.25	.05
☐ 14 Curt Young	.35	.17	.03
☐ 15 Ron Hassey	.35	.17	.03
☐ 16 Eric Plunk	.35	.17	.03
☐ 17 Luis Polonia	.50	.25	.05
☐ 18 Storm Davis	.50	.25	.05
☐ 19 Glenn Hubbard	.35	.17	.03
☐ 20 Greg Cadaret	.50	.25	.05
☐ 21 Stan Javier	.50	.25	.05
☐ 22 Felix Jose	.60	.30	.06
☐ 23 Mike Gallego	.35	.17	.03
☐ 24 Todd Burns	.50	.25	.05
☐ 25 Rick Honeycutt	.35	.17	.03
☐ 26 Gene Nelson	.35	.17	.03
☐ 27 A's Coaches	.35	.17	.03
☐ 28 Checklist Card	.35	.17	.03

1989 Mothers Cookies A's ROY's

The 1989 Mother's A's ROY's set contains 4 standard-size (2 1/2" by 3 1/2") cards with rounded corners. The fronts have borderless color photos, and the horizontally-oriented backs have biographical information. One card was included in each specially marked box of Mother's Cookies. On the first three cards in the set Rookie of the Year (and year) is mentioned under the player's name.

	MINT	EXC	G-VG
COMPLETE SET (4)	12.00	6.00	1.20
COMMON PLAYER (1-4)	3.00	1.50	.30
☐ 1 Jose Canseco 1986 ROY	5.00	2.50	.50
☐ 2 Mark McGwire 1987 ROY	4.00	2.00	.40
☐ 3 Walt Weiss 1988 ROY	3.00	1.50	.30
☐ 4 Walt Weiss, Mark McGwire, and Jose Canseco	4.00	2.00	.40

1989 Mother's Cookies Astros

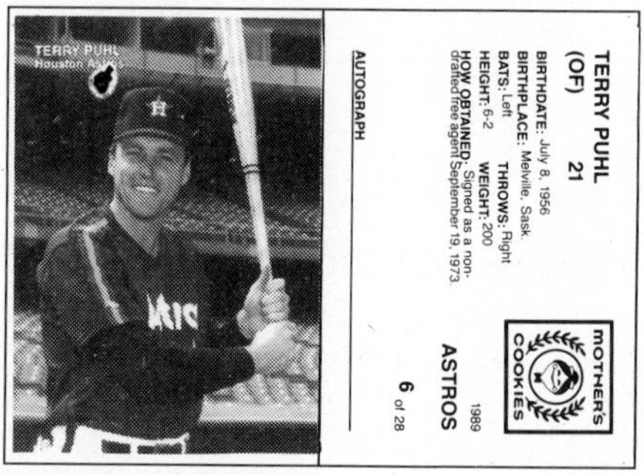

The 1989 Mother's Cookies Houston Astros set contains 28 standard-size (2 1/2" by 3 1/2") cards with rounded corners. The fronts have borderless color photos, and the horizontally-oriented backs have biographical information. Starter sets containing 20 of these cards were given away at an Astros home game during the 1989 season.

	MINT	EXC	G-VG
COMPLETE SET (28)	9.00	4.50	.90
COMMON PLAYER (1-28)	.35	.17	.03
☐ 1 Art Howe MG	.35	.17	.03
☐ 2 Mike Scott	.90	.45	.09
☐ 3 Gerald Young	.50	.25	.05
☐ 4 Bill Doran	.50	.25	.05
☐ 5 Billy Hatcher	.50	.25	.05
☐ 6 Terry Puhl	.50	.25	.05
☐ 7 Bob Knepper	.35	.17	.03
☐ 8 Kevin Bass	.50	.25	.05
☐ 9 Glenn Davis	1.00	.50	.10
☐ 10 Alan Ashby	.35	.17	.03
☐ 11 Bob Forsch	.35	.17	.03
☐ 12 Greg Gross	.35	.17	.03
☐ 13 Danny Darwin	.50	.25	.05
☐ 14 Craig Biggio	.90	.45	.09
☐ 15 Jim Clancy	.35	.17	.03
☐ 16 Rafael Ramirez	.35	.17	.03
☐ 17 Alex Trevino	.35	.17	.03

☐ 18 Craig Reynolds	.35	.17	.03
☐ 19 Dave Smith	.50	.25	.05
☐ 20 Larry Andersen	.35	.17	.03
☐ 21 Eric Yelding	.50	.25	.05
☐ 22 Jim Deshaies	.35	.17	.03
☐ 23 Juan Agosto	.35	.17	.03
☐ 24 Rick Rhoden	.35	.17	.03
☐ 25 Ken Caminiti	.35	.17	.03
☐ 26 Dave Meads	.35	.17	.03
☐ 27 Astros Coaches	.35	.17	.03
☐ 28 Checklist Card	.35	.17	.03

1989 Mother's Cookies Canseco

The 1989 Mother's Jose Canseco set contains 4 standard-size (2 1/2" by 3 1/2") cards with rounded corners. The fronts have borderless color photos, and the horizontally-oriented backs have biographical information. One card was included in each specially marked box of Mother's Cookies. Since all four cards picture Jose Canseco, the pose is identified parenthetically in the checklist below in order to distinguish the card fronts.

	MINT	EXC	G-VG
COMPLETE SET (4)	12.00	6.00	1.20
COMMON PLAYER (1-4)	3.50	1.75	.35
☐ 1 Jose Canseco (holding ball in hand)	3.50	1.75	.35
☐ 2 Jose Canseco (on one knee with bat)	3.50	1.75	.35
☐ 3 Jose Canseco (swinging at pitch)	3.50	1.75	.35
☐ 4 Jose Canseco (running toward second)	3.50	1.75	.35

1989 Mother's Cookies Will Clark

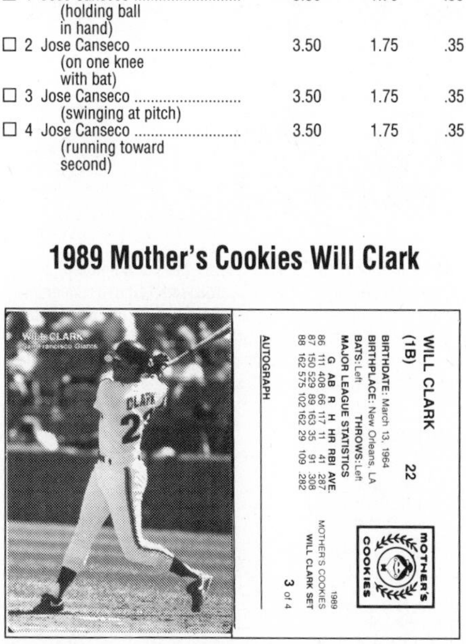

The 1989 Mother's Cookies Will Clark set contains 4 standard-size (2 1/2" by 3 1/2") cards with rounded corners. The fronts have borderless color photos, and the horizontally-oriented backs have biographical information. One card was included in each specially marked box of Mother's Cookies. Since all four cards picture Will Clark, the pose is identified parenthetically in the checklist below in order to distinguish the card fronts.

	MINT	EXC	G-VG
COMPLETE SET (4)	12.00	6.00	1.20
COMMON PLAYER (1-4)	3.50	1.75	.35
☐ 1 Will Clark (ball in glove)	3.50	1.75	.35
☐ 2 Will Clark (batting stance posed)	3.50	1.75	.35
☐ 3 Will Clark (swing follow through)	3.50	1.75	.35
☐ 4 Will Clark (starting toward first after hit, still holding bat)	3.50	1.75	.35

1989 Mother's Cookies Dodgers

The 1989 Mother's Los Angeles Dodgers set contains 28 standard-size (2 1/2" by 3 1/2") cards with rounded corners. The fronts have borderless color photos, and the horizontally-oriented backs have biographical information. Starter sets containing 20 of these cards were given away at a Dodgers home game during the 1989 season.

	MINT	EXC	G-VG
COMPLETE SET (28)	9.00	4.50	.90
COMMON PLAYER (1-28)	.35	.17	.03
☐ 1 Tom Lasorda MG	.50	.25	.05
☐ 2 Eddie Murray	.90	.45	.09
☐ 3 Mike Scioscia	.35	.17	.03
☐ 4 Fernando Valenzuela	.75	.35	.07
☐ 5 Mike Marshall	.50	.25	.05
☐ 6 Orel Hershiser	1.00	.50	.10
☐ 7 Alfredo Griffin	.35	.17	.03
☐ 8 Kirk Gibson	.75	.35	.07
☐ 9 John Tudor	.50	.25	.05
☐ 10 Willie Randolph	.50	.25	.05
☐ 11 Franklin Stubbs	.50	.25	.05
☐ 12 Mike Davis	.35	.17	.03
☐ 13 Mike Morgan	.35	.17	.03
☐ 14 John Shelby	.35	.17	.03
☐ 15 Rick Dempsey	.35	.17	.03
☐ 16 Jay Howell	.50	.25	.05
☐ 17 Dave Anderson	.35	.17	.03
☐ 18 Alejandro Pena	.35	.17	.03
☐ 19 Jeff Hamilton	.35	.17	.03
☐ 20 Ricky Horton	.35	.17	.03
☐ 21 Tim Leary	.50	.25	.05
☐ 22 Ray Searage	.35	.17	.03
☐ 23 Tim Belcher	.60	.30	.06
☐ 24 Tim Crews	.35	.17	.03
☐ 25 Mickey Hatcher	.35	.17	.03

☐ 26 Mariano Duncan	.50	.25	.05
☐ 27 Dodgers Coaches	.35	.17	.03
☐ 28 Checklist Card	.35	.17	.03

1989 Mother's Cookies Giants

The 1989 Mother's Cookies San Francisco Giants set contains 28 standard-size (2 1/2" by 3 1/2") cards with rounded corners. The fronts have borderless color photos, and the horizontally-oriented backs have biographical information. Starter sets containing 20 of these cards were given away at a Giants home game during the 1989 season.

	MINT	EXC	G-VG
COMPLETE SET (28)	12.00	6.00	1.20
COMMON PLAYER (1-28)	.35	.17	.03
☐ 1 Roger Craig MG	.50	.25	.05
☐ 2 Will Clark	2.50	1.25	.25
☐ 3 Kevin Mitchell	1.00	.50	.10
☐ 4 Kelly Downs	.50	.25	.05
☐ 5 Brett Butler	.60	.30	.06
☐ 6 Mike Krukow	.35	.17	.03
☐ 7 Candy Maldonado	.50	.25	.05
☐ 8 Terry Kennedy	.35	.17	.03
☐ 9 Dave Dravecky	.60	.30	.06
☐ 10 Robby Thompson	.50	.25	.05
☐ 11 Scott Garrelts	.50	.25	.05
☐ 12 Matt Williams	1.25	.60	.12
☐ 13 Jose Uribe	.35	.17	.03
☐ 14 Tracy Jones	.35	.17	.03
☐ 15 Rick Reuschel	.50	.25	.05
☐ 16 Ernest Riles	.35	.17	.03
☐ 17 Jeff Brantley	.50	.25	.05
☐ 18 Chris Speier	.35	.17	.03
☐ 19 Atlee Hammaker	.35	.17	.03
☐ 20 Ed Jurak	.35	.17	.03
☐ 21 Mike LaCoss	.35	.17	.03
☐ 22 Don Robinson	.35	.17	.03
☐ 23 Kirt Manwaring	.35	.17	.03
☐ 24 Craig Lefferts	.50	.25	.05
☐ 25 Donell Nixon	.35	.17	.03
☐ 26 Joe Price	.35	.17	.03
☐ 27 Rich Gossage	.50	.25	.05
☐ 28 Checklist Card	.35	.17	.03

1989 Mother's Cookies Griffey Jr.

The 1989 Mother's Cookies Ken Griffey Jr. set contains 4 standard-size (2 1/2" by 3 1/2") cards with rounded corners. The fronts have borderless color photos, and the horizontally-oriented backs have biographical information. One card was included in each specially marked box of Mother's Cookies. Since all four cards picture Ken Griffey Jr., the pose is identified parenthetically in the checklist below in order to distinguish the card fronts. Each card back provides a different aspect or background on Ken and his career. The photos were shot by noted sports photographer Barry Colla.

	MINT	EXC	G-VG
COMPLETE SET (4)	15.00	7.50	1.50
COMMON PLAYER (1-4)	4.00	2.00	.40
☐ 1 Ken Griffey Jr. (arms folded)	4.00	2.00	.40
☐ 2 Ken Griffey Jr. (baseball in hand)	4.00	2.00	.40
☐ 3 Ken Griffey Jr. (looking straight ahead with bat)	4.00	2.00	.40
☐ 4 Ken Griffey Jr. (looking over shoulder with bat)	4.00	2.00	.40

1989 Mother's Cookies Mariners

The 1989 Mother's Cookies Seattle Mariners set contains 28 standard-size (2 1/2" by 3 1/2") cards with rounded corners. The fronts have borderless color photos, and the horizontally-oriented backs have biographical information. Starter sets containing 20 of these cards were given away at a Mariners home game during the 1989 season.

	MINT	EXC	G-VG
COMPLETE SET (28)	14.00	7.00	1.40
COMMON PLAYER (1-28)	.35	.17	.03
☐ 1 Jim Lefebvre MG	.35	.17	.03
☐ 2 Alvin Davis	.60	.30	.06
☐ 3 Ken Griffey Jr.	7.00	3.50	.70
☐ 4 Jim Presley	.50	.25	.05
☐ 5 Mark Langston	.75	.35	.07
☐ 6 Henry Cotto	.35	.17	.03
☐ 7 Mickey Brantley	.35	.17	.03
☐ 8 Jeffrey Leonard	.50	.25	.05
☐ 9 Dave Valle	.35	.17	.03
☐ 10 Harold Reynolds	.50	.25	.05

☐ 11 Edgar Martinez	.60	.30	.06
☐ 12 Tom Niedenfuer	.35	.17	.03
☐ 13 Scott Bankhead	.50	.25	.05
☐ 14 Scott Bradley	.35	.17	.03
☐ 15 Omar Vizquel	.50	.25	.05
☐ 16 Erik Hanson	.75	.35	.07
☐ 17 Bill Swift	.50	.25	.05
☐ 18 Mike Campbell	.35	.17	.03
☐ 19 Mike Jackson	.35	.17	.03
☐ 20 Rich Renteria	.35	.17	.03
☐ 21 Mario Diaz	.35	.17	.03
☐ 22 Jerry Reed	.35	.17	.03
☐ 23 Darnell Coles	.35	.17	.03
☐ 24 Steve Trout	.35	.17	.03
☐ 25 Mike Schooler	.60	.30	.06
☐ 26 Julio Solano	.35	.17	.03
☐ 27 Mariners Coaches	.35	.17	.03
☐ 28 Checklist Card	.35	.17	.03

1989 Mother's Cookies McGwire

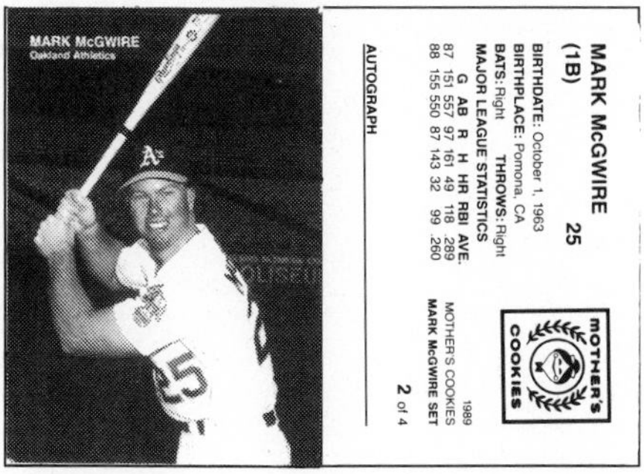

The 1989 Mother's Cookies Mark McGwire set contains 4 standard-size (2 1/2" by 3 1/2") cards with rounded corners. The fronts have borderless color photos, and the horizontally-oriented backs have biographical information. One card was included in each specially marked box of Mother's Cookies. Since all four cards picture Mark McGwire, the pose is identified parenthetically in the checklist below in order to distinguish the card fronts.

	MINT	EXC	G-VG
COMPLETE SET (4)	12.00	6.00	1.20
COMMON PLAYER (1-4)	3.50	1.75	.35
☐ 1 Mark McGwire (bat on shoulder)	3.50	1.75	.35
☐ 2 Mark McGwire (batting stance)	3.50	1.75	.35
☐ 3 Mark McGwire (holding bat in front)	3.50	1.75	.35
☐ 4 Mark McGwire (batting follow through)	3.50	1.75	.35

1989 Mother's Cookies Rangers

The 1989 Mother's Cookies Texas Rangers set contains 28 standard-size (2 1/2" by 3 1/2") cards with rounded corners. The fronts have borderless color photos, and the horizontally-oriented backs have biographical information. Starter sets containing 20 of these cards were given away at a Rangers home game during the 1989 season.

	MINT	EXC	G-VG
COMPLETE SET (28)	10.00	5.00	1.00
COMMON PLAYER (1-28)	.35	.17	.03

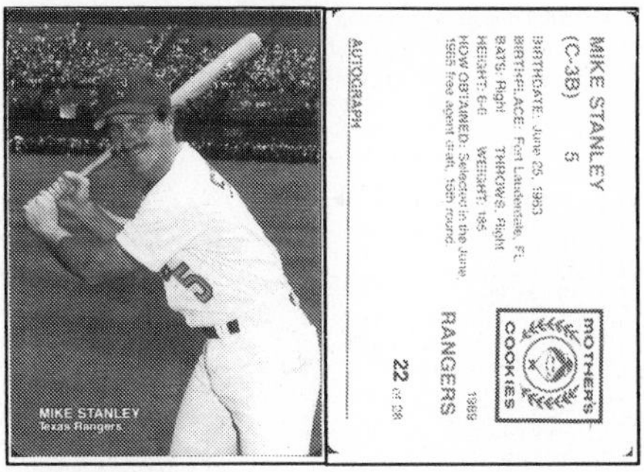

☐ 1 Bobby Valentine MG	.50	.25	.05
☐ 2 Nolan Ryan	2.50	1.25	.25
☐ 3 Julio Franco	.75	.35	.07
☐ 4 Charlie Hough	.50	.25	.05
☐ 5 Rafael Palmeiro	1.25	.60	.12
☐ 6 Jeff Russell	.50	.25	.05
☐ 7 Ruben Sierra	1.50	.75	.15
☐ 8 Steve Buechele	.35	.17	.03
☐ 9 Buddy Bell	.50	.25	.05
☐ 10 Pete Incaviglia	.50	.25	.05
☐ 11 Geno Petralli	.35	.17	.03
☐ 12 Cecil Espy	.35	.17	.03
☐ 13 Scott Fletcher	.35	.17	.03
☐ 14 Bobby Witt	.75	.35	.07
☐ 15 Brad Arnsberg	.50	.25	.05
☐ 16 Rick Leach	.35	.17	.03
☐ 17 Jamie Moyer	.35	.17	.03
☐ 18 Kevin Brown	.60	.30	.06
☐ 19 Jeff Kunkel	.35	.17	.03
☐ 20 Craig McMurtry	.35	.17	.03
☐ 21 Kenny Rogers	.50	.25	.05
☐ 22 Mike Stanley	.35	.17	.03
☐ 23 Cecilio Guante	.35	.17	.03
☐ 24 Jim Sundberg	.35	.17	.03
☐ 25 Jose Guzman	.35	.17	.03
☐ 26 Jeff Stone	.35	.17	.03
☐ 27 Rangers Coaches	.35	.17	.03
☐ 28 Checklist Card	.35	.17	.03

1990 Mother's Cookies Astros

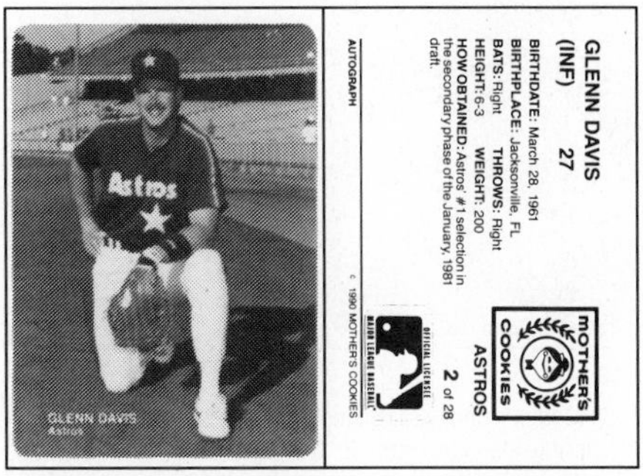

This standard-size, 2 1/2" by 3 1/2", 28-card set features members of the 1990 Houston Astros. This set features the traditional rounded corners and has biographical information about each player on the back. These Astros cards were given away on July 15th to the first 25,000 fans at the Astrodome. They were distributed in 20 card random packets at the game and eight more at the redemption booths. However, both groups of cards were random and there was no guarantee of getting a complete set in the cards. The promotional idea was that the only way one could finish the set was to trade for them.

The certificates of redemption for eight were redeemable at the major card show at the AstroArena on August 24-26, 1990.

	MINT	EXC	G-VG
COMPLETE SET (28)	9.00	4.50	.90
COMMON PLAYER (1-28)	.30	.15	.03
□ 1 Art Howe MG	.40	.20	.04
□ 2 Glenn Davis	1.00	.50	.10
□ 3 Eric Anthony	.75	.35	.07
□ 4 Mike Scott	.60	.30	.06
□ 5 Craig Biggio	.50	.25	.05
□ 6 Ken Caminiti	.40	.20	.04
□ 7 Bill Doran	.40	.20	.04
□ 8 Gerald Young	.40	.20	.04
□ 9 Terry Puhl	.30	.15	.03
□ 10 Mark Portugal	.30	.15	.03
□ 11 Mark Davidson	.30	.15	.03
□ 12 Jim Deshaies	.30	.15	.03
□ 13 Bill Gullickson	.30	.15	.03
□ 14 Franklin Stubbs	.40	.20	.04
□ 15 Danny Darwin	.40	.20	.04
□ 16 Ken Oberkfell	.30	.15	.03
□ 17 Dave Smith	.40	.20	.04
□ 18 Dan Schatzeder	.30	.15	.03
□ 19 Rafael Ramirez	.30	.15	.03
□ 20 Larry Andersen	.30	.15	.03
□ 21 Alex Trevino	.30	.15	.03
□ 22 Glenn Wilson	.30	.15	.03
□ 23 Jim Clancy	.30	.15	.03
□ 24 Eric Yelding	.40	.20	.04
□ 25 Casey Candaele	.30	.15	.03
□ 26 Juan Agosto	.30	.15	.03
□ 27 Coaches Matt Galante Billy Bowman Bob Cluck Phil Garner Ed Napoleon Rudy Jaramillo	.30	.15	.03
□ 28 Personnel Dave Labossiere TR Dennis Liborio EQ.MG Doc Ewell TR	.30	.15	.03

1990 Mother's Cookies Athletics

1990 Mother's Cookies Oakland Athletics set contains 28 cards measuring standard size, 2 1/2" by 3 1/2", with rounded corners. The envelope containing the cards honors the 1989 World Championship Oakland Athletics. The A's cards were released at the July 22nd game to the first 35,000 fans to walk through the gates. They were distributed in 20-card random packets at the game and eight more at the redemption booths. However, both groups of cards were random and there was no guarantee of getting a complete set in the cards. The promotional idea was that the only way one could finish the set was to trade for them. The redemption certificates were to be used at the Labor Day San Francisco card show. In addition to this the Mother's Giants cards were also redeemable at that show.

	MINT	EXC	G-VG
COMPLETE SET (28)	12.00	6.00	1.20
COMMON PLAYER (1-28)	.35	.17	.03
□ 1 Tony LaRussa MG	.50	.25	.05
□ 2 Mark McGwire	1.25	.60	.12
□ 3 Terry Steinbach	.50	.25	.05
□ 4 Rickey Henderson	2.00	1.00	.20
□ 5 Dave Stewart	.75	.35	.07
□ 6 Jose Canseco	2.00	1.00	.20
□ 7 Dennis Eckersley	.75	.35	.07
□ 8 Carney Lansford	.60	.30	.06
□ 9 Mike Moore	.50	.25	.05
□ 10 Walt Weiss	.60	.30	.06
□ 11 Scott Sanderson	.50	.25	.05
□ 12 Ron Hassey	.35	.17	.03
□ 13 Rick Honeycutt	.35	.17	.03
□ 14 Ken Phelps	.35	.17	.03
□ 15 Jamie Quirk	.35	.17	.03
□ 16 Bob Welch	.60	.30	.06
□ 17 Felix Jose	.60	.30	.06
□ 18 Dave Henderson	.50	.25	.05
□ 19 Mike Norris	.35	.17	.03
□ 20 Todd Burns	.35	.17	.03
□ 21 Lance Blankenship	.35	.17	.03
□ 22 Gene Nelson	.35	.17	.03
□ 23 Stan Javier	.50	.25	.05
□ 24 Curt Young	.35	.17	.03
□ 25 Mike Gallego	.35	.17	.03
□ 26 Joe Klink	.35	.17	.03
□ 27 A's Coaches Rene Lachemann Dave Duncan Merv Rettenmund Tommie Reynolds Art Kusnyer Dave McKay	.35	.17	.03
□ 28 Checklist Card A's Personnel Larry Davis, Trainer Steve Vuchinch, Visiting Club Mgr. Frank Cienscyk, Equipment Mgr. Barry Weinberg, Trainer	.35		

1990 Mother's Cookies Canseco

This is a standard Mother's Cookies set with four cards each measuring 2 1/2" by 3 1/2" with rounded corners issued to capitalize on Jose Canseco's popularity. This four-card set features Canseco in various batting poses.

	MINT	EXC	G-VG
COMPLETE SET (4)	12.00	6.00	1.20
COMMON PLAYER (1-4)	3.50	1.75	.35
□ 1 Jose Canseco (Sitting with bat over shoulders)	3.50	1.75	.35
□ 2 Jose Canseco (Standing with bat behind shoulders)	3.50	1.75	.35
□ 3 Jose Canseco (Batting Pose)	3.50	1.75	.35

☐ 4 Jose Canseco (Sitting on dugout steps)	3.50	1.75	.35

1990 Mother's Cookies Will Clark

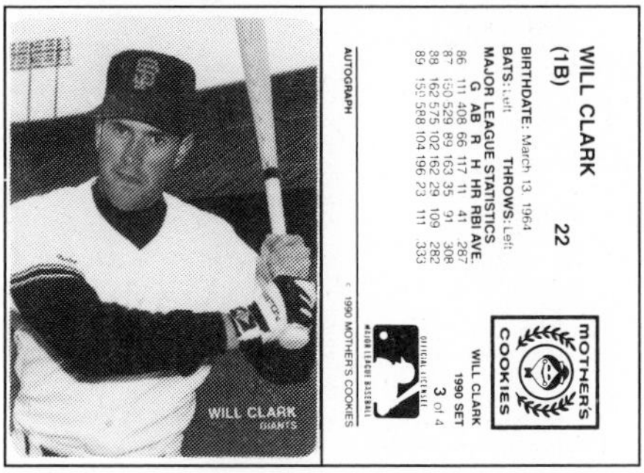

This is a standard Mother's Cookies set with four cards each measuring 2 1/2" by 3 1/2" with rounded corners issued to capitalize on Will Clark's popularity. This four-card set features Clark in various poses as indicated in the checklist below.

	MINT	EXC	G-VG
COMPLETE SET (4)	12.00	6.00	1.20
COMMON PLAYER (1-4)	3.50	1.75	.35
☐ 1 Will Clark (Batting pose looking over right shoulder)	3.50	1.75	.35
☐ 2 Will Clark (Holding bat on left shoulder)	3.50	1.75	.35
☐ 3 Will Clark (Holding bat ready to swing)	3.50	1.75	.35
☐ 4 Will Clark (Standing with bat behind shoulders)	3.50	1.75	.35

1990 Mother's Cookies Dodgers

The 1990 Mother's Cookies Los Angeles Dodgers set contains 28 cards (2 1/2" by 3 1/2") issued with rounded corners and beautiful full color fronts with biographical information on the back. These Dodgers cards were given away at Chavez Ravine to all fans fourteen and under at the August 19th game. They were distributed in 20-card random packets at the game and eight more at the redemption booths. However, both groups of cards were random and there was no guarantee of getting a complete set in the cards. The promotional idea was that the only way one could finish the set was to trade for them. The redemption for eight more cards was done at the 22nd Annual Labor Day card show at the Anaheim Convention Center.

	MINT	EXC	G-VG
COMPLETE SET (28)	9.00	4.50	.90
COMMON PLAYER (1-28)	.35	.17	.03
☐ 1 Tom Lasorda MG	.50	.25	.05
☐ 2 Fernando Valenzuela	.60	.30	.06
☐ 3 Kal Daniels	.60	.30	.06
☐ 4 Mike Scioscia	.35	.17	.03
☐ 5 Eddie Murray	.75	.35	.07
☐ 6 Mickey Hatcher	.35	.17	.03
☐ 7 Juan Samuel	.50	.25	.05
☐ 8 Alfredo Griffin	.35	.17	.03
☐ 9 Tim Belcher	.50	.25	.05
☐ 10 Hubie Brooks	.50	.25	.05
☐ 11 Jose Gonzalez	.50	.25	.05
☐ 12 Orel Hershiser	.90	.45	.09
☐ 13 Kirk Gibson	.75	.35	.07
☐ 14 Chris Gwynn	.50	.25	.05
☐ 15 Jay Howell	.50	.25	.05
☐ 16 Rick Dempsey	.35	.17	.03
☐ 17 Ramon Martinez	1.25	.60	.12
☐ 18 Lenny Harris	.50	.25	.05
☐ 19 John Wetteland	.50	.25	.05
☐ 20 Mike Sharperson	.35	.17	.03
☐ 21 Mike Morgan	.35	.17	.03
☐ 22 Ray Searage	.35	.17	.03
☐ 23 Jeff Hamilton	.35	.17	.03
☐ 24 Jim Gott	.35	.17	.03
☐ 25 John Shelby	.35	.17	.03
☐ 26 Tim Crews	.35	.17	.03
☐ 27 Don Aase	.35	.17	.03
☐ 28 Dodger Coaches (Joe Ferguson, Ron Perranoski, Mark Cresse, Ben Hines, Joe Amalfitano, Bill Russell, Manny Mota)	.35	.17	.03

1990 Mother's Cookies Giants

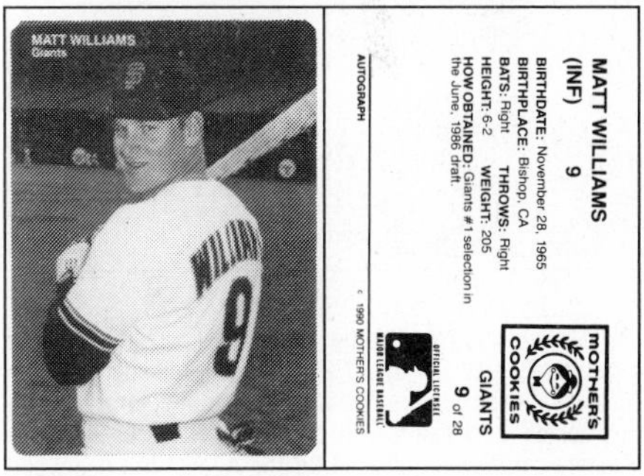

The 1990 Mother's Cookies San Francisco Giants set features cards with rounded corners measuring 2 1/2" by 3 1/2". The cards have full-color fronts and biographical information with no stats on the back. The Giants cards were given away at the July 29th game to the first 25,000 children 14 and under. They were distributed in 20-card random packets at the game and eight more at the redemption booths. However, both groups of cards were random and there was no guarantee of getting a complete set in the cards. The promotional idea was that the only way one could finish the set was to trade for them. The redemption certificates were to be used at the Labor Day San Francisco card show. In addition to this the Mother's A's cards were also redeemable at that show.

	MINT	EXC	G-VG
COMPLETE SET (28)	10.00	5.00	1.00
COMMON PLAYER (1-28)	.35	.17	.03
☐ 1 Roger Craig MG	.50	.25	.05
☐ 2 Will Clark	2.00	1.00	.20
☐ 3 Gary Carter	.75	.35	.07
☐ 4 Kelly Downs	.50	.25	.05
☐ 5 Kevin Mitchell	1.00	.50	.10
☐ 6 Steve Bedrosian	.50	.25	.05
☐ 7 Brett Butler	.60	.30	.06
☐ 8 Rick Reuschel	.50	.25	.05
☐ 9 Matt Williams	1.25	.60	.12
☐ 10 Robby Thompson	.50	.25	.05
☐ 11 Mike LaCoss	.35	.17	.03
☐ 12 Terry Kennedy	.35	.17	.03
☐ 13 Atlee Hammaker	.35	.17	.03
☐ 14 Rick Leach	.35	.17	.03
☐ 15 Ernest Riles	.35	.17	.03
☐ 16 Scott Garrelts	.50	.25	.05
☐ 17 Jose Uribe	.35	.17	.03
☐ 18 Greg Litton	.50	.25	.05
☐ 19 Dave Anderson	.35	.17	.03
☐ 20 Don Robinson	.35	.17	.03
☐ 21 Giants Coaches Dusty Baker Bob Lillis Bill Fahey Norm Sherry Wendall Kim	.35	.17	.03
☐ 22 Bill Bathe	.35	.17	.03
☐ 23 Randy O'Neal	.35	.17	.03
☐ 24 Kevin Bass	.50	.25	.05
☐ 25 Jeff Brantley	.50	.25	.05
☐ 26 John Burkett	.75	.35	.07
☐ 27 Ernie Camacho	.35	.17	.03
☐ 28 Checklist Card	.35	.17	.03

1990 Mother's Cookies Mariners

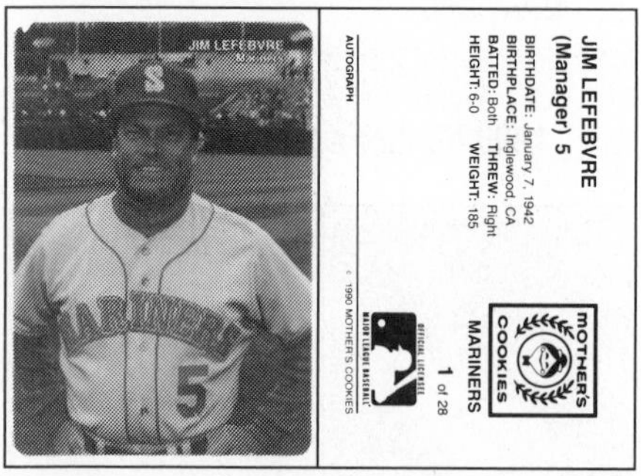

1990 Mother's Cookies Seattle Mariners set contains 28 cards in standard size (2 1/2" by 3 1/2") with the traditional Mother's Cookies rounded corners. The cards have full-color fronts and biographical information with no stats on the back. These Mariners cards were released for the August 5th game and given to the first 25,000 people who passed through the gates. They were distributed in 20-card random packets at the game and eight more at the redemption booths. However, both groups of cards were random and there was no guarantee of getting a complete set in the cards. The promotional idea was that the only way one could finish the set was to trade for them. The redemption for eight more cards were available at the Kingdome Card Show on August 12, 1990.

	MINT	EXC	G-VG
COMPLETE SET (28)	10.00	5.00	1.00
COMMON PLAYER (1-28)	.35	.17	.03
☐ 1 Jim Lefebvre MG	.50	.25	.05
☐ 2 Alvin Davis	.60	.30	.06
☐ 3 Ken Griffey Jr.	4.00	2.00	.40
☐ 4 Jeffrey Leonard	.50	.25	.05
☐ 5 David Valle	.35	.17	.03
☐ 6 Harold Reynolds	.50	.25	.05
☐ 7 Jay Buhner	.60	.30	.06
☐ 8 Erik Hanson	.60	.30	.06
☐ 9 Henry Cotto	.35	.17	.03
☐ 10 Edgar Martinez	.60	.30	.06
☐ 11 Bill Swift	.50	.25	.05
☐ 12 Omar Vizquel	.50	.25	.05
☐ 13 Randy Johnson	.50	.25	.05
☐ 14 Greg Briley	.60	.30	.06
☐ 15 Gene Harris	.50	.25	.05
☐ 16 Matt Young	.50	.25	.05
☐ 17 Pete O'Brien	.50	.25	.05
☐ 18 Brent Knackert	.50	.25	.05
☐ 19 Mike Jackson	.35	.17	.03
☐ 20 Brian Holman	.50	.25	.05
☐ 21 Mike Schooler	.50	.25	.05
☐ 22 Darnell Coles	.35	.17	.03
☐ 23 Keith Comstock	.35	.17	.03
☐ 24 Scott Bankhead	.50	.25	.05
☐ 25 Scott Bradley	.35	.17	.03
☐ 26 Mike Brumley	.35	.17	.03
☐ 27 Mariners Coaches Rusty Kuntz Gene Clines Bill Plummer Mike Paul Bob Didier	.35	.17	.03
☐ 28 Checklist Card Mariners Personnel Henry Genzale EQ.MG Tom Newberg ATR Rick Griffin TR	.35	.17	.03

1990 Mother's Cookies McGwire

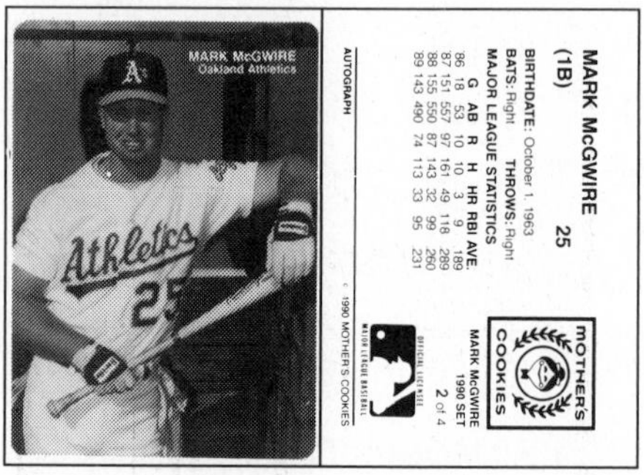

This is a standard Mother's Cookies set with four cards each measuring 2 1/2" by 3 1/2" with rounded corners issued to capitalize on Mark McGwire's popularity. This four-card set features McGwire in various poses as indicated in the checklist below.

	MINT	EXC	G-VG
COMPLETE SET (4)	12.00	6.00	1.20
COMMON PLAYER (1-4)	3.50	1.75	.35
☐ 1 Mark McGwire (Standing with bat on right shoulder)	3.50	1.75	.35
☐ 2 Mark McGwire (Standing in dugout with bat in front)	3.50	1.75	.35
☐ 3 Mark McGwire (Fielding Pose)	3.50	1.75	.35
☐ 4 Mark McGwire (Sitting on dugout steps)	3.50	1.75	.35

1990 Mother's Cookies Rangers

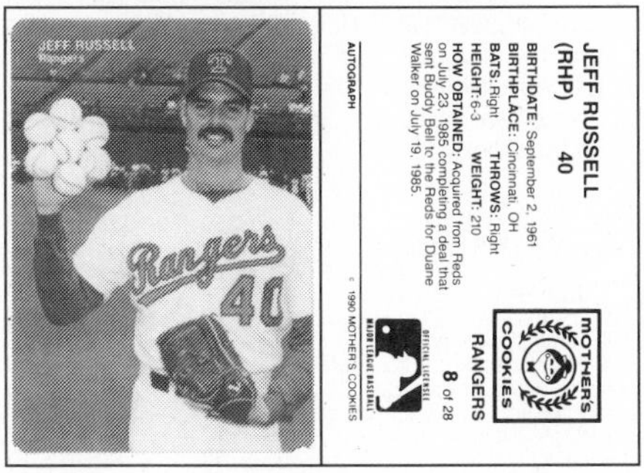

This 28-card, standard-size, 2 1/2" by 3 1/2", set features members of the 1990 Texas Rangers. The set has beautiful full-color photos on the front along with biographical information on the back. The set also features the now traditional Mother's Cookies rounded corners. The Rangers cards were distributed on July 22nd to the first 25,000 game attendees in Arlington. They were distributed in 20-card random packets at the game and eight more at the redemption booths. However, both groups of cards were random and there was no guarantee of getting a complete set in the cards. The promotional idea was that the only way one could finish the set was to trade for them. The certificates to redeem the cards for eigth more cards were able to be redeemed at the 17th annual Dallas Card Convention on August 18-19, 1990.

	MINT	EXC	G-VG
COMPLETE SET (28)	10.00	5.00	1.00
COMMON PLAYER (1-28)	.30	.15	.03
☐ 1 Bobby Valentine MG	.40	.20	.04
☐ 2 Nolan Ryan	2.00	1.00	.20
☐ 3 Ruben Sierra	1.00	.50	.10
☐ 4 Pete Incaviglia	.50	.25	.05
☐ 5 Charlie Hough	.40	.20	.04
☐ 6 Harold Baines	.50	.25	.05
☐ 7 Gino Petralli	.30	.15	.03
☐ 8 Jeff Russell	.40	.20	.04
☐ 9 Rafael Palmiero	.75	.35	.07
☐ 10 Julio Franco	.50	.25	.05
☐ 11 Jack Daugherty	.30	.15	.03
☐ 12 Gary Pettis	.30	.15	.03
☐ 13 Brian Bohanon	.40	.20	.04
☐ 14 Steve Buechele	.30	.15	.03
☐ 15 Bobby Witt	.60	.30	.06
☐ 16 Thad Bosley	.30	.15	.03
☐ 17 Gary Mielke	.30	.15	.03
☐ 18 Jeff Kunkel	.30	.15	.03
☐ 19 Mike Jeffcoat	.30	.15	.03
☐ 20 Mike Stanley	.30	.15	.03
☐ 21 Kevin Brown	.50	.25	.05
☐ 22 Kenny Rogers	.30	.15	.03
☐ 23 Jeff Huson	.30	.15	.03
☐ 24 Jamie Moyer	.30	.15	.03
☐ 25 Cecil Espy	.30	.15	.03
☐ 26 John Russell	.30	.15	.03
☐ 27 Coaches Dave Oliver Davey Lopes Tom Robson Tom House Toby Harrah	.30	.15	.03
☐ 28 Trainers Bill Zeigler TR Joe Macko EQ.MG. Marty Stajduhar, Strength and Cond. Danny Wheat ATR	.30	.15	.03

1990 Mother's Cookies Ryan

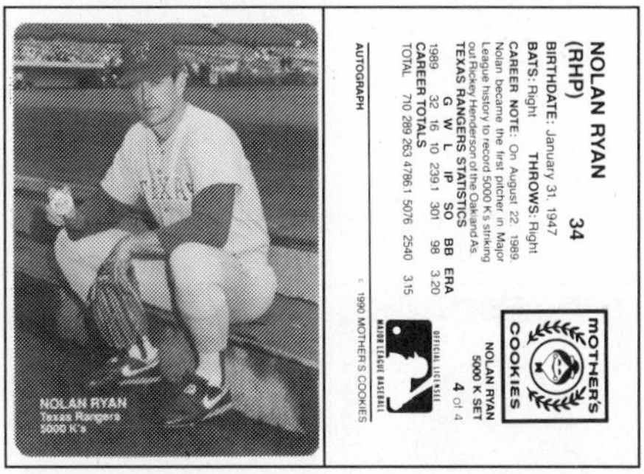

This is a typical Mother's Cookies set with four cartds each measuring the standard size of 2 1/2" by 3 1/2" with rounded corners honoring Ryan's more than 5,000 strikeouts over his career. This four-card set features Ryan in various pitching poses. The second card in the set is considered tougher to find than the other three in the set.

	MINT	EXC	G-VG
COMPLETE SET (4)	15.00	7.50	1.50
COMMON PLAYER (1-4)	3.50	1.75	.35
☐ 1 Nolan Ryan (Holding ball)	3.50	1.75	.35
☐ 2 Nolan Ryan (Dugout pose)	7.00	3.50	.70
☐ 3 Nolan Ryan (Holding ball behind waist)	3.50	1.75	.35
☐ 4 Nolan Ryan (Holding ball with 5,000 K's)	3.50	1.75	.35

1990 Mother's Cookies Matt Williams

This is a standard Mother's Cookies set with four cards each measuring 2 1/2" by 3 1/2" with rounded corners issued to capitalize on Matt Williams' popularity. This four-card set features Williams in various poses as indicated in the checklist below.

	MINT	EXC	G-VG
COMPLETE SET (4)	12.00	6.00	1.20
COMMON PLAYER (1-4)	3.50	1.75	.35
☐ 1 Matt Williams (Standing with bat on right shoulder)	3.50	1.75	.35

☐ 2 Matt Williams .... (Smiling batting pose)	3.50	1.75	.35
☐ 3 Matt Williams .... (Posing with glove)	3.50	1.75	.35
☐ 4 Matt Williams .... (Fielding pose with glove between legs)	3.50	1.75	.35

1976 Motorola Old Timers

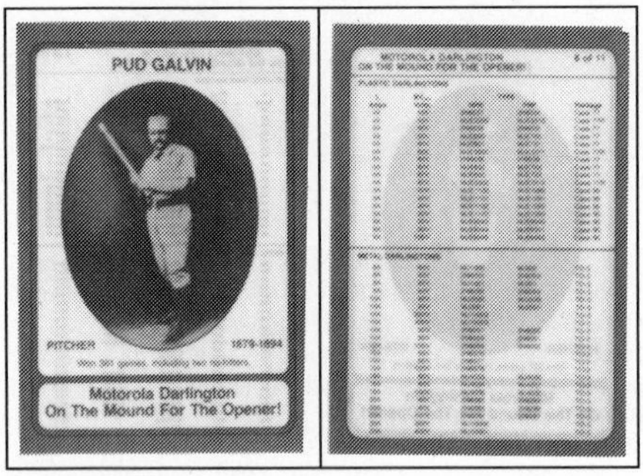

This 11-card, standard size, 2 1/2" by 3 1/2", set was issued by Motorola in 1976 and honored some of Baseball's all-time greats. The front of the cards were about the player while the backs of the cards talked in technical terms about Motorola products. The cards are also made on a thin (paper-like) card stock and are very flimsy.

	MINT	EXC	G-VG
COMPLETE SET (11)	20.00	10.00	2.00
COMMON PLAYER (1-11)	1.00	.50	.10
☐ 1 Honus Wagner	4.00	2.00	.40
☐ 2 Nap Lajoie	3.00	1.50	.30
☐ 3 Ty Cobb	5.00	2.50	.50
☐ 4 William Wambsganss	1.00	.50	.10
☐ 5 Three Fingers Brown	2.00	1.00	.20
☐ 6 Ray Schalk	2.00	1.00	.20
☐ 7 Frank Frisch	2.00	1.00	.20
☐ 8 Pud Galvin	2.00	1.00	.20
☐ 9 Babe Ruth	6.00	3.00	.60
☐ 10 Grover C. Alexander	2.00	1.00	.20
☐ 11 Frank L. Chance	2.00	1.00	.20

1989 MSA Superstars

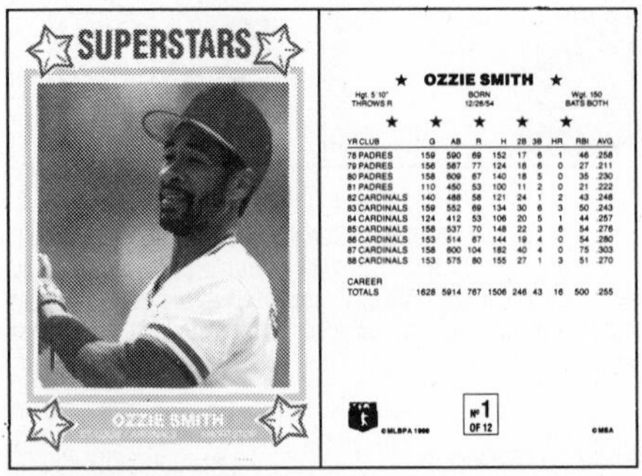

This 12-card, standard size, 2 1/2" by 3 1/2", set was issued by MSA (Michael Schechter Associates) and celebrated 12 of the leading players in the game as of 1989. The sets have an attractive design of stars in each of the front corners with the word Superstars on the top of the card and players name, team, and position underneath the full color photo of the player. Like most of the MSA sets there are no team logos used. The vertically-oriented backs show career statistics. Supposedly two cards were included in each specially-marked Ralston Purina cereal box.

	MINT	EXC	G-VG
COMPLETE SET (12)	7.50	3.75	.75
COMMON PLAYER (1-12)	.50	.25	.05
☐ 1 Ozzie Smith	.60	.30	.06
☐ 2 Andre Dawson	.60	.30	.06
☐ 3 Darryl Strawberry	.80	.40	.08
☐ 4 Mike Schmidt	1.00	.50	.10
☐ 5 Orel Hershiser	.60	.30	.06
☐ 6 Tim Raines	.60	.30	.06
☐ 7 Roger Clemens	.80	.40	.08
☐ 8 Kirby Puckett	.80	.40	.08
☐ 9 George Brett	.80	.40	.08
☐ 10 Alan Trammell	.50	.25	.05
☐ 11 Don Mattingly	1.00	.50	.10
☐ 12 Jose Canseco	1.00	.50	.10

1990 MSA Superstars

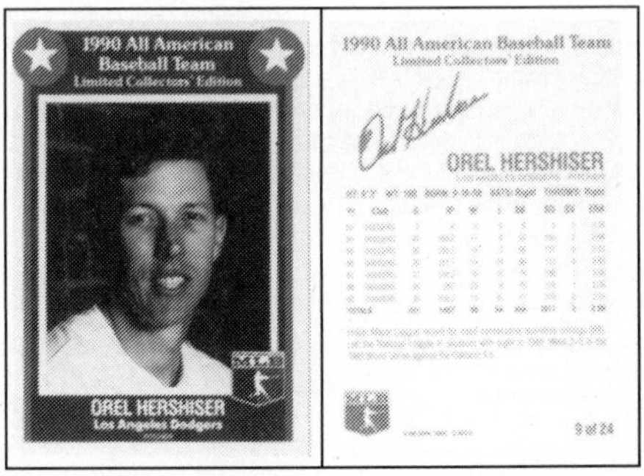

This 24-card, standard size, 2 1/2" by 3 1/2", set was issued by MSA (Michael Schechter Associates) for 7/11, Dr. Pepper, and other carbonated beverages (but there are no markings on the cards whatsoever to indicate who sponsored the set other than MSA). The fronts feature a red-white and blue design framing the players photos while the back has major league career statistics and a sentence of career highlights. The back also has a fascimile autograph of the player on the back. Like many of the sets sponsored by MSA there are no team logos on the cards as they have been airbrushed away.

	MINT	EXC	G-VG
COMPLETE SET (24)	30.00	15.00	3.00
COMMON PLAYER (1-24)	.60	.30	.06
☐ 1 George Brett	1.00	.50	.10
☐ 2 Mark McGwire	1.25	.60	.12
☐ 3 Wade Boggs	1.25	.60	.12
☐ 4 Cal Ripken	.75	.35	.07
☐ 5 Rickey Henderson	2.00	1.00	.20
☐ 6 Dwight Gooden	1.00	.50	.10
☐ 7 Bo Jackson	3.00	1.50	.30
☐ 8 Roger Clemens	1.25	.60	.12
☐ 9 Orel Hershiser	.75	.35	.07
☐ 10 Ozzie Smith	.75	.35	.07
☐ 11 Don Mattingly	2.00	1.00	.20
☐ 12 Kirby Puckett	1.25	.60	.12
☐ 13 Robin Yount	1.00	.50	.10
☐ 14 Tony Gwynn	1.00	.50	.10
☐ 15 Jose Canseco	1.50	.75	.15
☐ 16 Nolan Ryan	3.00	1.50	.30
☐ 17 Ken Griffey Jr.	3.00	1.50	.30
☐ 18 Will Clark	2.00	1.00	.20

☐ 19 Ryne Sandberg	2.00	1.00	.20
☐ 20 Kent Hrbek	.60	.30	.06
☐ 21 Carlton Fisk	.75	.35	.07
☐ 22 Paul Molitor	.60	.30	.06
☐ 23 Dave Winfield	.75	.35	.07
☐ 24 Andre Dawson	.75	.35	.07

1916 M101-4 Sporting News

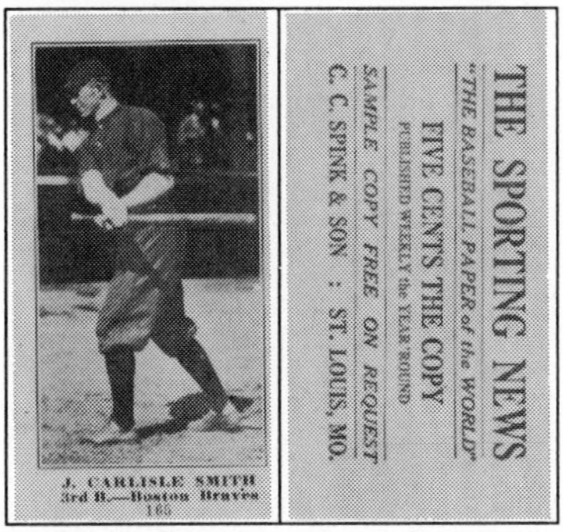

The cards in this 200-card set measure approximately 1 5/8" by 3". Issued in 1916 as a premium offer, the M101-4 set features black and white photos of current ballplayers. Each card is numbered and the reverse carries Sporting News advertising. The fronts are the same as D329, H801-9 and the unclassified Famous and Barr set. Most of the players in this also appear in the M101-5 set. Those cards which are asterisked in the checklist below are those cards which do not appear in the companion M101-5 set issued the year before.

	EX-MT	VG-E	GOOD
COMPLETE SET (200)	12000.00	5000.00	1250.00
COMMON PLAYER (1-200)	27.00	13.50	2.70
☐ 1 Babe Adams	27.00	13.50	2.70
☐ 2 Sam Agnew	27.00	13.50	2.70
☐ 3 Eddie Ainsmith	27.00	13.50	2.70
☐ 4 Grover Alexander	90.00	45.00	9.00
☐ 5 Leon Ames	27.00	13.50	2.70
☐ 6 Jimmy Archer	27.00	13.50	2.70
☐ 7 Jimmy Austin	27.00	13.50	2.70
☐ 8 H.D. Baird *	36.00	18.00	3.60
☐ 9 Frank Baker	75.00	37.50	7.50
☐ 10 Dave Bancroft	60.00	30.00	6.00
☐ 11 Jack Barry	27.00	13.50	2.70
☐ 12 Zinn Beck	27.00	13.50	2.70
☐ 13 Chief Bender *	75.00	37.50	7.50
☐ 14 Joe Benz	27.00	13.50	2.70
☐ 15 Bob Bescher	27.00	13.50	2.70
☐ 16 Al Betzel	27.00	13.50	2.70
☐ 17 Mordecai Brown	60.00	30.00	6.00
☐ 18 Eddie Burns	27.00	13.50	2.70
☐ 19 George Burns *	36.00	18.00	3.60
☐ 20 George J. Burns	27.00	13.50	2.70
☐ 21 Joe Bush	27.00	13.50	2.70
☐ 22 Donie Bush *	36.00	18.00	3.60
☐ 23 Art Butler	27.00	13.50	2.70
☐ 24 Bobbie Byrne	27.00	13.50	2.70
☐ 25 Forrest Cady *	36.00	18.00	3.60
☐ 26 Jim Callahan	27.00	13.50	2.70
☐ 27 Ray Caldwell	27.00	13.50	2.70
☐ 28 Max Carey	60.00	30.00	6.00
☐ 29 George Chalmers	27.00	13.50	2.70
☐ 30 Ray Chapman	45.00	22.50	4.50
☐ 31 Larry Cheney	27.00	13.50	2.70
☐ 32 Ed Cicotte	45.00	22.50	4.50
☐ 33 Tommy Clarke	27.00	13.50	2.70
☐ 34 Eddie Collins	75.00	37.50	7.50
☐ 35 Shano Collins	27.00	13.50	2.70
☐ 36 Charles Comiskey	75.00	37.50	7.50
☐ 37 Joe Connolly	27.00	13.50	2.70
☐ 38 Ty Cobb *	1500.00	600.00	150.00
☐ 39 Harry Coveleskie	27.00	13.50	2.70
☐ 40 Gabby Cravath	36.00	18.00	3.60
☐ 41 Sam Crawford	60.00	30.00	6.00
☐ 42 Jean Dale	27.00	13.50	2.70
☐ 43 Jake Daubert	36.00	18.00	3.60
☐ 44 Charles Deal	27.00	13.50	2.70
☐ 45 Frank Demaree	27.00	13.50	2.70
☐ 46 Josh Devore *	36.00	18.00	3.60
☐ 47 William Doak	27.00	13.50	2.70
☐ 48 Bill Donovan	27.00	13.50	2.70
☐ 49 Red Dooin	27.00	13.50	2.70
☐ 50 Mike Doolan	27.00	13.50	2.70
☐ 51 Larry Doyle	27.00	13.50	2.70
☐ 52 Jean Dubuc	27.00	13.50	2.70
☐ 53 Oscar J. Dugey	27.00	13.50	2.70
☐ 54 John Evers	60.00	30.00	6.00
☐ 55 Red Faber	60.00	30.00	6.00
☐ 56 Happy Felsch	45.00	22.50	4.50
☐ 57 Bill Fischer	27.00	13.50	2.70
☐ 58 Ray Fisher	27.00	13.50	2.70
☐ 59 Max Flack	27.00	13.50	2.70
☐ 60 Art Fletcher	27.00	13.50	2.70
☐ 61 Eddie Foster	27.00	13.50	2.70
☐ 62 Jacques Fournier	27.00	13.50	2.70
☐ 63 Del Gainer	27.00	13.50	2.70
☐ 64 Chick Gandil *	60.00	30.00	6.00
☐ 65 Larry Gardner	27.00	13.50	2.70
☐ 66 Joe Gedeon	27.00	13.50	2.70
☐ 67 Gus Getz	27.00	13.50	2.70
☐ 68 George Gibson	27.00	13.50	2.70
☐ 69 Wilbur Good	27.00	13.50	2.70
☐ 70 Hank Gowdy	27.00	13.50	2.70
☐ 71 Jack Graney	27.00	13.50	2.70
☐ 72 Clark Griffith *	90.00	45.00	9.00
☐ 73 Tommy Griffith	27.00	13.50	2.70
☐ 74 Heine Groh	36.00	18.00	3.60
☐ 75 Earl Hamilton	27.00	13.50	2.70
☐ 76 Bob Harmon	27.00	13.50	2.70
☐ 77 Roy Hartzell	27.00	13.50	2.70
☐ 78 Claude Hendrix	27.00	13.50	2.70
☐ 79 Olaf Henriksen	27.00	13.50	2.70
☐ 80 John Henry	27.00	13.50	2.70
☐ 81 Buck Herzog	27.00	13.50	2.70
☐ 82 Hugh High	27.00	13.50	2.70
☐ 83 Dick Hoblitzell	27.00	13.50	2.70
☐ 84 Harry Hooper	60.00	30.00	6.00
☐ 85 Ivan Howard	27.00	13.50	2.70
☐ 86 Miller Huggins	60.00	30.00	6.00
☐ 87 Joe Jackson	1500.00	750.00	150.00
☐ 88 William James	27.00	13.50	2.70
☐ 89 Harold Janvrin	27.00	13.50	2.70
☐ 90 Hughie Jennings	60.00	30.00	6.00
☐ 91 Walter Johnson	450.00	225.00	45.00
☐ 92 Fielder Jones	27.00	13.50	2.70
☐ 93 Joe Judge *	36.00	18.00	3.60
☐ 94 Benny Kauff	27.00	13.50	2.70
☐ 95 Bill Killifer	27.00	13.50	2.70
☐ 96 Ed Konetchy	27.00	13.50	2.70
☐ 97 Nap Lajoie	200.00	100.00	20.00
☐ 98 Jack Lapp	27.00	13.50	2.70
☐ 99 John Lavan	27.00	13.50	2.70
☐ 100 Jimmy Lavender	27.00	13.50	2.70
☐ 101 Nemo Leibold	27.00	13.50	2.70
☐ 102 Hub Leonard	27.00	13.50	2.70
☐ 103 Duffy Lewis	27.00	13.50	2.70
☐ 104 Hans Lobert	27.00	13.50	2.70
☐ 105 Tom Long	27.00	13.50	2.70
☐ 106 Fred Luderus	27.00	13.50	2.70
☐ 107 Connie Mack	150.00	75.00	15.00
☐ 108 Lee Magee	27.00	13.50	2.70
☐ 109 Sherry Magee *	36.00	18.00	3.60
☐ 110 Al Mamaux	27.00	13.50	2.70
☐ 111 Leslie Mann	27.00	13.50	2.70
☐ 112 Rabbit Maranville	60.00	30.00	6.00
☐ 113 Rube Marquard	60.00	30.00	6.00
☐ 114 J.E. Mayer	27.00	13.50	2.70
☐ 115 George McBride	27.00	13.50	2.70
☐ 116 John McGraw	90.00	45.00	9.00
☐ 117 Jack McInnis	36.00	18.00	3.60
☐ 118 Fred Merkle	36.00	18.00	3.60
☐ 119 Chief Meyers	27.00	13.50	2.70
☐ 120 Clyde Milan	27.00	13.50	2.70
☐ 121 John Miller *	36.00	18.00	3.60
☐ 122 Otto Miller	27.00	13.50	2.70
☐ 123 Willie Mitchell	27.00	13.50	2.70
☐ 124 Fred Mollwitz	27.00	13.50	2.70
☐ 125 Pat Moran	27.00	13.50	2.70
☐ 126 Ray Morgan	27.00	13.50	2.70
☐ 127 George Moriarty	27.00	13.50	2.70
☐ 128 Guy Morton	27.00	13.50	2.70
☐ 129 Mike Mowrey *	36.00	18.00	3.60
☐ 130 Eddie Murphy	27.00	13.50	2.70
☐ 131 Hy Myers	27.00	13.50	2.70
☐ 132 Bert Niehoff	27.00	13.50	2.70
☐ 133 Rube Oldring	27.00	13.50	2.70
☐ 134 Oliver O'Mara	27.00	13.50	2.70
☐ 135 Steve O'Neill	27.00	13.50	2.70

☐ 136 Dode Paskert	27.00	13.50	2.70
☐ 137 Roger Peckinpaugh	27.00	13.50	2.70
☐ 138 Walter Pipp	36.00	18.00	3.60
☐ 139 Del Pratt	27.00	13.50	2.70
☐ 140 Pat Ragan *	36.00	18.00	3.60
☐ 141 Bill Rariden	27.00	13.50	2.70
☐ 142 Eppa Rixey	60.00	30.00	6.00
☐ 143 Davey Robertson	27.00	13.50	2.70
☐ 144 Wilbert Robinson	90.00	45.00	9.00
☐ 145 Bob Roth	27.00	13.50	2.70
☐ 146 Eddie Roush	75.00	37.50	7.50
☐ 147 Clarence Rowland	27.00	13.50	2.70
☐ 148 Nap Rucker	27.00	13.50	2.70
☐ 149 Dick Rudolph	27.00	13.50	2.70
☐ 150 Reb Russell	27.00	13.50	2.70
☐ 151 Babe Ruth	3000.00	1200.00	300.00
☐ 152 Vic Saier	27.00	13.50	2.70
☐ 153 Slim Sallee	27.00	13.50	2.70
☐ 154 Ray Schalk	60.00	30.00	6.00
☐ 155 Wally Schang	27.00	13.50	2.70
☐ 156 Frank Schulte	27.00	13.50	2.70
☐ 157 Everett Scott	36.00	18.00	3.60
☐ 158 Jim Scott	27.00	13.50	2.70
☐ 159 Tom Seaton	27.00	13.50	2.70
☐ 160 Howard Shanks	27.00	13.50	2.70
☐ 161 Bob Shawkey	36.00	18.00	3.60
☐ 162 Ernie Shore	36.00	18.00	3.60
☐ 163 Bert Shotton	27.00	13.50	2.70
☐ 164 George Sisler	90.00	45.00	9.00
☐ 165 J.C. Smith	27.00	13.50	2.70
☐ 166 Fred Snodgrass	27.00	13.50	2.70
☐ 167 George Stallings	27.00	13.50	2.70
☐ 168 Oscar Stanage	27.00	13.50	2.70
☐ 169 Charles Stengel	450.00	225.00	45.00
☐ 170 Milton Stock	27.00	13.50	2.70
☐ 171 Amos Strunk	27.00	13.50	2.70
☐ 172 Billy Sullivan	36.00	18.00	3.60
☐ 173 Jeff Tesreau	27.00	13.50	2.70
☐ 174 Joe Tinker	60.00	30.00	6.00
☐ 175 Fred Toney	27.00	13.50	2.70
☐ 176 Terry Turner	27.00	13.50	2.70
☐ 177 George Tyler *	36.00	18.00	3.60
☐ 178 Jim Vaughn	27.00	13.50	2.70
☐ 179 Bobby Veach	27.00	13.50	2.70
☐ 180 James Viox	27.00	13.50	2.70
☐ 181 Oscar Vitt	27.00	13.50	2.70
☐ 182 Honus Wagner	450.00	225.00	45.00
☐ 183 Clarence Walker	27.00	13.50	2.70
☐ 184 Ed Walsh	60.00	30.00	6.00
☐ 185 Bill Wambsganss *	36.00	18.00	3.60
☐ 186 Buck Weaver	45.00	22.50	4.50
☐ 187 Carl Weilman	27.00	13.50	2.70
☐ 188 Zack Wheat	60.00	30.00	6.00
☐ 189 George Whitted	27.00	13.50	2.70
☐ 190 Fred Williams	27.00	13.50	2.70
☐ 191 Arthur Wilson	27.00	13.50	2.70
☐ 192 J.O. Wilson	27.00	13.50	2.70
☐ 193 Ivy Wingo	27.00	13.50	2.70
☐ 194 Meldon Wolfgang	27.00	13.50	2.70
☐ 195 Joe Wood	50.00	25.00	5.00
☐ 196 Steve Yerkes	27.00	13.50	2.70
☐ 197 Pep Young * (Detroit Tigers)	36.00	18.00	3.60
☐ 198 Rollie Zeider	27.00	13.50	2.70
☐ 199 Heine Zimmerman	27.00	13.50	2.70
☐ 200 Dutch Zwilling	27.00	13.50	2.70

1915 M101-5 Sporting News

The cards in this 200-card set measure 1 5/8 by 3". The 1915 M101-5 series of black and white, numbered baseball cards is very similar in style to M101-4. The set was offered as a marketing promotion by C.C. Spink and Son, publishers of The Sporting News ("The Baseball Paper of the World"). Most of the players in this also appear in the M101-4 set. Those cards which are asterisked in the checklist below are those cards which do not appear in the companion M101-4 set issued the next year.

	EX-MT	VG-E	GOOD
COMPLETE SET (200)	16500.00	7500.00	1800.00
COMMON PLAYER (1-200)	33.00	16.00	3.00
☐ 1 Babe Adams	33.00	16.00	3.00
☐ 2 Sam Agnew	33.00	16.00	3.00
☐ 3 Ed Ainsmith	33.00	16.00	3.00
☐ 4 Grover Alexander	100.00	50.00	10.00
☐ 5 Leon Ames	33.00	16.00	3.00
☐ 6 Jimmy Archer	33.00	16.00	3.00
☐ 7 Jimmy Austin	33.00	16.00	3.00
☐ 8 Frank Baker	80.00	40.00	8.00
☐ 9 Dave Bancroft	65.00	32.50	6.50
☐ 10 Jack Barry	33.00	16.00	3.00
☐ 11 Zinn Beck	33.00	16.00	3.00
☐ 12 Luke Boone *	40.00	20.00	4.00
☐ 13 Joe Benz	33.00	16.00	3.00
☐ 14 Bob Bescher	33.00	16.00	3.00
☐ 15 Al Betzel	33.00	16.00	3.00
☐ 16 Roger Bresnahan *	80.00	40.00	8.00
☐ 17 Eddie Burns	33.00	16.00	3.00
☐ 18 G.J. Burns	33.00	16.00	3.00
☐ 19 Joe Bush	33.00	16.00	3.00
☐ 20 Owen Bush *	40.00	20.00	4.00
☐ 21 Art Butler	33.00	16.00	3.00
☐ 22 Bobby Byrne	33.00	16.00	3.00
☐ 23 Mordecai Brown	65.00	32.50	6.50
☐ 24 Jimmy Callahan	33.00	16.00	3.00
☐ 25 Ray Caldwell	33.00	16.00	3.00
☐ 26 Max Carey	65.00	32.50	6.50
☐ 27 George Chalmers	33.00	16.00	3.00
☐ 28 Frank Chance *	100.00	50.00	10.00
☐ 29 Ray Chapman	50.00	25.00	5.00
☐ 30 Larry Cheney	33.00	16.00	3.00
☐ 31 Ed Cicotte	50.00	25.00	5.00
☐ 32 Tommy Clarke	33.00	16.00	3.00
☐ 33 Eddie Collins	80.00	40.00	8.00
☐ 34 Shano Collins	33.00	16.00	3.00
☐ 35 Charles Comiskey	80.00	40.00	8.00
☐ 36 Joe Connolly	33.00	16.00	3.00
☐ 37 L. Cook *	40.00	20.00	4.00
☐ 38 Jack Coombs *	80.00	40.00	8.00
☐ 39 Dan Costello *	40.00	20.00	4.00
☐ 40 Harry Coveleskie	33.00	16.00	3.00
☐ 41 Gavvy Cravath	40.00	20.00	4.00
☐ 42 Sam Crawford	65.00	32.50	6.50
☐ 43 Jean Dale	33.00	16.00	3.00
☐ 44 Jake Daubert	40.00	20.00	4.00
☐ 45 G.A. Davis Jr. *	40.00	20.00	4.00
☐ 46 Charles Deal	33.00	16.00	3.00
☐ 47 Frank Demaree	33.00	16.00	3.00
☐ 48 Bill Doak	33.00	16.00	3.00
☐ 49 Bill Donovan	33.00	16.00	3.00
☐ 50 Red Dooin	33.00	16.00	3.00
☐ 51 Mike Doolan	33.00	16.00	3.00
☐ 52 Larry Doyle	33.00	16.00	3.00
☐ 53 Jean Dubuc	33.00	16.00	3.00
☐ 54 Oscar Dugey	33.00	16.00	3.00
☐ 55 John Evers	65.00	32.50	6.50
☐ 56 Red Faber	65.00	32.50	6.50
☐ 57 Happy Felsch	50.00	25.00	5.00
☐ 58 Bill Fischer	33.00	16.00	3.00
☐ 59 Ray Fisher	33.00	16.00	3.00
☐ 60 Max Flack	33.00	16.00	3.00
☐ 61 Art Fletcher	33.00	16.00	3.00
☐ 62 Eddie Foster	33.00	16.00	3.00
☐ 63 Jacques Fournier	33.00	16.00	3.00
☐ 64 Del Gainer	33.00	16.00	3.00
☐ 65 Larry Gardner	33.00	16.00	3.00
☐ 66 Joe Gedeon	33.00	16.00	3.00
☐ 67 Gus Getz	33.00	16.00	3.00
☐ 68 George Gibson	33.00	16.00	3.00
☐ 69 Wilbur Good	33.00	16.00	3.00
☐ 70 Hank Gowdy	33.00	16.00	3.00
☐ 71 Jack Graney	33.00	16.00	3.00
☐ 72 Tommy Griffith	33.00	16.00	3.00
☐ 73 Heine Groh	40.00	20.00	4.00
☐ 74 Earl Hamilton	33.00	16.00	3.00
☐ 75 Bob Harmon	33.00	16.00	3.00
☐ 76 Roy Hartzell	33.00	16.00	3.00
☐ 77 Claude Hendrix	33.00	16.00	3.00
☐ 78 Olaf Henriksen	33.00	16.00	3.00

☐ 79 John Henry	33.00	16.00	3.00
☐ 80 Buck Herzog	33.00	16.00	3.00
☐ 81 Hugh High	33.00	16.00	3.00
☐ 82 Dick Hoblitzell	33.00	16.00	3.00
☐ 83 Harry Hooper	65.00	32.50	6.50
☐ 84 Ivan Howard	33.00	16.00	3.00
☐ 85 Miller Huggins	65.00	32.50	6.50
☐ 86 Joe Jackson	1650.00	750.00	175.00
☐ 87 William James	33.00	16.00	3.00
☐ 88 Harold Janvrin	33.00	16.00	3.00
☐ 89 Hughie Jennings	65.00	32.50	6.50
☐ 90 Walter Johnson	500.00	250.00	50.00
☐ 91 Fielder Jones	33.00	16.00	3.00
☐ 92 Benny Kauff	33.00	16.00	3.00
☐ 93 Bill Killefer	33.00	16.00	3.00
☐ 94 Ed Konetchy	33.00	16.00	3.00
☐ 95 Napoleon Lajoie	250.00	125.00	25.00
☐ 96 Jack Lapp	33.00	16.00	3.00
☐ 97 John Lavan	33.00	16.00	3.00
☐ 98 Jimmy Lavender	33.00	16.00	3.00
☐ 99 Nemo Leibold	33.00	16.00	3.00
☐ 100 Hub Leonard	33.00	16.00	3.00
☐ 101 Duffy Lewis	33.00	16.00	3.00
☐ 102 Hans Lobert	33.00	16.00	3.00
☐ 103 Tom Long	33.00	16.00	3.00
☐ 104 Fred Luderus	33.00	16.00	3.00
☐ 105 Connie Mack	165.00	75.00	15.00
☐ 106 Lee Magee	33.00	16.00	3.00
☐ 107 Al Mamaux	33.00	16.00	3.00
☐ 108 Leslie Mann	33.00	16.00	3.00
☐ 109 Rabbit Maranville	65.00	32.50	6.50
☐ 110 Rube Marquard	65.00	32.50	6.50
☐ 111 Armando Marsans *	40.00	20.00	4.00
☐ 112 J.E. Mayer	33.00	16.00	3.00
☐ 113 George McBride	33.00	16.00	3.00
☐ 114 John McGraw	100.00	50.00	10.00
☐ 115 Jack McInnis	40.00	20.00	4.00
☐ 116 Fred Merkle	40.00	20.00	4.00
☐ 117 Chief Meyers	33.00	16.00	3.00
☐ 118 Clyde Milan	33.00	16.00	3.00
☐ 119 Otto Miller	33.00	16.00	3.00
☐ 120 Willie Mitchell	33.00	16.00	3.00
☐ 121 Fred Mollwitz	33.00	16.00	3.00
☐ 122 J.H. Moran *	40.00	20.00	4.00
☐ 123 Pat Moran	33.00	16.00	3.00
☐ 124 Ray Morgan	33.00	16.00	3.00
☐ 125 George Moriarty	33.00	16.00	3.00
☐ 126 Guy Morton	33.00	16.00	3.00
☐ 127 Eddie Murphy	33.00	16.00	3.00
☐ 128 Jack Murray *	40.00	20.00	4.00
☐ 129 Hy Myers	33.00	16.00	3.00
☐ 130 Bert Niehoff	33.00	16.00	3.00
☐ 131 Les Nunamaker *	40.00	20.00	4.00
☐ 132 Rube Oldring	33.00	16.00	3.00
☐ 133 Oliver O'Mara	33.00	16.00	3.00
☐ 134 Steve O'Neill	33.00	16.00	3.00
☐ 135 Dode Paskert	33.00	16.00	3.00
☐ 136 Roger Peckinpaugh	33.00	16.00	3.00
☐ 137 E.J. Pfeffer *	40.00	20.00	4.00
☐ 138 George Pierce *	40.00	20.00	4.00
☐ 139 Walter Pipp	40.00	20.00	4.00
☐ 140 Del Pratt	33.00	16.00	3.00
☐ 141 Bill Rariden	33.00	16.00	3.00
☐ 142 Eppa Rixey	65.00	32.50	6.50
☐ 143 Davey Robertson	33.00	16.00	3.00
☐ 144 Wilbert Robinson	100.00	50.00	10.00
☐ 145 Bob Roth	33.00	16.00	3.00
☐ 146 Eddie Roush	80.00	40.00	8.00
☐ 147 Clarence Rowland	33.00	16.00	3.00
☐ 148 Nap Rucker	33.00	16.00	3.00
☐ 149 Dick Rudolph	33.00	16.00	3.00
☐ 150 Reb Russell	33.00	16.00	3.00
☐ 151 Babe Ruth	5000.00	2000.00	600.00
☐ 152 Vic Saier	33.00	16.00	3.00
☐ 153 Slim Sallee	33.00	16.00	3.00
☐ 154 Germany Schaefer *	40.00	20.00	4.00
☐ 155 Ray Schalk	65.00	32.50	6.50
☐ 156 Wally Schang	33.00	16.00	3.00
☐ 157 Chas. Schmidt *	40.00	20.00	4.00
☐ 158 Frank Schulte	33.00	16.00	3.00
☐ 159 Jim Scott	33.00	16.00	3.00
☐ 160 Everett Scott	40.00	20.00	4.00
☐ 161 Tom Seaton	33.00	16.00	3.00
☐ 162 Howard Shanks	33.00	16.00	3.00
☐ 163 Bob Shawkey	40.00	20.00	4.00
☐ 164 Ernie Shore	40.00	20.00	4.00
☐ 165 Bert Shotton	33.00	16.00	3.00
☐ 166 George Sisler	100.00	50.00	10.00
☐ 167 J.C. Smith	33.00	16.00	3.00
☐ 168 Fred Snodgrass	33.00	16.00	3.00
☐ 169 George Stallings	33.00	16.00	3.00
☐ 170 Oscar Stanage	33.00	16.00	3.00
☐ 171 Charles Stengel	500.00	250.00	50.00
☐ 172 Milton Stock	33.00	16.00	3.00
☐ 173 Amos Strunk	33.00	16.00	3.00
☐ 174 Billy Sullivan	40.00	20.00	4.00
☐ 175 Jeff Tesreau	33.00	16.00	3.00
☐ 176 Jim Thorpe *	2000.00	800.00	200.00
☐ 177 Joe Tinker	65.00	32.50	6.50
☐ 178 Fred Toney	33.00	16.00	3.00
☐ 179 Terry Turner	33.00	16.00	3.00
☐ 180 Jim Vaughn	33.00	16.00	3.00
☐ 181 Bobby Veach	33.00	16.00	3.00
☐ 182 James Viox	33.00	16.00	3.00
☐ 183 Oscar Vitt	33.00	16.00	3.00
☐ 184 Honus Wagner	500.00	250.00	50.00
☐ 185 Clarence Walker	33.00	16.00	3.00
☐ 186 Zack Wheat	65.00	32.50	6.50
☐ 187 Ed Walsh	65.00	32.50	6.50
☐ 188 Buck Weaver	50.00	25.00	5.00
☐ 189 Carl Weilman	33.00	16.00	3.00
☐ 190 George Whitted	33.00	16.00	3.00
☐ 191 Fred Williams	33.00	16.00	3.00
☐ 192 Arthur Wilson	33.00	16.00	3.00
☐ 193 J.O. Wilson	33.00	16.00	3.00
☐ 194 Ivy Wingo	33.00	16.00	3.00
☐ 195 Meldon Wolfgang	33.00	16.00	3.00
☐ 196 Joe Wood	55.00	27.50	5.50
☐ 197 Steve Yerkes	33.00	16.00	3.00
☐ 198 Rollie Zeider	33.00	16.00	3.00
☐ 199 Heinie Zimmerman	33.00	16.00	3.00
☐ 200 Dutch Zwilling	33.00	16.00	3.00

1911 M116 Sporting Life

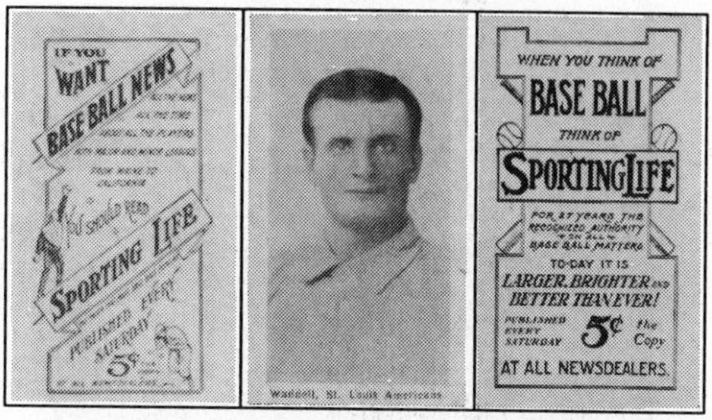

The cards in this 288-card set measure 1 1/2" by 2 5/8". The Sporting Life set was offered as a premium to the publication's subscribers in 1911. Each of the 24 series of 12 cards came in an envelope printed with a list of the players within. Cards marked with an asterisk are also found with a special blue background and are worth double the listed price. McConnell appears with both Boston AL (common) and Chicago White Sox (scarce); McQuillan appears with Phillies (common) and Cincinnati (scarce). Cards are numbered in the checklist below alphabetically within team. Teams are ordered alphabetically within league: Boston AL (1-19), Chicago AL (20-36), Cleveland (37-52), Detroit (53-73), New York AL (74-84), Philadelphia AL (85-105), St. Louis AL (106-120), Washington (121-134), Boston NL (135-147), Brooklyn (148-164), Chicago NL (165-185), Cincinnati (186-203), New York NL (204-223), Philadelphia NL (224-242), Pittsburgh (243-261), and St. Louis (262-279). Cards 280-288 feature minor leaguers and are somewhat more difficult to find since most are from the tougher higher series

	EX-MT	VG-E	GOOD
COMPLETE SET (290)	22500.00	9500.00	2500.00
COMMON MAJOR (1-279)	42.00	20.00	4.00
COMMON MINOR (280-288)	50.00	25.00	5.00
COMMON S21-S24	100.00	50.00	10.00
☐ 1 Frank Arellanes	42.00	20.00	4.00
☐ 2 Bill Carrigan	42.00	20.00	4.00
☐ 3 Ed Cicotte	60.00	30.00	6.00
☐ 4 Ray Collins S24	100.00	50.00	10.00
☐ 5 Pat Donahue	42.00	20.00	4.00
☐ 6 Donovan S21	100.00	50.00	10.00
☐ 7 Arthur Engle	42.00	20.00	4.00
☐ 8 Larry Gardner S24	100.00	50.00	10.00
☐ 9 Charles Hall	42.00	20.00	4.00

☐ 10	Harry Hooper S23	250.00	125.00	25.00
☐ 11	Edwin Karger	42.00	20.00	4.00
☐ 12	Harry Lord *	42.00	20.00	4.00
☐ 13	Thomas Madden S24	100.00	50.00	10.00
☐ 14A	Amby McConnell (Boston AL)	42.00	20.00	4.00
☐ 14B	Amby McConnell (Chicago AL)	1500.00	600.00	150.00
☐ 15	Tris Speaker S23	450.00	225.00	45.00
☐ 16	Jake Stahl	50.00	25.00	5.00
☐ 17	John Thoney	42.00	20.00	4.00
☐ 18	Heine Wagner	42.00	20.00	4.00
☐ 19	Joe Wood S23	150.00	75.00	15.00
☐ 20	Blackburn	42.00	20.00	4.00
☐ 21	James J. Block S21	100.00	50.00	10.00
☐ 22	Dougherty	42.00	20.00	4.00
☐ 23	Hugh Duffy	125.00	60.00	12.50
☐ 24	Ed Hahn	42.00	20.00	4.00
☐ 25	Paul Meloan S24	100.00	50.00	10.00
☐ 26	Fred Parent	42.00	20.00	4.00
☐ 27	Frederick Payne S21	100.00	50.00	10.00
☐ 28	William Purtell	42.00	20.00	4.00
☐ 29	James Scott S23	100.00	50.00	10.00
☐ 30	F. Smith	42.00	20.00	4.00
☐ 31	Sullivan	42.00	20.00	4.00
☐ 32	Tannehill	42.00	20.00	4.00
☐ 33	Ed Walsh	100.00	50.00	10.00
☐ 34	Guy (Doc) White	42.00	20.00	4.00
☐ 35	I. Young	42.00	20.00	4.00
☐ 36	Dutch Zwilling S24	100.00	50.00	10.00
☐ 37	Harry Bemis	42.00	20.00	4.00
☐ 38	Charles Berger	42.00	20.00	4.00
☐ 39	Joseph Birmingham	42.00	20.00	4.00
☐ 40	Hugh Bradley	42.00	20.00	4.00
☐ 41	Clarke	42.00	20.00	4.00
☐ 42	Falkenberg	42.00	20.00	4.00
☐ 43	Elmer Flick	125.00	60.00	12.50
☐ 44	Addie Joss	150.00	75.00	15.00
☐ 45	Napoleon Lajoie *	225.00	110.00	22.00
☐ 46	Frederick Linke S20	100.00	50.00	10.00
☐ 47	B. Lord	42.00	20.00	4.00
☐ 48	McGuire	42.00	20.00	4.00
☐ 49	Niles	42.00	20.00	4.00
☐ 50	Stovall	42.00	20.00	4.00
☐ 51	Turner	42.00	20.00	4.00
☐ 52	Cy Young	225.00	110.00	22.00
☐ 53	Beckendorf	42.00	20.00	4.00
☐ 54	Bush	42.00	20.00	4.00
☐ 55	Ty Cobb *	1800.00	800.00	200.00
☐ 56	Sam Crawford *	125.00	60.00	12.50
☐ 57	Jas. Delehanty	50.00	25.00	5.00
☐ 58	W. Donovan	42.00	20.00	4.00
☐ 59	Hugh Jennings *	100.00	50.00	10.00
☐ 60	D. Jones	42.00	20.00	4.00
☐ 61	T. Jones	42.00	20.00	4.00
☐ 62	Lathers S21	100.00	50.00	10.00
☐ 63	McIntyre	42.00	20.00	4.00
☐ 64	Moriarty	42.00	20.00	4.00
☐ 65	Mullin	42.00	20.00	4.00
☐ 66	O'Leary	42.00	20.00	4.00
☐ 67	Pernoll S23	100.00	50.00	10.00
☐ 68	Schmidt	42.00	20.00	4.00
☐ 69	Oscar Stanage	42.00	20.00	4.00
☐ 70	Stroud S21	100.00	50.00	10.00
☐ 71	Summers	42.00	20.00	4.00
☐ 72	Willett	42.00	20.00	4.00
☐ 73	Works	42.00	20.00	4.00
☐ 74	Austin S19	100.00	50.00	10.00
☐ 75	Hal Chase *	75.00	37.50	7.50
☐ 76	Cree	42.00	20.00	4.00
☐ 77	Criger	42.00	20.00	4.00
☐ 78	Ford S23	100.00	50.00	10.00
☐ 79	Gardner S23	100.00	50.00	10.00
☐ 80	Knight S19	100.00	50.00	10.00
☐ 81	LaPorte	42.00	20.00	4.00
☐ 82	Stallings	42.00	20.00	4.00
☐ 83	Sweeney S19	100.00	50.00	10.00
☐ 84	Wolter	42.00	20.00	4.00
☐ 85	Atkins S24	100.00	50.00	10.00
☐ 86	Frank Baker	125.00	60.00	12.50
☐ 87	Jack Barry	42.00	20.00	4.00
☐ 88	Chief Bender *	100.00	50.00	10.00
☐ 89	Eddie Collins *	125.00	60.00	12.50
☐ 90	Jack Coombs	60.00	30.00	6.00
☐ 91	H. Davis *	42.00	20.00	4.00
☐ 92	Dygert	42.00	20.00	4.00
☐ 93	Heitmuller	42.00	20.00	4.00
☐ 94	Hartsel	42.00	20.00	4.00
☐ 95	Krause	42.00	20.00	4.00
☐ 96	Lapp S24	100.00	50.00	10.00
☐ 97	Livingstone	42.00	20.00	4.00
☐ 98	Connie Mack	175.00	85.00	18.00
☐ 99	McInnes S24	100.00	50.00	10.00
☐ 100	Morgan	42.00	20.00	4.00

☐ 101	Murphy	42.00	20.00	4.00
☐ 102	Rube Oldring	42.00	20.00	4.00
☐ 103	Eddie Plank	175.00	85.00	18.00
☐ 104	Amos Strunk S24	100.00	50.00	10.00
☐ 105	Thomas *	42.00	20.00	4.00
☐ 106	Bailey	42.00	20.00	4.00
☐ 107	Criss S19	100.00	50.00	10.00
☐ 108	Graham	42.00	20.00	4.00
☐ 109	Hartzell	42.00	20.00	4.00
☐ 110	Hoffman	42.00	20.00	4.00
☐ 111	Howell	42.00	20.00	4.00
☐ 112	Lake S19	100.00	50.00	10.00
☐ 113	O'Conner	42.00	20.00	4.00
☐ 114	Pelty	42.00	20.00	4.00
☐ 115	Powell	42.00	20.00	4.00
☐ 116	Schweitzer	42.00	20.00	4.00
☐ 117	Stephens	42.00	20.00	4.00
☐ 118	Stone	42.00	20.00	4.00
☐ 119	Rube Waddell	125.00	60.00	12.50
☐ 120	Bobby Wallace	100.00	50.00	10.00
☐ 121	Conroy	42.00	20.00	4.00
☐ 122	Elberfeld	42.00	20.00	4.00
☐ 123	Foster	42.00	20.00	4.00
☐ 124	Gessler	42.00	20.00	4.00
☐ 125	Walter Johnson	500.00	250.00	50.00
☐ 126	Killifer S22	100.00	50.00	10.00
☐ 127	McAleer	42.00	20.00	4.00
☐ 128	McBride S21	100.00	50.00	10.00
☐ 129	Milan	42.00	20.00	4.00
☐ 130	Miller S23	100.00	50.00	10.00
☐ 131	Reisling	42.00	20.00	4.00
☐ 132	Schaefer	42.00	20.00	4.00
☐ 133	Street	42.00	20.00	4.00
☐ 134	Unglaub	42.00	20.00	4.00
☐ 135	Beck	42.00	20.00	4.00
☐ 136	Brown	42.00	20.00	4.00
☐ 137	Curtis S23	100.00	50.00	10.00
☐ 138	Ferguson	42.00	20.00	4.00
☐ 139	Samuel Frock S20	100.00	50.00	10.00
☐ 140	Graham	42.00	20.00	4.00
☐ 141	Buck Herzog	42.00	20.00	4.00
☐ 142	Lake	42.00	20.00	4.00
☐ 143	Bayard Sharpe S23	100.00	50.00	10.00
☐ 144	David Shean S20	100.00	50.00	10.00
☐ 145	C. Smith S22	100.00	50.00	10.00
☐ 146	H. Smith	42.00	20.00	4.00
☐ 147	Sweeney	42.00	20.00	4.00
☐ 148	Barger	42.00	20.00	4.00
☐ 149	Bell	42.00	20.00	4.00
☐ 150	Bergen	42.00	20.00	4.00
☐ 151	Burch	42.00	20.00	4.00
☐ 152	Dahlen	50.00	25.00	5.00
☐ 153	William Davidson S21	100.00	50.00	10.00
☐ 154	Frank Dessau S21	100.00	50.00	10.00
☐ 155	Erwin S20	100.00	50.00	10.00
☐ 156	Hummel	42.00	20.00	4.00
☐ 157	Hunter	42.00	20.00	4.00
☐ 158	Jordan *	42.00	20.00	4.00
☐ 159	Lennox	42.00	20.00	4.00
☐ 160	McElveen	42.00	20.00	4.00
☐ 161	McMillan	42.00	20.00	4.00
☐ 162	Nap Rucker	42.00	20.00	4.00
☐ 163	Scanlon	42.00	20.00	4.00
☐ 164	Wilhelm	42.00	20.00	4.00
☐ 165	Archer S22	100.00	50.00	10.00
☐ 166	Beaumont	42.00	20.00	4.00
☐ 167	Mordecai Brown *	125.00	60.00	12.50
☐ 168	Frank Chance *	150.00	75.00	15.00
☐ 169	Johnny Evers	125.00	60.00	12.50
☐ 170	Hofman	42.00	20.00	4.00
☐ 171	Kane	42.00	20.00	4.00
☐ 172	Kling	42.00	20.00	4.00
☐ 173	Kroh	42.00	20.00	4.00
☐ 174	McIntire	42.00	20.00	4.00
☐ 175	Needham	42.00	20.00	4.00
☐ 176	Overall	42.00	20.00	4.00
☐ 177	Pfeffer S23	100.00	50.00	10.00
☐ 178	Pfiester	42.00	20.00	4.00
☐ 179	Ed Reulbach	50.00	25.00	5.00
☐ 180	L. Richie	42.00	20.00	4.00
☐ 181	Schulte	42.00	20.00	4.00
☐ 182	Scheckard	42.00	20.00	4.00
☐ 183	Harry Steinfeldt	50.00	25.00	5.00
☐ 184	Joe Tinker	125.00	60.00	12.50
☐ 185	Zimmerman S19	100.00	50.00	10.00
☐ 186	Beebe	42.00	20.00	4.00
☐ 187	Bescher	42.00	20.00	4.00
☐ 188	Charles	42.00	20.00	4.00
☐ 189	Tommy Clarke S20	100.00	50.00	10.00
☐ 190	Downey	42.00	20.00	4.00
☐ 191	Doyle	42.00	20.00	4.00
☐ 192	Eagan	42.00	20.00	4.00
☐ 193	Fromme	42.00	20.00	4.00
☐ 194	Gaspar S19	100.00	50.00	10.00

☐ 195 Clark Griffith	100.00	50.00	10.00
☐ 196 Hoblitzel	42.00	20.00	4.00
☐ 197 Hans Lobert	42.00	20.00	4.00
☐ 198 McLean	42.00	20.00	4.00
☐ 199 Mitchell	42.00	20.00	4.00
☐ 200 Phelan S23	100.00	50.00	10.00
☐ 201 Rowan	42.00	20.00	4.00
☐ 202 Space	42.00	20.00	4.00
☐ 203 Suggs	42.00	20.00	4.00
☐ 204 Ames S22	100.00	50.00	10.00
☐ 205 Bridwell	42.00	20.00	4.00
☐ 206 Crandall	42.00	20.00	4.00
☐ 207 Devlin	42.00	20.00	4.00
☐ 208 Devore S19	100.00	50.00	10.00
☐ 209 Doyle *	42.00	20.00	4.00
☐ 210 Fletcher S22	100.00	50.00	10.00
☐ 211 Christy Mathewson	500.00	250.00	50.00
☐ 212 John McGraw	175.00	85.00	18.00
☐ 213 Fred Merkle	50.00	25.00	5.00
☐ 214 Murray	42.00	20.00	4.00
☐ 215 Myers S23	100.00	50.00	10.00
☐ 216 Raymond	42.00	20.00	4.00
☐ 217 Schlei	42.00	20.00	4.00
☐ 218 Seymour	42.00	20.00	4.00
☐ 219 Shafer S19	100.00	50.00	10.00
☐ 220 Fred Snodgrass	42.00	20.00	4.00
☐ 221 Tenney *	42.00	20.00	4.00
☐ 222 Wilson S23	100.00	50.00	10.00
☐ 223 G. Wiltse	42.00	20.00	4.00
☐ 224 Bates	42.00	20.00	4.00
☐ 225 Bransfeld	42.00	20.00	4.00
☐ 226 Dooin *	42.00	20.00	4.00
☐ 227 Doolan	42.00	20.00	4.00
☐ 228 Ewing	42.00	20.00	4.00
☐ 229 Foxen	42.00	20.00	4.00
☐ 230 Grant	42.00	20.00	4.00
☐ 231 Jacklitsch	42.00	20.00	4.00
☐ 232 Knabe	42.00	20.00	4.00
☐ 233 Sherry Magee	42.00	20.00	4.00
☐ 234A McQuillan * (Philadelphia NL)	42.00	20.00	4.00
☐ 234B McQuillan (Cincinnati NL)	1500.00	600.00	150.00
☐ 235 Moore	42.00	20.00	4.00
☐ 236 Moran	42.00	20.00	4.00
☐ 237 Moren	42.00	20.00	4.00
☐ 238 Dode Paskert S19	100.00	50.00	10.00
☐ 239 Schettler S20	100.00	50.00	10.00
☐ 240 Sparks	42.00	20.00	4.00
☐ 241 Titus S23	100.00	50.00	10.00
☐ 242A Jimmy Walsh S20 dark background	150.00	75.00	15.00
☐ 242B Jimmy Walsh S22 white background	150.00	75.00	15.00
☐ 243 Ed Abbaticchio	42.00	20.00	4.00
☐ 244 Adams	42.00	20.00	4.00
☐ 245 Byrne	42.00	20.00	4.00
☐ 246 Camnitz	42.00	20.00	4.00
☐ 247 Campbell S21	100.00	50.00	10.00
☐ 248 Fred Clarke	125.00	60.00	12.50
☐ 249 Flynn S20	100.00	50.00	10.00
☐ 250 Gibson *	42.00	20.00	4.00
☐ 251 Hyatt	42.00	20.00	4.00
☐ 252 Leach *	42.00	20.00	4.00
☐ 253 Leever	42.00	20.00	4.00
☐ 254 Leifield	42.00	20.00	4.00
☐ 255 Maddox	42.00	20.00	4.00
☐ 256 Miller	42.00	20.00	4.00
☐ 257 O'Conner	42.00	20.00	4.00
☐ 258 Deacon Phillipe	50.00	25.00	5.00
☐ 259 Simon S21	100.00	50.00	10.00
☐ 260 Hans Wagner *	500.00	250.00	50.00
☐ 261 Wilson	42.00	20.00	4.00
☐ 262 Bliss S21	100.00	50.00	10.00
☐ 263 Roger Bresnahan	100.00	50.00	10.00
☐ 264 Bachman	42.00	20.00	4.00
☐ 265 Corridon	42.00	20.00	4.00
☐ 266 Demmitt S22	100.00	50.00	10.00
☐ 267 Ellis	42.00	20.00	4.00
☐ 268 Evans S23	100.00	50.00	10.00
☐ 269 Harmon S20	100.00	50.00	10.00
☐ 270 Miller Huggins	100.00	50.00	10.00
☐ 271 Hulswitt	42.00	20.00	4.00
☐ 272 Konetchy	42.00	20.00	4.00
☐ 273 Lush	42.00	20.00	4.00
☐ 274 Mattern	42.00	20.00	4.00
☐ 275 Mowery S21	100.00	50.00	10.00
☐ 276 Rebel Oakes S24	100.00	50.00	10.00
☐ 277 Phelps	42.00	20.00	4.00
☐ 278 Sallee	42.00	20.00	4.00
☐ 279 Willis	42.00	20.00	4.00
☐ 280 Coveleskie: Louisville S22	125.00	60.00	12.50
☐ 281 Foster: Rochester S19	100.00	50.00	10.00
☐ 282 Frill: Jersey City S20	100.00	50.00	10.00
☐ 283 Hughes: Rochester S23	100.00	50.00	10.00
☐ 284 Krueger: Sacramento S20	100.00	50.00	10.00
☐ 285 Mitchell: Rochester S19	100.00	50.00	10.00
☐ 286 O'Hara: Toronto	50.00	25.00	5.00
☐ 287 Perring: Columbus S20	100.00	50.00	10.00
☐ 288 Ray: Western League S24	100.00	50.00	10.00

N28 Allen and Ginter

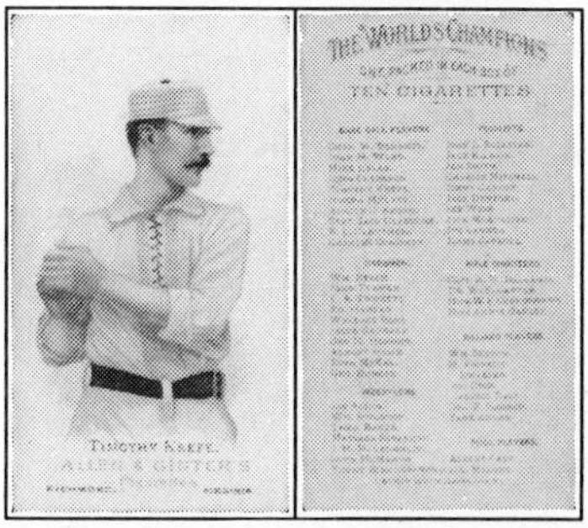

This 50-card set of The World's Champions was marketed by Allen and Ginter in 1887. The cards feature color lithographs of champion athletes from seven categories of sport, with baseball, rowing and boxing each having 10 individuals portrayed. Cards numbered 1 to 10 depict baseball players and cards numbered 11 to 20 depict popular boxers of the era. This set is called the first series although no such title appears on the cards. All 50 cards are checklisted on the reverse, and they are unnumbered. An album (ACC: A16) and an advertising banner (ACC: G20) were also issued in conjunction with this set.

	EX-MT	VG-E	GOOD
COMPLETE SET (50)	7500.00	3500.00	700.00
COMMON BASEBALL (1-10)	300.00	150.00	30.00
COMMON BOXERS (11-20)	75.00	37.50	7.50
COMMON OTHERS (21-50)	25.00	12.50	2.50
☐ 1 Adrian C. Anson	1500.00	600.00	150.00
☐ 2 Chas. W. Bennett	300.00	150.00	30.00
☐ 3 R.L. Caruthers	350.00	175.00	35.00
☐ 4 John Clarkson	700.00	350.00	70.00
☐ 5 Charles Comiskey	700.00	350.00	70.00
☐ 6 Capt. Jack Glasscock	350.00	175.00	35.00
☐ 7 Timothy Keefe	700.00	350.00	70.00
☐ 8 Mike Kelly	1000.00	500.00	90.00
☐ 9 Joseph Mulvey	300.00	150.00	30.00
☐ 10 John M. Ward	700.00	350.00	70.00
☐ 11 Jimmy Carney	75.00	37.50	7.50
☐ 12 Jimmy Carroll	75.00	37.50	7.50
☐ 13 Jack Dempsey	125.00	60.00	12.50
☐ 14 Jake Kilrain	100.00	50.00	10.00
☐ 15 Joe Lannon	75.00	37.50	7.50
☐ 16 Jack McAuliffe	75.00	37.50	7.50
☐ 17 Charlie Mitchell	100.00	50.00	10.00
☐ 18 Jem Smith	75.00	37.50	7.50
☐ 19 John L. Sullivan	150.00	75.00	15.00
☐ 20 Ike Weir	75.00	37.50	7.50
☐ 21 Wm. Beach	25.00	12.50	2.50
☐ 22 Geo. Bubear	25.00	12.50	2.50
☐ 23 Jacob Gaudaur	25.00	12.50	2.50
☐ 24 Albert Hamm	25.00	12.50	2.50
☐ 25 Ed. Hanlan	25.00	12.50	2.50
☐ 26 Geo. H. Hosmer	25.00	12.50	2.50
☐ 27 John McKay	25.00	12.50	2.50
☐ 28 Wallace Ross	25.00	12.50	2.50
☐ 29 John Teemer	25.00	12.50	2.50
☐ 30 E.A. Trickett	25.00	12.50	2.50
☐ 31 Joe Acton	25.00	12.50	2.50
☐ 32 Theo. Bauer	25.00	12.50	2.50

☐ 33 Young Bibby (Geo. Mehling)	25.00	12.50	2.50
☐ 34 J.F. McLaughlin	25.00	12.50	2.50
☐ 35 John McMahon	25.00	12.50	2.50
☐ 36 Wm. Muldoon	25.00	12.50	2.50
☐ 37 Matsada Sorakichi	25.00	12.50	2.50
☐ 38 Capt. A.H. Bogardus	25.00	12.50	2.50
☐ 39 Dr. W.F. Carver	25.00	12.50	2.50
☐ 40 Hon. W.F. Cody (Buffalo Bill)	100.00	50.00	10.00
☐ 41 Miss Annie Oakley	75.00	37.50	7.50
☐ 42 Yank Adams	25.00	12.50	2.50
☐ 43 Maurice Daly	25.00	12.50	2.50
☐ 44 Jos. Dion	25.00	12.50	2.50
☐ 45 J. Schaefer	25.00	12.50	2.50
☐ 46 Wm. Sexton	25.00	12.50	2.50
☐ 47 Geo. F. Slosson	25.00	12.50	2.50
☐ 48 M. Vignaux	25.00	12.50	2.50
☐ 49 Albert Frey	25.00	12.50	2.50
☐ 50 J.L. Malone	25.00	12.50	2.50

N29 Allen and Ginter

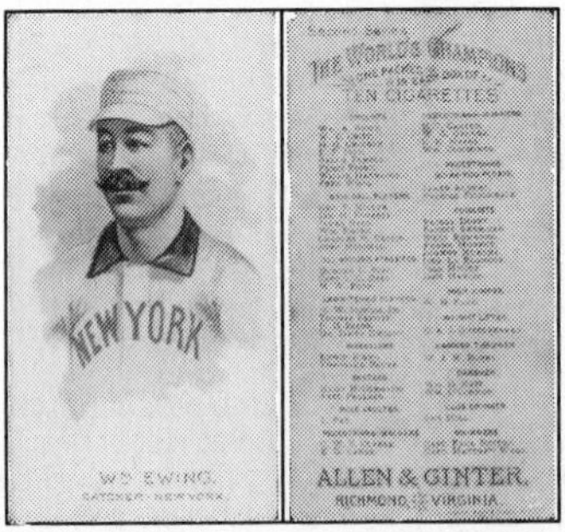

The second series of The World's Champions was probably issued in 1888. Like the first series, the cards are backlisted and unnumbered. However, there are 17 distinct categories of sports represented in this set, with only six baseball players portrayed (as opposed to 10 in the first series). Each card has a color lithograph of the individual set against a white background. An album (ACC: A17) and an advertising banner (ACC: G21) were issued in conjunction with the set. The numbering below is alphabetical within sport, e.g., baseball players (1-6), boxers (7-14), and other sports (15-50).

	EX-MT	VG-E	GOOD
COMPLETE SET (50)	9500.00	4500.00	950.00
COMMON BASEBALL (1-6)	900.00	450.00	90.00
COMMON BOXERS (7-14)	225.00	110.00	22.00
COMMON OTHERS (15-50)	75.00	37.50	7.50

☐ 1 Wm. Ewing	1800.00	800.00	160.00
☐ 2 Jas. H. Fogarty	900.00	450.00	90.00
☐ 3 Charles H. Getzin	900.00	450.00	90.00
☐ 4 Geo. F. Miller	900.00	450.00	90.00
☐ 5 John Morrell	900.00	450.00	90.00
☐ 6 James Ryan	900.00	450.00	90.00
☐ 7 Patsey Duffy	225.00	110.00	22.00
☐ 8 Billy Edwards	225.00	110.00	22.00
☐ 9 Jack Havlin	225.00	110.00	22.00
☐ 10 Patsey Kerrigan	225.00	110.00	22.00
☐ 11 Geo. La Blance	225.00	110.00	22.00
☐ 12 Jack McGee	225.00	110.00	22.00
☐ 13 Frank Murphy	225.00	110.00	22.00
☐ 14 Johnny Murphy	225.00	110.00	22.00
☐ 15 Capt. J.C. Daly	75.00	37.50	7.50
☐ 16 M.W. Ford	75.00	37.50	7.50
☐ 17 Duncan C. Ross	75.00	37.50	7.50
☐ 18 W.E. Crist	75.00	37.50	7.50
☐ 19 H.G. Crocken	75.00	37.50	7.50
☐ 20 Willie Harradon	75.00	37.50	7.50
☐ 21 F.F. Ives	75.00	37.50	7.50
☐ 22 Wm. A. Rowe	75.00	37.50	7.50
☐ 23 Percy Stone	75.00	37.50	7.50
☐ 24 Ralph Temple	75.00	37.50	7.50
☐ 25 Fred Wood	75.00	37.50	7.50
☐ 26 Dr. James Dwight	75.00	37.50	7.50
☐ 27 Thomas Pettit	75.00	37.50	7.50
☐ 28 R.D. Sears	75.00	37.50	7.50
☐ 29 H.W. Slocum Jr.	75.00	37.50	7.50
☐ 30 Theobaud Bauer	75.00	37.50	7.50
☐ 31 Edwin Bibby	75.00	37.50	7.50
☐ 32 Hugh McCormack	75.00	37.50	7.50
☐ 33 Axel Paulsen	75.00	37.50	7.50
☐ 34 T. Ray	75.00	37.50	7.50
☐ 35 C.W.V. Clarke	75.00	37.50	7.50
☐ 36 E.D. Lange	75.00	37.50	7.50
☐ 37 E.C. Carter	75.00	37.50	7.50
☐ 38 Wm. Cummings	75.00	37.50	7.50
☐ 39 W.G. George	75.00	37.50	7.50
☐ 40 L.E. Myers	75.00	37.50	7.50
☐ 41 James Albert	75.00	37.50	7.50
☐ 42 Patrick Fitzgerald	75.00	37.50	7.50
☐ 43 W.B. Page	75.00	37.50	7.50
☐ 44 C.A.J. Queckberner	75.00	37.50	7.50
☐ 45 W.J.M. Barry	75.00	37.50	7.50
☐ 46 Wm. G. East	75.00	37.50	7.50
☐ 47 Wm. O'Connor	75.00	37.50	7.50
☐ 48 Gus Hill	75.00	37.50	7.50
☐ 49 Capt. Paul Boyton	75.00	37.50	7.50
☐ 50 Capt. Matthew Webb	75.00	37.50	7.50

N43 Allen and Ginter

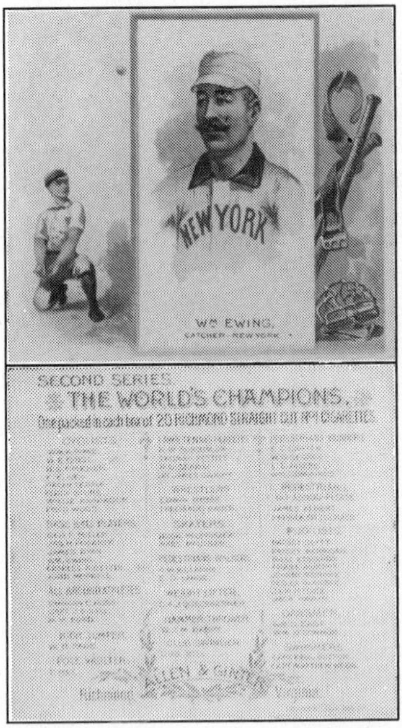

The primary designs of this 50-card set are identical to those of N29, but these are placed on a much larger card with extraneous background detail. The set was produced in 1888 by Allen and Ginter as inserts for a larger tobacco package than those in which sets N28 and N29 were marketed. Cards of this set, which is backlisted, are considered to be much scarcer than their counterparts in N29.

	EX-MT	VG-E	GOOD
COMPLETE SET (50)	12500.00	5500.00	1350.00
COMMON BASEBALL (1-6)	1200.00	500.00	125.00
COMMON BOXERS (7-14)	300.00	150.00	30.00
COMMON OTHERS (15-50)	100.00	50.00	10.00

☐ 1 William Ewing	2250.00	900.00	225.00
☐ 2 Jas. J. Fogarty	1200.00	500.00	125.00
☐ 3 Charles Getzein	1200.00	500.00	125.00
☐ 4 Geo. F. Miller	1200.00	500.00	125.00
☐ 5 John Morrell	1200.00	500.00	125.00

☐ 6 James Ryan	1200.00	500.00	125.00
☐ 7 Patsey Duffy	300.00	150.00	30.00
☐ 8 Billy Edwards	300.00	150.00	30.00
☐ 9 Jack Havlin	300.00	150.00	30.00
☐ 10 Patsey Kerrigan	300.00	150.00	30.00
☐ 11 George LaBlanche	300.00	150.00	30.00
☐ 12 Jack McGee	300.00	150.00	30.00
☐ 13 Frank Murphy	300.00	150.00	30.00
☐ 14 Johnny Murphy	300.00	150.00	30.00
☐ 15 James Albert	100.00	50.00	10.00
☐ 16 W.J.M. Barry	100.00	50.00	10.00
☐ 17 Theobaud Bauer	100.00	50.00	10.00
☐ 18 Edwin Bibby	100.00	50.00	10.00
☐ 19 Capt. Paul Boyton	100.00	50.00	10.00
☐ 20 E.C. Carter	100.00	50.00	10.00
☐ 21 C.W.V. Clarke	100.00	50.00	10.00
☐ 22 W.E. Crist	100.00	50.00	10.00
☐ 23 H.G. Crocker	100.00	50.00	10.00
☐ 24 Wm. Cummings	100.00	50.00	10.00
☐ 25 Capt. J.C. Daly	100.00	50.00	10.00
☐ 26 Dr. James Dwight	100.00	50.00	10.00
☐ 27 Wm. G. East	100.00	50.00	10.00
☐ 28 Patrick Fitzgerald	100.00	50.00	10.00
☐ 29 M.W. Ford	100.00	50.00	10.00
☐ 30 W.G. George	100.00	50.00	10.00
☐ 31 Willie Harradon	100.00	50.00	10.00
☐ 32 Gus Hill	100.00	50.00	10.00
☐ 33 F.F. Ives	100.00	50.00	10.00
☐ 34 E.D. Lange	100.00	50.00	10.00
☐ 35 Hugh McCormack	100.00	50.00	10.00
☐ 36 L.E. Myers	100.00	50.00	10.00
☐ 37 Wm. O'Connor	100.00	50.00	10.00
☐ 38 W.B. Page	100.00	50.00	10.00
☐ 39 Axel. Paulsen	100.00	50.00	10.00
☐ 40 Thomas Pettitt	100.00	50.00	10.00
☐ 41 C.A.J. Queckberner	100.00	50.00	10.00
☐ 42 T. Ray	100.00	50.00	10.00
☐ 43 Duncan C. Ross	100.00	50.00	10.00
☐ 44 Wm. A. Rowe	100.00	50.00	10.00
☐ 45 R.D. Sears	100.00	50.00	10.00
☐ 46 H.W. Slocum Jr.	100.00	50.00	10.00
☐ 47 Percy Stone	100.00	50.00	10.00
☐ 48 Ralph Temple	100.00	50.00	10.00
☐ 49 Capt. Matthew Webb	100.00	50.00	10.00
☐ 50 Fred Wood	100.00	50.00	10.00

N162 Goodwin

This 50-card set issued by Goodwin was one of the major competitors to the N28 and N29 sets marketed by Allen and Ginter. It contains individuals representing 18 sports, with eight baseball players pictured. Each color card is backlisted and bears advertising for "Old Judge" and "Gypsy Queen" cigarettes on the front. The set was released to the public in 1888 and an album (ACC: A36) is associated with it as a premium issue.

	EX-MT	VG-E	GOOD
COMPLETE SET (50)	10000.00	4500.00	1000.00
COMMON BASEBALL (1-8)	600.00	300.00	60.00
COMMON BOXER	150.00	75.00	15.00
COMMON OTHERS	50.00	25.00	5.00
☐ 1 Andrews: Phila.	600.00	300.00	60.00
☐ 2 Anson: Chicago	2250.00	1000.00	250.00
☐ 3 Brouthers: Detroit	1050.00	450.00	120.00
☐ 4 Caruthers: Brooklyn	650.00	325.00	65.00
☐ 5 Dunlap: Detroit	600.00	300.00	60.00
☐ 6 Glasscock: Indianapolis	650.00	325.00	65.00
☐ 7 Keefe: New York	1050.00	450.00	120.00
☐ 8 Kelly: Boston	1500.00	600.00	150.00
☐ 9 Acton (Wrestler)	50.00	25.00	5.00
☐ 10 Albert (Pedestrian)	50.00	25.00	5.00
☐ 11 Beach (Oarsman)	50.00	25.00	5.00
☐ 12 Beecher (Football)	600.00	300.00	60.00
☐ 13 Beeckman (Lawn Tennis)	50.00	25.00	5.00
☐ 14 Bogardus (Marksman)	50.00	25.00	5.00
☐ 15 Buffalo Bill (Wild West Hunter)	125.00	60.00	12.50
☐ 16 Daly (Billiards)	50.00	25.00	5.00
☐ 17 Dempsey (Pugilist)	250.00	125.00	25.00
☐ 18 D'oro (Pool)	50.00	25.00	5.00
☐ 19 Dwight (Lawn Tennis)	50.00	25.00	5.00
☐ 20 Fitzgerald (Pedestrian)	50.00	25.00	5.00
☐ 21 Garrison (Jockey)	50.00	25.00	5.00
☐ 22 Gaudaur (Oarsman)	50.00	25.00	5.00
☐ 23 Hanlan (Oarsman)	50.00	25.00	5.00
☐ 24 Kilrain (Pugilist)	200.00	100.00	20.00
☐ 25 MacKenzie (Chess)	50.00	25.00	5.00
☐ 26 McLaughlin (Jockey)	50.00	25.00	5.00
☐ 27 Mitchell (Pugilist)	200.00	100.00	20.00
☐ 28 Muldoon (Wrestler)	50.00	25.00	5.00
☐ 29 Murphy (Jockey)	50.00	25.00	5.00
☐ 30 Myers (Runner)	50.00	25.00	5.00
☐ 31 Page (High Jumper)	50.00	25.00	5.00
☐ 32 Prince (Bicyclist)	50.00	25.00	5.00
☐ 33 Ross (Broadswordsman)	50.00	25.00	5.00
☐ 34 Rowe (Bicyclist)	50.00	25.00	5.00
☐ 35 Rowell (Pedestrian)	50.00	25.00	5.00
☐ 36 Schaefer (Billiards)	50.00	25.00	5.00
☐ 37 Sears (Lawn Tennis)	50.00	25.00	5.00
☐ 38 Sexton (Billiards)	50.00	25.00	5.00
☐ 39 Slosson (Billiards)	50.00	25.00	5.00
☐ 40 Smith (Pugilist)	150.00	75.00	15.00
☐ 41 Steinitz (Chess)	50.00	25.00	5.00
☐ 42 Stevens (Bicyclist)	50.00	25.00	5.00
☐ 43 Sullivan (Pugilist)	300.00	150.00	30.00
☐ 44 Taylor (Lawn Tennis)	50.00	25.00	5.00
☐ 45 Teemer (Oarsman)	50.00	25.00	5.00
☐ 46 Vignaux (Billiards)	50.00	25.00	5.00
☐ 47 Voss (Strongest Man in the World)	50.00	25.00	5.00
☐ 48 Wood (Bicyclist)	50.00	25.00	5.00
☐ 49 Wood (Jockey)	50.00	25.00	5.00
☐ 50 Zukertort (Chess)	50.00	25.00	5.00

N172 Old Judge

The Goodwin Company's baseball series depicts hundreds of ballplayers from more than 40 major and minor league teams as well as boxers and wrestlers. The cards (approximately 1 1/2" by 2 1/2") are actually photographs from the Hall studio in New York which were pasted onto thick cardboard. The pictures are sepia in color with either a white or pink cast, and the cards are blank backed. They are found either numbered or unnumbered, with or without a copyright date, and with hand printed or machine printed names. All known cards have the name "Goodwin Co., New York" at the base. The cards were marketed during the period 1887-1890 in packs of "Old Judge" and "Gypsy Queen" cigarettes (cards marked with the latter brand are worth double the values listed below). They have been listed alphabetically and assigned numbers in the checklist below for simplicity's sake; the various poses known for some players also have not been listed for the same reason. Some of the players are pictured in horizontal (HOR) poses. In all, more than 2300 different Goodwin cards are known to collectors, with more being discovered every year. Cards from the "Spotted Tie" sub-series are denoted in the checklist below by SPOT.

	EX-MT	VG-E	GOOD
COMPLETE SET	105000.	45000.	10000.
COMMON PLAYER	100.00	50.00	10.00
COMMON PLAYER (DOUBLE)	150.00	75.00	15.00
COMMON BROWNS CHAMP	250.00	125.00	25.00
COMMON PLAYER (PCL)	1200.00	500.00	125.00
COMMON SPOTTED TIE	350.00	175.00	35.00
☐ 1 Gus Albert: Cleveland-Milwaukee	100.00	50.00	10.00
☐ 2 Charles Alcott: St. Louis Whites-Mansfield	100.00	50.00	10.00
☐ 3 Alexander: Des Moines	100.00	50.00	10.00
☐ 4 Myron Allen: K.C.	100.00	50.00	10.00
☐ 5 Bob Allen: Pitts.-Phila. N.L.	100.00	50.00	10.00
☐ 6 Uncle Bill Alvord: Toledo-Des Moines	100.00	50.00	10.00
☐ 7 Varney Anderson: St.Paul	100.00	50.00	10.00
☐ 8 Ed Andrews: Phila.	100.00	50.00	10.00
☐ 9 Andrews and Hoover: Philadelphia	150.00	75.00	15.00
☐ 10 Wally Andrews: Omaha	100.00	50.00	10.00
☐ 11 Bill Annis: Omaha-Worchester	100.00	50.00	10.00
☐ 12A Cap Anson: Chicago (in uniform)	6500.00	2700.00	750.00
☐ 12B Cap Anson: Chicago (not in uniform)	1650.00	750.00	175.00
☐ 13 Old Hoss Ardner: Kansas City-St. Joe	100.00	50.00	10.00
☐ 14 Tug Arundel: Indianapolis-Whites	100.00	50.00	10.00
☐ 15 Bakley: Jersey-Cleve.	100.00	50.00	10.00
☐ 16 Clarence Baldwin: Cincinnati	100.00	50.00	10.00
☐ 17 Mark (Fido) Baldwin: Chicago-Columbus	100.00	50.00	10.00
☐ 18 Lady Baldwin: Detroit	100.00	50.00	10.00
☐ 19 James Banning: Wash.	100.00	50.00	10.00
☐ 20 Samuel Barkley: Pittsburgh-K.C.	100.00	50.00	10.00
☐ 21 John Barnes: Mgr. St. Paul	100.00	50.00	10.00
☐ 22 Bald Billy Barnie: Mgr. Baltimore	150.00	75.00	15.00
☐ 23 Charles Bassett: Indianapolis-N.Y.	100.00	50.00	10.00
☐ 24 Charles Bastian: Phila.-Chicago	100.00	50.00	10.00
☐ 25 Bastian and Shriver: Philadelphia	150.00	75.00	15.00
☐ 26 Ollie Beard: Cinc.	100.00	50.00	10.00
☐ 27 Ebenezer Beatin: Cleve.	100.00	50.00	10.00
☐ 28 Jake Beckley: "Eagle Eye" Whites-Pittsburgh	500.00	250.00	50.00
☐ 29 Stephen Behel SPOT	450.00	225.00	45.00
☐ 30 Charles Bennett: Detroit-Boston	100.00	50.00	10.00
☐ 31 Louis Bierbauer: A's	100.00	50.00	10.00
☐ 32 Bierbauer and Gamble Athletics	150.00	75.00	15.00
☐ 33 Bill Bishop: Pittsburgh-Syracuse	100.00	50.00	10.00
☐ 34 William Blair: A's-Hamiltons	100.00	50.00	10.00
☐ 35 Ned Bligh: Columbus	100.00	50.00	10.00
☐ 36 Bogart: Indianapolis	100.00	50.00	10.00
☐ 37 Boyce: Washington	100.00	50.00	10.00
☐ 38 Jake Boyd: Maroons	150.00	75.00	15.00
☐ 39 Honest John Boyle: St. Louis-Chicago	100.00	50.00	10.00
☐ 40 Handsome Henry Boyle Indianapolis-N.Y.	100.00	50.00	10.00
☐ 41 Nick Bradley: K.C.- Worchester	100.00	50.00	10.00
☐ 42 George(Grin) Bradley Sioux City	100.00	50.00	10.00
☐ 43 Stephen Brady SPOT	450.00	225.00	45.00
☐ 44 Breckinridge: Sacramento PCL	1200.00	500.00	125.00
☐ 45 Jim Brennan: Kansas City- A's	100.00	50.00	10.00
☐ 46 Timothy Brosnan: Minn.-Sioux City	100.00	50.00	10.00
☐ 47 Cal Broughton: Detroit-Boston	100.00	50.00	10.00
☐ 48 Big Dan Brouthers: Detroit-Boston	450.00	225.00	45.00
☐ 49 Thomas Brown: Pittsburgh-Boston	100.00	50.00	10.00
☐ 50 Brown: California-N.Y.	100.00	50.00	10.00
☐ 51 Pete Browning: "Gladiator" Louisville	250.00	125.00	25.00
☐ 52 Charles Brynan: Chicago-Des Moines	100.00	50.00	10.00
☐ 53 Al Buckenberger: Mgr. Columbus	100.00	50.00	10.00
☐ 54 Dick Buckley: Indianapolis-N.Y.	100.00	50.00	10.00
☐ 55 Charles Buffington: Philadelphia	100.00	50.00	10.00
☐ 56 Ernest Burch: Brooklyn-Whites	100.00	50.00	10.00
☐ 57 Bill Burdick: Omaha-Indianapolis	100.00	50.00	10.00
☐ 58 Black Jack Burdock: Boston-Brooklyn	100.00	50.00	10.00
☐ 59 Robert Burks: Sioux City	100.00	50.00	10.00
☐ 60 George Burnham "Watch" Mgr. Indianapolis	150.00	75.00	15.00
☐ 61 Burns: Omaha	100.00	50.00	10.00
☐ 62 Jimmy Burns: K.C.	100.00	50.00	10.00
☐ 63 Tommy (Oyster) Burns Baltimore-Brooklyn	100.00	50.00	10.00
☐ 64 Thomas E. Burns: Chicago	100.00	50.00	10.00
☐ 65A Doc Bushong: Brook.	100.00	50.00	10.00
☐ 65B Doc Bushong: Browns Champ	250.00	125.00	25.00
☐ 66 Patsy Cahill: Ind.	100.00	50.00	10.00
☐ 67 Count Campau: Kansas City-Detroit	100.00	50.00	10.00
☐ 68 Jimmy Canavan: Omaha	100.00	50.00	10.00
☐ 69 Bart Cantz: Whites-Baltimore	100.00	50.00	10.00
☐ 70 Handsome Jack Carney Washington	100.00	50.00	10.00
☐ 71 Hick Carpenter Cincinnati	100.00	50.00	10.00
☐ 72 Cliff Carroll: Wash.	100.00	50.00	10.00
☐ 73 Scrappy Carroll: St.Paul-Chicago	100.00	50.00	10.00
☐ 74 Frederick Carroll: Pitts.	100.00	50.00	10.00
☐ 75 Jumbo Cartwright: Kansas City-St. Joe	100.00	50.00	10.00
☐ 76A Bob Caruthers: "Parisian" Brooklyn	150.00	75.00	15.00
☐ 76B Bob Caruthers: "Parisian" Browns Champs	300.00	150.00	30.00
☐ 77 Daniel Casey: Phila.	100.00	50.00	10.00
☐ 78 Icebox Chamberlain: St. Louis	100.00	50.00	10.00
☐ 79 Cupid Childs: Phila.-Syracuse	100.00	50.00	10.00

☐ 80	Bob Clark: Washington	100.00	50.00	10.00
☐ 81	Owen Clark: Washington	100.00	50.00	10.00
☐ 82	Clarke and Hughes: Brooklyn HOR	150.00	75.00	15.00
☐ 83	William(Dad) Clarke: Chicago-Omaha	100.00	50.00	10.00
☐ 84	John Clarkson: Chicago-Boston	450.00	225.00	45.00
☐ 85	Jack Clements: Philadelphia	100.00	50.00	10.00
☐ 86	Elmer Cleveland: Omaha-New York	100.00	50.00	10.00
☐ 87	Monk Cline: K.C.-Sioux City	100.00	50.00	10.00
☐ 88	Cody: Des Moines	100.00	50.00	10.00
☐ 89	John Coleman: Pittsburgh - A's	100.00	50.00	10.00
☐ 90	Bill Collins: New York-Newark	100.00	50.00	10.00
☐ 91	Hub Collins: Louisville-Brooklyn	100.00	50.00	10.00
☐ 92A	Charles Comiskey: Browns Champs	800.00	400.00	80.00
☐ 92B	Commy Comiskey: St. Louis-Chicago	500.00	250.00	50.00
☐ 93	Pete Connell: Des Moines	100.00	50.00	10.00
☐ 94A	Roger Connor: All-Star	500.00	250.00	50.00
☐ 94B	Roger Connor: New York	500.00	250.00	50.00
☐ 95	Richard Conway: Boston-Worchester	100.00	50.00	10.00
☐ 96	Peter Conway: Det.-Pitts.-Ind.	100.00	50.00	10.00
☐ 97	James Conway: K.C.	100.00	50.00	10.00
☐ 98	Paul Cook: Louisville	100.00	50.00	10.00
☐ 99	Jimmy Cooney: Omaha-Chicago	100.00	50.00	10.00
☐ 100	Larry Corcoran: Indianapolis-London	100.00	50.00	10.00
☐ 101	Pop Corkhill: Cincinnnati-Brooklyn	100.00	50.00	10.00
☐ 102	Roscoe Coughlin: Maroons-Chicago	150.00	75.00	15.00
☐ 103	Cannon Ball Crane: New York	100.00	50.00	10.00
☐ 104	Samuel Crane: Wash.	100.00	50.00	10.00
☐ 105	Jack Crogan: Maroons	150.00	75.00	15.00
☐ 106	John Crooks: Whites-Omaha	100.00	50.00	10.00
☐ 107	Lave Cross: Louisville-A's-Phila.	100.00	50.00	10.00
☐ 108	Bill Crossley: Milw.	100.00	50.00	10.00
☐ 109A	Joe Crotty SPOT	400.00	200.00	40.00
☐ 109B	Joe Crotty: Sioux City	100.00	50.00	10.00
☐ 110	Billy Crowell: Cleveland-St. Joe	100.00	50.00	10.00
☐ 111	Jim Cudworth: St. Louis-Worchester	100.00	50.00	10.00
☐ 112	Bert Cunningham: Baltimore-Phila.	100.00	50.00	10.00
☐ 113	Tacks Curtis: St. Joe	100.00	50.00	10.00
☐ 114A	Ed Cushman SPOT	450.00	225.00	45.00
☐ 114B	Ed Cushman: Toledo	300.00	150.00	30.00
☐ 115	Tony Cusick: Mil.	300.00	150.00	30.00
☐ 116	Dailey: Oakland PCL	1200.00	500.00	125.00
☐ 117	Edward Dailey: Phil.-Wash.-Columbus	100.00	50.00	10.00
☐ 118	Bill Daley: Boston	100.00	50.00	10.00
☐ 119	Con Daley: Boston-Indianapolis	100.00	50.00	10.00
☐ 120	Abner Dalrymple: Pittsburgh-Denver	100.00	50.00	10.00
☐ 121	Tom Daly: Chicago-Wash.-Cleve.	100.00	50.00	10.00
☐ 122	James Daly: Minn.	100.00	50.00	10.00
☐ 123	Law Daniels: K.C.	100.00	50.00	10.00
☐ 124	Dell Darling: Chicago	100.00	50.00	10.00
☐ 125	Wm. Darnbrough: Denver	100.00	50.00	10.00
☐ 126	D. Davin: Milwaukee	100.00	50.00	10.00
☐ 127	Jumbo Davis: K.C.	100.00	50.00	10.00
☐ 128	Pat Dealey: Wash.	100.00	50.00	10.00

☐ 129	Thomas Deasley: New York-Washington	100.00	50.00	10.00
☐ 130	Edward Decker: Phil.	100.00	50.00	10.00
☐ 131	Big Ed Delahanty: Philadelphia	900.00	450.00	90.00
☐ 132	Jeremiah Denny: Indianapolis-New York	100.00	50.00	10.00
☐ 133	James Devlin: St.L.	100.00	50.00	10.00
☐ 134	Thomas Dolan: Whites-St. Louis-Denver	100.00	50.00	10.00
☐ 135	Jack Donahue: San Francisco PCL	1200.00	500.00	125.00
☐ 136A	James Donahue SPOT	400.00	200.00	40.00
☐ 136B	James Donahue: K.C.	100.00	50.00	10.00
☐ 137	James Donnelly: Washington	100.00	50.00	10.00
☐ 138	Dooley: Oakland PCL	1200.00	500.00	125.00
☐ 139	J. Doran: Omaha	100.00	50.00	10.00
☐ 140	Michael Dorgan: N.Y.	100.00	50.00	10.00
☐ 141	Doyle: San Fran. PCL	1200.00	500.00	125.00
☐ 142	Homerun Duffe: St.L.	100.00	50.00	10.00
☐ 143	Hugh Duffy: Chicago	500.00	250.00	50.00
☐ 144	Dan Dugdale: Maroons-Minneapolis	150.00	75.00	15.00
☐ 145	Dugrahm: Maroons	150.00	75.00	15.00
☐ 146	Duck Duke: Minn.	100.00	50.00	10.00
☐ 147	Sure Shot Dunlap: Pittsburgh	100.00	50.00	10.00
☐ 148	J. Dunn: Maroons	150.00	75.00	15.00
☐ 149	Jesse(Cyclone)Duryea St. Paul-Cinc.	100.00	50.00	10.00
☐ 150	John Dwyer: Chicago-Maroons	150.00	75.00	15.00
☐ 151	Billy Earle: Cincinnati-St.Paul	100.00	50.00	10.00
☐ 152	Buck Ebright: Wash.	100.00	50.00	10.00
☐ 153	Red Ehret: Louisville	100.00	50.00	10.00
☐ 154	R. Emmerke: Des Moines	100.00	50.00	10.00
☐ 155	Dude Esterbrook: Louisville-Ind.-New York-All Star	100.00	50.00	10.00
☐ 156	Henry Esterday: K.C.-Columbus	100.00	50.00	10.00
☐ 157	Long John Ewing: Louisville-N.Y.	100.00	50.00	10.00
☐ 158	Buck Ewing: New York	450.00	225.00	45.00
☐ 159	Ewing and Mascot: New York	350.00	175.00	35.00
☐ 160	Jay Faatz: Cleveland	100.00	50.00	10.00
☐ 161	Clinkgers Fagan: Kansas City-Denver	100.00	50.00	10.00
☐ 162	William Farmer: Pittsburgh-St. Paul	100.00	50.00	10.00
☐ 163	Sidney Farrar: Philadelphia	100.00	50.00	10.00
☐ 164	John(Moose) Farrell: Wash.-Baltimore	100.00	50.00	10.00
☐ 165	Charles(Duke)Farrell Chicago	100.00	50.00	10.00
☐ 166	Frank Fennelly: Cincinnati-A's	100.00	50.00	10.00
☐ 167	Chas. Ferguson: Phila.	100.00	50.00	10.00
☐ 168	Colonel Ferson: Washington	100.00	50.00	10.00
☐ 169	Wallace Fessenden: Umpire National	150.00	75.00	15.00
☐ 170	Jocko Fields: Pitts.	100.00	50.00	10.00
☐ 171	Fischer: Maroons	150.00	75.00	15.00
☐ 172	Thomas Flanigan: Cleve.-Sioux City	100.00	50.00	10.00
☐ 173	Silver Flint: Chicago	100.00	50.00	10.00
☐ 174	Thomas Flood: St. Joe	100.00	50.00	10.00
☐ 175	Flynn: Omaha	900.00	450.00	90.00
☐ 176	James Fogarty: Philadelphia	100.00	50.00	10.00
☐ 177	Frank(Monkey)Foreman Baltimore-Cinc.	100.00	50.00	10.00
☐ 178	Thomas Forster: Milwaukee-Hartford	100.00	50.00	10.00
☐ 179A	Elmer E. Foster SPOT	400.00	200.00	40.00
☐ 179B	Elmer Foster: New York-Chicago	100.00	50.00	10.00
☐ 180	F.W. Foster SPOT T.W. Forster (sic)	450.00	225.00	45.00
☐ 181A	Scissors Foutz: Browns Champ	250.00	125.00	25.00

□ 181B Scissors Foutz: Brooklyn	100.00	50.00	10.00
□ 182 Julie Freeman: St.L.-Milwaukee	100.00	50.00	10.00
□ 183 Will Fry: St. Joe	100.00	50.00	10.00
□ 184 Fudger: Oakland PCL	1200.00	500.00	125.00
□ 185 William Fuller: Milwaukee	100.00	50.00	10.00
□ 186 Shorty Fuller: St.Louis	100.00	50.00	10.00
□ 187 Christopher Fullmer: Baltimore	100.00	50.00	10.00
□ 188 Fullmer and Tucker: Baltimore HOR	150.00	75.00	15.00
□ 189 Honest John Gaffney: Mgr. Washington	150.00	75.00	15.00
□ 190 Pud Galvin: Pitts.	500.00	250.00	50.00
□ 191 Robert Gamble: A's	100.00	50.00	10.00
□ 192 Charles Ganzel: Detroit-Boston	100.00	50.00	10.00
□ 193 Frank (Gid) Gardner: Phila.-Washington	100.00	50.00	10.00
□ 194 Gardner and Murray: Washington HOR	150.00	75.00	15.00
□ 195 Ed Gastfield: Omaha	100.00	50.00	10.00
□ 196 Hank Gastreich: Columbus	100.00	50.00	10.00
□ 197 Emil Geiss: Chicago	100.00	50.00	10.00
□ 198 Frenchy Genins: Sioux City	100.00	50.00	10.00
□ 199 William George: N.Y.	100.00	50.00	10.00
□ 200 Move Up Joe Gerhardt All Star-Jersey City	100.00	50.00	10.00
□ 201 Pretzels Getzein: Detroit-Ind.	100.00	50.00	10.00
□ 202 Robert Gilks: Cleve.	100.00	50.00	10.00
□ 203 Pete Gillespie: N.Y.	100.00	50.00	10.00
□ 204 Barney Gilligan Washington-Detroit	100.00	50.00	10.00
□ 205 Frank Gilmore: Wash.	100.00	50.00	10.00
□ 206 Lee Gisbon: A's	100.00	50.00	10.00
□ 207 Pebbly Jack Glasscock Indianapolis-N.Y.	150.00	75.00	15.00
□ 208 Kid Gleason: Phila.	100.00	50.00	10.00
□ 209A Brother Bill Gleason A's-Louisville	100.00	50.00	10.00
□ 209B William Bill Gleason Browns Champs	250.00	125.00	25.00
□ 210 Mouse Glenn: Sioux City	100.00	50.00	10.00
□ 211 Walt Goldsby: Balt.	100.00	50.00	10.00
□ 212 Michael Goodfellow: Cleveland-Detroit	100.00	50.00	10.00
□ 213 George Gore (Pianolegs) New York	100.00	50.00	10.00
□ 214 Frank Graves: Minn.	100.00	50.00	10.00
□ 215 William Greenwood: Baltimore-Columbus	100.00	50.00	10.00
□ 216 Michael Greer: Cleveland-Brooklyn	100.00	50.00	10.00
□ 217 Mike Griffin: Baltimore-Phila NL	100.00	50.00	10.00
□ 218 Clark Griffith: Milwaukee	550.00	275.00	55.00
□ 219 Henry Gruber: Cleve.	100.00	50.00	10.00
□ 220 Addison Gumbert: Chicago-Boston	100.00	50.00	10.00
□ 221 Thomas Gunning: Philadelphia-A's	100.00	50.00	10.00
□ 222 Joseph Gunson: K.C.	100.00	50.00	10.00
□ 223 George Haddock: Washington	100.00	50.00	10.00
□ 224 William Hafner: K.C.	100.00	50.00	10.00
□ 225 Willie Hahm: Chicago Mascot	100.00	50.00	10.00
□ 226 William Hallman: Philadelphia	100.00	50.00	10.00
□ 227 Charlie Hallstrom: Minn.	100.00	50.00	10.00
□ 228 Billy Hamilton: Kansas City-Phila.	550.00	275.00	55.00
□ 229 Hamm and Williamson:	150.00	75.00	15.00
□ 230A Frank Hankinson: SPOT	400.00	200.00	40.00
□ 230B Frank Hankinson: Kansas City	100.00	50.00	10.00
□ 231 Ned Hanlon: Det.-Boston-Pitts.	150.00	75.00	15.00
□ 232 William Hanrahan: Maroons-Minn.	150.00	75.00	15.00
□ 233 Hapeman: Sacramento PCL	1200.00	500.00	125.00

□ 234 Pa Harkins: Brooklyn-Baltimore	100.00	50.00	10.00
□ 235 William Hart: Cinc.-Des Moines	100.00	50.00	10.00
□ 236 Wm. Hasamdear: K.C.	100.00	50.00	10.00
□ 237 Colonel Hatfield: New York	100.00	50.00	10.00
□ 238 Egyptian Healey: Wash.-Indianapolis	100.00	50.00	10.00
□ 239 J.C. Healy: Omaha-Denver	100.00	50.00	10.00
□ 240 Guy Hecker: Louisville	100.00	50.00	10.00
□ 241 Tony Hellman: Sioux City	100.00	50.00	10.00
□ 242 Hardie Henderson: Brook.-Pitts.-Balt.	100.00	50.00	10.00
□ 243 Henderson and Greer: Brooklyn	150.00	75.00	15.00
□ 244 Moxie Hengle: Maroons-Minneapolis	150.00	75.00	15.00
□ 245 John Henry: Phila.	100.00	50.00	10.00
□ 246 Edward Herr: Whites-Milwaukee	100.00	50.00	10.00
□ 247 Hunkey Hines: Whites	100.00	50.00	10.00
□ 248 Paul Hines: Wash.-Indianapolis	100.00	50.00	10.00
□ 249 Texas Wonder Hoffman: Denver	100.00	50.00	10.00
□ 250 Eddie Hogan: Cleve.	100.00	50.00	10.00
□ 251A William Holbert SPOT	350.00	175.00	35.00
□ 251B William Holbert: Brooklyn-Mets-Jersey City	100.00	50.00	10.00
□ 252 James(Bugs) Holliday: Des Moines-Cinc.	100.00	50.00	10.00
□ 253 Charles Hoover: Maroons-Chi.-K.C.	150.00	75.00	15.00
□ 254 Buster Hoover: Phila.-Toronto	100.00	50.00	10.00
□ 255 Jack Horner: Milwaukee-New Haven	100.00	50.00	10.00
□ 256 Horner and Warner: Milwaukee	150.00	75.00	15.00
□ 257 Michael Horning: Boston-Balt.-N.Y.	100.00	50.00	10.00
□ 258 Pete Hotaling: Cleveland	100.00	50.00	10.00
□ 259 William Howes: Minn..-St. Paul	100.00	50.00	10.00
□ 260 Dummy Hoy: Washington	300.00	150.00	30.00
□ 261A Nat Hudson: Browns Champ	250.00	125.00	25.00
□ 261B Nat Hudson: St. Louis	100.00	50.00	10.00
□ 262 Mickey Hughes: Brk.	100.00	50.00	10.00
□ 263 Hungler: Sioux City	100.00	50.00	10.00
□ 264 Wild Bill Hutchinson: Chicago	100.00	50.00	10.00
□ 265 John Irwin: Wash.-Wilkes Barre	100.00	50.00	10.00
□ 266 Cutrate Irwin: Phila.-Boston-Wash.	100.00	50.00	10.00
□ 267 A.C. Jantzen: Minn.	100.00	50.00	10.00
□ 268 Frederick Jevne: Minn.-St. Paul	100.00	50.00	10.00
□ 269 John Johnson: K.C.-Columbus	100.00	50.00	10.00
□ 270 Richard Johnston: Boston	100.00	50.00	10.00
□ 271 Jordan: Minneapolis	100.00	50.00	10.00
□ 272 Heinie Kappell: Columbus-Cincinnati	100.00	50.00	10.00
□ 273 Keas: Milwaukee	100.00	50.00	10.00
□ 274 Sir Timothy Keefe: New York	450.00	225.00	45.00
□ 275 Keefe and Richardson Stealing 2nd Base New York HOR	350.00	175.00	35.00
□ 276 George Keefe: Wash.	100.00	50.00	10.00
□ 277 James Keenan: Cinc.	100.00	50.00	10.00
□ 278 Mike (King) Kelly "10,000" Chic-Boston	900.00	450.00	90.00
□ 279 Honest John Kelly: Mgr. Louisville	150.00	75.00	15.00
□ 280 Kelly: (Umpire) Western Association	150.00	75.00	15.00
□ 281 Charles Kelly: Philadelphia	100.00	50.00	10.00

☐ 282 Kelly and Powell: Umpire and Manager Sioux City	150.00	75.00	15.00
☐ 283A Rudolph Kemmler: Browns Champ	250.00	125.00	25.00
☐ 283B Rudolph Kemmler: St. Paul	100.00	50.00	10.00
☐ 284 Theodore Kennedy: Des Moines-Omaha	150.00	75.00	15.00
☐ 285 J.J. Kenyon: Whites-Des Moines	100.00	50.00	10.00
☐ 286 John Kerins: Louisville	100.00	50.00	10.00
☐ 287 Matthew Kilroy: Baltimore-Boston	100.00	50.00	10.00
☐ 288 Charles King: St.L.-Chi.	100.00	50.00	10.00
☐ 289 Aug. Kloff: Minn.-St.Joe	100.00	50.00	10.00
☐ 290 William Klusman: Milwaukee-Denver	100.00	50.00	10.00
☐ 291 Phillip Knell: St. Joe-Phila.	100.00	50.00	10.00
☐ 292 Fred Knouf: St. Louis	100.00	50.00	10.00
☐ 293 Charles Kremmeyer: Sacramento PCL	1200.00	500.00	125.00
☐ 294 William Krieg: Wash.-St. Joe-Minn.	100.00	50.00	10.00
☐ 295 Krieg and Kloff: Minneapolis	150.00	75.00	15.00
☐ 296 Gus Krock: Chicago	100.00	50.00	10.00
☐ 297 Willie Kuehne: Pittsburgh	100.00	50.00	10.00
☐ 298 Frederick Lange: Maroons	150.00	75.00	15.00
☐ 299 Ted Larkin: A's	100.00	50.00	10.00
☐ 300A Arlie Latham: Browns Champ	250.00	125.00	25.00
☐ 300B Arlie Latham: St. Louis-Chicago	150.00	75.00	15.00
☐ 301 John Lauer: Pittsburgh	100.00	50.00	10.00
☐ 302 Lawless: Columbus	100.00	50.00	10.00
☐ 303 John Leighton: Omaha	100.00	50.00	10.00
☐ 304 Levy: San Fran. PCL	1200.00	500.00	125.00
☐ 305 Tom Loftus MG: Whites-Cleveland	100.00	50.00	10.00
☐ 306 Lohbeck: Cleveland	100.00	50.00	10.00
☐ 307 Herman(Germany)Long Maroons-K.C.	200.00	100.00	20.00
☐ 308 Danny Long: Oak. PCL	1200.00	500.00	125.00
☐ 309 Tom Lovett: Omaha-Brooklyn	100.00	50.00	10.00
☐ 310 Bobby (Link) Lowe: Milwaukee	200.00	100.00	20.00
☐ 311A Jack Lynch SPOT	450.00	225.00	45.00
☐ 311B John Lynch: All Stars	100.00	50.00	10.00
☐ 312 Dennis Lyons: A's	100.00	50.00	10.00
☐ 313 Harry Lyons: St. L.	100.00	50.00	10.00
☐ 314 Connie Mack: Wash.	1350.00	600.00	150.00
☐ 315 Joe (Reddie) Mack: Louisville	100.00	50.00	10.00
☐ 316 James (Little Mack) Macullar: Des Moines-Milwaukee	100.00	50.00	10.00
☐ 317 Kid Madden: Boston	100.00	50.00	10.00
☐ 318 Daniel Mahoney: St. Joe	100.00	50.00	10.00
☐ 319 Willard(Grasshopper) Maines: St. Paul	100.00	50.00	10.00
☐ 320 Fred Mann: St.Louis-Hartford	100.00	50.00	10.00
☐ 321 Jimmy Manning: K.C.	100.00	50.00	10.00
☐ 322 Charles(Lefty) Marr: Col.-Cinc.	100.00	50.00	10.00
☐ 323 Mascot (Willie Breslin): New York	125.00	60.00	12.50
☐ 324 Samuel Maskery: Milwaukee-Des Moines	100.00	50.00	10.00
☐ 325 Bobby Mathews: A's	100.00	50.00	10.00
☐ 326 Michael Mattimore: New York-A's	100.00	50.00	10.00
☐ 327 Albert Maul: Pitts.	100.00	50.00	10.00
☐ 328A Albert Mays SPOT	350.00	175.00	35.00
☐ 328B Albert Mays: Columbus	100.00	50.00	10.00
☐ 329 James McAleer: Cleveland	100.00	50.00	10.00
☐ 330 Thomas McCarthy: Phila.-St. Louis	450.00	225.00	45.00
☐ 331 John McCarthy: K.C.	100.00	50.00	10.00
☐ 332 James McCauley: Maroons-Phila.	150.00	75.00	15.00
☐ 333 William McClellan: Brooklyn-Denver	100.00	50.00	10.00
☐ 334 John McCormack: Whites	100.00	50.00	10.00
☐ 335 Big Jim McCormick: Chicago-Pittsburgh	100.00	50.00	10.00
☐ 336 McCreachery: Mgr. Indianapolis	150.00	75.00	15.00
☐ 337 Thomas McCullum: Minneapolis	100.00	50.00	10.00
☐ 338 James(Chippy)McGarr: St. Louis-K.C.	100.00	50.00	10.00
☐ 339 Jack McGeachy: Ind.	100.00	50.00	10.00
☐ 340 John McGlone: Cleveland-Detroit	100.00	50.00	10.00
☐ 341 James(Deacon)McGuire Phila.-Toronto	100.00	50.00	10.00
☐ 342 Bill (Gunner) McGunnigle: Mgr. Brooklyn	150.00	75.00	15.00
☐ 343 Ed McKean: Cleveland	100.00	50.00	10.00
☐ 344 Alex McKinnon: Pittsburgh	100.00	50.00	10.00
☐ 345 Thomas McLaughlin SPOT	400.00	200.00	40.00
☐ 346 John (Bid) McPhee: Cincinnati	150.00	75.00	15.00
☐ 347 James McQuaid: Denver	100.00	50.00	10.00
☐ 348 John McQuaid: Umpire Amer. Assoc.	150.00	75.00	15.00
☐ 349 Jame McTamany: Brook.-Col.-K.C.	100.00	50.00	10.00
☐ 350 George McVey: Mil.-Denver-St. Joe	100.00	50.00	10.00
☐ 351 Meegan: San Fran. PCL	1200.00	500.00	125.00
☐ 352 John Messitt: Omaha	100.00	50.00	10.00
☐ 353 George(Doggie)Miller Pittsburgh	100.00	50.00	10.00
☐ 354 Joseph Miller: Omaha-Minneapolis	100.00	50.00	10.00
☐ 355 Jocko Milligan: St. Louis-Phila.	100.00	50.00	10.00
☐ 356 E.L. Mills: Milwaukee	100.00	50.00	10.00
☐ 357 Minnehan: Minneapolis	100.00	50.00	10.00
☐ 358 Samuel Moffet: Ind.	100.00	50.00	10.00
☐ 359 Honest Morrill: Boston-Washington	100.00	50.00	10.00
☐ 360 Ed Morris (Cannonball) Pittsburgh	100.00	50.00	10.00
☐ 361 Morrisey: St. Paul	100.00	50.00	10.00
☐ 362 Tony(Count) Mullane: Cincinnati	150.00	75.00	15.00
☐ 363 Joseph Mulvey: Philadelphia	100.00	50.00	10.00
☐ 364 P.L. Murphy: St. Paul	100.00	50.00	10.00
☐ 365 P.J. Murphy: New York	100.00	50.00	10.00
☐ 366 Miah Murray: Wash.	100.00	50.00	10.00
☐ 367 James (Truthful) Mutrie: Mgr. N.Y.	100.00	50.00	10.00
☐ 368 George Myers: Indianapolis-Phila.	100.00	50.00	10.00
☐ 369 Al (Cod) Myers: Washington	100.00	50.00	10.00
☐ 370 Thomas Nagle: Omaha-Chi.	100.00	50.00	10.00
☐ 371 Billy Nash: Boston	100.00	50.00	10.00
☐ 372 Jack(Candy) Nelson: SPOT	400.00	200.00	40.00
☐ 373 Kid Nichols: Omaha	650.00	325.00	65.00
☐ 374 Samuel Nichols: Pittsburgh	100.00	50.00	10.00
☐ 375 J.W. Nicholson Maroons-Minn.	150.00	75.00	15.00
☐ 376 Tom Nicholson (Parson) Whites-Cleveland	100.00	50.00	10.00
☐ 377A Nicholls Nicol Browns Champ	250.00	125.00	25.00
☐ 377B Hugh Nicol: Cinc.	100.00	50.00	10.00
☐ 378 Nicol and Reilly Cincinnati	150.00	75.00	15.00
☐ 379 Frederick Nyce Whites-Burlington	100.00	50.00	10.00
☐ 380 Doc Oberlander Cleveland-Syracuse	100.00	50.00	10.00

☐ 381	Jack O'Brien Brooklyn-Baltimore	100.00	50.00	10.00
☐ 382	William O'Brien: Washington	100.00	50.00	10.00
☐ 383	O'Brien and Irwin:	150.00	75.00	15.00
☐ 384	Darby O'Brien: Brooklyn	100.00	50.00	10.00
☐ 385	John O'Brien: Cleve.	100.00	50.00	10.00
☐ 386	P.J. O'Connell: Omaha-Des Moines	100.00	50.00	10.00
☐ 387	John O'Connor: Cincinnati-Columbus	100.00	50.00	10.00
☐ 388	Hank O'Day: Washington-New York	100.00	50.00	10.00
☐ 389A	James O'Neil: St. Louis-Chicago	100.00	50.00	10.00
☐ 389B	James O'Neil: Browns Champs	250.00	125.00	25.00
☐ 390	O'Neill: Oakland PCL	1200.00	500.00	125.00
☐ 391	Orator O'Rourke: New York	500.00	250.00	50.00
☐ 392	Thomas O'Rourke: Boston-Jersey City	100.00	50.00	10.00
☐ 393A	David Orr SPOT	350.00	175.00	35.00
☐ 393B	David Orr: All Star-Brooklyn-Columbus	100.00	50.00	10.00
☐ 394	Parsons: Minneapolis	100.00	50.00	10.00
☐ 395	Owen Patton: Minn.-Des Moines	100.00	50.00	10.00
☐ 396	James Peeples: Brooklyn-Columbus	100.00	50.00	10.00
☐ 397	Peeples and Henderson Brooklyn	150.00	75.00	15.00
☐ 398	Hip Perrier: San Francisco PCL	1200.00	500.00	125.00
☐ 399	Patrick Pettee: Milwaukee-London	100.00	50.00	10.00
☐ 400	Pettee and Lowe: Milwaukee	150.00	75.00	15.00
☐ 401	Bob Pettit: Chicago	100.00	50.00	10.00
☐ 402	Dandelion Pfeffer: Chi.	100.00	50.00	10.00
☐ 403	Dick Phelan: Des Moines	100.00	50.00	10.00
☐ 404	William Phillips: Brooklyn-Kansas City	100.00	50.00	10.00
☐ 405	Horace Phillips: Pittsburgh	100.00	50.00	10.00
☐ 406	John Pickett: St. Paul-K.C.-Phila.	100.00	50.00	10.00
☐ 407	George Pinkney: Brooklyn	100.00	50.00	10.00
☐ 408	Thomas Poorman: A's-Milwaukee	100.00	50.00	10.00
☐ 409	Henry Porter: Brooklyn-Kansas City	100.00	50.00	10.00
☐ 410	James Powell: Sioux City	100.00	50.00	10.00
☐ 411	Tom Powers: San Francisco PCL	1200.00	500.00	125.00
☐ 412	Bill Blonie Purcell: Baltimore-A's	100.00	50.00	10.00
☐ 413	Thomas Quinn: Baltimore	100.00	50.00	10.00
☐ 414	Joseph Quinn: Des Moines-Boston	100.00	50.00	10.00
☐ 415A	Old Hoss Radbourne: Boston (portrait)	750.00	375.00	75.00
☐ 415B	Old Hoss Radbourne: Boston (non-portrait)	500.00	250.00	50.00
☐ 416	Shorty Radford: Brooklyn-Cleveland	100.00	50.00	10.00
☐ 417	Tom Ramsey: Louisville	100.00	50.00	10.00
☐ 418	Rehse: Minneapolis	100.00	50.00	10.00
☐ 419	Long John Reilly: Cincinnati	100.00	50.00	10.00
☐ 420	Charles Reilly: (Princeton) St.Paul	100.00	50.00	10.00
☐ 421	Charles Reynolds: Kansas City	100.00	50.00	10.00
☐ 422	Hardie Richardson Detroit-Boston	100.00	50.00	10.00
☐ 423	Danny Richardson: New York	100.00	50.00	10.00
☐ 424	Frank Ringo: St. Paul	100.00	50.00	10.00
☐ 425	Charles Ripslager SPOT	400.00	200.00	40.00
☐ 426	John Roach: New York	100.00	50.00	10.00
☐ 427	Wilbert Robinson (Uncle Robbie): A's	550.00	275.00	55.00
☐ 428	M.C. Robinson: Minn.	100.00	50.00	10.00
☐ 429A	Yank Robinson: St. Louis	100.00	50.00	10.00
☐ 429B	Wm.(Yank) Robinson: Browns Champs	250.00	125.00	25.00
☐ 430	George Rooks: Maroons-Detroit	150.00	75.00	15.00
☐ 431	James(Chief) Roseman SPOT	400.00	200.00	40.00
☐ 432	Davis Rowe: Mgr. K.C.-Denver	100.00	50.00	10.00
☐ 433	Jack Rowe: Detroit-Pittsburgh	100.00	50.00	10.00
☐ 434	Amos (Hoosier Thunderbolt) Rusie: Ind.-New York	750.00	375.00	75.00
☐ 435	James Ryan: Chicago	100.00	50.00	10.00
☐ 436	Henry Sage: Des Moines-Toledo	100.00	50.00	10.00
☐ 437	Sage and Van Dyke: Des Moines-Toledo	150.00	75.00	15.00
☐ 438	Frank Salee Omaha-Boston	100.00	50.00	10.00
☐ 439	Sanders: Omaha	100.00	50.00	10.00
☐ 440	Al (Ben) Sanders: Philadelphia	100.00	50.00	10.00
☐ 441	Frank Scheibeck: Detroit	100.00	50.00	10.00
☐ 442	Albert Schellhase: St. Joseph	100.00	50.00	10.00
☐ 443	William Schenkle: Milwaukee	100.00	50.00	10.00
☐ 444	Bill Schildknecht: Des Moines-Milwaukee	100.00	50.00	10.00
☐ 445	Gus (Pink Whiskers) Schmelz Mgr. Cincinnati	100.00	50.00	10.00
☐ 446	R. F. Schoch: Wash.	100.00	50.00	10.00
☐ 447	Lewis Schoeneck (Jumbo): Maroons-Indianapolis	150.00	75.00	15.00
☐ 448	Pop Schriver: Phila.	100.00	50.00	10.00
☐ 449	John Seery: Ind.	100.00	50.00	10.00
☐ 450	William Serad Cincinnnati-Toronto	100.00	50.00	10.00
☐ 451	Edward Seward: A's	100.00	50.00	10.00
☐ 452	George(Orator)Shafer Des Moines	100.00	50.00	10.00
☐ 453	Frank Shafer: St. Paul	100.00	50.00	10.00
☐ 454	Daniel Shannon: Omaha-L'ville-Phila.	100.00	50.00	10.00
☐ 455	William Sharsig: Mgr. Athletics	150.00	75.00	15.00
☐ 456	Samuel Shaw: Baltimore-Newark	100.00	50.00	10.00
☐ 457	John Shaw: Minneapolis	100.00	50.00	10.00
☐ 458	William Shindle: Baltimore-Phila.	100.00	50.00	10.00
☐ 459	George Shock: Wash.	100.00	50.00	10.00
☐ 460	Otto Shomberg: Ind.	100.00	50.00	10.00
☐ 461	Lev Shreve: Ind.	100.00	50.00	10.00
☐ 462	Ed (Baldy) Silch: Brooklyn-Denver	100.00	50.00	10.00
☐ 463	Michael Slattery: New York	100.00	50.00	10.00
☐ 464	Sam(Skyrocket)Smith: Louisville	100.00	50.00	10.00
☐ 465A	John (Phenomenal) Smith (portrait)	750.00	375.00	75.00
☐ 465B	John (Phenomenal) Smith: Balt.-A's (non-portrait)	100.00	50.00	10.00
☐ 466	Elmer Smith: Cincinnati	100.00	50.00	10.00
☐ 467	Fred (Sam) Smith: Des Moines	100.00	50.00	10.00
☐ 468	George Smith (Germany) Brooklyn	100.00	50.00	10.00
☐ 469	Pop Smith: Pitt.-Bos.-Phila.	100.00	50.00	10.00
☐ 470	Nick Smith: St. Joe	100.00	50.00	10.00
☐ 471	Pop Snyder: Cleve.	100.00	50.00	10.00
☐ 472	P.T. Somers: St. Louis	100.00	50.00	10.00
☐ 473	Joe Sommer: Balt.	100.00	50.00	10.00
☐ 474	Pete Sommers: Chicago-New York	100.00	50.00	10.00
☐ 475	William Sowders: Boston-Pittsburgh	100.00	50.00	10.00

☐ 476	John Sowders: St. Paul-Kansas City	100.00	50.00	10.00
☐ 477	Charles Sprague: Maroons-Chi.-Cleve.	150.00	75.00	15.00
☐ 478	Edward Sproat: Whites	100.00	50.00	10.00
☐ 479	Harry Staley: Whites-Pittsburgh	100.00	50.00	10.00
☐ 480	Daniel Stearns: Des Moines-K.C.	100.00	50.00	10.00
☐ 481	Billy (Cannonball) Stemmyer: Boston-Cleveland	100.00	50.00	10.00
☐ 482	Stengel: Columbus	100.00	50.00	10.00
☐ 483	B.F. Stephens: Milw.	100.00	50.00	10.00
☐ 484	John C. Sterling: Minneapolis	100.00	50.00	10.00
☐ 485	Stockwell: S.F. PCL	1200.00	500.00	125.00
☐ 486	Harry Stovey: A's-Boston	250.00	125.00	25.00
☐ 487	C. Scott Stratton: Louisville	100.00	50.00	10.00
☐ 488	Joseph Straus: Omaha-Milwaukee	100.00	50.00	10.00
☐ 489	John (Cub) Stricker: Cleveland	100.00	50.00	10.00
☐ 490	J.O. Struck: Milw.	100.00	50.00	10.00
☐ 491	Marty Sullivan: Chicago-Ind.	100.00	50.00	10.00
☐ 492	Michael Sullivan: A's	100.00	50.00	10.00
☐ 493	Billy Sunday: Chicago-Pittsburgh	500.00	250.00	50.00
☐ 494	Sy Sutcliffe: Cleve.	100.00	50.00	10.00
☐ 495	Ezra Sutton: Boston-Milwaukee	100.00	50.00	10.00
☐ 496	Ed Cyrus Swartwood: Brook.-D.Moines-Ham.	100.00	50.00	10.00
☐ 497	Parke Swartzel: K.C.	100.00	50.00	10.00
☐ 498	Peter Sweeney: Wash.	100.00	50.00	10.00
☐ 499	Sylvester: Sacra. PCL	1200.00	500.00	125.00
☐ 500	Ed (Dimples) Tate: Boston-Baltimore	100.00	50.00	10.00
☐ 501	Patsy Tebeau: Chi.-Cleve.-Minn.	100.00	50.00	10.00
☐ 502	John Tener: Chicago	150.00	75.00	15.00
☐ 503	Bill (Adonis) Terry: Brooklyn	100.00	50.00	10.00
☐ 504	Big Sam Thompson: Detroit-Philadelphia	450.00	225.00	45.00
☐ 505	Silent Mike Tiernan: New York	100.00	50.00	10.00
☐ 506	Ledell Titcomb: N.Y.	100.00	50.00	10.00
☐ 507	Phillip Tomney: Louisville	100.00	50.00	10.00
☐ 508	Stephen Toole: Brooklyn-K.C.-Rochester	100.00	50.00	10.00
☐ 509	George Townsend: A's	100.00	50.00	10.00
☐ 510	William Traffley: Des Moines	100.00	50.00	10.00
☐ 511	George Treadway: St. Paul-Denver	100.00	50.00	10.00
☐ 512	Samuel Trott: Baltimore-Newark	100.00	50.00	10.00
☐ 513	Trott and Burns: Baltimore HOR	150.00	75.00	15.00
☐ 514	Tom(Foghorn) Tucker: Baltimore	100.00	50.00	10.00
☐ 515	William Tuckerman: St. Paul	100.00	50.00	10.00
☐ 516	Turner: Minneapolis	100.00	50.00	10.00
☐ 517	Lawrence Twitchell: Detroit-Cleveland	100.00	50.00	10.00
☐ 518	James Tyng: Phila.	100.00	50.00	10.00
☐ 519	William Van Dyke: Des Moines-Toledo	100.00	50.00	10.00
☐ 520	George Rip VanHaltren Chicago	100.00	50.00	10.00
☐ 521	Harry Vaughn: (Farmer) Louisville-New York	100.00	50.00	10.00
☐ 522	Peek-a-Boo Veach: St. Paul	300.00	150.00	30.00
☐ 523	Veach: Sacra. PCL	1200.00	500.00	125.00
☐ 524	Leon Viau: Cincinnati	100.00	50.00	10.00
☐ 525	William Vinton: Minneapolis	100.00	50.00	10.00
☐ 526	Joseph Visner: Brooklyn	100.00	50.00	10.00
☐ 527	Christian VonDer Ahe Owner Browns Champs	350.00	175.00	35.00
☐ 528	Joseph Walsh: Omaha	100.00	50.00	10.00
☐ 529	John (Monte) Ward: New York	450.00	225.00	45.00
☐ 530	E.H. Warner: Milwaukee	300.00	150.00	30.00
☐ 531	William Watkins: Mgr. Detroit-Kansas City	150.00	75.00	15.00
☐ 532	Bill Weaver: (Farmer) Louisville	100.00	50.00	10.00
☐ 533	Charles Weber: Sioux City	100.00	50.00	10.00
☐ 534	George Weidman (Stump): Detroit-New York	100.00	50.00	10.00
☐ 535	William Weidner: Columbus	100.00	50.00	10.00
☐ 536A	Curtis Welch: Browns Champ	250.00	125.00	25.00
☐ 536B	Curtis Welch: A's	100.00	50.00	10.00
☐ 537	Welch and Gleason: Athletics	150.00	75.00	15.00
☐ 538	Smilin'Mickey Welch: All Star-New York	500.00	250.00	50.00
☐ 539	Jake Wells: K.C.	100.00	50.00	10.00
☐ 540	Frank Wells: Des Moines-Mil.	150.00	75.00	15.00
☐ 541	Joseph Werrick: Louisville-St. Paul	100.00	50.00	10.00
☐ 542	Milton(Buck) West: Minneapolis	100.00	50.00	10.00
☐ 543	Gus (Cannonball) Weyhing: A's	100.00	50.00	10.00
☐ 544	John Weyhing: Athletics-Columbus	100.00	50.00	10.00
☐ 545	Bobby Wheelock: Boston-Detroit	100.00	50.00	10.00
☐ 546	Whitacre: A's	100.00	50.00	10.00
☐ 547	Pat Whitaker: Balt.	100.00	50.00	10.00
☐ 548	Deacon White: Detroit-Pittsburgh	100.00	50.00	10.00
☐ 549	William White: Louisville	100.00	50.00	10.00
☐ 550	Jim (Grasshopper) Whitney: Wash.-Indianapolis	100.00	50.00	10.00
☐ 551	Arthur Whitney: Pittsburgh-New York	100.00	50.00	10.00
☐ 552	G. Whitney: St. Joseph	100.00	50.00	10.00
☐ 553	James Williams: Mgr. Cleveland	150.00	75.00	15.00
☐ 554	Ned Williamson: Chi.	150.00	75.00	15.00
☐ 555	Williamson and Mascot	150.00	75.00	15.00
☐ 556	C.H. Willis: Omaha	100.00	50.00	10.00
☐ 557	Walt Wilmot: Washington-Chicago	100.00	50.00	10.00
☐ 558	George Winkleman: Minneapolis-Hartford	100.00	50.00	10.00
☐ 559	Samuel Wise: Boston-Washington	100.00	50.00	10.00
☐ 560	William Wolf (Chicken) Louisville	100.00	50.00	10.00
☐ 561	George (Dandy) Wood: Philadelphia	100.00	50.00	10.00
☐ 562	Peter Wood: Phila.	100.00	50.00	10.00
☐ 563	Harry Wright: Mgr. Philadelphia	1350.00	600.00	150.00
☐ 564	Charles Zimmer (Chief) Cleveland	100.00	50.00	10.00
☐ 565	Frank Zinn: Athletics	100.00	50.00	10.00

N184 Kimball's

This set of 50 color pictures of contemporary athletes was Kimball's answer to the sets produced by Allen , Ginter (N28 and N29) and Goodwin (N162). Issued in 1888, the cards are backlisted but are not numbered. The cards are listed below in alphabetical order without regard to sport. There are four baseball players in the set. An album (ACC: A42) was offered as a premium in exchange for coupons found in the tobacco packages. The baseball players are noted in the checklist below by BB after their name.

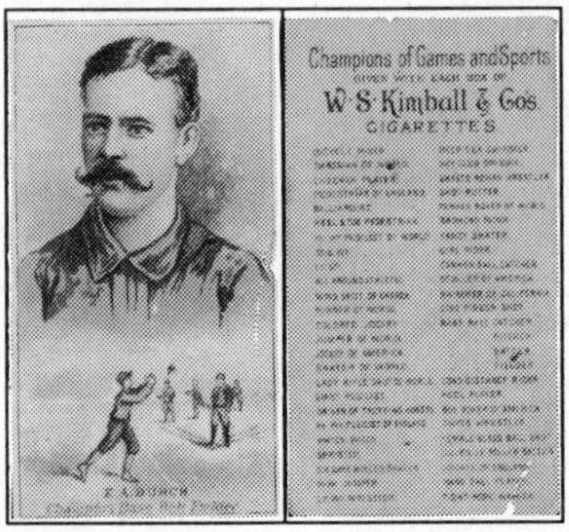

	EX-MT	VG-E	GOOD
COMPLETE SET (50)	4500.00	2000.00	450.00
COMMON BASEBALL	600.00	300.00	60.00
COMMON BOXER	150.00	75.00	15.00
COMMON OTHERS	50.00	25.00	5.00
☐ 1 Wm. Beach	50.00	25.00	5.00
☐ 2 Marve Beardsley	50.00	25.00	5.00
☐ 3 Chas. P. Blatt	50.00	25.00	5.00
☐ 4 Blondin	50.00	25.00	5.00
☐ 5 Paul Boynton	50.00	25.00	5.00
☐ 6 E.A.(Ernie) Burch BB	600.00	300.00	60.00
☐ 7 Patsy Cardiff	50.00	25.00	5.00
☐ 8 Phillip Casey	50.00	25.00	5.00
☐ 9 J.C. Cockburn	50.00	25.00	5.00
☐ 10 Dell Darling BB	600.00	300.00	60.00
☐ 11 Jack Dempsey BOX	225.00	110.00	22.00
☐ 12 Della Ferrell	50.00	25.00	5.00
☐ 13 Clarence Freeman	50.00	25.00	5.00
☐ 14 Louis George	50.00	25.00	5.00
☐ 15 W.G. George	50.00	25.00	5.00
☐ 16 George W. Hamilton	50.00	25.00	5.00
☐ 17 Edward Hanlan	50.00	25.00	5.00
☐ 18 C.H. Heins	50.00	25.00	5.00
☐ 19 Hardie Henderson BB	600.00	300.00	60.00
☐ 20 Thomas H. Hume	50.00	25.00	5.00
☐ 21 J.H. Jordon	50.00	25.00	5.00
☐ 22 Johnny Kane	50.00	25.00	5.00
☐ 23 James McLaughlin	50.00	25.00	5.00
☐ 24 John McPherson	50.00	25.00	5.00
☐ 25 Joseph Morsler	50.00	25.00	5.00
☐ 26 William Muldoon	50.00	25.00	5.00
☐ 27 S. Muller	50.00	25.00	5.00
☐ 28 Isaac Murphy	50.00	25.00	5.00
☐ 29 John Murphy	50.00	25.00	5.00
☐ 30 L.E. Myers	50.00	25.00	5.00
☐ 31 Annie Oakley	100.00	50.00	10.00
☐ 32 Daniel O'Leary	50.00	25.00	5.00
☐ 33 James O'Neil BB	700.00	350.00	70.00
☐ 34 Wm. Byrd Page	50.00	25.00	5.00
☐ 35 Axel Paulsen	50.00	25.00	5.00
☐ 36 Master Ray Perry	50.00	25.00	5.00
☐ 37 Duncan C. Ross	50.00	25.00	5.00
☐ 38 W.A. Rowe	50.00	25.00	5.00
☐ 39 Jacob Schaefer	50.00	25.00	5.00
☐ 40 M. Schloss	50.00	25.00	5.00
☐ 41 Jem Smith	50.00	25.00	5.00
☐ 42 Lillian Smith	50.00	25.00	5.00
☐ 43 Hattie Stewart	50.00	25.00	5.00
☐ 44 John L. Sullivan BOX	300.00	150.00	30.00
☐ 45 Arthur Wallace	50.00	25.00	5.00
☐ 46 Tommy Warren BOX	150.00	75.00	15.00
☐ 47 Ada Webb	50.00	25.00	5.00
☐ 48 John Wessels	50.00	25.00	5.00
☐ 49 Clarence Whistler	50.00	25.00	5.00
☐ 50 Charles Wood	50.00	25.00	5.00

N284 Buchner

The baseball players found in this Buchner set are a part of a larger group of cards portraying policemen, jockeys and actors, all of which were issued with the tobacco brand "Gold Coin." The set is comprised of three major groupings or types. In the first type, nine players from eight teams, plus three Brooklyn players, are all portrayed in identical poses according to position. In the second type, St. Louis has 14 players depicted in poses which are not repeated. The last group contains 53 additional cards which vary according to pose, team change, spelling, etc. These third type cards are indicated in the checklist below by an asterisk. In all, there are 116 individuals portrayed on 142 cards. The existence of an additional player in the set, McClellan of Brooklyn, has never been verified. The set was issued circa 1887. The cards are numbered below in alphabetical order within team with teams themselves listed in alphabetical order: Baltimore (1-4), Boston (5-13), Brooklyn (14-17), Chicago (18-26), Detroit (27-35), Indianapolis (36-47), LaCrosse (48-51), Milwaukee (52-55), New York Mets (56-63), New York (64-73), Philadelphia (74-83), Pittsburg (84-92), St. Louis (93-106), and Washington (107-117).

	EX-MT	VG-E	GOOD
COMPLETE SET	16000.00	7000.00	1500.00
COMMON PLAYERS	80.00	40.00	8.00
COMMON ST. LOUIS	120.00	60.00	12.00
COMMON PLAYERS *	120.00	60.00	12.00
☐ 1 Burns: Baltimore *	120.00	60.00	12.00
☐ 2 Fulmer: Baltimore *	120.00	60.00	12.00
☐ 3 Kilroy: Baltimore *	120.00	60.00	12.00
☐ 4 Purcell: Baltimore *	120.00	60.00	12.00
☐ 5 John Burdock: Boston	80.00	40.00	8.00
☐ 6 Bill Daley: Boston	80.00	40.00	8.00
☐ 7 Joe Hornung: Boston	80.00	40.00	8.00
☐ 8 Johnston: Boston	80.00	40.00	8.00
☐ 9A King Kelly: Boston (right field)	250.00	125.00	25.00
☐ 9B King Kelly: Boston (catcher) *	350.00	175.00	35.00
☐ 10A Morrill: Boston (both hands outstretched face high)	80.00	40.00	8.00
☐ 10B Morrill: Boston * (hands clasped near chin)	120.00	60.00	12.00
☐ 11A Hoss Radbourn: Boston	200.00	100.00	20.00
☐ 11B Hoss Radbourn: Boston * (hands together above waist)	300.00	150.00	30.00
☐ 12 Sutton: Boston	80.00	40.00	8.00
☐ 13 Wise: Boston	80.00	40.00	8.00
☐ 14 McClellan: Brooklyn (never confirmed)	00.00	00.00	0.00
☐ 15 Peoples: Brooklyn	80.00	40.00	8.00
☐ 16 Phillips: Brooklyn	80.00	40.00	8.00
☐ 17 Porter: Brooklyn	80.00	40.00	8.00
☐ 18A Adrian Anson: Chicago (both hands outstretched face high)	400.00	200.00	40.00

☐ 18B Adrian Anson: Chicago * (left hand on hip, right hand down)	600.00	300.00	60.00
☐ 19 Burns: Chicago	80.00	40.00	8.00
☐ 20A John Clarkson: Chicago	200.00	100.00	20.00
☐ 20B John Clarkson: Chicago * (right arm extended, left arm near side)	300.00	150.00	30.00
☐ 21 Silver Flint: Chicago	80.00	40.00	8.00
☐ 22 Pfeffer: Chicago	80.00	40.00	8.00
☐ 23 Ryan: Chicago	80.00	40.00	8.00
☐ 24 Billy Sullivan: Chicago	100.00	50.00	10.00
☐ 25 Billy Sunday: Chicago	200.00	100.00	20.00
☐ 26A Williamson: Chicago (shortstop)	80.00	40.00	8.00
☐ 26B Williamson: Chicago (second base) *	120.00	60.00	12.00
☐ 27 Bennett: Detroit	80.00	40.00	8.00
☐ 28A Dan Brouthers: Detroit (fielding)	200.00	100.00	20.00
☐ 28B Dan Brouthers: Detroit * (batting)	300.00	150.00	30.00
☐ 29 Dunlap: Detroit	80.00	40.00	8.00
☐ 30 Getzein: Detroit	80.00	40.00	8.00
☐ 31 Hanlon: Detroit	80.00	40.00	8.00
☐ 32 Manning: Detoit	80.00	40.00	8.00
☐ 33A Richardson: Detroit (hands together in front of chest)	80.00	40.00	8.00
☐ 33B Richardson: Detroit * (right hand holding ball above head)	120.00	60.00	12.00
☐ 34A Sam Thompson: Detroit (looking up with hands at waist)	200.00	100.00	20.00
☐ 34B Sam Thompson: Detroit * (hands chest high)	300.00	150.00	30.00
☐ 35 White: Detroit	80.00	40.00	8.00
☐ 36 Arundel: Indianapolis	80.00	40.00	8.00
☐ 37 Bassett: Indianapolis	80.00	40.00	8.00
☐ 38 Boyle: Indianapolis *	80.00	40.00	8.00
☐ 39 Cahill: Indianapolis *	120.00	60.00	12.00
☐ 40A Denny: Indianapolis (hands on knees, legs bent)	80.00	40.00	8.00
☐ 40B Denny: Indianapolis * (hands on knees, legs not bent)	120.00	60.00	12.00
☐ 41A Jack Glasscock: Indianapolis (crouching, catching a grounder)	100.00	50.00	10.00
☐ 41B Jack Glasscock: Indianapolis * (hands on knees)	150.00	75.00	15.00
☐ 42 Healy: Indianapolis	80.00	40.00	8.00
☐ 43 Meyers: Indianapolis *	120.00	60.00	12.00
☐ 44 McGeachy: Indianapolis	80.00	40.00	8.00
☐ 45 Polhemus: Indianapolis	80.00	40.00	8.00
☐ 46A Seery: Indianapolis (hands together in front of chest)	80.00	40.00	8.00
☐ 46B Seery: Indianapolis * (hands outstretched head high)	120.00	60.00	12.00
☐ 47 Shomberg: Indianapolis	80.00	40.00	8.00
☐ 48 Corbett: Lacrosse *	120.00	60.00	12.00
☐ 49 Crowley: Lacrosse *	120.00	60.00	12.00
☐ 50 Kennedy: Lacrosse *	120.00	60.00	12.00
☐ 51 Rooks: Lacrosse *	120.00	60.00	12.00
☐ 52 Forster: Milwaukee *	120.00	60.00	12.00
☐ 53 Hart: Milwaukee *	120.00	60.00	12.00
☐ 54 Morrissy: Milwaukee *	120.00	60.00	12.00
☐ 55 Strauss: Milwaukee *	120.00	60.00	12.00
☐ 56 Cushmann: NY Mets *	120.00	60.00	12.00
☐ 57 Jim Donohue: NY Mets *	120.00	60.00	12.00
☐ 58 Esterbrooke (sic): NY Mets *	120.00	60.00	12.00
☐ 59 Joe Gerhardt: NY Mets *	120.00	60.00	12.00
☐ 60 Frank Hankinson: NY Mets *	120.00	60.00	12.00
☐ 61 Jack Nelson: NY Mets *	120.00	60.00	12.00
☐ 62 Dave Orr: NY Mets *	120.00	60.00	12.00
☐ 63 James Rosemann: NY Mets *	120.00	60.00	12.00
☐ 64A Roger Connor: New York (both hands outstretched face high)	200.00	100.00	20.00
☐ 64B Roger Connor: New York * (hands outstretched, palms up)	300.00	150.00	30.00
☐ 65 Deasley: New York *	120.00	60.00	12.00
☐ 66A Mike Dorgan: New York (fielding)	80.00	40.00	8.00
☐ 66B Mike Dorgan: New York (batting) *	120.00	60.00	12.00
☐ 67A Buck Ewing: New York (ball in left hand, right arm out shoulder high)	200.00	100.00	20.00
☐ 67B Buck Ewing: New York * (appears ready to clap)	300.00	150.00	30.00
☐ 68A Pete Gillespie: New York (fielding)	80.00	40.00	8.00
☐ 68B Pete Gillespie: New York (batting) *	120.00	60.00	12.00
☐ 69 George Gore: New York	80.00	40.00	8.00
☐ 70A Tim Keefe: New York	200.00	100.00	20.00
☐ 70B Tim Keefe: New York * (ball just released from right hand)	300.00	150.00	30.00
☐ 71A Jim O'Rourke: New York (hands cupped in front, thigh high)	200.00	100.00	20.00
☐ 71B Jim O'Rourke: New York * (hands on knees, looking right)	300.00	150.00	30.00
☐ 72A Danny Richardson: New York (third base)	80.00	40.00	8.00
☐ 72B Danny Richardson: New York (second base) *	120.00	60.00	12.00
☐ 73A John M. Ward: New York (crouching, catching a grounder)	200.00	100.00	20.00
☐ 73B John M. Ward: New York * (hands by left knee)	300.00	150.00	30.00
☐ 73C John M. Ward: New York * (hands on knees)	300.00	150.00	30.00
☐ 74A Andrews: Philadelphia (hands together in front of neck)	80.00	40.00	8.00
☐ 74B Andrews: Philadelphia * (catching, hands waist high)	120.00	60.00	12.00
☐ 75 Bastian: Philadelphia	80.00	40.00	8.00
☐ 76 Dan Casey: Philadelphia *	120.00	60.00	12.00
☐ 77 Clements: Philadelphia	80.00	40.00	8.00
☐ 78 Sid Farrar: Philadelphia	80.00	40.00	8.00
☐ 79 Ferguson: Philadelphia	80.00	40.00	8.00
☐ 80 Fogerty: Philadelphia	80.00	40.00	8.00

☐ 81 Irwin: Philadelphia	80.00	40.00	8.00
☐ 82A Mulvey: Philadelphia (hands on knees)	80.00	40.00	8.00
☐ 82B Mulvey: Philadelphia * (hands together above head)	120.00	60.00	12.00
☐ 83A Pete Wood: Philadelphia (fielding)	80.00	40.00	8.00
☐ 83B Pete Wood: Philadelphia HOR (Stealing a Base) *	120.00	60.00	12.00
☐ 84 Barkley: Pittsburg	80.00	40.00	8.00
☐ 85 Beecher: Pittsburg	80.00	40.00	8.00
☐ 86 Brown: Pittsburg	80.00	40.00	8.00
☐ 87 Carroll: Pittsburg	80.00	40.00	8.00
☐ 88 Coleman: Pittsburg	80.00	40.00	8.00
☐ 89 McCormick: Pittsburg	80.00	40.00	8.00
☐ 90 Miller: Pittsburg	80.00	40.00	8.00
☐ 91 Smith: Pittsburg	80.00	40.00	8.00
☐ 92 Whitney: Pittsburg	80.00	40.00	8.00
☐ 93 Barkley: St. Louis	120.00	60.00	12.00
☐ 94 Bushong: St. Louis	120.00	60.00	12.00
☐ 95 Bob Carruthers (sic): St. Louis	150.00	75.00	15.00
☐ 96 Charles Comiskey: St. Louis	350.00	175.00	35.00
☐ 97 Dave Foutz: St. Louis	120.00	60.00	12.00
☐ 98 William Gleason: St. Louis	120.00	60.00	12.00
☐ 99 Arlie Latham: St. Louis	120.00	60.00	12.00
☐ 100 McGinnis: St. Louis	120.00	60.00	12.00
☐ 101 Hugh Nicol: St. Louis	120.00	60.00	12.00
☐ 102 James O'Neil: St. Louis	120.00	60.00	12.00
☐ 103 Robinson: St. Louis	120.00	60.00	12.00
☐ 104 Sullivan: St. Louis	120.00	60.00	12.00
☐ 105 Chris Von Der Ahe: St. Louis (actually a photo, rather than drawing)	350.00	175.00	35.00
☐ 106 Curt Welch: St. Louis	120.00	60.00	12.00
☐ 107 Carroll: Washington	80.00	40.00	8.00
☐ 108 Craig: Washington *	120.00	60.00	12.00
☐ 109 Crane: Washington *	120.00	60.00	12.00
☐ 110 Dailey: Washington	80.00	40.00	8.00
☐ 111 Donnelly: Washington	80.00	40.00	8.00
☐ 112A Farrell: Washington (ball in left hand, right arm out shoulder high)	80.00	40.00	8.00
☐ 112B Farrell: Washington * (ball in hands near right knee)	120.00	60.00	12.00
☐ 113 Gilligan: Washington	80.00	40.00	8.00
☐ 114A Hines: Washington (fielding)	80.00	40.00	8.00
☐ 114B Hines: Washington (batting) *	120.00	60.00	12.00
☐ 115 Myers: Washington	80.00	40.00	8.00
☐ 116 O'Brien: Washington	80.00	40.00	8.00
☐ 117 Whitney: Washington	80.00	40.00	8.00

N300 Mayo

The Mayo Tobacco Works of Richmond, Va., issued this set of 48 ballplayers about 1895. The cards contain sepia portraits although some pictures appear to be black and white. There are 40 different individuals known in the set; cards 1 to 28 appear in uniform, while the last twelve (29-40) appear in street clothes. Eight of the former also appear with variations in uniform. The player's name appears within the picture area and a "Mayo's Cut Plug" ad is printed in a panel at the base of the card.

	EX-MT	VG-E	GOOD
COMPLETE SET (48)	17500.00	7500.00	1500.00
COMMON PLAYERS (1-28)	250.00	125.00	25.00
COMMON PLAYERS (29-40)	250.00	125.00	25.00

☐ 1 Cap Anson: Chicago	1500.00	600.00	150.00
☐ 2 Bannon RF: Boston	250.00	125.00	25.00
☐ 3A Dan Brouthers 1B: Baltimore	600.00	300.00	60.00
☐ 3B Dan Brouthers 1B: Louisville	700.00	350.00	70.00
☐ 4 John Clarkson P: St. Louis	600.00	300.00	60.00
☐ 5 T.W. Corcoran SS: Brooklyn	250.00	125.00	25.00
☐ 6 Cross 2B: Philadelphia	250.00	125.00	25.00
☐ 7 Hugh Duffy CF: Boston	600.00	300.00	60.00
☐ 8A Buck Ewing RF: Cincinnati	650.00	325.00	65.00
☐ 8B Buck Ewing RF: Cleveland	650.00	325.00	65.00
☐ 9 Dave Foutz 1B: Brooklyn	250.00	125.00	25.00
☐ 10 Ganzel C: Boston	250.00	125.00	25.00
☐ 11A Glasscock SS: Pittsburgh	300.00	150.00	30.00
☐ 11B Glasscock SS: Louisville	300.00	150.00	30.00
☐ 12 Griffin CF: Brooklyn	250.00	125.00	25.00
☐ 13A Haddock P: Philadelphia	250.00	125.00	25.00
☐ 13B Haddock P: no team	250.00	125.00	25.00
☐ 14 Joyce CF: Brooklyn	250.00	125.00	25.00
☐ 15 Wm. Kennedy P: Brooklyn	250.00	125.00	25.00
☐ 16A Tom F. Kinslow C: Pitts.	250.00	125.00	25.00
☐ 16B Tom F. Kinslow C: no team	250.00	125.00	25.00
☐ 17 Arlie Latham 3B: Cincinnati	250.00	125.00	25.00
☐ 18 Long SS: Boston	300.00	150.00	30.00
☐ 19 Lovett P: Boston	250.00	125.00	25.00
☐ 20 Lowe 2B: Boston	300.00	150.00	30.00
☐ 21 McCarthy LF: Boston	600.00	300.00	60.00
☐ 22 Murphy SS: New York	250.00	125.00	25.00
☐ 23 Billy Nash 3B: Boston	250.00	125.00	25.00
☐ 24 Nicols P: Boston	250.00	125.00	25.00
☐ 25A Pfeffer 2B: Louisville	250.00	125.00	25.00
☐ 25B Pfeffer (retired)	250.00	125.00	25.00
☐ 26A Amos Rusie P: New York	900.00	450.00	90.00
☐ 26B Amos Russie (sic) P: New York	650.00	325.00	65.00
☐ 27 Tucker 1B: Boston	250.00	125.00	25.00
☐ 28A John Ward 2B: New York	600.00	300.00	60.00
☐ 28B John Ward (retired)	700.00	350.00	70.00
☐ 29 Chas. S. Abbey CF: Washington	250.00	125.00	25.00
☐ 30 E.W. Cartwright FB: Washington	250.00	125.00	25.00
☐ 31 W. F. Dahlen SS: Chicago	300.00	150.00	30.00
☐ 32 T.P. Daly SB: Brooklyn	250.00	125.00	25.00
☐ 33 E.J. Delehanty LF: Phila.	900.00	450.00	90.00
☐ 34 W.W. Hallman SB: Phila.	250.00	125.00	25.00
☐ 35 W.R. Hamilton CF: Phila.	600.00	300.00	60.00

☐ 36 W. Robinson C: Baltimore	600.00	300.00	60.00
☐ 37 James Ryan RF: Chicago	250.00	125.00	25.00
☐ 38 Wm. Shindle TB: Brooklyn	250.00	125.00	25.00
☐ 39 Geo. J. Smith SS: Cinc.	250.00	125.00	25.00
☐ 40 Otis H. Stockdale P: Washington	250.00	125.00	25.00

1986 National Photo Royals

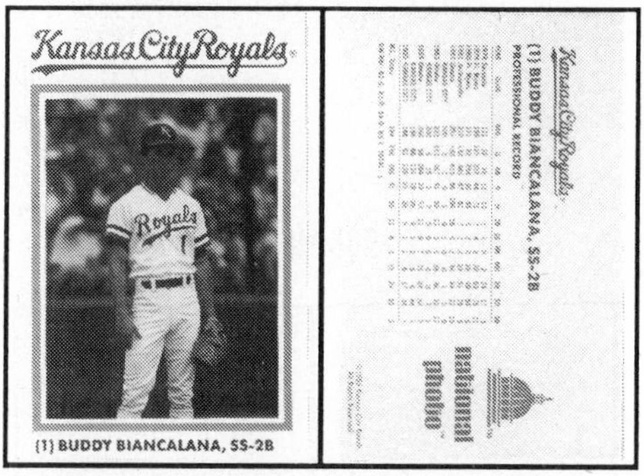

The set contains 24 cards which are numbered only by uniform number except for the checklist card and discount card, which entitles the bearer to a 40 percent discount at National Photo. Cards measure 2 7/8" by 4 1/4". Cards were distributed at the stadium on August 14th. The set was supposedly later available for 3.00 directly from the Royals.

	MINT	EXC	G-VG
COMPLETE SET (24)	10.00	5.00	1.00
COMMON PLAYER	.35	.17	.03
☐ 1 Buddy Biancalana	.35	.17	.03
☐ 3 Jorge Orta	.35	.17	.03
☐ 4 Greg Pryor	.35	.17	.03
☐ 5 George Brett	3.00	1.50	.30
☐ 6 Willie Wilson	.75	.35	.07
☐ 8 Jim Sundberg	.35	.17	.03
☐ 10 Dick Howser MG	.60	.30	.06
☐ 11 Hal McRae	.50	.25	.05
☐ 20 Frank White	.60	.30	.06
☐ 21 Lonnie Smith	.60	.30	.06
☐ 22 Dennis Leonard	.50	.25	.05
☐ 23 Mark Gubicza	1.00	.50	.10
☐ 24 Darryl Motley	.35	.17	.03
☐ 25 Danny Jackson	.60	.30	.06
☐ 26 Steve Farr	.35	.17	.03
☐ 29 Dan Quisenberry	.60	.30	.06
☐ 31 Bret Saberhagen	1.25	.60	.12
☐ 35 Lynn Jones	.35	.17	.03
☐ 37 Charlie Leibrandt	.50	.25	.05
☐ 38 Mark Huismann	.35	.17	.03
☐ 40 Buddy Black	.50	.25	.05
☐ 45 Steve Balboni	.50	.25	.05
☐ xx Discount card (unnumbered)	.35	.17	.03
☐ xx Checklist card (unnumbered)	.35	.17	.03

1984 Nestle Dream Team

The cards in this 22-card set measure 2 1/2" by 3 1/2". In conjunction with Topps, the Nestle Company issued this set entitled the Dream Team. The fronts have the Nestle trademark in the upper frameline, and the backs are identical to the Topps cards of this year except for the number and the Nestle's logo. Cards 1-11 feature stars of the American League while cards 12-22 show National League stars. Each league's "Dream Team" consists of eight position players and three pitchers. The cards were included with the Nestle chocolate bars as a pack of four (three player cards and a checklist header card. This set should not be confused with the Nestle 792-card (same player-number correspondence as 1984 Topps 792) set.

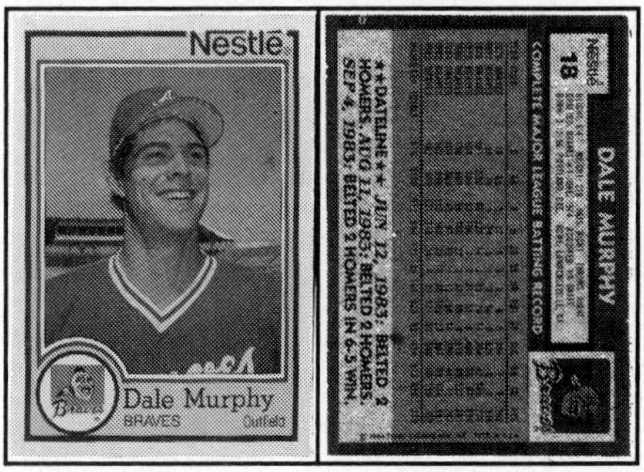

	MINT	EXC	G-VG
COMPLETE SET (22)	18.00	9.00	1.80
COMMON PLAYER (1-22)	.50	.25	.05
☐ 1 Eddie Murray	1.50	.75	.15
☐ 2 Lou Whitaker	.60	.30	.06
☐ 3 George Brett	2.50	1.25	.25
☐ 4 Cal Ripken	2.00	1.00	.20
☐ 5 Jim Rice	.75	.35	.07
☐ 6 Dave Winfield	1.00	.50	.10
☐ 7 Lloyd Moseby	.50	.25	.05
☐ 8 Lance Parrish	.60	.30	.06
☐ 9 LaMarr Hoyt	.50	.25	.05
☐ 10 Ron Guidry	.60	.30	.06
☐ 11 Dan Quisenberry	.60	.30	.06
☐ 12 Steve Garvey	1.25	.60	.12
☐ 13 Johnny Ray	.50	.25	.05
☐ 14 Mike Schmidt	4.00	2.00	.40
☐ 15 Ozzie Smith	1.00	.50	.10
☐ 16 Andre Dawson	1.00	.50	.10
☐ 17 Tim Raines	.80	.40	.08
☐ 18 Dale Murphy	2.00	1.00	.20
☐ 19 Tony Pena	.50	.25	.05
☐ 20 John Denny	.50	.25	.05
☐ 21 Steve Carlton	1.25	.60	.12
☐ 22 Al Holland	.50	.25	.05
☐ xx Checklist card (unnumbered)	.50	.25	.05

1984 Nestle 792

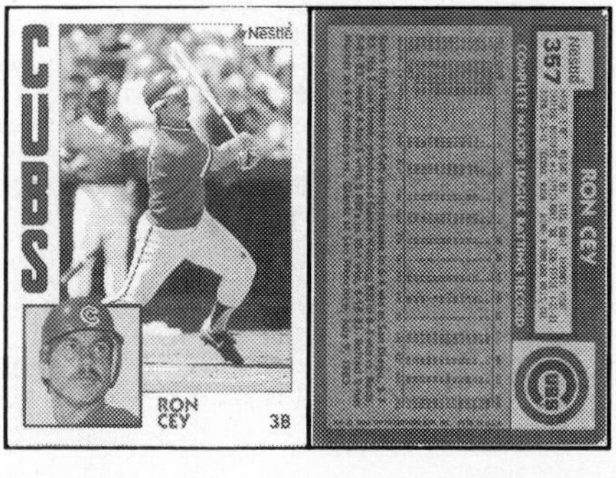

The cards in this 792-card set measure 2 1/2" by 3 1/2" and are extremely similar to the 1984 Topps regular issue (except for the Nestle logo instead of Topps logo on the front). In conjunction with Topps, the Nestle Company issued this set as six sheets available as a premium. The set was (as detailed on the back of the checklist card for the Nestle Dream Team cards) originally available from the Nestle Company in full sheets of 132 cards, 24" by 48", for 4.95 plus five Nestle candy wrappers per sheet. The backs are virtually identical to the Topps cards of this year, i.e., same player-number correspondence. These sheets have been cut up into individual cards and are available from a few dealers around the country. This is one of the few instances in this hobby where the complete uncut sheet is worth considerably less than the sum of the individual cards due to the expense required in having the sheet cut professionally (and precisely) into individual cards. Supposedly less than 5000 sets were printed. Since the checklist is exactly the same as that of the 1984 Topps, these Nestle cards are generally priced as a multiple of the corresponding Topps card. The list below shows only the two most expensive cards in the set. Cards not listed below are priced at five times the corresponding 1984 Topps price. Beware also on this set to look for fakes and forgeries. Cards billed as Nestle proofs in black and white are fakes. There are even a few counterfeits in color; the two cards listed below are the cards most likely to be reprinted illegally as they are the most valuable in the set.

	MINT	EXC	G-VG
COMPLETE CUT SET (792)	500.00	250.00	50.00
COMMON PLAYER (1-792)	.25	.12	.02
☐ 8 Don Mattingly	175.00	85.00	18.00
☐ 182 Darryl Strawberry	80.00	40.00	8.00

1987 Nestle Dream Team

This 33-card set is, in a sense, three sets: Golden Era (1-11 gold), AL Modern Era (12-22 red), and NL Modern Era (23-33 blue). Cards are 2 1/2" by 3 1/2" and have color coded borders by era. The first 11 card photos are in black and white. The Nestle set was apparently not licensed by Major League Baseball and hence the team logos are not shown in the photos. Six-packs of certain Nestle candy bars contained three cards; cards were also available through a send-in offer.

	MINT	EXC	G-VG
COMPLETE SET (33)	7.50	3.75	.75
COMMON PLAYER (1-33)	.15	.07	.01
☐ 1 Lou Gehrig	.75	.35	.07
☐ 2 Rogers Hornsby	.25	.12	.02
☐ 3 Pie Traynor	.15	.07	.01
☐ 4 Honus Wagner	.35	.17	.03
☐ 5 Babe Ruth	1.00	.50	.10
☐ 6 Tris Speaker	.25	.12	.02
☐ 7 Ty Cobb	.75	.35	.07
☐ 8 Mickey Cochrane	.25	.12	.02
☐ 9 Walter Johnson	.35	.17	.03
☐ 10 Carl Hubbell	.25	.12	.02
☐ 11 Jimmy Foxx	.25	.12	.02
☐ 12 Rod Carew	.35	.17	.03
☐ 13 Nellie Fox	.15	.07	.01
☐ 14 Brooks Robinson	.25	.12	.02
☐ 15 Luis Aparicio	.15	.07	.01
☐ 16 Frank Robinson	.25	.12	.02
☐ 17 Mickey Mantle	1.00	.50	.10
☐ 18 Ted Williams	.60	.30	.06
☐ 19 Yogi Berra	.40	.20	.04
☐ 20 Bob Feller	.35	.17	.03
☐ 21 Whitey Ford	.30	.15	.03
☐ 22 Harmon Killebrew	.25	.12	.02
☐ 23 Stan Musial	.40	.20	.04
☐ 24 Jackie Robinson	.50	.25	.05
☐ 25 Eddie Mathews	.25	.12	.02
☐ 26 Ernie Banks	.25	.12	.02
☐ 27 Roberto Clemente	.40	.20	.04
☐ 28 Willie Mays	.50	.25	.05
☐ 29 Hank Aaron	.50	.25	.05
☐ 30 Johnny Bench	.35	.17	.03
☐ 31 Bob Gibson	.25	.12	.02
☐ 32 Warren Spahn	.25	.12	.02
☐ 33 Duke Snider	.35	.17	.03

1988 Nestle

This 44-card set was produced for Nestle by Mike Schechter Associates and was printed in Canada. Cards are 2 1/2" by 3 1/2" and have yellow borders. The Nestle set was apparently not licensed by Major League Baseball and hence the team logos are not shown in the photos. The cards are numbered on the back. The backs are printed in red and blue on white card stock.

	MINT	EXC	G-VG
COMPLETE SET (44)	22.00	11.00	2.20
COMMON PLAYER (1-44)	.35	.17	.03
☐ 1 Roger Clemens	2.00	1.00	.20
☐ 2 Dale Murphy	1.00	.50	.10
☐ 3 Eric Davis	1.00	.50	.10
☐ 4 Gary Gaetti	.35	.17	.03
☐ 5 Ozzie Smith	.75	.35	.07
☐ 6 Mike Schmidt	2.00	1.00	.20
☐ 7 Ozzie Guillen	.50	.25	.05
☐ 8 John Franco	.35	.17	.03
☐ 9 Andre Dawson	.75	.35	.07
☐ 10 Mark McGwire	1.50	.75	.15
☐ 11 Bret Saberhagen	.75	.35	.07
☐ 12 Benny Santiago	.60	.30	.06
☐ 13 Jose Uribe	.35	.17	.03
☐ 14 Will Clark	2.00	1.00	.20
☐ 15 Don Mattingly	2.00	1.00	.20
☐ 16 Juan Samuel	.35	.17	.03
☐ 17 Jack Clark	.50	.25	.05
☐ 18 Darryl Strawberry	1.50	.75	.15
☐ 19 Bill Doran	.35	.17	.03
☐ 20 Pete Incaviglia	.50	.25	.05
☐ 21 Dwight Gooden	1.00	.50	.10
☐ 22 Willie Randolph	.35	.17	.03
☐ 23 Tim Wallach	.50	.25	.05
☐ 24 Pedro Guerrero	.50	.25	.05
☐ 25 Steve Bedrosian	.35	.17	.03
☐ 26 Gary Carter	.60	.30	.06
☐ 27 Jeff Reardon	.35	.17	.03
☐ 28 Dave Righetti	.50	.25	.05

☐ 29 Frank White	.35	.17	.03
☐ 30 Buddy Bell	.35	.17	.03
☐ 31 Tim Raines	.60	.30	.06
☐ 32 Wade Boggs	1.50	.75	.15
☐ 33 Dave Winfield	.60	.30	.06
☐ 34 George Bell	.60	.30	.06
☐ 35 Alan Trammell	.60	.30	.06
☐ 36 Joe Carter	.50	.25	.05
☐ 37 Jose Canseco	2.50	1.25	.25
☐ 38 Carlton Fisk	.75	.35	.07
☐ 39 Kirby Puckett	1.25	.60	.12
☐ 40 Tony Gwynn	.75	.35	.07
☐ 41 Matt Nokes	.35	.17	.03
☐ 42 Keith Hernandez	.50	.25	.05
☐ 43 Nolan Ryan	2.50	1.25	.25
☐ 44 Wally Joyner	.60	.30	.06

1954 N.Y. Journal American

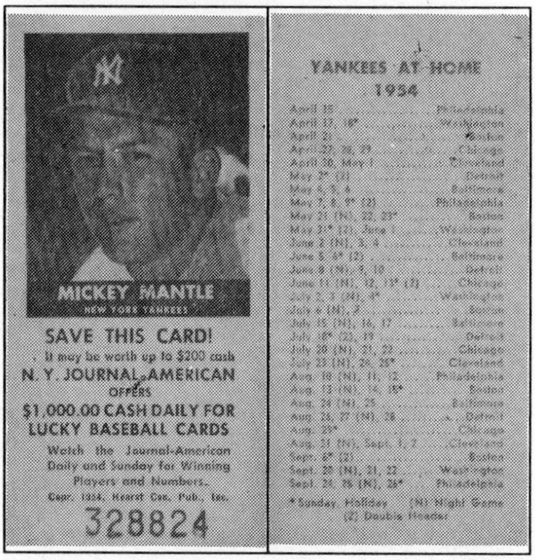

The cards in this 59-card set measure 2" by 4". The 1954 New York Journal American set contains black and white, unnumbered cards issued in conjunction with the newspaper. News stands were given boxes of cards to be distributed with purchases and each card had a serial number for redemption in the contest. The set spotlights New York teams only and carries game schedules on the reverse. The cards have been assigned numbers in the listing below alphabetically within team so that Brooklyn Dodgers are 1-19, New York Giants are 20-39, and New York Yankees are 40-59. There is speculation that a 20th Dodger card may exist. The catalog designation for this set is M127.

	NRMT	VG-E	GOOD
COMPLETE SET (59)	1750.00	375.00	75.00
COMMON PLAYER (1-59)	10.00	5.00	1.00
☐ 1 Joe Black	12.00	6.00	1.20
☐ 2 Roy Campanella	100.00	50.00	10.00
☐ 3 Billy Cox	10.00	5.00	1.00
☐ 4 Carl Erskine	14.00	7.00	1.40
☐ 5 Carl Furillo	17.00	8.50	1.70
☐ 6 Junior Gilliam	16.00	8.00	1.60
☐ 7 Gil Hodges	42.00	20.00	4.00
☐ 8 Jim Hughes	10.00	5.00	1.00
☐ 9 Clem Labine	10.00	5.00	1.00
☐ 10 Billy Loes	10.00	5.00	1.00
☐ 11 Russ Meyer	10.00	5.00	1.00
☐ 12 Don Newcombe	16.00	8.00	1.60
☐ 13 Ervin Palica	10.00	5.00	1.00
☐ 14 Pee Wee Reese	55.00	27.50	5.50
☐ 15 Jackie Robinson	125.00	60.00	12.50
☐ 16 Preacher Roe	16.00	8.00	1.60
☐ 17 George Shuba	10.00	5.00	1.00
☐ 18 Duke Snider	100.00	50.00	10.00
☐ 19 Dick Williams	12.00	6.00	1.20
☐ 20 John Antonelli	12.00	6.00	1.20
☐ 21 Alvin Dark	14.00	7.00	1.40
☐ 22 Marv Grissom	10.00	5.00	1.00
☐ 23 Ruben Gomez	10.00	5.00	1.00
☐ 24 Jim Hearn	10.00	5.00	1.00
☐ 25 Bobby Hofman	10.00	5.00	1.00
☐ 26 Monte Irvin	32.00	16.00	3.20
☐ 27 Larry Jansen	10.00	5.00	1.00
☐ 28 Ray Katt	10.00	5.00	1.00
☐ 29 Don Liddle	10.00	5.00	1.00
☐ 30 Whitey Lockman	10.00	5.00	1.00
☐ 31 Sal Maglie	16.00	8.00	1.60
☐ 32 Willie Mays	200.00	100.00	20.00
☐ 33 Don Mueller	12.00	6.00	1.20
☐ 34 Dusty Rhodes	12.00	6.00	1.20
☐ 35 Hank Thompson	12.00	6.00	1.20
☐ 36 Wes Westrum	10.00	5.00	1.00
☐ 37 Hoyt Wilhelm	35.00	17.50	3.50
☐ 38 Davey Williams	10.00	5.00	1.00
☐ 39 Al Worthington	10.00	5.00	1.00
☐ 40 Hank Bauer	16.00	8.00	1.60
☐ 41 Yogi Berra	100.00	50.00	10.00
☐ 42 Harry Byrd	10.00	5.00	1.00
☐ 43 Andy Carey	10.00	5.00	1.00
☐ 44 Jerry Coleman	10.00	5.00	1.00
☐ 45 Joe Collins	10.00	5.00	1.00
☐ 46 Whitey Ford	55.00	27.50	5.50
☐ 47 Steve Kraly	10.00	5.00	1.00
☐ 48 Bob Kuzava	10.00	5.00	1.00
☐ 49 Frank Leja	10.00	5.00	1.00
☐ 50 Ed Lopat	17.00	8.50	1.70
☐ 51 Mickey Mantle	400.00	200.00	40.00
☐ 52 Gil McDougald	16.00	8.00	1.60
☐ 53 Bill Miller	10.00	5.00	1.00
☐ 54 Tom Morgan	10.00	5.00	1.00
☐ 55 Irv Noren	10.00	5.00	1.00
☐ 56 Allie Reynolds	17.00	8.50	1.70
☐ 57 Phil Rizzuto	40.00	20.00	4.00
☐ 58 Eddie Robinson	10.00	5.00	1.00
☐ 59 Gene Woodling	12.00	6.00	1.20

1989 J.J. Nissen

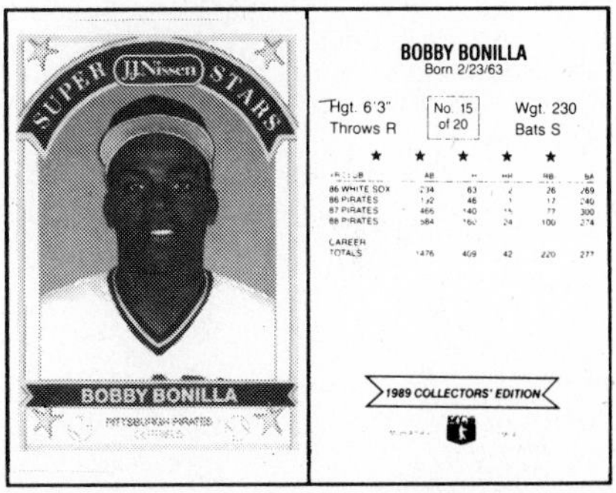

The 1989 J.J. Nissen set contains 20 standard-size (2 1/2" by 3 1/2") cards. The fronts have airbrushed facial photos with white and yellow borders and orange trim. The backs are white and feature career stats. The complete set price below does not include the error version of Mark Grace.

	MINT	EXC	G-VG
COMPLETE SET (20)	9.00	4.50	.90
COMMON PLAYER (1-20)	.30	.15	.03
☐ 1 Wally Joyner	.50	.25	.05
☐ 2 Wade Boggs	.90	.45	.09
☐ 3 Ellis Burks	.75	.35	.07
☐ 4 Don Mattingly	1.00	.50	.10
☐ 5 Jose Canseco	1.00	.50	.10
☐ 6 Mike Greenwell	.50	.25	.05
☐ 7 Eric Davis	.60	.30	.06
☐ 8 Kirby Puckett	.60	.30	.06
☐ 9 Kevin Seitzer	.40	.20	.04
☐ 10 Darryl Strawberry	.75	.35	.07
☐ 11 Gregg Jefferies	.75	.35	.07
☐ 12A Mark Grace ERR (photo actually Vance Law)	12.00	6.00	1.20
☐ 12B Mark Grace COR	1.00	.50	.10

□ 13 Matt Nokes	.30	.15	.03
□ 14 Mark McGwire	.75	.35	.07
□ 15 Bobby Bonilla	.50	.25	.05
□ 16 Roger Clemens	.90	.45	.09
□ 17 Frank Viola	.50	.25	.05
□ 18 Orel Hershiser	.50	.25	.05
□ 19 David Cone	.40	.20	.04
□ 20 Ted Williams	1.00	.50	.10

1960 Nu-Card Hi-Lites

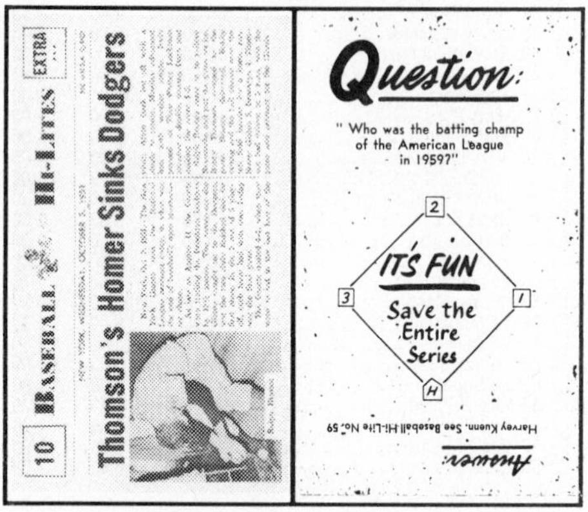

The cards in this 72-card set measure 3 1/4" by 5 3/8". In 1960, the Nu-Card Company introduced its Baseball Hi-Lites set of newspaper style cards. Each card singled out an individual baseball achievement with a picture and story. The reverses contain a baseball quiz. Cards 1-18 are more valuable if found printed totally in black on the front; these are copy-righted CVC as opposed to the NCI designation found on the red and black printed fronts.

	NRMT	VG-E	GOOD
COMPLETE SET (72)	225.00	110.00	22.00
COMMON PLAYER (1-72)	2.00	1.00	.20
□ 1 Babe Hits 3 Homers In A Series Game	10.00	5.00	1.00
□ 2 Podres Pitching Wins Series	2.00	1.00	.20
□ 3 Bevans Pitches No Hitter, Almost	2.00	1.00	.20
□ 4 Box Score Devised By Reporter	2.00	1.00	.20
□ 5 VanderMeer Pitches Two No Hitters	2.00	1.00	.20
□ 6 Indians Take Bums	2.00	1.00	.20
□ 7 DiMag Comes Thru	10.00	5.00	1.00
□ 8 Mathewson Pitches Three WS Shutouts	2.50	1.25	.25
□ 9 Haddix Pitches 12 Perfect Innings	2.00	1.00	.20
□ 10 Thomson's Homer Sinks Dodgers	2.50	1.25	.25
□ 11 Hubbell Strikes Out Five A.L. Stars	2.00	1.00	.20
□ 12 Pickoff Ends Series	2.00	1.00	.20
□ 13 Cards Take Series From Yanks	2.00	1.00	.20
□ 14 Dizzy And Daffy Dean Win Series	3.00	1.50	.30
□ 15 Owen Drops 3rd Strike	2.00	1.00	.20
□ 16 Ruth Calls Shot	10.00	5.00	1.00
□ 17 Merkle Pulls Boner	2.00	1.00	.20
□ 18 Larsen Hurls Perfect World Series Game	2.50	1.25	.25
□ 19 Bean Ball Ends Career of Mickey Cochrane	2.00	1.00	.20
□ 20 Banks Belts 47 Homers Earns MVP	3.50	1.75	.35
□ 21 Stan Musial Hits Five Homers in One Day	5.00	2.50	.50
□ 22 Mickey Mantle Hits Longest Homer	12.00	6.00	1.20
□ 23 Sievers Captures Home Run Title	2.00	1.00	.20
□ 24 Gehrig 2130 Consecutive Game Record Ends	6.00	3.00	.60
□ 25 Red Schoendienst Key Player Braves Pennant	2.50	1.25	.25
□ 26 Midget Pinch-Hits For St. Louis	2.50	1.25	.25
□ 27 Willie Mays Makes Greatest Catch	6.00	3.00	.60
□ 28 Homer by Yogi Berra Puts Yanks In 1st	4.00	2.00	.40
□ 29 Campy NL MVP	4.00	2.00	.40
□ 30 Bob Turley Hurls Yankees To WS Champions	2.00	1.00	.20
□ 31 Dodgers Take Series From Sox in Six	2.00	1.00	.20
□ 32 Furillo Hero as Dodgers Beat Chicago in 3rd WS Game	2.00	1.00	.20
□ 33 Adcock Gets 4 Homers And A Double	2.00	1.00	.20
□ 34 Dickey Chosen All-Star Catcher	2.00	1.00	.20
□ 35 Burdette Beats Yanks In Three WS Games	2.00	1.00	.20
□ 36 Umpires Clear White Sox Bench	2.00	1.00	.20
□ 37 Reese Honored As Greatest Dodger SS	3.00	1.50	.30
□ 38 Joe DiMaggio Hits In 56 Straight	10.00	5.00	1.00
□ 39 Ted Williams Hits .406 For Season	6.00	3.00	.60
□ 40 Walter Johnson Pitches 56 Straight	2.50	1.25	.25
□ 41 Hodges Hits 4 Home Runs In Nite Game	2.50	1.25	.25
□ 42 Greenberg Returns to Tigers From Army	2.50	1.25	.25
□ 43 Ty Cobb Named Best Player Of All Time	8.00	4.00	.80
□ 44 Robin Roberts Wins 28 Games	2.50	1.25	.25
□ 45 Rizzuto's Two Runs Save 1st Place	2.00	1.00	.20
□ 46 Tigers Beat Out Senators For Pennant	2.00	1.00	.20
□ 47 Babe Ruth Hits 60th Home Run	10.00	5.00	1.00
□ 48 Cy Young Honored	2.50	1.25	.25
□ 49 Killebrew Starts Spring Training	3.50	1.75	.35
□ 50 Mantle Hits Longest Homer at Stadium	12.00	6.00	1.20
□ 51 Braves Take Pennant	2.00	1.00	.20
□ 52 Ted Williams Hero Of All-Star Game	6.00	3.00	.60
□ 53 Robinson Saves Dodgers For Play-off Series	5.00	2.50	.50
□ 54 Snodgrass Muffs Fly	2.00	1.00	.20
□ 55 Snider Belts 2 Homers Ties Homer Record	3.50	1.75	.35
□ 56 Giants Win 26 Straight	2.00	1.00	.20
□ 57 Ted Kluszewski Stars In 1st Series Win	2.50	1.25	.25
□ 58 Ott Walks 5 Times In Single Game	2.00	1.00	.20
□ 59 Harvey Kuenn Takes A.L. Batting Title	2.00	1.00	.20
□ 60 Bob Feller Hurls 3rd No-Hitter of Career	3.50	1.75	.35
□ 61 Yanks Champs Again	2.00	1.00	.20
□ 62 Aaron's Bat Beats Yankees In Series	6.00	3.00	.60
□ 63 Warren Spahn Beats Yanks in W.S.	3.00	1.50	.30
□ 64 Ump's Wrong Call Helps Dodgers Beat Yanks	2.00	1.00	.20
□ 65 Kaline Hits 3 Homers Two In Same Inning	3.50	1.75	.35
□ 66 Bob Allison Named AL Rookie of the Year	2.00	1.00	.20
□ 67 McCovey Blasts Way Into Giant Lineup	3.50	1.75	.35
□ 68 Colavito Hits Four Homers in One Game	2.50	1.25	.25

☐ 69 Erskine Sets Strike Out Record in World Series	2.00	1.00	.20
☐ 70 Sal Maglie Pitches No-Hit Game	2.00	1.00	.20
☐ 71 Early Wynn Victory Crushes Yanks	2.50	1.25	.25
☐ 72 Nellie Fox AL MVP	2.50	1.25	.25

1961 Nu-Card Scoops

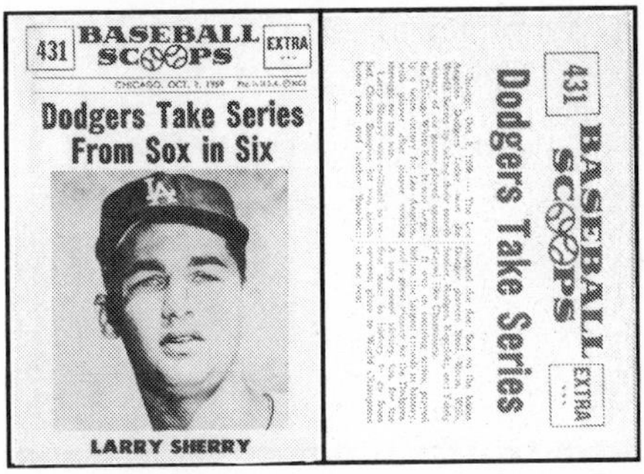

The cards in this 80-card set measure 2 1/2" by 3 1/2". This series depicts great moments in the history of individual ballplayers. Each card is designed as a miniature newspaper front-page, complete with data and picture. Both the number (401-480) and title are printed in red on the obverse, and the story is found on the back. An album was issued to hold the set. The set has been illegally reprinted, which has served to suppress the demand for the originals as well as the reprints.

	NRMT	VG-E	GOOD
COMPLETE SET (80)	110.00	55.00	11.00
COMMON PLAYER (401-480)	.75	.35	.07
☐ 401 Jim Gentile	.75	.35	.07
☐ 402 Warren Spahn (No-hitter)	3.00	1.50	.30
☐ 403 Bill Mazeroski	1.00	.50	.10
☐ 404 Willie Mays: (three triples)	6.00	3.00	.60
☐ 405 Woodie Held	.75	.35	.07
☐ 406 Vern Law	1.00	.50	.10
☐ 407 Pete Runnels	.75	.35	.07
☐ 408 Lew Burdette (No-hitter)	1.00	.50	.10
☐ 409 Dick Stuart	.75	.35	.07
☐ 410 Don Cardwell	.75	.35	.07
☐ 411 Camilo Pascual	.75	.35	.07
☐ 412 Ed Mathews	3.00	1.50	.30
☐ 413 Dick Groat	1.00	.50	.10
☐ 414 Gene Autry	2.00	1.00	.20
☐ 415 Bobby Richardson	1.50	.75	.15
☐ 416 Roger Maris	6.00	3.00	.60
☐ 417 Fred Merkle	.75	.35	.07
☐ 418 Don Larsen	1.00	.50	.10
☐ 419 Mickey Cochrane	1.05		
☐ 420 Ernie Banks	3.00	1.50	.30
☐ 421 Stan Musial	5.00	2.50	.50
☐ 422 Mickey Mantle (longest homer)	12.00	6.00	1.20
☐ 423 Roy Sievers	.75	.35	.07
☐ 424 Lou Gehrig	6.00	3.00	.60
☐ 425 Red Schoendienst	2.00	1.00	.20
☐ 426 Eddie Gaedel	1.50	.75	.15
☐ 427 Willie Mays (greatest catch)	6.00	3.00	.60
☐ 428 Jackie Robinson	5.00	2.50	.50
☐ 429 Roy Campanella	5.00	2.50	.50
☐ 430 Bob Turley	.75	.35	.07
☐ 431 Larry Sherry	.75	.35	.07
☐ 432 Carl Furillo	1.00	.50	.10
☐ 433 Joe Adcock	.75	.35	.07
☐ 434 Bill Dickey	1.00	.50	.10
☐ 435 Burdette 3 wins	.75	.35	.07
☐ 436 Umpire Clears Bench	.75	.35	.07
☐ 437 Pee Wee Reese	3.00	1.50	.30
☐ 438 Joe DiMaggio (56 Game Hit Streak)	9.00	4.50	.90
☐ 439 Ted Williams Hits .406	6.00	3.00	.60
☐ 440 Walter Johnson	3.00	1.50	.30
☐ 441 Gil Hodges	2.00	1.00	.20
☐ 442 Hank Greenberg	1.50	.75	.15
☐ 443 Ty Cobb	7.50	3.75	.75
☐ 444 Robin Roberts	2.50	1.25	.25
☐ 445 Phil Rizzuto	2.00	1.00	.20
☐ 446 Hal Newhouser	1.00	.50	.10
☐ 447 Babe Ruth 60th Homer	10.00	5.00	1.00
☐ 448 Cy Young	2.50	1.25	.25
☐ 449 Harmon Killebrew	3.00	1.50	.30
☐ 450 Mickey Mantle (longest homer)	10.00	5.00	1.00
☐ 451 Braves Take Pennant	.75	.35	.07
☐ 452 Ted Williams (All-Star Hero)	6.00	3.00	.60
☐ 453 Yogi Berra	5.00	2.50	.50
☐ 454 Fred Snodgrass	.75	.35	.07
☐ 455 Ruth 3 Homers	10.00	5.00	1.00
☐ 456 Giants 26 Game Streak	.75	.35	.07
☐ 457 Ted Kluszewski	1.25	.60	.12
☐ 458 Mel Ott	1.50	.75	.15
☐ 459 Harvey Kuenn	1.00	.50	.10
☐ 460 Bob Feller	3.50	1.75	.35
☐ 461 Casey Stengel	2.50	1.25	.25
☐ 462 Hank Aaron	6.00	3.00	.60
☐ 463 Spahn Beats Yanks	2.00	1.00	.20
☐ 464 Ump's Wrong Call	.75	.35	.07
☐ 465 Al Kaline	3.50	1.75	.35
☐ 466 Bob Allison	.75	.35	.07
☐ 467 Joe DiMaggio (Four Homers)	9.00	4.50	.90
☐ 468 Rocky Colavito	1.25	.60	.12
☐ 469 Carl Erskine	1.00	.50	.10
☐ 470 Sal Maglie	1.00	.50	.10
☐ 471 Early Wynn	2.00	1.00	.20
☐ 472 Nellie Fox	1.50	.75	.15
☐ 473 Marty Marion	1.00	.50	.10
☐ 474 Johnny Podres	.75	.35	.07
☐ 475 Mickey Owen	.75	.35	.07
☐ 476 Dean Brothers (Dizzy and Daffy)	2.50	1.25	.25
☐ 477 Christy Mathewson	2.50	1.25	.25
☐ 478 Harvey Haddix	.75	.35	.07
☐ 479 Carl Hubbell	1.00	.50	.10
☐ 480 Bobby Thomson	1.00	.50	.10

1952 Num Num

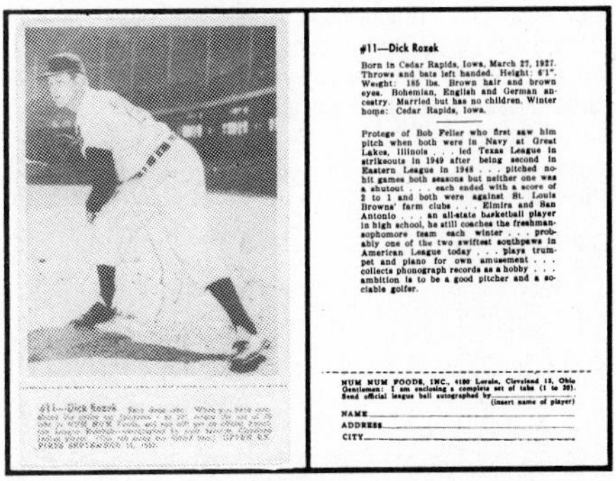

The cards in this 20-card set measure approximately 3 1/2" by 4 1/2". The 1952 Num Num Potato Chips issue features black and white, numbered cards of the Cleveland Indians. Cards came with and without coupons (tabs). The cards were issued without coupons directly by the Cleveland baseball club. When the complete set was obtained the tabs were cut off and exchanged for an autographed baseball. Card Number 16, Kennedy, is rather scarce. Cards with the tabs still intact are worth approximately 25 percent more than the values listed below. The catalog designation for this set is F337-2.

	NRMT	VG-E	GOOD
COMPLETE SET (20)	800.00	400.00	80.00
COMMON PLAYER (1-20)	20.00	10.00	2.00
☐ 1 Lou Brissie	20.00	10.00	2.00
☐ 2 Jim Hegan	20.00	10.00	2.00
☐ 3 Birdie Tebbetts	20.00	10.00	2.00
☐ 4 Bob Lemon	60.00	30.00	6.00
☐ 5 Bob Feller	100.00	50.00	10.00
☐ 6 Early Wynn	60.00	30.00	6.00
☐ 7 Mike Garcia	25.00	12.50	2.50
☐ 8 Steve Gromek	20.00	10.00	2.00
☐ 9 Bob Chakales	20.00	10.00	2.00
☐ 10 Al Rosen	40.00	20.00	4.00
☐ 11 Dick Rozek	20.00	10.00	2.00
☐ 12 Luke Easter	20.00	10.00	2.00
☐ 13 Ray Boone	20.00	10.00	2.00
☐ 14 Bobby Avila	20.00	10.00	2.00
☐ 15 Dale Mitchell	20.00	10.00	2.00
☐ 16 Bob Kennedy	400.00	200.00	40.00
☐ 17 Harry Simpson	20.00	10.00	2.00
☐ 18 Larry Doby	40.00	20.00	4.00
☐ 19 Sam Jones	25.00	12.50	2.50
☐ 20 Al Lopez MG	60.00	30.00	6.00

1986 Oh Henry Indians

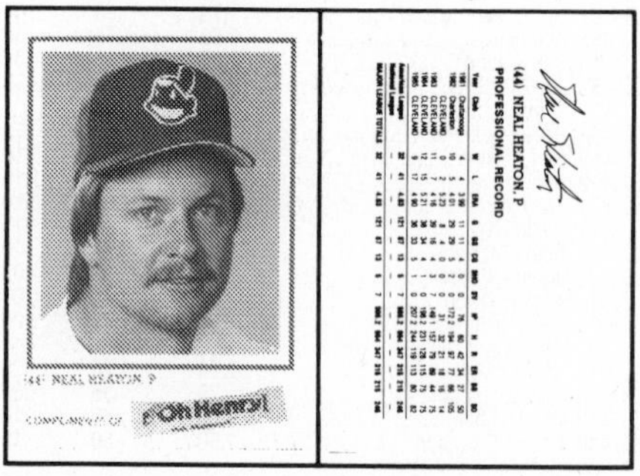

This 30-card set features Cleveland Indians and was distributed at the stadium to fans in attendance on Baseball Card Day. The cards were printed in one folded sheet which was perforated for easy separation into individual cards. The cards have white borders with a blue frame around each photo. The card backs include detailed career year-by-year statistics. The individual cards measure 2 1/4" by 3 1/8" and have full-color fronts.

	MINT	EXC	G-VG
COMPLETE SET (30)	12.50	6.25	1.25
COMMON PLAYER	.35	.17	.03
☐ 2 Brett Butler	.75	.35	.07
☐ 4 Tony Bernazard	.50	.25	.05
☐ 6 Andy Allanson	.35	.17	.03
☐ 7 Pat Corrales MG	.35	.17	.03
☐ 8 Carmen Castillo	.35	.17	.03
☐ 10 Pat Tabler	.60	.30	.06
☐ 13 Ernie Camacho	.50	.25	.05
☐ 14 Julio Franco	1.25	.60	.12
☐ 15 Dan Rohn	.35	.17	.03
☐ 18 Ken Schrom	.35	.17	.03
☐ 20 Otis Nixon	.35	.17	.03
☐ 22 Fran Mullins	.35	.17	.03
☐ 23 Chris Bando	.35	.17	.03
☐ 24 Ed Williams	.35	.17	.03
☐ 26 Brook Jacoby	.75	.35	.07
☐ 27 Mel Hall	.60	.30	.06
☐ 29 Andre Thornton	.75	.35	.07
☐ 30 Joe Carter	1.50	.75	.15
☐ 35 Phil Niekro	1.50	.75	.15
☐ 36 Jamie Easterly	.35	.17	.03
☐ 37 Don Schulze	.35	.17	.03
☐ 42 Rick Yett	.35	.17	.03
☐ 43 Scott Bailes	.35	.17	.03
☐ 44 Neal Heaton	.35	.17	.03
☐ 46 Jim Kern	.35	.17	.03
☐ 48 Dickie Noles	.35	.17	.03
☐ 49 Tom Candiotti	.50	.25	.05
☐ 53 Reggie Ritter	.35	.17	.03
☐ 54 Tom Waddell	.35	.17	.03
☐ xx Coaching Staff Jack Aker Bobby Bonds Doc Edwards John Goryl	.35	.17	.03

1980-83 Pacific Legends

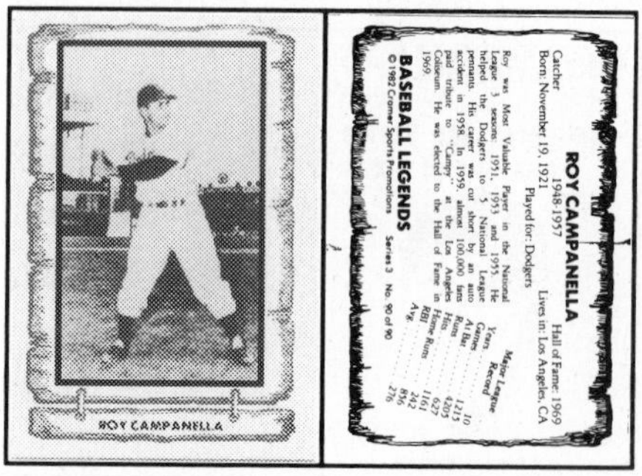

This 124-card set is actually four 30-card subsets plus a four-card wax box bottom panel. The set was distributed by series over several years beginning in 1980 with the first 30 cards. The set was produced by Pacific Trading Cards and is frequently referred to as Cramer Legends, for the founder of Pacific Trading cards, Mike Cramer. Cards are standard size, 2 1/2" by 3 1/2" and are golden-toned. Even though the wax box cards are numbered from 121-124 and called "series 5," the set is considered complete without them.

	MINT	EXC	G-VG
COMPLETE SET (120)	13.50	6.00	1.00
COMMON PLAYER (1-120)	.10	.05	.01
COMMON PLAYER (121-124)	.25	.12	.02
☐ 1 Babe Ruth	1.25	.60	.12
☐ 2 Heinie Manush	.10	.05	.01
☐ 3 Rabbit Maranville	.10	.05	.01
☐ 4 Earl Averill	.10	.05	.01
☐ 5 Joe DiMaggio	.75	.35	.07
☐ 6 Mickey Mantle	1.00	.50	.10
☐ 7 Hank Aaron	.40	.20	.04
☐ 8 Stan Musial	.30	.15	.03
☐ 9 Bill Terry	.10	.05	.01
☐ 10 Sandy Koufax	.30	.15	.03
☐ 11 Ernie Lombardi	.10	.05	.01
☐ 12 Dizzy Dean	.20	.10	.02
☐ 13 Lou Gehrig	.60	.30	.06
☐ 14 Walter Alston	.10	.05	.01
☐ 15 Jackie Robinson	.30	.15	.03
☐ 16 Jimmie Foxx	.10	.05	.01
☐ 17 Billy Southworth	.10	.05	.01
☐ 18 Honus Wagner	.25	.12	.02
☐ 19 Duke Snider	.25	.12	.02
☐ 20 Rogers Hornsby	.20	.10	.02
☐ 21 Paul Waner	.10	.05	.01
☐ 22 Luke Appling	.10	.05	.01
☐ 23 Billy Herman	.10	.05	.01
☐ 24 Lloyd Waner	.10	.05	.01
☐ 25 Fred Hutchinson	.10	.05	.01
☐ 26 Eddie Collins	.10	.05	.01
☐ 27 Lefty Grove	.20	.10	.02
☐ 28 Chuck Connors	.20	.10	.02
☐ 29 Lefty O'Doul	.10	.05	.01
☐ 30 Hank Greenberg	.20	.10	.02
☐ 31 Ty Cobb	.60	.30	.06
☐ 32 Enos Slaughter	.10	.05	.01
☐ 33 Ernie Banks	.25	.12	.02
☐ 34 Christy Mathewson	.20	.10	.02
☐ 35 Mel Ott	.10	.05	.01
☐ 36 Pie Traynor	.10	.05	.01
☐ 37 Clark Griffith	.10	.05	.01
☐ 38 Mickey Cochrane	.10	.05	.01

☐ 39 Joe Cronin	.10	.05	.01
☐ 40 Leo Durocher	.10	.05	.01
☐ 41 Home Run Baker	.10	.05	.01
☐ 42 Joe Tinker	.10	.05	.01
☐ 43 John McGraw	.10	.05	.01
☐ 44 Bill Dickey	.10	.05	.01
☐ 45 Walter Johnson	.20	.10	.02
☐ 46 Frankie Frisch	.10	.05	.01
☐ 47 Casey Stengel	.20	.10	.02
☐ 48 Willie Mays	.40	.20	.04
☐ 49 Johnny Mize	.10	.05	.01
☐ 50 Roberto Clemente	.30	.15	.03
☐ 51 Burleigh Grimes	.10	.05	.01
☐ 52 Pee Wee Reese	.20	.10	.02
☐ 53 Bob Feller	.20	.10	.02
☐ 54 Brooks Robinson	.20	.10	.02
☐ 55 Sam Crawford	.10	.05	.01
☐ 56 Robin Roberts	.15	.07	.01
☐ 57 Warren Spahn	.20	.10	.02
☐ 58 Joe McCarthy	.10	.05	.01
☐ 59 Jocko Conlan	.10	.05	.01
☐ 60 Satchel Paige	.25	.12	.02
☐ 61 Ted Williams	.30	.15	.03
☐ 62 George Kelly	.10	.05	.01
☐ 63 Gil Hodges	.10	.05	.01
☐ 64 Jim Bottomley	.10	.05	.01
☐ 65 Al Kaline	.20	.10	.02
☐ 66 Harvey Kuenn	.10	.05	.01
☐ 67 Yogi Berra	.25	.12	.02
☐ 68 Nellie Fox	.10	.05	.01
☐ 69 Harmon Killebrew	.15	.07	.01
☐ 70 Ed Roush	.10	.05	.01
☐ 71 Mordecai Brown	.10	.05	.01
☐ 72 Gabby Hartnett	.10	.05	.01
☐ 73 Early Wynn	.10	.05	.01
☐ 74 Nap Lajoie	.10	.05	.01
☐ 75 Charlie Grimm	.10	.05	.01
☐ 76 Joe Garagiola	.20	.10	.02
☐ 77 Ted Lyons	.10	.05	.01
☐ 78 Mickey Vernon	.10	.05	.01
☐ 79 Lou Boudreau	.10	.05	.01
☐ 80 Al Dark	.10	.05	.01
☐ 81 Ralph Kiner	.15	.07	.01
☐ 82 Phil Rizzuto	.15	.07	.01
☐ 83 Stan Hack	.10	.05	.01
☐ 84 Frank Chance	.10	.05	.01
☐ 85 Ray Schalk	.10	.05	.01
☐ 86 Bill McKechnie	.10	.05	.01
☐ 87 Travis Jackson	.10	.05	.01
☐ 88 Pete Reiser	.10	.05	.01
☐ 89 Carl Hubbell	.10	.05	.01
☐ 90 Roy Campanella	.25	.12	.02
☐ 91 Cy Young	.10	.05	.01
☐ 92 Kiki Cuyler	.10	.05	.01
☐ 93 Chief Bender	.10	.05	.01
☐ 94 Richie Ashburn	.20	.10	.02
☐ 95 Riggs Stephenson	.10	.05	.01
☐ 96 Minnie Minoso	.10	.05	.01
☐ 97 Hack Wilson	.10	.05	.01
☐ 98 Al Lopez	.10	.05	.01
☐ 99 Willie Keeler	.10	.05	.01
☐ 100 Fred Lindstrom	.10	.05	.01
☐ 101 Roger Maris	.25	.12	.02
☐ 102 Roger Bresnahan	.10	.05	.01
☐ 103 Monty Stratton	.10	.05	.01
☐ 104 Goose Goslin	.10	.05	.01
☐ 105 Earl Combs	.10	.05	.01
☐ 106 Pepper Martin	.10	.05	.01
☐ 107 Joe Jackson	.50	.25	.05
☐ 108 George Sisler	.10	.05	.01
☐ 109 Red Ruffing	.10	.05	.01
☐ 110 Johnny Vander Meer	.10	.05	.01
☐ 111 Herb Pennock	.10	.05	.01
☐ 112 Chuck Klein	.10	.05	.01
☐ 113 Paul Derringer	.10	.05	.01
☐ 114 Addie Joss	.10	.05	.01
☐ 115 Bobby Thomson	.10	.05	.01
☐ 116 Chick Hafey	.10	.05	.01
☐ 117 Lefty Gomez	.15	.07	.01
☐ 118 George Kell	.10	.05	.01
☐ 119 Al Simmons	.10	.05	.01
☐ 120 Bob Lemon	.10	.05	.01
☐ 121 Hoyt Wilhelm (wax box card)	.30	.15	.03
☐ 122 Arky Vaughan (wax box card)	.25	.12	.02
☐ 123 Frank Robinson (wax box card)	.35	.17	.03
☐ 124 Grover Alexander (wax box card)	.25	.12	.02

1988 Pacific Eight Men Out

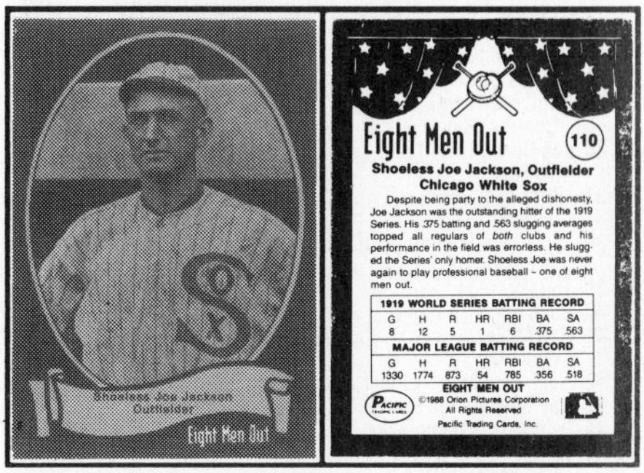

This set was produced by Mike Cramer's Pacific Trading Cards of Edmonds, Washington. The set was released in conjunction with the popular movie of the same name, which told the story of the "fix" of the 1919 World Series between the Cincinnati Reds and the Chicago "Black" Sox. The cards are standard size, 2 1/2" by 3 1/2" and have a raspberry-colored border on the card fronts as well as raspberry-colored print on the white card stock backs. The cards were available either as wax packs or as collated sets. Generally the cards relating to the movie (showing actors) are in full-color whereas the vintage photography showing the actual players involved is in a sepia tone.

	MINT	EXC	G-VG
COMPLETE SET (110)	10.00	5.00	1.00
COMMON PLAYER (1-110)	.10	.05	.01
☐ 1 We're Going To See The Sox	.10	.05	.01
☐ 2 White Sox Win The Pennant	.10	.05	.01
☐ 3 The Series	.10	.05	.01
☐ 4 1919 Chicago White Sox	.10	.05	.01
☐ 5 The Black Sox Scandal	.10	.05	.01
☐ 6 Eddie Cicotte 29-7 in 1919	.15	.07	.01
☐ 7 "Buck's Their Favorite"	.10	.05	.01
☐ 8 Eddie Collins	.20	.10	.02
☐ 9 Michael Rooker as Chick Gandil	.10	.05	.01
☐ 10 Charlie Sheen as Hap Felsch	.25	.12	.02
☐ 11 James Read as Lefty Williams	.10	.05	.01
☐ 12 John Cusak as Buck Weaver	.10	.05	.01
☐ 13 D.B. Sweeney as Joe Jackson	.15	.07	.01
☐ 14 David Strathairn as Eddie Cicotte	.10	.05	.01
☐ 15 Perry Lang as Fred McMullin	.10	.05	.01
☐ 16 Don Harvey as Swede Risberg	.10	.05	.01
☐ 17 The Gambler Burns And Maharg	.10	.05	.01
☐ 18 "Sleepy"Bill Burns	.10	.05	.01
☐ 19 The Key is Cicotte	.10	.05	.01
☐ 20 C'moan Betsy	.10	.05	.01
☐ 21 The Fix	.10	.05	.01
☐ 22 Chick Approaches Cicotte	.10	.05	.01
☐ 23 Kid Gleason	.10	.05	.01
☐ 24 Charles Comiskey Owner	.10	.05	.01
☐ 25 Chick Gandil 1st Baseman	.15	.07	.01
☐ 26 Swede Risberg	.10	.05	.01
☐ 27 Sport Sullivan	.10	.05	.01
☐ 28 Abe Attell And Arnold Rothstein	.10	.05	.01
☐ 29 Hugh Fullerton Sportswriter	.10	.05	.01

☐ 30 Ring Lardner Sportswriter	.10	.05	.01
☐ 31 "Shoeless"Joe His Batting Eye	.20	.10	.02
☐ 32 "Shoeless Joe"	.25	.12	.02
☐ 33 Buck Can't Sleep	.10	.05	.01
☐ 34 George"Buck" Weaver	.10	.05	.01
☐ 35 Hugh and Ring Confront Kid	.10	.05	.01
☐ 36 Joe Doesn't Want To Play	.10	.05	.01
☐ 37 "Shoeless" Joe Jackson	.25	.12	.02
☐ 38 "Sore Arm, Cicotte," "Old Man Cicotte"	.10	.05	.01
☐ 39 The Fix Is On	.10	.05	.01
☐ 40 Buck Plays To Win	.10	.05	.01
☐ 41 Hap Makes A Great Catch	.10	.05	.01
☐ 42 Hugh and Ring Suspect	.10	.05	.01
☐ 43 Ray Gets Things Going	.10	.05	.01
☐ 44 Lefty Loses Game Two	.10	.05	.01
☐ 45 Lefty Crosses Up Catcher Ray Schalk	.10	.05	.01
☐ 46 Chick's RBI Wins Game Three	.10	.05	.01
☐ 47 Dickie Kerr Wins Game Three	.10	.05	.01
☐ 48 Chick Leaves Buck At Third	.10	.05	.01
☐ 49 Williams Loses Game Five	.10	.05	.01
☐ 50 Ray Schalk	.10	.05	.01
☐ 51 Schalk Blocks The Plate	.10	.05	.01
☐ 52 Schalk Is Thrown Out	.10	.05	.01
☐ 53 Chicago Stickball Game	.10	.05	.01
☐ 54 I'm Forever Blowing Ball Games	.10	.05	.01
☐ 55 Felsch Scores Jackson	.20	.10	.02
☐ 56 Kerr Wins Game Six	.10	.05	.01
☐ 57 Where's The Money	.10	.05	.01
☐ 58 Cicotte Wins Game Seven	.10	.05	.01
☐ 59 Kid Watches Eddie	.10	.05	.01
☐ 60 Lefty Is Threatened	.10	.05	.01
☐ 61 James, Get Your Arm Ready, Fast	.10	.05	.01
☐ 62 Shoeless Joe's Home Run	.20	.10	.02
☐ 63 Buck Played His Best	.10	.05	.01
☐ 64 Hugh Exposes The Fix	.10	.05	.01
☐ 65 "Sign The Petition"	.10	.05	.01
☐ 66 Baseball Owners Hire A Commissioner	.10	.05	.01
☐ 67 Judge Kenesaw Mountain Landis	.10	.05	.01
☐ 68 Grand Jury Summoned	.10	.05	.01
☐ 69 "Say It Ain't So, Joe"	.15	.07	.01
☐ 70 The Swede's A Hard Guy	.10	.05	.01
☐ 71 Buck Loves The Game	.10	.05	.01
☐ 72 The Trial	.10	.05	.01
☐ 73 Kid Gleason Takes The Stand	.10	.05	.01
☐ 74 The Verdict	.10	.05	.01
☐ 75 Eight Men Out	.10	.05	.01
☐ 76 Oscar"Happy" Felsch	.20	.10	.02
☐ 77 Who's Joe Jackson	.20	.10	.02
☐ 78 Ban Johnson	.10	.05	.01
☐ 79 Judge Landis	.10	.05	.01
☐ 80 Charles Comiskey	.10	.05	.01
☐ 81 Heinie Groth	.10	.05	.01
☐ 82 Slim Sallee	.10	.05	.01
☐ 83 Dutch Ruether	.10	.05	.01
☐ 84 Edd Roush	.25	.12	.02
☐ 85 Morrie Rath	.10	.05	.01
☐ 86 Bill Rariden	.10	.05	.01
☐ 87 Jimmy Ring	.10	.05	.01
☐ 88 Greasy Neale	.10	.05	.01
☐ 89 Pat Moran	.10	.05	.01
☐ 90 Adolfo Luque	.10	.05	.01
☐ 91 Larry Kopf	.10	.05	.01
☐ 92 Ray Fisher	.10	.05	.01
☐ 93 Hod Eller	.10	.05	.01
☐ 94 Pat Duncan	.10	.05	.01
☐ 95 Jake Daubert	.10	.05	.01
☐ 96 Red Faber	.20	.10	.02
☐ 97 Dickie Kerr	.10	.05	.01
☐ 98 Shano Collins	.10	.05	.01
☐ 99 Eddie Collins	.20	.10	.02
☐ 100 Ray Schalk	.20	.10	.02
☐ 101 Nemo Leibold	.10	.05	.01
☐ 102 Kid Gleason	.10	.05	.01
☐ 103 Swede Risberg	.15	.07	.01
☐ 104 Eddie Cicotte	.15	.07	.01
☐ 105 Fred McMullin	.10	.05	.01
☐ 106 Chick Gandil	.15	.07	.01
☐ 107 Buck Weaver	.15	.07	.01
☐ 108 Lefty Williams	.15	.07	.01
☐ 109 Happy Felsch	.15	.07	.01
☐ 110 Joe Jackson	.50	.25	.05

1988 Pacific Legends

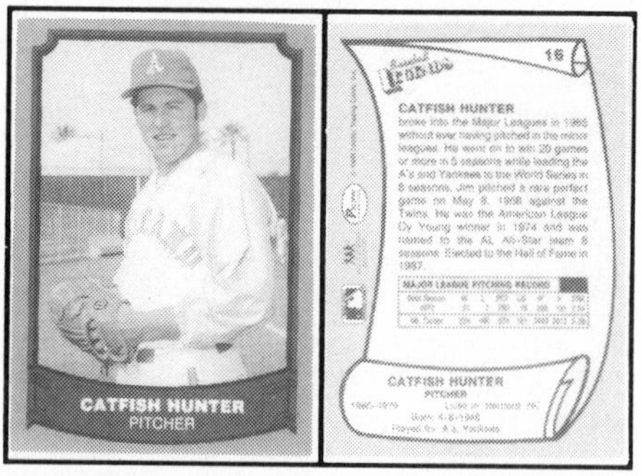

This attractive set of 110 full-color cards was produced by Mike Cramer's Pacific Trading Cards of Edmonds, Washington. The cards are silver bordered and are standard size, 2 1/2" by 3 1/2". Card backs are printed in yellow, black, and gray on white card stock. The cards were available either as wax packs or as collated sets. The players pictured in the set had retired many years before, but most are still well remembered. The statistics on the card backs give the player's career and "best season" statistics. The set was licensed by Major League Baseball Players Alumni.

	MINT	EXC	G-VG
COMPLETE SET (110)	10.00	5.00	1.00
COMMON PLAYER (1-110)	.05	.02	.00
☐ 1 Hank Aaron	.75	.35	.07
☐ 2 Red Schoendienst	.25	.12	.02
☐ 3 Brooks Robinson	.30	.15	.03
☐ 4 Luke Appling	.20	.10	.02
☐ 5 Gene Woodling	.05	.02	.00
☐ 6 Stan Musial	.60	.30	.06
☐ 7 Mickey Mantle	1.00	.50	.10
☐ 8 Richie Ashburn	.20	.10	.02
☐ 9 Ralph Kiner	.25	.12	.02
☐ 10 Phil Rizzuto	.20	.10	.02
☐ 11 Harvey Haddix	.05	.02	.00
☐ 12 Ken Boyer	.10	.05	.01
☐ 13 Clete Boyer	.05	.02	.00
☐ 14 Ken Harrelson	.10	.05	.01
☐ 15 Robin Roberts	.20	.10	.02
☐ 16 Catfish Hunter	.20	.10	.02
☐ 17 Frank Howard	.10	.05	.01
☐ 18 Jim Perry	.05	.02	.00
☐ 19A Elston Howard ERR (reversed negative)	.15	.07	.01
☐ 19B Elston Howard COR	.15	.07	.01
☐ 20 Jim Bouton	.10	.05	.01
☐ 21 Pee Wee Reese	.25	.12	.02
☐ 22A Mel Stottlemyre ERR (spelled Stottlemyer on card front)	.15	.07	.01
☐ 22B Mel Stottlemyre COR	.15	.07	.01
☐ 23 Hank Sauer	.05	.02	.00
☐ 24 Willie Mays	.75	.35	.07
☐ 25 Tom Tresh	.10	.05	.01
☐ 26 Roy Sievers	.05	.02	.00
☐ 27 Leo Durocher	.15	.07	.01
☐ 28 Al Dark	.05	.02	.00
☐ 29 Tony Kubek	.15	.07	.01
☐ 30 Johnny VanderMeer	.10	.05	.01
☐ 31 Joe Adcock	.05	.02	.00

☐ 32 Bob Lemon	.15	.07	.01
☐ 33 Don Newcombe	.10	.05	.01
☐ 34 Thurman Munson	.30	.15	.03
☐ 35 Earl Battey	.05	.02	.00
☐ 36 Ernie Banks	.30	.15	.03
☐ 37 Matty Alou	.05	.02	.00
☐ 38 Dave McNally	.05	.02	.00
☐ 39 Mickey Lolich	.10	.05	.01
☐ 40 Jackie Robinson	.40	.20	.04
☐ 41 Allie Reynolds	.10	.05	.01
☐ 42A Don Larsen ERR (misspelled Larson on card front)	.15	.07	.01
☐ 42B Don Larsen COR	.15	.07	.01
☐ 43 Fergie Jenkins	.20	.10	.02
☐ 44 Jim Gilliam	.10	.05	.01
☐ 45 Bobby Thomson	.10	.05	.01
☐ 46 Sparky Anderson	.10	.05	.01
☐ 47 Roy Campanella	.35	.17	.03
☐ 48 Marv Throneberry	.10	.05	.01
☐ 49 Bill Virdon	.05	.02	.00
☐ 50 Ted Williams	.50	.25	.05
☐ 51 Minnie Minoso	.15	.07	.01
☐ 52 Bob Turley	.05	.02	.00
☐ 53 Yogi Berra	.35	.17	.03
☐ 54 Juan Marichal	.20	.10	.02
☐ 55 Duke Snider	.35	.17	.03
☐ 56 Harvey Kuenn	.10	.05	.01
☐ 57 Nellie Fox	.15	.07	.01
☐ 58 Felipe Alou	.05	.02	.00
☐ 59 Tony Oliva	.10	.05	.01
☐ 60 Bill Mazeroski	.10	.05	.01
☐ 61 Bobby Shantz	.05	.02	.00
☐ 62 Mark Fidrych	.05	.02	.00
☐ 63 Johnny Mize	.20	.10	.02
☐ 64 Ralph Terry	.10	.05	.01
☐ 65 Gus Bell	.05	.02	.00
☐ 66 Jerry Koosman	.10	.05	.01
☐ 67 Mike McCormick	.05	.02	.00
☐ 68 Lou Burdette	.10	.05	.01
☐ 69 George Kell	.20	.10	.02
☐ 70 Vic Raschi	.10	.05	.01
☐ 71 Chuck Connors	.20	.10	.02
☐ 72 Ted Kluszewski	.15	.07	.01
☐ 73 Bobby Doerr	.20	.10	.02
☐ 74 Bobby Richardson	.15	.07	.01
☐ 75 Carl Erskine	.10	.05	.01
☐ 76 Hoyt Wilhelm	.20	.10	.02
☐ 77 Bob Purkey	.05	.02	.00
☐ 78 Bob Friend	.05	.02	.00
☐ 79 Monte Irvin	.20	.10	.02
☐ 80A Jim Lonborg ERR (misspelled Longborg on card front)	.15	.07	.01
☐ 80B Jim Lonborg COR	.15	.07	.01
☐ 81 Wally Moon	.05	.02	.00
☐ 82 Moose Skowron	.10	.05	.01
☐ 83 Tommy Davis	.10	.05	.01
☐ 84 Enos Slaughter	.20	.10	.02
☐ 85 Sal Maglie UER (1945-1917 on back)	.10	.05	.01
☐ 86 Harmon Killebrew	.20	.10	.02
☐ 87 Gil Hodges	.20	.10	.02
☐ 88 Jim Kaat	.10	.05	.01
☐ 89 Roger Maris	.40	.20	.04
☐ 90 Billy Williams	.20	.10	.02
☐ 91 Luis Aparicio	.20	.10	.02
☐ 92 Jim Bunning	.15	.07	.01
☐ 93 Bill Freehan	.10	.05	.01
☐ 94 Orlando Cepeda	.15	.07	.01
☐ 95 Early Wynn	.20	.10	.02
☐ 96 Tug McGraw	.10	.05	.01
☐ 97 Ron Santo	.10	.05	.01
☐ 98 Del Crandall	.05	.02	.00
☐ 99 Sal Bando	.05	.02	.00
☐ 100 Joe DiMaggio	.75	.35	.07
☐ 101 Bob Feller	.35	.17	.03
☐ 102 Larry Doby	.10	.05	.01
☐ 103 Rollie Fingers	.15	.07	.01
☐ 104 Al Kaline	.25	.12	.02
☐ 105 Johnny Podres	.10	.05	.01
☐ 106 Lou Boudreau	.20	.10	.02
☐ 107 Zoilo Versalles	.05	.02	.00
☐ 108 Dick Groat	.10	.05	.01
☐ 109 Warren Spahn	.25	.12	.02
☐ 110 Johnny Bench	.35	.17	.03

1989 Pacific Legends II

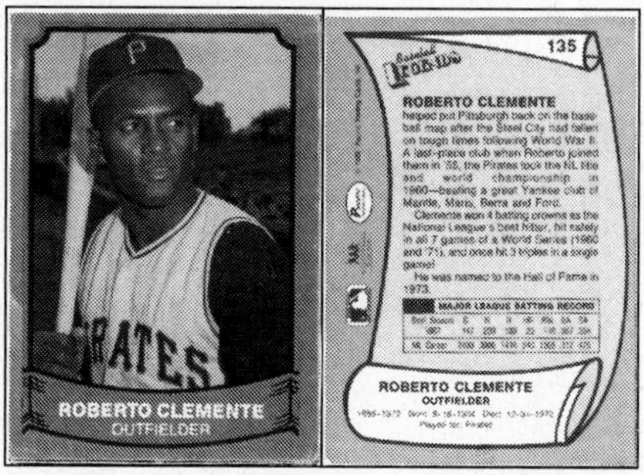

The 1989 Pacific Legends Series II set contains 110 standard-size (2 1/2" by 3 1/2") cards. The fronts have vintage color photos with silver borders. The backs are gray and feature career highlights and lifetime statistics. The cards were distributed as sets and in 10-card wax packs.

	MINT	EXC	G-VG
COMPLETE SET (110)	10.00	5.00	1.00
COMMON PLAYER (111-220)	.05	.02	.00
☐ 111 Reggie Jackson	.60	.30	.06
☐ 112 Rich Reese	.05	.02	.00
☐ 113 Frankie Frisch	.10	.05	.01
☐ 114 Ed Kranepool	.05	.02	.00
☐ 115 Al Hrabosky	.05	.02	.00
☐ 116 Eddie Mathews	.20	.10	.02
☐ 117 Ty Cobb	.50	.25	.05
☐ 118 Jim Davenport	.05	.02	.00
☐ 119 Buddy Lewis	.05	.02	.00
☐ 120 Virgil Trucks	.05	.02	.00
☐ 121 Del Ennis	.05	.02	.00
☐ 122 Dick Radatz	.05	.02	.00
☐ 123 Andy Pafko	.05	.02	.00
☐ 124 Wilbur Wood	.05	.02	.00
☐ 125 Joe Sewell	.10	.05	.01
☐ 126 Herb Score	.05	.02	.00
☐ 127 Paul Waner	.10	.05	.01
☐ 128 Lloyd Waner	.10	.05	.01
☐ 129 Brooks Robinson	.25	.12	.02
☐ 130 Bo Belinsky	.05	.02	.00
☐ 131 Phil Cavaretta	.05	.02	.00
☐ 132 Claude Osteen	.05	.02	.00
☐ 133 Tito Francona	.05	.02	.00
☐ 134 Billy Pierce	.05	.02	.00
☐ 135 Roberto Clemente	.35	.17	.03
☐ 136 Spud Chandler	.05	.02	.00
☐ 137 Enos Slaughter	.15	.07	.01
☐ 138 Ken Holtzman	.05	.02	.00
☐ 139 John Hopp	.05	.02	.00
☐ 140 Tony LaRussa	.05	.02	.00
☐ 141 Ryne Duren	.05	.02	.00
☐ 142 Glenn Beckert	.05	.02	.00
☐ 143 Ken Keltner	.05	.02	.00
☐ 144 Hank Bauer	.05	.02	.00
☐ 145 Roger Craig	.10	.05	.01
☐ 146 Frank Baker	.10	.05	.01
☐ 147 Jim O'Toole	.05	.02	.00
☐ 148 Rogers Hornsby	.20	.10	.02
☐ 149 Jose Cardenal	.05	.02	.00
☐ 150 Bobby Doerr	.15	.07	.01
☐ 151 Mickey Cochrane	.15	.07	.01
☐ 152 Gaylord Perry	.25	.12	.02
☐ 153 Frank Thomas	.05	.02	.00
☐ 154 Ted Williams	.50	.25	.05
☐ 155 Sam McDowell	.05	.02	.00
☐ 156 Bob Feller	.35	.17	.03
☐ 157 Bert Campaneris	.05	.02	.00
☐ 158 Thornton Lee UER (misspelled Thorton on card front)	.05	.02	.00
☐ 159 Gary Peters	.05	.02	.00
☐ 160 Joe Medwick	.15	.07	.01
☐ 161 Joe Nuxhall	.05	.02	.00
☐ 162 Joe Schultz	.05	.02	.00
☐ 163 Harmon Killebrew	.25	.12	.02
☐ 164 Bucky Walters	.05	.02	.00
☐ 165 Bob Allison	.05	.02	.00

☐ 166 Lou Boudreau	.15	.07	.01
☐ 167 Joe Cronin	.15	.07	.01
☐ 168 Mike Torrez	.05	.02	.00
☐ 169 Rich Rollins	.05	.02	.00
☐ 170 Tony Cuccinello	.05	.02	.00
☐ 171 Hoyt Wilhelm	.20	.10	.02
☐ 172 Ernie Harwell (announcer)	.10	.05	.01
☐ 173 George Foster	.10	.05	.01
☐ 174 Lou Gehrig	.50	.25	.05
☐ 175 Dave Kingman	.10	.05	.01
☐ 176 Babe Ruth	.80	.40	.08
☐ 177 Joe Black	.05	.02	.00
☐ 178 Roy Face	.05	.02	.00
☐ 179 Earl Weaver	.10	.05	.01
☐ 180 Johnny Mize	.15	.07	.01
☐ 181 Roger Cramer	.05	.02	.00
☐ 182 Jim Piersall	.05	.02	.00
☐ 183 Ned Garver	.05	.02	.00
☐ 184 Billy Williams	.15	.07	.01
☐ 185 Lefty Grove	.15	.07	.01
☐ 186 Jim Grant	.05	.02	.00
☐ 187 Elmer Valo	.05	.02	.00
☐ 188 Ewell Blackwell	.05	.02	.00
☐ 189 Mel Ott	.15	.07	.01
☐ 190 Harry Walker	.05	.02	.00
☐ 191 Bill Campbell	.05	.02	.00
☐ 192 Walter Johnson	.20	.10	.02
☐ 193 Catfish Hunter	.20	.10	.02
☐ 194 Charlie Keller	.05	.02	.00
☐ 195 Hank Greenberg	.15	.07	.01
☐ 196 Bobby Murcer	.10	.05	.01
☐ 197 Al Lopez	.15	.07	.01
☐ 198 Vida Blue	.05	.02	.00
☐ 199 Shag Crawford UMP	.05	.02	.00
☐ 200 Arky Vaughan	.15	.07	.01
☐ 201 Smoky Burgess	.05	.02	.00
☐ 202 Rip Sewell	.05	.02	.00
☐ 203 Earl Averill	.10	.05	.01
☐ 204 Milt Pappas	.05	.02	.00
☐ 205 Mel Harder	.05	.02	.00
☐ 206 Sam Jethroe	.05	.02	.00
☐ 207 Randy Hundley	.05	.02	.00
☐ 208 Jesse Haines	.05	.02	.00
☐ 209 Jack Brickhouse (announcer)	.05	.02	.00
☐ 210 Whitey Ford	.25	.12	.02
☐ 211 Honus Wagner	.30	.15	.03
☐ 212 Phil Niekro	.15	.07	.01
☐ 213 Gary Bell	.05	.02	.00
☐ 214 Jon Matlack	.05	.02	.00
☐ 215 Moe Drabowsky	.05	.02	.00
☐ 216 Edd Roush	.15	.07	.01
☐ 217 Joel Horlen	.05	.02	.00
☐ 218 Casey Stengel	.20	.10	.02
☐ 219 Burt Hooton	.05	.02	.00
☐ 220 Joe Jackson	.60	.30	.06

1989-90 Pacific Senior League

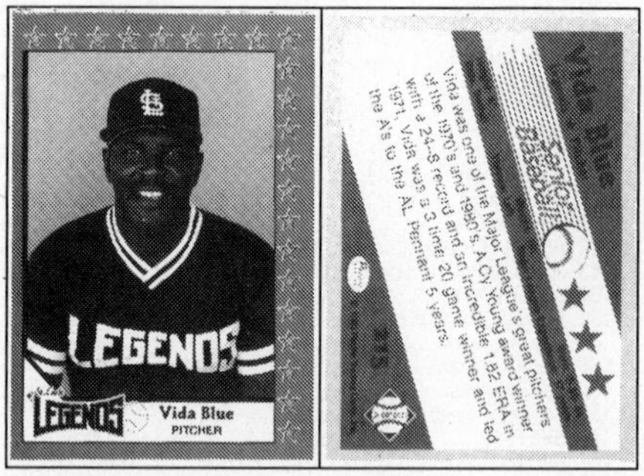

The 1989-90 Pacific Trading Cards Senior League set contains 220 standard-size (2 1/2" by 3 1/2") cards. The fronts feature color photos with silver borders and player names and positions at the bottom. The horizontally-oriented backs are red, white, and blue, and show vital statistics and career highlights. The cards were distributed as a boxed set with 15 card-sized logo stickers/puzzle pieces as well as in wax packs. There are several In Action cards in the set, designated by IA in the checklist below. The Nettles card was corrected very late according to the set's producer.

	MINT	EXC	G-VG
COMPLETE SET (220)	12.00	6.00	1.20
COMMON PLAYER (1-220)	.05	.02	.00
☐ 1 Bobby Tolan	.15	.07	.01
☐ 2 Sergio Ferrer	.05	.02	.00
☐ 3 David Rajsich	.05	.02	.00
☐ 4 Ron LeFlore	.15	.07	.01
☐ 5 Steve Henderson	.05	.02	.00
☐ 6 Jerry Martin	.05	.02	.00
☐ 7 Gary Rajsich	.05	.02	.00
☐ 8 Elias Sosa	.05	.02	.00
☐ 9 Jon Matlack	.10	.05	.01
☐ 10 Steve Kemp	.10	.05	.01
☐ 11 Lenny Randle	.05	.02	.00
☐ 12 Roy Howell	.05	.02	.00
☐ 13 Milt Wilcox	.05	.02	.00
☐ 14 Alan Bannister	.05	.02	.00
☐ 15 Dock Ellis	.05	.02	.00
☐ 16 Mike Williams	.05	.02	.00
☐ 17 Luis Gomez	.05	.02	.00
☐ 18 Joe Sambito	.05	.02	.00
☐ 19 Bake McBride	.05	.02	.00
☐ 20 Pat Zachry	.05	.02	.00
☐ 21 Dwight Lowry	.05	.02	.00
☐ 22 Ozzie Virgil Sr.	.05	.02	.00
☐ 23 Randy Lerch	.05	.02	.00
☐ 24 Butch Benton	.05	.02	.00
☐ 25 Tom Zimmer	.05	.02	.00
☐ 26 Al Holland UER (photo actually Sid Monge)	.15	.07	.01
☐ 27 Sammy Stewart	.05	.02	.00
☐ 28 Bill Lee	.10	.05	.01
☐ 29 Ferguson Jenkins	1.00	.50	.10
☐ 30 Leon Roberts	.05	.02	.00
☐ 31 Rick Wise	.10	.05	.01
☐ 32 Butch Hobson	.10	.05	.01
☐ 33 Pete LaCock	.05	.02	.00
☐ 34 Bill Campbell	.05	.02	.00
☐ 35 Doug Simunic	.05	.02	.00
☐ 36 Mario Guerrero	.05	.02	.00
☐ 37 Jim Willoughby	.05	.02	.00
☐ 38 Joe Pittman	.05	.02	.00
☐ 39 Mark Bomback	.05	.02	.00
☐ 40 Tommy McMillian	.05	.02	.00
☐ 41 Gary Allanson	.05	.02	.00
☐ 42 Cecil Cooper	.15	.07	.01
☐ 43 John LaRosa	.05	.02	.00
☐ 44 Darrell Brandon	.05	.02	.00
☐ 45 Bernie Carbo	.05	.02	.00
☐ 46 Mike Cuellar	.15	.07	.01
☐ 47 Al Bumbry	.05	.02	.00
☐ 48 Gene Richards	.05	.02	.00
☐ 49 Pedro Borbon	.05	.02	.00
☐ 50 Julio Solo	.05	.02	.00
☐ 51 Ed Nottle	.05	.02	.00
☐ 52 Jim Bibby	.05	.02	.00
☐ 53 Doug Griffin	.05	.02	.00
☐ 54 Ed Clements	.05	.02	.00
☐ 55 Dalton Jones	.05	.02	.00
☐ 56 Earl Weaver MG	.50	.25	.05
☐ 57 Jesus De La Rosa	.05	.02	.00
☐ 58 Paul Casanova	.05	.02	.00
☐ 59 Frank Riccelli	.05	.02	.00
☐ 60 Rafael Landestoy	.05	.02	.00
☐ 61 George Hendrick	.10	.05	.01
☐ 62 Cesar Cedeno	.15	.07	.01
☐ 63 Bert Campaneris	.15	.07	.01
☐ 64 Derrell Thomas	.05	.02	.00
☐ 65 Bobby Ramos	.05	.02	.00
☐ 66 Grant Jackson	.05	.02	.00
☐ 67 Steve Whitaker	.05	.02	.00
☐ 68 Pedro Ramos	.05	.02	.00
☐ 69 Joe Hicks	.05	.02	.00
☐ 70 Taylor Duncan	.05	.02	.00
☐ 71 Tom Shopay	.05	.02	.00
☐ 72 Ken Clay	.05	.02	.00
☐ 73 Mike Kekich	.05	.02	.00
☐ 74 Ed Halicki	.05	.02	.00
☐ 75 Ed Figueroa	.10	.05	.01
☐ 76 Paul Blair	.10	.05	.01
☐ 77 Luis Tiant	.25	.12	.02
☐ 78 Stan Bahnsen	.05	.02	.00
☐ 79 Rennie Stennett	.05	.02	.00
☐ 80 Bobby Molinaro	.05	.02	.00

☐ 81 Jim Gideon	.05	.02	.00
☐ 82 Orlando Gonzalez	.05	.02	.00
☐ 83 Amos Otis	.20	.10	.02
☐ 84 Dennis Leonard	.10	.05	.01
☐ 85 Pat Putman	.05	.02	.00
☐ 86 Rick Manning	.05	.02	.00
☐ 87 Pat Dobson	.10	.05	.01
☐ 88 Marty Castillo	.05	.02	.00
☐ 89 Steve McCatty	.05	.02	.00
☐ 90 Doug Bird	.05	.02	.00
☐ 91 Rick Waits	.05	.02	.00
☐ 92 Ron Jackson	.05	.02	.00
☐ 93 Tim Hosley	.05	.02	.00
☐ 94 Steve Luebber	.05	.02	.00
☐ 95 Rich Gale	.05	.02	.00
☐ 96 Champ Summers	.05	.02	.00
☐ 97 Dave LaRoche	.05	.02	.00
☐ 98 Bobby Jones	.05	.02	.00
☐ 99 Kim Allen	.05	.02	.00
☐ 100 Wayne Garland	.05	.02	.00
☐ 101 Tom Spencer	.05	.02	.00
☐ 102 Dan Driessen	.10	.05	.01
☐ 103 Ron Pruitt	.05	.02	.00
☐ 104 Tim Ireland	.05	.02	.00
☐ 105 Dan Driessen IA	.10	.05	.01
☐ 106 Pepe Frias	.05	.02	.00
☐ 107 Eric Rasmussen	.05	.02	.00
☐ 108 Don Hood	.05	.02	.00
☐ 109 Joe Coleman UER (photo actually Tony Torchia)	.05	.02	.00
☐ 110 Jim Slaton	.05	.02	.00
☐ 111 Clint Hurdie	.05	.02	.00
☐ 112 Larry Milbourne	.05	.02	.00
☐ 113 Al Holland	.05	.02	.00
☐ 114 George Foster	.15	.07	.01
☐ 115 Graig Nettles	.15	.07	.01
☐ 116 Oscar Gamble	.05	.02	.00
☐ 117 Ross Grimsley	.05	.02	.00
☐ 118 Bill Travers	.05	.02	.00
☐ 119 Jose Beniquez	.10	.05	.01
☐ 120 Jerry Grote IA	.05	.02	.00
☐ 121 John D'Acquisto	.05	.02	.00
☐ 122 Tom Murphy	.05	.02	.00
☐ 123 Walt Williams	.05	.02	.00
☐ 124 Roy Thomas	.05	.02	.00
☐ 125 Jerry Grote	.05	.02	.00
☐ 126A Jim Nettles ERR (writing on bat knob)	.50	.25	.05
☐ 126B Jim Nettles COR	1.00	.50	.10
☐ 127 Randy Niemann	.05	.02	.00
☐ 128 Bobby Bonds	.50	.25	.05
☐ 129 Ed Glynn	.05	.02	.00
☐ 130 Ed Hicks	.05	.02	.00
☐ 131 Ivan Murrell	.05	.02	.00
☐ 132 Graig Nettles	.25	.12	.02
☐ 133 Hal McRae	.15	.07	.01
☐ 134 Pat Kelly	.10	.05	.01
☐ 135 Sammy Stewart	.05	.02	.00
☐ 136 Bruce Kison	.05	.02	.00
☐ 137 Jim Morrison	.05	.02	.00
☐ 138 Omar Moreno	.05	.02	.00
☐ 139 Tom Brown	.05	.02	.00
☐ 140 Steve Dillard	.05	.02	.00
☐ 141 Gary Alexander	.05	.02	.00
☐ 142 Al Oliver	.25	.12	.02
☐ 143 Rick Lysander	.05	.02	.00
☐ 144 Tippy Martinez	.10	.05	.01
☐ 145 Al Cowens	.10	.05	.01
☐ 146 Gene Clines	.05	.02	.00
☐ 147 Willie Aikens	.10	.05	.01
☐ 148 Tommy Moore	.05	.02	.00
☐ 149 Clete Boyer	.10	.05	.01
☐ 150 Stan Cliburn	.05	.02	.00
☐ 151 Ken Kravec	.05	.02	.00
☐ 152 Garth Iorg	.05	.02	.00
☐ 153 Rick Peterson	.05	.02	.00
☐ 154 Wayne Nordhagen	.05	.02	.00
☐ 155 Danny Meyer	.05	.02	.00
☐ 156 Wayne Garrett	.05	.02	.00
☐ 157 Wayne Krenchicki	.05	.02	.00
☐ 158 Graig Nettles	.25	.12	.02
☐ 159 Earl Stephenson	.05	.02	.00
☐ 160 Carl Taylor	.05	.02	.00
☐ 161 Rollie Fingers	.60	.30	.06
☐ 162 Toby Harrah	.10	.05	.01
☐ 163 Mickey Rivers	.15	.07	.01
☐ 164 Dave Kingman	.15	.07	.01
☐ 165 Paul Mirabella	.05	.02	.00
☐ 166 Dick Williams	.10	.05	.01
☐ 167 Luis Pujols	.05	.02	.00
☐ 168 Tito Landrum	.10	.05	.01
☐ 169 Tom Underwood	.05	.02	.00
☐ 170 Mark Wagner	.05	.02	.00
☐ 171 Odell Jones	.05	.02	.00
☐ 172 Doug Capilla	.05	.02	.00
☐ 173 Allie Rondon	.05	.02	.00
☐ 174 Lowell Palmer	.05	.02	.00
☐ 175 Juan Eichelberger	.05	.02	.00
☐ 176 Wes Clements	.05	.02	.00
☐ 177 Rodney Scott	.05	.02	.00
☐ 178 Ron Washington	.10	.05	.01
☐ 179 Al Hrabosky	.10	.05	.01
☐ 180 Sid Monge	.05	.02	.00
☐ 181 Randy Johnson	.05	.02	.00
☐ 182 Tim Stoddard	.05	.02	.00
☐ 183 Dick Williams MG	.10	.05	.01
☐ 184 Lee Lacy	.10	.05	.01
☐ 185 Jerry White	.05	.02	.00
☐ 186 Dave Kingman	.15	.07	.01
☐ 187 Checklist 1-110	.05	.02	.00
☐ 188 Jose Cruz	.15	.07	.01
☐ 189 Jamie Easterly	.05	.02	.00
☐ 190 Ike Blessit	.05	.02	.00
☐ 191 Johnny Grubb	.05	.02	.00
☐ 192 Dave Cash	.05	.02	.00
☐ 193 Doug Corbett	.05	.02	.00
☐ 194 Bruce Bochy	.05	.02	.00
☐ 195 Mark Corey	.05	.02	.00
☐ 196 Gil Rondon	.05	.02	.00
☐ 197 Jerry Martin	.05	.02	.00
☐ 198 Gerry Pirtle	.05	.02	.00
☐ 199 Gates Brown	.10	.05	.01
☐ 200 Bob Galasso	.05	.02	.00
☐ 201 Bake McBride	.05	.02	.00
☐ 202 Wayne Granger	.05	.02	.00
☐ 203 Larry Milbourne	.05	.02	.00
☐ 204 Tom Paciorek	.10	.05	.01
☐ 205 U.L. Washington	.05	.02	.00
☐ 206 Larvell Blanks	.05	.02	.00
☐ 207 Bob Shirley	.05	.02	.00
☐ 208 Pete Falcone	.05	.02	.00
☐ 209 Sal Butera	.05	.02	.00
☐ 210 Roy Branch	.05	.02	.00
☐ 211 Dyar Miller	.05	.02	.00
☐ 212 Paul Siebert	.05	.02	.00
☐ 213 Ken Reitz	.05	.02	.00
☐ 214 Bill Madlock	.20	.10	.02
☐ 215 Vida Blue	.15	.07	.01
☐ 216 Dave Hilton	.05	.02	.00
☐ 217 Ramos and Bren	.05	.02	.00
☐ 218 Checklist 111-220	.05	.02	.00
☐ 219 Dobson and Weaver	.20	.10	.02
☐ 220 Curt Flood	.25	.12	.02

1990 Pacific Legends

The 1990 Pacific Legends set was a 110-card set issued by Pacific Trading Cards. The set numbering is basically arranged in two alphabetical sequences. This is a standard size (2 1/2" by 3 1/2") set which was available as factory set as well as in wax packs. The set does include some active players, Willie Wilson and Jesse Barfield, the last two players in the set.

	MINT	EXC	G-VG
COMPLETE SET (110)	9.00	4.50	.90
COMMON PLAYER (1-110)	.05	.02	.00

☐ 1 Hank Aaron	.60	.30	.06
☐ 2 Tommie Agee	.05	.02	.00
☐ 3 Luke Appling	.20	.10	.02
☐ 4 Sal Bando	.05	.02	.00
☐ 5 Ernie Banks	.30	.15	.03
☐ 6 Don Baylor	.10	.05	.01
☐ 7 Yogi Berra	.40	.20	.04
☐ 8 Vida Blue	.05	.02	.00
☐ 9 Lou Boudreau	.15	.07	.01
☐ 10 Clete Boyer	.05	.02	.00
☐ 11 George Bamberger	.05	.02	.00
☐ 12 Lou Brock	.20	.10	.02
☐ 13 Ralph Branca	.05	.02	.00
☐ 14 Carl Erskine	.05	.02	.00
☐ 15 Bert Campaneris	.05	.02	.00
☐ 16 Steve Carlton	.25	.12	.02
☐ 17 Rod Carew	.40	.20	.04
☐ 18 Rocky Colavito	.10	.05	.01
☐ 19 Frankie Crosetti	.10	.05	.01
☐ 20 Larry Doby	.10	.05	.01
☐ 21 Bobby Doerr	.15	.07	.01
☐ 22 Walt Dropo	.05	.02	.00
☐ 23 Rick Ferrell	.10	.05	.01
☐ 24 Joe Garagiola	.20	.10	.02
☐ 25 Ralph Garr	.05	.02	.00
☐ 26 Dick Groat	.05	.02	.00
☐ 27 Steve Garvey	.20	.10	.02
☐ 28 Bob Gibson	.20	.10	.02
☐ 29 Don Drysdale	.20	.10	.02
☐ 30 Billy Herman	.15	.07	.01
☐ 31 Bobby Grich	.05	.02	.00
☐ 32 Monte Irvin	.15	.07	.01
☐ 33 Dave Johnson	.05	.02	.00
☐ 34 Don Kessinger	.05	.02	.00
☐ 35 Harmon Killebrew	.20	.10	.02
☐ 36 Ralph Kiner	.20	.10	.02
☐ 37 Vern Law	.05	.02	.00
☐ 38 Ed Lopat	.10	.05	.01
☐ 39 Bill Mazeroski	.10	.05	.01
☐ 40 Rick Monday	.05	.02	.00
☐ 41 Manny Mota	.05	.02	.00
☐ 42 Don Newcombe	.10	.05	.01
☐ 43 Gaylord Perry	.20	.10	.02
☐ 44 Jim Piersall	.10	.05	.01
☐ 45 Johnny Podres	.10	.05	.01
☐ 46 Boog Powell	.10	.05	.01
☐ 47 Robin Roberts	.20	.10	.02
☐ 48 Ron Santo	.10	.05	.01
☐ 49 Herb Score	.10	.05	.01
☐ 50 Enos Slaughter	.15	.07	.01
☐ 51 Warren Spahn	.25	.12	.02
☐ 52 Rusty Staub	.10	.05	.01
☐ 53 Frank Torre	.05	.02	.00
☐ 54 Bob Horner	.05	.02	.00
☐ 55 Lee May	.05	.02	.00
☐ 56 Bill White	.10	.05	.01
☐ 57 Hoyt Wilhelm	.15	.07	.01
☐ 58 Billy Williams	.20	.10	.02
☐ 59 Ted Williams	.40	.20	.04
☐ 60 Tom Seaver	.40	.20	.04
☐ 61 Carl Yastrzemski	.50	.25	.05
☐ 62 Marv Throneberry	.05	.02	.00
☐ 63 Steve Stone	.05	.02	.00
☐ 64 Rico Petrocelli	.05	.02	.00
☐ 65 Orlando Cepeda	.15	.07	.01
☐ 66 Eddie Mathews	.20	.10	.02
☐ 67 Joe Sewell	.10	.05	.01
☐ 68 Catfish Hunter	.20	.10	.02
☐ 69 Alvin Dark	.10	.05	.01
☐ 70 Richie Ashburn	.15	.07	.01
☐ 71 Dusty Baker	.05	.02	.00
☐ 72 George Foster	.10	.05	.01
☐ 73 Eddie Yost	.05	.02	.00
☐ 74 Buddy Bell	.05	.02	.00
☐ 75 Manny Sanguillen	.05	.02	.00
☐ 76 Jim Bunning	.10	.05	.01
☐ 77 Smokey Burgess	.05	.02	.00
☐ 78 Al Rosen	.10	.05	.01
☐ 79 Gene Conley	.05	.02	.00
☐ 80 Dave Dravecky	.05	.02	.00
☐ 81 Charlie Gehringer	.15	.07	.01
☐ 82 Billy Pierce	.05	.02	.00
☐ 83 Willie Horton	.05	.02	.00
☐ 84 Ron Hunt	.05	.02	.00
☐ 85 Bob Feller	.25	.12	.02
☐ 86 George Kell	.15	.07	.01
☐ 87 Dave Kingman	.10	.05	.01
☐ 88 Jerry Koosman	.10	.05	.01
☐ 89 Clem Labine	.05	.02	.00
☐ 90 Tony LaRussa	.05	.02	.00
☐ 91 Dennis Leonard	.05	.02	.00
☐ 92 Dale Long	.05	.02	.00
☐ 93 Sparky Lyle	.10	.05	.01
☐ 94 Gil McDougald	.10	.05	.01
☐ 95 Don Mossi	.05	.02	.00
☐ 96 Phil Niekro	.20	.10	.02
☐ 97 Tom Paciorek	.05	.02	.00
☐ 98 Mel Parnell	.05	.02	.00
☐ 99 Lou Piniella	.10	.05	.01
☐ 100 Bobby Richardson	.10	.05	.01
☐ 101 Phil Rizzuto	.25	.12	.02
☐ 102 Brooks Robinson	.25	.12	.02
☐ 103 Pete Runnels	.05	.02	.00
☐ 104 Diego Segui	.05	.02	.00
☐ 105 Bobby Shantz	.05	.02	.00
☐ 106 Bobby Thomson	.10	.05	.01
☐ 107 Joe Torre	.15	.07	.01
☐ 108 Earl Weaver	.10	.05	.01
☐ 109 Willie Wilson	.10	.05	.01
☐ 110 Jesse Barfield	.10	.05	.01

1958 Packard Bell

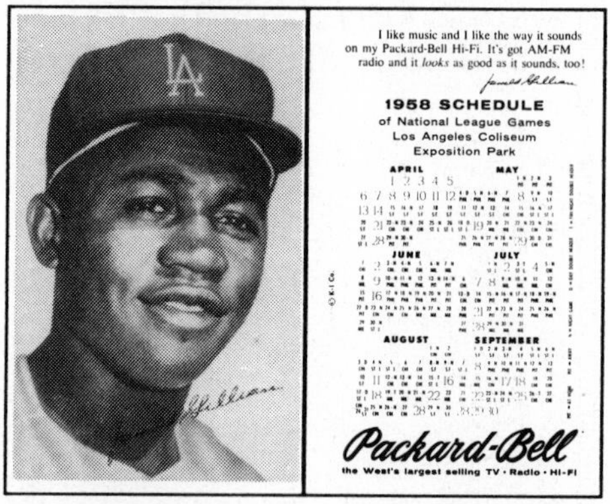

This seven-card set included members of the Los Angeles Dodgers and San Francisco Giants and was issued in both teams' first year on the West Coast. This black and white, unnumbered set features cards measuring approximately 3 3/8" by 5 3/8". The backs are advertisements for Packard Bell (a television and radio manufacturer) along with a schedule for either the Giants or Dodgers. There were four Giants printed and three Dodgers. The catalog designation for this set is H805-5.

	NRMT	VG-E	GOOD
COMPLETE SET (7)	400.00	200.00	40.00
COMMON CARD (1-7)	35.00	17.50	3.50
☐ 1 Walt Alston MG Los Angeles Dodgers	65.00	32.50	6.50
☐ 2 Johnny Antonelli San Francisco Giants	35.00	17.50	3.50
☐ 3 Jim Gilliam Los Angeles Dodgers	45.00	22.50	4.50
☐ 4 Gil Hodges Los Angeles Dodgers	90.00	45.00	9.00
☐ 5 Willie Mays San Francisco Giants	175.00	85.00	18.00
☐ 6 Bill Rigney MG San Francisco Giants	35.00	17.50	3.50
☐ 7 Hank Sauer San Francisco Giants	35.00	17.50	3.50

1977 Padres Schedule Cards

This 40-card set was issued in 1977 and was about members of the 1977 San Diego Padres. The cards measure approximately 2 1/4" by 3 3/8" and had black and white photos on the front of the cards with a schedule of the 1977 Padres special events on the back. The set is checklisted alphabetically in the list below.

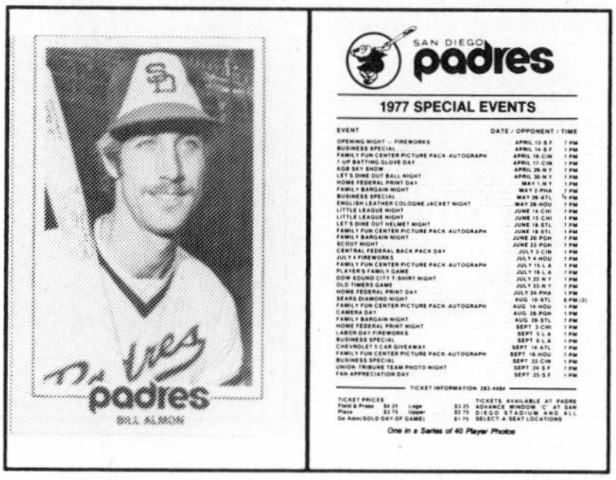

	NRMT	VG-E	GOOD
COMPLETE SET (40)	12.00	5.00	1.00
COMMON PLAYER (1-40)	.25	.12	.02
☐ 1 Bill Almon	.25	.12	.02
☐ 2 Joe Amalfitano CO	.25	.12	.02
☐ 3 Vic Bernal	.25	.12	.02
☐ 4 Buzzie Bavasi GM	.35	.17	.03
☐ 5 Mike Champion	.25	.12	.02
☐ 6 Champion And Almon	.25	.12	.02
☐ 7 Roger Craig CO	.50	.25	.05
☐ 8 John D'Acquisto	.25	.12	.02
☐ 9 Bob Davis	.25	.12	.02
☐ 10 Rollie Fingers	1.00	.50	.10
☐ 11 Dave Freisleben	.25	.12	.02
☐ 12 Tom Griffin	.25	.12	.02
☐ 13 George Hendrick	.35	.17	.03
☐ 14 Enzo Hernandez	.25	.12	.02
☐ 15 Mike Ivie	.25	.12	.02
☐ 16 Randy Jones Following Through	.35	.17	.03
☐ 17 Randy Jones Holding Cy Young Award	.35	.17	.03
☐ 18 John McNamara MG	.35	.17	.03
☐ 19 Luis Melendez	.25	.12	.02
☐ 20 Butch Metzger	.25	.12	.02
☐ 21 Bob Owchinko	.25	.12	.02
☐ 22 Doug Rader	.35	.17	.03
☐ 23 Gene Richards	.25	.12	.02
☐ 24 Dave Roberts	.25	.12	.02
☐ 25 Merv Rettenmund	.25	.12	.02
☐ 26 Rick Sawyer	.25	.12	.02
☐ 27 Bob Shirley	.25	.12	.02
☐ 28 Bob Skinner CO	.25	.12	.02
☐ 29 Dan Spillner	.25	.12	.02
☐ 30 Brent Strom	.25	.12	.02
☐ 31 Gary Sutherland	.25	.12	.02
☐ 32 Gene Tenace	.35	.17	.03
☐ 33 Dave Tomlin	.25	.12	.02
☐ 34 Jerry Turner	.25	.12	.02
☐ 35 Bobby Valentine	.35	.17	.03
☐ 36 Dave Wehrmeister	.25	.12	.02
☐ 37 Whitey Wietelmann CO	.25	.12	.02
☐ 38 Dave Winfield Bat on shoulders	2.00	1.00	.20
☐ 39 Dave Winfield Bat at Waist	2.00	1.00	.20
☐ 40 Don Williams CO	.25	.12	.02

1978 Padres Family Fun

This 39-card set features members of the 1978 San Diego Padres. These large cards measure approximately 3 1/2" by 5 1/2" and are framed in a style similar to the 1962 Topps set with wood-grain borders. The cards have full color photos on the front of the card along with the Padres logo and Family Fun Centers underneath the photo in circles and the name of the player on the bottom of the card. The backs of the card asked each person what their greatest thrill in Baseball was. This set is especially noteworthy for having one of the earliest Ozzie Smith cards printed. The set is checklisted alphabetically in the list below.

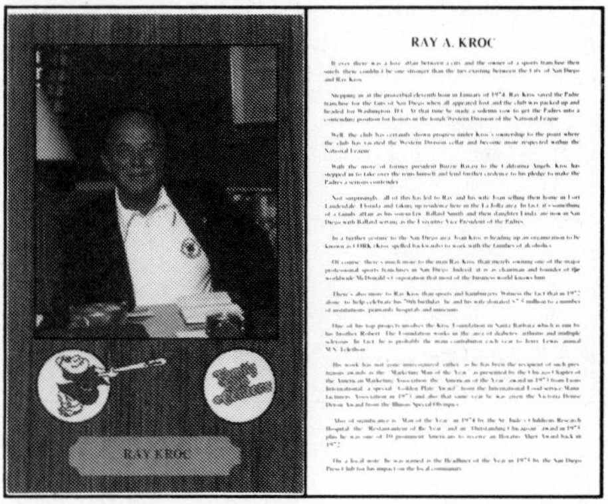

	MINT	EXC	G-VG
COMPLETE SET (39)	16.00	7.50	1.50
COMMON PLAYER (1-39)	.30	.15	.03
☐ 1 Bill Almon	.30	.15	.03
☐ 2 Tucker Ashford	.30	.15	.03
☐ 3 Chuck Baker	.30	.15	.03
☐ 4 Dave Campbell (announcer)	.30	.15	.03
☐ 5 Mike Champion	.30	.15	.03
☐ 6 Jerry Coleman (announcer)	.40	.20	.04
☐ 7 Roger Craig MG	.60	.30	.06
☐ 8 John D'Acquisto	.30	.15	.03
☐ 9 Bob Davis	.30	.15	.03
☐ 10 Chuck Estrada CO	.40	.20	.04
☐ 11 Rollie Fingers	1.00	.50	.10
☐ 12 Dave Freisleben	.30	.15	.03
☐ 13 Oscar Gamble	.40	.20	.04
☐ 14 Fernando Gonzalez	.30	.15	.03
☐ 15 Billy Herman CO	.60	.30	.06
☐ 16 Randy Jones	.40	.20	.04
☐ 17 Ray Kroc (Owner)	.50	.25	.05
☐ 18 Mark Lee	.30	.15	.03
☐ 19 Mickey Lolich	.50	.25	.05
☐ 20 Bob Owchinko	.30	.15	.03
☐ 21 Broderick Perkins	.30	.15	.03
☐ 22 Gaylord Perry	1.25	.60	.12
☐ 23 Eric Rasmussen	.30	.15	.03
☐ 24 Don Reynolds	.30	.15	.03
☐ 25 Gene Richards	.30	.15	.03
☐ 26 Dave Roberts	.30	.15	.03
☐ 27 Phil Roof CO	.30	.15	.03
☐ 28 Bob Shirley	.30	.15	.03
☐ 29 Ozzie Smith	7.50	3.75	.75
☐ 30 Dan Spillner	.30	.15	.03
☐ 31 Rick Sweet	.30	.15	.03
☐ 32 Gene Tenace	.40	.20	.04
☐ 33 Derrel Thomas	.30	.15	.03
☐ 34 Jerry Turner	.30	.15	.03
☐ 35 Dave Wehrmeister	.30	.15	.03
☐ 36 Whitey Wietelmann CO	.30	.15	.03
☐ 37 Don Williams CO	.30	.15	.03
☐ 38 Dave Winfield	2.00	1.00	.20
☐ 39 1978 All-Star Game	.30	.15	.03

1989 Padres Magazine Cards

These 2 1/2" by 3 1/2" cards came as an insert in issues of "Padres" magazine sold in San Diego. These cards were sponsored by San Diego Sports Collectibles, a major hobby dealer. The cards feature beautiful full-color photos on the front and interesting did-you-know facts on the back along with one line of career statistics. The cards of retired Padres feature an highlight of their career in San Diego. The suggested retail price of each of the six different Padres magazines was 1.50.

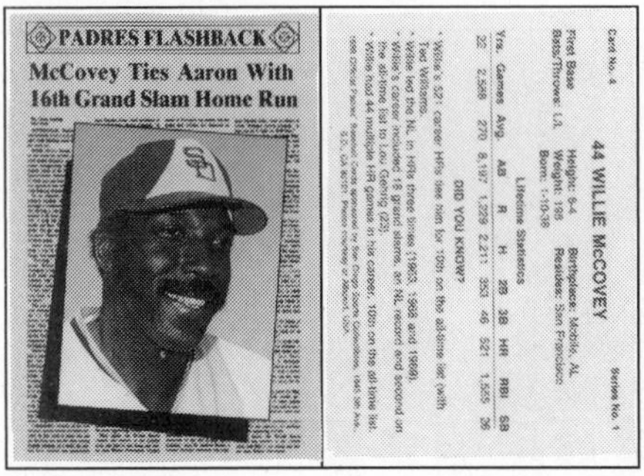

	MINT	EXC	G-VG
COMPLETE SET (24)	10.00	5.00	1.00
COMMON PLAYER (1-24)	.30	.15	.03
☐ 1 Jack McKeon MG	.30	.15	.03
☐ 2 Sandy Alomar Jr.	1.00	.50	.10
☐ 3 Tony Gwynn	1.00	.50	.10
☐ 4 Willie McCovey McCovey hits 16th career grand slam	1.00	.50	.10
☐ 5 John Kruk	.40	.20	.04
☐ 6 Jack Clark	.60	.30	.06
☐ 7 Eric Show	.40	.20	.04
☐ 8 Rollie Fingers Fingers wins NL Saves title for second time	.60	.30	.06
☐ 9 The Alomars Sandy Alomar Sr. Sandy Alomar Jr. Roberto Alomar	.75	.35	.07
☐ 10 Carmelo Martinez	.30	.15	.03
☐ 11 Benito Santiago	.75	.35	.07
☐ 12 Nate Colbert Colbert 5 HR's, 13 RBI's in Doubleheader	.30	.15	.03
☐ 13 Mark Davis	.40	.20	.04
☐ 14 Roberto Alomar	.75	.35	.07
☐ 15 Tim Flannery	.30	.15	.03
☐ 16 Randy Jones Jones wins Cy Young Award	.40	.20	.04
☐ 17 Dennis Rasmussen	.40	.20	.04
☐ 18 Greg W. Harris	.40	.20	.04
☐ 19 Garry Templeton	.40	.20	.04
☐ 20 Steve Garvey Garvey's HR ties NLCS	.60	.30	.06
☐ 21 Bruce Hurst	.40	.20	.04
☐ 22 Ed Whitson	.40	.20	.04
☐ 23 Chris James	.40	.20	.04
☐ 24 Gaylord Perry Perry Wins Cy Young Award in Both Leagues	.75	.35	.07

1988 Pepsi Tigers

This set of 25 cards features members of the Detroit Tigers and was sponsored by Pepsi Cola and Kroger. The cards are in full color on the fronts and measure approximately 2 7/8" by 4 1/4". The card backs contain complete Major and Minor League season-by-season statistics. The cards are unnumbered so they are listed below by uniform number, which is given on the card.

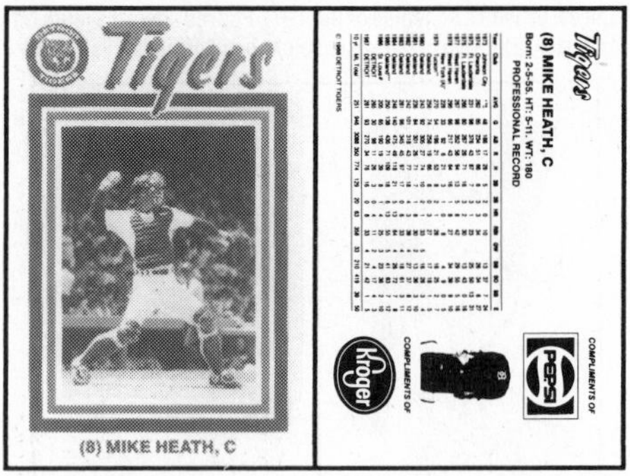

	MINT	EXC	G-VG
COMPLETE SET (25)	8.00	4.00	.80
COMMON PLAYER	.25	.12	.02
☐ 1 Lou Whitaker	.60	.30	.06
☐ 2 Alan Trammell	.80	.40	.08
☐ 8 Mike Heath	.25	.12	.02
☐ 11 Sparky Anderson MG	.35	.17	.03
☐ 12 Luis Salazar	.25	.12	.02
☐ 14 Dave Bergman	.25	.12	.02
☐ 15 Pat Sheridan	.25	.12	.02
☐ 16 Tom Brookens	.25	.12	.02
☐ 19 Doyle Alexander	.35	.17	.03
☐ 21 Guillermo Hernandez	.35	.17	.03
☐ 22 Ray Knight	.35	.17	.03
☐ 24 Gary Pettis	.35	.17	.03
☐ 25 Eric King	.35	.17	.03
☐ 26 Frank Tanana	.35	.17	.03
☐ 31 Larry Herndon	.25	.12	.02
☐ 32 Jim Walewander	.25	.12	.02
☐ 33 Matt Nokes	.35	.17	.03
☐ 34 Chet Lemon	.35	.17	.03
☐ 35 Walt Terrell	.35	.17	.03
☐ 39 Mike Henneman	.35	.17	.03
☐ 41 Darrell Evans	.50	.25	.05
☐ 44 Jeff Robinson	.35	.17	.03
☐ 47 Jack Morris	.50	.25	.05
☐ 48 Paul Gibson	.25	.12	.02
☐ xx Tigers Coaches Billy Consolo Alex Grammas Billy Muffett Vada Pinson Dick Tracewski	.25	.12	.02

1989 Pepsi McGwire

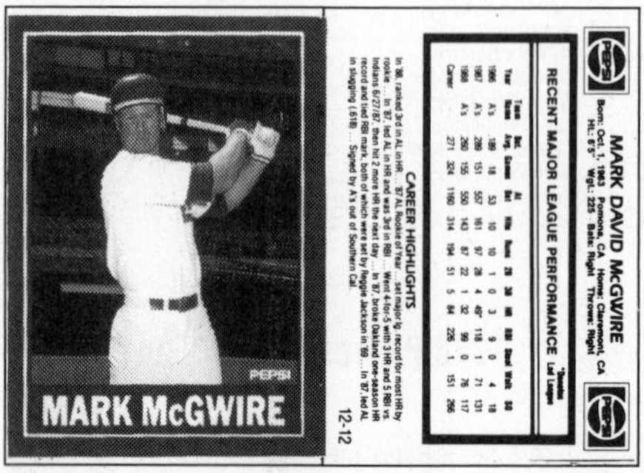

This set includes 12 cards each depicting Mark McGwire. The cards are standard size, 2 1/2" by 3 1/2" and are printed on rather thin card stock. The cards have a distinctive blue outer border. The cards are numbered on the back in the lower right corner. The Pepsi logo is shown on the front and back of each card. All the pictures used in the set are posed showing McGwire in a generic uniform with a Pepsi patch on his upper arm and his number 25 on his chest; in each case his cap or batting helmet is in the Oakland colors but without their logo. The card backs all contain exactly the same statistical and biographical information, only the card number is different. Supposedly cards were distributed inside specially marked 12-packs of Pepsi in the Northern California area.

	MINT	EXC	G-VG
COMPLETE SET (12)	30.00	15.00	3.00
COMMON PLAYER (1-12)	3.00	1.50	.30
☐ 1 Mark McGwire (batting stance with left foot lifted)	3.00	1.50	.30
☐ 2 Mark McGwire (fielding position at first base)	3.00	1.50	.30
☐ 3 Mark McGwire (reaching out with glove for ball)	3.00	1.50	.30
☐ 4 Mark McGwire (batting stance in empty stadium)	3.00	1.50	.30
☐ 5 Mark McGwire (on one knee with bat)	3.00	1.50	.30
☐ 6 Mark McGwire (stretching for ball at first base)	3.00	1.50	.30
☐ 7 Mark McGwire (smiling with bat on shoulder facing camera)	3.00	1.50	.30
☐ 8 Mark McGwire (holding bat in green windbreaker)	3.00	1.50	.30
☐ 9 Mark McGwire (Rawlings bat on left shoulder)	3.00	1.50	.30
☐ 10 Mark McGwire (holding bat parallel to ground in green windbreaker)	3.00	1.50	.30
☐ 11 Mark McGwire (holding bat parallel to ground in uniform, toothy smile)	3.00	1.50	.30
☐ 12 Mark McGwire (serious looking follow through)	3.00	1.50	.30

1990 Pepsi Jose Canseco

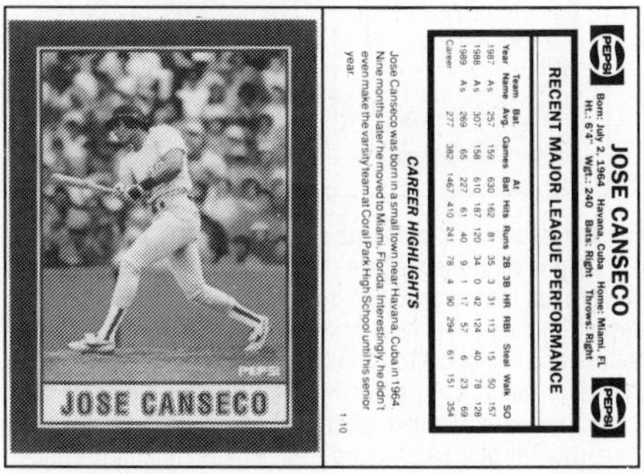

This 10-card, standard-size set of 2 1/2" by 3 1/2" cards was issued in conjuction with Pepsi-Cola. These blue-bordered cards do not have the team logos. This set is very similar in style to the Pepsi McGwire set issued the year before. All the pictures used in the set are posed showing Canseco in a generic uniform with a Pepsi patch.

	MINT	EXC	G-VG
COMPLETE SET (10)	18.00	9.00	1.80
COMMON PLAYER (1-10)	2.00	1.00	.20
☐ 1 Jose Canseco (Follow Through Waist)	2.00	1.00	.20
☐ 2 Jose Canseco (Follow Through Shoulder)	2.00	1.00	.20
☐ 3 Jose Canseco (Catching Ball)	2.00	1.00	.20
☐ 4 Jose Canseco (Batting Pose)	2.00	1.00	.20
☐ 5 Jose Canseco (Glove Over Chest)	2.00	1.00	.20
☐ 6 Jose Canseco (Action Follow Through)	2.00	1.00	.20
☐ 7 Jose Canseco (Sitting on Dugout Steps)	2.00	1.00	.20
☐ 8 Jose Canseco (Waiting for Pitch)	2.00	1.00	.20
☐ 9 Jose Canseco (Portrait/Bat at Waist)	2.00	1.00	.20
☐ 10 Jose Canseco (Portrait)	2.00	1.00	.20

1981 Perma-Graphic Credit Card

Perma-Graphic began their three-year foray into card manufacturing with this 32-card set of "credit cards" each measuring 2 1/8" by 3 3/8". The set featured 32 of the leading players of 1981. This set's design is split on the front between a full-color photo of the player and an identification of said player while the back has one line of career statistics and lines of career highlights. These sets (made of plastic) were issued with the cooperation of Topps Chewing Gum. This first set of Perma-Graphic cards seems to have been produced in greater quantities than the other five Perma-Graphic sets.

	MINT	EXC	G-VG
COMPLETE SET (32)	30.00	15.00	3.00
COMMON PLAYER (1-32)	.75	.35	.07
☐ 1 Johnny Bench	2.00	1.00	.20
☐ 2 Mike Schmidt	3.00	1.50	.30
☐ 3 George Brett	2.00	1.00	.20
☐ 4 Carl Yastrzemski	2.00	1.00	.20
☐ 5 Pete Rose	3.00	1.50	.30
☐ 6 Bob Horner	.75	.35	.07
☐ 7 Reggie Jackson	2.00	1.00	.20
☐ 8 Keith Hernandez	1.00	.50	.10
☐ 9 George Foster	.75	.35	.07
☐ 10 Garry Templeton	.75	.35	.07
☐ 11 Tom Seaver	2.00	1.00	.20
☐ 12 Steve Garvey	1.50	.75	.15
☐ 13 Dave Parker	1.25	.60	.12
☐ 14 Willie Stargell	1.50	.75	.15
☐ 15 Cecil Cooper	.75	.35	.07
☐ 16 Steve Carlton	2.00	1.00	.20
☐ 17 Ted Simmons	1.00	.50	.10
☐ 18 Dave Kingman	1.00	.50	.10
☐ 19 Rickey Henderson	3.00	1.50	.30
☐ 20 Fred Lynn	1.00	.50	.10
☐ 21 Dave Winfield	2.00	1.00	.20
☐ 22 Rod Carew	2.00	1.00	.20
☐ 23 Jim Rice	1.25	.60	.12
☐ 24 Bruce Sutter	.75	.35	.07

☐ 25 Cesar Cedeno	.75	.35	.07
☐ 26 Nolan Ryan	3.00	1.50	.30
☐ 27 Dusty Baker	.75	.35	.07
☐ 28 Jim Palmer	1.50	.75	.15
☐ 29 Gorman Thomas	.75	.35	.07
☐ 30 Ben Oglivie	.75	.35	.07
☐ 31 Willie Wilson	1.00	.50	.10
☐ 32 Gary Carter	1.25	.60	.12

1981 Perma-Graphic All-Stars

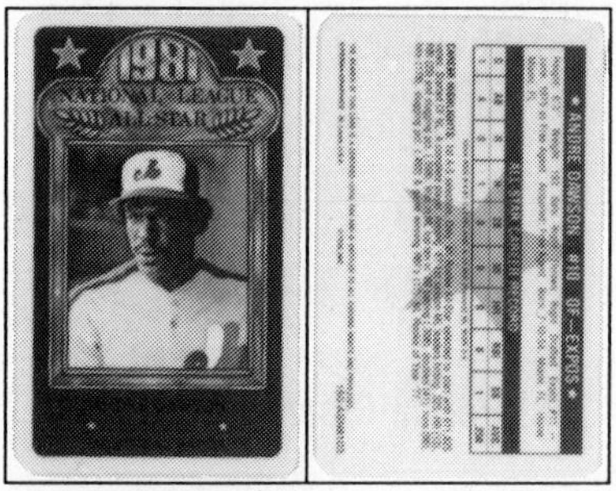

This set commemorates the starters of the 1981 All-Star game. This 18-card set measure 2 1/8" by 3 3/8" and has rounded corners. Because of the players strike of 1981 plenty of time was available to prepare the player's biography with appropriate notes. The set is framed on the front in red for the National League and Blue for the American league.

	MINT	EXC	G-VG
COMPLETE SET (18)	27.00	13.50	2.70
COMMON PLAYER (1-18)	1.00	.50	.10
☐ 1 Gary Carter	1.50	.75	.15
☐ 2 Dave Concepcion	1.25	.60	.12
☐ 3 Andre Dawson	1.50	.75	.15
☐ 4 George Foster	1.00	.50	.10
☐ 5 Davey Lopes	1.00	.50	.10
☐ 6 Dave Parker	1.25	.60	.12
☐ 7 Pete Rose	4.00	2.00	.40
☐ 8 Mike Schmidt	4.00	2.00	.40
☐ 9 Fernando Valenzuela	1.50	.75	.15
☐ 10 George Brett	3.00	1.50	.30
☐ 11 Rod Carew	2.00	1.00	.20
☐ 12 Bucky Dent	1.00	.50	.10
☐ 13 Carlton Fisk	1.50	.75	.15
☐ 14 Reggie Jackson	2.00	1.00	.20
☐ 15 Jack Morris	1.25	.60	.12
☐ 16 Willie Randolph	1.00	.50	.10
☐ 17 Ken Singleton	1.00	.50	.10
☐ 18 Dave Winfield	2.00	1.00	.20

1982 Perma-Graphic Credit Cards

For the second year Perma-Graphics, in association with Topps produced a high-quality set on plastic honoring the leading players in baseball of 1982. The players photo is on the front middle of the card and is framed by a brown border with many innovative designs. This 24-card set features plastic cards each measuring approximately 2 1/8" by 3 3/8". On the card back there is one line of career statistics along with career highlights. Perma-Graphics also issued the set in a limited "gold" edition, i.e., with a gold tint to the cards. The gold edition cards are valued at double the prices listed below. Again in 1982 Perma-Graphic issued these sets in conjuction and with the approval of Topps Chewing Gum.

	MINT	EXC	G-VG
COMPLETE SET (24)	35.00	17.50	3.50
COMMON PLAYER (1-24)	1.00	.50	.10
☐ 1 Johnny Bench	2.00	1.00	.20
☐ 2 Tom Seaver	2.00	1.00	.20
☐ 3 Mike Schmidt	3.00	1.50	.30
☐ 4 Gary Carter	1.50	.75	.15
☐ 5 Willie Stargell	1.50	.75	.15
☐ 6 Tim Raines	1.50	.75	.15
☐ 7 Bill Madlock	1.00	.50	.10
☐ 8 Keith Hernandez	1.25	.60	.12
☐ 9 Pete Rose	3.00	1.50	.30
☐ 10 Steve Carlton	2.00	1.00	.20
☐ 11 Steve Garvey	2.00	1.00	.20
☐ 12 Fernando Valenzuela	1.50	.75	.15
☐ 13 Carl Yastrzemski	3.00	1.50	.30
☐ 14 Dave Winfield	2.00	1.00	.20
☐ 15 Carney Lansford	1.00	.50	.10
☐ 16 Rollie Fingers	1.50	.75	.15
☐ 17 Tony Armas	1.00	.50	.10
☐ 18 Cecil Cooper	1.00	.50	.10
☐ 19 George Brett	3.00	1.50	.30
☐ 20 Reggie Jackson	2.00	1.00	.20
☐ 21 Rod Carew	2.00	1.00	.20
☐ 22 Eddie Murray	2.00	1.00	.20
☐ 23 Rickey Henderson	3.00	1.50	.30
☐ 24 Kirk Gibson	1.50	.75	.15

1982 Perma-Graphic All-Stars

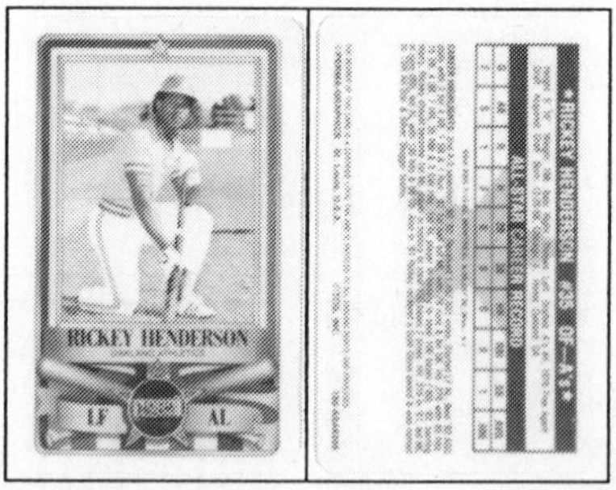

For the second time Perma-Graphic issued a special set commemorating the starters of the 1982 All-Star game. This 18-card set measures 2 1/8" by 3 3/8" and features a colorful design framing the players photo on the front The back again feature one line of complete All-Star game statistics including the 1982 game and career highlites. Perma-Graphics also issued the set in a limited "gold" edition, i.e., with a gold tint to the cards. The gold edition cards are valued at double the prices listed below.

	MINT	EXC	G-VG
COMPLETE SET (18)	27.00	13.50	2.70
COMMON PLAYER (1-18)	1.00	.50	.10
☐ 1 Dennis Eckersley	1.50	.75	.15
☐ 2 Cecil Cooper	1.00	.50	.10
☐ 3 Carlton Fisk	1.50	.75	.15
☐ 4 Robin Yount	2.00	1.00	.20
☐ 5 Bobby Grich	1.00	.50	.10
☐ 6 Rickey Henderson	3.00	1.50	.30
☐ 7 Reggie Jackson	2.00	1.00	.20
☐ 8 Fred Lynn	1.25	.60	.12

	MINT	EXC	G-VG
☐ 9 George Brett	2.00	1.00	.20
☐ 10 Gary Carter	1.50	.75	.15
☐ 11 Dave Concepcion	1.00	.50	.10
☐ 12 Andre Dawson	1.50	.75	.15
☐ 13 Tim Raines	1.50	.75	.15
☐ 14 Dale Murphy	2.00	1.00	.20
☐ 15 Steve Rogers	1.00	.50	.10
☐ 16 Pete Rose	3.00	1.50	.30
☐ 17 Mike Schmidt	3.00	1.50	.30
☐ 18 Manny Trillo	1.00	.50	.10

1983 Perma-Graphic Credit Cards

This set was the third straight year Perma-Graphic, with approval from Topps issued their high-quality plastic set. This 36-card set which measures 2 1/8" by 3 3/8" have the players photos framed by colorful backgrounds. The backs again feature one line of career statistics and several informative lines of career highlights. Perma-Graphics also issued the set in a limited "gold" edition, i.e., with a gold tint to the cards. The gold edition cards are valued at double the prices listed below.

	MINT	EXC	G-VG
COMPLETE SET (36)	40.00	20.00	4.00
COMMON PLAYER (1-36)	1.00	.50	.10
☐ 1 Bill Buckner	1.00	.50	.10
☐ 2 Steve Carlton	2.00	1.00	.20
☐ 3 Gary Carter	1.50	.75	.15
☐ 4 Andre Dawson	1.50	.75	.15
☐ 5 Pedro Guerrero	1.25	.60	.12
☐ 6 George Hendrick	1.00	.50	.10
☐ 7 Keith Hernandez	1.25	.60	.12
☐ 8 Bill Madlock	1.00	.50	.10
☐ 9 Dale Murphy	2.00	1.00	.20
☐ 10 Al Oliver	1.00	.50	.10
☐ 11 Dave Parker	1.50	.75	.15
☐ 12 Darrell Porter	1.00	.50	.10
☐ 13 Pete Rose	3.00	1.50	.30
☐ 14 Mike Schmidt	3.00	1.50	.30
☐ 15 Lonnie Smith	1.00	.50	.10
☐ 16 Ozzie Smith	1.50	.75	.15
☐ 17 Bruce Sutter	1.00	.50	.10
☐ 18 Fernando Valenzuela	1.25	.60	.12
☐ 19 George Brett	2.00	1.00	.20
☐ 20 Rod Carew	2.00	1.00	.20
☐ 21 Cecil Cooper	1.00	.50	.10
☐ 22 Doug DeCinces	1.00	.50	.10
☐ 23 Rollie Fingers	1.50	.75	.15
☐ 24 Damaso Garcia	1.00	.50	.10
☐ 25 Toby Harrah	1.00	.50	.10
☐ 26 Rickey Henderson	3.00	1.50	.30
☐ 27 Reggie Jackson	2.00	1.00	.20
☐ 28 Hal McRae	1.00	.50	.10
☐ 29 Eddie Murray	2.00	1.00	.20
☐ 30 Lance Parrish	1.50	.75	.15
☐ 31 Jim Rice	1.50	.75	.15
☐ 32 Gorman Thomas	1.25	.60	.12
☐ 33 Willie Wilson	1.25	.60	.12
☐ 34 Dave Winfield	2.00	1.00	.20
☐ 35 Carl Yastrzemski	3.00	1.50	.30
☐ 36 Robin Yount	2.00	1.00	.20

1983 Perma-Graphic All-Stars

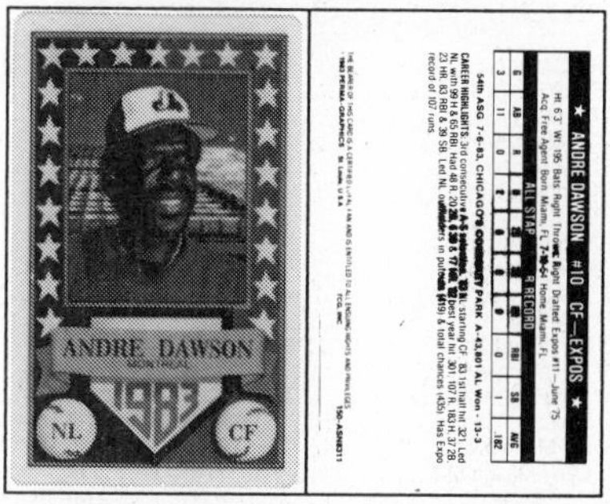

The 1983 All-Star Set was the third set Perma-Graphics issued commemorating the starters of the All-Star game. Again, Perma-Graphics used the Topps photos and issued their sets on plastics. This 18-card set features cards each measuring approximately 2 1/8" by 3 3/8". Perma-Graphics also issued the set in a limited "gold" edition, i.e., with a gold tint to the cards. The gold edition cards are valued at double the prices listed below.

	MINT	EXC	G-VG
COMPLETE SET (18)	27.00	13.50	2.70
COMMON PLAYER (1-18)	1.00	.50	.10
☐ 1 George Brett	2.00	1.00	.20
☐ 2 Rod Carew	2.00	1.00	.20
☐ 3 Fred Lynn	1.25	.60	.12
☐ 4 Jim Rice	1.50	.75	.15
☐ 5 Ted Simmons	1.25	.60	.12
☐ 6 Dave Stieb	1.50	.75	.15
☐ 7 Dave Winfield	2.00	1.00	.20
☐ 8 Manny Trillo	1.00	.50	.10
☐ 9 Robin Yount	2.00	1.00	.20
☐ 10 Gary Carter	1.50	.75	.15
☐ 11 Andre Dawson	1.50	.75	.15
☐ 12 Dale Murphy	2.00	1.00	.20
☐ 13 Al Oliver	1.00	.50	.10
☐ 14 Tim Raines	1.50	.75	.15
☐ 15 Steve Sax	1.25	.60	.12
☐ 16 Mike Schmidt	3.00	1.50	.30
☐ 17 Ozzie Smith	1.50	.75	.15
☐ 18 Mario Soto	1.00	.50	.10

1964 Philadelphia Bulletin

This 27-player set was produced by the Philadelphia Bulletin, a newspaper. The catalog designation for this set is M130-5. These large, approximately 8" by 10", photo cards are unnumbered and blank backed.

	NRMT	VG-E	GOOD
COMPLETE SET (27)	125.00	60.00	12.50
COMMON PLAYER (1-27)	4.50	2.25	.45
☐ 1 Rich Allen	12.00	6.00	1.20
☐ 2 Ruben Amaro	4.50	2.25	.45
☐ 3 Jack Baldschun	4.50	2.25	.45
☐ 4 Dennis Bennett	4.50	2.25	.45
☐ 5 John Boozer	4.50	2.25	.45
☐ 6 Johnny Briggs	4.50	2.25	.45
☐ 7 Jim Bunning (2)	10.00	5.00	1.00
☐ 8 Johnny Callison	6.00	3.00	.60
☐ 9 Danny Cater	4.50	2.25	.45
☐ 10 Wes Covington	6.00	3.00	.60
☐ 11 Ray Culp	4.50	2.25	.45
☐ 12 Clay Dalrymple	4.50	2.25	.45
☐ 13 Tony Gonzales	6.00	3.00	.60
☐ 14 John Herrnstein	4.50	2.25	.45
☐ 15 Alex Johnson	6.00	3.00	.60
☐ 16 Art Mahaffey	4.50	2.25	.45
☐ 17 Gene Mauch MG	7.50	3.75	.75
☐ 18 Vic Power	6.00	3.00	.60
☐ 19 Ed Roebuck	4.50	2.25	.45
☐ 20 Cookie Rojas	6.00	3.00	.60
☐ 21 Bobby Shantz	6.00	3.00	.60
☐ 22 Chris Short	6.00	3.00	.60
☐ 23 Tony Taylor	6.00	3.00	.60
☐ 24 Frank Thomas	6.00	3.00	.60
☐ 25 Gus Triandos	6.00	3.00	.60
☐ 26 Bobby Wine	6.00	3.00	.60
☐ 27 Rick Wise	6.00	3.00	.60

1939 Playball

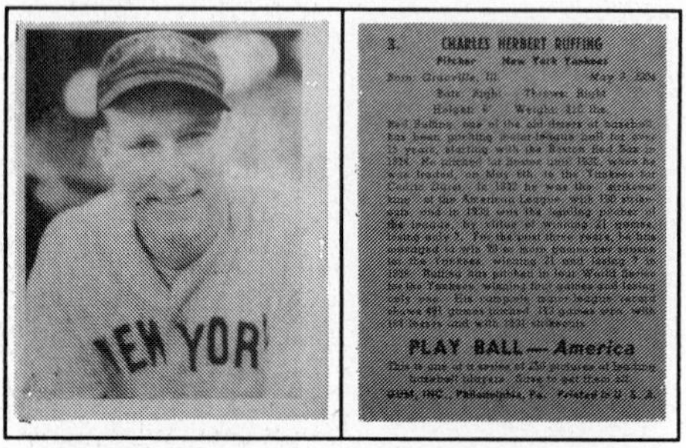

The cards in this 162-card set measure 2 1/2" by 3 1/8". Gum Incorporated introduced a brief (war-shortened) but innovative era of baseball card production with its set of 1939. The combination of actual player photos (black and white), large card size, and extensive biography proved extremely popular. Player names are found either entirely capitalized or with initial caps only, and a "sample card" overprint is not uncommon. Card number 126 was never issued, and cards 116-162 were produced in lesser quantities than 1-115. The catalog designation for this set is R334.

	EX-MT	VG-E	GOOD
COMPLETE SET	11000.00	5000.00	1250.00
COMMON PLAYER (1-115)	12.00	6.00	1.20
COMMON PLAYER (116-162)	120.00	60.00	12.00
☐ 1 Jake Powell	75.00	10.00	2.00
☐ 2 Lee Grissom	12.00	6.00	1.20
☐ 3 Red Ruffing	80.00	40.00	8.00
☐ 4 Eldon Auker	12.00	6.00	1.20
☐ 5 Luke Sewell	15.00	7.50	1.50
☐ 6 Leo Durocher	50.00	25.00	5.00
☐ 7 Bobby Doerr	80.00	40.00	8.00
☐ 8 Henry Pippen	12.00	6.00	1.20
☐ 9 James Tobin	12.00	6.00	1.20
☐ 10 James DeShong	12.00	6.00	1.20
☐ 11 Johnny Rizzo	12.00	6.00	1.20
☐ 12 Hershel Martin	12.00	6.00	1.20
☐ 13 Luke Hamlin	12.00	6.00	1.20
☐ 14 Jim Tabor	12.00	6.00	1.20
☐ 15 Paul Derringer	20.00	10.00	2.00
☐ 16 John Peacock	12.00	6.00	1.20
☐ 17 Emerson Dickman	12.00	6.00	1.20
☐ 18 Harry Danning	12.00	6.00	1.20
☐ 19 Paul Dean	20.00	10.00	2.00
☐ 20 Joe Heving	12.00	6.00	1.20
☐ 21 Dutch Leonard	16.00	8.00	1.60
☐ 22 Bucky Walters	16.00	8.00	1.60
☐ 23 Burgess Whitehead	12.00	6.00	1.20
☐ 24 Richard Coffman	12.00	6.00	1.20
☐ 25 George Selkirk	20.00	10.00	2.00
☐ 26 Joe DiMaggio	1600.00	750.00	200.00
☐ 27 Fred Ostermueller	12.00	6.00	1.20
☐ 28 Sylvester Johnson	12.00	6.00	1.20
☐ 29 John (Jack) Wilson	12.00	6.00	1.20
☐ 30 Bill Dickey	135.00	65.00	13.50
☐ 31 Sam West	12.00	6.00	1.20
☐ 32 Bob Seeds	12.00	6.00	1.20
☐ 33 Del Young	12.00	6.00	1.20
☐ 34 Frank Demaree	12.00	6.00	1.20
☐ 35 Bill Jurges	12.00	6.00	1.20
☐ 36 Frank McCormick	16.00	8.00	1.60
☐ 37 Virgil Davis	12.00	6.00	1.20
☐ 38 Billy Myers	12.00	6.00	1.20
☐ 39 Rick Ferrell	60.00	30.00	6.00
☐ 40 James Bagby Jr.	12.00	6.00	1.20
☐ 41 Lon Warneke	12.00	6.00	1.20
☐ 42 Arndt Jorgens	12.00	6.00	1.20
☐ 43 Melo Almada	12.00	6.00	1.20
☐ 44 Don Heffner	12.00	6.00	1.20
☐ 45 Merrill May	12.00	6.00	1.20
☐ 46 Morris Arnovich	12.00	6.00	1.20
☐ 47 Buddy Lewis	12.00	6.00	1.20
☐ 48 Lefty Gomez	110.00	55.00	11.00
☐ 49 Eddie Miller	12.00	6.00	1.20
☐ 50 Charlie Gehringer	110.00	55.00	11.00
☐ 51 Mel Ott	135.00	65.00	13.50
☐ 52 Tommy Henrich	25.00	12.50	2.50
☐ 53 Carl Hubbell	110.00	55.00	11.00
☐ 54 Harry Gumpert	12.00	6.00	1.20
☐ 55 Arky Vaughan	60.00	30.00	6.00
☐ 56 Hank Greenberg	135.00	65.00	13.50
☐ 57 Buddy Hassett	12.00	6.00	1.20
☐ 58 Lou Chiozza	12.00	6.00	1.20
☐ 59 Ken Chase	12.00	6.00	1.20
☐ 60 Schoolboy Rowe	16.00	8.00	1.60
☐ 61 Tony Cuccinello	12.00	6.00	1.20
☐ 62 Tom Carey	12.00	6.00	1.20
☐ 63 Emmett Mueller	12.00	6.00	1.20
☐ 64 Wally Moses	16.00	8.00	1.60
☐ 65 Harry Craft	12.00	6.00	1.20
☐ 66 Jimmy Ripple	12.00	6.00	1.20
☐ 67 Ed Joost	12.00	6.00	1.20
☐ 68 Fred Sington	12.00	6.00	1.20
☐ 69 Elbie Fletcher	12.00	6.00	1.20
☐ 70 Fred Frankhouse	12.00	6.00	1.20
☐ 71 Monte Pearson	12.00	6.00	1.20
☐ 72 Debs Garms	12.00	6.00	1.20
☐ 73 Hal Schumacher	12.00	6.00	1.20
☐ 74 Cookie Lavagetto	12.00	6.00	1.20
☐ 75 Stan Bordagaray	12.00	6.00	1.20
☐ 76 Goody Rosen	12.00	6.00	1.20
☐ 77 Lew Riggs	12.00	6.00	1.20
☐ 78 Julius Solters	12.00	6.00	1.20
☐ 79 Jo Jo Moore	12.00	6.00	1.20
☐ 80 Pete Fox	12.00	6.00	1.20
☐ 81 Babe Dahlgren	12.00	6.00	1.20
☐ 82 Chuck Klein	110.00	55.00	11.00
☐ 83 Gus Suhr	12.00	6.00	1.20
☐ 84 Skeeter Newsom	12.00	6.00	1.20
☐ 85 Johnny Cooney	12.00	6.00	1.20
☐ 86 Dolph Camilli	12.00	6.00	1.20
☐ 87 Milburn Shoffner	12.00	6.00	1.20
☐ 88 Charlie Keller	20.00	10.00	2.00
☐ 89 Lloyd Waner	60.00	30.00	6.00
☐ 90 Robert Klinger	12.00	6.00	1.20
☐ 91 John Knott	12.00	6.00	1.20
☐ 92 Ted Williams	1600.00	750.00	200.00
☐ 93 Charles Gelbert	12.00	6.00	1.20
☐ 94 Heinie Manush	60.00	30.00	6.00
☐ 95 Whit Wyatt	12.00	6.00	1.20
☐ 96 Babe Phelps	12.00	6.00	1.20
☐ 97 Bob Johnson	16.00	8.00	1.60
☐ 98 Pinky Whitney	12.00	6.00	1.20
☐ 99 Wally Berger	16.00	8.00	1.60
☐ 100 Charles Myer	12.00	6.00	1.20
☐ 101 Roger Cramer	16.00	8.00	1.60
☐ 102 Lem Young	12.00	6.00	1.20
☐ 103 Moe Berg	25.00	12.50	2.50
☐ 104 Tom Bridges	16.00	8.00	1.60
☐ 105 Rabbit McNair	12.00	6.00	1.20
☐ 106 Dolly Stark	12.00	6.00	1.20
☐ 107 Joe Vosmik	12.00	6.00	1.20
☐ 108 Frank Hayes	12.00	6.00	1.20
☐ 109 Myril Hoag	12.00	6.00	1.20
☐ 110 Fred Fitzsimmons	12.00	6.00	1.20
☐ 111 Van Lingle Mungo	16.00	8.00	1.60

☐ 112 Paul Waner	60.00	30.00	6.00
☐ 113 Al Schacht	16.00	8.00	1.60
☐ 114 Cecil Travis	12.00	6.00	1.20
☐ 115 Ralph Kress	12.00	6.00	1.20
☐ 116 Gene Desautels	120.00	60.00	12.00
☐ 117 Wayne Ambler	120.00	60.00	12.00
☐ 118 Lynn Nelson	120.00	60.00	12.00
☐ 119 Will Hershberger	120.00	60.00	12.00
☐ 120 Rabbit Warstler	120.00	60.00	12.00
☐ 121 Bill Posedel	120.00	60.00	12.00
☐ 122 George McQuinn	120.00	60.00	12.00
☐ 123 Ray T. Davis	120.00	60.00	12.00
☐ 124 Walter Brown	120.00	60.00	12.00
☐ 125 Cliff Melton	120.00	60.00	12.00
☐ 126 Not issued	000.00	00.00	00.00
☐ 127 Gil Brack	120.00	60.00	12.00
☐ 128 Joe Bowman	120.00	60.00	12.00
☐ 129 Bill Swift	120.00	60.00	12.00
☐ 130 Bill Brubaker	120.00	60.00	12.00
☐ 131 Mort Cooper	150.00	75.00	15.00
☐ 132 Jim Brown	120.00	60.00	12.00
☐ 133 Lynn Myers	120.00	60.00	12.00
☐ 134 Tot Presnell	120.00	60.00	12.00
☐ 135 Mickey Owen	150.00	75.00	15.00
☐ 136 Roy Bell	120.00	60.00	12.00
☐ 137 Pete Appleton	120.00	60.00	12.00
☐ 138 George Case	120.00	60.00	12.00
☐ 139 Vito Tamulis	120.00	60.00	12.00
☐ 140 Ray Hayworth	120.00	60.00	12.00
☐ 141 Pete Coscarart	120.00	60.00	12.00
☐ 142 Ira Hutchinson	120.00	60.00	12.00
☐ 143 Earl Averill	350.00	175.00	35.00
☐ 144 Zeke Bonura	120.00	60.00	12.00
☐ 145 Hugh Mulcahy	120.00	60.00	12.00
☐ 146 Tom Sunkel	120.00	60.00	12.00
☐ 147 George Coffman	120.00	60.00	12.00
☐ 148 Bill Trotter	120.00	60.00	12.00
☐ 149 Max West	120.00	60.00	12.00
☐ 150 James Walkup	120.00	60.00	12.00
☐ 151 Hugh Casey	150.00	75.00	15.00
☐ 152 Roy Weatherly	120.00	60.00	12.00
☐ 153 Paul Trout	150.00	75.00	15.00
☐ 154 Johnny Hudson	120.00	60.00	12.00
☐ 155 Jimmy Outlaw	120.00	60.00	12.00
☐ 156 Ray Berres	120.00	60.00	12.00
☐ 157 Don Padgett	120.00	60.00	12.00
☐ 158 Bud Thomas	120.00	60.00	12.00
☐ 159 Red Evans	120.00	60.00	12.00
☐ 160 Gene Moore	120.00	60.00	12.00
☐ 161 Lonnie Frey	120.00	60.00	12.00
☐ 162 Whitey Moore	150.00	75.00	15.00

1940 Playball

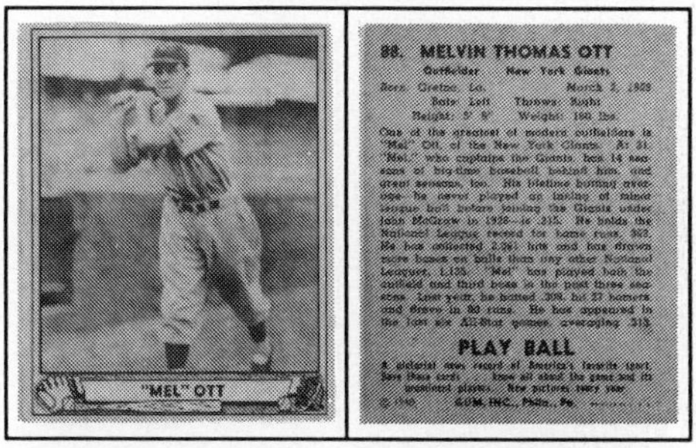

The cards in this 240-card series measure 2 1/2" by 3 1/8". Gum Inc. improved upon its 1939 design by enclosing the 1940 black and white player photo with a frame line and printing the player's name in a panel below the picture (often using a nickname). The set included many Hall of Famers and Old Timers. Cards 181-240 are scarcer than cards 1-180. The backs contain an extensive biography and a dated copyright line. The catalog number for this set is R335.

	EX-MT	VG-E	GOOD
COMPLETE SET (240)	15000.00	6500.00	1500.00
COMMON PLAYER (1-120)	13.50	6.25	1.25
COMMON PLAYER (121-180)	15.00	7.50	1.50
COMMON PLAYER (181-240)	65.00	32.50	6.50

☐ 1 Joe DiMaggio	2100.00	750.00	200.00
☐ 2 Art Jorgens	13.50	6.25	1.25
☐ 3 Babe Dahlgren	16.00	8.00	1.60
☐ 4 Tommy Henrich	25.00	12.50	2.50
☐ 5 Monte Pearson	16.00	8.00	1.60
☐ 6 Lefty Gomez	150.00	75.00	15.00
☐ 7 Bill Dickey	180.00	90.00	18.00
☐ 8 George Selkirk	20.00	10.00	2.00
☐ 9 Charlie Keller	25.00	12.50	2.50
☐ 10 Red Ruffing	80.00	40.00	8.00
☐ 11 Jake Powell	13.50	6.25	1.25
☐ 12 Johnny Schulte	13.50	6.25	1.25
☐ 13 Jack Knott	13.50	6.25	1.25
☐ 14 Rabbit McNair	13.50	6.25	1.25
☐ 15 George Case	16.00	8.00	1.60
☐ 16 Cecil Travis	13.50	6.25	1.25
☐ 17 Buddy Myer	13.50	6.25	1.25
☐ 18 Charlie Gelbert	13.50	6.25	1.25
☐ 19 Ken Chase	13.50	6.25	1.25
☐ 20 Buddy Lewis	13.50	6.25	1.25
☐ 21 Rick Ferrell	60.00	30.00	6.00
☐ 22 Sammy West	13.50	6.25	1.25
☐ 23 Dutch Leonard	16.00	8.00	1.60
☐ 24 Frank Hayes	13.50	6.25	1.25
☐ 25 Bob Johnson	16.00	8.00	1.60
☐ 26 Wally Moses	16.00	8.00	1.60
☐ 27 Ted Williams	1200.00	500.00	120.00
☐ 28 Gene Desautels	13.50	6.25	1.25
☐ 29 Doc Cramer	16.00	8.00	1.60
☐ 30 Moe Berg	25.00	12.50	2.50
☐ 31 Jack Wilson	13.50	6.25	1.25
☐ 32 Jim Bagby	13.50	6.25	1.25
☐ 33 Fritz Ostermueller	13.50	6.25	1.25
☐ 34 John Peacock	13.50	6.25	1.25
☐ 35 Joe Heving	13.50	6.25	1.25
☐ 36 Jim Tabor	13.50	6.25	1.25
☐ 37 Emerson Dickman	13.50	6.25	1.25
☐ 38 Bobby Doerr	70.00	35.00	7.00
☐ 39 Tom Carey	13.50	6.25	1.25
☐ 40 Hank Greenberg	160.00	80.00	16.00
☐ 41 Charley Gehringer	135.00	65.00	13.50
☐ 42 Bud Thomas	13.50	6.25	1.25
☐ 43 Pete Fox	13.50	6.25	1.25
☐ 44 Dizzy Trout	16.00	8.00	1.60
☐ 45 Red Kress	13.50	6.25	1.25
☐ 46 Earl Averill	80.00	40.00	8.00
☐ 47 Ol' Os Vitt	13.50	6.25	1.25
☐ 48 Luke Sewell	16.00	8.00	1.60
☐ 49 Stormy Weatherly	13.50	6.25	1.25
☐ 50 Hal Trosky	16.00	8.00	1.60
☐ 51 Don Heffner	13.50	6.25	1.25
☐ 52 Myril Hoag	13.50	6.25	1.25
☐ 53 Mac McQuinn	13.50	6.25	1.25
☐ 54 Bill Trotter	13.50	6.25	1.25
☐ 55 Slick Coffman	13.50	6.25	1.25
☐ 56 Eddie Miller	13.50	6.25	1.25
☐ 57 Max West	13.50	6.25	1.25
☐ 58 Bill Posedel	13.50	6.25	1.25
☐ 59 Rabbit Warstler	13.50	6.25	1.25
☐ 60 John Cooney	13.50	6.25	1.25
☐ 61 Tony Cuccinello	13.50	6.25	1.25
☐ 62 Buddy Hassett	13.50	6.25	1.25
☐ 63 Pete Coscarart	13.50	6.25	1.25
☐ 64 Van Lingle Mungo	16.00	8.00	1.60
☐ 65 Fitz Fitzsimmons	13.50	6.25	1.25
☐ 66 Babe Phelps	13.50	6.25	1.25
☐ 67 Whit Wyatt	16.00	8.00	1.60
☐ 68 Dolph Camilli	13.50	6.25	1.25
☐ 69 Cookie Lavagetto	13.50	6.25	1.25
☐ 70 Hot Potato Hamlin	13.50	6.25	1.25
☐ 71 Mel Almada	13.50	6.25	1.25
☐ 72 Chuck Dressen	16.00	8.00	1.60
☐ 73 Bucky Walters	16.00	8.00	1.60
☐ 74 Duke Derringer	20.00	10.00	2.00
☐ 75 Buck McCormick	16.00	8.00	1.60
☐ 76 Lonny Frey	13.50	6.25	1.25
☐ 77 Bill Hershberger	13.50	6.25	1.25
☐ 78 Lew Riggs	13.50	6.25	1.25
☐ 79 Harry Wildfire Craft	13.50	6.25	1.25
☐ 80 Billy Myers	13.50	6.25	1.25
☐ 81 Wally Berger	16.00	8.00	1.60
☐ 82 Hank Gowdy	13.50	6.25	1.25
☐ 83 Cliff Melton	13.50	6.25	1.25
☐ 84 Jo Jo Moore	13.50	6.25	1.25
☐ 85 Hal Schumacher	13.50	6.25	1.25
☐ 86 Harry Gumbert	13.50	6.25	1.25
☐ 87 Carl Hubbell	135.00	65.00	13.50
☐ 88 Mel Ott	160.00	80.00	16.00
☐ 89 Bill Jurges	13.50	6.25	1.25
☐ 90 Frank Demaree	13.50	6.25	1.25
☐ 91 Suitcase Seeds	13.50	6.25	1.25
☐ 92 Whitey Whitehead	13.50	6.25	1.25
☐ 93 Harry Danning	13.50	6.25	1.25
☐ 94 Gus Suhr	13.50	6.25	1.25

☐ 95 Mul Mulcahy	13.50	6.25	1.25
☐ 96 Heinie Mueller	13.50	6.25	1.25
☐ 97 Morry Arnovich	13.50	6.25	1.25
☐ 98 Pinky May	13.50	6.25	1.25
☐ 99 Syl Johnson	13.50	6.25	1.25
☐ 100 Hersh Martin	13.50	6.25	1.25
☐ 101 Del Young	13.50	6.25	1.25
☐ 102 Chuck Klein	110.00	55.00	11.00
☐ 103 Elbie Fletcher	13.50	6.25	1.25
☐ 104 Big Poison Waner	80.00	40.00	8.00
☐ 105 Little Poison Waner	80.00	40.00	8.00
☐ 106 Pep Young	13.50	6.25	1.25
☐ 107 Arky Vaughan	60.00	30.00	6.00
☐ 108 Johnny Rizzo	13.50	6.25	1.25
☐ 109 Don Padgett	13.50	6.25	1.25
☐ 110 Tom Sunkel	13.50	6.25	1.25
☐ 111 Mickey Owen	16.00	8.00	1.60
☐ 112 Jimmy Brown	13.50	6.25	1.25
☐ 113 Mort Cooper	16.00	8.00	1.60
☐ 114 Lon Warneke	13.50	6.25	1.25
☐ 115 Mike Gonzales	13.50	6.25	1.25
☐ 116 Al Schacht	16.00	8.00	1.60
☐ 117 Dolly Stark	16.00	8.00	1.60
☐ 118 Schoolboy Hoyt	80.00	40.00	8.00
☐ 119 Ol Pete Alexander	135.00	65.00	13.50
☐ 120 Walter Johnson	225.00	110.00	22.00
☐ 121 Atley Donald	15.00	7.50	1.50
☐ 122 Sandy Sundra	15.00	7.50	1.50
☐ 123 Hildy Hildebrand	15.00	7.50	1.50
☐ 124 Colonel Earle Combs	110.00	55.00	11.00
☐ 125 Art Fletcher	15.00	7.50	1.50
☐ 126 Jake Solters	15.00	7.50	1.50
☐ 127 Muddy Ruel	15.00	7.50	1.50
☐ 128 Pete Appleton	15.00	7.50	1.50
☐ 129 Bucky Harris	60.00	30.00	6.00
☐ 130 Deerfoot Milan	15.00	7.50	1.50
☐ 131 Zeke Bonura	15.00	7.50	1.50
☐ 132 Connie Mack	135.00	65.00	13.50
☐ 133 Jimmie Foxx	225.00	110.00	22.00
☐ 134 Joe Cronin	135.00	65.00	13.50
☐ 135 Line Drive Nelson	15.00	7.50	1.50
☐ 136 Cotton Pippen	15.00	7.50	1.50
☐ 137 Bing Miller	15.00	7.50	1.50
☐ 138 Beau Bell	15.00	7.50	1.50
☐ 139 Elden Auker	15.00	7.50	1.50
☐ 140 Dick Coffman	15.00	7.50	1.50
☐ 141 Casey Stengel	200.00	100.00	20.00
☐ 142 Highpockets Kelly	80.00	40.00	8.00
☐ 143 Gene Moore	15.00	7.50	1.50
☐ 144 Joe Vosmik	15.00	7.50	1.50
☐ 145 Vito Tamulis	15.00	7.50	1.50
☐ 146 Tot Pressnell	15.00	7.50	1.50
☐ 147 Johnny Hudson	15.00	7.50	1.50
☐ 148 Hugh Casey	15.00	7.50	1.50
☐ 149 Pinky Shoffner	15.00	7.50	1.50
☐ 150 Whitey Moore	15.00	7.50	1.50
☐ 151 Edwin Joost	15.00	7.50	1.50
☐ 152 Jimmy Wilson	15.00	7.50	1.50
☐ 153 Bill McKechnie	75.00	37.50	7.50
☐ 154 Jumbo Brown	15.00	7.50	1.50
☐ 155 Ray Hayworth	15.00	7.50	1.50
☐ 156 Daffy Dean	25.00	12.50	2.50
☐ 157 Lou Chiozza	15.00	7.50	1.50
☐ 158 Travis Jackson	80.00	40.00	8.00
☐ 159 Pancho Snyder	15.00	7.50	1.50
☐ 160 Hans Lobert	15.00	7.50	1.50
☐ 161 Debs Garms	15.00	7.50	1.50
☐ 162 Joe Bowman	15.00	7.50	1.50
☐ 163 Spud Davis	15.00	7.50	1.50
☐ 164 Ray Berres	15.00	7.50	1.50
☐ 165 Bob Klinger	15.00	7.50	1.50
☐ 166 Bill Brubaker	15.00	7.50	1.50
☐ 167 Frankie Frisch	110.00	55.00	11.00
☐ 168 Honus Wagner	250.00	125.00	25.00
☐ 169 Gabby Street	15.00	7.50	1.50
☐ 170 Tris Speaker	200.00	100.00	20.00
☐ 171 Harry Heilmann	110.00	55.00	11.00
☐ 172 Chief Bender	80.00	40.00	8.00
☐ 173 Larry Lajoie	200.00	100.00	20.00
☐ 174 Johnny Evers	80.00	40.00	8.00
☐ 175 Christy Mathewson	250.00	125.00	25.00
☐ 176 Heinie Manush	80.00	40.00	8.00
☐ 177 Homerun Baker	110.00	55.00	11.00
☐ 178 Max Carey	80.00	40.00	8.00
☐ 179 George Sisler	110.00	55.00	11.00
☐ 180 Mickey Cochrane	160.00	80.00	16.00
☐ 181 Spud Chandler	80.00	40.00	8.00
☐ 182 Knick Knickerbocker	65.00	32.50	6.50
☐ 183 Marvin Breuer	65.00	32.50	6.50
☐ 184 Mule Haas	65.00	32.50	6.50
☐ 185 Joe Kuhel	65.00	32.50	6.50
☐ 186 Taft Wright	65.00	32.50	6.50
☐ 187 Jimmy Dykes	80.00	40.00	8.00
☐ 188 Joe Krakauskas	65.00	32.50	6.50
☐ 189 Jim Bloodworth	65.00	32.50	6.50
☐ 190 Charley Berry	65.00	32.50	6.50
☐ 191 John Babich	65.00	32.50	6.50
☐ 192 Dick Siebert	65.00	32.50	6.50
☐ 193 Chubby Dean	65.00	32.50	6.50
☐ 194 Sam Chapman	65.00	32.50	6.50
☐ 195 Dee Miles	65.00	32.50	6.50
☐ 196 Nonny Nonnenkamp	65.00	32.50	6.50
☐ 197 Lou Finney	65.00	32.50	6.50
☐ 198 Denny Galehouse	65.00	32.50	6.50
☐ 199 Pinky Higgins	65.00	32.50	6.50
☐ 200 Soup Campbell	65.00	32.50	6.50
☐ 201 Barney McCosky	65.00	32.50	6.50
☐ 202 Al Milnar	65.00	32.50	6.50
☐ 203 Bad News Hale	65.00	32.50	6.50
☐ 204 Harry Eisenstat	65.00	32.50	6.50
☐ 205 Rollie Hemsley	65.00	32.50	6.50
☐ 206 Chet Laabs	65.00	32.50	6.50
☐ 207 Gus Mancuso	65.00	32.50	6.50
☐ 208 Lee Gamble	65.00	32.50	6.50
☐ 209 Hy Vandenberg	65.00	32.50	6.50
☐ 210 Bill Lohrman	65.00	32.50	6.50
☐ 211 Pop Joiner	65.00	32.50	6.50
☐ 212 Babe Young	65.00	32.50	6.50
☐ 213 John Rucker	65.00	32.50	6.50
☐ 214 Ken O'Dea	65.00	32.50	6.50
☐ 215 Johnnie McCarthy	65.00	32.50	6.50
☐ 216 Joe Marty	65.00	32.50	6.50
☐ 217 Walter Beck	65.00	32.50	6.50
☐ 218 Wally Millies	65.00	32.50	6.50
☐ 219 Russ Bauers	65.00	32.50	6.50
☐ 220 Mace Brown	65.00	32.50	6.50
☐ 221 Lee Handley	65.00	32.50	6.50
☐ 222 Max Butcher	65.00	32.50	6.50
☐ 223 Hugh Jennings	135.00	65.00	13.50
☐ 224 Pie Traynor	160.00	80.00	16.00
☐ 225 Shoeless Joe Jackson	1500.00	600.00	175.00
☐ 226 Harry Hooper	135.00	65.00	13.50
☐ 227 Pop Haines	135.00	65.00	13.50
☐ 228 Charley Grimm	80.00	40.00	8.00
☐ 229 Buck Herzog	65.00	32.50	6.50
☐ 230 Red Faber	135.00	65.00	13.50
☐ 231 Dolf Luque	65.00	32.50	6.50
☐ 232 Goose Goslin	135.00	65.00	13.50
☐ 233 Moose Earnshaw	65.00	32.50	6.50
☐ 234 Frank(Husk) Chance	160.00	80.00	16.00
☐ 235 John J. McGraw	180.00	90.00	18.00
☐ 236 Jim Bottomley	135.00	65.00	13.50
☐ 237 Wee Willie Keeler	180.00	90.00	18.00
☐ 238 Tony Lazzeri	100.00	50.00	10.00
☐ 239 George Uhle	65.00	32.50	6.50
☐ 240 Bill Atwood	80.00	40.00	8.00

1941 Playball

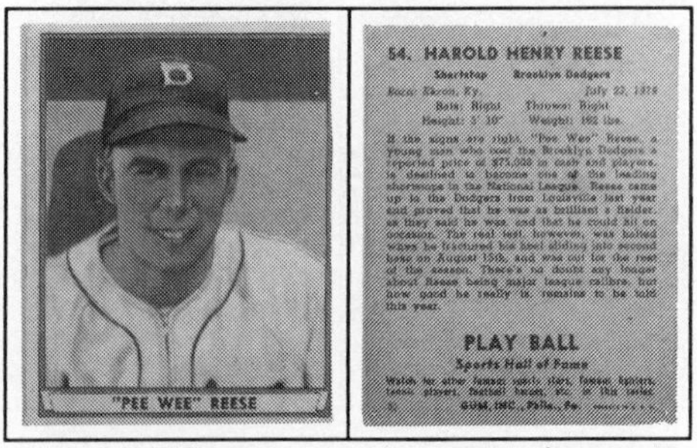

The cards in this 72-card set measure 2 1/2" by 3 1/8". Many of the cards in the 1941 Play Ball series are simply color versions of pictures appearing in the 1940 set. This was the only color baseball card set produced by Gum, Inc., and it carries the catalog designation R336. Card numbers 49-72 are slightly more difficult to obtain as they were not issued until 1942. In 1942, numbers 1-48 were also reissued but without the copyright date. The cards were also printed on paper without a cardboard backing; these are generally encountered in sheets or strips.

	EX-MT	VG-E	GOOD
COMPLETE SET	9500.00	4500.00	1000.00

COMMON PLAYER (1-48)	42.00	20.00	4.00
COMMON PLAYER (49-72)	70.00	35.00	7.00
☐ 1 Eddie Miller	125.00	25.00	5.00
☐ 2 Max West	42.00	20.00	4.00
☐ 3 Bucky Walters	50.00	25.00	5.00
☐ 4 Paul Derringer	50.00	25.00	5.00
☐ 5 Buck McCormick	50.00	25.00	5.00
☐ 6 Carl Hubbell	175.00	85.00	18.00
☐ 7 Harry Danning	42.00	20.00	4.00
☐ 8 Mel Ott	225.00	110.00	22.00
☐ 9 Pinky May	42.00	20.00	4.00
☐ 10 Arky Vaughan	90.00	45.00	9.00
☐ 11 Debs Garms	42.00	20.00	4.00
☐ 12 Jimmy Brown	42.00	20.00	4.00
☐ 13 Jimmy Foxx	350.00	175.00	35.00
☐ 14 Ted Williams	1200.00	500.00	120.00
☐ 15 Joe Cronin	110.00	55.00	11.00
☐ 16 Hal Trosky	50.00	25.00	5.00
☐ 17 Roy Weatherly	42.00	20.00	4.00
☐ 18 Hank Greenberg	200.00	100.00	20.00
☐ 19 Charlie Gehringer	175.00	85.00	18.00
☐ 20 Red Ruffing	110.00	55.00	11.00
☐ 21 Charlie Keller	65.00	32.50	6.50
☐ 22 Indian Bob Johnson	50.00	25.00	5.00
☐ 23 George McQuinn	42.00	20.00	4.00
☐ 24 Dutch Leonard	50.00	25.00	5.00
☐ 25 Gene Moore	42.00	20.00	4.00
☐ 26 Harry Gumpert	42.00	20.00	4.00
☐ 27 Babe Young	42.00	20.00	4.00
☐ 28 Joe Marty	42.00	20.00	4.00
☐ 29 Jack Wilson	42.00	20.00	4.00
☐ 30 Lou Finney	42.00	20.00	4.00
☐ 31 Joe Kuhel	42.00	20.00	4.00
☐ 32 Taft Wright	42.00	20.00	4.00
☐ 33 Al Milnar	42.00	20.00	4.00
☐ 34 Rollie Hemsley	42.00	20.00	4.00
☐ 35 Pinky Higgins	42.00	20.00	4.00
☐ 36 Barney McCosky	42.00	20.00	4.00
☐ 37 Bruce Campbell	42.00	20.00	4.00
☐ 38 Atley Donald	42.00	20.00	4.00
☐ 39 Tom Henrich	65.00	32.50	6.50
☐ 40 John Babich	42.00	20.00	4.00
☐ 41 Frank Blimp Hayes	42.00	20.00	4.00
☐ 42 Wally Moses	50.00	25.00	5.00
☐ 43 Al Brancato	42.00	20.00	4.00
☐ 44 Sam Chapman	42.00	20.00	4.00
☐ 45 Eldon Auker	42.00	20.00	4.00
☐ 46 Sid Hudson	42.00	20.00	4.00
☐ 47 Buddy Lewis	42.00	20.00	4.00
☐ 48 Cecil Travis	42.00	20.00	4.00
☐ 49 Babe Dahlgren	80.00	40.00	8.00
☐ 50 Johnny Cooney	70.00	35.00	7.00
☐ 51 Dolph Camilli	80.00	40.00	8.00
☐ 52 Kirby Higbe	70.00	35.00	7.00
☐ 53 Luke Hamlin	70.00	35.00	7.00
☐ 54 Pee Wee Reese	650.00	325.00	65.00
☐ 55 Whit Wyatt	80.00	40.00	8.00
☐ 56 Johnny VanderMeer	100.00	50.00	10.00
☐ 57 Moe Arnovich	70.00	35.00	7.00
☐ 58 Frank Demaree	70.00	35.00	7.00
☐ 59 Bill Jurges	70.00	35.00	7.00
☐ 60 Chuck Klein	175.00	85.00	18.00
☐ 61 Vince DiMaggio	225.00	110.00	22.00
☐ 62 Elbie Fletcher	70.00	35.00	7.00
☐ 63 Dom DiMaggio	225.00	110.00	22.00
☐ 64 Bobby Doerr	160.00	80.00	16.00
☐ 65 Tommy Bridges	80.00	40.00	8.00
☐ 66 Harland Clift	70.00	35.00	7.00
☐ 67 Walt Judnich	70.00	35.00	7.00
☐ 68 John Knott	70.00	35.00	7.00
☐ 69 George Case	70.00	35.00	7.00
☐ 70 Bill Dickey	450.00	225.00	45.00
☐ 71 Joe DiMaggio	2100.00	900.00	225.00
☐ 72 Lefty Gomez	400.00	100.00	20.00

1985 Polaroid Indians

This 32-card set features cards (each measuring 2 13/16" by 4 1/8") of the Cleveland Indians. The cards are unnumbered except for uniform number, as they are listed below. The set was also sponsored by J.C. Penney and was distributed at the stadium to fans in attendance on Baseball Card Day.

	MINT	EXC	G-VG
COMPLETE SET (32)	18.00	9.00	1.80
COMMON PLAYER	.45	.22	.04

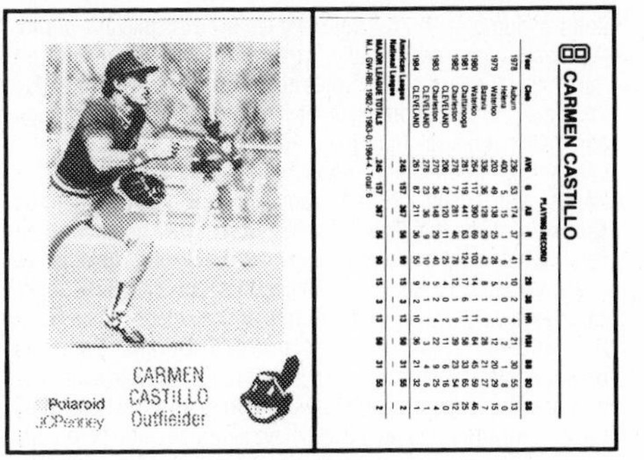

☐ 2 Brett Butler	.90	.45	.09
☐ 4 Tony Bernazard	.60	.30	.06
☐ 8 Carmen Castillo	.45	.22	.04
☐ 10 Pat Tabler	.60	.30	.06
☐ 12 Benny Ayala	.45	.22	.04
☐ 13 Ernie Camacho	.45	.22	.04
☐ 14 Julio Franco	1.50	.75	.15
☐ 16 Jerry Willard	.45	.22	.04
☐ 18 Pat Corrales MG	.45	.22	.04
☐ 20 Otis Nixon	.45	.22	.04
☐ 21 Mike Hargrove	.60	.30	.06
☐ 22 Mike Fischlin	.45	.22	.04
☐ 23 Chris Bando	.45	.22	.04
☐ 24 George Vukovich	.45	.22	.04
☐ 26 Brook Jacoby	.75	.35	.07
☐ 27 Mel Hall	.75	.35	.07
☐ 28 Bert Blyleven	1.25	.60	.12
☐ 29 Andre Thornton	.75	.35	.07
☐ 30 Joe Carter	1.50	.75	.15
☐ 32 Rick Behenna	.45	.22	.04
☐ 33 Roy Smith	.45	.22	.04
☐ 35 Jerry Reed	.45	.22	.04
☐ 36 Jamie Easterly	.45	.22	.04
☐ 38 Dave Von Ohlen	.45	.22	.04
☐ 41 Rich Thompson	.45	.22	.04
☐ 43 Bryan Clark	.45	.22	.04
☐ 44 Neal Heaton	.45	.22	.04
☐ 48 Vern Ruhle	.45	.22	.04
☐ 49 Jeff Barkley	.45	.22	.04
☐ 50 Ramon Romero	.45	.22	.04
☐ 54 Tom Waddell	.45	.22	.04
☐ xx Coaching Staff Bobby Bonds John Goryl Don McMahon Ed Napolean Dennis Sommers	.45	.22	.04

1979 Police Giants

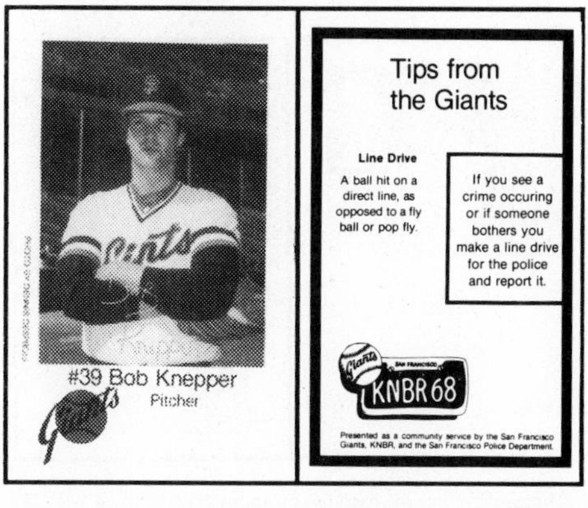
#39 Bob Knepper
Pitcher
Giants
Tips from the Giants
Line Drive
A ball hit on a direct line, as opposed to a fly ball or pop fly.
If you see a crime occuring or if someone bothers you make a line drive for the police and report it.
Giants
KNBR 68
Presented as a community service by the San Francisco Giants, KNBR, and the San Francisco Police Department.

The cards in this 30-card set measure 2 5/8" by 4 1/8". The 1979 Police Giants set features cards numbered by the player's uniform number. This full color set features the player's photo, the Giants' logo, and the player's name, number and position on the front of the cards. A facsimile autograph in an attractive blue ink is also contained on the front. The backs, printed in orange and black, feature Tips from the Giants, the Giants' and sponsoring radio station, KNBR, logos and a line listing the Giants, KNBR, and the San Francisco Police Department as sponsors of the set. The 15 cards which are shown with an asterisk below were available only from the Police. The other 15 cards were given away at the ballpark on June 17, 1979. These cards look very similar to the Giants police set issued in 1980, the following year. Both sets credit Dennis Desprois photographically on each card but this (1979) set seems to have a fuzzier focus on the pictures. The sets can be distinguished on the front since this set's cards have a number sign before the player's uniform number on the front. Also on the card backs the KNBR logo is usually left justified for the cards in the 1979 set whereas the 1980 set has the KNBR logo centered on the card back.

	NRMT	VG-E	GOOD
COMPLETE SET (30)	17.00	8.50	1.70
COMMON PLAYER	.45	.22	.04
☐ 1 Dave Bristol MG	.45	.22	.04
☐ 2 Marc Hill	.45	.22	.04
☐ 3 Mike Sadek *	.60	.30	.06
☐ 5 Tom Haller	.45	.22	.04
☐ 6 Joe Altobelli CO *	.60	.30	.06
☐ 8 Larry Shepard CO *	.60	.30	.06
☐ 9 Heity Cruz	.45	.22	.04
☐ 10 Johnnie LeMaster	.45	.22	.04
☐ 12 Jim Davenport	.60	.30	.06
☐ 14 Vida Blue	.60	.30	.06
☐ 15 Mike Ivie	.45	.22	.04
☐ 16 Roger Metzger	.45	.22	.04
☐ 17 Randy Moffitt	.45	.22	.04
☐ 18 Bill Madlock	.75	.35	.07
☐ 21 Rob Andrews *	.60	.30	.06
☐ 22 Jack Clark *	3.00	1.50	.30
☐ 25 Dave Roberts	.45	.22	.04
☐ 26 John Montefusco	.60	.30	.06
☐ 28 Ed Halicki *	.60	.30	.06
☐ 30 John Tamargo	.45	.22	.04
☐ 31 Larry Herndon	.45	.22	.04
☐ 36 Bill North *	.60	.30	.06
☐ 39 Bob Knepper *	.75	.35	.07
☐ 40 John Curtis *	.60	.30	.06
☐ 41 Darrell Evans *	1.25	.60	.12
☐ 43 Tom Griffin *	.60	.30	.06
☐ 44 Willie McCovey *	3.50	1.75	.35
☐ 45 Terry Whitfield *	.60	.30	.06
☐ 46 Gary Lavelle *	.60	.30	.06
☐ 49 Max Venable *	.60	.30	.06

1980 Police Dodgers

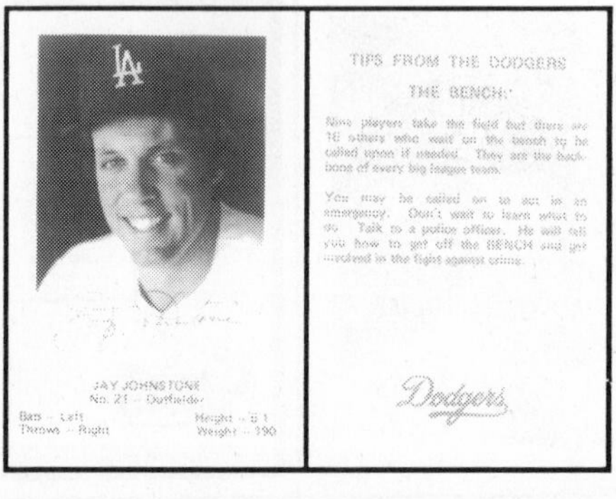

The cards in this 30-card set measure 2 13/16" by 4 1/8". The full color 1980 Police Los Angeles Dodgers set features the player's name, uniform number, position, and biographical data on the fronts in addition to the photo. The backs feature Tips from the Dodgers, the LAPD logo, and the Dodgers' logo. The cards are listed below according to uniform number.

	MINT	EXC	G-VG
COMPLETE SET (30)	11.00	5.50	1.10
COMMON PLAYER	.35	.17	.03
☐ 5 Johnny Oates	.35	.17	.03
☐ 6 Steve Garvey	1.25	.60	.12
☐ 7 Steve Yeager	.35	.17	.03
☐ 8 Reggie Smith	.50	.25	.05
☐ 9 Gary Thomasson	.35	.17	.03
☐ 10 Ron Cey	.50	.25	.05
☐ 12 Dusty Baker	.50	.25	.05
☐ 13 Joe Ferguson	.35	.17	.03
☐ 15 Davey Lopes	.50	.25	.05
☐ 16 Rick Monday	.50	.25	.05
☐ 18 Bill Russell	.50	.25	.05
☐ 20 Don Sutton	1.00	.50	.10
☐ 21 Jay Johnstone	.50	.25	.05
☐ 23 Teddy Martinez	.35	.17	.03
☐ 27 Joe Beckwith	.35	.17	.03
☐ 28 Pedro Guerrero	1.25	.60	.12
☐ 29 Don Stanhouse	.35	.17	.03
☐ 30 Derrel Thomas	.35	.17	.03
☐ 31 Doug Rau	.35	.17	.03
☐ 34 Ken Brett	.35	.17	.03
☐ 35 Bob Welch	1.00	.50	.10
☐ 37 Robert Castillo	.35	.17	.03
☐ 38 Dave Goltz	.35	.17	.03
☐ 41 Jerry Reuss	.50	.25	.05
☐ 43 Rick Sutcliffe	.75	.35	.07
☐ 44 Mickey Hatcher	.35	.17	.03
☐ 46 Burt Hooton	.35	.17	.03
☐ 49 Charlie Hough	.50	.25	.05
☐ xx Team Card (unnumbered)	.35	.17	.03

1980 Police Giants

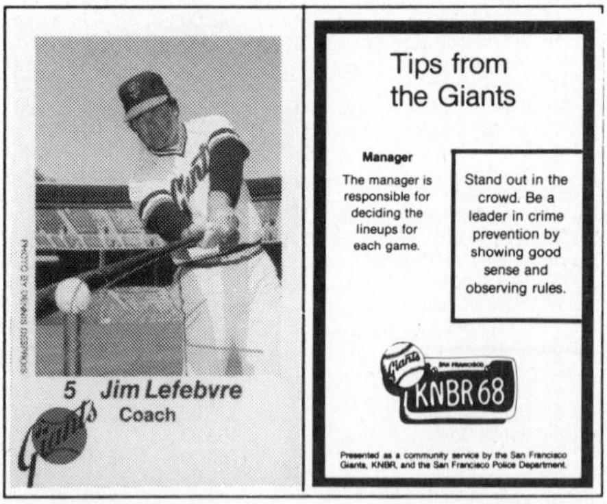

The cards in this 31-card set measure 2 5/8" by 4 1/8". The 1980 Police San Francisco Giants set features cards numbered by the player's uniform number. This full color set features the player's photo, the Giants' logo, and the player's name, number and position on the front of the cards. A facsimile autograph in an attractive blue ink is also contained on the front. The backs, printed in orange and black, feature Tips from the Giants, the Giants' and sponsoring radio station, KNBR, logos and a line listing the Giants, KNBR, and the San Francisco Police Department as sponsors of the set. The sets were given away at the ballpark on May 31, 1980.

	MINT	EXC	G-VG
COMPLETE SET (31)	11.00	5.50	1.10
COMMON PLAYER	.35	.17	.03
☐ 1 Dave Bristol MG	.35	.17	.03
☐ 2 Marc Hill	.35	.17	.03
☐ 3 Mike Sadek	.35	.17	.03
☐ 5 Jim Lefebvre	.50	.25	.05

☐ 6 Rennie Stennett	.35	.17	.03
☐ 7 Milt May	.35	.17	.03
☐ 8 Vern Benson CO	.35	.17	.03
☐ 9 Jim Wohlford	.35	.17	.03
☐ 10 Johnnie LeMaster	.35	.17	.03
☐ 12 Jim Davenport	.50	.25	.05
☐ 14 Vida Blue	.50	.25	.05
☐ 15 Mike Ivie	.35	.17	.03
☐ 16 Roger Metzger	.35	.17	.03
☐ 17 Randy Moffitt	.35	.17	.03
☐ 19 Al Holland	.35	.17	.03
☐ 20 Joe Strain	.35	.17	.03
☐ 22 Jack Clark	2.00	1.00	.20
☐ 26 John Montefusco	.50	.25	.05
☐ 28 Ed Halicki	.35	.17	.03
☐ 31 Larry Herndon	.35	.17	.03
☐ 32 Ed Whitson	.60	.30	.06
☐ 36 Bill North	.35	.17	.03
☐ 38 Greg Minton	.35	.17	.03
☐ 39 Bob Knepper	.50	.25	.05
☐ 41 Darrell Evans	1.00	.50	.10
☐ 42 John Van Ornum	.35	.17	.03
☐ 43 Tom Griffin	.35	.17	.03
☐ 44 Willie McCovey	2.50	1.25	.25
☐ 45 Terry Whitfield	.35	.17	.03
☐ 46 Gary Lavelle	.35	.17	.03
☐ 47 Don McMahon CO	.35	.17	.03

1981 Police Braves

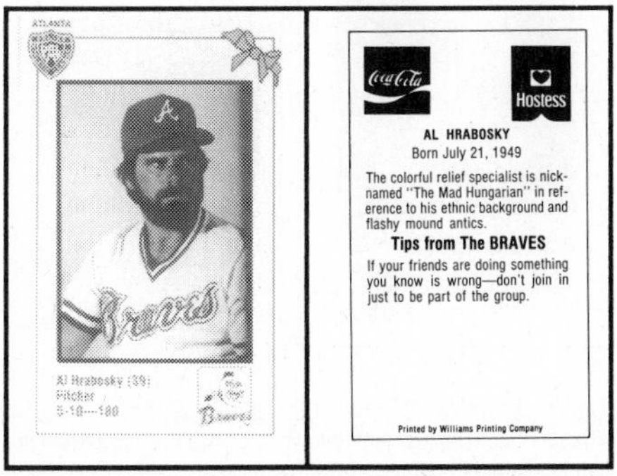
ATLANTA
Al Hrabosky (39)
Pitcher
5-10—180
Braves
Coca-Cola
Hostess
AL HRABOSKY
Born July 21, 1949
The colorful relief specialist is nicknamed "The Mad Hungarian" in reference to his ethnic background and flashy mound antics.
Tips from The BRAVES
If your friends are doing something you know is wrong—don't join in just to be part of the group.
Printed by Williams Printing Company

The cards in this 27-card set measure 2 5/8" by 4 1/8". This first Atlanta Police set features full color cards sponsored by the Braves, the Atlanta Police Department, Coca-Cola and Hostess. The cards are numbered by uniform number, which is contained on the front along with an Atlanta Police Athletic League logo, a black and white Braves logo, and a green bow in the upper right corner of the frameline. The backs feature brief player biographies, logos of Coke and Hostess, and Tips from the Braves. It is reported that 33,000 of these sets were printed. The Terry Harper card is supposed to be more difficult to obtain than other cards in the set.

	MINT	EXC	G-VG
COMPLETE SET (27)	10.00	5.00	1.00
COMMON PLAYER	.35	.17	.03
☐ 1 Jerry Royster	.35	.17	.03
☐ 3 Dale Murphy	3.00	1.50	.30
☐ 4 Biff Pocoroba	.35	.17	.03
☐ 5 Bob Horner	.90	.45	.09
☐ 6 Bobby Cox MG	.35	.17	.03
☐ 9 Luis Gomez	.35	.17	.03
☐ 10 Chris Chambliss	.50	.25	.05
☐ 15 Bill Nahorodny	.35	.17	.03
☐ 16 Rafael Ramirez	.50	.25	.05
☐ 17 Glenn Hubbard	.35	.17	.03
☐ 18 Claudell Washington	.50	.25	.05
☐ 19 Terry Harper	.75	.35	.07
☐ 20 Bruce Benedict	.35	.17	.03
☐ 24 John Montefusco	.50	.25	.05
☐ 25 Rufino Linares	.35	.17	.03
☐ 26 Gene Garber	.50	.25	.05
☐ 30 Brian Asselstine	.35	.17	.03
☐ 34 Larry Bradford	.35	.17	.03
☐ 35 Phil Niekro	1.75	.85	.17
☐ 37 Rick Camp	.35	.17	.03
☐ 39 Al Hrabosky	.50	.25	.05
☐ 40 Tommy Boggs	.35	.17	.03
☐ 42 Rick Mahler	.50	.25	.05
☐ 44 Hank Aaron CO	2.50	1.25	.25
☐ 45 Ed Miller	.35	.17	.03
☐ 46 Gaylord Perry	1.75	.85	.17
☐ 49 Preston Hanna	.35	.17	.03

1981 Police Dodgers

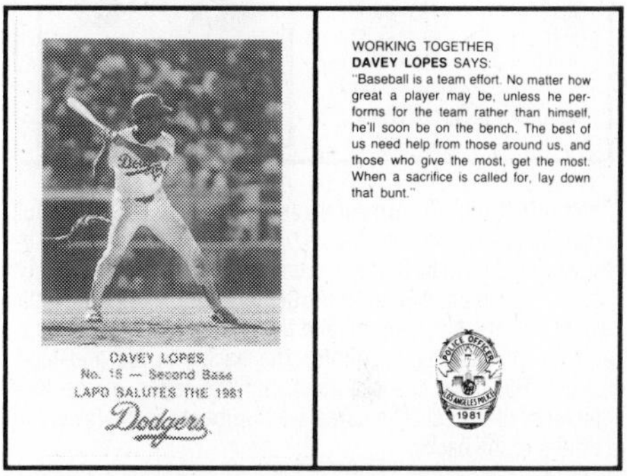
DAVEY LOPES
No. 15 — Second Base
LAPD SALUTES THE 1981
Dodgers
WORKING TOGETHER
DAVEY LOPES SAYS:
"Baseball is a team effort. No matter how great a player may be, unless he performs for the team rather than himself, he'll soon be on the bench. The best of us need help from those around us, and those who give the most, get the most. When a sacrifice is called for, lay down that bunt."
1981

The cards in this 32-card set measure 2 13/16" by 4 1/8". The full color set of 1981 Los Angeles Dodgers features the player's name, number, position and a line stating that the LAPD salutes the 1981 Dodgers, in addition to the player's photo. The backs feature the LAPD logo and short narratives, attributable to the player on the front of the card, revealing police associated tips. The cards of Ken Landreaux and Dave Stewart are reported to be more difficult to obtain than other cards in this set due to the fact that they are replacements for Stanhouse (released 4/17/81) and Hatcher (traded for Landreaux 3/30/81). The complete set price below refers to all 32 cards, i.e., including the variations.

	MINT	EXC	G-VG
COMPLETE SET (32)	12.00	6.00	1.20
COMMON PLAYER	.35	.17	.03
☐ 2 Tom Lasorda MG	.50	.25	.05
☐ 3 Rudy Law	.35	.17	.03
☐ 6 Steve Garvey	1.25	.60	.12
☐ 7 Steve Yeager	.35	.17	.03
☐ 8 Reggie Smith	.50	.25	.05
☐ 10 Ron Cey	.50	.25	.05
☐ 12 Dusty Baker	.50	.25	.05
☐ 13 Joe Ferguson	.35	.17	.03
☐ 14 Mike Scioscia	.35	.17	.03
☐ 15 Davey Lopes	.50	.25	.05
☐ 16 Rick Monday	.50	.25	.05
☐ 18 Bill Russell	.50	.25	.05
☐ 21 Jay Johnstone	.50	.25	.05
☐ 26 Don Stanhouse	.50	.25	.05
☐ 27 Joe Beckwith	.35	.17	.03
☐ 28 Pedro Guerrero	1.00	.50	.10
☐ 30 Derrel Thomas	.35	.17	.03
☐ 34 Fernando Valenzuela	2.00	1.00	.20
☐ 35 Bob Welch	.75	.35	.07
☐ 36 Pepe Frias	.35	.17	.03
☐ 37 Robert Castillo	.35	.17	.03
☐ 38 Dave Goltz	.35	.17	.03
☐ 41 Jerry Reuss	.35	.17	.03
☐ 43 Rick Sutcliffe	.75	.35	.07
☐ 44A Mickey Hatcher	.50	.25	.05
☐ 44B Ken Landreaux	1.25	.60	.12
☐ 46 Burt Hooton	.35	.17	.03
☐ 48 Dave Stewart	2.50	1.25	.25
☐ 51 Terry Forster	.50	.25	.05
☐ 57 Steve Howe	.35	.17	.03
☐ xx Team Photo (Checklist) (unnumbered)	.35	.17	.03
☐ xx Coaching Staff (unnumbered)	.35	.17	.03

1981 Police Mariners

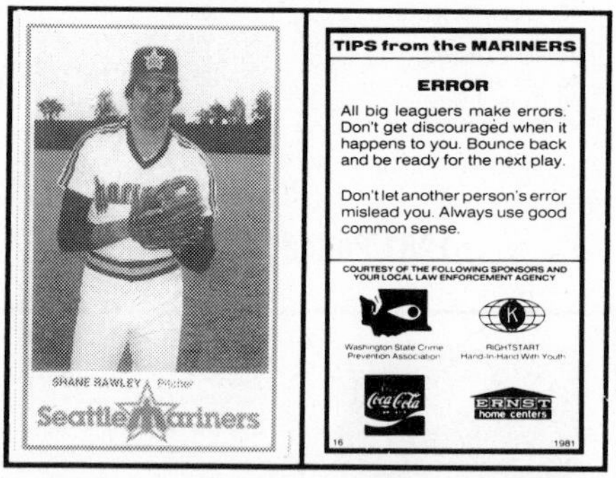

The cards in this 16-card set measure 2 5/8" by 4 1/8". The full color Seattle Mariners Police set of this year was sponsored by the Washington State Crime Prevention Association, the Kiwanis Club, Coca-Cola and Ernst Home Centers. The fronts feature the player's name, his position, and the Seattle Mariners name in addition to the player's photo. The backs, in red and blue, feature Tips from the Mariners and the logos of the four sponsors of the set. The cards are numbered in the lower left corners of the backs.

	MINT	EXC	G-VG
COMPLETE SET (16)	5.00	2.50	.50
COMMON PLAYER (1-16)	.35	.17	.03
☐ 1 Jeff Burroughs	.50	.25	.05
☐ 2 Floyd Bannister	.50	.25	.05
☐ 3 Glenn Abbott	.35	.17	.03
☐ 4 Jim Anderson	.35	.17	.03
☐ 5 Danny Meyer	.35	.17	.03
☐ 6 Julio Cruz	.50	.25	.05
☐ 7 Dave Edler	.35	.17	.03
☐ 8 Kenny Clay	.35	.17	.03
☐ 9 Lenny Randle	.35	.17	.03
☐ 10 Mike Parrott	.35	.17	.03
☐ 11 Tom Paciorek	.50	.25	.05
☐ 12 Jerry Narron	.35	.17	.03
☐ 13 Richie Zisk	.50	.25	.05
☐ 14 Maury Wills MG	.75	.35	.07
☐ 15 Joe Simpson	.35	.17	.03
☐ 16 Shane Rawley	.50	.25	.05

1981 Police Royals

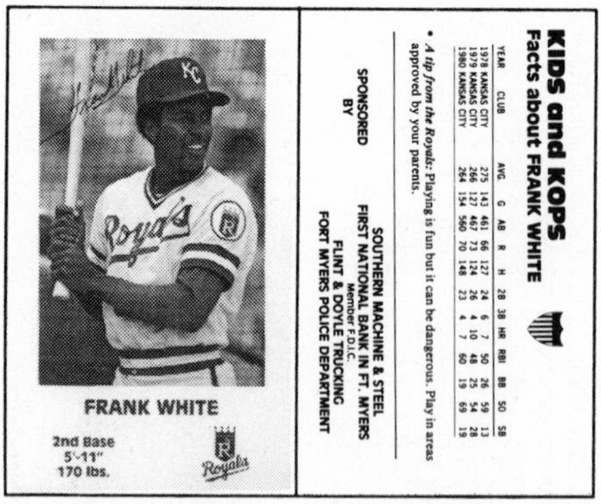

The cards in this 10-card set measure 2 1/2" by 4 1/8". The 1981 Police Kansas City Royals set features full color cards of Royals players. The fronts feature the player's name, position, height and weight, and the Royals' logo in addition to the photo and facsimile autograph of the player. The backs feature player statistics, Tips from the Royals, and identification of the sponsoring organizations.

	MINT	EXC	G-VG
COMPLETE SET (10)	35.00	17.50	3.50
COMMON PLAYER (1-10)	2.00	1.00	.20
☐ 1 Willie Aikens	2.00	1.00	.20
☐ 2 George Brett	20.00	10.00	2.00
☐ 3 Rich Gale	2.00	1.00	.20
☐ 4 Clint Hurdle	2.00	1.00	.20
☐ 5 Dennis Leonard	2.50	1.25	.25
☐ 6 Hal McRae	2.50	1.25	.25
☐ 7 Amos Otis	2.50	1.25	.25
☐ 8 U.L. Washington	2.00	1.00	.20
☐ 9 Frank White	4.00	2.00	.40
☐ 10 Willie Wilson	4.00	2.00	.40

1982 Police Braves

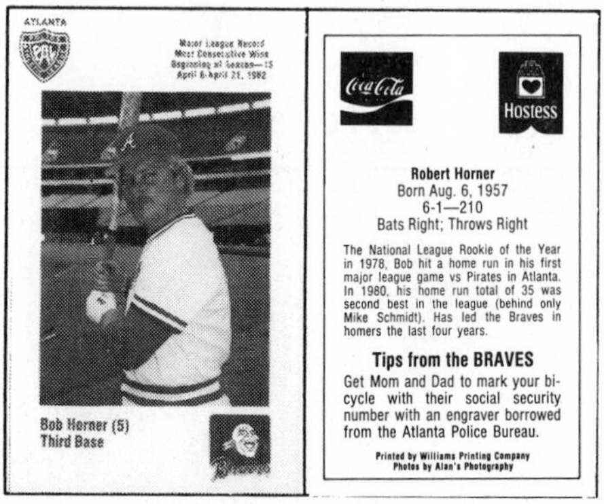

The cards in this 30-card set measure 2 5/8" by 4 1/8". The Atlanta Police Department followed up on their successful 1981 safety set by publishing a new Braves set for 1982. Featured in excellent color photos are manager Joe Torre, 24 players, and 5 coaches. The cards are numbered, by uniform number, on the front only, while the backs contain a short biography of the individual and a Tips from the Braves section. The logos for the Atlanta PAL and the Braves appear on the front; those of Coca-Cola and Hostess are found on the back. A line commemorating Atlanta's record-shattering, season-beginning win streak is located in the upper right corner on every card obverse. The player list on the reverse of the Torre card is a roster list and not a checklist for the set. There were 8,000 sets reportedly printed. The Bob Watson card is supposedly more difficult to obtain than others in this set.

	MINT	EXC	G-VG
COMPLETE SET (30)	17.00	8.50	1.70
COMMON PLAYER	.45	.22	.04
☐ 1 Jerry Royster	.45	.22	.04
☐ 3 Dale Murphy	5.00	2.50	.50
☐ 4 Biff Pocoroba	.45	.22	.04
☐ 5 Bob Horner	1.00	.50	.10
☐ 6 Randy Johnson	.45	.22	.04
☐ 8 Bob Watson	1.50	.75	.15
☐ 9 Joe Torre MG	1.00	.50	.10
☐ 10 Chris Chambliss	.60	.30	.06
☐ 15 Claudell Washington	.60	.30	.06
☐ 16 Rafael Ramirez	.45	.22	.04
☐ 17 Glenn Hubbard	.45	.22	.04
☐ 20 Bruce Benedict	.45	.22	.04
☐ 22 Brett Butler	1.00	.50	.10
☐ 23 Tommy Aaron CO	.60	.30	.06
☐ 25 Rufino Linares	.45	.22	.04
☐ 26 Gene Garber	.45	.22	.04
☐ 27 Larry McWilliams	.45	.22	.04

□ 28 Larry Whisenton	.45	.22	.04
□ 32 Steve Bedrosian	1.00	.50	.10
□ 35 Phil Niekro	2.50	1.25	.25
□ 37 Rick Camp	.45	.22	.04
□ 38 Joe Cowley	.45	.22	.04
□ 39 Al Hrabosky	.60	.30	.06
□ 42 Rick Mahler	.45	.22	.04
□ 43 Bob Walk	.60	.30	.06
□ 45 Bob Gibson CO	1.50	.75	.15
□ 49 Preston Hanna	.45	.22	.04
□ 52 Joe Pignatano CO	.45	.22	.04
□ 53 Dal Maxvill CO	.45	.22	.04
□ 54 Rube Walker CO	.45	.22	.04

□ 46 Jerry Augustine	.35	.17	.03
□ 47 Dwight Bernard	.35	.17	.03
□ 48 Mike Caldwell	.50	.25	.05
□ 50 Pete Vuckovich	.50	.25	.05
□ xx Team Card (unnumbered)	.35	.17	.03
□ xx Harry Dalton GM (unnumbered)	.35	.17	.03
□ xx Buck Rodgers MG (unnumbered)	.35	.17	.03
□ xx Brewer Coaches (unnumbered)	.35	.17	.03

1982 Police Brewers

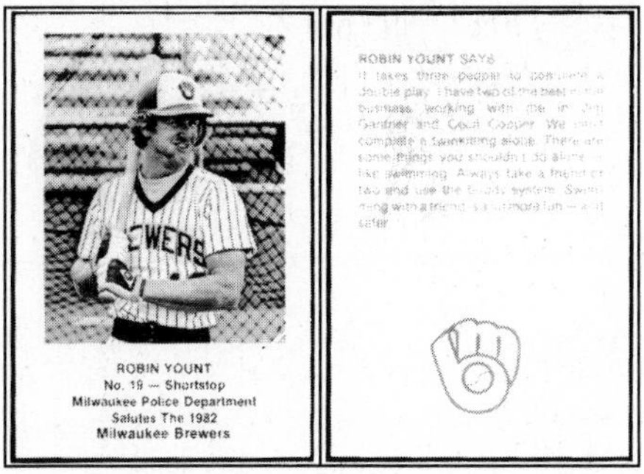

The cards in this 30-card set measure 2 13/16" by 4 1/8". The 1982 series of 30 Milwaukee Brewers baseball cards is noted for its excellent color photographs set upon a simple white background. The set was initially distributed at the stadium on May 5th, but was also handed out by several local police departments, and credit lines for the Wisconsin State Fair Park Police (no shield design on reverse), Milwaukee, Brookfield, and Wauwatosa PD's have already been found. The reverses feature advice concerning safety measures, social situations, and crime prevention (Romero card in both Spanish and English). The team card carries a checklist which lists the Brewer's coaches separately although they all appear on a single card; VP/GM Harry Dalton is not mentioned on this list but is included in the set.The prices below are for the basic set without regard to the Police Department listed on the backs. Cards from the more obscure corners and small towns of Wisconsin (where fewer cards were produced) will be valued higher.

	MINT	EXC	G-VG
COMPLETE SET (30)	14.00	7.00	1.40
COMMON PLAYER	.35	.17	.03
□ 4 Paul Molitor	1.50	.75	.15
□ 5 Ned Yost	.35	.17	.03
□ 7 Don Money	.35	.17	.03
□ 9 Larry Hisle	.50	.25	.05
□ 10 Bob McClure	.35	.17	.03
□ 11 Ed Romero	.35	.17	.03
□ 13 Roy Howell	.35	.17	.03
□ 15 Cecil Cooper	.60	.30	.06
□ 17 Jim Gantner	.60	.30	.06
□ 19 Robin Yount	3.00	1.50	.30
□ 20 Gorman Thomas	.60	.30	.06
□ 22 Charlie Moore	.35	.17	.03
□ 23 Ted Simmons	.75	.35	.07
□ 24 Ben Oglivie	.50	.25	.05
□ 26 Kevin Bass	.60	.30	.06
□ 28 Jamie Easterly	.35	.17	.03
□ 29 Mark Brouhard	.35	.17	.03
□ 30 Moose Haas	.35	.17	.03
□ 34 Rollie Fingers	1.00	.50	.10
□ 35 Randy Lerch	.35	.17	.03
□ 41 Jim Slaton	.35	.17	.03
□ 45 Doug Jones	.75	.35	.07

1982 Police Dodgers

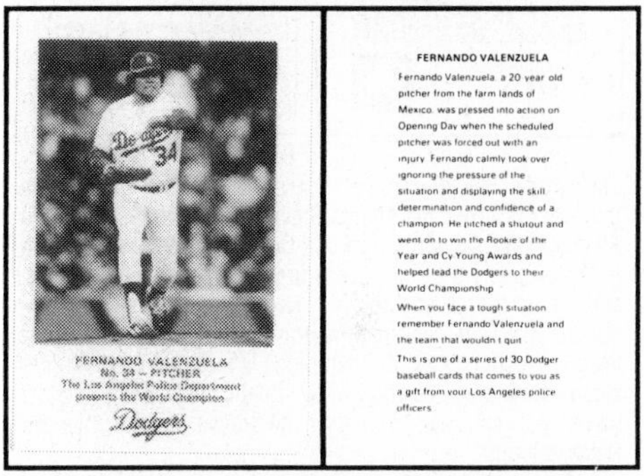

FERNANDO VALENZUELA
No. 34 — PITCHER
The Los Angeles Police Department
presents the World Champion
FERNANDO VALENZUELA
Fernando Valenzuela, a 20 year old pitcher from the farm lands of Mexico, was pressed into action on Opening Day when the scheduled pitcher was forced out with an injury. Fernando calmly took over ignoring the pressure of the situation and displaying the skill determination and confidence of a champion. He pitched a shutout and went on to win the Rookie of the Year and Cy Young Awards and helped lead the Dodgers to their World Championship.
When you face a tough situation remember Fernando Valenzuela and the team that wouldn't quit.
This is one of a series of 30 Dodger baseball cards that comes to you as a gift from your Los Angeles police officers.

The cards in this 30-card set measure 2 13/16" by 4 1/8". The 1982 Los Angeles Dodgers police set depicts the players and events of the 1981 season. There is a World Series trophy card, three cards commemorating the Division, League, and World Series wins, one manager card, and 25 player cards. The obverses have brilliant color photos set on white, and the player cards are numbered according to the uniform number of the individual. The reverses contain biographical material, information about stadium events, and a safety feature emphasizing "the team that wouldn't quit."

	MINT	EXC	G-VG
COMPLETE SET (30)	8.00	4.00	.80
COMMON PLAYER	.25	.12	.02
□ 2 Tom Lasorda MG	.35	.17	.03
□ 6 Steve Garvey	1.00	.50	.10
□ 7 Steve Yeager	.25	.12	.02
□ 8 Mark Belanger	.35	.17	.03
□ 10 Ron Cey	.35	.17	.03
□ 12 Dusty Baker	.35	.17	.03
□ 14 Mike Scioscia	.35	.17	.03
□ 16 Rick Monday	.35	.17	.03
□ 18 Bill Russell	.35	.17	.03
□ 21 Jay Johnstone	.35	.17	.03
□ 26 Alejandro Pena	.35	.17	.03
□ 28 Pedro Guerrero	1.00	.50	.10
□ 30 Derrel Thomas	.25	.12	.02
□ 31 Jorge Orta	.25	.12	.02
□ 34 Fernando Valenzuela	1.00	.50	.10
□ 35 Bob Welch	.60	.30	.06
□ 38 Dave Goltz	.25	.12	.02
□ 40 Ron Roenicke	.25	.12	.02
□ 41 Jerry Reuss	.25	.12	.02
□ 44 Ken Landreaux	.25	.12	.02
□ 46 Burt Hooton	.25	.12	.02
□ 48 Dave Stewart	.75	.35	.07
□ 49 Tom Niedenfuer	.25	.12	.02
□ 51 Terry Forster	.35	.17	.03
□ 52 Steve Sax	1.00	.50	.10
□ 57 Steve Howe	.25	.12	.02
□ xx World Series Trophy (checklist back) (unnumbered)	.25	.12	.02
□ xx World Series Commemorative (unnumbered)	.25	.12	.02
□ xx NL Champions (unnumbered)	.25	.12	.02
□ xx Division Champs (unnumbered)	.25	.12	.02

1983 Police Braves

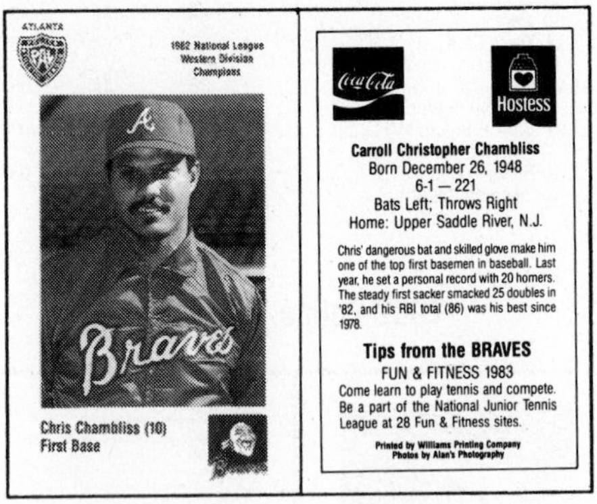

The cards in this 30-card set measure 2 5/8" by 4 1/8". For the third year in a row, the Atlanta Braves, in cooperation with the Atlanta Police Department, Coca-Cola, and Hostess, issued a full color safety set. The set features Joe Torre, five coaches, and 24 of the Atlanta Braves. Numbered only by uniform number, the statement that the Braves were the 1982 National League Western Division Champions is included on the fronts along with the Braves and Police Athletic biographies, a short narrative on the player, Tips from the Braves, and the Coke and Hostess logos.

	MINT	EXC	G-VG
COMPLETE SET (30)	12.00	6.00	1.20
COMMON PLAYER	.35	.17	.03
☐ 1 Jerry Royster	.35	.17	.03
☐ 3 Dale Murphy	3.50	1.75	.35
☐ 4 Biff Pocoroba	.35	.17	.03
☐ 5 Bob Horner	.90	.45	.09
☐ 6 Randy Johnson	.35	.17	.03
☐ 8 Bob Watson	.50	.25	.05
☐ 9 Joe Torre MG	.75	.35	.07
☐ 10 Chris Chambliss	.50	.25	.05
☐ 11 Ken Smith	.35	.17	.03
☐ 15 Claudell Washington	.50	.25	.05
☐ 16 Rafael Ramirez	.35	.17	.03
☐ 17 Glenn Hubbard	.35	.17	.03
☐ 19 Terry Harper	.35	.17	.03
☐ 20 Bruce Benedict	.35	.17	.03
☐ 22 Brett Butler	.75	.35	.07
☐ 24 Larry Owen	.35	.17	.03
☐ 26 Gene Garber	.35	.17	.03
☐ 27 Pascual Perez	.60	.30	.06
☐ 29 Craig McMurtry	.35	.17	.03
☐ 32 Steve Bedrosian	.75	.35	.07
☐ 33 Pete Falcone	.35	.17	.03
☐ 35 Phil Niekro	1.50	.75	.15
☐ 36 Sonny Jackson CO	.35	.17	.03
☐ 37 Rick Camp	.35	.17	.03
☐ 45 Bob Gibson CO	1.50	.75	.15
☐ 49 Rick Behenna	.35	.17	.03
☐ 51 Terry Forster	.50	.25	.05
☐ 52 Joe Pignatano CO	.35	.17	.03
☐ 53 Dal Maxvill CO	.35	.17	.03
☐ 54 Rube Walker CO	.35	.17	.03

1983 Police Brewers

The cards in this 30-card set measure 2 13/16" by 4 1/8". The 1983 Police Milwaukee Brewers set contains full color cards issued by the Milwaukee Police Department in conjunction with the Brewers. The cards are numbered on the fronts by the player uniform number and contain the line, "The Milwaukee Police Department Presents the 1983 Milwaukee Braves." The backs contain a brief narrative attributable to the player on the front, the Milwaukee Police logo, and a Milwaukee Brewers logo stating that they were the 1982 American League Champions. In all, 28 variations of these Police sets have been found to date. Prices below are for the basic set without regard to the Police Department listed on the backs of the cards; cards from the more obscure corners and small towns of Wisconsin (whose cards were produced in lesser quantities) will be valued higher.

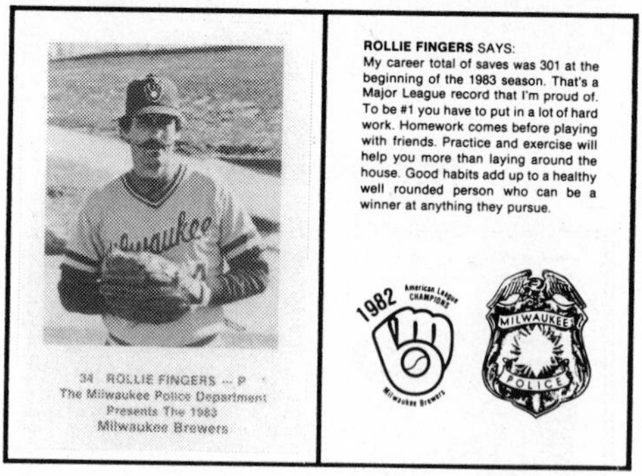

	MINT	EXC	G-VG
COMPLETE SET (30)	9.00	4.50	.90
COMMON PLAYER	.25	.12	.02
☐ 4 Paul Molitor	1.00	.50	.10
☐ 5 Ned Yost	.25	.12	.02
☐ 7 Don Money	.35	.17	.03
☐ 8 Rob Picciolo	.25	.12	.02
☐ 10 Bob McClure	.25	.12	.02
☐ 11 Ed Romero	.25	.12	.02
☐ 12 Larry Haney CO	.25	.12	.02
☐ 13 Roy Howell	.25	.12	.02
☐ 15 Cecil Cooper	.50	.25	.05
☐ 16 Marshall Edwards	.25	.12	.02
☐ 17 Jim Gantner	.35	.17	.03
☐ 18 Ron Hansen CO	.25	.12	.02
☐ 19 Robin Yount	2.00	1.00	.20
☐ 20 Gorman Thomas	.50	.25	.05
☐ 21 Don Sutton	1.00	.50	.10
☐ 22 Charlie Moore	.25	.12	.02
☐ 23 Ted Simmons	.60	.30	.06
☐ 24 Ben Oglivie	.35	.17	.03
☐ 26 Bob Skube	.25	.12	.02
☐ 27 Pete Ladd	.25	.12	.02
☐ 28 Jamie Easterly	.25	.12	.02
☐ 30 Moose Haas	.35	.17	.03
☐ 32 Harvey Kuenn MG	.50	.25	.05
☐ 34 Rollie Fingers	1.00	.50	.10
☐ 40 Bob L. Gibson	.25	.12	.02
☐ 41 Jim Slaton	.25	.12	.02
☐ 42 Tom Tellmann	.25	.12	.02
☐ 45 Pat Dobson CO	.35	.17	.03
☐ 46 Jerry Augustine	.25	.12	.02
☐ 48 Mike Caldwell	.35	.17	.03
☐ 50 Pete Vuckovich	.35	.17	.03
☐ xx Dave Garcia CO	.25	.12	.02
☐ xx Team Photo (Checklist back) (unnumbered)	.25	.12	.02

1983 Police Dodgers

The cards in this 30-card set measure 2 13/16" by 4 1/8". The full color Police Los Angeles Dodgers set of 1983 features the player's name and uniform number on the front along with the Dodger's logo, the year, and the player's photo. The backs feature a small insert portrait picture of the player, player biographies, and career statistics. The logo of the Los Angeles Police Department, the sponsor of the set, is found on the backs of the cards.

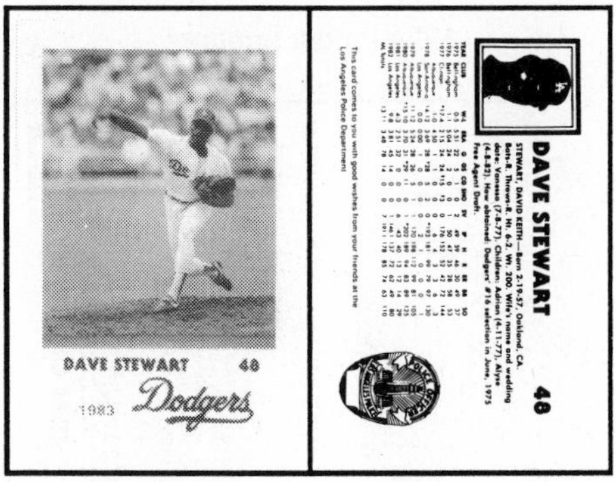

	MINT	EXC	G-VG
COMPLETE SET (30)	7.00	3.50	.70
COMMON PLAYER	.20	.10	.02
☐ 2 Tom Lasorda MG	.35	.17	.03
☐ 3 Steve Sax	.75	.35	.07
☐ 5 Mike Marshall	.50	.25	.05
☐ 7 Steve Yeager	.25	.12	.02
☐ 12 Dusty Baker	.30	.15	.03
☐ 14 Mike Scioscia	.30	.15	.03
☐ 16 Rick Monday	.30	.15	.03
☐ 17 Greg Brock	.25	.12	.02
☐ 18 Bill Russell	.30	.15	.03
☐ 20 Candy Maldonado	.35	.17	.03
☐ 21 Ricky Wright	.20	.10	.02
☐ 22 Mark Bradley	.20	.10	.02
☐ 23 Dave Sax	.20	.10	.02
☐ 26 Alejandro Pena	.25	.12	.02
☐ 27 Joe Beckwith	.20	.10	.02
☐ 28 Pedro Guerrero	.75	.35	.07
☐ 30 Derrel Thomas	.20	.10	.02
☐ 34 Fernando Valenzuela	.75	.35	.07
☐ 35 Bob Welch	.60	.30	.06
☐ 38 Pat Zachry	.20	.10	.02
☐ 40 Ron Roenicke	.20	.10	.02
☐ 41 Jerry Reuss	.25	.12	.02
☐ 43 Jose Morales	.20	.10	.02
☐ 44 Ken Landreaux	.20	.10	.02
☐ 46 Burt Hooton	.20	.10	.02
☐ 47 Larry White	.20	.10	.02
☐ 48 Dave Stewart	.75	.35	.07
☐ 49 Tom Niedenfuer	.25	.12	.02
☐ 57 Steve Howe	.20	.10	.02
☐ xx Coaching Staff (unnumbered)	.20	.10	.02

1983 Police Royals

The cards in this 10-card set measure 2 1/2" by 4 1/8". The 1983 Police Kansas City Royals set features full color cards of Royals players. The fronts feature the player's name, height and weight, and the Royals' logo in addition to the player's photo and a facsimile autograph. The backs feature Kids and Cops Facts about the players, Tips from the Royals, and identification of the sponsors of the set. The cards are unnumbered.

	MINT	EXC	G-VG
COMPLETE SET (10)	30.00	15.00	3.00
COMMON PLAYER (1-10)	1.75	.85	.17
☐ 1 Willie Aikens	1.75	.85	.17
☐ 2 George Brett	16.00	8.00	1.60
☐ 3 Dennis Leonard	2.50	1.25	.25
☐ 4 Hal McRae	2.50	1.25	.25
☐ 5 Amos Otis	2.50	1.25	.25
☐ 6 Dan Quisenberry	3.50	1.75	.35
☐ 7 U.L. Washington	1.75	.85	.17
☐ 8 John Wathan	2.50	1.25	.25
☐ 9 Frank White	4.00	2.00	.40
☐ 10 Willie Wilson	4.00	2.00	.40

1984 Police Braves

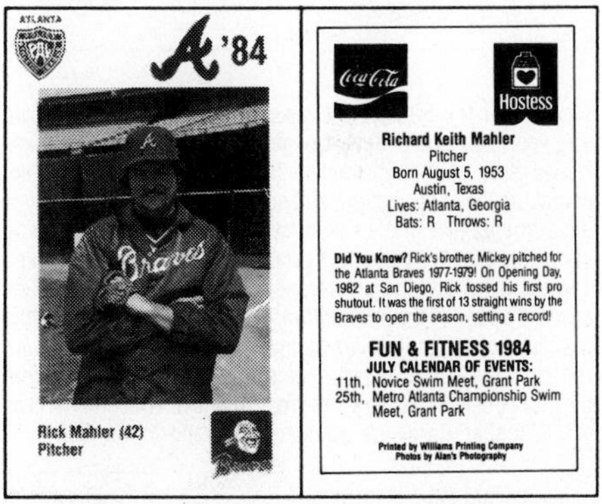

The cards in this 30-card set measure 2 5/8" by 4 1/8". For the fourth straight year, the Atlanta Police Department issued a full color set of Atlanta Braves. The cards were given out two per week by Atlanta police officers. In addition to the police department, the set was sponsored by Coke and Hostess. The backs of the cards of Perez and Ramirez are in Spanish. The Joe Torre card contains the checklist.

	MINT	EXC	G-VG
COMPLETE SET (30)	11.00	5.50	1.10
COMMON PLAYER	.30	.15	.03
☐ 1 Jerry Royster	.30	.15	.03
☐ 3 Dale Murphy	3.00	1.50	.30
☐ 5 Bob Horner	.75	.35	.07
☐ 6 Randy Johnson	.30	.15	.03
☐ 8 Bob Watson	.40	.20	.04
☐ 9 Joe Torre MG (checklist back)	.60	.30	.06
☐ 10 Chris Chambliss	.40	.20	.04
☐ 11 Mike Jorgensen	.30	.15	.03
☐ 15 Claudell Washington	.40	.20	.04
☐ 16 Rafael Ramirez	.30	.15	.03
☐ 17 Glenn Hubbard	.30	.15	.03
☐ 19 Terry Harper	.30	.15	.03
☐ 20 Bruce Benedict	.30	.15	.03
☐ 25 Alex Trevino	.30	.15	.03
☐ 26 Gene Garber	.30	.15	.03
☐ 27 Pascual Perez	.50	.25	.05
☐ 28 Gerald Perry	.60	.30	.06
☐ 29 Craig McMurtry	.30	.15	.03
☐ 31 Donnie Moore	.30	.15	.03
☐ 32 Steve Bedrosian	.75	.35	.07
☐ 33 Pete Falcone	.30	.15	.03
☐ 37 Rick Camp	.30	.15	.03
☐ 39 Len Barker	.30	.15	.03
☐ 42 Rick Mahler	.30	.15	.03
☐ 45 Bob Gibson CO	1.00	.50	.10
☐ 51 Terry Forster	.40	.20	.04
☐ 52 Joe Pignatano CO	.30	.15	.03

	MINT	EXC	G-VG
☐ 53 Dal Maxvill CO	.30	.15	.03
☐ 54 Rube Walker CO	.30	.15	.03
☐ 55 Luke Appling CO	.60	.30	.06

1984 Police Brewers

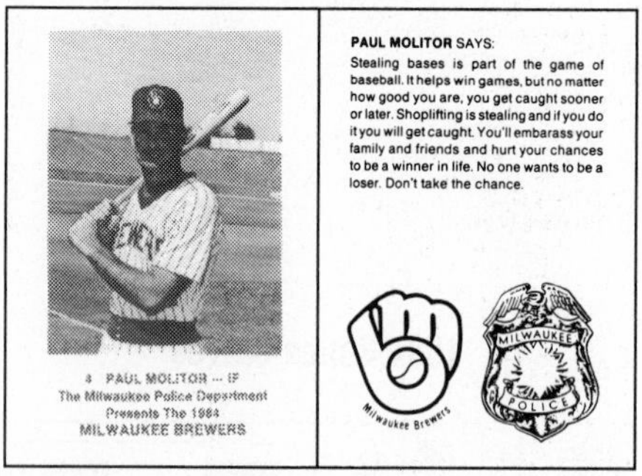
4 PAUL MOLITOR — IF
The Milwaukee Police Department
Presents The 1984
MILWAUKEE BREWERS
PAUL MOLITOR SAYS:
Stealing bases is part of the game of baseball. It helps win games, but no matter how good you are, you get caught sooner or later. Shoplifting is stealing and if you do it you will get caught. You'll embarass your family and friends and hurt your chances to be a winner in life. No one wants to be a loser. Don't take the chance.
MILWAUKEE
POLICE
Milwaukee Brewers

The cards in this 30-card set measure 2 13/16" by 4 1/8". Again this year, the police departments in and around Milwaukee issued sets of the Milwaukee Brewers. Although each set contained the same players and numbers, the individual police departments placed their own name on the fronts of cards to show that they were the particular jurisdiction issuing the set. The backs contain the Brewers logo, a safety tip, and in some cases, a badge of the jurisdiction. To date, 59 variations of this set have been found. Prices below are for the basic set without regard to the Police Department issuing the cards; cards from the more obscure corners and small towns of Wisconsin will be valued higher. Cards are numbered by uniform number.

	MINT	EXC	G-VG
COMPLETE SET (30)	7.00	3.50	.70
COMMON PLAYER	.20	.10	.02
☐ 2 Randy Ready	.25	.12	.02
☐ 4 Paul Molitor	.75	.35	.07
☐ 8 Jim Sundberg	.25	.12	.02
☐ 9 Rene Lachemann MG	.20	.10	.02
☐ 10 Bob McClure	.20	.10	.02
☐ 11 Ed Romero	.20	.10	.02
☐ 13 Roy Howell	.20	.10	.02
☐ 14 Dion James	.25	.12	.02
☐ 15 Cecil Cooper	.45	.22	.04
☐ 17 Jim Gantner	.30	.15	.03
☐ 19 Robin Yount	1.75	.85	.17
☐ 20 Don Sutton	.75	.35	.07
☐ 21 Bill Schroeder	.25	.12	.02
☐ 22 Charlie Moore	.20	.10	.02
☐ 23 Ted Simmons	.50	.25	.05
☐ 24 Ben Oglivie	.30	.15	.03
☐ 25 Bob Clark	.20	.10	.02
☐ 27 Pete Ladd	.20	.10	.02
☐ 28 Rick Manning	.20	.10	.02
☐ 29 Mark Brouhard	.20	.10	.02
☐ 30 Moose Haas	.20	.10	.02
☐ 34 Rollie Fingers	.75	.35	.07
☐ 42 Tom Tellmann	.20	.10	.02
☐ 43 Chuck Porter	.20	.10	.02
☐ 46 Jerry Augustine	.20	.10	.02
☐ 47 Jaime Cocanower	.20	.10	.02
☐ 48 Mike Caldwell	.25	.12	.02
☐ 50 Pete Vuckovich	.25	.12	.02
☐ xx Coaches Card (unnumbered)	.20	.10	.02
☐ xx Team Photo (Checklist back) (unnumbered)	.20	.10	.02

1984 Police Dodgers

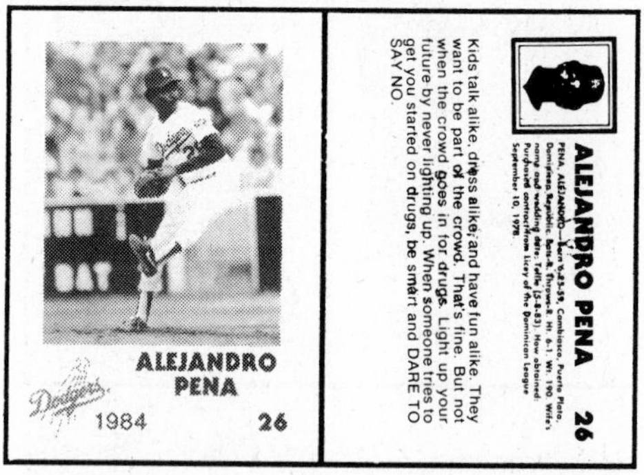

The cards in this 30-card set measure 2 13/16" by 4 1/8". For the fifth straight year, the Los Angeles Police Department sponsored a set of Dodger baseball cards. The set is numbered by player uniform number, which is featured on both the fronts and backs of the cards. The Dodgers' logo appears on the front, and the LAPD logo is superimposed on the backs of the cards. The backs are printed in Dodger blue ink and contain a small photo of the player on the front. Player biographical data and "Dare to Say No" antidrug information are featured on the back.

	MINT	EXC	G-VG
COMPLETE SET (30)	8.00	4.00	.80
COMMON PLAYER	.20	.10	.02
☐ 2 Tom Lasorda MG	.35	.17	.03
☐ 3 Steve Sax	.75	.35	.07
☐ 5 Mike Marshall	.50	.25	.05
☐ 7 Steve Yeager	.25	.12	.02
☐ 9 Greg Brock	.20	.10	.02
☐ 10 Dave Anderson	.20	.10	.02
☐ 14 Mike Scioscia	.25	.12	.02
☐ 16 Rick Monday	.25	.12	.02
☐ 17 Rafael Landestoy	.20	.10	.02
☐ 18 Bill Russell	.25	.12	.02
☐ 20 Candy Maldonado	.30	.15	.03
☐ 21 Bob Bailor	.20	.10	.02
☐ 25 German Rivera	.20	.10	.02
☐ 26 Alejandro Pena	.25	.12	.02
☐ 27 Carlos Diaz	.20	.10	.02
☐ 28 Pedro Guerrero	.75	.35	.07
☐ 31 Jack Fimple	.20	.10	.02
☐ 34 Fernando Valenzuela	.75	.35	.07
☐ 35 Bob Welch	.60	.30	.06
☐ 38 Pat Zachry	.20	.10	.02
☐ 40 Rick Honeycutt	.20	.10	.02
☐ 41 Jerry Reuss	.25	.12	.02
☐ 43 Jose Morales	.20	.10	.02
☐ 44 Ken Landreaux	.20	.10	.02
☐ 45 Terry Whitfield	.20	.10	.02
☐ 46 Burt Hooton	.20	.10	.02
☐ 49 Tom Niedenfuer	.25	.12	.02
☐ 55 Orel Hershiser	3.00	1.50	.30
☐ 56 Richard Rodas	.20	.10	.02
☐ xx Coaching Staff (unnumbered)	.20	.10	.02

1985 Police Braves

The cards in this 30-card set measure 2 5/8" by 4 1/8". For the fifth straight year, the Atlanta Police Department issued a full color set of Atlanta Braves. The set was also sponsored by Coca Cola and Hostess. In the upper right of the obverse is a logo commemorating the 20th anniversary of the Braves in Atlanta. Cards are numbered by uniform number. Cards feature a safety tip on the back. Each card except for Manager Haas has an interesting "Did You Know" fact about the player.

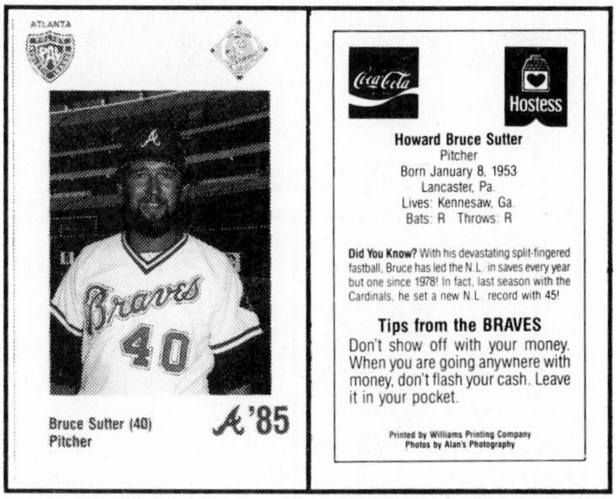

Born January 8, 1953
Lancaster, Pa.
Lives: Kennesaw, Ga.
Bats: R Throws: R
Did You Know? With his devastating split-fingered fastball, Bruce has led the N.L. in saves every year but one since 1978! In fact, last season with the Cardinals, he set a new N.L. record with 45!

Don't show off with your money. When you are going anywhere with money, don't flash your cash. Leave it in your pocket.

Photos by Alan's Photography

	MINT	EXC	G-VG
COMPLETE SET (30)	10.00	5.00	1.00
COMMON PLAYER	.30	.15	.03
☐ 2 Albert Hall	.40	.20	.04
☐ 3 Dale Murphy	3.00	1.50	.30
☐ 5 Rick Cerone	.30	.15	.03
☐ 7 Bobby Wine CO	.30	.15	.03
☐ 10 Chris Chambliss	.40	.20	.04
☐ 11 Bob Horner	.75	.35	.07
☐ 12 Paul Runge	.30	.15	.03
☐ 15 Claudell Washington	.40	.20	.04
☐ 16 Rafael Ramirez	.30	.15	.03
☐ 17 Glenn Hubbard	.30	.15	.03
☐ 18 Paul Zuvella	.30	.15	.03
☐ 19 Terry Harper	.30	.15	.03
☐ 20 Bruce Benedict	.30	.15	.03
☐ 22 Eddie Haas MG	.30	.15	.03
☐ 24 Ken Oberkfell	.30	.15	.03
☐ 26 Gene Garber	.30	.15	.03
☐ 27 Pascual Perez	.50	.25	.05
☐ 28 Gerald Perry	.50	.25	.05
☐ 29 Craig McMurtry	.30	.15	.03
☐ 32 Steve Bedrosian	.60	.30	.06
☐ 33 Johnny Sain CO	.50	.25	.05
☐ 34 Zane Smith	.60	.30	.06
☐ 36 Brad Komminsk	.40	.20	.04
☐ 37 Rick Camp	.30	.15	.03
☐ 39 Len Barker	.30	.15	.03
☐ 40 Bruce Sutter	.50	.25	.05
☐ 42 Rick Mahler	.30	.15	.03
☐ 51 Terry Forster	.40	.20	.04
☐ 52 Leo Mazzone CO	.30	.15	.03
☐ 53 Bobby Dews CO	.30	.15	.03

1985 Police Brewers

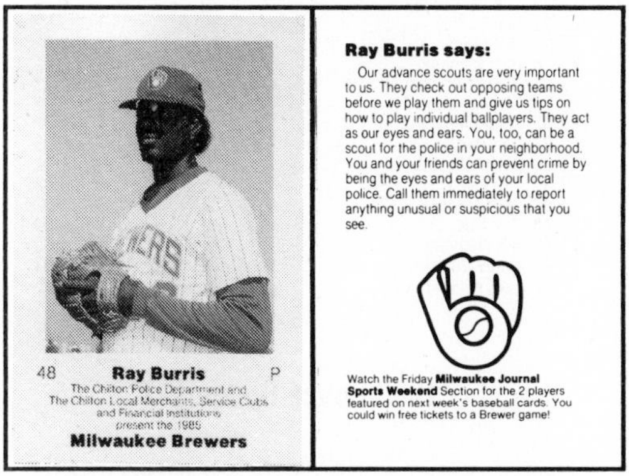
48 Ray Burris P
The Chilton Police Department and
The Chilton Local Merchants, Service Clubs and Financial Institutions present the 1985
Milwaukee Brewers
Ray Burris says:
Our advance scouts are very important to us. They check out opposing teams before we play them and give us tips on how to play individual ballplayers. They act as our eyes and ears. You, too, can be a scout for the police in your neighborhood. You and your friends can prevent crime by being the eyes and ears of your local police. Call them immediately to report anything unusual or suspicious that you see.
Watch the Friday Milwaukee Journal Sports Weekend Section for the 2 players featured on next week's baseball cards. You could win free tickets to a Brewer game!

The cards in this 30-card set measure 2 3/4" by 4 1/8". Again this year, the police departments in and around Milwaukee issued sets of the Milwaukee Brewers. The backs contain the Brewers logo, a safety tip, and in some cases, a badge of the jurisdiction.

Prices below are for the basic set without regard to the Police Department issuing the cards; cards from the more obscure corners and small towns of Wisconsin (smaller production) will be valued higher. Cards are numbered by uniform number.

	MINT	EXC	G-VG
COMPLETE SET (30)	7.00	3.50	.70
COMMON PLAYER	.20	.10	.02
☐ 2 Randy Ready	.25	.12	.02
☐ 4 Paul Molitor	.75	.35	.07
☐ 5 Doug Loman	.25	.12	.02
☐ 7 Paul Householder	.20	.10	.02
☐ 10 Bob McClure	.20	.10	.02
☐ 11 Ed Romero	.20	.10	.02
☐ 14 Dion James	.25	.12	.02
☐ 15 Cecil Cooper	.45	.22	.04
☐ 17 Jim Gantner	.30	.15	.03
☐ 18 Danny Darwin	.40	.20	.04
☐ 19 Robin Yount	1.75	.85	.17
☐ 21 Bill Schroeder	.25	.12	.02
☐ 22 Charlie Moore	.20	.10	.02
☐ 23 Ted Simmons	.45	.22	.04
☐ 24 Ben Oglivie	.30	.15	.03
☐ 26 Brian Giles	.20	.10	.02
☐ 27 Pete Ladd	.20	.10	.02
☐ 28 Rick Manning	.20	.10	.02
☐ 29 Mark Brouhard	.20	.10	.02
☐ 30 Moose Haas	.20	.10	.02
☐ 31 George Bamberger MG	.20	.10	.02
☐ 34 Rollie Fingers	.75	.35	.07
☐ 40 Bob L. Gibson	.20	.10	.02
☐ 41 Ray Searage	.20	.10	.02
☐ 47 Jaime Cocanower	.20	.10	.02
☐ 48 Ray Burris	.20	.10	.02
☐ 49 Ted Higuera	.75	.35	.07
☐ 50 Pete Vuckovich	.30	.15	.03
☐ xx Team Roster (unnumbered)	.20	.10	.02
☐ xx Coaches (unnumbered)	.20	.10	.02
☐ xx Newspaper Carrier (unnumbered)	.20	.10	.02

1986 Police Astros

This 26-card safety set was also sponsored by Kool-Aid. The backs contain a biographical paragraph above a "Tip from the Dugout". The front features a full-color photo of the player, his name, and uniform number. The cards are numbered on the back and measure 2 5/8" by 4 1/8". The backs are printed in orange and blue on white card stock. Sets were distributed at the Astrodome on June 14th as well as given away throughout the summer by the Houston Police.

	MINT	EXC	G-VG
COMPLETE SET (26)	8.00	4.00	.80
COMMON PLAYER (1-26)	.20	.10	.02
☐ 1 Jim Pankovits	.20	.10	.02
☐ 2 Nolan Ryan	2.50	1.25	.25
☐ 3 Mike Scott	.75	.35	.07
☐ 4 Kevin Bass	.40	.20	.04

☐ 5 Bill Doran	.40	.20	.04
☐ 6 Hal Lanier MG	.25	.12	.02
☐ 7 Denny Walling	.20	.10	.02
☐ 8 Alan Ashby	.20	.10	.02
☐ 9 Phil Garner	.25	.12	.02
☐ 10 Charlie Kerfeld	.20	.10	.02
☐ 11 Dave Smith	.35	.17	.03
☐ 12 Jose Cruz	.45	.22	.04
☐ 13 Craig Reynolds	.20	.10	.02
☐ 14 Mark Bailey	.20	.10	.02
☐ 15 Bob Knepper	.25	.12	.02
☐ 16 Julio Solano	.20	.10	.02
☐ 17 Dickie Thon	.25	.12	.02
☐ 18 Mike Madden	.20	.10	.02
☐ 19 Jeff Calhoun	.20	.10	.02
☐ 20 Tony Walker	.20	.10	.02
☐ 21 Terry Puhl	.30	.15	.03
☐ 22 Glenn Davis	1.25	.60	.12
☐ 23 Billy Hatcher	.35	.17	.03
☐ 24 Jim Deshaies	.25	.12	.02
☐ 25 Frank DiPino	.20	.10	.02
☐ 26 Coaching Staff	.20	.10	.02
☐ 49 Jeff Dedmon	.30	.15	.03
☐ 52 Al Monchak CO	.30	.15	.03

1986 Police Braves

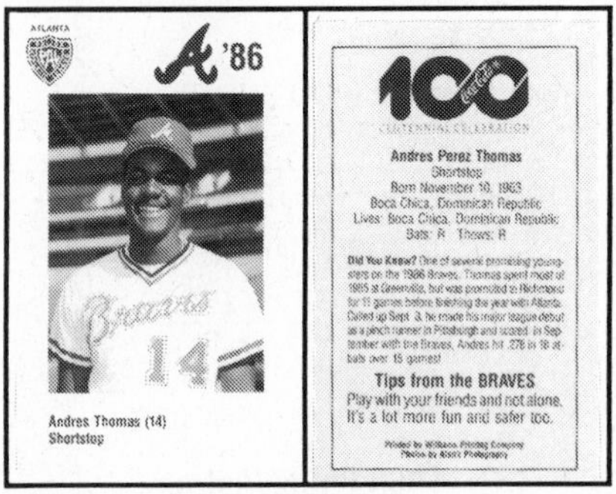

This 30-card safety set was also sponsored by Coca-Cola. The backs contain the usual biographical info and safety tip. The front features a full-color photo of the player, his name, and uniform number. The cards measure 2 5/8" by 4 1/8". Cards were freely distributed throughout the summer by the Police Departments in the Atlanta area. Cards are numbered below by uniform number.

	MINT	EXC	G-VG
COMPLETE SET (30)	10.00	5.00	1.00
COMMON PLAYER	.30	.15	.03
☐ 2 Russ Nixon CO	.30	.15	.03
☐ 3 Dale Murphy	2.50	1.25	.25
☐ 4 Bob Skinner CO	.40	.20	.04
☐ 5 Billy Sample	.30	.15	.03
☐ 7 Chuck Tanner MG	.40	.20	.04
☐ 8 Willie Stargell CO	1.00	.50	.10
☐ 9 Ozzie Virgil	.30	.15	.03
☐ 10 Chris Chambliss	.40	.20	.04
☐ 11 Bob Horner	.65	.30	.06
☐ 14 Andres Thomas	.40	.20	.04
☐ 15 Claudell Washington	.40	.20	.04
☐ 16 Rafael Ramirez	.30	.15	.03
☐ 17 Glenn Hubbard	.30	.15	.03
☐ 18 Omar Moreno	.30	.15	.03
☐ 19 Terry Harper	.30	.15	.03
☐ 20 Bruce Benedict	.30	.15	.03
☐ 23 Ted Simmons	.50	.25	.05
☐ 24 Ken Oberkfell	.30	.15	.03
☐ 26 Gene Garber	.30	.15	.03
☐ 29 Craig McMurtry	.30	.15	.03
☐ 30 Paul Assenmacher	.30	.15	.03
☐ 33 Johnny Sain CO	.50	.25	.05
☐ 34 Zane Smith	.50	.25	.05
☐ 38 Joe Johnson	.30	.15	.03
☐ 40 Bruce Sutter	.50	.25	.05
☐ 42 Rick Mahler	.40	.20	.04
☐ 46 David Palmer	.40	.20	.04
☐ 48 Duane Ward	.40	.20	.04

1986 Police Brewers

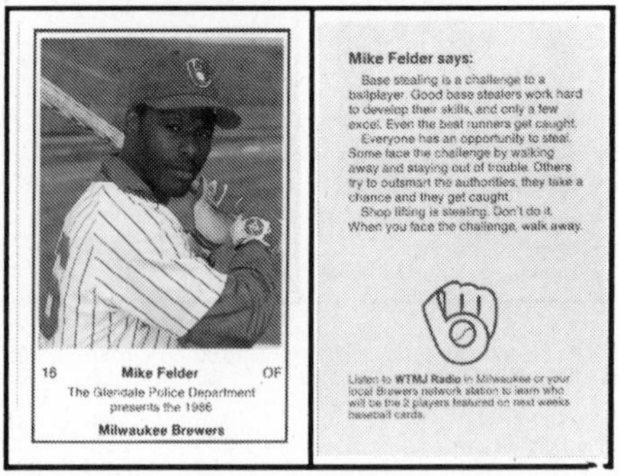
Mike Felder says:
Base stealing is a challenge to a ballplayer. Good base stealers work hard to develop their skills, and only a few excel. Even the best runners get caught.
Everyone has an opportunity to steal. Some face the challenge by walking away and staying out of trouble. Others try to outsmart the authorities, they take a chance and they get caught.
Shop lifting is stealing. Don't do it. When you face the challenge, walk away.
16
Mike Felder
OF
The Glendale Police Department presents the 1986
Milwaukee Brewers

This 32-card safety set was also sponsored by WTMJ Radio and Kinney Shoes. The backs contain the usual biographical info and safety tip. The front features a full-color photo of the player, his name, position, and uniform number. The cards measure 2 5/8" by 4 1/8". Cards were freely distributed throughout the summer by the Police Departments in the Milwaukee area. Cards are numbered below by uniform number.

	MINT	EXC	G-VG
COMPLETE SET (32)	6.00	3.00	.60
COMMON PLAYER	.20	.10	.02
☐ 1 Ernest Riles	.25	.12	.02
☐ 2 Randy Ready	.20	.10	.02
☐ 3 Juan Castillo	.20	.10	.02
☐ 4 Paul Molitor	.65	.30	.06
☐ 7 Paul Householder	.20	.10	.02
☐ 8 Andy Etchebarren CO	.20	.10	.02
☐ 10 Bob McClure	.20	.10	.02
☐ 11 Rick Cerone	.20	.10	.02
☐ 12 Larry Haney CO	.20	.10	.02
☐ 13 Billy Jo Robidoux	.25	.12	.02
☐ 15 Cecil Cooper	.35	.17	.03
☐ 16 Mike Felder	.25	.12	.02
☐ 17 Jim Gantner	.25	.12	.02
☐ 18 Danny Darwin	.30	.15	.03
☐ 19 Robin Yount	1.50	.75	.15
☐ 20 Juan Nieves	.25	.12	.02
☐ 21 Bill Schroeder	.25	.12	.02
☐ 22 Charlie Moore	.20	.10	.02
☐ 24 Ben Oglivie	.30	.15	.03
☐ 25 Mark Clear	.20	.10	.02
☐ 28 Rick Manning	.20	.10	.02
☐ 31 George Bamberger MG	.20	.10	.02
☐ 33 Frank Howard CO	.25	.12	.02
☐ 35 Tony Muser CO	.20	.10	.02
☐ 37 Dan Plesac	.35	.17	.03
☐ 38 Herm Starrette CO	.20	.10	.02
☐ 39 Tim Leary	.35	.17	.03
☐ 42 Tom Trebelhorn CO	.25	.12	.02
☐ 45 Rob Deer	.45	.22	.04
☐ 46 Bill Wegman	.25	.12	.02
☐ 47 Jaime Cocanower	.20	.10	.02
☐ 49 Teddy Higuera	.60	.30	.06

1986 Police Dodgers

This 30-card set features full-color cards each measuring 2 13/16" by 4 1/8". The cards are unnumbered except for uniform numbers. The backs give a safety tip as well as a short capsule biography. The sets were given away at Dodger Stadium on May 18th.

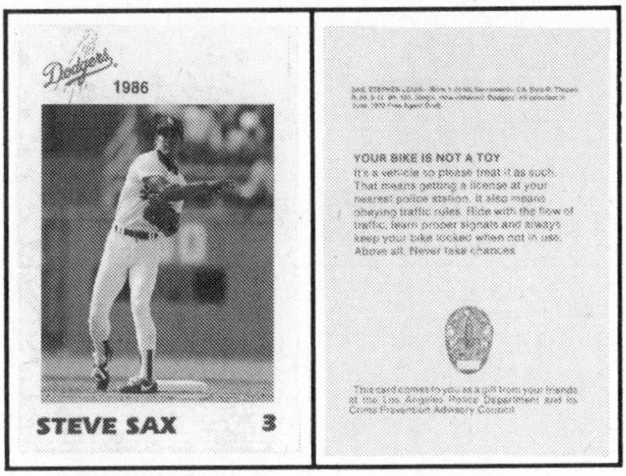

	MINT	EXC	G-VG
COMPLETE SET (30)	6.00	3.00	.60
COMMON PLAYER	.20	.10	.02
☐ 2 Tom Lasorda MG	.35	.17	.03
☐ 3 Steve Sax	.60	.30	.06
☐ 5 Mike Marshall	.50	.25	.05
☐ 9 Greg Brock	.20	.10	.02
☐ 10 Dave Anderson	.20	.10	.02
☐ 12 Bill Madlock	.30	.15	.03
☐ 14 Mike Scioscia	.30	.15	.03
☐ 17 Len Matuszek	.20	.10	.02
☐ 18 Bill Russell	.25	.12	.02
☐ 22 Franklin Stubbs	.30	.15	.03
☐ 23 Enos Cabell	.20	.10	.02
☐ 25 Mariano Duncan	.25	.12	.02
☐ 26 Alejandro Pena	.25	.12	.02
☐ 27 Carlos Diaz	.20	.10	.02
☐ 28 Pedro Guerrero	.75	.35	.07
☐ 29 Alex Trevino	.20	.10	.02
☐ 31 Ed VandeBerg	.20	.10	.02
☐ 34 Fernando Valenzuela	.75	.35	.07
☐ 35 Bob Welch	.50	.25	.05
☐ 40 Rick Honeycutt	.20	.10	.02
☐ 41 Jerry Reuss	.25	.12	.02
☐ 43 Ken Howell	.20	.10	.02
☐ 44 Ken Landreaux	.20	.10	.02
☐ 45 Terry Whitfield	.20	.10	.02
☐ 48 Dennis Powell	.20	.10	.02
☐ 49 Tom Niedenfuer	.20	.10	.02
☐ 51 Reggie Williams	.20	.10	.02
☐ 55 Orel Hershiser	1.25	.60	.12
☐ xx Coaching Staff (unnumbered) Don McMahon, Mark Cresse, Ben Hines, Ron Perranoski, Monty Basgall, Manny Mota, Joe Amalfitano	.20	.10	.02
☐ xx Team Photo (unnumbered) (checklist back)	.20	.10	.02

1987 Police Astros

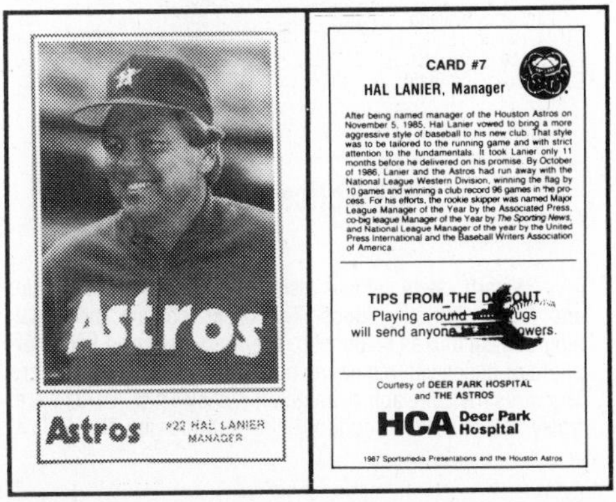

This 26-card safety set was sponsored by the Astros, Deer Park Hospital, and Sportsmedia Presentations. The backs contain a biographical paragraph above a "Tip from the Dugout". The front features a full-color photo of the player, his name, position, and uniform number. The cards are numbered on the back and measure 2 5/8" by 4 1/8". The first twelve cards were distributed at the Astrodome on July 14th and the rest were given away later in the summer by the Deer Park Hospital.

	MINT	EXC	G-VG
COMPLETE SET (26)	7.00	3.50	.70
COMMON PLAYER (1-26)	.20	.10	.02
☐ 1 Larry Andersen	.25	.12	.02
☐ 2 Mark Bailey	.20	.10	.02
☐ 3 Jose Cruz	.35	.17	.03
☐ 4 Danny Darwin	.30	.15	.03
☐ 5 Bill Doran	.45	.22	.04
☐ 6 Billy Hatcher	.35	.17	.03
☐ 7 Hal Lanier MG	.25	.12	.02
☐ 8 Davey Lopes	.30	.15	.03
☐ 9 Dave Meads	.20	.10	.02
☐ 10 Craig Reynolds	.20	.10	.02
☐ 11 Mike Scott	.75	.35	.07
☐ 12 Denny Walling	.20	.10	.02
☐ 13 Aurelio Lopez	.20	.10	.02
☐ 14 Dickie Thon	.25	.12	.02
☐ 15 Terry Puhl	.25	.12	.02
☐ 16 Nolan Ryan	2.50	1.25	.25
☐ 17 Dave Smith	.35	.17	.03
☐ 18 Julio Solano	.20	.10	.02
☐ 19 Jim Deshaies	.25	.12	.02
☐ 20 Bob Knepper	.25	.12	.02
☐ 21 Alan Ashby	.20	.10	.02
☐ 22 Kevin Bass	.35	.17	.03
☐ 23 Glenn Davis	.75	.35	.07
☐ 24 Phil Garner	.25	.12	.02
☐ 25 Jim Pankovits	.20	.10	.02
☐ 26 Coaching Staff	.20	.10	.02

1987 Police Brewers

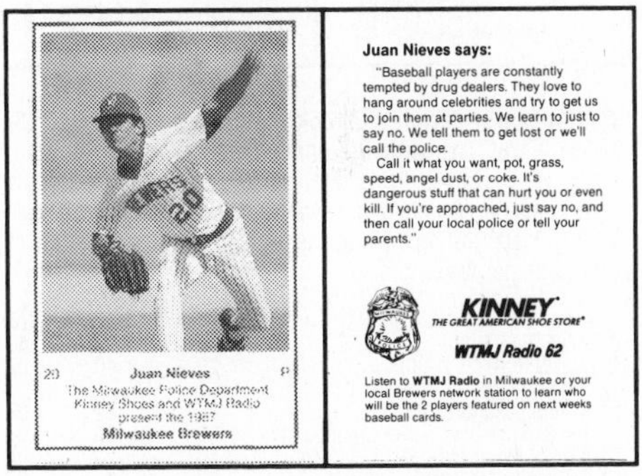

This 30-card safety set was also sponsored by WTMJ Radio and Kinney Shoes. The backs contain the usual biographical info and safety tip. The front features a full-color photo of the player, his name, position, and uniform number. The cards measure 2 5/8" by 4 1/8". Cards were freely distributed throughout the summer by the Police Departments in the Milwaukee area and throughout other parts of Wisconsin. Cards are numbered below by uniform number.

	MINT	EXC	G-VG
COMPLETE SET (30)	6.00	3.00	.60
COMMON PLAYER	.20	.10	.02
☐ 1 Ernest Riles	.25	.12	.02
☐ 2 Edgar Diaz	.25	.12	.02
☐ 3 Juan Castillo	.20	.10	.02
☐ 4 Paul Molitor	.75	.35	.07
☐ 5 B.J. Surhoff	.60	.30	.06
☐ 7 Dale Sveum	.25	.12	.02
☐ 9 Greg Brock	.25	.12	.02

	MINT	EXC	G-VG
☐ 13 Billy Jo Robidoux	.20	.10	.02
☐ 14 Jim Paciorek	.20	.10	.02
☐ 15 Cecil Cooper	.35	.17	.03
☐ 16 Mike Felder	.20	.10	.02
☐ 17 Jim Gantner	.30	.15	.03
☐ 19 Robin Yount	1.50	.75	.15
☐ 20 Juan Nieves	.25	.12	.02
☐ 21 Bill Schroeder	.25	.12	.02
☐ 25 Mark Clear	.20	.10	.02
☐ 26 Glenn Braggs	.35	.17	.03
☐ 28 Rick Manning	.20	.10	.02
☐ 29 Chris Bosio	.25	.12	.02
☐ 32 Chuck Crim	.20	.10	.02
☐ 34 Mark Ciardi	.20	.10	.02
☐ 37 Dan Plesac	.30	.15	.03
☐ 38 John Henry Johnson	.20	.10	.02
☐ 40 Mike Birkbeck	.25	.12	.02
☐ 42 Tom Trebelhorn MG	.25	.12	.02
☐ 45 Rob Deer	.35	.17	.03
☐ 46 Bill Wegman	.20	.10	.02
☐ 49 Teddy Higuera	.45	.22	.04
☐ xx Coaching Staff	.20	.10	.02
☐ xx Brewers Team (Checklist on back)	.20	.10	.02

1987 Police Dodgers

This 30-card set features full-color cards each measuring 2 13/16" by 4 1/8". The cards are unnumbered except for uniform numbers. The backs give a safety tip as well as a short capsule biography. Cards were given away at Dodger Stadium on April 24th and later during the summer by LAPD officers at a rate of two cards per week.

	MINT	EXC	G-VG
COMPLETE SET (30)	6.00	3.00	.60
COMMON PLAYER (1-30)	.20	.10	.02
☐ 1 Tom Lasorda MG 2	.35	.17	.03
☐ 2 Steve Sax 3	.60	.30	.06
☐ 3 Mike Marshall 5	.40	.20	.04
☐ 4 Dave Anderson 10	.20	.10	.02
☐ 5 Bill Madlock 12	.30	.15	.03
☐ 6 Mike Scioscia 14	.25	.12	.02
☐ 7 Gilberto Reyes 15	.20	.10	.02
☐ 8 Len Matuszek 17	.20	.10	.02
☐ 9 Reggie Williams 21	.20	.10	.02
☐ 10 Franklin Stubbs 22	.30	.15	.03
☐ 11 Tim Leary 23	.35	.17	.03
☐ 12 Mariano Duncan 25	.30	.15	.03
☐ 13 Alejandro Pena 26	.25	.12	.02
☐ 14 Pedro Guerrero 28	.75	.35	.07
☐ 15 Alex Trevino 29	.20	.10	.02
☐ 16 Jeff Hamilton 33	.25	.12	.02
☐ 17 Fernando Valenzuela 34	.75	.35	.07
☐ 18 Bob Welch 35	.50	.25	.05
☐ 19 Matt Young 36	.25	.12	.02
☐ 20 Rick Honeycutt 40	.20	.10	.02
☐ 21 Jerry Reuss 41	.25	.12	.02
☐ 22 Ken Howell 43	.25	.12	.02
☐ 23 Ken Landreaux 44	.20	.10	.02
☐ 24 Ralph Bryant 46	.20	.10	.02
☐ 25 Jose Gonzalez 47	.25	.12	.02
☐ 26 Tom Niedenfuer 49	.20	.10	.02
☐ 27 Brian Holton 51	.20	.10	.02
☐ 28 Orel Hershiser 55	1.00	.50	.10
☐ 29 Coaching Staff	.20	.10	.02
☐ 30 Dodgers Stadium (25th Anniversary)	.20	.10	.02

1988 Police Astros

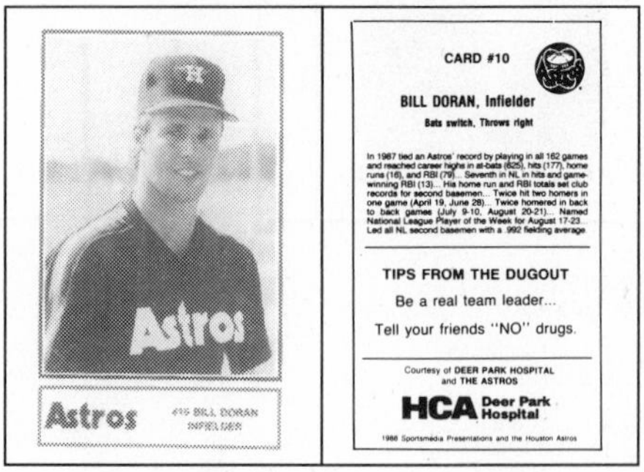

This 26-card safety set was sponsored by the Astros, Deer Park Hospital, and Sportsmedia Presentations. The backs contain a biographical paragraph above "Tips from the Dugout". The front features a full-color photo of the player, his name, position, and uniform number. The cards are numbered on the back and measure 2 5/8" by 4 1/8". The sets were supposedly distributed to the first 15,000 youngsters attending the New York Mets game against the Astros at the Astrodome on July 9th.

	MINT	EXC	G-VG
COMPLETE SET (26)	7.00	3.50	.70
COMMON PLAYER (1-26)	.25	.12	.02
☐ 1 Juan Agosto	.25	.12	.02
☐ 2 Larry Andersen	.25	.12	.02
☐ 3 Joaquin Andujar	.35	.17	.03
☐ 4 Alan Ashby	.25	.12	.02
☐ 5 Mark Bailey	.25	.12	.02
☐ 6 Kevin Bass	.45	.22	.04
☐ 7 Danny Darwin	.35	.17	.03
☐ 8 Glenn Davis	.75	.35	.07
☐ 9 Jim Deshaies	.35	.17	.03
☐ 10 Bill Doran	.45	.22	.04
☐ 11 Billy Hatcher	.35	.17	.03
☐ 12 Jeff Heathcock	.25	.12	.02
☐ 13 Steve Henderson	.25	.12	.02
☐ 14 Chuck Jackson	.25	.12	.02
☐ 15 Bob Knepper	.25	.12	.02
☐ 16 Jim Pankovits	.25	.12	.02
☐ 17 Terry Puhl	.35	.17	.03
☐ 18 Rafael Ramirez	.25	.12	.02
☐ 19 Craig Reynolds	.25	.12	.02
☐ 20 Nolan Ryan	2.50	1.25	.25
☐ 21 Mike Scott	.75	.35	.07
☐ 22 Dave Smith	.45	.22	.04
☐ 23 Denny Walling	.25	.12	.02
☐ 24 Gerald Young	.35	.17	.03
☐ 25 Hal Lanier MG	.25	.12	.02
☐ 26 Coaching Staff	.25	.12	.02

1988 Police Brewers

This 30-card safety set was also sponsored by WTMJ Radio and Stadia Athletic Shoes. The backs contain the usual biographical info and safety tip. The front features a full-color photo of the player, his name, position, and uniform number. The cards measure approximately 2 7/8" by 4 1/8". Cards were freely distributed throughout the summer by the Police

Departments in the Milwaukee area and throughout other parts of Wisconsin. Cards are numbered below by uniform number.

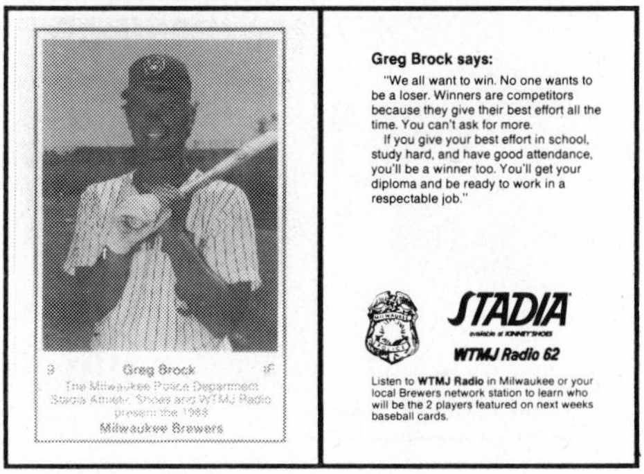
9
Greg Brock
1B
The Milwaukee Police Department
Stadia Athletic Shoes and WTMJ Radio
present the 1988
Milwaukee Brewers
Greg Brock says:
"We all want to win. No one wants to be a loser. Winners are competitors because they give their best effort all the time. You can't ask for more.
If you give your best effort in school, study hard, and have good attendance, you'll be a winner too. You'll get your diploma and be ready to work in a respectable job."
STADIA
WTMJ Radio 62
Listen to WTMJ Radio in Milwaukee or your local Brewers network station to learn who will be the 2 players featured on next weeks baseball cards.

	MINT	EXC	G-VG
COMPLETE SET (30)	6.00	3.00	.60
COMMON PLAYER	.20	.10	.02
☐ 1 Ernest Riles	.20	.10	.02
☐ 3 Juan Castillo	.20	.10	.02
☐ 4 Paul Molitor	.60	.30	.06
☐ 5 B.J. Surhoff	.35	.17	.03
☐ 7 Dale Sveum	.25	.12	.02
☐ 9 Greg Brock	.25	.12	.02
☐ 11 Charlie O'Brien	.20	.10	.02
☐ 14 Jim Adduci	.25	.12	.02
☐ 16 Mike Felder	.25	.12	.02
☐ 17 Jim Gantner	.30	.15	.03
☐ 19 Robin Yount	1.50	.75	.15
☐ 20 Juan Nieves	.25	.12	.02
☐ 21 Bill Schroeder	.25	.12	.02
☐ 23 Joey Meyer	.25	.12	.02
☐ 25 Mark Clear	.20	.10	.02
☐ 26 Glenn Braggs	.35	.17	.03
☐ 28 Odell Jones	.20	.10	.02
☐ 29 Chris Bosio	.25	.12	.02
☐ 30 Steve Kiefer	.20	.10	.02
☐ 32 Chuck Crim	.20	.10	.02
☐ 33 Jay Aldrich	.20	.10	.02
☐ 37 Dan Plesac	.30	.15	.03
☐ 40 Mike Birkbeck	.25	.12	.02
☐ 42 Tom Trebelhorn MG	.25	.12	.02
☐ 43 Dave Stapleton	.20	.10	.02
☐ 45 Rob Deer	.35	.17	.03
☐ 46 Bill Wegman	.20	.10	.02
☐ 49 Ted Higuera	.45	.22	.04
☐ x Team Photo HOR (unnumbered)	.20	.10	.02
☐ x Manager and Coaches HOR (unnumbered)	.20	.10	.02

1988 Police Dodgers

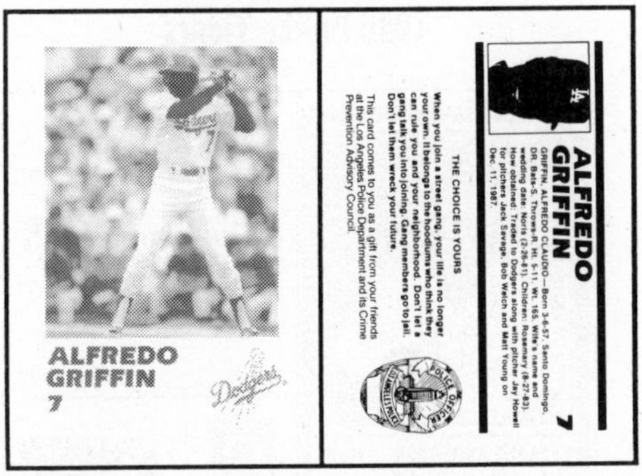

This 30-card set features full-color cards each measuring approximately 2 13/16" by 4 1/8". The cards are unnumbered except for uniform numbers. The backs give a safety tip as well as a short capsule biography. Cards were given during the summer by LAPD officers. The set is very similar to the 1987 set, the 1988 set is distinguished by the fact that it does not have the 25th anniversary (of Dodger Stadium) logo on the card front.

	MINT	EXC	G-VG
COMPLETE SET (30)	5.00	2.50	.50
COMMON PLAYER	.20	.10	.02
☐ 2 Tom Lasorda MG	.30	.15	.03
☐ 3 Steve Sax	.50	.25	.05
☐ 5 Mike Marshall	.40	.20	.04
☐ 7 Alfredo Griffin	.25	.12	.02
☐ 9 Mickey Hatcher	.20	.10	.02
☐ 10 Dave Anderson	.20	.10	.02
☐ 12 Danny Heep	.20	.10	.02
☐ 14 Mike Scioscia	.25	.12	.02
☐ 20 Don Sutton	.60	.30	.06
☐ 21 Tito Landrum and 17 Len Matuszak	.20	.10	.02
☐ 22 Franklin Stubbs	.30	.15	.03
☐ 23 Kirk Gibson	.75	.35	.07
☐ 25 Mariano Duncan	.25	.12	.02
☐ 26 Alejandro Pena	.20	.10	.02
☐ 27 Mike Sharperson and 52 Tim Crews	.20	.10	.02
☐ 28 Pedro Guerrero	.50	.25	.05
☐ 29 Alex Trevino	.20	.10	.02
☐ 31 John Shelby	.20	.10	.02
☐ 33 Jeff Hamilton	.25	.12	.02
☐ 34 Fernando Valenzuela	.50	.25	.05
☐ 37 Mike Davis	.20	.10	.02
☐ 41 Brad Havens	.20	.10	.02
☐ 43 Ken Howell	.25	.12	.02
☐ 47 Jesse Orosco	.20	.10	.02
☐ 49 Tim Belcher and 57 Shawn Hillegas	.35	.17	.03
☐ 50 Jay Howell	.30	.15	.03
☐ 51 Brian Holton	.20	.10	.02
☐ 54 Tim Leary	.35	.17	.03
☐ 55 Orel Hershiser	.90	.45	.09
☐ x Tom Lasorda MG and Coaches (unnumbered)	.30	.15	.03

1988 Police Tigers

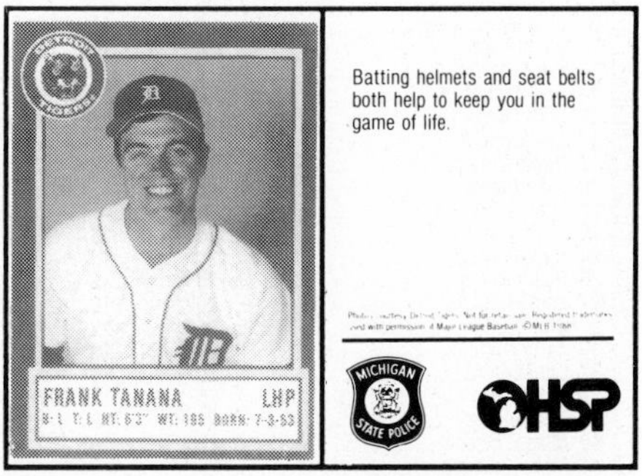

This set was sponsored by the Michigan State Police and the Detroit Tigers organization. There are 14 blue-bordered cards in the set; each card measures approximately 2 1/2" by 3 1/2". The cards are completely unnumbered as there is not even any reference to uniform numbers on the cards; the cards are listed below in alphabetical order.

	MINT	EXC	G-VG
COMPLETE SET (14)	35.00	17.50	3.50
COMMON PLAYER (1-14)	1.50	.75	.15
☐ 1 Doyle Alexander	2.00	1.00	.20

☐ 2 Sparky Anderson MG	3.50	1.75	.35
☐ 3 Dave Bergman	1.50	.75	.15
☐ 4 Tom Brookens	1.50	.75	.15
☐ 5 Darrell Evans	2.50	1.25	.25
☐ 6 Larry Herndon	1.50	.75	.15
☐ 7 Chet Lemon	2.00	1.00	.20
☐ 8 Jack Morris	3.50	1.75	.35
☐ 9 Matt Nokes	3.00	1.50	.30
☐ 10 Jeff Robinson	3.00	1.50	.30
☐ 11 Frank Tanana	2.00	1.00	.20
☐ 12 Walt Terrell	1.50	.75	.15
☐ 13 Alan Trammell	6.00	3.00	.60
☐ 14 Lou Whitaker	4.50	2.25	.45

1989 Police Brewers

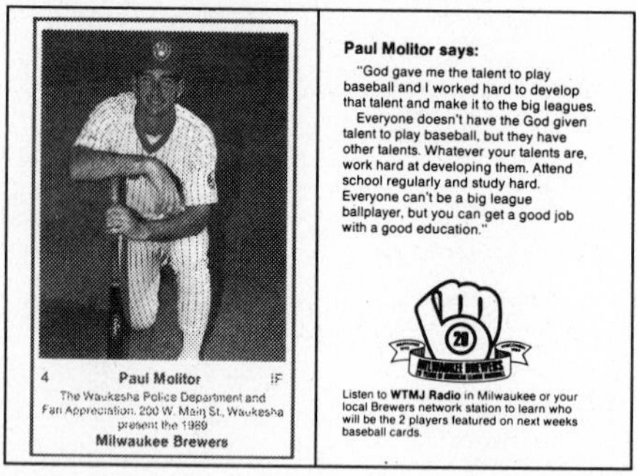
4 Paul Molitor IF
The Waukesha Police Department and Fan Appreciation, 200 W. Main St., Waukesha present the 1989
Milwaukee Brewers
Paul Molitor says:
"God gave me the talent to play baseball and I worked hard to develop that talent and make it to the big leagues.
Everyone doesn't have the God given talent to play baseball, but they have other talents. Whatever your talents are, work hard at developing them. Attend school regularly and study hard. Everyone can't be a big league ballplayer, but you can get a good job with a good education."
20
Listen to WTMJ Radio in Milwaukee or your local Brewers network station to learn who will be the 2 players featured on next weeks baseball cards.

The 1989 Police Milwaukee Brewers set contains 30 cards measuring approximately 2 3/4" by 4 1/4". The fronts have color photos with white borders; the backs feature safety tips. The unnumbered cards were given away by various local Wisconsin police departments. The cards are numbered below by uniform number.

	MINT	EXC	G-VG
COMPLETE SET (30)	6.00	3.00	.60
COMMON PLAYER	.20	.10	.02
☐ 1 Gary Sheffield	.75	.35	.07
☐ 4 Paul Molitor	.60	.30	.06
☐ 5 B.J. Surhoff	.30	.15	.03
☐ 6 Bill Spiers	.30	.15	.03
☐ 7 Dale Sveum	.20	.10	.02
☐ 9 Greg Brock	.20	.10	.02
☐ 14 Gus Polidor	.20	.10	.02
☐ 16 Mike Felder	.20	.10	.02
☐ 17 Jim Gantner	.25	.12	.02
☐ 19 Robin Yount	1.25	.60	.12
☐ 20 Juan Nieves	.25	.12	.02
☐ 22 Charlie O'Brien	.25	.12	.02
☐ 23 Joey Meyer	.25	.12	.02
☐ 25 Dave Engle	.20	.10	.02
☐ 26 Glenn Braggs	.25	.12	.02
☐ 27 Paul Mirabella	.20	.10	.02
☐ 29 Chris Bosio	.25	.12	.02
☐ 30 Terry Francona	.20	.10	.02
☐ 32 Chuck Crim	.20	.10	.02
☐ 37 Dan Plesac	.25	.12	.02
☐ 38 Don August	.25	.12	.02
☐ 40 Mike Birkbeck	.20	.10	.02
☐ 41 Mark Knudson	.20	.10	.02
☐ 42 Tom Trebelhorn MG	.25	.12	.02
☐ 45 Rob Deer	.30	.15	.03
☐ 46 Bill Wegman	.20	.10	.02
☐ 48 Bryan Clutterbuck	.20	.10	.02
☐ 49 Teddy Higuera	.35	.17	.03
☐ xx Team Card (checklist on back)	.20	.10	.02
☐ xx Coaches Card	.20	.10	.02

1989 Police Dodgers

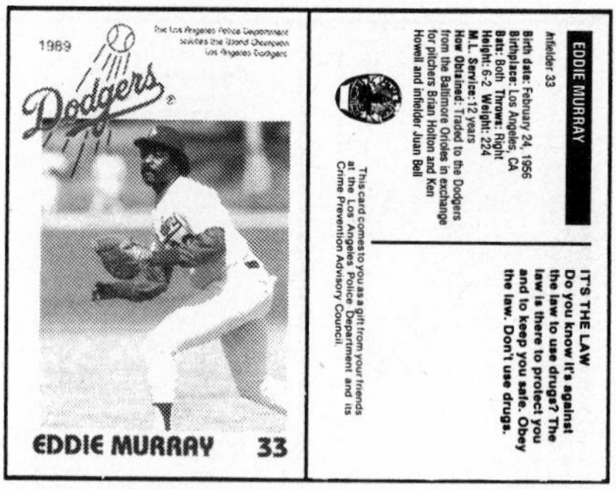

The 1989 Police Los Angeles Dodgers set contains 30 cards measuring approximately 2 5/8" by 4 1/4". The fronts have color photos with white borders; the backs feature safety tips and biographical information. The unnumbered cards were given away by various Los Angeles-area police departments.

	MINT	EXC	G-VG
COMPLETE SET (30)	5.00	2.50	.50
COMMON PLAYER	.20	.10	.02
☐ 1 Dodger Coaches	.20	.10	.02
☐ 2 Tom Lasorda MG	.30	.15	.03
☐ 3 Jeff Hamilton	.20	.10	.02
☐ 4 Mike Marshall	.35	.17	.03
☐ 5 Alfredo Griffin	.20	.10	.02
☐ 6 Mickey Hatcher	.20	.10	.02
☐ 7 Dave Anderson	.20	.10	.02
☐ 8 Willie Randolph	.30	.15	.03
☐ 9 Mike Scioscia	.25	.12	.02
☐ 10 Rick Dempsey	.20	.10	.02
☐ 11 Mike Davis	.20	.10	.02
☐ 12 Tracy Woodson	.25	.12	.02
☐ 13 Franklin Stubbs	.25	.12	.02
☐ 14 Kirk Gibson	.50	.25	.05
☐ 15 Mariano Duncan	.25	.12	.02
☐ 16 Alejandro Pena	.20	.10	.02
☐ 17 Mike Sharperson	.20	.10	.02
☐ 18 Ricky Horton	.20	.10	.02
☐ 19 John Tudor	.25	.12	.02
☐ 20 John Shelby	.20	.10	.02
☐ 21 Eddie Murray	.50	.25	.05
☐ 22 Fernando Valenzuela	.50	.25	.05
☐ 23 Mike Morgan	.20	.10	.02
☐ 24 Ramon Martinez	.75	.35	.07
☐ 25 Tim Belcher	.30	.15	.03
☐ 26 Jay Howell	.25	.12	.02
☐ 27 Tim Crews	.20	.10	.02
☐ 28 Tim Leary	.25	.12	.02
☐ 29 Orel Hershiser	.60	.30	.06
☐ 30 Ray Searage	.20	.10	.02

1989 Police Tigers

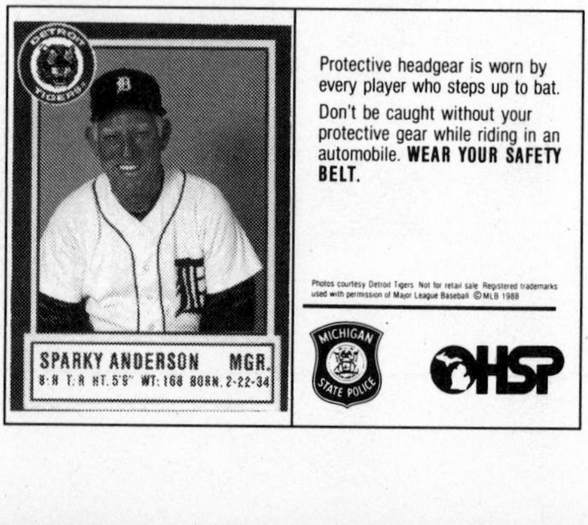
DETROIT TIGERS
SPARKY ANDERSON MGR.
B: R T: R HT: 5'9" WT: 168 BORN: 2-22-34
Protective headgear is worn by every player who steps up to bat.
Don't be caught without your protective gear while riding in an automobile. WEAR YOUR SAFETY BELT.
MICHIGAN STATE POLICE
OHSP

The 1989 Police Detroit Tigers set contains 14 standard-size (2 1/2" by 3 1/2") cards. The fronts have color photos with blue and orange borders; the backs feature safety tips. These unnumbered cards were given away by the Michigan state police. The cards are numbered below according to uniform number.

	MINT	EXC	G-VG
COMPLETE SET (14)	10.00	5.00	1.00
COMMON PLAYER	.50	.25	.05
☐ 1 Lou Whitaker	1.00	.50	.10
☐ 3 Alan Trammell	1.75	.85	.17
☐ 9 Fred Lynn	.60	.30	.06
☐ 14 Dave Bergman	.50	.25	.05
☐ 15 Pat Sheridan	.50	.25	.05
☐ 19 Doyle Alexander	.60	.30	.06
☐ 21 Guillermo Hernandez	.60	.30	.06
☐ 26 Frank Tanana	.60	.30	.06
☐ 33 Matt Nokes	.60	.30	.06
☐ 34 Chet Lemon	.60	.30	.06
☐ 39 Mike Henneman	.60	.30	.06
☐ 44 Jeff Robinson	.60	.30	.06
☐ 47 Jack Morris	.90	.45	.09
☐ xx Sparky Anderson MG	.75	.35	.07

1990 Police Brewers

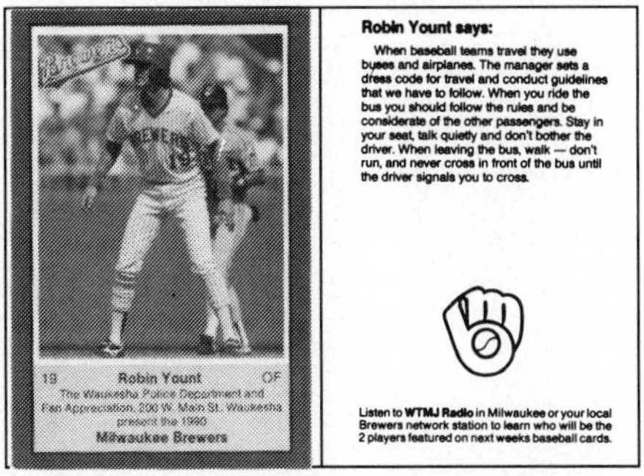

This 30-card police set was issued in conjunction with the Fan Appreciation store of Waukesha, Wisconsin and the Waukesha Police department. This set measures approximately 2 13/16" by 4 1/8" and is checklisted by uniform number. The front of the card is a full-color photo surrounded by a blue border while the back has anti-crime tips.

	MINT	EXC	G-VG
COMPLETE SET (30)	6.00	3.00	.60
COMMON PLAYER	.20	.10	.02
☐ 2 Edgar Diaz	.20	.10	.02
☐ 4 Paul Molitor	.60	.30	.06
☐ 7 Dale Sveum	.20	.10	.02
☐ 11 Gary Sheffield	.50	.25	.05
☐ 14 Gus Polidor	.20	.10	.02
☐ 16 Mike Felder	.20	.10	.02
☐ 17 Jim Gantner	.30	.15	.03
☐ 19 Robin Yount	.75	.35	.07
☐ 20 Juan Nieves	.25	.12	.02
☐ 22 Charlie O'Brien	.25	.12	.02
☐ 23 Greg Vaughn	.50	.25	.05
☐ 24 Darryl Hamilton	.30	.15	.03
☐ 26 Glenn Braggs	.25	.12	.02
☐ 27 Paul Mirabella	.20	.10	.02
☐ 28 Tom Filer	.20	.10	.02
☐ 29 Chris Bosio	.25	.12	.02
☐ 30 Terry Francona	.20	.10	.02
☐ 31 Jaime Navarro	.25	.12	.02
☐ 32 Chuck Crim	.20	.10	.02
☐ 34 Billy Bates	.25	.12	.02
☐ 36 Tony Fossas	.20	.10	.02
☐ 37 Dan Plesac	.25	.12	.02
☐ 38 Don August	.25	.12	.02
☐ 39 Dave Parker	.50	.25	.05
☐ 40 Mike Birkbeck	.20	.10	.02
☐ 41 Mark Knudson	.20	.10	.02
☐ 42 Tom Trebelhorn MG	.25	.12	.02
☐ 45 Rob Deer	.35	.17	.03
☐ 46 Bill Wegman	.20	.10	.02
☐ 47 Bill Krueger	.20	.10	.02
☐ 49 Teddy Higuera	.35	.17	.03
☐ xx Coaches	.20	.10	.02

Larry Haney 12
Don Baylor 25
Ray Burris 50
Andy Etchebarren 8
Duffy Dyer 10

1990 Police Dodgers

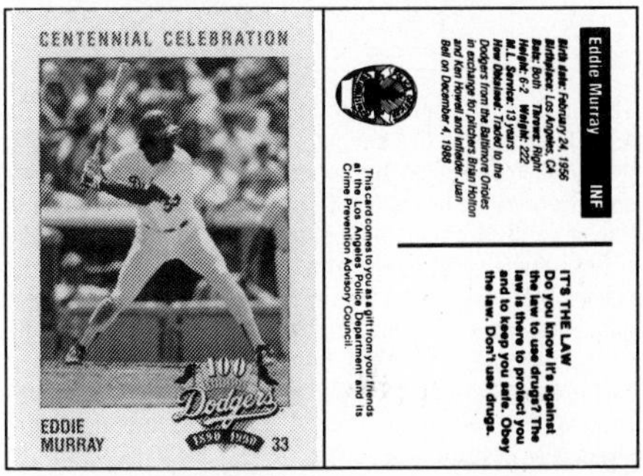

This 26-card set measures approximately 2 13/16" by 4 1/8" and was distributed by both the Los Angeles Police Department and at a pre-season Dodger-Angel exhibition game. This set also commemorated the 100th anniversary of the Dodgers existence. The front has a full-color photo of the player on the front while the back has a brief profile of the player with an anti-crime message. This set is checklisted below by uniform number.

	MINT	EXC	G-VG
COMPLETE SET (26)	5.00	2.50	.50
COMMON PLAYER	.20	.10	.02
☐ 1 Tommy Lasorda MG	.30	.15	.03
☐ 3 Jeff Hamilton	.20	.10	.02
☐ 7 Alfredo Griffin	.20	.10	.02
☐ 8 Mickey Hatcher	.20	.10	.02
☐ 10 Juan Samuel	.30	.15	.03
☐ 12 Willie Randolph	.30	.15	.03
☐ 14 Mike Scioscia	.30	.15	.03
☐ 15 Chris Gwynn	.30	.15	.03
☐ 17 Rick Dempsey	.20	.10	.02
☐ 21 Hubie Brooks	.30	.15	.03
☐ 22 Franklin Stubbs	.30	.15	.03
☐ 23 Kirk Gibson	.50	.25	.05
☐ 27 Mike Sharperson	.20	.10	.02
☐ 28 Kal Daniels	.40	.20	.04
☐ 29 Lenny Harris	.30	.15	.03
☐ 31 John Shelby	.20	.10	.02
☐ 33 Eddie Murray	.50	.25	.05
☐ 34 Fernando Valenzuela	.50	.25	.05
☐ 35 Jim Gott	.20	.10	.02
☐ 36 Mike Morgan	.30	.15	.03
☐ 38 Jose Gonzalez	.20	.10	.02
☐ 39 Jim Neidlinger	.30	.15	.03
☐ 46 Mike Hartley	.30	.15	.03
☐ 49 Tim Belcher	.30	.15	.03
☐ 50 Jay Howell	.25	.12	.02
☐ 52 Tim Crews	.20	.10	.02
☐ 55 Orel Hershiser	.50	.25	.05
☐ 57 John Wetteland	.30	.15	.03
☐ 59 Ray Searage	.20	.10	.02
☐ xx Coaches	.20	.10	.02

Ben Hines
Ron Perranowski
Mark Cresse
Manny Mota
Tommy Lasorda MG
Joe Amalfitano
Joe Ferguson
Bill Russell

1961 Post Cereal

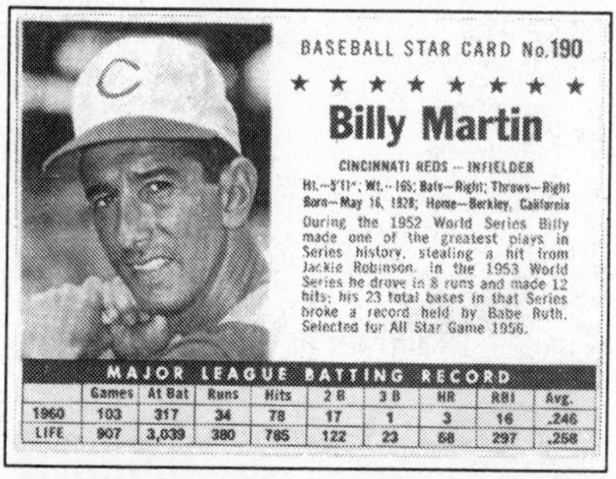
BASEBALL STAR CARD No. 190
Billy Martin
CINCINNATI REDS -- INFIELDER
Ht.--5'11"; Wt.--165; Bats--Right; Throws--Right
Born--May 16, 1928; Home--Berkley, California
During the 1952 World Series Billy made one of the greatest plays in Series history, stealing a hit from Jackie Robinson. In the 1953 World Series he drove in 8 runs and made 12 hits; his 23 total bases in that Series broke a record held by Babe Ruth. Selected for All Star Game 1956.
MAJOR LEAGUE BATTING RECORD
Games At Bat Runs Hits 2B 3B HR RBI Avg.
1960 103 317 34 78 17 1 3 16 .246
LIFE 907 3,039 380 785 122 23 68 297 .258

The cards in this 200-card set measure 2 1/2" by 3 1/2". The 1961 Post set was this company's first major set. The cards were available on thick cardbox stock, singly or in various panel sizes from cereal boxes (BOX), or in team sheets, printed on thinner cardboard stock, directly from the Post Cereal Company (COM). Many variations exist and are noted in the checklist below. There are many cards which were produced in lesser quantities; the prices below reflect the relative scarcity of the cards. Cards 10, 23, 70, 73, 94, 113, 135, 163, and 183 are examples of cards printed in limited quantities and hence commanding premium prices. The cards are numbered essentially in team groups, i.e., New York Yankees (1-18), Chicago White Sox (19-34), Detroit (35-46), Boston (47-56), Cleveland (57-67), Baltimore (68-80), Kansas City (81-90), Minnesota (91-100), Milwaukee (101-114), Philadelphia (115-124), Pittsburgh (125-140), San Francisco (141-155), Los Angeles Dodgers (156-170), St. Louis (171-180), Cincinnati (181-190), and Chicago Cubs (191-200). The catalog number is F278-33. The complete set prices refer to both ways of collecting the set, all variations (357) or one of each player (200). There was also an album produced by Post to hold the cards.

	NRMT	VG-E	GOOD
COMPLETE SET (357)	2100.00	1000.00	225.00
COMPLETE SET (200)	1300.00	600.00	135.00
COMMON PLAYER (1-200)	2.00	1.00	.20
☐ 1A Yogi Berra COM	20.00	10.00	2.00
☐ 1B Yogi Berra BOX	20.00	10.00	2.00
☐ 2A Elston Howard COM	3.00	1.50	.30
☐ 2B Elston Howard BOX	3.50	1.75	.35
☐ 3A Bill Skowron COM	3.00	1.50	.30
☐ 3B Bill Skowron BOX	2.00	1.00	.20
☐ 4A Mickey Mantle COM	100.00	50.00	10.00
☐ 4B Mickey Mantle BOX	100.00	50.00	10.00
☐ 5 Bob Turley COM only	15.00	7.50	1.50
☐ 6A Whitey Ford COM	7.50	3.75	.75
☐ 6B Whitey Ford BOX	7.50	3.75	.75
☐ 7A Roger Maris COM	25.00	12.50	2.50
☐ 7B Roger Maris BOX	25.00	12.50	2.50
☐ 8A B.Richardson COM	3.00	1.50	.30
☐ 8B B.Richardson BOX	2.00	1.00	.20
☐ 9A Tony Kubek COM	3.00	1.50	.30
☐ 9B Tony Kubek BOX	2.00	1.00	.20
☐ 10 G.McDougald BOX only	35.00	17.50	3.50
☐ 11 Cletis Boyer BOX only	2.00	1.00	.20
☐ 12A Hector Lopes COM	2.00	1.00	.20
☐ 12B Hector Lopes BOX	2.00	1.00	.20
☐ 13 Bob Cerv BOX only	2.00	1.00	.20
☐ 14 Ryne Duren BOX only	2.00	1.00	.20
☐ 15 Bobby Shantz BOX only	2.00	1.00	.20
☐ 16 Art Ditmar BOX only	2.00	1.00	.20
☐ 17 Jim Coates BOX only	2.00	1.00	.20
☐ 18 J.Blanchard BOX only	2.00	1.00	.20
☐ 19A Luis Aparicio COM	6.00	3.00	.60
☐ 19B Luis Aparicio BOX	5.00	2.50	.50
☐ 20A Nelson Fox COM	5.00	2.50	.50
☐ 20B Nelson Fox BOX	4.00	2.00	.40
☐ 21A Bill Pierce COM	3.00	1.50	.30
☐ 21B Bill Pierce BOX	5.00	2.50	.50
☐ 22A Early Wynn COM	8.00	4.00	.80
☐ 22B Early Wynn BOX	10.00	5.00	1.00
☐ 23 Bob Shaw BOX only	90.00	45.00	9.00
☐ 24A Al Smith COM	2.00	1.00	.20
☐ 24B Al Smith BOX	2.50	1.25	.25
☐ 25A Minnie Minoso COM	3.00	1.50	.30
☐ 25B Minnie Minoso BOX	2.50	1.25	.25
☐ 26A Roy Sievers COM	2.00	1.00	.20
☐ 26B Roy Sievers BOX	2.00	1.00	.20
☐ 27A Jim Landis COM	2.50	1.25	.25
☐ 27B Jim Landis BOX	2.50	1.25	.25
☐ 28A Sherm Lollar COM	2.50	1.25	.25
☐ 28B Sherm Lollar BOX	2.50	1.25	.25
☐ 29 Gerry Staley BOX only	2.00	1.00	.20
☐ 30A Gene Freese COM (Reds)	7.50	3.75	.75
☐ 30B Gene Freese BOX (White Sox)	2.00	1.00	.20
☐ 31 Ted Kluszewski BOX only	2.50	1.25	.25
☐ 32 Turk Lown BOX only	2.00	1.00	.20
☐ 33A Jim Rivera COM	2.00	1.00	.20
☐ 33B Jim Rivera BOX	2.00	1.00	.20
☐ 34 F.Baumann BOX only	2.00	1.00	.20
☐ 35A Al Kaline COM	15.00	7.50	1.50
☐ 35B Al Kaline BOX	15.00	7.50	1.50
☐ 36A Rocky Colavito COM	5.00	2.50	.50
☐ 36B Rocky Colavito BOX	4.00	2.00	.40
☐ 37A C.Maxwell COM	2.00	1.00	.20
☐ 37B C.Maxwell BOX	2.50	1.25	.25
☐ 38A Frank Lary COM	2.00	1.00	.20
☐ 38B Frank Lary BOX	2.00	1.00	.20
☐ 39A Jim Bunning COM	4.00	2.00	.40
☐ 39B Jim Bunning BOX	3.00	1.50	.30
☐ 40A Norm Cash COM	2.50	1.25	.25
☐ 40B Norm Cash BOX	2.00	1.00	.20
☐ 41A Frank Bolling COM (Braves, "Charlie Gehringer" in bio)	4.00	2.00	.40
☐ 41B Frank Bolling BOX (Tigers, "Charlie Derringer" in bio)	6.00	3.00	.60
☐ 42A Don Mossi COM	2.00	1.00	.20
☐ 42B Don Mossi BOX	2.00	1.00	.20
☐ 43A Lou Berberet COM	2.00	1.00	.20
☐ 43B Lou Berberet BOX	2.00	1.00	.20
☐ 44 Dave Sisler BOX only	2.00	1.00	.20
☐ 45 Ed Yost BOX only	2.00	1.00	.20
☐ 46 Pete Burnside BOX only	2.00	1.00	.20
☐ 47A Pete Runnels COM	2.00	1.00	.20
☐ 47B Pete Runnels BOX	3.00	1.50	.30
☐ 48A Frank Malzone COM	2.00	1.00	.20
☐ 48B Frank Malzone BOX	2.00	1.00	.20
☐ 49A Vic Wertz COM	4.00	2.00	.40
☐ 49B Vic Wertz BOX	4.00	2.00	.40
☐ 50A Tom Brewer COM	2.00	1.00	.20
☐ 50B Tom Brewer BOX	2.00	1.00	.20
☐ 51A Willie Tasby COM (Sold to Wash.)	5.00	2.50	.50
☐ 51B Willie Tasby BOX (no sale mention)	2.00	1.00	.20
☐ 52A Russ Nixon COM	2.00	1.00	.20
☐ 52B Russ Nixon BOX	2.00	1.00	.20
☐ 53A Don Buddin COM	2.00	1.00	.20
☐ 53B Don Buddin BOX	2.00	1.00	.20
☐ 54A B.Monbouquette COM	2.00	1.00	.20
☐ 54B B.Monbouquette BOX	2.00	1.00	.20
☐ 55A Frank Sullivan COM (Phillies)	7.50	3.75	.75
☐ 55B Frank Sullivan BOX (Red Sox)	2.00	1.00	.20
☐ 56A H.Sullivan COM	2.00	1.00	.20
☐ 56B H.Sullivan BOX	2.00	1.00	.20
☐ 57A Harvey Kuenn COM (Giants)	5.00	2.50	.50
☐ 57B Harvey Kuenn BOX (Indians)	3.00	1.50	.30
☐ 58A Gary Bell COM	3.00	1.50	.30
☐ 58B Gary Bell BOX	4.00	2.00	.40
☐ 59A Jim Perry COM	2.50	1.25	.25
☐ 59B Jim Perry BOX	2.00	1.00	.20
☐ 60A Jim Grant COM	2.00	1.00	.20
☐ 60B Jim Grant BOX	3.00	1.50	.30
☐ 61A Johnny Temple COM	2.00	1.00	.20
☐ 61B Johnny Temple BOX	2.00	1.00	.20
☐ 62A Paul Foytack COM	2.00	1.00	.20
☐ 62B Paul Foytack BOX	2.00	1.00	.20
☐ 63A Vic Power COM	2.00	1.00	.20
☐ 63B Vic Power BOX	2.00	1.00	.20
☐ 64A Tito Francona COM	2.00	1.00	.20
☐ 64B Tito Francona BOX	2.00	1.00	.20
☐ 65A Ken Aspromonte COM (Sold to L.A.)	6.00	3.00	.60

☐ 65B Ken Aspromonte BOX (no sale mention)	6.00	3.00	.60
☐ 66 Bob Wilson BOX only	2.00	1.00	.20
☐ 67A John Romano COM	2.00	1.00	.20
☐ 67B John Romano BOX	2.00	1.00	.20
☐ 68A Jim Gentile COM	2.50	1.25	.25
☐ 68B Jim Gentile BOX	2.00	1.00	.20
☐ 69A Gus Triandos COM	2.00	1.00	.20
☐ 69B Gus Triandos BOX	3.00	1.50	.30
☐ 70 G.Woodling BOX only	30.00	15.00	3.00
☐ 71A Milt Pappas COM	3.00	1.50	.30
☐ 71B Milt Pappas BOX	3.00	1.50	.30
☐ 72A Ron Hansen COM	2.00	1.00	.20
☐ 72B Ron Hansen BOX	2.00	1.00	.20
☐ 73 Chuck Estrada COM only	90.00	45.00	9.00
☐ 74A Steve Barber COM	2.00	1.00	.20
☐ 74B Steve Barber BOX	2.00	1.00	.20
☐ 75A B.Robinson COM	20.00	10.00	2.00
☐ 75B B.Robinson BOX	15.00	7.50	1.50
☐ 76A Jackie Brandt COM	2.00	1.00	.20
☐ 76B Jackie Brandt BOX	2.00	1.00	.20
☐ 77A Marv Breeding COM	2.00	1.00	.20
☐ 77B Marv Breeding BOX	2.00	1.00	.20
☐ 78 Hal Brown BOX only	2.00	1.00	.20
☐ 79 Billy Klaus BOX only	2.00	1.00	.20
☐ 80A Hoyt Wilhelm COM	8.00	4.00	.80
☐ 80B Hoyt Wilhelm BOX	5.00	2.50	.50
☐ 81A Jerry Lumpe COM	4.00	2.00	.40
☐ 81B Jerry Lumpe BOX	4.00	2.00	.40
☐ 82A Norm Siebern COM	2.00	1.00	.20
☐ 82B Norm Siebern BOX	2.00	1.00	.20
☐ 83A Bud Daley COM	3.00	1.50	.30
☐ 83B Bud Daley BOX	2.00	1.00	.20
☐ 84A Bill Tuttle COM	2.00	1.00	.20
☐ 84B Bill Tuttle BOX	2.00	1.00	.20
☐ 85A M.Throneberry COM	2.00	1.00	.20
☐ 85B M.Throneberry BOX	2.00	1.00	.20
☐ 86A Dick Williams COM	2.00	1.00	.20
☐ 86B Dick Williams BOX	2.00	1.00	.20
☐ 87A Ray Herbert COM	2.00	1.00	.20
☐ 87B Ray Herbert BOX	2.00	1.00	.20
☐ 88A Whitey Herzog COM	2.50	1.25	.25
☐ 88B Whitey Herzog BOX	2.00	1.00	.20
☐ 89A Ken Hamlin COM (Sold to L.A.)	15.00	7.50	1.50
☐ 89B Ken Hamlin BOX (no sale mention)	2.00	1.00	.20
☐ 90A Hank Bauer COM	2.50	1.25	.25
☐ 90B Hank Bauer BOX	2.00	1.00	.20
☐ 91A Bob Allison COM (Minnesota)	4.00	2.00	.40
☐ 91B Bob Allison BOX (Minneapolis)	4.00	2.00	.40
☐ 92A Harmon Killebrew (Minnesota) COM	30.00	15.00	3.00
☐ 92B Harmon Killebrew (Minneapolis) BOX	20.00	10.00	2.00
☐ 93A Jim Lemon COM (Minnesota)	15.00	7.50	1.50
☐ 93B Jim Lemon BOX (Minneapolis)	50.00	25.00	5.00
☐ 94A Chuck Stobbs (Minnesota) COM only	150.00	75.00	15.00
☐ 95A Reno Bertoia COM (Minnesota)	4.00	2.00	.40
☐ 95B Reno Bertoia BOX (Minneapolis)	2.00	1.00	.20
☐ 96A Billy Gardner COM (Minnesota)	4.00	2.00	.40
☐ 96B Billy Gardner BOX (Minneapolis)	2.00	1.00	.20
☐ 97A Earl Battey COM (Minnesota)	4.00	2.00	.40
☐ 97B Earl Battey BOX (Minneapolis)	2.00	1.00	.20
☐ 98A Pedro Ramos COM (Minnesota)	4.00	2.00	.40
☐ 98B Pedro Ramos BOX (Minneapolis)	2.00	1.00	.20
☐ 99A Camilo Pascual COM (Minnesota)	4.00	2.00	.40
☐ 99B Camilo Pascual BOX (Minneapolis)	2.00	1.00	.20
☐ 100A Billy Consolo COM (Minnesota)	4.00	2.00	.40
☐ 100B Billy Consolo BOX (Minneapolis)	2.00	1.00	.20
☐ 101A Warren Spahn COM	20.00	10.00	2.00
☐ 101B Warren Spahn BOX	15.00	7.50	1.50
☐ 102A Lew Burdette COM	3.00	1.50	.30
☐ 102B Lew Burdette BOX	2.50	1.25	.25
☐ 103A Bob Buhl COM	2.00	1.00	.20
☐ 103B Bob Buhl BOX	2.00	1.00	.20
☐ 104A Joe Adcock COM	3.00	1.50	.30
☐ 104B Joe Adcock BOX	3.00	1.50	.30
☐ 105A John Logan COM	3.00	1.50	.30
☐ 105B John Logan BOX	3.00	1.50	.30
☐ 106 Ed Mathews COM only	25.00	12.50	2.50
☐ 107A Hank Aaron COM	25.00	12.50	2.50
☐ 107B Hank Aaron BOX	20.00	10.00	2.00
☐ 108A Wes Covington COM	2.00	1.00	.20
☐ 108B Wes Covington BOX	2.00	1.00	.20
☐ 109A Bill Bruton COM (Tigers)	5.00	2.50	.50
☐ 109B Bill Bruton BOX (Braves)	5.00	2.50	.50
☐ 110A Del Crandall COM	3.00	1.50	.30
☐ 110B Del Crandall BOX	3.00	1.50	.30
☐ 111 Red Schoendienst BOX only	3.00	1.50	.30
☐ 112 Juan Pizarro BOX only	2.00	1.00	.20
☐ 113 Chuck Cottier BOX only	12.00	6.00	1.20
☐ 114 Al Spangler BOX only	2.00	1.00	.20
☐ 115A Dick Farrell COM	4.00	2.00	.40
☐ 115B Dick Farrell BOX	4.00	2.00	.40
☐ 116A Jim Owens COM	4.00	2.00	.40
☐ 116B Jim Owens BOX	4.00	2.00	.40
☐ 117A Robin Roberts COM	8.00	4.00	.80
☐ 117B Robin Roberts BOX	5.00	2.50	.50
☐ 118A Tony Taylor COM	2.00	1.00	.20
☐ 118B Tony Taylor BOX	2.00	1.00	.20
☐ 119A Lee Walls COM	2.00	1.00	.20
☐ 119B Lee Walls BOX	2.00	1.00	.20
☐ 120A Tony Curry COM	2.00	1.00	.20
☐ 120B Tony Curry BOX	2.00	1.00	.20
☐ 121A Pancho Herrera COM	2.00	1.00	.20
☐ 121B Pancho Herrera BOX	2.00	1.00	.20
☐ 122A Ken Walters COM	2.00	1.00	.20
☐ 122B Ken Walters BOX	2.00	1.00	.20
☐ 123A John Callison COM	2.00	1.00	.20
☐ 123B John Callison BOX	2.00	1.00	.20
☐ 124A Gene Conley COM (Red Sox)	8.00	4.00	.80
☐ 124B Gene Conley BOX (Phillies)	2.00	1.00	.20
☐ 125A Bob Friend COM	3.00	1.50	.30
☐ 125B Bob Friend BOX	3.00	1.50	.30
☐ 126A Vernon Law COM	3.00	1.50	.30
☐ 126B Vernon Law BOX	3.00	1.50	.30
☐ 127A Dick Stuart COM	2.00	1.00	.20
☐ 127B Dick Stuart BOX	2.00	1.00	.20
☐ 128A Bill Mazeroski COM	3.00	1.50	.30
☐ 128B Bill Mazeroski BOX	2.00	1.00	.20
☐ 129A Dick Groat COM	3.00	1.50	.30
☐ 129B Dick Groat BOX	2.00	1.00	.20
☐ 130A Don Hoak COM	2.00	1.00	.20
☐ 130B Don Hoak BOX	2.00	1.00	.20
☐ 131A Bob Skinner COM	2.00	1.00	.20
☐ 131B Bob Skinner BOX	2.00	1.00	.20
☐ 132A Bob Clemente COM	30.00	15.00	3.00
☐ 132B Bob Clemente BOX	25.00	12.50	2.50
☐ 133 Roy Face BOX only	2.50	1.25	.25
☐ 134 H.Haddix BOX only	2.00	1.00	.20
☐ 135 Bill Virdon BOX only	35.00	17.50	3.50
☐ 136A Gino Cimoli COM	2.00	1.00	.20
☐ 136B Gino Cimoli BOX	2.00	1.00	.20
☐ 137 Rocky Nelson BOX only	2.00	1.00	.20
☐ 138A Smoky Burgess COM	2.50	1.25	.25
☐ 138B Smoky Burgess BOX	2.00	1.00	.20
☐ 139 Hal Smith BOX only	2.00	1.00	.20
☐ 140 Wilmer Mizell BOX only	2.00	1.00	.20
☐ 141A M.McCormick COM	2.00	1.00	.20
☐ 141B M.McCormick BOX	2.00	1.00	.20
☐ 142A John Antonelli COM (Cleveland)	4.00	2.00	.40
☐ 142B John Antonelli BOX (San Francisco)	3.00	1.50	.30
☐ 143A Sam Jones COM	3.00	1.50	.30
☐ 143B Sam Jones BOX	4.00	2.00	.40
☐ 144A Orlando Cepeda COM	6.00	3.00	.60
☐ 144B Orlando Cepeda BOX	5.00	2.50	.50
☐ 145A Willie Mays COM	27.00	13.50	2.70
☐ 145B Willie Mays BOX	22.00	11.00	2.20
☐ 146A Willie Kirkland (Cleve.) COM	3.50	1.75	.35
☐ 146B Willie Kirkland (San Fran.) BOX	3.00	1.50	.30
☐ 147A Willie McCovey COM	10.00	5.00	1.00
☐ 147B Willie McCovey BOX	6.00	3.00	.60
☐ 148A Don Blasingame COM	2.00	1.00	.20
☐ 148B Don Blasingame BOX	2.00	1.00	.20
☐ 149A Jim Davenport COM	2.50	1.25	.25

☐ 149B Jim Davenport BOX	2.00	1.00	.20
☐ 150A Hobie Landrith COM	2.00	1.00	.20
☐ 150B Hobie Landrith BOX	2.00	1.00	.20
☐ 151 Bob Schmidt BOX only	2.00	1.00	.20
☐ 152A Ed Bressoud COM	2.00	1.00	.20
☐ 152B Ed Bressoud BOX	2.00	1.00	.20
☐ 153A Andre Rodgers	15.00	7.50	1.50
(no trade mention)			
BOX only			
☐ 153B Andre Rodgers	3.00	1.50	.30
(Traded to Milw.)			
BOX only			
☐ 154 Jack Sanford	2.00	1.00	.20
BOX only			
☐ 155 Billy O'Dell	2.00	1.00	.20
BOX only			
☐ 156A Norm Larker COM	2.00	1.00	.20
☐ 156B Norm Larker BOX	2.00	1.00	.20
☐ 157A Charlie Neal COM	2.00	1.00	.20
☐ 157B Charlie Neal BOX	2.00	1.00	.20
☐ 158A Jim Gilliam COM	4.00	2.00	.40
☐ 158B Jim Gilliam BOX	3.00	1.50	.30
☐ 159A Wally Moon COM	2.50	1.25	.25
☐ 159B Wally Moon BOX	2.00	1.00	.20
☐ 160A Don Drysdale COM	10.00	5.00	1.00
☐ 160B Don Drysdale BOX	7.50	3.75	.75
☐ 161A Larry Sherry COM	2.50	1.25	.25
☐ 161B Larry Sherry BOX	2.00	1.00	.20
☐ 162 Stan Williams	5.00	2.50	.50
BOX only			
☐ 163 Mel Roach BOX only	65.00	32.50	6.50
☐ 164A Maury Wills COM	5.00	2.50	.50
☐ 164B Maury Wills BOX	3.00	1.50	.30
☐ 165 Tommy Davis BOX only	2.00	1.00	.20
☐ 166A John Roseboro COM	2.00	1.00	.20
☐ 166B John Roseboro BOX	2.00	1.00	.20
☐ 167A Duke Snider COM	10.00	5.00	1.00
☐ 167B Duke Snider BOX	5.00	2.50	.50
☐ 168A Gil Hodges COM	8.00	4.00	.80
☐ 168B Gil Hodges BOX	5.00	2.50	.50
☐ 169 John Podres BOX only	2.00	1.00	.20
☐ 170 Ed Roebuck BOX only	2.00	1.00	.20
☐ 171A Ken Boyer COM	7.00	3.50	.70
☐ 171B Ken Boyer BOX	6.00	3.00	.60
☐ 172A J.Cunningham COM	2.00	1.00	.20
☐ 172B J.Cunningham BOX	2.00	1.00	.20
☐ 173A Daryl Spencer COM	2.00	1.00	.20
☐ 173B Daryl Spencer BOX	2.00	1.00	.20
☐ 174A Larry Jackson COM	2.00	1.00	.20
☐ 174B Larry Jackson BOX	2.00	1.00	.20
☐ 175A Lindy McDaniel COM	2.00	1.00	.20
☐ 175B Lindy McDaniel BOX	2.00	1.00	.20
☐ 176A Bill White COM	3.00	1.50	.30
☐ 176B Bill White BOX	2.00	1.00	.20
☐ 177A Alex Grammas COM	2.00	1.00	.20
☐ 177B Alex Grammas BOX	2.00	1.00	.20
☐ 178A Curt Flood COM	3.00	1.50	.30
☐ 178B Curt Flood BOX	2.00	1.00	.20
☐ 179A Ernie Broglio COM	2.00	1.00	.20
☐ 179B Ernie Broglio BOX	2.00	1.00	.20
☐ 180A Hal Smith COM	2.00	1.00	.20
☐ 180B Hal Smith BOX	2.00	1.00	.20
☐ 181A Vada Pinson COM	3.00	1.50	.30
☐ 181B Vada Pinson BOX	2.00	1.00	.20
☐ 182A Frank Robinson COM	30.00	15.00	3.00
☐ 182B Frank Robinson BOX	25.00	12.50	2.50
☐ 183 Roy McMillan	75.00	37.50	7.50
BOX only			
☐ 184A Bob Purkey COM	2.00	1.00	.20
☐ 184B Bob Purkey BOX	2.00	1.00	.20
☐ 185A Ed Kasko COM	2.00	1.00	.20
☐ 185B Ed Kasko BOX	2.00	1.00	.20
☐ 186A Gus Bell COM	2.00	1.00	.20
☐ 186B Gus Bell BOX	2.00	1.00	.20
☐ 187A Jerry Lynch COM	2.00	1.00	.20
☐ 187B Jerry Lynch BOX	2.00	1.00	.20
☐ 188A Ed Bailey COM	2.00	1.00	.20
☐ 188B Ed Bailey BOX	2.00	1.00	.20
☐ 189A Jim O'Toole COM	2.00	1.00	.20
☐ 189B Jim O'Toole BOX	2.00	1.00	.20
☐ 190A Billy Martin COM	7.50	3.75	.75
(Sold to Milw.)			
☐ 190B Billy Martin BOX	2.50	1.25	.25
(no sale mention)			
☐ 191A Ernie Banks COM	20.00	10.00	2.00
☐ 191B Ernie Banks BOX	15.00	7.50	1.50
☐ 192A Richie Ashburn COM	4.00	2.00	.40
☐ 192B Richie Ashburn BOX	3.00	1.50	.30
☐ 193A Frank Thomas COM	12.00	6.00	1.20
☐ 193B Frank Thomas BOX	30.00	15.00	3.00
☐ 194A Don Cardwell COM	2.00	1.00	.20
☐ 194B Don Cardwell BOX	2.00	1.00	.20
☐ 195A George Altman COM	2.00	1.00	.20
☐ 195B George Altman BOX	2.00	1.00	.20
☐ 196A Ron Santo COM	3.00	1.50	.30
☐ 196B Ron Santo BOX	2.00	1.00	.20
☐ 197A Glen Hobbie COM	2.00	1.00	.20
☐ 197B Glen Hobbie BOX	2.00	1.00	.20
☐ 198A Sam Taylor COM	2.00	1.00	.20
☐ 198B Sam Taylor BOX	2.00	1.00	.20
☐ 199A Jerry Kindall COM	2.00	1.00	.20
☐ 199B Jerry Kindall BOX	2.00	1.00	.20
☐ 200A Don Elston COM	2.00	1.00	.20
☐ 200B Don Elston BOX	2.00	1.00	.20

1962 Post Cereal

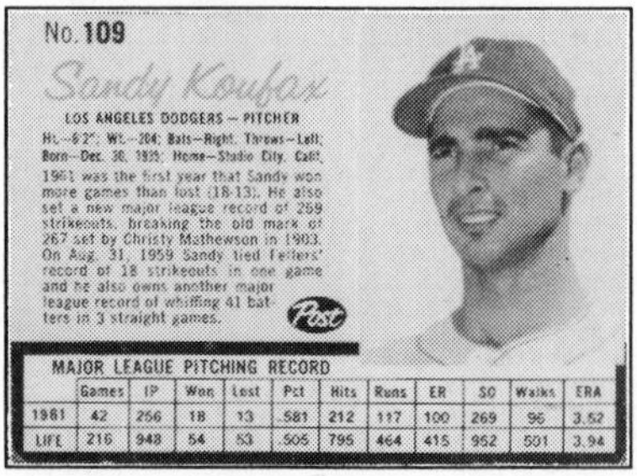

The cards in this 200-card series measure 2 1/2" by 3 1/2". The 1962 Post set is the easiest of the Post sets to complete. The cards are grouped numerically by team, for example, New York Yankees (1-13), Detroit (14-26), Baltimore (27-36), Cleveland (37-45), Chicago White Sox (46-55), Boston (56-64), Washington (65-73), Los Angeles Angels (74-82), Minnesota (83-91), Kansas City (92-100), Los Angeles Dodgers (101-115), Cincinnati (116-130), San Francisco (131-144), Milwaukee (145-157), St. Louis (158-168), Pittsburgh (169-181), Chicago Cubs (182-191), and Philadelphia (192-200). Cards 5B and 6B were printed on thin stock in a two card panel and distributed in a magazine promotion. The scarce cards are 55, 92, 101, 116, 121, and 140. The checklist for this set is the same as that of 1962 Jello and 1962 Post Canadian, but those sets are considered separate issues. The catalog number for this set is F278-37.

	NRMT	VG-E	GOOD
COMPLETE SET (208)	1400.00	650.00	160.00
COMMON PLAYER (1-200)	1.75	.85	.17
☐ 1 Bill Skowron	2.50	1.25	.25
☐ 2 Bobby Richardson	2.50	1.25	.25
☐ 3 Cletis Boyer	1.75	.85	.17
☐ 4 Tony Kubek	2.50	1.25	.25
☐ 5A Mickey Mantle	80.00	40.00	8.00
☐ 5B Mickey Mantle AD	80.00	40.00	8.00
☐ 6A Roger Maris	21.00	10.50	2.10
☐ 6B Roger Maris AD	21.00	10.50	2.10
☐ 7 Yogi Berra	16.00	8.00	1.60
☐ 8 Elston Howard	2.50	1.25	.25
☐ 9 Whitey Ford	8.00	4.00	.80
☐ 10 Ralph Terry	1.75	.85	.17
☐ 11 John Blanchard	1.75	.85	.17
☐ 12 Luis Arroyo	1.75	.85	.17
☐ 13 Bill Stafford	1.75	.85	.17
☐ 14A Norm Cash ERR	10.00	5.00	1.00
(Throws: right)			
☐ 14B Norm Cash COR	1.75	.85	.17
(Throws: left)			
☐ 15 Jake Wood	1.75	.85	.17
☐ 16 Steve Boros	1.75	.85	.17
☐ 17 Chico Fernandez	1.75	.85	.17
☐ 18 Bill Bruton	1.75	.85	.17
☐ 19 Rocky Colavito	2.50	1.25	.25
☐ 20 Al Kaline	12.00	6.00	1.20
☐ 21 Dick Brown	1.75	.85	.17
☐ 22 Frank Lary	1.75	.85	.17
☐ 23 Don Mossi	1.75	.85	.17
☐ 24 Phil Regan	1.75	.85	.17
☐ 25 Charley Maxwell	1.75	.85	.17
☐ 26 Jim Bunning	3.50	1.75	.35
☐ 27A Jim Gentile	2.50	1.25	.25
Home: Baltimore			

☐	27B Jim Gentile Home: San Lorenzo	12.00	6.00	1.20
☐	28 Marv Breeding	1.75	.85	.17
☐	29 Brooks Robinson	12.00	6.00	1.20
☐	30A Ron Hansen (At-Bats)	2.50	1.25	.25
☐	30B Ron Hansen (At Bats)	2.50	1.25	.25
☐	31 Jackie Brandt	1.75	.85	.17
☐	32 Dick Williams	1.75	.85	.17
☐	33 Gus Triandos	1.75	.85	.17
☐	34 Milt Pappas	1.75	.85	.17
☐	35 Hoyt Wilhelm	7.00	3.50	.70
☐	36 Chuck Estrada	6.00	3.00	.60
☐	37 Vic Power	1.75	.85	.17
☐	38 Johnny Temple	1.75	.85	.17
☐	39 Bubba Phillips	1.75	.85	.17
☐	40 Tito Francona	1.75	.85	.17
☐	41 Willie Kirkland	1.75	.85	.17
☐	42 John Romano	1.75	.85	.17
☐	43 Jim Perry	1.75	.85	.17
☐	44 Woodie Held	1.75	.85	.17
☐	45 Chuck Essegian	1.75	.85	.17
☐	46 Roy Sievers	1.75	.85	.17
☐	47 Nellie Fox	3.00	1.50	.30
☐	48 Al Smith	1.75	.85	.17
☐	49 Luis Aparicio	3.50	1.75	.35
☐	50 Jim Landis	1.75	.85	.17
☐	51 Minnie Minoso	2.50	1.25	.25
☐	52 Andy Carey	1.75	.85	.17
☐	53 Sherman Lollar	1.75	.85	.17
☐	54 Bill Pierce	2.50	1.25	.25
☐	55 Early Wynn	27.00	13.50	2.70
☐	56 Chuck Schilling	1.75	.85	.17
☐	57 Pete Runnels	1.75	.85	.17
☐	58 Frank Malzone	1.75	.85	.17
☐	59 Don Buddin	1.75	.85	.17
☐	60 Gary Geiger	1.75	.85	.17
☐	61 Carl Yastrzemski	36.00	18.00	3.60
☐	62 Jackie Jensen	1.75	.85	.17
☐	63 Jim Pagliaroni	1.75	.85	.17
☐	64 Don Schwall	1.75	.85	.17
☐	65 Dale Long	1.75	.85	.17
☐	66 Chuck Cottier	1.75	.85	.17
☐	67 Billy Klaus	1.75	.85	.17
☐	68 Coot Veal	1.75	.85	.17
☐	69 Marty Keough	32.00	16.00	3.20
☐	70 Willie Tasby	1.75	.85	.17
☐	71 Gene Woodling	1.75	.85	.17
☐	72 Gene Green	1.75	.85	.17
☐	73 Dick Donovan	1.75	.85	.17
☐	74 Steve Bilko	1.75	.85	.17
☐	75 Rocky Bridges	1.75	.85	.17
☐	76 Eddie Yost	1.75	.85	.17
☐	77 Leon Wagner	1.75	.85	.17
☐	78 Albie Pearson	1.75	.85	.17
☐	79 Ken Hunt	1.75	.85	.17
☐	80 Earl Averill Jr.	1.75	.85	.17
☐	81 Ryne Duren	1.75	.85	.17
☐	82 Ted Kluszewski	2.50	1.25	.25
☐	83 Bob Allison	25.00	12.50	2.50
☐	84 Billy Martin	3.00	1.50	.30
☐	85 Harmon Killebrew	8.00	4.00	.80
☐	86 Zoilo Versalles	1.75	.85	.17
☐	87 Lenny Green	1.75	.85	.17
☐	88 Bill Tuttle	1.75	.85	.17
☐	89 Jim Lemon	1.75	.85	.17
☐	90 Earl Battey	1.75	.85	.17
☐	91 Camilo Pascual	1.75	.85	.17
☐	92 Norm Sieburn	60.00	30.00	6.00
☐	93 Jerry Lumpe	1.75	.85	.17
☐	94 Dick Howser	2.50	1.25	.25
☐	95A Gene Stephens Born: Jan. 5	2.50	1.25	.25
☐	95B Gene Stephens Born: Jan. 20	12.00	6.00	1.20
☐	96 Leo Posada	1.75	.85	.17
☐	97 Joe Pignatano	1.75	.85	.17
☐	98 Jim Archer	1.75	.85	.17
☐	99 Haywood Sullivan	1.75	.85	.17
☐	100 Art Ditmar	1.75	.85	.17
☐	101 Gil Hodges	75.00	37.50	7.50
☐	102 Charlie Neal	1.75	.85	.17
☐	103 Daryl Spencer	24.00	12.00	2.40
☐	104 Maury Wills	4.00	2.00	.40
☐	105 Tommy Davis	2.50	1.25	.25
☐	106 Willie Davis	2.50	1.25	.25
☐	107 John Roseboro	1.75	.85	.17
☐	108 John Podres	2.50	1.25	.25
☐	109A Sandy Koufax	25.00	12.50	2.50
☐	109B Sandy Koufax (with blue lines)	60.00	30.00	6.00
☐	110 Don Drysdale	8.00	4.00	.80
☐	111 Larry Sherry	3.00	1.50	.30
☐	112 Jim Gilliam	2.50	1.25	.25
☐	113 Norm Larker	32.00	16.00	3.20
☐	114 Duke Snider	7.00	3.50	.70
☐	115 Stan Williams	1.75	.85	.17
☐	116 Gordy Coleman	75.00	37.50	7.50
☐	117 Don Blasingame	1.75	.85	.17
☐	118 Gene Freese	1.75	.85	.17
☐	119 Ed Kasko	1.75	.85	.17
☐	120 Gus Bell	1.75	.85	.17
☐	121 Vada Pinson	2.50	1.25	.25
☐	122 Frank Robinson	25.00	12.50	2.50
☐	123 Bob Purkey	1.75	.85	.17
☐	124A Joey Jay	2.50	1.25	.25
☐	124B Joey Jay (with blue lines)	12.00	6.00	1.20
☐	125 Jim Brosnan	27.00	13.50	2.70
☐	126 Jim O'Toole	1.75	.85	.17
☐	127 Jerry Lynch	50.00	25.00	5.00
☐	128 Wally Post	1.75	.85	.17
☐	129 Ken Hunt	1.75	.85	.17
☐	130 Jerry Zimmerman	1.75	.85	.17
☐	131 Willie McCovey	75.00	37.50	7.50
☐	132 Jose Pagan	1.75	.85	.17
☐	133 Felipe Alou	1.75	.85	.17
☐	134 Jim Davenport	1.75	.85	.17
☐	135 Harvey Kuenn	2.50	1.25	.25
☐	136 Orlando Cepeda	3.50	1.75	.35
☐	137 Ed Bailey	1.75	.85	.17
☐	138 Sam Jones	1.75	.85	.17
☐	139 Mike McCormick	1.75	.85	.17
☐	140 Juan Marichal	90.00	45.00	9.00
☐	141 Jack Sanford	1.75	.85	.17
☐	142 Willie Mays	30.00	15.00	3.00
☐	143 Stu Miller	6.00	3.00	.60
☐	144 Joe Amalfitano	15.00	7.50	1.50
☐	145A Joe Adcock	2.50	1.25	.25
☐	145B Joe Adock (sic) ERR	50.00	25.00	5.00
☐	146 Frank Bolling	1.75	.85	.17
☐	147 Ed Mathews	9.00	4.50	.90
☐	148 Roy McMillan	1.75	.85	.17
☐	149 Hank Aaron	30.00	15.00	3.00
☐	150 Gino Cimoli	1.75	.85	.17
☐	151 Frank Thomas	1.75	.85	.17
☐	152 Joe Torre	2.50	1.25	.25
☐	153 Lew Burdette	2.50	1.25	.25
☐	154 Bob Buhl	1.75	.85	.17
☐	155 Carlton Willey	1.75	.85	.17
☐	156 Lee Maye	1.75	.85	.17
☐	157 Al Spangler	1.75	.85	.17
☐	158 Bill White	40.00	20.00	4.00
☐	159 Ken Boyer	3.00	1.50	.30
☐	160 Joe Cunningham	1.75	.85	.17
☐	161 Carl Warwick	1.75	.85	.17
☐	162 Carl Sawatski	1.75	.85	.17
☐	163 Lindy McDaniel	1.75	.85	.17
☐	164 Ernie Broglio	1.75	.85	.17
☐	165 Larry Jackson	1.75	.85	.17
☐	166 Curt Flood	2.50	1.25	.25
☐	167 Curt Simmons	1.75	.85	.17
☐	168 Alex Grammas	1.75	.85	.17
☐	169 Dick Stuart	1.75	.85	.17
☐	170 Bill Mazeroski	2.50	1.25	.25
☐	171 Don Hoak	1.75	.85	.17
☐	172 Dick Groat	2.50	1.25	.25
☐	173A Roberto Clemente	20.00	10.00	2.00
☐	173B Roberto Clemente (with blue lines)	60.00	30.00	6.00
☐	174 Bob Skinner	1.75	.85	.17
☐	175 Bill Virdon	1.75	.85	.17
☐	176 Smoky Burgess	1.75	.85	.17
☐	177 Elroy Face	2.50	1.25	.25
☐	178 Bob Friend	1.75	.85	.17
☐	179 Vernon Law	1.75	.85	.17
☐	180 Harvey Haddix	1.75	.85	.17
☐	181 Hal Smith	1.75	.85	.17
☐	182 Ed Bouchee	1.75	.85	.17
☐	183 Don Zimmer	1.75	.85	.17
☐	184 Ron Santo	2.50	1.25	.25
☐	185 Andre Rodgers	1.75	.85	.17
☐	186 Richie Ashburn	3.50	1.75	.35
☐	187 George Altman	1.75	.85	.17
☐	188 Ernie Banks	12.00	6.00	1.20
☐	189 Sam Taylor	3.50	1.75	.35
☐	190 Don Elston	1.75	.85	.17
☐	191 Jerry Kindall	1.75	.85	.17
☐	192 Pancho Herrera	1.75	.85	.17
☐	193 Tony Taylor	1.75	.85	.17
☐	194 Ruben Amaro	1.75	.85	.17
☐	195 Don Demeter	1.75	.85	.17
☐	196 Bobby Gene Smith	1.75	.85	.17
☐	197 Clay Dalrymple	1.75	.85	.17
☐	198 Robin Roberts	6.00	3.00	.60
☐	199 Art Mahaffey	1.75	.85	.17
☐	200 John Buzhardt	1.75	.85	.17

1963 Post Cereal

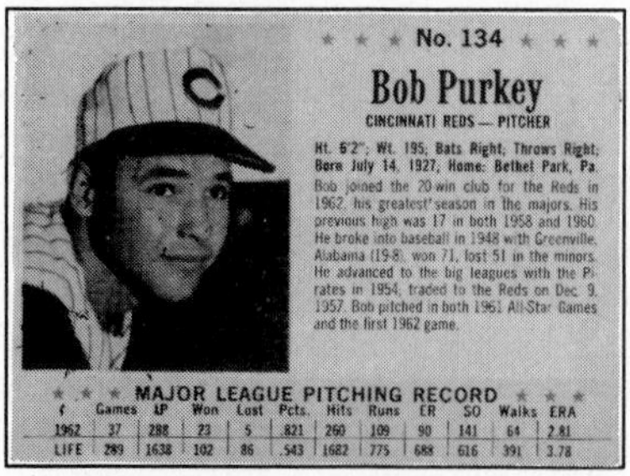

The cards in this 200-card set measure 2 1/2" by 3 1/2". The players are grouped by team with American Leaguers comprising 1-100 and National Leaguers 101-200. The ordering of teams is as follows: Minnesota (1-11), New York Yankees, Los Angeles Angels (24-34), Chicago White Sox (35-45), Detroit (46-56), Baltimore (57-66), Cleveland (67-76), Boston (77-84), Kansas City (85-92), Washington (93-100), San Francisco (101-112), Los Angeles Dodgers (113-124), Cincinnati (125-136), Pittsburgh (137-147), Milwaukee (148-157), St. Louis (158-168), Chicago Cubs (169-176), Philadelphia (177-184), Houston (185-192), and New York Mets (193-200). In contrast to the 1962 issue, the 1963 Post baseball card series is very difficult to complete. There are many card scarcities reflected in the price list below. Cards of the Post set are easily confused with those of the 1963 Jello set, which are 1/4" narrower (a difference which is often eliminated by bad cutting). The catalog designation is F278-38. There was also an album produced by Post to hold the cards.

	NRMT	VG-E	GOOD
COMPLETE SET (205)	3500.00	1600.00	375.00
COMMON PLAYER (1-200)	2.50	1.25	.25
☐ 1 Vic Power	2.50	1.25	.25
☐ 2 Bernie Allen	2.50	1.25	.25
☐ 3 Zoilo Versalles	2.50	1.25	.25
☐ 4 Rich Rollins	2.50	1.25	.25
☐ 5 Harmon Killebrew	16.00	8.00	1.60
☐ 6 Lenny Green	40.00	20.00	4.00
☐ 7 Bob Allison	2.50	1.25	.25
☐ 8 Earl Battey	2.50	1.25	.25
☐ 9 Camilo Pascual	2.50	1.25	.25
☐ 10 Jim Kaat	3.50	1.75	.35
☐ 11 Jack Kralick	2.50	1.25	.25
☐ 12 Bill Skowron	3.00	1.50	.30
☐ 13 Bobby Richardson	3.50	1.75	.35
☐ 14 Cletis Boyer	2.50	1.25	.25
☐ 15 Mickey Mantle	275.00	135.00	27.00
☐ 16 Roger Maris	150.00	75.00	15.00
☐ 17 Yogi Berra	16.00	8.00	1.60
☐ 18 Elston Howard	3.00	1.50	.30
☐ 19 Whitey Ford	10.00	5.00	1.00
☐ 20 Ralph Terry	2.50	1.25	.25
☐ 21 John Blanchard	2.50	1.25	.25
☐ 22 Bill Stafford	2.50	1.25	.25
☐ 23 Tom Tresh	2.50	1.25	.25
☐ 24 Steve Bilko	2.50	1.25	.25
☐ 25 Bill Moran	2.50	1.25	.25
☐ 26A Joe Koppe BA: .277	2.50	1.25	.25
☐ 26B Joe Koppe BA: .227	12.00	6.00	1.20
☐ 27 Felix Torres	2.50	1.25	.25
☐ 28A Leon Wagner BA: .278	2.50	1.25	.25
☐ 28B Leon Wagner BA: .272	12.00	6.00	1.20
☐ 29 Albie Pearson	2.50	1.25	.25
☐ 30 Lee Thomas UER (photo actually George Thomas)	80.00	40.00	8.00
☐ 31 Bob Rodgers	2.50	1.25	.25
☐ 32 Dean Chance	2.50	1.25	.25
☐ 33 Ken McBride	2.50	1.25	.25
☐ 34 George Thomas UER (photo actually Lee Thomas)	2.50	1.25	.25
☐ 35 Joe Cunningham	2.50	1.25	.25
☐ 36 Nelson Fox	3.50	1.75	.35
☐ 37 Luis Aparicio	5.00	2.50	.50
☐ 38 Al Smith	35.00	17.50	3.50
☐ 39 Floyd Robinson	100.00	50.00	10.00
☐ 40 Jim Landis	2.50	1.25	.25
☐ 41 Charlie Maxwell	2.50	1.25	.25
☐ 42 Sherman Lollar	2.50	1.25	.25
☐ 43 Early Wynn	6.00	3.00	.60
☐ 44 Juan Pizarro	2.50	1.25	.25
☐ 45 Ray Herbert	2.50	1.25	.25
☐ 46 Norm Cash	2.50	1.25	.25
☐ 47 Steve Boros	2.50	1.25	.25
☐ 48 Dick McAuliffe	21.00	10.50	2.10
☐ 49 Bill Bruton	3.00	1.50	.30
☐ 50 Rocky Colavito	4.00	2.00	.40
☐ 51 Al Kaline	18.00	9.00	1.80
☐ 52 Dick Brown	2.50	1.25	.25
☐ 53 Jim Bunning	150.00	75.00	15.00
☐ 54 Hank Aguirre	2.50	1.25	.25
☐ 55 Frank Lary	2.50	1.25	.25
☐ 56 Don Mossi	2.50	1.25	.25
☐ 57 Jim Gentile	2.50	1.25	.25
☐ 58 Jackie Brandt	2.50	1.25	.25
☐ 59 Brooks Robinson	20.00	10.00	2.00
☐ 60 Ron Hansen	3.00	1.50	.30
☐ 61 Jerry Adair	175.00	85.00	18.00
☐ 62 John (Boog) Powell	3.50	1.75	.35
☐ 63 Russ Snyder	2.50	1.25	.25
☐ 64 Steve Barber	2.50	1.25	.25
☐ 65 Milt Pappas	2.50	1.25	.25
☐ 66 Robin Roberts	6.00	3.00	.60
☐ 67 Tito Francona	2.50	1.25	.25
☐ 68 Jerry Kindall	2.50	1.25	.25
☐ 69 Woody Held	2.50	1.25	.25
☐ 70 Bubba Phillips	12.00	6.00	1.20
☐ 71 Chuck Essegian	2.50	1.25	.25
☐ 72 Willie Kirkland	2.50	1.25	.25
☐ 73 Al Luplow	2.50	1.25	.25
☐ 74 Ty Cline	2.50	1.25	.25
☐ 75 Dick Donovan	2.50	1.25	.25
☐ 76 John Romano	2.50	1.25	.25
☐ 77 Pete Runnels	2.50	1.25	.25
☐ 78 Ed Bressoud	2.50	1.25	.25
☐ 79 Frank Malzone	2.50	1.25	.25
☐ 80 Carl Yastrzemski	325.00	160.00	32.00
☐ 81 Gary Geiger	2.50	1.25	.25
☐ 82 Lou Clinton	2.50	1.25	.25
☐ 83 Earl Wilson	2.50	1.25	.25
☐ 84 Bill Monbouquette	2.50	1.25	.25
☐ 85 Norm Sieburn	2.50	1.25	.25
☐ 86 Jerry Lumpe	110.00	55.00	11.00
☐ 87 Manny Jimenez	110.00	55.00	11.00
☐ 88 Gino Cimoli	2.50	1.25	.25
☐ 89 Ed Charles	2.50	1.25	.25
☐ 90 Ed Rakow	2.50	1.25	.25
☐ 91 Bob Del Greco	2.50	1.25	.25
☐ 92 Haywood Sullivan	2.50	1.25	.25
☐ 93 Chuck Hinton	2.50	1.25	.25
☐ 94 Ken Retzer	2.50	1.25	.25
☐ 95 Harry Bright	2.50	1.25	.25
☐ 96 Bob Johnson	2.50	1.25	.25
☐ 97 Dave Stenhouse	12.00	6.00	1.20
☐ 98 Chuck Cottier	21.00	10.50	2.10
☐ 99 Tom Cheney	2.50	1.25	.25
☐ 100 Claude Osteen	12.00	6.00	1.20
☐ 101 Orlando Cepeda	4.00	2.00	.40
☐ 102 Charley Hiller	2.50	1.25	.25
☐ 103 Jose Pagan	2.50	1.25	.25
☐ 104 Jim Davenport	2.50	1.25	.25
☐ 105 Harvey Kuenn	3.50	1.75	.35
☐ 106 Willie Mays	40.00	20.00	4.00
☐ 107 Felipe Alou	2.50	1.25	.25
☐ 108 Tom Haller	100.00	50.00	10.00
☐ 109 Juan Marichal	6.00	3.00	.60
☐ 110 Jack Sanford	2.50	1.25	.25
☐ 111 Bill O'Dell	2.50	1.25	.25
☐ 112 Willie McCovey	7.00	3.50	.70
☐ 113 Lee Walls	2.50	1.25	.25
☐ 114 Jim Gilliam	3.00	1.50	.30
☐ 115 Maury Wills	3.50	1.75	.35
☐ 116 Ron Fairly	2.50	1.25	.25
☐ 117 Tommy Davis	2.50	1.25	.25
☐ 118 Duke Snider	8.00	4.00	.80
☐ 119 Willie Davis	175.00	85.00	18.00
☐ 120 John Roseboro	2.50	1.25	.25
☐ 121 Sandy Koufax	25.00	12.50	2.50
☐ 122 Stan Williams	2.50	1.25	.25
☐ 123 Don Drysdale	7.00	3.50	.70
☐ 124 Daryl Spencer	2.50	1.25	.25
☐ 125 Gordy Coleman	2.50	1.25	.25

☐ 126 Don Blasingame	2.50	1.25	.25
☐ 127 Leo Cardenas	2.50	1.25	.25
☐ 128 Eddie Kasko	175.00	85.00	18.00
☐ 129 Jerry Lynch	12.00	6.00	1.20
☐ 130 Vada Pinson	3.00	1.50	.30
☐ 131A Frank Robinson (no stripes)	15.00	7.50	1.50
☐ 131B Frank Robinson (stripes on hat)	30.00	15.00	3.00
☐ 132 John Edwards	2.50	1.25	.25
☐ 133 Joey Jay	2.50	1.25	.25
☐ 134 Bob Purkey	2.50	1.25	.25
☐ 135 Marty Keough	25.00	12.50	2.50
☐ 136 Jim O'Toole	2.50	1.25	.25
☐ 137 Dick Stuart	2.50	1.25	.25
☐ 138 Bill Mazeroski	3.00	1.50	.30
☐ 139 Dick Groat	3.00	1.50	.30
☐ 140 Don Hoak	30.00	15.00	3.00
☐ 141 Bob Skinner	15.00	7.50	1.50
☐ 142 Bill Virdon	3.00	1.50	.30
☐ 143 Roberto Clemente	27.00	13.50	2.70
☐ 144 Smoky Burgess	2.50	1.25	.25
☐ 145 Bob Friend	2.50	1.25	.25
☐ 146 Al McBean	2.50	1.25	.25
☐ 147 Elroy Face	3.00	1.50	.30
☐ 148 Joe Adcock	3.00	1.50	.30
☐ 149 Frank Bolling	2.50	1.25	.25
☐ 150 Roy McMillan	2.50	1.25	.25
☐ 151 Eddie Mathews	15.00	7.50	1.50
☐ 152 Hank Aaron	125.00	60.00	12.50
☐ 153 Del Crandall	32.00	16.00	3.20
☐ 154A Bob Shaw COR	2.50	1.25	.25
☐ 154B Bob Shaw ERR (two "in 1959" in same sentence)	12.00	6.00	1.20
☐ 155 Lew Burdette	3.00	1.50	.30
☐ 156 Joe Torre	3.00	1.50	.30
☐ 157 Tony Cloninger	2.50	1.25	.25
☐ 158A Bill White (Ht. 6'0")	3.50	1.75	.35
☐ 158B Bill White (Ht. 6';)	3.50	1.75	.35
☐ 159 Julian Javier	2.50	1.25	.25
☐ 160 Ken Boyer	3.50	1.75	.35
☐ 161 Julio Gotay	2.50	1.25	.25
☐ 162 Curt Flood	125.00	60.00	12.50
☐ 163 Charlie James	3.50	1.75	.35
☐ 164 Gene Oliver	2.50	1.25	.25
☐ 165 Ernie Broglio	2.50	1.25	.25
☐ 166 Bob Gibson	7.00	3.50	.70
☐ 167A Lindy McDaniel (no asterisk)	5.00	2.50	.50
☐ 167B Lindy McDaniel (asterisk traded line)	5.00	2.50	.50
☐ 168 Ray Washburn	2.50	1.25	.25
☐ 169 Ernie Banks	12.00	6.00	1.20
☐ 170 Ron Santo	3.00	1.50	.30
☐ 171 George Altman	2.50	1.25	.25
☐ 172 Billy Williams	150.00	75.00	15.00
☐ 173 Andre Rodgers	12.00	6.00	1.20
☐ 174 Ken Hubbs	25.00	12.50	2.50
☐ 175 Don Landrum	2.50	1.25	.25
☐ 176 Dick Bertell	16.00	8.00	1.60
☐ 177 Roy Sievers	2.50	1.25	.25
☐ 178 Tony Taylor	2.50	1.25	.25
☐ 179 John Callison	2.50	1.25	.25
☐ 180 Don Demeter	2.50	1.25	.25
☐ 181 Tony Gonzalez	12.00	6.00	1.20
☐ 182 Wes Covington	21.00	10.50	2.10
☐ 183 Art Mahaffey	2.50	1.25	.25
☐ 184 Clay Dalrymple	2.50	1.25	.25
☐ 185 Al Spangler	3.50	1.75	.35
☐ 186 Roman Mejias	2.50	1.25	.25
☐ 187 Bob Aspromonte	325.00	160.00	32.00
☐ 188 Norm Larker	32.00	16.00	3.20
☐ 189 Johnny Temple	2.50	1.25	.25
☐ 190 Carl Warwick	2.50	1.25	.25
☐ 191 Bob Lillis	2.50	1.25	.25
☐ 192 Dick Farrell	2.50	1.25	.25
☐ 193 Gil Hodges	7.00	3.50	.70
☐ 194 Marv Throneberry	2.50	1.25	.25
☐ 195 Charlie Neal	8.00	4.00	.80
☐ 196 Frank Thomas	175.00	85.00	18.00
☐ 197 Richie Ashburn	21.00	10.50	2.10
☐ 198 Felix Mantilla	2.50	1.25	.25
☐ 199 Rod Kanehl	16.00	8.00	1.60
☐ 200 Roger Craig	3.50	1.75	.35

1990 Post

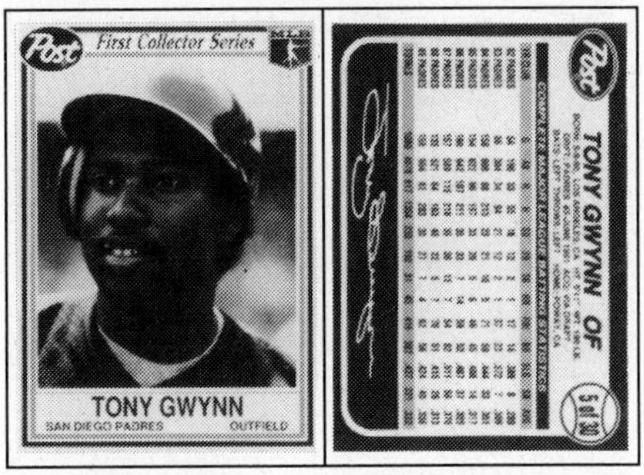

The 1990 Post Cereal set is a 30-card, standard-size (2 1/2" by 3 1/2") set issued with the assistance of Mike Schechter Associates. The sets do not have either team logos or other uniform identification on them. There is also a facsimile autograph on the back of the cards. The cards were inserted randomly as a cello pack (with three cards) inside specially marked boxes of Post cereals. The cards feature red, white, and blue fronts with the words, "First Collector Series". Card backs feature a facsimile autograph. The relatively high cost of the set is due to the fact that the cards were not available as a complete set as a part of any mail-in offer from the company.

	MINT	EXC	G-VG
COMPLETE SET (30)	25.00	12.50	2.50
COMMON PLAYER (1-30)	.60	.30	.06
☐ 1 Don Mattingly	2.50	1.25	.25
☐ 2 Roger Clemens	1.50	.75	.15
☐ 3 Kirby Puckett	1.00	.50	.10
☐ 4 George Brett	1.00	.50	.10
☐ 5 Tony Gwynn	.75	.35	.07
☐ 6 Ozzie Smith	.75	.35	.07
☐ 7 Will Clark	1.50	.75	.15
☐ 8 Orel Hershiser	.75	.35	.07
☐ 9 Ryne Sandberg	2.00	1.00	.20
☐ 10 Darryl Strawberry	1.50	.75	.15
☐ 11 Nolan Ryan	3.00	1.50	.30
☐ 12 Mark McGwire	1.50	.75	.15
☐ 13 Jim Abbott	.75	.35	.07
☐ 14 Bo Jackson	3.00	1.50	.30
☐ 15 Kevin Mitchell	.75	.35	.07
☐ 16 Jose Canseco	2.50	1.25	.25
☐ 17 Wade Boggs	1.50	.75	.15
☐ 18 Dale Murphy	1.00	.50	.10
☐ 19 Mark Grace	1.50	.75	.15
☐ 20 Mike Scott	.60	.30	.06
☐ 21 Cal Ripken Jr.	1.00	.50	.10
☐ 22 Pedro Guerrero	.60	.30	.06
☐ 23 Ken Griffey Jr.	3.00	1.50	.30
☐ 24 Eric Davis	1.00	.50	.10
☐ 25 Rickey Henderson	2.00	1.00	.20
☐ 26 Robin Yount	1.00	.50	.10
☐ 27 Von Hayes	.60	.30	.06
☐ 28 Alan Trammell	.60	.30	.06
☐ 29 Dwight Gooden	1.00	.50	.10
☐ 30 Joe Carter	.60	.30	.06

1986 Quaker Granola

This set of 33 cards was available in packages of Quaker Oats Chewy Granola, three player cards plus a complete set offer card in each package. The set was also available through a mail-in offer where anyone sending in four UPC seals from Chewy Granola (before 12/31/86) would receive a complete set. The cards were produced by Topps for Quaker Oats and are 2 1/2" by 3 1/2". Card backs are printed in red and blue on gray card stock. The cards are numbered on the front and the back.

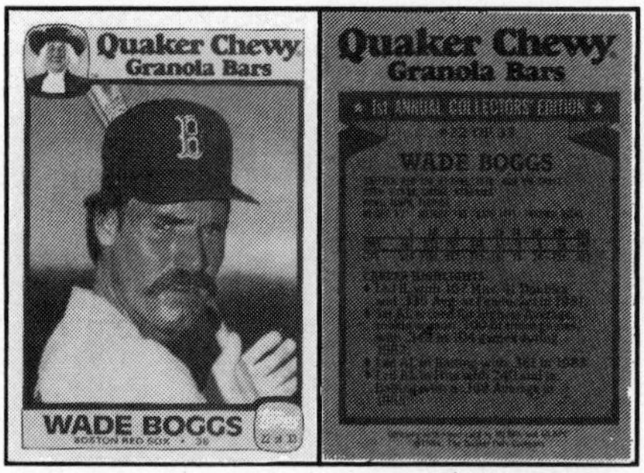

	MINT	EXC	G-VG
COMPLETE SET (33)	7.00	3.50	.70
COMMON PLAYER (1-33)	.20	.10	.02
☐ 1 Willie McGee	.25	.12	.02
☐ 2 Dwight Gooden	.60	.30	.06
☐ 3 Vince Coleman	.35	.17	.03
☐ 4 Gary Carter	.30	.15	.03
☐ 5 Jack Clark	.20	.10	.02
☐ 6 Steve Garvey	.35	.17	.03
☐ 7 Tony Gwynn	.50	.25	.05
☐ 8 Dale Murphy	.40	.20	.04
☐ 9 Dave Parker	.25	.12	.02
☐ 10 Tim Raines	.25	.12	.02
☐ 11 Pete Rose	.65	.30	.06
☐ 12 Nolan Ryan	1.25	.60	.12
☐ 13 Ryne Sandberg	.75	.35	.07
☐ 14 Mike Schmidt	.75	.35	.07
☐ 15 Ozzie Smith	.35	.17	.03
☐ 16 Darryl Strawberry	.50	.25	.05
☐ 17 Fernando Valenzuela	.25	.12	.02
☐ 18 Don Mattingly	1.00	.50	.10
☐ 19 Bret Saberhagen	.30	.15	.03
☐ 20 Ozzie Guillen	.20	.10	.02
☐ 21 Bert Blyleven	.20	.10	.02
☐ 22 Wade Boggs	.65	.30	.06
☐ 23 George Brett	.65	.30	.06
☐ 24 Darrell Evans	.20	.10	.02
☐ 25 Rickey Henderson	1.00	.50	.10
☐ 26 Reggie Jackson	.65	.30	.06
☐ 27 Eddie Murray	.45	.22	.04
☐ 28 Phil Niekro	.30	.15	.03
☐ 29 Dan Quisenberry	.20	.10	.02
☐ 30 Jim Rice	.25	.12	.02
☐ 31 Cal Ripken	.40	.20	.04
☐ 32 Tom Seaver	.40	.20	.04
☐ 33 Dave Winfield	.30	.15	.03
☐ 34 Offer Card for the complete set (unnumbered)	.03	.01	.00

1984 Ralston Purina

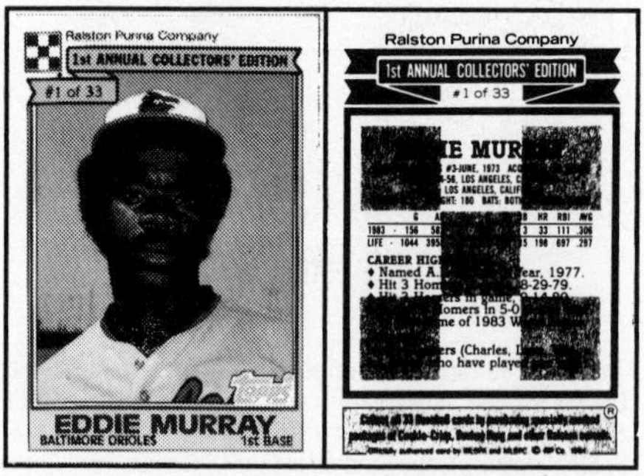

The cards in this 33-card set measure 2 1/2" by 3 1/2". In 1984 the Ralston Purina Company issued what it has entitled "The First Annual Collectors Edition of Baseball Cards." The cards feature portrait photos of the players rather than batting action shots. The Topps logo appears along with the Ralston logo on the front of the card. The backs are completely different from the Topps cards of this year; in fact, they contain neither a Topps logo nor a Topps copyright. Large quantities of these cards were obtained by card dealers for direct distribution into the organized hobby, hence the relatively low price of the set.

	MINT	EXC	G-VG
COMPLETE SET (33)	4.00	2.00	.40
COMMON PLAYER (1-33)	.10	.05	.01
☐ 1 Eddie Murray	.30	.15	.03
☐ 2 Ozzie Smith	.20	.10	.02
☐ 3 Ted Simmons	.10	.05	.01
☐ 4 Pete Rose	.50	.25	.05
☐ 5 Greg Luzinski	.10	.05	.01
☐ 6 Andre Dawson	.25	.12	.02
☐ 7 Dave Winfield	.20	.10	.02
☐ 8 Tom Seaver	.25	.12	.02
☐ 9 Jim Rice	.15	.07	.01
☐ 10 Fernando Valenzuela	.15	.07	.01
☐ 11 Wade Boggs	.40	.20	.04
☐ 12 Dale Murphy	.30	.15	.03
☐ 13 George Brett	.40	.20	.04
☐ 14 Nolan Ryan	.75	.35	.07
☐ 15 Rickey Henderson	.60	.30	.06
☐ 16 Steve Carlton	.25	.12	.02
☐ 17 Rod Carew	.30	.15	.03
☐ 18 Steve Garvey	.25	.12	.02
☐ 19 Reggie Jackson	.40	.20	.04
☐ 20 Dave Concepcion	.10	.05	.01
☐ 21 Robin Yount	.35	.17	.03
☐ 22 Mike Schmidt	.60	.30	.06
☐ 23 Jim Palmer	.25	.12	.02
☐ 24 Bruce Sutter	.10	.05	.01
☐ 25 Dan Quisenberry	.10	.05	.01
☐ 26 Bill Madlock	.10	.05	.01
☐ 27 Cecil Cooper	.10	.05	.01
☐ 28 Gary Carter	.15	.07	.01
☐ 29 Fred Lynn	.10	.05	.01
☐ 30 Pedro Guerrero	.15	.07	.01
☐ 31 Ron Guidry	.10	.05	.01
☐ 32 Keith Hernandez	.15	.07	.01
☐ 33 Carlton Fisk	.25	.12	.02

1987 Ralston Purina

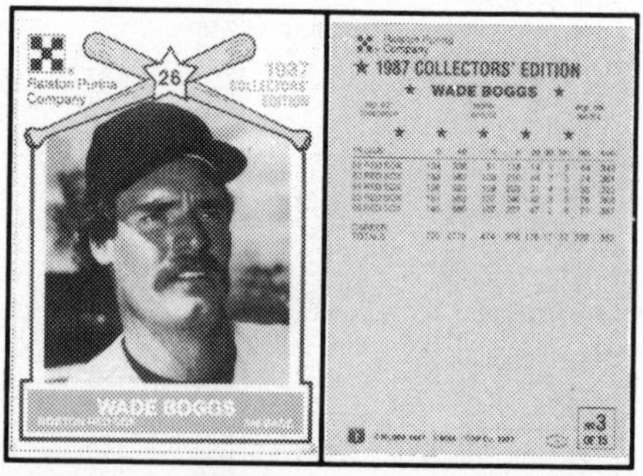

The Ralston Purina Company issued a set of 15 cards picturing players without their respective team logos. The cards measure approximately 2 1/2" by 3 3/8" and are in full-color on the front. The cards are numbered on the back in the lower right hand corner; the player's uniform number is prominently displayed on the front. The cards were distributed as inserts inside packages of certain flavors of Ralston Purina's breakfast cereals. Three cards and a contest card were packaged in cellophane and inserted within the cereal box. The set was also available as an uncut sheet through a mail-in offer. Since the uncut sheets are relatively common, the value of the sheet is essentially the same as the value of the sum of the individual cards. In fact there were two uncut sheets issued, one had "Honey Graham Chex" printed at the top and the other had "Cookie Crisp" printed at the top. Also cards were issued with and without the words "1987 Collectors Edition" printed in blue on the front. Supposedly 100,000 of the uncut sheets were given away free via instant win certificates inserted in with the cereal or collectors could send in two non-winning contest cards plus 1.00 for each uncut sheet.

	MINT	EXC	G-VG
COMPLETE SET (15)	10.00	5.00	1.00
COMMON PLAYER (1-15)	.50	.25	.05
☐ 1 Nolan Ryan	2.00	1.00	.20
☐ 2 Steve Garvey	.60	.30	.06
☐ 3 Wade Boggs	1.25	.60	.12
☐ 4 Dave Winfield	.60	.30	.06
☐ 5 Don Mattingly	2.00	1.00	.20
☐ 6 Don Sutton	.50	.25	.05
☐ 7 Dave Parker	.50	.25	.05
☐ 8 Eddie Murray	.75	.35	.07
☐ 9 Gary Carter	.60	.30	.06
☐ 10 Roger Clemens	1.25	.60	.12
☐ 11 Fernando Valenzuela	.60	.30	.06
☐ 12 Cal Ripken	.75	.35	.07
☐ 13 Ozzie Smith	.60	.30	.06
☐ 14 Mike Schmidt	1.25	.60	.12
☐ 15 Ryne Sandberg	1.25	.60	.12

1983 Rangers Affiliated Food

The cards in this 28-card set measure 2 3/8" by 3 1/2". The Affiliated Food Stores chain of Arlington, Texas, produced this set of Texas Rangers late during the 1983 baseball season. Complete sets were given to children 13 and under at the September 3, 1983, Rangers game. The cards are numbered by uniform number and feature the player's name, card number, and the words "1983 Rangers" on the bottom front. The backs contain biographical data, career totals, a small black and white insert picture of the player, and the Affiliated Food Stores' logo. The coaches card is unnumbered.

	MINT	EXC	G-VG
COMPLETE SET (28)	7.00	3.50	.70
COMMON PLAYER	.25	.12	.02
☐ 1 Bill Stein	.25	.12	.02
☐ 2 Mike Richardt	.25	.12	.02
☐ 3 Wayne Tolleson	.25	.12	.02
☐ 5 Billy Sample	.25	.12	.02
☐ 6 Bobby Jones	.25	.12	.02
☐ 7 Bucky Dent	.50	.25	.05
☐ 8 Bobby Johnson	.25	.12	.02
☐ 9 Pete O'Brien	.75	.35	.07
☐ 10 Jim Sundberg	.25	.12	.02
☐ 11 Doug Rader MG	.35	.17	.03
☐ 12 Dave Hostetler	.25	.12	.02
☐ 14 Larry Biittner	.25	.12	.02
☐ 15 Larry Parrish	.35	.17	.03
☐ 17 Mickey Rivers	.35	.17	.03
☐ 21 Odell Jones	.25	.12	.02
☐ 24 Dave Schmidt	.35	.17	.03
☐ 25 Buddy Bell	.50	.25	.05
☐ 26 George Wright	.25	.12	.02
☐ 28 Frank Tanana	.35	.17	.03
☐ 29 John Butcher	.25	.12	.02
☐ 32 John Matlack	.35	.17	.03
☐ 40 Rick Honeycutt	.25	.12	.02
☐ 41 Dave Tobik	.25	.12	.02
☐ 44 Danny Darwin	.35	.17	.03
☐ 46 Jim Anderson	.25	.12	.02
☐ 48 Mike Smithson	.25	.12	.02
☐ 49 Charlie Hough	.35	.17	.03
☐ xx Rangers Coaches: (unnumbered) Wayne Terwilliger 42, Merv Rettenmund 22, Dick Such 52, Glenn Ezell 18, Rich Donnelly 37	.25	.12	.02

1984 Rangers Jarvis Press

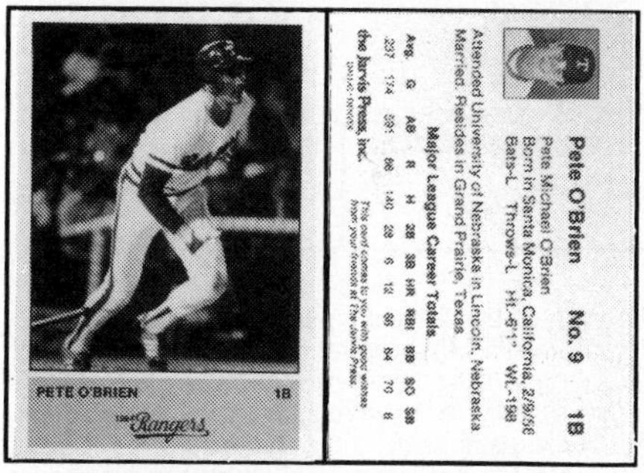

The cards in this 30-card set measure 2 1/2" by 3 1/2". The Jarvis Press of Dallas issued this full-color regional set of Texas Rangers. Cards are numbered on the front by the players uniform number. The cards were issued on an uncut sheet. Twenty-seven player cards, a manager card, a trainer card (unnumbered) and a coaches card (unnumbered) comprise this set. The backs are black and white and contain biographical information, statistics, and an additional photo of the player.

	MINT	EXC	G-VG
COMPLETE SET (30)	7.00	3.50	.70
COMMON PLAYER	.25	.12	.02
☐ 1 Bill Stein	.25	.12	.02
☐ 2 Alan Bannister	.25	.12	.02
☐ 3 Wayne Tolleson	.25	.12	.02
☐ 5 Billy Sample	.25	.12	.02
☐ 6 Bobby Jones	.25	.12	.02
☐ 7 Ned Yost	.25	.12	.02
☐ 9 Pete O'Brien	.50	.25	.05
☐ 11 Doug Rader MG	.35	.17	.03
☐ 13 Tommy Dunbar	.25	.12	.02
☐ 14 Jim Anderson	.25	.12	.02
☐ 15 Larry Parrish	.35	.17	.03
☐ 16 Mike Mason	.25	.12	.02
☐ 17 Mickey Rivers	.35	.17	.03
☐ 19 Curtis Wilkerson	.25	.12	.02
☐ 20 Jeff Kunkel	.35	.17	.03
☐ 21 Odell Jones	.25	.12	.02
☐ 24 Dave Schmidt	.35	.17	.03
☐ 25 Buddy Bell	.60	.30	.06
☐ 26 George Wright	.25	.12	.02
☐ 28 Frank Tanana	.35	.17	.03
☐ 30 Marv Foley	.25	.12	.02
☐ 31 Dave Stewart	1.00	.50	.10
☐ 32 Gary Ward	.25	.12	.02
☐ 36 Dickie Noles	.25	.12	.02
☐ 43 Donnie Scott	.25	.12	.02
☐ 44 Danny Darwin	.35	.17	.03
☐ 49 Charlie Hough	.35	.17	.03
☐ 53 Joey McLaughlin	.25	.12	.02

		MINT	EXC	G-VG
☐	xx Bill Ziegler (Trainer) (unnumbered)	.25	.12	.02
☐	xx Rangers Coaches: (unnumbered) Merv Rettenmund 22, Rich Donnelly 37, Glenn Ezell 18, Dick Such 52, Wayne Terwilliger 42	.25	.12	.02

1985 Rangers Performance

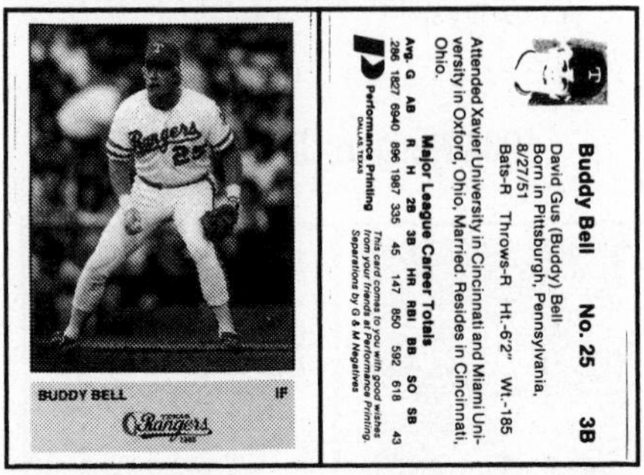

The cards in this 28-card set measure 2 3/8" by 3 1/2". Performance Printing sponsored this full-color regional set of Texas Rangers. Cards are numbered on the back by the players uniform number. The cards were also issued on an uncut sheet. Twenty-five player cards, a manager card, a trainer card (unnumbered) and a coaches card (unnumbered) comprise this set. The backs are black and white and contain biographical information, statistics, and an additional photo of the player.

		MINT	EXC	G-VG
	COMPLETE SET (28)	7.00	3.50	.70
	COMMON PLAYER	.25	.12	.02
☐	0 Oddibe McDowell	.50	.25	.05
☐	1 Bill Stein	.25	.12	.02
☐	2 Bobby Valentine MG	.35	.17	.03
☐	3 Wayne Tolleson	.25	.12	.02
☐	4 Don Slaught	.25	.12	.02
☐	5 Alan Bannister	.25	.12	.02
☐	6 Bobby Jones	.25	.12	.02
☐	7 Glenn Brummer	.25	.12	.02
☐	8 Luis Pujols	.25	.12	.02
☐	9 Pete O'Brien	.50	.25	.05
☐	11 Toby Harrah	.35	.17	.03
☐	13 Tommy Dunbar	.25	.12	.02
☐	15 Larry Parrish	.35	.17	.03
☐	16 Mike Mason	.25	.12	.02
☐	19 Curtis Wilkerson	.25	.12	.02
☐	24 Dave Schmidt	.35	.17	.03
☐	25 Buddy Bell	.50	.25	.05
☐	27 Greg Harris	.35	.17	.03
☐	30 Dave Rozema	.25	.12	.02
☐	32 Gary Ward	.25	.12	.02
☐	36 Dickie Noles	.25	.12	.02
☐	41 Chris Welsh	.25	.12	.02
☐	44 Cliff Johnson	.25	.12	.02
☐	46 Burt Hooton	.25	.12	.02
☐	48 Dave Stewart	.90	.45	.09
☐	49 Charlie Hough	.35	.17	.03
☐	xx Trainers: Bill Ziegler, Danny Wheat (unnumbered)	.25	.12	.02
☐	xx Rangers Coaches: (unnumbered) Art Howe 10, Rich Donnelly 37, Glenn Ezell 18, Tom House 35, Wayne Terwilliger 42	.25	.12	.02

1986 Rangers Performance

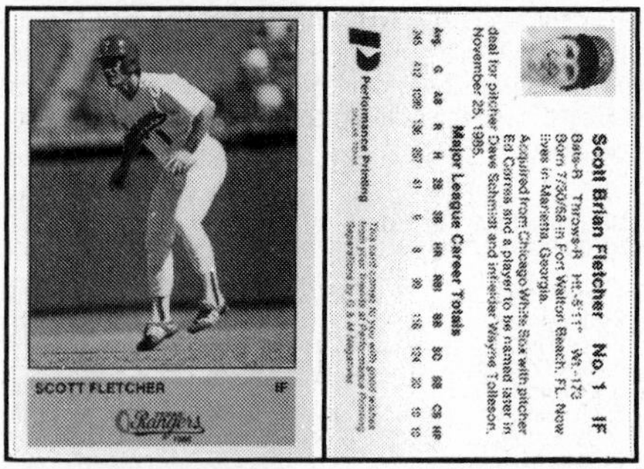

Performance Printing of Dallas produced a 28-card set of Texas Rangers which were given out at the stadium on August 23rd. Cards measure 2 3/8" by 3 1/2" and are in full color. The cards are unnumbered except for uniform number which is given on the card back. Card backs feature black printing on white card stock with a small picture of the player's head in the upper left corner. The set seems to be more desirable than the previous Ranger sets due to the Rangers' 1986 success which was directly related to their outstanding rookie crop.

		MINT	EXC	G-VG
	COMPLETE SET (28)	10.00	5.00	1.00
	COMMON PLAYER	.20	.10	.02
☐	0 Oddibe McDowell	.30	.15	.03
☐	1 Scott Fletcher	.30	.15	.03
☐	2 Bobby Valentine MG	.30	.15	.03
☐	3 Ruben Sierra	4.00	2.00	.40
☐	4 Don Slaught	.20	.10	.02
☐	9 Pete O'Brien	.40	.20	.04
☐	11 Toby Harrah	.30	.15	.03
☐	12 Geno Petralli	.20	.10	.02
☐	15 Larry Parrish	.30	.15	.03
☐	16 Mike Mason	.20	.10	.02
☐	17 Darrell Porter	.20	.10	.02
☐	18 Edwin Correa	.30	.15	.03
☐	19 Curtis Wilkerson	.20	.10	.02
☐	22 Steve Buechele	.30	.15	.03
☐	23 Jose Guzman	.30	.15	.03
☐	24 Ricky Wright	.20	.10	.02
☐	27 Greg Harris	.20	.10	.02
☐	28 Mitch Williams	.50	.25	.05
☐	29 Pete Incaviglia	1.00	.50	.10
☐	32 Gary Ward	.20	.10	.02
☐	34 Dale Mohorcic	.20	.10	.02
☐	40 Jeff Russell	.30	.15	.03
☐	44 Tom Paciorek	.20	.10	.02
☐	46 Mike Loynd	.30	.15	.03
☐	48 Bobby Witt	1.00	.50	.10
☐	49 Charlie Hough	.30	.15	.03
☐	xx Coaching Staff: (unnumbered) Art Howe 10, Joe Ferguson 13, Tim Foli 14, Tom Robson 31, Tom House 35	.20	.10	.02
☐	xx Trainers: (unnumbered) Bill Zeigler, Danny Wheat	.20	.10	.02

1954 Red Heart

The cards in this 33-card set measure 2 5/8" by 3 3/4". The 1954 Red Heart baseball series was marketed by Red Heart dog food, which, incidentally, was a subsidiary of Morrell Meats. The set consists of three series of eleven unnumbered cards each of which could be ordered from the company via an offer (two can labels plus ten cents for each series) on the can label. Each series has a specific color background (red, green or blue) behind the color player photo. Cards with red backgrounds are considered scarcer and are marked with an asterisk in the checklist (which has been alphabetized and numbered for reference). The catalog designation is F156.

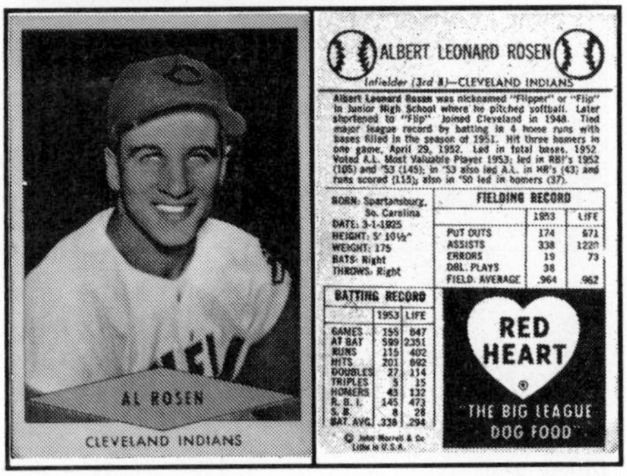

	NRMT	VG-E	GOOD
COMPLETE SET (33)	2000.00	900.00	200.00
COMMON PLAYER (1-33)	27.00	13.50	2.70
COMMON * (RED) PLAYER	35.00	17.50	3.50
☐ 1 Richie Ashburn *	60.00	30.00	6.00
☐ 2 Frank Baumholtz *	35.00	17.50	3.50
☐ 3 Gus Bell	27.00	13.50	2.70
☐ 4 Billy Cox	27.00	13.50	2.70
☐ 5 Alvin Dark	35.00	17.50	3.50
☐ 6 Carl Erskine *	45.00	22.50	4.50
☐ 7 Ferris Fain	27.00	13.50	2.70
☐ 8 Dee Fondy	27.00	13.50	2.70
☐ 9 Nelson Fox	50.00	25.00	5.00
☐ 10 Jim Gilliam	35.00	17.50	3.50
☐ 11 Jim Hegan *	35.00	17.50	3.50
☐ 12 George Kell	60.00	30.00	6.00
☐ 13 Ralph Kiner *	80.00	40.00	8.00
☐ 14 Ted Kluszewski *	60.00	30.00	6.00
☐ 15 Harvey Kuenn	35.00	17.50	3.50
☐ 16 Bob Lemon *	70.00	35.00	7.00
☐ 17 Sherman Lollar	27.00	13.50	2.70
☐ 18 Mickey Mantle	425.00	200.00	42.00
☐ 19 Billy Martin	60.00	30.00	6.00
☐ 20 Gil McDougald *	45.00	22.50	4.50
☐ 21 Roy McMillan	27.00	13.50	2.70
☐ 22 Minnie Minoso	35.00	17.50	3.50
☐ 23 Stan Musial *	300.00	150.00	30.00
☐ 24 Billy Pierce	35.00	17.50	3.50
☐ 25 Al Rosen *	45.00	22.50	4.50
☐ 26 Hank Sauer	27.00	13.50	2.70
☐ 27 Red Schoendienst *	70.00	35.00	7.00
☐ 28 Enos Slaughter	70.00	35.00	7.00
☐ 29 Duke Snider	110.00	55.00	11.00
☐ 30 Warren Spahn	60.00	30.00	6.00
☐ 31 Sammy White	27.00	13.50	2.70
☐ 32 Eddie Yost	27.00	13.50	2.70
☐ 33 Gus Zernial	27.00	13.50	2.70

1952 Red Man

The cards in this 52-card set measure 3 1/2" by 4" (or 3 1/2" by 3 5/8" without the tab). This Red Man issue was the first nationally available tobacco issue since the T cards of the teens early in this century. This 52 card set contains 26 top players from each league. Cards that have the tab (coupon) attached are generally worth two and a half times the price of cards with the tab removed. Card numbers are located on the tabs. The prices listed below refer to cards without tabs.

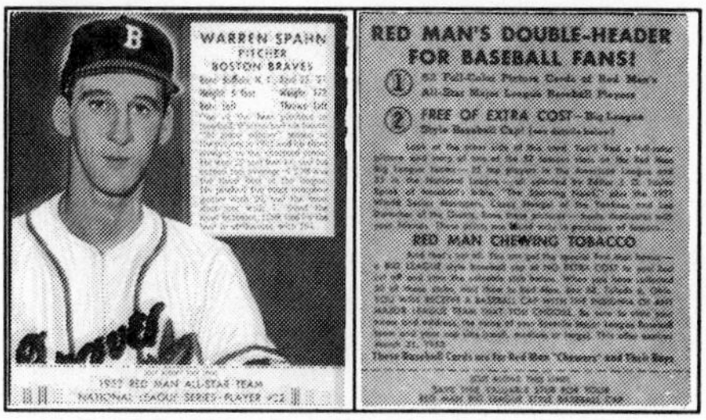

	NRMT	VG-E	GOOD
COMPLETE SET (52)	750.00	350.00	90.00
COMMON PLAYER	7.50	3.75	.75
☐ AL1 Casey Stengel MG	22.50	10.00	2.00
☐ AL2 Roberto Avila	7.50	3.75	.75
☐ AL3 Yogi Berra	35.00	17.50	3.50
☐ AL4 Gil Coan	7.50	3.75	.75
☐ AL5 Dom DiMaggio	10.00	5.00	1.00
☐ AL6 Larry Doby	9.00	4.50	.90
☐ AL7 Ferris Fain	7.50	3.75	.75
☐ AL8 Bob Feller	30.00	15.00	3.00
☐ AL9 Nelson Fox	13.50	6.00	1.00
☐ AL10 Johnny Groth	7.50	3.75	.75
☐ AL11 Jim Hegan	7.50	3.75	.75
☐ AL12 Eddie Joost	7.50	3.75	.75
☐ AL13 George Kell	17.00	8.50	1.70
☐ AL14 Gil McDougald	10.00	5.00	1.00
☐ AL15 Minnie Minoso	10.00	5.00	1.00
☐ AL16 Billy Pierce	9.00	4.50	.90
☐ AL17 Bob Porterfield	7.50	3.75	.75
☐ AL18 Eddie Robinson	7.50	3.75	.75
☐ AL19 Saul Rogovin	7.50	3.75	.75
☐ AL20 Bobby Shantz	7.50	3.75	.75
☐ AL21 Vern Stephens	7.50	3.75	.75
☐ AL22 Vic Wertz	7.50	3.75	.75
☐ AL23 Ted Williams	100.00	50.00	10.00
☐ AL24 Early Wynn	17.00	8.50	1.70
☐ AL25 Eddie Yost	7.50	3.75	.75
☐ AL26 Gus Zernial	7.50	3.75	.75
☐ NL1 Leo Durocher MG	17.00	8.50	1.70
☐ NL2 Richie Ashburn	15.00	7.50	1.50
☐ NL3 Ewell Blackwell	7.50	3.75	.75
☐ NL4 Cliff Chambers	7.50	3.75	.75
☐ NL5 Murray Dickson	7.50	3.75	.75
☐ NL6 Sid Gordon	7.50	3.75	.75
☐ NL7 Granny Hamner	7.50	3.75	.75
☐ NL8 Jim Hearn	7.50	3.75	.75
☐ NL9 Monte Irvin	15.00	7.50	1.50
☐ NL10 Larry Jansen	7.50	3.75	.75
☐ NL11 Willie Jones	7.50	3.75	.75
☐ NL12 Ralph Kiner	22.50	11.00	2.00
☐ NL13 Whitey Lockman	7.50	3.75	.75
☐ NL14 Sal Maglie	10.00	5.00	1.00
☐ NL15 Willie Mays	80.00	40.00	8.00
☐ NL16 Stan Musial	75.00	37.50	7.50
☐ NL17 Pee Wee Reese	30.00	15.00	3.00
☐ NL18 Robin Roberts	20.00	10.00	2.00
☐ NL19 Al Schoendienst	17.00	8.50	1.70
☐ NL20 Enos Slaughter	20.00	10.00	2.00
☐ NL21 Duke Snider	50.00	25.00	5.00
☐ NL22 Warren Spahn	20.00	10.00	2.00
☐ NL23 Ed Stanky	7.50	3.75	.75
☐ NL24 Bobby Thomson	10.00	5.00	1.00
☐ NL25 Earl Torgeson	7.50	3.75	.75
☐ NL26 Wes Westrum	7.50	3.75	.75

1953 Red Man

The cards in this 52-card set measure 3 1/2" by 4" (or 3 1/2" by 3 5/8" without the tab). The 1953 Red Man set contains 26 National League stars and 26 American League stars. Card numbers are located both on the write-up of the player and on the tab. Cards that have the tab (coupon) attached are generally worth two and a half times the price of cards with the tab removed. The prices listed below refer to cards without tabs.

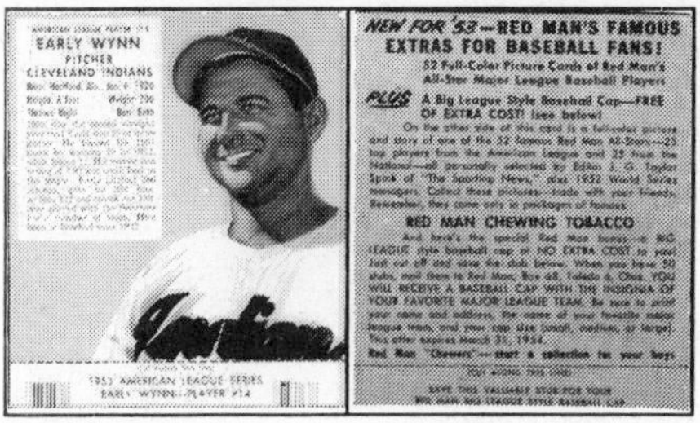

	NRMT	VG-E	GOOD
COMPLETE SET (52)	650.00	300.00	75.00
COMMON PLAYER	7.50	3.75	.75
☐ AL1 Casey Stengel MG	22.50	11.00	2.00
☐ AL2 Hank Bauer	10.00	5.00	1.00
☐ AL3 Yogi Berra	35.00	17.50	3.50
☐ AL4 Walt Dropo	7.50	3.75	.75
☐ AL5 Nelson Fox	13.50	6.00	1.00
☐ AL6 Jackie Jensen	10.00	5.00	1.00
☐ AL7 Eddie Joost	7.50	3.75	.75
☐ AL8 George Kell	17.00	8.50	1.70
☐ AL9 Dale Mitchell	7.50	3.75	.75
☐ AL10 Phil Rizzuto	17.00	8.50	1.70
☐ AL11 Eddie Robinson	7.50	3.75	.75
☐ AL12 Gene Woodling	9.00	4.50	.90
☐ AL13 Gus Zernial	7.50	3.75	.75
☐ AL14 Early Wynn	17.00	8.50	1.70
☐ AL15 Joe Dobson	7.50	3.75	.75
☐ AL16 Billy Pierce	9.00	4.50	.90
☐ AL17 Bob Lemon	17.00	8.50	1.70
☐ AL18 Johnny Mize	20.00	10.00	2.00
☐ AL19 Bob Porterfield	7.50	3.75	.75
☐ AL20 Bobby Shantz	7.50	3.75	.75
☐ AL21 Mickey Vernon	9.00	4.50	.90
☐ AL22 Dom DiMaggio	10.00	5.00	1.00
☐ AL23 Gil McDougald	10.00	5.00	1.00
☐ AL24 Al Rosen	10.00	5.00	1.00
☐ AL25 Mel Parnell	7.50	3.75	.75
☐ AL26 Bobby Avila	7.50	3.75	.75
☐ NL1 Charlie Dressen MG	7.50	3.75	.75
☐ NL2 Bobby Adams	7.50	3.75	.75
☐ NL3 Richie Ashburn	15.00	7.50	1.50
☐ NL4 Joe Black	9.00	4.50	.90
☐ NL5 Roy Campanella	50.00	25.00	5.00
☐ NL6 Ted Kluszewski	12.00	6.00	1.20
☐ NL7 Whitey Lockman	7.50	3.75	.75
☐ NL8 Sal Maglie	10.00	5.00	1.00
☐ NL9 Andy Pafko	7.50	3.75	.75
☐ NL10 Pee Wee Reese	30.00	15.00	3.00
☐ NL11 Robin Roberts	20.00	10.00	2.00
☐ NL12 Al Schoendienst	17.00	8.50	1.70
☐ NL13 Enos Slaughter	20.00	10.00	2.00
☐ NL14 Duke Snider	50.00	25.00	5.00
☐ NL15 Ralph Kiner	20.00	10.00	2.00
☐ NL16 Hank Sauer	7.50	3.75	.75
☐ NL17 Del Ennis	7.50	3.75	.75
☐ NL18 Granny Hamner	7.50	3.75	.75
☐ NL19 Warren Spahn	20.00	10.00	2.00
☐ NL20 Wes Westrum	7.50	3.75	.75
☐ NL21 Hoyt Wilhelm	17.00	8.50	1.70
☐ NL22 Murray Dickson	7.50	3.75	.75
☐ NL23 Warren Hacker	7.50	3.75	.75
☐ NL24 Gerry Staley	7.50	3.75	.75
☐ NL25 Bobby Thomson	10.00	5.00	1.00
☐ NL26 Stan Musial	75.00	37.50	7.50

1954 Red Man

The cards in this 50-card set measure 3 1/2" by 4" (or 3 1/2" by 3 5/8" without the tab). The 1954 Red Man set witnessed a reduction to 25 players from each league. George Kell, Sam Mele, and Dave Philley are known to exist with two different teams. Card number 19 of the National League exists as Enos Slaughter and as Gus Bell. Card numbers are on the write-ups of the players. Cards that have the tab (coupon) attached are generally worth two and a half times the price of cards with the tab removed. The prices listed below refer to cards without tabs. The complete set price below refers to all 54 cards including the four variations.

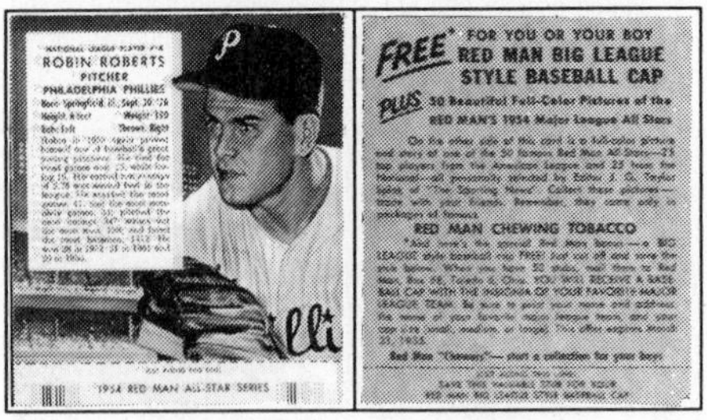

	NRMT	VG-E	GOOD
COMPLETE SET (54)	850.00	400.00	100.00
COMMON PLAYERS	7.50	3.75	.75
☐ AL1 Bobby Avila	7.50	3.75	.75
☐ AL2 Jim Busby	7.50	3.75	.75
☐ AL3 Nelson Fox	13.50	6.00	1.00
☐ AL4A George Kell (Boston)	25.00	12.50	2.50
☐ AL4B George Kell (Chicago)	50.00	25.00	5.00
☐ AL5 Sherman Lollar	7.50	3.75	.75
☐ AL6A Sam Mele (Baltimore)	10.00	5.00	1.00
☐ AL6B Sam Mele (Chicago)	30.00	15.00	3.00
☐ AL7 Minnie Minoso	10.00	5.00	1.00
☐ AL8 Mel Parnell	7.50	3.75	.75
☐ AL9A Dave Philley (Cleveland)	10.00	5.00	1.00
☐ AL9B Dave Philley (Philadelphia)	30.00	15.00	3.00
☐ AL10 Billy Pierce	9.00	4.50	.90
☐ AL11 Jim Piersall	10.00	5.00	1.00
☐ AL12 Al Rosen	10.00	5.00	1.00
☐ AL13 Mickey Vernon	9.00	4.50	.90
☐ AL14 Sammy White	7.50	3.75	.75
☐ AL15 Gene Woodling	9.00	4.50	.90
☐ AL16 Whitey Ford	30.00	15.00	3.00
☐ AL17 Phil Rizzuto	20.00	10.00	2.00
☐ AL18 Bob Porterfield	7.50	3.75	.75
☐ AL19 Chico Carrasquel	7.50	3.75	.75
☐ AL20 Yogi Berra	35.00	17.50	3.50
☐ AL21 Bob Lemon	17.00	8.50	1.70
☐ AL22 Ferris Fain	7.50	3.75	.75
☐ AL23 Hank Bauer	10.00	5.00	1.00
☐ AL24 Jim Delsing	7.50	3.75	.75
☐ AL25 Gil McDougald	10.00	5.00	1.00
☐ NL1 Richie Ashburn	15.00	7.50	1.50
☐ NL2 Billy Cox	7.50	3.75	.75
☐ NL3 Del Crandall	7.50	3.75	.75
☐ NL4 Carl Erskine	9.00	4.50	.90
☐ NL5 Monte Irvin	15.00	7.50	1.50
☐ NL6 Ted Kluszewski	12.00	6.00	1.20
☐ NL7 Don Mueller	7.50	3.75	.75
☐ NL8 Andy Pafko	7.50	3.75	.75
☐ NL9 Del Rice	7.50	3.75	.75
☐ NL10 Al Schoendienst	17.00	8.50	1.70
☐ NL11 Warren Spahn	20.00	10.00	2.00
☐ NL12 Curt Simmons	7.50	3.75	.75
☐ NL13 Roy Campanella	50.00	25.00	5.00
☐ NL14 Jim Gilliam	10.00	5.00	1.00
☐ NL15 Pee Wee Reese	30.00	15.00	3.00
☐ NL16 Duke Snider	50.00	25.00	5.00
☐ NL17 Rip Repulski	7.50	3.75	.75
☐ NL18 Robin Roberts	20.00	10.00	2.00
☐ NL19A Enos Slaughter	60.00	30.00	6.00
☐ NL19B Gus Bell	30.00	15.00	3.00
☐ NL20 Johnny Logan	7.50	3.75	.75
☐ NL21 John Antonelli	7.50	3.75	.75
☐ NL22 Gil Hodges	22.50	11.00	2.00
☐ NL23 Eddie Mathews	22.50	11.00	2.00
☐ NL24 Lew Burdette	9.00	4.50	.90
☐ NL25 Willie Mays	80.00	40.00	8.00

1955 Red Man

The cards in this 50-card set measure 3 1/2" by 4" (or 3 1/2" by 3 5/8" without the tab). The 1955 Red Man set contains 25 players from each league. Card numbers are on the write-ups of the players. Cards that have the tab (coupon) attached are generally worth two and a half times the price of cards with the tab removed. The prices listed below refer to cards without tabs.

	NRMT	VG-E	GOOD
COMPLETE SET (50)	600.00	275.00	75.00
COMMON PLAYER	7.50	3.75	.75
☐ AL1 Ray Boone	7.50	3.75	.75
☐ AL2 Jim Busby	7.50	3.75	.75
☐ AL3 Whitey Ford	30.00	15.00	3.00
☐ AL4 Nelson Fox	13.50	6.00	1.00
☐ AL5 Bob Grim	7.50	3.75	.75
☐ AL6 Jack Harshman	7.50	3.75	.75
☐ AL7 Jim Hegan	7.50	3.75	.75
☐ AL8 Bob Lemon	17.00	8.50	1.70
☐ AL9 Irv Noren	7.50	3.75	.75
☐ AL10 Bob Porterfield	7.50	3.75	.75
☐ AL11 Al Rosen	10.00	5.00	1.00
☐ AL12 Mickey Vernon	7.50	3.75	.75
☐ AL13 Vic Wertz	7.50	3.75	.75
☐ AL14 Early Wynn	17.00	8.50	1.70
☐ AL15 Bobby Avila	7.50	3.75	.75
☐ AL16 Yogi Berra	35.00	17.50	3.50
☐ AL17 Joe Coleman	7.50	3.75	.75
☐ AL18 Larry Doby	9.00	4.50	.90
☐ AL19 Jackie Jensen	7.50	3.75	.75
☐ AL20 Pete Runnels	7.50	3.75	.75
☐ AL21 Jim Piersall	10.00	5.00	1.00
☐ AL22 Hank Bauer	10.00	5.00	1.00
☐ AL23 Chico Carrasquel	7.50	3.75	.75
☐ AL24 Minnie Minoso	10.00	5.00	1.00
☐ AL25 Sandy Consuegra	7.50	3.75	.75
☐ NL1 Richie Ashburn	15.00	7.50	1.50
☐ NL2 Del Crandall	7.50	3.75	.75
☐ NL3 Gil Hodges	22.50	11.00	2.00
☐ NL4 Brooks Lawrence	7.50	3.75	.75
☐ NL5 Johnny Logan	7.50	3.75	.75
☐ NL6 Sal Maglie	9.00	4.50	.90
☐ NL7 Willie Mays	80.00	40.00	8.00
☐ NL8 Don Mueller	7.50	3.75	.75
☐ NL9 Bill Sarni	7.50	3.75	.75
☐ NL10 Warren Spahn	20.00	10.00	2.00
☐ NL11 Hank Thompson	7.50	3.75	.75
☐ NL12 Hoyt Wilhelm	17.00	8.50	1.70
☐ NL13 John Antonelli	7.50	3.75	.75
☐ NL14 Carl Erskine	9.00	4.50	.90
☐ NL15 Granny Hamner	7.50	3.75	.75
☐ NL16 Ted Kluszewski	12.00	6.00	1.20
☐ NL17 Pee Wee Reese	30.00	15.00	3.00
☐ NL18 Al Schoendienst	17.00	8.50	1.70
☐ NL19 Duke Snider	50.00	25.00	5.00
☐ NL20 Frank Thomas	7.50	3.75	.75
☐ NL21 Ray Jablonski	7.50	3.75	.75
☐ NL22 Dusty Rhodes	7.50	3.75	.75
☐ NL23 Gus Bell	7.50	3.75	.75
☐ NL24 Curt Simmons	7.50	3.75	.75
☐ NL25 Marv Grissom	7.50	3.75	.75

1955 Rodeo Meats

The cards in this 47-card set measure 2 1/2" by 3 1/2". The 1955 Rodeo Meats set contains unnumbered, color cards of the first Kansas City A's team. There are many background color variations noted in the checklist, and the card reverses carry a scrapbook offer. The Grimes and Kryhoski cards listed in the scrapbook album were apparently never issued. The catalog number for this set is F152-1. The cards have been arranged in alphabetical order and assigned numbers for reference.

	NRMT	VG-E	GOOD
COMPLETE SET (47)	4500.00	2200.00	500.00
COMMON PLAYER (1-47)	75.00	37.50	7.50
☐ 1 Joe Astroth	75.00	37.50	7.50
☐ 2 Harold Bevan	100.00	50.00	10.00
☐ 3 Charles Bishop	100.00	50.00	10.00
☐ 4 Don Bollweg	100.00	50.00	10.00
☐ 5 Lou Boudreau	225.00	110.00	22.00
☐ 6 Cloyd Boyer (salmon)	75.00	37.50	7.50
☐ 7 Cloyd Boyer (light blue)	125.00	60.00	12.50
☐ 8 Ed Burtschy	150.00	75.00	15.00
☐ 9 Art Ceccarelli	100.00	50.00	10.00
☐ 10 Joe DeMaestri (yellow)	75.00	37.50	7.50
☐ 11 Joe DeMaestri (green)	75.00	37.50	7.50
☐ 12 Art Ditmar	75.00	37.50	7.50
☐ 13 John Dixon	100.00	50.00	10.00
☐ 14 Jim Finigan	75.00	37.50	7.50
☐ 15 Marion Fricano	100.00	50.00	10.00
☐ 16 Tom Gorman	75.00	37.50	7.50
☐ 17 John Gray	100.00	50.00	10.00
☐ 18 Ray Herbert	75.00	37.50	7.50
☐ 19 Forest Jacobs	150.00	75.00	15.00
☐ 20 Alex Kellner	75.00	37.50	7.50
☐ 21 Harry Kraft	75.00	37.50	7.50
☐ 22 Jack Littrell	75.00	37.50	7.50
☐ 23 Hector Lopez	75.00	37.50	7.50
☐ 24 Oscar Melillo	75.00	37.50	7.50
☐ 25 Arnold Portocarrero (purple)	125.00	60.00	12.50
☐ 26 Arnold Portocarrero (gray)	75.00	37.50	7.50
☐ 27 Vic Power (yellow)	75.00	37.50	7.50
☐ 28 Vic Power (pink)	125.00	60.00	12.50
☐ 29 Vic Raschi	100.00	50.00	10.00
☐ 30 Bill Renna (lavender)	75.00	37.50	7.50
☐ 31 Bill Renna (dark pink)	125.00	60.00	12.50
☐ 32 Al Robertson	100.00	50.00	10.00
☐ 33 Johnny Sain	150.00	75.00	15.00
☐ 35 Bobby Schantz ERR (misspelling)	225.00	110.00	22.00
☐ 34 Bobby Shantz COR	150.00	75.00	15.00
☐ 36 Wilmer Shantz (orange)	75.00	37.50	7.50
☐ 37 Wilmer Shantz (lavender)	75.00	37.50	7.50
☐ 38 Harry Simpson	75.00	37.50	7.50
☐ 39 Enos Slaughter	250.00	125.00	25.00
☐ 40 Lou Sleator	75.00	37.50	7.50

☐ 41 George Susce	100.00	50.00	10.00
☐ 42 Bob Trice	100.00	50.00	10.00
☐ 43 Elmer Valo (yellow)	125.00	60.00	12.50
☐ 44 Elmer Valo (green sky)	75.00	37.50	7.50
☐ 45 Bill Wilson (yellow)	125.00	60.00	12.50
☐ 46 Bill Wilson (lavender sky)	75.00	37.50	7.50
☐ 47 Gus Zernial	75.00	37.50	7.50

1956 Rodeo Meats

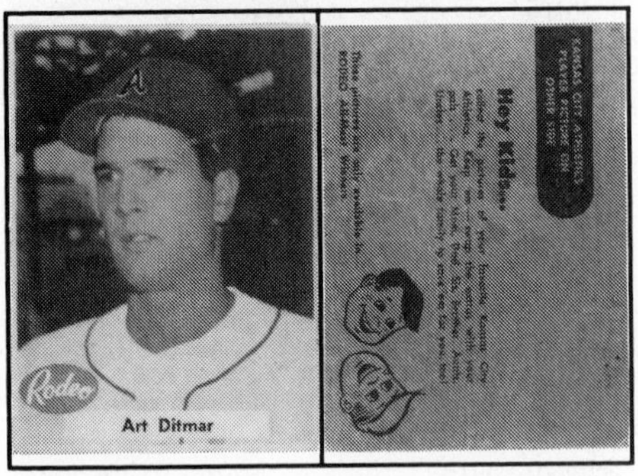

The cards in this 12-card set measure 2 1/2" by 3 1/2". The unnumbered, color cards of the 1956 Rodeo baseball series are easily distinguished from their 1955 counterparts by the absence of the scrapbook offer on the reverse. They were available only in packages of Rodeo All-Meat Wieners. The catalog designation for this set is F152-2, and the cards have been assigned numbers in alphabetical order in the checklist below.

	NRMT	VG-E	GOOD
COMPLETE SET (12)	1200.00	550.00	125.00
COMMON PLAYER (1-12)	75.00	37.50	7.50
☐ 1 Joe Astroth	75.00	37.50	7.50
☐ 2 Lou Boudreau	225.00	110.00	22.00
☐ 3 Joe DeMaestri	75.00	37.50	7.50
☐ 4 Art Ditmar	75.00	37.50	7.50
☐ 5 Jim Finigan	75.00	37.50	7.50
☐ 6 Hector Lopez	75.00	37.50	7.50
☐ 7 Vic Power	75.00	37.50	7.50
☐ 8 Bobby Shantz	125.00	60.00	12.50
☐ 9 Harry Simpson	75.00	37.50	7.50
☐ 10 Enos Slaughter	250.00	125.00	25.00
☐ 11 Elmer Valo	75.00	37.50	7.50
☐ 12 Gus Zernial	75.00	37.50	7.50

1958 S.F. Call-Bulletin

The cards in this 25-card set measure 2" by 4". The 1958 San Francisco Call-Bulletin set of unnumbered cards features black print on orange paper. These cards were given away as inserts in the San Francisco Call-Bulletin newspaper. The backs of the cards list the Giants home schedule and a radio station ad. The cards are entitled "Giant Payoff" and feature San Francisco Giant players only. The bottom part of the card (tab) could be detached as a ticket stub; hence, cards with the tab intact are worth approximately double the prices listed below. The catalog designation for this set is M126. The Tom Bowers card was issued in very short supply; also Bressoud, Jablonski, and Kirkland are somewhat tougher to find than the others. All of these tougher cards are asterisked in the checklist below.

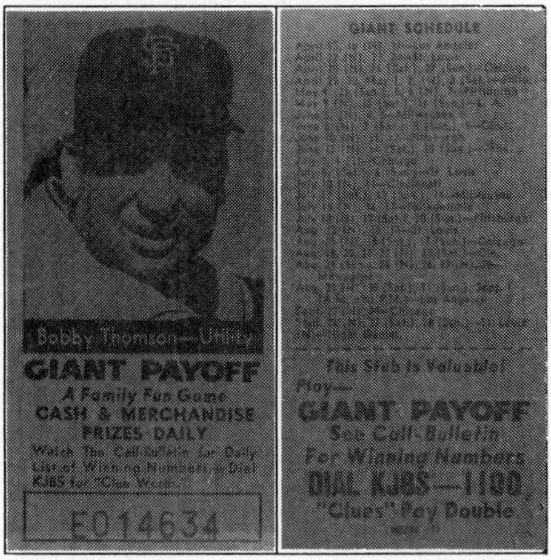

	NRMT	VG-E	GOOD
COMPLETE SET (25)	800.00	400.00	90.00
COMMON PLAYER (1-25)	6.00	3.00	.60
☐ 1 John Antonelli	7.50	3.75	.75
☐ 2 Curt Barclay	6.00	3.00	.60
☐ 3 Tom Bowers *	400.00	200.00	40.00
☐ 4 Ed Bressoud *	40.00	20.00	4.00
☐ 5 Orlando Cepeda	40.00	20.00	4.00
☐ 6 Ray Crone	6.00	3.00	.60
☐ 7 Jim Davenport	7.50	3.75	.75
☐ 8 Paul Giel	6.00	3.00	.60
☐ 9 Ruben Gomez	6.00	3.00	.60
☐ 10 Marv Grissom	6.00	3.00	.60
☐ 11 Ray Jablonski *	15.00	7.50	1.50
☐ 12 Willie Kirkland *	100.00	50.00	10.00
☐ 13 Whitey Lockman	6.00	3.00	.60
☐ 14 Willie Mays	175.00	85.00	18.00
☐ 15 Mike McCormick	7.50	3.75	.75
☐ 16 Stu Miller	7.50	3.75	.75
☐ 17 Ray Monzant	6.00	3.00	.60
☐ 18 Danny O'Connell	6.00	3.00	.60
☐ 19 Bill Rigney	7.50	3.75	.75
☐ 20 Hank Sauer	7.50	3.75	.75
☐ 21 Bob Schmidt	6.00	3.00	.60
☐ 22 Daryl Spencer	6.00	3.00	.60
☐ 23 Valmy Thomas	6.00	3.00	.60
☐ 24 Bobby Thomson	9.00	4.50	.90
☐ 25 Al Worthington	6.00	3.00	.60

1987-88 Score Test Samples

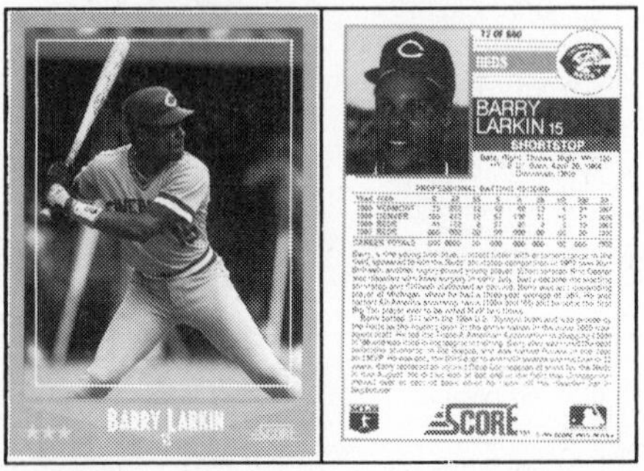

Late in 1987 near the end of the season, Score prepared some samples to show prospective dealers and buyers of the new Score cards what they would look like. These sample cards are distinguished by the fact that there is a row of zeroes for the 1987 season statistics since the season was not over when these sample cards were being printed. The cards are standard size, 2 1/2" by 3 1/2" and are virtually indistinguishable from the regular 1988 Score cards of the same players except for border color variations in a few instances.

	MINT	EXC	G-VG
COMPLETE SET (6)	15.00	7.50	1.50
COMMON PLAYER	2.50	1.25	.25
☐ 30 Mark Langston	3.50	1.75	.35
☐ 48 Tony Pena	2.50	1.25	.25
☐ 71 Keith Moreland	2.50	1.25	.25
☐ 72 Barry Larkin	5.00	2.50	.50
☐ 121 Dennis Boyd	3.00	1.50	.30
☐ 145 Denny Walling	2.50	1.25	.25

1988 Score

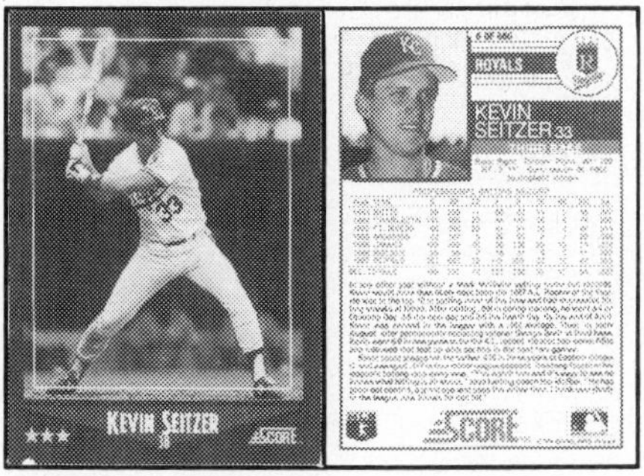

This 660-card set was distributed by Major League Marketing. Cards measure 2 1/2" by 3 1/2" and feature six distinctive border colors on the front. Highlights (652-660) and Rookie Prospects (623-647) are included in the set. Reggie Jackson's career is honored with a 5-card subset on cards 500-504. Card number 501, showing Reggie as a member of the Baltimore Orioles, is one of the few opportunities collectors have to visually remember (on a regular card) Reggie's one-year stay with the Orioles. The set is distinguished by the fact that each card back shows a full-color picture of the player. The key rookie cards in this set are Ellis Burks, Ron Gant, Gregg Jefferies, Roberto Kelly and Matt Williams. The company also produced a very limited "glossy" set, that is valued at eight times the value of the regular (non-glossy) set. Although exact production quantities of this glossy set are not known, it is generally accepted that the number of Score glossy sets produced in 1988 was much smaller (estimated only 10 percent to 15 percent as many) than the number of Topps Tiffany or Fleer Tin sets.

	MINT	EXC	G-VG
COMPLETE SET (660)	25.00	12.50	2.50
COMMON PLAYER (1-660)	.03	.01	.00
☐ 1 Don Mattingly	1.25	.25	.05
☐ 2 Wade Boggs	.45	.22	.04
☐ 3 Tim Raines	.15	.07	.01
☐ 4 Andre Dawson	.15	.07	.01
☐ 5 Mark McGwire	1.25	.60	.12
☐ 6 Kevin Seitzer	.45	.22	.04
☐ 7 Wally Joyner	.30	.15	.03
☐ 8 Jesse Barfield	.10	.05	.01
☐ 9 Pedro Guerrero	.12	.06	.01
☐ 10 Eric Davis	.40	.20	.04
☐ 11 George Brett	.30	.15	.03
☐ 12 Ozzie Smith	.15	.07	.01
☐ 13 Rickey Henderson	.40	.20	.04
☐ 14 Jim Rice	.15	.07	.01
☐ 15 Matt Nokes	.25	.12	.02
☐ 16 Mike Schmidt	.40	.20	.04
☐ 17 Dave Parker	.12	.06	.01
☐ 18 Eddie Murray	.15	.07	.01
☐ 19 Andres Galarraga	.12	.06	.01

☐ 20 Tony Fernandez	.10	.05	.01
☐ 21 Kevin McReynolds	.12	.06	.01
☐ 22 B.J. Surhoff	.12	.06	.01
☐ 23 Pat Tabler	.06	.03	.00
☐ 24 Kirby Puckett	.40	.20	.04
☐ 25 Benny Santiago	.40	.20	.04
☐ 26 Ryne Sandberg	.40	.20	.04
☐ 27 Kelly Downs (Will Clark in background, out of focus)	.08	.04	.01
☐ 28 Jose Cruz	.06	.03	.00
☐ 29 Pete O'Brien	.06	.03	.00
☐ 30 Mark Langston	.12	.06	.01
☐ 31 Lee Smith	.06	.03	.00
☐ 32 Juan Samuel	.08	.04	.01
☐ 33 Kevin Bass	.06	.03	.00
☐ 34 R.J. Reynolds	.03	.01	.00
☐ 35 Steve Sax	.12	.06	.01
☐ 36 John Kruk	.08	.04	.01
☐ 37 Alan Trammell	.12	.06	.01
☐ 38 Chris Bosio	.03	.01	.00
☐ 39 Brook Jacoby	.06	.03	.00
☐ 40 Willie McGee	.10	.05	.01
☐ 41 Dave Magadan	.15	.07	.01
☐ 42 Fred Lynn	.10	.05	.01
☐ 43 Kent Hrbek	.12	.06	.01
☐ 44 Brian Downing	.03	.01	.00
☐ 45 Jose Canseco	1.25	.60	.12
☐ 46 Jim Presley	.06	.03	.00
☐ 47 Mike Stanley	.03	.01	.00
☐ 48 Tony Pena	.06	.03	.00
☐ 49 David Cone	.65	.30	.06
☐ 50 Rick Sutcliffe	.08	.04	.01
☐ 51 Doug Drabek	.15	.07	.01
☐ 52 Bill Doran	.06	.03	.00
☐ 53 Mike Scioscia	.03	.01	.00
☐ 54 Candy Maldonado	.08	.04	.01
☐ 55 Dave Winfield	.18	.09	.01
☐ 56 Lou Whitaker	.10	.05	.01
☐ 57 Tom Henke	.06	.03	.00
☐ 58 Ken Gerhart	.03	.01	.00
☐ 59 Glenn Braggs	.06	.03	.00
☐ 60 Julio Franco	.10	.05	.01
☐ 61 Charlie Leibrandt	.03	.01	.00
☐ 62 Gary Gaetti	.10	.05	.01
☐ 63 Bob Boone	.08	.04	.01
☐ 64 Luis Polonia	.20	.10	.02
☐ 65 Dwight Evans	.10	.05	.01
☐ 66 Phil Bradley	.08	.04	.01
☐ 67 Mike Boddicker	.06	.03	.00
☐ 68 Vince Coleman	.15	.07	.01
☐ 69 Howard Johnson	.15	.07	.01
☐ 70 Tim Wallach	.08	.04	.01
☐ 71 Keith Moreland	.03	.01	.00
☐ 72 Barry Larkin	.35	.17	.03
☐ 73 Alan Ashby	.03	.01	.00
☐ 74 Rick Rhoden	.03	.01	.00
☐ 75 Darrell Evans	.06	.03	.00
☐ 76 Dave Stieb	.08	.04	.01
☐ 77 Dan Plesac	.03	.01	.00
☐ 78 Will Clark	1.10	.55	.11
☐ 79 Frank White	.06	.03	.00
☐ 80 Joe Carter	.15	.07	.01
☐ 81 Mike Witt	.03	.01	.00
☐ 82 Terry Steinbach	.18	.09	.01
☐ 83 Alvin Davis	.10	.05	.01
☐ 84 Tommy Herr (Will Clark shown sliding into second)	.08	.04	.01
☐ 85 Vance Law	.03	.01	.00
☐ 86 Kal Daniels	.15	.07	.01
☐ 87 Rick Honeycutt UER (wrong years for stats on back)	.03	.01	.00
☐ 88 Alfredo Griffin	.03	.01	.00
☐ 89 Bret Saberhagen	.15	.07	.01
☐ 90 Bert Blyleven	.10	.05	.01
☐ 91 Jeff Reardon	.08	.04	.01
☐ 92 Cory Snyder	.12	.06	.01
☐ 93A Greg Walker ERR (93 of 66)	5.00	2.50	.50
☐ 93B Greg Walker COR (93 of 660)	.08	.04	.01
☐ 94 Joe Magrane	.35	.17	.03
☐ 95 Rob Deer	.08	.04	.01
☐ 96 Ray Knight	.06	.03	.00
☐ 97 Casey Candaele	.03	.01	.00
☐ 98 John Cerutti	.03	.01	.00
☐ 99 Buddy Bell	.06	.03	.00
☐ 100 Jack Clark	.12	.06	.01
☐ 101 Eric Bell	.03	.01	.00
☐ 102 Willie Wilson	.08	.04	.01
☐ 103 Dave Schmidt	.03	.01	.00
☐ 104 Dennis Eckersley	.12	.06	.01

☐ 105	Don Sutton	.12	.06	.01
☐ 106	Danny Tartabull	.15	.07	.01
☐ 107	Fred McGriff	1.00	.50	.10
☐ 108	Les Straker	.06	.03	.00
☐ 109	Lloyd Moseby	.06	.03	.00
☐ 110	Roger Clemens	.50	.25	.05
☐ 111	Glenn Hubbard	.03	.01	.00
☐ 112	Ken Williams	.12	.06	.01
☐ 113	Ruben Sierra	.35	.17	.03
☐ 114	Stan Jefferson	.08	.04	.01
☐ 115	Milt Thompson	.03	.01	.00
☐ 116	Bobby Bonilla	.30	.15	.03
☐ 117	Wayne Tolleson	.03	.01	.00
☐ 118	Matt Williams	2.50	1.25	.25
☐ 119	Chet Lemon	.03	.01	.00
☐ 120	Dale Sveum	.03	.01	.00
☐ 121	Dennis Boyd	.06	.03	.00
☐ 122	Brett Butler	.08	.04	.01
☐ 123	Terry Kennedy	.03	.01	.00
☐ 124	Jack Howell	.03	.01	.00
☐ 125	Curt Young	.03	.01	.00
☐ 126A	Dave Valle ERR (misspelled Dale on card front)	.30	.15	.03
☐ 126B	Dave Valle COR	.10	.05	.01
☐ 127	Curt Wilkerson	.03	.01	.00
☐ 128	Tim Teufel	.03	.01	.00
☐ 129	Ozzie Virgil	.03	.01	.00
☐ 130	Brian Fisher	.03	.01	.00
☐ 131	Lance Parrish	.08	.04	.01
☐ 132	Tom Browning	.08	.04	.01
☐ 133A	Larry Andersen ERR (misspelled Anderson on card front)	.20	.10	.02
☐ 133B	Larry Andersen COR	.06	.03	.00
☐ 134A	Bob Brenly ERR (misspelled Brenley on card front)	.20	.10	.02
☐ 134B	Bob Brenly COR	.06	.03	.00
☐ 135	Mike Marshall	.08	.04	.01
☐ 136	Gerald Perry	.03	.01	.00
☐ 137	Bobby Meacham	.03	.01	.00
☐ 138	Larry Herndon	.03	.01	.00
☐ 139	Fred Manrique	.08	.04	.01
☐ 140	Charlie Hough	.03	.01	.00
☐ 141	Ron Darling	.08	.04	.01
☐ 142	Herm Winningham	.03	.01	.00
☐ 143	Mike Diaz	.03	.01	.00
☐ 144	Mike Jackson	.12	.06	.01
☐ 145	Denny Walling	.03	.01	.00
☐ 146	Robby Thompson	.03	.01	.00
☐ 147	Franklin Stubbs	.06	.03	.00
☐ 148	Albert Hall	.03	.01	.00
☐ 149	Bobby Witt	.15	.07	.01
☐ 150	Lance McCullers	.03	.01	.00
☐ 151	Scott Bradley	.03	.01	.00
☐ 152	Mark McLemore	.03	.01	.00
☐ 153	Tim Laudner	.03	.01	.00
☐ 154	Greg Swindell	.12	.06	.01
☐ 155	Marty Barrett	.06	.03	.00
☐ 156	Mike Heath	.03	.01	.00
☐ 157	Gary Ward	.03	.01	.00
☐ 158A	Lee Mazzilli ERR (misspelled Mazilli on card front)	.20	.10	.02
☐ 158B	Lee Mazzilli COR	.06	.03	.00
☐ 159	Tom Foley	.03	.01	.00
☐ 160	Robin Yount	.25	.12	.02
☐ 161	Steve Bedrosian	.08	.04	.01
☐ 162	Bob Walk	.03	.01	.00
☐ 163	Nick Esasky	.06	.03	.00
☐ 164	Ken Caminiti	.15	.07	.01
☐ 165	Jose Uribe	.03	.01	.00
☐ 166	Dave Anderson	.03	.01	.00
☐ 167	Ed Whitson	.06	.03	.00
☐ 168	Ernie Whitt	.03	.01	.00
☐ 169	Cecil Cooper	.08	.04	.01
☐ 170	Mike Pagliarulo	.03	.01	.00
☐ 171	Pat Sheridan	.03	.01	.00
☐ 172	Chris Bando	.03	.01	.00
☐ 173	Lee Lacy	.03	.01	.00
☐ 174	Steve Lombardozzi	.03	.01	.00
☐ 175	Mike Greenwell	1.00	.50	.10
☐ 176	Greg Minton	.03	.01	.00
☐ 177	Moose Haas	.03	.01	.00
☐ 178	Mike Kingery	.03	.01	.00
☐ 179	Greg Harris	.03	.01	.00
☐ 180	Bo Jackson	1.75	.85	.17
☐ 181	Carmelo Martinez	.03	.01	.00
☐ 182	Alex Trevino	.03	.01	.00
☐ 183	Ron Oester	.03	.01	.00
☐ 184	Danny Darwin	.06	.03	.00
☐ 185	Mike Krukow	.03	.01	.00
☐ 186	Rafael Palmeiro	.80	.40	.08
☐ 187	Tim Burke	.03	.01	.00
☐ 188	Roger McDowell	.06	.03	.00
☐ 189	Garry Templeton	.06	.03	.00
☐ 190	Terry Pendleton	.06	.03	.00
☐ 191	Larry Parrish	.03	.01	.00
☐ 192	Rey Quinones	.03	.01	.00
☐ 193	Joaquin Andujar	.06	.03	.00
☐ 194	Tom Brunansky	.08	.04	.01
☐ 195	Donnie Moore	.03	.01	.00
☐ 196	Dan Pasqua	.03	.01	.00
☐ 197	Jim Gantner	.03	.01	.00
☐ 198	Mark Eichhorn	.03	.01	.00
☐ 199	John Grubb	.03	.01	.00
☐ 200	Bill Ripken	.15	.07	.01
☐ 201	Sam Horn	.15	.07	.01
☐ 202	Todd Worrell	.10	.05	.01
☐ 203	Terry Leach	.06	.03	.00
☐ 204	Garth Iorg	.03	.01	.00
☐ 205	Brian Dayett	.03	.01	.00
☐ 206	Bo Diaz	.03	.01	.00
☐ 207	Craig Reynolds	.03	.01	.00
☐ 208	Brian Holton	.06	.03	.00
☐ 209	Marvell Wynne UER (misspelled Marvelle on card front)	.06	.03	.00
☐ 210	Dave Concepcion	.06	.03	.00
☐ 211	Mike Davis	.03	.01	.00
☐ 212	Devon White	.10	.05	.01
☐ 213	Mickey Brantley	.06	.03	.00
☐ 214	Greg Gagne	.03	.01	.00
☐ 215	Oddibe McDowell	.06	.03	.00
☐ 216	Jimmy Key	.06	.03	.00
☐ 217	Dave Bergman	.03	.01	.00
☐ 218	Calvin Schiraldi	.03	.01	.00
☐ 219	Larry Sheets	.06	.03	.00
☐ 220	Mike Easler	.03	.01	.00
☐ 221	Kurt Stillwell	.08	.04	.01
☐ 222	Chuck Jackson	.06	.03	.00
☐ 223	Dave Martinez	.06	.03	.00
☐ 224	Tim Leary	.08	.04	.01
☐ 225	Steve Garvey	.20	.10	.02
☐ 226	Greg Mathews	.03	.01	.00
☐ 227	Doug Sisk	.03	.01	.00
☐ 228	Dave Henderson	.06	.03	.00
☐ 229	Jimmy Dwyer	.03	.01	.00
☐ 230	Larry Owen	.03	.01	.00
☐ 231	Andre Thornton	.06	.03	.00
☐ 232	Mark Salas	.03	.01	.00
☐ 233	Tom Brookens	.03	.01	.00
☐ 234	Greg Brock	.03	.01	.00
☐ 235	Rance Mulliniks	.03	.01	.00
☐ 236	Bob Brower	.03	.01	.00
☐ 237	Joe Niekro	.06	.03	.00
☐ 238	Scott Bankhead	.06	.03	.00
☐ 239	Doug DeCinces	.03	.01	.00
☐ 240	Tommy John	.10	.05	.01
☐ 241	Rich Gedman	.03	.01	.00
☐ 242	Ted Power	.03	.01	.00
☐ 243	Dave Meads	.03	.01	.00
☐ 244	Jim Sundberg	.03	.01	.00
☐ 245	Ken Oberkfell	.03	.01	.00
☐ 246	Jimmy Jones	.08	.04	.01
☐ 247	Ken Landreaux	.03	.01	.00
☐ 248	Jose Oquendo	.03	.01	.00
☐ 249	John Mitchell	.08	.04	.01
☐ 250	Don Baylor	.08	.04	.01
☐ 251	Scott Fletcher	.03	.01	.00
☐ 252	Al Newman	.03	.01	.00
☐ 253	Carney Lansford	.08	.04	.01
☐ 254	Johnny Ray	.06	.03	.00
☐ 255	Gary Pettis	.03	.01	.00
☐ 256	Ken Phelps	.06	.03	.00
☐ 257	Rick Leach	.03	.01	.00
☐ 258	Tim Stoddard	.03	.01	.00
☐ 259	Ed Romero	.03	.01	.00
☐ 260	Sid Bream	.03	.01	.00
☐ 261A	Tom Niedenfuer ERR (misspelled Neidenfuer on card front)	.20	.10	.02
☐ 261B	Tom Niedenfuer COR	.06	.03	.00
☐ 262	Rick Dempsey	.03	.01	.00
☐ 263	Lonnie Smith	.08	.04	.01
☐ 264	Bob Forsch	.03	.01	.00
☐ 265	Barry Bonds	.45	.22	.04
☐ 266	Willie Randolph	.06	.03	.00
☐ 267	Mike Ramsey	.08	.04	.01
☐ 268	Don Slaught	.03	.01	.00
☐ 269	Mickey Tettleton	.06	.03	.00
☐ 270	Jerry Reuss	.03	.01	.00
☐ 271	Marc Sullivan	.03	.01	.00
☐ 272	Jim Morrison	.03	.01	.00
☐ 273	Steve Balboni	.03	.01	.00
☐ 274	Dick Schofield	.03	.01	.00
☐ 275	John Tudor	.08	.04	.01

☐ 276 Gene Larkin	.20	.10	.02
☐ 277 Harold Reynolds	.06	.03	.00
☐ 278 Jerry Browne	.03	.01	.00
☐ 279 Willie Upshaw	.03	.01	.00
☐ 280 Ted Higuera	.06	.03	.00
☐ 281 Terry McGriff	.06	.03	.00
☐ 282 Terry Puhl	.03	.01	.00
☐ 283 Mark Wasinger	.08	.04	.01
☐ 284 Luis Salazar	.03	.01	.00
☐ 285 Ted Simmons	.08	.04	.01
☐ 286 John Shelby	.03	.01	.00
☐ 287 John Smiley	.25	.12	.02
☐ 288 Curt Ford	.03	.01	.00
☐ 289 Steve Crawford	.03	.01	.00
☐ 290 Dan Quisenberry	.06	.03	.00
☐ 291 Alan Wiggins	.03	.01	.00
☐ 292 Randy Bush	.03	.01	.00
☐ 293 John Candelaria	.03	.01	.00
☐ 294 Tony Phillips	.03	.01	.00
☐ 295 Mike Morgan	.03	.01	.00
☐ 296 Bill Wegman	.03	.01	.00
☐ 297A Terry Francona ERR	.20	.10	.02
(misspelled Franconia			
on card front)			
☐ 297B Terry Francona COR	.06	.03	.00
☐ 298 Mickey Hatcher	.03	.01	.00
☐ 299 Andres Thomas	.03	.01	.00
☐ 300 Bob Stanley	.03	.01	.00
☐ 301 Al Pedrique	.06	.03	.00
☐ 302 Jim Lindeman	.03	.01	.00
☐ 303 Wally Backman	.03	.01	.00
☐ 304 Paul O'Neill	.12	.06	.01
☐ 305 Hubie Brooks	.08	.04	.01
☐ 306 Steve Buechele	.03	.01	.00
☐ 307 Bobby Thigpen	.12	.06	.01
☐ 308 George Hendrick	.03	.01	.00
☐ 309 John Moses	.03	.01	.00
☐ 310 Ron Guidry	.08	.04	.01
☐ 311 Bill Schroeder	.03	.01	.00
☐ 312 Jose Nunez	.10	.05	.01
☐ 313 Bud Black	.06	.03	.00
☐ 314 Joe Sambito	.03	.01	.00
☐ 315 Scott McGregor	.03	.01	.00
☐ 316 Rafael Santana	.03	.01	.00
☐ 317 Frank Williams	.03	.01	.00
☐ 318 Mike Fitzgerald	.03	.01	.00
☐ 319 Rick Mahler	.03	.01	.00
☐ 320 Jim Gott	.03	.01	.00
☐ 321 Mariano Duncan	.06	.03	.00
☐ 322 Jose Guzman	.03	.01	.00
☐ 323 Lee Guetterman	.03	.01	.00
☐ 324 Dan Gladden	.06	.03	.00
☐ 325 Gary Carter	.15	.07	.01
☐ 326 Tracy Jones	.06	.03	.00
☐ 327 Floyd Youmans	.03	.01	.00
☐ 328 Bill Dawley	.03	.01	.00
☐ 329 Paul Noce	.06	.03	.00
☐ 330 Angel Salazar	.03	.01	.00
☐ 331 Goose Gossage	.08	.04	.01
☐ 332 George Frazier	.03	.01	.00
☐ 333 Ruppert Jones	.03	.01	.00
☐ 334 Billy Jo Robidoux	.03	.01	.00
☐ 335 Mike Scott	.12	.06	.01
☐ 336 Randy Myers	.15	.07	.01
☐ 337 Bob Sebra	.03	.01	.00
☐ 338 Eric Show	.03	.01	.00
☐ 339 Mitch Williams	.06	.03	.00
☐ 340 Paul Molitor	.10	.05	.01
☐ 341 Gus Polidor	.03	.01	.00
☐ 342 Steve Trout	.03	.01	.00
☐ 343 Jerry Don Gleaton	.03	.01	.00
☐ 344 Bob Knepper	.03	.01	.00
☐ 345 Mitch Webster	.03	.01	.00
☐ 346 John Morris	.03	.01	.00
☐ 347 Andy Hawkins	.03	.01	.00
☐ 348 Dave Leiper	.03	.01	.00
☐ 349 Ernest Riles	.03	.01	.00
☐ 350 Dwight Gooden	.40	.20	.04
☐ 351 Dave Righetti	.08	.04	.01
☐ 352 Pat Dodson	.06	.03	.00
☐ 353 John Habyan	.03	.01	.00
☐ 354 Jim Deshaies	.03	.01	.00
☐ 355 Butch Wynegar	.03	.01	.00
☐ 356 Bryn Smith	.03	.01	.00
☐ 357 Matt Young	.03	.01	.00
☐ 358 Tom Pagnozzi	.08	.04	.01
☐ 359 Floyd Rayford	.03	.01	.00
☐ 360 Darryl Strawberry	.35	.17	.03
☐ 361 Sal Butera	.03	.01	.00
☐ 362 Domingo Ramos	.03	.01	.00
☐ 363 Chris Brown	.03	.01	.00
☐ 364 Jose Gonzalez	.08	.04	.01
☐ 365 Dave Smith	.03	.01	.00
☐ 366 Andy McGaffigan	.03	.01	.00

☐ 367 Stan Javier	.03	.01	.00
☐ 368 Henry Cotto	.03	.01	.00
☐ 369 Mike Birkbeck	.06	.03	.00
☐ 370 Len Dykstra	.18	.09	.01
☐ 371 Dave Collins	.03	.01	.00
☐ 372 Spike Owen	.03	.01	.00
☐ 373 Geno Petralli	.03	.01	.00
☐ 374 Ron Karkovice	.03	.01	.00
☐ 375 Shane Rawley	.03	.01	.00
☐ 376 DeWayne Buice	.06	.03	.00
☐ 377 Bill Pecota	.06	.03	.00
☐ 378 Leon Durham	.03	.01	.00
☐ 379 Ed Olwine	.03	.01	.00
☐ 380 Bruce Hurst	.08	.04	.01
☐ 381 Bob McClure	.03	.01	.00
☐ 382 Mark Thurmond	.03	.01	.00
☐ 383 Buddy Biancalana	.03	.01	.00
☐ 384 Tim Conroy	.03	.01	.00
☐ 385 Tony Gwynn	.30	.15	.03
☐ 386 Greg Gross	.03	.01	.00
☐ 387 Barry Lyons	.12	.06	.01
☐ 388 Mike Felder	.03	.01	.00
☐ 389 Pat Clements	.03	.01	.00
☐ 390 Ken Griffey	.10	.05	.01
☐ 391 Mark Davis	.10	.05	.01
☐ 392 Jose Rijo	.10	.05	.01
☐ 393 Mike Young	.03	.01	.00
☐ 394 Willie Fraser	.03	.01	.00
☐ 395 Dion James	.03	.01	.00
☐ 396 Steve Shields	.03	.01	.00
☐ 397 Randy St.Claire	.03	.01	.00
☐ 398 Danny Jackson	.06	.03	.00
☐ 399 Cecil Fielder	.40	.20	.04
☐ 400 Keith Hernandez	.12	.06	.01
☐ 401 Don Carman	.03	.01	.00
☐ 402 Chuck Crim	.06	.03	.00
☐ 403 Rob Woodward	.03	.01	.00
☐ 404 Junior Ortiz	.03	.01	.00
☐ 405 Glenn Wilson	.03	.01	.00
☐ 406 Ken Howell	.03	.01	.00
☐ 407 Jeff Kunkel	.03	.01	.00
☐ 408 Jeff Reed	.03	.01	.00
☐ 409 Chris James	.12	.06	.01
☐ 410 Zane Smith	.08	.04	.01
☐ 411 Ken Dixon	.03	.01	.00
☐ 412 Ricky Horton	.03	.01	.00
☐ 413 Frank DiPino	.03	.01	.00
☐ 414 Shane Mack	.12	.06	.01
☐ 415 Danny Cox	.03	.01	.00
☐ 416 Andy Van Slyke	.12	.06	.01
☐ 417 Danny Heep	.03	.01	.00
☐ 418 John Cangelosi	.03	.01	.00
☐ 419A John Christensen ERR	.20	.10	.02
(Christiansen			
on card front)			
☐ 419B John Christensen COR	.06	.03	.00
☐ 420 Joey Cora	.08	.04	.01
☐ 421 Mike LaValliere	.03	.01	.00
☐ 422 Kelly Gruber	.30	.15	.03
☐ 423 Bruce Benedict	.03	.01	.00
☐ 424 Len Matuszek	.03	.01	.00
☐ 425 Kent Tekulve	.03	.01	.00
☐ 426 Rafael Ramirez	.03	.01	.00
☐ 427 Mike Flanagan	.06	.03	.00
☐ 428 Mike Gallego	.03	.01	.00
☐ 429 Juan Castillo	.06	.03	.00
☐ 430 Neal Heaton	.03	.01	.00
☐ 431 Phil Garner	.03	.01	.00
☐ 432 Mike Dunne	.06	.03	.00
☐ 433 Wallace Johnson	.03	.01	.00
☐ 434 Jack O'Connor	.03	.01	.00
☐ 435 Steve Jeltz	.03	.01	.00
☐ 436 Donnell Nixon	.08	.04	.01
☐ 437 Jack Lazorko	.03	.01	.00
☐ 438 Keith Comstock	.06	.03	.00
☐ 439 Jeff Robinson	.03	.01	.00
(Pirates pitcher)			
☐ 440 Graig Nettles	.08	.04	.01
☐ 441 Mel Hall	.06	.03	.00
☐ 442 Gerald Young	.15	.07	.01
☐ 443 Gary Redus	.03	.01	.00
☐ 444 Charlie Moore	.03	.01	.00
☐ 445 Bill Madlock	.06	.03	.00
☐ 446 Mark Clear	.03	.01	.00
☐ 447 Greg Booker	.03	.01	.00
☐ 448 Rick Schu	.03	.01	.00
☐ 449 Ron Kittle	.08	.04	.01
☐ 450 Dale Murphy	.20	.10	.02
☐ 451 Bob Dernier	.03	.01	.00
☐ 452 Dale Mohorcic	.03	.01	.00
☐ 453 Rafael Belliard	.03	.01	.00
☐ 454 Charlie Puleo	.03	.01	.00
☐ 455 Dwayne Murphy	.03	.01	.00
☐ 456 Jim Eisenreich	.03	.01	.00

☐ 457	David Palmer	.03	.01	.00
☐ 458	Dave Stewart	.15	.07	.01
☐ 459	Pascual Perez	.06	.03	.00
☐ 460	Glenn Davis	.15	.07	.01
☐ 461	Dan Petry	.03	.01	.00
☐ 462	Jim Winn	.03	.01	.00
☐ 463	Darrell Miller	.03	.01	.00
☐ 464	Mike Moore	.06	.03	.00
☐ 465	Mike LaCoss	.03	.01	.00
☐ 466	Steve Farr	.06	.03	.00
☐ 467	Jerry Mumphrey	.03	.01	.00
☐ 468	Kevin Gross	.03	.01	.00
☐ 469	Bruce Bochy	.03	.01	.00
☐ 470	Orel Hershiser	.18	.09	.01
☐ 471	Eric King	.03	.01	.00
☐ 472	Ellis Burks	1.25	.60	.12
☐ 473	Darren Daulton	.06	.03	.00
☐ 474	Mookie Wilson	.06	.03	.00
☐ 475	Frank Viola	.18	.09	.01
☐ 476	Ron Robinson	.03	.01	.00
☐ 477	Bob Melvin	.03	.01	.00
☐ 478	Jeff Musselman	.06	.03	.00
☐ 479	Charlie Kerfeld	.03	.01	.00
☐ 480	Richard Dotson	.03	.01	.00
☐ 481	Kevin Mitchell	.40	.20	.04
☐ 482	Gary Roenicke	.03	.01	.00
☐ 483	Tim Flannery	.03	.01	.00
☐ 484	Rich Yett	.03	.01	.00
☐ 485	Pete Incaviglia	.10	.05	.01
☐ 486	Rick Cerone	.03	.01	.00
☐ 487	Tony Armas	.03	.01	.00
☐ 488	Jerry Reed	.03	.01	.00
☐ 489	Dave Lopes	.06	.03	.00
☐ 490	Frank Tanana	.06	.03	.00
☐ 491	Mike Loynd	.03	.01	.00
☐ 492	Bruce Ruffin	.03	.01	.00
☐ 493	Chris Speier	.03	.01	.00
☐ 494	Tom Hume	.03	.01	.00
☐ 495	Jesse Orosco	.03	.01	.00
☐ 496	Robbie Wine UER (misspelled Robby on card front)	.06	.03	.00
☐ 497	Jeff Montgomery	.20	.10	.02
☐ 498	Jeff Dedmon	.03	.01	.00
☐ 499	Luis Aguayo	.03	.01	.00
☐ 500	Reggie Jackson (Oakland A's)	.20	.10	.02
☐ 501	Reggie Jackson (Baltimore Orioles)	.25	.12	.02
☐ 502	Reggie Jackson (New York Yankees)	.20	.10	.02
☐ 503	Reggie Jackson (California Angels)	.20	.10	.02
☐ 504	Reggie Jackson (Oakland A's)	.20	.10	.02
☐ 505	Billy Hatcher	.03	.01	.00
☐ 506	Ed Lynch	.03	.01	.00
☐ 507	Willie Hernandez	.06	.03	.00
☐ 508	Jose DeLeon	.03	.01	.00
☐ 509	Joel Youngblood	.03	.01	.00
☐ 510	Bob Welch	.10	.05	.01
☐ 511	Steve Ontiveros	.03	.01	.00
☐ 512	Randy Ready	.03	.01	.00
☐ 513	Juan Nieves	.03	.01	.00
☐ 514	Jeff Russell	.03	.01	.00
☐ 515	Von Hayes	.08	.04	.01
☐ 516	Mark Gubicza	.08	.04	.01
☐ 517	Ken Dayley	.03	.01	.00
☐ 518	Don Aase	.03	.01	.00
☐ 519	Rick Reuschel	.08	.04	.01
☐ 520	Mike Henneman	.18	.09	.01
☐ 521	Rick Aguilera	.03	.01	.00
☐ 522	Jay Howell	.03	.01	.00
☐ 523	Ed Correa	.03	.01	.00
☐ 524	Manny Trillo	.03	.01	.00
☐ 525	Kirk Gibson	.15	.07	.01
☐ 526	Wally Ritchie	.03	.01	.00
☐ 527	Al Nipper	.03	.01	.00
☐ 528	Atlee Hammaker	.03	.01	.00
☐ 529	Shawon Dunston	.12	.06	.01
☐ 530	Jim Clancy	.03	.01	.00
☐ 531	Tom Paciorek	.03	.01	.00
☐ 532	Joel Skinner	.03	.01	.00
☐ 533	Scott Garrelts	.06	.03	.00
☐ 534	Tom O'Malley	.03	.01	.00
☐ 535	John Franco	.08	.04	.01
☐ 536	Paul Kilgus	.08	.04	.01
☐ 537	Darrell Porter	.03	.01	.00
☐ 538	Walt Terrell	.03	.01	.00
☐ 539	Bill Long	.08	.04	.01
☐ 540	George Bell	.15	.07	.01
☐ 541	Jeff Sellers	.03	.01	.00
☐ 542	Joe Boever	.10	.05	.01
☐ 543	Steve Howe	.03	.01	.00
☐ 544	Scott Sanderson	.06	.03	.00
☐ 545	Jack Morris	.10	.05	.01
☐ 546	Todd Benzinger	.20	.10	.02
☐ 547	Steve Henderson	.03	.01	.00
☐ 548	Eddie Milner	.03	.01	.00
☐ 549	Jeff Robinson (Tigers pitcher)	.20	.10	.02
☐ 550	Cal Ripken	.20	.10	.02
☐ 551	Jody Davis	.03	.01	.00
☐ 552	Kirk McCaskill	.03	.01	.00
☐ 553	Craig Lefferts	.03	.01	.00
☐ 554	Darnell Coles	.03	.01	.00
☐ 555	Phil Niekro	.12	.06	.01
☐ 556	Mike Aldrete	.03	.01	.00
☐ 557	Pat Perry	.03	.01	.00
☐ 558	Juan Agosto	.03	.01	.00
☐ 559	Rob Murphy	.03	.01	.00
☐ 560	Dennis Rasmussen	.03	.01	.00
☐ 561	Manny Lee	.03	.01	.00
☐ 562	Jeff Blauser	.18	.09	.01
☐ 563	Bob Ojeda	.06	.03	.00
☐ 564	Dave Dravecky	.08	.04	.01
☐ 565	Gene Garber	.03	.01	.00
☐ 566	Ron Roenicke	.03	.01	.00
☐ 567	Tommy Hinzo	.03	.01	.00
☐ 568	Eric Nolte	.03	.01	.00
☐ 569	Ed Hearn	.03	.01	.00
☐ 570	Mark Davidson	.06	.03	.00
☐ 571	Jim Walewander	.08	.04	.01
☐ 572	Donnie Hill	.03	.01	.00
☐ 573	Jamie Moyer	.03	.01	.00
☐ 574	Ken Schrom	.03	.01	.00
☐ 575	Nolan Ryan	.50	.25	.05
☐ 576	Jim Acker	.03	.01	.00
☐ 577	Jamie Quirk	.03	.01	.00
☐ 578	Jay Aldrich	.03	.01	.00
☐ 579	Claudell Washington	.06	.03	.00
☐ 580	Jeff Leonard	.06	.03	.00
☐ 581	Carmen Castillo	.03	.01	.00
☐ 582	Daryl Boston	.06	.03	.00
☐ 583	Jeff DeWillis	.03	.01	.00
☐ 584	John Marzano	.06	.03	.00
☐ 585	Bill Gullickson	.03	.01	.00
☐ 586	Andy Allanson	.03	.01	.00
☐ 587	Lee Tunnell	.03	.01	.00
☐ 588	Gene Nelson	.03	.01	.00
☐ 589	Dave LaPoint	.03	.01	.00
☐ 590	Harold Baines	.08	.04	.01
☐ 591	Bill Buckner	.06	.03	.00
☐ 592	Carlton Fisk	.15	.07	.01
☐ 593	Rick Manning	.03	.01	.00
☐ 594	Doug Jones	.25	.12	.02
☐ 595	Tom Candiotti	.06	.03	.00
☐ 596	Steve Lake	.03	.01	.00
☐ 597	Jose Lind	.25	.12	.02
☐ 598	Ross Jones	.03	.01	.00
☐ 599	Gary Matthews	.03	.01	.00
☐ 600	Fernando Valenzuela	.12	.06	.01
☐ 601	Dennis Martinez	.06	.03	.00
☐ 602	Les Lancaster	.10	.05	.01
☐ 603	Ozzie Guillen	.10	.05	.01
☐ 604	Tony Bernazard	.03	.01	.00
☐ 605	Chili Davis	.06	.03	.00
☐ 606	Roy Smalley	.03	.01	.00
☐ 607	Ivan Calderon	.06	.03	.00
☐ 608	Jay Tibbs	.03	.01	.00
☐ 609	Guy Hoffman	.03	.01	.00
☐ 610	Doyle Alexander	.03	.01	.00
☐ 611	Mike Bielecki	.03	.01	.00
☐ 612	Shawn Hillegas	.12	.06	.01
☐ 613	Keith Atherton	.03	.01	.00
☐ 614	Eric Plunk	.03	.01	.00
☐ 615	Sid Fernandez	.08	.04	.01
☐ 616	Dennis Lamp	.03	.01	.00
☐ 617	Dave Engle	.03	.01	.00
☐ 618	Harry Spilman	.03	.01	.00
☐ 619	Don Robinson	.03	.01	.00
☐ 620	John Farrell	.18	.09	.01
☐ 621	Nelson Liriano	.15	.07	.01
☐ 622	Floyd Bannister	.03	.01	.00
☐ 623	Randy Milligan	.90	.45	.09
☐ 624	Kevin Elster	.12	.06	.01
☐ 625	Jody Reed	.45	.22	.04
☐ 626	Shawn Abner	.10	.05	.01
☐ 627	Kurt Manwaring	.10	.05	.01
☐ 628	Pete Stanicek	.08	.04	.01
☐ 629	Rob Ducey	.15	.07	.01
☐ 630	Steve Kiefer	.03	.01	.00
☐ 631	Gary Thurman	.15	.07	.01
☐ 632	Darrel Akerfelds	.12	.06	.01
☐ 633	Dave Clark	.12	.06	.01
☐ 634	Roberto Kelly	.85	.40	.08
☐ 635	Keith Hughes	.10	.05	.01
☐ 636	John Davis	.08	.04	.01

☐ 637 Mike Devereaux	.18	.09	.01
☐ 638 Tom Glavine	.25	.12	.02
☐ 639 Keith Miller (New York Mets)	.15	.07	.01
☐ 640 Chris Gwynn UER (wrong batting and throwing on back)	.20	.10	.02
☐ 641 Tim Crews	.06	.03	.00
☐ 642 Mackey Sasser	.45	.22	.04
☐ 643 Vicente Palacios	.12	.06	.01
☐ 644 Kevin Romine	.06	.03	.00
☐ 645 Gregg Jefferies	2.75	1.35	.27
☐ 646 Jeff Treadway	.20	.10	.02
☐ 647 Ron Gant	1.50	.75	.15
☐ 648 Mark McGwire and Matt Nokes (Rookie Sluggers)	.15	.07	.01
☐ 649 Eric Davis and Tim Raines (Speed and Power)	.15	.07	.01
☐ 650 Don Mattingly and Jack Clark	.30	.15	.03
☐ 651 Tony Fernandez, Alan Trammell, and Cal Ripken	.10	.05	.01
☐ 652 Vince Coleman HL 100 Stolen Bases	.10	.05	.01
☐ 653 Kirby Puckett HL 10 Hits in a Row	.15	.07	.01
☐ 654 Benito Santiago HL Hitting Streak	.12	.06	.01
☐ 655 Juan Nieves HL No Hitter	.06	.03	.00
☐ 656 Steve Bedrosian HL Saves Record	.06	.03	.00
☐ 657 Mike Schmidt HL 500 Homers	.25	.12	.02
☐ 658 Don Mattingly HL Home Run Streak	.35	.17	.03
☐ 659 Mark McGwire HL Rookie HR Record	.30	.15	.03
☐ 660 Paul Molitor HL Hitting Streak	.10	.05	.01

.1988 Score Box Bottoms

There are six different wax box bottom panels each featuring three players and a trivia (related to a particular stadium for a given year) question. The players and trivia question cards are individually numbered. The trivia are numbered below with the prefix T in order to avoid confusion. The trivia cards are very unpopular with collectors since they do not picture any players. When panels of four are cut into individuals, the cards are standard size, 2/1/2" by 3 1/2". The card backs of the players feature the respective League logos most prominently.

	MINT	EXC	G-VG
COMPLETE SET (24)	5.00	2.50	.50
COMMON PLAYER (1-18)	.10	.05	.01
COMMON TRIVIA (T1-T6)	.05	.02	.00
☐ 1 Terry Kennedy	.10	.05	.01
☐ 2 Don Mattingly	.75	.35	.07
☐ 3 Willie Randolph	.15	.07	.01
☐ 4 Wade Boggs	.50	.25	.05
☐ 5 Cal Ripken	.35	.17	.03
☐ 6 George Bell	.20	.10	.02
☐ 7 Rickey Henderson	.75	.35	.07
☐ 8 Dave Winfield	.25	.12	.02
☐ 9 Bret Saberhagen	.25	.12	.02
☐ 10 Gary Carter	.20	.10	.02
☐ 11 Jack Clark	.15	.07	.01
☐ 12 Ryne Sandberg	.60	.30	.06
☐ 13 Mike Schmidt	.75	.35	.07
☐ 14 Ozzie Smith	.25	.12	.02
☐ 15 Eric Davis	.40	.20	.04
☐ 16 Andre Dawson	.25	.12	.02
☐ 17 Darryl Strawberry	.50	.25	.05
☐ 18 Mike Scott	.15	.07	.01
☐ T1 Fenway Park '60 Ted (Williams) Hits To The End	.10	.05	.01
☐ T2 Comiskey Park '83 Grand Slam (Fred Lynn) Breaks Jinx	.05	.02	.00
☐ T3 Anaheim Stadium '87 Old Rookie Record Falls (Mark McGwire)	.10	.05	.01
☐ T4 Wrigley Field '38 Gabby (Hartnett) Gets Pennant Homer	.05	.02	.00
☐ T5 Comiskey Park '50 Red (Schoendienst) Rips Winning HR	.05	.02	.00
☐ T6 County Stadium '87 Rookie (John Farrell) Stops Hit Streak (Paul Molitor)	.05	.02	.00

1988 Score Young Superstars I

This attractive high-gloss 40-card set of "Young Superstars" was distributed in a small blue box which had the checklist of the set on a side panel of the box. The cards were also distributed as an insert, one per rak pak. These attractive cards are in full color on the front and also have a full-color small portrait on the card back. The cards are standard size, 2 1/2" by 3 1/2". The cards in this series are distinguishable from the cards in Series II by the fact that this series has a blue and green border on the card front instead of the (Series II) blue and pink border.

	MINT	EXC	G-VG
COMPLETE SET (40)	9.00	4.50	.90
COMMON PLAYER (1-40)	.20	.10	.02
☐ 1 Mark McGwire	1.00	.50	.10
☐ 2 Benito Santiago	.50	.25	.05
☐ 3 Sam Horn	.25	.12	.02
☐ 4 Chris Bosio	.20	.10	.02
☐ 5 Matt Nokes	.25	.12	.02
☐ 6 Ken Williams	.20	.10	.02
☐ 7 Dion James	.20	.10	.02
☐ 8 B.J. Surhoff	.30	.15	.03
☐ 9 Joe Magrane	.25	.12	.02
☐ 10 Kevin Seitzer	.40	.20	.04
☐ 11 Stanley Jefferson	.20	.10	.02
☐ 12 Devon White	.25	.12	.02

□ 13 Nelson Liriano	.20	.10	.02
□ 14 Chris James	.25	.12	.02
□ 15 Mike Henneman	.20	.10	.02
□ 16 Terry Steinbach	.25	.12	.02
□ 17 John Kruk	.25	.12	.02
□ 18 Matt Williams	1.00	.50	.10
□ 19 Kelly Downs	.20	.10	.02
□ 20 Bill Ripken	.20	.10	.02
□ 21 Ozzie Guillen	.25	.12	.02
□ 22 Luis Polonia	.20	.10	.02
□ 23 Dave Magadan	.40	.20	.04
□ 24 Mike Greenwell	.60	.30	.06
□ 25 Will Clark	1.00	.50	.10
□ 26 Mike Dunn	.20	.10	.02
□ 27 Wally Joyner	.40	.20	.04
□ 28 Robby Thompson	.20	.10	.02
□ 29 Ken Caminiti	.20	.10	.02
□ 30 Jose Canseco	1.25	.60	.12
□ 31 Todd Benzinger	.25	.12	.02
□ 32 Pete Incaviglia	.30	.15	.03
□ 33 John Farrell	.25	.12	.02
□ 34 Casey Candaele	.20	.10	.02
□ 35 Mike Aldrete	.20	.10	.02
□ 36 Ruben Sierra	.75	.35	.07
□ 37 Ellis Burks	.75	.35	.07
□ 38 Tracy Jones	.20	.10	.02
□ 39 Kal Daniels	.35	.17	.03
□ 40 Cory Snyder	.30	.15	.03

1988 Score Young Superstars II

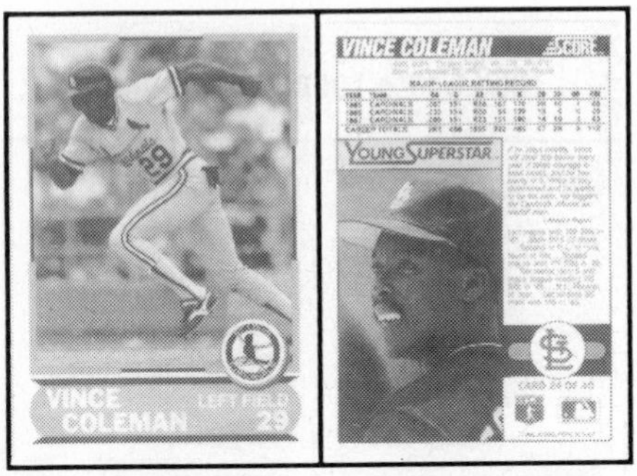

This attractive high-gloss 40-card set of "Young Superstars" was distributed in a small purple box which had the checklist of the set on a side panel of the box. The cards were not distributed as an insert with rak paks as the first series was, but were only available as a complete set from hobby dealers or through a mail-in offer direct from the company. These attractive cards are in full color on the front and also have a full-color small portrait on the card back. The cards are standard size, 2 1/2" by 3 1/2". The cards in this series are distinguishable from the cards in Series I by the fact that this series has a blue and pink border on the card front instead of the (Series I) blue and green border.

	MINT	EXC	G-VG
COMPLETE SET (40)	7.50	3.75	.75
COMMON PLAYER (1-40)	.20	.10	.02
□ 1 Eric Davis	.75	.35	.07
□ 2 Glenn Braggs	.25	.12	.02
□ 3 Dwight Gooden	.60	.30	.06
□ 4 Jose Lind	.25	.12	.02
□ 5 Danny Tartabull	.30	.15	.03
□ 6 Tony Fernandez	.25	.12	.02
□ 7 Julio Franco	.25	.12	.02
□ 8 Andres Galarraga	.30	.15	.03
□ 9 Bobby Bonilla	.50	.25	.05
□ 10 Rob Mallicoat	.20	.10	.02
□ 11 Gerald Young	.20	.10	.02
□ 12 Barry Bonds	.60	.30	.06
□ 13 Jerry Browne	.20	.10	.02
□ 14 Jeff Blauser	.20	.10	.02
□ 15 Mickey Brantley	.20	.10	.02
□ 16 Floyd Youmans	.20	.10	.02
□ 17 Bret Saberhagen	.30	.15	.03
□ 18 Shawon Dunston	.30	.15	.03
□ 19 Len Dykstra	.30	.15	.03
□ 20 Darryl Strawberry	.60	.30	.06
□ 21 Rick Aguilera	.20	.10	.02
□ 22 Ivan Calderon	.25	.12	.02
□ 23 Roger Clemens	.75	.35	.07
□ 24 Vince Coleman	.35	.17	.03
□ 25 Gary Thurman	.20	.10	.02
□ 26 Jeff Treadway	.20	.10	.02
□ 27 Oddibe McDowell	.25	.12	.02
□ 28 Fred McGriff	.50	.25	.05
□ 29 Mark McLemore	.20	.10	.02
□ 30 Jeff Musselman	.20	.10	.02
□ 31 Matt Williams	1.00	.50	.10
□ 32 Dan Plesac	.20	.10	.02
□ 33 Juan Nieves	.20	.10	.02
□ 34 Barry Larkin	.40	.20	.04
□ 35 Greg Matthews	.20	.10	.02
□ 36 Shane Mack	.20	.10	.02
□ 37 Scott Bankhead	.20	.10	.02
□ 38 Eric Bell	.20	.10	.02
□ 39 Greg Swindell	.25	.12	.02
□ 40 Kevin Elster	.20	.10	.02

1988 Score Traded

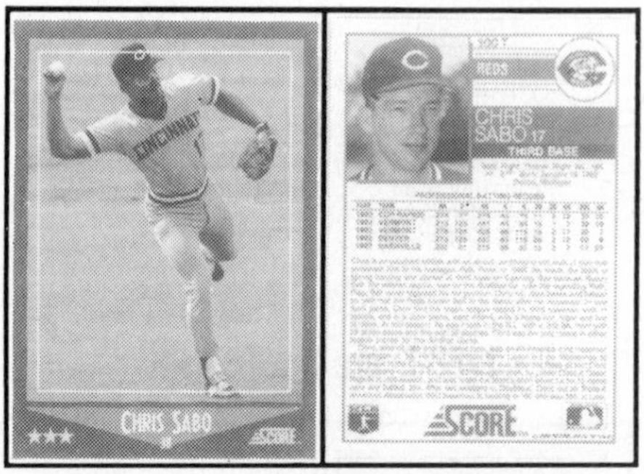

This 110-card set featured traded players (1-65) and rookies (66-110) for the 1988 season. The cards are distinguishable from the regular Score set by the orange borders and by the fact that the numbering on the back has a T suffix. The cards are standard size, 2 1/2" by 3 1/2", and were distributed by Score as a collated set in a special collector box along with some trivia cards. Score also produced a limited "glossy" Traded set, that is valued at one and a half times the value of the regular (non-glossy) set. It should be noted that the set itself (non-glossy) is now considered somewhat scarce. Apparently Score's first attempt at a Rookie/Traded set was produced very conservatively, resulting in a set which is now recognized as being much tougher to find than the other Rookie/Traded sets from the other major companies of that year. The key (extended) rookie cards in this set are Roberto Alomar, Craig Biggio, Mark Grace, Chris Sabo, and Walt Weiss.

	MINT	EXC	G-VG
COMPLETE SET (110)	65.00	32.50	6.50
COMMON PLAYER (1-65)	.12	.06	.01
COMMON PLAYER (66-110)	.12	.06	.01
□ 1T Jack Clark	.25	.12	.02
□ 2T Danny Jackson	.15	.07	.01
□ 3T Brett Butler	.20	.10	.02
□ 4T Kurt Stillwell	.25	.12	.02
□ 5T Tom Brunansky	.20	.10	.02
□ 6T Dennis Lamp	.12	.06	.01
□ 7T Jose DeLeon	.12	.06	.01
□ 8T Tom Herr	.12	.06	.01
□ 9T Keith Moreland	.12	.06	.01
□ 10T Kirk Gibson	.25	.12	.02
□ 11T Bud Black	.20	.10	.02
□ 12T Rafael Ramirez	.12	.06	.01

☐ 13T Luis Salazar	.12	.06	.01
☐ 14T Goose Gossage	.20	.10	.02
☐ 15T Bob Welch	.25	.12	.02
☐ 16T Vance Law	.12	.06	.01
☐ 17T Ray Knight	.20	.10	.02
☐ 18T Dan Quisenberry	.20	.10	.02
☐ 19T Don Slaught	.12	.06	.01
☐ 20T Lee Smith	.20	.10	.02
☐ 21T Rick Cerone	.12	.06	.01
☐ 22T Pat Tabler	.20	.10	.02
☐ 23T Larry McWilliams	.12	.06	.01
☐ 24T Ricky Horton	.12	.06	.01
☐ 25T Graig Nettles	.20	.10	.02
☐ 26T Dan Petry	.12	.06	.01
☐ 27T Jose Rijo	.25	.12	.02
☐ 28T Chili Davis	.20	.10	.02
☐ 29T Dickie Thon	.12	.06	.01
☐ 30T Mackey Sasser	.50	.25	.05
☐ 31T Mickey Tettleton	.25	.12	.02
☐ 32T Rick Dempsey	.12	.06	.01
☐ 33T Ron Hassey	.12	.06	.01
☐ 34T Phil Bradley	.20	.10	.02
☐ 35T Jay Howell	.12	.06	.01
☐ 36T Bill Buckner	.20	.10	.02
☐ 37T Alfredo Griffin	.12	.06	.01
☐ 38T Gary Pettis	.12	.06	.01
☐ 39T Calvin Schiraldi	.12	.06	.01
☐ 40T John Candelaria	.12	.06	.01
☐ 41T Joe Orsulak	.12	.06	.01
☐ 42T Willie Upshaw	.12	.06	.01
☐ 43T Herm Winningham	.12	.06	.01
☐ 44T Ron Kittle	.20	.10	.02
☐ 45T Bob Dernier	.12	.06	.01
☐ 46T Steve Balboni	.12	.06	.01
☐ 47T Steve Shields	.12	.06	.01
☐ 48T Henry Cotto	.12	.06	.01
☐ 49T Dave Henderson	.20	.10	.02
☐ 50T Dave Parker	.25	.12	.02
☐ 51T Mike Young	.12	.06	.01
☐ 52T Mark Salas	.12	.06	.01
☐ 53T Mike Davis	.12	.06	.01
☐ 54T Rafael Santana	.12	.06	.01
☐ 55T Don Baylor	.20	.10	.02
☐ 56T Dan Pasqua	.12	.06	.01
☐ 57T Ernest Riles	.12	.06	.01
☐ 58T Glenn Hubbard	.12	.06	.01
☐ 59T Mike Smithson	.12	.06	.01
☐ 60T Richard Dotson	.12	.06	.01
☐ 61T Jerry Reuss	.12	.06	.01
☐ 62T Mike Jackson	.12	.06	.01
☐ 63T Floyd Bannister	.12	.06	.01
☐ 64T Jesse Orosco	.12	.06	.01
☐ 65T Larry Parrish	.12	.06	.01
☐ 66T Jeff Bittiger	.20	.10	.02
☐ 67T Ray Hayward	.12	.06	.01
☐ 68T Ricky Jordan	1.75	.85	.17
☐ 69T Tommy Gregg	.30	.15	.03
☐ 70T Brady Anderson	.75	.35	.07
☐ 71T Jeff Montgomery	.35	.17	.03
☐ 72T Darryl Hamilton	.45	.22	.04
☐ 73T Cecil Espy	.20	.10	.02
☐ 74T Gregg Briley	1.50	.75	.15
☐ 75T Joey Meyer	.20	.10	.02
☐ 76T Mike MacFarlane	.40	.20	.04
☐ 77T Oswald Peraza	.20	.10	.02
☐ 78T Jack Armstrong	2.00	1.00	.20
☐ 79T Don Heinkel	.20	.10	.02
☐ 80T Mark Grace	25.00	12.50	2.50
☐ 81T Steve Curry	.20	.10	.02
☐ 82T Damon Berryhill	.90	.45	.09
☐ 83T Steve Ellsworth	.20	.10	.02
☐ 84T Pete Smith	.20	.10	.02
☐ 85T Jack McDowell	.75	.35	.07
☐ 86T Rob Dibble	2.00	1.00	.20
☐ 87T Bryan Harvey	.60	.30	.06
☐ 88T John Dopson	.50	.25	.05
☐ 89T Dave Gallagher	.40	.20	.04
☐ 90T Todd Stottlemyre	.75	.35	.07
☐ 91T Mike Schooler	1.00	.50	.10
☐ 92T Don Gordon	.20	.10	.02
☐ 93T Sil Campusano	.45	.22	.04
☐ 94T Jeff Pico	.20	.10	.02
☐ 95T Jay Buhner	1.50	.75	.15
☐ 96T Nelson Santovenia	.35	.17	.03
☐ 97T Al Leiter	.25	.12	.02
☐ 98T Luis Alicea	.20	.10	.02
☐ 99T Pat Borders	.75	.35	.07
☐ 100T Chris Sabo	8.00	4.00	.80
☐ 101T Tim Belcher	.60	.30	.06
☐ 102T Walt Weiss	2.75	1.35	.27
☐ 103T Craig Biggio	2.75	1.35	.27
☐ 104T Don August	.20	.10	.02
☐ 105T Roberto Alomar	7.50	3.75	.75
☐ 106T Todd Burns	.50	.25	.05
☐ 107T John Costello	.20	.10	.02
☐ 108T Melido Perez	.45	.22	.04
☐ 109T Darrin Jackson	.20	.10	.02
☐ 110T Orestes Destrade	.50	.25	.05

1989 Score

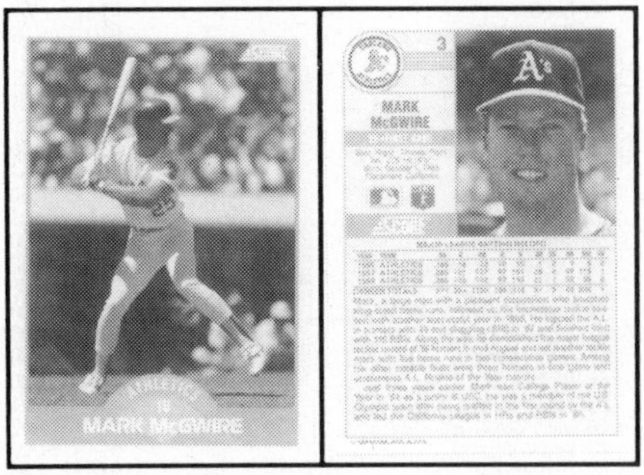

This 660-card set was distributed by Major League Marketing. Cards measure 2 1/2" by 3 1/2" and feature six distinctive inner border (inside a white outer border) colors on the front. Highlights (652-660) and Rookie Prospects (621-651) are included in the set. The set is distinguished by the fact that each card back shows a full-color picture (portrait) of the player. Score "missed" many of the mid-season and later trades; there are numerous examples of inconsistency with regard to the treatment of these players. Study as examples of this inconsistency on handling of late trades, cards numbered 49, 71, 77, 83, 106, 126, 139, 145, 173, 177, 242, 348, 384, 420, 439, 488, 494, and 525. The key rookie cards in this set are Sandy Alomar Jr., Ramon Martinez, and Gary Sheffield.

	MINT	EXC	G-VG
COMPLETE SET (660)	25.00	12.50	2.50
COMMON PLAYER (1-660)	.03	.01	.00
☐ 1 Jose Canseco	1.25	.35	.07
☐ 2 Andre Dawson	.15	.07	.01
☐ 3 Mark McGwire UER (bio says 116 RBI's, should be 118)	.35	.17	.03
☐ 4 Benito Santiago	.12	.06	.01
☐ 5 Rick Reuschel	.06	.03	.00
☐ 6 Fred McGriff	.18	.09	.01
☐ 7 Kal Daniels	.10	.05	.01
☐ 8 Gary Gaetti	.08	.04	.01
☐ 9 Ellis Burks	.25	.12	.02
☐ 10 Darryl Strawberry	.30	.15	.03
☐ 11 Julio Franco	.08	.04	.01
☐ 12 Lloyd Moseby	.06	.03	.00
☐ 13 Jeff Pico	.08	.04	.01
☐ 14 Johnny Ray	.03	.01	.00
☐ 15 Cal Ripken Jr.	.15	.07	.01
☐ 16 Dick Schofield	.03	.01	.00
☐ 17 Mel Hall	.06	.03	.00
☐ 18 Bill Ripken	.03	.01	.00
☐ 19 Brook Jacoby	.06	.03	.00
☐ 20 Kirby Puckett	.30	.15	.03
☐ 21 Bill Doran	.06	.03	.00
☐ 22 Pete O'Brien	.06	.03	.00
☐ 23 Matt Nokes	.06	.03	.00
☐ 24 Brian Fisher	.03	.01	.00
☐ 25 Jack Clark	.10	.05	.01
☐ 26 Gary Pettis	.03	.01	.00
☐ 27 Dave Valle	.03	.01	.00
☐ 28 Willie Wilson	.06	.03	.00
☐ 29 Curt Young	.03	.01	.00
☐ 30 Dale Murphy	.15	.07	.01
☐ 31 Barry Larkin	.15	.07	.01
☐ 32 Dave Stewart	.15	.07	.01
☐ 33 Mike LaValliere	.03	.01	.00
☐ 34 Glenn Hubbard	.03	.01	.00
☐ 35 Ryne Sandberg	.25	.12	.02
☐ 36 Tony Pena	.06	.03	.00

☐ 37 Greg Walker	.03	.01	.00
☐ 38 Von Hayes	.08	.04	.01
☐ 39 Kevin Mitchell	.30	.15	.03
☐ 40 Tim Raines	.12	.06	.01
☐ 41 Keith Hernandez	.10	.05	.01
☐ 42 Keith Moreland	.03	.01	.00
☐ 43 Ruben Sierra	.20	.10	.02
☐ 44 Chet Lemon	.03	.01	.00
☐ 45 Willie Randolph	.06	.03	.00
☐ 46 Andy Allanson	.03	.01	.00
☐ 47 Candy Maldonado	.06	.03	.00
☐ 48 Sid Bream	.03	.01	.00
☐ 49 Denny Walling	.03	.01	.00
☐ 50 Dave Winfield	.15	.07	.01
☐ 51 Alvin Davis	.08	.04	.01
☐ 52 Cory Snyder	.08	.04	.01
☐ 53 Hubie Brooks	.06	.03	.00
☐ 54 Chili Davis	.06	.03	.00
☐ 55 Kevin Seitzer	.10	.05	.01
☐ 56 Jose Uribe	.03	.01	.00
☐ 57 Tony Fernandez	.08	.04	.01
☐ 58 Tim Teufel	.03	.01	.00
☐ 59 Oddibe McDowell	.06	.03	.00
☐ 60 Les Lancaster	.03	.01	.00
☐ 61 Billy Hatcher	.06	.03	.00
☐ 62 Dan Gladden	.03	.01	.00
☐ 63 Marty Barrett	.03	.01	.00
☐ 64 Nick Esasky	.06	.03	.00
☐ 65 Wally Joyner	.12	.06	.01
☐ 66 Mike Greenwell	.25	.12	.02
☐ 67 Ken Williams	.03	.01	.00
☐ 68 Bob Horner	.06	.03	.00
☐ 69 Steve Sax	.08	.04	.01
☐ 70 Rickey Henderson	.25	.12	.02
☐ 71 Mitch Webster	.03	.01	.00
☐ 72 Rob Deer	.06	.03	.00
☐ 73 Jim Presley	.03	.01	.00
☐ 74 Albert Hall	.03	.01	.00
☐ 75A George Brett ERR	1.00	.50	.10
(at age 33)			
☐ 75B George Brett COR	.30	.15	.03
(at age 35)			
☐ 76 Brian Downing	.03	.01	.00
☐ 77 Dave Martinez	.03	.01	.00
☐ 78 Scott Fletcher	.03	.01	.00
☐ 79 Phil Bradley	.06	.03	.00
☐ 80 Ozzie Smith	.12	.06	.01
☐ 81 Larry Sheets	.03	.01	.00
☐ 82 Mike Aldrete	.03	.01	.00
☐ 83 Darnell Coles	.03	.01	.00
☐ 84 Len Dykstra	.12	.06	.01
☐ 85 Jim Rice	.10	.05	.01
☐ 86 Jeff Treadway	.03	.01	.00
☐ 87 Jose Lind	.03	.01	.00
☐ 88 Willie McGee	.10	.05	.01
☐ 89 Mickey Brantley	.03	.01	.00
☐ 90 Tony Gwynn	.15	.07	.01
☐ 91 R.J. Reynolds	.03	.01	.00
☐ 92 Milt Thompson	.03	.01	.00
☐ 93 Kevin McReynolds	.10	.05	.01
☐ 94 Eddie Murray UER	.15	.07	.01
('86 batting .025,			
should be .305)			
☐ 95 Lance Parrish	.08	.04	.01
☐ 96 Ron Kittle	.06	.03	.00
☐ 97 Gerald Young	.03	.01	.00
☐ 98 Ernie Whitt	.03	.01	.00
☐ 99 Jeff Reed	.03	.01	.00
☐ 100 Don Mattingly	.75	.35	.07
☐ 101 Gerald Perry	.03	.01	.00
☐ 102 Vance Law	.03	.01	.00
☐ 103 John Shelby	.03	.01	.00
☐ 104 Chris Sabo	1.00	.50	.10
☐ 105 Danny Tartabull	.08	.04	.01
☐ 106 Glenn Wilson	.03	.01	.00
☐ 107 Mark Davidson	.03	.01	.00
☐ 108 Dave Parker	.08	.04	.01
☐ 109 Eric Davis	.25	.12	.02
☐ 110 Alan Trammell	.12	.06	.01
☐ 111 Ozzie Virgil	.03	.01	.00
☐ 112 Frank Tanana	.03	.01	.00
☐ 113 Rafael Ramirez	.03	.01	.00
☐ 114 Dennis Martinez	.03	.01	.00
☐ 115 Jose DeLeon	.03	.01	.00
☐ 116 Bob Ojeda	.06	.03	.00
☐ 117 Doug Drabek	.10	.05	.01
☐ 118 Andy Hawkins	.03	.01	.00
☐ 119 Greg Maddux	.15	.07	.01
☐ 120 Cecil Fielder UER	.40	.20	.04
(photo on back			
reversed)			
☐ 121 Mike Scioscia	.03	.01	.00
☐ 122 Dan Petry	.03	.01	.00
☐ 123 Terry Kennedy	.03	.01	.00
☐ 124 Kelly Downs	.03	.01	.00
☐ 125 Greg Gross UER	.03	.01	.00
(Gregg on back)			
☐ 126 Fred Lynn	.08	.04	.01
☐ 127 Barry Bonds	.25	.12	.02
☐ 128 Harold Baines	.08	.04	.01
☐ 129 Doyle Alexander	.03	.01	.00
☐ 130 Kevin Elster	.06	.03	.00
☐ 131 Mike Heath	.03	.01	.00
☐ 132 Teddy Higuera	.06	.03	.00
☐ 133 Charlie Leibrandt	.03	.01	.00
☐ 134 Tim Laudner	.03	.01	.00
☐ 135A Ray Knight ERR	1.00	.50	.10
(reverse negative)			
☐ 135B Ray Knight COR	.10	.05	.01
☐ 136 Howard Johnson	.12	.06	.01
☐ 137 Terry Pendleton	.03	.01	.00
☐ 138 Andy McGaffigan	.03	.01	.00
☐ 139 Ken Oberkfell	.03	.01	.00
☐ 140 Butch Wynegar	.03	.01	.00
☐ 141 Rob Murphy	.03	.01	.00
☐ 142 Rich Renteria	.08	.04	.01
☐ 143 Jose Guzman	.03	.01	.00
☐ 144 Andres Galarraga	.08	.04	.01
☐ 145 Ricky Horton	.03	.01	.00
☐ 146 Frank DiPino	.03	.01	.00
☐ 147 Glenn Braggs	.03	.01	.00
☐ 148 John Kruk	.03	.01	.00
☐ 149 Mike Schmidt	.30	.15	.03
☐ 150 Lee Smith	.06	.03	.00
☐ 151 Robin Yount	.15	.07	.01
☐ 152 Mark Eichhorn	.03	.01	.00
☐ 153 DeWayne Buice	.03	.01	.00
☐ 154 B.J. Surhoff	.06	.03	.00
☐ 155 Vince Coleman	.12	.06	.01
☐ 156 Tony Phillips	.03	.01	.00
☐ 157 Willie Fraser	.03	.01	.00
☐ 158 Lance McCullers	.03	.01	.00
☐ 159 Greg Gagne	.03	.01	.00
☐ 160 Jesse Barfield	.08	.04	.01
☐ 161 Mark Langston	.10	.05	.01
☐ 162 Kurt Stillwell	.06	.03	.00
☐ 163 Dion James	.03	.01	.00
☐ 164 Glenn Davis	.12	.06	.01
☐ 165 Walt Weiss	.25	.12	.02
☐ 166 Dave Concepcion	.06	.03	.00
☐ 167 Alfredo Griffin	.03	.01	.00
☐ 168 Don Heinkel	.06	.03	.00
☐ 169 Luis Rivera	.03	.01	.00
☐ 170 Shane Rawley	.03	.01	.00
☐ 171 Darrell Evans	.06	.03	.00
☐ 172 Robby Thompson	.03	.01	.00
☐ 173 Jody Davis	.03	.01	.00
☐ 174 Andy Van Slyke	.10	.05	.01
☐ 175 Wade Boggs UER	.40	.20	.04
(bio says .364,			
should be .356)			
☐ 176 Garry Templeton	.06	.03	.00
('85 stats			
off-centered)			
☐ 177 Gary Redus	.03	.01	.00
☐ 178 Craig Lefferts	.03	.01	.00
☐ 179 Carney Lansford	.08	.04	.01
☐ 180 Ron Darling	.08	.04	.01
☐ 181 Kirk McCaskill	.03	.01	.00
☐ 182 Tony Armas	.03	.01	.00
☐ 183 Steve Farr	.03	.01	.00
☐ 184 Tom Brunansky	.08	.04	.01
☐ 185 Bryan Harvey UER	.15	.07	.01
('87 games 47,			
should be 3)			
☐ 186 Mike Marshall	.08	.04	.01
☐ 187 Bo Diaz	.03	.01	.00
☐ 188 Willie Upshaw	.03	.01	.00
☐ 189 Mike Pagliarulo	.03	.01	.00
☐ 190 Mike Krukow	.03	.01	.00
☐ 191 Tommy Herr	.06	.03	.00
☐ 192 Jim Pankovits	.03	.01	.00
☐ 193 Dwight Evans	.08	.04	.01
☐ 194 Kelly Gruber	.20	.10	.02
☐ 195 Bobby Bonilla	.20	.10	.02
☐ 196 Wallace Johnson	.03	.01	.00
☐ 197 Dave Stieb	.10	.05	.01
☐ 198 Pat Borders	.20	.10	.02
☐ 199 Rafael Palmeiro	.15	.07	.01
☐ 200 Dwight Gooden	.25	.12	.02
☐ 201 Pete Incaviglia	.08	.04	.01
☐ 202 Chris James	.06	.03	.00
☐ 203 Marvell Wynne	.03	.01	.00
☐ 204 Pat Sheridan	.03	.01	.00
☐ 205 Don Baylor	.08	.04	.01
☐ 206 Paul O'Neill	.10	.05	.01
☐ 207 Pete Smith	.10	.05	.01
☐ 208 Mark McLemore	.03	.01	.00

☐ 209 Henry Cotto	.03	.01	.00
☐ 210 Kirk Gibson	.12	.06	.01
☐ 211 Claudell Washington	.06	.03	.00
☐ 212 Randy Bush	.03	.01	.00
☐ 213 Joe Carter	.12	.06	.01
☐ 214 Bill Buckner	.06	.03	.00
☐ 215 Bert Blyleven UER	.08	.04	.01
(wrong birth year)			
☐ 216 Brett Butler	.08	.04	.01
☐ 217 Lee Mazzilli	.03	.01	.00
☐ 218 Spike Owen	.03	.01	.00
☐ 219 Bill Swift	.03	.01	.00
☐ 220 Tim Wallach	.08	.04	.01
☐ 221 David Cone	.12	.06	.01
☐ 222 Don Carman	.03	.01	.00
☐ 223 Rich Gossage	.08	.04	.01
☐ 224 Bob Walk	.03	.01	.00
☐ 225 Dave Righetti	.08	.04	.01
☐ 226 Kevin Bass	.06	.03	.00
☐ 227 Kevin Gross	.03	.01	.00
☐ 228 Tim Burke	.06	.03	.00
☐ 229 Rick Mahler	.03	.01	.00
☐ 230 Lou Whitaker UER	.08	.04	.01
(252 games in '85,			
should be 152)			
☐ 231 Luis Alicea	.06	.03	.00
☐ 232 Roberto Alomar	.50	.25	.05
☐ 233 Bob Boone	.06	.03	.00
☐ 234 Dickie Thon	.03	.01	.00
☐ 235 Shawon Dunston	.12	.06	.01
☐ 236 Pete Stanicek	.03	.01	.00
☐ 237 Craig Biggio	.30	.15	.03
(inconsistent design,			
portrait on front)			
☐ 238 Dennis Boyd	.06	.03	.00
☐ 239 Tom Candiotti	.03	.01	.00
☐ 240 Gary Carter	.10	.05	.01
☐ 241 Mike Stanley	.03	.01	.00
☐ 242 Ken Phelps	.03	.01	.00
☐ 243 Chris Bosio	.03	.01	.00
☐ 244 Les Straker	.03	.01	.00
☐ 245 Dave Smith	.03	.01	.00
☐ 246 John Candelaria	.03	.01	.00
☐ 247 Joe Orsulak	.03	.01	.00
☐ 248 Storm Davis	.06	.03	.00
☐ 249 Floyd Bannister UER	.03	.01	.00
(ML Batting Record)			
☐ 250 Jack Morris	.08	.04	.01
☐ 251 Bret Saberhagen	.15	.07	.01
☐ 252 Tom Niedenfuer	.03	.01	.00
☐ 253 Neal Heaton	.03	.01	.00
☐ 254 Eric Show	.03	.01	.00
☐ 255 Juan Samuel	.08	.04	.01
☐ 256 Dale Sveum	.03	.01	.00
☐ 257 Jim Gott	.03	.01	.00
☐ 258 Scott Garrelts	.03	.01	.00
☐ 259 Larry McWilliams	.03	.01	.00
☐ 260 Steve Bedrosian	.06	.03	.00
☐ 261 Jack Howell	.03	.01	.00
☐ 262 Jay Tibbs	.03	.01	.00
☐ 263 Jamie Moyer	.03	.01	.00
☐ 264 Doug Sisk	.03	.01	.00
☐ 265 Todd Worrell	.08	.04	.01
☐ 266 John Farrell	.03	.01	.00
☐ 267 Dave Collins	.03	.01	.00
☐ 268 Sid Fernandez	.08	.04	.01
☐ 269 Tom Brookens	.03	.01	.00
☐ 270 Shane Mack	.06	.03	.00
☐ 271 Paul Kilgus	.03	.01	.00
☐ 272 Chuck Crim	.03	.01	.00
☐ 273 Bob Knepper	.03	.01	.00
☐ 274 Mike Moore	.06	.03	.00
☐ 275 Guillermo Hernandez	.03	.01	.00
☐ 276 Dennis Eckersley	.12	.06	.01
☐ 277 Graig Nettles	.08	.04	.01
☐ 278 Rich Dotson	.03	.01	.00
☐ 279 Larry Herndon	.03	.01	.00
☐ 280 Gene Larkin	.03	.01	.00
☐ 281 Roger McDowell	.06	.03	.00
☐ 282 Greg Swindell	.08	.04	.01
☐ 283 Juan Agosto	.03	.01	.00
☐ 284 Jeff Robinson	.06	.03	.00
Detroit Tigers			
☐ 285 Mike Dunne	.03	.01	.00
☐ 286 Greg Mathews	.03	.01	.00
☐ 287 Kent Tekulve	.03	.01	.00
☐ 288 Jerry Mumphrey	.03	.01	.00
☐ 289 Jack McDowell	.12	.06	.01
☐ 290 Frank Viola	.12	.06	.01
☐ 291 Mark Gubicza	.06	.03	.00
☐ 292 Dave Schmidt	.03	.01	.00
☐ 293 Mike Henneman	.03	.01	.00
☐ 294 Jimmy Jones	.03	.01	.00
☐ 295 Charlie Hough	.03	.01	.00

☐ 296 Rafael Santana	.03	.01	.00
☐ 297 Chris Speier	.03	.01	.00
☐ 298 Mike Witt	.03	.01	.00
☐ 299 Pascual Perez	.06	.03	.00
☐ 300 Nolan Ryan	.50	.25	.05
☐ 301 Mitch Williams	.06	.03	.00
☐ 302 Mookie Wilson	.06	.03	.00
☐ 303 Mackey Sasser	.08	.04	.01
☐ 304 John Cerutti	.03	.01	.00
☐ 305 Jeff Reardon	.08	.04	.01
☐ 306 Randy Myers UER	.06	.03	.00
(6 hits in '87,			
should be 61)			
☐ 307 Greg Brock	.03	.01	.00
☐ 308 Bob Welch	.10	.05	.01
☐ 309 Jeff Robinson	.03	.01	.00
Pittsburgh Pirates			
☐ 310 Harold Reynolds	.06	.03	.00
☐ 311 Jim Walewander	.03	.01	.00
☐ 312 Dave Magadan	.12	.06	.01
☐ 313 Jim Gantner	.03	.01	.00
☐ 314 Walt Terrell	.03	.01	.00
☐ 315 Wally Backman	.03	.01	.00
☐ 316 Luis Salazar	.03	.01	.00
☐ 317 Rick Rhoden	.03	.01	.00
☐ 318 Tom Henke	.06	.03	.00
☐ 319 Mike Macfarlane	.12	.06	.01
☐ 320 Dan Plesac	.03	.01	.00
☐ 321 Calvin Schiraldi	.03	.01	.00
☐ 322 Stan Javier	.03	.01	.00
☐ 323 Devon White	.08	.04	.01
☐ 324 Scott Bradley	.03	.01	.00
☐ 325 Bruce Hurst	.06	.03	.00
☐ 326 Manny Lee	.03	.01	.00
☐ 327 Rick Aguilera	.03	.01	.00
☐ 328 Bruce Ruffin	.03	.01	.00
☐ 329 Ed Whitson	.06	.03	.00
☐ 330 Bo Jackson	.75	.35	.07
☐ 331 Ivan Calderon	.06	.03	.00
☐ 332 Mickey Hatcher	.03	.01	.00
☐ 333 Barry Jones	.06	.03	.00
☐ 334 Ron Hassey	.03	.01	.00
☐ 335 Bill Wegman	.03	.01	.00
☐ 336 Damon Berryhill	.15	.07	.01
☐ 337 Steve Ontiveros	.03	.01	.00
☐ 338 Dan Pasqua	.03	.01	.00
☐ 339 Bill Pecota	.03	.01	.00
☐ 340 Greg Cadaret	.08	.04	.01
☐ 341 Scott Bankhead	.06	.03	.00
☐ 342 Ron Guidry	.08	.04	.01
☐ 343 Danny Heep	.03	.01	.00
☐ 344 Bob Brower	.03	.01	.00
☐ 345 Rich Gedman	.03	.01	.00
☐ 346 Nelson Santovenia	.12	.06	.01
☐ 347 George Bell	.12	.06	.01
☐ 348 Ted Power	.03	.01	.00
☐ 349 Mark Grant	.03	.01	.00
☐ 350A Roger Clemens ERR	4.00	2.00	.40
(778 career wins)			
☐ 350B Roger Clemens COR	.50	.25	.05
(78 career wins)			
☐ 351 Bill Long	.03	.01	.00
☐ 352 Jay Bell	.10	.05	.01
☐ 353 Steve Balboni	.03	.01	.00
☐ 354 Bob Kipper	.03	.01	.00
☐ 355 Steve Jeltz	.03	.01	.00
☐ 356 Jesse Orosco	.03	.01	.00
☐ 357 Bob Dernier	.03	.01	.00
☐ 358 Mickey Tettleton	.06	.03	.00
☐ 359 Duane Ward	.03	.01	.00
☐ 360 Darrin Jackson	.08	.04	.01
☐ 361 Rey Quinones	.03	.01	.00
☐ 362 Mark Grace	1.00	.50	.10
☐ 363 Steve Lake	.03	.01	.00
☐ 364 Pat Perry	.03	.01	.00
☐ 365 Terry Steinbach	.08	.04	.01
☐ 366 Alan Ashby	.03	.01	.00
☐ 367 Jeff Montgomery	.08	.04	.01
☐ 368 Steve Buechele	.03	.01	.00
☐ 369 Chris Brown	.03	.01	.00
☐ 370 Orel Hershiser	.15	.07	.01
☐ 371 Todd Benzinger	.06	.03	.00
☐ 372 Ron Gant	.25	.12	.02
☐ 373 Paul Assenmacher	.03	.01	.00
☐ 374 Joey Meyer	.06	.03	.00
☐ 375 Neil Allen	.03	.01	.00
☐ 376 Mike Davis	.03	.01	.00
☐ 377 Jeff Parrett	.06	.03	.00
☐ 378 Jay Howell	.03	.01	.00
☐ 379 Rafael Belliard	.03	.01	.00
☐ 380 Luis Polonia UER	.06	.03	.00
(2 triples in '87,			
should be 10)			
☐ 381 Keith Atherton	.03	.01	.00

☐ 382 Kent Hrbek	.10	.05	.01
☐ 383 Bob Stanley	.03	.01	.00
☐ 384 Dave LaPoint	.03	.01	.00
☐ 385 Rance Mulliniks	.03	.01	.00
☐ 386 Melido Perez	.10	.05	.01
☐ 387 Doug Jones	.06	.03	.00
☐ 388 Steve Lyons	.03	.01	.00
☐ 389 Alejandro Pena	.03	.01	.00
☐ 390 Frank White	.06	.03	.00
☐ 391 Pat Tabler	.03	.01	.00
☐ 392 Eric Plunk	.03	.01	.00
☐ 393 Mike Maddux	.03	.01	.00
☐ 394 Allan Anderson	.06	.03	.00
☐ 395 Bob Brenly	.03	.01	.00
☐ 396 Rick Cerone	.03	.01	.00
☐ 397 Scott Terry	.03	.01	.00
☐ 398 Mike Jackson	.03	.01	.00
☐ 399 Bobby Thigpen UER	.10	.05	.01
(bio says 37 saves in			
'88, should be 34)			
☐ 400 Don Sutton	.10	.05	.01
☐ 401 Cecil Espy	.08	.04	.01
☐ 402 Junior Ortiz	.03	.01	.00
☐ 403 Mike Smithson	.03	.01	.00
☐ 404 Bud Black	.06	.03	.00
☐ 405 Tom Foley	.03	.01	.00
☐ 406 Andres Thomas	.03	.01	.00
☐ 407 Rick Sutcliffe	.08	.04	.01
☐ 408 Brian Harper	.06	.03	.00
☐ 409 John Smiley	.03	.01	.00
☐ 410 Juan Nieves	.03	.01	.00
☐ 411 Shawn Abner	.06	.03	.00
☐ 412 Wes Gardner	.06	.03	.00
☐ 413 Darren Daulton	.06	.03	.00
☐ 414 Juan Berenguer	.03	.01	.00
☐ 415 Charles Hudson	.03	.01	.00
☐ 416 Rick Honeycutt	.03	.01	.00
☐ 417 Greg Booker	.03	.01	.00
☐ 418 Tim Belcher	.12	.06	.01
☐ 419 Don August	.03	.01	.00
☐ 420 Dale Mohorcic	.03	.01	.00
☐ 421 Steve Lombardozzi	.03	.01	.00
☐ 422 Atlee Hammaker	.03	.01	.00
☐ 423 Jerry Don Gleaton	.03	.01	.00
☐ 424 Scott Bailes	.03	.01	.00
☐ 425 Bruce Sutter	.08	.04	.01
☐ 426 Randy Ready	.03	.01	.00
☐ 427 Jerry Reed	.03	.01	.00
☐ 428 Bryn Smith	.03	.01	.00
☐ 429 Tim Leary	.06	.03	.00
☐ 430 Mark Clear	.03	.01	.00
☐ 431 Terry Leach	.06	.03	.00
☐ 432 John Moses	.03	.01	.00
☐ 433 Ozzie Guillen	.08	.04	.01
☐ 434 Gene Nelson	.03	.01	.00
☐ 435 Gary Ward	.03	.01	.00
☐ 436 Luis Aguayo	.03	.01	.00
☐ 437 Fernando Valenzuela	.10	.05	.01
☐ 438 Jeff Russell	.03	.01	.00
☐ 439 Cecilio Guante	.03	.01	.00
☐ 440 Don Robinson	.03	.01	.00
☐ 441 Rick Anderson	.03	.01	.00
☐ 442 Tom Glavine	.06	.03	.00
☐ 443 Daryl Boston	.06	.03	.00
☐ 444 Joe Price	.03	.01	.00
☐ 445 Stewart Cliburn	.03	.01	.00
☐ 446 Manny Trillo	.03	.01	.00
☐ 447 Joel Skinner	.03	.01	.00
☐ 448 Charlie Puleo	.03	.01	.00
☐ 449 Carlton Fisk	.12	.06	.01
☐ 450 Will Clark	.60	.30	.06
☐ 451 Otis Nixon	.03	.01	.00
☐ 452 Rick Schu	.03	.01	.00
☐ 453 Todd Stottlemyre UER	.15	.07	.01
(ML Batting Record)			
☐ 454 Tim Birtsas	.03	.01	.00
☐ 455 Dave Gallagher	.12	.06	.01
☐ 456 Barry Lyons	.03	.01	.00
☐ 457 Fred Manrique	.03	.01	.00
☐ 458 Ernest Riles	.03	.01	.00
☐ 459 Doug Jennings	.15	.07	.01
☐ 460 Joe Magrane	.08	.04	.01
☐ 461 Jamie Quirk	.03	.01	.00
☐ 462 Jack Armstrong	.25	.12	.02
☐ 463 Bobby Witt	.10	.05	.01
☐ 464 Keith Miller	.03	.01	.00
New York Mets			
☐ 465 Todd Burns	.20	.10	.02
☐ 466 John Dopson	.20	.10	.02
☐ 467 Rich Yett	.03	.01	.00
☐ 468 Craig Reynolds	.03	.01	.00
☐ 469 Dave Bergman	.03	.01	.00
☐ 470 Rex Hudler	.06	.03	.00
☐ 471 Eric King	.03	.01	.00
☐ 472 Joaquin Andujar	.06	.03	.00
☐ 473 Sil Campusano	.20	.10	.02
☐ 474 Terry Mulholland	.03	.01	.00
☐ 475 Mike Flanagan	.03	.01	.00
☐ 476 Greg Harris	.03	.01	.00
Philadelphia Phillies			
☐ 477 Tommy John	.08	.04	.01
☐ 478 Dave Anderson	.03	.01	.00
☐ 479 Fred Toliver	.03	.01	.00
☐ 480 Jimmy Key	.06	.03	.00
☐ 481 Donell Nixon	.03	.01	.00
☐ 482 Mark Portugal	.03	.01	.00
☐ 483 Tom Pagnozzi	.03	.01	.00
☐ 484 Jeff Kunkel	.03	.01	.00
☐ 485 Frank Williams	.03	.01	.00
☐ 486 Jody Reed	.10	.05	.01
☐ 487 Roberto Kelly	.15	.07	.01
☐ 488 Shawn Hillegas UER	.03	.01	.00
(165 innings in '87,			
should be 165.2)			
☐ 489 Jerry Reuss	.03	.01	.00
☐ 490 Mark Davis	.10	.05	.01
☐ 491 Jeff Sellers	.03	.01	.00
☐ 492 Zane Smith	.06	.03	.00
☐ 493 Al Newman	.03	.01	.00
☐ 494 Mike Young	.03	.01	.00
☐ 495 Larry Parrish	.03	.01	.00
☐ 496 Herm Winningham	.03	.01	.00
☐ 497 Carmen Castillo	.03	.01	.00
☐ 498 Joe Hesketh	.03	.01	.00
☐ 499 Darrell Miller	.03	.01	.00
☐ 500 Mike LaCoss	.03	.01	.00
☐ 501 Charlie Lea	.03	.01	.00
☐ 502 Bruce Benedict	.03	.01	.00
☐ 503 Chuck Finley	.10	.05	.01
☐ 504 Brad Wellman	.03	.01	.00
☐ 505 Tim Crews	.03	.01	.00
☐ 506 Ken Gerhart	.03	.01	.00
☐ 507 Brian Holton UER	.08	.04	.01
(born 1/25/65 Denver,			
should be 11/29/59			
in McKeesport)			
☐ 508 Dennis Lamp	.03	.01	.00
☐ 509 Bobby Meacham UER	.06	.03	.00
('84 games 099)			
☐ 510 Tracy Jones	.03	.01	.00
☐ 511 Mike Fitzgerald	.03	.01	.00
Montreal Expos			
☐ 512 Jeff Bittiger	.10	.05	.01
☐ 513 Tim Flannery	.03	.01	.00
☐ 514 Ray Hayward	.03	.01	.00
☐ 515 Dave Leiper	.03	.01	.00
☐ 516 Rod Scurry	.03	.01	.00
☐ 517 Carmelo Martinez	.03	.01	.00
☐ 518 Curtis Wilkerson	.03	.01	.00
☐ 519 Stan Jefferson	.06	.03	.00
☐ 520 Dan Quisenberry	.08	.04	.01
☐ 521 Lloyd McClendon	.06	.03	.00
☐ 522 Steve Trout	.03	.01	.00
☐ 523 Larry Andersen	.03	.01	.00
☐ 524 Don Aase	.03	.01	.00
☐ 525 Bob Forsch	.03	.01	.00
☐ 526 Geno Petralli	.03	.01	.00
☐ 527 Angel Salazar	.03	.01	.00
☐ 528 Mike Schooler	.25	.12	.02
☐ 529 Jose Oquendo	.03	.01	.00
☐ 530 Jay Buhner	.12	.06	.01
☐ 531 Tom Bolton	.15	.07	.01
☐ 532 Al Nipper	.03	.01	.00
☐ 533 Dave Henderson	.06	.03	.00
☐ 534 John Costello	.06	.03	.00
☐ 535 Donnie Moore	.03	.01	.00
☐ 536 Mike Laga	.03	.01	.00
☐ 537 Mike Gallego	.03	.01	.00
☐ 538 Jim Clancy	.03	.01	.00
☐ 539 Joel Youngblood	.03	.01	.00
☐ 540 Rick Leach	.03	.01	.00
☐ 541 Kevin Romine	.03	.01	.00
☐ 542 Mark Salas	.03	.01	.00
☐ 543 Greg Minton	.03	.01	.00
☐ 544 Dave Palmer	.03	.01	.00
☐ 545 Dwayne Murphy UER	.03	.01	.00
(game-sinning)			
☐ 546 Jim Deshaies	.03	.01	.00
☐ 547 Don Gordon	.06	.03	.00
☐ 548 Ricky Jordan	.35	.17	.03
☐ 549 Mike Boddicker	.06	.03	.00
☐ 550 Mike Scott	.10	.05	.01
☐ 551 Jeff Ballard	.10	.05	.01
☐ 552A Jose Rijo ERR	1.00	.50	.10
(uniform listed as			
27 on back)			

□ 552B Jose Rijo COR (uniform listed as 24 on back)	.20	.10	.02
□ 553 Danny Darwin	.06	.03	.00
□ 554 Tom Browning	.06	.03	.00
□ 555 Danny Jackson	.06	.03	.00
□ 556 Rick Dempsey	.03	.01	.00
□ 557 Jeffrey Leonard	.06	.03	.00
□ 558 Jeff Musselman	.03	.01	.00
□ 559 Ron Robinson	.03	.01	.00
□ 560 John Tudor	.08	.04	.01
□ 561 Don Slaught	.03	.01	.00
□ 562 Dennis Rasmussen	.03	.01	.00
□ 563 Brady Anderson	.20	.10	.02
□ 564 Pedro Guerrero	.10	.05	.01
□ 565 Paul Molitor	.10	.05	.01
□ 566 Terry Clark	.08	.04	.01
□ 567 Terry Puhl	.03	.01	.00
□ 568 Mike Campbell	.08	.04	.01
□ 569 Paul Mirabella	.03	.01	.00
□ 570 Jeff Hamilton	.03	.01	.00
□ 571 Oswald Peraza	.08	.04	.01
□ 572 Bob McClure	.03	.01	.00
□ 573 Jose Bautista	.08	.04	.01
□ 574 Alex Trevino	.03	.01	.00
□ 575 John Franco	.06	.03	.00
□ 576 Mark Parent	.10	.05	.01
□ 577 Nelson Liriano	.03	.01	.00
□ 578 Steve Shields	.03	.01	.00
□ 579 Odell Jones	.03	.01	.00
□ 580 Al Leiter	.10	.05	.01
□ 581 Dave Stapleton	.08	.04	.01
□ 582 World Series '88 Orel Hershiser Jose Canseco Kirk Gibson Dave Stewart	.12	.06	.01
□ 583 Donnie Hill	.03	.01	.00
□ 584 Chuck Jackson	.03	.01	.00
□ 585 Rene Gonzales	.06	.03	.00
□ 586 Tracy Woodson	.06	.03	.00
□ 587 Jim Adduci	.03	.01	.00
□ 588 Mario Soto	.03	.01	.00
□ 589 Jeff Blauser	.03	.01	.00
□ 590 Jim Traber	.03	.01	.00
□ 591 Jon Perlman	.06	.03	.00
□ 592 Mark Williamson	.08	.04	.01
□ 593 Dave Meads	.03	.01	.00
□ 594 Jim Eisenreich	.03	.01	.00
□ 595A Paul Gibson P1	1.50	.75	.15
□ 595B Paul Gibson P2 (airbrushed leg on player in background)	.15	.07	.01
□ 596 Mike Birkbeck	.03	.01	.00
□ 597 Terry Francona	.03	.01	.00
□ 598 Paul Zuvella	.03	.01	.00
□ 599 Franklin Stubbs	.06	.03	.00
□ 600 Gregg Jefferies	.90	.45	.09
□ 601 John Cangelosi	.03	.01	.00
□ 602 Mike Sharperson	.03	.01	.00
□ 603 Mike Diaz	.03	.01	.00
□ 604 Gary Varsho	.10	.05	.01
□ 605 Terry Blocker	.10	.05	.01
□ 606 Charlie O'Brien	.08	.04	.01
□ 607 Jim Eppard	.06	.03	.00
□ 608 John Davis	.03	.01	.00
□ 609 Ken Griffey Sr.	.10	.05	.01
□ 610 Buddy Bell	.06	.03	.00
□ 611 Ted Simmons UER ('78 stats Cardinal)	.08	.04	.01
□ 612 Matt Williams	.30	.15	.03
□ 613 Danny Cox	.03	.01	.00
□ 614 Al Pedrique	.03	.01	.00
□ 615 Ron Oester	.03	.01	.00
□ 616 John Smoltz	.40	.20	.04
□ 617 Bob Melvin	.03	.01	.00
□ 618 Rob Dibble	.30	.15	.03
□ 619 Kirt Manwaring	.03	.01	.00
□ 620 Felix Fermin	.06	.03	.00
□ 621 Doug Dascenzo	.10	.05	.01
□ 622 Bill Brennan	.08	.04	.01
□ 623 Carlos Quintana	.45	.22	.04
□ 624 Mike Harkey UER (13 and 31 walks in '88, should be 35 and 33)	.40	.20	.04
□ 625 Gary Sheffield	1.25	.60	.12
□ 626 Tom Prince	.06	.03	.00
□ 627 Steve Searcy	.15	.07	.01
□ 628 Charlie Hayes (listed as outfielder)	.15	.07	.01
□ 629 Felix Jose	.25	.12	.02
□ 630 Sandy Alomar Jr.	1.00	.50	.10
□ 631 Derek Lilliquist	.15	.07	.01
□ 632 Geronimo Berroa	.10	.05	.01
□ 633 Luis Medina	.20	.10	.02
□ 634 Tom Gordon UER (height 6'0")	.60	.30	.06
□ 635 Ramon Martinez	1.25	.60	.12
□ 636 Craig Worthington	.20	.10	.02
□ 637 Edgar Martinez	.30	.15	.03
□ 638 Chad Kreuter	.12	.06	.01
□ 639 Ron Jones	.20	.10	.02
□ 640 Van Snider	.15	.07	.01
□ 641 Lance Blankenship	.10	.05	.01
□ 642 Dwight Smith UER (10 HR's in '87, should be 18)	.90	.45	.09
□ 643 Cameron Drew	.12	.06	.01
□ 644 Jerald Clark	.20	.10	.02
□ 645 Randy Johnson	.40	.20	.04
□ 646 Norm Charlton	.20	.10	.02
□ 647 Todd Frohwirth UER (southpaw on back)	.08	.04	.01
□ 648 Luis De Los Santos	.15	.07	.01
□ 649 Tim Jones	.10	.05	.01
□ 650 Dave West UER (ML hits 3, should be 6)	.20	.10	.02
□ 651 Bob Milacki	.20	.10	.02
□ 652 Wrigley Field HL (Let There Be Lights)	.03	.01	.00
□ 653 Orel Hershiser HL (The Streak)	.12	.06	.01
□ 654A Wade Boggs HL ERR (Wade Whacks 'Em) ("seaason" on back)	3.50	1.75	.35
□ 654B Wade Boggs HL COR (Wade Whacks 'Em)	.35	.17	.03
□ 655 Jose Canseco HL (One of a Kind)	.40	.20	.04
□ 656 Doug Jones HL (Doug Sets Saves)	.06	.03	.00
□ 657 Rickey Henderson HL (Rickey Rocks 'Em)	.25	.12	.02
□ 658 Tom Browning HL (Tom Perfect Pitches)	.06	.03	.00
□ 659 Mike Greenwell HL (Greenwell Gamers)	.15	.07	.01
□ 660 Boston Red Sox HL (Joe Morgan MG, Sox Sock 'Em)	.06	.03	.00

1989 Score Hottest 100 Rookies

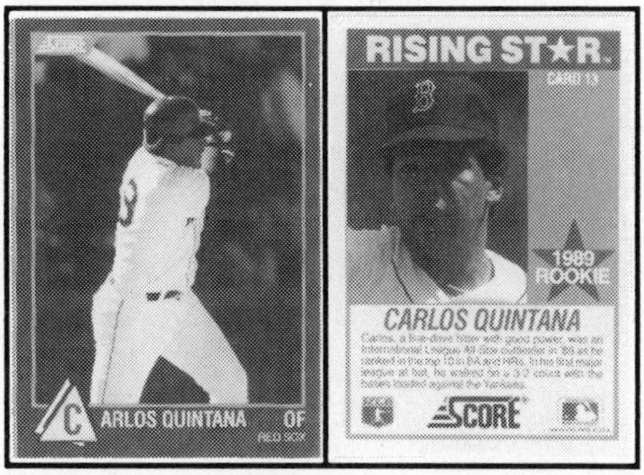

This set was distributed by Publications International in January 1989 through many retail stores and chains; the card set was packaged along with a colorful 48-page book for a suggested retail price of 12.95. Supposedly 225,000 sets were produced. The cards measure the standard 2 1/2" by 3 1/2" and show full color on both sides of the card. The cards were produced by Score as indicated on the card backs. The set is subtitled "Rising Star" on the reverse. The first six cards (1-6) of a 12-card set of Score's trivia cards, subtitled "Rookies to Remember" is included along with each set. The cards are numbered on the back. This set is distinguished by the sharp blue borders and the player's first initial inside a yellow triangle in the lower left corner of the obverse.

	MINT	EXC	G-VG
COMPLETE SET (100)	12.00	6.00	1.20
COMMON PLAYER (1-100)	.05	.02	.00
☐ 1 Gregg Jefferies	1.00	.50	.10
☐ 2 Vicente Palacios	.10	.05	.01
☐ 3 Cameron Drew	.10	.05	.01
☐ 4 Doug Dascenzo	.10	.05	.01
☐ 5 Luis Medina	.15	.07	.01
☐ 6 Craig Worthington	.20	.10	.02
☐ 7 Rob Ducey	.10	.05	.01
☐ 8 Hal Morris	.50	.25	.05
☐ 9 Bill Brennan	.10	.05	.01
☐ 10 Gary Sheffield	.75	.35	.07
☐ 11 Mike Devereaux	.15	.07	.01
☐ 12 Hensley Meulens	.60	.30	.06
☐ 13 Carlos Quintana	.35	.17	.03
☐ 14 Todd Frohwirth	.05	.02	.00
☐ 15 Scott Lusader	.05	.02	.00
☐ 16 Mark Carreon	.10	.05	.01
☐ 17 Torey Lovullo	.05	.02	.00
☐ 18 Randy Velarde	.05	.02	.00
☐ 19 Billy Bean	.05	.02	.00
☐ 20 Lance Blankenship	.05	.02	.00
☐ 21 Chris Gwynn	.10	.05	.01
☐ 22 Felix Jose	.20	.10	.02
☐ 23 Derek Lilliquist	.05	.02	.00
☐ 24 Gary Thurman	.10	.05	.01
☐ 25 Ron Jones	.15	.07	.01
☐ 26 Dave Justice	1.50	.75	.15
☐ 27 Johnny Paredes	.05	.02	.00
☐ 28 Tim Jones	.05	.02	.00
☐ 29 Jose Gonzales	.05	.02	.00
☐ 30 Geronimo Berroa	.05	.02	.00
☐ 31 Trevor Wilson	.10	.05	.01
☐ 32 Morris Madden	.05	.02	.00
☐ 33 Lance Johnson	.10	.05	.01
☐ 34 Marvin Freeman	.05	.02	.00
☐ 35 Jose Cecena	.05	.02	.00
☐ 36 Jim Corsi	.05	.02	.00
☐ 37 Rolando Roomes	.10	.05	.01
☐ 38 Scott Medvin	.05	.02	.00
☐ 39 Charlie Hayes	.10	.05	.01
☐ 40 Edgar Martinez	.25	.12	.02
☐ 41 Van Snider	.10	.05	.01
☐ 42 John Fishel	.05	.02	.00
☐ 43 Bruce Fields	.05	.02	.00
☐ 44 Darryl Hamilton	.10	.05	.01
☐ 45 Tom Prince	.05	.02	.00
☐ 46 Kirt Manwaring	.10	.05	.01
☐ 47 Steve Searcy	.10	.05	.01
☐ 48 Mike Harkey	.35	.17	.03
☐ 49 German Gonzalez	.05	.02	.00
☐ 50 Tony Perezchica	.05	.02	.00
☐ 51 Chad Kreuter	.05	.02	.00
☐ 52 Luis De los Santos	.10	.05	.01
☐ 53 Steve Curry	.05	.02	.00
☐ 54 Greg Briley	.25	.12	.02
☐ 55 Ramon Martinez	1.00	.50	.10
☐ 56 Ron Tingley	.05	.02	.00
☐ 57 Randy Kramer	.05	.02	.00
☐ 58 Alex Madrid	.05	.02	.00
☐ 59 Kevin Reimer	.10	.05	.01
☐ 60 Dave Otto	.10	.05	.01
☐ 61 Ken Patterson	.05	.02	.00
☐ 62 Keith Miller	.10	.05	.01
☐ 63 Randy Johnson	.25	.12	.02
☐ 64 Dwight Smith	.40	.20	.04
☐ 65 Eric Yelding	.15	.07	.01
☐ 66 Bob Geren	.10	.05	.01
☐ 67 Shane Turner	.15	.07	.01
☐ 68 Tom Gordon	.40	.20	.04
☐ 69 Jeff Huson	.10	.05	.01
☐ 70 Marty Brown	.10	.05	.01
☐ 71 Nelson Santovenia	.10	.05	.01
☐ 72 Roberto Alomar	.40	.20	.04
☐ 73 Mike Schooler	.20	.10	.02
☐ 74 Pete Smith	.10	.05	.01
☐ 75 John Costello	.10	.05	.01
☐ 76 Chris Sabo	.50	.25	.05
☐ 77 Damon Berryhill	.20	.10	.02
☐ 78 Mark Grace	1.00	.50	.10
☐ 79 Melido Perez	.15	.07	.01
☐ 80 Al Leiter	.10	.05	.01
☐ 81 Todd Stottlemyre	.15	.07	.01
☐ 82 Mackey Sasser	.15	.07	.01
☐ 83 Don August	.10	.05	.01
☐ 84 Jeff Treadway	.10	.05	.01
☐ 85 Jody Reed	.15	.07	.01
☐ 86 Mike Campbell	.10	.05	.01
☐ 87 Ron Gant	.75	.35	.07
☐ 88 Ricky Jordan	.25	.12	.02
☐ 89 Terry Clark	.05	.02	.00
☐ 90 Roberto Kelly	.50	.25	.05
☐ 91 Pat Borders	.10	.05	.01
☐ 92 Bryan Harvey	.10	.05	.01
☐ 93 Joey Meyer	.05	.02	.00
☐ 94 Tim Belcher	.15	.07	.01
☐ 95 Walt Weiss	.35	.17	.03
☐ 96 Dave Gallagher	.10	.05	.01
☐ 97 Mike Macfarlane	.10	.05	.01
☐ 98 Craig Biggio	.35	.17	.03
☐ 99 Jack Armstrong	.25	.12	.02
☐ 100 Todd Burns	.10	.05	.01

1989 Score Hottest 100 Stars

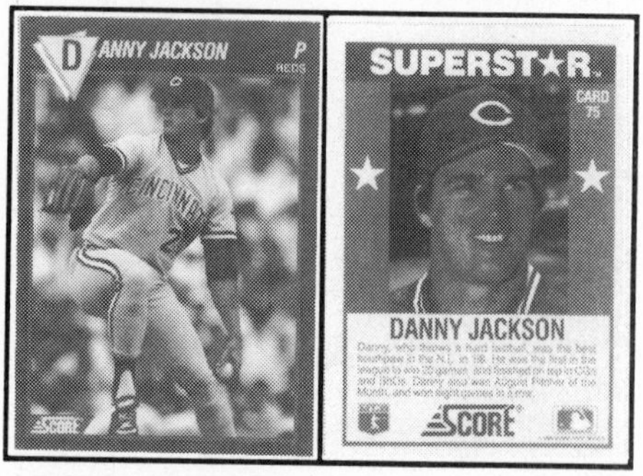

This set was distributed by Publications International in January 1989 through many retail stores and chains; the card set was packaged along with a colorful 48-page book for a suggested retail price of 12.95. Supposedly 225,000 sets were produced. The cards measure the standard 2 1/2" by 3 1/2" and show full color on both sides of the card. The cards were produced by Score as indicated on the card backs. The set is subtitled "Superstar" on the reverse. The last six cards (7-12) of a 12-card set of Score's trivia cards, subtitled "Rookies to Remember" is included along with each set. The cards are numbered on the back. This set is distinguished by the sharp red borders and the player's first initial inside a yellow triangle in the upper left corner of the obverse.

	MINT	EXC	G-VG
COMPLETE SET (100)	12.00	6.00	1.20
COMMON PLAYER (1-100)	.05	.02	.00
☐ 1 Jose Canseco	1.25	.60	.12
☐ 2 David Cone	.20	.10	.02
☐ 3 Dave Winfield	.20	.10	.02
☐ 4 George Brett	.35	.17	.03
☐ 5 Frank Viola	.15	.07	.01
☐ 6 Cory Snyder	.10	.05	.01
☐ 7 Alan Trammell	.20	.10	.02
☐ 8 Dwight Evans	.10	.05	.01
☐ 9 Tim Leary	.05	.02	.00
☐ 10 Don Mattingly	1.00	.50	.10
☐ 11 Kirby Puckett	.75	.35	.07
☐ 12 Carney Lansford	.15	.07	.01
☐ 13 Dennis Martinez	.05	.02	.00
☐ 14 Kent Hrbek	.15	.07	.01
☐ 15 Doc Gooden	.40	.20	.04
☐ 16 Dennis Eckersley	.20	.10	.02
☐ 17 Kevin Seitzer	.20	.10	.02
☐ 18 Lee Smith	.05	.02	.00
☐ 19 Danny Tartabull	.15	.07	.01
☐ 20 Gerald Perry	.05	.02	.00
☐ 21 Gary Gaetti	.10	.05	.01
☐ 22 Rick Reuschel	.10	.05	.01
☐ 23 Keith Hernandez	.15	.07	.01
☐ 24 Jeff Reardon	.10	.05	.01
☐ 25 Mark McGwire	.90	.45	.09
☐ 26 Juan Samuel	.10	.05	.01
☐ 27 Jack Clark	.10	.05	.01
☐ 28 Robin Yount	.40	.20	.04
☐ 29 Steve Bedrosian	.10	.05	.01
☐ 30 Kirk Gibson	.25	.12	.02
☐ 31 Barry Bonds	.50	.25	.05
☐ 32 Dan Plesac	.05	.02	.00

☐ 33 Steve Sax	.15	.07	.01
☐ 34 Jeff Robinson	.05	.02	.00
☐ 35 Orel Hershiser	.30	.15	.03
☐ 36 Julio Franco	.10	.05	.01
☐ 37 Dave Righetti	.10	.05	.01
☐ 38 Bob Knepper	.05	.02	.00
☐ 39 Carlton Fisk	.25	.12	.02
☐ 40 Tony Gwynn	.35	.17	.03
☐ 41 Doug Jones	.05	.02	.00
☐ 42 Bobby Bonilla	.35	.17	.03
☐ 43 Ellis Burks	.35	.17	.03
☐ 44 Pedro Guerrero	.15	.07	.01
☐ 45 Rickey Henderson	.75	.35	.07
☐ 46 Glenn Davis	.25	.12	.02
☐ 47 Benny Santiago	.25	.12	.02
☐ 48 Greg Maddux	.10	.05	.01
☐ 49 Teddy Higuera	.10	.05	.01
☐ 50 Darryl Strawberry	.60	.30	.06
☐ 51 Ozzie Guillen	.10	.05	.01
☐ 52 Barry Larkin	.25	.12	.02
☐ 53 Tony Fernandez	.10	.05	.01
☐ 54 Ryne Sandberg	.60	.30	.06
☐ 55 Joe Carter	.20	.10	.02
☐ 56 Rafael Palmeiro	.20	.10	.02
☐ 57 Paul Molitor	.15	.07	.01
☐ 58 Eric Davis	.60	.30	.06
☐ 59 Mike Henneman	.05	.02	.00
☐ 60 Mike Scott	.10	.05	.01
☐ 61 Tom Browning	.10	.05	.01
☐ 62 Mark Davis	.10	.05	.01
☐ 63 Tom Henke	.05	.02	.00
☐ 64 Nolan Ryan	1.25	.60	.12
☐ 65 Fred McGriff	.50	.25	.05
☐ 66 Dale Murphy	.35	.17	.03
☐ 67 Mark Langston	.10	.05	.01
☐ 68 Bobby Thigpen	.20	.10	.02
☐ 69 Mark Gubicza	.10	.05	.01
☐ 70 Mike Greenwell	.40	.20	.04
☐ 71 Ron Darling	.10	.05	.01
☐ 72 Gerald Young	.10	.05	.01
☐ 73 Wally Joyner	.20	.10	.02
☐ 74 Andres Galarraga	.20	.10	.02
☐ 75 Danny Jackson	.10	.05	.01
☐ 76 Mike Schmidt	.75	.35	.07
☐ 77 Cal Ripken Jr.	.30	.15	.03
☐ 78 Alvin Davis	.10	.05	.01
☐ 79 Bruce Hurst	.10	.05	.01
☐ 80 Andre Dawson	.20	.10	.02
☐ 81 Bob Boone	.10	.05	.01
☐ 82 Harold Reynolds	.10	.05	.01
☐ 83 Eddie Murray	.30	.15	.03
☐ 84 Robby Thompson	.05	.02	.00
☐ 85 Will Clark	1.00	.50	.10
☐ 86 Vince Coleman	.20	.10	.02
☐ 87 Doug Drabek	.20	.10	.02
☐ 88 Ozzie Smith	.25	.12	.02
☐ 89 Bob Welch	.20	.10	.02
☐ 90 Roger Clemens	.75	.35	.07
☐ 91 George Bell	.20	.10	.02
☐ 92 Andy Van Slyke	.15	.07	.01
☐ 93 Willie McGee	.20	.10	.02
☐ 94 Todd Worrell	.10	.05	.01
☐ 95 Tim Raines	.25	.12	.02
☐ 96 Kevin McReynolds	.25	.12	.02
☐ 97 John Franco	.10	.05	.01
☐ 98 Jim Gott	.05	.02	.00
☐ 99 Johnny Ray	.05	.02	.00
☐ 100 Wade Boggs	.60	.30	.06

1989 Score Young Superstars I

The 1989 Score Young Superstars set I contains 42 standard-size (2 1/2" by 3 1/2") cards. The fronts are pink, white and blue. The vertically-oriented backs have color facial shots, 1988 and career stats, and biographical information. One card was included in each 1989 Score rack pack, and the cards were also distributed as a boxed set with five Magic Motion trivia cards.

	MINT	EXC	G-VG
COMPLETE SET (42)	7.50	3.75	.75
COMMON PLAYER (1-42)	.20	.10	.02
☐ 1 Gregg Jefferies	.75	.35	.07
☐ 2 Jody Reed	.25	.12	.02
☐ 3 Mark Grace	.90	.45	.09
☐ 4 Dave Gallagher	.20	.10	.02

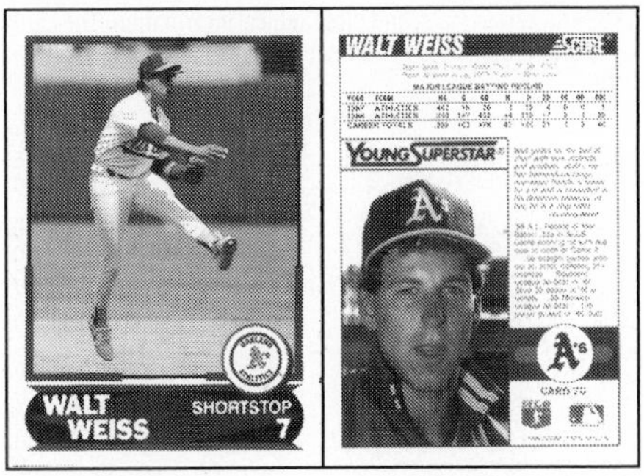

☐ 5 Bo Jackson	1.00	.50	.10
☐ 6 Jay Buhner	.25	.12	.02
☐ 7 Melido Perez	.20	.10	.02
☐ 8 Bobby Witt	.25	.12	.02
☐ 9 David Cone	.25	.12	.02
☐ 10 Chris Sabo	.35	.17	.03
☐ 11 Pat Borders	.25	.12	.02
☐ 12 Mark Grant	.20	.10	.02
☐ 13 Mike Macfarlane	.20	.10	.02
☐ 14 Mike Jackson	.20	.10	.02
☐ 15 Ricky Jordan	.25	.12	.02
☐ 16 Ron Gant	.50	.25	.05
☐ 17 Al Leiter	.20	.10	.02
☐ 18 Jeff Parrett	.20	.10	.02
☐ 19 Pete Smith	.20	.10	.02
☐ 20 Walt Weiss	.25	.12	.02
☐ 21 Doug Drabek	.25	.12	.02
☐ 22 Kirt Manwaring	.20	.10	.02
☐ 23 Keith Miller	.20	.10	.02
☐ 24 Damon Berryhill	.25	.12	.02
☐ 25 Gary Sheffield	.60	.30	.06
☐ 26 Brady Anderson	.25	.12	.02
☐ 27 Mitch Williams	.20	.10	.02
☐ 28 Roberto Alomar	.35	.17	.03
☐ 29 Bobby Thigpen	.30	.15	.03
☐ 30 Bryan Harvey UER (47 games in '87)	.25	.12	.02
☐ 31 Jose Rijo	.25	.12	.02
☐ 32 Dave West	.25	.12	.02
☐ 33 Joey Meyer	.20	.10	.02
☐ 34 Allan Anderson	.20	.10	.02
☐ 35 Rafael Palmeiro	.30	.15	.03
☐ 36 Tim Belcher	.25	.12	.02
☐ 37 John Smiley	.20	.10	.02
☐ 38 Mackey Sasser	.25	.12	.02
☐ 39 Greg Maddux	.25	.12	.02
☐ 40 Ramon Martinez	.50	.25	.05
☐ 41 Randy Myers	.20	.10	.02
☐ 42 Scott Bankhead	.20	.10	.02

1989 Score Young Superstars II

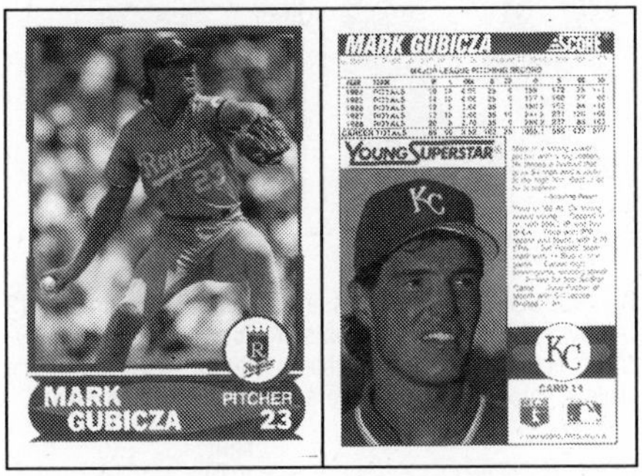

The 1989 Score Young Superstars II set contains 42 standard-size (2 1/2" by 3 1/2") cards. The fronts are orange, white and purple. The vertically-oriented backs have color facial shots,

1988 and career stats, and biographical information. The cards were distributed as a boxed set with five Magic Motion trivia cards.

	MINT	EXC	G-VG
COMPLETE SET (42)	6.00	3.00	.60
COMMON PLAYER (1-42)	.20	.10	.02
☐ 1 Sandy Alomar Jr.	.75	.35	.07
☐ 2 Tom Gordon	.50	.25	.05
☐ 3 Ron Jones	.20	.10	.02
☐ 4 Todd Burns	.20	.10	.02
☐ 5 Paul O'Neill	.30	.15	.03
☐ 6 Gene Larkin	.20	.10	.02
☐ 7 Eric King	.20	.10	.02
☐ 8 Jeff Robinson	.20	.10	.02
☐ 9 Bill Wegman	.20	.10	.02
☐ 10 Cecil Espy	.20	.10	.02
☐ 11 Jose Guzman	.20	.10	.02
☐ 12 Kelly Gruber	.35	.17	.03
☐ 13 Duane Ward	.20	.10	.02
☐ 14 Mark Gubicza	.25	.12	.02
☐ 15 Norm Charlton	.30	.15	.03
☐ 16 Jose Oquendo	.20	.10	.02
☐ 17 Geronimo Berroa	.20	.10	.02
☐ 18 Ken Griffey Jr.	1.25	.60	.12
☐ 19 Lance McCullers	.20	.10	.02
☐ 20 Todd Stottlemyre	.25	.12	.02
☐ 21 Craig Worthington	.25	.12	.02
☐ 22 Mike Devereaux	.25	.12	.02
☐ 23 Tom Glavine	.25	.12	.02
☐ 24 Dale Sveum	.20	.10	.02
☐ 25 Roberto Kelly	.50	.25	.05
☐ 26 Luis Medina	.25	.12	.02
☐ 27 Steve Searcy	.25	.12	.02
☐ 28 Don August	.20	.10	.02
☐ 29 Shawn Hillegas	.20	.10	.02
☐ 30 Mike Campbell	.20	.10	.02
☐ 31 Mike Harkey	.35	.17	.03
☐ 32 Randy Johnson	.25	.12	.02
☐ 33 Craig Biggio	.35	.17	.03
☐ 34 Mike Schooler	.25	.12	.02
☐ 35 Andres Thomas	.20	.10	.02
☐ 36 Jerome Walton	.60	.30	.06
☐ 37 Cris Carpenter	.20	.10	.02
☐ 38 Kevin Mitchell	.50	.25	.05
☐ 39 Eddie Williams	.20	.10	.02
☐ 40 Chad Kreuter	.20	.10	.02
☐ 41 Danny Jackson	.20	.10	.02
☐ 42 Kurt Stillwell	.25	.12	.02

1989 Score Scoremasters

The 1989 Score Scoremasters set contains 42 standard-size (2 1/2" by 3 1/2") cards. The fronts are "pure" with attractively-drawn action portraits. The backs feature write-ups of the players' careers. The cards were distributed as a boxed set.

	MINT	EXC	G-VG
COMPLETE SET (42)	10.00	5.00	1.00
COMMON PLAYER (1-42)	.20	.10	.02
☐ 1 Bo Jackson	1.00	.50	.10
☐ 2 Jerome Walton	.60	.30	.06
☐ 3 Cal Ripken Jr.	.40	.20	.04
☐ 4 Mike Scott	.25	.12	.02
☐ 5 Nolan Ryan	1.00	.50	.10
☐ 6 Don Mattingly	1.00	.50	.10
☐ 7 Tom Gordon	.40	.20	.04
☐ 8 Jack Morris	.20	.10	.02
☐ 9 Carlton Fisk	.40	.20	.04
☐ 10 Will Clark	.90	.45	.09
☐ 11 George Brett	.50	.25	.05
☐ 12 Kevin Mitchell	.50	.25	.05
☐ 13 Mark Langston	.25	.12	.02
☐ 14 Dave Stewart	.30	.15	.03
☐ 15 Dale Murphy	.40	.20	.04
☐ 16 Gary Gaetti	.25	.12	.02
☐ 17 Wade Boggs	.90	.45	.09
☐ 18 Eric Davis	.60	.30	.06
☐ 19 Kirby Puckett	.75	.35	.07
☐ 20 Roger Clemens	.90	.45	.09
☐ 21 Orel Hershiser	.40	.20	.04
☐ 22 Mark Grace	.90	.45	.09
☐ 23 Ryne Sandberg	.75	.35	.07
☐ 24 Barry Larkin	.35	.17	.03
☐ 25 Ellis Burks	.45	.22	.04
☐ 26 Dwight Gooden	.40	.20	.04
☐ 27 Ozzie Smith	.30	.15	.03
☐ 28 Andre Dawson	.30	.15	.03
☐ 29 Julio Franco	.20	.10	.02
☐ 30 Ken Griffey Jr.	1.50	.75	.15
☐ 31 Ruben Sierra	.60	.30	.06
☐ 32 Mark McGwire	.90	.45	.09
☐ 33 Andres Galarraga	.25	.12	.02
☐ 34 Joe Carter	.25	.12	.02
☐ 35 Vince Coleman	.30	.15	.03
☐ 36 Mike Greenwell	.45	.22	.04
☐ 37 Tony Gwynn	.50	.25	.05
☐ 38 Andy Van Slyke	.20	.10	.02
☐ 39 Gregg Jefferies	.75	.35	.07
☐ 40 Jose Canseco	1.00	.50	.10
☐ 41 Dave Winfield	.30	.15	.03
☐ 42 Darryl Strawberry	.60	.30	.06

1989 Score Nat West Yankees

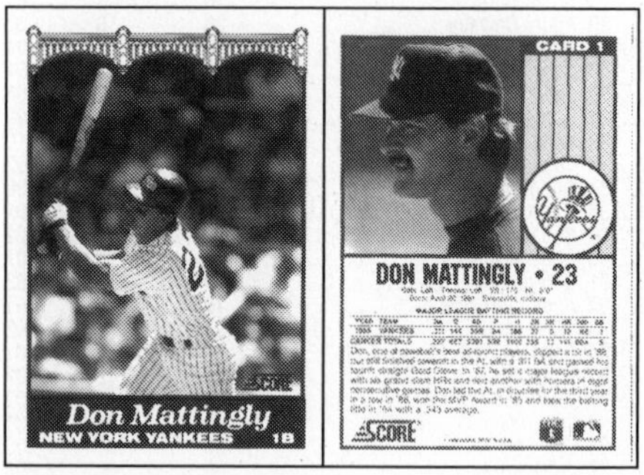

The 1989 Score Nat West New York Yankees set features 33 standard-size (2 1/2" by 3 1/2") cards. The fronts and backs are navy; the backs have color mug shots, 1988 and career stats. The set was given away at a 1989 Yankees' home game.

	MINT	EXC	G-VG
COMPLETE SET (33)	15.00	7.50	1.50
COMMON PLAYER (1-33)	.30	.15	.03
☐ 1 Don Mattingly	2.50	1.25	.25
☐ 2 Steve Sax	.75	.35	.07
☐ 3 Alvaro Espinoza	.30	.15	.03
☐ 4 Luis Polonia	.40	.20	.04
☐ 5 Jesse Barfield	.50	.25	.05
☐ 6 Dave Righetti	.50	.25	.05
☐ 7 Dave Winfield	.90	.45	.09
☐ 8 John Candelaria	.30	.15	.03
☐ 9 Wayne Tolleson	.30	.15	.03
☐ 10 Ken Phelps	.30	.15	.03
☐ 11 Rafael Santana	.30	.15	.03
☐ 12 Don Slaught	.30	.15	.03
☐ 13 Mike Pagliarulo	.30	.15	.03
☐ 14 Lance McCullers	.30	.15	.03
☐ 15 Dave LaPoint	.30	.15	.03

☐ 16 Dale Mohorcic	.30	.15	.03
☐ 17 Steve Balboni	.30	.15	.03
☐ 18 Roberto Kelly	.75	.35	.07
☐ 19 Andy Hawkins	.40	.20	.04
☐ 20 Mel Hall	.40	.20	.04
☐ 21 Tom Brookens	.30	.15	.03
☐ 22 Deion Sanders	1.25	.60	.12
☐ 23 Richard Dotson	.30	.15	.03
☐ 24 Lee Guetterman	.30	.15	.03
☐ 25 Bob Geren	.40	.20	.04
☐ 26 Jimmy Jones	.30	.15	.03
☐ 27 Chuck Cary	.40	.20	.04
☐ 28 Ron Guidry	.60	.30	.06
☐ 29 Hal Morris	.90	.45	.09
☐ 30 Clay Parker	.40	.20	.04
☐ 31 Dallas Green MG	.40	.20	.04
☐ 32 Thurman Munson (memorial)	2.50	1.25	.25
☐ 33 Yankees Team Card	.50	.25	.05

1989 Score Traded

The 1989 Score Traded set contains 110 standard-size (2 1/2" by 3 1/2") cards. The fronts have coral green borders with pink diamonds at the bottom. The vertically-oriented backs have color facial shots, career stats, and biographical information. Cards 1-80 feature traded players; cards 81-110 feature 1989 rookies. The set was distributed in a blue box with 10 Magic Motion trivia cards. The key rookie cards in this set are Jim Abbott, Junior Felix, Ken Griffey Jr., and Jerome Walton.

	MINT	EXC	G-VG
COMPLETE SET (110)	12.00	6.00	1.20
COMMON PLAYER (1-80)	.05	.02	.00
COMMON PLAYER (81-110)	.08	.04	.01

☐ 1 Rafael Palmeiro	.20	.06	.01
☐ 2 Nolan Ryan	1.25	.60	.12
☐ 3 Jack Clark	.12	.06	.01
☐ 4 Dave LaPoint	.05	.02	.00
☐ 5 Mike Moore	.10	.05	.01
☐ 6 Pete O'Brien	.10	.05	.01
☐ 7 Jeffrey Leonard	.10	.05	.01
☐ 8 Rob Murphy	.05	.02	.00
☐ 9 Tom Herr	.10	.05	.01
☐ 10 Claudell Washington	.10	.05	.01
☐ 11 Mike Pagliarulo	.05	.02	.00
☐ 12 Steve Lake	.05	.02	.00
☐ 13 Spike Owen	.05	.02	.00
☐ 14 Andy Hawkins	.05	.02	.00
☐ 15 Todd Benzinger	.05	.02	.00
☐ 16 Mookie Wilson	.10	.05	.01
☐ 17 Bert Blyleven	.12	.06	.01
☐ 18 Jeff Treadway	.05	.02	.00
☐ 19 Bruce Hurst	.10	.05	.01
☐ 20 Steve Sax	.12	.06	.01
☐ 21 Juan Samuel	.12	.06	.01
☐ 22 Jesse Barfield	.12	.06	.01
☐ 23 Carmen Castillo	.05	.02	.00
☐ 24 Terry Leach	.05	.02	.00
☐ 25 Mark Langston	.12	.06	.01
☐ 26 Eric King	.10	.05	.01
☐ 27 Steve Balboni	.05	.02	.00
☐ 28 Len Dykstra	.15	.07	.01
☐ 29 Keith Moreland	.05	.02	.00
☐ 30 Terry Kennedy	.05	.02	.00
☐ 31 Eddie Murray	.15	.07	.01
☐ 32 Mitch Williams	.10	.05	.01
☐ 33 Jeff Parrett	.10	.05	.01
☐ 34 Wally Backman	.05	.02	.00
☐ 35 Julio Franco	.12	.06	.01
☐ 36 Lance Parrish	.15	.07	.01
☐ 37 Nick Esasky	.10	.05	.01
☐ 38 Luis Polonia	.05	.02	.00
☐ 39 Kevin Gross	.05	.02	.00
☐ 40 John Dopson	.10	.05	.01
☐ 41 Willie Randolph	.10	.05	.01
☐ 42 Jim Clancy	.05	.02	.00
☐ 43 Tracy Jones	.05	.02	.00
☐ 44 Phil Bradley	.10	.05	.01
☐ 45 Milt Thompson	.05	.02	.00
☐ 46 Chris James	.10	.05	.01
☐ 47 Scott Fletcher	.05	.02	.00
☐ 48 Kal Daniels	.15	.07	.01
☐ 49 Steve Bedrosian	.10	.05	.01
☐ 50 Rickey Henderson	.50	.25	.05
☐ 51 Dion James	.05	.02	.00
☐ 52 Tim Leary	.10	.05	.01
☐ 53 Roger McDowell	.10	.05	.01
☐ 54 Mel Hall	.10	.05	.01
☐ 55 Dickie Thon	.05	.02	.00
☐ 56 Zane Smith	.10	.05	.01
☐ 57 Danny Heep	.05	.02	.00
☐ 58 Bob McClure	.05	.02	.00
☐ 59 Brian Holton	.05	.02	.00
☐ 60 Randy Ready	.05	.02	.00
☐ 61 Bob Melvin	.05	.02	.00
☐ 62 Harold Baines	.12	.06	.01
☐ 63 Lance McCullers	.05	.02	.00
☐ 64 Jody Davis	.05	.02	.00
☐ 65 Darrell Evans	.10	.05	.01
☐ 66 Joel Youngblood	.05	.02	.00
☐ 67 Frank Viola	.20	.10	.02
☐ 68 Mike Aldrete	.05	.02	.00
☐ 69 Greg Cadaret	.10	.05	.01
☐ 70 John Kruk	.10	.05	.01
☐ 71 Pat Sheridan	.05	.02	.00
☐ 72 Oddibe McDowell	.10	.05	.01
☐ 73 Tom Brookens	.05	.02	.00
☐ 74 Bob Boone	.15	.07	.01
☐ 75 Walt Terrell	.05	.02	.00
☐ 76 Joel Skinner	.05	.02	.00
☐ 77 Randy Johnson	.15	.07	.01
☐ 78 Felix Fermin	.05	.02	.00
☐ 79 Rick Mahler	.05	.02	.00
☐ 80 Richard Dotson	.05	.02	.00
☐ 81 Cris Carpenter	.15	.07	.01
☐ 82 Bill Spiers	.20	.10	.02
☐ 83 Junior Felix	1.00	.50	.10
☐ 84 Joe Girardi	.25	.12	.02
☐ 85 Jerome Walton	1.50	.75	.15
☐ 86 Greg Litton	.20	.10	.02
☐ 87 Greg W.Harris	.20	.10	.02
☐ 88 Jim Abbott	.90	.45	.09
☐ 89 Kevin Brown	.25	.12	.02
☐ 90 John Wetteland	.25	.12	.02
☐ 91 Gary Wayne	.12	.06	.01
☐ 92 Rich Monteleone	.12	.06	.01
☐ 93 Bob Geren	.20	.10	.02
☐ 94 Clay Parker	.12	.06	.01
☐ 95 Steve Finley	.25	.12	.02
☐ 96 Gregg Olson	.90	.45	.09
☐ 97 Ken Patterson	.12	.06	.01
☐ 98 Ken Hill	.20	.10	.02
☐ 99 Scott Scudder	.30	.15	.03
☐ 100 Ken Griffey Jr.	6.50	3.25	.65
☐ 101 Jeff Brantley	.25	.12	.02
☐ 102 Donn Pall	.12	.06	.01
☐ 103 Carlos Martinez	.20	.10	.02
☐ 104 Joe Oliver	.35	.17	.03
☐ 105 Omar Vizquel	.15	.07	.01
☐ 106 Joey Belle	.45	.22	.04
☐ 107 Kenny Rogers	.20	.10	.02
☐ 108 Mark Carreon	.15	.07	.01
☐ 109 Rolando Roomes	.15	.07	.01
☐ 110 Pete Harnisch	.15	.07	.01

1990 Score

The 1990 Score set contains 704 standard-size (2 1/2" by 3 1/2") cards. The front borders are red, blue, green or white. The vertically-oriented backs are white with borders that match the fronts, and feature color mugshots. Cards numbered 661-682 contain the first round draft picks subset noted as DC for "draft choice" in the checklist below. Cards numbered 683-695 contain the "Dream Team" subset noted by DT in the checklist below. The key rookie cards in this set are Juan Gonzalez, Dave Justice, Kevin Maas, Ben McDonald, John Olerud, and Frank Thomas.

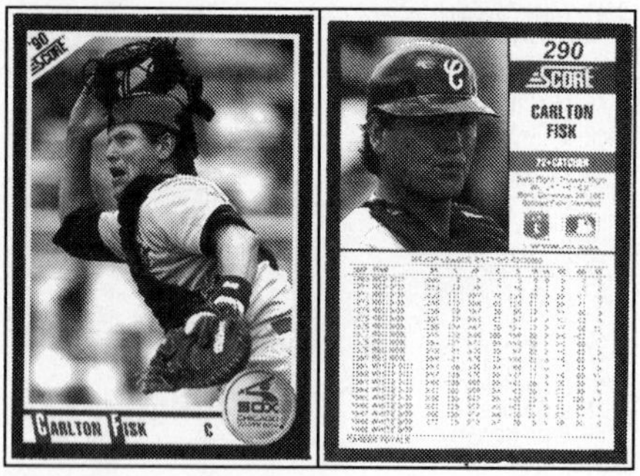

	MINT	EXC	G-VG
COMPLETE SET (704)	26.00	13.00	2.60
COMMON PLAYER (1-704)	.03	.01	.00
☐ 1 Don Mattingly	.45	.22	.04
☐ 2 Cal Ripken	.12	.06	.01
☐ 3 Dwight Evans	.08	.04	.01
☐ 4 Barry Bonds	.20	.10	.02
☐ 5 Kevin McReynolds	.08	.04	.01
☐ 6 Ozzie Guillen	.06	.03	.00
☐ 7 Terry Kennedy	.03	.01	.00
☐ 8 Bryan Harvey	.03	.01	.00
☐ 9 Alan Trammell	.08	.04	.01
☐ 10 Cory Snyder	.08	.04	.01
☐ 11 Jody Reed	.06	.03	.00
☐ 12 Roberto Alomar	.12	.06	.01
☐ 13 Pedro Guerrero	.08	.04	.01
☐ 14 Gary Redus	.03	.01	.00
☐ 15 Marty Barrett	.03	.01	.00
☐ 16 Ricky Jordan	.12	.06	.01
☐ 17 Joe Magrane	.08	.04	.01
☐ 18 Sid Fernandez	.08	.04	.01
☐ 19 Richard Dotson	.03	.01	.00
☐ 20 Jack Clark	.08	.04	.01
☐ 21 Bob Walk	.03	.01	.00
☐ 22 Ron Karkovice	.03	.01	.00
☐ 23 Lenny Harris	.12	.06	.01
☐ 24 Phil Bradley	.06	.03	.00
☐ 25 Andres Galarraga	.08	.04	.01
☐ 26 Brian Downing	.03	.01	.00
☐ 27 Dave Martinez	.03	.01	.00
☐ 28 Eric King	.03	.01	.00
☐ 29 Barry Lyons	.03	.01	.00
☐ 30 Dave Schmidt	.03	.01	.00
☐ 31 Mike Boddicker	.03	.01	.00
☐ 32 Tom Foley	.03	.01	.00
☐ 33 Brady Anderson	.03	.01	.00
☐ 34 Jim Presley	.03	.01	.00
☐ 35 Lance Parrish	.08	.04	.01
☐ 36 Von Hayes	.08	.04	.01
☐ 37 Lee Smith	.06	.03	.00
☐ 38 Herm Winningham	.03	.01	.00
☐ 39 Alejandro Pena	.03	.01	.00
☐ 40 Mike Scott	.08	.04	.01
☐ 41 Joe Orsulak	.03	.01	.00
☐ 42 Rafael Ramirez	.03	.01	.00
☐ 43 Gerald Young	.03	.01	.00
☐ 44 Dick Schofield	.03	.01	.00
☐ 45 Dave Smith	.03	.01	.00
☐ 46 Dave Magadan	.08	.04	.01
☐ 47 Dennis Martinez	.03	.01	.00
☐ 48 Greg Minton	.03	.01	.00
☐ 49 Milt Thompson	.03	.01	.00
☐ 50 Orel Hershiser	.08	.04	.01
☐ 51 Bip Roberts	.06	.03	.00
☐ 52 Jerry Browne	.03	.01	.00
☐ 53 Bob Ojeda	.06	.03	.00
☐ 54 Fernando Valenzuela	.08	.04	.01
☐ 55 Matt Nokes	.06	.03	.00
☐ 56 Brook Jacoby	.06	.03	.00
☐ 57 Frank Tanana	.03	.01	.00
☐ 58 Scott Fletcher	.03	.01	.00
☐ 59 Ron Oester	.03	.01	.00
☐ 60 Bob Boone	.06	.03	.00
☐ 61 Dan Gladden	.03	.01	.00
☐ 62 Darnell Coles	.03	.01	.00
☐ 63 Gregg Olson	.25	.12	.02
☐ 64 Todd Burns	.06	.03	.00
☐ 65 Todd Benzinger	.03	.01	.00
☐ 66 Dale Murphy	.12	.06	.01
☐ 67 Mike Flanagan	.03	.01	.00
☐ 68 Jose Oquendo	.03	.01	.00
☐ 69 Cecil Espy	.03	.01	.00
☐ 70 Chris Sabo	.20	.10	.02
☐ 71 Shane Rawley	.03	.01	.00
☐ 72 Tom Brunansky	.08	.04	.01
☐ 73 Vance Law	.03	.01	.00
☐ 74 B.J. Surhoff	.06	.03	.00
☐ 75 Lou Whitaker	.08	.04	.01
☐ 76 Ken Caminiti UER (Euclid, Ohio should be Hanford, California)	.03	.01	.00
☐ 77 Nelson Liriano	.03	.01	.00
☐ 78 Tommy Gregg	.06	.03	.00
☐ 79 Don Slaught	.03	.01	.00
☐ 80 Eddie Murray	.12	.06	.01
☐ 81 Joe Boever	.03	.01	.00
☐ 82 Charlie Leibrandt	.03	.01	.00
☐ 83 Jose Lind	.03	.01	.00
☐ 84 Tony Phillips	.03	.01	.00
☐ 85 Mitch Webster	.03	.01	.00
☐ 86 Dan Plesac	.03	.01	.00
☐ 87 Rick Mahler	.03	.01	.00
☐ 88 Steve Lyons	.03	.01	.00
☐ 89 Tony Fernandez	.08	.04	.01
☐ 90 Ryne Sandberg	.20	.10	.02
☐ 91 Nick Esasky	.06	.03	.00
☐ 92 Luis Salazar	.03	.01	.00
☐ 93 Pete Incaviglia	.06	.03	.00
☐ 94 Ivan Calderon	.06	.03	.00
☐ 95 Jeff Treadway	.03	.01	.00
☐ 96 Kurt Stillwell	.06	.03	.00
☐ 97 Gary Sheffield	.25	.12	.02
☐ 98 Jeffrey Leonard	.06	.03	.00
☐ 99 Andres Thomas	.03	.01	.00
☐ 100 Roberto Kelly	.10	.05	.01
☐ 101 Alvaro Espinoza	.03	.01	.00
☐ 102 Greg Gagne	.03	.01	.00
☐ 103 John Farrell	.03	.01	.00
☐ 104 Willie Wilson	.06	.03	.00
☐ 105 Glenn Braggs	.06	.03	.00
☐ 106 Chet Lemon	.03	.01	.00
☐ 107A Jamie Moyer ERR (scintilating)	.12	.06	.01
☐ 107B Jamie Moyer COR (scintillating)	.40	.20	.04
☐ 108 Chuck Crim	.03	.01	.00
☐ 109 Dave Valle	.03	.01	.00
☐ 110 Walt Weiss	.08	.04	.01
☐ 111 Larry Sheets	.03	.01	.00
☐ 112 Don Robinson	.03	.01	.00
☐ 113 Danny Heep	.03	.01	.00
☐ 114 Carmelo Martinez	.03	.01	.00
☐ 115 Dave Gallagher	.03	.01	.00
☐ 116 Mike LaValliere	.03	.01	.00
☐ 117 Bob McClure	.03	.01	.00
☐ 118 Rene Gonzales	.03	.01	.00
☐ 119 Mark Parent	.03	.01	.00
☐ 120 Wally Joyner	.08	.04	.01
☐ 121 Mark Gubicza	.06	.03	.00
☐ 122 Tony Pena	.06	.03	.00
☐ 123 Carmen Castillo	.03	.01	.00
☐ 124 Howard Johnson	.08	.04	.01
☐ 125 Steve Sax	.08	.04	.01
☐ 126 Tim Belcher	.06	.03	.00
☐ 127 Tim Burke	.06	.03	.00
☐ 128 Al Newman	.03	.01	.00
☐ 129 Dennis Rasmussen	.03	.01	.00
☐ 130 Doug Jones	.06	.03	.00
☐ 131 Fred Lynn	.08	.04	.01
☐ 132 Jeff Hamilton	.03	.01	.00
☐ 133 German Gonzalez	.03	.01	.00
☐ 134 John Morris	.03	.01	.00
☐ 135 Dave Parker	.08	.04	.01
☐ 136 Gary Pettis	.03	.01	.00
☐ 137 Dennis Boyd	.06	.03	.00
☐ 138 Candy Maldonado	.06	.03	.00
☐ 139 Rick Cerone	.03	.01	.00
☐ 140 George Brett	.15	.07	.01
☐ 141 Dave Clark	.03	.01	.00
☐ 142 Dickie Thon	.03	.01	.00
☐ 143 Junior Ortiz	.03	.01	.00
☐ 144 Don August	.03	.01	.00
☐ 145 Gary Gaetti	.08	.04	.01

☐ 146 Kirt Manwaring	.03	.01	.00
☐ 147 Jeff Reed	.03	.01	.00
☐ 148 Jose Alvarez	.03	.01	.00
☐ 149 Mike Schooler	.06	.03	.00
☐ 150 Mark Grace	.25	.12	.02
☐ 151 Geronimo Berroa	.03	.01	.00
☐ 152 Barry Jones	.03	.01	.00
☐ 153 Geno Petralli	.03	.01	.00
☐ 154 Jim Deshaies	.03	.01	.00
☐ 155 Barry Larkin	.12	.06	.01
☐ 156 Alfredo Griffin	.03	.01	.00
☐ 157 Tom Henke	.06	.03	.00
☐ 158 Mike Jeffcoat	.03	.01	.00
☐ 159 Bob Welch	.08	.04	.01
☐ 160 Julio Franco	.06	.03	.00
☐ 161 Henry Cotto	.03	.01	.00
☐ 162 Terry Steinbach	.06	.03	.00
☐ 163 Damon Berryhill	.08	.04	.01
☐ 164 Tim Crews	.03	.01	.00
☐ 165 Tom Browning	.06	.03	.00
☐ 166 Fred Manrique	.03	.01	.00
☐ 167 Harold Reynolds	.06	.03	.00
☐ 168A Ron Hassey ERR (27 on back)	.12	.06	.01
☐ 168B Ron Hassey COR (24 on back)	2.00	1.00	.20
☐ 169 Shawon Dunston	.10	.05	.01
☐ 170 Bobby Bonilla	.15	.07	.01
☐ 171 Tommy Herr	.06	.03	.00
☐ 172 Mike Heath	.03	.01	.00
☐ 173 Rich Gedman	.03	.01	.00
☐ 174 Bill Ripken	.03	.01	.00
☐ 175 Pete O'Brien	.06	.03	.00
☐ 176A Lloyd McClendon ERR (uniform number on back listed as 1)	1.25	.60	.12
☐ 176B Lloyd McClendon COR (uniform number on back listed as 10)	.08	.04	.01
☐ 177 Brian Holton	.03	.01	.00
☐ 178 Jeff Blauser	.03	.01	.00
☐ 179 Jim Eisenreich	.03	.01	.00
☐ 180 Bert Blyleven	.08	.04	.01
☐ 181 Rob Murphy	.03	.01	.00
☐ 182 Bill Doran	.06	.03	.00
☐ 183 Curt Ford	.03	.01	.00
☐ 184 Mike Henneman	.03	.01	.00
☐ 185 Eric Davis	.18	.09	.01
☐ 186 Lance McCullers	.03	.01	.00
☐ 187 Steve Davis	.12	.06	.01
☐ 188 Bill Wegman	.03	.01	.00
☐ 189 Brian Harper	.03	.01	.00
☐ 190 Mike Moore	.06	.03	.00
☐ 191 Dale Mohorcic	.03	.01	.00
☐ 192 Tim Wallach	.06	.03	.00
☐ 193 Keith Hernandez	.08	.04	.01
☐ 194 Dave Righetti	.08	.04	.01
☐ 195A Bret Saberhagen ERR (joke)	.15	.07	.01
☐ 195B Bret Saberhagen COR (joker)	.50	.25	.05
☐ 196 Paul Kilgus	.03	.01	.00
☐ 197 Bud Black	.03	.01	.00
☐ 198 Juan Samuel	.06	.03	.00
☐ 199 Kevin Seitzer	.08	.04	.01
☐ 200 Darryl Strawberry	.20	.10	.02
☐ 201 Dave Stieb	.08	.04	.01
☐ 202 Charlie Hough	.03	.01	.00
☐ 203 Jack Morris	.08	.04	.01
☐ 204 Rance Mulliniks	.03	.01	.00
☐ 205 Alvin Davis	.08	.04	.01
☐ 206 Jack Howell	.03	.01	.00
☐ 207 Ken Patterson	.06	.03	.00
☐ 208 Terry Pendleton	.03	.01	.00
☐ 209 Craig Lefferts	.03	.01	.00
☐ 210 Kevin Brown	.10	.05	.01
☐ 211 Dan Petry	.03	.01	.00
☐ 212 Dave Leiper	.03	.01	.00
☐ 213 Daryl Boston	.06	.03	.00
☐ 214 Kevin Hickey	.03	.01	.00
☐ 215 Mike Krukow	.03	.01	.00
☐ 216 Terry Francona	.03	.01	.00
☐ 217 Kirk McCaskill	.03	.01	.00
☐ 218 Scott Bailes	.03	.01	.00
☐ 219 Bob Forsch	.03	.01	.00
☐ 220A Mike Aldrete ERR (25 on back)	.12	.06	.01
☐ 220B Mike Aldrete COR (24 on back)	.40	.20	.04
☐ 221 Steve Buechele	.03	.01	.00
☐ 222 Jesse Barfield	.08	.04	.01
☐ 223 Juan Berenguer	.03	.01	.00
☐ 224 Andy McGaffigan	.03	.01	.00
☐ 225 Pete Smith	.03	.01	.00
☐ 226 Mike Witt	.03	.01	.00
☐ 227 Jay Howell	.03	.01	.00
☐ 228 Scott Bradley	.03	.01	.00
☐ 229 Jerome Walton	.45	.22	.04
☐ 230 Greg Swindell	.06	.03	.00
☐ 231 Atlee Hammaker	.03	.01	.00
☐ 232A Mike Devereaux ERR (RF on front)	.12	.06	.01
☐ 232B Mike Devereaux COR (CF on front)	2.00	1.00	.20
☐ 233 Ken Hill	.08	.04	.01
☐ 234 Craig Worthington	.08	.04	.01
☐ 235 Scott Terry	.03	.01	.00
☐ 236 Brett Butler	.06	.03	.00
☐ 237 Doyle Alexander	.03	.01	.00
☐ 238 Dave Anderson	.03	.01	.00
☐ 239 Bob Milacki	.06	.03	.00
☐ 240 Dwight Smith	.15	.07	.01
☐ 241 Otis Nixon	.03	.01	.00
☐ 242 Pat Tabler	.03	.01	.00
☐ 243 Derek Lilliquist	.06	.03	.00
☐ 244 Danny Tartabull	.08	.04	.01
☐ 245 Wade Boggs	.20	.10	.02
☐ 246 Scott Garrelts (should say Relief Pitcher on front)	.06	.03	.00
☐ 247 Spike Owen	.03	.01	.00
☐ 248 Norm Charlton	.06	.03	.00
☐ 249 Gerald Perry	.03	.01	.00
☐ 250 Nolan Ryan	.40	.20	.04
☐ 251 Kevin Gross	.03	.01	.00
☐ 252 Randy Milligan	.08	.04	.01
☐ 253 Mike LaCoss	.03	.01	.00
☐ 254 Dave Bergman	.03	.01	.00
☐ 255 Tony Gwynn	.15	.07	.01
☐ 256 Felix Fermin	.03	.01	.00
☐ 257 Greg Harris	.10	.05	.01
☐ 258 Junior Felix	.35	.17	.03
☐ 259 Mark Davis	.08	.04	.01
☐ 260 Vince Coleman	.08	.04	.01
☐ 261 Paul Gibson	.03	.01	.00
☐ 262 Mitch Williams	.03	.01	.00
☐ 263 Jeff Russell	.03	.01	.00
☐ 264 Omar Vizquel	.08	.04	.01
☐ 265 Andre Dawson	.10	.05	.01
☐ 266 Storm Davis	.06	.03	.00
☐ 267 Guillermo Hernandez	.03	.01	.00
☐ 268 Mike Felder	.03	.01	.00
☐ 269 Tom Candiotti	.03	.01	.00
☐ 270 Bruce Hurst	.06	.03	.00
☐ 271 Fred McGriff	.12	.06	.01
☐ 272 Glenn Davis	.10	.05	.01
☐ 273 John Franco	.06	.03	.00
☐ 274 Rich Yett	.03	.01	.00
☐ 275 Craig Biggio	.08	.04	.01
☐ 276 Gene Larkin	.03	.01	.00
☐ 277 Rob Dibble	.08	.04	.01
☐ 278 Randy Bush	.03	.01	.00
☐ 279 Kevin Bass	.06	.03	.00
☐ 280A Bo Jackson ERR (Watham)	.80	.40	.08
☐ 280B Bo Jackson COR (Wathan)	1.75	.85	.17
☐ 281 Wally Backman	.03	.01	.00
☐ 282 Larry Andersen	.03	.01	.00
☐ 283 Chris Bosio	.03	.01	.00
☐ 284 Juan Agosto	.03	.01	.00
☐ 285 Ozzie Smith	.10	.05	.01
☐ 286 George Bell	.08	.04	.01
☐ 287 Rex Hudler	.03	.01	.00
☐ 288 Pat Borders	.06	.03	.00
☐ 289 Danny Jackson	.06	.03	.00
☐ 290 Carlton Fisk	.10	.05	.01
☐ 291 Tracy Jones	.03	.01	.00
☐ 292 Allan Anderson	.03	.01	.00
☐ 293 Johnny Ray	.03	.01	.00
☐ 294 Lee Guetterman	.03	.01	.00
☐ 295 Paul O'Neill	.08	.04	.01
☐ 296 Carney Lansford	.08	.04	.01
☐ 297 Tom Brookens	.03	.01	.00
☐ 298 Claudell Washington	.03	.01	.00
☐ 299 Hubie Brooks	.06	.03	.00
☐ 300 Will Clark	.45	.22	.04
☐ 301 Kenny Rogers	.10	.05	.01
☐ 302 Darrell Evans	.06	.03	.00
☐ 303 Greg Briley	.15	.07	.01
☐ 304 Donn Pall	.06	.03	.00
☐ 305 Teddy Higuera	.06	.03	.00
☐ 306 Dan Pasqua	.03	.01	.00
☐ 307 Dave Winfield	.10	.05	.01
☐ 308 Dennis Powell	.03	.01	.00
☐ 309 Jose DeLeon	.03	.01	.00

☐ 310	Roger Clemens UER (dominate, should say dominant)	.20	.10	.02
☐ 311	Melido Perez	.06	.03	.00
☐ 312	Devon White	.06	.03	.00
☐ 313	Dwight Gooden	.18	.09	.01
☐ 314	Carlos Martinez	.08	.04	.01
☐ 315	Dennis Eckersley	.10	.05	.01
☐ 316	Clay Parker	.06	.03	.00
☐ 317	Rick Honeycutt	.03	.01	.00
☐ 318	Tim Laudner	.03	.01	.00
☐ 319	Joe Carter	.10	.05	.01
☐ 320	Robin Yount	.15	.07	.01
☐ 321	Felix Jose	.08	.04	.01
☐ 322	Mickey Tettleton	.06	.03	.00
☐ 323	Mike Gallego	.03	.01	.00
☐ 324	Edgar Martinez	.10	.05	.01
☐ 325	Dave Henderson	.06	.03	.00
☐ 326	Chili Davis	.06	.03	.00
☐ 327	Steve Balboni	.03	.01	.00
☐ 328	Jody Davis	.03	.01	.00
☐ 329	Shawn Hillegas	.03	.01	.00
☐ 330	Jim Abbott	.30	.15	.03
☐ 331	John Dopson	.06	.03	.00
☐ 332	Mark Williamson	.03	.01	.00
☐ 333	Jeff Robinson	.03	.01	.00
☐ 334	John Smiley	.03	.01	.00
☐ 335	Bobby Thigpen	.08	.04	.01
☐ 336	Garry Templeton	.06	.03	.00
☐ 337	Marvell Wynne	.03	.01	.00
☐ 338A	Ken Griffey Sr. ERR (uniform number on back listed as 25)	.12	.06	.01
☐ 338B	Ken Griffey Sr. COR (uniform number on back listed as 30)	5.00	2.50	.50
☐ 339	Steve Finley	.12	.06	.01
☐ 340	Ellis Burks	.15	.07	.01
☐ 341	Frank Williams	.03	.01	.00
☐ 342	Mike Morgan	.03	.01	.00
☐ 343	Kevin Mitchell	.20	.10	.02
☐ 344	Joel Youngblood	.03	.01	.00
☐ 345	Mike Greenwell	.15	.07	.01
☐ 346	Glenn Wilson	.03	.01	.00
☐ 347	John Costello	.03	.01	.00
☐ 348	Wes Gardner	.03	.01	.00
☐ 349	Jeff Ballard	.03	.01	.00
☐ 350	Mark Thurmond UER (ERA is 192, should be 1.92)	.03	.01	.00
☐ 351	Randy Myers	.06	.03	.00
☐ 352	Shawn Abner	.03	.01	.00
☐ 353	Jesse Orosco	.03	.01	.00
☐ 354	Greg Walker	.03	.01	.00
☐ 355	Pete Harnisch	.06	.03	.00
☐ 356	Steve Farr	.03	.01	.00
☐ 357	Dave LaPoint	.03	.01	.00
☐ 358	Willie Fraser	.03	.01	.00
☐ 359	Mickey Hatcher	.03	.01	.00
☐ 360	Rickey Henderson	.25	.12	.02
☐ 361	Mike Fitzgerald	.03	.01	.00
☐ 362	Bill Schroeder	.03	.01	.00
☐ 363	Mark Carreon	.06	.03	.00
☐ 364	Ron Jones	.06	.03	.00
☐ 365	Jeff Montgomery	.06	.03	.00
☐ 366	Bill Krueger	.03	.01	.00
☐ 367	John Cangelosi	.03	.01	.00
☐ 368	Jose Gonzalez	.03	.01	.00
☐ 369	Greg Hibbard	.20	.10	.02
☐ 370	John Smoltz	.08	.04	.01
☐ 371	Jeff Brantley	.15	.07	.01
☐ 372	Frank White	.06	.03	.00
☐ 373	Ed Whitson	.03	.01	.00
☐ 374	Willie McGee	.08	.04	.01
☐ 375	Jose Canseco	.50	.25	.05
☐ 376	Randy Ready	.03	.01	.00
☐ 377	Don Aase	.03	.01	.00
☐ 378	Tony Armas	.03	.01	.00
☐ 379	Steve Bedrosian	.06	.03	.00
☐ 380	Chuck Finley	.08	.04	.01
☐ 381	Kent Hrbek	.08	.04	.01
☐ 382	Jim Gantner	.03	.01	.00
☐ 383	Mel Hall	.06	.03	.00
☐ 384	Mike Marshall	.08	.04	.01
☐ 385	Mark McGwire	.25	.12	.02
☐ 386	Wayne Tolleson	.03	.01	.00
☐ 387	Brian Holman	.10	.05	.01
☐ 388	John Wetteland	.15	.07	.01
☐ 389	Darren Daulton	.06	.03	.00
☐ 390	Rob Deer	.06	.03	.00
☐ 391	John Moses	.03	.01	.00
☐ 392	Todd Worrell	.06	.03	.00
☐ 393	Chuck Cary	.06	.03	.00
☐ 394	Stan Javier	.03	.01	.00
☐ 395	Willie Randolph	.06	.03	.00
☐ 396	Bill Buckner	.06	.03	.00
☐ 397	Robby Thompson	.03	.01	.00
☐ 398	Mike Scioscia	.03	.01	.00
☐ 399	Lonnie Smith	.06	.03	.00
☐ 400	Kirby Puckett	.25	.12	.02
☐ 401	Mark Langston	.08	.04	.01
☐ 402	Danny Darwin	.03	.01	.00
☐ 403	Greg Maddux	.06	.03	.00
☐ 404	Lloyd Moseby	.06	.03	.00
☐ 405	Rafael Palmeiro	.12	.06	.01
☐ 406	Chad Kreuter	.03	.01	.00
☐ 407	Jimmy Key	.06	.03	.00
☐ 408	Tim Birtsas	.03	.01	.00
☐ 409	Tim Raines	.08	.04	.01
☐ 410	Dave Stewart	.10	.05	.01
☐ 411	Eric Yelding	.20	.10	.02
☐ 412	Kent Anderson	.10	.05	.01
☐ 413	Les Lancaster	.03	.01	.00
☐ 414	Rick Dempsey	.03	.01	.00
☐ 415	Randy Johnson	.06	.03	.00
☐ 416	Gary Carter	.08	.04	.01
☐ 417	Rolando Roomes	.06	.03	.00
☐ 418	Dan Schatzeder	.03	.01	.00
☐ 419	Bryn Smith	.03	.01	.00
☐ 420	Ruben Sierra	.15	.07	.01
☐ 421	Steve Jeltz	.03	.01	.00
☐ 422	Ken Oberkfell	.03	.01	.00
☐ 423	Sid Bream	.03	.01	.00
☐ 424	Jim Clancy	.03	.01	.00
☐ 425	Kelly Gruber	.12	.06	.01
☐ 426	Rick Leach	.03	.01	.00
☐ 427	Len Dykstra	.10	.05	.01
☐ 428	Jeff Pico	.03	.01	.00
☐ 429	John Cerutti	.03	.01	.00
☐ 430	David Cone	.08	.04	.01
☐ 431	Jeff Kunkel	.03	.01	.00
☐ 432	Luis Aquino	.03	.01	.00
☐ 433	Ernie Whitt	.03	.01	.00
☐ 434	Bo Diaz	.03	.01	.00
☐ 435	Steve Lake	.03	.01	.00
☐ 436	Pat Perry	.03	.01	.00
☐ 437	Mike Davis	.03	.01	.00
☐ 438	Cecilio Guante	.03	.01	.00
☐ 439	Duane Ward	.03	.01	.00
☐ 440	Andy Van Slyke	.08	.04	.01
☐ 441	Gene Nelson	.03	.01	.00
☐ 442	Luis Polonia	.03	.01	.00
☐ 443	Kevin Elster	.06	.03	.00
☐ 444	Keith Moreland	.03	.01	.00
☐ 445	Roger McDowell	.06	.03	.00
☐ 446	Ron Darling	.08	.04	.01
☐ 447	Ernest Riles	.03	.01	.00
☐ 448	Mookie Wilson	.06	.03	.00
☐ 449A	Billy Spiers ERR (no birth year)	1.25	.60	.12
☐ 449B	Billy Spiers COR (born in 1966)	.15	.07	.01
☐ 450	Rick Sutcliffe	.06	.03	.00
☐ 451	Nelson Santovenia	.03	.01	.00
☐ 452	Andy Allanson	.03	.01	.00
☐ 453	Bob Melvin	.03	.01	.00
☐ 454	Benito Santiago	.12	.06	.01
☐ 455	Jose Uribe	.03	.01	.00
☐ 456	Bill Landrum	.03	.01	.00
☐ 457	Bobby Witt	.08	.04	.01
☐ 458	Kevin Romine	.03	.01	.00
☐ 459	Lee Mazzilli	.03	.01	.00
☐ 460	Paul Molitor	.08	.04	.01
☐ 461	Ramon Martinez	.40	.20	.04
☐ 462	Frank DiPino	.03	.01	.00
☐ 463	Walt Terrell	.03	.01	.00
☐ 464	Bob Geren	.08	.04	.01
☐ 465	Rick Reuschel	.06	.03	.00
☐ 466	Mark Grant	.03	.01	.00
☐ 467	John Kruk	.03	.01	.00
☐ 468	Gregg Jefferies	.30	.15	.03
☐ 469	R.J. Reynolds	.03	.01	.00
☐ 470	Harold Baines	.08	.04	.01
☐ 471	Dennis Lamp	.03	.01	.00
☐ 472	Tom Gordon	.15	.07	.01
☐ 473	Terry Puhl	.03	.01	.00
☐ 474	Curt Wilkerson	.03	.01	.00
☐ 475	Dan Quisenberry	.06	.03	.00
☐ 476	Oddibe McDowell	.06	.03	.00
☐ 477	Zane Smith	.06	.03	.00
☐ 478	Franklin Stubbs	.06	.03	.00
☐ 479	Wallace Johnson	.03	.01	.00
☐ 480	Jay Tibbs	.03	.01	.00
☐ 481	Tom Glavine	.06	.03	.00
☐ 482	Manny Lee	.03	.01	.00
☐ 483	Joe Hesketh UER (says Rookiess on back, should say Rookies)	.03	.01	.00

☐ 484 Mike Bielecki	.03	.01	.00
☐ 485 Greg Brock	.03	.01	.00
☐ 486 Pascual Perez	.06	.03	.00
☐ 487 Kirk Gibson	.08	.04	.01
☐ 488 Scott Sanderson	.03	.01	.00
☐ 489 Domingo Ramos	.03	.01	.00
☐ 490 Kal Daniels	.08	.04	.01
☐ 491A David Wells ERR (reverse negative photo on card back)	3.00	1.50	.30
☐ 491B David Wells COR	.12	.06	.01
☐ 492 Jerry Reed	.03	.01	.00
☐ 493 Eric Show	.03	.01	.00
☐ 494 Mike Pagliarulo	.03	.01	.00
☐ 495 Ron Robinson	.03	.01	.00
☐ 496 Brad Komminsk	.03	.01	.00
☐ 497 Greg Litton	.12	.06	.01
☐ 498 Chris James	.06	.03	.00
☐ 499 Luis Quinones	.03	.01	.00
☐ 500 Frank Viola	.08	.04	.01
☐ 501 Tim Teufel	.03	.01	.00
☐ 502 Terry Leach	.03	.01	.00
☐ 503 Matt Williams	.20	.10	.02
☐ 504 Tim Leary	.06	.03	.00
☐ 505 Doug Drabek	.08	.04	.01
☐ 506 Mariano Duncan	.03	.01	.00
☐ 507 Charlie Hayes	.06	.03	.00
☐ 508 Joey Belle	.20	.10	.02
☐ 509 Pat Sheridan	.03	.01	.00
☐ 510 Mackey Sasser	.06	.03	.00
☐ 511 Jose Rijo	.06	.03	.00
☐ 512 Mike Smithson	.03	.01	.00
☐ 513 Gary Ward	.03	.01	.00
☐ 514 Dion James	.03	.01	.00
☐ 515 Jim Gott	.03	.01	.00
☐ 516 Drew Hall	.03	.01	.00
☐ 517 Doug Bair	.03	.01	.00
☐ 518 Scott Scudder	.15	.07	.01
☐ 519 Rick Aguilera	.03	.01	.00
☐ 520 Rafael Belliard	.03	.01	.00
☐ 521 Jay Buhner	.06	.03	.00
☐ 522 Jeff Reardon	.06	.03	.00
☐ 523 Steve Rosenberg	.08	.04	.01
☐ 524 Randy Velarde	.06	.03	.00
☐ 525 Jeff Musselman	.03	.01	.00
☐ 526 Bill Long	.03	.01	.00
☐ 527 Gary Wayne	.10	.05	.01
☐ 528 Dave Johnson (P)	.12	.06	.01
☐ 529 Ron Kittle	.06	.03	.00
☐ 530 Erik Hanson UER (5th line on back says seson, should say season)	.20	.10	.02
☐ 531 Steve Wilson	.08	.04	.01
☐ 532 Joey Meyer	.06	.03	.00
☐ 533 Curt Young	.03	.01	.00
☐ 534 Kelly Downs	.03	.01	.00
☐ 535 Joe Girardi	.08	.04	.01
☐ 536 Lance Blankenship	.03	.01	.00
☐ 537 Greg Mathews	.03	.01	.00
☐ 538 Donell Nixon	.03	.01	.00
☐ 539 Mark Knudson	.06	.03	.00
☐ 540 Jeff Wetherby	.10	.05	.01
☐ 541 Darrin Jackson	.03	.01	.00
☐ 542 Terry Mulholland	.03	.01	.00
☐ 543 Eric Hetzel	.06	.03	.00
☐ 544 Rick Reed	.12	.06	.01
☐ 545 Dennis Cook	.10	.05	.01
☐ 546 Mike Jackson	.03	.01	.00
☐ 547 Brian Fisher	.03	.01	.00
☐ 548 Gene Harris	.12	.06	.01
☐ 549 Jeff King	.12	.06	.01
☐ 550 Dave Dravecky	.08	.04	.01
☐ 551 Randy Kutcher	.03	.01	.00
☐ 552 Mark Portugal	.03	.01	.00
☐ 553 Jim Corsi	.06	.03	.00
☐ 554 Todd Stottlemyre	.06	.03	.00
☐ 555 Scott Bankhead	.06	.03	.00
☐ 556 Ken Dayley	.03	.01	.00
☐ 557 Rick Wrona	.12	.06	.01
☐ 558 Sammy Sosa	.50	.25	.05
☐ 559 Keith Miller	.03	.01	.00
☐ 560 Ken Griffey Jr.	2.50	1.25	.25
☐ 561A Ryne Sandberg HL ERR (position on front listed as 3B)	10.00	5.00	1.00
☐ 561B Ryne Sandberg HL COR	.35	.17	.03
☐ 562 Billy Hatcher	.06	.03	.00
☐ 563 Jay Bell	.03	.01	.00
☐ 564 Jack Daugherty	.10	.05	.01
☐ 565 Rich Monteleone	.08	.04	.01
☐ 566 Bo Jackson AS-MVP	.50	.25	.05
☐ 567 Tony Fossas	.08	.04	.01
☐ 568 Roy Smith	.03	.01	.00

☐ 569 Jaime Navarro	.15	.07	.01
☐ 570 Lance Johnson	.08	.04	.01
☐ 571 Mike Dyer	.12	.06	.01
☐ 572 Kevin Ritz	.10	.05	.01
☐ 573 Dave West	.06	.03	.00
☐ 574 Gary Mielke	.10	.05	.01
☐ 575 Scott Lusader	.03	.01	.00
☐ 576 Joe Oliver	.15	.07	.01
☐ 577 Sandy Alomar Jr.	.35	.17	.03
☐ 578 Andy Benes UER (extra comma between day and year)	.30	.15	.03
☐ 579 Tim Jones	.03	.01	.00
☐ 580 Randy McCament	.10	.05	.01
☐ 581 Curt Schilling	.06	.03	.00
☐ 582 John Orton	.12	.06	.01
☐ 583A Milt Cuyler ERR (998 games)	1.50	.75	.15
☐ 583B Milt Cuyler COR (98 games)	.35	.17	.03
☐ 584 Eric Anthony	.75	.35	.07
☐ 585 Greg Vaughn	.60	.30	.06
☐ 586 Deion Sanders	.30	.15	.03
☐ 587 Jose DeJesus	.03	.01	.00
☐ 588 Chip Hale	.10	.05	.01
☐ 589 John Olerud	2.50	1.25	.25
☐ 590 Steve Olin	.10	.05	.01
☐ 591 Marquis Grissom	.50	.25	.05
☐ 592 Moises Alou	.35	.17	.03
☐ 593 Mark Lemke	.06	.03	.00
☐ 594 Dean Palmer	.20	.10	.02
☐ 595 Robin Ventura	.30	.15	.03
☐ 596 Tino Martinez	.75	.35	.07
☐ 597 Mike Huff	.20	.10	.02
☐ 598 Scott Hemond	.25	.12	.02
☐ 599 Wally Whitehurst	.10	.05	.01
☐ 600 Todd Zeile	.75	.35	.07
☐ 601 Glenallen Hill	.15	.07	.01
☐ 602 Hal Morris	.45	.22	.04
☐ 603 Juan Bell	.12	.06	.01
☐ 604 Bobby Rose	.20	.10	.02
☐ 605 Matt Merullo	.12	.06	.01
☐ 606 Kevin Maas	3.00	1.50	.30
☐ 607 Randy Nosek	.12	.06	.01
☐ 608 Billy Bates	.12	.06	.01
☐ 609 Mike Stanton	.12	.06	.01
☐ 610 Mauro Gozzo	.12	.06	.01
☐ 611 Charles Nagy	.25	.12	.02
☐ 612 Scott Coolbaugh	.18	.09	.01
☐ 613 Jose Vizcaino	.15	.07	.01
☐ 614 Greg Smith	.15	.07	.01
☐ 615 Jeff Huson	.12	.06	.01
☐ 616 Mickey Weston	.10	.05	.01
☐ 617 John Pawlowski	.08	.04	.01
☐ 618A Joe Skalski ERR (27 on back)	.15	.07	.01
☐ 618B Joe Skalski COR (67 on back)	2.00	1.00	.20
☐ 619 Bernie Williams	.40	.20	.04
☐ 620 Shawn Holman	.12	.06	.01
☐ 621 Gary Eave	.12	.06	.01
☐ 622 Darrin Fletcher UER (Elmhurst, should be Elmhurst)	.25	.12	.02
☐ 623 Pat Combs	.12	.06	.01
☐ 624 Mike Blowers	.20	.10	.02
☐ 625 Kevin Appier	.30	.15	.03
☐ 626 Pat Austin	.12	.06	.01
☐ 627 Kelly Mann	.12	.06	.01
☐ 628 Matt Kinzer	.10	.05	.01
☐ 629 Chris Hammond	.25	.12	.02
☐ 630 Dean Wilkins	.15	.07	.01
☐ 631 Larry Walker	.40	.20	.04
☐ 632 Blaine Beatty	.12	.06	.01
☐ 633A Tommy Barrett ERR (29 on back)	.12	.06	.01
☐ 633B Tommy Barrett COR (14 on back)	4.00	2.00	.40
☐ 634 Stan Belinda	.15	.07	.01
☐ 635 Mike (Tex) Smith	.12	.06	.01
☐ 636 Hensley Meulens	.35	.17	.03
☐ 637 Juan Gonzalez	2.00	1.00	.20
☐ 638 Lenny Webster	.15	.07	.01
☐ 639 Mark Gardner	.20	.10	.02
☐ 640 Tommy Greene	.30	.15	.03
☐ 641 Mike Hartley	.15	.07	.01
☐ 642 Phil Stephenson	.12	.06	.01
☐ 643 Kevin Mmahat	.15	.07	.01
☐ 644 Ed Whited	.18	.09	.01
☐ 645 Delino DeShields	.75	.35	.07
☐ 646 Kevin Blankenship	.06	.03	.00
☐ 647 Paul Sorrento	.12	.06	.01
☐ 648 Mike Roesler	.12	.06	.01
☐ 649 Jason Grimsley	.12	.06	.01

		MINT	EXC	G-VG
☐ 650	Dave Justice	3.25	1.60	.32
☐ 651	Scott Cooper	.35	.17	.03
☐ 652	Dave Eiland	.08	.04	.01
☐ 653	Mike Munoz	.12	.06	.01
☐ 654	Jeff Fischer	.10	.05	.01
☐ 655	Terry Jorgenson	.12	.06	.01
☐ 656	George Canale	.12	.06	.01
☐ 657	Brian Dubois	.12	.06	.01
☐ 658	Carlos Quintana	.06	.03	.00
☐ 659	Luis De Los Santos	.03	.01	.00
☐ 660	Jerald Clark	.03	.01	.00
☐ 661	Donald Harris DC	.20	.10	.02
☐ 662	Paul Coleman DC	.30	.15	.03
☐ 663	Frank Thomas DC	3.25	1.60	.32
☐ 664	Brent Mayne DC	.20	.10	.02
☐ 665	Eddie Zosky DC	.35	.17	.03
☐ 666	Steve Hosey DC	.35	.17	.03
☐ 667	Scott Bryant DC	.25	.12	.02
☐ 668	Tom Goodwin DC	.40	.20	.04
☐ 669	Cal Eldred DC	.20	.10	.02
☐ 670	Earl Cunningham DC	.30	.15	.03
☐ 671	Alan Zinter DC	.25	.12	.02
☐ 672	Chuck Knoblauch DC	.25	.12	.02
☐ 673	Kyle Abbott DC	.25	.12	.02
☐ 674	Roger Salkeld DC	.45	.22	.04
☐ 675	Maurice Vaughn DC	1.35	.65	.13
☐ 676	Keith (Kiki) Jones DC	.60	.30	.06
☐ 677	Tyler Houston DC	.35	.17	.03
☐ 678	Jeff Jackson DC	.15	.07	.01
☐ 679	Greg Gohr DC	.20	.10	.02
☐ 680	Ben McDonald DC	1.50	.75	.15
☐ 681	Greg Blosser DC	.50	.25	.05
☐ 682	Willie Green DC	.25	.12	.02
☐ 683	Wade Boggs DT	.15	.07	.01
☐ 684	Will Clark DT	.30	.15	.03
☐ 685	Tony Gwynn DT	.10	.05	.01
☐ 686	Rickey Henderson DT	.25	.12	.02
☐ 687	Bo Jackson DT	.50	.25	.05
☐ 688	Mark Langston DT	.08	.04	.01
☐ 689	Barry Larkin DT	.10	.05	.01
☐ 690	Kirby Puckett DT	.18	.09	.01
☐ 691	Ryne Sandberg DT	.20	.10	.02
☐ 692	Mike Scott DT	.08	.04	.01
☐ 693A	Terry Steinbach DT ERR (cathers)	.10	.05	.01
☐ 693B	Terry Steinbach DT COR (catchers)	.40	.20	.04
☐ 694	Bobby Thigpen DT	.08	.04	.01
☐ 695	Mitch Williams DT	.06	.03	.00
☐ 696	Nolan Ryan HL	.30	.15	.03
☐ 697	Bo Jackson FB/BB	7.50	3.75	.75
☐ 698	Rickey Henderson ALCS-MVP	.20	.10	.02
☐ 699	Will Clark NLCS-MVP	.20	.10	.02
☐ 700	WS Games 1/2	.06	.03	.00
☐ 701	Candlestick	.15	.07	.01
☐ 702	WS Game 3	.06	.03	.00
☐ 703	WS Wrap-up	.06	.03	.00
☐ 704	Wade Boggs	.15	.07	.01

1990 Score Dream Team Rookies

The 1990 Score Dream Team Rookies Insert contains ten standard-size (2 1/2" by 3 1/2") cards. The ten cards represent one player for each position and Bart Giamatti. The sets were inserted in the Score factory collated sets hobby dealers received early in 1990, but not the retail sets issued later in 1990. Card B1 is a special commemorative card of the late Commissioner A. Bartlett Giamatti.

	MINT	EXC	G-VG
COMPLETE SET (10)	10.00	5.00	1.00
COMMON PLAYER (B1-B10)	.35	.17	.03

☐ B1	A.Bartlett Giamatti (late Commissioner)	3.50	1.75	.35
☐ B2	Pat Combs	.60	.30	.06
☐ B3	Todd Zeile	1.25	.60	.12
☐ B4	Luis De Los Santos	.35	.17	.03
☐ B5	Mark Lemke	.35	.17	.03
☐ B6	Robin Ventura	1.00	.50	.10
☐ B7	Jeff Huson	.35	.17	.03
☐ B8	Greg Vaughn	1.00	.50	.10
☐ B9	Marquis Grissom	1.00	.50	.10
☐ B10	Eric Anthony	1.25	.60	.12

1990 Score Commemorative Nolan Ryan card

This 2 1/2" by 3 1/2" card was issued by Optigraphics (producer of Score and Sportflics) to commemorate the 11th National Sports Card Collectors Convention held in Arlington, Texas in July of 1990. This card featured a Score front similar to the Ryan 1990 Score highlight card except for the 11th National Convention Logo on the bottom right of the card. On the other side a Ryan Sportflics card was printed that stated (reflected) either Sportflics or 1990 National Sports Collectors Convention on the bottom of the card This issue was limited to a printing of 600 cards with Ryan himself destroying the presses.

		MINT	EXC	G-VG
☐ xx	Nolan Ryan (no number on back; card back is actually another front in Sportflics style)	750.00	300.00	75.00

1990 Score Young Superstars I

1990 Score Young Superstars I are glossy full color cards featuring 42 of the most popular young players. The first series was issued with Score rak packs while the second series was available only via a mailaway from the Company. The set contains standard-size (2 1/2" by 3 1/2") cards.

	MINT	EXC	G-VG
COMPLETE SET (42)	6.00	3.00	.60
COMMON PLAYER (1-42)	.20	.10	.02

☐ 1 Bo Jackson	1.00	.50	.10
☐ 2 Dwight Smith	.30	.15	.03
☐ 3 Joey Belle	.30	.15	.03
☐ 4 Gregg Olson	.30	.15	.03
☐ 5 Jim Abbott	.40	.20	.04
☐ 6 Felix Fermin	.20	.10	.02
☐ 7 Brian Holman	.25	.12	.02
☐ 8 Clay Parker	.20	.10	.02
☐ 9 Junior Felix	.30	.15	.03
☐ 10 Joe Oliver	.20	.10	.02
☐ 11 Steve Finley	.25	.12	.02
☐ 12 Greg Briley	.30	.15	.03
☐ 13 Greg Vaughn	.40	.20	.04
☐ 14 Bill Spiers	.20	.10	.02
☐ 15 Eric Yelding	.25	.12	.02
☐ 16 Jose Gonzalez	.20	.10	.02
☐ 17 Mark Carreon	.20	.10	.02
☐ 18 Greg Harris	.20	.10	.02
☐ 19 Felix Jose	.25	.12	.02
☐ 20 Bob Milacki	.20	.10	.02
☐ 21 Kenny Rogers	.20	.10	.02
☐ 22 Rolando Roomes	.20	.10	.02
☐ 23 Bip Roberts	.20	.10	.02
☐ 24 Jeff Brantley	.20	.10	.02
☐ 25 Jeff Ballard	.20	.10	.02
☐ 26 John Dopson	.20	.10	.02
☐ 27 Ken Patterson	.20	.10	.02
☐ 28 Omar Vizquel	.20	.10	.02
☐ 29 Kevin Brown	.25	.12	.02
☐ 30 Derek Lilliquist	.20	.10	.02
☐ 31 David Wells	.20	.10	.02
☐ 32 Ken Hill	.20	.10	.02
☐ 33 Greg Litton	.20	.10	.02
☐ 34 Rob Ducey	.20	.10	.02
☐ 35 Carlos Martinez	.20	.10	.02
☐ 36 John Smoltz	.25	.12	.02
☐ 37 Lenny Harris	.25	.12	.02
☐ 38 Charlie Hayes	.25	.12	.02
☐ 39 Tommy Gregg	.20	.10	.02
☐ 40 John Wetteland	.25	.12	.02
☐ 41 Jeff Huson	.20	.10	.02
☐ 42 Eric Anthony	.40	.20	.04

1990 Score Young Superstars II

1990 Score Young Superstars II are glossy full color cards featuring 42 of the most popular young players. Whereas the first series was issued with Score rak packs, this second series was available only via a mailaway from the Company. The set contains standard-size (2 1/2" by 3 1/2") cards.

	MINT	EXC	G-VG
COMPLETE SET (42)	6.00	3.00	.60
COMMON PLAYER (1-42)	.20	.10	.02
☐ 1 Todd Zeile	.40	.20	.04
☐ 2 Ben McDonald	.60	.30	.06
☐ 3 Delino DeShields	.50	.25	.05
☐ 4 Pat Combs	.30	.15	.03
☐ 5 John Olerud	.75	.35	.07
☐ 6 Marquis Grissom	.35	.17	.03
☐ 7 Mike Stanton	.20	.10	.02
☐ 8 Robin Ventura	.35	.17	.03
☐ 9 Larry Walker	.30	.15	.03
☐ 10 Dante Bichette	.25	.12	.02
☐ 11 Jack Armstrong	.25	.12	.02
☐ 12 Jay Bell	.20	.10	.02
☐ 13 Andy Benes	.30	.15	.03
☐ 14 Joey Cora	.20	.10	.02
☐ 15 Rob Dibble	.30	.15	.03
☐ 16 Jeff King	.20	.10	.02
☐ 17 Jeff Hamilton	.20	.10	.02
☐ 18 Erik Hanson	.30	.15	.03
☐ 19 Pete Harnisch	.20	.10	.02
☐ 20 Greg Hibbard	.20	.10	.02
☐ 21 Stan Javier	.20	.10	.02
☐ 22 Mark Lemke	.20	.10	.02
☐ 23 Steve Olin	.20	.10	.02
☐ 24 Tommy Greene	.20	.10	.02
☐ 25 Sammy Sosa	.30	.15	.03
☐ 26 Gary Wayne	.20	.10	.02
☐ 27 Deion Sanders	.30	.15	.03
☐ 28 Steve Wilson	.20	.10	.02
☐ 29 Joe Girardi	.20	.10	.02
☐ 30 John Orton	.20	.10	.02
☐ 31 Kevin Tapani	.30	.15	.03
☐ 32 Carlos Baerga	.30	.15	.03
☐ 33 Glenallen Hill	.30	.15	.03
☐ 34 Mike Blowers	.25	.12	.02
☐ 35 Dave Hollins	.25	.12	.02
☐ 36 Lance Blankenship	.20	.10	.02
☐ 37 Hal Morris	.35	.17	.03
☐ 38 Lance Johnson	.25	.12	.02
☐ 39 Chris Gwynn	.20	.10	.02
☐ 40 Doug Dascenzo	.20	.10	.02
☐ 41 Jerald Clark	.20	.10	.02
☐ 42 Carlos Quintana	.30	.15	.03

1990 Score Nat West Yankees

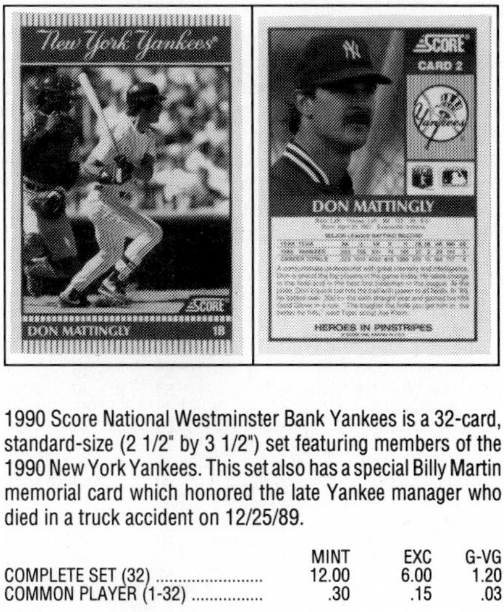

1990 Score National Westminster Bank Yankees is a 32-card, standard-size (2 1/2" by 3 1/2") set featuring members of the 1990 New York Yankees. This set also has a special Billy Martin memorial card which honored the late Yankee manager who died in a truck accident on 12/25/89.

	MINT	EXC	G-VG
COMPLETE SET (32)	12.00	6.00	1.20
COMMON PLAYER (1-32)	.30	.15	.03

☐ 1 Stump Merrill MG	.40	.20	.04
☐ 2 Don Mattingly	1.50	.75	.15
☐ 3 Steve Sax	.60	.30	.06
☐ 4 Alvaro Espinoza	.30	.15	.03
☐ 5 Jesse Barfield	.50	.25	.05
☐ 6 Roberto Kelly	.75	.35	.07
☐ 7 Mel Hall	.40	.20	.04
☐ 8 Claudell Washington	.40	.20	.04
☐ 9 Bob Geren	.40	.20	.04
☐ 10 Jim Leyritz	.40	.20	.04
☐ 11 Pascual Perez	.40	.20	.04
☐ 12 Dave LaPoint	.30	.15	.03
☐ 13 Tim Leary	.40	.20	.04
☐ 14 Mike Witt	.30	.15	.03
☐ 15 Chuck Cary	.30	.15	.03
☐ 16 Dave Righetti	.50	.25	.05
☐ 17 Lee Guetterman	.30	.15	.03
☐ 18 Andy Hawkins	.30	.15	.03
☐ 19 Greg Cadaret	.30	.15	.03
☐ 20 Eric Plunk	.30	.15	.03
☐ 21 Jimmy Jones	.30	.15	.03
☐ 22 Deion Sanders	.60	.30	.06
☐ 23 Jeff Robinson	.30	.15	.03
☐ 24 Matt Nokes	.40	.20	.04
☐ 25 Steve Balboni	.30	.15	.03
☐ 26 Wayne Tolleson	.30	.15	.03
☐ 27 Randy Velarde	.30	.15	.03
☐ 28 Rick Cerone	.30	.15	.03
☐ 29 Alan Mills	.40	.20	.04
☐ 30 Billy Martin (memorial)	.60	.30	.06
☐ 31 Stadium Card	.30	.15	.03
☐ 32 All-Time Yankee Record	.30	.15	.03

1990 Score Pepsi Red Sox

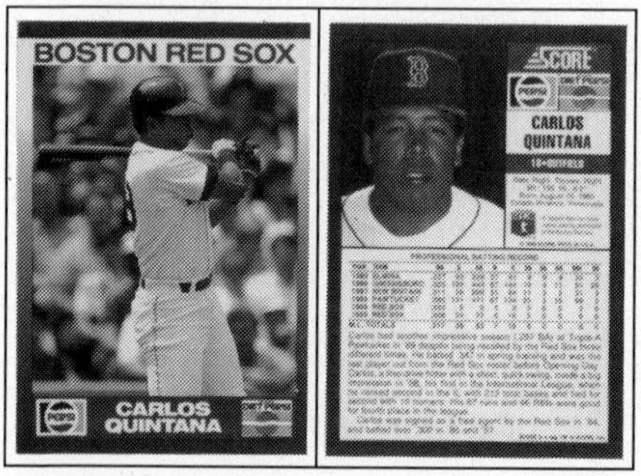

The Score Pepsi Boston Red Sox is a 20-card standard-size set, 2 1/2" by 3 1/2", which is checklisted alphabetically below. This set was apparently prepared very early in the 1990 season as Bill Buckner and Lee Smith are still members of the Red Sox in this set. The top of the front of the card have Boston Red Sox printed while the bottom of the card has the players name surrounded by the Pepsi and the Diet Pepsi logo. The backs of the cards have the Score feel to them except the Pepsi and Diet Pepsi logos are again featured prominently on the back of the cards .

	MINT	EXC	G-VG
COMPLETE SET (20)	15.00	7.50	1.50
COMMON PLAYER (1-20)	.50	.25	.05
☐ 1 Marty Barrett	.60	.30	.06
☐ 2 Mike Boddicker	.60	.30	.06
☐ 3 Wade Boggs	1.75	.85	.17
☐ 4 Bill Buckner	.60	.30	.06
☐ 5 Ellis Burks	1.25	.60	.12
☐ 6 Roger Clemens	1.75	.85	.17
☐ 7 John Dopson	.60	.30	.06
☐ 8 Dwight Evans	1.00	.50	.10
☐ 9 Wes Gardner	.50	.25	.05
☐ 10 Rich Gedman	.50	.25	.05
☐ 11 Mike Greenwell	1.00	.50	.10
☐ 12 Dennis Lamp	.50	.25	.05
☐ 13 Rob Murphy	.50	.25	.05
☐ 14 Tony Pena	.60	.30	.06
☐ 15 Carlos Quintana	.75	.35	.07
☐ 16 Jeff Reardon	.60	.30	.06
☐ 17 Jody Reed	.75	.35	.07
☐ 18 Luis Rivera	.50	.25	.05
☐ 19 Kevin Romine	.50	.25	.05
☐ 20 Lee Smith	.60	.30	.06

1990 Score 100 Rising Stars

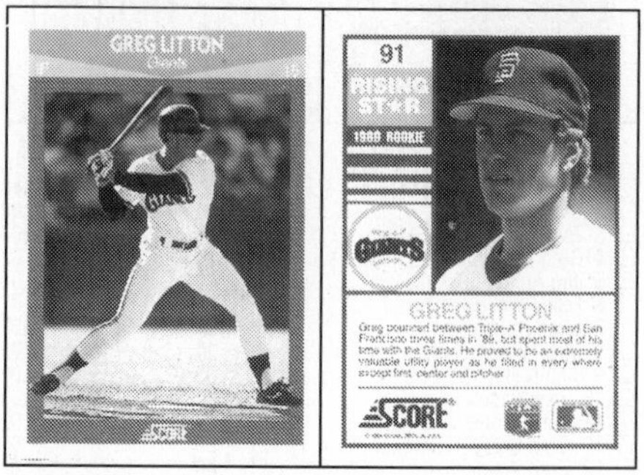

The 1990 Score Rising Stars set contains 100 standard size (2 1/2" by 3 1/2") cards. The fronts are green, blue and white. The vertically-oriented backs feature a large color facial shot and career highlights. The cards were distributed as a set in a blister pack, which also included a full color booklet with more information about each player.

	MINT	EXC	G-VG
COMPLETE SET (100)	12.00	6.00	1.20
COMMON PLAYER (1-100)	.05	.02	.00
☐ 1 Tom Gordon	.30	.15	.03
☐ 2 Jerome Walton	.60	.30	.06
☐ 3 Ken Griffey Jr.	1.00	.50	.10
☐ 4 Dwight Smith	.25	.12	.02
☐ 5 Jim Abbott	.50	.25	.05
☐ 6 Todd Zeile	.60	.30	.06
☐ 7 Donn Pall	.05	.02	.00
☐ 8 Rick Reed	.05	.02	.00
☐ 9 Joey Belle	.20	.10	.02
☐ 10 Gregg Jefferies	.50	.25	.05
☐ 11 Kevin Ritz	.10	.05	.01
☐ 12 Charlie Hayes	.10	.05	.01
☐ 13 Kevin Appier	.20	.10	.02
☐ 14 Jeff Huson	.05	.02	.00
☐ 15 Gary Wayne	.10	.05	.01
☐ 16 Eric Yelding	.10	.05	.01
☐ 17 Clay Parker	.05	.02	.00
☐ 18 Junior Felix	.35	.17	.03
☐ 19 Derek Lilliquist	.10	.05	.01
☐ 20 Gary Sheffield	.40	.20	.04
☐ 21 Craig Worthington	.10	.05	.01
☐ 22 Jeff Brantley	.15	.07	.01
☐ 23 Eric Hetzel	.10	.05	.01
☐ 24 Greg W.Harris	.10	.05	.01
☐ 25 John Wetteland	.15	.07	.01
☐ 26 Joe Oliver	.15	.07	.01
☐ 27 Kevin Maas	1.50	.75	.15
☐ 28 Kevin Brown	.15	.07	.01
☐ 29 Mike Stanton	.10	.05	.01
☐ 30 Greg Vaughn	.45	.22	.04
☐ 31 Ron Jones	.15	.07	.01
☐ 32 Gregg Olson	.35	.17	.03
☐ 33 Joe Girardi	.15	.07	.01
☐ 34 Ken Hill	.10	.05	.01
☐ 35 Sammy Sosa	.40	.20	.04
☐ 36 Geronimo Berroa	.05	.02	.00
☐ 37 Omar Vizquel	.10	.05	.01
☐ 38 Dean Palmer	.15	.07	.01
☐ 39 John Olerud	1.25	.60	.12
☐ 40 Deion Sanders	.50	.25	.05
☐ 41 Randy Kramer	.10	.05	.01
☐ 42 Scott Lusader	.05	.02	.00
☐ 43 Dave Johnson (P)	.10	.05	.01
☐ 44 Jeff Wetherby	.10	.05	.01

□ 45 Eric Anthony	.50	.25	.05
□ 46 Kenny Rogers	.10	.05	.01
□ 47 Matt Winters	.15	.07	.01
□ 48 Mauro Gozzo	.10	.05	.01
□ 49 Carlos Quintana	.20	.10	.02
□ 50 Bob Geren	.10	.05	.01
□ 51 Chad Kreuter	.10	.05	.01
□ 52 Randy Johnson	.15	.07	.01
□ 53 Hensley Meulens	.40	.20	.04
□ 54 Gene Harris	.10	.05	.01
□ 55 Bill Spiers	.10	.05	.01
□ 56 Kelly Mann	.10	.05	.01
□ 57 Tom McCarthy	.10	.05	.01
□ 58 Steve Finley	.10	.05	.01
□ 59 Ramon Martinez	.40	.20	.04
□ 60 Greg Briley	.20	.10	.02
□ 61 Jack Daugherty	.10	.05	.01
□ 62 Tim Jones	.05	.02	.00
□ 63 Doug Strange	.10	.05	.01
□ 64 John Orton	.10	.05	.01
□ 65 Scott Scudder	.15	.07	.01
□ 66 Mark Gardner	.10	.05	.01
□ 67 Mark Carreon	.10	.05	.01
□ 68 Bob Milacki	.10	.05	.01
□ 69 Andy Benes	.40	.20	.04
□ 70 Carlos Martinez	.10	.05	.01
□ 71 Jeff King	.10	.05	.01
□ 72 Brad Arnsberg	.10	.05	.01
□ 73 Rick Wrona	.10	.05	.01
□ 74 Cris Carpenter	.10	.05	.01
□ 75 Dennis Cook	.10	.05	.01
□ 76 Pete Harnisch	.05	.02	.00
□ 77 Greg Hibbard	.10	.05	.01
□ 78 Ed Whited	.15	.07	.01
□ 79 Scott Coolbaugh	.15	.07	.01
□ 80 Billy Bates	.10	.05	.01
□ 81 German Gonzalez	.05	.02	.00
□ 82 Lance Blankenship	.05	.02	.00
□ 83 Lenny Harris	.15	.07	.01
□ 84 Milt Cuyler	.20	.10	.02
□ 85 Erik Hanson	.20	.10	.02
□ 86 Kent Anderson	.10	.05	.01
□ 87 Hal Morris	.40	.20	.04
□ 88 Mike Brumley	.10	.05	.01
□ 89 Ken Patterson	.10	.05	.01
□ 90 Mike Devereaux	.10	.05	.01
□ 91 Greg Litton	.10	.05	.01
□ 92 Rolando Roomes	.10	.05	.01
□ 93 Ben McDonald	.90	.45	.09
□ 94 Curt Schilling	.10	.05	.01
□ 95 Jose DeJesus	.15	.07	.01
□ 96 Robin Ventura	.40	.20	.04
□ 97 Steve Searcy	.15	.07	.01
□ 98 Chip Hale	.10	.05	.01
□ 99 Marquis Grissom	.35	.17	.03
□ 100 Luis de los Santos	.10	.05	.01

1990 Score 100 Superstars

The 1990 Score Superstars set contains 100 standard size (2 1/2" by 3 1/2") cards. The fronts are red, white, blue and purple. The vertically-oriented backs feature a large color facial shot and career highlights. The cards were distributed as a set in a blister pack, which also included a full color booklet with more information about each player.

	MINT	EXC	G-VG
COMPLETE SET (100)	12.00	6.00	1.20
COMMON PLAYER (1-100)	.05	.02	.00
□ 1 Kirby Puckett	.45	.22	.04
□ 2 Steve Sax	.15	.07	.01
□ 3 Tony Gwynn	.30	.15	.03
□ 4 Willie Randolph	.10	.05	.01
□ 5 Jose Canseco	1.00	.50	.10
□ 6 Ozzie Smith	.20	.10	.02
□ 7 Rick Reuschel	.10	.05	.01
□ 8 Bill Doran	.05	.02	.00
□ 9 Mickey Tettleton	.10	.05	.01
□ 10 Don Mattingly	1.00	.50	.10
□ 11 Greg Swindell	.10	.05	.01
□ 12 Bert Blyleven	.10	.05	.01
□ 13 Dave Stewart	.20	.10	.02
□ 14 Andres Galarraga	.15	.07	.01
□ 15 Darryl Strawberry	.50	.25	.05
□ 16 Ellis Burks	.35	.17	.03
□ 17 Paul O'Neill	.20	.10	.02
□ 18 Bruce Hurst	.10	.05	.01
□ 19 Dave Smith	.05	.02	.00
□ 20 Carney Lansford	.10	.05	.01
□ 21 Robby Thompson	.05	.02	.00
□ 22 Gary Gaetti	.10	.05	.01
□ 23 Jeff Russell	.05	.02	.00
□ 24 Chuck Finley	.15	.07	.01
□ 25 Mark McGwire	.75	.35	.07
□ 26 Alvin Davis	.10	.05	.01
□ 27 George Bell	.15	.07	.01
□ 28 Cory Snyder	.10	.05	.01
□ 29 Keith Hernandez	.10	.05	.01
□ 30 Will Clark	.90	.45	.09
□ 31 Steve Bedrosian	.10	.05	.01
□ 32 Ryne Sandberg	.60	.30	.06
□ 33 Tom Browning	.10	.05	.01
□ 34 Tim Burke	.10	.05	.01
□ 35 John Smoltz	.15	.07	.01
□ 36 Phil Bradley	.10	.05	.01
□ 37 Bobby Bonilla	.25	.12	.02
□ 38 Kirk McCaskill	.05	.02	.00
□ 39 Dave Righetti	.10	.05	.01
□ 40 Bo Jackson	1.00	.50	.10
□ 41 Alan Trammell	.15	.07	.01
□ 42 Mike Moore	.05	.02	.00
□ 43 Harold Reynolds	.10	.05	.01
□ 44 Nolan Ryan	1.00	.50	.10
□ 45 Fred McGriff	.35	.17	.03
□ 46 Brian Downing	.05	.02	.00
□ 47 Brett Butler	.10	.05	.01
□ 48 Mike Scioscia	.05	.02	.00
□ 49 John Franco	.05	.02	.00
□ 50 Kevin Mitchell	.45	.22	.04
□ 51 Mark Davis	.10	.05	.01
□ 52 Glenn Davis	.15	.07	.01
□ 53 Barry Bonds	.35	.17	.03
□ 54 Dwight Evans	.15	.07	.01
□ 55 Terry Steinbach	.10	.05	.01
□ 56 Dave Gallagher	.05	.02	.00
□ 57 Roberto Kelly	.30	.15	.03
□ 58 Rafael Palmeiro	.20	.10	.02
□ 59 Joe Carter	.20	.10	.02
□ 60 Mark Grace	.90	.45	.09
□ 61 Pedro Guerrero	.15	.07	.01
□ 62 Von Hayes	.10	.05	.01
□ 63 Benito Santiago	.30	.15	.03
□ 64 Dale Murphy	.40	.20	.04
□ 65 John Smiley	.05	.02	.00
□ 66 Cal Ripken Jr.	.35	.17	.03
□ 67 Mike Greenwell	.30	.15	.03
□ 68 Devon White	.10	.05	.01
□ 69 Ed Whitson	.05	.02	.00
□ 70 Carlton Fisk	.20	.10	.02
□ 71 Lou Whitaker	.10	.05	.01
□ 72 Danny Tartabull	.15	.07	.01
□ 73 Vince Coleman	.20	.10	.02
□ 74 Andre Dawson	.25	.12	.02
□ 75 Tim Raines	.20	.10	.02
□ 76 George Brett	.35	.17	.03
□ 77 Tom Herr	.05	.02	.00
□ 78 Andy Van Slyke	.10	.05	.01
□ 79 Roger Clemens	.60	.30	.06
□ 80 Wade Boggs	.60	.30	.06
□ 81 Wally Joyner	.25	.12	.02
□ 82 Lonnie Smith	.10	.05	.01
□ 83 Howard Johnson	.15	.07	.01
□ 84 Julio Franco	.10	.05	.01
□ 85 Ruben Sierra	.40	.20	.04
□ 86 Dan Plesac	.05	.02	.00
□ 87 Bobby Thigpen	.15	.07	.01
□ 88 Kevin Seitzer	.20	.10	.02
□ 89 Dave Stieb	.15	.07	.01
□ 90 Rickey Henderson	.75	.35	.07

☐ 91 Jeffrey Leonard	.10	.05	.01
☐ 92 Robin Yount	.40	.20	.04
☐ 93 Mitch Williams	.10	.05	.01
☐ 94 Orel Hershiser	.25	.12	.02
☐ 95 Eric Davis	.45	.22	.04
☐ 96 Mark Langston	.10	.05	.01
☐ 97 Mike Scott	.15	.07	.01
☐ 98 Paul Molitor	.10	.05	.01
☐ 99 Dwight Gooden	.35	.17	.03
☐ 100 Kevin Bass	.10	.05	.01

1990 Score Traded

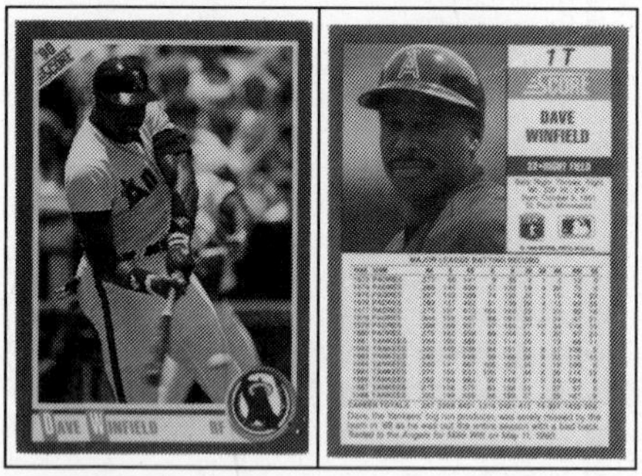

The 1990 Score Rookie/Traded set marks the fourth consecutive year Score has issued an end of the year set to mark trades and give rookies early cards. This now-standard set consists of 110 cards; cards measure the standard size of 2 1/2" by 3 1/2". The first 66 cards are traded players while the last 44 cards are rookie cards. Included in the rookie part of the set are cross-athletes Eric Lindros (hockey) and D.J. Dozier (football).

	MINT	EXC	G-VG
COMPLETE SET (110)	12.00	6.00	1.20
COMMON PLAYER (1-66)	.06	.03	.00
COMMON PLAYER (67-110)	.06	.03	.00
☐ 1T Dave Winfield	.12	.06	.01
☐ 2T Kevin Bass	.10	.05	.01
☐ 3T Nick Esasky	.10	.05	.01
☐ 4T Mitch Webster	.06	.03	.00
☐ 5T Pascual Perez	.10	.05	.01
☐ 6T Gary Pettis	.06	.03	.00
☐ 7T Tony Pena	.10	.05	.01
☐ 8T Candy Maldonado	.10	.05	.01
☐ 9T Cecil Fielder	.50	.25	.05
☐ 10T Carmelo Martinez	.06	.03	.00
☐ 11T Mark Langston	.10	.05	.01
☐ 12T Dave Parker	.10	.05	.01
☐ 13T Don Slaught	.06	.03	.00
☐ 14T Tony Phillips	.06	.03	.00
☐ 15T John Franco	.10	.05	.01
☐ 16T Randy Myers	.10	.05	.01
☐ 17T Jeff Reardon	.10	.05	.01
☐ 18T Sandy Alomar Jr.	.30	.15	.03
☐ 19T Joe Carter	.12	.06	.01
☐ 20T Fred Lynn	.10	.05	.01
☐ 21T Storm Davis	.10	.05	.01
☐ 22T Craig Lefferts	.06	.03	.00
☐ 23T Pete O'Brien	.10	.05	.01
☐ 24T Dennis Boyd	.10	.05	.01
☐ 25T Lloyd Moseby	.10	.05	.01
☐ 26T Mark Davis	.10	.05	.01
☐ 27T Tim Leary	.10	.05	.01
☐ 28T Gerald Perry	.06	.03	.00
☐ 29T Don Aase	.06	.03	.00
☐ 30T Ernie Whitt	.06	.03	.00
☐ 31T Mike Marshall	.10	.05	.01
☐ 32T Alejandro Pena	.06	.03	.00
☐ 33T Juan Samuel	.10	.05	.01
☐ 34T Hubie Brooks	.10	.05	.01
☐ 35T Gary Carter	.10	.05	.01
☐ 36T Jim Presley	.06	.03	.00
☐ 37T Wally Backman	.06	.03	.00
☐ 38T Matt Nokes	.10	.05	.01
☐ 39T Dan Petry	.06	.03	.00
☐ 40T Franklin Stubbs	.10	.05	.01
☐ 41T Jeff Huson	.10	.05	.01
☐ 42T Billy Hatcher	.10	.05	.01
☐ 43T Terry Leach	.10	.05	.01
☐ 44T Fred Manrique	.06	.03	.00
☐ 45T Claudell Washington	.10	.05	.01
☐ 46T Luis Polonia	.06	.03	.00
☐ 47T Daryl Boston	.10	.05	.01
☐ 48T Lee Smith	.10	.05	.01
☐ 49T Tom Brunansky	.12	.06	.01
☐ 50T Mike Witt	.06	.03	.00
☐ 51T Willie Randolph	.10	.05	.01
☐ 52T Stan Javier	.06	.03	.00
☐ 53T Brad Komminsk	.06	.03	.00
☐ 54T Cecilio Guante	.06	.03	.00
☐ 55T Bryn Smith	.06	.03	.00
☐ 56T Glenn Braggs	.10	.05	.01
☐ 57T Keith Hernandez	.12	.06	.01
☐ 58T Ken Oberkfell	.06	.03	.00
☐ 59T Steve Jeltz	.06	.03	.00
☐ 60T Chris James	.10	.05	.01
☐ 61T Scott Sanderson	.10	.05	.01
☐ 62T Bill Long	.06	.03	.00
☐ 63T Rick Cerone	.06	.03	.00
☐ 64T Scott Bailes	.06	.03	.00
☐ 65T Larry Sheets	.06	.03	.00
☐ 66T Junior Ortiz	.06	.03	.00
☐ 67T Francisco Cabrera	.20	.10	.02
☐ 68T Gary DiSarcina	.15	.07	.01
☐ 69T Greg Olson	.25	.12	.02
☐ 70T Beau Allred	.15	.07	.01
☐ 71T Oscar Azocar	.30	.15	.03
☐ 72T Kent Mercker	.20	.10	.02
☐ 73T John Burkett	.25	.12	.02
☐ 74T Carlos Baerga	.40	.20	.04
☐ 75T Dave Hollins	.25	.12	.02
☐ 76T Todd Hundley	.20	.10	.02
☐ 77T Rick Parker	.12	.06	.01
☐ 78T Steve Cummings	.12	.06	.01
☐ 79T Bill Sampen	.20	.10	.02
☐ 80T Jerry Kutzler	.12	.06	.01
☐ 81T Derek Bell	.35	.17	.03
☐ 82T Kevin Tapani	.25	.12	.02
☐ 83T Jim Leyritz	.25	.12	.02
☐ 84T Ray Lankford	.90	.45	.09
☐ 85T Wayne Edwards	.15	.07	.01
☐ 86T Frank Thomas	1.75	.85	.17
☐ 87T Tim Naehring	.30	.15	.03
☐ 88T Willie Blair	.10	.05	.01
☐ 89T Alan Mills	.15	.07	.01
☐ 90T Scott Radinsky	.20	.10	.02
☐ 91T Howard Farmer	.15	.07	.01
☐ 92T Julio Machado	.12	.06	.01
☐ 93T Rafael Valdez	.15	.07	.01
☐ 94T Shawn Boskie	.20	.10	.02
☐ 95T David Segui	.40	.20	.04
☐ 96T Chris Hoiles	.25	.12	.02
☐ 97T D.J. Dozier	.50	.25	.05
☐ 98T Hector Villanueva	.25	.12	.02
☐ 99T Eric Gunderson	.15	.07	.01
☐ 100T Eric Lindros	3.00	1.50	.30
☐ 101T Dave Otto	.10	.05	.01
☐ 102T Dana Kiecker	.20	.10	.02
☐ 103T Tim Drummond	.12	.06	.01
☐ 104T Mickey Pina	.35	.17	.03
☐ 105T Craig Grebeck	.15	.07	.01
☐ 106T Bernard Gilkey	.45	.22	.04
☐ 107T Tim Layana	.20	.10	.02
☐ 108T Scott Chiamparino	.40	.20	.04
☐ 109T Steve Avery	.30	.15	.03
☐ 110T Terry Shumpert	.15	.07	.01

1991 Score I

The 1991 Score Series 1 contains 441 cards. The cards feature a solid color border framing the full-color photo of the cards. The cards measure the standard card size of 2 1/2" by 3 1/2" and also feature Score trademark full-color photos on the back. The backs also include a brief biography on each player. This set marks the fourth consecutive year that Score has issued a major set but the first time Score issued the set in two series. Score also reused their successful Dream Team concept by using non-baseball photos of Today's stars. Series 1 has the Annie Leibowitz photo of Jose Canseco used in American Express ads. This first series also includes 49 Rookie prospects,

12 1st Round Draft Picks and 5 each of the Master Blaster, K-Man and Rifleman subsets. The All-Star sets are all American Leaguers (which are all caricatures) and five highlight cards.

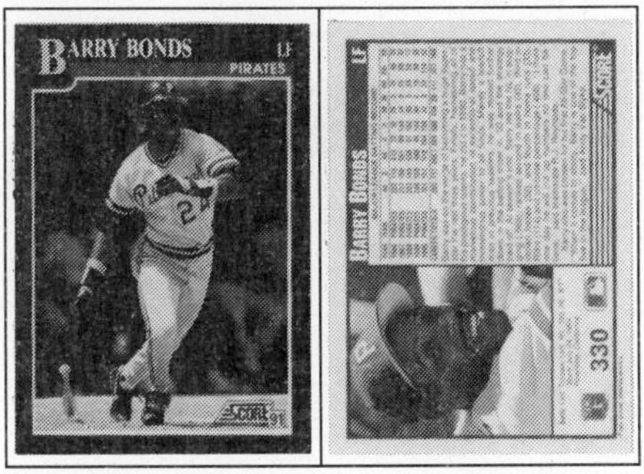

	MINT	EXC	G-VG
COMPLETE SET (441)	15.00	7.50	1.50
COMMON PLAYER (1-441)	.03	.01	.00
☐ 1 Jose Canseco	.30	.15	.03
☐ 2 Ken Griffey Jr.	.75	.35	.07
☐ 3 Ryne Sandberg	.15	.07	.01
☐ 4 Nolan Ryan	.25	.12	.02
☐ 5 Bo Jackson	.30	.15	.03
☐ 6 Bret Saberhagen	.08	.04	.01
☐ 7 Will Clark	.25	.12	.02
☐ 8 Ellis Burks	.10	.05	.01
☐ 9 Joe Carter	.08	.04	.01
☐ 10 Rickey Henderson	.20	.10	.02
☐ 11 Ozzie Guillen	.06	.03	.00
☐ 12 Wade Boggs	.15	.07	.01
☐ 13 Jerome Walton	.20	.10	.02
☐ 14 John Franco	.06	.03	.00
☐ 15 Ricky Jordan	.06	.03	.00
☐ 16 Wally Backman	.03	.01	.00
☐ 17 Rob Dibble	.06	.03	.00
☐ 18 Glenn Braggs	.03	.01	.00
☐ 19 Cory Snyder	.08	.04	.01
☐ 20 Kal Daniels	.08	.04	.01
☐ 21 Mark Langston	.08	.04	.01
☐ 22 Kevin Gross	.03	.01	.00
☐ 23 Don Mattingly	.25	.12	.02
☐ 24 Dave Righetti	.06	.03	.00
☐ 25 Roberto Alomar	.08	.04	.01
☐ 26 Robby Thompson	.03	.01	.00
☐ 27 Jack McDowell	.06	.03	.00
☐ 28 Bip Roberts	.06	.03	.00
☐ 29 Jay Howell	.03	.01	.00
☐ 30 Dave Stieb	.08	.04	.01
☐ 31 Johnny Ray	.03	.01	.00
☐ 32 Steve Sax	.08	.04	.01
☐ 33 Terry Mulholland	.03	.01	.00
☐ 34 Lee Guetterman	.03	.01	.00
☐ 35 Tim Raines	.08	.04	.01
☐ 36 Scott Fletcher	.03	.01	.00
☐ 37 Lance Parrish	.08	.04	.01
☐ 38 Tony Phillips	.03	.01	.00
☐ 39 Todd Stottlemyre	.06	.03	.00
☐ 40 Alan Trammell	.08	.04	.01
☐ 41 Todd Burns	.03	.01	.00
☐ 42 Mookie Wilson	.06	.03	.00
☐ 43 Chris Bosio	.03	.01	.00
☐ 44 Jeffrey Leonard	.06	.03	.00
☐ 45 Doug Jones	.06	.03	.00
☐ 46 Mike Scott	.08	.04	.01
☐ 47 Andy Hawkins	.03	.01	.00
☐ 48 Harold Reynolds	.06	.03	.00
☐ 49 Paul Molitor	.08	.04	.01
☐ 50 John Farrell	.03	.01	.00
☐ 51 Danny Darwin	.03	.01	.00
☐ 52 Jeff Blauser	.03	.01	.00
☐ 53 John Tudor	.06	.03	.00
☐ 54 Milt Thompson	.03	.01	.00
☐ 55 Dave Justice	.65	.30	.06
☐ 56 Greg Olson	.10	.05	.01
☐ 57 Willie Blair	.03	.01	.00
☐ 58 Rick Parker	.03	.01	.00
☐ 59 Shawn Boskie	.06	.03	.00
☐ 60 Kevin Tapani	.08	.04	.01
☐ 61 Dave Hollins	.10	.05	.01
☐ 62 Scott Radinsky	.06	.03	.00
☐ 63 Francisco Cabrera	.06	.03	.00
☐ 64 Tim Layana	.06	.03	.00
☐ 65 Jim Leyritz	.10	.05	.01
☐ 66 Wayne Edwards	.06	.03	.00
☐ 67 Lee Stevens	.15	.07	.01
☐ 68 Bill Sampen	.06	.03	.00
☐ 69 Craig Grebeck	.03	.01	.00
☐ 70 John Burkett	.06	.03	.00
☐ 71 Hector Villanueva	.10	.05	.01
☐ 72 Oscar Azocar	.12	.06	.01
☐ 73 Alan Mills	.06	.03	.00
☐ 74 Carlos Baerga	.15	.07	.01
☐ 75 Charles Nagy	.12	.06	.01
☐ 76 Tim Drummond	.03	.01	.00
☐ 77 Dana Kiecker	.06	.03	.00
☐ 78 Tom Edens	.10	.05	.01
☐ 79 Kent Mercker	.06	.03	.00
☐ 80 Steve Avery	.15	.07	.01
☐ 81 Lee Smith	.06	.03	.00
☐ 82 Dave Martinez	.03	.01	.00
☐ 83 Dave Winfield	.10	.05	.01
☐ 84 Bill Spiers	.03	.01	.00
☐ 85 Dan Pasqua	.03	.01	.00
☐ 86 Randy Milligan	.08	.04	.01
☐ 87 Tracy Jones	.03	.01	.00
☐ 88 Greg Myers	.03	.01	.00
☐ 89 Keith Hernandez	.08	.04	.01
☐ 90 Todd Benzinger	.03	.01	.00
☐ 91 Mike Jackson	.03	.01	.00
☐ 92 Mike Stanley	.03	.01	.00
☐ 93 Candy Maldonado	.06	.03	.00
☐ 94 John Kruk	.03	.01	.00
☐ 95 Cal Ripken Jr.	.12	.06	.01
☐ 96 Willie Fraser	.03	.01	.00
☐ 97 Mike Felder	.03	.01	.00
☐ 98 Bill Landrum	.03	.01	.00
☐ 99 Chuck Crim	.03	.01	.00
☐ 100 Chuck Finley	.08	.04	.01
☐ 101 Kirk Manwaring	.03	.01	.00
☐ 102 Jaime Navarro	.06	.03	.00
☐ 103 Dickie Thon	.03	.01	.00
☐ 104 Brian Downing	.03	.01	.00
☐ 105 Jim Abbott	.12	.06	.01
☐ 106 Tom Brookens	.03	.01	.00
☐ 107 Darryl Hamilton	.03	.01	.00
☐ 108 Bryan Harvey	.03	.01	.00
☐ 109 Greg Harris	.03	.01	.00
☐ 110 Greg Swindell	.06	.03	.00
☐ 111 Juan Berenguer	.03	.01	.00
☐ 112 Mike Heath	.03	.01	.00
☐ 113 Scott Bradley	.03	.01	.00
☐ 114 Jack Morris	.06	.03	.00
☐ 115 Barry Jones	.03	.01	.00
☐ 116 Kevin Romine	.03	.01	.00
☐ 117 Garry Templeton	.03	.01	.00
☐ 118 Scott Sanderson	.03	.01	.00
☐ 119 Roberto Kelly	.08	.04	.01
☐ 120 George Brett	.12	.06	.01
☐ 121 Oddibe McDowell	.06	.03	.00
☐ 122 Jim Acker	.03	.01	.00
☐ 123 Bill Swift	.03	.01	.00
☐ 124 Eric King	.03	.01	.00
☐ 125 Jay Buhner	.06	.03	.00
☐ 126 Matt Young	.03	.01	.00
☐ 127 Alvaro Espinoza	.03	.01	.00
☐ 128 Greg Hibbard	.03	.01	.00
☐ 129 Jeff Robinson	.03	.01	.00
☐ 130 Mike Greenwell	.12	.06	.01
☐ 131 Dion James	.03	.01	.00
☐ 132 Donn Pall	.03	.01	.00
☐ 133 Lloyd Moseby	.06	.03	.00
☐ 134 Randy Velarde	.03	.01	.00
☐ 135 Allan Anderson	.03	.01	.00
☐ 136 Mark Davis	.08	.04	.01
☐ 137 Eric Davis	.12	.06	.01
☐ 138 Phil Stephenson	.03	.01	.00
☐ 139 Felix Fermin	.03	.01	.00
☐ 140 Pedro Guerrero	.08	.04	.01
☐ 141 Charlie Hough	.03	.01	.00
☐ 142 Mike Henneman	.03	.01	.00
☐ 143 Jeff Montgomery	.06	.03	.00
☐ 144 Lenny Harris	.06	.03	.00
☐ 145 Bruce Hurst	.06	.03	.00
☐ 146 Eric Anthony	.15	.07	.01
☐ 147 Paul Assenmacher	.03	.01	.00
☐ 148 Jesse Barfield	.08	.04	.01
☐ 149 Carlos Quintana	.08	.04	.01
☐ 150 Dave Stewart	.10	.05	.01
☐ 151 Roy Smith	.03	.01	.00
☐ 152 Paul Gibson	.03	.01	.00
☐ 153 Mickey Hatcher	.03	.01	.00
☐ 154 Jim Eisenreich	.03	.01	.00
☐ 155 Kenny Rogers	.03	.01	.00

☐ 156 Dave Schmidt	.03	.01	.00
☐ 157 Lance Johnson	.03	.01	.00
☐ 158 Dave West	.03	.01	.00
☐ 159 Steve Balboni	.03	.01	.00
☐ 160 Jeff Brantley	.06	.03	.00
☐ 161 Craig Biggio	.06	.03	.00
☐ 162 Brook Jacoby	.06	.03	.00
☐ 163 Dan Gladden	.03	.01	.00
☐ 164 Jeff Reardon	.06	.03	.00
☐ 165 Mark Carreon	.03	.01	.00
☐ 166 Mel Hall	.03	.01	.00
☐ 167 Gary Mielke	.03	.01	.00
☐ 168 Cecil Fielder	.20	.10	.02
☐ 169 Darrin Jackson	.03	.01	.00
☐ 170 Rick Aguilera	.03	.01	.00
☐ 171 Walt Weiss	.06	.03	.00
☐ 172 Steve Farr	.03	.01	.00
☐ 173 Jody Reed	.06	.03	.00
☐ 174 Mike Jeffcoat	.03	.01	.00
☐ 175 Mark Grace	.15	.07	.01
☐ 176 Larry Sheets	.03	.01	.00
☐ 177 Bill Gullickson	.03	.01	.00
☐ 178 Chris Gwynn	.03	.01	.00
☐ 179 Melido Perez	.06	.03	.00
☐ 180 Sid Fernandez	.06	.03	.00
☐ 181 Tim Burke	.06	.03	.00
☐ 182 Gary Pettis	.03	.01	.00
☐ 183 Rob Murphy	.03	.01	.00
☐ 184 Craig Lefferts	.03	.01	.00
☐ 185 Howard Johnson	.08	.04	.01
☐ 186 Ken Caminiti	.03	.01	.00
☐ 187 Tim Belcher	.06	.03	.00
☐ 188 Greg Cadaret	.03	.01	.00
☐ 189 Matt Williams	.12	.06	.01
☐ 190 Dave Magadan	.08	.04	.01
☐ 191 Geno Petralli	.03	.01	.00
☐ 192 Jeff Robinson	.03	.01	.00
☐ 193 Jim Deshaies	.03	.01	.00
☐ 194 Willie Randolph	.06	.03	.00
☐ 195 George Bell	.08	.04	.01
☐ 196 Hubie Brooks	.06	.03	.00
☐ 197 Tom Gordon	.10	.05	.01
☐ 198 Mike Fitzgerald	.03	.01	.00
☐ 199 Mike Pagliarulo	.03	.01	.00
☐ 200 Kirby Puckett	.15	.07	.01
☐ 201 Shawon Dunston	.08	.04	.01
☐ 202 Dennis Boyd	.06	.03	.00
☐ 203 Junior Felix	.10	.05	.01
☐ 204 Alejandro Pena	.03	.01	.00
☐ 205 Pete Smith	.03	.01	.00
☐ 206 Tom Glavine	.03	.01	.00
☐ 207 Luis Salazar	.03	.01	.00
☐ 208 John Smoltz	.06	.03	.00
☐ 209 Doug Dascenzo	.03	.01	.00
☐ 210 Tim Wallach	.06	.03	.00
☐ 211 Greg Gagne	.03	.01	.00
☐ 212 Mark Gubicza	.06	.03	.00
☐ 213 Mark Parent	.03	.01	.00
☐ 214 Ken Oberkfell	.03	.01	.00
☐ 215 Gary Carter	.08	.04	.01
☐ 216 Rafael Palmeiro	.08	.04	.01
☐ 217 Tom Niedenfuer	.03	.01	.00
☐ 218 Dave LaPoint	.03	.01	.00
☐ 219 Jeff Treadway	.03	.01	.00
☐ 220 Mitch Williams	.03	.01	.00
☐ 221 Jose DeLeon	.03	.01	.00
☐ 222 Mike LaValliere	.03	.01	.00
☐ 223 Darrel Akerfelds	.03	.01	.00
☐ 224 Kent Anderson	.03	.01	.00
☐ 225 Dwight Evans	.08	.04	.01
☐ 226 Gary Redus	.03	.01	.00
☐ 227 Paul O'Neill	.08	.04	.01
☐ 228 Marty Barrett	.03	.01	.00
☐ 229 Tom Browning	.06	.03	.00
☐ 230 Terry Pendleton	.03	.01	.00
☐ 231 Jack Armstrong	.06	.03	.00
☐ 232 Mike Boddicker	.03	.01	.00
☐ 233 Neal Heaton	.03	.01	.00
☐ 234 Marquis Grissom	.12	.06	.01
☐ 235 Bert Blyleven	.06	.03	.00
☐ 236 Curt Young	.03	.01	.00
☐ 237 Don Carman	.03	.01	.00
☐ 238 Charlie Hayes	.03	.01	.00
☐ 239 Mark Knudson	.03	.01	.00
☐ 240 Todd Zeile	.15	.07	.01
☐ 241 Larry Walker	.10	.05	.01
☐ 242 Jerald Clark	.03	.01	.00
☐ 243 Jeff Ballard	.03	.01	.00
☐ 244 Jeff King	.06	.03	.00
☐ 245 Tom Brunansky	.08	.04	.01
☐ 246 Darren Daulton	.06	.03	.00
☐ 247 Scott Terry	.03	.01	.00
☐ 248 Rob Deer	.06	.03	.00
☐ 249 Brady Anderson	.06	.03	.00
☐ 250 Lenny Dykstra	.08	.04	.01
☐ 251 Greg Harris	.03	.01	.00
☐ 252 Mike Hartley	.03	.01	.00
☐ 253 Joey Cora	.03	.01	.00
☐ 254 Ivan Calderon	.06	.03	.00
☐ 255 Ted Power	.03	.01	.00
☐ 256 Sammy Sosa	.15	.07	.01
☐ 257 Steve Buechele	.03	.01	.00
☐ 258 Mike Devereaux	.03	.01	.00
☐ 259 Brad Komminsk	.03	.01	.00
☐ 260 Teddy Higuera	.06	.03	.00
☐ 261 Shawn Abner	.06	.03	.00
☐ 262 Dave Valle	.03	.01	.00
☐ 263 Jeff Huson	.03	.01	.00
☐ 264 Edgar Martinez	.08	.04	.01
☐ 265 Carlton Fisk	.10	.05	.01
☐ 266 Steve Finley	.06	.03	.00
☐ 267 John Wetteland	.06	.03	.00
☐ 268 Kevin Appier	.08	.04	.01
☐ 269 Steve Lyons	.03	.01	.00
☐ 270 Mickey Tettleton	.06	.03	.00
☐ 271 Luis Rivera	.03	.01	.00
☐ 272 Steve Jeltz	.03	.01	.00
☐ 273 R.J. Reynolds	.03	.01	.00
☐ 274 Carlos Martinez	.03	.01	.00
☐ 275 Dan Plesac	.03	.01	.00
☐ 276 Mike Morgan	.03	.01	.00
☐ 277 Jeff Russell	.03	.01	.00
☐ 278 Pete Incaviglia	.06	.03	.00
☐ 279 Kevin Seitzer	.08	.04	.01
☐ 280 Bobby Thigpen	.08	.04	.01
☐ 281 Stan Javier	.03	.01	.00
☐ 282 Henry Cotto	.03	.01	.00
☐ 283 Gary Wayne	.03	.01	.00
☐ 284 Shane Mack	.06	.03	.00
☐ 285 Brian Holman	.06	.03	.00
☐ 286 Gerald Perry	.03	.01	.00
☐ 287 Steve Crawford	.03	.01	.00
☐ 288 Nelson Liriano	.03	.01	.00
☐ 289 Don Aase	.03	.01	.00
☐ 290 Randy Johnson	.06	.03	.00
☐ 291 Harold Baines	.08	.04	.01
☐ 292 Kent Hrbek	.08	.04	.01
☐ 293 Les Lancaster	.03	.01	.00
☐ 294 Jeff Musselman	.03	.01	.00
☐ 295 Kurt Stillwell	.06	.03	.00
☐ 296 Stan Belinda	.06	.03	.00
☐ 297 Lou Whitaker	.06	.03	.00
☐ 298 Glenn Wilson	.03	.01	.00
☐ 299 Omar Vizquel	.03	.01	.00
☐ 300 Ramon Martinez	.15	.07	.01
☐ 301 Dwight Smith	.08	.04	.01
☐ 302 Tim Crews	.03	.01	.00
☐ 303 Lance Blankenship	.03	.01	.00
☐ 304 Sid Bream	.03	.01	.00
☐ 305 Rafael Ramirez	.03	.01	.00
☐ 306 Steve Wilson	.03	.01	.00
☐ 307 Mackey Sasser	.06	.03	.00
☐ 308 Franklin Stubbs	.06	.03	.00
☐ 309 Jack Daugherty	.03	.01	.00
☐ 310 Eddie Murray	.10	.05	.01
☐ 311 Bob Welch	.08	.04	.01
☐ 312 Brian Harper	.03	.01	.00
☐ 313 Lance McCullers	.03	.01	.00
☐ 314 Dave Smith	.03	.01	.00
☐ 315 Bobby Bonilla	.12	.06	.01
☐ 316 Jerry Don Gleaton	.03	.01	.00
☐ 317 Greg Maddux	.06	.03	.00
☐ 318 Keith Miller	.03	.01	.00
☐ 319 Mark Portugal	.03	.01	.00
☐ 320 Robin Ventura	.15	.07	.01
☐ 321 Bob Ojeda	.06	.03	.00
☐ 322 Mike Harkey	.08	.04	.01
☐ 323 Jay Bell	.03	.01	.00
☐ 324 Mark McGwire	.20	.10	.02
☐ 325 Gary Gaetti	.08	.04	.01
☐ 326 Jeff Pico	.03	.01	.00
☐ 327 Kevin McReynolds	.08	.04	.01
☐ 328 Frank Tanana	.03	.01	.00
☐ 329 Eric Yelding	.06	.03	.00
☐ 330 Barry Bonds	.15	.07	.01
☐ 331 Brian McRae RP	.60	.30	.06
☐ 332 Pedro Munoz RP	.15	.07	.01
☐ 333 Daryl Irvine RP	.10	.05	.01
☐ 334 Chris Hoiles RP	.12	.06	.01
☐ 335 Thomas Howard RP	.15	.07	.01
☐ 336 Jeff Schulz RP	.10	.05	.01
☐ 337 Jeff Manto RP	.06	.03	.00
☐ 338 Beau Allred RP	.06	.03	.00
☐ 339 Mike Bordick RP	.10	.05	.01
☐ 340 Todd Hundley RP	.12	.06	.01
☐ 341 Jim Vatcher RP	.15	.07	.01
☐ 342 Luis Sojo RP	.08	.04	.01
☐ 343 Jose Offerman RP	.35	.17	.03

☐	344 Pete Coachman RP	.25	.12	.02
☐	345 Mike Benjamin RP	.10	.05	.01
☐	346 Ozzie Canseco RP	.15	.07	.01
☐	347 Tim McIntosh RP	.08	.04	.01
☐	348 Phil Plantier RP	.50	.25	.05
☐	349 Terry Shumpert RP	.06	.03	.00
☐	350 Darren Lewis RP	.30	.15	.03
☐	351 David Walsh RP	.10	.05	.01
☐	352 Scott Chiamparino RP	.25	.12	.02
☐	353 Julio Valera RP	.10	.05	.01
☐	354 Anthony Telford RP	.10	.05	.01
☐	355 Kevin Wickander RP	.06	.03	.00
☐	356 Tim Naehring RP	.20	.10	.02
☐	357 Jim Poole RP	.10	.05	.01
☐	358 Mark Whiten RP	.30	.15	.03
☐	359 Terry Wells RP	.10	.05	.01
☐	360 Rafael Valdez RP	.06	.03	.00
☐	361 Mel Stottlemyre RP	.08	.04	.01
☐	362 David Segui RP	.25	.12	.02
☐	363 Paul Abbott RP	.15	.07	.01
☐	364 Steve Howard RP	.08	.04	.01
☐	365 Karl Rhodes RP	.10	.05	.01
☐	366 Rafael Novoa RP	.10	.05	.01
☐	367 Joe Grahe RP	.10	.05	.01
☐	368 Darren Reed RP	.08	.04	.01
☐	369 Jeff McKnight RP	.10	.05	.01
☐	370 Scott Leius RP	.08	.04	.01
☐	371 Mark Dewey RP	.10	.05	.01
☐	372 Mark Lee RP	.10	.05	.01
☐	373 Rosario Rodriguez RP	.10	.05	.01
☐	374 Chuck McElroy RP	.08	.04	.01
☐	375 Mike Bell RP	.10	.05	.01
☐	376 Mickey Morandini RP	.15	.07	.01
☐	377 Bill Haselman RP	.10	.05	.01
☐	378 Dave Pavlas RP	.10	.05	.01
☐	379 Derrick May RP	.35	.17	.03
☐	380 Jeromy Burnitz FDP	.35	.17	.03
☐	381 Donald Peters FDP	.15	.07	.01
☐	382 Alex Fernandez FDP	1.00	.50	.10
☐	383 Michael Mussina FDP	.35	.17	.03
☐	384 Daniel Smith FDP	.15	.07	.01
☐	385 Lane Dickson FDP	.25	.12	.02
☐	386 Carl Everett FDP	.30	.15	.03
☐	387 Thomas Nevers FDP	.15	.07	.01
☐	388 Adam Hyzdu FDP	.25	.12	.02
☐	389 Todd Van Poppel FDP	1.25	.60	.12
☐	390 Rondell White FDP	.30	.15	.03
☐	391 Marc Newfield FDP	.25	.12	.02
☐	392 Julio Franco AS	.06	.03	.00
☐	393 Wade Boggs AS	.10	.05	.01
☐	394 Ozzie Guillen AS	.06	.03	.00
☐	395 Cecil Fielder AS	.12	.06	.01
☐	396 Ken Griffey Jr. AS	.35	.17	.03
☐	397 Rickey Henderson AS	.12	.06	.01
☐	398 Jose Canseco AS	.25	.12	.02
☐	399 Roger Clemens AS	.12	.06	.01
☐	400 Sandy Alomar Jr. AS	.10	.05	.01
☐	401 Bobby Thigpen AS	.06	.03	.00
☐	402 Bobby Bonilla MB	.10	.05	.01
☐	403 Eric Davis MB	.10	.05	.01
☐	404 Fred McGriff MB	.10	.05	.01
☐	405 Glenn Davis MB	.08	.04	.01
☐	406 Kevin Mitchell MB	.12	.06	.01
☐	407 Rob Dibble KM	.06	.03	.00
☐	408 Ramon Martinez KM	.12	.06	.01
☐	409 David Cone KM	.08	.04	.01
☐	410 Bobby Witt KM	.08	.04	.01
☐	411 Mark Langston KM	.08	.04	.01
☐	412 Bo Jackson RIF	.25	.12	.02
☐	413 Shawon Dunston RIF	.08	.04	.01
☐	414 Jesse Barfield RIF	.08	.04	.01
☐	415 Ken Caminiti RIF	.06	.03	.00
☐	416 Benito Santiago RIF	.08	.04	.01
☐	417 Nolan Ryan HL	.25	.12	.02
☐	418 Bobby Thigpen HL	.06	.03	.00
☐	419 Ramon Martinez HL	.12	.06	.01
☐	420 Bo Jackson HL	.25	.12	.02
☐	421 Carlton Fisk HL	.08	.04	.01
☐	422 Jimmy Key	.06	.03	.00
☐	423 Junior Noboa	.03	.01	.00
☐	424 Al Newman	.03	.01	.00
☐	425 Pat Borders	.06	.03	.00
☐	426 Von Hayes	.06	.03	.00
☐	427 Tim Teufel	.03	.01	.00
☐	428 Eric Plunk	.03	.01	.00
☐	429 John Moses	.03	.01	.00
☐	430 Mike Witt	.03	.01	.00
☐	431 Otis Nixon	.03	.01	.00
☐	432 Tony Fernandez	.06	.03	.00
☐	433 Rance Mulliniks	.03	.01	.00
☐	434 Dan Petry	.03	.01	.00
☐	435 Bob Geren	.03	.01	.00
☐	436 Steve Frey	.08	.04	.01
☐	437 Jamie Moyer	.03	.01	.00
☐	438 Junior Ortiz	.03	.01	.00
☐	439 Tom O'Malley	.03	.01	.00
☐	440 Pat Combs	.06	.03	.00
☐	441 Jose Canseco DT	2.50	.80	.15

1991 Score II

This series was issued approximately three months after the release of the Score Series One. This 459-card, standard size, 2 1/2" by 3 1/2", card set included many of the special cards Score is noted for, e.g., the continuation of the Dream Team set begun in Series One, All-Star Cartoons featuring National Leaguers, a continuation of the 1990 first round draft picks, and 61 rookie prospects. There are many other special subsets in this year as well. This set marks the first time Score has issued their set in two different series.

		MINT	EXC	G-VG
	COMPLETE SET (459)	15.00	7.50	1.50
	COMMON PLAYER (442-900)	.03	.01	.00
☐	442 Alfredo Griffin	.03	.01	.00
☐	443 Andres Galarraga	.06	.03	.00
☐	444 Bryn Smith	.03	.01	.00
☐	445 Andre Dawson	.10	.05	.01
☐	446 Juan Samuel	.06	.03	.00
☐	447 Mike Aldrete	.03	.01	.00
☐	448 Ron Gant	.10	.05	.01
☐	449 Fernando Valenzuela	.08	.04	.01
☐	450 Vince Coleman	.08	.04	.01
☐	451 Kevin Mitchell	.12	.06	.01
☐	452 Spike Owen	.03	.01	.00
☐	453 Mike Bielecki	.03	.01	.00
☐	454 Dennis Martinez	.03	.01	.00
☐	455 Brett Butler	.06	.03	.00
☐	456 Ron Darling	.06	.03	.00
☐	457 Dennis Rasmussen	.03	.01	.00
☐	458 Ken Howell	.03	.01	.00
☐	459 Steve Bedrosian	.06	.03	.00
☐	460 Frank Viola	.08	.04	.01
☐	461 Jose Lind	.03	.01	.00
☐	462 Chris Sabo	.10	.05	.01
☐	463 Dante Bichette	.10	.05	.01
☐	464 Rick Mahler	.03	.01	.00
☐	465 John Smiley	.03	.01	.00
☐	466 Devon White	.06	.03	.00
☐	467 John Orton	.03	.01	.00
☐	468 Mike Stanton	.03	.01	.00
☐	469 Billy Hatcher	.06	.03	.00
☐	470 Wally Joyner	.08	.04	.01
☐	471 Gene Larkin	.03	.01	.00
☐	472 Doug Drabek	.08	.04	.01
☐	473 Gary Sheffield	.12	.06	.01
☐	474 David Wells	.03	.01	.00
☐	475 Andy Van Slyke	.08	.04	.01
☐	476 Mike Gallego	.03	.01	.00
☐	477 B.J. Surhoff	.06	.03	.00
☐	478 Gene Nelson	.03	.01	.00
☐	479 Mariano Duncan	.03	.01	.00
☐	480 Fred McGriff	.10	.05	.01
☐	481 Jerry Browne	.03	.01	.00
☐	482 Alvin Davis	.06	.03	.00
☐	483 Bill Wegman	.03	.01	.00
☐	484 Dave Parker	.08	.04	.01

☐	485	Dennis Eckersley	.08	.04	.01
☐	486	Erik Hanson	.06	.03	.00
☐	487	Bill Ripken	.03	.01	.00
☐	488	Tom Candiotti	.03	.01	.00
☐	489	Mike Schooler	.03	.01	.00
☐	490	Gregg Olson	.10	.05	.01
☐	491	Chris James	.03	.01	.00
☐	492	Pete Harnisch	.03	.01	.00
☐	493	Julio Franco	.06	.03	.00
☐	494	Greg Briley	.06	.03	.00
☐	495	Ruben Sierra	.12	.06	.01
☐	496	Steve Olin	.03	.01	.00
☐	497	Mike Fetters	.08	.04	.01
☐	498	Mark Williams	.10	.05	.01
☐	499	Bob Tewksbury	.08	.04	.01
☐	500	Tony Gwynn	.12	.06	.01
☐	501	Randy Myers	.06	.03	.00
☐	502	Keith Comstock	.03	.01	.00
☐	503	Craig Worthington	.06	.03	.00
☐	504	Mark Eichhorn	.03	.01	.00
☐	505	Barry Larkin	.10	.05	.01
☐	506	Dave Johnson	.03	.01	.00
☐	507	Bobby Witt	.06	.03	.00
☐	508	Joe Orsulak	.03	.01	.00
☐	509	Pete O'Brien	.03	.01	.00
☐	510	Brad Arnsberg	.08	.04	.01
☐	511	Storm Davis	.03	.01	.00
☐	512	Bob Milacki	.03	.01	.00
☐	513	Bill Pecota	.03	.01	.00
☐	514	Glenallen Hill	.06	.03	.00
☐	515	Danny Tartabull	.06	.03	.00
☐	516	Mike Moore	.03	.01	.00
☐	517	Ron Robinson	.03	.01	.00
☐	518	Mark Gardner	.03	.01	.00
☐	519	Rick Wrona	.03	.01	.00
☐	520	Mike Scioscia	.03	.01	.00
☐	521	Frank Wills	.08	.04	.01
☐	522	Greg Brock	.03	.01	.00
☐	523	Jack Clark	.08	.04	.01
☐	524	Bruce Ruffin	.03	.01	.00
☐	525	Robin Yount	.12	.06	.01
☐	526	Tom Foley	.03	.01	.00
☐	527	Pat Perry	.03	.01	.00
☐	528	Greg Vaughn	.12	.06	.01
☐	529	Wally Whitehurst	.03	.01	.00
☐	530	Norm Charlton	.06	.03	.00
☐	531	Marvell Wynne	.03	.01	.00
☐	532	Jim Gantner	.03	.01	.00
☐	533	Greg Litton	.03	.01	.00
☐	534	Manny Lee	.03	.01	.00
☐	535	Scott Bailes	.03	.01	.00
☐	536	Charlie Leibrandt	.03	.01	.00
☐	537	Roger McDowell	.03	.01	.00
☐	538	Andy Benes	.10	.05	.01
☐	539	Rick Honeycutt	.03	.01	.00
☐	540	Dwight Gooden	.12	.06	.01
☐	541	Scott Garrelts	.03	.01	.00
☐	542	Dave Clark	.03	.01	.00
☐	543	Lonnie Smith	.06	.03	.00
☐	544	Rick Reuschel	.06	.03	.00
☐	545	Delino DeShields	.20	.10	.02
☐	546	Mike Sharperson	.03	.01	.00
☐	547	Mike Kingery	.03	.01	.00
☐	548	Terry Kennedy	.03	.01	.00
☐	549	David Cone	.08	.04	.01
☐	550	Orel Hershiser	.10	.05	.01
☐	551	Matt Nokes	.06	.03	.00
☐	552	Eddie Williams	.08	.04	.01
☐	553	Frank DiPino	.03	.01	.00
☐	554	Fred Lynn	.06	.03	.00
☐	555	Alex Cole	.30	.15	.03
☐	556	Terry Leach	.03	.01	.00
☐	557	Chet Lemon	.03	.01	.00
☐	558	Paul Mirabella	.03	.01	.00
☐	559	Bill Long	.03	.01	.00
☐	560	Phil Bradley	.06	.03	.00
☐	561	Duane Ward	.03	.01	.00
☐	562	Dave Bergman	.03	.01	.00
☐	563	Eric Show	.03	.01	.00
☐	564	Xavier Hernandez	.08	.04	.01
☐	565	Jeff Parrett	.03	.01	.00
☐	566	Chuck Cary	.03	.01	.00
☐	567	Ken Hill	.03	.01	.00
☐	568	Bob Welch	.08	.04	.01
☐	569	John Mitchell	.03	.01	.00
☐	570	Travis Fryman	.40	.20	.04
☐	571	Derek Lilliquist	.03	.01	.00
☐	572	Steve Lake	.03	.01	.00
☐	573	John Barfield	.10	.05	.01
☐	574	Randy Bush	.03	.01	.00
☐	575	Joe Magrane	.06	.03	.00
☐	576	Eddie Diaz	.08	.04	.01
☐	577	Casey Candaele	.03	.01	.00
☐	578	Jesse Orosco	.03	.01	.00
☐	579	Tom Henke	.06	.03	.00
☐	580	Rick Cerone	.03	.01	.00
☐	581	Drew Hall	.03	.01	.00
☐	582	Tony Castillo	.08	.04	.01
☐	583	Jimmy Jones	.03	.01	.00
☐	584	Rick Reed	.03	.01	.00
☐	585	Joe Girardi	.03	.01	.00
☐	586	Jeff Gray	.10	.05	.01
☐	587	Luis Polonia	.03	.01	.00
☐	588	Joe Klink	.08	.04	.01
☐	589	Rex Hudler	.03	.01	.00
☐	590	Kirk McCaskill	.03	.01	.00
☐	591	Juan Agosto	.03	.01	.00
☐	592	Wes Gardner	.03	.01	.00
☐	593	Rich Rodriguez	.10	.05	.01
☐	594	Mitch Webster	.03	.01	.00
☐	595	Kelly Gruber	.10	.05	.01
☐	596	Dale Mohorcic	.03	.01	.00
☐	597	Willie McGee	.08	.04	.01
☐	598	Bill Krueger	.03	.01	.00
☐	599	Bob Walk	.03	.01	.00
☐	600	Kevin Maas	.40	.20	.04
☐	601	Danny Jackson	.06	.03	.00
☐	602	Craig McMurtry	.03	.01	.00
☐	603	Curtis Wilkerson	.03	.01	.00
☐	604	Adam Peterson	.08	.04	.01
☐	605	Sam Horn	.06	.03	.00
☐	606	Tommy Gregg	.03	.01	.00
☐	607	Ken Dayley	.03	.01	.00
☐	608	Carmelo Castillo	.03	.01	.00
☐	609	John Shelby	.03	.01	.00
☐	610	Don Slaught	.03	.01	.00
☐	611	Calvin Schiraldi	.03	.01	.00
☐	612	Dennis Lamp	.03	.01	.00
☐	613	Andres Thomas	.03	.01	.00
☐	614	Jose Gonzalez	.03	.01	.00
☐	615	Randy Ready	.03	.01	.00
☐	616	Kevin Bass	.06	.03	.00
☐	617	Mike Marshall	.06	.03	.00
☐	618	Daryl Boston	.06	.03	.00
☐	619	Andy McGaffigan	.03	.01	.00
☐	620	Joe Oliver	.06	.03	.00
☐	621	Jim Gott	.03	.01	.00
☐	622	Jose Oquendo	.03	.01	.00
☐	623	Jose DeJesus	.03	.01	.00
☐	624	Mike Brumley	.08	.04	.01
☐	625	John Olerud	.35	.17	.03
☐	626	Ernest Riles	.03	.01	.00
☐	627	Gene Harris	.03	.01	.00
☐	628	Jose Uribe	.03	.01	.00
☐	629	Darnell Coles	.03	.01	.00
☐	630	Carney Lansford	.06	.03	.00
☐	631	Tim Leary	.03	.01	.00
☐	632	Tim Hulett	.03	.01	.00
☐	633	Kevin Elster	.03	.01	.00
☐	634	Tony Fossas	.03	.01	.00
☐	635	Francisco Oliveras	.08	.04	.01
☐	636	Bob Patterson	.08	.04	.01
☐	637	Gary Ward	.03	.01	.00
☐	638	Rene Gonzales	.03	.01	.00
☐	639	Don Robinson	.03	.01	.00
☐	640	Darryl Strawberry	.15	.07	.01
☐	641	Dave Anderson	.03	.01	.00
☐	642	Scott Scudder	.03	.01	.00
☐	643	Reggie Harris	.12	.06	.01
☐	644	Dave Henderson	.03	.01	.00
☐	645	Ben McDonald	.25	.12	.02
☐	646	Bob Kipper	.03	.01	.00
☐	647	Hal Morris	.12	.06	.01
☐	648	Tim Birtsas	.03	.01	.00
☐	649	Steve Searcy	.03	.01	.00
☐	650	Dale Murphy	.10	.05	.01
☐	651	Ron Oester	.03	.01	.00
☐	652	Mike LaCoss	.03	.01	.00
☐	653	Ron Jones	.06	.03	.00
☐	654	Kelly Downs	.03	.01	.00
☐	655	Roger Clemens	.15	.07	.01
☐	656	Herm Winningham	.03	.01	.00
☐	657	Trevor Wilson	.08	.04	.01
☐	658	Jose Rijo	.06	.03	.00
☐	659	Dann Bilardello	.03	.01	.00
☐	660	Gregg Jefferies	.15	.07	.01
☐	661	Doug Drabek AS	.06	.03	.00
☐	662	Randy Myers AS	.06	.03	.00
☐	663	Benny Santiago AS	.08	.04	.01
☐	664	Will Clark AS	.15	.07	.01
☐	665	Ryne Sandberg AS	.12	.06	.01
☐	666	Barry Larkin AS	.08	.04	.01
☐	667	Matt Williams AS	.10	.05	.01
☐	668	Barry Bonds AS	.10	.05	.01
☐	669	Eric Davis AS	.10	.05	.01
☐	670	Bobby Bonilla AS	.10	.05	.01
☐	671	Chipper Jones FDP	.60	.30	.06

☐	672 Eric Christopherson FDP	.15	.07	.01
☐	673 Robbie Beckett FDP	.15	.07	.01
☐	674 Shane Andrews FDP	.15	.07	.01
☐	675 Steve Karsay FDP	.30	.15	.03
☐	676 Aaron Holbert FDP	.15	.07	.01
☐	677 Donovan Osborne FDP	.15	.07	.01
☐	678 Todd Ritchie FDP	.15	.07	.01
☐	679 Ron Walden FDP	.15	.07	.01
☐	680 Tim Costo FDP	.40	.20	.04
☐	681 Dan Wilson FDP	.15	.07	.01
☐	682 Kurt Miller FDP	.15	.07	.01
☐	683 Mike Lieberthal FDP	.25	.12	.02
☐	684 Roger Clemens KM	.12	.06	.01
☐	685 Doc Gooden KM	.12	.06	.01
☐	686 Nolan Ryan KM	.25	.12	.02
☐	687 Frank Viola KM	.08	.04	.01
☐	688 Erik Hanson KM	.06	.03	.00
☐	689 Matt Williams MB	.10	.05	.01
☐	690 Jose Canseco MB	.25	.12	.02
☐	691 Darryl Strawberry MB	.12	.06	.01
☐	692 Bo Jackson MB	.25	.12	.02
☐	693 Cecil Fielder MB	.20	.10	.02
☐	694 Sandy Alomar Jr. RF	.10	.05	.01
☐	695 Cory Snyder RF	.06	.03	.00
☐	696 Eric Davis RF	.10	.05	.01
☐	697 Ken Griffey Jr RF	.35	.17	.03
☐	698 Andy Van Slyke RF	.08	.04	.01
☐	699 Langston/Witt NH	.06	.03	.00
☐	700 Randy Johnson NH	.06	.03	.00
☐	701 Nolan Ryan NH	.25	.12	.02
☐	702 Dave Stewart NH	.10	.05	.01
☐	703 Fernando Valenzuela NH	.08	.04	.01
☐	704 Andy Hawkins NH	.06	.03	.00
☐	705 Melido Perez NH	.03	.01	.00
☐	706 Terry Mulholland NH	.03	.01	.00
☐	707 Dave Stieb NH	.06	.03	.00
☐	708 Brian Barnes RP	.10	.05	.01
☐	709 Bernard Gilkey RP	.20	.10	.02
☐	710 Steve Decker RP	.30	.15	.03
☐	711 Paul Faries RP	.10	.05	.01
☐	712 Paul Marak RP	.10	.05	.01
☐	713 Wes Chamberlain RP	.30	.15	.03
☐	714 Kevin Belcher RP	.15	.07	.01
☐	715 Dan Boone RP	.08	.04	.01
☐	716 Steve Adkins RP	.10	.05	.01
☐	717 Geronimo Pena RP	.12	.06	.01
☐	718 Howard Farmer RP	.10	.05	.01
☐	719 Mark Leonard RP	.20	.10	.02
☐	720 Tom Lampkin RP	.08	.04	.01
☐	721 Mike Gardiner RP	.12	.06	.01
☐	722 Jeff Conine RP	.50	.25	.05
☐	723 Efrain Valdez RP	.10	.05	.01
☐	724 Chuck Malone RP	.08	.04	.01
☐	725 Leo Gomez RP	.40	.20	.04
☐	726 Paul McClellan RP	.10	.05	.01
☐	727 Mark Leiter RP	.10	.05	.01
☐	728 Rich DeLucia RP	.10	.05	.01
☐	729 Mel Rojas RP	.08	.04	.01
☐	730 Hector Wagner RP	.12	.06	.01
☐	731 Ray Lankford RP	.30	.15	.03
☐	732 Turner Ward RP	.20	.10	.02
☐	733 Gerald Alexander RP	.10	.05	.01
☐	734 Scott Anderson RP	.10	.05	.01
☐	735 Tony Perezchica P	.08	.04	.01
☐	736 Jimmy Kremers RP	.10	.05	.01
☐	737 American Flag (Pray for Peace)	.08	.04	.01
☐	738 Mike York RP	.10	.05	.01
☐	739 Mike Rochford RP	.08	.04	.01
☐	740 Scott Aldred RP	.10	.05	.01
☐	741 Rico Brogna RP	.20	.10	.02
☐	742 Dave Burba RP	.10	.05	.01
☐	743 Ray Stephens RP	.10	.05	.01
☐	744 Eric Gunderson RP	.10	.05	.01
☐	745 Troy Afenir RP	.10	.05	.01
☐	746 Jeff Shaw RP	.12	.06	.01
☐	747 Orlando Merced RP	.12	.06	.01
☐	748 Omar Olivares RP	.10	.05	.01
☐	749 Jerry Kutzler RP	.03	.01	.00
☐	750 Mo Vaughn RP	.30	.15	.03
☐	751 Matt Stark RP	.20	.10	.02
☐	752 Randy Hennis RP	.10	.05	.01
☐	753 Andujar Cedeno RP	.50	.25	.05
☐	754 Kelvin Torve RP	.10	.05	.01
☐	755 Joe Kraemer RP	.10	.05	.01
☐	756 Phil Clark RP	.20	.10	.02
☐	757 Ed Vosberg RP	.10	.05	.01
☐	758 Mike Perez RP	.10	.05	.01
☐	759 Scott Lewis RP	.12	.06	.01
☐	760 Steve Chitren RP	.10	.05	.01
☐	761 Ray Young RP	.10	.05	.01
☐	762 Andres Santana RP	.15	.07	.01

☐	763 Rodney McCray RP	.10	.05	.01
☐	764 Sean Berry RP	.20	.10	.02
☐	765 Brent Mayne RP	.06	.03	.00
☐	766 Mike Simms RP	.10	.05	.01
☐	767 Glenn Sutko RP	.12	.06	.01
☐	768 Gary DiSarcina RP	.03	.01	.00
☐	769 George Brett HL	.10	.05	.01
☐	770 Cecil Fielder HL	.15	.07	.01
☐	771 Jim Presley	.03	.01	.00
☐	772 John Dopson	.03	.01	.00
☐	773 Bo Jackson RB	.25	.12	.02
☐	774 Brent Knackert	.12	.06	.01
☐	775 Bill Doran	.06	.03	.00
☐	776 Dick Schofield	.03	.01	.00
☐	777 Nelson Santovenia	.03	.01	.00
☐	778 Mark Guthrie	.08	.04	.01
☐	779 Mark Lemke	.03	.01	.00
☐	780 Terry Steinbach	.06	.03	.00
☐	781 Tom Bolton	.03	.01	.00
☐	782 Randy Tomlin	.10	.05	.01
☐	783 Jeff Kunkel	.03	.01	.00
☐	784 Felix Jose	.06	.03	.00
☐	785 Rick Sutcliffe	.06	.03	.00
☐	786 John Cerutti	.03	.01	.00
☐	787 Jose Vizcaino	.06	.03	.00
☐	788 Curt Schilling	.03	.01	.00
☐	789 Ed Whitson	.03	.01	.00
☐	790 Tony Pena	.06	.03	.00
☐	791 John Candelaria	.03	.01	.00
☐	792 Carmelo Martinez	.03	.01	.00
☐	793 Sandy Alomar Jr.	.15	.07	.01
☐	794 Jim Neidlinger	.15	.07	.01
☐	795 Barry Larkin WS	.08	.04	.01
☐	796 Paul Sorrento	.03	.01	.00
☐	797 Tom Pagnozzi	.03	.01	.00
☐	798 Tino Martinez	.30	.15	.03
☐	799 Scott Ruskin	.10	.05	.01
☐	800 Kirk Gibson	.08	.04	.01
☐	801 Walt Terrell	.03	.01	.00
☐	802 John Tussell	.03	.01	.00
☐	803 Chili Davis	.06	.03	.00
☐	804 Chris Nabholz	.15	.07	.01
☐	805 Juan Gonzales	.25	.12	.02
☐	806 Ron Hassey	.03	.01	.00
☐	807 Todd Worrell	.06	.03	.00
☐	808 Tommy Greene	.03	.01	.00
☐	809 Joel Skinner	.03	.01	.00
☐	810 Benito Santiago	.08	.04	.01
☐	811 Pat Tabler	.03	.01	.00
☐	812 Scott Erickson	.15	.07	.01
☐	813 Moises Alou	.10	.05	.01
☐	814 Dale Sveum	.03	.01	.00
☐	815 Ryne Sandberg MANYR	.15	.07	.01
☐	816 Rick Dempsey	.03	.01	.00
☐	817 Scott Bankhead	.03	.01	.00
☐	818 Jason Grimsley	.03	.01	.00
☐	819 Doug Jennings	.03	.01	.00
☐	820 Tom Herr	.06	.03	.00
☐	821 Rob Ducey	.03	.01	.00
☐	822 Luis Quinones	.03	.01	.00
☐	823 Greg Minton	.03	.01	.00
☐	824 Mark Grant	.03	.01	.00
☐	825 Ozzie Smith	.08	.04	.01
☐	826 Dave Eiland	.03	.01	.00
☐	827 Danny Heep	.03	.01	.00
☐	828 Hensely Meulens	.15	.07	.01
☐	829 Charlie O'Brien	.03	.01	.00
☐	830 Glenn Davis	.08	.04	.01
☐	831 John Marzano	.03	.01	.00
☐	832 Steve Ontiveros	.03	.01	.00
☐	833 Ron Karkovice	.03	.01	.00
☐	834 Jerry Goff	.08	.04	.01
☐	835 Ken Griffey Sr.	.06	.03	.00
☐	836 Kevin Reimer	.08	.04	.01
☐	837 Randy Kutcher	.03	.01	.00
☐	838 Mike Blowers	.06	.03	.00
☐	839 Mike Macfarlane	.03	.01	.00
☐	840 Frank Thomas	.75	.35	.07
☐	841 Greg Smith	.06	.03	.00
☐	842 Jack Howell	.03	.01	.00
☐	843 Goose Gozzo	.03	.01	.00
☐	844 Gerald Young	.03	.01	.00
☐	845 Zane Smith	.06	.03	.00
☐	846 Kevin Brown	.06	.03	.00
☐	847 Sil Campusano	.03	.01	.00
☐	848 Larry Andersen	.03	.01	.00
☐	849 Cal Ripken Jr. FRAN	.12	.06	.01
☐	850 Roger Clemens FRAN	.15	.07	.01
☐	851 Sandy Alomar Jr. FRAN	.15	.07	.01
☐	852 Alan Trammell FRAN	.10	.05	.01
☐	853 George Brett FRAN	.12	.06	.01
☐	854 Robin Yount FRAN	.12	.06	.01
☐	855 Kirby Puckett FRAN	.15	.07	.01
☐	856 Don Mattingly FRAN	.25	.12	.02

☐ 857 Rickey Henderson FRAN	.20	.10	.02
☐ 858 Ken Griffey Jr FRAN	.75	.35	.07
☐ 859 Ruben Sierra FRAN	.12	.06	.01
☐ 860 John Olerud FRAN	.35	.17	.03
☐ 861 Dave Justice FRAN	.65	.30	.06
☐ 862 Ryne Sandberg FRAN	.15	.07	.01
☐ 863 Eric Davis FRAN	.12	.06	.01
☐ 864 Darryl Strawberry FRAN	.20	.10	.02
☐ 865 Tim Wallach FRAN	.06	.03	.00
☐ 866 Doc Gooden FRAN	.15	.07	.01
☐ 867 Len Dykstra FRAN	.08	.04	.01
☐ 868 Barry Bonds FRAN	.15	.07	.01
☐ 869 Todd Zeile FRAN	.15	.07	.01
☐ 870 Benito Santiago FRAN	.10	.05	.01
☐ 871 Will Clark FRAN	.25	.12	.02
☐ 872 Glenn Davis FRAN	.10	.05	.01
☐ 873 Wally Joyner FRAN	.08	.04	.01
☐ 874 Frank Thomas FRAN	.75	.35	.07
☐ 875 Rickey Henderson MVP	.12	.06	.01
☐ 876 Barry Bonds MVP	.10	.05	.01
☐ 877 Bob Welch CY	.06	.03	.00
☐ 878 Doug Drabek CY	.06	.03	.00
☐ 879 Sandy Alomar Jr ROY	.12	.06	.01
☐ 880 Dave Justice ROY	.30	.15	.03
☐ 881 Damon Berryhill DT	.06	.03	.00
☐ 882 Frank Viola DT	.12	.06	.01
☐ 883 Dave Stewart DT	.15	.07	.01
☐ 884 Doug Jones DT	.06	.03	.00
☐ 885 Randy Myers DT	.06	.03	.00
☐ 886 Will Clark DT	.35	.17	.03
☐ 887 Roberto Alomar DT	.15	.07	.01
☐ 888 Barry Larkin DT	.15	.07	.01
☐ 889 Wade Boggs DT	.20	.10	.02
☐ 890 Rickey Henderson DT	.60	.30	.06
☐ 891 Kirby Puckett DT	.20	.10	.02
☐ 892 Ken Griffey Jr DT	1.00	.50	.10
☐ 893 Benny Santiago DT	.15	.07	.01
☐ 894 Wade Boggs BONUS	.20	.10	.02
☐ 895 Rickey Henderson BONUS	.25	.12	.02
☐ 896 Ken Griffey Jr. BONUS	.50	.25	.05
☐ 897 Will Clark BONUS	.25	.12	.02
☐ 898 George Brett BONUS	.20	.10	.02
☐ 899 Barry Larkin BONUS	.15	.07	.01
☐ 900 Nolan Ryan BONUS	.35	.17	.03

1991 Score 100 Superstars

The 1991 Score 100 Superstars sets were issued by Score with or without special books which goes with the cards. The cards, which feature 100 of the most popular superstars, are the standard size 2 1/2" by 3 1/2". The fronts of the cards feature beautiful full-color photos surrounded by red, white and blue borders while the backs are surrounded by red and blue borders and feature a full-color photo on the back along with a brief biography. The sets (with the special book with brief biography on the players) are marketed for retail purposes at a suggested price of 12.95.

	MINT	VG-E	F-G
COMPLETE SET (1-100)	12.00	6.00	1.20
COMMON PLAYER (1-100)	.05	.02	.00
☐ 1 Jose Canseco	1.00	.50	.10
☐ 2 Bo Jackson	1.00	.50	.10
☐ 3 Wade Boggs	.50	.25	.05
☐ 4 Will Clark	.75	.35	.07
☐ 5 Ken Griffey Jr.	1.00	.50	.10
☐ 6 Doug Drabek	.15	.07	.01
☐ 7 Kirby Puckett	.35	.17	.03
☐ 8 Joe Orsulak	.05	.02	.00
☐ 9 Eric Davis	.35	.17	.03
☐ 10 Rickey Henderson	.75	.35	.07
☐ 11 Lenny Dykstra	.15	.07	.01
☐ 12 Ruben Sierra	.30	.15	.03
☐ 13 Paul Molitor	.10	.05	.01
☐ 14 Ron Gant	.20	.10	.02
☐ 15 Ozzie Guillen	.10	.05	.01
☐ 16 Ramon Martinez	.25	.12	.02
☐ 17 Edgar Martinez	.10	.05	.01
☐ 18 Ozzie Smith	.15	.07	.01
☐ 19 Charlie Hayes	.10	.05	.01
☐ 20 Barry Larkin	.20	.10	.02
☐ 21 Cal Ripken	.30	.15	.03
☐ 22 Andy Van Slyke	.10	.05	.01
☐ 23 Don Mattingly	1.00	.50	.10
☐ 24 Dave Stewart	.15	.07	.01
☐ 25 Nolan Ryan	1.00	.50	.10
☐ 26 Barry Bonds	.40	.20	.04
☐ 27 Gregg Olson	.25	.12	.02
☐ 28 Chris Sabo	.30	.15	.03
☐ 29 John Franco	.10	.05	.01
☐ 30 Gary Sheffield	.25	.12	.02
☐ 31 Jeff Treadway	.05	.02	.00
☐ 32 Tom Browning	.05	.02	.00
☐ 33 Jose Lind	.05	.02	.00
☐ 34 Dave Magadan	.15	.07	.01
☐ 35 Dale Murphy	.30	.15	.03
☐ 36 Tom Candiotti	.05	.02	.00
☐ 37 Willie McGee	.15	.07	.01
☐ 38 Robin Yount	.30	.15	.03
☐ 39 Mark McGwire	.50	.25	.05
☐ 40 George Bell	.15	.07	.01
☐ 41 Carlton Fisk	.25	.12	.02
☐ 42 Bobby Bonilla	.25	.12	.02
☐ 43 Randy Milligan	.10	.05	.01
☐ 44 Dave Parker	.15	.07	.01
☐ 45 Shawon Dunston	.15	.07	.01
☐ 46 Brian Harper	.05	.02	.00
☐ 47 John Tudor	.05	.02	.00
☐ 48 Ellis Burks	.30	.15	.03
☐ 49 Bob Welch	.15	.07	.01
☐ 50 Roger Clemens	.50	.25	.05
☐ 51 Mike Henneman	.05	.02	.00
☐ 52 Eddie Murray	.20	.10	.02
☐ 53 Kal Daniels	.15	.07	.01
☐ 54 Doug Jones	.05	.02	.00
☐ 55 Craig Biggio	.10	.05	.01
☐ 56 Rafael Palmeiro	.15	.07	.01
☐ 57 Wally Joyner	.15	.07	.01
☐ 58 Tim Wallach	.10	.05	.01
☐ 59 Bret Saberhagen	.15	.07	.01
☐ 60 Ryne Sandberg	.60	.30	.06
☐ 61 Benito Santiago	.15	.07	.01
☐ 62 Darryl Strawberry	.40	.20	.04
☐ 63 Alan Trammell	.15	.07	.01
☐ 64 Kelly Gruber	.15	.07	.01
☐ 65 Dwight Gooden	.30	.15	.03
☐ 66 Dave Winfield	.15	.07	.01
☐ 67 Rick Aguilera	.05	.02	.00
☐ 68 Dave Righetti	.10	.05	.01
☐ 69 Jim Abbott	.25	.12	.02
☐ 70 Frank Viola	.15	.07	.01
☐ 71 Fred McGriff	.20	.10	.02
☐ 72 Steve Sax	.10	.05	.01
☐ 73 Dennis Eckersley	.15	.07	.01
☐ 74 Cory Snyder	.10	.05	.01
☐ 75 Mackey Sasser	.10	.05	.01
☐ 76 Candy Maldonado	.10	.05	.01
☐ 77 Matt Williams	.30	.15	.03
☐ 78 Kent Hrbek	.10	.05	.01
☐ 79 Randy Myers	.05	.02	.00
☐ 80 Gregg Jefferies	.30	.15	.03
☐ 81 Joe Carter	.15	.07	.01
☐ 82 Mike Greenwell	.35	.17	.03
☐ 83 Jack Armstong	.15	.07	.01
☐ 84 Julio Franco	.10	.05	.01
☐ 85 George Brett	.30	.15	.03
☐ 86 Howard Johnson	.15	.07	.01
☐ 87 Andre Dawson	.20	.10	.02
☐ 88 Cecil Fielder	.40	.20	.04
☐ 89 Tim Raines	.15	.07	.01
☐ 90 Chuck Finley	.10	.05	.01
☐ 91 Mark Grace	.50	.25	.05
☐ 92 Brook Jacoby	.10	.05	.01
☐ 93 Dave Stieb	.15	.07	.01
☐ 94 Tony Gwynn	.30	.15	.03
☐ 95 Bobby Thigpen	.15	.07	.01

		MINT	VG-E	F-G
☐ 96	Roberto Kelly	.25	.12	.02
☐ 97	Kevin Seitzer	.15	.07	.01
☐ 98	Kevin Mitchell	.30	.15	.03
☐ 99	Dwight Evans	.10	.05	.01
☐ 100	Roberto Alomar	.20	.10	.02

1991 Score 100 Rising Stars

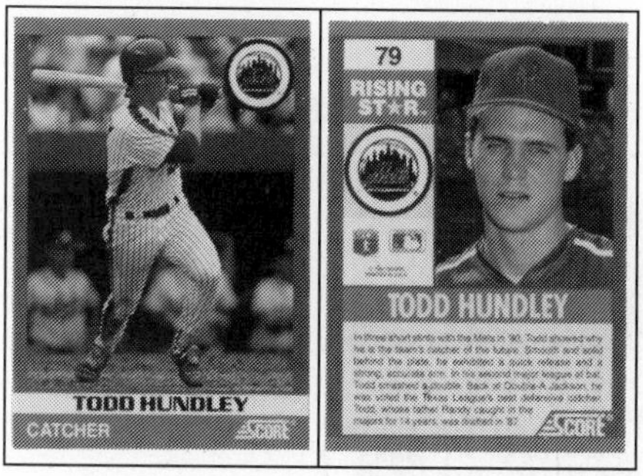

The 1991 Score 100 Rising Stars sets were issued by Score with or without special books which goes with the cards. The cards, which feature 100 of the most popular rising stars, are the standard size 2 1/2" by 3 1/2". The fronts of the cards are beautiful full-color photos surrounded by blue and green borders while the backs have a full color photo on the back and give a brief biography of the player. The sets (with the special book with brief biography on the players) are marketed for retail purposes at a suggested price of 12.95.

		MINT	VG-E	F-G
COMPLETE SET (100)		12.00	6.00	1.20
COMMON PLAYER (1-100)		.05	.02	.00
☐ 1	Sandy Alomar Jr.	.30	.15	.03
☐ 2	Tom Edens	.10	.05	.01
☐ 3	Terry Shumpert	.10	.05	.01
☐ 4	Shawn Boskie	.10	.05	.01
☐ 5	Steve Avery	.20	.10	.02
☐ 6	Deion Sanders	.30	.15	.03
☐ 7	John Burkett	.15	.07	.01
☐ 8	Stan Belinda	.10	.05	.01
☐ 9	Thomas Howard	.10	.05	.01
☐ 10	Wayne Edwards	.10	.05	.01
☐ 11	Rick Parker	.10	.05	.01
☐ 12	Randy Veres	.10	.05	.01
☐ 13	Alex Cole	.40	.20	.04
☐ 14	Scott Chiamparino	.20	.10	.02
☐ 15	Greg Olson	.15	.07	.01
☐ 16	Jose DeJesus	.10	.05	.01
☐ 17	Mike Blowers	.15	.07	.01
☐ 18	Jeff Huson	.05	.02	.00
☐ 19	Willie Blair	.05	.02	.00
☐ 20	Howard Farmer	.10	.05	.01
☐ 21	Larry Walker	.15	.07	.01
☐ 22	Scott Hemond	.15	.07	.01
☐ 23	Mel Stottlemyre	.15	.07	.01
☐ 24	Mark Whiten	.30	.15	.03
☐ 25	Jeff Schulz	.10	.05	.01
☐ 26	Gary DiSarcina	.10	.05	.01
☐ 27	George Canale	.10	.05	.01
☐ 28	Dean Palmer	.15	.07	.01
☐ 29	Jim Leyritz	.10	.05	.01
☐ 30	Carlos Baerga	.30	.15	.03
☐ 31	Rafael Valdez	.10	.05	.01
☐ 32	Derek Bell	.25	.12	.02
☐ 33	Francisco Cabrera	.15	.07	.01
☐ 34	Chris Hoiles	.15	.07	.01
☐ 35	Craig Grebeck	.10	.05	.01
☐ 36	Scogg Coolbaugh	.10	.05	.01
☐ 37	Kevin Wickander	.10	.05	.01
☐ 38	Marquis Grissom	.20	.10	.02
☐ 39	Chip Hale	.10	.05	.01
☐ 40	Kevin Maas	.60	.30	.06
☐ 41	Juan Gonzalez	.50	.25	.05
☐ 42	Eric Anthony	.30	.15	.03
☐ 43	Luis Sojo	.10	.05	.01
☐ 44	Paul Sorrento	.10	.05	.01
☐ 45	Dave Justice	.60	.30	.06
☐ 46	Oscar Azocar	.15	.07	.01
☐ 47	Charles Nagy	.10	.05	.01
☐ 48	Robin Ventura	.30	.15	.03
☐ 49	Reggie Harris	.15	.07	.01
☐ 50	Ben McDonald	.40	.20	.04
☐ 51	Hector Villanueva	.15	.07	.01
☐ 52	Kevin Tapani	.15	.07	.01
☐ 53	Brian Bohanon	.15	.07	.01
☐ 54	Tim Layana	.10	.05	.01
☐ 55	Delino DeShields	.30	.15	.03
☐ 56	Beau Allred	.10	.05	.01
☐ 57	Eric Gunderson	.10	.05	.01
☐ 58	Kent Mercker	.10	.05	.01
☐ 59	Juan Bell	.10	.05	.01
☐ 60	Glenallen Hill	.10	.05	.01
☐ 61	David Segui	.30	.15	.03
☐ 62	Alan Mills	.15	.07	.01
☐ 63	Mike Harkey	.20	.10	.02
☐ 64	Bill Sampen	.10	.05	.01
☐ 65	Greg Vaughn	.30	.15	.03
☐ 66	Alex Fernandez	.60	.30	.06
☐ 67	Mike Hartley	.10	.05	.01
☐ 68	Travis Fryman	.40	.20	.04
☐ 69	Dave Rohde	.10	.05	.01
☐ 70	Tom Lampkin	.05	.02	.00
☐ 71	Mark Gardner	.10	.05	.01
☐ 72	Pat Combs	.15	.07	.01
☐ 73	Kevin Appier	.15	.07	.01
☐ 74	Mike Fetters	.10	.05	.01
☐ 75	Greg Myers	.10	.05	.01
☐ 76	Steve Searcy	.10	.05	.01
☐ 77	Tim Naehring	.20	.10	.02
☐ 78	Frank Thomas	.60	.30	.06
☐ 79	Todd Hundley	.10	.05	.01
☐ 80	Ed Vosberg	.10	.05	.01
☐ 81	Todd Zeile	.20	.10	.02
☐ 82	Lee Stevens	.15	.07	.01
☐ 83	Scott Radinsky	.10	.05	.01
☐ 84	Hensley Meulens	.30	.15	.03
☐ 85	Brian DuBois	.10	.05	.01
☐ 86	Steve Olin	.10	.05	.01
☐ 87	Julio Machado	.10	.05	.01
☐ 88	Jose Vizcaino	.10	.05	.01
☐ 89	Mark Lemke	.10	.05	.01
☐ 90	Felix Jose	.20	.10	.02
☐ 91	Wally Whitehurst	.10	.05	.01
☐ 92	Dana Kiecker	.15	.07	.01
☐ 93	Mike Munoz	.15	.07	.01
☐ 94	Adam Peterson	.10	.05	.01
☐ 95	Tim Drummond	.10	.05	.01
☐ 96	Dave Hollins	.20	.10	.02
☐ 97	Craig Wilson	.15	.07	.01
☐ 98	Hal Morris	.25	.12	.02
☐ 99	Jose Offerman	.40	.20	.04
☐ 100	John Olerud	.40	.20	.04

1985 7-Eleven Twins

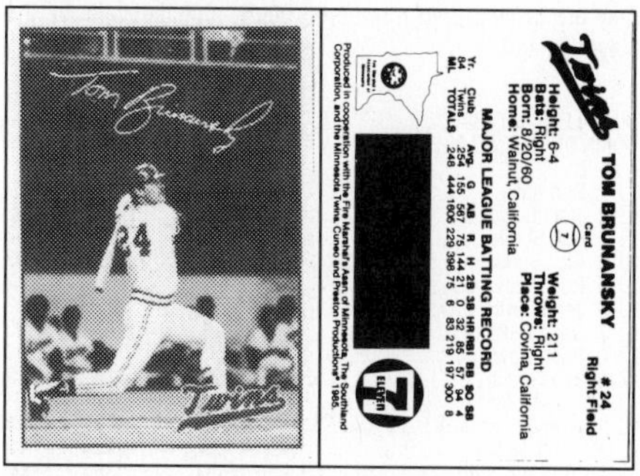

This 13-card set of Minnesota Twins was produced and distributed by the Twins in conjunction with the 7-Eleven stores and the Fire Marshall's Association. The cards measure approximately 2 1/2" by 3 1/2" and are in full color. Supposedly 20,000 sets of cards were distributed during the promotion which began on June 2nd and lasted throughout the month of July. The card backs have some statistics and a fire safety tip.

	MINT	EXC	G-VG
COMPLETE SET (13)	8.00	4.00	.80
COMMON PLAYER (1-13)	.30	.15	.03
☐ 1 Kirby Puckett	4.00	2.00	.40
☐ 2 Frank Viola	1.00	.50	.10
☐ 3 Mickey Hatcher	.30	.15	.03
☐ 4 Kent Hrbek	1.00	.50	.10
☐ 5 John Butcher	.30	.15	.03
☐ 6 Roy Smalley	.30	.15	.03
☐ 7 Tom Brunansky	.60	.30	.06
☐ 8 Ron Davis	.30	.15	.03
☐ 9 Gary Gaetti	.90	.45	.09
☐ 10 Tim Teufel	.30	.15	.03
☐ 11 Mike Smithson	.30	.15	.03
☐ 12 Tim Laudner	.30	.15	.03
☐ xx Checklist Card	.30	.15	.03

1984 Smokey Angels

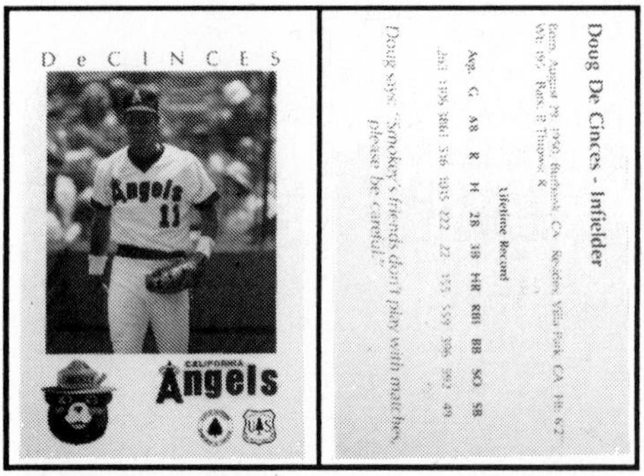

The cards in this 32-card set measure 2 1/2" by 3 3/4" and feature the California Angels in full color. Sets were given out to persons 15 and under attending the June 16th game against the Indians. Unlike the Padres set of this year, Smokey the Bear is not featured on these cards. The player's photo, the Angels' logo, and the Smokey the Bear logo appear on the front, in addition to the California Department of Forestry and the U.S. Forest Service logos. The abbreviated backs contain short biographical data, career statistics, and an anti-wildfire hint from the player on the front. Since the cards are unnumbered, they are ordered and numbered below alphabetically by the player's name.

	MINT	EXC	G-VG
COMPLETE SET (32)	8.00	4.00	.80
COMMON PLAYER (1-32)	.25	.12	.02
☐ 1 Don Aase	.25	.12	.02
☐ 2 Juan Beniquez	.25	.12	.02
☐ 3 Bob Boone	.50	.25	.05
☐ 4 Rick Burleson	.35	.17	.03
☐ 5 Rod Carew	1.25	.60	.12
☐ 6 John Curtis	.25	.12	.02
☐ 7 Doug DeCinces	.35	.17	.03
☐ 8 Brian Downing	.35	.17	.03
☐ 9 Ken Forsch	.25	.12	.02
☐ 10 Bobby Grich	.35	.17	.03
☐ 11 Reggie Jackson	1.50	.75	.15
☐ 12 Ron Jackson	.25	.12	.02
☐ 13 Tommy John	.60	.30	.06
☐ 14 Curt Kaufman	.25	.12	.02
☐ 15 Bruce Kison	.25	.12	.02
☐ 16 Frank LaCorte	.25	.12	.02
☐ 17 Logo Card (Forestry Dept.)	.25	.12	.02
☐ 18 Fred Lynn	.35	.17	.03
☐ 19 John McNamara MG	.35	.17	.03
☐ 20 Jerry Narron	.25	.12	.02
☐ 21 Gary Pettis	.35	.17	.03
☐ 22 Rob Picciolo	.25	.12	.02
☐ 23 Ron Romanick	.25	.12	.02
☐ 24 Luis Sanchez	.25	.12	.02
☐ 25 Dick Schofield	.35	.17	.03
☐ 26 Daryl Sconiers	.25	.12	.02
☐ 27 Jim Slaton	.25	.12	.02
☐ 28 Smokey the Bear	.25	.12	.02
☐ 29 Ellis Valentine	.25	.12	.02
☐ 30 Rob Wilfong	.25	.12	.02
☐ 31 Mike Witt	.35	.17	.03
☐ 32 Geoff Zahn	.25	.12	.02

1984 Smokey Dodgers

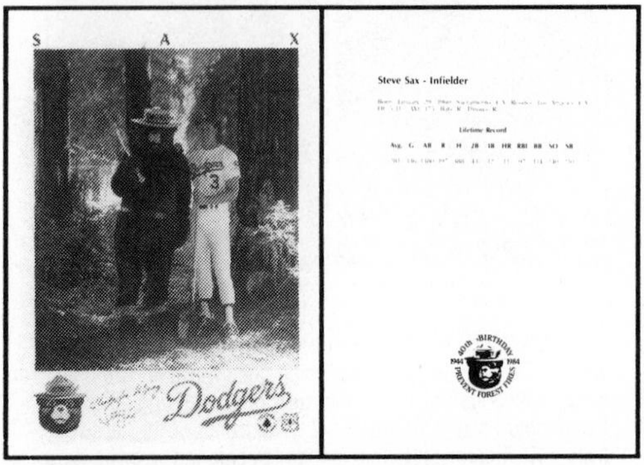

This four-card set was not widely distributed and has not proven to be very popular with collectors. Cards were supposedly distributed by fire agencies in Southern California at fairs, mall displays, and special events. Cards are approximately 5" by 7" and feature a color picture of Smokey the Bear with a Dodger. The cards were printed on relatively thin card stock; printing on the back is black on white.

	MINT	EXC	G-VG
COMPLETE SET (4)	12.00	6.00	1.20
COMMON PLAYER (1-4)	1.50	.75	.15
☐ 1 Ken Landreaux with Smokey	2.50	1.25	.25
☐ 2 Tom Niedenfuer with Smokey	2.50	1.25	.25
☐ 3 Steve Sax with Smokey	7.50	3.75	.75
☐ 4 Smokey the Bear (batting pose)	1.50	.75	.15

1984 Smokey Padres

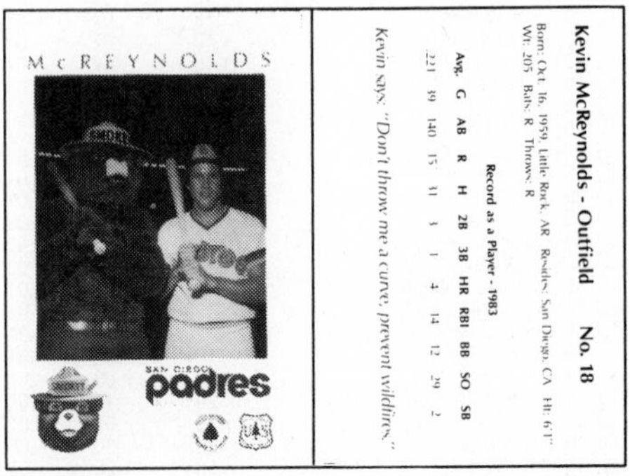

The cards in this 29-card set measure 2 1/2" by 3 3/4". This unnumbered, full color set features the Fire Prevention Bear and a Padres player, coach, manager, or associate on each card. The set was given out at the ballpark at the May 14th game against the Expos. Logos of the California Department of Forestry and the U.S. Forest Service appear in conjunction with a Smokey the Bear logo on the obverse. The set commemorates the 40th birthday of Smokey the Bear. The backs contain short biographical data, statistics and a fire prevention hint from the player pictured on the front.

	MINT	EXC	G-VG
COMPLETE SET (29)	10.00	5.00	1.00
COMMON PLAYER (1-29)	.30	.15	.03
☐ 1 Kurt Bevacqua	.30	.15	.03
☐ 2 Bobby Brown	.30	.15	.03
☐ 3 Dave Campbell (Broadcast Team)	.30	.15	.03
☐ 4 The Chicken (Mascot)	.60	.30	.06
☐ 5 Jerry Coleman (Broadcast Team)	.30	.15	.03
☐ 6 Luis DeLeon	.30	.15	.03
☐ 7 Dave Dravecky	.75	.35	.07
☐ 8 Harry Dunlop CO	.30	.15	.03
☐ 9 Tim Flannery	.30	.15	.03
☐ 10 Steve Garvey	1.25	.60	.12
☐ 11 Doug Gwosdz	.30	.15	.03
☐ 12 Tony Gwynn	1.75	.85	.17
☐ 13 Harold (Doug) Harvey (ex-UMP)	.30	.15	.03
☐ 14 Terry Kennedy	.30	.15	.03
☐ 15 Jack Krol CO	.30	.15	.03
☐ 16 Tim Lollar	.30	.15	.03
☐ 17 Jack McKeon (VP for Baseball Operations)	.50	.25	.05
☐ 18 Kevin McReynolds	1.75	.85	.17
☐ 19 Sid Monge	.30	.15	.03
☐ 20 Luis Salazar	.40	.20	.04
☐ 21 Norm Sherry CO	.30	.15	.03
☐ 22 Eric Show	.40	.20	.04
☐ 23 Smokey the Bear	.30	.15	.03
☐ 24 Garry Templeton	.40	.20	.04
☐ 25 Mark Thurmond	.30	.15	.03
☐ 26 Ozzie Virgil CO	.30	.15	.03
☐ 27 Ed Whitson	.40	.20	.04
☐ 28 Alan Wiggins	.30	.15	.03
☐ 29 Dick Williams MG	.40	.20	.04

1985 Smokey Angels

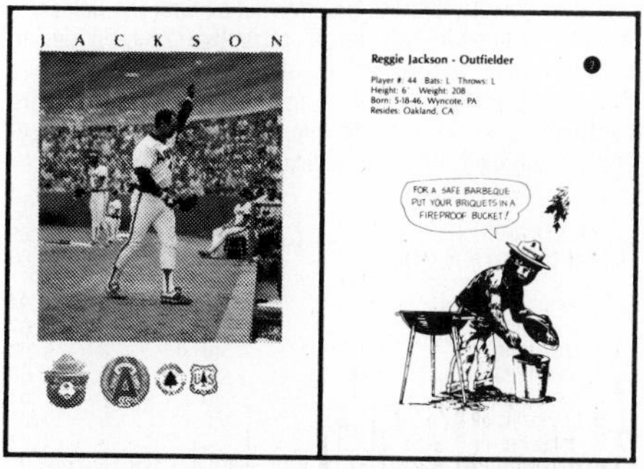

The cards in this 24-card set measure 4 1/4" by 6" and feature the California Angels in full color. The player's photo, the Angels' logo, and the Smokey the Bear logo appear on the front, in addition to the California Department of Forestry and the U.S. Forest Service logos. The abbreviated backs contain short biographical data and an anti-wildfire hint.

	MINT	EXC	G-VG
COMPLETE SET (24)	7.00	3.50	.70
COMMON PLAYER (1-24)	.25	.12	.02
☐ 1 Mike Witt	.35	.17	.03
☐ 2 Reggie Jackson	1.25	.60	.12
☐ 3 Bob Boone	.50	.25	.05
☐ 4 Mike Brown	.25	.12	.02
☐ 5 Rod Carew	1.00	.50	.10
☐ 6 Doug DeCinces	.35	.17	.03
☐ 7 Brian Downing	.35	.17	.03
☐ 8 Ken Forsch	.25	.12	.02
☐ 9 Gary Pettis	.35	.17	.03
☐ 10 Jerry Narron	.25	.12	.02
☐ 11 Ron Romanick	.25	.12	.02
☐ 12 Bobby Grich	.35	.17	.03
☐ 13 Dick Schofield	.35	.17	.03
☐ 14 Juan Beniquez	.25	.12	.02
☐ 15 Geoff Zahn	.25	.12	.02
☐ 16 Luis Sanchez	.25	.12	.02
☐ 17 Jim Slaton	.25	.12	.02
☐ 18 Doug Corbett	.25	.12	.02
☐ 19 Ruppert Jones	.25	.12	.02
☐ 20 Rob Wilfong	.25	.12	.02
☐ 21 Donnie Moore	.25	.12	.02
☐ 22 Pat Clements	.25	.12	.02
☐ 23 Tommy John	.50	.25	.05
☐ 24 Gene Mauch MG	.25	.12	.02

1986 Smokey Angels

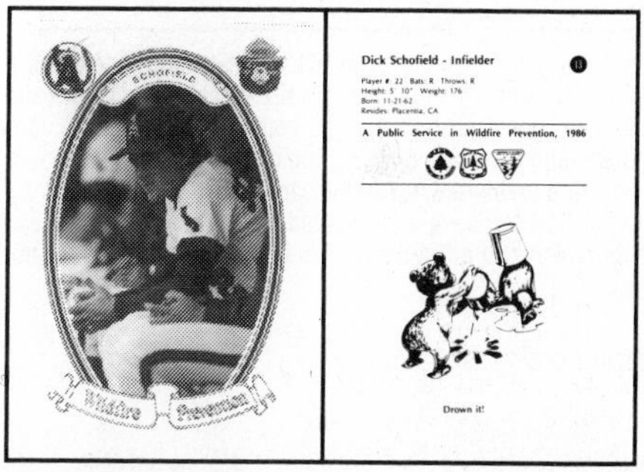

The Forestry Service (in conjunction with the California Angels) produced this large, attractive 24-card set. The cards feature Smokey the Bear pictured in the upper right corner of the card. The card backs give a fire safety tip. The set was given out free at Anaheim Stadium on August 9th. The cards measure 4 1/4" by 6" and are subtitled "Wildfire Prevention" on the front.

	MINT	EXC	G-VG
COMPLETE SET (24)	8.00	4.00	.80
COMMON PLAYER (1-24)	.25	.12	.02
☐ 1 Mike Witt	.35	.17	.03
☐ 2 Reggie Jackson	1.00	.50	.10
☐ 3 Bob Boone	.50	.25	.05
☐ 4 Don Sutton	.65	.30	.06
☐ 5 Kirk McCaskill	.35	.17	.03
☐ 6 Doug DeCinces	.35	.17	.03
☐ 7 Brian Downing	.35	.17	.03
☐ 8 Doug Corbett	.25	.12	.02
☐ 9 Gary Pettis	.35	.17	.03
☐ 10 Jerry Narron	.25	.12	.02
☐ 11 Ron Romanick	.25	.12	.02
☐ 12 Bobby Grich	.35	.17	.03
☐ 13 Dick Schofield	.35	.17	.03
☐ 14 George Hendrick	.35	.17	.03
☐ 15 Rick Burleson	.35	.17	.03
☐ 16 John Candelaria	.35	.17	.03
☐ 17 Jim Slaton	.25	.12	.02
☐ 18 Darrell Miller	.25	.12	.02
☐ 19 Ruppert Jones	.25	.12	.02
☐ 20 Rob Wilfong	.25	.12	.02
☐ 21 Donnie Moore	.25	.12	.02
☐ 22 Wally Joyner	1.50	.75	.15
☐ 23 Terry Forster	.25	.12	.02
☐ 24 Gene Mauch MG	.25	.12	.02

1987 Smokey A's Colorgrams

These cards are actually pages of a booklet featuring members of the Oakland A's and Smokey's fire safety tips. The booklet has 12 pages each containing a black and white photo card (approximately 2 1/2" by 3 3/4") and a black and white player caricature (oversized head) postcard (approximately 3 3/4" by 5 5/8"). The cards are unnumbered but they have biographical information and a fire-prevention cartoon on the back of the card.

	MINT	EXC	G-VG
COMPLETE SET (12)	10.00	5.00	1.00
COMMON PLAYER (1-12)	.50	.25	.05
☐ 1 Joaquin Andujar	.50	.25	.05
☐ 2 Jose Canseco	3.00	1.50	.30
☐ 3 Mike Davis	.50	.25	.05
☐ 4 Alfredo Griffin	.50	.25	.05
☐ 5 Moose Haas	.50	.25	.05
☐ 6 Jay Howell	.75	.35	.07
☐ 7 Reggie Jackson	1.50	.75	.15
☐ 8 Carney Lansford	1.00	.50	.10
☐ 9 Dwayne Murphy	.60	.30	.06
☐ 10 Tony Phillips	.60	.30	.06
☐ 11 Dave Stewart	1.25	.60	.12
☐ 12 Curt Young	.50	.25	.05

1987 Smokey AL

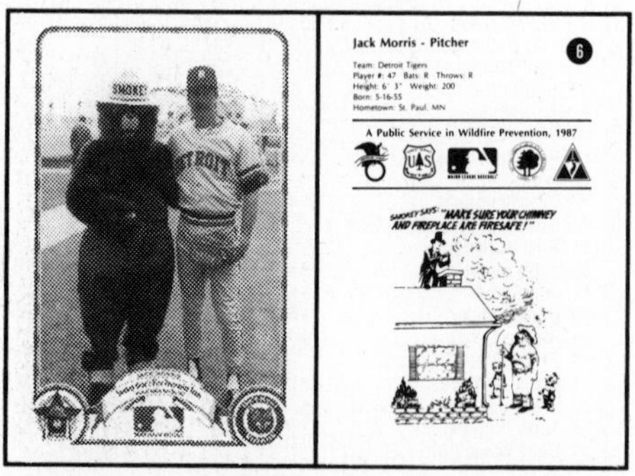

The U.S. Forestry Service (in conjunction with Major League Baseball) produced this large, attractive 14 player card set to commemorate the 43rd birthday of Smokey. The cards feature Smokey the Bear pictured on every card with the player. The card backs give a fire safety tip. The cards measure 4" by 6" and are subtitled "National Smokey Bear Day 1987" on the front. The cards were printed on an uncut (but perforated) sheet that measured 18" by 24".

	MINT	EXC	G-VG
COMPLETE SET (16)	6.00	3.00	.60
COMMON PLAYER (1-16)	.25	.12	.02
☐ 1 Jose Canseco	2.00	1.00	.20
☐ 2 Dennis Oil Can Boyd	.25	.12	.02
☐ 3 John Candelaria	.25	.12	.02
☐ 4 Harold Baines	.35	.17	.03
☐ 5 Joe Carter	.50	.25	.05
☐ 6 Jack Morris	.35	.17	.03
☐ 7 Buddy Biancalana	.25	.12	.02
☐ 8 Kirby Puckett	1.25	.60	.12
☐ 9 Mike Pagliarulo	.25	.12	.02
☐ 10 Larry Sheets	.25	.12	.02
☐ 11 Mike Moore	.35	.17	.03
☐ 12 Charlie Hough	.25	.12	.02
☐ 13 National Smokey Bear Day 1987	.25	.12	.02
☐ 14 Tom Henke	.25	.12	.02
☐ 15 Jim Gantner	.25	.12	.02
☐ 16 American League Smokey Bear Day 1987	.25	.12	.02

1987 Smokey Angels

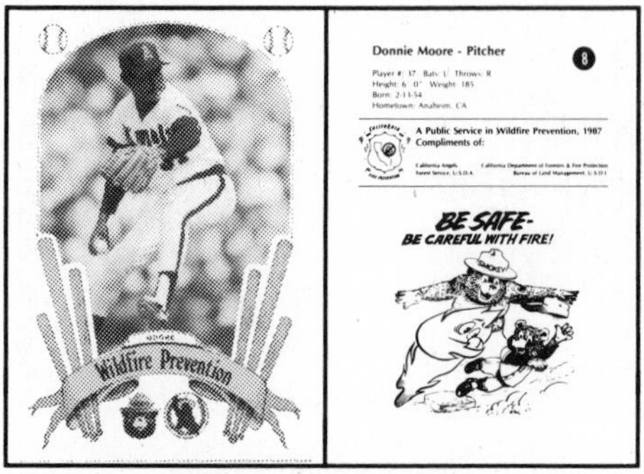

The U.S. Forestry Service (in conjunction with the California Angels) produced this large, attractive 24-card set to commemorate the 43rd birthday of Smokey. The cards feature Smokey the Bear pictured at the bottom of every card. The card backs give a cartoon fire safety tip. The cards measure 4" by 6" and are subtitled "Wildfire Prevention" on the front.

	MINT	EXC	G-VG
COMPLETE SET (24)	8.00	4.00	.80
COMMON PLAYER (1-24)	.30	.15	.03
☐ 1 John Candelaria	.40	.20	.04
☐ 2 Don Sutton	.75	.35	.07
☐ 3 Mike Witt	.40	.20	.04
☐ 4 Gary Lucas	.30	.15	.03
☐ 5 Kirk McCaskill	.40	.20	.04
☐ 6 Chuck Finley	.60	.30	.06
☐ 7 Willie Fraser	.30	.15	.03
☐ 8 Donnie Moore	.30	.15	.03
☐ 9 Urbano Lugo	.30	.15	.03
☐ 10 Butch Wynegar	.30	.15	.03
☐ 11 Darrell Miller	.30	.15	.03
☐ 12 Wally Joyner	1.00	.50	.10
☐ 13 Mark McLemore	.30	.15	.03
☐ 14 Mark Ryal	.30	.15	.03
☐ 15 Dick Schofield	.40	.20	.04
☐ 16 Jack Howell	.40	.20	.04
☐ 17 Doug DeCinces	.40	.20	.04
☐ 18 Gus Polidor	.30	.15	.03
☐ 19 Brian Downing	.40	.20	.04
☐ 20 Gary Pettis	.40	.20	.04
☐ 21 Ruppert Jones	.30	.15	.03
☐ 22 George Hendrick	.30	.15	.03
☐ 23 Devon White	.90	.45	.09
☐ 24 Checklist Card	.30	.15	.03

1987 Smokey Braves

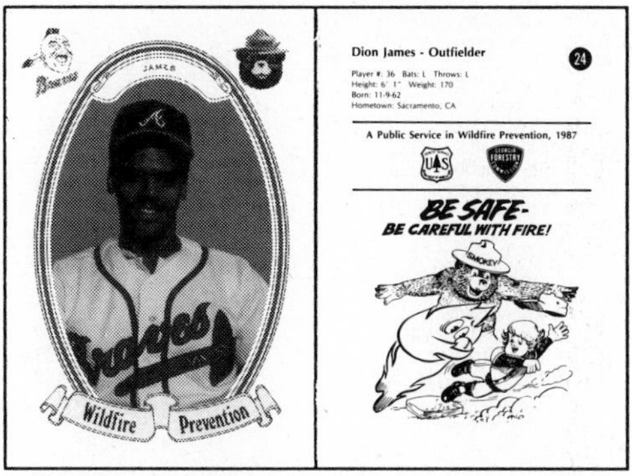

The U.S. Forestry Service (in conjunction with the Atlanta Braves) produced this large, attractive 27-card set to commemorate the 43rd birthday of Smokey. The cards feature Smokey the Bear pictured in the top right corner of every card. The card backs give a cartoon fire safety tip. The cards measure 4" by 6" and are subtitled "Wildfire Prevention" on the front. Distribution of the cards was gradual at the stadium throughout the summer. These large cards are numbered on the back.

	MINT	EXC	G-VG
COMPLETE SET (27)	15.00	7.50	1.50
COMMON PLAYER (1-26)	.50	.25	.05
☐ 1 Zane Smith	.75	.35	.07
☐ 2 Charlie Puleo	.50	.25	.05
☐ 3 Randy O'Neal	.50	.25	.05
☐ 4 David Palmer	.60	.30	.06
☐ 5 Rick Mahler	.60	.30	.06
☐ 6 Ed Olwine	.50	.25	.05
☐ 7 Jeff Dedmon	.50	.25	.05
☐ 8 Paul Assenmacher	.50	.25	.05
☐ 9 Gene Garber	.50	.25	.05
☐ 10 Jim Acker	.50	.25	.05
☐ 11 Bruce Benedict	.50	.25	.05
☐ 12 Ozzie Virgil	.50	.25	.05
☐ 13 Ted Simmons	.90	.45	.09
☐ 14 Dale Murphy	2.00	1.00	.20
☐ 15 Graig Nettles	.75	.35	.07
☐ 16 Ken Oberkfell	.50	.25	.05
☐ 17 Gerald Perry	.60	.30	.06
☐ 18 Rafael Ramirez	.50	.25	.05
☐ 19 Ken Griffey	.75	.35	.07
☐ 20 Andres Thomas	.60	.30	.06
☐ 21 Glenn Hubbard	.50	.25	.05
☐ 22 Damaso Garcia	.50	.25	.05
☐ 23 Gary Roenicke	.50	.25	.05
☐ 24 Dion James	.50	.25	.05
☐ 25 Albert Hall	.50	.25	.05
☐ 26 Chuck Tanner MG	.50	.25	.05
☐ xx Smokey/Checklist (unnumbered)	.50	.25	.05

1987 Smokey Cardinals

The U.S. Forestry Service (in conjunction with the St. Louis Cardinals) produced this large, attractive 25-card set to commemorate the 43rd birthday of Smokey. The cards feature Smokey the Bear pictured in the top right corner of every card. The card backs give a cartoon fire safety tip. The cards measure 4" by 6" and are subtitled "Wildfire Prevention" on the front. Sets were supposedly available from the Cardinals team for 3.50 postpaid. Also a limited number of 8 1/2" by 12" full-color team photos were available from the team to those who sent in a large SASE. The large team photo is not considered part of the complete set.

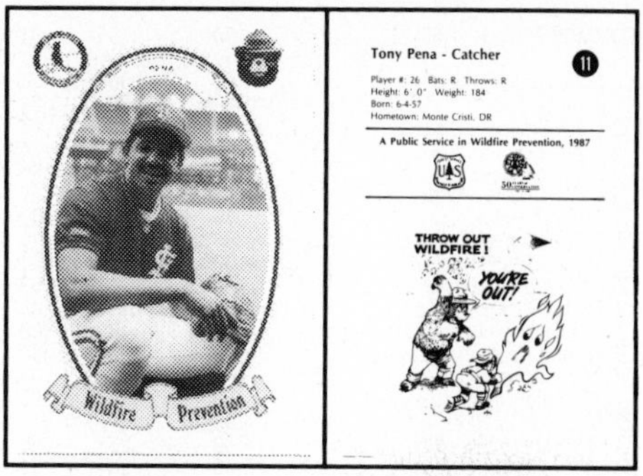

	MINT	EXC	G-VG
COMPLETE SET (25)	12.00	6.00	1.20
COMMON PLAYER (1-25)	.40	.20	.04
☐ 1 Ray Soff	.40	.20	.04
☐ 2 Todd Worrell	.60	.30	.06
☐ 3 John Tudor	.50	.25	.05
☐ 4 Pat Perry	.40	.20	.04
☐ 5 Rick Horton	.40	.20	.04
☐ 6 Danny Cox	.50	.25	.05
☐ 7 Bob Forsch	.40	.20	.04
☐ 8 Greg Matthews	.40	.20	.04
☐ 9 Bill Dawley	.40	.20	.04
☐ 10 Steve Lake	.40	.20	.04
☐ 11 Tony Pena	.50	.25	.05
☐ 12 Tom Pagnozzi	.40	.20	.04
☐ 13 Jack Clark	.75	.35	.07
☐ 14 Jim Lindeman	.40	.20	.04
☐ 15 Mike Laga	.40	.20	.04
☐ 16 Terry Pendleton	.50	.25	.05
☐ 17 Ozzie Smith	1.00	.50	.10
☐ 18 Jose Oquendo	.50	.25	.05
☐ 19 Tom Lawless	.40	.20	.04
☐ 20 Tom Herr	.50	.25	.05
☐ 21 Curt Ford	.40	.20	.04
☐ 22 Willie McGee	.60	.30	.06
☐ 23 Tito Landrum	.40	.20	.04
☐ 24 Vince Coleman	1.00	.50	.10
☐ 25 Whitey Herzog MG	.50	.25	.05
☐ xx Team Photo (large)	1.00	.50	.10

1987 Smokey Dodger All-Stars

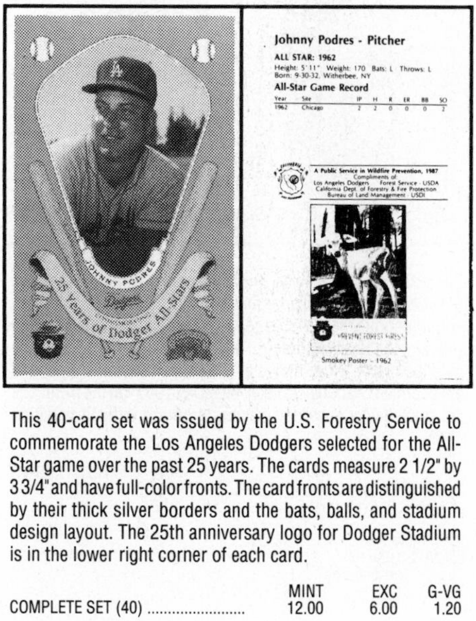

This 40-card set was issued by the U.S. Forestry Service to commemorate the Los Angeles Dodgers selected for the All-Star game over the past 25 years. The cards measure 2 1/2" by 3 3/4" and have full-color fronts. The card fronts are distinguished by their thick silver borders and the bats, balls, and stadium design layout. The 25th anniversary logo for Dodger Stadium is in the lower right corner of each card.

	MINT	EXC	G-VG
COMPLETE SET (40)	12.00	6.00	1.20

COMMON PLAYER (1-40)	.30	.15	.03
☐ 1 Walt Alston MG	.60	.30	.06
☐ 2 Dusty Baker	.40	.20	.04
☐ 3 Jim Brewer	.30	.15	.03
☐ 4 Ron Cey	.40	.20	.04
☐ 5 Tommy Davis	.40	.20	.04
☐ 6 Willie Davis	.40	.20	.04
☐ 7 Don Drysdale	.80	.40	.08
☐ 8 Steve Garvey	.80	.40	.08
☐ 9 Bill Grabarkewitz	.30	.15	.03
☐ 10 Pedro Guerrero	.60	.30	.06
☐ 11 Tom Haller	.30	.15	.03
☐ 12 Orel Hershiser	.80	.40	.08
☐ 13 Burt Hooton	.30	.15	.03
☐ 14 Steve Howe	.30	.15	.03
☐ 15 Tommy John	.50	.25	.05
☐ 16 Sandy Koufax	1.00	.50	.10
☐ 17 Tom Lasorda MG	.50	.25	.05
☐ 18 Jim Lefebvre	.40	.20	.04
☐ 19 Davey Lopes	.40	.20	.04
☐ 20 Mike Marshall (pitcher)	.40	.20	.04
☐ 21 Mike Marshall (outfielder)	.40	.20	.04
☐ 22 Andy Messersmith	.30	.15	.03
☐ 23 Rick Monday	.30	.15	.03
☐ 24 Manny Mota	.40	.20	.04
☐ 25 Claude Osteen	.30	.15	.03
☐ 26 Johnny Podres	.40	.20	.04
☐ 27 Phil Regan	.30	.15	.03
☐ 28 Jerry Reuss	.30	.15	.03
☐ 29 Rick Rhoden	.30	.15	.03
☐ 30 John Roseboro	.30	.15	.03
☐ 31 Bill Russell	.40	.20	.04
☐ 32 Steve Sax	.50	.25	.05
☐ 33 Bill Singer	.30	.15	.03
☐ 34 Reggie Smith	.40	.20	.04
☐ 35 Don Sutton	.80	.40	.08
☐ 36 Fernando Valenzuela	.60	.30	.06
☐ 37 Bob Welch	.50	.25	.05
☐ 38 Maury Wills	.50	.25	.05
☐ 39 Jim Wynn	.30	.15	.03
☐ 40 Checklist Card	.30	.15	.03

1987 Smokey National League

The U.S. Forestry Service (in conjunction with Major League Baseball) produced this large, attractive 14 player card set to commemorate the 43rd birthday of Smokey. The cards feature Smokey the Bear pictured on every card with the player. The card backs give a fire safety tip. The cards measure 4" by 6" and are subtitled "National Smokey Bear Day 1987" on the front. The set price below does not include the more difficult variation cards.

	MINT	EXC	G-VG
COMPLETE SET (15)	6.00	3.00	.60
COMMON PLAYER (1-15)	.25	.12	.02
☐ 1 Steve Sax	.50	.25	.05
☐ 2A Dale Murphy (holding bat)	2.00	1.00	.20
☐ 2B Dale Murphy (no bat, arm around Smokey)	12.50	6.25	1.25
☐ 3A Jody Davis (kneeling with Smokey)	.50	.25	.05
☐ 3B Jody Davis (standing, shaking Smokey's hand)	8.00	4.00	.80
☐ 4 Bill Gullickson	.25	.12	.02
☐ 5 Mike Scott	.50	.25	.05
☐ 6 Roger McDowell	.35	.17	.03
☐ 7 Steve Bedrosian	.35	.17	.03
☐ 8 Johnny Ray	.25	.12	.02
☐ 9 Ozzie Smith	.75	.35	.07
☐ 10 Steve Garvey	.75	.35	.07
☐ 11 National Smokey Bear Day	.25	.12	.02
☐ 12 Mike Krukow	.25	.12	.02
☐ 13 Smokey the Bear	.25	.12	.02
☐ 14 Mike Fitzgerald	.25	.12	.02
☐ 15 National League Logo	.25	.12	.02

1987 Smokey Rangers

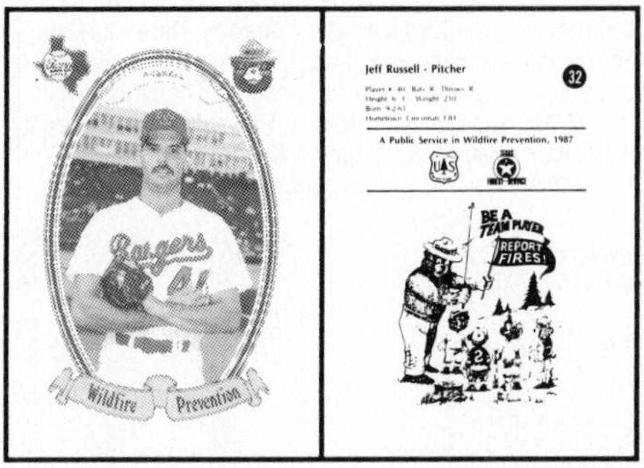

The U.S. Forestry Service (in conjunction with the Texas Rangers) produced this large, attractive 32-card set. The cards feature Smokey the Bear pictured in the upper-right corner of every player's card. The card backs give a cartoon fire safety tip. The cards measure approximately 4 1/4" by 6" and are subtitled "Wildfire Prevention" on the front. These large cards are numbered on the back. Cards 4 Mike Mason and 14 Tom Paciorek were withdrawn and were never formally released as part of the set and hence are quite scarce.

	MINT	EXC	G-VG
COMPLETE SET (32)	75.00	37.50	7.50
COMMON PLAYER (1-32)	.35	.17	.03
☐ 1 Charlie Hough	.60	.30	.06
☐ 2 Greg Harris	.35	.17	.03
☐ 3 Jose Guzman	.50	.25	.05
☐ 4 Mike Mason SP	30.00	15.00	3.00
☐ 5 Dale Mohorcic	.35	.17	.03
☐ 6 Bobby Witt	1.25	.60	.12
☐ 7 Mitch Williams	.60	.30	.06
☐ 8 Geno Petralli	.35	.17	.03
☐ 9 Don Slaught	.35	.17	.03
☐ 10 Darrell Porter	.35	.17	.03
☐ 11 Steve Buechele	.50	.25	.05
☐ 12 Pete O'Brien	.50	.25	.05
☐ 13 Scott Fletcher	.35	.17	.03
☐ 14 Tom Paciorek SP	30.00	15.00	3.00
☐ 15 Pete Incaviglia	.90	.45	.09
☐ 16 Oddibe McDowell	.50	.25	.05
☐ 17 Ruben Sierra	2.50	1.25	.25
☐ 18 Larry Parrish	.50	.25	.05
☐ 19 Bobby Valentine MG	.50	.25	.05
☐ 20 Tom House CO	.35	.17	.03
☐ 21 Tom Robson CO	.35	.17	.03
☐ 22 Edwin Correa	.35	.17	.03
☐ 23 Mike Stanley	.35	.17	.03
☐ 24 Joe Ferguson CO	.35	.17	.03
☐ 25 Art Howe CO	.50	.25	.05

	MINT	EXC	G-VG
☐ 26 Bob Brower	.35	.17	.03
☐ 27 Mike Loynd	.35	.17	.03
☐ 28 Curtis Wilkerson	.35	.17	.03
☐ 29 Tim Foli CO	.35	.17	.03
☐ 30 Dave Oliver	.35	.17	.03
☐ 31 Jerry Browne	.50	.25	.05
☐ 32 Jeff Russell	.50	.25	.05

1988 Smokey Angels

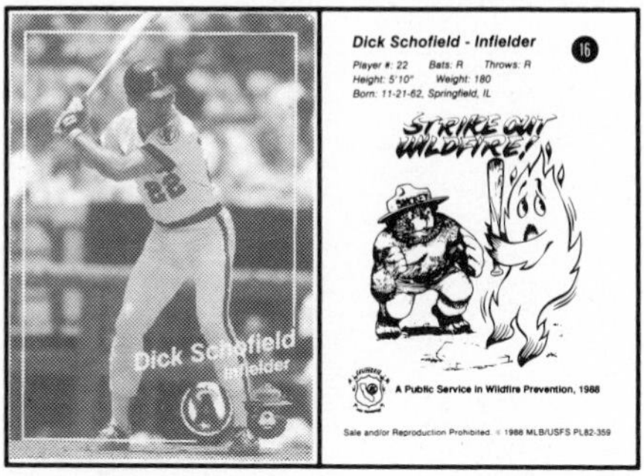

The U.S. Forestry Service (in conjunction with the California Angels) produced this attractive 25-card set. The cards feature Smokey the Bear pictured at the bottom of every card. The card backs give a cartoon fire safety tip. The cards measure approximately 2 1/2" by 3 1/2" and are in full color. The cards are numbered on the back. They were distributed during promotions on August 28, September 4, and September 18.

	MINT	EXC	G-VG
COMPLETE SET (25)	10.00	5.00	1.00
COMMON PLAYER (1-24)	.35	.17	.03
☐ 1 Cookie Rojas MG	.35	.17	.03
☐ 2 Johnny Ray	.50	.25	.05
☐ 3 Jack Howell	.50	.25	.05
☐ 4 Mike Witt	.35	.17	.03
☐ 5 Tony Armas	.50	.25	.05
☐ 6 Gus Polidor	.35	.17	.03
☐ 7 DeWayne Buice	.35	.17	.03
☐ 8 Dan Petry	.50	.25	.05
☐ 9 Bob Boone	.60	.30	.06
☐ 10 Chili Davis	.50	.25	.05
☐ 11 Greg Minton	.35	.17	.03
☐ 12 Kirk McCaskell	.50	.25	.05
☐ 13 Devon White	.75	.35	.07
☐ 14 Willie Fraser	.35	.17	.03
☐ 15 Chuck Finley	.75	.35	.07
☐ 16 Dick Schofield	.50	.25	.05
☐ 17 Wally Joyner	.90	.45	.09
☐ 18 Brian Downing	.50	.25	.05
☐ 19 Stewart Cliburn	.35	.17	.03
☐ 20 Donnie Moore	.35	.17	.03
☐ 21 Bryan Harvey	.50	.25	.05
☐ 22 Mark McLemore	.35	.17	.03
☐ 23 Butch Wynegar	.35	.17	.03
☐ 24 George Hendrick	.35	.17	.03
☐ xx Checklist/Logo Card	.35	.17	.03

1988 Smokey Cardinals

The U.S. Forestry Service (in conjunction with the St. Louis Cardinals) produced this attractive 25-card set. The cards feature Smokey the Bear pictured in the lower right corner of every card. The card backs give a cartoon fire safety tip. The cards measure approximately 3" by 5" and are in full color. The cards are numbered on the backs. The sets were distributed on July 19th during the Cardinals' game against the Los Angeles Dodgers to fans 15 years of age and under.

	MINT	EXC	G-VG
COMPLETE SET (25)	12.00	6.00	1.20
COMMON PLAYER (1-25)	.40	.20	.04
☐ 1 Whitey Herzog MG	.50	.25	.05
☐ 2 Danny Cox	.50	.25	.05
☐ 3 Ken Dayley	.40	.20	.04
☐ 4 Jose DeLeon	.50	.25	.05
☐ 5 Bob Forsch	.40	.20	.04
☐ 6 Joe Magrane	.60	.30	.06
☐ 7 Greg Mathews	.40	.20	.04
☐ 8 Scott Terry	.40	.20	.04
☐ 9 John Tudor	.50	.25	.05
☐ 10 Todd Worrell	.50	.25	.05
☐ 11 Steve Lake	.40	.20	.04
☐ 12 Tom Pagnozzi	.40	.20	.04
☐ 13 Tony Pena	.50	.25	.05
☐ 14 Bob Horner	.50	.25	.05
☐ 15 Tom Lawless	.40	.20	.04
☐ 16 Jose Oquendo	.50	.25	.05
☐ 17 Terry Pendleton	.50	.25	.05
☐ 18 Ozzie Smith	1.00	.50	.10
☐ 19 Vince Coleman	1.00	.50	.10
☐ 20 Curt Ford	.40	.20	.04
☐ 21 Willie McGee	.75	.35	.07
☐ 22 Larry McWilliams	.40	.20	.04
☐ 23 Steve Peters	.50	.25	.05
☐ 24 Luis Alicea	.40	.20	.04
☐ 25 Tom Brunansky	.60	.30	.06

1988 Smokey Dodgers

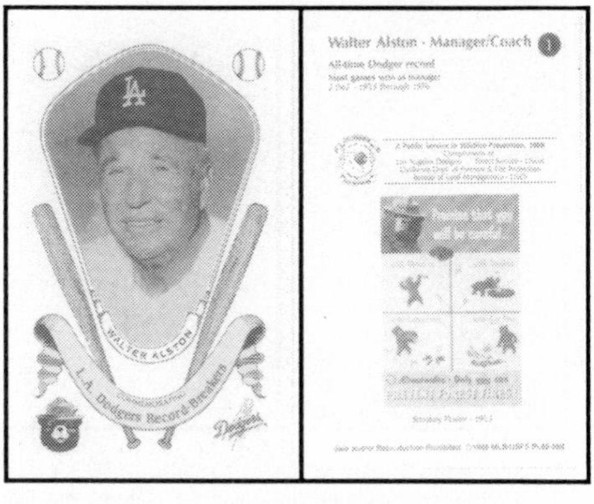

This 32-card set was issued by the U.S. Forestry Service as a perforated sheet that could be separated into individual cards. The set commemorates Los Angeles Dodgers who hold various team and league records, i.e., "L.A. Dodgers Record-Breakers." The cards measure approximately 2 1/2" by 4" and have full-color fronts. The card fronts are distinguished by their thick light blue borders and the bats, balls, and stadium design layout. The sheets of cards were distributed at the Dodgers' Smokey Bear Day game on September 9th.

	MINT	EXC	G-VG
COMPLETE SET (32)	10.00	5.00	1.00
COMMON PLAYER (1-32)	.30	.15	.03
☐ 1 Walter Alston MG	.50	.25	.05
☐ 2 John Roseboro	.30	.15	.03
☐ 3 Frank Howard	.40	.20	.04
☐ 4 Sandy Koufax	.75	.35	.07
☐ 5 Manny Mota	.40	.20	.04
☐ 6 Sandy Koufax, Jerry Reuss, and Bill Singer	.40	.20	.04
☐ 7 Maury Wills	.50	.25	.05
☐ 8 Tommy Davis	.40	.20	.04
☐ 9 Phil Regan	.30	.15	.03
☐ 10 Wes Parker	.30	.15	.03
☐ 11 Don Drysdale	.60	.30	.06
☐ 12 Willie Davis	.40	.20	.04
☐ 13 Bill Russell	.30	.15	.03
☐ 14 Jim Brewer	.30	.15	.03
☐ 15 Steve Garvey, Davey Lopes, Bill Russell, and Ron Cey	.40	.20	.04
☐ 16 Mike Marshall	.40	.20	.04
☐ 17 Steve Garvey	.60	.30	.06
☐ 18 Davey Lopes	.40	.20	.04
☐ 19 Burt Hooton	.30	.15	.03
☐ 20 Jim Wynn	.30	.15	.03
☐ 21 Dusty Baker, Ron Cey, Steve Garvey, and Reggie Smith	.40	.20	.04
☐ 22 Dusty Baker	.40	.20	.04
☐ 23 Tommy Lasorda MG	.50	.25	.05
☐ 24 Fernando Valenzuela	.60	.30	.06
☐ 25 Steve Sax	.50	.25	.05
☐ 26 Dodger Stadium	.30	.15	.03
☐ 27 Ron Cey	.40	.20	.04
☐ 28 Pedro Guerrero	.60	.30	.06
☐ 29 Mike Marshall	.40	.20	.04
☐ 30 Don Sutton	.60	.30	.06
☐ xx Checklist Card (unnumbered)	.30	.15	.03
☐ xx Smokey Bear (unnumbered)	.30	.15	.03

1988 Smokey Padres

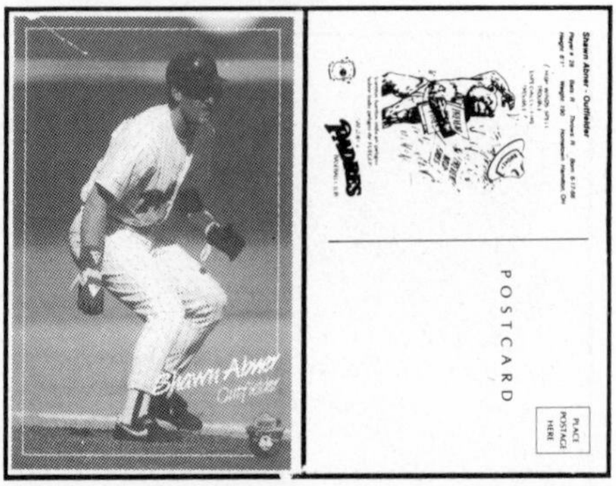

The cards in this 31-card set measure approximately 3 3/4" by 5 3/4". This unnumbered, full color set features the Fire Prevention Bear, Smokey, and a Padres player, coach, manager, or associate on each card. The set was given out at Jack Murphy Stadium to fans under the age of 14 during the Smokey Bear Day game promotion. The logo of the California Department of Forestry appears on the reverse in conjunction with a Smokey the Bear logo on the obverse. The backs contain short biographical data and a fire prevention hint from Smokey. The set is numbered below in alphabetical order. The card backs are actually postcards that can be addressed and mailed. Cards of Larry Bowa and Candy Sierra were printed but were not officially released since they were no longer members of the Padres by the time the cards were to be distributed.

	MINT	EXC	G-VG
COMPLETE SET (31)	20.00	10.00	2.00
COMMON PLAYER (1-31)	.50	.25	.05
☐ 1 Shawn Abner	.75	.35	.07
☐ 2 Roberto Alomar	2.00	1.00	.20
☐ 3 Sandy Alomar CO	.60	.30	.06
☐ 4 Greg Booker	.50	.25	.05
☐ 5 Chris Brown	.50	.25	.05
☐ 6 Mark Davis	.90	.45	.09
☐ 7 Pat Dobson CO	.60	.30	.06
☐ 8 Tim Flannery	.50	.25	.05
☐ 9 Mark Grant	.50	.25	.05
☐ 10 Tony Gwynn	2.00	1.00	.20
☐ 11 Andy Hawkins	.60	.30	.06
☐ 12 Stan Jefferson	.60	.30	.06
☐ 13 Jimmy Jones	.60	.30	.06
☐ 14 John Kruk	.60	.30	.06
☐ 15 Dave Leiper	.50	.25	.05
☐ 16 Shane Mack	.75	.35	.07
☐ 17 Carmelo Martinez	.60	.30	.06
☐ 18 Lance McCullers	.50	.25	.05
☐ 19 Keith Moreland	.50	.25	.05
☐ 20 Eric Nolte	.50	.25	.05
☐ 21 Amos Otis CO	.50	.25	.05
☐ 22 Mark Parent	.50	.25	.05
☐ 23 Randy Ready	.50	.25	.05
☐ 24 Greg Riddoch	.60	.30	.06
☐ 25 Benito Santiago	1.50	.75	.15
☐ 26 Eric Show	.60	.30	.06
☐ 27 Denny Sommers CO	.50	.25	.05
☐ 28 Garry Templeton	.60	.30	.06
☐ 29 Dickie Thon	.60	.30	.06
☐ 30 Ed Whitson	.60	.30	.06
☐ 31 Marvell Wynne	.50	.25	.05

1988 Smokey Rangers

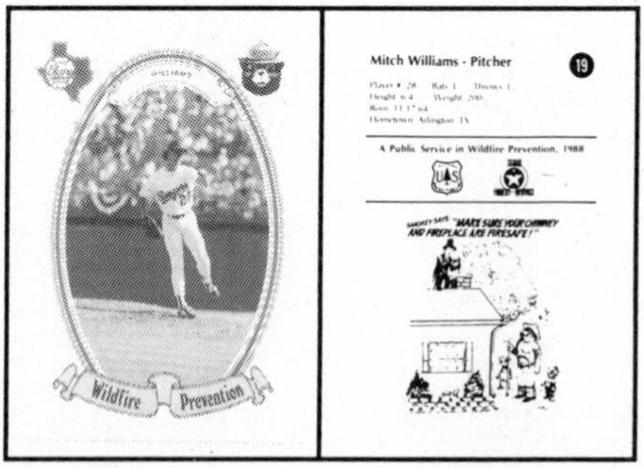

The cards in this 21-card set measure approximately 3 1/2" by 5". This numbered, full color set features the Fire Prevention Bear, Smokey, and a Rangers player (or manager) on each card. The set was given out at Arlington Stadium to fans during the Smokey Bear Day game promotion on August 7th. The logos of the Texas Forest Service and the U.S. Forestry Service appear on the reverse in conjunction with a Smokey the Bear logo on the obverse. The backs contain short biographical data and a fire prevention hint from Smokey.

	MINT	EXC	G-VG
COMPLETE SET (21)	12.00	6.00	1.20
COMMON PLAYER (1-21)	.50	.25	.05
☐ 1 Tom O'Malley	.50	.25	.05

☐ 2 Pete O'Brien	.60	.30	.06
☐ 3 Geno Petralli	.50	.25	.05
☐ 4 Pete Incaviglia	.75	.35	.07
☐ 5 Oddibe McDowell	.60	.30	.06
☐ 6 Dal Mohorcic	.50	.25	.05
☐ 7 Bobby Witt	.90	.45	.09
☐ 8 Bobby Valentine MG	.60	.30	.06
☐ 9 Ruben Sierra	2.00	1.00	.20
☐ 10 Scott Fletcher	.50	.25	.05
☐ 11 Mike Stanley	.50	.25	.05
☐ 12 Steve Buechele	.50	.25	.05
☐ 13 Charlie Hough	.60	.30	.06
☐ 14 Larry Parrish	.60	.30	.06
☐ 15 Jerry Browne	.50	.25	.05
☐ 16 Bob Brower	.50	.25	.05
☐ 17 Jeff Russell	.60	.30	.06
☐ 18 Edwin Correa	.50	.25	.05
☐ 19 Mitch Williams	.60	.30	.06
☐ 20 Jose Guzman	.50	.25	.05
☐ 21 Curtis Wilkerson	.50	.25	.05

1988 Smokey Royals

This set of 28 cards features caricatures of the Kansas City Royals players. The cards are nunmbered on the back except for the unnumbered title/checklist card. The card set was distributed as a giveaway item at the stadium on August 14th to kids age 14 and under. The cards are approximately 3" by 5" and are in full color on the card fronts. The Smokey logo is in the upper right corner of every obverse.

	MINT	EXC	G-VG
COMPLETE SET (28)	12.00	6.00	1.20
COMMON PLAYER (1-27)	.40	.20	.04
☐ 1 John Wathan MG	.50	.25	.05
☐ 2 Royals Coaches	.40	.20	.04
☐ 3 Willie Wilson	.60	.30	.06
☐ 4 Danny Tartabull	.90	.45	.09
☐ 5 Bo Jackson	2.50	1.25	.25
☐ 6 Gary Thurman	.50	.25	.05
☐ 7 Jerry Don Gleaton	.40	.20	.04
☐ 8 Floyd Bannister	.40	.20	.04
☐ 9 Buddy Black	.50	.25	.05
☐ 10 Steve Farr	.50	.25	.05
☐ 11 Gene Garber	.40	.20	.04
☐ 12 Mark Gubicza	.75	.35	.07
☐ 13 Charlie Liebrandt	.50	.25	.05
☐ 14 Ted Power	.40	.20	.04
☐ 15 Dan Quisenberry	.60	.30	.06
☐ 16 Bret Saberhagen	1.00	.50	.10
☐ 17 Mike Macfarlane	.50	.25	.05
☐ 18 Scotti Madison	.40	.20	.04
☐ 19 Jamie Quirk	.40	.20	.04
☐ 20 George Brett	1.25	.60	.12
☐ 21 Kevin Seitzer	.75	.35	.07
☐ 22 Bill Pecota	.40	.20	.04
☐ 23 Kurt Stillwell	.50	.25	.05
☐ 24 Brad Wellman	.40	.20	.04
☐ 25 Frank White	.50	.25	.05
☐ 26 Jim Eisenreich	.50	.25	.05
☐ 27 Smokey Bear	.40	.20	.04
☐ xx Checklist Card	.40	.20	.04

1988 Smokey Twins Colorgrams

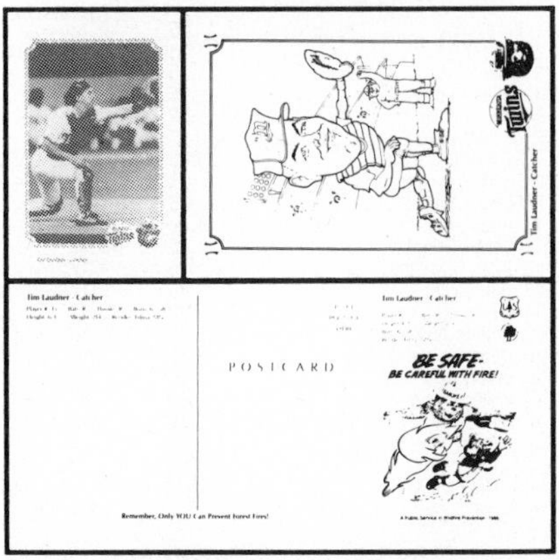

These cards are actually pages of a booklet featuring members of the Minnesota Twins and Smokey's fire safety tips. The booklet has 12 pages each containing a black and white photo card (approximately 2 1/2" by 3 3/4") and a black and white player caricature (oversized head) postcard (approximately 3 3/4" by 5 5/8"). The cards are unnumbered but they have biographical information and a fire-prevention cartoon on the back of the card.

	MINT	EXC	G-VG
COMPLETE SET (12)	12.00	6.00	1.20
COMMON PLAYER (1-12)	.65	.30	.06
☐ 1 Frank Viola	1.50	.75	.15
☐ 2 Gary Gaetti	1.25	.60	.12
☐ 3 Kent Hrbek	1.25	.60	.12
☐ 4 Jeff Reardon	.90	.45	.09
☐ 5 Gene Larkin	.65	.30	.06
☐ 6 Bert Blyleven	1.25	.60	.12
☐ 7 Tim Laudner	.65	.30	.06
☐ 8 Greg Gagne	.65	.30	.06
☐ 9 Randy Bush	.65	.30	.06
☐ 10 Dan Gladden	.65	.30	.06
☐ 11 Al Newman	.65	.30	.06
☐ 12 Kirby Puckett	2.50	1.25	.25

1989 Smokey Angels All-Stars

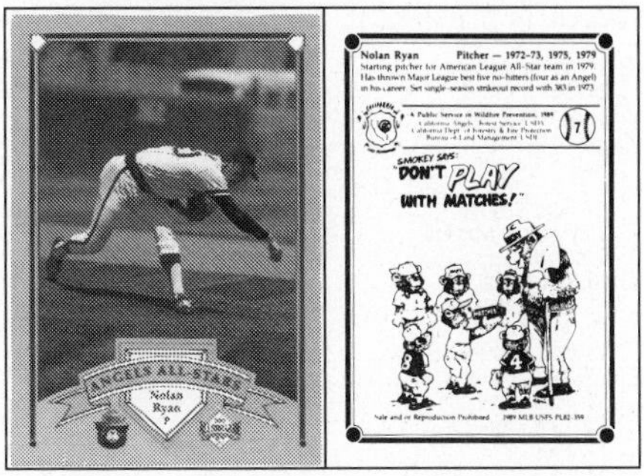

The 1989 Smokey Angels All-Stars set contains 20 standard-size (2 1/2 by 3 1/2 inch) cards. The fronts have red and white borders. The backs are blue and red and feature career highlights. This set, which depicts current and former Angels who appeared in the All-Star game, was given away at the June 25, 1989 Angels home game.

	MINT	EXC	G-VG
COMPLETE SET (20)	6.00	3.00	.60
COMMON PLAYER (1-20)	.25	.12	.02
☐ 1 Bill Rigney	.25	.12	.02
☐ 2 Dean Chance	.35	.17	.03
☐ 3 Jim Fregosi	.35	.17	.03
☐ 4 Bobby Knoop	.25	.12	.02
☐ 5 Don Mincher	.25	.12	.02
☐ 6 Clyde Wright	.25	.12	.02
☐ 7 Nolan Ryan	1.50	.75	.15
☐ 8 Frank Robinson	.75	.35	.07
☐ 9 Frank Tanana	.35	.17	.03
☐ 10 Rod Carew	1.00	.50	.10
☐ 11 Bobby Grich	.35	.17	.03
☐ 12 Brian Downing	.35	.17	.03
☐ 13 Don Baylor	.35	.17	.03
☐ 14 Fred Lynn	.35	.17	.03
☐ 15 Reggie Jackson	1.00	.50	.10
☐ 16 Doug DeCinces	.35	.17	.03
☐ 17 Bob Boone	.50	.25	.05
☐ 18 Wally Joyner	.75	.35	.07
☐ 19 Mike Witt	.35	.17	.03
☐ 20 Johnny Ray	.25	.12	.02

1989 Smokey Cardinals

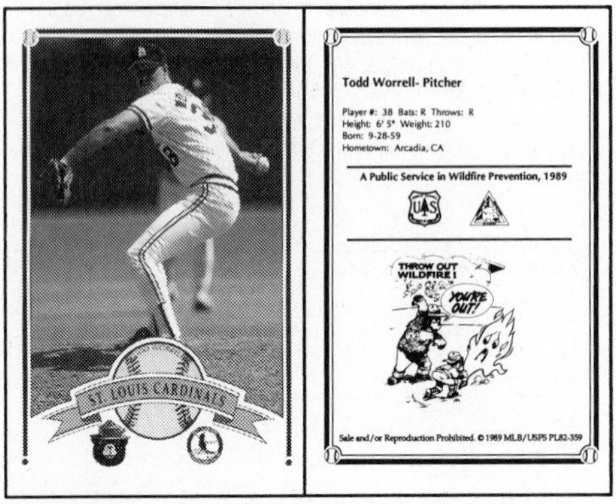

The 1989 Smokey Cardinals set contains 24 cards measuring 4" by 6". The fronts have color photos with white and red borders. The backs feature biographical information. The cards are unnumbered so they are listed below in alphabetical order for reference.

	MINT	EXC	G-VG
COMPLETE SET (24)	10.00	5.00	1.00
COMMON PLAYER (1-24)	.30	.15	.03
☐ 1 Tom Brunansky	.60	.30	.06
☐ 2 Vince Coleman	.80	.40	.08
☐ 3 John Costello	.40	.20	.04
☐ 4 Ken Dayley	.30	.15	.03
☐ 5 Jose DeLeon	.40	.20	.04
☐ 6 Frank DiPino	.30	.15	.03
☐ 7 Pedro Guerrero	.80	.40	.08
☐ 8 Whitey Herzog MG	.40	.20	.04
☐ 9 Ken Hill	.40	.20	.04
☐ 10 Tim Jones	.30	.15	.03
☐ 11 Jim Lindeman	.30	.15	.03
☐ 12 Joe Magrane	.40	.20	.04
☐ 13 Willie McGee	.60	.30	.06
☐ 14 John Morris	.30	.15	.03
☐ 15 Jose Oquendo	.40	.20	.04
☐ 16 Tom Pagnozzi	.30	.15	.03
☐ 17 Tony Pena	.40	.20	.04
☐ 18 Terry Pendleton	.40	.20	.04
☐ 19 Dan Quisenberry	.50	.25	.05
☐ 20 Ozzie Smith	.80	.40	.08
☐ 21 Scott Terry	.30	.15	.03
☐ 22 Milt Thompson	.30	.15	.03
☐ 23 Denny Walling	.30	.15	.03
☐ 24 Todd Worrell	.40	.20	.04

1989 Smokey Colt .45s

The 1989 Smokey Houston Colt .45s set contains 29 standard-size (2 1/2" by 3 1/2") cards. The fronts have black and white photos with white and light blue borders. This set depicts old Houston Colt .45s' players from their inaugural 1962 season.

	MINT	EXC	G-VG
COMPLETE SET (29)	6.00	3.00	.60
COMMON PLAYER (1-29)	.25	.12	.02
☐ 1 Bob Bruce	.25	.12	.02
☐ 2 Al Cicotte	.25	.12	.02
☐ 3 Dave Giusti	.35	.17	.03
☐ 4 Jim Golden	.25	.12	.02
☐ 5 Ken Johnson	.25	.12	.02
☐ 6 Tom Borland	.25	.12	.02
☐ 7 Bobby Shantz	.35	.17	.03
☐ 8 Dick Farrell	.35	.17	.03
☐ 9 Jim Umbricht	.25	.12	.02
☐ 10 Hal Woodeshick	.25	.12	.02
☐ 11 Merritt Ranew	.25	.12	.02
☐ 12 Hal Smith	.25	.12	.02
☐ 13 Jim Campbell	.25	.12	.02
☐ 14 Norm Larker	.25	.12	.02
☐ 15 Joe Amalfitano	.25	.12	.02
☐ 16 Bob Aspromonte	.25	.12	.02
☐ 17 Bob Lillis	.35	.17	.03
☐ 18 Dick Gernert	.25	.12	.02
☐ 19 Don Buddin	.25	.12	.02
☐ 20 Pidge Browne	.25	.12	.02
☐ 21 Von McDaniel	.25	.12	.02
☐ 22 Don Taussig	.25	.12	.02
☐ 23 Al Spangler	.25	.12	.02
☐ 24 Al Heist	.25	.12	.02
☐ 25 Jim Pendleton	.25	.12	.02
☐ 26 Johnny Weekly	.25	.12	.02
☐ 27 Harry Craft	.25	.12	.02
☐ 28 Colt Coaches	.25	.12	.02
☐ 29 1962 Houston Colt 45s	.25	.12	.02

1989 Smokey Dodger Greats

The 1989 Smokey Dodger Greats set contains 104 standard-size (2 1/2" by 3 1/2") cards. The fronts and backs have white and blue borders. The backs are vertically-oriented and feature career totals and fire prevention cartoons. The set depicts notable Dodgers of all eras, and was distributed in perforated sheet format.

	MINT	EXC	G-VG
COMPLETE SET (104)	15.00	7.50	1.50
COMMON PLAYER (1-104)	.10	.05	.01
☐ 1 Walter Alston	.25	.12	.02
☐ 2 David Bancroft	.20	.10	.02
☐ 3 Dan Brouthers	.20	.10	.02
☐ 4 Roy Campanella	.40	.20	.04
☐ 5 Max Carey	.20	.10	.02
☐ 6 Hazen"KiKi" Cuyler	.20	.10	.02
☐ 7 Don Drysdale	.30	.15	.03
☐ 8 Burleigh Grimes	.20	.10	.02
☐ 9 Billy Herman	.20	.10	.02
☐ 10 Waite Hoyt	.20	.10	.02
☐ 11 Hughie Jennings	.20	.10	.02
☐ 12 Willie Keeler	.20	.10	.02
☐ 13 Joseph Kelley	.20	.10	.02
☐ 14 George Kelly	.20	.10	.02
☐ 15 Sandy Koufax	.40	.20	.04
☐ 16 Henry"Heinie" Manush	.20	.10	.02
☐ 17 Juan Marichal	.25	.12	.02
☐ 18 Rabbit Maranville	.20	.10	.02
☐ 19 Rube Marquard	.20	.10	.02
☐ 20 Thomas McCarthy	.20	.10	.02
☐ 21 Joseph McGinnity	.20	.10	.02
☐ 22 Joe Medwick	.20	.10	.02
☐ 23 Pee Wee Reese	.30	.15	.03
☐ 24 Frank Robinson	.30	.15	.03
☐ 25 Jackie Robinson	.60	.30	.06
☐ 26 George"Babe" Ruth	.60	.30	.06
☐ 27 Duke Snider	.35	.17	.03
☐ 28 Casey Stengel	.35	.17	.03
☐ 29 Dazzy Vance	.20	.10	.02
☐ 30 Arky Vaughan	.20	.10	.02
☐ 31 Mike Scioscia	.10	.05	.01
☐ 32 Lloyd Waner	.20	.10	.02
☐ 33 John"Monte" Ward	.20	.10	.02
☐ 34 Zack Wheat	.20	.10	.02
☐ 35 Hoyt Wilhelm	.20	.10	.02
☐ 36 Hack Wilson	.20	.10	.02
☐ 37 Tony Cuccinello	.10	.05	.01
☐ 38 Al Lopez	.20	.10	.02
☐ 39 Leo Durocher	.20	.10	.02
☐ 40 Cookie Lavagetto	.10	.05	.01
☐ 41 Babe Phelps	.10	.05	.01
☐ 42 Dolph Camilli	.10	.05	.01
☐ 43 Whitlow Wyatt	.10	.05	.01
☐ 44 Mickey Owen	.10	.05	.01
☐ 45 Van Mungo	.10	.05	.01
☐ 46 Pete Coscarart	.10	.05	.01
☐ 47 Pete Reiser	.10	.05	.01
☐ 48 Augie Galan	.10	.05	.01
☐ 49 Dixie Walker	.10	.05	.01
☐ 50 Kirby Higbe	.10	.05	.01
☐ 51 Ralph Branca	.20	.10	.02
☐ 52 Bruce Edwards	.10	.05	.01
☐ 53 Eddie Stanky	.10	.05	.01
☐ 54 Gil Hodges	.20	.10	.02
☐ 55 Don Newcombe	.20	.10	.02
☐ 56 Preacher Roe	.20	.10	.02
☐ 57 Willie Randolph	.10	.05	.01
☐ 58 Carl Furillo	.20	.10	.02
☐ 59 Charlie Dressen	.10	.05	.01
☐ 60 Carl Erskine	.20	.10	.02
☐ 61 Clem Labine	.10	.05	.01
☐ 62 Gino Cimoli	.10	.05	.01
☐ 63 Johnny Podres	.20	.10	.02
☐ 64 Johnny Roseboro	.10	.05	.01
☐ 65 Wally Moon	.10	.05	.01
☐ 66 Charlie Neal	.10	.05	.01
☐ 67 Norm Larker	.10	.05	.01
☐ 68 Stan Williams	.10	.05	.01
☐ 69 Maury Wills	.20	.10	.02
☐ 70 Tommy Davis	.20	.10	.02
☐ 71 Jim Lefebvre	.15	.07	.01
☐ 72 Phil Regan	.10	.05	.01
☐ 73 Claude Osteen	.10	.05	.01
☐ 74 Tom Haller	.10	.05	.01
☐ 75 Bill Singer	.10	.05	.01
☐ 76 Bill Grabarkewitz	.10	.05	.01
☐ 77 Willie Davis	.10	.05	.01
☐ 78 Don Sutton	.25	.12	.02
☐ 79 Jim Brewer	.10	.05	.01
☐ 80 Manny Mota	.15	.07	.01
☐ 81 Bill Russell	.15	.07	.01
☐ 82 Ron Cey	.15	.07	.01
☐ 83 Steve Garvey	.30	.15	.03
☐ 84 Mike G. Marshall	.10	.05	.01
☐ 85 Andy Messersmith	.10	.05	.01
☐ 86 Jimmy Wynn	.10	.05	.01
☐ 87 Rick Rhoden	.10	.05	.01
☐ 88 Reggie Smith	.15	.07	.01
☐ 89 Jay Howell	.15	.07	.01
☐ 90 Rick Monday	.10	.05	.01
☐ 91 Tommy John	.20	.10	.02
☐ 92 Bob Welch	.20	.10	.02
☐ 93 Dusty Baker	.15	.07	.01
☐ 94 Pedro Guerrero	.20	.10	.02
☐ 95 Burt Hooton	.10	.05	.01
☐ 96 Davey Lopes	.15	.07	.01
☐ 97 Fernando Valenzuela	.20	.10	.02
☐ 98 Steve Howe	.10	.05	.01
☐ 99 Steve Sax	.20	.10	.02
☐ 100 Orel Hershiser	.25	.12	.02
☐ 101 Mike A. Marshall	.20	.10	.02
☐ 102 Ernie Lombardi	.20	.10	.02
☐ 103 Fred Lindstrom	.20	.10	.02
☐ 104 Wilbert Robinson	.20	.10	.02

1989 Smokey Rangers

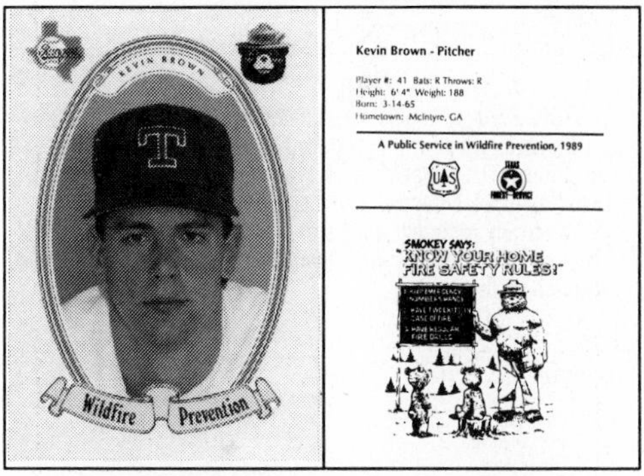

The 1989 Smokey Rangers set features 34 unnumbered cards measuring approximately 4 1/4" by 6". The fronts feature mugshot photos with white borders. The backs feature biographical information and fire prevention tips. The set was given away at a 1989 Rangers' home game.

	MINT	EXC	G-VG
COMPLETE SET (34)	15.00	7.50	1.50
COMMON PLAYER (1-34)	.40	.20	.04
☐ 1 Darrel Akerfelds	.40	.20	.04
☐ 2 Brad Arnsberg	.40	.20	.04
☐ 3 Buddy Bell	.60	.30	.06
☐ 4 Kevin Brown	.75	.35	.07
☐ 5 Steve Buechele	.40	.20	.04
☐ 6 Dick Egan CO	.40	.20	.04
☐ 7 Cecil Espy	.40	.20	.04
☐ 8 Scott Fletcher	.40	.20	.04
☐ 9 Julio Franco	.75	.35	.07
☐ 10 Cecilio Guante	.40	.20	.04
☐ 11 Jose Guzman	.50	.25	.05
☐ 12 Drew Hall	.40	.20	.04
☐ 13 Toby Harrah	.50	.25	.05
☐ 14 Charlie Hough	.50	.25	.05
☐ 15 Tom House CO	.40	.20	.04
☐ 16 Pete Incaviglia	.75	.35	.07
☐ 17 Chad Kreuter	.40	.20	.04
☐ 18 Jeff Kunkel	.40	.20	.04
☐ 19 Rick Leach	.40	.20	.04
☐ 20 Davey Lopes	.50	.25	.05
☐ 21 Craig McMurtry	.40	.20	.04
☐ 22 Jamie Moyer	.40	.20	.04
☐ 23 Dave Oliver CO	.40	.20	.04
☐ 24 Rafael Palmeiro	.75	.35	.07
☐ 25 Geno Petralli	.40	.20	.04
☐ 26 Tom Robson CO	.40	.20	.04
☐ 27 Kenny Rogers	.50	.25	.05
☐ 28 Jeff Russell	.50	.25	.05

☐ 29 Nolan Ryan	2.50	1.25	.25
☐ 30 Ruben Sierra	2.50	1.25	.25
☐ 31 Mike Stanley	.40	.20	.04
☐ 32 Jim Sundberg	.50	.25	.05
☐ 33 Bobby Valentine MG	.50	.25	.05
☐ 34 Bobby Witt	.75	.35	.07

1990 Smokey Angels

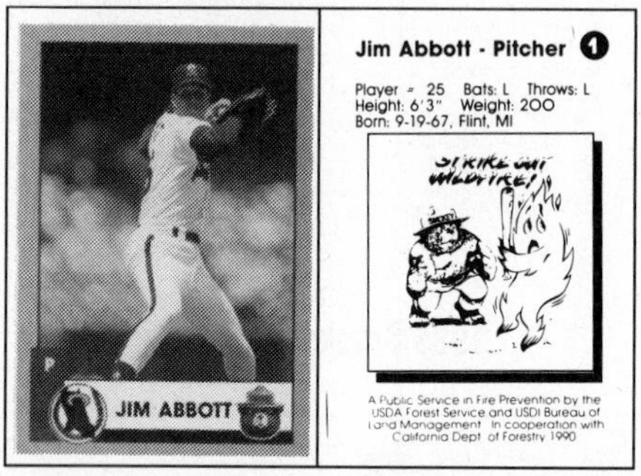

The 1990 Smokey Angels set contains standard-size (2 1/2" by 3 1/2") cards which were produced by the U.S. Forest Service and Bureau of Land Management in conjuction with the California Department of Forestry. The first 18 cards in the set are alphabetically arranged. Bailes and McClure were apparently added to the checklist later than these 18, after they were acquired by the Angels.

	MINT	EXC	G-VG
COMPLETE SET (20)	6.00	3.00	.60
COMMON PLAYER (1-20)	.30	.15	.03
☐ 1 Jim Abbott	.75	.35	.07
☐ 2 Bert Blyleven	.50	.25	.05
☐ 3 Chili Davis	.40	.20	.04
☐ 4 Brian Downing	.40	.20	.04
☐ 5 Chuck Finley	.50	.25	.05
☐ 6 Willie Fraser	.30	.15	.03
☐ 7 Bryan Harvey	.40	.20	.04
☐ 8 Jack Howell	.40	.20	.04
☐ 9 Wally Joyner	.75	.35	.07
☐ 10 Mark Langston	.50	.25	.05
☐ 11 Kirk McCaskill	.40	.20	.04
☐ 12 Mark McLemore	.30	.15	.03
☐ 13 Lance Parrish	.50	.25	.05
☐ 14 Johnny Ray	.40	.20	.04
☐ 15 Dick Schofield	.40	.20	.04
☐ 16 Mike Witt	.30	.15	.03
☐ 17 Claudell Washington	.40	.20	.04
☐ 18 Devon White	.50	.25	.05
☐ 19 Scott Bailes	.30	.15	.03
☐ 20 Bob McClure	.30	.15	.03

1990 Smokey Cardinals

This 27-card, approximately 3" by 5", set was issued about the 1990 St. Louis Cardinals in conjuction with the US Forest Service which was using the popular character Smokey the Bear. The set has full color action photos of the Cardinals on the front of the card while the back of the card has fire safety tips on the bottom of the card. The set has been checklisted alphabetically for reference. The cards are unnumbered; not even uniform numbers are displayed prominently.

	MINT	EXC	G-VG
COMPLETE SET (27)	12.00	6.00	1.20
COMMON PLAYER (1-27)	.40	.20	.04

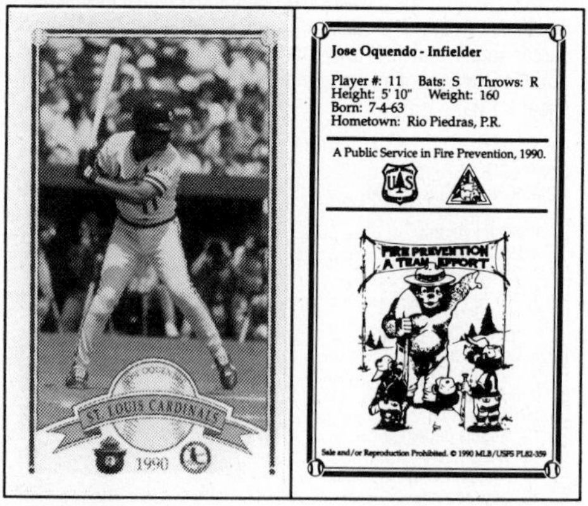

☐ 1 Vince Coleman	.80	.40	.08
☐ 2 Dave Collins	.40	.20	.04
☐ 3 Danny Cox	.40	.20	.04
☐ 4 Ken Dayley	.40	.20	.04
☐ 5 Frank DiPino	.40	.20	.04
☐ 6 Jose DeLeon	.50	.25	.05
☐ 7 Pedro Guerrero	.60	.30	.06
☐ 8 Whitey Herzog MG	.50	.25	.05
☐ 9 Rick Horton	.40	.20	.04
☐ 10 Rex Hudler	.50	.25	.05
☐ 11 Tim Jones	.40	.20	.04
☐ 12 Joe Magrane	.50	.25	.05
☐ 13 Greg Mathews	.40	.20	.04
☐ 14 Willie McGee	.60	.30	.06
☐ 15 John Morris	.40	.20	.04
☐ 16 Tom Niedenfuer	.40	.20	.04
☐ 17 Jose Oquendo	.40	.20	.04
☐ 18 Tom Pagnozzi	.40	.20	.04
☐ 19 Terry Pendleton	.50	.25	.05
☐ 20 Bryn Smith	.50	.25	.05
☐ 21 Lee Smith	.50	.25	.05
☐ 22 Ozzie Smith	.80	.40	.08
☐ 23 Scott Terry	.40	.20	.04
☐ 24 Milt Thompson	.40	.20	.04
☐ 25 John Tudor	.50	.25	.05
☐ 26 Denny Walling	.40	.20	.04
☐ 27 Todd Zeile	.80	.40	.08

1989 Socko Orel Hershiser

The 1989 Socko Orel Hershiser set contains seven unnumbered standard-size (2 1/2" by 3 1/2") cards. The fronts are blue, green and yellow, and feature full color photos of Hershiser with the Dodger logos airbrushed out. The backs are white and include "Tips from Orel." The cards were distributed as a promotional set through Socko beverages.

	MINT	EXC	G-VG
COMPLETE SET (7)	12.50	6.25	1.25
COMMON PLAYER (1-7)	2.00	1.00	.20
☐ 1 Orel Hershiser The Kick	2.00	1.00	.20
☐ 2 Orel Hershiser The Follow-Through	2.00	1.00	.20
☐ 3 Orel Hershiser The Release	2.00	1.00	.20
☐ 4 Orel Hershiser Backing Up The Catcher	2.00	1.00	.20
☐ 5 Orel Hershiser Barehanding the Ball	2.00	1.00	.20
☐ 6 Orel Hershiser The Grip	2.00	1.00	.20
☐ 7 Orel Hershiser Pitching from the Stretch	2.00	1.00	.20

1957 Sohio Indians

The 1957 Sohio Cleveland Indians set consists of 18 perforated photos, approximately 5" by 7", in black and white with facsimile autographs on the front which were designed to be pasted into a special photo album issued by SOHIO (Standard Oil of Ohio). The set features one of the earliest Roger Maris cards.

	NRMT	VG-E	GOOD
COMPLETE SET (18)	200.00	100.00	20.00
COMMON PLAYER (1-18)	5.00	2.50	.50
☐ 1 Bob Avila	6.00	3.00	.60
☐ 2 Jim Busby	5.00	2.50	.50
☐ 3 Chico Carrasquel	5.00	2.50	.50
☐ 4 Rocky Colavito	15.00	7.50	1.50
☐ 5 Mike Garcia	6.00	3.00	.60
☐ 6 Jim Hegan	6.00	3.00	.60
☐ 7 Bob Lemon	15.00	7.50	1.50
☐ 8 Roger Maris	100.00	50.00	10.00
☐ 9 Don Mossi	6.00	3.00	.60
☐ 10 Ray Narleski	5.00	2.50	.50
☐ 11 Russ Nixon	6.00	3.00	.60
☐ 12 Herb Score	7.50	3.75	.75
☐ 13 Al Smith	5.00	2.50	.50
☐ 14 George Strickland	5.00	2.50	.50
☐ 15 Bob Usher	5.00	2.50	.50
☐ 16 Vic Wertz	6.00	3.00	.60
☐ 17 Gene Woodling	6.00	3.00	.60
☐ 18 Early Wynn	15.00	7.50	1.50

1957 Sohio Reds

The 1957 Sohio Cincinnati Reds set consists of 18 perforated photos, approximately 5" by 7", in black and white with facsimile autographs on the front which were designed to be pasted into a special photo album issued by SOHIO (Standard Oil of Ohio).

	NRMT	VG-E	GOOD
COMPLETE SET (18)	150.00	75.00	15.00
COMMON PLAYER (1-18)	5.00	2.50	.50
☐ 1 Ed Bailey	5.00	2.50	.50
☐ 2 Gus Bell	6.00	3.00	.60
☐ 3 Rocky Bridges	5.00	2.50	.50
☐ 4 Smoky Burgess	6.00	3.00	.60
☐ 5 Hersh Freeman	5.00	2.50	.50
☐ 6 Alex Grammas	5.00	2.50	.50
☐ 7 Don Gross	5.00	2.50	.50
☐ 8 Warren Hacker	5.00	2.50	.50
☐ 9 Don Hoak	5.00	2.50	.50
☐ 10 Hal Jeffcoat	5.00	2.50	.50
☐ 11 Johnny Klippstein	5.00	2.50	.50
☐ 12 Ted Kluszewski	15.00	7.50	1.50
☐ 13 Brooks Lawrence	5.00	2.50	.50
☐ 14 Roy McMillan	5.00	2.50	.50
☐ 15 Joe Nuxhall	6.00	3.00	.60
☐ 16 Wally Post	6.00	3.00	.60
☐ 17 Frank Robinson	75.00	37.50	7.50
☐ 18 John Temple	6.00	3.00	.60

1953-54 Spic and Span 3x5

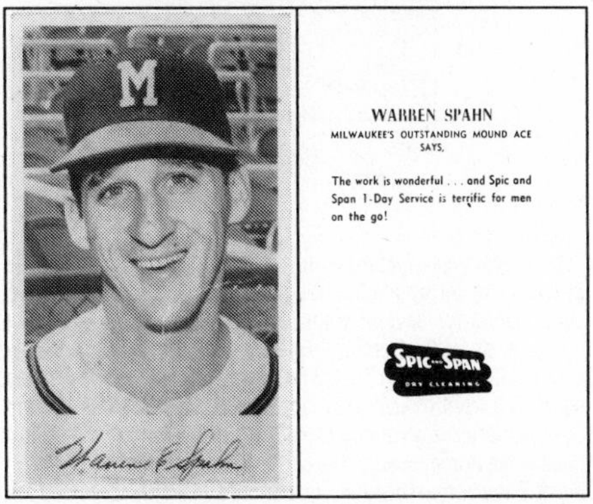
WARREN SPAHN
MILWAUKEE'S OUTSTANDING MOUND ACE SAYS,
The work is wonderful . . . and Spic and Span 1-Day Service is terrific for men on the go!

This 27-card set features only members of the Milwaukee Braves. The cards are black and white and approximately 3 1/

4" by 5 1/2". Some of the photos in the set are posed against blank backgrounds, but most are posed against seats and a chain link fence, hence the set is sometimes referred to as the "chain link fence" set. There is a facsimile autograph at the bottom of the card. The set was probably issued in 1953 and 1954 since Hank Aaron is not included in the set and Don Liddle, Ebba St.Claire, and Johnny Antonelli were traded from the Braves on February 1, 1954 for Bobby Thomson (who is also in the set). Cards can be found either blank back or with player's name, comment, and logo in blue on the back

	NRMT	VG-E	GOOD
COMPLETE SET (27)	800.00	375.00	80.00
COMMON PLAYER (1-27)	25.00	12.50	2.50
☐ 1 Joe Adcock	35.00	17.50	3.50
☐ 2 Johnny Antonelli	30.00	15.00	3.00
☐ 3 Vern Bickford	25.00	12.50	2.50
☐ 4 Bill Bruton	30.00	15.00	3.00
☐ 5 Bob Buhl	30.00	15.00	3.00
☐ 6 Lew Burdette	35.00	17.50	3.50
☐ 7 Dick Cole	25.00	12.50	2.50
☐ 8 Walker Cooper	25.00	12.50	2.50
☐ 9 Del Crandall	30.00	15.00	3.00
☐ 10 George Crowe	25.00	12.50	2.50
☐ 11 Jack Dittmer	25.00	12.50	2.50
☐ 12 Sid Gordon	25.00	12.50	2.50
☐ 13 Ernie Johnson	30.00	15.00	3.00
☐ 14 Dave Jolly	25.00	12.50	2.50
☐ 15 Don Liddle	25.00	12.50	2.50
☐ 16 John Logan	30.00	15.00	3.00
☐ 17 Ed Mathews	100.00	50.00	10.00
☐ 18 Danny O'Connell	25.00	12.50	2.50
☐ 19 Andy Pafko	25.00	12.50	2.50
☐ 20 Jim Pendleton	25.00	12.50	2.50
☐ 21 Ebba St.Claire	25.00	12.50	2.50
☐ 22 Warren Spahn	100.00	50.00	10.00
☐ 23 Max Surkont	25.00	12.50	2.50
☐ 24 Bob Thomson	35.00	17.50	3.50
☐ 25 Bob Thorpe	25.00	12.50	2.50
☐ 26 Roberto Vargas	25.00	12.50	2.50
☐ 27 Jim Wilson	25.00	12.50	2.50

1953-56 Spic and Span 7x10

This 13-card set features only members of the Milwaukee Braves. The set was issued beginning in 1953 but may have been issued for several years as they seem to be the most common of all the Spic and Span issues. In addition, Danny O'Connell and Bobby Thomson were not on the '53 Braves team. The front of each card shows the logo, "Spic and Span Dry Cleaners ... the Choice of Your Favorite Braves." There is a thick white border around the cards with facsimile autograph in black in the bottom border. The cards have blank backs and are approximately 7" by 10".

	NRMT	VG-E	GOOD
COMPLETE SET (13)	150.00	75.00	15.00
COMMON PLAYER (1-13)	7.50	3.75	.75
☐ 1 Joe Adcock	15.00	7.50	1.50
☐ 2 William H. Bruton	10.00	5.00	1.00
☐ 3 Robert Buhl	10.00	5.00	1.00
☐ 4 Lou Burdette	15.00	7.50	1.50
☐ 5 Del Crandall	10.00	5.00	1.00
☐ 6 Jack Dittmer	7.50	3.75	.75
☐ 7 Johnny Logan	10.00	5.00	1.00
☐ 8 Edwin L.Mathews, Jr.	40.00	20.00	4.00
☐ 9 Chet Nichols	7.50	3.75	.75
☐ 10 Danny O'Connell	7.50	3.75	.75
☐ 11 Andy Pafko	7.50	3.75	.75
☐ 12 Warren Spahn	40.00	20.00	4.00
☐ 13 Bob Thomson	15.00	7.50	1.50

1954 Spic and Span Postcards

This black and white set features only members of the Milwaukee Braves. The cards have postcard backs and measure approximately 3 11/16" by 6". The postcards were issued beginning in 1954. There is a facsimile autograph on the front in black or white ink. The set apparently was also issued with white borders in a 5" by 7" size. The catalog designation for this set is PC756. The front of each card shows the logo, "Spic and Span Dry Cleaners ... the Choice of Your Favorite Braves."

	NRMT	VG-E	GOOD
COMPLETE SET (18)	450.00	225.00	45.00
COMMON PLAYER (1-18)	12.50	6.25	1.25
☐ 1 Henry Aaron	150.00	75.00	15.00
☐ 2 Joe Adcock	20.00	10.00	2.00
☐ 3 Billy Bruton	15.00	7.50	1.50
☐ 4 Bob Buhl	15.00	7.50	1.50
☐ 5 Lew Burdette	20.00	10.00	2.00
☐ 6 Gene Conley	12.50	6.25	1.25
☐ 7 Del Crandall	15.00	7.50	1.50
☐ 8 Ray Crone	12.50	6.25	1.25
☐ 9 Jack Dittmer	12.50	6.25	1.25
☐ 10 Ernie Johnson	15.00	7.50	1.50
☐ 11 Dave Jolly	12.50	6.25	1.25
☐ 12 Johnny Logan	15.00	7.50	1.50
☐ 13 Edwin L. Mathews, Jr.	60.00	30.00	6.00
☐ 14 Chet Nichols	12.50	6.25	1.25
☐ 15 Danny O'Connell	12.50	6.25	1.25
☐ 16 Andy Pafko	12.50	6.25	1.25
☐ 17 Warren Spahn	60.00	30.00	6.00
☐ 18 Bob Thomson	20.00	10.00	2.00

1955 Spic and Span Die-Cut

This 18-card, die-cut, set features only members of the Milwaukee Braves. Each player measures differently according to the pose but they are, on average, approximately 8" by 8". The cards could be folded together to stand up. Each card contains a logo in the middle at the bottom and a copyright notice, "1955 Spic and Span Cleaners" in the lower right corner.

	NRMT	VG-E	GOOD
COMPLETE SET (18)	2500.00	1000.00	200.00
COMMON PLAYER (1-18)	100.00	50.00	10.00
☐ 1 Hank Aaron	600.00	300.00	60.00
☐ 2 Joe Adcock	150.00	75.00	15.00
☐ 3 William H. Bruton	120.00	60.00	12.00
☐ 4 Robert Buhl	120.00	60.00	12.00
☐ 5 Lou Burdette	150.00	75.00	15.00
☐ 6 Gene Conley	100.00	50.00	10.00
☐ 7 Del Crandall	120.00	60.00	12.00
☐ 8 Jack Dittmer	100.00	50.00	10.00
☐ 9 Ernie Johnson	120.00	60.00	12.00
☐ 10 Dave Jolly	100.00	50.00	10.00
☐ 11 Johnny Logan	120.00	60.00	12.00
☐ 12 Edwin L. Mathews	300.00	150.00	30.00
☐ 13 Chet Nichols	100.00	50.00	10.00
☐ 14 Danny O'Connell	100.00	50.00	10.00
☐ 15 Andy Pafko	100.00	50.00	10.00
☐ 16 Warren E. Spahn	300.00	150.00	30.00
☐ 17 Bob Thomson	150.00	75.00	15.00
☐ 18 Jim Wilson	100.00	50.00	10.00

1957 Spic and Span 4x5

This set contains 20 black and white photos each with a blue-printed message such as "Stay in There and Pitch" and blue facsimile autograph The set features only members of the Milwaukee Braves. Red Schoendienst was traded to the Braves on June 15, 1957 in exchange for Danny O'Connell, Ray Crone, and Bobby Thomson. Wes Covington, Felix Mantilla, and Bob Trowbridge are also listed as shorter-printed (SP) cards as they were apparently mid-season call-ups. The cards are approximately 4 5/16" by 5" with a thick white border and are blank backed. Spic and Span appears in blue in the white border in the lower right corner of the card.

	NRMT	VG-E	GOOD
COMPLETE SET (20)	400.00	200.00	40.00
COMMON PLAYER (1-20)	9.00	4.50	.90
COMMON PLAYER SP	20.00	10.00	2.00
☐ 1 Henry Aaron	125.00	60.00	12.50
☐ 2 Joe Adcock	15.00	7.50	1.50
☐ 3 Billy Bruton	11.00	5.50	1.10
☐ 4 Bob Buhl	11.00	5.50	1.10
☐ 5 Lou Burdette	15.00	7.50	1.50
☐ 6 Gene Conley	9.00	4.50	.90
☐ 7 Wes Covington SP	20.00	10.00	2.00
☐ 7 Del Crandall	11.00	5.50	1.10
☐ 8 Ray Crone	9.00	4.50	.90
☐ 9 Fred Haney MG	9.00	4.50	.90
☐ 10 Ernie Johnson	11.00	5.50	1.10
☐ 11 Johnny Logan	11.00	5.50	1.10
☐ 12 Felix Mantilla SP	20.00	10.00	2.00
☐ 12 Ed Mathews	50.00	25.00	5.00
☐ 13 Danny O'Connell	9.00	4.50	.90
☐ 14 Andy Pafko	9.00	4.50	.90
☐ 15 Red Schoendienst SP	50.00	25.00	5.00
☐ 15 Warren Spahn	50.00	25.00	5.00
☐ 16 Bob Thomson	15.00	7.50	1.50
☐ 16 Bob Trowbridge SP	20.00	10.00	2.00

1960 Spic and Span

This 26-card set features only members of the Milwaukee Braves. These small cards each measure approximately 2 13/16" by 3 1/16". The cards have a thin white border around a black and white photo with no other writing or words on the front. The card backs have the Spic and Span logo at the bottom along with "Photographed and Autographed Exclusively for Spic and Span". A message and facsimile autograph from the player is presented inside a square box all in blue on the card back.

	NRMT	VG-E	GOOD
COMPLETE SET (27)	500.00	250.00	50.00
COMMON PLAYER (1-26)	9.00	4.50	.90
☐ 1 Henry Aaron	125.00	60.00	12.50
☐ 2 Joe Adcock	15.00	7.50	1.50
☐ 3 Billy Bruton	11.00	5.50	1.10
☐ 4 Bob Buhl	11.00	5.50	1.10
☐ 5 Lou Burdette	15.00	7.50	1.50
☐ 6 Chuck Cottier	9.00	4.50	.90
☐ 7A Del Crandall ERR (reversed negative)	50.00	25.00	5.00
☐ 7B Del Crandall COR	15.00	7.50	1.50
☐ 8 Charlie Dressen MG	11.00	5.50	1.10
☐ 9 Joey Jay	9.00	4.50	.90
☐ 10 Johnny Logan	11.00	5.50	1.10
☐ 11 Felix Mantilla	9.00	4.50	.90
☐ 12 Ed Mathews	50.00	25.00	5.00

□ 13 Lee Maye	9.00	4.50	.90
□ 14 Don McMahon	9.00	4.50	.90
□ 15 George Myatt CO	9.00	4.50	.90
□ 16 Andy Pafko	9.00	4.50	.90
□ 17 Juan Pizarro	9.00	4.50	.90
□ 18 Mel Roach	9.00	4.50	.90
□ 19 Bob Rush	9.00	4.50	.90
□ 20 Bob Scheffing CO	9.00	4.50	.90
□ 21 Red Schoendienst	35.00	17.50	3.50
□ 22 Warren Spahn	50.00	25.00	5.00
□ 23 Al Spangler	9.00	4.50	.90
□ 24 Frank Torre	11.00	5.50	1.10
□ 25 Carl Willey	9.00	4.50	.90
□ 26 Whit Wyatt CO	11.00	5.50	1.10

1985-86 Sportflics Prototypes

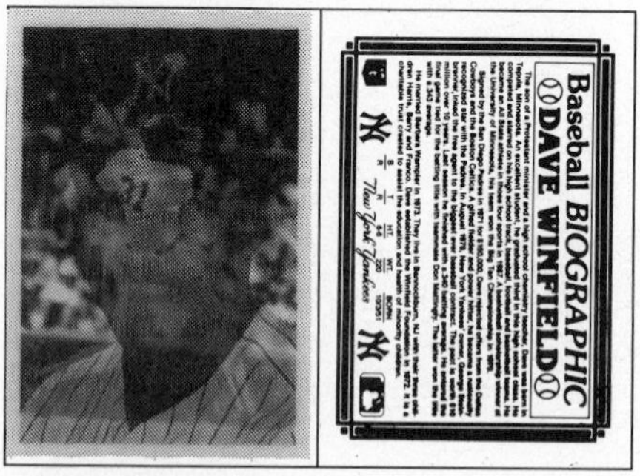

The 1985-86 Sportflics Proof set contains four standard-size (2 1/2" by 3 1/2") unnumbered cards, one mini (1 5/16" by 1 5/16") Joe DiMaggio card, and one trivia card (1 3/4" by 2"). The standard-size cards resemble regular 1986 Sportflics cards, but have different photos and stats only through 1984. One of the Winfield cards has a bio only; unfortunately the biographical statements on the back are incorrect in several instances. The DiMaggio card has black and white photos on the front, and career totals on the back. The trivia card is the same as those distributed with 1986 Sportflics, except it shows the major league baseball logo on the front. These test cards were apparently produced in limited quantity to show Major League Baseball and the Major League Baseball Players Association what Sportflics was proposing in order to be a new licensee for producing cards. These cards are very difficult to find. These cards are considerably rarer than the Sportflics Test cards which were given out after the Sportflics license had been granted.

	MINT	EXC	G-VG
COMPLETE SET (5)	100.00	50.00	10.00
COMMON PLAYER (1-5)	10.00	5.00	1.00
□ 1 Joe DiMaggio (small size)	25.00	12.50	2.50
□ 2 Mike Schmidt (stats on back)	40.00	20.00	4.00
□ 3 Bruce Sutter (stats on back)	10.00	5.00	1.00
□ 4 Dave Winfield (biographical back)	16.00	8.00	1.60
□ 5 Dave Winfield (stats on back)	25.00	12.50	2.50

1985-86 Sportflics Test

This three card pack was a test, distributed freely by salesmen to potential buyers to show them what the new Sportflics product would look like. The set is sometimes referred to as the Vendor Sample Kit. Some of these packs even found their way to the retail counters. They are not rare although they are obviously much less common than the regular issue of Sportflics. The cards show statistics only up through 1984. The copyright date on the card backs shows 1986. The cards are standard size, 2 1/2" by 3 1/2".

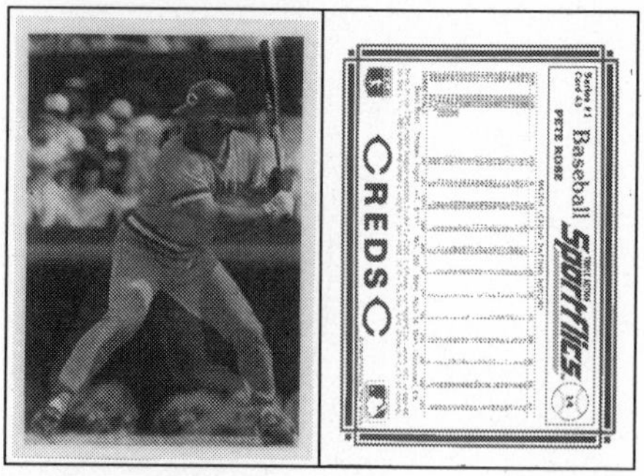

	MINT	EXC	G-VG
COMPLETE SET (3)	21.00	10.50	2.10
COMMON PLAYER	6.00	3.00	.60
□ 1 RBI Sluggers Mike Schmidt Dale Murphy Jim Rice	6.00	3.00	.60
□ 43 Pete Rose (pictured with batting helmet; Pete is number 50 in regular 1986 set)	12.00	6.00	1.20
□ 45 Tom Seaver (Tom is number 25 in regular 1986 set)	9.00	4.50	.90

1986 Sportflics

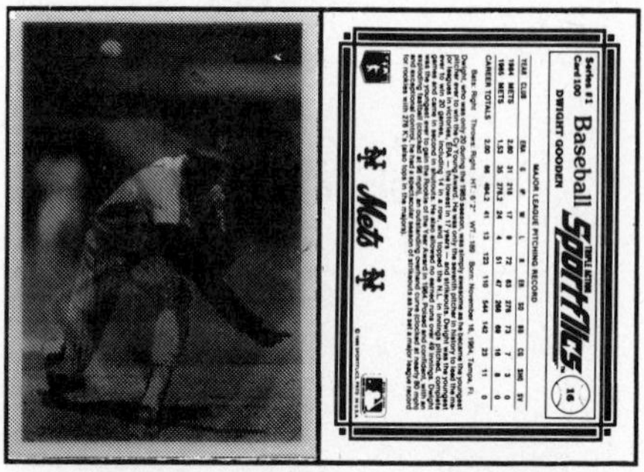

This 200-card set was marketed with 133 small trivia cards. This inaugural set for Sportflics was initially fairly well received by the public. Sportflics was distributed by Major League Marketing; the company is also affiliated with Wrigley and Amurol. The set features 139 single player "magic motion" cards (which can be tilted to show three different pictures of the same player), 50 "Tri-Stars" (which show three different players), 10 "Big Six" cards (which show six players who share similar achievements), and one World Champs card featuring 12 members of the victorious Kansas City Royals. All cards measure 2 1/2" by 3 1/2". Some of the cards also have (limited production and rarely seen) proof versions with some player selection differences; a proof version of number 178 includes Jim Wilson instead of Mark Funderburk. Also a proof of number 179 with Karl Best, Mark Funderburk, Andres Galarraga, Dwayne Henry, Pete Incaviglia, and Todd Worrell was produced.

	MINT	EXC	G-VG
COMPLETE SET (200)	37.50	16.00	3.00
COMMON PLAYER (1-200)	.12	.06	.01
☐ 1 George Brett	1.25	.60	.12
☐ 2 Don Mattingly	4.50	2.25	.45
☐ 3 Wade Boggs	2.50	1.25	.25
☐ 4 Eddie Murray	.50	.25	.05
☐ 5 Dale Murphy	.60	.30	.06
☐ 6 Rickey Henderson	1.50	.75	.15
☐ 7 Harold Baines	.12	.06	.01
☐ 8 Cal Ripken	.75	.35	.07
☐ 9 Orel Hershiser	.75	.35	.07
☐ 10 Bret Saberhagen	.50	.25	.05
☐ 11 Tim Raines	.40	.20	.04
☐ 12 Fernando Valenzuela	.30	.15	.03
☐ 13 Tony Gwynn	.75	.35	.07
☐ 14 Pedro Guerrero	.25	.12	.02
☐ 15 Keith Hernandez	.25	.12	.02
☐ 16 Ernie Riles	.20	.10	.02
☐ 17 Jim Rice	.30	.15	.03
☐ 18 Ron Guidry	.25	.12	.02
☐ 19 Willie McGee	.25	.12	.02
☐ 20 Ryne Sandberg	1.50	.75	.15
☐ 21 Kirk Gibson	.30	.15	.03
☐ 22 Ozzie Guillen	.60	.30	.06
☐ 23 Dave Parker	.25	.12	.02
☐ 24 Vince Coleman	2.00	1.00	.20
☐ 25 Tom Seaver	.50	.25	.05
☐ 26 Brett Butler	.25	.12	.02
☐ 27 Steve Carlton	.40	.20	.04
☐ 28 Gary Carter	.35	.17	.03
☐ 29 Cecil Cooper	.20	.10	.02
☐ 30 Jose Cruz	.15	.07	.01
☐ 31 Alvin Davis	.20	.10	.02
☐ 32 Dwight Evans	.25	.12	.02
☐ 33 Julio Franco	.25	.12	.02
☐ 34 Damaso Garcia	.12	.06	.01
☐ 35 Steve Garvey	.50	.25	.05
☐ 36 Kent Hrbek	.25	.12	.02
☐ 37 Reggie Jackson	.65	.30	.06
☐ 38 Fred Lynn	.20	.10	.02
☐ 39 Paul Molitor	.15	.07	.01
☐ 40 Jim Presley	.15	.07	.01
☐ 41 Dave Righetti	.20	.10	.02
☐ 42 Robin Yount	.90	.45	.09
☐ 43 Nolan Ryan	2.00	1.00	.20
☐ 44 Mike Schmidt	1.50	.75	.15
☐ 45 Lee Smith	.12	.06	.01
☐ 46 Rick Sutcliffe	.20	.10	.02
☐ 47 Bruce Sutter	.15	.07	.01
☐ 48 Lou Whitaker	.20	.10	.02
☐ 49 Dave Winfield	.45	.22	.04
☐ 50 Pete Rose	1.25	.60	.12
☐ 51 NL MVP's	.75	.35	.07
Ryne Sandberg			
Steve Garvey			
Pete Rose			
☐ 52 Slugging Stars	.40	.20	.04
George Brett			
Harold Baines			
Jim Rice			
☐ 53 No-Hitters	.20	.10	.02
Phil Niekro			
Jerry Reuss			
Mike Witt			
☐ 54 Big Hitters	1.25	.60	.12
Don Mattingly			
Cal Ripken			
Robin Yount			
☐ 55 Bullpen Aces	.20	.10	.02
Dan Quisenberry			
Goose Gossage			
Lee Smith			
☐ 56 Rookies of The Year	1.00	.50	.10
Darryl Strawberry			
Steve Sax			
Pete Rose			
☐ 57 AL MVP's	.50	.25	.05
Cal Ripken			
Don Baylor			
Reggie Jackson			
☐ 58 Repeat Batting Champs	.75	.35	.07
Dave Parker			
Bill Madlock			
Pete Rose			
☐ 59 Cy Young Winners	.15	.07	.01
LaMarr Hoyt			
Mike Flanagan			
Ron Guidry			
☐ 60 Double Award Winners	.30	.15	.03
Fernando Valenzuela			
Rick Sutcliffe			
Tom Seaver			
☐ 61 Home Run Champs	.65	.30	.06
Reggie Jackson			
Jim Rice			
Tony Armas			
☐ 62 NL MVP's	.75	.35	.07
Keith Hernandez			
Dale Murphy			
Mike Schmidt			
☐ 63 AL MVP's	.60	.30	.06
Robin Yount			
George Brett			
Fred Lynn			
☐ 64 Comeback Players	.15	.07	.01
Bert Blyleven			
Jerry Koosman			
John Denny			
☐ 65 Cy Young Relievers	.20	.10	.02
Willie Hernandez			
Rollie Fingers			
Bruce Sutter			
☐ 66 Rookies of The Year	.20	.10	.02
Bob Horner			
Andre Dawson			
Gary Matthews			
☐ 67 Rookies of The Year	.35	.17	.03
Ron Kittle			
Carlton Fisk			
Tom Seaver			
☐ 68 Home Run Champs	.35	.17	.03
Mike Schmidt			
George Foster			
Dave Kingman			
☐ 69 Double Award Winners	1.00	.50	.10
Cal Ripken			
Rod Carew			
Pete Rose			
☐ 70 Cy Young Winners	.40	.20	.04
Rick Sutcliffe			
Steve Carlton			
Tom Seaver			
☐ 71 Top Sluggers	.50	.25	.05
Reggie Jackson			
Fred Lynn			
Robin Yount			
☐ 72 Rookies of The Year	.25	.12	.02
Dave Righetti			
Fernando Valenzuela			
Rick Sutcliffe			
☐ 73 Rookies of The Year	.50	.25	.05
Fred Lynn			
Eddie Murray			
Cal Ripken			
☐ 74 Rookies of The Year	.25	.12	.02
Alvin Davis			
Lou Whitaker			
Rod Carew			
☐ 75 Batting Champs	1.25	.60	.12
Don Mattingly			
Wade Boggs			
Carney Lansford			
☐ 76 Jesse Barfield	.20	.10	.02
☐ 77 Phil Bradley	.20	.10	.02
☐ 78 Chris Brown	.15	.07	.01
☐ 79 Tom Browning	.20	.10	.02
☐ 80 Tom Brunansky	.20	.10	.02
☐ 81 Bill Buckner	.15	.07	.01
☐ 82 Chili Davis	.15	.07	.01
☐ 83 Mike Davis	.12	.06	.01
☐ 84 Rich Gedman	.12	.06	.01
☐ 85 Willie Hernandez	.15	.07	.01
☐ 86 Ron Kittle	.20	.10	.02
☐ 87 Lee Lacy	.12	.06	.01
☐ 88 Bill Madlock	.15	.07	.01
☐ 89 Mike Marshall	.20	.10	.02
☐ 90 Keith Moreland	.12	.06	.01
☐ 91 Graig Nettles	.20	.10	.02
☐ 92 Lance Parrish	.25	.12	.02
☐ 93 Kirby Puckett	2.50	1.25	.25
☐ 94 Juan Samuel	.25	.12	.02
☐ 95 Steve Sax	.25	.12	.02
☐ 96 Dave Stieb	.25	.12	.02
☐ 97 Darryl Strawberry	1.50	.75	.15
☐ 98 Willie Upshaw	.12	.06	.01
☐ 99 Frank Viola	.35	.17	.03
☐ 100 Dwight Gooden	1.50	.75	.15
☐ 101 Joaquin Andujar	.12	.06	.01
☐ 102 George Bell	.30	.15	.03

☐ 103 Bert Blyleven	.25	.12	.02
☐ 104 Mike Boddicker	.12	.06	.01
☐ 105 Britt Burns	.12	.06	.01
☐ 106 Rod Carew	.45	.22	.04
☐ 107 Jack Clark	.25	.12	.02
☐ 108 Danny Cox	.15	.07	.01
☐ 109 Ron Darling	.20	.10	.02
☐ 110 Andre Dawson	.40	.20	.04
☐ 111 Leon Durham	.12	.06	.01
☐ 112 Tony Fernandez	.20	.10	.02
☐ 113 Tommy Herr	.12	.06	.01
☐ 114 Teddy Higuera	.25	.12	.02
☐ 115 Bob Horner	.15	.07	.01
☐ 116 Dave Kingman	.15	.07	.01
☐ 117 Jack Morris	.20	.10	.02
☐ 118 Dan Quisenberry	.15	.07	.01
☐ 119 Jeff Reardon	.15	.07	.01
☐ 120 Bryn Smith	.12	.06	.01
☐ 121 Ozzie Smith	.30	.15	.03
☐ 122 John Tudor	.15	.07	.01
☐ 123 Tim Wallach	.15	.07	.01
☐ 124 Willie Wilson	.15	.07	.01
☐ 125 Carlton Fisk	.35	.17	.03
☐ 126 RBI Sluggers	.20	.10	.02
Gary Carter			
Al Oliver			
George Foster			
☐ 127 Run Scorers	.45	.22	.04
Tim Raines			
Ryne Sandberg			
Keith Hernandez			
☐ 128 Run Scorers	.35	.17	.03
Paul Molitor			
Cal Ripken			
Willie Wilson			
☐ 129 No-Hitters	.15	.07	.01
John Candelaria			
Dennis Eckersley			
Bob Forsch			
☐ 130 World Series MVP's	.60	.30	.06
Pete Rose			
Ron Cey			
Rollie Fingers			
☐ 131 All-Star Game MVP's	.15	.07	.01
Dave Concepcion			
George Foster			
Bill Madlock			
☐ 132 Cy Young Winners	.15	.07	.01
John Denny			
Fernando Valenzuela			
Vida Blue			
☐ 133 Comeback Players	.15	.07	.01
Rich Dotson			
Joaquin Andujar			
Doyle Alexander			
☐ 134 Big Winners	.35	.17	.03
Rick Sutcliffe			
Tom Seaver			
John Denny			
☐ 135 Veteran Pitchers	.50	.25	.05
Tom Seaver			
Phil Niekro			
Don Sutton			
☐ 136 Rookies of The Year	.75	.35	.07
Dwight Gooden			
Vince Coleman			
Alfredo Griffin			
☐ 137 All-Star Game MVP's	.40	.20	.04
Gary Carter			
Fred Lynn			
Steve Garvey			
☐ 138 Veteran Hitters	.60	.30	.06
Tony Perez			
Rusty Staub			
Pete Rose			
☐ 139 Power Hitters	.50	.25	.05
Mike Schmidt			
Jim Rice			
George Foster			
☐ 140 Batting Champs	.25	.12	.02
Tony Gwynn			
Al Oliver			
Bill Buckner			
☐ 141 No-Hitters	1.00	.50	.10
Nolan Ryan			
Jack Morris			
Dave Righetti			
☐ 142 No-Hitters	.30	.15	.03
Tom Seaver			
Bert Blyleven			
Vida Blue			
☐ 143 Strikeout Kings	1.25	.60	.12
Nolan Ryan			
Fernando Valenzuela			
Dwight Gooden			
☐ 144 Base Stealers	.20	.10	.02
Tim Raines			
Willie Wilson			
Davey Lopes			
☐ 145 RBI Sluggers	.20	.10	.02
Tony Armas			
Cecil Cooper			
Eddie Murray			
☐ 146 AL MVP's	.40	.20	.04
Rod Carew			
Jim Rice			
Rollie Fingers			
☐ 147 World Series MVP's	.40	.20	.04
Alan Trammell			
Rick Dempsey			
Reggie Jackson			
☐ 148 World Series MVP's	.40	.20	.04
Darrell Porter			
Pedro Guerrero			
Mike Schmidt			
☐ 149 ERA Leaders	.15	.07	.01
Mike Boddicker			
Rick Sutcliffe			
Ron Guidry			
☐ 150 Comeback Players	.35	.17	.03
Reggie Jackson			
Dave Kingman			
Fred Lynn			
☐ 151 Buddy Bell	.15	.07	.01
☐ 152 Dennis Boyd	.15	.07	.01
☐ 153 Dave Concepcion	.15	.07	.01
☐ 154 Brian Downing	.12	.06	.01
☐ 155 Shawon Dunston	.50	.25	.05
☐ 156 John Franco	.25	.12	.02
☐ 157 Scott Garrelts	.20	.10	.02
☐ 158 Bob James	.12	.06	.01
☐ 159 Charlie Leibrandt	.12	.06	.01
☐ 160 Oddibe McDowell	.20	.10	.02
☐ 161 Roger McDowell	.20	.10	.02
☐ 162 Mike Moore	.20	.10	.02
☐ 163 Phil Niekro	.30	.15	.03
☐ 164 Al Oliver	.15	.07	.01
☐ 165 Tony Pena	.20	.10	.02
☐ 166 Ted Power	.12	.06	.01
☐ 167 Mike Scioscia	.12	.06	.01
☐ 168 Mario Soto	.12	.06	.01
☐ 169 Bob Stanley	.12	.06	.01
☐ 170 Gary Templeton	.15	.07	.01
☐ 171 Andre Thornton	.12	.06	.01
☐ 172 Alan Trammell	.30	.15	.03
☐ 173 Doug DeCinces	.15	.07	.01
☐ 174 Greg Walker	.12	.06	.01
☐ 175 Don Sutton	.25	.12	.02
☐ 176 1985 Award Winners	1.00	.50	.10
Ozzie Guillen			
Bret Saberhagen			
Don Mattingly			
Vince Coleman			
Dwight Gooden			
Willie McGee			
☐ 177 1985 Hot Rookies	.35	.17	.03
Stew Cliburn			
Brian Fisher			
Joe Hesketh			
Joe Orsulak			
Mark Salas			
Larry Sheets			
☐ 178 1986 Rookies To Watch	12.00	6.00	1.20
Jose Canseco			
Mark Funderburk			
Mike Greenwell			
Steve Lombardozzi			
Billy Joe Robidoux			
Danny Tartabull			
☐ 179 1985 Gold Glovers	.75	.35	.07
George Brett			
Ron Guidry			
Keith Hernandez			
Don Mattingly			
Willie McGee			
Dale Murphy			
☐ 180 Active Lifetime .300	.75	.35	.07
Wade Boggs			
George Brett			
Rod Carew			
Cecil Cooper			
Don Mattingly			
Willie Wilson			
☐ 181 Active Lifetime .300	.60	.30	.06

Tony Gwynn			
Bill Madlock			
Pedro Guerrero			
Dave Parker			
Pete Rose			
Keith Hernandez			
☐ 182 1985 Milestones	.75	.35	.07
Rod Carew			
Phil Niekro			
Pete Rose			
Nolan Ryan			
Tom Seaver			
Matt Tallman (fan)			
☐ 183 1985 Triple Crown	.75	.35	.07
Wade Boggs			
Darrell Evans			
Don Mattingly			
Willie McGee			
Dale Murphy			
Dave Parker			
☐ 184 1985 Highlights	.75	.35	.07
Wade Boggs			
Dwight Gooden			
Rickey Henderson			
Don Mattingly			
Willie McGee			
John Tudor			
☐ 185 1985 20 Game Winners	.75	.35	.07
Dwight Gooden			
Ron Guidry			
John Tudor			
Joaquin Andujar			
Bret Saberhagen			
Tom Browning			
☐ 186 World Series Champs	.35	.17	.03
L. Smith, Dane Iorg			
W. Wilson, Leibrandt			
G. Brett, Saberhagen			
Motley, Quisenberry			
D. Jackson, Sundberg			
S. Balboni, F. White			
☐ 187 Hubie Brooks	.25	.12	.02
☐ 188 Glenn Davis	1.00	.50	.10
☐ 189 Darrell Evans	.20	.10	.02
☐ 190 Rich Gossage	.20	.10	.02
☐ 191 Andy Hawkins	.15	.07	.01
☐ 192 Jay Howell	.12	.06	.01
☐ 193 LaMarr Hoyt	.12	.06	.01
☐ 194 Davey Lopes	.12	.06	.01
☐ 195 Mike Scott	.30	.15	.03
☐ 196 Ted Simmons	.20	.10	.02
☐ 197 Gary Ward	.12	.06	.01
☐ 198 Bob Welch	.30	.15	.03
☐ 199 Mike Young	.12	.06	.01
☐ 200 Buddy Biancalana	.12	.06	.01

1986 Sportflics Decade Greats

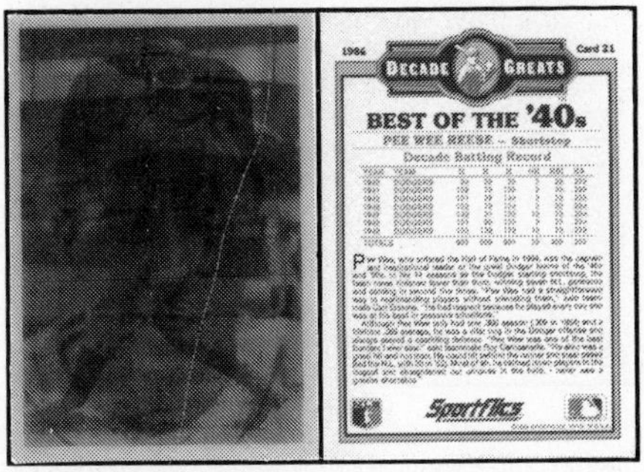

This set of 75 three-phase "animated" cards was produced by Sportflics and manufactured by Opti-Graphics of Arlington, Texas. Cards are standard size, 2 1/2" by 3 1/2", and feature both sepia (players of the '30s and '40s) and full color cards. The concept of the set was that the best players at each position for each decade (from the '30s to the '80s) were chosen. The bios were written by Les Woodcock. Also included with the set in the specially designed collector box are 51 trivia cards with historical questions about the six decades of All-Star games.

	MINT	EXC	G-VG
COMPLETE SET (75)	15.00	7.50	1.50
COMMON PLAYER (1-75)	.15	.07	.01
☐ 1 Babe Ruth	3.00	1.50	.30
☐ 2 Jimmie Foxx	.35	.17	.03
☐ 3 Lefty Grove	.35	.17	.03
☐ 4 Hank Greenberg	.35	.17	.03
☐ 5 Al Simmons	.25	.12	.02
☐ 6 Carl Hubbell	.25	.12	.02
☐ 7 Joe Cronin	.25	.12	.02
☐ 8 Mel Ott	.35	.17	.03
☐ 9 Lefty Gomez	.25	.12	.02
☐ 10 Lou Gehrig	1.00	.50	.10
(Best '30s Player)			
☐ 11 Pie Traynor	.25	.12	.02
☐ 12 Charlie Gehringer	.25	.12	.02
☐ 13 Best '30s Catchers	.25	.12	.02
Bill Dickey			
Mickey Cochrane			
Gabby Hartnett			
☐ 14 Best '30s Pitchers	.25	.12	.02
Dizzy Dean			
Red Ruffing			
Paul Derringer			
☐ 15 Best '30s Outfielders	.15	.07	.01
Paul Waner			
Joe Medwick			
Earl Averill			
☐ 16 Bob Feller	.75	.35	.07
☐ 17 Lou Boudreau	.25	.12	.02
☐ 18 Enos Slaughter	.35	.17	.03
☐ 19 Hal Newhouser	.15	.07	.01
☐ 20 Joe DiMaggio	1.50	.75	.15
☐ 21 Pee Wee Reese	.50	.25	.05
☐ 22 Phil Rizzuto	.40	.20	.04
☐ 23 Ernie Lombardi	.15	.07	.01
☐ 24 Best '40s Infielders	.25	.12	.02
Johnny Mize			
Joe Gordon			
George Kell			
☐ 25 Ted Williams	1.00	.50	.10
(Best '40s Player)			
☐ 26 Mickey Mantle	3.00	1.50	.30
☐ 27 Warren Spahn	.35	.17	.03
☐ 28 Jackie Robinson	.75	.35	.07
☐ 29 Ernie Banks	.35	.17	.03
☐ 30 Stan Musial	.75	.35	.07
(Best '50s Player)			
☐ 31 Yogi Berra	.75	.35	.07
☐ 32 Duke Snider	.75	.35	.07
☐ 33 Roy Campanella	.75	.35	.07
☐ 34 Eddie Mathews	.35	.17	.03
☐ 35 Ralph Kiner	.25	.12	.02
☐ 36 Early Wynn	.25	.12	.02
☐ 37 Double Play Duo	.25	.12	.02
Nellie Fox			
Luis Aparicio			
☐ 38 Best '50s First Base	.15	.07	.01
Gil Hodges			
Ted Kluszewski			
Mickey Vernon			
☐ 39 Best '50s Pitchers	.15	.07	.01
Bob Lemon			
Don Newcombe			
Robin Roberts			
☐ 40 Henry Aaron	1.00	.50	.10
☐ 41 Frank Robinson	.35	.17	.03
☐ 42 Bob Gibson	.35	.17	.03
☐ 43 Roberto Clemente	.90	.45	.09
☐ 44 Whitey Ford	.45	.22	.04
☐ 45 Brooks Robinson	.50	.25	.05
☐ 46 Juan Marichal	.25	.12	.02
☐ 47 Carl Yastrzemski	1.00	.50	.10
☐ 48 Best '60s First Base	.25	.12	.02
Willie McCovey			
Harmon Killebrew			
Orlando Cepeda			
☐ 49 Best '60s Catchers	.15	.07	.01
Joe Torre			
Elston Howard			
Bill Freehan			
☐ 50 Willie Mays	1.00	.50	.10
(Best '50s Player)			
☐ 51 Best '60s Outfielders	.25	.12	.02
Al Kaline			
Tony Oliva			
Billy Williams			
☐ 52 Tom Seaver	.75	.35	.07
☐ 53 Reggie Jackson	1.00	.50	.10

☐ 54 Steve Carlton	.75	.35	.07
☐ 55 Mike Schmidt	1.25	.60	.12
☐ 56 Joe Morgan	.45	.22	.04
☐ 57 Jim Rice	.25	.12	.02
☐ 58 Jim Palmer	.45	.22	.04
☐ 59 Lou Brock	.35	.17	.03
☐ 60 Pete Rose (Best '70s Player)	1.25	.60	.12
☐ 61 Steve Garvey	.50	.25	.05
☐ 62 Best '70s Catchers: Thurman Munson, Carlton Fisk, Ted Simmons	.35	.17	.03
☐ 63 Best '70s Pitchers: Vida Blue, Catfish Hunter, Nolan Ryan	.50	.25	.05
☐ 64 George Brett	1.00	.50	.10
☐ 65 Don Mattingly	1.50	.75	.15
☐ 66 Fernando Valenzuela	.25	.12	.02
☐ 67 Dale Murphy	.75	.35	.07
☐ 68 Wade Boggs	1.00	.50	.10
☐ 69 Rickey Henderson	1.25	.60	.12
☐ 70 Eddie Murray (Best '80s Player)	.60	.30	.06
☐ 71 Ron Guidry	.15	.07	.01
☐ 72 Best '80s Catchers: Gary Carter, Lance Parrish, Tony Pena	.25	.12	.02
☐ 73 Best '80s Infielders: Cal Ripken, Lou Whitaker, Robin Yount	.25	.12	.02
☐ 74 Best '80s Outfielders: Pedro Guerrero, Tim Raines, Dave Winfield	.25	.12	.02
☐ 75 Dwight Gooden	.75	.35	.07

1986 Sportflics Rookies

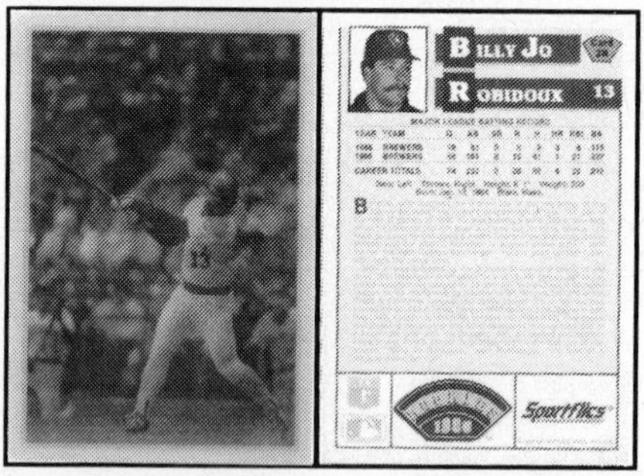

This set of 50 three-phase "animated" cards features top rookies of 1986 as well as a few outstanding rookies from the past. These "Magic Motion" cards are standard size, 2 1/2" by 3 1/2", and feature a distinctive light blue border on the front of the card. Cards were distributed in a light blue box, which also contained 34 trivia cards, each measuring 1 3/4" by 2". There are 47 single player cards along with two Tri-Stars and one Big Six.

	MINT	EXC	G-VG
COMPLETE SET (50)	20.00	10.00	2.00
COMMON PLAYER (1-50)	.12	.06	.01
☐ 1 John Kruk	.30	.15	.03
☐ 2 Edwin Correa	.15	.07	.01
☐ 3 Pete Incaviglia	.70	.35	.07
☐ 4 Dale Sveum	.15	.07	.01
☐ 5 Juan Nieves	.15	.07	.01
☐ 6 Will Clark	6.50	3.25	.65
☐ 7 Wally Joyner	1.75	.85	.17
☐ 8 Lance McCullers	.15	.07	.01
☐ 9 Scott Bailes	.15	.07	.01
☐ 10 Dan Plesac	.20	.10	.02
☐ 11 Jose Canseco	6.50	3.25	.65
☐ 12 Bobby Witt	.60	.30	.06
☐ 13 Barry Bonds	2.50	1.25	.25
☐ 14 Andres Thomas	.15	.07	.01
☐ 15 Jim Deshaies	.15	.07	.01
☐ 16 Ruben Sierra	2.50	1.25	.25
☐ 17 Steve Lombardozzi	.12	.06	.01
☐ 18 Cory Snyder	.75	.35	.07
☐ 19 Reggie Williams	.12	.06	.01
☐ 20 Mitch Williams	.20	.10	.02
☐ 21 Glenn Braggs	.25	.12	.02
☐ 22 Danny Tartabull	.50	.25	.05
☐ 23 Charlie Kerfeld	.15	.07	.01
☐ 24 Paul Assenmacher	.12	.06	.01
☐ 25 Robby Thompson	.20	.10	.02
☐ 26 Bobby Bonilla	1.75	.85	.17
☐ 27 Andres Galarraga	.60	.30	.06
☐ 28 Billy Jo Robidoux	.15	.07	.01
☐ 29 Bruce Ruffin	.15	.07	.01
☐ 30 Greg Swindell	.50	.25	.05
☐ 31 John Cangelosi	.12	.06	.01
☐ 32 Jim Traber	.12	.06	.01
☐ 33 Russ Morman	.12	.06	.01
☐ 34 Barry Larkin	2.00	1.00	.20
☐ 35 Todd Worrell	.40	.20	.04
☐ 36 John Cerutti	.15	.07	.01
☐ 37 Mike Kingery	.12	.06	.01
☐ 38 Mark Eichhorn	.12	.06	.01
☐ 39 Scott Bankhead	.20	.10	.02
☐ 40 Bo Jackson	6.00	3.00	.60
☐ 41 Greg Mathews	.15	.07	.01
☐ 42 Eric King	.20	.10	.02
☐ 43 Kal Daniels	.75	.35	.07
☐ 44 Calvin Schiraldi	.15	.07	.01
☐ 45 Mickey Brantley	.20	.10	.02
☐ 46 Tri-Stars: Willie Mays, Pete Rose, Fred Lynn	.50	.25	.05
☐ 47 Tri-Stars: Tom Seaver, Fern. Valenzuela, Dwight Gooden	.50	.25	.05
☐ 48 Big Six: Eddie Murray, Lou Whitaker, Dave Righetti, Steve Sax, Cal Ripken Jr., Darryl Strawberry	.50	.25	.05
☐ 49 Kevin Mitchell	2.50	1.25	.25
☐ 50 Mike Diaz	.15	.07	.01

1987 Sportflics

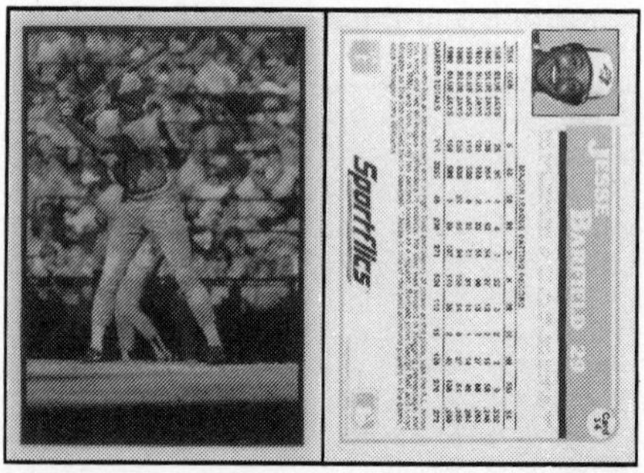

This 200-card set was produced by Sportflics and again features three sequence action pictures on each card. Cards measure 2 1/2" by 3 1/2" and are in full color. Also included with the cards were 136 small team logo and trivia cards. There are 165 individual players, 20 Tri-Stars (the top three players in each league at each position), and 15 other miscellaneous multi-player cards. The cards feature a red border on the front. A full-color face shot of the player is printed on the back of the card.

Cards are numbered on the back in the upper right corner. The cards in the factory-collated sets are copyrighted 1986, while the cards in the wax packs are copyrighted 1987 or show no copyright year on the back. Cards from wax packs with 1987 copyright are 1-35, 41-75, 81-115, 121-155, and 161-195; the rest of the numbers (when taken from wax packs) are found without a copyright year.

	MINT	EXC	G-VG
COMPLETE SET (200)	35.00	17.50	3.50
COMMON PLAYER (1-200)	.12	.06	.01
☐ 1 Don Mattingly	3.00	1.50	.30
☐ 2 Wade Boggs	1.00	.50	.10
☐ 3 Dale Murphy	.40	.20	.04
☐ 4 Rickey Henderson	1.00	.50	.10
☐ 5 George Brett	.60	.30	.06
☐ 6 Eddie Murray	.40	.20	.04
☐ 7 Kirby Puckett	1.25	.60	.12
☐ 8 Ryne Sandberg	1.00	.50	.10
☐ 9 Cal Ripken	.50	.25	.05
☐ 10 Roger Clemens	1.25	.60	.12
☐ 11 Ted Higuera	.15	.07	.01
☐ 12 Steve Sax	.15	.07	.01
☐ 13 Chris Brown	.12	.06	.01
☐ 14 Jesse Barfield	.15	.07	.01
☐ 15 Kent Hrbek	.20	.10	.02
☐ 16 Robin Yount	.50	.25	.05
☐ 17 Glenn Davis	.40	.20	.04
☐ 18 Hubie Brooks	.15	.07	.01
☐ 19 Mike Scott	.15	.07	.01
☐ 20 Darryl Strawberry	.90	.45	.09
☐ 21 Alvin Davis	.20	.10	.02
☐ 22 Eric Davis	.90	.45	.09
☐ 23 Danny Tartabull	.35	.17	.03
☐ 24A Cory Snyder ERR '86 (photo on front is Pat Tabler)	3.00	1.50	.30
☐ 24B Cory Snyder ERR '87 (photos on front and back are Pat Tabler)	2.00	1.00	.20
☐ 24C Cory Snyder COR '86	2.00	1.00	.20
☐ 25 Pete Rose	.90	.45	.09
☐ 26 Wally Joyner	.90	.45	.09
☐ 27 Pedro Guerrero	.25	.12	.02
☐ 28 Tom Seaver	.45	.22	.04
☐ 29 Bob Knepper	.15	.07	.01
☐ 30 Mike Schmidt	1.00	.50	.10
☐ 31 Tony Gwynn	.75	.35	.07
☐ 32 Don Slaught	.12	.06	.01
☐ 33 Todd Worrell	.20	.10	.02
☐ 34 Tim Raines	.20	.10	.02
☐ 35 Dave Parker	.20	.10	.02
☐ 36 Bob Ojeda	.15	.07	.01
☐ 37 Pete Incaviglia	.60	.30	.06
☐ 38 Bruce Hurst	.20	.10	.02
☐ 39 Bobby Witt	.50	.25	.05
☐ 40 Steve Garvey	.40	.20	.04
☐ 41 Dave Winfield	.35	.17	.03
☐ 42 Jose Cruz	.15	.07	.01
☐ 43 Orel Hershiser	.40	.20	.04
☐ 44 Reggie Jackson	.60	.30	.06
☐ 45 Chili Davis	.12	.06	.01
☐ 46 Robby Thompson	.15	.07	.01
☐ 47 Dennis Boyd	.12	.06	.01
☐ 48 Kirk Gibson	.25	.12	.02
☐ 49 Fred Lynn	.15	.07	.01
☐ 50 Gary Carter	.25	.12	.02
☐ 51 George Bell	.30	.15	.03
☐ 52 Pete O'Brien	.12	.06	.01
☐ 53 Ron Darling	.15	.07	.01
☐ 54 Paul Molitor	.15	.07	.01
☐ 55 Mike Pagliarulo	.12	.06	.01
☐ 56 Mike Boddicker	.15	.07	.01
☐ 57 Dave Righetti	.20	.10	.02
☐ 58 Len Dykstra	.50	.25	.05
☐ 59 Mike Witt	.15	.07	.01
☐ 60 Tony Bernazard	.12	.06	.01
☐ 61 John Kruk	.20	.10	.02
☐ 62 Mike Krukow	.12	.06	.01
☐ 63 Sid Fernandez	.15	.07	.01
☐ 64 Gary Gaetti	.15	.07	.01
☐ 65 Vince Coleman	.50	.25	.05
☐ 66 Pat Tabler	.15	.07	.01
☐ 67 Mike Scioscia	.12	.06	.01
☐ 68 Scott Garrelts	.12	.06	.01
☐ 69 Brett Butler	.15	.07	.01
☐ 70 Bill Buckner	.15	.07	.01
☐ 71A Dennis Rasmussen ERR '86 copyright (photo on back is John Montefusco)	1.00	.50	.10
☐ 71B Dennis Rasmussen COR '87 copyright (photo with mustache)	.50	.25	.05
☐ 72 Tim Wallach	.15	.07	.01
☐ 73 Bob Horner	.15	.07	.01
☐ 74 Willie McGee	.15	.07	.01
☐ 75 Tri-Stars Don Mattingly Wally Joyner Eddie Murray	1.00	.50	.10
☐ 76A Jesse Orosco COR '86 copyright	.35	.17	.03
☐ 76B Jesse Orosco ERR '87 copyright (number on back is 96)	.15	.07	.01
☐ 77 Tri-Stars Todd Worrell Jeff Reardon Lee Smith	.15	.07	.01
☐ 78 Candy Maldonado	.15	.07	.01
☐ 79 Tri-Stars Ozzie Smith Hubie Brooks Shawon Dunston	.25	.12	.02
☐ 80 Tri-Stars George Bell Jose Canseco Jim Rice	.90	.45	.09
☐ 81 Bert Blyleven	.20	.10	.02
☐ 82 Mike Marshall	.15	.07	.01
☐ 83 Ron Guidry	.20	.10	.02
☐ 84 Julio Franco	.20	.10	.02
☐ 85 Willie Wilson	.20	.10	.02
☐ 86 Lee Lacy	.12	.06	.01
☐ 87 Jack Morris	.15	.07	.01
☐ 88 Ray Knight	.15	.07	.01
☐ 89 Phil Bradley	.15	.07	.01
☐ 90 Jose Canseco	3.00	1.50	.30
☐ 91 Gary Ward	.12	.06	.01
☐ 92 Mike Easler	.12	.06	.01
☐ 93 Tony Pena	.15	.07	.01
☐ 94 Dave Smith	.12	.06	.01
☐ 95 Will Clark	3.00	1.50	.30
☐ 96 Lloyd Moseby (See also 76B)	.15	.07	.01
☐ 97 Jim Rice	.20	.10	.02
☐ 98 Shawon Dunston	.25	.12	.02
☐ 99 Don Sutton	.20	.10	.02
☐ 100 Dwight Gooden	.90	.45	.09
☐ 101 Lance Parrish	.20	.10	.02
☐ 102 Mark Langston	.15	.07	.01
☐ 103 Floyd Youmans	.12	.06	.01
☐ 104 Lee Smith	.12	.06	.01
☐ 105 Willie Hernandez	.15	.07	.01
☐ 106 Doug DeCinces	.12	.06	.01
☐ 107 Ken Schrom	.12	.06	.01
☐ 108 Don Carman	.12	.06	.01
☐ 109 Brook Jacoby	.15	.07	.01
☐ 110 Steve Bedrosian	.20	.10	.02
☐ 111 Tri-Stars Roger Clemens Jack Morris Ted Higuera	.50	.25	.05
☐ 112 Tri-Stars Marty Barrett Tony Bernazard Lou Whitaker	.15	.07	.01
☐ 113 Tri-Stars Cal Ripken Scott Fletcher Tony Fernandez	.25	.12	.02
☐ 114 Tri-Stars Wade Boggs George Brett Gary Gaetti	.75	.35	.07
☐ 115 Tri-Stars Mike Schmidt Chris Brown Tim Wallach	.50	.25	.05
☐ 116 Tri-Stars Ryne Sandberg Johnny Ray Bill Doran	.30	.15	.03
☐ 117 Tri-Stars Dave Parker Tony Gwynn Kevin Bass	.20	.10	.02
☐ 118 Big Six Rookies Ty Gainey Terry Steinbach Dave Clark Pat Dodson Phil Lombardi Benito Santiago	1.25	.60	.12

☐ 119 Hi-Lite Tri-Stars	.20	.10	.02
Dave Righetti			
Fernando Valenzuela			
Mike Scott			
☐ 120 Tri-Stars	.50	.25	.05
Fernando Valenzuela			
Mike Scott			
Dwight Gooden			
☐ 121 Johnny Ray	.12	.06	.01
☐ 122 Keith Moreland	.12	.06	.01
☐ 123 Juan Samuel	.20	.10	.02
☐ 124 Wally Backman	.12	.06	.01
☐ 125 Nolan Ryan	1.50	.75	.15
☐ 126 Greg Harris	.12	.06	.01
☐ 127 Kirk McCaskill	.12	.06	.01
☐ 128 Dwight Evans	.20	.10	.02
☐ 129 Rick Rhoden	.12	.06	.01
☐ 130 Bill Madlock	.12	.06	.01
☐ 131 Oddibe McDowell	.15	.07	.01
☐ 132 Darrell Evans	.20	.10	.02
☐ 133 Keith Hernandez	.15	.07	.01
☐ 134 Tom Brunansky	.15	.07	.01
☐ 135 Kevin McReynolds	.25	.12	.02
☐ 136 Scott Fletcher	.12	.06	.01
☐ 137 Lou Whitaker	.15	.07	.01
☐ 138 Carney Lansford	.15	.07	.01
☐ 139 Andre Dawson	.40	.20	.04
☐ 140 Carlton Fisk	.30	.15	.03
☐ 141 Buddy Bell	.15	.07	.01
☐ 142 Ozzie Smith	.30	.15	.03
☐ 143 Dan Pasqua	.15	.07	.01
☐ 144 Kevin Mitchell	.90	.45	.09
☐ 145 Bret Saberhagen	.25	.12	.02
☐ 146 Charlie Kerfeld	.12	.06	.01
☐ 147 Phil Niekro	.20	.10	.02
☐ 148 John Candelaria	.12	.06	.01
☐ 149 Rich Gedman	.12	.06	.01
☐ 150 Fernando Valenzuela	.20	.10	.02
☐ 151 Tri-Stars	.15	.07	.01
Gary Carter			
Mike Scioscia			
Tony Pena			
☐ 152 Tri-Stars	.30	.15	.03
Tim Raines			
Jose Cruz			
Vince Coleman			
☐ 153 Tri-Stars	.20	.10	.02
Jesse Barfield			
Harold Baines			
Dave Winfield			
☐ 154 Tri-Stars	.15	.07	.01
Lance Parrish			
Don Slaught			
Rich Gedman			
☐ 155 Tri-Stars	.65	.30	.06
Dale Murphy			
Kevin McReynolds			
Eric Davis			
☐ 156 Hi-Lite Tri-Stars	.45	.22	.04
Don Sutton			
Mike Schmidt			
Jim Deshaies			
☐ 157 Speedburners	.40	.20	.04
Rickey Henderson			
John Cangelosi			
Gary Pettis			
☐ 158 Big Six Rookies	1.25	.60	.12
Randy Asadoor			
Casey Candaele			
Kevin Seitzer			
Rafael Palmeiro			
Tim Pyznarski			
Dave Cochrane			
☐ 159 Big Six	1.50	.75	.15
Don Mattingly			
Rickey Henderson			
Roger Clemens			
Dale Murphy			
Eddie Murray			
Dwight Gooden			
☐ 160 Roger McDowell	.15	.07	.01
☐ 161 Brian Downing	.12	.06	.01
☐ 162 Bill Doran	.15	.07	.01
☐ 163 Don Baylor	.15	.07	.01
☐ 164A Alfredo Griffin ERR (no uniform number on card back) '87	.25	.12	.02
☐ 164B Alfredo Griffin COR '86	.25	.12	.02
☐ 165 Don Aase	.12	.06	.01
☐ 166 Glenn Wilson	.12	.06	.01
☐ 167 Dan Quisenberry	.20	.10	.02
☐ 168 Frank White	.12	.06	.01
☐ 169 Cecil Cooper	.12	.06	.01
☐ 170 Jody Davis	.12	.06	.01
☐ 171 Harold Baines	.20	.10	.02
☐ 172 Rob Deer	.15	.07	.01
☐ 173 John Tudor	.15	.07	.01
☐ 174 Larry Parrish	.12	.06	.01
☐ 175 Kevin Bass	.15	.07	.01
☐ 176 Joe Carter	.35	.17	.03
☐ 177 Mitch Webster	.12	.06	.01
☐ 178 Dave Kingman	.15	.07	.01
☐ 179 Jim Presley	.12	.06	.01
☐ 180 Mel Hall	.15	.07	.01
☐ 181 Shane Rawley	.12	.06	.01
☐ 182 Marty Barrett	.15	.07	.01
☐ 183 Damaso Garcia	.12	.06	.01
☐ 184 Bobby Grich	.15	.07	.01
☐ 185 Leon Durham	.12	.06	.01
☐ 186 Ozzie Guillen	.25	.12	.02
☐ 187 Tony Fernandez	.15	.07	.01
☐ 188 Alan Trammell	.20	.10	.02
☐ 189 Jim Clancy	.12	.06	.01
☐ 190 Bo Jackson	3.00	1.50	.30
☐ 191 Bob Forsch	.12	.06	.01
☐ 192 John Franco	.20	.10	.02
☐ 193 Von Hayes	.20	.10	.02
☐ 194 Tri-Stars	.15	.07	.01
Don Aase			
Dave Righetti			
Mark Eichhorn			
☐ 195 Tri-Stars	.60	.30	.06
Keith Hernandez			
Will Clark			
Glenn Davis			
☐ 196 Hi-Lite Tri-Stars	.45	.22	.04
Roger Clemens			
Joe Cowley			
Bob Horner			
☐ 197 Big Six	.75	.35	.07
George Brett			
Hubie Brooks			
Tony Gwynn			
Ryne Sandberg			
Tim Raines			
Wade Boggs			
☐ 198 Tri-Stars	.60	.30	.06
Kirby Puckett			
Rickey Henderson			
Fred Lynn			
☐ 199 Speedburners	.60	.30	.06
Tim Raines			
Vince Coleman			
Eric Davis			
☐ 200 Steve Carlton	.35	.17	.03

1987 Sportflics Dealer Panels

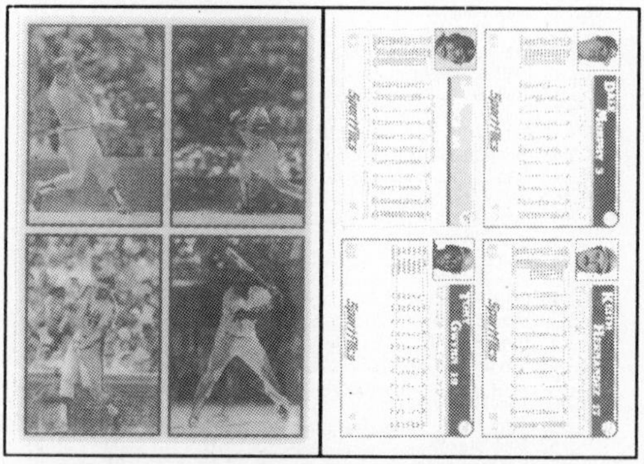

These "Magic Motion" card panels of four were issued only to dealers who were ordering other Sportflics product in quantity. If cut into individual cards, the interior white borders will be slightly narrower than the regular issue Sportflics since the panels of four measure a shade under 4 7/8" by 6 7/8". The cards have a 1986 copyright on the back same as the factory collated sets. Other than the slight difference in size, these cards are essentially styled the same as the regular issue of 1987 Sportflics.

This set of sixteen top players was accompanied by the inclusion of four smaller panels of four team logo/team fact cards. The 16 small team cards correspond directly to the 16 players in the sets. The checklist below prices the panels and gives the card number for each player, which is the same as the player's card number in the Sportflics regular set.

	MINT	EXC	G-VG
COMPLETE SET (4)	12.00	6.00	1.20
COMMON PANEL (1-4)	3.00	1.50	.30
☐ 1 Don Mattingly 1 Roger Clemens 10 Mike Schmidt 30 Tim Raines 34	5.00	2.50	.50
☐ 2 Wade Boggs 2 Eddie Murray 6 Wally Joyner 26 Fern.Valenzuela 150	3.50	1.75	.35
☐ 3 Dale Murphy 3 Tony Gwynn 31 Jim Rice 97 Keith Hernandez 133	3.00	1.50	.30
☐ 4 Rickey Henderson 4 George Brett 5 Cal Ripken 9 Dwight Gooden 100	4.00	2.00	.40

1987 Sportflics Team Preview

This 26-card set features a card for each Major League team. Each card shows 12 different players on that team via four "Magic Motion" trios. The cards are numbered on the backs. The narrative on the back gives Outlook, Newcomers to Watch, and Summary for each team. The list of players appearing on the front is given at the bottom of the reverse of each card. Cards are standard size, 2 1/2" by 3 1/2". The was distributed as a complete set in its own box along with 26 team logo trivia cards measuring 1 3/4" by 2".

	MINT	EXC	G-VG
COMPLETE SET (26)	6.00	3.00	.60
COMMON PLAYER (1-26)	.30	.15	.03
☐ 1 Texas Rangers	.30	.15	.03
☐ 2 New York Mets	.40	.20	.04
☐ 3 Cleveland Indians	.30	.15	.03
☐ 4 Cincinnati Reds	.40	.20	.04
☐ 5 Toronto Blue Jays	.30	.15	.03
☐ 6 Philadelphia Phillies	.30	.15	.03
☐ 7 New York Yankees	.40	.20	.04
☐ 8 Houston Astros	.30	.15	.03
☐ 9 Boston Red Sox	.40	.20	.04
☐ 10 San Francisco Giants	.30	.15	.03
☐ 11 California Angels	.30	.15	.03
☐ 12 St. Louis Cardinals	.40	.20	.04
☐ 13 Kansas City Royals	.40	.20	.04
☐ 14 Los Angeles Dodgers	.40	.20	.04
☐ 15 Detroit Tigers	.40	.20	.04
☐ 16 San Diego Padres	.30	.15	.03
☐ 17 Minnesota Twins	.40	.20	.04
☐ 18 Pittsburgh Pirates	.30	.15	.03
☐ 19 Milwaukee Brewers	.30	.15	.03
☐ 20 Montreal Expos	.30	.15	.03
☐ 21 Baltimore Orioles	.40	.20	.04
☐ 22 Chicago Cubs	.30	.15	.03
☐ 23 Oakland Athletics	.40	.20	.04
☐ 24 Atlanta Braves	.30	.15	.03
☐ 25 Seattle Mariners	.30	.15	.03
☐ 26 Chicago White Sox	.30	.15	.03

1987 Sportflics Rookie Packs

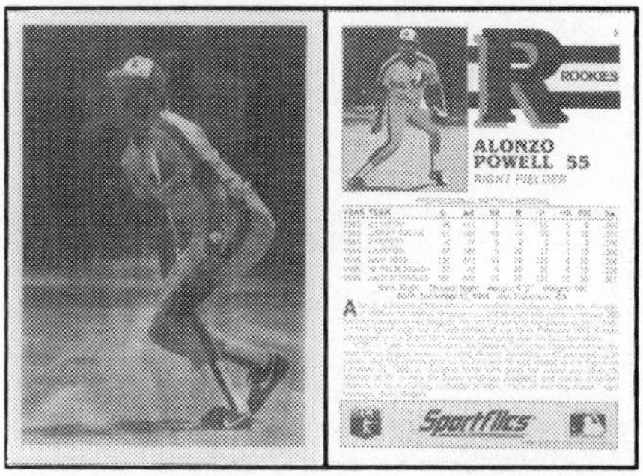

This two pack set consists of 10 "rookie" players and 2 trivia cards. Each of the two different packs had half the set and the outside of the wrapper told which cards were inside. The cards are all 2 1/2" by 3 1/2". The set includes the first major league baseball cards ever of Alonzo Powell, John Smiley, and Brick Smith. Dealers received one rookie pack with every Team Preview set they ordered. The card backs also feature a full-color small photo of the player.

	MINT	EXC	G-VG
COMPLETE SET (10)	7.50	3.75	.75
COMMON PLAYER (1-10)	.40	.20	.04
☐ 1 Terry Steinbach (pack two)	1.25	.60	.12
☐ 2 Rafael Palmeiro (pack one)	1.50	.75	.15
☐ 3 Dave Magadan (pack two)	1.25	.60	.12
☐ 4 Marvin Freeman (pack two)	.40	.20	.04
☐ 5 Brick Smith (pack two)	.40	.20	.04
☐ 6 B.J. Surhoff (pack one)	.80	.40	.08
☐ 7 John Smiley (pack one)	.80	.40	.08
☐ 8 Alonzo Powell (pack two)	.40	.20	.04
☐ 9 Benny Santiago (pack one)	2.50	1.25	.25
☐ 10 Devon White (pack one)	1.25	.60	.12

1987 Sportflics Rookies I

These "Magic Motion" cards were issued as a series of 25 cards packaged in its own complete set box, along with 17 trivia cards. Cards are 2 1/2" by 3 1/2." The three front photos show the player in two action poses and one portrait pose. The card backs also provide a full-color photo (1 3/8" by 2 1/4") of the player as well as the usual statistics and biographical notes. The front photos are framed by a wide, round-cornered, red border and have the player's name and uniform number at the bottom.

	MINT	EXC	G-VG
COMPLETE SET (25)	9.00	4.50	.90
COMMON PLAYER (1-25)	.12	.06	.01
☐ 1 Eric Bell	.12	.06	.01
☐ 2 Chris Bosio	.25	.12	.02
☐ 3 Bob Brower	.12	.06	.01
☐ 4 Jerry Browne	.20	.10	.02
☐ 5 Ellis Burks	1.75	.85	.17
☐ 6 Casey Candaele	.12	.06	.01
☐ 7 Ken Gerhart	.12	.06	.01
☐ 8 Mike Greenwell	1.75	.85	.17
☐ 9 Stan Jefferson	.20	.10	.02
☐ 10 Dave Magadan	.50	.25	.05
☐ 11 Joe Magrane	.40	.20	.04
☐ 12 Fred McGriff	1.25	.60	.12
☐ 13 Mark McGwire	2.00	1.00	.20
☐ 14 Mark McLemore	.12	.06	.01
☐ 15 Jeff Musselman	.12	.06	.01
☐ 16 Matt Nokes	.35	.17	.03
☐ 17 Paul O'Neill	.40	.20	.04
☐ 18 Luis Polonia	.20	.10	.02
☐ 19 Benny Santiago	1.00	.50	.10
☐ 20 Kevin Seitzer	.90	.45	.09
☐ 21 John Smiley	.30	.15	.03
☐ 22 Terry Steinbach	.45	.22	.04
☐ 23 B.J. Surhoff	.30	.15	.03
☐ 24 Devon White	.30	.15	.03
☐ 25 Matt Williams	2.75	1.35	.27

1987 Sportflics Rookies II

These "Magic Motion" cards were issued as a series of 25 cards packaged in its own complete set box along with 17 trivia cards. Cards are 2 1/2" by 3 1/2." In this second set the card numbering begins with number 26. The three front photos show the player in two action poses and one portrait pose. The card backs also provide a full-color photo (1 3/8" by 2 1/4") of the player as well as the usual statistics and biographical notes. The front photos are framed by a wide, round-cornered, red border and have the player's name and uniform number at the bottom.

	MINT	EXC	G-VG
COMPLETE SET (25)	4.50	2.25	.45
COMMON PLAYER (26-50)	.12	.06	.01
☐ 26 DeWayne Buice	.12	.06	.01
☐ 27 Willie Fraser	.12	.06	.01
☐ 28 Billy Ripken	.20	.10	.02
☐ 29 Mike Henneman	.20	.10	.02
☐ 30 Shawn Hillegas	.12	.06	.01
☐ 31 Shane Mack	.20	.10	.02
☐ 32 Rafael Palmeiro	.75	.35	.07
☐ 33 Mike Jackson	.12	.06	.01
☐ 34 Gene Larkin	.20	.10	.02
☐ 35 Jimmy Jones	.15	.07	.01
☐ 36 Gerald Young	.20	.10	.02
☐ 37 Ken Caminiti	.20	.10	.02
☐ 38 Sam Horn	.20	.10	.02
☐ 39 David Cone	.85	.40	.08
☐ 40 Mike Dunne	.12	.06	.01
☐ 41 Ken Williams	.20	.10	.02
☐ 42 John Morris	.12	.06	.01
☐ 43 Jim Lindeman	.12	.06	.01
☐ 44 Todd Benzinger	.25	.12	.02
☐ 45 Mike Stanley	.12	.06	.01
☐ 46 Les Straker	.12	.06	.01
☐ 47 Jeff Robinson	.20	.10	.02
☐ 48 Jeff Blauser	.20	.10	.02
☐ 49 John Marzano	.15	.07	.01
☐ 50 Keith Miller	.25	.12	.02

1988 Sportflics

This 225-card set was produced by Sportflics and again features three sequence action pictures on each card. Cards measure 2 1/2" by 3 1/2" and are in full color. There are 219 individual players, 3 Highlights trios, and 3 Rookie Prospect trio cards. The cards feature a red border on the front. A full-color action picture of the player is printed on the back of the card. Cards are numbered on the back in the lower right corner.

	MINT	EXC	G-VG
COMPLETE SET (225)	36.00	18.00	3.60
COMMON PLAYER (1-225)	.12	.06	.01
☐ 1 Don Mattingly	1.50	.50	.10
☐ 2 Tim Raines	.20	.10	.02
☐ 3 Andre Dawson	.25	.12	.02
☐ 4 George Bell	.20	.10	.02
☐ 5 Joe Carter	.30	.15	.03
☐ 6 Matt Nokes	.20	.10	.02
☐ 7 Dave Winfield	.30	.15	.03
☐ 8 Kirby Puckett	.75	.35	.07
☐ 9 Will Clark	1.75	.85	.17
☐ 10 Eric Davis	.75	.35	.07
☐ 11 Rickey Henderson	.60	.30	.06
☐ 12 Ryne Sandberg	.60	.30	.06
☐ 13 Jesse Barfield UER (misspelled Jessie on card back)	.25	.12	.02
☐ 14 Ozzie Guillen	.20	.10	.02
☐ 15 Bret Saberhagen	.20	.10	.02
☐ 16 Tony Gwynn	.50	.25	.05
☐ 17 Kevin Seitzer	.40	.20	.04
☐ 18 Jack Clark	.15	.07	.01
☐ 19 Danny Tartabull	.20	.10	.02

☐	20	Ted Higuera	.15	.07	.01
☐	21	Charlie Leibrandt UER (misspelled Liebrandt on card front)	.15	.07	.01
☐	22	Benny Santiago	.50	.25	.05
☐	23	Fred Lynn	.20	.10	.02
☐	24	Robby Thompson	.15	.07	.01
☐	25	Alan Trammell	.15	.07	.01
☐	26	Tony Fernandez	.15	.07	.01
☐	27	Rick Sutcliffe	.15	.07	.01
☐	28	Gary Carter	.20	.10	.02
☐	29	Cory Snyder	.20	.10	.02
☐	30	Lou Whitaker	.15	.07	.01
☐	31	Keith Hernandez	.15	.07	.01
☐	32	Mike Witt	.15	.07	.01
☐	33	Harold Baines	.15	.07	.01
☐	34	Robin Yount	.45	.22	.04
☐	35	Mike Schmidt	.80	.40	.08
☐	36	Dion James	.12	.06	.01
☐	37	Tom Candiotti	.12	.06	.01
☐	38	Tracy Jones	.15	.07	.01
☐	39	Nolan Ryan	1.00	.50	.10
☐	40	Fernando Valenzuela	.20	.10	.02
☐	41	Vance Law	.12	.06	.01
☐	42	Roger McDowell	.15	.07	.01
☐	43	Carlton Fisk	.30	.15	.03
☐	44	Scott Garrelts	.15	.07	.01
☐	45	Lee Guetterman	.12	.06	.01
☐	46	Mark Langston	.15	.07	.01
☐	47	Willie Randolph	.15	.07	.01
☐	48	Bill Doran	.15	.07	.01
☐	49	Larry Parrish	.12	.06	.01
☐	50	Wade Boggs	.75	.35	.07
☐	51	Shane Rawley	.12	.06	.01
☐	52	Alvin Davis	.15	.07	.01
☐	53	Jeff Reardon	.15	.07	.01
☐	54	Jim Presley	.12	.06	.01
☐	55	Kevin Bass	.12	.06	.01
☐	56	Kevin McReynolds	.20	.10	.02
☐	57	B.J. Surhoff	.20	.10	.02
☐	58	Julio Franco	.15	.07	.01
☐	59	Eddie Murray	.30	.15	.03
☐	60	Jody Davis	.12	.06	.01
☐	61	Todd Worrell	.15	.07	.01
☐	62	Von Hayes	.20	.10	.02
☐	63	Billy Hatcher	.15	.07	.01
☐	64	John Kruk	.20	.10	.02
☐	65	Tom Henke	.15	.07	.01
☐	66	Mike Scott	.20	.10	.02
☐	67	Vince Coleman	.25	.12	.02
☐	68	Ozzie Smith	.25	.12	.02
☐	69	Ken Williams	.15	.07	.01
☐	70	Steve Bedrosian	.15	.07	.01
☐	71	Luis Polonia	.20	.10	.02
☐	72	Brook Jacoby	.15	.07	.01
☐	73	Ron Darling	.15	.07	.01
☐	74	Lloyd Moseby	.12	.06	.01
☐	75	Wally Joyner	.30	.15	.03
☐	76	Dan Quisenberry	.15	.07	.01
☐	77	Scott Fletcher	.12	.06	.01
☐	78	Kirk McCaskill	.12	.06	.01
☐	79	Paul Molitor	.20	.10	.02
☐	80	Mike Aldrete	.12	.06	.01
☐	81	Neal Heaton	.12	.06	.01
☐	82	Jeffrey Leonard	.12	.06	.01
☐	83	Dave Magadan	.25	.12	.02
☐	84	Danny Cox	.12	.06	.01
☐	85	Lance McCullers	.12	.06	.01
☐	86	Jay Howell	.12	.06	.01
☐	87	Charlie Hough	.12	.06	.01
☐	88	Gene Garber	.12	.06	.01
☐	89	Jesse Orosco	.12	.06	.01
☐	90	Don Robinson	.12	.06	.01
☐	91	Willie McGee	.15	.07	.01
☐	92	Bert Blyleven	.15	.07	.01
☐	93	Phil Bradley	.15	.07	.01
☐	94	Terry Kennedy	.12	.06	.01
☐	95	Kent Hrbek	.15	.07	.01
☐	96	Juan Samuel	.15	.07	.01
☐	97	Pedro Guerrero	.15	.07	.01
☐	98	Sid Bream	.12	.06	.01
☐	99	Devon White	.20	.10	.02
☐	100	Mark McGwire	.90	.45	.09
☐	101	Dave Parker	.15	.07	.01
☐	102	Glenn Davis	.25	.12	.02
☐	103	Greg Walker	.12	.06	.01
☐	104	Rick Rhoden	.12	.06	.01
☐	105	Mitch Webster	.12	.06	.01
☐	106	Lenny Dykstra	.20	.10	.02
☐	107	Gene Larkin	.12	.06	.01
☐	108	Floyd Youmans	.12	.06	.01
☐	109	Andy Van Slyke	.20	.10	.02
☐	110	Mike Scioscia	.12	.06	.01
☐	111	Kirk Gibson	.25	.12	.02
☐	112	Kal Daniels	.20	.10	.02
☐	113	Ruben Sierra	.90	.45	.09
☐	114	Sam Horn	.20	.10	.02
☐	115	Ray Knight	.15	.07	.01
☐	116	Jimmy Key	.12	.06	.01
☐	117	Bo Diaz	.12	.06	.01
☐	118	Mike Greenwell	1.00	.50	.10
☐	119	Barry Bonds	.65	.30	.06
☐	120	Reggie Jackson UER (463 lifetime homers)	.75	.35	.07
☐	121	Mike Pagliarulo	.12	.06	.01
☐	122	Tommy John	.25	.12	.02
☐	123	Bill Madlock	.12	.06	.01
☐	124	Ken Caminiti	.20	.10	.02
☐	125	Gary Ward	.12	.06	.01
☐	126	Candy Maldonado	.15	.07	.01
☐	127	Harold Reynolds	.12	.06	.01
☐	128	Joe Magrane	.25	.12	.02
☐	129	Mike Henneman	.20	.10	.02
☐	130	Jim Gantner	.12	.06	.01
☐	131	Bobby Bonilla	.40	.20	.04
☐	132	John Farrell	.20	.10	.02
☐	133	Frank Tanana	.15	.07	.01
☐	134	Zane Smith	.15	.07	.01
☐	135	Dave Righetti	.15	.07	.01
☐	136	Rick Reuschel	.15	.07	.01
☐	137	Dwight Evans	.20	.10	.02
☐	138	Howard Johnson	.30	.15	.03
☐	139	Terry Leach	.12	.06	.01
☐	140	Casey Candaele	.12	.06	.01
☐	141	Tom Herr	.12	.06	.01
☐	142	Tony Pena	.20	.10	.02
☐	143	Lance Parrish	.25	.12	.02
☐	144	Ellis Burks	1.00	.50	.10
☐	145	Pete O'Brien	.15	.07	.01
☐	146	Mike Boddicker	.15	.07	.01
☐	147	Buddy Bell	.15	.07	.01
☐	148	Bo Jackson	2.00	1.00	.20
☐	149	Frank White	.15	.07	.01
☐	150	George Brett	.40	.20	.04
☐	151	Tim Wallach	.15	.07	.01
☐	152	Cal Ripken Jr.	.35	.17	.03
☐	153	Brett Butler	.15	.07	.01
☐	154	Gary Gaetti	.15	.07	.01
☐	155	Darryl Strawberry	.75	.35	.07
☐	156	Alredo Griffin	.12	.06	.01
☐	157	Marty Barrett	.12	.06	.01
☐	158	Jim Rice	.20	.10	.02
☐	159	Terry Pendleton	.15	.07	.01
☐	160	Orel Hershiser	.35	.17	.03
☐	161	Larry Sheets	.12	.06	.01
☐	162	Dave Stewart UER (Braves logo)	.35	.17	.03
☐	163	Shawon Dunston	.25	.12	.02
☐	164	Keith Moreland	.12	.06	.01
☐	165	Ken Oberkfell	.12	.06	.01
☐	166	Ivan Calderon	.20	.10	.02
☐	167	Bob Welch	.25	.12	.02
☐	168	Fred McGriff	.40	.20	.04
☐	169	Pete Incaviglia	.20	.10	.02
☐	170	Dale Murphy	.35	.17	.03
☐	171	Mike Dunne	.12	.06	.01
☐	172	Chili Davis	.15	.07	.01
☐	173	Milt Thompson	.12	.06	.01
☐	174	Terry Steinbach	.20	.10	.02
☐	175	Oddibe McDowell	.15	.07	.01
☐	176	Jack Morris	.15	.07	.01
☐	177	Sid Fernandez	.15	.07	.01
☐	178	Ken Griffey	.20	.10	.02
☐	179	Lee Smith	.12	.06	.01
☐	180	Highlights 1987 Kirby Puckett Juan Nieves Mike Schmidt	.50	.25	.05
☐	181	Brian Downing	.12	.06	.01
☐	182	Andres Galarraga	.20	.10	.02
☐	183	Rob Deer	.20	.10	.02
☐	184	Greg Brock	.12	.06	.01
☐	185	Doug DeCinces	.12	.06	.01
☐	186	Johnny Ray	.12	.06	.01
☐	187	Hubie Brooks	.15	.07	.01
☐	188	Darrell Evans	.12	.06	.01
☐	189	Mel Hall	.12	.06	.01
☐	190	Jim Deshaies	.12	.06	.01
☐	191	Dan Plesac	.12	.06	.01
☐	192	Willie Wilson	.15	.07	.01
☐	193	Mike LaValliere	.12	.06	.01
☐	194	Tom Brunansky	.15	.07	.01
☐	195	John Franco	.15	.07	.01
☐	196	Frank Viola	.25	.12	.02
☐	197	Bruce Hurst	.20	.10	.02
☐	198	John Tudor	.15	.07	.01
☐	199	Bob Forsch	.12	.06	.01
☐	200	Dwight Gooden	.65	.30	.06

☐ 201 Jose Canseco	2.25	1.10	.22
☐ 202 Carney Lansford	.15	.07	.01
☐ 203 Kelly Downs	.12	.06	.01
☐ 204 Glenn Wilson	.12	.06	.01
☐ 205 Pat Tabler	.12	.06	.01
☐ 206 Mike Davis	.12	.06	.01
☐ 207 Roger Clemens	.80	.40	.08
☐ 208 Dave Smith	.12	.06	.01
☐ 209 Curt Young	.12	.06	.01
☐ 210 Mark Eichhorn	.12	.06	.01
☐ 211 Juan Nieves	.12	.06	.01
☐ 212 Bob Boone	.15	.07	.01
☐ 213 Don Sutton	.15	.07	.01
☐ 214 Willie Upshaw	.12	.06	.01
☐ 215 Jim Clancy	.12	.06	.01
☐ 216 Bill Ripken	.20	.10	.02
☐ 217 Ozzie Virgil	.12	.06	.01
☐ 218 Dave Concepcion	.15	.07	.01
☐ 219 Alan Ashby	.12	.06	.01
☐ 220 Mike Marshall	.15	.07	.01
☐ 221 Highlights 1987 Mark McGwire Paul Molitor Vince Coleman	.50	.25	.05
☐ 222 Highlights 1987 Benito Santiago Steve Bedrosian Don Mattingly	.75	.35	.07
☐ 223 Rookie Prospects Shawn Abner Jay Buhner Gary Thurman	.30	.15	.03
☐ 224 Rookie Prospects Tim Crews Vincente Palacios John Davis	.15	.07	.01
☐ 225 Rookie Prospects Jody Reed Jeff Treadway Keith Miller	.60	.30	.06

1988 Sportflics Gamewinners

This 25-card set of "Gamewinners" was distributed in a green and yellow box along with 17 trivia cards by Weiser Card Company of New Jersey. The 25 players selected for the set show a strong New York preference. The set was ostensibly produced for use as a youth organizational fund raiser. The cards are the standard size, 2 1/2" by 3 1/2" and are done in the typical Sportflics' Magic Motion (three picture) style. The cards are numbered on the back.

	MINT	EXC	G-VG
COMPLETE SET (25)	9.00	4.50	.90
COMMON PLAYER (1-25)	.20	.10	.02
☐ 1 Don Mattingly	1.25	.60	.12
☐ 2 Mark McGwire	.90	.45	.09
☐ 3 Wade Boggs	.90	.45	.09
☐ 4 Will Clark	.90	.45	.09
☐ 5 Eric Davis	.75	.35	.07
☐ 6 Willie Randolph	.20	.10	.02
☐ 7 Dave Winfield	.40	.20	.04
☐ 8 Rickey Henderson	.90	.45	.09
☐ 9 Dwight Gooden	.50	.25	.05
☐ 10 Benny Santiago	.50	.25	.05
☐ 11 Keith Hernandez	.30	.15	.03
☐ 12 Juan Samuel	.25	.12	.02
☐ 13 Kevin Seitzer	.35	.17	.03
☐ 14 Gary Carter	.40	.20	.04
☐ 15 Darryl Strawberry	.90	.45	.09
☐ 16 Rick Rhoden	.20	.10	.02
☐ 17 Howard Johnson	.40	.20	.04
☐ 18 Matt Nokes	.25	.12	.02
☐ 19 Dave Righetti	.30	.15	.03
☐ 20 Roger Clemens	.90	.45	.09
☐ 21 Mike Schmidt	1.00	.50	.10
☐ 22 Kevin McReynolds	.35	.17	.03
☐ 23 Mike Pagliarulo	.20	.10	.02
☐ 24 Kevin Elster	.20	.10	.02
☐ 25 Jack Clark	.30	.15	.03

1989 Sportflics

This 225-card set was produced by Sportflics (distributed by Major League Marketing) and again features three sequence action pictures on each card. Cards measure 2 1/2" by 3 1/2" and are in full color. There are 220 individual players, 2 Highlights trios, and 3 Rookie Prospect trio cards. The cards feature a white border on the front with red and blue inner trim colors. A full-color action picture of the player is printed on the back of the card. Cards are numbered on the back in the lower right corner.

	MINT	EXC	G-VG
COMPLETE SET (225)	37.50	16.00	3.00
COMMON PLAYER (1-225)	.12	.06	.01
☐ 1 Jose Canseco	1.75	.85	.17
☐ 2 Wally Joyner	.25	.12	.02
☐ 3 Roger Clemens	.50	.25	.05
☐ 4 Greg Swindell	.20	.10	.02
☐ 5 Jack Morris	.15	.07	.01
☐ 6 Mickey Brantley	.12	.06	.01
☐ 7 Jim Presley	.12	.06	.01
☐ 8 Pete O'Brien	.15	.07	.01
☐ 9 Jesse Barfield	.15	.07	.01
☐ 10 Frank Viola	.20	.10	.02
☐ 11 Kevin Bass	.12	.06	.01
☐ 12 Glenn Wilson	.12	.06	.01
☐ 13 Chris Sabo	.35	.17	.03
☐ 14 Fred McGriff	.30	.15	.03
☐ 15 Mark Grace	1.75	.85	.17
☐ 16 Devon White	.15	.07	.01
☐ 17 Juan Samuel	.15	.07	.01
☐ 18 Lou Whitaker	.15	.07	.01
☐ 19 Greg Walker	.12	.06	.01
☐ 20 Roberto Alomar	.50	.25	.05
☐ 21 Mike Schmidt	.75	.35	.07
☐ 22 Benny Santiago	.30	.15	.03
☐ 23 Dave Stewart	.20	.10	.02
☐ 24 Dave Winfield	.20	.10	.02
☐ 25 George Bell	.15	.07	.01
☐ 26 Jack Clark	.15	.07	.01
☐ 27 Doug Drabek	.20	.10	.02
☐ 28 Ron Gant	.40	.20	.04
☐ 29 Glenn Braggs	.15	.07	.01
☐ 30 Rafael Palmeiro	.25	.12	.02
☐ 31 Brett Butler	.15	.07	.01

☐	32 Ron Darling	.15	.07	.01
☐	33 Alvin Davis	.15	.07	.01
☐	34 Bob Walk	.12	.06	.01
☐	35 Dave Stieb	.20	.10	.02
☐	36 Orel Hershiser	.30	.15	.03
☐	37 John Farrell	.15	.07	.01
☐	38 Doug Jones	.15	.07	.01
☐	39 Kelly Downs	.15	.07	.01
☐	40 Bob Boone	.15	.07	.01
☐	41 Gary Sheffield	1.25	.60	.12
☐	42 Doug Dascenzo	.15	.07	.01
☐	43 Chad Kreuter	.15	.07	.01
☐	44 Ricky Jordan	.40	.20	.04
☐	45 Dave West	.20	.10	.02
☐	46 Danny Tartabull	.20	.10	.02
☐	47 Teddy Higuera	.15	.07	.01
☐	48 Gary Gaetti	.15	.07	.01
☐	49 Dave Parker	.15	.07	.01
☐	50 Don Mattingly	1.00	.50	.10
☐	51 David Cone	.20	.10	.02
☐	52 Kal Daniels	.15	.07	.01
☐	53 Carney Lansford	.15	.07	.01
☐	54 Mike Marshall	.15	.07	.01
☐	55 Kevin Seitzer	.15	.07	.01
☐	56 Mike Henneman	.15	.07	.01
☐	57 Bill Doran	.15	.07	.01
☐	58 Steve Sax	.15	.07	.01
☐	59 Lance Parrish	.15	.07	.01
☐	60 Keith Hernandez	.15	.07	.01
☐	61 Jose Uribe	.12	.06	.01
☐	62 Jose Lind	.12	.06	.01
☐	63 Steve Bedrosian	.15	.07	.01
☐	64 George Brett	.25	.12	.02
☐	65 Kirk Gibson	.20	.10	.02
☐	66 Cal Ripken Jr.	.25	.12	.02
☐	67 Mitch Webster	.12	.06	.01
☐	68 Fred Lynn	.15	.07	.01
☐	69 Eric Davis	.40	.20	.04
☐	70 Bo Jackson	1.75	.85	.17
☐	71 Kevin Elster	.15	.07	.01
☐	72 Rick Reuschel	.15	.07	.01
☐	73 Tim Burke	.15	.07	.01
☐	74 Mark Davis	.15	.07	.01
☐	75 Claudell Washington	.15	.07	.01
☐	76 Lance McCullers	.12	.06	.01
☐	77 Mike Moore	.15	.07	.01
☐	78 Robby Thompson	.15	.07	.01
☐	79 Roger McDowell	.15	.07	.01
☐	80 Danny Jackson	.15	.07	.01
☐	81 Tim Leary	.15	.07	.01
☐	82 Bobby Witt	.20	.10	.02
☐	83 Jim Gott	.12	.06	.01
☐	84 Andy Hawkins	.12	.06	.01
☐	85 Ozzie Guillen	.20	.10	.02
☐	86 John Tudor	.15	.07	.01
☐	87 Todd Burns	.15	.07	.01
☐	88 Dave Gallagher	.12	.06	.01
☐	89 Jay Buhner	.15	.07	.01
☐	90 Gregg Jefferies	.90	.45	.09
☐	91 Bob Welch	.20	.10	.02
☐	92 Charlie Hough	.12	.06	.01
☐	93 Tony Fernandez	.15	.07	.01
☐	94 Ozzie Virgil	.12	.06	.01
☐	95 Andre Dawson	.25	.12	.02
☐	96 Hubie Brooks	.15	.07	.01
☐	97 Kevin McReynolds	.15	.07	.01
☐	98 Mike LaValliere	.12	.06	.01
☐	99 Terry Pendleton	.15	.07	.01
☐	100 Wade Boggs	.60	.30	.06
☐	101 Dennis Eckersley	.20	.10	.02
☐	102 Mark Gubicza	.15	.07	.01
☐	103 Frank Tanana	.15	.07	.01
☐	104 Joe Carter	.25	.12	.02
☐	105 Ozzie Smith	.20	.10	.02
☐	106 Dennis Martinez	.12	.06	.01
☐	107 Jeff Treadway	.15	.07	.01
☐	108 Greg Maddux	.20	.10	.02
☐	109 Bret Saberhagen	.25	.12	.02
☐	110 Dale Murphy	.40	.20	.04
☐	111 Rob Deer	.15	.07	.01
☐	112 Pete Incaviglia	.15	.07	.01
☐	113 Vince Coleman	.20	.10	.02
☐	114 Tim Wallach	.15	.07	.01
☐	115 Nolan Ryan	1.25	.60	.12
☐	116 Walt Weiss	.20	.10	.02
☐	117 Brian Downing	.12	.06	.01
☐	118 Melido Perez	.15	.07	.01
☐	119 Terry Steinbach	.15	.07	.01
☐	120 Mike Scott	.15	.07	.01
☐	121 Tim Belcher	.15	.07	.01
☐	122 Mike Boddicker	.12	.06	.01
☐	123 Len Dykstra	.20	.10	.02
☐	124 Fernando Valenzuela	.15	.07	.01
☐	125 Gerald Young	.12	.06	.01
☐	126 Tom Henke	.15	.07	.01
☐	127 Dave Henderson	.12	.06	.01
☐	128 Dan Plesac	.12	.06	.01
☐	129 Chili Davis	.15	.07	.01
☐	130 Bryan Harvey	.15	.07	.01
☐	131 Don August	.12	.06	.01
☐	132 Mike Harkey	.35	.17	.03
☐	133 Luis Polonia	.15	.07	.01
☐	134 Craig Worthington	.20	.10	.02
☐	135 Joey Meyer	.12	.06	.01
☐	136 Barry Larkin	.30	.15	.03
☐	137 Glenn Davis	.20	.10	.02
☐	138 Mike Scioscia	.12	.06	.01
☐	139 Andres Galarraga	.15	.07	.01
☐	140 Dwight Gooden	.40	.20	.04
☐	141 Keith Moreland	.12	.06	.01
☐	142 Kevin Mitchell	.60	.30	.06
☐	143 Mike Greenwell	.40	.20	.04
☐	144 Mel Hall	.12	.06	.01
☐	145 Rickey Henderson	.60	.30	.06
☐	146 Barry Bonds	.45	.22	.04
☐	147 Eddie Murray	.25	.12	.02
☐	148 Lee Smith	.15	.07	.01
☐	149 Julio Franco	.15	.07	.01
☐	150 Tim Raines	.15	.07	.01
☐	151 Mitch Williams	.12	.06	.01
☐	152 Tim Laudner	.12	.06	.01
☐	153 Mike Pagliarulo	.12	.06	.01
☐	154 Floyd Bannister	.12	.06	.01
☐	155 Gary Carter	.15	.07	.01
☐	156 Kirby Puckett	.60	.30	.06
☐	157 Harold Baines	.15	.07	.01
☐	158 Dave Righetti	.15	.07	.01
☐	159 Mark Langston	.15	.07	.01
☐	160 Tony Gwynn	.35	.17	.03
☐	161 Tom Brunansky	.15	.07	.01
☐	162 Vance Law	.12	.06	.01
☐	163 Kelly Gruber	.25	.12	.02
☐	164 Gerald Perry	.12	.06	.01
☐	165 Harold Reynolds	.12	.06	.01
☐	166 Andy Van Slyke	.15	.07	.01
☐	167 Jimmy Key	.12	.06	.01
☐	168 Jeff Reardon	.15	.07	.01
☐	169 Milt Thompson	.12	.06	.01
☐	170 Will Clark	1.50	.75	.15
☐	171 Chet Lemon	.12	.06	.01
☐	172 Pat Tabler	.12	.06	.01
☐	173 Jim Rice	.15	.07	.01
☐	174 Billy Hatcher	.15	.07	.01
☐	175 Bruce Hurst	.15	.07	.01
☐	176 John Franco	.15	.07	.01
☐	177 Van Snider	.15	.07	.01
☐	178 Ron Jones	.15	.07	.01
☐	179 Jerald Clark	.15	.07	.01
☐	180 Tom Browning	.15	.07	.01
☐	181 Von Hayes	.15	.07	.01
☐	182 Bobby Bonilla	.30	.15	.03
☐	183 Todd Worrell	.15	.07	.01
☐	184 John Kruk	.15	.07	.01
☐	185 Scott Fletcher	.12	.06	.01
☐	186 Willie Wilson	.15	.07	.01
☐	187 Jody Davis	.12	.06	.01
☐	188 Kent Hrbek	.15	.07	.01
☐	189 Ruben Sierra	.40	.20	.04
☐	190 Shawon Dunston	.20	.10	.02
☐	191 Ellis Burks	.40	.20	.04
☐	192 Brook Jacoby	.15	.07	.01
☐	193 Jeff Robinson Detroit Tigers	.15	.07	.01
☐	194 Rich Dotson	.12	.06	.01
☐	195 Johnny Ray	.12	.06	.01
☐	196 Cory Snyder	.20	.10	.02
☐	197 Mike Witt	.12	.06	.01
☐	198 Marty Barrett	.12	.06	.01
☐	199 Robin Yount	.35	.17	.03
☐	200 Mark McGwire	.60	.30	.06
☐	201 Ryne Sandberg	.50	.25	.05
☐	202 John Candelaria	.12	.06	.01
☐	203 Matt Nokes	.15	.07	.01
☐	204 Dwight Evans	.20	.10	.02
☐	205 Darryl Strawberry	.55	.27	.05
☐	206 Willie McGee	.15	.07	.01
☐	207 Bobby Thigpen	.20	.10	.02
☐	208 B.J. Surhoff	.15	.07	.01
☐	209 Paul Molitor	.15	.07	.01
☐	210 Jody Reed	.15	.07	.01
☐	211 Doyle Alexander	.12	.06	.01
☐	212 Dennis Rasmussen	.12	.06	.01
☐	213 Kevin Gross	.12	.06	.01
☐	214 Kirk McCaskill	.12	.06	.01
☐	215 Alan Trammell	.15	.07	.01
☐	216 Damon Berryhill	.15	.07	.01
☐	217 Rick Sutcliffe	.15	.07	.01
☐	218 Don Slaught	.12	.06	.01

		MINT	EXC	G-VG
☐ 219	Carlton Fisk	.20	.10	.02
☐ 220	Allan Anderson	.15	.07	.01
☐ 221	Jose Canseco Wade Boggs Mike Greenwell	1.25	.60	.12
☐ 222	Orel Hershiser Dennis Eckersley Tom Browning	.35	.17	.03
☐ 223	Gary Sheffield Gregg Jefferies Sandy Alomar Jr.	4.00	2.00	.40
☐ 224	Bob Milacki Randy Johnson Ramon Martinez	1.00	.50	.10
☐ 225	Cameron Drew Geronimo Berroa Ron Jones	.20	.10	.02

1990 Sportflics

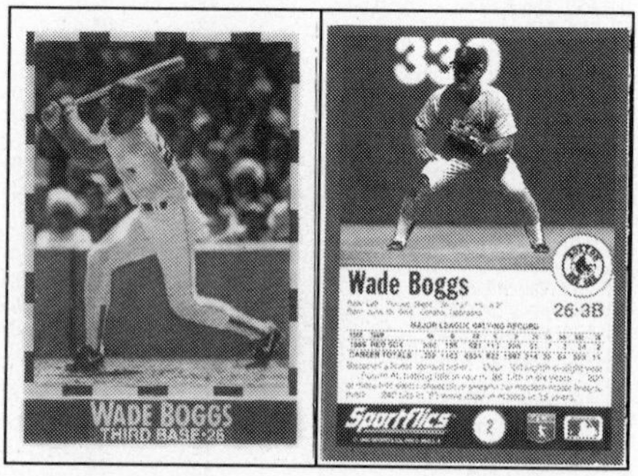

The 1990 Sportflics set contains 225 standard-size (2 1/2" by 3 1/2") cards. On the fronts, the black, white, orange, and yellow borders surround two photos, which can each be seen depending on the angle. The set is considered an improvement over the previous years' versions by many collectors due to the increased clarity of the fronts, caused by having two images rather than three. The backs are dominated by large color photos.

	MINT	EXC	G-VG
COMPLETE SET (225)	36.00	18.00	3.60
COMMON PLAYER (1-225)	.12	.06	.01

		MINT	EXC	G-VG
☐ 1	Kevin Mitchell	.30	.15	.03
☐ 2	Wade Boggs	.40	.20	.04
☐ 3	Cory Snyder	.15	.07	.01
☐ 4	Paul O'Neill	.15	.07	.01
☐ 5	Will Clark	.75	.35	.07
☐ 6	Tony Fernandez	.15	.07	.01
☐ 7	Ken Griffey Jr.	2.50	1.25	.25
☐ 8	Nolan Ryan	1.00	.50	.10
☐ 9	Rafael Palmeiro	.20	.10	.02
☐ 10	Jesse Barfield	.15	.07	.01
☐ 11	Kirby Puckett	.40	.20	.04
☐ 12	Steve Sax	.15	.07	.01
☐ 13	Fred McGriff	.20	.10	.02
☐ 14	Gregg Jefferies	.45	.22	.04
☐ 15	Mark Grace	.45	.22	.04
☐ 16	Ozzie Smith	.15	.07	.01
☐ 17	George Bell	.15	.07	.01
☐ 18	Robin Yount	.25	.12	.02
☐ 19	Glenn Davis	.15	.07	.01
☐ 20	Jeffrey Leonard	.12	.06	.01
☐ 21	Chili Davis	.12	.06	.01
☐ 22	Craig Biggio	.15	.07	.01
☐ 23	Jose Canseco	1.00	.50	.10
☐ 24	Derek Lilliquist	.12	.06	.01
☐ 25	Chris Bosio	.12	.06	.01
☐ 26	Dave Stieb	.15	.07	.01
☐ 27	Bobby Thigpen	.15	.07	.01
☐ 28	Jack Clark	.15	.07	.01
☐ 29	Kevin Ritz	.15	.07	.01
☐ 30	Tom Gordon	.25	.12	.02
☐ 31	Bryan Harvey	.15	.07	.01
☐ 32	Jim Deshaies	.12	.06	.01
☐ 33	Terry Steinbach	.15	.07	.01
☐ 34	Tom Glavine	.12	.06	.01
☐ 35	Bob Welch	.15	.07	.01
☐ 36	Charlie Hayes	.15	.07	.01
☐ 37	Jeff Reardon	.15	.07	.01
☐ 38	Joe Orsulak	.12	.06	.01
☐ 39	Scott Garrelts	.15	.07	.01
☐ 40	Bob Boone	.15	.07	.01
☐ 41	Scott Bankhead	.15	.07	.01
☐ 42	Tom Henke	.15	.07	.01
☐ 43	Greg Briley	.15	.07	.01
☐ 44	Teddy Higuera	.15	.07	.01
☐ 45	Pat Borders	.15	.07	.01
☐ 46	Kevin Seitzer	.15	.07	.01
☐ 47	Bruce Hurst	.15	.07	.01
☐ 48	Ozzie Guillen	.15	.07	.01
☐ 49	Wally Joyner	.15	.07	.01
☐ 50	Mike Greenwell	.25	.12	.02
☐ 51	Gary Gaetti	.15	.07	.01
☐ 52	Gary Sheffield	.40	.20	.04
☐ 53	Dennis Martinez	.12	.06	.01
☐ 54	Ryne Sandberg	.50	.25	.05
☐ 55	Mike Scott	.15	.07	.01
☐ 56	Todd Benzinger	.15	.07	.01
☐ 57	Kelly Gruber	.20	.10	.02
☐ 58	Jose Lind	.12	.06	.01
☐ 59	Allan Anderson	.12	.06	.01
☐ 60	Robby Thompson	.12	.06	.01
☐ 61	John Smoltz	.15	.07	.01
☐ 62	Mark Davis	.15	.07	.01
☐ 63	Tom Herr	.12	.06	.01
☐ 64	Randy Johnson	.15	.07	.01
☐ 65	Lonnie Smith	.15	.07	.01
☐ 66	Pedro Guerrero	.15	.07	.01
☐ 67	Jerome Walton	.80	.40	.08
☐ 68	Ramon Martinez	.50	.25	.05
☐ 69	Tim Raines	.15	.07	.01
☐ 70	Matt Williams	.30	.15	.03
☐ 71	Joe Oliver	.20	.10	.02
☐ 72	Nick Esasky	.15	.07	.01
☐ 73	Kevin Brown	.15	.07	.01
☐ 74	Walt Weiss	.15	.07	.01
☐ 75	Roger McDowell	.12	.06	.01
☐ 76	Jose DeLeon	.12	.06	.01
☐ 77	Brian Downing	.12	.06	.01
☐ 78	Jay Howell	.12	.06	.01
☐ 79	Jose Uribe	.12	.06	.01
☐ 80	Ellis Burks	.25	.12	.02
☐ 81	Sammy Sosa	.50	.25	.05
☐ 82	Johnny Ray	.12	.06	.01
☐ 83	Danny Darwin	.12	.06	.01
☐ 84	Carney Lansford	.15	.07	.01
☐ 85	Jose Oquendo	.12	.06	.01
☐ 86	John Cerutti	.12	.06	.01
☐ 87	Dave Winfield	.20	.10	.02
☐ 88	Dave Righetti	.15	.07	.01
☐ 89	Danny Jackson	.12	.06	.01
☐ 90	Andy Benes	.40	.20	.04
☐ 91	Tom Browning	.15	.07	.01
☐ 92	Pete O'Brien	.12	.06	.01
☐ 93	Roberto Alomar	.20	.10	.02
☐ 94	Bret Saberhagen	.20	.10	.02
☐ 95	Phil Bradley	.15	.07	.01
☐ 96	Doug Jones	.15	.07	.01
☐ 97	Eric Davis	.25	.12	.02
☐ 98	Tony Gwynn	.30	.15	.03
☐ 99	Jim Abbott	.50	.25	.05
☐ 100	Cal Ripken	.25	.12	.02
☐ 101	Andy Van Slyke	.15	.07	.01
☐ 102	Dan Plesac	.12	.06	.01
☐ 103	Lou Whitaker	.15	.07	.01
☐ 104	Steve Bedrosian	.15	.07	.01
☐ 105	Dave Gallagher	.15	.07	.01
☐ 106	Keith Hernandez	.15	.07	.01
☐ 107	Duane Ward	.12	.06	.01
☐ 108	Andre Dawson	.20	.10	.02
☐ 109	Howard Johnson	.15	.07	.01
☐ 110	Mark Langston	.15	.07	.01
☐ 111	Jerry Browne	.12	.06	.01
☐ 112	Alvin Davis	.15	.07	.01
☐ 113	Sid Fernandez	.15	.07	.01
☐ 114	Mike Devereaux	.12	.06	.01
☐ 115	Benito Santiago	.20	.10	.02
☐ 116	Bip Roberts	.15	.07	.01
☐ 117	Craig Worthington	.15	.07	.01
☐ 118	Kevin Elster	.12	.06	.01
☐ 119	Harold Reynolds	.12	.06	.01
☐ 120	Joe Carter	.20	.10	.02
☐ 121	Brian Harper	.12	.06	.01
☐ 122	Frank Viola	.15	.07	.01
☐ 123	Jeff Ballard	.12	.06	.01
☐ 124	John Kruk	.12	.06	.01
☐ 125	Harold Baines	.15	.07	.01
☐ 126	Tom Candiotti	.12	.06	.01
☐ 127	Kevin McReynolds	.15	.07	.01

☐ 128 Mookie Wilson	.12	.06	.01
☐ 129 Danny Tartabull	.15	.07	.01
☐ 130 Craig Lefferts	.12	.06	.01
☐ 131 Jose DeJesus	.12	.06	.01
☐ 132 John Orton	.20	.10	.02
☐ 133 Curt Schilling	.12	.06	.01
☐ 134 Marquis Grissom	.45	.22	.04
☐ 135 Greg Vaughn	.75	.35	.07
☐ 136 Brett Butler	.15	.07	.01
☐ 137 Rob Deer	.15	.07	.01
☐ 138 John Franco	.15	.07	.01
☐ 139 Keith Moreland	.12	.06	.01
☐ 140 Dave Smith	.12	.06	.01
☐ 141 Mark McGwire	.40	.20	.04
☐ 142 Vince Coleman	.20	.10	.02
☐ 143 Barry Bonds	.35	.17	.03
☐ 144 Mike Henneman	.12	.06	.01
☐ 145 Dwight Gooden	.30	.15	.03
☐ 146 Darryl Strawberry	.35	.17	.03
☐ 147 Von Hayes	.15	.07	.01
☐ 148 Andres Galarraga	.15	.07	.01
☐ 149 Roger Clemens	.40	.20	.04
☐ 150 Don Mattingly	.75	.35	.07
☐ 151 Joe Magrane	.15	.07	.01
☐ 152 Dwight Smith	.25	.12	.02
☐ 153 Ricky Jordan	.15	.07	.01
☐ 154 Alan Trammell	.15	.07	.01
☐ 155 Brook Jacoby	.15	.07	.01
☐ 156 Len Dykstra	.15	.07	.01
☐ 157 Mike LaValliere	.12	.06	.01
☐ 158 Julio Franco	.15	.07	.01
☐ 159 Joey Belle	.20	.10	.02
☐ 160 Barry Larkin	.25	.12	.02
☐ 161 Rick Reuschel	.15	.07	.01
☐ 162 Nelson Santovenia	.12	.06	.01
☐ 163 Mike Scioscia	.12	.06	.01
☐ 164 Damon Berryhill	.15	.07	.01
☐ 165 Todd Worrell	.15	.07	.01
☐ 166 Jim Eisenreich	.12	.06	.01
☐ 167 Ivan Calderon	.15	.07	.01
☐ 168 Mauro Gozzo	.15	.07	.01
☐ 169 Kirk McCaskill	.12	.06	.01
☐ 170 Dennis Eckersley	.20	.10	.02
☐ 171 Mickey Tettleton	.15	.07	.01
☐ 172 Chuck Finley	.15	.07	.01
☐ 173 Dave Magadan	.15	.07	.01
☐ 174 Terry Pendleton	.12	.06	.01
☐ 175 Willie Randolph	.15	.07	.01
☐ 176 Jeff Huson	.15	.07	.01
☐ 177 Todd Zeile	.90	.45	.09
☐ 178 Steve Olin	.15	.07	.01
☐ 179 Eric Anthony	.75	.35	.07
☐ 180 Scott Coolbaugh	.25	.12	.02
☐ 181 Rick Sutcliffe	.15	.07	.01
☐ 182 Tim Wallach	.15	.07	.01
☐ 183 Paul Molitor	.15	.07	.01
☐ 184 Roberto Kelly	.20	.10	.02
☐ 185 Mike Moore	.15	.07	.01
☐ 186 Junior Felix	.35	.17	.03
☐ 187 Mike Schooler	.15	.07	.01
☐ 188 Ruben Sierra	.25	.12	.02
☐ 189 Dale Murphy	.20	.10	.02
☐ 190 Dan Gladden	.12	.06	.01
☐ 191 John Smiley	.12	.06	.01
☐ 192 Jeff Russell	.12	.06	.01
☐ 193 Bert Blyleven	.15	.07	.01
☐ 194 Dave Stewart	.15	.07	.01
☐ 195 Bobby Bonilla	.25	.12	.02
☐ 196 Mitch Williams	.12	.06	.01
☐ 197 Orel Hershiser	.20	.10	.02
☐ 198 Kevin Bass	.12	.06	.01
☐ 199 Tim Burke	.12	.06	.01
☐ 200 Bo Jackson	1.25	.60	.12
☐ 201 David Cone	.15	.07	.01
☐ 202 Gary Pettis	.12	.06	.01
☐ 203 Kent Hrbek	.15	.07	.01
☐ 204 Carlton Fisk	.20	.10	.02
☐ 205 Bob Geren	.15	.07	.01
☐ 206 Bill Spiers	.15	.07	.01
☐ 207 Oddibe McDowell	.12	.06	.01
☐ 208 Rickey Henderson	.50	.25	.05
☐ 209 Ken Caminiti	.15	.07	.01
☐ 210 Devon White	.15	.07	.01
☐ 211 Greg Maddux	.15	.07	.01
☐ 212 Ed Whitson	.12	.06	.01
☐ 213 Carlos Martinez	.15	.07	.01
☐ 214 George Brett	.35	.17	.03
☐ 215 Gregg Olson	.40	.20	.04
☐ 216 Kenny Rogers	.15	.07	.01
☐ 217 Dwight Evans	.15	.07	.01
☐ 218 Pat Tabler	.12	.06	.01
☐ 219 Jeff Treadway	.12	.06	.01
☐ 220 Scott Fletcher	.12	.06	.01
☐ 221 Deion Sanders	.50	.25	.05
☐ 222 Robin Ventura	.40	.20	.04
☐ 223 Chip Hale	.15	.07	.01
☐ 224 Tommy Greene	.30	.15	.03
☐ 225 Dean Palmer	.25	.12	.02

1981 Squirt

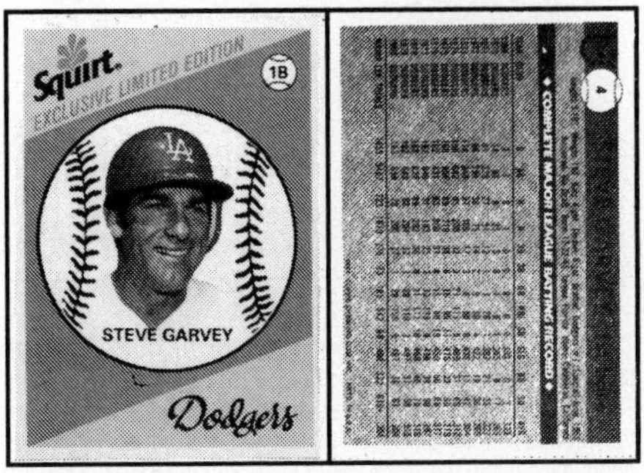

The cards in this 22-panel set consist of 33 different individual cards, each measuring 2 1/2" by 3 1/2" while the panels measure 2 1/2" by 10 1/2" as the 1981 Squirt cards were issued individually as well as in two card panels. Cards numbered 1-11 appear twice, whereas cards 12-33 appear only once in the 22-panel set. The pattern for pairings was 1/12 and 1/23, 2/13 and 2/24, 3/14 and 3/25, and so forth on up to 11/22 and 11/33. Two card panels have a value equal to the sum of the individual cards on the panel. Supposedly panels 4/15, 4/26, 5/27, and 6/28 are more difficult to find than the other panels and are marked as SP in the checklist below.

	MINT	EXC	G-VG
COMPLETE PANEL SET	22.50	10.00	2.00
COMPLETE IND. SET	11.00	5.00	1.00
COMMON PANEL	.40	.20	.04
COMMON PLAYER (1-11) DP	.20	.10	.02
COMMON PLAYER (12-33)	.20	.10	.02
☐ 1 George Brett DP	.60	.30	.06
☐ 2 George Foster DP	.20	.10	.02
☐ 3 Ben Oglivie DP	.20	.10	.02
☐ 4 Steve Garvey DP	.75	.35	.07
☐ 5 Reggie Jackson DP	.75	.35	.07
☐ 6 Bill Buckner DP	.20	.10	.02
☐ 7 Jim Rice DP	.25	.12	.02
☐ 8 Mike Schmidt DP	.90	.45	.09
☐ 9 Rod Carew DP	.60	.30	.06
☐ 10 Dave Parker DP	.30	.15	.03
☐ 11 Pete Rose DP	.90	.45	.09
☐ 12 Garry Templeton	.20	.10	.02
☐ 13 Rick Burleson	.20	.10	.02
☐ 14 Dave Kingman	.20	.10	.02
☐ 15 Eddie Murray SP	3.50	1.75	.35
☐ 16 Don Sutton	.60	.30	.06
☐ 17 Dusty Baker	.20	.10	.02
☐ 18 Jack Clark	.50	.25	.05
☐ 19 Dave Winfield	1.00	.50	.10
☐ 20 Johnny Bench	1.25	.60	.12
☐ 21 Lee Mazzilli	.20	.10	.02
☐ 22 Al Oliver	.20	.10	.02
☐ 23 Jerry Mumphrey	.20	.10	.02
☐ 24 Tony Armas	.20	.10	.02
☐ 25 Fred Lynn	.30	.15	.03
☐ 26 Ron LeFlore SP	1.00	.50	.10
☐ 27 Steve Kemp SP	1.00	.50	.10
☐ 28 Rickey Henderson SP	7.50	3.75	.75
☐ 29 John Castino	.20	.10	.02
☐ 30 Cecil Cooper	.20	.10	.02
☐ 31 Bruce Bochte	.20	.10	.02
☐ 32 Joe Charboneau	.20	.10	.02
☐ 33 Chet Lemon	.20	.10	.02

1982 Squirt

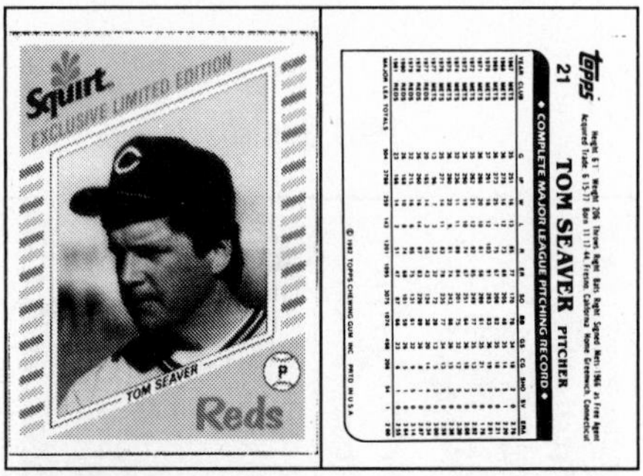

The cards in this 22-card set measure 2 1/2" by 3 1/2". Although the 1982 "Exclusive Limited Edition" was prepared for Squirt by Topps, the format and pictures are completely different from the regular Topps cards of this year. Each color picture is obliquely cut and the word Squirt is printed in red in the top left corner. The cards are numbered 1 through 22 and the reverses are yellow and black on white. The cards were issued on four types of panels: (1) yellow attachment card at top with picture card in center and scratch-off game at bottom; (2) yellow attachment card at top with scratch-off game in center and picture card at bottom; (3) white attachment card at top with "Collect all 22" panel in center and picture card at bottom; (4) two card panel with attachment card at top. The two card panels have parallel cards; that is, numbers 1 and 12 together, numbers 2 and 13 together, etc. Two card panels have a value equal to the sum of the individual cards on the panel. The two types (1 and 2) with the scratch-off games are more slightly difficult to obtain than the other two types and hence command prices double those below.

	MINT	EXC	G-VG
COMPLETE SET (22)	7.50	3.75	.75
COMMON PLAYER (1-22)	.20	.10	.02
☐ 1 Cecil Cooper	.20	.10	.02
☐ 2 Jerry Remy	.20	.10	.02
☐ 3 George Brett	.90	.45	.09
☐ 4 Alan Trammell	.40	.20	.04
☐ 5 Reggie Jackson	.90	.45	.09
☐ 6 Kirk Gibson	.45	.22	.04
☐ 7 Dave Winfield	.45	.22	.04
☐ 8 Carlton Fisk	.40	.20	.04
☐ 9 Ron Guidry	.20	.10	.02
☐ 10 Dennis Leonard	.20	.10	.02
☐ 11 Rollie Fingers	.30	.15	.03
☐ 12 Pete Rose	1.00	.50	.10
☐ 13 Phil Garner	.20	.10	.02
☐ 14 Mike Schmidt	1.00	.50	.10
☐ 15 Dave Concepcion	.20	.10	.02
☐ 16 George Hendrick	.20	.10	.02
☐ 17 Andre Dawson	.35	.17	.03
☐ 18 George Foster	.25	.12	.02
☐ 19 Gary Carter	.40	.20	.04
☐ 20 Fernando Valenzuela	.30	.15	.03
☐ 21 Tom Seaver	.75	.35	.07
☐ 22 Bruce Sutter	.25	.12	.02

1976 SSPC

The cards in this 630-card set measure 2 1/2" by 3 1/2". The 1976 "Pure Card" set issued by TCMA derives its name from the lack of borders, logos, signatures, etc., which often clutter up the picture areas of some baseball sets. It differs from other sets produced by this company in that it cannot be re-issued due to an agreement entered into by the manufacturer. Thus, while not technically a legitimate issue, it is significant because it cannot be reprinted, unlike other collector issues. There are no scarcities known. The cards are numbered in team groups, i.e., Atlanta (1-21), Cincinnati (22-46), Houston (47-65), Los Angeles (66-91), San Francisco (92-113), San Diego (114-133), Chicago White Sox (134-158), Kansas City (159-195), California (186-204), Minnesota (205-225), Milwaukee (226-251), Texas (252-273), St. Louis (274-300), Chicago Cubs (301-321), Montreal (322-351), Detroit (352-373), Baltimore (374-401), Boston (402-424), New York Yankees (425-455), Philadelphia (456-477), Oakland (478-503), Cleveland (504-532), New York Mets (533-560), and Pittsburgh (561-586). The rest of the numbers are filled in with checklists (589-595), miscellaneous players, and a heavy dose of coaches.

CINCINNATI REDS
10
Manager
5'9". 170 lbs.
Bn. 2/22/34
BR-TR
GEORGE LEE (SPARKY) ANDERSON
Prior to '75, Sparky had all kinds of success as Red's skipper - 3 divisional titles and 2 N.L. Championships in 5 seasons, but he'd never reached his goal of a World's Championship. Finally, last year, he guided Cincinnati to 108 wins, a sweep in the playoffs, and a 7-game Series victory over Boston. A second baseman in his playing days, he started in the Dodgers' chain in '53, and spent '59 as the Phillies' regular second sacker, finishing with a .218 average in his only big league season. Returned to the minors and became a skipper in '64, and won 4 titles before joining the Padres as a coach in '69. Joined Reds in '70.
CARD # 22
SSPC 1975
CINCINNATI

	NRMT	VG-E	GOOD
COMPLETE SET (630)	90.00	40.00	8.00
COMMON PLAYER (1-630)	.10	.05	.01
☐ 1 Buzz Capra	.10	.05	.01
☐ 2 Tom House	.15	.07	.01
☐ 3 Max Leon	.10	.05	.01
☐ 4 Carl Morton	.10	.05	.01
☐ 5 Phil Niekro	2.00	1.00	.20
☐ 6 Mike Thompson	.10	.05	.01
☐ 7 Elias Sosa	.10	.05	.01
☐ 8 Larvell Blanks	.10	.05	.01
☐ 9 Darrell Evans	.35	.17	.03
☐ 10 Rod Gilbreath	.10	.05	.01
☐ 11 Mike Lum	.10	.05	.01
☐ 12 Craig Robinson	.10	.05	.01
☐ 13 Earl Williams	.10	.05	.01
☐ 14 Vic Correll	.10	.05	.01
☐ 15 Biff Pocoroba	.10	.05	.01
☐ 16 Dusty Baker	.20	.10	.02
☐ 17 Ralph Garr	.15	.07	.01
☐ 18 Cito Gaston	.30	.15	.03
☐ 19 Dave May	.10	.05	.01
☐ 20 Rowland Office	.10	.05	.01
☐ 21 Bob Beall	.10	.05	.01
☐ 22 Sparky Anderson MG	.40	.20	.04
☐ 23 Jack Billingham	.10	.05	.01
☐ 24 Pedro Borbon	.10	.05	.01
☐ 25 Clay Carroll	.10	.05	.01
☐ 26 Pat Darcy	.10	.05	.01
☐ 27 Don Gullett	.15	.07	.01
☐ 28 Clay Kirby	.10	.05	.01
☐ 29 Gary Nolan	.10	.05	.01
☐ 30 Fred Norman	.10	.05	.01
☐ 31 Johnny Bench	6.50	3.25	.65
☐ 32 Bill Plummer	.10	.05	.01
☐ 33 Darrel Chaney	.10	.05	.01
☐ 34 Dave Concepcion	.25	.12	.02
☐ 35 Terry Crowley	.10	.05	.01
☐ 36 Dan Driessen	.15	.07	.01
☐ 37 Doug Flynn	.10	.05	.01
☐ 38 Joe Morgan	4.00	2.00	.40
☐ 39 Tony Perez	.90	.45	.09
☐ 40 Ken Griffey	.35	.17	.03
☐ 41 Pete Rose	10.00	5.00	1.00
☐ 42 Ed Armbrister	.10	.05	.01
☐ 43 John Vukovich	.10	.05	.01
☐ 44 George Foster	.90	.45	.09
☐ 45 Cesar Geronimo	.10	.05	.01

☐ 46 Merv Rettenmund	.10	.05	.01
☐ 47 Jim Crawford	.10	.05	.01
☐ 48 Ken Forsch	.10	.05	.01
☐ 49 Doug Konieczny	.10	.05	.01
☐ 50 Joe Niekro	.30	.15	.03
☐ 51 Cliff Johnson	.10	.05	.01
☐ 52 Skip Jutze	.10	.05	.01
☐ 53 Milt May	.10	.05	.01
☐ 54 Rob Andrews	.10	.05	.01
☐ 55 Ken Boswell	.10	.05	.01
☐ 56 Tommy Helms	.15	.07	.01
☐ 57 Roger Metzger	.10	.05	.01
☐ 58 Larry Milbourne	.10	.05	.01
☐ 59 Doug Rader	.20	.10	.02
☐ 60 Bob Watson	.20	.10	.02
☐ 61 Enos Cabell	.10	.05	.01
☐ 62 Jose Cruz	.30	.15	.03
☐ 63 Cesar Cedeno	.20	.10	.02
☐ 64 Greg Gross	.10	.05	.01
☐ 65 Wilbur Howard	.10	.05	.01
☐ 66 Al Downing	.10	.05	.01
☐ 67 Burt Hooton	.10	.05	.01
☐ 68 Charlie Hough	.20	.10	.02
☐ 69 Tommy John	.75	.35	.07
☐ 70 Andy Messersmith	.15	.07	.01
☐ 71 Doug Rau	.10	.05	.01
☐ 72 Rick Rhoden	.15	.07	.01
☐ 73 Don Sutton	1.25	.60	.12
☐ 74 Rick Auerbach	.10	.05	.01
☐ 75 Ron Cey	.40	.20	.04
☐ 76 Ivan DeJesus	.10	.05	.01
☐ 77 Steve Garvey	4.00	2.00	.40
☐ 78 Lee Lacy	.10	.05	.01
☐ 79 Dave Lopes	.20	.10	.02
☐ 80 Ken McMullen	.10	.05	.01
☐ 81 Joe Ferguson	.10	.05	.01
☐ 82 Paul Powell	.10	.05	.01
☐ 83 Steve Yeager	.10	.05	.01
☐ 84 Willie Crawford	.10	.05	.01
☐ 85 Henry Cruz	.10	.05	.01
☐ 86 Charlie Manuel	.10	.05	.01
☐ 87 Manny Mota	.15	.07	.01
☐ 88 Tom Paciorek	.10	.05	.01
☐ 89 Jim Wynn	.15	.07	.01
☐ 90 Walt Alston MG	.75	.35	.07
☐ 91 Bill Buckner	.40	.20	.04
☐ 92 Jim Barr	.10	.05	.01
☐ 93 Mike Caldwell	.15	.07	.01
☐ 94 John D'Acquisto	.10	.05	.01
☐ 95 Dave Heaverlo	.10	.05	.01
☐ 96 Gary Lavelle	.10	.05	.01
☐ 97 John Montefusco	.15	.07	.01
☐ 98 Charlie Williams	.10	.05	.01
☐ 99 Chris Arnold	.10	.05	.01
☐ 100 Marc Hill	.10	.05	.01
☐ 101 Dave Rader	.10	.05	.01
☐ 102 Bruce Miller	.10	.05	.01
☐ 103 Willie Montanez	.10	.05	.01
☐ 104 Steve Ontiveros	.10	.05	.01
☐ 105 Chris Speier	.10	.05	.01
☐ 106 Derrel Thomas	.10	.05	.01
☐ 107 Gary Thomasson	.10	.05	.01
☐ 108 Glenn Adams	.10	.05	.01
☐ 109 Von Joshua	.10	.05	.01
☐ 110 Gary Matthews	.20	.10	.02
☐ 111 Bobby Murcer	.40	.20	.04
☐ 112 Horace Speed	.10	.05	.01
☐ 113 Wes Westrum MG	.10	.05	.01
☐ 114 Rich Folkers	.10	.05	.01
☐ 115 Alan Foster	.10	.05	.01
☐ 116 Dave Freisleben	.10	.05	.01
☐ 117 Dan Frisella	.10	.05	.01
☐ 118 Randy Jones	.15	.07	.01
☐ 119 Dan Spillner	.10	.05	.01
☐ 120 Larry Hardy	.10	.05	.01
☐ 121 Randy Hundley	.10	.05	.01
☐ 122 Fred Kendall	.10	.05	.01
☐ 123 John McNamara MG	.15	.07	.01
☐ 124 Tito Fuentes	.10	.05	.01
☐ 125 Enzo Hernandez	.10	.05	.01
☐ 126 Steve Huntz	.10	.05	.01
☐ 127 Mike Ivie	.10	.05	.01
☐ 128 Hector Torres	.10	.05	.01
☐ 129 Ted Kubiak	.10	.05	.01
☐ 130 John Grubb	.10	.05	.01
☐ 131 John Scott	.10	.05	.01
☐ 132 Bob Tolan	.10	.05	.01
☐ 133 Dave Winfield	4.00	2.00	.40
☐ 134 Bill Gogolewski	.10	.05	.01
☐ 135 Dan Osborn	.10	.05	.01
☐ 136 Jim Kaat	.60	.30	.06
☐ 137 Claude Osteen	.15	.07	.01
☐ 138 Cecil Upshaw	.10	.05	.01
☐ 139 Wilbur Wood	.15	.07	.01
☐ 140 Lloyd Allen	.10	.05	.01
☐ 141 Brian Downing	.25	.12	.02
☐ 142 Jim Essian	.10	.05	.01
☐ 143 Bucky Dent	.40	.20	.04
☐ 144 Jorge Orta	.10	.05	.01
☐ 145 Lee Richard	.10	.05	.01
☐ 146 Bill Stein	.10	.05	.01
☐ 147 Ken Henderson	.10	.05	.01
☐ 148 Carlos May	.10	.05	.01
☐ 149 Nyls Nyman	.10	.05	.01
☐ 150 Bob Coluccio	.10	.05	.01
☐ 151 Chuck Tanner MG	.15	.07	.01
☐ 152 Pat Kelly	.10	.05	.01
☐ 153 Jerry Hairston	.10	.05	.01
☐ 154 Pete Varney	.10	.05	.01
☐ 155 Bill Melton	.10	.05	.01
☐ 156 Rich Gossage	.90	.45	.09
☐ 157 Terry Forster	.15	.07	.01
☐ 158 Rich Hinton	.10	.05	.01
☐ 159 Nelson Briles	.10	.05	.01
☐ 160 Al Fitzmorris	.10	.05	.01
☐ 161 Steve Mingori	.10	.05	.01
☐ 162 Marty Pattin	.10	.05	.01
☐ 163 Paul Splittorff	.15	.07	.01
☐ 164 Dennis Leonard	.20	.10	.02
☐ 165 Buck Martinez	.10	.05	.01
☐ 166 Bob Stinson	.10	.05	.01
☐ 167 George Brett	12.00	6.00	1.20
☐ 168 Harmon Killebrew	2.50	1.25	.25
☐ 169 John Mayberry	.15	.07	.01
☐ 170 Fred Patek	.10	.05	.01
☐ 171 Cookie Rojas	.10	.05	.01
☐ 172 Rodney Scott	.10	.05	.01
☐ 173 Tony Solaita	.10	.05	.01
☐ 174 Frank White	.25	.12	.02
☐ 175 Al Cowens	.10	.05	.01
☐ 176 Hal McRae	.20	.10	.02
☐ 177 Amos Otis	.25	.12	.02
☐ 178 Vada Pinson	.35	.17	.03
☐ 179 Jim Wohlford	.10	.05	.01
☐ 180 Doug Bird	.10	.05	.01
☐ 181 Mark Littell	.10	.05	.01
☐ 182 Bob McClure	.10	.05	.01
☐ 183 Steve Busby	.15	.07	.01
☐ 184 Fran Healy	.10	.05	.01
☐ 185 Whitey Herzog MG	.25	.12	.02
☐ 186 Andy Hassler	.10	.05	.01
☐ 187 Nolan Ryan	12.00	6.00	1.20
☐ 188 Bill Singer	.10	.05	.01
☐ 189 Frank Tanana	.15	.07	.01
☐ 190 Ed Figueroa	.10	.05	.01
☐ 191 Dave Collins	.15	.07	.01
☐ 192 Dick Williams MG	.15	.07	.01
☐ 193 Ellie Rodriguez	.10	.05	.01
☐ 194 Dave Chalk	.10	.05	.01
☐ 195 Winston Llenas	.10	.05	.01
☐ 196 Rudy Meoli	.10	.05	.01
☐ 197 Orlando Ramirez	.10	.05	.01
☐ 198 Jerry Remy	.10	.05	.01
☐ 199 Billy Smith	.10	.05	.01
☐ 200 Bruce Bochte	.10	.05	.01
☐ 201 Joe Lahoud	.10	.05	.01
☐ 202 Morris Nettles	.10	.05	.01
☐ 203 Mickey Rivers	.15	.07	.01
☐ 204 Leroy Stanton	.10	.05	.01
☐ 205 Vic Albury	.10	.05	.01
☐ 206 Tom Burgmeier	.10	.05	.01
☐ 207 Bill Butler	.10	.05	.01
☐ 208 Bill Campbell	.10	.05	.01
☐ 209 Ray Corbin	.10	.05	.01
☐ 210 Joe Decker	.10	.05	.01
☐ 211 Jim Hughes	.10	.05	.01
☐ 212 Ed Bane UER (photo actually Mike Pazik)	.10	.05	.01
☐ 213 Glenn Borgmann	.10	.05	.01
☐ 214 Rod Carew	6.00	3.00	.60
☐ 215 Steve Brye	.10	.05	.01
☐ 216 Dan Ford	.10	.05	.01
☐ 217 Tony Oliva	.90	.45	.09
☐ 218 Dave Goltz	.10	.05	.01
☐ 219 Bert Blyleven	.75	.35	.07
☐ 220 Larry Hisle	.10	.05	.01
☐ 221 Steve Braun	.10	.05	.01
☐ 222 Jerry Terrell	.10	.05	.01
☐ 223 Eric Soderholm	.10	.05	.01
☐ 224 Phil Roof	.10	.05	.01
☐ 225 Danny Thompson	.10	.05	.01
☐ 226 Jim Colborn	.10	.05	.01
☐ 227 Tom Murphy	.10	.05	.01
☐ 228 Ed Rodriquez	.10	.05	.01
☐ 229 Jim Slaton	.10	.05	.01
☐ 230 Ed Sprague	.10	.05	.01
☐ 231 Charlie Moore	.10	.05	.01

☐ 232	Darrell Porter	.10	.05	.01
☐ 233	Kurt Bevacqua	.10	.05	.01
☐ 234	Pedro Garcia	.10	.05	.01
☐ 235	Mike Hegan	.10	.05	.01
☐ 236	Don Money	.10	.05	.01
☐ 237	George Scott	.15	.07	.01
☐ 238	Robin Yount	12.00	6.00	1.20
☐ 239	Hank Aaron	8.00	4.00	.80
☐ 240	Rob Ellis	.10	.05	.01
☐ 241	Sixto Lezcano	.10	.05	.01
☐ 242	Bob Mitchell	.10	.05	.01
☐ 243	Gorman Thomas	.25	.12	.02
☐ 244	Bill Travers	.10	.05	.01
☐ 245	Pete Broberg	.10	.05	.01
☐ 246	Bill Sharp	.10	.05	.01
☐ 247	Bobby Darwin	.10	.05	.01
☐ 248	Rick Austin UER (photo actually Larry Anderson)	.10	.05	.01
☐ 249	Larry Anderson UER (photo actually Rick Austin)	.10	.05	.01
☐ 250	Tom Bianco	.10	.05	.01
☐ 251	Lafayette Currence	.10	.05	.01
☐ 252	Steve Foucault	.10	.05	.01
☐ 253	Bill Hands	.10	.05	.01
☐ 254	Steve Hargan	.10	.05	.01
☐ 255	Fergie Jenkins	2.50	1.25	.25
☐ 256	Bob Sheldon	.10	.05	.01
☐ 257	Jim Umbarger	.10	.05	.01
☐ 258	Clyde Wright	.10	.05	.01
☐ 259	Bill Fahey	.10	.05	.01
☐ 260	Jim Sundberg	.15	.07	.01
☐ 261	Leo Cardenas	.10	.05	.01
☐ 262	Jim Fregosi	.20	.10	.02
☐ 263	Mike Hargrove	.15	.07	.01
☐ 264	Toby Harrah	.15	.07	.01
☐ 265	Roy Howell	.10	.05	.01
☐ 266	Lenny Randle	.10	.05	.01
☐ 267	Roy Smalley	.15	.07	.01
☐ 268	Jim Spencer	.10	.05	.01
☐ 269	Jeff Burroughs	.15	.07	.01
☐ 270	Tom Grieve	.20	.10	.02
☐ 271	Joe Lovitto	.10	.05	.01
☐ 272	Frank Lucchesi MG	.10	.05	.01
☐ 273	Dave Nelson	.10	.05	.01
☐ 274	Ted Simmons	.60	.30	.06
☐ 275	Lou Brock	3.50	1.75	.35
☐ 276	Ron Fairly	.10	.05	.01
☐ 277	Bake McBride	.10	.05	.01
☐ 278	Reggie Smith	.25	.12	.02
☐ 279	Willie Davis	.15	.07	.01
☐ 280	Ken Reitz	.10	.05	.01
☐ 281	Buddy Bradford	.10	.05	.01
☐ 282	Luis Melendez	.10	.05	.01
☐ 283	Mike Tyson	.10	.05	.01
☐ 284	Ted Sizemore	.10	.05	.01
☐ 285	Mario Guerrero	.10	.05	.01
☐ 286	Larry Lintz	.10	.05	.01
☐ 287	Ken Rudolph	.10	.05	.01
☐ 288	Dick Billings	.10	.05	.01
☐ 289	Jerry Mumphrey	.10	.05	.01
☐ 290	Mike Wallace	.10	.05	.01
☐ 291	Al Hrabosky	.15	.07	.01
☐ 292	Ken Reynolds	.10	.05	.01
☐ 293	Mike Garman	.10	.05	.01
☐ 294	Bob Forsch	.15	.07	.01
☐ 295	John Denny	.20	.10	.02
☐ 296	Harry Rasmussen	.10	.05	.01
☐ 297	Lynn McGlothen	.10	.05	.01
☐ 298	Mike Barlow	.10	.05	.01
☐ 299	Greg Terlecky	.10	.05	.01
☐ 300	Red Schoendienst MG	.60	.30	.06
☐ 301	Rick Reuschel	.40	.20	.04
☐ 302	Steve Stone	.20	.10	.02
☐ 303	Bill Bonham	.10	.05	.01
☐ 304	Oscar Zamora	.10	.05	.01
☐ 305	Ken Frailing	.10	.05	.01
☐ 306	Milt Wilcox	.10	.05	.01
☐ 307	Darold Knowles	.10	.05	.01
☐ 308	Jim Marshall	.10	.05	.01
☐ 309	Bill Madlock	.75	.35	.07
☐ 310	Jose Cardenal	.10	.05	.01
☐ 311	Rick Monday	.15	.07	.01
☐ 312	Jerry Morales	.10	.05	.01
☐ 313	Tim Hosley	.10	.05	.01
☐ 314	Gene Hiser	.10	.05	.01
☐ 315	Don Kessinger	.20	.10	.02
☐ 316	Manny Trillo	.10	.05	.01
☐ 317	Pete LaCock	.10	.05	.01
☐ 318	George Mitterwald	.10	.05	.01
☐ 319	Steve Swisher	.10	.05	.01
☐ 320	Rob Sperring	.10	.05	.01
☐ 321	Vic Harris	.10	.05	.01
☐ 322	Ron Dunn	.10	.05	.01
☐ 323	Jose Morales	.10	.05	.01
☐ 324	Pete Mackanin	.10	.05	.01
☐ 325	Jim Cox	.10	.05	.01
☐ 326	Larry Parrish	.30	.15	.03
☐ 327	Mike Jorgensen	.10	.05	.01
☐ 328	Tim Foli	.10	.05	.01
☐ 329	Hal Breeden	.10	.05	.01
☐ 330	Nate Colbert	.10	.05	.01
☐ 331	Pepe Frias	.10	.05	.01
☐ 332	Pat Scanlon	.10	.05	.01
☐ 333	Bob Bailey	.10	.05	.01
☐ 334	Gary Carter	4.00	2.00	.40
☐ 335	Pepe Mangual	.10	.05	.01
☐ 336	Larry Biittner	.10	.05	.01
☐ 337	Jim Lyttle	.10	.05	.01
☐ 338	Gary Roenicke	.10	.05	.01
☐ 339	Tony Scott	.10	.05	.01
☐ 340	Jerry White	.10	.05	.01
☐ 341	Jim Dwyer	.10	.05	.01
☐ 342	Ellis Valentine	.10	.05	.01
☐ 343	Fred Scherman	.10	.05	.01
☐ 344	Dennis Blair	.10	.05	.01
☐ 345	Woodie Fryman	.10	.05	.01
☐ 346	Chuck Taylor	.10	.05	.01
☐ 347	Dan Warthen	.10	.05	.01
☐ 348	Dan Carrithers	.10	.05	.01
☐ 349	Steve Rogers	.15	.07	.01
☐ 350	Dale Murray	.10	.05	.01
☐ 351	Duke Snider CO	2.50	1.25	.25
☐ 352	Ralph Houk MG	.20	.10	.02
☐ 353	John Hiller	.15	.07	.01
☐ 354	Mickey Lolich	.35	.17	.03
☐ 355	Dave Lemancyzk	.10	.05	.01
☐ 356	Lerrin LaGrow	.10	.05	.01
☐ 357	Fred Arroyo	.10	.05	.01
☐ 358	Joe Coleman	.10	.05	.01
☐ 359	Ben Oglivie	.20	.10	.02
☐ 360	Willie Horton	.15	.07	.01
☐ 361	John Knox	.10	.05	.01
☐ 362	Leon Roberts	.10	.05	.01
☐ 363	Ron LeFlore	.15	.07	.01
☐ 364	Gary Sutherland	.10	.05	.01
☐ 365	Dan Meyer	.10	.05	.01
☐ 366	Aurelio Rodriguez	.10	.05	.01
☐ 367	Tom Veryzer	.10	.05	.01
☐ 368	Jack Pierce	.10	.05	.01
☐ 369	Gene Michael	.15	.07	.01
☐ 370	Billy Baldwin	.10	.05	.01
☐ 371	Gates Brown	.15	.07	.01
☐ 372	Mickey Stanley	.15	.07	.01
☐ 373	Terry Humphrey	.10	.05	.01
☐ 374	Doyle Alexander	.20	.10	.02
☐ 375	Mike Cuellar	.15	.07	.01
☐ 376	Wayne Garland	.10	.05	.01
☐ 377	Ross Grimsley	.10	.05	.01
☐ 378	Grant Jackson	.10	.05	.01
☐ 379	Dyar Miller	.10	.05	.01
☐ 380	Jim Palmer	4.00	2.00	.40
☐ 381	Mike Torrez	.10	.05	.01
☐ 382	Mike Willis	.10	.05	.01
☐ 383	Dave Duncan	.10	.05	.01
☐ 384	Ellie Hendricks	.10	.05	.01
☐ 385	Jim Hutto	.10	.05	.01
☐ 386	Bob Bailor	.10	.05	.01
☐ 387	Doug DeCinces	.30	.15	.03
☐ 388	Bob Grich	.25	.12	.02
☐ 389	Lee May	.20	.10	.02
☐ 390	Tony Muser	.10	.05	.01
☐ 391	Tim Nordbrook	.10	.05	.01
☐ 392	Brooks Robinson	4.00	2.00	.40
☐ 393	Royle Stillman	.10	.05	.01
☐ 394	Don Baylor	.35	.17	.03
☐ 395	Paul Blair	.15	.07	.01
☐ 396	Al Bumbry	.10	.05	.01
☐ 397	Larry Harlow	.10	.05	.01
☐ 398	Tommy Davis	.15	.07	.01
☐ 399	Jim Northrup	.15	.07	.01
☐ 400	Ken Singleton	.25	.12	.02
☐ 401	Tom Shopay	.10	.05	.01
☐ 402	Fred Lynn	.90	.45	.09
☐ 403	Carlton Fisk	2.50	1.25	.25
☐ 404	Cecil Cooper	.50	.25	.05
☐ 405	Jim Rice	3.00	1.50	.30
☐ 406	Juan Beniquez	.15	.07	.01
☐ 407	Denny Doyle	.10	.05	.01
☐ 408	Dwight Evans	1.00	.50	.10
☐ 409	Carl Yastrzemski	8.00	4.00	.80
☐ 410	Rick Burleson	.15	.07	.01
☐ 411	Bernie Carbo	.10	.05	.01
☐ 412	Doug Griffin	.10	.05	.01
☐ 413	Rico Petrocelli	.15	.07	.01
☐ 414	Bob Montgomery	.10	.05	.01
☐ 415	Tim Blackwell	.10	.05	.01

☐	416 Rick Miller	.10	.05	.01
☐	417 Darrell Johnson MG	.10	.05	.01
☐	418 Jim Burton	.10	.05	.01
☐	419 Jim Willoughby	.10	.05	.01
☐	420 Rogelio Moret	.10	.05	.01
☐	421 Bill Lee	.15	.07	.01
☐	422 Dick Drago	.10	.05	.01
☐	423 Diego Segui	.10	.05	.01
☐	424 Luis Tiant	.30	.15	.03
☐	425 Jim Hunter	2.50	1.25	.25
☐	426 Rick Sawyer	.10	.05	.01
☐	427 Rudy May	.10	.05	.01
☐	428 Dick Tidrow	.10	.05	.01
☐	429 Sparky Lyle	.35	.17	.03
☐	430 Doc Medich	.10	.05	.01
☐	431 Pat Dobson	.15	.07	.01
☐	432 Dave Pagan	.10	.05	.01
☐	433 Thurman Munson	4.00	2.00	.40
☐	434 Chris Chambliss	.20	.10	.02
☐	435 Roy White	.15	.07	.01
☐	436 Walt Williams	.10	.05	.01
☐	437 Graig Nettles	.75	.35	.07
☐	438 Rick Dempsey	.15	.07	.01
☐	439 Bobby Bonds	.45	.22	.04
☐	440 Ed Herrmann	.10	.05	.01
☐	441 Sandy Alomar	.10	.05	.01
☐	442 Fred Stanley	.10	.05	.01
☐	443 Terry Whitfield	.10	.05	.01
☐	444 Rich Bladt	.10	.05	.01
☐	445 Lou Piniella	.50	.25	.05
☐	446 Rich Coggins	.10	.05	.01
☐	447 Ed Brinkman	.10	.05	.01
☐	448 Jim Mason	.10	.05	.01
☐	449 Larry Murray	.10	.05	.01
☐	450 Ron Blomberg	.10	.05	.01
☐	451 Elliott Maddox	.10	.05	.01
☐	452 Kerry Dineen	.10	.05	.01
☐	453 Billy Martin MG	1.00	.50	.10
☐	454 Dave Bergman	.10	.05	.01
☐	455 Otto Velez	.10	.05	.01
☐	456 Joe Hoerner	.10	.05	.01
☐	457 Tug McGraw	.40	.20	.04
☐	458 Gene Garber	.15	.07	.01
☐	459 Steve Carlton	3.50	1.75	.35
☐	460 Larry Christenson	.10	.05	.01
☐	461 Tom Underwood	.10	.05	.01
☐	462 Jim Lonborg	.15	.07	.01
☐	463 Jay Johnstone	.15	.07	.01
☐	464 Larry Bowa	.35	.17	.03
☐	465 Dave Cash	.10	.05	.01
☐	466 Ollie Brown	.10	.05	.01
☐	467 Greg Luzinski	.25	.12	.02
☐	468 Johnny Oates	.10	.05	.01
☐	469 Mike Anderson	.10	.05	.01
☐	470 Mike Schmidt	12.00	6.00	1.20
☐	471 Bob Boone	.50	.25	.05
☐	472 Tom Hutton	.10	.05	.01
☐	473 Rich Allen	.40	.20	.04
☐	474 Tony Taylor	.10	.05	.01
☐	475 Jerry Martin	.10	.05	.01
☐	476 Danny Ozark MG	.10	.05	.01
☐	477 Dick Ruthven	.10	.05	.01
☐	478 Jim Todd	.10	.05	.01
☐	479 Paul Lindblad	.10	.05	.01
☐	480 Rollie Fingers	1.50	.75	.15
☐	481 Vida Blue	.25	.12	.02
☐	482 Ken Holtzman	.15	.07	.01
☐	483 Dick Bosman	.10	.05	.01
☐	484 Sonny Siebert	.10	.05	.01
☐	485 Glenn Abbott	.10	.05	.01
☐	486 Stan Bahnsen	.10	.05	.01
☐	487 Mike Norris	.15	.07	.01
☐	488 Alvin Dark MG	.10	.05	.01
☐	489 Claudell Washington	.20	.10	.02
☐	490 Joe Rudi	.15	.07	.01
☐	491 Bill North	.10	.05	.01
☐	492 Bert Campaneris	.15	.07	.01
☐	493 Gene Tenace	.15	.07	.01
☐	494 Reggie Jackson	9.00	4.50	.90
☐	495 Phil Garner	.15	.07	.01
☐	496 Billy Williams	2.50	1.25	.25
☐	497 Sal Bando	.20	.10	.02
☐	498 Jim Holt	.10	.05	.01
☐	499 Ted Martinez	.10	.05	.01
☐	500 Ray Fosse	.10	.05	.01
☐	501 Matt Alexander	.10	.05	.01
☐	502 Larry Haney	.10	.05	.01
☐	503 Angel Mangual	.10	.05	.01
☐	504 Fred Beene	.10	.05	.01
☐	505 Tom Buskey	.10	.05	.01
☐	506 Dennis Eckersley	5.00	2.50	.50
☐	507 Roric Harrison	.10	.05	.01
☐	508 Don Hood	.10	.05	.01
☐	509 Jim Kern	.10	.05	.01

☐	510 Dave LaRoche	.10	.05	.01
☐	511 Fritz Peterson	.10	.05	.01
☐	512 Jim Strickland	.10	.05	.01
☐	513 Rick Waits	.10	.05	.01
☐	514 Alan Ashby	.10	.05	.01
☐	515 John Ellis	.10	.05	.01
☐	516 Rick Cerone	.10	.05	.01
☐	517 Buddy Bell	.40	.20	.04
☐	518 Jack Brohamer	.10	.05	.01
☐	519 Rico Carty	.15	.07	.01
☐	520 Ed Crosby	.10	.05	.01
☐	521 Frank Duffy	.10	.05	.01
☐	522 Duane Kuiper UER (photo actually Rick Manning)	.10	.05	.01
☐	523 Joe Lis	.10	.05	.01
☐	524 Boog Powell	.60	.30	.06
☐	525 Frank Robinson	3.00	1.50	.30
☐	526 Oscar Gamble	.15	.07	.01
☐	527 George Hendrick	.15	.07	.01
☐	528 John Lowenstein	.10	.05	.01
☐	529 Rick Manning UER (photo actually Duane Kuiper)	.10	.05	.01
☐	530 Tommy Smith	.10	.05	.01
☐	531 Charlie Spikes	.10	.05	.01
☐	532 Steve Kline	.10	.05	.01
☐	533 Ed Kranepool	.15	.07	.01
☐	534 Mike Vail	.10	.05	.01
☐	535 Del Unser	.10	.05	.01
☐	536 Felix Millan	.10	.05	.01
☐	537 Rusty Staub	.35	.17	.03
☐	538 Jesus Alou	.10	.05	.01
☐	539 Wayne Garrett	.10	.05	.01
☐	540 Mike Phillips	.10	.05	.01
☐	541 Joe Torre	.50	.25	.05
☐	542 Dave Kingman	.70	.35	.07
☐	543 Gene Clines	.10	.05	.01
☐	544 Jack Heidemann	.10	.05	.01
☐	545 Bud Harrelson	.20	.10	.02
☐	546 John Stearns	.15	.07	.01
☐	547 John Milner	.10	.05	.01
☐	548 Bob Apodaca	.10	.05	.01
☐	549 Skip Lockwood	.10	.05	.01
☐	550 Ken Sanders	.10	.05	.01
☐	551 Tom Seaver	5.00	2.50	.50
☐	552 Rick Baldwin	.10	.05	.01
☐	553 Hank Webb	.10	.05	.01
☐	554 Jon Matlack	.15	.07	.01
☐	555 Randy Tate	.10	.05	.01
☐	556 Tom Hall	.10	.05	.01
☐	557 George Stone	.10	.05	.01
☐	558 Craig Swan	.15	.07	.01
☐	559 Jerry Cram	.10	.05	.01
☐	560 Roy Staiger	.10	.05	.01
☐	561 Kent Tekulve	.20	.10	.02
☐	562 Jerry Reuss	.15	.07	.01
☐	563 John Candelaria	.25	.12	.02
☐	564 Larry Demery	.10	.05	.01
☐	565 Dave Giusti	.15	.07	.01
☐	566 Jim Rooker	.10	.05	.01
☐	567 Ramon Hernandez	.10	.05	.01
☐	568 Bruce Kison	.10	.05	.01
☐	569 Ken Brett	.10	.05	.01
☐	570 Bob Moose	.15	.07	.01
☐	571 Manny Sanguillen	.20	.10	.02
☐	572 Dave Parker	2.50	1.25	.25
☐	573 Willie Stargell	3.50	1.75	.35
☐	574 Richie Zisk	.15	.07	.01
☐	575 Rennie Stennett	.10	.05	.01
☐	576 Al Oliver	.70	.35	.07
☐	577 Bill Robinson	.25	.12	.02
☐	578 Bob Robertson	.10	.05	.01
☐	579 Rich Hebner	.10	.05	.01
☐	580 Ed Kirkpatrick	.10	.05	.01
☐	581 Duffy Dyer	.10	.05	.01
☐	582 Craig Reynolds	.10	.05	.01
☐	583 Frank Taveras	.10	.05	.01
☐	584 Willie Randolph	1.00	.50	.10
☐	585 Art Howe	.25	.12	.02
☐	586 Danny Murtaugh MG	.10	.05	.01
☐	587 Rick McKinney	.10	.05	.01
☐	588 Ed Goodson	.10	.05	.01
☐	589 Checklist 1 George Brett Al Cowens	1.25	.60	.12
☐	590 Checklist 2 Keith Hernandez Lou Brock	1.00	.50	.10
☐	591 Checklist 3 Jerry Koosman Duke Snider	.60	.30	.06

		NRMT	VG-E	GOOD
☐ 592	Checklist 4 Maury Wills John Knox	.25	.12	.02
☐ 593A	Checklist 5 ERR Jim Hunter Nolan Ryan (Noland on front)	100.00	50.00	10.00
☐ 593B	Checklist 5 COR Jim Hunter Nolan Ryan	5.00	2.50	.50
☐ 594	Checklist 6 Ralph Branca Carl Erskine Pee Wee Reese	.30	.15	.03
☐ 595	Checklist 7 Willie Mays Herb Score	.75	.35	.07
☐ 596	Larry Cox	.10	.05	.01
☐ 597	Gene Mauch MG	.15	.07	.01
☐ 598	Whitey Wietelmann CO	.10	.05	.01
☐ 599	Wayne Simpson	.10	.05	.01
☐ 600	Mel Thomason	.10	.05	.01
☐ 601	Ike Hampton	.10	.05	.01
☐ 602	Ken Crosby	.10	.05	.01
☐ 603	Ralph Rowe	.10	.05	.01
☐ 604	Jim Tyrone	.10	.05	.01
☐ 605	Mick Kelleher	.10	.05	.01
☐ 606	Mario Mendoza	.10	.05	.01
☐ 607	Mike Rogodzinski	.10	.05	.01
☐ 608	Bob Gallagher	.10	.05	.01
☐ 609	Jerry Koosman	.20	.10	.02
☐ 610	Joe Frazier MG	.10	.05	.01
☐ 611	Karl Kuehl MG	.10	.05	.01
☐ 612	Frank LaCorte	.10	.05	.01
☐ 613	Ray Bare	.10	.05	.01
☐ 614	Billy Muffett CO	.10	.05	.01
☐ 615	Bill Laxton	.10	.05	.01
☐ 616	Willie Mays CO	6.00	3.00	.60
☐ 617	Phil Cavarretta CO	.15	.07	.01
☐ 618	Ted Kluszewski CO	.35	.17	.03
☐ 619	Elston Howard CO	.35	.17	.03
☐ 620	Alex Grammas CO	.10	.05	.01
☐ 621	Mickey Vernon CO	.15	.07	.01
☐ 622	Dick Sisler CO	.10	.05	.01
☐ 623	Harvey Haddix CO	.15	.07	.01
☐ 624	Bobby Winkles CO	.10	.05	.01
☐ 625	John Pesky CO	.10	.05	.01
☐ 626	Jim Davenport CO	.15	.07	.01
☐ 627	Dave Tomlin	.10	.05	.01
☐ 628	Roger Craig CO	.35	.17	.03
☐ 629	Joe Amalfitano CO	.10	.05	.01
☐ 630	Jim Reese CO	.15	.07	.01

1953 Stahl Meyer

The cards in this 9-card set measure approximately 3 1/4" by 4 1/2". The 1953 Stahl Meyer set of full color, unnumbered cards includes three players from each of the three New York teams. The cards have white borders. The Lockman card is the most plentiful of any card in the set. Some batting and fielding statistics and short biography are included on the back. The cards are ordered in the checklist below by alphabetical order without regard to team affiliation.

	NRMT	VG-E	GOOD
COMPLETE SET	3500.00	1500.00	375.00
COMMON PLAYER (1-9)	125.00	60.00	12.50
☐ 1 Hank Bauer	150.00	75.00	15.00
☐ 2 Roy Campanella	600.00	300.00	60.00
☐ 3 Gil Hodges	300.00	150.00	30.00
☐ 4 Monte Irvin	200.00	100.00	20.00
☐ 5 Whitey Lockman	125.00	60.00	12.50
☐ 6 Mickey Mantle	2000.00	800.00	200.00
☐ 7 Phil Rizzuto	300.00	150.00	30.00
☐ 8 Duke Snider	600.00	300.00	60.00
☐ 9 Bobby Thomson	150.00	75.00	15.00

1954 Stahl Meyer

The cards in this 12-card set measure approximately 3 1/4" by 4 1/2". The 1954 Stahl Meyer set of full color, unnumbered cards includes four players from each of the three New York teams. The cards have yellow borders and the backs, oriented horizontally, include an ad for a baseball kit and the player's statistics. No player biography is included on the back. The cards are ordered in the checklist below by alphabetical order without regard to team affiliation.

	NRMT	VG-E	GOOD
COMPLETE SET	5400.00	2500.00	600.00
COMMON PLAYER (1-12)	150.00	75.00	15.00
☐ 1 Hank Bauer	175.00	85.00	18.00
☐ 2 Carl Erskine	175.00	85.00	18.00
☐ 3 Gil Hodges	300.00	150.00	30.00
☐ 4 Monte Irvin	250.00	125.00	25.00
☐ 5 Whitey Lockman	150.00	75.00	15.00
☐ 6 Mickey Mantle	2400.00	1000.00	250.00
☐ 7 Willie Mays	1200.00	500.00	125.00
☐ 8 Gil McDougald	175.00	85.00	18.00
☐ 9 Don Mueller	150.00	75.00	15.00
☐ 10 Don Newcombe	175.00	85.00	18.00
☐ 11 Phil Rizzuto	300.00	150.00	30.00
☐ 12 Duke Snider	600.00	300.00	60.00

1955 Stahl Meyer

The cards in this 12 card set measure approximately 3 1/4" by 4 1/2". The 1955 Stahl Meyer set of full color, unnumbered cards contains four players each from the three New York teams. As in the 1954 set, the cards have yellow borders; however, the back of the cards contain a sketch of Mickey Mantle with an ad for a baseball cap or a pennant. The cards are ordered in the checklist below by alphabetical order without regard to team affiliation.

	NRMT	VG-E	GOOD
COMPLETE SET	4200.00	2000.00	450.00
COMMON PLAYER (1-12)	150.00	75.00	15.00
☐ 1 Hank Bauer	175.00	85.00	18.00
☐ 2 Carl Erskine	175.00	85.00	18.00
☐ 3 Gil Hodges	300.00	150.00	30.00
☐ 4 Monte Irvin	250.00	125.00	25.00
☐ 5 Whitey Lockman	150.00	75.00	15.00
☐ 6 Mickey Mantle	2400.00	1000.00	250.00
☐ 7 Gil McDougald	175.00	85.00	18.00
☐ 8 Don Mueller	150.00	75.00	15.00
☐ 9 Don Newcombe	175.00	85.00	18.00
☐ 10 Dusty Rhodes	150.00	75.00	15.00
☐ 11 Phil Rizzuto	300.00	150.00	30.00
☐ 12 Duke Snider	600.00	300.00	60.00

1990 Starline Long John Silver

The 1990 Starline Long John Silver set was issued over an eight-week promotion, five cards at a time within a cello pack. The set was initially available only through the Long John Silver seafood fast-food chain with one pack being given to each customer who ordered a meal with a 32-ounce Coke. However after the promotion was over, leftover sets found their way into the organized card-collecting hobby. This 40-card, standard-size (2 1/2" by 3 1/2") set was featured the best of today's players. There are several cards for some of the players in the set. After the promotion at Long John Silver had been completed, there were reportedly more than 100,000 sets left over that were released into the organized hobby.

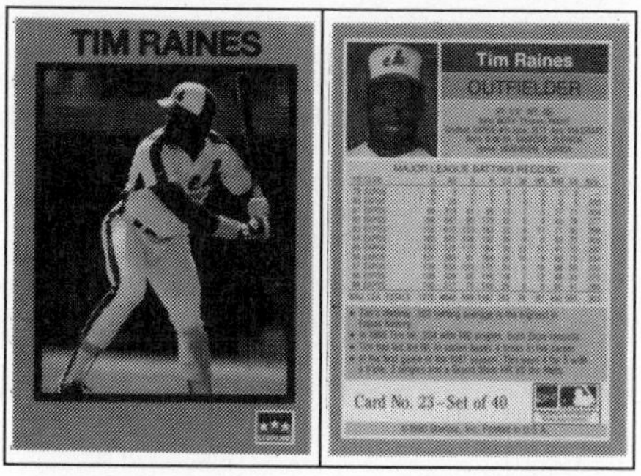

	MINT	EXC	G-VG
COMPLETE SET (40)	10.00	5.00	1.00
COMMON PLAYER (1-40)	.20	.10	.02
☐ 1 Don Mattingly	.75	.35	.07
☐ 2 Mark Grace	.50	.25	.05
☐ 3 Eric Davis	.40	.20	.04
☐ 4 Tony Gwynn	.40	.20	.04
☐ 5 Bobby Bonilla	.35	.17	.03
☐ 6 Wade Boggs	.50	.25	.05
☐ 7 Frank Viola	.30	.15	.03
☐ 8 Ruben Sierra	.35	.17	.03
☐ 9 Mark McGwire	.60	.30	.06
☐ 10 Alan Trammell	.30	.15	.03
☐ 11 Mark McGwire	.60	.30	.06
☐ 12 Gregg Jefferies	.50	.25	.05
☐ 13 Nolan Ryan	.75	.35	.07
☐ 14 John Smoltz	.20	.10	.02
☐ 15 Glenn Davis	.25	.12	.02
☐ 16 Mark Grace	.50	.25	.05
☐ 17 Wade Boggs	.50	.25	.05
☐ 18 Frank Viola	.30	.15	.03
☐ 19 Bret Saberhagen	.30	.15	.03
☐ 20 Chris Sabo	.30	.15	.03
☐ 21 Darryl Strawberry	.50	.25	.05
☐ 22 Wade Boggs	.50	.25	.05
☐ 23 Tim Raines	.30	.15	.03
☐ 24 Alan Trammell	.30	.15	.03
☐ 25 Chris Sabo	.30	.15	.03
☐ 26 Nolan Ryan	.75	.35	.07
☐ 27 Mark McGwire	.60	.30	.06
☐ 28 Don Mattingly	.75	.35	.07
☐ 29 Tony Gwynn	.40	.20	.04
☐ 30 Glenn Davis	.25	.12	.02
☐ 31 Bobby Bonilla	.35	.17	.03
☐ 32 Gregg Jefferies	.50	.25	.05
☐ 33 Ruben Sierra	.35	.17	.03
☐ 34 John Smoltz	.20	.10	.02
☐ 35 Don Mattingly	.75	.35	.07
☐ 36 Bret Saberhagen	.30	.15	.03
☐ 37 Darryl Strawberry	.50	.25	.05
☐ 38 Eric Davis	.40	.20	.04
☐ 39 Tim Raines	.30	.15	.03
☐ 40 Mark Grace	.50	.25	.05

1962 Sugardale

The cards in this 22-card set measure 3 3/4" by 5 1/8". The 1962 Sugardale Meats set of black and white, numbered and lettered cards features the Cleveland Indians and the Pittsburgh Pirates. The Indians are numbered while the Pirates are lettered. The backs, in red print, give player tips. The Bob Nieman card was just recently discovered and is quite scarce. The catalog designation is F174-1.

	NRMT	VG-E	GOOD
COMPLETE SET (22)	1800.00	800.00	200.00
COMMON PLAYER (1-19)	45.00	22.50	4.50
COMMON PLAYER (A-D)	75.00	37.50	7.50
☐ 1 Barry Latman	45.00	22.50	4.50
☐ 2 Gary Bell	45.00	22.50	4.50
☐ 3 Dick Donovan	45.00	22.50	4.50
☐ 4 Frank Funk	45.00	22.50	4.50
☐ 5 Jim Perry	75.00	37.50	7.50
☐ 6 not issued	00.00	.00	.00
☐ 7 John Romano	45.00	22.50	4.50
☐ 8 Ty Cline	45.00	22.50	4.50
☐ 9 Tito Francona	45.00	22.50	4.50
☐ 10 Bob Nieman	250.00	125.00	25.00
☐ 11 Willie Kirkland	45.00	22.50	4.50
☐ 12 Woody Held	45.00	22.50	4.50
☐ 13 Jerry Kindall	45.00	22.50	4.50
☐ 14 Bubba Phillips	45.00	22.50	4.50
☐ 15 Mel Harder	45.00	22.50	4.50
☐ 16 Salty Parker	45.00	22.50	4.50
☐ 17 Ray Katt	45.00	22.50	4.50
☐ 18 Mel McGaha	45.00	22.50	4.50
☐ 19 Pedro Ramos	45.00	22.50	4.50
☐ A Dick Groat	90.00	45.00	9.00
☐ B Robert Clemente	800.00	400.00	80.00
☐ C Don Hoak	75.00	37.50	7.50
☐ D Dick Stuart	90.00	45.00	9.00

1963 Sugardale

The cards in this 31-card set measure 3 3/4" by 5 1/8". The 1963 Sugardale Meats set of 31 black and white, numbered cards features the Cleveland Indians and Pittsburgh Pirates. The backs are printed in red and give player tips. The 1963 Sugardale set can be distinguished from the 1962 Sugardale set by examining the biographies on the card for mention of the 1962 season. The Perry and Skinner cards were withdrawn after June trades and are difficult to obtain.

	NRMT	VG-E	GOOD
COMPLETE SET (31)	1800.00	800.00	200.00
COMMON PLAYER (1-33)	45.00	22.50	4.50
COMMON PLAYER (34-38)	75.00	37.50	7.50
☐ 1 Barry Latman	45.00	22.50	4.50
☐ 2 Gary Bell	45.00	22.50	4.50
☐ 3 Dick Donovan	45.00	22.50	4.50
☐ 4 Joe Adcock	75.00	37.50	7.50
☐ 5 Jim Perry	175.00	85.00	18.00
☐ 6 Not issued	00.00	00.00	0.00
☐ 7 John Romano	45.00	22.50	4.50
☐ 8 Mike de la Hoz	45.00	22.50	4.50
☐ 9 Tito Francona	45.00	22.50	4.50
☐ 10 Gene Green	45.00	22.50	4.50
☐ 11 Willie Kirkland	45.00	22.50	4.50
☐ 12 Woody Held	45.00	22.50	4.50
☐ 13 Jerry Kindall	45.00	22.50	4.50
☐ 14 Max Alvis	45.00	22.50	4.50
☐ 15 Mel Harder	45.00	22.50	4.50
☐ 16 George Strickland	45.00	22.50	4.50
☐ 17 Elmer Valo	45.00	22.50	4.50
☐ 18 Birdie Tebbetts	45.00	22.50	4.50
☐ 19 Pedro Ramos	45.00	22.50	4.50
☐ 20 Al Luplow	45.00	22.50	4.50
☐ 21 Not issued	00.00	00.00	0.00
☐ 22 Not issued	00.00	00.00	0.00
☐ 23 Jim Grant	45.00	22.50	4.50
☐ 24 Victor Davalillo	45.00	22.50	4.50
☐ 25 Jerry Walker	45.00	22.50	4.50
☐ 26 Sam McDowell	75.00	37.50	7.50
☐ 27 Fred Whitfield	45.00	22.50	4.50
☐ 28 Jack Kralick	45.00	22.50	4.50
☐ 29 Not issued	00.00	00.00	0.00
☐ 30 Not issued	00.00	00.00	0.00
☐ 31 Not issued	00.00	00.00	0.00
☐ 32 Not issued	00.00	00.00	0.00
☐ 33 Bob Allen	45.00	22.50	4.50
☐ 34 Don Cardwell	75.00	37.50	7.50
☐ 35 Bob Skinner	250.00	125.00	25.00
☐ 36 Don Schwall	75.00	37.50	7.50
☐ 37 Jim Pagliaroni	75.00	37.50	7.50
☐ 38 Dick Schofield	75.00	37.50	7.50

1990 Sunflower Seeds

This 24-card, standard-size, 2 1/2" by 3 1/2" set is an attractive set which frames the players photo by solid blue borders. In the upper left hand of the card the description, Jumbo California Sunflower Seeds, was placed and underneath the photo is the player's name in red and the team name in very small printing in white. The back of the card features the complete major league record of the player and a short write up as well. This set was issued by Stagi and Scriven Farms Inc. with the cooperation of Michael Schechter Associates (MSA) and features some of the big-name stars in baseball at the time of printing of the set. The set was an attempt by the company to promote sunflower seeds as an alternative to chewing tobacco in the dugout. Three cards were available as an insert in each specially marked bag of Jumbo California Sunflower Seeds.

	MINT	EXC	G-VG
COMPLETE SET (24)	20.00	10.00	2.00
COMMON PLAYER (1-24)	.50	.25	.05
☐ 1 Kevin Mitchell	.75	.35	.07
☐ 2 Ken Griffey Jr.	3.00	1.50	.30
☐ 3 Howard Johnson	.50	.25	.05
☐ 4 Bo Jackson	2.50	1.25	.25
☐ 5 Kirby Puckett	1.00	.50	.10
☐ 6 Robin Yount	.75	.35	.07
☐ 7 Dave Stieb	.50	.25	.05
☐ 8 Don Mattingly	2.00	1.00	.20
☐ 9 Barry Bonds	1.00	.50	.10
☐ 10 Pedro Guerrero	.50	.25	.05
☐ 11 Tony Gwynn	1.00	.50	.10
☐ 12 Von Hayes	.50	.25	.05
☐ 13 Rickey Henderson	2.00	1.00	.20
☐ 14 Tim Raines	.75	.35	.07
☐ 15 Alan Trammell	.75	.35	.07
☐ 16 Dave Stewart	.75	.35	.07
☐ 17 Will Clark	2.00	1.00	.20
☐ 18 Roger Clemens	1.50	.75	.15
☐ 19 Wally Joyner	.75	.35	.07
☐ 20 Ryne Sandberg	2.00	1.00	.20
☐ 21 Eric Davis	1.00	.50	.10
☐ 22 Mike Scott	.50	.25	.05
☐ 23 Cal Ripken Jr.	1.00	.50	.10
☐ 24 Eddie Murray	.75	.35	.07

1948 Swell Sport Thrills

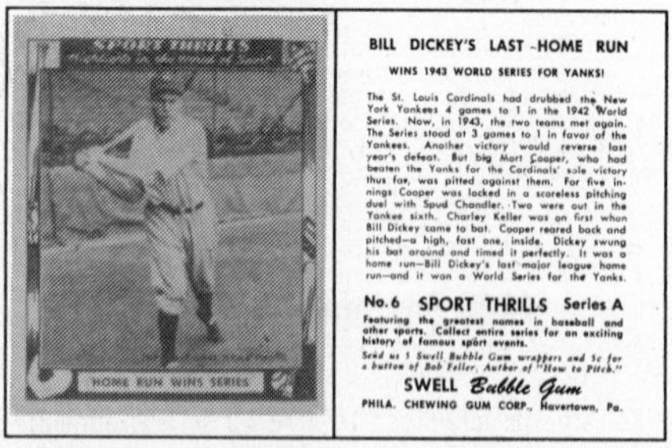

The cards in this 20-card set measure approximately 2 7/16" by 3". The 1948 Swell Gum Sports Thrills set of black and white, numbered cards highlights events from baseball history. The cards have picture framed borders with the title "Sports Thrills Highlights in the World of Sport" on the front. The backs of the cards give the story of the event pictured on the front. Cards numbered 9, 11, 16, and 20 are more difficult to obtain than the other cards in this set. The catalog designation is R448.

	NRMT	VG-E	GOOD
COMPLETE SET (20)	850.00	425.00	85.00
COMMON PLAYER (1-20)	15.00	7.50	1.50
☐ 1 Greatest Single Inning: Athletics' 10 Run Rally	15.00	7.50	1.50
☐ 2 Amazing Record: Reiser's Debut With Dodgers	15.00	7.50	1.50
☐ 3 Dramatic Debut: Jackie Robinson ROY	125.00	60.00	12.50
☐ 4 Greatest Pitcher of Them All: W.Johnson	50.00	25.00	5.00
☐ 5 Three Strikes Not Out: Lost Third Strike Changes Tide of 1941 World Series	15.00	7.50	1.50
☐ 6 Home Run Wins Series: Bill Dickey's Last Home Run	25.00	12.50	2.50
☐ 7 Never Say Die Pitcher: Schumacher Pitching	15.00	7.50	1.50
☐ 8 Five Strikeouts: Nationals Lose All Star Game (Hubbell)	25.00	12.50	2.50
☐ 9 Greatest Catch: Al Gionfriddo's Catch	25.00	12.50	2.50
☐ 10 No Hits No Runs: VanderMeer Comes Back	25.00	12.50	2.50
☐ 11 Bases Loaded: Alexander The Great	40.00	20.00	4.00
☐ 12 Most Dramatic Homer: Babe Ruth Points	150.00	75.00	15.00
☐ 13 Winning Run: Bridges' Pitching and Goslin's Single Wins 1935 World Series	15.00	7.50	1.50
☐ 14 Great Slugging: Lou Gehrig's Four Homers	100.00	50.00	10.00
☐ 15 Four Men To Stop Him: DiMaggio's Bat Streak	40.00	20.00	4.00
☐ 16 Three Run Homer in Ninth: Williams' Homer	150.00	75.00	15.00
☐ 17 Football Block: Lindell's Football Block Paves Way For Yank's Series Victory	15.00	7.50	1.50
☐ 18 Home Run To Fame: Reese's Grand Slam	40.00	20.00	4.00
☐ 19 Strikeout Record: Feller Whiffs Five	40.00	20.00	4.00
☐ 20 Rifle Arm: Furillo	40.00	20.00	4.00

1989 Swell Baseball Greats

The 1989 Swell Baseball Greats set contains 135 standard-size (2 1/2" by 3 1/2") cards. The fronts have vintage color photos with beige, red and white borders. The horizontally-oriented backs are white and scarlet, and feature career highlights and lifetime stats. The set was produced by Philadelphia Chewing Gum Corporation.

	MINT	EXC	G-VG
COMPLETE SET (135)	10.00	5.00	1.00
COMMON PLAYER (1-135)	.05	.02	.00
☐ 1 Babe Ruth	1.00	.50	.10
☐ 2 Ty Cobb	.60	.30	.06
☐ 3 Walter Johnson	.35	.17	.03
☐ 4 Honus Wagner	.35	.17	.03
☐ 5 Cy Young	.20	.10	.02

☐ 6	Joe Adcock	.05	.02	.00
☐ 7	Jim Bunning	.10	.05	.01
☐ 8	Orlando Cepeda	.10	.05	.01
☐ 9	Harvey Kuenn	.05	.02	.00
☐ 10	Jim Hunter	.20	.10	.02
☐ 11	Johnny VanderMeer	.10	.05	.01
☐ 12	Tony Oliva	.10	.05	.01
☐ 13	Harvey Haddix UER (reverse negative)	.10	.05	.01
☐ 14	Dick McAuliffe	.05	.02	.00
☐ 15	Lefty Grove	.20	.10	.02
☐ 16	Bo Belinsky	.05	.02	.00
☐ 17	Claude Osteen	.05	.02	.00
☐ 18	Doc Medich	.05	.02	.00
☐ 19	Del Ennis	.05	.02	.00
☐ 20	Rogers Hornsby	.25	.12	.02
☐ 21	Bob Buhl	.05	.02	.00
☐ 22	Phil Niekro	.20	.10	.02
☐ 23	Don Zimmer	.10	.05	.01
☐ 24	Greg Luzinski	.05	.02	.00
☐ 25	Lou Gehrig	.60	.30	.06
☐ 26	Ken Singleton	.10	.05	.01
☐ 27	Bob Allison	.05	.02	.00
☐ 28	Ed Kranepool	.05	.02	.00
☐ 29	Manny Sanguillen	.05	.02	.00
☐ 30	Luke Appling	.20	.10	.02
☐ 31	Ralph Terry	.05	.02	.00
☐ 32	Smoky Burgess	.05	.02	.00
☐ 33	Gil Hodges	.20	.10	.02
☐ 34	Harry Walker	.05	.02	.00
☐ 35	Edd Roush	.15	.07	.01
☐ 36	Ron Santo	.10	.05	.01
☐ 37	Jim Perry	.05	.02	.00
☐ 38	Jose Morales	.05	.02	.00
☐ 39	Stan Bahnsen	.05	.02	.00
☐ 40	Al Kaline	.30	.15	.03
☐ 41	Mel Harder	.05	.02	.00
☐ 42	Ralph Houk	.05	.02	.00
☐ 43	Jack Billingham	.05	.02	.00
☐ 44	Carl Erskine	.10	.05	.01
☐ 45	Hoyt Wilhelm	.20	.10	.02
☐ 46	Dick Radatz	.05	.02	.00
☐ 47	Roy Sievers	.05	.02	.00
☐ 48	Jim Lonborg	.05	.02	.00
☐ 49	Bobby Richardson	.10	.05	.01
☐ 50	Whitey Ford	.30	.15	.03
☐ 51	Roy Face	.10	.05	.01
☐ 52	Tom Tresh	.05	.02	.00
☐ 53	Joe Nuxhall	.05	.02	.00
☐ 54	Mickey Vernon	.05	.02	.00
☐ 55	Johnny Mize	.20	.10	.02
☐ 56	Scott McGregor	.05	.02	.00
☐ 57	Billy Pierce	.10	.05	.01
☐ 58	Dave Giusti	.05	.02	.00
☐ 59	Minnie Minoso	.10	.05	.01
☐ 60	Early Wynn	.15	.07	.01
☐ 61	Jose Cardenal	.05	.02	.00
☐ 62	Sam Jethroe	.05	.02	.00
☐ 63	Sal Bando	.05	.02	.00
☐ 64	Elrod Hendricks	.05	.02	.00
☐ 65	Enos Slaughter	.20	.10	.02
☐ 66	Jim Bouton	.05	.02	.00
☐ 67	Bill Mazeroski	.10	.05	.01
☐ 68	Tony Kubek	.10	.05	.01
☐ 69	Joe Black	.05	.02	.00
☐ 70	Harmon Killebrew	.20	.10	.02
☐ 71	Sam McDowell	.05	.02	.00
☐ 72	Bucky Dent	.10	.05	.01
☐ 73	Virgil Trucks	.05	.02	.00
☐ 74	Andy Pafko	.05	.02	.00
☐ 75	Bob Feller	.30	.15	.03
☐ 76	Tito Francona	.05	.02	.00
☐ 77	Al Dark	.05	.02	.00
☐ 78	Larry Dierker	.05	.02	.00
☐ 79	Nellie Briles	.05	.02	.00
☐ 80	Lou Boudreau	.15	.07	.01
☐ 81	Wally Moon	.05	.02	.00
☐ 82	Hank Bauer	.05	.02	.00
☐ 83	Jim Piersall	.05	.02	.00
☐ 84	Jim Grant	.05	.02	.00
☐ 85	Richie Ashburn	.15	.07	.01
☐ 86	Bob Friend	.05	.02	.00
☐ 87	Ken Keltner	.05	.02	.00
☐ 88	Jim Kaat	.10	.05	.01
☐ 89	Dean Chance	.05	.02	.00
☐ 90	Al Lopez	.15	.07	.01
☐ 91	Dick Groat	.10	.05	.01
☐ 92	Johnny Blanchard	.05	.02	.00
☐ 93	Chuck Hinton	.05	.02	.00
☐ 94	Clete Boyer	.05	.02	.00
☐ 95	Steve Carlton	.25	.12	.02
☐ 96	Tug McGraw	.10	.05	.01
☐ 97	Mickey Lolich	.10	.05	.01
☐ 98	Earl Weaver	.10	.05	.01
☐ 99	Sal Maglie	.10	.05	.01
☐ 100	Ted Williams	.60	.30	.06
☐ 101	Allie Reynolds UER (photo actually Marius Russo)	.20	.10	.02
☐ 102	Gene Woodling UER (photo actually Irv Noren)	.20	.10	.02
☐ 103	Moe Drabowsky	.05	.02	.00
☐ 104	Mickey Stanley	.05	.02	.00
☐ 105	Jim Palmer	.25	.12	.02
☐ 106	Bill Freehan	.10	.05	.01
☐ 107	Bob Robertson	.05	.02	.00
☐ 108	Walt Dropo	.05	.02	.00
☐ 109	Jerry Koosman	.10	.05	.01
☐ 110	Bobby Doerr	.20	.10	.02
☐ 111	Phil Rizzuto	.25	.12	.02
☐ 112	Don Kessinger	.10	.05	.01
☐ 113	Milt Pappas	.10	.05	.01
☐ 114	Herb Score	.10	.05	.01
☐ 115	Larry Doby	.10	.05	.01
☐ 116	Glenn Beckert	.05	.02	.00
☐ 117	Andre Thornton	.05	.02	.00
☐ 118	Gary Matthews	.05	.02	.00
☐ 119	Bill Virdon	.10	.05	.01
☐ 120	Billy Williams	.20	.10	.02
☐ 121	Johnny Sain	.10	.05	.01
☐ 122	Don Newcombe	.10	.05	.01
☐ 123	Rico Petrocelli	.05	.02	.00
☐ 124	Dick Bosman	.05	.02	.00
☐ 125	Roberto Clemente	.40	.20	.04
☐ 126	Rocky Colavito	.10	.05	.01
☐ 127	Wilbur Wood	.05	.02	.00
☐ 128	Duke Sims	.05	.02	.00
☐ 129	Ken Holtzman	.05	.02	.00
☐ 130	Casey Stengel	.20	.10	.02
☐ 131	Bobby Shantz	.10	.05	.01
☐ 132	Del Crandall	.10	.05	.01
☐ 133	Bobby Thomson	.10	.05	.01
☐ 134	Brooks Robinson	.30	.15	.03
☐ 135	Checklist Card	.05	.02	.00

1990 Swell Baseball Greats

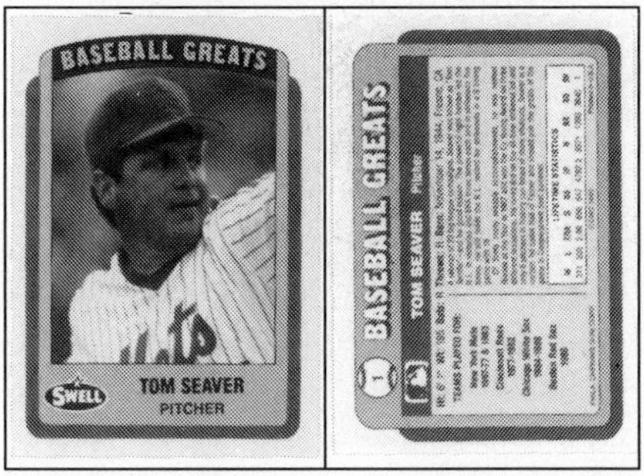

The 1990 Swell Baseball Greats set is a standard-size (2 1/2" by 3 1/2"), 135-card set. The words Baseball Greats is boldly proclaimed on the top of the card. This set was issued by Swell in both complete set form and in 10-card wax packs.

	MINT	EXC	G-VG
COMPLETE SET (135)	10.00	5.00	1.00
COMMON PLAYER (1-135)	.05	.02	.00
☐ 1 Tom Seaver	.40	.20	.04
☐ 2 Hank Aaron	.50	.25	.05
☐ 3 Mickey Cochrane	.15	.07	.01
☐ 4 Rod Carew	.40	.20	.04
☐ 5 Carl Yastrzemski	.45	.22	.04
☐ 6 Dizzy Dean	.20	.10	.02
☐ 7 Sal Bando	.05	.02	.00
☐ 8 Whitey Ford	.25	.12	.02
☐ 9 Bill White	.10	.05	.01
☐ 10 Babe Ruth	1.00	.50	.10
☐ 11 Robin Roberts	.20	.10	.02
☐ 12 Warren Spahn	.25	.12	.02
☐ 13 Billy Williams	.20	.10	.02
☐ 14 Joe Garagiola	.20	.10	.02
☐ 15 Ty Cobb	.60	.30	.06
☐ 16 Boog Powell	.10	.05	.01
☐ 17 Tom Tresh	.05	.02	.00
☐ 18 Luke Appling	.20	.10	.02
☐ 19 Tommie Agee	.05	.02	.00
☐ 20 Roberto Clemente	.50	.25	.05
☐ 21 Bobby Thomson	.10	.05	.01
☐ 22 Charlie Keller	.10	.05	.01
☐ 23 George Bamberger	.05	.02	.00
☐ 24 Eddie Lopat	.10	.05	.01
☐ 25 Lou Gehrig	.60	.30	.06
☐ 26 Manny Mota	.05	.02	.00
☐ 27 Steve Stone	.05	.02	.00
☐ 28 Orlando Cepeda	.15	.07	.01
☐ 29 Al Bumbry	.05	.02	.00
☐ 30 Grover Alexander	.15	.07	.01
☐ 31 Lou Boudreau	.15	.07	.01
☐ 32 Herb Score	.10	.05	.01
☐ 33 Harry Walker	.05	.02	.00
☐ 34 Deron Johnson	.05	.02	.00
☐ 35 Edd Roush	.10	.05	.01
☐ 36 Carl Erskine	.10	.05	.01
☐ 37 Ken Forsch	.05	.02	.00
☐ 38 Sal Maglie	.10	.05	.01
☐ 39 Al Rosen	.10	.05	.01
☐ 40 Casey Stengel	.20	.10	.02
☐ 41 Cesar Cedeno	.05	.02	.00
☐ 42 Roy White	.05	.02	.00
☐ 43 Larry Doby	.10	.05	.01
☐ 44 Rod Kanehl	.05	.02	.00
☐ 45 Tris Speaker	.20	.10	.02
☐ 46 Ralph Garr	.05	.02	.00
☐ 47 Andre Thornton	.05	.02	.00
☐ 48 Frankie Crosetti	.10	.05	.01
☐ 49 Dick Groat	.10	.05	.01
☐ 50 Honus Wagner	.25	.12	.02
☐ 51 Rogers Hornsby	.25	.12	.02
☐ 52 Ken Brett	.05	.02	.00
☐ 53 Lenny Randle	.05	.02	.00
☐ 54 Enos Slaughter	.20	.10	.02
☐ 55 Mel Ott	.20	.10	.02
☐ 56 Rico Petrocelli	.05	.02	.00
☐ 57 Walt Dropo	.05	.02	.00
☐ 58 Bob Grich	.05	.02	.00
☐ 59 Billy Herman	.10	.05	.01
☐ 60 Bob Feller	.25	.12	.02
☐ 61 Davey Johnson	.10	.05	.01
☐ 62 Don Drysdale	.20	.10	.02
☐ 63 Lary Sorensen	.05	.02	.00
☐ 64 Ron Santo	.10	.05	.01
☐ 65 Eddie Mathews	.20	.10	.02
☐ 66 Gaylord Perry	.20	.10	.02
☐ 67 Lee May	.05	.02	.00
☐ 68 Johnnie LeMaster	.05	.02	.00
☐ 69 Don Kessinger	.10	.05	.01
☐ 70 Lefty Grove	.20	.10	.02
☐ 71 Lou Brock	.25	.12	.02
☐ 72 Don Cardwell	.05	.02	.00
☐ 73 Harvey Haddix	.05	.02	.00
☐ 74 Frank Torre	.05	.02	.00
☐ 75 Walter Johnson	.25	.12	.02
☐ 76 Don Newcombe	.10	.05	.01
☐ 77 Marv Throneberry	.05	.02	.00
☐ 78 Jim Northrup	.05	.02	.00
☐ 79 Fritz Peterson	.05	.02	.00
☐ 80 Ralph Kiner	.20	.10	.02
☐ 81 Mickey Lolich	.10	.05	.01
☐ 82 Donn Clendenon	.05	.02	.00
☐ 83 Pete Vuckovich	.05	.02	.00
☐ 84 Lefty Gomez	.20	.10	.02
☐ 85 Monte Irvin	.15	.07	.01
☐ 86 Rick Ferrell	.10	.05	.01
☐ 87 Tommy Hutton	.05	.02	.00
☐ 88 Julio Cruz	.05	.02	.00
☐ 89 Vida Blue	.10	.05	.01
☐ 90 Jonnie Mize	.20	.10	.02
☐ 91 Rusty Staub	.10	.05	.01
☐ 92 Jimmy Piersall	.10	.05	.01
☐ 93 Bill Mazeroski	.10	.05	.01
☐ 94 Lee Lacy	.05	.02	.00
☐ 95 Ernie Banks	.25	.12	.02
☐ 96 Bobby Doerr	.20	.10	.02
☐ 97 George Foster	.10	.05	.01
☐ 98 Eric Soderholm	.05	.02	.00
☐ 99 Johnny Vander Meer	.10	.05	.01
☐ 100 Cy Young	.25	.12	.02
☐ 101 Jimmie Foxx	.30	.15	.03
☐ 102 Clete Boyer	.10	.05	.01
☐ 103 Steve Garvey	.25	.12	.02
☐ 104 Johnny Podres	.10	.05	.01
☐ 105 Yogi Berra	.40	.20	.04
☐ 106 Bill Monbouquette	.05	.02	.00
☐ 107 Milt Pappas	.05	.02	.00
☐ 108 Dave LaRoche	.05	.02	.00
☐ 109 Elliott Maddox	.05	.02	.00
☐ 110 Steve Carlton	.30	.15	.03
☐ 111 Bud Harrelson	.10	.05	.01
☐ 112 Mark Littell	.05	.02	.00
☐ 113 Frank Thomas	.05	.02	.00
☐ 114 Bill Robinson	.10	.05	.01
☐ 115 Satchel Paige	.30	.15	.03
☐ 116 John Denny	.05	.02	.00
☐ 117 Clyde King	.05	.02	.00
☐ 118 Billy Sample	.05	.02	.00
☐ 119 Rocky Colavito	.15	.07	.01
☐ 120 Bob Gibson	.25	.12	.02
☐ 121 Bert Campaneris	.05	.02	.00
☐ 122 Mark Fidrych	.10	.05	.01
☐ 123 Ed Charles	.05	.02	.00
☐ 124 Jim Lonborg	.10	.05	.01
☐ 125 Ted Williams	.50	.25	.05
☐ 126 Manny Sanguillen	.10	.05	.01
☐ 127 Matt Keough	.05	.02	.00
☐ 128 Vern Ruhle	.05	.02	.00
☐ 129 Bob Skinner	.05	.02	.00
☐ 130 Joe Torre	.15	.07	.01
☐ 131 Ralph Houk	.05	.02	.00
☐ 132 Gil Hodges	.25	.12	.02
☐ 133 Ralph Branca	.10	.05	.01
☐ 134 Christy Mathewson	.25	.12	.02
☐ 135 Checklist Card	.05	.02	.00

1991 Swell Baseball Greats

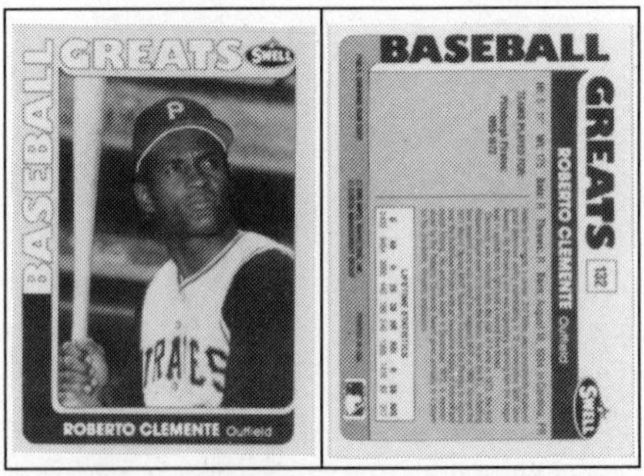

This set marks the third year Philadelphia Chewing Gum (using the Swell trade name) issued a set honoring famous and other important retired players. The front of the cards feature yellow and red borders framing the full-color photo of the player(where full color was available) The cards were issued with cooperation from Impel Marketing. This 150-card set measures the now-standard size of 2 1/2" by 3 1/2" and is sequenced in several alphabetical orders.

	MINT	EXC	G-VG
COMPLETE SET (150)	10.00	5.00	1.00
COMMON PLAYER (1-150)	.05	.02	.00
☐ 1 Tommie Agee	.05	.02	.00

☐ 2 Matty Alou	.05	.02	.00
☐ 3 Luke Appling	.20	.10	.02
☐ 4 Richie Ashburn	.15	.07	.01
☐ 5 Ernie Banks	.25	.12	.02
☐ 6 Don Baylor	.10	.05	.01
☐ 7 Buddy Bell	.10	.05	.01
☐ 8 Yogi Berra	.35	.17	.03
☐ 9 Joe Black	.10	.05	.01
☐ 10 Vida Blue	.10	.05	.01
☐ 11 Bobby Bonds	.10	.05	.01
☐ 12 Lou Boudreau	.15	.07	.01
☐ 13 Lou Brock	.20	.10	.02
☐ 14 Ralph Branca	.10	.05	.01
☐ 15 Bobby Brown	.10	.05	.01
☐ 16 Lou Burdette	.10	.05	.01
☐ 17 Steve Carlton	.30	.15	.03
☐ 18 Rico Carty	.10	.05	.01
☐ 19 Jerry Coleman	.10	.05	.01
☐ 20 Frankie Crosetti	.10	.05	.01
☐ 21 Julio Cruz	.05	.02	.00
☐ 22 Alvin Dark	.05	.02	.00
☐ 23 Doug DeCinces	.05	.02	.00
☐ 24 Larry Doby	.10	.05	.01
☐ 25 Bobby Doerr	.20	.10	.02
☐ 26 Don Drysdale	.20	.10	.02
☐ 27 Carl Erskine	.10	.05	.01
☐ 28 Elroy Face	.10	.05	.01
☐ 29 Rick Ferrell	.10	.05	.01
☐ 30 Rollie Fingers	.15	.07	.01
☐ 31 Joe Garagiola	.20	.10	.02
☐ 32 Steve Garvey	.30	.15	.03
☐ 33 Bob Gibson	.20	.10	.02
☐ 34 Mudcat Grant	.05	.02	.00
☐ 35 Dick Groat	.10	.05	.01
☐ 36 Jerry Grote	.05	.02	.00
☐ 37 Toby Harrah	.05	.02	.00
☐ 38 Bud Harrelson	.10	.05	.01
☐ 39 Billy Herman	.15	.07	.01
☐ 40 Ken Holtzman	.05	.02	.00
☐ 41 Willie Horton	.05	.02	.00
☐ 42 Ralph Houk	.05	.02	.00
☐ 43 Al Hrabosky	.05	.02	.00
☐ 44 Monte Irvin	.20	.10	.02
☐ 45 Fergie Jenkins	.20	.10	.02
☐ 46 Davey Johnson	.05	.02	.00
☐ 47 George Kell	.15	.07	.01
☐ 48 Charlie Keller	.10	.05	.01
☐ 49 Harmon Killebrew	.25	.12	.02
☐ 50 Ralph Kiner	.25	.12	.02
☐ 51 Clyde King	.05	.02	.00
☐ 52 Dave Kingman	.10	.05	.01
☐ 53 Al Kaline	.30	.15	.03
☐ 54 Clem Labine	.10	.05	.01
☐ 55 Vern Law	.10	.05	.01
☐ 56 Mickey Lolich	.10	.05	.01
☐ 57 Jim Lonborg	.10	.05	.01
☐ 58 Eddie Lopat	.10	.05	.01
☐ 59 Sal Maglie	.10	.05	.01
☐ 60 Bill Mazeroski	.10	.05	.01
☐ 61 Johnny VanderMeer	.10	.05	.01
☐ 62 Johnny Mize	.20	.10	.02
☐ 63 Manny Mota	.05	.02	.00
☐ 64 Wally Moon	.05	.02	.00
☐ 65 Rick Monday	.05	.02	.00
☐ 66 Tom Tresh	.10	.05	.01
☐ 67 Graig Nettles	.10	.05	.01
☐ 68 Don Newcombe	.10	.05	.01
☐ 69 Milt Pappas	.05	.02	.00
☐ 70 Gaylord Perry	.20	.10	.02
☐ 71 Rico Petrocelli	.05	.02	.00
☐ 72 Jimmy Piersall	.10	.05	.01
☐ 73 Johnny Podres	.10	.05	.01
☐ 74 Boog Powell	.10	.05	.01
☐ 75 Bobby Richardson	.10	.05	.01
☐ 76 Vern Ruhle	.05	.02	.00
☐ 77 Robin Roberts	.20	.10	.02
☐ 78 Al Rosen	.10	.05	.01
☐ 79 Billy Sample	.05	.02	.00
☐ 80 Manny Sanguillen	.10	.05	.01
☐ 81 Ron Santo	.10	.05	.01
☐ 82 Herb Score	.10	.05	.01
☐ 83 Bobby Shantz	.10	.05	.01
☐ 84 Enos Slaughter	.20	.10	.02
☐ 85 Eric Soderholm	.05	.02	.00
☐ 86 Warren Spahn	.25	.12	.02
☐ 87 Rusty Staub	.10	.05	.01
☐ 88 Bobby Thomson	.10	.05	.01
☐ 89 Marv Throneberry	.05	.02	.00
☐ 90 Luis Tiant	.10	.05	.01
☐ 91 Frank Torre	.05	.02	.00
☐ 92 Joe Torre	.15	.07	.01
☐ 93 Bill Virdon	.10	.05	.01
☐ 94 Harry Walker	.05	.02	.00
☐ 95 Earl Weaver	.10	.05	.01
☐ 96 Bill White	.10	.05	.01
☐ 97 Roy White	.05	.02	.00
☐ 98 Billy Williams	.20	.10	.02
☐ 99 Dick Williams	.05	.02	.00
☐ 100 Ted Williams	.50	.25	.05
☐ 101 Gene Woodling	.10	.05	.01
☐ 102 Hank Aaron	.50	.25	.05
☐ 103 Rod Carew	.40	.20	.04
☐ 104 Cesar Cedeno	.10	.05	.01
☐ 105 Orlando Cepeda	.15	.07	.01
☐ 106 Willie Mays	.50	.25	.05
☐ 107 Tom Seaver	.40	.20	.04
☐ 108 Carl Yastrzemski	.40	.20	.04
☐ 109 Clete Boyer	.10	.05	.01
☐ 110 Bert Campaneris	.05	.02	.00
☐ 111 Walt Dropo	.05	.02	.00
☐ 112 George Foster	.10	.05	.01
☐ 113 Phil Garner	.05	.02	.00
☐ 114 Harvey Kuenn	.10	.05	.01
☐ 115 Don Kessinger	.10	.05	.01
☐ 116 Rocky Colavito	.15	.07	.01
☐ 117 Bobby Murcer	.10	.05	.01
☐ 118 Mel Purcell	.05	.02	.00
☐ 119 Ken Reitz	.05	.02	.00
☐ 120 Earl Wilson	.05	.02	.00
☐ 121 Wilbur Wood	.05	.02	.00
☐ 122 Ed Yost	.05	.02	.00
☐ 123 Jim Bouton	.10	.05	.01
☐ 124 Babe Ruth	1.00	.50	.10
☐ 125 Lou Gehrig	.60	.30	.06
☐ 126 Honus Wagner	.25	.12	.02
☐ 127 Ty Cobb	.60	.30	.06
☐ 128 Grover C. Alexander	.20	.10	.02
☐ 129 Lefty Gomez	.20	.10	.02
☐ 130 Walter Johnson	.25	.12	.02
☐ 131 Gil Hodges	.20	.10	.02
☐ 132 Roberto Clemente	.45	.22	.04
☐ 133 Satchel Paige	.30	.15	.03
☐ 134 Edd Roush	.15	.07	.01
☐ 135 Cy Young	.20	.10	.02
☐ 136 Casey Stengel	.25	.12	.02
☐ 137 Rogers Hornsby	.25	.12	.02
☐ 138 Dizzy Dean	.30	.15	.03
☐ 139 Lefty Grove	.20	.10	.02
☐ 140 Tris Speaker	.20	.10	.02
☐ 141 Christy Mathewson	.25	.12	.02
☐ 142 Mickey Cochrane	.15	.07	.01
☐ 143 Jimmie Foxx	.30	.15	.03
☐ 144 Mel Ott	.20	.10	.02
☐ 145 Bob Feller	.30	.15	.03
☐ 146 Brooks Robinson	.20	.10	.02
☐ 147 Eddie Mathews	.20	.10	.02
☐ 148 Pie Traynor	.15	.07	.01
☐ 149 Thurman Munson	.25	.12	.02
☐ 150 Checklist Card	.05	.02	.00

1957 Swifts Franks

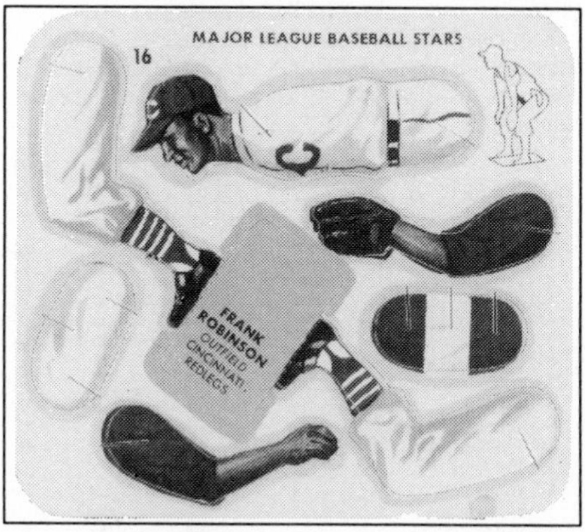

The cards in this 18-card set measure 3 1/2" by 4". These full color, numbered cards issued in 1957 by the Swift Company are die-cut. Each card consists of several pieces which can be punched out and assembled to form a stand-up model of the player. The cards and a game board were available directly from the company. The company-direct set consisted of three panels each containing six cards; sets found in this "uncut" state carry a value 25 percent higher than the values listed below. The catalog designation for this set is F162.

	NRMT	VG-E	GOOD
COMPLETE SET (18)	1600.00	750.00	175.00
COMMON PLAYER (1-18)	45.00	22.50	4.50
☐ 1 John Podres	60.00	30.00	6.00
☐ 2 Gus Triandos	45.00	22.50	4.50
☐ 3 Dale Long	45.00	22.50	4.50
☐ 4 Billy Pierce	60.00	30.00	6.00
☐ 5 Ed Bailey	45.00	22.50	4.50
☐ 6 Vic Wertz	45.00	22.50	4.50
☐ 7 Nelson Fox	100.00	50.00	10.00
☐ 8 Ken Boyer	90.00	45.00	9.00
☐ 9 Gil McDougald	75.00	37.50	7.50
☐ 10 Junior Gilliam	75.00	37.50	7.50
☐ 11 Eddie Yost	45.00	22.50	4.50
☐ 12 Johnny Logan	45.00	22.50	4.50
☐ 13 Hank Aaron	500.00	250.00	50.00
☐ 14 Bill Tuttle	45.00	22.50	4.50
☐ 15 Jackie Jensen	75.00	37.50	7.50
☐ 16 Frank Robinson	160.00	80.00	16.00
☐ 17 Richie Ashburn	125.00	60.00	12.50
☐ 18 Rocky Colavito	100.00	50.00	10.00

1990 Target Dodgers

The 1990 Target Dodgers is one of the largest sets ever made. This over-1,000 card set features cards each measuring approximately 2" by 3" individually and was issued in large perforated sheets of 15 cards. Players in the set played at one time or another for one of the Dodgers franchises. As such many of the players in the set are older and relatively unknown to today's younger collectors. The set was apparently intended to be arranged in alphabetical order. There were several numbers not used (408, 458, 463, 792, 902, 907, 969, 996, 1031, 1054, 1061, and 1098) as well as a few instances of duplicated numbers.

	MINT	EXC	G-VG
COMPLETE SET	60.00	30.00	6.00
COMMON PLAYER	.10	.05	.01
☐ 1 Bert Abbey	.10	.05	.01
☐ 2 Cal Abrams	.10	.05	.01
☐ 3 Hank Aguirre	.10	.05	.01
☐ 4 Eddie Ainsmith	.10	.05	.01
☐ 5 Ed Albosta	.10	.05	.01
☐ 6 Luis Alcaraz	.10	.05	.01
☐ 7 Doyle Alexander	.10	.05	.01
☐ 8 Dick Allen	.20	.10	.02
☐ 9 Frank Allen	.10	.05	.01
☐ 10 Johnny Allen	.10	.05	.01
☐ 11 Mel Almada	.10	.05	.01
☐ 12 Walter Alston	.30	.15	.03
☐ 13 Ed Amelung	.10	.05	.01
☐ 14 Sandy Amoros	.10	.05	.01
☐ 15 Dave Anderson	.10	.05	.01
☐ 16 Ferrell Anderson	.10	.05	.01
☐ 17 John Anderson	.10	.05	.01
☐ 18 Stan Andrews	.10	.05	.01
☐ 19 Bill Antonello	.10	.05	.01
☐ 20 Jimmy Archer	.10	.05	.01
☐ 21 Bob Aspromonte	.10	.05	.01
☐ 22 Rick Auerbach	.10	.05	.01
☐ 23 Charlie Babb	.10	.05	.01
☐ 24 Johnny Babich	.10	.05	.01
☐ 25 Bob Bailey	.10	.05	.01
☐ 26 Bob Bailor	.10	.05	.01
☐ 27 Dusty Baker	.20	.10	.02
☐ 28 Tom Baker	.10	.05	.01
☐ 29 Dave Bancroft	.20	.10	.02
☐ 30 Dan Bankhead	.10	.05	.01
☐ 31 Jack Banta	.10	.05	.01
☐ 32 Jim Barbieri	.10	.05	.01
☐ 33 Red Barkley	.10	.05	.01
☐ 34 Jesse Barnes	.10	.05	.01
☐ 35 Rex Barney	.10	.05	.01
☐ 36 Billy Barnie	.10	.05	.01
☐ 37 Bob Barrett	.10	.05	.01
☐ 38 Jim Baxes	.10	.05	.01
☐ 39 Billy Bean	.10	.05	.01
☐ 40 BoomBoom Beck	.10	.05	.01
☐ 41 Joe Beckwith	.10	.05	.01
☐ 42 Hank Behrman	.10	.05	.01
☐ 43 Mark Belanger	.20	.10	.02
☐ 44 Wayne Belardi	.10	.05	.01
☐ 45 Tim Belcher	.20	.10	.02
☐ 46 George Bell	.10	.05	.01
☐ 47 Ray Benge	.10	.05	.01
☐ 48 Moe Berg	.20	.10	.02
☐ 49 Bill Bergen	.10	.05	.01
☐ 50 Ray Berries	.10	.05	.01
☐ 51 Don Bessent	.10	.05	.01
☐ 52 Steve Bilko	.10	.05	.01
☐ 53 Jack Billingham	.10	.05	.01
☐ 54 Babe Birrer	.10	.05	.01
☐ 55 Del Bissonette	.10	.05	.01
☐ 56 Joe Black	.20	.10	.02
☐ 57 Lu Blue	.10	.05	.01
☐ 58 George Boehler	.10	.05	.01
☐ 59 Sammy Bohne	.10	.05	.01
☐ 60 John Bolling	.10	.05	.01
☐ 61 Ike Boone	.10	.05	.01
☐ 62 Frenchy Bordagaray	.10	.05	.01
☐ 63 Ken Boyer	.20	.10	.02
☐ 64 Buzz Boyle	.10	.05	.01
☐ 65 Mark Bradley	.10	.05	.01
☐ 66 Bobby Bragan	.10	.05	.01
☐ 67 Ralph Branca	.20	.10	.02
☐ 68 Ed Brandt	.10	.05	.01
☐ 69 Sid Bream	.10	.05	.01
☐ 70 Marv Breeding	.10	.05	.01
☐ 71 Tom Brennan	.10	.05	.01
☐ 72 William Brennan	.10	.05	.01
☐ 73 Rube Bressler	.10	.05	.01
☐ 74 Ken Brett	.10	.05	.01
☐ 75 Jim Brewer	.10	.05	.01
☐ 76 Tony Brewer	.10	.05	.01
☐ 77 Rocky Bridges	.10	.05	.01
☐ 78 Greg Brock	.10	.05	.01
☐ 79 Dan Brouthers	.30	.15	.03
☐ 80 Eddie Brown	.10	.05	.01
☐ 81 Elmer Brown	.10	.05	.01
☐ 82 Lindsay Brown	.10	.05	.01
☐ 83 Lloyd Brown	.10	.05	.01
☐ 84 Mace Brown	.10	.05	.01
☐ 85 Tommy Brown	.10	.05	.01
☐ 86 Pete Browning	.20	.10	.02
☐ 87 Ralph Bryant	.10	.05	.01
☐ 88 Jim Bucher	.10	.05	.01
☐ 89 Bill Buckner	.20	.10	.02
☐ 90 Jim Bunning	.30	.15	.03
☐ 91 Jack Burdock	.10	.05	.01
☐ 92 Glenn Burke	.10	.05	.01
☐ 93 Buster Burrell	.10	.05	.01
☐ 94 Larry Burright	.10	.05	.01
☐ 95 Doc Bushong	.10	.05	.01
☐ 96 Max Butcher	.10	.05	.01
☐ 97 Johnny Butler	.10	.05	.01
☐ 98 Enos Cabell	.10	.05	.01
☐ 99 Leon Cadore	.10	.05	.01
☐ 100 Bruce Caldwell	.10	.05	.01
☐ 101 Dick Calmus	.10	.05	.01
☐ 102 Dolf Camilli	.10	.05	.01
☐ 103 Doug Camilli	.10	.05	.01
☐ 104 Roy Campanella	.50	.25	.05
☐ 105 Al Campanis	.20	.10	.02
☐ 106 Jim Campanis	.10	.05	.01
☐ 107A Leo Callahan	.10	.05	.01
☐ 107B Gilly Campbell	.10	.05	.01
☐ 108 Jimmy Canavan	.10	.05	.01
☐ 109 Chris Cannizzaro	.10	.05	.01
☐ 110 Guy Cantrell	.10	.05	.01
☐ 111 Ben Cantwell	.10	.05	.01
☐ 112 Andy Carey	.10	.05	.01
☐ 113 Max Carey	.30	.15	.03
☐ 114 Tex Carleton	.10	.05	.01

☐ 115	Ownie Carroll	.10	.05	.01
☐ 116	Bob Caruthers	.10	.05	.01
☐ 117	Doc Casey	.10	.05	.01
☐ 118	Hugh Casey	.10	.05	.01
☐ 119	Bobby Castillo	.10	.05	.01
☐ 120	Cesar Cedeno	.10	.05	.01
☐ 121	Ron Cey	.20	.10	.02
☐ 122	Ed Chandler	.10	.05	.01
☐ 123	Ben Chapman	.10	.05	.01
☐ 124	Larry Cheney	.10	.05	.01
☐ 125	Bob Chipman	.10	.05	.01
☐ 126	Chuck Churn	.10	.05	.01
☐ 127	Gino Cimoli	.10	.05	.01
☐ 128	Moose Clabaugh	.10	.05	.01
☐ 129	Bud Clancy	.10	.05	.01
☐ 130	Bob Clark	.10	.05	.01
☐ 131	Watty Clark	.10	.05	.01
☐ 132	Alta Cohen	.10	.05	.01
☐ 133	Rocky Colavito	.30	.15	.03
☐ 134	Jackie Collum	.10	.05	.01
☐ 135	Chuck Connors	.30	.15	.03
☐ 136	Jack Combs	.20	.10	.02
☐ 137	Johnny Cooney	.10	.05	.01
☐ 138	Tommy Corcoran	.10	.05	.01
☐ 139	Pop Corkhill	.10	.05	.01
☐ 140	John Corriden	.10	.05	.01
☐ 141	Pete Coscarart	.10	.05	.01
☐ 142	Wes Covington	.10	.05	.01
☐ 143	Billy Cox	.20	.10	.02
☐ 144	Roger Craig	.20	.10	.02
☐ 146	Willie Crawford	.10	.05	.01
☐ 147	Tim Crews	.10	.05	.01
☐ 148	John Cronin	.10	.05	.01
☐ 149	Lave Cross	.10	.05	.01
☐ 150	Bill Crouch	.10	.05	.01
☐ 151	Don Crow	.10	.05	.01
☐ 152	Henry Cruz	.10	.05	.01
☐ 153	Tony Cuccinello	.10	.05	.01
☐ 154	Roy Cullenbine	.10	.05	.01
☐ 155	George Culver	.10	.05	.01
☐ 156	Nick Cullop	.10	.05	.01
☐ 157	George Cutshaw	.10	.05	.01
☐ 158	Kiki Cuyler	.30	.15	.03
☐ 159	Bill Dahlen	.20	.10	.02
☐ 160	Babe Dahlgren	.10	.05	.01
☐ 161	Jack Dalton	.10	.05	.01
☐ 162	Tom Daly	.10	.05	.01
☐ 163	Cliff Dapper	.10	.05	.01
☐ 164	Bob Darnell	.10	.05	.01
☐ 165	Bobby Darwin	.10	.05	.01
☐ 166	Jake Daubert	.20	.10	.02
☐ 167	Vic Davalillo	.10	.05	.01
☐ 168	Curt Davis	.10	.05	.01
☐ 169	Mike Davis	.10	.05	.01
☐ 170	Ron Davis	.10	.05	.01
☐ 171	Tommy Davis	.20	.10	.02
☐ 172	Willie Davis	.20	.10	.02
☐ 173	Pea Ridge Day	.10	.05	.01
☐ 174	Tommy Dean	.10	.05	.01
☐ 175	Hank Deberry	.10	.05	.01
☐ 176	Art Decatur	.10	.05	.01
☐ 177	Raoul DeDeaux	.10	.05	.01
☐ 178	Ivan DeJesus	.10	.05	.01
☐ 179	Don Demeter	.10	.05	.01
☐ 180	Gene DeMontreville	.10	.05	.01
☐ 181	Rick Dempsey	.10	.05	.01
☐ 182	Eddie Dent	.10	.05	.01
☐ 183	Mike Devereaux	.10	.05	.01
☐ 184	Carlos Diaz	.10	.05	.01
☐ 185	Dick Dietz	.10	.05	.01
☐ 186	Pop Dillon	.10	.05	.01
☐ 187	Bill Doak	.10	.05	.01
☐ 188	John Dobbs	.10	.05	.01
☐ 189	George Dockins	.10	.05	.01
☐ 190	Cozy Dolan	.10	.05	.01
☐ 191	Patsy Donovan	.10	.05	.01
☐ 192	Wild Bill Donovan	.10	.05	.01
☐ 193	Mickey Doolan	.10	.05	.01
☐ 194	Jack Doscher	.10	.05	.01
☐ 195	Phil Douglas	.10	.05	.01
☐ 196	Snooks Dowd	.10	.05	.01
☐ 197	Al Downing	.10	.05	.01
☐ 198	Red Downs	.10	.05	.01
☐ 199	Jack Doyle	.10	.05	.01
☐ 200	Solly Drake	.10	.05	.01
☐ 201	Tom Drake	.10	.05	.01
☐ 202	Chuck Dressen	.20	.10	.02
☐ 203	Don Drysdale	.30	.15	.03
☐ 204	Clise Dudley	.10	.05	.01
☐ 205	Mariano Duncan	.20	.10	.02
☐ 206	Jack Dunn	.10	.05	.01
☐ 207	Bull Durham	.10	.05	.01
☐ 208	Leo Durocher	.30	.15	.03
☐ 209	Billy Earle	.10	.05	.01
☐ 210	George Earnshaw	.10	.05	.01
☐ 211	Ox Eckhardt	.10	.05	.01
☐ 212	Bruce Edwards	.10	.05	.01
☐ 213	Hank Edwards	.10	.05	.01
☐ 214	Dick W. Egan	.10	.05	.01
☐ 215	Harry Eisenstat	.10	.05	.01
☐ 216	Kid Elberfeld	.10	.05	.01
☐ 217	Jumbo Elliot	.10	.05	.01
☐ 218	Don Elston	.10	.05	.01
☐ 219	Gil English	.10	.05	.01
☐ 220	Johnny Enzmann	.10	.05	.01
☐ 221	Al Epperly	.10	.05	.01
☐ 222	Carl Erskine	.20	.10	.02
☐ 223	Tex Erwin	.10	.05	.01
☐ 224	Cecil Espy	.10	.05	.01
☐ 225	Chuck Essegian	.10	.05	.01
☐ 226	Dude Esterbrook	.10	.05	.01
☐ 227	Red Evans	.10	.05	.01
☐ 228	Bunny Fabrique	.10	.05	.01
☐ 229	Jim Fairey	.10	.05	.01
☐ 230	Ron Fairly	.20	.10	.02
☐ 231	George Fallon	.10	.05	.01
☐ 232	Turk Farrell	.10	.05	.01
☐ 233	Duke Farrel	.10	.05	.01
☐ 234	Jim Faulkner	.10	.05	.01
☐ 235	Alex Ferguson	.10	.05	.01
☐ 236	Joe Ferguson	.10	.05	.01
☐ 237	Chico Fernandez	.10	.05	.01
☐ 238	Sid Fernandez	.20	.10	.02
☐ 239	Al Ferrara	.10	.05	.01
☐ 240	Wes Ferrell	.20	.10	.02
☐ 241	Lou Fette	.10	.05	.01
☐ 242	Chick Fewster	.10	.05	.01
☐ 243	Jack Fimple	.10	.05	.01
☐ 244	Neal Mickey Finn	.10	.05	.01
☐ 245	Bob Fisher	.10	.05	.01
☐ 246	Freddie Fitzsimmons	.10	.05	.01
☐ 247	Tim Flood	.10	.05	.01
☐ 248	Jake Flowers	.10	.05	.01
☐ 249	Hod Ford	.10	.05	.01
☐ 250	Terry Forster	.20	.10	.02
☐ 251	Alan Foster	.10	.05	.01
☐ 252	Jack Fournier	.10	.05	.01
☐ 253	Dave Foutz	.10	.05	.01
☐ 254	Art Fowler	.10	.05	.01
☐ 255	Fred Frankhouse	.10	.05	.01
☐ 256	Herman Franks	.10	.05	.01
☐ 257	Johnny Frederick	.10	.05	.01
☐ 258	Larry French	.10	.05	.01
☐ 259	Lonny Frey	.10	.05	.01
☐ 260	Pepe Frias	.10	.05	.01
☐ 261	Charlie Fuchs	.10	.05	.01
☐ 262	Carl Furillo	.20	.10	.02
☐ 263	Len Gabrielson	.10	.05	.01
☐ 264	Augie Galan	.10	.05	.01
☐ 265	Joe Gallagher	.10	.05	.01
☐ 266	Phil Gallivan	.10	.05	.01
☐ 267	Balvino Galvez	.10	.05	.01
☐ 268	Mike Garman	.10	.05	.01
☐ 269	Phil Garner	.10	.05	.01
☐ 270	Steve Garvey	.30	.15	.03
☐ 271	Ned Garvin	.10	.05	.01
☐ 272	Hank Gastright	.10	.05	.01
☐ 273	Sid Gautreaux	.10	.05	.01
☐ 274	Jim Gentile	.10	.05	.01
☐ 275	Greek George	.10	.05	.01
☐ 276	Ben Geraghty	.10	.05	.01
☐ 277	Gus Getz	.10	.05	.01
☐ 278	Bob Giallombardo	.10	.05	.01
☐ 279	Kirk Gibson	.30	.15	.03
☐ 280	Charlie Gilbert	.10	.05	.01
☐ 281	Jim Gilliam	.20	.10	.02
☐ 282	Al Gionfriddo	.10	.05	.01
☐ 283	Tony Giuliani	.10	.05	.01
☐ 284	Al Glossop	.10	.05	.01
☐ 285	John Gochnaur	.10	.05	.01
☐ 286	Jim Golden	.10	.05	.01
☐ 287	Dave Goltz	.10	.05	.01
☐ 288	Jose Gonzales	.10	.05	.01
☐ 289	Johnny Gooch	.10	.05	.01
☐ 290	Ed Goodson	.10	.05	.01
☐ 291	Billy Grabarkewitz	.10	.05	.01
☐ 292	Jack Graham	.10	.05	.01
☐ 293	Mudcat Grant	.10	.05	.01
☐ 294	Dick Gray	.10	.05	.01
☐ 295	Kent Greenfield	.10	.05	.01
☐ 296	Hal Gregg	.10	.05	.01
☐ 297	Alfredo Griffin	.10	.05	.01
☐ 298	Mike Griffin	.10	.05	.01
☐ 299	Derrel Griffith	.10	.05	.01
☐ 300	Tommy Griffith	.10	.05	.01
☐ 301	Burleigh Grimes	.30	.15	.03
☐ 302	Lee Grissom	.10	.05	.01
☐ 303	Jerry Grote	.10	.05	.01

☐ 304 Pedro Guerrero	.30	.15	.03
☐ 305 Brad Gulden	.10	.05	.01
☐ 306 Ad Gumbert	.10	.05	.01
☐ 307 Chris Gwynn	.20	.10	.02
☐ 308 Bert Haas	.10	.05	.01
☐ 309 John Hale	.10	.05	.01
☐ 310 Tom Haller	.10	.05	.01
☐ 311 Bill Hallman	.10	.05	.01
☐ 312 Jeff Hamilton	.10	.05	.01
☐ 313 Luke Hamlin	.10	.05	.01
☐ 314 Ned Hanlon	.10	.05	.01
☐ 315 Gerald Hannahs	.10	.05	.01
☐ 316 Charlie Hargreaves	.10	.05	.01
☐ 317 Tim Harkiness	.10	.05	.01
☐ 318 Harry Harper	.10	.05	.01
☐ 319 Joe Harris	.10	.05	.01
☐ 320 Lenny Harris	.20	.10	.02
☐ 321 Bill F. Hart	.10	.05	.01
☐ 322 Buddy Hassett	.10	.05	.01
☐ 323 Mickey Hatcher	.10	.05	.01
☐ 324 Joe Hatten	.10	.05	.01
☐ 325 Phil Haugstad	.10	.05	.01
☐ 326 Brad Havens	.10	.05	.01
☐ 327 Ray Hayworth	.10	.05	.01
☐ 328 Ed Head	.10	.05	.01
☐ 329 Danny Heep	.10	.05	.01
☐ 330 Fred Heimach	.10	.05	.01
☐ 331 Harvey Hendrick	.10	.05	.01
☐ 332 Weldon Henley	.10	.05	.01
☐ 333 Butch Henline	.10	.05	.01
☐ 334 Dutch Henry	.10	.05	.01
☐ 335 Roy Henshaw	.10	.05	.01
☐ 336 Babe Herman	.20	.10	.02
☐ 337 Billy Herman	.30	.15	.03
☐ 338 Gene Hermanski	.10	.05	.01
☐ 339 Enzo Hernandez	.10	.05	.01
☐ 340 Art Herring	.10	.05	.01
☐ 341 Orel Hershiser	.30	.15	.03
☐ 342 Dave J. Hickman	.10	.05	.01
☐ 343 Jim Hickman	.10	.05	.01
☐ 344 Kirby Higbe	.10	.05	.01
☐ 345 Andy High	.10	.05	.01
☐ 346 George Hildebrand	.10	.05	.01
☐ 347 Hunkey Hines	.10	.05	.01
☐ 348 Don Hoak	.10	.05	.01
☐ 349 Oris Hockett	.10	.05	.01
☐ 350 Gil Hodges	.30	.15	.03
☐ 351 Glenn Hoffman	.10	.05	.01
☐ 352 Al Hollingsworth	.10	.05	.01
☐ 353 Tommy Holmes	.20	.10	.02
☐ 354 Brian Holton	.10	.05	.01
☐ 355 Rick Honeycutt	.10	.05	.01
☐ 356 Burt Hooton	.10	.05	.01
☐ 357 Gail Hopkins	.10	.05	.01
☐ 358 Johnny Hopp	.10	.05	.01
☐ 359 Charlie Hough	.20	.10	.02
☐ 360 Frank Howard	.20	.10	.02
☐ 361 Steve Howe	.10	.05	.01
☐ 362 Dixie Howell	.10	.05	.01
☐ 363 Harry Howell	.10	.05	.01
☐ 364 Jay Howell	.20	.10	.02
☐ 365 Ken Howell	.20	.10	.02
☐ 366 Waite Hoyt	.30	.15	.03
☐ 367 Johnny Hudson	.10	.05	.01
☐ 368 Jim J. Hughes	.10	.05	.01
☐ 369 Jim R. Hughes	.10	.05	.01
☐ 370 Mickey Hughes	.10	.05	.01
☐ 371 John Hummel	.10	.05	.01
☐ 372 Ron Hunt	.10	.05	.01
☐ 373 Willard Hunter	.10	.05	.01
☐ 374 Ira Hutchinson	.10	.05	.01
☐ 375 Tom Hutton	.10	.05	.01
☐ 376 Charlie Irwin	.10	.05	.01
☐ 377 Fred Jacklitsch	.10	.05	.01
☐ 378 Randy Jackson	.10	.05	.01
☐ 379 Merwin Jacobson	.10	.05	.01
☐ 380 Cleo James	.10	.05	.01
☐ 381 Hal Janvrin	.10	.05	.01
☐ 382 Roy Jarvis	.10	.05	.01
☐ 383 George Jeffcoat	.10	.05	.01
☐ 384 Jack Jenkins	.10	.05	.01
☐ 385 Hughie Jennings	.30	.15	.03
☐ 386 Tommy John	.20	.10	.02
☐ 387 Lou Johnson	.10	.05	.01
☐ 388 Fred Ivy Johnston	.10	.05	.01
☐ 389 Jimmy Johnston	.10	.05	.01
☐ 390 Jay Johnstone	.20	.10	.02
☐ 391 Fielder Jones	.10	.05	.01
☐ 392 Oscar Jones	.10	.05	.01
☐ 393 Tim Jordan	.10	.05	.01
☐ 394 Spider Jorgensen	.10	.05	.01
☐ 395 Von Joshua	.10	.05	.01
☐ 396 Bill Joyce	.10	.05	.01
☐ 397 Joe Judge	.10	.05	.01

☐ 398 Alex Kampouris	.10	.05	.01
☐ 399 Willie Keeler	.30	.15	.03
☐ 400 Mike Kekich	.10	.05	.01
☐ 401 John Kelleher	.10	.05	.01
☐ 402 Frank Kellert	.10	.05	.01
☐ 403 Joe Kelley	.30	.15	.03
☐ 404 George Kelly	.30	.15	.03
☐ 405 Bob Kennedy	.10	.05	.01
☐ 406 Brickyard Kennedy	.10	.05	.01
☐ 407 John Kennedy	.10	.05	.01
☐ 408 Not issued	.00	.00	.00
☐ 409 Newt Kimball	.10	.05	.01
☐ 410 Clyde King	.10	.05	.01
☐ 411 Enos Kirkpatrick	.10	.05	.01
☐ 412 Frank Kitson	.10	.05	.01
☐ 413 Johnny Klippstein	.10	.05	.01
☐ 414 Elmer Klumpp	.10	.05	.01
☐ 415 Len Koenecke	.10	.05	.01
☐ 416 Ed Konetchy	.10	.05	.01
☐ 417 Andy Kosco	.10	.05	.01
☐ 418 Sandy Koufax	.50	.25	.05
☐ 419 Ernie Koy	.10	.05	.01
☐ 420 Charlie Kress	.10	.05	.01
☐ 421 Bill Krueger	.10	.05	.01
☐ 422 Ernie Krueger	.10	.05	.01
☐ 423 Clem Labine	.10	.05	.01
☐ 424 Candy LaChance	.10	.05	.01
☐ 425 Lee Lacy	.10	.05	.01
☐ 426 Lerrin LaGrow	.10	.05	.01
☐ 427 Bill Lamar	.10	.05	.01
☐ 428 Wayne LaMaster	.10	.05	.01
☐ 429 Ray Lamb	.10	.05	.01
☐ 430 Rafael Landestoy	.10	.05	.01
☐ 431 Ken Landreaux	.10	.05	.01
☐ 432 Tito Landrum	.10	.05	.01
☐ 433 Norm Larker	.10	.05	.01
☐ 434 Lyn Lary	.10	.05	.01
☐ 435 Tom Lasorda	.30	.15	.03
☐ 436 Cookie Lavagetto	.10	.05	.01
☐ 437 Rudy Law	.10	.05	.01
☐ 438 Tony Lazzeri	.20	.10	.02
☐ 439 Tim Leary	.20	.10	.02
☐ 440 Bob Lee	.10	.05	.01
☐ 441 Hal Lee	.10	.05	.01
☐ 442 Leron Lee	.10	.05	.01
☐ 443 Jim Lefebvre	.20	.10	.02
☐ 444 Ken Lehman	.10	.05	.01
☐ 445 Don LeJohn	.10	.05	.01
☐ 446 Steve Lembo	.10	.05	.01
☐ 447 Ed Lennox	.10	.05	.01
☐ 448 Dutch Leonard	.20	.10	.02
☐ 449 Jeffery Leonard	.10	.05	.01
☐ 451 Dennis Lewallyn	.10	.05	.01
☐ 452 Bob Lillis	.10	.05	.01
☐ 453 Jim Lindsey	.10	.05	.01
☐ 454 Fred Lindstrom	.30	.15	.03
☐ 455 Billy Loes	.10	.05	.01
☐ 456 Bob Logan	.10	.05	.01
☐ 457 Bill Lohrman	.10	.05	.01
☐ 458 Not issued	.00	.00	.00
☐ 459 Vic Lombardi	.10	.05	.01
☐ 460 Davey Lopes	.20	.10	.02
☐ 461 Al Lopez	.30	.15	.03
☐ 462 Ray Lucas	.10	.05	.01
☐ 463 Not issued	.00	.00	.00
☐ 464 Harry Lumley	.10	.05	.01
☐ 465 Don Lund	.10	.05	.01
☐ 466 Dolf Luque	.10	.05	.01
☐ 467 Jim Lyttle	.10	.05	.01
☐ 468 Max Macon	.10	.05	.01
☐ 469 Bill Madlock	.20	.10	.02
☐ 470 Lee Magee	.10	.05	.01
☐ 471 Sal Maglie	.20	.10	.02
☐ 472 George Magoon	.10	.05	.01
☐ 473 Duster Mails	.10	.05	.01
☐ 474 Candy Maldonado	.20	.10	.02
☐ 475 Tony Malinosky	.10	.05	.01
☐ 476 Lew Malone	.10	.05	.01
☐ 477 Al Mamaux	.10	.05	.01
☐ 478 Gus Mancuso	.10	.05	.01
☐ 479 Charlie Manuel	.10	.05	.01
☐ 480 Heinie Manush	.30	.15	.03
☐ 481 Rabbit Maranville	.30	.15	.03
☐ 482 Juan Marichal	.40	.20	.04
☐ 483 Rube Marquard	.30	.15	.03
☐ 484 Bill Marriott	.10	.05	.01
☐ 485 Buck Marrow	.10	.05	.01
☐ 486 Mike A. Marshall	.20	.10	.02
☐ 487 Mike G. Marshall	.20	.10	.02
☐ 488 Morrie Martin	.10	.05	.01
☐ 489 Ramon Martinez	.50	.25	.05
☐ 490 Teddy Martinez	.10	.05	.01
☐ 491 Earl Mattingly	.10	.05	.01
☐ 492 Len Matuszek	.10	.05	.01

☐ 493 Gene Mauch	.20	.10	.02
☐ 494 Al Maul	.10	.05	.01
☐ 495 Carmen Mauro	.10	.05	.01
☐ 496 Alvin McBean	.10	.05	.01
☐ 497 Bill McCarren	.10	.05	.01
☐ 498 Jack McCarthy	.10	.05	.01
☐ 499 Tommy McCarthy	.10	.05	.01
☐ 500 Lew McCarty	.10	.05	.01
☐ 501 Mike J. McCormick	.10	.05	.01
☐ 502 Judge McCreedie	.10	.05	.01
☐ 503 Tom McCreery	.10	.05	.01
☐ 504 Danny McDevitt	.10	.05	.01
☐ 505 Chappie McFarland	.10	.05	.01
☐ 506 Joe McGinnity	.30	.15	.03
☐ 507 Bob McGraw	.10	.05	.01
☐ 508 Deacon McGuire	.10	.05	.01
☐ 509 Bill McGunnigle	.10	.05	.01
☐ 510 Harry McIntyre	.10	.05	.01
☐ 511 Cal McLish	.10	.05	.01
☐ 512 Ken McMullen	.10	.05	.01
☐ 513 Dough McWeeny	.10	.05	.01
☐ 514 Joe Medwick	.30	.15	.03
☐ 515 Rube Melton	.10	.05	.01
☐ 516 Fred Merkle	.20	.10	.02
☐ 517 Orland Mercado	.10	.05	.01
☐ 518 Andy Messersmith	.20	.10	.02
☐ 519 Irish Meusel	.10	.05	.01
☐ 520 Benny Meyer	.10	.05	.01
☐ 521 Russ Meyer	.10	.05	.01
☐ 522 Chief Meyers	.10	.05	.01
☐ 523 Gene Michael	.20	.10	.02
☐ 524 Pete Mikkelsen	.10	.05	.01
☐ 525 Eddie Miksis	.10	.05	.01
☐ 526 Johnny Miljus	.10	.05	.01
☐ 527 Bob Miller	.10	.05	.01
☐ 528 Larry Miller	.10	.05	.01
☐ 529 Otto Miller	.10	.05	.01
☐ 530 Ralph Miller	.10	.05	.01
☐ 531 Walt Miller	.10	.05	.01
☐ 532 Wally Millies	.10	.05	.01
☐ 533 Bob Milliken	.10	.05	.01
☐ 534 Buster Mills	.10	.05	.01
☐ 535 Paul Minner	.10	.05	.01
☐ 536 Bobby Mitchell	.10	.05	.01
☐ 537 Clarence Mitchell	.10	.05	.01
☐ 538 Dale Mitchell	.10	.05	.01
☐ 539 Fred Mitchell	.10	.05	.01
☐ 540 Johnny Mitchell	.10	.05	.01
☐ 541 Joe Moeller	.10	.05	.01
☐ 542 Rick Monday	.10	.05	.01
☐ 543 Wally Moon	.10	.05	.01
☐ 544 Cy Moore	.10	.05	.01
☐ 545 Dee Moore	.10	.05	.01
☐ 546 Eddie Moore	.10	.05	.01
☐ 547 Gene Moore	.10	.05	.01
☐ 548 Randy Moore	.10	.05	.01
☐ 549 Ray Moore	.10	.05	.01
☐ 550 Jose Morales	.10	.05	.01
☐ 551 Bobby Morgan	.10	.05	.01
☐ 552 Eddie Morgan	.10	.05	.01
☐ 553 Mike Morgan	.10	.05	.01
☐ 554 Johnny Morrison	.10	.05	.01
☐ 555 Walt Moryn	.10	.05	.01
☐ 556 Ray Moss	.10	.05	.01
☐ 557 Manny Mota	.20	.10	.02
☐ 558 Joe Mulvey	.10	.05	.01
☐ 559 Van Lingle Mungo	.10	.05	.01
☐ 560 Les Munns	.10	.05	.01
☐ 561 Mike Munoz	.20	.10	.02
☐ 562 Simmy Murch	.10	.05	.01
☐ 563 Eddie Murray	.40	.20	.04
☐ 564 Hy Myers	.10	.05	.01
☐ 565 Sam Nahem	.10	.05	.01
☐ 566 Earl Naylor	.10	.05	.01
☐ 567 Charlie Neal	.10	.05	.01
☐ 568 Ron Negray	.10	.05	.01
☐ 569 Bernie Neis	.10	.05	.01
☐ 570 Rocky Nelson	.10	.05	.01
☐ 571 Dick Nen	.10	.05	.01
☐ 572 Don Newcombe	.20	.10	.02
☐ 573 Bobo Newsom	.20	.10	.02
☐ 574 Doc Newton	.10	.05	.01
☐ 575 Tom Niedenfuer	.10	.05	.01
☐ 576 Otho Nitcholas	.10	.05	.01
☐ 577 Al Nixon	.10	.05	.01
☐ 578 Jerry Nops	.10	.05	.01
☐ 579 Irv Noren	.10	.05	.01
☐ 580 Fred Norman	.10	.05	.01
☐ 581 Bill North	.10	.05	.01
☐ 582 Johnny Oates	.10	.05	.01
☐ 583 Bob O'Brien	.10	.05	.01
☐ 584 John O'Brien	.10	.05	.01
☐ 585 Lefty O'Doul	.20	.10	.02
☐ 586 Joe Oeschger	.10	.05	.01

☐ 587 Al Oliver	.20	.10	.02
☐ 588 Nate Oliver	.10	.05	.01
☐ 589 Luis Olmo	.10	.05	.01
☐ 590 Ivy Olson	.10	.05	.01
☐ 591 Mickey O'Neil	.10	.05	.01
☐ 592 Joe Orengo	.10	.05	.01
☐ 593 Jesse Orosco	.10	.05	.01
☐ 594 Frank O'Rourke	.10	.05	.01
☐ 595 Jorge Orta	.10	.05	.01
☐ 596 Phil Ortega	.10	.05	.01
☐ 597 Claude Osteen	.20	.10	.02
☐ 598 Fritz Ostermueller	.10	.05	.01
☐ 599 Mickey Owen	.20	.10	.02
☐ 600 Tom Paciorek	.10	.05	.01
☐ 601 Don Padgett	.10	.05	.01
☐ 602 Andy Pafko	.10	.05	.01
☐ 603 Erv Palica	.10	.05	.01
☐ 604 Ed Palmquist	.10	.05	.01
☐ 605 Wes Parker	.20	.10	.02
☐ 606 Jay Partridge	.10	.05	.01
☐ 607 Camilio Pascual	.20	.10	.02
☐ 608 Kevin Pasley	.10	.05	.01
☐ 609 Dave Patterson	.10	.05	.01
☐ 610 Harley Payne	.10	.05	.01
☐ 611 Johnny Peacock	.10	.05	.01
☐ 612 Hal Peck	.10	.05	.01
☐ 613 Stu Pederson	.10	.05	.01
☐ 614 Alejandro Pena	.20	.10	.02
☐ 615 Jose Pena	.10	.05	.01
☐ 616 Jack Perconte	.10	.05	.01
☐ 617 Charlie Perkins	.10	.05	.01
☐ 618 Ron Perranoski	.20	.10	.02
☐ 619 Jim Peterson	.10	.05	.01
☐ 620 Jesse Petty	.10	.05	.01
☐ 621 Jeff Pfeffer	.10	.05	.01
☐ 622 Babe Phelps	.10	.05	.01
☐ 623 Val Picinich	.10	.05	.01
☐ 624 Joe Pignatano	.10	.05	.01
☐ 625 George Pinckney	.10	.05	.01
☐ 626 Ed Pipgras	.10	.05	.01
☐ 627 Bud Podbielan	.10	.05	.01
☐ 628 Johnny Podres	.20	.10	.02
☐ 629 Boots Poffenberger	.10	.05	.01
☐ 630 Nick Polly	.10	.05	.01
☐ 631 Paul Popovich	.10	.05	.01
☐ 632 Bill Posedel	.10	.05	.01
☐ 633 Boog Powell	.20	.10	.02
☐ 634 Dennis Powell	.10	.05	.01
☐ 635 Paul Ray Powell	.10	.05	.01
☐ 636 Ted Power	.10	.05	.01
☐ 637 Tot Pressnell	.10	.05	.01
☐ 638 John Purdin	.10	.05	.01
☐ 639 Jack Quinn	.10	.05	.01
☐ 640 Marv Rackley	.10	.05	.01
☐ 641 Jack Radtke	.10	.05	.01
☐ 642 Pat Ragan	.10	.05	.01
☐ 643 Ed Rakow	.10	.05	.01
☐ 644 Bob Ramazzotti	.10	.05	.01
☐ 645 Willie Ramsdell	.10	.05	.01
☐ 646 Mike James Ramsey	.10	.05	.01
☐ 647 Mike Jeffery Ramsey	.10	.05	.01
☐ 648 Willie Randolph	.20	.10	.02
☐ 649 Doug Rau	.10	.05	.01
☐ 650 Lance Rautzhan	.10	.05	.01
☐ 651 Howie Reed	.10	.05	.01
☐ 652 Pee Wee Reese	.40	.20	.04
☐ 653 Phil Regan	.20	.10	.02
☐ 654 Bill Reidy	.10	.05	.01
☐ 655 Bobby Reis	.10	.05	.01
☐ 656 Pete Reiser	.20	.10	.02
☐ 657 Rip Repulski	.10	.05	.01
☐ 658 Ed Reulbach	.20	.10	.02
☐ 659 Jerry Reuss	.10	.05	.01
☐ 660 R.J. Reynolds	.10	.05	.01
☐ 661 Billy Rhiel	.10	.05	.01
☐ 662 Rick Rhoden	.10	.05	.01
☐ 663 Paul Richards	.20	.10	.02
☐ 664 Danny Richardson	.10	.05	.01
☐ 665 Pete Richert	.10	.05	.01
☐ 666 Harry Riconda	.10	.05	.01
☐ 667 Joe Riggert	.10	.05	.01
☐ 668 Lew Riggs	.10	.05	.01
☐ 669 Jimmy Ripple	.10	.05	.01
☐ 670 Lou Ritter	.10	.05	.01
☐ 671 German Rivera	.10	.05	.01
☐ 672 Johnny Rizzo	.10	.05	.01
☐ 673 Jim Roberts	.10	.05	.01
☐ 674 Earl Robinson	.10	.05	.01
☐ 675 Frank Robinson	.40	.20	.04
☐ 676 Jackie Robinson	.50	.25	.05
☐ 677A Wilbert Robinson	.30	.15	.03
☐ 678B Sergio Robles	.10	.05	.01
☐ 678 Rich Rodas	.10	.05	.01
☐ 679 Ellie Rodriguez	.10	.05	.01

☐ 680	Preacher Roe	.20	.10	.02
☐ 681	Ed Roebuck	.10	.05	.01
☐ 682	Ron Roenicke	.10	.05	.01
☐ 683	Oscar Roettger	.10	.05	.01
☐ 684	Lee Rogers	.10	.05	.01
☐ 685	Packy Rogers	.10	.05	.01
☐ 686	Stan Rojek	.10	.05	.01
☐ 687	Vicente Romo	.10	.05	.01
☐ 688	Johnny Roseboro	.10	.05	.01
☐ 689	Goody Rosen	.10	.05	.01
☐ 690	Don Ross	.10	.05	.01
☐ 691	Ken Rowe	.10	.05	.01
☐ 692	Schoolboy Rowe	.20	.10	.02
☐ 693	Luther Roy	.10	.05	.01
☐ 694	Jerry Royster	.10	.05	.01
☐ 695	Nap Rucker	.10	.05	.01
☐ 696	Dutch Ruether	.10	.05	.01
☐ 697	Bill Russell	.20	.10	.02
☐ 698	Jim Russell	.10	.05	.01
☐ 699	John Russell UER (photo actually current catcher John Russell)	.10	.05	.01
☐ 700	Johnny Rutherford	.10	.05	.01
☐ 701	John Ryan	.10	.05	.01
☐ 702	Rosy Ryan	.10	.05	.01
☐ 703	Mike Sandlock	.10	.05	.01
☐ 704	Ted Savage	.10	.05	.01
☐ 705	Dave Sax	.10	.05	.01
☐ 706	Steve Sax	.20	.10	.02
☐ 707	Bill Sayles	.10	.05	.01
☐ 708	Bill Schardt	.10	.05	.01
☐ 709	Johnny Schmitz	.10	.05	.01
☐ 710	Dick Schofield	.10	.05	.01
☐ 711	Howie Schultz	.10	.05	.01
☐ 712	Ferdie Schupp	.10	.05	.01
☐ 713	Mike Scioscia	.20	.10	.02
☐ 714	Dick Scott	.10	.05	.01
☐ 715	Tom Seats	.10	.05	.01
☐ 716	Jimmy Sebring	.10	.05	.01
☐ 717	Larry See	.10	.05	.01
☐ 718	Dave Sells	.10	.05	.01
☐ 719	Greg Shanahan	.10	.05	.01
☐ 720	Mike Sharperson	.10	.05	.01
☐ 721	Joe Shaute	.10	.05	.01
☐ 722	Merv Shea	.10	.05	.01
☐ 723	Jimmy Sheckhard	.10	.05	.01
☐ 724	Jack Sheehan	.10	.05	.01
☐ 725	John Shelby	.10	.05	.01
☐ 726	Vince Sherlock	.10	.05	.01
☐ 727	Larry Sherry	.20	.10	.02
☐ 728	Norm Sherry	.10	.05	.01
☐ 729	Bill Shindle	.10	.05	.01
☐ 730	Craig Shipley	.10	.05	.01
☐ 731	Bart Shirley	.10	.05	.01
☐ 732	Steve Shirley	.10	.05	.01
☐ 733	Burt Shotton	.10	.05	.01
☐ 734	George Shuba	.10	.05	.01
☐ 735	Dick Siebert	.10	.05	.01
☐ 736	Joe Simpson	.10	.05	.01
☐ 737	Duke Sims	.10	.05	.01
☐ 738	Bill Singer	.10	.05	.01
☐ 739	Fred Sington	.10	.05	.01
☐ 740	Ted Sizemore	.10	.05	.01
☐ 741	Frank Skaff	.10	.05	.01
☐ 742	Bill Skowron	.20	.10	.02
☐ 743	Gordon Slade	.10	.05	.01
☐ 744	Dwain Lefty Sloat	.10	.05	.01
☐ 745	Charley Smith	.10	.05	.01
☐ 746	Dick Smith	.10	.05	.01
☐ 747	George Smith	.10	.05	.01
☐ 748	Germany Smith	.10	.05	.01
☐ 749	Jack Smith	.10	.05	.01
☐ 750	Reggie Smith	.20	.10	.02
☐ 751	Sherry Smith	.10	.05	.01
☐ 752	Harry Smythe	.10	.05	.01
☐ 753	Duke Snider	.50	.25	.05
☐ 754	Eddie Solomon	.10	.05	.01
☐ 755	Elias Sosa	.10	.05	.01
☐ 756	Daryl Spencer	.10	.05	.01
☐ 757	Roy Spencer	.10	.05	.01
☐ 758	Karl Spooner	.10	.05	.01
☐ 759	Eddie Stack	.10	.05	.01
☐ 760	Tuck Stainback	.10	.05	.01
☐ 761	George Stallings	.10	.05	.01
☐ 762	Jerry Standaert	.10	.05	.01
☐ 763	Don Stanhouse	.10	.05	.01
☐ 764	Eddie Stanky	.20	.10	.02
☐ 765	Dolly Stark	.20	.10	.02
☐ 766	Jigger Statz	.10	.05	.01
☐ 767	Casey Stengel	.40	.20	.04
☐ 768	Jerry Stephenson	.10	.05	.01
☐ 769	Ed Stevens	.10	.05	.01
☐ 770	Dave Stewart	.30	.15	.03
☐ 771	Stuffy Stewart	.10	.05	.01
☐ 772	Bob Stinson	.10	.05	.01
☐ 773	Milt Stock	.10	.05	.01
☐ 774	Harry Stovey	.20	.10	.02
☐ 775	Mike Strahler	.10	.05	.01
☐ 776	Sammy Strang	.10	.05	.01
☐ 777	Elmer Stricklett	.10	.05	.01
☐ 778	Joe Stripp	.10	.05	.01
☐ 779	Dick Stuart	.20	.10	.02
☐ 780	Franklin Stubbs	.20	.10	.02
☐ 781	Bill Sudakis	.10	.05	.01
☐ 782	Clyde Sukeforth	.10	.05	.01
☐ 783	Billy Sullivan	.20	.10	.02
☐ 784	Tom Sunkel	.10	.05	.01
☐ 785	Rick Sutcliffe	.20	.10	.02
☐ 786	Don Sutton	.30	.15	.03
☐ 787	Bill Swift	.10	.05	.01
☐ 788	Vito Tamulis	.10	.05	.01
☐ 789	Danny Taylor	.10	.05	.01
☐ 790	Harry Taylor	.10	.05	.01
☐ 791	Zack Taylor	.10	.05	.01
☐ 792	Not issued	.00	.00	.00
☐ 793	Chuck Templeton	.10	.05	.01
☐ 794	Wayne Terwilliger	.10	.05	.01
☐ 795	Derrell Thomas	.10	.05	.01
☐ 796	Fay Thomas	.10	.05	.01
☐ 797	Gary Thomasson	.10	.05	.01
☐ 798	Don Thompson	.10	.05	.01
☐ 799	Fresco Thompson	.10	.05	.01
☐ 800	Tim Thompson	.10	.05	.01
☐ 801	Hank Thormahlen	.10	.05	.01
☐ 802	Sloppy Thurston	.10	.05	.01
☐ 803	Cotton Tierney	.10	.05	.01
☐ 804	Al Todd	.10	.05	.01
☐ 805	Bert Tooley	.10	.05	.01
☐ 806	Jeff Torborg	.20	.10	.02
☐ 807	Dick Tracewski	.10	.05	.01
☐ 808	Nick Tremark	.10	.05	.01
☐ 809	Alex Trevino	.10	.05	.01
☐ 810	Tommy Tucker	.10	.05	.01
☐ 811	John Tudor	.20	.10	.02
☐ 812	Mike Vail	.10	.05	.01
☐ 813	Rene Valdes	.10	.05	.01
☐ 814	Bobby Valentine	.20	.10	.02
☐ 815	Fernando Valenzuela	.30	.15	.03
☐ 816	Elmer Valo	.10	.05	.01
☐ 817	Dazzy Vance	.30	.15	.03
☐ 818	Sandy Vance	.10	.05	.01
☐ 819	Chris Van Cuyk	.10	.05	.01
☐ 820	Ed Vande Berg	.10	.05	.01
☐ 821	Arky Vaughan	.30	.15	.03
☐ 822	Zoilo Versalles	.20	.10	.02
☐ 823	Joe Vosmik	.10	.05	.01
☐ 824	Ben Wade	.10	.05	.01
☐ 825	Dixie Walker	.10	.05	.01
☐ 826	Rube Walker	.10	.05	.01
☐ 827	Stan Wall	.10	.05	.01
☐ 828	Lee Walls	.10	.05	.01
☐ 829	Danny Walton	.10	.05	.01
☐ 830	Lloyd Waner	.30	.15	.03
☐ 831	Paul Waner	.30	.15	.03
☐ 832	Chuck Ward	.10	.05	.01
☐ 833	John Monte Ward	.30	.15	.03
☐ 834	Preston Ward	.10	.05	.01
☐ 835	Jack Warner	.10	.05	.01
☐ 836	Tommy Warren	.10	.05	.01
☐ 837	Carl Warwick	.10	.05	.01
☐ 838	Jimmy Wasdell	.10	.05	.01
☐ 839	Ron Washington	.10	.05	.01
☐ 840	George Watkins	.10	.05	.01
☐ 841	Hank Webb	.10	.05	.01
☐ 842	Les Webber	.10	.05	.01
☐ 843	Gary Weiss	.10	.05	.01
☐ 844	Bob Welch	.30	.15	.03
☐ 845	Brad Wellman	.10	.05	.01
☐ 846	John Werhas	.10	.05	.01
☐ 847	Max West	.10	.05	.01
☐ 848	Gus Weyhing	.10	.05	.01
☐ 849	Mack Wheat	.10	.05	.01
☐ 850	Zack Wheat	.30	.15	.03
☐ 851	Ed Wheeler	.10	.05	.01
☐ 852	Larry White	.10	.05	.01
☐ 853	Myron White	.10	.05	.01
☐ 854	Terry Whitfield	.10	.05	.01
☐ 855	Dick Whitman	.10	.05	.01
☐ 856	Possum Whitted	.10	.05	.01
☐ 857	Kemp Wicker	.10	.05	.01
☐ 858	Hoyt Wilhelm	.30	.15	.03
☐ 859	Kaiser Wilhelm	.10	.05	.01
☐ 860	Nick Willhite	.10	.05	.01
☐ 861	Dick Williams	.10	.05	.01
☐ 862	Reggie Williams	.10	.05	.01
☐ 863	Stan Williams	.10	.05	.01
☐ 864	Woody Williams	.10	.05	.01

☐	865 Maury Wills	.30	.15	.03
☐	866 Hack Wilson	.30	.15	.03
☐	867 Robert Wilson	.10	.05	.01
☐	868 Gordon Windhorn	.10	.05	.01
☐	869 Jim Winford	.10	.05	.01
☐	870 Lave Winham	.10	.05	.01
☐	871 Tom Winsett	.10	.05	.01
☐	872 Hank Winston	.10	.05	.01
☐	873 Whitney Witt	.10	.05	.01
☐	874 Pete Wojey	.10	.05	.01
☐	875 Tracy Woodson	.10	.05	.01
☐	876 Clarence Wright	.10	.05	.01
☐	877 Glenn Wright	.10	.05	.01
☐	878 Ricky Wright	.10	.05	.01
☐	879 Whit Wyatt	.10	.05	.01
☐	880 Jimmy Wynn	.10	.05	.01
☐	881 Joe Yeager	.10	.05	.01
☐	882 Steve Yeager	.10	.05	.01
☐	883 Matt Young	.10	.05	.01
☐	884 Tom Zachary	.10	.05	.01
☐	885 Pat Zachry	.10	.05	.01
☐	886 Geoff Zahn	.10	.05	.01
☐	887 Don Zimmer	.20	.10	.02
☐	888 Morrie Aderholt	.10	.05	.01
☐	889 Raleigh Aitchison	.10	.05	.01
☐	890 Whitey Alperman	.10	.05	.01
☐	891 Orlando Alvarez	.10	.05	.01
☐	892 Pat Ankeman	.10	.05	.01
☐	893 Ed Appleton	.10	.05	.01
☐	894 Doug Baird	.10	.05	.01
☐	895 Lady Baldwin	.10	.05	.01
☐	896 Win Ballou	.10	.05	.01
☐	897 Bob Barr	.10	.05	.01
☐	898 Boyd Bartley	.10	.05	.01
☐	899 Eddie Basinski	.10	.05	.01
☐	900 Erve Beck	.10	.05	.01
☐	901 Ralph Birkofer	.10	.05	.01
☐	902 Not issued	.00	.00	.00
☐	903 Joe Bradshaw	.10	.05	.01
☐	904 Bruce Brubaker	.10	.05	.01
☐	905 Oyster Burns	.10	.05	.01
☐	906 John Butler	.10	.05	.01
☐	907 Not issued	.00	.00	.00
☐	908 Kid Carsey	.10	.05	.01
☐	909 Pete Cassidy	.10	.05	.01
☐	910 Tom Catterson	.10	.05	.01
☐	911 Glenn Chapman	.10	.05	.01
☐	912 Paul Chervinko	.10	.05	.01
☐	913 George Cisar	.10	.05	.01
☐	914 Wally Clement	.10	.05	.01
☐	915 Bill Collins	.10	.05	.01
☐	916 Chuck Corgan	.10	.05	.01
☐	917 Dick Cox	.10	.05	.01
☐	918 George Crable	.10	.05	.01
☐	919 Sam Crane	.10	.05	.01
☐	920 Cliff Curtis	.10	.05	.01
☐	921 Fats Dantonio	.10	.05	.01
☐	922 Con Daily	.10	.05	.01
☐	923 Jud Daley	.10	.05	.01
☐	924 Jake Daniel	.10	.05	.01
☐	925 Kal Daniels	.20	.10	.02
☐	926 Dan Daub	.10	.05	.01
☐	927 Lindsay Deal	.10	.05	.01
☐	928 Artie Dede	.10	.05	.01
☐	929 Pat Deisel	.10	.05	.01
☐	930 Bert Delmas	.10	.05	.01
☐	931 Rube Dessau	.10	.05	.01
☐	932 Leo Dickerman	.10	.05	.01
☐	933 John Douglas	.10	.05	.01
☐	934 Red Downey	.10	.05	.01
☐	935 Carl Doyle	.10	.05	.01
☐	936 John Duffie	.10	.05	.01
☐	937 Dick Durning	.10	.05	.01
☐	938 Red Durrett	.10	.05	.01
☐	939 Mal Eason	.10	.05	.01
☐	940 Charlie Ebbetts	.10	.05	.01
☐	941 Rube Ehardt	.10	.05	.01
☐	942 Rowdy Elliot	.10	.05	.01
☐	943 Bones Ely	.10	.05	.01
☐	944 Woody English	.10	.05	.01
☐	945 Roy Evans	.10	.05	.01
☐	946 Gus Felix	.10	.05	.01
☐	947 Bill Fischer	.10	.05	.01
☐	948 Jeff Fischer	.10	.05	.01
☐	949 Chauncey Fisher	.10	.05	.01
☐	950 Tom Fitzsimmons	.10	.05	.01
☐	951 Darrin Fletcher	.20	.10	.02
☐	952 Wes Flowers	.10	.05	.01
☐	953 Howard Freigau	.10	.05	.01
☐	954 Nig Fuller	.10	.05	.01
☐	955 John Gaddy	.10	.05	.01
☐	956 Welcome Gaston	.10	.05	.01
☐	957 Frank Gatins	.10	.05	.01
☐	958 Pete Gilbert	.10	.05	.01
☐	959 Wally Gilbert	.10	.05	.01
☐	960 Carden Gillenwater	.10	.05	.01
☐	961 Roy Gleason	.10	.05	.01
☐	962 Harvey Green	.10	.05	.01
☐	963 Nelson Greene	.10	.05	.01
☐	964 John Grim	.10	.05	.01
☐	965 Dan Griner	.10	.05	.01
☐	967 Bill Hall	.10	.05	.01
☐	968 Johnny Hall	.10	.05	.01
☐	969 Not issued	.00	.00	.00
☐	970 Pat Hanifin	.10	.05	.01
☐	971 Bill Harris	.10	.05	.01
☐	972 Bill W. Hart	.10	.05	.01
☐	973 Chris Hartje	.10	.05	.01
☐	974 Mike Hartley	.20	.10	.02
☐	975 Gil Hatfield	.10	.05	.01
☐	976 Chris Haughey	.10	.05	.01
☐	977 Hugh Hearne	.10	.05	.01
☐	978 Mike Hechinger	.10	.05	.01
☐	979 Jake Hehl	.10	.05	.01
☐	980 Bob Higgins	.10	.05	.01
☐	981 Still Bill Hill	.10	.05	.01
☐	982 Shawn Hillegas	.20	.10	.02
☐	983 Wally Hood	.10	.05	.01
☐	984 Lefty Hopper	.10	.05	.01
☐	985 Ricky Horton	.10	.05	.01
☐	986 Ed Householder	.10	.05	.01
☐	987 Bill Hubbell	.10	.05	.01
☐	988 Al Humphrey	.10	.05	.01
☐	989 Bernie Hungling	.10	.05	.01
☐	990 George Hunter	.10	.05	.01
☐	991 Pat Hurley	.10	.05	.01
☐	992 Joe Hutcheson	.10	.05	.01
☐	993 Roy Hutson	.10	.05	.01
☐	994 Bert Inks	.10	.05	.01
☐	995 Dutch Jordan	.10	.05	.01
☐	996 Not issued	.00	.00	.00
☐	997 Frank Kane	.10	.05	.01
☐	998 Chet Kehn	.10	.05	.01
☐	999 Maury Kent	.10	.05	.01
☐	1000 Tom Kinslow	.10	.05	.01
☐	1001 Fred Kipp	.10	.05	.01
☐	1002 Joe Klugman	.10	.05	.01
☐	1003 Elmer Knetzer	.10	.05	.01
☐	1004 Barney Koch	.10	.05	.01
☐	1005 Jim Korwan	.10	.05	.01
☐	1006 Joe Koukalik	.10	.05	.01
☐	1007 Lou Koupal	.10	.05	.01
☐	1008 Joe Kustus	.10	.05	.01
☐	1009 Frank Lamanske	.10	.05	.01
☐	1010 Tacks Latimer	.10	.05	.01
☐	1011 Bill Leard	.10	.05	.01
☐	1012 Phil Lewis	.10	.05	.01
☐	1013 Mickey Livingston	.10	.05	.01
☐	1014 Dick Loftus	.10	.05	.01
☐	1015 Charlie Loudenslager	.10	.05	.01
☐	1016 Tom Lovett	.10	.05	.01
☐	1017 Charlie Malay	.10	.05	.01
☐	1018 Mal Mallette	.10	.05	.01
☐	1019 Ralph Mauriello	.10	.05	.01
☐	1020 Bill McCabe	.10	.05	.01
☐	1021 Gene McCann	.10	.05	.01
☐	1022 Mike W. McCormick	.10	.05	.01
☐	1023 Terry McDermott	.10	.05	.01
☐	1024 John McDougal	.10	.05	.01
☐	1025 Pryor McElveen	.10	.05	.01
☐	1026 Dan McGann	.10	.05	.01
☐	1027 Pat McGlothin	.10	.05	.01
☐	1028 Doc McJames	.10	.05	.01
☐	1029 Kit McKenna	.10	.05	.01
☐	1030 Sadie McMahon	.10	.05	.01
☐	1031 Not issued	.00	.00	.00
☐	1032 Tommy McMillan	.10	.05	.01
☐	1033 Glenn Mickens	.10	.05	.01
☐	1034 Don Miles	.10	.05	.01
☐	1035 Hack Miller	.10	.05	.01
☐	1036 John Miller	.10	.05	.01
☐	1037 Lemmie Miller	.10	.05	.01
☐	1038 George Mohart	.10	.05	.01
☐	1039 Gary Moore	.10	.05	.01
☐	1040 Herbie Moran	.10	.05	.01
☐	1041 Earl Mossor	.10	.05	.01
☐	1042 Glen Moulder	.10	.05	.01
☐	1043 Billy Mullen	.10	.05	.01
☐	1045 Curly Onis	.10	.05	.01
☐	1046 Tiny Osborne	.10	.05	.01
☐	1047 Jim Pastorius	.10	.05	.01
☐	1048 Art Parks	.10	.05	.01
☐	1049 Chink Outen	.10	.05	.01
☐	1050 Jimmy Pattison	.10	.05	.01
☐	1051 Norman Plitt	.10	.05	.01
☐	1052 Doc Reisling	.10	.05	.01
☐	1053 Gilberto Reyes	.10	.05	.01
☐	1054 Not issued	.00	.00	.00

☐ 1055 Lou Rochelli	.10	.05	.01
☐ 1056 Jim Romano	.10	.05	.01
☐ 1057 Max Rosenfeld	.10	.05	.01
☐ 1058 Andy Rush	.10	.05	.01
☐ 1059 Jack Ryan	.10	.05	.01
☐ 1060 Jack Savage	.10	.05	.01
☐ 1061 Not issued	.00	.00	.00
☐ 1062 Ray Schmandt	.10	.05	.01
☐ 1063 Henry Schmidt	.10	.05	.01
☐ 1064 Charlie Schmutz	.10	.05	.01
☐ 1065 Joe Schultz	.10	.05	.01
☐ 1066 Ray Searage	.10	.05	.01
☐ 1067 Elmer Sexauer	.10	.05	.01
☐ 1068 George Sharrott	.10	.05	.01
☐ 1069 Tommy Sheehan	.10	.05	.01
☐ 1071 George Shoch	.10	.05	.01
☐ 1072 Broadway Aleck Smith	.10	.05	.01
☐ 1073 Hap Smith	.10	.05	.01
☐ 1074 Red Smith	.10	.05	.01
☐ 1075 Tony Smith	.10	.05	.01
☐ 1076 Gene Snyder	.10	.05	.01
☐ 1077 Denny Sothern	.10	.05	.01
☐ 1078 Bill Steele	.10	.05	.01
☐ 1080 Farmer Steelman	.10	.05	.01
☐ 1081 Dutch Stryker	.10	.05	.01
☐ 1082 Tommy Tatum	.10	.05	.01
☐ 1084 Adonis Terry	.10	.05	.01
☐ 1085 Ray Thomas	.10	.05	.01
☐ 1086 George Treadway	.10	.05	.01
☐ 1087 Overton Tremper	.10	.05	.01
☐ 1088 Ty Tyson	.10	.05	.01
☐ 1089 Rube Vickers	.10	.05	.01
☐ 1090 Jose Vizcaino	.10	.05	.01
☐ 1091 Bull Wagner	.10	.05	.01
☐ 1092 Butts Wagner	.10	.05	.01
☐ 1093 Rube Ward	.10	.05	.01
☐ 1094 John Wetteland	.20	.10	.02
☐ 1095 Eddie Wilson	.10	.05	.01
☐ 1096 Tex Wilson	.10	.05	.01
☐ 1097 Zeke Wrigley	.10	.05	.01
☐ 1098 Not issued	.00	.00	.00
☐ 1099 Rube Yarrison	.10	.05	.01
☐ 1100 Earl Yingling	.10	.05	.01
☐ 1101 Chink Zachary	.10	.05	.01
☐ 1102 Lefty Davis	.10	.05	.01
☐ 1103 Bob Hall	.10	.05	.01
☐ 1104 Darby O'Brien	.10	.05	.01
☐ 1105 Larry LeJeune	.10	.05	.01
☐ 1144 Hub Northen	.10	.05	.01

1984 Tastykake Phillies

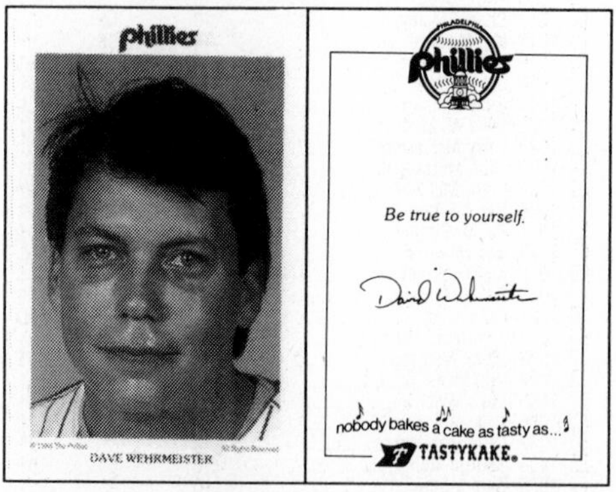
phillies
DAVE WEHRMEISTER
Be true to yourself.
nobody bakes a cake as tasty as...
TASTYKAKE

This set features the Philadelphia Phillies and was sponsored by Tastykake. The card fronts feature a colorful picture of the player or subject inside a white border. The cards measure approximately 3 1/2" by 5 1/4". The set was distributed to fans attending a specific game. There were four additional cards which were put out late in the year updating new players (after the first 40 had been out for some time). The update cards are numbered 41-44 after the first group. The card backs contain a brief message (tip) from the player with his facsimile autograph. The cards are unnumbered but the title card gives a numbering system essentially by position; that system is used below for the first 40 cards.

	MINT	VG-E	F-G
COMPLETE SET (44)	10.00	5.00	1.00
COMMON PLAYER (1-40)	.20	.10	.02
COMMON PLAYER (41-44)	.40	.20	.04
☐ 1 Logo Card/Checklist	.20	.10	.02
☐ 2 Team Photo	.20	.10	.02
☐ 3 Phillie Phanatic	.20	.10	.02
☐ 4 Veterans Stadium	.20	.10	.02
☐ 5 Steve Carlton Hall of Fame	1.00	.50	.10
☐ 6 Mike Schmidt Hall of Fame	1.50	.75	.15
☐ 7 Phillies Broadcasters	.20	.10	.02
☐ 8 Paul Owens MG	.20	.10	.02
☐ 9 Dave Bristol CO	.20	.10	.02
☐ 10 John Felske CO	.20	.10	.02
☐ 11 Deron Johnson CO	.20	.10	.02
☐ 12 Claude Osteen CO	.20	.10	.02
☐ 13 Mike Ryan CO	.20	.10	.02
☐ 14 Larry Andersen	.20	.10	.02
☐ 15 Marty Bystrom	.20	.10	.02
☐ 16 Bill Campbell	.20	.10	.02
☐ 17 Steve Carlton	1.00	.50	.10
☐ 18 John Denny	.30	.15	.03
☐ 19 Tony Ghelfi	.20	.10	.02
☐ 20 Kevin Gross	.20	.10	.02
☐ 21 Al Holland	.20	.10	.02
☐ 22 Charles Hudson	.20	.10	.02
☐ 23 Jerry Koosman	.30	.15	.03
☐ 24 Tug McGraw	.40	.20	.04
☐ 25 Bo Diaz	.20	.10	.02
☐ 26 Ozzie Virgil	.20	.10	.02
☐ 27 John Wockenfuss	.20	.10	.02
☐ 28 Luis Aguayo	.20	.10	.02
☐ 29 Ivan DeJesus	.20	.10	.02
☐ 30 Kiko Garcia	.20	.10	.02
☐ 31 Len Matuszek	.20	.10	.02
☐ 32 Juan Samuel	.30	.15	.03
☐ 33 Mike Schmidt	1.50	.75	.15
☐ 34 Tim Corcoran	.20	.10	.02
☐ 35 Greg Gross	.20	.10	.02
☐ 36 Von Hayes	.50	.25	.05
☐ 37 Joe Lefebvre	.20	.10	.02
☐ 38 Sixto Lezcano	.20	.10	.02
☐ 39 Garry Maddox	.30	.15	.03
☐ 40 Glenn Wilson	.20	.10	.02
☐ 41 Don Carman	.40	.20	.04
☐ 42 John Russell	.40	.20	.04
☐ 43 Jeff Stone	.40	.20	.04
☐ 44 Dave Wehrmeister	.40	.20	.04

1985 Tastykake Phillies

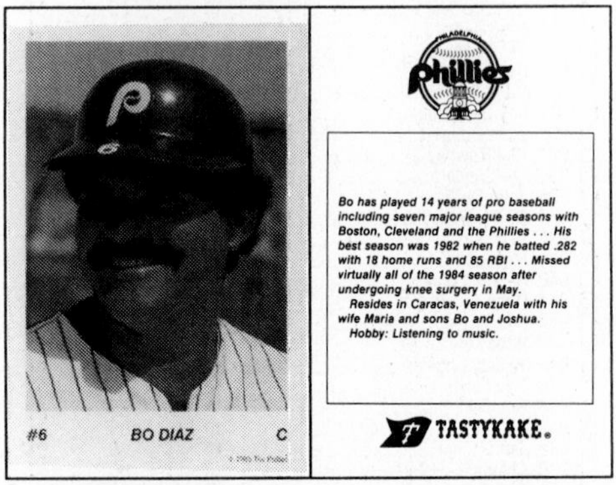
Bo has played 14 years of pro baseball including seven major league seasons with Boston, Cleveland and the Phillies . . . His best season was 1982 when he batted .282 with 18 home runs and 85 RBI . . . Missed virtually all of the 1984 season after undergoing knee surgery in May.
Resides in Caracas, Venezuela with his wife Maria and sons Bo and Joshua.
Hobby: Listening to music.
#6
BO DIAZ
C
TASTYKAKE

The 1985 Tastykake Philadelphia Phillies set consists of 47 cards, each measuring approximately 3 1/2" by 5 1/4". They feature a color photo of the player framed against white borders. The group shots of the various parts of the teams were posed after the other cards were issued so there are stylistic differences between the group shots and the individual shots. The backs feature brief biographies of the players.

	MINT	VG-E	F-G
COMPLETE SET (47)	10.00	5.00	1.00
COMMON PLAYER (1-47)	.20	.10	.02
☐ 1 Checklist	.20	.10	.02
☐ 2 John Felske MG	.20	.10	.02
☐ 3 Dave Bristol CO	.20	.10	.02
☐ 4 Lee Elia CO	.20	.10	.02
☐ 5 Claude Osteen CO	.20	.10	.02
☐ 6 Mike Ryan CO	.20	.10	.02
☐ 7 Del Unser CO	.20	.10	.02
☐ 8 John Felske MG and Del Unser CO Dave Bristol CO Lee Elia CO Mike Ryan CO Hank King CO Claude Osteen CO	.20	.10	.02
☐ 9 Pitching Staff Zachry, Andersen, Hudson, Rawley, Denny, Carlton, Gross, Holland, Koosman, Carman, Bill Campbell	.20	.10	.02
☐ 10 Catchers Darren Daulton, Bo Diaz, Ozzie Virgil	.20	.10	.02
☐ 11 Infielders Schmidt, Jeltz, Ivan DeJesus, Samuel, Aguayo, Russell	.20	.10	.02
☐ 12 Outfielders Corcoran, Gross, Hayes, Lefebvre, Stone, Wilson	.20	.10	.02
☐ 13 Larry Andersen	.30	.15	.03
☐ 14 Steve Carlton	1.00	.50	.10
☐ 15 Don Carman	.20	.10	.02
☐ 16 John Denny	.30	.15	.03
☐ 17 Tony Ghelfi	.20	.10	.02
☐ 18 Kevin Gross	.30	.15	.03
☐ 19 Al Holland	.20	.10	.02
☐ 20 Charles Hudson	.20	.10	.02
☐ 21 Jerry Koosman	.30	.15	.03
☐ 22 Shane Rawley	.20	.10	.02
☐ 23 Pat Zachry	.20	.10	.02
☐ 24 Darren Daulton	.50	.25	.05
☐ 25 Bo Diaz	.20	.10	.02
☐ 26 Ozzie Virgil	.20	.10	.02
☐ 27 John Wockenfuss	.20	.10	.02
☐ 28 Luis Aguayo	.20	.10	.02
☐ 29 Kiko Garcia	.20	.10	.02
☐ 30 Steve Jeltz	.20	.10	.02
☐ 31 John Russell	.20	.10	.02
☐ 32 Juan Samuel	.40	.20	.04
☐ 33 Mike Schmidt	1.50	.75	.15
☐ 34 Tim Corcoran	.20	.10	.02
☐ 35 Greg Gross	.20	.10	.02
☐ 36 Von Hayes	.50	.25	.05
☐ 37 Joe Lefebvre	.20	.10	.02
☐ 38 Garry Maddox	.30	.15	.03
☐ 39 Jeff Stone	.20	.10	.02
☐ 40 Glenn Wilson	.20	.10	.02
☐ 41 Ramon Caraballo and Mike Diaz	.20	.10	.02
☐ 42 Mike Maddux and Rodger Cole	.20	.10	.02
☐ 43 Rick Schu and Chris James	.30	.15	.03
☐ 44 Francisco Melendez and Ken Jackson	.20	.10	.02
☐ 45 Randy Salava and Rocky Childress	.20	.10	.02
☐ 46 Rich Surhoff and Ralph Citarella	.20	.10	.02
☐ 47 Team Photo	.20	.10	.02

1986 Tastykake Phillies

The 1986 Tastykake Philadelphia Phillies set consists of 47 cards, which measure approximately 3 1/2" by 5 1/4". This set features members of the 1986 Philadelphia Phillies. The front of the cards features a full-color photo of the player against white borders while the back has brief biographies. The set has been checklisted for reference below in order by uniform number.

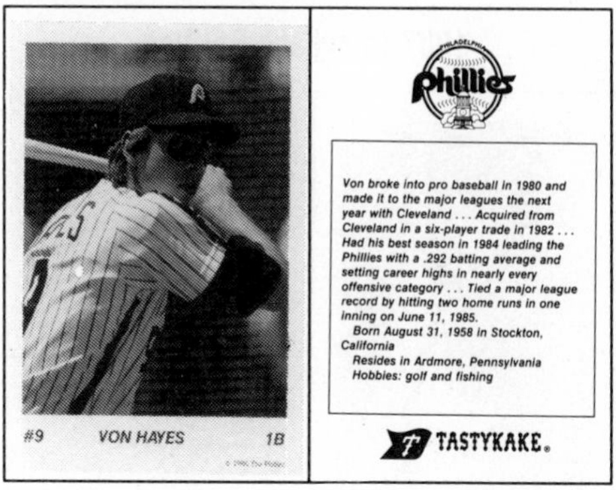
#9
VON HAYES
1B
Phillies
Von broke into pro baseball in 1980 and made it to the major leagues the next year with Cleveland . . . Acquired from Cleveland in a six-player trade in 1982 . . . Had his best season in 1984 leading the Phillies with a .292 batting average and setting career highs in nearly every offensive category . . . Tied a major league record by hitting two home runs in one inning on June 11, 1985.
Born August 31, 1958 in Stockton, California
Resides in Ardmore, Pennsylvania
Hobbies: golf and fishing
TASTYKAKE.

	MINT	VG-E	F-G
COMPLETE SET (47)	10.00	5.00	1.00
COMMON PLAYER	.20	.10	.02
☐ 2 Jim Davenport CO	.30	.15	.03
☐ 3 Claude Osteen CO	.20	.10	.02
☐ 4 Lee Elia CO	.20	.10	.02
☐ 5 Mike Ryan CO	.20	.10	.02
☐ 6 John Russell	.20	.10	.02
☐ 7 John Felske MG	.20	.10	.02
☐ 8 Juan Samuel	.40	.20	.04
☐ 9 Von Hayes	.50	.25	.05
☐ 10 Darren Daulton	.50	.25	.05
☐ 11 Tom Foley	.20	.10	.02
☐ 12 Glenn Wilson	.20	.10	.02
☐ 14 Jeff Stone	.20	.10	.02
☐ 15 Rick Schu	.20	.10	.02
☐ 16 Luis Aguayo	.20	.10	.02
☐ 20 Mike Schmidt	1.50	.75	.15
☐ 21 Greg Gross	.20	.10	.02
☐ 22 Gary Redus	.30	.15	.03
☐ 23 Joe Lefebvre	.20	.10	.02
☐ 24 Milt Thompson	.30	.15	.03
☐ 25 Del Unser CO	.20	.10	.02
☐ 26 Chris James	.40	.20	.04
☐ 27 Kent Tekulve	.30	.15	.03
☐ 28 Shane Rawley	.20	.10	.02
☐ 29 Ronn Reynolds	.20	.10	.02
☐ 30 Steve Jeltz	.20	.10	.02
☐ 31 Garry Maddox	.30	.15	.03
☐ 32 Steve Carlton	1.00	.50	.10
☐ 33 David Shipanoff	.20	.10	.02
☐ 35 Randy Lerch	.20	.10	.02
☐ 36 Robin Roberts	.75	.35	.07
☐ 39 Dave Rucker	.20	.10	.02
☐ 40 Steve Bedrosian	.40	.20	.04
☐ 41 Tom Hume	.20	.10	.02
☐ 42 Don Carman	.20	.10	.02
☐ 43 Fred Toliver	.20	.10	.02
☐ 46 Kevin Gross	.30	.15	.03
☐ 47 Larry Andersen	.30	.15	.03
☐ 48 Dave Stewart	1.00	.50	.10
☐ 49 Charles Hudson	.20	.10	.02
☐ 50 Rocky Childress	.20	.10	.02
☐ xx Future Phillies Ramon Caraballo Joe Cipolloni	.20	.10	.02
☐ xx Future Phillies Arturo Gonzalez Mike Maddux	.20	.10	.02
☐ xx Future Phillies Francisco Melendez Ricky Jordan	.30	.15	.03
☐ xx Future Phillies Kevin Ward Randy Day	.20	.10	.02
☐ xx Night to Remember 26-7, June 11, 1985	.20	.10	.02
☐ xx Pennant Winning Team 1915 Phillies	.20	.10	.02
☐ xx Pennant Winning Team 1950 Phillies	.20	.10	.02

☐ xx Pennant Winning Team 1980 Phillies	.20	.10	.02
☐ xx Pennant Winning Team 1983 Phillies	.20	.10	.02

1987 Tastykake Phillies

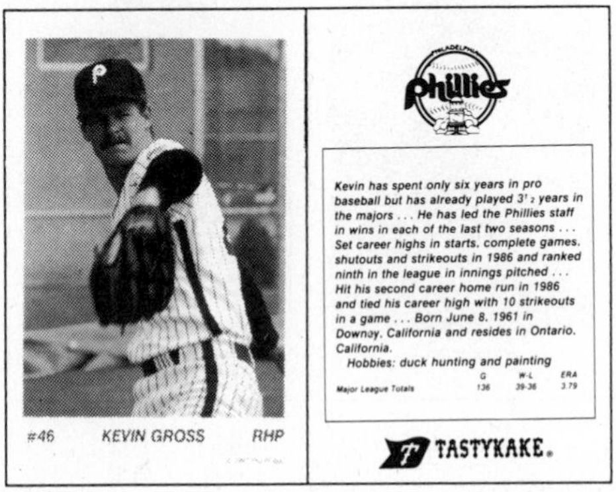
Phillies
Kevin has spent only six years in pro baseball but has already played 3½ years in the majors . . . He has led the Phillies staff in wins in each of the last two seasons . . . Set career highs in starts, complete games, shutouts and strikeouts in 1986 and ranked ninth in the league in innings pitched . . . Hit his second career home run in 1986 and tied his career high with 10 strikeouts in a game . . . Born June 8, 1961 in Downey, California and resides in Ontario, California.
Hobbies: duck hunting and painting
G W-L ERA
Major League Totals 136 39-36 3.79
#46 KEVIN GROSS RHP
TASTYKAKE

The 1987 Tastykake Philadelphia Phillies set consists of 47 cards which measure approximately 3 1/2" by 5 1/4". The sets again feature full-color photos against a solid white background. There were two number 39s in this set as the Phillies changed personnel during the season, Joe Cowley and Bob Scanlon. For convenience uniform numbers are used below as a basis for numbering and checklisting this set.

	MINT	VG-E	F-G
COMPLETE SET (47)	10.00	5.00	1.00
COMMON PLAYER	.20	.10	.02
☐ 6 John Russell	.20	.10	.02
☐ 7 John Felske MG	.20	.10	.02
☐ 8 Juan Samuel	.40	.20	.04
☐ 9 Von Hayes	.50	.25	.05
☐ 10 Darren Daulton	.40	.20	.04
☐ 11 Greg Legg	.20	.10	.02
☐ 12 Glenn Wilson	.20	.10	.02
☐ 13 Lance Parrish	.50	.25	.05
☐ 14 Jeff Stone	.20	.10	.02
☐ 15 Rick Schu	.20	.10	.02
☐ 16 Luis Aguayo	.20	.10	.02
☐ 17 Ron Roenicke	.20	.10	.02
☐ 18 Chris James	.40	.20	.04
☐ 20 Mike Schmidt	1.50	.75	.15
☐ 21 Greg Gross	.20	.10	.02
☐ 23 Joe Cipolloni	.20	.10	.02
☐ 24 Milt Thompson	.30	.15	.03
☐ 27 Kent Tekulve	.30	.15	.03
☐ 28 Shane Rawley	.20	.10	.02
☐ 29 Ronn Reynolds	.20	.10	.02
☐ 30 Steve Jeltz	.20	.10	.02
☐ 33 Mike Jackson	.20	.10	.02
☐ 34 Mike Easler	.20	.10	.02
☐ 35 Dan Schatzeder	.20	.10	.02
☐ 37 Ken Howell	.30	.15	.03
☐ 38 Jim Olander	.20	.10	.02
☐ 39A Joe Cowley	.20	.10	.02
☐ 39B Bob Scanlan	.20	.10	.02
☐ 40 Steve Bedrosian	.30	.15	.03
☐ 41 Tom Hume	.20	.10	.02
☐ 42 Don Carman	.20	.10	.02
☐ 43 Freddie Toliver	.20	.10	.02
☐ 44 Mike Maddux	.20	.10	.02
☐ 45 Greg Jelks	.20	.10	.02
☐ 46 Kevin Gross	.30	.15	.03
☐ 47 Bruce Ruffin	.20	.10	.02
☐ 48 Marvin Freeman	.20	.10	.02
☐ 49 Len Watts	.20	.10	.02
☐ 50 Tom Newell	.20	.10	.02
☐ 51 Ken Jackson	.20	.10	.02
☐ 52 Todd Frohwirth	.20	.10	.02
☐ 58 Doug Bair	.20	.10	.02
☐ xx Phillie Phanatic (team mascot)	.20	.10	.02
☐ xx Team Photo	.20	.10	.02
☐ xx Shawn Barton and Rick Lundblade	.20	.10	.02
☐ xx Jeff Kaye and Darren Loy	.20	.10	.02
☐ xx Coaches Card Claude Osteen CO Del Unser CO Jim Davenport CO Mike Ryan CO Lee Elia CO	.20	.10	.02

1988 Tastykake Phillies

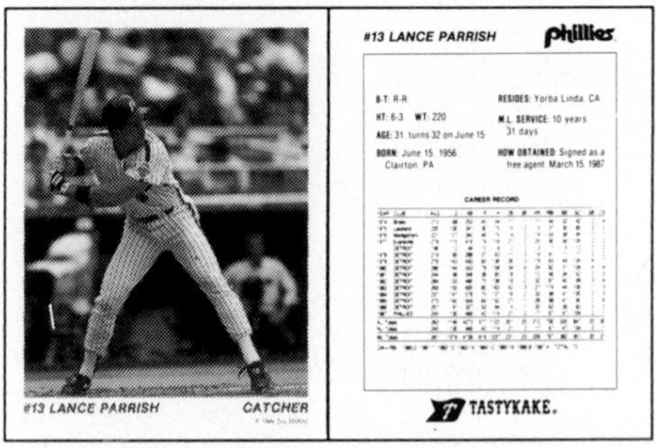

The 1988 Tastykake Philadelphia Phillies set is a 30-card set measuring approximately 4 7/8" by 6 1/4". This set is listed below alphabetically by player. The cards have a full-color photo front and complete player history on the back. There was also a nine-card update set issued later in the year which included a Ricky Jordan card; the update cards are numbered as 31-39 and are blank backed.

	MINT	EXC	G-VG
COMPLETE SET (39)	10.00	5.00	1.00
COMMON PLAYER (1-30)	.20	.10	.02
COMMON PLAYER (31-39)	.20	.10	.02
☐ 1 Luis Aguayo	.20	.10	.02
☐ 2 Bill Almon	.20	.10	.02
☐ 3 Steve Bedrosian	.30	.15	.03
☐ 4 Phil Bradley	.30	.15	.03
☐ 5 Jeff Calhoun	.20	.10	.02
☐ 6 Don Carman	.20	.10	.02
☐ 7 Darren Daulton	.40	.20	.04
☐ 8 Bob Dernier	.20	.10	.02
☐ 9 Lee Elia	.20	.10	.02
☐ 10 Todd Frohwirth	.20	.10	.02
☐ 11 Greg Gross	.20	.10	.02
☐ 12 Kevin Gross	.30	.15	.03
☐ 13 Von Hayes	.50	.25	.05
☐ 14 Chris James	.30	.15	.03
☐ 15 Steve Jeltz	.20	.10	.02
☐ 16 Mike Maddux	.20	.10	.02
☐ 17 Dave Palmer	.30	.15	.03
☐ 18 Lance Parrish	.50	.25	.05
☐ 19 Shane Rawley	.20	.10	.02
☐ 20 Wally Ritchie	.20	.10	.02
☐ 21 Bruce Ruffin	.20	.10	.02
☐ 22 Juan Samuel	.40	.20	.04
☐ 23 Mike Schmidt	1.50	.75	.15
☐ 24 Kent Tekulve	.30	.15	.03
☐ 25 Milt Thompson	.30	.15	.03
☐ 26 Mike Young	.20	.10	.02
☐ 27 Phillies Prospects Tom Barrett Brad Brink Steve DeAngelis Ron Jones Keith Miller Brad Moore Howard Nichols Shane Turner	.20	.10	.02
☐ 28 Team Card	.20	.10	.02

☐ 29 Phillies Coaches	.20	.10	.02
Claude Osteen			
Del Unser			
John Vuckovich			
Dave Bristol			
Tony Taylor			
Mike Ryan			
☐ 30 Phillie Phanatic (Mascot)	.20	.10	.02
☐ 31 Larry Bowa CO	.30	.15	.03
☐ 32 Lee Elia CO	.20	.10	.02
☐ 33 Jackie Gutierrez	.20	.10	.02
☐ 34 Greg Harris	.30	.15	.03
☐ 35 Ricky Jordan	.30	.15	.03
☐ 36 Keith Miller	.30	.15	.03
☐ 37 John Russell	.20	.10	.02
☐ 38 John Vuckovich CO	.20	.10	.02
☐ 39 Phillies Announcers	.30	.15	.03
Garry Maddox			
Richie Ashburn			
Chris Wheeler			
Harry Kalas			
Andy Musser			

1989 Tastykake Phillies

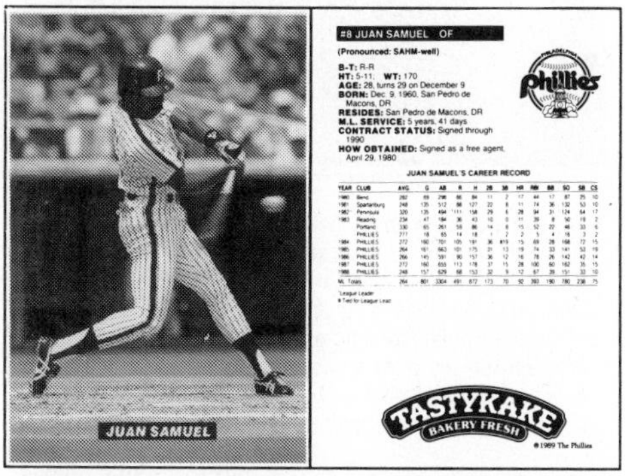

This set was a 36-card set of Philadelphia Phillies measuring approximately 4 1/8" by 6" featuring full-color fronts with complete biographical information and career stats on the back. The set is checklisted alphabetically in the list below. The set was a give away at a Phillies game in May and was later available from a mail-away offer. There was also a nine-player extended set issued later during the 1989 season; the extended players are numbered below in alphabetical order, numbers 37-45.

	MINT	EXC	G-VG
COMPLETE SET (45)	12.00	6.00	1.20
COMMON PLAYER (1-36)	.20	.10	.02
COMMON PLAYER (37-45)	.30	.15	.03
☐ 1 Steve Bedrosian	.30	.15	.03
☐ 2 Larry Bowa CO	.30	.15	.03
☐ 3 Don Carman	.20	.10	.02
☐ 4 Darren Daulton	.40	.20	.04
☐ 5 Bob Dernier	.20	.10	.02
☐ 6 Curt Ford	.20	.10	.02
☐ 7 Todd Frohwirth	.20	.10	.02
☐ 8 Greg Harris	.30	.15	.03
☐ 9 Von Hayes	.50	.25	.05
☐ 10 Tom Herr	.30	.15	.03
☐ 11 Ken Howell	.30	.15	.03
☐ 12 Chris James	.30	.15	.03
☐ 13 Steve Jeltz	.20	.10	.02
☐ 14 Ron Jones	.20	.10	.02
☐ 15 Ricky Jordan	.30	.15	.03
☐ 16 Darold Knowles CO	.20	.10	.02
☐ 17 Steve Lake	.20	.10	.02
☐ 18 Nick Levya MG	.20	.10	.02
☐ 19 Mike Maddux	.20	.10	.02
☐ 20 Alex Madrid	.20	.10	.02
☐ 21 Larry McWilliams	.20	.10	.02
☐ 22 Denis Menke CO	.20	.10	.02
☐ 23 Dwayne Murphy	.20	.10	.02
☐ 24 Tom Nieto	.20	.10	.02
☐ 25 Randy O'Neal	.20	.10	.02
☐ 26 Steve Ontiveros	.20	.10	.02
☐ 27 Jeff Parrett	.20	.10	.02
☐ 28 Bruce Ruffin	.20	.10	.02
☐ 29 Mike Ryal	.20	.10	.02
☐ 30 Mike Ryan CO	.20	.10	.02
☐ 31 Juan Samuel	.40	.20	.04
☐ 32 Mike Schmidt	1.50	.75	.15
☐ 33 Tony Taylor CO	.20	.10	.02
☐ 34 Dickie Thon	.30	.15	.03
☐ 35 John Vuckovich CO	.20	.10	.02
☐ 36 Floyd Youmans	.20	.10	.02
☐ 37 Jim Adduci	.30	.15	.03
☐ 38 Eric Bullock	.30	.15	.03
☐ 39 Dennis Cook	.40	.20	.04
☐ 40 Lenny Dykstra	.75	.35	.07
☐ 41 Charlie Hayes	.40	.20	.04
☐ 42 John Kruk	.40	.20	.04
☐ 43 Roger McDowell	.40	.20	.04
☐ 44 Terry Mulholland	.40	.20	.04
☐ 45 Randy Ready	.30	.15	.03

1990 Tastykake Phillies

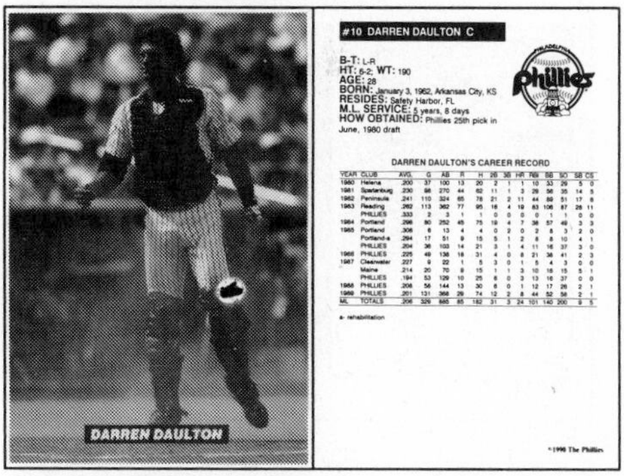

The 1990 Tastykake Philadelphia Phillies set is a 36-card set measuring approximately 4 1/8" by 6" which features players, coaches and manager, four players who have had their uniform numbers retired, broadcasters, and even the Phillies Mascot. The set is checklisted alphabetically, with complete biography and complete stats on the back.

	MINT	EXC	G-VG
COMPLETE SET (36)	8.00	4.00	.80
COMMON PLAYER (1-36)	.20	.10	.02
☐ 1 Darrel Akerfelds	.20	.10	.02
☐ 2 Rod Booker	.20	.10	.02
☐ 3 Sil Campusano	.30	.15	.03
☐ 4 Don Carman	.20	.10	.02
☐ 5 Pat Combs	.40	.20	.04
☐ 6 Dennis Cook	.30	.15	.03
☐ 7 Darren Daulton	.30	.15	.03
☐ 8 Lenny Dykstra	.60	.30	.06
☐ 9 Curt Ford	.20	.10	.02
☐ 10 Jason Grimsley	.20	.10	.02
☐ 11 Charlie Hayes	.30	.15	.03
☐ 12 Von Hayes	.40	.20	.04
☐ 13 Tommy Herr	.30	.15	.03
☐ 14 Dave Hollins	.40	.20	.04
☐ 15 Ken Howell	.30	.15	.03
☐ 16 Ron Jones	.30	.15	.03
☐ 17 Ricky Jordan	.30	.15	.03
☐ 18 John Kruk	.30	.15	.03
☐ 19 Steve Lake	.20	.10	.02
☐ 20 Nick Levya MG	.20	.10	.02
☐ 21 Carmelo Martinez	.20	.10	.02
☐ 22 Roger McDowell	.30	.15	.03
☐ 23 Chuck McElroy	.20	.10	.02
☐ 24 Terry Mulholland	.30	.15	.03
☐ 25 Jeff Parrett	.20	.10	.02
☐ 26 Randy Ready	.20	.10	.02
☐ 27 Bruce Ruffin	.20	.10	.02

☐ 28 Dickie Thon	.30	.15	.03
☐ 29 Richie Ashburn	.50	.25	.05
☐ 30 Steve Carlton	1.00	.50	.10
☐ 31 Robin Roberts	.75	.35	.07
☐ 32 Mike Schmidt	1.50	.75	.15
☐ 33 Phillie Phanatic (Mascot)	.20	.10	.02
☐ 34 Phillie Coaches Denis Menke Mike Ryan John Vuckovich Hal Lanier Darold Knowles Larry Bowa	.20	.10	.02
☐ 35 Phillies Broadcasters Chris Wheeler Andy Musser Harry Kalas Richie Ashburn	.20	.10	.02
☐ 36 Phillies Broadcasters Mike Schmidt Jim Barniak Garry Maddox	.30	.15	.03

1986 Texas Gold Reds

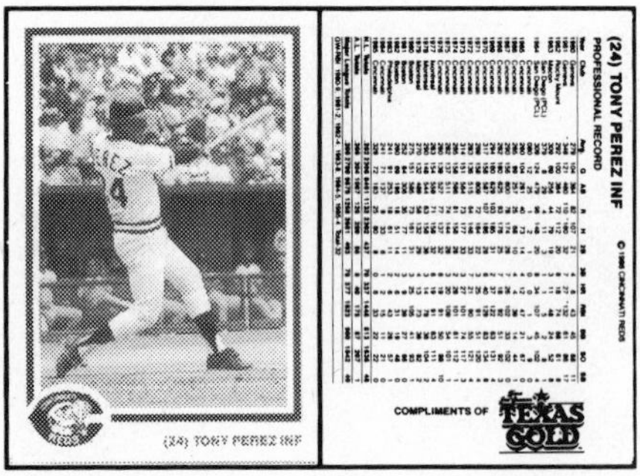

Texas Gold Ice Cream is the sponsor of this 28-card set of Cincinnati Reds. The cards are 2 1/2" by 3 1/2" and feature player photos in full color with a red and white border on the front of the card. The set was distributed to fans attending the Reds game at Riverfront Stadium on September 19th. The card backs contain the player's career statistics, uniform number, name, position, and the Texas Gold logo.

	MINT	EXC	G-VG
COMPLETE SET (28)	30.00	15.00	3.00
COMMON PLAYER	.50	.25	.05
☐ 6 Bo Diaz	.50	.25	.05
☐ 9 Max Venable	.50	.25	.05
☐ 11 Kurt Stillwell	.60	.30	.06
☐ 12 Nick Esasky	.60	.30	.06
☐ 13 Dave Concepcion	.60	.30	.06
☐ 14A Pete Rose INF	3.00	1.50	.30
☐ 14B Pete Rose MG	3.00	1.50	.30
☐ 14C Pete Rose (commemorative)	3.00	1.50	.30
☐ 16 Ron Oester	.50	.25	.05
☐ 20 Eddie Milner	.50	.25	.05
☐ 22 Sal Butera	.50	.25	.05
☐ 24 Tony Perez	.90	.45	.09
☐ 25 Buddy Bell	.60	.30	.06
☐ 28 Kal Daniels	2.50	1.25	.25
☐ 29 Tracy Jones	.60	.30	.06
☐ 31 John Franco	.90	.45	.09
☐ 32 Tom Browning	.90	.45	.09
☐ 33 Ron Robinson	.60	.30	.06
☐ 34 Bill Gullickson	.50	.25	.05
☐ 36 Mario Soto	.60	.30	.06
☐ 39 Dave Parker	1.00	.50	.10
☐ 40 John Denny	.60	.30	.06
☐ 44 Eric Davis	7.50	3.75	.75
☐ 45 Chris Welsh	.50	.25	.05
☐ 48 Ted Power	.50	.25	.05
☐ 49 Joe Price	.50	.25	.05

☐ xx Reds Coaches George Scherger Bruce Kimm Billy DeMars Tommy Helms Scott Breeden Jim Lett	.50	.25	.05
☐ xx Preferred Customer Card (Discount Coupon)	.50	.25	.05

1971 Ticketron Dodgers

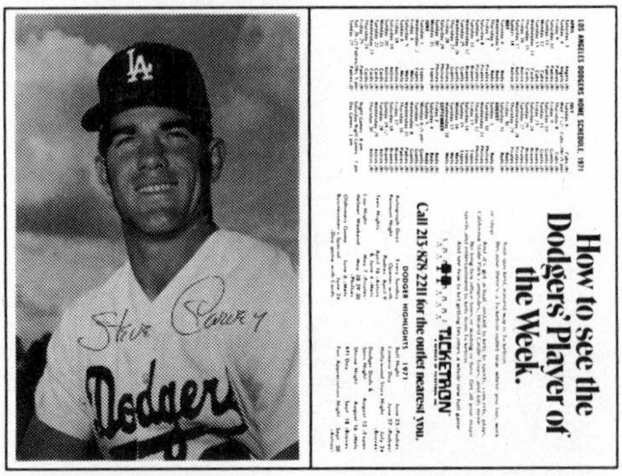

The 1971 Ticketron Los Angeles Dodgers set is a 20-card set with cards measuring approximately 4" by 6". This set has a 1971 Garvey rookie year card as well as 18 other players including Richie Allen in his only year as a Dodger. The fronts are beautiful full-color photos which also have a facsimile autograph on the front and are borderless while the backs contain an advertisement for Ticketron, the 1971 Dodger home schedule and a list of promotional events scheduled for 1971.

	NRMT	VG-E	GOOD
COMPLETE SET (20)	90.00	45.00	9.00
COMMON PLAYER (1-20)	2.50	1.25	.25
☐ 1 Richie Allen	5.00	2.50	.50
☐ 2 Walter Alston MG	6.00	3.00	.60
☐ 3 Jim Brewer	2.50	1.25	.25
☐ 4 Willie Crawford	2.50	1.25	.25
☐ 5 Willie Davis	3.50	1.75	.35
☐ 6 Steve Garvey	30.00	15.00	3.00
☐ 7 Bill Grabarkewitz	2.50	1.25	.25
☐ 8 Jim Lefebvre	3.50	1.75	.35
☐ 9 Pete Mikkelsen	2.50	1.25	.25
☐ 10 Joe Moeller	2.50	1.25	.25
☐ 11 Manny Mota	3.50	1.75	.35
☐ 12 Claude Osteen	3.50	1.75	.35
☐ 13 Wes Parker	3.50	1.75	.35
☐ 14 Bill Russell	3.50	1.75	.35
☐ 15 Duke Sims	2.50	1.25	.25
☐ 16 Bill Singer	2.50	1.25	.25
☐ 17 Bill Sudakis	2.50	1.25	.25
☐ 18 Don Sutton	6.00	3.00	.60
☐ 19 Maury Wills	5.00	2.50	.50
☐ 20 Vic Scully and Jerry Doggett (announcers)	2.50	1.25	.25

1971 Ticketron Giants

The 1971 Ticketron San Francisco Giants set is a 10-card set featuring members of the division-winning 1971 San Francisco Giants. The set measures approximately 3 7/8" by 6" and features an attractive full-color photo framed by white borders on the front along with a facsimile autograph. The back contains an ad for Ticketron as well as the 1971 Giants home schedule.

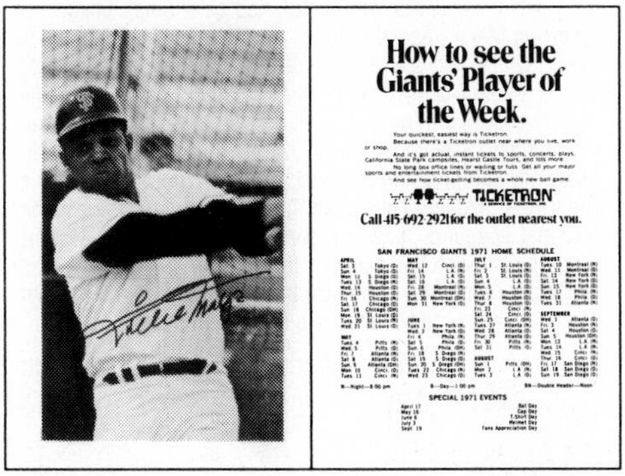

	NRMT	VG-E	GOOD
COMPLETE SET (10)	70.00	30.00	6.00
COMMON PLAYER (1-10)	2.50	1.25	.25
☐ 1 Bobby Bonds	5.00	2.50	.50
☐ 2 Dick Dietz	2.50	1.25	.25
☐ 3 Charles Fox MG	2.50	1.25	.25
☐ 4 Tito Fuentes	2.50	1.25	.25
☐ 5 Ken Henderson	2.50	1.25	.25
☐ 6 Juan Marichal	10.00	4.50	.90
☐ 7 Willie Mays	35.00	15.00	3.00
☐ 8 Willie McCovey	15.00	6.00	1.20
☐ 9 Don McMahon	2.50	1.25	.25
☐ 10 Gaylord Perry	10.00	4.50	.90

1947 Tip Top

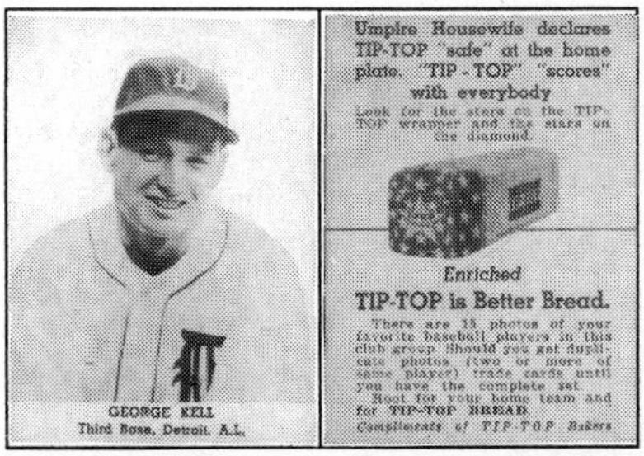

The cards in this 163-card set measure approximately 2 1/4" by 3". The 1947 Tip Top Bread issue contains unnumbered cards with black and white player photos. The set is of interest to baseball historians in that it contains cards of many players not appearing in any other card sets. The cards were issued locally for the eleven following teams: Red Sox (1-15), White Sox (16-30), Tigers (31-45), Yankees (46-60), Browns (61-75), Braves (76-90), Dodgers (91-104), Cubs (105-119), Giants (120-135), Pirates (136-149), and Cardinals (150-164). Players of the Red Sox, Tigers, White Sox, Braves, and the Cubs are scarcer than those of the other teams; players from these tougher teams are marked by SP below to indicate their scarcity. The catalog designation is D323.

	NRMT	VG-E	GOOD
COMPLETE SET (163)	10500.00	4500.00	1000.00
COMMON PLAYER (1-164)	25.00	12.50	2.50
COMMON SP PLAYER	80.00	40.00	8.00
☐ 1 Leon Culberson SP	80.00	40.00	8.00
☐ 2 Dom DiMaggio SP	135.00	65.00	13.50
☐ 3 Joe Dobson SP	80.00	40.00	8.00
☐ 4 Bob Doerr SP	250.00	125.00	25.00
☐ 5 Dave(Boo) Ferris SP	80.00	40.00	8.00
☐ 6 Mickey Harris SP	80.00	40.00	8.00
☐ 7 Frank Hayes SP	80.00	40.00	8.00
☐ 8 Cecil Hughson SP	80.00	40.00	8.00
☐ 9 Earl Johnson SP	80.00	40.00	8.00
☐ 10 Roy Partee SP	80.00	40.00	8.00
☐ 11 Johnny Pesky SP	90.00	45.00	9.00
☐ 12 Rip Russell SP	80.00	40.00	8.00
☐ 13 Hal Wagner SP	80.00	40.00	8.00
☐ 14 Rudy York SP	100.00	50.00	10.00
☐ 15 Bill Zuber SP	80.00	40.00	8.00
☐ 16 Floyd Baker SP	80.00	40.00	8.00
☐ 17 Earl Caldwell SP	80.00	40.00	8.00
☐ 18 Lloyd Christopher SP	80.00	40.00	8.00
☐ 19 George Dickey SP	80.00	40.00	8.00
☐ 20 Ralph Hodgin SP	80.00	40.00	8.00
☐ 21 Bob Kennedy SP	80.00	40.00	8.00
☐ 22 Joe Kuhel SP	80.00	40.00	8.00
☐ 23 Thornton Lee SP	80.00	40.00	8.00
☐ 24 Ed Lopat SP	135.00	65.00	13.50
☐ 25 Cass Michaels SP	80.00	40.00	8.00
☐ 26 John Rigney SP	80.00	40.00	8.00
☐ 27 Mike Tresh SP	80.00	40.00	8.00
☐ 28 Thurman Tucker SP	80.00	40.00	8.00
☐ 29 Jack Wallasca SP	80.00	40.00	8.00
☐ 30 Taft Wright SP	80.00	40.00	8.00
☐ 31 Walter(Hoot)Evers SP	80.00	40.00	8.00
☐ 32 John Gorsica SP	80.00	40.00	8.00
☐ 33 Fred Hutchinson SP	100.00	50.00	10.00
☐ 34 George Kell SP	350.00	175.00	35.00
☐ 35 Eddie Lake SP	80.00	40.00	8.00
☐ 36 Ed Mayo SP	80.00	40.00	8.00
☐ 37 Arthur Mills SP	80.00	40.00	8.00
☐ 38 Pat Mullin SP	80.00	40.00	8.00
☐ 39 James Outlaw SP	80.00	40.00	8.00
☐ 40 Frank Overmire SP	80.00	40.00	8.00
☐ 41 Bob Swift SP	80.00	40.00	8.00
☐ 42 Birdie Tebbetts SP	80.00	40.00	8.00
☐ 43 Paul(Diz) Trout SP	90.00	45.00	9.00
☐ 44 Virgil Trucks SP	90.00	45.00	9.00
☐ 45 Dick Wakefield SP	80.00	40.00	8.00
☐ 46 Larry Berra	350.00	175.00	35.00
☐ 47 Floyd(Bill) Bevans	25.00	12.50	2.50
☐ 48 Bobby Brown	45.00	22.50	4.50
☐ 49 Thomas Byrne	25.00	12.50	2.50
☐ 50 Frank Crosetti	40.00	20.00	4.00
☐ 51 Tom Henrich	40.00	20.00	4.00
☐ 52 Charlie Keller	35.00	17.50	3.50
☐ 53 Johnny Lindell	25.00	12.50	2.50
☐ 54 Joe Page	25.00	12.50	2.50
☐ 55 Mel Queen	25.00	12.50	2.50
☐ 56 Allie Reynolds	45.00	22.50	4.50
☐ 57 Phil Rizzuto	135.00	65.00	13.50
☐ 58 Aaron Robinson	25.00	12.50	2.50
☐ 59 George Stirnweiss	25.00	12.50	2.50
☐ 60 Charles Wensloff	25.00	12.50	2.50
☐ 61 John Berardino	25.00	12.50	2.50
☐ 62 Clifford Fannin	25.00	12.50	2.50
☐ 63 Dennis Galehouse	25.00	12.50	2.50
☐ 64 Jeff Heath	25.00	12.50	2.50
☐ 65 Walter Judnich	25.00	12.50	2.50
☐ 66 Jack Kramer	25.00	12.50	2.50
☐ 67 Paul Lehner	25.00	12.50	2.50
☐ 68 Lester Moss	25.00	12.50	2.50
☐ 69 Bob Muncrief	25.00	12.50	2.50
☐ 70 Nelson Potter	25.00	12.50	2.50
☐ 71 Fred Sanford	25.00	12.50	2.50
☐ 72 Joe Schultz	25.00	12.50	2.50
☐ 73 Vern Stephens	35.00	17.50	3.50
☐ 74 Jerry Witte	25.00	12.50	2.50
☐ 75 Al Zarilla	25.00	12.50	2.50
☐ 76 Charles Barrett SP	80.00	40.00	8.00
☐ 77 Hank Camelli SP	80.00	40.00	8.00
☐ 78 Dick Culler SP	80.00	40.00	8.00
☐ 79 Nanny Fernandez SP	80.00	40.00	8.00
☐ 80 Si Johnson SP	80.00	40.00	8.00
☐ 81 Danny Litwhiler SP	80.00	40.00	8.00
☐ 82 Phil Masi SP	80.00	40.00	8.00
☐ 83 Carvel Rowell SP	80.00	40.00	8.00
☐ 84 Connie Ryan SP	80.00	40.00	8.00
☐ 85 John Sain SP	135.00	65.00	13.50
☐ 86 Ray Sanders SP	80.00	40.00	8.00
☐ 87 Sibby Sisti SP	80.00	40.00	8.00
☐ 88 Billy Southworth SP	80.00	40.00	8.00
☐ 89 Warren Spahn SP	450.00	225.00	45.00
☐ 90 Ed Wright SP	80.00	40.00	8.00
☐ 91 Bob Bragan	25.00	12.50	2.50
☐ 92 Ralph Branca	35.00	17.50	3.50
☐ 93 Hugh Casey	25.00	12.50	2.50
☐ 94 Bruce Edwards	25.00	12.50	2.50
☐ 95 Hal Gregg	25.00	12.50	2.50
☐ 96 Joe Hatten	25.00	12.50	2.50
☐ 97 Gene Hermanski	25.00	12.50	2.50
☐ 98 John Jorgensen	25.00	12.50	2.50

☐ 99 Harry Lavagetto	25.00	12.50	2.50
☐ 100 Vic Lombardi	25.00	12.50	2.50
☐ 101 Frank Melton	25.00	12.50	2.50
☐ 102 Ed Miksis	25.00	12.50	2.50
☐ 103 Marv Rackley	25.00	12.50	2.50
☐ 104 Ed Stevens	25.00	12.50	2.50
☐ 105 Phil Cavarretta SP	135.00	65.00	13.50
☐ 106 Bob Chipman SP	80.00	40.00	8.00
☐ 107 Stanley Hack SP	90.00	45.00	9.00
☐ 108 Don Johnson SP	80.00	40.00	8.00
☐ 109 Emil Kush SP	80.00	40.00	8.00
☐ 110 Bill Lee SP	80.00	40.00	8.00
☐ 111 Mickey Livingston SP	80.00	40.00	8.00
☐ 112 Harry Lowrey SP	80.00	40.00	8.00
☐ 113 Clyde McCullough SP	80.00	40.00	8.00
☐ 114 Andy Pafko SP	90.00	45.00	9.00
☐ 115 Marv Rickert SP	80.00	40.00	8.00
☐ 116 John Schmitz SP	80.00	40.00	8.00
☐ 117 Bobby Sturgeon SP	80.00	40.00	8.00
☐ 118 Ed Waitkus SP	80.00	40.00	8.00
☐ 119 Henry Wyse SP	80.00	40.00	8.00
☐ 120 Bill Ayers	25.00	12.50	2.50
☐ 121 Robert Blattner	25.00	12.50	2.50
☐ 122 Mike Budnick	25.00	12.50	2.50
☐ 123 Sid Gordon	25.00	12.50	2.50
☐ 124 Clinton Hartung	25.00	12.50	2.50
☐ 125 Monte Kennedy	25.00	12.50	2.50
☐ 126 Dave Koslo	25.00	12.50	2.50
☐ 127 Carroll Lockman	25.00	12.50	2.50
☐ 128 Jack Lohrke	25.00	12.50	2.50
☐ 129 Ernie Lombardi	80.00	40.00	8.00
☐ 130 Willard Marshall	25.00	12.50	2.50
☐ 131 John Mize	100.00	50.00	10.00
☐ 132 Eugene Thompson (does not exist)	00.00	00.00	0.00
☐ 133 Ken Trinkle	25.00	12.50	2.50
☐ 134 Bill Voiselle	25.00	12.50	2.50
☐ 135 Mickey Witek	25.00	12.50	2.50
☐ 136 Eddie Basinski	25.00	12.50	2.50
☐ 137 Ernie Bonham	25.00	12.50	2.50
☐ 138 Billy Cox	35.00	17.50	3.50
☐ 139 Elbie Fletcher	25.00	12.50	2.50
☐ 140 Frank Gustine	25.00	12.50	2.50
☐ 141 Kirby Higbe	25.00	12.50	2.50
☐ 142 Leroy Jarvis	25.00	12.50	2.50
☐ 143 Ralph Kiner	100.00	50.00	10.00
☐ 144 Fred Ostermueller	25.00	12.50	2.50
☐ 145 Preacher Roe	45.00	22.50	4.50
☐ 146 Jim Russell	25.00	12.50	2.50
☐ 147 Rip Sewell	25.00	12.50	2.50
☐ 148 Nick Strincevich	25.00	12.50	2.50
☐ 149 Honus Wagner	125.00	60.00	12.50
☐ 150 Alpha Brazle	25.00	12.50	2.50
☐ 151 Ken Burkhart	25.00	12.50	2.50
☐ 152 Bernard Creger	25.00	12.50	2.50
☐ 153 Joffre Cross	25.00	12.50	2.50
☐ 154 Charles E. Diering	25.00	12.50	2.50
☐ 155 Ervin Dusak	25.00	12.50	2.50
☐ 156 Joe Garagiola	100.00	50.00	10.00
☐ 157 Tony Kaufmann	25.00	12.50	2.50
☐ 158 George Kurowski	25.00	12.50	2.50
☐ 159 Marty Marion	50.00	25.00	5.00
☐ 160 George Munger	25.00	12.50	2.50
☐ 161 Del Rice	25.00	12.50	2.50
☐ 162 Dick Sisler	25.00	12.50	2.50
☐ 163 Enos Slaughter	100.00	50.00	10.00
☐ 164 Ted Wilks	25.00	12.50	2.50

1988 T/M Umpire Cards

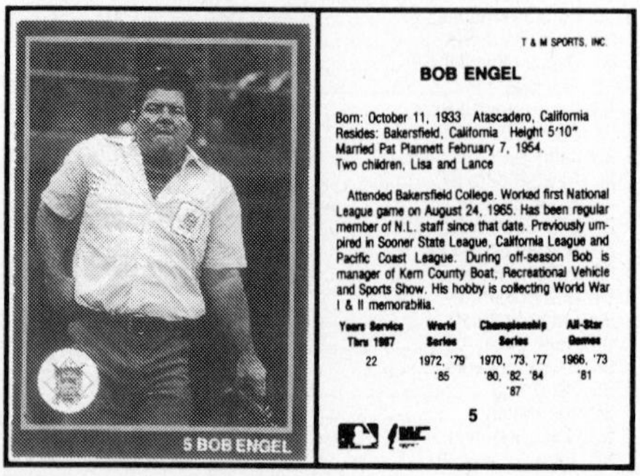
T & M SPORTS, INC.
BOB ENGEL
Born: October 11, 1933 Atascadero, California
Resides: Bakersfield, California Height 5'10"
Married Pat Plannett February 7, 1954.
Two children, Lisa and Lance
Attended Bakersfield College. Worked first National League game on August 24, 1965. Has been regular member of N.L. staff since that date. Previously umpired in Sooner State League, California League and Pacific Coast League. During off-season Bob is manager of Kern County Boat, Recreational Vehicle and Sports Show. His hobby is collecting World War I & II memorabilia.
Years Service Thru 1987
World Series
Championship Series
All-Star Games
22
1972, '79 '85
1970, '73, '77 '80, '82, '84 '87
1966, '73 '81
5
5 BOB ENGEL

This set of 64 cards was distributed as a small boxed set featuring Major League umpires exclusively. The box itself is blank, white, and silver. The set was produced by T and M Sports under licenses from Major League Baseball and the Major League Umpires Association. The cards are in color and are standard size, 2 1/2" by 3 1/2". Card backs are printed in black on light blue. All the cards are black bordered, but the American Leaguers have a red thin inner border, whereas the National Leaguers have a green thin inner border. A short biographical sketch is given on the back for each umpire. The cards are numbered on the back; the number on the front of each card refers to the umpire's uniform number.

	MINT	EXC	G-VG
COMPLETE SET (64)	9.00	4.50	.90
COMMON PLAYER (1-64)	.25	.12	.02
☐ 1 Doug Harvey	.35	.17	.03
☐ 2 Lee Weyer	.25	.12	.02
☐ 3 Billy Williams	.25	.12	.02
☐ 4 John Kibler	.25	.12	.02
☐ 5 Bob Engel	.25	.12	.02
☐ 6 Harry Wendelstedt	.35	.17	.03
☐ 7 Larry Barnett	.25	.12	.02
☐ 8 Don Denkinger	.35	.17	.03
☐ 9 Dave Phillips	.35	.17	.03
☐ 10 Larry McCoy	.25	.12	.02
☐ 11 Bruce Froemming	.35	.17	.03
☐ 12 John McSherry	.35	.17	.03
☐ 13 Jim Evans	.25	.12	.02
☐ 14 Frank Pulli	.25	.12	.02
☐ 15 Joe Brinkman	.25	.12	.02
☐ 16 Terry Tata	.25	.12	.02
☐ 17 Paul Runge	.25	.12	.02
☐ 18 Dutch Rennert	.25	.12	.02
☐ 19 Nick Bremigan	.25	.12	.02
☐ 20 Jim McKean	.25	.12	.02
☐ 21 Terry Cooney	.25	.12	.02
☐ 22 Rich Garcia	.25	.12	.02
☐ 23 Dale Ford	.25	.12	.02
☐ 24 Al Clark	.25	.12	.02
☐ 25 Greg Kose	.25	.12	.02
☐ 26 Jim Quick	.25	.12	.02
☐ 27 Ed Montague	.25	.12	.02
☐ 28 Jerry Crawford	.25	.12	.02
☐ 29 Steve Palermo	.25	.12	.02
☐ 30 Durwood Merrill	.25	.12	.02
☐ 31 Ken Kaiser	.35	.17	.03
☐ 32 Vic Voltaggio	.25	.12	.02
☐ 33 Mike Reilly	.25	.12	.02
☐ 34 Eric Gregg	.45	.22	.04
☐ 35 Ted Hendry	.25	.12	.02
☐ 36 Joe West	.25	.12	.02
☐ 37 Dave Pallone	.35	.17	.03
☐ 38 Fred Brocklander	.25	.12	.02
☐ 39 John Shulock	.25	.12	.02
☐ 40 Derryl Cousins	.25	.12	.02
☐ 41 Charlie Williams	.25	.12	.02
☐ 42 Rocky Roe	.25	.12	.02
☐ 43 Randy Marsh	.25	.12	.02
☐ 44 Bob Davidson	.25	.12	.02
☐ 45 Drew Coble	.25	.12	.02
☐ 46 Tim McClelland	.25	.12	.02
☐ 47 Dan Morrison	.25	.12	.02
☐ 48 Rick Reed	.25	.12	.02
☐ 49 Steve Rippley	.25	.12	.02
☐ 50 John Hirshbeck	.25	.12	.02
☐ 51 Mark Johnson	.25	.12	.02
☐ 52 Gerry Davis	.25	.12	.02
☐ 53 Dana DeMuth	.25	.12	.02
☐ 54 Larry Young	.25	.12	.02
☐ 55 Tim Welke	.25	.12	.02
☐ 56 Greg Bonin	.25	.12	.02
☐ 57 Tom Hallion	.25	.12	.02
☐ 58 Dale Scott	.25	.12	.02
☐ 59 Tim Tschida	.25	.12	.02
☐ 60 Dick Stello	.25	.12	.02
☐ 61 All-Star Game	.25	.12	.02
☐ 62 World Series	.25	.12	.02
☐ 63 Jocko Conlan	.60	.30	.06
☐ 64 Checklist Card	.25	.12	.02

1989 T/M Umpires

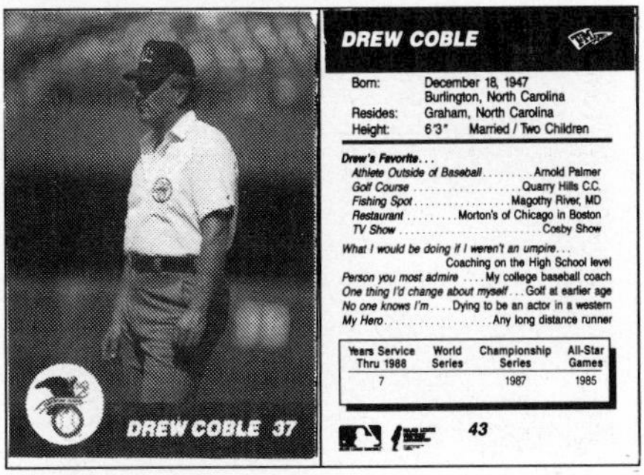

The 1989 Umpires set contains 63 standard-size (2 1/2 by 3 1/2 inch) cards. The fronts have borderless color photos with AL or NL logos. The backs are grey and include biographical information. The cards were distributed as a boxed set along with a custom album.

	MINT	EXC	G-VG
COMPLETE SET (63)	9.00	4.50	.90
COMMON PLAYER (1-63)	.25	.12	.02
☐ 1 Doug Harvey	.35	.17	.03
☐ 2 John Kibler	.25	.12	.02
☐ 3 Bob Engel	.25	.12	.02
☐ 4 Harry Wendelstedt	.35	.17	.03
☐ 5 Larry Barnett	.25	.12	.02
☐ 6 Don Denkinger	.35	.17	.03
☐ 7 Dave Phillips	.35	.17	.03
☐ 8 Larry McCoy	.25	.12	.02
☐ 9 Bruce Froemming	.35	.17	.03
☐ 10 John McSherry	.35	.17	.03
☐ 11 Jim Evans	.25	.12	.02
☐ 12 Frank Pulli	.25	.12	.02
☐ 13 Joe Brinkman	.25	.12	.02
☐ 14 Terry Tata	.25	.12	.02
☐ 15 Nick Bremigan	.25	.12	.02
☐ 16 Jim McKean	.25	.12	.02
☐ 17 Paul Runge	.25	.12	.02
☐ 18 Dutch Rennert	.25	.12	.02
☐ 19 Terry Cooney	.25	.12	.02
☐ 20 Rich Garcia	.25	.12	.02
☐ 21 Dale Ford	.25	.12	.02
☐ 22 Al Clark	.25	.12	.02
☐ 23 Greg Kosc	.25	.12	.02
☐ 24 Jim Quick	.25	.12	.02
☐ 25 Eddie Montague	.25	.12	.02
☐ 26 Jerry Crawford	.25	.12	.02
☐ 27 Steve Palermo	.25	.12	.02
☐ 28 Durwood Merrill	.25	.12	.02
☐ 29 Ken Kaiser	.35	.17	.03
☐ 30 Vic Voltaggio	.25	.12	.02
☐ 31 Mike Reilly	.25	.12	.02
☐ 32 Eric Gregg	.45	.22	.04
☐ 33 Ted Hendry	.25	.12	.02
☐ 34 Joe West	.25	.12	.02
☐ 35 Dave Pallone	.35	.17	.03
☐ 36 Fred Brocklander	.25	.12	.02
☐ 37 John Shulock	.25	.12	.02
☐ 38 Derryl Cousins	.25	.12	.02
☐ 39 Charlie Williams	.25	.12	.02
☐ 40 Rocky Roe	.25	.12	.02
☐ 41 Randy Marsh	.25	.12	.02
☐ 42 Bob Davidson	.25	.12	.02
☐ 43 Drew Coble	.25	.12	.02
☐ 44 Tim McClelland	.25	.12	.02
☐ 45 Dan Morrison	.25	.12	.02
☐ 46 Rick Reed	.25	.12	.02
☐ 47 Steve Rippley	.25	.12	.02
☐ 48 John Hirschbeck	.25	.12	.02
☐ 49 Mark Johnson	.25	.12	.02
☐ 50 Gerry Davis	.25	.12	.02
☐ 51 Dana DeMuth	.25	.12	.02
☐ 52 Larry Young	.25	.12	.02
☐ 53 Tim Welke	.25	.12	.02
☐ 54 Greg Bonin	.25	.12	.02
☐ 55 Tom Hallion	.25	.12	.02
☐ 56 Dale Scott	.25	.12	.02
☐ 57 Tim Tschida	.25	.12	.02
☐ 58 Gary Darling	.25	.12	.02
☐ 59 Mark Hirschbeck	.25	.12	.02
☐ 60 All Star	.25	.12	.02
☐ 61 World Series	.25	.12	.02
☐ 62 Lee Weyer	.25	.12	.02
☐ 63 Connolly/Klem	.50	.25	.05

1989-90 T/M Senior League

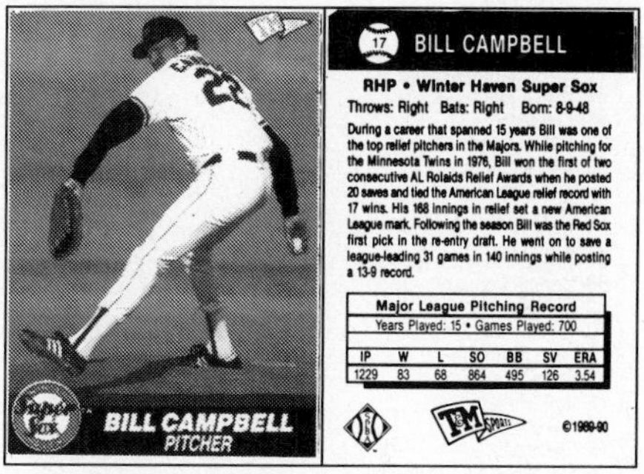

The 1989-90 T/M Senior League set contains 120 standard-size (2 1/2" by 3 1/2") cards depicting members of the new Senior League. The fronts are borderless, with full color photos and black bands at the bottom with player names and positions. The vertically-oriented backs are gray and red, and show career major league totals and highlights. The cards were distributed as a boxed set with a checklist card and eight card-sized puzzle pieces.

	MINT	EXC	G-VG
COMPLETE SET (120)	9.00	4.50	.90
COMMON PLAYER (1-120)	.10	.05	.01
☐ 1 Curt Flood (commissioner)	.30	.15	.03
☐ 2 Willie Aikens	.20	.10	.02
☐ 3 Gary Allenson	.10	.05	.01
☐ 4 Stan Bahnsen	.10	.05	.01
☐ 5 Alan Bannister	.10	.05	.01
☐ 6 Juan Beniquez	.10	.05	.01
☐ 7 Jim Bibby	.10	.05	.01
☐ 8 Paul Blair	.20	.10	.02
☐ 9 Vida Blue	.20	.10	.02
☐ 10 Bobby Bonds	.30	.15	.03
☐ 11 Pedro Borbon	.10	.05	.01
☐ 12 Clete Boyer	.20	.10	.02
☐ 13 Gates Brown	.20	.10	.02
☐ 14 Al Bumbry	.10	.05	.01
☐ 15 Sal Butera	.10	.05	.01
☐ 16 Bert Campaneris	.20	.10	.02
☐ 17 Bill Campbell	.10	.05	.01
☐ 18 Bernie Carbo	.10	.05	.01
☐ 19 Dave Cash	.10	.05	.01
☐ 20 Cesar Cedeno	.20	.10	.02
☐ 21 Gene Clines	.10	.05	.01
☐ 22 Dave Collins	.20	.10	.02
☐ 23 Cecil Cooper	.20	.10	.02
☐ 24 Doug Corbett	.10	.05	.01
☐ 25 Al Cowens	.20	.10	.02
☐ 26 Jose Cruz	.20	.10	.02
☐ 27 Mike Cuellar	.20	.10	.02
☐ 28 Pat Dobson	.20	.10	.02
☐ 29 Dick Drago	.10	.05	.01
☐ 30 Dan Driessen	.20	.10	.02
☐ 31 Jamie Easterly	.10	.05	.01
☐ 32 Juan Eichelberger	.10	.05	.01
☐ 33 Dock Ellis	.10	.05	.01
☐ 34 Ed Figueroa	.10	.05	.01
☐ 35 Rollie Fingers	.60	.30	.06
☐ 36 George Foster	.30	.15	.03
☐ 37 Oscar Gamble	.20	.10	.02
☐ 38 Wayne Garland	.10	.05	.01
☐ 39 Wayne Garrett	.10	.05	.01
☐ 40 Ross Grimsley	.10	.05	.01
☐ 41 Jerry Grote	.10	.05	.01
☐ 42 Johnny Grubb	.10	.05	.01

☐ 43 Mario Guerrero	.10	.05	.01
☐ 44 Toby Harrah	.20	.10	.02
☐ 45 Steve Henderson	.10	.05	.01
☐ 46 George Hendrick	.20	.10	.02
☐ 47 Butch Hobson	.10	.05	.01
☐ 48 Roy Howell	.10	.05	.01
☐ 49 Al Hrabosky	.20	.10	.02
☐ 50 Clint Hurdle	.10	.05	.01
☐ 51 Garth Iorg	.10	.05	.01
☐ 52 Tim Ireland	.10	.05	.01
☐ 53 Grant Jackson	.10	.05	.01
☐ 54 Ron Jackson	.10	.05	.01
☐ 55 Ferguson Jenkins	.75	.35	.07
☐ 56 Odell Jones	.10	.05	.01
☐ 57 Mike Kekich	.10	.05	.01
☐ 58 Steve Kemp	.20	.10	.02
☐ 59 Dave Kingman	.30	.15	.03
☐ 60 Bruce Kison	.10	.05	.01
☐ 61 Lee Lacy	.10	.05	.01
☐ 62 Rafael Landestoy	.10	.05	.01
☐ 63 Ken Landreaux	.20	.10	.02
☐ 64 Tito Landrum	.10	.05	.01
☐ 65 Dave LaRoche	.10	.05	.01
☐ 66 Bill Lee	.20	.10	.02
☐ 67 Ron LeFlore	.20	.10	.02
☐ 68 Dennis Leonard	.20	.10	.02
☐ 69 Bill Madlock	.30	.15	.03
☐ 70 Mickey Mahler	.10	.05	.01
☐ 71 Rich Manning	.10	.05	.01
☐ 72 Tippy Martinez	.10	.05	.01
☐ 73 Jon Matlack	.20	.10	.02
☐ 74 Bake McBride	.10	.05	.01
☐ 75 Steve McCatty	.10	.05	.01
☐ 76 Hal McRae	.20	.10	.02
☐ 77 Dan Meyer	.10	.05	.01
☐ 78 Felix Millan	.10	.05	.01
☐ 79 Paul Mirabella	.10	.05	.01
☐ 80 Omar Moreno	.10	.05	.01
☐ 81 Jim Morrison	.10	.05	.01
☐ 82 Graig Nettles	.30	.15	.03
☐ 83 Al Oliver	.30	.15	.03
☐ 84 Amos Otis	.20	.10	.02
☐ 85 Tom Paciorek	.10	.05	.01
☐ 86 Lowell Palmer	.10	.05	.01
☐ 87 Pat Putnam	.10	.05	.01
☐ 88 Lenny Randle	.10	.05	.01
☐ 89 Ken Reitz	.10	.05	.01
☐ 90 Gene Richards	.10	.05	.01
☐ 91 Mickey Rivers	.20	.10	.02
☐ 92 Leon Roberts	.10	.05	.01
☐ 93 Joe Sambito	.10	.05	.01
☐ 94 Rodney Scott	.10	.05	.01
☐ 95 Bob Shirley	.10	.05	.01
☐ 96 Jim Slaton	.10	.05	.01
☐ 97 Elias Sosa	.10	.05	.01
☐ 98 Fred Stanley	.10	.05	.01
☐ 99 Bill Stein	.10	.05	.01
☐ 100 Rennie Stennett	.10	.05	.01
☐ 101 Sammy Stewart	.10	.05	.01
☐ 102 Tim Stoddard	.10	.05	.01
☐ 103 Champ Summers	.10	.05	.01
☐ 104 Derrel Thomas	.10	.05	.01
☐ 105 Luis Tiant	.30	.15	.03
☐ 106 Bobby Tolan	.20	.10	.02
☐ 107 Bill Travers	.10	.05	.01
☐ 108 Tom Underwood	.10	.05	.01
☐ 109 Ricks Waits	.10	.05	.01
☐ 110 Ron Washington	.10	.05	.01
☐ 111 U.L. Washington	.10	.05	.01
☐ 112 Earl Weaver MG	.30	.15	.03
☐ 113 Jerry White	.10	.05	.01
☐ 114 Milt Wilcox	.10	.05	.01
☐ 115 Dick Williams MG	.20	.10	.02
☐ 116 Walt Williams	.10	.05	.01
☐ 117 Rick Wise	.10	.05	.01
☐ 118 Favorite Suns Luis Tiant Cesar Cedeno	.15	.07	.01
☐ 119 Home Run Legends George Foster Bobby Bonds	.30	.15	.03
☐ 120 Sunshine Skippers Earl Weaver Dick Williams	.10	.05	.01
☐ 121 Checklist 1-120 (unnumbered)	.10	.05	.01

1990 T/M Umpires

The 1990 T/M Umpires set is a standard-size (2 1/2" by 3 1/2") set which features a picture of each umpire on the front of the card with a baseball rules question on the back of the card. The set was issued as a boxed set as well as in packs.

	MINT	EXC	G-VG
COMPLETE SET (70)	8.00	4.00	.80
COMMON PLAYER (1-70)	.20	.10	.02
☐ 1 Doug Harvey	.30	.15	.03
☐ 2 John Kibler	.20	.10	.02
☐ 3 Bob Engel	.20	.10	.02
☐ 4 Harry Wendelstedt	.30	.15	.03
☐ 5 Larry Barnett	.20	.10	.02
☐ 6 Don Denkinger	.30	.15	.03
☐ 7 Dave Phillips	.30	.15	.03
☐ 8 Larry McCoy	.20	.10	.02
☐ 9 Bruce Froemming	.30	.15	.03
☐ 10 John McSherry	.20	.10	.02
☐ 11 Jim Evans	.20	.10	.02
☐ 12 Frank Pulli	.20	.10	.02
☐ 13 Joe Brinkman	.20	.10	.02
☐ 14 Terry Tata	.20	.10	.02
☐ 15 Jim McKean	.20	.10	.02
☐ 16 Dutch Rennert	.20	.10	.02
☐ 17 Paul Runge	.20	.10	.02
☐ 18 Terry Cooney	.20	.10	.02
☐ 19 Rich Garcia	.20	.10	.02
☐ 20 Dale Ford	.20	.10	.02
☐ 21 Al Clark	.20	.10	.02
☐ 22 Greg Kosc	.20	.10	.02
☐ 23 Jim Quick	.20	.10	.02
☐ 24 Eddie Montague	.20	.10	.02
☐ 25 Jerry Crawford	.20	.10	.02
☐ 26 Steve Palermo	.20	.10	.02
☐ 27 Durwood Merrill	.20	.10	.02
☐ 28 Ken Kaiser	.30	.15	.03
☐ 29 Vic Voltaggio	.20	.10	.02
☐ 30 Mike Reilly	.20	.10	.02
☐ 31 Eric Gregg	.40	.20	.04
☐ 32 Ted Hendry	.20	.10	.02
☐ 33 Joe West	.20	.10	.02
☐ 34 Fred Brocklander	.20	.10	.02
☐ 35 John Shulock	.20	.10	.02
☐ 36 Derryl Cousins	.20	.10	.02
☐ 37 Charlie Williams	.20	.10	.02
☐ 38 Rocky Roe	.20	.10	.02
☐ 39 Randy Marsh	.20	.10	.02
☐ 40 Bob Davidson	.20	.10	.02
☐ 41 Drew Coble	.20	.10	.02
☐ 42 Tim McClelland	.20	.10	.02
☐ 43 Dan Morrison	.20	.10	.02
☐ 44 Rick Reed	.20	.10	.02
☐ 45 Steve Ripley	.20	.10	.02
☐ 46 John Hirschbeck	.20	.10	.02
☐ 47 Mark Johnson	.20	.10	.02
☐ 48 Gerry Davis	.20	.10	.02
☐ 49 Dana DeMuth	.20	.10	.02
☐ 50 Larry Young	.20	.10	.02
☐ 51 Tim Welke	.20	.10	.02
☐ 52 Greg Bonin	.20	.10	.02
☐ 53 Tom Hallion	.20	.10	.02
☐ 54 Dale Scott	.20	.10	.02
☐ 55 Tim Tschida	.20	.10	.02
☐ 56 Gary Darling	.20	.10	.02
☐ 57 Mark Hirschbeck	.20	.10	.02
☐ 58 Jerry Layne	.20	.10	.02

☐ 59 Jim Joyce	.20	.10	.02
☐ 60 Bill Hohn	.20	.10	.02
☐ 61 All-Star Game	.20	.10	.02
☐ 62 World Series	.20	.10	.02
☐ 63 Nick Bremigan	.20	.10	.02
☐ 64 The Runges	.30	.15	.03
☐ 65 A.Bartlett Giamatti (memorial)	.50	.25	.05
☐ 66 Puzzle Piece 1	.20	.10	.02
☐ 67 Puzzle Piece 2	.20	.10	.02
☐ 68 Puzzle Piece 3	.20	.10	.02
☐ 69 Puzzle Piece 4	.20	.10	.02
☐ 70 Checklist Card	.20	.10	.02
☐ 71 Al Barlick	1.00	.50	.10

1951 Topps Blue Backs

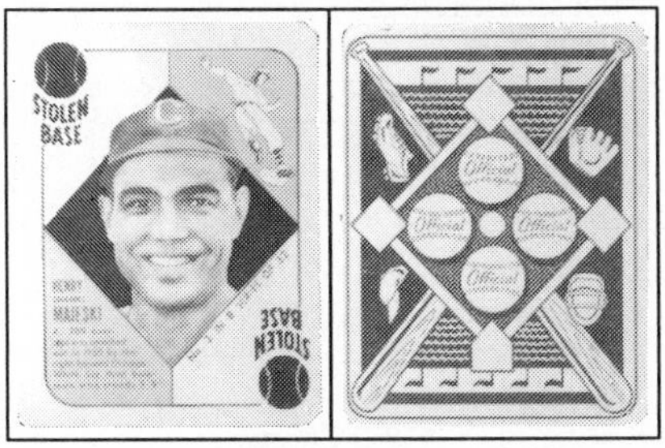

The cards in this 52-card set measure 2" by 2 5/8". The 1951 Topps series of blue backed baseball cards could be used to play a baseball game by shuffling the cards and drawing them from a pile. These cards were marketed with a piece of caramel candy, which often melted or was squashed in such a way as to damage the card and wrapper (despite the fact that a paper shield was inserted between candy and card). Blue Backs are more difficult to obtain than the similarly styled Red Backs. The set is denoted on the cards as "Set B" and the Red Back set is correspondingly Set A. Appropriately leading off the set is Eddie Yost.

	NRMT	VG-E	GOOD
COMPLETE SET (52)	1800.00	800.00	200.00
COMMON PLAYER (1-52)	33.00	16.00	3.00
☐ 1 Eddie Yost	36.00	18.00	3.60
☐ 2 Hank Majeski	33.00	16.00	3.00
☐ 3 Richie Ashburn	85.00	42.50	8.50
☐ 4 Del Ennis	33.00	16.00	3.00
☐ 5 Johnny Pesky	33.00	16.00	3.00
☐ 6 Red Schoendienst	90.00	45.00	9.00
☐ 7 Gerry Staley	33.00	16.00	3.00
☐ 8 Dick Sisler	33.00	16.00	3.00
☐ 9 Johnny Sain	45.00	22.50	4.50
☐ 10 Joe Page	36.00	18.00	3.60
☐ 11 Johnny Groth	33.00	16.00	3.00
☐ 12 Sam Jethroe	33.00	16.00	3.00
☐ 13 Mickey Vernon	36.00	18.00	3.60
☐ 14 Red Munger	33.00	16.00	3.00
☐ 15 Eddie Joost	33.00	16.00	3.00
☐ 16 Murry Dickson	33.00	16.00	3.00
☐ 17 Roy Smalley	33.00	16.00	3.00
☐ 18 Ned Garver	33.00	16.00	3.00
☐ 19 Phil Masi	33.00	16.00	3.00
☐ 20 Ralph Branca	40.00	20.00	4.00
☐ 21 Billy Johnson	33.00	16.00	3.00
☐ 22 Bob Kuzava	33.00	16.00	3.00
☐ 23 Dizzy Trout	33.00	16.00	3.00
☐ 24 Sherman Lollar	33.00	16.00	3.00
☐ 25 Sam Mele	33.00	16.00	3.00
☐ 26 Chico Carrasquel	33.00	16.00	3.00
☐ 27 Andy Pafko	33.00	16.00	3.00
☐ 28 Harry Brecheen	33.00	16.00	3.00
☐ 29 Granville Hamner	33.00	16.00	3.00
☐ 30 Enos Slaughter	110.00	55.00	11.00
☐ 31 Lou Brissie	33.00	16.00	3.00
☐ 32 Bob Elliott	33.00	16.00	3.00
☐ 33 Don Lenhardt	33.00	16.00	3.00
☐ 34 Earl Torgeson	33.00	16.00	3.00
☐ 35 Tommy Byrne	33.00	16.00	3.00
☐ 36 Cliff Fannin	33.00	16.00	3.00
☐ 37 Bobby Doerr	90.00	45.00	9.00
☐ 38 Irv Noren	33.00	16.00	3.00
☐ 39 Ed Lopat	45.00	22.50	4.50
☐ 40 Vic Wertz	36.00	18.00	3.60
☐ 41 Johnny Schmitz	33.00	16.00	3.00
☐ 42 Bruce Edwards	33.00	16.00	3.00
☐ 43 Willie Jones	33.00	16.00	3.00
☐ 44 Johnny Wyrostek	33.00	16.00	3.00
☐ 45 Billy Pierce	40.00	20.00	4.00
☐ 46 Gerry Priddy	33.00	16.00	3.00
☐ 47 Herman Wehmeier	33.00	16.00	3.00
☐ 48 Billy Cox	36.00	18.00	3.60
☐ 49 Hank Sauer	36.00	18.00	3.60
☐ 50 Johnny Mize	120.00	60.00	12.00
☐ 51 Eddie Waitkus	33.00	16.00	3.00
☐ 52 Sam Chapman	36.00	18.00	3.60

1951 Topps Red Backs

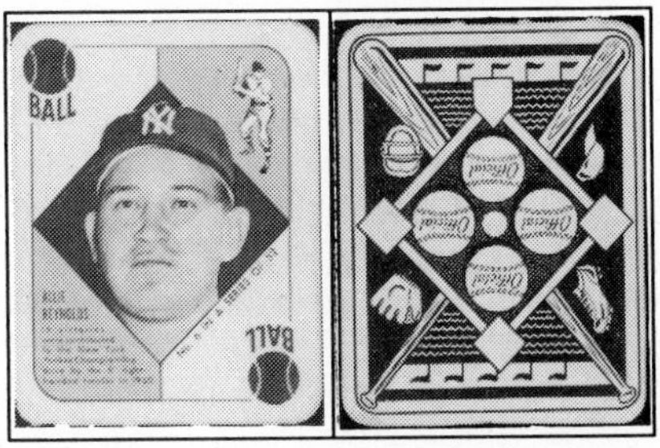

The cards in this 52-card set measure 2" by 2 5/8". The 1951 Topps Red Back set is identical in style to the Blue Back set of the same year. The cards have rounded corners and were designed to be used as a baseball game. Zernial, number 36, is listed with either the White Sox or Athletics, and Holmes, number 52, with either the Braves or Hartford. The set is denoted on the cards as "Set A" and the Blue Back set is correspondingly Set B.

	NRMT	VG-E	GOOD
COMPLETE SET (54)	625.00	275.00	50.00
COMMON PLAYER (1-52)	6.00	3.00	.60
☐ 1 Yogi Berra	100.00	25.00	5.00
☐ 2 Sid Gordon	6.00	3.00	.60
☐ 3 Ferris Fain	7.00	3.50	.70
☐ 4 Vern Stephens	6.00	3.00	.60
☐ 5 Phil Rizzuto	27.00	13.50	2.70
☐ 6 Allie Reynolds	11.00	5.50	1.10
☐ 7 Howie Pollet	6.00	3.00	.60
☐ 8 Early Wynn	20.00	10.00	2.00
☐ 9 Roy Sievers	7.00	3.50	.70
☐ 10 Mel Parnell	7.00	3.50	.70
☐ 11 Gene Hermanski	6.00	3.00	.60
☐ 12 Jim Hegan	6.00	3.00	.60
☐ 13 Dale Mitchell	6.00	3.00	.60
☐ 14 Wayne Terwilliger	6.00	3.00	.60
☐ 15 Ralph Kiner	27.00	13.50	2.70
☐ 16 Preacher Roe	9.00	4.50	.90
☐ 17 Dave (Gus) Bell	8.00	4.00	.80
☐ 18 Gerry Coleman	8.00	4.00	.80
☐ 19 Dick Kokos	6.00	3.00	.60
☐ 20 Dom DiMaggio	10.00	5.00	1.00
☐ 21 Larry Jansen	6.00	3.00	.60
☐ 22 Bob Feller	40.00	20.00	4.00
☐ 23 Ray Boone	8.00	4.00	.80
☐ 24 Hank Bauer	12.00	6.00	1.20
☐ 25 Cliff Chambers	6.00	3.00	.60
☐ 26 Luke Easter	6.00	3.00	.60
☐ 27 Wally Westlake	6.00	3.00	.60
☐ 28 Elmer Valo	6.00	3.00	.60
☐ 29 Bob Kennedy	6.00	3.00	.60
☐ 30 Warren Spahn	40.00	20.00	4.00
☐ 31 Gil Hodges	27.00	13.50	2.70
☐ 32 Henry Thompson	7.00	3.50	.70
☐ 33 William Werle	6.00	3.00	.60
☐ 34 Grady Hatton	6.00	3.00	.60

☐ 35 Al Rosen	12.00	6.00	1.20
☐ 36A Gus Zernial (Chicago)	25.00	12.50	2.50
☐ 36B Gus Zernial (Philadelphia)	20.00	10.00	2.00
☐ 37 Wes Westrum	6.00	3.00	.60
☐ 38 Duke Snider	75.00	37.50	7.50
☐ 39 Ted Kluszewski	13.50	6.00	1.20
☐ 40 Mike Garcia	7.00	3.50	.70
☐ 41 Whitey Lockman	7.00	3.50	.70
☐ 42 Ray Scarborough	6.00	3.00	.60
☐ 43 Maurice McDermott	6.00	3.00	.60
☐ 44 Sid Hudson	6.00	3.00	.60
☐ 45 Andy Seminick	6.00	3.00	.60
☐ 46 Billy Goodman	7.00	3.50	.70
☐ 47 Tommy Glaviano	6.00	3.00	.60
☐ 48 Eddie Stanky	8.00	4.00	.80
☐ 49 Al Zarilla	6.00	3.00	.60
☐ 50 Monte Irvin	36.00	18.00	3.60
☐ 51 Eddie Robinson	6.00	3.00	.60
☐ 52A Tommy Holmes (Boston)	25.00	12.50	2.50
☐ 52B Tommy Holmes (Hartford)	20.00	10.00	2.00

1951 Topps Teams

The cards in this 9-card set measure 2 1/16" by 5 1/4". These unnumbered team cards issued by Topps in 1951 carry black and white photographs framed by a yellow border. They are found with or without "1950" printed in the name panel before the team name (no difference in value for either variety). These cards were issued in the same 5 cent wrapper as the Connie Mack and Current All Stars. They have been assigned reference numbers in the checklist alphabetically by team city and name.

	NRMT	VG-E	GOOD
COMPLETE SET (9)	1700.00	750.00	200.00
COMMON TEAM (1-9)	150.00	75.00	15.00
☐ 1 Boston Red Sox	300.00	150.00	30.00
☐ 2 Brooklyn Dodgers	225.00	110.00	22.00
☐ 3 Chicago White Sox	180.00	90.00	18.00
☐ 4 Cincinnati Reds	150.00	75.00	15.00
☐ 5 New York Giants	180.00	90.00	18.00
☐ 6 Philadelphia Athletics	150.00	75.00	15.00
☐ 7 Philadelphia Phillies	150.00	75.00	15.00
☐ 8 St. Louis Cardinals	300.00	150.00	30.00
☐ 9 Washington Senators	150.00	75.00	15.00

1951 Topps Connie Mack

The cards in this 11-card set measure 2 1/16" by 5 1/4". The series of die-cut cards which comprise the set entitled Connie Mack All-Stars was one of Topps' most distinctive and fragile card designs. Printed on thin cardboard, these elegant cards were protected in the wrapper by panels of accompanying Red Backs, but once removed were easily damaged (after all, they were intended to be folded and used as toy figures). Cards without tops have a value less than one-half of that listed below. The cards are unnumbered and are listed below in alphabetical order.

	NRMT	VG-E	GOOD
COMPLETE SET (11)	5000.00	2200.00	500.00
COMMON PLAYER (1-11)	125.00	60.00	12.50
☐ 1 Grover C. Alexander	350.00	175.00	35.00
☐ 2 Mickey Cochrane	250.00	125.00	25.00
☐ 3 Ed Collins	125.00	60.00	12.50
☐ 4 Jimmy Collins	125.00	60.00	12.50
☐ 5 Lou Gehrig	1500.00	600.00	150.00
☐ 6 Walter Johnson	500.00	250.00	50.00
☐ 7 Connie Mack	250.00	125.00	25.00
☐ 8 Christy Mathewson	250.00	125.00	25.00
☐ 9 Babe Ruth	2000.00	800.00	200.00
☐ 10 Tris Speaker	125.00	60.00	12.50
☐ 11 Honus Wagner	250.00	125.00	25.00

1951 Topps Current AS

The cards in this 11-card set measure 2 1/16" by 5 1/4". The 1951 Topps Current All-Star series is probably the rarest of all legitimate, nationally issued, post war baseball issues. The set price listed below does not include the prices for the cards of Konstanty, Roberts and Stanky, which likely never were released to the public in gum packs. These three cards (SP in the checklist below) were probably obtained directly from the company and exist in extremely limited numbers. As with the Connie Mack set, cards without the die-cut background are worth half of the value listed below. The cards are unnumbered and are listed below in alphabetical order.

	NRMT	VG-E	GOOD
COMPLETE SET (8)	3500.00	1500.00	350.00
COMMON PLAYER (1-11)	150.00	75.00	15.00
☐ 1 Yogi Berra	1000.00	400.00	100.00
☐ 2 Larry Doby	200.00	100.00	20.00
☐ 3 Walt Dropo	250.00	125.00	25.00
☐ 4 Hoot Evers	150.00	75.00	15.00
☐ 5 George Kell	450.00	225.00	45.00
☐ 6 Ralph Kiner	600.00	300.00	60.00
☐ 7 Jim Konstanty SP	10000.00	5000.00	1000.00
☐ 8 Bob Lemon	500.00	250.00	50.00
☐ 9 Phil Rizzuto	500.00	250.00	50.00
☐ 10 Robin Roberts SP	12000.00	6000.00	1200.00
☐ 11 Eddie Stanky SP	10000.00	5000.00	1000.00

1952 Topps

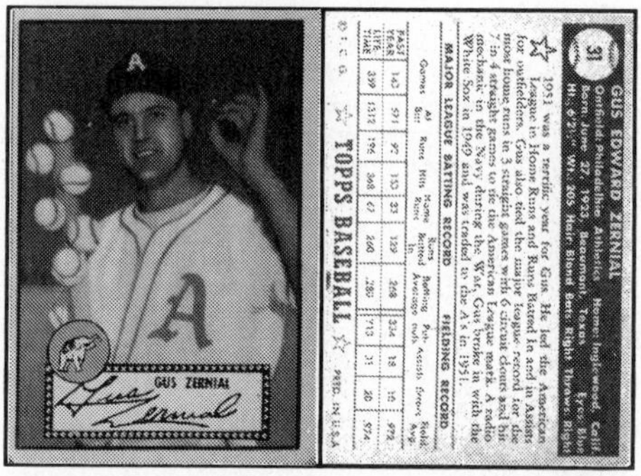

The cards in this 407-card set measure 2 5/8" by 3 3/4". The 1952 Topps set is Topps' first truly major set. Card numbers 1 to 80 were issued with red or black backs, both of which are less plentiful than card numbers 81 to 250. In fact, the first series is considered the most difficult with respect to finding perfect condition cards. Card number 48 (Joe Page) and number 49 (Johnny Sain) can be found with each other's write-up on their back. Card numbers 251 to 310 are somewhat scarce and numbers 311 to 407 are quite scarce. Cards 281-300 were single printed compared to the other cards in the next to last series. Cards 311-313 were double printed on the last high number printing sheet. The key card in the set is obviously Mickey Mantle, number 311, Mickey's first of many Topps cards. Although rarely seen, there exist salesman sample panels of three cards containing the fronts of regular cards with ad information on the back. Two such panels seen are Bob Mahoney/Robin Roberts/Sid Hudson and Wally Westlake/Dizzy Trout/Irv Noren. The key rookies in this set are Billy Martin, Eddie Mathews, and Hoyt Wilhelm.

	NRMT	VG-E	GOOD
COMPLETE SET (407)	40000.	18000.	6000.
COMMON PLAYER (1-80)	48.00	22.00	4.50
COMMON PLAYER (81-250)	25.00	12.50	2.50
COMMON PLAYER (251-280)	40.00	20.00	4.00
COMMON PLAYER (281-300)	48.00	22.00	4.50

COMMON PLAYER (301-310)	40.00	20.00	4.00
COMMON PLAYER (311-407)	150.00	75.00	15.00
☐ 1 Andy Pafko	1200.00	75.00	15.00
☐ 2 Pete Runnels	55.00	27.50	5.50
☐ 3 Hank Thompson	55.00	27.50	5.50
☐ 4 Don Lenhardt	48.00	22.00	4.50
☐ 5 Larry Jansen	48.00	22.00	4.50
☐ 6 Grady Hatton	48.00	22.00	4.50
☐ 7 Wayne Terwilliger	48.00	22.00	4.50
☐ 8 Fred Marsh	48.00	22.00	4.50
☐ 9 Robert Hogue	48.00	22.00	4.50
☐ 10 Al Rosen	75.00	37.50	7.50
☐ 11 Phil Rizzuto	175.00	85.00	18.00
☐ 12 Romanus Basgall	48.00	22.00	4.50
☐ 13 Johnny Wyrostek	48.00	22.00	4.50
☐ 14 Bob Elliott	55.00	27.50	5.50
☐ 15 Johnny Pesky	55.00	27.50	5.50
☐ 16 Gene Hermanski	48.00	22.00	4.50
☐ 17 Jim Hegan	55.00	27.50	5.50
☐ 18 Merrill Combs	48.00	22.00	4.50
☐ 19 Johnny Bucha	48.00	22.00	4.50
☐ 20 Billy Loes	90.00	45.00	9.00
☐ 21 Ferris Fain	55.00	27.50	5.50
☐ 22 Dom DiMaggio	80.00	40.00	8.00
☐ 23 Billy Goodman	55.00	27.50	5.50
☐ 24 Luke Easter	55.00	27.50	5.50
☐ 25 Johnny Groth	48.00	22.00	4.50
☐ 26 Monte Irvin	100.00	50.00	10.00
☐ 27 Sam Jethroe	48.00	22.00	4.50
☐ 28 Jerry Priddy	48.00	22.00	4.50
☐ 29 Ted Kluszewski	80.00	40.00	8.00
☐ 30 Mel Parnell	55.00	27.50	5.50
☐ 31 Gus Zernial	60.00	30.00	6.00
☐ 32 Eddie Robinson	48.00	22.00	4.50
☐ 33 Warren Spahn	250.00	125.00	25.00
☐ 34 Elmer Valo	48.00	22.00	4.50
☐ 35 Hank Sauer	65.00	32.50	6.50
☐ 36 Gil Hodges	150.00	75.00	15.00
☐ 37 Duke Snider	275.00	135.00	27.00
☐ 38 Wally Westlake	48.00	22.00	4.50
☐ 39 Dizzy Trout	48.00	22.00	4.50
☐ 40 Irv Noren	48.00	22.00	4.50
☐ 41 Bob Wellman	48.00	22.00	4.50
☐ 42 Lou Kretlow	48.00	22.00	4.50
☐ 43 Ray Scarborough	48.00	22.00	4.50
☐ 44 Con Dempsey	48.00	22.00	4.50
☐ 45 Eddie Joost	48.00	22.00	4.50
☐ 46 Gordon Goldsberry	48.00	22.00	4.50
☐ 47 Willie Jones	48.00	22.00	4.50
☐ 48A Joe Page COR	65.00	32.50	6.50
☐ 48B Joe Page ERR (bio for Sain)	300.00	150.00	30.00
☐ 49A Johnny Sain COR	90.00	45.00	9.00
☐ 49B Johnny Sain ERR (bio for Page)	300.00	150.00	30.00
☐ 50 Marv Rickert	48.00	22.00	4.50
☐ 51 Jim Russell	48.00	22.00	4.50
☐ 52 Don Mueller	60.00	30.00	6.00
☐ 53 Chris Van Cuyk	48.00	22.00	4.50
☐ 54 Leo Kiely	48.00	22.00	4.50
☐ 55 Ray Boone	55.00	27.50	5.50
☐ 56 Tommy Glaviano	48.00	22.00	4.50
☐ 57 Ed Lopat	100.00	50.00	10.00
☐ 58 Bob Mahoney	48.00	22.00	4.50
☐ 59 Robin Roberts	125.00	60.00	12.50
☐ 60 Sid Hudson	48.00	22.00	4.50
☐ 61 Tookie Gilbert	48.00	22.00	4.50
☐ 62 Chuck Stobbs	48.00	22.00	4.50
☐ 63 Howie Pollet	48.00	22.00	4.50
☐ 64 Roy Sievers	55.00	27.50	5.50
☐ 65 Enos Slaughter	125.00	60.00	12.50
☐ 66 Preacher Roe	100.00	50.00	10.00
☐ 67 Allie Reynolds	100.00	50.00	10.00
☐ 68 Cliff Chambers	48.00	22.00	4.50
☐ 69 Virgil Stallcup	48.00	22.00	4.50
☐ 70 Al Zarilla	48.00	22.00	4.50
☐ 71 Tom Upton	48.00	22.00	4.50
☐ 72 Karl Olson	48.00	22.00	4.50
☐ 73 Bill Werle	48.00	22.00	4.50
☐ 74 Andy Hansen	48.00	22.00	4.50
☐ 75 Wes Westrum	48.00	22.00	4.50
☐ 76 Eddie Stanky	60.00	30.00	6.00
☐ 77 Bob Kennedy	48.00	22.00	4.50
☐ 78 Ellis Kinder	48.00	22.00	4.50
☐ 79 Jerald Staley	48.00	22.00	4.50
☐ 80 Herman Wehmeier	48.00	22.00	4.50
☐ 81 Vernon Law	30.00	15.00	3.00
☐ 82 Duane Pillette	25.00	12.50	2.50
☐ 83 Billy Johnson	25.00	12.50	2.50
☐ 84 Vern Stephens	30.00	15.00	3.00
☐ 85 Bob Kuzava	25.00	12.50	2.50
☐ 86 Ted Gray	25.00	12.50	2.50
☐ 87 Dale Coogan	25.00	12.50	2.50
☐ 88 Bob Feller	135.00	65.00	13.50
☐ 89 Johnny Lipon	25.00	12.50	2.50
☐ 90 Mickey Grasso	25.00	12.50	2.50
☐ 91 Red Schoendienst	75.00	37.50	7.50
☐ 92 Dale Mitchell	30.00	15.00	3.00
☐ 93 Al Sima	25.00	12.50	2.50
☐ 94 Sam Mele	25.00	12.50	2.50
☐ 95 Ken Holcombe	25.00	12.50	2.50
☐ 96 Willard Marshall	25.00	12.50	2.50
☐ 97 Earl Torgeson	25.00	12.50	2.50
☐ 98 Billy Pierce	30.00	15.00	3.00
☐ 99 Gene Woodling	50.00	25.00	5.00
☐ 100 Del Rice	25.00	12.50	2.50
☐ 101 Max Lanier	25.00	12.50	2.50
☐ 102 Bill Kennedy	25.00	12.50	2.50
☐ 103 Cliff Mapes	25.00	12.50	2.50
☐ 104 Don Kolloway	25.00	12.50	2.50
☐ 105 Johnny Pramesa	25.00	12.50	2.50
☐ 106 Mickey Vernon	30.00	15.00	3.00
☐ 107 Connie Ryan	25.00	12.50	2.50
☐ 108 Jim Konstanty	30.00	15.00	3.00
☐ 109 Ted Wilks	25.00	12.50	2.50
☐ 110 Dutch Leonard	25.00	12.50	2.50
☐ 111 Peanuts Lowrey	25.00	12.50	2.50
☐ 112 Hank Majeski	25.00	12.50	2.50
☐ 113 Dick Sisler	25.00	12.50	2.50
☐ 114 Willard Ramsdell	25.00	12.50	2.50
☐ 115 Red Munger	25.00	12.50	2.50
☐ 116 Carl Scheib	25.00	12.50	2.50
☐ 117 Sherm Lollar	30.00	15.00	3.00
☐ 118 Ken Raffensberger	25.00	12.50	2.50
☐ 119 Mickey McDermott	25.00	12.50	2.50
☐ 120 Bob Chakales	25.00	12.50	2.50
☐ 121 Gus Niarhos	25.00	12.50	2.50
☐ 122 Jackie Jensen	70.00	35.00	7.00
☐ 123 Eddie Yost	25.00	12.50	2.50
☐ 124 Monte Kennedy	25.00	12.50	2.50
☐ 125 Bill Rigney	25.00	12.50	2.50
☐ 126 Fred Hutchinson	30.00	15.00	3.00
☐ 127 Paul Minner	25.00	12.50	2.50
☐ 128 Don Bollweg	25.00	12.50	2.50
☐ 129 Johnny Mize	75.00	37.50	7.50
☐ 130 Sheldon Jones	25.00	12.50	2.50
☐ 131 Morrie Martin	25.00	12.50	2.50
☐ 132 Clyde Klutz	25.00	12.50	2.50
☐ 133 Al Widmar	25.00	12.50	2.50
☐ 134 Joe Tipton	25.00	12.50	2.50
☐ 135 Dixie Howell	25.00	12.50	2.50
☐ 136 Johnny Schmitz	25.00	12.50	2.50
☐ 137 Roy McMillan	25.00	12.50	2.50
☐ 138 Bill MacDonald	25.00	12.50	2.50
☐ 139 Ken Wood	25.00	12.50	2.50
☐ 140 Johnny Antonelli	30.00	15.00	3.00
☐ 141 Clint Hartung	25.00	12.50	2.50
☐ 142 Harry Perkowski	25.00	12.50	2.50
☐ 143 Les Moss	25.00	12.50	2.50
☐ 144 Ed Blake	25.00	12.50	2.50
☐ 145 Joe Haynes	25.00	12.50	2.50
☐ 146 Frank House	25.00	12.50	2.50
☐ 147 Bob Young	25.00	12.50	2.50
☐ 148 Johnny Klippstein	25.00	12.50	2.50
☐ 149 Dick Kryhoski	25.00	12.50	2.50
☐ 150 Ted Beard	25.00	12.50	2.50
☐ 151 Wally Post	30.00	15.00	3.00
☐ 152 Al Evans	25.00	12.50	2.50
☐ 153 Bob Rush	25.00	12.50	2.50
☐ 154 Joe Muir	25.00	12.50	2.50
☐ 155 Frank Overmire	25.00	12.50	2.50
☐ 156 Frank Hiller	25.00	12.50	2.50
☐ 157 Bob Usher	25.00	12.50	2.50
☐ 158 Eddie Waitkus	25.00	12.50	2.50
☐ 159 Saul Rogovin	25.00	12.50	2.50
☐ 160 Owen Friend	25.00	12.50	2.50
☐ 161 Bud Byerly	25.00	12.50	2.50
☐ 162 Del Crandall	30.00	15.00	3.00
☐ 163 Stan Rojek	25.00	12.50	2.50
☐ 164 Walt Dubiel	25.00	12.50	2.50
☐ 165 Eddie Kazak	25.00	12.50	2.50
☐ 166 Paul LaPalme	25.00	12.50	2.50
☐ 167 Bill Howerton	25.00	12.50	2.50
☐ 168 Charlie Silvera	30.00	15.00	3.00
☐ 169 Howie Judson	25.00	12.50	2.50
☐ 170 Gus Bell	30.00	15.00	3.00
☐ 171 Ed Erautt	25.00	12.50	2.50
☐ 172 Eddie Miksis	25.00	12.50	2.50
☐ 173 Roy Smalley	25.00	12.50	2.50
☐ 174 Clarence Marshall	25.00	12.50	2.50
☐ 175 Billy Martin	300.00	150.00	30.00
☐ 176 Hank Edwards	25.00	12.50	2.50
☐ 177 Bill Wight	25.00	12.50	2.50
☐ 178 Cass Michaels	25.00	12.50	2.50
☐ 179 Frank Smith	25.00	12.50	2.50
☐ 180 Charley Maxwell	30.00	15.00	3.00
☐ 181 Bob Swift	25.00	12.50	2.50

☐ 182 Billy Hitchcock	25.00	12.50	2.50
☐ 183 Erv Dusak	25.00	12.50	2.50
☐ 184 Bob Ramazotti	25.00	12.50	2.50
☐ 185 Bill Nicholson	25.00	12.50	2.50
☐ 186 Walt Masterson	25.00	12.50	2.50
☐ 187 Bob Miller	25.00	12.50	2.50
☐ 188 Clarence Podbielan	25.00	12.50	2.50
☐ 189 Pete Reiser	35.00	17.50	3.50
☐ 190 Don Johnson	25.00	12.50	2.50
☐ 191 Yogi Berra	350.00	175.00	35.00
☐ 192 Myron Ginsberg	25.00	12.50	2.50
☐ 193 Harry Simpson	25.00	12.50	2.50
☐ 194 Joe Hatton	25.00	12.50	2.50
☐ 195 Minnie Minoso	80.00	40.00	8.00
☐ 196 Solly Hemus	25.00	12.50	2.50
☐ 197 George Strickland	25.00	12.50	2.50
☐ 198 Phil Haugstad	25.00	12.50	2.50
☐ 199 George Zuverink	25.00	12.50	2.50
☐ 200 Ralph Houk	65.00	32.50	6.50
☐ 201 Alex Kellner	25.00	12.50	2.50
☐ 202 Joe Collins	35.00	17.50	3.50
☐ 203 Curt Simmons	30.00	15.00	3.00
☐ 204 Ron Northey	25.00	12.50	2.50
☐ 205 Clyde King	25.00	12.50	2.50
☐ 206 Joe Ostrowski	25.00	12.50	2.50
☐ 207 Mickey Harris	25.00	12.50	2.50
☐ 208 Marlin Stuart	25.00	12.50	2.50
☐ 209 Howie Fox	25.00	12.50	2.50
☐ 210 Dick Fowler	25.00	12.50	2.50
☐ 211 Ray Coleman	25.00	12.50	2.50
☐ 212 Ned Garver	25.00	12.50	2.50
☐ 213 Nippy Jones	25.00	12.50	2.50
☐ 214 Johnny Hopp	30.00	15.00	3.00
☐ 215 Hank Bauer	40.00	20.00	4.00
☐ 216 Richie Ashburn	80.00	40.00	8.00
☐ 217 Snuffy Stirnweiss	30.00	15.00	3.00
☐ 218 Clyde McCullough	25.00	12.50	2.50
☐ 219 Bobby Shantz	35.00	17.50	3.50
☐ 220 Joe Presko	25.00	12.50	2.50
☐ 221 Granny Hamner	25.00	12.50	2.50
☐ 222 Hoot Evers	25.00	12.50	2.50
☐ 223 Del Ennis	30.00	15.00	3.00
☐ 224 Bruce Edwards	25.00	12.50	2.50
☐ 225 Frank Baumholtz	25.00	12.50	2.50
☐ 226 Dave Philley	25.00	12.50	2.50
☐ 227 Joe Garagiola	110.00	55.00	11.00
☐ 228 Al Brazle	25.00	12.50	2.50
☐ 229 Gene Bearden	30.00	15.00	3.00
☐ 230 Matt Batts	25.00	12.50	2.50
☐ 231 Sam Zoldak	25.00	12.50	2.50
☐ 232 Billy Cox	30.00	15.00	3.00
☐ 233 Bob Friend	30.00	15.00	3.00
☐ 234 Steve Souchock	25.00	12.50	2.50
☐ 235 Walt Dropo	30.00	15.00	3.00
☐ 236 Ed Fitzgerald	25.00	12.50	2.50
☐ 237 Jerry Coleman	30.00	15.00	3.00
☐ 238 Art Houtteman	25.00	12.50	2.50
☐ 239 Rocky Bridges	25.00	12.50	2.50
☐ 240 Jack Phillips	25.00	12.50	2.50
☐ 241 Tommy Byrne	25.00	12.50	2.50
☐ 242 Tom Poholsky	25.00	12.50	2.50
☐ 243 Larry Doby	40.00	20.00	4.00
☐ 244 Vic Wertz	30.00	15.00	3.00
☐ 245 Sherry Robertson	25.00	12.50	2.50
☐ 246 George Kell	65.00	32.50	6.50
☐ 247 Randy Gumpert	25.00	12.50	2.50
☐ 248 Frank Shea	25.00	12.50	2.50
☐ 249 Bobby Adams	25.00	12.50	2.50
☐ 250 Carl Erskine	50.00	25.00	5.00
☐ 251 Chico Carrasquel	40.00	20.00	4.00
☐ 252 Vern Bickford	40.00	20.00	4.00
☐ 253 Johnny Berardino	45.00	22.50	4.50
☐ 254 Joe Dobson	40.00	20.00	4.00
☐ 255 Clyde Vollmer	40.00	20.00	4.00
☐ 256 Pete Suder	40.00	20.00	4.00
☐ 257 Bobby Avila	45.00	22.50	4.50
☐ 258 Steve Gromek	40.00	20.00	4.00
☐ 259 Bob Addis	40.00	20.00	4.00
☐ 260 Pete Castiglione	40.00	20.00	4.00
☐ 261 Willie Mays	1150.00	500.00	125.00
☐ 262 Virgil Trucks	45.00	22.50	4.50
☐ 263 Harry Brecheen	45.00	22.50	4.50
☐ 264 Roy Hartsfield	40.00	20.00	4.00
☐ 265 Chuck Diering	40.00	20.00	4.00
☐ 266 Murry Dickson	40.00	20.00	4.00
☐ 267 Sid Gordon	40.00	20.00	4.00
☐ 268 Bob Lemon	150.00	75.00	15.00
☐ 269 Willard Nixon	40.00	20.00	4.00
☐ 270 Lou Brissie	40.00	20.00	4.00
☐ 271 Jim Delsing	40.00	20.00	4.00
☐ 272 Mike Garcia	50.00	25.00	5.00
☐ 273 Erv Palica	40.00	20.00	4.00
☐ 274 Ralph Branca	80.00	40.00	8.00
☐ 275 Pat Mullin	40.00	20.00	4.00
☐ 276 Jim Wilson	40.00	20.00	4.00
☐ 277 Early Wynn	150.00	75.00	15.00
☐ 278 Allie Clark	40.00	20.00	4.00
☐ 279 Eddie Stewart	40.00	20.00	4.00
☐ 280 Cloyd Boyer	45.00	22.50	4.50
☐ 281 Tommy Brown SP	48.00	22.00	4.50
☐ 282 Birdie Tebbetts SP	55.00	27.50	5.50
☐ 283 Phil Masi SP	48.00	22.00	4.50
☐ 284 Hank Arft SP	48.00	22.00	4.50
☐ 285 Cliff Fannin SP	48.00	22.00	4.50
☐ 286 Joe DeMaestri SP	48.00	22.00	4.50
☐ 287 Steve Bilko SP	48.00	22.00	4.50
☐ 288 Chet Nichols SP	48.00	22.00	4.50
☐ 289 Tommy Holmes SP	55.00	27.50	5.50
☐ 290 Joe Astroth SP	48.00	22.00	4.50
☐ 291 Gil Coan SP	48.00	22.00	4.50
☐ 292 Floyd Baker SP	48.00	22.00	4.50
☐ 293 Sibby Sisti SP	48.00	22.00	4.50
☐ 294 Walker Cooper SP	48.00	22.00	4.50
☐ 295 Phil Cavarretta SP	55.00	27.50	5.50
☐ 296 Red Rolfe SP	55.00	27.50	5.50
☐ 297 Andy Seminick SP	48.00	22.00	4.50
☐ 298 Bob Ross SP	48.00	22.00	4.50
☐ 299 Ray Murray SP	48.00	22.00	4.50
☐ 300 Barney McCosky SP	48.00	22.00	4.50
☐ 301 Bob Porterfield	40.00	20.00	4.00
☐ 302 Max Surkont	40.00	20.00	4.00
☐ 303 Harry Dorish	40.00	20.00	4.00
☐ 304 Sam Dente	40.00	20.00	4.00
☐ 305 Paul Richards	50.00	25.00	5.00
☐ 306 Lou Sleater	40.00	20.00	4.00
☐ 307 Frank Campos	40.00	20.00	4.00
☐ 308 Luis Aloma	40.00	20.00	4.00
☐ 309 Jim Busby	40.00	20.00	4.00
☐ 310 George Metkovich	55.00	27.50	5.50
☐ 311 Mickey Mantle DP	7500.00	3000.00	750.00
☐ 312 Jackie Robinson DP	850.00	425.00	85.00
☐ 313 Bobby Thomson DP	175.00	85.00	18.00
☐ 314 Roy Campanella	1300.00	500.00	125.00
☐ 315 Leo Durocher	275.00	135.00	27.00
☐ 316 Dave Williams	175.00	85.00	18.00
☐ 317 Conrado Marrero	150.00	75.00	15.00
☐ 318 Harold Gregg	150.00	75.00	15.00
☐ 319 Al Walker	150.00	75.00	15.00
☐ 320 John Rutherford	150.00	75.00	15.00
☐ 321 Joe Black	225.00	110.00	22.00
☐ 322 Randy Jackson	150.00	75.00	15.00
☐ 323 Bubba Church	150.00	75.00	15.00
☐ 324 Warren Hacker	150.00	75.00	15.00
☐ 325 Bill Serena	150.00	75.00	15.00
☐ 326 George Shuba	175.00	85.00	18.00
☐ 327 Al Wilson	150.00	75.00	15.00
☐ 328 Bob Borkowski	150.00	75.00	15.00
☐ 329 Ike Delock	150.00	75.00	15.00
☐ 330 Turk Lown	150.00	75.00	15.00
☐ 331 Tom Morgan	150.00	75.00	15.00
☐ 332 Anthony Bartirome	150.00	75.00	15.00
☐ 333 Pee Wee Reese	800.00	400.00	80.00
☐ 334 Wilmer Mizell	150.00	75.00	15.00
☐ 335 Ted Lepcio	150.00	75.00	15.00
☐ 336 Dave Koslo	150.00	75.00	15.00
☐ 337 Jim Hearn	150.00	75.00	15.00
☐ 338 Sal Yvars	150.00	75.00	15.00
☐ 339 Russ Meyer	150.00	75.00	15.00
☐ 340 Bob Hooper	150.00	75.00	15.00
☐ 341 Hal Jeffcoat	150.00	75.00	15.00
☐ 342 Clem Labine	175.00	85.00	18.00
☐ 343 Dick Gernert	150.00	75.00	15.00
☐ 344 Ewell Blackwell	175.00	85.00	18.00
☐ 345 Sammy White	150.00	75.00	15.00
☐ 346 George Spencer	150.00	75.00	15.00
☐ 347 Joe Adcock	200.00	100.00	20.00
☐ 348 Robert Kelly	150.00	75.00	15.00
☐ 349 Bob Cain	150.00	75.00	15.00
☐ 350 Cal Abrams	150.00	75.00	15.00
☐ 351 Alvin Dark	200.00	100.00	20.00
☐ 352 Karl Drews	150.00	75.00	15.00
☐ 353 Bobby Del Greco	150.00	75.00	15.00
☐ 354 Fred Hatfield	150.00	75.00	15.00
☐ 355 Bobby Morgan	150.00	75.00	15.00
☐ 356 Toby Atwell	150.00	75.00	15.00
☐ 357 Smoky Burgess	175.00	85.00	18.00
☐ 358 John Kucab	150.00	75.00	15.00
☐ 359 Dee Fondy	150.00	75.00	15.00
☐ 360 George Crowe	150.00	75.00	15.00
☐ 361 William Posedel CO	150.00	75.00	15.00
☐ 362 Ken Heintzelman	150.00	75.00	15.00
☐ 363 Dick Rozek	150.00	75.00	15.00
☐ 364 Clyde Sukeforth CO	150.00	75.00	15.00
☐ 365 Cookie Lavagetto CO	150.00	75.00	15.00
☐ 366 Dave Madison	150.00	75.00	15.00
☐ 367 Ben Thorpe	150.00	75.00	15.00
☐ 368 Ed Wright	150.00	75.00	15.00
☐ 369 Dick Groat	250.00	125.00	25.00

□ 370 Billy Hoeft	150.00	75.00	15.00
□ 371 Bobby Hofman	150.00	75.00	15.00
□ 372 Gil McDougald	275.00	135.00	27.00
□ 373 Jim Turner CO	175.00	85.00	18.00
□ 374 John Benton	150.00	75.00	15.00
□ 375 John Merson	150.00	75.00	15.00
□ 376 Faye Throneberry	150.00	75.00	15.00
□ 377 Chuck Dressen MG	175.00	85.00	18.00
□ 378 Leroy Fusselman	150.00	75.00	15.00
□ 379 Joe Rossi	150.00	75.00	15.00
□ 380 Clem Koshorek	150.00	75.00	15.00
□ 381 Milton Stock CO	150.00	75.00	15.00
□ 382 Sam Jones	175.00	85.00	18.00
□ 383 Del Wilber	150.00	75.00	15.00
□ 384 Frank Crosetti CO	250.00	125.00	25.00
□ 385 Herman Franks	175.00	85.00	18.00
□ 386 John Yuhas	150.00	75.00	15.00
□ 387 Billy Meyer	150.00	75.00	15.00
□ 388 Bob Chipman	150.00	75.00	15.00
□ 389 Ben Wade	150.00	75.00	15.00
□ 390 Glenn Nelson	150.00	75.00	15.00
□ 391 Ben Chapman UER (photo actually Sam Chapman)	150.00	75.00	15.00
□ 392 Hoyt Wilhelm	500.00	250.00	50.00
□ 393 Ebba St.Claire	150.00	75.00	15.00
□ 394 Billy Herman CO	250.00	125.00	25.00
□ 395 Jake Pitler CO	150.00	75.00	15.00
□ 396 Dick Williams	250.00	125.00	25.00
□ 397 Forrest Main	150.00	75.00	15.00
□ 398 Hal Rice	150.00	75.00	15.00
□ 399 Jim Fridley	150.00	75.00	15.00
□ 400 Bill Dickey CO	500.00	250.00	50.00
□ 401 Bob Schultz	150.00	75.00	15.00
□ 402 Earl Harrist	150.00	75.00	15.00
□ 403 Bill Miller	150.00	75.00	15.00
□ 404 Dick Brodowski	150.00	75.00	15.00
□ 405 Eddie Pellagrini	150.00	75.00	15.00
□ 406 Joe Nuxhall	200.00	100.00	20.00
□ 407 Eddie Mathews	1750.00	600.00	150.00

1953 Topps

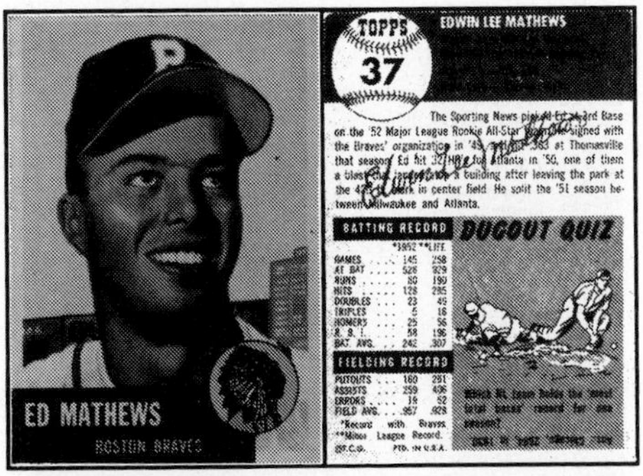

The cards in this 274-card set measure 2 5/8" by 3 3/4". Although the last card is numbered 280, there are only 274 cards in the set since numbers 253, 261, 267, 268, 271, and 275 were never issued. The 1953 Topps series contains line drawings of players in full color. The name and team panel at the card base is easily damaged, making it very difficult to complete a mint set. The high number series, 221 to 280, was produced in shorter supply late in the year and hence is more difficult to complete than the lower numbers. The key cards in the set are Mickey Mantle (82) and Willie Mays (244). The key rookies in this set are Roy Face, Jim Gilliam, and Johnny Podres, all from the last series. There are a number of double-printed cards (actually not double but 50 percent more of each of these numbers were printed compared to the other cards in the series) indicated by DP in the checklist below. In addition, there are five numbers which were printed in with the more plentiful series 166-220; these cards (94, 107, 131, 145, and 156) are also indicated by DP in the checklist below. There were some three-card advertising panels produced by Topps; the players include Johnny Mize/Clem Koshorek/Toby Atwell and Mickey Mantle/Johnny Wyrostek/Sal Yvars. When cut apart, these advertising cards are distinguished by the non-standard card back, i.e., part of an advertisement for the 1953 Topps set instead of the typical statistics and biographical information about the player pictured.

	NRMT	VG-E	GOOD
COMPLETE SET (274)	12500.00	5500.00	1250.00
COMMON PLAYER (1-165)	22.50	10.00	2.00
COMMON DP (1-165)	16.00	8.00	1.60
COMMON PLAYER (166-220)	16.00	8.00	1.60
COMMON PLAYER (221-280)	80.00	40.00	8.00
COMMON DP (221-280)	40.00	20.00	4.00

□ 1 Jackie Robinson DP	600.00	175.00	40.00
□ 2 Luke Easter DP	16.00	8.00	1.60
□ 3 George Crowe	22.50	10.00	2.00
□ 4 Ben Wade	22.50	10.00	2.00
□ 5 Joe Dobson	22.50	10.00	2.00
□ 6 Sam Jones	22.50	10.00	2.00
□ 7 Bob Borkowski DP	16.00	8.00	1.60
□ 8 Clem Koshorek DP	16.00	8.00	1.60
□ 9 Joe Collins	30.00	15.00	3.00
□ 10 Smoky Burgess	25.00	12.50	2.50
□ 11 Sal Yvars	22.50	10.00	2.00
□ 12 Howie Judson DP	16.00	8.00	1.60
□ 13 Conrado Marrero DP	16.00	8.00	1.60
□ 14 Clem Labine DP	22.50	10.00	2.00
□ 15 Bobo Newsom DP	20.00	10.00	2.00
□ 16 Peanuts Lowrey DP	16.00	8.00	1.60
□ 17 Billy Hitchcock	22.50	10.00	2.00
□ 18 Ted Lepcio DP	16.00	8.00	1.60
□ 19 Mel Parnell DP	22.50	10.00	2.00
□ 20 Hank Thompson	25.00	12.50	2.50
□ 21 Billy Johnson	22.50	10.00	2.00
□ 22 Howie Fox	22.50	10.00	2.00
□ 23 Toby Atwell DP	16.00	8.00	1.60
□ 24 Ferris Fain	25.00	12.50	2.50
□ 25 Ray Boone	25.00	12.50	2.50
□ 26 Dale Mitchell DP	18.00	9.00	1.80
□ 27 Roy Campanella DP	200.00	100.00	20.00
□ 28 Eddie Pellagrini	22.50	10.00	2.00
□ 29 Hal Jeffcoat	22.50	10.00	2.00
□ 30 Willard Nixon	22.50	10.00	2.00
□ 31 Ewell Blackwell	37.50	15.00	3.00
□ 32 Clyde Vollmer	22.50	10.00	2.00
□ 33 Bob Kennedy DP	16.00	8.00	1.60
□ 34 George Shuba	25.00	12.50	2.50
□ 35 Irv Noren DP	16.00	8.00	1.60
□ 36 Johnny Groth DP	16.00	8.00	1.60
□ 37 Eddie Mathews DP	110.00	55.00	11.00
□ 38 Jim Hearn DP	16.00	8.00	1.60
□ 39 Eddie Miksis	22.50	10.00	2.00
□ 40 John Lipon	22.50	10.00	2.00
□ 41 Enos Slaughter	75.00	37.50	7.50
□ 42 Gus Zernial DP	16.00	8.00	1.60
□ 43 Gil McDougald	40.00	20.00	4.00
□ 44 Ellis Kinder	22.50	10.00	2.00
□ 45 Grady Hatton DP	16.00	8.00	1.60
□ 46 Johnny Klippstein DP	16.00	8.00	1.60
□ 47 Bubba Church DP	16.00	8.00	1.60
□ 48 Bob Del Greco DP	16.00	8.00	1.60
□ 49 Faye Throneberry DP	16.00	8.00	1.60
□ 50 Chuck Dressen MG DP	20.00	10.00	2.00
□ 51 Frank Campos DP	16.00	8.00	1.60
□ 52 Ted Gray DP	16.00	8.00	1.60
□ 53 Sherm Lollar DP	18.00	9.00	1.80
□ 54 Bob Feller DP	100.00	50.00	10.00
□ 55 Maurice McDermott DP	16.00	8.00	1.60
□ 56 Jerry Staley DP	16.00	8.00	1.60
□ 57 Carl Scheib	22.50	10.00	2.00
□ 58 George Metkovich	22.50	10.00	2.00
□ 59 Karl Drews DP	16.00	8.00	1.60
□ 60 Cloyd Boyer DP	16.00	8.00	1.60
□ 61 Early Wynn	75.00	37.50	7.50
□ 62 Monte Irvin DP	42.00	18.00	4.00
□ 63 Gus Niarhos DP	16.00	8.00	1.60
□ 64 Dave Philley	22.50	10.00	2.00
□ 65 Earl Harrist	22.50	10.00	2.00
□ 66 Minnie Minoso	40.00	20.00	4.00
□ 67 Roy Sievers DP	18.00	9.00	1.80
□ 68 Del Rice	22.50	10.00	2.00
□ 69 Dick Brodowski	22.50	10.00	2.00
□ 70 Ed Yuhas	22.50	10.00	2.00
□ 71 Tony Bartirome	22.50	10.00	2.00
□ 72 Fred Hutchinson	25.00	12.50	2.50
□ 73 Eddie Robinson	22.50	10.00	2.00
□ 74 Joe Rossi	22.50	10.00	2.00
□ 75 Mike Garcia	25.00	12.50	2.50
□ 76 Pee Wee Reese	125.00	60.00	12.50
□ 77 Johnny Mize DP	60.00	30.00	6.00
□ 78 Red Schoendienst	60.00	30.00	6.00

□ 79 Johnny Wyrostek	22.50	10.00	2.00
□ 80 Jim Hegan	25.00	12.50	2.50
□ 81 Joe Black	55.00	27.50	5.50
□ 82 Mickey Mantle	1900.00	750.00	200.00
□ 83 Howie Pollet	22.50	10.00	2.00
□ 84 Bob Hooper DP	16.00	8.00	1.60
□ 85 Bobby Morgan DP	16.00	8.00	1.60
□ 86 Billy Martin	125.00	60.00	12.50
□ 87 Ed Lopat	40.00	20.00	4.00
□ 88 Willie Jones DP	16.00	8.00	1.60
□ 89 Chuck Stobbs DP	16.00	8.00	1.60
□ 90 Hank Edwards DP	16.00	8.00	1.60
□ 91 Ebba St.Claire DP	16.00	8.00	1.60
□ 92 Paul Minner DP	16.00	8.00	1.60
□ 93 Hal Rice DP	16.00	8.00	1.60
□ 94 Bill Kennedy DP	16.00	8.00	1.60
□ 95 Willard Marshall DP	16.00	8.00	1.60
□ 96 Virgil Trucks	25.00	12.50	2.50
□ 97 Don Kolloway DP	16.00	8.00	1.60
□ 98 Cal Abrams DP	16.00	8.00	1.60
□ 99 Dave Madison	22.50	10.00	2.00
□ 100 Bill Miller	22.50	10.00	2.00
□ 101 Ted Wilks	22.50	10.00	2.00
□ 102 Connie Ryan DP	16.00	8.00	1.60
□ 103 Joe Astroth DP	16.00	8.00	1.60
□ 104 Yogi Berra	200.00	100.00	20.00
□ 105 Joe Nuxhall DP	18.00	9.00	1.80
□ 106 Johnny Antonelli	25.00	12.50	2.50
□ 107 Danny O'Connell DP	16.00	8.00	1.60
□ 108 Bob Porterfield DP	16.00	8.00	1.60
□ 109 Alvin Dark	30.00	15.00	3.00
□ 110 Herman Wehmeier DP	16.00	8.00	1.60
□ 111 Hank Sauer DP	18.00	9.00	1.80
□ 112 Ned Garver DP	16.00	8.00	1.60
□ 113 Jerry Priddy	22.50	10.00	2.00
□ 114 Phil Rizzuto	100.00	50.00	10.00
□ 115 George Spencer	22.50	10.00	2.00
□ 116 Frank Smith DP	16.00	8.00	1.60
□ 117 Sid Gordon DP	16.00	8.00	1.60
□ 118 Gus Bell DP	18.00	9.00	1.80
□ 119 Johnny Sain	40.00	20.00	4.00
□ 120 Davey Williams	30.00	15.00	3.00
□ 121 Walt Dropo	25.00	12.50	2.50
□ 122 Elmer Valo	22.50	10.00	2.00
□ 123 Tommy Byrne DP	18.00	9.00	1.80
□ 124 Sibby Sisti DP	16.00	8.00	1.60
□ 125 Dick Williams DP	20.00	10.00	2.00
□ 126 Bill Connelly DP	16.00	8.00	1.60
□ 127 Clint Courtney DP	16.00	8.00	1.60
□ 128 Wilmer Mizell DP	16.00	8.00	1.60
□ 129 Keith Thomas	22.50	10.00	2.00
□ 130 Turk Lown DP	16.00	8.00	1.60
□ 131 Harry Byrd DP	16.00	8.00	1.60
□ 132 Tom Morgan	22.50	10.00	2.00
□ 133 Gil Coan	22.50	10.00	2.00
□ 134 Rube Walker	25.00	12.50	2.50
□ 135 Al Rosen DP	35.00	17.50	3.50
□ 136 Ken Heintzelman DP	16.00	8.00	1.60
□ 137 John Rutherford DP	16.00	8.00	1.60
□ 138 George Kell	50.00	25.00	5.00
□ 139 Sammy White	22.50	10.00	2.00
□ 140 Tommy Glaviano	22.50	10.00	2.00
□ 141 Allie Reynolds DP	35.00	17.50	3.50
□ 142 Vic Wertz	25.00	12.50	2.50
□ 143 Billy Pierce	30.00	15.00	3.00
□ 144 Bob Schultz DP	16.00	8.00	1.60
□ 145 Harry Dorish DP	16.00	8.00	1.60
□ 146 Granny Hamner	22.50	10.00	2.00
□ 147 Warren Spahn	125.00	60.00	12.50
□ 148 Mickey Grasso	22.50	10.00	2.00
□ 149 Dom DiMaggio DP	35.00	17.50	3.50
□ 150 Harry Simpson DP	16.00	8.00	1.60
□ 151 Hoyt Wilhelm	60.00	30.00	6.00
□ 152 Bob Adams DP	16.00	8.00	1.60
□ 153 Andy Seminick DP	16.00	8.00	1.60
□ 154 Dick Groat	35.00	17.50	3.50
□ 155 Dutch Leonard	22.50	10.00	2.00
□ 156 Jim Rivera DP	16.00	8.00	1.60
□ 157 Bob Addis DP	16.00	8.00	1.60
□ 158 Johnny Logan	25.00	12.50	2.50
□ 159 Wayne Terwilliger DP	16.00	8.00	1.60
□ 160 Bob Young	22.50	10.00	2.00
□ 161 Vern Bickford DP	16.00	8.00	1.60
□ 162 Ted Kluszewski	37.50	15.00	3.00
□ 163 Fred Hatfield DP	16.00	8.00	1.60
□ 164 Frank Shea DP	16.00	8.00	1.60
□ 165 Billy Hoeft	22.50	10.00	2.00
□ 166 Billy Hunter	16.00	8.00	1.60
□ 167 Art Schult	16.00	8.00	1.60
□ 168 Willard Schmidt	16.00	8.00	1.60
□ 169 Dizzy Trout	16.00	8.00	1.60
□ 170 Bill Werle	16.00	8.00	1.60
□ 171 Bill Glynn	16.00	8.00	1.60
□ 172 Rip Repulski	16.00	8.00	1.60
□ 173 Preston Ward	16.00	8.00	1.60
□ 174 Billy Loes	18.00	9.00	1.80
□ 175 Ron Kline	16.00	8.00	1.60
□ 176 Don Hoak	20.00	10.00	2.00
□ 177 Jim Dyck	16.00	8.00	1.60
□ 178 Jim Waugh	16.00	8.00	1.60
□ 179 Gene Hermanski	16.00	8.00	1.60
□ 180 Virgil Stallcup	16.00	8.00	1.60
□ 181 Al Zarilla	16.00	8.00	1.60
□ 182 Bobby Hofman	16.00	8.00	1.60
□ 183 Stu Miller	16.00	8.00	1.60
□ 184 Hal Brown	16.00	8.00	1.60
□ 185 Jim Pendleton	16.00	8.00	1.60
□ 186 Charlie Bishop	16.00	8.00	1.60
□ 187 Jim Fridley	16.00	8.00	1.60
□ 188 Andy Carey	20.00	10.00	2.00
□ 189 Ray Jablonski	16.00	8.00	1.60
□ 190 Dixie Walker	16.00	8.00	1.60
□ 191 Ralph Kiner	45.00	22.50	4.50
□ 192 Wally Westlake	16.00	8.00	1.60
□ 193 Mike Clark	16.00	8.00	1.60
□ 194 Eddie Kazak	16.00	8.00	1.60
□ 195 Ed McGhee	16.00	8.00	1.60
□ 196 Bob Keegan	16.00	8.00	1.60
□ 197 Del Crandall	18.00	9.00	1.80
□ 198 Forrest Main	16.00	8.00	1.60
□ 199 Marion Fricano	16.00	8.00	1.60
□ 200 Gordon Goldsberry	16.00	8.00	1.60
□ 201 Paul LaPalme	16.00	8.00	1.60
□ 202 Carl Sawatski	16.00	8.00	1.60
□ 203 Cliff Fannin	16.00	8.00	1.60
□ 204 Dick Bokelman	16.00	8.00	1.60
□ 205 Vern Benson	16.00	8.00	1.60
□ 206 Ed Bailey	18.00	9.00	1.80
□ 207 Whitey Ford	150.00	75.00	15.00
□ 208 Jim Wilson	16.00	8.00	1.60
□ 209 Jim Greengrass	16.00	8.00	1.60
□ 210 Bob Cerv	20.00	10.00	2.00
□ 211 J.W. Porter	16.00	8.00	1.60
□ 212 Jack Dittmer	16.00	8.00	1.60
□ 213 Ray Scarborough	16.00	8.00	1.60
□ 214 Bill Bruton	18.00	9.00	1.80
□ 215 Gene Conley	18.00	9.00	1.80
□ 216 Jim Hughes	16.00	8.00	1.60
□ 217 Murray Wall	16.00	8.00	1.60
□ 218 Les Fusselman	16.00	8.00	1.60
□ 219 Pete Runnels UER (photo actually Don Johnson)	18.00	9.00	1.80
□ 220 Satchel Paige UER (misspelled Satchell on card front)	400.00	200.00	40.00
□ 221 Bob Milliken	80.00	40.00	8.00
□ 222 Vic Janowicz DP	45.00	22.50	4.50
□ 223 Johnny O'Brien DP	45.00	22.50	4.50
□ 224 Lou Sleater DP	40.00	20.00	4.00
□ 225 Bobby Shantz	90.00	45.00	9.00
□ 226 Ed Erautt	80.00	40.00	8.00
□ 227 Morrie Martin	80.00	40.00	8.00
□ 228 Hal Newhouser	100.00	50.00	10.00
□ 229 Rockey Krsnich	80.00	40.00	8.00
□ 230 Johnny Lindell DP	40.00	20.00	4.00
□ 231 Solly Hemus DP	40.00	20.00	4.00
□ 232 Dick Kokos	80.00	40.00	8.00
□ 233 Al Aber	80.00	40.00	8.00
□ 234 Ray Murray DP	40.00	20.00	4.00
□ 235 John Hetki DP	40.00	20.00	4.00
□ 236 Harry Perkowski DP	40.00	20.00	4.00
□ 237 Bud Podbielan DP	40.00	20.00	4.00
□ 238 Cal Hogue DP	40.00	20.00	4.00
□ 239 Jim Delsing	80.00	40.00	8.00
□ 240 Fred Marsh	80.00	40.00	8.00
□ 241 Al Sima DP	40.00	20.00	4.00
□ 242 Charlie Silvera	80.00	40.00	8.00
□ 243 Carlos Bernier DP	40.00	20.00	4.00
□ 244 Willie Mays	1600.00	650.00	175.00
□ 245 Bill Norman	80.00	40.00	8.00
□ 246 Roy Face DP	85.00	42.50	8.50
□ 247 Mike Sandlock DP	40.00	20.00	4.00
□ 248 Gene Stephens DP	40.00	20.00	4.00
□ 249 Eddie O'Brien	80.00	40.00	8.00
□ 250 Bob Wilson	80.00	40.00	8.00
□ 251 Sid Hudson	80.00	40.00	8.00
□ 252 Hank Foiles	80.00	40.00	8.00
□ 253 Does not exist	00.00	00.00	0.00
□ 254 Preacher Roe DP	85.00	42.50	8.50
□ 255 Dixie Howell	80.00	40.00	8.00
□ 256 Les Peden	80.00	40.00	8.00
□ 257 Bob Boyd	80.00	40.00	8.00
□ 258 Jim Gilliam	300.00	150.00	30.00
□ 259 Roy McMillan DP	45.00	22.50	4.50
□ 260 Sam Calderone	80.00	40.00	8.00
□ 261 Does not exist	00.00	00.00	0.00
□ 262 Bob Oldis	80.00	40.00	8.00

☐ 263 Johnny Podres	250.00	125.00	25.00
☐ 264 Gene Woodling DP	60.00	30.00	6.00
☐ 265 Jackie Jensen	100.00	50.00	10.00
☐ 266 Bob Cain	80.00	40.00	8.00
☐ 267 Does not exist	00.00	00.00	0.00
☐ 268 Does not exist	00.00	00.00	0.00
☐ 269 Duane Pillette	80.00	40.00	8.00
☐ 270 Vern Stephens	90.00	45.00	9.00
☐ 271 Does not exist	00.00	00.00	0.00
☐ 272 Bill Antonello	80.00	40.00	8.00
☐ 273 Harvey Haddix	100.00	50.00	10.00
☐ 274 John Riddle	80.00	40.00	8.00
☐ 275 Does not exist	00.00	00.00	0.00
☐ 276 Ken Raffensberger	80.00	40.00	8.00
☐ 277 Don Lund	80.00	40.00	8.00
☐ 278 Willie Miranda	80.00	40.00	8.00
☐ 279 Joe Coleman DP	40.00	20.00	4.00
☐ 280 Milt Bolling	325.00	50.00	10.00

1954 Topps

The cards in this 250-card set measure 2 5/8" by 3 3/4". Each of the cards in the 1954 Topps set contains a large "head" shot of the player in color plus a smaller full-length photo in black and white set against a color background. This series contains the rookie cards of Hank Aaron, Ernie Banks, and Al Kaline and two separate cards of Ted Williams (number 1 and number 250). Conspicuous by his absence is Mickey Mantle who apparently was the exclusive property of Bowman during 1954 (and 1955).

	NRMT	VG-E	GOOD
COMPLETE SET (250)	7500.00	3500.00	750.00
COMMON PLAYER (1-50)	11.00	5.50	1.10
COMMON PLAYER (51-75)	28.00	14.00	2.80
COMMON PLAYER (76-125)	11.00	5.50	1.10
COMMON PLAYER (126-250)	12.50	6.25	1.25
☐ 1 Ted Williams	600.00	200.00	40.00
☐ 2 Gus Zernial	12.00	6.00	1.20
☐ 3 Monte Irvin	30.00	15.00	3.00
☐ 4 Hank Sauer	12.00	6.00	1.20
☐ 5 Ed Lopat	18.00	9.00	1.80
☐ 6 Pete Runnels	12.00	6.00	1.20
☐ 7 Ted Kluszewski	21.00	10.50	2.10
☐ 8 Bob Young	11.00	5.50	1.10
☐ 9 Harvey Haddix	12.00	6.00	1.20
☐ 10 Jackie Robinson	240.00	100.00	20.00
☐ 11 Paul Leslie Smith	11.00	5.50	1.10
☐ 12 Del Crandall	12.00	6.00	1.20
☐ 13 Billy Martin	75.00	37.50	7.50
☐ 14 Preacher Roe	18.00	9.00	1.80
☐ 15 Al Rosen	18.00	9.00	1.80
☐ 16 Vic Janowicz	12.00	6.00	1.20
☐ 17 Phil Rizzuto	65.00	32.50	6.50
☐ 18 Walt Dropo	12.00	6.00	1.20
☐ 19 Johnny Lipon	11.00	5.50	1.10
☐ 20 Warren Spahn	90.00	45.00	9.00
☐ 21 Bobby Shantz	12.00	6.00	1.20
☐ 22 Jim Greengrass	11.00	5.50	1.10
☐ 23 Luke Easter	11.00	5.50	1.10
☐ 24 Granny Hamner	11.00	5.50	1.10
☐ 25 Harvey Kuenn	30.00	15.00	3.00
☐ 26 Ray Jablonski	11.00	5.50	1.10
☐ 27 Ferris Fain	12.00	6.00	1.20
☐ 28 Paul Minner	11.00	5.50	1.10
☐ 29 Jim Hegan	12.00	6.00	1.20
☐ 30 Eddie Mathews	90.00	45.00	9.00
☐ 31 Johnny Klippstein	11.00	5.50	1.10
☐ 32 Duke Snider	125.00	60.00	12.50
☐ 33 Johnny Schmitz	11.00	5.50	1.10
☐ 34 Jim Rivera	11.00	5.50	1.10
☐ 35 Jim Gilliam	20.00	10.00	2.00
☐ 36 Hoyt Wilhelm	35.00	17.50	3.50
☐ 37 Whitey Ford	90.00	45.00	9.00
☐ 38 Eddie Stanky	12.00	6.00	1.20
☐ 39 Sherm Lollar	12.00	6.00	1.20
☐ 40 Mel Parnell	12.00	6.00	1.20
☐ 41 Willie Jones	11.00	5.50	1.10
☐ 42 Don Mueller	12.00	6.00	1.20
☐ 43 Dick Groat	13.50	6.25	1.25
☐ 44 Ned Garver	11.00	5.50	1.10
☐ 45 Richie Ashburn	32.00	16.00	3.20
☐ 46 Ken Raffensberger	11.00	5.50	1.10
☐ 47 Ellis Kinder	11.00	5.50	1.10
☐ 48 Billy Hunter	11.00	5.50	1.10
☐ 49 Ray Murray	11.00	5.50	1.10
☐ 50 Yogi Berra	225.00	110.00	22.00
☐ 51 Johnny Lindell	28.00	14.00	2.80
☐ 52 Vic Power	28.00	14.00	2.80
☐ 53 Jack Dittmer	28.00	14.00	2.80
☐ 54 Vern Stephens	33.00	16.00	3.00
☐ 55 Phil Cavarretta	33.00	16.00	3.00
☐ 56 Willie Miranda	28.00	14.00	2.80
☐ 57 Luis Aloma	28.00	14.00	2.80
☐ 58 Bob Wilson	28.00	14.00	2.80
☐ 59 Gene Conley	33.00	16.00	3.00
☐ 60 Frank Baumholtz	28.00	14.00	2.80
☐ 61 Bob Cain	28.00	14.00	2.80
☐ 62 Eddie Robinson	33.00	16.00	3.00
☐ 63 Johnny Pesky	33.00	16.00	3.00
☐ 64 Hank Thompson	33.00	16.00	3.00
☐ 65 Bob Swift	28.00	14.00	2.80
☐ 66 Ted Lepcio	28.00	14.00	2.80
☐ 67 Jim Willis	28.00	14.00	2.80
☐ 68 Sam Calderone	28.00	14.00	2.80
☐ 69 Bud Podbielan	28.00	14.00	2.80
☐ 70 Larry Doby	50.00	25.00	5.00
☐ 71 Frank Smith	28.00	14.00	2.80
☐ 72 Preston Ward	28.00	14.00	2.80
☐ 73 Wayne Terwilliger	28.00	14.00	2.80
☐ 74 Bill Taylor	28.00	14.00	2.80
☐ 75 Fred Haney	28.00	14.00	2.80
☐ 76 Bob Scheffing	11.00	5.50	1.10
☐ 77 Ray Boone	12.00	6.00	1.20
☐ 78 Ted Kazanski	11.00	5.50	1.10
☐ 79 Andy Pafko	12.00	6.00	1.20
☐ 80 Jackie Jensen	18.00	9.00	1.80
☐ 81 Dave Hoskins	11.00	5.50	1.10
☐ 82 Milt Bolling	11.00	5.50	1.10
☐ 83 Joe Collins	13.50	6.25	1.25
☐ 84 Dick Cole	11.00	5.50	1.10
☐ 85 Bob Turley	25.00	12.50	2.50
☐ 86 Billy Herman	20.00	10.00	2.00
☐ 87 Roy Face	13.50	6.25	1.25
☐ 88 Matt Batts	11.00	5.50	1.10
☐ 89 Howie Pollet	11.00	5.50	1.10
☐ 90 Willie Mays	375.00	175.00	37.00
☐ 91 Bob Oldis	11.00	5.50	1.10
☐ 92 Wally Westlake	11.00	5.50	1.10
☐ 93 Sid Hudson	11.00	5.50	1.10
☐ 94 Ernie Banks	650.00	325.00	65.00
☐ 95 Hal Rice	11.00	5.50	1.10
☐ 96 Charlie Silvera	11.00	5.50	1.10
☐ 97 Jerald Hal Lane	11.00	5.50	1.10
☐ 98 Joe Black	18.00	9.00	1.80
☐ 99 Bobby Hofman	11.00	5.50	1.10
☐ 100 Bob Keegan	11.00	5.50	1.10
☐ 101 Gene Woodling	18.00	9.00	1.80
☐ 102 Gil Hodges	75.00	37.50	7.50
☐ 103 Jim Lemon	12.00	6.00	1.20
☐ 104 Mike Sandlock	11.00	5.50	1.10
☐ 105 Andy Carey	13.50	6.25	1.25
☐ 106 Dick Kokos	11.00	5.50	1.10
☐ 107 Duane Pillette	11.00	5.50	1.10
☐ 108 Thornton Kipper	11.00	5.50	1.10
☐ 109 Bill Bruton	12.00	6.00	1.20
☐ 110 Harry Dorish	11.00	5.50	1.10
☐ 111 Jim Delsing	11.00	5.50	1.10
☐ 112 Bill Renna	11.00	5.50	1.10
☐ 113 Bob Boyd	11.00	5.50	1.10
☐ 114 Dean Stone	11.00	5.50	1.10
☐ 115 Rip Repulski	11.00	5.50	1.10
☐ 116 Steve Bilko	11.00	5.50	1.10
☐ 117 Solly Hemus	11.00	5.50	1.10
☐ 118 Carl Scheib	11.00	5.50	1.10
☐ 119 Johnny Antonelli	13.50	6.25	1.25
☐ 120 Roy McMillan	11.00	5.50	1.10
☐ 121 Clem Labine	13.50	6.25	1.25
☐ 122 Johnny Logan	12.00	6.00	1.20
☐ 123 Bobby Adams	11.00	5.50	1.10

☐ 124	Marion Fricano	11.00	5.50	1.10
☐ 125	Harry Perkowski	11.00	5.50	1.10
☐ 126	Ben Wade	12.50	6.25	1.25
☐ 127	Steve O'Neill	12.50	6.25	1.25
☐ 128	Hank Aaron	1350.00	600.00	150.00
☐ 129	Forrest Jacobs	12.50	6.25	1.25
☐ 130	Hank Bauer	24.00	12.00	2.40
☐ 131	Reno Bertoia	12.50	6.25	1.25
☐ 132	Tom Lasorda	160.00	80.00	16.00
☐ 133	Dave Baker	12.50	6.25	1.25
☐ 134	Cal Hogue	12.50	6.25	1.25
☐ 135	Joe Presko	12.50	6.25	1.25
☐ 136	Connie Ryan	12.50	6.25	1.25
☐ 137	Wally Moon	25.00	12.50	2.50
☐ 138	Bob Borkowski	12.50	6.25	1.25
☐ 139	The O'Briens Johnny O'Brien Eddie O'Brien	27.00	13.50	2.70
☐ 140	Tom Wright	12.50	6.25	1.25
☐ 141	Joey Jay	14.00	7.00	1.40
☐ 142	Tom Poholsky	12.50	6.25	1.25
☐ 143	Ralston Hemsley CO	12.50	6.25	1.25
☐ 144	Bill Werle	12.50	6.25	1.25
☐ 145	Elmer Valo	12.50	6.25	1.25
☐ 146	Don Johnson	12.50	6.25	1.25
☐ 147	Johnny Riddle CO	12.50	6.25	1.25
☐ 148	Bob Trice	12.50	6.25	1.25
☐ 149	Al Robertson	12.50	6.25	1.25
☐ 150	Dick Kryhoski	12.50	6.25	1.25
☐ 151	Alex Grammas	12.50	6.25	1.25
☐ 152	Michael Blyzka	12.50	6.25	1.25
☐ 153	Al Walker	14.00	7.00	1.40
☐ 154	Mike Fornieles	12.50	6.25	1.25
☐ 155	Bob Kennedy	12.50	6.25	1.25
☐ 156	Joe Coleman	12.50	6.25	1.25
☐ 157	Don Lenhardt	12.50	6.25	1.25
☐ 158	Peanuts Lowrey	12.50	6.25	1.25
☐ 159	Dave Philley	12.50	6.25	1.25
☐ 160	Ralph Kress CO	12.50	6.25	1.25
☐ 161	John Hetki	12.50	6.25	1.25
☐ 162	Herman Wehmeier	12.50	6.25	1.25
☐ 163	Frank House	12.50	6.25	1.25
☐ 164	Stu Miller	12.50	6.25	1.25
☐ 165	Jim Pendleton	12.50	6.25	1.25
☐ 166	Johnny Podres	24.00	12.00	2.40
☐ 167	Don Lund	12.50	6.25	1.25
☐ 168	Morrie Martin	12.50	6.25	1.25
☐ 169	Jim Hughes	12.50	6.25	1.25
☐ 170	James(Dusty) Rhodes	15.00	7.50	1.50
☐ 171	Leo Kiely	12.50	6.25	1.25
☐ 172	Harold Brown	12.50	6.25	1.25
☐ 173	Jack Harshman	12.50	6.25	1.25
☐ 174	Tom Qualters	12.50	6.25	1.25
☐ 175	Frank Leja	14.00	7.00	1.40
☐ 176	Robert Keeley	12.50	6.25	1.25
☐ 177	Bob Milliken	12.50	6.25	1.25
☐ 178	Bill Glynn	12.50	6.25	1.25
☐ 179	Gair Allie	12.50	6.25	1.25
☐ 180	Wes Westrum	12.50	6.25	1.25
☐ 181	Mel Roach	12.50	6.25	1.25
☐ 182	Chuck Harmon	12.50	6.25	1.25
☐ 183	Earle Combs CO	20.00	10.00	2.00
☐ 184	Ed Bailey	14.00	7.00	1.40
☐ 185	Chuck Stobbs	12.50	6.25	1.25
☐ 186	Karl Olson	12.50	6.25	1.25
☐ 187	Henry Manush CO	20.00	10.00	2.00
☐ 188	Dave Jolly	12.50	6.25	1.25
☐ 189	Floyd Ross	12.50	6.25	1.25
☐ 190	Ray Herbert	12.50	6.25	1.25
☐ 191	John(Dick) Schofield	14.00	7.00	1.40
☐ 192	Ellis Deal CO	12.50	6.25	1.25
☐ 193	Johnny Hopp CO	14.00	7.00	1.40
☐ 194	Bill Sarni	12.50	6.25	1.25
☐ 195	Billy Consolo	12.50	6.25	1.25
☐ 196	Stan Jok	12.50	6.25	1.25
☐ 197	Lynwood Rowe CO ("Schoolboy")	14.00	7.00	1.40
☐ 198	Carl Sawatski	12.50	6.25	1.25
☐ 199	Glenn(Rocky) Nelson	12.50	6.25	1.25
☐ 200	Larry Jansen	14.00	7.00	1.40
☐ 201	Al Kaline	650.00	325.00	65.00
☐ 202	Bob Purkey	12.50	6.25	1.25
☐ 203	Harry Brecheen CO	14.00	7.00	1.40
☐ 204	Angel Scull	12.50	6.25	1.25
☐ 205	Johnny Sain	25.00	12.50	2.50
☐ 206	Ray Crone	12.50	6.25	1.25
☐ 207	Tom Oliver CO	12.50	6.25	1.25
☐ 208	Grady Hatton	12.50	6.25	1.25
☐ 209	Chuck Thompson	12.50	6.25	1.25
☐ 210	Bob Buhl	14.00	7.00	1.40
☐ 211	Don Hoak	14.00	7.00	1.40
☐ 212	Bob Micelotta	12.50	6.25	1.25
☐ 213	Johnny Fitzpatrick	12.50	6.25	1.25
☐ 214	Arnie Portocarrero	12.50	6.25	1.25
☐ 215	Warren McGhee	12.50	6.25	1.25
☐ 216	Al Sima	12.50	6.25	1.25
☐ 217	Paul Schreiber CO	12.50	6.25	1.25
☐ 218	Fred Marsh	12.50	6.25	1.25
☐ 219	Chuck Kress	12.50	6.25	1.25
☐ 220	Ruben Gomez	12.50	6.25	1.25
☐ 221	Dick Brodowski	12.50	6.25	1.25
☐ 222	Bill Wilson	12.50	6.25	1.25
☐ 223	Joe Haynes	12.50	6.25	1.25
☐ 224	Dick Weik	12.50	6.25	1.25
☐ 225	Don Liddle	12.50	6.25	1.25
☐ 226	Jehosie Heard	12.50	6.25	1.25
☐ 227	Colonel Mills CO	12.50	6.25	1.25
☐ 228	Gene Hermanski	12.50	6.25	1.25
☐ 229	Bob Talbot	12.50	6.25	1.25
☐ 230	Bob Kuzava	14.00	7.00	1.40
☐ 231	Roy Smalley	12.50	6.25	1.25
☐ 232	Lou Limmer	12.50	6.25	1.25
☐ 233	Augie Galan CO	12.50	6.25	1.25
☐ 234	Jerry Lynch	14.00	7.00	1.40
☐ 235	Vernon Law	14.00	7.00	1.40
☐ 236	Paul Penson	12.50	6.25	1.25
☐ 237	Dominic Ryba CO	12.50	6.25	1.25
☐ 238	Al Aber	12.50	6.25	1.25
☐ 239	Bill Skowron	65.00	32.50	6.50
☐ 240	Sam Mele	12.50	6.25	1.25
☐ 241	Robert Miller	12.50	6.25	1.25
☐ 242	Curt Roberts	12.50	6.25	1.25
☐ 243	Ray Blades CO	12.50	6.25	1.25
☐ 244	Leroy Wheat	12.50	6.25	1.25
☐ 245	Roy Sievers	14.00	7.00	1.40
☐ 246	Howie Fox	12.50	6.25	1.25
☐ 247	Ed Mayo CO	12.50	6.25	1.25
☐ 248	Al Smith	14.00	7.00	1.40
☐ 249	Wilmer Mizell	14.00	7.00	1.40
☐ 250	Ted Williams	700.00	225.00	50.00

1955 Topps

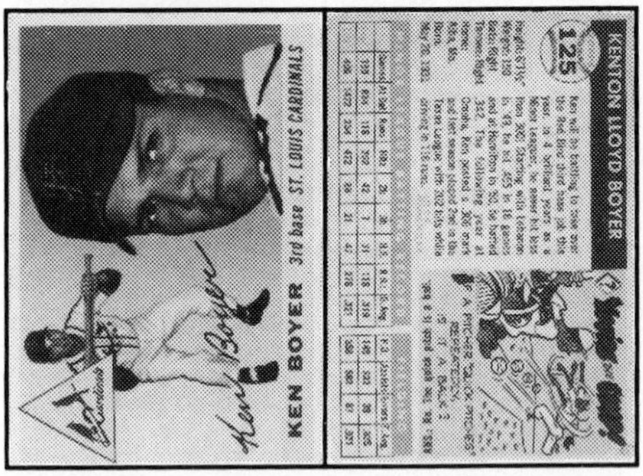

The cards in this 206-card set measure 2 5/8" by 3 3/4". Both the large "head" shot and the smaller full-length photos used on each card of the 1955 Topps set are in color. The card fronts were designed horizontally for the first time in Topps' history. The first card features Dusty Rhodes, hitting star for the Giants' 1954 World Series sweep over the Indians. A "high" series, 161 to 210, is more difficult to find than cards 1 to 160. Numbers 175, 186, 203, and 209 were never issued. To fill in for the four cards not issued in the high number series, Topps double printed four players, those appearing on cards 170, 172, 184, and 188. The key rookies in this set are Ken Boyer, Roberto Clemente, Harmon Killebrew, and Sandy Koufax.

	NRMT	VG-E	GOOD
COMPLETE SET (206)	5800.00	2750.00	600.00
COMMON PLAYER (1-150)	6.50	3.25	.65
COMMON PLAYER (151-160)	15.00	7.50	1.50
COMMON PLAYER (161-210)	20.00	10.00	2.00

☐ 1	Dusty Rhodes	40.00	5.00	1.00
☐ 2	Ted Williams	350.00	175.00	35.00
☐ 3	Art Fowler	6.50	3.25	.65
☐ 4	Al Kaline	175.00	85.00	18.00
☐ 5	Jim Gilliam	12.00	6.00	1.20

□ 6 Stan Hack	7.50	3.75	.75
□ 7 Jim Hegan	7.50	3.75	.75
□ 8 Harold Smith	6.50	3.25	.65
□ 9 Robert Miller	6.50	3.25	.65
□ 10 Bob Keegan	6.50	3.25	.65
□ 11 Ferris Fain	7.50	3.75	.75
□ 12 Vernon Thies	6.50	3.25	.65
□ 13 Fred Marsh	6.50	3.25	.65
□ 14 Jim Finigan	6.50	3.25	.65
□ 15 Jim Pendleton	6.50	3.25	.65
□ 16 Roy Sievers	7.50	3.75	.75
□ 17 Bobby Hofman	6.50	3.25	.65
□ 18 Russ Kemmerer	6.50	3.25	.65
□ 19 Billy Herman CO	12.00	6.00	1.20
□ 20 Andy Carey	8.00	4.00	.80
□ 21 Alex Grammas	6.50	3.25	.65
□ 22 Bill Skowron	14.00	7.00	1.40
□ 23 Jack Parks	6.50	3.25	.65
□ 24 Hal Newhouser	12.00	6.00	1.20
□ 25 Johnny Podres	14.00	7.00	1.40
□ 26 Dick Groat	9.00	4.50	.90
□ 27 Billy Gardner	7.50	3.75	.75
□ 28 Ernie Banks	175.00	85.00	18.00
□ 29 Herman Wehmeier	6.50	3.25	.65
□ 30 Vic Power	6.50	3.25	.65
□ 31 Warren Spahn	75.00	37.50	7.50
□ 32 Warren McGhee	6.50	3.25	.65
□ 33 Tom Qualters	6.50	3.25	.65
□ 34 Wayne Terwilliger	6.50	3.25	.65
□ 35 Dave Jolly	6.50	3.25	.65
□ 36 Leo Kiely	6.50	3.25	.65
□ 37 Joe Cunningham	7.50	3.75	.75
□ 38 Bob Turley	12.00	6.00	1.20
□ 39 Bill Glynn	6.50	3.25	.65
□ 40 Don Hoak	7.50	3.75	.75
□ 41 Chuck Stobbs	6.50	3.25	.65
□ 42 John(Windy) McCall	6.50	3.25	.65
□ 43 Harvey Haddix	7.50	3.75	.75
□ 44 Harold Valentine	6.50	3.25	.65
□ 45 Hank Sauer	7.50	3.75	.75
□ 46 Ted Kazanski	6.50	3.25	.65
□ 47 Hank Aaron UER (birth incorrectly listed as 2/10)	325.00	160.00	32.00
□ 48 Bob Kennedy	6.50	3.25	.65
□ 49 J.W. Porter	6.50	3.25	.65
□ 50 Jackie Robinson	200.00	100.00	20.00
□ 51 Jim Hughes	6.50	3.25	.65
□ 52 Bill Tremel	6.50	3.25	.65
□ 53 Bill Taylor	6.50	3.25	.65
□ 54 Lou Limmer	6.50	3.25	.65
□ 55 Rip Repulski	6.50	3.25	.65
□ 56 Ray Jablonski	6.50	3.25	.65
□ 57 Billy O'Dell	6.50	3.25	.65
□ 58 Jim Rivera	6.50	3.25	.65
□ 59 Gair Allie	6.50	3.25	.65
□ 60 Dean Stone	6.50	3.25	.65
□ 61 Forrest Jacobs	6.50	3.25	.65
□ 62 Thornton Kipper	6.50	3.25	.65
□ 63 Joe Collins	8.00	4.00	.80
□ 64 Gus Triandos	8.00	4.00	.80
□ 65 Ray Boone	7.50	3.75	.75
□ 66 Ron Jackson	6.50	3.25	.65
□ 67 Wally Moon	7.50	3.75	.75
□ 68 Jim Davis	6.50	3.25	.65
□ 69 Ed Bailey	7.50	3.75	.75
□ 70 Al Rosen	11.00	5.50	1.10
□ 71 Ruben Gomez	6.50	3.25	.65
□ 72 Karl Olson	6.50	3.25	.65
□ 73 Jack Shepard	6.50	3.25	.65
□ 74 Bob Borkowski	6.50	3.25	.65
□ 75 Sandy Amoros	13.50	6.25	1.25
□ 76 Howie Pollet	6.50	3.25	.65
□ 77 Arnie Portocarrero	6.50	3.25	.65
□ 78 Gordon Jones	6.50	3.25	.65
□ 79 Clyde Schell	6.50	3.25	.65
□ 80 Bob Grim	13.50	6.25	1.25
□ 81 Gene Conley	7.50	3.75	.75
□ 82 Chuck Harmon	6.50	3.25	.65
□ 83 Tom Brewer	6.50	3.25	.65
□ 84 Camilo Pascual	9.00	4.50	.90
□ 85 Don Mossi	9.00	4.50	.90
□ 86 Bill Wilson	6.50	3.25	.65
□ 87 Frank House	6.50	3.25	.65
□ 88 Bob Skinner	7.50	3.75	.75
□ 89 Joe Frazier	6.50	3.25	.65
□ 90 Karl Spooner	10.00	5.00	1.00
□ 91 Milt Bolling	6.50	3.25	.65
□ 92 Don Zimmer	30.00	15.00	3.00
□ 93 Steve Bilko	6.50	3.25	.65
□ 94 Reno Bertoia	6.50	3.25	.65
□ 95 Preston Ward	6.50	3.25	.65
□ 96 Chuck Bishop	6.50	3.25	.65
□ 97 Carlos Paula	6.50	3.25	.65
□ 98 John Riddle	6.50	3.25	.65
□ 99 Frank Leja	6.50	3.25	.65
□ 100 Monte Irvin	24.00	12.00	2.40
□ 101 Johnny Gray	6.50	3.25	.65
□ 102 Wally Westlake	6.50	3.25	.65
□ 103 Chuck White	6.50	3.25	.65
□ 104 Jack Harshman	6.50	3.25	.65
□ 105 Chuck Diering	6.50	3.25	.65
□ 106 Frank Sullivan	6.50	3.25	.65
□ 107 Curt Roberts	6.50	3.25	.65
□ 108 Al Walker	6.50	3.25	.65
□ 109 Ed Lopat	12.00	6.00	1.20
□ 110 Gus Zernial	7.50	3.75	.75
□ 111 Bob Milliken	6.50	3.25	.65
□ 112 Nelson King	6.50	3.25	.65
□ 113 Harry Brecheen	7.50	3.75	.75
□ 114 Louis Ortiz	6.50	3.25	.65
□ 115 Ellis Kinder	6.50	3.25	.65
□ 116 Tom Hurd	6.50	3.25	.65
□ 117 Mel Roach	6.50	3.25	.65
□ 118 Bob Purkey	6.50	3.25	.65
□ 119 Bob Lennon	6.50	3.25	.65
□ 120 Ted Kluszewski	15.00	7.50	1.50
□ 121 Bill Renna	6.50	3.25	.65
□ 122 Carl Sawatski	6.50	3.25	.65
□ 123 Sandy Koufax	900.00	450.00	90.00
□ 124 Harmon Killebrew	300.00	150.00	30.00
□ 125 Ken Boyer	50.00	25.00	5.00
□ 126 Dick Hall	6.50	3.25	.65
□ 127 Dale Long	7.50	3.75	.75
□ 128 Ted Lepcio	6.50	3.25	.65
□ 129 Elvin Tappe	6.50	3.25	.65
□ 130 Mayo Smith MG	6.50	3.25	.65
□ 131 Grady Hatton	6.50	3.25	.65
□ 132 Bob Trice	6.50	3.25	.65
□ 133 Dave Hoskins	6.50	3.25	.65
□ 134 Joey Jay	6.50	3.25	.65
□ 135 Johnny O'Brien	6.50	3.25	.65
□ 136 Vernon Stewart	6.50	3.25	.65
□ 137 Harry Elliott	6.50	3.25	.65
□ 138 Ray Herbert	6.50	3.25	.65
□ 139 Steve Kraly	6.50	3.25	.65
□ 140 Mel Parnell	8.00	4.00	.80
□ 141 Tom Wright	6.50	3.25	.65
□ 142 Jerry Lynch	6.50	3.25	.65
□ 143 John(Dick) Schofield	6.50	3.25	.65
□ 144 John(Joe) Amalfitano	6.50	3.25	.65
□ 145 Elmer Valo	6.50	3.25	.65
□ 146 Dick Donovan	6.50	3.25	.65
□ 147 Hugh Pepper	6.50	3.25	.65
□ 148 Hector Brown	6.50	3.25	.65
□ 149 Ray Crone	6.50	3.25	.65
□ 150 Mike Higgins	6.50	3.25	.65
□ 151 Ralph Kress	15.00	7.50	1.50
□ 152 Harry Agganis	75.00	37.50	7.50
□ 153 Bud Podbielan	15.00	7.50	1.50
□ 154 Willie Miranda	15.00	7.50	1.50
□ 155 Eddie Mathews	100.00	50.00	10.00
□ 156 Joe Black	22.00	11.00	2.20
□ 157 Robert Miller	15.00	7.50	1.50
□ 158 Tommy Carroll	18.00	9.00	1.80
□ 159 Johnny Schmitz	15.00	7.50	1.50
□ 160 Ray Narleski	18.00	9.00	1.80
□ 161 Chuck Tanner	30.00	15.00	3.00
□ 162 Joe Coleman	20.00	10.00	2.00
□ 163 Faye Throneberry	20.00	10.00	2.00
□ 164 Roberto Clemente	1100.00	500.00	125.00
□ 165 Don Johnson	20.00	10.00	2.00
□ 166 Hank Bauer	35.00	17.50	3.50
□ 167 Thomas Casagrande	20.00	10.00	2.00
□ 168 Duane Pillette	20.00	10.00	2.00
□ 169 Bob Oldis	20.00	10.00	2.00
□ 170 Jim Pearce DP	10.00	5.00	1.00
□ 171 Dick Brodowski	20.00	10.00	2.00
□ 172 Frank Baumholtz DP	10.00	5.00	1.00
□ 173 Johnny Kline	20.00	10.00	2.00
□ 174 Rudy Minarcin	20.00	10.00	2.00
□ 175 Does not exist	00.00	00.00	0.00
□ 176 Norm Zauchin	20.00	10.00	2.00
□ 177 Al Robertson	20.00	10.00	2.00
□ 178 Bobby Adams	20.00	10.00	2.00
□ 179 Jim Bolger	20.00	10.00	2.00
□ 180 Clem Labine	25.00	12.50	2.50
□ 181 Roy McMillan	20.00	10.00	2.00
□ 182 Humberto Robinson	20.00	10.00	2.00
□ 183 Anthony Jacobs	20.00	10.00	2.00
□ 184 Harry Perkowski DP	10.00	5.00	1.00
□ 185 Don Ferrarese	20.00	10.00	2.00
□ 186 Does not exist	00.00	00.00	0.00
□ 187 Gil Hodges	135.00	65.00	13.50
□ 188 Charlie Silvera DP	10.00	5.00	1.00
□ 189 Phil Rizzuto	125.00	60.00	12.50
□ 190 Gene Woodling	25.00	12.50	2.50
□ 191 Eddie Stanky	25.00	12.50	2.50

☐ 192 Jim Delsing	20.00	10.00	2.00
☐ 193 Johnny Sain	30.00	15.00	3.00
☐ 194 Willie Mays	425.00	200.00	42.00
☐ 195 Ed Roebuck	25.00	12.50	2.50
☐ 196 Gale Wade	20.00	10.00	2.00
☐ 197 Al Smith	20.00	10.00	2.00
☐ 198 Yogi Berra	250.00	125.00	25.00
☐ 199 Odbert Hamric	20.00	10.00	2.00
☐ 200 Jackie Jensen	45.00	22.50	4.50
☐ 201 Sherm Lollar	25.00	12.50	2.50
☐ 202 Jim Owens	20.00	10.00	2.00
☐ 203 Does not exist	00.00	00.00	0.00
☐ 204 Frank Smith	20.00	10.00	2.00
☐ 205 Gene Freese	20.00	10.00	2.00
☐ 206 Pete Daley	20.00	10.00	2.00
☐ 207 Billy Consolo	20.00	10.00	2.00
☐ 208 Ray Moore	20.00	10.00	2.00
☐ 209 Does not exist	00.00	00.00	0.00
☐ 210 Duke Snider	500.00	125.00	25.00

1955 Topps Double Header

The cards in ths 66-card set measure 2 1/16" by 4 7/8". Borrowing a design from the T201 Mecca series, Topps issued a 132-player "Double Header" set in a separate wrapper in 1955. Each player is numbered in the biographical section on the reverse. When open, with perforated flap up, one player is revealed; when the flap is lowered, or closed, the player design on top incorporates a portion of the inside player artwork. When the cards are placed side by side, a continuous ballpark background is formed. Some cards have been found without perforations, and all players pictured appear in the low series of the 1955 regular issue.

	NRMT	VG-E	GOOD
COMPLETE SET (66)	3200.00	1500.00	350.00
COMMON PAIR (1-132)	30.00	15.00	3.00
☐ 1 Al Rosen and 2 Chuck Diering	40.00	20.00	4.00
☐ 3 Monte Irvin and 4 Russ Kemmerer	45.00	22.50	4.50
☐ 5 Ted Kazanski and 6 Gordon Jones	30.00	15.00	3.00
☐ 7 Bill Taylor and 8 Billy O'Dell	30.00	15.00	3.00
☐ 9 J.W. Porter and 10 Thornton Kipper	30.00	15.00	3.00
☐ 11 Curt Roberts and 12 Arnie Portocarrero	30.00	15.00	3.00
☐ 13 Wally Westlake and 14 Frank House	30.00	15.00	3.00
☐ 15 Rube Walker and 16 Lou Limmer	30.00	15.00	3.00
☐ 17 Dean Stone and 18 Charlie White	30.00	15.00	3.00
☐ 19 Karl Spooner and 20 Jim Hughes	30.00	15.00	3.00
☐ 21 Bill Skowron and 22 Frank Sullivan	40.00	20.00	4.00
☐ 23 Jack Shepard and 24 Stan Hack	30.00	15.00	3.00
☐ 25 Jackie Robinson and 26 Don Hoak	175.00	85.00	18.00
☐ 27 Dusty Rhodes and 28 Jim Davis	30.00	15.00	3.00
☐ 29 Vic Power and 30 Ed Bailey	30.00	15.00	3.00
☐ 31 Howie Pollet and 32 Ernie Banks	150.00	75.00	15.00
☐ 33 Jim Pendleton and 34 Gene Conley	30.00	15.00	3.00
☐ 35 Karl Olson and 36 Andy Carey	30.00	15.00	3.00
☐ 37 Wally Moon and 38 Joe Cunningham	30.00	15.00	3.00
☐ 39 Freddie Marsh and 40 Vernon Thies	30.00	15.00	3.00
☐ 41 Eddie Lopat and 42 Harvey Haddix	40.00	20.00	4.00
☐ 43 Leo Kiely and 44 Chuck Stobbs	30.00	15.00	3.00
☐ 45 Al Kaline and 46 Harold Valentine	175.00	85.00	18.00
☐ 47 Forrest Jacobs and 48 Johnny Gray	30.00	15.00	3.00
☐ 49 Ron Jackson and 50 Jim Finigan	30.00	15.00	3.00
☐ 51 Ray Jablonski and 52 Bob Keegan	30.00	15.00	3.00
☐ 53 Billy Herman and 54 Sandy Amoros	45.00	22.50	4.50
☐ 55 Chuck Harmon and 56 Bob Skinner	30.00	15.00	3.00
☐ 57 Dick Hall and 58 Bob Grim	30.00	15.00	3.00
☐ 59 Billy Glynn and 60 Bob Miller	30.00	15.00	3.00
☐ 61 Billy Gardner and 62 John Hetki	30.00	15.00	3.00
☐ 63 Bob Borkowski and 64 Bob Turley	40.00	20.00	4.00
☐ 65 Joe Collins and 66 Jack Harshman	30.00	15.00	3.00
☐ 67 Jim Hegan and 68 Jack Parks	30.00	15.00	3.00
☐ 69 Ted Williams and 70 Mayo Smith MG	300.00	150.00	30.00
☐ 71 Gair Allie and 72 Grady Hatton	30.00	15.00	3.00
☐ 73 Jerry Lynch and 74 Harry Brecheen	30.00	15.00	3.00
☐ 75 Tom Wright and 76 Vernon Stewart	30.00	15.00	3.00
☐ 77 Dave Hoskins and 78 Warren McGhee	30.00	15.00	3.00
☐ 79 Roy Sievers and 80 Art Fowler	30.00	15.00	3.00
☐ 81 Danny Schell and 82 Gus Triandos	30.00	15.00	3.00
☐ 83 Joe Frazier and 84 Don Mossi	30.00	15.00	3.00
☐ 85 Elmer Valo and 86 Hector Brown	30.00	15.00	3.00
☐ 87 Bob Kennedy and 88 Windy McCall	30.00	15.00	3.00
☐ 89 Ruben Gomez and 90 Jim Rivera	30.00	15.00	3.00
☐ 91 Louis Ortiz and 92 Milt Bolling	30.00	15.00	3.00
☐ 93 Carl Sawatski and 94 El Tappe	30.00	15.00	3.00
☐ 95 Dave Jolly and 96 Bobby Hofman	30.00	15.00	3.00
☐ 97 Preston Ward and 98 Don Zimmer	40.00	20.00	4.00
☐ 99 Bill Renna and 100 Dick Groat	40.00	20.00	4.00
☐ 101 Bill Wilson and 102 Bill Tremel	30.00	15.00	3.00
☐ 103 Hank Sauer and 104 Camilo Pascual	40.00	20.00	4.00
☐ 105 Hank Aaron and 106 Ray Herbert	350.00	175.00	35.00
☐ 107 Alex Grammas and 108 Tom Qualters	30.00	15.00	3.00
☐ 109 Hal Newhouser and 110 Chuck Bishop	40.00	20.00	4.00

☐ 111 Harmon Killebrew	150.00	75.00	15.00
112 John Podres			
☐ 113 Ray Boone and	30.00	15.00	3.00
114 Bob Purkey			
☐ 115 Dale Long and	30.00	15.00	3.00
116 Ferris Fain			
☐ 117 Steve Bilko and	30.00	15.00	3.00
118 Bob Milliken			
☐ 119 Mel Parnell and	30.00	15.00	3.00
120 Tom Hurd			
☐ 121 Ted Kluszewski and	45.00	22.50	4.50
122 Jim Owens			
☐ 123 Gus Zernial and	30.00	15.00	3.00
124 Bob Trice			
☐ 125 Rip Repulski and	30.00	15.00	3.00
126 Ted Lepcio			
☐ 127 Warren Spahn and	120.00	60.00	12.00
128 Tom Brewer			
☐ 129 Jim Gilliam and	40.00	20.00	4.00
130 Ellis Kinder			
☐ 131 Herm Wehmeier and	30.00	15.00	3.00
132 Wayne Terwilliger			

1956 Topps

The cards in this 340-card set measure 2 5/8" by 3 3/4". Following up with another horizontally oriented card in 1956, Topps improved the format by layering the color "head" shot onto an actual action sequence involving the player. Cards 1 to 180 come with either white or gray backs: in the 1 to 100 sequence, gray backs are less common (worth about 10 percent more) and in the 101 to 180 sequence, white backs are less common (worth 30 percent more). The team cards, used for the first time in a regular set by Topps, are found dated 1955, or undated, with the team name appearing on either side. The dated team cards in the first series were not printed on the gray stock. The two unnumbered checklist cards are highly prized (must be unmarked to qualify as excellent or mint). The complete set price below does not include the unnumbered checklist cards or any of the variations. The key rookies in this set are Walt Alston, Luis Aparicio, and Roger Craig. There are ten double-printed cards in the first series as evidenced by the discovery of an uncut sheet of 110 cards (10 by 11); these DP's are listed below.

	NRMT	VG-E	GOOD
COMPLETE SET (340)	6250.00	3000.00	750.00
COMMON PLAYER (1-100)	6.00	3.00	.60
COMMON PLAYER (101-180)	8.00	4.00	.80
COMMON PLAYER (181-260)	13.00	6.50	1.30
COMMON PLAYER (261-340)	10.00	5.00	1.00
☐ 1 William Harridge	125.00	15.00	3.00
(AL President)			
☐ 2 Warren Giles	15.00	7.50	1.50
(NL President)			
☐ 3 Elmer Valo	6.00	3.00	.60
☐ 4 Carlos Paula	6.00	3.00	.60
☐ 5 Ted Williams	250.00	125.00	25.00
☐ 6 Ray Boone	6.00	3.00	.60
☐ 7 Ron Negray	6.00	3.00	.60
☐ 8 Walter Alston MG	32.00	16.00	3.20
☐ 9 Ruben Gomez DP	6.00	3.00	.60
☐ 10 Warren Spahn	65.00	32.50	6.50
☐ 11A Chicago Cubs	21.00	10.50	2.10
(centered)			
☐ 11B Cubs Team	50.00	25.00	5.00
(dated 1955)			
☐ 11C Cubs Team	21.00	10.50	2.10
(name at far left)			
☐ 12 Andy Carey	7.00	3.50	.70
☐ 13 Roy Face	8.00	4.00	.80
☐ 14 Ken Boyer DP	12.00	6.00	1.20
☐ 15 Ernie Banks DP	75.00	37.50	7.50
☐ 16 Hector Lopez	6.00	3.00	.60
☐ 17 Gene Conley	6.00	3.00	.60
☐ 18 Dick Donovan	6.00	3.00	.60
☐ 19 Chuck Diering	6.00	3.00	.60
☐ 20 Al Kaline	85.00	42.50	8.50
☐ 21 Joe Collins DP	7.00	3.50	.70
☐ 22 Jim Finigan	6.00	3.00	.60
☐ 23 Fred Marsh	6.00	3.00	.60
☐ 24 Dick Groat	8.00	4.00	.80
☐ 25 Ted Kluszewski	14.00	7.00	1.40
☐ 26 Grady Hatton	6.00	3.00	.60
☐ 27 Nelson Burbrink	6.00	3.00	.60
☐ 28 Bobby Hofman	6.00	3.00	.60
☐ 29 Jack Harshman	6.00	3.00	.60
☐ 30 Jackie Robinson DP	150.00	75.00	15.00
☐ 31 Hank Aaron UER	200.00	100.00	20.00
(small photo			
actually W.Mays)			
☐ 32 Frank House	6.00	3.00	.60
☐ 33 Roberto Clemente	300.00	150.00	30.00
☐ 34 Tom Brewer	6.00	3.00	.60
☐ 35 Al Rosen	9.00	4.50	.90
☐ 36 Rudy Minarcin	6.00	3.00	.60
☐ 37 Alex Grammas	6.00	3.00	.60
☐ 38 Bob Kennedy	6.00	3.00	.60
☐ 39 Don Mossi	7.00	3.50	.70
☐ 40 Bob Turley	9.00	4.50	.90
☐ 41 Hank Sauer	7.00	3.50	.70
☐ 42 Sandy Amoros	8.00	4.00	.80
☐ 43 Ray Moore	6.00	3.00	.60
☐ 44 Windy McCall	6.00	3.00	.60
☐ 45 Gus Zernial	6.00	3.00	.60
☐ 46 Gene Freese DP	6.00	3.00	.60
☐ 47 Art Fowler	6.00	3.00	.60
☐ 48 Jim Hegan	6.00	3.00	.60
☐ 49 Pedro Ramos	6.00	3.00	.60
☐ 50 Dusty Rhodes	7.00	3.50	.70
☐ 51 Ernie Oravetz	6.00	3.00	.60
☐ 52 Bob Grim	8.00	4.00	.80
☐ 53 Arnie Portocarrero	6.00	3.00	.60
☐ 54 Bob Keegan	6.00	3.00	.60
☐ 55 Wally Moon	8.00	4.00	.80
☐ 56 Dale Long	7.00	3.50	.70
☐ 57 Duke Maas	6.00	3.00	.60
☐ 58 Ed Roebuck	7.00	3.50	.70
☐ 59 Jose Santiago	6.00	3.00	.60
☐ 60 Mayo Smith MG DP	6.00	3.00	.60
☐ 61 Bill Skowron	12.00	6.00	1.20
☐ 62 Hal Smith	6.00	3.00	.60
☐ 63 Roger Craig	27.00	13.50	2.70
☐ 64 Luis Arroyo	7.00	3.50	.70
☐ 65 Johnny O'Brien	6.00	3.00	.60
☐ 66 Bob Speake	6.00	3.00	.60
☐ 67 Vic Power	6.00	3.00	.60
☐ 68 Chuck Stobbs	6.00	3.00	.60
☐ 69 Chuck Tanner	8.00	4.00	.80
☐ 70 Jim Rivera	6.00	3.00	.60
☐ 71 Frank Sullivan	6.00	3.00	.60
☐ 72A Phillies Team	21.00	10.50	2.10
(centered)			
☐ 72B Phillies Team	50.00	25.00	5.00
(dated 1955)			
☐ 72C Phillies Team	21.00	10.50	2.10
(name at far left)			
☐ 73 Wayne Terwilliger	6.00	3.00	.60
☐ 74 Jim King	6.00	3.00	.60
☐ 75 Roy Sievers DP	7.00	3.50	.70
☐ 76 Ray Crone	6.00	3.00	.60
☐ 77 Harvey Haddix	7.00	3.50	.70
☐ 78 Herman Wehmeier	6.00	3.00	.60
☐ 79 Sandy Koufax	300.00	150.00	30.00
☐ 80 Gus Triandos DP	7.00	3.50	.70
☐ 81 Wally Westlake	6.00	3.00	.60
☐ 82 Bill Renna	6.00	3.00	.60
☐ 83 Karl Spooner	8.00	4.00	.80
☐ 84 Babe Birrer	6.00	3.00	.60
☐ 85A Cleveland Indians	21.00	10.50	2.10
(centered)			
☐ 85B Indians Team	50.00	25.00	5.00
(dated 1955)			

85C Indians Team (name at far left)	21.00	10.50	2.10
86 Ray Jablonski DP	6.00	3.00	.60
87 Dean Stone	6.00	3.00	.60
88 Johnny Kucks	7.00	3.50	.70
89 Norm Zauchin	6.00	3.00	.60
90A Cincinnati Redlegs Team (centered)	21.00	10.50	2.10
90B Reds Team (dated 1955)	50.00	25.00	5.00
90C Reds Team (name at far left)	21.00	10.50	2.10
91 Gail Harris	6.00	3.00	.60
92 Bob(Red) Wilson	6.00	3.00	.60
93 George Susce	6.00	3.00	.60
94 Ron Kline	6.00	3.00	.60
95A Milwaukee Braves Team (centered)	21.00	10.50	2.10
95B Braves Team (dated 1955)	50.00	25.00	5.00
95C Braves Team (name at far left)	21.00	10.50	2.10
96 Bill Tremel	6.00	3.00	.60
97 Jerry Lynch	6.00	3.00	.60
98 Camilo Pascual	8.00	4.00	.80
99 Don Zimmer	15.00	7.50	1.50
100A Baltimore Orioles Team (centered)	21.00	10.50	2.10
100B Orioles Team (dated 1955)	50.00	25.00	5.00
100C Orioles Team (name at far left)	21.00	10.50	2.10
101 Roy Campanella	125.00	60.00	12.50
102 Jim Davis	8.00	4.00	.80
103 Willie Miranda	8.00	4.00	.80
104 Bob Lennon	8.00	4.00	.80
105 Al Smith	8.00	4.00	.80
106 Joe Astroth	8.00	4.00	.80
107 Eddie Mathews	55.00	27.50	5.50
108 Laurin Pepper	8.00	4.00	.80
109 Enos Slaughter	25.00	12.50	2.50
110 Yogi Berra	130.00	65.00	13.00
111 Boston Red Sox Team Card	24.00	12.00	2.40
112 Dee Fondy	8.00	4.00	.80
113 Phil Rizzuto	50.00	25.00	5.00
114 Jim Owens	8.00	4.00	.80
115 Jackie Jensen	12.00	6.00	1.20
116 Eddie O'Brien	8.00	4.00	.80
117 Virgil Trucks	9.00	4.50	.90
118 Nellie Fox	22.00	11.00	2.20
119 Larry Jackson	9.00	4.50	.90
120 Richie Ashburn	25.00	12.50	2.50
121 Pittsburgh Pirates Team Card	24.00	12.00	2.40
122 Willard Nixon	8.00	4.00	.80
123 Roy McMillan	8.00	4.00	.80
124 Don Kaiser	8.00	4.00	.80
125 Minnie Minoso	16.00	8.00	1.60
126 Jim Brady	8.00	4.00	.80
127 Willie Jones	8.00	4.00	.80
128 Eddie Yost	8.00	4.00	.80
129 Jake Martin	8.00	4.00	.80
130 Willie Mays	250.00	125.00	25.00
131 Bob Roselli	8.00	4.00	.80
132 Bobby Avila	9.00	4.50	.90
133 Ray Narleski	8.00	4.00	.80
134 St. Louis Cardinals Team Card	24.00	12.00	2.40
135 Mickey Mantle	800.00	350.00	75.00
136 Johnny Logan	9.00	4.50	.90
137 Al Silvera	8.00	4.00	.80
138 Johnny Antonelli	9.00	4.50	.90
139 Tommy Carroll	8.00	4.00	.80
140 Herb Score	20.00	10.00	2.00
141 Joe Frazier	8.00	4.00	.80
142 Gene Baker	8.00	4.00	.80
143 Jim Piersall	11.00	5.50	1.10
144 Leroy Powell	8.00	4.00	.80
145 Gil Hodges	45.00	22.50	4.50
146 Washington Nationals Team Card	21.00	10.50	2.10
147 Earl Torgeson	8.00	4.00	.80
148 Alvin Dark	10.00	5.00	1.00
149 Dixie Howell	8.00	4.00	.80
150 Duke Snider	120.00	60.00	12.00
151 Spook Jacobs	8.00	4.00	.80
152 Billy Hoeft	8.00	4.00	.80
153 Frank Thomas	9.00	4.50	.90
154 Dave Pope	8.00	4.00	.80
155 Harvey Kuenn	11.00	5.50	1.10
156 Wes Westrum	8.00	4.00	.80
157 Dick Brodowski	8.00	4.00	.80
158 Wally Post	9.00	4.50	.90
159 Clint Courtney	8.00	4.00	.80
160 Billy Pierce	10.00	5.00	1.00
161 Joe DeMaestri	8.00	4.00	.80
162 Dave(Gus) Bell	9.00	4.50	.90
163 Gene Woodling	10.00	5.00	1.00
164 Harmon Killebrew	110.00	55.00	11.00
165 Red Schoendienst	25.00	12.50	2.50
166 Brooklyn Dodgers Team Card	180.00	90.00	18.00
167 Harry Dorish	8.00	4.00	.80
168 Sammy White	8.00	4.00	.80
169 Bob Nelson	8.00	4.00	.80
170 Bill Virdon	12.00	6.00	1.20
171 Jim Wilson	8.00	4.00	.80
172 Frank Torre	9.00	4.50	.90
173 Johnny Podres	14.00	7.00	1.40
174 Glen Gorbous	8.00	4.00	.80
175 Del Crandall	9.00	4.50	.90
176 Alex Kellner	8.00	4.00	.80
177 Hank Bauer	15.00	7.50	1.50
178 Joe Black	10.00	5.00	1.00
179 Harry Chiti	8.00	4.00	.80
180 Robin Roberts	25.00	12.50	2.50
181 Billy Martin	85.00	42.50	8.50
182 Paul Minner	13.00	6.50	1.30
183 Stan Lopata	13.00	6.50	1.30
184 Don Bessent	13.00	6.50	1.30
185 Bill Bruton	14.00	7.00	1.40
186 Ron Jackson	13.00	6.50	1.30
187 Early Wynn	32.00	16.00	3.20
188 Chicago White Sox Team Card	27.00	13.50	2.70
189 Ned Garver	13.00	6.50	1.30
190 Carl Furillo	20.00	10.00	2.00
191 Frank Lary	15.00	7.50	1.50
192 Smoky Burgess	15.00	7.50	1.50
193 Wilmer Mizell	13.00	6.50	1.30
194 Monte Irvin	27.00	13.50	2.70
195 George Kell	27.00	13.50	2.70
196 Tom Poholsky	13.00	6.50	1.30
197 Granny Hamner	13.00	6.50	1.30
198 Ed Fitzgerald	13.00	6.50	1.30
199 Hank Thompson	15.00	7.50	1.50
200 Bob Feller	110.00	55.00	11.00
201 Rip Repulski	13.00	6.50	1.30
202 Jim Hearn	13.00	6.50	1.30
203 Bill Tuttle	13.00	6.50	1.30
204 Art Swanson	13.00	6.50	1.30
205 Whitey Lockman	15.00	7.50	1.50
206 Erv Palica	13.00	6.50	1.30
207 Jim Small	13.00	6.50	1.30
208 Elston Howard	35.00	17.50	3.50
209 Max Surkont	13.00	6.50	1.30
210 Mike Garcia	15.00	7.50	1.50
211 Murry Dickson	13.00	6.50	1.30
212 Johnny Temple	15.00	7.50	1.50
213 Detroit Tigers Team Card	40.00	20.00	4.00
214 Bob Rush	13.00	6.50	1.30
215 Tommy Byrne	15.00	7.50	1.50
216 Jerry Schoonmaker	13.00	6.50	1.30
217 Billy Klaus	13.00	6.50	1.30
218 Joe Nuxall (sic, Nuxhall)	15.00	7.50	1.50
219 Lew Burdette	18.00	9.00	1.80
220 Del Ennis	15.00	7.50	1.50
221 Bob Friend	15.00	7.50	1.50
222 Dave Philley	13.00	6.50	1.30
223 Randy Jackson	13.00	6.50	1.30
224 Bud Podbielan	13.00	6.50	1.30
225 Gil McDougald	22.00	11.00	2.20
226 New York Giants Team Card	65.00	32.50	6.50
227 Russ Meyer	13.00	6.50	1.30
228 Mickey Vernon	15.00	7.50	1.50
229 Harry Brecheen	15.00	7.50	1.50
230 Chico Carrasquel	13.00	6.50	1.30
231 Bob Hale	13.00	6.50	1.30
232 Toby Atwell	13.00	6.50	1.30
233 Carl Erskine	18.00	9.00	1.80
234 Pete Runnels	15.00	7.50	1.50
235 Don Newcombe	35.00	17.50	3.50
236 Kansas City Athletics Team Card	22.00	11.00	2.20
237 Jose Valdivielso	13.00	6.50	1.30
238 Walt Dropo	15.00	7.50	1.50
239 Harry Simpson	13.00	6.50	1.30
240 Whitey Ford	110.00	55.00	11.00
241 Don Mueller UER (6" tall)	15.00	7.50	1.50
242 Hershell Freeman	13.00	6.50	1.30
243 Sherm Lollar	15.00	7.50	1.50
244 Bob Buhl	13.00	6.50	1.30
245 Billy Goodman	15.00	7.50	1.50

☐ 246 Tom Gorman	13.00	6.50	1.30
☐ 247 Bill Sarni	13.00	6.50	1.30
☐ 248 Bob Porterfield	13.00	6.50	1.30
☐ 249 Johnny Klippstein	13.00	6.50	1.30
☐ 250 Larry Doby	17.00	8.50	1.70
☐ 251 New York Yankees Team Card	200.00	100.00	20.00
☐ 252 Vern Law	15.00	7.50	1.50
☐ 253 Irv Noren	15.00	7.50	1.50
☐ 254 George Crowe	13.00	6.50	1.30
☐ 255 Bob Lemon	33.00	16.00	3.00
☐ 256 Tom Hurd	13.00	6.50	1.30
☐ 257 Bobby Thomson	17.00	8.50	1.70
☐ 258 Art Ditmar	15.00	7.50	1.50
☐ 259 Sam Jones	15.00	7.50	1.50
☐ 260 Pee Wee Reese	125.00	60.00	12.50
☐ 261 Bobby Shantz	13.00	6.50	1.30
☐ 262 Howie Pollet	10.00	5.00	1.00
☐ 263 Bob Miller	10.00	5.00	1.00
☐ 264 Ray Monzant	10.00	5.00	1.00
☐ 265 Sandy Consuegra	10.00	5.00	1.00
☐ 266 Don Ferrarese	10.00	5.00	1.00
☐ 267 Bob Nieman	10.00	5.00	1.00
☐ 268 Dale Mitchell	12.00	6.00	1.20
☐ 269 Jack Meyer	10.00	5.00	1.00
☐ 270 Billy Loes	11.00	5.50	1.10
☐ 271 Foster Castleman	10.00	5.00	1.00
☐ 272 Danny O'Connell	10.00	5.00	1.00
☐ 273 Walker Cooper	10.00	5.00	1.00
☐ 274 Frank Baumholtz	10.00	5.00	1.00
☐ 275 Jim Greengrass	10.00	5.00	1.00
☐ 276 George Zuverink	10.00	5.00	1.00
☐ 277 Daryl Spencer	10.00	5.00	1.00
☐ 278 Chet Nichols	10.00	5.00	1.00
☐ 279 Johnny Groth	10.00	5.00	1.00
☐ 280 Jim Gilliam	16.00	8.00	1.60
☐ 281 Art Houtteman	10.00	5.00	1.00
☐ 282 Warren Hacker	10.00	5.00	1.00
☐ 283 Hal Smith	10.00	5.00	1.00
☐ 284 Ike Delock	10.00	5.00	1.00
☐ 285 Eddie Miksis	10.00	5.00	1.00
☐ 286 Bill Wight	10.00	5.00	1.00
☐ 287 Bobby Adams	10.00	5.00	1.00
☐ 288 Bob Cerv	20.00	10.00	2.00
☐ 289 Hal Jeffcoat	10.00	5.00	1.00
☐ 290 Curt Simmons	13.00	6.50	1.30
☐ 291 Frank Kellert	10.00	5.00	1.00
☐ 292 Luis Aparicio	125.00	60.00	12.50
☐ 293 Stu Miller	11.00	5.50	1.10
☐ 294 Ernie Johnson	12.00	6.00	1.20
☐ 295 Clem Labine	12.00	6.00	1.20
☐ 296 Andy Seminick	10.00	5.00	1.00
☐ 297 Bob Skinner	12.00	6.00	1.20
☐ 298 Johnny Schmitz	10.00	5.00	1.00
☐ 299 Charlie Neal	20.00	10.00	2.00
☐ 300 Vic Wertz	12.00	6.00	1.20
☐ 301 Marv Grissom	10.00	5.00	1.00
☐ 302 Eddie Robinson	10.00	5.00	1.00
☐ 303 Jim Dyck	10.00	5.00	1.00
☐ 304 Frank Malzone	16.00	8.00	1.60
☐ 305 Brooks Lawrence	10.00	5.00	1.00
☐ 306 Curt Roberts	10.00	5.00	1.00
☐ 307 Hoyt Wilhelm	30.00	15.00	3.00
☐ 308 Chuck Harmon	10.00	5.00	1.00
☐ 309 Don Blasingame	10.00	5.00	1.00
☐ 310 Steve Gromek	10.00	5.00	1.00
☐ 311 Hal Naragon	10.00	5.00	1.00
☐ 312 Andy Pafko	11.00	5.50	1.10
☐ 313 Gene Stephens	10.00	5.00	1.00
☐ 314 Hobie Landrith	10.00	5.00	1.00
☐ 315 Milt Bolling	10.00	5.00	1.00
☐ 316 Jerry Coleman	13.00	6.50	1.30
☐ 317 Al Aber	10.00	5.00	1.00
☐ 318 Fred Hatfield	10.00	5.00	1.00
☐ 319 Jack Crimian	10.00	5.00	1.00
☐ 320 Joe Adcock	13.00	6.50	1.30
☐ 321 Jim Konstanty	12.00	6.00	1.20
☐ 322 Karl Olson	10.00	5.00	1.00
☐ 323 Willard Schmidt	10.00	5.00	1.00
☐ 324 Rocky Bridges	10.00	5.00	1.00
☐ 325 Don Liddle	10.00	5.00	1.00
☐ 326 Connie Johnson	10.00	5.00	1.00
☐ 327 Bob Wiesler	10.00	5.00	1.00
☐ 328 Preston Ward	10.00	5.00	1.00
☐ 329 Lou Berberet	10.00	5.00	1.00
☐ 330 Jim Busby	10.00	5.00	1.00
☐ 331 Dick Hall	10.00	5.00	1.00
☐ 332 Don Larsen	27.00	13.50	2.70
☐ 333 Rube Walker	12.00	6.00	1.20
☐ 334 Bob Miller	10.00	5.00	1.00
☐ 335 Don Hoak	11.00	5.50	1.10
☐ 336 Ellis Kinder	10.00	5.00	1.00
☐ 337 Bobby Morgan	10.00	5.00	1.00
☐ 338 Jim Delsing	10.00	5.00	1.00
☐ 339 Rance Pless	10.00	5.00	1.00
☐ 340 Mickey McDermott	50.00	7.50	1.50
☐ 341 Checklist 1/3 (unnumbered)	225.00	30.00	5.00
☐ 342 Checklist 2/4 (unnumbered)	225.00	30.00	5.00

1957 Topps

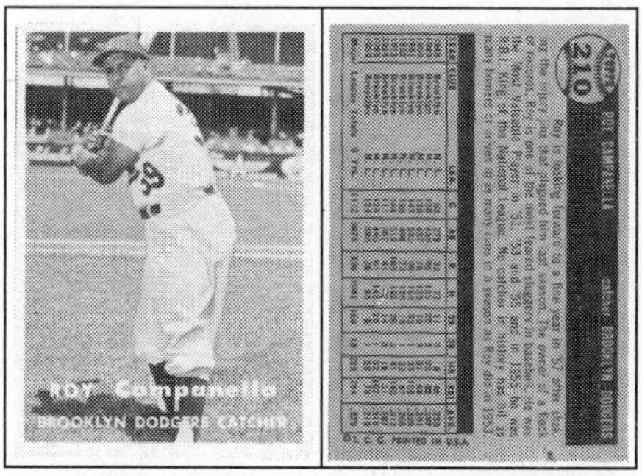

The cards in this 407-card set measure 2 1/2" by 3 1/2". In 1957, Topps returned to the vertical obverse, adopted what we now call the standard card size, and used a large, uncluttered color photo for the first time since 1952. Cards in the series 265 to 352 and the unnumbered checklist cards are scarcer than other cards in the set. However within this scarce series (265-352) there are 22 cards which were printed in double the quantity of the other cards in the series; these 22 double prints are indicated by DP in the checklist below. The first star combination cards, cards 400 and 407, are quite popular with collectors. They feature the big stars of the previous season's World Series teams, the Dodgers (Furillo, Hodges, Campanella, and Snider) and Yankees (Berra and Mantle). The complete set price below does not include the unnumbered checklist cards. The key rookies in this set are Jim Bunning, Rocky Colavito, Don Drysdale, Whitey Herzog, Tony Kubek, Bobby Richardson, Brooks Robinson, and Frank Robinson.

	NRMT	VG-E	GOOD
COMPLETE SET (407)	7000.00	3350.00	750.00
COMMON PLAYER (1-88)	6.50	3.25	.65
COMMON PLAYER (89-176)	5.00	2.50	.50
COMMON PLAYER (177-264)	3.75	1.85	.37
COMMON PLAYER (265-352)	18.00	9.00	1.80
COMMON DP (265-352)	10.00	5.00	1.00
COMMON PLAYER (353-407)	5.00	2.50	.50

☐ 1 Ted Williams	450.00	125.00	25.00
☐ 2 Yogi Berra	135.00	65.00	13.50
☐ 3 Dale Long	7.50	3.75	.75
☐ 4 Johnny Logan	7.50	3.75	.75
☐ 5 Sal Maglie	10.00	5.00	1.00
☐ 6 Hector Lopez	6.50	3.25	.65
☐ 7 Luis Aparicio	30.00	15.00	3.00
☐ 8 Don Mossi	7.50	3.75	.75
☐ 9 Johnny Temple	7.50	3.75	.75
☐ 10 Willie Mays	210.00	90.00	18.00
☐ 11 George Zuverink	6.50	3.25	.65
☐ 12 Dick Groat	10.00	5.00	1.00
☐ 13 Wally Burnette	6.50	3.25	.65
☐ 14 Bob Nieman	6.50	3.25	.65
☐ 15 Robin Roberts	24.00	12.00	2.40
☐ 16 Walt Moryn	6.50	3.25	.65
☐ 17 Billy Gardner	7.50	3.75	.75
☐ 18 Don Drysdale	200.00	90.00	20.00
☐ 19 Bob Wilson	6.50	3.25	.65
☐ 20 Hank Aaron UER (reverse negative photo on front)	250.00	100.00	25.00
☐ 21 Frank Sullivan	6.50	3.25	.65
☐ 22 Jerry Snyder UER (photo actually Ed Fitzgerald)	6.50	3.25	.65

☐ 23 Sherm Lollar	7.50	3.75	.75
☐ 24 Bill Mazeroski	36.00	18.00	3.60
☐ 25 Whitey Ford	60.00	30.00	6.00
☐ 26 Bob Boyd	6.50	3.25	.65
☐ 27 Ted Kazanski	6.50	3.25	.65
☐ 28 Gene Conley	6.50	3.25	.65
☐ 29 Whitey Herzog	22.00	11.00	2.20
☐ 30 Pee Wee Reese	55.00	27.50	5.50
☐ 31 Ron Northey	6.50	3.25	.65
☐ 32 Hershell Freeman	6.50	3.25	.65
☐ 33 Jim Small	6.50	3.25	.65
☐ 34 Tom Sturdivant	6.50	3.25	.65
☐ 35 Frank Robinson	250.00	100.00	25.00
☐ 36 Bob Grim	7.50	3.75	.75
☐ 37 Frank Torre	7.50	3.75	.75
☐ 38 Nellie Fox	16.00	8.00	1.60
☐ 39 Al Worthington	6.50	3.25	.65
☐ 40 Early Wynn	18.00	9.00	1.80
☐ 41 Hal W. Smith	6.50	3.25	.65
☐ 42 Dee Fondy	6.50	3.25	.65
☐ 43 Connie Johnson	6.50	3.25	.65
☐ 44 Joe DeMaestri	6.50	3.25	.65
☐ 45 Carl Furillo	10.00	5.00	1.00
☐ 46 Robert J. Miller	6.50	3.25	.65
☐ 47 Don Blasingame	6.50	3.25	.65
☐ 48 Bill Bruton	7.50	3.75	.75
☐ 49 Daryl Spencer	6.50	3.25	.65
☐ 50 Herb Score	10.00	5.00	1.00
☐ 51 Clint Courtney	6.50	3.25	.65
☐ 52 Lee Walls	6.50	3.25	.65
☐ 53 Clem Labine	7.50	3.75	.75
☐ 54 Elmer Valo	6.50	3.25	.65
☐ 55 Ernie Banks	85.00	42.50	8.50
☐ 56 Dave Sisler	6.50	3.25	.65
☐ 57 Jim Lemon	7.50	3.75	.75
☐ 58 Ruben Gomez	6.50	3.25	.65
☐ 59 Dick Williams	7.50	3.75	.75
☐ 60 Billy Hoeft	6.50	3.25	.65
☐ 61 James"Dusty" Rhodes	7.50	3.75	.75
☐ 62 Billy Martin	45.00	22.50	4.50
☐ 63 Ike Delock	6.50	3.25	.65
☐ 64 Pete Runnels	7.50	3.75	.75
☐ 65 Wally Moon	7.50	3.75	.75
☐ 66 Brooks Lawrence	6.50	3.25	.65
☐ 67 Chico Carrasquel	6.50	3.25	.65
☐ 68 Ray Crone	6.50	3.25	.65
☐ 69 Roy McMillan	6.50	3.25	.65
☐ 70 Richie Ashburn	16.00	8.00	1.60
☐ 71 Murry Dickson	6.50	3.25	.65
☐ 72 Bill Tuttle	6.50	3.25	.65
☐ 73 George Crowe	6.50	3.25	.65
☐ 74 Vito Valentinetti	6.50	3.25	.65
☐ 75 Jim Piersall	10.00	5.00	1.00
☐ 76 Roberto Clemente	200.00	100.00	20.00
☐ 77 Paul Foytack	6.50	3.25	.65
☐ 78 Vic Wertz	7.50	3.75	.75
☐ 79 Lindy McDaniel	7.50	3.75	.75
☐ 80 Gil Hodges	37.50	16.00	3.00
☐ 81 Herman Wehmeier	6.50	3.25	.65
☐ 82 Elston Howard	14.00	7.00	1.40
☐ 83 Lou Skizas	6.50	3.25	.65
☐ 84 Moe Drabowsky	6.50	3.25	.65
☐ 85 Larry Doby	10.00	5.00	1.00
☐ 86 Bill Sarni	6.50	3.25	.65
☐ 87 Tom Gorman	6.50	3.25	.65
☐ 88 Harvey Kuenn	10.00	5.00	1.00
☐ 89 Roy Sievers	6.00	3.00	.60
☐ 90 Warren Spahn	65.00	32.50	6.50
☐ 91 Mack Burk	5.00	2.50	.50
☐ 92 Mickey Vernon	6.00	3.00	.60
☐ 93 Hal Jeffcoat	5.00	2.50	.50
☐ 94 Bobby Del Greco	5.00	2.50	.50
☐ 95 Mickey Mantle	800.00	300.00	75.00
☐ 96 Hank Aguirre	5.00	2.50	.50
☐ 97 New York Yankees Team Card	40.00	20.00	4.00
☐ 98 Alvin Dark	7.50	3.75	.75
☐ 99 Bob Keegan	5.00	2.50	.50
☐ 100 Giles and Harridge League Presidents	10.00	5.00	1.00
☐ 101 Chuck Stobbs	5.00	2.50	.50
☐ 102 Ray Boone	6.00	3.00	.60
☐ 103 Joe Nuxhall	6.00	3.00	.60
☐ 104 Hank Foiles	5.00	2.50	.50
☐ 105 Johnny Antonelli	6.00	3.00	.60
☐ 106 Ray Moore	5.00	2.50	.50
☐ 107 Jim Rivera	5.00	2.50	.50
☐ 108 Tommy Byrne	6.00	3.00	.60
☐ 109 Hank Thompson	6.00	3.00	.60
☐ 110 Bill Virdon	7.00	3.50	.70
☐ 111 Hal R. Smith	5.00	2.50	.50
☐ 112 Tom Brewer	5.00	2.50	.50
☐ 113 Wilmer Mizell	5.00	2.50	.50
☐ 114 Milwaukee Braves Team Card	15.00	7.50	1.50
☐ 115 Jim Gilliam	11.00	5.50	1.10
☐ 116 Mike Fornieles	5.00	2.50	.50
☐ 117 Joe Adcock	7.00	3.50	.70
☐ 118 Bob Porterfield	5.00	2.50	.50
☐ 119 Stan Lopata	5.00	2.50	.50
☐ 120 Bob Lemon	18.00	9.00	1.80
☐ 121 Clete Boyer	12.00	6.00	1.20
☐ 122 Ken Boyer	11.00	5.50	1.10
☐ 123 Steve Ridzik	5.00	2.50	.50
☐ 124 Dave Philley	5.00	2.50	.50
☐ 125 Al Kaline	75.00	37.50	7.50
☐ 126 Bob Wiesler	5.00	2.50	.50
☐ 127 Bob Buhl	6.00	3.00	.60
☐ 128 Ed Bailey	6.00	3.00	.60
☐ 129 Saul Rogovin	5.00	2.50	.50
☐ 130 Don Newcombe	12.00	6.00	1.20
☐ 131 Milt Bolling	5.00	2.50	.50
☐ 132 Art Ditmar	6.00	3.00	.60
☐ 133 Del Crandall	6.00	3.00	.60
☐ 134 Don Kaiser	5.00	2.50	.50
☐ 135 Bill Skowron	11.00	5.50	1.10
☐ 136 Jim Hegan	6.00	3.00	.60
☐ 137 Bob Rush	5.00	2.50	.50
☐ 138 Minnie Minoso	11.00	5.50	1.10
☐ 139 Lou Kretlow	5.00	2.50	.50
☐ 140 Frank Thomas	6.00	3.00	.60
☐ 141 Al Aber	5.00	2.50	.50
☐ 142 Charley Thompson	5.00	2.50	.50
☐ 143 Andy Pafko	6.00	3.00	.60
☐ 144 Ray Narleski	5.00	2.50	.50
☐ 145 Al Smith	5.00	2.50	.50
☐ 146 Don Ferrarese	5.00	2.50	.50
☐ 147 Al Walker	5.00	2.50	.50
☐ 148 Don Mueller	6.00	3.00	.60
☐ 149 Bob Kennedy	5.00	2.50	.50
☐ 150 Bob Friend	6.00	3.00	.60
☐ 151 Willie Miranda	5.00	2.50	.50
☐ 152 Jack Harshman	5.00	2.50	.50
☐ 153 Karl Olson	5.00	2.50	.50
☐ 154 Red Schoendienst	18.00	9.00	1.80
☐ 155 Jim Brosnan	6.00	3.00	.60
☐ 156 Gus Triandos	6.00	3.00	.60
☐ 157 Wally Post	6.00	3.00	.60
☐ 158 Curt Simmons	6.00	3.00	.60
☐ 159 Solly Drake	5.00	2.50	.50
☐ 160 Billy Pierce	7.00	3.50	.70
☐ 161 Pittsburgh Pirates Team Card	10.00	5.00	1.00
☐ 162 Jack Meyer	5.00	2.50	.50
☐ 163 Sammy White	5.00	2.50	.50
☐ 164 Tommy Carroll	5.00	2.50	.50
☐ 165 Ted Kluszewski	16.00	8.00	1.60
☐ 166 Roy Face	7.00	3.50	.70
☐ 167 Vic Power	6.00	3.00	.60
☐ 168 Frank Lary	6.00	3.00	.60
☐ 169 Herb Plews	5.00	2.50	.50
☐ 170 Duke Snider	100.00	50.00	10.00
☐ 171 Boston Red Sox Team Card	11.00	5.50	1.10
☐ 172 Gene Woodling	7.00	3.50	.70
☐ 173 Roger Craig	12.00	6.00	1.20
☐ 174 Willie Jones	5.00	2.50	.50
☐ 175 Don Larsen	12.00	6.00	1.20
☐ 176A Gene Baker ERR (misspelled Bakep on card back)	300.00	150.00	30.00
☐ 176B Gene Baker COR	5.00	2.50	.50
☐ 177 Eddie Yost	3.75	1.85	.37
☐ 178 Don Bessent	3.75	1.85	.37
☐ 179 Ernie Oravetz	3.75	1.85	.37
☐ 180 Gus Bell	5.00	2.50	.50
☐ 181 Dick Donovan	3.75	1.85	.37
☐ 182 Hobie Landrith	3.75	1.85	.37
☐ 183 Chicago Cubs Team Card	10.00	5.00	1.00
☐ 184 Tito Francona	5.00	2.50	.50
☐ 185 Johnny Kucks	5.00	2.50	.50
☐ 186 Jim King	3.75	1.85	.37
☐ 187 Virgil Trucks	5.00	2.50	.50
☐ 188 Felix Mantilla	3.75	1.85	.37
☐ 189 Willard Nixon	3.75	1.85	.37
☐ 190 Randy Jackson	3.75	1.85	.37
☐ 191 Joe Margoneri	3.75	1.85	.37
☐ 192 Jerry Coleman	5.00	2.50	.50
☐ 193 Del Rice	3.75	1.85	.37
☐ 194 Hal Brown	3.75	1.85	.37
☐ 195 Bobby Avila	3.75	1.85	.37
☐ 196 Larry Jackson	3.75	1.85	.37
☐ 197 Hank Sauer	5.00	2.50	.50
☐ 198 Detroit Tigers Team Card	10.00	5.00	1.00
☐ 199 Vern Law	5.00	2.50	.50

☐ 200	Gil McDougald	11.00	5.50	1.10
☐ 201	Sandy Amoros	5.00	2.50	.50
☐ 202	Dick Gernert	3.75	1.85	.37
☐ 203	Hoyt Wilhelm	18.00	9.00	1.80
☐ 204	Kansas City Athletics Team Card	9.00	4.50	.90
☐ 205	Charlie Maxwell	3.75	1.85	.37
☐ 206	Willard Schmidt	3.75	1.85	.37
☐ 207	Gordon(Billy) Hunter	3.75	1.85	.37
☐ 208	Lou Burdette	6.50	3.25	.65
☐ 209	Bob Skinner	5.00	2.50	.50
☐ 210	Roy Campanella	100.00	50.00	10.00
☐ 211	Camilo Pascual	6.00	3.00	.60
☐ 212	Rocco Colavito	75.00	37.50	7.50
☐ 213	Les Moss	3.75	1.85	.37
☐ 214	Philadelphia Phillies Team Card	10.00	5.00	1.00
☐ 215	Enos Slaughter	20.00	10.00	2.00
☐ 216	Marv Grissom	3.75	1.85	.37
☐ 217	Gene Stephens	3.75	1.85	.37
☐ 218	Ray Jablonski	3.75	1.85	.37
☐ 219	Tom Acker	3.75	1.85	.37
☐ 220	Jackie Jensen	10.00	5.00	1.00
☐ 221	Dixie Howell	3.75	1.85	.37
☐ 222	Alex Grammas	3.75	1.85	.37
☐ 223	Frank House	3.75	1.85	.37
☐ 224	Marv Blaylock	3.75	1.85	.37
☐ 225	Harry Simpson	3.75	1.85	.37
☐ 226	Preston Ward	3.75	1.85	.37
☐ 227	Jerry Staley	3.75	1.85	.37
☐ 228	Smoky Burgess	5.00	2.50	.50
☐ 229	George Susce	3.75	1.85	.37
☐ 230	George Kell	15.00	7.50	1.50
☐ 231	Solly Hemus	3.75	1.85	.37
☐ 232	Whitey Lockman	5.00	2.50	.50
☐ 233	Art Fowler	3.75	1.85	.37
☐ 234	Dick Cole	3.75	1.85	.37
☐ 235	Tom Poholsky	3.75	1.85	.37
☐ 236	Joe Ginsberg	3.75	1.85	.37
☐ 237	Foster Castleman	3.75	1.85	.37
☐ 238	Eddie Robinson	3.75	1.85	.37
☐ 239	Tom Morgan	3.75	1.85	.37
☐ 240	Hank Bauer	10.00	5.00	1.00
☐ 241	Joe Lonnett	3.75	1.85	.37
☐ 242	Charlie Neal	5.00	2.50	.50
☐ 243	St. Louis Cardinals Team Card	10.00	5.00	1.00
☐ 244	Billy Loes	5.00	2.50	.50
☐ 245	Rip Repulski	3.75	1.85	.37
☐ 246	Jose Valdivielso	3.75	1.85	.37
☐ 247	Turk Lown	3.75	1.85	.37
☐ 248	Jim Finigan	3.75	1.85	.37
☐ 249	Dave Pope	3.75	1.85	.37
☐ 250	Eddie Mathews	35.00	17.50	3.50
☐ 251	Baltimore Orioles Team Card	10.00	5.00	1.00
☐ 252	Carl Erskine	10.00	5.00	1.00
☐ 253	Gus Zernial	5.00	2.50	.50
☐ 254	Ron Negray	3.75	1.85	.37
☐ 255	Charlie Silvera	3.75	1.85	.37
☐ 256	Ron Kline	3.75	1.85	.37
☐ 257	Walt Dropo	5.00	2.50	.50
☐ 258	Steve Gromek	3.75	1.85	.37
☐ 259	Eddie O'Brien	3.75	1.85	.37
☐ 260	Del Ennis	5.00	2.50	.50
☐ 261	Bob Chakales	3.75	1.85	.37
☐ 262	Bobby Thomson	10.00	5.00	1.00
☐ 263	George Strickland	3.75	1.85	.37
☐ 264	Bob Turley	10.00	5.00	1.00
☐ 265	Harvey Haddix DP	15.00	7.50	1.50
☐ 266	Ken Kuhn DP	10.00	5.00	1.00
☐ 267	Danny Kravitz	18.00	9.00	1.80
☐ 268	Jack Collum	18.00	9.00	1.80
☐ 269	Bob Cerv	21.00	10.50	2.10
☐ 270	Washington Senators Team Card	36.00	18.00	3.60
☐ 271	Danny O'Connell DP	10.00	5.00	1.00
☐ 272	Bobby Shantz	24.00	12.00	2.40
☐ 273	Jim Davis	18.00	9.00	1.80
☐ 274	Don Hoak	21.00	10.50	2.10
☐ 275	Cleveland Indians Team Card	36.00	18.00	3.60
☐ 276	Jim Pyburn	18.00	9.00	1.80
☐ 277	Johnny Podres DP	50.00	25.00	5.00
☐ 278	Fred Hatfield DP	10.00	5.00	1.00
☐ 279	Bob Thurman	18.00	9.00	1.80
☐ 280	Alex Kellner	18.00	9.00	1.80
☐ 281	Gail Harris	18.00	9.00	1.80
☐ 282	Jack Dittmer DP	10.00	5.00	1.00
☐ 283	Wes Covington DP	12.00	6.00	1.20
☐ 284	Don Zimmer	25.00	12.50	2.50
☐ 285	Ned Garver	18.00	9.00	1.80
☐ 286	Bobby Richardson	100.00	50.00	10.00
☐ 287	Sam Jones	21.00	10.50	2.10

☐ 288	Ted Lepcio	18.00	9.00	1.80
☐ 289	Jim Bolger DP	10.00	5.00	1.00
☐ 290	Andy Carey DP	15.00	7.50	1.50
☐ 291	Windy McCall	18.00	9.00	1.80
☐ 292	Billy Klaus	18.00	9.00	1.80
☐ 293	Ted Abernathy	18.00	9.00	1.80
☐ 294	Rocky Bridges DP	10.00	5.00	1.00
☐ 295	Joe Collins DP	15.00	7.50	1.50
☐ 296	Johnny Klippstein	18.00	9.00	1.80
☐ 297	Jack Crimian	18.00	9.00	1.80
☐ 298	Irv Noren DP	10.00	5.00	1.00
☐ 299	Chuck Harmon	18.00	9.00	1.80
☐ 300	Mike Garcia	21.00	10.50	2.10
☐ 301	Sammy Esposito DP	10.00	5.00	1.00
☐ 302	Sandy Koufax DP	325.00	160.00	32.00
☐ 303	Billy Goodman	21.00	10.50	2.10
☐ 304	Joe Cunningham	21.00	10.50	2.10
☐ 305	Chico Fernandez	18.00	9.00	1.80
☐ 306	Darrell Johnson DP	15.00	7.50	1.50
☐ 307	Jack D. Phillips DP	10.00	5.00	1.00
☐ 308	Dick Hall	18.00	9.00	1.80
☐ 309	Jim Busby DP	10.00	5.00	1.00
☐ 310	Max Surkont DP	10.00	5.00	1.00
☐ 311	Al Pilarcik DP	10.00	5.00	1.00
☐ 312	Tony Kubek DP	110.00	55.00	11.00
☐ 313	Mel Parnell	21.00	10.50	2.10
☐ 314	Ed Bouchee DP	10.00	5.00	1.00
☐ 315	Lou Berberet DP	10.00	5.00	1.00
☐ 316	Billy O'Dell	18.00	9.00	1.80
☐ 317	New York Giants Team Card	50.00	25.00	5.00
☐ 318	Mickey McDermott	18.00	9.00	1.80
☐ 319	Gino Cimoli	21.00	10.50	2.10
☐ 320	Neil Chrisley	18.00	9.00	1.80
☐ 321	John (Red) Murff	18.00	9.00	1.80
☐ 322	Cincinnati Reds Team Card	50.00	25.00	5.00
☐ 323	Wes Westrum	21.00	10.50	2.10
☐ 324	Brooklyn Dodgers Team Card	100.00	50.00	10.00
☐ 325	Frank Bolling	18.00	9.00	1.80
☐ 326	Pedro Ramos	18.00	9.00	1.80
☐ 327	Jim Pendleton	18.00	9.00	1.80
☐ 328	Brooks Robinson	350.00	175.00	35.00
☐ 329	Chicago White Sox Team Card	36.00	18.00	3.60
☐ 330	Jim Wilson	18.00	9.00	1.80
☐ 331	Ray Katt	18.00	9.00	1.80
☐ 332	Bob Bowman	18.00	9.00	1.80
☐ 333	Ernie Johnson	21.00	10.50	2.10
☐ 334	Jerry Schoonmaker	18.00	9.00	1.80
☐ 335	Granny Hamner	18.00	9.00	1.80
☐ 336	Haywood Sullivan	21.00	10.50	2.10
☐ 337	Rene Valdes	18.00	9.00	1.80
☐ 338	Jim Bunning	125.00	60.00	12.50
☐ 339	Bob Speake	18.00	9.00	1.80
☐ 340	Bill Wight	18.00	9.00	1.80
☐ 341	Don Gross	18.00	9.00	1.80
☐ 342	Gene Mauch	21.00	10.50	2.10
☐ 343	Taylor Phillips	18.00	9.00	1.80
☐ 344	Paul LaPalme	18.00	9.00	1.80
☐ 345	Paul Smith	18.00	9.00	1.80
☐ 346	Dick Littlefield	18.00	9.00	1.80
☐ 347	Hal Naragon	18.00	9.00	1.80
☐ 348	Jim Hearn	18.00	9.00	1.80
☐ 349	Nellie King	18.00	9.00	1.80
☐ 350	Eddie Miksis	18.00	9.00	1.80
☐ 351	Dave Hillman	18.00	9.00	1.80
☐ 352	Ellis Kinder	18.00	9.00	1.80
☐ 353	Cal Neeman	5.00	2.50	.50
☐ 354	W. (Rip) Coleman	5.00	2.50	.50
☐ 355	Frank Malzone	6.00	3.00	.60
☐ 356	Faye Throneberry	5.00	2.50	.50
☐ 357	Earl Torgeson	5.00	2.50	.50
☐ 358	Jerry Lynch	5.00	2.50	.50
☐ 359	Tom Cheney	5.00	2.50	.50
☐ 360	Johnny Groth	5.00	2.50	.50
☐ 361	Curt Barclay	5.00	2.50	.50
☐ 362	Roman Mejias	5.00	2.50	.50
☐ 363	Eddie Kasko	5.00	2.50	.50
☐ 364	Cal McLish	5.00	2.50	.50
☐ 365	Ozzie Virgil	5.00	2.50	.50
☐ 366	Ken Lehman	5.00	2.50	.50
☐ 367	Ed Fitzgerald	5.00	2.50	.50
☐ 368	Bob Purkey	5.00	2.50	.50
☐ 369	Milt Graff	5.00	2.50	.50
☐ 370	Warren Hacker	5.00	2.50	.50
☐ 371	Bob Lennon	5.00	2.50	.50
☐ 372	Norm Zauchin	5.00	2.50	.50
☐ 373	Pete Whisenant	5.00	2.50	.50
☐ 374	Don Cardwell	5.00	2.50	.50
☐ 375	Jim Landis	5.00	2.50	.50
☐ 376	Don Elston	5.00	2.50	.50
☐ 377	Andre Rodgers	5.00	2.50	.50

☐ 378 Elmer Singleton	5.00	2.50	.50
☐ 379 Don Lee	5.00	2.50	.50
☐ 380 Walker Cooper	5.00	2.50	.50
☐ 381 Dean Stone	5.00	2.50	.50
☐ 382 Jim Brideweser	5.00	2.50	.50
☐ 383 Juan Pizarro	5.00	2.50	.50
☐ 384 Bobby G. Smith	5.00	2.50	.50
☐ 385 Art Houtteman	5.00	2.50	.50
☐ 386 Lyle Luttrell	5.00	2.50	.50
☐ 387 Jack Sanford	7.50	3.75	.75
☐ 388 Pete Daley	5.00	2.50	.50
☐ 389 Dave Jolly	5.00	2.50	.50
☐ 390 Reno Bertoia	5.00	2.50	.50
☐ 391 Ralph Terry	10.00	5.00	1.00
☐ 392 Chuck Tanner	7.50	3.75	.75
☐ 393 Raul Sanchez	5.00	2.50	.50
☐ 394 Luis Arroyo	6.00	3.00	.60
☐ 395 J.M.(Bubba) Phillips	5.00	2.50	.50
☐ 396 K. (Casey) Wise	5.00	2.50	.50
☐ 397 Roy Smalley	5.00	2.50	.50
☐ 398 Al Cicotte	6.00	3.00	.60
☐ 399 Billy Consolo	5.00	2.50	.50
☐ 400 Dodgers' Sluggers Carl Furillo Gil Hodges Roy Campanella Duke Snider	175.00	85.00	18.00
☐ 401 Earl Battey	6.00	3.00	.60
☐ 402 Jim Pisoni	5.00	2.50	.50
☐ 403 Dick Hyde	5.00	2.50	.50
☐ 404 Harry Anderson	5.00	2.50	.50
☐ 405 Duke Maas	5.00	2.50	.50
☐ 406 Bob Hale	5.00	2.50	.50
☐ 407 Yankee Power Hitters Mickey Mantle Yogi Berra	350.00	175.00	35.00
☐ 408 Checklist 1/2 (unnumbered)	150.00	20.00	5.00
☐ 409 Checklist 2/3 (unnumbered)	300.00	40.00	10.00
☐ 410 Checklist 3/4 (unnumbered)	450.00	60.00	15.00
☐ 411 Checklist 4/5 (unnumbered)	600.00	80.00	20.00

1958 Topps

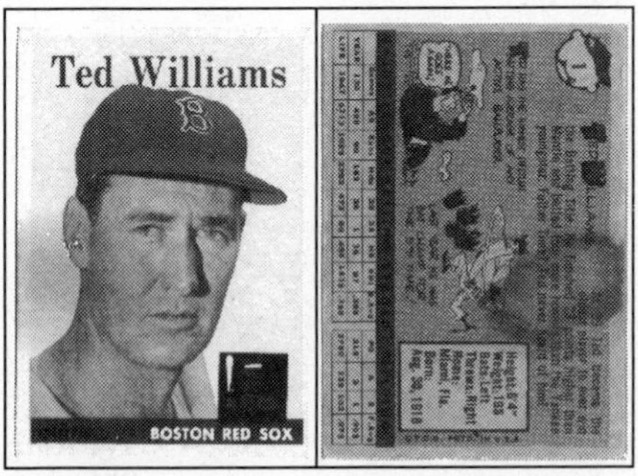

The cards in this 494-card set measure 2 1/2" by 3 1/2". Although the last card is numbered 495, number 145 was not issued, bringing the set total to 494 cards. The 1958 Topps set contains the first Sport Magazine All-Star Selection series (475-495) and expanded use of combination cards. The team cards carried series checklists on back (Milwaukee, Detroit, Baltimore, and Cincinnati are also found with players listed alphabetically). Cards with the scarce yellow name (YL) or team (YT) lettering, as opposed to the common white lettering, are noted in the checklist. In the last series, cards of Stan Musial and Mickey Mantle were triple printed; the cards they replaced (443, 446, 450, and 462) on the printing sheet were hence printed in shorter supply than other cards in the last series and are marked with an SP in the list below. Technically the New York Giants team card (18) is an error as the Giants had already moved to San Francisco. The key rookies in this set are Orlando Cepeda, Roger Maris, and Vada Pinson.

	NRMT	VG-E	GOOD
COMPLETE SET (494)	4200.00	2000.00	450.00
COMMON PLAYER (1-110)	6.00	3.00	.60
COMMON PLAYER (111-198)	4.50	2.25	.45
COMMON PLAYER (199-352)	3.50	1.75	.35
COMMON PLAYER (353-440)	3.00	1.50	.30
COMMON PLAYER (441-474)	2.50	1.25	.25
COMMON PLAYER (475-495)	3.00	1.50	.30

☐ 1 Ted Williams	350.00	100.00	25.00
☐ 2A Bob Lemon	16.00	8.00	1.60
☐ 2B Bob Lemon YT	35.00	17.50	3.50
☐ 3 Alex Kellner	6.00	3.00	.60
☐ 4 Hank Foiles	6.00	3.00	.60
☐ 5 Willie Mays	165.00	75.00	15.00
☐ 6 George Zuverink	6.00	3.00	.60
☐ 7 Dale Long	7.00	3.50	.70
☐ 8A Eddie Kasko	6.00	3.00	.60
☐ 8B Eddie Kasko YL	24.00	12.00	2.40
☐ 9 Hank Bauer	9.00	4.50	.90
☐ 10 Lou Burdette	8.00	4.00	.80
☐ 11A Jim Rivera	6.00	3.00	.60
☐ 11B Jim Rivera YT	18.00	9.00	1.80
☐ 12 George Crowe	6.00	3.00	.60
☐ 13A Billy Hoeft	6.00	3.00	.60
☐ 13B Billy Hoeft YL	24.00	12.00	2.40
☐ 14 Rip Repulski	6.00	3.00	.60
☐ 15 Jim Lemon	7.00	3.50	.70
☐ 16 Charlie Neal	7.00	3.50	.70
☐ 17 Felix Mantilla	6.00	3.00	.60
☐ 18 Frank Sullivan	6.00	3.00	.60
☐ 19 New York Giants Team Card (checklist on back)	25.00	6.00	1.25
☐ 20A Gil McDougald	9.00	4.50	.90
☐ 20B Gil McDougald YL	25.00	12.50	2.50
☐ 21 Curt Barclay	6.00	3.00	.60
☐ 22 Hal Naragon	6.00	3.00	.60
☐ 23A Bill Tuttle	6.00	3.00	.60
☐ 23B Bill Tuttle YL	24.00	12.00	2.40
☐ 24A Hobie Landrith	6.00	3.00	.60
☐ 24B Hobie Landrith YL	24.00	12.00	2.40
☐ 25 Don Drysdale	50.00	25.00	5.00
☐ 26 Ron Jackson	6.00	3.00	.60
☐ 27 Bud Freeman	6.00	3.00	.60
☐ 28 Jim Busby	6.00	3.00	.60
☐ 29 Ted Lepcio	6.00	3.00	.60
☐ 30A Hank Aaron	165.00	75.00	15.00
☐ 30B Hank Aaron YL	300.00	150.00	30.00
☐ 31 Tex Clevenger	6.00	3.00	.60
☐ 32A J.W. Porter	6.00	3.00	.60
☐ 32B J.W. Porter YL	24.00	12.00	2.40
☐ 33A Cal Neeman	6.00	3.00	.60
☐ 33B Cal Neeman YT	18.00	9.00	1.80
☐ 34 Bob Thurman	6.00	3.00	.60
☐ 35A Don Mossi	7.00	3.50	.70
☐ 35B Don Mossi YT	20.00	10.00	2.00
☐ 36 Ted Kazanski	6.00	3.00	.60
☐ 37 Mike McCormick UER (photo actually Ray Monzant)	9.00	4.50	.90
☐ 38 Dick Gernert	6.00	3.00	.60
☐ 39 Bob Martyn	6.00	3.00	.60
☐ 40 George Kell	13.50	6.25	1.25
☐ 41 Dave Hillman	6.00	3.00	.60
☐ 42 John Roseboro	9.00	4.50	.90
☐ 43 Sal Maglie	8.00	4.00	.80
☐ 44 Washington Senators Team Card (checklist on back)	12.50	4.00	1.00
☐ 45 Dick Groat	8.00	4.00	.80
☐ 46A Lou Sleater	6.00	3.00	.60
☐ 46B Lou Sleater YL	24.00	12.00	2.40
☐ 47 Roger Maris	300.00	150.00	30.00
☐ 48 Chuck Harmon	6.00	3.00	.60
☐ 49 Smoky Burgess	7.00	3.50	.70
☐ 50A Billy Pierce	8.00	4.00	.80
☐ 50B Billy Pierce YT	20.00	10.00	2.00
☐ 51 Del Rice	6.00	3.00	.60
☐ 52A Bob Clemente	140.00	70.00	14.00
☐ 52B Bob Clemente YT	225.00	110.00	22.00
☐ 53A Morrie Martin	6.00	3.00	.60
☐ 53B Morrie Martin YL	24.00	12.00	2.40
☐ 54 Norm Siebern	6.00	3.00	.60
☐ 55 Chico Carrasquel	6.00	3.00	.60
☐ 56 Bill Fischer	6.00	3.00	.60
☐ 57A Tim Thompson	6.00	3.00	.60
☐ 57B Tim Thompson YL	24.00	12.00	2.40
☐ 58A Art Schult	6.00	3.00	.60
☐ 58B Art Schult YT	18.00	9.00	1.80

☐ 59 Dave Sisler	6.00	3.00	.60
☐ 60A Del Ennis	7.00	3.50	.70
☐ 60B Del Ennis YL	24.00	12.00	2.40
☐ 61A Darrell Johnson	7.00	3.50	.70
☐ 61B Darrell Johnson YL	24.00	12.00	2.40
☐ 62 Joe DeMaestri	6.00	3.00	.60
☐ 63 Joe Nuxhall	7.00	3.50	.70
☐ 64 Joe Lonnett	6.00	3.00	.60
☐ 65A Von McDaniel	6.00	3.00	.60
☐ 65B Von McDaniel YL	24.00	12.00	2.40
☐ 66 Lee Walls	6.00	3.00	.60
☐ 67 Joe Ginsberg	6.00	3.00	.60
☐ 68 Daryl Spencer	6.00	3.00	.60
☐ 69 Wally Burnette	6.00	3.00	.60
☐ 70A Al Kaline	70.00	35.00	7.00
☐ 70B Al Kaline YL	125.00	60.00	12.50
☐ 71 Dodgers Team (checklist on back)	30.00	7.50	1.50
☐ 72 Bud Byerly	6.00	3.00	.60
☐ 73 Pete Daley	6.00	3.00	.60
☐ 74 Roy Face	8.00	4.00	.80
☐ 75 Gus Bell	7.00	3.50	.70
☐ 76A Dick Farrell	7.00	3.50	.70
☐ 76B Dick Farrell YT	20.00	10.00	2.00
☐ 77A Don Zimmer	8.00	4.00	.80
☐ 77B Don Zimmer YT	20.00	10.00	2.00
☐ 78A Ernie Johnson	7.00	3.50	.70
☐ 78B Ernie Johnson YL	24.00	12.00	2.40
☐ 79A Dick Williams	7.00	3.50	.70
☐ 79B Dick Williams YT	20.00	10.00	2.00
☐ 80 Dick Drott	6.00	3.00	.60
☐ 81A Steve Boros	7.00	3.50	.70
☐ 81B Steve Boros YT	20.00	10.00	2.00
☐ 82 Ron Kline	6.00	3.00	.60
☐ 83 Bob Hazle	7.00	3.50	.70
☐ 84 Billy O'Dell	6.00	3.00	.60
☐ 85A Luis Aparicio	22.00	11.00	2.20
☐ 85B Luis Aparicio YT	40.00	20.00	4.00
☐ 86 Valmy Thomas	6.00	3.00	.60
☐ 87 Johnny Kucks	7.00	3.50	.70
☐ 88 Duke Snider	70.00	35.00	7.00
☐ 89 Billy Klaus	6.00	3.00	.60
☐ 90 Robin Roberts	16.00	8.00	1.60
☐ 91 Chuck Tanner	7.00	3.50	.70
☐ 92A Clint Courtney	6.00	3.00	.60
☐ 92B Clint Courtney YL	24.00	12.00	2.40
☐ 93 Sandy Amoros	7.00	3.50	.70
☐ 94 Bob Skinner	7.00	3.50	.70
☐ 95 Frank Bolling	6.00	3.00	.60
☐ 96 Joe Durham	6.00	3.00	.60
☐ 97A Larry Jackson	6.00	3.00	.60
☐ 97B Larry Jackson YL	24.00	12.00	2.40
☐ 98A Billy Hunter	6.00	3.00	.60
☐ 98B Billy Hunter YL	24.00	12.00	2.40
☐ 99 Bobby Adams	6.00	3.00	.60
☐ 100A Early Wynn	16.00	8.00	1.60
☐ 100B Early Wynn YT	35.00	17.50	3.50
☐ 101A Bobby Richardson	15.00	7.50	1.50
☐ 101B Bobby Richardson YL	35.00	17.50	3.50
☐ 102 George Strickland	6.00	3.00	.60
☐ 103 Jerry Lynch	6.00	3.00	.60
☐ 104 Jim Pendleton	6.00	3.00	.60
☐ 105 Billy Gardner	6.00	3.00	.60
☐ 106 Dick Schofield	6.00	3.00	.60
☐ 107 Ossie Virgil	6.00	3.00	.60
☐ 108A Jim Landis	6.00	3.00	.60
☐ 108B Jim Landis YT	18.00	9.00	1.80
☐ 109 Herb Plews	6.00	3.00	.60
☐ 110 Johnny Logan	7.00	3.50	.70
☐ 111 Stu Miller	4.50	2.25	.45
☐ 112 Gus Zernial	4.50	2.25	.45
☐ 113 Jerry Walker	4.50	2.25	.45
☐ 114 Irv Noren	4.50	2.25	.45
☐ 115 Jim Bunning	15.00	7.50	1.50
☐ 116 Dave Philley	4.50	2.25	.45
☐ 117 Frank Torre	5.50	2.75	.55
☐ 118 Harvey Haddix	5.50	2.75	.55
☐ 119 Harry Chiti	4.50	2.25	.45
☐ 120 Johnny Podres	8.00	4.00	.80
☐ 121 Eddie Miksis	4.50	2.25	.45
☐ 122 Walt Moryn	4.50	2.25	.45
☐ 123 Dick Tomanek	4.50	2.25	.45
☐ 124 Bobby Usher	4.50	2.25	.45
☐ 125 Alvin Dark	6.50	3.25	.65
☐ 126 Stan Palys	4.50	2.25	.45
☐ 127 Tom Sturdivant	5.50	2.75	.55
☐ 128 Willie Kirkland	4.50	2.25	.45
☐ 129 Jim Derrington	4.50	2.25	.45
☐ 130 Jackie Jensen	8.00	4.00	.80
☐ 131 Bob Henrich	4.50	2.25	.45
☐ 132 Vern Law	5.50	2.75	.55
☐ 133 Russ Nixon	6.50	3.25	.65
☐ 134 Philadelphia Phillies Team Card (checklist on back)	10.00	2.50	.50
☐ 135 Mike(Moe) Drabowsky	5.50	2.75	.55
☐ 136 Jim Finigan	4.50	2.25	.45
☐ 137 Russ Kemmerer	4.50	2.25	.45
☐ 138 Earl Torgeson	4.50	2.25	.45
☐ 139 George Brunet	4.50	2.25	.45
☐ 140 Wes Covington	5.50	2.75	.55
☐ 141 Ken Lehman	4.50	2.25	.45
☐ 142 Enos Slaughter	20.00	10.00	2.00
☐ 143 Billy Muffett	4.50	2.25	.45
☐ 144 Bobby Morgan	4.50	2.25	.45
☐ 145 Never issued	0.00	.00	.00
☐ 146 Dick Gray	4.50	2.25	.45
☐ 147 Don McMahon	5.50	2.75	.55
☐ 148 Billy Consolo	4.50	2.25	.45
☐ 149 Tom Acker	4.50	2.25	.45
☐ 150 Mickey Mantle	500.00	250.00	50.00
☐ 151 Buddy Pritchard	4.50	2.25	.45
☐ 152 Johnny Antonelli	5.50	2.75	.55
☐ 153 Les Moss	4.50	2.25	.45
☐ 154 Harry Byrd	4.50	2.25	.45
☐ 155 Hector Lopez	4.50	2.25	.45
☐ 156 Dick Hyde	4.50	2.25	.45
☐ 157 Dee Fondy	4.50	2.25	.45
☐ 158 Cleveland Indians Team Card (checklist on back)	10.00	2.50	.50
☐ 159 Taylor Phillips	4.50	2.25	.45
☐ 160 Don Hoak	5.50	2.75	.55
☐ 161 Don Larsen	8.00	4.00	.80
☐ 162 Gil Hodges	20.00	10.00	2.00
☐ 163 Jim Wilson	4.50	2.25	.45
☐ 164 Bob Taylor	4.50	2.25	.45
☐ 165 Bob Nieman	4.50	2.25	.45
☐ 166 Danny O'Connell	4.50	2.25	.45
☐ 167 Frank Baumann	4.50	2.25	.45
☐ 168 Joe Cunningham	5.50	2.75	.55
☐ 169 Ralph Terry	6.50	3.25	.65
☐ 170 Vic Wertz	5.50	2.75	.55
☐ 171 Harry Anderson	4.50	2.25	.45
☐ 172 Don Gross	4.50	2.25	.45
☐ 173 Eddie Yost	4.50	2.25	.45
☐ 174 Athletics Team (checklist on back)	10.00	2.50	.50
☐ 175 Marv Throneberry	9.00	4.50	.90
☐ 176 Bob Buhl	4.50	2.25	.45
☐ 177 Al Smith	4.50	2.25	.45
☐ 178 Ted Kluszewski	8.00	4.00	.80
☐ 179 Willie Miranda	4.50	2.25	.45
☐ 180 Lindy McDaniel	5.50	2.75	.55
☐ 181 Willie Jones	4.50	2.25	.45
☐ 182 Joe Caffie	4.50	2.25	.45
☐ 183 Dave Jolly	4.50	2.25	.45
☐ 184 Elvin Tappe	4.50	2.25	.45
☐ 185 Ray Boone	5.50	2.75	.55
☐ 186 Jack Meyer	4.50	2.25	.45
☐ 187 Sandy Koufax	135.00	65.00	13.50
☐ 188 Milt Bolling UER (photo actually Lou Berberet)	4.50	2.25	.45
☐ 189 George Susce	4.50	2.25	.45
☐ 190 Red Schoendienst	16.00	8.00	1.60
☐ 191 Art Ceccarelli	4.50	2.25	.45
☐ 192 Milt Graff	4.50	2.25	.45
☐ 193 Jerry Lumpe	4.50	2.25	.45
☐ 194 Roger Craig	8.00	4.00	.80
☐ 195 Whitey Lockman	5.50	2.75	.55
☐ 196 Mike Garcia	5.50	2.75	.55
☐ 197 Haywood Sullivan	5.50	2.75	.55
☐ 198 Bill Virdon	5.50	2.75	.55
☐ 199 Don Blasingame	3.50	1.75	.35
☐ 200 Bob Keegan	3.50	1.75	.35
☐ 201 Jim Bolger	3.50	1.75	.35
☐ 202 Woody Held	3.50	1.75	.35
☐ 203 Al Walker	3.50	1.75	.35
☐ 204 Leo Kiely	3.50	1.75	.35
☐ 205 Johnny Temple	4.50	2.25	.45
☐ 206 Bob Shaw	3.50	1.75	.35
☐ 207 Solly Hemus	3.50	1.75	.35
☐ 208 Cal McLish	3.50	1.75	.35
☐ 209 Bob Anderson	3.50	1.75	.35
☐ 210 Wally Moon	4.50	2.25	.45
☐ 211 Pete Burnside	3.50	1.75	.35
☐ 212 Bubba Phillips	3.50	1.75	.35
☐ 213 Red Wilson	3.50	1.75	.35
☐ 214 Willard Schmidt	3.50	1.75	.35
☐ 215 Jim Gilliam	8.00	4.00	.80
☐ 216 St. Louis Cardinals Team Card (checklist on back)	10.00	2.50	.50
☐ 217 Jack Harshman	3.50	1.75	.35
☐ 218 Dick Rand	3.50	1.75	.35

☐ 219	Camilo Pascual	4.50	2.25	.45
☐ 220	Tom Brewer	3.50	1.75	.35
☐ 221	Jerry Kindall	4.50	2.25	.45
☐ 222	Bud Daley	3.50	1.75	.35
☐ 223	Andy Pafko	4.50	2.25	.45
☐ 224	Bob Grim	4.50	2.25	.45
☐ 225	Billy Goodman	4.50	2.25	.45
☐ 226	Bob Smith	3.50	1.75	.35
☐ 227	Gene Stephens	3.50	1.75	.35
☐ 228	Duke Maas	3.50	1.75	.35
☐ 229	Frank Zupo	3.50	1.75	.35
☐ 230	Richie Ashburn	13.00	6.50	1.30
☐ 231	Lloyd Merritt	3.50	1.75	.35
☐ 232	Reno Bertoia	3.50	1.75	.35
☐ 233	Mickey Vernon	4.50	2.25	.45
☐ 234	Carl Sawatski	3.50	1.75	.35
☐ 235	Tom Gorman	3.50	1.75	.35
☐ 236	Ed Fitzgerald	3.50	1.75	.35
☐ 237	Bill Wight	3.50	1.75	.35
☐ 238	Bill Mazeroski	10.00	5.00	1.00
☐ 239	Chuck Stobbs	3.50	1.75	.35
☐ 240	Bill Skowron	10.00	5.00	1.00
☐ 241	Dick Littlefield	3.50	1.75	.35
☐ 242	Johnny Klippstein	3.50	1.75	.35
☐ 243	Larry Raines	3.50	1.75	.35
☐ 244	Don Demeter	3.50	1.75	.35
☐ 245	Frank Lary	4.50	2.25	.45
☐ 246	New York Yankees	36.00	10.00	2.00
	Team Card			
	(checklist on back)			
☐ 247	Casey Wise	3.50	1.75	.35
☐ 248	Herman Wehmeier	3.50	1.75	.35
☐ 249	Ray Moore	3.50	1.75	.35
☐ 250	Roy Sievers	4.50	2.25	.45
☐ 251	Warren Hacker	3.50	1.75	.35
☐ 252	Bob Trowbridge	3.50	1.75	.35
☐ 253	Don Mueller	4.50	2.25	.45
☐ 254	Alex Grammas	3.50	1.75	.35
☐ 255	Bob Turley	8.00	4.00	.80
☐ 256	Chicago White Sox	10.00	2.50	.50
	Team Card			
	(checklist on back)			
☐ 257	Hal Smith	3.50	1.75	.35
☐ 258	Carl Erskine	6.50	3.25	.65
☐ 259	Al Pilarcik	3.50	1.75	.35
☐ 260	Frank Malzone	4.50	2.25	.45
☐ 261	Turk Lown	3.50	1.75	.35
☐ 262	Johnny Groth	3.50	1.75	.35
☐ 263	Eddie Bressoud	3.50	1.75	.35
☐ 264	Jack Sanford	4.50	2.25	.45
☐ 265	Pete Runnels	4.50	2.25	.45
☐ 266	Connie Johnson	3.50	1.75	.35
☐ 267	Sherm Lollar	4.50	2.25	.45
☐ 268	Granny Hamner	3.50	1.75	.35
☐ 269	Paul Smith	3.50	1.75	.35
☐ 270	Warren Spahn	45.00	22.50	4.50
☐ 271	Billy Martin	16.00	8.00	1.60
☐ 272	Ray Crone	3.50	1.75	.35
☐ 273	Hal Smith	3.50	1.75	.35
☐ 274	Rocky Bridges	3.50	1.75	.35
☐ 275	Elston Howard	10.00	5.00	1.00
☐ 276	Bobby Avila	3.50	1.75	.35
☐ 277	Virgil Trucks	3.50	1.75	.35
☐ 278	Mack Burk	3.50	1.75	.35
☐ 279	Bob Boyd	3.50	1.75	.35
☐ 280	Jim Piersall	6.00	3.00	.60
☐ 281	Sammy Taylor	3.50	1.75	.35
☐ 282	Paul Foytack	3.50	1.75	.35
☐ 283	Ray Shearer	3.50	1.75	.35
☐ 284	Ray Katt	3.50	1.75	.35
☐ 285	Frank Robinson	75.00	37.50	7.50
☐ 286	Gino Cimoli	3.50	1.75	.35
☐ 287	Sam Jones	3.50	1.75	.35
☐ 288	Harmon Killebrew	65.00	32.50	6.50
☐ 289	Series Hurling Rivals	5.00	2.50	.50
	Lou Burdette			
	Bobby Shantz			
☐ 290	Dick Donovan	3.50	1.75	.35
☐ 291	Don Landrum	3.50	1.75	.35
☐ 292	Ned Garver	3.50	1.75	.35
☐ 293	Gene Freese	3.50	1.75	.35
☐ 294	Hal Jeffcoat	3.50	1.75	.35
☐ 295	Minnie Minoso	8.00	4.00	.80
☐ 296	Ryne Duren	8.00	4.00	.80
☐ 297	Don Buddin	3.50	1.75	.35
☐ 298	Jim Hearn	3.50	1.75	.35
☐ 299	Harry Simpson	3.50	1.75	.35
☐ 300	Harridge and Giles	7.00	3.50	.70
	League Presidents			
☐ 301	Randy Jackson	3.50	1.75	.35
☐ 302	Mike Baxes	3.50	1.75	.35
☐ 303	Neil Chrisley	3.50	1.75	.35

☐ 304	Tigers' Big Bats	12.00	6.00	1.20
	Harvey Kuenn			
	Al Kaline			
☐ 305	Clem Labine	4.50	2.25	.45
☐ 306	Whammy Douglas	3.50	1.75	.35
☐ 307	Brooks Robinson	80.00	40.00	8.00
☐ 308	Paul Giel	3.50	1.75	.35
☐ 309	Gail Harris	3.50	1.75	.35
☐ 310	Ernie Banks	70.00	35.00	7.00
☐ 311	Bob Purkey	3.50	1.75	.35
☐ 312	Boston Red Sox	10.00	2.50	.50
	Team Card			
	(checklist on back)			
☐ 313	Bob Rush	3.50	1.75	.35
☐ 314	Dodgers' Boss and	16.00	8.00	1.60
	Power: Duke Snider			
	Walt Alston			
☐ 315	Bob Friend	4.50	2.25	.45
☐ 316	Tito Francona	3.50	1.75	.35
☐ 317	Albie Pearson	4.50	2.25	.45
☐ 318	Frank House	3.50	1.75	.35
☐ 319	Lou Skizas	3.50	1.75	.35
☐ 320	Whitey Ford	45.00	22.50	4.50
☐ 321	Sluggers Supreme	33.00	15.00	3.00
	Ted Kluszewski			
	Ted Williams			
☐ 322	Harding Peterson	3.50	1.75	.35
☐ 323	Elmer Valo	3.50	1.75	.35
☐ 324	Hoyt Wilhelm	16.00	8.00	1.60
☐ 325	Joe Adcock	4.50	2.25	.45
☐ 326	Bob Miller	3.50	1.75	.35
☐ 327	Chicago Cubs	10.00	2.50	.50
	Team Card			
	(checklist on back)			
☐ 328	Ike Delock	3.50	1.75	.35
☐ 329	Bob Cerv	4.50	2.25	.45
☐ 330	Ed Bailey	4.50	2.25	.45
☐ 331	Pedro Ramos	3.50	1.75	.35
☐ 332	Jim King	3.50	1.75	.35
☐ 333	Andy Carey	4.50	2.25	.45
☐ 334	Mound Aces	4.50	2.25	.45
	Bob Friend			
	Billy Pierce			
☐ 335	Ruben Gomez	3.50	1.75	.35
☐ 336	Bert Hamric	3.50	1.75	.35
☐ 337	Hank Aguirre	3.50	1.75	.35
☐ 338	Walt Dropo	3.50	1.75	.35
☐ 339	Fred Hatfield	3.50	1.75	.35
☐ 340	Don Newcombe	8.00	4.00	.80
☐ 341	Pittsburgh Pirates	10.00	2.50	.50
	Team Card			
	(checklist on back)			
☐ 342	Jim Brosnan	4.50	2.25	.45
☐ 343	Orlando Cepeda	65.00	32.50	6.50
☐ 344	Bob Porterfield	3.50	1.75	.35
☐ 345	Jim Hegan	3.50	1.75	.35
☐ 346	Steve Bilko	3.50	1.75	.35
☐ 347	Don Rudolph	3.50	1.75	.35
☐ 348	Chico Fernandez	3.50	1.75	.35
☐ 349	Murry Dickson	3.50	1.75	.35
☐ 350	Ken Boyer	8.00	4.00	.80
☐ 351	Braves Fence Busters	24.00	12.00	2.40
	Del Crandall			
	Eddie Mathews			
	Hank Aaron			
	Joe Adcock			
☐ 352	Herb Score	6.00	3.00	.60
☐ 353	Stan Lopata	3.00	1.50	.30
☐ 354	Art Ditmar	3.00	1.50	.30
☐ 355	Bill Bruton	4.00	2.00	.40
☐ 356	Bob Malkmus	3.00	1.50	.30
☐ 357	Danny McDevitt	3.00	1.50	.30
☐ 358	Gene Baker	3.00	1.50	.30
☐ 359	Billy Loes	3.00	1.50	.30
☐ 360	Roy McMillan	3.00	1.50	.30
☐ 361	Mike Fornieles	3.00	1.50	.30
☐ 362	Ray Jablonski	3.00	1.50	.30
☐ 363	Don Elston	3.00	1.50	.30
☐ 364	Earl Battey	4.00	2.00	.40
☐ 365	Tom Morgan	3.00	1.50	.30
☐ 366	Gene Green	3.00	1.50	.30
☐ 367	Jack Urban	3.00	1.50	.30
☐ 368	Rocky Colavito	16.00	8.00	1.60
☐ 369	Ralph Lumenti	3.00	1.50	.30
☐ 370	Yogi Berra	80.00	40.00	8.00
☐ 371	Marty Keough	3.00	1.50	.30
☐ 372	Don Cardwell	3.00	1.50	.30
☐ 373	Joe Pignatano	3.00	1.50	.30
☐ 374	Brooks Lawrence	3.00	1.50	.30
☐ 375	Pee Wee Reese	42.00	20.00	4.00
☐ 376	Charley Rabe	3.00	1.50	.30
☐ 377A	Milwaukee Braves	10.00	3.00	.75
	Team Card			
	(alphabetical)			

☐ 377B Milwaukee Team numerical checklist	65.00	10.00	2.00
☐ 378 Hank Sauer	4.00	2.00	.40
☐ 379 Ray Herbert	3.00	1.50	.30
☐ 380 Charley Maxwell	4.00	2.00	.40
☐ 381 Hal Brown	3.00	1.50	.30
☐ 382 Al Cicotte	3.00	1.50	.30
☐ 383 Lou Berberet	3.00	1.50	.30
☐ 384 John Goryl	3.00	1.50	.30
☐ 385 Wilmer Mizell	3.00	1.50	.30
☐ 386 Birdie's Sluggers Ed Bailey Birdie Tebbetts Frank Robinson	7.00	3.50	.70
☐ 387 Wally Post	4.00	2.00	.40
☐ 388 Billy Moran	3.00	1.50	.30
☐ 389 Bill Taylor	3.00	1.50	.30
☐ 390 Del Crandall	4.00	2.00	.40
☐ 391 Dave Melton	3.00	1.50	.30
☐ 392 Bennie Daniels	3.00	1.50	.30
☐ 393 Tony Kubek	16.00	8.00	1.60
☐ 394 Jim Grant	4.00	2.00	.40
☐ 395 Willard Nixon	3.00	1.50	.30
☐ 396 Dutch Dotterer	3.00	1.50	.30
☐ 397A Detroit Tigers Team Card (alphabetical)	10.00	3.00	.75
☐ 397B Detroit Team numerical checklist	65.00	10.00	2.00
☐ 398 Gene Woodling	4.00	2.00	.40
☐ 399 Marv Grissom	3.00	1.50	.30
☐ 400 Nellie Fox	11.00	5.50	1.10
☐ 401 Don Bessent	3.00	1.50	.30
☐ 402 Bobby Gene Smith	3.00	1.50	.30
☐ 403 Steve Korcheck	3.00	1.50	.30
☐ 404 Curt Simmons	4.00	2.00	.40
☐ 405 Ken Aspromonte	3.00	1.50	.30
☐ 406 Vic Power	3.00	1.50	.30
☐ 407 Carlton Willey	3.00	1.50	.30
☐ 408A Baltimore Orioles Team Card (alphabetical)	10.00	3.00	.75
☐ 408B Baltimore Team numerical checklist	65.00	10.00	2.00
☐ 409 Frank Thomas	4.00	2.00	.40
☐ 410 Murray Wall	3.00	1.50	.30
☐ 411 Tony Taylor	3.00	1.50	.30
☐ 412 Jerry Staley	3.00	1.50	.30
☐ 413 Jim Davenport	4.00	2.00	.40
☐ 414 Sammy White	3.00	1.50	.30
☐ 415 Bob Bowman	3.00	1.50	.30
☐ 416 Foster Castleman	3.00	1.50	.30
☐ 417 Carl Furillo	7.00	3.50	.70
☐ 418 World Series Batting Foes: Mickey Mantle Hank Aaron	135.00	65.00	13.50
☐ 419 Bobby Shantz	5.00	2.50	.50
☐ 420 Vada Pinson	18.00	9.00	1.80
☐ 421 Dixie Howell	3.00	1.50	.30
☐ 422 Norm Zauchin	3.00	1.50	.30
☐ 423 Phil Clark	3.00	1.50	.30
☐ 424 Larry Doby	5.00	2.50	.50
☐ 425 Sammy Esposito	3.00	1.50	.30
☐ 426 Johnny O'Brien	3.00	1.50	.30
☐ 427 Al Worthington	3.00	1.50	.30
☐ 428A Cincinnati Reds Team Card (alphabetical)	10.00	3.00	.75
☐ 428B Cincinnati Team numerical checklist	65.00	10.00	2.00
☐ 429 Gus Triandos	4.00	2.00	.40
☐ 430 Bobby Thomson	5.00	2.50	.50
☐ 431 Gene Conley	4.00	2.00	.40
☐ 432 John Powers	3.00	1.50	.30
☐ 433A Pancho Herrer ERR	500.00	250.00	50.00
☐ 433B Pancho Herrera COR	3.00	1.50	.30
☐ 434 Harvey Kuenn	6.00	3.00	.60
☐ 435 Ed Roebuck	4.00	2.00	.40
☐ 436 Rival Fence Busters Willie Mays Duke Snider	50.00	25.00	5.00
☐ 437 Bob Speake	3.00	1.50	.30
☐ 438 Whitey Herzog	6.00	3.00	.60
☐ 439 Ray Narleski	3.00	1.50	.30
☐ 440 Eddie Mathews	30.00	15.00	3.00
☐ 441 Jim Marshall	2.50	1.25	.25
☐ 442 Phil Paine	2.50	1.25	.25
☐ 443 Billy Harrell SP	10.00	5.00	1.00
☐ 444 Danny Kravitz	2.50	1.25	.25
☐ 445 Bob Smith	2.50	1.25	.25
☐ 446 Carroll Hardy SP	10.00	5.00	1.00
☐ 447 Ray Monzant	2.50	1.25	.25
☐ 448 Charlie Lau	6.00	3.00	.60
☐ 449 Gene Fodge	2.50	1.25	.25
☐ 450 Preston Ward SP	10.00	5.00	1.00
☐ 451 Joe Taylor	2.50	1.25	.25
☐ 452 Roman Mejias	2.50	1.25	.25
☐ 453 Tom Qualters	2.50	1.25	.25
☐ 454 Harry Hanebrink	2.50	1.25	.25
☐ 455 Hal Griggs	2.50	1.25	.25
☐ 456 Dick Brown	2.50	1.25	.25
☐ 457 Milt Pappas	6.00	3.00	.60
☐ 458 Julio Becquer	2.50	1.25	.25
☐ 459 Ron Blackburn	2.50	1.25	.25
☐ 460 Chuck Essegian	2.50	1.25	.25
☐ 461 Ed Mayer	2.50	1.25	.25
☐ 462 Gary Geiger SP	10.00	5.00	1.00
☐ 463 Vito Valentinetti	2.50	1.25	.25
☐ 464 Curt Flood	15.00	7.50	1.50
☐ 465 Arnie Portocarrero	2.50	1.25	.25
☐ 466 Pete Whisenant	2.50	1.25	.25
☐ 467 Glen Hobbie	2.50	1.25	.25
☐ 468 Bob Schmidt	2.50	1.25	.25
☐ 469 Don Ferrarese	2.50	1.25	.25
☐ 470 R.C. Stevens	2.50	1.25	.25
☐ 471 Lenny Green	2.50	1.25	.25
☐ 472 Joey Jay	3.50	1.75	.35
☐ 473 Bill Renna	2.50	1.25	.25
☐ 474 Roman Semproch	2.50	1.25	.25
☐ 475 Haney/Stengel AS (checklist back)	15.00	5.00	1.00
☐ 476 Stan Musial AS TP	30.00	15.00	3.00
☐ 477 Bill Skowron AS	4.50	2.25	.45
☐ 478 Johnny Temple AS	3.00	1.50	.30
☐ 479 Nellie Fox AS	6.50	3.25	.65
☐ 480 Eddie Mathews AS	12.00	6.00	1.20
☐ 481 Frank Malzone AS	3.00	1.50	.30
☐ 482 Ernie Banks AS	16.00	8.00	1.60
☐ 483 Luis Aparicio AS	10.00	5.00	1.00
☐ 484 Frank Robinson AS	16.00	8.00	1.60
☐ 485 Ted Williams AS	60.00	30.00	6.00
☐ 486 Willie Mays AS	36.00	18.00	3.60
☐ 487 Mickey Mantle AS TP	90.00	45.00	9.00
☐ 488 Hank Aaron AS	36.00	18.00	3.60
☐ 489 Jackie Jensen AS	3.50	1.75	.35
☐ 490 Ed Bailey AS	3.00	1.50	.30
☐ 491 Sherm Lollar AS	3.00	1.50	.30
☐ 492 Bob Friend AS	3.00	1.50	.30
☐ 493 Bob Turley AS	3.50	1.75	.35
☐ 494 Warren Spahn AS	14.00	7.00	1.40
☐ 495 Herb Score AS	6.00	1.75	.35

1959 Topps

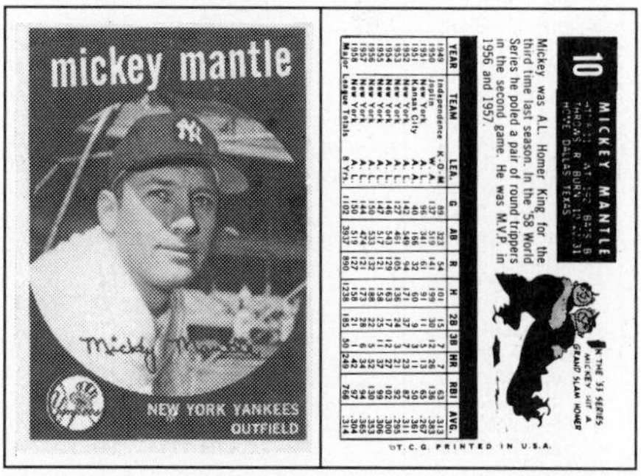

The cards in this 572-card set measure 2 1/2" by 3 1/2". The 1959 Topps set contains bust pictures of the players in a colored circle. Card numbers 551 to 572 are Sporting News All-Star Selections. High numbers 507 to 572 have the card number in a black background on the reverse rather than a green background as in the lower numbers. The high numbers are more difficult to obtain. Several cards in the 300s exist with or without an extra traded or option line on the back of the card. Cards 199 to 286 exist with either white or gray backs. Cards 461 to 470 contain "Highlights" while cards 116 to 146 give an alphabetically ordered listing of "Rookie Prospects." These Rookie Prospects (RP) were Topps' first organized inclusion of untested "Rookie" cards. Card 440 features Lew Burdette erroneously posing as a left-handed pitcher. There were some three-card advertising panels produced by Topps; the players included are from the first series; one panel shows Don McMahon, Red Wilson, and Bob Boyd on the front with Ted Kluszewski's reverse on one of the backs. Another panel shows Billy Hunter, Chuck Stobbs, and Carl Sawatski on the front with Nellie Fox's reverse on one of the backs. When cut apart, these advertising cards are distinguished by the non-standard card back, i.e., part of an advertisement for the 1959 Topps set instead of the typical statistics and biographical information about the player pictured. The key rookies in this set are Sparky Anderson, Bob Gibson, and Bill White.

	NRMT	VG-E	GOOD
COMPLETE SET (572)	4000.00	1800.00	500.00
COMMON PLAYER (1-110)	4.00	2.00	.40
COMMON PLAYER (111-506)	2.50	1.25	.25
COMMON PLAYER (507-550)	10.00	5.00	1.00
COMMON PLAYER (551-572)	12.00	6.00	1.20

	NRMT	VG-E	GOOD
☐ 1 Ford Frick	50.00	7.50	1.50
☐ 2 Eddie Yost	4.00	2.00	.40
☐ 3 Don McMahon	4.00	2.00	.40
☐ 4 Albie Pearson	4.00	2.00	.40
☐ 5 Dick Donovan	4.00	2.00	.40
☐ 6 Alex Grammas	4.00	2.00	.40
☐ 7 Al Pilarcik	4.00	2.00	.40
☐ 8 Phillies Team	15.00	3.00	.75
(checklist on back)			
☐ 9 Paul Giel	4.00	2.00	.40
☐ 10 Mickey Mantle	325.00	160.00	32.00
☐ 11 Billy Hunter	4.00	2.00	.40
☐ 12 Vern Law	5.00	2.50	.50
☐ 13 Dick Gernert	4.00	2.00	.40
☐ 14 Pete Whisenant	4.00	2.00	.40
☐ 15 Dick Drott	4.00	2.00	.40
☐ 16 Joe Pignatano	4.00	2.00	.40
☐ 17 Danny's Stars	5.00	2.50	.50
Frank Thomas			
Danny Murtaugh			
Ted Kluszewski			
☐ 18 Jack Urban	4.00	2.00	.40
☐ 19 Eddie Bressoud	4.00	2.00	.40
☐ 20 Duke Snider	50.00	25.00	5.00
☐ 21 Connie Johnson	4.00	2.00	.40
☐ 22 Al Smith	4.00	2.00	.40
☐ 23 Murry Dickson	4.00	2.00	.40
☐ 24 Red Wilson	4.00	2.00	.40
☐ 25 Don Hoak	4.00	2.00	.40
☐ 26 Chuck Stobbs	4.00	2.00	.40
☐ 27 Andy Pafko	4.00	2.00	.40
☐ 28 Al Worthington	4.00	2.00	.40
☐ 29 Jim Bolger	4.00	2.00	.40
☐ 30 Nellie Fox	11.00	5.50	1.10
☐ 31 Ken Lehman	4.00	2.00	.40
☐ 32 Don Buddin	4.00	2.00	.40
☐ 33 Ed Fitzgerald	4.00	2.00	.40
☐ 34 Pitchers Beware	9.00	4.50	.90
Al Kaline			
Charley Maxwell			
☐ 35 Ted Kluszewski	7.00	3.50	.70
☐ 36 Hank Aguirre	4.00	2.00	.40
☐ 37 Gene Green	4.00	2.00	.40
☐ 38 Morrie Martin	4.00	2.00	.40
☐ 39 Ed Bouchee	4.00	2.00	.40
☐ 40 Warren Spahn	45.00	22.50	4.50
☐ 41 Bob Martyn	4.00	2.00	.40
☐ 42 Murray Wall	4.00	2.00	.40
☐ 43 Steve Bilko	4.00	2.00	.40
☐ 44 Vito Valentinetti	4.00	2.00	.40
☐ 45 Andy Carey	5.00	2.50	.50
☐ 46 Bill R. Henry	4.00	2.00	.40
☐ 47 Jim Finigan	4.00	2.00	.40
☐ 48 Orioles Team	12.50	3.00	.75
(checklist on back)			
☐ 49 Bill Hall	4.00	2.00	.40
☐ 50 Willie Mays	135.00	65.00	13.50
☐ 51 Rip Coleman	4.00	2.00	.40
☐ 52 Coot Veal	4.00	2.00	.40
☐ 53 Stan Williams	4.00	2.00	.40
☐ 54 Mel Roach	4.00	2.00	.40
☐ 55 Tom Brewer	4.00	2.00	.40
☐ 56 Carl Sawatski	4.00	2.00	.40
☐ 57 Al Cicotte	4.00	2.00	.40
☐ 58 Eddie Miksis	4.00	2.00	.40
☐ 59 Irv Noren	4.00	2.00	.40
☐ 60 Bob Turley	7.00	3.50	.70
☐ 61 Dick Brown	4.00	2.00	.40
☐ 62 Tony Taylor	4.00	2.00	.40
☐ 63 Jim Hearn	4.00	2.00	.40
☐ 64 Joe DeMaestri	4.00	2.00	.40
☐ 65 Frank Torre	4.00	2.00	.40
☐ 66 Joe Ginsberg	4.00	2.00	.40
☐ 67 Brooks Lawrence	4.00	2.00	.40
☐ 68 Dick Schofield	4.00	2.00	.40
☐ 69 Giants Team	12.50	3.00	.75
(checklist on back)			
☐ 70 Harvey Kuenn	6.00	3.00	.60
☐ 71 Don Bessent	4.00	2.00	.40
☐ 72 Bill Renna	4.00	2.00	.40
☐ 73 Ron Jackson	4.00	2.00	.40
☐ 74 Directing Power	5.00	2.50	.50
Jim Lemon			
Cookie Lavagetto			
Roy Sievers			
☐ 75 Sam Jones	4.00	2.00	.40
☐ 76 Bobby Richardson	10.00	5.00	1.00
☐ 77 John Goryl	4.00	2.00	.40
☐ 78 Pedro Ramos	4.00	2.00	.40
☐ 79 Harry Chiti	4.00	2.00	.40
☐ 80 Minnie Minoso	7.00	3.50	.70
☐ 81 Hal Jeffcoat	4.00	2.00	.40
☐ 82 Bob Boyd	4.00	2.00	.40
☐ 83 Bob Smith	4.00	2.00	.40
☐ 84 Reno Bertoia	4.00	2.00	.40
☐ 85 Harry Anderson	4.00	2.00	.40
☐ 86 Bob Keegan	4.00	2.00	.40
☐ 87 Danny O'Connell	4.00	2.00	.40
☐ 88 Herb Score	6.00	3.00	.60
☐ 89 Billy Gardner	4.00	2.00	.40
☐ 90 Bill Skowron	9.00	4.50	.90
☐ 91 Herb Moford	4.00	2.00	.40
☐ 92 Dave Philley	4.00	2.00	.40
☐ 93 Julio Becquer	4.00	2.00	.40
☐ 94 White Sox Team	12.50	3.00	.75
(checklist on back)			
☐ 95 Carl Willey	4.00	2.00	.40
☐ 96 Lou Berberet	4.00	2.00	.40
☐ 97 Jerry Lynch	4.00	2.00	.40
☐ 98 Arnie Portocarrero	4.00	2.00	.40
☐ 99 Ted Kazanski	4.00	2.00	.40
☐ 100 Bob Cerv	5.00	2.50	.50
☐ 101 Alex Kellner	4.00	2.00	.40
☐ 102 Felipe Alou	10.00	5.00	1.00
☐ 103 Billy Goodman	5.00	2.50	.50
☐ 104 Del Rice	4.00	2.00	.40
☐ 105 Lee Walls	4.00	2.00	.40
☐ 106 Hal Woodeshick	4.00	2.00	.40
☐ 107 Norm Larker	5.00	2.50	.50
☐ 108 Zack Monroe	4.00	2.00	.40
☐ 109 Bob Schmidt	4.00	2.00	.40
☐ 110 George Witt	4.00	2.00	.40
☐ 111 Redlegs Team	8.00	2.00	.40
(checklist on back)			
☐ 112 Billy Consolo	2.50	1.25	.25
☐ 113 Taylor Phillips	2.50	1.25	.25
☐ 114 Earl Battey	2.50	1.25	.25
☐ 115 Mickey Vernon	3.50	1.75	.35
☐ 116 Bob Allison RP	5.00	2.50	.50
☐ 117 John Blanchard RP	3.50	1.75	.35
☐ 118 John Buzhardt RP	2.50	1.25	.25
☐ 119 John Callison RP	4.50	2.25	.45
☐ 120 Chuck Coles RP	2.50	1.25	.25
☐ 121 Bob Conley RP	2.50	1.25	.25
☐ 122 Bennie Daniels RP	2.50	1.25	.25
☐ 123 Don Dillard RP	2.50	1.25	.25
☐ 124 Dan Dobbek RP	2.50	1.25	.25
☐ 125 Ron Fairly RP	4.50	2.25	.45
☐ 126 Ed Haas RP	2.50	1.25	.25
☐ 127 Kent Hadley RP	2.50	1.25	.25
☐ 128 Bob Hartman RP	2.50	1.25	.25
☐ 129 Frank Herrera RP	2.50	1.25	.25
☐ 130 Lou Jackson RP	2.50	1.25	.25
☐ 131 Deron Johnson RP	3.50	1.75	.35
☐ 132 Don Lee RP	2.50	1.25	.25
☐ 133 Bob Lillis RP	3.50	1.75	.35
☐ 134 Jim McDaniel RP	2.50	1.25	.25
☐ 135 Gene Oliver RP	2.50	1.25	.25
☐ 136 Jim O'Toole RP	3.50	1.75	.35
☐ 137 Dick Ricketts RP	2.50	1.25	.25
☐ 138 John Romano RP	3.50	1.75	.35
☐ 139 Ed Sadowski RP	2.50	1.25	.25
☐ 140 Charlie Secrest RP	2.50	1.25	.25
☐ 141 Joe Shipley RP	2.50	1.25	.25
☐ 142 Dick Stigman RP	2.50	1.25	.25
☐ 143 Willie Tasby RP	2.50	1.25	.25
☐ 144 Jerry Walker RP	2.50	1.25	.25
☐ 145 Dom Zanni RP	2.50	1.25	.25
☐ 146 Jerry Zimmerman RP	2.50	1.25	.25
☐ 147 Cubs Clubbers	9.00	4.50	.90
Dale Long			
Ernie Banks			
Walt Moryn			
☐ 148 Mike McCormick	3.50	1.75	.35

☐ 149	Jim Bunning	10.00	5.00	1.00
☐ 150	Stan Musial	135.00	65.00	13.50
☐ 151	Bob Malkmus	2.50	1.25	.25
☐ 152	Johnny Klippstein	2.50	1.25	.25
☐ 153	Jim Marshall	2.50	1.25	.25
☐ 154	Ray Herbert	2.50	1.25	.25
☐ 155	Enos Slaughter	16.00	8.00	1.60
☐ 156	Ace Hurlers	4.00	2.00	.40
	Billy Pierce			
	Robin Roberts			
☐ 157	Felix Mantilla	2.50	1.25	.25
☐ 158	Walt Dropo	2.50	1.25	.25
☐ 159	Bob Shaw	2.50	1.25	.25
☐ 160	Dick Groat	4.00	2.00	.40
☐ 161	Frank Baumann	2.50	1.25	.25
☐ 162	Bobby G. Smith	2.50	1.25	.25
☐ 163	Sandy Koufax	125.00	60.00	12.50
☐ 164	Johnny Groth	2.50	1.25	.25
☐ 165	Bill Bruton	2.50	1.25	.25
☐ 166	Destruction Crew	5.00	2.50	.50
	Minnie Minoso			
	Rocky Colavito			
	(misspelled Colovito			
	on card back)			
	Larry Doby			
☐ 167	Duke Maas	2.50	1.25	.25
☐ 168	Carroll Hardy	2.50	1.25	.25
☐ 169	Ted Abernathy	2.50	1.25	.25
☐ 170	Gene Woodling	3.50	1.75	.35
☐ 171	Willard Schmidt	2.50	1.25	.25
☐ 172	Athletics Team	8.00	2.00	.40
	(checklist on back)			
☐ 173	Bill Monbouquette	2.50	1.25	.25
☐ 174	Jim Pendleton	2.50	1.25	.25
☐ 175	Dick Farrell	2.50	1.25	.25
☐ 176	Preston Ward	2.50	1.25	.25
☐ 177	John Briggs	2.50	1.25	.25
☐ 178	Ruben Amaro	2.50	1.25	.25
☐ 179	Don Rudolph	2.50	1.25	.25
☐ 180	Yogi Berra	65.00	32.50	6.50
☐ 181	Bob Porterfield	2.50	1.25	.25
☐ 182	Milt Graff	2.50	1.25	.25
☐ 183	Stu Miller	2.50	1.25	.25
☐ 184	Harvey Haddix	3.50	1.75	.35
☐ 185	Jim Busby	2.50	1.25	.25
☐ 186	Mudcat Grant	2.50	1.25	.25
☐ 187	Bubba Phillips	2.50	1.25	.25
☐ 188	Juan Pizarro	2.50	1.25	.25
☐ 189	Neil Chrisley	2.50	1.25	.25
☐ 190	Bill Virdon	3.50	1.75	.35
☐ 191	Russ Kemmerer	2.50	1.25	.25
☐ 192	Charlie Beamon	2.50	1.25	.25
☐ 193	Sammy Taylor	2.50	1.25	.25
☐ 194	Jim Brosnan	2.50	1.25	.25
☐ 195	Rip Repulski	2.50	1.25	.25
☐ 196	Billy Moran	2.50	1.25	.25
☐ 197	Ray Semproch	2.50	1.25	.25
☐ 198	Jim Davenport	3.50	1.75	.35
☐ 199	Leo Kiely	2.50	1.25	.25
☐ 200	Warren Giles	4.50	2.25	.45
	(NL President)			
☐ 201	Tom Acker	2.50	1.25	.25
☐ 202	Roger Maris	135.00	65.00	13.50
☐ 203	Ossie Virgil	2.50	1.25	.25
☐ 204	Casey Wise	2.50	1.25	.25
☐ 205	Don Larsen	4.00	2.00	.40
☐ 206	Carl Furillo	5.00	2.50	.50
☐ 207	George Strickland	2.50	1.25	.25
☐ 208	Willie Jones	2.50	1.25	.25
☐ 209	Lenny Green	2.50	1.25	.25
☐ 210	Ed Bailey	2.50	1.25	.25
☐ 211	Bob Blaylock	2.50	1.25	.25
☐ 212	Fence Busters	30.00	15.00	3.00
	Hank Aaron			
	Eddie Mathews			
☐ 213	Jim Rivera	2.50	1.25	.25
☐ 214	Marcelino Solis	2.50	1.25	.25
☐ 215	Jim Lemon	3.50	1.75	.35
☐ 216	Andre Rodgers	2.50	1.25	.25
☐ 217	Carl Erskine	3.50	1.75	.35
☐ 218	Roman Mejias	2.50	1.25	.25
☐ 219	George Zuverink	2.50	1.25	.25
☐ 220	Frank Malzone	3.50	1.75	.35
☐ 221	Bob Bowman	2.50	1.25	.25
☐ 222	Bobby Shantz	3.50	1.75	.35
☐ 223	Cardinals Team	8.00	2.00	.40
	(checklist on back)			
☐ 224	Claude Osteen	3.50	1.75	.35
☐ 225	Johnny Logan	3.50	1.75	.35
☐ 226	Art Ceccarelli	2.50	1.25	.25
☐ 227	Hal W. Smith	2.50	1.25	.25
☐ 228	Don Gross	2.50	1.25	.25
☐ 229	Vic Power	2.50	1.25	.25
☐ 230	Bill Fischer	2.50	1.25	.25

☐ 231	Ellis Burton	2.50	1.25	.25
☐ 232	Eddie Kasko	2.50	1.25	.25
☐ 233	Paul Foytack	2.50	1.25	.25
☐ 234	Chuck Tanner	3.50	1.75	.35
☐ 235	Valmy Thomas	2.50	1.25	.25
☐ 236	Ted Bowsfield	2.50	1.25	.25
☐ 237	Run Preventers	5.00	2.50	.50
	Gil McDougald			
	Bob Turley			
	Bobby Richardson			
☐ 238	Gene Baker	2.50	1.25	.25
☐ 239	Bob Trowbridge	2.50	1.25	.25
☐ 240	Hank Bauer	4.50	2.25	.45
☐ 241	Billy Muffett	2.50	1.25	.25
☐ 242	Ron Samford	2.50	1.25	.25
☐ 243	Marv Grissom	2.50	1.25	.25
☐ 244	Ted Gray	2.50	1.25	.25
☐ 245	Ned Garver	2.50	1.25	.25
☐ 246	J.W. Porter	2.50	1.25	.25
☐ 247	Don Ferrarese	2.50	1.25	.25
☐ 248	Red Sox Team	9.00	2.00	.40
	(checklist on back)			
☐ 249	Bobby Adams	2.50	1.25	.25
☐ 250	Billy O'Dell	2.50	1.25	.25
☐ 251	Clete Boyer	3.50	1.75	.35
☐ 252	Ray Boone	2.50	1.25	.25
☐ 253	Seth Morehead	2.50	1.25	.25
☐ 254	Zeke Bella	2.50	1.25	.25
☐ 255	Del Ennis	2.50	1.25	.25
☐ 256	Jerry Davie	2.50	1.25	.25
☐ 257	Leon Wagner	2.50	1.25	.25
☐ 258	Fred Kipp	2.50	1.25	.25
☐ 259	Jim Pisoni	2.50	1.25	.25
☐ 260	Early Wynn	12.00	6.00	1.20
☐ 261	Gene Stephens	2.50	1.25	.25
☐ 262	Hitters' Foes	4.50	2.25	.45
	Johnny Podres			
	Clem Labine			
	Don Drysdale			
☐ 263	Bud Daley	2.50	1.25	.25
☐ 264	Chico Carrasquel	2.50	1.25	.25
☐ 265	Ron Kline	2.50	1.25	.25
☐ 266	Woody Held	2.50	1.25	.25
☐ 267	John Romonosky	2.50	1.25	.25
☐ 268	Tito Francona	2.50	1.25	.25
☐ 269	Jack Meyer	2.50	1.25	.25
☐ 270	Gil Hodges	16.00	8.00	1.60
☐ 271	Orlando Pena	2.50	1.25	.25
☐ 272	Jerry Lumpe	2.50	1.25	.25
☐ 273	Joey Jay	2.50	1.25	.25
☐ 274	Jerry Kindall	2.50	1.25	.25
☐ 275	Jack Sanford	2.50	1.25	.25
☐ 276	Pete Daley	2.50	1.25	.25
☐ 277	Turk Lown	2.50	1.25	.25
☐ 278	Chuck Essegian	2.50	1.25	.25
☐ 279	Ernie Johnson	2.50	1.25	.25
☐ 280	Frank Bolling	2.50	1.25	.25
☐ 281	Walt Craddock	2.50	1.25	.25
☐ 282	R.C. Stevens	2.50	1.25	.25
☐ 283	Russ Heman	2.50	1.25	.25
☐ 284	Steve Korcheck	2.50	1.25	.25
☐ 285	Joe Cunningham	2.50	1.25	.25
☐ 286	Dean Stone	2.50	1.25	.25
☐ 287	Don Zimmer	4.00	2.00	.40
☐ 288	Dutch Dotterer	2.50	1.25	.25
☐ 289	Johnny Kucks	2.50	1.25	.25
☐ 290	Wes Covington	2.50	1.25	.25
☐ 291	Pitching Partners	3.50	1.75	.35
	Pedro Ramos			
	Camilo Pascual			
☐ 292	Dick Williams	3.50	1.75	.35
☐ 293	Ray Moore	2.50	1.25	.25
☐ 294	Hank Foiles	2.50	1.25	.25
☐ 295	Billy Martin	12.00	6.00	1.20
☐ 296	Ernie Broglio	3.50	1.75	.35
☐ 297	Jackie Brandt	2.50	1.25	.25
☐ 298	Tex Clevenger	2.50	1.25	.25
☐ 299	Billy Klaus	2.50	1.25	.25
☐ 300	Richie Ashburn	10.00	5.00	1.00
☐ 301	Earl Averill	2.50	1.25	.25
☐ 302	Don Mossi	3.50	1.75	.35
☐ 303	Marty Keough	2.50	1.25	.25
☐ 304	Cubs Team	8.00	2.00	.40
	(checklist on back)			
☐ 305	Curt Raydon	2.50	1.25	.25
☐ 306	Jim Gilliam	5.00	2.50	.50
☐ 307	Curt Barclay	2.50	1.25	.25
☐ 308	Norm Siebern	2.50	1.25	.25
☐ 309	Sal Maglie	4.00	2.00	.40
☐ 310	Luis Aparicio	16.00	8.00	1.60
☐ 311	Norm Zauchin	2.50	1.25	.25
☐ 312	Don Newcombe	4.00	2.00	.40
☐ 313	Frank House	2.50	1.25	.25
☐ 314	Don Cardwell	2.50	1.25	.25

□ 315 Joe Adcock	3.50	1.75	.35
□ 316A Ralph Lumenti UER	2.50	1.25	.25
(option)			
(photo actually			
Camilo Pascual)			
□ 316B Ralph Lumenti UER	85.00	42.50	8.50
(no option)			
(photo actually			
Camilo Pascual)			
□ 317 Hitting Kings	16.00	8.00	1.60
Willie Mays			
Richie Ashburn			
□ 318 Rocky Bridges	2.50	1.25	.25
□ 319 Dave Hillman	2.50	1.25	.25
□ 320 Bob Skinner	3.50	1.75	.35
□ 321A Bob Giallombardo	2.50	1.25	.25
(option)			
□ 321B Bob Giallombardo	85.00	42.50	8.50
(no option)			
□ 322A Harry Hanebrink	2.50	1.25	.25
(traded)			
□ 322B Harry Hanebrink	85.00	42.50	8.50
(no trade)			
□ 323 Frank Sullivan	2.50	1.25	.25
□ 324 Don Demeter	2.50	1.25	.25
□ 325 Ken Boyer	6.00	3.00	.60
□ 326 Marv Throneberry	3.50	1.75	.35
□ 327 Gary Bell	2.50	1.25	.25
□ 328 Lou Skizas	2.50	1.25	.25
□ 329 Tigers Team	9.00	2.00	.40
(checklist on back)			
□ 330 Gus Triandos	3.50	1.75	.35
□ 331 Steve Boros	2.50	1.25	.25
□ 332 Ray Monzant	2.50	1.25	.25
□ 333 Harry Simpson	2.50	1.25	.25
□ 334 Glen Hobbie	2.50	1.25	.25
□ 335 Johnny Temple	2.50	1.25	.25
□ 336A Billy Loes	2.50	1.25	.25
(with traded line)			
□ 336B Billy Loes	85.00	42.50	8.50
(no trade)			
□ 337 George Crowe	2.50	1.25	.25
□ 338 Sparky Anderson	20.00	10.00	2.00
□ 339 Roy Face	4.00	2.00	.40
□ 340 Roy Sievers	3.50	1.75	.35
□ 341 Tom Qualters	2.50	1.25	.25
□ 342 Ray Jablonski	2.50	1.25	.25
□ 343 Billy Hoeft	2.50	1.25	.25
□ 344 Russ Nixon	2.50	1.25	.25
□ 345 Gil McDougald	5.00	2.50	.50
□ 346 Batter Bafflers	2.50	1.25	.25
Dave Sisler			
Tom Brewer			
□ 347 Bob Buhl	2.50	1.25	.25
□ 348 Ted Lepcio	2.50	1.25	.25
□ 349 Hoyt Wilhelm	14.00	7.00	1.40
□ 350 Ernie Banks	60.00	30.00	6.00
□ 351 Earl Torgeson	2.50	1.25	.25
□ 352 Robin Roberts	14.00	7.00	1.40
□ 353 Curt Flood	4.00	2.00	.40
□ 354 Pete Burnside	2.50	1.25	.25
□ 355 Jim Piersall	3.50	1.75	.35
□ 356 Bob Mabe	2.50	1.25	.25
□ 357 Dick Stuart	4.00	2.00	.40
□ 358 Ralph Terry	3.50	1.75	.35
□ 359 Bill White	16.00	8.00	1.60
□ 360 Al Kaline	50.00	25.00	5.00
□ 361 Willard Nixon	2.50	1.25	.25
□ 362A Dolan Nichols	2.50	1.25	.25
(with option line)			
□ 362B Dolan Nichols	85.00	42.50	8.50
(no option)			
□ 363 Bobby Avila	2.50	1.25	.25
□ 364 Danny McDevitt	2.50	1.25	.25
□ 365 Gus Bell	2.50	1.25	.25
□ 366 Humberto Robinson	2.50	1.25	.25
□ 367 Cal Neeman	2.50	1.25	.25
□ 368 Don Mueller	3.50	1.75	.35
□ 369 Dick Tomanek	2.50	1.25	.25
□ 370 Pete Runnels	3.50	1.75	.35
□ 371 Dick Brodowski	2.50	1.25	.25
□ 372 Jim Hegan	2.50	1.25	.25
□ 373 Herb Plews	2.50	1.25	.25
□ 374 Art Ditmar	2.50	1.25	.25
□ 375 Bob Nieman	2.50	1.25	.25
□ 376 Hal Naragon	2.50	1.25	.25
□ 377 John Antonelli	3.50	1.75	.35
□ 378 Gail Harris	2.50	1.25	.25
□ 379 Bob Miller	2.50	1.25	.25
□ 380 Hank Aaron	110.00	55.00	11.00
□ 381 Mike Baxes	2.50	1.25	.25
□ 382 Curt Simmons	3.50	1.75	.35
□ 383 Words of Wisdom	6.50	3.25	.65
Don Larsen			
Casey Stengel			
□ 384 Dave Sisler	2.50	1.25	.25
□ 385 Sherm Lollar	2.50	1.25	.25
□ 386 Jim Delsing	2.50	1.25	.25
□ 387 Don Drysdale	32.00	16.00	3.20
□ 388 Bob Will	2.50	1.25	.25
□ 389 Joe Nuxhall	3.50	1.75	.35
□ 390 Orlando Cepeda	16.00	8.00	1.60
□ 391 Milt Pappas	3.50	1.75	.35
□ 392 Whitey Herzog	4.00	2.00	.40
□ 393 Frank Lary	3.50	1.75	.35
□ 394 Randy Jackson	2.50	1.25	.25
□ 395 Elston Howard	5.00	2.50	.50
□ 396 Bob Rush	2.50	1.25	.25
□ 397 Senators Team	7.50	2.00	.40
(checklist on back)			
□ 398 Wally Post	2.50	1.25	.25
□ 399 Larry Jackson	2.50	1.25	.25
□ 400 Jackie Jensen	4.00	2.00	.40
□ 401 Ron Blackburn	2.50	1.25	.25
□ 402 Hector Lopez	2.50	1.25	.25
□ 403 Clem Labine	3.50	1.75	.35
□ 404 Hank Sauer	3.50	1.75	.35
□ 405 Roy McMillan	2.50	1.25	.25
□ 406 Solly Drake	2.50	1.25	.25
□ 407 Moe Drabowsky	2.50	1.25	.25
□ 408 Keystone Combo	6.50	3.25	.65
Nellie Fox			
Luis Aparicio			
□ 409 Gus Zernial	2.50	1.25	.25
□ 410 Billy Pierce	3.50	1.75	.35
□ 411 Whitey Lockman	2.50	1.25	.25
□ 412 Stan Lopata	2.50	1.25	.25
□ 413 Camilo Pascual UER	3.50	1.75	.35
(listed as Camillo			
on front and Pasqual			
on back)			
□ 414 Dale Long	3.50	1.75	.35
□ 415 Bill Mazeroski	4.50	2.25	.45
□ 416 Haywood Sullivan	2.50	1.25	.25
□ 417 Virgil Trucks	2.50	1.25	.25
□ 418 Gino Cimoli	2.50	1.25	.25
□ 419 Braves Team	8.00	2.00	.40
(checklist on back)			
□ 420 Rocky Colavito	8.00	4.00	.80
□ 421 Herman Wehmeier	2.50	1.25	.25
□ 422 Hobie Landrith	2.50	1.25	.25
□ 423 Bob Grim	2.50	1.25	.25
□ 424 Ken Aspromonte	2.50	1.25	.25
□ 425 Del Crandall	2.50	1.25	.25
□ 426 Jerry Staley	2.50	1.25	.25
□ 427 Charlie Neal	2.50	1.25	.25
□ 428 Buc Hill Aces	3.50	1.75	.35
Ron Kline			
Bob Friend			
Vernon Law			
Roy Face			
□ 429 Bobby Thomson	3.50	1.75	.35
□ 430 Whitey Ford	36.00	18.00	3.60
□ 431 Whammy Douglas	2.50	1.25	.25
□ 432 Smoky Burgess	3.50	1.75	.35
□ 433 Billy Harrell	2.50	1.25	.25
□ 434 Hal Griggs	2.50	1.25	.25
□ 435 Frank Robinson	40.00	20.00	4.00
□ 436 Granny Hamner	2.50	1.25	.25
□ 437 Ike Delock	2.50	1.25	.25
□ 438 Sammy Esposito	2.50	1.25	.25
□ 439 Brooks Robinson	42.00	20.00	4.00
□ 440 Lou Burdette	6.00	3.00	.60
(posing as if			
lefthanded)			
□ 441 John Roseboro	3.50	1.75	.35
□ 442 Ray Narleski	2.50	1.25	.25
□ 443 Daryl Spencer	2.50	1.25	.25
□ 444 Ron Hansen	2.50	1.25	.25
□ 445 Cal McLish	2.50	1.25	.25
□ 446 Rocky Nelson	2.50	1.25	.25
□ 447 Bob Anderson	2.50	1.25	.25
□ 448 Vada Pinson	4.50	2.25	.45
□ 449 Tom Gorman	2.50	1.25	.25
□ 450 Eddie Mathews	28.00	14.00	2.80
□ 451 Jimmy Constable	2.50	1.25	.25
□ 452 Chico Fernandez	2.50	1.25	.25
□ 453 Les Moss	2.50	1.25	.25
□ 454 Phil Clark	2.50	1.25	.25
□ 455 Larry Doby	4.00	2.00	.40
□ 456 Jerry Casale	2.50	1.25	.25
□ 457 Dodgers Team	13.50	4.00	1.00
(checklist on back)			
□ 458 Gordon Jones	2.50	1.25	.25
□ 459 Bill Tuttle	2.50	1.25	.25
□ 460 Bob Friend	3.50	1.75	.35

☐ 461	Mantle Hits Homer	36.00	18.00	3.60
☐ 462	Colavito's Catch	4.50	2.25	.45
☐ 463	Kaline Batting Champ	10.00	5.00	1.00
☐ 464	Mays' Series Catch	16.00	8.00	1.60
☐ 465	Sievers Sets Mark	3.50	1.75	.35
☐ 466	Pierce All-Star	3.50	1.75	.35
☐ 467	Aaron Clubs Homer	16.00	8.00	1.60
☐ 468	Snider's Play	10.00	5.00	1.00
☐ 469	Hustler Banks	10.00	5.00	1.00
☐ 470	Musial's 3000 Hit	14.00	7.00	1.40
☐ 471	Tom Sturdivant	2.50	1.25	.25
☐ 472	Gene Freese	2.50	1.25	.25
☐ 473	Mike Fornieles	2.50	1.25	.25
☐ 474	Moe Thacker	2.50	1.25	.25
☐ 475	Jack Harshman	2.50	1.25	.25
☐ 476	Indians Team	8.00	2.00	.40
	(checklist on back)			
☐ 477	Barry Latman	2.50	1.25	.25
☐ 478	Bob Clemente	100.00	50.00	10.00
☐ 479	Lindy McDaniel	2.50	1.25	.25
☐ 480	Red Schoendienst	12.00	6.00	1.20
☐ 481	Charlie Maxwell	2.50	1.25	.25
☐ 482	Russ Meyer	2.50	1.25	.25
☐ 483	Clint Courtney	2.50	1.25	.25
☐ 484	Willie Kirkland	2.50	1.25	.25
☐ 485	Ryne Duren	3.50	1.75	.35
☐ 486	Sammy White	2.50	1.25	.25
☐ 487	Hal Brown	2.50	1.25	.25
☐ 488	Walt Moryn	2.50	1.25	.25
☐ 489	John Powers	2.50	1.25	.25
☐ 490	Frank Thomas	2.50	1.25	.25
☐ 491	Don Blasingame	2.50	1.25	.25
☐ 492	Gene Conley	2.50	1.25	.25
☐ 493	Jim Landis	2.50	1.25	.25
☐ 494	Don Pavletich	2.50	1.25	.25
☐ 495	Johnny Podres	4.00	2.00	.40
☐ 496	Wayne Terwilliger UER	2.50	1.25	.25
	(Athlftics on front)			
☐ 497	Hal R. Smith	2.50	1.25	.25
☐ 498	Dick Hyde	2.50	1.25	.25
☐ 499	Johnny O'Brien	2.50	1.25	.25
☐ 500	Vic Wertz	2.50	1.25	.25
☐ 501	Bob Tiefenauer	2.50	1.25	.25
☐ 502	Alvin Dark	3.50	1.75	.35
☐ 503	Jim Owens	2.50	1.25	.25
☐ 504	Ossie Alvarez	2.50	1.25	.25
☐ 505	Tony Kubek	8.00	4.00	.80
☐ 506	Bob Purkey	2.50	1.25	.25
☐ 507	Bob Hale	10.00	5.00	1.00
☐ 508	Art Fowler	10.00	5.00	1.00
☐ 509	Norm Cash	35.00	17.50	3.50
☐ 510	Yankees Team	50.00	10.00	2.00
	(checklist on back)			
☐ 511	George Susce	10.00	5.00	1.00
☐ 512	George Altman	10.00	5.00	1.00
☐ 513	Tommy Carroll	10.00	5.00	1.00
☐ 514	Bob Gibson	350.00	175.00	35.00
☐ 515	Harmon Killebrew	110.00	55.00	11.00
☐ 516	Mike Garcia	12.00	6.00	1.20
☐ 517	Joe Koppe	10.00	5.00	1.00
☐ 518	Mike Cueller UER	15.00	7.50	1.50
	(sic, Cuellar)			
☐ 519	Infield Power	12.00	6.00	1.20
	Pete Runnels			
	Dick Gernert			
	Frank Malzone			
☐ 520	Don Elston	10.00	5.00	1.00
☐ 521	Gary Geiger	10.00	5.00	1.00
☐ 522	Gene Snyder	10.00	5.00	1.00
☐ 523	Harry Bright	10.00	5.00	1.00
☐ 524	Larry Osborne	10.00	5.00	1.00
☐ 525	Jim Coates	10.00	5.00	1.00
☐ 526	Bob Speake	10.00	5.00	1.00
☐ 527	Solly Hemus	10.00	5.00	1.00
☐ 528	Pirates Team	32.00	7.50	1.50
	(checklist on back)			
☐ 529	George Bamberger	12.00	6.00	1.20
☐ 530	Wally Moon	12.00	6.00	1.20
☐ 531	Ray Webster	10.00	5.00	1.00
☐ 532	Mark Freeman	10.00	5.00	1.00
☐ 533	Darrell Johnson	12.00	6.00	1.20
☐ 534	Faye Throneberry	10.00	5.00	1.00
☐ 535	Ruben Gomez	10.00	5.00	1.00
☐ 536	Danny Kravitz	10.00	5.00	1.00
☐ 537	Rudolph Arias	10.00	5.00	1.00
☐ 538	Chick King	10.00	5.00	1.00
☐ 539	Gary Blaylock	10.00	5.00	1.00
☐ 540	Willie Miranda	10.00	5.00	1.00
☐ 541	Bob Thurman	10.00	5.00	1.00
☐ 542	Jim Perry	16.00	8.00	1.60
☐ 543	Corsair Trio	50.00	25.00	5.00
	Bob Skinner			
	Bill Virdon			
	Roberto Clemente			
☐ 544	Lee Tate	10.00	5.00	1.00
☐ 545	Tom Morgan	10.00	5.00	1.00
☐ 546	Al Schroll	10.00	5.00	1.00
☐ 547	Jim Baxes	10.00	5.00	1.00
☐ 548	Elmer Singleton	10.00	5.00	1.00
☐ 549	Howie Nunn	10.00	5.00	1.00
☐ 550	Roy Campanella	135.00	65.00	13.50
	(Symbol of Courage)			
☐ 551	Fred Haney MG AS	12.00	6.00	1.20
☐ 552	Casey Stengel MG AS	25.00	12.50	2.50
☐ 553	Orlando Cepeda AS	16.00	8.00	1.60
☐ 554	Bill Skowron AS	13.50	6.25	1.25
☐ 555	Bill Mazeroski AS	13.50	6.25	1.25
☐ 556	Nellie Fox AS	16.00	8.00	1.60
☐ 557	Ken Boyer AS	13.50	6.25	1.25
☐ 558	Frank Malzone AS	12.00	6.00	1.20
☐ 559	Ernie Banks AS	35.00	17.50	3.50
☐ 560	Luis Aparicio AS	20.00	10.00	2.00
☐ 561	Hank Aaron AS	100.00	50.00	10.00
☐ 562	Al Kaline AS	35.00	17.50	3.50
☐ 563	Willie Mays AS	100.00	50.00	10.00
☐ 564	Mickey Mantle AS	200.00	100.00	20.00
☐ 565	Wes Covington AS	12.00	6.00	1.20
☐ 566	Roy Sievers AS	12.00	6.00	1.20
☐ 567	Del Crandall AS	12.00	6.00	1.20
☐ 568	Gus Triandos AS	12.00	6.00	1.20
☐ 569	Bob Friend AS	12.00	6.00	1.20
☐ 570	Bob Turley AS	12.00	6.00	1.20
☐ 571	Warren Spahn AS	30.00	15.00	3.00
☐ 572	Billy Pierce AS	16.00	7.00	1.40

1960 Topps

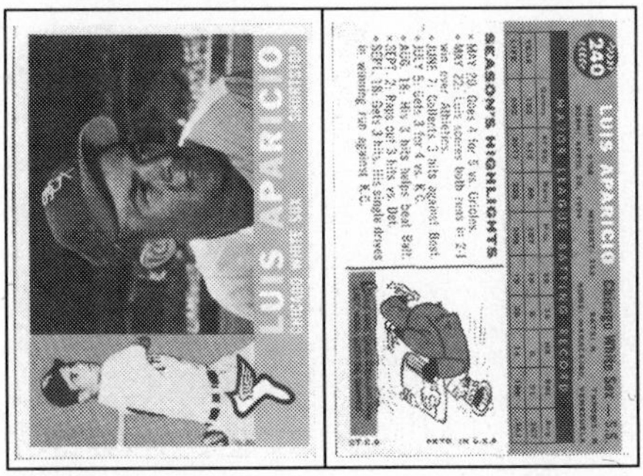

The cards in this 572-card set measure 2 1/2" by 3 1/2". The 1960 Topps set is the only Topps standard size issue to use a horizontally oriented front. World Series cards appeared for the first time (385 to 391), and there is a Rookie Prospect (RP) series (117-148), the most famous of which is Carl Yastrzemski, and a Sport Magazine All-Star Selection (AS) series (553-572). There are 16 manager cards listed alphabetically from 212 through 227. The coaching staff of each team was also afforded their own card in a 16-card subset (455-470). Cards 375 to 440 come with either gray or white backs, and the high series (507-572) were printed on a more limited basis than the rest of the set. The team cards have series checklists on the reverse. The key rookies in this set are Willie McCovey and Carl Yastrzemski.

	NRMT	VG-E	GOOD
COMPLETE SET (572)	3600.00	1650.00	375.00
COMMON PLAYER (1-110)	1.75	.85	.17
COMMON PLAYER (111-198)	1.75	.85	.17
COMMON PLAYER (199-286)	2.00	1.00	.20
COMMON PLAYER (287-440)	2.25	1.10	.22
COMMON PLAYER (441-506)	3.50	1.75	.35
COMMON PLAYER (507-552)	10.00	5.00	1.00
COMMON PLAYER (553-572)	12.00	6.00	1.20

☐ 1	Early Wynn	35.00	7.00	1.25
☐ 2	Roman Mejias	1.75	.85	.17
☐ 3	Joe Adcock	2.25	1.10	.22
☐ 4	Bob Purkey	1.75	.85	.17
☐ 5	Wally Moon	2.25	1.10	.22
☐ 6	Lou Berberet	1.75	.85	.17

☐ 7 Master and Mentor	12.00	5.00	1.00
Willie Mays			
Bill Rigney			
☐ 8 Bud Daley	1.75	.85	.17
☐ 9 Faye Throneberry	1.75	.85	.17
☐ 10 Ernie Banks	40.00	20.00	4.00
☐ 11 Norm Siebern	1.75	.85	.17
☐ 12 Milt Pappas	2.25	1.10	.22
☐ 13 Wally Post	1.75	.85	.17
☐ 14 Jim Grant	1.75	.85	.17
☐ 15 Pete Runnels	2.25	1.10	.22
☐ 16 Ernie Broglio	2.25	1.10	.22
☐ 17 Johnny Callison	2.25	1.10	.22
☐ 18 Dodgers Team	10.00	2.50	.50
(checklist on back)			
☐ 19 Felix Mantilla	1.75	.85	.17
☐ 20 Roy Face	3.00	1.50	.30
☐ 21 Dutch Dotterer	1.75	.85	.17
☐ 22 Rocky Bridges	1.75	.85	.17
☐ 23 Eddie Fisher	1.75	.85	.17
☐ 24 Dick Gray	1.75	.85	.17
☐ 25 Roy Sievers	2.25	1.10	.22
☐ 26 Wayne Terwilliger	1.75	.85	.17
☐ 27 Dick Drott	1.75	.85	.17
☐ 28 Brooks Robinson	36.00	18.00	3.60
☐ 29 Clem Labine	2.25	1.10	.22
☐ 30 Tito Francona	1.75	.85	.17
☐ 31 Sammy Esposito	1.75	.85	.17
☐ 32 Sophomore Stalwarts	2.25	1.10	.22
Jim O'Toole			
Vada Pinson			
☐ 33 Tom Morgan	1.75	.85	.17
☐ 34 George Anderson	5.00	2.50	.50
☐ 35 Whitey Ford	33.00	15.00	3.00
☐ 36 Russ Nixon	2.25	1.10	.22
☐ 37 Bill Bruton	1.75	.85	.17
☐ 38 Jerry Casale	1.75	.85	.17
☐ 39 Earl Averill	1.75	.85	.17
☐ 40 Joe Cunningham	1.75	.85	.17
☐ 41 Barry Latman	1.75	.85	.17
☐ 42 Hobie Landrith	1.75	.85	.17
☐ 43 Senators Team	5.00	1.50	.30
(checklist on back)			
☐ 44 Bobby Locke	1.75	.85	.17
☐ 45 Roy McMillan	1.75	.85	.17
☐ 46 Jerry Fisher	1.75	.85	.17
☐ 47 Don Zimmer	3.50	1.75	.35
☐ 48 Hal W. Smith	1.75	.85	.17
☐ 49 Curt Raydon	1.75	.85	.17
☐ 50 Al Kaline	33.00	15.00	3.00
☐ 51 Jim Coates	1.75	.85	.17
☐ 52 Dave Philley	1.75	.85	.17
☐ 53 Jackie Brandt	1.75	.85	.17
☐ 54 Mike Fornieles	1.75	.85	.17
☐ 55 Bill Mazeroski	4.00	2.00	.40
☐ 56 Steve Korcheck	1.75	.85	.17
☐ 57 Win Savers	2.25	1.10	.22
Turk Lown			
Jerry Staley			
☐ 58 Gino Cimoli	1.75	.85	.17
☐ 59 Juan Pizarro	1.75	.85	.17
☐ 60 Gus Triandos	2.25	1.10	.22
☐ 61 Eddie Kasko	1.75	.85	.17
☐ 62 Roger Craig	4.00	2.00	.40
☐ 63 George Strickland	1.75	.85	.17
☐ 64 Jack Meyer	1.75	.85	.17
☐ 65 Elston Howard	4.00	2.00	.40
☐ 66 Bob Trowbridge	1.75	.85	.17
☐ 67 Jose Pagan	1.75	.85	.17
☐ 68 Dave Hillman	1.75	.85	.17
☐ 69 Billy Goodman	2.25	1.10	.22
☐ 70 Lew Burdette	3.00	1.50	.30
☐ 71 Marty Keough	1.75	.85	.17
☐ 72 Tigers Team	7.50	2.00	.40
(checklist on back)			
☐ 73 Bob Gibson	42.00	20.00	4.00
☐ 74 Walt Moryn	1.75	.85	.17
☐ 75 Vic Power	1.75	.85	.17
☐ 76 Bill Fischer	1.75	.85	.17
☐ 77 Hank Foiles	1.75	.85	.17
☐ 78 Bob Grim	1.75	.85	.17
☐ 79 Walt Dropo	1.75	.85	.17
☐ 80 Johnny Antonelli	2.25	1.10	.22
☐ 81 Russ Snyder	1.75	.85	.17
☐ 82 Ruben Gomez	1.75	.85	.17
☐ 83 Tony Kubek	5.00	2.50	.50
☐ 84 Hal R. Smith	1.75	.85	.17
☐ 85 Frank Lary	2.25	1.10	.22
☐ 86 Dick Gernert	1.75	.85	.17
☐ 87 John Romonosky	1.75	.85	.17
☐ 88 John Roseboro	2.25	1.10	.22
☐ 89 Hal Brown	1.75	.85	.17
☐ 90 Bobby Avila	1.75	.85	.17
☐ 91 Bennie Daniels	1.75	.85	.17

☐ 92 Whitey Herzog	3.50	1.75	.35
☐ 93 Art Schult	1.75	.85	.17
☐ 94 Leo Kiely	1.75	.85	.17
☐ 95 Frank Thomas	1.75	.85	.17
☐ 96 Ralph Terry	2.50	1.25	.25
☐ 97 Ted Lepcio	1.75	.85	.17
☐ 98 Gordon Jones	1.75	.85	.17
☐ 99 Lenny Green	1.75	.85	.17
☐ 100 Nellie Fox	6.50	3.25	.65
☐ 101 Bob Miller	1.75	.85	.17
☐ 102 Kent Hadley	1.75	.85	.17
☐ 103 Dick Farrell	1.75	.85	.17
☐ 104 Dick Schofield	1.75	.85	.17
☐ 105 Larry Sherry	2.50	1.25	.25
☐ 106 Billy Gardner	1.75	.85	.17
☐ 107 Carlton Willey	1.75	.85	.17
☐ 108 Pete Daley	1.75	.85	.17
☐ 109 Clete Boyer	2.50	1.25	.25
☐ 110 Cal McLish	1.75	.85	.17
☐ 111 Vic Wertz	2.25	1.10	.22
☐ 112 Jack Harshman	1.75	.85	.17
☐ 113 Bob Skinner	2.25	1.10	.22
☐ 114 Ken Aspromonte	1.75	.85	.17
☐ 115 Fork and Knuckler	4.00	2.00	.40
Roy Face			
Hoyt Wilhelm			
☐ 116 Jim Rivera	1.75	.85	.17
☐ 117 Tom Borland RP	1.75	.85	.17
☐ 118 Bob Bruce RP	1.75	.85	.17
☐ 119 Chico Cardenas RP	2.25	1.10	.22
☐ 120 Duke Carmel RP	1.75	.85	.17
☐ 121 Camilo Carreon RP	1.75	.85	.17
☐ 122 Don Dillard RP	1.75	.85	.17
☐ 123 Dan Dobbek RP	1.75	.85	.17
☐ 124 Jim Donohue RP	1.75	.85	.17
☐ 125 Dick Ellsworth RP	3.00	1.50	.30
☐ 126 Chuck Estrada RP	3.00	1.50	.30
☐ 127 Ron Hansen RP	1.75	.85	.17
☐ 128 Bill Harris RP	1.75	.85	.17
☐ 129 Bob Hartman RP	1.75	.85	.17
☐ 130 Frank Herrera RP	1.75	.85	.17
☐ 131 Ed Hobaugh RP	1.75	.85	.17
☐ 132 Frank Howard RP	12.00	6.00	1.20
☐ 133 Manuel Javier RP	3.00	1.50	.30
(sic, Julian)			
☐ 134 Deron Johnson RP	2.25	1.10	.22
☐ 135 Ken Johnson RP	1.75	.85	.17
☐ 136 Jim Kaat RP	25.00	12.50	2.50
☐ 137 Lou Klimchock RP	1.75	.85	.17
☐ 138 Art Mahaffey RP	2.25	1.10	.22
☐ 139 Carl Mathias RP	1.75	.85	.17
☐ 140 Julio Navarro RP	2.25	1.10	.22
☐ 141 Jim Proctor RP	1.75	.85	.17
☐ 142 Bill Short RP	2.25	1.10	.22
☐ 143 Al Spangler RP	1.75	.85	.17
☐ 144 Al Stieglitz RP	1.75	.85	.17
☐ 145 Jim Umbricht RP	1.75	.85	.17
☐ 146 Ted Wieand RP	1.75	.85	.17
☐ 147 Bob Will RP	1.75	.85	.17
☐ 148 Carl Yastrzemski RP	350.00	175.00	35.00
☐ 149 Bob Nieman	1.75	.85	.17
☐ 150 Billy Pierce	2.50	1.25	.25
☐ 151 Giants Team	6.00	1.75	.35
(checklist on back)			
☐ 152 Gail Harris	1.75	.85	.17
☐ 153 Bobby Thomson	3.00	1.50	.30
☐ 154 Jim Davenport	2.25	1.10	.22
☐ 155 Charlie Neal	2.25	1.10	.22
☐ 156 Art Ceccarelli	1.75	.85	.17
☐ 157 Rocky Nelson	1.75	.85	.17
☐ 158 Wes Covington	2.25	1.10	.22
☐ 159 Jim Piersall	3.00	1.50	.30
☐ 160 Rival All-Stars	33.00	15.00	3.00
Mickey Mantle			
Ken Boyer			
☐ 161 Ray Narleski	1.75	.85	.17
☐ 162 Sammy Taylor	1.75	.85	.17
☐ 163 Hector Lopez	1.75	.85	.17
☐ 164 Reds Team	6.00	1.75	.35
(checklist on back)			
☐ 165 Jack Sanford	2.25	1.10	.22
☐ 166 Chuck Essegian	1.75	.85	.17
☐ 167 Valmy Thomas	1.75	.85	.17
☐ 168 Alex Grammas	1.75	.85	.17
☐ 169 Jake Striker	1.75	.85	.17
☐ 170 Del Crandall	2.25	1.10	.22
☐ 171 Johnny Groth	1.75	.85	.17
☐ 172 Willie Kirkland	1.75	.85	.17
☐ 173 Billy Martin	10.00	5.00	1.00
☐ 174 Indians Team	5.00	1.75	.35
(checklist on back)			
☐ 175 Pedro Ramos	1.75	.85	.17
☐ 176 Vada Pinson	3.50	1.75	.35
☐ 177 Johnny Kucks	1.75	.85	.17

☐	178	Woody Held	1.75	.85	.17
☐	179	Rip Coleman	1.75	.85	.17
☐	180	Harry Simpson	1.75	.85	.17
☐	181	Billy Loes	1.75	.85	.17
☐	182	Glen Hobbie	1.75	.85	.17
☐	183	Eli Grba	1.75	.85	.17
☐	184	Gary Geiger	1.75	.85	.17
☐	185	Jim Owens	1.75	.85	.17
☐	186	Dave Sisler	1.75	.85	.17
☐	187	Jay Hook	1.75	.85	.17
☐	188	Dick Williams	2.50	1.25	.25
☐	189	Don McMahon	1.75	.85	.17
☐	190	Gene Woodling	2.25	1.10	.22
☐	191	Johnny Klippstein	1.75	.85	.17
☐	192	Danny O'Connell	1.75	.85	.17
☐	193	Dick Hyde	1.75	.85	.17
☐	194	Bobby Gene Smith	1.75	.85	.17
☐	195	Lindy McDaniel	2.25	1.10	.22
☐	196	Andy Carey	2.25	1.10	.22
☐	197	Ron Kline	1.75	.85	.17
☐	198	Jerry Lynch	1.75	.85	.17
☐	199	Dick Donovan	2.00	1.00	.20
☐	200	Willie Mays	100.00	50.00	10.00
☐	201	Larry Osborne	2.00	1.00	.20
☐	202	Fred Kipp	2.00	1.00	.20
☐	203	Sammy White	2.00	1.00	.20
☐	204	Ryne Duren	3.00	1.50	.30
☐	205	Johnny Logan	3.00	1.50	.30
☐	206	Claude Osteen	3.00	1.50	.30
☐	207	Bob Boyd	2.00	1.00	.20
☐	208	White Sox Team	5.00	1.75	.35
		(checklist on back)			
☐	209	Ron Blackburn	2.00	1.00	.20
☐	210	Harmon Killebrew	25.00	12.50	2.50
☐	211	Taylor Phillips	2.00	1.00	.20
☐	212	Walt Alston MG	10.00	5.00	1.00
☐	213	Chuck Dressen MG	2.00	1.00	.20
☐	214	Jimmy Dykes MG	2.00	1.00	.20
☐	215	Bob Elliott MG	2.00	1.00	.20
☐	216	Joe Gordon MG	2.00	1.00	.20
☐	217	Charlie Grimm MG	2.00	1.00	.20
☐	218	Solly Hemus MG	2.00	1.00	.20
☐	219	Fred Hutchinson MG	2.00	1.00	.20
☐	220	Billy Jurges MG	2.00	1.00	.20
☐	221	Cookie Lavagetto MG	2.00	1.00	.20
☐	222	Al Lopez MG	6.00	3.00	.60
☐	223	Danny Murtaugh MG	2.00	1.00	.20
☐	224	Paul Richards MG	2.00	1.00	.20
☐	225	Bill Rigney MG	2.00	1.00	.20
☐	226	Eddie Sawyer MG	2.00	1.00	.20
☐	227	Casey Stengel MG	15.00	7.50	1.50
☐	228	Ernie Johnson	2.00	1.00	.20
☐	229	Joe M. Morgan	5.00	2.50	.50
☐	230	Mound Magicians	5.00	2.50	.50
		Lou Burdette			
		Warren Spahn			
		Bob Buhl			
☐	231	Hal Naragon	2.00	1.00	.20
☐	232	Jim Busby	2.00	1.00	.20
☐	233	Don Elston	2.00	1.00	.20
☐	234	Don Demeter	2.00	1.00	.20
☐	235	Gus Bell	2.00	1.00	.20
☐	236	Dick Ricketts	2.00	1.00	.20
☐	237	Elmer Valo	2.00	1.00	.20
☐	238	Danny Kravitz	2.00	1.00	.20
☐	239	Joe Shipley	2.00	1.00	.20
☐	240	Luis Aparicio	12.50	6.25	1.25
☐	241	Albie Pearson	2.00	1.00	.20
☐	242	Cardinals Team	6.00	1.75	.35
		(checklist on back)			
☐	243	Bubba Phillips	2.00	1.00	.20
☐	244	Hal Griggs	2.00	1.00	.20
☐	245	Eddie Yost	2.00	1.00	.20
☐	246	Lee Maye	2.00	1.00	.20
☐	247	Gil McDougald	4.00	2.00	.40
☐	248	Del Rice	2.00	1.00	.20
☐	249	Earl Wilson	3.00	1.50	.30
☐	250	Stan Musial	90.00	45.00	9.00
☐	251	Bob Malkmus	2.00	1.00	.20
☐	252	Ray Herbert	2.00	1.00	.20
☐	253	Eddie Bressoud	2.00	1.00	.20
☐	254	Arnie Portocarrero	2.00	1.00	.20
☐	255	Jim Gilliam	4.00	2.00	.40
☐	256	Dick Brown	2.00	1.00	.20
☐	257	Gordy Coleman	3.00	1.50	.30
☐	258	Dick Groat	4.00	2.00	.40
☐	259	George Altman	2.00	1.00	.20
☐	260	Power Plus	3.00	1.50	.30
		Rocky Colavito			
		Tito Francona			
☐	261	Pete Burnside	2.00	1.00	.20
☐	262	Hank Bauer	3.00	1.50	.30
☐	263	Darrell Johnson	2.00	1.00	.20
☐	264	Robin Roberts	11.00	5.50	1.10
☐	265	Rip Repulski	2.00	1.00	.20
☐	266	Joey Jay	2.00	1.00	.20
☐	267	Jim Marshall	2.00	1.00	.20
☐	268	Al Worthington	2.00	1.00	.20
☐	269	Gene Green	2.00	1.00	.20
☐	270	Bob Turley	3.00	1.50	.30
☐	271	Julio Becquer	2.00	1.00	.20
☐	272	Fred Green	2.00	1.00	.20
☐	273	Neil Chrisley	2.00	1.00	.20
☐	274	Tom Acker	2.00	1.00	.20
☐	275	Curt Flood	3.50	1.75	.35
☐	276	Ken McBride	2.00	1.00	.20
☐	277	Harry Bright	2.00	1.00	.20
☐	278	Stan Williams	2.00	1.00	.20
☐	279	Chuck Tanner	3.00	1.50	.30
☐	280	Frank Sullivan	2.00	1.00	.20
☐	281	Ray Boone	2.00	1.00	.20
☐	282	Joe Nuxhall	3.00	1.50	.30
☐	283	John Blanchard	3.00	1.50	.30
☐	284	Don Gross	2.00	1.00	.20
☐	285	Harry Anderson	2.00	1.00	.20
☐	286	Ray Semproch	2.00	1.00	.20
☐	287	Felipe Alou	3.00	1.50	.30
☐	288	Bob Mabe	2.25	1.10	.22
☐	289	Willie Jones	2.25	1.10	.22
☐	290	Jerry Lumpe	2.25	1.10	.22
☐	291	Bob Keegan	2.25	1.10	.22
☐	292	Dodger Backstops	3.00	1.50	.30
		Joe Pignatano			
		John Roseboro			
☐	293	Gene Conley	2.25	1.10	.22
☐	294	Tony Taylor	2.25	1.10	.22
☐	295	Gil Hodges	14.00	7.00	1.40
☐	296	Nelson Chittum	2.25	1.10	.22
☐	297	Reno Bertoia	2.25	1.10	.22
☐	298	George Witt	2.25	1.10	.22
☐	299	Earl Torgeson	2.25	1.10	.22
☐	300	Hank Aaron	100.00	50.00	10.00
☐	301	Jerry Davie	2.25	1.10	.22
☐	302	Phillies Team	5.00	1.75	.35
		(checklist on back)			
☐	303	Billy O'Dell	2.25	1.10	.22
☐	304	Joe Ginsberg	2.25	1.10	.22
☐	305	Richie Ashburn	7.00	3.50	.70
☐	306	Frank Baumann	2.25	1.10	.22
☐	307	Gene Oliver	2.25	1.10	.22
☐	308	Dick Hall	2.25	1.10	.22
☐	309	Bob Hale	2.25	1.10	.22
☐	310	Frank Malzone	3.00	1.50	.30
☐	311	Raul Sanchez	2.25	1.10	.22
☐	312	Charley Lau	3.00	1.50	.30
☐	313	Turk Lown	2.25	1.10	.22
☐	314	Chico Fernandez	2.25	1.10	.22
☐	315	Bobby Shantz	3.50	1.75	.35
☐	316	Willie McCovey	200.00	100.00	20.00
☐	317	Pumpsie Green	2.25	1.10	.22
☐	318	Jim Baxes	2.25	1.10	.22
☐	319	Joe Koppe	2.25	1.10	.22
☐	320	Bob Allison	3.00	1.50	.30
☐	321	Ron Fairly	3.00	1.50	.30
☐	322	Willie Tasby	2.25	1.10	.22
☐	323	John Romano	2.25	1.10	.22
☐	324	Jim Perry	3.50	1.75	.35
☐	325	Jim O'Toole	3.00	1.50	.30
☐	326	Bob Clemente	90.00	45.00	9.00
☐	327	Ray Sadecki	2.25	1.10	.22
☐	328	Earl Battey	2.25	1.10	.22
☐	329	Zack Monroe	2.25	1.10	.22
☐	330	Harvey Kuenn	3.50	1.75	.35
☐	331	Henry Mason	2.25	1.10	.22
☐	332	Yankees Team	20.00	6.00	1.25
		(checklist on back)			
☐	333	Danny McDevitt	2.25	1.10	.22
☐	334	Ted Abernathy	2.25	1.10	.22
☐	335	Red Schoendienst	10.00	5.00	1.00
☐	336	Ike Delock	2.25	1.10	.22
☐	337	Cal Neeman	2.25	1.10	.22
☐	338	Ray Monzant	2.25	1.10	.22
☐	339	Harry Chiti	2.25	1.10	.22
☐	340	Harvey Haddix	3.00	1.50	.30
☐	341	Carroll Hardy	2.25	1.10	.22
☐	342	Casey Wise	2.25	1.10	.22
☐	343	Sandy Koufax	100.00	50.00	10.00
☐	344	Clint Courtney	2.25	1.10	.22
☐	345	Don Newcombe	3.50	1.75	.35
☐	346	J.C. Martin UER	2.25	1.10	.22
		(face actually			
		Gary Peters)			
☐	347	Ed Bouchee	2.25	1.10	.22
☐	348	Barry Shetrone	2.25	1.10	.22
☐	349	Moe Drabowsky	2.25	1.10	.22
☐	350	Mickey Mantle	300.00	150.00	30.00
☐	351	Don Nottebart	2.25	1.10	.22

☐ 352	Cincy Clouters	4.00	2.00	.40
	Gus Bell			
	Frank Robinson			
	Jerry Lynch			
☐ 353	Don Larsen	3.00	1.50	.30
☐ 354	Bob Lillis	3.00	1.50	.30
☐ 355	Bill White	4.00	2.00	.40
☐ 356	Joe Amalfitano	2.25	1.10	.22
☐ 357	Al Schroll	2.25	1.10	.22
☐ 358	Joe DeMaestri	2.25	1.10	.22
☐ 359	Buddy Gilbert	2.25	1.10	.22
☐ 360	Herb Score	3.00	1.50	.30
☐ 361	Bob Oldis	2.25	1.10	.22
☐ 362	Russ Kemmerer	2.25	1.10	.22
☐ 363	Gene Stephens	2.25	1.10	.22
☐ 364	Paul Foytack	2.25	1.10	.22
☐ 365	Minnie Minoso	4.00	2.00	.40
☐ 366	Dallas Green	9.00	4.50	.90
☐ 367	Bill Tuttle	2.25	1.10	.22
☐ 368	Daryl Spencer	2.25	1.10	.22
☐ 369	Billy Hoeft	2.25	1.10	.22
☐ 370	Bill Skowron	5.00	2.50	.50
☐ 371	Bud Byerly	2.25	1.10	.22
☐ 372	Frank House	2.25	1.10	.22
☐ 373	Don Hoak	2.25	1.10	.22
☐ 374	Bob Buhl	2.25	1.10	.22
☐ 375	Dale Long	3.00	1.50	.30
☐ 376	John Briggs	2.25	1.10	.22
☐ 377	Roger Maris	100.00	50.00	10.00
☐ 378	Stu Miller	2.25	1.10	.22
☐ 379	Red Wilson	2.25	1.10	.22
☐ 380	Bob Shaw	2.25	1.10	.22
☐ 381	Braves Team	5.00	1.75	.35
	(checklist on back)			
☐ 382	Ted Bowsfield	2.25	1.10	.22
☐ 383	Leon Wagner	2.25	1.10	.22
☐ 384	Don Cardwell	2.25	1.10	.22
☐ 385	World Series Game 1	4.50	2.25	.45
	Neal Steals Second			
☐ 386	World Series Game 2	4.50	2.25	.45
	Neal Belts 2nd Homer			
☐ 387	World Series Game 3	4.50	2.25	.45
	Furillo Breaks Game			
☐ 388	World Series Game 4	6.00	3.00	.60
	Hodges' Homer			
☐ 389	World Series Game 5	6.00	3.00	.60
	Luis Swipes Base			
☐ 390	World Series Game 6	4.50	2.25	.45
	Scrambling After Ball			
☐ 391	World Series Summary	4.50	2.25	.45
	The Champs Celebrate			
☐ 392	Tex Clevenger	2.25	1.10	.22
☐ 393	Smoky Burgess	3.00	1.50	.30
☐ 394	Norm Larker	2.25	1.10	.22
☐ 395	Hoyt Wilhelm	11.00	5.50	1.10
☐ 396	Steve Bilko	2.25	1.10	.22
☐ 397	Don Blasingame	2.25	1.10	.22
☐ 398	Mike Cuellar	3.00	1.50	.30
☐ 399	Young Hill Stars	3.00	1.50	.30
	Milt Pappas			
	Jack Fisher			
	Jerry Walker			
☐ 400	Rocky Colavito	6.50	3.25	.65
☐ 401	Bob Duliba	2.25	1.10	.22
☐ 402	Dick Stuart	3.00	1.50	.30
☐ 403	Ed Sadowski	2.25	1.10	.22
☐ 404	Bob Rush	2.25	1.10	.22
☐ 405	Bobby Richardson	5.00	2.50	.50
☐ 406	Billy Klaus	2.25	1.10	.22
☐ 407	Gary Peters UER	3.00	1.50	.30
	(face actually			
	J.C. Martin)			
☐ 408	Carl Furillo	4.00	2.00	.40
☐ 409	Ron Samford	2.25	1.10	.22
☐ 410	Sam Jones	2.25	1.10	.22
☐ 411	Ed Bailey	2.25	1.10	.22
☐ 412	Bob Anderson	2.25	1.10	.22
☐ 413	Athletics Team	5.00	1.75	.35
	(checklist on back)			
☐ 414	Don Williams	2.25	1.10	.22
☐ 415	Bob Cerv	3.00	1.50	.30
☐ 416	Humberto Robinson	2.25	1.10	.22
☐ 417	Chuck Cottier	3.00	1.50	.30
☐ 418	Don Mossi	3.00	1.50	.30
☐ 419	George Crowe	2.25	1.10	.22
☐ 420	Eddie Mathews	28.00	14.00	2.80
☐ 421	Duke Maas	2.25	1.10	.22
☐ 422	John Powers	2.25	1.10	.22
☐ 423	Ed Fitzgerald	2.25	1.10	.22
☐ 424	Pete Whisenant	2.25	1.10	.22
☐ 425	Johnny Podres	3.50	1.75	.35
☐ 426	Ron Jackson	2.25	1.10	.22
☐ 427	Al Grunwald	2.25	1.10	.22
☐ 428	Al Smith	2.25	1.10	.22

☐ 429	AL Kings	4.00	2.00	.40
	Nellie Fox			
	Harvey Kuenn			
☐ 430	Art Ditmar	2.25	1.10	.22
☐ 431	Andre Rodgers	2.25	1.10	.22
☐ 432	Chuck Stobbs	2.25	1.10	.22
☐ 433	Irv Noren	2.25	1.10	.22
☐ 434	Brooks Lawrence	2.25	1.10	.22
☐ 435	Gene Freese	2.25	1.10	.22
☐ 436	Marv Throneberry	3.00	1.50	.30
☐ 437	Bob Friend	3.00	1.50	.30
☐ 438	Jim Coker	2.25	1.10	.22
☐ 439	Tom Brewer	2.25	1.10	.22
☐ 440	Jim Lemon	3.00	1.50	.30
☐ 441	Gary Bell	3.50	1.75	.35
☐ 442	Joe Pignatano	3.50	1.75	.35
☐ 443	Charley Maxwell	3.50	1.75	.35
☐ 444	Jerry Kindall	3.50	1.75	.35
☐ 445	Warren Spahn	36.00	18.00	3.60
☐ 446	Ellis Burton	3.50	1.75	.35
☐ 447	Ray Moore	3.50	1.75	.35
☐ 448	Jim Gentile	6.00	3.00	.60
☐ 449	Jim Brosnan	3.50	1.75	.35
☐ 450	Orlando Cepeda	10.00	5.00	1.00
☐ 451	Curt Simmons	4.50	2.25	.45
☐ 452	Ray Webster	3.50	1.75	.35
☐ 453	Vern Law	4.50	2.25	.45
☐ 454	Hal Woodeshick	3.50	1.75	.35
☐ 455	Baltimore Coaches	4.50	2.25	.45
	Eddie Robinson			
	Harry Brecheen			
	Luman Harris			
☐ 456	Red Sox Coaches	6.00	3.00	.60
	Rudy York			
	Billy Herman			
	Sal Maglie			
	Del Baker			
☐ 457	Cubs Coaches	4.50	2.25	.45
	Charlie Root			
	Lou Klein			
	Elvin Tappe			
☐ 458	White Sox Coaches	4.50	2.25	.45
	Johnny Cooney			
	Don Gutteridge			
	Tony Cuccinello			
	Ray Berres			
☐ 459	Reds Coaches	4.50	2.25	.45
	Reggie Otero			
	Cot Deal			
	Wally Moses			
☐ 460	Indians Coaches	6.00	3.00	.60
	Mel Harder			
	Jo-Jo White			
	Bob Lemon			
	Ralph(Red) Kress			
☐ 461	Tigers Coaches	6.00	3.00	.60
	Tom Ferrick			
	Luke Appling			
	Billy Hitchcock			
☐ 462	Athletics Coaches	4.50	2.25	.45
	Fred Fitzsimmons			
	Don Heffner			
	Walker Cooper			
☐ 463	Dodgers Coaches	6.00	3.00	.60
	Bobby Bragan			
	Pete Reiser			
	Joe Becker			
	Greg Mulleavy			
☐ 464	Braves Coaches	4.50	2.25	.45
	Bob Scheffing			
	Whitlow Wyatt			
	Andy Pafko			
	George Myatt			
☐ 465	Yankees Coaches	10.00	5.00	1.00
	Bill Dickey			
	Ralph Houk			
	Frank Crosetti			
	Ed Lopat			
☐ 466	Phillies Coaches	4.50	2.25	.45
	Ken Silvestri			
	Dick Carter			
	Andy Cohen			
☐ 467	Pirates Coaches	4.50	2.25	.45
	Mickey Vernon			
	Frank Oceak			
	Sam Narron			
	Bill Burwell			
☐ 468	Cardinals Coaches	4.50	2.25	.45
	Johnny Keane			
	Howie Pollet			
	Ray Katt			
	Harry Walker			

□ 469 Giants Coaches	4.50	2.25	.45
Wes Westrum			
Salty Parker			
Bill Posedel			
□ 470 Senators Coaches	4.50	2.25	.45
Bob Swift			
Ellis Clary			
Sam Mele			
□ 471 Ned Garver	3.50	1.75	.35
□ 472 Alvin Dark	4.50	2.25	.45
□ 473 Al Cicotte	3.50	1.75	.35
□ 474 Haywood Sullivan	3.50	1.75	.35
□ 475 Don Drysdale	30.00	15.00	3.00
□ 476 Lou Johnson	4.50	2.25	.45
□ 477 Don Ferrarese	3.50	1.75	.35
□ 478 Frank Torre	3.50	1.75	.35
□ 479 Georges Maranda	3.50	1.75	.35
□ 480 Yogi Berra	55.00	27.50	5.50
□ 481 Wes Stock	3.50	1.75	.35
□ 482 Frank Bolling	3.50	1.75	.35
□ 483 Camilo Pascual	4.50	2.25	.45
□ 484 Pirates Team	12.50	4.00	1.00
(checklist on back)			
□ 485 Ken Boyer	6.00	3.00	.60
□ 486 Bobby Del Greco	3.50	1.75	.35
□ 487 Tom Sturdivant	3.50	1.75	.35
□ 488 Norm Cash	6.00	3.00	.60
□ 489 Steve Ridzik	3.50	1.75	.35
□ 490 Frank Robinson	40.00	20.00	4.00
□ 491 Mel Roach	3.50	1.75	.35
□ 492 Larry Jackson	3.50	1.75	.35
□ 493 Duke Snider	42.00	20.00	4.00
□ 494 Orioles Team	8.00	2.00	.40
(checklist on back)			
□ 495 Sherm Lollar	4.50	2.25	.45
□ 496 Bill Virdon	5.00	2.50	.50
□ 497 John Tsitouris	3.50	1.75	.35
□ 498 Al Pilarcik	3.50	1.75	.35
□ 499 Johnny James	3.50	1.75	.35
□ 500 Johnny Temple	3.50	1.75	.35
□ 501 Bob Schmidt	3.50	1.75	.35
□ 502 Jim Bunning	9.00	4.50	.90
□ 503 Don Lee	3.50	1.75	.35
□ 504 Seth Morehead	3.50	1.75	.35
□ 505 Ted Kluszewski	5.00	2.50	.50
□ 506 Lee Walls	3.50	1.75	.35
□ 507 Dick Stigman	10.00	5.00	1.00
□ 508 Billy Consolo	10.00	5.00	1.00
□ 509 Tommy Davis	16.00	8.00	1.60
□ 510 Jerry Staley	10.00	5.00	1.00
□ 511 Ken Walters	10.00	5.00	1.00
□ 512 Joe Gibbon	10.00	5.00	1.00
□ 513 Chicago Cubs	27.00	8.00	2.00
Team Card			
(checklist on back)			
□ 514 Steve Barber	10.00	5.00	1.00
□ 515 Stan Lopata	10.00	5.00	1.00
□ 516 Marty Kutyna	10.00	5.00	1.00
□ 517 Charlie James	10.00	5.00	1.00
□ 518 Tony Gonzalez	10.00	5.00	1.00
□ 519 Ed Roebuck	10.00	5.00	1.00
□ 520 Don Buddin	10.00	5.00	1.00
□ 521 Mike Lee	10.00	5.00	1.00
□ 522 Ken Hunt	10.00	5.00	1.00
□ 523 Clay Dalrymple	10.00	5.00	1.00
□ 524 Bill Henry	10.00	5.00	1.00
□ 525 Marv Breeding	10.00	5.00	1.00
□ 526 Paul Giel	10.00	5.00	1.00
□ 527 Jose Valdivielso	10.00	5.00	1.00
□ 528 Ben Johnson	10.00	5.00	1.00
□ 529 Norm Sherry	11.00	5.50	1.10
□ 530 Mike McCormick	11.00	5.50	1.10
□ 531 Sandy Amoros	11.00	5.50	1.10
□ 532 Mike Garcia	12.00	6.00	1.20
□ 533 Lu Clinton	10.00	5.00	1.00
□ 534 Ken MacKenzie	10.00	5.00	1.00
□ 535 Whitey Lockman	11.00	5.50	1.10
□ 536 Wynn Hawkins	10.00	5.00	1.00
□ 537 Boston Red Sox	27.00	8.00	2.00
Team Card			
(checklist on back)			
□ 538 Frank Barnes	10.00	5.00	1.00
□ 539 Gene Baker	10.00	5.00	1.00
□ 540 Jerry Walker	10.00	5.00	1.00
□ 541 Tony Curry	10.00	5.00	1.00
□ 542 Ken Hamlin	10.00	5.00	1.00
□ 543 Elio Chacon	10.00	5.00	1.00
□ 544 Bill Monbouquette	11.00	5.50	1.10
□ 545 Carl Sawatski	10.00	5.00	1.00
□ 546 Hank Aguirre	10.00	5.00	1.00
□ 547 Bob Aspromonte	10.00	5.00	1.00
□ 548 Don Mincher	12.00	6.00	1.20
□ 549 John Buzhardt	10.00	5.00	1.00
□ 550 Jim Landis	10.00	5.00	1.00
□ 551 Ed Rakow	10.00	5.00	1.00
□ 552 Walt Bond	10.00	5.00	1.00
□ 553 Bill Skowron AS	13.50	6.25	1.25
□ 554 Willie McCovey AS	50.00	25.00	5.00
□ 555 Nellie Fox AS	15.00	7.50	1.50
□ 556 Charlie Neal AS	12.00	6.00	1.20
□ 557 Frank Malzone AS	12.00	6.00	1.20
□ 558 Eddie Mathews AS	24.00	12.00	2.40
□ 559 Luis Aparicio AS	18.00	9.00	1.80
□ 560 Ernie Banks AS	35.00	17.50	3.50
□ 561 Al Kaline AS	35.00	17.50	3.50
□ 562 Joe Cunningham AS	12.00	6.00	1.20
□ 563 Mickey Mantle AS	200.00	100.00	20.00
□ 564 Willie Mays AS	100.00	50.00	10.00
□ 565 Roger Maris AS	100.00	50.00	10.00
□ 566 Hank Aaron AS	100.00	50.00	10.00
□ 567 Sherm Lollar AS	12.00	6.00	1.20
□ 568 Del Crandall AS	12.00	6.00	1.20
□ 569 Camilo Pascual AS	12.00	6.00	1.20
□ 570 Don Drysdale AS	20.00	10.00	2.00
□ 571 Billy Pierce AS	12.00	6.00	1.20
□ 572 Johnny Antonelli AS	16.00	7.00	1.50

1961 Topps

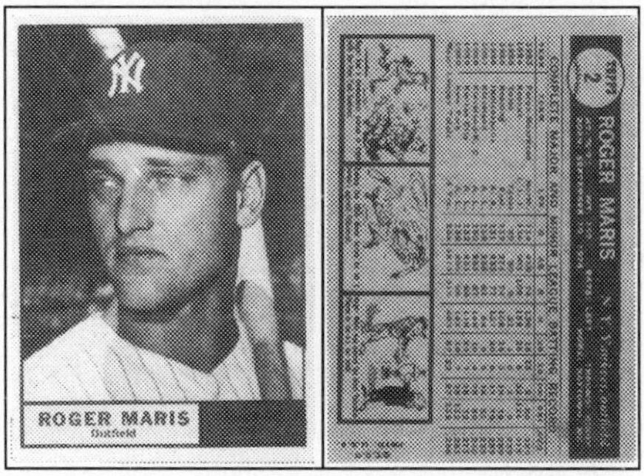

The cards in this 587-card set measure 2 1/2" by 3 1/2". In 1961, Topps returned to the vertical obverse format. Introduced for the first time were "League Leaders" (41 to 50) and separate, numbered checklist cards. Two number 463s exist: the Braves team card carrying that number was meant to be number 426. There are three versions of the second series checklist card number 98; the variations are distinguished by the color of the "CHECKLIST" headline on the front of the card, the color of the printing of the card number on the bottom of the reverse, and the presence of the copyright notice running vertically on the card back. There are two groups of managers (131-139 and 219-226) as well as separate series of World Series cards (306-313), Baseball Thrills (401 to 410), previous MVP's (AL 471-478 and NL 479-486) and Sporting News All-Stars (566 to 589). The usual last series scarcity (523 to 589) exists. The set actually totals 587 cards since numbers 587 and 588 were never issued. The key rookies in this set are ex-Cubs Ron Santo and Billy Williams.

	NRMT	VG-E	GOOD
COMPLETE SET (587)	5000.00	2300.00	500.00
COMMON PLAYER (1-110)	1.50	.75	.15
COMMON PLAYER (111-370)	1.75	.85	.17
COMMON PLAYER (371-446)	2.50	1.25	.25
COMMON PLAYER (447-522)	3.00	1.50	.30
COMMON PLAYER (523-565)	27.00	13.50	2.70
COMMON PLAYER (566-589)	30.00	15.00	3.00
□ 1 Dick Groat	16.00	1.75	.35
□ 2 Roger Maris	125.00	40.00	8.00
□ 3 John Buzhardt	1.50	.75	.15
□ 4 Lenny Green	1.50	.75	.15
□ 5 John Romano	1.50	.75	.15
□ 6 Ed Roebuck	1.50	.75	.15
□ 7 White Sox Team	3.50	1.75	.35
□ 8 Dick Williams	2.00	1.00	.20

☐ 9	Bob Purkey	1.50	.75	.15
☐ 10	Brooks Robinson	30.00	15.00	3.00
☐ 11	Curt Simmons	2.00	1.00	.20
☐ 12	Moe Thacker	1.50	.75	.15
☐ 13	Chuck Cottier	1.50	.75	.15
☐ 14	Don Mossi	2.00	1.00	.20
☐ 15	Willie Kirkland	1.50	.75	.15
☐ 16	Billy Muffett	1.50	.75	.15
☐ 17	Checklist 1	9.00	.90	.20
☐ 18	Jim Grant	1.50	.75	.15
☐ 19	Clete Boyer	2.00	1.00	.20
☐ 20	Robin Roberts	10.00	5.00	1.00
☐ 21	Zorro Versalles	2.00	1.00	.20
	(first name should			
	be Zoilo)			
☐ 22	Clem Labine	2.00	1.00	.20
☐ 23	Don Demeter	1.50	.75	.15
☐ 24	Ken Johnson	1.50	.75	.15
☐ 25	Reds' Heavy Artillery	4.50	2.25	.45
	Vada Pinson			
	Gus Bell			
	Frank Robinson			
☐ 26	Wes Stock	1.50	.75	.15
☐ 27	Jerry Kindall	1.50	.75	.15
☐ 28	Hector Lopez	1.50	.75	.15
☐ 29	Don Nottebart	1.50	.75	.15
☐ 30	Nellie Fox	6.00	3.00	.60
☐ 31	Bob Schmidt	1.50	.75	.15
☐ 32	Ray Sadecki	1.50	.75	.15
☐ 33	Gary Geiger	1.50	.75	.15
☐ 34	Wynn Hawkins	1.50	.75	.15
☐ 35	Ron Santo	25.00	12.50	2.50
☐ 36	Jack Kralick	1.50	.75	.15
☐ 37	Charley Maxwell	1.50	.75	.15
☐ 38	Bob Lillis	1.50	.75	.15
☐ 39	Leo Posada	1.50	.75	.15
☐ 40	Bob Turley	2.50	1.25	.25
☐ 41	NL Batting Leaders	5.00	2.50	.50
	Dick Groat			
	Norm Larker			
	Willie Mays			
	Roberto Clemente			
☐ 42	AL Batting Leaders	2.50	1.25	.25
	Pete Runnels			
	Al Smith			
	Minnie Minoso			
	Bill Skowron			
☐ 43	NL Home Run Leaders	7.00	3.50	.70
	Ernie Banks			
	Hank Aaron			
	Ed Mathews			
	Ken Boyer			
☐ 44	AL Home Run Leaders	18.00	9.00	1.80
	Mickey Mantle			
	Roger Maris			
	Jim Lemon			
	Rocky Colavito			
☐ 45	NL ERA Leaders	2.50	1.25	.25
	Mike McCormick			
	Ernie Broglio			
	Don Drysdale			
	Bob Friend			
	Stan Williams			
☐ 46	AL ERA Leaders	2.50	1.25	.25
	Frank Baumann			
	Jim Bunning			
	Art Ditmar			
	H. Brown			
☐ 47	NL Pitching Leaders	2.50	1.25	.25
	Ernie Broglio			
	Warren Spahn			
	Vern Law			
	Lou Burdette			
☐ 48	AL Pitching Leaders	2.50	1.25	.25
	Chuck Estrada			
	Jim Perry			
	Bud Daley			
	Art Ditmar			
	Frank Lary			
	Milt Pappas			
☐ 49	NL Strikeout Leaders	4.00	2.00	.40
	Don Drysdale			
	Sandy Koufax			
	Sam Jones			
	Ernie Broglio			
☐ 50	AL Strikeout Leaders	2.50	1.25	.25
	Jim Bunning			
	Pedro Ramos			
	Early Wynn			
	Frank Lary			
☐ 51	Detroit Tigers	3.50	1.75	.35
	Team Card			
☐ 52	George Crowe	1.50	.75	.15
☐ 53	Russ Nixon	2.00	1.00	.20
☐ 54	Earl Francis	1.50	.75	.15
☐ 55	Jim Davenport	2.00	1.00	.20
☐ 56	Russ Kemmerer	1.50	.75	.15
☐ 57	Marv Throneberry	2.00	1.00	.20
☐ 58	Joe Schaffernoth	1.50	.75	.15
☐ 59	Jim Woods	1.50	.75	.15
☐ 60	Woody Held	1.50	.75	.15
☐ 61	Ron Piche	1.50	.75	.15
☐ 62	Al Pilarcik	1.50	.75	.15
☐ 63	Jim Kaat	7.50	3.75	.75
☐ 64	Alex Grammas	1.50	.75	.15
☐ 65	Ted Kluszewski	3.50	1.75	.35
☐ 66	Billy Henry	1.50	.75	.15
☐ 67	Ossie Virgil	1.50	.75	.15
☐ 68	Deron Johnson	2.00	1.00	.20
☐ 69	Earl Wilson	1.50	.75	.15
☐ 70	Bill Virdon	2.50	1.25	.25
☐ 71	Jerry Adair	1.50	.75	.15
☐ 72	Stu Miller	1.50	.75	.15
☐ 73	Al Spangler	1.50	.75	.15
☐ 74	Joe Pignatano	1.50	.75	.15
☐ 75	Lindy Shows Larry	2.00	1.00	.20
	Lindy McDaniel			
	Larry Jackson			
☐ 76	Harry Anderson	1.50	.75	.15
☐ 77	Dick Stigman	1.50	.75	.15
☐ 78	Lee Walls	1.50	.75	.15
☐ 79	Joe Ginsberg	1.50	.75	.15
☐ 80	Harmon Killebrew	20.00	10.00	2.00
☐ 81	Tracy Stallard	1.50	.75	.15
☐ 82	Joe Christopher	1.50	.75	.15
☐ 83	Bob Bruce	1.50	.75	.15
☐ 84	Lee Maye	1.50	.75	.15
☐ 85	Jerry Walker	1.50	.75	.15
☐ 86	Los Angeles Dodgers	4.00	2.00	.40
	Team Card			
☐ 87	Joe Amalfitano	1.50	.75	.15
☐ 88	Richie Ashburn	6.50	3.25	.65
☐ 89	Billy Martin	6.50	3.25	.65
☐ 90	Jerry Staley	1.50	.75	.15
☐ 91	Walt Moryn	1.50	.75	.15
☐ 92	Hal Naragon	1.50	.75	.15
☐ 93	Tony Gonzalez	1.50	.75	.15
☐ 94	Johnny Kucks	1.50	.75	.15
☐ 95	Norm Cash	3.50	1.75	.35
☐ 96	Billy O'Dell	1.50	.75	.15
☐ 97	Jerry Lynch	1.50	.75	.15
☐ 98A	Checklist 2	9.00	.90	.20
	(red "Checklist",			
	98 black on white)			
☐ 98B	Checklist 2	9.00	.90	.20
	(yellow "Checklist",			
	98 black on white)			
☐ 98C	Checklist 2	9.00	.90	.20
	(yellow "Checklist",			
	98 white on black,			
	no copyright)			
☐ 99	Don Buddin UER	1.50	.75	.15
	(66 HR's)			
☐ 100	Harvey Haddix	2.50	1.25	.25
☐ 101	Bubba Phillips	1.50	.75	.15
☐ 102	Gene Stephens	1.50	.75	.15
☐ 103	Ruben Amaro	1.50	.75	.15
☐ 104	John Blanchard	2.00	1.00	.20
☐ 105	Carl Willey	1.50	.75	.15
☐ 106	Whitey Herzog	3.00	1.50	.30
☐ 107	Seth Morehead	1.50	.75	.15
☐ 108	Dan Dobbek	1.50	.75	.15
☐ 109	Johnny Podres	2.50	1.25	.25
☐ 110	Vada Pinson	3.00	1.50	.30
☐ 111	Jack Meyer	1.75	.85	.17
☐ 112	Chico Fernandez	1.75	.85	.17
☐ 113	Mike Fornieles	1.75	.85	.17
☐ 114	Hobie Landrith	1.75	.85	.17
☐ 115	Johnny Antonelli	2.25	1.10	.22
☐ 116	Joe DeMaestri	1.75	.85	.17
☐ 117	Dale Long	2.25	1.10	.22
☐ 118	Chris Cannizzaro	1.75	.85	.17
☐ 119	A's Big Armor	2.25	1.10	.22
	Norm Siebern			
	Hank Bauer			
	Jerry Lumpe			
☐ 120	Eddie Mathews	22.00	11.00	2.20
☐ 121	Eli Grba	1.75	.85	.17
☐ 122	Chicago Cubs	3.50	1.75	.35
	Team Card			
☐ 123	Billy Gardner	2.25	1.10	.22
☐ 124	J.C. Martin	1.75	.85	.17
☐ 125	Steve Barber	1.75	.85	.17
☐ 126	Dick Stuart	2.25	1.10	.22
☐ 127	Ron Kline	1.75	.85	.17
☐ 128	Rip Repulski	1.75	.85	.17
☐ 129	Ed Hobaugh	1.75	.85	.17
☐ 130	Norm Larker	1.75	.85	.17

☐ 131 Paul Richards MG	1.75	.85	.17
☐ 132 Al Lopez MG	4.00	2.00	.40
☐ 133 Ralph Houk MG	3.00	1.50	.30
☐ 134 Mickey Vernon MG	2.25	1.10	.22
☐ 135 Fred Hutchinson MG	2.25	1.10	.22
☐ 136 Walt Alston MG	5.00	2.50	.50
☐ 137 Chuck Dressen MG	1.75	.85	.17
☐ 138 Danny Murtaugh MG	1.75	.85	.17
☐ 139 Solly Hemus MG	1.75	.85	.17
☐ 140 Gus Triandos	2.25	1.10	.22
☐ 141 Billy Williams	120.00	60.00	12.00
☐ 142 Luis Arroyo	2.25	1.10	.22
☐ 143 Russ Snyder	1.75	.85	.17
☐ 144 Jim Coker	1.75	.85	.17
☐ 145 Bob Buhl	1.75	.85	.17
☐ 146 Marty Keough	1.75	.85	.17
☐ 147 Ed Rakow	1.75	.85	.17
☐ 148 Julian Javier	1.75	.85	.17
☐ 149 Bob Oldis	1.75	.85	.17
☐ 150 Willie Mays	100.00	50.00	10.00
☐ 151 Jim Donohue	1.75	.85	.17
☐ 152 Earl Torgeson	1.75	.85	.17
☐ 153 Don Lee	1.75	.85	.17
☐ 154 Bobby Del Greco	1.75	.85	.17
☐ 155 Johnny Temple	2.25	1.10	.22
☐ 156 Ken Hunt	1.75	.85	.17
☐ 157 Cal McLish	1.75	.85	.17
☐ 158 Pete Daley	1.75	.85	.17
☐ 159 Orioles Team	3.50	1.75	.35
☐ 160 Whitey Ford UER (incorrectly listed as 5'0" tall)	33.00	15.00	3.00
☐ 161 Sherman Jones UER (photo actually Eddie Fisher)	1.75	.85	.17
☐ 162 Jay Hook	1.75	.85	.17
☐ 163 Ed Sadowski	1.75	.85	.17
☐ 164 Felix Mantilla	1.75	.85	.17
☐ 165 Gino Cimoli	1.75	.85	.17
☐ 166 Danny Kravitz	1.75	.85	.17
☐ 167 San Francisco Giants Team Card	3.50	1.75	.35
☐ 168 Tommy Davis	4.00	2.00	.40
☐ 169 Don Elston	1.75	.85	.17
☐ 170 Al Smith	1.75	.85	.17
☐ 171 Paul Foytack	1.75	.85	.17
☐ 172 Don Dillard	1.75	.85	.17
☐ 173 Beantown Bombers Frank Malzone Vic Wertz Jackie Jensen	2.25	1.10	.22
☐ 174 Ray Semproch	1.75	.85	.17
☐ 175 Gene Freese	1.75	.85	.17
☐ 176 Ken Aspromonte	1.75	.85	.17
☐ 177 Don Larsen	2.50	1.25	.25
☐ 178 Bob Nieman	1.75	.85	.17
☐ 179 Joe Koppe	1.75	.85	.17
☐ 180 Bobby Richardson	5.00	2.50	.50
☐ 181 Fred Green	1.75	.85	.17
☐ 182 Dave Nicholson	1.75	.85	.17
☐ 183 Andre Rodgers	1.75	.85	.17
☐ 184 Steve Bilko	1.75	.85	.17
☐ 185 Herb Score	2.25	1.10	.22
☐ 186 Elmer Valo	1.75	.85	.17
☐ 187 Billy Klaus	1.75	.85	.17
☐ 188 Jim Marshall	1.75	.85	.17
☐ 189A Checklist 3 (copyright symbol almost adjacent to 263 Ken Hamlin)	9.00	.90	.20
☐ 189B Checklist 3 (copyright symbol adjacent to 264 Glen Hobbie)	9.00	.90	.20
☐ 190 Stan Williams	1.75	.85	.17
☐ 191 Mike De La Hoz	1.75	.85	.17
☐ 192 Dick Brown	1.75	.85	.17
☐ 193 Gene Conley	1.75	.85	.17
☐ 194 Gordy Coleman	2.25	1.10	.22
☐ 195 Jerry Casale	1.75	.85	.17
☐ 196 Ed Bouchee	1.75	.85	.17
☐ 197 Dick Hall	1.75	.85	.17
☐ 198 Carl Sawatski	1.75	.85	.17
☐ 199 Bob Boyd	1.75	.85	.17
☐ 200 Warren Spahn	25.00	12.50	2.50
☐ 201 Pete Whisenant	1.75	.85	.17
☐ 202 Al Neiger	1.75	.85	.17
☐ 203 Eddie Bressoud	1.75	.85	.17
☐ 204 Bob Skinner	2.25	1.10	.22
☐ 205 Billy Pierce	2.50	1.25	.25
☐ 206 Gene Green	1.75	.85	.17
☐ 207 Dodger Southpaws Sandy Koufax Johnny Podres	16.00	8.00	1.60
☐ 208 Larry Osborne	1.75	.85	.17
☐ 209 Ken McBride	1.75	.85	.17
☐ 210 Pete Runnels	2.25	1.10	.22
☐ 211 Bob Gibson	32.00	16.00	3.20
☐ 212 Haywood Sullivan	1.75	.85	.17
☐ 213 Bill Stafford	1.75	.85	.17
☐ 214 Danny Murphy	1.75	.85	.17
☐ 215 Gus Bell	2.25	1.10	.22
☐ 216 Ted Bowsfield	1.75	.85	.17
☐ 217 Mel Roach	1.75	.85	.17
☐ 218 Hal Brown	1.75	.85	.17
☐ 219 Gene Mauch MG	2.25	1.10	.22
☐ 220 Alvin Dark MG	2.25	1.10	.22
☐ 221 Mike Higgins MG	1.75	.85	.17
☐ 222 Jimmy Dykes MG	1.75	.85	.17
☐ 223 Bob Scheffing MG	1.75	.85	.17
☐ 224 Joe Gordon MG	1.75	.85	.17
☐ 225 Bill Rigney MG	1.75	.85	.17
☐ 226 Harry Lavagetto MG	1.75	.85	.17
☐ 227 Juan Pizarro	1.75	.85	.17
☐ 228 New York Yankees Team Card	17.00	8.50	1.70
☐ 229 Rudy Hernandez	1.75	.85	.17
☐ 230 Don Hoak	1.75	.85	.17
☐ 231 Dick Drott	1.75	.85	.17
☐ 232 Bill White	4.00	2.00	.40
☐ 233 Joey Jay	1.75	.85	.17
☐ 234 Ted Lepcio	1.75	.85	.17
☐ 235 Camilo Pascual	2.25	1.10	.22
☐ 236 Don Gile	1.75	.85	.17
☐ 237 Billy Loes	1.75	.85	.17
☐ 238 Jim Gilliam	3.00	1.50	.30
☐ 239 Dave Sisler	1.75	.85	.17
☐ 240 Ron Hansen	1.75	.85	.17
☐ 241 Al Cicotte	1.75	.85	.17
☐ 242 Hal Smith	1.75	.85	.17
☐ 243 Frank Lary	2.25	1.10	.22
☐ 244 Chico Cardenas	1.75	.85	.17
☐ 245 Joe Adcock	2.25	1.10	.22
☐ 246 Bob Davis	1.75	.85	.17
☐ 247 Billy Goodman	2.25	1.10	.22
☐ 248 Ed Keegan	1.75	.85	.17
☐ 249 Cincinnati Reds Team Card	3.50	1.75	.35
☐ 250 Buc Hill Aces Vern Law Roy Face	2.25	1.10	.22
☐ 251 Bill Bruton	1.75	.85	.17
☐ 252 Bill Short	1.75	.85	.17
☐ 253 Sammy Taylor	1.75	.85	.17
☐ 254 Ted Sadowski	1.75	.85	.17
☐ 255 Vic Power	1.75	.85	.17
☐ 256 Billy Hoeft	1.75	.85	.17
☐ 257 Carroll Hardy	1.75	.85	.17
☐ 258 Jack Sanford	2.25	1.10	.22
☐ 259 John Schaive	1.75	.85	.17
☐ 260 Don Drysdale	22.00	11.00	2.20
☐ 261 Charlie Lau	2.25	1.10	.22
☐ 262 Tony Curry	1.75	.85	.17
☐ 263 Ken Hamlin	1.75	.85	.17
☐ 264 Glen Hobbie	1.75	.85	.17
☐ 265 Tony Kubek	6.00	3.00	.60
☐ 266 Lindy McDaniel	1.75	.85	.17
☐ 267 Norm Siebern	1.75	.85	.17
☐ 268 Ike Delock	1.75	.85	.17
☐ 269 Harry Chiti	1.75	.85	.17
☐ 270 Bob Friend	2.25	1.10	.22
☐ 271 Jim Landis	1.75	.85	.17
☐ 272 Tom Morgan	1.75	.85	.17
☐ 273A Checklist 4 (copyright symbol adjacent to 336 Don Mincher)	12.00	1.20	.20
☐ 273B Checklist 4 (copyright symbol adjacent to 339 Gene Baker)	9.00	.90	.20
☐ 274 Gary Bell	1.75	.85	.17
☐ 275 Gene Woodling	2.25	1.10	.22
☐ 276 Ray Rippelmeyer	1.75	.85	.17
☐ 277 Hank Foiles	1.75	.85	.17
☐ 278 Don McMahon	1.75	.85	.17
☐ 279 Jose Pagan	1.75	.85	.17
☐ 280 Frank Howard	4.00	2.00	.40
☐ 281 Frank Sullivan	1.75	.85	.17
☐ 282 Faye Throneberry	1.75	.85	.17
☐ 283 Bob Anderson	1.75	.85	.17
☐ 284 Dick Gernert	1.75	.85	.17
☐ 285 Sherm Lollar	2.25	1.10	.22
☐ 286 George Witt	1.75	.85	.17
☐ 287 Carl Yastrzemski	165.00	75.00	15.00
☐ 288 Albie Pearson	1.75	.85	.17
☐ 289 Ray Moore	1.75	.85	.17
☐ 290 Stan Musial	85.00	42.50	8.50

☐ 291 Tex Clevenger	1.75	.85	.17
☐ 292 Jim Baumer	1.75	.85	.17
☐ 293 Tom Sturdivant	1.75	.85	.17
☐ 294 Don Blasingame	1.75	.85	.17
☐ 295 Milt Pappas	2.25	1.10	.22
☐ 296 Wes Covington	1.75	.85	.17
☐ 297 Athletics Team	3.50	1.75	.35
☐ 298 Jim Golden	1.75	.85	.17
☐ 299 Clay Dalrymple	1.75	.85	.17
☐ 300 Mickey Mantle	300.00	150.00	30.00
☐ 301 Chet Nichols	1.75	.85	.17
☐ 302 Al Heist	1.75	.85	.17
☐ 303 Gary Peters	2.25	1.10	.22
☐ 304 Rocky Nelson	1.75	.85	.17
☐ 305 Mike McCormick	2.25	1.10	.22
☐ 306 World Series Game 1	5.00	2.50	.50
Virdon Saves Game			
☐ 307 World Series Game 2	30.00	15.00	3.00
Mantle 2 Homers			
☐ 308 World Series Game 3	6.00	3.00	.60
Richardson is Hero			
☐ 309 World Series Game 4	5.00	2.50	.50
Cimoli Safe			
☐ 310 World Series Game 5	5.00	2.50	.50
Face Saves the Day			
☐ 311 World Series Game 6	7.50	3.75	.75
Ford Second Shutout			
☐ 312 World Series Game 7	7.50	3.75	.75
Mazeroski's Homer			
☐ 313 World Series Summary	5.00	2.50	.50
Pirates Celebrate			
☐ 314 Bob Miller	1.75	.85	.17
☐ 315 Earl Battey	1.75	.85	.17
☐ 316 Bobby Gene Smith	1.75	.85	.17
☐ 317 Jim Brewer	1.75	.85	.17
☐ 318 Danny O'Connell	1.75	.85	.17
☐ 319 Valmy Thomas	1.75	.85	.17
☐ 320 Lou Burdette	2.50	1.25	.25
☐ 321 Marv Breeding	1.75	.85	.17
☐ 322 Bill Kunkel	2.25	1.10	.22
☐ 323 Sammy Esposito	1.75	.85	.17
☐ 324 Hank Aguirre	1.75	.85	.17
☐ 325 Wally Moon	2.25	1.10	.22
☐ 326 Dave Hillman	1.75	.85	.17
☐ 327 Matty Alou	5.00	2.50	.50
☐ 328 Jim O'Toole	2.25	1.10	.22
☐ 329 Julio Becquer	1.75	.85	.17
☐ 330 Rocky Colavito	6.00	3.00	.60
☐ 331 Ned Garver	1.75	.85	.17
☐ 332 Dutch Dotterer UER	1.75	.85	.17
(photo actually			
Tommy Dotterer,			
Dutch's brother)			
☐ 333 Fritz Brickell	1.75	.85	.17
☐ 334 Walt Bond	1.75	.85	.17
☐ 335 Frank Bolling	1.75	.85	.17
☐ 336 Don Mincher	2.25	1.10	.22
☐ 337 Al's Aces	4.50	2.25	.45
Early Wynn			
Al Lopez			
Herb Score			
☐ 338 Don Landrum	1.75	.85	.17
☐ 339 Gene Baker	1.75	.85	.17
☐ 340 Vic Wertz	2.25	1.10	.22
☐ 341 Jim Owens	1.75	.85	.17
☐ 342 Clint Courtney	1.75	.85	.17
☐ 343 Earl Robinson	1.75	.85	.17
☐ 344 Sandy Koufax	90.00	45.00	9.00
☐ 345 Jim Piersall	2.50	1.25	.25
☐ 346 Howie Nunn	1.75	.85	.17
☐ 347 St. Louis Cardinals	3.50	1.75	.35
Team Card			
☐ 348 Steve Boros	1.75	.85	.17
☐ 349 Danny McDevitt	1.75	.85	.17
☐ 350 Ernie Banks	35.00	17.50	3.50
☐ 351 Jim King	1.75	.85	.17
☐ 352 Bob Shaw	1.75	.85	.17
☐ 353 Howie Bedell	1.75	.85	.17
☐ 354 Billy Harrell	1.75	.85	.17
☐ 355 Bob Allison	2.25	1.10	.22
☐ 356 Ryne Duren	2.25	1.10	.22
☐ 357 Daryl Spencer	1.75	.85	.17
☐ 358 Earl Averill	1.75	.85	.17
☐ 359 Dallas Green	4.00	2.00	.40
☐ 360 Frank Robinson	37.50	16.00	3.00
☐ 361A Checklist 5	9.00	.90	.20
(no ad on back)			
☐ 361B Checklist 5	12.00	1.20	.20
(Special Feature			
ad on back)			
☐ 362 Frank Funk	1.75	.85	.17
☐ 363 John Roseboro	2.25	1.10	.22
☐ 364 Moe Drabowsky	1.75	.85	.17
☐ 365 Jerry Lumpe	1.75	.85	.17
☐ 366 Eddie Fisher	1.75	.85	.17
☐ 367 Jim Rivera	1.75	.85	.17
☐ 368 Bennie Daniels	1.75	.85	.17
☐ 369 Dave Philley	1.75	.85	.17
☐ 370 Roy Face	2.50	1.25	.25
☐ 371 Bill Skowron SP	24.00	12.00	2.40
☐ 372 Bob Hendley	2.50	1.25	.25
☐ 373 Boston Red Sox	5.00	2.50	.50
Team Card			
☐ 374 Paul Giel	2.50	1.25	.25
☐ 375 Ken Boyer	4.00	2.00	.40
☐ 376 Mike Roarke	2.50	1.25	.25
☐ 377 Ruben Gomez	2.50	1.25	.25
☐ 378 Wally Post	3.00	1.50	.30
☐ 379 Bobby Shantz	3.00	1.50	.30
☐ 380 Minnie Minoso	3.50	1.75	.35
☐ 381 Dave Wickersham	2.50	1.25	.25
☐ 382 Frank Thomas	3.00	1.50	.30
☐ 383 Frisco First Liners	3.00	1.50	.30
Mike McCormick			
Jack Sanford			
Billy O'Dell			
☐ 384 Chuck Essegian	2.50	1.25	.25
☐ 385 Jim Perry	3.50	1.75	.35
☐ 386 Joe Hicks	2.50	1.25	.25
☐ 387 Duke Maas	2.50	1.25	.25
☐ 388 Bob Clemente	85.00	42.50	8.50
☐ 389 Ralph Terry	3.50	1.75	.35
☐ 390 Del Crandall	3.00	1.50	.30
☐ 391 Winston Brown	2.50	1.25	.25
☐ 392 Reno Bertoia	2.50	1.25	.25
☐ 393 Batter Bafflers	2.50	1.25	.25
Don Cardwell			
Glen Hobbie			
☐ 394 Ken Walters	2.50	1.25	.25
☐ 395 Chuck Estrada	2.50	1.25	.25
☐ 396 Bob Aspromonte	2.50	1.25	.25
☐ 397 Hal Woodeshick	2.50	1.25	.25
☐ 398 Hank Bauer	3.00	1.50	.30
☐ 399 Cliff Cook	2.50	1.25	.25
☐ 400 Vern Law	3.00	1.50	.30
☐ 401 Ruth 60th Homer	20.00	10.00	2.00
☐ 402 Perfect Game	12.00	6.00	1.20
(Don Larsen)			
☐ 403 26 Inning Tie	5.00	2.50	.50
☐ 404 Hornsby .424 Average	6.00	3.00	.60
☐ 405 Gehrig's Streak	15.00	7.50	1.50
☐ 406 Mantle 565 Ft. Homer	40.00	20.00	4.00
☐ 407 Chesbro Wins 41	5.00	2.50	.50
☐ 408 Mathewson Fans 267	6.00	3.00	.60
☐ 409 Johnson Shutouts	6.00	3.00	.60
☐ 410 Haddix 12 Perfect	5.00	2.50	.50
Innings			
☐ 411 Tony Taylor	2.50	1.25	.25
☐ 412 Larry Sherry	3.00	1.50	.30
☐ 413 Eddie Yost	2.50	1.25	.25
☐ 414 Dick Donovan	2.50	1.25	.25
☐ 415 Hank Aaron	100.00	50.00	10.00
☐ 416 Dick Howser	8.00	4.00	.80
☐ 417 Juan Marichal	125.00	60.00	12.50
☐ 418 Ed Bailey	2.50	1.25	.25
☐ 419 Tom Borland	2.50	1.25	.25
☐ 420 Ernie Broglio	3.00	1.50	.30
☐ 421 Ty Cline	2.50	1.25	.25
☐ 422 Bud Daley	2.50	1.25	.25
☐ 423 Charlie Neal SP	5.00	2.50	.50
☐ 424 Turk Lown	2.50	1.25	.25
☐ 425 Yogi Berra	65.00	32.50	6.50
☐ 426 Milwaukee Braves	6.50	3.25	.65
Team Card			
(back numbered 463)			
☐ 427 Dick Ellsworth	3.00	1.50	.30
☐ 428 Ray Barker SP	4.50	2.25	.45
☐ 429 Al Kaline	36.00	18.00	3.60
☐ 430 Bill Mazeroski SP	18.00	9.00	1.80
☐ 431 Chuck Stobbs	2.50	1.25	.25
☐ 432 Coot Veal	2.50	1.25	.25
☐ 433 Art Mahaffey	2.50	1.25	.25
☐ 434 Tom Brewer	2.50	1.25	.25
☐ 435 Orlando Cepeda	9.00	4.50	.90
☐ 436 Jim Maloney	6.00	3.00	.60
☐ 437A Checklist 6	10.00	1.00	.20
440 Louis Aparicio			
☐ 437B Checklist 6	10.00	1.00	.20
440 Luis Aparicio			
☐ 438 Curt Flood	3.50	1.75	.35
☐ 439 Phil Regan	3.00	1.50	.30
☐ 440 Luis Aparicio	12.00	6.00	1.20
☐ 441 Dick Bertell	2.50	1.25	.25
☐ 442 Gordon Jones	2.50	1.25	.25
☐ 443 Duke Snider	40.00	20.00	4.00
☐ 444 Joe Nuxhall	3.00	1.50	.30
☐ 445 Frank Malzone	3.00	1.50	.30
☐ 446 Bob Taylor	2.50	1.25	.25

☐ 447	Harry Bright	3.00	1.50	.30
☐ 448	Del Rice	3.00	1.50	.30
☐ 449	Bob Bolin	3.00	1.50	.30
☐ 450	Jim Lemon	3.50	1.75	.35
☐ 451	Power for Ernie	3.50	1.75	.35
	Daryl Spencer			
	Bill White			
	Ernie Broglio			
☐ 452	Bob Allen	3.00	1.50	.30
☐ 453	Dick Schofield	3.00	1.50	.30
☐ 454	Pumpsie Green	3.00	1.50	.30
☐ 455	Early Wynn	12.00	6.00	1.20
☐ 456	Hal Bevan	3.00	1.50	.30
☐ 457	Johnny James	3.00	1.50	.30
☐ 458	Willie Tasby	3.00	1.50	.30
☐ 459	Terry Fox	3.00	1.50	.30
☐ 460	Gil Hodges	14.00	7.00	1.40
☐ 461	Smoky Burgess	3.50	1.75	.35
☐ 462	Lou Klimchock	3.00	1.50	.30
☐ 463	Jack Fisher	3.50	1.75	.35
	(See also 426)			
☐ 464	Lee Thomas	4.50	2.25	.45
☐ 465	Roy McMillan	3.00	1.50	.30
☐ 466	Ron Moeller	3.00	1.50	.30
☐ 467	Cleveland Indians	6.00	3.00	.60
	Team Card			
☐ 468	John Callison	3.50	1.75	.35
☐ 469	Ralph Lumenti	3.00	1.50	.30
☐ 470	Roy Sievers	3.50	1.75	.35
☐ 471	Phil Rizzuto MVP	13.00	6.50	1.30
☐ 472	Yogi Berra MVP	35.00	17.50	3.50
☐ 473	Bob Shantz MVP	3.50	1.75	.35
☐ 474	Al Rosen MVP	4.00	2.00	.40
☐ 475	Mickey Mantle MVP	100.00	50.00	10.00
☐ 476	Jackie Jensen MVP	4.00	2.00	.40
☐ 477	Nellie Fox MVP	5.00	2.50	.50
☐ 478	Roger Maris MVP	35.00	17.50	3.50
☐ 479	Jim Konstanty MVP	3.50	1.75	.35
☐ 480	Roy Campanella MVP	25.00	12.50	2.50
☐ 481	Hank Sauer MVP	3.50	1.75	.35
☐ 482	Willie Mays MVP	35.00	17.50	3.50
☐ 483	Don Newcombe MVP	3.50	1.75	.35
☐ 484	Hank Aaron MVP	35.00	17.50	3.50
☐ 485	Ernie Banks MVP	20.00	10.00	2.00
☐ 486	Dick Groat MVP	3.50	1.75	.35
☐ 487	Gene Oliver	3.00	1.50	.30
☐ 488	Joe McClain	3.00	1.50	.30
☐ 489	Walt Dropo	3.00	1.50	.30
☐ 490	Jim Bunning	8.00	4.00	.80
☐ 491	Philadelphia Phillies	6.00	3.00	.60
	Team Card			
☐ 492	Ron Fairly	3.50	1.75	.35
☐ 493	Don Zimmer UER	4.50	2.25	.45
	(Brooklyn A.L.)			
☐ 494	Tom Cheney	3.00	1.50	.30
☐ 495	Elston Howard	5.00	2.50	.50
☐ 496	Ken MacKenzie	3.00	1.50	.30
☐ 497	Willie Jones	3.00	1.50	.30
☐ 498	Ray Herbert	3.00	1.50	.30
☐ 499	Chuck Schilling	3.00	1.50	.30
☐ 500	Harvey Kuenn	4.00	2.00	.40
☐ 501	John DeMerit	3.00	1.50	.30
☐ 502	Clarence Coleman	3.00	1.50	.30
☐ 503	Tito Francona	3.00	1.50	.30
☐ 504	Billy Consolo	3.00	1.50	.30
☐ 505	Red Schoendienst	14.00	7.00	1.40
☐ 506	Willie Davis	10.00	5.00	1.00
☐ 507	Pete Burnside	3.00	1.50	.30
☐ 508	Rocky Bridges	3.00	1.50	.30
☐ 509	Camilo Carreon	3.00	1.50	.30
☐ 510	Art Ditmar	3.00	1.50	.30
☐ 511	Joe M. Morgan	4.00	2.00	.40
☐ 512	Bob Will	3.00	1.50	.30
☐ 513	Jim Brosnan	3.50	1.75	.35
☐ 514	Jake Wood	3.00	1.50	.30
☐ 515	Jackie Brandt	3.00	1.50	.30
☐ 516	Checklist 7	10.00	1.00	.20
☐ 517	Willie McCovey	55.00	27.50	5.50
☐ 518	Andy Carey	3.50	1.75	.35
☐ 519	Jim Pagliaroni	3.00	1.50	.30
☐ 520	Joe Cunningham	3.50	1.75	.35
☐ 521	Brother Battery	3.50	1.75	.35
	Norm Sherry			
	Larry Sherry			
☐ 522	Dick Farrell	3.50	1.75	.35
☐ 523	Joe Gibbon	27.00	13.50	2.70
☐ 524	Johnny Logan	30.00	15.00	3.00
☐ 525	Ron Perranoski	30.00	15.00	3.00
☐ 526	R.C. Stevens	27.00	13.50	2.70
☐ 527	Gene Leek	27.00	13.50	2.70
☐ 528	Pedro Ramos	27.00	13.50	2.70
☐ 529	Bob Roselli	27.00	13.50	2.70
☐ 530	Bob Malkmus	27.00	13.50	2.70
☐ 531	Jim Coates	27.00	13.50	2.70
☐ 532	Bob Hale	27.00	13.50	2.70
☐ 533	Jack Curtis	27.00	13.50	2.70
☐ 534	Eddie Kasko	27.00	13.50	2.70
☐ 535	Larry Jackson	27.00	13.50	2.70
☐ 536	Bill Tuttle	27.00	13.50	2.70
☐ 537	Bobby Locke	27.00	13.50	2.70
☐ 538	Chuck Hiller	27.00	13.50	2.70
☐ 539	Johnny Klippstein	27.00	13.50	2.70
☐ 540	Jackie Jensen	33.00	16.00	3.00
☐ 541	Roland Sheldon	27.00	13.50	2.70
☐ 542	Minnesota Twins	50.00	25.00	5.00
	Team Card			
☐ 543	Roger Craig	33.00	16.00	3.00
☐ 544	George Thomas	27.00	13.50	2.70
☐ 545	Hoyt Wilhelm	55.00	27.50	5.50
☐ 546	Marty Kutyna	27.00	13.50	2.70
☐ 547	Leon Wagner	27.00	13.50	2.70
☐ 548	Ted Wills	27.00	13.50	2.70
☐ 549	Hal R. Smith	27.00	13.50	2.70
☐ 550	Frank Baumann	27.00	13.50	2.70
☐ 551	George Altman	27.00	13.50	2.70
☐ 552	Jim Archer	27.00	13.50	2.70
☐ 553	Bill Fischer	27.00	13.50	2.70
☐ 554	Pittsburgh Pirates	50.00	25.00	5.00
	Team Card			
☐ 555	Sam Jones	27.00	13.50	2.70
☐ 556	Ken R. Hunt	27.00	13.50	2.70
☐ 557	Jose Valdivielso	27.00	13.50	2.70
☐ 558	Don Ferrarese	27.00	13.50	2.70
☐ 559	Jim Gentile	30.00	15.00	3.00
☐ 560	Barry Latman	27.00	13.50	2.70
☐ 561	Charley James	27.00	13.50	2.70
☐ 562	Bill Monbouquette	30.00	15.00	3.00
☐ 563	Bob Cerv	30.00	15.00	3.00
☐ 564	Don Cardwell	27.00	13.50	2.70
☐ 565	Felipe Alou	30.00	15.00	3.00
☐ 566	Paul Richards MG AS	30.00	15.00	3.00
☐ 567	Danny Murtaugh MG AS	30.00	15.00	3.00
☐ 568	Bill Skowron AS	33.00	16.00	3.00
☐ 569	Frank Herrera AS	30.00	15.00	3.00
☐ 570	Nellie Fox AS	36.00	18.00	3.60
☐ 571	Bill Mazeroski AS	33.00	16.00	3.00
☐ 572	Brooks Robinson AS	85.00	42.50	8.50
☐ 573	Ken Boyer AS	33.00	16.00	3.00
☐ 574	Luis Aparicio AS	42.00	20.00	4.00
☐ 575	Ernie Banks AS	85.00	42.50	8.50
☐ 576	Roger Maris AS	120.00	60.00	12.00
☐ 577	Hank Aaron AS	150.00	75.00	15.00
☐ 578	Mickey Mantle AS	325.00	160.00	32.00
☐ 579	Willie Mays AS	150.00	75.00	15.00
☐ 580	Al Kaline AS	85.00	42.50	8.50
☐ 581	Frank Robinson AS	85.00	42.50	8.50
☐ 582	Earl Battey AS	30.00	15.00	3.00
☐ 583	Del Crandall AS	30.00	15.00	3.00
☐ 584	Jim Perry AS	30.00	15.00	3.00
☐ 585	Bob Friend AS	30.00	15.00	3.00
☐ 586	Whitey Ford AS	85.00	42.50	8.50
☐ 587	Does not exist	00.00	00.00	0.00
☐ 588	Does not exist	00.00	00.00	0.00
☐ 589	Warren Spahn AS	125.00	45.00	9.00

1962 Topps

The cards in this 598-card set measure 2 1/2" by 3 1/2". The 1962 Topps set contains a mini-series spotlighting Babe Ruth (135-144). Other subsets in the set include League Leaders

(51-60), World Series cards (232-237), In Action cards (311-319), NL All Stars (390-399), AL All Stars (466-475), and Rookie Prospects (591-598). The All-Star selections were again provided by Sport Magazine, as in 1958 and 1960. The second series had two distinct printings which are distinguishable by numerous color and pose variations. Card number 139 exists as A: Babe Ruth Special card, B: Hal Reniff with arms over head, or C: Hal Reniff in the same pose as card number 159. In addition, two poses exist for players depicted on card numbers 129, 132, 134, 147, 174, 176, and 190. The high number series, 523 to 598, is somewhat more difficult to obtain than other cards in the set. Within the last series (523-598) there are 43 cards which were printed in lesser quantities; these are marked SP in the checklist below. The set price listed does not include the pose variations (see checklist below for individual values). The key rookies in this set are Lou Brock, Tim McCarver, Gaylord Perry, and Bob Uecker.

	NRMT	VG-E	GOOD
COMPLETE SET	4300.00	2100.00	450.00
COMMON PLAYER (1-109)	1.25	.60	.12
COMMON PLAYER (110-196)	1.50	.75	.15
COMMON PLAYER (197-283)	1.75	.85	.17
COMMON PLAYER (284-370)	2.25	1.10	.22
COMMON PLAYER (371-446)	3.25	1.60	.32
COMMON PLAYER (447-522)	4.00	2.00	.40
COMMON PLAYER (523-590)	12.00	6.00	1.20
COMMON SP (523-590)	20.00	10.00	2.00
COMMON PLAYER (591-598)	20.00	10.00	2.00

☐ 1 Roger Maris	200.00	50.00	10.00
☐ 2 Jim Brosnan	1.25	.60	.12
☐ 3 Pete Runnels	1.25	.60	.12
☐ 4 John DeMerit	1.25	.60	.12
☐ 5 Sandy Koufax UER (struck ou 18)	100.00	50.00	10.00
☐ 6 Marv Breeding	1.25	.60	.12
☐ 7 Frank Thomas	1.25	.60	.12
☐ 8 Ray Herbert	1.25	.60	.12
☐ 9 Jim Davenport	1.25	.60	.12
☐ 10 Bob Clemente	90.00	45.00	9.00
☐ 11 Tom Morgan	1.25	.60	.12
☐ 12 Harry Craft MG	1.25	.60	.12
☐ 13 Dick Howser	2.00	1.00	.20
☐ 14 Bill White	3.50	1.75	.35
☐ 15 Dick Donovan	1.25	.60	.12
☐ 16 Darrell Johnson	1.25	.60	.12
☐ 17 John Callison	1.50	.75	.15
☐ 18 Managers' Dream Mickey Mantle Willie Mays	100.00	50.00	10.00
☐ 19 Ray Washburn	1.25	.60	.12
☐ 20 Rocky Colavito	4.50	2.25	.45
☐ 21 Jim Kaat	5.00	2.50	.50
☐ 22A Checklist 1 COR	6.50	.60	.12
☐ 22B Checklist 1 ERR (121-176 on back)	6.50	.60	.12
☐ 23 Norm Larker	1.25	.60	.12
☐ 24 Tigers Team	4.00	2.00	.40
☐ 25 Ernie Banks	33.00	15.00	3.00
☐ 26 Chris Cannizzaro	1.25	.60	.12
☐ 27 Chuck Cottier	1.25	.60	.12
☐ 28 Minnie Minoso	3.00	1.50	.30
☐ 29 Casey Stengel MG	14.00	7.00	1.40
☐ 30 Eddie Mathews	18.00	9.00	1.80
☐ 31 Tom Tresh	10.00	5.00	1.00
☐ 32 John Roseboro	1.50	.75	.15
☐ 33 Don Larsen	2.00	1.00	.20
☐ 34 Johnny Temple	1.25	.60	.12
☐ 35 Don Schwall	1.25	.60	.12
☐ 36 Don Leppert	1.25	.60	.12
☐ 37 Tribe Hill Trio Barry Latman Dick Stigman Jim Perry	1.50	.75	.15
☐ 38 Gene Stephens	1.25	.60	.12
☐ 39 Joe Koppe	1.25	.60	.12
☐ 40 Orlando Cepeda	6.00	3.00	.60
☐ 41 Cliff Cook	1.25	.60	.12
☐ 42 Jim King	1.25	.60	.12
☐ 43 Los Angeles Dodgers Team Card	4.00	2.00	.40
☐ 44 Don Taussig	1.25	.60	.12
☐ 45 Brooks Robinson	30.00	15.00	3.00
☐ 46 Jack Baldschun	1.25	.60	.12
☐ 47 Bob Will	1.25	.60	.12
☐ 48 Ralph Terry	1.75	.85	.17
☐ 49 Hal Jones	1.25	.60	.12
☐ 50 Stan Musial	85.00	42.50	8.50
☐ 51 AL Batting Leaders Norm Cash Jim Piersall Al Kaline Elston Howard	2.25	1.10	.22
☐ 52 NL Batting Leaders Bob Clemente Vada Pinson Ken Boyer Wally Moon	4.50	2.25	.45
☐ 53 AL Home Run Leaders Roger Maris Mickey Mantle Jim Gentile Harmon Killebrew	25.00	12.50	2.50
☐ 54 NL Home Run Leaders Orlando Cepeda Willie Mays Frank Robinson	4.50	2.25	.45
☐ 55 AL ERA Leaders Dick Donovan Bill Stafford Don Mossi Milt Pappas	2.25	1.10	.22
☐ 56 NL ERA Leaders Warren Spahn Jim O'Toole Curt Simmons Mike McCormick	3.00	1.50	.30
☐ 57 AL Wins Leaders Whitey Ford Frank Lary Steve Barber Jim Bunning	3.00	1.50	.30
☐ 58 NL Wins Leaders Warren Spahn Joe Jay Jim O'Toole	3.00	1.50	.30
☐ 59 AL Strikeout Leaders Camilo Pascual Whitey Ford Jim Bunning Juan Pizzaro	2.25	1.10	.22
☐ 60 NL Strikeout Leaders Sandy Koufax Stan Williams Don Drysdale Jim O'Toole	4.50	2.25	.45
☐ 61 Cardinals Team	4.00	2.00	.40
☐ 62 Steve Boros	1.50	.75	.15
☐ 63 Tony Cloninger	1.25	.60	.12
☐ 64 Russ Snyder	1.25	.60	.12
☐ 65 Bobby Richardson	5.00	2.50	.50
☐ 66 Cuno Barragon	1.25	.60	.12
☐ 67 Harvey Haddix	1.75	.85	.17
☐ 68 Ken Hunt	1.25	.60	.12
☐ 69 Phil Ortega	1.25	.60	.12
☐ 70 Harmon Killebrew	18.00	9.00	1.80
☐ 71 Dick LeMay	1.25	.60	.12
☐ 72 Bob's Pupils Steve Boros Bob Scheffing Jake Wood	1.25	.60	.12
☐ 73 Nellie Fox	5.00	2.50	.50
☐ 74 Bob Lillis	1.25	.60	.12
☐ 75 Milt Pappas	1.50	.75	.15
☐ 76 Howie Bedell	1.25	.60	.12
☐ 77 Tony Taylor	1.25	.60	.12
☐ 78 Gene Green	1.25	.60	.12
☐ 79 Ed Hobaugh	1.25	.60	.12
☐ 80 Vada Pinson	2.50	1.25	.25
☐ 81 Jim Pagliaroni	1.25	.60	.12
☐ 82 Deron Johnson	1.25	.60	.12
☐ 83 Larry Jackson	1.25	.60	.12
☐ 84 Lenny Green	1.25	.60	.12
☐ 85 Gil Hodges	12.00	6.00	1.20
☐ 86 Donn Clendenon	1.50	.75	.15
☐ 87 Mike Roarke	1.25	.60	.12
☐ 88 Ralph Houk MG (Berra in background)	2.50	1.25	.25
☐ 89 Barney Schultz	1.25	.60	.12
☐ 90 Jim Piersall	2.00	1.00	.20
☐ 91 J.C. Martin	1.25	.60	.12
☐ 92 Sam Jones	1.25	.60	.12
☐ 93 John Blanchard	1.50	.75	.15
☐ 94 Jay Hook	1.25	.60	.12
☐ 95 Don Hoak	1.25	.60	.12
☐ 96 Eli Grba	1.25	.60	.12
☐ 97 Tito Francona	1.25	.60	.12
☐ 98 Checklist 2	6.50	.60	.12
☐ 99 John (Boog) Powell	13.50	6.00	1.25
☐ 100 Warren Spahn	30.00	15.00	3.00
☐ 101 Carroll Hardy	1.25	.60	.12

☐ 102 Al Schroll	1.25	.60	.12
☐ 103 Don Blasingame	1.25	.60	.12
☐ 104 Ted Savage	1.25	.60	.12
☐ 105 Don Mossi	1.50	.75	.15
☐ 106 Carl Sawatski	1.25	.60	.12
☐ 107 Mike McCormick	1.50	.75	.15
☐ 108 Willie Davis	2.00	1.00	.20
☐ 109 Bob Shaw	1.25	.60	.12
☐ 110 Bill Skowron	3.50	1.75	.35
☐ 111 Dallas Green	3.50	1.75	.35
☐ 112 Hank Foiles	1.50	.75	.15
☐ 113 Chicago White Sox	3.50	1.75	.35
Team Card			
☐ 114 Howie Koplitz	1.50	.75	.15
☐ 115 Bob Skinner	1.50	.75	.15
☐ 116 Herb Score	2.00	1.00	.20
☐ 117 Gary Geiger	1.50	.75	.15
☐ 118 Julian Javier	1.50	.75	.15
☐ 119 Danny Murphy	1.50	.75	.15
☐ 120 Bob Purkey	1.50	.75	.15
☐ 121 Billy Hitchcock MG	1.50	.75	.15
☐ 122 Norm Bass	1.50	.75	.15
☐ 123 Mike De La Hoz	1.50	.75	.15
☐ 124 Bill Pleis	1.50	.75	.15
☐ 125 Gene Woodling	2.00	1.00	.20
☐ 126 Al Cicotte	1.50	.75	.15
☐ 127 Pride of A's	2.00	1.00	.20
Norm Siebern			
Hank Bauer			
Jerry Lumpe			
☐ 128 Art Fowler	1.50	.75	.15
☐ 129A Lee Walls	1.50	.75	.15
(facing right)			
☐ 129B Lee Walls	18.00	9.00	1.80
(facing left)			
☐ 130 Frank Bolling	1.50	.75	.15
☐ 131 Pete Richert	1.50	.75	.15
☐ 132A Angels Team	4.00	2.00	.40
(without photo)			
☐ 132B Angels Team	18.00	9.00	1.80
(with photo)			
☐ 133 Felipe Alou	2.50	1.25	.25
☐ 134A Billy Hoeft	1.50	.75	.15
(facing right)			
☐ 134B Billy Hoeft	18.00	9.00	1.80
(facing straight)			
☐ 135 Babe Ruth Special 1	8.00	4.00	.80
Babe as a Boy			
☐ 136 Babe Ruth Special 2	8.00	4.00	.80
Babe Joins Yanks			
☐ 137 Babe Ruth Special 3	8.00	4.00	.80
Babe with Huggins			
☐ 138 Babe Ruth Special 4	8.00	4.00	.80
Famous Slugger			
☐ 139A Babe Ruth Special 5	10.00	5.00	1.00
☐ 139B Hal Reniff PORT	10.00	5.00	1.00
☐ 139C Hal Reniff	50.00	25.00	5.00
(pitching)			
☐ 140 Babe Ruth Special 6	10.00	5.00	1.00
Gehrig and Ruth			
☐ 141 Babe Ruth Special 7	8.00	4.00	.80
Twilight Years			
☐ 142 Babe Ruth Special 8	8.00	4.00	.80
Coaching Dodgers			
☐ 143 Babe Ruth Special 9	8.00	4.00	.80
Greatest Sports Hero			
☐ 144 Babe Ruth Special 10	8.00	4.00	.80
Farewell Speech			
☐ 145 Barry Latman	1.50	.75	.15
☐ 146 Don Demeter	1.50	.75	.15
☐ 147A Bill Kunkel PORT	1.50	.75	.15
☐ 147B Bill Kunkel	18.00	9.00	1.80
(pitching pose)			
☐ 148 Wally Post	1.50	.75	.15
☐ 149 Bob Duliba	1.50	.75	.15
☐ 150 Al Kaline	27.00	13.50	2.70
☐ 151 Johnny Klippstein	1.50	.75	.15
☐ 152 Mickey Vernon MG	1.50	.75	.15
☐ 153 Pumpsie Green	1.50	.75	.15
☐ 154 Lee Thomas	2.00	1.00	.20
☐ 155 Stu Miller	1.50	.75	.15
☐ 156 Merritt Ranew	1.50	.75	.15
☐ 157 Wes Covington	1.50	.75	.15
☐ 158 Braves Team	4.00	2.00	.40
☐ 159 Hal Reniff	2.00	1.00	.20
☐ 160 Dick Stuart	2.00	1.00	.20
☐ 161 Frank Baumann	1.50	.75	.15
☐ 162 Sammy Drake	1.50	.75	.15
☐ 163 Hot Corner Guard	2.00	1.00	.20
Billy Gardner			
Cletis Boyer			
☐ 164 Hal Naragon	1.50	.75	.15
☐ 165 Jackie Brandt	1.50	.75	.15
☐ 166 Don Lee	1.50	.75	.15

☐ 167 Tim McCarver	24.00	12.00	2.40
☐ 168 Leo Posada	1.50	.75	.15
☐ 169 Bob Cerv	2.00	1.00	.20
☐ 170 Ron Santo	6.00	3.00	.60
☐ 171 Dave Sisler	1.50	.75	.15
☐ 172 Fred Hutchinson MG	2.00	1.00	.20
☐ 173 Chico Fernandez	1.50	.75	.15
☐ 174A Carl Willey	1.50	.75	.15
(capless)			
☐ 174B Carl Willey	18.00	9.00	1.80
(with cap)			
☐ 175 Frank Howard	3.00	1.50	.30
☐ 176A Eddie Yost PORT	1.50	.75	.15
☐ 176B Eddie Yost BATTING	18.00	9.00	1.80
☐ 177 Bobby Shantz	2.00	1.00	.20
☐ 178 Camilo Carreon	1.50	.75	.15
☐ 179 Tom Sturdivant	1.50	.75	.15
☐ 180 Bob Allison	2.00	1.00	.20
☐ 181 Paul Brown	1.50	.75	.15
☐ 182 Bob Nieman	1.50	.75	.15
☐ 183 Roger Craig	2.50	1.25	.25
☐ 184 Haywood Sullivan	1.50	.75	.15
☐ 185 Roland Sheldon	1.50	.75	.15
☐ 186 Mack Jones	1.50	.75	.15
☐ 187 Gene Conley	1.50	.75	.15
☐ 188 Chuck Hiller	1.50	.75	.15
☐ 189 Dick Hall	1.50	.75	.15
☐ 190A Wally Moon PORT	2.00	1.00	.20
☐ 190B Wally Moon BATTING	18.00	9.00	1.80
☐ 191 Jim Brewer	1.50	.75	.15
☐ 192A Checklist 3	6.50	.60	.12
(without comma)			
☐ 192B Checklist 3	7.50	.75	.15
(comma after			
Checklist)			
☐ 193 Eddie Kasko	1.50	.75	.15
☐ 194 Dean Chance	2.00	1.00	.20
☐ 195 Joe Cunningham	1.50	.75	.15
☐ 196 Terry Fox	1.50	.75	.15
☐ 197 Daryl Spencer	1.75	.85	.17
☐ 198 Johnny Keane MG	2.25	1.10	.22
☐ 199 Gaylord Perry	125.00	60.00	12.50
☐ 200 Mickey Mantle	375.00	175.00	37.00
☐ 201 Ike Delock	1.75	.85	.17
☐ 202 Carl Warwick	1.75	.85	.17
☐ 203 Jack Fisher	1.75	.85	.17
☐ 204 Johnny Weekly	1.75	.85	.17
☐ 205 Gene Freese	1.75	.85	.17
☐ 206 Senators Team	3.50	1.75	.35
☐ 207 Pete Burnside	1.75	.85	.17
☐ 208 Billy Martin	6.00	3.00	.60
☐ 209 Jim Fregosi	5.00	2.50	.50
☐ 210 Roy Face	2.50	1.25	.25
☐ 211 Midway Masters	1.75	.85	.17
Frank Bolling			
Roy McMillan			
☐ 212 Jim Owens	1.75	.85	.17
☐ 213 Richie Ashburn	6.00	3.00	.60
☐ 214 Dom Zanni	1.75	.85	.17
☐ 215 Woody Held	1.75	.85	.17
☐ 216 Ron Kline	1.75	.85	.17
☐ 217 Walt Alston MG	4.50	2.25	.45
☐ 218 Joe Torre	15.00	7.50	1.50
☐ 219 Al Downing	3.50	1.75	.35
☐ 220 Roy Sievers	2.25	1.10	.22
☐ 221 Bill Short	1.75	.85	.17
☐ 222 Jerry Zimmerman	1.75	.85	.17
☐ 223 Alex Grammas	1.75	.85	.17
☐ 224 Don Rudolph	1.75	.85	.17
☐ 225 Frank Malzone	2.25	1.10	.22
☐ 226 San Francisco Giants	4.00	2.00	.40
Team Card			
☐ 227 Bob Tiefenauer	1.75	.85	.17
☐ 228 Dale Long	2.25	1.10	.22
☐ 229 Jesus McFarlane	1.75	.85	.17
☐ 230 Camilo Pascual	2.25	1.10	.22
☐ 231 Ernie Bowman	1.75	.85	.17
☐ 232 World Series Game 1	4.00	2.00	.40
Yanks win opener			
☐ 233 World Series Game 2	4.00	2.00	.40
Jay ties it up			
☐ 234 World Series Game 3	10.00	5.00	1.00
Maris wins in 9th			
☐ 235 World Series Game 4	6.00	3.00	.60
Ford sets new mark			
☐ 236 World Series Game 5	4.00	2.00	.40
Yanks crush Reds			
☐ 237 World Series Summary	4.00	2.00	.40
Yanks celebrate			
☐ 238 Norm Sherry	1.75	.85	.17
☐ 239 Cecil Butler	1.75	.85	.17
☐ 240 George Altman	1.75	.85	.17
☐ 241 Johnny Kucks	1.75	.85	.17
☐ 242 Mel McGaha MG	1.75	.85	.17

☐ 243 Robin Roberts	10.00	5.00	1.00
☐ 244 Don Gile	1.75	.85	.17
☐ 245 Ron Hansen	1.75	.85	.17
☐ 246 Art Ditmar	1.75	.85	.17
☐ 247 Joe Pignatano	1.75	.85	.17
☐ 248 Bob Aspromonte	1.75	.85	.17
☐ 249 Ed Keegan	1.75	.85	.17
☐ 250 Norm Cash	3.50	1.75	.35
☐ 251 New York Yankees Team Card	14.00	7.00	1.40
☐ 252 Earl Francis	1.75	.85	.17
☐ 253 Harry Chiti MG	1.75	.85	.17
☐ 254 Gordon Windhorn	1.75	.85	.17
☐ 255 Juan Pizarro	1.75	.85	.17
☐ 256 Elio Chacon	1.75	.85	.17
☐ 257 Jack Spring	1.75	.85	.17
☐ 258 Marty Keough	1.75	.85	.17
☐ 259 Lou Klimchock	1.75	.85	.17
☐ 260 Billy Pierce	2.50	1.25	.25
☐ 261 George Alusik	1.75	.85	.17
☐ 262 Bob Schmidt	1.75	.85	.17
☐ 263 The Right Pitch Bob Purkey Jim Turner Joe Jay	1.75	.85	.17
☐ 264 Dick Ellsworth	1.75	.85	.17
☐ 265 Joe Adcock	2.25	1.10	.22
☐ 266 John Anderson	1.75	.85	.17
☐ 267 Dan Dobbek	1.75	.85	.17
☐ 268 Ken McBride	1.75	.85	.17
☐ 269 Bob Oldis	1.75	.85	.17
☐ 270 Dick Groat	3.00	1.50	.30
☐ 271 Ray Rippelmeyer	1.75	.85	.17
☐ 272 Earl Robinson	1.75	.85	.17
☐ 273 Gary Bell	1.75	.85	.17
☐ 274 Sammy Taylor	1.75	.85	.17
☐ 275 Norm Siebern	1.75	.85	.17
☐ 276 Hal Kolstad	1.75	.85	.17
☐ 277 Checklist 4	6.50	.60	.12
☐ 278 Ken Johnson	1.75	.85	.17
☐ 279 Hobie Landrith UER (wrong birthdate)	1.75	.85	.17
☐ 280 Johnny Podres	3.00	1.50	.30
☐ 281 Jake Gibbs	1.75	.85	.17
☐ 282 Dave Hillman	1.75	.85	.17
☐ 283 Charlie Smith	1.75	.85	.17
☐ 284 Ruben Amaro	2.25	1.10	.22
☐ 285 Curt Simmons	3.00	1.50	.30
☐ 286 Al Lopez MG	3.50	1.75	.35
☐ 287 George Witt	2.25	1.10	.22
☐ 288 Billy Williams	32.00	16.00	3.20
☐ 289 Mike Krsnich	2.25	1.10	.22
☐ 290 Jim Gentile	3.00	1.50	.30
☐ 291 Hal Stowe	2.25	1.10	.22
☐ 292 Jerry Kindall	2.25	1.10	.22
☐ 293 Bob Miller	2.25	1.10	.22
☐ 294 Phillies Team	4.50	2.25	.45
☐ 295 Vern Law	3.00	1.50	.30
☐ 296 Ken Hamlin	2.25	1.10	.22
☐ 297 Ron Perranoski	3.00	1.50	.30
☐ 298 Bill Tuttle	2.25	1.10	.22
☐ 299 Don Wert	2.25	1.10	.22
☐ 300 Willie Mays	125.00	60.00	12.50
☐ 301 Galen Cisco	2.25	1.10	.22
☐ 302 Johnny Edwards	2.25	1.10	.22
☐ 303 Frank Torre	2.25	1.10	.22
☐ 304 Dick Farrell	2.25	1.10	.22
☐ 305 Jerry Lumpe	2.25	1.10	.22
☐ 306 Redbird Rippers Lindy McDaniel Larry Jackson	3.00	1.50	.30
☐ 307 Jim Grant	2.25	1.10	.22
☐ 308 Neil Chrisley	2.25	1.10	.22
☐ 309 Moe Morhardt	2.25	1.10	.22
☐ 310 Whitey Ford	27.00	13.50	2.70
☐ 311 Tony Kubek IA	3.50	1.75	.35
☐ 312 Warren Spahn IA	7.00	3.50	.70
☐ 313 Roger Maris IA	14.00	7.00	1.40
☐ 314 Rocky Colavito IA	3.50	1.75	.35
☐ 315 Whitey Ford IA	8.00	4.00	.80
☐ 316 Harmon Killebrew IA	7.00	3.50	.70
☐ 317 Stan Musial IA	14.00	7.00	1.40
☐ 318 Mickey Mantle IA	42.00	20.00	4.00
☐ 319 Mike McCormick IA	3.00	1.50	.30
☐ 320 Hank Aaron	125.00	60.00	12.50
☐ 321 Lee Stange	2.25	1.10	.22
☐ 322 Alvin Dark MG	3.00	1.50	.30
☐ 323 Don Landrum	2.25	1.10	.22
☐ 324 Joe McClain	2.25	1.10	.22
☐ 325 Luis Aparicio	12.00	6.00	1.20
☐ 326 Tom Parsons	2.25	1.10	.22
☐ 327 Ozzie Virgil	2.25	1.10	.22
☐ 328 Ken Walters	2.25	1.10	.22
☐ 329 Bob Bolin	2.25	1.10	.22

☐ 330 John Romano	2.25	1.10	.22
☐ 331 Moe Drabowsky	2.25	1.10	.22
☐ 332 Don Buddin	2.25	1.10	.22
☐ 333 Frank Cipriani	2.25	1.10	.22
☐ 334 Boston Red Sox Team Card	4.50	2.25	.45
☐ 335 Bill Bruton	2.25	1.10	.22
☐ 336 Billy Muffett	2.25	1.10	.22
☐ 337 Jim Marshall	2.25	1.10	.22
☐ 338 Billy Gardner	2.25	1.10	.22
☐ 339 Jose Valdivielso	2.25	1.10	.22
☐ 340 Don Drysdale	32.00	16.00	3.20
☐ 341 Mike Hershberger	2.25	1.10	.22
☐ 342 Ed Rakow	2.25	1.10	.22
☐ 343 Albie Pearson	2.25	1.10	.22
☐ 344 Ed Bauta	2.25	1.10	.22
☐ 345 Chuck Schilling	2.25	1.10	.22
☐ 346 Jack Kralick	2.25	1.10	.22
☐ 347 Chuck Hinton	2.25	1.10	.22
☐ 348 Larry Burright	2.25	1.10	.22
☐ 349 Paul Foytack	2.25	1.10	.22
☐ 350 Frank Robinson	36.00	18.00	3.60
☐ 351 Braves' Backstops Joe Torre Del Crandall	3.50	1.75	.35
☐ 352 Frank Sullivan	2.25	1.10	.22
☐ 353 Bill Mazeroski	4.00	2.00	.40
☐ 354 Roman Mejias	2.25	1.10	.22
☐ 355 Steve Barber	2.25	1.10	.22
☐ 356 Tom Haller	3.00	1.50	.30
☐ 357 Jerry Walker	2.25	1.10	.22
☐ 358 Tommy Davis	3.50	1.75	.35
☐ 359 Bobby Locke	2.25	1.10	.22
☐ 360 Yogi Berra	60.00	30.00	6.00
☐ 361 Bob Hendley	2.25	1.10	.22
☐ 362 Ty Cline	2.25	1.10	.22
☐ 363 Bob Roselli	2.25	1.10	.22
☐ 364 Ken Hunt	2.25	1.10	.22
☐ 365 Charlie Neal	3.00	1.50	.30
☐ 366 Phil Regan	3.00	1.50	.30
☐ 367 Checklist 5	6.50	.60	.12
☐ 368 Bob Tillman	2.25	1.10	.22
☐ 369 Ted Bowsfield	2.25	1.10	.22
☐ 370 Ken Boyer	5.00	2.50	.50
☐ 371 Earl Battey	3.25	1.60	.32
☐ 372 Jack Curtis	3.25	1.60	.32
☐ 373 Al Heist	3.25	1.60	.32
☐ 374 Gene Mauch MG	4.00	2.00	.40
☐ 375 Ron Fairly	4.00	2.00	.40
☐ 376 Bud Daley	3.25	1.60	.32
☐ 377 John Orsino	3.25	1.60	.32
☐ 378 Bennie Daniels	3.25	1.60	.32
☐ 379 Chuck Essegian	3.25	1.60	.32
☐ 380 Lou Burdette	4.00	2.00	.40
☐ 381 Chico Cardenas	3.25	1.60	.32
☐ 382 Dick Williams	4.00	2.00	.40
☐ 383 Ray Sadecki	3.25	1.60	.32
☐ 384 K.C. Athletics Team Card	6.50	3.25	.65
☐ 385 Early Wynn	13.00	6.50	1.30
☐ 386 Don Mincher	4.00	2.00	.40
☐ 387 Lou Brock	150.00	75.00	15.00
☐ 388 Ryne Duren	4.00	2.00	.40
☐ 389 Smokey Burgess	4.00	2.00	.40
☐ 390 Orlando Cepeda AS	5.50	2.75	.55
☐ 391 Bill Mazeroski AS	4.50	2.25	.45
☐ 392 Ken Boyer AS	4.50	2.25	.45
☐ 393 Roy McMillan AS	4.00	2.00	.40
☐ 394 Hank Aaron AS	30.00	15.00	3.00
☐ 395 Willie Mays AS	30.00	15.00	3.00
☐ 396 Frank Robinson AS	14.00	7.00	1.40
☐ 397 John Roseboro AS	4.00	2.00	.40
☐ 398 Don Drysdale AS	8.00	4.00	.80
☐ 399 Warren Spahn AS	9.00	4.50	.90
☐ 400 Elston Howard	7.00	3.50	.70
☐ 401 AL/NL Homer Kings Roger Maris Orlando Cepeda	32.00	16.00	3.20
☐ 402 Gino Cimoli	3.25	1.60	.32
☐ 403 Chet Nichols	3.25	1.60	.32
☐ 404 Tim Harkness	3.25	1.60	.32
☐ 405 Jim Perry	4.00	2.00	.40
☐ 406 Bob Taylor	3.25	1.60	.32
☐ 407 Hank Aguirre	3.25	1.60	.32
☐ 408 Gus Bell	4.00	2.00	.40
☐ 409 Pittsburgh Pirates Team Card	6.50	3.25	.65
☐ 410 Al Smith	3.25	1.60	.32
☐ 411 Danny O'Connell	3.25	1.60	.32
☐ 412 Charlie James	3.25	1.60	.32
☐ 413 Matty Alou	4.00	2.00	.40
☐ 414 Joe Gaines	3.25	1.60	.32
☐ 415 Bill Virdon	4.50	2.25	.45
☐ 416 Bob Scheffing MG	3.25	1.60	.32

☐ 417 Joe Azcue	3.25	1.60	.32
☐ 418 Andy Carey	3.25	1.60	.32
☐ 419 Bob Bruce	3.25	1.60	.32
☐ 420 Gus Triandos	4.00	2.00	.40
☐ 421 Ken MacKenzie	3.25	1.60	.32
☐ 422 Steve Bilko	3.25	1.60	.32
☐ 423 Rival League Relief Aces: Roy Face Hoyt Wilhelm	4.50	2.25	.45
☐ 424 Al McBean	3.25	1.60	.32
☐ 425 Carl Yastrzemski	200.00	100.00	20.00
☐ 426 Bob Farley	3.25	1.60	.32
☐ 427 Jake Wood	3.25	1.60	.32
☐ 428 Joe Hicks	3.25	1.60	.32
☐ 429 Billy O'Dell	3.25	1.60	.32
☐ 430 Tony Kubek	9.00	4.50	.90
☐ 431 Bob Rodgers	6.00	3.00	.60
☐ 432 Jim Pendleton	3.25	1.60	.32
☐ 433 Jim Archer	3.25	1.60	.32
☐ 434 Clay Dalrymple	3.25	1.60	.32
☐ 435 Larry Sherry	4.00	2.00	.40
☐ 436 Felix Mantilla	3.25	1.60	.32
☐ 437 Ray Moore	3.25	1.60	.32
☐ 438 Dick Brown	3.25	1.60	.32
☐ 439 Jerry Buchek	3.25	1.60	.32
☐ 440 Joey Jay	3.25	1.60	.32
☐ 441 Checklist 6	6.50	.60	.12
☐ 442 Wes Stock	4.00	2.00	.40
☐ 443 Del Crandall	4.00	2.00	.40
☐ 444 Ted Wills	3.25	1.60	.32
☐ 445 Vic Power	3.25	1.60	.32
☐ 446 Don Elston	3.25	1.60	.32
☐ 447 Willie Kirkland	4.00	2.00	.40
☐ 448 Joe Gibbon	4.00	2.00	.40
☐ 449 Jerry Adair	4.00	2.00	.40
☐ 450 Jim O'Toole	4.00	2.00	.40
☐ 451 Jose Tartabull	4.00	2.00	.40
☐ 452 Earl Averill	4.00	2.00	.40
☐ 453 Cal McLish	4.00	2.00	.40
☐ 454 Floyd Robinson	4.00	2.00	.40
☐ 455 Luis Arroyo	4.00	2.00	.40
☐ 456 Joe Amalfitano	4.00	2.00	.40
☐ 457 Lou Clinton	4.00	2.00	.40
☐ 458A Bob Buhl (Braves emblem on cap)	4.00	2.00	.40
☐ 458B Bob Buhl (no emblem on cap)	40.00	20.00	4.00
☐ 459 Ed Bailey	4.00	2.00	.40
☐ 460 Jim Bunning	9.00	4.50	.90
☐ 461 Ken Hubbs	12.00	6.00	1.20
☐ 462A Willie Tasby (Senators emblem on cap)	4.00	2.00	.40
☐ 462B Willie Tasby (no emblem on cap)	40.00	20.00	4.00
☐ 463 Hank Bauer MG	5.00	2.50	.50
☐ 464 Al Jackson	4.00	2.00	.40
☐ 465 Reds Team	8.00	4.00	.80
☐ 466 Norm Cash AS	5.00	2.50	.50
☐ 467 Chuck Schilling AS	4.00	2.00	.40
☐ 468 Brooks Robinson AS	14.00	7.00	1.40
☐ 469 Luis Aparicio AS	8.00	4.00	.80
☐ 470 Al Kaline AS	14.00	7.00	1.40
☐ 471 Mickey Mantle AS	100.00	50.00	10.00
☐ 472 Rocky Colavito AS	5.00	2.50	.50
☐ 473 Elston Howard AS	5.00	2.50	.50
☐ 474 Frank Lary AS	4.50	2.25	.45
☐ 475 Whitey Ford AS	12.00	6.00	1.20
☐ 476 Orioles Team	8.00	4.00	.80
☐ 477 Andre Rodgers	4.00	2.00	.40
☐ 478 Don Zimmer	5.00	2.50	.50
☐ 479 Joel Horlen	4.00	2.00	.40
☐ 480 Harvey Kuenn	5.50	2.75	.55
☐ 481 Vic Wertz	4.50	2.25	.45
☐ 482 Sam Mele MG	4.00	2.00	.40
☐ 483 Don McMahon	4.00	2.00	.40
☐ 484 Dick Schofield	4.00	2.00	.40
☐ 485 Pedro Ramos	4.00	2.00	.40
☐ 486 Jim Gilliam	6.00	3.00	.60
☐ 487 Jerry Lynch	4.00	2.00	.40
☐ 488 Hal Brown	4.00	2.00	.40
☐ 489 Julio Gotay	4.00	2.00	.40
☐ 490 Clete Boyer	5.50	2.75	.55
☐ 491 Leon Wagner	4.00	2.00	.40
☐ 492 Hal W. Smith	4.00	2.00	.40
☐ 493 Danny McDevitt	4.00	2.00	.40
☐ 494 Sammy White	4.00	2.00	.40
☐ 495 Don Cardwell	4.00	2.00	.40
☐ 496 Wayne Causey	4.00	2.00	.40
☐ 497 Ed Bouchee	4.00	2.00	.40
☐ 498 Jim Donohue	4.00	2.00	.40
☐ 499 Zoilo Versalles	4.00	2.00	.40

☐ 500 Duke Snider	42.00	20.00	4.00
☐ 501 Claude Osteen	4.50	2.25	.45
☐ 502 Hector Lopez	4.00	2.00	.40
☐ 503 Danny Murtaugh MG	4.00	2.00	.40
☐ 504 Eddie Bressoud	4.00	2.00	.40
☐ 505 Juan Marichal	35.00	17.50	3.50
☐ 506 Charlie Maxwell	4.00	2.00	.40
☐ 507 Ernie Broglio	4.00	2.00	.40
☐ 508 Gordy Coleman	4.50	2.25	.45
☐ 509 Dave Giusti	5.00	2.50	.50
☐ 510 Jim Lemon	4.50	2.25	.45
☐ 511 Bubba Phillips	4.00	2.00	.40
☐ 512 Mike Fornieles	4.00	2.00	.40
☐ 513 Whitey Herzog	5.50	2.75	.55
☐ 514 Sherm Lollar	4.50	2.25	.45
☐ 515 Stan Williams	4.00	2.00	.40
☐ 516 Checklist 7	12.00	1.20	.20
☐ 517 Dave Wickersham	4.00	2.00	.40
☐ 518 Lee Maye	4.00	2.00	.40
☐ 519 Bob Johnson	4.00	2.00	.40
☐ 520 Bob Friend	4.50	2.25	.45
☐ 521 Jacke Davis UER (listed as OF on front and P on back)	4.00	2.00	.40
☐ 522 Lindy McDaniel	4.50	2.25	.45
☐ 523 Russ Nixon SP	20.00	10.00	2.00
☐ 524 Howie Nunn SP	20.00	10.00	2.00
☐ 525 George Thomas	12.00	6.00	1.20
☐ 526 Hal Woodeshick SP	20.00	10.00	2.00
☐ 527 Dick McAuliffe	14.00	7.00	1.40
☐ 528 Turk Lown	12.00	6.00	1.20
☐ 529 John Schaive SP	20.00	10.00	2.00
☐ 530 Bob Gibson SP	135.00	65.00	13.50
☐ 531 Bobby G. Smith	12.00	6.00	1.20
☐ 532 Dick Stigman	12.00	6.00	1.20
☐ 533 Charley Lau SP	20.00	10.00	2.00
☐ 534 Tony Gonzalez SP	20.00	10.00	2.00
☐ 535 Ed Roebuck	12.00	6.00	1.20
☐ 536 Dick Gernert	12.00	6.00	1.20
☐ 537 Cleveland Indians Team Card	24.00	12.00	2.40
☐ 538 Jack Sanford	14.00	7.00	1.40
☐ 539 Billy Moran	12.00	6.00	1.20
☐ 540 Jim Landis SP	20.00	10.00	2.00
☐ 541 Don Nottebart SP	20.00	10.00	2.00
☐ 542 Dave Philley	12.00	6.00	1.20
☐ 543 Bob Allen SP	20.00	10.00	2.00
☐ 544 Willie McCovey SP	135.00	65.00	13.50
☐ 545 Hoyt Wilhelm SP	50.00	25.00	5.00
☐ 546 Moe Thacker SP	20.00	10.00	2.00
☐ 547 Don Ferrarese	12.00	6.00	1.20
☐ 548 Bobby Del Greco	12.00	6.00	1.20
☐ 549 Bill Rigney MG SP	20.00	10.00	2.00
☐ 550 Art Mahaffey SP	20.00	10.00	2.00
☐ 551 Harry Bright	12.00	6.00	1.20
☐ 552 Chicago Cubs SP Team Card	40.00	20.00	4.00
☐ 553 Jim Coates	12.00	6.00	1.20
☐ 554 Bubba Morton SP	20.00	10.00	2.00
☐ 555 John Buzhardt SP	20.00	10.00	2.00
☐ 556 Al Spangler	12.00	6.00	1.20
☐ 557 Bob Anderson SP	20.00	10.00	2.00
☐ 558 John Goryl	12.00	6.00	1.20
☐ 559 Mike Higgins MG	12.00	6.00	1.20
☐ 560 Chuck Estrada SP	20.00	10.00	2.00
☐ 561 Gene Oliver SP	20.00	10.00	2.00
☐ 562 Bill Henry	12.00	6.00	1.20
☐ 563 Ken Aspromonte	12.00	6.00	1.20
☐ 564 Bob Grim	12.00	6.00	1.20
☐ 565 Jose Pagan	12.00	6.00	1.20
☐ 566 Marty Kutyna SP	20.00	10.00	2.00
☐ 567 Tracy Stallard SP	20.00	10.00	2.00
☐ 568 Jim Golden	12.00	6.00	1.20
☐ 569 Ed Sadowski SP	20.00	10.00	2.00
☐ 570 Bill Stafford SP	20.00	10.00	2.00
☐ 571 Billy Klaus SP	20.00	10.00	2.00
☐ 572 Bob G. Miller SP	20.00	10.00	2.00
☐ 573 Johnny Logan	14.00	7.00	1.40
☐ 574 Dean Stone	12.00	6.00	1.20
☐ 575 Red Schoendienst SP	42.00	20.00	4.00
☐ 576 Russ Kemmerer SP	20.00	10.00	2.00
☐ 577 Dave Nicholson SP	20.00	10.00	2.00
☐ 578 Jim Duffalo	12.00	6.00	1.20
☐ 579 Jim Schaffer SP	20.00	10.00	2.00
☐ 580 Bill Monbouquette	12.00	6.00	1.20
☐ 581 Mel Roach	12.00	6.00	1.20
☐ 582 Ron Piche	12.00	6.00	1.20
☐ 583 Larry Osborne	12.00	6.00	1.20
☐ 584 Minnesota Twins SP Team Card	40.00	20.00	4.00
☐ 585 Glen Hobbie SP	20.00	10.00	2.00
☐ 586 Sammy Esposito SP	20.00	10.00	2.00
☐ 587 Frank Funk SP	20.00	10.00	2.00
☐ 588 Birdie Tebbetts MG	12.00	6.00	1.20

☐ 589 Bob Turley	16.00	8.00	1.60
☐ 590 Curt Flood	18.00	9.00	1.80
☐ 591 Rookie Pitchers SP Sam McDowell Ron Taylor Ron Nischwitz Art Quirk Dick Radatz	35.00	17.50	3.50
☐ 592 Rookie Pitchers SP Dan Pfister Bo Belinsky Dave Stenhouse Jim Bouton Joe Bonikowski	45.00	22.50	4.50
☐ 593 Rookie Pitchers SP Jack Lamabe Craig Anderson Jack Hamilton Bob Moorhead Bob Veale	25.00	12.50	2.50
☐ 594 Rookie Catchers SP Doc Edwards Ken Retzer Bob Uecker Doug Camilli Don Pavletich	125.00	60.00	12.50
☐ 595 Rookie Infielders SP Bob Sadowski Felix Torres Marlan Coughtry Ed Charles	20.00	10.00	2.00
☐ 596 Rookie Infielders SP Bernie Allen Joe Pepitone Phil Linz Rich Rollins	36.00	18.00	3.60
☐ 597 Rookie Infielders SP Jim McKnight Rod Kanehl Amado Samuel Denis Menke	20.00	10.00	2.00
☐ 598 Rookie Outfielders SP Al Luplow Manny Jimenez Howie Goss Jim Hickman Ed Olivares	45.00	22.50	4.50

1963 Topps

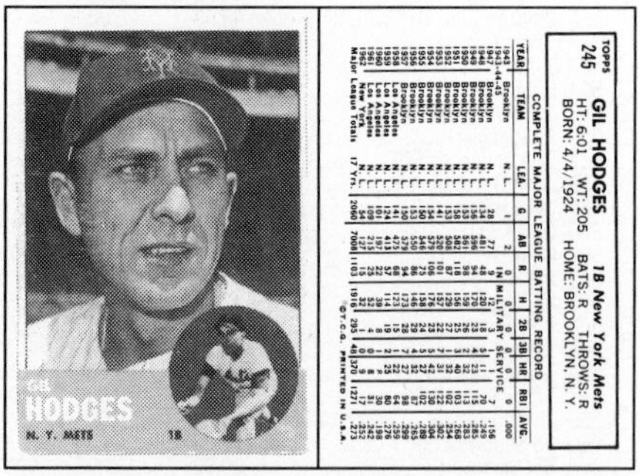

The cards in this 576-card set measure 2 1/2" by 3 1/2". The sharp color photographs of the 1963 set are a vivid contrast to the drab pictures of 1962. In addition to the "League Leaders" series (1-10) and World Series cards (142-148), the seventh and last series of cards (523-576) contains seven rookie cards (each depicting four players). There were some three-card advertising panels produced by Topps; the players included are from the first series; one panel shows Hoyt Wilhelm, Don Lock, and Bob Duliba on the front with a Stan Musial ad/endorsement on one of the backs. This set has gained special prominence in recent years since it contains the rookie card of Pete Rose (537). Other key rookies in this set are Tony Oliva, Willie Stargell, and Rusty Staub.

	NRMT	VG-E	GOOD
COMPLETE SET (576)	4300.00	2100.00	450.00
COMMON PLAYER (1-109)	1.00	.50	.10
COMMON PLAYER (110-196)	1.25	.60	.12
COMMON PLAYER (197-283)	1.50	.75	.15
COMMON PLAYER (284-446)	2.25	1.10	.22
COMMON PLAYER (447-522)	11.00	5.50	1.10
COMMON PLAYER (523-576)	6.50	3.25	.65
☐ 1 NL Batting Leaders Tommy Davis Frank Robinson Stan Musial Hank Aaron Bill White	30.00	5.00	1.00
☐ 2 AL Batting Leaders Pete Runnels Mickey Mantle Floyd Robinson Norm Siebern Chuck Hinton	10.00	5.00	1.00
☐ 3 NL Home Run Leaders Willie Mays Hank Aaron Frank Robinson Orlando Cepeda Ernie Banks	12.00	6.00	1.20
☐ 4 AL Home Run Leaders Harmon Killebrew Norm Cash Rocky Colavito Roger Maris Jim Gentile Leon Wagner	3.00	1.50	.30
☐ 5 NL ERA Leaders Sandy Koufax Bob Shaw Bob Purkey Bob Gibson Don Drysdale	4.50	2.25	.45
☐ 6 AL ERA Leaders Hank Aguirre Robin Roberts Whitey Ford Eddie Fisher Dean Chance	2.50	1.25	.25
☐ 7 AL Pitching Leaders Don Drysdale Jack Sanford Bob Purkey Billy O'Dell Art Mahaffey Joe Jay	2.00	1.00	.20
☐ 8 AL Pitching Leaders Ralph Terry Dick Donovan Ray Herbert Jim Bunning Camilo Pascual	2.00	1.00	.20
☐ 9 NL Strikeout Leaders Don Drysdale Sandy Koufax Bob Gibson Billy O'Dell Dick Farrell	4.50	2.25	.45
☐ 10 AL Strikeout Leaders Camilo Pascual Jim Bunning Ralph Terry Juan Pizarro Jim Kaat	2.00	1.00	.20
☐ 11 Lee Walls	1.00	.50	.10
☐ 12 Steve Barber	1.00	.50	.10
☐ 13 Philadelphia Phillies Team Card	2.00	1.00	.20
☐ 14 Pedro Ramos	1.00	.50	.10
☐ 15 Ken Hubbs	2.00	1.00	.20
☐ 16 Al Smith	1.00	.50	.10
☐ 17 Ryne Duren	1.50	.75	.15
☐ 18 Buc Blasters Smoky Burgess Dick Stuart Bob Clemente Bob Skinner	8.00	4.00	.80
☐ 19 Pete Burnside	1.00	.50	.10
☐ 20 Tony Kubek	3.00	1.50	.30
☐ 21 Marty Keough	1.00	.50	.10
☐ 22 Curt Simmons	1.50	.75	.15
☐ 23 Ed Lopat MG	1.50	.75	.15
☐ 24 Bob Bruce	1.00	.50	.10
☐ 25 Al Kaline	25.00	12.50	2.50
☐ 26 Ray Moore	1.00	.50	.10
☐ 27 Choo Choo Coleman	1.00	.50	.10
☐ 28 Mike Fornieles	1.00	.50	.10

☐ 29A	1962 Rookie Stars	4.50	2.25	.45
	Sammy Ellis			
	Ray Culp			
	John Boozer			
	Jesse Gonder			
☐ 29B	1963 Rookie Stars	2.00	1.00	.20
	Sammy Ellis			
	Ray Culp			
	John Boozer			
	Jesse Gonder			
☐ 30	Harvey Kuenn	2.00	1.00	.20
☐ 31	Cal Koonce	1.00	.50	.10
☐ 32	Tony Gonzalez	1.00	.50	.10
☐ 33	Bo Belinsky	1.50	.75	.15
☐ 34	Dick Schofield	1.00	.50	.10
☐ 35	John Buzhardt	1.00	.50	.10
☐ 36	Jerry Kindall	1.00	.50	.10
☐ 37	Jerry Lynch	1.00	.50	.10
☐ 38	Bud Daley	1.00	.50	.10
☐ 39	Angels Team	2.00	1.00	.20
☐ 40	Vic Power	1.00	.50	.10
☐ 41	Charley Lau	1.50	.75	.15
☐ 42	Stan Williams	1.00	.50	.10
	(listed as Yankee on			
	card but LA cap)			
☐ 43	Veteran Masters	3.50	1.75	.35
	Casey Stengel			
	Gene Woodling			
☐ 44	Terry Fox	1.00	.50	.10
☐ 45	Bob Aspromonte	1.00	.50	.10
☐ 46	Tommy Aaron	1.50	.75	.15
☐ 47	Don Lock	1.00	.50	.10
☐ 48	Birdie Tebbetts MG	1.00	.50	.10
☐ 49	Dal Maxvill	1.00	.50	.10
☐ 50	Billy Pierce	1.50	.75	.15
☐ 51	George Alusik	1.00	.50	.10
☐ 52	Chuck Schilling	1.00	.50	.10
☐ 53	Joe Moeller	1.00	.50	.10
☐ 54A	1962 Rookie Stars	7.50	3.75	.75
	Nelson Mathews			
	Harry Fanok			
	Jack Cullen			
	Dave DeBusschere			
☐ 54B	1963 Rookie Stars	3.50	1.75	.35
	Nelson Mathews			
	Harry Fanok			
	Jack Cullen			
	Dave DeBusschere			
☐ 55	Bill Virdon	1.50	.75	.15
☐ 56	Dennis Bennett	1.00	.50	.10
☐ 57	Billy Moran	1.00	.50	.10
☐ 58	Bob Will	1.00	.50	.10
☐ 59	Craig Anderson	1.00	.50	.10
☐ 60	Elston Howard	4.50	2.25	.45
☐ 61	Ernie Bowman	1.00	.50	.10
☐ 62	Bob Hendley	1.00	.50	.10
☐ 63	Reds Team	2.00	1.00	.20
☐ 64	Dick McAuliffe	1.00	.50	.10
☐ 65	Jackie Brandt	1.00	.50	.10
☐ 66	Mike Joyce	1.00	.50	.10
☐ 67	Ed Charles	1.00	.50	.10
☐ 68	Friendly Foes	8.00	4.00	.80
	Duke Snider			
	Gil Hodges			
☐ 69	Bud Zipfel	1.00	.50	.10
☐ 70	Jim O'Toole	1.00	.50	.10
☐ 71	Bobby Wine	1.00	.50	.10
☐ 72	Johnny Romano	1.00	.50	.10
☐ 73	Bobby Bragan MG	1.00	.50	.10
☐ 74	Denny Lemaster	1.00	.50	.10
☐ 75	Bob Allison	1.50	.75	.15
☐ 76	Earl Wilson	1.00	.50	.10
☐ 77	Al Spangler	1.00	.50	.10
☐ 78	Marv Throneberry	1.50	.75	.15
☐ 79	Checklist 1	5.50	.50	.10
☐ 80	Jim Gilliam	2.00	1.00	.20
☐ 81	Jim Schaffer	1.00	.50	.10
☐ 82	Ed Rakow	1.00	.50	.10
☐ 83	Charley James	1.00	.50	.10
☐ 84	Ron Kline	1.00	.50	.10
☐ 85	Tom Haller	1.00	.50	.10
☐ 86	Charley Maxwell	1.00	.50	.10
☐ 87	Bob Veale	1.50	.75	.15
☐ 88	Ron Hansen	1.00	.50	.10
☐ 89	Dick Stigman	1.00	.50	.10
☐ 90	Gordy Coleman	1.00	.50	.10
☐ 91	Dallas Green	2.00	1.00	.20
☐ 92	Hector Lopez	1.00	.50	.10
☐ 93	Galen Cisco	1.00	.50	.10
☐ 94	Bob Schmidt	1.00	.50	.10
☐ 95	Larry Jackson	1.00	.50	.10
☐ 96	Lou Clinton	1.00	.50	.10
☐ 97	Bob Duliba	1.00	.50	.10
☐ 98	George Thomas	1.00	.50	.10
☐ 99	Jim Umbricht	1.00	.50	.10
☐ 100	Joe Cunningham	1.00	.50	.10
☐ 101	Joe Gibbon	1.00	.50	.10
☐ 102A	Checklist 2	5.50	.50	.10
	(red on yellow)			
☐ 102B	Checklist 2	7.50	.75	.15
	(white on red)			
☐ 103	Chuck Essegian	1.00	.50	.10
☐ 104	Lew Krausse	1.00	.50	.10
☐ 105	Ron Fairly	1.50	.75	.15
☐ 106	Bobby Bolin	1.00	.50	.10
☐ 107	Jim Hickman	1.00	.50	.10
☐ 108	Hoyt Wilhelm	8.50	4.25	.85
☐ 109	Lee Maye	1.00	.50	.10
☐ 110	Rich Rollins	1.25	.60	.12
☐ 111	Al Jackson	1.25	.60	.12
☐ 112	Dick Brown	1.25	.60	.12
☐ 113	Don Landrum UER	1.75	.85	.17
	(photo actually			
	Ron Santo)			
☐ 114	Dan Osinski	1.25	.60	.12
☐ 115	Carl Yastrzemski	85.00	42.50	8.50
☐ 116	Jim Brosnan	1.25	.60	.12
☐ 117	Jacke Davis	1.25	.60	.12
☐ 118	Sherm Lollar	1.25	.60	.12
☐ 119	Bob Lillis	1.25	.60	.12
☐ 120	Roger Maris	55.00	27.50	5.50
☐ 121	Jim Hannan	1.25	.60	.12
☐ 122	Julio Gotay	1.25	.60	.12
☐ 123	Frank Howard	2.25	1.10	.22
☐ 124	Dick Howser	1.75	.85	.17
☐ 125	Robin Roberts	10.00	5.00	1.00
☐ 126	Bob Uecker	30.00	15.00	3.00
☐ 127	Bill Tuttle	1.25	.60	.12
☐ 128	Matty Alou	1.75	.85	.17
☐ 129	Gary Bell	1.25	.60	.12
☐ 130	Dick Groat	1.75	.85	.17
☐ 131	Washington Senators	2.00	1.00	.20
	Team Card			
☐ 132	Jack Hamilton	1.25	.60	.12
☐ 133	Gene Freese	1.25	.60	.12
☐ 134	Bob Scheffing MG	1.25	.60	.12
☐ 135	Richie Ashburn	6.00	3.00	.60
☐ 136	Ike Delock	1.25	.60	.12
☐ 137	Mack Jones	1.25	.60	.12
☐ 138	Pride of NL	30.00	15.00	3.00
	Willie Mays			
	Stan Musial			
☐ 139	Earl Averill	1.25	.60	.12
☐ 140	Frank Lary	1.75	.85	.17
☐ 141	Manny Mota	5.00	2.50	.50
☐ 142	World Series Game 1	4.50	2.25	.45
	Ford wins			
	series opener			
☐ 143	World Series Game 2	3.00	1.50	.30
	Sanford flashes			
	shutout magic			
☐ 144	World Series Game 3	8.00	4.00	.80
	Maris sparks			
	Yankee rally			
☐ 145	World Series Game 4	3.00	1.50	.30
	Hiller blasts			
	grand slammer			
☐ 146	World Series Game 5	3.00	1.50	.30
	Tresh's homer			
	defeats Giants			
☐ 147	World Series Game 6	3.00	1.50	.30
	Pierce stars in			
	3 hit victory			
☐ 148	World Series Game 7	3.00	1.50	.30
	Yanks celebrate			
	as Terry wins			
☐ 149	Marv Breeding	1.25	.60	.12
☐ 150	Johnny Podres	2.00	1.00	.20
☐ 151	Pirates Team	2.00	1.00	.20
☐ 152	Ron Nischwitz	1.25	.60	.12
☐ 153	Hal Smith	1.25	.60	.12
☐ 154	Walt Alston MG	3.50	1.75	.35
☐ 155	Bill Stafford	1.25	.60	.12
☐ 156	Roy McMillan	1.25	.60	.12
☐ 157	Diego Segui	1.25	.60	.12
☐ 158	Rookie Stars	1.75	.85	.17
	Rogelio Alvares			
	Dave Roberts			
	Tommy Harper			
	Bob Saverine			
☐ 159	Jim Pagliaroni	1.25	.60	.12
☐ 160	Juan Pizarro	1.25	.60	.12
☐ 161	Frank Torre	1.25	.60	.12
☐ 162	Twins Team	2.00	1.00	.20
☐ 163	Don Larsen	1.75	.85	.17
☐ 164	Bubba Morton	1.25	.60	.12
☐ 165	Jim Kaat	4.00	2.00	.40
☐ 166	Johnny Keane MG	1.75	.85	.17

☐ 167 Jim Fregosi	2.00	1.00	.20
☐ 168 Russ Nixon	1.75	.85	.17
☐ 169 Rookie Stars	30.00	12.00	2.50
Dick Egan			
Julio Navarro			
Tommie Sisk			
Gaylord Perry			
☐ 170 Joe Adcock	1.75	.85	.17
☐ 171 Steve Hamilton	1.25	.60	.12
☐ 172 Gene Oliver	1.25	.60	.12
☐ 173 Bombers' Best	50.00	25.00	5.00
Tom Tresh			
Mickey Mantle			
Bobby Richardson			
☐ 174 Larry Burright	1.25	.60	.12
☐ 175 Bob Buhl	1.25	.60	.12
☐ 176 Jim King	1.25	.60	.12
☐ 177 Bubba Phillips	1.25	.60	.12
☐ 178 Johnny Edwards	1.25	.60	.12
☐ 179 Ron Piche	1.25	.60	.12
☐ 180 Bill Skowron	2.00	1.00	.20
☐ 181 Sammy Esposito	1.25	.60	.12
☐ 182 Albie Pearson	1.25	.60	.12
☐ 183 Joe Pepitone	2.50	1.25	.25
☐ 184 Vern Law	1.75	.85	.17
☐ 185 Chuck Hiller	1.25	.60	.12
☐ 186 Jerry Zimmerman	1.25	.60	.12
☐ 187 Willie Kirkland	1.25	.60	.12
☐ 188 Eddie Bressoud	1.25	.60	.12
☐ 189 Dave Giusti	1.75	.85	.17
☐ 190 Minnie Minoso	2.50	1.25	.25
☐ 191 Checklist 3	5.50	.50	.10
☐ 192 Clay Dalrymple	1.25	.60	.12
☐ 193 Andre Rodgers	1.25	.60	.12
☐ 194 Joe Nuxhall	1.75	.85	.17
☐ 195 Manny Jimenez	1.25	.60	.12
☐ 196 Doug Camilli	1.25	.60	.12
☐ 197 Roger Craig	2.50	1.25	.25
☐ 198 Lenny Green	1.50	.75	.15
☐ 199 Joe Amalfitano	1.50	.75	.15
☐ 200 Mickey Mantle	325.00	160.00	32.00
☐ 201 Cecil Butler	1.50	.75	.15
☐ 202 Boston Red Sox	3.50	1.75	.35
Team Card			
☐ 203 Chico Cardenas	1.50	.75	.15
☐ 204 Don Nottebart	1.50	.75	.15
☐ 205 Luis Aparicio	12.00	6.00	1.20
☐ 206 Ray Washburn	1.50	.75	.15
☐ 207 Ken Hunt	1.50	.75	.15
☐ 208 Rookie Stars	1.50	.75	.15
Ron Herbel			
John Miller			
Wally Wolf			
Ron Taylor			
☐ 209 Hobie Landrith	1.50	.75	.15
☐ 210 Sandy Koufax	125.00	60.00	12.50
☐ 211 Fred Whitfield	1.50	.75	.15
☐ 212 Glen Hobbie	1.50	.75	.15
☐ 213 Billy Hitchcock MG	1.50	.75	.15
☐ 214 Orlando Pena	1.50	.75	.15
☐ 215 Bob Skinner	1.50	.75	.15
☐ 216 Gene Conley	1.50	.75	.15
☐ 217 Joe Christopher	1.50	.75	.15
☐ 218 Tiger Twirlers	2.50	1.25	.25
Frank Lary			
Don Mossi			
Jim Bunning			
☐ 219 Chuck Cottier	1.50	.75	.15
☐ 220 Camilo Pascual	2.00	1.00	.20
☐ 221 Cookie Rojas	2.00	1.00	.20
☐ 222 Cubs Team	3.00	1.50	.30
☐ 223 Eddie Fisher	1.50	.75	.15
☐ 224 Mike Roarke	1.50	.75	.15
☐ 225 Joey Jay	1.50	.75	.15
☐ 226 Julian Javier	1.50	.75	.15
☐ 227 Jim Grant	1.50	.75	.15
☐ 228 Rookie Stars	33.00	15.00	3.00
Max Alvis			
Bob Bailey			
Tony Oliva			
(listed as Pedro)			
Ed Kranepool			
☐ 229 Willie Davis	2.00	1.00	.20
☐ 230 Pete Runnels	1.50	.75	.15
☐ 231 Eli Grba UER	1.50	.75	.15
(large photo is			
Ryne Duren)			
☐ 232 Frank Malzone	2.00	1.00	.20
☐ 233 Casey Stengel MG	15.00	7.50	1.50
☐ 234 Dave Nicholson	1.50	.75	.15
☐ 235 Billy O'Dell	1.50	.75	.15
☐ 236 Bill Bryan	1.50	.75	.15
☐ 237 Jim Coates	1.50	.75	.15
☐ 238 Lou Johnson	1.50	.75	.15
☐ 239 Harvey Haddix	2.00	1.00	.20
☐ 240 Rocky Colavito	4.50	2.25	.45
☐ 241 Bob Smith	1.50	.75	.15
☐ 242 Power Plus	25.00	12.50	2.50
Ernie Banks			
Hank Aaron			
☐ 243 Don Leppert	1.50	.75	.15
☐ 244 John Tsitouris	1.50	.75	.15
☐ 245 Gil Hodges	16.00	8.00	1.60
☐ 246 Lee Stange	1.50	.75	.15
☐ 247 Yankees Team	10.00	5.00	1.00
☐ 248 Tito Francona	1.50	.75	.15
☐ 249 Leo Burke	1.50	.75	.15
☐ 250 Stan Musial	100.00	50.00	10.00
☐ 251 Jack Lamabe	1.50	.75	.15
☐ 252 Ron Santo	4.50	2.25	.45
☐ 253 Rookie Stars	1.50	.75	.15
Len Gabrielson			
Pete Jernigan			
John Wojcik			
Deacon Jones			
☐ 254 Mike Hershberger	1.50	.75	.15
☐ 255 Bob Shaw	1.50	.75	.15
☐ 256 Jerry Lumpe	1.50	.75	.15
☐ 257 Hank Aguirre	1.50	.75	.15
☐ 258 Alvin Dark MG	2.00	1.00	.20
☐ 259 Johnny Logan	2.00	1.00	.20
☐ 260 Jim Gentile	2.00	1.00	.20
☐ 261 Bob Miller	1.50	.75	.15
☐ 262 Ellis Burton	1.50	.75	.15
☐ 263 Dave Stenhouse	1.50	.75	.15
☐ 264 Phil Linz	2.00	1.00	.20
☐ 265 Vada Pinson	3.50	1.75	.35
☐ 266 Bob Allen	1.50	.75	.15
☐ 267 Carl Sawatski	1.50	.75	.15
☐ 268 Don Demeter	1.50	.75	.15
☐ 269 Don Mincher	2.00	1.00	.20
☐ 270 Felipe Alou	2.00	1.00	.20
☐ 271 Dean Stone	1.50	.75	.15
☐ 272 Danny Murphy	1.50	.75	.15
☐ 273 Sammy Taylor	1.50	.75	.15
☐ 274 Checklist 4	5.50	.50	.10
☐ 275 Eddie Mathews	18.00	9.00	1.80
☐ 276 Barry Shetrone	1.50	.75	.15
☐ 277 Dick Farrell	1.50	.75	.15
☐ 278 Chico Fernandez	1.50	.75	.15
☐ 279 Wally Moon	2.00	1.00	.20
☐ 280 Bob Rodgers	2.00	1.00	.20
☐ 281 Tom Sturdivant	1.50	.75	.15
☐ 282 Bobby Del Greco	1.50	.75	.15
☐ 283 Roy Sievers	2.00	1.00	.20
☐ 284 Dave Sisler	2.25	1.10	.22
☐ 285 Dick Stuart	3.00	1.50	.30
☐ 286 Stu Miller	2.25	1.10	.22
☐ 287 Dick Bertell	2.25	1.10	.22
☐ 288 Chicago White Sox	4.00	2.00	.40
Team Card			
☐ 289 Hal Brown	2.25	1.10	.22
☐ 290 Bill White	4.00	2.00	.40
☐ 291 Don Rudolph	2.25	1.10	.22
☐ 292 Pumpsie Green	2.25	1.10	.22
☐ 293 Bill Pleis	2.25	1.10	.22
☐ 294 Bill Rigney MG	2.25	1.10	.22
☐ 295 Ed Roebuck	2.25	1.10	.22
☐ 296 Doc Edwards	2.25	1.10	.22
☐ 297 Jim Golden	2.25	1.10	.22
☐ 298 Don Dillard	2.25	1.10	.22
☐ 299 Rookie Stars	2.25	1.10	.22
Dave Morehead			
Bob Dustal			
Tom Butters			
Dan Schneider			
☐ 300 Willie Mays	125.00	60.00	12.50
☐ 301 Bill Fischer	2.25	1.10	.22
☐ 302 Whitey Herzog	3.50	1.75	.35
☐ 303 Earl Francis	2.25	1.10	.22
☐ 304 Harry Bright	2.25	1.10	.22
☐ 305 Don Hoak	2.25	1.10	.22
☐ 306 Star Receivers	3.00	1.50	.30
Earl Battey			
Elston Howard			
☐ 307 Chet Nichols	2.25	1.10	.22
☐ 308 Camilo Carreon	2.25	1.10	.22
☐ 309 Jim Brewer	2.25	1.10	.22
☐ 310 Tommy Davis	3.50	1.75	.35
☐ 311 Joe McClain	2.25	1.10	.22
☐ 312 Houston Colts	8.00	4.00	.80
Team Card			
☐ 313 Ernie Broglio	2.25	1.10	.22
☐ 314 John Goryl	2.25	1.10	.22
☐ 315 Ralph Terry	3.00	1.50	.30
☐ 316 Norm Sherry	2.25	1.10	.22
☐ 317 Sam McDowell	3.50	1.75	.35
☐ 318 Gene Mauch MG	3.00	1.50	.30

☐ 319	Joe Gaines	2.25	1.10	.22
☐ 320	Warren Spahn	33.00	15.00	3.00
☐ 321	Gino Cimoli	2.25	1.10	.22
☐ 322	Bob Turley	3.00	1.50	.30
☐ 323	Bill Mazeroski	3.50	1.75	.35
☐ 324	Rookie Stars George Williams Pete Ward Phil Roof Vic Davalillo	3.00	1.50	.30
☐ 325	Jack Sanford	2.25	1.10	.22
☐ 326	Hank Foiles	2.25	1.10	.22
☐ 327	Paul Foytack	2.25	1.10	.22
☐ 328	Dick Williams	3.00	1.50	.30
☐ 329	Lindy McDaniel	3.00	1.50	.30
☐ 330	Chuck Hinton	2.25	1.10	.22
☐ 331	Series Foes Bill Stafford Bill Pierce	3.00	1.50	.30
☐ 332	Joel Horlen	2.25	1.10	.22
☐ 333	Carl Warwick	2.25	1.10	.22
☐ 334	Wynn Hawkins	2.25	1.10	.22
☐ 335	Leon Wagner	2.25	1.10	.22
☐ 336	Ed Bauta	2.25	1.10	.22
☐ 337	Dodgers Team	8.00	4.00	.80
☐ 338	Russ Kemmerer	2.25	1.10	.22
☐ 339	Ted Bowsfield	2.25	1.10	.22
☐ 340	Yogi Berra (player/coach)	65.00	32.50	6.50
☐ 341	Jack Baldschun	2.25	1.10	.22
☐ 342	Gene Woodling	3.00	1.50	.30
☐ 343	Johnny Pesky MG	3.00	1.50	.30
☐ 344	Don Schwall	3.00	1.50	.30
☐ 345	Brooks Robinson	40.00	20.00	4.00
☐ 346	Billy Hoeft	2.25	1.10	.22
☐ 347	Joe Torre	5.00	2.50	.50
☐ 348	Vic Wertz	2.25	1.10	.22
☐ 349	Zoilo Versalles	2.25	1.10	.22
☐ 350	Bob Purkey	2.25	1.10	.22
☐ 351	Al Luplow	2.25	1.10	.22
☐ 352	Ken Johnson	2.25	1.10	.22
☐ 353	Billy Williams	22.00	11.00	2.20
☐ 354	Dom Zanni	2.25	1.10	.22
☐ 355	Dean Chance	3.00	1.50	.30
☐ 356	John Schaive	2.25	1.10	.22
☐ 357	George Altman	2.25	1.10	.22
☐ 358	Milt Pappas	3.00	1.50	.30
☐ 359	Haywood Sullivan	2.25	1.10	.22
☐ 360	Don Drysdale	28.00	14.00	2.80
☐ 361	Clete Boyer	3.50	1.75	.35
☐ 362	Checklist 5	5.50	.50	.10
☐ 363	Dick Radatz	3.50	1.75	.35
☐ 364	Howie Goss	2.25	1.10	.22
☐ 365	Jim Bunning	7.00	3.50	.70
☐ 366	Tony Taylor	2.25	1.10	.22
☐ 367	Tony Cloninger	2.25	1.10	.22
☐ 368	Ed Bailey	2.25	1.10	.22
☐ 369	Jim Lemon MG	3.00	1.50	.30
☐ 370	Dick Donovan	2.25	1.10	.22
☐ 371	Rod Kanehl	2.25	1.10	.22
☐ 372	Don Lee	2.25	1.10	.22
☐ 373	Jim Campbell	2.25	1.10	.22
☐ 374	Claude Osteen	3.00	1.50	.30
☐ 375	Ken Boyer	5.00	2.50	.50
☐ 376	John Wyatt	2.25	1.10	.22
☐ 377	Baltimore Orioles Team Card	4.50	2.25	.45
☐ 378	Bill Henry	2.25	1.10	.22
☐ 379	Bob Anderson	2.25	1.10	.22
☐ 380	Ernie Banks	40.00	20.00	4.00
☐ 381	Frank Baumann	2.25	1.10	.22
☐ 382	Ralph Houk MG	3.00	1.50	.30
☐ 383	Pete Richert	2.25	1.10	.22
☐ 384	Bob Tillman	2.25	1.10	.22
☐ 385	Art Mahaffey	2.25	1.10	.22
☐ 386	Rookie Stars Ed Kirkpatrick John Bateman Larry Bearnarth Garry Roggenburk	3.00	1.50	.30
☐ 387	Al McBean	2.25	1.10	.22
☐ 388	Jim Davenport	3.00	1.50	.30
☐ 389	Frank Sullivan	2.25	1.10	.22
☐ 390	Hank Aaron	125.00	60.00	12.50
☐ 391	Bill Dailey	2.25	1.10	.22
☐ 392	Tribe Thumpers Johnny Romano Tito Francona	3.00	1.50	.30
☐ 393	Ken MacKenzie	2.25	1.10	.22
☐ 394	Tim McCarver	9.00	4.50	.90
☐ 395	Don McMahon	2.25	1.10	.22
☐ 396	Joe Koppe	2.25	1.10	.22
☐ 397	Kansas City Athletics Team Card	4.00	2.00	.40
☐ 398	Boog Powell	11.00	5.50	1.10
☐ 399	Dick Ellsworth	3.00	1.50	.30
☐ 400	Frank Robinson	40.00	20.00	4.00
☐ 401	Jim Bouton	5.00	2.50	.50
☐ 402	Mickey Vernon MG	2.25	1.10	.22
☐ 403	Ron Perranoski	3.00	1.50	.30
☐ 404	Bob Oldis	2.25	1.10	.22
☐ 405	Floyd Robinson	2.25	1.10	.22
☐ 406	Howie Koplitz	2.25	1.10	.22
☐ 407	Rookie Stars Frank Kostro Chico Ruiz Larry Elliot Dick Simpson	2.25	1.10	.22
☐ 408	Billy Gardner	2.25	1.10	.22
☐ 409	Roy Face	3.50	1.75	.35
☐ 410	Earl Battey	2.25	1.10	.22
☐ 411	Jim Constable	2.25	1.10	.22
☐ 412	Dodger Big Three Johnny Podres Don Drysdale Sandy Koufax	28.00	14.00	2.80
☐ 413	Jerry Walker	2.25	1.10	.22
☐ 414	Ty Cline	2.25	1.10	.22
☐ 415	Bob Gibson	33.00	15.00	3.00
☐ 416	Alex Grammas	2.25	1.10	.22
☐ 417	Giants Team	4.50	2.25	.45
☐ 418	John Orsino	2.25	1.10	.22
☐ 419	Tracy Stallard	2.25	1.10	.22
☐ 420	Bobby Richardson	6.50	3.25	.65
☐ 421	Tom Morgan	2.25	1.10	.22
☐ 422	Fred Hutchinson MG	3.00	1.50	.30
☐ 423	Ed Hobaugh	2.25	1.10	.22
☐ 424	Charlie Smith	2.25	1.10	.22
☐ 425	Smoky Burgess	3.00	1.50	.30
☐ 426	Barry Latman	2.25	1.10	.22
☐ 427	Bernie Allen	2.25	1.10	.22
☐ 428	Carl Boles	2.25	1.10	.22
☐ 429	Lou Burdette	3.50	1.75	.35
☐ 430	Norm Siebern	2.25	1.10	.22
☐ 431A	Checklist 6 (white on red)	5.50	.50	.10
☐ 431B	Checklist 6 (black on orange)	10.00	1.00	.20
☐ 432	Roman Mejias	2.25	1.10	.22
☐ 433	Denis Menke	2.25	1.10	.22
☐ 434	John Callison	3.00	1.50	.30
☐ 435	Woody Held	2.25	1.10	.22
☐ 436	Tim Harkness	2.25	1.10	.22
☐ 437	Bill Bruton	2.25	1.10	.22
☐ 438	Wes Stock	2.25	1.10	.22
☐ 439	Don Zimmer	3.00	1.50	.30
☐ 440	Juan Marichal	22.00	11.00	2.20
☐ 441	Lee Thomas	3.00	1.50	.30
☐ 442	J.C. Hartman	2.25	1.10	.22
☐ 443	Jim Piersall	3.50	1.75	.35
☐ 444	Jim Maloney	3.00	1.50	.30
☐ 445	Norm Cash	3.50	1.75	.35
☐ 446	Whitey Ford	33.00	15.00	3.00
☐ 447	Felix Mantilla	11.00	5.50	1.10
☐ 448	Jack Kralick	11.00	5.50	1.10
☐ 449	Jose Tartabull	11.00	5.50	1.10
☐ 450	Bob Friend	12.50	6.25	1.25
☐ 451	Indians Team	20.00	10.00	2.00
☐ 452	Barney Schultz	11.00	5.50	1.10
☐ 453	Jake Wood	11.00	5.50	1.10
☐ 454A	Art Fowler (card number on white background)	11.00	5.50	1.10
☐ 454B	Art Fowler (card number on orange background)	15.00	7.50	1.50
☐ 455	Ruben Amaro	11.00	5.50	1.10
☐ 456	Jim Coker	11.00	5.50	1.10
☐ 457	Tex Clevenger	11.00	5.50	1.10
☐ 458	Al Lopez MG	15.00	7.50	1.50
☐ 459	Dick LeMay	11.00	5.50	1.10
☐ 460	Del Crandall	12.50	6.25	1.25
☐ 461	Norm Bass	11.00	5.50	1.10
☐ 462	Wally Post	11.00	5.50	1.10
☐ 463	Joe Schaffernoth	11.00	5.50	1.10
☐ 464	Ken Aspromonte	11.00	5.50	1.10
☐ 465	Chuck Estrada	12.50	6.25	1.25
☐ 466	Rookie Stars SP Nate Oliver Tony Martinez Bill Freehan Jerry Robinson	30.00	15.00	3.00
☐ 467	Phil Ortega	11.00	5.50	1.10
☐ 468	Carroll Hardy	11.00	5.50	1.10
☐ 469	Jay Hook	11.00	5.50	1.10
☐ 470	Tom Tresh SP	30.00	15.00	3.00
☐ 471	Ken Retzer	11.00	5.50	1.10
☐ 472	Lou Brock	125.00	60.00	12.50

☐ 473 New York Mets Team Card	50.00	25.00	5.00
☐ 474 Jack Fisher	11.00	5.50	1.10
☐ 475 Gus Triandos	12.50	6.25	1.25
☐ 476 Frank Funk	11.00	5.50	1.10
☐ 477 Donn Clendenon	12.50	6.25	1.25
☐ 478 Paul Brown	11.00	5.50	1.10
☐ 479 Ed Brinkman	11.00	5.50	1.10
☐ 480 Bill Monbouquette	11.00	5.50	1.10
☐ 481 Bob Taylor	11.00	5.50	1.10
☐ 482 Felix Torres	11.00	5.50	1.10
☐ 483 Jim Owens	11.00	5.50	1.10
☐ 484 Dale Long SP	20.00	10.00	2.00
☐ 485 Jim Landis	11.00	5.50	1.10
☐ 486 Ray Sadecki	11.00	5.50	1.10
☐ 487 John Roseboro	12.50	6.25	1.25
☐ 488 Jerry Adair	11.00	5.50	1.10
☐ 489 Paul Toth	11.00	5.50	1.10
☐ 490 Willie McCovey	100.00	50.00	10.00
☐ 491 Harry Craft MG	11.00	5.50	1.10
☐ 492 Dave Wickersham	11.00	5.50	1.10
☐ 493 Walt Bond	11.00	5.50	1.10
☐ 494 Phil Regan	12.50	6.25	1.25
☐ 495 Frank Thomas SP	20.00	10.00	2.00
☐ 496 Rookie Stars	12.50	6.25	1.25
Steve Dalkowski			
Fred Newman			
Jack Smith			
Carl Bouldin			
☐ 497 Bennie Daniels	11.00	5.50	1.10
☐ 498 Eddie Kasko	11.00	5.50	1.10
☐ 499 J.C. Martin	11.00	5.50	1.10
☐ 500 Harmon Killebrew SP	90.00	45.00	9.00
☐ 501 Joe Azcue	11.00	5.50	1.10
☐ 502 Daryl Spencer	11.00	5.50	1.10
☐ 503 Braves Team	20.00	10.00	2.00
☐ 504 Bob Johnson	11.00	5.50	1.10
☐ 505 Curt Flood	17.00	8.50	1.70
☐ 506 Gene Green	11.00	5.50	1.10
☐ 507 Roland Sheldon	11.00	5.50	1.10
☐ 508 Ted Savage	11.00	5.50	1.10
☐ 509A Checklist 7 (copyright centered)	16.00	2.00	.40
☐ 509B Checklist 7 (copyright to right)	16.00	2.00	.40
☐ 510 Ken McBride	11.00	5.50	1.10
☐ 511 Charlie Neal	11.00	5.50	1.10
☐ 512 Cal McLish	11.00	5.50	1.10
☐ 513 Gary Geiger	11.00	5.50	1.10
☐ 514 Larry Osborne	11.00	5.50	1.10
☐ 515 Don Elston	11.00	5.50	1.10
☐ 516 Purnell Goldy	11.00	5.50	1.10
☐ 517 Hal Woodeshick	11.00	5.50	1.10
☐ 518 Don Blasingame	11.00	5.50	1.10
☐ 519 Claude Raymond	11.00	5.50	1.10
☐ 520 Orlando Cepeda	18.00	9.00	1.80
☐ 521 Dan Pfister	11.00	5.50	1.10
☐ 522 Rookie Stars	11.00	5.50	1.10
Mel Nelson			
Gary Peters			
Jim Roland			
Art Quirk			
☐ 523 Bill Kunkel	6.50	3.25	.65
☐ 524 Cardinals Team	13.50	6.25	1.25
☐ 525 Nellie Fox	13.50	6.25	1.25
☐ 526 Dick Hall	6.50	3.25	.65
☐ 527 Ed Sadowski	6.50	3.25	.65
☐ 528 Carl Willey	6.50	3.25	.65
☐ 529 Wes Covington	6.50	3.25	.65
☐ 530 Don Mossi	7.50	3.75	.75
☐ 531 Sam Mele MG	6.50	3.25	.65
☐ 532 Steve Boros	6.50	3.25	.65
☐ 533 Bobby Shantz	7.50	3.75	.75
☐ 534 Ken Walters	6.50	3.25	.65
☐ 535 Jim Perry	8.50	4.25	.85
☐ 536 Norm Larker	6.50	3.25	.65
☐ 537 Rookie Stars	650.00	325.00	65.00
Pedro Gonzales			
Ken McMullen			
Al Weis			
Pete Rose			
☐ 538 George Brunet	6.50	3.25	.65
☐ 539 Wayne Causey	6.50	3.25	.65
☐ 540 Bob Clemente	180.00	90.00	18.00
☐ 541 Ron Moeller	6.50	3.25	.65
☐ 542 Lou Klimchock	6.50	3.25	.65
☐ 543 Russ Snyder	6.50	3.25	.65
☐ 544 Rookie Stars	30.00	15.00	3.00
Duke Carmel			
Bill Haas			
Rusty Staub			
Dick Phillips			
☐ 545 Jose Pagan	6.50	3.25	.65
☐ 546 Hal Reniff	6.50	3.25	.65
☐ 547 Gus Bell	6.50	3.25	.65
☐ 548 Tom Satriano	6.50	3.25	.65
☐ 549 Rookie Stars	6.50	3.25	.65
Marcelino Lopez			
Pete Lovrich			
Paul Ratliff			
Elmo Plaskett			
☐ 550 Duke Snider	65.00	32.50	6.50
☐ 551 Billy Klaus	6.50	3.25	.65
☐ 552 Detroit Tigers Team Card	20.00	10.00	2.00
☐ 553 Rookie Stars	250.00	125.00	25.00
Brock Davis			
Jim Gosger			
Willie Stargell			
John Herrnstein			
☐ 554 Hank Fischer	6.50	3.25	.65
☐ 555 John Blanchard	7.50	3.75	.75
☐ 556 Al Worthington	6.50	3.25	.65
☐ 557 Cuno Barragan	6.50	3.25	.65
☐ 558 Rookie Stars	6.50	3.25	.65
Bill Faul			
Ron Hunt			
Al Moran			
Bob Lipski			
☐ 559 Danny Murtaugh MG	6.50	3.25	.65
☐ 560 Ray Herbert	6.50	3.25	.65
☐ 561 Mike De La Hoz	6.50	3.25	.65
☐ 562 Rookie Stars	11.00	5.50	1.10
Randy Cardinal			
Dave McNally			
Ken Rowe			
Don Rowe			
☐ 563 Mike McCormick	7.50	3.75	.75
☐ 564 George Banks	6.50	3.25	.65
☐ 565 Larry Sherry	7.50	3.75	.75
☐ 566 Cliff Cook	6.50	3.25	.65
☐ 567 Jim Duffalo	6.50	3.25	.65
☐ 568 Bob Sadowski	6.50	3.25	.65
☐ 569 Luis Arroyo	7.50	3.75	.75
☐ 570 Frank Bolling	6.50	3.25	.65
☐ 571 Johnny Klippstein	6.50	3.25	.65
☐ 572 Jack Spring	6.50	3.25	.65
☐ 573 Coot Veal	6.50	3.25	.65
☐ 574 Hal Kolstad	6.50	3.25	.65
☐ 575 Don Cardwell	6.50	3.25	.65
☐ 576 Johnny Temple	9.00	3.50	.70

1964 Topps

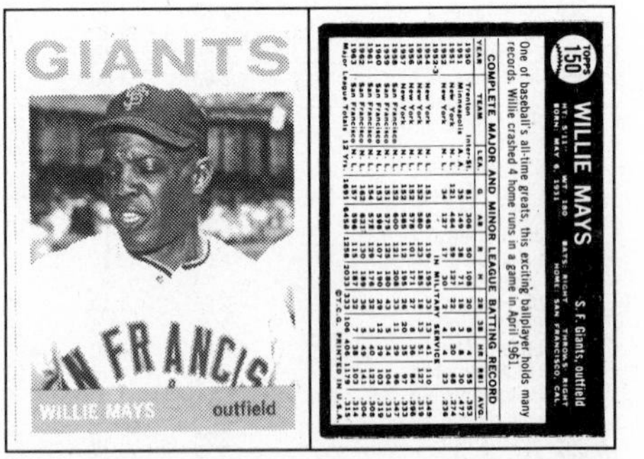

The cards in this 587-card set measure 2 1/2" by 3 1/2". Players in the 1964 Topps baseball series were easy to sort by team due to the giant block lettering found at the top of each card. The name and position of the player are found underneath the picture, and the card is numbered in a ball design on the orange-colored back. The usual last series scarcity holds for this set (523 to 587). Subsets within this set include League Leaders (1-12) and World Series cards (136-140). There were some three-card advertising panels produced by Topps; the players included are from the first series; one panel shows Walt Alston, Bill Henry, and Vada Pinson on the front with a Mickey Mantle card back on one of the backs. Another panel shows Carl Willey, White Sox Rookies, and Bob Friend on the front with a Mickey

Mantle card back on one of the backs. The key rookie cards in this set are Richie Allen, Tommy John, Lou Piniella, and Phil Niekro.

	NRMT	VG-E	GOOD
COMPLETE SET (587)	2600.00	1250.00	275.00
COMMON PLAYER (1-196)	1.00	.50	.10
COMMON PLAYER (197-370)	1.25	.60	.12
COMMON PLAYER (371-522)	2.50	1.25	.25
COMMON PLAYER (523-587)	6.50	3.25	.65
☐ 1 NL ERA Leaders	15.00	3.00	.60
Sandy Koufax			
Dick Ellsworth			
Bob Friend			
☐ 2 AL ERA Leaders	2.00	1.00	.20
Gary Peters			
Juan Pizarro			
Camilo Pascual			
☐ 3 NL Pitching Leaders	7.00	3.50	.70
Sandy Koufax			
Juan Marichal			
Warren Spahn			
Jim Maloney			
☐ 4 AL Pitching Leaders	2.50	1.25	.25
Whitey Ford			
Camilo Pascual			
Jim Bouton			
☐ 5 NL Strikeout Leaders	6.00	3.00	.60
Sandy Koufax			
Jim Maloney			
Don Drysdale			
☐ 6 AL Strikeout Leaders	2.00	1.00	.20
Camilo Pascual			
Jim Bunning			
Dick Stigman			
☐ 7 NL Batting Leaders	4.00	2.00	.40
Tommy Davis			
Bob Clemente			
Dick Groat			
Hank Aaron			
☐ 8 AL Batting Leaders	5.00	2.50	.50
Carl Yastrzemski			
Al Kaline			
Rich Rollins			
☐ 9 NL Home Run Leaders	10.00	5.00	1.00
Hank Aaron			
Willie McCovey			
Willie Mays			
Orlando Cepeda			
☐ 10 AL Home Run Leaders	2.00	1.00	.20
Harmon Killebrew			
Dick Stuart			
Bob Allison			
☐ 11 NL RBI Leaders	3.50	1.75	.35
Hank Aaron			
Ken Boyer			
Bill White			
☐ 12 AL RBI Leaders	2.50	1.25	.25
Dick Stuart			
Al Kaline			
Harmon Killebrew			
☐ 13 Hoyt Wilhelm	8.00	4.00	.80
☐ 14 Dodgers Rookies	1.00	.50	.10
Dick Nen			
Nick Willhite			
☐ 15 Zoilo Versalles	1.00	.50	.10
☐ 16 John Boozer	1.00	.50	.10
☐ 17 Willie Kirkland	1.00	.50	.10
☐ 18 Billy O'Dell	1.00	.50	.10
☐ 19 Don Wert	1.00	.50	.10
☐ 20 Bob Friend	1.50	.75	.15
☐ 21 Yogi Berra MG	32.00	16.00	3.20
☐ 22 Jerry Adair	1.00	.50	.10
☐ 23 Chris Zachary	1.00	.50	.10
☐ 24 Carl Sawatski	1.00	.50	.10
☐ 25 Bill Monbouquette	1.00	.50	.10
☐ 26 Gino Cimoli	1.00	.50	.10
☐ 27 New York Mets	4.00	2.00	.40
Team Card			
☐ 28 Claude Osteen	1.50	.75	.15
☐ 29 Lou Brock	30.00	15.00	3.00
☐ 30 Ron Perranoski	1.50	.75	.15
☐ 31 Dave Nicholson	1.00	.50	.10
☐ 32 Dean Chance	1.50	.75	.15
☐ 33 Reds Rookies	1.50	.75	.15
Sammy Ellis			
Mel Queen			
☐ 34 Jim Perry	1.50	.75	.15
☐ 35 Eddie Mathews	17.00	8.50	1.70
☐ 36 Hal Reniff	1.00	.50	.10
☐ 37 Smokey Burgess	1.50	.75	.15
☐ 38 Jim Wynn	3.00	1.50	.30
☐ 39 Hank Aguirre	1.00	.50	.10
☐ 40 Dick Groat	1.50	.75	.15
☐ 41 Friendly Foes	3.00	1.50	.30
Willie McCovey			
Leon Wagner			
☐ 42 Moe Drabowsky	1.00	.50	.10
☐ 43 Roy Sievers	1.50	.75	.15
☐ 44 Duke Carmel	1.00	.50	.10
☐ 45 Milt Pappas	1.50	.75	.15
☐ 46 Ed Brinkman	1.00	.50	.10
☐ 47 Giants Rookies	1.50	.75	.15
Jesus Alou			
Ron Herbel			
☐ 48 Bob Perry	1.00	.50	.10
☐ 49 Bill Henry	1.00	.50	.10
☐ 50 Mickey Mantle	200.00	100.00	20.00
☐ 51 Pete Richert	1.00	.50	.10
☐ 52 Chuck Hinton	1.00	.50	.10
☐ 53 Denis Menke	1.00	.50	.10
☐ 54 Sam Mele MG	1.00	.50	.10
☐ 55 Ernie Banks	25.00	12.50	2.50
☐ 56 Hal Brown	1.00	.50	.10
☐ 57 Tim Harkness	1.00	.50	.10
☐ 58 Don Demeter	1.00	.50	.10
☐ 59 Ernie Broglio	1.00	.50	.10
☐ 60 Frank Malzone	1.50	.75	.15
☐ 61 Angel Backstops	1.50	.75	.15
Bob Rodgers			
Ed Sadowski			
☐ 62 Ted Savage	1.00	.50	.10
☐ 63 John Orsino	1.00	.50	.10
☐ 64 Ted Abernathy	1.00	.50	.10
☐ 65 Felipe Alou	1.50	.75	.15
☐ 66 Eddie Fisher	1.00	.50	.10
☐ 67 Tigers Team	2.50	1.25	.25
☐ 68 Willie Davis	1.50	.75	.15
☐ 69 Clete Boyer	1.50	.75	.15
☐ 70 Joe Torre	2.50	1.25	.25
☐ 71 Jack Spring	1.00	.50	.10
☐ 72 Chico Cardenas	1.00	.50	.10
☐ 73 Jimmie Hall	1.50	.75	.15
☐ 74 Pirates Rookies	1.00	.50	.10
Bob Priddy			
Tom Butters			
☐ 75 Wayne Causey	1.00	.50	.10
☐ 76 Checklist 1	5.00	.50	.10
☐ 77 Jerry Walker	1.00	.50	.10
☐ 78 Merritt Ranew	1.00	.50	.10
☐ 79 Bob Heffner	1.00	.50	.10
☐ 80 Vada Pinson	2.50	1.25	.25
☐ 81 All-Star Vets	5.00	2.50	.50
Nellie Fox			
Harmon Killebrew			
☐ 82 Jim Davenport	1.50	.75	.15
☐ 83 Gus Triandos	1.50	.75	.15
☐ 84 Carl Willey	1.00	.50	.10
☐ 85 Pete Ward	1.00	.50	.10
☐ 86 Al Downing	1.50	.75	.15
☐ 87 St. Louis Cardinals	2.50	1.25	.25
Team Card			
☐ 88 John Roseboro	1.50	.75	.15
☐ 89 Boog Powell	4.00	2.00	.40
☐ 90 Earl Battey	1.00	.50	.10
☐ 91 Bob Bailey	1.00	.50	.10
☐ 92 Steve Ridzik	1.00	.50	.10
☐ 93 Gary Geiger	1.00	.50	.10
☐ 94 Braves Rookies	1.00	.50	.10
Jim Britton			
Larry Maxie			
☐ 95 George Altman	1.00	.50	.10
☐ 96 Bob Buhl	1.00	.50	.10
☐ 97 Jim Fregosi	1.50	.75	.15
☐ 98 Bill Bruton	1.00	.50	.10
☐ 99 Al Stanek	1.00	.50	.10
☐ 100 Elston Howard	3.50	1.75	.35
☐ 101 Walt Alston MG	3.50	1.75	.35
☐ 102 Checklist 2	5.00	.50	.10
☐ 103 Curt Flood	2.50	1.25	.25
☐ 104 Art Mahaffey	1.00	.50	.10
☐ 105 Woody Held	1.00	.50	.10
☐ 106 Joe Nuxhall	1.50	.75	.15
☐ 107 White Sox Rookies	1.00	.50	.10
Bruce Howard			
Frank Kreutzer			
☐ 108 John Wyatt	1.00	.50	.10
☐ 109 Rusty Staub	6.00	3.00	.60
☐ 110 Albie Pearson	1.00	.50	.10
☐ 111 Don Elston	1.00	.50	.10
☐ 112 Bob Tillman	1.00	.50	.10
☐ 113 Grover Powell	1.00	.50	.10
☐ 114 Don Lock	1.00	.50	.10
☐ 115 Frank Bolling	1.00	.50	.10

☐ 116	Twins Rookies	11.00	5.50	1.10
	Jay Ward			
	Tony Oliva			
☐ 117	Earl Francis	1.00	.50	.10
☐ 118	John Blanchard	1.50	.75	.15
☐ 119	Gary Kolb	1.00	.50	.10
☐ 120	Don Drysdale	15.00	7.50	1.50
☐ 121	Pete Runnels	1.50	.75	.15
☐ 122	Don McMahon	1.00	.50	.10
☐ 123	Jose Pagan	1.00	.50	.10
☐ 124	Orlando Pena	1.00	.50	.10
☐ 125	Pete Rose	175.00	85.00	18.00
☐ 126	Russ Snyder	1.00	.50	.10
☐ 127	Angels Rookies	1.00	.50	.10
	Aubrey Gatewood			
	Dick Simpson			
☐ 128	Mickey Lolich	12.00	6.00	1.20
☐ 129	Amado Samuel	1.00	.50	.10
☐ 130	Gary Peters	1.00	.50	.10
☐ 131	Steve Boros	1.00	.50	.10
☐ 132	Braves Team	2.50	1.25	.25
☐ 133	Jim Grant	1.00	.50	.10
☐ 134	Don Zimmer	1.50	.75	.15
☐ 135	Johnny Callison	1.50	.75	.15
☐ 136	World Series Game 1	10.00	5.00	1.00
	Koufax strikes out 15			
☐ 137	World Series Game 2	3.00	1.50	.30
	Davis sparks rally			
☐ 138	World Series Game 3	3.00	1.50	.30
	LA 3 straight			
☐ 139	World Series Game 4	3.00	1.50	.30
	Sealing Yanks doom			
☐ 140	World Series Summary	3.00	1.50	.30
	Dodgers celebrate			
☐ 141	Danny Murtaugh MG	1.00	.50	.10
☐ 142	John Bateman	1.00	.50	.10
☐ 143	Bubba Phillips	1.00	.50	.10
☐ 144	Al Worthington	1.00	.50	.10
☐ 145	Norm Siebern	1.00	.50	.10
☐ 146	Indians Rookies	55.00	27.50	5.50
	Tommy John			
	Bob Chance			
☐ 147	Ray Sadecki	1.00	.50	.10
☐ 148	J.C. Martin	1.00	.50	.10
☐ 149	Paul Foytack	1.00	.50	.10
☐ 150	Willie Mays	85.00	42.50	8.50
☐ 151	Athletics Team	2.00	1.00	.20
☐ 152	Denny Lemaster	1.00	.50	.10
☐ 153	Dick Williams	1.50	.75	.15
☐ 154	Dick Tracewski	1.00	.50	.10
☐ 155	Duke Snider	28.00	14.00	2.80
☐ 156	Bill Dailey	1.00	.50	.10
☐ 157	Gene Mauch MG	1.50	.75	.15
☐ 158	Ken Johnson	1.00	.50	.10
☐ 159	Charlie Dees	1.00	.50	.10
☐ 160	Ken Boyer	4.50	2.25	.45
☐ 161	Dave McNally	2.00	1.00	.20
☐ 162	Hitting Area	1.50	.75	.15
	Dick Sisler			
	Vada Pinson			
☐ 163	Donn Clendenon	1.50	.75	.15
☐ 164	Bud Daley	1.00	.50	.10
☐ 165	Jerry Lumpe	1.00	.50	.10
☐ 166	Marty Keough	1.00	.50	.10
☐ 167	Senators Rookies	21.00	10.50	2.10
	Mike Brumley			
	Lou Piniella			
☐ 168	Al Weis	1.00	.50	.10
☐ 169	Del Crandall	1.50	.75	.15
☐ 170	Dick Radatz	1.50	.75	.15
☐ 171	Ty Cline	1.00	.50	.10
☐ 172	Indians Team	2.00	1.00	.20
☐ 173	Ryne Duren	1.50	.75	.15
☐ 174	Doc Edwards	1.50	.75	.15
☐ 175	Billy Williams	14.00	7.00	1.40
☐ 176	Tracy Stallard	1.00	.50	.10
☐ 177	Harmon Killebrew	17.00	8.50	1.70
☐ 178	Hank Bauer MG	1.50	.75	.15
☐ 179	Carl Warwick	1.00	.50	.10
☐ 180	Tommy Davis	2.00	1.00	.20
☐ 181	Dave Wickersham	1.00	.50	.10
☐ 182	Sox Sockers	10.00	5.00	1.00
	Carl Yastrzemski			
	Chuck Schilling			
☐ 183	Ron Taylor	1.00	.50	.10
☐ 184	Al Luplow	1.00	.50	.10
☐ 185	Jim O'Toole	1.00	.50	.10
☐ 186	Roman Mejias	1.00	.50	.10
☐ 187	Ed Roebuck	1.00	.50	.10
☐ 188	Checklist 3	5.00	.50	.10
☐ 189	Bob Hendley	1.00	.50	.10
☐ 190	Bobby Richardson	4.00	2.00	.40
☐ 191	Clay Dalrymple	1.00	.50	.10
☐ 192	Cubs Rookies	1.00	.50	.10
	John Boccabella			
	Billy Cowan			
☐ 193	Jerry Lynch	1.00	.50	.10
☐ 194	John Goryl	1.00	.50	.10
☐ 195	Floyd Robinson	1.00	.50	.10
☐ 196	Jim Gentile	1.50	.75	.15
☐ 197	Frank Lary	1.75	.85	.17
☐ 198	Len Gabrielson	1.25	.60	.12
☐ 199	Joe Azcue	1.25	.60	.12
☐ 200	Sandy Koufax	85.00	42.50	8.50
☐ 201	Orioles Rookies	2.25	1.10	.22
	Sam Bowens			
	Wally Bunker			
☐ 202	Galen Cisco	1.25	.60	.12
☐ 203	John Kennedy	1.25	.60	.12
☐ 204	Matty Alou	1.75	.85	.17
☐ 205	Nellie Fox	4.00	2.00	.40
☐ 206	Steve Hamilton	1.25	.60	.12
☐ 207	Fred Hutchinson MG	1.75	.85	.17
☐ 208	Wes Covington	1.25	.60	.12
☐ 209	Bob Allen	1.25	.60	.12
☐ 210	Carl Yastrzemski	85.00	42.50	8.50
☐ 211	Jim Coker	1.25	.60	.12
☐ 212	Pete Lovrich	1.25	.60	.12
☐ 213	Angels Team	2.50	1.25	.25
☐ 214	Ken McMullen	1.25	.60	.12
☐ 215	Ray Herbert	1.25	.60	.12
☐ 216	Mike De La Hoz	1.25	.60	.12
☐ 217	Jim King	1.25	.60	.12
☐ 218	Hank Fischer	1.25	.60	.12
☐ 219	Young Aces	2.00	1.00	.20
	Al Downing			
	Jim Bouton			
☐ 220	Dick Ellsworth	1.75	.85	.17
☐ 221	Bob Saverine	1.25	.60	.12
☐ 222	Billy Pierce	1.75	.85	.17
☐ 223	George Banks	1.25	.60	.12
☐ 224	Tommie Sisk	1.25	.60	.12
☐ 225	Roger Maris	55.00	27.50	5.50
☐ 226	Colts Rookies	1.25	.60	.12
	Gerald Grote			
	Larry Yellen			
☐ 227	Barry Latman	1.25	.60	.12
☐ 228	Felix Mantilla	1.25	.60	.12
☐ 229	Charley Lau	1.75	.85	.17
☐ 230	Brooks Robinson	28.00	14.00	2.80
☐ 231	Dick Calmus	1.25	.60	.12
☐ 232	Al Lopez MG	2.50	1.25	.25
☐ 233	Hal Smith	1.25	.60	.12
☐ 234	Gary Bell	1.25	.60	.12
☐ 235	Ron Hunt	1.25	.60	.12
☐ 236	Bill Faul	1.25	.60	.12
☐ 237	Cubs Team	2.50	1.25	.25
☐ 238	Roy McMillan	1.25	.60	.12
☐ 239	Herm Starrette	1.25	.60	.12
☐ 240	Bill White	2.50	1.25	.25
☐ 241	Jim Owens	1.25	.60	.12
☐ 242	Harvey Kuenn	2.00	1.00	.20
☐ 243	Phillies Rookies	14.00	7.00	1.40
	Richie Allen			
	John Herrnstein			
☐ 244	Tony LaRussa	11.00	5.50	1.10
☐ 245	Dick Stigman	1.25	.60	.12
☐ 246	Manny Mota	1.75	.85	.17
☐ 247	Dave DeBusschere	2.50	1.25	.25
☐ 248	Johnny Pesky MG	1.75	.85	.17
☐ 249	Doug Camilli	1.25	.60	.12
☐ 250	Al Kaline	25.00	12.50	2.50
☐ 251	Choo Choo Coleman	1.25	.60	.12
☐ 252	Ken Aspromonte	1.25	.60	.12
☐ 253	Wally Post	1.25	.60	.12
☐ 254	Don Hoak	1.25	.60	.12
☐ 255	Lee Thomas	1.75	.85	.17
☐ 256	Johnny Weekly	1.25	.60	.12
☐ 257	San Francisco Giants	2.50	1.25	.25
	Team Card			
☐ 258	Garry Roggenburk	1.25	.60	.12
☐ 259	Harry Bright	1.25	.60	.12
☐ 260	Frank Robinson	22.00	11.00	2.20
☐ 261	Jim Hannan	1.25	.60	.12
☐ 262	Cards Rookies	4.00	2.00	.40
	Mike Shannon			
	Harry Fanok			
☐ 263	Chuck Estrada	1.75	.85	.17
☐ 264	Jim Landis	1.25	.60	.12
☐ 265	Jim Bunning	4.50	2.25	.45
☐ 266	Gene Freese	1.25	.60	.12
☐ 267	Wilbur Wood	1.75	.85	.17
☐ 268	Bill's Got It	1.75	.85	.17
	Danny Murtaugh			
	Bill Virdon			
☐ 269	Ellis Burton	1.25	.60	.12
☐ 270	Rich Rollins	1.75	.85	.17

☐ 271	Bob Sadowski	1.25	.60	.12
☐ 272	Jake Wood	1.25	.60	.12
☐ 273	Mel Nelson	1.25	.60	.12
☐ 274	Checklist 4	5.00	.50	.10
☐ 275	John Tsitouris	1.25	.60	.12
☐ 276	Jose Tartabull	1.25	.60	.12
☐ 277	Ken Retzer	1.25	.60	.12
☐ 278	Bobby Shantz	1.75	.85	.17
☐ 279	Joe Koppe (glove	1.75	.85	.17
	on wrong hand) UER			
☐ 280	Juan Marichal	10.00	5.00	1.00
☐ 281	Yankees Rookies	2.00	1.00	.20
	Jake Gibbs			
	Tom Metcalf			
☐ 282	Bob Bruce	1.25	.60	.12
☐ 283	Tom McCraw	1.25	.60	.12
☐ 284	Dick Schofield	1.25	.60	.12
☐ 285	Robin Roberts	8.00	4.00	.80
☐ 286	Don Landrum	1.25	.60	.12
☐ 287	Red Sox Rookies	22.00	11.00	2.20
	Tony Conigliaro			
	Bill Spanswick			
☐ 288	Al Moran	1.25	.60	.12
☐ 289	Frank Funk	1.25	.60	.12
☐ 290	Bob Allison	1.75	.85	.17
☐ 291	Phil Ortega	1.25	.60	.12
☐ 292	Mike Roarke	1.25	.60	.12
☐ 293	Phillies Team	2.50	1.25	.25
☐ 294	Ken L. Hunt	1.25	.60	.12
☐ 295	Roger Craig	2.25	1.10	.22
☐ 296	Ed Kirkpatrick	1.25	.60	.12
☐ 297	Ken MacKenzie	1.25	.60	.12
☐ 298	Harry Craft MG	1.25	.60	.12
☐ 299	Bill Stafford	1.25	.60	.12
☐ 300	Hank Aaron	85.00	42.50	8.50
☐ 301	Larry Brown	1.25	.60	.12
☐ 302	Dan Pfister	1.25	.60	.12
☐ 303	Jim Campbell	1.25	.60	.12
☐ 304	Bob Johnson	1.25	.60	.12
☐ 305	Jack Lamabe	1.25	.60	.12
☐ 306	Giant Gunners	16.00	8.00	1.60
	Willie Mays			
	Orlando Cepeda			
☐ 307	Joe Gibbon	1.25	.60	.12
☐ 308	Gene Stephens	1.25	.60	.12
☐ 309	Paul Toth	1.25	.60	.12
☐ 310	Jim Gilliam	2.25	1.10	.22
☐ 311	Tom Brown	1.25	.60	.12
☐ 312	Tigers Rookies	1.25	.60	.12
	Fritz Fisher			
	Fred Gladding			
☐ 313	Chuck Hiller	1.25	.60	.12
☐ 314	Jerry Buchek	1.25	.60	.12
☐ 315	Bo Belinsky	1.75	.85	.17
☐ 316	Gene Oliver	1.25	.60	.12
☐ 317	Al Smith	1.25	.60	.12
☐ 318	Minnesota Twins	2.50	1.25	.25
	Team Card			
☐ 319	Paul Brown	1.25	.60	.12
☐ 320	Rocky Colavito	4.50	2.25	.45
☐ 321	Bob Lillis	1.25	.60	.12
☐ 322	George Brunet	1.25	.60	.12
☐ 323	John Buzhardt	1.25	.60	.12
☐ 324	Casey Stengel MG	11.00	5.50	1.10
☐ 325	Hector Lopez	1.25	.60	.12
☐ 326	Ron Brand	1.25	.60	.12
☐ 327	Don Blasingame	1.25	.60	.12
☐ 328	Bob Shaw	1.25	.60	.12
☐ 329	Russ Nixon	1.75	.85	.17
☐ 330	Tommy Harper	1.75	.85	.17
☐ 331	AL Bombers	75.00	37.50	7.50
	Roger Maris			
	Norm Cash			
	Mickey Mantle			
	Al Kaline			
☐ 332	Ray Washburn	1.25	.60	.12
☐ 333	Billy Moran	1.25	.60	.12
☐ 334	Lew Krausse	1.25	.60	.12
☐ 335	Don Mossi	1.25	.60	.12
☐ 336	Andre Rodgers	1.25	.60	.12
☐ 337	Dodgers Rookies	5.00	2.50	.50
	Al Ferrara			
	Jeff Torborg			
☐ 338	Jack Kralick	1.25	.60	.12
☐ 339	Walt Bond	1.25	.60	.12
☐ 340	Joe Cunningham	1.25	.60	.12
☐ 341	Jim Roland	1.25	.60	.12
☐ 342	Willie Stargell	42.00	20.00	4.00
☐ 343	Senators Team	2.25	1.10	.22
☐ 344	Phil Linz	1.75	.85	.17
☐ 345	Frank Thomas	1.75	.85	.17
☐ 346	Joey Jay	1.25	.60	.12
☐ 347	Bobby Wine	1.25	.60	.12
☐ 348	Ed Lopat MG	1.75	.85	.17
☐ 349	Art Fowler	1.25	.60	.12
☐ 350	Willie McCovey	22.00	11.00	2.20
☐ 351	Dan Schneider	1.25	.60	.12
☐ 352	Eddie Bressoud	1.25	.60	.12
☐ 353	Wally Moon	1.75	.85	.17
☐ 354	Dave Giusti	1.75	.85	.17
☐ 355	Vic Power	1.25	.60	.12
☐ 356	Reds Rookies	1.75	.85	.17
	Bill McCool			
	Chico Ruiz			
☐ 357	Charley James	1.25	.60	.12
☐ 358	Ron Kline	1.25	.60	.12
☐ 359	Jim Schaffer	1.25	.60	.12
☐ 360	Joe Pepitone	2.25	1.10	.22
☐ 361	Jay Hook	1.25	.60	.12
☐ 362	Checklist 5	5.00	.50	.10
☐ 363	Dick McAuliffe	1.75	.85	.17
☐ 364	Joe Gaines	1.25	.60	.12
☐ 365	Cal McLish	1.25	.60	.12
☐ 366	Nelson Mathews	1.25	.60	.12
☐ 367	Fred Whitfield	1.25	.60	.12
☐ 368	White Sox Rookies	1.75	.85	.17
	Fritz Ackley			
	Don Buford			
☐ 369	Jerry Zimmerman	1.25	.60	.12
☐ 370	Hal Woodeshick	1.25	.60	.12
☐ 371	Frank Howard	3.50	1.75	.35
☐ 372	Howie Koplitz	2.50	1.25	.25
☐ 373	Pirates Team	5.00	2.50	.50
☐ 374	Bobby Bolin	2.50	1.25	.25
☐ 375	Ron Santo	4.00	2.00	.40
☐ 376	Dave Morehead	2.50	1.25	.25
☐ 377	Bob Skinner	2.50	1.25	.25
☐ 378	Braves Rookies	3.50	1.75	.35
	Woody Woodward			
	Jack Smith			
☐ 379	Tony Gonzalez	2.50	1.25	.25
☐ 380	Whitey Ford	25.00	12.50	2.50
☐ 381	Bob Taylor	2.50	1.25	.25
☐ 382	Wes Stock	2.50	1.25	.25
☐ 383	Bill Rigney MG	2.50	1.25	.25
☐ 384	Ron Hansen	2.50	1.25	.25
☐ 385	Curt Simmons	3.50	1.75	.35
☐ 386	Lenny Green	2.50	1.25	.25
☐ 387	Terry Fox	2.50	1.25	.25
☐ 388	A's Rookies	2.50	1.25	.25
	John O'Donoghue			
	George Williams			
☐ 389	Jim Umbricht	2.50	1.25	.25
	(card back mentions			
	his death)			
☐ 390	Orlando Cepeda	6.50	3.25	.65
☐ 391	Sam McDowell	3.50	1.75	.35
☐ 392	Jim Pagliaroni	2.50	1.25	.25
☐ 393	Casey Teaches	4.50	2.25	.45
	Casey Stengel			
	Ed Kranepool			
☐ 394	Bob Miller	2.50	1.25	.25
☐ 395	Tom Tresh	3.50	1.75	.35
☐ 396	Dennis Bennett	2.50	1.25	.25
☐ 397	Chuck Cottier	2.50	1.25	.25
☐ 398	Mets Rookies	2.50	1.25	.25
	Bill Haas			
	Dick Smith			
☐ 399	Jackie Brandt	2.50	1.25	.25
☐ 400	Warren Spahn	25.00	12.50	2.50
☐ 401	Charlie Maxwell	2.50	1.25	.25
☐ 402	Tom Sturdivant	2.50	1.25	.25
☐ 403	Reds Team	5.00	2.50	.50
☐ 404	Tony Martinez	2.50	1.25	.25
☐ 405	Ken McBride	2.50	1.25	.25
☐ 406	Al Spangler	2.50	1.25	.25
☐ 407	Bill Freehan	4.00	2.00	.40
☐ 408	Cubs Rookies	2.50	1.25	.25
	Jim Stewart			
	Fred Burdette			
☐ 409	Bill Fischer	2.50	1.25	.25
☐ 410	Dick Stuart	3.50	1.75	.35
☐ 411	Lee Walls	2.50	1.25	.25
☐ 412	Ray Culp	2.50	1.25	.25
☐ 413	Johnny Keane MG	2.50	1.25	.25
☐ 414	Jack Sanford	2.50	1.25	.25
☐ 415	Tony Kubek	5.00	2.50	.50
☐ 416	Lee Maye	2.50	1.25	.25
☐ 417	Don Cardwell	2.50	1.25	.25
☐ 418	Orioles Rookies	3.50	1.75	.35
	Darold Knowles			
	Les Narum			
☐ 419	Ken Harrelson	6.00	3.00	.60
☐ 420	Jim Maloney	3.50	1.75	.35
☐ 421	Camilo Carreon	2.50	1.25	.25
☐ 422	Jack Fisher	2.50	1.25	.25

☐ 423	Tops in NL	75.00	37.50	7.50
	Hank Aaron			
	Willie Mays			
☐ 424	Dick Bertell	2.50	1.25	.25
☐ 425	Norm Cash	4.00	2.00	.40
☐ 426	Bob Rodgers	3.50	1.75	.35
☐ 427	Don Rudolph	2.50	1.25	.25
☐ 428	Red Sox Rookies	2.50	1.25	.25
	Archie Skeen			
	Pete Smith			
	(back states Archie			
	has retired)			
☐ 429	Tim McCarver	6.00	3.00	.60
☐ 430	Juan Pizarro	2.50	1.25	.25
☐ 431	George Alusik	2.50	1.25	.25
☐ 432	Ruben Amaro	2.50	1.25	.25
☐ 433	Yankees Team	11.00	5.50	1.10
☐ 434	Don Nottebart	2.50	1.25	.25
☐ 435	Vic Davalillo	2.50	1.25	.25
☐ 436	Charlie Neal	2.50	1.25	.25
☐ 437	Ed Bailey	2.50	1.25	.25
☐ 438	Checklist 6	7.50	.75	.15
☐ 439	Harvey Haddix	3.50	1.75	.35
☐ 440	Bob Clemente	90.00	45.00	9.00
☐ 441	Bob Duliba	2.50	1.25	.25
☐ 442	Pumpsie Green	2.50	1.25	.25
☐ 443	Chuck Dressen MG	2.00	1.00	.20
☐ 444	Larry Jackson	2.50	1.25	.25
☐ 445	Bill Skowron	3.50	1.75	.35
☐ 446	Julian Javier	2.50	1.25	.25
☐ 447	Ted Bowsfield	2.50	1.25	.25
☐ 448	Cookie Rojas	2.50	1.25	.25
☐ 449	Deron Johnson	2.50	1.25	.25
☐ 450	Steve Barber	2.50	1.25	.25
☐ 451	Joe Amalfitano	2.50	1.25	.25
☐ 452	Giants Rookies	3.50	1.75	.35
	Gil Garrido			
	Jim Ray Hart			
☐ 453	Frank Baumann	2.50	1.25	.25
☐ 454	Tommie Aaron	3.50	1.75	.35
☐ 455	Bernie Allen	2.50	1.25	.25
☐ 456	Dodgers Rookies	3.50	1.75	.35
	Wes Parker			
	John Werhas			
☐ 457	Jesse Gonder	2.50	1.25	.25
☐ 458	Ralph Terry	3.50	1.75	.35
☐ 459	Red Sox Rookies	2.50	1.25	.25
	Pete Charton			
	Dalton Jones			
☐ 460	Bob Gibson	27.00	13.50	2.70
☐ 461	George Thomas	2.50	1.25	.25
☐ 462	Birdie Tebbetts MG	2.50	1.25	.25
☐ 463	Don Leppert	2.50	1.25	.25
☐ 464	Dallas Green	3.50	1.75	.35
☐ 465	Mike Hershberger	2.50	1.25	.25
☐ 466	A's Rookies	2.50	1.25	.25
	Dick Green			
	Aurelio Monteagudo			
☐ 467	Bob Aspromonte	2.50	1.25	.25
☐ 468	Gaylord Perry	30.00	15.00	3.00
☐ 469	Cubs Rookies	2.50	1.25	.25
	Fred Norman			
	Sterling Slaughter			
☐ 470	Jim Bouton	4.00	2.00	.40
☐ 471	Gates Brown	3.50	1.75	.35
☐ 472	Vern Law	3.50	1.75	.35
☐ 473	Baltimore Orioles	5.00	2.50	.50
	Team Card			
☐ 474	Larry Sherry	3.50	1.75	.35
☐ 475	Ed Charles	2.50	1.25	.25
☐ 476	Braves Rookies	6.00	3.00	.60
	Rico Carty			
	Dick Kelley			
☐ 477	Mike Joyce	2.50	1.25	.25
☐ 478	Dick Howser	3.50	1.75	.35
☐ 479	Cardinals Rookies	2.50	1.25	.25
	Dave Bakenhaster			
	Johnny Lewis			
☐ 480	Bob Purkey	2.50	1.25	.25
☐ 481	Chuck Schilling	2.50	1.25	.25
☐ 482	Phillies Rookies	3.50	1.75	.35
	John Briggs			
	Danny Cater			
☐ 483	Fred Valentine	2.50	1.25	.25
☐ 484	Bill Pleis	2.50	1.25	.25
☐ 485	Tom Haller	2.50	1.25	.25
☐ 486	Bob Kennedy MG	2.50	1.25	.25
☐ 487	Mike McCormick	3.50	1.75	.35
☐ 488	Yankees Rookies	2.50	1.25	.25
	Pete Mikkelsen			
	Bob Meyer			
☐ 489	Julio Navarro	2.50	1.25	.25
☐ 490	Ron Fairly	3.50	1.75	.35
☐ 491	Ed Rakow	2.50	1.25	.25
☐ 492	Colts Rookies	2.50	1.25	.25
	Jim Beauchamp			
	Mike White			
☐ 493	Don Lee	2.50	1.25	.25
☐ 494	Al Jackson	2.50	1.25	.25
☐ 495	Bill Virdon	3.50	1.75	.35
☐ 496	White Sox Team	5.00	2.50	.50
☐ 497	Jeoff Long	2.50	1.25	.25
☐ 498	Dave Stenhouse	2.50	1.25	.25
☐ 499	Indians Rookies	2.50	1.25	.25
	Chico Salmon			
	Gordon Seyfried			
☐ 500	Camilo Pascual	3.50	1.75	.35
☐ 501	Bob Veale	3.50	1.75	.35
☐ 502	Angels Rookies	3.50	1.75	.35
	Bobby Knoop			
	Bob Lee			
☐ 503	Earl Wilson	2.50	1.25	.25
☐ 504	Claude Raymond	2.50	1.25	.25
☐ 505	Stan Williams	2.50	1.25	.25
☐ 506	Bobby Bragan MG	2.50	1.25	.25
☐ 507	Johnny Edwards	2.50	1.25	.25
☐ 508	Diego Segui	2.50	1.25	.25
☐ 509	Pirates Rookies	3.50	1.75	.35
	Gene Alley			
	Orlando McFarlane			
☐ 510	Lindy McDaniel	2.50	1.25	.25
☐ 511	Lou Jackson	2.50	1.25	.25
☐ 512	Tigers Rookies	6.00	3.00	.60
	Willie Horton			
	Joe Sparma			
☐ 513	Don Larsen	3.50	1.75	.35
☐ 514	Jim Hickman	2.50	1.25	.25
☐ 515	Johnny Romano	2.50	1.25	.25
☐ 516	Twins Rookies	2.50	1.25	.25
	Jerry Arrigo			
	Dwight Siebler			
☐ 517A	Checklist 7 ERR	20.00	2.00	.40
	(incorrect numbering			
	sequence on back)			
☐ 517B	Checklist 7 COR	10.00	1.00	.20
	(correct numbering			
	on back)			
☐ 518	Carl Bouldin	2.50	1.25	.25
☐ 519	Charlie Smith	2.50	1.25	.25
☐ 520	Jack Baldschun	2.50	1.25	.25
☐ 521	Tom Satriano	2.50	1.25	.25
☐ 522	Bob Tiefenauer	2.50	1.25	.25
☐ 523	Lou Burdette UER	9.00	4.50	.90
	(pitching lefty)			
☐ 524	Reds Rookies	6.50	3.25	.65
	Jim Dickson			
	Bobby Klaus			
☐ 525	Al McBean	6.50	3.25	.65
☐ 526	Lou Clinton	6.50	3.25	.65
☐ 527	Larry Bearnarth	6.50	3.25	.65
☐ 528	A's Rookies	7.50	3.75	.75
	Dave Duncan			
	Tommie Reynolds			
☐ 529	Alvin Dark MG	7.50	3.75	.75
☐ 530	Leon Wagner	6.50	3.25	.65
☐ 531	Los Angeles Dodgers	15.00	7.50	1.50
	Team Card			
☐ 532	Twins Rookies	6.50	3.25	.65
	Bud Bloomfield			
	(Bloomfield photo			
	actually Jay Ward)			
	Joe Nossek			
☐ 533	Johnny Klippstein	6.50	3.25	.65
☐ 534	Gus Bell	6.50	3.25	.65
☐ 535	Phil Regan	6.50	3.25	.65
☐ 536	Mets Rookies	6.50	3.25	.65
	Larry Elliot			
	John Stephenson			
☐ 537	Dan Osinski	6.50	3.25	.65
☐ 538	Minnie Minoso	9.00	4.50	.90
☐ 539	Roy Face	8.00	4.00	.80
☐ 540	Luis Aparicio	16.00	8.00	1.60
☐ 541	Braves Rookies	160.00	80.00	16.00
	Phil Roof			
	Phil Niekro			
☐ 542	Don Mincher	7.50	3.75	.75
☐ 543	Bob Uecker	60.00	30.00	6.00
☐ 544	Colts Rookies	6.50	3.25	.65
	Steve Hertz			
	Joe Hoerner			
☐ 545	Max Alvis	6.50	3.25	.65
☐ 546	Joe Christopher	6.50	3.25	.65
☐ 547	Gil Hodges	12.50	6.25	1.25
☐ 548	NL Rookies	6.50	3.25	.65
	Wayne Schurr			
	Paul Speckenbach			
☐ 549	Joe Moeller	6.50	3.25	.65

☐ 550 Ken Hubbs (in memoriam)	15.00	7.50	1.50
☐ 551 Billy Hoeft	6.50	3.25	.65
☐ 552 Indians Rookies Tom Kelley Sonny Siebert	7.50	3.75	.75
☐ 553 Jim Brewer	6.50	3.25	.65
☐ 554 Hank Foiles	6.50	3.25	.65
☐ 555 Lee Stange	6.50	3.25	.65
☐ 556 Mets Rookies Steve Dillon Ron Locke	6.50	3.25	.65
☐ 557 Leo Burke	6.50	3.25	.65
☐ 558 Don Schwall	6.50	3.25	.65
☐ 559 Dick Phillips	6.50	3.25	.65
☐ 560 Dick Farrell	6.50	3.25	.65
☐ 561 Phillies Rookies UER Dave Bennett (19 ... is 18) Rick Wise	10.00	5.00	1.00
☐ 562 Pedro Ramos	6.50	3.25	.65
☐ 563 Dal Maxvill	6.50	3.25	.65
☐ 564 AL Rookies Joe McCabe Jerry McNertney	6.50	3.25	.65
☐ 565 Stu Miller	6.50	3.25	.65
☐ 566 Ed Kranepool	8.00	4.00	.80
☐ 567 Jim Kaat	12.00	6.00	1.20
☐ 568 NL Rookies Phil Gagliano Cap Peterson	6.50	3.25	.65
☐ 569 Fred Newman	6.50	3.25	.65
☐ 570 Bill Mazeroski	8.00	4.00	.80
☐ 571 Gene Conley	6.50	3.25	.65
☐ 572 AL Rookies Dave Gray Dick Egan	6.50	3.25	.65
☐ 573 Jim Duffalo	6.50	3.25	.65
☐ 574 Manny Jimenez	6.50	3.25	.65
☐ 575 Tony Cloninger	6.50	3.25	.65
☐ 576 Mets Rookies Jerry Hinsley Bill Wakefield	6.50	3.25	.65
☐ 577 Gordy Coleman	6.50	3.25	.65
☐ 578 Glen Hobbie	6.50	3.25	.65
☐ 579 Red Sox Team	15.00	7.50	1.50
☐ 580 Johnny Podres	8.00	4.00	.80
☐ 581 Yankees Rookies Pedro Gonzalez Archie Moore	6.50	3.25	.65
☐ 582 Rod Kanehl	6.50	3.25	.65
☐ 583 Tito Francona	6.50	3.25	.65
☐ 584 Joel Horlen	6.50	3.25	.65
☐ 585 Tony Taylor	6.50	3.25	.65
☐ 586 Jim Piersall	8.00	4.00	.80
☐ 587 Bennie Daniels	9.00	3.50	.70

1964 Topps Giants

The cards in this 60-card set measure 3 1/8" by 5 1/4". The 1964 Topps Giants are postcard size cards containing color player photographs. They are numbered on the backs, which also contain biographical information presented in a newspaper format. These "giant size" cards were distributed in both cellophane and waxed gum packs apart from the Topps regular issue of 1964. Cards 3, 28, 42, 45, 47, 51 and 60 slightly more difficult to find and are indicated by SP in the checklist below.

	NRMT	VG-E	GOOD
COMPLETE SET (60)	90.00	45.00	9.00
COMMON PLAYER (1-60)	.15	.07	.01
☐ 1 Gary Peters	.15	.07	.01
☐ 2 Ken Johnson	.15	.07	.01
☐ 3 Sandy Koufax SP	18.00	9.00	1.80
☐ 4 Bob Bailey	.15	.07	.01
☐ 5 Milt Pappas	.15	.07	.01
☐ 6 Ron Hunt	.15	.07	.01
☐ 7 Whitey Ford	2.00	1.00	.20
☐ 8 Roy McMillan	.15	.07	.01
☐ 9 Rocky Colavito	.35	.17	.03
☐ 10 Jim Bunning	.50	.25	.05
☐ 11 Bob Clemente	4.00	2.00	.40
☐ 12 Al Kaline	2.50	1.25	.25
☐ 13 Nellie Fox	.50	.25	.05
☐ 14 Tony Gonzalez	.15	.07	.01
☐ 15 Jim Gentile	.15	.07	.01
☐ 16 Dean Chance	.15	.07	.01
☐ 17 Dick Ellsworth	.15	.07	.01
☐ 18 Jim Fregosi	.15	.07	.01
☐ 19 Dick Groat	.25	.12	.02
☐ 20 Chuck Hinton	.15	.07	.01
☐ 21 Elston Howard	.30	.15	.03
☐ 22 Dick Farrell	.15	.07	.01
☐ 23 Albie Pearson	.15	.07	.01
☐ 24 Frank Howard	.25	.12	.02
☐ 25 Mickey Mantle	12.00	6.00	1.20
☐ 26 Joe Torre	.25	.12	.02
☐ 27 Eddie Brinkman	.15	.07	.01
☐ 28 Bob Friend SP	5.00	2.50	.50
☐ 29 Frank Robinson	2.00	1.00	.20
☐ 30 Bill Freehan	.15	.07	.01
☐ 31 Warren Spahn	1.50	.75	.15
☐ 32 Camilo Pascual	.15	.07	.01
☐ 33 Pete Ward	.15	.07	.01
☐ 34 Jim Maloney	.15	.07	.01
☐ 35 Dave Wickersham	.15	.07	.01
☐ 36 Johnny Callison	.15	.07	.01
☐ 37 Juan Marichal	1.50	.75	.15
☐ 38 Harmon Killebrew	1.50	.75	.15
☐ 39 Luis Aparicio	1.50	.75	.15
☐ 40 Dick Radatz	.15	.07	.01
☐ 41 Bob Gibson	1.50	.75	.15
☐ 42 Dick Stuart SP	5.00	2.50	.50
☐ 43 Tommy Davis	.15	.07	.01
☐ 44 Tony Oliva	.30	.15	.03
☐ 45 Wayne Causey SP	5.00	2.50	.50
☐ 46 Max Alvis	.15	.07	.01
☐ 47 Galen Cisco SP	5.00	2.50	.50
☐ 48 Carl Yastrzemski	4.00	2.00	.40
☐ 49 Hank Aaron	4.00	2.00	.40
☐ 50 Brooks Robinson	3.00	1.50	.30
☐ 51 Willie Mays SP	18.00	9.00	1.80
☐ 52 Billy Williams	1.50	.75	.15
☐ 53 Juan Pizarro	.15	.07	.01
☐ 54 Leon Wagner	.15	.07	.01
☐ 55 Orlando Cepeda	.50	.25	.05
☐ 56 Vada Pinson	.25	.12	.02
☐ 57 Ken Boyer	.25	.12	.02
☐ 58 Ron Santo	.25	.12	.02
☐ 59 John Romano	.15	.07	.01
☐ 60 Bill Skowron SP	5.00	2.50	.50

1964 Topps Stand Ups

In 1964 Topps produced a die-cut "Stand-Up" card design for the first time since their Connie Mack and Current All Stars of 1951. The cards have full-length, color player photos set against a green and yellow background. Of the 77 cards in the set, 22 were single printed and these are marked in the checklist below with an SP. These unnumbered cards are standard-size (2 1/2" by 3 1/2"), blank backed, and have been numbered here for reference in alphabetical order of players.

	NRMT	VG-E	GOOD
COMPLETE SET (77)	2100.00	50.00	10.00

COMMON PLAYER (1-77)	4.50	2.25	.45
COMMON PLAYER SP	22.00	11.00	2.20
☐ 1 Hank Aaron	100.00	50.00	10.00
☐ 2 Hank Aguirre	4.50	2.25	.45
☐ 3 George Altman	4.50	2.25	.45
☐ 4 Max Alvis	4.50	2.25	.45
☐ 5 Bob Aspromonte	4.50	2.25	.45
☐ 6 Jack Baldschun SP	22.00	11.00	2.20
☐ 7 Ernie Banks	45.00	22.50	4.50
☐ 8 Steve Barber	4.50	2.25	.45
☐ 9 Earl Battey	4.50	2.25	.45
☐ 10 Ken Boyer	6.00	3.00	.60
☐ 11 Ernie Broglio	4.50	2.25	.45
☐ 12 John Callison	4.50	2.25	.45
☐ 13 Norm Cash SP	27.00	13.50	2.70
☐ 14 Wayne Causey	4.50	2.25	.45
☐ 15 Orlando Cepeda	7.50	3.75	.75
☐ 16 Ed Charles	4.50	2.25	.45
☐ 17 Bob Clemente	80.00	40.00	8.00
☐ 18 Donn Clendenon SP	22.00	11.00	2.20
☐ 19 Rocky Colavito	7.50	3.75	.75
☐ 20 Ray Culp SP	22.00	11.00	2.20
☐ 21 Tommy Davis	6.00	3.00	.60
☐ 22 Don Drysdale SP	80.00	40.00	8.00
☐ 23 Dick Ellsworth	4.50	2.25	.45
☐ 24 Dick Farrell	4.50	2.25	.45
☐ 25 Jim Fregosi	6.00	3.00	.60
☐ 26 Bob Friend	4.50	2.25	.45
☐ 27 Jim Gentile	4.50	2.25	.45
☐ 28 Jesse Gonder SP	22.00	11.00	2.20
☐ 29 Tony Gonzalez SP	22.00	11.00	2.20
☐ 30 Dick Groat	6.00	3.00	.60
☐ 31 Woody Held	4.50	2.25	.45
☐ 32 Chuck Hinton	4.50	2.25	.45
☐ 33 Elston Howard	6.00	3.00	.60
☐ 34 Frank Howard SP	27.00	13.50	2.70
☐ 35 Ron Hunt	4.50	2.25	.45
☐ 36 Al Jackson	4.50	2.25	.45
☐ 37 Ken Johnson	4.50	2.25	.45
☐ 38 Al Kaline	50.00	25.00	5.00
☐ 39 Harmon Killebrew	35.00	17.50	3.50
☐ 40 Sandy Koufax	80.00	40.00	8.00
☐ 41 Don Lock SP	22.00	11.00	2.20
☐ 42 Jerry Lumpe SP	22.00	11.00	2.20
☐ 43 Jim Maloney	4.50	2.25	.45
☐ 44 Frank Malzone	4.50	2.25	.45
☐ 45 Mickey Mantle	400.00	200.00	40.00
☐ 46 Juan Marichal SP	80.00	40.00	8.00
☐ 47 Eddie Mathews SP	90.00	45.00	9.00
☐ 48 Willie Mays	100.00	50.00	10.00
☐ 49 Bill Mazeroski	6.00	3.00	.60
☐ 50 Ken McBride	4.50	2.25	.45
☐ 51 Willie McCovey SP	90.00	45.00	9.00
☐ 52 Claude Osteen	4.50	2.25	.45
☐ 53 Jim O'Toole	4.50	2.25	.45
☐ 54 Camilo Pascual	4.50	2.25	.45
☐ 55 Albie Pearson SP	22.00	11.00	2.20
☐ 56 Gary Peters	4.50	2.25	.45
☐ 57 Vada Pinson	6.00	3.00	.60
☐ 58 Juan Pizarro	4.50	2.25	.45
☐ 59 Boog Powell	6.00	3.00	.60
☐ 60 Bobby Richardson	7.50	3.75	.75
☐ 61 Brooks Robinson	45.00	22.50	4.50
☐ 62 Floyd Robinson	4.50	2.25	.45
☐ 63 Frank Robinson	35.00	17.50	3.50
☐ 64 Ed Roebuck SP	22.00	11.00	2.20
☐ 65 Rich Rollins	4.50	2.25	.45
☐ 66 John Romano	4.50	2.25	.45
☐ 67 Ron Santo SP	27.00	13.50	2.70
☐ 68 Norm Siebern	4.50	2.25	.45
☐ 69 Warren Spahn SP	90.00	45.00	9.00
☐ 70 Dick Stuart SP	22.00	11.00	2.20
☐ 71 Lee Thomas	4.50	2.25	.45
☐ 72 Joe Torre	7.50	3.75	.75
☐ 73 Pete Ward	4.50	2.25	.45
☐ 74 Bill White SP	27.00	13.50	2.70
☐ 75 Billy Williams SP	80.00	40.00	8.00
☐ 76 Hal Woodeshick SP	22.00	11.00	2.20
☐ 77 Carl Yastrzemski SP	350.00	175.00	35.00

1965 Topps

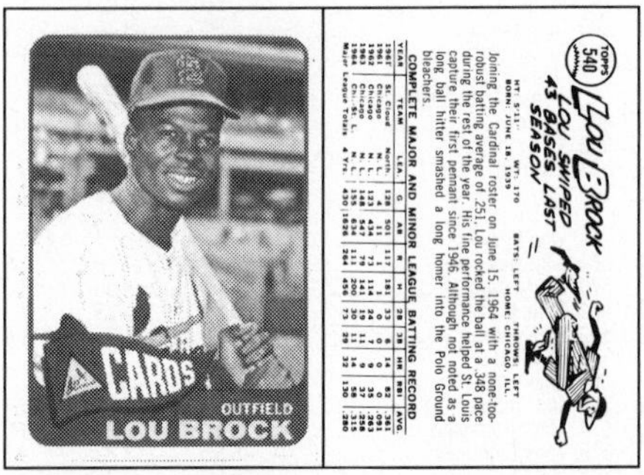

The cards in this 598-card set measure 2 1/2" by 3 1/2". The cards comprising the 1965 Topps set have team names located within a distinctive pennant design below the picture. The cards have blue borders on the reverse and were issued by series. Cards 523 to 598 are more difficult to obtain than all other series. Within this last series there are 44 cards that were printed in lesser quantities than the other cards in that series; these shorter-printed cards are marked by SP in the checklist below. In addition, the sixth series (447-522) is more difficult to obtain than series one through five. Featured subsets within this set include League Leaders (1-12) and World Series cards (132-139). Key cards in this set include Steve Carlton's rookie, Mickey Mantle, and Pete Rose. Other key rookies in this set are Jim Hunter, Joe Morgan, and Tony Perez.

	NRMT	VG-E	GOOD
COMPLETE SET (598)	3400.00	1600.00	350.00
COMMON PLAYER (1-196)	.90	.45	.09
COMMON PLAYER (197-283)	1.10	.55	.11
COMMON PLAYER (284-370)	1.75	.85	.17
COMMON PLAYER (371-446)	2.50	1.25	.25
COMMON PLAYER (447-522)	4.00	2.00	.40
COMMON PLAYER (523-598)	5.00	2.50	.50
COMMON SP (523-598)	9.00	4.50	.90
☐ 1 AL Batting Leaders Tony Oliva Elston Howard Brooks Robinson	12.50	2.00	.40
☐ 2 NL Batting Leaders Bob Clemente Hank Aaron Rico Carty	6.00	3.00	.60
☐ 3 AL Home Run Leaders Harmon Killebrew Mickey Mantle Boog Powell	10.00	5.00	1.00
☐ 4 NL Home Run Leaders Willie Mays Billy Williams Jim Ray Hart Orlando Cepeda Johnny Callison	5.00	2.50	.50
☐ 5 AL RBI Leaders Brooks Robinson Harmon Killebrew Mickey Mantle Dick Stuart	9.00	4.50	.90

☐ 6 NL RBI Leaders	3.00	1.50	.30
Ken Boyer			
Willie Mays			
Ron Santo			
☐ 7 AL ERA Leaders	1.75	.85	.17
Dean Chance			
Joel Horlen			
☐ 8 NL ERA Leaders	6.00	3.00	.60
Sandy Koufax			
Don Drysdale			
☐ 9 AL Pitching Leaders	1.75	.85	.17
Dean Chance			
Gary Peters			
Dave Wickersham			
Juan Pizarro			
Wally Bunker			
☐ 10 NL Pitching Leaders	1.75	.85	.17
Larry Jackson			
Ray Sadecki			
Juan Marichal			
☐ 11 AL Strikeout Leaders	1.75	.85	.17
Al Downing			
Dean Chance			
Camilo Pascual			
☐ 12 NL Strikeout Leaders	2.50	1.25	.25
Bob Veale			
Don Drysdale			
Bob Gibson			
☐ 13 Pedro Ramos	.90	.45	.09
☐ 14 Len Gabrielson	.90	.45	.09
☐ 15 Robin Roberts	7.00	3.50	.70
☐ 16 Houston Rookies	180.00	90.00	18.00
Joe Morgan			
Sonny Jackson			
☐ 17 Johnny Romano	.90	.45	.09
☐ 18 Bill McCool	.90	.45	.09
☐ 19 Gates Brown	1.25	.60	.12
☐ 20 Jim Bunning	3.50	1.75	.35
☐ 21 Don Blasingame	.90	.45	.09
☐ 22 Charlie Smith	.90	.45	.09
☐ 23 Bob Tiefenauer	.90	.45	.09
☐ 24 Minnesota Twins	2.50	1.25	.25
Team Card			
☐ 25 Al McBean	.90	.45	.09
☐ 26 Bobby Knoop	.90	.45	.09
☐ 27 Dick Bertell	.90	.45	.09
☐ 28 Barney Schultz	.90	.45	.09
☐ 29 Felix Mantilla	.90	.45	.09
☐ 30 Jim Bouton	1.75	.85	.17
☐ 31 Mike White	.90	.45	.09
☐ 32 Herman Franks MG	.90	.45	.09
☐ 33 Jackie Brandt	.90	.45	.09
☐ 34 Cal Koonce	.90	.45	.09
☐ 35 Ed Charles	.90	.45	.09
☐ 36 Bobby Wine	.90	.45	.09
☐ 37 Fred Gladding	.90	.45	.09
☐ 38 Jim King	.90	.45	.09
☐ 39 Gerry Arrigo	.90	.45	.09
☐ 40 Frank Howard	1.75	.85	.17
☐ 41 White Sox Rookies	.90	.45	.09
Bruce Howard			
Marv Staehle			
☐ 42 Earl Wilson	.90	.45	.09
☐ 43 Mike Shannon	1.25	.60	.12
☐ 44 Wade Blasingame	.90	.45	.09
☐ 45 Roy McMillan	.90	.45	.09
☐ 46 Bob Lee	.90	.45	.09
☐ 47 Tommy Harper	1.25	.60	.12
☐ 48 Claude Raymond	.90	.45	.09
☐ 49 Orioles Rookies	1.50	.75	.15
Curt Blefary			
John Miller			
☐ 50 Juan Marichal	9.00	4.50	.90
☐ 51 Bill Bryan	.90	.45	.09
☐ 52 Ed Roebuck	.90	.45	.09
☐ 53 Dick McAuliffe	1.25	.60	.12
☐ 54 Joe Gibbon	.90	.45	.09
☐ 55 Tony Conigliaro	7.50	3.75	.75
☐ 56 Ron Kline	.90	.45	.09
☐ 57 Cardinals Team	2.00	1.00	.20
☐ 58 Fred Talbot	.90	.45	.09
☐ 59 Nate Oliver	.90	.45	.09
☐ 60 Jim O'Toole	.90	.45	.09
☐ 61 Chris Cannizzaro	.90	.45	.09
☐ 62 Jim Katt UER	4.50	2.25	.45
(sic, Kaat)			
☐ 63 Ty Cline	.90	.45	.09
☐ 64 Lou Burdette	1.50	.75	.15
☐ 65 Tony Kubek	3.00	1.50	.30
☐ 66 Bill Rigney MG	.90	.45	.09
☐ 67 Harvey Haddix	1.25	.60	.12
☐ 68 Del Crandall	1.25	.60	.12
☐ 69 Bill Virdon	1.50	.75	.15
☐ 70 Bill Skowron	1.50	.75	.15

☐ 71 John O'Donoghue	.90	.45	.09
☐ 72 Tony Gonzalez	.90	.45	.09
☐ 73 Dennis Ribant	.90	.45	.09
☐ 74 Red Sox Rookies	4.00	2.00	.40
Rico Petrocelli			
Jerry Stephenson			
☐ 75 Deron Johnson	1.25	.60	.12
☐ 76 Sam McDowell	1.25	.60	.12
☐ 77 Doug Camilli	.90	.45	.09
☐ 78 Dal Maxvill	.90	.45	.09
☐ 79 Checklist 1	4.50	.45	.09
☐ 80 Turk Farrell	.90	.45	.09
☐ 81 Don Buford	.90	.45	.09
☐ 82 Braves Rookies	1.50	.75	.15
Santos Alomar			
John Braun			
☐ 83 George Thomas	.90	.45	.09
☐ 84 Ron Herbel	.90	.45	.09
☐ 85 Willie Smith	.90	.45	.09
☐ 86 Les Narum	.90	.45	.09
☐ 87 Nelson Mathews	.90	.45	.09
☐ 88 Jack Lamabe	.90	.45	.09
☐ 89 Mike Hershberger	.90	.45	.09
☐ 90 Rich Rollins	1.25	.60	.12
☐ 91 Cubs Team	2.00	1.00	.20
☐ 92 Dick Howser	1.50	.75	.15
☐ 93 Jack Fisher	.90	.45	.09
☐ 94 Charlie Lau	1.25	.60	.12
☐ 95 Bill Mazeroski	2.00	1.00	.20
☐ 96 Sonny Siebert	1.25	.60	.12
☐ 97 Pedro Gonzalez	.90	.45	.09
☐ 98 Bob Miller	.90	.45	.09
☐ 99 Gil Hodges MG	6.00	3.00	.60
☐ 100 Ken Boyer	2.50	1.25	.25
☐ 101 Fred Newman	.90	.45	.09
☐ 102 Steve Boros	1.25	.60	.12
☐ 103 Harvey Kuenn	1.75	.85	.17
☐ 104 Checklist 2	4.50	.45	.09
☐ 105 Chico Salmon	.90	.45	.09
☐ 106 Gene Oliver	.90	.45	.09
☐ 107 Phillies Rookies	1.50	.75	.15
Pat Corrales			
Costen Shockley			
☐ 108 Don Mincher	1.25	.60	.12
☐ 109 Walt Bond	.90	.45	.09
☐ 110 Ron Santo	2.50	1.25	.25
☐ 111 Lee Thomas	1.25	.60	.12
☐ 112 Derrell Griffith	.90	.45	.09
☐ 113 Steve Barber	.90	.45	.09
☐ 114 Jim Hickman	.90	.45	.09
☐ 115 Bobby Richardson	2.50	1.25	.25
☐ 116 Cardinals Rookies	1.50	.75	.15
Dave Dowling			
Bob Tolan			
☐ 117 Wes Stock	.90	.45	.09
☐ 118 Hal Lanier	1.50	.75	.15
☐ 119 John Kennedy	.90	.45	.09
☐ 120 Frank Robinson	22.00	11.00	2.20
☐ 121 Gene Alley	1.25	.60	.12
☐ 122 Bill Pleis	.90	.45	.09
☐ 123 Frank Thomas	1.25	.60	.12
☐ 124 Tom Satriano	.90	.45	.09
☐ 125 Juan Pizarro	.90	.45	.09
☐ 126 Dodgers Team	3.50	1.75	.35
☐ 127 Frank Lary	1.25	.60	.12
☐ 128 Vic Davalillo	.90	.45	.09
☐ 129 Bennie Daniels	.90	.45	.09
☐ 130 Al Kaline	22.00	11.00	2.20
☐ 131 Johnny Keane MG	1.25	.60	.12
☐ 132 World Series Game 1	2.50	1.25	.25
Cards take opener			
☐ 133 World Series Game 2	2.50	1.25	.25
Stottlemyre wins			
☐ 134 World Series Game 3	25.00	12.50	2.50
Mantle's homer			
☐ 135 World Series Game 4	3.00	1.50	.30
Boyer's grand-slam			
☐ 136 World Series Game 5	2.50	1.25	.25
10th inning triumph			
☐ 137 World Series Game 6	3.00	1.50	.30
Bouton wins again			
☐ 138 World Series Game 7	5.00	2.50	.50
Gibson wins finale			
☐ 139 World Series Summary	2.50	1.25	.25
Cards celebrate			
☐ 140 Dean Chance	1.25	.60	.12
☐ 141 Charlie James	.90	.45	.09
☐ 142 Bill Monbouquette	.90	.45	.09
☐ 143 Pirates Rookies	.90	.45	.09
John Gelnar			
Jerry May			
☐ 144 Ed Kranepool	1.50	.75	.15
☐ 145 Luis Tiant	7.50	3.75	.75
☐ 146 Ron Hansen	.90	.45	.09

□ 147	Dennis Bennett	.90	.45	.09
□ 148	Willie Kirkland	.90	.45	.09
□ 149	Wayne Schurr	.90	.45	.09
□ 150	Brooks Robinson	22.00	11.00	2.20
□ 151	Athletics Team	2.00	1.00	.20
□ 152	Phil Ortega	.90	.45	.09
□ 153	Norm Cash	2.25	1.10	.22
□ 154	Bob Humphreys	.90	.45	.09
□ 155	Roger Maris	45.00	22.50	4.50
□ 156	Bob Sadowski	.90	.45	.09
□ 157	Zoilo Versalles	1.25	.60	.12
□ 158	Dick Sisler	.90	.45	.09
□ 159	Jim Duffalo	.90	.45	.09
□ 160	Bob Clemente UER	70.00	35.00	7.00
	(1960 Pittsburfh)			
□ 161	Frank Baumann	.90	.45	.09
□ 162	Russ Nixon	1.25	.60	.12
□ 163	Johnny Briggs	.90	.45	.09
□ 164	Al Spangler	.90	.45	.09
□ 165	Dick Ellsworth	1.25	.60	.12
□ 166	Indians Rookies	1.50	.75	.15
	George Culver			
	Tommie Agee			
□ 167	Bill Wakefield	.90	.45	.09
□ 168	Dick Green	.90	.45	.09
□ 169	Dave Vineyard	.90	.45	.09
□ 170	Hank Aaron	75.00	37.50	7.50
□ 171	Jim Roland	.90	.45	.09
□ 172	Jim Piersall	1.50	.75	.15
□ 173	Detroit Tigers	2.50	1.25	.25
	Team Card			
□ 174	Joey Jay	.90	.45	.09
□ 175	Bob Aspromonte	.90	.45	.09
□ 176	Willie McCovey	15.00	7.50	1.50
□ 177	Pete Mikkelsen	.90	.45	.09
□ 178	Dalton Jones	.90	.45	.09
□ 179	Hal Woodeshick	.90	.45	.09
□ 180	Bob Allison	1.25	.60	.12
□ 181	Senators Rookies	.90	.45	.09
	Don Loun			
	Joe McCabe			
□ 182	Mike De La Hoz	.90	.45	.09
□ 183	Dave Nicholson	.90	.45	.09
□ 184	John Boozer	.90	.45	.09
□ 185	Max Alvis	.90	.45	.09
□ 186	Billy Cowan	.90	.45	.09
□ 187	Casey Stengel MG	11.00	5.50	1.10
□ 188	Sam Bowens	.90	.45	.09
□ 189	Checklist 3	4.50	.45	.09
□ 190	Bill White	2.00	1.00	.20
□ 191	Phil Regan	1.25	.60	.12
□ 192	Jim Coker	.90	.45	.09
□ 193	Gaylord Perry	15.00	7.50	1.50
□ 194	Rookie Stars	1.25	.60	.12
	Bill Kelso			
	Rick Reichardt			
□ 195	Bob Veale	1.25	.60	.12
□ 196	Ron Fairly	1.25	.60	.12
□ 197	Diego Segui	1.10	.55	.11
□ 198	Smoky Burgess	1.50	.75	.15
□ 199	Bob Heffner	1.10	.55	.11
□ 200	Joe Torre	2.00	1.00	.20
□ 201	Twins Rookies	1.50	.75	.15
	Sandy Valdespino			
	Cesar Tovar			
□ 202	Leo Burke	1.10	.55	.11
□ 203	Dallas Green	2.00	1.00	.20
□ 204	Russ Snyder	1.10	.55	.11
□ 205	Warren Spahn	18.00	9.00	1.80
□ 206	Willie Horton	2.00	1.00	.20
□ 207	Pete Rose	150.00	75.00	15.00
□ 208	Tommy John	12.00	6.00	1.20
□ 209	Pirates Team	2.50	1.25	.25
□ 210	Jim Fregosi	1.75	.85	.17
□ 211	Steve Ridzik	1.10	.55	.11
□ 212	Ron Brand	1.10	.55	.11
□ 213	Jim Davenport	1.50	.75	.15
□ 214	Bob Purkey	1.10	.55	.11
□ 215	Pete Ward	1.10	.55	.11
□ 216	Al Worthington	1.10	.55	.11
□ 217	Walt Alston MG	3.50	1.75	.35
□ 218	Dick Schofield	1.10	.55	.11
□ 219	Bob Meyer	1.10	.55	.11
□ 220	Billy Williams	11.00	5.50	1.10
□ 221	John Tsitouris	1.10	.55	.11
□ 222	Bob Tillman	1.10	.55	.11
□ 223	Dan Osinski	1.10	.55	.11
□ 224	Bob Chance	1.10	.55	.11
□ 225	Bo Belinsky	1.50	.75	.15
□ 226	Yankees Rookies	1.50	.75	.15
	Elvio Jimenez			
	Jake Gibbs			
□ 227	Bobby Klaus	1.10	.55	.11
□ 228	Jack Sanford	1.50	.75	.15
□ 229	Lou Clinton	1.10	.55	.11
□ 230	Ray Sadecki	1.10	.55	.11
□ 231	Jerry Adair	1.10	.55	.11
□ 232	Steve Blass	2.00	1.00	.20
□ 233	Don Zimmer	1.50	.75	.15
□ 234	White Sox Team	2.25	1.10	.22
□ 235	Chuck Hinton	1.10	.55	.11
□ 236	Denny McLain	15.00	7.50	1.50
□ 237	Bernie Allen	1.10	.55	.11
□ 238	Joe Moeller	1.10	.55	.11
□ 239	Doc Edwards	1.50	.75	.15
□ 240	Bob Bruce	1.10	.55	.11
□ 241	Mack Jones	1.10	.55	.11
□ 242	George Brunet	1.10	.55	.11
□ 243	Reds Rookies	2.50	1.25	.25
	Ted Davidson			
	Tommy Helms			
□ 244	Lindy McDaniel	1.50	.75	.15
□ 245	Joe Pepitone	2.00	1.00	.20
□ 246	Tom Butters	1.10	.55	.11
□ 247	Wally Moon	1.50	.75	.15
□ 248	Gus Triandos	1.50	.75	.15
□ 249	Dave McNally	2.00	1.00	.20
□ 250	Willie Mays	100.00	50.00	10.00
□ 251	Billy Herman MG	2.00	1.00	.20
□ 252	Pete Richert	1.10	.55	.11
□ 253	Danny Cater	1.50	.75	.15
□ 254	Roland Sheldon	1.10	.55	.11
□ 255	Camilo Pascual	1.50	.75	.15
□ 256	Tito Francona	1.10	.55	.11
□ 257	Jim Wynn	1.75	.85	.17
□ 258	Larry Bearnarth	1.10	.55	.11
□ 259	Tigers Rookies	2.50	1.25	.25
	Jim Northrup			
	Ray Oyler			
□ 260	Don Drysdale	16.00	8.00	1.60
□ 261	Duke Carmel	1.10	.55	.11
□ 262	Bud Daley	1.10	.55	.11
□ 263	Marty Keough	1.10	.55	.11
□ 264	Bob Buhl	1.10	.55	.11
□ 265	Jim Pagliaroni	1.10	.55	.11
□ 266	Bert Campaneris	3.50	1.75	.35
□ 267	Senators Team	2.25	1.10	.22
□ 268	Ken McBride	1.10	.55	.11
□ 269	Frank Bolling	1.10	.55	.11
□ 270	Milt Pappas	1.50	.75	.15
□ 271	Don Wert	1.10	.55	.11
□ 272	Chuck Schilling	1.10	.55	.11
□ 273	Checklist 4	4.50	.45	.09
□ 274	Lum Harris MG	1.10	.55	.11
□ 275	Dick Groat	1.75	.85	.17
□ 276	Hoyt Wilhelm	7.50	3.75	.75
□ 277	Johnny Lewis	1.10	.55	.11
□ 278	Ken Retzer	1.10	.55	.11
□ 279	Dick Tracewski	1.10	.55	.11
□ 280	Dick Stuart	1.50	.75	.15
□ 281	Bill Stafford	1.10	.55	.11
□ 282	Giants Rookies	2.00	1.00	.20
	Dick Estelle			
	Masanori Murakami			
□ 283	Fred Whitfield	1.10	.55	.11
□ 284	Nick Willhite	1.75	.85	.17
□ 285	Ron Hunt	1.75	.85	.17
□ 286	Athletics Rookies	1.75	.85	.17
	Jim Dickson			
	Aurelio Monteagudo			
□ 287	Gary Kolb	1.75	.85	.17
□ 288	Jack Hamilton	1.75	.85	.17
□ 289	Gordy Coleman	2.25	1.10	.22
□ 290	Wally Bunker	2.25	1.10	.22
□ 291	Jerry Lynch	1.75	.85	.17
□ 292	Larry Yellen	1.75	.85	.17
□ 293	Angels Team	3.50	1.75	.35
□ 294	Tim McCarver	3.50	1.75	.35
□ 295	Dick Radatz	2.25	1.10	.22
□ 296	Tony Taylor	1.75	.85	.17
□ 297	Dave DeBusschere	2.50	1.25	.25
□ 298	Jim Stewart	1.75	.85	.17
□ 299	Jerry Zimmerman	1.75	.85	.17
□ 300	Sandy Koufax	100.00	50.00	10.00
□ 301	Birdie Tebbetts MG	1.75	.85	.17
□ 302	Al Stanek	1.75	.85	.17
□ 303	John Orsino	1.75	.85	.17
□ 304	Dave Stenhouse	1.75	.85	.17
□ 305	Rico Carty	2.50	1.25	.25
□ 306	Bubba Phillips	1.75	.85	.17
□ 307	Barry Latman	1.75	.85	.17
□ 308	Mets Rookies	2.25	1.10	.22
	Cleon Jones			
	Tom Parsons			
□ 309	Steve Hamilton	1.75	.85	.17
□ 310	Johnny Callison	2.25	1.10	.22
□ 311	Orlando Pena	1.75	.85	.17
□ 312	Joe Nuxhall	2.25	1.10	.22

☐ 313 Jim Schaffer	1.75	.85	.17
☐ 314 Sterling Slaughter	1.75	.85	.17
☐ 315 Frank Malzone	2.25	1.10	.22
☐ 316 Reds Team	3.50	1.75	.35
☐ 317 Don McMahon	1.75	.85	.17
☐ 318 Matty Alou	2.25	1.10	.22
☐ 319 Ken McMullen	1.75	.85	.17
☐ 320 Bob Gibson	22.00	11.00	2.20
☐ 321 Rusty Staub	3.50	1.75	.35
☐ 322 Rick Wise	2.25	1.10	.22
☐ 323 Hank Bauer MG	2.25	1.10	.22
☐ 324 Bobby Locke	1.75	.85	.17
☐ 325 Donn Clendenon	2.25	1.10	.22
☐ 326 Dwight Siebler	1.75	.85	.17
☐ 327 Denis Menke	1.75	.85	.17
☐ 328 Eddie Fisher	1.75	.85	.17
☐ 329 Hawk Taylor	1.75	.85	.17
☐ 330 Whitey Ford	22.00	11.00	2.20
☐ 331 Dodgers Rookies	2.25	1.10	.22
Al Ferrara			
John Purdin			
☐ 332 Ted Abernathy	1.75	.85	.17
☐ 333 Tom Reynolds	1.75	.85	.17
☐ 334 Vic Roznovsky	1.75	.85	.17
☐ 335 Mickey Lolich	3.50	1.75	.35
☐ 336 Woody Held	1.75	.85	.17
☐ 337 Mike Cuellar	2.25	1.10	.22
☐ 338 Philadelphia Phillies	3.50	1.75	.35
Team Card			
☐ 339 Ryne Duren	2.25	1.10	.22
☐ 340 Tony Oliva	6.00	3.00	.60
☐ 341 Bob Bolin	1.75	.85	.17
☐ 342 Bob Rodgers	2.25	1.10	.22
☐ 343 Mike McCormick	2.25	1.10	.22
☐ 344 Wes Parker	2.25	1.10	.22
☐ 345 Floyd Robinson	1.75	.85	.17
☐ 346 Bobby Bragan MG	1.75	.85	.17
☐ 347 Roy Face	2.50	1.25	.25
☐ 348 George Banks	1.75	.85	.17
☐ 349 Larry Miller	1.75	.85	.17
☐ 350 Mickey Mantle	375.00	175.00	37.00
☐ 351 Jim Perry	2.50	1.25	.25
☐ 352 Alex Johnson	2.50	1.25	.25
☐ 353 Jerry Lumpe	1.75	.85	.17
☐ 354 Cubs Rookies	1.75	.85	.17
Billy Ott			
Jack Warner			
☐ 355 Vada Pinson	2.50	1.25	.25
☐ 356 Bill Spanswick	1.75	.85	.17
☐ 357 Carl Warwick	1.75	.85	.17
☐ 358 Albie Pearson	1.75	.85	.17
☐ 359 Ken Johnson	1.75	.85	.17
☐ 360 Orlando Cepeda	5.00	2.50	.50
☐ 361 Checklist 5	4.50	.45	.09
☐ 362 Don Schwall	1.75	.85	.17
☐ 363 Bob Johnson	1.75	.85	.17
☐ 364 Galen Cisco	1.75	.85	.17
☐ 365 Jim Gentile	2.25	1.10	.22
☐ 366 Dan Schneider	1.75	.85	.17
☐ 367 Leon Wagner	1.75	.85	.17
☐ 368 White Sox Rookies	2.25	1.10	.22
Ken Berry			
Joel Gibson			
☐ 369 Phil Linz	2.25	1.10	.22
☐ 370 Tommy Davis	2.50	1.25	.25
☐ 371 Frank Kreutzer	2.50	1.25	.25
☐ 372 Clay Dalrymple	2.50	1.25	.25
☐ 373 Curt Simmons	3.00	1.50	.30
☐ 374 Angels Rookies	3.50	1.75	.35
Jose Cardenal			
Dick Simpson			
☐ 375 Dave Wickersham	2.50	1.25	.25
☐ 376 Jim Landis	2.50	1.25	.25
☐ 377 Willie Stargell	25.00	12.50	2.50
☐ 378 Chuck Estrada	3.00	1.50	.30
☐ 379 Giants Team	5.00	2.50	.50
☐ 380 Rocky Colavito	4.00	2.00	.40
☐ 381 Al Jackson	2.50	1.25	.25
☐ 382 J.C. Martin	2.50	1.25	.25
☐ 383 Felipe Alou	3.50	1.75	.35
☐ 384 Johnny Klippstein	2.50	1.25	.25
☐ 385 Carl Yastrzemski	90.00	45.00	9.00
☐ 386 Cubs Rookies	2.50	1.25	.25
Paul Jaeckel			
Fred Norman			
☐ 387 Johnny Podres	3.50	1.75	.35
☐ 388 John Blanchard	3.00	1.50	.30
☐ 389 Don Larsen	3.00	1.50	.30
☐ 390 Bill Freehan	3.50	1.75	.35
☐ 391 Mel McGaha MG	2.50	1.25	.25
☐ 392 Bob Friend	3.00	1.50	.30
☐ 393 Ed Kirkpatrick	2.50	1.25	.25
☐ 394 Jim Hannan	2.50	1.25	.25
☐ 395 Jim Ray Hart	3.50	1.75	.35

☐ 396 Frank Bertaina	2.50	1.25	.25
☐ 397 Jerry Buchek	2.50	1.25	.25
☐ 398 Reds Rookies	3.00	1.50	.30
Dan Neville			
Art Shamsky			
☐ 399 Ray Herbert	2.50	1.25	.25
☐ 400 Harmon Killebrew	22.00	11.00	2.20
☐ 401 Carl Willey	2.50	1.25	.25
☐ 402 Joe Amalfitano	2.50	1.25	.25
☐ 403 Boston Red Sox	5.00	2.50	.50
Team Card			
☐ 404 Stan Williams	2.50	1.25	.25
(listed as Indian			
but Yankee cap)			
☐ 405 John Roseboro	3.00	1.50	.30
☐ 406 Ralph Terry	3.00	1.50	.30
☐ 407 Lee Maye	2.50	1.25	.25
☐ 408 Larry Sherry	3.00	1.50	.30
☐ 409 Astros Rookies	3.50	1.75	.35
Jim Beauchamp			
Larry Dierker			
☐ 410 Luis Aparicio	9.00	4.50	.90
☐ 411 Roger Craig	3.50	1.75	.35
☐ 412 Bob Bailey	2.50	1.25	.25
☐ 413 Hal Reniff	2.50	1.25	.25
☐ 414 Al Lopez MG	3.50	1.75	.35
☐ 415 Curt Flood	4.50	2.25	.45
☐ 416 Jim Brewer	2.50	1.25	.25
☐ 417 Ed Brinkman	2.50	1.25	.25
☐ 418 Johnny Edwards	2.50	1.25	.25
☐ 419 Ruben Amaro	2.50	1.25	.25
☐ 420 Larry Jackson	2.50	1.25	.25
☐ 421 Twins Rookies	2.50	1.25	.25
Gary Dotter			
Jay Ward			
☐ 422 Aubrey Gatewood	2.50	1.25	.25
☐ 423 Jesse Gonder	2.50	1.25	.25
☐ 424 Gary Bell	2.50	1.25	.25
☐ 425 Wayne Causey	2.50	1.25	.25
☐ 426 Braves Team	5.00	2.50	.50
☐ 427 Bob Saverine	2.50	1.25	.25
☐ 428 Bob Shaw	2.50	1.25	.25
☐ 429 Don Demeter	2.50	1.25	.25
☐ 430 Gary Peters	3.00	1.50	.30
☐ 431 Cards Rookies	3.50	1.75	.35
Nelson Briles			
Wayne Spiezio			
☐ 432 Jim Grant	2.50	1.25	.25
☐ 433 John Bateman	2.50	1.25	.25
☐ 434 Dave Morehead	2.50	1.25	.25
☐ 435 Willie Davis	3.50	1.75	.35
☐ 436 Don Elston	2.50	1.25	.25
☐ 437 Chico Cardenas	2.50	1.25	.25
☐ 438 Harry Walker MG	2.50	1.25	.25
☐ 439 Moe Drabowsky	2.50	1.25	.25
☐ 440 Tom Tresh	3.50	1.75	.35
☐ 441 Denny Lemaster	2.50	1.25	.25
☐ 442 Vic Power	2.50	1.25	.25
☐ 443 Checklist 6	7.50	.75	.15
☐ 444 Bob Hendley	2.50	1.25	.25
☐ 445 Don Lock	2.50	1.25	.25
☐ 446 Art Mahaffey	2.50	1.25	.25
☐ 447 Julian Javier	4.00	2.00	.40
☐ 448 Lee Stange	4.00	2.00	.40
☐ 449 Mets Rookies	4.00	2.00	.40
Jerry Hinsley			
Gary Kroll			
☐ 450 Elston Howard	6.00	3.00	.60
☐ 451 Jim Owens	4.00	2.00	.40
☐ 452 Gary Geiger	4.00	2.00	.40
☐ 453 Dodgers Rookies	5.00	2.50	.50
Willie Crawford			
John Werhas			
☐ 454 Ed Rakow	4.00	2.00	.40
☐ 455 Norm Siebern	4.00	2.00	.40
☐ 456 Bill Henry	4.00	2.00	.40
☐ 457 Bob Kennedy MG	4.00	2.00	.40
☐ 458 John Buzhardt	4.00	2.00	.40
☐ 459 Frank Kostro	4.00	2.00	.40
☐ 460 Richie Allen	7.50	3.75	.75
☐ 461 Braves Rookies	50.00	25.00	5.00
Clay Carroll			
Phil Niekro			
☐ 462 Lew Krausse UER	4.00	2.00	.40
(photo actually			
Pete Lovrich)			
☐ 463 Manny Mota	5.00	2.50	.50
☐ 464 Ron Piche	4.00	2.00	.40
☐ 465 Tom Haller	4.00	2.00	.40
☐ 466 Senators Rookies	4.00	2.00	.40
Pete Craig			
Dick Nen			
☐ 467 Ray Washburn	4.00	2.00	.40
☐ 468 Larry Brown	4.00	2.00	.40

☐ 469	Don Nottebart	4.00	2.00	.40
☐ 470	Yogi Berra MG	50.00	25.00	5.00
☐ 471	Billy Hoeft	4.00	2.00	.40
☐ 472	Don Pavletich	4.00	2.00	.40
☐ 473	Orioles Rookies	12.00	6.00	1.20
	Paul Blair			
	Dave Johnson			
☐ 474	Cookie Rojas	5.00	2.50	.50
☐ 475	Clete Boyer	5.00	2.50	.50
☐ 476	Billy O'Dell	4.00	2.00	.40
☐ 477	Cards Rookies	450.00	225.00	45.00
	Fritz Ackley			
	Steve Carlton			
☐ 478	Wilbur Wood	5.00	2.50	.50
☐ 479	Ken Harrelson	6.00	3.00	.60
☐ 480	Joel Horlen	5.00	2.50	.50
☐ 481	Cleveland Indians	8.00	4.00	.80
	Team Card			
☐ 482	Bob Priddy	4.00	2.00	.40
☐ 483	George Smith	4.00	2.00	.40
☐ 484	Ron Perranoski	5.00	2.50	.50
☐ 485	Nellie Fox	9.00	4.50	.90
☐ 486	Angels Rookies	4.00	2.00	.40
	Tom Egan			
	Pat Rogan			
☐ 487	Woody Woodward	5.00	2.50	.50
☐ 488	Ted Wills	4.00	2.00	.40
☐ 489	Gene Mauch MG	5.00	2.50	.50
☐ 490	Earl Battey	4.00	2.00	.40
☐ 491	Tracy Stallard	4.00	2.00	.40
☐ 492	Gene Freese	4.00	2.00	.40
☐ 493	Tigers Rookies	4.00	2.00	.40
	Bill Roman			
	Bruce Brubaker			
☐ 494	Jay Ritchie	4.00	2.00	.40
☐ 495	Joe Christopher	4.00	2.00	.40
☐ 496	Joe Cunningham	4.00	2.00	.40
☐ 497	Giants Rookies	5.00	2.50	.50
	Ken Henderson			
	Jack Hiatt			
☐ 498	Gene Stephens	4.00	2.00	.40
☐ 499	Stu Miller	4.00	2.00	.40
☐ 500	Eddie Mathews	28.00	14.00	2.80
☐ 501	Indians Rookies	4.00	2.00	.40
	Ralph Gagliano			
	Jim Rittwage			
☐ 502	Don Cardwell	4.00	2.00	.40
☐ 503	Phil Gagliano	4.00	2.00	.40
☐ 504	Jerry Grote	4.00	2.00	.40
☐ 505	Ray Culp	4.00	2.00	.40
☐ 506	Sam Mele MG	4.00	2.00	.40
☐ 507	Sammy Ellis	4.00	2.00	.40
☐ 508	Checklist 7	10.00	1.00	.20
☐ 509	Red Sox Rookies	4.00	2.00	.40
	Bob Guindon			
	Gerry Vezendy			
☐ 510	Ernie Banks	50.00	25.00	5.00
☐ 511	Ron Locke	4.00	2.00	.40
☐ 512	Cap Peterson	4.00	2.00	.40
☐ 513	New York Yankees	11.00	5.50	1.10
	Team Card			
☐ 514	Joe Azcue	4.00	2.00	.40
☐ 515	Vern Law	5.00	2.50	.50
☐ 516	Al Weis	4.00	2.00	.40
☐ 517	Angels Rookies	4.00	2.00	.40
	Paul Schaal			
	Jack Warner			
☐ 518	Ken Rowe	4.00	2.00	.40
☐ 519	Bob Uecker UER	42.00	20.00	4.00
	(posing as a left-handed batter)			
☐ 520	Tony Cloninger	4.00	2.00	.40
☐ 521	Phillies Rookies	4.00	2.00	.40
	Dave Bennett			
	Morrie Stevens			
☐ 522	Hank Aguirre	4.00	2.00	.40
☐ 523	Mike Brumley SP	9.00	4.50	.90
☐ 524	Dave Giusti SP	9.00	4.50	.90
☐ 525	Eddie Bressoud	5.00	2.50	.50
☐ 526	Athletics Rookies SP	175.00	85.00	18.00
	Rene Lachemann			
	Johnny Odom			
	Jim Hunter ERR			
	("Tim" on back)			
	Skip Lockwood			
☐ 527	Jeff Torborg SP	12.00	6.00	1.20
☐ 528	George Altman	5.00	2.50	.50
☐ 529	Jerry Fosnow SP	9.00	4.50	.90
☐ 530	Jim Maloney	7.00	3.50	.70
☐ 531	Chuck Hiller	5.00	2.50	.50
☐ 532	Hector Lopez	5.00	2.50	.50
☐ 533	Mets Rookies SP	24.00	12.00	2.40
	Dan Napoleon			
	Ron Swoboda			
	Tug McGraw			
	Jim Bethke			
☐ 534	John Herrnstein	5.00	2.50	.50
☐ 535	Jack Kralick SP	9.00	4.50	.90
☐ 536	Andre Rodgers SP	9.00	4.50	.90
☐ 537	Angels Rookies	6.00	3.00	.60
	Marcelino Lopes			
	Phil Roof			
	Rudy May			
☐ 538	Chuck Dressen MG SP	9.00	4.50	.90
☐ 539	Herm Starrette	5.00	2.50	.50
☐ 540	Lou Brock SP	50.00	25.00	5.00
☐ 541	White Sox Rookies	5.00	2.50	.50
	Greg Bollo			
	Bob Locker			
☐ 542	Lou Klimchock	5.00	2.50	.50
☐ 543	Ed Connolly SP	9.00	4.50	.90
☐ 544	Howie Reed	5.00	2.50	.50
☐ 545	Jesus Alou SP	9.00	4.50	.90
☐ 546	Indians Rookies	5.00	2.50	.50
	Bill Davis			
	Mike Hedlund			
	Ray Barker			
	Floyd Weaver			
☐ 547	Jake Wood SP	9.00	4.50	.90
☐ 548	Dick Stigman	5.00	2.50	.50
☐ 549	Cubs Rookies SP	15.00	7.50	1.50
	Roberto Pena			
	Glenn Beckert			
☐ 550	Mel Stottlemyre SP	25.00	12.50	2.50
☐ 551	New York Mets SP	18.00	9.00	1.80
	Team Card			
☐ 552	Julio Gotay	5.00	2.50	.50
☐ 553	Astros Rookies	5.00	2.50	.50
	Dan Coombs			
	Gene Ratliff			
	Jack McClure			
☐ 554	Chico Ruiz SP	9.00	4.50	.90
☐ 555	Jack Baldschun SP	9.00	4.50	.90
☐ 556	Red Schoendienst	17.00	8.50	1.70
	MG SP			
☐ 557	Jose Santiago	5.00	2.50	.50
☐ 558	Tommie Sisk	5.00	2.50	.50
☐ 559	Ed Bailey SP	9.00	4.50	.90
☐ 560	Boog Powell SP	12.00	6.00	1.20
☐ 561	Dodgers Rookies	12.00	6.00	1.20
	Dennis Daboll			
	Mike Kekich			
	Hector Valle			
	Jim Lefebvre			
☐ 562	Billy Moran	5.00	2.50	.50
☐ 563	Julio Navarro	5.00	2.50	.50
☐ 564	Mel Nelson	5.00	2.50	.50
☐ 565	Ernie Broglio SP	9.00	4.50	.90
☐ 566	Yankees Rookies SP	9.00	4.50	.90
	Gil Blanco			
	Ross Moschitto			
	Art Lopez			
☐ 567	Tommie Aaron	6.00	3.00	.60
☐ 568	Ron Taylor SP	9.00	4.50	.90
☐ 569	Gino Cimoli SP	9.00	4.50	.90
☐ 570	Claude Osteen SP	10.00	5.00	1.00
☐ 571	Ossie Virgil SP	9.00	4.50	.90
☐ 572	Baltimore Orioles SP	16.00	8.00	1.60
	Team Card			
☐ 573	Red Sox Rookies SP	16.00	8.00	1.60
	Jim Lonborg			
	Gerry Moses			
	Bill Schlesinger			
	Mike Ryan			
☐ 574	Roy Sievers	6.00	3.00	.60
☐ 575	Jose Pagan	5.00	2.50	.50
☐ 576	Terry Fox SP	9.00	4.50	.90
☐ 577	AL Rookie Stars SP	10.00	5.00	1.00
	Darold Knowles			
	Don Buschhorn			
	Richie Scheinblum			
☐ 578	Camilo Carreon SP	9.00	4.50	.90
☐ 579	Dick Smith SP	9.00	4.50	.90
☐ 580	Jimmie Hall SP	10.00	5.00	1.00
☐ 581	NL Rookie Stars SP	110.00	55.00	11.00
	Tony Perez			
	Dave Ricketts			
	Kevin Collins			
☐ 582	Bob Schmidt SP	9.00	4.50	.90
☐ 583	Wes Covington SP	10.00	5.00	1.00
☐ 584	Harry Bright	5.00	2.50	.50
☐ 585	Hank Fischer	5.00	2.50	.50
☐ 586	Tom McCraw SP	9.00	4.50	.90
☐ 587	Joe Sparma	5.00	2.50	.50
☐ 588	Lenny Green	5.00	2.50	.50

☐ 589 Giants Rookies SP	9.00	4.50	.90
Frank Linzy			
Bob Schroder			
☐ 590 John Wyatt	5.00	2.50	.50
☐ 591 Bob Skinner SP	9.00	4.50	.90
☐ 592 Frank Bork SP	9.00	4.50	.90
☐ 593 Tigers Rookies SP	9.00	4.50	.90
Jackie Moore			
John Sullivan			
☐ 594 Joe Gaines	5.00	2.50	.50
☐ 595 Don Lee	5.00	2.50	.50
☐ 596 Don Landrum SP	9.00	4.50	.90
☐ 597 Twins Rookies	5.00	2.50	.50
Joe Nossek			
John Sevcik			
Dick Reese			
☐ 598 Al Downing SP	15.00	5.00	1.00

1966 Topps

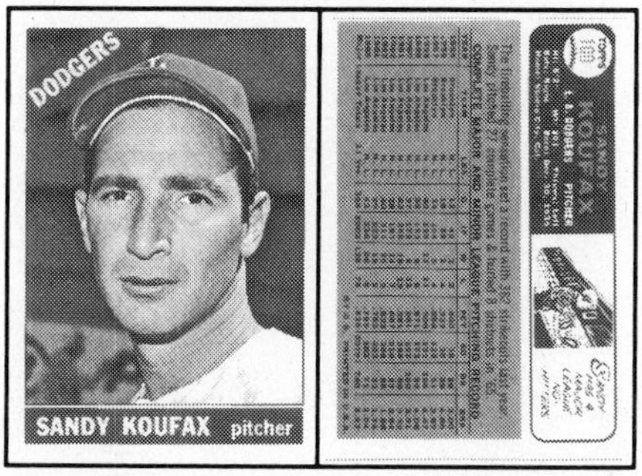

The cards in this 598-card set measure 2 1/2" by 3 1/2". There are the same number of cards as in the 1965 set. Once again, the seventh series cards (523 to 598) are considered more difficult to obtain than the cards of any other series in the set. Within this last series there are 43 cards that were printed in lesser quantities than the other cards in that series; these shorter-printed cards are marked by SP in the checklist below. The only featured subset within this set is League Leaders (215-226). Noteworthy rookie cards in the set include Jim Palmer (126), Ferguson Jenkins (254), and Don Sutton (288). Palmer is described in the bio (on his card back) as a left-hander.

	NRMT	VG-E	GOOD
COMPLETE SET (598)	3800.00	1800.00	400.00
COMMON PLAYER (1-109)	.80	.40	.08
COMMON PLAYER (110-283)	1.00	.50	.10
COMMON PLAYER (284-370)	1.35	.65	.13
COMMON PLAYER (371-446)	2.25	1.10	.22
COMMON PLAYER (447-522)	4.00	2.00	.40
COMMON PLAYER (523-598)	13.00	6.50	1.30
COMMON SP (523-598)	26.00	13.00	2.60
☐ 1 Willie Mays	150.00	50.00	10.00
☐ 2 Ted Abernathy	.80	.40	.08
☐ 3 Sam Mele MG	.80	.40	.08
☐ 4 Ray Culp	.80	.40	.08
☐ 5 Jim Fregosi	1.00	.50	.10
☐ 6 Chuck Schilling	.80	.40	.08
☐ 7 Tracy Stallard	.80	.40	.08
☐ 8 Floyd Robinson	.80	.40	.08
☐ 9 Clete Boyer	1.00	.50	.10
☐ 10 Tony Cloninger	.80	.40	.08
☐ 11 Senators Rookies	.80	.40	.08
Brant Alyea			
Pete Craig			
☐ 12 John Tsitouris	.80	.40	.08
☐ 13 Lou Johnson	.80	.40	.08
☐ 14 Norm Siebern	.80	.40	.08
☐ 15 Vern Law	1.00	.50	.10
☐ 16 Larry Brown	.80	.40	.08
☐ 17 John Stephenson	.80	.40	.08
☐ 18 Roland Sheldon	.80	.40	.08
☐ 19 San Francisco Giants	2.00	1.00	.20
Team Card			
☐ 20 Willie Horton	1.25	.60	.12
☐ 21 Don Nottebart	.80	.40	.08
☐ 22 Joe Nossek	.80	.40	.08
☐ 23 Jack Sanford	1.00	.50	.10
☐ 24 Don Kessinger	2.00	1.00	.20
☐ 25 Pete Ward	.80	.40	.08
☐ 26 Ray Sadecki	.80	.40	.08
☐ 27 Orioles Rookies	1.25	.60	.12
Darold Knowles			
Andy Etchebarren			
☐ 28 Phil Niekro	14.00	7.00	1.40
☐ 29 Mike Brumley	.80	.40	.08
☐ 30 Pete Rose	65.00	32.50	6.50
☐ 31 Jack Cullen	.80	.40	.08
☐ 32 Adolfo Phillips	.80	.40	.08
☐ 33 Jim Pagliaroni	.80	.40	.08
☐ 34 Checklist 1	4.00	.40	.08
☐ 35 Ron Swoboda	1.25	.60	.12
☐ 36 Jim Hunter	30.00	15.00	3.00
☐ 37 Billy Herman MG	1.50	.75	.15
☐ 38 Ron Nischwitz	.80	.40	.08
☐ 39 Ken Henderson	.80	.40	.08
☐ 40 Jim Grant	.80	.40	.08
☐ 41 Don LeJohn	.80	.40	.08
☐ 42 Aubrey Gatewood	.80	.40	.08
☐ 43 Don Landrum	.80	.40	.08
☐ 44 Indians Rookies	.80	.40	.08
Bill Davis			
Tom Kelley			
☐ 45 Jim Gentile	1.25	.60	.12
☐ 46 Howie Koplitz	.80	.40	.08
☐ 47 J.C. Martin	.80	.40	.08
☐ 48 Paul Blair	1.25	.60	.12
☐ 49 Woody Woodward	1.00	.50	.10
☐ 50 Mickey Mantle	180.00	90.00	18.00
☐ 51 Gordon Richardson	.80	.40	.08
☐ 52 Power Plus	1.25	.60	.12
Wes Covington			
Johnny Callison			
☐ 53 Bob Duliba	.80	.40	.08
☐ 54 Jose Pagan	.80	.40	.08
☐ 55 Ken Harrelson	1.25	.60	.12
☐ 56 Sandy Valdespino	.80	.40	.08
☐ 57 Jim Lefebvre	1.50	.75	.15
☐ 58 Dave Wickersham	.80	.40	.08
☐ 59 Reds Team	2.00	1.00	.20
☐ 60 Curt Flood	1.75	.85	.17
☐ 61 Bob Bolin	.80	.40	.08
☐ 62A Merritt Ranew	.80	.40	.08
(with sold line)			
☐ 62B Merritt Ranew	30.00	15.00	3.00
(without sold line)			
☐ 63 Jim Stewart	.80	.40	.08
☐ 64 Bob Bruce	.80	.40	.08
☐ 65 Leon Wagner	.80	.40	.08
☐ 66 Al Weis	.80	.40	.08
☐ 67 Mets Rookies	1.00	.50	.10
Cleon Jones			
Dick Selma			
☐ 68 Hal Reniff	.80	.40	.08
☐ 69 Ken Hamlin	.80	.40	.08
☐ 70 Carl Yastrzemski	55.00	27.50	5.50
☐ 71 Frank Carpin	.80	.40	.08
☐ 72 Tony Perez	17.00	8.50	1.70
☐ 73 Jerry Zimmerman	.80	.40	.08
☐ 74 Don Mossi	1.00	.50	.10
☐ 75 Tommy Davis	1.50	.75	.15
☐ 76 Red Schoendienst MG	4.00	2.00	.40
☐ 77 John Orsino	.80	.40	.08
☐ 78 Frank Linzy	.80	.40	.08
☐ 79 Joe Pepitone	1.50	.75	.15
☐ 80 Richie Allen	3.00	1.50	.30
☐ 81 Ray Oyler	.80	.40	.08
☐ 82 Bob Hendley	.80	.40	.08
☐ 83 Albie Pearson	.80	.40	.08
☐ 84 Braves Rookies	.80	.40	.08
Jim Beauchamp			
Dick Kelley			
☐ 85 Eddie Fisher	.80	.40	.08
☐ 86 John Bateman	.80	.40	.08
☐ 87 Dan Napoleon	.80	.40	.08
☐ 88 Fred Whitfield	.80	.40	.08
☐ 89 Ted Davidson	.80	.40	.08
☐ 90 Luis Aparicio	6.50	3.25	.65
☐ 91A Bob Uecker	21.00	10.50	2.10
(with traded line)			
☐ 91B Bob Uecker	60.00	30.00	6.00
(no traded line)			
☐ 92 Yankees Team	3.50	1.75	.35
☐ 93 Jim Lonborg	1.75	.85	.17
☐ 94 Matty Alou	1.00	.50	.10
☐ 95 Pete Richert	.80	.40	.08
☐ 96 Felipe Alou	1.25	.60	.12
☐ 97 Jim Merritt	.80	.40	.08

☐ 98 Don Demeter	.80	.40	.08
☐ 99 Buc Belters	3.50	1.75	.35
Willie Stargell			
Donn Clendenon			
☐ 100 Sandy Koufax	85.00	42.50	8.50
☐ 101A Checklist 2	5.00	.50	.10
(115 Bill Henry)			
☐ 101B Checklist 2	12.00	1.20	.20
(115 W. Spahn)			
☐ 102 Ed Kirkpatrick	.80	.40	.08
☐ 103A Dick Groat	1.50	.75	.15
(with traded line)			
☐ 103B Dick Groat	30.00	15.00	3.00
(no traded line)			
☐ 104A Alex Johnson	1.25	.60	.12
(with traded line)			
☐ 104B Alex Johnson	30.00	15.00	3.00
(no traded line)			
☐ 105 Milt Pappas	1.25	.60	.12
☐ 106 Rusty Staub	2.00	1.00	.20
☐ 107 A's Rookies	.80	.40	.08
Larry Stahl			
Ron Tompkins			
☐ 108 Bobby Klaus	.80	.40	.08
☐ 109 Ralph Terry	1.25	.60	.12
☐ 110 Ernie Banks	18.00	9.00	1.80
☐ 111 Gary Peters	1.25	.60	.12
☐ 112 Manny Mota	1.50	.75	.15
☐ 113 Hank Aguirre	1.00	.50	.10
☐ 114 Jim Gosger	1.00	.50	.10
☐ 115 Bill Henry	1.00	.50	.10
☐ 116 Walt Alston MG	3.00	1.50	.30
☐ 117 Jake Gibbs	1.00	.50	.10
☐ 118 Mike McCormick	1.25	.60	.12
☐ 119 Art Shamsky	1.00	.50	.10
☐ 120 Harmon Killebrew	16.00	8.00	1.60
☐ 121 Ray Herbert	1.00	.50	.10
☐ 122 Joe Gaines	1.00	.50	.10
☐ 123 Pirates Rookies	1.00	.50	.10
Frank Bork			
Jerry May			
☐ 124 Tug McGraw	3.00	1.50	.30
☐ 125 Lou Brock	18.00	9.00	1.80
☐ 126 Jim Palmer UER	225.00	110.00	22.00
(described as a			
lefthander on			
card back)			
☐ 127 Ken Berry	1.00	.50	.10
☐ 128 Jim Landis	1.00	.50	.10
☐ 129 Jack Kralick	1.00	.50	.10
☐ 130 Joe Torre	2.00	1.00	.20
☐ 131 Angels Team	2.25	1.10	.22
☐ 132 Orlando Cepeda	4.50	2.25	.45
☐ 133 Don McMahon	1.00	.50	.10
☐ 134 Wes Parker	1.50	.75	.15
☐ 135 Dave Morehead	1.00	.50	.10
☐ 136 Woody Held	1.00	.50	.10
☐ 137 Pat Corrales	1.50	.75	.15
☐ 138 Roger Repoz	1.00	.50	.10
☐ 139 Cubs Rookies	1.00	.50	.10
Byron Browne			
Don Young			
☐ 140 Jim Maloney	1.50	.75	.15
☐ 141 Tom McCraw	1.00	.50	.10
☐ 142 Don Dennis	1.00	.50	.10
☐ 143 Jose Tartabull	1.00	.50	.10
☐ 144 Don Schwall	1.00	.50	.10
☐ 145 Bill Freehan	2.00	1.00	.20
☐ 146 George Altman	1.00	.50	.10
☐ 147 Lum Harris MG	1.00	.50	.10
☐ 148 Bob Johnson	1.00	.50	.10
☐ 149 Dick Nen	1.00	.50	.10
☐ 150 Rocky Colavito	3.00	1.50	.30
☐ 151 Gary Wagner	1.00	.50	.10
☐ 152 Frank Malzone	1.25	.60	.12
☐ 153 Rico Carty	1.75	.85	.17
☐ 154 Chuck Hiller	1.00	.50	.10
☐ 155 Marcelino Lopez	1.00	.50	.10
☐ 156 Double Play Combo	1.25	.60	.12
Dick Schofield			
Hal Lanier			
☐ 157 Rene Lachemann	1.50	.75	.15
☐ 158 Jim Brewer	1.00	.50	.10
☐ 159 Chico Ruiz	1.00	.50	.10
☐ 160 Whitey Ford	18.00	9.00	1.80
☐ 161 Jerry Lumpe	1.00	.50	.10
☐ 162 Lee Maye	1.00	.50	.10
☐ 163 Tito Francona	1.00	.50	.10
☐ 164 White Sox Rookies	1.25	.60	.12
Tommie Agee			
Marv Staehle			
☐ 165 Don Lock	1.00	.50	.10
☐ 166 Chris Krug	1.00	.50	.10
☐ 167 Boog Powell	3.00	1.50	.30
☐ 168 Dan Osinski	1.00	.50	.10
☐ 169 Duke Sims	1.00	.50	.10
☐ 170 Cookie Rojas	1.25	.60	.12
☐ 171 Nick Willhite	1.00	.50	.10
☐ 172 Mets Team	2.50	1.25	.25
☐ 173 Al Spangler	1.00	.50	.10
☐ 174 Ron Taylor	1.00	.50	.10
☐ 175 Bert Campaneris	1.50	.75	.15
☐ 176 Jim Davenport	1.25	.60	.12
☐ 177 Hector Lopez	1.00	.50	.10
☐ 178 Bob Tillman	1.00	.50	.10
☐ 179 Cards Rookies	1.25	.60	.12
Dennis Aust			
Bob Tolan			
☐ 180 Vada Pinson	1.75	.85	.17
☐ 181 Al Worthington	1.00	.50	.10
☐ 182 Jerry Lynch	1.00	.50	.10
☐ 183 Checklist 3	4.00	.40	.08
☐ 184 Denis Menke	1.00	.50	.10
☐ 185 Bob Buhl	1.00	.50	.10
☐ 186 Ruben Amaro	1.00	.50	.10
☐ 187 Chuck Dressen MG	1.25	.60	.12
☐ 188 Al Luplow	1.00	.50	.10
☐ 189 John Roseboro	1.25	.60	.12
☐ 190 Jimmie Hall	1.25	.60	.12
☐ 191 Darrell Sutherland	1.00	.50	.10
☐ 192 Vic Power	1.00	.50	.10
☐ 193 Dave McNally	1.50	.75	.15
☐ 194 Senators Team	2.00	1.00	.20
☐ 195 Joe Morgan	40.00	20.00	4.00
☐ 196 Don Pavletich	1.00	.50	.10
☐ 197 Sonny Siebert	1.25	.60	.12
☐ 198 Mickey Stanley	2.00	1.00	.20
☐ 199 Chisox Clubbers	1.50	.75	.15
Bill Skowron			
Johnny Romano			
Floyd Robinson			
☐ 200 Eddie Mathews	11.00	5.50	1.10
☐ 201 Jim Dickson	1.00	.50	.10
☐ 202 Clay Dalrymple	1.00	.50	.10
☐ 203 Jose Santiago	1.00	.50	.10
☐ 204 Cubs Team	2.00	1.00	.20
☐ 205 Tom Tresh	1.75	.85	.17
☐ 206 Al Jackson	1.00	.50	.10
☐ 207 Frank Quilici	1.00	.50	.10
☐ 208 Bob Miller	1.00	.50	.10
☐ 209 Tigers Rookies	2.00	1.00	.20
Fritz Fisher			
John Hiller			
☐ 210 Bill Mazeroski	1.75	.85	.17
☐ 211 Frank Kreutzer	1.00	.50	.10
☐ 212 Ed Kranepool	1.50	.75	.15
☐ 213 Fred Newman	1.00	.50	.10
☐ 214 Tommy Harper	1.25	.60	.12
☐ 215 NL Batting Leaders	14.00	7.00	1.40
Bob Clemente			
Hank Aaron			
Willie Mays			
☐ 216 AL Batting Leaders	3.50	1.75	.35
Tony Oliva			
Carl Yastrzemski			
Vic Davalillo			
☐ 217 NL Home Run Leaders	9.00	4.50	.90
Willie Mays			
Willie McCovey			
Billy Williams			
☐ 218 AL Home Run Leaders	2.00	1.00	.20
Tony Conigliaro			
Norm Cash			
Willie Horton			
☐ 219 NL RBI Leaders	3.50	1.75	.35
Deron Johnson			
Frank Robinson			
Willie Mays			
☐ 220 AL RBI Leaders	2.00	1.00	.20
Rocky Colavito			
Willie Horton			
Tony Oliva			
☐ 221 NL ERA Leaders	3.50	1.75	.35
Sandy Koufax			
Juan Marichal			
Vern Law			
☐ 222 AL ERA Leaders	2.00	1.00	.20
Sam McDowell			
Eddie Fisher			
Sonny Siebert			
☐ 223 NL Pitching Leaders	3.50	1.75	.35
Sandy Koufax			
Tony Cloninger			
Don Drysdale			
☐ 224 AL Pitching Leaders	2.00	1.00	.20
Jim Grant			
Mel Stottlemyre			
Jim Kaat			

☐ 225	NL Strikeout Leaders	3.50	1.75	.35
	Sandy Koufax			
	Bob Veale			
	Bob Gibson			
☐ 226	AL Strikeout Leaders	2.00	1.00	.20
	Sam McDowell			
	Mickey Lolich			
	Dennis McLain			
	Sonny Siebert			
☐ 227	Russ Nixon	1.25	.60	.12
☐ 228	Larry Dierker	1.25	.60	.12
☐ 229	Hank Bauer MG	1.25	.60	.12
☐ 230	Johnny Callison	1.25	.60	.12
☐ 231	Floyd Weaver	1.00	.50	.10
☐ 232	Glenn Beckert	1.50	.75	.15
☐ 233	Dom Zanni	1.00	.50	.10
☐ 234	Yankees Rookies	4.00	2.00	.40
	Rich Beck			
	Roy White			
☐ 235	Don Cardwell	1.00	.50	.10
☐ 236	Mike Hershberger	1.00	.50	.10
☐ 237	Billy O'Dell	1.00	.50	.10
☐ 238	Dodgers Team	2.50	1.25	.25
☐ 239	Orlando Pena	1.00	.50	.10
☐ 240	Earl Battey	1.00	.50	.10
☐ 241	Dennis Ribant	1.00	.50	.10
☐ 242	Jesus Alou	1.00	.50	.10
☐ 243	Nelson Briles	1.50	.75	.15
☐ 244	Astros Rookies	1.00	.50	.10
	Chuck Harrison			
	Sonny Jackson			
☐ 245	John Buzhardt	1.00	.50	.10
☐ 246	Ed Bailey	1.00	.50	.10
☐ 247	Carl Warwick	1.00	.50	.10
☐ 248	Pete Mikkelsen	1.00	.50	.10
☐ 249	Bill Rigney MG	1.00	.50	.10
☐ 250	Sammy Ellis	1.00	.50	.10
☐ 251	Ed Brinkman	1.00	.50	.10
☐ 252	Denny Lemaster	1.00	.50	.10
☐ 253	Don Wert	1.00	.50	.10
☐ 254	Phillies Rookies	90.00	40.00	7.50
	Ferguson Jenkins			
	Bill Sorrell			
☐ 255	Willie Stargell	16.00	8.00	1.60
☐ 256	Lew Krausse	1.00	.50	.10
☐ 257	Jeff Torborg	1.75	.85	.17
☐ 258	Dave Giusti	1.25	.60	.12
☐ 259	Boston Red Sox	2.50	1.25	.25
	Team Card			
☐ 260	Bob Shaw	1.00	.50	.10
☐ 261	Ron Hansen	1.00	.50	.10
☐ 262	Jack Hamilton	1.00	.50	.10
☐ 263	Tom Egan	1.00	.50	.10
☐ 264	Twins Rookies	1.00	.50	.10
	Andy Kosco			
	Ted Uhlaender			
☐ 265	Stu Miller	1.00	.50	.10
☐ 266	Pedro Gonzalez UER	1.00	.50	.10
	(misspelled Gonzales			
	on card back)			
☐ 267	Joe Sparma	1.00	.50	.10
☐ 268	John Blanchard	1.25	.60	.12
☐ 269	Don Heffner MG	1.00	.50	.10
☐ 270	Claude Osteen	1.25	.60	.12
☐ 271	Hal Lanier	1.25	.60	.12
☐ 272	Jack Baldschun	1.00	.50	.10
☐ 273	Astro Aces	1.50	.75	.15
	Bob Aspromonte			
	Rusty Staub			
☐ 274	Buster Narum	1.00	.50	.10
☐ 275	Tim McCarver	2.50	1.25	.25
☐ 276	Jim Bouton	1.75	.85	.17
☐ 277	George Thomas	1.00	.50	.10
☐ 278	Cal Koonce	1.00	.50	.10
☐ 279	Checklist 4	4.00	.40	.08
☐ 280	Bobby Knoop	1.00	.50	.10
☐ 281	Bruce Howard	1.00	.50	.10
☐ 282	Johnny Lewis	1.00	.50	.10
☐ 283	Jim Perry	1.50	.75	.15
☐ 284	Bobby Wine	1.35	.65	.13
☐ 285	Luis Tiant	2.25	1.10	.22
☐ 286	Gary Geiger	1.35	.65	.13
☐ 287	Jack Aker	1.35	.65	.13
☐ 288	Dodgers Rookies	110.00	55.00	11.00
	Bill Singer			
	Don Sutton			
☐ 289	Larry Sherry	1.75	.85	.17
☐ 290	Ron Santo	2.50	1.25	.25
☐ 291	Moe Drabowsky	1.35	.65	.13
☐ 292	Jim Coker	1.35	.65	.13
☐ 293	Mike Shannon	1.75	.85	.17
☐ 294	Steve Ridzik	1.35	.65	.13
☐ 295	Jim Ray Hart	1.75	.85	.17
☐ 296	Johnny Keane MG	1.75	.85	.17
☐ 297	Jim Owens	1.35	.65	.13
☐ 298	Rico Petrocelli	1.75	.85	.17
☐ 299	Lou Burdette	1.75	.85	.17
☐ 300	Bob Clemente	75.00	37.50	7.50
☐ 301	Greg Bollo	1.35	.65	.13
☐ 302	Ernie Bowman	1.35	.65	.13
☐ 303	Cleveland Indians	2.50	1.25	.25
	Team Card			
☐ 304	John Herrnstein	1.35	.65	.13
☐ 305	Camilo Pascual	1.75	.85	.17
☐ 306	Ty Cline	1.35	.65	.13
☐ 307	Clay Carroll	1.35	.65	.13
☐ 308	Tom Haller	1.75	.85	.17
☐ 309	Diego Segui	1.35	.65	.13
☐ 310	Frank Robinson	33.00	15.00	3.00
☐ 311	Reds Rookies	1.75	.85	.17
	Tommy Helms			
	Dick Simpson			
☐ 312	Bob Saverine	1.35	.65	.13
☐ 313	Chris Zachary	1.35	.65	.13
☐ 314	Hector Valle	1.35	.65	.13
☐ 315	Norm Cash	2.50	1.25	.25
☐ 316	Jack Fisher	1.35	.65	.13
☐ 317	Dalton Jones	1.35	.65	.13
☐ 318	Harry Walker MG	1.35	.65	.13
☐ 319	Gene Freese	1.35	.65	.13
☐ 320	Bob Gibson	17.00	8.50	1.70
☐ 321	Rick Reichardt	1.35	.65	.13
☐ 322	Bill Faul	1.35	.65	.13
☐ 323	Ray Barker	1.35	.65	.13
☐ 324	John Boozer	1.35	.65	.13
☐ 325	Vic Davalillo	1.35	.65	.13
☐ 326	Braves Team	2.50	1.25	.25
☐ 327	Bernie Allen	1.35	.65	.13
☐ 328	Jerry Grote	1.35	.65	.13
☐ 329	Pete Charton	1.35	.65	.13
☐ 330	Ron Fairly	1.75	.85	.17
☐ 331	Ron Herbel	1.35	.65	.13
☐ 332	Bill Bryan	1.35	.65	.13
☐ 333	Senators Rookies	1.35	.65	.13
	Joe Coleman			
	Jim French			
☐ 334	Marty Keough	1.35	.65	.13
☐ 335	Juan Pizarro	1.35	.65	.13
☐ 336	Gene Alley	1.75	.85	.17
☐ 337	Fred Gladding	1.35	.65	.13
☐ 338	Dal Maxvill	1.35	.65	.13
☐ 339	Del Crandall	1.75	.85	.17
☐ 340	Dean Chance	1.75	.85	.17
☐ 341	Wes Westrum MG	1.35	.65	.13
☐ 342	Bob Humphreys	1.35	.65	.13
☐ 343	Joe Christopher	1.35	.65	.13
☐ 344	Steve Blass	1.75	.85	.17
☐ 345	Bob Allison	1.75	.85	.17
☐ 346	Mike De La Hoz	1.35	.65	.13
☐ 347	Phil Regan	1.75	.85	.17
☐ 348	Orioles Team	2.50	1.25	.25
☐ 349	Cap Peterson	1.35	.65	.13
☐ 350	Mel Stottlemyre	3.00	1.50	.30
☐ 351	Fred Valentine	1.35	.65	.13
☐ 352	Bob Aspromonte	1.35	.65	.13
☐ 353	Al McBean	1.35	.65	.13
☐ 354	Smoky Burgess	1.75	.85	.17
☐ 355	Wade Blasingame	1.35	.65	.13
☐ 356	Red Sox Rookies	1.35	.65	.13
	Owen Johnson			
	Ken Sanders			
☐ 357	Gerry Arrigo	1.35	.65	.13
☐ 358	Charlie Smith	1.35	.65	.13
☐ 359	Johnny Briggs	1.35	.65	.13
☐ 360	Ron Hunt	1.35	.65	.13
☐ 361	Tom Satriano	1.35	.65	.13
☐ 362	Gates Brown	1.75	.85	.17
☐ 363	Checklist 5	5.00	.50	.10
☐ 364	Nate Oliver	1.35	.65	.13
☐ 365	Roger Maris	50.00	25.00	5.00
☐ 366	Wayne Causey	1.35	.65	.13
☐ 367	Mel Nelson	1.35	.65	.13
☐ 368	Charlie Lau	1.75	.85	.17
☐ 369	Jim King	1.35	.65	.13
☐ 370	Chico Cardenas	1.35	.65	.13
☐ 371	Lee Stange	2.25	1.10	.22
☐ 372	Harvey Kuenn	3.00	1.50	.30
☐ 373	Giants Rookies	2.25	1.10	.22
	Jack Hiatt			
	Dick Estelle			
☐ 374	Bob Locker	2.25	1.10	.22
☐ 375	Donn Clendenon	3.00	1.50	.30
☐ 376	Paul Schaal	2.25	1.10	.22
☐ 377	Turk Farrell	2.25	1.10	.22
☐ 378	Dick Tracewski	2.25	1.10	.22
☐ 379	Cardinal Team	4.50	2.25	.45
☐ 380	Tony Conigliaro	5.50	2.75	.55
☐ 381	Hank Fischer	2.25	1.10	.22

☐ 382 Phil Roof	2.25	1.10	.22
☐ 383 Jackie Brandt	2.25	1.10	.22
☐ 384 Al Downing	3.00	1.50	.30
☐ 385 Ken Boyer	3.50	1.75	.35
☐ 386 Gil Hodges MG	4.50	2.25	.45
☐ 387 Howie Reed	2.25	1.10	.22
☐ 388 Don Mincher	3.00	1.50	.30
☐ 389 Jim O'Toole	3.00	1.50	.30
☐ 390 Brooks Robinson	22.00	11.00	2.20
☐ 391 Chuck Hinton	2.25	1.10	.22
☐ 392 Cubs Rookies	3.00	1.50	.30
Bill Hands			
Randy Hundley			
☐ 393 George Brunet	2.25	1.10	.22
☐ 394 Ron Brand	2.25	1.10	.22
☐ 395 Len Gabrielson	2.25	1.10	.22
☐ 396 Jerry Stephenson	2.25	1.10	.22
☐ 397 Bill White	3.50	1.75	.35
☐ 398 Danny Cater	2.25	1.10	.22
☐ 399 Ray Washburn	2.25	1.10	.22
☐ 400 Zoilo Versalles	2.25	1.10	.22
☐ 401 Ken McMullen	2.25	1.10	.22
☐ 402 Jim Hickman	2.25	1.10	.22
☐ 403 Fred Talbot	2.25	1.10	.22
☐ 404 Pittsburgh Pirates	4.50	2.25	.45
Team Card			
☐ 405 Elston Howard	3.50	1.75	.35
☐ 406 Joey Jay	2.25	1.10	.22
☐ 407 John Kennedy	2.25	1.10	.22
☐ 408 Lee Thomas	3.00	1.50	.30
☐ 409 Billy Hoeft	2.25	1.10	.22
☐ 410 Al Kaline	22.00	11.00	2.20
☐ 411 Gene Mauch MG	3.00	1.50	.30
☐ 412 Sam Bowens	2.25	1.10	.22
☐ 413 Johnny Romano	2.25	1.10	.22
☐ 414 Dan Coombs	2.25	1.10	.22
☐ 415 Max Alvis	2.25	1.10	.22
☐ 416 Phil Ortega	2.25	1.10	.22
☐ 417 Angels Rookies	2.25	1.10	.22
Jim McGlothlin			
Ed Sukla			
☐ 418 Phil Gagliano	2.25	1.10	.22
☐ 419 Mike Ryan	2.25	1.10	.22
☐ 420 Juan Marichal	11.00	5.50	1.10
☐ 421 Roy McMillan	2.25	1.10	.22
☐ 422 Ed Charles	2.25	1.10	.22
☐ 423 Ernie Broglio	2.25	1.10	.22
☐ 424 Reds Rookies	4.00	2.00	.40
Lee May			
Darrell Osteen			
☐ 425 Bob Veale	3.00	1.50	.30
☐ 426 White Sox Team	4.50	2.25	.45
☐ 427 John Miller	2.25	1.10	.22
☐ 428 Sandy Alomar	3.00	1.50	.30
☐ 429 Bill Monbouquette	2.25	1.10	.22
☐ 430 Don Drysdale	16.00	8.00	1.60
☐ 431 Walt Bond	2.25	1.10	.22
☐ 432 Bob Heffner	2.25	1.10	.22
☐ 433 Alvin Dark MG	3.00	1.50	.30
☐ 434 Willie Kirkland	2.25	1.10	.22
☐ 435 Jim Bunning	5.00	2.50	.50
☐ 436 Julian Javier	2.25	1.10	.22
☐ 437 Al Stanek	2.25	1.10	.22
☐ 438 Willie Smith	2.25	1.10	.22
☐ 439 Pedro Ramos	2.25	1.10	.22
☐ 440 Deron Johnson	2.25	1.10	.22
☐ 441 Tommie Sisk	2.25	1.10	.22
☐ 442 Orioles Rookies	2.25	1.10	.22
Ed Barnowski			
Eddie Watt			
☐ 443 Bill Wakefield	2.25	1.10	.22
☐ 444 Checklist 6	7.50	.75	.15
☐ 445 Jim Kaat	5.50	2.75	.55
☐ 446 Mack Jones	2.25	1.10	.22
☐ 447 Dick Ellsworth UER	5.00	2.50	.50
(photo actually			
Ken Hubbs)			
☐ 448 Eddie Stanky MG	5.00	2.50	.50
☐ 449 Joe Moeller	4.00	2.00	.40
☐ 450 Tony Oliva	6.50	3.25	.65
☐ 451 Barry Latman	4.00	2.00	.40
☐ 452 Joe Azcue	4.00	2.00	.40
☐ 453 Ron Kline	4.00	2.00	.40
☐ 454 Jerry Buchek	4.00	2.00	.40
☐ 455 Mickey Lolich	6.00	3.00	.60
☐ 456 Red Sox Rookies	4.00	2.00	.40
Darrell Brandon			
Joe Foy			
☐ 457 Joe Gibbon	4.00	2.00	.40
☐ 458 Manny Jiminez	4.00	2.00	.40
☐ 459 Bill McCool	4.00	2.00	.40
☐ 460 Curt Blefary	5.00	2.50	.50
☐ 461 Roy Face	5.00	2.50	.50
☐ 462 Bob Rodgers	5.00	2.50	.50
☐ 463 Philadelphia Phillies	8.00	4.00	.80
Team Card			
☐ 464 Larry Bearnarth	4.00	2.00	.40
☐ 465 Don Buford	5.00	2.50	.50
☐ 466 Ken Johnson	4.00	2.00	.40
☐ 467 Vic Roznovsky	4.00	2.00	.40
☐ 468 Johnny Podres	6.00	3.00	.60
☐ 469 Yankees Rookies	14.00	7.00	1.40
Bobby Murcer			
Dooley Womack			
☐ 470 Sam McDowell	5.00	2.50	.50
☐ 471 Bob Skinner	5.00	2.50	.50
☐ 472 Terry Fox	4.00	2.00	.40
☐ 473 Rich Rollins	5.00	2.50	.50
☐ 474 Dick Schofield	4.00	2.00	.40
☐ 475 Dick Radatz	5.00	2.50	.50
☐ 476 Bobby Bragan MG	4.00	2.00	.40
☐ 477 Steve Barber	4.00	2.00	.40
☐ 478 Tony Gonzalez	4.00	2.00	.40
☐ 479 Jim Hannan	4.00	2.00	.40
☐ 480 Dick Stuart	5.00	2.50	.50
☐ 481 Bob Lee	4.00	2.00	.40
☐ 482 Cubs Rookies	4.00	2.00	.40
John Boccabella			
Dave Dowling			
☐ 483 Joe Nuxhall	5.00	2.50	.50
☐ 484 Wes Covington	4.00	2.00	.40
☐ 485 Bob Bailey	4.00	2.00	.40
☐ 486 Tommy John	11.00	5.50	1.10
☐ 487 Al Ferrara	4.00	2.00	.40
☐ 488 George Banks	4.00	2.00	.40
☐ 489 Curt Simmons	5.00	2.50	.50
☐ 490 Bobby Richardson	9.00	4.50	.90
☐ 491 Dennis Bennett	4.00	2.00	.40
☐ 492 Athletics Team	8.00	4.00	.80
☐ 493 Johnny Klippstein	4.00	2.00	.40
☐ 494 Gordy Coleman	5.00	2.50	.50
☐ 495 Dick McAuliffe	5.00	2.50	.50
☐ 496 Lindy McDaniel	4.00	2.00	.40
☐ 497 Chris Cannizzaro	4.00	2.00	.40
☐ 498 Pirates Rookies	5.00	2.50	.50
Luke Walker			
Woody Fryman			
☐ 499 Wally Bunker	4.00	2.00	.40
☐ 500 Hank Aaron	85.00	42.50	8.50
☐ 501 John O'Donoghue	4.00	2.00	.40
☐ 502 Lenny Green	4.00	2.00	.40
☐ 503 Steve Hamilton	4.00	2.00	.40
☐ 504 Grady Hatton MG	4.00	2.00	.40
☐ 505 Jose Cardenal	4.00	2.00	.40
☐ 506 Bo Belinsky	4.00	2.00	.40
☐ 507 Johnny Edwards	4.00	2.00	.40
☐ 508 Steve Hargan	4.00	2.00	.40
☐ 509 Jake Wood	4.00	2.00	.40
☐ 510 Hoyt Wilhelm	13.00	6.50	1.30
☐ 511 Giants Rookies	4.00	2.00	.40
Bob Barton			
Tito Fuentes			
☐ 512 Dick Stigman	4.00	2.00	.40
☐ 513 Camilo Carreon	4.00	2.00	.40
☐ 514 Hal Woodeshick	4.00	2.00	.40
☐ 515 Frank Howard	5.50	2.75	.55
☐ 516 Eddie Bressoud	4.00	2.00	.40
☐ 517A Checklist 7	12.00	1.20	.20
529 White Sox Rookies			
544 Cardinals Rookies			
☐ 517B Checklist 7	12.00	1.20	.20
529 W. Sox Rookies			
544 Cards Rookies			
☐ 518 Braves Rookies	4.00	2.00	.40
Herb Hippauf			
Arnie Umbach			
☐ 519 Bob Friend	5.00	2.50	.50
☐ 520 Jim Wynn	5.00	2.50	.50
☐ 521 John Wyatt	4.00	2.00	.40
☐ 522 Phil Linz	5.00	2.50	.50
☐ 523 Bob Sadowski	13.00	6.50	1.30
☐ 524 Giants Rookies SP	26.00	13.00	2.60
Ollie Brown			
Don Mason			
☐ 525 Gary Bell SP	26.00	13.00	2.60
☐ 526 Twins Team SP	60.00	30.00	6.00
☐ 527 Julio Navarro	13.00	6.50	1.30
☐ 528 Jesse Gonder SP	26.00	13.00	2.60
☐ 529 White Sox Rookies	16.00	8.00	1.60
Lee Elia			
Dennis Higgins			
Bill Voss			
☐ 530 Robin Roberts	36.00	18.00	3.60
☐ 531 Joe Cunningham	13.00	6.50	1.30
☐ 532 Aurelio Monteagudo SP	26.00	13.00	2.60
☐ 533 Jerry Adair SP	26.00	13.00	2.60

☐ 534 Mets Rookies	13.00	6.50	1.30
Dave Eilers			
Rob Gardner			
☐ 535 Willie Davis SP	35.00	17.50	3.50
☐ 536 Dick Egan	13.00	6.50	1.30
☐ 537 Herman Franks MG	13.00	6.50	1.30
☐ 538 Bob Allen SP	26.00	13.00	2.60
☐ 539 Astros Rookies	13.00	6.50	1.30
Bill Heath			
Carroll Sembera			
☐ 540 Denny McLain SP	50.00	25.00	5.00
☐ 541 Gene Oliver SP	26.00	13.00	2.60
☐ 542 George Smith	13.00	6.50	1.30
☐ 543 Roger Craig SP	35.00	17.50	3.50
☐ 544 Cardinals Rookies SP	26.00	13.00	2.60
Joe Hoerner			
George Kernek			
Jimmy Williams			
☐ 545 Dick Green SP	26.00	13.00	2.60
☐ 546 Dwight Siebler	13.00	6.50	1.30
☐ 547 Horace Clarke SP	40.00	20.00	4.00
☐ 548 Gary Kroll SP	26.00	13.00	2.60
☐ 549 Senators Rookies	13.00	6.50	1.30
Al Closter			
Casey Cox			
☐ 550 Willie McCovey SP	100.00	50.00	10.00
☐ 551 Bob Purkey SP	26.00	13.00	2.60
☐ 552 Birdie Tebbetts MG SP	26.00	13.00	2.60
☐ 553 Rookie Stars	13.00	6.50	1.30
Pat Garrett			
Jackie Warner			
☐ 554 Jim Northrup SP	30.00	15.00	3.00
☐ 555 Ron Perranoski SP	30.00	15.00	3.00
☐ 556 Mel Queen SP	26.00	13.00	2.60
☐ 557 Felix Mantilla SP	26.00	13.00	2.60
☐ 558 Red Sox Rookies	20.00	10.00	2.00
Guido Grilli			
Pete Magrini			
George Scott			
☐ 559 Roberto Pena SP	26.00	13.00	2.60
☐ 560 Joel Horlen	13.00	6.50	1.30
☐ 561 ChooChoo Coleman SP	40.00	20.00	4.00
☐ 562 Russ Snyder	13.00	6.50	1.30
☐ 563 Twins Rookies	13.00	6.50	1.30
Pete Cimino			
Cesar Tovar			
☐ 564 Bob Chance SP	26.00	13.00	2.60
☐ 565 Jim Piersall SP	35.00	17.50	3.50
☐ 566 Mike Cuellar SP	30.00	15.00	3.00
☐ 567 Dick Howser SP	30.00	15.00	3.00
☐ 568 Athletics Rookies	13.00	6.50	1.30
Paul Lindblad			
Ron Stone			
☐ 569 Orlando McFarlane SP	26.00	13.00	2.60
☐ 570 Art Mahaffey SP	26.00	13.00	2.60
☐ 571 Dave Roberts SP	26.00	13.00	2.60
☐ 572 Bob Priddy	13.00	6.50	1.30
☐ 573 Derrell Griffith	13.00	6.50	1.30
☐ 574 Mets Rookies	13.00	6.50	1.30
Bill Hepler			
Bill Murphy			
☐ 575 Earl Wilson	13.00	6.50	1.30
☐ 576 Dave Nicholson SP	26.00	13.00	2.60
☐ 577 Jack Lamabe SP	26.00	13.00	2.60
☐ 578 Chi Chi Olivo SP	26.00	13.00	2.60
☐ 579 Orioles Rookies	20.00	10.00	2.00
Frank Bertaina			
Gene Brabender			
Dave Johnson			
☐ 580 Billy Williams SP	85.00	42.50	8.50
☐ 581 Tony Martinez	13.00	6.50	1.30
☐ 582 Garry Roggenburk	13.00	6.50	1.30
☐ 583 Tigers Team SP	120.00	60.00	12.00
☐ 584 Yankees Rookies	13.00	6.50	1.30
Frank Fernandez			
Fritz Peterson			
☐ 585 Tony Taylor	13.00	6.50	1.30
☐ 586 Claude Raymond SP	26.00	13.00	2.60
☐ 587 Dick Bertell	13.00	6.50	1.30
☐ 588 Athletics Rookies	13.00	6.50	1.30
Chuck Dobson			
Ken Suarez			
☐ 589 Lou Klimchock SP	26.00	13.00	2.60
☐ 590 Bill Skowron SP	40.00	20.00	4.00
☐ 591 NL Rookies SP	30.00	15.00	3.00
Bart Shirley			
Grant Jackson			
☐ 592 Andre Rodgers	13.00	6.50	1.30
☐ 593 Doug Camilli SP	26.00	13.00	2.60
☐ 594 Chico Salmon	13.00	6.50	1.30
☐ 595 Larry Jackson	13.00	6.50	1.30
☐ 596 Astros Rookies SP	26.00	13.00	2.60
Nate Colbert			
Greg Sims			
☐ 597 John Sullivan	13.00	6.50	1.30
☐ 598 Gaylord Perry SP	250.00	50.00	10.00

1967 Topps

The cards in this 609-card set measure 2 1/2" by 3 1/2". The 1967 Topps series is considered by some collectors to be one of the company's finest accomplishments in baseball card production. Excellent color photographs are combined with easy-to-read backs. Cards 458 to 533 are slightly harder to find than numbers 1 to 457, and the inevitable (difficult to find) high series (534 to 609) exists. Each checklist card features a small circular picture of a popular player included in that series. Printing discrepancies resulted in some high series cards being in shorter supply. The checklist below identifies (by DP) 22 double-printed high numbers; of the 76 cards in the last series, 54 cards were short printed and the other 22 cards are much more plentiful. Featured subsets within this set include World Series cards (151-155) and League Leaders (233-244). Although there are several relatively expensive cards in this popular set, the key cards in the set are undoubtedly the Tom Seaver rookie card (581) and the Rod Carew rookie card (569). Although rarely seen, there exists a salesman's sample panel of three cards, that pictures Earl Battey, Manny Mota, and Gene Brabender with ad information on the back about the "new" Topps cards.

	NRMT	VG-E	GOOD
COMPLETE SET (609)	4600.00	2250.00	500.00
COMMON PLAYER (1-109)	.80	.40	.08
COMMON PLAYER (110-283)	1.10	.55	.11
COMMON PLAYER (284-370)	1.25	.60	.12
COMMON PLAYER (371-457)	2.00	1.00	.20
COMMON PLAYER (458-533)	5.00	2.50	.50
COMMON PLAYER (534-609)	16.00	8.00	1.60
COMMON DP (534-609)	7.00	3.50	.70
☐ 1 The Champs	18.00	2.50	.50
Frank Robinson			
Hank Bauer			
Brooks Robinson			
☐ 2 Jack Hamilton	.80	.40	.08
☐ 3 Duke Sims	.80	.40	.08
☐ 4 Hal Lanier	1.00	.50	.10
☐ 5 Whitey Ford UER	16.00	8.00	1.60
(1953 listed as 1933 in stats on back)			
☐ 6 Dick Simpson	.80	.40	.08
☐ 7 Don McMahon	.80	.40	.08
☐ 8 Chuck Harrison	.80	.40	.08
☐ 9 Ron Hansen	.80	.40	.08
☐ 10 Matty Alou	1.00	.50	.10
☐ 11 Barry Moore	.80	.40	.08
☐ 12 Dodgers Rookies	1.00	.50	.10
Jim Campanis			
Bill Singer			
☐ 13 Joe Sparma	.80	.40	.08

☐ 14	Phil Linz	1.00	.50	.10
☐ 15	Earl Battey	.80	.40	.08
☐ 16	Bill Hands	.80	.40	.08
☐ 17	Jim Gosger	.80	.40	.08
☐ 18	Gene Oliver	.80	.40	.08
☐ 19	Jim McGlothlin	.80	.40	.08
☐ 20	Orlando Cepeda	5.50	2.75	.55
☐ 21	Dave Bristol MG	.80	.40	.08
☐ 22	Gene Brabender	.80	.40	.08
☐ 23	Larry Elliot	.80	.40	.08
☐ 24	Bob Allen	.80	.40	.08
☐ 25	Elston Howard	2.50	1.25	.25
☐ 26A	Bob Priddy	30.00	15.00	3.00
	(no traded line)			
☐ 26B	Bob Priddy	.80	.40	.08
	(with traded line)			
☐ 27	Bob Saverine	.80	.40	.08
☐ 28	Barry Latman	.80	.40	.08
☐ 29	Tom McCraw	.80	.40	.08
☐ 30	Al Kaline	17.00	8.50	1.70
☐ 31	Jim Brewer	.80	.40	.08
☐ 32	Bob Bailey	.80	.40	.08
☐ 33	Athletic Rookies	2.00	1.00	.20
	Sal Bando			
	Randy Schwartz			
☐ 34	Pete Cimino	.80	.40	.08
☐ 35	Rico Carty	1.25	.60	.12
☐ 36	Bob Tillman	.80	.40	.08
☐ 37	Rick Wise	1.00	.50	.10
☐ 38	Bob Johnson	.80	.40	.08
☐ 39	Curt Simmons	1.00	.50	.10
☐ 40	Rick Reichardt	.80	.40	.08
☐ 41	Joe Hoerner	.80	.40	.08
☐ 42	Mets Team	2.50	1.25	.25
☐ 43	Chico Salmon	.80	.40	.08
☐ 44	Joe Nuxhall	1.00	.50	.10
☐ 45	Roger Maris	37.50	16.00	3.50
☐ 46	Lindy McDaniel	1.00	.50	.10
☐ 47	Ken McMullen	.80	.40	.08
☐ 48	Bill Freehan	1.75	.85	.17
☐ 49	Roy Face	1.50	.75	.15
☐ 50	Tony Oliva	3.50	1.75	.35
☐ 51	Astros Rookies	.80	.40	.08
	Dave Adlesh			
	Wes Bales			
☐ 52	Dennis Higgins	.80	.40	.08
☐ 53	Clay Dalrymple	.80	.40	.08
☐ 54	Dick Green	.80	.40	.08
☐ 55	Don Drysdale	11.00	5.50	1.10
☐ 56	Jose Tartabull	.80	.40	.08
☐ 57	Pat Jarvis	.80	.40	.08
☐ 58	Paul Schaal	.80	.40	.08
☐ 59	Ralph Terry	1.25	.60	.12
☐ 60	Luis Aparicio	6.00	3.00	.60
☐ 61	Gordy Coleman	.80	.40	.08
☐ 62	Checklist 1	4.00	.40	.08
	Frank Robinson			
☐ 63	Cards' Clubbers	5.00	2.50	.50
	Lou Brock			
	Curt Flood			
☐ 64	Fred Valentine	.80	.40	.08
☐ 65	Tom Haller	.80	.40	.08
☐ 66	Manny Mota	1.00	.50	.10
☐ 67	Ken Berry	.80	.40	.08
☐ 68A	Bob Buhl ERR	30.00	15.00	3.00
	(listed as Rbaves			
	on card back)			
☐ 68B	Bob Buhl COR	.80	.40	.08
	(Braves on card back)			
☐ 69	Vic Davalillo	.80	.40	.08
☐ 70	Ron Santo	2.50	1.25	.25
☐ 71	Camilo Pascual	1.00	.50	.10
☐ 72	Tigers Rookies	.80	.40	.08
	George Korince			
	(Photo actually			
	James Murray Brown)			
	John (Tom) Matchick			
☐ 73	Rusty Staub	1.75	.85	.17
☐ 74	Wes Stock	.80	.40	.08
☐ 75	George Scott	1.50	.75	.15
☐ 76	Jim Barbieri	.80	.40	.08
☐ 77	Dooley Womack	.80	.40	.08
☐ 78	Pat Corrales	1.00	.50	.10
☐ 79	Bubba Morton	.80	.40	.08
☐ 80	Jim Maloney	1.25	.60	.12
☐ 81	Eddie Stanky MG	1.00	.50	.10
☐ 82	Steve Barber	.80	.40	.08
☐ 83	Ollie Brown	.80	.40	.08
☐ 84	Tommie Sisk	.80	.40	.08
☐ 85	Johnny Callison	1.00	.50	.10
☐ 86A	Mike McCormick	30.00	15.00	3.00
	(no traded line;			
	Senators on front			
	but Giants on back)			
☐ 86B	Mike McCormick	1.25	.60	.12
	(with traded line			
	at end of bio;			
	Senators on front			
	but Giants on back)			
☐ 87	George Altman	.80	.40	.08
☐ 88	Mickey Lolich	2.50	1.25	.25
☐ 89	Felix Millan	.80	.40	.08
☐ 90	Jim Nash	.80	.40	.08
☐ 91	Johnny Lewis	.80	.40	.08
☐ 92	Ray Washburn	.80	.40	.08
☐ 93	Yankees Rookies	2.50	1.25	.25
	Stan Bahnsen			
	Bobby Murcer			
☐ 94	Ron Fairly	1.00	.50	.10
☐ 95	Sonny Siebert	1.00	.50	.10
☐ 96	Art Shamsky	.80	.40	.08
☐ 97	Mike Cuellar	1.00	.50	.10
☐ 98	Rich Rollins	1.00	.50	.10
☐ 99	Lee Stange	.80	.40	.08
☐ 100	Frank Robinson	16.00	8.00	1.60
☐ 101	Ken Johnson	.80	.40	.08
☐ 102	Philadelphia Phillies	2.00	1.00	.20
	Team Card			
☐ 103	Checklist 2	6.00	1.00	.20
	Mickey Mantle			
☐ 104	Minnie Rojas	.80	.40	.08
☐ 105	Ken Boyer	1.75	.85	.17
☐ 106	Randy Hundley	.80	.40	.08
☐ 107	Joel Horlen	1.00	.50	.10
☐ 108	Alex Johnson	1.00	.50	.10
☐ 109	Tribe Thumpers	1.50	.75	.15
	Rocky Colavito			
	Leon Wagner			
☐ 110	Jack Aker	1.10	.55	.11
☐ 111	John Kennedy	1.10	.55	.11
☐ 112	Dave Wickersham	1.10	.55	.11
☐ 113	Dave Nicholson	1.10	.55	.11
☐ 114	Jack Baldschun	1.10	.55	.11
☐ 115	Paul Casanova	1.10	.55	.11
☐ 116	Herman Franks MG	1.10	.55	.11
☐ 117	Darrell Brandon	1.10	.55	.11
☐ 118	Bernie Allen	1.10	.55	.11
☐ 119	Wade Blasingame	1.10	.55	.11
☐ 120	Floyd Robinson	1.10	.55	.11
☐ 121	Eddie Bressoud	1.10	.55	.11
☐ 122	George Brunet	1.10	.55	.11
☐ 123	Pirates Rookies	1.10	.55	.11
	Jim Price			
	Luke Walker			
☐ 124	Jim Stewart	1.10	.55	.11
☐ 125	Moe Drabowsky	1.10	.55	.11
☐ 126	Tony Taylor	1.10	.55	.11
☐ 127	John O'Donoghue	1.10	.55	.11
☐ 128	Ed Spiezio	1.10	.55	.11
☐ 129	Phil Roof	1.10	.55	.11
☐ 130	Phil Regan	1.50	.75	.15
☐ 131	Yankees Team	4.00	2.00	.40
☐ 132	Ozzie Virgil	1.10	.55	.11
☐ 133	Ron Kline	1.10	.55	.11
☐ 134	Gates Brown	1.50	.75	.15
☐ 135	Deron Johnson	1.50	.75	.15
☐ 136	Carroll Sembera	1.10	.55	.11
☐ 137	Twins Rookies	1.10	.55	.11
	Ron Clark			
	Jim Ollum			
☐ 138	Dick Kelley	1.10	.55	.11
☐ 139	Dalton Jones	1.10	.55	.11
☐ 140	Willie Stargell	16.00	8.00	1.60
☐ 141	John Miller	1.10	.55	.11
☐ 142	Jackie Brandt	1.10	.55	.11
☐ 143	Sox Sockers	1.10	.55	.11
	Pete Ward			
	Don Buford			
☐ 144	Bill Hepler	1.10	.55	.11
☐ 145	Larry Brown	1.10	.55	.11
☐ 146	Steve Carlton	100.00	50.00	10.00
☐ 147	Tom Egan	1.10	.55	.11
☐ 148	Adolfo Phillips	1.10	.55	.11
☐ 149	Joe Moeller	1.10	.55	.11
☐ 150	Mickey Mantle	200.00	100.00	20.00
☐ 151	World Series Game 1	2.25	1.10	.22
	Moe mows down 11			
☐ 152	World Series Game 2	4.50	2.25	.45
	Palmer blanks Dodgers			
☐ 153	World Series Game 3	2.25	1.10	.22
	Blair's homer			
	defeats L.A.			
☐ 154	World Series Game 4	2.25	1.10	.22
	Orioles 4 straight			
☐ 155	World Series Summary	2.25	1.10	.22
	Winners celebrate			
☐ 156	Ron Herbel	1.10	.55	.11
☐ 157	Danny Cater	1.10	.55	.11

☐ 158 Jimmie Coker	1.10	.55	.11
☐ 159 Bruce Howard	1.10	.55	.11
☐ 160 Willie Davis	1.75	.85	.17
☐ 161 Dick Williams MG	1.50	.75	.15
☐ 162 Billy O'Dell	1.10	.55	.11
☐ 163 Vic Roznovsky	1.10	.55	.11
☐ 164 Dwight Siebler	1.10	.55	.11
☐ 165 Cleon Jones	1.10	.55	.11
☐ 166 Eddie Mathews	11.00	5.50	1.10
☐ 167 Senators Rookies	1.10	.55	.11
Joe Coleman			
Tim Cullen			
☐ 168 Ray Culp	1.10	.55	.11
☐ 169 Horace Clarke	1.10	.55	.11
☐ 170 Dick McAuliffe	1.50	.75	.15
☐ 171 Cal Koonce	1.10	.55	.11
☐ 172 Bill Heath	1.10	.55	.11
☐ 173 St. Louis Cardinals	2.25	1.10	.22
Team Card			
☐ 174 Dick Radatz	1.50	.75	.15
☐ 175 Bobby Knoop	1.10	.55	.11
☐ 176 Sammy Ellis	1.10	.55	.11
☐ 177 Tito Fuentes	1.10	.55	.11
☐ 178 John Buzhardt	1.10	.55	.11
☐ 179 Braves Rookies	1.10	.55	.11
Charles Vaughan			
Cecil Upshaw			
☐ 180 Curt Blefary	1.10	.55	.11
☐ 181 Terry Fox	1.10	.55	.11
☐ 182 Ed Charles	1.10	.55	.11
☐ 183 Jim Pagliaroni	1.10	.55	.11
☐ 184 George Thomas	1.10	.55	.11
☐ 185 Ken Holtzman	2.00	1.00	.20
☐ 186 Mets Maulers	1.50	.75	.15
Ed Kranepool			
Ron Swoboda			
☐ 187 Pedro Ramos	1.10	.55	.11
☐ 188 Ken Harrelson	1.50	.75	.15
☐ 189 Chuck Hinton	1.10	.55	.11
☐ 190 Turk Farrell	1.10	.55	.11
☐ 191A Checklist 3	4.00	.40	.08
(214 Tom Kelley)			
(Willie Mays)			
☐ 191B Checklist 3	8.00	.75	.15
(214 Dick Kelley)			
(Willie Mays)			
☐ 192 Fred Gladding	1.10	.55	.11
☐ 193 Jose Cardenal	1.10	.55	.11
☐ 194 Bob Allison	1.50	.75	.15
☐ 195 Al Jackson	1.10	.55	.11
☐ 196 Johnny Romano	1.10	.55	.11
☐ 197 Ron Perranoski	1.50	.75	.15
☐ 198 Chuck Hiller	1.10	.55	.11
☐ 199 Billy Hitchcock MG	1.10	.55	.11
☐ 200 Willie Mays UER	80.00	40.00	8.00
('63 Sna Francisco			
on card back stats)			
☐ 201 Hal Reniff	1.10	.55	.11
☐ 202 Johnny Edwards	1.10	.55	.11
☐ 203 Al McBean	1.10	.55	.11
☐ 204 Orioles Rookies	1.50	.75	.15
Mike Epstein			
Tom Phoebus			
☐ 205 Dick Groat	1.75	.85	.17
☐ 206 Dennis Bennett	1.10	.55	.11
☐ 207 John Orsino	1.10	.55	.11
☐ 208 Jack Lamabe	1.10	.55	.11
☐ 209 Joe Nossek	1.10	.55	.11
☐ 210 Bob Gibson	16.00	8.00	1.60
☐ 211 Twins Team	2.25	1.10	.22
☐ 212 Chris Zachary	1.10	.55	.11
☐ 213 Jay Johnstone	1.50	.75	.15
☐ 214 Dick Kelley	1.10	.55	.11
☐ 215 Ernie Banks	16.00	8.00	1.60
☐ 216 Bengal Belters	6.00	3.00	.60
Norm Cash			
Al Kaline			
☐ 217 Rob Gardner	1.10	.55	.11
☐ 218 Wes Parker	1.50	.75	.15
☐ 219 Clay Carroll	1.10	.55	.11
☐ 220 Jim Ray Hart	1.50	.75	.15
☐ 221 Woodie Fryman	1.10	.55	.11
☐ 222 Reds Rookies	1.75	.85	.17
Darrell Osteen			
Lee May			
☐ 223 Mike Ryan	1.10	.55	.11
☐ 224 Walt Bond	1.10	.55	.11
☐ 225 Mel Stottlemyre	2.00	1.00	.20
☐ 226 Julian Javier	1.10	.55	.11
☐ 227 Paul Lindblad	1.10	.55	.11
☐ 228 Gil Hodges MG	4.00	2.00	.40
☐ 229 Larry Jackson	1.10	.55	.11
☐ 230 Boog Powell	2.50	1.25	.25
☐ 231 John Bateman	1.10	.55	.11
☐ 232 Don Buford	1.10	.55	.11
☐ 233 AL ERA Leaders	1.75	.85	.17
Gary Peters			
Joel Horlen			
Steve Hargan			
☐ 234 NL ERA Leaders	5.00	2.50	.50
Sandy Koufax			
Mike Cuellar			
Juan Marichal			
☐ 235 AL Pitching Leaders	1.75	.85	.17
Jim Kaat			
Denny McLain			
Earl Wilson			
☐ 236 NL Pitching Leaders	10.00	5.00	1.00
Sandy Koufax			
Juan Marichal			
Bob Gibson			
Gaylord Perry			
☐ 237 AL Strikeout Leaders	1.75	.85	.17
Sam McDowell			
Jim Kaat			
Earl Wilson			
☐ 238 NL Strikeout Leaders	3.00	1.50	.30
Sandy Koufax			
Jim Bunning			
Bob Veale			
☐ 239 AL Batting Leaders	4.00	2.00	.40
Frank Robinson			
Tony Oliva			
Al Kaline			
☐ 240 NL Batting Leaders	1.75	.85	.17
Matty Alou			
Felipe Alou			
Rico Carty			
☐ 241 AL RBI Leaders	3.50	1.75	.35
Frank Robinson			
Harmon Killebrew			
Boog Powell			
☐ 242 NL RBI Leaders	6.00	3.00	.60
Hank Aaron			
Bob Clemente			
Richie Allen			
☐ 243 AL Home Run Leaders	3.50	1.75	.35
Frank Robinson			
Harmon Killebrew			
Boog Powell			
☐ 244 NL Home Run Leaders	6.00	3.00	.60
Hank Aaron			
Richie Allen			
Willie Mays			
☐ 245 Curt Flood	1.75	.85	.17
☐ 246 Jim Perry	1.50	.75	.15
☐ 247 Jerry Lumpe	1.10	.55	.11
☐ 248 Gene Mauch MG	1.50	.75	.15
☐ 249 Nick Willhite	1.10	.55	.11
☐ 250 Hank Aaron	80.00	40.00	8.00
☐ 251 Woody Held	1.10	.55	.11
☐ 252 Bob Bolin	1.10	.55	.11
☐ 253 Indians Rookies	1.10	.55	.11
Bill Davis			
Gus Gil			
☐ 254 Milt Pappas	1.50	.75	.15
☐ 255 Frank Howard	1.75	.85	.17
☐ 256 Bob Hendley	1.10	.55	.11
☐ 257 Charlie Smith	1.10	.55	.11
☐ 258 Lee Maye	1.10	.55	.11
☐ 259 Don Dennis	1.10	.55	.11
☐ 260 Jim Lefebvre	1.50	.75	.15
☐ 261 John Wyatt	1.10	.55	.11
☐ 262 Athletics Team	2.00	1.00	.20
☐ 263 Hank Aguirre	1.10	.55	.11
☐ 264 Ron Swoboda	1.50	.75	.15
☐ 265 Lou Burdette	1.75	.85	.17
☐ 266 Pitt Power	3.50	1.75	.35
Willie Stargell			
Donn Clendenon			
☐ 267 Don Schwall	1.10	.55	.11
☐ 268 Johnny Briggs	1.10	.55	.11
☐ 269 Don Nottebart	1.10	.55	.11
☐ 270 Zoilo Versalles	1.10	.55	.11
☐ 271 Eddie Watt	1.10	.55	.11
☐ 272 Cubs Rookies	1.10	.55	.11
Bill Connors			
Dave Dowling			
☐ 273 Dick Lines	1.10	.55	.11
☐ 274 Bob Aspromonte	1.10	.55	.11
☐ 275 Fred Whitfield	1.10	.55	.11
☐ 276 Bruce Brubaker	1.10	.55	.11
☐ 277 Steve Whitaker	1.10	.55	.11
☐ 278 Checklist 4	4.00	.40	.08
Jim Kaat			
☐ 279 Frank Linzy	1.10	.55	.11
☐ 280 Tony Conigliaro	4.50	2.25	.45
☐ 281 Bob Rodgers	1.50	.75	.15

☐	282 John Odom	1.10	.55	.11
☐	283 Gene Alley	1.50	.75	.15
☐	284 Johnny Podres	1.75	.85	.17
☐	285 Lou Brock	16.00	8.00	1.60
☐	286 Wayne Causey	1.25	.60	.12
☐	287 Mets Rookies	1.25	.60	.12
	Greg Goossen			
	Bart Shirley			
☐	288 Denny Lemaster	1.25	.60	.12
☐	289 Tom Tresh	1.75	.85	.17
☐	290 Bill White	2.00	1.00	.20
☐	291 Jim Hannan	1.25	.60	.12
☐	292 Don Pavletich	1.25	.60	.12
☐	293 Ed Kirkpatrick	1.25	.60	.12
☐	294 Walt Alston MG	2.50	1.25	.25
☐	295 Sam McDowell	1.75	.85	.17
☐	296 Glenn Beckert	1.75	.85	.17
☐	297 Dave Morehead	1.25	.60	.12
☐	298 Ron Davis	1.25	.60	.12
☐	299 Norm Siebern	1.25	.60	.12
☐	300 Jim Kaat	3.50	1.75	.35
☐	301 Jesse Gonder	1.25	.60	.12
☐	302 Orioles Team	2.50	1.25	.25
☐	303 Gil Blanco	1.25	.60	.12
☐	304 Phil Gagliano	1.25	.60	.12
☐	305 Earl Wilson	1.25	.60	.12
☐	306 Bud Harrelson	1.75	.85	.17
☐	307 Jim Beauchamp	1.25	.60	.12
☐	308 Al Downing	1.75	.85	.17
☐	309 Hurlers Beware	1.75	.85	.17
	Johnny Callison			
	Richie Allen			
☐	310 Gary Peters	1.75	.85	.17
☐	311 Ed Brinkman	1.25	.60	.12
☐	312 Don Mincher	1.75	.85	.17
☐	313 Bob Lee	1.25	.60	.12
☐	314 Red Sox Rookies	3.50	1.75	.35
	Mike Andrews			
	Reggie Smith			
☐	315 Billy Williams	10.00	5.00	1.00
☐	316 Jack Kralick	1.25	.60	.12
☐	317 Cesar Tovar	1.25	.60	.12
☐	318 Dave Giusti	1.75	.85	.17
☐	319 Paul Blair	1.75	.85	.17
☐	320 Gaylord Perry	11.00	5.00	1.00
☐	321 Mayo Smith MG	1.25	.60	.12
☐	322 Jose Pagan	1.25	.60	.12
☐	323 Mike Hershberger	1.25	.60	.12
☐	324 Hal Woodeshick	1.25	.60	.12
☐	325 Chico Cardenas	1.25	.60	.12
☐	326 Bob Uecker	20.00	10.00	2.00
☐	327 California Angels	2.25	1.10	.22
	Team Card			
☐	328 Clete Boyer	1.75	.85	.17
☐	329 Charlie Lau	1.75	.85	.17
☐	330 Claude Osteen	1.75	.85	.17
☐	331 Joe Foy	1.25	.60	.12
☐	332 Jesus Alou	1.25	.60	.12
☐	333 Fergie Jenkins	15.00	6.00	1.25
☐	334 Twin Terrors	3.50	1.75	.35
	Bob Allison			
	Harmon Killebrew			
☐	335 Bob Veale	1.75	.85	.17
☐	336 Joe Azcue	1.25	.60	.12
☐	337 Joe Morgan	25.00	12.50	2.50
☐	338 Bob Locker	1.25	.60	.12
☐	339 Chico Ruiz	1.25	.60	.12
☐	340 Joe Pepitone	2.00	1.00	.20
☐	341 Giants Rookies	1.25	.60	.12
	Dick Dietz			
	Bill Sorrell			
☐	342 Hank Fischer	1.25	.60	.12
☐	343 Tom Satriano	1.25	.60	.12
☐	344 Ossie Chavarria	1.25	.60	.12
☐	345 Stu Miller	1.25	.60	.12
☐	346 Jim Hickman	1.25	.60	.12
☐	347 Grady Hatton MG	1.25	.60	.12
☐	348 Tug McGraw	2.00	1.00	.20
☐	349 Bob Chance	1.25	.60	.12
☐	350 Joe Torre	2.00	1.00	.20
☐	351 Vern Law	1.75	.85	.17
☐	352 Ray Oyler	1.25	.60	.12
☐	353 Bill McCool	1.25	.60	.12
☐	354 Cubs Team	2.50	1.25	.25
☐	355 Carl Yastrzemski	100.00	50.00	10.00
☐	356 Larry Jaster	1.25	.60	.12
☐	357 Bill Skowron	2.00	1.00	.20
☐	358 Ruben Amaro	1.25	.60	.12
☐	359 Dick Ellsworth	1.75	.85	.17
☐	360 Leon Wagner	1.25	.60	.12
☐	361 Checklist 5	5.00	.50	.10
	Roberto Clemente			
☐	362 Darold Knowles	1.25	.60	.12
☐	363 Dave Johnson	2.00	1.00	.20
☐	364 Claude Raymond	1.25	.60	.12
☐	365 John Roseboro	1.75	.85	.17
☐	366 Andy Kosco	1.25	.60	.12
☐	367 Angels Rookies	1.25	.60	.12
	Bill Kelso			
	Don Wallace			
☐	368 Jack Hiatt	1.25	.60	.12
☐	369 Jim Hunter	16.00	8.00	1.60
☐	370 Tommy Davis	1.75	.85	.17
☐	371 Jim Lonborg	3.00	1.50	.30
☐	372 Mike De La Hoz	2.00	1.00	.20
☐	373 White Sox Rookies	2.00	1.00	.20
	Duane Josephson			
	Fred Klages			
☐	374 Mel Queen	2.00	1.00	.20
☐	375 Jake Gibbs	2.00	1.00	.20
☐	376 Don Lock	2.00	1.00	.20
☐	377 Luis Tiant	3.00	1.50	.30
☐	378 Detroit Tigers	4.00	2.00	.40
	Team Card			
☐	379 Jerry May	2.00	1.00	.20
☐	380 Dean Chance	2.50	1.25	.25
☐	381 Dick Schofield	2.00	1.00	.20
☐	382 Dave McNally	2.50	1.25	.25
☐	383 Ken Henderson	2.00	1.00	.20
☐	384 Cardinals Rookies	2.00	1.00	.20
	Jim Cosman			
	Dick Hughes			
☐	385 Jim Fregosi	2.50	1.25	.25
	(batting wrong)			
☐	386 Dick Selma	2.00	1.00	.20
☐	387 Cap Peterson	2.00	1.00	.20
☐	388 Arnold Earley	2.00	1.00	.20
☐	389 Alvin Dark MG	2.50	1.25	.25
☐	390 Jim Wynn	2.50	1.25	.25
☐	391 Wilbur Wood	2.50	1.25	.25
☐	392 Tommy Harper	2.50	1.25	.25
☐	393 Jim Bouton	3.00	1.50	.30
☐	394 Jake Wood	2.00	1.00	.20
☐	395 Chris Short	2.00	1.00	.20
☐	396 Atlanta Aces	2.00	1.00	.20
	Denis Menke			
	Tony Cloninger			
☐	397 Willie Smith	2.00	1.00	.20
☐	398 Jeff Torborg	3.00	1.50	.30
☐	399 Al Worthington	2.00	1.00	.20
☐	400 Bob Clemente	60.00	30.00	6.00
☐	401 Jim Coates	2.00	1.00	.20
☐	402 Phillies Rookies	2.00	1.00	.20
	Grant Jackson			
	Billy Wilson			
☐	403 Dick Nen	2.00	1.00	.20
☐	404 Nelson Briles	2.50	1.25	.25
☐	405 Russ Snyder	2.00	1.00	.20
☐	406 Lee Elia	2.50	1.25	.25
☐	407 Reds Team	4.00	2.00	.40
☐	408 Jim Northrup	2.50	1.25	.25
☐	409 Ray Sadecki	2.00	1.00	.20
☐	410 Lou Johnson	2.00	1.00	.20
☐	411 Dick Howser	2.50	1.25	.25
☐	412 Astros Rookies	3.00	1.50	.30
	Norm Miller			
	Doug Rader			
☐	413 Jerry Grote	2.00	1.00	.20
☐	414 Casey Cox	2.00	1.00	.20
☐	415 Sonny Jackson	2.00	1.00	.20
☐	416 Roger Repoz	2.00	1.00	.20
☐	417A Bob Bruce ERR	30.00	15.00	3.00
	(RBAVES on back)			
☐	417B Bob Bruce COR	2.00	1.00	.20
☐	418 Sam Mele MG	2.00	1.00	.20
☐	419 Don Kessinger	2.50	1.25	.25
☐	420 Denny McLain	4.00	2.00	.40
☐	421 Dal Maxvill	2.00	1.00	.20
☐	422 Hoyt Wilhelm	8.00	4.00	.80
☐	423 Fence Busters	18.00	9.00	1.80
	Willie Mays			
	Willie McCovey			
☐	424 Pedro Gonzalez	2.00	1.00	.20
☐	425 Pete Mikkelsen	2.00	1.00	.20
☐	426 Lou Clinton	2.00	1.00	.20
☐	427 Ruben Gomez	2.00	1.00	.20
☐	428 Dodgers Rookies	2.50	1.25	.25
	Tom Hutton			
	Gene Michael			
☐	429 Garry Roggenburk	2.00	1.00	.20
☐	430 Pete Rose	75.00	37.50	7.50
☐	431 Ted Uhlaender	2.00	1.00	.20
☐	432 Jimmie Hall	2.50	1.25	.25
☐	433 Al Luplow	2.00	1.00	.20
☐	434 Eddie Fisher	2.00	1.00	.20
☐	435 Mack Jones	2.00	1.00	.20
☐	436 Pete Ward	2.00	1.00	.20
☐	437 Senators Team	4.00	2.00	.40

☐ 438 Chuck Dobson	2.00	1.00	.20
☐ 439 Byron Browne	2.00	1.00	.20
☐ 440 Steve Hargan	2.00	1.00	.20
☐ 441 Jim Davenport	2.50	1.25	.25
☐ 442 Yankees Rookies	3.50	1.75	.35
Bill Robinson			
Joe Verbanic			
☐ 443 Tito Francona	2.00	1.00	.20
☐ 444 George Smith	2.00	1.00	.20
☐ 445 Don Sutton	27.00	13.50	2.70
☐ 446 Russ Nixon	2.50	1.25	.25
☐ 447 Bo Belinsky	2.50	1.25	.25
☐ 448 Harry Walker MG	2.00	1.00	.20
☐ 449 Orlando Pena	2.00	1.00	.20
☐ 450 Richie Allen	3.50	1.75	.35
☐ 451 Fred Newman	2.00	1.00	.20
☐ 452 Ed Kranepool	2.50	1.25	.25
☐ 453 Aurelio Monteagudo	2.00	1.00	.20
☐ 454A Checklist 6	5.00	.50	.10
Juan Marichal			
(missing left ear)			
☐ 454B Checklist 6	10.00	1.00	.20
Juan Marichal			
(left ear showing)			
☐ 455 Tommy Agee	2.50	1.25	.25
☐ 456 Phil Niekro	12.00	6.00	1.20
☐ 457 Andy Etchebarren	2.00	1.00	.20
☐ 458 Lee Thomas	6.00	3.00	.60
☐ 459 Senators Rookies	5.00	2.50	.50
Dick Bosman			
Pete Craig			
☐ 460 Harmon Killebrew	40.00	20.00	4.00
☐ 461 Bob Miller	5.00	2.50	.50
☐ 462 Bob Barton	5.00	2.50	.50
☐ 463 Hill Aces	6.00	3.00	.60
Sam McDowell			
Sonny Siebert			
☐ 464 Dan Coombs	5.00	2.50	.50
☐ 465 Willie Horton	6.00	3.00	.60
☐ 466 Bobby Wine	5.00	2.50	.50
☐ 467 Jim O'Toole	5.00	2.50	.50
☐ 468 Ralph Houk MG	6.00	3.00	.60
☐ 469 Len Gabrielson	5.00	2.50	.50
☐ 470 Bob Shaw	5.00	2.50	.50
☐ 471 Rene Lachemann	6.00	3.00	.60
☐ 472 Rookies Pirates	5.00	2.50	.50
John Gelnar			
George Spriggs			
☐ 473 Jose Santiago	5.00	2.50	.50
☐ 474 Bob Tolan	6.00	3.00	.60
☐ 475 Jim Palmer	100.00	50.00	10.00
☐ 476 Tony Perez SP	60.00	30.00	6.00
☐ 477 Braves Team	10.00	5.00	1.00
☐ 478 Bob Humphreys	5.00	2.50	.50
☐ 479 Gary Bell	5.00	2.50	.50
☐ 480 Willie McCovey	28.00	14.00	2.80
☐ 481 Leo Durocher MG	8.00	4.00	.80
☐ 482 Bill Monbouquette	5.00	2.50	.50
☐ 483 Jim Landis	5.00	2.50	.50
☐ 484 Jerry Adair	5.00	2.50	.50
☐ 485 Tim McCarver	14.00	7.00	1.40
☐ 486 Twins Rookies	5.00	2.50	.50
Rich Reese			
Bill Whitby			
☐ 487 Tommie Reynolds	5.00	2.50	.50
☐ 488 Gerry Arrigo	5.00	2.50	.50
☐ 489 Doug Clemens	5.00	2.50	.50
☐ 490 Tony Cloninger	5.00	2.50	.50
☐ 491 Sam Bowens	5.00	2.50	.50
☐ 492 Pittsburgh Pirates	10.00	5.00	1.00
Team Card			
☐ 493 Phil Ortega	5.00	2.50	.50
☐ 494 Bill Rigney MG	5.00	2.50	.50
☐ 495 Fritz Peterson	5.00	2.50	.50
☐ 496 Orlando McFarlane	5.00	2.50	.50
☐ 497 Ron Campbell	5.00	2.50	.50
☐ 498 Larry Dierker	5.00	2.50	.50
☐ 499 Indians Rookies	5.00	2.50	.50
George Culver			
Jose Vidal			
☐ 500 Juan Marichal	20.00	10.00	2.00
☐ 501 Jerry Zimmerman	5.00	2.50	.50
☐ 502 Derrell Griffith	5.00	2.50	.50
☐ 503 Los Angeles Dodgers	12.00	6.00	1.20
Team Card			
☐ 504 Orlando Martinez	5.00	2.50	.50
☐ 505 Tommy Helms	6.00	3.00	.60
☐ 506 Smoky Burgess	6.00	3.00	.60
☐ 507 Orioles Rookies	5.00	2.50	.50
Ed Barnowski			
Larry Haney			
☐ 508 Dick Hall	5.00	2.50	.50
☐ 509 Jim King	5.00	2.50	.50
☐ 510 Bill Mazeroski	10.00	5.00	1.00
☐ 511 Don Wert	5.00	2.50	.50
☐ 512 Red Schoendienst MG	10.00	5.00	1.00
☐ 513 Marcelino Lopez	5.00	2.50	.50
☐ 514 John Werhas	5.00	2.50	.50
☐ 515 Bert Campaneris	6.00	3.00	.60
☐ 516 Giants Team	10.00	5.00	1.00
☐ 517 Fred Talbot	5.00	2.50	.50
☐ 518 Denis Menke	5.00	2.50	.50
☐ 519 Ted Davidson	5.00	2.50	.50
☐ 520 Max Alvis	5.00	2.50	.50
☐ 521 Bird Bombers	7.00	3.50	.70
Boog Powell			
Curt Blefary			
☐ 522 John Stephenson	5.00	2.50	.50
☐ 523 Jim Merritt	5.00	2.50	.50
☐ 524 Felix Mantilla	5.00	2.50	.50
☐ 525 Ron Hunt	5.00	2.50	.50
☐ 526 Tigers Rookies	7.00	3.50	.70
Pat Dobson			
George Korince			
(See 67T-72)			
☐ 527 Dennis Ribant	5.00	2.50	.50
☐ 528 Rico Petrocelli	6.00	3.00	.60
☐ 529 Gary Wagner	5.00	2.50	.50
☐ 530 Felipe Alou	6.00	3.00	.60
☐ 531 Checklist 7	11.00	1.00	.20
Brooks Robinson			
☐ 532 Jim Hicks	5.00	2.50	.50
☐ 533 Jack Fisher	5.00	2.50	.50
☐ 534 Hank Bauer MG DP	8.00	4.00	.80
☐ 535 Donn Clendenon	21.00	10.50	2.10
☐ 536 Cubs Rookies	32.00	16.00	3.20
Joe Niekro			
Paul Popovich			
☐ 537 Chuck Estrada DP	7.00	3.50	.70
☐ 538 J.C. Martin	16.00	8.00	1.60
☐ 539 Dick Egan DP	7.00	3.50	.70
☐ 540 Norm Cash	30.00	15.00	3.00
☐ 541 Joe Gibbon	16.00	8.00	1.60
☐ 542 Athletics Rookies DP	10.00	5.00	1.00
Rick Monday			
Tony Pierce			
☐ 543 Dan Schneider	16.00	8.00	1.60
☐ 544 Cleveland Indians	30.00	15.00	3.00
Team Card			
☐ 545 Jim Grant	16.00	8.00	1.60
☐ 546 Woody Woodward	16.00	8.00	1.60
☐ 547 Red Sox Rookies DP	7.00	3.50	.70
Russ Gibson			
Bill Rohr			
☐ 548 Tony Gonzalez DP	7.00	3.50	.70
☐ 549 Jack Sanford	16.00	8.00	1.60
☐ 550 Vada Pinson DP	9.00	4.50	.90
☐ 551 Doug Camilli DP	7.00	3.50	.70
☐ 552 Ted Savage	16.00	8.00	1.60
☐ 553 Yankees Rookies	25.00	12.50	2.50
Mike Hegan			
Thad Tillotson			
☐ 554 Andre Rodgers DP	7.00	3.50	.70
☐ 555 Don Cardwell	16.00	8.00	1.60
☐ 556 Al Weis DP	7.00	3.50	.70
☐ 557 Al Ferrara	16.00	8.00	1.60
☐ 558 Orioles Rookies	40.00	20.00	4.00
Mark Belanger			
Bill Dillman			
☐ 559 Dick Tracewski DP	7.00	3.50	.70
☐ 560 Jim Bunning	45.00	22.50	4.50
☐ 561 Sandy Alomar	16.00	8.00	1.60
☐ 562 Steve Blass DP	7.00	3.50	.70
☐ 563 Joe Adcock	21.00	10.50	2.10
☐ 564 Astros Rookies DP	7.00	3.50	.70
Alonzo Harris			
Aaron Pointer			
☐ 565 Lew Krausse	16.00	8.00	1.60
☐ 566 Gary Geiger DP	7.00	3.50	.70
☐ 567 Steve Hamilton	16.00	8.00	1.60
☐ 568 John Sullivan	16.00	8.00	1.60
☐ 569 AL Rookies DP	475.00	225.00	47.00
Rod Carew			
Hank Allen			
☐ 570 Maury Wills	100.00	50.00	10.00
☐ 571 Larry Sherry	16.00	8.00	1.60
☐ 572 Don Demeter	16.00	8.00	1.60
☐ 573 Chicago White Sox	30.00	15.00	3.00
Team Card UER			
(Indians team			
stats on back)			
☐ 574 Jerry Buchek	16.00	8.00	1.60
☐ 575 Dave Boswell	16.00	8.00	1.60
☐ 576 NL Rookies	21.00	10.50	2.10
Ramon Hernandez			
Norm Gigon			
☐ 577 Bill Short	16.00	8.00	1.60
☐ 578 John Boccabella	16.00	8.00	1.60

☐ 579 Bill Henry	16.00	8.00	1.60
☐ 580 Rocky Colavito	45.00	22.50	4.50
☐ 581 Mets Rookies	1100.00	450.00	90.00
Bill Denehy			
Tom Seaver			
☐ 582 Jim Owens DP	7.00	3.50	.70
☐ 583 Ray Barker	16.00	8.00	1.60
☐ 584 Jim Piersall	22.00	11.00	2.20
☐ 585 Wally Bunker	16.00	8.00	1.60
☐ 586 Manny Jimenez	16.00	8.00	1.60
☐ 587 NL Rookies	21.00	10.50	2.10
Don Shaw			
Gary Sutherland			
☐ 588 Johnny Klippstein DP	7.00	3.50	.70
☐ 589 Dave Ricketts DP	7.00	3.50	.70
☐ 590 Pete Richert	16.00	8.00	1.60
☐ 591 Ty Cline	16.00	8.00	1.60
☐ 592 NL Rookies	21.00	10.50	2.10
Jim Shellenback			
Ron Willis			
☐ 593 Wes Westrum MG	21.00	10.50	2.10
☐ 594 Dan Osinski	16.00	8.00	1.60
☐ 595 Cookie Rojas	21.00	10.50	2.10
☐ 596 Galen Cisco DP	7.00	3.50	.70
☐ 597 Ted Abernathy	16.00	8.00	1.60
☐ 598 White Sox Rookies	21.00	10.50	2.10
Walt Williams			
Ed Stroud			
☐ 599 Bob Duliba DP	7.00	3.50	.70
☐ 600 Brooks Robinson	225.00	110.00	22.00
☐ 601 Bill Bryan DP	7.00	3.50	.70
☐ 602 Juan Pizarro	16.00	8.00	1.60
☐ 603 Athletics Rookies	16.00	8.00	1.60
Tim Talton			
Ramon Webster			
☐ 604 Red Sox Team	100.00	50.00	10.00
☐ 605 Mike Shannon	40.00	20.00	4.00
☐ 606 Ron Taylor	16.00	8.00	1.60
☐ 607 Mickey Stanley	30.00	15.00	3.00
☐ 608 Cubs Rookies DP	7.00	3.50	.70
Rich Nye			
John Upham			
☐ 609 Tommy John	110.00	25.00	5.00

1968 Topps

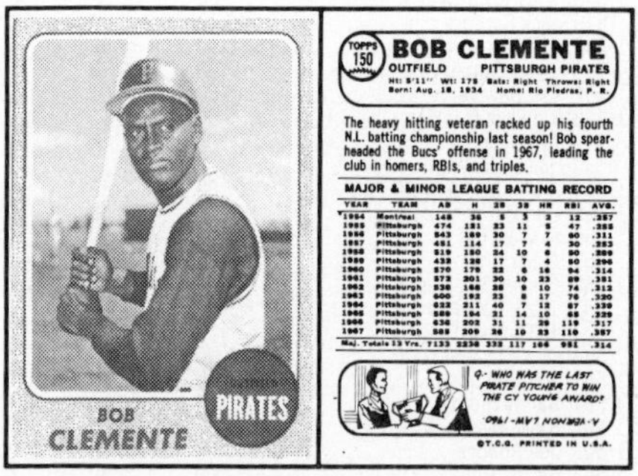

The cards in this 598-card set measure 2 1/2" by 3 1/2". The 1968 Topps set includes Sporting News All-Star Selections as card numbers 361 to 380. Other subsets in the set include League Leaders (1-12) and World Series cards (151-158). The front of each checklist card features a picture of a popular player inside a circle. High numbers 534 to 598 are slightly more difficult to obtain. The first series looks different from the other series, as it has a lighter, wider mesh background on the card front. The later series all had a much darker, finer mesh pattern. Key cards in the set are the rookie cards of Johnny Bench (247) and Nolan Ryan (177).

	NRMT	VG-E	GOOD
COMPLETE SET (598)	2800.00	1350.00	300.00
COMMON PLAYER (1-109)	.80	.40	.08
COMMON PLAYER (110-196)	.80	.40	.08
COMMON PLAYER (197-457)	.80	.40	.08
COMMON PLAYER (458-533)	1.50	.75	.15
COMMON PLAYER (534-598)	1.75	.85	.17
☐ 1 NL Batting Leaders	10.00	2.00	.40
Bob Clemente			
Tony Gonzales			
Matty Alou			
☐ 2 AL Batting Leaders	6.50	3.25	.65
Carl Yastrzemski			
Frank Robinson			
Al Kaline			
☐ 3 NL RBI Leaders	4.00	2.00	.40
Orlando Cepeda			
Bob Clemente			
Hank Aaron			
☐ 4 AL RBI Leaders	6.50	3.25	.65
Carl Yastrzemski			
Harmon Killebrew			
Frank Robinson			
☐ 5 NL Home Run Leaders	3.50	1.75	.35
Hank Aaron			
Jim Wynn			
Ron Santo			
Willie McCovey			
☐ 6 NL Home Run Leaders	4.00	2.00	.40
Carl Yastrzemski			
Harmon Killebrew			
Frank Howard			
☐ 7 NL ERA Leaders	1.50	.75	.15
Phil Niekro			
Jim Bunning			
Chris Short			
☐ 8 AL ERA Leaders	1.50	.75	.15
Joel Horlen			
Gary Peters			
Sonny Siebert			
☐ 9 NL Pitching Leaders	1.50	.75	.15
Mike McCormick			
Ferguson Jenkins			
Jim Bunning			
Claude Osteen			
☐ 10A AL Pitching Leaders	1.50	.75	.15
Jim Lonborg ERR			
(misspelled Lonberg			
on card back)			
Earl Wilson			
Dean Chance			
☐ 10B AL Pitching Leaders	1.50	.75	.15
Jim Lonborg COR			
Earl Wilson			
Dean Chance			
☐ 11 NL Strikeout Leaders	1.50	.75	.15
Jim Bunning			
Ferguson Jenkins			
Gaylord Perry			
☐ 12 AL Strikeout Leaders	1.50	.75	.15
Jim Lonborg UER			
(misspelled Longberg			
on card back)			
Sam McDowell			
Dean Chance			
☐ 13 Chuck Hartenstein	.80	.40	.08
☐ 14 Jerry McNertney	.80	.40	.08
☐ 15 Ron Hunt	.80	.40	.08
☐ 16 Indians Rookies	3.50	1.75	.35
Lou Piniella			
Richie Scheinblum			
☐ 17 Dick Hall	.80	.40	.08
☐ 18 Mike Hershberger	.80	.40	.08
☐ 19 Juan Pizarro	.80	.40	.08
☐ 20 Brooks Robinson	17.00	8.50	1.70
☐ 21 Ron Davis	.80	.40	.08
☐ 22 Pat Dobson	1.00	.50	.10
☐ 23 Chico Cardenas	.80	.40	.08
☐ 24 Bobby Locke	.80	.40	.08
☐ 25 Julian Javier	.80	.40	.08
☐ 26 Darrell Brandon	.80	.40	.08
☐ 27 Gil Hodges MG	5.50	2.75	.55
☐ 28 Ted Uhlaender	.80	.40	.08
☐ 29 Joe Verbanic	.80	.40	.08
☐ 30 Joe Torre	1.50	.75	.15
☐ 31 Ed Stroud	.80	.40	.08
☐ 32 Joe Gibbon	.80	.40	.08
☐ 33 Pete Ward	.80	.40	.08
☐ 34 Al Ferrara	.80	.40	.08
☐ 35 Steve Hargan	.80	.40	.08
☐ 36 Pirates Rookies	1.25	.60	.12
Bob Moose			
Bob Robertson			
☐ 37 Billy Williams	8.00	4.00	.80
☐ 38 Tony Pierce	.80	.40	.08
☐ 39 Cookie Rojas	1.00	.50	.10
☐ 40 Denny McLain	6.50	3.25	.65
☐ 41 Julio Gotay	.80	.40	.08
☐ 42 Larry Haney	.80	.40	.08

☐ 43 Gary Bell	.80	.40	.08
☐ 44 Frank Kostro	.80	.40	.08
☐ 45 Tom Seaver	175.00	85.00	18.00
☐ 46 Dave Ricketts	.80	.40	.08
☐ 47 Ralph Houk MG	1.00	.50	.10
☐ 48 Ted Davidson	.80	.40	.08
☐ 49A Eddie Brinkman	.80	.40	.08
(white team name)			
☐ 49B Eddie Brinkman	40.00	20.00	4.00
(yellow team name)			
☐ 50 Willie Mays	65.00	32.50	6.50
☐ 51 Bob Locker	.80	.40	.08
☐ 52 Hawk Taylor	.80	.40	.08
☐ 53 Gene Alley	1.00	.50	.10
☐ 54 Stan Williams	.80	.40	.08
☐ 55 Felipe Alou	1.00	.50	.10
☐ 56 Orioles Rookies	.80	.40	.08
Dave Leonhard			
Dave May			
☐ 57 Dan Schneider	.80	.40	.08
☐ 58 Eddie Mathews	8.00	4.00	.80
☐ 59 Don Lock	.80	.40	.08
☐ 60 Ken Holtzman	1.25	.60	.12
☐ 61 Reggie Smith	1.50	.75	.15
☐ 62 Chuck Dobson	.80	.40	.08
☐ 63 Dick Kenworthy	.80	.40	.08
☐ 64 Jim Merritt	.80	.40	.08
☐ 65 John Roseboro	.80	.40	.08
☐ 66A Casey Cox	.80	.40	.08
(white team name)			
☐ 66B Casey Cox	100.00	50.00	10.00
(yellow team name)			
☐ 67 Checklist 1	3.50	.40	.08
Jim Kaat			
☐ 68 Ron Willis	.80	.40	.08
☐ 69 Tom Tresh	1.25	.60	.12
☐ 70 Bob Veale	1.00	.50	.10
☐ 71 Vern Fuller	.80	.40	.08
☐ 72 Tommy John	4.00	2.00	.40
☐ 73 Jim Ray Hart	1.00	.50	.10
☐ 74 Milt Pappas	1.00	.50	.10
☐ 75 Don Mincher	1.00	.50	.10
☐ 76 Braves Rookies	1.00	.50	.10
Jim Britton			
Ron Reed			
☐ 77 Don Wilson	.80	.40	.08
☐ 78 Jim Northrup	1.25	.60	.12
☐ 79 Ted Kubiak	.80	.40	.08
☐ 80 Rod Carew	125.00	60.00	12.50
☐ 81 Larry Jackson	.80	.40	.08
☐ 82 Sam Bowens	.80	.40	.08
☐ 83 John Stephenson	.80	.40	.08
☐ 84 Bob Tolan	1.00	.50	.10
☐ 85 Gaylord Perry	9.00	4.00	.80
☐ 86 Willie Stargell	10.00	5.00	1.00
☐ 87 Dick Williams MG	1.00	.50	.10
☐ 88 Phil Regan	1.00	.50	.10
☐ 89 Jake Gibbs	.80	.40	.08
☐ 90 Vada Pinson	1.50	.75	.15
☐ 91 Jim Ollom	.80	.40	.08
☐ 92 Ed Kranepool	1.00	.50	.10
☐ 93 Tony Cloninger	.80	.40	.08
☐ 94 Lee Maye	.80	.40	.08
☐ 95 Bob Aspromonte	.80	.40	.08
☐ 96 Senator Rookies	.80	.40	.08
Frank Coggins			
Dick Nold			
☐ 97 Tom Phoebus	.80	.40	.08
☐ 98 Gary Sutherland	.80	.40	.08
☐ 99 Rocky Colavito	2.50	1.25	.25
☐ 100 Bob Gibson	16.00	8.00	1.60
☐ 101 Glenn Beckert	1.00	.50	.10
☐ 102 Jose Cardenal	.80	.40	.08
☐ 103 Don Sutton	8.00	4.00	.80
☐ 104 Dick Dietz	.80	.40	.08
☐ 105 Al Downing	1.00	.50	.10
☐ 106 Dalton Jones	.80	.40	.08
☐ 107A Checklist 2	3.50	.40	.08
Juan Marichal			
(tan wide mesh)			
☐ 107B Checklist 2	3.50	.40	.08
Juan Marichal			
(brown fine mesh)			
☐ 108 Don Pavletich	.80	.40	.08
☐ 109 Bert Campaneris	1.00	.50	.10
☐ 110 Hank Aaron	65.00	32.50	6.50
☐ 111 Rich Reese	.80	.40	.08
☐ 112 Woodie Fryman	.80	.40	.08
☐ 113 Tigers Rookies	.80	.40	.08
Tom Matchick			
Daryl Patterson			
☐ 114 Ron Swoboda	1.00	.50	.10
☐ 115 Sam McDowell	1.00	.50	.10
☐ 116 Ken McMullen	.80	.40	.08
☐ 117 Larry Jaster	.80	.40	.08
☐ 118 Mark Belanger	1.00	.50	.10
☐ 119 Ted Savage	.80	.40	.08
☐ 120 Mel Stottlemyre	1.50	.75	.15
☐ 121 Jimmie Hall	.80	.40	.08
☐ 122 Gene Mauch MG	1.00	.50	.10
☐ 123 Jose Santiago	.80	.40	.08
☐ 124 Nate Oliver	.80	.40	.08
☐ 125 Joel Horlen	.80	.40	.08
☐ 126 Bobby Etheridge	.80	.40	.08
☐ 127 Paul Lindblad	.80	.40	.08
☐ 128 Astros Rookies	.80	.40	.08
Tom Dukes			
Alonzo Harris			
☐ 129 Mickey Stanley	1.25	.60	.12
☐ 130 Tony Perez	7.00	3.50	.70
☐ 131 Frank Bertaina	.80	.40	.08
☐ 132 Bud Harrelson	1.25	.60	.12
☐ 133 Fred Whitfield	.80	.40	.08
☐ 134 Pat Jarvis	.80	.40	.08
☐ 135 Paul Blair	1.00	.50	.10
☐ 136 Randy Hundley	1.00	.50	.10
☐ 137 Twins Team	2.00	1.00	.20
☐ 138 Ruben Amaro	.80	.40	.08
☐ 139 Chris Short	.80	.40	.08
☐ 140 Tony Conigliaro	3.50	1.75	.35
☐ 141 Dal Maxvill	.80	.40	.08
☐ 142 White Sox Rookies	.80	.40	.08
Buddy Bradford			
Bill Voss			
☐ 143 Pete Cimino	.80	.40	.08
☐ 144 Joe Morgan	16.00	8.00	1.60
☐ 145 Don Drysdale	9.00	4.50	.90
☐ 146 Sal Bando	1.25	.60	.12
☐ 147 Frank Linzy	.80	.40	.08
☐ 148 Dave Bristol MG	.80	.40	.08
☐ 149 Bob Saverine	.80	.40	.08
☐ 150 Bob Clemente	45.00	22.50	4.50
☐ 151 World Series Game 1	5.00	2.50	.50
Brock socks 4 hits			
in opener			
☐ 152 World Series Game 2	7.50	3.75	.75
Yaz smashes 2 homers			
☐ 153 World Series Game 3	2.50	1.25	.25
Briles cools Boston			
☐ 154 World Series Game 4	5.00	2.50	.50
Gibson hurls shutout			
☐ 155 World Series Game 5	2.50	1.25	.25
Lonborg wins again			
☐ 156 World Series Game 6	2.50	1.25	.25
Petrocelli 2 homers			
☐ 157 World Series Game 7	2.50	1.25	.25
St. Louis wins it			
☐ 158 World Series Summary	2.50	1.25	.25
Cardinals celebrate			
☐ 159 Don Kessinger	1.00	.50	.10
☐ 160 Earl Wilson	.80	.40	.08
☐ 161 Norm Miller	.80	.40	.08
☐ 162 Cards Rookies	1.25	.60	.12
Hal Gilson			
Mike Torrez			
☐ 163 Gene Brabender	.80	.40	.08
☐ 164 Ramon Webster	.80	.40	.08
☐ 165 Tony Oliva	3.00	1.50	.30
☐ 166 Claude Raymond	.80	.40	.08
☐ 167 Elston Howard	2.25	1.10	.22
☐ 168 Dodgers Team	2.00	1.00	.20
☐ 169 Bob Bolin	.80	.40	.08
☐ 170 Jim Fregosi	1.25	.60	.12
☐ 171 Don Nottebart	.80	.40	.08
☐ 172 Walt Williams	.80	.40	.08
☐ 173 John Boozer	.80	.40	.08
☐ 174 Bob Tillman	.80	.40	.08
☐ 175 Maury Wills	3.50	1.75	.35
☐ 176 Bob Allen	.80	.40	.08
☐ 177 Mets Rookies	1200.00	450.00	100.00
Jerry Koosman			
Nolan Ryan			
☐ 178 Don Wert	.80	.40	.08
☐ 179 Bill Stoneman	.80	.40	.08
☐ 180 Curt Flood	1.50	.75	.15
☐ 181 Jerry Zimmerman	.80	.40	.08
☐ 182 Dave Giusti	1.00	.50	.10
☐ 183 Bob Kennedy MG	.80	.40	.08
☐ 184 Lou Johnson	.80	.40	.08
☐ 185 Tom Haller	.80	.40	.08
☐ 186 Eddie Watt	.80	.40	.08
☐ 187 Sonny Jackson	.80	.40	.08
☐ 188 Cap Peterson	.80	.40	.08
☐ 189 Bill Landis	.80	.40	.08
☐ 190 Bill White	1.50	.75	.15
☐ 191 Dan Frisella	.80	.40	.08
☐ 192 Checklist 3	3.50	.40	.08
Carl Yastrzemski			

☐ 193 Jack Hamilton	.80	.40	.08
☐ 194 Don Buford	1.00	.50	.10
☐ 195 Joe Pepitone	1.50	.75	.15
☐ 196 Gary Nolan	1.00	.50	.10
☐ 197 Larry Brown	.80	.40	.08
☐ 198 Roy Face	1.50	.75	.15
☐ 199 A's Rookies	.80	.40	.08
Roberto Rodriquez			
Darrell Osteen			
☐ 200 Orlando Cepeda	4.00	2.00	.40
☐ 201 Mike Marshall	1.50	.75	.15
☐ 202 Adolfo Phillips	.80	.40	.08
☐ 203 Dick Kelley	.80	.40	.08
☐ 204 Andy Etchebarren	.80	.40	.08
☐ 205 Juan Marichal	7.00	3.50	.70
☐ 206 Cal Ermer MG	.80	.40	.08
☐ 207 Carroll Sembera	.80	.40	.08
☐ 208 Willie Davis	1.25	.60	.12
☐ 209 Tim Cullen	.80	.40	.08
☐ 210 Gary Peters	1.00	.50	.10
☐ 211 J.C. Martin	.80	.40	.08
☐ 212 Dave Morehead	.80	.40	.08
☐ 213 Chico Ruiz	.80	.40	.08
☐ 214 Yankees Rookies	1.00	.50	.10
Stan Bahnsen			
Frank Fernandez			
☐ 215 Jim Bunning	3.50	1.75	.35
☐ 216 Bubba Morton	.80	.40	.08
☐ 217 Turk Farrell	.80	.40	.08
☐ 218 Ken Suarez	.80	.40	.08
☐ 219 Rob Gardner	.80	.40	.08
☐ 220 Harmon Killebrew	13.00	6.50	1.30
☐ 221 Braves Team	1.75	.85	.17
☐ 222 Jim Hardin	.80	.40	.08
☐ 223 Ollie Brown	.80	.40	.08
☐ 224 Jack Aker	.80	.40	.08
☐ 225 Richie Allen	2.00	1.00	.20
☐ 226 Jimmie Price	.80	.40	.08
☐ 227 Joe Hoerner	.80	.40	.08
☐ 228 Dodgers Rookies	.80	.40	.08
Jack Billingham			
Jim Fairey			
☐ 229 Fred Klages	.80	.40	.08
☐ 230 Pete Rose	50.00	25.00	5.00
☐ 231 Dave Baldwin	.80	.40	.08
☐ 232 Denis Menke	.80	.40	.08
☐ 233 George Scott	1.00	.50	.10
☐ 234 Bill Monbouquette	.80	.40	.08
☐ 235 Ron Santo	2.00	1.00	.20
☐ 236 Tug McGraw	2.00	1.00	.20
☐ 237 Alvin Dark MG	1.00	.50	.10
☐ 238 Tom Satriano	.80	.40	.08
☐ 239 Bill Henry	.80	.40	.08
☐ 240 Al Kaline	17.00	8.50	1.70
☐ 241 Felix Millan	.80	.40	.08
☐ 242 Moe Drabowsky	.80	.40	.08
☐ 243 Rich Rollins	.80	.40	.08
☐ 244 John Donaldson	.80	.40	.08
☐ 245 Tony Gonzalez	.80	.40	.08
☐ 246 Fritz Peterson	.80	.40	.08
☐ 247 Reds Rookies	400.00	200.00	40.00
Johnny Bench			
Ron Tompkins			
☐ 248 Fred Valentine	.80	.40	.08
☐ 249 Bill Singer	1.00	.50	.10
☐ 250 Carl Yastrzemski	40.00	20.00	4.00
☐ 251 Manny Sanguillen	2.50	1.25	.25
☐ 252 Angels Team	1.75	.85	.17
☐ 253 Dick Hughes	.80	.40	.08
☐ 254 Cleon Jones	.80	.40	.08
☐ 255 Dean Chance	1.00	.50	.10
☐ 256 Norm Cash	2.50	1.25	.25
☐ 257 Phil Niekro	5.00	2.50	.50
☐ 258 Cubs Rookies	.80	.40	.08
Jose Arcia			
Bill Schlesinger			
☐ 259 Ken Boyer	1.50	.75	.15
☐ 260 Jim Wynn	1.25	.60	.12
☐ 261 Dave Duncan	1.00	.50	.10
☐ 262 Rick Wise	1.00	.50	.10
☐ 263 Horace Clarke	.80	.40	.08
☐ 264 Ted Abernathy	.80	.40	.08
☐ 265 Tommy Davis	1.25	.60	.12
☐ 266 Paul Popovich	.80	.40	.08
☐ 267 Herman Franks MG	.80	.40	.08
☐ 268 Bob Humphreys	.80	.40	.08
☐ 269 Bob Tiefenauer	.80	.40	.08
☐ 270 Matty Alou	1.00	.50	.10
☐ 271 Bobby Knoop	.80	.40	.08
☐ 272 Ray Culp	.80	.40	.08
☐ 273 Dave Johnson	1.25	.60	.12
☐ 274 Mike Cuellar	1.00	.50	.10
☐ 275 Tim McCarver	2.00	1.00	.20
☐ 276 Jim Roland	.80	.40	.08
☐ 277 Jerry Buchek	.80	.40	.08
☐ 278 Checklist 4	3.50	.40	.08
Orlando Cepeda			
☐ 279 Bill Hands	.80	.40	.08
☐ 280 Mickey Mantle	180.00	90.00	18.00
☐ 281 Jim Campanis	.80	.40	.08
☐ 282 Rick Monday	1.25	.60	.12
☐ 283 Mel Queen	.80	.40	.08
☐ 284 Johnny Briggs	.80	.40	.08
☐ 285 Dick McAuliffe	1.00	.50	.10
☐ 286 Cecil Upshaw	.80	.40	.08
☐ 287 White Sox Rookies	.80	.40	.08
Mickey Abarbanel			
Cisco Carlos			
☐ 288 Dave Wickersham	.80	.40	.08
☐ 289 Woody Held	.80	.40	.08
☐ 290 Willie McCovey	9.00	4.50	.90
☐ 291 Dick Lines	.80	.40	.08
☐ 292 Art Shamsky	.80	.40	.08
☐ 293 Bruce Howard	.80	.40	.08
☐ 294 Red Schoendienst MG	3.50	1.75	.35
☐ 295 Sonny Siebert	1.00	.50	.10
☐ 296 Byron Browne	.80	.40	.08
☐ 297 Russ Gibson	.80	.40	.08
☐ 298 Jim Brewer	.80	.40	.08
☐ 299 Gene Michael	1.25	.60	.12
☐ 300 Rusty Staub	1.75	.85	.17
☐ 301 Twins Rookies	.80	.40	.08
George Mitterwald			
Rick Renick			
☐ 302 Gerry Arrigo	.80	.40	.08
☐ 303 Dick Green	.80	.40	.08
☐ 304 Sandy Valdespino	.80	.40	.08
☐ 305 Minnie Rojas	.80	.40	.08
☐ 306 Mike Ryan	.80	.40	.08
☐ 307 John Hiller	1.00	.50	.10
☐ 308 Pirates Team	1.75	.85	.17
☐ 309 Ken Henderson	.80	.40	.08
☐ 310 Luis Aparicio	5.00	2.50	.50
☐ 311 Jack Lamabe	.80	.40	.08
☐ 312 Curt Blefary	.80	.40	.08
☐ 313 Al Weis	.80	.40	.08
☐ 314 Red Sox Rookies	.80	.40	.08
Bill Rohr			
George Spriggs			
☐ 315 Zoilo Versalles	.80	.40	.08
☐ 316 Steve Barber	.80	.40	.08
☐ 317 Ron Brand	.80	.40	.08
☐ 318 Chico Salmon	.80	.40	.08
☐ 319 George Culver	.80	.40	.08
☐ 320 Frank Howard	1.50	.75	.15
☐ 321 Leo Durocher MG	1.75	.85	.17
☐ 322 Dave Boswell	.80	.40	.08
☐ 323 Deron Johnson	.80	.40	.08
☐ 324 Jim Nash	.80	.40	.08
☐ 325 Manny Mota	1.00	.50	.10
☐ 326 Dennis Ribant	.80	.40	.08
☐ 327 Tony Taylor	.80	.40	.08
☐ 328 Angels Rookies	.80	.40	.08
Chuck Vinson			
Jim Weaver			
☐ 329 Duane Josephson	.80	.40	.08
☐ 330 Roger Maris	32.00	16.00	3.20
☐ 331 Dan Osinski	.80	.40	.08
☐ 332 Doug Rader	1.25	.60	.12
☐ 333 Ron Herbel	.80	.40	.08
☐ 334 Orioles Team	1.75	.85	.17
☐ 335 Bob Allison	1.00	.50	.10
☐ 336 John Purdin	.80	.40	.08
☐ 337 Bill Robinson	1.50	.75	.15
☐ 338 Bob Johnson	.80	.40	.08
☐ 339 Rich Nye	.80	.40	.08
☐ 340 Max Alvis	.80	.40	.08
☐ 341 Jim Lemon MG	.80	.40	.08
☐ 342 Ken Johnson	.80	.40	.08
☐ 343 Jim Gosger	.80	.40	.08
☐ 344 Donn Clendenon	1.00	.50	.10
☐ 345 Bob Hendley	.80	.40	.08
☐ 346 Jerry Adair	.80	.40	.08
☐ 347 George Brunet	.80	.40	.08
☐ 348 Phillies Rookies	.80	.40	.08
Larry Colton			
Dick Thoenen			
☐ 349 Ed Spiezio	.80	.40	.08
☐ 350 Hoyt Wilhelm	5.50	2.75	.55
☐ 351 Bob Barton	.80	.40	.08
☐ 352 Jackie Hernandez	.80	.40	.08
☐ 353 Mack Jones	.80	.40	.08
☐ 354 Pete Richert	.80	.40	.08
☐ 355 Ernie Banks	14.00	7.00	1.40
☐ 356A Checklist 5	3.50	.40	.08
Ken Holtzman			
(head centered			
within circle)			

☐ 356B Checklist 5 Ken Holtzman (head shifted right within circle)	3.50	.40	.08
☐ 357 Len Gabrielson	.80	.40	.08
☐ 358 Mike Epstein	.80	.40	.08
☐ 359 Joe Moeller	.80	.40	.08
☐ 360 Willie Horton	1.25	.60	.12
☐ 361 Harmon Killebrew AS	6.00	3.00	.60
☐ 362 Orlando Cepeda AS	1.75	.85	.17
☐ 363 Rod Carew AS	13.00	6.50	1.30
☐ 364 Joe Morgan AS	6.50	3.25	.65
☐ 365 Brooks Robinson AS	6.50	3.25	.65
☐ 366 Ron Santo AS	1.25	.60	.12
☐ 367 Jim Fregosi AS	1.00	.50	.10
☐ 368 Gene Alley AS	1.00	.50	.10
☐ 369 Carl Yastrzemski AS	12.00	6.00	1.20
☐ 370 Hank Aaron AS	12.00	6.00	1.20
☐ 371 Tony Oliva AS	1.50	.75	.15
☐ 372 Lou Brock AS	6.50	3.25	.65
☐ 373 Frank Robinson AS	6.50	3.25	.65
☐ 374 Bob Clemente AS	10.00	5.00	1.00
☐ 375 Bill Freehan AS	1.25	.60	.12
☐ 376 Tim McCarver AS	1.25	.60	.12
☐ 377 Joel Horlen AS	1.00	.50	.10
☐ 378 Bob Gibson AS	6.50	3.25	.65
☐ 379 Gary Peters AS	1.00	.50	.10
☐ 380 Ken Holtzman AS	1.00	.50	.10
☐ 381 Boog Powell	2.00	1.00	.20
☐ 382 Ramon Hernandez	.80	.40	.08
☐ 383 Steve Whitaker	.80	.40	.08
☐ 384 Reds Rookies Bill Henry Hal McRae	6.00	3.00	.60
☐ 385 Jim Hunter	12.00	6.00	1.20
☐ 386 Greg Goossen	.80	.40	.08
☐ 387 Joe Foy	.80	.40	.08
☐ 388 Ray Washburn	.80	.40	.08
☐ 389 Jay Johnstone	1.00	.50	.10
☐ 390 Bill Mazeroski	1.50	.75	.15
☐ 391 Bob Priddy	.80	.40	.08
☐ 392 Grady Hatton MG	.80	.40	.08
☐ 393 Jim Perry	1.00	.50	.10
☐ 394 Tommie Aaron	1.00	.50	.10
☐ 395 Camilo Pascual	1.00	.50	.10
☐ 396 Bobby Wine	.80	.40	.08
☐ 397 Vic Davalillo	.80	.40	.08
☐ 398 Jim Grant	.80	.40	.08
☐ 399 Ray Oyler	.80	.40	.08
☐ 400A Mike McCormick (yellow letters)	1.00	.50	.10
☐ 400B Mike McCormick (team name in white letters)	100.00	50.00	10.00
☐ 401 Mets Team	2.25	1.10	.22
☐ 402 Mike Hegan	.80	.40	.08
☐ 403 John Buzhardt	.80	.40	.08
☐ 404 Floyd Robinson	.80	.40	.08
☐ 405 Tommy Helms	.80	.40	.08
☐ 406 Dick Ellsworth	1.00	.50	.10
☐ 407 Gary Kolb	.80	.40	.08
☐ 408 Steve Carlton	45.00	22.50	4.50
☐ 409 Orioles Rookies Frank Peters Ron Stone	.80	.40	.08
☐ 410 Fergie Jenkins	10.00	4.00	.80
☐ 411 Ron Hansen	.80	.40	.08
☐ 412 Clay Carroll	.80	.40	.08
☐ 413 Tom McCraw	.80	.40	.08
☐ 414 Mickey Lolich	3.00	1.50	.30
☐ 415 Johnny Callison	1.00	.50	.10
☐ 416 Bill Rigney MG	.80	.40	.08
☐ 417 Willie Crawford	.80	.40	.08
☐ 418 Eddie Fisher	.80	.40	.08
☐ 419 Jack Hiatt	.80	.40	.08
☐ 420 Cesar Tovar	.80	.40	.08
☐ 421 Ron Taylor	.80	.40	.08
☐ 422 Rene Lachemann	1.00	.50	.10
☐ 423 Fred Gladding	.80	.40	.08
☐ 424 Chicago White Sox Team Card	1.75	.85	.17
☐ 425 Jim Maloney	1.25	.60	.12
☐ 426 Hank Allen	.80	.40	.08
☐ 427 Dick Calmus	.80	.40	.08
☐ 428 Vic Roznovsky	.80	.40	.08
☐ 429 Tommie Sisk	.80	.40	.08
☐ 430 Rico Petrocelli	1.25	.60	.12
☐ 431 Dooley Womack	.80	.40	.08
☐ 432 Indians Rookies Bill Davis Jose Vidal	.80	.40	.08
☐ 433 Bob Rodgers	1.25	.60	.12
☐ 434 Ricardo Joseph	.80	.40	.08
☐ 435 Ron Perranoski	1.00	.50	.10
☐ 436 Hal Lanier	1.00	.50	.10
☐ 437 Don Cardwell	.80	.40	.08
☐ 438 Lee Thomas	1.00	.50	.10
☐ 439 Lum Harris MG	.80	.40	.08
☐ 440 Claude Osteen	1.00	.50	.10
☐ 441 Alex Johnson	1.00	.50	.10
☐ 442 Dick Bosman	.80	.40	.08
☐ 443 Joe Azcue	.80	.40	.08
☐ 444 Jack Fisher	.80	.40	.08
☐ 445 Mike Shannon	1.25	.60	.12
☐ 446 Ron Kline	.80	.40	.08
☐ 447 Tigers Rookies George Korince Fred Lasher	.80	.40	.08
☐ 448 Gary Wagner	.80	.40	.08
☐ 449 Gene Oliver	.80	.40	.08
☐ 450 Jim Kaat	3.50	1.75	.35
☐ 451 Al Spangler	.80	.40	.08
☐ 452 Jesus Alou	.80	.40	.08
☐ 453 Sammy Ellis	.80	.40	.08
☐ 454A Checklist 6 Frank Robinson (cap complete within circle)	3.50	.40	.08
☐ 454B Checklist 6 Frank Robinson (cap partially within circle)	3.50	.40	.08
☐ 455 Rico Carty	1.25	.60	.12
☐ 456 John O'Donoghue	.80	.40	.08
☐ 457 Jim Lefebvre	1.25	.60	.12
☐ 458 Lew Krausse	1.50	.75	.15
☐ 459 Dick Simpson	1.50	.75	.15
☐ 460 Jim Lonborg	2.00	1.00	.20
☐ 461 Chuck Hiller	1.50	.75	.15
☐ 462 Barry Moore	1.50	.75	.15
☐ 463 Jim Schaffer	1.50	.75	.15
☐ 464 Don McMahon	1.50	.75	.15
☐ 465 Tommie Agee	1.50	.75	.15
☐ 466 Bill Dillman	1.50	.75	.15
☐ 467 Dick Howser	2.00	1.00	.20
☐ 468 Larry Sherry	1.50	.75	.15
☐ 469 Ty Cline	1.50	.75	.15
☐ 470 Bill Freehan	2.50	1.25	.25
☐ 471 Orlando Pena	1.50	.75	.15
☐ 472 Walt Alston MG	2.50	1.25	.25
☐ 473 Al Worthington	1.50	.75	.15
☐ 474 Paul Schaal	1.50	.75	.15
☐ 475 Joe Niekro	2.50	1.25	.25
☐ 476 Woody Woodward	2.00	1.00	.20
☐ 477 Philadelphia Phillies Team Card	3.00	1.50	.30
☐ 478 Dave McNally	2.00	1.00	.20
☐ 479 Phil Gagliano	1.50	.75	.15
☐ 480 Manager's Dream Tony Oliva Chico Cardenas Bob Clemente	21.00	10.50	2.10
☐ 481 John Wyatt	1.50	.75	.15
☐ 482 Jose Pagan	1.50	.75	.15
☐ 483 Darold Knowles	1.50	.75	.15
☐ 484 Phil Roof	1.50	.75	.15
☐ 485 Ken Berry	1.50	.75	.15
☐ 486 Cal Koonce	1.50	.75	.15
☐ 487 Lee May	2.00	1.00	.20
☐ 488 Dick Tracewski	1.50	.75	.15
☐ 489 Wally Bunker	1.50	.75	.15
☐ 490 Super Stars Harmon Killebrew Willie Mays Mickey Mantle	65.00	32.50	6.50
☐ 491 Denny Lemaster	1.50	.75	.15
☐ 492 Jeff Torborg	2.00	1.00	.20
☐ 493 Jim McGlothlin	1.50	.75	.15
☐ 494 Ray Sadecki	1.50	.75	.15
☐ 495 Leon Wagner	1.50	.75	.15
☐ 496 Steve Hamilton	1.50	.75	.15
☐ 497 Cards Team	3.00	1.50	.30
☐ 498 Bill Bryan	1.50	.75	.15
☐ 499 Steve Blass	2.00	1.00	.20
☐ 500 Frank Robinson	17.00	8.50	1.70
☐ 501 John Odom	1.50	.75	.15
☐ 502 Mike Andrews	1.50	.75	.15
☐ 503 Al Jackson	1.50	.75	.15
☐ 504 Russ Snyder	1.50	.75	.15
☐ 505 Joe Sparma	1.50	.75	.15
☐ 506 Clarence Jones	1.50	.75	.15
☐ 507 Wade Blasingame	1.50	.75	.15
☐ 508 Duke Sims	1.50	.75	.15
☐ 509 Dennis Higgins	1.50	.75	.15
☐ 510 Ron Fairly	2.00	1.00	.20
☐ 511 Bill Kelso	1.50	.75	.15
☐ 512 Grant Jackson	1.50	.75	.15
☐ 513 Hank Bauer MG	2.00	1.00	.20

☐ 514 Al McBean	1.50	.75	.15
☐ 515 Russ Nixon	2.00	1.00	.20
☐ 516 Pete Mikkelsen	1.50	.75	.15
☐ 517 Diego Segui	1.50	.75	.15
☐ 518A Checklist 7 (539 ML Rookies) (Clete Boyer)	5.00	.50	.10
☐ 518B Checklist 7 (539 AL Rookies) (Clete Boyer)	10.00	1.00	.20
☐ 519 Jerry Stephenson	1.50	.75	.15
☐ 520 Lou Brock	17.00	8.50	1.70
☐ 521 Don Shaw	1.50	.75	.15
☐ 522 Wayne Causey	1.50	.75	.15
☐ 523 John Tsitouris	1.50	.75	.15
☐ 524 Andy Kosco	1.50	.75	.15
☐ 525 Jim Davenport	2.00	1.00	.20
☐ 526 Bill Denehy	1.50	.75	.15
☐ 527 Tito Francona	1.50	.75	.15
☐ 528 Tigers Team	32.00	16.00	3.20
☐ 529 Bruce Von Hoff	1.50	.75	.15
☐ 530 Bird Belters Brooks Robinson Frank Robinson	8.00	4.00	.80
☐ 531 Chuck Hinton	1.50	.75	.15
☐ 532 Luis Tiant	2.50	1.25	.25
☐ 533 Wes Parker	2.00	1.00	.20
☐ 534 Bob Miller	1.75	.85	.17
☐ 535 Danny Cater	1.75	.85	.17
☐ 536 Bill Short	1.75	.85	.17
☐ 537 Norm Siebern	1.75	.85	.17
☐ 538 Manny Jimenez	1.75	.85	.17
☐ 539 Major League Rookies Jim Ray Mike Ferraro	2.25	1.10	.22
☐ 540 Nelson Briles	1.75	.85	.17
☐ 541 Sandy Alomar	1.75	.85	.17
☐ 542 John Boccabella	1.75	.85	.17
☐ 543 Bob Lee	1.75	.85	.17
☐ 544 Mayo Smith MG	1.75	.85	.17
☐ 545 Lindy McDaniel	1.75	.85	.17
☐ 546 Roy White	2.25	1.10	.22
☐ 547 Dan Coombs	1.75	.85	.17
☐ 548 Bernie Allen	1.75	.85	.17
☐ 549 Orioles Rookies Curt Motton Roger Nelson	1.75	.85	.17
☐ 550 Clete Boyer	2.25	1.10	.22
☐ 551 Darrell Sutherland	1.75	.85	.17
☐ 552 Ed Kirkpatrick	1.75	.85	.17
☐ 553 Hank Aguirre	1.75	.85	.17
☐ 554 A's Team	3.50	1.75	.35
☐ 555 Jose Tartabull	1.75	.85	.17
☐ 556 Dick Selma	1.75	.85	.17
☐ 557 Frank Quilici	1.75	.85	.17
☐ 558 Johnny Edwards	1.75	.85	.17
☐ 559 Pirates Rookies Carl Taylor Luke Walker	2.25	1.10	.22
☐ 560 Paul Casanova	1.75	.85	.17
☐ 561 Lee Elia	2.25	1.10	.22
☐ 562 Jim Bouton	2.50	1.25	.25
☐ 563 Ed Charles	1.75	.85	.17
☐ 564 Eddie Stanky MG	2.25	1.10	.22
☐ 565 Larry Dierker	2.25	1.10	.22
☐ 566 Ken Harrelson	2.25	1.10	.22
☐ 567 Clay Dalrymple	1.75	.85	.17
☐ 568 Willie Smith	1.75	.85	.17
☐ 569 NL Rookies Ivan Murrell Les Rohr	1.75	.85	.17
☐ 570 Rick Reichardt	1.75	.85	.17
☐ 571 Tony LaRussa	3.00	1.50	.30
☐ 572 Don Bosch	1.75	.85	.17
☐ 573 Joe Coleman	1.75	.85	.17
☐ 574 Cincinnati Reds Team Card	3.50	1.75	.35
☐ 575 Jim Palmer	45.00	22.50	4.50
☐ 576 Dave Adlesh	1.75	.85	.17
☐ 577 Fred Talbot	1.75	.85	.17
☐ 578 Orlando Martinez	1.75	.85	.17
☐ 579 NL Rookies Larry Hisle Mike Lum	2.50	1.25	.25
☐ 580 Bob Bailey	1.75	.85	.17
☐ 581 Garry Roggenburk	1.75	.85	.17
☐ 582 Jerry Grote	1.75	.85	.17
☐ 583 Gates Brown	2.25	1.10	.22
☐ 584 Larry Shepard MG	1.75	.85	.17
☐ 585 Wilbur Wood	2.25	1.10	.22
☐ 586 Jim Pagliaroni	1.75	.85	.17
☐ 587 Roger Repoz	1.75	.85	.17
☐ 588 Dick Schofield	1.75	.85	.17
☐ 589 Twins Rookies Ron Clark Moe Ogier	1.75	.85	.17
☐ 590 Tommy Harper	2.25	1.10	.22
☐ 591 Dick Nen	1.75	.85	.17
☐ 592 John Bateman	1.75	.85	.17
☐ 593 Lee Stange	1.75	.85	.17
☐ 594 Phil Linz	2.25	1.10	.22
☐ 595 Phil Ortega	1.75	.85	.17
☐ 596 Charlie Smith	1.75	.85	.17
☐ 597 Bill McCool	1.75	.85	.17
☐ 598 Jerry May	2.25	1.10	.22

1968 Topps Game

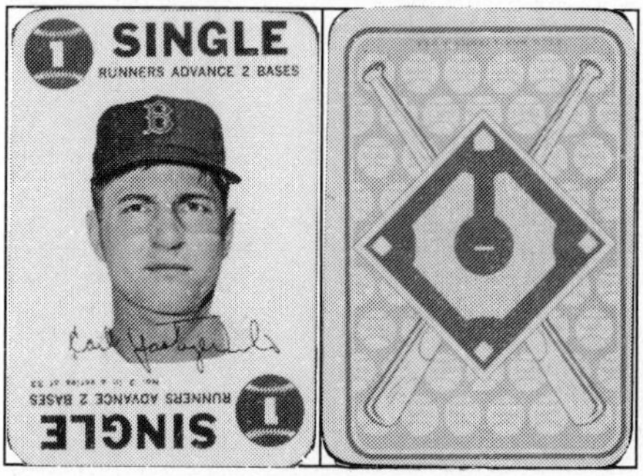

The cards in this 33-card set measure 2 1/4" by 3 1/4". This "Game" card set of players, issued as inserts with the regular 1968 Topps baseball series, was patterned directly after the Red Back and Blue Back sets of 1951. Each card has a color player photo set upon a pure white background, with a facsimile autograph underneath the picture. The cards have blue backs, and were also sold in boxed sets on a limited basis.

	NRMT	VG-E	GOOD
COMPLETE SET (33)	70.00	35.00	7.00
COMMON PLAYER (1-33)	.40	.20	.04
☐ 1 Matty Alou	.40	.20	.04
☐ 2 Mickey Mantle	16.00	8.00	1.60
☐ 3 Carl Yastrzemski	10.00	5.00	1.00
☐ 4 Hank Aaron	7.50	3.75	.75
☐ 5 Harmon Killebrew	2.50	1.25	.25
☐ 6 Roberto Clemente	6.00	3.00	.60
☐ 7 Frank Robinson	3.50	1.75	.35
☐ 8 Willie Mays	7.50	3.75	.75
☐ 9 Brooks Robinson	3.50	1.75	.35
☐ 10 Tommy Davis	.40	.20	.04
☐ 11 Bill Freehan	.40	.20	.04
☐ 12 Claude Osteen	.40	.20	.04
☐ 13 Gary Peters	.40	.20	.04
☐ 14 Jim Lonborg	.40	.20	.04
☐ 15 Steve Hargan	.40	.20	.04
☐ 16 Dean Chance	.40	.20	.04
☐ 17 Mike McCormick	.40	.20	.04
☐ 18 Tim McCarver	.60	.30	.06
☐ 19 Ron Santo	.60	.30	.06
☐ 20 Tony Gonzalez	.40	.20	.04
☐ 21 Frank Howard	.50	.25	.05
☐ 22 George Scott	.40	.20	.04
☐ 23 Rich Allen	.50	.25	.05
☐ 24 Jim Wynn	.40	.20	.04
☐ 25 Gene Alley	.40	.20	.04
☐ 26 Rick Monday	.40	.20	.04
☐ 27 Al Kaline	4.00	2.00	.40
☐ 28 Rusty Staub	.60	.30	.06
☐ 29 Rod Carew	5.00	2.50	.50
☐ 30 Pete Rose	10.00	5.00	1.00
☐ 31 Joe Torre	.60	.30	.06
☐ 32 Orlando Cepeda	.60	.30	.06
☐ 33 Jim Fregosi	.50	.25	.05

1969 Topps

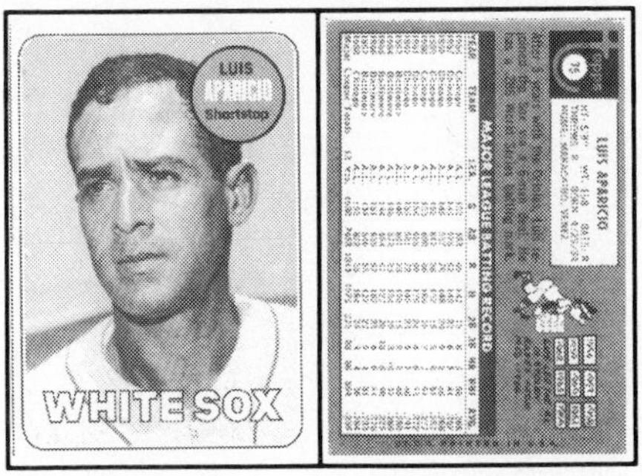

The cards in this 664-card set measure 2 1/2" by 3 1/2". The 1969 Topps set includes Sporting News All-Star Selections as card numbers 416 to 435. Other popular subsets within this set include League Leaders (1-12) and World Series cards (162-169). The fifth series contains several variations; the more difficult variety consists of cards with the player's first name, last name, and/or position in white letters instead of lettering in some other color. These are designated in the checklist below by WL (white letters). Each checklist card features a different popular player's picture inside a circle on the front of the checklist card. Two different poses of Clay Dalrymple and Donn Clendenon exist, as indicated in the checklist. The key rookie cards in this set are Rollie Fingers, Reggie Jackson, and Graig Nettles. This was the last year that Topps issued multi-player special star cards, ending a 13-year tradition, which they had begun in 1957. There were cropping differences in checklist cards 57, 214, and 412, due to their each being printed with two different series. The differences are difficult to explain and have not been greatly sought by collectors; hence they are not listed explicitly in the list below.

	NRMT	VG-E	GOOD
COMPLETE SET (664)	2200.00	1000.00	250.00
COMMON PLAYER (1-218)	.75	.35	.07
COMMON PLAYER (219-327)	1.10	.55	.11
COMMON PLAYER (328-512)	.75	.35	.07
COMMON PLAYER (513-588)	.90	.45	.09
COMMON PLAYER (589-664)	1.10	.55	.11

☐ 1 AL Batting Leaders	8.00	1.50	.30
Carl Yastrzemski			
Danny Cater			
Tony Oliva			
☐ 2 NL Batting Leaders	3.50	1.75	.35
Pete Rose			
Matty Alou			
Felipe Alou			
☐ 3 AL RBI Leaders	1.50	.75	.15
Ken Harrelson			
Frank Howard			
Jim Northrup			
☐ 4 NL RBI Leaders	3.00	1.50	.30
Willie McCovey			
Ron Santo			
Billy Williams			
☐ 5 AL Home Run Leaders	1.50	.75	.15
Frank Howard			
Willie Horton			
Ken Harrelson			
☐ 6 NL Home Run Leaders	3.00	1.50	.30
Willie McCovey			
Richie Allen			
Ernie Banks			
☐ 7 AL ERA Leaders	1.50	.75	.15
Luis Tiant			
Sam McDowell			
Dave McNally			
☐ 8 NL ERA Leaders	1.50	.75	.15
Bob Gibson			
Bobby Bolin			
Bob Veale			
☐ 9 AL Pitching Leaders	1.50	.75	.15
Denny McLain			
Dave McNally			
Luis Tiant			
Mel Stottlemyre			
☐ 10 NL Pitching Leaders	3.00	1.50	.30
Juan Marichal			
Bob Gibson			
Fergie Jenkins			
☐ 11 AL Strikeout Leaders	1.50	.75	.15
Sam McDowell			
Denny McLain			
Luis Tiant			
☐ 12 NL Strikeout Leaders	1.50	.75	.15
Bob Gibson			
Fergie Jenkins			
Bill Singer			
☐ 13 Mickey Stanley	1.00	.50	.10
☐ 14 Al McBean	.75	.35	.07
☐ 15 Boog Powell	1.50	.75	.15
☐ 16 Giants Rookies	.75	.35	.07
Cesar Gutierrez			
Rich Robertson			
☐ 17 Mike Marshall	1.00	.50	.10
☐ 18 Dick Schofield	.75	.35	.07
☐ 19 Ken Suarez	.75	.35	.07
☐ 20 Ernie Banks	14.00	7.00	1.40
☐ 21 Jose Santiago	.75	.35	.07
☐ 22 Jesus Alou	.75	.35	.07
☐ 23 Lew Krausse	.75	.35	.07
☐ 24 Walt Alston MG	1.75	.85	.17
☐ 25 Roy White	1.00	.50	.10
☐ 26 Clay Carroll	.75	.35	.07
☐ 27 Bernie Allen	.75	.35	.07
☐ 28 Mike Ryan	.75	.35	.07
☐ 29 Dave Morehead	.75	.35	.07
☐ 30 Bob Allison	1.00	.50	.10
☐ 31 Mets Rookies	1.75	.85	.17
Gary Gentry			
Amos Otis			
☐ 32 Sammy Ellis	.75	.35	.07
☐ 33 Wayne Causey	.75	.35	.07
☐ 34 Gary Peters	1.00	.50	.10
☐ 35 Joe Morgan	12.00	6.00	1.20
☐ 36 Luke Walker	.75	.35	.07
☐ 37 Curt Motton	.75	.35	.07
☐ 38 Zoilo Versalles	.75	.35	.07
☐ 39 Dick Hughes	.75	.35	.07
☐ 40 Mayo Smith MG	.75	.35	.07
☐ 41 Bob Barton	.75	.35	.07
☐ 42 Tommy Harper	1.00	.50	.10
☐ 43 Joe Niekro	1.25	.60	.12
☐ 44 Danny Cater	.75	.35	.07
☐ 45 Maury Wills	2.00	1.00	.20
☐ 46 Fritz Peterson	.75	.35	.07
☐ 47A Paul Popovich	.75	.35	.07
(no helmet emblem)			
☐ 47B Paul Popovich	15.00	7.50	1.50
(C emblem on helmet)			
☐ 48 Brant Alyea	.75	.35	.07
☐ 49A Royals Rookies	.75	.35	.07
Steve Jones			
E. Rodriguez "g"			
☐ 49B Royals Rookies	15.00	7.50	1.50
Steve Jones			
E. Rodriquez "q"			
☐ 50 Bob Clemente UER	40.00	20.00	4.00
(Bats Right			
listed twice)			
☐ 51 Woodie Fryman	.75	.35	.07
☐ 52 Mike Andrews	.75	.35	.07
☐ 53 Sonny Jackson	.75	.35	.07
☐ 54 Cisco Carlos	.75	.35	.07
☐ 55 Jerry Grote	.75	.35	.07
☐ 56 Rich Reese	.75	.35	.07
☐ 57 Checklist 1	3.00	.40	.08
Denny McLain			
☐ 58 Fred Gladding	.75	.35	.07
☐ 59 Jay Johnstone	1.00	.50	.10
☐ 60 Nelson Briles	.75	.35	.07
☐ 61 Jimmie Hall	.75	.35	.07
☐ 62 Chico Salmon	.75	.35	.07
☐ 63 Jim Hickman	.75	.35	.07
☐ 64 Bill Monbouquette	.75	.35	.07
☐ 65 Willie Davis	1.00	.50	.10
☐ 66 Orioles Rookies	1.00	.50	.10
Mike Adamson			
Merv Rettenmund			
☐ 67 Bill Stoneman	.75	.35	.07
☐ 68 Dave Duncan	.75	.35	.07
☐ 69 Steve Hamilton	.75	.35	.07
☐ 70 Tommy Helms	1.00	.50	.10
☐ 71 Steve Whitaker	.75	.35	.07
☐ 72 Ron Taylor	.75	.35	.07

☐ 73 Johnny Briggs	.75	.35	.07
☐ 74 Preston Gomez MG	.75	.35	.07
☐ 75 Luis Aparicio	5.00	2.50	.50
☐ 76 Norm Miller	.75	.35	.07
☐ 77A Ron Perranoski	1.00	.50	.10
(no emblem on cap)			
☐ 77B Ron Perranoski	15.00	7.50	1.50
(LA on cap)			
☐ 78 Tom Satriano	.75	.35	.07
☐ 79 Milt Pappas	1.00	.50	.10
☐ 80 Norm Cash	1.75	.85	.17
☐ 81 Mel Queen	.75	.35	.07
☐ 82 Pirates Rookies	8.00	4.00	.80
Rich Hebner			
Al Oliver			
☐ 83 Mike Ferraro	1.00	.50	.10
☐ 84 Bob Humphreys	.75	.35	.07
☐ 85 Lou Brock	14.00	7.00	1.40
☐ 86 Pete Richert	.75	.35	.07
☐ 87 Horace Clarke	.75	.35	.07
☐ 88 Rich Nye	.75	.35	.07
☐ 89 Russ Gibson	.75	.35	.07
☐ 90 Jerry Koosman	3.50	1.75	.35
☐ 91 Alvin Dark MG	1.00	.50	.10
☐ 92 Jack Billingham	.75	.35	.07
☐ 93 Joe Foy	.75	.35	.07
☐ 94 Hank Aguirre	.75	.35	.07
☐ 95 Johnny Bench	175.00	85.00	18.00
☐ 96 Denny Lemaster	.75	.35	.07
☐ 97 Buddy Bradford	.75	.35	.07
☐ 98 Dave Giusti	1.00	.50	.10
☐ 99A Twins Rookies	15.00	7.50	1.50
Danny Morris			
Graig Nettles			
(no loop)			
☐ 99B Twins Rookies	30.00	15.00	3.00
(errant loop in			
upper left corner			
of obverse)			
☐ 100 Hank Aaron	50.00	25.00	5.00
☐ 101 Daryl Patterson	.75	.35	.07
☐ 102 Jim Davenport	1.00	.50	.10
☐ 103 Roger Repoz	.75	.35	.07
☐ 104 Steve Blass	1.00	.50	.10
☐ 105 Rick Monday	1.00	.50	.10
☐ 106 Jim Hannan	.75	.35	.07
☐ 107A Checklist 2	3.00	.40	.08
(161 Jim Purdin)			
(Bob Gibson)			
☐ 107B Checklist 2	6.00	.50	.10
(161 John Purdin)			
(Bob Gibson)			
☐ 108 Tony Taylor	.75	.35	.07
☐ 109 Jim Lonborg	1.25	.60	.12
☐ 110 Mike Shannon	1.00	.50	.10
☐ 111 Johnny Morris	.75	.35	.07
☐ 112 J.C. Martin	.75	.35	.07
☐ 113 Dave May	.75	.35	.07
☐ 114 Yankees Rookies	.75	.35	.07
Alan Closter			
John Cumberland			
☐ 115 Bill Hands	.75	.35	.07
☐ 116 Chuck Harrison	.75	.35	.07
☐ 117 Jim Fairey	.75	.35	.07
☐ 118 Stan Williams	.75	.35	.07
☐ 119 Doug Rader	1.25	.60	.12
☐ 120 Pete Rose	35.00	17.50	3.50
☐ 121 Joe Grzenda	.75	.35	.07
☐ 122 Ron Fairly	1.00	.50	.10
☐ 123 Wilbur Wood	1.00	.50	.10
☐ 124 Hank Bauer MG	1.00	.50	.10
☐ 125 Ray Sadecki	.75	.35	.07
☐ 126 Dick Tracewski	.75	.35	.07
☐ 127 Kevin Collins	.75	.35	.07
☐ 128 Tommie Aaron	1.00	.50	.10
☐ 129 Bill McCool	.75	.35	.07
☐ 130 Carl Yastrzemski	33.00	15.00	3.00
☐ 131 Chris Cannizzaro	.75	.35	.07
☐ 132 Dave Baldwin	.75	.35	.07
☐ 133 Johnny Callison	1.00	.50	.10
☐ 134 Jim Weaver	.75	.35	.07
☐ 135 Tommy Davis	1.25	.60	.12
☐ 136 Cards Rookies	1.00	.50	.10
Steve Huntz			
Mike Torrez			
☐ 137 Wally Bunker	.75	.35	.07
☐ 138 John Bateman	.75	.35	.07
☐ 139 Andy Kosco	.75	.35	.07
☐ 140 Jim Lefebvre	1.25	.60	.12
☐ 141 Bill Dillman	.75	.35	.07
☐ 142 Woody Woodward	1.00	.50	.10
☐ 143 Joe Nossek	.75	.35	.07
☐ 144 Bob Hendley	.75	.35	.07
☐ 145 Max Alvis	.75	.35	.07

☐ 146 Jim Perry	1.00	.50	.10
☐ 147 Leo Durocher MG	1.75	.85	.17
☐ 148 Lee Stange	.75	.35	.07
☐ 149 Ollie Brown	.75	.35	.07
☐ 150 Denny McLain	3.50	1.75	.35
☐ 151A Clay Dalrymple	.75	.35	.07
(Portrait, Orioles)			
☐ 151B Clay Dalrymple	15.00	7.50	1.50
(Catching, Phillies)			
☐ 152 Tommie Sisk	.75	.35	.07
☐ 153 Ed Brinkman	.75	.35	.07
☐ 154 Jim Britton	.75	.35	.07
☐ 155 Pete Ward	.75	.35	.07
☐ 156 Houston Rookies	.75	.35	.07
Hal Gilson			
Leon McFadden			
☐ 157 Bob Rodgers	1.00	.50	.10
☐ 158 Joe Gibbon	.75	.35	.07
☐ 159 Jerry Adair	.75	.35	.07
☐ 160 Vada Pinson	1.50	.75	.15
☐ 161 John Purdin	.75	.35	.07
☐ 162 World Series Game 1	4.00	2.00	.40
Gibson fans 17			
☐ 163 World Series Game 2	2.25	1.10	.22
Tiger homers			
deck the Cards			
☐ 164 World Series Game 3	3.00	1.50	.30
McCarver's homer			
☐ 165 World Series Game 4	4.00	2.00	.40
Brock lead-off homer			
☐ 166 World Series Game 5	5.00	2.50	.50
Kaline's key hit			
☐ 167 World Series Game 6	2.25	1.10	.22
Northrup grandslam			
☐ 168 World Series Game 7	4.00	2.00	.40
Lolich outduels			
Bob Gibson			
☐ 169 World Series Summary	2.25	1.10	.22
Tigers celebrate			
☐ 170 Frank Howard	1.50	.75	.15
☐ 171 Glenn Beckert	1.00	.50	.10
☐ 172 Jerry Stephenson	.75	.35	.07
☐ 173 White Sox Rookies	.75	.35	.07
Bob Christian			
Gerry Nyman			
☐ 174 Grant Jackson	.75	.35	.07
☐ 175 Jim Bunning	2.50	1.25	.25
☐ 176 Joe Azcue	.75	.35	.07
☐ 177 Ron Reed	.75	.35	.07
☐ 178 Ray Oyler	.75	.35	.07
☐ 179 Don Pavletich	.75	.35	.07
☐ 180 Willie Horton	1.00	.50	.10
☐ 181 Mel Nelson	.75	.35	.07
☐ 182 Bill Rigney MG	.75	.35	.07
☐ 183 Don Shaw	.75	.35	.07
☐ 184 Roberto Pena	.75	.35	.07
☐ 185 Tom Phoebus	.75	.35	.07
☐ 186 Johnny Edwards	.75	.35	.07
☐ 187 Leon Wagner	.75	.35	.07
☐ 188 Rick Wise	1.00	.50	.10
☐ 189 Red Sox Rookies	.75	.35	.07
Joe Lahoud			
John Thibodeau			
☐ 190 Willie Mays	50.00	25.00	5.00
☐ 191 Lindy McDaniel	.75	.35	.07
☐ 192 Jose Pagan	.75	.35	.07
☐ 193 Don Cardwell	.75	.35	.07
☐ 194 Ted Uhlaender	.75	.35	.07
☐ 195 John Odom	.75	.35	.07
☐ 196 Lum Harris MG	.75	.35	.07
☐ 197 Dick Selma	.75	.35	.07
☐ 198 Willie Smith	.75	.35	.07
☐ 199 Jim French	.75	.35	.07
☐ 200 Bob Gibson	10.00	5.00	1.00
☐ 201 Russ Snyder	.75	.35	.07
☐ 202 Don Wilson	.75	.35	.07
☐ 203 Dave Johnson	1.00	.50	.10
☐ 204 Jack Hiatt	.75	.35	.07
☐ 205 Rick Reichardt	.75	.35	.07
☐ 206 Phillies Rookies	1.00	.50	.10
Larry Hisle			
Barry Lersch			
☐ 207 Roy Face	1.25	.60	.12
☐ 208A Donn Clendenon	1.00	.50	.10
(Houston)			
☐ 208B Donn Clendenon	15.00	7.50	1.50
(Expos)			
☐ 209 Larry Haney UER	.75	.35	.07
(reverse negative)			
☐ 210 Felix Millan	.75	.35	.07
☐ 211 Galen Cisco	.75	.35	.07
☐ 212 Tom Tresh	1.25	.60	.12
☐ 213 Gerry Arrigo	.75	.35	.07

☐ 214 Checklist 3	3.00	.40	.08
With 69T deckle CL			
on back (no player)			
☐ 215 Rico Petrocelli	1.00	.50	.10
☐ 216 Don Sutton	6.00	3.00	.60
☐ 217 John Donaldson	.75	.35	.07
☐ 218 John Roseboro	1.00	.50	.10
☐ 219 Freddie Patek	1.50	.75	.15
☐ 220 Sam McDowell	1.50	.75	.15
☐ 221 Art Shamsky	1.10	.55	.11
☐ 222 Duane Josephson	1.10	.55	.11
☐ 223 Tom Dukes	1.10	.55	.11
☐ 224 Angels Rookies	1.10	.55	.11
Bill Harrelson			
Steve Kealey			
☐ 225 Don Kessinger	1.50	.75	.15
☐ 226 Bruce Howard	1.10	.55	.11
☐ 227 Frank Johnson	1.10	.55	.11
☐ 228 Dave Leonhard	1.10	.55	.11
☐ 229 Don Lock	1.10	.55	.11
☐ 230 Rusty Staub	2.25	1.10	.22
☐ 231 Pat Dobson	1.50	.75	.15
☐ 232 Dave Ricketts	1.10	.55	.11
☐ 233 Steve Barber	1.10	.55	.11
☐ 234 Dave Bristol MG	1.10	.55	.11
☐ 235 Jim Hunter	12.00	6.00	1.20
☐ 236 Manny Mota	1.50	.75	.15
☐ 237 Bobby Cox	1.50	.75	.15
☐ 238 Ken Johnson	1.10	.55	.11
☐ 239 Bob Taylor	1.10	.55	.11
☐ 240 Ken Harrelson	1.75	.85	.17
☐ 241 Jim Brewer	1.10	.55	.11
☐ 242 Frank Kostro	1.10	.55	.11
☐ 243 Ron Kline	1.10	.55	.11
☐ 244 Indians Rookies	1.75	.85	.17
Ray Fosse			
George Woodson			
☐ 245 Ed Charles	1.10	.55	.11
☐ 246 Joe Coleman	1.10	.55	.11
☐ 247 Gene Oliver	1.10	.55	.11
☐ 248 Bob Priddy	1.10	.55	.11
☐ 249 Ed Spiezio	1.10	.55	.11
☐ 250 Frank Robinson	20.00	10.00	2.00
☐ 251 Ron Herbel	1.10	.55	.11
☐ 252 Chuck Cottier	1.10	.55	.11
☐ 253 Jerry Johnson	1.10	.55	.11
☐ 254 Joe Schultz	1.10	.55	.11
☐ 255 Steve Carlton	45.00	22.50	4.50
☐ 256 Gates Brown	1.50	.75	.15
☐ 257 Jim Ray	1.10	.55	.11
☐ 258 Jackie Hernandez	1.10	.55	.11
☐ 259 Bill Short	1.10	.55	.11
☐ 260 Reggie Jackson	450.00	225.00	45.00
☐ 261 Bob Johnson	1.10	.55	.11
☐ 262 Mike Kekich	1.10	.55	.11
☐ 263 Jerry May	1.10	.55	.11
☐ 264 Bill Landis	1.10	.55	.11
☐ 265 Chico Cardenas	1.10	.55	.11
☐ 266 Dodger Rookies	1.10	.55	.11
Tom Hutton			
Alan Foster			
☐ 267 Vicente Romo	1.10	.55	.11
☐ 268 Al Spangler	1.10	.55	.11
☐ 269 Al Weis	1.10	.55	.11
☐ 270 Mickey Lolich	2.25	1.10	.22
☐ 271 Larry Stahl	1.10	.55	.11
☐ 272 Ed Stroud	1.10	.55	.11
☐ 273 Ron Willis	1.10	.55	.11
☐ 274 Clyde King MG	1.10	.55	.11
☐ 275 Vic Davalillo	1.10	.55	.11
☐ 276 Gary Wagner	1.10	.55	.11
☐ 277 Elrod Hendricks	1.10	.55	.11
☐ 278 Gary Geiger UER	1.10	.55	.11
(Batting wrong)			
☐ 279 Roger Nelson	1.10	.55	.11
☐ 280 Alex Johnson	1.50	.75	.15
☐ 281 Ted Kubiak	1.10	.55	.11
☐ 282 Pat Jarvis	1.10	.55	.11
☐ 283 Sandy Alomar	1.50	.75	.15
☐ 284 Expos Rookies	1.10	.55	.11
Jerry Robertson			
Mike Wegener			
☐ 285 Don Mincher	1.50	.75	.15
☐ 286 Dock Ellis	1.50	.75	.15
☐ 287 Jose Tartabull	1.10	.55	.11
☐ 288 Ken Holtzman	1.50	.75	.15
☐ 289 Bart Shirley	1.10	.55	.11
☐ 290 Jim Kaat	3.50	1.75	.35
☐ 291 Vern Fuller	1.10	.55	.11
☐ 292 Al Downing	1.50	.75	.15
☐ 293 Dick Dietz	1.10	.55	.11
☐ 294 Jim Lemon MG	1.10	.55	.11
☐ 295 Tony Perez	7.50	3.75	.75
☐ 296 Andy Messersmith	1.75	.85	.17
☐ 297 Deron Johnson	1.50	.75	.15
☐ 298 Dave Nicholson	1.10	.55	.11
☐ 299 Mark Belanger	1.50	.75	.15
☐ 300 Felipe Alou	1.50	.75	.15
☐ 301 Darrell Brandon	1.10	.55	.11
☐ 302 Jim Pagliaroni	1.10	.55	.11
☐ 303 Cal Koonce	1.10	.55	.11
☐ 304 Padres Rookies	4.00	2.00	.40
Bill Davis			
Clarence Gaston			
☐ 305 Dick McAuliffe	1.50	.75	.15
☐ 306 Jim Grant	1.10	.55	.11
☐ 307 Gary Kolb	1.10	.55	.11
☐ 308 Wade Blasingame	1.10	.55	.11
☐ 309 Walt Williams	1.10	.55	.11
☐ 310 Tom Haller	1.10	.55	.11
☐ 311 Sparky Lyle	10.00	5.00	1.00
☐ 312 Lee Elia	1.50	.75	.15
☐ 313 Bill Robinson	1.75	.85	.17
☐ 314 Checklist 4	3.00	.40	.08
Don Drysdale			
☐ 315 Eddie Fisher	1.10	.55	.11
☐ 316 Hal Lanier	1.50	.75	.15
☐ 317 Bruce Look	1.10	.55	.11
☐ 318 Jack Fisher	1.10	.55	.11
☐ 319 Ken McMullen	1.10	.55	.11
☐ 320 Dal Maxvill	1.10	.55	.11
☐ 321 Jim McAndrew	1.10	.55	.11
☐ 322 Jose Vidal	1.10	.55	.11
☐ 323 Larry Miller	1.10	.55	.11
☐ 324 Tiger Rookies	1.10	.55	.11
Les Cain			
Dave Campbell			
☐ 325 Jose Cardenal	1.10	.55	.11
☐ 326 Gary Sutherland	1.10	.55	.11
☐ 327 Willie Crawford	1.10	.55	.11
☐ 328 Joel Horlen	1.00	.50	.10
☐ 329 Rick Joseph	.75	.35	.07
☐ 330 Tony Conigliaro	2.50	1.25	.25
☐ 331 Braves Rookies	1.25	.60	.12
Gil Garrido			
Tom House			
☐ 332 Fred Talbot	.75	.35	.07
☐ 333 Ivan Murrell	.75	.35	.07
☐ 334 Phil Roof	.75	.35	.07
☐ 335 Bill Mazeroski	1.25	.60	.12
☐ 336 Jim Roland	.75	.35	.07
☐ 337 Marty Martinez	.75	.35	.07
☐ 338 Del Unser	.75	.35	.07
☐ 339 Reds Rookies	.75	.35	.07
Steve Mingori			
Jose Pena			
☐ 340 Dave McNally	1.25	.60	.12
☐ 341 Dave Adlesh	.75	.35	.07
☐ 342 Bubba Morton	.75	.35	.07
☐ 343 Dan Frisella	.75	.35	.07
☐ 344 Tom Matchick	.75	.35	.07
☐ 345 Frank Linzy	.75	.35	.07
☐ 346 Wayne Comer	.75	.35	.07
☐ 347 Randy Hundley	1.00	.50	.10
☐ 348 Steve Hargan	.75	.35	.07
☐ 349 Dick Williams MG	1.00	.50	.10
☐ 350 Richie Allen	1.50	.75	.15
☐ 351 Carroll Sembera	.75	.35	.07
☐ 352 Paul Schaal	.75	.35	.07
☐ 353 Jeff Torborg	1.00	.50	.10
☐ 354 Nate Oliver	.75	.35	.07
☐ 355 Phil Niekro	4.50	2.25	.45
☐ 356 Frank Quilici MG	.75	.35	.07
☐ 357 Carl Taylor	.75	.35	.07
☐ 358 Athletics Rookies	.75	.35	.07
George Lauzerique			
Roberto Rodriquez			
☐ 359 Dick Kelley	.75	.35	.07
☐ 360 Jim Wynn	1.25	.60	.12
☐ 361 Gary Holman	.75	.35	.07
☐ 362 Jim Maloney	1.00	.50	.10
☐ 363 Russ Nixon	1.00	.50	.10
☐ 364 Tommie Agee	1.00	.50	.10
☐ 365 Jim Fregosi	1.25	.60	.12
☐ 366 Bo Belinsky	1.00	.50	.10
☐ 367 Lou Johnson	.75	.35	.07
☐ 368 Vic Roznovsky	.75	.35	.07
☐ 369 Bob Skinner	1.00	.50	.10
☐ 370 Juan Marichal	6.00	3.00	.60
☐ 371 Sal Bando	1.00	.50	.10
☐ 372 Adolfo Phillips	.75	.35	.07
☐ 373 Fred Lasher	.75	.35	.07
☐ 374 Bob Tillman	.75	.35	.07
☐ 375 Harmon Killebrew	16.00	8.00	1.60
☐ 376 Royals Rookies	1.00	.50	.10
Mike Fiore			
Jim Rooker			
☐ 377 Gary Bell	.75	.35	.07

☐ 378 Jose Herrera	.75	.35	.07
☐ 379 Ken Boyer	1.25	.60	.12
☐ 380 Stan Bahnsen	.75	.35	.07
☐ 381 Ed Kranepool	1.00	.50	.10
☐ 382 Pat Corrales	1.00	.50	.10
☐ 383 Casey Cox	.75	.35	.07
☐ 384 Larry Shepard MG	.75	.35	.07
☐ 385 Orlando Cepeda	2.50	1.25	.25
☐ 386 Jim McGlothlin	.75	.35	.07
☐ 387 Bobby Klaus	.75	.35	.07
☐ 388 Tom McCraw	.75	.35	.07
☐ 389 Dan Coombs	.75	.35	.07
☐ 390 Bill Freehan	1.25	.60	.12
☐ 391 Ray Culp	.75	.35	.07
☐ 392 Bob Burda	.75	.35	.07
☐ 393 Gene Brabender	.75	.35	.07
☐ 394 Pilots Rookies	3.50	1.75	.35
Lou Piniella			
Marv Staehle			
☐ 395 Chris Short	.75	.35	.07
☐ 396 Jim Campanis	.75	.35	.07
☐ 397 Chuck Dobson	.75	.35	.07
☐ 398 Tito Francona	.75	.35	.07
☐ 399 Bob Bailey	.75	.35	.07
☐ 400 Don Drysdale	8.00	4.00	.80
☐ 401 Jake Gibbs	.75	.35	.07
☐ 402 Ken Boswell	.75	.35	.07
☐ 403 Bob Miller	.75	.35	.07
☐ 404 Cubs Rookies	.75	.35	.07
Vic LaRose			
Gary Ross			
☐ 405 Lee May	1.00	.50	.10
☐ 406 Phil Ortega	.75	.35	.07
☐ 407 Tom Egan	.75	.35	.07
☐ 408 Nate Colbert	.75	.35	.07
☐ 409 Bob Moose	.75	.35	.07
☐ 410 Al Kaline	15.00	7.50	1.50
☐ 411 Larry Dierker	1.00	.50	.10
☐ 412 Checklist 5	6.50	.75	.15
Mickey Mantle			
☐ 413 Roland Sheldon	.75	.35	.07
☐ 414 Duke Sims	.75	.35	.07
☐ 415 Ray Washburn	.75	.35	.07
☐ 416 Willie McCovey AS	5.50	2.75	.55
☐ 417 Ken Harrelson AS	1.00	.50	.10
☐ 418 Tommy Helms AS	1.00	.50	.10
☐ 419 Rod Carew AS	8.50	4.25	.85
☐ 420 Ron Santo AS	1.25	.60	.12
☐ 421 Brooks Robinson AS	5.50	2.75	.55
☐ 422 Don Kessinger AS	1.00	.50	.10
☐ 423 Bert Campaneris AS	1.00	.50	.10
☐ 424 Pete Rose AS	12.00	6.00	1.20
☐ 425 Carl Yastrzemski AS	12.00	6.00	1.20
☐ 426 Curt Flood AS	1.00	.50	.10
☐ 427 Tony Oliva AS	1.25	.60	.12
☐ 428 Lou Brock AS	5.50	2.75	.55
☐ 429 Willie Horton AS	1.00	.50	.10
☐ 430 Johnny Bench AS	13.50	6.50	1.25
☐ 431 Bill Freehan AS	1.00	.50	.10
☐ 432 Bob Gibson AS	4.50	2.25	.45
☐ 433 Denny McLain AS	1.25	.60	.12
☐ 434 Jerry Koosman AS	1.00	.50	.10
☐ 435 Sam McDowell AS	1.00	.50	.10
☐ 436 Gene Alley	1.00	.50	.10
☐ 437 Luis Alcaraz	.75	.35	.07
☐ 438 Gary Waslewski	.75	.35	.07
☐ 439 White Sox Rookies	.75	.35	.07
Ed Herrmann			
Dan Lazar			
☐ 440A Willie McCovey	16.00	8.00	1.60
☐ 440B Willie McCovey WL	90.00	45.00	9.00
(McCovey white)			
☐ 441A Dennis Higgins	.75	.35	.07
☐ 441B Dennis Higgins WL	20.00	10.00	2.00
(Higgins white)			
☐ 442 Ty Cline	.75	.35	.07
☐ 443 Don Wert	.75	.35	.07
☐ 444A Joe Moeller	.75	.35	.07
☐ 444B Joe Moeller WL	20.00	10.00	2.00
(Moeller white)			
☐ 445 Bobby Knoop	.75	.35	.07
☐ 446 Claude Raymond	.75	.35	.07
☐ 447A Ralph Houk MG	1.00	.50	.10
☐ 447B Ralph Houk WL MG	20.00	10.00	2.00
(Houk white)			
☐ 448 Bob Tolan	1.00	.50	.10
☐ 449 Paul Lindblad	.75	.35	.07
☐ 450 Billy Williams	6.50	3.25	.65
☐ 451A Rich Rollins	1.00	.50	.10
☐ 451B Rich Rollins WL	20.00	10.00	2.00
(Rich and 3B white)			
☐ 452A Al Ferrara	.75	.35	.07
☐ 452B Al Ferrara WL	20.00	10.00	2.00
(Al and OF white)			
☐ 453 Mike Cuellar	1.25	.60	.12
☐ 454A Phillies Rookies	1.00	.50	.10
Larry Colton			
Don Money			
☐ 454B Phillies Rookies WL	20.00	10.00	2.00
Larry Colton			
Don Money			
(names in white)			
☐ 455 Sonny Siebert	1.00	.50	.10
☐ 456 Bud Harrelson	1.25	.60	.12
☐ 457 Dalton Jones	.75	.35	.07
☐ 458 Curt Blefary	1.00	.50	.10
☐ 459 Dave Boswell	.75	.35	.07
☐ 460 Joe Torre	1.00	.50	.10
☐ 461A Mike Epstein	.50	.25	.05
☐ 461B Mike Epstein WL	15.00	7.50	1.50
(Epstein white)			
☐ 462 Red Schoendienst MG	2.50	1.25	.25
☐ 463 Dennis Ribant	.50	.25	.05
☐ 464A Dave Marshall	.50	.25	.05
☐ 464B Dave Marshall WL	15.00	7.50	1.50
(Marshall white)			
☐ 465 Tommy John	3.50	1.75	.35
☐ 466 John Boccabella	.50	.25	.05
☐ 467 Tommie Reynolds	.50	.25	.05
☐ 468A Pirates Rookies	.50	.25	.05
Bruce Dal Canton			
Bob Robertson			
☐ 468B Pirates Rookies WL	15.00	7.50	1.50
Bruce Dal Canton			
Bob Robertson			
(names in white)			
☐ 469 Chico Ruiz	.75	.35	.07
☐ 470A Mel Stottlemyre	1.50	.75	.15
☐ 470B Mel Stottlemyre WL	25.00	12.50	2.50
(Stottlemyre white)			
☐ 471A Ted Savage	.75	.35	.07
☐ 471B Ted Savage WL	20.00	10.00	2.00
(Savage white)			
☐ 472 Jim Price	.75	.35	.07
☐ 473A Jose Arcia	.75	.35	.07
☐ 473B Jose Arcia WL	20.00	10.00	2.00
(Jose and 2B white)			
☐ 474 Tom Murphy	.75	.35	.07
☐ 475 Tim McCarver	1.75	.85	.17
☐ 476A Boston Rookies	1.00	.50	.10
Ken Brett			
Gerry Moses			
☐ 476B Boston Rookies WL	20.00	10.00	2.00
Ken Brett			
Gerry Moses			
(names in white)			
☐ 477 Jeff James	.75	.35	.07
☐ 478 Don Buford	1.00	.50	.10
☐ 479 Richie Scheinblum	.75	.35	.07
☐ 480 Tom Seaver	110.00	55.00	11.00
☐ 481 Bill Melton	.75	.35	.07
☐ 482A Jim Gosger	.75	.35	.07
☐ 482B Jim Gosger WL	20.00	10.00	2.00
(Jim and OF white)			
☐ 483 Ted Abernathy	.75	.35	.07
☐ 484 Joe Gordon MG	1.00	.50	.10
☐ 485A Gaylord Perry	9.00	4.00	.80
☐ 485B Gaylord Perry WL	60.00	30.00	6.00
(Perry white)			
☐ 486A Paul Casanova	.75	.35	.07
☐ 486B Paul Casanova WL	20.00	10.00	2.00
(Casanova white)			
☐ 487 Denis Menke	.75	.35	.07
☐ 488 Joe Sparma	.75	.35	.07
☐ 489 Clete Boyer	1.25	.60	.12
☐ 490 Matty Alou	1.00	.50	.10
☐ 491A Twins Rookies	.75	.35	.07
Jerry Crider			
George Mitterwald			
☐ 491B Twins Rookies WL	20.00	10.00	2.00
Jerry Crider			
George Mitterwald			
(names in white)			
☐ 492 Tony Cloninger	.75	.35	.07
☐ 493A Wes Parker	1.00	.50	.10
☐ 493B Wes Parker WL	20.00	10.00	2.00
(Parker white)			
☐ 494 Ken Berry	.75	.35	.07
☐ 495 Bert Campaneris	1.00	.50	.10
☐ 496 Larry Jaster	.75	.35	.07
☐ 497 Julian Javier	.75	.35	.07
☐ 498 Juan Pizarro	.75	.35	.07
☐ 499 Astro Rookies	.75	.35	.07
Don Bryant			
Steve Shea			
☐ 500A Mickey Mantle	180.00	90.00	18.00
(no Topps copy-right on card back)			

☐ 500B Mickey Mantle WL	550.00	275.00	55.00
(Mantle in white; no Topps copyright on card back)			
☐ 501A Tony Gonzalez	.75	.35	.07
☐ 501B Tony Gonzalez WL	20.00	10.00	2.00
(Tony and OF white)			
☐ 502 Minnie Rojas	.75	.35	.07
☐ 503 Larry Brown	.75	.35	.07
☐ 504 Checklist 6	3.00	.40	.08
Brooks Robinson			
☐ 505A Bobby Bolin	.75	.35	.07
☐ 505B Bobby Bolin WL	20.00	10.00	2.00
(Bolin white)			
☐ 506 Paul Blair	1.00	.50	.10
☐ 507 Cookie Rojas	1.00	.50	.10
☐ 508 Moe Drabowsky	.75	.35	.07
☐ 509 Manny Sanguillen	1.25	.60	.12
☐ 510 Rod Carew	65.00	32.50	6.50
☐ 511A Diego Segui	.75	.35	.07
☐ 511B Diego Segui WL	20.00	10.00	2.00
(Diego and P white)			
☐ 512 Cleon Jones	.75	.35	.07
☐ 513 Camilo Pascual	1.25	.60	.12
☐ 514 Mike Lum	.90	.45	.09
☐ 515 Dick Green	.90	.45	.09
☐ 516 Earl Weaver MG	6.00	3.00	.60
☐ 517 Mike McCormick	1.25	.60	.12
☐ 518 Fred Whitfield	.90	.45	.09
☐ 519 Yankees Rookies	.90	.45	.09
Gerry Kenney			
Len Boehmer			
☐ 520 Bob Veale	1.25	.60	.12
☐ 521 George Thomas	.90	.45	.09
☐ 522 Joe Hoerner	.90	.45	.09
☐ 523 Bob Chance	.90	.45	.09
☐ 524 Expos Rookies	.90	.45	.09
Jose Laboy			
Floyd Wicker			
☐ 525 Earl Wilson	.90	.45	.09
☐ 526 Hector Torres	.90	.45	.09
☐ 527 Al Lopez MG	2.50	1.25	.25
☐ 528 Claude Osteen	1.25	.60	.12
☐ 529 Ed Kirkpatrick	.90	.45	.09
☐ 530 Cesar Tovar	.90	.45	.09
☐ 531 Dick Farrell	.90	.45	.09
☐ 532 Bird Hill Aces	1.25	.60	.12
Tom Phoebus			
Jim Hardin			
Dave McNally			
Mike Cuellar			
☐ 533 Nolan Ryan	375.00	175.00	37.00
☐ 534 Jerry McNertney	.90	.45	.09
☐ 535 Phil Regan	1.25	.60	.12
☐ 536 Padres Rookies	.90	.45	.09
Danny Breeden			
Dave Roberts			
☐ 537 Mike Paul	.90	.45	.09
☐ 538 Charlie Smith	.90	.45	.09
☐ 539 Ted Shows How	4.50	2.25	.45
Mike Epstein			
Ted Williams			
☐ 540 Curt Flood	1.50	.75	.15
☐ 541 Joe Verbanic	.90	.45	.09
☐ 542 Bob Aspromonte	.90	.45	.09
☐ 543 Fred Newman	.90	.45	.09
☐ 544 Tigers Rookies	.90	.45	.09
Mike Kilkenny			
Ron Woods			
☐ 545 Willie Stargell	12.00	6.00	1.20
☐ 546 Jim Nash	.90	.45	.09
☐ 547 Billy Martin MG	5.00	2.50	.50
☐ 548 Bob Locker	.90	.45	.09
☐ 549 Ron Brand	.90	.45	.09
☐ 550 Brooks Robinson	15.00	7.50	1.50
☐ 551 Wayne Granger	.90	.45	.09
☐ 552 Dodgers Rookies	1.25	.60	.12
Ted Sizemore			
Bill Sudakis			
☐ 553 Ron Davis	.90	.45	.09
☐ 554 Frank Bertaina	.90	.45	.09
☐ 555 Jim Ray Hart	1.25	.60	.12
☐ 556 A's Stars	1.25	.60	.12
Sal Bando			
Bert Campaneris			
Danny Cater			
☐ 557 Frank Fernandez	.90	.45	.09
☐ 558 Tom Burgmeier	1.25	.60	.12
☐ 559 Cardinals Rookies	.90	.45	.09
Joe Hague			
Jim Hicks			
☐ 560 Luis Tiant	1.50	.75	.15
☐ 561 Ron Clark	.90	.45	.09
☐ 562 Bob Watson	2.50	1.25	.25
☐ 563 Marty Pattin	.90	.45	.09
☐ 564 Gil Hodges MG	7.00	3.50	.70
☐ 565 Hoyt Wilhelm	6.00	3.00	.60
☐ 566 Ron Hansen	.90	.45	.09
☐ 567 Pirates Rookies	.90	.45	.09
Elvio Jimenez			
Jim Shellenback			
☐ 568 Cecil Upshaw	.90	.45	.09
☐ 569 Billy Harris	.90	.45	.09
☐ 570 Ron Santo	2.50	1.25	.25
☐ 571 Cap Peterson	.90	.45	.09
☐ 572 Giants Heroes	8.00	4.00	.80
Willie McCovey			
Juan Marichal			
☐ 573 Jim Palmer	33.00	15.00	3.00
☐ 574 George Scott	1.25	.60	.12
☐ 575 Bill Singer	1.25	.60	.12
☐ 576 Phillies Rookies	.90	.45	.09
Ron Stone			
Bill Wilson			
☐ 577 Mike Hegan	.90	.45	.09
☐ 578 Don Bosch	.90	.45	.09
☐ 579 Dave Nelson	1.25	.60	.12
☐ 580 Jim Northrup	1.25	.60	.12
☐ 581 Gary Nolan	.90	.45	.09
☐ 582A Checklist 7	3.00	.40	.08
(white circle on back)			
(Tony Oliva)			
☐ 582B Checklist 7	6.00	.60	.12
(red circle on back)			
(Tony Oliva)			
☐ 583 Clyde Wright	.90	.45	.09
☐ 584 Don Mason	.90	.45	.09
☐ 585 Ron Swoboda	1.25	.60	.12
☐ 586 Tim Cullen	.90	.45	.09
☐ 587 Joe Rudi	2.50	1.25	.25
☐ 588 Bill White	1.75	.85	.17
☐ 589 Joe Pepitone	1.50	.75	.15
☐ 590 Rico Carty	1.50	.75	.15
☐ 591 Mike Hedlund	1.10	.55	.11
☐ 592 Padres Rookies	1.10	.55	.11
Rafael Robles			
Al Santorini			
☐ 593 Don Nottebart	1.10	.55	.11
☐ 594 Dooley Womack	1.10	.55	.11
☐ 595 Lee Maye	1.10	.55	.11
☐ 596 Chuck Hartenstein	1.10	.55	.11
☐ 597 A.L. Rookies	75.00	37.50	7.50
Bob Floyd			
Larry Burchart			
Rollie Fingers			
☐ 598 Ruben Amaro	1.10	.55	.11
☐ 599 John Boozer	1.10	.55	.11
☐ 600 Tony Oliva	3.50	1.75	.35
☐ 601 Tug McGraw	2.00	1.00	.20
☐ 602 Cubs Rookies	1.10	.55	.11
Alec Distaso			
Don Young			
Jim Qualls			
☐ 603 Joe Keough	1.10	.55	.11
☐ 604 Bobby Etheridge	1.10	.55	.11
☐ 605 Dick Ellsworth	1.50	.75	.15
☐ 606 Gene Mauch MG	1.50	.75	.15
☐ 607 Dick Bosman	1.10	.55	.11
☐ 608 Dick Simpson	1.10	.55	.11
☐ 609 Phil Gagliano	1.10	.55	.11
☐ 610 Jim Hardin	1.10	.55	.11
☐ 611 Braves Rookies	1.75	.85	.17
Bob Didier			
Walt Hriniak			
Gary Neibauer			
☐ 612 Jack Aker	1.10	.55	.11
☐ 613 Jim Beauchamp	1.10	.55	.11
☐ 614 Houston Rookies	1.10	.55	.11
Tom Griffin			
Skip Guinn			
☐ 615 Len Gabrielson	1.10	.55	.11
☐ 616 Don McMahon	1.10	.55	.11
☐ 617 Jesse Gonder	1.10	.55	.11
☐ 618 Ramon Webster	1.10	.55	.11
☐ 619 Royals Rookies	1.50	.75	.15
Bill Butler			
Pat Kelly			
Juan Rios			
☐ 620 Dean Chance	1.50	.75	.15
☐ 621 Bill Voss	1.10	.55	.11
☐ 622 Dan Osinski	1.10	.55	.11
☐ 623 Hank Allen	1.10	.55	.11
☐ 624 NL Rookies	1.10	.55	.11
Darrel Chaney			
Duffy Dyer			
Terry Harmon			
☐ 625 Mack Jones UER	1.10	.55	.11
(Batting wrong)			

☐ 626 Gene Michael	1.50	.75	.15
☐ 627 George Stone	1.10	.55	.11
☐ 628 Red Sox Rookies	1.50	.75	.15
Bill Conigliaro			
Syd O'Brien			
Fred Wenz			
☐ 629 Jack Hamilton	1.10	.55	.11
☐ 630 Bobby Bonds	18.00	9.00	1.80
☐ 631 John Kennedy	1.10	.55	.11
☐ 632 Jon Warden	1.10	.55	.11
☐ 633 Harry Walker MG	1.10	.55	.11
☐ 634 Andy Etchebarren	1.10	.55	.11
☐ 635 George Culver	1.10	.55	.11
☐ 636 Woody Held	1.10	.55	.11
☐ 637 Padres Rookies	1.10	.55	.11
Jerry DaVanon			
Frank Reberger			
Clay Kirby			
☐ 638 Ed Sprague	1.10	.55	.11
☐ 639 Barry Moore	1.10	.55	.11
☐ 640 Fergie Jenkins	8.00	3.50	.65
☐ 641 NL Rookies	1.10	.55	.11
Bobby Darwin			
John Miller			
Tommy Dean			
☐ 642 John Hiller	1.50	.75	.15
☐ 643 Billy Cowan	1.10	.55	.11
☐ 644 Chuck Hinton	1.10	.55	.11
☐ 645 George Brunet	1.10	.55	.11
☐ 646 Expos Rookies	1.10	.55	.11
Dan McGinn			
Carl Morton			
☐ 647 Dave Wickersham	1.10	.55	.11
☐ 648 Bobby Wine	1.10	.55	.11
☐ 649 Al Jackson	1.10	.55	.11
☐ 650 Ted Williams MG	10.00	5.00	1.00
☐ 651 Gus Gil	1.10	.55	.11
☐ 652 Eddie Watt	1.10	.55	.11
☐ 653 Aurelio Rodriguez	1.75	.85	.17
(photo actually Angels' batboy)			
☐ 654 White Sox Rookies	1.50	.75	.15
Carlos May			
Don Secrist			
Rich Morales			
☐ 655 Mike Hershberger	1.10	.55	.11
☐ 656 Dan Schneider	1.10	.55	.11
☐ 657 Bobby Murcer	2.00	1.00	.20
☐ 658 AL Rookies	1.10	.55	.11
Tom Hall			
Bill Burbach			
Jim Miles			
☐ 659 Johnny Podres	1.75	.85	.17
☐ 660 Reggie Smith	1.75	.85	.17
☐ 661 Jim Merritt	1.10	.55	.11
☐ 662 Royals Rookies	1.50	.75	.15
Dick Drago			
George Spriggs			
Bob Oliver			
☐ 663 Dick Radatz	1.50	.75	.15
☐ 664 Ron Hunt	1.50	.75	.15

1969 Topps Deckle

The cards in this 33-card set measure 2 1/4" by 3 1/4". This unusual black and white insert set derives its name from the serrated border, or edge, of the cards. The cards were included as inserts in the regularly issued Topps baseball series of 1969. Card number 11 is found with either Hoyt Wilhelm or Jim Wynn, and number 22 with either Rusty Staub or Joe Foy. The set price below does include all variations.

	NRMT	VG-E	GOOD
COMPLETE SET (35)	70.00	35.00	7.00
COMMON PLAYER (1-33)	.40	.20	.04
☐ 1 Brooks Robinson	4.00	2.00	.40
☐ 2 Boog Powell	.60	.30	.06
☐ 3 Ken Harrelson	.50	.25	.05
☐ 4 Carl Yastrzemski	6.00	3.00	.60
☐ 5 Jim Fregosi	.50	.25	.05
☐ 6 Luis Aparicio	1.25	.60	.12
☐ 7 Luis Tiant	.50	.25	.05
☐ 8 Denny McLain	.50	.25	.05
☐ 9 Willie Horton	.50	.25	.05
☐ 10 Bill Freehan	.50	.25	.05
☐ 11A Hoyt Wilhelm	5.00	2.50	.50
☐ 11B Jim Wynn	6.00	3.00	.60
☐ 12 Rod Carew	5.00	2.50	.50
☐ 13 Mel Stottlemyre	.40	.20	.04
☐ 14 Rick Monday	.40	.20	.04
☐ 15 Tommy Davis	.50	.25	.05
☐ 16 Frank Howard	.50	.25	.05
☐ 17 Felipe Alou	.40	.20	.04
☐ 18 Don Kessinger	.40	.20	.04
☐ 19 Ron Santo	.60	.30	.06
☐ 20 Tommy Helms	.40	.20	.04
☐ 21 Pete Rose	9.00	4.50	.90
☐ 22A Rusty Staub	2.50	1.25	.25
☐ 22B Joe Foy	6.00	3.00	.60
☐ 23 Tom Haller	.40	.20	.04
☐ 24 Maury Wills	.60	.30	.06
☐ 25 Jerry Koosman	.50	.25	.05
☐ 26 Richie Allen	.50	.25	.05
☐ 27 Bob Clemente	6.00	3.00	.60
☐ 28 Curt Flood	.50	.25	.05
☐ 29 Bob Gibson	2.00	1.00	.20
☐ 30 Al Ferrara	.40	.20	.04
☐ 31 Willie McCovey	3.00	1.50	.30
☐ 32 Juan Marichal	2.50	1.25	.25
☐ 33 Willie Mays	7.50	3.75	.75

1969 Topps Super

The cards in this 66-card set measure 2 1/4" by 3 1/4". This beautiful Topps set was released independently of the regular baseball series of 1969. It is referred to as "Super Baseball" on the back of the card, a title which was also used for the postcard-size cards issued in 1970 and 1971. Complete sheets, and cards with square corners cut from these sheets, are sometimes encountered.

	NRMT	VG-E	GOOD
COMPLETE SET (66)	4000.00	1800.00	400.00
COMMON PLAYER (1-66)	10.00	5.00	1.00
☐ 1 Dave McNally	12.00	6.00	1.20
☐ 2 Frank Robinson	150.00	75.00	15.00
☐ 3 Brooks Robinson	200.00	100.00	20.00

☐ 4 Ken Harrelson	12.00	6.00	1.20
☐ 5 Carl Yastrzemski	400.00	200.00	40.00
☐ 6 Ray Culp	10.00	5.00	1.00
☐ 7 Jim Fregosi	10.00	5.00	1.00
☐ 8 Rick Reichardt	10.00	5.00	1.00
☐ 9 Vic Davalillo	10.00	5.00	1.00
☐ 10 Luis Aparicio	75.00	37.50	7.50
☐ 11 Pete Ward	10.00	5.00	1.00
☐ 12 Joe Horlen	10.00	5.00	1.00
☐ 13 Luis Tiant	12.00	6.00	1.20
☐ 14 Sam McDowell	10.00	5.00	1.00
☐ 15 Jose Cardenal	10.00	5.00	1.00
☐ 16 Willie Horton	10.00	5.00	1.00
☐ 17 Denny McLain	14.00	7.00	1.40
☐ 18 Bill Freehan	12.00	6.00	1.20
☐ 19 Harmon Killebrew	100.00	50.00	10.00
☐ 20 Tony Oliva	16.00	8.00	1.60
☐ 21 Dean Chance	10.00	5.00	1.00
☐ 22 Joe Foy	10.00	5.00	1.00
☐ 23 Roger Nelson	10.00	5.00	1.00
☐ 24 Mickey Mantle	750.00	375.00	75.00
☐ 25 Mel Stottlemyre	12.00	6.00	1.20
☐ 26 Roy White	10.00	5.00	1.00
☐ 27 Rick Monday	10.00	5.00	1.00
☐ 28 Reggie Jackson	600.00	300.00	60.00
☐ 29 Bert Campaneris	10.00	5.00	1.00
☐ 30 Frank Howard	12.00	6.00	1.20
☐ 31 Camilo Pascual	10.00	5.00	1.00
☐ 32 Tommy Davis	12.00	6.00	1.20
☐ 33 Don Mincher	10.00	5.00	1.00
☐ 34 Hank Aaron	400.00	200.00	40.00
☐ 35 Felipe Alou	10.00	5.00	1.00
☐ 36 Joe Torre	16.00	8.00	1.60
☐ 37 Fergie Jenkins	75.00	37.50	7.50
☐ 38 Ron Santo	12.00	6.00	1.20
☐ 39 Billy Williams	75.00	37.50	7.50
☐ 40 Tommy Helms	10.00	5.00	1.00
☐ 41 Pete Rose	500.00	250.00	50.00
☐ 42 Joe Morgan	100.00	50.00	10.00
☐ 43 Jim Wynn	10.00	5.00	1.00
☐ 44 Curt Blefary	10.00	5.00	1.00
☐ 45 Willie Davis	10.00	5.00	1.00
☐ 46 Don Drysdale	75.00	37.50	7.50
☐ 47 Tom Haller	10.00	5.00	1.00
☐ 48 Rusty Staub	14.00	7.00	1.40
☐ 49 Maury Wills	16.00	8.00	1.60
☐ 50 Cleon Jones	10.00	5.00	1.00
☐ 51 Jerry Koosman	12.00	6.00	1.20
☐ 52 Tom Seaver	300.00	150.00	30.00
☐ 53 Richie Allen	14.00	7.00	1.40
☐ 54 Chris Short	10.00	5.00	1.00
☐ 55 Cookie Rojas	10.00	5.00	1.00
☐ 56 Matty Alou	10.00	5.00	1.00
☐ 57 Steve Blass	10.00	5.00	1.00
☐ 58 Bob Clemente	250.00	125.00	25.00
☐ 59 Curt Flood	14.00	7.00	1.40
☐ 60 Bob Gibson	100.00	50.00	10.00
☐ 61 Tim McCarver	16.00	8.00	1.60
☐ 62 Dick Selma	10.00	5.00	1.00
☐ 63 Ollie Brown	10.00	5.00	1.00
☐ 64 Juan Marichal	100.00	50.00	10.00
☐ 65 Willie Mays	400.00	200.00	40.00
☐ 66 Willie McCovey	125.00	60.00	12.50

1970 Topps

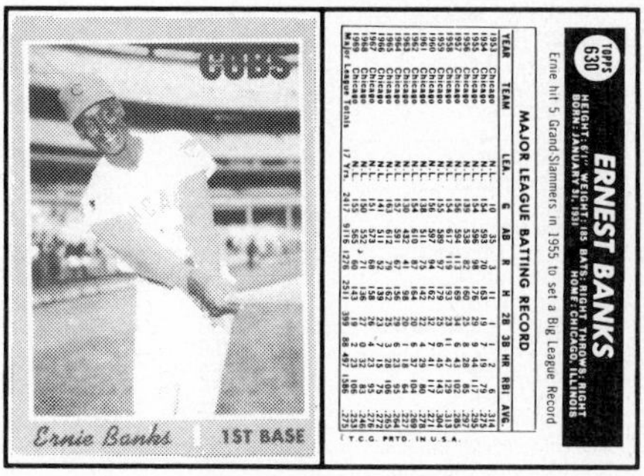

The cards in this 720-card set measure 2 1/2" by 3 1/2". The Topps set for 1970 has color photos surrounded by white frame lines and gray borders. The backs have a blue biographical section and a yellow record section. All-Star selections are featured on cards 450 to 469. Other topical subsets within this set include League Leaders (61-72), Playoffs cards (195-202), and World Series cards (305-310). There are graduations of scarcity, terminating in the high series (634-720), which are outlined in the value summary. The key rookie card in this set is Thurman Munson.

	NRMT	VG-E	GOOD
COMPLETE SET (720)	1800.00	850.00	200.00
COMMON PLAYER (1-132)	.40	.20	.04
COMMON PLAYER (133-263)	.50	.25	.05
COMMON PLAYER (264-459)	.55	.27	.05
COMMON PLAYER (460-546)	.80	.40	.08
COMMON PLAYER (547-633)	1.50	.75	.15
COMMON PLAYER (634-720)	3.50	1.75	.35
☐ 1 New York Mets Team Card	10.00	1.25	.25
☐ 2 Diego Segui	.40	.20	.04
☐ 3 Darrel Chaney	.40	.20	.04
☐ 4 Tom Egan	.40	.20	.04
☐ 5 Wes Parker	.60	.30	.06
☐ 6 Grant Jackson	.40	.20	.04
☐ 7 Indians Rookies Gary Boyd Russ Nagelson	.40	.20	.04
☐ 8 Jose Martinez	.40	.20	.04
☐ 9 Checklist 1	3.00	.30	.06
☐ 10 Carl Yastrzemski	33.00	15.00	3.00
☐ 11 Nate Colbert	.40	.20	.04
☐ 12 John Hiller	.60	.30	.06
☐ 13 Jack Hiatt	.40	.20	.04
☐ 14 Hank Allen	.40	.20	.04
☐ 15 Larry Dierker	.60	.30	.06
☐ 16 Charlie Metro MG	.40	.20	.04
☐ 17 Hoyt Wilhelm	3.50	1.75	.35
☐ 18 Carlos May	.40	.20	.04
☐ 19 John Boccabella	.40	.20	.04
☐ 20 Dave McNally	.60	.30	.06
☐ 21 A's Rookies Vida Blue Gene Tenace	3.50	1.75	.35
☐ 22 Ray Washburn	.40	.20	.04
☐ 23 Bill Robinson	.60	.30	.06
☐ 24 Dick Selma	.40	.20	.04
☐ 25 Cesar Tovar	.40	.20	.04
☐ 26 Tug McGraw	1.25	.60	.12
☐ 27 Chuck Hinton	.40	.20	.04
☐ 28 Billy Wilson	.40	.20	.04
☐ 29 Sandy Alomar	.40	.20	.04
☐ 30 Matty Alou	.60	.30	.06
☐ 31 Marty Pattin	.40	.20	.04
☐ 32 Harry Walker MG	.40	.20	.04
☐ 33 Don Wert	.40	.20	.04
☐ 34 Willie Crawford	.40	.20	.04
☐ 35 Joel Horlen	.40	.20	.04
☐ 36 Red Rookies Danny Breeden Bernie Carbo	.60	.30	.06
☐ 37 Dick Drago	.40	.20	.04
☐ 38 Mack Jones	.40	.20	.04
☐ 39 Mike Nagy	.40	.20	.04
☐ 40 Rich Allen	1.25	.60	.12
☐ 41 George Lauzerique	.40	.20	.04
☐ 42 Tito Fuentes	.40	.20	.04
☐ 43 Jack Aker	.40	.20	.04
☐ 44 Roberto Pena	.40	.20	.04
☐ 45 Dave Johnson	.75	.35	.07
☐ 46 Ken Rudolph	.40	.20	.04
☐ 47 Bob Miller	.40	.20	.04
☐ 48 Gil Garrido	.40	.20	.04
☐ 49 Tim Cullen	.40	.20	.04
☐ 50 Tommie Agee	.60	.30	.06
☐ 51 Bob Christian	.40	.20	.04
☐ 52 Bruce Dal Canton	.40	.20	.04
☐ 53 John Kennedy	.40	.20	.04
☐ 54 Jeff Torborg	.60	.30	.06
☐ 55 John Odom	.40	.20	.04
☐ 56 Phillies Rookies Joe Lis Scott Reid	.40	.20	.04
☐ 57 Pat Kelly	.40	.20	.04
☐ 58 Dave Marshall	.40	.20	.04
☐ 59 Dick Ellsworth	.60	.30	.06
☐ 60 Jim Wynn	.60	.30	.06

☐ 61 NL Batting Leaders	3.50	1.75	.35
Pete Rose			
Bob Clemente			
Cleon Jones			
☐ 62 AL Batting Leaders	1.50	.75	.15
Rod Carew			
Reggie Smith			
Tony Oliva			
☐ 63 NL RBI Leaders	1.50	.75	.15
Willie McCovey			
Ron Santo			
Tony Perez			
☐ 64 AL RBI Leaders	2.50	1.25	.25
Harmon Killebrew			
Boog Powell			
Reggie Jackson			
☐ 65 NL Home Run Leaders	2.50	1.25	.25
Willie McCovey			
Hank Aaron			
Lee May			
☐ 66 AL Home Run Leaders	2.50	1.25	.25
Harmon Killebrew			
Frank Howard			
Reggie Jackson			
☐ 67 NL ERA Leaders	3.50	1.75	.35
Juan Marichal			
Steve Carlton			
Bob Gibson			
☐ 68 AL ERA Leaders	1.50	.75	.15
Dick Bosman			
Jim Palmer			
Mike Cuellar			
☐ 69 NL Pitching Leaders	2.50	1.25	.25
Tom Seaver			
Phil Niekro			
Fergie Jenkins			
Juan Marichal			
☐ 70 AL Pitching Leaders	1.50	.75	.15
Dennis McLain			
Mike Cuellar			
Dave Boswell			
Dave McNally			
Jim Perry			
Mel Stottlemyre			
☐ 71 NL Strikeout Leaders	1.50	.75	.15
Fergie Jenkins			
Bob Gibson			
Bill Singer			
☐ 72 AL Strikeout Leaders	1.50	.75	.15
Sam McDowell			
Mickey Lolich			
Andy Messersmith			
☐ 73 Wayne Granger	.40	.20	.04
☐ 74 Angels Rookies	.40	.20	.04
Greg Washburn			
Wally Wolf			
☐ 75 Jim Kaat	2.00	1.00	.20
☐ 76 Carl Taylor	.40	.20	.04
☐ 77 Frank Linzy	.40	.20	.04
☐ 78 Joe Lahoud	.40	.20	.04
☐ 79 Clay Kirby	.40	.20	.04
☐ 80 Don Kessinger	.60	.30	.06
☐ 81 Dave May	.40	.20	.04
☐ 82 Frank Fernandez	.40	.20	.04
☐ 83 Don Cardwell	.40	.20	.04
☐ 84 Paul Casanova	.40	.20	.04
☐ 85 Max Alvis	.40	.20	.04
☐ 86 Lum Harris MG	.40	.20	.04
☐ 87 Steve Renko	.40	.20	.04
☐ 88 Pilots Rookies	.40	.20	.04
Miguel Fuentes			
Dick Baney			
☐ 89 Juan Rios	.40	.20	.04
☐ 90 Tim McCarver	1.00	.50	.10
☐ 91 Rich Morales	.40	.20	.04
☐ 92 George Culver	.40	.20	.04
☐ 93 Rick Renick	.40	.20	.04
☐ 94 Freddie Patek	.60	.30	.06
☐ 95 Earl Wilson	.40	.20	.04
☐ 96 Cardinals Rookies	2.00	1.00	.20
Leron Lee			
Jerry Reuss			
☐ 97 Joe Moeller	.40	.20	.04
☐ 98 Gates Brown	.60	.30	.06
☐ 99 Bobby Pfeil	.40	.20	.04
☐ 100 Mel Stottlemyre	1.00	.50	.10
☐ 101 Bobby Floyd	.40	.20	.04
☐ 102 Joe Rudi	.75	.35	.07
☐ 103 Frank Reberger	.40	.20	.04
☐ 104 Gerry Moses	.40	.20	.04
☐ 105 Tony Gonzalez	.40	.20	.04
☐ 106 Darold Knowles	.40	.20	.04
☐ 107 Bobby Etheridge	.40	.20	.04
☐ 108 Tom Burgmeier	.40	.20	.04

☐ 109 Expos Rookies	.60	.30	.06
Garry Jestadt			
Carl Morton			
☐ 110 Bob Moose	.40	.20	.04
☐ 111 Mike Hegan	.40	.20	.04
☐ 112 Dave Nelson	.40	.20	.04
☐ 113 Jim Ray	.40	.20	.04
☐ 114 Gene Michael	.60	.30	.06
☐ 115 Alex Johnson	.60	.30	.06
☐ 116 Sparky Lyle	1.25	.60	.12
☐ 117 Don Young	.40	.20	.04
☐ 118 George Mitterwald	.40	.20	.04
☐ 119 Chuck Taylor	.40	.20	.04
☐ 120 Sal Bando	.75	.35	.07
☐ 121 Orioles Rookies	.60	.30	.06
Fred Beene			
Terry Crowley			
☐ 122 George Stone	.40	.20	.04
☐ 123 Don Gutteridge	.40	.20	.04
☐ 124 Larry Jaster	.40	.20	.04
☐ 125 Deron Johnson	.60	.30	.06
☐ 126 Marty Martinez	.40	.20	.04
☐ 127 Joe Coleman	.40	.20	.04
☐ 128 Checklist 2	3.00	.30	.06
☐ 129 Jimmie Price	.40	.20	.04
☐ 130 Ollie Brown	.40	.20	.04
☐ 131 Dodgers Rookies	.40	.20	.04
Ray Lamb			
Bob Stinson			
☐ 132 Jim McGlothlin	.40	.20	.04
☐ 133 Clay Carroll	.50	.25	.05
☐ 134 Danny Walton	.50	.25	.05
☐ 135 Dick Dietz	.50	.25	.05
☐ 136 Steve Hargan	.50	.25	.05
☐ 137 Art Shamsky	.50	.25	.05
☐ 138 Joe Foy	.50	.25	.05
☐ 139 Rich Nye	.50	.25	.05
☐ 140 Reggie Jackson	120.00	60.00	12.00
☐ 141 Pirates Rookies	.75	.35	.07
Dave Cash			
Johnny Jeter			
☐ 142 Fritz Peterson	.50	.25	.05
☐ 143 Phil Gagliano	.50	.25	.05
☐ 144 Ray Culp	.50	.25	.05
☐ 145 Rico Carty	.75	.35	.07
☐ 146 Danny Murphy	.50	.25	.05
☐ 147 Angel Hermoso	.50	.25	.05
☐ 148 Earl Weaver MG	1.25	.60	.12
☐ 149 Billy Champion	.50	.25	.05
☐ 150 Harmon Killebrew	6.50	3.25	.65
☐ 151 Dave Roberts	.50	.25	.05
☐ 152 Ike Brown	.50	.25	.05
☐ 153 Gary Gentry	.50	.25	.05
☐ 154 Senators Rookies	.50	.25	.05
Jim Miles			
Jan Dukes			
☐ 155 Denis Menke	.50	.25	.05
☐ 156 Eddie Fisher	.50	.25	.05
☐ 157 Manny Mota	.75	.35	.07
☐ 158 Jerry McNertney	.50	.25	.05
☐ 159 Tommy Helms	.75	.35	.07
☐ 160 Phil Niekro	3.50	1.75	.35
☐ 161 Richie Scheinblum	.50	.25	.05
☐ 162 Jerry Johnson	.50	.25	.05
☐ 163 Syd O'Brien	.50	.25	.05
☐ 164 Ty Cline	.50	.25	.05
☐ 165 Ed Kirkpatrick	.50	.25	.05
☐ 166 Al Oliver	2.00	1.00	.20
☐ 167 Bill Burbach	.50	.25	.05
☐ 168 Dave Watkins	.50	.25	.05
☐ 169 Tom Hall	.50	.25	.05
☐ 170 Billy Williams	5.50	2.75	.55
☐ 171 Jim Nash	.50	.25	.05
☐ 172 Braves Rookies	1.50	.75	.15
Garry Hill			
Ralph Garr			
☐ 173 Jim Hicks	.50	.25	.05
☐ 174 Ted Sizemore	.75	.35	.07
☐ 175 Dick Bosman	.50	.25	.05
☐ 176 Jim Ray Hart	.75	.35	.07
☐ 177 Jim Northrup	.75	.35	.07
☐ 178 Denny Lemaster	.50	.25	.05
☐ 179 Ivan Murrell	.50	.25	.05
☐ 180 Tommy John	2.50	1.25	.25
☐ 181 Sparky Anderson MG	1.00	.50	.10
☐ 182 Dick Hall	.50	.25	.05
☐ 183 Jerry Grote	.50	.25	.05
☐ 184 Ray Fosse	.50	.25	.05
☐ 185 Don Mincher	.75	.35	.07
☐ 186 Rick Joseph	.50	.25	.05
☐ 187 Mike Hedlund	.50	.25	.05
☐ 188 Manny Sanguillen	.75	.35	.07

☐ 189	Yankees Rookies Thurman Munson Dave McDonald	100.00	50.00	10.00
☐ 190	Joe Torre	1.25	.60	.12
☐ 191	Vicente Romo	.50	.25	.05
☐ 192	Jim Qualls	.50	.25	.05
☐ 193	Mike Wegener	.50	.25	.05
☐ 194	Chuck Manuel	.50	.25	.05
☐ 195	NL Playoff Game 1 Seaver wins opener	4.50	2.25	.45
☐ 196	NL Playoff Game 2 Mets show muscle	1.50	.75	.15
☐ 197	NL Playoff Game 3 Ryan saves the day	7.50	3.75	.75
☐ 198	NL Playoff Summary Mets celebrate	1.50	.75	.15
☐ 199	AL Playoff Game 1 Orioles win squeaker (Cuellar)	1.50	.75	.15
☐ 200	AL Playoff Game 2 Powell scores winning run	1.50	.75	.15
☐ 201	AL Playoff Game 3 Birds wrap it up	1.50	.75	.15
☐ 202	AL Playoff Summary Orioles celebrate	1.50	.75	.15
☐ 203	Rudy May	.50	.25	.05
☐ 204	Len Gabrielson	.50	.25	.05
☐ 205	Bert Campaneris	.75	.35	.07
☐ 206	Clete Boyer	.75	.35	.07
☐ 207	Tigers Rookies Norman McRae Bob Reed	.50	.25	.05
☐ 208	Fred Gladding	.50	.25	.05
☐ 209	Ken Suarez	.50	.25	.05
☐ 210	Juan Marichal	5.00	2.50	.50
☐ 211	Ted Williams MG	6.50	3.25	.65
☐ 212	Al Santorini	.50	.25	.05
☐ 213	Andy Etchebarren	.50	.25	.05
☐ 214	Ken Boswell	.50	.25	.05
☐ 215	Reggie Smith	1.25	.60	.12
☐ 216	Chuck Hartenstein	.50	.25	.05
☐ 217	Ron Hansen	.50	.25	.05
☐ 218	Ron Stone	.50	.25	.05
☐ 219	Jerry Kenney	.50	.25	.05
☐ 220	Steve Carlton	25.00	12.50	2.50
☐ 221	Ron Brand	.50	.25	.05
☐ 222	Jim Rooker	.50	.25	.05
☐ 223	Nate Oliver	.50	.25	.05
☐ 224	Steve Barber	.50	.25	.05
☐ 225	Lee May	.75	.35	.07
☐ 226	Ron Perranoski	.75	.35	.07
☐ 227	Astros Rookies John Mayberry Bob Watkins	1.00	.50	.10
☐ 228	Aurelio Rodriguez	.50	.25	.05
☐ 229	Rich Robertson	.50	.25	.05
☐ 230	Brooks Robinson	11.00	5.50	1.10
☐ 231	Luis Tiant	1.25	.60	.12
☐ 232	Bob Didier	.50	.25	.05
☐ 233	Lew Krausse	.50	.25	.05
☐ 234	Tommy Dean	.50	.25	.05
☐ 235	Mike Epstein	.50	.25	.05
☐ 236	Bob Veale	.75	.35	.07
☐ 237	Russ Gibson	.50	.25	.05
☐ 238	Jose Laboy	.50	.25	.05
☐ 239	Ken Berry	.50	.25	.05
☐ 240	Fergie Jenkins	6.00	2.50	.50
☐ 241	Royals Rookies Al Fitzmorris Scott Northey	.50	.25	.05
☐ 242	Walter Alston MG	1.50	.75	.15
☐ 243	Joe Sparma	.50	.25	.05
☐ 244A	Checklist 3 (red bat on front)	3.00	.30	.06
☐ 244B	Checklist 3 (brown bat on front)	3.00	.30	.06
☐ 245	Leo Cardenas	.50	.25	.05
☐ 246	Jim McAndrew	.50	.25	.05
☐ 247	Lou Klimchock	.50	.25	.05
☐ 248	Jesus Alou	.50	.25	.05
☐ 249	Bob Locker	.50	.25	.05
☐ 250	Willie McCovey	8.00	4.00	.80
☐ 251	Dick Schofield	.50	.25	.05
☐ 252	Lowell Palmer	.50	.25	.05
☐ 253	Ron Woods	.50	.25	.05
☐ 254	Camilo Pascual	.75	.35	.07
☐ 255	Jim Spencer	.50	.25	.05
☐ 256	Vic Davalillo	.50	.25	.05
☐ 257	Dennis Higgins	.50	.25	.05
☐ 258	Paul Popovich	.50	.25	.05
☐ 259	Tommie Reynolds	.50	.25	.05
☐ 260	Claude Osteen	.75	.35	.07
☐ 261	Curt Motton	.50	.25	.05
☐ 262	Padres Rookies Jerry Morales Jim Williams	.75	.35	.07
☐ 263	Duane Josephson	.50	.25	.05
☐ 264	Rich Hebner	.75	.35	.07
☐ 265	Randy Hundley	.75	.35	.07
☐ 266	Wally Bunker	.55	.27	.05
☐ 267	Twins Rookies Herman Hill Paul Ratliff	.55	.27	.05
☐ 268	Claude Raymond	.55	.27	.05
☐ 269	Cesar Gutierrez	.55	.27	.05
☐ 270	Chris Short	.55	.27	.05
☐ 271	Greg Goossen	.55	.27	.05
☐ 272	Hector Torres	.55	.27	.05
☐ 273	Ralph Houk MG	.75	.35	.07
☐ 274	Gerry Arrigo	.55	.27	.05
☐ 275	Duke Sims	.55	.27	.05
☐ 276	Ron Hunt	.55	.27	.05
☐ 277	Paul Doyle	.55	.27	.05
☐ 278	Tommie Aaron	.75	.35	.07
☐ 279	Bill Lee	1.00	.50	.10
☐ 280	Donn Clendenon	.75	.35	.07
☐ 281	Casey Cox	.55	.27	.05
☐ 282	Steve Huntz	.55	.27	.05
☐ 283	Angel Bravo	.55	.27	.05
☐ 284	Jack Baldschun	.55	.27	.05
☐ 285	Paul Blair	.75	.35	.07
☐ 286	Dodgers Rookies Jack Jenkins Bill Buckner	7.50	3.75	.75
☐ 287	Fred Talbot	.55	.27	.05
☐ 288	Larry Hisle	.75	.35	.07
☐ 289	Gene Brabender	.55	.27	.05
☐ 290	Rod Carew	38.00	17.00	3.50
☐ 291	Leo Durocher MG	1.25	.60	.12
☐ 292	Eddie Leon	.55	.27	.05
☐ 293	Bob Bailey	.55	.27	.05
☐ 294	Jose Azcue	.55	.27	.05
☐ 295	Cecil Upshaw	.55	.27	.05
☐ 296	Woody Woodward	.75	.35	.07
☐ 297	Curt Blefary	.55	.27	.05
☐ 298	Ken Henderson	.55	.27	.05
☐ 299	Buddy Bradford	.55	.27	.05
☐ 300	Tom Seaver	70.00	35.00	7.00
☐ 301	Chico Salmon	.55	.27	.05
☐ 302	Jeff James	.55	.27	.05
☐ 303	Brant Alyea	.55	.27	.05
☐ 304	Bill Russell	1.75	.85	.17
☐ 305	World Series Game 1 Buford leadoff homer	1.50	.75	.15
☐ 306	World Series Game 2 Clendenon's homer breaks ice	1.50	.75	.15
☐ 307	World Series Game 3 Agee's catch saves the day	1.50	.75	.15
☐ 308	World Series Game 4 Martin's bunt ends deadlock	1.50	.75	.15
☐ 309	World Series Game 5 Koosman shuts door	1.50	.75	.15
☐ 310	World Series Summary Mets whoop it up	1.50	.75	.15
☐ 311	Dick Green	.55	.27	.05
☐ 312	Mike Torrez	.75	.35	.07
☐ 313	Mayo Smith MG	.55	.27	.05
☐ 314	Bill McCool	.55	.27	.05
☐ 315	Luis Aparicio	3.50	1.75	.35
☐ 316	Skip Guinn	.55	.27	.05
☐ 317	Red Sox Rookies Billy Conigliaro Luis Alvarado	.75	.35	.07
☐ 318	Willie Smith	.55	.27	.05
☐ 319	Clay Dalrymple	.55	.27	.05
☐ 320	Jim Maloney	.75	.35	.07
☐ 321	Lou Piniella	1.75	.85	.17
☐ 322	Luke Walker	.55	.27	.05
☐ 323	Wayne Comer	.55	.27	.05
☐ 324	Tony Taylor	.55	.27	.05
☐ 325	Dave Boswell	.55	.27	.05
☐ 326	Bill Voss	.55	.27	.05
☐ 327	Hal King	.55	.27	.05
☐ 328	George Brunet	.55	.27	.05
☐ 329	Chris Cannizzaro	.55	.27	.05
☐ 330	Lou Brock	8.00	4.00	.80
☐ 331	Chuck Dobson	.55	.27	.05
☐ 332	Bobby Wine	.55	.27	.05
☐ 333	Bobby Murcer	1.00	.50	.10
☐ 334	Phil Regan	.50	.25	.05
☐ 335	Bill Freehan	1.00	.50	.10
☐ 336	Del Unser	.55	.27	.05
☐ 337	Mike McCormick	.75	.35	.07
☐ 338	Paul Schaal	.55	.27	.05

☐ 339 Johnny Edwards	.55	.27	.05
☐ 340 Tony Conigliaro	1.50	.75	.15
☐ 341 Bill Sudakis	.55	.27	.05
☐ 342 Wilbur Wood	.75	.35	.07
☐ 343A Checklist 4	3.00	.30	.06
(red bat on front)			
☐ 343B Checklist 4	3.00	.30	.06
(brown bat on front)			
☐ 344 Marcelino Lopez	.55	.27	.05
☐ 345 Al Ferrara	.55	.27	.05
☐ 346 Red Schoendienst MG	1.75	.85	.17
☐ 347 Russ Snyder	.55	.27	.05
☐ 348 Mets Rookies	.75	.35	.07
Mike Jorgensen			
Jesse Hudson			
☐ 349 Steve Hamilton	.55	.27	.05
☐ 350 Roberto Clemente	40.00	20.00	4.00
☐ 351 Tom Murphy	.55	.27	.05
☐ 352 Bob Barton	.55	.27	.05
☐ 353 Stan Williams	.75	.35	.07
☐ 354 Amos Otis	1.00	.50	.10
☐ 355 Doug Rader	.75	.35	.07
☐ 356 Fred Lasher	.55	.27	.05
☐ 357 Bob Burda	.55	.27	.05
☐ 358 Pedro Borbon	.55	.27	.05
☐ 359 Phil Roof	.55	.27	.05
☐ 360 Curt Flood	1.00	.50	.10
☐ 361 Ray Jarvis	.55	.27	.05
☐ 362 Joe Hague	.55	.27	.05
☐ 363 Tom Shopay	.55	.27	.05
☐ 364 Dan McGinn	.55	.27	.05
☐ 365 Zoilo Versalles	.55	.27	.05
☐ 366 Barry Moore	.55	.27	.05
☐ 367 Mike Lum	.55	.27	.05
☐ 368 Ed Herrmann	.55	.27	.05
☐ 369 Alan Foster	.55	.27	.05
☐ 370 Tommy Harper	.75	.35	.07
☐ 371 Rod Gaspar	.55	.27	.05
☐ 372 Dave Giusti	.75	.35	.07
☐ 373 Roy White	1.00	.50	.10
☐ 374 Tommie Sisk	.55	.27	.05
☐ 375 Johnny Callison	.75	.35	.07
☐ 376 Lefty Phillips MG	.55	.27	.05
☐ 377 Bill Butler	.55	.27	.05
☐ 378 Jim Davenport	.75	.35	.07
☐ 379 Tom Tischinski	.55	.27	.05
☐ 380 Tony Perez	3.50	1.75	.35
☐ 381 Athletics Rookies	.55	.27	.05
Bobby Brooks			
Mike Olivo			
☐ 382 Jack DiLauro	.55	.27	.05
☐ 383 Mickey Stanley	.75	.35	.07
☐ 384 Gary Neibauer	.55	.27	.05
☐ 385 George Scott	.75	.35	.07
☐ 386 Bill Dillman	.55	.27	.05
☐ 387 Baltimore Orioles	1.25	.60	.12
Team Card			
☐ 388 Byron Browne	.55	.27	.05
☐ 389 Jim Shellenback	.55	.27	.05
☐ 390 Willie Davis	1.00	.50	.10
☐ 391 Larry Brown	.55	.27	.05
☐ 392 Walt Hriniak	.75	.35	.07
☐ 393 John Gelnar	.55	.27	.05
☐ 394 Gil Hodges MG	3.50	1.75	.35
☐ 395 Walt Williams	.55	.27	.05
☐ 396 Steve Blass	.75	.35	.07
☐ 397 Roger Repoz	.55	.27	.05
☐ 398 Bill Stoneman	.55	.27	.05
☐ 399 New York Yankees	1.50	.75	.15
Team Card			
☐ 400 Denny McLain	1.25	.60	.12
☐ 401 Giants Rookies	.55	.27	.05
John Harrell			
Bernie Williams			
☐ 402 Ellie Rodriguez	.55	.27	.05
☐ 403 Jim Bunning	2.50	1.25	.25
☐ 404 Rich Reese	.75	.35	.07
☐ 405 Bill Hands	.55	.27	.05
☐ 406 Mike Andrews	.55	.27	.05
☐ 407 Bob Watson	1.00	.50	.10
☐ 408 Paul Lindblad	.55	.27	.05
☐ 409 Bob Tolan	.75	.35	.07
☐ 410 Boog Powell	2.50	1.25	.25
☐ 411 Los Angeles Dodgers	1.75	.85	.17
Team Card			
☐ 412 Larry Burchart	.55	.27	.05
☐ 413 Sonny Jackson	.55	.27	.05
☐ 414 Paul Edmondson	.55	.27	.05
☐ 415 Julian Javier	.75	.35	.07
☐ 416 Joe Verbanic	.55	.27	.05
☐ 417 John Bateman	.55	.27	.05
☐ 418 John Donaldson	.55	.27	.05
☐ 419 Ron Taylor	.55	.27	.05
☐ 420 Ken McMullen	.55	.27	.05
☐ 421 Pat Dobson	.75	.35	.07
☐ 422 Royals Team	1.50	.75	.15
☐ 423 Jerry May	.55	.27	.05
☐ 424 Mike Kilkenny	.55	.27	.05
(inconsistent design,			
card number in			
white circle)			
☐ 425 Bobby Bonds	4.50	2.25	.45
☐ 426 Bill Rigney MG	.55	.27	.05
☐ 427 Fred Norman	.55	.27	.05
☐ 428 Don Buford	.75	.35	.07
☐ 429 Cubs Rookies	.55	.27	.05
Randy Bobb			
Jim Cosman			
☐ 430 Andy Messersmith	.75	.35	.07
☐ 431 Ron Swoboda	.75	.35	.07
☐ 432A Checklist 5	3.00	.30	.06
("Baseball" in			
yellow letters)			
☐ 432B Checklist 5	3.00	.30	.06
("Baseball" in			
white letters)			
☐ 433 Ron Bryant	.55	.27	.05
☐ 434 Felipe Alou	.75	.35	.07
☐ 435 Nelson Briles	.75	.35	.07
☐ 436 Philadelphia Phillies	1.25	.60	.12
Team Card			
☐ 437 Danny Cater	.55	.27	.05
☐ 438 Pat Jarvis	.55	.27	.05
☐ 439 Lee Maye	.55	.27	.05
☐ 440 Bill Mazeroski	1.25	.60	.12
☐ 441 John O'Donoghue	.55	.27	.05
☐ 442 Gene Mauch MG	.75	.35	.07
☐ 443 Al Jackson	.55	.27	.05
☐ 444 White Sox Rookies	.55	.27	.05
Billy Farmer			
John Matias			
☐ 445 Vada Pinson	1.25	.60	.12
☐ 446 Billy Grabarkewitz	.55	.27	.05
☐ 447 Lee Stange	.55	.27	.05
☐ 448 Houston Astros	1.25	.60	.12
Team Card			
☐ 449 Jim Palmer	17.00	8.50	1.70
☐ 450 Willie McCovey AS	4.00	2.00	.40
☐ 451 Boog Powell AS	1.00	.50	.10
☐ 452 Felix Millan AS	.75	.35	.07
☐ 453 Rod Carew AS	5.50	2.75	.55
☐ 454 Ron Santo AS	1.00	.50	.10
☐ 455 Brooks Robinson AS	4.50	2.25	.45
☐ 456 Don Kessinger AS	.75	.35	.07
☐ 457 Rico Petrocelli AS	.75	.35	.07
☐ 458 Pete Rose AS	12.00	6.00	1.20
☐ 459 Reggie Jackson AS	14.00	7.00	1.40
☐ 460 Matty Alou AS	1.00	.50	.10
☐ 461 Carl Yastrzemski AS	10.00	5.00	1.00
☐ 462 Hank Aaron AS	10.00	5.00	1.00
☐ 463 Frank Robinson AS	5.00	2.50	.50
☐ 464 Johnny Bench AS	11.00	5.50	1.10
☐ 465 Bill Freehan AS	1.00	.50	.10
☐ 466 Juan Marichal AS	3.75	1.85	.37
☐ 467 Denny McLain AS	1.00	.50	.10
☐ 468 Jerry Koosman AS	1.00	.50	.10
☐ 469 Sam McDowell AS	1.00	.50	.10
☐ 470 Willie Stargell	9.00	4.50	.90
☐ 471 Chris Zachary	.80	.40	.08
☐ 472 Braves Team	1.75	.85	.17
☐ 473 Don Bryant	.80	.40	.08
☐ 474 Dick Kelley	.80	.40	.08
☐ 475 Dick McAuliffe	1.00	.50	.10
☐ 476 Don Shaw	.80	.40	.08
☐ 477 Orioles Rookies	.80	.40	.08
Al Severinsen			
Roger Freed			
☐ 478 Bobby Heise	.80	.40	.08
☐ 479 Dick Woodson	.80	.40	.08
☐ 480 Glenn Beckert	1.00	.50	.10
☐ 481 Jose Tartabull	.80	.40	.08
☐ 482 Tom Hilgendorf	.80	.40	.08
☐ 483 Gail Hopkins	.80	.40	.08
☐ 484 Gary Nolan	1.00	.50	.10
☐ 485 Jay Johnstone	1.00	.50	.10
☐ 486 Terry Harmon	.80	.40	.08
☐ 487 Cisco Carlos	.80	.40	.08
☐ 488 J.C. Martin	.80	.40	.08
☐ 489 Eddie Kasko MG	.80	.40	.08
☐ 490 Bill Singer	1.00	.50	.10
☐ 491 Graig Nettles	4.00	2.00	.40
☐ 492 Astros Rookies	.80	.40	.08
Keith Lampard			
Scipio Spinks			
☐ 493 Lindy McDaniel	.80	.40	.08
☐ 494 Larry Stahl	.80	.40	.08
☐ 495 Dave Morehead	.80	.40	.08
☐ 496 Steve Whitaker	.80	.40	.08

☐ 497	Eddie Watt	.80	.40	.08
☐ 498	Al Weis	.80	.40	.08
☐ 499	Skip Lockwood	.80	.40	.08
☐ 500	Hank Aaron	36.00	18.00	3.60
☐ 501	Chicago White Sox	1.75	.85	.17
	Team Card			
☐ 502	Rollie Fingers	16.00	8.00	1.60
☐ 503	Dal Maxvill	.80	.40	.08
☐ 504	Don Pavletich	.80	.40	.08
☐ 505	Ken Holtzman	1.00	.50	.10
☐ 506	Ed Stroud	.80	.40	.08
☐ 507	Pat Corrales	1.00	.50	.10
☐ 508	Joe Niekro	1.25	.60	.12
☐ 509	Montreal Expos	1.75	.85	.17
	Team Card			
☐ 510	Tony Oliva	2.25	1.10	.22
☐ 511	Joe Hoerner	.80	.40	.08
☐ 512	Billy Harris	.80	.40	.08
☐ 513	Preston Gomez MG	.80	.40	.08
☐ 514	Steve Hovley	.80	.40	.08
☐ 515	Don Wilson	.80	.40	.08
☐ 516	Yankees Rookies	.80	.40	.08
	John Ellis			
	Jim Lyttle			
☐ 517	Joe Gibbon	.80	.40	.08
☐ 518	Bill Melton	.80	.40	.08
☐ 519	Don McMahon	.80	.40	.08
☐ 520	Willie Horton	1.25	.60	.12
☐ 521	Cal Koonce	.80	.40	.08
☐ 522	Angels Team	1.75	.85	.17
☐ 523	Jose Pena	.80	.40	.08
☐ 524	Alvin Dark MG	1.00	.50	.10
☐ 525	Jerry Adair	.80	.40	.08
☐ 526	Ron Herbel	.80	.40	.08
☐ 527	Don Bosch	.80	.40	.08
☐ 528	Elrod Hendricks	.80	.40	.08
☐ 529	Bob Aspromonte	.80	.40	.08
☐ 530	Bob Gibson	9.00	4.50	.90
☐ 531	Ron Clark	.80	.40	.08
☐ 532	Danny Murtaugh MG	.80	.40	.08
☐ 533	Buzz Stephen	.80	.40	.08
☐ 534	Twins Team	1.75	.85	.17
☐ 535	Andy Kosco	.80	.40	.08
☐ 536	Mike Kekich	.80	.40	.08
☐ 537	Joe Morgan	9.00	4.50	.90
☐ 538	Bob Humphreys	.80	.40	.08
☐ 539	Phillies Rookies	4.00	2.00	.40
	Dennis Doyle			
	Larry Bowa			
☐ 540	Gary Peters	1.00	.50	.10
☐ 541	Bill Heath	.80	.40	.08
☐ 542	Checklist 6	3.00	.30	.06
☐ 543	Clyde Wright	.80	.40	.08
☐ 544	Cincinnati Reds	2.00	1.00	.20
	Team Card			
☐ 545	Ken Harrelson	1.25	.60	.12
☐ 546	Ron Reed	1.00	.50	.10
☐ 547	Rick Monday	2.00	1.00	.20
☐ 548	Howie Reed	1.50	.75	.15
☐ 549	Cardinals Team	3.00	1.50	.30
☐ 550	Frank Howard	2.50	1.25	.25
☐ 551	Dock Ellis	1.50	.75	.15
☐ 552	Royals Rookies	1.50	.75	.15
	Don O'Riley			
	Dennis Paepke			
	Fred Rico			
☐ 553	Jim Lefebvre	2.00	1.00	.20
☐ 554	Tom Timmermann	1.50	.75	.15
☐ 555	Orlando Cepeda	4.00	2.00	.40
☐ 556	Dave Bristol MG	1.50	.75	.15
☐ 557	Ed Kranepool	2.00	1.00	.20
☐ 558	Vern Fuller	1.50	.75	.15
☐ 559	Tommy Davis	2.00	1.00	.20
☐ 560	Gaylord Perry	9.00	4.50	.90
☐ 561	Tom McCraw	1.50	.75	.15
☐ 562	Ted Abernathy	1.50	.75	.15
☐ 563	Boston Red Sox	3.00	1.50	.30
	Team Card			
☐ 564	Johnny Briggs	1.50	.75	.15
☐ 565	Jim Hunter	9.00	4.50	.90
☐ 566	Gene Alley	2.00	1.00	.20
☐ 567	Bob Oliver	1.50	.75	.15
☐ 568	Stan Bahnsen	1.50	.75	.15
☐ 569	Cookie Rojas	2.00	1.00	.20
☐ 570	Jim Fregosi	2.00	1.00	.20
☐ 571	Jim Brewer	1.50	.75	.15
☐ 572	Frank Quilici MG	1.50	.75	.15
☐ 573	Padres Rookies	1.50	.75	.15
	Mike Corkins			
	Rafael Robles			
	Ron Slocum			
☐ 574	Bobby Bolin	1.50	.75	.15
☐ 575	Cleon Jones	1.50	.75	.15
☐ 576	Milt Pappas	2.00	1.00	.20
☐ 577	Bernie Allen	1.50	.75	.15
☐ 578	Tom Griffin	1.50	.75	.15
☐ 579	Detroit Tigers	3.00	1.50	.30
	Team Card			
☐ 580	Pete Rose	75.00	37.50	7.50
☐ 581	Tom Satriano	1.50	.75	.15
☐ 582	Mike Paul	1.50	.75	.15
☐ 583	Hal Lanier	2.00	1.00	.20
☐ 584	Al Downing	2.00	1.00	.20
☐ 585	Rusty Staub	2.50	1.25	.25
☐ 586	Rickey Clark	1.50	.75	.15
☐ 587	Jose Arcia	1.50	.75	.15
☐ 588A	Checklist 7	7.00	.75	.15
	(666 Adolfo)			
☐ 588B	Checklist 7	3.50	.35	.07
	(666 Adolpho)			
☐ 589	Joe Keough	1.50	.75	.15
☐ 590	Mike Cuellar	2.00	1.00	.20
☐ 591	Mike Ryan	1.50	.75	.15
☐ 592	Daryl Patterson	1.50	.75	.15
☐ 593	Chicago Cubs	3.00	1.50	.30
	Team Card			
☐ 594	Jake Gibbs	1.50	.75	.15
☐ 595	Maury Wills	2.50	1.25	.25
☐ 596	Mike Hershberger	1.50	.75	.15
☐ 597	Sonny Siebert	2.00	1.00	.20
☐ 598	Joe Pepitone	2.00	1.00	.20
☐ 599	Senators Rookies	1.50	.75	.15
	Dick Stelmaszek			
	Gene Martin			
	Dick Such			
☐ 600	Willie Mays	55.00	27.50	5.50
☐ 601	Pete Richert	1.50	.75	.15
☐ 602	Ted Savage	1.50	.75	.15
☐ 603	Ray Oyler	1.50	.75	.15
☐ 604	Clarence Gaston	2.50	1.25	.25
☐ 605	Rick Wise	2.00	1.00	.20
☐ 606	Chico Ruiz	1.50	.75	.15
☐ 607	Gary Waslewski	1.50	.75	.15
☐ 608	Pittsburgh Pirates	3.00	1.50	.30
	Team Card			
☐ 609	Buck Martinez	1.50	.75	.15
	(inconsistent design,			
	card number in			
	white circle)			
☐ 610	Jerry Koosman	2.50	1.25	.25
☐ 611	Norm Cash	2.50	1.25	.25
☐ 612	Jim Hickman	1.50	.75	.15
☐ 613	Dave Baldwin	1.50	.75	.15
☐ 614	Mike Shannon	2.00	1.00	.20
☐ 615	Mark Belanger	2.00	1.00	.20
☐ 616	Jim Merritt	1.50	.75	.15
☐ 617	Jim French	1.50	.75	.15
☐ 618	Billy Wynne	1.50	.75	.15
☐ 619	Norm Miller	1.50	.75	.15
☐ 620	Jim Perry	2.50	1.25	.25
☐ 621	Braves Rookies	17.00	8.50	1.70
	Mike McQueen			
	Darrell Evans			
	Rick Kester			
☐ 622	Don Sutton	8.00	4.00	.80
☐ 623	Horace Clarke	1.50	.75	.15
☐ 624	Clyde King MG	1.50	.75	.15
☐ 625	Dean Chance	2.00	1.00	.20
☐ 626	Dave Ricketts	1.50	.75	.15
☐ 627	Gary Wagner	1.50	.75	.15
☐ 628	Wayne Garrett	1.50	.75	.15
☐ 629	Merv Rettenmund	1.50	.75	.15
☐ 630	Ernie Banks	25.00	12.50	2.50
☐ 631	Oakland Athletics	3.00	1.50	.30
	Team Card			
☐ 632	Gary Sutherland	1.50	.75	.15
☐ 633	Roger Nelson	1.50	.75	.15
☐ 634	Bud Harrelson	4.50	2.25	.45
☐ 635	Bob Allison	4.50	2.25	.45
☐ 636	Jim Stewart	3.50	1.75	.35
☐ 637	Cleveland Indians	7.00	3.50	.70
	Team Card			
☐ 638	Frank Bertaina	3.50	1.75	.35
☐ 639	Dave Campbell	3.50	1.75	.35
☐ 640	Al Kaline	40.00	20.00	4.00
☐ 641	Al McBean	3.50	1.75	.35
☐ 642	Angels Rookies	3.50	1.75	.35
	Greg Garrett			
	Gordon Lund			
	Jarvis Tatum			
☐ 643	Jose Pagan	3.50	1.75	.35
☐ 644	Gerry Nyman	3.50	1.75	.35
☐ 645	Don Money	3.50	1.75	.35
☐ 646	Jim Britton	3.50	1.75	.35
☐ 647	Tom Matchick	3.50	1.75	.35
☐ 648	Larry Haney	3.50	1.75	.35
☐ 649	Jimmie Hall	3.50	1.75	.35
☐ 650	Sam McDowell	4.50	2.25	.45

☐ 651 Jim Gosger	3.50	1.75	.35
☐ 652 Rich Rollins	3.50	1.75	.35
☐ 653 Moe Drabowsky	3.50	1.75	.35
☐ 654 NL Rookies	4.50	2.25	.45
Oscar Gamble			
Boots Day			
Angel Mangual			
☐ 655 John Roseboro	3.50	1.75	.35
☐ 656 Jim Hardin	3.50	1.75	.35
☐ 657 San Diego Padres	7.00	3.50	.70
Team Card			
☐ 658 Ken Tatum	3.50	1.75	.35
☐ 659 Pete Ward	3.50	1.75	.35
☐ 660 Johnny Bench	165.00	75.00	15.00
☐ 661 Jerry Robertson	3.50	1.75	.35
☐ 662 Frank Lucchesi MG	3.50	1.75	.35
☐ 663 Tito Francona	3.50	1.75	.35
☐ 664 Bob Robertson	3.50	1.75	.35
☐ 665 Jim Lonborg	4.50	2.25	.45
☐ 666 Adolpho Phillips	3.50	1.75	.35
☐ 667 Bob Meyer	3.50	1.75	.35
☐ 668 Bob Tillman	3.50	1.75	.35
☐ 669 White Sox Rookies	3.50	1.75	.35
Bart Johnson			
Dan Lazar			
Mickey Scott			
☐ 670 Ron Santo	5.50	2.75	.55
☐ 671 Jim Campanis	3.50	1.75	.35
☐ 672 Leon McFadden	3.50	1.75	.35
☐ 673 Ted Uhlaender	3.50	1.75	.35
☐ 674 Dave Leonhard	3.50	1.75	.35
☐ 675 Jose Cardenal	3.50	1.75	.35
☐ 676 Senators Team	7.00	3.50	.70
☐ 677 Woodie Fryman	3.50	1.75	.35
☐ 678 Dave Duncan	3.50	1.75	.35
☐ 679 Ray Sadecki	3.50	1.75	.35
☐ 680 Rico Petrocelli	4.50	2.25	.45
☐ 681 Bob Garibaldi	3.50	1.75	.35
☐ 682 Dalton Jones	3.50	1.75	.35
☐ 683 Reds Rookies	4.50	2.25	.45
Vern Geishert			
Hal McRae			
Wayne Simpson			
☐ 684 Jack Fisher	3.50	1.75	.35
☐ 685 Tom Haller	3.50	1.75	.35
☐ 686 Jackie Hernandez	3.50	1.75	.35
☐ 687 Bob Priddy	3.50	1.75	.35
☐ 688 Ted Kubiak	3.50	1.75	.35
☐ 689 Frank Tepedino	3.50	1.75	.35
☐ 690 Ron Fairly	3.50	1.75	.35
☐ 691 Joe Grzenda	3.50	1.75	.35
☐ 692 Duffy Dyer	3.50	1.75	.35
☐ 693 Bob Johnson	3.50	1.75	.35
☐ 694 Gary Ross	3.50	1.75	.35
☐ 695 Bobby Knoop	3.50	1.75	.35
☐ 696 San Francisco Giants	7.00	3.50	.70
Team Card			
☐ 697 Jim Hannan	3.50	1.75	.35
☐ 698 Tom Tresh	4.50	2.25	.45
☐ 699 Hank Aguirre	3.50	1.75	.35
☐ 700 Frank Robinson	37.50	16.00	3.50
☐ 701 Jack Billingham	3.50	1.75	.35
☐ 702 AL Rookies	3.50	1.75	.35
Bob Johnson			
Ron Klimkowski			
Bill Zepp			
☐ 703 Lou Marone	3.50	1.75	.35
☐ 704 Frank Baker	3.50	1.75	.35
☐ 705 Tony Cloninger	3.50	1.75	.35
☐ 706 John McNamara MG	7.50	3.75	.75
☐ 707 Kevin Collins	3.50	1.75	.35
☐ 708 Jose Santiago	3.50	1.75	.35
☐ 709 Mike Fiore	3.50	1.75	.35
☐ 710 Felix Millan	3.50	1.75	.35
☐ 711 Ed Brinkman	3.50	1.75	.35
☐ 712 Nolan Ryan	325.00	160.00	32.00
☐ 713 Pilots Team	15.00	7.50	1.50
☐ 714 Al Spangler	3.50	1.75	.35
☐ 715 Mickey Lolich	5.00	2.50	.50
☐ 716 Cardinals Rookies	3.50	1.75	.35
Sal Campisi			
Reggie Cleveland			
Santiago Guzman			
☐ 717 Tom Phoebus	3.50	1.75	.35
☐ 718 Ed Spiezio	3.50	1.75	.35
☐ 719 Jim Roland	3.50	1.75	.35
☐ 720 Rick Reichardt	4.50	2.25	.45

1971 Topps

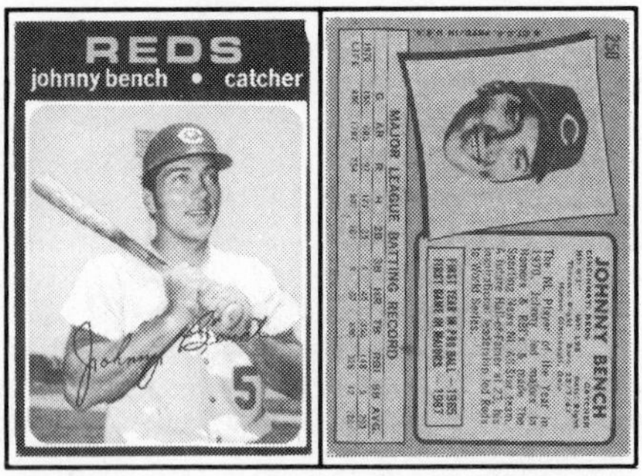

The cards in this 752-card set measure 2 1/2" by 3 1/2". The 1971 Topps set is a challenge to complete in strict mint condition because the black obverse border is easily scratched and damaged. An unusual feature of this set is that the player is also pictured in black and white on the back of the card. Featured subsets within this set include League Leaders (61-72), Playoffs cards (195-202), and World Series cards (327-332). Cards 524-643 and the last series (644-752) are somewhat scarce. The last series was printed in two sheets of 132. On the printing sheets 44 cards were printed in 50 percent greater quantity than the other 66 cards. These 66 (slightly) shorter-printed numbers are identified in the checklist below by SP. The key rookie cards in this set are the multi-player rookie cards of Dusty Baker and Don Baylor and the card of Steve Garvey.

	NRMT	VG-E	GOOD
COMPLETE SET (752)	1750.00	750.00	175.00
COMMON PLAYER (1-263)	.40	.20	.04
COMMON PLAYER (264-393)	.50	.25	.05
COMMON PLAYER (394-523)	.75	.35	.07
COMMON PLAYER (524-643)	1.75	.85	.17
COMMON PLAYER (644-752)	4.00	2.00	.40
COMMON SP (644-752)	5.00	2.50	.50
☐ 1 Baltimore Orioles	10.00	1.25	.25
Team Card			
☐ 2 Dock Ellis	.40	.20	.04
☐ 3 Dick McAuliffe	.60	.30	.06
☐ 4 Vic Davalillo	.40	.20	.04
☐ 5 Thurman Munson	30.00	15.00	3.00
☐ 6 Ed Spiezio	.40	.20	.04
☐ 7 Jim Holt	.40	.20	.04
☐ 8 Mike McQueen	.40	.20	.04
☐ 9 George Scott	.60	.30	.06
☐ 10 Claude Osteen	.60	.30	.06
☐ 11 Elliott Maddox	.40	.20	.04
☐ 12 Johnny Callison	.60	.30	.06
☐ 13 White Sox Rookies	.40	.20	.04
Charlie Brinkman			
Dick Moloney			
☐ 14 Dave Concepcion	10.00	5.00	1.00
☐ 15 Andy Messersmith	.60	.30	.06
☐ 16 Ken Singleton	2.00	1.00	.20
☐ 17 Billy Sorrell	.40	.20	.04
☐ 18 Norm Miller	.40	.20	.04
☐ 19 Skip Pitlock	.40	.20	.04
☐ 20 Reggie Jackson	65.00	32.50	6.50
☐ 21 Dan McGinn	.40	.20	.04
☐ 22 Phil Roof	.40	.20	.04
☐ 23 Oscar Gamble	.60	.30	.06
☐ 24 Rich Hand	.40	.20	.04
☐ 25 Clarence Gaston	.75	.35	.07
☐ 26 Bert Blyleven	30.00	15.00	3.00
☐ 27 Pirates Rookies	.40	.20	.04
Fred Cambria			
Gene Clines			
☐ 28 Ron Klimkowski	.40	.20	.04
☐ 29 Don Buford	.60	.30	.06
☐ 30 Phil Niekro	3.50	1.75	.35
☐ 31 Eddie Kasko MG	.40	.20	.04
☐ 32 Jerry DaVanon	.40	.20	.04
☐ 33 Del Unser	.40	.20	.04
☐ 34 Sandy Vance	.40	.20	.04
☐ 35 Lou Piniella	1.25	.60	.12

☐ 36 Dean Chance	.60	.30	.06
☐ 37 Rich McKinney	.40	.20	.04
☐ 38 Jim Colborn	.40	.20	.04
☐ 39 Tiger Rookies	.40	.20	.04
Lerrin LaGrow			
Gene Lamont			
☐ 40 Lee May	.60	.30	.06
☐ 41 Rick Austin	.40	.20	.04
☐ 42 Boots Day	.40	.20	.04
☐ 43 Steve Kealey	.40	.20	.04
☐ 44 Johnny Edwards	.40	.20	.04
☐ 45 Jim Hunter	6.00	3.00	.60
☐ 46 Dave Campbell	.40	.20	.04
☐ 47 Johnny Jeter	.40	.20	.04
☐ 48 Dave Baldwin	.40	.20	.04
☐ 49 Don Money	.40	.20	.04
☐ 50 Willie McCovey	7.00	3.50	.70
☐ 51 Steve Kline	.40	.20	.04
☐ 52 Braves Rookies	.60	.30	.06
Oscar Brown			
Earl Williams			
☐ 53 Paul Blair	.60	.30	.06
☐ 54 Checklist 1	3.00	.30	.06
☐ 55 Steve Carlton	22.00	11.00	2.20
☐ 56 Duane Josephson	.40	.20	.04
☐ 57 Von Joshua	.40	.20	.04
☐ 58 Bill Lee	.60	.30	.06
☐ 59 Gene Mauch MG	.60	.30	.06
☐ 60 Dick Bosman	.40	.20	.04
☐ 61 AL Batting Leaders	2.25	1.10	.22
Alex Johnson			
Carl Yastrzemski			
Tony Oliva			
☐ 62 NL Batting Leaders	1.25	.60	.12
Rico Carty			
Joe Torre			
Manny Sanguillen			
☐ 63 AL RBI Leaders	1.25	.60	.12
Frank Howard			
Tony Conigliaro			
Boog Powell			
☐ 64 NL RBI Leaders	2.25	1.10	.22
Johnny Bench			
Tony Perez			
Billy Williams			
☐ 65 AL HR Leaders	2.25	1.10	.22
Frank Howard			
Harmon Killebrew			
Carl Yastrzemski			
☐ 66 NL HR Leaders	2.25	1.10	.22
Johnny Bench			
Billy Williams			
Tony Perez			
☐ 67 AL ERA Leaders	1.25	.60	.12
Diego Segui			
Jim Palmer			
Clyde Wright			
☐ 68 NL ERA Leaders	1.25	.60	.12
Tom Seaver			
Wayne Simpson			
Luke Walker			
☐ 69 AL Pitching Leaders	1.25	.60	.12
Mike Cuellar			
Dave McNally			
Jim Perry			
☐ 70 NL Pitching Leaders	2.25	1.10	.22
Bob Gibson			
Gaylord Perry			
Fergie Jenkins			
☐ 71 AL Strikeout Leaders	1.25	.60	.12
Sam McDowell			
Mickey Lolich			
Bob Johnson			
☐ 72 NL Strikeout Leaders	2.25	1.10	.22
Tom Seaver			
Bob Gibson			
Fergie Jenkins			
☐ 73 George Brunet	.40	.20	.04
☐ 74 Twins Rookies	.40	.20	.04
Pete Hamm			
Jim Nettles			
☐ 75 Gary Nolan	.60	.30	.06
☐ 76 Ted Savage	.40	.20	.04
☐ 77 Mike Compton	.40	.20	.04
☐ 78 Jim Spencer	.40	.20	.04
☐ 79 Wade Blasingame	.40	.20	.04
☐ 80 Bill Melton	.40	.20	.04
☐ 81 Felix Millan	.40	.20	.04
☐ 82 Casey Cox	.40	.20	.04
☐ 83 Met Rookies	.60	.30	.06
Tim Foli			
Randy Bobb			
☐ 84 Marcel Lachemann	.60	.30	.06
☐ 85 Billy Grabarkewitz	.40	.20	.04
☐ 86 Mike Kilkenny	.40	.20	.04
☐ 87 Jack Heidemann	.40	.20	.04
☐ 88 Hal King	.40	.20	.04
☐ 89 Ken Brett	.60	.30	.06
☐ 90 Joe Pepitone	.75	.35	.07
☐ 91 Bob Lemon MG	1.50	.75	.15
☐ 92 Fred Wenz	.40	.20	.04
☐ 93 Senators Rookies	.40	.20	.04
Norm McRae			
Denny Riddleberger			
☐ 94 Don Hahn	.40	.20	.04
☐ 95 Luis Tiant	.75	.35	.07
☐ 96 Joe Hague	.40	.20	.04
☐ 97 Floyd Wicker	.40	.20	.04
☐ 98 Joe Decker	.40	.20	.04
☐ 99 Mark Belanger	.60	.30	.06
☐ 100 Pete Rose	45.00	22.50	4.50
☐ 101 Les Cain	.40	.20	.04
☐ 102 Astros Rookies	1.00	.50	.10
Ken Forsch			
Larry Howard			
☐ 103 Rich Severson	.40	.20	.04
☐ 104 Dan Frisella	.40	.20	.04
☐ 105 Tony Conigliaro	1.00	.50	.10
☐ 106 Tom Dukes	.40	.20	.04
☐ 107 Roy Foster	.40	.20	.04
☐ 108 John Cumberland	.40	.20	.04
☐ 109 Steve Hovley	.40	.20	.04
☐ 110 Bill Mazeroski	.75	.35	.07
☐ 111 Yankee Rookies	.40	.20	.04
Loyd Colson			
Bobby Mitchell			
☐ 112 Manny Mota	.60	.30	.06
☐ 113 Jerry Crider	.40	.20	.04
☐ 114 Billy Conigliaro	.60	.30	.06
☐ 115 Donn Clendenon	.60	.30	.06
☐ 116 Ken Sanders	.40	.20	.04
☐ 117 Ted Simmons	10.00	5.00	1.00
☐ 118 Cookie Rojas	.60	.30	.06
☐ 119 Frank Lucchesi MG	.40	.20	.04
☐ 120 Willie Horton	.60	.30	.06
☐ 121 Cubs Rookies	.40	.20	.04
Jim Dunegan			
Roe Skidmore			
☐ 122 Eddie Watt	.40	.20	.04
☐ 123A Checklist 2	3.00	.30	.06
(card number			
at bottom right)			
☐ 123B Checklist 2	3.00	.30	.06
(card number			
centered)			
☐ 124 Don Gullett	.75	.35	.07
☐ 125 Ray Fosse	.40	.20	.04
☐ 126 Danny Coombs	.40	.20	.04
☐ 127 Danny Thompson	.40	.20	.04
☐ 128 Frank Johnson	.40	.20	.04
☐ 129 Aurelio Monteagudo	.40	.20	.04
☐ 130 Denis Menke	.40	.20	.04
☐ 131 Curt Blefary	.40	.20	.04
☐ 132 Jose Laboy	.40	.20	.04
☐ 133 Mickey Lolich	1.00	.50	.10
☐ 134 Jose Arcia	.40	.20	.04
☐ 135 Rick Monday	.60	.30	.06
☐ 136 Duffy Dyer	.40	.20	.04
☐ 137 Marcelino Lopez	.40	.20	.04
☐ 138 Phillies Rookies	.60	.30	.06
Joe Lis			
Willie Montanez			
☐ 139 Paul Casanova	.40	.20	.04
☐ 140 Gaylord Perry	6.00	2.50	.50
☐ 141 Frank Quilici	.40	.20	.04
☐ 142 Mack Jones	.40	.20	.04
☐ 143 Steve Blass	.60	.30	.06
☐ 144 Jackie Hernandez	.40	.20	.04
☐ 145 Bill Singer	.60	.30	.06
☐ 146 Ralph Houk MG	.60	.30	.06
☐ 147 Bob Priddy	.40	.20	.04
☐ 148 John Mayberry	.60	.30	.06
☐ 149 Mike Hershberger	.40	.20	.04
☐ 150 Sam McDowell	.60	.30	.06
☐ 151 Tommy Davis	.60	.30	.06
☐ 152 Angels Rookies	.40	.20	.04
Lloyd Allen			
Winston Llenas			
☐ 153 Gary Ross	.40	.20	.04
☐ 154 Cesar Gutierrez	.40	.20	.04
☐ 155 Ken Henderson	.40	.20	.04
☐ 156 Bart Johnson	.40	.20	.04
☐ 157 Bob Bailey	.40	.20	.04
☐ 158 Jerry Reuss	.75	.35	.07
☐ 159 Jarvis Tatum	.40	.20	.04
☐ 160 Tom Seaver	42.00	20.00	4.00
☐ 161 Coin Checklist	3.00	.30	.06
☐ 162 Jack Billingham	.40	.20	.04

☐	163	Buck Martinez	.40	.20	.04
☐	164	Reds Rookies	.60	.30	.06
		Frank Duffy			
		Milt Wilcox			
☐	165	Cesar Tovar	.40	.20	.04
☐	166	Joe Hoerner	.40	.20	.04
☐	167	Tom Grieve	1.00	.50	.10
☐	168	Bruce Dal Canton	.40	.20	.04
☐	169	Ed Herrmann	.40	.20	.04
☐	170	Mike Cuellar	.60	.30	.06
☐	171	Bobby Wine	.40	.20	.04
☐	172	Duke Sims	.40	.20	.04
☐	173	Gil Garrido	.40	.20	.04
☐	174	Dave LaRoche	.40	.20	.04
☐	175	Jim Hickman	.40	.20	.04
☐	176	Red Sox Rookies	.40	.20	.04
		Bob Montgomery			
		Doug Griffin			
☐	177	Hal McRae	.75	.35	.07
☐	178	Dave Duncan	.40	.20	.04
☐	179	Mike Corkins	.40	.20	.04
☐	180	Al Kaline UER	15.00	7.50	1.50
		(Home instead			
		of Birth)			
☐	181	Hal Lanier	.60	.30	.06
☐	182	Al Downing	.60	.30	.06
☐	183	Gil Hodges MG	3.00	1.50	.30
☐	184	Stan Bahnsen	.40	.20	.04
☐	185	Julian Javier	.40	.20	.04
☐	186	Bob Spence	.40	.20	.04
☐	187	Ted Abernathy	.40	.20	.04
☐	188	Dodgers Rookies	2.25	1.10	.22
		Bob Valentine			
		Mike Strahler			
☐	189	George Mitterwald	.40	.20	.04
☐	190	Bob Tolan	.60	.30	.06
☐	191	Mike Andrews	.40	.20	.04
☐	192	Billy Wilson	.40	.20	.04
☐	193	Bob Grich	3.00	1.50	.30
☐	194	Mike Lum	.40	.20	.04
☐	195	AL Playoff Game 1	1.75	.85	.17
		Powell muscles Twins			
☐	196	AL Playoff Game 2	1.75	.85	.17
		McNally makes it			
		two straight			
☐	197	AL Playoff Game 3	3.00	1.50	.30
		Palmer mows'em down			
☐	198	AL Playoff Summary	1.75	.85	.17
		Orioles celebrate			
☐	199	NL Playoff Game 1	1.75	.85	.17
		Cline pinch-triple			
		decides it			
☐	200	NL Playoff Game 2	1.75	.85	.17
		Tolan scores for			
		third time			
☐	201	NL Playoff Game 3	1.75	.85	.17
		Cline scores			
		winning run			
☐	202	NL Playoff Summary	1.75	.85	.17
		Reds celebrate			
☐	203	Larry Gura	.75	.35	.07
☐	204	Brewers Rookies	.40	.20	.04
		Bernie Smith			
		George Kopacz			
☐	205	Gerry Moses	.40	.20	.04
☐	206	Checklist 3	3.00	.30	.06
☐	207	Alan Foster	.40	.20	.04
☐	208	Billy Martin MG	3.00	1.50	.30
☐	209	Steve Renko	.40	.20	.04
☐	210	Rod Carew	33.00	15.00	3.00
☐	211	Phil Hennigan	.40	.20	.04
☐	212	Rich Hebner	.60	.30	.06
☐	213	Frank Baker	.40	.20	.04
☐	214	Al Ferrara	.60	.30	.06
☐	215	Diego Segui	.40	.20	.04
☐	216	Cards Rookies	.40	.20	.04
		Reggie Cleveland			
		Luis Melendez			
☐	217	Ed Stroud	.40	.20	.04
☐	218	Tony Cloninger	.40	.20	.04
☐	219	Elrod Hendricks	.40	.20	.04
☐	220	Ron Santo	1.50	.75	.15
☐	221	Dave Morehead	.40	.20	.04
☐	222	Bob Watson	.60	.30	.06
☐	223	Cecil Upshaw	.40	.20	.04
☐	224	Alan Gallagher	.40	.20	.04
☐	225	Gary Peters	.60	.30	.06
☐	226	Bill Russell	.75	.35	.07
☐	227	Floyd Weaver	.40	.20	.04
☐	228	Wayne Garrett	.40	.20	.04
☐	229	Jim Hannan	.40	.20	.04
☐	230	Willie Stargell	8.50	4.25	.85
☐	231	Indians Rookies	.60	.30	.06
		Vince Colbert			
		John Lowenstein			
☐	232	John Strohmayer	.40	.20	.04
☐	233	Larry Bowa	1.75	.85	.17
☐	234	Jim Lyttle	.40	.20	.04
☐	235	Nate Colbert	.40	.20	.04
☐	236	Bob Humphreys	.40	.20	.04
☐	237	Cesar Cedeno	2.00	1.00	.20
☐	238	Chuck Dobson	.40	.20	.04
☐	239	Red Schoendienst MG	1.25	.60	.12
☐	240	Clyde Wright	.40	.20	.04
☐	241	Dave Nelson	.40	.20	.04
☐	242	Jim Ray	.40	.20	.04
☐	243	Carlos May	.40	.20	.04
☐	244	Bob Tillman	.40	.20	.04
☐	245	Jim Kaat	2.00	1.00	.20
☐	246	Tony Taylor	.40	.20	.04
☐	247	Royals Rookies	.75	.35	.07
		Jerry Cram			
		Paul Splittorff			
☐	248	Hoyt Wilhelm	3.50	1.75	.35
☐	249	Chico Salmon	.40	.20	.04
☐	250	Johnny Bench	45.00	22.50	4.50
☐	251	Frank Reberger	.40	.20	.04
☐	252	Eddie Leon	.40	.20	.04
☐	253	Bill Sudakis	.40	.20	.04
☐	254	Cal Koonce	.40	.20	.04
☐	255	Bob Robertson	.40	.20	.04
☐	256	Tony Gonzalez	.40	.20	.04
☐	257	Nelson Briles	.60	.30	.06
☐	258	Dick Green	.40	.20	.04
☐	259	Dave Marshall	.40	.20	.04
☐	260	Tommy Harper	.60	.30	.06
☐	261	Darold Knowles	.40	.20	.04
☐	262	Padres Rookies	.40	.20	.04
		Jim Williams			
		Dave Robinson			
☐	263	John Ellis	.40	.20	.04
☐	264	Joe Morgan	8.50	4.25	.85
☐	265	Jim Northrup	.75	.35	.07
☐	266	Bill Stoneman	.50	.25	.05
☐	267	Rich Morales	.50	.25	.05
☐	268	Phillies Team	1.25	.60	.12
☐	269	Gail Hopkins	.50	.25	.05
☐	270	Rico Carty	.75	.35	.07
☐	271	Bill Zepp	.50	.25	.05
☐	272	Tommy Helms	.75	.35	.07
☐	273	Pete Richert	.50	.25	.05
☐	274	Ron Slocum	.50	.25	.05
☐	275	Vada Pinson	1.25	.60	.12
☐	276	Giants Rookies	6.00	3.00	.60
		Mike Davison			
		George Foster			
☐	277	Gary Waslewski	.50	.25	.05
☐	278	Jerry Grote	.50	.25	.05
☐	279	Lefty Phillips MG	.50	.25	.05
☐	280	Fergie Jenkins	6.00	2.50	.50
☐	281	Danny Walton	.50	.25	.05
☐	282	Jose Pagan	.50	.25	.05
☐	283	Dick Such	.50	.25	.05
☐	284	Jim Gosger	.50	.25	.05
☐	285	Sal Bando	.75	.35	.07
☐	286	Jerry McNertney	.50	.25	.05
☐	287	Mike Fiore	.50	.25	.05
☐	288	Joe Moeller	.50	.25	.05
☐	289	White Sox Team	1.25	.60	.12
☐	290	Tony Oliva	2.25	1.10	.22
☐	291	George Culver	.50	.25	.05
☐	292	Jay Johnstone	.75	.35	.07
☐	293	Pat Corrales	.75	.35	.07
☐	294	Steve Dunning	.50	.25	.05
☐	295	Bobby Bonds	3.50	1.75	.35
☐	296	Tom Timmermann	.50	.25	.05
☐	297	Johnny Briggs	.50	.25	.05
☐	298	Jim Nelson	.50	.25	.05
☐	299	Ed Kirkpatrick	.50	.25	.05
☐	300	Brooks Robinson	12.00	6.00	1.20
☐	301	Earl Wilson	.50	.25	.05
☐	302	Phil Gagliano	.50	.25	.05
☐	303	Lindy McDaniel	.50	.25	.05
☐	304	Ron Brand	.50	.25	.05
☐	305	Reggie Smith	1.00	.50	.10
☐	306	Jim Nash	.50	.25	.05
☐	307	Don Wert	.50	.25	.05
☐	308	St. Louis Cardinals	1.25	.60	.12
		Team Card			
☐	309	Dick Ellsworth	.75	.35	.07
☐	310	Tommie Agee	.50	.25	.05
☐	311	Lee Stange	.50	.25	.05
☐	312	Harry Walker MG	.50	.25	.05
☐	313	Tom Hall	.50	.25	.05
☐	314	Jeff Torborg	.75	.35	.07
☐	315	Ron Fairly	.75	.35	.07

☐ 316	Fred Scherman	.50	.25	.05
☐ 317	Athletic Rookies	.50	.25	.05
	Jim Driscoll			
	Angel Mangual			
☐ 318	Rudy May	.50	.25	.05
☐ 319	Ty Cline	.50	.25	.05
☐ 320	Dave McNally	.75	.35	.07
☐ 321	Tom Matchick	.50	.25	.05
☐ 322	Jim Beauchamp	.50	.25	.05
☐ 323	Billy Champion	.50	.25	.05
☐ 324	Graig Nettles	2.25	1.10	.22
☐ 325	Juan Marichal	5.00	2.50	.50
☐ 326	Richie Scheinblum	.50	.25	.05
☐ 327	World Series Game 1	1.75	.85	.17
	Powell homers to			
	opposite field			
☐ 328	World Series Game 2	1.75	.85	.17
	Don Buford			
☐ 329	World Series Game 3	2.50	1.25	.25
	Frank Robinson			
	shows muscle			
☐ 330	World Series Game 4	1.75	.85	.17
	Reds stay alive			
☐ 331	World Series Game 5	2.50	1.25	.25
	Brooks Robinson			
	commits robbery			
☐ 332	World Series Summary	1.75	.85	.17
	Orioles celebrate			
☐ 333	Clay Kirby	.50	.25	.05
☐ 334	Roberto Pena	.50	.25	.05
☐ 335	Jerry Koosman	1.25	.60	.12
☐ 336	Detroit Tigers	1.25	.60	.12
	Team Card			
☐ 337	Jesus Alou	.50	.25	.05
☐ 338	Gene Tenace	.75	.35	.07
☐ 339	Wayne Simpson	.50	.25	.05
☐ 340	Rico Petrocelli	.75	.35	.07
☐ 341	Steve Garvey	85.00	42.50	8.50
☐ 342	Frank Tepedino	.50	.25	.05
☐ 343	Pirates Rookies	.50	.25	.05
	Ed Acosta			
	Milt May			
☐ 344	Ellie Rodriguez	.50	.25	.05
☐ 345	Joel Horlen	.50	.25	.05
☐ 346	Lum Harris MG	.50	.25	.05
☐ 347	Ted Uhlaender	.50	.25	.05
☐ 348	Fred Norman	.50	.25	.05
☐ 349	Rich Reese	.50	.25	.05
☐ 350	Billy Williams	5.00	2.50	.50
☐ 351	Jim Shellenback	.50	.25	.05
☐ 352	Denny Doyle	.50	.25	.05
☐ 353	Carl Taylor	.50	.25	.05
☐ 354	Don McMahon	.50	.25	.05
☐ 355	Bud Harrelson	.75	.35	.07
☐ 356	Bob Locker	.50	.25	.05
☐ 357	Reds Team	1.25	.60	.12
☐ 358	Danny Cater	.50	.25	.05
☐ 359	Ron Reed	.50	.25	.05
☐ 360	Jim Fregosi	.75	.35	.07
☐ 361	Don Sutton	4.50	2.25	.45
☐ 362	Orioles Rookies	.50	.25	.05
	Mike Adamson			
	Roger Freed			
☐ 363	Mike Nagy	.50	.25	.05
☐ 364	Tommy Dean	.50	.25	.05
☐ 365	Bob Johnson	.50	.25	.05
☐ 366	Ron Stone	.50	.25	.05
☐ 367	Dalton Jones	.50	.25	.05
☐ 368	Bob Veale	.75	.35	.07
☐ 369	Checklist 4	3.00	.30	.06
☐ 370	Joe Torre	2.50	1.25	.25
☐ 371	Jack Hiatt	.50	.25	.05
☐ 372	Lew Krausse	.50	.25	.05
☐ 373	Tom McCraw	.50	.25	.05
☐ 374	Clete Boyer	.75	.35	.07
☐ 375	Steve Hargan	.50	.25	.05
☐ 376	Expos Rookies	.50	.25	.05
	Clyde Mashore			
	Ernie McAnally			
☐ 377	Greg Garrett	.50	.25	.05
☐ 378	Tito Fuentes	.50	.25	.05
☐ 379	Wayne Granger	.50	.25	.05
☐ 380	Ted Williams MG	5.00	2.50	.50
☐ 381	Fred Gladding	.50	.25	.05
☐ 382	Jake Gibbs	.50	.25	.05
☐ 383	Rod Gaspar	.50	.25	.05
☐ 384	Rollie Fingers	9.00	4.50	.90
☐ 385	Maury Wills	1.75	.85	.17
☐ 386	Red Sox Team	1.25	.60	.12
☐ 387	Ron Herbel	.50	.25	.05
☐ 388	Al Oliver	1.75	.85	.17
☐ 389	Ed Brinkman	.50	.25	.05
☐ 390	Glenn Beckert	.75	.35	.07
☐ 391	Twins Rookies	.75	.35	.07
	Steve Brye			
	Cotton Nash			
☐ 392	Grant Jackson	.50	.25	.05
☐ 393	Merv Rettenmund	.50	.25	.05
☐ 394	Clay Carroll	.75	.35	.07
☐ 395	Roy White	1.00	.50	.10
☐ 396	Dick Schofield	.75	.35	.07
☐ 397	Alvin Dark MG	1.00	.50	.10
☐ 398	Howie Reed	.75	.35	.07
☐ 399	Jim French	.75	.35	.07
☐ 400	Hank Aaron	37.50	16.00	3.00
☐ 401	Tom Murphy	.75	.35	.07
☐ 402	Dodgers Team	1.75	.85	.17
☐ 403	Joe Coleman	.75	.35	.07
☐ 404	Astros Rookies	.75	.35	.07
	Buddy Harris			
	Roger Metzger			
☐ 405	Leo Cardenas	.75	.35	.07
☐ 406	Ray Sadecki	.75	.35	.07
☐ 407	Joe Rudi	1.00	.50	.10
☐ 408	Rafael Robles	.75	.35	.07
☐ 409	Don Pavletich	.75	.35	.07
☐ 410	Ken Holtzman	1.00	.50	.10
☐ 411	George Spriggs	.75	.35	.07
☐ 412	Jerry Johnson	.75	.35	.07
☐ 413	Pat Kelly	.75	.35	.07
☐ 414	Woodie Fryman	.75	.35	.07
☐ 415	Mike Hegan	.75	.35	.07
☐ 416	Gene Alley	1.00	.50	.10
☐ 417	Dick Hall	.75	.35	.07
☐ 418	Adolfo Phillips	.75	.35	.07
☐ 419	Ron Hansen	.75	.35	.07
☐ 420	Jim Merritt	.75	.35	.07
☐ 421	John Stephenson	.75	.35	.07
☐ 422	Frank Bertaina	.75	.35	.07
☐ 423	Tigers Rookies	.75	.35	.07
	Dennis Saunders			
	Tim Marting			
☐ 424	R. Rodriquez	.75	.35	.07
☐ 425	Doug Rader	1.25	.60	.12
☐ 426	Chris Cannizzaro	.75	.35	.07
☐ 427	Bernie Allen	.75	.35	.07
☐ 428	Jim McAndrew	.75	.35	.07
☐ 429	Chuck Hinton	.75	.35	.07
☐ 430	Wes Parker	1.00	.50	.10
☐ 431	Tom Burgmeier	.75	.35	.07
☐ 432	Bob Didier	.75	.35	.07
☐ 433	Skip Lockwood	.75	.35	.07
☐ 434	Gary Sutherland	.75	.35	.07
☐ 435	Jose Cardenal	.75	.35	.07
☐ 436	Wilbur Wood	1.00	.50	.10
☐ 437	Danny Murtaugh MG	.75	.35	.07
☐ 438	Mike McCormick	1.00	.50	.10
☐ 439	Phillies Rookies	2.25	1.10	.22
	Greg Luzinski			
	Scott Reid			
☐ 440	Bert Campaneris	1.00	.50	.10
☐ 441	Milt Pappas	1.00	.50	.10
☐ 442	California Angels	1.50	.75	.15
	Team Card			
☐ 443	Rich Robertson	.75	.35	.07
☐ 444	Jimmie Price	.75	.35	.07
☐ 445	Art Shamsky	.75	.35	.07
☐ 446	Bobby Bolin	.75	.35	.07
☐ 447	Cesar Geronimo	.75	.35	.07
☐ 448	Dave Roberts	.75	.35	.07
☐ 449	Brant Alyea	.75	.35	.07
☐ 450	Bob Gibson	8.50	4.25	.85
☐ 451	Joe Keough	.75	.35	.07
☐ 452	John Boccabella	.75	.35	.07
☐ 453	Terry Crowley	.75	.35	.07
☐ 454	Mike Paul	.75	.35	.07
☐ 455	Don Kessinger	1.00	.50	.10
☐ 456	Bob Meyer	.75	.35	.07
☐ 457	Willie Smith	.75	.35	.07
☐ 458	White Sox Rookies	.75	.35	.07
	Ron Lolich			
	Dave Lemonds			
☐ 459	Jim Lefebvre	1.25	.60	.12
☐ 460	Fritz Peterson	.75	.35	.07
☐ 461	Jim Ray Hart	1.00	.50	.10
☐ 462	Senators Team	1.50	.75	.15
☐ 463	Tom Kelley	.75	.35	.07
☐ 464	Aurelio Rodriguez	.75	.35	.07
☐ 465	Tim McCarver	1.50	.75	.15
☐ 466	Ken Berry	.75	.35	.07
☐ 467	Al Santorini	.75	.35	.07
☐ 468	Frank Fernandez	.75	.35	.07
☐ 469	Bob Aspromonte	.75	.35	.07
☐ 470	Bob Oliver	.75	.35	.07
☐ 471	Tom Griffin	.75	.35	.07
☐ 472	Ken Rudolph	.75	.35	.07
☐ 473	Gary Wagner	.75	.35	.07

☐ 474 Jim Fairey	.75	.35	.07
☐ 475 Ron Perranoski	1.00	.50	.10
☐ 476 Dal Maxvill	.75	.35	.07
☐ 477 Earl Weaver MG	1.50	.75	.15
☐ 478 Bernie Carbo	.75	.35	.07
☐ 479 Dennis Higgins	.75	.35	.07
☐ 480 Manny Sanguillen	1.25	.60	.12
☐ 481 Daryl Patterson	.75	.35	.07
☐ 482 Padres Team	1.50	.75	.15
☐ 483 Gene Michael	1.00	.50	.10
☐ 484 Don Wilson	.75	.35	.07
☐ 485 Ken McMullen	.75	.35	.07
☐ 486 Steve Huntz	.75	.35	.07
☐ 487 Paul Schaal	.75	.35	.07
☐ 488 Jerry Stephenson	.75	.35	.07
☐ 489 Luis Alvarado	.75	.35	.07
☐ 490 Deron Johnson	1.00	.50	.10
☐ 491 Jim Hardin	.75	.35	.07
☐ 492 Ken Boswell	.75	.35	.07
☐ 493 Dave May	.75	.35	.07
☐ 494 Braves Rookies	1.00	.50	.10
Ralph Garr			
Rick Kester			
☐ 495 Felipe Alou	1.00	.50	.10
☐ 496 Woody Woodward	1.00	.50	.10
☐ 497 Horacio Pina	.75	.35	.07
☐ 498 John Kennedy	.75	.35	.07
☐ 499 Checklist 5	3.00	.30	.06
☐ 500 Jim Perry	1.25	.60	.12
☐ 501 Andy Etchebarren	.75	.35	.07
☐ 502 Cubs Team	1.75	.85	.17
☐ 503 Gates Brown	1.00	.50	.10
☐ 504 Ken Wright	.75	.35	.07
☐ 505 Ollie Brown	.75	.35	.07
☐ 506 Bobby Knoop	.75	.35	.07
☐ 507 George Stone	.75	.35	.07
☐ 508 Roger Repoz	.75	.35	.07
☐ 509 Jim Grant	.75	.35	.07
☐ 510 Ken Harrelson	1.25	.60	.12
☐ 511 Chris Short	.75	.35	.07
☐ 512 Red Sox Rookies	.75	.35	.07
Dick Mills			
Mike Garman			
☐ 513 Nolan Ryan	150.00	75.00	15.00
☐ 514 Ron Woods	.75	.35	.07
☐ 515 Carl Morton	.75	.35	.07
☐ 516 Ted Kubiak	.75	.35	.07
☐ 517 Charlie Fox MG	.75	.35	.07
☐ 518 Joe Grzenda	.75	.35	.07
☐ 519 Willie Crawford	.75	.35	.07
☐ 520 Tommy John	3.00	1.50	.30
☐ 521 Leron Lee	.75	.35	.07
☐ 522 Twins Team	1.50	.75	.15
☐ 523 John Odom	.75	.35	.07
☐ 524 Mickey Stanley	2.25	1.10	.22
☐ 525 Ernie Banks	27.00	13.50	2.70
☐ 526 Ray Jarvis	1.75	.85	.17
☐ 527 Cleon Jones	1.75	.85	.17
☐ 528 Wally Bunker	1.75	.85	.17
☐ 529 NL Rookie Infielders	4.00	2.00	.40
Enzo Hernandez			
Bill Buckner			
Marty Perez			
☐ 530 Carl Yastrzemski	42.00	20.00	4.00
☐ 531 Mike Torrez	1.75	.85	.17
☐ 532 Bill Rigney MG	1.75	.85	.17
☐ 533 Mike Ryan	1.75	.85	.17
☐ 534 Luke Walker	1.75	.85	.17
☐ 535 Curt Flood	2.50	1.25	.25
☐ 536 Claude Raymond	1.75	.85	.17
☐ 537 Tom Egan	1.75	.85	.17
☐ 538 Angel Bravo	1.75	.85	.17
☐ 539 Larry Brown	1.75	.85	.17
☐ 540 Larry Dierker	2.25	1.10	.22
☐ 541 Bob Burda	1.75	.85	.17
☐ 542 Bob Miller	1.75	.85	.17
☐ 543 New York Yankees	3.50	1.75	.35
Team Card			
☐ 544 Vida Blue	4.00	2.00	.40
☐ 545 Dick Dietz	1.75	.85	.17
☐ 546 John Matias	1.75	.85	.17
☐ 547 Pat Dobson	1.75	.85	.17
☐ 548 Don Mason	1.75	.85	.17
☐ 549 Jim Brewer	1.75	.85	.17
☐ 550 Harmon Killebrew	16.00	8.00	1.60
☐ 551 Frank Linzy	1.75	.85	.17
☐ 552 Buddy Bradford	1.75	.85	.17
☐ 553 Kevin Collins	1.75	.85	.17
☐ 554 Lowell Palmer	1.75	.85	.17
☐ 555 Walt Williams	1.75	.85	.17
☐ 556 Jim McGlothlin	1.75	.85	.17
☐ 557 Tom Satriano	1.75	.85	.17
☐ 558 Hector Torres	1.75	.85	.17
☐ 559 AL Rookie Pitchers	1.75	.85	.17
Terry Cox			
Bill Gogolewski			
Gary Jones			
☐ 560 Rusty Staub	3.00	1.50	.30
☐ 561 Syd O'Brien	1.75	.85	.17
☐ 562 Dave Giusti	1.75	.85	.17
☐ 563 Giants Team	3.50	1.75	.35
☐ 564 Al Fitzmorris	1.75	.85	.17
☐ 565 Jim Wynn	2.50	1.25	.25
☐ 566 Tim Cullen	1.75	.85	.17
☐ 567 Walt Alston MG	3.00	1.50	.30
☐ 568 Sal Campisi	1.75	.85	.17
☐ 569 Ivan Murrell	1.75	.85	.17
☐ 570 Jim Palmer	25.00	12.50	2.50
☐ 571 Ted Sizemore	1.75	.85	.17
☐ 572 Jerry Kenney	1.75	.85	.17
☐ 573 Ed Kranepool	2.25	1.10	.22
☐ 574 Jim Bunning	3.50	1.75	.35
☐ 575 Bill Freehan	2.50	1.25	.25
☐ 576 Cubs Rookies	1.75	.85	.17
Adrian Garrett			
Brock Davis			
Garry Jestadt			
☐ 577 Jim Lonborg	2.50	1.25	.25
☐ 578 Ron Hunt	1.75	.85	.17
☐ 579 Marty Pattin	1.75	.85	.17
☐ 580 Tony Perez	5.00	2.50	.50
☐ 581 Roger Nelson	1.75	.85	.17
☐ 582 Dave Cash	1.75	.85	.17
☐ 583 Ron Cook	1.75	.85	.17
☐ 584 Indians Team	3.50	1.75	.35
☐ 585 Willie Davis	2.50	1.25	.25
☐ 586 Dick Woodson	1.75	.85	.17
☐ 587 Sonny Jackson	1.75	.85	.17
☐ 588 Tom Bradley	1.75	.85	.17
☐ 589 Bob Barton	1.75	.85	.17
☐ 590 Alex Johnson	1.75	.85	.17
☐ 591 Jackie Brown	1.75	.85	.17
☐ 592 Randy Hundley	1.75	.85	.17
☐ 593 Jack Aker	1.75	.85	.17
☐ 594 Cards Rookies	3.00	1.50	.30
Bob Chlupsa			
Bob Stinson			
Al Hrabosky			
☐ 595 Dave Johnson	3.00	1.50	.30
☐ 596 Mike Jorgensen	1.75	.85	.17
☐ 597 Ken Suarez	1.75	.85	.17
☐ 598 Rick Wise	2.25	1.10	.22
☐ 599 Norm Cash	3.00	1.50	.30
☐ 600 Willie Mays	65.00	32.50	6.50
☐ 601 Ken Tatum	1.75	.85	.17
☐ 602 Marty Martinez	1.75	.85	.17
☐ 603 Pirates Team	3.50	1.75	.35
☐ 604 John Gelnar	1.75	.85	.17
☐ 605 Orlando Cepeda	4.50	2.25	.45
☐ 606 Chuck Taylor	1.75	.85	.17
☐ 607 Paul Ratliff	1.75	.85	.17
☐ 608 Mike Wegener	1.75	.85	.17
☐ 609 Leo Durocher MG	3.00	1.50	.30
☐ 610 Amos Otis	2.25	1.10	.22
☐ 611 Tom Phoebus	1.75	.85	.17
☐ 612 Indians Rookies	1.75	.85	.17
Lou Camilli			
Ted Ford			
Steve Mingori			
☐ 613 Pedro Borbon	1.75	.85	.17
☐ 614 Billy Cowan	1.75	.85	.17
☐ 615 Mel Stottlemyre	2.50	1.25	.25
☐ 616 Larry Hisle	1.75	.85	.17
☐ 617 Clay Dalrymple	1.75	.85	.17
☐ 618 Tug McGraw	3.00	1.50	.30
☐ 619A Checklist 6	3.00	.30	.06
(copyright on back)			
☐ 619B Checklist 6	4.00	.40	.08
(no copyright)			
☐ 620 Frank Howard	3.00	1.50	.30
☐ 621 Ron Bryant	1.75	.85	.17
☐ 622 Joe Lahoud	1.75	.85	.17
☐ 623 Pat Jarvis	1.75	.85	.17
☐ 624 Athletics Team	3.50	1.75	.35
☐ 625 Lou Brock	18.00	9.00	1.80
☐ 626 Freddie Patek	2.25	1.10	.22
☐ 627 Steve Hamilton	1.75	.85	.17
☐ 628 John Bateman	1.75	.85	.17
☐ 629 John Hiller	2.25	1.10	.22
☐ 630 Roberto Clemente	45.00	22.50	4.50
☐ 631 Eddie Fisher	1.75	.85	.17
☐ 632 Darrel Chaney	1.75	.85	.17
☐ 633 AL Rookie Outfielders	1.75	.85	.17
Bobby Brooks			
Pete Koegel			
Scott Northey			
☐ 634 Phil Regan	2.25	1.10	.22

☐ 635 Bobby Murcer	3.50	1.75	.35
☐ 636 Denny Lemaster	1.75	.85	.17
☐ 637 Dave Bristol MG	1.75	.85	.17
☐ 638 Stan Williams	1.75	.85	.17
☐ 639 Tom Haller	1.75	.85	.17
☐ 640 Frank Robinson	33.00	15.00	3.00
☐ 641 New York Mets	4.00	2.00	.40
Team Card			
☐ 642 Jim Roland	1.75	.85	.17
☐ 643 Rick Reichardt	1.75	.85	.17
☐ 644 Jim Stewart SP	5.00	2.50	.50
☐ 645 Jim Maloney SP	5.00	2.50	.50
☐ 646 Bobby Floyd SP	5.00	2.50	.50
☐ 647 Juan Pizarro	4.00	2.00	.40
☐ 648 Mets Rookies SP	8.00	4.00	.80
Rich Folkers			
Ted Martinez			
John Matlack			
☐ 649 Sparky Lyle SP	8.00	4.00	.80
☐ 650 Rich Allen SP	12.00	6.00	1.20
☐ 651 Jerry Robertson SP	5.00	2.50	.50
☐ 652 Braves Team	8.00	4.00	.80
☐ 653 Russ Snyder SP	5.00	2.50	.50
☐ 654 Don Shaw SP	5.00	2.50	.50
☐ 655 Mike Epstein SP	5.00	2.50	.50
☐ 656 Gerry Nyman SP	5.00	2.50	.50
☐ 657 Jose Azcue	4.00	2.00	.40
☐ 658 Paul Lindblad SP	5.00	2.50	.50
☐ 659 Byron Browne SP	5.00	2.50	.50
☐ 660 Ray Culp	4.00	2.00	.40
☐ 661 Chuck Tanner MG SP	5.00	2.50	.50
☐ 662 Mike Hedlund SP	5.00	2.50	.50
☐ 663 Marv Staehle	4.00	2.00	.40
☐ 664 Rookie Pitchers SP	5.00	2.50	.50
Archie Reynolds			
Bob Reynolds			
Ken Reynolds			
☐ 665 Ron Swoboda SP	5.00	2.50	.50
☐ 666 Gene Brabender SP	5.00	2.50	.50
☐ 667 Pete Ward	4.00	2.00	.40
☐ 668 Gary Neibauer	4.00	2.00	.40
☐ 669 Ike Brown SP	5.00	2.50	.50
☐ 670 Bill Hands	4.00	2.00	.40
☐ 671 Bill Voss SP	5.00	2.50	.50
☐ 672 Ed Crosby SP	5.00	2.50	.50
☐ 673 Gerry Janeski SP	5.00	2.50	.50
☐ 674 Montreal Expos	8.00	4.00	.80
Team Card			
☐ 675 Dave Boswell	4.00	2.00	.40
☐ 676 Tommie Reynolds	4.00	2.00	.40
☐ 677 Jack DiLauro SP	5.00	2.50	.50
☐ 678 George Thomas	4.00	2.00	.40
☐ 679 Don O'Riley	4.00	2.00	.40
☐ 680 Don Mincher SP	5.00	2.50	.50
☐ 681 Bill Butler	4.00	2.00	.40
☐ 682 Terry Harmon	4.00	2.00	.40
☐ 683 Bill Burbach SP	5.00	2.50	.50
☐ 684 Curt Motton	4.00	2.00	.40
☐ 685 Moe Drabowsky	4.00	2.00	.40
☐ 686 Chico Ruiz SP	5.00	2.50	.50
☐ 687 Ron Taylor SP	5.00	2.50	.50
☐ 688 Sparky Anderson MG SP	10.00	5.00	1.00
☐ 689 Frank Baker	4.00	2.00	.40
☐ 690 Bob Moose	4.00	2.00	.40
☐ 691 Bobby Heise	4.00	2.00	.40
☐ 692 AL Rookie Pitchers SP	5.00	2.50	.50
Hal Haydel			
Rogelio Moret			
Wayne Twitchell			
☐ 693 Jose Pena SP	5.00	2.50	.50
☐ 694 Rick Renick SP	5.00	2.50	.50
☐ 695 Joe Niekro	5.00	2.50	.50
☐ 696 Jerry Morales	4.00	2.00	.40
☐ 697 Rickey Clark SP	5.00	2.50	.50
☐ 698 Milwaukee Brewers SP	10.00	5.00	1.00
Team Card			
☐ 699 Jim Britton	4.00	2.00	.40
☐ 700 Boog Powell SP	10.00	5.00	1.00
☐ 701 Bob Garibaldi	4.00	2.00	.40
☐ 702 Milt Ramirez	4.00	2.00	.40
☐ 703 Mike Kekich	4.00	2.00	.40
☐ 704 J.C. Martin SP	5.00	2.50	.50
☐ 705 Dick Selma SP	5.00	2.50	.50
☐ 706 Joe Foy SP	5.00	2.50	.50
☐ 707 Fred Lasher	4.00	2.00	.40
☐ 708 Russ Nagelson SP	5.00	2.50	.50
☐ 709 Rookie Outfielders SP	30.00	15.00	3.00
Dusty Baker			
Don Baylor			
Tom Paciorek			
☐ 710 Sonny Siebert	4.00	2.00	.40
☐ 711 Larry Stahl SP	5.00	2.50	.50
☐ 712 Jose Martinez	4.00	2.00	.40
☐ 713 Mike Marshall SP	6.00	3.00	.60
☐ 714 Dick Williams MG SP	6.00	3.00	.60
☐ 715 Horace Clarke SP	5.00	2.50	.50
☐ 716 Dave Leonhard	4.00	2.00	.40
☐ 717 Tommie Aaron SP	6.00	3.00	.60
☐ 718 Billy Wynne	4.00	2.00	.40
☐ 719 Jerry May SP	5.00	2.50	.50
☐ 720 Matty Alou	4.00	2.00	.40
☐ 721 John Morris	4.00	2.00	.40
☐ 722 Houston Astros SP	10.00	5.00	1.00
Team Card			
☐ 723 Vicente Romo SP	5.00	2.50	.50
☐ 724 Tom Tischinski SP	5.00	2.50	.50
☐ 725 Gary Gentry SP	5.00	2.50	.50
☐ 726 Paul Popovich	4.00	2.00	.40
☐ 727 Ray Lamb SP	5.00	2.50	.50
☐ 728 NL Rookie Outfielders	4.00	2.00	.40
Wayne Redmond			
Keith Lampard			
Bernie Williams			
☐ 729 Dick Billings	4.00	2.00	.40
☐ 730 Jim Rooker	4.00	2.00	.40
☐ 731 Jim Qualls SP	5.00	2.50	.50
☐ 732 Bob Reed	4.00	2.00	.40
☐ 733 Lee Maye SP	5.00	2.50	.50
☐ 734 Rob Gardner SP	5.00	2.50	.50
☐ 735 Mike Shannon SP	6.00	3.00	.60
☐ 736 Mel Queen SP	5.00	2.50	.50
☐ 737 Preston Gomez MG SP	5.00	2.50	.50
☐ 738 Russ Gibson SP	5.00	2.50	.50
☐ 739 Barry Lersch SP	5.00	2.50	.50
☐ 740 Luis Aparicio SP	15.00	7.50	1.50
☐ 741 Skip Guinn	4.00	2.00	.40
☐ 742 Kansas City Royals	8.00	4.00	.80
Team Card			
☐ 743 John O'Donoghue SP	5.00	2.50	.50
☐ 744 Chuck Manuel SP	5.00	2.50	.50
☐ 745 Sandy Alomar SP	5.00	2.50	.50
☐ 746 Andy Kosco	4.00	2.00	.40
☐ 747 NL Rookie Pitchers	4.00	2.00	.40
Al Severinsen			
Scipio Spinks			
Balor Moore			
☐ 748 John Purdin SP	5.00	2.50	.50
☐ 749 Ken Szotkiewicz	4.00	2.00	.40
☐ 750 Denny McLain SP	10.00	5.00	1.00
☐ 751 Al Weis SP	6.00	3.00	.60
☐ 752 Dick Drago	4.00	2.00	.40

1972 Topps

The cards in this 787-card set measure 2 1/2" by 3 1/2". The 1972 Topps set contained the most cards ever for a Topps set to that point in time. Features appearing for the first time were "Boyhood Photos" (KP: 341-348 and 491-498), Awards and Trophy cards (621-626), "In Action" (distributed throughout the set), and "Traded Cards" (TR: 751-757). Other subsets included League Leaders (85-96), Playoffs cards (221-222), and World Series cards (223-230). The curved lines of the color picture are a departure from the rectangular designs of other years. There is a series of intermediate scarcity (526-656) and the usual high numbers (657-787). The key rookie card in this set is Carlton Fisk.

	NRMT	VG-E	GOOD
COMPLETE SET (787)	1600.00	750.00	160.00
COMMON PLAYER (1-132)	.35	.17	.03
COMMON PLAYER (133-263)	.40	.20	.04
COMMON PLAYER (264-394)	.50	.25	.05
COMMON PLAYER (395-525)	.65	.30	.06
COMMON PLAYER (526-656)	1.75	.85	.17
COMMON PLAYER (657-787)	3.50	1.75	.35
☐ 1 Pittsburgh Pirates	6.00	1.00	.20
Team Card			
☐ 2 Ray Culp	.35	.17	.03
☐ 3 Bob Tolan	.50	.25	.05
☐ 4 Checklist 1	2.00	.20	.04
☐ 5 John Bateman	.35	.17	.03
☐ 6 Fred Scherman	.35	.17	.03
☐ 7 Enzo Hernandez	.35	.17	.03
☐ 8 Ron Swoboda	.50	.25	.05
☐ 9 Stan Williams	.35	.17	.03
☐ 10 Amos Otis	.50	.25	.05
☐ 11 Bobby Valentine	.75	.35	.07
☐ 12 Jose Cardenal	.35	.17	.03
☐ 13 Joe Grzenda	.35	.17	.03
☐ 14 Phillies Rookies	.35	.17	.03
Pete Koegel			
Mike Anderson			
Wayne Twitchell			
☐ 15 Walt Williams	.35	.17	.03
☐ 16 Mike Jorgensen	.35	.17	.03
☐ 17 Dave Duncan	.35	.17	.03
☐ 18A Juan Pizarro	.35	.17	.03
(yellow underline			
C and S of Cubs)			
☐ 18B Juan Pizarro	5.00	2.50	.50
(green underline			
C and S of Cubs)			
☐ 19 Billy Cowan	.35	.17	.03
☐ 20 Don Wilson	.35	.17	.03
☐ 21 Braves Team	1.00	.50	.10
☐ 22 Rob Gardner	.35	.17	.03
☐ 23 Ted Kubiak	.35	.17	.03
☐ 24 Ted Ford	.35	.17	.03
☐ 25 Bill Singer	.50	.25	.05
☐ 26 Andy Etchebarren	.35	.17	.03
☐ 27 Bob Johnson	.35	.17	.03
☐ 28 Twins Rookies	.35	.17	.03
Bob Gebhard			
Steve Brye			
Hal Haydel			
☐ 29A Bill Bonham	.35	.17	.03
(yellow underline			
C and S of Cubs)			
☐ 29B Bill Bonham	5.00	2.50	.50
(green underline			
C and S of Cubs)			
☐ 30 Rico Petrocelli	.50	.25	.05
☐ 31 Cleon Jones	.35	.17	.03
☐ 32 Jones In Action	.35	.17	.03
☐ 33 Billy Martin MG	3.00	1.50	.30
☐ 34 Martin In Action	1.25	.60	.12
☐ 35 Jerry Johnson	.35	.17	.03
☐ 36 Johnson In Action	.35	.17	.03
☐ 37 Carl Yastrzemski	18.00	9.00	1.80
☐ 38 Yastrzemski In Action	8.00	4.00	.80
☐ 39 Bob Barton	.35	.17	.03
☐ 40 Barton In Action	.35	.17	.03
☐ 41 Tommy Davis	.50	.25	.05
☐ 42 Davis In Action	.35	.17	.03
☐ 43 Rick Wise	.35	.17	.03
☐ 44 Wise In Action	.35	.17	.03
☐ 45A Glenn Beckert	.50	.25	.05
(yellow underline			
C and S of Cubs)			
☐ 45B Glenn Beckert	5.00	2.50	.50
(green underline			
C and S of Cubs)			
☐ 46 Beckert In Action	.35	.17	.03
☐ 47 John Ellis	.35	.17	.03
☐ 48 Ellis In Action	.35	.17	.03
☐ 49 Willie Mays	25.00	12.50	2.50
☐ 50 Mays In Action	12.00	6.00	1.20
☐ 51 Harmon Killebrew	4.50	2.25	.45
☐ 52 Killebrew In Action	2.00	1.00	.20
☐ 53 Bud Harrelson	.50	.25	.05
☐ 54 Harrelson In Action	.35	.17	.03
☐ 55 Clyde Wright	.35	.17	.03
☐ 56 Rich Chiles	.35	.17	.03
☐ 57 Bob Oliver	.35	.17	.03
☐ 58 Ernie McAnally	.35	.17	.03
☐ 59 Fred Stanley	.35	.17	.03
☐ 60 Manny Sanguillen	.50	.25	.05
☐ 61 Cubs Rookies	.75	.35	.07
Burt Hooton			
Gene Hiser			
Earl Stephenson			
☐ 62 Angel Mangual	.35	.17	.03
☐ 63 Duke Sims	.35	.17	.03
☐ 64 Pete Broberg	.35	.17	.03
☐ 65 Cesar Cedeno	.75	.35	.07
☐ 66 Ray Corbin	.35	.17	.03
☐ 67 Red Schoendienst MG	1.25	.60	.12
☐ 68 Jim York	.35	.17	.03
☐ 69 Roger Freed	.35	.17	.03
☐ 70 Mike Cuellar	.50	.25	.05
☐ 71 Angels Team	1.00	.50	.10
☐ 72 Bruce Kison	.75	.35	.07
☐ 73 Steve Huntz	.35	.17	.03
☐ 74 Cecil Upshaw	.35	.17	.03
☐ 75 Bert Campaneris	.50	.25	.05
☐ 76 Don Carrithers	.35	.17	.03
☐ 77 Ron Theobald	.35	.17	.03
☐ 78 Steve Arlin	.35	.17	.03
☐ 79 Red Sox Rookies	150.00	75.00	15.00
Mike Garman			
Cecil Cooper			
Carlton Fisk			
☐ 80 Tony Perez	2.50	1.25	.25
☐ 81 Mike Hedlund	.35	.17	.03
☐ 82 Ron Woods	.35	.17	.03
☐ 83 Dalton Jones	.35	.17	.03
☐ 84 Vince Colbert	.35	.17	.03
☐ 85 NL Batting Leaders	1.00	.50	.10
Joe Torre			
Ralph Garr			
Glenn Beckert			
☐ 86 AL Batting Leaders	1.00	.50	.10
Tony Oliva			
Bobby Murcer			
Merv Rettenmund			
☐ 87 NL RBI Leaders	2.00	1.00	.20
Joe Torre			
Willie Stargell			
Hank Aaron			
☐ 88 AL RBI Leaders	2.00	1.00	.20
Harmon Killebrew			
Frank Robinson			
Reggie Smith			
☐ 89 NL Home Run Leaders	2.00	1.00	.20
Willie Stargell			
Hank Aaron			
Lee May			
☐ 90 AL Home Run Leaders	1.50	.75	.15
Bill Melton			
Norm Cash			
Reggie Jackson			
☐ 91 NL ERA Leaders	1.50	.75	.15
Tom Seaver			
Dave Roberts UER			
(photo actually			
Danny Coombs)			
Don Wilson			
☐ 92 AL ERA Leaders	1.00	.50	.10
Vida Blue			
Wilbur Wood			
Jim Palmer			
☐ 93 NL Pitching Leaders	2.00	1.00	.20
Fergie Jenkins			
Steve Carlton			
Al Downing			
Tom Seaver			
☐ 94 AL Pitching Leaders	1.00	.50	.10
Mickey Lolich			
Vida Blue			
Wilbur Wood			
☐ 95 NL Strikeout Leaders	1.50	.75	.15
Tom Seaver			
Fergie Jenkins			
Bill Stoneman			
☐ 96 AL Strikeout Leaders	1.00	.50	.10
Mickey Lolich			
Vida Blue			
Joe Coleman			
☐ 97 Tom Kelley	.35	.17	.03
☐ 98 Chuck Tanner MG	.50	.25	.05
☐ 99 Ross Grimsley	.35	.17	.03
☐ 100 Frank Robinson	5.00	2.50	.50
☐ 101 Astros Rookies	1.50	.75	.15
Bill Greif			
J.R. Richard			
Ray Busse			
☐ 102 Lloyd Allen	.35	.17	.03
☐ 103 Checklist 2	2.00	.20	.04
☐ 104 Toby Harrah	1.25	.60	.12
☐ 105 Gary Gentry	.35	.17	.03
☐ 106 Brewers Team	1.00	.50	.10

☐ 107	Jose Cruz	1.50	.75	.15
☐ 108	Gary Waslewski	.35	.17	.03
☐ 109	Jerry May	.35	.17	.03
☐ 110	Ron Hunt	.35	.17	.03
☐ 111	Jim Grant	.35	.17	.03
☐ 112	Greg Luzinski	1.00	.50	.10
☐ 113	Rogelio Moret	.35	.17	.03
☐ 114	Bill Buckner	1.75	.85	.17
☐ 115	Jim Fregosi	.50	.25	.05
☐ 116	Ed Farmer	.35	.17	.03
☐ 117A	Cleo James	.35	.17	.03
	(yellow underline			
	C and S of Cubs)			
☐ 117B	Cleo James	5.00	2.50	.50
	(green underline			
	C and S of Cubs)			
☐ 118	Skip Lockwood	.35	.17	.03
☐ 119	Marty Perez	.35	.17	.03
☐ 120	Bill Freehan	.75	.35	.07
☐ 121	Ed Sprague	.35	.17	.03
☐ 122	Larry Biittner	.35	.17	.03
☐ 123	Ed Acosta	.35	.17	.03
☐ 124	Yankees Rookies	.35	.17	.03
	Alan Closter			
	Rusty Torres			
	Roger Hambright			
☐ 125	Dave Cash	.35	.17	.03
☐ 126	Bart Johnson	.35	.17	.03
☐ 127	Duffy Dyer	.35	.17	.03
☐ 128	Eddie Watt	.35	.17	.03
☐ 129	Charlie Fox MG	.35	.17	.03
☐ 130	Bob Gibson	5.00	2.50	.50
☐ 131	Jim Nettles	.35	.17	.03
☐ 132	Joe Morgan	5.00	2.50	.50
☐ 133	Joe Keough	.40	.20	.04
☐ 134	Carl Morton	.40	.20	.04
☐ 135	Vada Pinson	.75	.35	.07
☐ 136	Darrell Chaney	.40	.20	.04
☐ 137	Dick Williams MG	.60	.30	.06
☐ 138	Mike Kekich	.40	.20	.04
☐ 139	Tim McCarver	.75	.35	.07
☐ 140	Pat Dobson	.60	.30	.06
☐ 141	Mets Rookies	.60	.30	.06
	Buzz Capra			
	Leroy Stanton			
	Jon Matlack			
☐ 142	Chris Chambliss	1.50	.75	.15
☐ 143	Garry Jestadt	.40	.20	.04
☐ 144	Marty Pattin	.40	.20	.04
☐ 145	Don Kessinger	.60	.30	.06
☐ 146	Steve Kealey	.40	.20	.04
☐ 147	Dave Kingman	6.00	3.00	.60
☐ 148	Dick Billings	.40	.20	.04
☐ 149	Gary Neibauer	.40	.20	.04
☐ 150	Norm Cash	1.00	.50	.10
☐ 151	Jim Brewer	.40	.20	.04
☐ 152	Gene Clines	.40	.20	.04
☐ 153	Rick Auerbach	.40	.20	.04
☐ 154	Ted Simmons	2.25	1.10	.22
☐ 155	Larry Dierker	.60	.30	.06
☐ 156	Minnesota Twins	1.00	.50	.10
	Team Card			
☐ 157	Don Gullett	.60	.30	.06
☐ 158	Jerry Kenney	.40	.20	.04
☐ 159	John Boccabella	.40	.20	.04
☐ 160	Andy Messersmith	.60	.30	.06
☐ 161	Brock Davis	.40	.20	.04
☐ 162	Brewers Rookies UER	.75	.35	.07
	Jerry Bell			
	Darrell Porter			
	Bob Reynolds			
	(Porter and Bell			
	photos switched)			
☐ 163	Tug McGraw	.75	.35	.07
☐ 164	McGraw In Action	.60	.30	.06
☐ 165	Chris Speier	.60	.30	.06
☐ 166	Speier In Action	.40	.20	.04
☐ 167	Deron Johnson	.40	.20	.04
☐ 168	Johnson In Action	.40	.20	.04
☐ 169	Vida Blue	.75	.35	.07
☐ 170	Blue In Action	.60	.30	.06
☐ 171	Darrell Evans	1.50	.75	.15
☐ 172	Evans In Action	.75	.35	.07
☐ 173	Clay Kirby	.40	.20	.04
☐ 174	Kirby In Action	.40	.20	.04
☐ 175	Tom Haller	.40	.20	.04
☐ 176	Haller In Action	.40	.20	.04
☐ 177	Paul Schaal	.40	.20	.04
☐ 178	Schaal In Action	.40	.20	.04
☐ 179	Dock Ellis	.40	.20	.04
☐ 180	Ellis In Action	.40	.20	.04
☐ 181	Ed Kranepool	.60	.30	.06
☐ 182	Kranepool In Action	.40	.20	.04
☐ 183	Bill Melton	.40	.20	.04

☐ 184	Melton In Action	.40	.20	.04
☐ 185	Ron Bryant	.40	.20	.04
☐ 186	Bryant In Action	.40	.20	.04
☐ 187	Gates Brown	.60	.30	.06
☐ 188	Frank Lucchesi MG	.40	.20	.04
☐ 189	Gene Tenace	.60	.30	.06
☐ 190	Dave Giusti	.60	.30	.06
☐ 191	Jeff Burroughs	.75	.35	.07
☐ 192	Cubs Team	1.00	.50	.10
☐ 193	Kurt Bevacqua	.40	.20	.04
☐ 194	Fred Norman	.40	.20	.04
☐ 195	Orlando Cepeda	2.00	1.00	.20
☐ 196	Mel Queen	.40	.20	.04
☐ 197	Johnny Briggs	.40	.20	.04
☐ 198	Dodgers Rookies	2.25	1.10	.22
	Charlie Hough			
	Bob O'Brien			
	Mike Strahler			
☐ 199	Mike Fiore	.40	.20	.04
☐ 200	Lou Brock	5.00	2.50	.50
☐ 201	Phil Roof	.40	.20	.04
☐ 202	Scipio Spinks	.40	.20	.04
☐ 203	Ron Blomberg	.40	.20	.04
☐ 204	Tommy Helms	.60	.30	.06
☐ 205	Dick Drago	.40	.20	.04
☐ 206	Dal Maxvill	.40	.20	.04
☐ 207	Tom Egan	.40	.20	.04
☐ 208	Milt Pappas	.60	.30	.06
☐ 209	Joe Rudi	.60	.30	.06
☐ 210	Denny McLain	1.00	.50	.10
☐ 211	Gary Sutherland	.40	.20	.04
☐ 212	Grant Jackson	.40	.20	.04
☐ 213	Angels Rookies	.40	.20	.04
	Billy Parker			
	Art Kusnyer			
	Tom Silverio			
☐ 214	Mike McQueen	.40	.20	.04
☐ 215	Alex Johnson	.40	.20	.04
☐ 216	Joe Niekro	.75	.35	.07
☐ 217	Roger Metzger	.40	.20	.04
☐ 218	Eddie Kasko MG	.40	.20	.04
☐ 219	Rennie Stennett	.60	.30	.06
☐ 220	Jim Perry	.75	.35	.07
☐ 221	NL Playoffs	1.00	.50	.10
	Bucs champs			
☐ 222	AL Playoffs	1.50	.75	.15
	Orioles champs			
	(Brooks Robinson)			
☐ 223	World Series Game 1	1.00	.50	.10
	(McNally pitching)			
☐ 224	World Series Game 2	1.00	.50	.10
	(Dave Johnson and			
	Mark Belanger)			
☐ 225	World Series Game 3	1.00	.50	.10
	(Sanguillen scoring)			
☐ 226	World Series Game 4	2.50	1.25	.25
	(Clemente on 2nd)			
☐ 227	World Series Game 5	1.00	.50	.10
	(Briles pitching)			
☐ 228	World Series Game 6	1.25	.60	.12
	(Frank Robinson and			
	Manny Sanguillen)			
☐ 229	World Series Game 7	1.00	.50	.10
	(Blass pitching)			
☐ 230	World Series Summary	1.00	.50	.10
	Pirates celebrate			
☐ 231	Casey Cox	.40	.20	.04
☐ 232	Giants Rookies	.40	.20	.04
	Chris Arnold			
	Jim Barr			
	Dave Rader			
☐ 233	Jay Johnstone	.60	.30	.06
☐ 234	Ron Taylor	.40	.20	.04
☐ 235	Merv Rettenmund	.40	.20	.04
☐ 236	Jim McGlothlin	.40	.20	.04
☐ 237	Yankees Team	1.25	.60	.12
☐ 238	Leron Lee	.40	.20	.04
☐ 239	Tom Timmermann	.40	.20	.04
☐ 240	Rich Allen	2.50	1.25	.25
☐ 241	Rollie Fingers	5.50	2.75	.55
☐ 242	Don Mincher	.60	.30	.06
☐ 243	Frank Linzy	.40	.20	.04
☐ 244	Steve Braun	.40	.20	.04
☐ 245	Tommie Agee	.60	.30	.06
☐ 246	Tom Burgmeier	.40	.20	.04
☐ 247	Milt May	.40	.20	.04
☐ 248	Tom Bradley	.40	.20	.04
☐ 249	Harry Walker MG	.40	.20	.04
☐ 250	Boog Powell	1.00	.50	.10
☐ 251	Checklist 3	2.00	.20	.04
☐ 252	Ken Reynolds	.40	.20	.04
☐ 253	Sandy Alomar	.40	.20	.04
☐ 254	Boots Day	.40	.20	.04
☐ 255	Jim Lonborg	.75	.35	.07

☐ 256	George Foster	1.50	.75	.15
☐ 257	Tigers Rookies	.40	.20	.04
	Jim Foor			
	Tim Hosley			
	Paul Jata			
☐ 258	Randy Hundley	.60	.30	.06
☐ 259	Sparky Lyle	.75	.35	.07
☐ 260	Ralph Garr	.60	.30	.06
☐ 261	Steve Mingori	.40	.20	.04
☐ 262	San Diego Padres	1.00	.50	.10
	Team Card			
☐ 263	Felipe Alou	.60	.30	.06
☐ 264	Tommy John	2.00	1.00	.20
☐ 265	Wes Parker	.60	.30	.06
☐ 266	Bobby Bolin	.40	.20	.04
☐ 267	Dave Concepcion	1.75	.85	.17
☐ 268	A's Rookies	.40	.20	.04
	Dwain Anderson			
	Chris Floethe			
☐ 269	Don Hahn	.40	.20	.04
☐ 270	Jim Palmer	11.00	5.50	1.10
☐ 271	Ken Rudolph	.40	.20	.04
☐ 272	Mickey Rivers	1.00	.50	.10
☐ 273	Bobby Floyd	.40	.20	.04
☐ 274	Al Severinsen	.40	.20	.04
☐ 275	Cesar Tovar	.40	.20	.04
☐ 276	Gene Mauch MG	.60	.30	.06
☐ 277	Elliott Maddox	.40	.20	.04
☐ 278	Dennis Higgins	.40	.20	.04
☐ 279	Larry Brown	.40	.20	.04
☐ 280	Willie McCovey	5.00	2.50	.50
☐ 281	Bill Parsons	.40	.20	.04
☐ 282	Astros Team	1.00	.50	.10
☐ 283	Darrell Brandon	.40	.20	.04
☐ 284	Ike Brown	.40	.20	.04
☐ 285	Gaylord Perry	6.00	2.50	.50
☐ 286	Gene Alley	.60	.30	.06
☐ 287	Jim Hardin	.40	.20	.04
☐ 288	Johnny Jeter	.40	.20	.04
☐ 289	Syd O'Brien	.40	.20	.04
☐ 290	Sonny Siebert	.60	.30	.06
☐ 291	Hal McRae	.75	.35	.07
☐ 292	McRae In Action	.60	.30	.06
☐ 293	Dan Frisella	.40	.20	.04
☐ 294	Frisella In Action	.40	.20	.04
☐ 295	Dick Dietz	.40	.20	.04
☐ 296	Dietz In Action	.40	.20	.04
☐ 297	Claude Osteen	.60	.30	.06
☐ 298	Osteen In Action	.40	.20	.04
☐ 299	Hank Aaron	25.00	12.50	2.50
☐ 300	Aaron in Action	12.00	6.00	1.20
☐ 301	George Mitterwald	.40	.20	.04
☐ 302	Mitterwald In Action	.40	.20	.04
☐ 303	Joe Pepitone	.75	.35	.07
☐ 304	Pepitone In Action	.60	.30	.06
☐ 305	Ken Boswell	.40	.20	.04
☐ 306	Boswell In Action	.40	.20	.04
☐ 307	Steve Renko	.40	.20	.04
☐ 308	Renko In Action	.40	.20	.04
☐ 309	Roberto Clemente	25.00	12.50	2.50
☐ 310	Clemente In Action	12.00	6.00	1.20
☐ 311	Clay Carroll	.40	.20	.04
☐ 312	Carroll In Action	.40	.20	.04
☐ 313	Luis Aparicio	3.00	1.50	.30
☐ 314	Aparicio In Action	1.25	.60	.12
☐ 315	Paul Splittorff	.60	.30	.06
☐ 316	Cardinals Rookies	.60	.30	.06
	Jim Bibby			
	Jorge Roque			
	Santiago Guzman			
☐ 317	Rich Hand	.40	.20	.04
☐ 318	Sonny Jackson	.40	.20	.04
☐ 319	Aurelio Rodriguez	.40	.20	.04
☐ 320	Steve Blass	.60	.30	.06
☐ 321	Joe Lahoud	.40	.20	.04
☐ 322	Jose Pena	.40	.20	.04
☐ 323	Earl Weaver MG	.75	.35	.07
☐ 324	Mike Ryan	.40	.20	.04
☐ 325	Mel Stottlemyre	.75	.35	.07
☐ 326	Pat Kelly	.40	.20	.04
☐ 327	Steve Stone	1.00	.50	.10
☐ 328	Red Sox Team	1.25	.60	.12
☐ 329	Roy Foster	.40	.20	.04
☐ 330	Jim Hunter	4.00	2.00	.40
☐ 331	Stan Swanson	.40	.20	.04
☐ 332	Buck Martinez	.40	.20	.04
☐ 333	Steve Barber	.40	.20	.04
☐ 334	Rangers Rookies	.40	.20	.04
	Bill Fahey			
	Jim Mason			
	Tom Ragland			
☐ 335	Bill Hands	.40	.20	.04
☐ 336	Marty Martinez	.40	.20	.04
☐ 337	Mike Kilkenny	.40	.20	.04
☐ 338	Bob Grich	.75	.35	.07
☐ 339	Ron Cook	.40	.20	.04
☐ 340	Roy White	.60	.30	.06
☐ 341	KP: Joe Torre	.60	.30	.06
☐ 342	KP: Wilbur Wood	.40	.20	.04
☐ 343	KP: Willie Stargell	1.00	.50	.10
☐ 344	KP: Dave McNally	.40	.20	.04
☐ 345	KP: Rick Wise	.40	.20	.04
☐ 346	KP: Jim Fregosi	.60	.30	.06
☐ 347	KP: Tom Seaver	1.75	.85	.17
☐ 348	KP: Sal Bando	.40	.20	.04
☐ 349	Al Fitzmorris	.40	.20	.04
☐ 350	Frank Howard	.75	.35	.07
☐ 351	Braves Rookies	.60	.30	.06
	Tom House			
	Rick Kester			
	Jimmy Britton			
☐ 352	Dave LaRoche	.40	.20	.04
☐ 353	Art Shamsky	.40	.20	.04
☐ 354	Tom Murphy	.40	.20	.04
☐ 355	Bob Watson	.60	.30	.06
☐ 356	Gerry Moses	.40	.20	.04
☐ 357	Woodie Fryman	.40	.20	.04
☐ 358	Sparky Anderson MG	1.00	.50	.10
☐ 359	Don Pavletich	.40	.20	.04
☐ 360	Dave Roberts	.40	.20	.04
☐ 361	Mike Andrews	.40	.20	.04
☐ 362	New York Mets	1.25	.60	.12
	Team Card			
☐ 363	Ron Klimkowski	.40	.20	.04
☐ 364	Johnny Callison	.60	.30	.06
☐ 365	Dick Bosman	.40	.20	.04
☐ 366	Jimmy Rosario	.40	.20	.04
☐ 367	Ron Perranoski	.60	.30	.06
☐ 368	Danny Thompson	.60	.30	.06
☐ 369	Jim Lefebvre	.75	.35	.07
☐ 370	Don Buford	.60	.30	.06
☐ 371	Denny Lemaster	.40	.20	.04
☐ 372	Royals Rookies	.40	.20	.04
	Lance Clemons			
	Monty Montgomery			
☐ 373	John Mayberry	.60	.30	.06
☐ 374	Jack Heidemann	.40	.20	.04
☐ 375	Reggie Cleveland	.40	.20	.04
☐ 376	Andy Kosco	.40	.20	.04
☐ 377	Terry Harmon	.40	.20	.04
☐ 378	Checklist 4	2.00	.20	.04
☐ 379	Ken Berry	.40	.20	.04
☐ 380	Earl Williams	.40	.20	.04
☐ 381	Chicago White Sox	1.00	.50	.10
	Team Card			
☐ 382	Joe Gibbon	.40	.20	.04
☐ 383	Brant Alyea	.40	.20	.04
☐ 384	Dave Campbell	.40	.20	.04
☐ 385	Mickey Stanley	.60	.30	.06
☐ 386	Jim Colborn	.40	.20	.04
☐ 387	Horace Clarke	.40	.20	.04
☐ 388	Charlie Williams	.40	.20	.04
☐ 389	Bill Rigney MG	.40	.20	.04
☐ 390	Willie Davis	.60	.30	.06
☐ 391	Ken Sanders	.40	.20	.04
☐ 392	Pirates Rookies	.60	.30	.06
	Fred Cambria			
	Richie Zisk			
☐ 393	Curt Motton	.40	.20	.04
☐ 394	Ken Forsch	.60	.30	.06
☐ 395	Matty Alou	1.00	.50	.10
☐ 396	Paul Lindblad	.75	.35	.07
☐ 397	Philadelphia Phillies	1.50	.75	.15
	Team Card			
☐ 398	Larry Hisle	1.00	.50	.10
☐ 399	Milt Wilcox	.75	.35	.07
☐ 400	Tony Oliva	1.75	.85	.17
☐ 401	Jim Nash	.75	.35	.07
☐ 402	Bobby Heise	.75	.35	.07
☐ 403	John Cumberland	.75	.35	.07
☐ 404	Jeff Torborg	1.00	.50	.10
☐ 405	Ron Fairly	.75	.35	.07
☐ 406	George Hendrick	1.00	.50	.10
☐ 407	Chuck Taylor	.75	.35	.07
☐ 408	Jim Northrup	1.00	.50	.10
☐ 409	Frank Baker	.75	.35	.07
☐ 410	Fergie Jenkins	4.00	1.75	.35
☐ 411	Bob Montgomery	.75	.35	.07
☐ 412	Dick Kelley	.75	.35	.07
☐ 413	White Sox Rookies	.75	.35	.07
	Don Eddy			
	Dave Lemonds			
☐ 414	Bob Miller	.75	.35	.07
☐ 415	Cookie Rojas	.75	.35	.07
☐ 416	Johnny Edwards	.75	.35	.07
☐ 417	Tom Hall	.75	.35	.07
☐ 418	Tom Shopay	.75	.35	.07
☐ 419	Jim Spencer	.75	.35	.07

☐	420 Steve Carlton	18.00	9.00	1.80
☐	421 Ellie Rodriguez	.75	.35	.07
☐	422 Ray Lamb	.75	.35	.07
☐	423 Oscar Gamble	.75	.35	.07
☐	424 Bill Gogolewski	.75	.35	.07
☐	425 Ken Singleton	1.00	.50	.10
☐	426 Singleton In Action	.75	.35	.07
☐	427 Tito Fuentes	.75	.35	.07
☐	428 Fuentes In Action	.75	.35	.07
☐	429 Bob Robertson	.75	.35	.07
☐	430 Robertson In Action	.75	.35	.07
☐	431 Clarence Gaston	1.25	.60	.12
☐	432 Gaston In Action	1.00	.50	.10
☐	433 Johnny Bench	35.00	17.50	3.50
☐	434 Bench In Action	15.00	7.50	1.50
☐	435 Reggie Jackson	35.00	17.50	3.50
☐	436 Jackson In Action	15.00	7.50	1.50
☐	437 Maury Wills	1.25	.60	.12
☐	438 Wills In Action	1.00	.50	.10
☐	439 Billy Williams	3.50	1.75	.35
☐	440 Williams In Action	1.50	.75	.15
☐	441 Thurman Munson	16.00	8.00	1.60
☐	442 Munson In Action	7.50	3.75	.75
☐	443 Ken Henderson	.75	.35	.07
☐	444 Henderson In Action	.75	.35	.07
☐	445 Tom Seaver	25.00	12.50	2.50
☐	446 Seaver In Action	12.00	6.00	1.20
☐	447 Willie Stargell	5.00	2.50	.50
☐	448 Stargell In Action	2.00	1.00	.20
☐	449 Bob Lemon MG	1.25	.60	.12
☐	450 Mickey Lolich	1.25	.60	.12
☐	451 Tony LaRussa	1.25	.60	.12
☐	452 Ed Herrmann	.75	.35	.07
☐	453 Barry Lersch	.75	.35	.07
☐	454 Oakland A's	1.50	.75	.15
	Team Card			
☐	455 Tommy Harper	1.00	.50	.10
☐	456 Mark Belanger	1.00	.50	.10
☐	457 Padres Rookies	.75	.35	.07
	Darcy Fast			
	Derrel Thomas			
	Mike Ivie			
☐	458 Aurelio Monteagudo	.75	.35	.07
☐	459 Rick Renick	.75	.35	.07
☐	460 Al Downing	1.00	.50	.10
☐	461 Tim Cullen	.75	.35	.07
☐	462 Rickey Clark	.75	.35	.07
☐	463 Bernie Carbo	.75	.35	.07
☐	464 Jim Roland	.75	.35	.07
☐	465 Gil Hodges MG	2.50	1.25	.25
☐	466 Norm Miller	.75	.35	.07
☐	467 Steve Kline	.75	.35	.07
☐	468 Richie Scheinblum	.75	.35	.07
☐	469 Ron Herbel	.75	.35	.07
☐	470 Ray Fosse	1.00	.50	.10
☐	471 Luke Walker	.75	.35	.07
☐	472 Phil Gagliano	.75	.35	.07
☐	473 Dan McGinn	.75	.35	.07
☐	474 Orioles Rookies	3.00	1.50	.30
	Don Baylor			
	Roric Harrison			
	Johnny Oates			
☐	475 Gary Nolan	1.00	.50	.10
☐	476 Lee Richard	.75	.35	.07
☐	477 Tom Phoebus	.75	.35	.07
☐	478 Checklist 5	2.00	.20	.04
☐	479 Don Shaw	.75	.35	.07
☐	480 Lee May	1.00	.50	.10
☐	481 Billy Conigliaro	.75	.35	.07
☐	482 Joe Hoerner	.75	.35	.07
☐	483 Ken Suarez	.75	.35	.07
☐	484 Lum Harris MG	.75	.35	.07
☐	485 Phil Regan	1.00	.50	.10
☐	486 John Lowenstein	.75	.35	.07
☐	487 Tigers Team	1.50	.75	.15
☐	488 Mike Nagy	.75	.35	.07
☐	489 Expos Rookies	.75	.35	.07
	Terry Humphrey			
	Keith Lampard			
☐	490 Dave McNally	1.00	.50	.10
☐	491 KP: Lou Piniella	1.00	.50	.10
☐	492 KP: Mel Stottlemyre	1.00	.50	.10
☐	493 KP: Bob Bailey	.75	.35	.07
☐	494 KP: Willie Horton	.75	.35	.07
☐	495 KP: Bill Melton	.75	.35	.07
☐	496 KP: Bud Harrelson	.75	.35	.07
☐	497 KP: Jim Perry	.75	.35	.07
☐	498 KP: Brooks Robinson	1.50	.75	.15
☐	499 Vicente Romo	.75	.35	.07
☐	500 Joe Torre	1.25	.60	.12
☐	501 Pete Hamm	.75	.35	.07
☐	502 Jackie Hernandez	.75	.35	.07
☐	503 Gary Peters	.75	.35	.07
☐	504 Ed Spiezio	.75	.35	.07
☐	505 Mike Marshall	1.00	.50	.10
☐	506 Indians Rookies	1.00	.50	.10
	Terry Ley			
	Jim Moyer			
	Dick Tidrow			
☐	507 Fred Gladding	.75	.35	.07
☐	508 Elrod Hendricks	.75	.35	.07
☐	509 Don McMahon	.75	.35	.07
☐	510 Ted Williams MG	6.00	3.00	.60
☐	511 Tony Taylor	.75	.35	.07
☐	512 Paul Popovich	.75	.35	.07
☐	513 Lindy McDaniel	.75	.35	.07
☐	514 Ted Sizemore	.75	.35	.07
☐	515 Bert Blyleven	11.00	5.50	1.10
☐	516 Oscar Brown	.75	.35	.07
☐	517 Ken Brett	.75	.35	.07
☐	518 Wayne Garrett	.75	.35	.07
☐	519 Ted Abernathy	.75	.35	.07
☐	520 Larry Bowa	1.50	.75	.15
☐	521 Alan Foster	.75	.35	.07
☐	522 Dodgers Team	1.75	.85	.17
☐	523 Chuck Dobson	.75	.35	.07
☐	524 Reds Rookies	.75	.35	.07
	Ed Armbrister			
	Mel Behney			
☐	525 Carlos May	.75	.35	.07
☐	526 Bob Bailey	1.75	.85	.17
☐	527 Dave Leonhard	1.75	.85	.17
☐	528 Ron Stone	1.75	.85	.17
☐	529 Dave Nelson	1.75	.85	.17
☐	530 Don Sutton	4.00	2.00	.40
☐	531 Freddie Patek	2.25	1.10	.22
☐	532 Fred Kendall	1.75	.85	.17
☐	533 Ralph Houk MG	2.25	1.10	.22
☐	534 Jim Hickman	1.75	.85	.17
☐	535 Ed Brinkman	1.75	.85	.17
☐	536 Doug Rader	2.25	1.10	.22
☐	537 Bob Locker	1.75	.85	.17
☐	538 Charlie Sands	1.75	.85	.17
☐	539 Terry Forster	2.25	1.10	.22
☐	540 Felix Millan	1.75	.85	.17
☐	541 Roger Repoz	1.75	.85	.17
☐	542 Jack Billingham	1.75	.85	.17
☐	543 Duane Josephson	1.75	.85	.17
☐	544 Ted Martinez	1.75	.85	.17
☐	545 Wayne Granger	1.75	.85	.17
☐	546 Joe Hague	1.75	.85	.17
☐	547 Indians Team	3.50	1.75	.35
☐	548 Frank Reberger	1.75	.85	.17
☐	549 Dave May	1.75	.85	.17
☐	550 Brooks Robinson	18.00	9.00	1.80
☐	551 Ollie Brown	1.75	.85	.17
☐	552 Brown In Action	1.75	.85	.17
☐	553 Wilbur Wood	1.75	.85	.17
☐	554 Wood In Action	1.75	.85	.17
☐	555 Ron Santo	3.00	1.50	.30
☐	556 Santo In Action	2.25	1.10	.22
☐	557 John Odom	1.75	.85	.17
☐	558 Odom In Action	1.75	.85	.17
☐	559 Pete Rose	60.00	30.00	6.00
☐	560 Rose In Action	25.00	12.50	2.50
☐	561 Leo Cardenas	1.75	.85	.17
☐	562 Cardenas In Action	1.75	.85	.17
☐	563 Ray Sadecki	1.75	.85	.17
☐	564 Sadecki In Action	1.75	.85	.17
☐	565 Reggie Smith	2.25	1.10	.22
☐	566 Smith In Action	1.75	.85	.17
☐	567 Juan Marichal	6.00	3.00	.60
☐	568 Marichal In Action	2.50	1.25	.25
☐	569 Ed Kirkpatrick	1.75	.85	.17
☐	570 Kirkpatrick In Action	1.75	.85	.17
☐	571 Nate Colbert	1.75	.85	.17
☐	572 Colbert In Action	1.75	.85	.17
☐	573 Fritz Peterson	1.75	.85	.17
☐	574 Peterson In Action	1.75	.85	.17
☐	575 Al Oliver	2.25	1.10	.22
☐	576 Leo Durocher MG	2.25	1.10	.22
☐	577 Mike Paul	1.75	.85	.17
☐	578 Billy Grabarkewitz	1.75	.85	.17
☐	579 Doyle Alexander	3.00	1.50	.30
☐	580 Lou Piniella	3.00	1.50	.30
☐	581 Wade Blasingame	1.75	.85	.17
☐	582 Montreal Expos	3.50	1.75	.35
	Team Card			
☐	583 Darold Knowles	1.75	.85	.17
☐	584 Jerry McNertney	1.75	.85	.17
☐	585 George Scott	2.25	1.10	.22
☐	586 Denis Menke	1.75	.85	.17
☐	587 Billy Wilson	1.75	.85	.17
☐	588 Jim Holt	1.75	.85	.17
☐	589 Hal Lanier	2.25	1.10	.22
☐	590 Graig Nettles	3.00	1.50	.30
☐	591 Paul Casanova	1.75	.85	.17
☐	592 Lew Krausse	1.75	.85	.17

☐ 593 Rich Morales	1.75	.85	.17
☐ 594 Jim Beauchamp	1.75	.85	.17
☐ 595 Nolan Ryan	125.00	60.00	12.50
☐ 596 Manny Mota	2.25	1.10	.22
☐ 597 Jim Magnuson	1.75	.85	.17
☐ 598 Hal King	1.75	.85	.17
☐ 599 Billy Champion	1.75	.85	.17
☐ 600 Al Kaline	18.00	9.00	1.80
☐ 601 George Stone	1.75	.85	.17
☐ 602 Dave Bristol MG	1.75	.85	.17
☐ 603 Jim Ray	1.75	.85	.17
☐ 604A Checklist 6	4.00	.40	.08
(copyright on back			
bottom right)			
☐ 604B Checklist 6	6.00	.60	.12
(copyright on back			
bottom left)			
☐ 605 Nelson Briles	1.75	.85	.17
☐ 606 Luis Melendez	1.75	.85	.17
☐ 607 Frank Duffy	1.75	.85	.17
☐ 608 Mike Corkins	1.75	.85	.17
☐ 609 Tom Grieve	2.25	1.10	.22
☐ 610 Bill Stoneman	1.75	.85	.17
☐ 611 Rich Reese	1.75	.85	.17
☐ 612 Joe Decker	1.75	.85	.17
☐ 613 Mike Ferraro	2.25	1.10	.22
☐ 614 Ted Uhlaender	1.75	.85	.17
☐ 615 Steve Hargan	1.75	.85	.17
☐ 616 Joe Ferguson	1.75	.85	.17
☐ 617 Kansas City Royals	3.50	1.75	.35
Team Card			
☐ 618 Rich Robertson	1.75	.85	.17
☐ 619 Rich McKinney	1.75	.85	.17
☐ 620 Phil Niekro	4.00	2.00	.40
☐ 621 Commissioners Award	2.50	1.25	.25
☐ 622 MVP Award	2.50	1.25	.25
☐ 623 Cy Young Award	2.50	1.25	.25
☐ 624 Minor League Player	2.50	1.25	.25
☐ 625 Rookie of the Year	2.50	1.25	.25
☐ 626 Babe Ruth Award	3.00	1.50	.30
☐ 627 Moe Drabowsky	1.75	.85	.17
☐ 628 Terry Crowley	1.75	.85	.17
☐ 629 Paul Doyle	1.75	.85	.17
☐ 630 Rich Hebner	1.75	.85	.17
☐ 631 John Strohmayer	1.75	.85	.17
☐ 632 Mike Hegan	1.75	.85	.17
☐ 633 Jack Hiatt	1.75	.85	.17
☐ 634 Dick Woodson	1.75	.85	.17
☐ 635 Don Money	1.75	.85	.17
☐ 636 Bill Lee	2.25	1.10	.22
☐ 637 Preston Gomez MG	1.75	.85	.17
☐ 638 Ken Wright	1.75	.85	.17
☐ 639 J.C. Martin	1.75	.85	.17
☐ 640 Joe Coleman	1.75	.85	.17
☐ 641 Mike Lum	1.75	.85	.17
☐ 642 Dennis Riddleberger	1.75	.85	.17
☐ 643 Russ Gibson	1.75	.85	.17
☐ 644 Bernie Allen	1.75	.85	.17
☐ 645 Jim Maloney	2.25	1.10	.22
☐ 646 Chico Salmon	1.75	.85	.17
☐ 647 Bob Moose	1.75	.85	.17
☐ 648 Jim Lyttle	1.75	.85	.17
☐ 649 Pete Richert	1.75	.85	.17
☐ 650 Sal Bando	2.25	1.10	.22
☐ 651 Cincinnati Reds	3.50	1.75	.35
Team Card			
☐ 652 Marcelino Lopez	1.75	.85	.17
☐ 653 Jim Fairey	1.75	.85	.17
☐ 654 Horacio Pina	1.75	.85	.17
☐ 655 Jerry Grote	1.75	.85	.17
☐ 656 Rudy May	1.75	.85	.17
☐ 657 Bobby Wine	3.50	1.75	.35
☐ 658 Steve Dunning	3.50	1.75	.35
☐ 659 Bob Aspromonte	3.50	1.75	.35
☐ 660 Paul Blair	4.50	2.25	.45
☐ 661 Bill Virdon	4.50	2.25	.45
☐ 662 Stan Bahnsen	3.50	1.75	.35
☐ 663 Fran Healy	3.50	1.75	.35
☐ 664 Bobby Knoop	3.50	1.75	.35
☐ 665 Chris Short	3.50	1.75	.35
☐ 666 Hector Torres	3.50	1.75	.35
☐ 667 Ray Newman	3.50	1.75	.35
☐ 668 Texas Rangers	7.00	3.50	.70
Team Card			
☐ 669 Willie Crawford	3.50	1.75	.35
☐ 670 Ken Holtzman	4.50	2.25	.45
☐ 671 Donn Clendenon	4.50	2.25	.45
☐ 672 Archie Reynolds	3.50	1.75	.35
☐ 673 Dave Marshall	3.50	1.75	.35
☐ 674 John Kennedy	3.50	1.75	.35
☐ 675 Pat Jarvis	3.50	1.75	.35
☐ 676 Danny Cater	3.50	1.75	.35
☐ 677 Ivan Murrell	3.50	1.75	.35
☐ 678 Steve Luebber	3.50	1.75	.35
☐ 679 Astros Rookies	3.50	1.75	.35
Bob Fenwick			
Bob Stinson			
☐ 680 Dave Johnson	4.50	2.25	.45
☐ 681 Bobby Pfeil	3.50	1.75	.35
☐ 682 Mike McCormick	4.50	2.25	.45
☐ 683 Steve Hovley	3.50	1.75	.35
☐ 684 Hal Breeden	3.50	1.75	.35
☐ 685 Joel Horlen	3.50	1.75	.35
☐ 686 Steve Garvey	80.00	40.00	8.00
☐ 687 Del Unser	3.50	1.75	.35
☐ 688 St. Louis Cardinals	7.00	3.50	.70
Team Card			
☐ 689 Eddie Fisher	3.50	1.75	.35
☐ 690 Willie Montanez	3.50	1.75	.35
☐ 691 Curt Blefary	3.50	1.75	.35
☐ 692 Blefary In Action	3.50	1.75	.35
☐ 693 Alan Gallagher	3.50	1.75	.35
☐ 694 Gallagher In Action	3.50	1.75	.35
☐ 695 Rod Carew	80.00	40.00	8.00
☐ 696 Carew In Action	36.00	18.00	3.60
☐ 697 Jerry Koosman	8.00	4.00	.80
☐ 698 Koosman In Action	5.00	2.50	.50
☐ 699 Bobby Murcer	8.00	4.00	.80
☐ 700 Murcer In Action	5.00	2.50	.50
☐ 701 Jose Pagan	3.50	1.75	.35
☐ 702 Pagan In Action	3.50	1.75	.35
☐ 703 Doug Griffin	3.50	1.75	.35
☐ 704 Griffin In Action	3.50	1.75	.35
☐ 705 Pat Corrales	4.50	2.25	.45
☐ 706 Corrales In Action	3.50	1.75	.35
☐ 707 Tim Foli	3.50	1.75	.35
☐ 708 Foli In Action	3.50	1.75	.35
☐ 709 Jim Kaat	11.00	5.50	1.10
☐ 710 Kaat In Action	7.00	3.50	.70
☐ 711 Bobby Bonds	11.00	5.50	1.10
☐ 712 Bonds In Action	7.00	3.50	.70
☐ 713 Gene Michael	3.50	1.75	.35
☐ 714 Michael In Action	3.50	1.75	.35
☐ 715 Mike Epstein	3.50	1.75	.35
☐ 716 Jesus Alou	3.50	1.75	.35
☐ 717 Bruce Dal Canton	3.50	1.75	.35
☐ 718 Del Rice MG	3.50	1.75	.35
☐ 719 Cesar Geronimo	3.50	1.75	.35
☐ 720 Sam McDowell	4.50	2.25	.45
☐ 721 Eddie Leon	3.50	1.75	.35
☐ 722 Bill Sudakis	3.50	1.75	.35
☐ 723 Al Santorini	3.50	1.75	.35
☐ 724 AL Rookie Pitchers	4.50	2.25	.45
John Curtis			
Rich Hinton			
Mickey Scott			
☐ 725 Dick McAuliffe	4.50	2.25	.45
☐ 726 Dick Selma	3.50	1.75	.35
☐ 727 Jose LaBoy	3.50	1.75	.35
☐ 728 Gail Hopkins	3.50	1.75	.35
☐ 729 Bob Veale	4.50	2.25	.45
☐ 730 Rick Monday	4.50	2.25	.45
☐ 731 Baltimore Orioles	7.00	3.50	.70
Team Card			
☐ 732 George Culver	3.50	1.75	.35
☐ 733 Jim Ray Hart	4.50	2.25	.45
☐ 734 Bob Burda	3.50	1.75	.35
☐ 735 Diego Segui	3.50	1.75	.35
☐ 736 Bill Russell	5.00	2.50	.50
☐ 737 Len Randle	3.50	1.75	.35
☐ 738 Jim Merritt	3.50	1.75	.35
☐ 739 Don Mason	3.50	1.75	.35
☐ 740 Rico Carty	4.50	2.25	.45
☐ 741 Rookie First Basemen	4.50	2.25	.45
Tom Hutton			
John Milner			
Rick Miller			
☐ 742 Jim Rooker	3.50	1.75	.35
☐ 743 Cesar Gutierrez	3.50	1.75	.35
☐ 744 Jim Slaton	3.50	1.75	.35
☐ 745 Julian Javier	3.50	1.75	.35
☐ 746 Lowell Palmer	3.50	1.75	.35
☐ 747 Jim Stewart	3.50	1.75	.35
☐ 748 Phil Hennigan	3.50	1.75	.35
☐ 749 Walter Alston MG	8.00	4.00	.80
☐ 750 Willie Horton	4.50	2.25	.45
☐ 751 Steve Carlton TR	42.00	20.00	4.00
☐ 752 Joe Morgan TR	36.00	18.00	3.60
☐ 753 Denny McLain TR	8.00	4.00	.80
☐ 754 Frank Robinson TR	27.00	13.50	2.70
☐ 755 Jim Fregosi TR	4.50	2.25	.45
☐ 756 Rick Wise TR	4.50	2.25	.45
☐ 757 Jose Cardenal TR	4.50	2.25	.45
☐ 758 Gil Garrido	3.50	1.75	.35
☐ 759 Chris Cannizzaro	3.50	1.75	.35
☐ 760 Bill Mazeroski	6.00	3.00	.60

☐ 761	Rookie Outfielders	12.00	6.00	1.20
	Ben Oglivie			
	Ron Cey			
	Bernie Williams			
☐ 762	Wayne Simpson	3.50	1.75	.35
☐ 763	Ron Hansen	3.50	1.75	.35
☐ 764	Dusty Baker	4.50	2.25	.45
☐ 765	Ken McMullen	3.50	1.75	.35
☐ 766	Steve Hamilton	3.50	1.75	.35
☐ 767	Tom McCraw	3.50	1.75	.35
☐ 768	Denny Doyle	3.50	1.75	.35
☐ 769	Jack Aker	3.50	1.75	.35
☐ 770	Jim Wynn	4.50	2.25	.45
☐ 771	San Francisco Giants	7.00	3.50	.70
	Team Card			
☐ 772	Ken Tatum	3.50	1.75	.35
☐ 773	Ron Brand	3.50	1.75	.35
☐ 774	Luis Alvarado	3.50	1.75	.35
☐ 775	Jerry Reuss	4.50	2.25	.45
☐ 776	Bill Voss	3.50	1.75	.35
☐ 777	Hoyt Wilhelm	15.00	7.50	1.50
☐ 778	Twins Rookies	5.00	2.50	.50
	Vic Albury			
	Rick Dempsey			
	Jim Strickland			
☐ 779	Tony Cloninger	3.50	1.75	.35
☐ 780	Dick Green	3.50	1.75	.35
☐ 781	Jim McAndrew	3.50	1.75	.35
☐ 782	Larry Stahl	3.50	1.75	.35
☐ 783	Les Cain	3.50	1.75	.35
☐ 784	Ken Aspromonte	3.50	1.75	.35
☐ 785	Vic Davalillo	3.50	1.75	.35
☐ 786	Chuck Brinkman	3.50	1.75	.35
☐ 787	Ron Reed	4.50	2.25	.45

1973 Topps

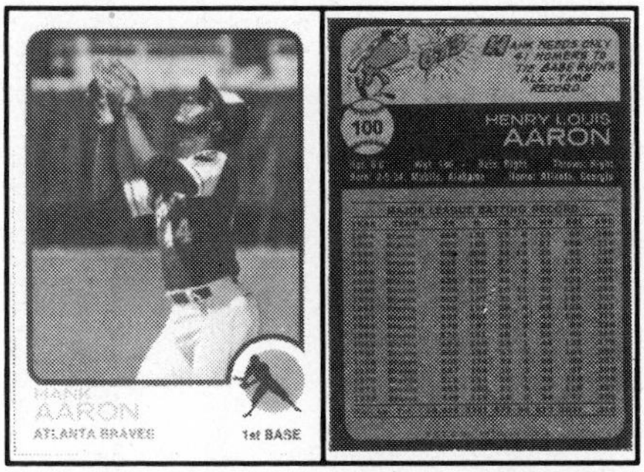

The cards in this 660-card set measure 2 1/2" by 3 1/2". The 1973 Topps set marked the last year in which Topps marketed baseball cards in consecutive series. The last series (529-660) is more difficult to obtain. Beginning in 1974, all Topps cards were printed at the same time, thus eliminating the "high number" factor. The set features team leader cards with small individual pictures of the coaching staff members and a larger picture of the manager. The "background" variations below with respect to these leader cards are subtle and are best understood after a side-by-side comparison of the two varieties. An "All-Time Leaders" series (471-478) appeared for the first time in this set. Kid Pictures appeared again for the second year in a row (341-346). Other topical subsets within the set included League Leaders (61-68), Playoffs cards (201-202), World Series cards (203-210), and Rookie Prospects (601-616). The key rookie cards in this set are Bob Boone, Dwight Evans, and Mike Schmidt.

	NRMT	VG-E	GOOD
COMPLETE SET (660)	1000.00	400.00	80.00
COMMON PLAYER (1-264)	.30	.15	.03
COMMON PLAYER (265-396)	.40	.20	.04
COMMON PLAYER (397-528)	.75	.35	.07
COMMON PLAYER (529-660)	1.75	.85	.17

☐ 1	All-Time HR Leaders	20.00	5.00	1.00
	Babe Ruth 714			
	Hank Aaron 673			
	Willie Mays 654			
☐ 2	Rich Hebner	.30	.15	.03
☐ 3	Jim Lonborg	.50	.25	.05
☐ 4	John Milner	.30	.15	.03
☐ 5	Ed Brinkman	.30	.15	.03
☐ 6	Mac Scarce	.30	.15	.03
☐ 7	Texas Rangers Team	.75	.35	.07
☐ 8	Tom Hall	.30	.15	.03
☐ 9	Johnny Oates	.30	.15	.03
☐ 10	Don Sutton	2.25	1.10	.22
☐ 11	Chris Chambliss	.50	.25	.05
☐ 12A	Padres Leaders	.50	.25	.05
	Don Zimmer MG			
	Dave Garcia CO			
	Johnny Podres CO			
	Bob Skinner CO			
	Whitey Wietelmann CO			
	(Podres no right ear)			
☐ 12B	Padres Leaders	1.00	.50	.10
	(Podres has right ear)			
☐ 13	George Hendrick	.50	.25	.05
☐ 14	Sonny Siebert	.30	.15	.03
☐ 15	Ralph Garr	.30	.15	.03
☐ 16	Steve Braun	.30	.15	.03
☐ 17	Fred Gladding	.30	.15	.03
☐ 18	Leroy Stanton	.30	.15	.03
☐ 19	Tim Foli	.30	.15	.03
☐ 20	Stan Bahnsen	.30	.15	.03
☐ 21	Randy Hundley	.30	.15	.03
☐ 22	Ted Abernathy	.30	.15	.03
☐ 23	Dave Kingman	1.50	.75	.15
☐ 24	Al Santorini	.30	.15	.03
☐ 25	Roy White	.50	.25	.05
☐ 26	Pittsburgh Pirates	.75	.35	.07
	Team Card			
☐ 27	Bill Gogolewski	.30	.15	.03
☐ 28	Hal McRae	.50	.25	.05
☐ 29	Tony Taylor	.30	.15	.03
☐ 30	Tug McGraw	.75	.35	.07
☐ 31	Buddy Bell	4.00	2.00	.40
☐ 32	Fred Norman	.30	.15	.03
☐ 33	Jim Breazeale	.30	.15	.03
☐ 34	Pat Dobson	.30	.15	.03
☐ 35	Willie Davis	.50	.25	.05
☐ 36	Steve Barber	.30	.15	.03
☐ 37	Bill Robinson	.50	.25	.05
☐ 38	Mike Epstein	.30	.15	.03
☐ 39	Dave Roberts	.30	.15	.03
☐ 40	Reggie Smith	.60	.30	.06
☐ 41	Tom Walker	.30	.15	.03
☐ 42	Mike Andrews	.30	.15	.03
☐ 43	Randy Moffitt	.30	.15	.03
☐ 44	Rick Monday	.50	.25	.05
☐ 45	Ellie Rodriguez UER	.30	.15	.03
	(photo actually			
	John Felske)			
☐ 46	Lindy McDaniel	.30	.15	.03
☐ 47	Luis Melendez	.30	.15	.03
☐ 48	Paul Splittorff	.30	.15	.03
☐ 49A	Twins Leaders	.50	.25	.05
	Frank Quilici MG			
	Vern Morgan CO			
	Bob Rodgers CO			
	Ralph Rowe CO			
	Al Worthington CO			
	(solid backgrounds)			
☐ 49B	Twins Leaders	1.00	.50	.10
	(natural backgrounds)			
☐ 50	Roberto Clemente	25.00	12.50	2.50
☐ 51	Chuck Seelbach	.30	.15	.03
☐ 52	Denis Menke	.30	.15	.03
☐ 53	Steve Dunning	.30	.15	.03
☐ 54	Checklist 1	1.50	.15	.03
☐ 55	Jon Matlack	.50	.25	.05
☐ 56	Merv Rettenmund	.30	.15	.03
☐ 57	Derrel Thomas	.30	.15	.03
☐ 58	Mike Paul	.30	.15	.03
☐ 59	Steve Yeager	.60	.30	.06
☐ 60	Ken Holtzman	.50	.25	.05
☐ 61	Batting Leaders	1.75	.85	.17
	Billy Williams			
	Rod Carew			
☐ 62	Home Run Leaders	1.50	.75	.15
	Johnny Bench			
	Dick Allen			
☐ 63	RBI Leaders	1.50	.75	.15
	Johnny Bench			
	Dick Allen			
☐ 64	Stolen Base Leaders	1.00	.50	.10
	Lou Brock			
	Bert Campaneris			

☐ 65 ERA Leaders	1.00	.50	.10
Steve Carlton			
Luis Tiant			
☐ 66 Victory Leaders	1.00	.50	.10
Steve Carlton			
Gaylord Perry			
Wilbur Wood			
☐ 67 Strikeout Leaders	5.00	2.50	.50
Steve Carlton			
Nolan Ryan			
☐ 68 Leading Firemen	1.00	.50	.10
Clay Carroll			
Sparky Lyle			
☐ 69 Phil Gagliano	.30	.15	.03
☐ 70 Milt Pappas	.50	.25	.05
☐ 71 Johnny Briggs	.30	.15	.03
☐ 72 Ron Reed	.30	.15	.03
☐ 73 Ed Herrmann	.30	.15	.03
☐ 74 Billy Champion	.30	.15	.03
☐ 75 Vada Pinson	.60	.30	.06
☐ 76 Doug Rader	.50	.25	.05
☐ 77 Mike Torrez	.30	.15	.03
☐ 78 Richie Scheinblum	.30	.15	.03
☐ 79 Jim Willoughby	.30	.15	.03
☐ 80 Tony Oliva UER	1.25	.60	.12
(Minnseota on front)			
☐ 81A Cubs Leaders	.50	.25	.05
Whitey Lockman MG			
Hank Aguirre CO			
Ernie Banks CO			
Larry Jansen CO			
Pete Reiser CO			
(solid backgrounds)			
☐ 81B Cubs Leaders	1.00	.50	.10
(natural backgrounds)			
☐ 82 Fritz Peterson	.30	.15	.03
☐ 83 Leron Lee	.30	.15	.03
☐ 84 Rollie Fingers	4.00	2.00	.40
☐ 85 Ted Simmons	1.50	.75	.15
☐ 86 Tom McCraw	.30	.15	.03
☐ 87 Ken Boswell	.30	.15	.03
☐ 88 Mickey Stanley	.50	.25	.05
☐ 89 Jack Billingham	.30	.15	.03
☐ 90 Brooks Robinson	4.50	2.25	.45
☐ 91 Dodgers Team	.75	.35	.07
☐ 92 Jerry Bell	.30	.15	.03
☐ 93 Jesus Alou	.30	.15	.03
☐ 94 Dick Billings	.30	.15	.03
☐ 95 Steve Blass	.50	.25	.05
☐ 96 Doug Griffin	.30	.15	.03
☐ 97 Willie Montanez	.30	.15	.03
☐ 98 Dick Woodson	.30	.15	.03
☐ 99 Carl Taylor	.30	.15	.03
☐ 100 Hank Aaron	18.00	9.00	1.80
☐ 101 Ken Henderson	.30	.15	.03
☐ 102 Rudy May	.30	.15	.03
☐ 103 Celerino Sanchez	.30	.15	.03
☐ 104 Reggie Cleveland	.30	.15	.03
☐ 105 Carlos May	.30	.15	.03
☐ 106 Terry Humphrey	.30	.15	.03
☐ 107 Phil Hennigan	.30	.15	.03
☐ 108 Bill Russell	.50	.25	.05
☐ 109 Doyle Alexander	.75	.35	.07
☐ 110 Bob Watson	.50	.25	.05
☐ 111 Dave Nelson	.30	.15	.03
☐ 112 Gary Ross	.30	.15	.03
☐ 113 Jerry Grote	.30	.15	.03
☐ 114 Lynn McGlothen	.30	.15	.03
☐ 115 Ron Santo	.75	.35	.07
☐ 116A Yankees Leaders	.60	.30	.06
Ralph Houk MG			
Jim Hegan CO			
Elston Howard CO			
Dick Howser CO			
Jim Turner CO			
(solid backgrounds)			
☐ 116B Yankees Leaders	1.00	.50	.10
(natural backgrounds)			
☐ 117 Ramon Hernandez	.30	.15	.03
☐ 118 John Mayberry	.50	.25	.05
☐ 119 Larry Bowa	.85	.40	.08
☐ 120 Joe Coleman	.30	.15	.03
☐ 121 Dave Rader	.30	.15	.03
☐ 122 Jim Strickland	.30	.15	.03
☐ 123 Sandy Alomar	.30	.15	.03
☐ 124 Jim Hardin	.30	.15	.03
☐ 125 Ron Fairly	.30	.15	.03
☐ 126 Jim Brewer	.30	.15	.03
☐ 127 Brewers Team	.75	.35	.07
☐ 128 Ted Sizemore	.30	.15	.03
☐ 129 Terry Forster	.50	.25	.05
☐ 130 Pete Rose	20.00	10.00	2.00
☐ 131A Red Sox Leaders	.50	.25	.05
Eddie Kasko MG			
Doug Camilli CO			
Don Lenhardt CO			
Eddie Popowski CO			
(no right ear)			
Lee Stange CO			
☐ 131B Red Sox Leaders	1.00	.50	.10
(Popowski has right			
ear showing)			
☐ 132 Matty Alou	.50	.25	.05
☐ 133 Dave Roberts	.30	.15	.03
☐ 134 Milt Wilcox	.30	.15	.03
☐ 135 Lee May UER	.50	.25	.05
(career average .000)			
☐ 136A Orioles Leaders	.75	.35	.07
Earl Weaver MG			
George Bamberger CO			
Jim Frey CO			
Billy Hunter CO			
George Staller CO			
(orange backgrounds)			
☐ 136B Orioles Leaders	1.25	.60	.12
(dark pale			
backgrounds)			
☐ 137 Jim Beauchamp	.30	.15	.03
☐ 138 Horacio Pina	.30	.15	.03
☐ 139 Carmen Fanzone	.30	.15	.03
☐ 140 Lou Piniella	.85	.40	.08
☐ 141 Bruce Kison	.30	.15	.03
☐ 142 Thurman Munson	9.00	4.50	.90
☐ 143 John Curtis	.30	.15	.03
☐ 144 Marty Perez	.30	.15	.03
☐ 145 Bobby Bonds	1.00	.50	.10
☐ 146 Woodie Fryman	.30	.15	.03
☐ 147 Mike Anderson	.30	.15	.03
☐ 148 Dave Goltz	.30	.15	.03
☐ 149 Ron Hunt	.30	.15	.03
☐ 150 Wilbur Wood	.50	.25	.05
☐ 151 Wes Parker	.50	.25	.05
☐ 152 Dave May	.30	.15	.03
☐ 153 Al Hrabosky	.50	.25	.05
☐ 154 Jeff Torborg	.50	.25	.05
☐ 155 Sal Bando	.50	.25	.05
☐ 156 Cesar Geronimo	.30	.15	.03
☐ 157 Denny Riddleberger	.30	.15	.03
☐ 158 Astros Team	.75	.35	.07
☐ 159 Clarence Gaston	.75	.35	.07
☐ 160 Jim Palmer	8.00	4.00	.80
☐ 161 Ted Martinez	.30	.15	.03
☐ 162 Pete Broberg	.30	.15	.03
☐ 163 Vic Davalillo	.30	.15	.03
☐ 164 Monty Montgomery	.30	.15	.03
☐ 165 Luis Aparicio	2.50	1.25	.25
☐ 166 Terry Harmon	.30	.15	.03
☐ 167 Steve Stone	.50	.25	.05
☐ 168 Jim Northrup	.50	.25	.05
☐ 169 Ron Schueler	.30	.15	.03
☐ 170 Harmon Killebrew	4.00	2.00	.40
☐ 171 Bernie Carbo	.30	.15	.03
☐ 172 Steve Kline	.30	.15	.03
☐ 173 Hal Breeden	.30	.15	.03
☐ 174 Rich Gossage	10.00	5.00	1.00
☐ 175 Frank Robinson	4.50	2.25	.45
☐ 176 Chuck Taylor	.30	.15	.03
☐ 177 Bill Plummer	.30	.15	.03
☐ 178 Don Rose	.30	.15	.03
☐ 179A A's Leaders	.50	.25	.05
Dick Williams MG			
Jerry Adair CO			
Vern Hoscheit CO			
Irv Noren CO			
Wes Stock CO			
(Hoscheit left ear			
showing)			
☐ 179B A's Leaders	1.00	.50	.10
(Hoscheit left ear			
not showing)			
☐ 180 Fergie Jenkins	2.50	1.10	.22
☐ 181 Jack Brohamer	.30	.15	.03
☐ 182 Mike Caldwell	.50	.25	.05
☐ 183 Don Buford	.30	.15	.03
☐ 184 Jerry Koosman	.85	.40	.08
☐ 185 Jim Wynn	.50	.25	.05
☐ 186 Bill Fahey	.30	.15	.03
☐ 187 Luke Walker	.30	.15	.03
☐ 188 Cookie Rojas	.30	.15	.03
☐ 189 Greg Luzinski	.85	.40	.08
☐ 190 Bob Gibson	3.50	1.75	.35
☐ 191 Tigers Team	.75	.35	.07
☐ 192 Pat Jarvis	.30	.15	.03
☐ 193 Carlton Fisk	30.00	15.00	3.00
☐ 194 Jorge Orta	.30	.15	.03
☐ 195 Clay Carroll	.30	.15	.03

☐ 196	Ken McMullen	.30	.15	.03
☐ 197	Ed Goodson	.30	.15	.03
☐ 198	Horace Clarke	.30	.15	.03
☐ 199	Bert Blyleven	4.50	2.25	.45
☐ 200	Billy Williams	3.00	1.50	.30
☐ 201	A.L. Playoffs	.80	.40	.08
	A's over Tigers;			
	Hendrick scores			
	winning run			
☐ 202	N.L. Playoffs	.80	.40	.08
	Reds over Pirates			
	Foster's run decides			
☐ 203	World Series Game 1	.80	.40	.08
	Tenace the Menace			
☐ 204	World Series Game 2	.80	.40	.08
	A's two straight			
☐ 205	World Series Game 3	.80	.40	.08
	Reds win squeeker			
☐ 206	World Series Game 4	.80	.40	.08
	Tenace singles			
	in ninth			
☐ 207	World Series Game 5	.80	.40	.08
	Odom out at plate			
☐ 208	World Series Game 6	.80	.40	.08
	Reds' slugging			
	ties series			
☐ 209	World Series Game 7	.80	.40	.08
	Campy stars			
	winning rally			
☐ 210	World Series Summary	.80	.40	.08
	World champions:			
	A's Win			
☐ 211	Balor Moore	.30	.15	.03
☐ 212	Joe Lahoud	.30	.15	.03
☐ 213	Steve Garvey	15.00	7.50	1.50
☐ 214	Steve Hamilton	.30	.15	.03
☐ 215	Dusty Baker	.60	.30	.06
☐ 216	Toby Harrah	.50	.25	.05
☐ 217	Don Wilson	.30	.15	.03
☐ 218	Aurelio Rodriguez	.30	.15	.03
☐ 219	Cardinals Team	.75	.35	.07
☐ 220	Nolan Ryan	55.00	27.50	5.50
☐ 221	Fred Kendall	.30	.15	.03
☐ 222	Rob Gardner	.30	.15	.03
☐ 223	Bud Harrelson	.50	.25	.05
☐ 224	Bill Lee	.30	.15	.03
☐ 225	Al Oliver	1.00	.50	.10
☐ 226	Ray Fosse	.30	.15	.03
☐ 227	Wayne Twitchell	.30	.15	.03
☐ 228	Bobby Darwin	.30	.15	.03
☐ 229	Roric Harrison	.30	.15	.03
☐ 230	Joe Morgan	4.50	2.25	.45
☐ 231	Bill Parsons	.30	.15	.03
☐ 232	Ken Singleton	.50	.25	.05
☐ 233	Ed Kirkpatrick	.30	.15	.03
☐ 234	Bill North	.30	.15	.03
☐ 235	Jim Hunter	3.50	1.75	.35
☐ 236	Tito Fuentes	.30	.15	.03
☐ 237A	Braves Leaders	1.00	.50	.10
	Eddie Mathews MG			
	Lew Burdette CO			
	Jim Busby CO			
	Roy Hartsfield CO			
	Ken Silvestri CO			
	(Burdette right ear			
	showing)			
☐ 237B	Braves Leaders	1.75	.85	.17
	(Burdette right ear			
	not showing)			
☐ 238	Tony Muser	.30	.15	.03
☐ 239	Pete Richert	.30	.15	.03
☐ 240	Bobby Murcer	.60	.30	.06
☐ 241	Dwain Anderson	.30	.15	.03
☐ 242	George Culver	.30	.15	.03
☐ 243	Angels Team	.75	.35	.07
☐ 244	Ed Acosta	.30	.15	.03
☐ 245	Carl Yastrzemski	14.00	7.00	1.40
☐ 246	Ken Sanders	.30	.15	.03
☐ 247	Del Unser	.30	.15	.03
☐ 248	Jerry Johnson	.30	.15	.03
☐ 249	Larry Biittner	.30	.15	.03
☐ 250	Manny Sanguillen	.50	.25	.05
☐ 251	Roger Nelson	.30	.15	.03
☐ 252A	Giants Leaders	.50	.25	.05
	Charlie Fox MG			
	Joe Amalfitano CO			
	Andy Gilbert CO			
	Don McMahon CO			
	John McNamara CO			
	(orange backgrounds)			
☐ 252B	Giants Leaders	1.00	.50	.10
	(dark pale			
	backgrounds)			
☐ 253	Mark Belanger	.50	.25	.05
☐ 254	Bill Stoneman	.30	.15	.03
☐ 255	Reggie Jackson	22.00	11.00	2.20
☐ 256	Chris Zachary	.30	.15	.03
☐ 257A	Mets Leaders	1.50	.75	.15
	Yogi Berra MG			
	Roy McMillan CO			
	Joe Pignatano CO			
	Rube Walker CO			
	Eddie Yost CO			
	(orange backgrounds)			
☐ 257B	Mets Leaders	2.25	1.10	.22
	(dark pale			
	backgrounds)			
☐ 258	Tommy John	1.50	.75	.15
☐ 259	Jim Holt	.30	.15	.03
☐ 260	Gary Nolan	.50	.25	.05
☐ 261	Pat Kelly	.30	.15	.03
☐ 262	Jack Aker	.30	.15	.03
☐ 263	George Scott	.50	.25	.05
☐ 264	Checklist 2	1.50	.15	.03
☐ 265	Gene Michael	.60	.30	.06
☐ 266	Mike Lum	.40	.20	.04
☐ 267	Lloyd Allen	.40	.20	.04
☐ 268	Jerry Morales	.40	.20	.04
☐ 269	Tim McCarver	.80	.40	.08
☐ 270	Luis Tiant	.80	.40	.08
☐ 271	Tom Hutton	.40	.20	.04
☐ 272	Ed Farmer	.40	.20	.04
☐ 273	Chris Speier	.40	.20	.04
☐ 274	Darold Knowles	.40	.20	.04
☐ 275	Tony Perez	2.00	1.00	.20
☐ 276	Joe Lovitto	.40	.20	.04
☐ 277	Bob Miller	.40	.20	.04
☐ 278	Baltimore Orioles	.80	.40	.08
	Team Card			
☐ 279	Mike Strahler	.40	.20	.04
☐ 280	Al Kaline	5.00	2.50	.50
☐ 281	Mike Jorgensen	.40	.20	.04
☐ 282	Steve Hovley	.40	.20	.04
☐ 283	Ray Sadecki	.40	.20	.04
☐ 284	Glenn Borgmann	.40	.20	.04
☐ 285	Don Kessinger	.60	.30	.06
☐ 286	Frank Linzy	.40	.20	.04
☐ 287	Eddie Leon	.40	.20	.04
☐ 288	Gary Gentry	.40	.20	.04
☐ 289	Bob Oliver	.40	.20	.04
☐ 290	Cesar Cedeno	.60	.30	.06
☐ 291	Rogelio Moret	.40	.20	.04
☐ 292	Jose Cruz	.80	.40	.08
☐ 293	Bernie Allen	.40	.20	.04
☐ 294	Steve Arlin	.40	.20	.04
☐ 295	Bert Campaneris	.60	.30	.06
☐ 296	Reds Leaders	.80	.40	.08
	Sparky Anderson MG			
	Alex Grammas CO			
	Ted Kluszewski CO			
	George Scherger CO			
	Larry Shepard CO			
☐ 297	Walt Williams	.40	.20	.04
☐ 298	Ron Bryant	.40	.20	.04
☐ 299	Ted Ford	.40	.20	.04
☐ 300	Steve Carlton	12.00	6.00	1.20
☐ 301	Billy Grabarkewitz	.40	.20	.04
☐ 302	Terry Crowley	.40	.20	.04
☐ 303	Nelson Briles	.40	.20	.04
☐ 304	Duke Sims	.40	.20	.04
☐ 305	Willie Mays	25.00	12.50	2.50
☐ 306	Tom Burgmeier	.40	.20	.04
☐ 307	Boots Day	.40	.20	.04
☐ 308	Skip Lockwood	.40	.20	.04
☐ 309	Paul Popovich	.40	.20	.04
☐ 310	Dick Allen	.80	.40	.08
☐ 311	Joe Decker	.40	.20	.04
☐ 312	Oscar Brown	.40	.20	.04
☐ 313	Jim Ray	.40	.20	.04
☐ 314	Ron Swoboda	.60	.30	.06
☐ 315	John Odom	.40	.20	.04
☐ 316	San Diego Padres	.80	.40	.08
	Team Card			
☐ 317	Danny Cater	.40	.20	.04
☐ 318	Jim McGlothlin	.40	.20	.04
☐ 319	Jim Spencer	.40	.20	.04
☐ 320	Lou Brock	4.50	2.25	.45
☐ 321	Rich Hinton	.40	.20	.04
☐ 322	Garry Maddox	1.00	.50	.10
☐ 323	Tigers Leaders	1.00	.50	.10
	Billy Martin MG			
	Art Fowler CO			
	Charlie Silvera CO			
	Dick Tracewski CO			
☐ 324	Al Downing	.60	.30	.06
☐ 325	Boog Powell	.80	.40	.08
☐ 326	Darrell Brandon	.40	.20	.04
☐ 327	John Lowenstein	.40	.20	.04

☐ 328 Bill Bonham	.40	.20	.04
☐ 329 Ed Kranepool	.60	.30	.06
☐ 330 Rod Carew	15.00	7.50	1.50
☐ 331 Carl Morton	.40	.20	.04
☐ 332 John Felske	.40	.20	.04
☐ 333 Gene Clines	.40	.20	.04
☐ 334 Freddie Patek	.40	.20	.04
☐ 335 Bob Tolan	.40	.20	.04
☐ 336 Tom Bradley	.40	.20	.04
☐ 337 Dave Duncan	.40	.20	.04
☐ 338 Checklist 3	1.50	.15	.03
☐ 339 Dick Tidrow	.40	.20	.04
☐ 340 Nate Colbert	.40	.20	.04
☐ 341 KP: Jim Palmer	1.25	.60	.12
☐ 342 KP: Sam McDowell	.60	.30	.06
☐ 343 KP: Bobby Murcer	.60	.30	.06
☐ 344 KP: Jim Hunter	.80	.40	.08
☐ 345 KP: Chris Speier	.40	.20	.04
☐ 346 KP: Gaylord Perry	.80	.40	.08
☐ 347 Kansas City Royals	.80	.40	.08
Team Card			
☐ 348 Rennie Stennett	.40	.20	.04
☐ 349 Dick McAuliffe	.60	.30	.06
☐ 350 Tom Seaver	18.00	9.00	1.80
☐ 351 Jimmy Stewart	.40	.20	.04
☐ 352 Don Stanhouse	.40	.20	.04
☐ 353 Steve Brye	.40	.20	.04
☐ 354 Billy Parker	.40	.20	.04
☐ 355 Mike Marshall	.60	.30	.06
☐ 356 White Sox Leaders	.60	.30	.06
Chuck Tanner MG			
Joe Lonnett CO			
Jim Mahoney CO			
Al Monchak CO			
Johnny Sain CO			
☐ 357 Ross Grimsley	.40	.20	.04
☐ 358 Jim Nettles	.40	.20	.04
☐ 359 Cecil Upshaw	.40	.20	.04
☐ 360 Joe Rudi UER	.60	.30	.06
(photo actually			
Gene Tenace)			
☐ 361 Fran Healy	.40	.20	.04
☐ 362 Eddie Watt	.40	.20	.04
☐ 363 Jackie Hernandez	.40	.20	.04
☐ 364 Rick Wise	.60	.30	.06
☐ 365 Rico Petrocelli	.60	.30	.06
☐ 366 Brock Davis	.40	.20	.04
☐ 367 Burt Hooton	.60	.30	.06
☐ 368 Bill Buckner	.80	.40	.08
☐ 369 Lerrin LaGrow	.40	.20	.04
☐ 370 Willie Stargell	4.50	2.25	.45
☐ 371 Mike Kekich	.40	.20	.04
☐ 372 Oscar Gamble	.60	.30	.06
☐ 373 Clyde Wright	.40	.20	.04
☐ 374 Darrell Evans	.80	.40	.08
☐ 375 Larry Dierker	.60	.30	.06
☐ 376 Frank Duffy	.40	.20	.04
☐ 377 Expos Leaders	.60	.30	.06
Gene Mauch MG			
Dave Bristol CO			
Larry Doby CO			
Cal McLish CO			
Jerry Zimmerman CO			
☐ 378 Len Randle	.40	.20	.04
☐ 379 Cy Acosta	.40	.20	.04
☐ 380 Johnny Bench	20.00	10.00	2.00
☐ 381 Vicente Romo	.40	.20	.04
☐ 382 Mike Hegan	.40	.20	.04
☐ 383 Diego Segui	.40	.20	.04
☐ 384 Don Baylor	1.25	.60	.12
☐ 385 Jim Perry	.60	.30	.06
☐ 386 Don Money	.40	.20	.04
☐ 387 Jim Barr	.40	.20	.04
☐ 388 Ben Oglivie	.60	.30	.06
☐ 389 New York Mets	2.00	1.00	.20
Team Card			
☐ 390 Mickey Lolich	.80	.40	.08
☐ 391 Lee Lacy	.60	.30	.06
☐ 392 Dick Drago	.40	.20	.04
☐ 393 Jose Cardenal	.40	.20	.04
☐ 394 Sparky Lyle	.60	.30	.06
☐ 395 Roger Metzger	.40	.20	.04
☐ 396 Grant Jackson	.40	.20	.04
☐ 397 Dave Cash	.75	.35	.07
☐ 398 Rich Hand	.75	.35	.07
☐ 399 George Foster	1.50	.75	.15
☐ 400 Gaylord Perry	4.00	1.75	.35
☐ 401 Clyde Mashore	.75	.35	.07
☐ 402 Jack Hiatt	.75	.35	.07
☐ 403 Sonny Jackson	.75	.35	.07
☐ 404 Chuck Brinkman	.75	.35	.07
☐ 405 Cesar Tovar	.75	.35	.07
☐ 406 Paul Lindblad	.75	.35	.07
☐ 407 Felix Millan	.75	.35	.07
☐ 408 Jim Colborn	.75	.35	.07
☐ 409 Ivan Murrell	.75	.35	.07
☐ 410 Willie McCovey	4.50	2.25	.45
(Bench behind plate)			
☐ 411 Ray Corbin	.75	.35	.07
☐ 412 Manny Mota	1.00	.50	.10
☐ 413 Tom Timmermann	.75	.35	.07
☐ 414 Ken Rudolph	.75	.35	.07
☐ 415 Marty Pattin	.75	.35	.07
☐ 416 Paul Schaal	.75	.35	.07
☐ 417 Scipio Spinks	.75	.35	.07
☐ 418 Bob Grich	1.00	.50	.10
☐ 419 Casey Cox	.75	.35	.07
☐ 420 Tommie Agee	.75	.35	.07
☐ 421A Angels Leaders	1.00	.50	.10
Bobby Winkles MG			
Tom Morgan CO			
Salty Parker CO			
Jimmie Reese CO			
John Roseboro CO			
(orange backgrounds)			
☐ 421B Angels Leaders	1.50	.75	.15
(dark pale			
backgrounds)			
☐ 422 Bob Robertson	.75	.35	.07
☐ 423 Johnny Jeter	.75	.35	.07
☐ 424 Denny Doyle	.75	.35	.07
☐ 425 Alex Johnson	.75	.35	.07
☐ 426 Dave LaRoche	.75	.35	.07
☐ 427 Rick Auerbach	.75	.35	.07
☐ 428 Wayne Simpson	.75	.35	.07
☐ 429 Jim Fairey	.75	.35	.07
☐ 430 Vida Blue	1.00	.50	.10
☐ 431 Gerry Moses	.75	.35	.07
☐ 432 Dan Frisella	.75	.35	.07
☐ 433 Willie Horton	1.00	.50	.10
☐ 434 San Francisco Giants	1.50	.75	.15
Team Card			
☐ 435 Rico Carty	1.00	.50	.10
☐ 436 Jim McAndrew	.75	.35	.07
☐ 437 John Kennedy	.75	.35	.07
☐ 438 Enzo Hernandez	.75	.35	.07
☐ 439 Eddie Fisher	.75	.35	.07
☐ 440 Glenn Beckert	1.00	.50	.10
☐ 441 Gail Hopkins	.75	.35	.07
☐ 442 Dick Dietz	.75	.35	.07
☐ 443 Danny Thompson	.75	.35	.07
☐ 444 Ken Brett	.75	.35	.07
☐ 445 Ken Berry	.75	.35	.07
☐ 446 Jerry Reuss	1.00	.50	.10
☐ 447 Joe Hague	.75	.35	.07
☐ 448 John Hiller	1.00	.50	.10
☐ 449A Indians Leaders	1.00	.50	.10
Ken Aspromonte MG			
Rocky Colavito CO			
Joe Lutz CO			
Warren Spahn CO			
(Spahn's right			
ear pointed)			
☐ 449B Indians Leaders	1.50	.75	.15
(Spahn's right			
ear round)			
☐ 450 Joe Torre	1.25	.60	.12
☐ 451 John Vukovich	.75	.35	.07
☐ 452 Paul Casanova	.75	.35	.07
☐ 453 Checklist 4	1.50	.15	.03
☐ 454 Tom Haller	.75	.35	.07
☐ 455 Bill Melton	.75	.35	.07
☐ 456 Dick Green	.75	.35	.07
☐ 457 John Strohmayer	.75	.35	.07
☐ 458 Jim Mason	.75	.35	.07
☐ 459 Jimmy Howarth	.75	.35	.07
☐ 460 Bill Freehan	1.25	.60	.12
☐ 461 Mike Corkins	.75	.35	.07
☐ 462 Ron Blomberg	.75	.35	.07
☐ 463 Ken Tatum	.75	.35	.07
☐ 464 Chicago Cubs	1.50	.75	.15
Team Card			
☐ 465 Dave Giusti	1.00	.50	.10
☐ 466 Jose Arcia	.75	.35	.07
☐ 467 Mike Ryan	.75	.35	.07
☐ 468 Tom Griffin	.75	.35	.07
☐ 469 Dan Monzon	.75	.35	.07
☐ 470 Mike Cuellar	1.00	.50	.10
☐ 471 Hits Leaders	3.50	1.75	.35
Ty Cobb 4191			
☐ 472 Grand Slam Leaders	3.50	1.75	.35
Lou Gehrig 23			
☐ 473 Total Bases Leaders	3.50	1.75	.35
Hank Aaron 6172			
☐ 474 RBI Leaders	6.00	3.00	.60
Babe Ruth 2209			
☐ 475 Batting Leaders	3.50	1.75	.35
Ty Cobb .367			

☐	476	Shutout Leaders	1.50	.75	.15
		Walter Johnson 113			
☐	477	Victory Leaders	1.50	.75	.15
		Cy Young 511			
☐	478	Strikeout Leaders	1.50	.75	.15
		Walter Johnson 3508			
☐	479	Hal Lanier	1.00	.50	.10
☐	480	Juan Marichal	3.50	1.75	.35
☐	481	Chicago White Sox	1.50	.75	.15
		Team Card			
☐	482	Rick Reuschel	6.00	3.00	.60
☐	483	Dal Maxvill	.75	.35	.07
☐	484	Ernie McAnally	.75	.35	.07
☐	485	Norm Cash	1.25	.60	.12
☐	486A	Phillies Leaders	1.00	.50	.10
		Danny Ozark MG			
		Carroll Beringer CO			
		Billy DeMars CO			
		Ray Rippelmeyer CO			
		Bobby Wine CO			
		(orange backgrounds)			
☐	486B	Phillies Leaders	1.50	.75	.15
		(dark pale			
		backgrounds)			
☐	487	Bruce Dal Canton	.75	.35	.07
☐	488	Dave Campbell	.75	.35	.07
☐	489	Jeff Burroughs	1.00	.50	.10
☐	490	Claude Osteen	1.00	.50	.10
☐	491	Bob Montgomery	.75	.35	.07
☐	492	Pedro Borbon	.75	.35	.07
☐	493	Duffy Dyer	.75	.35	.07
☐	494	Rich Morales	.75	.35	.07
☐	495	Tommy Helms	1.00	.50	.10
☐	496	Ray Lamb	.75	.35	.07
☐	497A	Cardinals Leaders	1.00	.50	.10
		Red Schoendienst MG			
		Vern Benson CO			
		George Kissell CO			
		Barney Schultz CO			
		(orange backgrounds)			
☐	497B	Cardinals Leaders	1.50	.75	.15
		(dark pale			
		backgrounds)			
☐	498	Graig Nettles	2.25	1.10	.22
☐	499	Bob Moose	.75	.35	.07
☐	500	Oakland A's Team	1.50	.75	.15
☐	501	Larry Gura	1.00	.50	.10
☐	502	Bobby Valentine	1.25	.60	.12
☐	503	Phil Niekro	3.50	1.75	.35
☐	504	Earl Williams	.75	.35	.07
☐	505	Bob Bailey	.75	.35	.07
☐	506	Bart Johnson	.75	.35	.07
☐	507	Darrel Chaney	.75	.35	.07
☐	508	Gates Brown	1.00	.50	.10
☐	509	Jim Nash	.75	.35	.07
☐	510	Amos Otis	1.00	.50	.10
☐	511	Sam McDowell	1.00	.50	.10
☐	512	Dalton Jones	.75	.35	.07
☐	513	Dave Marshall	.75	.35	.07
☐	514	Jerry Kenney	.75	.35	.07
☐	515	Andy Messersmith	1.00	.50	.10
☐	516	Danny Walton	.75	.35	.07
☐	517A	Pirates Leaders	1.00	.50	.10
		Bill Virdon MG			
		Don Leppert CO			
		Bill Mazeroski CO			
		Dave Ricketts CO			
		Mel Wright CO			
		(Mazeroski has			
		no right ear)			
☐	517B	Pirates Leaders	1.50	.75	.15
		(Mazeroski has			
		right ear)			
☐	518	Bob Veale	1.00	.50	.10
☐	519	Johnny Edwards	.75	.35	.07
☐	520	Mel Stottlemyre	1.25	.60	.12
☐	521	Atlanta Braves	1.50	.75	.15
		Team Card			
☐	522	Leo Cardenas	.75	.35	.07
☐	523	Wayne Granger	.75	.35	.07
☐	524	Gene Tenace	1.00	.50	.10
☐	525	Jim Fregosi	1.00	.50	.10
☐	526	Ollie Brown	.75	.35	.07
☐	527	Dan McGinn	.75	.35	.07
☐	528	Paul Blair	1.00	.50	.10
☐	529	Milt May	1.75	.85	.17
☐	530	Jim Kaat	3.50	1.75	.35
☐	531	Ron Woods	1.75	.85	.17
☐	532	Steve Mingori	1.75	.85	.17
☐	533	Larry Stahl	1.75	.85	.17
☐	534	Dave Lemonds	1.75	.85	.17
☐	535	Johnny Callison	2.25	1.10	.22
☐	536	Philadelphia Phillies	3.50	1.75	.35
		Team Card			
☐	537	Bill Slayback	1.75	.85	.17
☐	538	Jim Ray Hart	2.25	1.10	.22
☐	539	Tom Murphy	1.75	.85	.17
☐	540	Cleon Jones	2.25	1.10	.22
☐	541	Bob Bolin	1.75	.85	.17
☐	542	Pat Corrales	2.25	1.10	.22
☐	543	Alan Foster	1.75	.85	.17
☐	544	Von Joshua	1.75	.85	.17
☐	545	Orlando Cepeda	4.00	2.00	.40
☐	546	Jim York	1.75	.85	.17
☐	547	Bobby Heise	1.75	.85	.17
☐	548	Don Durham	1.75	.85	.17
☐	549	Rangers Leaders	3.00	1.50	.30
		Whitey Herzog MG			
		Chuck Estrada CO			
		Chuck Hiller CO			
		Jackie Moore CO			
☐	550	Dave Johnson	2.50	1.25	.25
☐	551	Mike Kilkenny	1.75	.85	.17
☐	552	J.C. Martin	1.75	.85	.17
☐	553	Mickey Scott	1.75	.85	.17
☐	554	Dave Concepcion	3.50	1.75	.35
☐	555	Bill Hands	1.75	.85	.17
☐	556	New York Yankees	4.00	2.00	.40
		Team Card			
☐	557	Bernie Williams	1.75	.85	.17
☐	558	Jerry May	1.75	.85	.17
☐	559	Barry Lersch	1.75	.85	.17
☐	560	Frank Howard	3.00	1.50	.30
☐	561	Jim Geddes	1.75	.85	.17
☐	562	Wayne Garrett	1.75	.85	.17
☐	563	Larry Haney	1.75	.85	.17
☐	564	Mike Thompson	1.75	.85	.17
☐	565	Jim Hickman	1.75	.85	.17
☐	566	Lew Krausse	1.75	.85	.17
☐	567	Bob Fenwick	1.75	.85	.17
☐	568	Ray Newman	1.75	.85	.17
☐	569	Dodgers Leaders	3.00	1.50	.30
		Walt Alston MG			
		Red Adams CO			
		Monty Basgall CO			
		Jim Gilliam CO			
		Tom Lasorda CO			
☐	570	Bill Singer	2.25	1.10	.22
☐	571	Rusty Torres	1.75	.85	.17
☐	572	Gary Sutherland	1.75	.85	.17
☐	573	Fred Beene	1.75	.85	.17
☐	574	Bob Didier	1.75	.85	.17
☐	575	Dock Ellis	1.75	.85	.17
☐	576	Montreal Expos	3.50	1.75	.35
		Team Card			
☐	577	Eric Soderholm	1.75	.85	.17
☐	578	Ken Wright	1.75	.85	.17
☐	579	Tom Grieve	2.25	1.10	.22
☐	580	Joe Pepitone	2.25	1.10	.22
☐	581	Steve Kealey	1.75	.85	.17
☐	582	Darrell Porter	1.75	.85	.17
☐	583	Bill Grief	1.75	.85	.17
☐	584	Chris Arnold	1.75	.85	.17
☐	585	Joe Niekro	2.50	1.25	.25
☐	586	Bill Sudakis	1.75	.85	.17
☐	587	Rich McKinney	1.75	.85	.17
☐	588	Checklist 5	14.00	1.50	.30
☐	589	Ken Forsch	2.25	1.10	.22
☐	590	Deron Johnson	1.75	.85	.17
☐	591	Mike Hedlund	1.75	.85	.17
☐	592	John Boccabella	1.75	.85	.17
☐	593	Royals Leaders	2.50	1.25	.25
		Jack McKeon MG			
		Galen Cisco CO			
		Harry Dunlop CO			
		Charlie Lau CO			
☐	594	Vic Harris	1.75	.85	.17
☐	595	Don Gullett	2.50	1.25	.25
☐	596	Red Sox Team	3.50	1.75	.35
☐	597	Mickey Rivers	2.50	1.25	.25
☐	598	Phil Roof	1.75	.85	.17
☐	599	Ed Crosby	1.75	.85	.17
☐	600	Dave McNally	2.25	1.10	.22
☐	601	Rookie Catchers	1.75	.85	.17
		Sergio Robles			
		George Pena			
		Rick Stelmaszek			
☐	602	Rookie Pitchers	1.75	.85	.17
		Mel Behney			
		Ralph Garcia			
		Doug Rau			
☐	603	Rookie 3rd Basemen	1.75	.85	.17
		Terry Hughes			
		Bill McNulty			
		Ken Reitz			

☐ 604 Rookie Pitchers	1.75	.85	.17
Jesse Jefferson			
Dennis O'Toole			
Bob Strampe			
☐ 605 Rookie 1st Basemen	1.75	.85	.17
Enos Cabell			
Pat Bourque			
Gonzalo Marquez			
☐ 606 Rookie Outfielders	3.50	1.75	.35
Gary Matthews			
Tom Paciorek			
Jorge Roque			
☐ 607 Rookie Shortstops	1.75	.85	.17
Pepe Frias			
Ray Busse			
Mario Guerrero			
☐ 608 Rookie Pitchers	1.75	.85	.17
Steve Busby			
Dick Colpaert			
George Medich			
☐ 609 Rookie 2nd Basemen	4.00	2.00	.40
Larvell Blanks			
Pedro Garcia			
Dave Lopes			
☐ 610 Rookie Pitchers	2.50	1.25	.25
Jimmy Freeman			
Charlie Hough			
Hank Webb			
☐ 611 Rookie Outfielders	1.75	.85	.17
Rich Coggins			
Jim Wohlford			
Richie Zisk			
☐ 612 Rookie Pitchers	1.75	.85	.17
Steve Lawson			
Bob Reynolds			
Brent Strom			
☐ 613 Rookie Catchers	35.00	17.50	3.50
Bob Boone			
Skip Jutze			
Mike Ivie			
☐ 614 Rookie Outfielders	65.00	32.50	6.50
Al Bumbry			
Dwight Evans			
Charlie Spikes			
☐ 615 Rookie 3rd Basemen	425.00	150.00	30.00
Ron Cey			
John Hilton			
Mike Schmidt			
☐ 616 Rookie Pitchers	1.75	.85	.17
Norm Angelini			
Steve Blateric			
Mike Garman			
☐ 617 Rich Chiles	1.75	.85	.17
☐ 618 Andy Etchebarren	1.75	.85	.17
☐ 619 Billy Wilson	1.75	.85	.17
☐ 620 Tommy Harper	2.25	1.10	.22
☐ 621 Joe Ferguson	2.25	1.10	.22
☐ 622 Larry Hisle	2.25	1.10	.22
☐ 623 Steve Renko	1.75	.85	.17
☐ 624 Astros Leaders	2.50	1.25	.25
Leo Durocher MG			
Preston Gomez CO			
Grady Hatton CO			
Hub Kittle CO			
Jim Owens CO			
☐ 625 Angel Mangual	1.75	.85	.17
☐ 626 Bob Barton	1.75	.85	.17
☐ 627 Luis Alvarado	1.75	.85	.17
☐ 628 Jim Slaton	1.75	.85	.17
☐ 629 Indians Team	3.50	1.75	.35
☐ 630 Denny McLain	4.00	2.00	.40
☐ 631 Tom Matchick	1.75	.85	.17
☐ 632 Dick Selma	1.75	.85	.17
☐ 633 Ike Brown	1.75	.85	.17
☐ 634 Alan Closter	1.75	.85	.17
☐ 635 Gene Alley	2.25	1.10	.22
☐ 636 Rickey Clark	1.75	.85	.17
☐ 637 Norm Miller	1.75	.85	.17
☐ 638 Ken Reynolds	1.75	.85	.17
☐ 639 Willie Crawford	1.75	.85	.17
☐ 640 Dick Bosman	1.75	.85	.17
☐ 641 Cincinnati Reds	3.50	1.75	.35
Team Card			
☐ 642 Jose LaBoy	1.75	.85	.17
☐ 643 Al Fitzmorris	1.75	.85	.17
☐ 644 Jack Heidemann	1.75	.85	.17
☐ 645 Bob Locker	1.75	.85	.17
☐ 646 Brewers Leaders	2.25	1.10	.22
Del Crandall MG			
Harvey Kuenn CO			
Joe Nossek CO			
Bob Shaw CO			
Jim Walton CO			
☐ 647 George Stone	1.75	.85	.17
☐ 648 Tom Egan	1.75	.85	.17
☐ 649 Rich Folkers	1.75	.85	.17
☐ 650 Felipe Alou	2.25	1.10	.22
☐ 651 Don Carrithers	1.75	.85	.17
☐ 652 Ted Kubiak	1.75	.85	.17
☐ 653 Joe Hoerner	1.75	.85	.17
☐ 654 Twins Team	3.50	1.75	.35
☐ 655 Clay Kirby	1.75	.85	.17
☐ 656 John Ellis	1.75	.85	.17
☐ 657 Bob Johnson	1.75	.85	.17
☐ 658 Elliott Maddox	1.75	.85	.17
☐ 659 Jose Pagan	1.75	.85	.17
☐ 660 Fred Scherman	2.50	1.25	.25

1974 Topps

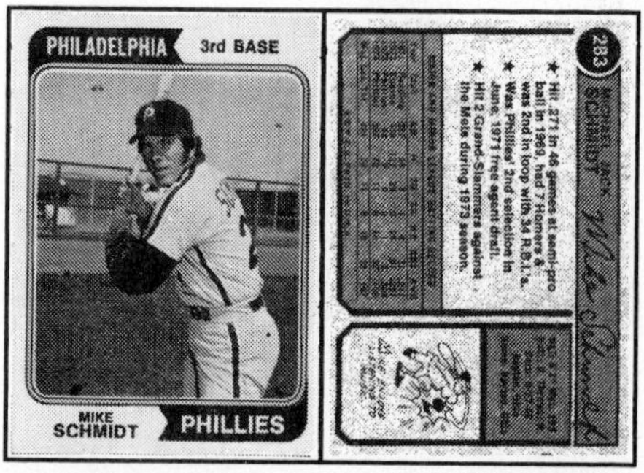

The cards in this 660-card set measure 2 1/2" by 3 1/2". This year marked the first time Topps issued all the cards of its baseball set at the same time rather than in series. Some interesting variations were created by the rumored move of the San Diego Padres to Washington. Fifteen cards (13 players, the team card, and the rookie card (599) of the Padres were printed either as "San Diego" (SD) or "Washington." The latter are the scarcer variety and are denoted in the checklist below by WAS. Each team's manager and his coaches again have a combined card with small pictures of each coach below the larger photo of the team's manager. The first six cards in the set (1-6) feature Hank Aaron and his illustrious career. Other topical subsets included in the set are League Leaders (201-208), All-Star selections (331-339), Playoffs cards (470-471), World Series cards (472-479), and Rookie Prospects (596-608). The card backs for the All-Stars (331-339) have no statistics, but form a picture puzzle of Bobby Bonds, the 1973 All-Star Game MVP. The key rookies in this set are Ken Griffey Sr., Dave Parker, and Dave Winfield.

	NRMT	VG-E	GOOD
COMPLETE SET (660)	500.00	250.00	50.00
COMMON PLAYER (1-660)	.30	.15	.03
☐ 1 Hank Aaron	25.00	5.00	1.00
Complete ML record			
☐ 2 Aaron Special 54-57	5.00	2.50	.50
Records on back			
☐ 3 Aaron Special 58-61	5.00	2.50	.50
Memorable homers			
☐ 4 Aaron Special 62-65	5.00	2.50	.50
Life in ML's 1954-63			
☐ 5 Aaron Special 66-69	5.00	2.50	.50
Life in ML's 1964-73			
☐ 6 Aaron Special 70-73	5.00	2.50	.50
Milestone homers			
☐ 7 Jim Hunter	4.00	2.00	.40
☐ 8 George Theodore	.30	.15	.03
☐ 9 Mickey Lolich	.60	.30	.06
☐ 10 Johnny Bench	14.00	7.00	1.40
☐ 11 Jim Bibby	.30	.15	.03
☐ 12 Dave May	.30	.15	.03
☐ 13 Tom Hilgendorf	.30	.15	.03
☐ 14 Paul Popovich	.30	.15	.03
☐ 15 Joe Torre	.75	.35	.07

☐ 16 Baltimore Orioles	.65	.30	.06
Team Card			
☐ 17 Doug Bird	.30	.15	.03
☐ 18 Gary Thomasson	.30	.15	.03
☐ 19 Gerry Moses	.30	.15	.03
☐ 20 Nolan Ryan	36.00	18.00	3.60
☐ 21 Bob Gallagher	.30	.15	.03
☐ 22 Cy Acosta	.30	.15	.03
☐ 23 Craig Robinson	.30	.15	.03
☐ 24 John Hiller	.50	.25	.05
☐ 25 Ken Singleton	.50	.25	.05
☐ 26 Bill Campbell	.30	.15	.03
☐ 27 George Scott	.50	.25	.05
☐ 28 Manny Sanguillen	.50	.25	.05
☐ 29 Phil Niekro	2.25	1.10	.22
☐ 30 Bobby Bonds	.75	.35	.07
☐ 31 Astros Leaders	.50	.25	.05
Preston Gomez MG			
Roger Craig CO			
Hub Kittle CO			
Grady Hatton CO			
Bob Lillis CO			
☐ 32A Johnny Grubb SD	.30	.15	.03
☐ 32B Johnny Grubb WAS	4.50	2.25	.45
☐ 33 Don Newhauser	.30	.15	.03
☐ 34 Andy Kosco	.30	.15	.03
☐ 35 Gaylord Perry	3.00	1.25	.25
☐ 36 St. Louis Cardinals	.65	.30	.06
Team Card			
☐ 37 Dave Sells	.30	.15	.03
☐ 38 Don Kessinger	.50	.25	.05
☐ 39 Ken Suarez	.30	.15	.03
☐ 40 Jim Palmer	6.50	3.25	.65
☐ 41 Bobby Floyd	.30	.15	.03
☐ 42 Claude Osteen	.50	.25	.05
☐ 43 Jim Wynn	.50	.25	.05
☐ 44 Mel Stottlemyre	.60	.30	.06
☐ 45 Dave Johnson	.60	.30	.06
☐ 46 Pat Kelly	.30	.15	.03
☐ 47 Dick Ruthven	.30	.15	.03
☐ 48 Dick Sharon	.30	.15	.03
☐ 49 Steve Renko	.30	.15	.03
☐ 50 Rod Carew	11.00	5.50	1.10
☐ 51 Bobby Heise	.30	.15	.03
☐ 52 Al Oliver	.90	.45	.09
☐ 53A Fred Kendall SD	.30	.15	.03
☐ 53B Fred Kendall WAS	4.50	2.25	.45
☐ 54 Elias Sosa	.30	.15	.03
☐ 55 Frank Robinson	4.00	2.00	.40
☐ 56 New York Mets Team	.75	.35	.07
☐ 57 Darold Knowles	.30	.15	.03
☐ 58 Charlie Spikes	.30	.15	.03
☐ 59 Ross Grimsley	.30	.15	.03
☐ 60 Lou Brock	4.00	2.00	.40
☐ 61 Luis Aparicio	2.00	1.00	.20
☐ 62 Bob Locker	.30	.15	.03
☐ 63 Bill Sudakis	.30	.15	.03
☐ 64 Doug Rau	.30	.15	.03
☐ 65 Amos Otis	.50	.25	.05
☐ 66 Sparky Lyle	.50	.25	.05
☐ 67 Tommy Helms	.50	.25	.05
☐ 68 Grant Jackson	.30	.15	.03
☐ 69 Del Unser	.30	.15	.03
☐ 70 Dick Allen	.60	.30	.06
☐ 71 Dan Frisella	.30	.15	.03
☐ 72 Aurelio Rodriguez	.30	.15	.03
☐ 73 Mike Marshall	.50	.25	.05
☐ 74 Twins Team	.65	.30	.06
☐ 75 Jim Colborn	.30	.15	.03
☐ 76 Mickey Rivers	.50	.25	.05
☐ 77A Rich Troedson SD	.30	.15	.03
☐ 77B Rich Troedson WAS	4.50	2.25	.45
☐ 78 Giants Leaders	.50	.25	.05
Charlie Fox MG			
John McNamara CO			
Joe Amalfitano CO			
Andy Gilbert CO			
Don McMahon CO			
☐ 79 Gene Tenace	.50	.25	.05
☐ 80 Tom Seaver	13.00	6.50	1.30
☐ 81 Frank Duffy	.30	.15	.03
☐ 82 Dave Giusti	.30	.15	.03
☐ 83 Orlando Cepeda	1.00	.50	.10
☐ 84 Rick Wise	.30	.15	.03
☐ 85 Joe Morgan	4.00	2.00	.40
☐ 86 Joe Ferguson	.30	.15	.03
☐ 87 Fergie Jenkins	2.00	.85	.17
☐ 88 Freddie Patek	.30	.15	.03
☐ 89 Jackie Brown	.30	.15	.03
☐ 90 Bobby Murcer	.60	.30	.06
☐ 91 Ken Forsch	.30	.15	.03
☐ 92 Paul Blair	.50	.25	.05
☐ 93 Rod Gilbreath	.30	.15	.03
☐ 94 Tigers Team	.65	.30	.06

☐ 95 Steve Carlton	8.00	4.00	.80
☐ 96 Jerry Hairston	.30	.15	.03
☐ 97 Bob Bailey	.30	.15	.03
☐ 98 Bert Blyleven	2.50	1.25	.25
☐ 99 Brewers Leaders	.50	.25	.05
Del Crandall MG			
Harvey Kuenn CO			
Joe Nossek CO			
Jim Walton CO			
Al Widmar CO			
☐ 100 Willie Stargell	3.50	1.75	.35
☐ 101 Bobby Valentine	.60	.30	.06
☐ 102A Bill Greif SD	.30	.15	.03
☐ 102B Bill Greif WAS	4.50	2.25	.45
☐ 103 Sal Bando	.50	.25	.05
☐ 104 Ron Bryant	.30	.15	.03
☐ 105 Carlton Fisk	15.00	7.50	1.50
☐ 106 Harry Parker	.30	.15	.03
☐ 107 Alex Johnson	.30	.15	.03
☐ 108 Al Hrabosky	.30	.15	.03
☐ 109 Bob Grich	.50	.25	.05
☐ 110 Billy Williams	3.00	1.50	.30
☐ 111 Clay Carroll	.30	.15	.03
☐ 112 Dave Lopes	.50	.25	.05
☐ 113 Dick Drago	.30	.15	.03
☐ 114 Angels Team	.65	.30	.06
☐ 115 Willie Horton	.50	.25	.05
☐ 116 Jerry Reuss	.50	.25	.05
☐ 117 Ron Blomberg	.30	.15	.03
☐ 118 Bill Lee	.30	.15	.03
☐ 119 Phillies Leaders	.50	.25	.05
Danny Ozark MG			
Ray Ripplemeyer CO			
Bobby Wine CO			
Carroll Beringer CO			
Billy DeMars CO			
☐ 120 Wilbur Wood	.30	.15	.03
☐ 121 Larry Lintz	.30	.15	.03
☐ 122 Jim Holt	.30	.15	.03
☐ 123 Nelson Briles	.30	.15	.03
☐ 124 Bobby Coluccio	.30	.15	.03
☐ 125A Nate Colbert SD	.30	.15	.03
☐ 125B Nate Colbert WAS	4.50	2.25	.45
☐ 126 Checklist 1	1.50	.15	.03
☐ 127 Tom Paciorek	.30	.15	.03
☐ 128 John Ellis	.30	.15	.03
☐ 129 Chris Speier	.30	.15	.03
☐ 130 Reggie Jackson	15.00	7.50	1.50
☐ 131 Bob Boone	2.50	1.25	.25
☐ 132 Felix Millan	.30	.15	.03
☐ 133 David Clyde	.30	.15	.03
☐ 134 Denis Menke	.30	.15	.03
☐ 135 Roy White	.50	.25	.05
☐ 136 Rick Reuschel	1.75	.85	.17
☐ 137 Al Bumbry	.30	.15	.03
☐ 138 Eddie Brinkman	.30	.15	.03
☐ 139 Aurelio Monteagudo	.30	.15	.03
☐ 140 Darrell Evans	.60	.30	.06
☐ 141 Pat Bourque	.30	.15	.03
☐ 142 Pedro Garcia	.30	.15	.03
☐ 143 Dick Woodson	.30	.15	.03
☐ 144 Dodgers Leaders	1.25	.60	.12
Walter Alston MG			
Tom Lasorda CO			
Jim Gilliam CO			
Red Adams CO			
Monty Basgall CO			
☐ 145 Dock Ellis	.30	.15	.03
☐ 146 Ron Fairly	.30	.15	.03
☐ 147 Bart Johnson	.30	.15	.03
☐ 148A Dave Hilton SD	.30	.15	.03
☐ 148B Dave Hilton WAS	4.50	2.25	.45
☐ 149 Mac Scarce	.30	.15	.03
☐ 150 John Mayberry	.50	.25	.05
☐ 151 Diego Segui	.30	.15	.03
☐ 152 Oscar Gamble	.50	.25	.05
☐ 153 Jon Matlack	.30	.15	.03
☐ 154 Astros Team	.65	.30	.06
☐ 155 Bert Campaneris	.50	.25	.05
☐ 156 Randy Moffitt	.30	.15	.03
☐ 157 Vic Harris	.30	.15	.03
☐ 158 Jack Billingham	.30	.15	.03
☐ 159 Jim Ray Hart	.30	.15	.03
☐ 160 Brooks Robinson	4.50	2.25	.45
☐ 161 Ray Burris UER	.50	.25	.05
(card number is			
printed sideways)			
☐ 162 Bill Freehan	.60	.30	.06
☐ 163 Ken Berry	.30	.15	.03
☐ 164 Tom House	.30	.15	.03
☐ 165 Willie Davis	.50	.25	.05

☐ 166 Royals Leaders	.50	.25	.05
Jack McKeon MG			
Charlie Lau CO			
Harry Dunlop CO			
Galen Cisco CO			
☐ 167 Luis Tiant	.60	.30	.06
☐ 168 Danny Thompson	.30	.15	.03
☐ 169 Steve Rogers	.60	.30	.06
☐ 170 Bill Melton	.30	.15	.03
☐ 171 Eduardo Rodriguez	.30	.15	.03
☐ 172 Gene Clines	.30	.15	.03
☐ 173A Randy Jones SD	.75	.35	.07
☐ 173B Randy Jones WAS	5.50	2.75	.55
☐ 174 Bill Robinson	.50	.25	.05
☐ 175 Reggie Cleveland	.30	.15	.03
☐ 176 John Lowenstein	.30	.15	.03
☐ 177 Dave Roberts	.30	.15	.03
☐ 178 Garry Maddox	.50	.25	.05
☐ 179 Mets Leaders	1.25	.60	.12
Yogi Berra MG			
Rube Walker CO			
Eddie Yost CO			
Roy McMillan CO			
Joe Pignatano CO			
☐ 180 Ken Holtzman	.50	.25	.05
☐ 181 Cesar Geronimo	.30	.15	.03
☐ 182 Lindy McDaniel	.30	.15	.03
☐ 183 Johnny Oates	.30	.15	.03
☐ 184 Texas Rangers	.65	.30	.06
Team Card			
☐ 185 Jose Cardenal	.30	.15	.03
☐ 186 Fred Scherman	.30	.15	.03
☐ 187 Don Baylor	1.00	.50	.10
☐ 188 Rudy Meoli	.30	.15	.03
☐ 189 Jim Brewer	.30	.15	.03
☐ 190 Tony Oliva	1.00	.50	.10
☐ 191 Al Fitzmorris	.30	.15	.03
☐ 192 Mario Guerrero	.30	.15	.03
☐ 193 Tom Walker	.30	.15	.03
☐ 194 Darrell Porter	.30	.15	.03
☐ 195 Carlos May	.30	.15	.03
☐ 196 Jim Fregosi	.50	.25	.05
☐ 197A Vicente Romo SD	.30	.15	.03
☐ 197B Vicente Romo WAS	4.50	2.25	.45
☐ 198 Dave Cash	.30	.15	.03
☐ 199 Mike Kekich	.30	.15	.03
☐ 200 Cesar Cedeno	.50	.25	.05
☐ 201 Batting Leaders	3.50	1.75	.35
Rod Carew			
Pete Rose			
☐ 202 Home Run Leaders	2.25	1.10	.22
Reggie Jackson			
Willie Stargell			
☐ 203 RBI Leaders	2.25	1.10	.22
Reggie Jackson			
Willie Stargell			
☐ 204 Stolen Base Leaders	.75	.35	.07
Tommy Harper			
Lou Brock			
☐ 205 Victory Leaders	.65	.30	.06
Wilbur Wood			
Ron Bryant			
☐ 206 ERA Leaders	2.50	1.25	.25
Jim Palmer			
Tom Seaver			
☐ 207 Strikeout Leaders	5.00	2.50	.50
Nolan Ryan			
Tom Seaver			
☐ 208 Leading Firemen	.65	.30	.06
John Hiller			
Mike Marshall			
☐ 209 Ted Sizemore	.30	.15	.03
☐ 210 Bill Singer	.30	.15	.03
☐ 211 Chicago Cubs Team	.65	.30	.06
☐ 212 Rollie Fingers	3.50	1.75	.35
☐ 213 Dave Rader	.30	.15	.03
☐ 214 Billy Grabarkewitz	.30	.15	.03
☐ 215 Al Kaline UER	4.50	2.25	.45
(no copyright on back)			
☐ 216 Ray Sadecki	.30	.15	.03
☐ 217 Tim Foli	.30	.15	.03
☐ 218 Johnny Briggs	.30	.15	.03
☐ 219 Doug Griffin	.30	.15	.03
☐ 220 Don Sutton	2.00	1.00	.20
☐ 221 White Sox Leaders	.50	.25	.05
Chuck Tanner MG			
Jim Mahoney CO			
Alex Monchak CO			
Johnny Sain CO			
Joe Lonnett CO			
☐ 222 Ramon Hernandez	.30	.15	.03
☐ 223 Jeff Burroughs	.50	.25	.05
☐ 224 Roger Metzger	.30	.15	.03
☐ 225 Paul Splittorff	.30	.15	.03

☐ 226A Padres Team SD	1.00	.50	.10
☐ 226B Padres Team WAS	5.00	2.50	.50
☐ 227 Mike Lum	.30	.15	.03
☐ 228 Ted Kubiak	.30	.15	.03
☐ 229 Fritz Peterson	.30	.15	.03
☐ 230 Tony Perez	1.50	.75	.15
☐ 231 Dick Tidrow	.30	.15	.03
☐ 232 Steve Brye	.30	.15	.03
☐ 233 Jim Barr	.30	.15	.03
☐ 234 John Milner	.30	.15	.03
☐ 235 Dave McNally	.50	.25	.05
☐ 236 Cardinals Leaders	.65	.30	.06
Red Schoendienst MG			
Barney Schultz CO			
George Kissell CO			
Johnny Lewis CO			
Vern Benson CO			
☐ 237 Ken Brett	.30	.15	.03
☐ 238 Fran Healy HOR	.50	.25	.05
(Munson sliding			
in background)			
☐ 239 Bill Russell	.50	.25	.05
☐ 240 Joe Coleman	.30	.15	.03
☐ 241A Glenn Beckert SD	.50	.25	.05
☐ 241B Glenn Beckert WAS	5.00	2.50	.50
☐ 242 Bill Gogolewski	.30	.15	.03
☐ 243 Bob Oliver	.30	.15	.03
☐ 244 Carl Morton	.30	.15	.03
☐ 245 Cleon Jones	.30	.15	.03
☐ 246 Athletics Team	.65	.30	.06
☐ 247 Rick Miller	.30	.15	.03
☐ 248 Tom Hall	.30	.15	.03
☐ 249 George Mitterwald	.30	.15	.03
☐ 250A Willie McCovey SD	4.00	2.00	.40
☐ 250B Willie McCovey WAS	25.00	12.50	2.50
☐ 251 Graig Nettles	1.50	.75	.15
☐ 252 Dave Parker	38.00	17.00	3.50
☐ 253 John Boccabella	.30	.15	.03
☐ 254 Stan Bahnsen	.30	.15	.03
☐ 255 Larry Bowa	.75	.35	.07
☐ 256 Tom Griffin	.30	.15	.03
☐ 257 Buddy Bell	1.25	.60	.12
☐ 258 Jerry Morales	.30	.15	.03
☐ 259 Bob Reynolds	.30	.15	.03
☐ 260 Ted Simmons	1.25	.60	.12
☐ 261 Jerry Bell	.30	.15	.03
☐ 262 Ed Kirkpatrick	.30	.15	.03
☐ 263 Checklist 2	1.50	.15	.03
☐ 264 Joe Rudi	.50	.25	.05
☐ 265 Tug McGraw	.75	.35	.07
☐ 266 Jim Northrup	.50	.25	.05
☐ 267 Andy Messersmith	.50	.25	.05
☐ 268 Tom Grieve	.50	.25	.05
☐ 269 Bob Johnson	.30	.15	.03
☐ 270 Ron Santo	.75	.35	.07
☐ 271 Bill Hands	.30	.15	.03
☐ 272 Paul Casanova	.30	.15	.03
☐ 273 Checklist 3	1.50	.15	.03
☐ 274 Fred Beene	.30	.15	.03
☐ 275 Ron Hunt	.30	.15	.03
☐ 276 Angels Leaders	.50	.25	.05
Bobby Winkles MG			
John Roseboro CO			
Tom Morgan CO			
Jimmie Reese CO			
Salty Parker CO			
☐ 277 Gary Nolan	.30	.15	.03
☐ 278 Cookie Rojas	.30	.15	.03
☐ 279 Jim Crawford	.30	.15	.03
☐ 280 Carl Yastrzemski	14.00	7.00	1.40
☐ 281 Giants Team	.65	.30	.06
☐ 282 Doyle Alexander	.60	.30	.06
☐ 283 Mike Schmidt	125.00	60.00	12.50
☐ 284 Dave Duncan	.30	.15	.03
☐ 285 Reggie Smith	.60	.30	.06
☐ 286 Tony Muser	.30	.15	.03
☐ 287 Clay Kirby	.30	.15	.03
☐ 288 Gorman Thomas	2.00	1.00	.20
☐ 289 Rick Auerbach	.30	.15	.03
☐ 290 Vida Blue	.60	.30	.06
☐ 291 Don Hahn	.30	.15	.03
☐ 292 Chuck Seelbach	.30	.15	.03
☐ 293 Milt May	.30	.15	.03
☐ 294 Steve Foucault	.30	.15	.03
☐ 295 Rick Monday	.50	.25	.05
☐ 296 Ray Corbin	.30	.15	.03
☐ 297 Hal Breeden	.30	.15	.03
☐ 298 Roric Harrison	.30	.15	.03
☐ 299 Gene Michael	.50	.25	.05
☐ 300 Pete Rose	16.00	8.00	1.60
☐ 301 Bob Montgomery	.30	.15	.03
☐ 302 Rudy May	.30	.15	.03
☐ 303 George Hendrick	.50	.25	.05
☐ 304 Don Wilson	.30	.15	.03

☐ 305 Tito Fuentes	.30	.15	.03
☐ 306 Orioles Leaders	.75	.35	.07
Earl Weaver MG			
Jim Frey CO			
George Bamberger CO			
Billy Hunter CO			
George Staller CO			
☐ 307 Luis Melendez	.30	.15	.03
☐ 308 Bruce Dal Canton	.30	.15	.03
☐ 309A Dave Roberts SD	.30	.15	.03
☐ 309B Dave Roberts WAS	6.50	3.25	.65
☐ 310 Terry Forster	.50	.25	.05
☐ 311 Jerry Grote	.30	.15	.03
☐ 312 Deron Johnson	.30	.15	.03
☐ 313 Barry Lersch	.30	.15	.03
☐ 314 Milwaukee Brewers	.65	.30	.06
Team Card			
☐ 315 Ron Cey	1.00	.50	.10
☐ 316 Jim Perry	.50	.25	.05
☐ 317 Richie Zisk	.30	.15	.03
☐ 318 Jim Merritt	.30	.15	.03
☐ 319 Randy Hundley	.30	.15	.03
☐ 320 Dusty Baker	.50	.25	.05
☐ 321 Steve Braun	.30	.15	.03
☐ 322 Ernie McAnally	.30	.15	.03
☐ 323 Richie Scheinblum	.30	.15	.03
☐ 324 Steve Kline	.30	.15	.03
☐ 325 Tommy Harper	.50	.25	.05
☐ 326 Reds Leaders	.75	.35	.07
Sparky Anderson MG			
Larry Shephard CO			
George Scherger CO			
Alex Grammas CO			
Ted Kluszewski CO			
☐ 327 Tom Timmermann	.30	.15	.03
☐ 328 Skip Jutze	.30	.15	.03
☐ 329 Mark Belanger	.50	.25	.05
☐ 330 Juan Marichal	2.50	1.25	.25
☐ 331 All-Star Catchers	3.00	1.50	.30
Carlton Fisk			
Johnny Bench			
☐ 332 All-Star 1B	2.00	1.00	.20
Dick Allen			
Hank Aaron			
☐ 333 All-Star 2B	2.50	1.25	.25
Rod Carew			
Joe Morgan			
☐ 334 All-Star 3B	1.25	.60	.12
Brooks Robinson			
Ron Santo			
☐ 335 All-Star SS	.50	.25	.05
Bert Campaneris			
Chris Speier			
☐ 336 All-Star LF	2.50	1.25	.25
Bobby Murcer			
Pete Rose			
☐ 337 All-Star CF	.50	.25	.05
Amos Otis			
Cesar Cedeno			
☐ 338 All-Star RF	3.00	1.50	.30
Reggie Jackson			
Billy Williams			
☐ 339 All-Star Pitchers	.60	.30	.06
Jim Hunter			
Rick Wise			
☐ 340 Thurman Munson	7.50	3.75	.75
☐ 341 Dan Driessen	.75	.35	.07
☐ 342 Jim Lonborg	.50	.25	.05
☐ 343 Royals Team	.65	.30	.06
☐ 344 Mike Caldwell	.50	.25	.05
☐ 345 Bill North	.30	.15	.03
☐ 346 Ron Reed	.30	.15	.03
☐ 347 Sandy Alomar	.30	.15	.03
☐ 348 Pete Richert	.30	.15	.03
☐ 349 John Vukovich	.30	.15	.03
☐ 350 Bob Gibson	3.50	1.75	.35
☐ 351 Dwight Evans	14.00	7.00	1.40
☐ 352 Bill Stoneman	.30	.15	.03
☐ 353 Rich Coggins	.30	.15	.03
☐ 354 Cubs Leaders	.50	.25	.05
Whitey Lockman MG			
J.C. Martin CO			
Hank Aguirre CO			
Al Spangler CO			
Jim Marshall CO			
☐ 355 Dave Nelson	.30	.15	.03
☐ 356 Jerry Koosman	.75	.35	.07
☐ 357 Buddy Bradford	.30	.15	.03
☐ 358 Dal Maxvill	.30	.15	.03
☐ 359 Brent Strom	.30	.15	.03
☐ 360 Greg Luzinski	.75	.35	.07
☐ 361 Don Carrithers	.30	.15	.03
☐ 362 Hal King	.30	.15	.03
☐ 363 Yankees Team	.75	.35	.07

☐ 364A Cito Gaston SD	.75	.35	.07
☐ 364B Cito Gaston WAS	7.50	3.75	.75
☐ 365 Steve Busby	.50	.25	.05
☐ 366 Larry Hisle	.50	.25	.05
☐ 367 Norm Cash	.75	.35	.07
☐ 368 Manny Mota	.50	.25	.05
☐ 369 Paul Lindblad	.30	.15	.03
☐ 370 Bob Watson	.50	.25	.05
☐ 371 Jim Slaton	.30	.15	.03
☐ 372 Ken Reitz	.30	.15	.03
☐ 373 John Curtis	.30	.15	.03
☐ 374 Marty Perez	.30	.15	.03
☐ 375 Earl Williams	.30	.15	.03
☐ 376 Jorge Orta	.30	.15	.03
☐ 377 Ron Woods	.30	.15	.03
☐ 378 Burt Hooton	.50	.25	.05
☐ 379 Rangers Leaders	1.00	.50	.10
Billy Martin MG			
Frank Lucchesi CO			
Art Fowler CO			
Charlie Silvera CO			
Jackie Moore CO			
☐ 380 Bud Harrelson	.50	.25	.05
☐ 381 Charlie Sands	.30	.15	.03
☐ 382 Bob Moose	.30	.15	.03
☐ 383 Phillies Team	.65	.30	.06
☐ 384 Chris Chambliss	.50	.25	.05
☐ 385 Don Gullett	.50	.25	.05
☐ 386 Gary Matthews	.50	.25	.05
☐ 387A Rich Morales SD	.30	.15	.03
☐ 387B Rich Morales WAS	6.50	3.25	.65
☐ 388 Phil Roof	.30	.15	.03
☐ 389 Gates Brown	.50	.25	.05
☐ 390 Lou Piniella	.75	.35	.07
☐ 391 Billy Champion	.30	.15	.03
☐ 392 Dick Green	.30	.15	.03
☐ 393 Orlando Pena	.30	.15	.03
☐ 394 Ken Henderson	.30	.15	.03
☐ 395 Doug Rader	.50	.25	.05
☐ 396 Tommy Davis	.50	.25	.05
☐ 397 George Stone	.30	.15	.03
☐ 398 Duke Sims	.30	.15	.03
☐ 399 Mike Paul	.30	.15	.03
☐ 400 Harmon Killebrew	4.00	2.00	.40
☐ 401 Elliott Maddox	.30	.15	.03
☐ 402 Jim Rooker	.30	.15	.03
☐ 403 Red Sox Leaders	.50	.25	.05
Darrell Johnson MG			
Eddie Popowski CO			
Lee Stange CO			
Don Zimmer CO			
Don Bryant CO			
☐ 404 Jim Howarth	.30	.15	.03
☐ 405 Ellie Rodriguez	.30	.15	.03
☐ 406 Steve Arlin	.30	.15	.03
☐ 407 Jim Wohlford	.30	.15	.03
☐ 408 Charlie Hough	.60	.30	.06
☐ 409 Ike Brown	.30	.15	.03
☐ 410 Pedro Borbon	.30	.15	.03
☐ 411 Frank Baker	.30	.15	.03
☐ 412 Chuck Taylor	.30	.15	.03
☐ 413 Don Money	.30	.15	.03
☐ 414 Checklist 4	1.50	.15	.03
☐ 415 Gary Gentry	.30	.15	.03
☐ 416 White Sox Team	.65	.30	.06
☐ 417 Rich Folkers	.30	.15	.03
☐ 418 Walt Williams	.30	.15	.03
☐ 419 Wayne Twitchell	.30	.15	.03
☐ 420 Ray Fosse	.30	.15	.03
☐ 421 Dan Fife	.30	.15	.03
☐ 422 Gonzalo Marquez	.30	.15	.03
☐ 423 Fred Stanley	.30	.15	.03
☐ 424 Jim Beauchamp	.30	.15	.03
☐ 425 Pete Broberg	.30	.15	.03
☐ 426 Rennie Stennett	.30	.15	.03
☐ 427 Bobby Bolin	.30	.15	.03
☐ 428 Gary Sutherland	.30	.15	.03
☐ 429 Dick Lange	.30	.15	.03
☐ 430 Matty Alou	.50	.25	.05
☐ 431 Gene Garber	.50	.25	.05
☐ 432 Chris Arnold	.30	.15	.03
☐ 433 Lerrin LaGrow	.30	.15	.03
☐ 434 Ken McMullen	.30	.15	.03
☐ 435 Dave Concepcion	1.00	.50	.10
☐ 436 Don Hood	.30	.15	.03
☐ 437 Jim Lyttle	.30	.15	.03
☐ 438 Ed Herrmann	.30	.15	.03
☐ 439 Norm Miller	.30	.15	.03
☐ 440 Jim Kaat	1.00	.50	.10
☐ 441 Tom Ragland	.30	.15	.03
☐ 442 Alan Foster	.30	.15	.03
☐ 443 Tom Hutton	.30	.15	.03
☐ 444 Vic Davalillo	.30	.15	.03
☐ 445 George Medich	.30	.15	.03

☐ 446	Len Randle	.30	.15	.03
☐ 447	Twins Leaders	.50	.25	.05
	Frank Quilici MG			
	Ralph Rowe CO			
	Bob Rodgers CO			
	Vern Morgan CO			
☐ 448	Ron Hodges	.30	.15	.03
☐ 449	Tom McCraw	.30	.15	.03
☐ 450	Rich Hebner	.30	.15	.03
☐ 451	Tommy John	1.50	.75	.15
☐ 452	Gene Hiser	.30	.15	.03
☐ 453	Balor Moore	.30	.15	.03
☐ 454	Kurt Bevacqua	.30	.15	.03
☐ 455	Tom Bradley	.30	.15	.03
☐ 456	Dave Winfield	50.00	25.00	5.00
☐ 457	Chuck Goggin	.30	.15	.03
☐ 458	Jim Ray	.30	.15	.03
☐ 459	Cincinnati Reds	.65	.30	.06
	Team Card			
☐ 460	Boog Powell	.75	.35	.07
☐ 461	John Odom	.30	.15	.03
☐ 462	Luis Alvarado	.30	.15	.03
☐ 463	Pat Dobson	.30	.15	.03
☐ 464	Jose Cruz	.50	.25	.05
☐ 465	Dick Bosman	.30	.15	.03
☐ 466	Dick Billings	.30	.15	.03
☐ 467	Winston Llenas	.30	.15	.03
☐ 468	Pepe Frias	.30	.15	.03
☐ 469	Joe Decker	.30	.15	.03
☐ 470	AL Playoffs	3.00	1.50	.30
	A's over Orioles			
	(Reggie Jackson)			
☐ 471	NL Playoffs	.75	.35	.07
	Mets over Reds			
	(Matlack pitching)			
☐ 472	World Series Game 1	.75	.35	.07
	(Knowles pitching)			
☐ 473	World Series Game 2	3.00	1.50	.30
	(Willie Mays batting)			
☐ 474	World Series Game 3	.75	.35	.07
	(Campaneris stealing)			
☐ 475	World Series Game 4	.75	.35	.07
	(Staub batting)			
☐ 476	World Series Game 5	.75	.35	.07
	Cleon Jones scoring)			
☐ 477	World Series Game 6	3.00	1.50	.30
	(Reggie Jackson)			
☐ 478	World Series Game 7	.75	.35	.07
	(Campaneris batting)			
☐ 479	World Series Summary	.75	.35	.07
	A's celebrate; win			
	2nd consecutive			
	championship			
☐ 480	Willie Crawford	.30	.15	.03
☐ 481	Jerry Terrell	.30	.15	.03
☐ 482	Bob Didier	.30	.15	.03
☐ 483	Atlanta Braves	.65	.30	.06
	Team Card			
☐ 484	Carmen Fanzone	.30	.15	.03
☐ 485	Felipe Alou	.50	.25	.05
☐ 486	Steve Stone	.50	.25	.05
☐ 487	Ted Martinez	.30	.15	.03
☐ 488	Andy Etchebarren	.30	.15	.03
☐ 489	Pirates Leaders	.50	.25	.05
	Danny Murtaugh MG			
	Don Osborn CO			
	Don Leppert CO			
	Bill Mazeroski CO			
	Bob Skinner CO			
☐ 490	Vada Pinson	.75	.35	.07
☐ 491	Roger Nelson	.30	.15	.03
☐ 492	Mike Rogodzinski	.30	.15	.03
☐ 493	Joe Hoerner	.30	.15	.03
☐ 494	Ed Goodson	.30	.15	.03
☐ 495	Dick McAuliffe	.50	.25	.05
☐ 496	Tom Murphy	.30	.15	.03
☐ 497	Bobby Mitchell	.30	.15	.03
☐ 498	Pat Corrales	.50	.25	.05
☐ 499	Rusty Torres	.30	.15	.03
☐ 500	Lee May	.50	.25	.05
☐ 501	Eddie Leon	.30	.15	.03
☐ 502	Dave LaRoche	.30	.15	.03
☐ 503	Eric Soderholm	.30	.15	.03
☐ 504	Joe Niekro	.50	.25	.05
☐ 505	Bill Buckner	.75	.35	.07
☐ 506	Ed Farmer	.30	.15	.03
☐ 507	Larry Stahl	.30	.15	.03
☐ 508	Expos Team	.65	.30	.06
☐ 509	Jesse Jefferson	.30	.15	.03
☐ 510	Wayne Garrett	.30	.15	.03
☐ 511	Toby Harrah	.50	.25	.05
☐ 512	Joe Lahoud	.30	.15	.03
☐ 513	Jim Campanis	.30	.15	.03
☐ 514	Paul Schaal	.30	.15	.03
☐ 515	Willie Montanez	.30	.15	.03
☐ 516	Horacio Pina	.30	.15	.03
☐ 517	Mike Hegan	.30	.15	.03
☐ 518	Derrel Thomas	.30	.15	.03
☐ 519	Bill Sharp	.30	.15	.03
☐ 520	Tim McCarver	.75	.35	.07
☐ 521	Indians Leaders	.50	.25	.05
	Ken Aspromonte MG			
	Clay Bryant CO			
	Tony Pacheco CO			
☐ 522	J.R. Richard	.50	.25	.05
☐ 523	Cecil Cooper	2.00	1.00	.20
☐ 524	Bill Plummer	.30	.15	.03
☐ 525	Clyde Wright	.30	.15	.03
☐ 526	Frank Tepedino	.30	.15	.03
☐ 527	Bobby Darwin	.30	.15	.03
☐ 528	Bill Bonham	.30	.15	.03
☐ 529	Horace Clarke	.30	.15	.03
☐ 530	Mickey Stanley	.50	.25	.05
☐ 531	Expos Leaders	.50	.25	.05
	Gene Mauch MG			
	Dave Bristol CO			
	Cal McLish CO			
	Larry Doby CO			
	Jerry Zimmerman CO			
☐ 532	Skip Lockwood	.30	.15	.03
☐ 533	Mike Phillips	.30	.15	.03
☐ 534	Eddie Watt	.30	.15	.03
☐ 535	Bob Tolan	.30	.15	.03
☐ 536	Duffy Dyer	.30	.15	.03
☐ 537	Steve Mingori	.30	.15	.03
☐ 538	Cesar Tovar	.30	.15	.03
☐ 539	Lloyd Allen	.30	.15	.03
☐ 540	Bob Robertson	.30	.15	.03
☐ 541	Cleveland Indians	.65	.30	.06
	Team Card			
☐ 542	Rich Gossage	2.25	1.10	.22
☐ 543	Danny Cater	.30	.15	.03
☐ 544	Ron Schueler	.30	.15	.03
☐ 545	Billy Conigliaro	.30	.15	.03
☐ 546	Mike Corkins	.30	.15	.03
☐ 547	Glenn Borgmann	.30	.15	.03
☐ 548	Sonny Siebert	.30	.15	.03
☐ 549	Mike Jorgensen	.30	.15	.03
☐ 550	Sam McDowell	.50	.25	.05
☐ 551	Von Joshua	.30	.15	.03
☐ 552	Denny Doyle	.30	.15	.03
☐ 553	Jim Willoughby	.30	.15	.03
☐ 554	Tim Johnson	.30	.15	.03
☐ 555	Woodie Fryman	.30	.15	.03
☐ 556	Dave Campbell	.30	.15	.03
☐ 557	Jim McGlothlin	.30	.15	.03
☐ 558	Bill Fahey	.30	.15	.03
☐ 559	Darrell Chaney	.30	.15	.03
☐ 560	Mike Cuellar	.50	.25	.05
☐ 561	Ed Kranepool	.50	.25	.05
☐ 562	Jack Aker	.30	.15	.03
☐ 563	Hal McRae	.50	.25	.05
☐ 564	Mike Ryan	.30	.15	.03
☐ 565	Milt Wilcox	.30	.15	.03
☐ 566	Jackie Hernandez	.30	.15	.03
☐ 567	Red Sox Team	.65	.30	.06
☐ 568	Mike Torrez	.50	.25	.05
☐ 569	Rick Dempsey	.50	.25	.05
☐ 570	Ralph Garr	.50	.25	.05
☐ 571	Rich Hand	.30	.15	.03
☐ 572	Enzo Hernandez	.30	.15	.03
☐ 573	Mike Adams	.30	.15	.03
☐ 574	Bill Parsons	.30	.15	.03
☐ 575	Steve Garvey	14.00	7.00	1.40
☐ 576	Scipio Spinks	.30	.15	.03
☐ 577	Mike Sadek	.30	.15	.03
☐ 578	Ralph Houk MG	.50	.25	.05
☐ 579	Cecil Upshaw	.30	.15	.03
☐ 580	Jim Spencer	.30	.15	.03
☐ 581	Fred Norman	.30	.15	.03
☐ 582	Bucky Dent	1.75	.85	.17
☐ 583	Marty Pattin	.30	.15	.03
☐ 584	Ken Rudolph	.30	.15	.03
☐ 585	Merv Rettenmund	.30	.15	.03
☐ 586	Jack Brohamer	.30	.15	.03
☐ 587	Larry Christenson	.30	.15	.03
☐ 588	Hal Lanier	.50	.25	.05
☐ 589	Boots Day	.30	.15	.03
☐ 590	Roger Moret	.30	.15	.03
☐ 591	Sonny Jackson	.30	.15	.03
☐ 592	Ed Bane	.30	.15	.03
☐ 593	Steve Yeager	.50	.25	.05
☐ 594	Leroy Stanton	.30	.15	.03
☐ 595	Steve Blass	.50	.25	.05

☐ 596 Rookie Pitchers	.50	.25	.05
Wayne Garland			
Fred Holdsworth			
Mark Littell			
Dick Pole			
☐ 597 Rookie Shortstops	.50	.25	.05
Dave Chalk			
John Gamble			
Pete MacKanin			
Manny Trillo			
☐ 598 Rookie Outfielders	16.00	8.00	1.60
Dave Augustine			
Ken Griffey			
Steve Ontiveros			
Jim Tyrone			
☐ 599A Rookie Pitchers WAS	.60	.30	.06
Ron Diorio			
Dave Freisleben			
Frank Riccelli			
Greg Shanahan			
☐ 599B Rookie Pitchers SD	3.00	1.50	.30
(SD in large print)			
☐ 599C Rookie Pitchers SD	4.50	2.25	.45
(SD in small print)			
☐ 600 Rookie Infielders	5.00	2.50	.50
Ron Cash			
Jim Cox			
Bill Madlock			
Reggie Sanders			
☐ 601 Rookie Outfielders	2.75	1.35	.27
Ed Armbrister			
Rich Bladt			
Brian Downing			
Bake McBride			
☐ 602 Rookie Pitchers	.50	.25	.05
Glen Abbott			
Rick Henninger			
Craig Swan			
Dan Vossler			
☐ 603 Rookie Catchers	.50	.25	.05
Barry Foote			
Tom Lundstedt			
Charlie Moore			
Sergio Robles			
☐ 604 Rookie Infielders	4.50	2.25	.45
Terry Hughes			
John Knox			
Andy Thornton			
Frank White			
☐ 605 Rookie Pitchers	2.00	1.00	.20
Vic Albury			
Ken Frailing			
Kevin Kobel			
Frank Tanana			
☐ 606 Rookie Outfielders	.30	.15	.03
Jim Fuller			
Wilbur Howard			
Tommy Smith			
Otto Velez			
☐ 607 Rookie Shortstops	.30	.15	.03
Leo Foster			
Tom Heintzelman			
Dave Rosello			
Frank Taveras			
☐ 608A Rookie Pitchers: ERR	2.00	1.00	.20
Bob Apodaco (sic)			
Dick Baney			
John D'Acquisto			
Mike Wallace			
☐ 608B Rookie Pitchers: COR	.30	.15	.03
Bob Apodaca			
Dick Baney			
John D'Acquisto			
Mike Wallace			
☐ 609 Rico Petrocelli	.50	.25	.05
☐ 610 Dave Kingman	1.00	.50	.10
☐ 611 Rich Stelmaszek	.30	.15	.03
☐ 612 Luke Walker	.30	.15	.03
☐ 613 Dan Monzon	.30	.15	.03
☐ 614 Adrian Devine	.30	.15	.03
☐ 615 Johnny Jeter	.30	.15	.03
☐ 616 Larry Gura	.50	.25	.05
☐ 617 Ted Ford	.30	.15	.03
☐ 618 Jim Mason	.30	.15	.03
☐ 619 Mike Anderson	.30	.15	.03
☐ 620 Al Downing	.50	.25	.05
☐ 621 Bernie Carbo	.30	.15	.03
☐ 622 Phil Gagliano	.30	.15	.03
☐ 623 Celerino Sanchez	.30	.15	.03
☐ 624 Bob Miller	.30	.15	.03
☐ 625 Ollie Brown	.30	.15	.03
☐ 626 Pittsburgh Pirates	.65	.30	.06
Team Card			
☐ 627 Carl Taylor	.30	.15	.03
☐ 628 Ivan Murrell	.30	.15	.03
☐ 629 Rusty Staub	.75	.35	.07
☐ 630 Tommy Agee	.50	.25	.05
☐ 631 Steve Barber	.30	.15	.03
☐ 632 George Culver	.30	.15	.03
☐ 633 Dave Hamilton	.30	.15	.03
☐ 634 Braves Leaders	1.00	.50	.10
Eddie Mathews MG			
Herm Starrette CO			
Connie Ryan CO			
Jim Busby CO			
Ken Silvestri CO			
☐ 635 Johnny Edwards	.30	.15	.03
☐ 636 Dave Goltz	.30	.15	.03
☐ 637 Checklist 5	1.50	.15	.03
☐ 638 Ken Sanders	.30	.15	.03
☐ 639 Joe Lovitto	.30	.15	.03
☐ 640 Milt Pappas	.50	.25	.05
☐ 641 Chuck Brinkman	.30	.15	.03
☐ 642 Terry Harmon	.30	.15	.03
☐ 643 Dodgers Team	.75	.35	.07
☐ 644 Wayne Granger	.30	.15	.03
☐ 645 Ken Boswell	.30	.15	.03
☐ 646 George Foster	1.25	.60	.12
☐ 647 Juan Beniquez	.60	.30	.06
☐ 648 Terry Crowley	.30	.15	.03
☐ 649 Fernando Gonzalez	.30	.15	.03
☐ 650 Mike Epstein	.30	.15	.03
☐ 651 Leron Lee	.30	.15	.03
☐ 652 Gail Hopkins	.30	.15	.03
☐ 653 Bob Stinson	.30	.15	.03
☐ 654A Jesus Alou ERR	6.00	3.00	.60
(no position)			
☐ 654B Jesus Alou COR	.50	.25	.05
(outfield)			
☐ 655 Mike Tyson	.30	.15	.03
☐ 656 Adrian Garrett	.30	.15	.03
☐ 657 Jim Shellenback	.30	.15	.03
☐ 658 Lee Lacy	.30	.15	.03
☐ 659 Joe Lis	.30	.15	.03
☐ 660 Larry Dierker	.60	.30	.06

1974 Topps Traded

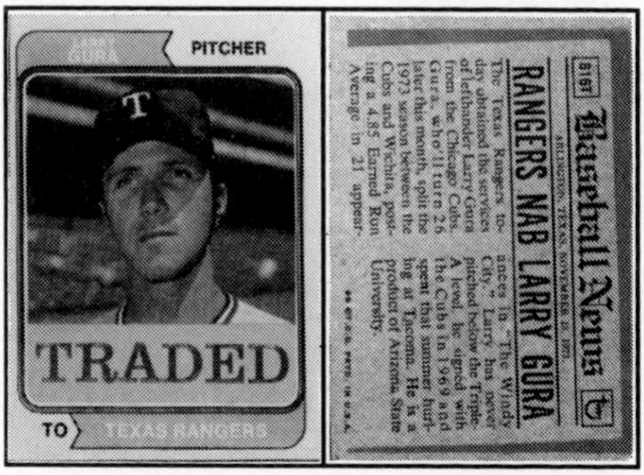

The cards in this 44-card set measure 2 1/2" by 3 1/2". The 1974 Topps Traded set contains 43 player cards and one unnumbered checklist card. The obverses have the word "traded" in block letters and the backs are designed in newspaper style. Card numbers are the same as in the regular set except they are followed by a "T." No known scarcities exist for this set.

	NRMT	VG-E	GOOD
COMPLETE SET (44)	7.50	3.75	.75
COMMON PLAYER	.15	.07	.01
☐ 23T Craig Robinson	.15	.07	.01
☐ 42T Claude Osteen	.25	.12	.02
☐ 43T Jim Wynn	.25	.12	.02
☐ 51T Bobby Heise	.15	.07	.01
☐ 59T Ross Grimsley	.15	.07	.01
☐ 62T Bob Locker	.15	.07	.01
☐ 63T Bill Sudakis	.15	.07	.01
☐ 73T Mike Marshall	.35	.17	.03
☐ 123T Nelson Briles	.25	.12	.02
☐ 139T Aurelio Monteagudo	.15	.07	.01

151T	Diego Segui	.15	.07	.01
165T	Willie Davis	.25	.12	.02
175T	Reggie Cleveland	.15	.07	.01
182T	Lindy McDaniel	.15	.07	.01
186T	Fred Scherman	.15	.07	.01
249T	George Mitterwald	.15	.07	.01
262T	Ed Kirkpatrick	.15	.07	.01
269T	Bob Johnson	.15	.07	.01
270T	Ron Santo	.50	.25	.05
313T	Barry Lersch	.15	.07	.01
319T	Randy Hundley	.15	.07	.01
330T	Juan Marichal	1.50	.75	.15
348T	Pete Richert	.15	.07	.01
373T	John Curtis	.15	.07	.01
390T	Lou Piniella	.50	.25	.05
428T	Gary Sutherland	.15	.07	.01
454T	Kurt Bevacqua	.15	.07	.01
458T	Jim Ray	.15	.07	.01
485T	Felipe Alou	.25	.12	.02
486T	Steve Stone	.25	.12	.02
496T	Tom Murphy	.15	.07	.01
516T	Horacio Pina	.15	.07	.01
534T	Eddie Watt	.15	.07	.01
538T	Cesar Tovar	.15	.07	.01
544T	Ron Schueler	.15	.07	.01
579T	Cecil Upshaw	.15	.07	.01
585T	Merv Rettenmund	.15	.07	.01
612T	Luke Walker	.15	.07	.01
616T	Larry Gura	.20	.10	.02
618T	Jim Mason	.15	.07	.01
630T	Tommie Agee	.15	.07	.01
648T	Terry Crowley	.15	.07	.01
649T	Fernando Gonzalez	.15	.07	.01
xxxT	Traded Checklist (unnumbered)	.60	.06	.01

1975 Topps

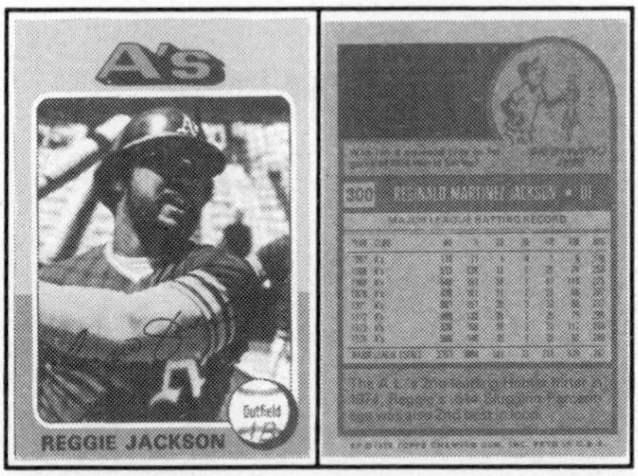

The cards in the 1975 Topps set were issued in two different sizes: a regular standard size (2 1/2" by 3 1/2") and a mini size (2 1/2" by 3 1/8") which was issued as a test in certain areas of the country. The 660-card Topps baseball set for 1975 was radically different in appearance from sets of the preceding years. The most prominent change was the use of a two-color frame surrounding the picture area rather than a single, subdued color. A facsimile autograph appears on the picture, and the backs are printed in red and green on gray. Cards 189-212 depict the MVP's of both leagues from 1951 through 1974. The first seven cards (1-7) feature players breaking records or achieving milestones during the previous season. Cards 306-313 picture league leaders in various statistical categories. Cards 459-466 depict the results of post-season action. Team cards feature a checklist back for players on that team and show a small inset photo of the manager on the front. The Phillies Team card number 46 erroneously lists Terry Harmon as number 339 instead of number 399. This set is quite popular with collectors, at least in part due to the fact that the rookie cards of Robin Yount, George Brett, Gary Carter, Jim Rice, Fred Lynn, and Keith Hernandez are all in the set. Topps minis have the same checklist and are worth approximately double the prices listed below.

	NRMT	VG-E	GOOD
COMPLETE SET (660)	700.00	350.00	70.00
COMMON PLAYER (1-132)	.30	.15	.03
COMMON PLAYER (133-264)	.30	.15	.03
COMMON PLAYER (265-660)	.30	.15	.03
1 RB: Hank Aaron Sets Homer Mark	20.00	5.00	1.00
2 RB: Lou Brock 118 Stolen Bases	2.50	1.25	.25
3 RB: Bob Gibson 3000th Strikeout	2.50	1.25	.25
4 RB: Al Kaline 3000 Hit Club	2.50	1.25	.25
5 RB: Nolan Ryan Fans 300 for 3rd Year in a Row	8.50	4.25	.85
6 RB: Mike Marshall Hurls 106 Games	.50	.25	.05
7 No Hitters Steve Busby Dick Bosman Nolan Ryan	1.25	.60	.12
8 Rogelio Moret	.30	.15	.03
9 Frank Tepedino	.30	.15	.03
10 Willie Davis	.50	.25	.05
11 Bill Melton	.30	.15	.03
12 David Clyde	.30	.15	.03
13 Gene Locklear	.30	.15	.03
14 Milt Wilcox	.30	.15	.03
15 Jose Cardenal	.30	.15	.03
16 Frank Tanana	.75	.35	.07
17 Dave Concepcion	1.00	.50	.10
18 Tigers: Team/Mgr. Ralph Houk (checklist back)	.75	.35	.07
19 Jerry Koosman	.60	.30	.06
20 Thurman Munson	7.00	3.50	.70
21 Rollie Fingers	2.50	1.25	.25
22 Dave Cash	.30	.15	.03
23 Bill Russell	.50	.25	.05
24 Al Fitzmorris	.30	.15	.03
25 Lee May	.50	.25	.05
26 Dave McNally	.50	.25	.05
27 Ken Reitz	.30	.15	.03
28 Tom Murphy	.30	.15	.03
29 Dave Parker	12.00	6.00	1.20
30 Bert Blyleven	2.50	1.25	.25
31 Dave Rader	.30	.15	.03
32 Reggie Cleveland	.30	.15	.03
33 Dusty Baker	.50	.25	.05
34 Steve Renko	.30	.15	.03
35 Ron Santo	.60	.30	.06
36 Joe Lovitto	.30	.15	.03
37 Dave Freisleben	.30	.15	.03
38 Buddy Bell	.75	.35	.07
39 Andre Thornton	.50	.25	.05
40 Bill Singer	.30	.15	.03
41 Cesar Geronimo	.30	.15	.03
42 Joe Coleman	.30	.15	.03
43 Cleon Jones	.30	.15	.03
44 Pat Dobson	.30	.15	.03
45 Joe Rudi	.50	.25	.05
46 Phillies: Team/Mgr. Danny Ozark (checklist back)	.75	.35	.07
47 Tommy John	1.25	.60	.12
48 Freddie Patek	.30	.15	.03
49 Larry Dierker	.30	.15	.03
50 Brooks Robinson	4.50	2.25	.45
51 Bob Forsch	1.00	.50	.10
52 Darrell Porter	.30	.15	.03
53 Dave Giusti	.30	.15	.03
54 Eric Soderholm	.30	.15	.03
55 Bobby Bonds	.75	.35	.07
56 Rick Wise	.30	.15	.03
57 Dave Johnson	.50	.25	.05
58 Chuck Taylor	.30	.15	.03
59 Ken Henderson	.30	.15	.03
60 Fergie Jenkins	2.00	.85	.17
61 Dave Winfield	14.00	7.00	1.40
62 Fritz Peterson	.30	.15	.03
63 Steve Swisher	.30	.15	.03
64 Dave Chalk	.30	.15	.03
65 Don Gullett	.50	.25	.05
66 Willie Horton	.50	.25	.05
67 Tug McGraw	.60	.30	.06
68 Ron Blomberg	.30	.15	.03
69 John Odom	.30	.15	.03
70 Mike Schmidt	55.00	27.50	5.50
71 Charlie Hough	.50	.25	.05
72 Royals: Team/Mgr. Jack McKeon (checklist back)	.75	.35	.07

☐ 73	J.R. Richard	.50	.25	.05
☐ 74	Mark Belanger	.50	.25	.05
☐ 75	Ted Simmons	1.25	.60	.12
☐ 76	Ed Sprague	.30	.15	.03
☐ 77	Richie Zisk	.30	.15	.03
☐ 78	Ray Corbin	.30	.15	.03
☐ 79	Gary Matthews	.50	.25	.05
☐ 80	Carlton Fisk	9.00	4.50	.90
☐ 81	Ron Reed	.30	.15	.03
☐ 82	Pat Kelly	.30	.15	.03
☐ 83	Jim Merritt	.30	.15	.03
☐ 84	Enzo Hernandez	.30	.15	.03
☐ 85	Bill Bonham	.30	.15	.03
☐ 86	Joe Lis	.30	.15	.03
☐ 87	George Foster	1.25	.60	.12
☐ 88	Tom Egan	.30	.15	.03
☐ 89	Jim Ray	.30	.15	.03
☐ 90	Rusty Staub	.60	.30	.06
☐ 91	Dick Green	.30	.15	.03
☐ 92	Cecil Upshaw	.30	.15	.03
☐ 93	Dave Lopes	.50	.25	.05
☐ 94	Jim Lonborg	.50	.25	.05
☐ 95	John Mayberry	.50	.25	.05
☐ 96	Mike Cosgrove	.30	.15	.03
☐ 97	Earl Williams	.30	.15	.03
☐ 98	Rich Folkers	.30	.15	.03
☐ 99	Mike Hegan	.30	.15	.03
☐ 100	Willie Stargell	3.50	1.75	.35
☐ 101	Expos: Team/Mgr. Gene Mauch (checklist back)	.75	.35	.07
☐ 102	Joe Decker	.30	.15	.03
☐ 103	Rick Miller	.30	.15	.03
☐ 104	Bill Madlock	1.25	.60	.12
☐ 105	Buzz Capra	.30	.15	.03
☐ 106	Mike Hargrove	.75	.35	.07
☐ 107	Jim Barr	.30	.15	.03
☐ 108	Tom Hall	.30	.15	.03
☐ 109	George Hendrick	.50	.25	.05
☐ 110	Wilbur Wood	.50	.25	.05
☐ 111	Wayne Garrett	.30	.15	.03
☐ 112	Larry Hardy	.30	.15	.03
☐ 113	Elliott Maddox	.30	.15	.03
☐ 114	Dick Lange	.30	.15	.03
☐ 115	Joe Ferguson	.30	.15	.03
☐ 116	Lerrin LaGrow	.30	.15	.03
☐ 117	Orioles: Team/Mgr. Earl Weaver (checklist back)	.75	.35	.07
☐ 118	Mike Anderson	.30	.15	.03
☐ 119	Tommy Helms	.50	.25	.05
☐ 120	Steve Busby (photo actually Fran Healy)	.50	.25	.05
☐ 121	Bill North	.30	.15	.03
☐ 122	Al Hrabosky	.30	.15	.03
☐ 123	Johnny Briggs	.30	.15	.03
☐ 124	Jerry Reuss	.50	.25	.05
☐ 125	Ken Singleton	.50	.25	.05
☐ 126	Checklist 1-132	1.50	.15	.03
☐ 127	Glenn Borgmann	.30	.15	.03
☐ 128	Bill Lee	.50	.25	.05
☐ 129	Rick Monday	.50	.25	.05
☐ 130	Phil Niekro	2.25	1.10	.22
☐ 131	Toby Harrah	.50	.25	.05
☐ 132	Randy Moffitt	.30	.15	.03
☐ 133	Dan Driessen	.50	.25	.05
☐ 134	Ron Hodges	.30	.15	.03
☐ 135	Charlie Spikes	.30	.15	.03
☐ 136	Jim Mason	.30	.15	.03
☐ 137	Terry Forster	.50	.25	.05
☐ 138	Del Unser	.30	.15	.03
☐ 139	Horacio Pina	.30	.15	.03
☐ 140	Steve Garvey	8.00	4.00	.80
☐ 141	Mickey Stanley	.50	.25	.05
☐ 142	Bob Reynolds	.30	.15	.03
☐ 143	Cliff Johnson	.30	.15	.03
☐ 144	Jim Wohlford	.30	.15	.03
☐ 145	Ken Holtzman	.50	.25	.05
☐ 146	Padres: Team/Mgr. John McNamara (checklist back)	.75	.35	.07
☐ 147	Pedro Garcia	.30	.15	.03
☐ 148	Jim Rooker	.30	.15	.03
☐ 149	Tim Foli	.30	.15	.03
☐ 150	Bob Gibson	3.50	1.75	.35
☐ 151	Steve Brye	.30	.15	.03
☐ 152	Mario Guerrero	.30	.15	.03
☐ 153	Rick Reuschel	.75	.35	.07
☐ 154	Mike Lum	.30	.15	.03
☐ 155	Jim Bibby	.50	.25	.05
☐ 156	Dave Kingman	1.00	.50	.10
☐ 157	Pedro Borbon	.30	.15	.03
☐ 158	Jerry Grote	.30	.15	.03
☐ 159	Steve Arlin	.30	.15	.03
☐ 160	Graig Nettles	1.25	.60	.12
☐ 161	Stan Bahnsen	.30	.15	.03
☐ 162	Willie Montanez	.30	.15	.03
☐ 163	Jim Brewer	.30	.15	.03
☐ 164	Mickey Rivers	.50	.25	.05
☐ 165	Doug Rader	.50	.25	.05
☐ 166	Woodie Fryman	.30	.15	.03
☐ 167	Rich Coggins	.30	.15	.03
☐ 168	Bill Greif	.30	.15	.03
☐ 169	Cookie Rojas	.30	.15	.03
☐ 170	Bert Campaneris	.50	.25	.05
☐ 171	Ed Kirkpatrick	.30	.15	.03
☐ 172	Red Sox: Team/Mgr. Darrell Johnson (checklist back)	.75	.35	.07
☐ 173	Steve Rogers	.50	.25	.05
☐ 174	Bake McBride	.50	.25	.05
☐ 175	Don Money	.30	.15	.03
☐ 176	Burt Hooton	.30	.15	.03
☐ 177	Vic Correll	.30	.15	.03
☐ 178	Cesar Tovar	.30	.15	.03
☐ 179	Tom Bradley	.30	.15	.03
☐ 180	Joe Morgan	6.00	3.00	.60
☐ 181	Fred Beene	.30	.15	.03
☐ 182	Don Hahn	.30	.15	.03
☐ 183	Mel Stottlemyre	.60	.30	.06
☐ 184	Jorge Orta	.30	.15	.03
☐ 185	Steve Carlton	6.00	3.00	.60
☐ 186	Willie Crawford	.30	.15	.03
☐ 187	Denny Doyle	.30	.15	.03
☐ 188	Tom Griffin	.30	.15	.03
☐ 189	1951 MVP's Larry (Yogi) Berra Roy Campanella (Campy never issued)	1.50	.75	.15
☐ 190	1952 MVP's Bobby Shantz Hank Sauer	.50	.25	.05
☐ 191	1953 MVP's Al Rosen Roy Campanella	.75	.35	.07
☐ 192	1954 MVP's Yogi Berra Willie Mays	1.50	.75	.15
☐ 193	1955 MVP's Yogi Berra Roy Campanella (Campy card never issued, pictured with LA cap, sic)	1.50	.75	.15
☐ 194	1956 MVP's Mickey Mantle Don Newcombe	4.50	2.25	.45
☐ 195	1957 MVP's Mickey Mantle Hank Aaron	6.00	3.00	.60
☐ 196	1958 MVP's Jackie Jensen Ernie Banks	.60	.30	.06
☐ 197	1959 MVP's Nellie Fox Ernie Banks	.60	.30	.06
☐ 198	1960 MVP's Roger Maris Dick Groat	.75	.35	.07
☐ 199	1961 MVP's Roger Maris Frank Robinson	1.50	.75	.15
☐ 200	1962 MVP's Mickey Mantle Maury Wills (Wills never issued)	4.50	2.25	.45
☐ 201	1963 MVP's Elston Howard Sandy Koufax	.75	.35	.07
☐ 202	1964 MVP's Brooks Robinson Ken Boyer	.60	.30	.06
☐ 203	1965 MVP's Zoilo Versalles Willie Mays	.75	.35	.07
☐ 204	1966 MVP's Frank Robinson Bob Clemente	1.00	.50	.10
☐ 205	1967 MVP's Carl Yastrzemski Orlando Cepeda	1.00	.50	.10
☐ 206	1968 MVP's Denny McLain Bob Gibson	.75	.35	.07
☐ 207	1969 MVP's Harmon Killebrew Willie McCovey	.75	.35	.07

☐ 208	1970 MVP's Boog Powell Johnny Bench	.75	.35	.07
☐ 209	1971 MVP's Vida Blue Joe Torre	.50	.25	.05
☐ 210	1972 MVP's Rich Allen Johnny Bench	.75	.35	.07
☐ 211	1973 MVP's Reggie Jackson Pete Rose	3.00	1.50	.30
☐ 212	1974 MVP's Jeff Burroughs Steve Garvey	.60	.30	.06
☐ 213	Oscar Gamble	.50	.25	.05
☐ 214	Harry Parker	.30	.15	.03
☐ 215	Bobby Valentine	.60	.30	.06
☐ 216	Giants: Team/Mgr. Wes Westrum (checklist back)	.75	.35	.07
☐ 217	Lou Piniella	.75	.35	.07
☐ 218	Jerry Johnson	.30	.15	.03
☐ 219	Ed Herrmann	.30	.15	.03
☐ 220	Don Sutton	2.00	1.00	.20
☐ 221	Aurelio Rodriguez	.30	.15	.03
☐ 222	Dan Spillner	.30	.15	.03
☐ 223	Robin Yount	140.00	70.00	14.00
☐ 224	Ramon Hernandez	.30	.15	.03
☐ 225	Bob Grich	.50	.25	.05
☐ 226	Bill Campbell	.30	.15	.03
☐ 227	Bob Watson	.50	.25	.05
☐ 228	George Brett	160.00	80.00	16.00
☐ 229	Barry Foote	.30	.15	.03
☐ 230	Jim Hunter	3.00	1.50	.30
☐ 231	Mike Tyson	.30	.15	.03
☐ 232	Diego Segui	.30	.15	.03
☐ 233	Billy Grabarkewitz	.30	.15	.03
☐ 234	Tom Grieve	.50	.25	.05
☐ 235	Jack Billingham	.30	.15	.03
☐ 236	Angels: Team/Mgr. Dick Williams (checklist back)	.75	.35	.07
☐ 237	Carl Morton	.30	.15	.03
☐ 238	Dave Duncan	.30	.15	.03
☐ 239	George Stone	.30	.15	.03
☐ 240	Garry Maddox	.50	.25	.05
☐ 241	Dick Tidrow	.30	.15	.03
☐ 242	Jay Johnstone	.50	.25	.05
☐ 243	Jim Kaat	1.00	.50	.10
☐ 244	Bill Buckner	.60	.30	.06
☐ 245	Mickey Lolich	.60	.30	.06
☐ 246	Cardinals: Team/Mgr. Red Schoendienst (checklist back)	.75	.35	.07
☐ 247	Enos Cabell	.30	.15	.03
☐ 248	Randy Jones	.50	.25	.05
☐ 249	Danny Thompson	.30	.15	.03
☐ 250	Ken Brett	.30	.15	.03
☐ 251	Fran Healy	.30	.15	.03
☐ 252	Fred Scherman	.30	.15	.03
☐ 253	Jesus Alou	.30	.15	.03
☐ 254	Mike Torrez	.30	.15	.03
☐ 255	Dwight Evans	6.00	3.00	.60
☐ 256	Billy Champion	.30	.15	.03
☐ 257	Checklist: 133-264	1.50	.15	.03
☐ 258	Dave LaRoche	.30	.15	.03
☐ 259	Len Randle	.30	.15	.03
☐ 260	Johnny Bench	12.00	6.00	1.20
☐ 261	Andy Hassler	.30	.15	.03
☐ 262	Rowland Office	.30	.15	.03
☐ 263	Jim Perry	.50	.25	.05
☐ 264	John Milner	.30	.15	.03
☐ 265	Ron Bryant	.30	.15	.03
☐ 266	Sandy Alomar	.30	.15	.03
☐ 267	Dick Ruthven	.30	.15	.03
☐ 268	Hal McRae	.50	.25	.05
☐ 269	Doug Rau	.30	.15	.03
☐ 270	Ron Fairly	.30	.15	.03
☐ 271	Gerry Moses	.30	.15	.03
☐ 272	Lynn McGlothen	.30	.15	.03
☐ 273	Steve Braun	.30	.15	.03
☐ 274	Vicente Romo	.30	.15	.03
☐ 275	Paul Blair	.50	.25	.05
☐ 276	White Sox Team/Mgr. Chuck Tanner (checklist back)	.75	.35	.07
☐ 277	Frank Taveras	.30	.15	.03
☐ 278	Paul Lindblad	.30	.15	.03
☐ 279	Milt May	.30	.15	.03
☐ 280	Carl Yastrzemski	11.00	5.50	1.10
☐ 281	Jim Slaton	.30	.15	.03
☐ 282	Jerry Morales	.30	.15	.03
☐ 283	Steve Foucault	.30	.15	.03
☐ 284	Ken Griffey	3.00	1.50	.30
☐ 285	Ellie Rodriguez	.30	.15	.03
☐ 286	Mike Jorgensen	.30	.15	.03
☐ 287	Roric Harrison	.30	.15	.03
☐ 288	Bruce Ellingsen	.30	.15	.03
☐ 289	Ken Rudolph	.30	.15	.03
☐ 290	Jon Matlack	.50	.25	.05
☐ 291	Bill Sudakis	.30	.15	.03
☐ 292	Ron Schueler	.30	.15	.03
☐ 293	Dick Sharon	.30	.15	.03
☐ 294	Geoff Zahn	.30	.15	.03
☐ 295	Vada Pinson	.60	.30	.06
☐ 296	Alan Foster	.30	.15	.03
☐ 297	Craig Kusick	.30	.15	.03
☐ 298	Johnny Grubb	.30	.15	.03
☐ 299	Bucky Dent	.75	.35	.07
☐ 300	Reggie Jackson	14.00	7.00	1.40
☐ 301	Dave Roberts	.30	.15	.03
☐ 302	Rick Burleson	.60	.30	.06
☐ 303	Grant Jackson	.30	.15	.03
☐ 304	Pirates: Team/Mgr. Danny Murtaugh (checklist back)	.75	.35	.07
☐ 305	Jim Colborn	.30	.15	.03
☐ 306	Batting Leaders Rod Carew Ralph Garr	.75	.35	.07
☐ 307	Home Run Leaders Dick Allen Mike Schmidt	1.75	.85	.17
☐ 308	RBI Leaders Jeff Burroughs Johnny Bench	.75	.35	.07
☐ 309	Stolen Base Leaders Bill North Lou Brock	.75	.35	.07
☐ 310	Victory Leaders Jim Hunter Fergie Jenkins Andy Messersmith Phil Niekro	.75	.35	.07
☐ 311	ERA Leaders Jim Hunter Buzz Capra	.75	.35	.07
☐ 312	Strikeout Leaders Nolan Ryan Steve Carlton	4.50	2.25	.45
☐ 313	Leading Firemen Terry Forster Mike Marshall	.60	.30	.06
☐ 314	Buck Martinez	.30	.15	.03
☐ 315	Don Kessinger	.50	.25	.05
☐ 316	Jackie Brown	.30	.15	.03
☐ 317	Joe Lahoud	.30	.15	.03
☐ 318	Ernie McAnally	.30	.15	.03
☐ 319	Johnny Oates	.30	.15	.03
☐ 320	Pete Rose	15.00	7.50	1.50
☐ 321	Rudy May	.30	.15	.03
☐ 322	Ed Goodson	.30	.15	.03
☐ 323	Fred Holdsworth	.30	.15	.03
☐ 324	Ed Kranepool	.50	.25	.05
☐ 325	Tony Oliva	.75	.35	.07
☐ 326	Wayne Twitchell	.30	.15	.03
☐ 327	Jerry Hairston	.30	.15	.03
☐ 328	Sonny Siebert	.30	.15	.03
☐ 329	Ted Kubiak	.30	.15	.03
☐ 330	Mike Marshall	.50	.25	.05
☐ 331	Indians: Team/Mgr. Frank Robinson (checklist back)	.75	.35	.07
☐ 332	Fred Kendall	.30	.15	.03
☐ 333	Dick Drago	.30	.15	.03
☐ 334	Greg Gross	.30	.15	.03
☐ 335	Jim Palmer	6.00	3.00	.60
☐ 336	Rennie Stennett	.30	.15	.03
☐ 337	Kevin Kobel	.30	.15	.03
☐ 338	Rich Stelmaszek	.30	.15	.03
☐ 339	Jim Fregosi	.50	.25	.05
☐ 340	Paul Splittorff	.30	.15	.03
☐ 341	Hal Breeden	.30	.15	.03
☐ 342	Leroy Stanton	.30	.15	.03
☐ 343	Danny Frisella	.30	.15	.03
☐ 344	Ben Oglivie	.50	.25	.05
☐ 345	Clay Carroll	.30	.15	.03
☐ 346	Bobby Darwin	.30	.15	.03
☐ 347	Mike Caldwell	.30	.15	.03
☐ 348	Tony Muser	.30	.15	.03
☐ 349	Ray Sadecki	.30	.15	.03
☐ 350	Bobby Murcer	.60	.30	.06
☐ 351	Bob Boone	1.25	.60	.12
☐ 352	Darold Knowles	.30	.15	.03
☐ 353	Luis Melendez	.30	.15	.03
☐ 354	Dick Bosman	.30	.15	.03
☐ 355	Chris Cannizzaro	.30	.15	.03

☐	356	Rico Petrocelli	.50	.25	.05
☐	357	Ken Forsch	.30	.15	.03
☐	358	Al Bumbry	.30	.15	.03
☐	359	Paul Popovich	.30	.15	.03
☐	360	George Scott	.50	.25	.05
☐	361	Dodgers: Team/Mgr.	1.00	.50	.10
		Walter Alston			
		(checklist back)			
☐	362	Steve Hargan	.30	.15	.03
☐	363	Carmen Fanzone	.30	.15	.03
☐	364	Doug Bird	.30	.15	.03
☐	365	Bob Bailey	.30	.15	.03
☐	366	Ken Sanders	.30	.15	.03
☐	367	Craig Robinson	.30	.15	.03
☐	368	Vic Albury	.30	.15	.03
☐	369	Merv Rettenmund	.30	.15	.03
☐	370	Tom Seaver	10.00	5.00	1.00
☐	371	Gates Brown	.50	.25	.05
☐	372	John D'Acquisto	.30	.15	.03
☐	373	Bill Sharp	.30	.15	.03
☐	374	Eddie Watt	.30	.15	.03
☐	375	Roy White	.50	.25	.05
☐	376	Steve Yeager	.50	.25	.05
☐	377	Tom Hilgendorf	.30	.15	.03
☐	378	Derrel Thomas	.30	.15	.03
☐	379	Bernie Carbo	.30	.15	.03
☐	380	Sal Bando	.50	.25	.05
☐	381	John Curtis	.30	.15	.03
☐	382	Don Baylor	1.00	.50	.10
☐	383	Jim York	.30	.15	.03
☐	384	Brewers: Team/Mgr.	.75	.35	.07
		Del Crandall			
		(checklist back)			
☐	385	Dock Ellis	.30	.15	.03
☐	386	Checklist: 265-396	1.50	.15	.03
☐	387	Jim Spencer	.30	.15	.03
☐	388	Steve Stone	.50	.25	.05
☐	389	Tony Solaita	.30	.15	.03
☐	390	Ron Cey	.75	.35	.07
☐	391	Don DeMola	.30	.15	.03
☐	392	Bruce Bochte	.50	.25	.05
☐	393	Gary Gentry	.30	.15	.03
☐	394	Larvell Blanks	.30	.15	.03
☐	395	Bud Harrelson	.50	.25	.05
☐	396	Fred Norman	.30	.15	.03
☐	397	Bill Freehan	.60	.30	.06
☐	398	Elias Sosa	.30	.15	.03
☐	399	Terry Harmon	.30	.15	.03
☐	400	Dick Allen	.60	.30	.06
☐	401	Mike Wallace	.30	.15	.03
☐	402	Bob Tolan	.30	.15	.03
☐	403	Tom Buskey	.30	.15	.03
☐	404	Ted Sizemore	.30	.15	.03
☐	405	John Montague	.30	.15	.03
☐	406	Bob Gallagher	.30	.15	.03
☐	407	Herb Washington	.30	.15	.03
☐	408	Clyde Wright	.30	.15	.03
☐	409	Bob Robertson	.30	.15	.03
☐	410	Mike Cueller UER	.50	.25	.05
		(sic, Cuellar)			
☐	411	George Mitterwald	.30	.15	.03
☐	412	Bill Hands	.30	.15	.03
☐	413	Marty Pattin	.30	.15	.03
☐	414	Manny Mota	.50	.25	.05
☐	415	John Hiller	.50	.25	.05
☐	416	Larry Lintz	.30	.15	.03
☐	417	Skip Lockwood	.30	.15	.03
☐	418	Leo Foster	.30	.15	.03
☐	419	Dave Goltz	.30	.15	.03
☐	420	Larry Bowa	.60	.30	.06
☐	421	Mets: Team/Mgr.	1.00	.50	.10
		Yogi Berra			
		(checklist back)			
☐	422	Brian Downing	.60	.30	.06
☐	423	Clay Kirby	.30	.15	.03
☐	424	John Lowenstein	.30	.15	.03
☐	425	Tito Fuentes	.30	.15	.03
☐	426	George Medich	.30	.15	.03
☐	427	Clarence Gaston	.60	.30	.06
☐	428	Dave Hamilton	.30	.15	.03
☐	429	Jim Dwyer	.30	.15	.03
☐	430	Luis Tiant	.60	.30	.06
☐	431	Rod Gilbreath	.30	.15	.03
☐	432	Ken Berry	.30	.15	.03
☐	433	Larry Demery	.30	.15	.03
☐	434	Bob Locker	.30	.15	.03
☐	435	Dave Nelson	.30	.15	.03
☐	436	Ken Frailing	.30	.15	.03
☐	437	Al Cowens	.50	.25	.05
☐	438	Don Carrithers	.30	.15	.03
☐	439	Ed Brinkman	.30	.15	.03
☐	440	Andy Messersmith	.50	.25	.05
☐	441	Bobby Heise	.30	.15	.03
☐	442	Maximino Leon	.30	.15	.03
☐	443	Twins: Team/Mgr.	.75	.35	.07
		Frank Quilici			
		(checklist back)			
☐	444	Gene Garber	.30	.15	.03
☐	445	Felix Millan	.30	.15	.03
☐	446	Bart Johnson	.30	.15	.03
☐	447	Terry Crowley	.30	.15	.03
☐	448	Frank Duffy	.30	.15	.03
☐	449	Charlie Williams	.30	.15	.03
☐	450	Willie McCovey	3.50	1.75	.35
☐	451	Rick Dempsey	.50	.25	.05
☐	452	Angel Mangual	.30	.15	.03
☐	453	Claude Osteen	.50	.25	.05
☐	454	Doug Griffin	.30	.15	.03
☐	455	Don Wilson	.30	.15	.03
☐	456	Bob Coluccio	.30	.15	.03
☐	457	Mario Mendoza	.30	.15	.03
☐	458	Ross Grimsley	.30	.15	.03
☐	459	1974 AL Champs	.60	.30	.06
		A's over Orioles			
		(2B action pictured)			
☐	460	1974 NL Champs	.75	.35	.07
		Dodgers over Pirates			
		(Taveras/Garvey at 2B)			
☐	461	World Series Game 1	2.00	1.00	.20
		(Reggie Jackson)			
☐	462	World Series Game 2	.60	.30	.06
		(Dodger dugout)			
☐	463	World Series Game 3	.75	.35	.07
		(Fingers pitching)			
☐	464	World Series Game 4	.60	.30	.06
		(A's batter)			
☐	465	World Series Game 5	.60	.30	.06
		(Rudi rounding third)			
☐	466	World Series Summary	.60	.30	.06
		A's do it again;			
		win third straight			
		(A's group picture)			
☐	467	Ed Halicki	.30	.15	.03
☐	468	Bobby Mitchell	.30	.15	.03
☐	469	Tom Dettore	.30	.15	.03
☐	470	Jeff Burroughs	.50	.25	.05
☐	471	Bob Stinson	.30	.15	.03
☐	472	Bruce Dal Canton	.30	.15	.03
☐	473	Ken McMullen	.30	.15	.03
☐	474	Luke Walker	.30	.15	.03
☐	475	Darrell Evans	.60	.30	.06
☐	476	Ed Figueroa	.30	.15	.03
☐	477	Tom Hutton	.30	.15	.03
☐	478	Tom Burgmeier	.30	.15	.03
☐	479	Ken Boswell	.30	.15	.03
☐	480	Carlos May	.30	.15	.03
☐	481	Will McEnaney	.30	.15	.03
☐	482	Tom McCraw	.30	.15	.03
☐	483	Steve Ontiveros	.30	.15	.03
☐	484	Glenn Beckert	.50	.25	.05
☐	485	Sparky Lyle	.60	.30	.06
☐	486	Ray Fosse	.30	.15	.03
☐	487	Astros: Team/Mgr.	.75	.35	.07
		Preston Gomez			
		(checklist back)			
☐	488	Bill Travers	.30	.15	.03
☐	489	Cecil Cooper	1.25	.60	.12
☐	490	Reggie Smith	.60	.30	.06
☐	491	Doyle Alexander	.50	.25	.05
☐	492	Rich Hebner	.30	.15	.03
☐	493	Don Stanhouse	.30	.15	.03
☐	494	Pete LaCock	.30	.15	.03
☐	495	Nelson Briles	.30	.15	.03
☐	496	Pepe Frias	.30	.15	.03
☐	497	Jim Nettles	.30	.15	.03
☐	498	Al Downing	.50	.25	.05
☐	499	Marty Perez	.30	.15	.03
☐	500	Nolan Ryan	40.00	20.00	4.00
☐	501	Bill Robinson	.50	.25	.05
☐	502	Pat Bourque	.30	.15	.03
☐	503	Fred Stanley	.30	.15	.03
☐	504	Buddy Bradford	.30	.15	.03
☐	505	Chris Speier	.30	.15	.03
☐	506	Leron Lee	.30	.15	.03
☐	507	Tom Carroll	.30	.15	.03
☐	508	Bob Hansen	.30	.15	.03
☐	509	Dave Hilton	.30	.15	.03
☐	510	Vida Blue	.60	.30	.06
☐	511	Rangers: Team/Mgr.	1.00	.50	.10
		Billy Martin			
		(checklist back)			
☐	512	Larry Milbourne	.30	.15	.03
☐	513	Dick Pole	.30	.15	.03
☐	514	Jose Cruz	.50	.25	.05
☐	515	Manny Sanguillen	.50	.25	.05
☐	516	Don Hood	.30	.15	.03
☐	517	Checklist: 397-528	1.50	.15	.03
☐	518	Leo Cardenas	.30	.15	.03

☐ 519	Jim Todd	.30	.15	.03
☐ 520	Amos Otis	.50	.25	.05
☐ 521	Dennis Blair	.30	.15	.03
☐ 522	Gary Sutherland	.30	.15	.03
☐ 523	Tom Paciorek	.30	.15	.03
☐ 524	John Doherty	.30	.15	.03
☐ 525	Tom House	.30	.15	.03
☐ 526	Larry Hisle	.30	.15	.03
☐ 527	Mac Scarce	.30	.15	.03
☐ 528	Eddie Leon	.30	.15	.03
☐ 529	Gary Thomasson	.30	.15	.03
☐ 530	Gaylord Perry	3.00	1.25	.25
☐ 531	Reds: Team/Mgr.	1.00	.50	.10
	Sparky Anderson			
	(checklist back)			
☐ 532	Gorman Thomas	.60	.30	.06
☐ 533	Rudy Meoli	.30	.15	.03
☐ 534	Alex Johnson	.30	.15	.03
☐ 535	Gene Tenace	.50	.25	.05
☐ 536	Bob Moose	.30	.15	.03
☐ 537	Tommy Harper	.50	.25	.05
☐ 538	Duffy Dyer	.30	.15	.03
☐ 539	Jesse Jefferson	.30	.15	.03
☐ 540	Lou Brock	3.50	1.75	.35
☐ 541	Roger Metzger	.30	.15	.03
☐ 542	Pete Broberg	.30	.15	.03
☐ 543	Larry Biittner	.30	.15	.03
☐ 544	Steve Mingori	.30	.15	.03
☐ 545	Billy Williams	3.00	1.50	.30
☐ 546	John Knox	.30	.15	.03
☐ 547	Von Joshua	.30	.15	.03
☐ 548	Charlie Sands	.30	.15	.03
☐ 549	Bill Butler	.30	.15	.03
☐ 550	Ralph Garr	.30	.15	.03
☐ 551	Larry Christenson	.30	.15	.03
☐ 552	Jack Brohamer	.30	.15	.03
☐ 553	John Boccabella	.30	.15	.03
☐ 554	Rich Gossage	1.50	.75	.15
☐ 555	Al Oliver	.75	.35	.07
☐ 556	Tim Johnson	.30	.15	.03
☐ 557	Larry Gura	.50	.25	.05
☐ 558	Dave Roberts	.30	.15	.03
☐ 559	Bob Montgomery	.30	.15	.03
☐ 560	Tony Perez	1.25	.60	.12
☐ 561	A's: Team/Mgr.	.75	.35	.07
	Alvin Dark			
	(checklist back)			
☐ 562	Gary Nolan	.30	.15	.03
☐ 563	Wilbur Howard	.30	.15	.03
☐ 564	Tommy Davis	.50	.25	.05
☐ 565	Joe Torre	.75	.35	.07
☐ 566	Ray Burris	.30	.15	.03
☐ 567	Jim Sundberg	.75	.35	.07
☐ 568	Dale Murray	.30	.15	.03
☐ 569	Frank White	.75	.35	.07
☐ 570	Jim Wynn	.50	.25	.05
☐ 571	Dave Lemanczyk	.30	.15	.03
☐ 572	Roger Nelson	.30	.15	.03
☐ 573	Orlando Pena	.30	.15	.03
☐ 574	Tony Taylor	.30	.15	.03
☐ 575	Gene Clines	.30	.15	.03
☐ 576	Phil Roof	.30	.15	.03
☐ 577	John Morris	.30	.15	.03
☐ 578	Dave Tomlin	.30	.15	.03
☐ 579	Skip Pitlock	.30	.15	.03
☐ 580	Frank Robinson	4.00	2.00	.40
☐ 581	Darrel Chaney	.30	.15	.03
☐ 582	Eduardo Rodriguez	.30	.15	.03
☐ 583	Andy Etchebarren	.30	.15	.03
☐ 584	Mike Garman	.30	.15	.03
☐ 585	Chris Chambliss	.50	.25	.05
☐ 586	Tim McCarver	.60	.30	.06
☐ 587	Chris Ward	.30	.15	.03
☐ 588	Rick Auerbach	.30	.15	.03
☐ 589	Braves: Team/Mgr.	.75	.35	.07
	Clyde King			
	(checklist back)			
☐ 590	Cesar Cedeno	.50	.25	.05
☐ 591	Glenn Abbott	.30	.15	.03
☐ 592	Balor Moore	.30	.15	.03
☐ 593	Gene Lamont	.30	.15	.03
☐ 594	Jim Fuller	.30	.15	.03
☐ 595	Joe Niekro	.50	.25	.05
☐ 596	Ollie Brown	.30	.15	.03
☐ 597	Winston Llenas	.30	.15	.03
☐ 598	Bruce Kison	.30	.15	.03
☐ 599	Nate Colbert	.30	.15	.03
☐ 600	Rod Carew	9.00	4.00	.80
☐ 601	Juan Beniquez	.50	.25	.05
☐ 602	John Vukovich	.30	.15	.03
☐ 603	Lew Krausse	.30	.15	.03
☐ 604	Oscar Zamora	.30	.15	.03
☐ 605	John Ellis	.30	.15	.03
☐ 606	Bruce Miller	.30	.15	.03

☐ 607	Jim Holt	.30	.15	.03
☐ 608	Gene Michael	.50	.25	.05
☐ 609	Elrod Hendricks	.30	.15	.03
☐ 610	Ron Hunt	.30	.15	.03
☐ 611	Yankees: Team/Mgr.	1.00	.50	.10
	Bill Virdon			
	(checklist back)			
☐ 612	Terry Hughes	.30	.15	.03
☐ 613	Bill Parsons	.30	.15	.03
☐ 614	Rookie Pitchers	.30	.15	.03
	Jack Kucek			
	Dyar Miller			
	Vern Ruhle			
	Paul Siebert			
☐ 615	Rookie Pitchers	1.00	.50	.10
	Pat Darcy			
	Dennis Leonard			
	Tom Underwood			
	Hank Webb			
☐ 616	Rookie Outfielders	30.00	15.00	3.00
	Dave Augustine			
	Pepe Mangual			
	Jim Rice			
	John Scott			
☐ 617	Rookie Infielders	1.75	.85	.17
	Mike Cubbage			
	Doug DeCinces			
	Reggie Sanders			
	Manny Trillo			
☐ 618	Rookie Pitchers	2.50	1.25	.25
	Jamie Easterly			
	Tom Johnson			
	Scott McGregor			
	Rick Rhoden			
☐ 619	Rookie Outfielders	.30	.15	.03
	Benny Ayala			
	Nyls Nyman			
	Tommy Smith			
	Jerry Turner			
☐ 620	Rookie Catcher/OF	35.00	17.50	3.50
	Gary Carter			
	Marc Hill			
	Danny Meyer			
	Leon Roberts			
☐ 621	Rookie Pitchers	.75	.35	.07
	John Denny			
	Rawly Eastwick			
	Jim Kern			
	Juan Veintidos			
☐ 622	Rookie Outfielders	12.00	6.00	1.20
	Ed Armbrister			
	Fred Lynn			
	Tom Poquette			
	Terry Whitfield UER			
	(listed as Ney York)			
☐ 623	Rookie Infielders	22.00	11.00	2.20
	Phil Garner			
	Keith Hernandez UER			
	(sic, bats right)			
	Bob Sheldon			
	Tom Veryzer			
☐ 624	Rookie Pitchers	.30	.15	.03
	Doug Konieczny			
	Gary Lavelle			
	Jim Otten			
	Eddie Solomon			
☐ 625	Boog Powell	.60	.30	.06
☐ 626	Larry Haney UER	.30	.15	.03
	(photo actually			
	Dave Duncan)			
☐ 627	Tom Walker	.30	.15	.03
☐ 628	Ron LeFlore	.50	.25	.05
☐ 629	Joe Hoerner	.30	.15	.03
☐ 630	Greg Luzinski	.60	.30	.06
☐ 631	Lee Lacy	.30	.15	.03
☐ 632	Morris Nettles	.30	.15	.03
☐ 633	Paul Casanova	.30	.15	.03
☐ 634	Cy Acosta	.30	.15	.03
☐ 635	Chuck Dobson	.30	.15	.03
☐ 636	Charlie Moore	.30	.15	.03
☐ 637	Ted Martinez	.30	.15	.03
☐ 638	Cubs: Team/Mgr.	.75	.35	.07
	Jim Marshall			
	(checklist back)			
☐ 639	Steve Kline	.30	.15	.03
☐ 640	Harmon Killebrew	4.00	2.00	.40
☐ 641	Jim Northrup	.50	.25	.05
☐ 642	Mike Phillips	.30	.15	.03
☐ 643	Brent Strom	.30	.15	.03
☐ 644	Bill Fahey	.30	.15	.03
☐ 645	Danny Cater	.30	.15	.03
☐ 646	Checklist: 529-660	1.50	.15	.03
☐ 647	Claudell Washington	2.50	1.25	.25
☐ 648	Dave Pagan	.30	.15	.03

☐ 649 Jack Heidemann	.30	.15	.03
☐ 650 Dave May	.30	.15	.03
☐ 651 John Morlan	.30	.15	.03
☐ 652 Lindy McDaniel	.30	.15	.03
☐ 653 Lee Richard UER (listed as Richards on card front)	.30	.15	.03
☐ 654 Jerry Terrell	.30	.15	.03
☐ 655 Rico Carty	.50	.25	.05
☐ 656 Bill Plummer	.30	.15	.03
☐ 657 Bob Oliver	.30	.15	.03
☐ 658 Vic Harris	.30	.15	.03
☐ 659 Bob Apodaca	.30	.15	.03
☐ 660 Hank Aaron	20.00	5.00	1.00

1976 Topps

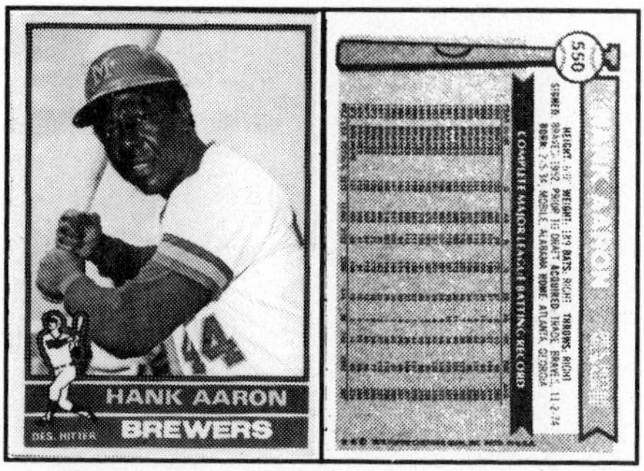

The 1976 Topps set of 660 cards (measuring 2 1/2" by 3 1/2") is known for its sharp color photographs and interesting presentation of subjects. Team cards feature a checklist back for players on that team and show a small inset photo of the manager on the front. A "Father and Son" series (66-70) spotlights five Major Leaguers whose fathers also made the "Big Show." Other subseries include "All Time All Stars" (341-350), "Record Breakers" from the previous season (1-6), League Leaders (191-205), Post-season cards (461-462), and Rookie Prospects (589-599). The key rookies in this set are Dennis Eckersley and Willie Randolph.

	NRMT	VG-E	GOOD
COMPLETE SET (660)	375.00	175.00	37.00
COMMON PLAYER (1-660)	.22	.11	.02
☐ 1 RB: Hank Aaron Most RBI's, 2262	12.00	2.50	.50
☐ 2 RB: Bobby Bonds Most leadoff HR's 32; plus three seasons 30 homers/30 steals	.50	.25	.05
☐ 3 RB: Mickey Lolich Lefthander, Most Strikeouts, 2679	.50	.25	.05
☐ 4 RB: Dave Lopes Most Consecutive SB attempts, 38	.35	.17	.03
☐ 5 RB: Tom Seaver Most Cons. seasons with 200 SO's, 8	2.25	1.10	.22
☐ 6 RB: Rennie Stennett Most Hits in a 9 inning game, 7	.35	.17	.03
☐ 7 Jim Umbarger	.22	.11	.02
☐ 8 Tito Fuentes	.22	.11	.02
☐ 9 Paul Lindblad	.22	.11	.02
☐ 10 Lou Brock	2.75	1.35	.27
☐ 11 Jim Hughes	.22	.11	.02
☐ 12 Richie Zisk	.35	.17	.03
☐ 13 John Wockenfuss	.22	.11	.02
☐ 14 Gene Garber	.22	.11	.02
☐ 15 George Scott	.35	.17	.03
☐ 16 Bob Apodaca	.22	.11	.02
☐ 17 New York Yankees Team Card; Billy Martin MG (checklist back)	1.00	.50	.10
☐ 18 Dale Murray	.22	.11	.02
☐ 19 George Brett	40.00	20.00	4.00
☐ 20 Bob Watson	.35	.17	.03
☐ 21 Dave LaRoche	.22	.11	.02
☐ 22 Bill Russell	.35	.17	.03
☐ 23 Brian Downing	.50	.25	.05
☐ 24 Cesar Geronimo	.22	.11	.02
☐ 25 Mike Torrez	.22	.11	.02
☐ 26 Andre Thornton	.35	.17	.03
☐ 27 Ed Figueroa	.22	.11	.02
☐ 28 Dusty Baker	.50	.25	.05
☐ 29 Rick Burleson	.35	.17	.03
☐ 30 John Montefusco	.35	.17	.03
☐ 31 Len Randle	.22	.11	.02
☐ 32 Danny Frisella	.22	.11	.02
☐ 33 Bill North	.22	.11	.02
☐ 34 Mike Garman	.22	.11	.02
☐ 35 Tony Oliva	.75	.35	.07
☐ 36 Frank Taveras	.22	.11	.02
☐ 37 John Hiller	.35	.17	.03
☐ 38 Garry Maddox	.35	.17	.03
☐ 39 Pete Broberg	.22	.11	.02
☐ 40 Dave Kingman	.75	.35	.07
☐ 41 Tippy Martinez	.35	.17	.03
☐ 42 Barry Foote	.22	.11	.02
☐ 43 Paul Splittorff	.22	.11	.02
☐ 44 Doug Rader	.35	.17	.03
☐ 45 Boog Powell	.50	.25	.05
☐ 46 Dodgers Team Walter Alston MG (checklist back)	.75	.35	.07
☐ 47 Jesse Jefferson	.22	.11	.02
☐ 48 Dave Concepcion	.60	.30	.06
☐ 49 Dave Duncan	.22	.11	.02
☐ 50 Fred Lynn	2.25	1.10	.22
☐ 51 Ray Burris	.22	.11	.02
☐ 52 Dave Chalk	.22	.11	.02
☐ 53 Mike Beard	.22	.11	.02
☐ 54 Dave Rader	.22	.11	.02
☐ 55 Gaylord Perry	2.50	1.10	.22
☐ 56 Bob Tolan	.22	.11	.02
☐ 57 Phil Garner	.35	.17	.03
☐ 58 Ron Reed	.22	.11	.02
☐ 59 Larry Hisle	.35	.17	.03
☐ 60 Jerry Reuss	.35	.17	.03
☐ 61 Ron LeFlore	.35	.17	.03
☐ 62 Johnny Oates	.22	.11	.02
☐ 63 Bobby Darwin	.22	.11	.02
☐ 64 Jerry Koosman	.50	.25	.05
☐ 65 Chris Chambliss	.35	.17	.03
☐ 66 Father and Son Gus Bell Buddy Bell	.35	.17	.03
☐ 67 Father and Son Ray Boone Bob Boone	.50	.25	.05
☐ 68 Father and Son Joe Coleman Joe Coleman Jr.	.22	.11	.02
☐ 69 Father and Son Jim Hegan Mike Hegan	.22	.11	.02
☐ 70 Father and Son Roy Smalley Roy Smalley Jr.	.22	.11	.02
☐ 71 Steve Rogers	.35	.17	.03
☐ 72 Hal McRae	.35	.17	.03
☐ 73 Baltimore Orioles Team Card Earl Weaver MG (checklist back)	.75	.35	.07
☐ 74 Oscar Gamble	.35	.17	.03
☐ 75 Larry Dierker	.35	.17	.03
☐ 76 Willie Crawford	.22	.11	.02
☐ 77 Pedro Borbon	.22	.11	.02
☐ 78 Cecil Cooper	.90	.45	.09
☐ 79 Jerry Morales	.22	.11	.02
☐ 80 Jim Kaat	.75	.35	.07
☐ 81 Darrell Evans	.60	.30	.06
☐ 82 Von Joshua	.22	.11	.02
☐ 83 Jim Spencer	.22	.11	.02
☐ 84 Brent Strom	.22	.11	.02
☐ 85 Mickey Rivers	.35	.17	.03
☐ 86 Mike Tyson	.22	.11	.02
☐ 87 Tom Burgmeier	.22	.11	.02
☐ 88 Duffy Dyer	.22	.11	.02
☐ 89 Vern Ruhle	.22	.11	.02
☐ 90 Sal Bando	.50	.25	.05
☐ 91 Tom Hutton	.22	.11	.02
☐ 92 Eduardo Rodriguez	.22	.11	.02

☐	93	Mike Phillips	.22	.11	.02
☐	94	Jim Dwyer	.22	.11	.02
☐	95	Brooks Robinson	3.50	1.75	.35
☐	96	Doug Bird	.22	.11	.02
☐	97	Wilbur Howard	.22	.11	.02
☐	98	Dennis Eckersley	24.00	12.00	2.40
☐	99	Lee Lacy	.22	.11	.02
☐	100	Jim Hunter	2.50	1.25	.25
☐	101	Pete LaCock	.22	.11	.02
☐	102	Jim Willoughby	.22	.11	.02
☐	103	Biff Pocoroba	.22	.11	.02
☐	104	Reds Team	.75	.35	.07
		Sparky Anderson MG			
		(checklist back)			
☐	105	Gary Lavelle	.22	.11	.02
☐	106	Tom Grieve	.35	.17	.03
☐	107	Dave Roberts	.22	.11	.02
☐	108	Don Kirkwood	.22	.11	.02
☐	109	Larry Lintz	.22	.11	.02
☐	110	Carlos May	.22	.11	.02
☐	111	Danny Thompson	.22	.11	.02
☐	112	Kent Tekulve	1.00	.50	.10
☐	113	Gary Sutherland	.22	.11	.02
☐	114	Jay Johnstone	.35	.17	.03
☐	115	Ken Holtzman	.35	.17	.03
☐	116	Charlie Moore	.22	.11	.02
☐	117	Mike Jorgensen	.22	.11	.02
☐	118	Red Sox Team	.75	.35	.07
		Darrell Johnson MG			
		(checklist back)			
☐	119	Checklist 1-132	1.00	.10	.02
☐	120	Rusty Staub	.50	.25	.05
☐	121	Tony Solaita	.22	.11	.02
☐	122	Mike Cosgrove	.22	.11	.02
☐	123	Walt Williams	.22	.11	.02
☐	124	Doug Rau	.22	.11	.02
☐	125	Don Baylor	.70	.35	.07
☐	126	Tom Dettore	.22	.11	.02
☐	127	Larvell Blanks	.22	.11	.02
☐	128	Ken Griffey	1.50	.75	.15
☐	129	Andy Etchebarren	.22	.11	.02
☐	130	Luis Tiant	.50	.25	.05
☐	131	Bill Stein	.22	.11	.02
☐	132	Don Hood	.22	.11	.02
☐	133	Gary Matthews	.35	.17	.03
☐	134	Mike Ivie	.22	.11	.02
☐	135	Bake McBride	.35	.17	.03
☐	136	Dave Goltz	.22	.11	.02
☐	137	Bill Robinson	.35	.17	.03
☐	138	Lerrin LaGrow	.22	.11	.02
☐	139	Gorman Thomas	.50	.25	.05
☐	140	Vida Blue	.50	.25	.05
☐	141	Larry Parrish	1.00	.50	.10
☐	142	Dick Drago	.22	.11	.02
☐	143	Jerry Grote	.22	.11	.02
☐	144	Al Fitzmorris	.22	.11	.02
☐	145	Larry Bowa	.60	.30	.06
☐	146	George Medich	.22	.11	.02
☐	147	Astros Team	.75	.35	.07
		Bill Virdon MG			
		(checklist back)			
☐	148	Stan Thomas	.22	.11	.02
☐	149	Tommy Davis	.35	.17	.03
☐	150	Steve Garvey	5.50	2.75	.55
☐	151	Bill Bonham	.22	.11	.02
☐	152	Leroy Stanton	.22	.11	.02
☐	153	Buzz Capra	.22	.11	.02
☐	154	Bucky Dent	.60	.30	.06
☐	155	Jack Billingham	.22	.11	.02
☐	156	Rico Carty	.35	.17	.03
☐	157	Mike Caldwell	.35	.17	.03
☐	158	Ken Reitz	.22	.11	.02
☐	159	Jerry Terrell	.22	.11	.02
☐	160	Dave Winfield	7.50	3.75	.75
☐	161	Bruce Kison	.22	.11	.02
☐	162	Jack Pierce	.22	.11	.02
☐	163	Jim Slaton	.22	.11	.02
☐	164	Pepe Mangual	.22	.11	.02
☐	165	Gene Tenace	.35	.17	.03
☐	166	Skip Lockwood	.22	.11	.02
☐	167	Freddie Patek	.22	.11	.02
☐	168	Tom Hilgendorf	.22	.11	.02
☐	169	Graig Nettles	1.00	.50	.10
☐	170	Rick Wise	.35	.17	.03
☐	171	Greg Gross	.22	.11	.02
☐	172	Rangers Team	.75	.35	.07
		Frank Lucchesi MG			
		(checklist back)			
☐	173	Steve Swisher	.22	.11	.02
☐	174	Charlie Hough	.35	.17	.03
☐	175	Ken Singleton	.35	.17	.03
☐	176	Dick Lange	.22	.11	.02
☐	177	Marty Perez	.22	.11	.02
☐	178	Tom Buskey	.22	.11	.02
☐	179	George Foster	1.00	.50	.10
☐	180	Rich Gossage	1.25	.60	.12
☐	181	Willie Montanez	.22	.11	.02
☐	182	Harry Rasmussen	.22	.11	.02
☐	183	Steve Braun	.22	.11	.02
☐	184	Bill Greif	.22	.11	.02
☐	185	Dave Parker	6.50	3.25	.65
☐	186	Tom Walker	.22	.11	.02
☐	187	Pedro Garcia	.22	.11	.02
☐	188	Fred Scherman	.22	.11	.02
☐	189	Claudell Washington	.60	.30	.06
☐	190	Jon Matlack	.35	.17	.03
☐	191	NL Batting Leaders	.50	.25	.05
		Bill Madlock			
		Ted Simmons			
		Manny Sanguillen			
☐	192	AL Batting Leaders	1.50	.75	.15
		Rod Carew			
		Fred Lynn			
		Thurman Munson			
☐	193	NL Home Run Leaders	1.00	.50	.10
		Mike Schmidt			
		Dave Kingman			
		Greg Luzinski			
☐	194	AL Home Run Leaders	1.00	.50	.10
		Reggie Jackson			
		George Scott			
		John Mayberry			
☐	195	NL RBI Leaders	1.00	.50	.10
		Greg Luzinski			
		Johnny Bench			
		Tony Perez			
☐	196	AL RBI Leaders	.50	.25	.05
		George Scott			
		John Mayberry			
		Fred Lynn			
☐	197	NL Steals Leaders	1.00	.50	.10
		Dave Lopes			
		Joe Morgan			
		Lou Brock			
☐	198	AL Steals Leaders	.50	.25	.05
		Mickey Rivers			
		Claudell Washington			
		Amos Otis			
☐	199	NL Victory Leaders	.75	.35	.07
		Tom Seaver			
		Randy Jones			
		Andy Messersmith			
☐	200	AL Victory Leaders	1.25	.60	.12
		Jim Hunter			
		Jim Palmer			
		Vida Blue			
☐	201	NL ERA Leaders	.50	.25	.05
		Randy Jones			
		Andy Messersmith			
		Tom Seaver			
☐	202	AL ERA Leaders	2.00	1.00	.20
		Jim Palmer			
		Jim Hunter			
		Dennis Eckersley			
☐	203	NL Strikeout Leaders	.75	.35	.07
		Tom Seaver			
		John Montefusco			
		Andy Messersmith			
☐	204	AL Strikeout Leaders	.50	.25	.05
		Frank Tanana			
		Bert Blyleven			
		Gaylord Perry			
☐	205	Leading Firemen	.50	.25	.05
		Al Hrabosky			
		Rich Gossage			
☐	206	Manny Trillo	.22	.11	.02
☐	207	Andy Hassler	.22	.11	.02
☐	208	Mike Lum	.22	.11	.02
☐	209	Alan Ashby	.35	.17	.03
☐	210	Lee May	.35	.17	.03
☐	211	Clay Carroll	.22	.11	.02
☐	212	Pat Kelly	.22	.11	.02
☐	213	Dave Heaverlo	.22	.11	.02
☐	214	Eric Soderholm	.22	.11	.02
☐	215	Reggie Smith	.50	.25	.05
☐	216	Expos Team	.65	.30	.06
		Karl Kuehl MG			
		(checklist back)			
☐	217	Dave Freisleben	.22	.11	.02
☐	218	John Knox	.22	.11	.02
☐	219	Tom Murphy	.22	.11	.02
☐	220	Manny Sanguillen	.35	.17	.03
☐	221	Jim Todd	.22	.11	.02
☐	222	Wayne Garrett	.22	.11	.02
☐	223	Ollie Brown	.22	.11	.02
☐	224	Jim York	.22	.11	.02
☐	225	Roy White	.35	.17	.03
☐	226	Jim Sundberg	.35	.17	.03

☐ 227	Oscar Zamora	.22	.11	.02
☐ 228	John Hale	.22	.11	.02
☐ 229	Jerry Remy	.35	.17	.03
☐ 230	Carl Yastrzemski	9.00	4.50	.90
☐ 231	Tom House	.22	.11	.02
☐ 232	Frank Duffy	.22	.11	.02
☐ 233	Grant Jackson	.22	.11	.02
☐ 234	Mike Sadek	.22	.11	.02
☐ 235	Bert Blyleven	1.75	.85	.17
☐ 236	Kansas City Royals	.75	.35	.07
	Team Card			
	Whitey Herzog MG			
	(checklist back)			
☐ 237	Dave Hamilton	.22	.11	.02
☐ 238	Larry Biittner	.22	.11	.02
☐ 239	John Curtis	.22	.11	.02
☐ 240	Pete Rose	15.00	7.50	1.50
☐ 241	Hector Torres	.22	.11	.02
☐ 242	Dan Meyer	.22	.11	.02
☐ 243	Jim Rooker	.22	.11	.02
☐ 244	Bill Sharp	.22	.11	.02
☐ 245	Felix Millan	.22	.11	.02
☐ 246	Cesar Tovar	.22	.11	.02
☐ 247	Terry Harmon	.22	.11	.02
☐ 248	Dick Tidrow	.22	.11	.02
☐ 249	Cliff Johnson	.22	.11	.02
☐ 250	Fergie Jenkins	1.50	.60	.12
☐ 251	Rick Monday	.35	.17	.03
☐ 252	Tim Nordbrook	.22	.11	.02
☐ 253	Bill Buckner	.50	.25	.05
☐ 254	Rudy Meoli	.22	.11	.02
☐ 255	Fritz Peterson	.22	.11	.02
☐ 256	Rowland Office	.22	.11	.02
☐ 257	Ross Grimsley	.22	.11	.02
☐ 258	Nyls Nyman	.22	.11	.02
☐ 259	Darrel Chaney	.22	.11	.02
☐ 260	Steve Busby	.35	.17	.03
☐ 261	Gary Thomasson	.22	.11	.02
☐ 262	Checklist 133-264	1.00	.10	.02
☐ 263	Lyman Bostock	.50	.25	.05
☐ 264	Steve Renko	.22	.11	.02
☐ 265	Willie Davis	.35	.17	.03
☐ 266	Alan Foster	.22	.11	.02
☐ 267	Aurelio Rodriguez	.22	.11	.02
☐ 268	Del Unser	.22	.11	.02
☐ 269	Rick Austin	.22	.11	.02
☐ 270	Willie Stargell	3.00	1.50	.30
☐ 271	Jim Lonborg	.35	.17	.03
☐ 272	Rick Dempsey	.35	.17	.03
☐ 273	Joe Niekro	.35	.17	.03
☐ 274	Tommy Harper	.35	.17	.03
☐ 275	Rick Manning	.22	.11	.02
☐ 276	Mickey Scott	.22	.11	.02
☐ 277	Cubs Team	.75	.35	.07
	Jim Marshall MG			
	(checklist back)			
☐ 278	Bernie Carbo	.22	.11	.02
☐ 279	Roy Howell	.22	.11	.02
☐ 280	Burt Hooton	.35	.17	.03
☐ 281	Dave May	.22	.11	.02
☐ 282	Dan Osborn	.22	.11	.02
☐ 283	Merv Rettenmund	.22	.11	.02
☐ 284	Steve Ontiveros	.22	.11	.02
☐ 285	Mike Cuellar	.35	.17	.03
☐ 286	Jim Wohlford	.22	.11	.02
☐ 287	Pete Mackanin	.22	.11	.02
☐ 288	Bill Campbell	.22	.11	.02
☐ 289	Enzo Hernandez	.22	.11	.02
☐ 290	Ted Simmons	.75	.35	.07
☐ 291	Ken Sanders	.22	.11	.02
☐ 292	Leon Roberts	.22	.11	.02
☐ 293	Bill Castro	.22	.11	.02
☐ 294	Ed Kirkpatrick	.22	.11	.02
☐ 295	Dave Cash	.22	.11	.02
☐ 296	Pat Dobson	.22	.11	.02
☐ 297	Roger Metzger	.22	.11	.02
☐ 298	Dick Bosman	.22	.11	.02
☐ 299	Champ Summers	.22	.11	.02
☐ 300	Johnny Bench	9.00	4.50	.90
☐ 301	Jackie Brown	.22	.11	.02
☐ 302	Rick Miller	.22	.11	.02
☐ 303	Steve Foucault	.22	.11	.02
☐ 304	Angels Team	.75	.35	.07
	Dick Williams MG			
	(checklist back)			
☐ 305	Andy Messersmith	.35	.17	.03
☐ 306	Rod Gilbreath	.22	.11	.02
☐ 307	Al Bumbry	.22	.11	.02
☐ 308	Jim Barr	.22	.11	.02
☐ 309	Bill Melton	.22	.11	.02
☐ 310	Randy Jones	.35	.17	.03
☐ 311	Cookie Rojas	.22	.11	.02
☐ 312	Don Carrithers	.22	.11	.02
☐ 313	Dan Ford	.22	.11	.02
☐ 314	Ed Kranepool	.35	.17	.03
☐ 315	Al Hrabosky	.35	.17	.03
☐ 316	Robin Yount	33.00	15.00	3.00
☐ 317	John Candelaria	3.00	1.50	.30
☐ 318	Bob Boone	.80	.40	.08
☐ 319	Larry Gura	.35	.17	.03
☐ 320	Willie Horton	.35	.17	.03
☐ 321	Jose Cruz	.35	.17	.03
☐ 322	Glenn Abbott	.22	.11	.02
☐ 323	Rob Sperring	.22	.11	.02
☐ 324	Jim Bibby	.22	.11	.02
☐ 325	Tony Perez	.90	.45	.09
☐ 326	Dick Pole	.22	.11	.02
☐ 327	Dave Moates	.22	.11	.02
☐ 328	Carl Morton	.22	.11	.02
☐ 329	Joe Ferguson	.22	.11	.02
☐ 330	Nolan Ryan	27.00	13.50	2.70
☐ 331	San Diego Padres	.75	.35	.07
	Team Card			
	John McNamara MG			
	(checklist back)			
☐ 332	Charlie Williams	.22	.11	.02
☐ 333	Bob Coluccio	.22	.11	.02
☐ 334	Dennis Leonard	.35	.17	.03
☐ 335	Bob Grich	.35	.17	.03
☐ 336	Vic Albury	.22	.11	.02
☐ 337	Bud Harrelson	.35	.17	.03
☐ 338	Bob Bailey	.22	.11	.02
☐ 339	John Denny	.35	.17	.03
☐ 340	Jim Rice	8.00	4.00	.80
☐ 341	All-Time 1B	3.50	1.75	.35
	Lou Gehrig			
☐ 342	All-Time 2B	1.75	.85	.17
	Rogers Hornsby			
☐ 343	All-Time 3B	.75	.35	.07
	Pie Traynor			
☐ 344	All-Time SS	1.75	.85	.17
	Honus Wagner			
☐ 345	All-Time OF	6.00	3.00	.60
	Babe Ruth			
☐ 346	All-Time OF	3.50	1.75	.35
	Ty Cobb			
☐ 347	All-Time OF	3.50	1.75	.35
	Ted Williams			
☐ 348	All-Time C	.75	.35	.07
	Mickey Cochrane			
☐ 349	All-Time RHP	1.50	.75	.15
	Walter Johnson			
☐ 350	All-Time LHP	1.25	.60	.12
	Lefty Grove			
☐ 351	Randy Hundley	.22	.11	.02
☐ 352	Dave Giusti	.22	.11	.02
☐ 353	Sixto Lezcano	.22	.11	.02
☐ 354	Ron Blomberg	.22	.11	.02
☐ 355	Steve Carlton	5.00	2.50	.50
☐ 356	Ted Martinez	.22	.11	.02
☐ 357	Ken Forsch	.22	.11	.02
☐ 358	Buddy Bell	.50	.25	.05
☐ 359	Rick Reuschel	.60	.30	.06
☐ 360	Jeff Burroughs	.35	.17	.03
☐ 361	Detroit Tigers	.75	.35	.07
	Team Card			
	Ralph Houk MG			
	(checklist back)			
☐ 362	Will McEnaney	.22	.11	.02
☐ 363	Dave Collins	.75	.35	.07
☐ 364	Elias Sosa	.22	.11	.02
☐ 365	Carlton Fisk	6.00	3.00	.60
☐ 366	Bobby Valentine	.35	.17	.03
☐ 367	Bruce Miller	.22	.11	.02
☐ 368	Wilbur Wood	.22	.11	.02
☐ 369	Frank White	.50	.25	.05
☐ 370	Ron Cey	.60	.30	.06
☐ 371	Elrod Hendricks	.22	.11	.02
☐ 372	Rick Baldwin	.22	.11	.02
☐ 373	Johnny Briggs	.22	.11	.02
☐ 374	Dan Warthen	.22	.11	.02
☐ 375	Ron Fairly	.35	.17	.03
☐ 376	Rich Hebner	.22	.11	.02
☐ 377	Mike Hegan	.22	.11	.02
☐ 378	Steve Stone	.35	.17	.03
☐ 379	Ken Boswell	.22	.11	.02
☐ 380	Bobby Bonds	.50	.25	.05
☐ 381	Denny Doyle	.22	.11	.02
☐ 382	Matt Alexander	.22	.11	.02
☐ 383	John Ellis	.22	.11	.02
☐ 384	Phillies Team	.75	.35	.07
	Danny Ozark MG			
	(checklist back)			
☐ 385	Mickey Lolich	.50	.25	.05
☐ 386	Ed Goodson	.22	.11	.02
☐ 387	Mike Miley	.22	.11	.02
☐ 388	Stan Perzanowski	.22	.11	.02
☐ 389	Glenn Adams	.22	.11	.02

☐ 390 Don Gullett	.35	.17	.03
☐ 391 Jerry Hairston	.22	.11	.02
☐ 392 Checklist 265-396	1.00	.10	.02
☐ 393 Paul Mitchell	.22	.11	.02
☐ 394 Fran Healy	.22	.11	.02
☐ 395 Jim Wynn	.35	.17	.03
☐ 396 Bill Lee	.35	.17	.03
☐ 397 Tim Foli	.22	.11	.02
☐ 398 Dave Tomlin	.22	.11	.02
☐ 399 Luis Melendez	.22	.11	.02
☐ 400 Rod Carew	7.00	3.25	.65
☐ 401 Ken Brett	.22	.11	.02
☐ 402 Don Money	.22	.11	.02
☐ 403 Geoff Zahn	.22	.11	.02
☐ 404 Enos Cabell	.22	.11	.02
☐ 405 Rollie Fingers	2.00	1.00	.20
☐ 406 Ed Herrmann	.22	.11	.02
☐ 407 Tom Underwood	.22	.11	.02
☐ 408 Charlie Spikes	.22	.11	.02
☐ 409 Dave Lemanczyk	.22	.11	.02
☐ 410 Ralph Garr	.22	.11	.02
☐ 411 Bill Singer	.22	.11	.02
☐ 412 Toby Harrah	.35	.17	.03
☐ 413 Pete Varney	.22	.11	.02
☐ 414 Wayne Garland	.22	.11	.02
☐ 415 Vada Pinson	.50	.25	.05
☐ 416 Tommy John	1.00	.50	.10
☐ 417 Gene Clines	.22	.11	.02
☐ 418 Jose Morales	.22	.11	.02
☐ 419 Reggie Cleveland	.22	.11	.02
☐ 420 Joe Morgan	5.00	2.50	.50
☐ 421 A's Team	.75	.35	.07
(no MG on front;			
checklist back)			
☐ 422 Johnny Grubb	.22	.11	.02
☐ 423 Ed Halicki	.22	.11	.02
☐ 424 Phil Roof	.22	.11	.02
☐ 425 Rennie Stennett	.22	.11	.02
☐ 426 Bob Forsch	.22	.11	.02
☐ 427 Kurt Bevacqua	.22	.11	.02
☐ 428 Jim Crawford	.22	.11	.02
☐ 429 Fred Stanley	.22	.11	.02
☐ 430 Jose Cardenal	.22	.11	.02
☐ 431 Dick Ruthven	.22	.11	.02
☐ 432 Tom Veryzer	.22	.11	.02
☐ 433 Rick Waits	.22	.11	.02
☐ 434 Morris Nettles	.22	.11	.02
☐ 435 Phil Niekro	1.75	.85	.17
☐ 436 Bill Fahey	.22	.11	.02
☐ 437 Terry Forster	.35	.17	.03
☐ 438 Doug DeCinces	.60	.30	.06
☐ 439 Rick Rhoden	.50	.25	.05
☐ 440 John Mayberry	.35	.17	.03
☐ 441 Gary Carter	9.00	4.50	.90
☐ 442 Hank Webb	.22	.11	.02
☐ 443 Giants Team	.75	.35	.07
(no MG on front;			
checklist back)			
☐ 444 Gary Nolan	.22	.11	.02
☐ 445 Rico Petrocelli	.35	.17	.03
☐ 446 Larry Haney	.22	.11	.02
☐ 447 Gene Locklear	.22	.11	.02
☐ 448 Tom Johnson	.22	.11	.02
☐ 449 Bob Robertson	.22	.11	.02
☐ 450 Jim Palmer	5.00	2.50	.50
☐ 451 Buddy Bradford	.22	.11	.02
☐ 452 Tom Hausman	.22	.11	.02
☐ 453 Lou Piniella	.60	.30	.06
☐ 454 Tom Griffin	.22	.11	.02
☐ 455 Dick Allen	.50	.25	.05
☐ 456 Joe Coleman	.22	.11	.02
☐ 457 Ed Crosby	.22	.11	.02
☐ 458 Earl Williams	.22	.11	.02
☐ 459 Jim Brewer	.22	.11	.02
☐ 460 Cesar Cedeno	.35	.17	.03
☐ 461 NL and AL Champs	.50	.25	.05
Reds sweep Bucs,			
Bosox surprise A's			
☐ 462 '75 World Series	.50	.25	.05
Reds Champs			
☐ 463 Steve Hargan	.22	.11	.02
☐ 464 Ken Henderson	.22	.11	.02
☐ 465 Mike Marshall	.35	.17	.03
☐ 466 Bob Stinson	.22	.11	.02
☐ 467 Woodie Fryman	.22	.11	.02
☐ 468 Jesus Alou	.22	.11	.02
☐ 469 Rawly Eastwick	.22	.11	.02
☐ 470 Bobby Murcer	.50	.25	.05
☐ 471 Jim Burton	.22	.11	.02
☐ 472 Bob Davis	.22	.11	.02
☐ 473 Paul Blair	.35	.17	.03
☐ 474 Ray Corbin	.22	.11	.02
☐ 475 Joe Rudi	.35	.17	.03
☐ 476 Bob Moose	.22	.11	.02
☐ 477 Indians Team	.75	.35	.07
Frank Robinson MG			
(checklist back)			
☐ 478 Lynn McGlothen	.22	.11	.02
☐ 479 Bobby Mitchell	.22	.11	.02
☐ 480 Mike Schmidt	30.00	15.00	3.00
☐ 481 Rudy May	.22	.11	.02
☐ 482 Tim Hosley	.22	.11	.02
☐ 483 Mickey Stanley	.35	.17	.03
☐ 484 Eric Raich	.22	.11	.02
☐ 485 Mike Hargrove	.35	.17	.03
☐ 486 Bruce Dal Canton	.22	.11	.02
☐ 487 Leron Lee	.22	.11	.02
☐ 488 Claude Osteen	.35	.17	.03
☐ 489 Skip Jutze	.22	.11	.02
☐ 490 Frank Tanana	.35	.17	.03
☐ 491 Terry Crowley	.22	.11	.02
☐ 492 Marty Pattin	.22	.11	.02
☐ 493 Derrel Thomas	.22	.11	.02
☐ 494 Craig Swan	.35	.17	.03
☐ 495 Nate Colbert	.22	.11	.02
☐ 496 Juan Beniquez	.22	.11	.02
☐ 497 Joe McIntosh	.22	.11	.02
☐ 498 Glenn Borgmann	.22	.11	.02
☐ 499 Mario Guerrero	.22	.11	.02
☐ 500 Reggie Jackson	12.00	6.00	1.20
☐ 501 Billy Champion	.22	.11	.02
☐ 502 Tim McCarver	.50	.25	.05
☐ 503 Elliott Maddox	.22	.11	.02
☐ 504 Pirates Team	.75	.35	.07
Danny Murtaugh MG			
(checklist back)			
☐ 505 Mark Belanger	.35	.17	.03
☐ 506 George Mitterwald	.22	.11	.02
☐ 507 Ray Bare	.22	.11	.02
☐ 508 Duane Kuiper	.22	.11	.02
☐ 509 Bill Hands	.22	.11	.02
☐ 510 Amos Otis	.35	.17	.03
☐ 511 Jamie Easterley	.22	.11	.02
☐ 512 Ellie Rodriguez	.22	.11	.02
☐ 513 Bart Johnson	.22	.11	.02
☐ 514 Dan Driessen	.35	.17	.03
☐ 515 Steve Yeager	.22	.11	.02
☐ 516 Wayne Granger	.22	.11	.02
☐ 517 John Milner	.22	.11	.02
☐ 518 Doug Flynn	.22	.11	.02
☐ 519 Steve Brye	.22	.11	.02
☐ 520 Willie McCovey	2.75	1.35	.27
☐ 521 Jim Colborn	.22	.11	.02
☐ 522 Ted Sizemore	.22	.11	.02
☐ 523 Bob Montgomery	.22	.11	.02
☐ 524 Pete Falcone	.22	.11	.02
☐ 525 Billy Williams	2.25	1.10	.22
☐ 526 Checklist 397-528	1.00	.10	.02
☐ 527 Mike Anderson	.22	.11	.02
☐ 528 Dock Ellis	.22	.11	.02
☐ 529 Deron Johnson	.22	.11	.02
☐ 530 Don Sutton	1.50	.75	.15
☐ 531 New York Mets	1.00	.50	.10
Team Card			
Joe Frazier MG			
(checklist back)			
☐ 532 Milt May	.22	.11	.02
☐ 533 Lee Richard	.22	.11	.02
☐ 534 Stan Bahnsen	.22	.11	.02
☐ 535 Dave Nelson	.22	.11	.02
☐ 536 Mike Thompson	.22	.11	.02
☐ 537 Tony Muser	.22	.11	.02
☐ 538 Pat Darcy	.22	.11	.02
☐ 539 John Balaz	.22	.11	.02
☐ 540 Bill Freehan	.50	.25	.05
☐ 541 Steve Mingori	.22	.11	.02
☐ 542 Keith Hernandez	7.00	3.50	.70
☐ 543 Wayne Twitchell	.22	.11	.02
☐ 544 Pepe Frias	.22	.11	.02
☐ 545 Sparky Lyle	.50	.25	.05
☐ 546 Dave Rosello	.22	.11	.02
☐ 547 Roric Harrison	.22	.11	.02
☐ 548 Manny Mota	.35	.17	.03
☐ 549 Randy Tate	.22	.11	.02
☐ 550 Hank Aaron	14.00	7.00	1.40
☐ 551 Jerry DaVanon	.22	.11	.02
☐ 552 Terry Humphrey	.22	.11	.02
☐ 553 Randy Moffitt	.22	.11	.02
☐ 554 Ray Fosse	.22	.11	.02
☐ 555 Dyar Miller	.22	.11	.02
☐ 556 Twins Team	.75	.35	.07
Gene Mauch MG			
(checklist back)			
☐ 557 Dan Spillner	.22	.11	.02
☐ 558 Clarence Gaston	.50	.25	.05
☐ 559 Clyde Wright	.22	.11	.02
☐ 560 Jorge Orta	.22	.11	.02
☐ 561 Tom Carroll	.22	.11	.02

☐ 562 Adrian Garrett	.22	.11	.02
☐ 563 Larry Demery	.22	.11	.02
☐ 564 Bubble Gum Champ Kurt Bevacqua	.22	.11	.02
☐ 565 Tug McGraw	.50	.25	.05
☐ 566 Ken McMullen	.22	.11	.02
☐ 567 George Stone	.22	.11	.02
☐ 568 Rob Andrews	.22	.11	.02
☐ 569 Nelson Briles	.22	.11	.02
☐ 570 George Hendrick	.35	.17	.03
☐ 571 Don DeMola	.22	.11	.02
☐ 572 Rich Coggins	.22	.11	.02
☐ 573 Bill Travers	.22	.11	.02
☐ 574 Don Kessinger	.35	.17	.03
☐ 575 Dwight Evans	3.50	1.75	.35
☐ 576 Maximino Leon	.22	.11	.02
☐ 577 Marc Hill	.22	.11	.02
☐ 578 Ted Kubiak	.22	.11	.02
☐ 579 Clay Kirby	.22	.11	.02
☐ 580 Bert Campaneris	.35	.17	.03
☐ 581 Cardinals Team Red Schoendienst MG (checklist back)	.75	.35	.07
☐ 582 Mike Kekich	.22	.11	.02
☐ 583 Tommy Helms	.35	.17	.03
☐ 584 Stan Wall	.22	.11	.02
☐ 585 Joe Torre	.60	.30	.06
☐ 586 Ron Schueler	.22	.11	.02
☐ 587 Leo Cardenas	.22	.11	.02
☐ 588 Kevin Kobel	.22	.11	.02
☐ 589 Rookie Pitchers Santo Alcala Mike Flanagan Joe Pactwa Pablo Torrealba	2.00	1.00	.20
☐ 590 Rookie Outfielders Henry Cruz Chet Lemon Ellis Valentine Terry Whitfield	1.00	.50	.10
☐ 591 Rookie Pitchers Steve Grilli Craig Mitchell Jose Sosa George Throop	.22	.11	.02
☐ 592 Rookie Infielders Willie Randolph Dave McKay Jerry Royster Roy Staiger	5.00	2.50	.50
☐ 593 Rookie Pitchers Larry Anderson Ken Crosby Mark Littell Butch Metzger	.35	.17	.03
☐ 594 Rookie Catchers/OF Andy Merchant Ed Ott Royle Stillman Jerry White	.35	.17	.03
☐ 595 Rookie Pitchers Art DeFillipis Randy Lerch Sid Monge Steve Barr	.35	.17	.03
☐ 596 Rookie Infielders Craig Reynolds Lamar Johnson Johnnie LeMaster Jerry Manuel	.50	.25	.05
☐ 597 Rookie Pitchers Don Aase Jack Kucek Frank LaCorte Mike Pazik	.60	.30	.06
☐ 598 Rookie Outfielders Hector Cruz Jamie Quirk Jerry Turner Joe Wallis	.35	.17	.03
☐ 599 Rookie Pitchers Rob Dressler Ron Guidry Bob McClure Pat Zachry	11.00	5.50	1.10
☐ 600 Tom Seaver	8.00	4.00	.80
☐ 601 Ken Rudolph	.22	.11	.02
☐ 602 Doug Konieczny	.22	.11	.02
☐ 603 Jim Holt	.22	.11	.02
☐ 604 Joe Lovitto	.22	.11	.02
☐ 605 Al Downing	.35	.17	.03
☐ 606 Milwaukee Brewers Team Card Alex Grammas MG (checklist back)	.75	.35	.07
☐ 607 Rich Hinton	.22	.11	.02
☐ 608 Vic Correll	.22	.11	.02
☐ 609 Fred Norman	.22	.11	.02
☐ 610 Greg Luzinski	.50	.25	.05
☐ 611 Rich Folkers	.22	.11	.02
☐ 612 Joe Lahoud	.22	.11	.02
☐ 613 Tim Johnson	.22	.11	.02
☐ 614 Fernando Arroyo	.22	.11	.02
☐ 615 Mike Cubbage	.22	.11	.02
☐ 616 Buck Martinez	.22	.11	.02
☐ 617 Darold Knowles	.22	.11	.02
☐ 618 Jack Brohamer	.22	.11	.02
☐ 619 Bill Butler	.22	.11	.02
☐ 620 Al Oliver	.50	.25	.05
☐ 621 Tom Hall	.22	.11	.02
☐ 622 Rick Auerbach	.22	.11	.02
☐ 623 Bob Allietta	.22	.11	.02
☐ 624 Tony Taylor	.22	.11	.02
☐ 625 J.R. Richard	.35	.17	.03
☐ 626 Bob Sheldon	.22	.11	.02
☐ 627 Bill Plummer	.22	.11	.02
☐ 628 John D'Acquisto	.22	.11	.02
☐ 629 Sandy Alomar	.22	.11	.02
☐ 630 Chris Speier	.22	.11	.02
☐ 631 Braves Team Dave Bristol MG (checklist back)	.75	.35	.07
☐ 632 Rogelio Moret	.22	.11	.02
☐ 633 John Stearns	.35	.17	.03
☐ 634 Larry Christenson	.22	.11	.02
☐ 635 Jim Fregosi	.35	.17	.03
☐ 636 Joe Decker	.22	.11	.02
☐ 637 Bruce Bochte	.22	.11	.02
☐ 638 Doyle Alexander	.35	.17	.03
☐ 639 Fred Kendall	.22	.11	.02
☐ 640 Bill Madlock	1.00	.50	.10
☐ 641 Tom Paciorek	.22	.11	.02
☐ 642 Dennis Blair	.22	.11	.02
☐ 643 Checklist 529-660	1.00	.10	.02
☐ 644 Tom Bradley	.22	.11	.02
☐ 645 Darrell Porter	.22	.11	.02
☐ 646 John Lowenstein	.22	.11	.02
☐ 647 Ramon Hernandez	.22	.11	.02
☐ 648 Al Cowens	.35	.17	.03
☐ 649 Dave Roberts	.22	.11	.02
☐ 650 Thurman Munson	6.50	3.25	.65
☐ 651 John Odom	.22	.11	.02
☐ 652 Ed Armbrister	.22	.11	.02
☐ 653 Mike Norris	.35	.17	.03
☐ 654 Doug Griffin	.22	.11	.02
☐ 655 Mike Vail	.22	.11	.02
☐ 656 Chicago White Sox Team Card Chuck Tanner MG (checklist back)	.75	.35	.07
☐ 657 Roy Smalley	.50	.25	.05
☐ 658 Jerry Johnson	.22	.11	.02
☐ 659 Ben Oglivie	.35	.17	.03
☐ 660 Dave Lopes	.75	.20	.04

1976 Topps Traded

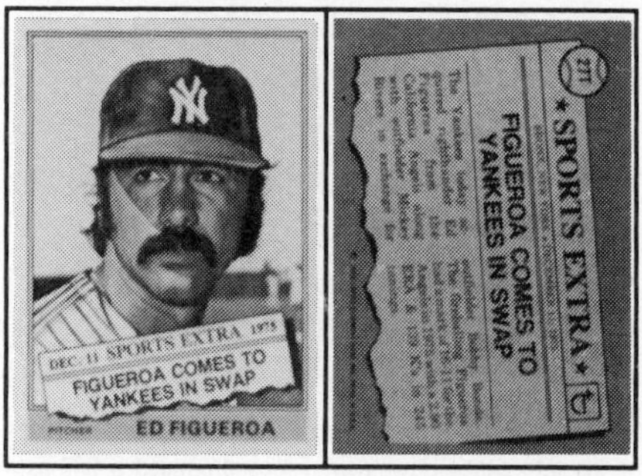

The cards in this 44-card set measure 2 1/2" by 3 1/2". The 1976 Topps Traded set contains 43 players and one unnumbered checklist card. The individuals pictured were traded after the Topps regular set was printed. A "Sports Extra" heading design is found on each picture and is also used to introduce the biographical section of the reverse. Each card is numbered according to the player's regular 1976 card with the addition of "T" to indicate his new status.

	NRMT	VG-E	GOOD
COMPLETE SET (44)	7.50	3.75	.75
COMMON PLAYER	.15	.07	.01
☐ 27T Ed Figueroa	.15	.07	.01
☐ 28T Dusty Baker	.30	.15	.03
☐ 44T Doug Rader	.25	.12	.02
☐ 58T Ron Reed	.15	.07	.01
☐ 74T Oscar Gamble	.25	.12	.02
☐ 80T Jim Kaat	.90	.45	.09
☐ 83T Jim Spencer	.15	.07	.01
☐ 85T Mickey Rivers	.20	.10	.02
☐ 99T Lee Lacy	.20	.10	.02
☐ 120T Rusty Staub	.50	.25	.05
☐ 127T Larvell Blanks	.15	.07	.01
☐ 146T George Medich	.15	.07	.01
☐ 158T Ken Reitz	.15	.07	.01
☐ 208T Mike Lum	.15	.07	.01
☐ 211T Clay Carroll	.15	.07	.01
☐ 231T Tom House	.15	.07	.01
☐ 250T Fergie Jenkins	1.25	.60	.12
☐ 259T Darrel Chaney	.15	.07	.01
☐ 292T Leon Roberts	.15	.07	.01
☐ 296T Pat Dobson	.15	.07	.01
☐ 309T Bill Melton	.15	.07	.01
☐ 338T Bob Bailey	.15	.07	.01
☐ 380T Bobby Bonds	.50	.25	.05
☐ 383T John Ellis	.15	.07	.01
☐ 385T Mickey Lolich	.40	.20	.04
☐ 401T Ken Brett	.15	.07	.01
☐ 410T Ralph Garr	.15	.07	.01
☐ 411T Bill Singer	.15	.07	.01
☐ 428T Jim Crawford	.15	.07	.01
☐ 434T Morris Nettles	.15	.07	.01
☐ 464T Ken Henderson	.15	.07	.01
☐ 497T Joe McIntosh	.15	.07	.01
☐ 524T Pete Falcone	.15	.07	.01
☐ 527T Mike Anderson	.15	.07	.01
☐ 528T Dock Ellis	.15	.07	.01
☐ 532T Milt May	.15	.07	.01
☐ 554T Ray Fosse	.15	.07	.01
☐ 579T Clay Kirby	.15	.07	.01
☐ 583T Tommy Helms	.15	.07	.01
☐ 592T Willie Randolph	1.25	.60	.12
☐ 618T Jack Brohamer	.15	.07	.01
☐ 632T Rogelio Moret	.15	.07	.01
☐ 649T Dave Roberts	.15	.07	.01
☐ xxxT Traded Checklist (unnumbered)	.60	.06	.01

1977 Topps

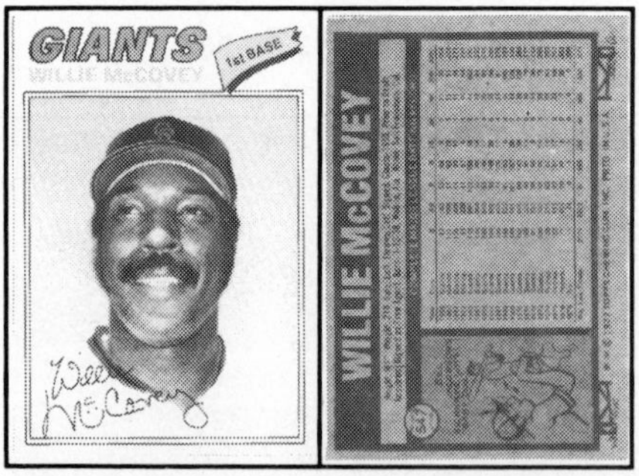

The cards in this 660-card set measure 2 1/2" by 3 1/2". In 1977 for the fifth consecutive year, Topps produced a 660-card baseball set. The player's name, team affiliation, and his position are compactly arranged over the picture area and a facsimile autograph appears on the photo. Team cards feature a checklist of that team's players in the set and a small picture of the manager on the front of the card. Appearing for the first time are the series "Brothers" (631-634) and "Turn Back the Clock" (433-437). Other subseries in the set are League Leaders (1-8), Record Breakers (231-234), Playoffs cards (276-277), World Series cards (411-413), and Rookie Prospects (472-479 and 487-494). The key cards in the set are the rookie cards of Dale Murphy (476) and Andre Dawson (473). Cards numbered 23 or lower, that feature Yankees and do not follow the numbering checklisted below, are not necessarily error cards. They are probably Burger King cards, a separate set with its own pricing and mass distribution. Burger King cards are indistinguishable from the corresponding Topps cards except for the card numbering difference and the fact that Burger King cards do not have a printing sheet designation (such as A through F like the regular Topps) anywhere on the card back in very small print. There was an aluminum version of the Dale Murphy rookie card number 476 produced (legally) in the early '80s; proceeds from the sales (originally priced at 10.00) of this "card" went to the Huntington's Disease Foundation.

	NRMT	VG-E	GOOD
COMPLETE SET (660)	375.00	175.00	37.00
COMMON PLAYER (1-660)	.18	.09	.01
☐ 1 Batting Leaders George Brett Bill Madlock	3.00	.60	.12
☐ 2 Home Run Leaders Graig Nettles Mike Schmidt	.75	.35	.07
☐ 3 RBI Leaders Lee May George Foster	.30	.15	.03
☐ 4 Stolen Base Leaders Bill North Dave Lopes	.30	.15	.03
☐ 5 Victory Leaders Jim Palmer Randy Jones	.40	.20	.04
☐ 6 Strikeout Leaders Nolan Ryan Tom Seaver	3.75	1.85	.37
☐ 7 ERA Leaders Mark Fidrych John Denny	.30	.15	.03
☐ 8 Leading Firemen Bill Campbell Rawly Eastwick	.30	.15	.03
☐ 9 Doug Rader	.30	.15	.03
☐ 10 Reggie Jackson	9.00	4.50	.90
☐ 11 Rob Dressler	.18	.09	.01
☐ 12 Larry Haney	.18	.09	.01
☐ 13 Luis Gomez	.18	.09	.01
☐ 14 Tommy Smith	.18	.09	.01
☐ 15 Don Gullett	.30	.15	.03
☐ 16 Bob Jones	.18	.09	.01
☐ 17 Steve Stone	.30	.15	.03
☐ 18 Indians Team/Mgr. Frank Robinson (checklist back)	.65	.30	.06
☐ 19 John D'Acquisto	.18	.09	.01
☐ 20 Graig Nettles	.75	.35	.07
☐ 21 Ken Forsch	.18	.09	.01
☐ 22 Bill Freehan	.30	.15	.03
☐ 23 Dan Driessen	.30	.15	.03
☐ 24 Carl Morton	.18	.09	.01
☐ 25 Dwight Evans	2.50	1.25	.25
☐ 26 Ray Sadecki	.18	.09	.01
☐ 27 Bill Buckner	.40	.20	.04
☐ 28 Woodie Fryman	.18	.09	.01
☐ 29 Bucky Dent	.40	.20	.04
☐ 30 Greg Luzinski	.40	.20	.04
☐ 31 Jim Todd	.18	.09	.01
☐ 32 Checklist 1	.90	.09	.02
☐ 33 Wayne Garland	.18	.09	.01
☐ 34 Angels Team/Mgr. Norm Sherry (checklist back)	.65	.30	.06
☐ 35 Rennie Stennett	.18	.09	.01
☐ 36 John Ellis	.18	.09	.01
☐ 37 Steve Hargan	.18	.09	.01
☐ 38 Craig Kusick	.18	.09	.01
☐ 39 Tom Griffin	.18	.09	.01
☐ 40 Bobby Murcer	.40	.20	.04
☐ 41 Jim Kern	.18	.09	.01
☐ 42 Jose Cruz	.30	.15	.03
☐ 43 Ray Bare	.18	.09	.01
☐ 44 Bud Harrelson	.30	.15	.03
☐ 45 Rawly Eastwick	.18	.09	.01

☐ 46 Buck Martinez	.18	.09	.01
☐ 47 Lynn McGlothen	.18	.09	.01
☐ 48 Tom Paciorek	.18	.09	.01
☐ 49 Grant Jackson	.18	.09	.01
☐ 50 Ron Cey	.40	.20	.04
☐ 51 Brewers Team/Mgr.	.65	.30	.06
Alex Grammas			
(checklist back)			
☐ 52 Ellis Valentine	.18	.09	.01
☐ 53 Paul Mitchell	.18	.09	.01
☐ 54 Sandy Alomar	.18	.09	.01
☐ 55 Jeff Burroughs	.30	.15	.03
☐ 56 Rudy May	.18	.09	.01
☐ 57 Marc Hill	.18	.09	.01
☐ 58 Chet Lemon	.30	.15	.03
☐ 59 Larry Christenson	.18	.09	.01
☐ 60 Jim Rice	4.50	2.25	.45
☐ 61 Manny Sanguillen	.30	.15	.03
☐ 62 Eric Raich	.18	.09	.01
☐ 63 Tito Fuentes	.18	.09	.01
☐ 64 Larry Biittner	.18	.09	.01
☐ 65 Skip Lockwood	.18	.09	.01
☐ 66 Roy Smalley	.30	.15	.03
☐ 67 Joaquin Andujar	.75	.35	.07
☐ 68 Bruce Bochte	.18	.09	.01
☐ 69 Jim Crawford	.18	.09	.01
☐ 70 Johnny Bench	6.50	3.25	.65
☐ 71 Dock Ellis	.18	.09	.01
☐ 72 Mike Anderson	.18	.09	.01
☐ 73 Charlie Williams	.18	.09	.01
☐ 74 A's Team/Mgr.	.65	.30	.06
Jack McKeon			
(checklist back)			
☐ 75 Dennis Leonard	.30	.15	.03
☐ 76 Tim Foli	.18	.09	.01
☐ 77 Dyar Miller	.18	.09	.01
☐ 78 Bob Davis	.18	.09	.01
☐ 79 Don Money	.18	.09	.01
☐ 80 Andy Messersmith	.30	.15	.03
☐ 81 Juan Beniquez	.18	.09	.01
☐ 82 Jim Rooker	.18	.09	.01
☐ 83 Kevin Bell	.18	.09	.01
☐ 84 Ollie Brown	.18	.09	.01
☐ 85 Duane Kuiper	.18	.09	.01
☐ 86 Pat Zachry	.18	.09	.01
☐ 87 Glenn Borgmann	.18	.09	.01
☐ 88 Stan Wall	.18	.09	.01
☐ 89 Butch Hobson	.30	.15	.03
☐ 90 Cesar Cedeno	.30	.15	.03
☐ 91 John Verhoeven	.18	.09	.01
☐ 92 Dave Rosello	.18	.09	.01
☐ 93 Tom Poquette	.18	.09	.01
☐ 94 Craig Swan	.18	.09	.01
☐ 95 Keith Hernandez	3.50	1.75	.35
☐ 96 Lou Piniella	.40	.20	.04
☐ 97 Dave Heaverlo	.18	.09	.01
☐ 98 Milt May	.18	.09	.01
☐ 99 Tom Hausman	.18	.09	.01
☐ 100 Joe Morgan	2.50	1.25	.25
☐ 101 Dick Bosman	.18	.09	.01
☐ 102 Jose Morales	.18	.09	.01
☐ 103 Mike Bacsik	.18	.09	.01
☐ 104 Omar Moreno	.30	.15	.03
☐ 105 Steve Yeager	.30	.15	.03
☐ 106 Mike Flanagan	.40	.20	.04
☐ 107 Bill Melton	.18	.09	.01
☐ 108 Alan Foster	.18	.09	.01
☐ 109 Jorge Orta	.18	.09	.01
☐ 110 Steve Carlton	4.50	2.25	.45
☐ 111 Rico Petrocelli	.30	.15	.03
☐ 112 Bill Greif	.18	.09	.01
☐ 113 Blue Jays Leaders	.50	.25	.05
Roy Hartsfield MG			
Don Leppert CO			
Bob Miller CO			
Jackie Moore CO			
Harry Warner CO			
(checklist back)			
☐ 114 Bruce Dal Canton	.18	.09	.01
☐ 115 Rick Manning	.18	.09	.01
☐ 116 Joe Niekro	.30	.15	.03
☐ 117 Frank White	.30	.15	.03
☐ 118 Rick Jones	.18	.09	.01
☐ 119 John Stearns	.18	.09	.01
☐ 120 Rod Carew	6.50	3.25	.65
☐ 121 Gary Nolan	.18	.09	.01
☐ 122 Ben Oglivie	.30	.15	.03
☐ 123 Fred Stanley	.18	.09	.01
☐ 124 George Mitterwald	.18	.09	.01
☐ 125 Bill Travers	.18	.09	.01
☐ 126 Rod Gilbreath	.18	.09	.01
☐ 127 Ron Fairly	.18	.09	.01
☐ 128 Tommy John	1.00	.50	.10
☐ 129 Mike Sadek	.18	.09	.01
☐ 130 Al Oliver	.40	.20	.04
☐ 131 Orlando Ramirez	.18	.09	.01
☐ 132 Chip Lang	.18	.09	.01
☐ 133 Ralph Garr	.30	.15	.03
☐ 134 Padres Team/Mgr.	.65	.30	.06
John McNamara			
(checklist back)			
☐ 135 Mark Belanger	.30	.15	.03
☐ 136 Jerry Mumphrey	.30	.15	.03
☐ 137 Jeff Terpko	.18	.09	.01
☐ 138 Bob Stinson	.18	.09	.01
☐ 139 Fred Norman	.18	.09	.01
☐ 140 Mike Schmidt	21.00	10.50	2.10
☐ 141 Mark Littell	.18	.09	.01
☐ 142 Steve Dillard	.18	.09	.01
☐ 143 Ed Herrmann	.18	.09	.01
☐ 144 Bruce Sutter	3.00	1.50	.30
☐ 145 Tom Veryzer	.18	.09	.01
☐ 146 Dusty Baker	.30	.15	.03
☐ 147 Jackie Brown	.18	.09	.01
☐ 148 Fran Healy	.18	.09	.01
☐ 149 Mike Cubbage	.18	.09	.01
☐ 150 Tom Seaver	6.50	3.25	.65
☐ 151 Johnny LeMaster	.18	.09	.01
☐ 152 Gaylord Perry	2.00	1.00	.20
☐ 153 Ron Jackson	.18	.09	.01
☐ 154 Dave Giusti	.18	.09	.01
☐ 155 Joe Rudi	.30	.15	.03
☐ 156 Pete Mackanin	.18	.09	.01
☐ 157 Ken Brett	.18	.09	.01
☐ 158 Ted Kubiak	.18	.09	.01
☐ 159 Bernie Carbo	.18	.09	.01
☐ 160 Will McEnaney	.18	.09	.01
☐ 161 Garry Templeton	1.50	.75	.15
☐ 162 Mike Cuellar	.30	.15	.03
☐ 163 Dave Hilton	.18	.09	.01
☐ 164 Tug McGraw	.40	.20	.04
☐ 165 Jim Wynn	.30	.15	.03
☐ 166 Bill Campbell	.18	.09	.01
☐ 167 Rich Hebner	.18	.09	.01
☐ 168 Charlie Spikes	.18	.09	.01
☐ 169 Darold Knowles	.18	.09	.01
☐ 170 Thurman Munson	4.50	2.25	.45
☐ 171 Ken Sanders	.18	.09	.01
☐ 172 John Milner	.18	.09	.01
☐ 173 Chuck Scrivener	.18	.09	.01
☐ 174 Nelson Briles	.18	.09	.01
☐ 175 Butch Wynegar	.40	.20	.04
☐ 176 Bob Robertson	.18	.09	.01
☐ 177 Bart Johnson	.18	.09	.01
☐ 178 Bombo Rivera	.18	.09	.01
☐ 179 Paul Hartzell	.18	.09	.01
☐ 180 Dave Lopes	.30	.15	.03
☐ 181 Ken McMullen	.18	.09	.01
☐ 182 Dan Spillner	.18	.09	.01
☐ 183 Cardinals Team/Mgr.	.65	.30	.06
Vern Rapp			
(checklist back)			
☐ 184 Bo McLaughlin	.18	.09	.01
☐ 185 Sixto Lezcano	.18	.09	.01
☐ 186 Doug Flynn	.18	.09	.01
☐ 187 Dick Pole	.18	.09	.01
☐ 188 Bob Tolan	.18	.09	.01
☐ 189 Rick Dempsey	.30	.15	.03
☐ 190 Ray Burris	.18	.09	.01
☐ 191 Doug Griffin	.18	.09	.01
☐ 192 Clarence Gaston	.40	.20	.04
☐ 193 Larry Gura	.30	.15	.03
☐ 194 Gary Matthews	.30	.15	.03
☐ 195 Ed Figueroa	.18	.09	.01
☐ 196 Len Randle	.18	.09	.01
☐ 197 Ed Ott	.18	.09	.01
☐ 198 Wilbur Wood	.30	.15	.03
☐ 199 Pepe Frias	.18	.09	.01
☐ 200 Frank Tanana	.30	.15	.03
☐ 201 Ed Kranepool	.30	.15	.03
☐ 202 Tom Johnson	.18	.09	.01
☐ 203 Ed Armbrister	.18	.09	.01
☐ 204 Jeff Newman	.18	.09	.01
☐ 205 Pete Falcone	.18	.09	.01
☐ 206 Boog Powell	.40	.20	.04
☐ 207 Glenn Abbott	.18	.09	.01
☐ 208 Checklist 2	.90	.09	.02
☐ 209 Rob Andrews	.18	.09	.01
☐ 210 Fred Lynn	1.75	.85	.17
☐ 211 Giants Team/Mgr.	.65	.30	.06
Joe Altobelli			
(checklist back)			
☐ 212 Jim Mason	.18	.09	.01
☐ 213 Maximino Leon	.18	.09	.01
☐ 214 Darrell Porter	.18	.09	.01
☐ 215 Butch Metzger	.18	.09	.01
☐ 216 Doug DeCinces	.30	.15	.03
☐ 217 Tom Underwood	.18	.09	.01

☐	218 John Wathan	1.50	.75	.15
☐	219 Joe Coleman	.18	.09	.01
☐	220 Chris Chambliss	.30	.15	.03
☐	221 Bob Bailey	.18	.09	.01
☐	222 Francisco Barrios	.18	.09	.01
☐	223 Earl Williams	.18	.09	.01
☐	224 Rusty Torres	.18	.09	.01
☐	225 Bob Apodaca	.18	.09	.01
☐	226 Leroy Stanton	.18	.09	.01
☐	227 Joe Sambito	.30	.15	.03
☐	228 Twins Team/Mgr. Gene Mauch (checklist back)	.65	.30	.06
☐	229 Don Kessinger	.30	.15	.03
☐	230 Vida Blue	.30	.15	.03
☐	231 RB: George Brett Most cons. games with 3 or more hits	4.50	2.25	.45
☐	232 RB: Minnie Minoso Oldest to hit safely	.30	.15	.03
☐	233 RB: Jose Morales, Most pinch-hits, season	.30	.15	.03
☐	234 RB: Nolan Ryan Most seasons, 300 or more strikeouts	6.50	3.25	.65
☐	235 Cecil Cooper	.50	.25	.05
☐	236 Tom Buskey	.18	.09	.01
☐	237 Gene Clines	.18	.09	.01
☐	238 Tippy Martinez	.30	.15	.03
☐	239 Bill Plummer	.18	.09	.01
☐	240 Ron LeFlore	.30	.15	.03
☐	241 Dave Tomlin	.18	.09	.01
☐	242 Ken Henderson	.18	.09	.01
☐	243 Ron Reed	.18	.09	.01
☐	244 John Mayberry (cartoon mentions T206 Wagner)	.40	.20	.04
☐	245 Rick Rhoden	.30	.15	.03
☐	246 Mike Vail	.18	.09	.01
☐	247 Chris Knapp	.18	.09	.01
☐	248 Wilbur Howard	.18	.09	.01
☐	249 Pete Redfern	.18	.09	.01
☐	250 Bill Madlock	.60	.30	.06
☐	251 Tony Muser	.18	.09	.01
☐	252 Dale Murray	.18	.09	.01
☐	253 John Hale	.18	.09	.01
☐	254 Doyle Alexander	.30	.15	.03
☐	255 George Scott	.30	.15	.03
☐	256 Joe Hoerner	.18	.09	.01
☐	257 Mike Miley	.18	.09	.01
☐	258 Luis Tiant	.40	.20	.04
☐	259 Mets Team/Mgr. Joe Frazier (checklist back)	.75	.35	.07
☐	260 J.R. Richard	.30	.15	.03
☐	261 Phil Garner	.30	.15	.03
☐	262 Al Cowens	.30	.15	.03
☐	263 Mike Marshall	.30	.15	.03
☐	264 Tom Hutton	.18	.09	.01
☐	265 Mark Fidrych	.75	.35	.07
☐	266 Derrel Thomas	.18	.09	.01
☐	267 Ray Fosse	.18	.09	.01
☐	268 Rick Sawyer	.18	.09	.01
☐	269 Joe Lis	.18	.09	.01
☐	270 Dave Parker	4.50	2.25	.45
☐	271 Terry Forster	.30	.15	.03
☐	272 Lee Lacy	.18	.09	.01
☐	273 Eric Soderholm	.18	.09	.01
☐	274 Don Stanhouse	.18	.09	.01
☐	275 Mike Hargrove	.30	.15	.03
☐	276 AL Champs Chambliss' homer decides it	.40	.20	.04
☐	277 NL Champs Reds sweep Phillies	.40	.20	.04
☐	278 Danny Frisella	.18	.09	.01
☐	279 Joe Wallis	.18	.09	.01
☐	280 Jim Hunter	2.00	1.00	.20
☐	281 Roy Staiger	.18	.09	.01
☐	282 Sid Monge	.18	.09	.01
☐	283 Jerry DaVanon	.18	.09	.01
☐	284 Mike Norris	.18	.09	.01
☐	285 Brooks Robinson	2.50	1.25	.25
☐	286 Johnny Grubb	.18	.09	.01
☐	287 Reds Team/Mgr. Sparky Anderson (checklist back)	.75	.35	.07
☐	288 Bob Montgomery	.18	.09	.01
☐	289 Gene Garber	.18	.09	.01
☐	290 Amos Otis	.30	.15	.03
☐	291 Jason Thompson	.30	.15	.03
☐	292 Rogelio Moret	.18	.09	.01
☐	293 Jack Brohamer	.18	.09	.01
☐	294 George Medich	.18	.09	.01
☐	295 Gary Carter	5.00	2.50	.50
☐	296 Don Hood	.18	.09	.01
☐	297 Ken Reitz	.18	.09	.01
☐	298 Charlie Hough	.30	.15	.03
☐	299 Otto Velez	.18	.09	.01
☐	300 Jerry Koosman	.40	.20	.04
☐	301 Toby Harrah	.30	.15	.03
☐	302 Mike Garman	.18	.09	.01
☐	303 Gene Tenace	.30	.15	.03
☐	304 Jim Hughes	.18	.09	.01
☐	305 Mickey Rivers	.30	.15	.03
☐	306 Rick Waits	.18	.09	.01
☐	307 Gary Sutherland	.18	.09	.01
☐	308 Gene Pentz	.18	.09	.01
☐	309 Red Sox Team/Mgr. Don Zimmer (checklist back)	.65	.30	.06
☐	310 Larry Bowa	.40	.20	.04
☐	311 Vern Ruhle	.18	.09	.01
☐	312 Rob Belloir	.18	.09	.01
☐	313 Paul Blair	.30	.15	.03
☐	314 Steve Mingori	.18	.09	.01
☐	315 Dave Chalk	.18	.09	.01
☐	316 Steve Rogers	.30	.15	.03
☐	317 Kurt Bevacqua	.18	.09	.01
☐	318 Duffy Dyer	.18	.09	.01
☐	319 Rich Gossage	.90	.45	.09
☐	320 Ken Griffey	1.00	.50	.10
☐	321 Dave Goltz	.18	.09	.01
☐	322 Bill Russell	.30	.15	.03
☐	323 Larry Lintz	.18	.09	.01
☐	324 John Curtis	.18	.09	.01
☐	325 Mike Ivie	.18	.09	.01
☐	326 Jesse Jefferson	.18	.09	.01
☐	327 Astros Team/Mgr. Bill Virdon (checklist back)	.65	.30	.06
☐	328 Tommy Boggs	.18	.09	.01
☐	329 Ron Hodges	.18	.09	.01
☐	330 George Hendrick	.30	.15	.03
☐	331 Jim Colborn	.18	.09	.01
☐	332 Elliott Maddox	.18	.09	.01
☐	333 Paul Reuschel	.18	.09	.01
☐	334 Bill Stein	.18	.09	.01
☐	335 Bill Robinson	.30	.15	.03
☐	336 Denny Doyle	.18	.09	.01
☐	337 Ron Schueler	.18	.09	.01
☐	338 Dave Duncan	.18	.09	.01
☐	339 Adrian Devine	.18	.09	.01
☐	340 Hal McRae	.30	.15	.03
☐	341 Joe Kerrigan	.18	.09	.01
☐	342 Jerry Remy	.18	.09	.01
☐	343 Ed Halicki	.18	.09	.01
☐	344 Brian Downing	.30	.15	.03
☐	345 Reggie Smith	.30	.15	.03
☐	346 Bill Singer	.18	.09	.01
☐	347 George Foster	1.25	.60	.12
☐	348 Brent Strom	.18	.09	.01
☐	349 Jim Holt	.18	.09	.01
☐	350 Larry Dierker	.18	.09	.01
☐	351 Jim Sundberg	.30	.15	.03
☐	352 Mike Phillips	.18	.09	.01
☐	353 Stan Thomas	.18	.09	.01
☐	354 Pirates Team/Mgr. Chuck Tanner (checklist back)	.65	.30	.06
☐	355 Lou Brock	2.50	1.25	.25
☐	356 Checklist 3	.90	.09	.02
☐	357 Tim McCarver	.40	.20	.04
☐	358 Tom House	.18	.09	.01
☐	359 Willie Randolph	1.25	.60	.12
☐	360 Rick Monday	.30	.15	.03
☐	361 Eduardo Rodriguez	.18	.09	.01
☐	362 Tommy Davis	.30	.15	.03
☐	363 Dave Roberts	.18	.09	.01
☐	364 Vic Correll	.18	.09	.01
☐	365 Mike Torrez	.18	.09	.01
☐	366 Ted Sizemore	.18	.09	.01
☐	367 Dave Hamilton	.18	.09	.01
☐	368 Mike Jorgensen	.18	.09	.01
☐	369 Terry Humphrey	.18	.09	.01
☐	370 John Montefusco	.30	.15	.03
☐	371 Royals Team/Mgr. Whitey Herzog (checklist back)	.65	.30	.06
☐	372 Rich Folkers	.18	.09	.01
☐	373 Bert Campaneris	.30	.15	.03
☐	374 Kent Tekulve	.30	.15	.03
☐	375 Larry Hisle	.18	.09	.01
☐	376 Nino Espinosa	.18	.09	.01
☐	377 Dave McKay	.18	.09	.01
☐	378 Jim Umbarger	.18	.09	.01
☐	379 Larry Cox	.18	.09	.01
☐	380 Lee May	.30	.15	.03

☐ 381	Bob Forsch	.25	.12	.02
☐ 382	Charlie Moore	.18	.09	.01
☐ 383	Stan Bahnsen	.18	.09	.01
☐ 384	Darrel Chaney	.18	.09	.01
☐ 385	Dave LaRoche	.18	.09	.01
☐ 386	Manny Mota	.30	.15	.03
☐ 387	Yankees Team (checklist back)	.75	.35	.07
☐ 388	Terry Harmon	.18	.09	.01
☐ 389	Ken Kravec	.18	.09	.01
☐ 390	Dave Winfield	5.00	2.50	.50
☐ 391	Dan Warthen	.18	.09	.01
☐ 392	Phil Roof	.18	.09	.01
☐ 393	John Lowenstein	.18	.09	.01
☐ 394	Bill Laxton	.18	.09	.01
☐ 395	Manny Trillo	.18	.09	.01
☐ 396	Tom Murphy	.18	.09	.01
☐ 397	Larry Herndon	.30	.15	.03
☐ 398	Tom Burgmeier	.18	.09	.01
☐ 399	Bruce Boisclair	.18	.09	.01
☐ 400	Steve Garvey	4.00	2.00	.40
☐ 401	Mickey Scott	.18	.09	.01
☐ 402	Tommy Helms	.30	.15	.03
☐ 403	Tom Grieve	.30	.15	.03
☐ 404	Eric Rasmussen	.18	.09	.01
☐ 405	Claudell Washington	.40	.20	.04
☐ 406	Tim Johnson	.18	.09	.01
☐ 407	Dave Freisleben	.18	.09	.01
☐ 408	Cesar Tovar	.18	.09	.01
☐ 409	Pete Broberg	.18	.09	.01
☐ 410	Willie Montanez	.18	.09	.01
☐ 411	W.S. Games 1 and 2 Morgan homers opener; Bench stars as Reds take 2nd game	.60	.30	.06
☐ 412	W.S. Games 3 and 4 Reds stop Yankees; Bench's two homers wrap it up	.60	.30	.06
☐ 413	World Series Summary Cincy wins 2nd straight series	.50	.25	.05
☐ 414	Tommy Harper	.30	.15	.03
☐ 415	Jay Johnstone	.30	.15	.03
☐ 416	Chuck Hartenstein	.18	.09	.01
☐ 417	Wayne Garrett	.18	.09	.01
☐ 418	White Sox Team/Mgr. Bob Lemon (checklist back)	.65	.30	.06
☐ 419	Steve Swisher	.18	.09	.01
☐ 420	Rusty Staub	.40	.20	.04
☐ 421	Doug Rau	.18	.09	.01
☐ 422	Freddie Patek	.18	.09	.01
☐ 423	Gary Lavelle	.18	.09	.01
☐ 424	Steve Brye	.18	.09	.01
☐ 425	Joe Torre	.50	.25	.05
☐ 426	Dick Drago	.18	.09	.01
☐ 427	Dave Rader	.18	.09	.01
☐ 428	Rangers Team/Mgr. Frank Lucchesi (checklist back)	.65	.30	.06
☐ 429	Ken Boswell	.18	.09	.01
☐ 430	Fergie Jenkins	1.25	.50	.10
☐ 431	Dave Collins UER (photo actually Bobby Jones)	.30	.15	.03
☐ 432	Buzz Capra	.18	.09	.01
☐ 433	Turn back clock 1972 Nate Colbert	.30	.15	.03
☐ 434	Turn back clock 1967 Yaz Triple Crown	2.00	1.00	.20
☐ 435	Turn back clock 1962 Wills 104 steals	.40	.20	.04
☐ 436	Turn back clock 1957 Keegan hurls Majors' only no-hitter	.30	.15	.03
☐ 437	Turn back clock 1952 Kiner leads NL HR's 7th straight year	.50	.25	.05
☐ 438	Marty Perez	.18	.09	.01
☐ 439	Gorman Thomas	.40	.20	.04
☐ 440	Jon Matlack	.30	.15	.03
☐ 441	Larvell Blanks	.18	.09	.01
☐ 442	Braves Team/Mgr. Dave Bristol (checklist back)	.65	.30	.06
☐ 443	Lamar Johnson	.18	.09	.01
☐ 444	Wayne Twitchell	.18	.09	.01
☐ 445	Ken Singleton	.30	.15	.03
☐ 446	Bill Bonham	.18	.09	.01
☐ 447	Jerry Turner	.18	.09	.01
☐ 448	Ellie Rodriguez	.18	.09	.01
☐ 449	Al Fitzmorris	.18	.09	.01
☐ 450	Pete Rose	9.00	4.50	.90
☐ 451	Checklist 4	.90	.09	.02
☐ 452	Mike Caldwell	.18	.09	.01
☐ 453	Pedro Garcia	.18	.09	.01
☐ 454	Andy Etchebarren	.18	.09	.01
☐ 455	Rick Wise	.18	.09	.01
☐ 456	Leon Roberts	.18	.09	.01
☐ 457	Steve Luebber	.18	.09	.01
☐ 458	Leo Foster	.18	.09	.01
☐ 459	Steve Foucault	.18	.09	.01
☐ 460	Willie Stargell	2.50	1.25	.25
☐ 461	Dick Tidrow	.18	.09	.01
☐ 462	Don Baylor	.60	.30	.06
☐ 463	Jamie Quirk	.18	.09	.01
☐ 464	Randy Moffitt	.18	.09	.01
☐ 465	Rico Carty	.30	.15	.03
☐ 466	Fred Holdsworth	.18	.09	.01
☐ 467	Phillies Team/Mgr. Danny Ozark (checklist back)	.65	.30	.06
☐ 468	Ramon Hernandez	.18	.09	.01
☐ 469	Pat Kelly	.18	.09	.01
☐ 470	Ted Simmons	.60	.30	.06
☐ 471	Del Unser	.18	.09	.01
☐ 472	Rookie Pitchers Don Aase, Bob McClure, Gil Patterson, Dave Wehrmeister	.40	.20	.04
☐ 473	Rookie Outfielders Andre Dawson, Gene Richards, John Scott, Denny Walling	50.00	25.00	5.00
☐ 474	Rookie Shortstops Bob Bailor, Kiko Garcia, Craig Reynolds, Alex Taveras	.30	.15	.03
☐ 475	Rookie Pitchers Chris Batton, Rick Camp, Scott McGregor, Manny Sarmiento	.40	.20	.04
☐ 476	Rookie Catchers Gary Alexander, Rick Cerone, Dale Murphy, Kevin Pasley	50.00	25.00	5.00
☐ 477	Rookie Infielders Doug Ault, Rich Dauer, Orlando Gonzalez, Phil Mankowski	.30	.15	.03
☐ 478	Rookie Pitchers Jim Gideon, Leon Hooten, Dave Johnson, Mark Lemongello	.30	.15	.03
☐ 479	Rookie Outfielders Brian Asselstine, Wayne Gross, Sam Mejias, Alvis Woods	.30	.15	.03
☐ 480	Carl Yastrzemski	6.00	3.00	.60
☐ 481	Roger Metzger	.18	.09	.01
☐ 482	Tony Solaita	.18	.09	.01
☐ 483	Richie Zisk	.18	.09	.01
☐ 484	Burt Hooton	.18	.09	.01
☐ 485	Roy White	.30	.15	.03
☐ 486	Ed Bane	.18	.09	.01
☐ 487	Rookie Pitchers Larry Anderson, Ed Glynn, Joe Henderson, Greg Terlecky	.18	.09	.01
☐ 488	Rookie Outfielders Jack Clark, Ruppert Jones, Lee Mazzilli, Dan Thomas	18.00	9.00	1.80
☐ 489	Rookie Pitchers Len Barker, Randy Lerch, Greg Minton, Mike Overy	.40	.20	.04
☐ 490	Rookie Shortstops Billy Almon, Mickey Klutts, Tommy McMillan, Mark Wagner	.30	.15	.03

☐ 491	Rookie Pitchers	2.50	1.25	.25
	Mike Dupree			
	Denny Martinez			
	Craig Mitchell			
	Bob Sykes			
☐ 492	Rookie Outfielders	.90	.45	.09
	Tony Armas			
	Steve Kemp			
	Carlos Lopez			
	Gary Woods			
☐ 493	Rookie Pitchers	.75	.35	.07
	Mike Krukow			
	Jim Otten			
	Gary Wheelock			
	Mike Willis			
☐ 494	Rookie Infielders	.50	.25	.05
	Juan Bernhardt			
	Mike Champion			
	Jim Gantner			
	Bump Wills			
☐ 495	Al Hrabosky	.30	.15	.03
☐ 496	Gary Thomasson	.18	.09	.01
☐ 497	Clay Carroll	.18	.09	.01
☐ 498	Sal Bando	.30	.15	.03
☐ 499	Pablo Torrealba	.18	.09	.01
☐ 500	Dave Kingman	.60	.30	.06
☐ 501	Jim Bibby	.18	.09	.01
☐ 502	Randy Hundley	.18	.09	.01
☐ 503	Bill Lee	.30	.15	.03
☐ 504	Dodgers Team/Mgr.	.75	.35	.07
	Tom Lasorda			
	(checklist back)			
☐ 505	Oscar Gamble	.30	.15	.03
☐ 506	Steve Grilli	.18	.09	.01
☐ 507	Mike Hegan	.18	.09	.01
☐ 508	Dave Pagan	.18	.09	.01
☐ 509	Cookie Rojas	.18	.09	.01
☐ 510	John Candelaria	.75	.35	.07
☐ 511	Bill Fahey	.18	.09	.01
☐ 512	Jack Billingham	.18	.09	.01
☐ 513	Jerry Terrell	.18	.09	.01
☐ 514	Cliff Johnson	.18	.09	.01
☐ 515	Chris Speier	.18	.09	.01
☐ 516	Bake McBride	.18	.09	.01
☐ 517	Pete Vuckovich	.50	.25	.05
☐ 518	Cubs Team/Mgr.	.65	.30	.06
	Herman Franks			
	(checklist back)			
☐ 519	Don Kirkwood	.18	.09	.01
☐ 520	Garry Maddox	.30	.15	.03
☐ 521	Bob Grich	.30	.15	.03
☐ 522	Enzo Hernandez	.18	.09	.01
☐ 523	Rollie Fingers	1.50	.75	.15
☐ 524	Rowland Office	.18	.09	.01
☐ 525	Dennis Eckersley	6.00	3.00	.60
☐ 526	Larry Parrish	.30	.15	.03
☐ 527	Dan Meyer	.18	.09	.01
☐ 528	Bill Castro	.18	.09	.01
☐ 529	Jim Essian	.18	.09	.01
☐ 530	Rick Reuschel	.60	.30	.06
☐ 531	Lyman Bostock	.30	.15	.03
☐ 532	Jim Willoughby	.18	.09	.01
☐ 533	Mickey Stanley	.30	.15	.03
☐ 534	Paul Splittorff	.18	.09	.01
☐ 535	Cesar Geronimo	.18	.09	.01
☐ 536	Vic Albury	.18	.09	.01
☐ 537	Dave Roberts	.18	.09	.01
☐ 538	Frank Taveras	.18	.09	.01
☐ 539	Mike Wallace	.18	.09	.01
☐ 540	Bob Watson	.30	.15	.03
☐ 541	John Denny	.30	.15	.03
☐ 542	Frank Duffy	.18	.09	.01
☐ 543	Ron Blomberg	.18	.09	.01
☐ 544	Gary Ross	.18	.09	.01
☐ 545	Bob Boone	.60	.30	.06
☐ 546	Orioles Team/Mgr.	.75	.35	.07
	Earl Weaver			
	(checklist back)			
☐ 547	Willie McCovey	2.50	1.25	.25
☐ 548	Joel Youngblood	.18	.09	.01
☐ 549	Jerry Royster	.18	.09	.01
☐ 550	Randy Jones	.30	.15	.03
☐ 551	Bill North	.18	.09	.01
☐ 552	Pepe Mangual	.18	.09	.01
☐ 553	Jack Heidemann	.18	.09	.01
☐ 554	Bruce Kimm	.18	.09	.01
☐ 555	Dan Ford	.18	.09	.01
☐ 556	Doug Bird	.18	.09	.01
☐ 557	Jerry White	.18	.09	.01
☐ 558	Elias Sosa	.18	.09	.01
☐ 559	Alan Bannister	.18	.09	.01
☐ 560	Dave Concepcion	.40	.20	.04
☐ 561	Pete LaCock	.18	.09	.01
☐ 562	Checklist 5	.90	.09	.02
☐ 563	Bruce Kison	.18	.09	.01
☐ 564	Alan Ashby	.18	.09	.01
☐ 565	Mickey Lolich	.40	.20	.04
☐ 566	Rick Miller	.18	.09	.01
☐ 567	Enos Cabell	.18	.09	.01
☐ 568	Carlos May	.18	.09	.01
☐ 569	Jim Lonborg	.30	.15	.03
☐ 570	Bobby Bonds	.40	.20	.04
☐ 571	Darrell Evans	.50	.25	.05
☐ 572	Ross Grimsley	.18	.09	.01
☐ 573	Joe Ferguson	.18	.09	.01
☐ 574	Aurelio Rodriguez	.18	.09	.01
☐ 575	Dick Ruthven	.18	.09	.01
☐ 576	Fred Kendall	.18	.09	.01
☐ 577	Jerry Augustine	.18	.09	.01
☐ 578	Bob Randall	.18	.09	.01
☐ 579	Don Carrithers	.18	.09	.01
☐ 580	George Brett	22.00	11.00	2.20
☐ 581	Pedro Borbon	.18	.09	.01
☐ 582	Ed Kirkpatrick	.18	.09	.01
☐ 583	Paul Lindblad	.18	.09	.01
☐ 584	Ed Goodson	.18	.09	.01
☐ 585	Rick Burleson	.30	.15	.03
☐ 586	Steve Renko	.18	.09	.01
☐ 587	Rick Baldwin	.18	.09	.01
☐ 588	Dave Moates	.18	.09	.01
☐ 589	Mike Cosgrove	.18	.09	.01
☐ 590	Buddy Bell	.50	.25	.05
☐ 591	Chris Arnold	.18	.09	.01
☐ 592	Dan Briggs	.18	.09	.01
☐ 593	Dennis Blair	.18	.09	.01
☐ 594	Biff Pocoroba	.18	.09	.01
☐ 595	John Hiller	.30	.15	.03
☐ 596	Jerry Martin	.18	.09	.01
☐ 597	Mariners Leaders	.50	.25	.05
	Darrell Johnson MG			
	Don Bryant CO			
	Jim Busby CO			
	Vada Pinson CO			
	Wes Stock CO			
	(checklist back)			
☐ 598	Sparky Lyle	.50	.25	.05
☐ 599	Mike Tyson	.18	.09	.01
☐ 600	Jim Palmer	3.00	1.50	.30
☐ 601	Mike Lum	.18	.09	.01
☐ 602	Andy Hassler	.18	.09	.01
☐ 603	Willie Davis	.30	.15	.03
☐ 604	Jim Slaton	.18	.09	.01
☐ 605	Felix Millan	.18	.09	.01
☐ 606	Steve Braun	.18	.09	.01
☐ 607	Larry Demery	.18	.09	.01
☐ 608	Roy Howell	.18	.09	.01
☐ 609	Jim Barr	.18	.09	.01
☐ 610	Jose Cardenal	.18	.09	.01
☐ 611	Dave Lemanczyk	.18	.09	.01
☐ 612	Barry Foote	.18	.09	.01
☐ 613	Reggie Cleveland	.18	.09	.01
☐ 614	Greg Gross	.18	.09	.01
☐ 615	Phil Niekro	1.50	.75	.15
☐ 616	Tommy Sandt	.18	.09	.01
☐ 617	Bobby Darwin	.18	.09	.01
☐ 618	Pat Dobson	.18	.09	.01
☐ 619	Johnny Oates	.18	.09	.01
☐ 620	Don Sutton	1.50	.75	.15
☐ 621	Tigers Team/Mgr.	.75	.35	.07
	Ralph Houk			
	(checklist back)			
☐ 622	Jim Wohlford	.18	.09	.01
☐ 623	Jack Kucek	.18	.09	.01
☐ 624	Hector Cruz	.18	.09	.01
☐ 625	Ken Holtzman	.30	.15	.03
☐ 626	Al Bumbry	.18	.09	.01
☐ 627	Bob Myrick	.18	.09	.01
☐ 628	Mario Guerrero	.18	.09	.01
☐ 629	Bobby Valentine	.30	.15	.03
☐ 630	Bert Blyleven	1.25	.60	.12
☐ 631	Big League Brothers	2.25	1.10	.22
	George Brett			
	Ken Brett			
☐ 632	Big League Brothers	.30	.15	.03
	Bob Forsch			
	Ken Forsch			
☐ 633	Big League Brothers	.30	.15	.03
	Lee May			
	Carlos May			
☐ 634	Big League Brothers	.30	.15	.03
	Paul Reuschel			
	Rick Reuschel UER			
	(photos switched)			
☐ 635	Robin Yount	18.00	9.00	1.80
☐ 636	Santo Alcala	.18	.09	.01
☐ 637	Alex Johnson	.18	.09	.01
☐ 638	Jim Kaat	.60	.30	.06
☐ 639	Jerry Morales	.18	.09	.01

		NRMT	VG-E	GOOD
☐ 640	Carlton Fisk	5.00	2.50	.50
☐ 641	Dan Larson	.18	.09	.01
☐ 642	Willie Crawford	.18	.09	.01
☐ 643	Mike Pazik	.18	.09	.01
☐ 644	Matt Alexander	.18	.09	.01
☐ 645	Jerry Reuss	.30	.15	.03
☐ 646	Andres Mora	.18	.09	.01
☐ 647	Expos Team/Mgr. Dick Williams (checklist back)	.65	.30	.06
☐ 648	Jim Spencer	.18	.09	.01
☐ 649	Dave Cash	.18	.09	.01
☐ 650	Nolan Ryan	22.00	11.00	2.20
☐ 651	Von Joshua	.18	.09	.01
☐ 652	Tom Walker	.18	.09	.01
☐ 653	Diego Segui	.18	.09	.01
☐ 654	Ron Pruitt	.18	.09	.01
☐ 655	Tony Perez	.80	.40	.08
☐ 656	Ron Guidry	3.00	1.50	.30
☐ 657	Mick Kelleher	.18	.09	.01
☐ 658	Marty Pattin	.18	.09	.01
☐ 659	Merv Rettenmund	.18	.09	.01
☐ 660	Willie Horton	.30	.15	.03

1978 Topps

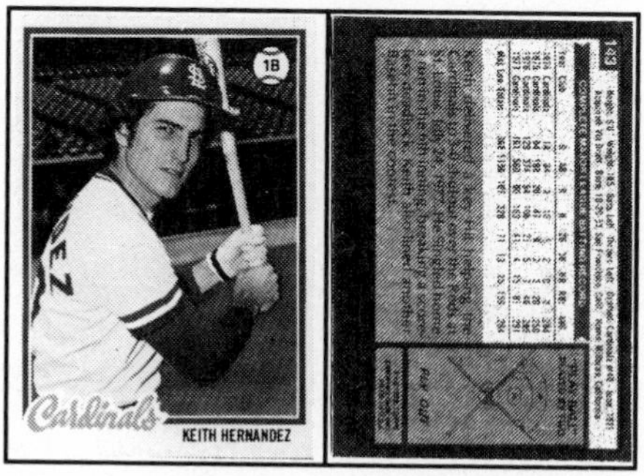

The cards in this 726-card set measure 2 1/2" by 3 1/2". The 1978 Topps set experienced an increase in number of cards from the previous five regular issue sets of 660. Cards 1 through 7 feature Record Breakers (RB) of the 1977 season. Other subsets within this set include League Leaders (201-208), Post-season cards (411-413), and Rookie Prospects (701-711). The key rookie cards in this set are the multi-player rookie card of Paul Molitor and Alan Trammell, Jack Morris, Eddie Murray, Lance Parrish, and Lou Whitaker. The manager cards in the set feature a "then and now" format on the card front showing the manager as he looked many years before, e.g., during his playing days. While no scarcities exist, 66 of the cards are more abundant in supply, as they were "double printed." These 66 double-printed cards are noted in the checklist by DP. Team cards again feature a checklist of that team's players in the set on the back. Cards numbered 23 or lower, that feature Astros, Rangers, Tigers, or Yankees and do not follow the numbering checklisted below, are not necessarily error cards. They are probably Burger King cards, a separate set with its own pricing and mass distribution. Burger King cards are indistinguishable from the corresponding Topps cards except for the card numbering difference and the fact that Burger King cards do not have a printing sheet designation (such as A through F like the regular Topps) anywhere on the card back in very small print.

		NRMT	VG-E	GOOD
	COMPLETE SET (726)	280.00	120.00	25.00
	COMMON PLAYER (1-726)	.14	.07	.01
	COMMON DP's (1-726)	.07	.03	.01
☐ 1	RB: Lou Brock Most steals, lifetime	2.00	.50	.10
☐ 2	RB: Sparky Lyle Most games, pure relief, lifetime	.25	.12	.02
☐ 3	RB: Willie McCovey Most times, 2 HR's in inning, lifetime	1.00	.50	.10
☐ 4	RB: Brooks Robinson Most consecutive seasons with one club	1.00	.50	.10
☐ 5	RB: Pete Rose Most hits, switch hitter, lifetime	2.25	1.10	.22
☐ 6	RB: Nolan Ryan Most games with 10 or more strikeouts, lifetime	4.50	2.25	.45
☐ 7	RB: Reggie Jackson Most homers, one World Series	2.50	1.25	.25
☐ 8	Mike Sadek	.14	.07	.01
☐ 9	Doug DeCinces	.25	.12	.02
☐ 10	Phil Niekro	1.25	.60	.12
☐ 11	Rick Manning	.14	.07	.01
☐ 12	Don Aase	.25	.12	.02
☐ 13	Art Howe	.50	.25	.05
☐ 14	Lerrin LaGrow	.14	.07	.01
☐ 15	Tony Perez DP	.35	.17	.03
☐ 16	Roy White	.25	.12	.02
☐ 17	Mike Krukow	.25	.12	.02
☐ 18	Bob Grich	.25	.12	.02
☐ 19	Darrell Porter	.14	.07	.01
☐ 20	Pete Rose DP	4.00	2.00	.40
☐ 21	Steve Kemp	.25	.12	.02
☐ 22	Charlie Hough	.25	.12	.02
☐ 23	Bump Wills	.14	.07	.01
☐ 24	Don Money DP	.07	.03	.01
☐ 25	Jon Matlack	.25	.12	.02
☐ 26	Rich Hebner	.14	.07	.01
☐ 27	Geoff Zahn	.14	.07	.01
☐ 28	Ed Ott	.14	.07	.01
☐ 29	Bob Lacey	.14	.07	.01
☐ 30	George Hendrick	.25	.12	.02
☐ 31	Glenn Abbott	.14	.07	.01
☐ 32	Garry Templeton	.35	.17	.03
☐ 33	Dave Lemanczyk	.14	.07	.01
☐ 34	Willie McCovey	2.00	1.00	.20
☐ 35	Sparky Lyle	.35	.17	.03
☐ 36	Eddie Murray	50.00	25.00	5.00
☐ 37	Rick Waits	.14	.07	.01
☐ 38	Willie Montanez	.14	.07	.01
☐ 39	Floyd Bannister	1.00	.50	.10
☐ 40	Carl Yastrzemski	4.50	2.25	.45
☐ 41	Burt Hooton	.14	.07	.01
☐ 42	Jorge Orta	.14	.07	.01
☐ 43	Bill Atkinson	.14	.07	.01
☐ 44	Toby Harrah	.25	.12	.02
☐ 45	Mark Fidrych	.35	.17	.03
☐ 46	Al Cowens	.14	.07	.01
☐ 47	Jack Billingham	.14	.07	.01
☐ 48	Don Baylor	.50	.25	.05
☐ 49	Ed Kranepool	.25	.12	.02
☐ 50	Rick Reuschel	.45	.22	.04
☐ 51	Charlie Moore DP	.07	.03	.01
☐ 52	Jim Lonborg	.25	.12	.02
☐ 53	Phil Garner DP	.07	.03	.01
☐ 54	Tom Johnson	.14	.07	.01
☐ 55	Mitchell Page	.14	.07	.01
☐ 56	Randy Jones	.14	.07	.01
☐ 57	Dan Meyer	.14	.07	.01
☐ 58	Bob Forsch	.25	.12	.02
☐ 59	Otto Velez	.14	.07	.01
☐ 60	Thurman Munson	3.50	1.75	.35
☐ 61	Larvell Blanks	.14	.07	.01
☐ 62	Jim Barr	.14	.07	.01
☐ 63	Don Zimmer MG	.25	.12	.02
☐ 64	Gene Pentz	.14	.07	.01
☐ 65	Ken Singleton	.25	.12	.02
☐ 66	White Sox Team (checklist back)	.50	.25	.05
☐ 67	Claudell Washington	.25	.12	.02
☐ 68	Steve Foucault DP	.07	.03	.01
☐ 69	Mike Vail	.14	.07	.01
☐ 70	Rich Gossage	.75	.35	.07
☐ 71	Terry Humphrey	.14	.07	.01
☐ 72	Andre Dawson	11.00	5.50	1.10
☐ 73	Andy Hassler	.14	.07	.01
☐ 74	Checklist 1	.75	.07	.01
☐ 75	Dick Ruthven	.14	.07	.01
☐ 76	Steve Ontiveros	.14	.07	.01
☐ 77	Ed Kirkpatrick	.14	.07	.01
☐ 78	Pablo Torrealba	.14	.07	.01
☐ 79	Darrell Johnson DP	.07	.03	.01
☐ 80	Ken Griffey	.75	.35	.07
☐ 81	Pete Redfern	.14	.07	.01

☐ 82	Giants Team (checklist back)	.50	.25	.05
☐ 83	Bob Montgomery	.14	.07	.01
☐ 84	Kent Tekulve	.25	.12	.02
☐ 85	Ron Fairly	.14	.07	.01
☐ 86	Dave Tomlin	.14	.07	.01
☐ 87	John Lowenstein	.14	.07	.01
☐ 88	Mike Phillips	.14	.07	.01
☐ 89	Ken Clay	.14	.07	.01
☐ 90	Larry Bowa	.35	.17	.03
☐ 91	Oscar Zamora	.14	.07	.01
☐ 92	Adrian Devine	.14	.07	.01
☐ 93	Bobby Cox DP	.07	.03	.01
☐ 94	Chuck Scrivener	.14	.07	.01
☐ 95	Jamie Quirk	.14	.07	.01
☐ 96	Orioles Team (checklist back)	.50	.25	.05
☐ 97	Stan Bahnsen	.14	.07	.01
☐ 98	Jim Essian	.14	.07	.01
☐ 99	Willie Hernandez	.90	.45	.09
☐ 100	George Brett	11.00	5.50	1.10
☐ 101	Sid Monge	.14	.07	.01
☐ 102	Matt Alexander	.14	.07	.01
☐ 103	Tom Murphy	.14	.07	.01
☐ 104	Lee Lacy	.14	.07	.01
☐ 105	Reggie Cleveland	.14	.07	.01
☐ 106	Bill Plummer	.14	.07	.01
☐ 107	Ed Halicki	.14	.07	.01
☐ 108	Von Joshua	.14	.07	.01
☐ 109	Joe Torre	.35	.17	.03
☐ 110	Richie Zisk	.14	.07	.01
☐ 111	Mike Tyson	.14	.07	.01
☐ 112	Astros Team (checklist back)	.50	.25	.05
☐ 113	Don Carrithers	.14	.07	.01
☐ 114	Paul Blair	.25	.12	.02
☐ 115	Gary Nolan	.14	.07	.01
☐ 116	Tucker Ashford	.14	.07	.01
☐ 117	John Montague	.14	.07	.01
☐ 118	Terry Harmon	.14	.07	.01
☐ 119	Denny Martinez	.35	.17	.03
☐ 120	Gary Carter	3.00	1.50	.30
☐ 121	Alvis Woods	.14	.07	.01
☐ 122	Dennis Eckersley	3.50	1.75	.35
☐ 123	Manny Trillo	.14	.07	.01
☐ 124	Dave Rozema	.14	.07	.01
☐ 125	George Scott	.25	.12	.02
☐ 126	Paul Moskau	.14	.07	.01
☐ 127	Chet Lemon	.25	.12	.02
☐ 128	Bill Russell	.25	.12	.02
☐ 129	Jim Colborn	.14	.07	.01
☐ 130	Jeff Burroughs	.25	.12	.02
☐ 131	Bert Blyleven	1.00	.50	.10
☐ 132	Enos Cabell	.14	.07	.01
☐ 133	Jerry Augustine	.14	.07	.01
☐ 134	Steve Henderson	.14	.07	.01
☐ 135	Ron Guidry DP	.75	.35	.07
☐ 136	Ted Sizemore	.14	.07	.01
☐ 137	Craig Kusick	.14	.07	.01
☐ 138	Larry Demery	.14	.07	.01
☐ 139	Wayne Gross	.14	.07	.01
☐ 140	Rollie Fingers	1.25	.60	.12
☐ 141	Ruppert Jones	.14	.07	.01
☐ 142	John Montefusco	.25	.12	.02
☐ 143	Keith Hernandez	2.50	1.25	.25
☐ 144	Jesse Jefferson	.14	.07	.01
☐ 145	Rick Monday	.25	.12	.02
☐ 146	Doyle Alexander	.25	.12	.02
☐ 147	Lee Mazzilli	.14	.07	.01
☐ 148	Andre Thornton	.25	.12	.02
☐ 149	Dale Murray	.14	.07	.01
☐ 150	Bobby Bonds	.35	.17	.03
☐ 151	Milt Wilcox	.14	.07	.01
☐ 152	Ivan DeJesus	.14	.07	.01
☐ 153	Steve Stone	.25	.12	.02
☐ 154	Cecil Cooper DP	.25	.12	.02
☐ 155	Butch Hobson	.14	.07	.01
☐ 156	Andy Messersmith	.25	.12	.02
☐ 157	Pete LaCock DP	.07	.03	.01
☐ 158	Joaquin Andujar	.35	.17	.03
☐ 159	Lou Piniella	.35	.17	.03
☐ 160	Jim Palmer	3.00	1.50	.30
☐ 161	Bob Boone	.50	.25	.05
☐ 162	Paul Thormodsgard	.14	.07	.01
☐ 163	Bill North	.14	.07	.01
☐ 164	Bob Owchinko	.14	.07	.01
☐ 165	Rennie Stennett	.14	.07	.01
☐ 166	Carlos Lopez	.14	.07	.01
☐ 167	Tim Foli	.14	.07	.01
☐ 168	Reggie Smith	.35	.17	.03
☐ 169	Jerry Johnson	.14	.07	.01
☐ 170	Lou Brock	2.25	1.10	.22
☐ 171	Pat Zachry	.14	.07	.01
☐ 172	Mike Hargrove	.25	.12	.02
☐ 173	Robin Yount	9.00	4.50	.90
☐ 174	Wayne Garland	.14	.07	.01
☐ 175	Jerry Morales	.14	.07	.01
☐ 176	Milt May	.14	.07	.01
☐ 177	Gene Garber DP	.07	.03	.01
☐ 178	Dave Chalk	.14	.07	.01
☐ 179	Dick Tidrow	.14	.07	.01
☐ 180	Dave Concepcion	.35	.17	.03
☐ 181	Ken Forsch	.14	.07	.01
☐ 182	Jim Spencer	.14	.07	.01
☐ 183	Doug Bird	.14	.07	.01
☐ 184	Checklist 2	.75	.07	.01
☐ 185	Ellis Valentine	.14	.07	.01
☐ 186	Bob Stanley DP	.25	.12	.02
☐ 187	Jerry Royster DP	.07	.03	.01
☐ 188	Al Bumbry	.14	.07	.01
☐ 189	Tom Lasorda MG	.35	.17	.03
☐ 190	John Candelaria	.35	.17	.03
☐ 191	Rodney Scott	.14	.07	.01
☐ 192	Padres Team (checklist back)	.50	.25	.05
☐ 193	Rich Chiles	.14	.07	.01
☐ 194	Derrel Thomas	.14	.07	.01
☐ 195	Larry Dierker	.14	.07	.01
☐ 196	Bob Bailor	.14	.07	.01
☐ 197	Nino Espinosa	.14	.07	.01
☐ 198	Ron Pruitt	.14	.07	.01
☐ 199	Craig Reynolds	.14	.07	.01
☐ 200	Reggie Jackson	5.00	2.50	.50
☐ 201	Batting Leaders Dave Parker Rod Carew	.90	.45	.09
☐ 202	Home Run Leaders DP George Foster Jim Rice	.14	.07	.01
☐ 203	RBI Leaders George Foster Larry Hisle	.25	.12	.02
☐ 204	Steals Leaders DP Frank Taveras Freddie Patek	.14	.07	.01
☐ 205	Victory Leaders Steve Carlton Dave Goltz Dennis Leonard Jim Palmer	.60	.30	.06
☐ 206	Strikeout Leaders DP Phil Niekro Nolan Ryan	.75	.35	.07
☐ 207	ERA Leaders DP John Candelaria Frank Tanana	.14	.07	.01
☐ 208	Top Firemen Rollie Fingers Bill Campbell	.25	.12	.02
☐ 209	Dock Ellis	.14	.07	.01
☐ 210	Jose Cardenal	.14	.07	.01
☐ 211	Earl Weaver MG DP	.14	.07	.01
☐ 212	Mike Caldwell	.14	.07	.01
☐ 213	Alan Bannister	.14	.07	.01
☐ 214	Angels Team (checklist back)	.50	.25	.05
☐ 215	Darrell Evans	.35	.17	.03
☐ 216	Mike Paxton	.14	.07	.01
☐ 217	Rod Gilbreath	.14	.07	.01
☐ 218	Marty Pattin	.14	.07	.01
☐ 219	Mike Cubbage	.14	.07	.01
☐ 220	Pedro Borbon	.14	.07	.01
☐ 221	Chris Speier	.14	.07	.01
☐ 222	Jerry Martin	.14	.07	.01
☐ 223	Bruce Kison	.14	.07	.01
☐ 224	Jerry Tabb	.14	.07	.01
☐ 225	Don Gullett DP	.14	.07	.01
☐ 226	Joe Ferguson	.14	.07	.01
☐ 227	Al Fitzmorris	.14	.07	.01
☐ 228	Manny Mota DP	.14	.07	.01
☐ 229	Leo Foster	.14	.07	.01
☐ 230	Al Hrabosky	.14	.07	.01
☐ 231	Wayne Nordhagen	.14	.07	.01
☐ 232	Mickey Stanley	.25	.12	.02
☐ 233	Dick Pole	.14	.07	.01
☐ 234	Herman Franks MG	.14	.07	.01
☐ 235	Tim McCarver	.35	.17	.03
☐ 236	Terry Whitfield	.14	.07	.01
☐ 237	Rich Dauer	.14	.07	.01
☐ 238	Juan Beniquez	.14	.07	.01
☐ 239	Dyar Miller	.14	.07	.01
☐ 240	Gene Tenace	.25	.12	.02
☐ 241	Pete Vuckovich	.25	.12	.02
☐ 242	Barry Bonnell DP	.14	.07	.01
☐ 243	Bob McClure	.14	.07	.01
☐ 244	Expos Team DP (checklist back)	.25	.12	.02
☐ 245	Rick Burleson	.25	.12	.02

☐ 246	Dan Driessen	.14	.07	.01
☐ 247	Larry Christenson	.14	.07	.01
☐ 248	Frank White DP	.14	.07	.01
☐ 249	Dave Goltz DP	.07	.03	.01
☐ 250	Graig Nettles DP	.25	.12	.02
☐ 251	Don Kirkwood	.14	.07	.01
☐ 252	Steve Swisher DP	.07	.03	.01
☐ 253	Jim Kern	.14	.07	.01
☐ 254	Dave Collins	.14	.07	.01
☐ 255	Jerry Reuss	.25	.12	.02
☐ 256	Joe Altobelli MG	.14	.07	.01
☐ 257	Hector Cruz	.14	.07	.01
☐ 258	John Hiller	.25	.12	.02
☐ 259	Dodgers Team	.50	.25	.05
	(checklist back)			
☐ 260	Bert Campaneris	.25	.12	.02
☐ 261	Tim Hosley	.14	.07	.01
☐ 262	Rudy May	.14	.07	.01
☐ 263	Danny Walton	.14	.07	.01
☐ 264	Jamie Easterly	.14	.07	.01
☐ 265	Sal Bando DP	.14	.07	.01
☐ 266	Bob Shirley	.14	.07	.01
☐ 267	Doug Ault	.14	.07	.01
☐ 268	Gil Flores	.14	.07	.01
☐ 269	Wayne Twitchell	.14	.07	.01
☐ 270	Carlton Fisk	3.50	1.75	.35
☐ 271	Randy Lerch DP	.07	.03	.01
☐ 272	Royle Stillman	.14	.07	.01
☐ 273	Fred Norman	.14	.07	.01
☐ 274	Freddie Patek	.14	.07	.01
☐ 275	Dan Ford	.14	.07	.01
☐ 276	Bill Bonham DP	.07	.03	.01
☐ 277	Bruce Boisclair	.14	.07	.01
☐ 278	Enrique Romo	.14	.07	.01
☐ 279	Bill Virdon MG	.25	.12	.02
☐ 280	Buddy Bell	.35	.17	.03
☐ 281	Eric Rasmussen DP	.07	.03	.01
☐ 282	Yankees Team	.60	.30	.06
	(checklist back)			
☐ 283	Omar Moreno	.14	.07	.01
☐ 284	Randy Moffitt	.14	.07	.01
☐ 285	Steve Yeager DP	.14	.07	.01
☐ 286	Ben Oglivie	.25	.12	.02
☐ 287	Kiko Garcia	.14	.07	.01
☐ 288	Dave Hamilton	.14	.07	.01
☐ 289	Checklist 3	.75	.07	.01
☐ 290	Willie Horton	.25	.12	.02
☐ 291	Gary Ross	.14	.07	.01
☐ 292	Gene Richards	.14	.07	.01
☐ 293	Mike Willis	.14	.07	.01
☐ 294	Larry Parrish	.25	.12	.02
☐ 295	Bill Lee	.25	.12	.02
☐ 296	Biff Pocoroba	.14	.07	.01
☐ 297	Warren Brusstar DP	.07	.03	.01
☐ 298	Tony Armas	.25	.12	.02
☐ 299	Whitey Herzog MG	.25	.12	.02
☐ 300	Joe Morgan	2.25	1.10	.22
☐ 301	Buddy Schultz	.14	.07	.01
☐ 302	Cubs Team	.50	.25	.05
	(checklist back)			
☐ 303	Sam Hinds	.14	.07	.01
☐ 304	John Milner	.14	.07	.01
☐ 305	Rico Carty	.25	.12	.02
☐ 306	Joe Niekro	.25	.12	.02
☐ 307	Glenn Borgmann	.14	.07	.01
☐ 308	Jim Rooker	.14	.07	.01
☐ 309	Cliff Johnson	.14	.07	.01
☐ 310	Don Sutton	1.25	.60	.12
☐ 311	Jose Baez DP	.07	.03	.01
☐ 312	Greg Minton	.25	.12	.02
☐ 313	Andy Etchebarren	.14	.07	.01
☐ 314	Paul Lindblad	.14	.07	.01
☐ 315	Mark Belanger	.25	.12	.02
☐ 316	Henry Cruz DP	.07	.03	.01
☐ 317	Dave Johnson	.25	.12	.02
☐ 318	Tom Griffin	.14	.07	.01
☐ 319	Alan Ashby	.14	.07	.01
☐ 320	Fred Lynn	1.00	.50	.10
☐ 321	Santo Alcala	.14	.07	.01
☐ 322	Tom Paciorek	.14	.07	.01
☐ 323	Jim Fregosi DP	.14	.07	.01
☐ 324	Vern Rapp MG	.14	.07	.01
☐ 325	Bruce Sutter	.75	.35	.07
☐ 326	Mike Lum DP	.07	.03	.01
☐ 327	Rick Langford DP	.07	.03	.01
☐ 328	Milwaukee Brewers	.50	.25	.05
	Team Card			
	(checklist back)			
☐ 329	John Verhoeven	.14	.07	.01
☐ 330	Bob Watson	.25	.12	.02
☐ 331	Mark Littell	.14	.07	.01
☐ 332	Duane Kuiper	.14	.07	.01
☐ 333	Jim Todd	.14	.07	.01
☐ 334	John Stearns	.14	.07	.01
☐ 335	Bucky Dent	.35	.17	.03
☐ 336	Steve Busby	.14	.07	.01
☐ 337	Tom Grieve	.25	.12	.02
☐ 338	Dave Heaverlo	.14	.07	.01
☐ 339	Mario Guerrero	.14	.07	.01
☐ 340	Bake McBride	.14	.07	.01
☐ 341	Mike Flanagan	.35	.17	.03
☐ 342	Aurelio Rodriguez	.14	.07	.01
☐ 343	John Wathan DP	.14	.07	.01
☐ 344	Sam Ewing	.14	.07	.01
☐ 345	Luis Tiant	.35	.17	.03
☐ 346	Larry Biittner	.14	.07	.01
☐ 347	Terry Forster	.25	.12	.02
☐ 348	Del Unser	.14	.07	.01
☐ 349	Rick Camp DP	.07	.03	.01
☐ 350	Steve Garvey	3.50	1.75	.35
☐ 351	Jeff Torborg	.25	.12	.02
☐ 352	Tony Scott	.14	.07	.01
☐ 353	Doug Bair	.14	.07	.01
☐ 354	Cesar Geronimo	.14	.07	.01
☐ 355	Bill Travers	.14	.07	.01
☐ 356	New York Mets	.50	.25	.05
	Team Card			
	(checklist back)			
☐ 357	Tom Poquette	.14	.07	.01
☐ 358	Mark Lemongello	.14	.07	.01
☐ 359	Marc Hill	.14	.07	.01
☐ 360	Mike Schmidt	11.00	5.50	1.10
☐ 361	Chris Knapp	.14	.07	.01
☐ 362	Dave May	.14	.07	.01
☐ 363	Bob Randall	.14	.07	.01
☐ 364	Jerry Turner	.14	.07	.01
☐ 365	Ed Figueroa	.14	.07	.01
☐ 366	Larry Milbourne DP	.07	.03	.01
☐ 367	Rick Dempsey	.14	.07	.01
☐ 368	Balor Moore	.14	.07	.01
☐ 369	Tim Nordbrook	.14	.07	.01
☐ 370	Rusty Staub	.35	.17	.03
☐ 371	Ray Burris	.14	.07	.01
☐ 372	Brian Asselstine	.14	.07	.01
☐ 373	Jim Willoughby	.14	.07	.01
☐ 374	Jose Morales	.14	.07	.01
☐ 375	Tommy John	.80	.40	.08
☐ 376	Jim Wohlford	.14	.07	.01
☐ 377	Manny Sarmiento	.14	.07	.01
☐ 378	Bobby Winkles MG	.14	.07	.01
☐ 379	Skip Lockwood	.14	.07	.01
☐ 380	Ted Simmons	.50	.25	.05
☐ 381	Phillies Team	.50	.25	.05
	(checklist back)			
☐ 382	Joe Lahoud	.14	.07	.01
☐ 383	Mario Mendoza	.14	.07	.01
☐ 384	Jack Clark	4.00	2.00	.40
☐ 385	Tito Fuentes	.14	.07	.01
☐ 386	Bob Gorinski	.14	.07	.01
☐ 387	Ken Holtzman	.25	.12	.02
☐ 388	Bill Fahey DP	.07	.03	.01
☐ 389	Julio Gonzalez	.14	.07	.01
☐ 390	Oscar Gamble	.14	.07	.01
☐ 391	Larry Haney	.14	.07	.01
☐ 392	Billy Almon	.14	.07	.01
☐ 393	Tippy Martinez	.14	.07	.01
☐ 394	Roy Howell DP	.07	.03	.01
☐ 395	Jim Hughes	.14	.07	.01
☐ 396	Bob Stinson DP	.07	.03	.01
☐ 397	Greg Gross	.14	.07	.01
☐ 398	Don Hood	.14	.07	.01
☐ 399	Pete Mackanin	.14	.07	.01
☐ 400	Nolan Ryan	17.00	8.50	1.70
☐ 401	Sparky Anderson MG	.25	.12	.02
☐ 402	Dave Campbell	.14	.07	.01
☐ 403	Bud Harrelson	.25	.12	.02
☐ 404	Tigers Team	.50	.25	.05
	(checklist back)			
☐ 405	Rawly Eastwick	.14	.07	.01
☐ 406	Mike Jorgensen	.14	.07	.01
☐ 407	Odell Jones	.14	.07	.01
☐ 408	Joe Zdeb	.14	.07	.01
☐ 409	Ron Schueler	.14	.07	.01
☐ 410	Bill Madlock	.50	.25	.05
☐ 411	AL Champs	.50	.25	.05
	Yankees rally to			
	defeat Royals			
☐ 412	NL Champs	.50	.25	.05
	Dodgers overpower			
	Phillies in four			
☐ 413	World Series	2.00	1.00	.20
	Reggie and Yankees			
	reign supreme			
☐ 414	Darold Knowles DP	.07	.03	.01
☐ 415	Ray Fosse	.14	.07	.01
☐ 416	Jack Brohamer	.14	.07	.01
☐ 417	Mike Garman DP	.07	.03	.01
☐ 418	Tony Muser	.14	.07	.01

☐ 419	Jerry Garvin	.14	.07	.01
☐ 420	Greg Luzinski	.35	.17	.03
☐ 421	Junior Moore	.14	.07	.01
☐ 422	Steve Braun	.14	.07	.01
☐ 423	Dave Rosello	.14	.07	.01
☐ 424	Boston Red Sox Team Card (checklist back)	.50	.25	.05
☐ 425	Steve Rogers DP	.14	.07	.01
☐ 426	Fred Kendall	.14	.07	.01
☐ 427	Mario Soto	.60	.30	.06
☐ 428	Joel Youngblood	.14	.07	.01
☐ 429	Mike Barlow	.14	.07	.01
☐ 430	Al Oliver	.35	.17	.03
☐ 431	Butch Metzger	.14	.07	.01
☐ 432	Terry Bulling	.14	.07	.01
☐ 433	Fernando Gonzalez	.14	.07	.01
☐ 434	Mike Norris	.14	.07	.01
☐ 435	Checklist 4	.75	.07	.01
☐ 436	Vic Harris DP	.07	.03	.01
☐ 437	Bo McLaughlin	.14	.07	.01
☐ 438	John Ellis	.14	.07	.01
☐ 439	Ken Kravec	.14	.07	.01
☐ 440	Dave Lopes	.25	.12	.02
☐ 441	Larry Gura	.14	.07	.01
☐ 442	Elliott Maddox	.14	.07	.01
☐ 443	Darrel Chaney	.14	.07	.01
☐ 444	Roy Hartsfield MG	.14	.07	.01
☐ 445	Mike Ivie	.14	.07	.01
☐ 446	Tug McGraw	.35	.17	.03
☐ 447	Leroy Stanton	.14	.07	.01
☐ 448	Bill Castro	.14	.07	.01
☐ 449	Tim Blackwell DP	.07	.03	.01
☐ 450	Tom Seaver	4.00	2.00	.40
☐ 451	Minnesota Twins Team Card (checklist back)	.50	.25	.05
☐ 452	Jerry Mumphrey	.14	.07	.01
☐ 453	Doug Flynn	.14	.07	.01
☐ 454	Dave LaRoche	.14	.07	.01
☐ 455	Bill Robinson	.25	.12	.02
☐ 456	Vern Ruhle	.14	.07	.01
☐ 457	Bob Bailey	.14	.07	.01
☐ 458	Jeff Newman	.14	.07	.01
☐ 459	Charlie Spikes	.14	.07	.01
☐ 460	Jim Hunter	1.50	.75	.15
☐ 461	Rob Andrews DP	.07	.03	.01
☐ 462	Rogelio Moret	.14	.07	.01
☐ 463	Kevin Bell	.14	.07	.01
☐ 464	Jerry Grote	.14	.07	.01
☐ 465	Hal McRae	.25	.12	.02
☐ 466	Dennis Blair	.14	.07	.01
☐ 467	Alvin Dark MG	.14	.07	.01
☐ 468	Warren Cromartie	.35	.17	.03
☐ 469	Rick Cerone	.25	.12	.02
☐ 470	J.R. Richard	.25	.12	.02
☐ 471	Roy Smalley	.14	.07	.01
☐ 472	Ron Reed	.14	.07	.01
☐ 473	Bill Buckner	.35	.17	.03
☐ 474	Jim Slaton	.14	.07	.01
☐ 475	Gary Matthews	.25	.12	.02
☐ 476	Bill Stein	.14	.07	.01
☐ 477	Doug Capilla	.14	.07	.01
☐ 478	Jerry Remy	.14	.07	.01
☐ 479	Cardinals Team (checklist back)	.50	.25	.05
☐ 480	Ron LeFlore	.14	.07	.01
☐ 481	Jackson Todd	.14	.07	.01
☐ 482	Rick Miller	.14	.07	.01
☐ 483	Ken Macha	.14	.07	.01
☐ 484	Jim Norris	.14	.07	.01
☐ 485	Chris Chambliss	.25	.12	.02
☐ 486	John Curtis	.14	.07	.01
☐ 487	Jim Tyrone	.14	.07	.01
☐ 488	Dan Spillner	.14	.07	.01
☐ 489	Rudy Meoli	.14	.07	.01
☐ 490	Amos Otis	.25	.12	.02
☐ 491	Scott McGregor	.25	.12	.02
☐ 492	Jim Sundberg	.14	.07	.01
☐ 493	Steve Renko	.14	.07	.01
☐ 494	Chuck Tanner MG	.14	.07	.01
☐ 495	Dave Cash	.14	.07	.01
☐ 496	Jim Clancy DP	.25	.12	.02
☐ 497	Glenn Adams	.14	.07	.01
☐ 498	Joe Sambito	.14	.07	.01
☐ 499	Seattle Mariners Team Card (checklist back)	.50	.25	.05
☐ 500	George Foster	.75	.35	.07
☐ 501	Dave Roberts	.14	.07	.01
☐ 502	Pat Rockett	.14	.07	.01
☐ 503	Ike Hampton	.14	.07	.01
☐ 504	Roger Freed	.14	.07	.01
☐ 505	Felix Millan	.14	.07	.01

☐ 506	Ron Blomberg	.14	.07	.01
☐ 507	Willie Crawford	.14	.07	.01
☐ 508	Johnny Oates	.14	.07	.01
☐ 509	Brent Strom	.14	.07	.01
☐ 510	Willie Stargell	2.25	1.10	.22
☐ 511	Frank Duffy	.14	.07	.01
☐ 512	Larry Herndon	.14	.07	.01
☐ 513	Barry Foote	.14	.07	.01
☐ 514	Rob Sperring	.14	.07	.01
☐ 515	Tim Corcoran	.14	.07	.01
☐ 516	Gary Beare	.14	.07	.01
☐ 517	Andres Mora	.14	.07	.01
☐ 518	Tommy Boggs DP	.07	.03	.01
☐ 519	Brian Downing	.25	.12	.02
☐ 520	Larry Hisle	.14	.07	.01
☐ 521	Steve Staggs	.14	.07	.01
☐ 522	Dick Williams MG	.14	.07	.01
☐ 523	Donnie Moore	.25	.12	.02
☐ 524	Bernie Carbo	.14	.07	.01
☐ 525	Jerry Terrell	.14	.07	.01
☐ 526	Reds Team (checklist back)	.50	.25	.05
☐ 527	Vic Correll	.14	.07	.01
☐ 528	Rob Picciolo	.14	.07	.01
☐ 529	Paul Hartzell	.14	.07	.01
☐ 530	Dave Winfield	3.00	1.50	.30
☐ 531	Tom Underwood	.14	.07	.01
☐ 532	Skip Jutze	.14	.07	.01
☐ 533	Sandy Alomar	.14	.07	.01
☐ 534	Wilbur Howard	.14	.07	.01
☐ 535	Checklist 5	.75	.07	.01
☐ 536	Roric Harrison	.14	.07	.01
☐ 537	Bruce Bochte	.14	.07	.01
☐ 538	Johnny LeMaster	.14	.07	.01
☐ 539	Vic Davalillo DP	.07	.03	.01
☐ 540	Steve Carlton	3.50	1.75	.35
☐ 541	Larry Cox	.14	.07	.01
☐ 542	Tim Johnson	.14	.07	.01
☐ 543	Larry Harlow DP	.07	.03	.01
☐ 544	Len Randle DP	.07	.03	.01
☐ 545	Bill Campbell	.14	.07	.01
☐ 546	Ted Martinez	.14	.07	.01
☐ 547	John Scott	.14	.07	.01
☐ 548	Billy Hunter MG DP	.07	.03	.01
☐ 549	Joe Kerrigan	.14	.07	.01
☐ 550	John Mayberry	.25	.12	.02
☐ 551	Atlanta Braves Team Card (checklist back)	.50	.25	.05
☐ 552	Francisco Barrios	.14	.07	.01
☐ 553	Terry Puhl	.50	.25	.05
☐ 554	Joe Coleman	.14	.07	.01
☐ 555	Butch Wynegar	.14	.07	.01
☐ 556	Ed Armbrister	.14	.07	.01
☐ 557	Tony Solaita	.14	.07	.01
☐ 558	Paul Mitchell	.14	.07	.01
☐ 559	Phil Mankowski	.14	.07	.01
☐ 560	Dave Parker	3.50	1.75	.35
☐ 561	Charlie Williams	.14	.07	.01
☐ 562	Glenn Burke	.14	.07	.01
☐ 563	Dave Rader	.14	.07	.01
☐ 564	Mick Kelleher	.14	.07	.01
☐ 565	Jerry Koosman	.35	.17	.03
☐ 566	Merv Rettenmund	.14	.07	.01
☐ 567	Dick Drago	.14	.07	.01
☐ 568	Tom Hutton	.14	.07	.01
☐ 569	Lary Sorensen	.14	.07	.01
☐ 570	Dave Kingman	.60	.30	.06
☐ 571	Buck Martinez	.14	.07	.01
☐ 572	Rick Wise	.14	.07	.01
☐ 573	Luis Gomez	.14	.07	.01
☐ 574	Bob Lemon MG	.35	.17	.03
☐ 575	Pat Dobson	.14	.07	.01
☐ 576	Sam Mejias	.14	.07	.01
☐ 577	Oakland A's Team Card (checklist back)	.50	.25	.05
☐ 578	Buzz Capra	.14	.07	.01
☐ 579	Rance Mulliniks	.25	.12	.02
☐ 580	Rod Carew	3.50	1.75	.35
☐ 581	Lynn McGlothen	.14	.07	.01
☐ 582	Fran Healy	.14	.07	.01
☐ 583	George Medich	.14	.07	.01
☐ 584	John Hale	.14	.07	.01
☐ 585	Woodie Fryman DP	.07	.03	.01
☐ 586	Ed Goodson	.14	.07	.01
☐ 587	John Urrea	.14	.07	.01
☐ 588	Jim Mason	.14	.07	.01
☐ 589	Bob Knepper	1.25	.60	.12
☐ 590	Bobby Murcer	.35	.17	.03
☐ 591	George Zeber	.14	.07	.01
☐ 592	Bob Apodaca	.14	.07	.01
☐ 593	Dave Skaggs	.14	.07	.01
☐ 594	Dave Freisleben	.14	.07	.01

☐ 595	Sixto Lezcano	.14	.07	.01
☐ 596	Gary Wheelock	.14	.07	.01
☐ 597	Steve Dillard	.14	.07	.01
☐ 598	Eddie Solomon	.14	.07	.01
☐ 599	Gary Woods	.14	.07	.01
☐ 600	Frank Tanana	.25	.12	.02
☐ 601	Gene Mauch MG	.14	.07	.01
☐ 602	Eric Soderholm	.14	.07	.01
☐ 603	Will McEnaney	.14	.07	.01
☐ 604	Earl Williams	.14	.07	.01
☐ 605	Rick Rhoden	.25	.12	.02
☐ 606	Pirates Team	.50	.25	.05
	(checklist back)			
☐ 607	Fernando Arroyo	.14	.07	.01
☐ 608	Johnny Grubb	.14	.07	.01
☐ 609	John Denny	.25	.12	.02
☐ 610	Garry Maddox	.25	.12	.02
☐ 611	Pat Scanlon	.14	.07	.01
☐ 612	Ken Henderson	.14	.07	.01
☐ 613	Marty Perez	.14	.07	.01
☐ 614	Joe Wallis	.14	.07	.01
☐ 615	Clay Carroll	.14	.07	.01
☐ 616	Pat Kelly	.14	.07	.01
☐ 617	Joe Nolan	.14	.07	.01
☐ 618	Tommy Helms	.25	.12	.02
☐ 619	Thad Bosley DP	.14	.07	.01
☐ 620	Willie Randolph	.35	.17	.03
☐ 621	Craig Swan DP	.14	.07	.01
☐ 622	Champ Summers	.14	.07	.01
☐ 623	Eduardo Rodriguez	.14	.07	.01
☐ 624	Gary Alexander DP	.07	.03	.01
☐ 625	Jose Cruz	.25	.12	.02
☐ 626	Blue Jays Team DP	.25	.12	.02
	(checklist back)			
☐ 627	David Johnson	.14	.07	.01
☐ 628	Ralph Garr	.14	.07	.01
☐ 629	Don Stanhouse	.14	.07	.01
☐ 630	Ron Cey	.35	.17	.03
☐ 631	Danny Ozark MG	.14	.07	.01
☐ 632	Rowland Office	.14	.07	.01
☐ 633	Tom Veryzer	.14	.07	.01
☐ 634	Len Barker	.14	.07	.01
☐ 635	Joe Rudi	.25	.12	.02
☐ 636	Jim Bibby	.14	.07	.01
☐ 637	Duffy Dyer	.14	.07	.01
☐ 638	Paul Splittorff	.14	.07	.01
☐ 639	Gene Clines	.14	.07	.01
☐ 640	Lee May DP	.14	.07	.01
☐ 641	Doug Rau	.14	.07	.01
☐ 642	Denny Doyle	.14	.07	.01
☐ 643	Tom House	.14	.07	.01
☐ 644	Jim Dwyer	.14	.07	.01
☐ 645	Mike Torrez	.14	.07	.01
☐ 646	Rick Auerbach DP	.07	.03	.01
☐ 647	Steve Dunning	.14	.07	.01
☐ 648	Gary Thomasson	.14	.07	.01
☐ 649	Moose Haas	.25	.12	.02
☐ 650	Cesar Cedeno	.25	.12	.02
☐ 651	Doug Rader	.25	.12	.02
☐ 652	Checklist 6	.75	.07	.01
☐ 653	Ron Hodges DP	.07	.03	.01
☐ 654	Pepe Frias	.14	.07	.01
☐ 655	Lyman Bostock	.25	.12	.02
☐ 656	Dave Garcia MG	.14	.07	.01
☐ 657	Bombo Rivera	.14	.07	.01
☐ 658	Manny Sanguillen	.25	.12	.02
☐ 659	Rangers Team	.50	.25	.05
	(checklist back)			
☐ 660	Jason Thompson	.25	.12	.02
☐ 661	Grant Jackson	.14	.07	.01
☐ 662	Paul Dade	.14	.07	.01
☐ 663	Paul Reuschel	.14	.07	.01
☐ 664	Fred Stanley	.14	.07	.01
☐ 665	Dennis Leonard	.25	.12	.02
☐ 666	Billy Smith	.14	.07	.01
☐ 667	Jeff Byrd	.14	.07	.01
☐ 668	Dusty Baker	.25	.12	.02
☐ 669	Pete Falcone	.14	.07	.01
☐ 670	Jim Rice	3.75	1.85	.37
☐ 671	Gary Lavelle	.14	.07	.01
☐ 672	Don Kessinger	.25	.12	.02
☐ 673	Steve Brye	.14	.07	.01
☐ 674	Ray Knight	1.75	.85	.17
☐ 675	Jay Johnstone	.25	.12	.02
☐ 676	Bob Myrick	.14	.07	.01
☐ 677	Ed Herrmann	.14	.07	.01
☐ 678	Tom Burgmeier	.14	.07	.01
☐ 679	Wayne Garrett	.14	.07	.01
☐ 680	Vida Blue	.25	.12	.02
☐ 681	Rob Belloir	.14	.07	.01
☐ 682	Ken Brett	.14	.07	.01
☐ 683	Mike Champion	.14	.07	.01
☐ 684	Ralph Houk MG	.25	.12	.02
☐ 685	Frank Taveras	.14	.07	.01
☐ 686	Gaylord Perry	2.00	1.00	.20
☐ 687	Julio Cruz	.25	.12	.02
☐ 688	George Mitterwald	.14	.07	.01
☐ 689	Indians Team	.50	.25	.05
	(checklist back)			
☐ 690	Mickey Rivers	.25	.12	.02
☐ 691	Ross Grimsley	.14	.07	.01
☐ 692	Ken Reitz	.14	.07	.01
☐ 693	Lamar Johnson	.14	.07	.01
☐ 694	Elias Sosa	.14	.07	.01
☐ 695	Dwight Evans	1.50	.75	.15
☐ 696	Steve Mingori	.14	.07	.01
☐ 697	Roger Metzger	.14	.07	.01
☐ 698	Juan Bernhardt	.14	.07	.01
☐ 699	Jackie Brown	.14	.07	.01
☐ 700	Johnny Bench	4.50	2.25	.45
☐ 701	Rookie Pitchers	.35	.17	.03
	Tom Hume			
	Larry Landreth			
	Steve McCatty			
	Bruce Taylor			
☐ 702	Rookie Catchers	.25	.12	.02
	Bill Nahordony			
	Kevin Pasley			
	Rick Sweet			
	Don Werner			
☐ 703	Rookie Pitchers DP	6.50	3.25	.65
	Larry Andersen			
	Tim Jones			
	Mickey Mahler			
	Jack Morris			
☐ 704	Rookie 2nd Basemen	12.50	6.25	1.25
	Garth Iorg			
	Dave Oliver			
	Sam Perlozzo			
	Lou Whitaker			
☐ 705	Rookie Outfielders	.50	.25	.05
	Dave Bergman			
	Miguel Dilone			
	Clint Hurdle			
	Willie Norwood			
☐ 706	Rookie 1st Basemen	.25	.12	.02
	Wayne Cage			
	Ted Cox			
	Pat Putnam			
	Dave Revering			
☐ 707	Rookie Shortstops	50.00	25.00	5.00
	Mickey Klutts			
	Paul Molitor			
	Alan Trammell			
	U.L. Washington			
☐ 708	Rookie Catchers	25.00	12.50	2.50
	Bo Diaz			
	Dale Murphy			
	Lance Parrish			
	Ernie Whitt			
☐ 709	Rookie Pitchers	.35	.17	.03
	Steve Burke			
	Matt Keough			
	Lance Rautzhan			
	Dan Schatzeder			
☐ 710	Rookie Outfielders	.60	.30	.06
	Dell Alston			
	Rick Bosetti			
	Mike Easler			
	Keith Smith			
☐ 711	Rookie Pitchers DP	.14	.07	.01
	Cardell Camper			
	Dennis Lamp			
	Craig Mitchell			
	Roy Thomas			
☐ 712	Bobby Valentine	.25	.12	.02
☐ 713	Bob Davis	.14	.07	.01
☐ 714	Mike Anderson	.14	.07	.01
☐ 715	Jim Kaat	.60	.30	.06
☐ 716	Clarence Gaston	.35	.17	.03
☐ 717	Nelson Briles	.14	.07	.01
☐ 718	Ron Jackson	.14	.07	.01
☐ 719	Randy Elliott	.14	.07	.01
☐ 720	Fergie Jenkins	1.00	.40	.07
☐ 721	Billy Martin MG	.60	.30	.06
☐ 722	Pete Broberg	.14	.07	.01
☐ 723	John Wockenfuss	.14	.07	.01
☐ 724	Kansas City Royals	.50	.25	.05
	Team Card			
	(checklist back)			
☐ 725	Kurt Bevacqua	.14	.07	.01
☐ 726	Wilbur Wood	.25	.12	.02

1979 Topps

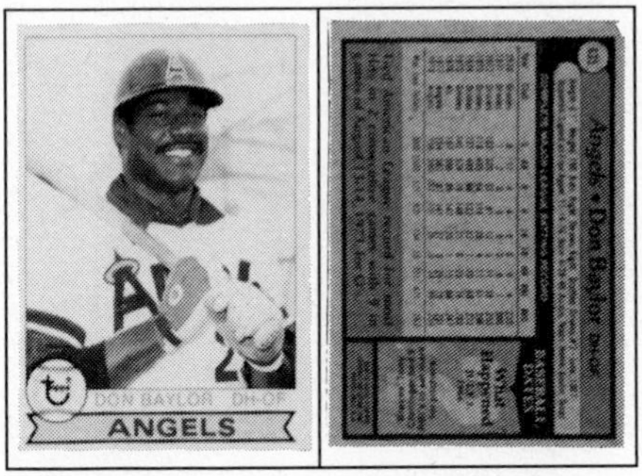

The cards in this 726-card set measure 2 1/2" by 3 1/2". Topps continued with the same number of cards as in 1978. Various series spotlight League Leaders (1-8), "Season and Career Record Holders" (411-418), "Record Breakers of 1978" (201-206), and one "Prospects" card for each team (701-726). Team cards feature a checklist on back of that team's players in the set and a small picture of the manager on the front of the card. There are 66 cards that were double printed and these are noted in the checklist by the abbreviation DP. Bump Wills was initially depicted in a Ranger uniform but with a Blue Jays affiliation; later printings correctly labeled him with Texas. The set price listed does not include the scarcer Wills (Rangers) card. The key rookie cards in this set are Pedro Guerrero, Carney Lansford, Ozzie Smith, and Bob Welch. Cards numbered 23 or lower, which feature Phillies or Yankees and do not follow the numbering checklisted below, are not necessarily error cards. They are probably Burger King cards, a separate set with its own pricing and mass distribution. Burger King cards are indistinguishable from the corresponding Topps cards except for the card numbering difference and the fact that Burger King cards do not have a printing sheet designation (such as A through F like the regular Topps) anywhere on the card back in very small print.

	NRMT	VG-E	GOOD
COMPLETE SET (726)	225.00	110.00	22.00
COMMON PLAYER (1-726)	.11	.05	.01
COMMON DP's (1-726)	.06	.03	.00
☐ 1 Batting Leaders	2.00	.50	.10
Rod Carew			
Dave Parker			
☐ 2 Home Run Leaders	.30	.15	.03
Jim Rice			
George Foster			
☐ 3 RBI Leaders	.30	.15	.03
Jim Rice			
George Foster			
☐ 4 Stolen Base Leaders	.20	.10	.02
Ron LeFlore			
Omar Moreno			
☐ 5 Victory Leaders	.30	.15	.03
Ron Guidry			
Gaylord Perry			
☐ 6 Strikeout Leaders	2.00	1.00	.20
Nolan Ryan			
J.R. Richard			
☐ 7 ERA Leaders	.20	.10	.02
Ron Guidry			
Craig Swan			
☐ 8 Leading Firemen	.30	.15	.03
Rich Gossage			
Rollie Fingers			
☐ 9 Dave Campbell	.11	.05	.01
☐ 10 Lee May	.20	.10	.02
☐ 11 Marc Hill	.11	.05	.01
☐ 12 Dick Drago	.11	.05	.01
☐ 13 Paul Dade	.11	.05	.01
☐ 14 Rafael Landestoy	.11	.05	.01
☐ 15 Ross Grimsley	.11	.05	.01
☐ 16 Fred Stanley	.11	.05	.01
☐ 17 Donnie Moore	.11	.05	.01
☐ 18 Tony Solaita	.11	.05	.01
☐ 19 Larry Gura DP	.11	.05	.01
☐ 20 Joe Morgan DP	.85	.40	.08
☐ 21 Kevin Kobel	.11	.05	.01
☐ 22 Mike Jorgensen	.11	.05	.01
☐ 23 Terry Forster	.20	.10	.02
☐ 24 Paul Molitor	4.00	2.00	.40
☐ 25 Steve Carlton	2.50	1.25	.25
☐ 26 Jamie Quirk	.11	.05	.01
☐ 27 Dave Goltz	.11	.05	.01
☐ 28 Steve Brye	.11	.05	.01
☐ 29 Rick Langford	.11	.05	.01
☐ 30 Dave Winfield	2.50	1.25	.25
☐ 31 Tom House DP	.11	.05	.01
☐ 32 Jerry Mumphrey	.11	.05	.01
☐ 33 Dave Rozema	.11	.05	.01
☐ 34 Rob Andrews	.11	.05	.01
☐ 35 Ed Figueroa	.11	.05	.01
☐ 36 Alan Ashby	.11	.05	.01
☐ 37 Joe Kerrigan DP	.06	.03	.00
☐ 38 Bernie Carbo	.11	.05	.01
☐ 39 Dale Murphy	9.00	4.50	.90
☐ 40 Dennis Eckersley	2.00	1.00	.20
☐ 41 Twins Team/Mgr.	.40	.20	.04
Gene Mauch			
(checklist back)			
☐ 42 Ron Blomberg	.11	.05	.01
☐ 43 Wayne Twitchell	.11	.05	.01
☐ 44 Kurt Bevacqua	.11	.05	.01
☐ 45 Al Hrabosky	.11	.05	.01
☐ 46 Ron Hodges	.11	.05	.01
☐ 47 Fred Norman	.11	.05	.01
☐ 48 Merv Rettenmund	.11	.05	.01
☐ 49 Vern Ruhle	.11	.05	.01
☐ 50 Steve Garvey DP	1.25	.60	.12
☐ 51 Ray Fosse DP	.06	.03	.00
☐ 52 Randy Lerch	.11	.05	.01
☐ 53 Mick Kelleher	.11	.05	.01
☐ 54 Dell Alston DP	.06	.03	.00
☐ 55 Willie Stargell	2.25	1.10	.22
☐ 56 John Hale	.11	.05	.01
☐ 57 Eric Rasmussen	.11	.05	.01
☐ 58 Bob Randall DP	.06	.03	.00
☐ 59 John Denny DP	.11	.05	.01
☐ 60 Mickey Rivers	.20	.10	.02
☐ 61 Bo Diaz	.20	.10	.02
☐ 62 Randy Moffitt	.11	.05	.01
☐ 63 Jack Brohamer	.11	.05	.01
☐ 64 Tom Underwood	.11	.05	.01
☐ 65 Mark Belanger	.20	.10	.02
☐ 66 Tigers Team/Mgr.	.40	.20	.04
Les Moss			
(checklist back)			
☐ 67 Jim Mason DP	.06	.03	.00
☐ 68 Joe Niekro DP	.11	.05	.01
☐ 69 Elliott Maddox	.11	.05	.01
☐ 70 John Candelaria	.30	.15	.03
☐ 71 Brian Downing	.20	.10	.02
☐ 72 Steve Mingori	.11	.05	.01
☐ 73 Ken Henderson	.11	.05	.01
☐ 74 Shane Rawley	.90	.45	.09
☐ 75 Steve Yeager	.11	.05	.01
☐ 76 Warren Cromartie	.11	.05	.01
☐ 77 Dan Briggs DP	.06	.03	.00
☐ 78 Elias Sosa	.11	.05	.01
☐ 79 Ted Cox	.11	.05	.01
☐ 80 Jason Thompson	.11	.05	.01
☐ 81 Roger Erickson	.11	.05	.01
☐ 82 Mets Team/Mgr.	.40	.20	.04
Joe Torre			
(checklist back)			
☐ 83 Fred Kendall	.11	.05	.01
☐ 84 Greg Minton	.11	.05	.01
☐ 85 Gary Matthews	.20	.10	.02
☐ 86 Rodney Scott	.11	.05	.01
☐ 87 Pete Falcone	.11	.05	.01
☐ 88 Bob Molinaro	.11	.05	.01
☐ 89 Dick Tidrow	.11	.05	.01
☐ 90 Bob Boone	.40	.20	.04
☐ 91 Terry Crowley	.11	.05	.01
☐ 92 Jim Bibby	.11	.05	.01
☐ 93 Phil Mankowski	.11	.05	.01
☐ 94 Len Barker	.11	.05	.01
☐ 95 Robin Yount	8.00	4.00	.80
☐ 96 Indians Team/Mgr.	.40	.20	.04
Jeff Torborg			
(checklist back)			
☐ 97 Sam Mejias	.11	.05	.01
☐ 98 Ray Burris	.11	.05	.01
☐ 99 John Wathan	.30	.15	.03
☐ 100 Tom Seaver DP	2.25	1.10	.22
☐ 101 Roy Howell	.11	.05	.01
☐ 102 Mike Anderson	.11	.05	.01

☐ 103 Jim Todd	.11	.05	.01
☐ 104 Johnny Oates DP	.06	.03	.00
☐ 105 Rick Camp DP	.06	.03	.00
☐ 106 Frank Duffy	.11	.05	.01
☐ 107 Jesus Alou DP	.06	.03	.00
☐ 108 Eduardo Rodriguez	.11	.05	.01
☐ 109 Joel Youngblood	.11	.05	.01
☐ 110 Vida Blue	.20	.10	.02
☐ 111 Roger Freed	.11	.05	.01
☐ 112 Phillies Team/Mgr. Danny Ozark (checklist back)	.40	.20	.04
☐ 113 Pete Redfern	.11	.05	.01
☐ 114 Cliff Johnson	.11	.05	.01
☐ 115 Nolan Ryan	14.00	7.00	1.40
☐ 116 Ozzie Smith	45.00	22.50	4.50
☐ 117 Grant Jackson	.11	.05	.01
☐ 118 Bud Harrelson	.20	.10	.02
☐ 119 Don Stanhouse	.11	.05	.01
☐ 120 Jim Sundberg	.11	.05	.01
☐ 121 Checklist 1 DP	.20	.02	.00
☐ 122 Mike Paxton	.11	.05	.01
☐ 123 Lou Whitaker	3.50	1.75	.35
☐ 124 Dan Schatzeder	.11	.05	.01
☐ 125 Rick Burleson	.20	.10	.02
☐ 126 Doug Bair	.11	.05	.01
☐ 127 Thad Bosley	.11	.05	.01
☐ 128 Ted Martinez	.11	.05	.01
☐ 129 Marty Pattin DP	.06	.03	.00
☐ 130 Bob Watson DP	.11	.05	.01
☐ 131 Jim Clancy	.11	.05	.01
☐ 132 Rowland Office	.11	.05	.01
☐ 133 Bill Castro	.11	.05	.01
☐ 134 Alan Bannister	.11	.05	.01
☐ 135 Bobby Murcer	.30	.15	.03
☐ 136 Jim Kaat	.40	.20	.04
☐ 137 Larry Wolfe DP	.06	.03	.00
☐ 138 Mark Lee	.11	.05	.01
☐ 139 Luis Pujols	.11	.05	.01
☐ 140 Don Gullett	.20	.10	.02
☐ 141 Tom Paciorek	.11	.05	.01
☐ 142 Charlie Williams	.11	.05	.01
☐ 143 Tony Scott	.11	.05	.01
☐ 144 Sandy Alomar	.11	.05	.01
☐ 145 Rick Rhoden	.20	.10	.02
☐ 146 Duane Kuiper	.11	.05	.01
☐ 147 Dave Hamilton	.11	.05	.01
☐ 148 Bruce Boisclair	.11	.05	.01
☐ 149 Manny Sarmiento	.11	.05	.01
☐ 150 Wayne Cage	.11	.05	.01
☐ 151 John Hiller	.20	.10	.02
☐ 152 Rick Cerone	.20	.10	.02
☐ 153 Dennis Lamp	.11	.05	.01
☐ 154 Jim Gantner DP	.11	.05	.01
☐ 155 Dwight Evans	1.25	.60	.12
☐ 156 Buddy Solomon	.11	.05	.01
☐ 157 U.L. Washington UER (sic, bats left, should be right)	.11	.05	.01
☐ 158 Joe Sambito	.11	.05	.01
☐ 159 Roy White	.20	.10	.02
☐ 160 Mike Flanagan	.30	.15	.03
☐ 161 Barry Foote	.11	.05	.01
☐ 162 Tom Johnson	.11	.05	.01
☐ 163 Glenn Burke	.11	.05	.01
☐ 164 Mickey Lolich	.30	.15	.03
☐ 165 Frank Taveras	.11	.05	.01
☐ 166 Leon Roberts	.11	.05	.01
☐ 167 Roger Metzger DP	.06	.03	.00
☐ 168 Dave Freisleben	.11	.05	.01
☐ 169 Bill Nahorodny	.11	.05	.01
☐ 170 Don Sutton	1.25	.60	.12
☐ 171 Gene Clines	.11	.05	.01
☐ 172 Mike Bruhert	.11	.05	.01
☐ 173 John Lowenstein	.11	.05	.01
☐ 174 Rick Auerbach	.11	.05	.01
☐ 175 George Hendrick	.20	.10	.02
☐ 176 Aurelio Rodriguez	.11	.05	.01
☐ 177 Ron Reed	.11	.05	.01
☐ 178 Alvis Woods	.11	.05	.01
☐ 179 Jim Beattie DP	.11	.05	.01
☐ 180 Larry Hisle	.11	.05	.01
☐ 181 Mike Garman	.11	.05	.01
☐ 182 Tim Johnson	.11	.05	.01
☐ 183 Paul Splittorff	.11	.05	.01
☐ 184 Darrel Chaney	.11	.05	.01
☐ 185 Mike Torrez	.11	.05	.01
☐ 186 Eric Soderholm	.11	.05	.01
☐ 187 Mark Lemongello	.11	.05	.01
☐ 188 Pat Kelly	.11	.05	.01
☐ 189 Eddie Whitson	1.50	.75	.15
☐ 190 Ron Cey	.35	.17	.03
☐ 191 Mike Norris	.11	.05	.01

☐ 192 Cardinals Team/Mgr. Ken Boyer (checklist back)	.40	.20	.04
☐ 193 Glenn Adams	.11	.05	.01
☐ 194 Randy Jones	.11	.05	.01
☐ 195 Bill Madlock	.40	.20	.04
☐ 196 Steve Kemp DP	.11	.05	.01
☐ 197 Bob Apodaca	.11	.05	.01
☐ 198 Johnny Grubb	.11	.05	.01
☐ 199 Larry Milbourne	.11	.05	.01
☐ 200 Johnny Bench DP	2.00	1.00	.20
☐ 201 RB: Mike Edwards Most unassisted DP's, second basemen	.11	.05	.01
☐ 202 RB: Ron Guidry, Most strikeouts, lefthander, nine inning game	.30	.15	.03
☐ 203 RB: J.R. Richard Most strikeouts, season, righthander	.20	.10	.02
☐ 204 RB: Pete Rose Most consecutive games batting safely	1.50	.75	.15
☐ 205 RB: John Stearns Most SB's by catcher, season	.11	.05	.01
☐ 206 RB: Sammy Stewart 7 straight SO's, first ML game	.11	.05	.01
☐ 207 Dave Lemanczyk	.11	.05	.01
☐ 208 Clarence Gaston	.20	.10	.02
☐ 209 Reggie Cleveland	.11	.05	.01
☐ 210 Larry Bowa	.30	.15	.03
☐ 211 Denny Martinez	.30	.15	.03
☐ 212 Carney Lansford	7.50	3.75	.75
☐ 213 Bill Travers	.11	.05	.01
☐ 214 Red Sox Team/Mgr. Don Zimmer (checklist back)	.40	.20	.04
☐ 215 Willie McCovey	1.75	.85	.17
☐ 216 Wilbur Wood	.20	.10	.02
☐ 217 Steve Dillard	.11	.05	.01
☐ 218 Dennis Leonard	.20	.10	.02
☐ 219 Roy Smalley	.11	.05	.01
☐ 220 Cesar Geronimo	.11	.05	.01
☐ 221 Jesse Jefferson	.11	.05	.01
☐ 222 Bob Beall	.11	.05	.01
☐ 223 Kent Tekulve	.20	.10	.02
☐ 224 Dave Revering	.11	.05	.01
☐ 225 Rich Gossage	.60	.30	.06
☐ 226 Ron Pruitt	.11	.05	.01
☐ 227 Steve Stone	.20	.10	.02
☐ 228 Vic Davalillo	.11	.05	.01
☐ 229 Doug Flynn	.11	.05	.01
☐ 230 Bob Forsch	.11	.05	.01
☐ 231 John Wockenfuss	.11	.05	.01
☐ 232 Jimmy Sexton	.11	.05	.01
☐ 233 Paul Mitchell	.11	.05	.01
☐ 234 Toby Harrah	.20	.10	.02
☐ 235 Steve Rogers	.11	.05	.01
☐ 236 Jim Dwyer	.11	.05	.01
☐ 237 Billy Smith	.11	.05	.01
☐ 238 Balor Moore	.11	.05	.01
☐ 239 Willie Horton	.20	.10	.02
☐ 240 Rick Reuschel	.40	.20	.04
☐ 241 Checklist 2 DP	.20	.02	.00
☐ 242 Pablo Torrealba	.11	.05	.01
☐ 243 Buck Martinez DP	.06	.03	.00
☐ 244 Pirates Team/Mgr. Chuck Tanner (checklist back)	.40	.20	.04
☐ 245 Jeff Burroughs	.20	.10	.02
☐ 246 Darrell Jackson	.11	.05	.01
☐ 247 Tucker Ashford DP	.06	.03	.00
☐ 248 Pete LaCock	.11	.05	.01
☐ 249 Paul Thormodsgard	.11	.05	.01
☐ 250 Willie Randolph	.30	.15	.03
☐ 251 Jack Morris	2.50	1.25	.25
☐ 252 Bob Stinson	.11	.05	.01
☐ 253 Rick Wise	.20	.10	.02
☐ 254 Luis Gomez	.11	.05	.01
☐ 255 Tommy John	.70	.35	.07
☐ 256 Mike Sadek	.11	.05	.01
☐ 257 Adrian Devine	.11	.05	.01
☐ 258 Mike Phillips	.11	.05	.01
☐ 259 Reds Team/Mgr. Sparky Anderson (checklist back)	.40	.20	.04
☐ 260 Richie Zisk	.11	.05	.01
☐ 261 Mario Guerrero	.11	.05	.01
☐ 262 Nelson Briles	.11	.05	.01
☐ 263 Oscar Gamble	.11	.05	.01
☐ 264 Don Robinson	1.00	.50	.10
☐ 265 Don Money	.11	.05	.01

☐ 266	Jim Willoughby	.11	.05	.01
☐ 267	Joe Rudi	.20	.10	.02
☐ 268	Julio Gonzalez	.11	.05	.01
☐ 269	Woodie Fryman	.11	.05	.01
☐ 270	Butch Hobson	.11	.05	.01
☐ 271	Rawly Eastwick	.11	.05	.01
☐ 272	Tim Corcoran	.11	.05	.01
☐ 273	Jerry Terrell	.11	.05	.01
☐ 274	Willie Norwood	.11	.05	.01
☐ 275	Junior Moore	.11	.05	.01
☐ 276	Jim Colborn	.11	.05	.01
☐ 277	Tom Grieve	.20	.10	.02
☐ 278	Andy Messersmith	.20	.10	.02
☐ 279	Jerry Grote DP	.06	.03	.00
☐ 280	Andre Thornton	.20	.10	.02
☐ 281	Vic Correll DP	.06	.03	.00
☐ 282	Blue Jays Team/Mgr.	.30	.15	.03
	Roy Hartsfield			
	(checklist back)			
☐ 283	Ken Kravec	.11	.05	.01
☐ 284	Johnnie LeMaster	.11	.05	.01
☐ 285	Bobby Bonds	.35	.17	.03
☐ 286	Duffy Dyer	.11	.05	.01
☐ 287	Andres Mora	.11	.05	.01
☐ 288	Milt Wilcox	.11	.05	.01
☐ 289	Jose Cruz	.20	.10	.02
☐ 290	Dave Lopes	.20	.10	.02
☐ 291	Tom Griffin	.11	.05	.01
☐ 292	Don Reynolds	.11	.05	.01
☐ 293	Jerry Garvin	.11	.05	.01
☐ 294	Pepe Frias	.11	.05	.01
☐ 295	Mitchell Page	.11	.05	.01
☐ 296	Preston Hanna	.11	.05	.01
☐ 297	Ted Sizemore	.11	.05	.01
☐ 298	Rich Gale	.11	.05	.01
☐ 299	Steve Ontiveros	.11	.05	.01
☐ 300	Rod Carew	2.50	1.25	.25
☐ 301	Tom Hume	.11	.05	.01
☐ 302	Braves Team/Mgr.	.40	.20	.04
	Bobby Cox			
	(checklist back)			
☐ 303	Lary Sorensen	.11	.05	.01
☐ 304	Steve Swisher	.11	.05	.01
☐ 305	Willie Montanez	.11	.05	.01
☐ 306	Floyd Bannister	.20	.10	.02
☐ 307	Larvell Blanks	.11	.05	.01
☐ 308	Bert Blyleven	.75	.35	.07
☐ 309	Ralph Garr	.20	.10	.02
☐ 310	Thurman Munson	2.50	1.25	.25
☐ 311	Gary Lavelle	.11	.05	.01
☐ 312	Bob Robertson	.11	.05	.01
☐ 313	Dyar Miller	.11	.05	.01
☐ 314	Larry Harlow	.11	.05	.01
☐ 315	Jon Matlack	.20	.10	.02
☐ 316	Milt May	.11	.05	.01
☐ 317	Jose Cardenal	.11	.05	.01
☐ 318	Bob Welch	15.00	7.50	1.50
☐ 319	Wayne Garrett	.11	.05	.01
☐ 320	Carl Yastrzemski	3.50	1.75	.35
☐ 321	Gaylord Perry	1.50	.75	.15
☐ 322	Danny Goodwin	.11	.05	.01
☐ 323	Lynn McGlothen	.11	.05	.01
☐ 324	Mike Tyson	.11	.05	.01
☐ 325	Cecil Cooper	.45	.22	.04
☐ 326	Pedro Borbon	.11	.05	.01
☐ 327	Art Howe	.20	.10	.02
☐ 328	Oakland A's Team/Mgr.	.40	.20	.04
	Jack McKeon			
	(checklist back)			
☐ 329	Joe Coleman	.11	.05	.01
☐ 330	George Brett	8.00	4.00	.80
☐ 331	Mickey Mahler	.11	.05	.01
☐ 332	Gary Alexander	.11	.05	.01
☐ 333	Chet Lemon	.20	.10	.02
☐ 334	Craig Swan	.11	.05	.01
☐ 335	Chris Chambliss	.20	.10	.02
☐ 336	Bobby Thompson	.11	.05	.01
☐ 337	John Montague	.11	.05	.01
☐ 338	Vic Harris	.11	.05	.01
☐ 339	Ron Jackson	.11	.05	.01
☐ 340	Jim Palmer	2.25	1.10	.22
☐ 341	Willie Upshaw	.45	.22	.04
☐ 342	Dave Roberts	.11	.05	.01
☐ 343	Ed Glynn	.11	.05	.01
☐ 344	Jerry Royster	.11	.05	.01
☐ 345	Tug McGraw	.30	.15	.03
☐ 346	Bill Buckner	.30	.15	.03
☐ 347	Doug Rau	.11	.05	.01
☐ 348	Andre Dawson	7.50	3.75	.75
☐ 349	Jim Wright	.11	.05	.01
☐ 350	Garry Templeton	.20	.10	.02
☐ 351	Wayne Nordhagen	.11	.05	.01
☐ 352	Steve Renko	.11	.05	.01
☐ 353	Checklist 3	.50	.05	.01

☐ 354	Bill Bonham	.11	.05	.01
☐ 355	Lee Mazzilli	.11	.05	.01
☐ 356	Giants Team/Mgr.	.40	.20	.04
	Joe Altobelli			
	(checklist back)			
☐ 357	Jerry Augustine	.11	.05	.01
☐ 358	Alan Trammell	10.00	5.00	1.00
☐ 359	Dan Spillner DP	.06	.03	.00
☐ 360	Amos Otis	.20	.10	.02
☐ 361	Tom Dixon	.11	.05	.01
☐ 362	Mike Cubbage	.11	.05	.01
☐ 363	Craig Skok	.11	.05	.01
☐ 364	Gene Richards	.11	.05	.01
☐ 365	Sparky Lyle	.30	.15	.03
☐ 366	Juan Bernhardt	.11	.05	.01
☐ 367	Dave Skaggs	.11	.05	.01
☐ 368	Don Aase	.11	.05	.01
☐ 369A	Bump Wills ERR	3.00	1.50	.30
	(Blue Jays)			
☐ 369B	Bump Wills COR	3.50	1.75	.35
	(Rangers)			
☐ 370	Dave Kingman	.40	.20	.04
☐ 371	Jeff Holly	.11	.05	.01
☐ 372	Lamar Johnson	.11	.05	.01
☐ 373	Lance Rautzhan	.11	.05	.01
☐ 374	Ed Herrmann	.11	.05	.01
☐ 375	Bill Campbell	.11	.05	.01
☐ 376	Gorman Thomas	.30	.15	.03
☐ 377	Paul Moskau	.11	.05	.01
☐ 378	Rob Picciolo DP	.06	.03	.00
☐ 379	Dale Murray	.11	.05	.01
☐ 380	John Mayberry	.20	.10	.02
☐ 381	Astros Team/Mgr.	.40	.20	.04
	Bill Virdon			
	(checklist back)			
☐ 382	Jerry Martin	.11	.05	.01
☐ 383	Phil Garner	.11	.05	.01
☐ 384	Tommy Boggs	.11	.05	.01
☐ 385	Dan Ford	.11	.05	.01
☐ 386	Francisco Barrios	.11	.05	.01
☐ 387	Gary Thomasson	.11	.05	.01
☐ 388	Jack Billingham	.11	.05	.01
☐ 389	Joe Zdeb	.11	.05	.01
☐ 390	Rollie Fingers	1.00	.50	.10
☐ 391	Al Oliver	.30	.15	.03
☐ 392	Doug Ault	.11	.05	.01
☐ 393	Scott McGregor	.20	.10	.02
☐ 394	Randy Stein	.11	.05	.01
☐ 395	Dave Cash	.11	.05	.01
☐ 396	Bill Plummer	.11	.05	.01
☐ 397	Sergio Ferrer	.11	.05	.01
☐ 398	Ivan DeJesus	.11	.05	.01
☐ 399	David Clyde	.11	.05	.01
☐ 400	Jim Rice	2.50	1.25	.25
☐ 401	Ray Knight	.30	.15	.03
☐ 402	Paul Hartzell	.11	.05	.01
☐ 403	Tim Foli	.11	.05	.01
☐ 404	White Sox Team/Mgr	.40	.20	.04
	Don Kessinger			
	(checklist back)			
☐ 405	Butch Wynegar DP	.06	.03	.00
☐ 406	Joe Wallis DP	.06	.03	.00
☐ 407	Pete Vuckovich	.11	.05	.01
☐ 408	Charlie Moore DP	.06	.03	.00
☐ 409	Willie Wilson	2.00	1.00	.20
☐ 410	Darrell Evans	.30	.15	.03
☐ 411	Hits Record	.40	.20	.04
	Season: G.Sisler			
	Career: Ty Cobb			
☐ 412	RBI Record	.40	.20	.04
	Season: Hack Wilson			
	Career: Hank Aaron			
☐ 413	Home Run Record	.60	.30	.06
	Season: Roger Maris			
	Career: Hank Aaron			
☐ 414	Batting Record	.40	.20	.04
	Season: R.Hornsby			
	Career: Ty Cobb			
☐ 415	Steals Record	.40	.20	.04
	Season: Lou Brock			
	Career: Lou Brock			
☐ 416	Wins Record	.20	.10	.02
	Season: Jack Chesbro			
	Career: Cy Young			
☐ 417	Strikeout Record DP	.20	.10	.02
	Season: Nolan Ryan			
	Career: W.Johnson			
☐ 418	ERA Record DP	.11	.05	.01
	Season: Dutch Leonard			
	Career: W.Johnson			
☐ 419	Dick Ruthven	.11	.05	.01
☐ 420	Ken Griffey	.50	.25	.05
☐ 421	Doug DeCinces	.20	.10	.02
☐ 422	Ruppert Jones	.11	.05	.01

☐ 423 Bob Montgomery	.11	.05	.01
☐ 424 Angels Team/Mgr.	.40	.20	.04
Jim Fregosi			
(checklist back)			
☐ 425 Rick Manning	.11	.05	.01
☐ 426 Chris Speier	.11	.05	.01
☐ 427 Andy Replogle	.11	.05	.01
☐ 428 Bobby Valentine	.20	.10	.02
☐ 429 John Urrea DP	.06	.03	.00
☐ 430 Dave Parker	2.00	1.00	.20
☐ 431 Glenn Borgmann	.11	.05	.01
☐ 432 Dave Heaverlo	.11	.05	.01
☐ 433 Larry Biittner	.11	.05	.01
☐ 434 Ken Clay	.11	.05	.01
☐ 435 Gene Tenace	.11	.05	.01
☐ 436 Hector Cruz	.11	.05	.01
☐ 437 Rick Williams	.11	.05	.01
☐ 438 Horace Speed	.11	.05	.01
☐ 439 Frank White	.20	.10	.02
☐ 440 Rusty Staub	.30	.15	.03
☐ 441 Lee Lacy	.11	.05	.01
☐ 442 Doyle Alexander	.20	.10	.02
☐ 443 Bruce Bochte	.11	.05	.01
☐ 444 Aurelio Lopez	.20	.10	.02
☐ 445 Steve Henderson	.11	.05	.01
☐ 446 Jim Lonborg	.20	.10	.02
☐ 447 Manny Sanguillen	.20	.10	.02
☐ 448 Moose Haas	.11	.05	.01
☐ 449 Bombo Rivera	.11	.05	.01
☐ 450 Dave Concepcion	.30	.15	.03
☐ 451 Royals Team/Mgr.	.40	.20	.04
Whitey Herzog			
(checklist back)			
☐ 452 Jerry Morales	.11	.05	.01
☐ 453 Chris Knapp	.11	.05	.01
☐ 454 Len Randle	.11	.05	.01
☐ 455 Bill Lee DP	.11	.05	.01
☐ 456 Chuck Baker	.11	.05	.01
☐ 457 Bruce Sutter	.70	.35	.07
☐ 458 Jim Essian	.11	.05	.01
☐ 459 Sid Monge	.11	.05	.01
☐ 460 Graig Nettles	.50	.25	.05
☐ 461 Jim Barr DP	.06	.03	.00
☐ 462 Otto Velez	.11	.05	.01
☐ 463 Steve Comer	.11	.05	.01
☐ 464 Joe Nolan	.11	.05	.01
☐ 465 Reggie Smith	.20	.10	.02
☐ 466 Mark Littell	.11	.05	.01
☐ 467 Don Kessinger DP	.11	.05	.01
☐ 468 Stan Bahnsen DP	.06	.03	.00
☐ 469 Lance Parrish	3.50	1.75	.35
☐ 470 Garry Maddox DP	.11	.05	.01
☐ 471 Joaquin Andujar	.20	.10	.02
☐ 472 Craig Kusick	.11	.05	.01
☐ 473 Dave Roberts	.11	.05	.01
☐ 474 Dick Davis	.11	.05	.01
☐ 475 Dan Driessen	.11	.05	.01
☐ 476 Tom Poquette	.11	.05	.01
☐ 477 Bob Grich	.20	.10	.02
☐ 478 Juan Beniquez	.11	.05	.01
☐ 479 Padres Team/Mgr.	.40	.20	.04
Roger Craig			
(checklist back)			
☐ 480 Fred Lynn	.75	.35	.07
☐ 481 Skip Lockwood	.11	.05	.01
☐ 482 Craig Reynolds	.11	.05	.01
☐ 483 Checklist 4 DP	.20	.02	.00
☐ 484 Rick Waits	.11	.05	.01
☐ 485 Bucky Dent	.30	.15	.03
☐ 486 Bob Knepper	.20	.10	.02
☐ 487 Miguel Dilone	.11	.05	.01
☐ 488 Bob Owchinko	.11	.05	.01
☐ 489 Larry Cox UER	.11	.05	.01
(photo actually			
Dave Rader)			
☐ 490 Al Cowens	.11	.05	.01
☐ 491 Tippy Martinez	.11	.05	.01
☐ 492 Bob Bailor	.11	.05	.01
☐ 493 Larry Christenson	.11	.05	.01
☐ 494 Jerry White	.11	.05	.01
☐ 495 Tony Perez	.60	.30	.06
☐ 496 Barry Bonnell DP	.06	.03	.00
☐ 497 Glenn Abbott	.11	.05	.01
☐ 498 Rich Chiles	.11	.05	.01
☐ 499 Rangers Team/Mgr.	.40	.20	.04
Pat Corrales			
(checklist back)			
☐ 500 Ron Guidry	1.25	.60	.12
☐ 501 Junior Kennedy	.11	.05	.01
☐ 502 Steve Braun	.11	.05	.01
☐ 503 Terry Humphrey	.11	.05	.01
☐ 504 Larry McWilliams	.30	.15	.03
☐ 505 Ed Kranepool	.11	.05	.01
☐ 506 John D'Acquisto	.11	.05	.01
☐ 507 Tony Armas	.20	.10	.02
☐ 508 Charlie Hough	.20	.10	.02
☐ 509 Mario Mendoza	.11	.05	.01
☐ 510 Ted Simmons	.40	.20	.04
☐ 511 Paul Reuschel DP	.06	.03	.00
☐ 512 Jack Clark	2.50	1.25	.25
☐ 513 Dave Johnson	.20	.10	.02
☐ 514 Mike Proly	.11	.05	.01
☐ 515 Enos Cabell	.11	.05	.01
☐ 516 Champ Summers DP	.06	.03	.00
☐ 517 Al Bumbry	.11	.05	.01
☐ 518 Jim Umbarger	.11	.05	.01
☐ 519 Ben Oglivie	.20	.10	.02
☐ 520 Gary Carter	2.50	1.25	.25
☐ 521 Sam Ewing	.11	.05	.01
☐ 522 Ken Holtzman	.20	.10	.02
☐ 523 John Milner	.11	.05	.01
☐ 524 Tom Burgmeier	.11	.05	.01
☐ 525 Freddie Patek	.11	.05	.01
☐ 526 Dodgers Team/Mgr.	.50	.25	.05
Tom Lasorda			
(checklist back)			
☐ 527 Lerrin LaGrow	.11	.05	.01
☐ 528 Wayne Gross DP	.06	.03	.00
☐ 529 Brian Asselstine	.11	.05	.01
☐ 530 Frank Tanana	.20	.10	.02
☐ 531 Fernando Gonzalez	.11	.05	.01
☐ 532 Buddy Schultz	.11	.05	.01
☐ 533 Leroy Stanton	.11	.05	.01
☐ 534 Ken Forsch	.11	.05	.01
☐ 535 Ellis Valentine	.11	.05	.01
☐ 536 Jerry Reuss	.20	.10	.02
☐ 537 Tom Veryzer	.11	.05	.01
☐ 538 Mike Ivie DP	.06	.03	.00
☐ 539 John Ellis	.11	.05	.01
☐ 540 Greg Luzinski	.30	.15	.03
☐ 541 Jim Slaton	.11	.05	.01
☐ 542 Rick Bosetti	.11	.05	.01
☐ 543 Kiko Garcia	.11	.05	.01
☐ 544 Fergie Jenkins	.75	.30	.06
☐ 545 John Stearns	.11	.05	.01
☐ 546 Bill Russell	.20	.10	.02
☐ 547 Clint Hurdle	.11	.05	.01
☐ 548 Enrique Romo	.11	.05	.01
☐ 549 Bob Bailey	.11	.05	.01
☐ 550 Sal Bando	.20	.10	.02
☐ 551 Cubs Team/Mgr.	.40	.20	.04
Herman Franks			
(checklist back)			
☐ 552 Jose Morales	.11	.05	.01
☐ 553 Denny Walling	.11	.05	.01
☐ 554 Matt Keough	.11	.05	.01
☐ 555 Biff Pocoroba	.11	.05	.01
☐ 556 Mike Lum	.11	.05	.01
☐ 557 Ken Brett	.11	.05	.01
☐ 558 Jay Johnstone	.20	.10	.02
☐ 559 Greg Pryor	.11	.05	.01
☐ 560 John Montefusco	.20	.10	.02
☐ 561 Ed Ott	.11	.05	.01
☐ 562 Dusty Baker	.30	.15	.03
☐ 563 Roy Thomas	.11	.05	.01
☐ 564 Jerry Turner	.11	.05	.01
☐ 565 Rico Carty	.20	.10	.02
☐ 566 Nino Espinosa	.11	.05	.01
☐ 567 Richie Hebner	.11	.05	.01
☐ 568 Carlos Lopez	.11	.05	.01
☐ 569 Bob Sykes	.11	.05	.01
☐ 570 Cesar Cedeno	.20	.10	.02
☐ 571 Darrell Porter	.11	.05	.01
☐ 572 Rod Gilbreath	.11	.05	.01
☐ 573 Jim Kern	.11	.05	.01
☐ 574 Claudell Washington	.20	.10	.02
☐ 575 Luis Tiant	.30	.15	.03
☐ 576 Mike Parrott	.11	.05	.01
☐ 577 Brewers Team/Mgr.	.40	.20	.04
George Bamberger			
(checklist back)			
☐ 578 Pete Broberg	.11	.05	.01
☐ 579 Greg Gross	.11	.05	.01
☐ 580 Ron Fairly	.11	.05	.01
☐ 581 Darold Knowles	.11	.05	.01
☐ 582 Paul Blair	.11	.05	.01
☐ 583 Julio Cruz	.11	.05	.01
☐ 584 Jim Rooker	.11	.05	.01
☐ 585 Hal McRae	.20	.10	.02
☐ 586 Bob Horner	1.50	.75	.15
☐ 587 Ken Reitz	.11	.05	.01
☐ 588 Tom Murphy	.11	.05	.01
☐ 589 Terry Whitfield	.11	.05	.01
☐ 590 J.R. Richard	.20	.10	.02
☐ 591 Mike Hargrove	.20	.10	.02
☐ 592 Mike Krukow	.20	.10	.02
☐ 593 Rick Dempsey	.11	.05	.01
☐ 594 Bob Shirley	.11	.05	.01

☐ 595 Phil Niekro	1.25	.60	.12
☐ 596 Jim Wohlford	.11	.05	.01
☐ 597 Bob Stanley	.11	.05	.01
☐ 598 Mark Wagner	.11	.05	.01
☐ 599 Jim Spencer	.11	.05	.01
☐ 600 George Foster	.60	.30	.06
☐ 601 Dave LaRoche	.11	.05	.01
☐ 602 Checklist 5	.50	.05	.01
☐ 603 Rudy May	.11	.05	.01
☐ 604 Jeff Newman	.11	.05	.01
☐ 605 Rick Monday DP	.11	.05	.01
☐ 606 Expos Team/Mgr.	.40	.20	.04
Dick Williams			
(checklist back)			
☐ 607 Omar Moreno	.11	.05	.01
☐ 608 Dave McKay	.11	.05	.01
☐ 609 Silvio Martinez	.11	.05	.01
☐ 610 Mike Schmidt	8.00	4.00	.80
☐ 611 Jim Norris	.11	.05	.01
☐ 612 Rick Honeycutt	.60	.30	.06
☐ 613 Mike Edwards	.11	.05	.01
☐ 614 Willie Hernandez	.35	.17	.03
☐ 615 Ken Singleton	.20	.10	.02
☐ 616 Billy Almon	.11	.05	.01
☐ 617 Terry Puhl	.11	.05	.01
☐ 618 Jerry Remy	.11	.05	.01
☐ 619 Ken Landreaux	.30	.15	.03
☐ 620 Bert Campaneris	.20	.10	.02
☐ 621 Pat Zachry	.11	.05	.01
☐ 622 Dave Collins	.11	.05	.01
☐ 623 Bob McClure	.11	.05	.01
☐ 624 Larry Herndon	.11	.05	.01
☐ 625 Mark Fidrych	.20	.10	.02
☐ 626 Yankees Team/Mgr.	.50	.25	.05
Bob Lemon			
(checklist back)			
☐ 627 Gary Serum	.11	.05	.01
☐ 628 Del Unser	.11	.05	.01
☐ 629 Gene Garber	.11	.05	.01
☐ 630 Bake McBride	.11	.05	.01
☐ 631 Jorge Orta	.11	.05	.01
☐ 632 Don Kirkwood	.11	.05	.01
☐ 633 Rob Wilfong DP	.06	.03	.00
☐ 634 Paul Lindblad	.11	.05	.01
☐ 635 Don Baylor	1.00	.50	.10
☐ 636 Wayne Garland	.11	.05	.01
☐ 637 Bill Robinson	.20	.10	.02
☐ 638 Al Fitzmorris	.11	.05	.01
☐ 639 Manny Trillo	.11	.05	.01
☐ 640 Eddie Murray	11.00	5.50	1.10
☐ 641 Bobby Castillo	.11	.05	.01
☐ 642 Wilbur Howard DP	.06	.03	.00
☐ 643 Tom Hausman	.11	.05	.01
☐ 644 Manny Mota	.20	.10	.02
☐ 645 George Scott DP	.11	.05	.01
☐ 646 Rick Sweet	.11	.05	.01
☐ 647 Bob Lacey	.11	.05	.01
☐ 648 Lou Piniella	.30	.15	.03
☐ 649 John Curtis	.11	.05	.01
☐ 650 Pete Rose	4.50	2.25	.45
☐ 651 Mike Caldwell	.11	.05	.01
☐ 652 Stan Papi	.11	.05	.01
☐ 653 Warren Brusstar DP	.06	.03	.00
☐ 654 Rick Miller	.11	.05	.01
☐ 655 Jerry Koosman	.30	.15	.03
☐ 656 Hosken Powell	.11	.05	.01
☐ 657 George Medich	.11	.05	.01
☐ 658 Taylor Duncan	.11	.05	.01
☐ 659 Mariners Team/Mgr.	.40	.20	.04
Darrell Johnson			
(checklist back)			
☐ 660 Ron LeFlore DP	.11	.05	.01
☐ 661 Bruce Kison	.11	.05	.01
☐ 662 Kevin Bell	.11	.05	.01
☐ 663 Mike Vail	.11	.05	.01
☐ 664 Doug Bird	.11	.05	.01
☐ 665 Lou Brock	1.75	.85	.17
☐ 666 Rich Dauer	.11	.05	.01
☐ 667 Don Hood	.11	.05	.01
☐ 668 Bill North	.11	.05	.01
☐ 669 Checklist 6	.50	.05	.01
☐ 670 Jim Hunter DP	.65	.30	.06
☐ 671 Joe Ferguson DP	.06	.03	.00
☐ 672 Ed Halicki	.11	.05	.01
☐ 673 Tom Hutton	.11	.05	.01
☐ 674 Dave Tomlin	.11	.05	.01
☐ 675 Tim McCarver	.30	.15	.03
☐ 676 Johnny Sutton	.11	.05	.01
☐ 677 Larry Parrish	.20	.10	.02
☐ 678 Geoff Zahn	.11	.05	.01
☐ 679 Derrel Thomas	.11	.05	.01
☐ 680 Carlton Fisk	3.00	1.50	.30
☐ 681 John Henry Johnson	.11	.05	.01
☐ 682 Dave Chalk	.11	.05	.01
☐ 683 Dan Meyer DP	.06	.03	.00
☐ 684 Jamie Easterly DP	.06	.03	.00
☐ 685 Sixto Lezcano	.11	.05	.01
☐ 686 Ron Schueler DP	.06	.03	.00
☐ 687 Rennie Stennett	.11	.05	.01
☐ 688 Mike Willis	.11	.05	.01
☐ 689 Orioles Team/Mgr.	.50	.25	.05
Earl Weaver			
(checklist back)			
☐ 690 Buddy Bell DP	.11	.05	.01
☐ 691 Dock Ellis DP	.06	.03	.00
☐ 692 Mickey Stanley	.11	.05	.01
☐ 693 Dave Rader	.11	.05	.01
☐ 694 Burt Hooton	.11	.05	.01
☐ 695 Keith Hernandez	2.25	1.10	.22
☐ 696 Andy Hassler	.11	.05	.01
☐ 697 Dave Bergman	.11	.05	.01
☐ 698 Bill Stein	.11	.05	.01
☐ 699 Hal Dues	.11	.05	.01
☐ 700 Reggie Jackson DP	2.50	1.25	.25
☐ 701 Orioles Prospects	.20	.10	.02
Mark Corey			
John Flinn			
Sammy Stewart			
☐ 702 Red Sox Prospects	.20	.10	.02
Joel Finch			
Garry Hancock			
Allen Ripley			
☐ 703 Angels Prospects	.11	.05	.01
Jim Anderson			
Dave Frost			
Bob Slater			
☐ 704 White Sox Prospects	.11	.05	.01
Ross Baumgarten			
Mike Colbern			
Mike Squires			
☐ 705 Indians Prospects	1.00	.50	.10
Alfredo Griffin			
Tim Norrid			
Dave Oliver			
☐ 706 Tigers Prospects	.11	.05	.01
Dave Stegman			
Dave Tobik			
Kip Young			
☐ 707 Royals Prospects	.30	.15	.03
Randy Bass			
Jim Gaudet			
Randy McGilberry			
☐ 708 Brewers Prospects	1.25	.60	.12
Kevin Bass			
Eddie Romero			
Ned Yost			
☐ 709 Twins Prospects	.11	.05	.01
Sam Perlozzo			
Rick Sofield			
Kevin Stanfield			
☐ 710 Yankees Prospects	.30	.15	.03
Brian Doyle			
Mike Heath			
Dave Rajsich			
☐ 711 A's Prospects	.30	.15	.03
Dwayne Murphy			
Bruce Robinson			
Alan Wirth			
☐ 712 Mariners Prospects	.11	.05	.01
Bud Anderson			
Greg Biercevicz			
Byron McLaughlin			
☐ 713 Rangers Prospects	1.00	.50	.10
Danny Darwin			
Pat Putnam			
Billy Sample			
☐ 714 Blue Jays Prospects	.30	.15	.03
Victor Cruz			
Pat Kelly			
Ernie Whitt			
☐ 715 Braves Prospects	.30	.15	.03
Bruce Benedict			
Glenn Hubbard			
Larry Whisenton			
☐ 716 Cubs Prospects	.11	.05	.01
Dave Geisel			
Karl Pagel			
Scot Thompson			
☐ 717 Reds Prospects	.60	.30	.06
Mike LaCoss			
Ron Oester			
Harry Spilman			
☐ 718 Astros Prospects	.11	.05	.01
Bruce Bochy			
Mike Fischlin			
Don Pisker			

□ 719 Dodgers Prospects Pedro Guerrero Rudy Law Joe Simpson	11.00	5.50	1.10
□ 720 Expos Prospects Jerry Fry Jerry Pirtle Scott Sanderson	1.00	.50	.10
□ 721 Mets Prospects Juan Berenguer Dwight Bernard Dan Norman	.30	.15	.03
□ 722 Phillies Prospects Jim Morrison Lonnie Smith Jim Wright	2.25	1.10	.22
□ 723 Pirates Prospects Dale Berra Eugenio Cotes Ben Wiltbank	.30	.15	.03
□ 724 Cardinals Prospects Tom Bruno George Frazier Terry Kennedy	.60	.30	.06
□ 725 Padres Prospects Jim Beswick Steve Mura Broderick Perkins	.11	.05	.01
□ 726 Giants Prospects Greg Johnston Joe Strain John Tamargo	.20	.10	.02

1980 Topps

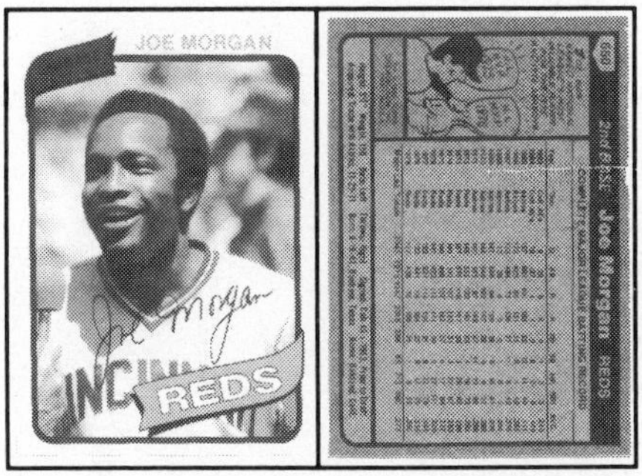

The cards in this 726-card set measure 2 1/2" by 3 1/2". In 1980 Topps released another set of the same size and number of cards as the previous two years. As with those sets, Topps again has produced 66 double-printed cards in the set; they are noted by DP in the checklist below. The player's name appears over the picture and his position and team are found in pennant design. Every card carries a facsimile autograph. Team cards feature a team checklist of players in the set on the back and the manager's name on the front. Cards 1-6 show Highlights (HL) of the 1979 season, cards 201-207 are League Leaders, and cards 661-686 feature American and National League rookie "Future Stars," one card for each team showing three young prospects. The key rookie cards in this set are Rickey Henderson, Dave Stieb, and Rick Sutcliffe.

	MINT	EXC	G-VG
COMPLETE SET (726)	275.00	135.00	27.00
COMMON PLAYER (1-726)	.10	.05	.01
COMMON DP's (1-726)	.05	.02	.00
□ 1 HL: Brock and Yaz, Enter 3000 hit circle	1.50	.75	.15
□ 2 HL: Willie McCovey, 512th homer sets new mark for NL lefties	.75	.35	.07
□ 3 HL: Manny Mota, All- time pinch-hits, 145	.20	.10	.02
□ 4 HL: Pete Rose, Career Record 10th season with 200 or more hits	2.00	1.00	.20
□ 5 HL: Garry Templeton, First with 100 hits from each side of plate	.20	.10	.02
□ 6 HL: Del Unser, 3rd cons. pinch homer sets new ML standard	.10	.05	.01
□ 7 Mike Lum	.10	.05	.01
□ 8 Craig Swan	.10	.05	.01
□ 9 Steve Braun	.10	.05	.01
□ 10 Denny Martinez	.20	.10	.02
□ 11 Jimmy Sexton	.10	.05	.01
□ 12 John Curtis DP	.05	.02	.00
□ 13 Ron Pruitt	.10	.05	.01
□ 14 Dave Cash	.10	.05	.01
□ 15 Bill Campbell	.10	.05	.01
□ 16 Jerry Narron	.10	.05	.01
□ 17 Bruce Sutter	.50	.25	.05
□ 18 Ron Jackson	.10	.05	.01
□ 19 Balor Moore	.10	.05	.01
□ 20 Dan Ford	.10	.05	.01
□ 21 Manny Sarmiento	.10	.05	.01
□ 22 Pat Putnam	.10	.05	.01
□ 23 Derrel Thomas	.10	.05	.01
□ 24 Jim Slaton	.10	.05	.01
□ 25 Lee Mazzilli	.10	.05	.01
□ 26 Marty Pattin	.10	.05	.01
□ 27 Del Unser	.10	.05	.01
□ 28 Bruce Kison	.10	.05	.01
□ 29 Mark Wagner	.10	.05	.01
□ 30 Vida Blue	.20	.10	.02
□ 31 Jay Johnstone	.15	.07	.01
□ 32 Julio Cruz DP	.10	.05	.01
□ 33 Tony Scott	.10	.05	.01
□ 34 Jeff Newman DP	.05	.02	.00
□ 35 Luis Tiant	.20	.10	.02
□ 36 Rusty Torres	.10	.05	.01
□ 37 Kiko Garcia	.10	.05	.01
□ 38 Dan Spillner DP	.05	.02	.00
□ 39 Rowland Office	.10	.05	.01
□ 40 Carlton Fisk	2.50	1.25	.25
□ 41 Rangers Team/Mgr. Pat Corrales (checklist back)	.35	.17	.03
□ 42 David Palmer	.35	.17	.03
□ 43 Bombo Rivera	.10	.05	.01
□ 44 Bill Fahey	.10	.05	.01
□ 45 Frank White	.30	.15	.03
□ 46 Rico Carty	.20	.10	.02
□ 47 Bill Bonham DP	.05	.02	.00
□ 48 Rick Miller	.10	.05	.01
□ 49 Mario Guerrero	.10	.05	.01
□ 50 J.R. Richard	.20	.10	.02
□ 51 Joe Ferguson DP	.05	.02	.00
□ 52 Warren Brusstar	.10	.05	.01
□ 53 Ben Oglivie	.20	.10	.02
□ 54 Dennis Lamp	.10	.05	.01
□ 55 Bill Madlock	.35	.17	.03
□ 56 Bobby Valentine	.20	.10	.02
□ 57 Pete Vuckovich	.10	.05	.01
□ 58 Doug Flynn	.10	.05	.01
□ 59 Eddy Putman	.10	.05	.01
□ 60 Bucky Dent	.30	.15	.03
□ 61 Gary Serum	.10	.05	.01
□ 62 Mike Ivie	.10	.05	.01
□ 63 Bob Stanley	.10	.05	.01
□ 64 Joe Nolan	.10	.05	.01
□ 65 Al Bumbry	.10	.05	.01
□ 66 Royals Team/Mgr. Jim Frey (checklist back)	.35	.17	.03
□ 67 Doyle Alexander	.15	.07	.01
□ 68 Larry Harlow	.10	.05	.01
□ 69 Rick Williams	.10	.05	.01
□ 70 Gary Carter	2.00	1.00	.20
□ 71 John Milner DP	.05	.02	.00
□ 72 Fred Howard DP	.05	.02	.00
□ 73 Dave Collins	.10	.05	.01
□ 74 Sid Monge	.10	.05	.01
□ 75 Bill Russell	.15	.07	.01
□ 76 John Stearns	.10	.05	.01
□ 77 Dave Stieb	10.00	5.00	1.00
□ 78 Ruppert Jones	.10	.05	.01
□ 79 Bob Owchinko	.10	.05	.01
□ 80 Ron LeFlore	.10	.05	.01
□ 81 Ted Sizemore	.10	.05	.01
□ 82 Astros Team/Mgr. Bill Virdon (checklist back)	.35	.17	.03
□ 83 Steve Trout	.25	.12	.02
□ 84 Gary Lavelle	.10	.05	.01
□ 85 Ted Simmons	.40	.20	.04

☐ 86 Dave Hamilton	.10	.05	.01
☐ 87 Pepe Frias	.10	.05	.01
☐ 88 Ken Landreaux	.10	.05	.01
☐ 89 Don Hood	.10	.05	.01
☐ 90 Manny Trillo	.10	.05	.01
☐ 91 Rick Dempsey	.10	.05	.01
☐ 92 Rick Rhoden	.15	.07	.01
☐ 93 Dave Roberts DP	.05	.02	.00
☐ 94 Neil Allen	.35	.17	.03
☐ 95 Cecil Cooper	.30	.15	.03
☐ 96 A's Team/Mgr.	.35	.17	.03
Jim Marshall			
(checklist back)			
☐ 97 Bill Lee	.15	.07	.01
☐ 98 Jerry Terrell	.10	.05	.01
☐ 99 Victor Cruz	.10	.05	.01
☐ 100 Johnny Bench	3.00	1.50	.30
☐ 101 Aurelio Lopez	.10	.05	.01
☐ 102 Rich Dauer	.10	.05	.01
☐ 103 Bill Caudill	.25	.12	.02
☐ 104 Manny Mota	.15	.07	.01
☐ 105 Frank Tanana	.15	.07	.01
☐ 106 Jeff Leonard	1.50	.75	.15
☐ 107 Francisco Barrios	.10	.05	.01
☐ 108 Bob Horner	.65	.30	.06
☐ 109 Bill Travers	.10	.05	.01
☐ 110 Fred Lynn DP	.30	.15	.03
☐ 111 Bob Knepper	.20	.10	.02
☐ 112 White Sox Team/Mgr.	.35	.17	.03
Tony LaRussa			
(checklist back)			
☐ 113 Geoff Zahn	.10	.05	.01
☐ 114 Juan Beniquez	.10	.05	.01
☐ 115 Sparky Lyle	.20	.10	.02
☐ 116 Larry Cox	.10	.05	.01
☐ 117 Dock Ellis	.10	.05	.01
☐ 118 Phil Garner	.10	.05	.01
☐ 119 Sammy Stewart	.10	.05	.01
☐ 120 Greg Luzinski	.20	.10	.02
☐ 121 Checklist 1	.35	.03	.00
☐ 122 Dave Rosello DP	.05	.02	.00
☐ 123 Lynn Jones	.10	.05	.01
☐ 124 Dave Lemanczyk	.10	.05	.01
☐ 125 Tony Perez	.50	.25	.05
☐ 126 Dave Tomlin	.10	.05	.01
☐ 127 Gary Thomasson	.10	.05	.01
☐ 128 Tom Burgmeier	.10	.05	.01
☐ 129 Craig Reynolds	.10	.05	.01
☐ 130 Amos Otis	.20	.10	.02
☐ 131 Paul Mitchell	.10	.05	.01
☐ 132 Biff Pocoroba	.10	.05	.01
☐ 133 Jerry Turner	.10	.05	.01
☐ 134 Matt Keough	.10	.05	.01
☐ 135 Bill Buckner	.30	.15	.03
☐ 136 Dick Ruthven	.10	.05	.01
☐ 137 John Castino	.10	.05	.01
☐ 138 Ross Baumgarten	.10	.05	.01
☐ 139 Dane Iorg	.20	.10	.02
☐ 140 Rich Gossage	.50	.25	.05
☐ 141 Gary Alexander	.10	.05	.01
☐ 142 Phil Huffman	.10	.05	.01
☐ 143 Bruce Bochte DP	.10	.05	.01
☐ 144 Steve Comer	.10	.05	.01
☐ 145 Darrell Evans	.30	.15	.03
☐ 146 Bob Welch	2.50	1.25	.25
☐ 147 Terry Puhl	.15	.07	.01
☐ 148 Manny Sanguillen	.15	.07	.01
☐ 149 Tom Hume	.10	.05	.01
☐ 150 Jason Thompson	.10	.05	.01
☐ 151 Tom Hausman DP	.05	.02	.00
☐ 152 John Fulgham	.10	.05	.01
☐ 153 Tim Blackwell	.10	.05	.01
☐ 154 Lary Sorensen	.10	.05	.01
☐ 155 Jerry Remy	.10	.05	.01
☐ 156 Tony Brizzolara	.10	.05	.01
☐ 157 Willie Wilson DP	.20	.10	.02
☐ 158 Rob Picciolo DP	.05	.02	.00
☐ 159 Ken Clay	.10	.05	.01
☐ 160 Eddie Murray	5.00	2.50	.50
☐ 161 Larry Christenson	.10	.05	.01
☐ 162 Bob Randall	.10	.05	.01
☐ 163 Steve Swisher	.10	.05	.01
☐ 164 Greg Pryor	.10	.05	.01
☐ 165 Omar Moreno	.10	.05	.01
☐ 166 Glenn Abbott	.10	.05	.01
☐ 167 Jack Clark	2.00	1.00	.20
☐ 168 Rick Waits	.10	.05	.01
☐ 169 Luis Gomez	.10	.05	.01
☐ 170 Burt Hooton	.10	.05	.01
☐ 171 Fernando Gonzalez	.10	.05	.01
☐ 172 Ron Hodges	.10	.05	.01
☐ 173 John Henry Johnson	.10	.05	.01
☐ 174 Ray Knight	.20	.10	.02
☐ 175 Rick Reuschel	.35	.17	.03
☐ 176 Champ Summers	.10	.05	.01
☐ 177 Dave Heaverlo	.10	.05	.01
☐ 178 Tim McCarver	.30	.15	.03
☐ 179 Ron Davis	.20	.10	.02
☐ 180 Warren Cromartie	.10	.05	.01
☐ 181 Moose Haas	.10	.05	.01
☐ 182 Ken Reitz	.10	.05	.01
☐ 183 Jim Anderson DP	.05	.02	.00
☐ 184 Steve Renko DP	.05	.02	.00
☐ 185 Hal McRae	.20	.10	.02
☐ 186 Junior Moore	.10	.05	.01
☐ 187 Alan Ashby	.10	.05	.01
☐ 188 Terry Crowley	.10	.05	.01
☐ 189 Kevin Kobel	.10	.05	.01
☐ 190 Buddy Bell	.30	.15	.03
☐ 191 Ted Martinez	.10	.05	.01
☐ 192 Braves Team/Mgr.	.35	.17	.03
Bobby Cox			
(checklist back)			
☐ 193 Dave Goltz	.10	.05	.01
☐ 194 Mike Easler	.15	.07	.01
☐ 195 John Montefusco	.15	.07	.01
☐ 196 Lance Parrish	2.00	1.00	.20
☐ 197 Byron McLaughlin	.10	.05	.01
☐ 198 Dell Alston DP	.05	.02	.00
☐ 199 Mike LaCoss	.20	.10	.02
☐ 200 Jim Rice	1.25	.60	.12
☐ 201 Batting Leaders	.30	.15	.03
Keith Hernandez			
Fred Lynn			
☐ 202 Home Run Leaders	.20	.10	.02
Dave Kingman			
Gorman Thomas			
☐ 203 RBI Leaders	.30	.15	.03
Dave Winfield			
Don Baylor			
☐ 204 Stolen Base Leaders	.20	.10	.02
Omar Moreno			
Willie Wilson			
☐ 205 Victory Leaders	.20	.10	.02
Joe Niekro			
Phil Niekro			
Mike Flanagan			
☐ 206 Strikeout Leaders	1.50	.75	.15
J.R. Richard			
Nolan Ryan			
☐ 207 ERA Leaders	.20	.10	.02
J.R. Richard			
Ron Guidry			
☐ 208 Wayne Cage	.10	.05	.01
☐ 209 Von Joshua	.10	.05	.01
☐ 210 Steve Carlton	2.50	1.25	.25
☐ 211 Dave Skaggs DP	.05	.02	.00
☐ 212 Dave Roberts	.10	.05	.01
☐ 213 Mike Jorgensen DP	.05	.02	.00
☐ 214 Angels Team/Mgr.	.35	.17	.03
Jim Fregosi			
(checklist back)			
☐ 215 Sixto Lezcano	.10	.05	.01
☐ 216 Phil Mankowski	.10	.05	.01
☐ 217 Ed Halicki	.10	.05	.01
☐ 218 Jose Morales	.10	.05	.01
☐ 219 Steve Mingori	.10	.05	.01
☐ 220 Dave Concepcion	.30	.15	.03
☐ 221 Joe Cannon	.10	.05	.01
☐ 222 Ron Hassey	.40	.20	.04
☐ 223 Bob Sykes	.10	.05	.01
☐ 224 Willie Montanez	.10	.05	.01
☐ 225 Lou Piniella	.30	.15	.03
☐ 226 Bill Stein	.10	.05	.01
☐ 227 Len Barker	.10	.05	.01
☐ 228 Johnny Oates	.10	.05	.01
☐ 229 Jim Bibby	.10	.05	.01
☐ 230 Dave Winfield	2.25	1.10	.22
☐ 231 Steve McCatty	.10	.05	.01
☐ 232 Alan Trammell	3.50	1.75	.35
☐ 233 LaRue Washington	.10	.05	.01
☐ 234 Vern Ruhle	.10	.05	.01
☐ 235 Andre Dawson	3.75	1.85	.37
☐ 236 Marc Hill	.10	.05	.01
☐ 237 Scott McGregor	.20	.10	.02
☐ 238 Rob Wilfong	.10	.05	.01
☐ 239 Don Aase	.10	.05	.01
☐ 240 Dave Kingman	.35	.17	.03
☐ 241 Checklist 2	.35	.03	.00
☐ 242 Lamar Johnson	.10	.05	.01
☐ 243 Jerry Augustine	.10	.05	.01
☐ 244 Cardinals Team/Mgr.	.35	.17	.03
Ken Boyer			
(checklist back)			
☐ 245 Phil Niekro	.90	.45	.09
☐ 246 Tim Foli DP	.05	.02	.00
☐ 247 Frank Riccelli	.10	.05	.01
☐ 248 Jamie Quirk	.10	.05	.01

☐ 249	Jim Clancy	.10	.05	.01
☐ 250	Jim Kaat	.40	.20	.04
☐ 251	Kip Young	.10	.05	.01
☐ 252	Ted Cox	.10	.05	.01
☐ 253	John Montague	.10	.05	.01
☐ 254	Paul Dade DP	.05	.02	.00
☐ 255	Dusty Baker DP	.10	.05	.01
☐ 256	Roger Erickson	.10	.05	.01
☐ 257	Larry Herndon	.10	.05	.01
☐ 258	Paul Moskau	.10	.05	.01
☐ 259	Mets Team/Mgr.	.40	.20	.04
	Joe Torre			
	(checklist back)			
☐ 260	Al Oliver	.30	.15	.03
☐ 261	Dave Chalk	.10	.05	.01
☐ 262	Benny Ayala	.10	.05	.01
☐ 263	Dave LaRoche DP	.05	.02	.00
☐ 264	Bill Robinson	.20	.10	.02
☐ 265	Robin Yount	5.00	2.50	.50
☐ 266	Bernie Carbo	.10	.05	.01
☐ 267	Dan Schatzeder	.10	.05	.01
☐ 268	Rafael Landestoy	.10	.05	.01
☐ 269	Dave Tobik	.10	.05	.01
☐ 270	Mike Schmidt DP	3.50	1.75	.35
☐ 271	Dick Drago DP	.05	.02	.00
☐ 272	Ralph Garr	.10	.05	.01
☐ 273	Eduardo Rodriguez	.10	.05	.01
☐ 274	Dale Murphy	6.50	3.25	.65
☐ 275	Jerry Koosman	.30	.15	.03
☐ 276	Tom Veryzer	.10	.05	.01
☐ 277	Rick Bosetti	.10	.05	.01
☐ 278	Jim Spencer	.10	.05	.01
☐ 279	Rob Andrews	.10	.05	.01
☐ 280	Gaylord Perry	1.00	.50	.10
☐ 281	Paul Blair	.10	.05	.01
☐ 282	Mariners Team/Mgr.	.35	.17	.03
	Darrell Johnson			
	(checklist back)			
☐ 283	John Ellis	.10	.05	.01
☐ 284	Larry Murray DP	.05	.02	.00
☐ 285	Don Baylor	.40	.20	.04
☐ 286	Darold Knowles DP	.05	.02	.00
☐ 287	John Lowenstein	.10	.05	.01
☐ 288	Dave Rozema	.10	.05	.01
☐ 289	Bruce Bochy	.10	.05	.01
☐ 290	Steve Garvey	2.00	1.00	.20
☐ 291	Randy Scarberry	.10	.05	.01
☐ 292	Dale Berra	.10	.05	.01
☐ 293	Elias Sosa	.10	.05	.01
☐ 294	Charlie Spikes	.10	.05	.01
☐ 295	Larry Gura	.10	.05	.01
☐ 296	Dave Rader	.10	.05	.01
☐ 297	Tim Johnson	.10	.05	.01
☐ 298	Ken Holtzman	.15	.07	.01
☐ 299	Steve Henderson	.10	.05	.01
☐ 300	Ron Guidry	.75	.35	.07
☐ 301	Mike Edwards	.10	.05	.01
☐ 302	Dodgers Team/Mgr.	.50	.25	.05
	Tom Lasorda			
	(checklist back)			
☐ 303	Bill Castro	.10	.05	.01
☐ 304	Butch Wynegar	.10	.05	.01
☐ 305	Randy Jones	.10	.05	.01
☐ 306	Denny Walling	.10	.05	.01
☐ 307	Rick Honeycutt	.15	.07	.01
☐ 308	Mike Hargrove	.15	.07	.01
☐ 309	Larry McWilliams	.10	.05	.01
☐ 310	Dave Parker	1.50	.75	.15
☐ 311	Roger Metzger	.10	.05	.01
☐ 312	Mike Barlow	.10	.05	.01
☐ 313	Johnny Grubb	.10	.05	.01
☐ 314	Tim Stoddard	.15	.07	.01
☐ 315	Steve Kemp	.15	.07	.01
☐ 316	Bob Lacey	.10	.05	.01
☐ 317	Mike Anderson DP	.05	.02	.00
☐ 318	Jerry Reuss	.15	.07	.01
☐ 319	Chris Speier	.10	.05	.01
☐ 320	Dennis Eckersley	1.25	.60	.12
☐ 321	Keith Hernandez	1.50	.75	.15
☐ 322	Claudell Washington	.20	.10	.02
☐ 323	Mick Kelleher	.10	.05	.01
☐ 324	Tom Underwood	.10	.05	.01
☐ 325	Dan Driessen	.10	.05	.01
☐ 326	Bo McLaughlin	.10	.05	.01
☐ 327	Ray Fosse DP	.05	.02	.00
☐ 328	Twins Team/Mgr.	.35	.17	.03
	Gene Mauch			
	(checklist back)			
☐ 329	Bert Roberge	.10	.05	.01
☐ 330	Al Cowens	.10	.05	.01
☐ 331	Richie Hebner	.10	.05	.01
☐ 332	Enrique Romo	.10	.05	.01
☐ 333	Jim Norris DP	.05	.02	.00
☐ 334	Jim Beattie	.10	.05	.01

☐ 335	Willie McCovey	1.50	.75	.15
☐ 336	George Medich	.10	.05	.01
☐ 337	Carney Lansford	1.75	.85	.17
☐ 338	John Wockenfuss	.10	.05	.01
☐ 339	John D'Acquisto	.10	.05	.01
☐ 340	Ken Singleton	.15	.07	.01
☐ 341	Jim Essian	.10	.05	.01
☐ 342	Odell Jones	.10	.05	.01
☐ 343	Mike Vail	.10	.05	.01
☐ 344	Randy Lerch	.10	.05	.01
☐ 345	Larry Parrish	.15	.07	.01
☐ 346	Buddy Solomon	.10	.05	.01
☐ 347	Harry Chappas	.10	.05	.01
☐ 348	Checklist 3	.35	.03	.00
☐ 349	Jack Brohamer	.10	.05	.01
☐ 350	George Hendrick	.15	.07	.01
☐ 351	Bob Davis	.10	.05	.01
☐ 352	Dan Briggs	.10	.05	.01
☐ 353	Andy Hassler	.10	.05	.01
☐ 354	Rick Auerbach	.10	.05	.01
☐ 355	Gary Matthews	.15	.07	.01
☐ 356	Padres Team/Mgr.	.35	.17	.03
	Jerry Coleman			
	(checklist back)			
☐ 357	Bob McClure	.10	.05	.01
☐ 358	Lou Whitaker	1.50	.75	.15
☐ 359	Randy Moffitt	.10	.05	.01
☐ 360	Darrell Porter DP	.10	.05	.01
☐ 361	Wayne Garland	.10	.05	.01
☐ 362	Danny Goodwin	.10	.05	.01
☐ 363	Wayne Gross	.10	.05	.01
☐ 364	Ray Burris	.10	.05	.01
☐ 365	Bobby Murcer	.30	.15	.03
☐ 366	Rob Dressler	.10	.05	.01
☐ 367	Billy Smith	.10	.05	.01
☐ 368	Willie Aikens	.25	.12	.02
☐ 369	Jim Kern	.10	.05	.01
☐ 370	Cesar Cedeno	.20	.10	.02
☐ 371	Jack Morris	1.00	.50	.10
☐ 372	Joel Youngblood	.10	.05	.01
☐ 373	Dan Petry DP	.50	.25	.05
☐ 374	Jim Gantner	.20	.10	.02
☐ 375	Ross Grimsley	.10	.05	.01
☐ 376	Gary Allenson	.10	.05	.01
☐ 377	Junior Kennedy	.10	.05	.01
☐ 378	Jerry Mumphrey	.10	.05	.01
☐ 379	Kevin Bell	.10	.05	.01
☐ 380	Garry Maddox	.15	.07	.01
☐ 381	Cubs Team/Mgr.	.35	.17	.03
	Preston Gomez			
	(checklist back)			
☐ 382	Dave Freisleben	.10	.05	.01
☐ 383	Ed Ott	.10	.05	.01
☐ 384	Joey McLaughlin	.10	.05	.01
☐ 385	Enos Cabell	.10	.05	.01
☐ 386	Darrell Jackson	.10	.05	.01
☐ 387A	Fred Stanley	1.00	.50	.10
	(yellow name on front)			
☐ 387B	Fred Stanley	.10	.05	.01
	(red name on front)			
☐ 388	Mike Paxton	.10	.05	.01
☐ 389	Pete LaCock	.10	.05	.01
☐ 390	Fergie Jenkins	.60	.22	.04
☐ 391	Tony Armas DP	.10	.05	.01
☐ 392	Milt Wilcox	.10	.05	.01
☐ 393	Ozzie Smith	8.00	4.00	.80
☐ 394	Reggie Cleveland	.10	.05	.01
☐ 395	Ellis Valentine	.10	.05	.01
☐ 396	Dan Meyer	.10	.05	.01
☐ 397	Roy Thomas DP	.05	.02	.00
☐ 398	Barry Foote	.10	.05	.01
☐ 399	Mike Proly DP	.05	.02	.00
☐ 400	George Foster	.50	.25	.05
☐ 401	Pete Falcone	.10	.05	.01
☐ 402	Merv Rettenmund	.10	.05	.01
☐ 403	Pete Redfern DP	.05	.02	.00
☐ 404	Orioles Team/Mgr.	.40	.20	.04
	Earl Weaver			
	(checklist back)			
☐ 405	Dwight Evans	1.00	.50	.10
☐ 406	Paul Molitor	1.50	.75	.15
☐ 407	Tony Solaita	.10	.05	.01
☐ 408	Bill North	.10	.05	.01
☐ 409	Paul Splittorff	.10	.05	.01
☐ 410	Bobby Bonds	.35	.17	.03
☐ 411	Frank LaCorte	.10	.05	.01
☐ 412	Thad Bosley	.10	.05	.01
☐ 413	Allen Ripley	.10	.05	.01
☐ 414	George Scott	.10	.05	.01
☐ 415	Bill Atkinson	.10	.05	.01
☐ 416	Tom Brookens	.10	.05	.01
☐ 417	Craig Chamberlain DP	.05	.02	.00
☐ 418	Roger Freed DP	.05	.02	.00
☐ 419	Vic Correll	.10	.05	.01

☐ 420 Butch Hobson	.10	.05	.01
☐ 421 Doug Bird	.10	.05	.01
☐ 422 Larry Milbourne	.10	.05	.01
☐ 423 Dave Frost	.10	.05	.01
☐ 424 Yankees Team/Mgr. Dick Howser (checklist back)	.40	.20	.04
☐ 425 Mark Belanger	.15	.07	.01
☐ 426 Grant Jackson	.10	.05	.01
☐ 427 Tom Hutton DP	.05	.02	.00
☐ 428 Pat Zachry	.10	.05	.01
☐ 429 Duane Kuiper	.10	.05	.01
☐ 430 Larry Hisle DP	.10	.05	.01
☐ 431 Mike Krukow	.15	.07	.01
☐ 432 Willie Norwood	.10	.05	.01
☐ 433 Rich Gale	.10	.05	.01
☐ 434 Johnnie LeMaster	.10	.05	.01
☐ 435 Don Gullett	.20	.10	.02
☐ 436 Billy Almon	.10	.05	.01
☐ 437 Joe Niekro	.25	.12	.02
☐ 438 Dave Revering	.10	.05	.01
☐ 439 Mike Phillips	.10	.05	.01
☐ 440 Don Sutton	1.00	.50	.10
☐ 441 Eric Soderholm	.10	.05	.01
☐ 442 Jorge Orta	.10	.05	.01
☐ 443 Mike Parrott	.10	.05	.01
☐ 444 Alvis Woods	.10	.05	.01
☐ 445 Mark Fidrych	.20	.10	.02
☐ 446 Duffy Dyer	.10	.05	.01
☐ 447 Nino Espinosa	.10	.05	.01
☐ 448 Jim Wohlford	.10	.05	.01
☐ 449 Doug Bair	.10	.05	.01
☐ 450 George Brett	6.50	3.25	.65
☐ 451 Indians Team/Mgr. Dave Garcia (checklist back)	.35	.17	.03
☐ 452 Steve Dillard	.10	.05	.01
☐ 453 Mike Bacsik	.10	.05	.01
☐ 454 Tom Donohue	.10	.05	.01
☐ 455 Mike Torrez	.10	.05	.01
☐ 456 Frank Taveras	.10	.05	.01
☐ 457 Bert Blyleven	.60	.30	.06
☐ 458 Billy Sample	.10	.05	.01
☐ 459 Mickey Lolich DP	.10	.05	.01
☐ 460 Willie Randolph	.30	.15	.03
☐ 461 Dwayne Murphy	.10	.05	.01
☐ 462 Mike Sadek DP	.05	.02	.00
☐ 463 Jerry Royster	.10	.05	.01
☐ 464 John Denny	.15	.07	.01
☐ 465 Rick Monday	.15	.07	.01
☐ 466 Mike Squires	.10	.05	.01
☐ 467 Jesse Jefferson	.10	.05	.01
☐ 468 Aurelio Rodriguez	.10	.05	.01
☐ 469 Randy Niemann DP	.05	.02	.00
☐ 470 Bob Boone	.40	.20	.04
☐ 471 Hosken Powell DP	.05	.02	.00
☐ 472 Willie Hernandez	.20	.10	.02
☐ 473 Bump Wills	.10	.05	.01
☐ 474 Steve Busby	.10	.05	.01
☐ 475 Cesar Geronimo	.10	.05	.01
☐ 476 Bob Shirley	.10	.05	.01
☐ 477 Buck Martinez	.10	.05	.01
☐ 478 Gil Flores	.10	.05	.01
☐ 479 Expos Team/Mgr. Dick Williams (checklist back)	.30	.15	.03
☐ 480 Bob Watson	.15	.07	.01
☐ 481 Tom Paciorek	.10	.05	.01
☐ 482 Rickey Henderson	180.00	90.00	18.00
☐ 483 Bo Diaz	.10	.05	.01
☐ 484 Checklist 4	.35	.03	.00
☐ 485 Mickey Rivers	.15	.07	.01
☐ 486 Mike Tyson DP	.05	.02	.00
☐ 487 Wayne Nordhagen	.10	.05	.01
☐ 488 Roy Howell	.10	.05	.01
☐ 489 Preston Hanna DP	.05	.02	.00
☐ 490 Lee May	.10	.05	.01
☐ 491 Steve Mura DP	.05	.02	.00
☐ 492 Todd Cruz	.10	.05	.01
☐ 493 Jerry Martin	.10	.05	.01
☐ 494 Craig Minetto	.10	.05	.01
☐ 495 Bake McBride	.10	.05	.01
☐ 496 Silvio Martinez	.10	.05	.01
☐ 497 Jim Mason	.10	.05	.01
☐ 498 Danny Darwin	.25	.12	.02
☐ 499 Giants Team/Mgr. Dave Bristol (checklist back)	.35	.17	.03
☐ 500 Tom Seaver	2.50	1.25	.25
☐ 501 Rennie Stennett	.10	.05	.01
☐ 502 Rich Wortham DP	.05	.02	.00
☐ 503 Mike Cubbage	.10	.05	.01
☐ 504 Gene Garber	.10	.05	.01
☐ 505 Bert Campaneris	.15	.07	.01
☐ 506 Tom Buskey	.10	.05	.01
☐ 507 Leon Roberts	.10	.05	.01
☐ 508 U.L. Washington	.10	.05	.01
☐ 509 Ed Glynn	.10	.05	.01
☐ 510 Ron Cey	.30	.15	.03
☐ 511 Eric Wilkins	.10	.05	.01
☐ 512 Jose Cardenal	.10	.05	.01
☐ 513 Tom Dixon DP	.05	.02	.00
☐ 514 Steve Ontiveros	.10	.05	.01
☐ 515 Mike Caldwell	.10	.05	.01
☐ 516 Hector Cruz	.10	.05	.01
☐ 517 Don Stanhouse	.10	.05	.01
☐ 518 Nelson Norman	.10	.05	.01
☐ 519 Steve Nicosia	.10	.05	.01
☐ 520 Steve Rogers	.10	.05	.01
☐ 521 Ken Brett	.10	.05	.01
☐ 522 Jim Morrison	.10	.05	.01
☐ 523 Ken Henderson	.10	.05	.01
☐ 524 Jim Wright DP	.05	.02	.00
☐ 525 Clint Hurdle	.10	.05	.01
☐ 526 Phillies Team/Mgr. Dallas Green (checklist back)	.40	.20	.04
☐ 527 Doug Rau DP	.05	.02	.00
☐ 528 Adrian Devine	.10	.05	.01
☐ 529 Jim Barr	.10	.05	.01
☐ 530 Jim Sundberg DP	.10	.05	.01
☐ 531 Eric Rasmussen	.10	.05	.01
☐ 532 Willie Horton	.15	.07	.01
☐ 533 Checklist 5	.35	.03	.00
☐ 534 Andre Thornton	.15	.07	.01
☐ 535 Bob Forsch	.10	.05	.01
☐ 536 Lee Lacy	.10	.05	.01
☐ 537 Alex Trevino	.20	.10	.02
☐ 538 Joe Strain	.10	.05	.01
☐ 539 Rudy May	.10	.05	.01
☐ 540 Pete Rose	4.00	2.00	.40
☐ 541 Miguel Dilone	.10	.05	.01
☐ 542 Joe Coleman	.10	.05	.01
☐ 543 Pat Kelly	.10	.05	.01
☐ 544 Rick Sutcliffe	3.25	1.60	.32
☐ 545 Jeff Burroughs	.10	.05	.01
☐ 546 Rick Langford	.10	.05	.01
☐ 547 John Wathan	.20	.10	.02
☐ 548 Dave Rajsich	.10	.05	.01
☐ 549 Larry Wolfe	.10	.05	.01
☐ 550 Ken Griffey	.45	.22	.04
☐ 551 Pirates Team/Mgr. Chuck Tanner (checklist back)	.35	.17	.03
☐ 552 Bill Nahorodny	.10	.05	.01
☐ 553 Dick Davis	.10	.05	.01
☐ 554 Art Howe	.20	.10	.02
☐ 555 Ed Figueroa	.10	.05	.01
☐ 556 Joe Rudi	.15	.07	.01
☐ 557 Mark Lee	.10	.05	.01
☐ 558 Alfredo Griffin	.20	.10	.02
☐ 559 Dale Murray	.10	.05	.01
☐ 560 Dave Lopes	.15	.07	.01
☐ 561 Eddie Whitson	.20	.10	.02
☐ 562 Joe Wallis	.10	.05	.01
☐ 563 Will McEnaney	.10	.05	.01
☐ 564 Rick Manning	.10	.05	.01
☐ 565 Dennis Leonard	.15	.07	.01
☐ 566 Bud Harrelson	.15	.07	.01
☐ 567 Skip Lockwood	.10	.05	.01
☐ 568 Gary Roenicke	.15	.07	.01
☐ 569 Terry Kennedy	.20	.10	.02
☐ 570 Roy Smalley	.10	.05	.01
☐ 571 Joe Sambito	.10	.05	.01
☐ 572 Jerry Morales DP	.05	.02	.00
☐ 573 Kent Tekulve	.15	.07	.01
☐ 574 Scot Thompson	.10	.05	.01
☐ 575 Ken Kravec	.10	.05	.01
☐ 576 Jim Dwyer	.10	.05	.01
☐ 577 Blue Jays Team/Mgr. Bobby Mattick (checklist back)	.30	.15	.03
☐ 578 Scott Sanderson	.25	.12	.02
☐ 579 Charlie Moore	.10	.05	.01
☐ 580 Nolan Ryan	12.00	6.00	1.20
☐ 581 Bob Bailor	.10	.05	.01
☐ 582 Brian Doyle	.10	.05	.01
☐ 583 Bob Stinson	.10	.05	.01
☐ 584 Kurt Bevacqua	.10	.05	.01
☐ 585 Al Hrabosky	.15	.07	.01
☐ 586 Mitchell Page	.10	.05	.01
☐ 587 Garry Templeton	.20	.10	.02
☐ 588 Greg Minton	.10	.05	.01
☐ 589 Chet Lemon	.10	.05	.01
☐ 590 Jim Palmer	2.25	1.10	.22
☐ 591 Rick Cerone	.10	.05	.01
☐ 592 Jon Matlack	.15	.07	.01
☐ 593 Jesus Alou	.10	.05	.01

☐ 594 Dick Tidrow	.10	.05	.01
☐ 595 Don Money	.10	.05	.01
☐ 596 Rick Matula	.10	.05	.01
☐ 597 Tom Poquette	.10	.05	.01
☐ 598 Fred Kendall DP	.05	.02	.00
☐ 599 Mike Norris	.10	.05	.01
☐ 600 Reggie Jackson	3.50	1.75	.35
☐ 601 Buddy Schultz	.10	.05	.01
☐ 602 Brian Downing	.15	.07	.01
☐ 603 Jack Billingham DP	.05	.02	.00
☐ 604 Glenn Adams	.10	.05	.01
☐ 605 Terry Forster	.15	.07	.01
☐ 606 Reds Team/Mgr. John McNamara (checklist back)	.35	.17	.03
☐ 607 Woodie Fryman	.10	.05	.01
☐ 608 Alan Bannister	.10	.05	.01
☐ 609 Ron Reed	.10	.05	.01
☐ 610 Willie Stargell	1.50	.75	.15
☐ 611 Jerry Garvin DP	.05	.02	.00
☐ 612 Cliff Johnson	.10	.05	.01
☐ 613 Randy Stein	.10	.05	.01
☐ 614 John Hiller	.15	.07	.01
☐ 615 Doug DeCinces	.15	.07	.01
☐ 616 Gene Richards	.10	.05	.01
☐ 617 Joaquin Andujar	.15	.07	.01
☐ 618 Bob Montgomery DP	.05	.02	.00
☐ 619 Sergio Ferrer	.10	.05	.01
☐ 620 Richie Zisk	.10	.05	.01
☐ 621 Bob Grich	.20	.10	.02
☐ 622 Mario Soto	.15	.07	.01
☐ 623 Gorman Thomas	.20	.10	.02
☐ 624 Lerrin LaGrow	.10	.05	.01
☐ 625 Chris Chambliss	.15	.07	.01
☐ 626 Tigers Team/Mgr. Sparky Anderson (checklist back)	.40	.20	.04
☐ 627 Pedro Borbon	.10	.05	.01
☐ 628 Doug Capilla	.10	.05	.01
☐ 629 Jim Todd	.10	.05	.01
☐ 630 Larry Bowa	.30	.15	.03
☐ 631 Mark Littell	.10	.05	.01
☐ 632 Barry Bonnell	.10	.05	.01
☐ 633 Bob Apodaca	.10	.05	.01
☐ 634 Glenn Borgmann DP	.05	.02	.00
☐ 635 John Candelaria	.25	.12	.02
☐ 636 Toby Harrah	.15	.07	.01
☐ 637 Joe Simpson	.10	.05	.01
☐ 638 Mark Clear	.20	.10	.02
☐ 639 Larry Biittner	.10	.05	.01
☐ 640 Mike Flanagan	.20	.10	.02
☐ 641 Ed Kranepool	.10	.05	.01
☐ 642 Ken Forsch DP	.10	.05	.01
☐ 643 John Mayberry	.15	.07	.01
☐ 644 Charlie Hough	.15	.07	.01
☐ 645 Rick Burleson	.20	.10	.02
☐ 646 Checklist 6	.35	.03	.00
☐ 647 Milt May	.10	.05	.01
☐ 648 Roy White	.15	.07	.01
☐ 649 Tom Griffin	.10	.05	.01
☐ 650 Joe Morgan	2.00	1.00	.20
☐ 651 Rollie Fingers	.75	.35	.07
☐ 652 Mario Mendoza	.10	.05	.01
☐ 653 Stan Bahnsen	.10	.05	.01
☐ 654 Bruce Boisclair DP	.05	.02	.00
☐ 655 Tug McGraw	.30	.15	.03
☐ 656 Larvell Blanks	.10	.05	.01
☐ 657 Dave Edwards	.10	.05	.01
☐ 658 Chris Knapp	.10	.05	.01
☐ 659 Brewers Team/Mgr. George Bamberger (checklist back)	.35	.17	.03
☐ 660 Rusty Staub	.30	.15	.03
☐ 661 Orioles Rookies Mark Corey Dave Ford Wayne Krenchicki	.15	.07	.01
☐ 662 Red Sox Rookies Joel Finch Mike O'Berry Chuck Rainey	.15	.07	.01
☐ 663 Angels Rookies Ralph Botting Bob Clark Dickie Thon	.75	.35	.07
☐ 664 White Sox Rookies Mike Colbern Guy Hoffman Dewey Robinson	.15	.07	.01
☐ 665 Indians Rookies Larry Andersen Bobby Cuellar Sandy Wihtol	.40	.20	.04
☐ 666 Tigers Rookies Mike Chris Al Greene Bruce Robbins	.15	.07	.01
☐ 667 Royals Rookies Renie Martin Bill Paschall Dan Quisenberry	1.50	.75	.15
☐ 668 Brewers Rookies Danny Boitano Willie Mueller Lenn Sakata	.15	.07	.01
☐ 669 Twins Rookies Dan Graham Rick Sofield Gary Ward	.50	.25	.05
☐ 670 Yankees Rookies Bobby Brown Brad Gulden Darryl Jones	.15	.07	.01
☐ 671 A's Rookies Derek Bryant Brian Kingman Mike Morgan	.75	.35	.07
☐ 672 Mariners Rookies Charlie Beamon Rodney Craig Rafael Vasquez	.15	.07	.01
☐ 673 Rangers Rookies Brian Allard Jerry Don Gleaton Greg Mahlberg	.15	.07	.01
☐ 674 Blue Jays Rookies Butch Edge Pat Kelly Ted Wilborn	.15	.07	.01
☐ 675 Braves Rookies Bruce Benedict Larry Bradford Eddie Miller	.15	.07	.01
☐ 676 Cubs Rookies Dave Geisel Steve Macko Karl Pagel	.15	.07	.01
☐ 677 Reds Rookies Art DeFreites Frank Pastore Harry Spilman	.15	.07	.01
☐ 678 Astros Rookies Reggie Baldwin Alan Knicely Pete Ladd	.15	.07	.01
☐ 679 Dodgers Rookies Joe Beckwith Mickey Hatcher Dave Patterson	.45	.22	.04
☐ 680 Expos Rookies Tony Bernazard Randy Miller John Tamargo	.40	.20	.04
☐ 681 Mets Rookies Dan Norman Jesse Orosco Mike Scott	9.00	4.50	.90
☐ 682 Phillies Rookies Ramon Aviles Dickie Noles Kevin Saucier	.20	.10	.02
☐ 683 Pirates Rookies Dorian Boyland Alberto Lois Harry Saferight	.15	.07	.01
☐ 684 Cardinals Rookies George Frazier Tom Herr Dan O'Brien	1.50	.75	.15
☐ 685 Padres Rookies Tim Flannery Brian Greer Jim Wilhelm	.30	.15	.03
☐ 686 Giants Rookies Greg Johnston Dennis Littlejohn Phil Nastu	.15	.07	.01
☐ 687 Mike Heath DP	.05	.02	.00
☐ 688 Steve Stone	.15	.07	.01
☐ 689 Red Sox Team/Mgr. Don Zimmer (checklist back)	.40	.20	.04
☐ 690 Tommy John	.50	.25	.05
☐ 691 Ivan DeJesus	.10	.05	.01
☐ 692 Rawly Eastwick DP	.05	.02	.00
☐ 693 Craig Kusick	.10	.05	.01
☐ 694 Jim Rooker	.10	.05	.01

☐ 695 Reggie Smith	.20	.10	.02
☐ 696 Julio Gonzalez	.10	.05	.01
☐ 697 David Clyde	.10	.05	.01
☐ 698 Oscar Gamble	.10	.05	.01
☐ 699 Floyd Bannister	.10	.05	.01
☐ 700 Rod Carew DP	1.25	.60	.12
☐ 701 Ken Oberkfell	.30	.15	.03
☐ 702 Ed Farmer	.10	.05	.01
☐ 703 Otto Velez	.10	.05	.01
☐ 704 Gene Tenace	.15	.07	.01
☐ 705 Freddie Patek	.10	.05	.01
☐ 706 Tippy Martinez	.10	.05	.01
☐ 707 Elliott Maddox	.10	.05	.01
☐ 708 Bob Tolan	.10	.05	.01
☐ 709 Pat Underwood	.10	.05	.01
☐ 710 Graig Nettles	.30	.15	.03
☐ 711 Bob Galasso	.10	.05	.01
☐ 712 Rodney Scott	.10	.05	.01
☐ 713 Terry Whitfield	.10	.05	.01
☐ 714 Fred Norman	.10	.05	.01
☐ 715 Sal Bando	.15	.07	.01
☐ 716 Lynn McGlothen	.10	.05	.01
☐ 717 Mickey Klutts DP	.05	.02	.00
☐ 718 Greg Gross	.10	.05	.01
☐ 719 Don Robinson	.20	.10	.02
☐ 720 Carl Yastrzemski DP	1.75	.85	.17
☐ 721 Paul Hartzell	.10	.05	.01
☐ 722 Jose Cruz	.15	.07	.01
☐ 723 Shane Rawley	.15	.07	.01
☐ 724 Jerry White	.10	.05	.01
☐ 725 Rick Wise	.10	.05	.01
☐ 726 Steve Yeager	.15	.07	.01

1981 Topps

The cards in this 726-card set measure 2 1/2" by 3 1/2". League Leaders (1-8), Record Breakers (201-208), and Post-season cards (401-404) are topical subsets found in this set marketed by Topps in 1981. The team cards are all grouped together (661-686) and feature team checklist backs and a very small photo of the team's manager in the upper right corner of the obverse. The obverses carry the player's position and team in a baseball cap design, and the company name is printed in a small baseball. The backs are red and gray. The 66 double-printed cards are noted in the checklist by DP. The set is quite popular with collectors partly due to the presence of rookie cards of Fernando Valenzuela, Tim Raines, Kirk Gibson, Harold Baines, John Tudor, Lloyd Moseby, Hubie Brooks, Mike Boddicker, and Tony Pena.

	MINT	EXC	G-VG
COMPLETE SET (726)	110.00	55.00	11.00
COMMON PLAYER (1-726)	.08	.04	.01
COMMON DP's (1-726)	.04	.02	.00
☐ 1 Batting Leaders	.90	.25	.05
George Brett			
Bill Buckner			
☐ 2 Home Run Leaders	.40	.20	.04
Reggie Jackson			
Ben Oglivie			
Mike Schmidt			
☐ 3 RBI Leaders	.25	.12	.02
Cecil Cooper			
Mike Schmidt			
☐ 4 Stolen Base Leaders	.90	.45	.09
Rickey Henderson			
Ron LeFlore			
☐ 5 Victory Leaders	.15	.07	.01
Steve Stone			
Steve Carlton			
☐ 6 Strikeout Leaders	.15	.07	.01
Len Barker			
Steve Carlton			
☐ 7 ERA Leaders	.12	.06	.01
Rudy May			
Don Sutton			
☐ 8 Leading Firemen	.12	.06	.01
Dan Quisenberry			
Rollie Fingers			
Tom Hume			
☐ 9 Pete LaCock DP	.04	.02	.00
☐ 10 Mike Flanagan	.12	.06	.01
☐ 11 Jim Wohlford DP	.04	.02	.00
☐ 12 Mark Clear	.08	.04	.01
☐ 13 Joe Charboneau	.12	.06	.01
☐ 14 John Tudor	2.00	1.00	.20
☐ 15 Larry Parrish	.12	.06	.01
☐ 16 Ron Davis	.08	.04	.01
☐ 17 Cliff Johnson	.08	.04	.01
☐ 18 Glenn Adams	.08	.04	.01
☐ 19 Jim Clancy	.08	.04	.01
☐ 20 Jeff Burroughs	.12	.06	.01
☐ 21 Ron Oester	.12	.06	.01
☐ 22 Danny Darwin	.15	.07	.01
☐ 23 Alex Trevino	.08	.04	.01
☐ 24 Don Stanhouse	.08	.04	.01
☐ 25 Sixto Lezcano	.08	.04	.01
☐ 26 U.L. Washington	.08	.04	.01
☐ 27 Champ Summers DP	.04	.02	.00
☐ 28 Enrique Romo	.08	.04	.01
☐ 29 Gene Tenace	.12	.06	.01
☐ 30 Jack Clark	.70	.35	.07
☐ 31 Checklist 1-121 DP	.10	.01	.00
☐ 32 Ken Oberkfell	.08	.04	.01
☐ 33 Rick Honeycutt	.08	.04	.01
☐ 34 Aurelio Rodriguez	.08	.04	.01
☐ 35 Mitchell Page	.08	.04	.01
☐ 36 Ed Farmer	.08	.04	.01
☐ 37 Gary Roenicke	.08	.04	.01
☐ 38 Win Remmerswaal	.08	.04	.01
☐ 39 Tom Veryzer	.08	.04	.01
☐ 40 Tug McGraw	.15	.07	.01
☐ 41 Ranger Rookies	.12	.06	.01
Bob Babcock			
John Butcher			
Jerry Don Gleaton			
☐ 42 Jerry White DP	.04	.02	.00
☐ 43 Jose Morales	.08	.04	.01
☐ 44 Larry McWilliams	.08	.04	.01
☐ 45 Enos Cabell	.08	.04	.01
☐ 46 Rick Bosetti	.08	.04	.01
☐ 47 Ken Brett	.08	.04	.01
☐ 48 Dave Skaggs	.08	.04	.01
☐ 49 Bob Shirley	.08	.04	.01
☐ 50 Dave Lopes	.15	.07	.01
☐ 51 Bill Robinson DP	.08	.04	.01
☐ 52 Hector Cruz	.08	.04	.01
☐ 53 Kevin Saucier	.08	.04	.01
☐ 54 Ivan DeJesus	.08	.04	.01
☐ 55 Mike Norris	.08	.04	.01
☐ 56 Buck Martinez	.08	.04	.01
☐ 57 Dave Roberts	.08	.04	.01
☐ 58 Joel Youngblood	.08	.04	.01
☐ 59 Dan Petry	.12	.06	.01
☐ 60 Willie Randolph	.15	.07	.01
☐ 61 Butch Wynegar	.08	.04	.01
☐ 62 Joe Pettini	.08	.04	.01
☐ 63 Steve Renko DP	.04	.02	.00
☐ 64 Brian Asselstine	.08	.04	.01
☐ 65 Scott McGregor	.12	.06	.01
☐ 66 Royals Rookies	.12	.06	.01
Manny Castillo			
Tim Ireland			
Mike Jones			
☐ 67 Ken Kravec	.08	.04	.01
☐ 68 Matt Alexander DP	.04	.02	.00
☐ 69 Ed Halicki	.08	.04	.01
☐ 70 Al Oliver DP	.12	.06	.01
☐ 71 Hal Dues	.08	.04	.01
☐ 72 Barry Evans DP	.04	.02	.00
☐ 73 Doug Bair	.08	.04	.01
☐ 74 Mike Hargrove	.12	.06	.01
☐ 75 Reggie Smith	.15	.07	.01
☐ 76 Mario Mendoza	.08	.04	.01
☐ 77 Mike Barlow	.08	.04	.01

☐	78 Steve Dillard	.08	.04	.01
☐	79 Bruce Robbins	.08	.04	.01
☐	80 Rusty Staub	.20	.10	.02
☐	81 Dave Stapleton	.12	.06	.01
☐	82 Astros Rookies DP	.12	.06	.01
	Danny Heep			
	Alan Knicely			
	Bobby Sprowl			
☐	83 Mike Proly	.08	.04	.01
☐	84 Johnnie LeMaster	.08	.04	.01
☐	85 Mike Caldwell	.08	.04	.01
☐	86 Wayne Gross	.08	.04	.01
☐	87 Rick Camp	.08	.04	.01
☐	88 Joe Lefebvre	.12	.06	.01
☐	89 Darrell Jackson	.08	.04	.01
☐	90 Bake McBride	.08	.04	.01
☐	91 Tim Stoddard DP	.08	.04	.01
☐	92 Mike Easler	.12	.06	.01
☐	93 Ed Glynn DP	.04	.02	.00
☐	94 Harry Spilman DP	.04	.02	.00
☐	95 Jim Sundberg	.12	.06	.01
☐	96 A's Rookies	.15	.07	.01
	Dave Beard			
	Ernie Camacho			
	Pat Dempsey			
☐	97 Chris Speier	.08	.04	.01
☐	98 Clint Hurdle	.08	.04	.01
☐	99 Eric Wilkins	.08	.04	.01
☐	100 Rod Carew	1.75	.85	.17
☐	101 Benny Ayala	.08	.04	.01
☐	102 Dave Tobik	.08	.04	.01
☐	103 Jerry Martin	.08	.04	.01
☐	104 Terry Forster	.12	.06	.01
☐	105 Jose Cruz	.12	.06	.01
☐	106 Don Money	.08	.04	.01
☐	107 Rich Wortham	.08	.04	.01
☐	108 Bruce Benedict	.08	.04	.01
☐	109 Mike Scott	1.50	.75	.15
☐	110 Carl Yastrzemski	1.75	.85	.17
☐	111 Greg Minton	.08	.04	.01
☐	112 White Sox Rookies	.12	.06	.01
	Rusty Kuntz			
	Fran Mullin			
	Leo Sutherland			
☐	113 Mike Phillips	.08	.04	.01
☐	114 Tom Underwood	.08	.04	.01
☐	115 Roy Smalley	.08	.04	.01
☐	116 Joe Simpson	.08	.04	.01
☐	117 Pete Falcone	.08	.04	.01
☐	118 Kurt Bevacqua	.08	.04	.01
☐	119 Tippy Martinez	.08	.04	.01
☐	120 Larry Bowa	.15	.07	.01
☐	121 Larry Harlow	.08	.04	.01
☐	122 John Denny	.12	.06	.01
☐	123 Al Cowens	.08	.04	.01
☐	124 Jerry Garvin	.08	.04	.01
☐	125 Andre Dawson	2.00	1.00	.20
☐	126 Charlie Leibrandt	.40	.20	.04
☐	127 Rudy Law	.08	.04	.01
☐	128 Gary Allenson DP	.04	.02	.00
☐	129 Art Howe	.15	.07	.01
☐	130 Larry Gura	.08	.04	.01
☐	131 Keith Moreland	.35	.17	.03
☐	132 Tommy Boggs	.08	.04	.01
☐	133 Jeff Cox	.08	.04	.01
☐	134 Steve Mura	.08	.04	.01
☐	135 Gorman Thomas	.20	.10	.02
☐	136 Doug Capilla	.08	.04	.01
☐	137 Hosken Powell	.08	.04	.01
☐	138 Rich Dotson DP	.20	.10	.02
☐	139 Oscar Gamble	.12	.06	.01
☐	140 Bob Forsch	.12	.06	.01
☐	141 Miguel Dilone	.08	.04	.01
☐	142 Jackson Todd	.08	.04	.01
☐	143 Dan Meyer	.08	.04	.01
☐	144 Allen Ripley	.08	.04	.01
☐	145 Mickey Rivers	.12	.06	.01
☐	146 Bobby Castillo	.08	.04	.01
☐	147 Dale Berra	.08	.04	.01
☐	148 Randy Niemann	.08	.04	.01
☐	149 Joe Nolan	.08	.04	.01
☐	150 Mark Fidrych	.15	.07	.01
☐	151 Claudell Washington	.15	.07	.01
☐	152 John Urrea	.08	.04	.01
☐	153 Tom Poquette	.08	.04	.01
☐	154 Rick Langford	.08	.04	.01
☐	155 Chris Chambliss	.12	.06	.01
☐	156 Bob McClure	.08	.04	.01
☐	157 John Wathan	.12	.06	.01
☐	158 Fergie Jenkins	.30	.15	.03
☐	159 Brian Doyle	.08	.04	.01
☐	160 Garry Maddox	.12	.06	.01
☐	161 Dan Graham	.08	.04	.01
☐	162 Doug Corbett	.08	.04	.01
☐	163 Bill Almon	.08	.04	.01
☐	164 LaMarr Hoyt	.25	.12	.02
☐	165 Tony Scott	.08	.04	.01
☐	166 Floyd Bannister	.08	.04	.01
☐	167 Terry Whitfield	.08	.04	.01
☐	168 Don Robinson DP	.08	.04	.01
☐	169 John Mayberry	.12	.06	.01
☐	170 Ross Grimsley	.08	.04	.01
☐	171 Gene Richards	.08	.04	.01
☐	172 Gary Woods	.08	.04	.01
☐	173 Bump Wills	.08	.04	.01
☐	174 Doug Rau	.08	.04	.01
☐	175 Dave Collins	.08	.04	.01
☐	176 Mike Krukow	.12	.06	.01
☐	177 Rick Peters	.08	.04	.01
☐	178 Jim Essian DP	.04	.02	.00
☐	179 Rudy May	.08	.04	.01
☐	180 Pete Rose	3.50	1.75	.35
☐	181 Elias Sosa	.08	.04	.01
☐	182 Bob Grich	.15	.07	.01
☐	183 Dick Davis DP	.04	.02	.00
☐	184 Jim Dwyer	.08	.04	.01
☐	185 Dennis Leonard	.12	.06	.01
☐	186 Wayne Nordhagen	.08	.04	.01
☐	187 Mike Parrott	.08	.04	.01
☐	188 Doug DeCinces	.12	.06	.01
☐	189 Craig Swan	.08	.04	.01
☐	190 Cesar Cedeno	.15	.07	.01
☐	191 Rick Sutcliffe	.60	.30	.06
☐	192 Braves Rookies	.30	.15	.03
	Terry Harper			
	Ed Miller			
	Rafael Ramirez			
☐	193 Pete Vuckovich	.12	.06	.01
☐	194 Rod Scurry	.08	.04	.01
☐	195 Rich Murray	.08	.04	.01
☐	196 Duffy Dyer	.08	.04	.01
☐	197 Jim Kern	.08	.04	.01
☐	198 Jerry Dybzinski	.08	.04	.01
☐	199 Chuck Rainey	.08	.04	.01
☐	200 George Foster	.25	.12	.02
☐	201 RB: Johnny Bench	.40	.20	.04
	Most homers,			
	lifetime, catcher			
☐	202 RB: Steve Carlton	.40	.20	.04
	Most strikeouts,			
	lefthander, lifetime			
☐	203 RB: Bill Gullickson	.12	.06	.01
	Most strikeouts,			
	game, rookie			
☐	204 RB: Ron LeFlore and	.12	.06	.01
	Rodney Scott			
	Most stolen bases,			
	teammates, season			
☐	205 RB: Pete Rose	.75	.35	.07
	Most cons. seasons			
	600 or more at-bats			
☐	206 RB: Mike Schmidt	.75	.35	.07
	Most homers, third			
	baseman, season			
☐	207 RB: Ozzie Smith	.20	.10	.02
	Most assists			
	season, shortstop			
☐	208 RB: Willie Wilson	.12	.06	.01
	Most at-bats, season			
☐	209 Dickie Thon DP	.12	.06	.01
☐	210 Jim Palmer	1.50	.75	.15
☐	211 Derrel Thomas	.08	.04	.01
☐	212 Steve Nicosia	.08	.04	.01
☐	213 Al Holland	.12	.06	.01
☐	214 Angels Rookies	.08	.04	.01
	Ralph Botting			
	Jim Dorsey			
	John Harris			
☐	215 Larry Hisle	.08	.04	.01
☐	216 John Henry Johnson	.08	.04	.01
☐	217 Rich Hebner	.08	.04	.01
☐	218 Paul Splittorff	.08	.04	.01
☐	219 Ken Landreaux	.08	.04	.01
☐	220 Tom Seaver	1.75	.85	.17
☐	221 Bob Davis	.08	.04	.01
☐	222 Jorge Orta	.08	.04	.01
☐	223 Roy Lee Jackson	.08	.04	.01
☐	224 Pat Zachry	.08	.04	.01
☐	225 Ruppert Jones	.08	.04	.01
☐	226 Manny Sanguillen DP	.08	.04	.01
☐	227 Fred Martinez	.08	.04	.01
☐	228 Tom Paciorek	.08	.04	.01
☐	229 Rollie Fingers	.75	.35	.07
☐	230 George Hendrick	.12	.06	.01
☐	231 Joe Beckwith	.08	.04	.01
☐	232 Mickey Klutts	.08	.04	.01
☐	233 Skip Lockwood	.08	.04	.01
☐	234 Lou Whitaker	.60	.30	.06

☐ 235	Scott Sanderson	.15	.07	.01
☐ 236	Mike Ivie	.08	.04	.01
☐ 237	Charlie Moore	.08	.04	.01
☐ 238	Willie Hernandez	.15	.07	.01
☐ 239	Rick Miller DP	.04	.02	.00
☐ 240	Nolan Ryan	5.00	2.50	.50
☐ 241	Checklist 122-242 DP	.10	.01	.00
☐ 242	Chet Lemon	.08	.04	.01
☐ 243	Sal Butera	.08	.04	.01
☐ 244	Cardinals Rookies	.15	.07	.01
	Tito Landrum			
	Al Olmsted			
	Andy Rincon			
☐ 245	Ed Figueroa	.08	.04	.01
☐ 246	Ed Ott DP	.04	.02	.00
☐ 247	Glenn Hubbard DP	.04	.02	.00
☐ 248	Joey McLaughlin	.08	.04	.01
☐ 249	Larry Cox	.08	.04	.01
☐ 250	Ron Guidry	.50	.25	.05
☐ 251	Tom Brookens	.08	.04	.01
☐ 252	Victor Cruz	.08	.04	.01
☐ 253	Dave Bergman	.08	.04	.01
☐ 254	Ozzie Smith	2.50	1.25	.25
☐ 255	Mark Littell	.08	.04	.01
☐ 256	Bombo Rivera	.08	.04	.01
☐ 257	Rennie Stennett	.08	.04	.01
☐ 258	Joe Price	.12	.06	.01
☐ 259	Mets Rookies	2.50	1.25	.25
	Juan Berenguer			
	Hubie Brooks			
	Mookie Wilson			
☐ 260	Ron Cey	.25	.12	.02
☐ 261	Rickey Henderson	30.00	15.00	3.00
☐ 262	Sammy Stewart	.08	.04	.01
☐ 263	Brian Downing	.12	.06	.01
☐ 264	Jim Norris	.08	.04	.01
☐ 265	John Candelaria	.12	.06	.01
☐ 266	Tom Herr	.15	.07	.01
☐ 267	Stan Bahnsen	.08	.04	.01
☐ 268	Jerry Royster	.08	.04	.01
☐ 269	Ken Forsch	.08	.04	.01
☐ 270	Greg Luzinski	.20	.10	.02
☐ 271	Bill Castro	.08	.04	.01
☐ 272	Bruce Kimm	.08	.04	.01
☐ 273	Stan Papi	.08	.04	.01
☐ 274	Craig Chamberlain	.08	.04	.01
☐ 275	Dwight Evans	.50	.25	.05
☐ 276	Dan Spillner	.08	.04	.01
☐ 277	Alfredo Griffin	.12	.06	.01
☐ 278	Rick Sofield	.08	.04	.01
☐ 279	Bob Knepper	.15	.07	.01
☐ 280	Ken Griffey	.30	.15	.03
☐ 281	Fred Stanley	.08	.04	.01
☐ 282	Mariners Rookies	.12	.06	.01
	Rick Anderson			
	Greg Biercevicz			
	Rodney Craig			
☐ 283	Billy Sample	.08	.04	.01
☐ 284	Brian Kingman	.08	.04	.01
☐ 285	Jerry Turner	.08	.04	.01
☐ 286	Dave Frost	.08	.04	.01
☐ 287	Lenn Sakata	.08	.04	.01
☐ 288	Bob Clark	.08	.04	.01
☐ 289	Mickey Hatcher	.12	.06	.01
☐ 290	Bob Boone DP	.12	.06	.01
☐ 291	Aurelio Lopez	.08	.04	.01
☐ 292	Mike Squires	.08	.04	.01
☐ 293	Charlie Lea	.18	.09	.01
☐ 294	Mike Tyson DP	.04	.02	.00
☐ 295	Hal McRae	.12	.06	.01
☐ 296	Bill Nahorodny DP	.04	.02	.00
☐ 297	Bob Bailor	.08	.04	.01
☐ 298	Buddy Solomon	.08	.04	.01
☐ 299	Elliott Maddox	.08	.04	.01
☐ 300	Paul Molitor	.60	.30	.06
☐ 301	Matt Keough	.08	.04	.01
☐ 302	Dodgers Rookies	8.00	4.00	.80
	Jack Perconte			
	Mike Scioscia			
	Fernando Valenzuela			
☐ 303	Johnny Oates	.08	.04	.01
☐ 304	John Castino	.08	.04	.01
☐ 305	Ken Clay	.08	.04	.01
☐ 306	Juan Beniquez DP	.04	.02	.00
☐ 307	Gene Garber	.08	.04	.01
☐ 308	Rick Manning	.08	.04	.01
☐ 309	Luis Salazar	.25	.12	.02
☐ 310	Vida Blue DP	.12	.06	.01
☐ 311	Freddie Patek	.08	.04	.01
☐ 312	Rick Rhoden	.12	.06	.01
☐ 313	Luis Pujols	.08	.04	.01
☐ 314	Rich Dauer	.08	.04	.01
☐ 315	Kirk Gibson	6.50	3.25	.65
☐ 316	Craig Minetto	.08	.04	.01
☐ 317	Lonnie Smith	.20	.10	.02
☐ 318	Steve Yeager	.08	.04	.01
☐ 319	Rowland Office	.08	.04	.01
☐ 320	Tom Burgmeier	.08	.04	.01
☐ 321	Leon Durham	.35	.17	.03
☐ 322	Neil Allen	.12	.06	.01
☐ 323	Jim Morrison DP	.08	.04	.01
☐ 324	Mike Willis	.08	.04	.01
☐ 325	Ray Knight	.20	.10	.02
☐ 326	Biff Pocoroba	.08	.04	.01
☐ 327	Moose Haas	.12	.06	.01
☐ 328	Twins Rookies	.20	.10	.02
	Dave Engle			
	Greg Johnston			
	Gary Ward			
☐ 329	Joaquin Andujar	.15	.07	.01
☐ 330	Frank White	.15	.07	.01
☐ 331	Dennis Lamp	.08	.04	.01
☐ 332	Lee Lacy DP	.08	.04	.01
☐ 333	Sid Monge	.08	.04	.01
☐ 334	Dane Iorg	.08	.04	.01
☐ 335	Rick Cerone	.08	.04	.01
☐ 336	Eddie Whitson	.12	.06	.01
☐ 337	Lynn Jones	.08	.04	.01
☐ 338	Checklist 243-363	.20	.02	.00
☐ 339	John Ellis	.08	.04	.01
☐ 340	Bruce Kison	.08	.04	.01
☐ 341	Dwayne Murphy	.08	.04	.01
☐ 342	Eric Rasmussen DP	.04	.02	.00
☐ 343	Frank Taveras	.08	.04	.01
☐ 344	Byron McLaughlin	.08	.04	.01
☐ 345	Warren Cromartie	.08	.04	.01
☐ 346	Larry Christenson DP	.04	.02	.00
☐ 347	Harold Baines	4.50	2.25	.45
☐ 348	Bob Sykes	.08	.04	.01
☐ 349	Glenn Hoffman	.08	.04	.01
☐ 350	J.R. Richard	.15	.07	.01
☐ 351	Otto Velez	.08	.04	.01
☐ 352	Dick Tidrow DP	.04	.02	.00
☐ 353	Terry Kennedy	.12	.06	.01
☐ 354	Mario Soto	.15	.07	.01
☐ 355	Bob Horner	.25	.12	.02
☐ 356	Padres Rookies	.08	.04	.01
	George Stablein			
	Craig Stimac			
	Tom Tellmann			
☐ 357	Jim Slaton	.08	.04	.01
☐ 358	Mark Wagner	.08	.04	.01
☐ 359	Tom Hausman	.08	.04	.01
☐ 360	Willie Wilson	.25	.12	.02
☐ 361	Joe Strain	.08	.04	.01
☐ 362	Bo Diaz	.08	.04	.01
☐ 363	Geoff Zahn	.08	.04	.01
☐ 364	Mike Davis	.25	.12	.02
☐ 365	Graig Nettles DP	.12	.06	.01
☐ 366	Mike Ramsey	.08	.04	.01
☐ 367	Dennis Martinez	.15	.07	.01
☐ 368	Leon Roberts	.08	.04	.01
☐ 369	Frank Tanana	.12	.06	.01
☐ 370	Dave Winfield	1.25	.60	.12
☐ 371	Charlie Hough	.12	.06	.01
☐ 372	Jay Johnstone	.12	.06	.01
☐ 373	Pat Underwood	.08	.04	.01
☐ 374	Tommy Hutton	.08	.04	.01
☐ 375	Dave Concepcion	.15	.07	.01
☐ 376	Ron Reed	.08	.04	.01
☐ 377	Jerry Morales	.08	.04	.01
☐ 378	Dave Rader	.08	.04	.01
☐ 379	Lary Sorensen	.08	.04	.01
☐ 380	Willie Stargell	1.00	.50	.10
☐ 381	Cubs Rookies	.12	.06	.01
	Carlos Lezcano			
	Steve Macko			
	Randy Martz			
☐ 382	Paul Mirabella	.08	.04	.01
☐ 383	Eric Soderholm DP	.04	.02	.00
☐ 384	Mike Sadek	.08	.04	.01
☐ 385	Joe Sambito	.08	.04	.01
☐ 386	Dave Edwards	.08	.04	.01
☐ 387	Phil Niekro	.70	.35	.07
☐ 388	Andre Thornton	.12	.06	.01
☐ 389	Marty Pattin	.08	.04	.01
☐ 390	Cesar Geronimo	.08	.04	.01
☐ 391	Dave Lemanczyk DP	.04	.02	.00
☐ 392	Lance Parrish	.75	.35	.07
☐ 393	Broderick Perkins	.08	.04	.01
☐ 394	Woodie Fryman	.08	.04	.01
☐ 395	Scot Thompson	.08	.04	.01
☐ 396	Bill Campbell	.08	.04	.01
☐ 397	Julio Cruz	.08	.04	.01
☐ 398	Ross Baumgarten	.08	.04	.01
☐ 399	Orioles Rookies	2.50	1.25	.25
	Mike Boddicker			
	Mark Corey			
	Floyd Rayford			

☐ 400	Reggie Jackson	1.75	.85	.17
☐ 401	AL Champs	.60	.30	.06
	Royals sweep Yanks			
	(Brett swinging)			
☐ 402	NL Champs	.20	.10	.02
	Phillies squeak			
	past Astros			
☐ 403	1980 World Series	.20	.10	.02
	Phillies beat			
	Royals in six			
☐ 404	1980 World Series	.20	.10	.02
	Phillies win first			
	World Series			
☐ 405	Nino Espinosa	.08	.04	.01
☐ 406	Dickie Noles	.08	.04	.01
☐ 407	Ernie Whitt	.12	.06	.01
☐ 408	Fernando Arroyo	.08	.04	.01
☐ 409	Larry Herndon	.08	.04	.01
☐ 410	Bert Campaneris	.12	.06	.01
☐ 411	Terry Puhl	.12	.06	.01
☐ 412	Britt Burns	.20	.10	.02
☐ 413	Tony Bernazard	.12	.06	.01
☐ 414	John Pacella DP	.04	.02	.00
☐ 415	Ben Oglivie	.12	.06	.01
☐ 416	Gary Alexander	.08	.04	.01
☐ 417	Dan Schatzeder	.08	.04	.01
☐ 418	Bobby Brown	.08	.04	.01
☐ 419	Tom Hume	.08	.04	.01
☐ 420	Keith Hernandez	.75	.35	.07
☐ 421	Bob Stanley	.08	.04	.01
☐ 422	Dan Ford	.08	.04	.01
☐ 423	Shane Rawley	.08	.04	.01
☐ 424	Yankees Rookies	.08	.04	.01
	Tim Lollar			
	Bruce Robinson			
	Dennis Werth			
☐ 425	Al Bumbry	.08	.04	.01
☐ 426	Warren Brusstar	.08	.04	.01
☐ 427	John D'Acquisto	.08	.04	.01
☐ 428	John Stearns	.08	.04	.01
☐ 429	Mick Kelleher	.08	.04	.01
☐ 430	Jim Bibby	.08	.04	.01
☐ 431	Dave Roberts	.08	.04	.01
☐ 432	Len Barker	.08	.04	.01
☐ 433	Rance Mulliniks	.08	.04	.01
☐ 434	Roger Erickson	.08	.04	.01
☐ 435	Jim Spencer	.08	.04	.01
☐ 436	Gary Lucas	.08	.04	.01
☐ 437	Mike Heath DP	.04	.02	.00
☐ 438	John Montefusco	.12	.06	.01
☐ 439	Denny Walling	.08	.04	.01
☐ 440	Jerry Reuss	.12	.06	.01
☐ 441	Ken Reitz	.08	.04	.01
☐ 442	Ron Pruitt	.08	.04	.01
☐ 443	Jim Beattie DP	.04	.02	.00
☐ 444	Garth Iorg	.08	.04	.01
☐ 445	Ellis Valentine	.08	.04	.01
☐ 446	Checklist 364-484	.20	.02	.00
☐ 447	Junior Kennedy DP	.04	.02	.00
☐ 448	Tim Corcoran	.08	.04	.01
☐ 449	Paul Mitchell	.08	.04	.01
☐ 450	Dave Kingman DP	.12	.06	.01
☐ 451	Indians Rookies	.12	.06	.01
	Chris Bando			
	Tom Brennan			
	Sandy Wihtol			
☐ 452	Renie Martin	.08	.04	.01
☐ 453	Rob Wilfong DP	.04	.02	.00
☐ 454	Andy Hassler	.08	.04	.01
☐ 455	Rick Burleson	.12	.06	.01
☐ 456	Jeff Reardon	1.50	.75	.15
☐ 457	Mike Lum	.08	.04	.01
☐ 458	Randy Jones	.08	.04	.01
☐ 459	Greg Gross	.08	.04	.01
☐ 460	Rich Gossage	.35	.17	.03
☐ 461	Dave McKay	.08	.04	.01
☐ 462	Jack Brohamer	.08	.04	.01
☐ 463	Milt May	.08	.04	.01
☐ 464	Adrian Devine	.08	.04	.01
☐ 465	Bill Russell	.12	.06	.01
☐ 466	Bob Molinaro	.08	.04	.01
☐ 467	Dave Stieb	1.50	.75	.15
☐ 468	John Wockenfuss	.08	.04	.01
☐ 469	Jeff Leonard	.25	.12	.02
☐ 470	Manny Trillo	.08	.04	.01
☐ 471	Mike Vail	.08	.04	.01
☐ 472	Dyar Miller DP	.04	.02	.00
☐ 473	Jose Cardenal	.08	.04	.01
☐ 474	Mike LaCoss	.08	.04	.01
☐ 475	Buddy Bell	.20	.10	.02
☐ 476	Jerry Koosman	.15	.07	.01
☐ 477	Luis Gomez	.08	.04	.01
☐ 478	Juan Eichelberger	.08	.04	.01
☐ 479	Expos Rookies	9.00	4.50	.90
	Tim Raines			
	Roberto Ramos			
	Bobby Pate			
☐ 480	Carlton Fisk	1.25	.60	.12
☐ 481	Bob Lacey DP	.04	.02	.00
☐ 482	Jim Gantner	.08	.04	.01
☐ 483	Mike Griffin	.08	.04	.01
☐ 484	Max Venable DP	.04	.02	.00
☐ 485	Garry Templeton	.15	.07	.01
☐ 486	Marc Hill	.08	.04	.01
☐ 487	Dewey Robinson	.08	.04	.01
☐ 488	Damaso Garcia	.15	.07	.01
☐ 489	John Littlefield	.08	.04	.01
☐ 490	Eddie Murray	2.00	1.00	.20
☐ 491	Gordy Pladson	.08	.04	.01
☐ 492	Barry Foote	.08	.04	.01
☐ 493	Dan Quisenberry	.25	.12	.02
☐ 494	Bob Walk	.40	.20	.04
☐ 495	Dusty Baker	.12	.06	.01
☐ 496	Paul Dade	.08	.04	.01
☐ 497	Fred Norman	.08	.04	.01
☐ 498	Pat Putnam	.08	.04	.01
☐ 499	Frank Pastore	.08	.04	.01
☐ 500	Jim Rice	.65	.30	.06
☐ 501	Tim Foli DP	.04	.02	.00
☐ 502	Giants Rookies	.08	.04	.01
	Chris Bourjos			
	Al Hargesheimer			
	Mike Rowland			
☐ 503	Steve McCatty	.08	.04	.01
☐ 504	Dale Murphy	2.50	1.25	.25
☐ 505	Jason Thompson	.08	.04	.01
☐ 506	Phil Huffman	.08	.04	.01
☐ 507	Jamie Quirk	.08	.04	.01
☐ 508	Rob Dressler	.08	.04	.01
☐ 509	Pete Mackanin	.08	.04	.01
☐ 510	Lee Mazzilli	.08	.04	.01
☐ 511	Wayne Garland	.08	.04	.01
☐ 512	Gary Thomasson	.08	.04	.01
☐ 513	Frank LaCorte	.08	.04	.01
☐ 514	George Riley	.08	.04	.01
☐ 515	Robin Yount	2.50	1.25	.25
☐ 516	Doug Bird	.08	.04	.01
☐ 517	Richie Zisk	.08	.04	.01
☐ 518	Grant Jackson	.08	.04	.01
☐ 519	John Tamargo DP	.04	.02	.00
☐ 520	Steve Stone	.12	.06	.01
☐ 521	Sam Mejias	.08	.04	.01
☐ 522	Mike Colbern	.08	.04	.01
☐ 523	John Fulgham	.08	.04	.01
☐ 524	Willie Aikens	.12	.06	.01
☐ 525	Mike Torrez	.08	.04	.01
☐ 526	Phillies Rookies	.15	.07	.01
	Marty Bystrom			
	Jay Loviglio			
	Jim Wright			
☐ 527	Danny Goodwin	.08	.04	.01
☐ 528	Gary Matthews	.12	.06	.01
☐ 529	Dave LaRoche	.08	.04	.01
☐ 530	Steve Garvey	1.25	.60	.12
☐ 531	John Curtis	.08	.04	.01
☐ 532	Bill Stein	.08	.04	.01
☐ 533	Jesus Figueroa	.08	.04	.01
☐ 534	Dave Smith	.75	.35	.07
☐ 535	Omar Moreno	.08	.04	.01
☐ 536	Bob Owchinko DP	.04	.02	.00
☐ 537	Ron Hodges	.08	.04	.01
☐ 538	Tom Griffin	.08	.04	.01
☐ 539	Rodney Scott	.08	.04	.01
☐ 540	Mike Schmidt DP	2.25	1.10	.22
☐ 541	Steve Swisher	.08	.04	.01
☐ 542	Larry Bradford DP	.04	.02	.00
☐ 543	Terry Crowley	.08	.04	.01
☐ 544	Rich Gale	.08	.04	.01
☐ 545	Johnny Grubb	.08	.04	.01
☐ 546	Paul Moskau	.08	.04	.01
☐ 547	Mario Guerrero	.08	.04	.01
☐ 548	Dave Goltz	.08	.04	.01
☐ 549	Jerry Remy	.08	.04	.01
☐ 550	Tommy John	.35	.17	.03
☐ 551	Pirates Rookies	2.25	1.10	.22
	Vance Law			
	Tony Pena			
	Pascual Perez			
☐ 552	Steve Trout	.12	.06	.01
☐ 553	Tim Blackwell	.08	.04	.01
☐ 554	Bert Blyleven UER	.50	.25	.05
	(1 is missing from			
	1980 on card back)			
☐ 555	Cecil Cooper	.25	.12	.02
☐ 556	Jerry Mumphrey	.08	.04	.01
☐ 557	Chris Knapp	.08	.04	.01
☐ 558	Barry Bonnell	.08	.04	.01

☐ 559	Willie Montanez	.08	.04	.01
☐ 560	Joe Morgan	.90	.45	.09
☐ 561	Dennis Littlejohn	.08	.04	.01
☐ 562	Checklist 485-605	.20	.02	.00
☐ 563	Jim Kaat	.25	.12	.02
☐ 564	Ron Hassey DP	.08	.04	.01
☐ 565	Burt Hooton	.08	.04	.01
☐ 566	Del Unser	.08	.04	.01
☐ 567	Mark Bomback	.08	.04	.01
☐ 568	Dave Revering	.08	.04	.01
☐ 569	Al Williams DP	.04	.02	.00
☐ 570	Ken Singleton	.15	.07	.01
☐ 571	Todd Cruz	.08	.04	.01
☐ 572	Jack Morris	.55	.27	.05
☐ 573	Phil Garner	.08	.04	.01
☐ 574	Bill Caudill	.08	.04	.01
☐ 575	Tony Perez	.30	.15	.03
☐ 576	Reggie Cleveland	.08	.04	.01
☐ 577	Blue Jays Rookies	.15	.07	.01
	Luis Leal			
	Brian Milner			
	Ken Schrom			
☐ 578	Bill Gullickson	.30	.15	.03
☐ 579	Tim Flannery	.08	.04	.01
☐ 580	Don Baylor	.25	.12	.02
☐ 581	Roy Howell	.08	.04	.01
☐ 582	Gaylord Perry	.55	.27	.05
☐ 583	Larry Milbourne	.08	.04	.01
☐ 584	Randy Lerch	.08	.04	.01
☐ 585	Amos Otis	.15	.07	.01
☐ 586	Silvio Martinez	.08	.04	.01
☐ 587	Jeff Newman	.08	.04	.01
☐ 588	Gary Lavelle	.08	.04	.01
☐ 589	Lamar Johnson	.08	.04	.01
☐ 590	Bruce Sutter	.25	.12	.02
☐ 591	John Lowenstein	.08	.04	.01
☐ 592	Steve Comer	.08	.04	.01
☐ 593	Steve Kemp	.12	.06	.01
☐ 594	Preston Hanna DP	.04	.02	.00
☐ 595	Butch Hobson	.08	.04	.01
☐ 596	Jerry Augustine	.08	.04	.01
☐ 597	Rafael Landestoy	.08	.04	.01
☐ 598	George Vukovich DP	.04	.02	.00
☐ 599	Dennis Kinney	.08	.04	.01
☐ 600	Johnny Bench	1.75	.85	.17
☐ 601	Don Aase	.08	.04	.01
☐ 602	Bobby Murcer	.15	.07	.01
☐ 603	John Verhoeven	.08	.04	.01
☐ 604	Rob Picciolo	.08	.04	.01
☐ 605	Don Sutton	.60	.30	.06
☐ 606	Reds Rookies DP	.08	.04	.01
	Bruce Berenyi			
	Geoff Combe			
	Paul Householder			
☐ 607	David Palmer	.12	.06	.01
☐ 608	Greg Pryor	.08	.04	.01
☐ 609	Lynn McGlothen	.08	.04	.01
☐ 610	Darrell Porter	.08	.04	.01
☐ 611	Rick Matula DP	.04	.02	.00
☐ 612	Duane Kuiper	.08	.04	.01
☐ 613	Jim Anderson	.08	.04	.01
☐ 614	Dave Rozema	.08	.04	.01
☐ 615	Rick Dempsey	.08	.04	.01
☐ 616	Rick Wise	.08	.04	.01
☐ 617	Craig Reynolds	.08	.04	.01
☐ 618	John Milner	.08	.04	.01
☐ 619	Steve Henderson	.08	.04	.01
☐ 620	Dennis Eckersley	.75	.35	.07
☐ 621	Tom Donohue	.08	.04	.01
☐ 622	Randy Moffitt	.08	.04	.01
☐ 623	Sal Bando	.12	.06	.01
☐ 624	Bob Welch	.75	.35	.07
☐ 625	Bill Buckner	.20	.10	.02
☐ 626	Tigers Rookies	.12	.06	.01
	Dave Steffen			
	Jerry Ujdur			
	Roger Weaver			
☐ 627	Luis Tiant	.15	.07	.01
☐ 628	Vic Correll	.08	.04	.01
☐ 629	Tony Armas	.12	.06	.01
☐ 630	Steve Carlton	1.50	.75	.15
☐ 631	Ron Jackson	.08	.04	.01
☐ 632	Alan Bannister	.08	.04	.01
☐ 633	Bill Lee	.12	.06	.01
☐ 634	Doug Flynn	.08	.04	.01
☐ 635	Bobby Bonds	.15	.07	.01
☐ 636	Al Hrabosky	.12	.06	.01
☐ 637	Jerry Narron	.08	.04	.01
☐ 638	Checklist 606-726	.20	.02	.00
☐ 639	Carney Lansford	.45	.22	.04
☐ 640	Dave Parker	.65	.30	.06
☐ 641	Mark Belanger	.12	.06	.01
☐ 642	Vern Ruhle	.08	.04	.01
☐ 643	Lloyd Moseby	1.25	.60	.12
☐ 644	Ramon Aviles DP	.04	.02	.00
☐ 645	Rick Reuschel	.25	.12	.02
☐ 646	Marvis Foley	.08	.04	.01
☐ 647	Dick Drago	.08	.04	.01
☐ 648	Darrell Evans	.25	.12	.02
☐ 649	Manny Sarmiento	.08	.04	.01
☐ 650	Bucky Dent	.18	.09	.01
☐ 651	Pedro Guerrero	2.50	1.25	.25
☐ 652	John Montague	.08	.04	.01
☐ 653	Bill Fahey	.08	.04	.01
☐ 654	Ray Burris	.08	.04	.01
☐ 655	Dan Driessen	.08	.04	.01
☐ 656	Jon Matlack	.08	.04	.01
☐ 657	Mike Cubbage DP	.04	.02	.00
☐ 658	Milt Wilcox	.08	.04	.01
☐ 659	Brewers Rookies	.12	.06	.01
	John Flinn			
	Ed Romero			
	Ned Yost			
☐ 660	Gary Carter	1.50	.75	.15
☐ 661	Orioles Team/Mgr.	.25	.12	.02
	Earl Weaver			
	(checklist back)			
☐ 662	Red Sox Team/Mgr.	.20	.10	.02
	Ralph Houk			
	(checklist back)			
☐ 663	Angels Team/Mgr.	.20	.10	.02
	Jim Fregosi			
	(checklist back)			
☐ 664	White Sox Team/Mgr.	.20	.10	.02
	Tony LaRussa			
	(checklist back)			
☐ 665	Indians Team/Mgr.	.20	.10	.02
	Dave Garcia			
	(checklist back)			
☐ 666	Tigers Team/Mgr.	.25	.12	.02
	Sparky Anderson			
	(checklist back)			
☐ 667	Royals Team/Mgr.	.20	.10	.02
	Jim Frey			
	(checklist back)			
☐ 668	Brewers Team/Mgr.	.20	.10	.02
	Bob Rodgers			
	(checklist back)			
☐ 669	Twins Team/Mgr.	.20	.10	.02
	John Goryl			
	(checklist back)			
☐ 670	Yankees Team/Mgr.	.25	.12	.02
	Gene Michael			
	(checklist back)			
☐ 671	A's Team/Mgr.	.25	.12	.02
	Billy Martin			
	(checklist back)			
☐ 672	Mariners Team/Mgr.	.20	.10	.02
	Maury Wills			
	(checklist back)			
☐ 673	Rangers Team/Mgr.	.20	.10	.02
	Don Zimmer			
	(checklist back)			
☐ 674	Blue Jays Team/Mgr.	.20	.10	.02
	Bobby Mattick			
	(checklist back)			
☐ 675	Braves Team/Mgr.	.20	.10	.02
	Bobby Cox			
	(checklist back)			
☐ 676	Cubs Team/Mgr.	.20	.10	.02
	Joe Amalfitano			
	(checklist back)			
☐ 677	Reds Team/Mgr.	.20	.10	.02
	John McNamara			
	(checklist back)			
☐ 678	Astros Team/Mgr.	.20	.10	.02
	Bill Virdon			
	(checklist back)			
☐ 679	Dodgers Team/Mgr.	.25	.12	.02
	Tom Lasorda			
	(checklist back)			
☐ 680	Expos Team/Mgr.	.20	.10	.02
	Dick Williams			
	(checklist back)			
☐ 681	Mets Team/Mgr.	.25	.12	.02
	Joe Torre			
	(checklist back)			
☐ 682	Phillies Team/Mgr.	.20	.10	.02
	Dallas Green			
	(checklist back)			
☐ 683	Pirates Team/Mgr.	.20	.10	.02
	Chuck Tanner			
	(checklist back)			
☐ 684	Cardinals Team/Mgr.	.20	.10	.02
	Whitey Herzog			
	(checklist back)			

☐	685 Padres Team/Mgr. Frank Howard (checklist back)	.20	.10	.02
☐	686 Giants Team/Mgr. Dave Bristol (checklist back)	.20	.10	.02
☐	687 Jeff Jones	.08	.04	.01
☐	688 Kiko Garcia	.08	.04	.01
☐	689 Red Sox Rookies Bruce Hurst Keith MacWhorter Reid Nichols	2.50	1.25	.25
☐	690 Bob Watson	.12	.06	.01
☐	691 Dick Ruthven	.08	.04	.01
☐	692 Lenny Randle	.08	.04	.01
☐	693 Steve Howe	.12	.06	.01
☐	694 Bud Harrelson DP	.08	.04	.01
☐	695 Kent Tekulve	.12	.06	.01
☐	696 Alan Ashby	.08	.04	.01
☐	697 Rick Waits	.08	.04	.01
☐	698 Mike Jorgensen	.08	.04	.01
☐	699 Glenn Abbott	.08	.04	.01
☐	700 George Brett	3.25	1.60	.32
☐	701 Joe Rudi	.12	.06	.01
☐	702 George Medich	.08	.04	.01
☐	703 Alvis Woods	.08	.04	.01
☐	704 Bill Travers DP	.04	.02	.00
☐	705 Ted Simmons	.25	.12	.02
☐	706 Dave Ford	.08	.04	.01
☐	707 Dave Cash	.08	.04	.01
☐	708 Doyle Alexander	.12	.06	.01
☐	709 Alan Trammell DP	.40	.20	.04
☐	710 Ron LeFlore DP	.08	.04	.01
☐	711 Joe Ferguson	.08	.04	.01
☐	712 Bill Bonham	.08	.04	.01
☐	713 Bill North	.08	.04	.01
☐	714 Pete Redfern	.08	.04	.01
☐	715 Bill Madlock	.15	.07	.01
☐	716 Glenn Borgmann	.08	.04	.01
☐	717 Jim Barr DP	.04	.02	.00
☐	718 Larry Biittner	.08	.04	.01
☐	719 Sparky Lyle	.15	.07	.01
☐	720 Fred Lynn	.30	.15	.03
☐	721 Toby Harrah	.12	.06	.01
☐	722 Joe Niekro	.12	.06	.01
☐	723 Bruce Bochte	.08	.04	.01
☐	724 Lou Piniella	.15	.07	.01
☐	725 Steve Rogers	.12	.06	.01
☐	726 Rick Monday	.20	.10	.02

1981 Topps Traded

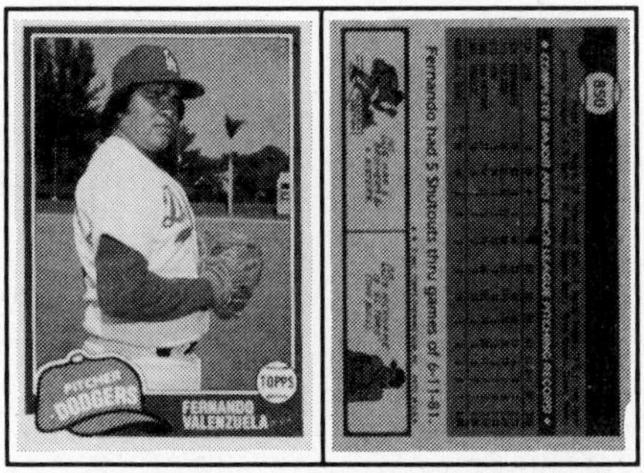

The cards in this 132-card set measure 2 1/2" by 3 1/2". For the first time since 1976, Topps issued a "traded" set in 1981. Unlike the small traded sets of 1974 and 1976, this set contains a larger number of cards and was sequentially numbered, alphabetically, from 727 to 858. Thus, this set gives the impression it is a continuation of their regular issue of this year. The sets were issued only through hobby card dealers and were boxed in complete sets of 132 cards. There are no key rookie cards in this set.

	MINT	EXC	G-VG
COMPLETE SET (132)	27.00	13.50	2.70
COMMON PLAYER (727-858)	.09	.04	.01

☐	727 Danny Ainge	.85	.25	.05
☐	728 Doyle Alexander	.20	.10	.02
☐	729 Gary Alexander	.09	.04	.01
☐	730 Bill Almon	.09	.04	.01
☐	731 Joaquin Andujar	.15	.07	.01
☐	732 Bob Bailor	.09	.04	.01
☐	733 Juan Beniquez	.09	.04	.01
☐	734 Dave Bergman	.09	.04	.01
☐	735 Tony Bernazard	.15	.07	.01
☐	736 Larry Biittner	.09	.04	.01
☐	737 Doug Bird	.09	.04	.01
☐	738 Bert Blyleven	1.25	.60	.12
☐	739 Mark Bomback	.09	.04	.01
☐	740 Bobby Bonds	.30	.15	.03
☐	741 Rick Bosetti	.09	.04	.01
☐	742 Hubie Brooks	1.75	.85	.17
☐	743 Rick Burleson	.15	.07	.01
☐	744 Ray Burris	.09	.04	.01
☐	745 Jeff Burroughs	.15	.07	.01
☐	746 Enos Cabell	.09	.04	.01
☐	747 Ken Clay	.09	.04	.01
☐	748 Mark Clear	.09	.04	.01
☐	749 Larry Cox	.09	.04	.01
☐	750 Hector Cruz	.09	.04	.01
☐	751 Victor Cruz	.09	.04	.01
☐	752 Mike Cubbage	.09	.04	.01
☐	753 Dick Davis	.09	.04	.01
☐	754 Brian Doyle	.09	.04	.01
☐	755 Dick Drago	.09	.04	.01
☐	756 Leon Durham	.20	.10	.02
☐	757 Jim Dwyer	.09	.04	.01
☐	758 Dave Edwards	.09	.04	.01
☐	759 Jim Essian	.09	.04	.01
☐	760 Bill Fahey	.09	.04	.01
☐	761 Rollie Fingers	1.25	.60	.12
☐	762 Carlton Fisk	4.00	2.00	.40
☐	763 Barry Foote	.09	.04	.01
☐	764 Ken Forsch	.09	.04	.01
☐	765 Kiko Garcia	.09	.04	.01
☐	766 Cesar Geronimo	.09	.04	.01
☐	767 Gary Gray	.09	.04	.01
☐	768 Mickey Hatcher	.20	.10	.02
☐	769 Steve Henderson	.09	.04	.01
☐	770 Marc Hill	.09	.04	.01
☐	771 Butch Hobson	.09	.04	.01
☐	772 Rick Honeycutt	.09	.04	.01
☐	773 Roy Howell	.09	.04	.01
☐	774 Mike Ivie	.09	.04	.01
☐	775 Roy Lee Jackson	.09	.04	.01
☐	776 Cliff Johnson	.09	.04	.01
☐	777 Randy Jones	.15	.07	.01
☐	778 Ruppert Jones	.09	.04	.01
☐	779 Mick Kelleher	.09	.04	.01
☐	780 Terry Kennedy	.15	.07	.01
☐	781 Dave Kingman	.35	.17	.03
☐	782 Bob Knepper	.15	.07	.01
☐	783 Ken Kravec	.09	.04	.01
☐	784 Bob Lacey	.09	.04	.01
☐	785 Dennis Lamp	.09	.04	.01
☐	786 Rafael Landestoy	.09	.04	.01
☐	787 Ken Landreaux	.15	.07	.01
☐	788 Carney Lansford	1.50	.75	.15
☐	789 Dave LaRoche	.09	.04	.01
☐	790 Joe Lefebvre	.09	.04	.01
☐	791 Ron LeFlore	.15	.07	.01
☐	792 Randy Lerch	.09	.04	.01
☐	793 Sixto Lezcano	.09	.04	.01
☐	794 John Littlefield	.09	.04	.01
☐	795 Mike Lum	.09	.04	.01
☐	796 Greg Luzinski	.25	.12	.02
☐	797 Fred Lynn	.50	.25	.05
☐	798 Jerry Martin	.09	.04	.01
☐	799 Buck Martinez	.09	.04	.01
☐	800 Gary Matthews	.15	.07	.01
☐	801 Mario Mendoza	.09	.04	.01
☐	802 Larry Milbourne	.09	.04	.01
☐	803 Rick Miller	.09	.04	.01
☐	804 John Montefusco	.15	.07	.01
☐	805 Jerry Morales	.09	.04	.01
☐	806 Jose Morales	.09	.04	.01
☐	807 Joe Morgan	1.75	.85	.17
☐	808 Jerry Mumphrey	.09	.04	.01
☐	809 Gene Nelson	.20	.10	.02
☐	810 Ed Ott	.09	.04	.01
☐	811 Bob Owchinko	.09	.04	.01
☐	812 Gaylord Perry	1.25	.60	.12
☐	813 Mike Phillips	.09	.04	.01
☐	814 Darrell Porter	.15	.07	.01
☐	815 Mike Proly	.09	.04	.01
☐	816 Tim Raines	8.00	4.00	.80
☐	817 Lenny Randle	.09	.04	.01
☐	818 Doug Rau	.09	.04	.01
☐	819 Jeff Reardon	.75	.35	.07
☐	820 Ken Reitz	.09	.04	.01

☐ 821 Steve Renko	.09	.04	.01
☐ 822 Rick Reuschel	.40	.20	.04
☐ 823 Dave Revering	.09	.04	.01
☐ 824 Dave Roberts	.09	.04	.01
☐ 825 Leon Roberts	.09	.04	.01
☐ 826 Joe Rudi	.15	.07	.01
☐ 827 Kevin Saucier	.09	.04	.01
☐ 828 Tony Scott	.09	.04	.01
☐ 829 Bob Shirley	.09	.04	.01
☐ 830 Ted Simmons	.50	.25	.05
☐ 831 Lary Sorensen	.09	.04	.01
☐ 832 Jim Spencer	.09	.04	.01
☐ 833 Harry Spilman	.09	.04	.01
☐ 834 Fred Stanley	.09	.04	.01
☐ 835 Rusty Staub	.25	.12	.02
☐ 836 Bill Stein	.09	.04	.01
☐ 837 Joe Strain	.09	.04	.01
☐ 838 Bruce Sutter	.40	.20	.04
☐ 839 Don Sutton	1.25	.60	.12
☐ 840 Steve Swisher	.09	.04	.01
☐ 841 Frank Tanana	.20	.10	.02
☐ 842 Gene Tenace	.15	.07	.01
☐ 843 Jason Thompson	.09	.04	.01
☐ 844 Dickie Thon	.30	.15	.03
☐ 845 Bill Travers	.09	.04	.01
☐ 846 Tom Underwood	.09	.04	.01
☐ 847 John Urrea	.09	.04	.01
☐ 848 Mike Vail	.09	.04	.01
☐ 849 Ellis Valentine	.09	.04	.01
☐ 850 Fernando Valenzuela	5.00	2.50	.50
☐ 851 Pete Vuckovich	.15	.07	.01
☐ 852 Mark Wagner	.09	.04	.01
☐ 853 Bob Walk	.20	.10	.02
☐ 854 Claudell Washington	.20	.10	.02
☐ 855 Dave Winfield	3.50	1.75	.35
☐ 856 Geoff Zahn	.09	.04	.01
☐ 857 Richie Zisk	.15	.07	.01
☐ 858 Checklist 727-858	.09	.01	.00

1982 Topps

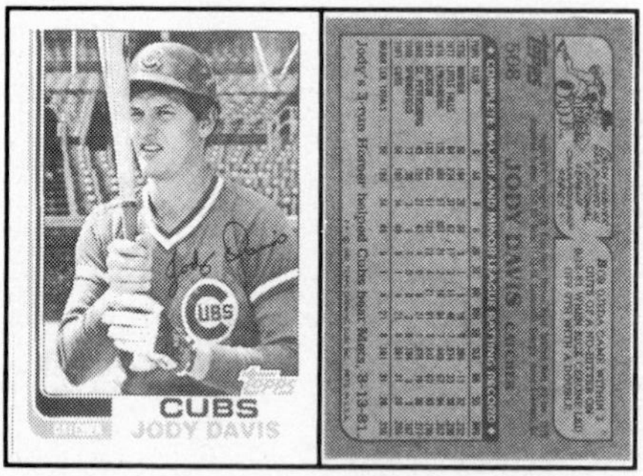

The cards in this 792-card set measure 2 1/2" by 3 1/2". The 1982 baseball series is the largest set Topps has ever issued at one printing. The 66-card increase from the previous year's total eliminated the "double print" practice, that had occurred in every regular issue since 1978. Cards 1-6 depict Highlights (HL) of the 1981 season, cards 161-168 picture League Leaders, and there are mini-series of AL (547-557) and NL (337-347) All-Stars (AS). The abbreviation "SA" in the checklist is given for the 40 "Super Action" cards introduced in this set. The team cards are actually Team Leader (TL) cards picturing the batting and pitching leader for that team with a checklist back. The key rookie cards in this set are George Bell, Cal Ripken Jr., and Dave Stewart.

	MINT	EXC	G-VG
COMPLETE SET (792)	100.00	50.00	10.00
COMMON PLAYER (1-792)	.07	.03	.01
☐ 1 HL: Steve Carlton Sets new NL strikeout record	.50	.25	.05
☐ 2 HL: Ron Davis Fans 8 straight in relief	.10	.05	.01
☐ 3 HL: Tim Raines Swipes 71 bases as rookie	.30	.15	.03
☐ 4 HL: Pete Rose Sets NL career hits mark	.75	.35	.07
☐ 5 HL: Nolan Ryan Pitches fifth career no-hitter	1.25	.60	.12
☐ 6 HL: Fern. Valenzuela 8 shutouts as rookie	.25	.12	.02
☐ 7 Scott Sanderson	.10	.05	.01
☐ 8 Rich Dauer	.07	.03	.01
☐ 9 Ron Guidry	.35	.17	.03
☐ 10 SA: Ron Guidry	.15	.07	.01
☐ 11 Gary Alexander	.07	.03	.01
☐ 12 Moose Haas	.07	.03	.01
☐ 13 Lamar Johnson	.07	.03	.01
☐ 14 Steve Howe	.07	.03	.01
☐ 15 Ellis Valentine	.07	.03	.01
☐ 16 Steve Comer	.07	.03	.01
☐ 17 Darrell Evans	.15	.07	.01
☐ 18 Fernando Arroyo	.07	.03	.01
☐ 19 Ernie Whitt	.07	.03	.01
☐ 20 Garry Maddox	.10	.05	.01
☐ 21 Orioles Rookies Bob Bonner Cal Ripken Jeff Schneider	25.00	12.50	2.50
☐ 22 Jim Beattie	.07	.03	.01
☐ 23 Willie Hernandez	.15	.07	.01
☐ 24 Dave Frost	.07	.03	.01
☐ 25 Jerry Remy	.07	.03	.01
☐ 26 Jorge Orta	.07	.03	.01
☐ 27 Tom Herr	.15	.07	.01
☐ 28 John Urrea	.07	.03	.01
☐ 29 Dwayne Murphy	.07	.03	.01
☐ 30 Tom Seaver	1.25	.60	.12
☐ 31 SA: Tom Seaver	.50	.25	.05
☐ 32 Gene Garber	.07	.03	.01
☐ 33 Jerry Morales	.07	.03	.01
☐ 34 Joe Sambito	.07	.03	.01
☐ 35 Willie Aikens	.07	.03	.01
☐ 36 Rangers TL Mgr. Don Zimmer Batting: Al Oliver Pitching: Doc Medich	.15	.07	.01
☐ 37 Dan Graham	.07	.03	.01
☐ 38 Charlie Lea	.07	.03	.01
☐ 39 Lou Whitaker	.40	.20	.04
☐ 40 Dave Parker	.40	.20	.04
☐ 41 SA: Dave Parker	.15	.07	.01
☐ 42 Rick Sofield	.07	.03	.01
☐ 43 Mike Cubbage	.07	.03	.01
☐ 44 Britt Burns	.07	.03	.01
☐ 45 Rick Cerone	.07	.03	.01
☐ 46 Jerry Augustine	.07	.03	.01
☐ 47 Jeff Leonard	.10	.05	.01
☐ 48 Bobby Castillo	.07	.03	.01
☐ 49 Alvis Woods	.07	.03	.01
☐ 50 Buddy Bell	.15	.07	.01
☐ 51 Cubs Rookies Jay Howell Carlos Lezcano Ty Waller	.50	.25	.05
☐ 52 Larry Andersen	.07	.03	.01
☐ 53 Greg Gross	.07	.03	.01
☐ 54 Ron Hassey	.07	.03	.01
☐ 55 Rick Burleson	.10	.05	.01
☐ 56 Mark Littell	.07	.03	.01
☐ 57 Craig Reynolds	.07	.03	.01
☐ 58 John D'Acquisto	.07	.03	.01
☐ 59 Rich Gedman	.50	.25	.05
☐ 60 Tony Armas	.10	.05	.01
☐ 61 Tommy Boggs	.07	.03	.01
☐ 62 Mike Tyson	.07	.03	.01
☐ 63 Mario Soto	.10	.05	.01
☐ 64 Lynn Jones	.07	.03	.01
☐ 65 Terry Kennedy	.07	.03	.01
☐ 66 Astros TL Mgr. Bill Virdon Batting: Art Howe Pitching: Nolan Ryan	.20	.10	.02
☐ 67 Rich Gale	.07	.03	.01
☐ 68 Roy Howell	.07	.03	.01
☐ 69 Al Williams	.07	.03	.01
☐ 70 Tim Raines	2.25	1.10	.22
☐ 71 Roy Lee Jackson	.07	.03	.01
☐ 72 Rick Auerbach	.07	.03	.01
☐ 73 Buddy Solomon	.07	.03	.01
☐ 74 Bob Clark	.07	.03	.01

☐ 75 Tommy John	.25	.12	.02
☐ 76 Greg Pryor	.07	.03	.01
☐ 77 Miguel Dilone	.07	.03	.01
☐ 78 George Medich	.07	.03	.01
☐ 79 Bob Bailor	.07	.03	.01
☐ 80 Jim Palmer	1.00	.50	.10
☐ 81 SA: Jim Palmer	.40	.20	.04
☐ 82 Bob Welch	.60	.30	.06
☐ 83 Yankees Rookies	.40	.20	.04
Steve Balboni			
Andy McGaffigan			
Andre Robertson			
☐ 84 Rennie Stennett	.07	.03	.01
☐ 85 Lynn McGlothen	.07	.03	.01
☐ 86 Dane Iorg	.07	.03	.01
☐ 87 Matt Keough	.07	.03	.01
☐ 88 Biff Pocoroba	.07	.03	.01
☐ 89 Steve Henderson	.07	.03	.01
☐ 90 Nolan Ryan	4.50	2.25	.45
☐ 91 Carney Lansford	.30	.15	.03
☐ 92 Brad Havens	.07	.03	.01
☐ 93 Larry Hisle	.07	.03	.01
☐ 94 Andy Hassler	.07	.03	.01
☐ 95 Ozzie Smith	1.25	.60	.12
☐ 96 Royals TL	.25	.12	.02
Mgr. Jim Frey			
Batting: George Brett			
Pitching: Larry Gura			
☐ 97 Paul Moskau	.07	.03	.01
☐ 98 Terry Bulling	.07	.03	.01
☐ 99 Barry Bonnell	.07	.03	.01
☐ 100 Mike Schmidt	2.75	1.35	.27
☐ 101 SA: Mike Schmidt	1.10	.55	.11
☐ 102 Dan Briggs	.07	.03	.01
☐ 103 Bob Lacey	.07	.03	.01
☐ 104 Rance Mulliniks	.07	.03	.01
☐ 105 Kirk Gibson	1.25	.60	.12
☐ 106 Enrique Romo	.07	.03	.01
☐ 107 Wayne Krenchicki	.07	.03	.01
☐ 108 Bob Sykes	.07	.03	.01
☐ 109 Dave Revering	.07	.03	.01
☐ 110 Carlton Fisk	1.00	.50	.10
☐ 111 SA: Carlton Fisk	.40	.20	.04
☐ 112 Billy Sample	.07	.03	.01
☐ 113 Steve McCatty	.07	.03	.01
☐ 114 Ken Landreaux	.07	.03	.01
☐ 115 Gaylord Perry	.40	.20	.04
☐ 116 Jim Wohlford	.07	.03	.01
☐ 117 Rawly Eastwick	.07	.03	.01
☐ 118 Expos Rookies	.75	.35	.07
Terry Francona			
Brad Mills			
Bryn Smith			
☐ 119 Joe Pittman	.07	.03	.01
☐ 120 Gary Lucas	.07	.03	.01
☐ 121 Ed Lynch	.07	.03	.01
☐ 122 Jamie Easterly UER	.07	.03	.01
(photo actually			
Reggie Cleveland)			
☐ 123 Danny Goodwin	.07	.03	.01
☐ 124 Reid Nichols	.07	.03	.01
☐ 125 Danny Ainge	.40	.20	.04
☐ 126 Braves TL	.15	.07	.01
Mgr. Bobby Cox			
Batting: C.Washington			
Pitching: Rick Mahler			
☐ 127 Lonnie Smith	.15	.07	.01
☐ 128 Frank Pastore	.07	.03	.01
☐ 129 Checklist 1-132	.10	.01	.00
☐ 130 Julio Cruz	.07	.03	.01
☐ 131 Stan Bahnsen	.07	.03	.01
☐ 132 Lee May	.10	.05	.01
☐ 133 Pat Underwood	.07	.03	.01
☐ 134 Dan Ford	.07	.03	.01
☐ 135 Andy Rincon	.07	.03	.01
☐ 136 Lenn Sakata	.07	.03	.01
☐ 137 George Cappuzzello	.07	.03	.01
☐ 138 Tony Pena	.35	.17	.03
☐ 139 Jeff Jones	.07	.03	.01
☐ 140 Ron LeFlore	.10	.05	.01
☐ 141 Indians Rookies	2.00	1.00	.20
Chris Bando			
Tom Brennan			
Von Hayes			
☐ 142 Dave LaRoche	.07	.03	.01
☐ 143 Mookie Wilson	.20	.10	.02
☐ 144 Fred Breining	.07	.03	.01
☐ 145 Bob Horner	.20	.10	.02
☐ 146 Mike Griffin	.07	.03	.01
☐ 147 Denny Walling	.07	.03	.01
☐ 148 Mickey Klutts	.07	.03	.01
☐ 149 Pat Putnam	.07	.03	.01
☐ 150 Ted Simmons	.20	.10	.02
☐ 151 Dave Edwards	.07	.03	.01

☐ 152 Ramon Aviles	.07	.03	.01
☐ 153 Roger Erickson	.07	.03	.01
☐ 154 Dennis Werth	.07	.03	.01
☐ 155 Otto Velez	.07	.03	.01
☐ 156 Oakland A's TL	.40	.20	.04
Mgr. Billy Martin			
Batting: R.Henderson			
Pitching: S. McCatty			
☐ 157 Steve Crawford	.07	.03	.01
☐ 158 Brian Downing	.10	.05	.01
☐ 159 Larry Biittner	.07	.03	.01
☐ 160 Luis Tiant	.15	.07	.01
☐ 161 Batting Leaders	.15	.07	.01
Bill Madlock			
Carney Lansford			
☐ 162 Home Run Leaders	.30	.15	.03
Mike Schmidt			
Tony Armas			
Dwight Evans			
Bobby Grich			
Eddie Murray			
☐ 163 RBI Leaders	.50	.25	.05
Mike Schmidt			
Eddie Murray			
☐ 164 Stolen Base Leaders	.60	.30	.06
Tim Raines			
Rickey Henderson			
☐ 165 Victory Leaders	.15	.07	.01
Tom Seaver			
Denny Martinez			
Steve McCatty			
Jack Morris			
Pete Vuckovich			
☐ 166 Strikeout Leaders	.15	.07	.01
Fernando Valenzuela			
Len Barker			
☐ 167 ERA Leaders	.60	.30	.06
Nolan Ryan			
Steve McCatty			
☐ 168 Leading Firemen	.15	.07	.01
Bruce Sutter			
Rollie Fingers			
☐ 169 Charlie Leibrandt	.07	.03	.01
☐ 170 Jim Bibby	.07	.03	.01
☐ 171 Giants Rookies	1.00	.50	.10
Bob Brenly			
Chili Davis			
Bob Tufts			
☐ 172 Bill Gullickson	.07	.03	.01
☐ 173 Jamie Quirk	.07	.03	.01
☐ 174 Dave Ford	.07	.03	.01
☐ 175 Jerry Mumphrey	.07	.03	.01
☐ 176 Dewey Robinson	.07	.03	.01
☐ 177 John Ellis	.07	.03	.01
☐ 178 Dyar Miller	.07	.03	.01
☐ 179 Steve Garvey	.90	.45	.09
☐ 180 SA: Steve Garvey	.40	.20	.04
☐ 181 Silvio Martinez	.07	.03	.01
☐ 182 Larry Herndon	.07	.03	.01
☐ 183 Mike Proly	.07	.03	.01
☐ 184 Mick Kelleher	.07	.03	.01
☐ 185 Phil Niekro	.50	.25	.05
☐ 186 Cardinals TL	.15	.07	.01
Mgr. Whitey Herzog			
Batting K. Hernandez			
Pitching Bob Forsch			
☐ 187 Jeff Newman	.07	.03	.01
☐ 188 Randy Martz	.07	.03	.01
☐ 189 Glenn Hoffman	.07	.03	.01
☐ 190 J.R. Richard	.10	.05	.01
☐ 191 Tim Wallach	2.50	1.25	.25
☐ 192 Broderick Perkins	.07	.03	.01
☐ 193 Darrell Jackson	.07	.03	.01
☐ 194 Mike Vail	.07	.03	.01
☐ 195 Paul Molitor	.40	.20	.04
☐ 196 Willie Upshaw	.07	.03	.01
☐ 197 Shane Rawley	.07	.03	.01
☐ 198 Chris Speier	.07	.03	.01
☐ 199 Don Aase	.07	.03	.01
☐ 200 George Brett	2.50	1.25	.25
☐ 201 SA: George Brett	1.00	.50	.10
☐ 202 Rick Manning	.07	.03	.01
☐ 203 Blue Jays Rookies	3.50	1.75	.35
Jesse Barfield			
Brian Milner			
Boomer Wells			
☐ 204 Gary Roenicke	.07	.03	.01
☐ 205 Neil Allen	.10	.05	.01
☐ 206 Tony Bernazard	.07	.03	.01
☐ 207 Rod Scurry	.07	.03	.01
☐ 208 Bobby Murcer	.15	.07	.01
☐ 209 Gary Lavelle	.07	.03	.01
☐ 210 Keith Hernandez	.60	.30	.06
☐ 211 Dan Petry	.07	.03	.01

☐ 212	Mario Mendoza	.07	.03	.01
☐ 213	Dave Stewart	11.00	5.50	1.10
☐ 214	Brian Asselstine	.07	.03	.01
☐ 215	Mike Krukow	.10	.05	.01
☐ 216	White Sox TL	.15	.07	.01
	Mgr. Tony LaRussa			
	Batting: Chet Lemon			
	Pitching: Dennis Lamp			
☐ 217	Bo McLaughlin	.07	.03	.01
☐ 218	Dave Roberts	.07	.03	.01
☐ 219	John Curtis	.07	.03	.01
☐ 220	Manny Trillo	.07	.03	.01
☐ 221	Jim Slaton	.07	.03	.01
☐ 222	Butch Wynegar	.07	.03	.01
☐ 223	Lloyd Moseby	.25	.12	.02
☐ 224	Bruce Bochte	.07	.03	.01
☐ 225	Mike Torrez	.07	.03	.01
☐ 226	Checklist 133-264	.10	.01	.00
☐ 227	Ray Burris	.07	.03	.01
☐ 228	Sam Mejias	.07	.03	.01
☐ 229	Geoff Zahn	.07	.03	.01
☐ 230	Willie Wilson	.20	.10	.02
☐ 231	Phillies Rookies	1.25	.60	.12
	Mark Davis			
	Bob Dernier			
	Ozzie Virgil			
☐ 232	Terry Crowley	.07	.03	.01
☐ 233	Duane Kuiper	.07	.03	.01
☐ 234	Ron Hodges	.07	.03	.01
☐ 235	Mike Easler	.10	.05	.01
☐ 236	John Martin	.07	.03	.01
☐ 237	Rusty Kuntz	.07	.03	.01
☐ 238	Kevin Saucier	.07	.03	.01
☐ 239	Jon Matlack	.07	.03	.01
☐ 240	Bucky Dent	.15	.07	.01
☐ 241	SA: Bucky Dent	.10	.05	.01
☐ 242	Milt May	.07	.03	.01
☐ 243	Bob Owchinko	.07	.03	.01
☐ 244	Rufino Linares	.07	.03	.01
☐ 245	Ken Reitz	.07	.03	.01
☐ 246	New York Mets TL	.20	.10	.02
	Mgr. Joe Torre			
	Batting: Hubie Brooks			
	Pitching: Mike Scott			
☐ 247	Pedro Guerrero	1.00	.50	.10
☐ 248	Frank LaCorte	.07	.03	.01
☐ 249	Tim Flannery	.07	.03	.01
☐ 250	Tug McGraw	.15	.07	.01
☐ 251	Fred Lynn	.30	.15	.03
☐ 252	SA: Fred Lynn	.15	.07	.01
☐ 253	Chuck Baker	.07	.03	.01
☐ 254	Jorge Bell	10.00	5.00	1.00
☐ 255	Tony Perez	.25	.12	.02
☐ 256	SA: Tony Perez	.10	.05	.01
☐ 257	Larry Harlow	.07	.03	.01
☐ 258	Bo Diaz	.07	.03	.01
☐ 259	Rodney Scott	.07	.03	.01
☐ 260	Bruce Sutter	.20	.10	.02
☐ 261	Tigers Rookies UER	.10	.05	.01
	Howard Bailey			
	Marty Castillo			
	Dave Rucker			
	(Rucker photo act-			
	ally Roger Weaver)			
☐ 262	Doug Bair	.07	.03	.01
☐ 263	Victor Cruz	.07	.03	.01
☐ 264	Dan Quisenberry	.20	.10	.02
☐ 265	Al Bumbry	.07	.03	.01
☐ 266	Rick Leach	.07	.03	.01
☐ 267	Kurt Bevacqua	.07	.03	.01
☐ 268	Rickey Keeton	.07	.03	.01
☐ 269	Jim Essian	.07	.03	.01
☐ 270	Rusty Staub	.15	.07	.01
☐ 271	Larry Bradford	.07	.03	.01
☐ 272	Bump Wills	.07	.03	.01
☐ 273	Doug Bird	.07	.03	.01
☐ 274	Bob Ojeda	1.00	.50	.10
☐ 275	Bob Watson	.10	.05	.01
☐ 276	Angels TL	.20	.10	.02
	Mgr. Gene Mauch			
	Batting: Rod Carew			
	Pitching: Ken Forsch			
☐ 277	Terry Puhl	.07	.03	.01
☐ 278	John Littlefield	.07	.03	.01
☐ 279	Bill Russell	.10	.05	.01
☐ 280	Ben Oglivie	.10	.05	.01
☐ 281	John Verhoeven	.07	.03	.01
☐ 282	Ken Macha	.07	.03	.01
☐ 283	Brian Allard	.07	.03	.01
☐ 284	Bob Grich	.10	.05	.01
☐ 285	Sparky Lyle	.15	.07	.01
☐ 286	Bill Fahey	.07	.03	.01
☐ 287	Alan Bannister	.07	.03	.01
☐ 288	Garry Templeton	.10	.05	.01

☐ 289	Bob Stanley	.07	.03	.01
☐ 290	Ken Singleton	.10	.05	.01
☐ 291	Pirates Rookies	1.25	.60	.12
	Vance Law			
	Bob Long			
	Johnny Ray			
☐ 292	David Palmer	.07	.03	.01
☐ 293	Rob Picciolo	.07	.03	.01
☐ 294	Mike LaCoss	.07	.03	.01
☐ 295	Jason Thompson	.07	.03	.01
☐ 296	Bob Walk	.10	.05	.01
☐ 297	Clint Hurdle	.07	.03	.01
☐ 298	Danny Darwin	.10	.05	.01
☐ 299	Steve Trout	.07	.03	.01
☐ 300	Reggie Jackson	1.50	.75	.15
☐ 301	SA: Reggie Jackson	.65	.30	.06
☐ 302	Doug Flynn	.07	.03	.01
☐ 303	Bill Caudill	.07	.03	.01
☐ 304	Johnnie LeMaster	.07	.03	.01
☐ 305	Don Sutton	.50	.25	.05
☐ 306	SA: Don Sutton	.20	.10	.02
☐ 307	Randy Bass	.10	.05	.01
☐ 308	Charlie Moore	.07	.03	.01
☐ 309	Pete Redfern	.07	.03	.01
☐ 310	Mike Hargrove	.10	.05	.01
☐ 311	Dodgers TL	.15	.07	.01
	Mgr. Tom Lasorda			
	Batting: Dusty Baker			
	Pitching: Burt Hooton			
☐ 312	Lenny Randle	.07	.03	.01
☐ 313	John Harris	.07	.03	.01
☐ 314	Buck Martinez	.07	.03	.01
☐ 315	Burt Hooton	.07	.03	.01
☐ 316	Steve Braun	.07	.03	.01
☐ 317	Dick Ruthven	.07	.03	.01
☐ 318	Mike Heath	.07	.03	.01
☐ 319	Dave Rozema	.07	.03	.01
☐ 320	Chris Chambliss	.10	.05	.01
☐ 321	SA: Chris Chambliss	.07	.03	.01
☐ 322	Garry Hancock	.07	.03	.01
☐ 323	Bill Lee	.10	.05	.01
☐ 324	Steve Dillard	.07	.03	.01
☐ 325	Jose Cruz	.10	.05	.01
☐ 326	Pete Falcone	.07	.03	.01
☐ 327	Joe Nolan	.07	.03	.01
☐ 328	Ed Farmer	.07	.03	.01
☐ 329	U.L. Washington	.07	.03	.01
☐ 330	Rick Wise	.07	.03	.01
☐ 331	Benny Ayala	.07	.03	.01
☐ 332	Don Robinson	.10	.05	.01
☐ 333	Brewers Rookies	.10	.05	.01
	Frank DiPino			
	Marshall Edwards			
	Chuck Porter			
☐ 334	Aurelio Rodriguez	.07	.03	.01
☐ 335	Jim Sundberg	.07	.03	.01
☐ 336	Mariners TL	.10	.05	.01
	Mgr. Rene Lachemann			
	Batting: Tom Paciorek			
	Pitching: Glenn Abbott			
☐ 337	Pete Rose AS	.75	.35	.07
☐ 338	Dave Lopes AS	.10	.05	.01
☐ 339	Mike Schmidt AS	.50	.25	.05
☐ 340	Dave Concepcion AS	.10	.05	.01
☐ 341	Andre Dawson AS	.25	.12	.02
☐ 342A	George Foster AS	.25	.12	.02
	(with autograph)			
☐ 342B	George Foster AS	1.75	.85	.17
	(w/o autograph)			
☐ 343	Dave Parker AS	.20	.10	.02
☐ 344	Gary Carter AS	.25	.12	.02
☐ 345	Fern. Valenzuela AS	.20	.10	.02
☐ 346A	Tom Seaver AS ERR	1.00	.50	.10
	("t ed")			
☐ 346B	Tom Seaver AS COR	.30	.15	.03
	("tied")			
☐ 347	Bruce Sutter AS	.10	.05	.01
☐ 348	Derrel Thomas	.07	.03	.01
☐ 349	George Frazier	.07	.03	.01
☐ 350	Thad Bosley	.07	.03	.01
☐ 351	Reds Rookies	.10	.05	.01
	Scott Brown			
	Geoff Coumbe			
	Paul Householder			
☐ 352	Dick Davis	.07	.03	.01
☐ 353	Jack O'Connor	.07	.03	.01
☐ 354	Roberto Ramos	.07	.03	.01
☐ 355	Dwight Evans	.35	.17	.03
☐ 356	Denny Lewallyn	.07	.03	.01
☐ 357	Butch Hobson	.07	.03	.01
☐ 358	Mike Parrott	.07	.03	.01
☐ 359	Jim Dwyer	.07	.03	.01
☐ 360	Len Barker	.07	.03	.01
☐ 361	Rafael Landestoy	.07	.03	.01

☐ 362	Jim Wright UER	.07	.03	.01
	(wrong Jim Wright			
	pictured)			
☐ 363	Bob Molinaro	.07	.03	.01
☐ 364	Doyle Alexander	.10	.05	.01
☐ 365	Bill Madlock	.15	.07	.01
☐ 366	Padres TL	.10	.05	.01
	Mgr. Frank Howard			
	Batting: Luis Salazar			
	Pitching: Eichelberger			
☐ 367	Jim Kaat	.15	.07	.01
☐ 368	Alex Trevino	.07	.03	.01
☐ 369	Champ Summers	.07	.03	.01
☐ 370	Mike Norris	.07	.03	.01
☐ 371	Jerry Don Gleaton	.07	.03	.01
☐ 372	Luis Gomez	.07	.03	.01
☐ 373	Gene Nelson	.10	.05	.01
☐ 374	Tim Blackwell	.07	.03	.01
☐ 375	Dusty Baker	.10	.05	.01
☐ 376	Chris Welsh	.07	.03	.01
☐ 377	Kiko Garcia	.07	.03	.01
☐ 378	Mike Caldwell	.07	.03	.01
☐ 379	Rob Wilfong	.07	.03	.01
☐ 380	Dave Stieb	.80	.40	.08
☐ 381	Red Sox Rookies	.80	.40	.08
	Bruce Hurst			
	Dave Schmidt			
	Julio Valdez			
☐ 382	Joe Simpson	.07	.03	.01
☐ 383A	Pascual Perez ERR	30.00	15.00	3.00
	(no position			
	on front)			
☐ 383B	Pascual Perez COR	.25	.12	.02
☐ 384	Keith Moreland	.07	.03	.01
☐ 385	Ken Forsch	.07	.03	.01
☐ 386	Jerry White	.07	.03	.01
☐ 387	Tom Veryzer	.07	.03	.01
☐ 388	Joe Rudi	.10	.05	.01
☐ 389	George Vukovich	.07	.03	.01
☐ 390	Eddie Murray	1.50	.75	.15
☐ 391	Dave Tobik	.07	.03	.01
☐ 392	Rick Bosetti	.07	.03	.01
☐ 393	Al Hrabosky	.10	.05	.01
☐ 394	Checklist 265-396	.10	.01	.00
☐ 395	Omar Moreno	.07	.03	.01
☐ 396	Twins TL	.10	.05	.01
	Mgr. Billy Gardner			
	Batting: John Castino			
	Pitching: F. Arroyo			
☐ 397	Ken Brett	.07	.03	.01
☐ 398	Mike Squires	.07	.03	.01
☐ 399	Pat Zachry	.07	.03	.01
☐ 400	Johnny Bench	1.25	.60	.12
☐ 401	SA: Johnny Bench	.50	.25	.05
☐ 402	Bill Stein	.07	.03	.01
☐ 403	Jim Tracy	.07	.03	.01
☐ 404	Dickie Thon	.10	.05	.01
☐ 405	Rick Reuschel	.20	.10	.02
☐ 406	Al Holland	.07	.03	.01
☐ 407	Danny Boone	.07	.03	.01
☐ 408	Ed Romero	.07	.03	.01
☐ 409	Don Cooper	.07	.03	.01
☐ 410	Ron Cey	.15	.07	.01
☐ 411	SA: Ron Cey	.10	.05	.01
☐ 412	Luis Leal	.07	.03	.01
☐ 413	Dan Meyer	.07	.03	.01
☐ 414	Elias Sosa	.07	.03	.01
☐ 415	Don Baylor	.15	.07	.01
☐ 416	Marty Bystrom	.07	.03	.01
☐ 417	Pat Kelly	.07	.03	.01
☐ 418	Rangers Rookies	.25	.12	.02
	John Butcher			
	Bobby Johnson			
	Dave Schmidt			
☐ 419	Steve Stone	.10	.05	.01
☐ 420	George Hendrick	.10	.05	.01
☐ 421	Mark Clear	.07	.03	.01
☐ 422	Cliff Johnson	.07	.03	.01
☐ 423	Stan Papi	.07	.03	.01
☐ 424	Bruce Benedict	.07	.03	.01
☐ 425	John Candelaria	.10	.05	.01
☐ 426	Orioles TL	.20	.10	.02
	Mgr. Earl Weaver			
	Batting: Eddie Murray			
	Pitching: Sam Stewart			
☐ 427	Ron Oester	.07	.03	.01
☐ 428	LaMarr Hoyt	.10	.05	.01
☐ 429	John Wathan	.07	.03	.01
☐ 430	Vida Blue	.10	.05	.01
☐ 431	SA: Vida Blue	.07	.03	.01
☐ 432	Mike Scott	.65	.30	.06
☐ 433	Alan Ashby	.07	.03	.01
☐ 434	Joe Lefebvre	.07	.03	.01
☐ 435	Robin Yount	2.00	1.00	.20
☐ 436	Joe Strain	.07	.03	.01
☐ 437	Juan Berenguer	.07	.03	.01
☐ 438	Pete Mackanin	.07	.03	.01
☐ 439	Dave Righetti	2.00	1.00	.20
☐ 440	Jeff Burroughs	.10	.05	.01
☐ 441	Astros Rookies	.10	.05	.01
	Danny Heep			
	Billy Smith			
	Bobby Sprowl			
☐ 442	Bruce Kison	.07	.03	.01
☐ 443	Mark Wagner	.07	.03	.01
☐ 444	Terry Forster	.10	.05	.01
☐ 445	Larry Parrish	.10	.05	.01
☐ 446	Wayne Garland	.07	.03	.01
☐ 447	Darrell Porter	.07	.03	.01
☐ 448	SA: Darrell Porter	.07	.03	.01
☐ 449	Luis Aguayo	.07	.03	.01
☐ 450	Jack Morris	.45	.22	.04
☐ 451	Ed Miller	.07	.03	.01
☐ 452	Lee Smith	1.00	.50	.10
☐ 453	Art Howe	.10	.05	.01
☐ 454	Rick Langford	.07	.03	.01
☐ 455	Tom Burgmeier	.07	.03	.01
☐ 456	Chicago Cubs TL	.10	.05	.01
	Mgr. Joe Amalfitano			
	Batting: Bill Buckner			
	Pitching: Randy Martz			
☐ 457	Tim Stoddard	.07	.03	.01
☐ 458	Willie Montanez	.07	.03	.01
☐ 459	Bruce Berenyi	.07	.03	.01
☐ 460	Jack Clark	.45	.22	.04
☐ 461	Rich Dotson	.07	.03	.01
☐ 462	Dave Chalk	.07	.03	.01
☐ 463	Jim Kern	.07	.03	.01
☐ 464	Juan Bonilla	.07	.03	.01
☐ 465	Lee Mazzilli	.07	.03	.01
☐ 466	Randy Lerch	.07	.03	.01
☐ 467	Mickey Hatcher	.07	.03	.01
☐ 468	Floyd Bannister	.07	.03	.01
☐ 469	Ed Ott	.07	.03	.01
☐ 470	John Mayberry	.10	.05	.01
☐ 471	Royals Rookies	.20	.10	.02
	Atlee Hammaker			
	Mike Jones			
	Darryl Motley			
☐ 472	Oscar Gamble	.07	.03	.01
☐ 473	Mike Stanton	.07	.03	.01
☐ 474	Ken Oberkfell	.07	.03	.01
☐ 475	Alan Trammell	.65	.30	.06
☐ 476	Brian Kingman	.07	.03	.01
☐ 477	Steve Yeager	.07	.03	.01
☐ 478	Ray Searage	.07	.03	.01
☐ 479	Rowland Office	.07	.03	.01
☐ 480	Steve Carlton	1.25	.60	.12
☐ 481	SA: Steve Carlton	.50	.25	.05
☐ 482	Glenn Hubbard	.07	.03	.01
☐ 483	Gary Woods	.07	.03	.01
☐ 484	Ivan DeJesus	.07	.03	.01
☐ 485	Kent Tekulve	.10	.05	.01
☐ 486	Yankees TL	.15	.07	.01
	Mgr. Bob Lemon			
	Batting: J. Mumphrey			
	Pitching: Tommy John			
☐ 487	Bob McClure	.07	.03	.01
☐ 488	Ron Jackson	.07	.03	.01
☐ 489	Rick Dempsey	.07	.03	.01
☐ 490	Dennis Eckersley	.50	.25	.05
☐ 491	Checklist 397-528	.10	.01	.00
☐ 492	Joe Price	.07	.03	.01
☐ 493	Chet Lemon	.10	.05	.01
☐ 494	Hubie Brooks	.50	.25	.05
☐ 495	Dennis Leonard	.10	.05	.01
☐ 496	Johnny Grubb	.07	.03	.01
☐ 497	Jim Anderson	.07	.03	.01
☐ 498	Dave Bergman	.07	.03	.01
☐ 499	Paul Mirabella	.07	.03	.01
☐ 500	Rod Carew	1.00	.50	.10
☐ 501	SA: Rod Carew	.40	.20	.04
☐ 502	Braves Rookies	2.25	1.10	.22
	Steve Bedrosian UER			
	(photo actually			
	Larry Owen)			
	Brett Butler			
	Larry Owen			
☐ 503	Julio Gonzalez	.07	.03	.01
☐ 504	Rick Peters	.07	.03	.01
☐ 505	Graig Nettles	.20	.10	.02
☐ 506	SA: Graig Nettles	.10	.05	.01
☐ 507	Terry Harper	.07	.03	.01
☐ 508	Jody Davis	.50	.25	.05
☐ 509	Harry Spilman	.07	.03	.01
☐ 510	Fernando Valenzuela	1.50	.75	.15
☐ 511	Ruppert Jones	.07	.03	.01
☐ 512	Jerry Dybzinski	.07	.03	.01

☐ 513	Rick Rhoden	.10	.05	.01
☐ 514	Joe Ferguson	.07	.03	.01
☐ 515	Larry Bowa	.15	.07	.01
☐ 516	SA: Larry Bowa	.10	.05	.01
☐ 517	Mark Brouhard	.07	.03	.01
☐ 518	Garth Iorg	.07	.03	.01
☐ 519	Glenn Adams	.07	.03	.01
☐ 520	Mike Flanagan	.10	.05	.01
☐ 521	Bill Almon	.07	.03	.01
☐ 522	Chuck Rainey	.07	.03	.01
☐ 523	Gary Gray	.07	.03	.01
☐ 524	Tom Hausman	.07	.03	.01
☐ 525	Ray Knight	.12	.06	.01
☐ 526	Expos TL	.10	.05	.01
	Mgr. Jim Fanning			
	Batting: W.Cromartie			
	Pitching: B.Gullickson			
☐ 527	John Henry Johnson	.07	.03	.01
☐ 528	Matt Alexander	.07	.03	.01
☐ 529	Allen Ripley	.07	.03	.01
☐ 530	Dickie Noles	.07	.03	.01
☐ 531	A's Rookies	.10	.05	.01
	Rich Bordi			
	Mark Budaska			
	Kelvin Moore			
☐ 532	Toby Harrah	.10	.05	.01
☐ 533	Joaquin Andujar	.10	.05	.01
☐ 534	Dave McKay	.07	.03	.01
☐ 535	Lance Parrish	.40	.20	.04
☐ 536	Rafael Ramirez	.07	.03	.01
☐ 537	Doug Capilla	.07	.03	.01
☐ 538	Lou Piniella	.15	.07	.01
☐ 539	Vern Ruhle	.07	.03	.01
☐ 540	Andre Dawson	1.10	.55	.11
☐ 541	Barry Evans	.07	.03	.01
☐ 542	Ned Yost	.07	.03	.01
☐ 543	Bill Robinson	.10	.05	.01
☐ 544	Larry Christenson	.07	.03	.01
☐ 545	Reggie Smith	.10	.05	.01
☐ 546	SA: Reggie Smith	.07	.03	.01
☐ 547	Rod Carew AS	.30	.15	.03
☐ 548	Willie Randolph AS	.10	.05	.01
☐ 549	George Brett AS	.50	.25	.05
☐ 550	Bucky Dent AS	.10	.05	.01
☐ 551	Reggie Jackson AS	.45	.22	.04
☐ 552	Ken Singleton AS	.07	.03	.01
☐ 553	Dave Winfield AS	.30	.15	.03
☐ 554	Carlton Fisk AS	.20	.10	.02
☐ 555	Scott McGregor AS	.07	.03	.01
☐ 556	Jack Morris AS	.10	.05	.01
☐ 557	Rich Gossage AS	.10	.05	.01
☐ 558	John Tudor	.50	.25	.05
☐ 559	Indians TL	.10	.05	.01
	Mgr. Dave Garcia			
	Batting: Mike Hargrove			
	Pitching: Bert Blyleven			
☐ 560	Doug Corbett	.07	.03	.01
☐ 561	Cardinals Rookies	.10	.05	.01
	Glenn Brummer			
	Luis DeLeon			
	Gene Roof			
☐ 562	Mike O'Berry	.07	.03	.01
☐ 563	Ross Baumgarten	.07	.03	.01
☐ 564	Doug DeCinces	.10	.05	.01
☐ 565	Jackson Todd	.07	.03	.01
☐ 566	Mike Jorgensen	.07	.03	.01
☐ 567	Bob Babcock	.07	.03	.01
☐ 568	Joe Pettini	.07	.03	.01
☐ 569	Willie Randolph	.10	.05	.01
☐ 570	SA: Willie Randolph	.07	.03	.01
☐ 571	Glenn Abbott	.07	.03	.01
☐ 572	Juan Beniquez	.07	.03	.01
☐ 573	Rick Waits	.07	.03	.01
☐ 574	Mike Ramsey	.07	.03	.01
☐ 575	Al Cowens	.07	.03	.01
☐ 576	Giants TL	.10	.05	.01
	Mgr. Frank Robinson			
	Batting: Milt May			
	Pitching: Vida Blue			
☐ 577	Rick Monday	.10	.05	.01
☐ 578	Shooty Babitt	.07	.03	.01
☐ 579	Rick Mahler	.30	.15	.03
☐ 580	Bobby Bonds	.15	.07	.01
☐ 581	Ron Reed	.07	.03	.01
☐ 582	Luis Pujols	.07	.03	.01
☐ 583	Tippy Martinez	.07	.03	.01
☐ 584	Hosken Powell	.07	.03	.01
☐ 585	Rollie Fingers	.40	.20	.04
☐ 586	SA: Rollie Fingers	.15	.07	.01
☐ 587	Tim Lollar	.07	.03	.01
☐ 588	Dale Berra	.07	.03	.01
☐ 589	Dave Stapleton	.07	.03	.01
☐ 590	Al Oliver	.15	.07	.01
☐ 591	SA: Al Oliver	.10	.05	.01
☐ 592	Craig Swan	.07	.03	.01
☐ 593	Billy Smith	.07	.03	.01
☐ 594	Renie Martin	.07	.03	.01
☐ 595	Dave Collins	.07	.03	.01
☐ 596	Damaso Garcia	.10	.05	.01
☐ 597	Wayne Nordhagen	.07	.03	.01
☐ 598	Bob Galasso	.07	.03	.01
☐ 599	White Sox Rookies	.07	.03	.01
	Jay Loviglio			
	Reggie Patterson			
	Leo Sutherland			
☐ 600	Dave Winfield	.75	.35	.07
☐ 601	Sid Monge	.07	.03	.01
☐ 602	Freddie Patek	.07	.03	.01
☐ 603	Rich Hebner	.07	.03	.01
☐ 604	Orlando Sanchez	.07	.03	.01
☐ 605	Steve Rogers	.07	.03	.01
☐ 606	Blue Jays TL	.10	.05	.01
	Mgr. Bobby Mattick			
	Batting: J.Mayberry			
	Pitching: Dave Stieb			
☐ 607	Leon Durham	.10	.05	.01
☐ 608	Jerry Royster	.07	.03	.01
☐ 609	Rick Sutcliffe	.25	.12	.02
☐ 610	Rickey Henderson	9.00	4.50	.90
☐ 611	Joe Niekro	.15	.07	.01
☐ 612	Gary Ward	.10	.05	.01
☐ 613	Jim Gantner	.07	.03	.01
☐ 614	Juan Eichelberger	.07	.03	.01
☐ 615	Bob Boone	.15	.07	.01
☐ 616	SA: Bob Boone	.10	.05	.01
☐ 617	Scott McGregor	.10	.05	.01
☐ 618	Tim Foli	.07	.03	.01
☐ 619	Bill Campbell	.07	.03	.01
☐ 620	Ken Griffey	.25	.12	.02
☐ 621	SA: Ken Griffey	.10	.05	.01
☐ 622	Dennis Lamp	.07	.03	.01
☐ 623	Mets Rookies	.90	.45	.09
	Ron Gardenhire			
	Terry Leach			
	Tim Leary			
☐ 624	Fergie Jenkins	.20	.10	.02
☐ 625	Hal McRae	.10	.05	.01
☐ 626	Randy Jones	.07	.03	.01
☐ 627	Enos Cabell	.07	.03	.01
☐ 628	Bill Travers	.07	.03	.01
☐ 629	John Wockenfuss	.07	.03	.01
☐ 630	Joe Charboneau	.10	.05	.01
☐ 631	Gene Tenace	.07	.03	.01
☐ 632	Bryan Clark	.07	.03	.01
☐ 633	Mitchell Page	.07	.03	.01
☐ 634	Checklist 529-660	.10	.01	.00
☐ 635	Ron Davis	.07	.03	.01
☐ 636	Phillies TL	.40	.20	.04
	Mgr. Dallas Green			
	Batting: Pete Rose			
	Pitching: S.Carlton			
☐ 637	Rick Camp	.07	.03	.01
☐ 638	John Milner	.07	.03	.01
☐ 639	Ken Kravec	.07	.03	.01
☐ 640	Cesar Cedeno	.10	.05	.01
☐ 641	Steve Mura	.07	.03	.01
☐ 642	Mike Scioscia	.10	.05	.01
☐ 643	Pete Vuckovich	.10	.05	.01
☐ 644	John Castino	.07	.03	.01
☐ 645	Frank White	.10	.05	.01
☐ 646	SA: Frank White	.07	.03	.01
☐ 647	Warren Brusstar	.07	.03	.01
☐ 648	Jose Morales	.07	.03	.01
☐ 649	Ken Clay	.07	.03	.01
☐ 650	Carl Yastrzemski	1.50	.75	.15
☐ 651	SA: Carl Yastrzemski	.60	.30	.06
☐ 652	Steve Nicosia	.07	.03	.01
☐ 653	Angels Rookies	3.00	1.50	.30
	Tom Brunansky			
	Luis Sanchez			
	Daryl Sconiers			
☐ 654	Jim Morrison	.07	.03	.01
☐ 655	Joel Youngblood	.07	.03	.01
☐ 656	Eddie Whitson	.12	.06	.01
☐ 657	Tom Poquette	.07	.03	.01
☐ 658	Tito Landrum	.07	.03	.01
☐ 659	Fred Martinez	.07	.03	.01
☐ 660	Dave Concepcion	.15	.07	.01
☐ 661	SA: Dave Concepcion	.10	.05	.01
☐ 662	Luis Salazar	.10	.05	.01
☐ 663	Hector Cruz	.07	.03	.01
☐ 664	Dan Spillner	.07	.03	.01
☐ 665	Jim Clancy	.07	.03	.01
☐ 666	Tigers TL	.10	.05	.01
	Mgr. Sparky Anderson			
	Batting: Steve Kemp			
	Pitching: Dan Petry			
☐ 667	Jeff Reardon	.35	.17	.03

☐ 668 Dale Murphy	2.00	1.00	.20
☐ 669 Larry Milbourne	.07	.03	.01
☐ 670 Steve Kemp	.10	.05	.01
☐ 671 Mike Davis	.10	.05	.01
☐ 672 Bob Knepper	.10	.05	.01
☐ 673 Keith Drumwright	.07	.03	.01
☐ 674 Dave Goltz	.07	.03	.01
☐ 675 Cecil Cooper	.20	.10	.02
☐ 676 Sal Butera	.07	.03	.01
☐ 677 Alfredo Griffin	.10	.05	.01
☐ 678 Tom Paciorek	.07	.03	.01
☐ 679 Sammy Stewart	.07	.03	.01
☐ 680 Gary Matthews	.10	.05	.01
☐ 681 Dodgers Rookies	5.00	2.50	.50
Mike Marshall			
Ron Roenicke			
Steve Sax			
☐ 682 Jesse Jefferson	.07	.03	.01
☐ 683 Phil Garner	.07	.03	.01
☐ 684 Harold Baines	.75	.35	.07
☐ 685 Bert Blyleven	.30	.15	.03
☐ 686 Gary Allenson	.07	.03	.01
☐ 687 Greg Minton	.07	.03	.01
☐ 688 Leon Roberts	.07	.03	.01
☐ 689 Lary Sorensen	.07	.03	.01
☐ 690 Dave Kingman	.20	.10	.02
☐ 691 Dan Schatzeder	.07	.03	.01
☐ 692 Wayne Gross	.07	.03	.01
☐ 693 Cesar Geronimo	.07	.03	.01
☐ 694 Dave Wehrmeister	.07	.03	.01
☐ 695 Warren Cromartie	.07	.03	.01
☐ 696 Pirates TL	.10	.05	.01
Mgr. Chuck Tanner			
Batting: Bill Madlock			
Pitching:Eddie Solomon			
☐ 697 John Montefusco	.10	.05	.01
☐ 698 Tony Scott	.07	.03	.01
☐ 699 Dick Tidrow	.07	.03	.01
☐ 700 George Foster	.25	.12	.02
☐ 701 SA: George Foster	.10	.05	.01
☐ 702 Steve Renko	.07	.03	.01
☐ 703 Brewers TL	.10	.05	.01
Mgr. Bob Rodgers			
Batting: Cecil Cooper			
Pitching: P.Vuckovich			
☐ 704 Mickey Rivers	.10	.05	.01
☐ 705 SA: Mickey Rivers	.07	.03	.01
☐ 706 Barry Foote	.07	.03	.01
☐ 707 Mark Bomback	.07	.03	.01
☐ 708 Gene Richards	.07	.03	.01
☐ 709 Don Money	.07	.03	.01
☐ 710 Jerry Reuss	.10	.05	.01
☐ 711 Mariners Rookies	1.75	.85	.17
Dave Edler			
Dave Henderson			
Reggie Walton			
☐ 712 Dennis Martinez	.10	.05	.01
☐ 713 Del Unser	.07	.03	.01
☐ 714 Jerry Koosman	.15	.07	.01
☐ 715 Willie Stargell	.60	.30	.06
☐ 716 SA: Willie Stargell	.25	.12	.02
☐ 717 Rick Miller	.07	.03	.01
☐ 718 Charlie Hough	.10	.05	.01
☐ 719 Jerry Narron	.07	.03	.01
☐ 720 Greg Luzinski	.15	.07	.01
☐ 721 SA: Greg Luzinski	.10	.05	.01
☐ 722 Jerry Martin	.07	.03	.01
☐ 723 Junior Kennedy	.07	.03	.01
☐ 724 Dave Rosello	.07	.03	.01
☐ 725 Amos Otis	.10	.05	.01
☐ 726 SA: Amos Otis	.07	.03	.01
☐ 727 Sixto Lezcano	.07	.03	.01
☐ 728 Aurelio Lopez	.07	.03	.01
☐ 729 Jim Spencer	.07	.03	.01
☐ 730 Gary Carter	.80	.40	.08
☐ 731 Padres Rookies	.07	.03	.01
Mike Armstrong			
Doug Gwosdz			
Fred Kuhaulua			
☐ 732 Mike Lum	.07	.03	.01
☐ 733 Larry McWilliams	.07	.03	.01
☐ 734 Mike Ivie	.07	.03	.01
☐ 735 Rudy May	.07	.03	.01
☐ 736 Jerry Turner	.07	.03	.01
☐ 737 Reggie Cleveland	.07	.03	.01
☐ 738 Dave Engle	.07	.03	.01
☐ 739 Joey McLaughlin	.07	.03	.01
☐ 740 Dave Lopes	.10	.05	.01
☐ 741 SA: Dave Lopes	.07	.03	.01
☐ 742 Dick Drago	.07	.03	.01
☐ 743 John Stearns	.07	.03	.01
☐ 744 Mike Witt	.90	.45	.09
☐ 745 Bake McBride	.07	.03	.01
☐ 746 Andre Thornton	.10	.05	.01

☐ 747 John Lowenstein	.07	.03	.01
☐ 748 Marc Hill	.07	.03	.01
☐ 749 Bob Shirley	.07	.03	.01
☐ 750 Jim Rice	.60	.30	.06
☐ 751 Rick Honeycutt	.07	.03	.01
☐ 752 Lee Lacy	.07	.03	.01
☐ 753 Tom Brookens	.07	.03	.01
☐ 754 Joe Morgan	.60	.30	.06
☐ 755 SA: Joe Morgan	.25	.12	.02
☐ 756 Reds TL	.30	.15	.03
Mgr. John McNamara			
Batting: Ken Griffey			
Pitching: Tom Seaver			
☐ 757 Tom Underwood	.07	.03	.01
☐ 758 Claudell Washington	.10	.05	.01
☐ 759 Paul Splittorff	.07	.03	.01
☐ 760 Bill Buckner	.15	.07	.01
☐ 761 Dave Smith	.12	.06	.01
☐ 762 Mike Phillips	.07	.03	.01
☐ 763 Tom Hume	.07	.03	.01
☐ 764 Steve Swisher	.07	.03	.01
☐ 765 Gorman Thomas	.15	.07	.01
☐ 766 Twins Rookies	6.00	3.00	.60
Lenny Faedo			
Kent Hrbek			
Tim Laudner			
☐ 767 Roy Smalley	.07	.03	.01
☐ 768 Jerry Garvin	.07	.03	.01
☐ 769 Richie Zisk	.10	.05	.01
☐ 770 Rich Gossage	.25	.12	.02
☐ 771 SA: Rich Gossage	.10	.05	.01
☐ 772 Bert Campaneris	.10	.05	.01
☐ 773 John Denny	.10	.05	.01
☐ 774 Jay Johnstone	.10	.05	.01
☐ 775 Bob Forsch	.07	.03	.01
☐ 776 Mark Belanger	.10	.05	.01
☐ 777 Tom Griffin	.07	.03	.01
☐ 778 Kevin Hickey	.07	.03	.01
☐ 779 Grant Jackson	.07	.03	.01
☐ 780 Pete Rose	2.25	1.10	.22
☐ 781 SA: Pete Rose	.90	.45	.09
☐ 782 Frank Taveras	.07	.03	.01
☐ 783 Greg Harris	.35	.17	.03
☐ 784 Milt Wilcox	.07	.03	.01
☐ 785 Dan Driessen	.07	.03	.01
☐ 786 Red Sox TL	.10	.05	.01
Mgr. Ralph Houk			
Batting: C.Lansford			
Pitching: Mike Torrez			
☐ 787 Fred Stanley	.07	.03	.01
☐ 788 Woodie Fryman	.07	.03	.01
☐ 789 Checklist 661-792	.10	.01	.00
☐ 790 Larry Gura	.07	.03	.01
☐ 791 Bobby Brown	.07	.03	.01
☐ 792 Frank Tanana	.15	.07	.01

1982 Topps Traded

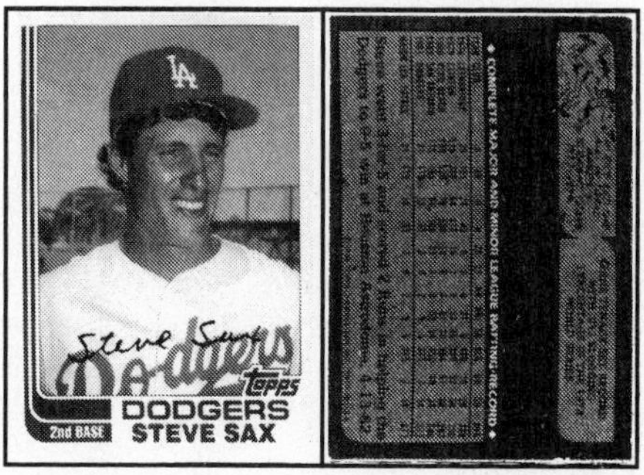

The cards in this 132-card set measure 2 1/2" by 3 1/2". The 1982 Topps Traded or extended series is distinguished by a "T" printed after the number (located on the reverse). This was the first time Topps began a new tradition of newly numbering (and alphabetizing) their traded series from 1T to 132T. Of the total cards, 70 players represent the American League and 61 represent the National League, with the remaining card a numbered checklist (132T). The Cubs lead the pack with 12 changes, while the Red Sox are the only team in either league to have no new additions. All 131 player photos used in the set are completely new. Of this total, 112 individuals are seen in the uniform of their new team, 11 others have been elevated to single card status from "Future Stars" cards, and eight more are entirely new to the 1982 Topps lineup. The backs are almost completely red in color with black print. There are no key rookie cards in this set. Although the Cal Ripken card is this set's most valuable card, it is not his Rookie Card since he had already been included in the 1982 regualr set, albeit on a multi-player card.

	MINT	EXC	G-VG
COMPLETE SET (132)	51.00	24.00	4.00
COMMON PLAYER (1-132)	.09	.04	.01
□ 1T Doyle Alexander	.15	.07	.01
□ 2T Jesse Barfield	1.75	.85	.17
□ 3T Ross Baumgarten	.09	.04	.01
□ 4T Steve Bedrosian	.75	.35	.07
□ 5T Mark Belanger	.15	.07	.01
□ 6T Kurt Bevacqua	.09	.04	.01
□ 7T Tim Blackwell	.09	.04	.01
□ 8T Vida Blue	.15	.07	.01
□ 9T Bob Boone	.30	.15	.03
□ 10T Larry Bowa	.20	.10	.02
□ 11T Dan Briggs	.09	.04	.01
□ 12T Bobby Brown	.09	.04	.01
□ 13T Tom Brunansky	1.75	.85	.17
□ 14T Jeff Burroughs	.15	.07	.01
□ 15T Enos Cabell	.09	.04	.01
□ 16T Bill Campbell	.09	.04	.01
□ 17T Bobby Castillo	.09	.04	.01
□ 18T Bill Caudill	.09	.04	.01
□ 19T Cesar Cedeno	.20	.10	.02
□ 20T Dave Collins	.09	.04	.01
□ 21T Doug Corbett	.09	.04	.01
□ 22T Al Cowens	.09	.04	.01
□ 23T Chili Davis	1.25	.60	.12
□ 24T Dick Davis	.09	.04	.01
□ 25T Ron Davis	.09	.04	.01
□ 26T Doug DeCinces	.20	.10	.02
□ 27T Ivan DeJesus	.09	.04	.01
□ 28T Bob Dernier	.15	.07	.01
□ 29T Bo Diaz	.09	.04	.01
□ 30T Roger Erickson	.09	.04	.01
□ 31T Jim Essian	.09	.04	.01
□ 32T Ed Farmer	.09	.04	.01
□ 33T Doug Flynn	.09	.04	.01
□ 34T Tim Foli	.09	.04	.01
□ 35T Dan Ford	.09	.04	.01
□ 36T George Foster	.35	.17	.03
□ 37T Dave Frost	.09	.04	.01
□ 38T Rich Gale	.09	.04	.01
□ 39T Ron Gardenhire	.15	.07	.01
□ 40T Ken Griffey	.50	.25	.05
□ 41T Greg Harris	.20	.10	.02
□ 42T Von Hayes	1.75	.85	.17
□ 43T Larry Herndon	.09	.04	.01
□ 44T Kent Hrbek	6.00	3.00	.60
□ 45T Mike Ivie	.09	.04	.01
□ 46T Grant Jackson	.09	.04	.01
□ 47T Reggie Jackson	4.50	2.25	.45
□ 48T Ron Jackson	.09	.04	.01
□ 49T Fergie Jenkins	.50	.25	.05
□ 50T Lamar Johnson	.09	.04	.01
□ 51T Randy Johnson	.09	.04	.01
□ 52T Jay Johnstone	.20	.10	.02
□ 53T Mick Kelleher	.09	.04	.01
□ 54T Steve Kemp	.15	.07	.01
□ 55T Junior Kennedy	.09	.04	.01
□ 56T Jim Kern	.09	.04	.01
□ 57T Ray Knight	.25	.12	.02
□ 58T Wayne Krenchicki	.09	.04	.01
□ 59T Mike Krukow	.15	.07	.01
□ 60T Duane Kuiper	.09	.04	.01
□ 61T Mike LaCoss	.09	.04	.01
□ 62T Chet Lemon	.15	.07	.01
□ 63T Sixto Lezcano	.09	.04	.01
□ 64T Dave Lopes	.20	.10	.02
□ 65T Jerry Martin	.09	.04	.01
□ 66T Renie Martin	.09	.04	.01
□ 67T John Mayberry	.15	.07	.01
□ 68T Lee Mazzilli	.09	.04	.01
□ 69T Bake McBride	.09	.04	.01
□ 70T Dan Meyer	.09	.04	.01
□ 71T Larry Milbourne	.09	.04	.01
□ 72T Eddie Milner	.15	.07	.01
□ 73T Sid Monge	.09	.04	.01
□ 74T John Montefusco	.15	.07	.01
□ 75T Jose Morales	.09	.04	.01
□ 76T Keith Moreland	.15	.07	.01
□ 77T Jim Morrison	.09	.04	.01
□ 78T Rance Mulliniks	.09	.04	.01
□ 79T Steve Mura	.09	.04	.01
□ 80T Gene Nelson	.15	.07	.01
□ 81T Joe Nolan	.09	.04	.01
□ 82T Dickie Noles	.09	.04	.01
□ 83T Al Oliver	.20	.10	.02
□ 84T Jorge Orta	.09	.04	.01
□ 85T Tom Paciorek	.09	.04	.01
□ 86T Larry Parrish	.15	.07	.01
□ 87T Jack Perconte	.09	.04	.01
□ 88T Gaylord Perry	1.00	.50	.10
□ 89T Rob Picciolo	.09	.04	.01
□ 90T Joe Pittman	.09	.04	.01
□ 91T Hosken Powell	.09	.04	.01
□ 92T Mike Proly	.09	.04	.01
□ 93T Greg Pryor	.09	.04	.01
□ 94T Charlie Puleo	.15	.07	.01
□ 95T Shane Rawley	.15	.07	.01
□ 96T Johnny Ray	.90	.45	.09
□ 97T Dave Revering	.09	.04	.01
□ 98T Cal Ripken	30.00	15.00	3.00
□ 99T Allen Ripley	.09	.04	.01
□ 100T Bill Robinson	.15	.07	.01
□ 101T Aurelio Rodriguez	.09	.04	.01
□ 102T Joe Rudi	.15	.07	.01
□ 103T Steve Sax	6.00	3.00	.60
□ 104T Dan Schatzeder	.09	.04	.01
□ 105T Bob Shirley	.09	.04	.01
□ 106T Eric Show	.90	.45	.09
□ 107T Roy Smalley	.15	.07	.01
□ 108T Lonnie Smith	.25	.12	.02
□ 109T Ozzie Smith	7.50	3.75	.75
□ 110T Reggie Smith	.20	.10	.02
□ 111T Lary Sorensen	.09	.04	.01
□ 112T Elias Sosa	.09	.04	.01
□ 113T Mike Stanton	.09	.04	.01
□ 114T Steve Stroughter	.09	.04	.01
□ 115T Champ Summers	.09	.04	.01
□ 116T Rick Sutcliffe	.50	.25	.05
□ 117T Frank Tanana	.15	.07	.01
□ 118T Frank Taveras	.09	.04	.01
□ 119T Garry Templeton	.15	.07	.01
□ 120T Alex Trevino	.09	.04	.01
□ 121T Jerry Turner	.09	.04	.01
□ 122T Ed VandeBerg	.15	.07	.01
□ 123T Tom Veryzer	.09	.04	.01
□ 124T Ron Washington	.15	.07	.01
□ 125T Bob Watson	.15	.07	.01
□ 126T Dennis Werth	.09	.04	.01
□ 127T Eddie Whitson	.25	.12	.02
□ 128T Rob Wilfong	.09	.04	.01
□ 129T Bump Wills	.09	.04	.01
□ 130T Gary Woods	.09	.04	.01
□ 131T Butch Wynegar	.15	.07	.01
□ 132T Checklist: 1-132	.09	.01	.00

1983 Topps

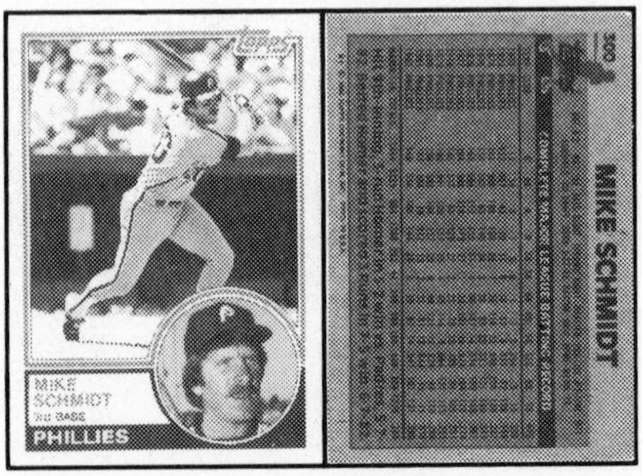

The cards in this 792-card set measure 2 1/2" by 3 1/2". Each regular card of the Topps set for 1983 features a large action shot of a player with a small cameo portrait at bottom right. There are special series for AL and NL All Stars (386-407),

League Leaders (701-708), and Record Breakers (1-6). In addition, there are 34 "Super Veteran" (SV) cards and six numbered checklist cards. The Super Veteran cards are oriented horizontally and show two pictures of the featured player, a recent picture and a picture showing the player as a rookie when he broke in. The cards are numbered on the reverse at the upper left corner. The team cards are actually Team Leader (TL) cards picturing the batting and pitching leader for that team with a checklist back. The key rookie cards in this set are Wade Boggs, Tony Gwynn, Ryne Sandberg, and Frank Viola.

	MINT	EXC	G-VG
COMPLETE SET (792)	135.00	65.00	13.50
COMMON PLAYER (1-792)	.07	.03	.01
☐ 1 RB: Tony Armas	.12	.06	.01
11 putouts by rightfielder			
☐ 2 RB: Rickey Henderson	.90	.45	.09
Sets modern record for steals, season			
☐ 3 RB: Greg Minton	.10	.05	.01
269 1/3 homerless innings streak			
☐ 4 RB: Lance Parrish	.15	.07	.01
Threw out three baserunners in All-Star game			
☐ 5 RB: Manny Trillo	.10	.05	.01
479 consecutive errorless chances, second baseman			
☐ 6 RB: John Wathan	.10	.05	.01
ML steals record for catchers, 31			
☐ 7 Gene Richards	.07	.03	.01
☐ 8 Steve Balboni	.10	.05	.01
☐ 9 Joey McLaughlin	.07	.03	.01
☐ 10 Gorman Thomas	.15	.07	.01
☐ 11 Billy Gardner MG	.07	.03	.01
☐ 12 Paul Mirabella	.07	.03	.01
☐ 13 Larry Herndon	.07	.03	.01
☐ 14 Frank LaCorte	.07	.03	.01
☐ 15 Ron Cey	.15	.07	.01
☐ 16 George Vukovich	.07	.03	.01
☐ 17 Kent Tekulve	.10	.05	.01
☐ 18 SV: Kent Tekulve	.07	.03	.01
☐ 19 Oscar Gamble	.07	.03	.01
☐ 20 Carlton Fisk	.75	.35	.07
☐ 21 Baltimore Orioles TL	.40	.20	.04
BA: Eddie Murray			
ERA: Jim Palmer			
☐ 22 Randy Martz	.07	.03	.01
☐ 23 Mike Heath	.07	.03	.01
☐ 24 Steve Mura	.07	.03	.01
☐ 25 Hal McRae	.10	.05	.01
☐ 26 Jerry Royster	.07	.03	.01
☐ 27 Doug Corbett	.07	.03	.01
☐ 28 Bruce Bochte	.07	.03	.01
☐ 29 Randy Jones	.07	.03	.01
☐ 30 Jim Rice	.40	.20	.04
☐ 31 Bill Gullickson	.10	.05	.01
☐ 32 Dave Bergman	.07	.03	.01
☐ 33 Jack O'Connor	.07	.03	.01
☐ 34 Paul Householder	.07	.03	.01
☐ 35 Rollie Fingers	.35	.17	.03
☐ 36 SV: Rollie Fingers	.15	.07	.01
☐ 37 Darrell Johnson MG	.07	.03	.01
☐ 38 Tim Flannery	.07	.03	.01
☐ 39 Terry Puhl	.07	.03	.01
☐ 40 Fernando Valenzuela	.65	.30	.06
☐ 41 Jerry Turner	.07	.03	.01
☐ 42 Dale Murray	.07	.03	.01
☐ 43 Bob Dernier	.07	.03	.01
☐ 44 Don Robinson	.07	.03	.01
☐ 45 John Mayberry	.10	.05	.01
☐ 46 Richard Dotson	.10	.05	.01
☐ 47 Dave McKay	.07	.03	.01
☐ 48 Lary Sorensen	.07	.03	.01
☐ 49 Willie McGee	5.00	2.50	.50
☐ 50 Bob Horner UER	.20	.10	.02
('82 RBI total 7)			
☐ 51 Chicago Cubs TL	.15	.07	.01
BA: Leon Durham			
ERA: Fergie Jenkins			
☐ 52 Onix Concepcion	.07	.03	.01
☐ 53 Mike Witt	.15	.07	.01
☐ 54 Jim Maler	.07	.03	.01
☐ 55 Mookie Wilson	.15	.07	.01
☐ 56 Chuck Rainey	.07	.03	.01
☐ 57 Tim Blackwell	.07	.03	.01
☐ 58 Al Holland	.07	.03	.01
☐ 59 Benny Ayala	.07	.03	.01
☐ 60 Johnny Bench	1.00	.50	.10
☐ 61 SV: Johnny Bench	.40	.20	.04
☐ 62 Bob McClure	.07	.03	.01
☐ 63 Rick Monday	.10	.05	.01
☐ 64 Bill Stein	.07	.03	.01
☐ 65 Jack Morris	.30	.15	.03
☐ 66 Bob Lillis MG	.07	.03	.01
☐ 67 Sal Butera	.07	.03	.01
☐ 68 Eric Show	.35	.17	.03
☐ 69 Lee Lacy	.07	.03	.01
☐ 70 Steve Carlton	.75	.35	.07
☐ 71 SV: Steve Carlton	.30	.15	.03
☐ 72 Tom Paciorek	.07	.03	.01
☐ 73 Allen Ripley	.07	.03	.01
☐ 74 Julio Gonzalez	.07	.03	.01
☐ 75 Amos Otis	.10	.05	.01
☐ 76 Rick Mahler	.07	.03	.01
☐ 77 Hosken Powell	.07	.03	.01
☐ 78 Bill Caudill	.07	.03	.01
☐ 79 Mick Kelleher	.07	.03	.01
☐ 80 George Foster	.20	.10	.02
☐ 81 Yankees TL	.15	.07	.01
BA: Jerry Mumphrey			
ERA: Dave Righetti			
☐ 82 Bruce Hurst	.30	.15	.03
☐ 83 Ryne Sandberg	45.00	22.50	4.50
☐ 84 Milt May	.07	.03	.01
☐ 85 Ken Singleton	.10	.05	.01
☐ 86 Tom Hume	.07	.03	.01
☐ 87 Joe Rudi	.10	.05	.01
☐ 88 Jim Gantner	.07	.03	.01
☐ 89 Leon Roberts	.07	.03	.01
☐ 90 Jerry Reuss	.10	.05	.01
☐ 91 Larry Milbourne	.07	.03	.01
☐ 92 Mike LaCoss	.07	.03	.01
☐ 93 John Castino	.07	.03	.01
☐ 94 Dave Edwards	.07	.03	.01
☐ 95 Alan Trammell	.50	.25	.05
☐ 96 Dick Howser MG	.10	.05	.01
☐ 97 Ross Baumgarten	.07	.03	.01
☐ 98 Vance Law	.12	.06	.01
☐ 99 Dickie Noles	.07	.03	.01
☐ 100 Pete Rose	2.00	1.00	.20
☐ 101 SV: Pete Rose	.80	.40	.08
☐ 102 Dave Beard	.07	.03	.01
☐ 103 Darrell Porter	.07	.03	.01
☐ 104 Bob Walk	.07	.03	.01
☐ 105 Don Baylor	.15	.07	.01
☐ 106 Gene Nelson	.07	.03	.01
☐ 107 Mike Jorgensen	.07	.03	.01
☐ 108 Glenn Hoffman	.07	.03	.01
☐ 109 Luis Leal	.07	.03	.01
☐ 110 Ken Griffey	.20	.10	.02
☐ 111 Montreal Expos TL	.10	.05	.01
BA: Al Oliver			
ERA: Steve Rogers			
☐ 112 Bob Shirley	.07	.03	.01
☐ 113 Ron Roenicke	.07	.03	.01
☐ 114 Jim Slaton	.07	.03	.01
☐ 115 Chili Davis	.20	.10	.02
☐ 116 Dave Schmidt	.10	.05	.01
☐ 117 Alan Knicely	.07	.03	.01
☐ 118 Chris Welsh	.07	.03	.01
☐ 119 Tom Brookens	.07	.03	.01
☐ 120 Len Barker	.07	.03	.01
☐ 121 Mickey Hatcher	.07	.03	.01
☐ 122 Jimmy Smith	.07	.03	.01
☐ 123 George Frazier	.07	.03	.01
☐ 124 Marc Hill	.07	.03	.01
☐ 125 Leon Durham	.07	.03	.01
☐ 126 Joe Torre MG	.12	.06	.01
☐ 127 Preston Hanna	.07	.03	.01
☐ 128 Mike Ramsey	.07	.03	.01
☐ 129 Checklist: 1-132	.10	.01	.00
☐ 130 Dave Stieb	.45	.22	.04
☐ 131 Ed Ott	.07	.03	.01
☐ 132 Todd Cruz	.07	.03	.01
☐ 133 Jim Barr	.07	.03	.01
☐ 134 Hubie Brooks	.25	.12	.02
☐ 135 Dwight Evans	.35	.17	.03
☐ 136 Willie Aikens	.07	.03	.01
☐ 137 Woodie Fryman	.07	.03	.01
☐ 138 Rick Dempsey	.07	.03	.01
☐ 139 Bruce Berenyi	.07	.03	.01
☐ 140 Willie Randolph	.10	.05	.01
☐ 141 Indians TL	.10	.05	.01
BA: Toby Harrah			
ERA: Rick Sutcliffe			
☐ 142 Mike Caldwell	.07	.03	.01
☐ 143 Joe Pettini	.07	.03	.01
☐ 144 Mark Wagner	.07	.03	.01
☐ 145 Don Sutton	.40	.20	.04

☐ 146	SV: Don Sutton	.20	.10	.02
☐ 147	Rick Leach	.07	.03	.01
☐ 148	Dave Roberts	.07	.03	.01
☐ 149	Johnny Ray	.12	.06	.01
☐ 150	Bruce Sutter	.20	.10	.02
☐ 151	SV: Bruce Sutter	.10	.05	.01
☐ 152	Jay Johnstone	.10	.05	.01
☐ 153	Jerry Koosman	.10	.05	.01
☐ 154	Johnnie LeMaster	.07	.03	.01
☐ 155	Dan Quisenberry	.15	.07	.01
☐ 156	Billy Martin MG	.15	.07	.01
☐ 157	Steve Bedrosian	.25	.12	.02
☐ 158	Rob Wilfong	.07	.03	.01
☐ 159	Mike Stanton	.07	.03	.01
☐ 160	Dave Kingman	.15	.07	.01
☐ 161	SV: Dave Kingman	.10	.05	.01
☐ 162	Mark Clear	.07	.03	.01
☐ 163	Cal Ripken	5.50	2.75	.55
☐ 164	David Palmer	.07	.03	.01
☐ 165	Dan Driessen	.07	.03	.01
☐ 166	John Pacella	.07	.03	.01
☐ 167	Mark Brouhard	.07	.03	.01
☐ 168	Juan Eichelberger	.07	.03	.01
☐ 169	Doug Flynn	.07	.03	.01
☐ 170	Steve Howe	.07	.03	.01
☐ 171	Giants TL	.15	.07	.01
	BA: Joe Morgan			
	ERA: Bill Laskey			
☐ 172	Vern Ruhle	.07	.03	.01
☐ 173	Jim Morrison	.07	.03	.01
☐ 174	Jerry Ujdur	.07	.03	.01
☐ 175	Bo Diaz	.07	.03	.01
☐ 176	Dave Righetti	.35	.17	.03
☐ 177	Harold Baines	.40	.20	.04
☐ 178	Luis Tiant	.10	.05	.01
☐ 179	SV: Luis Tiant	.07	.03	.01
☐ 180	Rickey Henderson	6.50	3.25	.65
☐ 181	Terry Felton	.07	.03	.01
☐ 182	Mike Fischlin	.07	.03	.01
☐ 183	Ed VandeBerg	.07	.03	.01
☐ 184	Bob Clark	.07	.03	.01
☐ 185	Tim Lollar	.07	.03	.01
☐ 186	Whitey Herzog MG	.10	.05	.01
☐ 187	Terry Leach	.12	.06	.01
☐ 188	Rick Miller	.07	.03	.01
☐ 189	Dan Schatzeder	.07	.03	.01
☐ 190	Cecil Cooper	.15	.07	.01
☐ 191	Joe Price	.07	.03	.01
☐ 192	Floyd Rayford	.07	.03	.01
☐ 193	Harry Spilman	.07	.03	.01
☐ 194	Cesar Geronimo	.07	.03	.01
☐ 195	Bob Stoddard	.07	.03	.01
☐ 196	Bill Fahey	.07	.03	.01
☐ 197	Jim Eisenreich	.75	.35	.07
☐ 198	Kiko Garcia	.07	.03	.01
☐ 199	Marty Bystrom	.07	.03	.01
☐ 200	Rod Carew	.75	.35	.07
☐ 201	SV: Rod Carew	.30	.15	.03
☐ 202	Blue Jays TL	.12	.06	.01
	BA: Damaso Garcia			
	ERA: Dave Stieb			
☐ 203	Mike Morgan	.10	.05	.01
☐ 204	Junior Kennedy	.07	.03	.01
☐ 205	Dave Parker	.35	.17	.03
☐ 206	Ken Oberkfell	.07	.03	.01
☐ 207	Rick Camp	.07	.03	.01
☐ 208	Dan Meyer	.07	.03	.01
☐ 209	Mike Moore	1.35	.65	.13
☐ 210	Jack Clark	.35	.17	.03
☐ 211	John Denny	.10	.05	.01
☐ 212	John Stearns	.07	.03	.01
☐ 213	Tom Burgmeier	.07	.03	.01
☐ 214	Jerry White	.07	.03	.01
☐ 215	Mario Soto	.10	.05	.01
☐ 216	Tony LaRussa MG	.10	.05	.01
☐ 217	Tim Stoddard	.07	.03	.01
☐ 218	Roy Howell	.07	.03	.01
☐ 219	Mike Armstrong	.07	.03	.01
☐ 220	Dusty Baker	.10	.05	.01
☐ 221	Joe Niekro	.10	.05	.01
☐ 222	Damaso Garcia	.07	.03	.01
☐ 223	John Montefusco	.07	.03	.01
☐ 224	Mickey Rivers	.10	.05	.01
☐ 225	Enos Cabell	.07	.03	.01
☐ 226	Enrique Romo	.07	.03	.01
☐ 227	Chris Bando	.07	.03	.01
☐ 228	Joaquin Andujar	.10	.05	.01
☐ 229	Phillies TL	.15	.07	.01
	BA: Bo Diaz			
	ERA: Steve Carlton			
☐ 230	Fergie Jenkins	.20	.10	.02
☐ 231	SV: Fergie Jenkins	.10	.05	.01
☐ 232	Tom Brunansky	.60	.30	.06
☐ 233	Wayne Gross	.07	.03	.01
☐ 234	Larry Andersen	.07	.03	.01
☐ 235	Claudell Washington	.10	.05	.01
☐ 236	Steve Renko	.07	.03	.01
☐ 237	Dan Norman	.07	.03	.01
☐ 238	Bud Black	.80	.40	.08
☐ 239	Dave Stapleton	.07	.03	.01
☐ 240	Rich Gossage	.25	.12	.02
☐ 241	SV: Rich Gossage	.10	.05	.01
☐ 242	Joe Nolan	.07	.03	.01
☐ 243	Duane Walker	.07	.03	.01
☐ 244	Dwight Bernard	.07	.03	.01
☐ 245	Steve Sax	.75	.35	.07
☐ 246	George Bamberger MG	.07	.03	.01
☐ 247	Dave Smith	.10	.05	.01
☐ 248	Bake McBride	.07	.03	.01
☐ 249	Checklist: 133-264	.10	.01	.00
☐ 250	Bill Buckner	.15	.07	.01
☐ 251	Alan Wiggins	.10	.05	.01
☐ 252	Luis Aguayo	.07	.03	.01
☐ 253	Larry McWilliams	.07	.03	.01
☐ 254	Rick Cerone	.07	.03	.01
☐ 255	Gene Garber	.07	.03	.01
☐ 256	SV: Gene Garber	.07	.03	.01
☐ 257	Jesse Barfield	.60	.30	.06
☐ 258	Manny Castillo	.07	.03	.01
☐ 259	Jeff Jones	.07	.03	.01
☐ 260	Steve Kemp	.07	.03	.01
☐ 261	Tigers TL	.10	.05	.01
	BA: Larry Herndon			
	ERA: Dan Petry			
☐ 262	Ron Jackson	.07	.03	.01
☐ 263	Renie Martin	.07	.03	.01
☐ 264	Jamie Quirk	.07	.03	.01
☐ 265	Joel Youngblood	.07	.03	.01
☐ 266	Paul Boris	.07	.03	.01
☐ 267	Terry Francona	.07	.03	.01
☐ 268	Storm Davis	.90	.45	.09
☐ 269	Ron Oester	.07	.03	.01
☐ 270	Dennis Eckersley	.40	.20	.04
☐ 271	Ed Romero	.07	.03	.01
☐ 272	Frank Tanana	.10	.05	.01
☐ 273	Mark Belanger	.10	.05	.01
☐ 274	Terry Kennedy	.07	.03	.01
☐ 275	Ray Knight	.10	.05	.01
☐ 276	Gene Mauch MG	.07	.03	.01
☐ 277	Rance Mulliniks	.07	.03	.01
☐ 278	Kevin Hickey	.07	.03	.01
☐ 279	Greg Gross	.07	.03	.01
☐ 280	Bert Blyleven	.25	.12	.02
☐ 281	Andre Robertson	.07	.03	.01
☐ 282	Reggie Smith	.15	.07	.01
	(Ryne Sandberg			
	ducking back)			
☐ 283	SV: Reggie Smith	.07	.03	.01
☐ 284	Jeff Lahti	.07	.03	.01
☐ 285	Lance Parrish	.35	.17	.03
☐ 286	Rick Langford	.07	.03	.01
☐ 287	Bobby Brown	.07	.03	.01
☐ 288	Joe Cowley	.07	.03	.01
☐ 289	Jerry Dybzinski	.07	.03	.01
☐ 290	Jeff Reardon	.20	.10	.02
☐ 291	Pirates TL	.10	.05	.01
	BA: Bill Madlock			
	ERA: John Candelaria			
☐ 292	Craig Swan	.07	.03	.01
☐ 293	Glenn Gulliver	.07	.03	.01
☐ 294	Dave Engle	.07	.03	.01
☐ 295	Jerry Remy	.07	.03	.01
☐ 296	Greg Harris	.07	.03	.01
☐ 297	Ned Yost	.07	.03	.01
☐ 298	Floyd Chiffer	.07	.03	.01
☐ 299	George Wright	.07	.03	.01
☐ 300	Mike Schmidt	2.50	1.25	.25
☐ 301	SV: Mike Schmidt	1.00	.50	.10
☐ 302	Ernie Whitt	.07	.03	.01
☐ 303	Miguel Dilone	.07	.03	.01
☐ 304	Dave Rucker	.07	.03	.01
☐ 305	Larry Bowa	.10	.05	.01
☐ 306	Tom Lasorda MG	.10	.05	.01
☐ 307	Lou Piniella	.10	.05	.01
☐ 308	Jesus Vega	.07	.03	.01
☐ 309	Jeff Leonard	.10	.05	.01
☐ 310	Greg Luzinski	.12	.06	.01
☐ 311	Glenn Brummer	.07	.03	.01
☐ 312	Brian Kingman	.07	.03	.01
☐ 313	Gary Gray	.07	.03	.01
☐ 314	Ken Dayley	.10	.05	.01
☐ 315	Rick Burleson	.10	.05	.01
☐ 316	Paul Splittorff	.07	.03	.01
☐ 317	Gary Rajsich	.07	.03	.01
☐ 318	John Tudor	.30	.15	.03
☐ 319	Lenn Sakata	.07	.03	.01
☐ 320	Steve Rogers	.07	.03	.01

☐ 321	Brewers TL	.15	.07	.01
	BA: Robin Yount			
	ERA: Pete Vuckovich			
☐ 322	Dave Van Gorder	.07	.03	.01
☐ 323	Luis DeLeon	.07	.03	.01
☐ 324	Mike Marshall	.30	.15	.03
☐ 325	Von Hayes	.40	.20	.04
☐ 326	Garth Iorg	.07	.03	.01
☐ 327	Bobby Castillo	.07	.03	.01
☐ 328	Craig Reynolds	.07	.03	.01
☐ 329	Randy Niemann	.07	.03	.01
☐ 330	Buddy Bell	.15	.07	.01
☐ 331	Mike Krukow	.10	.05	.01
☐ 332	Glenn Wilson	.40	.20	.04
☐ 333	Dave LaRoche	.07	.03	.01
☐ 334	SV: Dave LaRoche	.07	.03	.01
☐ 335	Steve Henderson	.07	.03	.01
☐ 336	Rene Lachemann MG	.07	.03	.01
☐ 337	Tito Landrum	.07	.03	.01
☐ 338	Bob Owchinko	.07	.03	.01
☐ 339	Terry Harper	.07	.03	.01
☐ 340	Larry Gura	.07	.03	.01
☐ 341	Doug DeCinces	.10	.05	.01
☐ 342	Atlee Hammaker	.07	.03	.01
☐ 343	Bob Bailor	.07	.03	.01
☐ 344	Roger LaFrancois	.07	.03	.01
☐ 345	Jim Clancy	.07	.03	.01
☐ 346	Joe Pittman	.07	.03	.01
☐ 347	Sammy Stewart	.07	.03	.01
☐ 348	Alan Bannister	.07	.03	.01
☐ 349	Checklist: 265-396	.10	.01	.00
☐ 350	Robin Yount	1.25	.60	.12
☐ 351	Reds TL	.10	.05	.01
	BA: Cesar Cedeno			
	ERA: Mario Soto			
☐ 352	Mike Scioscia	.10	.05	.01
☐ 353	Steve Comer	.07	.03	.01
☐ 354	Randy Johnson	.07	.03	.01
☐ 355	Jim Bibby	.07	.03	.01
☐ 356	Gary Woods	.07	.03	.01
☐ 357	Len Matuszek	.07	.03	.01
☐ 358	Jerry Garvin	.07	.03	.01
☐ 359	Dave Collins	.07	.03	.01
☐ 360	Nolan Ryan	4.00	2.00	.40
☐ 361	SV: Nolan Ryan	1.25	.60	.12
☐ 362	Bill Almon	.07	.03	.01
☐ 363	John Stuper	.07	.03	.01
☐ 364	Brett Butler	.25	.12	.02
☐ 365	Dave Lopes	.10	.05	.01
☐ 366	Dick Williams MG	.07	.03	.01
☐ 367	Bud Anderson	.07	.03	.01
☐ 368	Richie Zisk	.07	.03	.01
☐ 369	Jesse Orosco	.07	.03	.01
☐ 370	Gary Carter	.55	.27	.05
☐ 371	Mike Richardt	.07	.03	.01
☐ 372	Terry Crowley	.07	.03	.01
☐ 373	Kevin Saucier	.07	.03	.01
☐ 374	Wayne Krenchicki	.07	.03	.01
☐ 375	Pete Vuckovich	.10	.05	.01
☐ 376	Ken Landreaux	.07	.03	.01
☐ 377	Lee May	.10	.05	.01
☐ 378	SV: Lee May	.07	.03	.01
☐ 379	Guy Sularz	.07	.03	.01
☐ 380	Ron Davis	.07	.03	.01
☐ 381	Red Sox TL	.15	.07	.01
	BA: Jim Rice			
	ERA: Bob Stanley			
☐ 382	Bob Knepper	.10	.05	.01
☐ 383	Ozzie Virgil	.07	.03	.01
☐ 384	Dave Dravecky	.85	.40	.08
☐ 385	Mike Easler	.10	.05	.01
☐ 386	Rod Carew AS	.25	.12	.02
☐ 387	Bob Grich AS	.10	.05	.01
☐ 388	George Brett AS	.35	.17	.03
☐ 389	Robin Yount AS	.30	.15	.03
☐ 390	Reggie Jackson AS	.30	.15	.03
☐ 391	Rickey Henderson AS	.90	.45	.09
☐ 392	Fred Lynn AS	.10	.05	.01
☐ 393	Carlton Fisk AS	.20	.10	.02
☐ 394	Pete Vuckovich AS	.07	.03	.01
☐ 395	Larry Gura AS	.07	.03	.01
☐ 396	Dan Quisenberry AS	.10	.05	.01
☐ 397	Pete Rose AS	.50	.25	.05
☐ 398	Manny Trillo AS	.07	.03	.01
☐ 399	Mike Schmidt AS	.45	.22	.04
☐ 400	Dave Concepcion AS	.07	.03	.01
☐ 401	Dale Murphy AS	.35	.17	.03
☐ 402	Andre Dawson AS	.25	.12	.02
☐ 403	Tim Raines AS	.20	.10	.02
☐ 404	Gary Carter AS	.20	.10	.02
☐ 405	Steve Rogers AS	.07	.03	.01
☐ 406	Steve Carlton AS	.20	.10	.02
☐ 407	Bruce Sutter AS	.10	.05	.01
☐ 408	Rudy May	.07	.03	.01

☐ 409	Marvis Foley	.07	.03	.01
☐ 410	Phil Niekro	.40	.20	.04
☐ 411	SV: Phil Niekro	.15	.07	.01
☐ 412	Rangers TL	.10	.05	.01
	BA: Buddy Bell			
	ERA: Charlie Hough			
☐ 413	Matt Keough	.07	.03	.01
☐ 414	Julio Cruz	.07	.03	.01
☐ 415	Bob Forsch	.07	.03	.01
☐ 416	Joe Ferguson	.07	.03	.01
☐ 417	Tom Hausman	.07	.03	.01
☐ 418	Greg Pryor	.07	.03	.01
☐ 419	Steve Crawford	.07	.03	.01
☐ 420	Al Oliver	.10	.05	.01
☐ 421	SV: Al Oliver	.07	.03	.01
☐ 422	George Cappuzzello	.07	.03	.01
☐ 423	Tom Lawless	.10	.05	.01
☐ 424	Jerry Augustine	.07	.03	.01
☐ 425	Pedro Guerrero	.50	.25	.05
☐ 426	Earl Weaver MG	.10	.05	.01
☐ 427	Roy Lee Jackson	.07	.03	.01
☐ 428	Champ Summers	.07	.03	.01
☐ 429	Eddie Whitson	.10	.05	.01
☐ 430	Kirk Gibson	.50	.25	.05
☐ 431	Gary Gaetti	4.50	2.25	.45
☐ 432	Porfirio Altamirano	.07	.03	.01
☐ 433	Dale Berra	.07	.03	.01
☐ 434	Dennis Lamp	.07	.03	.01
☐ 435	Tony Armas	.10	.05	.01
☐ 436	Bill Campbell	.07	.03	.01
☐ 437	Rick Sweet	.07	.03	.01
☐ 438	Dave LaPoint	.50	.25	.05
☐ 439	Rafael Ramirez	.07	.03	.01
☐ 440	Ron Guidry	.30	.15	.03
☐ 441	Astros TL	.10	.05	.01
	BA: Ray Knight			
	ERA: Joe Niekro			
☐ 442	Brian Downing	.10	.05	.01
☐ 443	Don Hood	.07	.03	.01
☐ 444	Wally Backman	.30	.15	.03
☐ 445	Mike Flanagan	.10	.05	.01
☐ 446	Reid Nichols	.07	.03	.01
☐ 447	Bryn Smith	.15	.07	.01
☐ 448	Darrell Evans	.15	.07	.01
☐ 449	Eddie Milner	.10	.05	.01
☐ 450	Ted Simmons	.15	.07	.01
☐ 451	SV: Ted Simmons	.10	.05	.01
☐ 452	Lloyd Moseby	.10	.05	.01
☐ 453	Lamar Johnson	.07	.03	.01
☐ 454	Bob Welch	.40	.20	.04
☐ 455	Sixto Lezcano	.07	.03	.01
☐ 456	Lee Elia MG	.07	.03	.01
☐ 457	Milt Wilcox	.07	.03	.01
☐ 458	Ron Washington	.07	.03	.01
☐ 459	Ed Farmer	.07	.03	.01
☐ 460	Roy Smalley	.07	.03	.01
☐ 461	Steve Trout	.07	.03	.01
☐ 462	Steve Nicosia	.07	.03	.01
☐ 463	Gaylord Perry	.35	.17	.03
☐ 464	SV: Gaylord Perry	.15	.07	.01
☐ 465	Lonnie Smith	.15	.07	.01
☐ 466	Tom Underwood	.07	.03	.01
☐ 467	Rufino Linares	.07	.03	.01
☐ 468	Dave Goltz	.07	.03	.01
☐ 469	Ron Gardenhire	.07	.03	.01
☐ 470	Greg Minton	.07	.03	.01
☐ 471	K.C. Royals TL	.10	.05	.01
	BA: Willie Wilson			
	ERA: Vida Blue			
☐ 472	Gary Allenson	.07	.03	.01
☐ 473	John Lowenstein	.07	.03	.01
☐ 474	Ray Burris	.07	.03	.01
☐ 475	Cesar Cedeno	.10	.05	.01
☐ 476	Rob Picciolo	.07	.03	.01
☐ 477	Tom Niedenfuer	.07	.03	.01
☐ 478	Phil Garner	.07	.03	.01
☐ 479	Charlie Hough	.10	.05	.01
☐ 480	Toby Harrah	.10	.05	.01
☐ 481	Scot Thompson	.07	.03	.01
☐ 482	Tony Gwynn UER	22.50	10.00	2.00
	(no Topps logo under			
	card number on back)			
☐ 483	Lynn Jones	.07	.03	.01
☐ 484	Dick Ruthven	.07	.03	.01
☐ 485	Omar Moreno	.07	.03	.01
☐ 486	Clyde King MG	.07	.03	.01
☐ 487	Jerry Hairston	.07	.03	.01
☐ 488	Alfredo Griffin	.10	.05	.01
☐ 489	Tom Herr	.10	.05	.01
☐ 490	Jim Palmer	.75	.35	.07
☐ 491	SV: Jim Palmer	.30	.15	.03
☐ 492	Paul Serna	.07	.03	.01
☐ 493	Steve McCatty	.07	.03	.01
☐ 494	Bob Brenly	.07	.03	.01

☐ 495	Warren Cromartie	.07	.03	.01
☐ 496	Tom Veryzer	.07	.03	.01
☐ 497	Rick Sutcliffe	.25	.12	.02
☐ 498	Wade Boggs	35.00	17.50	3.50
☐ 499	Jeff Little	.07	.03	.01
☐ 500	Reggie Jackson	1.25	.60	.12
☐ 501	SV: Reggie Jackson	.50	.25	.05
☐ 502	Atlanta Braves TL	.30	.15	.03
	BA: Dale Murphy			
	ERA: Phil Niekro			
☐ 503	Moose Haas	.07	.03	.01
☐ 504	Don Werner	.07	.03	.01
☐ 505	Garry Templeton	.10	.05	.01
☐ 506	Jim Gott	.35	.17	.03
☐ 507	Tony Scott	.07	.03	.01
☐ 508	Tom Filer	.12	.06	.01
☐ 509	Lou Whitaker	.35	.17	.03
☐ 510	Tug McGraw	.15	.07	.01
☐ 511	SV: Tug McGraw	.10	.05	.01
☐ 512	Doyle Alexander	.10	.05	.01
☐ 513	Fred Stanley	.07	.03	.01
☐ 514	Rudy Law	.07	.03	.01
☐ 515	Gene Tenace	.07	.03	.01
☐ 516	Bill Virdon MG	.07	.03	.01
☐ 517	Gary Ward	.07	.03	.01
☐ 518	Bill Laskey	.07	.03	.01
☐ 519	Terry Bulling	.07	.03	.01
☐ 520	Fred Lynn	.25	.12	.02
☐ 521	Bruce Benedict	.07	.03	.01
☐ 522	Pat Zachry	.07	.03	.01
☐ 523	Carney Lansford	.25	.12	.02
☐ 524	Tom Brennan	.07	.03	.01
☐ 525	Frank White	.10	.05	.01
☐ 526	Checklist: 397-528	.10	.01	.00
☐ 527	Larry Biittner	.07	.03	.01
☐ 528	Jamie Easterly	.07	.03	.01
☐ 529	Tim Laudner	.07	.03	.01
☐ 530	Eddie Murray	1.00	.50	.10
☐ 531	Oakland A's TL	.35	.17	.03
	BA: Rickey Henderson			
	ERA: Rick Langford			
☐ 532	Dave Stewart	2.50	1.25	.25
☐ 533	Luis Salazar	.10	.05	.01
☐ 534	John Butcher	.07	.03	.01
☐ 535	Manny Trillo	.07	.03	.01
☐ 536	John Wockenfuss	.07	.03	.01
☐ 537	Rod Scurry	.07	.03	.01
☐ 538	Danny Heep	.07	.03	.01
☐ 539	Roger Erickson	.07	.03	.01
☐ 540	Ozzie Smith	.80	.40	.08
☐ 541	Britt Burns	.07	.03	.01
☐ 542	Jody Davis	.10	.05	.01
☐ 543	Alan Fowlkes	.07	.03	.01
☐ 544	Larry Whisenton	.07	.03	.01
☐ 545	Floyd Bannister	.07	.03	.01
☐ 546	Dave Garcia MG	.07	.03	.01
☐ 547	Geoff Zahn	.07	.03	.01
☐ 548	Brian Giles	.07	.03	.01
☐ 549	Charlie Puleo	.07	.03	.01
☐ 550	Carl Yastrzemski	1.25	.60	.12
☐ 551	SV: Carl Yastrzemski	.50	.25	.05
☐ 552	Tim Wallach	.40	.20	.04
☐ 553	Dennis Martinez	.10	.05	.01
☐ 554	Mike Vail	.07	.03	.01
☐ 555	Steve Yeager	.07	.03	.01
☐ 556	Willie Upshaw	.07	.03	.01
☐ 557	Rick Honeycutt	.07	.03	.01
☐ 558	Dickie Thon	.10	.05	.01
☐ 559	Pete Redfern	.07	.03	.01
☐ 560	Ron LeFlore	.10	.05	.01
☐ 561	Cardinals TL	.10	.05	.01
	BA: Lonnie Smith			
	ERA: Joaquin Andujar			
☐ 562	Dave Rozema	.07	.03	.01
☐ 563	Juan Bonilla	.07	.03	.01
☐ 564	Sid Monge	.07	.03	.01
☐ 565	Bucky Dent	.15	.07	.01
☐ 566	Manny Sarmiento	.07	.03	.01
☐ 567	Joe Simpson	.07	.03	.01
☐ 568	Willie Hernandez	.10	.05	.01
☐ 569	Jack Perconte	.07	.03	.01
☐ 570	Vida Blue	.10	.05	.01
☐ 571	Mickey Klutts	.07	.03	.01
☐ 572	Bob Watson	.10	.05	.01
☐ 573	Andy Hassler	.07	.03	.01
☐ 574	Glenn Adams	.07	.03	.01
☐ 575	Neil Allen	.07	.03	.01
☐ 576	Frank Robinson MG	.15	.07	.01
☐ 577	Luis Aponte	.07	.03	.01
☐ 578	David Green	.07	.03	.01
☐ 579	Rich Dauer	.07	.03	.01
☐ 580	Tom Seaver	1.00	.50	.10
☐ 581	SV: Tom Seaver	.40	.20	.04
☐ 582	Marshall Edwards	.07	.03	.01
☐ 583	Terry Forster	.10	.05	.01
☐ 584	Dave Hostetler	.07	.03	.01
☐ 585	Jose Cruz	.10	.05	.01
☐ 586	Frank Viola	10.00	5.00	1.00
☐ 587	Ivan DeJesus	.07	.03	.01
☐ 588	Pat Underwood	.07	.03	.01
☐ 589	Alvis Woods	.07	.03	.01
☐ 590	Tony Pena	.25	.12	.02
☐ 591	White Sox TL	.10	.05	.01
	BA: Greg Luzinski			
	ERA: LaMarr Hoyt			
☐ 592	Shane Rawley	.07	.03	.01
☐ 593	Broderick Perkins	.07	.03	.01
☐ 594	Eric Rasmussen	.07	.03	.01
☐ 595	Tim Raines	.90	.45	.09
☐ 596	Randy Johnson	.07	.03	.01
☐ 597	Mike Proly	.07	.03	.01
☐ 598	Dwayne Murphy	.07	.03	.01
☐ 599	Don Aase	.07	.03	.01
☐ 600	George Brett	1.75	.85	.17
☐ 601	Ed Lynch	.07	.03	.01
☐ 602	Rich Gedman	.07	.03	.01
☐ 603	Joe Morgan	.50	.25	.05
☐ 604	SV: Joe Morgan	.20	.10	.02
☐ 605	Gary Roenicke	.07	.03	.01
☐ 606	Bobby Cox MG	.07	.03	.01
☐ 607	Charlie Leibrandt	.07	.03	.01
☐ 608	Don Money	.07	.03	.01
☐ 609	Danny Darwin	.10	.05	.01
☐ 610	Steve Garvey	.75	.35	.07
☐ 611	Bert Roberge	.07	.03	.01
☐ 612	Steve Swisher	.07	.03	.01
☐ 613	Mike Ivie	.07	.03	.01
☐ 614	Ed Glynn	.07	.03	.01
☐ 615	Garry Maddox	.10	.05	.01
☐ 616	Bill Nahorodny	.07	.03	.01
☐ 617	Butch Wynegar	.07	.03	.01
☐ 618	LaMarr Hoyt	.10	.05	.01
☐ 619	Keith Moreland	.07	.03	.01
☐ 620	Mike Norris	.07	.03	.01
☐ 621	New York Mets TL	.10	.05	.01
	BA: Mookie Wilson			
	ERA: Craig Swan			
☐ 622	Dave Edler	.07	.03	.01
☐ 623	Luis Sanchez	.07	.03	.01
☐ 624	Glenn Hubbard	.07	.03	.01
☐ 625	Ken Forsch	.07	.03	.01
☐ 626	Jerry Martin	.07	.03	.01
☐ 627	Doug Bair	.07	.03	.01
☐ 628	Julio Valdez	.07	.03	.01
☐ 629	Charlie Lea	.07	.03	.01
☐ 630	Paul Molitor	.30	.15	.03
☐ 631	Tippy Martinez	.07	.03	.01
☐ 632	Alex Trevino	.07	.03	.01
☐ 633	Vicente Romo	.07	.03	.01
☐ 634	Max Venable	.07	.03	.01
☐ 635	Graig Nettles	.15	.07	.01
☐ 636	SV: Graig Nettles	.10	.05	.01
☐ 637	Pat Corrales MG	.07	.03	.01
☐ 638	Dan Petry	.07	.03	.01
☐ 639	Art Howe	.10	.05	.01
☐ 640	Andre Thornton	.10	.05	.01
☐ 641	Billy Sample	.07	.03	.01
☐ 642	Checklist: 529-660	.10	.01	.00
☐ 643	Bump Wills	.07	.03	.01
☐ 644	Joe Lefebvre	.07	.03	.01
☐ 645	Bill Madlock	.10	.05	.01
☐ 646	Jim Essian	.07	.03	.01
☐ 647	Bobby Mitchell	.07	.03	.01
☐ 648	Jeff Burroughs	.10	.05	.01
☐ 649	Tommy Boggs	.07	.03	.01
☐ 650	George Hendrick	.10	.05	.01
☐ 651	Angels TL	.20	.10	.02
	BA: Rod Carew			
	ERA: Mike Witt			
☐ 652	Butch Hobson	.07	.03	.01
☐ 653	Ellis Valentine	.07	.03	.01
☐ 654	Bob Ojeda	.15	.07	.01
☐ 655	Al Bumbry	.07	.03	.01
☐ 656	Dave Frost	.07	.03	.01
☐ 657	Mike Gates	.07	.03	.01
☐ 658	Frank Pastore	.07	.03	.01
☐ 659	Charlie Moore	.07	.03	.01
☐ 660	Mike Hargrove	.10	.05	.01
☐ 661	Bill Russell	.10	.05	.01
☐ 662	Joe Sambito	.07	.03	.01
☐ 663	Tom O'Malley	.07	.03	.01
☐ 664	Bob Molinaro	.07	.03	.01
☐ 665	Jim Sundberg	.07	.03	.01
☐ 666	Sparky Anderson MG	.10	.05	.01
☐ 667	Dick Davis	.07	.03	.01
☐ 668	Larry Christenson	.07	.03	.01
☐ 669	Mike Squires	.07	.03	.01
☐ 670	Jerry Mumphrey	.07	.03	.01

☐ 671	Lenny Faedo	.07	.03	.01
☐ 672	Jim Kaat	.15	.07	.01
☐ 673	SV: Jim Kaat	.10	.05	.01
☐ 674	Kurt Bevacqua	.07	.03	.01
☐ 675	Jim Beattie	.07	.03	.01
☐ 676	Biff Pocoroba	.07	.03	.01
☐ 677	Dave Revering	.07	.03	.01
☐ 678	Juan Beniquez	.07	.03	.01
☐ 679	Mike Scott	.45	.22	.04
☐ 680	Andre Dawson	.90	.45	.09
☐ 681	Dodgers Leaders	.25	.12	.02
	BA: Pedro Guerrero			
	ERA: Fern.Valenzuela			
☐ 682	Bob Stanley	.07	.03	.01
☐ 683	Dan Ford	.07	.03	.01
☐ 684	Rafael Landestoy	.07	.03	.01
☐ 685	Lee Mazzilli	.07	.03	.01
☐ 686	Randy Lerch	.07	.03	.01
☐ 687	U.L. Washington	.07	.03	.01
☐ 688	Jim Wohlford	.07	.03	.01
☐ 689	Ron Hassey	.07	.03	.01
☐ 690	Kent Hrbek	.75	.35	.07
☐ 691	Dave Tobik	.07	.03	.01
☐ 692	Denny Walling	.07	.03	.01
☐ 693	Sparky Lyle	.10	.05	.01
☐ 694	SV: Sparky Lyle	.07	.03	.01
☐ 695	Ruppert Jones	.07	.03	.01
☐ 696	Chuck Tanner MG	.07	.03	.01
☐ 697	Barry Foote	.07	.03	.01
☐ 698	Tony Bernazard	.10	.05	.01
☐ 699	Lee Smith	.15	.07	.01
☐ 700	Keith Hernandez	.50	.25	.05
☐ 701	Batting Leaders	.10	.05	.01
	AL: Willie Wilson			
	NL: Al Oliver			
☐ 702	Home Run Leaders	.15	.07	.01
	AL: Reggie Jackson			
	AL: Gorman Thomas			
	NL: Dave Kingman			
☐ 703	RBI Leaders	.15	.07	.01
	AL: Hal McRae			
	NL: Dale Murphy			
	NL: Al Oliver			
☐ 704	SB Leaders	.35	.17	.03
	AL: Rickey Henderson			
	NL: Tim Raines			
☐ 705	Victory Leaders	.12	.06	.01
	AL: LaMarr Hoyt			
	NL: Steve Carlton			
☐ 706	Strikeout Leaders	.12	.06	.01
	AL: Floyd Bannister			
	NL: Steve Carlton			
☐ 707	ERA Leaders	.10	.05	.01
	AL: Rick Sutcliffe			
	NL: Steve Rogers			
☐ 708	Leading Firemen	.10	.05	.01
	AL: Dan Quisenberry			
	NL: Bruce Sutter			
☐ 709	Jimmy Sexton	.07	.03	.01
☐ 710	Willie Wilson	.15	.07	.01
☐ 711	Mariners TL	.10	.05	.01
	BA: Bruce Bochte			
	ERA: Jim Beattie			
☐ 712	Bruce Kison	.07	.03	.01
☐ 713	Ron Hodges	.07	.03	.01
☐ 714	Wayne Nordhagen	.07	.03	.01
☐ 715	Tony Perez	.20	.10	.02
☐ 716	SV: Tony Perez	.10	.05	.01
☐ 717	Scott Sanderson	.10	.05	.01
☐ 718	Jim Dwyer	.07	.03	.01
☐ 719	Rich Gale	.07	.03	.01
☐ 720	Dave Concepcion	.15	.07	.01
☐ 721	John Martin	.07	.03	.01
☐ 722	Jorge Orta	.07	.03	.01
☐ 723	Randy Moffitt	.07	.03	.01
☐ 724	Johnny Grubb	.07	.03	.01
☐ 725	Dan Spillner	.07	.03	.01
☐ 726	Harvey Kuenn MG	.10	.05	.01
☐ 727	Chet Lemon	.07	.03	.01
☐ 728	Ron Reed	.07	.03	.01
☐ 729	Jerry Morales	.07	.03	.01
☐ 730	Jason Thompson	.07	.03	.01
☐ 731	Al Williams	.07	.03	.01
☐ 732	Dave Henderson	.35	.17	.03
☐ 733	Buck Martinez	.07	.03	.01
☐ 734	Steve Braun	.07	.03	.01
☐ 735	Tommy John	.20	.10	.02
☐ 736	SV: Tommy John	.10	.05	.01
☐ 737	Mitchell Page	.07	.03	.01
☐ 738	Tim Foli	.07	.03	.01
☐ 739	Rick Ownbey	.07	.03	.01
☐ 740	Rusty Staub	.15	.07	.01
☐ 741	SV: Rusty Staub	.10	.05	.01
☐ 742	Padres TL	.10	.05	.01
	BA: Terry Kennedy			
	ERA: Tim Lollar			
☐ 743	Mike Torrez	.07	.03	.01
☐ 744	Brad Mills	.07	.03	.01
☐ 745	Scott McGregor	.10	.05	.01
☐ 746	John Wathan	.10	.05	.01
☐ 747	Fred Breining	.07	.03	.01
☐ 748	Derrel Thomas	.07	.03	.01
☐ 749	Jon Matlack	.07	.03	.01
☐ 750	Ben Oglivie	.10	.05	.01
☐ 751	Brad Havens	.07	.03	.01
☐ 752	Luis Pujols	.07	.03	.01
☐ 753	Elias Sosa	.07	.03	.01
☐ 754	Bill Robinson	.10	.05	.01
☐ 755	John Candelaria	.10	.05	.01
☐ 756	Russ Nixon MG	.07	.03	.01
☐ 757	Rick Manning	.07	.03	.01
☐ 758	Aurelio Rodriguez	.07	.03	.01
☐ 759	Doug Bird	.07	.03	.01
☐ 760	Dale Murphy	1.75	.85	.17
☐ 761	Gary Lucas	.07	.03	.01
☐ 762	Cliff Johnson	.07	.03	.01
☐ 763	Al Cowens	.07	.03	.01
☐ 764	Pete Falcone	.07	.03	.01
☐ 765	Bob Boone	.18	.09	.01
☐ 766	Barry Bonnell	.07	.03	.01
☐ 767	Duane Kuiper	.07	.03	.01
☐ 768	Chris Speier	.07	.03	.01
☐ 769	Checklist: 661-792	.10	.01	.00
☐ 770	Dave Winfield	.60	.30	.06
☐ 771	Twins TL	.10	.05	.01
	BA: Kent Hrbek			
	ERA: Bobby Castillo			
☐ 772	Jim Kern	.07	.03	.01
☐ 773	Larry Hisle	.07	.03	.01
☐ 774	Alan Ashby	.07	.03	.01
☐ 775	Burt Hooton	.07	.03	.01
☐ 776	Larry Parrish	.10	.05	.01
☐ 777	John Curtis	.07	.03	.01
☐ 778	Rich Hebner	.07	.03	.01
☐ 779	Rick Waits	.07	.03	.01
☐ 780	Gary Matthews	.10	.05	.01
☐ 781	Rick Rhoden	.10	.05	.01
☐ 782	Bobby Murcer	.10	.05	.01
☐ 783	SV: Bobby Murcer	.07	.03	.01
☐ 784	Jeff Newman	.07	.03	.01
☐ 785	Dennis Leonard	.10	.05	.01
☐ 786	Ralph Houk MG	.07	.03	.01
☐ 787	Dick Tidrow	.07	.03	.01
☐ 788	Dane Iorg	.07	.03	.01
☐ 789	Bryan Clark	.07	.03	.01
☐ 790	Bob Grich	.10	.05	.01
☐ 791	Gary Lavelle	.07	.03	.01
☐ 792	Chris Chambliss	.15	.07	.01

1983 Topps Traded

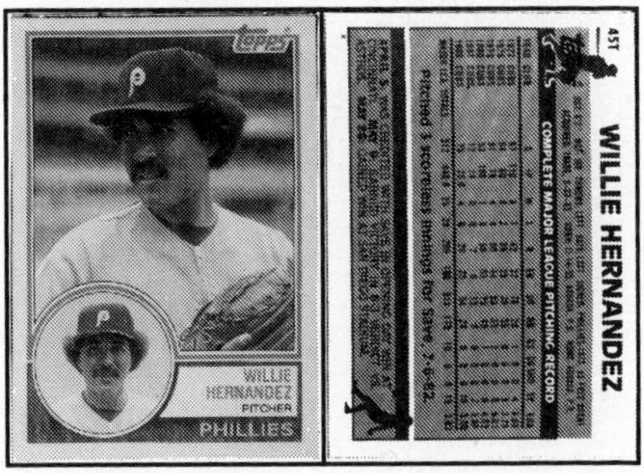

The cards in this 132-card set measure 2 1/2" by 3 1/2". For the third year in a row, Topps issued a 132-card Traded (or extended) set featuring some of the year's top rookies and players who had changed teams during the year, but were featured with their old team in the Topps regular issue of 1983. The cards were available through hobby dealers only and were printed in Ireland by the Topps affiliate in that country. The set is numbered alphabetically by the last name of the player of the card. The Darryl Strawberry card number 108 can be found with either one or two asterisks (in the lower left corner of the reverse). The key (extended) rookie card in this set is obviously Darryl Strawberry.

	MINT	EXC	G-VG
COMPLETE SET (132)	105.00	45.00	9.00
COMMON PLAYER (1-132)	.09	.04	.01

☐ 1T Neil Allen	.20	.10	.02
☐ 2T Bill Almon	.09	.04	.01
☐ 3T Joe Altobelli MG	.09	.04	.01
☐ 4T Tony Armas	.15	.07	.01
☐ 5T Doug Bair	.09	.04	.01
☐ 6T Steve Baker	.09	.04	.01
☐ 7T Floyd Bannister	.15	.07	.01
☐ 8T Don Baylor	.25	.12	.02
☐ 9T Tony Bernazard	.15	.07	.01
☐ 10T Larry Biittner	.09	.04	.01
☐ 11T Dann Bilardello	.09	.04	.01
☐ 12T Doug Bird	.09	.04	.01
☐ 13T Steve Boros MG	.09	.04	.01
☐ 14T Greg Brock	.25	.12	.02
☐ 15T Mike Brown (Red Sox pitcher)	.15	.07	.01
☐ 16T Tom Burgmeier	.09	.04	.01
☐ 17T Randy Bush	.25	.12	.02
☐ 18T Bert Campaneris	.15	.07	.01
☐ 19T Ron Cey	.20	.10	.02
☐ 20T Chris Codiroli	.15	.07	.01
☐ 21T Dave Collins	.09	.04	.01
☐ 22T Terry Crowley	.09	.04	.01
☐ 23T Julio Cruz	.09	.04	.01
☐ 24T Mike Davis	.15	.07	.01
☐ 25T Frank DiPino	.09	.04	.01
☐ 26T Bill Doran	2.50	1.25	.25
☐ 27T Jerry Dybzinski	.09	.04	.01
☐ 28T Jamie Easterly	.09	.04	.01
☐ 29T Juan Eichelberger	.09	.04	.01
☐ 30T Jim Essian	.09	.04	.01
☐ 31T Pete Falcone	.09	.04	.01
☐ 32T Mike Ferraro MG	.09	.04	.01
☐ 33T Terry Forster	.15	.07	.01
☐ 34T Julio Franco	5.00	2.50	.50
☐ 35T Rich Gale	.09	.04	.01
☐ 36T Kiko Garcia	.09	.04	.01
☐ 37T Steve Garvey	1.50	.75	.15
☐ 38T Johnny Grubb	.09	.04	.01
☐ 39T Mel Hall	1.00	.50	.10
☐ 40T Von Hayes	1.00	.50	.10
☐ 41T Danny Heep	.15	.07	.01
☐ 42T Steve Henderson	.09	.04	.01
☐ 43T Keith Hernandez	1.00	.50	.10
☐ 44T Leo Hernandez	.15	.07	.01
☐ 45T Willie Hernandez	.20	.10	.02
☐ 46T Al Holland	.09	.04	.01
☐ 47T Frank Howard MG	.15	.07	.01
☐ 48T Bobby Johnson	.09	.04	.01
☐ 49T Cliff Johnson	.09	.04	.01
☐ 50T Odell Jones	.09	.04	.01
☐ 51T Mike Jorgensen	.09	.04	.01
☐ 52T Bob Kearney	.09	.04	.01
☐ 53T Steve Kemp	.15	.07	.01
☐ 54T Matt Keough	.09	.04	.01
☐ 55T Ron Kittle	1.00	.50	.10
☐ 56T Mickey Klutts	.09	.04	.01
☐ 57T Alan Knicely	.09	.04	.01
☐ 58T Mike Krukow	.15	.07	.01
☐ 59T Rafael Landestoy	.09	.04	.01
☐ 60T Carney Lansford	.65	.30	.06
☐ 61T Joe Lefebvre	.09	.04	.01
☐ 62T Bryan Little	.09	.04	.01
☐ 63T Aurelio Lopez	.09	.04	.01
☐ 64T Mike Madden	.09	.04	.01
☐ 65T Rick Manning	.09	.04	.01
☐ 66T Billy Martin MG	.30	.15	.03
☐ 67T Lee Mazzilli	.09	.04	.01
☐ 68T Andy McGaffigan	.09	.04	.01
☐ 69T Craig McMurtry	.15	.07	.01
☐ 70T John McNamara MG	.15	.07	.01
☐ 71T Orlando Mercado	.15	.07	.01
☐ 72T Larry Milbourne	.09	.04	.01
☐ 73T Randy Moffitt	.09	.04	.01
☐ 74T Sid Monge	.09	.04	.01
☐ 75T Jose Morales	.09	.04	.01
☐ 76T Omar Moreno	.09	.04	.01
☐ 77T Joe Morgan	2.00	1.00	.20
☐ 78T Mike Morgan	.20	.10	.02
☐ 79T Dale Murray	.09	.04	.01
☐ 80T Jeff Newman	.09	.04	.01
☐ 81T Pete O'Brien	1.00	.50	.10
☐ 82T Jorge Orta	.09	.04	.01
☐ 83T Alejandro Pena	.60	.30	.06
☐ 84T Pascual Perez	.30	.15	.03
☐ 85T Tony Perez	.65	.30	.06
☐ 86T Broderick Perkins	.09	.04	.01
☐ 87T Tony Phillips	.35	.17	.03
☐ 88T Charlie Puleo	.09	.04	.01
☐ 89T Pat Putnam	.09	.04	.01
☐ 90T Jamie Quirk	.09	.04	.01
☐ 91T Doug Rader MG	.15	.07	.01
☐ 92T Chuck Rainey	.09	.04	.01
☐ 93T Bobby Ramos	.09	.04	.01
☐ 94T Gary Redus	.35	.17	.03
☐ 95T Steve Renko	.09	.04	.01
☐ 96T Leon Roberts	.09	.04	.01
☐ 97T Aurelio Rodriguez	.09	.04	.01
☐ 98T Dick Ruthven	.09	.04	.01
☐ 99T Daryl Sconiers	.09	.04	.01
☐ 100T Mike Scott	1.25	.60	.12
☐ 101T Tom Seaver	3.50	1.75	.35
☐ 102T John Shelby	.25	.12	.02
☐ 103T Bob Shirley	.09	.04	.01
☐ 104T Joe Simpson	.09	.04	.01
☐ 105T Doug Sisk	.15	.07	.01
☐ 106T Mike Smithson	.15	.07	.01
☐ 107T Elias Sosa	.09	.04	.01
☐ 108T Darryl Strawberry	90.00	45.00	9.00
☐ 109T Tom Tellmann	.09	.04	.01
☐ 110T Gene Tenace	.15	.07	.01
☐ 111T Gorman Thomas	.20	.10	.02
☐ 112T Dick Tidrow	.09	.04	.01
☐ 113T Dave Tobik	.09	.04	.01
☐ 114T Wayne Tolleson	.15	.07	.01
☐ 115T Mike Torrez	.09	.04	.01
☐ 116T Manny Trillo	.09	.04	.01
☐ 117T Steve Trout	.09	.04	.01
☐ 118T Lee Tunnell	.15	.07	.01
☐ 119T Mike Vail	.09	.04	.01
☐ 120T Ellis Valentine	.09	.04	.01
☐ 121T Tom Veryzer	.09	.04	.01
☐ 122T George Vukovich	.09	.04	.01
☐ 123T Rick Waits	.09	.04	.01
☐ 124T Greg Walker	.45	.22	.04
☐ 125T Chris Welsh	.09	.04	.01
☐ 126T Len Whitehouse	.09	.04	.01
☐ 127T Eddie Whitson	.15	.07	.01
☐ 128T Jim Wohlford	.09	.04	.01
☐ 129T Matt Young	.15	.07	.01
☐ 130T Joel Youngblood	.09	.04	.01
☐ 131T Pat Zachry	.09	.04	.01
☐ 132T Checklist 1T-132T	.09	.01	.00

1983 Topps Glossy 40

The cards in this 40-card set measure 2 1/2" by 3 1/2". The 1983 Topps "Collector's Edition" or "All-Star Set" (popularly known as "Glossies") consists of color ballplayer picture cards with shiny, glazed surfaces. The player's name appears in small print outside the frame line at bottom left. The backs contain no biography or record and list only the set titles, the player's name, team, position, and the card number.

	MINT	EXC	G-VG
COMPLETE SET (40)	12.00	6.00	1.20
COMMON PLAYER (1-40)	.20	.10	.02

☐ 1 Carl Yastrzemski	1.25	.60	.12
☐ 2 Mookie Wilson	.20	.10	.02
☐ 3 Andre Thornton	.20	.10	.02
☐ 4 Keith Hernandez	.30	.15	.03
☐ 5 Robin Yount	.90	.45	.09
☐ 6 Terry Kennedy	.20	.10	.02
☐ 7 Dave Winfield	.50	.25	.05
☐ 8 Mike Schmidt	1.25	.60	.12
☐ 9 Buddy Bell	.20	.10	.02
☐ 10 Fernando Valenzuela	.35	.17	.03
☐ 11 Rich Gossage	.20	.10	.02
☐ 12 Bob Horner	.20	.10	.02
☐ 13 Toby Harrah	.20	.10	.02
☐ 14 Pete Rose	1.25	.60	.12
☐ 15 Cecil Cooper	.20	.10	.02
☐ 16 Dale Murphy	.90	.45	.09
☐ 17 Carlton Fisk	.45	.22	.04
☐ 18 Ray Knight	.25	.12	.02
☐ 19 Jim Palmer	.60	.30	.06
☐ 20 Gary Carter	.45	.22	.04
☐ 21 Richie Zisk	.20	.10	.02
☐ 22 Dusty Baker	.20	.10	.02
☐ 23 Willie Wilson	.25	.12	.02
☐ 24 Bill Buckner	.20	.10	.02
☐ 25 Dave Stieb	.25	.12	.02
☐ 26 Bill Madlock	.20	.10	.02
☐ 27 Lance Parrish	.30	.15	.03
☐ 28 Nolan Ryan	1.50	.75	.15
☐ 29 Rod Carew	.90	.45	.09
☐ 30 Al Oliver	.25	.12	.02
☐ 31 George Brett	1.00	.50	.10
☐ 32 Jack Clark	.30	.15	.03
☐ 33 Ricky Henderson	1.25	.60	.12
☐ 34 Dave Concepcion	.25	.12	.02
☐ 35 Kent Hrbek	.40	.20	.04
☐ 36 Steve Carlton	.60	.30	.06
☐ 37 Eddie Murray	.90	.45	.09
☐ 38 Ruppert Jones	.20	.10	.02
☐ 39 Reggie Jackson	1.00	.50	.10
☐ 40 Bruce Sutter	.25	.12	.02

1983 Topps Gaylord Perry

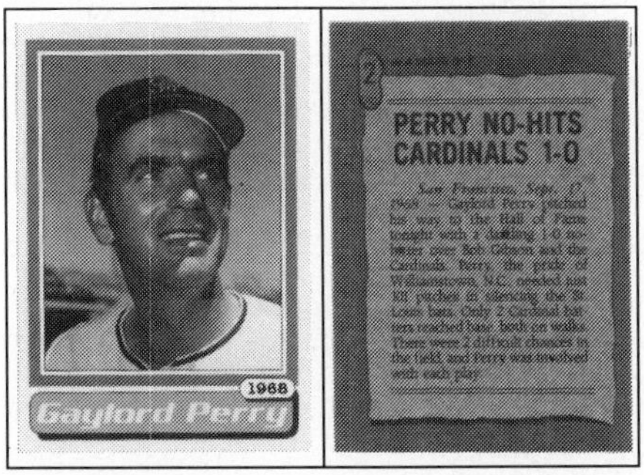

This six-card, standard-size, 2 1/2" by 3 1/2" set depicts Gaylord Perry during various parts of his career. These cards have the looks of Topps cards and were produced by Topps but have no Topps logo on either the front or the back of the card.

	MINT	EXC	G-VG
COMPLETE SET (6)	12.00	6.00	1.20
COMMON PLAYER (1-6)	2.50	1.25	.25
☐ 1 Gaylord Perry San Francisco Giants (Perry wins first game in 1962)	2.50	1.25	.25
☐ 2 Gaylord Perry San Francisco Giants (Perry pitches no-hitter in 1968)	2.50	1.25	.25
☐ 3 Gaylord Perry Cleveland Indians (Perry wins Cy Young Award in 1972)	2.50	1.25	.25
☐ 4 Gaylord Perry Texas Rangers (Perry strikes out 2,500th in 1975)	2.50	1.25	.25
☐ 5 Gaylord Perry San Diego Padres (Perry wins second Cy Young and strikes out 3,000th in 1978)	2.50	1.25	.25
☐ 6 Gaylord Perry Seattle Mariners (Perry wins 300th)	2.50	1.25	.25

1984 Topps

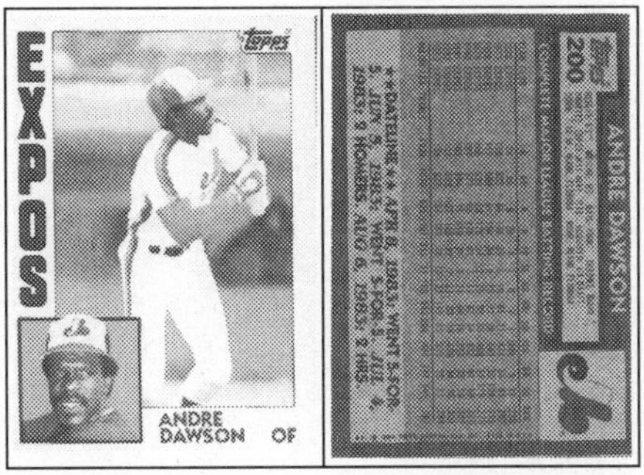

The cards in this 792-card set measure 2 1/2" by 3 1/2". For the second year in a row, Topps utilized a dual picture on the front of the card. A portrait is shown in a square insert and an action shot is featured in the main photo. Card numbers 1-6 feature 1983 Highlights (HL), cards 131-138 depict League Leaders, card numbers 386-407 feature All-Stars, and card numbers 701-718 feature active Major League career leaders in various statistical categories. Each team leader (TL) card features the team's leading hitter and pitcher pictured on the front with a team checklist back. There are six numerical checklist cards in the set. The player cards feature team logos in the upper right corner of the reverse. The key rookie cards in this set are Don Mattingly, Darryl Strawberry, and Andy Van Slyke. Topps also produced a specially boxed "glossy" edition, frequently referred to as the Topps Tiffany set. There were supposedly only 10,000 sets of the Tiffany cards produced; they were marketed to hobby dealers. The checklist of cards (792 regular and 132 Traded) is identical to that of the normal non-glossy cards. There are two primary distinguishing features of the Tiffany cards, white card stock reverses and high gloss obverses. These Tiffany cards are valued at approximately five times the values listed below. Topps tested a special send-in offer in Michigan and a few other states whereby collectors could obtain direct from Topps ten cards of their choice. Needless to say most people ordered the key (most valuable) players necessitating the printing of a special sheet to keep up with the demand. The special sheet had five cards of Darryl Strawberry, three cards of Don Mattingly, etc. The test was apparently a failure in Topps' eyes as they have never tried it again.

	MINT	EXC	G-VG
COMPLETE SET (792)	110.00	55.00	11.00
COMMON PLAYER (1-792)	.06	.03	.00
☐ 1 HL: Steve Carlton 300th win and all-time SO king	.30	.15	.03
☐ 2 HL: Rickey Henderson 100 stolen bases, three times	.65	.30	.06
☐ 3 HL: Dan Quisenberry Sets save record	.10	.05	.01

☐ 4 HL: Nolan Ryan,	.40	.20	.04
Steve Carlton, and			
Gaylord Perry			
(All surpass Johnson)			
☐ 5 HL: Dave Righetti,	.10	.05	.01
Bob Forsch,			
and Mike Warren			
(All pitch no-hitters)			
☐ 6 HL: Johnny Bench,	.30	.15	.03
Gaylord Perry, and			
Carl Yastrzemski			
(Superstars retire)			
☐ 7 Gary Lucas	.06	.03	.00
☐ 8 Don Mattingly	27.00	13.50	2.70
☐ 9 Jim Gott	.10	.05	.01
☐ 10 Robin Yount	.75	.35	.07
☐ 11 Minnesota Twins TL	.10	.05	.01
Kent Hrbek			
Ken Schrom			
☐ 12 Billy Sample	.06	.03	.00
☐ 13 Scott Holman	.06	.03	.00
☐ 14 Tom Brookens	.06	.03	.00
☐ 15 Burt Hooton	.06	.03	.00
☐ 16 Omar Moreno	.06	.03	.00
☐ 17 John Denny	.06	.03	.00
☐ 18 Dale Berra	.06	.03	.00
☐ 19 Ray Fontenot	.08	.04	.01
☐ 20 Greg Luzinski	.10	.05	.01
☐ 21 Joe Altobelli MG	.06	.03	.00
☐ 22 Bryan Clark	.06	.03	.00
☐ 23 Keith Moreland	.06	.03	.00
☐ 24 John Martin	.06	.03	.00
☐ 25 Glenn Hubbard	.06	.03	.00
☐ 26 Bud Black	.10	.05	.01
☐ 27 Daryl Sconiers	.06	.03	.00
☐ 28 Frank Viola	1.50	.75	.15
☐ 29 Danny Heep	.06	.03	.00
☐ 30 Wade Boggs	6.00	3.00	.60
☐ 31 Andy McGaffigan	.06	.03	.00
☐ 32 Bobby Ramos	.06	.03	.00
☐ 33 Tom Burgmeier	.06	.03	.00
☐ 34 Eddie Milner	.06	.03	.00
☐ 35 Don Sutton	.30	.15	.03
☐ 36 Denny Walling	.06	.03	.00
☐ 37 Texas Rangers TL	.10	.05	.01
Buddy Bell			
Rick Honeycutt			
☐ 38 Luis DeLeon	.06	.03	.00
☐ 39 Garth Iorg	.06	.03	.00
☐ 40 Dusty Baker	.10	.05	.01
☐ 41 Tony Bernazard	.06	.03	.00
☐ 42 Johnny Grubb	.06	.03	.00
☐ 43 Ron Reed	.06	.03	.00
☐ 44 Jim Morrison	.06	.03	.00
☐ 45 Jerry Mumphrey	.06	.03	.00
☐ 46 Ray Smith	.06	.03	.00
☐ 47 Rudy Law	.06	.03	.00
☐ 48 Julio Franco	2.00	1.00	.20
☐ 49 John Stuper	.06	.03	.00
☐ 50 Chris Chambliss	.10	.05	.01
☐ 51 Jim Frey MG	.06	.03	.00
☐ 52 Paul Splittorff	.06	.03	.00
☐ 53 Juan Beniquez	.06	.03	.00
☐ 54 Jesse Orosco	.06	.03	.00
☐ 55 Dave Concepcion	.10	.05	.01
☐ 56 Gary Allenson	.06	.03	.00
☐ 57 Dan Schatzeder	.06	.03	.00
☐ 58 Max Venable	.06	.03	.00
☐ 59 Sammy Stewart	.06	.03	.00
☐ 60 Paul Molitor	.20	.10	.02
☐ 61 Chris Codiroli	.06	.03	.00
☐ 62 Dave Hostetler	.06	.03	.00
☐ 63 Ed VandeBerg	.06	.03	.00
☐ 64 Mike Scioscia	.06	.03	.00
☐ 65 Kirk Gibson	.35	.17	.03
☐ 66 Houston Astros TL	.30	.15	.03
Jose Cruz			
Nolan Ryan			
☐ 67 Gary Ward	.06	.03	.00
☐ 68 Luis Salazar	.06	.03	.00
☐ 69 Rod Scurry	.06	.03	.00
☐ 70 Gary Matthews	.06	.03	.00
☐ 71 Leo Hernandez	.06	.03	.00
☐ 72 Mike Squires	.06	.03	.00
☐ 73 Jody Davis	.10	.05	.01
☐ 74 Jerry Martin	.06	.03	.00
☐ 75 Bob Forsch	.06	.03	.00
☐ 76 Alfredo Griffin	.06	.03	.00
☐ 77 Brett Butler	.15	.07	.01
☐ 78 Mike Torrez	.06	.03	.00
☐ 79 Rob Wilfong	.06	.03	.00
☐ 80 Steve Rogers	.06	.03	.00
☐ 81 Billy Martin MG	.15	.07	.01
☐ 82 Doug Bird	.06	.03	.00

☐ 83 Richie Zisk	.06	.03	.00
☐ 84 Lenny Faedo	.06	.03	.00
☐ 85 Atlee Hammaker	.06	.03	.00
☐ 86 John Shelby	.18	.09	.01
☐ 87 Frank Pastore	.06	.03	.00
☐ 88 Rob Picciolo	.06	.03	.00
☐ 89 Mike Smithson	.06	.03	.00
☐ 90 Pedro Guerrero	.40	.20	.04
☐ 91 Dan Spillner	.06	.03	.00
☐ 92 Lloyd Moseby	.10	.05	.01
☐ 93 Bob Knepper	.06	.03	.00
☐ 94 Mario Ramirez	.06	.03	.00
☐ 95 Aurelio Lopez	.06	.03	.00
☐ 96 K.C. Royals TL	.10	.05	.01
Hal McRae			
Larry Gura			
☐ 97 LaMarr Hoyt	.06	.03	.00
☐ 98 Steve Nicosia	.06	.03	.00
☐ 99 Craig Lefferts	.30	.15	.03
☐ 100 Reggie Jackson	.80	.40	.08
☐ 101 Porfirio Altamirano	.06	.03	.00
☐ 102 Ken Oberkfell	.06	.03	.00
☐ 103 Dwayne Murphy	.06	.03	.00
☐ 104 Ken Dayley	.06	.03	.00
☐ 105 Tony Armas	.06	.03	.00
☐ 106 Tim Stoddard	.06	.03	.00
☐ 107 Ned Yost	.06	.03	.00
☐ 108 Randy Moffitt	.06	.03	.00
☐ 109 Brad Wellman	.06	.03	.00
☐ 110 Ron Guidry	.25	.12	.02
☐ 111 Bill Virdon MG	.06	.03	.00
☐ 112 Tom Niedenfuer	.06	.03	.00
☐ 113 Kelly Paris	.06	.03	.00
☐ 114 Checklist 1-132	.08	.01	.00
☐ 115 Andre Thornton	.10	.05	.01
☐ 116 George Bjorkman	.06	.03	.00
☐ 117 Tom Veryzer	.06	.03	.00
☐ 118 Charlie Hough	.10	.05	.01
☐ 119 John Wockenfuss	.06	.03	.00
☐ 120 Keith Hernandez	.35	.17	.03
☐ 121 Pat Sheridan	.18	.09	.01
☐ 122 Cecilio Guante	.06	.03	.00
☐ 123 Butch Wynegar	.06	.03	.00
☐ 124 Damaso Garcia	.06	.03	.00
☐ 125 Britt Burns	.06	.03	.00
☐ 126 Atlanta Braves TL	.15	.07	.01
Dale Murphy			
Craig McMurtry			
☐ 127 Mike Madden	.06	.03	.00
☐ 128 Rick Manning	.06	.03	.00
☐ 129 Bill Laskey	.06	.03	.00
☐ 130 Ozzie Smith	.45	.22	.04
☐ 131 Batting Leaders	.25	.12	.02
Bill Madlock			
Wade Boggs			
☐ 132 Home Run Leaders	.25	.12	.02
Mike Schmidt			
Jim Rice			
☐ 133 RBI Leaders	.20	.10	.02
Dale Murphy			
Cecil Cooper			
Jim Rice			
☐ 134 Stolen Base Leaders	.40	.20	.04
Tim Raines			
Rickey Henderson			
☐ 135 Victory Leaders	.10	.05	.01
John Denny			
LaMarr Hoyt			
☐ 136 Strikeout Leaders	.18	.09	.01
Steve Carlton			
Jack Morris			
☐ 137 ERA Leaders	.10	.05	.01
Atlee Hammaker			
Rick Honeycutt			
☐ 138 Leading Firemen	.10	.05	.01
Al Holland			
Dan Quisenberry			
☐ 139 Bert Campaneris	.10	.05	.01
☐ 140 Storm Davis	.10	.05	.01
☐ 141 Pat Corrales MG	.06	.03	.00
☐ 142 Rich Gale	.06	.03	.00
☐ 143 Jose Morales	.06	.03	.00
☐ 144 Brian Harper	.45	.22	.04
☐ 145 Gary Lavelle	.06	.03	.00
☐ 146 Ed Romero	.06	.03	.00
☐ 147 Dan Petry	.06	.03	.00
☐ 148 Joe Lefebvre	.06	.03	.00
☐ 149 Jon Matlack	.06	.03	.00
☐ 150 Dale Murphy	1.00	.50	.10
☐ 151 Steve Trout	.06	.03	.00
☐ 152 Glenn Brummer	.06	.03	.00
☐ 153 Dick Tidrow	.06	.03	.00
☐ 154 Dave Henderson	.20	.10	.02
☐ 155 Frank White	.10	.05	.01

☐ 156	Oakland A's TL	.25	.12	.02
	Rickey Henderson			
	Tim Conroy			
☐ 157	Gary Gaetti	.65	.30	.06
☐ 158	John Curtis	.06	.03	.00
☐ 159	Darryl Cias	.06	.03	.00
☐ 160	Mario Soto	.06	.03	.00
☐ 161	Junior Ortiz	.06	.03	.00
☐ 162	Bob Ojeda	.10	.05	.01
☐ 163	Lorenzo Gray	.06	.03	.00
☐ 164	Scott Sanderson	.10	.05	.01
☐ 165	Ken Singleton	.10	.05	.01
☐ 166	Jamie Nelson	.06	.03	.00
☐ 167	Marshall Edwards	.06	.03	.00
☐ 168	Juan Bonilla	.06	.03	.00
☐ 169	Larry Parrish	.06	.03	.00
☐ 170	Jerry Reuss	.06	.03	.00
☐ 171	Frank Robinson MG	.15	.07	.01
☐ 172	Frank DiPino	.06	.03	.00
☐ 173	Marvell Wynne	.10	.05	.01
☐ 174	Juan Berenguer	.06	.03	.00
☐ 175	Graig Nettles	.15	.07	.01
☐ 176	Lee Smith	.10	.05	.01
☐ 177	Jerry Hairston	.06	.03	.00
☐ 178	Bill Krueger	.06	.03	.00
☐ 179	Buck Martinez	.06	.03	.00
☐ 180	Manny Trillo	.06	.03	.00
☐ 181	Roy Thomas	.06	.03	.00
☐ 182	Darryl Strawberry	18.00	9.00	1.80
☐ 183	Al Williams	.06	.03	.00
☐ 184	Mike O'Berry	.06	.03	.00
☐ 185	Sixto Lezcano	.06	.03	.00
☐ 186	Cardinal TL	.10	.05	.01
	Lonnie Smith			
	John Stuper			
☐ 187	Luis Aponte	.06	.03	.00
☐ 188	Bryan Little	.06	.03	.00
☐ 189	Tim Conroy	.06	.03	.00
☐ 190	Ben Oglivie	.06	.03	.00
☐ 191	Mike Boddicker	.10	.05	.01
☐ 192	Nick Esasky	.65	.30	.06
☐ 193	Darrell Brown	.06	.03	.00
☐ 194	Domingo Ramos	.06	.03	.00
☐ 195	Jack Morris	.15	.07	.01
☐ 196	Don Slaught	.15	.07	.01
☐ 197	Garry Hancock	.06	.03	.00
☐ 198	Bill Doran	.75	.35	.07
☐ 199	Willie Hernandez	.15	.07	.01
☐ 200	Andre Dawson	.50	.25	.05
☐ 201	Bruce Kison	.06	.03	.00
☐ 202	Bobby Cox MG	.06	.03	.00
☐ 203	Matt Keough	.06	.03	.00
☐ 204	Bobby Meacham	.06	.03	.00
☐ 205	Greg Minton	.06	.03	.00
☐ 206	Andy Van Slyke	2.50	1.25	.25
☐ 207	Donnie Moore	.06	.03	.00
☐ 208	Jose Oquendo	.50	.25	.05
☐ 209	Manny Sarmiento	.06	.03	.00
☐ 210	Joe Morgan	.40	.20	.04
☐ 211	Rick Sweet	.06	.03	.00
☐ 212	Broderick Perkins	.06	.03	.00
☐ 213	Bruce Hurst	.15	.07	.01
☐ 214	Paul Householder	.06	.03	.00
☐ 215	Tippy Martinez	.06	.03	.00
☐ 216	White Sox TL	.15	.07	.01
	Carlton Fisk			
	Richard Dotson			
☐ 217	Alan Ashby	.06	.03	.00
☐ 218	Rick Waits	.06	.03	.00
☐ 219	Joe Simpson	.06	.03	.00
☐ 220	Fernando Valenzuela	.30	.15	.03
☐ 221	Cliff Johnson	.06	.03	.00
☐ 222	Rick Honeycutt	.06	.03	.00
☐ 223	Wayne Krenchicki	.06	.03	.00
☐ 224	Sid Monge	.06	.03	.00
☐ 225	Lee Mazzilli	.06	.03	.00
☐ 226	Juan Eichelberger	.06	.03	.00
☐ 227	Steve Braun	.06	.03	.00
☐ 228	John Rabb	.06	.03	.00
☐ 229	Paul Owens MG	.06	.03	.00
☐ 230	Rickey Henderson	4.50	2.25	.45
☐ 231	Gary Woods	.06	.03	.00
☐ 232	Tim Wallach	.20	.10	.02
☐ 233	Checklist 133-264	.08	.01	.00
☐ 234	Rafael Ramirez	.06	.03	.00
☐ 235	Matt Young	.06	.03	.00
☐ 236	Ellis Valentine	.06	.03	.00
☐ 237	John Castino	.06	.03	.00
☐ 238	Reid Nichols	.06	.03	.00
☐ 239	Jay Howell	.06	.03	.00
☐ 240	Eddie Murray	.75	.35	.07
☐ 241	Bill Almon	.06	.03	.00
☐ 242	Alex Trevino	.06	.03	.00
☐ 243	Pete Ladd	.06	.03	.00
☐ 244	Candy Maldonado	.60	.30	.06
☐ 245	Rick Sutcliffe	.25	.12	.02
☐ 246	New York Mets TL	.20	.10	.02
	Mookie Wilson			
	Tom Seaver			
☐ 247	Onix Concepcion	.06	.03	.00
☐ 248	Bill Dawley	.06	.03	.00
☐ 249	Jay Johnstone	.10	.05	.01
☐ 250	Bill Madlock	.10	.05	.01
☐ 251	Tony Gwynn	3.25	1.60	.32
☐ 252	Larry Christenson	.06	.03	.00
☐ 253	Jim Wohlford	.06	.03	.00
☐ 254	Shane Rawley	.06	.03	.00
☐ 255	Bruce Benedict	.06	.03	.00
☐ 256	Dave Geisel	.06	.03	.00
☐ 257	Julio Cruz	.06	.03	.00
☐ 258	Luis Sanchez	.06	.03	.00
☐ 259	Sparky Anderson MG	.06	.03	.00
☐ 260	Scott McGregor	.06	.03	.00
☐ 261	Bobby Brown	.06	.03	.00
☐ 262	Tom Candiotti	.45	.22	.04
☐ 263	Jack Fimple	.06	.03	.00
☐ 264	Doug Frobel	.06	.03	.00
☐ 265	Donnie Hill	.06	.03	.00
☐ 266	Steve Lubratich	.06	.03	.00
☐ 267	Carmelo Martinez	.30	.15	.03
☐ 268	Jack O'Connor	.06	.03	.00
☐ 269	Aurelio Rodriguez	.06	.03	.00
☐ 270	Jeff Russell	.50	.25	.05
☐ 271	Moose Haas	.06	.03	.00
☐ 272	Rick Dempsey	.06	.03	.00
☐ 273	Charlie Puleo	.06	.03	.00
☐ 274	Rick Monday	.06	.03	.00
☐ 275	Len Matuszek	.06	.03	.00
☐ 276	Angels TL	.15	.07	.01
	Rod Carew			
	Geoff Zahn			
☐ 277	Eddie Whitson	.10	.05	.01
☐ 278	Jorge Bell	1.25	.60	.12
☐ 279	Ivan DeJesus	.06	.03	.00
☐ 280	Floyd Bannister	.06	.03	.00
☐ 281	Larry Milbourne	.06	.03	.00
☐ 282	Jim Barr	.06	.03	.00
☐ 283	Larry Biittner	.06	.03	.00
☐ 284	Howard Bailey	.06	.03	.00
☐ 285	Darrell Porter	.06	.03	.00
☐ 286	Lary Sorensen	.06	.03	.00
☐ 287	Warren Cromartie	.06	.03	.00
☐ 288	Jim Beattie	.06	.03	.00
☐ 289	Randy Johnson	.06	.03	.00
☐ 290	Dave Dravecky	.20	.10	.02
☐ 291	Chuck Tanner MG	.06	.03	.00
☐ 292	Tony Scott	.06	.03	.00
☐ 293	Ed Lynch	.06	.03	.00
☐ 294	U.L. Washington	.06	.03	.00
☐ 295	Mike Flanagan	.10	.05	.01
☐ 296	Jeff Newman	.06	.03	.00
☐ 297	Bruce Berenyi	.06	.03	.00
☐ 298	Jim Gantner	.06	.03	.00
☐ 299	John Butcher	.06	.03	.00
☐ 300	Pete Rose	1.25	.60	.12
☐ 301	Frank LaCorte	.06	.03	.00
☐ 302	Barry Bonnell	.06	.03	.00
☐ 303	Marty Castillo	.06	.03	.00
☐ 304	Warren Brusstar	.06	.03	.00
☐ 305	Roy Smalley	.06	.03	.00
☐ 306	Dodgers TL	.12	.06	.01
	Pedro Guerrero			
	Bob Welch			
☐ 307	Bobby Mitchell	.06	.03	.00
☐ 308	Ron Hassey	.06	.03	.00
☐ 309	Tony Phillips	.25	.12	.02
☐ 310	Willie McGee	.45	.22	.04
☐ 311	Jerry Koosman	.10	.05	.01
☐ 312	Jorge Orta	.06	.03	.00
☐ 313	Mike Jorgensen	.06	.03	.00
☐ 314	Orlando Mercado	.06	.03	.00
☐ 315	Bob Grich	.10	.05	.01
☐ 316	Mark Bradley	.06	.03	.00
☐ 317	Greg Pryor	.06	.03	.00
☐ 318	Bill Gullickson	.06	.03	.00
☐ 319	Al Bumbry	.06	.03	.00
☐ 320	Bob Stanley	.06	.03	.00
☐ 321	Harvey Kuenn MG	.06	.03	.00
☐ 322	Ken Schrom	.06	.03	.00
☐ 323	Alan Knicely	.06	.03	.00
☐ 324	Alejandro Pena	.25	.12	.02
☐ 325	Darrell Evans	.15	.07	.01
☐ 326	Bob Kearney	.06	.03	.00
☐ 327	Ruppert Jones	.06	.03	.00
☐ 328	Vern Ruhle	.06	.03	.00
☐ 329	Pat Tabler	.20	.10	.02
☐ 330	John Candelaria	.10	.05	.01
☐ 331	Bucky Dent	.10	.05	.01

☐	332 Kevin Gross	.30	.15	.03
☐	333 Larry Herndon	.06	.03	.00
☐	334 Chuck Rainey	.06	.03	.00
☐	335 Don Baylor	.12	.06	.01
☐	336 Seattle Mariners TL	.10	.05	.01
	Pat Putnam			
	Matt Young			
☐	337 Kevin Hagen	.06	.03	.00
☐	338 Mike Warren	.10	.05	.01
☐	339 Roy Lee Jackson	.06	.03	.00
☐	340 Hal McRae	.10	.05	.01
☐	341 Dave Tobik	.06	.03	.00
☐	342 Tim Foli	.06	.03	.00
☐	343 Mark Davis	.15	.07	.01
☐	344 Rick Miller	.06	.03	.00
☐	345 Kent Hrbek	.45	.22	.04
☐	346 Kurt Bevacqua	.06	.03	.00
☐	347 Allan Ramirez	.06	.03	.00
☐	348 Toby Harrah	.06	.03	.00
☐	349 Bob L. Gibson	.06	.03	.00
	(Brewers Pitcher)			
☐	350 George Foster	.15	.07	.01
☐	351 Russ Nixon MG	.06	.03	.00
☐	352 Dave Stewart	1.25	.60	.12
☐	353 Jim Anderson	.06	.03	.00
☐	354 Jeff Burroughs	.06	.03	.00
☐	355 Jason Thompson	.06	.03	.00
☐	356 Glenn Abbott	.06	.03	.00
☐	357 Ron Cey	.10	.05	.01
☐	358 Bob Dernier	.06	.03	.00
☐	359 Jim Acker	.06	.03	.00
☐	360 Willie Randolph	.10	.05	.01
☐	361 Dave Smith	.10	.05	.01
☐	362 David Green	.06	.03	.00
☐	363 Tim Laudner	.06	.03	.00
☐	364 Scott Fletcher	.20	.10	.02
☐	365 Steve Bedrosian	.15	.07	.01
☐	366 Padres TL	.10	.05	.01
	Terry Kennedy			
	Dave Dravecky			
☐	367 Jamie Easterly	.06	.03	.00
☐	368 Hubie Brooks	.15	.07	.01
☐	369 Steve McCatty	.06	.03	.00
☐	370 Tim Raines	.50	.25	.05
☐	371 Dave Gumpert	.06	.03	.00
☐	372 Gary Roenicke	.06	.03	.00
☐	373 Bill Scherrer	.06	.03	.00
☐	374 Don Money	.06	.03	.00
☐	375 Dennis Leonard	.08	.04	.01
☐	376 Dave Anderson	.15	.07	.01
☐	377 Danny Darwin	.10	.05	.01
☐	378 Bob Brenly	.06	.03	.00
☐	379 Checklist 265-396	.08	.01	.00
☐	380 Steve Garvey	.50	.25	.05
☐	381 Ralph Houk MG	.06	.03	.00
☐	382 Chris Nyman	.06	.03	.00
☐	383 Terry Puhl	.06	.03	.00
☐	384 Lee Tunnell	.10	.05	.01
☐	385 Tony Perez	.20	.10	.02
☐	386 George Hendrick AS	.10	.05	.01
☐	387 Johnny Ray AS	.10	.05	.01
☐	388 Mike Schmidt AS	.40	.20	.04
☐	389 Ozzie Smith AS	.15	.07	.01
☐	390 Tim Raines AS	.15	.07	.01
☐	391 Dale Murphy AS	.30	.15	.03
☐	392 Andre Dawson AS	.20	.10	.02
☐	393 Gary Carter AS	.15	.07	.01
☐	394 Steve Rogers AS	.10	.05	.01
☐	395 Steve Carlton AS	.20	.10	.02
☐	396 Jesse Orosco AS	.10	.05	.01
☐	397 Eddie Murray AS	.20	.10	.02
☐	398 Lou Whitaker AS	.10	.05	.01
☐	399 George Brett AS	.30	.15	.03
☐	400 Cal Ripken AS	.25	.12	.02
☐	401 Jim Rice AS	.15	.07	.01
☐	402 Dave Winfield AS	.15	.07	.01
☐	403 Lloyd Moseby AS	.10	.05	.01
☐	404 Ted Simmons AS	.10	.05	.01
☐	405 LaMarr Hoyt AS	.10	.05	.01
☐	406 Ron Guidry AS	.10	.05	.01
☐	407 Dan Quisenberry AS	.10	.05	.01
☐	408 Lou Piniella	.10	.05	.01
☐	409 Juan Agosto	.12	.06	.01
☐	410 Claudell Washington	.10	.05	.01
☐	411 Houston Jimenez	.06	.03	.00
☐	412 Doug Rader MG	.06	.03	.00
☐	413 Spike Owen	.30	.15	.03
☐	414 Mitchell Page	.06	.03	.00
☐	415 Tommy John	.18	.09	.01
☐	416 Dane Iorg	.06	.03	.00
☐	417 Mike Armstrong	.06	.03	.00
☐	418 Ron Hodges	.06	.03	.00
☐	419 John Henry Johnson	.06	.03	.00
☐	420 Cecil Cooper	.12	.06	.01
☐	421 Charlie Lea	.06	.03	.00
☐	422 Jose Cruz	.10	.05	.01
☐	423 Mike Morgan	.10	.05	.01
☐	424 Dann Bilardello	.06	.03	.00
☐	425 Steve Howe	.06	.03	.00
☐	426 Orioles TL	.20	.10	.02
	Cal Ripken			
	Mike Boddicker			
☐	427 Rick Leach	.06	.03	.00
☐	428 Fred Breining	.06	.03	.00
☐	429 Randy Bush	.20	.10	.02
☐	430 Rusty Staub	.10	.05	.01
☐	431 Chris Bando	.06	.03	.00
☐	432 Charles Hudson	.12	.06	.01
☐	433 Rich Hebner	.06	.03	.00
☐	434 Harold Baines	.30	.15	.03
☐	435 Neil Allen	.06	.03	.00
☐	436 Rick Peters	.06	.03	.00
☐	437 Mike Proly	.06	.03	.00
☐	438 Biff Pocoroba	.06	.03	.00
☐	439 Bob Stoddard	.06	.03	.00
☐	440 Steve Kemp	.06	.03	.00
☐	441 Bob Lillis MG	.06	.03	.00
☐	442 Byron McLaughlin	.06	.03	.00
☐	443 Benny Ayala	.06	.03	.00
☐	444 Steve Renko	.06	.03	.00
☐	445 Jerry Remy	.06	.03	.00
☐	446 Luis Pujols	.06	.03	.00
☐	447 Tom Brunansky	.30	.15	.03
☐	448 Ben Hayes	.06	.03	.00
☐	449 Joe Pettini	.06	.03	.00
☐	450 Gary Carter	.40	.20	.04
☐	451 Bob Jones	.06	.03	.00
☐	452 Chuck Porter	.06	.03	.00
☐	453 Willie Upshaw	.06	.03	.00
☐	454 Joe Beckwith	.06	.03	.00
☐	455 Terry Kennedy	.06	.03	.00
☐	456 Chicago Cubs TL	.10	.05	.01
	Keith Moreland			
	Fergie Jenkins			
☐	457 Dave Rozema	.06	.03	.00
☐	458 Kiko Garcia	.06	.03	.00
☐	459 Kevin Hickey	.06	.03	.00
☐	460 Dave Winfield	.45	.22	.04
☐	461 Jim Maler	.06	.03	.00
☐	462 Lee Lacy	.06	.03	.00
☐	463 Dave Engle	.06	.03	.00
☐	464 Jeff A. Jones	.06	.03	.00
	(A's Pitcher)			
☐	465 Mookie Wilson	.10	.05	.01
☐	466 Gene Garber	.06	.03	.00
☐	467 Mike Ramsey	.06	.03	.00
☐	468 Geoff Zahn	.06	.03	.00
☐	469 Tom O'Malley	.06	.03	.00
☐	470 Nolan Ryan	3.50	1.75	.35
☐	471 Dick Howser MG	.06	.03	.00
☐	472 Mike Brown	.06	.03	.00
	(Red Sox Pitcher)			
☐	473 Jim Dwyer	.06	.03	.00
☐	474 Greg Bargar	.06	.03	.00
☐	475 Gary Redus	.20	.10	.02
☐	476 Tom Tellmann	.06	.03	.00
☐	477 Rafael Landestoy	.06	.03	.00
☐	478 Alan Bannister	.06	.03	.00
☐	479 Frank Tanana	.10	.05	.01
☐	480 Ron Kittle	.30	.15	.03
☐	481 Mark Thurmond	.10	.05	.01
☐	482 Enos Cabell	.06	.03	.00
☐	483 Fergie Jenkins	.25	.12	.02
☐	484 Ozzie Virgil	.06	.03	.00
☐	485 Rick Rhoden	.06	.03	.00
☐	486 N.Y. Yankees TL	.10	.05	.01
	Don Baylor			
	Ron Guidry			
☐	487 Ricky Adams	.06	.03	.00
☐	488 Jesse Barfield	.25	.12	.02
☐	489 Dave Von Ohlen	.06	.03	.00
☐	490 Cal Ripken	2.00	1.00	.20
☐	491 Bobby Castillo	.06	.03	.00
☐	492 Tucker Ashford	.06	.03	.00
☐	493 Mike Norris	.06	.03	.00
☐	494 Chili Davis	.20	.10	.02
☐	495 Rollie Fingers	.20	.10	.02
☐	496 Terry Francona	.06	.03	.00
☐	497 Bud Anderson	.06	.03	.00
☐	498 Rich Gedman	.06	.03	.00
☐	499 Mike Witt	.10	.05	.01
☐	500 George Brett	1.00	.50	.10
☐	501 Steve Henderson	.06	.03	.00
☐	502 Joe Torre MG	.10	.05	.01
☐	503 Elias Sosa	.06	.03	.00
☐	504 Mickey Rivers	.06	.03	.00
☐	505 Pete Vuckovich	.06	.03	.00
☐	506 Ernie Whitt	.06	.03	.00

☐ 507 Mike LaCoss	.06	.03	.00
☐ 508 Mel Hall	.40	.20	.04
☐ 509 Brad Havens	.06	.03	.00
☐ 510 Alan Trammell	.40	.20	.04
☐ 511 Marty Bystrom	.06	.03	.00
☐ 512 Oscar Gamble	.06	.03	.00
☐ 513 Dave Beard	.06	.03	.00
☐ 514 Floyd Rayford	.06	.03	.00
☐ 515 Gorman Thomas	.10	.05	.01
☐ 516 Montreal Expos TL	.10	.05	.01
Al Oliver			
Charlie Lea			
☐ 517 John Moses	.06	.03	.00
☐ 518 Greg Walker	.25	.12	.02
☐ 519 Ron Davis	.06	.03	.00
☐ 520 Bob Boone	.12	.06	.01
☐ 521 Pete Falcone	.06	.03	.00
☐ 522 Dave Bergman	.06	.03	.00
☐ 523 Glenn Hoffman	.06	.03	.00
☐ 524 Carlos Diaz	.06	.03	.00
☐ 525 Willie Wilson	.12	.06	.01
☐ 526 Ron Oester	.06	.03	.00
☐ 527 Checklist 397-528	.08	.01	.00
☐ 528 Mark Brouhard	.06	.03	.00
☐ 529 Keith Atherton	.06	.03	.00
☐ 530 Dan Ford	.06	.03	.00
☐ 531 Steve Boros MG	.06	.03	.00
☐ 532 Eric Show	.06	.03	.00
☐ 533 Ken Landreaux	.06	.03	.00
☐ 534 Pete O'Brien	.50	.25	.05
☐ 535 Bo Diaz	.06	.03	.00
☐ 536 Doug Bair	.06	.03	.00
☐ 537 Johnny Ray	.10	.05	.01
☐ 538 Kevin Bass	.10	.05	.01
☐ 539 George Frazier	.06	.03	.00
☐ 540 George Hendrick	.06	.03	.00
☐ 541 Dennis Lamp	.06	.03	.00
☐ 542 Duane Kuiper	.06	.03	.00
☐ 543 Craig McMurtry	.06	.03	.00
☐ 544 Cesar Geronimo	.06	.03	.00
☐ 545 Bill Buckner	.10	.05	.01
☐ 546 Indians TL	.10	.05	.01
Mike Hargrove			
Lary Sorensen			
☐ 547 Mike Moore	.20	.10	.02
☐ 548 Ron Jackson	.06	.03	.00
☐ 549 Walt Terrell	.25	.12	.02
☐ 550 Jim Rice	.25	.12	.02
☐ 551 Scott Ullger	.06	.03	.00
☐ 552 Ray Burris	.06	.03	.00
☐ 553 Joe Nolan	.06	.03	.00
☐ 554 Ted Power	.06	.03	.00
☐ 555 Greg Brock	.12	.06	.01
☐ 556 Joey McLaughlin	.06	.03	.00
☐ 557 Wayne Tolleson	.06	.03	.00
☐ 558 Mike Davis	.06	.03	.00
☐ 559 Mike Scott	.30	.15	.03
☐ 560 Carlton Fisk	.45	.22	.04
☐ 561 Whitey Herzog MG	.06	.03	.00
☐ 562 Manny Castillo	.06	.03	.00
☐ 563 Glenn Wilson	.06	.03	.00
☐ 564 Al Holland	.06	.03	.00
☐ 565 Leon Durham	.06	.03	.00
☐ 566 Jim Bibby	.06	.03	.00
☐ 567 Mike Heath	.06	.03	.00
☐ 568 Pete Filson	.06	.03	.00
☐ 569 Bake McBride	.06	.03	.00
☐ 570 Dan Quisenberry	.12	.06	.01
☐ 571 Bruce Bochy	.06	.03	.00
☐ 572 Jerry Royster	.06	.03	.00
☐ 573 Dave Kingman	.15	.07	.01
☐ 574 Brian Downing	.06	.03	.00
☐ 575 Jim Clancy	.06	.03	.00
☐ 576 Giants TL	.10	.05	.01
Jeff Leonard			
Atlee Hammaker			
☐ 577 Mark Clear	.06	.03	.00
☐ 578 Lenn Sakata	.06	.03	.00
☐ 579 Bob James	.10	.05	.01
☐ 580 Lonnie Smith	.12	.06	.01
☐ 581 Jose DeLeon	.30	.15	.03
☐ 582 Bob McClure	.06	.03	.00
☐ 583 Derrel Thomas	.06	.03	.00
☐ 584 Dave Schmidt	.06	.03	.00
☐ 585 Dan Driessen	.06	.03	.00
☐ 586 Joe Niekro	.10	.05	.01
☐ 587 Von Hayes	.18	.09	.01
☐ 588 Milt Wilcox	.06	.03	.00
☐ 589 Mike Easler	.06	.03	.00
☐ 590 Dave Stieb	.20	.10	.02
☐ 591 Tony LaRussa MG	.06	.03	.00
☐ 592 Andre Robertson	.06	.03	.00
☐ 593 Jeff Lahti	.06	.03	.00
☐ 594 Gene Richards	.06	.03	.00
☐ 595 Jeff Reardon	.15	.07	.01
☐ 596 Ryne Sandberg	8.00	4.00	.80
☐ 597 Rick Camp	.06	.03	.00
☐ 598 Rusty Kuntz	.06	.03	.00
☐ 599 Doug Sisk	.08	.04	.01
☐ 600 Rod Carew	.60	.30	.06
☐ 601 John Tudor	.15	.07	.01
☐ 602 John Wathan	.06	.03	.00
☐ 603 Renie Martin	.06	.03	.00
☐ 604 John Lowenstein	.06	.03	.00
☐ 605 Mike Caldwell	.06	.03	.00
☐ 606 Blue Jays TL	.12	.06	.01
Lloyd Moseby			
Dave Stieb			
☐ 607 Tom Hume	.06	.03	.00
☐ 608 Bobby Johnson	.06	.03	.00
☐ 609 Dan Meyer	.06	.03	.00
☐ 610 Steve Sax	.35	.17	.03
☐ 611 Chet Lemon	.06	.03	.00
☐ 612 Harry Spilman	.06	.03	.00
☐ 613 Greg Gross	.06	.03	.00
☐ 614 Len Barker	.06	.03	.00
☐ 615 Garry Templeton	.06	.03	.00
☐ 616 Don Robinson	.06	.03	.00
☐ 617 Rick Cerone	.06	.03	.00
☐ 618 Dickie Noles	.06	.03	.00
☐ 619 Jerry Dybzinski	.06	.03	.00
☐ 620 Al Oliver	.10	.05	.01
☐ 621 Frank Howard MG	.06	.03	.00
☐ 622 Al Cowens	.06	.03	.00
☐ 623 Ron Washington	.06	.03	.00
☐ 624 Terry Harper	.06	.03	.00
☐ 625 Larry Gura	.06	.03	.00
☐ 626 Bob Clark	.06	.03	.00
☐ 627 Dave LaPoint	.06	.03	.00
☐ 628 Ed Jurak	.06	.03	.00
☐ 629 Rick Langford	.06	.03	.00
☐ 630 Ted Simmons	.12	.06	.01
☐ 631 Dennis Martinez	.10	.05	.01
☐ 632 Tom Foley	.06	.03	.00
☐ 633 Mike Krukow	.06	.03	.00
☐ 634 Mike Marshall	.18	.09	.01
☐ 635 Dave Righetti	.18	.09	.01
☐ 636 Pat Putnam	.06	.03	.00
☐ 637 Phillies TL	.10	.05	.01
Gary Matthews			
John Denny			
☐ 638 George Vukovich	.06	.03	.00
☐ 639 Rick Lysander	.06	.03	.00
☐ 640 Lance Parrish	.25	.12	.02
☐ 641 Mike Richardt	.06	.03	.00
☐ 642 Tom Underwood	.06	.03	.00
☐ 643 Mike Brown	.06	.03	.00
(Angels OF)			
☐ 644 Tim Lollar	.06	.03	.00
☐ 645 Tony Pena	.15	.07	.01
☐ 646 Checklist 529-660	.08	.01	.00
☐ 647 Ron Roenicke	.06	.03	.00
☐ 648 Len Whitehouse	.06	.03	.00
☐ 649 Tom Herr	.10	.05	.01
☐ 650 Phil Niekro	.20	.10	.02
☐ 651 John McNamara MG	.06	.03	.00
☐ 652 Rudy May	.06	.03	.00
☐ 653 Dave Stapleton	.06	.03	.00
☐ 654 Bob Bailor	.06	.03	.00
☐ 655 Amos Otis	.10	.05	.01
☐ 656 Bryn Smith	.10	.05	.01
☐ 657 Thad Bosley	.06	.03	.00
☐ 658 Jerry Augustine	.06	.03	.00
☐ 659 Duane Walker	.06	.03	.00
☐ 660 Ray Knight	.10	.05	.01
☐ 661 Steve Yeager	.06	.03	.00
☐ 662 Tom Brennan	.06	.03	.00
☐ 663 Johnnie LeMaster	.06	.03	.00
☐ 664 Dave Stegman	.06	.03	.00
☐ 665 Buddy Bell	.12	.06	.01
☐ 666 Detroit Tigers TL	.15	.07	.01
Lou Whitaker			
Jack Morris			
☐ 667 Vance Law	.06	.03	.00
☐ 668 Larry McWilliams	.06	.03	.00
☐ 669 Dave Lopes	.10	.05	.01
☐ 670 Rich Gossage	.18	.09	.01
☐ 671 Jamie Quirk	.06	.03	.00
☐ 672 Ricky Nelson	.06	.03	.00
☐ 673 Mike Walters	.06	.03	.00
☐ 674 Tim Flannery	.06	.03	.00
☐ 675 Pascual Perez	.15	.07	.01
☐ 676 Brian Giles	.06	.03	.00
☐ 677 Doyle Alexander	.10	.05	.01
☐ 678 Chris Speier	.06	.03	.00
☐ 679 Art Howe	.10	.05	.01
☐ 680 Fred Lynn	.15	.07	.01
☐ 681 Tom Lasorda MG	.10	.05	.01

□ 682 Dan Morogiello	.06	.03	.00
□ 683 Marty Barrett	.65	.30	.06
□ 684 Bob Shirley	.06	.03	.00
□ 685 Willie Aikens	.06	.03	.00
□ 686 Joe Price	.06	.03	.00
□ 687 Roy Howell	.06	.03	.00
□ 688 George Wright	.06	.03	.00
□ 689 Mike Fischlin	.06	.03	.00
□ 690 Jack Clark	.25	.12	.02
□ 691 Steve Lake	.06	.03	.00
□ 692 Dickie Thon	.06	.03	.00
□ 693 Alan Wiggins	.06	.03	.00
□ 694 Mike Stanton	.06	.03	.00
□ 695 Lou Whitaker	.30	.15	.03
□ 696 Pirates TL	.10	.05	.01
Bill Madlock			
Rick Rhoden			
□ 697 Dale Murray	.06	.03	.00
□ 698 Marc Hill	.06	.03	.00
□ 699 Dave Rucker	.06	.03	.00
□ 700 Mike Schmidt	1.75	.85	.17
□ 701 NL Active Batting	.20	.10	.02
Bill Madlock			
Pete Rose			
Dave Parker			
□ 702 NL Active Hits	.20	.10	.02
Pete Rose			
Rusty Staub			
Tony Perez			
□ 703 NL Active Home Run	.20	.10	.02
Mike Schmidt			
Tony Perez			
Dave Kingman			
□ 704 NL Active RBI	.10	.05	.01
Tony Perez			
Rusty Staub			
Al Oliver			
□ 705 NL Active Steals	.10	.05	.01
Joe Morgan			
Cesar Cedeno			
Larry Bowa			
□ 706 NL Active Victory	.20	.10	.02
Steve Carlton			
Fergie Jenkins			
Tom Seaver			
□ 707 NL Active Strikeout	.40	.20	.04
Steve Carlton			
Nolan Ryan			
Tom Seaver			
□ 708 NL Active ERA	.20	.10	.02
Tom Seaver			
Steve Carlton			
Steve Rogers			
□ 709 NL Active Save	.10	.05	.01
Bruce Sutter			
Tug McGraw			
Gene Garber			
□ 710 AL Active Batting	.20	.10	.02
Rod Carew			
George Brett			
Cecil Cooper			
□ 711 AL Active Hits	.20	.10	.02
Rod Carew			
Bert Campaneris			
Reggie Jackson			
□ 712 AL Active Home Run	.18	.09	.01
Reggie Jackson			
Graig Nettles			
Greg Luzinski			
□ 713 AL Active RBI	.15	.07	.01
Reggie Jackson			
Ted Simmons			
Graig Nettles			
□ 714 AL Active Steals	.10	.05	.01
Bert Campaneris			
Dave Lopes			
Omar Moreno			
□ 715 AL Active Victory	.20	.10	.02
Jim Palmer			
Don Sutton			
Tommy John			
□ 716 AL Active Strikeout	.10	.05	.01
Don Sutton			
Bert Blyleven			
Jerry Koosman			
□ 717 AL Active ERA	.15	.07	.01
Jim Palmer			
Rollie Fingers			
Ron Guidry			
□ 718 AL Active Save	.12	.06	.01
Rollie Fingers			
Rich Gossage			
Dan Quisenberry			
□ 719 Andy Hassler	.06	.03	.00
□ 720 Dwight Evans	.25	.12	.02
□ 721 Del Crandall MG	.06	.03	.00
□ 722 Bob Welch	.20	.10	.02
□ 723 Rich Dauer	.06	.03	.00
□ 724 Eric Rasmussen	.06	.03	.00
□ 725 Cesar Cedeno	.10	.05	.01
□ 726 Brewers TL	.10	.05	.01
Ted Simmons			
Moose Haas			
□ 727 Joel Youngblood	.06	.03	.00
□ 728 Tug McGraw	.10	.05	.01
□ 729 Gene Tenace	.06	.03	.00
□ 730 Bruce Sutter	.15	.07	.01
□ 731 Lynn Jones	.06	.03	.00
□ 732 Terry Crowley	.06	.03	.00
□ 733 Dave Collins	.06	.03	.00
□ 734 Odell Jones	.06	.03	.00
□ 735 Rick Burleson	.06	.03	.00
□ 736 Dick Ruthven	.06	.03	.00
□ 737 Jim Essian	.06	.03	.00
□ 738 Bill Schroeder	.10	.05	.01
□ 739 Bob Watson	.10	.05	.01
□ 740 Tom Seaver	.75	.35	.07
□ 741 Wayne Gross	.06	.03	.00
□ 742 Dick Williams MG	.06	.03	.00
□ 743 Don Hood	.06	.03	.00
□ 744 Jamie Allen	.06	.03	.00
□ 745 Dennis Eckersley	.30	.15	.03
□ 746 Mickey Hatcher	.06	.03	.00
□ 747 Pat Zachry	.06	.03	.00
□ 748 Jeff Leonard	.10	.05	.01
□ 749 Doug Flynn	.06	.03	.00
□ 750 Jim Palmer	.65	.30	.06
□ 751 Charlie Moore	.06	.03	.00
□ 752 Phil Garner	.06	.03	.00
□ 753 Doug Gwosdz	.06	.03	.00
□ 754 Kent Tekulve	.06	.03	.00
□ 755 Garry Maddox	.06	.03	.00
□ 756 Reds TL	.10	.05	.01
Ron Oester			
Mario Soto			
□ 757 Larry Bowa	.10	.05	.01
□ 758 Bill Stein	.06	.03	.00
□ 759 Richard Dotson	.06	.03	.00
□ 760 Bob Horner	.15	.07	.01
□ 761 John Montefusco	.06	.03	.00
□ 762 Rance Mulliniks	.06	.03	.00
□ 763 Craig Swan	.06	.03	.00
□ 764 Mike Hargrove	.06	.03	.00
□ 765 Ken Forsch	.06	.03	.00
□ 766 Mike Vail	.06	.03	.00
□ 767 Carney Lansford	.15	.07	.01
□ 768 Champ Summers	.06	.03	.00
□ 769 Bill Caudill	.06	.03	.00
□ 770 Ken Griffey	.15	.07	.01
□ 771 Billy Gardner MG	.06	.03	.00
□ 772 Jim Slaton	.06	.03	.00
□ 773 Todd Cruz	.06	.03	.00
□ 774 Tom Gorman	.06	.03	.00
□ 775 Dave Parker	.25	.12	.02
□ 776 Craig Reynolds	.06	.03	.00
□ 777 Tom Paciorek	.06	.03	.00
□ 778 Andy Hawkins	.40	.20	.04
□ 779 Jim Sundberg	.06	.03	.00
□ 780 Steve Carlton	.50	.25	.05
□ 781 Checklist 661-792	.08	.01	.00
□ 782 Steve Balboni	.06	.03	.00
□ 783 Luis Leal	.06	.03	.00
□ 784 Leon Roberts	.06	.03	.00
□ 785 Joaquin Andujar	.10	.05	.01
□ 786 Red Sox TL	.25	.12	.02
Wade Boggs			
Bob Ojeda			
□ 787 Bill Campbell	.06	.03	.00
□ 788 Milt May	.06	.03	.00
□ 789 Bert Blyleven	.26		
□ 790 Doug DeCinces	.10	.05	.01
□ 791 Terry Forster	.06	.03	.00
□ 792 Bill Russell	.15	.07	.01

1984 Topps Traded

The cards in this 132-card set measure 2 1/2" by 3 1/2". In its now standard procedure, Topps issued its Traded (or extended) set for the fourth year in a row. Because all photos and statistics of its regular set for the year were developed during the fall and winter months of the preceding year, players who changed teams during the fall, winter, and spring months are portrayed with the teams they were with in 1983. The Traded set amends the shortcomings of the regular set by presenting the players with their proper teams for the current year. Rookies not contained in the regular set are also picked up in the Traded set. The key (extended) rookie cards in this set are Alvin Davis, Dwight Gooden, Mark Langston, Jose Rijo, and Bret Saberhagen. Again this year, the Topps affiliate in Ireland printed the cards, and the cards were available through hobby channels only. Topps also produced a specially boxed "glossy" edition, frequently referred to as the Topps Traded Tiffany set. There were supposedly only 10,000 sets of the Tiffany cards produced; they were marketed to hobby dealers. The checklist of cards is identical to that of the normal non-glossy cards. There are two primary distinguishing features of the Tiffany cards, white card stock reverses and high gloss obverses. These Tiffany cards are valued at approximately five times the values listed below.

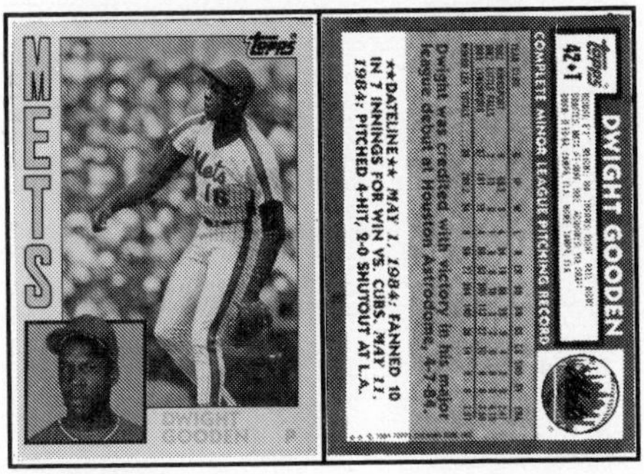

	MINT	EXC	G-VG
COMPLETE SET (132)	100.00	50.00	10.00
COMMON PLAYER (1-132)	.11	.05	.01

☐ 1T Willie Aikens	.20	.10	.02
☐ 2T Luis Aponte	.11	.05	.01
☐ 3T Mike Armstrong	.11	.05	.01
☐ 4T Bob Bailor	.11	.05	.01
☐ 5T Dusty Baker	.20	.10	.02
☐ 6T Steve Balboni	.15	.07	.01
☐ 7T Alan Bannister	.11	.05	.01
☐ 8T Dave Beard	.11	.05	.01
☐ 9T Joe Beckwith	.11	.05	.01
☐ 10T Bruce Berenyi	.11	.05	.01
☐ 11T Dave Bergman	.11	.05	.01
☐ 12T Tony Bernazard	.15	.07	.01
☐ 13T Yogi Berra MG	.40	.20	.04
☐ 14T Barry Bonnell	.11	.05	.01
☐ 15T Phil Bradley	1.75	.85	.17
☐ 16T Fred Breining	.11	.05	.01
☐ 17T Bill Buckner	.25	.12	.02
☐ 18T Ray Burris	.11	.05	.01
☐ 19T John Butcher	.11	.05	.01
☐ 20T Brett Butler	.35	.17	.03
☐ 21T Enos Cabell	.11	.05	.01
☐ 22T Bill Campbell	.11	.05	.01
☐ 23T Bill Caudill	.11	.05	.01
☐ 24T Bob Clark	.11	.05	.01
☐ 25T Bryan Clark	.11	.05	.01
☐ 26T Jaime Cocanower	.15	.07	.01
☐ 27T Ron Darling	4.00	2.00	.40
☐ 28T Alvin Davis	7.50	3.75	.75
☐ 29T Ken Dayley	.20	.10	.02
☐ 30T Jeff Dedmon	.15	.07	.01
☐ 31T Bob Dernier	.15	.07	.01
☐ 32T Carlos Diaz	.11	.05	.01
☐ 33T Mike Easler	.11	.05	.01
☐ 34T Dennis Eckersley	.75	.35	.07
☐ 35T Jim Essian	.11	.05	.01
☐ 36T Darrell Evans	.30	.15	.03
☐ 37T Mike Fitzgerald	.15	.07	.01
☐ 38T Tim Foli	.11	.05	.01
☐ 39T George Frazier	.11	.05	.01
☐ 40T Rich Gale	.11	.05	.01
☐ 41T Barbaro Garbey	.15	.07	.01
☐ 42T Dwight Gooden	45.00	22.50	4.50
☐ 43T Rich Gossage	.35	.17	.03
☐ 44T Wayne Gross	.11	.05	.01
☐ 45T Mark Gubicza	3.50	1.75	.35
☐ 46T Jackie Gutierrez	.15	.07	.01
☐ 47T Mel Hall	.30	.15	.03
☐ 48T Toby Harrah	.15	.07	.01
☐ 49T Ron Hassey	.15	.07	.01
☐ 50T Rich Hebner	.11	.05	.01
☐ 51T Willie Hernandez	.25	.12	.02
☐ 52T Ricky Horton	.25	.12	.02
☐ 53T Art Howe	.15	.07	.01
☐ 54T Dane Iorg	.11	.05	.01
☐ 55T Brook Jacoby	2.25	1.10	.22
☐ 56T Mike Jeffcoat	.20	.10	.02
☐ 57T Dave Johnson MG	.25	.12	.02
☐ 58T Lynn Jones	.11	.05	.01
☐ 59T Ruppert Jones	.11	.05	.01
☐ 60T Mike Jorgensen	.11	.05	.01
☐ 61T Bob Kearney	.11	.05	.01
☐ 62T Jimmy Key	2.25	1.10	.22
☐ 63T Dave Kingman	.30	.15	.03
☐ 64T Jerry Koosman	.30	.15	.03
☐ 65T Wayne Krenchicki	.11	.05	.01
☐ 66T Rusty Kuntz	.11	.05	.01
☐ 67T Rene Lachemann MG	.11	.05	.01
☐ 68T Frank LaCorte	.11	.05	.01
☐ 69T Dennis Lamp	.11	.05	.01
☐ 70T Mark Langston	11.00	5.50	1.10
☐ 71T Rick Leach	.11	.05	.01
☐ 72T Craig Lefferts	.30	.15	.03
☐ 73T Gary Lucas	.11	.05	.01
☐ 74T Jerry Martin	.11	.05	.01
☐ 75T Carmelo Martinez	.20	.10	.02
☐ 76T Mike Mason	.15	.07	.01
☐ 77T Gary Matthews	.15	.07	.01
☐ 78T Andy McGaffigan	.11	.05	.01
☐ 79T Larry Milbourne	.11	.05	.01
☐ 80T Sid Monge	.11	.05	.01
☐ 81T Jackie Moore MG	.11	.05	.01
☐ 82T Joe Morgan	2.50	1.25	.25
☐ 83T Graig Nettles	.40	.20	.04
☐ 84T Phil Niekro	1.00	.50	.10
☐ 85T Ken Oberkfell	.11	.05	.01
☐ 86T Mike O'Berry	.11	.05	.01
☐ 87T Al Oliver	.30	.15	.03
☐ 88T Jorge Orta	.11	.05	.01
☐ 89T Amos Otis	.20	.10	.02
☐ 90T Dave Parker	1.50	.75	.15
☐ 91T Tony Perez	.60	.30	.06
☐ 92T Gerald Perry	.75	.35	.07
☐ 93T Gary Pettis	.40	.20	.04
☐ 94T Rob Picciolo	.11	.05	.01
☐ 95T Vern Rapp MG	.11	.05	.01
☐ 96T Floyd Rayford	.11	.05	.01
☐ 97T Randy Ready	.35	.17	.03
☐ 98T Ron Reed	.11	.05	.01
☐ 99T Gene Richards	.11	.05	.01
☐ 100T Jose Rijo	4.50	2.25	.45
☐ 101T Jeff Robinson (Giants pitcher)	.25	.12	.02
☐ 102T Ron Romanick	.15	.07	.01
☐ 103T Pete Rose	7.50	3.75	.75
☐ 104T Bret Saberhagen	21.00	10.50	2.10
☐ 105T Juan Samuel	2.75	1.35	.27
☐ 106T Scott Sanderson	.30	.15	.03
☐ 107T Dick Schofield	.35	.17	.03
☐ 108T Tom Seaver	4.00	2.00	.40
☐ 109T Jim Slaton	.11	.05	.01
☐ 110T Mike Smithson	.15	.07	.01
☐ 111T Lary Sorensen	.11	.05	.01
☐ 112T Tim Stoddard	.11	.05	.01
☐ 113T Champ Summers	.11	.05	.01
☐ 114T Jim Sundberg	.11	.05	.01
☐ 115T Rick Sutcliffe	.50	.25	.05
☐ 116T Craig Swan	.11	.05	.01
☐ 117T Tim Teufel	.35	.17	.03
☐ 118T Derrel Thomas	.11	.05	.01
☐ 119T Gorman Thomas	.30	.15	.03
☐ 120T Alex Trevino	.11	.05	.01
☐ 121T Manny Trillo	.11	.05	.01
☐ 122T John Tudor	.30	.15	.03
☐ 123T Tom Underwood	.11	.05	.01
☐ 124T Mike Vail	.11	.05	.01
☐ 125T Tom Waddell	.15	.07	.01
☐ 126T Gary Ward	.15	.07	.01
☐ 127T Curt Wilkerson	.15	.07	.01
☐ 128T Frank Williams	.20	.10	.02
☐ 129T Glenn Wilson	.15	.07	.01
☐ 130T John Wockenfuss	.11	.05	.01
☐ 131T Ned Yost	.11	.05	.01
☐ 132T Checklist 1-132	.11	.01	.00

1984 Topps Glossy 22

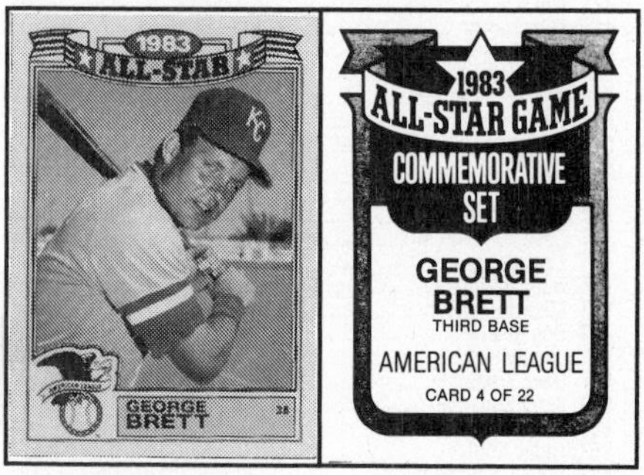

The cards in this 22-card set measure 2 1/2" by 3 1/2". Unlike the 1983 Topps Glossy set which was not distributed with its regular baseball cards, the 1984 Topps Glossy set was distributed as inserts in Topps Rak-Paks. The set features the nine American and National League All-Stars who started in the 1983 All Star game in Chicago. The managers and team captains (Yastrzemski and Bench) complete the set. The cards are numbered on the back and are ordered by position within league (AL: 1-11 and NL: 12-22).

	MINT	EXC	G-VG
COMPLETE SET (22)	3.50	1.75	.35
COMMON PLAYER (1-22)	.10	.05	.01
☐ 1 Harvey Kuenn MG	.10	.05	.01
☐ 2 Rod Carew	.50	.25	.05
☐ 3 Manny Trillo	.10	.05	.01
☐ 4 George Brett	.60	.30	.06
☐ 5 Robin Yount	.50	.25	.05
☐ 6 Jim Rice	.20	.10	.02
☐ 7 Fred Lynn	.15	.07	.01
☐ 8 Dave Winfield	.30	.15	.03
☐ 9 Ted Simmons	.15	.07	.01
☐ 10 Dave Stieb	.15	.07	.01
☐ 11 Carl Yastrzemski CAPT	.45	.22	.04
☐ 12 Whitey Herzog MG	.10	.05	.01
☐ 13 Al Oliver	.15	.07	.01
☐ 14 Steve Sax	.25	.12	.02
☐ 15 Mike Schmidt	.90	.45	.09
☐ 16 Ozzie Smith	.35	.17	.03
☐ 17 Tim Raines	.30	.15	.03
☐ 18 Andre Dawson	.35	.17	.03
☐ 19 Dale Murphy	.65	.30	.06
☐ 20 Gary Carter	.30	.15	.03
☐ 21 Mario Soto	.10	.05	.01
☐ 22 Johnny Bench CAPT	.30	.15	.03

1984 Topps Glossy 40

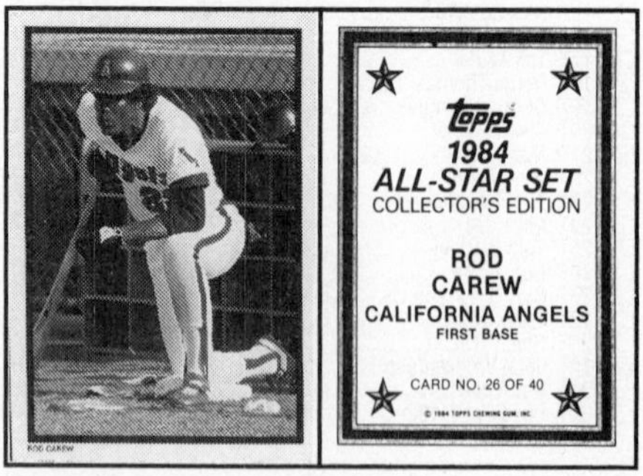

The cards in this 40-card set measure 2 1/2" by 3 1/2". Similar to last year's glossy set, this set was issued as a bonus prize to Topps All-Star Baseball Game cards found in wax packs. Twenty-five bonus runs from the game cards were necessary to obtain a five card subset of the series. There were eight different subsets of five cards. The cards are numbered and contain 20 stars from each league.

	MINT	EXC	G-VG
COMPLETE SET (40)	12.00	6.00	1.20
COMMON PLAYER (1-40)	.20	.10	.02
☐ 1 Pete Rose	1.25	.60	.12
☐ 2 Lance Parrish	.30	.15	.03
☐ 3 Steve Rogers	.20	.10	.02
☐ 4 Eddie Murray	.75	.35	.07
☐ 5 Johnny Ray	.20	.10	.02
☐ 6 Rickey Henderson	1.25	.60	.12
☐ 7 Atlee Hammaker	.20	.10	.02
☐ 8 Wade Boggs	1.00	.50	.10
☐ 9 Gary Carter	.35	.17	.03
☐ 10 Jack Morris	.25	.12	.02
☐ 11 Darrell Evans	.20	.10	.02
☐ 12 George Brett	1.00	.50	.10
☐ 13 Bob Horner	.25	.12	.02
☐ 14 Ron Guidry	.25	.12	.02
☐ 15 Nolan Ryan	1.25	.60	.12
☐ 16 Dave Winfield	.50	.25	.05
☐ 17 Ozzie Smith	.35	.17	.03
☐ 18 Ted Simmons	.20	.10	.02
☐ 19 Bill Madlock	.25	.12	.02
☐ 20 Tony Armas	.20	.10	.02
☐ 21 Al Oliver	.25	.12	.02
☐ 22 Jim Rice	.30	.15	.03
☐ 23 George Hendrick	.20	.10	.02
☐ 24 Dave Stieb	.25	.12	.02
☐ 25 Pedro Guerrero	.35	.17	.03
☐ 26 Rod Carew	.90	.45	.09
☐ 27 Steve Carlton	.60	.30	.06
☐ 28 Dave Righetti	.20	.10	.02
☐ 29 Darryl Strawberry	1.50	.75	.15
☐ 30 Lou Whitaker	.25	.12	.02
☐ 31 Dale Murphy	.90	.45	.09
☐ 32 LaMarr Hoyt	.20	.10	.02
☐ 33 Jesse Orosco	.20	.10	.02
☐ 34 Cecil Cooper	.20	.10	.02
☐ 35 Andre Dawson	.35	.17	.03
☐ 36 Robin Yount	.75	.35	.07
☐ 37 Tim Raines	.35	.17	.03
☐ 38 Dan Quisenberry	.25	.12	.02
☐ 39 Mike Schmidt	1.25	.60	.12
☐ 40 Carlton Fisk	.40	.20	.04

1984 Topps Cereal

The cards in this 33 card-set measure 2 1/2" by 3 1/2". The cards are numbered both on the front and the back. The 1984 Topps Cereal Series is exactly the same as the Ralston-Purina issue of this year except for a Topps logo and the words "Cereal Series" on the tops of the fronts of the cards in place of the Ralston checkerboard background. The checkerboard background is absent from the reverse, and a Topps logo is on the reverse of the cereal cards. These cards were distributed in unmarked boxes of Ralston-Purina cereal with a pack of four cards (three players and a checklist) being inside random cereal boxes. The back of the checklist details an offer to obtain any twelve cards direct from the issuer for only 1.50.

	MINT	EXC	G-VG
COMPLETE SET (34)	12.00	6.00	1.20
COMMON PLAYER (1-33)	.20	.10	.02
□ 1 Eddie Murray	.90	.45	.09
□ 2 Ozzie Smith	.40	.20	.04
□ 3 Ted Simmons	.25	.12	.02
□ 4 Pete Rose	1.25	.60	.12
□ 5 Greg Luzinski	.20	.10	.02
□ 6 Andre Dawson	.35	.17	.03
□ 7 Dave Winfield	.45	.22	.04
□ 8 Tom Seaver	.65	.30	.06
□ 9 Jim Rice	.30	.15	.03
□ 10 Fernando Valenzuela	.35	.17	.03
□ 11 Wade Boggs	1.00	.50	.10
□ 12 Dale Murphy	.90	.45	.09
□ 13 George Brett	1.00	.50	.10
□ 14 Nolan Ryan	1.25	.60	.12
□ 15 Rickey Henderson	1.25	.60	.12
□ 16 Steve Carlton	.60	.30	.06
□ 17 Rod Carew	.75	.35	.07
□ 18 Steve Garvey	.50	.25	.05
□ 19 Reggie Jackson	1.00	.50	.10
□ 20 Dave Concepcion	.20	.10	.02
□ 21 Robin Yount	.90	.45	.09
□ 22 Mike Schmidt	1.25	.60	.12
□ 23 Jim Palmer	.50	.25	.05
□ 24 Bruce Sutter	.25	.12	.02
□ 25 Dan Quisenberry	.25	.12	.02
□ 26 Bill Madlock	.20	.10	.02
□ 27 Cecil Cooper	.20	.10	.02
□ 28 Gary Carter	.40	.20	.04
□ 29 Fred Lynn	.25	.12	.02
□ 30 Pedro Guerrero	.35	.17	.03
□ 31 Ron Guidry	.25	.12	.02
□ 32 Keith Hernandez	.30	.15	.03
□ 33 Carlton Fisk	.40	.20	.04
□ 34 Checklist card (unnumbered)	.25	.12	.02

1985 Topps

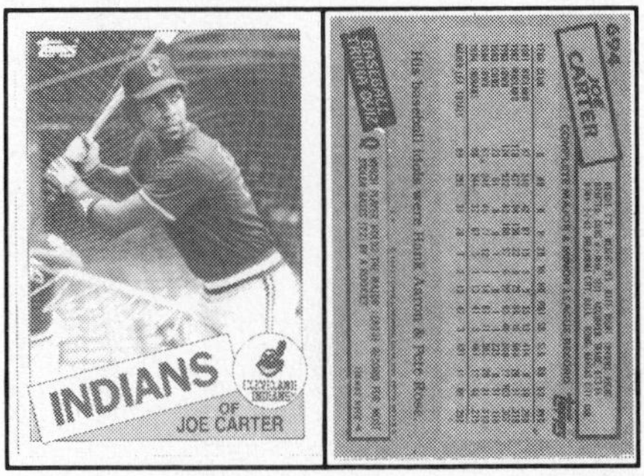

The cards in this 792-card set measure 2 1/2" by 3 1/2". The 1985 Topps set contains full color cards. The fronts feature both the Topps and team logos along with the team name, player's name, and his position. The backs feature player statistics with ink colors of light green and maroon on a gray stock. A trivia quiz is included on the lower portion of the backs. The first ten cards (1-10) are Record Breakers (RB), cards 131-143 are Father and Son (FS) cards, and cards 701 to 722 portray All-Star selections (AS). Cards 271 to 282 represent "First Draft Picks" still active in the Major Leagues and cards 389-404 feature the coach and players on the 1984 U.S. Olympic Baseball Team. The manager cards in the set are important in that they contain the checklist of that team's players on the back. The key rookie cards in this set are Roger Clemens, Eric Davis, Shawon Dunston, Dwight Gooden, Orel Hershiser, Mark Langston, Mark McGwire, Kirby Puckett, Jose Rijo, and Bret Saberhagen. Topps also produced a specially boxed "glossy" edition, frequently referred to as the Topps Tiffany set. There were supposedly only 8,000 sets of the Tiffany cards produced; they were marketed to hobby dealers. The checklist of cards (792 regular and 132 Traded) is identical to that of the normal non-glossy cards. There are two primary distinguishing features of the Tiffany cards, white card stock reverses and high gloss obverses. These Tiffany cards are valued at approximately five times the values listed below.

	MINT	EXC	G-VG
COMPLETE SET (792)	105.00	45.00	9.00
COMMON PLAYER (1-792)	.05	.02	.00
□ 1 Carlton Fisk RB Longest game by catcher	.25	.06	.01
□ 2 Steve Garvey RB Consecutive error-less games, 1B	.20	.10	.02
□ 3 Dwight Gooden RB Most strikeouts, rookie, season	.75	.35	.07
□ 4 Cliff Johnson RB Most pinch homers, lifetime	.05	.02	.00
□ 5 Joe Morgan RB Most homers, 2B, lifetime	.12	.06	.01
□ 6 Pete Rose RB Most singles, lifetime	.50	.25	.05
□ 7 Nolan Ryan RB Most strikeouts, lifetime	.75	.35	.07
□ 8 Juan Samuel RB Most stolen bases, rookie, season	.12	.06	.01
□ 9 Bruce Sutter RB Most saves, season, NL	.08	.04	.01
□ 10 Don Sutton RB Most seasons, 100 or more K's	.10	.05	.01
□ 11 Ralph Houk MG (checklist back)	.08	.04	.01
□ 12 Dave Lopes	.08	.04	.01
□ 13 Tim Lollar	.05	.02	.00
□ 14 Chris Bando	.05	.02	.00
□ 15 Jerry Koosman	.08	.04	.01
□ 16 Bobby Meacham	.05	.02	.00
□ 17 Mike Scott	.25	.12	.02
□ 18 Mickey Hatcher	.05	.02	.00
□ 19 George Frazier	.05	.02	.00
□ 20 Chet Lemon	.05	.02	.00
□ 21 Lee Tunnell	.05	.02	.00
□ 22 Duane Kuiper	.05	.02	.00
□ 23 Bret Saberhagen	4.00	2.00	.40
□ 24 Jesse Barfield	.20	.10	.02
□ 25 Steve Bedrosian	.15	.07	.01
□ 26 Roy Smalley	.05	.02	.00
□ 27 Bruce Berenyi	.05	.02	.00
□ 28 Dann Bilardello	.05	.02	.00
□ 29 Odell Jones	.05	.02	.00
□ 30 Cal Ripken	.80	.40	.08
□ 31 Terry Whitfield	.05	.02	.00
□ 32 Chuck Porter	.05	.02	.00
□ 33 Tito Landrum	.05	.02	.00
□ 34 Ed Nunez	.05	.02	.00
□ 35 Graig Nettles	.10	.05	.01
□ 36 Fred Breining	.05	.02	.00
□ 37 Reid Nichols	.05	.02	.00
□ 38 Jackie Moore MG (checklist back)	.08	.04	.01
□ 39 John Wockenfuss	.05	.02	.00
□ 40 Phil Niekro	.18	.09	.01
□ 41 Mike Fischlin	.05	.02	.00
□ 42 Luis Sanchez	.05	.02	.00
□ 43 Andre David	.05	.02	.00
□ 44 Dickie Thon	.05	.02	.00
□ 45 Greg Minton	.05	.02	.00
□ 46 Gary Woods	.05	.02	.00
□ 47 Dave Rozema	.05	.02	.00
□ 48 Tony Fernandez	1.25	.60	.12
□ 49 Butch Davis	.05	.02	.00
□ 50 John Candelaria	.08	.04	.01
□ 51 Bob Watson	.08	.04	.01

☐ 52	Jerry Dybzinski	.05	.02	.00
☐ 53	Tom Gorman	.05	.02	.00
☐ 54	Cesar Cedeno	.08	.04	.01
☐ 55	Frank Tanana	.08	.04	.01
☐ 56	Jim Dwyer	.05	.02	.00
☐ 57	Pat Zachry	.05	.02	.00
☐ 58	Orlando Mercado	.05	.02	.00
☐ 59	Rick Waits	.05	.02	.00
☐ 60	George Hendrick	.08	.04	.01
☐ 61	Curt Kaufman	.05	.02	.00
☐ 62	Mike Ramsey	.05	.02	.00
☐ 63	Steve McCatty	.05	.02	.00
☐ 64	Mark Bailey	.05	.02	.00
☐ 65	Bill Buckner	.10	.05	.01
☐ 66	Dick Williams MG (checklist back)	.08	.04	.01
☐ 67	Rafael Santana	.12	.06	.01
☐ 68	Von Hayes	.18	.09	.01
☐ 69	Jim Winn	.05	.02	.00
☐ 70	Don Baylor	.10	.05	.01
☐ 71	Tim Laudner	.05	.02	.00
☐ 72	Rick Sutcliffe	.10	.05	.01
☐ 73	Rusty Kuntz	.05	.02	.00
☐ 74	Mike Krukow	.05	.02	.00
☐ 75	Willie Upshaw	.05	.02	.00
☐ 76	Alan Bannister	.05	.02	.00
☐ 77	Joe Beckwith	.05	.02	.00
☐ 78	Scott Fletcher	.05	.02	.00
☐ 79	Rick Mahler	.05	.02	.00
☐ 80	Keith Hernandez	.30	.15	.03
☐ 81	Lenn Sakata	.05	.02	.00
☐ 82	Joe Price	.05	.02	.00
☐ 83	Charlie Moore	.05	.02	.00
☐ 84	Spike Owen	.05	.02	.00
☐ 85	Mike Marshall	.12	.06	.01
☐ 86	Don Aase	.05	.02	.00
☐ 87	David Green	.05	.02	.00
☐ 88	Bryn Smith	.08	.04	.01
☐ 89	Jackie Gutierrez	.08	.04	.01
☐ 90	Rich Gossage	.12	.06	.01
☐ 91	Jeff Burroughs	.05	.02	.00
☐ 92	Paul Owens MG (checklist back)	.08	.04	.01
☐ 93	Don Schulze	.05	.02	.00
☐ 94	Toby Harrah	.05	.02	.00
☐ 95	Jose Cruz	.08	.04	.01
☐ 96	Johnny Ray	.08	.04	.01
☐ 97	Pete Filson	.05	.02	.00
☐ 98	Steve Lake	.05	.02	.00
☐ 99	Milt Wilcox	.05	.02	.00
☐ 100	George Brett	.60	.30	.06
☐ 101	Jim Acker	.05	.02	.00
☐ 102	Tommy Dunbar	.05	.02	.00
☐ 103	Randy Lerch	.05	.02	.00
☐ 104	Mike Fitzgerald	.05	.02	.00
☐ 105	Ron Kittle	.12	.06	.01
☐ 106	Pascual Perez	.10	.05	.01
☐ 107	Tom Foley	.05	.02	.00
☐ 108	Darnell Coles	.12	.06	.01
☐ 109	Gary Roenicke	.05	.02	.00
☐ 110	Alejandro Pena	.08	.04	.01
☐ 111	Doug DeCinces	.08	.04	.01
☐ 112	Tom Tellmann	.05	.02	.00
☐ 113	Tom Herr	.08	.04	.01
☐ 114	Bob James	.05	.02	.00
☐ 115	Rickey Henderson	2.00	1.00	.20
☐ 116	Dennis Boyd	.35	.17	.03
☐ 117	Greg Gross	.05	.02	.00
☐ 118	Eric Show	.08	.04	.01
☐ 119	Pat Corrales MG (checklist back)	.08	.04	.01
☐ 120	Steve Kemp	.05	.02	.00
☐ 121	Checklist: 1-132	.08	.01	.00
☐ 122	Tom Brunansky	.18	.09	.01
☐ 123	Dave Smith	.08	.04	.01
☐ 124	Rich Hebner	.05	.02	.00
☐ 125	Kent Tekulve	.05	.02	.00
☐ 126	Ruppert Jones	.05	.02	.00
☐ 127	Mark Gubicza	.90	.45	.09
☐ 128	Ernie Whitt	.05	.02	.00
☐ 129	Gene Garber	.05	.02	.00
☐ 130	Al Oliver	.10	.05	.01
☐ 131	Buddy/Gus Bell FS	.08	.04	.01
☐ 132	Dale/Yogi Berra FS	.15	.07	.01
☐ 133	Bob/Ray Boone FS	.08	.04	.01
☐ 134	Terry/Tito Francona FS	.05	.02	.00
☐ 135	Terry/Bob Kennedy FS	.05	.02	.00
☐ 136	Jeff/Jim Kunkel FS	.05	.02	.00
☐ 137	Vance/Vern Law FS	.05	.02	.00
☐ 138	Dick/Dick Schofield FS	.05	.02	.00
☐ 139	Joel/Bob Skinner FS	.05	.02	.00
☐ 140	Roy/Roy Smalley FS	.05	.02	.00
☐ 141	Mike/D.Stenhouse FS	.05	.02	.00
☐ 142	Steve/Dizzy Trout FS	.05	.02	.00
☐ 143	Ozzie/Ozzie Virgil FS	.05	.02	.00
☐ 144	Ron Gardenhire	.05	.02	.00
☐ 145	Alvin Davis	1.75	.85	.17
☐ 146	Gary Redus	.05	.02	.00
☐ 147	Bill Swaggerty	.05	.02	.00
☐ 148	Steve Yeager	.05	.02	.00
☐ 149	Dickie Noles	.05	.02	.00
☐ 150	Jim Rice	.20	.10	.02
☐ 151	Moose Haas	.05	.02	.00
☐ 152	Steve Braun	.05	.02	.00
☐ 153	Frank LaCorte	.05	.02	.00
☐ 154	Argenis Salazar	.05	.02	.00
☐ 155	Yogi Berra MG (checklist back)	.15	.07	.01
☐ 156	Craig Reynolds	.05	.02	.00
☐ 157	Tug McGraw	.10	.05	.01
☐ 158	Pat Tabler	.08	.04	.01
☐ 159	Carlos Diaz	.05	.02	.00
☐ 160	Lance Parrish	.18	.09	.01
☐ 161	Ken Schrom	.05	.02	.00
☐ 162	Benny Distefano	.08	.04	.01
☐ 163	Dennis Eckersley	.15	.07	.01
☐ 164	Jorge Orta	.05	.02	.00
☐ 165	Dusty Baker	.08	.04	.01
☐ 166	Keith Atherton	.05	.02	.00
☐ 167	Rufino Linares	.05	.02	.00
☐ 168	Garth Iorg	.05	.02	.00
☐ 169	Dan Spillner	.05	.02	.00
☐ 170	George Foster	.10	.05	.01
☐ 171	Bill Stein	.05	.02	.00
☐ 172	Jack Perconte	.05	.02	.00
☐ 173	Mike Young	.08	.04	.01
☐ 174	Rick Honeycutt	.05	.02	.00
☐ 175	Dave Parker	.18	.09	.01
☐ 176	Bill Schroeder	.05	.02	.00
☐ 177	Dave Von Ohlen	.05	.02	.00
☐ 178	Miguel Dilone	.05	.02	.00
☐ 179	Tommy John	.15	.07	.01
☐ 180	Dave Winfield	.35	.17	.03
☐ 181	Roger Clemens	14.00	7.00	1.40
☐ 182	Tim Flannery	.05	.02	.00
☐ 183	Larry McWilliams	.05	.02	.00
☐ 184	Carmen Castillo	.05	.02	.00
☐ 185	Al Holland	.05	.02	.00
☐ 186	Bob Lillis MG (checklist back)	.08	.04	.01
☐ 187	Mike Walters	.05	.02	.00
☐ 188	Greg Pryor	.05	.02	.00
☐ 189	Warren Brusstar	.05	.02	.00
☐ 190	Rusty Staub	.10	.05	.01
☐ 191	Steve Nicosia	.05	.02	.00
☐ 192	Howard Johnson	4.00	2.00	.40
☐ 193	Jimmy Key	.75	.35	.07
☐ 194	Dave Stegman	.05	.02	.00
☐ 195	Glenn Hubbard	.05	.02	.00
☐ 196	Pete O'Brien	.10	.05	.01
☐ 197	Mike Warren	.05	.02	.00
☐ 198	Eddie Milner	.05	.02	.00
☐ 199	Dennis Martinez	.08	.04	.01
☐ 200	Reggie Jackson	.50	.25	.05
☐ 201	Burt Hooton	.05	.02	.00
☐ 202	Gorman Thomas	.10	.05	.01
☐ 203	Bob McClure	.05	.02	.00
☐ 204	Art Howe	.08	.04	.01
☐ 205	Steve Rogers	.05	.02	.00
☐ 206	Phil Garner	.05	.02	.00
☐ 207	Mark Clear	.05	.02	.00
☐ 208	Champ Summers	.05	.02	.00
☐ 209	Bill Campbell	.05	.02	.00
☐ 210	Gary Matthews	.08	.04	.01
☐ 211	Clay Christiansen	.05	.02	.00
☐ 212	George Vukovich	.05	.02	.00
☐ 213	Billy Gardner MG (checklist back)	.08	.04	.01
☐ 214	John Tudor	.12	.06	.01
☐ 215	Bob Brenly	.05	.02	.00
☐ 216	Jerry Don Gleaton	.05	.02	.00
☐ 217	Leon Roberts	.05	.02	.00
☐ 218	Doyle Alexander	.05	.02	.00
☐ 219	Gerald Perry	.30	.15	.03
☐ 220	Fred Lynn	.15	.07	.01
☐ 221	Ron Reed	.05	.02	.00
☐ 222	Hubie Brooks	.15	.07	.01
☐ 223	Tom Hume	.05	.02	.00
☐ 224	Al Cowens	.05	.02	.00
☐ 225	Mike Boddicker	.10	.05	.01
☐ 226	Juan Beniquez	.05	.02	.00
☐ 227	Danny Darwin	.08	.04	.01
☐ 228	Dion James	.10	.05	.01
☐ 229	Dave LaPoint	.05	.02	.00
☐ 230	Gary Carter	.35	.17	.03
☐ 231	Dwayne Murphy	.05	.02	.00
☐ 232	Dave Beard	.05	.02	.00
☐ 233	Ed Jurak	.05	.02	.00

☐ 234 Jerry Narron	.05	.02	.00
☐ 235 Garry Maddox	.05	.02	.00
☐ 236 Mark Thurmond	.05	.02	.00
☐ 237 Julio Franco	.45	.22	.04
☐ 238 Jose Rijo	1.25	.60	.12
☐ 239 Tim Teufel	.12	.06	.01
☐ 240 Dave Stieb	.15	.07	.01
☐ 241 Jim Frey MG (checklist back)	.08	.04	.01
☐ 242 Greg Harris	.05	.02	.00
☐ 243 Barbaro Garbey	.05	.02	.00
☐ 244 Mike Jones	.05	.02	.00
☐ 245 Chili Davis	.10	.05	.01
☐ 246 Mike Norris	.05	.02	.00
☐ 247 Wayne Tolleson	.05	.02	.00
☐ 248 Terry Forster	.05	.02	.00
☐ 249 Harold Baines	.18	.09	.01
☐ 250 Jesse Orosco	.05	.02	.00
☐ 251 Brad Gulden	.05	.02	.00
☐ 252 Dan Ford	.05	.02	.00
☐ 253 Sid Bream	.35	.17	.03
☐ 254 Pete Vuckovich	.05	.02	.00
☐ 255 Lonnie Smith	.08	.04	.01
☐ 256 Mike Stanton	.05	.02	.00
☐ 257 Bryan Little	.05	.02	.00
☐ 258 Mike Brown (Angels OF)	.05	.02	.00
☐ 259 Gary Allenson	.05	.02	.00
☐ 260 Dave Righetti	.12	.06	.01
☐ 261 Checklist: 133-264	.08	.01	.00
☐ 262 Greg Booker	.05	.02	.00
☐ 263 Mel Hall	.10	.05	.01
☐ 264 Joe Sambito	.05	.02	.00
☐ 265 Juan Samuel	.45	.22	.04
☐ 266 Frank Viola	.40	.20	.04
☐ 267 Henry Cotto	.12	.06	.01
☐ 268 Chuck Tanner MG (checklist back)	.08	.04	.01
☐ 269 Doug Baker	.05	.02	.00
☐ 270 Dan Quisenberry	.10	.05	.01
☐ 271 Tim Foli FDP68	.05	.02	.00
☐ 272 Jeff Burroughs FDP69	.05	.02	.00
☐ 273 Bill Almon FDP74	.05	.02	.00
☐ 274 Floyd Bannister FDP76	.05	.02	.00
☐ 275 Harold Baines FDP77	.12	.06	.01
☐ 276 Bob Horner FDP78	.10	.05	.01
☐ 277 Al Chambers FDP79	.05	.02	.00
☐ 278 D.Strawberry FDP80	1.25	.60	.12
☐ 279 Mike Moore FDP81	.10	.05	.01
☐ 280 Sh.Dunston FDP82	2.75	1.35	.27
☐ 281 Tim Belcher FDP83	1.00	.50	.10
☐ 282 Shawn Abner FDP84	.30	.15	.03
☐ 283 Fran Mullins	.05	.02	.00
☐ 284 Marty Bystrom	.05	.02	.00
☐ 285 Dan Driessen	.05	.02	.00
☐ 286 Rudy Law	.05	.02	.00
☐ 287 Walt Terrell	.05	.02	.00
☐ 288 Jeff Kunkel	.08	.04	.01
☐ 289 Tom Underwood	.05	.02	.00
☐ 290 Cecil Cooper	.10	.05	.01
☐ 291 Bob Welch	.15	.07	.01
☐ 292 Brad Komminsk	.05	.02	.00
☐ 293 Curt Young	.18	.09	.01
☐ 294 Tom Nieto	.05	.02	.00
☐ 295 Joe Niekro	.08	.04	.01
☐ 296 Ricky Nelson	.05	.02	.00
☐ 297 Gary Lucas	.05	.02	.00
☐ 298 Marty Barrett	.10	.05	.01
☐ 299 Andy Hawkins	.08	.04	.01
☐ 300 Rod Carew	.45	.22	.04
☐ 301 John Montefusco	.05	.02	.00
☐ 302 Tim Corcoran	.05	.02	.00
☐ 303 Mike Jeffcoat	.05	.02	.00
☐ 304 Gary Gaetti	.25	.12	.02
☐ 305 Dale Berra	.05	.02	.00
☐ 306 Rick Reuschel	.10	.05	.01
☐ 307 Sparky Anderson MG (checklist back)	.08	.04	.01
☐ 308 John Wathan	.05	.02	.00
☐ 309 Mike Witt	.08	.04	.01
☐ 310 Manny Trillo	.05	.02	.00
☐ 311 Jim Gott	.05	.02	.00
☐ 312 Marc Hill	.05	.02	.00
☐ 313 Dave Schmidt	.05	.02	.00
☐ 314 Ron Oester	.05	.02	.00
☐ 315 Doug Sisk	.05	.02	.00
☐ 316 John Lowenstein	.05	.02	.00
☐ 317 Jack Lazorko	.05	.02	.00
☐ 318 Ted Simmons	.10	.05	.01
☐ 319 Jeff Jones	.05	.02	.00
☐ 320 Dale Murphy	.60	.30	.06
☐ 321 Ricky Horton	.18	.09	.01
☐ 322 Dave Stapleton	.05	.02	.00
☐ 323 Andy McGaffigan	.05	.02	.00
☐ 324 Bruce Bochy	.05	.02	.00
☐ 325 John Denny	.05	.02	.00
☐ 326 Kevin Bass	.10	.05	.01
☐ 327 Brook Jacoby	.35	.17	.03
☐ 328 Bob Shirley	.05	.02	.00
☐ 329 Ron Washington	.05	.02	.00
☐ 330 Leon Durham	.05	.02	.00
☐ 331 Bill Laskey	.05	.02	.00
☐ 332 Brian Harper	.15	.07	.01
☐ 333 Willie Hernandez	.10	.05	.01
☐ 334 Dick Howser MG (checklist back)	.08	.04	.01
☐ 335 Bruce Benedict	.05	.02	.00
☐ 336 Rance Mulliniks	.05	.02	.00
☐ 337 Billy Sample	.05	.02	.00
☐ 338 Britt Burns	.05	.02	.00
☐ 339 Danny Heep	.05	.02	.00
☐ 340 Robin Yount	.50	.25	.05
☐ 341 Floyd Rayford	.05	.02	.00
☐ 342 Ted Power	.05	.02	.00
☐ 343 Bill Russell	.05	.02	.00
☐ 344 Dave Henderson	.12	.06	.01
☐ 345 Charlie Lea	.05	.02	.00
☐ 346 Terry Pendleton	.50	.25	.05
☐ 347 Rick Langford	.05	.02	.00
☐ 348 Bob Boone	.10	.05	.01
☐ 349 Domingo Ramos	.05	.02	.00
☐ 350 Wade Boggs	3.00	1.50	.30
☐ 351 Juan Agosto	.05	.02	.00
☐ 352 Joe Morgan	.25	.12	.02
☐ 353 Julio Solano	.05	.02	.00
☐ 354 Andre Robertson	.05	.02	.00
☐ 355 Bert Blyleven	.15	.07	.01
☐ 356 Dave Meier	.05	.02	.00
☐ 357 Rich Bordi	.05	.02	.00
☐ 358 Tony Pena	.10	.05	.01
☐ 359 Pat Sheridan	.05	.02	.00
☐ 360 Steve Carlton	.40	.20	.04
☐ 361 Alfredo Griffin	.05	.02	.00
☐ 362 Craig McMurtry	.05	.02	.00
☐ 363 Ron Hodges	.05	.02	.00
☐ 364 Richard Dotson	.05	.02	.00
☐ 365 Danny Ozark MG (checklist back)	.08	.04	.01
☐ 366 Todd Cruz	.05	.02	.00
☐ 367 Keefe Cato	.05	.02	.00
☐ 368 Dave Bergman	.05	.02	.00
☐ 369 R.J. Reynolds	.25	.12	.02
☐ 370 Bruce Sutter	.10	.05	.01
☐ 371 Mickey Rivers	.05	.02	.00
☐ 372 Roy Howell	.05	.02	.00
☐ 373 Mike Moore	.10	.05	.01
☐ 374 Brian Downing	.07	.03	.01
☐ 375 Jeff Reardon	.10	.05	.01
☐ 376 Jeff Newman	.05	.02	.00
☐ 377 Checklist: 265-396	.08	.01	.00
☐ 378 Alan Wiggins	.05	.02	.00
☐ 379 Charles Hudson	.05	.02	.00
☐ 380 Ken Griffey	.12	.06	.01
☐ 381 Roy Smith	.05	.02	.00
☐ 382 Denny Walling	.05	.02	.00
☐ 383 Rick Lysander	.05	.02	.00
☐ 384 Jody Davis	.08	.04	.01
☐ 385 Jose DeLeon	.08	.04	.01
☐ 386 Dan Gladden	.40	.20	.04
☐ 387 Buddy Biancalana	.08	.04	.01
☐ 388 Bert Roberge	.05	.02	.00
☐ 389 Rod Dedeaux OLY CO	.05	.02	.00
☐ 390 Sid Akins OLY	.08	.04	.01
☐ 391 Flavio Alfaro OLY	.08	.04	.01
☐ 392 Don August OLY	.25	.12	.02
☐ 393 Scott Bankhead OLY	.65	.30	.06
☐ 394 Bob Caffrey OLY	.08	.04	.01
☐ 395 Mike Dunne OLY	.25	.12	.02
☐ 396 Gary Green OLY	.10	.05	.01
☐ 397 John Hoover OLY	.10	.05	.01
☐ 398 Shane Mack OLY	.50	.25	.05
☐ 399 John Marzano OLY	.25	.12	.02
☐ 400 Oddibe McDowell OLY	.60	.30	.06
☐ 401 Mark McGwire OLY	20.00	10.00	2.00
☐ 402 Pat Pacillo OLY	.15	.07	.01
☐ 403 Cory Snyder OLY	3.00	1.50	.30
☐ 404 Billy Swift OLY	.25	.12	.02
☐ 405 Tom Veryzer	.05	.02	.00
☐ 406 Len Whitehouse	.05	.02	.00
☐ 407 Bobby Ramos	.05	.02	.00
☐ 408 Sid Monge	.05	.02	.00
☐ 409 Brad Wellman	.05	.02	.00
☐ 410 Bob Horner	.10	.05	.01
☐ 411 Bobby Cox MG (checklist back)	.08	.04	.01
☐ 412 Bud Black	.08	.04	.01
☐ 413 Vance Law	.05	.02	.00
☐ 414 Gary Ward	.05	.02	.00

☐	415 Ron Darling UER (no trivia answer)	.60	.30	.06
☐	416 Wayne Gross	.05	.02	.00
☐	417 John Franco	1.25	.60	.12
☐	418 Ken Landreaux	.05	.02	.00
☐	419 Mike Caldwell	.05	.02	.00
☐	420 Andre Dawson	.35	.17	.03
☐	421 Dave Rucker	.05	.02	.00
☐	422 Carney Lansford	.12	.06	.01
☐	423 Barry Bonnell	.05	.02	.00
☐	424 Al Nipper	.10	.05	.01
☐	425 Mike Hargrove	.05	.02	.00
☐	426 Vern Ruhle	.05	.02	.00
☐	427 Mario Ramirez	.05	.02	.00
☐	428 Larry Andersen	.05	.02	.00
☐	429 Rick Cerone	.05	.02	.00
☐	430 Ron Davis	.05	.02	.00
☐	431 U.L. Washington	.05	.02	.00
☐	432 Thad Bosley	.05	.02	.00
☐	433 Jim Morrison	.05	.02	.00
☐	434 Gene Richards	.05	.02	.00
☐	435 Dan Petry	.05	.02	.00
☐	436 Willie Aikens	.05	.02	.00
☐	437 Al Jones	.05	.02	.00
☐	438 Joe Torre MG (checklist back)	.08	.04	.01
☐	439 Junior Ortiz	.05	.02	.00
☐	440 Fernando Valenzuela	.25	.12	.02
☐	441 Duane Walker	.05	.02	.00
☐	442 Ken Forsch	.05	.02	.00
☐	443 George Wright	.05	.02	.00
☐	444 Tony Phillips	.05	.02	.00
☐	445 Tippy Martinez	.05	.02	.00
☐	446 Jim Sundberg	.05	.02	.00
☐	447 Jeff Lahti	.05	.02	.00
☐	448 Derrel Thomas	.05	.02	.00
☐	449 Phil Bradley	.65	.30	.06
☐	450 Steve Garvey	.40	.20	.04
☐	451 Bruce Hurst	.12	.06	.01
☐	452 John Castino	.05	.02	.00
☐	453 Tom Waddell	.05	.02	.00
☐	454 Glenn Wilson	.05	.02	.00
☐	455 Bob Knepper	.05	.02	.00
☐	456 Tim Foli	.05	.02	.00
☐	457 Cecilio Guante	.05	.02	.00
☐	458 Randy Johnson	.05	.02	.00
☐	459 Charlie Leibrandt	.05	.02	.00
☐	460 Ryne Sandberg	2.50	1.25	.25
☐	461 Marty Castillo	.05	.02	.00
☐	462 Gary Lavelle	.05	.02	.00
☐	463 Dave Collins	.05	.02	.00
☐	464 Mike Mason	.05	.02	.00
☐	465 Bob Grich	.08	.04	.01
☐	466 Tony LaRussa MG (checklist back)	.08	.04	.01
☐	467 Ed Lynch	.05	.02	.00
☐	468 Wayne Krenchicki	.05	.02	.00
☐	469 Sammy Stewart	.05	.02	.00
☐	470 Steve Sax	.30	.15	.03
☐	471 Pete Ladd	.05	.02	.00
☐	472 Jim Essian	.05	.02	.00
☐	473 Tim Wallach	.12	.06	.01
☐	474 Kurt Kepshire	.07	.03	.01
☐	475 Andre Thornton	.07	.03	.01
☐	476 Jeff Stone	.10	.05	.01
☐	477 Bob Ojeda	.10	.05	.01
☐	478 Kurt Bevacqua	.05	.02	.00
☐	479 Mike Madden	.05	.02	.00
☐	480 Lou Whitaker	.18	.09	.01
☐	481 Dale Murray	.05	.02	.00
☐	482 Harry Spilman	.05	.02	.00
☐	483 Mike Smithson	.05	.02	.00
☐	484 Larry Bowa	.08	.04	.01
☐	485 Matt Young	.05	.02	.00
☐	486 Steve Balboni	.05	.02	.00
☐	487 Frank Williams	.08	.04	.01
☐	488 Joel Skinner	.08	.04	.01
☐	489 Bryan Clark	.05	.02	.00
☐	490 Jason Thompson	.05	.02	.00
☐	491 Rick Camp	.05	.02	.00
☐	492 Dave Johnson MG (checklist back)	.08	.04	.01
☐	493 Orel Hershiser	4.00	2.00	.40
☐	494 Rich Dauer	.05	.02	.00
☐	495 Mario Soto	.05	.02	.00
☐	496 Donnie Scott	.05	.02	.00
☐	497 Gary Pettis UER (photo actually Gary's little brother, Lynn)	.20	.10	.02
☐	498 Ed Romero	.05	.02	.00
☐	499 Danny Cox	.15	.07	.01
☐	500 Mike Schmidt	1.00	.50	.10
☐	501 Dan Schatzeder	.05	.02	.00
☐	502 Rick Miller	.05	.02	.00
☐	503 Tim Conroy	.05	.02	.00
☐	504 Jerry Willard	.05	.02	.00
☐	505 Jim Beattie	.05	.02	.00
☐	506 Franklin Stubbs	.40	.20	.04
☐	507 Ray Fontenot	.05	.02	.00
☐	508 John Shelby	.05	.02	.00
☐	509 Milt May	.05	.02	.00
☐	510 Kent Hrbek	.30	.15	.03
☐	511 Lee Smith	.08	.04	.01
☐	512 Tom Brookens	.05	.02	.00
☐	513 Lynn Jones	.05	.02	.00
☐	514 Jeff Cornell	.05	.02	.00
☐	515 Dave Concepcion	.08	.04	.01
☐	516 Roy Lee Jackson	.05	.02	.00
☐	517 Jerry Martin	.05	.02	.00
☐	518 Chris Chambliss	.08	.04	.01
☐	519 Doug Rader MG (checklist back)	.08	.04	.01
☐	520 LaMarr Hoyt	.08	.04	.01
☐	521 Rick Dempsey	.05	.02	.00
☐	522 Paul Molitor	.15	.07	.01
☐	523 Candy Maldonado	.18	.09	.01
☐	524 Rob Wilfong	.05	.02	.00
☐	525 Darrell Porter	.05	.02	.00
☐	526 David Palmer	.05	.02	.00
☐	527 Checklist: 397-528	.08	.01	.00
☐	528 Bill Krueger	.05	.02	.00
☐	529 Rich Gedman	.05	.02	.00
☐	530 Dave Dravecky	.10	.05	.01
☐	531 Joe Lefebvre	.05	.02	.00
☐	532 Frank DiPino	.05	.02	.00
☐	533 Tony Bernazard	.05	.02	.00
☐	534 Brian Dayett	.05	.02	.00
☐	535 Pat Putnam	.05	.02	.00
☐	536 Kirby Puckett	14.00	7.00	1.40
☐	537 Don Robinson	.05	.02	.00
☐	538 Keith Moreland	.05	.02	.00
☐	539 Aurelio Lopez	.05	.02	.00
☐	540 Claudell Washington	.08	.04	.01
☐	541 Mark Davis	.10	.05	.01
☐	542 Don Slaught	.05	.02	.00
☐	543 Mike Squires	.05	.02	.00
☐	544 Bruce Kison	.05	.02	.00
☐	545 Lloyd Moseby	.10	.05	.01
☐	546 Brent Gaff	.05	.02	.00
☐	547 Pete Rose MG (checklist back)	.45	.22	.04
☐	548 Larry Parrish	.05	.02	.00
☐	549 Mike Scioscia	.05	.02	.00
☐	550 Scott McGregor	.05	.02	.00
☐	551 Andy Van Slyke	.45	.22	.04
☐	552 Chris Codiroli	.05	.02	.00
☐	553 Bob Clark	.05	.02	.00
☐	554 Doug Flynn	.05	.02	.00
☐	555 Bob Stanley	.05	.02	.00
☐	556 Sixto Lezcano	.05	.02	.00
☐	557 Len Barker	.05	.02	.00
☐	558 Carmelo Martinez	.05	.02	.00
☐	559 Jay Howell	.05	.02	.00
☐	560 Bill Madlock	.08	.04	.01
☐	561 Darryl Motley	.05	.02	.00
☐	562 Houston Jimenez	.05	.02	.00
☐	563 Dick Ruthven	.05	.02	.00
☐	564 Alan Ashby	.05	.02	.00
☐	565 Kirk Gibson	.30	.15	.03
☐	566 Ed VandeBerg	.05	.02	.00
☐	567 Joel Youngblood	.05	.02	.00
☐	568 Cliff Johnson	.05	.02	.00
☐	569 Ken Oberkfell	.05	.02	.00
☐	570 Darryl Strawberry	3.75	1.85	.37
☐	571 Charlie Hough	.08	.04	.01
☐	572 Tom Paciorek	.05	.02	.00
☐	573 Jay Tibbs	.08	.04	.01
☐	574 Joe Altobelli MG (checklist back)	.08	.04	.01
☐	575 Pedro Guerrero	.25	.12	.02
☐	576 Jaime Cocanower	.05	.02	.00
☐	577 Chris Speier	.05	.02	.00
☐	578 Terry Francona	.05	.02	.00
☐	579 Ron Romanick	.05	.02	.00
☐	580 Dwight Evans	.15	.07	.01
☐	581 Mark Wagner	.05	.02	.00
☐	582 Ken Phelps	.15	.07	.01
☐	583 Bobby Brown	.05	.02	.00
☐	584 Kevin Gross	.05	.02	.00
☐	585 Butch Wynegar	.05	.02	.00
☐	586 Bill Scherrer	.05	.02	.00
☐	587 Doug Frobel	.05	.02	.00
☐	588 Bobby Castillo	.05	.02	.00
☐	589 Bob Dernier	.05	.02	.00
☐	590 Ray Knight	.08	.04	.01
☐	591 Larry Herndon	.05	.02	.00
☐	592 Jeff Robinson (Giants pitcher)	.18	.09	.01
☐	593 Rick Leach	.05	.02	.00

☐ 594 Curt Wilkerson	.05	.02	.00
☐ 595 Larry Gura	.05	.02	.00
☐ 596 Jerry Hairston	.05	.02	.00
☐ 597 Brad Lesley	.05	.02	.00
☐ 598 Jose Oquendo	.08	.04	.01
☐ 599 Storm Davis	.10	.05	.01
☐ 600 Pete Rose	1.00	.50	.10
☐ 601 Tom Lasorda MG (checklist back)	.08	.04	.01
☐ 602 Jeff Dedmon	.05	.02	.00
☐ 603 Rick Manning	.05	.02	.00
☐ 604 Daryl Sconiers	.05	.02	.00
☐ 605 Ozzie Smith	.25	.12	.02
☐ 606 Rich Gale	.05	.02	.00
☐ 607 Bill Almon	.05	.02	.00
☐ 608 Craig Lefferts	.08	.04	.01
☐ 609 Broderick Perkins	.05	.02	.00
☐ 610 Jack Morris	.15	.07	.01
☐ 611 Ozzie Virgil	.05	.02	.00
☐ 612 Mike Armstrong	.05	.02	.00
☐ 613 Terry Puhl	.05	.02	.00
☐ 614 Al Williams	.05	.02	.00
☐ 615 Marvell Wynne	.05	.02	.00
☐ 616 Scott Sanderson	.05	.02	.00
☐ 617 Willie Wilson	.10	.05	.01
☐ 618 Pete Falcone	.05	.02	.00
☐ 619 Jeff Leonard	.08	.04	.01
☐ 620 Dwight Gooden	9.00	4.50	.90
☐ 621 Marvis Foley	.05	.02	.00
☐ 622 Luis Leal	.05	.02	.00
☐ 623 Greg Walker	.08	.04	.01
☐ 624 Benny Ayala	.05	.02	.00
☐ 625 Mark Langston	2.25	1.10	.22
☐ 626 German Rivera	.05	.02	.00
☐ 627 Eric Davis	13.50	6.50	1.25
☐ 628 Rene Lachemann MG (checklist back)	.08	.04	.01
☐ 629 Dick Schofield	.15	.07	.01
☐ 630 Tim Raines	.35	.17	.03
☐ 631 Bob Forsch	.05	.02	.00
☐ 632 Bruce Bochte	.05	.02	.00
☐ 633 Glenn Hoffman	.05	.02	.00
☐ 634 Bill Dawley	.05	.02	.00
☐ 635 Terry Kennedy	.05	.02	.00
☐ 636 Shane Rawley	.05	.02	.00
☐ 637 Brett Butler	.10	.05	.01
☐ 638 Mike Pagliarulo	.60	.30	.06
☐ 639 Ed Hodge	.05	.02	.00
☐ 640 Steve Henderson	.05	.02	.00
☐ 641 Rod Scurry	.05	.02	.00
☐ 642 Dave Owen	.05	.02	.00
☐ 643 Johnny Grubb	.05	.02	.00
☐ 644 Mark Huismann	.05	.02	.00
☐ 645 Damaso Garcia	.05	.02	.00
☐ 646 Scot Thompson	.05	.02	.00
☐ 647 Rafael Ramirez	.05	.02	.00
☐ 648 Bob Jones	.05	.02	.00
☐ 649 Sid Fernandez	.85	.40	.08
☐ 650 Greg Luzinski	.10	.05	.01
☐ 651 Jeff Russell	.12	.06	.01
☐ 652 Joe Nolan	.05	.02	.00
☐ 653 Mark Brouhard	.05	.02	.00
☐ 654 Dave Anderson	.05	.02	.00
☐ 655 Joaquin Andujar	.08	.04	.01
☐ 656 Chuck Cottier MG (checklist back)	.08	.04	.01
☐ 657 Jim Slaton	.05	.02	.00
☐ 658 Mike Stenhouse	.08	.04	.01
☐ 659 Checklist: 529-660	.08	.01	.00
☐ 660 Tony Gwynn	1.25	.60	.12
☐ 661 Steve Crawford	.05	.02	.00
☐ 662 Mike Heath	.05	.02	.00
☐ 663 Luis Aguayo	.05	.02	.00
☐ 664 Steve Farr	.20	.10	.02
☐ 665 Don Mattingly	9.00	4.50	.90
☐ 666 Mike LaCoss	.05	.02	.00
☐ 667 Dave Engle	.05	.02	.00
☐ 668 Steve Trout	.05	.02	.00
☐ 669 Lee Lacy	.05	.02	.00
☐ 670 Tom Seaver	.40	.20	.04
☐ 671 Dane Iorg	.05	.02	.00
☐ 672 Juan Berenguer	.05	.02	.00
☐ 673 Buck Martinez	.05	.02	.00
☐ 674 Atlee Hammaker	.05	.02	.00
☐ 675 Tony Perez	.15	.07	.01
☐ 676 Albert Hall	.08	.04	.01
☐ 677 Wally Backman	.05	.02	.00
☐ 678 Joey McLaughlin	.05	.02	.00
☐ 679 Bob Kearney	.05	.02	.00
☐ 680 Jerry Reuss	.05	.02	.00
☐ 681 Ben Oglivie	.08	.04	.01
☐ 682 Doug Corbett	.05	.02	.00
☐ 683 Whitey Herzog MG (checklist back)	.08	.04	.01

☐ 684 Bill Doran	.10	.05	.01
☐ 685 Bill Caudill	.05	.02	.00
☐ 686 Mike Easler	.05	.02	.00
☐ 687 Bill Gullickson	.05	.02	.00
☐ 688 Len Matuszek	.05	.02	.00
☐ 689 Luis DeLeon	.05	.02	.00
☐ 690 Alan Trammell	.30	.15	.03
☐ 691 Dennis Rasmussen	.25	.12	.02
☐ 692 Randy Bush	.05	.02	.00
☐ 693 Tim Stoddard	.05	.02	.00
☐ 694 Joe Carter	3.00	1.50	.30
☐ 695 Rick Rhoden	.08	.04	.01
☐ 696 John Rabb	.05	.02	.00
☐ 697 Onix Concepcion	.05	.02	.00
☐ 698 Jorge Bell	.50	.25	.05
☐ 699 Donnie Moore	.05	.02	.00
☐ 700 Eddie Murray	.45	.22	.04
☐ 701 Eddie Murray AS	.20	.10	.02
☐ 702 Damaso Garcia AS	.05	.02	.00
☐ 703 George Brett AS	.25	.12	.02
☐ 704 Cal Ripken AS	.20	.10	.02
☐ 705 Dave Winfield AS	.15	.07	.01
☐ 706 Rickey Henderson AS	.50	.25	.05
☐ 707 Tony Armas AS	.05	.02	.00
☐ 708 Lance Parrish AS	.10	.05	.01
☐ 709 Mike Boddicker AS	.05	.02	.00
☐ 710 Frank Viola AS	.10	.05	.01
☐ 711 Dan Quisenberry AS	.08	.04	.01
☐ 712 Keith Hernandez AS	.12	.06	.01
☐ 713 Ryne Sandberg AS	.50	.25	.05
☐ 714 Mike Schmidt AS	.35	.17	.03
☐ 715 Ozzie Smith AS	.15	.07	.01
☐ 716 Dale Murphy AS	.25	.12	.02
☐ 717 Tony Gwynn AS	.25	.12	.02
☐ 718 Jeff Leonard AS	.05	.02	.00
☐ 719 Gary Carter AS	.15	.07	.01
☐ 720 Rick Sutcliffe AS	.08	.04	.01
☐ 721 Bob Knepper AS	.05	.02	.00
☐ 722 Bruce Sutter AS	.08	.04	.01
☐ 723 Dave Stewart	.40	.20	.04
☐ 724 Oscar Gamble	.05	.02	.00
☐ 725 Floyd Bannister	.05	.02	.00
☐ 726 Al Bumbry	.05	.02	.00
☐ 727 Frank Pastore	.05	.02	.00
☐ 728 Bob Bailor	.05	.02	.00
☐ 729 Don Sutton	.25	.12	.02
☐ 730 Dave Kingman	.10	.05	.01
☐ 731 Neil Allen	.05	.02	.00
☐ 732 John McNamara MG (checklist back)	.08	.04	.01
☐ 733 Tony Scott	.05	.02	.00
☐ 734 John Henry Johnson	.05	.02	.00
☐ 735 Garry Templeton	.08	.04	.01
☐ 736 Jerry Mumphrey	.05	.02	.00
☐ 737 Bo Diaz	.05	.02	.00
☐ 738 Omar Moreno	.05	.02	.00
☐ 739 Ernie Camacho	.05	.02	.00
☐ 740 Jack Clark	.25	.12	.02
☐ 741 John Butcher	.05	.02	.00
☐ 742 Ron Hassey	.05	.02	.00
☐ 743 Frank White	.08	.04	.01
☐ 744 Doug Bair	.05	.02	.00
☐ 745 Buddy Bell	.10	.05	.01
☐ 746 Jim Clancy	.05	.02	.00
☐ 747 Alex Trevino	.05	.02	.00
☐ 748 Lee Mazzilli	.05	.02	.00
☐ 749 Julio Cruz	.05	.02	.00
☐ 750 Rollie Fingers	.15	.07	.01
☐ 751 Kelvin Chapman	.05	.02	.00
☐ 752 Bob Owchinko	.05	.02	.00
☐ 753 Greg Brock	.05	.02	.00
☐ 754 Larry Milbourne	.05	.02	.00
☐ 755 Ken Singleton	.08	.04	.01
☐ 756 Rob Picciolo	.05	.02	.00
☐ 757 Willie McGee	.30	.15	.03
☐ 758 Ray Burris	.05	.02	.00
☐ 759 Jim Fanning MG (checklist back)	.08	.04	.01
☐ 760 Nolan Ryan	2.00	1.00	.20
☐ 761 Jerry Remy	.05	.02	.00
☐ 762 Eddie Whitson	.08	.04	.01
☐ 763 Kiko Garcia	.05	.02	.00
☐ 764 Jamie Easterly	.05	.02	.00
☐ 765 Willie Randolph	.08	.04	.01
☐ 766 Paul Mirabella	.05	.02	.00
☐ 767 Darrell Brown	.05	.02	.00
☐ 768 Ron Cey	.10	.05	.01
☐ 769 Joe Cowley	.05	.02	.00
☐ 770 Carlton Fisk	.30	.15	.03
☐ 771 Geoff Zahn	.05	.02	.00
☐ 772 Johnnie LeMaster	.05	.02	.00
☐ 773 Hal McRae	.08	.04	.01
☐ 774 Dennis Lamp	.05	.02	.00
☐ 775 Mookie Wilson	.08	.04	.01

	MINT	EXC	G-VG
☐ 776 Jerry Royster	.05	.02	.00
☐ 777 Ned Yost	.05	.02	.00
☐ 778 Mike Davis	.05	.02	.00
☐ 779 Nick Esasky	.12	.06	.01
☐ 780 Mike Flanagan	.08	.04	.01
☐ 781 Jim Gantner	.05	.02	.00
☐ 782 Tom Niedenfuer	.05	.02	.00
☐ 783 Mike Jorgensen	.05	.02	.00
☐ 784 Checklist: 661-792	.08	.01	.00
☐ 785 Tony Armas	.08	.04	.01
☐ 786 Enos Cabell	.05	.02	.00
☐ 787 Jim Wohlford	.05	.02	.00
☐ 788 Steve Comer	.05	.02	.00
☐ 789 Luis Salazar	.05	.02	.00
☐ 790 Ron Guidry	.15	.07	.01
☐ 791 Ivan DeJesus	.05	.02	.00
☐ 792 Darrell Evans	.15	.07	.01

1985 Topps Glossy 22

The cards in this 22-card set measure 2 1/2" by 3 1/2". Similar in design, both front and back, to last year's Glossy set, this edition features the managers, starting nine players and honorary captains of the National and American League teams in the 1984 All-Star game. The set is numbered on the reverse with plyers essentially ordered by position within league, NL: 1-11 and AL: 12-22.

	MINT	EXC	G-VG
COMPLETE SET (22)	3.50	1.75	.35
COMMON PLAYER (1-22)	.10	.05	.01
☐ 1 Paul Owens MG	.10	.05	.01
☐ 2 Steve Garvey	.40	.20	.04
☐ 3 Ryne Sandberg	.60	.30	.06
☐ 4 Mike Schmidt	.75	.35	.07
☐ 5 Ozzie Smith	.25	.12	.02
☐ 6 Tony Gwynn	.40	.20	.04
☐ 7 Dale Murphy	.60	.30	.06
☐ 8 Darryl Strawberry	.75	.35	.07
☐ 9 Gary Carter	.25	.12	.02
☐ 10 Charlie Lea	.10	.05	.01
☐ 11 Willie McCovey CAPT	.20	.10	.02
☐ 12 Joe Altobelli MG	.10	.05	.01
☐ 13 Rod Carew	.50	.25	.05
☐ 14 Lou Whitaker	.15	.07	.01
☐ 15 George Brett	.60	.30	.06
☐ 16 Cal Ripken	.40	.20	.04
☐ 17 Dave Winfield	.30	.15	.03
☐ 18 Chet Lemon	.10	.05	.01
☐ 19 Reggie Jackson	.60	.30	.06
☐ 20 Lance Parrish	.20	.10	.02
☐ 21 Dave Stieb	.15	.07	.01
☐ 22 Hank Greenberg CAPT	.15	.07	.01

1985 Topps Glossy 40

The cards in this 40-card set measure 2 1/2" by 3 1/2". Similar to last year's glossy set, this set was issued as a bonus prize to Topps All-Star Baseball Game cards found in wax packs. The set could be obtained by sending in the "Bonus Runs" from the "Winning Pitch" game insert cards. For 25 runs and 75 cents, a collector could send in for one of the eight different five card series plus automatically be entered in the Grand Prize Sweepstakes for a chance at a free trip to the All-Star game. The cards are numbered and contain 20 stars from each league.

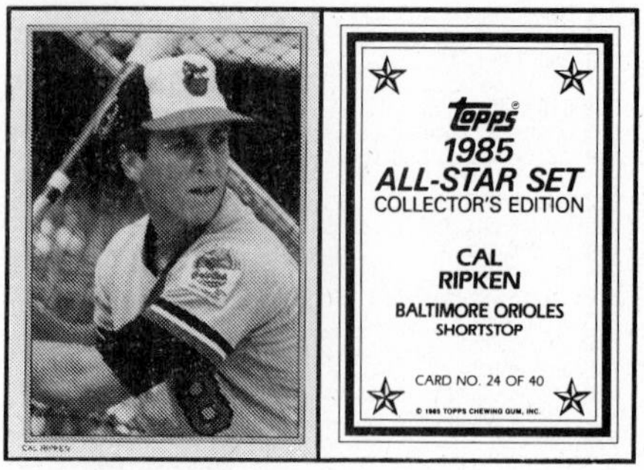

	MINT	EXC	G-VG
COMPLETE SET (40)	12.00	6.00	1.20
COMMON PLAYER (1-40)	.20	.10	.02
☐ 1 Dale Murphy	.90	.45	.09
☐ 2 Jesse Orosco	.20	.10	.02
☐ 3 Bob Brenly	.20	.10	.02
☐ 4 Mike Boddicker	.20	.10	.02
☐ 5 Dave Kingman	.25	.12	.02
☐ 6 Jim Rice	.30	.15	.03
☐ 7 Frank Viola	.35	.17	.03
☐ 8 Alvin Davis	.30	.15	.03
☐ 9 Rick Sutcliffe	.25	.12	.02
☐ 10 Pete Rose	1.25	.60	.12
☐ 11 Leon Durham	.20	.10	.02
☐ 12 Joaquin Andujar	.20	.10	.02
☐ 13 Keith Hernandez	.30	.15	.03
☐ 14 Dave Winfield	.45	.22	.04
☐ 15 Reggie Jackson	1.00	.50	.10
☐ 16 Alan Trammell	.35	.17	.03
☐ 17 Bert Blyleven	.25	.12	.02
☐ 18 Tony Armas	.20	.10	.02
☐ 19 Rich Gossage	.25	.12	.02
☐ 20 Jose Cruz	.20	.10	.02
☐ 21 Ryne Sandberg	.75	.35	.07
☐ 22 Bruce Sutter	.25	.12	.02
☐ 23 Mike Schmidt	1.25	.60	.12
☐ 24 Cal Ripken	.90	.45	.09
☐ 25 Dan Petry	.20	.10	.02
☐ 26 Jack Morris	.25	.12	.02
☐ 27 Don Mattingly	1.75	.85	.17
☐ 28 Eddie Murray	.60	.30	.06
☐ 29 Tony Gwynn	.60	.30	.06
☐ 30 Charlie Lea	.20	.10	.02
☐ 31 Juan Samuel	.25	.12	.02
☐ 32 Phil Niekro	.35	.17	.03
☐ 33 Alejandro Pena	.20	.10	.02
☐ 34 Harold Baines	.30	.15	.03
☐ 35 Dan Quisenberry	.25	.12	.02
☐ 36 Gary Carter	.40	.20	.04
☐ 37 Mario Soto	.20	.10	.02
☐ 38 Dwight Gooden	1.00	.50	.10
☐ 39 Tom Brunansky	.25	.12	.02
☐ 40 Dave Stieb	.25	.12	.02

1985 Topps Traded

The cards in this 132-card set measure 2 1/2" by 3 1/2". In its now standard procedure, Topps issued its Traded (or extended) set for the fifth year in a row. Because all photos and statistics of its regular set for the year were developed during the fall and winter months of the preceding year, players who changed teams during the fall, winter, and spring months are portrayed in the 1985 regular issue set with the teams they were with in 1984. The Traded set amends the shortcomings of the regular set by presenting the players with their proper teams for the current year. Rookies not contained in the regular set are also picked up in the Traded set. The key (extended) rookie cards in this set are Vince Coleman and Ozzie Guillen. Again this year, the Topps affiliate in Ireland printed the cards, and the cards were available through hobby channels only. Topps also produced a specially boxed "glossy" edition, frequently referred to as the Topps Traded Tiffany set. There were supposedly only 8,000 sets of the Tiffany cards produced; they were marketed to hobby dealers. The checklist of cards is identical to that of the normal non-glossy cards. There are two primary distinguishing features of the Tiffany cards, white card stock reverses and high gloss obverses. These Tiffany cards are valued at approximately five times the values listed below.

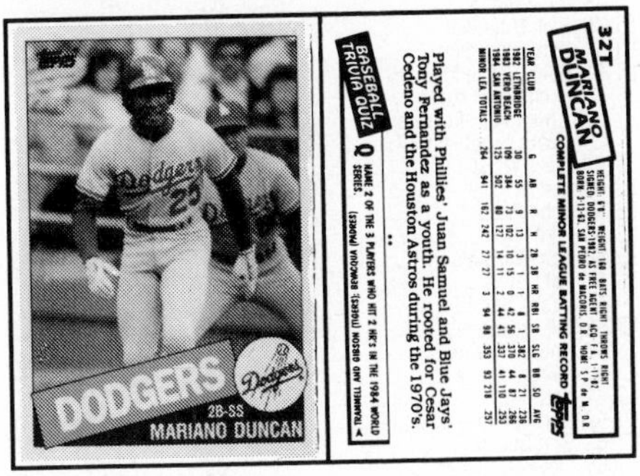

	MINT	EXC	G-VG
COMPLETE SET (132)	18.00	9.00	1.80
COMMON PLAYER (1-132)	.07	.03	.01
☐ 1T Don Aase	.15	.07	.01
☐ 2T Bill Almon	.07	.03	.01
☐ 3T Benny Ayala	.07	.03	.01
☐ 4T Dusty Baker	.10	.05	.01
☐ 5T Geo.Bamberger MG	.10	.05	.01
☐ 6T Dale Berra	.07	.03	.01
☐ 7T Rich Bordi	.07	.03	.01
☐ 8T Daryl Boston	.30	.15	.03
☐ 9T Hubie Brooks	.35	.17	.03
☐ 10T Chris Brown	.15	.07	.01
☐ 11T Tom Browning	1.25	.60	.12
☐ 12T Al Bumbry	.07	.03	.01
☐ 13T Ray Burris	.07	.03	.01
☐ 14T Jeff Burroughs	.10	.05	.01
☐ 15T Bill Campbell	.07	.03	.01
☐ 16T Don Carman	.20	.10	.02
☐ 17T Gary Carter	.75	.35	.07
☐ 18T Bobby Castillo	.07	.03	.01
☐ 19T Bill Caudill	.07	.03	.01
☐ 20T Rick Cerone	.07	.03	.01
☐ 21T Bryan Clark	.07	.03	.01
☐ 22T Jack Clark	.35	.17	.03
☐ 23T Pat Clements	.10	.05	.01
☐ 24T Vince Coleman	7.00	3.50	.70
☐ 25T Dave Collins	.07	.03	.01
☐ 26T Danny Darwin	.10	.05	.01
☐ 27T Jim Davenport MG	.07	.03	.01
☐ 28T Jerry Davis	.07	.03	.01
☐ 29T Brian Dayett	.07	.03	.01
☐ 30T Ivan DeJesus	.07	.03	.01
☐ 31T Ken Dixon	.10	.05	.01
☐ 32T Mariano Duncan	.80	.40	.08
☐ 33T John Felske MG	.07	.03	.01
☐ 34T Mike Fitzgerald	.07	.03	.01
☐ 35T Ray Fontenot	.07	.03	.01
☐ 36T Greg Gagne	.25	.12	.02
☐ 37T Oscar Gamble	.07	.03	.01
☐ 38T Scott Garrelts	.60	.30	.06
☐ 39T Bob L. Gibson	.07	.03	.01
☐ 40T Jim Gott	.10	.05	.01
☐ 41T David Green	.07	.03	.01
☐ 42T Alfredo Griffin	.07	.03	.01
☐ 43T Ozzie Guillen	2.50	1.25	.25
☐ 44T Eddie Haas MG	.07	.03	.01
☐ 45T Terry Harper	.07	.03	.01
☐ 46T Toby Harrah	.10	.05	.01
☐ 47T Greg Harris	.07	.03	.01
☐ 48T Ron Hassey	.07	.03	.01
☐ 49T Rickey Henderson	3.50	1.75	.35
☐ 50T Steve Henderson	.07	.03	.01
☐ 51T George Hendrick	.10	.05	.01
☐ 52T Joe Hesketh	.15	.07	.01
☐ 53T Teddy Higuera	2.00	1.00	.20
☐ 54T Donnie Hill	.10	.05	.01
☐ 55T Al Holland	.07	.03	.01
☐ 56T Burt Hooton	.07	.03	.01
☐ 57T Jay Howell	.10	.05	.01
☐ 58T Ken Howell	.20	.10	.02
☐ 59T LaMarr Hoyt	.10	.05	.01
☐ 60T Tim Hulett	.10	.05	.01
☐ 61T Bob James	.10	.05	.01
☐ 62T Steve Jeltz	.10	.05	.01
☐ 63T Cliff Johnson	.07	.03	.01
☐ 64T Howard Johnson	2.25	1.10	.22
☐ 65T Ruppert Jones	.07	.03	.01
☐ 66T Steve Kemp	.07	.03	.01
☐ 67T Bruce Kison	.07	.03	.01
☐ 68T Alan Knicely	.07	.03	.01
☐ 69T Mike LaCoss	.07	.03	.01
☐ 70T Lee Lacy	.07	.03	.01
☐ 71T Dave LaPoint	.07	.03	.01
☐ 72T Gary Lavelle	.07	.03	.01
☐ 73T Vance Law	.10	.05	.01
☐ 74T Johnnie LeMaster	.07	.03	.01
☐ 75T Sixto Lezcano	.07	.03	.01
☐ 76T Tim Lollar	.07	.03	.01
☐ 77T Fred Lynn	.25	.12	.02
☐ 78T Billy Martin MG	.20	.10	.02
☐ 79T Ron Mathis	.07	.03	.01
☐ 80T Len Matuszek	.07	.03	.01
☐ 81T Gene Mauch MG	.07	.03	.01
☐ 82T Oddibe McDowell	.50	.25	.05
☐ 83T Roger McDowell	.80	.40	.08
☐ 84T John McNamara MG	.10	.05	.01
☐ 85T Donnie Moore	.07	.03	.01
☐ 86T Gene Nelson	.07	.03	.01
☐ 87T Steve Nicosia	.07	.03	.01
☐ 88T Al Oliver	.15	.07	.01
☐ 89T Joe Orsulak	.35	.17	.03
☐ 90T Rob Picciolo	.07	.03	.01
☐ 91T Chris Pittaro	.10	.05	.01
☐ 92T Jim Presley	.75	.35	.07
☐ 93T Rick Reuschel	.20	.10	.02
☐ 94T Bert Roberge	.07	.03	.01
☐ 95T Bob Rodgers MG	.07	.03	.01
☐ 96T Jerry Royster	.07	.03	.01
☐ 97T Dave Rozema	.07	.03	.01
☐ 98T Dave Rucker	.07	.03	.01
☐ 99T Vern Ruhle	.07	.03	.01
☐ 100T Paul Runge	.10	.05	.01
☐ 101T Mark Salas	.10	.05	.01
☐ 102T Luis Salazar	.07	.03	.01
☐ 103T Joe Sambito	.07	.03	.01
☐ 104T Rick Schu	.12	.06	.01
☐ 105T Donnie Scott	.07	.03	.01
☐ 106T Larry Sheets	.25	.12	.02
☐ 107T Don Slaught	.07	.03	.01
☐ 108T Roy Smalley	.07	.03	.01
☐ 109T Lonnie Smith	.15	.07	.01
☐ 110T Nate Snell UER (headings on back for a batter)	.10	.05	.01
☐ 111T Chris Speier	.07	.03	.01
☐ 112T Mike Stenhouse	.10	.05	.01
☐ 113T Tim Stoddard	.07	.03	.01
☐ 114T Jim Sundberg	.07	.03	.01
☐ 115T Bruce Sutter	.20	.10	.02
☐ 116T Don Sutton	.50	.25	.05
☐ 117T Kent Tekulve	.10	.05	.01
☐ 118T Tom Tellmann	.07	.03	.01
☐ 119T Walt Terrell	.10	.05	.01
☐ 120T Mickey Tettleton	.90	.45	.09
☐ 121T Derrel Thomas	.07	.03	.01
☐ 122T Rich Thompson	.10	.05	.01
☐ 123T Alex Trevino	.07	.03	.01
☐ 124T John Tudor	.20	.10	.02
☐ 125T Jose Uribe	.25	.12	.02
☐ 126T Bobby Valentine MG	.10	.05	.01
☐ 127T Dave Von Ohlen	.07	.03	.01
☐ 128T U.L. Washington	.07	.03	.01
☐ 129T Earl Weaver MG	.10	.05	.01
☐ 130T Eddie Whitson	.10	.05	.01
☐ 131T Herm Winningham	.15	.07	.01
☐ 132T Checklist 1-132	.07	.01	.00

1986 Topps

The cards in this 792-card set are standard-size (2 1/2" by 3 1/2"). The first seven cards are a tribute to Pete Rose and his career. Cards 2-7 show small photos of Pete's Topps cards of the given years on the front with biographical information pertaining to those years on the back. The team leader cards were done differently with a simple player action shot on a white background; the player pictured is dubbed the "Dean" of that team, i.e., the player with the longest continuous service with that team. Topps again features a "Turn Back the Clock" series (401-405). Record breakers of the previous year are acknowledged on cards 201 to 207. Cards 701-722 feature All-Star selections from each league. Manager cards feature the team checklist on the reverse. Ryne Sandberg (690) is the only player card in the set without a Topps logo on the front of the card; this omission was never corrected by Topps. There are two other uncorrected errors involving misnumbered cards; see card numbers 51, 57, 141, and 171 in the checklist below. The backs of all the cards have a distinctive red background. The key rookie cards in this set are Vince Coleman, Len Dykstra and Cecil Fielder. Topps also produced a specially boxed "glossy" edition, frequently referred to as the Topps Tiffany set. There were supposedly only 5,000 sets of the Tiffany cards produced; they were marketed to hobby dealers. The checklist of cards (792 regular and 132 Traded) is identical to that of the normal non-glossy cards. There are two primary distinguishing features of the Tiffany cards, white card stock reverses and high gloss obverses. These Tiffany cards are valued at approximately five times the values listed below.

	MINT	EXC	G-VG
COMPLETE SET (792)	42.00	19.00	4.00
COMMON PLAYER (1-792)	.03	.01	.00
☐ 1 Pete Rose	1.00	.50	.10
☐ 2 Rose Special: '63-'66	.30	.15	.03
☐ 3 Rose Special: '67-'70	.30	.15	.03
☐ 4 Rose Special: '71-'74	.30	.15	.03
☐ 5 Rose Special: '75-'78	.30	.15	.03
☐ 6 Rose Special: '79-'82	.30	.15	.03
☐ 7 Rose Special: '83-'85	.30	.15	.03
☐ 8 Dwayne Murphy	.03	.01	.00
☐ 9 Roy Smith	.03	.01	.00
☐ 10 Tony Gwynn	.60	.30	.06
☐ 11 Bob Ojeda	.06	.03	.00
☐ 12 Jose Uribe	.20	.10	.02
☐ 13 Bob Kearney	.03	.01	.00
☐ 14 Julio Cruz	.03	.01	.00
☐ 15 Eddie Whitson	.06	.03	.00
☐ 16 Rick Schu	.06	.03	.00
☐ 17 Mike Stenhouse	.03	.01	.00
☐ 18 Brent Gaff	.03	.01	.00
☐ 19 Rich Hebner	.03	.01	.00
☐ 20 Lou Whitaker	.12	.06	.01
☐ 21 G.Bamberger MG (checklist back)	.06	.03	.00
☐ 22 Duane Walker	.03	.01	.00
☐ 23 Manny Lee	.10	.05	.01
☐ 24 Len Barker	.03	.01	.00
☐ 25 Willie Wilson	.10	.05	.01
☐ 26 Frank DiPino	.03	.01	.00
☐ 27 Ray Knight	.06	.03	.00
☐ 28 Eric Davis	2.25	1.10	.22
☐ 29 Tony Phillips	.03	.01	.00
☐ 30 Eddie Murray	.35	.17	.03
☐ 31 Jamie Easterly	.03	.01	.00
☐ 32 Steve Yeager	.03	.01	.00
☐ 33 Jeff Lahti	.03	.01	.00
☐ 34 Ken Phelps	.06	.03	.00
☐ 35 Jeff Reardon	.08	.04	.01
☐ 36 Tigers Leaders Lance Parrish	.08	.04	.01
☐ 37 Mark Thurmond	.03	.01	.00
☐ 38 Glenn Hoffman	.03	.01	.00
☐ 39 Dave Rucker	.03	.01	.00
☐ 40 Ken Griffey	.10	.05	.01
☐ 41 Brad Wellman	.03	.01	.00
☐ 42 Geoff Zahn	.03	.01	.00
☐ 43 Dave Engle	.03	.01	.00
☐ 44 Lance McCullers	.20	.10	.02
☐ 45 Damaso Garcia	.03	.01	.00
☐ 46 Billy Hatcher	.20	.10	.02
☐ 47 Juan Berenguer	.03	.01	.00
☐ 48 Bill Almon	.03	.01	.00
☐ 49 Rick Manning	.03	.01	.00
☐ 50 Dan Quisenberry	.10	.05	.01
☐ 51 Bobby Wine MG ERR (checklist back) (number of card on back is actually 57)	.08	.04	.01
☐ 52 Chris Welsh	.03	.01	.00
☐ 53 Len Dykstra	2.25	1.10	.22
☐ 54 John Franco	.12	.06	.01
☐ 55 Fred Lynn	.12	.06	.01
☐ 56 Tom Niedenfuer	.03	.01	.00
☐ 57 Bill Doran (see also 51)	.08	.04	.01
☐ 58 Bill Krueger	.03	.01	.00
☐ 59 Andre Thornton	.06	.03	.00
☐ 60 Dwight Evans	.12	.06	.01
☐ 61 Karl Best	.06	.03	.00
☐ 62 Bob Boone	.08	.04	.01
☐ 63 Ron Roenicke	.03	.01	.00
☐ 64 Floyd Bannister	.03	.01	.00
☐ 65 Dan Driessen	.03	.01	.00
☐ 66 Cardinals Leaders Bob Forsch	.03	.01	.00
☐ 67 Carmelo Martinez	.03	.01	.00
☐ 68 Ed Lynch	.03	.01	.00
☐ 69 Luis Aguayo	.03	.01	.00
☐ 70 Dave Winfield	.25	.12	.02
☐ 71 Ken Schrom	.03	.01	.00
☐ 72 Shawon Dunston	.50	.25	.05
☐ 73 Randy O'Neal	.03	.01	.00
☐ 74 Rance Mulliniks	.03	.01	.00
☐ 75 Jose DeLeon	.06	.03	.00
☐ 76 Dion James	.03	.01	.00
☐ 77 Charlie Leibrandt	.03	.01	.00
☐ 78 Bruce Benedict	.03	.01	.00
☐ 79 Dave Schmidt	.03	.01	.00
☐ 80 Darryl Strawberry	1.25	.60	.12
☐ 81 Gene Mauch MG (checklist back)	.06	.03	.00
☐ 82 Tippy Martinez	.03	.01	.00
☐ 83 Phil Garner	.03	.01	.00
☐ 84 Curt Young	.03	.01	.00
☐ 85 Tony Perez (Eric Davis also shown on card)	.20	.10	.02
☐ 86 Tom Waddell	.03	.01	.00
☐ 87 Candy Maldonado	.10	.05	.01
☐ 88 Tom Nieto	.03	.01	.00
☐ 89 Randy St.Claire	.03	.01	.00
☐ 90 Garry Templeton	.06	.03	.00
☐ 91 Steve Crawford	.03	.01	.00
☐ 92 Al Cowens	.03	.01	.00
☐ 93 Scot Thompson	.03	.01	.00
☐ 94 Rich Bordi	.03	.01	.00
☐ 95 Ozzie Virgil	.03	.01	.00
☐ 96 Blue Jays Leaders Jim Clancy	.03	.01	.00
☐ 97 Gary Gaetti	.12	.06	.01
☐ 98 Dick Ruthven	.03	.01	.00
☐ 99 Buddy Biancalana	.03	.01	.00
☐ 100 Nolan Ryan	1.50	.75	.15
☐ 101 Dave Bergman	.03	.01	.00
☐ 102 Joe Orsulak	.25	.12	.02
☐ 103 Luis Salazar	.03	.01	.00
☐ 104 Sid Fernandez	.15	.07	.01
☐ 105 Gary Ward	.03	.01	.00
☐ 106 Ray Burris	.03	.01	.00
☐ 107 Rafael Ramirez	.03	.01	.00
☐ 108 Ted Power	.03	.01	.00
☐ 109 Len Matuszek	.03	.01	.00

□ 110	Scott McGregor	.03	.01	.00
□ 111	Roger Craig MG	.06	.03	.00
	(checklist back)			
□ 112	Bill Campbell	.03	.01	.00
□ 113	U.L. Washington	.03	.01	.00
□ 114	Mike Brown	.03	.01	.00
	(Pirates OF)			
□ 115	Jay Howell	.03	.01	.00
□ 116	Brook Jacoby	.08	.04	.01
□ 117	Bruce Kison	.03	.01	.00
□ 118	Jerry Royster	.03	.01	.00
□ 119	Barry Bonnell	.03	.01	.00
□ 120	Steve Carlton	.25	.12	.02
□ 121	Nelson Simmons	.06	.03	.00
□ 122	Pete Filson	.03	.01	.00
□ 123	Greg Walker	.03	.01	.00
□ 124	Luis Sanchez	.03	.01	.00
□ 125	Dave Lopes	.06	.03	.00
□ 126	Mets Leaders	.06	.03	.00
	Mookie Wilson			
□ 127	Jack Howell	.15	.07	.01
□ 128	John Wathan	.03	.01	.00
□ 129	Jeff Dedmon	.03	.01	.00
□ 130	Alan Trammell	.20	.10	.02
□ 131	Checklist: 1-132	.06	.01	.00
□ 132	Razor Shines	.03	.01	.00
□ 133	Andy McGaffigan	.03	.01	.00
□ 134	Carney Lansford	.08	.04	.01
□ 135	Joe Niekro	.06	.03	.00
□ 136	Mike Hargrove	.03	.01	.00
□ 137	Charlie Moore	.03	.01	.00
□ 138	Mark Davis	.12	.06	.01
□ 139	Daryl Boston	.25	.12	.02
□ 140	John Candelaria	.06	.03	.00
□ 141	Chuck Cottier MG	.08	.04	.01
	(checklist back)			
	(see also 171)			
□ 142	Bob Jones	.03	.01	.00
□ 143	Dave Van Gorder	.03	.01	.00
□ 144	Doug Sisk	.03	.01	.00
□ 145	Pedro Guerrero	.15	.07	.01
□ 146	Jack Perconte	.03	.01	.00
□ 147	Larry Sheets	.10	.05	.01
□ 148	Mike Heath	.03	.01	.00
□ 149	Brett Butler	.10	.05	.01
□ 150	Joaquin Andujar	.06	.03	.00
□ 151	Dave Stapleton	.03	.01	.00
□ 152	Mike Morgan	.06	.03	.00
□ 153	Ricky Adams	.03	.01	.00
□ 154	Bert Roberge	.03	.01	.00
□ 155	Bob Grich	.06	.03	.00
□ 156	White Sox Leaders	.03	.01	.00
	Richard Dotson			
□ 157	Ron Hassey	.03	.01	.00
□ 158	Derrel Thomas	.03	.01	.00
□ 159	Orel Hershiser UER	.75	.35	.07
	(82 Alburquerque)			
□ 160	Chet Lemon	.03	.01	.00
□ 161	Lee Tunnell	.03	.01	.00
□ 162	Greg Gagne	.10	.05	.01
□ 163	Pete Ladd	.03	.01	.00
□ 164	Steve Balboni	.03	.01	.00
□ 165	Mike Davis	.03	.01	.00
□ 166	Dickie Thon	.03	.01	.00
□ 167	Zane Smith	.25	.12	.02
□ 168	Jeff Burroughs	.03	.01	.00
□ 169	George Wright	.03	.01	.00
□ 170	Gary Carter	.25	.12	.02
□ 171	Bob Rodgers MG ERR	.08	.04	.01
	(checklist back)			
	(number of card on			
	back actually 141)			
□ 172	Jerry Reed	.03	.01	.00
□ 173	Wayne Gross	.03	.01	.00
□ 174	Brian Snyder	.03	.01	.00
□ 175	Steve Sax	.15	.07	.01
□ 176	Jay Tibbs	.03	.01	.00
□ 177	Joel Youngblood	.03	.01	.00
□ 178	Ivan DeJesus	.03	.01	.00
□ 179	Stu Cliburn	.06	.03	.00
□ 180	Don Mattingly	2.75	1.35	.27
□ 181	Al Nipper	.03	.01	.00
□ 182	Bobby Brown	.03	.01	.00
□ 183	Larry Andersen	.03	.01	.00
□ 184	Tim Laudner	.03	.01	.00
□ 185	Rollie Fingers	.12	.06	.01
□ 186	Astros Leaders	.03	.01	.00
	Jose Cruz			
□ 187	Scott Fletcher	.03	.01	.00
□ 188	Bob Dernier	.03	.01	.00
□ 189	Mike Mason	.03	.01	.00
□ 190	George Hendrick	.03	.01	.00
□ 191	Wally Backman	.03	.01	.00
□ 192	Milt Wilcox	.03	.01	.00

□ 193	Daryl Sconiers	.03	.01	.00
□ 194	Craig McMurtry	.03	.01	.00
□ 195	Dave Concepcion	.06	.03	.00
□ 196	Doyle Alexander	.03	.01	.00
□ 197	Enos Cabell	.03	.01	.00
□ 198	Ken Dixon	.03	.01	.00
□ 199	Dick Howser MG	.06	.03	.00
	(checklist back)			
□ 200	Mike Schmidt	.75	.35	.07
□ 201	RB: Vince Coleman	.20	.10	.02
	Most stolen bases,			
	season, rookie			
□ 202	RB: Dwight Gooden	.30	.15	.03
	Youngest 20 game			
	winner			
□ 203	RB: Keith Hernandez	.12	.06	.01
	Most game-winning			
	RBI's			
□ 204	RB: Phil Niekro	.10	.05	.01
	Oldest shutout			
	pitcher			
□ 205	RB: Tony Perez	.10	.05	.01
	Oldest grand slammer			
□ 206	RB: Pete Rose	.35	.17	.03
	Most hits, lifetime			
□ 207	RB: Fern.Valenzuela	.12	.06	.01
	Most cons. innings,			
	start of season,			
	no earned runs			
□ 208	Ramon Romero	.03	.01	.00
□ 209	Randy Ready	.10	.05	.01
□ 210	Calvin Schiraldi	.06	.03	.00
□ 211	Ed Wojna	.03	.01	.00
□ 212	Chris Speier	.03	.01	.00
□ 213	Bob Shirley	.03	.01	.00
□ 214	Randy Bush	.03	.01	.00
□ 215	Frank White	.06	.03	.00
□ 216	A's Leaders	.03	.01	.00
	Dwayne Murphy			
□ 217	Bill Scherrer	.03	.01	.00
□ 218	Randy Hunt	.03	.01	.00
□ 219	Dennis Lamp	.03	.01	.00
□ 220	Bob Horner	.10	.05	.01
□ 221	Dave Henderson	.08	.04	.01
□ 222	Craig Gerber	.03	.01	.00
□ 223	Atlee Hammaker	.03	.01	.00
□ 224	Cesar Cedeno	.06	.03	.00
□ 225	Ron Darling	.15	.07	.01
□ 226	Lee Lacy	.03	.01	.00
□ 227	Al Jones	.03	.01	.00
□ 228	Tom Lawless	.03	.01	.00
□ 229	Bill Gullickson	.03	.01	.00
□ 230	Terry Kennedy	.03	.01	.00
□ 231	Jim Frey MG	.06	.03	.00
	(checklist back)			
□ 232	Rick Rhoden	.03	.01	.00
□ 233	Steve Lyons	.06	.03	.00
□ 234	Doug Corbett	.03	.01	.00
□ 235	Butch Wynegar	.03	.01	.00
□ 236	Frank Eufemia	.03	.01	.00
□ 237	Ted Simmons	.08	.04	.01
□ 238	Larry Parrish	.03	.01	.00
□ 239	Joel Skinner	.03	.01	.00
□ 240	Tommy John	.12	.06	.01
□ 241	Tony Fernandez	.20	.10	.02
□ 242	Rich Thompson	.03	.01	.00
□ 243	Johnny Grubb	.03	.01	.00
□ 244	Craig Lefferts	.06	.03	.00
□ 245	Jim Sundberg	.03	.01	.00
□ 246	Phillies Leaders	.12	.06	.01
	Steve Carlton			
□ 247	Terry Harper	.03	.01	.00
□ 248	Spike Owen	.03	.01	.00
□ 249	Rob Deer	.45	.22	.04
□ 250	Dwight Gooden	1.75	.85	.17
□ 251	Rich Dauer	.03	.01	.00
□ 252	Bobby Castillo	.03	.01	.00
□ 253	Dann Bilardello	.03	.01	.00
□ 254	Ozzie Guillen	1.00	.50	.10
□ 255	Tony Armas	.03	.01	.00
□ 256	Kurt Kepshire	.03	.01	.00
□ 257	Doug DeCinces	.06	.03	.00
□ 258	Tim Burke	.25	.12	.02
□ 259	Dan Pasqua	.15	.07	.01
□ 260	Tony Pena	.08	.04	.01
□ 261	Bobby Valentine MG	.06	.03	.00
	(checklist back)			
□ 262	Mario Ramirez	.03	.01	.00
□ 263	Checklist: 133-264	.06	.01	.00
□ 264	Darren Daulton	.35	.17	.03
□ 265	Ron Davis	.03	.01	.00
□ 266	Keith Moreland	.03	.01	.00
□ 267	Paul Molitor	.12	.06	.01
□ 268	Mike Scott	.20	.10	.02

☐	269	Dane Iorg	.03	.01	.00
☐	270	Jack Morris	.12	.06	.01
☐	271	Dave Collins	.03	.01	.00
☐	272	Tim Tolman	.03	.01	.00
☐	273	Jerry Willard	.03	.01	.00
☐	274	Ron Gardenhire	.03	.01	.00
☐	275	Charlie Hough	.03	.01	.00
☐	276	Yankees Leaders	.03	.01	.00
		Willie Randolph			
☐	277	Jaime Cocanower	.03	.01	.00
☐	278	Sixto Lezcano	.03	.01	.00
☐	279	Al Pardo	.03	.01	.00
☐	280	Tim Raines	.25	.12	.02
☐	281	Steve Mura	.03	.01	.00
☐	282	Jerry Mumphrey	.03	.01	.00
☐	283	Mike Fischlin	.03	.01	.00
☐	284	Brian Dayett	.03	.01	.00
☐	285	Buddy Bell	.06	.03	.00
☐	286	Luis DeLeon	.03	.01	.00
☐	287	John Christensen	.03	.01	.00
☐	288	Don Aase	.03	.01	.00
☐	289	Johnnie LeMaster	.03	.01	.00
☐	290	Carlton Fisk	.30	.15	.03
☐	291	Tom Lasorda MG	.10	.05	.01
		(checklist back)			
☐	292	Chuck Porter	.03	.01	.00
☐	293	Chris Chambliss	.06	.03	.00
☐	294	Danny Cox	.06	.03	.00
☐	295	Kirk Gibson	.25	.12	.02
☐	296	Geno Petralli	.03	.01	.00
☐	297	Tim Lollar	.03	.01	.00
☐	298	Craig Reynolds	.03	.01	.00
☐	299	Bryn Smith	.03	.01	.00
☐	300	George Brett	.50	.25	.05
☐	301	Dennis Rasmussen	.06	.03	.00
☐	302	Greg Gross	.03	.01	.00
☐	303	Curt Wardle	.03	.01	.00
☐	304	Mike Gallego	.03	.01	.00
☐	305	Phil Bradley	.06	.03	.00
☐	306	Padres Leaders	.03	.01	.00
		Terry Kennedy			
☐	307	Dave Sax	.03	.01	.00
☐	308	Ray Fontenot	.03	.01	.00
☐	309	John Shelby	.03	.01	.00
☐	310	Greg Minton	.03	.01	.00
☐	311	Dick Schofield	.03	.01	.00
☐	312	Tom Filer	.03	.01	.00
☐	313	Joe DeSa	.03	.01	.00
☐	314	Frank Pastore	.03	.01	.00
☐	315	Mookie Wilson	.06	.03	.00
☐	316	Sammy Khalifa	.03	.01	.00
☐	317	Ed Romero	.03	.01	.00
☐	318	Terry Whitfield	.03	.01	.00
☐	319	Rick Camp	.03	.01	.00
☐	320	Jim Rice	.18	.09	.01
☐	321	Earl Weaver MG	.06	.03	.00
		(checklist back)			
☐	322	Bob Forsch	.03	.01	.00
☐	323	Jerry Davis	.03	.01	.00
☐	324	Dan Schatzeder	.03	.01	.00
☐	325	Juan Beniquez	.03	.01	.00
☐	326	Kent Tekulve	.03	.01	.00
☐	327	Mike Pagliarulo	.08	.04	.01
☐	328	Pete O'Brien	.08	.04	.01
☐	329	Kirby Puckett	2.50	1.25	.25
☐	330	Rick Sutcliffe	.10	.05	.01
☐	331	Alan Ashby	.03	.01	.00
☐	332	Darryl Motley	.03	.01	.00
☐	333	Tom Henke	.18	.09	.01
☐	334	Ken Oberkfell	.03	.01	.00
☐	335	Don Sutton	.15	.07	.01
☐	336	Indians Leaders	.03	.01	.00
		Andre Thornton			
☐	337	Darnell Coles	.03	.01	.00
☐	338	Jorge Bell	.25	.12	.02
☐	339	Bruce Berenyi	.03	.01	.00
☐	340	Cal Ripken	.50	.25	.05
☐	341	Frank Williams	.03	.01	.00
☐	342	Gary Redus	.03	.01	.00
☐	343	Carlos Diaz	.03	.01	.00
☐	344	Jim Wohlford	.03	.01	.00
☐	345	Donnie Moore	.03	.01	.00
☐	346	Bryan Little	.03	.01	.00
☐	347	Teddy Higuera	.90	.45	.09
☐	348	Cliff Johnson	.03	.01	.00
☐	349	Mark Clear	.03	.01	.00
☐	350	Jack Clark	.20	.10	.02
☐	351	Chuck Tanner MG	.06	.03	.00
		(checklist back)			
☐	352	Harry Spilman	.03	.01	.00
☐	353	Keith Atherton	.03	.01	.00
☐	354	Tony Bernazard	.03	.01	.00
☐	355	Lee Smith	.06	.03	.00
☐	356	Mickey Hatcher	.03	.01	.00

☐	357	Ed VandeBerg	.03	.01	.00
☐	358	Rick Dempsey	.03	.01	.00
☐	359	Mike LaCoss	.03	.01	.00
☐	360	Lloyd Moseby	.06	.03	.00
☐	361	Shane Rawley	.03	.01	.00
☐	362	Tom Paciorek	.03	.01	.00
☐	363	Terry Forster	.06	.03	.00
☐	364	Reid Nichols	.03	.01	.00
☐	365	Mike Flanagan	.06	.03	.00
☐	366	Reds Leaders	.03	.01	.00
		Dave Concepcion			
☐	367	Aurelio Lopez	.03	.01	.00
☐	368	Greg Brock	.03	.01	.00
☐	369	Al Holland	.03	.01	.00
☐	370	Vince Coleman	2.25	1.10	.22
☐	371	Bill Stein	.03	.01	.00
☐	372	Ben Oglivie	.06	.03	.00
☐	373	Urbano Lugo	.03	.01	.00
☐	374	Terry Francona	.03	.01	.00
☐	375	Rich Gedman	.03	.01	.00
☐	376	Bill Dawley	.03	.01	.00
☐	377	Joe Carter	.40	.20	.04
☐	378	Bruce Bochte	.03	.01	.00
☐	379	Bobby Meacham	.03	.01	.00
☐	380	LaMarr Hoyt	.06	.03	.00
☐	381	Ray Miller MG	.06	.03	.00
		(checklist back)			
☐	382	Ivan Calderon	.90	.45	.09
☐	383	Chris Brown	.10	.05	.01
☐	384	Steve Trout	.03	.01	.00
☐	385	Cecil Cooper	.08	.04	.01
☐	386	Cecil Fielder	6.50	3.25	.65
☐	387	Steve Kemp	.03	.01	.00
☐	388	Dickie Noles	.03	.01	.00
☐	389	Glenn Davis	3.00	1.50	.30
☐	390	Tom Seaver	.35	.17	.03
☐	391	Julio Franco	.20	.10	.02
☐	392	John Russell	.03	.01	.00
☐	393	Chris Pittaro	.03	.01	.00
☐	394	Checklist: 265-396	.06	.01	.00
☐	395	Scott Garrelts	.25	.12	.02
☐	396	Red Sox Leaders	.08	.04	.01
		Dwight Evans			
☐	397	Steve Buechele	.18	.09	.01
☐	398	Earnie Riles	.15	.07	.01
☐	399	Bill Swift	.06	.03	.00
☐	400	Rod Carew	.35	.17	.03
☐	401	Turn Back 5 Years	.10	.05	.01
		Fern.Valenzuela '81			
☐	402	Turn Back 10 Years	.15	.07	.01
		Tom Seaver '76			
☐	403	Turn Back 15 Years	.15	.07	.01
		Willie Mays '71			
☐	404	Turn Back 20 Years	.10	.05	.01
		Frank Robinson '66			
☐	405	Turn Back 25 Years	.15	.07	.01
		Roger Maris '61			
☐	406	Scott Sanderson	.06	.03	.00
☐	407	Sal Butera	.03	.01	.00
☐	408	Dave Smith	.06	.03	.00
☐	409	Paul Runge	.03	.01	.00
☐	410	Dave Kingman	.08	.04	.01
☐	411	Sparky Anderson MG	.06	.03	.00
		(checklist back)			
☐	412	Jim Clancy	.03	.01	.00
☐	413	Tim Flannery	.03	.01	.00
☐	414	Tom Gorman	.03	.01	.00
☐	415	Hal McRae	.06	.03	.00
☐	416	Dennis Martinez	.06	.03	.00
☐	417	R.J. Reynolds	.03	.01	.00
☐	418	Alan Knicely	.03	.01	.00
☐	419	Frank Wills	.03	.01	.00
☐	420	Von Hayes	.08	.04	.01
☐	421	David Palmer	.03	.01	.00
☐	422	Mike Jorgensen	.03	.01	.00
☐	423	Dan Spillner	.03	.01	.00
☐	424	Rick Miller	.03	.01	.00
☐	425	Larry McWilliams	.03	.01	.00
☐	426	Brewers Leaders	.03	.01	.00
		Charlie Moore			
☐	427	Joe Cowley	.03	.01	.00
☐	428	Max Venable	.03	.01	.00
☐	429	Greg Booker	.03	.01	.00
☐	430	Kent Hrbek	.15	.07	.01
☐	431	George Frazier	.03	.01	.00
☐	432	Mark Bailey	.03	.01	.00
☐	433	Chris Codiroli	.03	.01	.00
☐	434	Curt Wilkerson	.03	.01	.00
☐	435	Bill Caudill	.03	.01	.00
☐	436	Doug Flynn	.03	.01	.00
☐	437	Rick Mahler	.03	.01	.00
☐	438	Clint Hurdle	.03	.01	.00
☐	439	Rick Honeycutt	.03	.01	.00
☐	440	Alvin Davis	.15	.07	.01

☐ 441	Whitey Herzog MG	.06	.03	.00
	(checklist back)			
☐ 442	Ron Robinson	.12	.06	.01
☐ 443	Bill Buckner	.06	.03	.00
☐ 444	Alex Trevino	.03	.01	.00
☐ 445	Bert Blyleven	.10	.05	.01
☐ 446	Lenn Sakata	.03	.01	.00
☐ 447	Jerry Don Gleaton	.03	.01	.00
☐ 448	Herm Winningham	.10	.05	.01
☐ 449	Rod Scurry	.03	.01	.00
☐ 450	Graig Nettles	.10	.05	.01
☐ 451	Mark Brown	.03	.01	.00
☐ 452	Bob Clark	.03	.01	.00
☐ 453	Steve Jeltz	.03	.01	.00
☐ 454	Burt Hooton	.03	.01	.00
☐ 455	Willie Randolph	.06	.03	.00
☐ 456	Braves Leaders	.12	.06	.01
	Dale Murphy			
☐ 457	Mickey Tettleton	.45	.22	.04
☐ 458	Kevin Bass	.08	.04	.01
☐ 459	Luis Leal	.03	.01	.00
☐ 460	Leon Durham	.03	.01	.00
☐ 461	Walt Terrell	.03	.01	.00
☐ 462	Domingo Ramos	.03	.01	.00
☐ 463	Jim Gott	.06	.03	.00
☐ 464	Ruppert Jones	.03	.01	.00
☐ 465	Jesse Orosco	.03	.01	.00
☐ 466	Tom Foley	.03	.01	.00
☐ 467	Bob James	.03	.01	.00
☐ 468	Mike Scioscia	.03	.01	.00
☐ 469	Storm Davis	.06	.03	.00
☐ 470	Bill Madlock	.08	.04	.01
☐ 471	Bobby Cox MG	.06	.03	.00
	(checklist back)			
☐ 472	Joe Hesketh	.06	.03	.00
☐ 473	Mark Brouhard	.03	.01	.00
☐ 474	John Tudor	.10	.05	.01
☐ 475	Juan Samuel	.10	.05	.01
☐ 476	Ron Mathis	.03	.01	.00
☐ 477	Mike Easler	.03	.01	.00
☐ 478	Andy Hawkins	.06	.03	.00
☐ 479	Bob Melvin	.08	.04	.01
☐ 480	Oddibe McDowell	.12	.06	.01
☐ 481	Scott Bradley	.10	.05	.01
☐ 482	Rick Lysander	.03	.01	.00
☐ 483	George Vukovich	.03	.01	.00
☐ 484	Donnie Hill	.03	.01	.00
☐ 485	Gary Matthews	.03	.01	.00
☐ 486	Angels Leaders	.03	.01	.00
	Bobby Grich			
☐ 487	Bret Saberhagen	.65	.30	.06
☐ 488	Lou Thornton	.06	.03	.00
☐ 489	Jim Winn	.03	.01	.00
☐ 490	Jeff Leonard	.06	.03	.00
☐ 491	Pascual Perez	.08	.04	.01
☐ 492	Kelvin Chapman	.03	.01	.00
☐ 493	Gene Nelson	.03	.01	.00
☐ 494	Gary Roenicke	.03	.01	.00
☐ 495	Mark Langston	.25	.12	.02
☐ 496	Jay Johnstone	.06	.03	.00
☐ 497	John Stuper	.03	.01	.00
☐ 498	Tito Landrum	.03	.01	.00
☐ 499	Bob L. Gibson	.03	.01	.00
☐ 500	Rickey Henderson	1.00	.50	.10
☐ 501	Dave Johnson MG	.06	.03	.00
	(checklist back)			
☐ 502	Glen Cook	.03	.01	.00
☐ 503	Mike Fitzgerald	.03	.01	.00
☐ 504	Denny Walling	.03	.01	.00
☐ 505	Jerry Koosman	.06	.03	.00
☐ 506	Bill Russell	.03	.01	.00
☐ 507	Steve Ontiveros	.08	.04	.01
☐ 508	Alan Wiggins	.03	.01	.00
☐ 509	Ernie Camacho	.03	.01	.00
☐ 510	Wade Boggs	1.50	.75	.15
☐ 511	Ed Nunez	.03	.01	.00
☐ 512	Thad Bosley	.03	.01	.00
☐ 513	Ron Washington	.03	.01	.00
☐ 514	Mike Jones	.03	.01	.00
☐ 515	Darrell Evans	.08	.04	.01
☐ 516	Giants Leaders	.03	.01	.00
	Greg Minton			
☐ 517	Milt Thompson	.20	.10	.02
☐ 518	Buck Martinez	.03	.01	.00
☐ 519	Danny Darwin	.03	.01	.00
☐ 520	Keith Hernandez	.20	.10	.02
☐ 521	Nate Snell	.03	.01	.00
☐ 522	Bob Bailor	.03	.01	.00
☐ 523	Joe Price	.03	.01	.00
☐ 524	Darrell Miller	.06	.03	.00
☐ 525	Marvell Wynne	.03	.01	.00
☐ 526	Charlie Lea	.03	.01	.00
☐ 527	Checklist: 397-528	.06	.01	.00
☐ 528	Terry Pendleton	.06	.03	.00
☐ 529	Marc Sullivan	.03	.01	.00
☐ 530	Rich Gossage	.10	.05	.01
☐ 531	Tony LaRussa MG	.06	.03	.00
	(checklist back)			
☐ 532	Don Carman	.18	.09	.01
☐ 533	Billy Sample	.03	.01	.00
☐ 534	Jeff Calhoun	.03	.01	.00
☐ 535	Toby Harrah	.03	.01	.00
☐ 536	Jose Rijo	.15	.07	.01
☐ 537	Mark Salas	.03	.01	.00
☐ 538	Dennis Eckersley	.15	.07	.01
☐ 539	Glenn Hubbard	.03	.01	.00
☐ 540	Dan Petry	.03	.01	.00
☐ 541	Jorge Orta	.03	.01	.00
☐ 542	Don Schulze	.03	.01	.00
☐ 543	Jerry Narron	.03	.01	.00
☐ 544	Eddie Milner	.03	.01	.00
☐ 545	Jimmy Key	.10	.05	.01
☐ 546	Mariners Leaders	.03	.01	.00
	Dave Henderson			
☐ 547	Roger McDowell	.30	.15	.03
☐ 548	Mike Young	.03	.01	.00
☐ 549	Bob Welch	.12	.06	.01
☐ 550	Tom Herr	.06	.03	.00
☐ 551	Dave LaPoint	.03	.01	.00
☐ 552	Marc Hill	.03	.01	.00
☐ 553	Jim Morrison	.03	.01	.00
☐ 554	Paul Householder	.03	.01	.00
☐ 555	Hubie Brooks	.10	.05	.01
☐ 556	John Denny	.03	.01	.00
☐ 557	Gerald Perry	.08	.04	.01
☐ 558	Tim Stoddard	.03	.01	.00
☐ 559	Tommy Dunbar	.03	.01	.00
☐ 560	Dave Righetti	.10	.05	.01
☐ 561	Bob Lillis MG	.06	.03	.00
	(checklist back)			
☐ 562	Joe Beckwith	.03	.01	.00
☐ 563	Alejandro Sanchez	.03	.01	.00
☐ 564	Warren Brusstar	.03	.01	.00
☐ 565	Tom Brunansky	.12	.06	.01
☐ 566	Alfredo Griffin	.03	.01	.00
☐ 567	Jeff Barkley	.03	.01	.00
☐ 568	Donnie Scott	.03	.01	.00
☐ 569	Jim Acker	.03	.01	.00
☐ 570	Rusty Staub	.08	.04	.01
☐ 571	Mike Jeffcoat	.03	.01	.00
☐ 572	Paul Zuvella	.03	.01	.00
☐ 573	Tom Hume	.03	.01	.00
☐ 574	Ron Kittle	.10	.05	.01
☐ 575	Mike Boddicker	.08	.04	.01
☐ 576	Expos Leaders	.10	.05	.01
	Andre Dawson			
☐ 577	Jerry Reuss	.03	.01	.00
☐ 578	Lee Mazzilli	.03	.01	.00
☐ 579	Jim Slaton	.03	.01	.00
☐ 580	Willie McGee	.15	.07	.01
☐ 581	Bruce Hurst	.10	.05	.01
☐ 582	Jim Gantner	.03	.01	.00
☐ 583	Al Bumbry	.03	.01	.00
☐ 584	Brian Fisher	.12	.06	.01
☐ 585	Garry Maddox	.03	.01	.00
☐ 586	Greg Harris	.03	.01	.00
☐ 587	Rafael Santana	.03	.01	.00
☐ 588	Steve Lake	.03	.01	.00
☐ 589	Sid Bream	.03	.01	.00
☐ 590	Bob Knepper	.03	.01	.00
☐ 591	Jackie Moore MG	.06	.03	.00
	(checklist back)			
☐ 592	Frank Tanana	.06	.03	.00
☐ 593	Jesse Barfield	.12	.06	.01
☐ 594	Chris Bando	.03	.01	.00
☐ 595	Dave Parker	.15	.07	.01
☐ 596	Onix Concepcion	.03	.01	.00
☐ 597	Sammy Stewart	.03	.01	.00
☐ 598	Jim Presley	.15	.07	.01
☐ 599	Rick Aguilera	.30	.15	.03
☐ 600	Dale Murphy	.30	.15	.03
☐ 601	Gary Lucas	.03	.01	.00
☐ 602	Mariano Duncan	.30	.15	.03
☐ 603	Bill Laskey	.03	.01	.00
☐ 604	Gary Pettis	.06	.03	.00
☐ 605	Dennis Boyd	.08	.04	.01
☐ 606	Royals Leaders	.03	.01	.00
	Hal McRae			
☐ 607	Ken Dayley	.03	.01	.00
☐ 608	Bruce Bochy	.03	.01	.00
☐ 609	Barbaro Garbey	.03	.01	.00
☐ 610	Ron Guidry	.10	.05	.01
☐ 611	Gary Woods	.03	.01	.00
☐ 612	Richard Dotson	.03	.01	.00
☐ 613	Roy Smalley	.03	.01	.00
☐ 614	Rick Waits	.03	.01	.00
☐ 615	Johnny Ray	.06	.03	.00
☐ 616	Glenn Brummer	.03	.01	.00

☐ 617	Lonnie Smith	.08	.04	.01
☐ 618	Jim Pankovits	.03	.01	.00
☐ 619	Danny Heep	.03	.01	.00
☐ 620	Bruce Sutter	.10	.05	.01
☐ 621	John Felske MG (checklist back)	.06	.03	.00
☐ 622	Gary Lavelle	.03	.01	.00
☐ 623	Floyd Rayford	.03	.01	.00
☐ 624	Steve McCatty	.03	.01	.00
☐ 625	Bob Brenly	.03	.01	.00
☐ 626	Roy Thomas	.03	.01	.00
☐ 627	Ron Oester	.03	.01	.00
☐ 628	Kirk McCaskill	.35	.17	.03
☐ 629	Mitch Webster	.20	.10	.02
☐ 630	Fernando Valenzuela	.20	.10	.02
☐ 631	Steve Braun	.03	.01	.00
☐ 632	Dave Von Ohlen	.03	.01	.00
☐ 633	Jackie Gutierrez	.03	.01	.00
☐ 634	Roy Lee Jackson	.03	.01	.00
☐ 635	Jason Thompson	.03	.01	.00
☐ 636	Cubs Leaders Lee Smith	.03	.01	.00
☐ 637	Rudy Law	.03	.01	.00
☐ 638	John Butcher	.03	.01	.00
☐ 639	Bo Diaz	.03	.01	.00
☐ 640	Jose Cruz	.06	.03	.00
☐ 641	Wayne Tolleson	.03	.01	.00
☐ 642	Ray Searage	.03	.01	.00
☐ 643	Tom Brookens	.03	.01	.00
☐ 644	Mark Gubicza	.18	.09	.01
☐ 645	Dusty Baker	.06	.03	.00
☐ 646	Mike Moore	.08	.04	.01
☐ 647	Mel Hall	.08	.04	.01
☐ 648	Steve Bedrosian	.10	.05	.01
☐ 649	Ronn Reynolds	.03	.01	.00
☐ 650	Dave Stieb	.12	.06	.01
☐ 651	Billy Martin MG (checklist back)	.12	.06	.01
☐ 652	Tom Browning	.25	.12	.02
☐ 653	Jim Dwyer	.03	.01	.00
☐ 654	Ken Howell	.10	.05	.01
☐ 655	Manny Trillo	.03	.01	.00
☐ 656	Brian Harper	.08	.04	.01
☐ 657	Juan Agosto	.03	.01	.00
☐ 658	Rob Wilfong	.03	.01	.00
☐ 659	Checklist: 529-660	.06	.01	.00
☐ 660	Steve Garvey	.35	.17	.03
☐ 661	Roger Clemens	2.50	1.25	.25
☐ 662	Bill Schroeder	.03	.01	.00
☐ 663	Neil Allen	.03	.01	.00
☐ 664	Tim Corcoran	.03	.01	.00
☐ 665	Alejandro Pena	.03	.01	.00
☐ 666	Rangers Leaders Charlie Hough	.03	.01	.00
☐ 667	Tim Teufel	.03	.01	.00
☐ 668	Cecilio Guante	.03	.01	.00
☐ 669	Ron Cey	.06	.03	.00
☐ 670	Willie Hernandez	.06	.03	.00
☐ 671	Lynn Jones	.03	.01	.00
☐ 672	Rob Picciolo	.03	.01	.00
☐ 673	Ernie Whitt	.03	.01	.00
☐ 674	Pat Tabler	.08	.04	.01
☐ 675	Claudell Washington	.06	.03	.00
☐ 676	Matt Young	.03	.01	.00
☐ 677	Nick Esasky	.08	.04	.01
☐ 678	Dan Gladden	.06	.03	.00
☐ 679	Britt Burns	.03	.01	.00
☐ 680	George Foster	.10	.05	.01
☐ 681	Dick Williams MG (checklist back)	.06	.03	.00
☐ 682	Junior Ortiz	.03	.01	.00
☐ 683	Andy Van Slyke	.20	.10	.02
☐ 684	Bob McClure	.03	.01	.00
☐ 685	Tim Wallach	.10	.05	.01
☐ 686	Jeff Stone	.03	.01	.00
☐ 687	Mike Trujillo	.03	.01	.00
☐ 688	Larry Herndon	.03	.01	.00
☐ 689	Dave Stewart	.35	.17	.03
☐ 690	Ryne Sandberg UER (no Topps logo on front)	1.50	.75	.15
☐ 691	Mike Madden	.03	.01	.00
☐ 692	Dale Berra	.03	.01	.00
☐ 693	Tom Tellmann	.03	.01	.00
☐ 694	Garth Iorg	.03	.01	.00
☐ 695	Mike Smithson	.03	.01	.00
☐ 696	Dodgers Leaders Bill Russell	.03	.01	.00
☐ 697	Bud Black	.06	.03	.00
☐ 698	Brad Komminsk	.03	.01	.00
☐ 699	Pat Corrales MG (checklist back)	.06	.03	.00
☐ 700	Reggie Jackson	.35	.17	.03
☐ 701	Keith Hernandez AS	.10	.05	.01
☐ 702	Tom Herr AS	.06	.03	.00
☐ 703	Tim Wallach AS	.06	.03	.00
☐ 704	Ozzie Smith AS	.10	.05	.01
☐ 705	Dale Murphy AS	.18	.09	.01
☐ 706	Pedro Guerrero AS	.10	.05	.01
☐ 707	Willie McGee AS	.08	.04	.01
☐ 708	Gary Carter AS	.15	.07	.01
☐ 709	Dwight Gooden AS	.30	.15	.03
☐ 710	John Tudor AS	.06	.03	.00
☐ 711	Jeff Reardon AS	.06	.03	.00
☐ 712	Don Mattingly AS	.75	.35	.07
☐ 713	Damaso Garcia AS	.06	.03	.00
☐ 714	George Brett AS	.25	.12	.02
☐ 715	Cal Ripken AS	.20	.10	.02
☐ 716	Rickey Henderson AS	.30	.15	.03
☐ 717	Dave Winfield AS	.15	.07	.01
☐ 718	George Bell AS	.10	.05	.01
☐ 719	Carlton Fisk AS	.12	.06	.01
☐ 720	Bret Saberhagen AS	.10	.05	.01
☐ 721	Ron Guidry AS	.06	.03	.00
☐ 722	Dan Quisenberry AS	.06	.03	.00
☐ 723	Marty Bystrom	.03	.01	.00
☐ 724	Tim Hulett	.03	.01	.00
☐ 725	Mario Soto	.03	.01	.00
☐ 726	Orioles Leaders Rick Dempsey	.03	.01	.00
☐ 727	David Green	.03	.01	.00
☐ 728	Mike Marshall	.10	.05	.01
☐ 729	Jim Beattie	.03	.01	.00
☐ 730	Ozzie Smith	.18	.09	.01
☐ 731	Don Robinson	.03	.01	.00
☐ 732	Floyd Youmans	.15	.07	.01
☐ 733	Ron Romanick	.03	.01	.00
☐ 734	Marty Barrett	.06	.03	.00
☐ 735	Dave Dravecky	.08	.04	.01
☐ 736	Glenn Wilson	.03	.01	.00
☐ 737	Pete Vuckovich	.03	.01	.00
☐ 738	Andre Robertson	.03	.01	.00
☐ 739	Dave Rozema	.03	.01	.00
☐ 740	Lance Parrish	.12	.06	.01
☐ 741	Pete Rose MG (checklist back)	.35	.17	.03
☐ 742	Frank Viola	.25	.12	.02
☐ 743	Pat Sheridan	.03	.01	.00
☐ 744	Lary Sorensen	.03	.01	.00
☐ 745	Willie Upshaw	.03	.01	.00
☐ 746	Denny Gonzalez	.03	.01	.00
☐ 747	Rick Cerone	.03	.01	.00
☐ 748	Steve Henderson	.03	.01	.00
☐ 749	Ed Jurak	.03	.01	.00
☐ 750	Gorman Thomas	.06	.03	.00
☐ 751	Howard Johnson	.30	.15	.03
☐ 752	Mike Krukow	.03	.01	.00
☐ 753	Dan Ford	.03	.01	.00
☐ 754	Pat Clements	.06	.03	.00
☐ 755	Harold Baines	.10	.05	.01
☐ 756	Pirates Leaders Rick Rhoden	.03	.01	.00
☐ 757	Darrell Porter	.03	.01	.00
☐ 758	Dave Anderson	.03	.01	.00
☐ 759	Moose Haas	.03	.01	.00
☐ 760	Andre Dawson	.35	.17	.03
☐ 761	Don Slaught	.03	.01	.00
☐ 762	Eric Show	.03	.01	.00
☐ 763	Terry Puhl	.03	.01	.00
☐ 764	Kevin Gross	.03	.01	.00
☐ 765	Don Baylor	.10	.05	.01
☐ 766	Rick Langford	.03	.01	.00
☐ 767	Jody Davis	.06	.03	.00
☐ 768	Vern Ruhle	.03	.01	.00
☐ 769	Harold Reynolds	.60	.30	.06
☐ 770	Vida Blue	.06	.03	.00
☐ 771	John McNamara MG (checklist back)	.06	.03	.00
☐ 772	Brian Downing	.03	.01	.00
☐ 773	Greg Pryor	.03	.01	.00
☐ 774	Terry Leach	.06	.03	.00
☐ 775	Al Oliver	.08	.04	.01
☐ 776	Gene Garber	.03	.01	.00
☐ 777	Wayne Krenchicki	.03	.01	.00
☐ 778	Jerry Hairston	.03	.01	.00
☐ 779	Rick Reuschel	.10	.05	.01
☐ 780	Robin Yount	.35	.17	.03
☐ 781	Joe Nolan	.03	.01	.00
☐ 782	Ken Landreaux	.03	.01	.00
☐ 783	Ricky Horton	.03	.01	.00
☐ 784	Alan Bannister	.03	.01	.00
☐ 785	Bob Stanley	.03	.01	.00
☐ 786	Twins Leaders Mickey Hatcher	.03	.01	.00
☐ 787	Vance Law	.03	.01	.00
☐ 788	Marty Castillo	.03	.01	.00
☐ 789	Kurt Bevacqua	.03	.01	.00
☐ 790	Phil Niekro	.15	.07	.01

		MINT	EXC	G-VG
☐ 791	Checklist: 661-792	.06	.01	.00
☐ 792	Charles Hudson	.06	.03	.00

1986 Topps Wax Box Cards

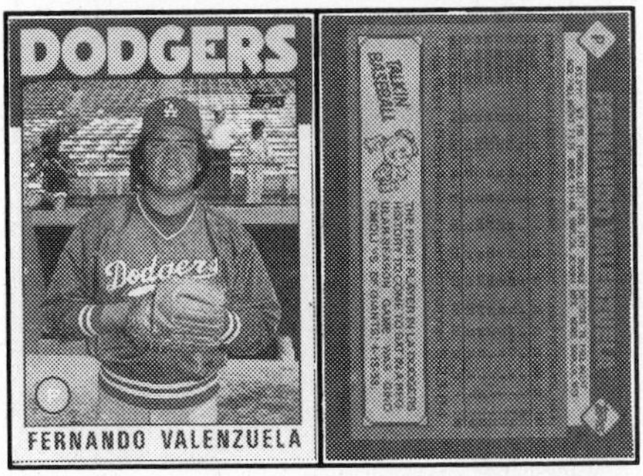

Topps printed cards (each measuring the standard 2 1/2" by 3 1/2") on the bottoms of their wax pack boxes for their regular issue cards; there are four different boxes, each with four cards. These sixteen cards ("numbered" A through P) are listed below; they are not considered an integral part of the regular set but are considered a separate set. They are styled almost exactly like the 1986 Topps regular issue cards.

	MINT	EXC	G-VG
COMPLETE SET (16)	6.00	3.00	.60
COMMON PLAYER (A-P)	.10	.05	.01
☐ A Jorge Bell	.25	.12	.02
☐ B Wade Boggs	.75	.35	.07
☐ C George Brett	.50	.25	.05
☐ D Vince Coleman	1.00	.50	.10
☐ E Carlton Fisk	.30	.15	.03
☐ F Dwight Gooden	.75	.35	.07
☐ G Pedro Guerrero	.20	.10	.02
☐ H Ron Guidry	.15	.07	.01
☐ I Reggie Jackson	.50	.25	.05
☐ J Don Mattingly	1.25	.60	.12
☐ K Oddibe McDowell	.15	.07	.01
☐ L Willie McGee	.20	.10	.02
☐ M Dale Murphy	.50	.25	.05
☐ N Pete Rose	1.00	.50	.10
☐ O Bret Saberhagen	.35	.17	.03
☐ P Fernando Valenzuela	.15	.07	.01

1986 Topps Glossy 22

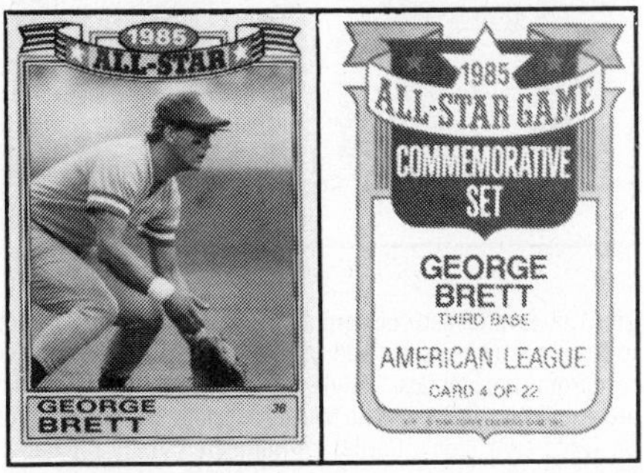

This 22-card set was distributed as an insert, one card per rak pack. The players featured are the starting lineups of the 1985 All-Star Game played in Minnesota. Cards are very colorful with a high gloss finish and are standard-size, 2 1/2" by 3 1/2". Cards are numbered on the back.

	MINT	EXC	G-VG
COMPLETE SET (22)	3.50	1.75	.35
COMMON PLAYER (1-22)	.10	.05	.01
☐ 1 Sparky Anderson MG	.10	.05	.01
☐ 2 Eddie Murray	.25	.12	.02
☐ 3 Lou Whitaker	.15	.07	.01
☐ 4 George Brett	.40	.20	.04
☐ 5 Cal Ripken	.35	.17	.03
☐ 6 Jim Rice	.25	.12	.02
☐ 7 Rickey Henderson	.50	.25	.05
☐ 8 Dave Winfield	.30	.15	.03
☐ 9 Carlton Fisk	.30	.15	.03
☐ 10 Jack Morris	.15	.07	.01
☐ 11 AL Team Photo	.10	.05	.01
☐ 12 Dick Williams MG	.10	.05	.01
☐ 13 Steve Garvey	.30	.15	.03
☐ 14 Tom Herr	.10	.05	.01
☐ 15 Graig Nettles	.15	.07	.01
☐ 16 Ozzie Smith	.25	.12	.02
☐ 17 Tony Gwynn	.45	.22	.04
☐ 18 Dale Murphy	.45	.22	.04
☐ 19 Darryl Strawberry	.50	.25	.05
☐ 20 Terry Kennedy	.10	.05	.01
☐ 21 LaMarr Hoyt	.10	.05	.01
☐ 22 NL Team Photo	.10	.05	.01

1986 Topps Glossy 60

This 60-card glossy set was produced by Topps and distributed ten cards at a time based on the offer found on the wax packs. Cards measure the standard 2 1/2" by 3 1/2". Each series of ten cards was available by sending in 1.00 plus six "special offer" cards inserted one per wax pack. The card backs are printed in red and blue on white card stock. The card fronts feature a white border and a green frame surrounding a full-color photo of the player.

	MINT	EXC	G-VG
COMPLETE SET (60)	12.00	6.00	1.20
COMMON PLAYER (1-60)	.20	.10	.02
☐ 1 Oddibe McDowell	.20	.10	.02
☐ 2 Reggie Jackson	.60	.30	.06
☐ 3 Fernando Valenzuela	.30	.15	.03
☐ 4 Jack Clark	.30	.15	.03
☐ 5 Rickey Henderson	.75	.35	.07
☐ 6 Steve Balboni	.20	.10	.02
☐ 7 Keith Hernandez	.25	.12	.02
☐ 8 Lance Parrish	.25	.12	.02
☐ 9 Willie McGee	.25	.12	.02
☐ 10 Chris Brown	.20	.10	.02
☐ 11 Darryl Strawberry	.60	.30	.06
☐ 12 Ron Guidry	.25	.12	.02
☐ 13 Dave Parker	.30	.15	.03
☐ 14 Cal Ripken	.35	.17	.03
☐ 15 Tim Raines	.30	.15	.03
☐ 16 Rod Carew	.45	.22	.04
☐ 17 Mike Schmidt	.75	.35	.07
☐ 18 George Brett	.60	.30	.06

☐	19 Joe Hesketh	.20	.10	.02
☐	20 Dan Pasqua	.20	.10	.02
☐	21 Vince Coleman	.50	.25	.05
☐	22 Tom Seaver	.40	.20	.04
☐	23 Gary Carter	.30	.15	.03
☐	24 Orel Hershiser	.50	.25	.05
☐	25 Pedro Guerrero	.30	.15	.03
☐	26 Wade Boggs	.75	.35	.07
☐	27 Bret Saberhagen	.35	.17	.03
☐	28 Carlton Fisk	.35	.17	.03
☐	29 Kirk Gibson	.35	.17	.03
☐	30 Brian Fisher	.20	.10	.02
☐	31 Don Mattingly	1.25	.60	.12
☐	32 Tom Herr	.20	.10	.02
☐	33 Eddie Murray	.45	.22	.04
☐	34 Ryne Sandberg	.75	.35	.07
☐	35 Dan Quisenberry	.25	.12	.02
☐	36 Jim Rice	.30	.15	.03
☐	37 Dale Murphy	.50	.25	.05
☐	38 Steve Garvey	.40	.20	.04
☐	39 Roger McDowell	.20	.10	.02
☐	40 Earnie Riles	.20	.10	.02
☐	41 Dwight Gooden	.75	.35	.07
☐	42 Dave Winfield	.35	.17	.03
☐	43 Dave Stieb	.25	.12	.02
☐	44 Bob Horner	.25	.12	.02
☐	45 Nolan Ryan	1.25	.60	.12
☐	46 Ozzie Smith	.30	.15	.03
☐	47 Jorge Bell	.30	.15	.03
☐	48 Gorman Thomas	.20	.10	.02
☐	49 Tom Browning	.25	.12	.02
☐	50 Larry Sheets	.20	.10	.02
☐	51 Pete Rose	1.00	.50	.10
☐	52 Brett Butler	.25	.12	.02
☐	53 John Tudor	.25	.12	.02
☐	54 Phil Bradley	.20	.10	.02
☐	55 Jeff Reardon	.20	.10	.02
☐	56 Rich Gossage	.25	.12	.02
☐	57 Tony Gwynn	.50	.25	.05
☐	58 Ozzie Guillen	.25	.12	.02
☐	59 Glenn Davis	.40	.20	.04
☐	60 Darrell Evans	.20	.10	.02

1986 Topps Mini Leaders

The 1986 Topps Mini set of Major League Leaders features 66 cards of leaders of the various statistical categories for the 1985 season. The cards are numbered on the back and measure 2 1/8" by 2 15/16". They are very similar in design to the Team Leader "Dean" cards in the 1986 Topps regular issue.

		MINT	EXC	G-VG
	COMPLETE SET (66)	7.00	3.50	.70
	COMMON PLAYER (1-66)	.05	.02	.00
☐	1 Eddie Murray	.30	.15	.03
☐	2 Cal Ripken	.30	.15	.03
☐	3 Wade Boggs	.50	.25	.05
☐	4 Dennis Boyd	.05	.02	.00
☐	5 Dwight Evans	.15	.07	.01
☐	6 Bruce Hurst	.10	.05	.01
☐	7 Gary Pettis	.05	.02	.00
☐	8 Harold Baines	.10	.05	.01
☐	9 Floyd Bannister	.05	.02	.00
☐	10 Britt Burns	.05	.02	.00
☐	11 Carlton Fisk	.20	.10	.02
☐	12 Brett Butler	.10	.05	.01
☐	13 Darrell Evans	.10	.05	.01
☐	14 Jack Morris	.10	.05	.01
☐	15 Lance Parrish	.15	.07	.01
☐	16 Walt Terrell	.05	.02	.00
☐	17 Steve Balboni	.05	.02	.00
☐	18 George Brett	.30	.15	.03
☐	19 Charlie Leibrandt	.05	.02	.00
☐	20 Bret Saberhagen	.20	.10	.02
☐	21 Lonnie Smith	.10	.05	.01
☐	22 Willie Wilson	.10	.05	.01
☐	23 Bert Blyleven	.10	.05	.01
☐	24 Mike Smithson	.05	.02	.00
☐	25 Frank Viola	.20	.10	.02
☐	26 Ron Guidry	.10	.05	.01
☐	27 Rickey Henderson	.50	.25	.05
☐	28 Don Mattingly	.90	.45	.09
☐	29 Dave Winfield	.25	.12	.02
☐	30 Mike Moore	.10	.05	.01
☐	31 Gorman Thomas	.10	.05	.01
☐	32 Toby Harrah	.05	.02	.00
☐	33 Charlie Hough	.05	.02	.00
☐	34 Doyle Alexander	.10	.05	.01
☐	35 Jimmy Key	.05	.02	.00
☐	36 Dave Stieb	.10	.05	.01
☐	37 Dale Murphy	.25	.12	.02
☐	38 Keith Moreland	.05	.02	.00
☐	39 Ryne Sandberg	.50	.25	.05
☐	40 Tom Browning	.05	.02	.00
☐	41 Dave Parker	.15	.07	.01
☐	42 Mario Soto	.05	.02	.00
☐	43 Nolan Ryan	.90	.45	.09
☐	44 Pedro Guerrero	.15	.07	.01
☐	45 Orel Hershiser	.25	.12	.02
☐	46 Mike Scioscia	.05	.02	.00
☐	47 Fernando Valenzuela	.20	.10	.02
☐	48 Bob Welch	.10	.05	.01
☐	49 Tim Raines	.20	.10	.02
☐	50 Gary Carter	.20	.10	.02
☐	51 Sid Fernandez	.10	.05	.01
☐	52 Dwight Gooden	.40	.20	.04
☐	53 Keith Hernandez	.15	.07	.01
☐	54 Juan Samuel	.10	.05	.01
☐	55 Mike Schmidt	.90	.45	.09
☐	56 Glenn Wilson	.05	.02	.00
☐	57 Rick Reuschel	.10	.05	.01
☐	58 Joaquin Andujar	.05	.02	.00
☐	59 Jack Clark	.15	.07	.01
☐	60 Vince Coleman	.30	.15	.03
☐	61 Danny Cox	.05	.02	.00
☐	62 Tom Herr	.05	.02	.00
☐	63 Willie McGee	.15	.07	.01
☐	64 John Tudor	.10	.05	.01
☐	65 Tony Gwynn	.35	.17	.03
☐	66 Checklist Card	.05	.02	.00

1986 Topps Traded

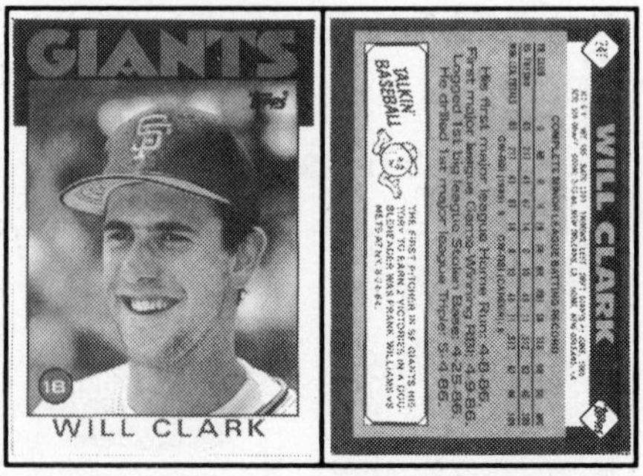

This 132-card Traded or extended set was distributed by Topps to dealers in a special red and white box as a complete set. The card fronts are identical in style to the Topps regular issue and are also 2 1/2" by 3 1/2". The backs are printed in red and black on white card stock. Cards are numbered (with a T suffix) alphabetically according to the name of the player. The key (extended) rookie cards in this set are Barry Bonds, Bobby Bonilla, Jose Canseco, Will Clark, and Kevin Mitchell. Topps also produced a specially boxed "glossy" edition frequently referred to as the Topps Traded Tiffany set. There were supposedly only 5,000 sets of the Tiffany cards produced; they were marketed to hobby dealers. The checklist of cards is identical to that of the normal non-glossy cards. There are two primary distinguishing features of the Tiffany cards, white card stock reverses and high gloss obverses. These Tiffany cards are valued at approximately five times the values listed below.

	MINT	EXC	G-VG
COMPLETE SET (132)	32.00	16.00	3.20
COMMON PLAYER (1-132)	.06	.03	.00
□ 1T Andy Allanson	.12	.06	.01
□ 2T Neil Allen	.06	.03	.00
□ 3T Joaquin Andujar	.10	.05	.01
□ 4T Paul Assenmacher	.12	.06	.01
□ 5T Scott Bailes	.12	.06	.01
□ 6T Don Baylor	.10	.05	.01
□ 7T Steve Bedrosian	.12	.06	.01
□ 8T Juan Beniquez	.06	.03	.00
□ 9T Juan Berenguer	.06	.03	.00
□ 10T Mike Bielecki	.20	.10	.02
□ 11T Barry Bonds	3.00	1.50	.30
□ 12T Bobby Bonilla	2.00	1.00	.20
□ 13T Juan Bonilla	.06	.03	.00
□ 14T Rich Bordi	.06	.03	.00
□ 15T Steve Boros MG	.06	.03	.00
□ 16T Rick Burleson	.10	.05	.01
□ 17T Bill Campbell	.06	.03	.00
□ 18T Tom Candiotti	.10	.05	.01
□ 19T John Cangelosi	.10	.05	.01
□ 20T Jose Canseco	9.00	4.50	.90
□ 21T Carmen Castillo	.06	.03	.00
□ 22T Rick Cerone	.06	.03	.00
□ 23T John Cerutti	.15	.07	.01
□ 24T Will Clark	9.00	4.50	.90
□ 25T Mark Clear	.06	.03	.00
□ 26T Darnell Coles	.10	.05	.01
□ 27T Dave Collins	.06	.03	.00
□ 28T Tim Conroy	.06	.03	.00
□ 29T Joe Cowley	.06	.03	.00
□ 30T Joel Davis	.10	.05	.01
□ 31T Rob Deer	.20	.10	.02
□ 32T John Denny	.10	.05	.01
□ 33T Mike Easler	.06	.03	.00
□ 34T Mark Eichhorn	.10	.05	.01
□ 35T Steve Farr	.10	.05	.01
□ 36T Scott Fletcher	.06	.03	.00
□ 37T Terry Forster	.10	.05	.01
□ 38T Terry Francona	.06	.03	.00
□ 39T Jim Fregosi MG	.06	.03	.00
□ 40T Andres Galarraga	.90	.45	.09
□ 41T Ken Griffey	.25	.12	.02
□ 42T Bill Gullickson	.06	.03	.00
□ 43T Jose Guzman	.15	.07	.01
□ 44T Moose Haas	.06	.03	.00
□ 45T Billy Hatcher	.25	.12	.02
□ 46T Mike Heath	.06	.03	.00
□ 47T Tom Hume	.06	.03	.00
□ 48T Pete Incaviglia	.80	.40	.08
□ 49T Dane Iorg	.06	.03	.00
□ 50T Bo Jackson	9.00	4.50	.90
□ 51T Wally Joyner	1.75	.85	.17
□ 52T Charlie Kerfeld	.10	.05	.01
□ 53T Eric King	.25	.12	.02
□ 54T Bob Kipper	.06	.03	.00
□ 55T Wayne Krenchicki	.06	.03	.00
□ 56T John Kruk	.30	.15	.03
□ 57T Mike LaCoss	.06	.03	.00
□ 58T Pete Ladd	.06	.03	.00
□ 59T Mike Laga	.10	.05	.01
□ 60T Hal Lanier MG	.06	.03	.00
□ 61T Dave LaPoint	.06	.03	.00
□ 62T Rudy Law	.06	.03	.00
□ 63T Rick Leach	.06	.03	.00
□ 64T Tim Leary	.15	.07	.01
□ 65T Dennis Leonard	.10	.05	.01
□ 66T Jim Leyland MG	.10	.05	.01
□ 67T Steve Lyons	.10	.05	.01
□ 68T Mickey Mahler	.06	.03	.00
□ 69T Candy Maldonado	.20	.10	.02
□ 70T Roger Mason	.10	.05	.01
□ 71T Bob McClure	.06	.03	.00
□ 72T Andy McGaffigan	.06	.03	.00
□ 73T Gene Michael MG	.06	.03	.00
□ 74T Kevin Mitchell	3.50	1.75	.35
□ 75T Omar Moreno	.06	.03	.00
□ 76T Jerry Mumphrey	.06	.03	.00
□ 77T Phil Niekro	.30	.15	.03
□ 78T Randy Niemann	.06	.03	.00
□ 79T Juan Nieves	.10	.05	.01
□ 80T Otis Nixon	.10	.05	.01
□ 81T Bob Ojeda	.10	.05	.01
□ 82T Jose Oquendo	.10	.05	.01
□ 83T Tom Paciorek	.06	.03	.00
□ 84T David Palmer	.06	.03	.00
□ 85T Frank Pastore	.06	.03	.00
□ 86T Lou Piniella MG	.10	.05	.01
□ 87T Dan Plesac	.15	.07	.01
□ 88T Darrell Porter	.06	.03	.00
□ 89T Rey Quinones	.10	.05	.01
□ 90T Gary Redus	.06	.03	.00
□ 91T Bip Roberts	.35	.17	.03
□ 92T Billy Jo Robidoux	.10	.05	.01
□ 93T Jeff Robinson (Giants pitcher)	.10	.05	.01
□ 94T Gary Roenicke	.06	.03	.00
□ 95T Ed Romero	.06	.03	.00
□ 96T Argenis Salazar	.06	.03	.00
□ 97T Joe Sambito	.06	.03	.00
□ 98T Billy Sample	.06	.03	.00
□ 99T Dave Schmidt	.10	.05	.01
□ 100T Ken Schrom	.06	.03	.00
□ 101T Tom Seaver	.60	.30	.06
□ 102T Ted Simmons	.15	.07	.01
□ 103T Sammy Stewart	.06	.03	.00
□ 104T Kurt Stillwell	.35	.17	.03
□ 105T Franklin Stubbs	.15	.07	.01
□ 106T Dale Sveum	.15	.07	.01
□ 107T Chuck Tanner MG	.06	.03	.00
□ 108T Danny Tartabull	.65	.30	.06
□ 109T Tim Teufel	.10	.05	.01
□ 110T Bob Tewksbury	.12	.06	.01
□ 111T Andres Thomas	.15	.07	.01
□ 112T Milt Thompson	.10	.05	.01
□ 113T Robby Thompson	.25	.12	.02
□ 114T Jay Tibbs	.06	.03	.00
□ 115T Wayne Tolleson	.06	.03	.00
□ 116T Alex Trevino	.06	.03	.00
□ 117T Manny Trillo	.06	.03	.00
□ 118T Ed VandeBerg	.06	.03	.00
□ 119T Ozzie Virgil	.06	.03	.00
□ 120T Bob Walk	.06	.03	.00
□ 121T Gene Walter	.06	.03	.00
□ 122T Claudell Washington	.10	.05	.01
□ 123T Bill Wegman	.10	.05	.01
□ 124T Dick Williams MG	.06	.03	.00
□ 125T Mitch Williams	.25	.12	.02
□ 126T Bobby Witt	.75	.35	.07
□ 127T Todd Worrell	.35	.17	.03
□ 128T George Wright	.06	.03	.00
□ 129T Ricky Wright	.06	.03	.00
□ 130T Steve Yeager	.06	.03	.00
□ 131T Paul Zuvella	.06	.03	.00
□ 132T Checklist 1-132	.06	.01	.00

1987 Topps

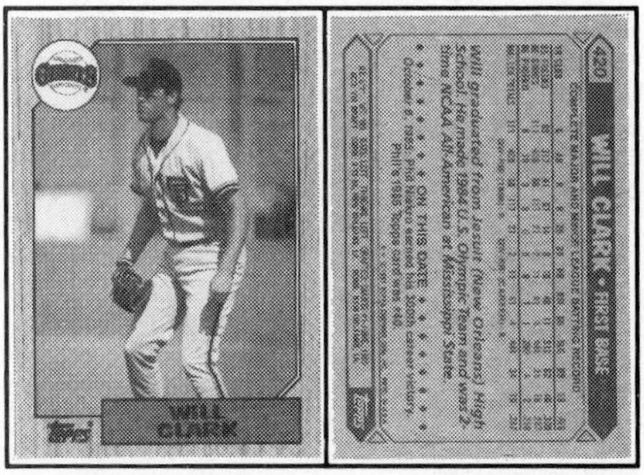

This 792-card set is reminiscent of the 1962 Topps baseball cards with their simulated wood grain borders. The backs are printed in yellow and blue on gray card stock. The manager cards contain a checklist of the respective team's players on the back. Subsets in the set include Record Breakers (1-7), Turn Back the Clock (311-315), and All-Star selections (595-616). The Team Leader cards typically show players conferring on the mound inside a white cloud. The wax pack wrapper gives details of "Spring Fever Baseball" where a lucky collector can win a trip for four to Spring Training. The key rookie cards in this set are Barry Bonds, Bobby Bonilla, Will Clark, Mike Greenwell, Bo Jackson, Barry Larkin, Dave Magadan, Kevin Mitchell, Rafael Palmiero, and Ruben Sierra. Topps also produced a specially boxed "glossy" edition, frequently referred to as the Topps Tiffany set. This year Topps did not disclose the number of sets they produced or sold. It is apparent from the availability that there were many more sets produced this year compared to the 1984-86 Tiffany sets, perhaps 30,000 sets, more than three times as many. The checklist of cards (792 regular and 132 Traded) is identical to that of the normal non-glossy cards. There are two primary distinguishing features of the Tiffany cards, white card stock reverses and high gloss obverses. These Tiffany cards are valued at approximately three times the values listed below.

	MINT	EXC	G-VG
COMPLETE SET (792)	40.00	20.00	4.00
COMMON PLAYER (1-792)	.03	.01	.00
☐ 1 RB: Roger Clemens	.30	.10	.02
Most strikeouts,			
nine inning game			
☐ 2 RB: Jim Deshaies	.06	.03	.00
Most cons. K's,			
start of game			
☐ 3 RB: Dwight Evans	.08	.04	.01
Earliest home run,			
season			
☐ 4 RB: Davey Lopes	.06	.03	.00
Most steals, season,			
40-year-old			
☐ 5 RB: Dave Righetti	.08	.04	.01
Most saves, season			
☐ 6 RB: Ruben Sierra	.20	.10	.02
Youngest player to			
switch hit homers			
in game			
☐ 7 RB: Todd Worrell	.08	.04	.01
Most saves,			
season, rookie			
☐ 8 Terry Pendleton	.06	.03	.00
☐ 9 Jay Tibbs	.03	.01	.00
☐ 10 Cecil Cooper	.08	.04	.01
☐ 11 Indians Team	.03	.01	.00
(mound conference)			
☐ 12 Jeff Sellers	.08	.04	.01
☐ 13 Nick Esasky	.10	.05	.01
☐ 14 Dave Stewart	.20	.10	.02
☐ 15 Claudell Washington	.06	.03	.00
☐ 16 Pat Clements	.03	.01	.00
☐ 17 Pete O'Brien	.06	.03	.00
☐ 18 Dick Howser MG	.06	.03	.00
(checklist back)			
☐ 19 Matt Young	.03	.01	.00
☐ 20 Gary Carter	.18	.09	.01
☐ 21 Mark Davis	.12	.06	.01
☐ 22 Doug DeCinces	.06	.03	.00
☐ 23 Lee Smith	.06	.03	.00
☐ 24 Tony Walker	.06	.03	.00
☐ 25 Bert Blyleven	.10	.05	.01
☐ 26 Greg Brock	.03	.01	.00
☐ 27 Joe Cowley	.03	.01	.00
☐ 28 Rick Dempsey	.03	.01	.00
☐ 29 Jimmy Key	.06	.03	.00
☐ 30 Tim Raines	.15	.07	.01
☐ 31 Braves Team	.03	.01	.00
(Hubbard/Ramirez)			
☐ 32 Tim Leary	.06	.03	.00
☐ 33 Andy Van Slyke	.15	.07	.01
☐ 34 Jose Rijo	.12	.06	.01
☐ 35 Sid Bream	.03	.01	.00
☐ 36 Eric King	.20	.10	.02
☐ 37 Marvell Wynne	.03	.01	.00
☐ 38 Dennis Leonard	.03	.01	.00
☐ 39 Marty Barrett	.06	.03	.00
☐ 40 Dave Righetti	.10	.05	.01
☐ 41 Bo Diaz	.03	.01	.00
☐ 42 Gary Redus	.03	.01	.00
☐ 43 Gene Michael MG	.06	.03	.00
(checklist back)			
☐ 44 Greg Harris	.03	.01	.00
☐ 45 Jim Presley	.06	.03	.00
☐ 46 Dan Gladden	.06	.03	.00
☐ 47 Dennis Powell	.03	.01	.00
☐ 48 Wally Backman	.03	.01	.00
☐ 49 Terry Harper	.03	.01	.00
☐ 50 Dave Smith	.06	.03	.00
☐ 51 Mel Hall	.06	.03	.00
☐ 52 Keith Atherton	.03	.01	.00
☐ 53 Ruppert Jones	.03	.01	.00
☐ 54 Bill Dawley	.03	.01	.00
☐ 55 Tim Wallach	.08	.04	.01
☐ 56 Brewers Team	.03	.01	.00
(mound conference)			
☐ 57 Scott Nielsen	.10	.05	.01
☐ 58 Thad Bosley	.03	.01	.00
☐ 59 Ken Dayley	.03	.01	.00
☐ 60 Tony Pena	.08	.04	.01
☐ 61 Bobby Thigpen	.65	.30	.06
☐ 62 Bobby Meacham	.03	.01	.00
☐ 63 Fred Toliver	.03	.01	.00
☐ 64 Harry Spilman	.03	.01	.00
☐ 65 Tom Browning	.10	.05	.01
☐ 66 Marc Sullivan	.03	.01	.00
☐ 67 Bill Swift	.03	.01	.00
☐ 68 Tony LaRussa MG	.06	.03	.00
(checklist back)			
☐ 69 Lonnie Smith	.08	.04	.01
☐ 70 Charlie Hough	.06	.03	.00
☐ 71 Mike Aldrete	.08	.04	.01
☐ 72 Walt Terrell	.03	.01	.00
☐ 73 Dave Anderson	.03	.01	.00
☐ 74 Dan Pasqua	.06	.03	.00
☐ 75 Ron Darling	.12	.06	.01
☐ 76 Rafael Ramirez	.03	.01	.00
☐ 77 Bryan Oelkers	.03	.01	.00
☐ 78 Tom Foley	.03	.01	.00
☐ 79 Juan Nieves	.06	.03	.00
☐ 80 Wally Joyner	.90	.45	.09
☐ 81 Padres Team	.03	.01	.00
(Hawkins/Kennedy)			
☐ 82 Rob Murphy	.12	.06	.01
☐ 83 Mike Davis	.03	.01	.00
☐ 84 Steve Lake	.03	.01	.00
☐ 85 Kevin Bass	.06	.03	.00
☐ 86 Nate Snell	.03	.01	.00
☐ 87 Mark Salas	.03	.01	.00
☐ 88 Ed Wojna	.03	.01	.00
☐ 89 Ozzie Guillen	.20	.10	.02
☐ 90 Dave Stieb	.12	.06	.01
☐ 91 Harold Reynolds	.06	.03	.00
☐ 92A Urbano Lugo	.20	.10	.02
ERR (no trademark)			
☐ 92B Urbano Lugo COR	.06	.03	.00
☐ 93 Jim Leyland MG	.06	.03	.00
(checklist back)			
☐ 94 Calvin Schiraldi	.06	.03	.00
☐ 95 Oddibe McDowell	.06	.03	.00
☐ 96 Frank Williams	.03	.01	.00
☐ 97 Glenn Wilson	.03	.01	.00
☐ 98 Bill Scherrer	.03	.01	.00
☐ 99 Darryl Motley	.03	.01	.00
☐ 100 Steve Garvey	.20	.10	.02
☐ 101 Carl Willis	.03	.01	.00
☐ 102 Paul Zuvella	.03	.01	.00
☐ 103 Rick Aguilera	.03	.01	.00
☐ 104 Billy Sample	.03	.01	.00
☐ 105 Floyd Youmans	.03	.01	.00
☐ 106 Blue Jays Team	.12	.06	.01
(Bell/Barfield)			
☐ 107 John Butcher	.03	.01	.00
☐ 108 Jim Gantner UER	.06	.03	.00
(Brewers logo			
reversed)			
☐ 109 R.J. Reynolds	.03	.01	.00
☐ 110 John Tudor	.10	.05	.01
☐ 111 Alfredo Griffin	.03	.01	.00
☐ 112 Alan Ashby	.03	.01	.00
☐ 113 Neil Allen	.03	.01	.00
☐ 114 Billy Beane	.03	.01	.00
☐ 115 Donnie Moore	.03	.01	.00
☐ 116 Bill Russell	.03	.01	.00
☐ 117 Jim Beattie	.03	.01	.00
☐ 118 Bobby Valentine MG	.06	.03	.00
(checklist back)			
☐ 119 Ron Robinson	.06	.03	.00
☐ 120 Eddie Murray	.25	.12	.02
☐ 121 Kevin Romine	.08	.04	.01
☐ 122 Jim Clancy	.03	.01	.00
☐ 123 John Kruk	.25	.12	.02
☐ 124 Ray Fontenot	.03	.01	.00
☐ 125 Bob Brenly	.03	.01	.00
☐ 126 Mike Loynd	.03	.01	.00
☐ 127 Vance Law	.03	.01	.00
☐ 128 Checklist 1-132	.06	.01	.00
☐ 129 Rick Cerone	.03	.01	.00
☐ 130 Dwight Gooden	.65	.30	.06
☐ 131 Pirates Team	.03	.01	.00
(Bream/Pena)			

☐ 132	Paul Assenmacher	.03	.01	.00
☐ 133	Jose Oquendo	.03	.01	.00
☐ 134	Rich Yett	.03	.01	.00
☐ 135	Mike Easler	.03	.01	.00
☐ 136	Ron Romanick	.03	.01	.00
☐ 137	Jerry Willard	.03	.01	.00
☐ 138	Roy Lee Jackson	.03	.01	.00
☐ 139	Devon White	.45	.22	.04
☐ 140	Bret Saberhagen	.20	.10	.02
☐ 141	Herm Winningham	.03	.01	.00
☐ 142	Rick Sutcliffe	.08	.04	.01
☐ 143	Steve Boros MG (checklist back)	.06	.03	.00
☐ 144	Mike Scioscia	.03	.01	.00
☐ 145	Charlie Kerfeld	.03	.01	.00
☐ 146	Tracy Jones	.10	.05	.01
☐ 147	Randy Niemann	.03	.01	.00
☐ 148	Dave Collins	.03	.01	.00
☐ 149	Ray Searage	.03	.01	.00
☐ 150	Wade Boggs	.75	.35	.07
☐ 151	Mike LaCoss	.03	.01	.00
☐ 152	Toby Harrah	.03	.01	.00
☐ 153	Duane Ward	.12	.06	.01
☐ 154	Tom O'Malley	.03	.01	.00
☐ 155	Eddie Whitson	.06	.03	.00
☐ 156	Mariners Team (mound conference)	.03	.01	.00
☐ 157	Danny Darwin	.06	.03	.00
☐ 158	Tim Teufel	.03	.01	.00
☐ 159	Ed Olwine	.03	.01	.00
☐ 160	Julio Franco	.12	.06	.01
☐ 161	Steve Ontiveros	.03	.01	.00
☐ 162	Mike LaValliere	.15	.07	.01
☐ 163	Kevin Gross	.03	.01	.00
☐ 164	Sammy Khalifa	.03	.01	.00
☐ 165	Jeff Reardon	.08	.04	.01
☐ 166	Bob Boone	.08	.04	.01
☐ 167	Jim Deshaies	.15	.07	.01
☐ 168	Lou Piniella MG (checklist back)	.08	.04	.01
☐ 169	Ron Washington	.03	.01	.00
☐ 170	Bo Jackson	4.50	2.25	.45
☐ 171	Chuck Cary	.15	.07	.01
☐ 172	Ron Oester	.03	.01	.00
☐ 173	Alex Trevino	.03	.01	.00
☐ 174	Henry Cotto	.03	.01	.00
☐ 175	Bob Stanley	.03	.01	.00
☐ 176	Steve Buechele	.03	.01	.00
☐ 177	Keith Moreland	.03	.01	.00
☐ 178	Cecil Fielder	1.50	.75	.15
☐ 179	Bill Wegman	.06	.03	.00
☐ 180	Chris Brown	.03	.01	.00
☐ 181	Cardinals Team (mound conference)	.03	.01	.00
☐ 182	Lee Lacy	.03	.01	.00
☐ 183	Andy Hawkins	.03	.01	.00
☐ 184	Bobby Bonilla	1.50	.75	.15
☐ 185	Roger McDowell	.06	.03	.00
☐ 186	Bruce Benedict	.03	.01	.00
☐ 187	Mark Huismann	.03	.01	.00
☐ 188	Tony Phillips	.03	.01	.00
☐ 189	Joe Hesketh	.03	.01	.00
☐ 190	Jim Sundberg	.03	.01	.00
☐ 191	Charles Hudson	.03	.01	.00
☐ 192	Cory Snyder	.35	.17	.03
☐ 193	Roger Craig MG (checklist back)	.06	.03	.00
☐ 194	Kirk McCaskill	.03	.01	.00
☐ 195	Mike Pagliarulo	.06	.03	.00
☐ 196	Randy O'Neal UER (wrong ML career W-L totals)	.03	.01	.00
☐ 197	Mark Bailey	.03	.01	.00
☐ 198	Lee Mazzilli	.03	.01	.00
☐ 199	Mariano Duncan	.08	.04	.01
☐ 200	Pete Rose	.45	.22	.04
☐ 201	John Cangelosi	.06	.03	.00
☐ 202	Ricky Wright	.03	.01	.00
☐ 203	Mike Kingery	.06	.03	.00
☐ 204	Sammy Stewart	.03	.01	.00
☐ 205	Graig Nettles	.08	.04	.01
☐ 206	Twins Team (Frank Viola and Tim Laudner)	.06	.03	.00
☐ 207	George Frazier	.03	.01	.00
☐ 208	John Shelby	.03	.01	.00
☐ 209	Rick Schu	.03	.01	.00
☐ 210	Lloyd Moseby	.06	.03	.00
☐ 211	John Morris	.03	.01	.00
☐ 212	Mike Fitzgerald	.03	.01	.00
☐ 213	Randy Myers	.45	.22	.04
☐ 214	Omar Moreno	.03	.01	.00
☐ 215	Mark Langston	.18	.09	.01
☐ 216	B.J. Surhoff	.35	.17	.03
☐ 217	Chris Codiroli	.03	.01	.00
☐ 218	Sparky Anderson MG (checklist back)	.06	.03	.00
☐ 219	Cecilio Guante	.03	.01	.00
☐ 220	Joe Carter	.25	.12	.02
☐ 221	Vern Ruhle	.03	.01	.00
☐ 222	Denny Walling	.03	.01	.00
☐ 223	Charlie Leibrandt	.03	.01	.00
☐ 224	Wayne Tolleson	.03	.01	.00
☐ 225	Mike Smithson	.03	.01	.00
☐ 226	Max Venable	.03	.01	.00
☐ 227	Jamie Moyer	.08	.04	.01
☐ 228	Curt Wilkerson	.03	.01	.00
☐ 229	Mike Birkbeck	.08	.04	.01
☐ 230	Don Baylor	.08	.04	.01
☐ 231	Giants Team (Bob Brenly and Jim Gott)	.03	.01	.00
☐ 232	Reggie Williams	.03	.01	.00
☐ 233	Russ Morman	.08	.04	.01
☐ 234	Pat Sheridan	.03	.01	.00
☐ 235	Alvin Davis	.10	.05	.01
☐ 236	Tommy John	.10	.05	.01
☐ 237	Jim Morrison	.03	.01	.00
☐ 238	Bill Krueger	.03	.01	.00
☐ 239	Juan Espino	.03	.01	.00
☐ 240	Steve Balboni	.03	.01	.00
☐ 241	Danny Heep	.03	.01	.00
☐ 242	Rick Mahler	.03	.01	.00
☐ 243	Whitey Herzog MG (checklist back)	.06	.03	.00
☐ 244	Dickie Noles	.03	.01	.00
☐ 245	Willie Upshaw	.03	.01	.00
☐ 246	Jim Dwyer	.03	.01	.00
☐ 247	Jeff Reed	.03	.01	.00
☐ 248	Gene Walter	.03	.01	.00
☐ 249	Jim Pankovits	.03	.01	.00
☐ 250	Teddy Higuera	.10	.05	.01
☐ 251	Rob Wilfong	.03	.01	.00
☐ 252	Dennis Martinez	.06	.03	.00
☐ 253	Eddie Milner	.03	.01	.00
☐ 254	Bob Tewksbury	.08	.04	.01
☐ 255	Juan Samuel	.10	.05	.01
☐ 256	Royals Team (Brett/F.White)	.10	.05	.01
☐ 257	Bob Forsch	.03	.01	.00
☐ 258	Steve Yeager	.03	.01	.00
☐ 259	Mike Greenwell	2.50	1.25	.25
☐ 260	Vida Blue	.06	.03	.00
☐ 261	Ruben Sierra	2.50	1.25	.25
☐ 262	Jim Winn	.03	.01	.00
☐ 263	Stan Javier	.06	.03	.00
☐ 264	Checklist 133-264	.06	.01	.00
☐ 265	Darrell Evans	.08	.04	.01
☐ 266	Jeff Hamilton	.12	.06	.01
☐ 267	Howard Johnson	.20	.10	.02
☐ 268	Pat Corrales MG (checklist back)	.06	.03	.00
☐ 269	Cliff Speck	.03	.01	.00
☐ 270	Jody Davis	.03	.01	.00
☐ 271	Mike Brown (Mariners pitcher)	.03	.01	.00
☐ 272	Andres Galarraga	.40	.20	.04
☐ 273	Gene Nelson	.03	.01	.00
☐ 274	Jeff Hearron UER (duplicate 1986 stat line on back)	.06	.03	.00
☐ 275	LaMarr Hoyt	.03	.01	.00
☐ 276	Jackie Gutierrez	.03	.01	.00
☐ 277	Juan Agosto	.03	.01	.00
☐ 278	Gary Pettis	.03	.01	.00
☐ 279	Dan Plesac	.15	.07	.01
☐ 280	Jeff Leonard	.06	.03	.00
☐ 281	Reds Team (Pete Rose, Bo Diaz, and Bill Gullickson)	.10	.05	.01
☐ 282	Jeff Calhoun	.03	.01	.00
☐ 283	Doug Drabek	.75	.35	.07
☐ 284	John Moses	.03	.01	.00
☐ 285	Dennis Boyd	.06	.03	.00
☐ 286	Mike Woodard	.03	.01	.00
☐ 287	Dave Von Ohlen	.03	.01	.00
☐ 288	Tito Landrum	.03	.01	.00
☐ 289	Bob Kipper	.03	.01	.00
☐ 290	Leon Durham	.03	.01	.00
☐ 291	Mitch Williams	.20	.10	.02
☐ 292	Franklin Stubbs	.03	.01	.00
☐ 293	Bob Rodgers MG (checklist back)	.06	.03	.00
☐ 294	Steve Jeltz	.03	.01	.00
☐ 295	Len Dykstra	.30	.15	.03
☐ 296	Andres Thomas	.10	.05	.01
☐ 297	Don Schulze	.03	.01	.00
☐ 298	Larry Herndon	.03	.01	.00

☐ 299	Joel Davis	.03	.01	.00
☐ 300	Reggie Jackson	.30	.15	.03
☐ 301	Luis Aquino UER (no trademark, never corrected)	.06	.03	.00
☐ 302	Bill Schroeder	.03	.01	.00
☐ 303	Juan Berenguer	.03	.01	.00
☐ 304	Phil Garner	.03	.01	.00
☐ 305	John Franco	.08	.04	.01
☐ 306	Red Sox Team (Tom Seaver, John McNamara, and Rich Gedman)	.08	.04	.01
☐ 307	Lee Guetterman	.10	.05	.01
☐ 308	Don Slaught	.03	.01	.00
☐ 309	Mike Young	.03	.01	.00
☐ 310	Frank Viola	.25	.12	.02
☐ 311	Turn Back 1982 Rickey Henderson	.25	.12	.02
☐ 312	Turn Back 1977 Reggie Jackson	.15	.07	.01
☐ 313	Turn Back 1972 Roberto Clemente	.12	.06	.01
☐ 314	Turn Back 1967 UER Carl Yastrzemski (sic, 112 RBI's on back)	.12	.06	.01
☐ 315	Turn Back 1962 Maury Wills	.06	.03	.00
☐ 316	Brian Fisher	.03	.01	.00
☐ 317	Clint Hurdle	.03	.01	.00
☐ 318	Jim Fregosi MG (checklist back)	.06	.03	.00
☐ 319	Greg Swindell	.90	.45	.09
☐ 320	Barry Bonds	2.50	1.25	.25
☐ 321	Mike Laga	.03	.01	.00
☐ 322	Chris Bando	.03	.01	.00
☐ 323	Al Newman	.06	.03	.00
☐ 324	David Palmer	.03	.01	.00
☐ 325	Garry Templeton	.06	.03	.00
☐ 326	Mark Gubicza	.10	.05	.01
☐ 327	Dale Sveum	.12	.06	.01
☐ 328	Bob Welch	.12	.06	.01
☐ 329	Ron Roenicke	.03	.01	.00
☐ 330	Mike Scott	.18	.09	.01
☐ 331	Mets Team (Gary Carter and Darryl Strawberry)	.18	.09	.01
☐ 332	Joe Price	.03	.01	.00
☐ 333	Ken Phelps	.06	.03	.00
☐ 334	Ed Correa	.08	.04	.01
☐ 335	Candy Maldonado	.10	.05	.01
☐ 336	Allan Anderson	.20	.10	.02
☐ 337	Darrell Miller	.03	.01	.00
☐ 338	Tim Conroy	.03	.01	.00
☐ 339	Donnie Hill	.03	.01	.00
☐ 340	Roger Clemens	.90	.45	.09
☐ 341	Mike Brown (Pirates OF)	.03	.01	.00
☐ 342	Bob James	.03	.01	.00
☐ 343	Hal Lanier MG (checklist back)	.06	.03	.00
☐ 344A	Joe Niekro (copyright inside righthand border)	.10	.05	.01
☐ 344B	Joe Niekro (copyright outside righthand border)	.50	.25	.05
☐ 345	Andre Dawson	.30	.15	.03
☐ 346	Shawon Dunston	.18	.09	.01
☐ 347	Mickey Brantley	.10	.05	.01
☐ 348	Carmelo Martinez	.03	.01	.00
☐ 349	Storm Davis	.06	.03	.00
☐ 350	Keith Hernandez	.15	.07	.01
☐ 351	Gene Garber	.03	.01	.00
☐ 352	Mike Felder	.06	.03	.00
☐ 353	Ernie Camacho	.03	.01	.00
☐ 354	Jamie Quirk	.03	.01	.00
☐ 355	Don Carman	.03	.01	.00
☐ 356	White Sox Team (mound conference)	.03	.01	.00
☐ 357	Steve Fireovid	.03	.01	.00
☐ 358	Sal Butera	.03	.01	.00
☐ 359	Doug Corbett	.03	.01	.00
☐ 360	Pedro Guerrero	.12	.06	.01
☐ 361	Mark Thurmond	.03	.01	.00
☐ 362	Luis Quinones	.06	.03	.00
☐ 363	Jose Guzman	.06	.03	.00
☐ 364	Randy Bush	.03	.01	.00
☐ 365	Rick Rhoden	.03	.01	.00
☐ 366	Mark McGwire	2.50	1.25	.25
☐ 367	Jeff Lahti	.03	.01	.00
☐ 368	John McNamara MG (checklist back)	.06	.03	.00
☐ 369	Brian Dayett	.03	.01	.00
☐ 370	Fred Lynn	.10	.05	.01
☐ 371	Mark Eichhorn	.06	.03	.00
☐ 372	Jerry Mumphrey	.03	.01	.00
☐ 373	Jeff Dedmon	.03	.01	.00
☐ 374	Glenn Hoffman	.03	.01	.00
☐ 375	Ron Guidry	.10	.05	.01
☐ 376	Scott Bradley	.03	.01	.00
☐ 377	John Henry Johnson	.03	.01	.00
☐ 378	Rafael Santana	.03	.01	.00
☐ 379	John Russell	.03	.01	.00
☐ 380	Rich Gossage	.08	.04	.01
☐ 381	Expos Team (mound conference)	.03	.01	.00
☐ 382	Rudy Law	.03	.01	.00
☐ 383	Ron Davis	.03	.01	.00
☐ 384	Johnny Grubb	.03	.01	.00
☐ 385	Orel Hershiser	.20	.10	.02
☐ 386	Dickie Thon	.03	.01	.00
☐ 387	T.R. Bryden	.03	.01	.00
☐ 388	Geno Petralli	.03	.01	.00
☐ 389	Jeff Robinson (Giants pitcher)	.06	.03	.00
☐ 390	Gary Matthews	.03	.01	.00
☐ 391	Jay Howell	.03	.01	.00
☐ 392	Checklist 265-396	.06	.01	.00
☐ 393	Pete Rose MG (checklist back)	.35	.17	.03
☐ 394	Mike Bielecki	.08	.04	.01
☐ 395	Damaso Garcia	.03	.01	.00
☐ 396	Tim Lollar	.03	.01	.00
☐ 397	Greg Walker	.03	.01	.00
☐ 398	Brad Havens	.03	.01	.00
☐ 399	Curt Ford	.03	.01	.00
☐ 400	George Brett	.30	.15	.03
☐ 401	Billy Jo Robidoux	.06	.03	.00
☐ 402	Mike Trujillo	.03	.01	.00
☐ 403	Jerry Royster	.03	.01	.00
☐ 404	Doug Sisk	.03	.01	.00
☐ 405	Brook Jacoby	.08	.04	.01
☐ 406	Yankees Team (Henderson/Mattingly)	.30	.15	.03
☐ 407	Jim Acker	.03	.01	.00
☐ 408	John Mizerock	.03	.01	.00
☐ 409	Milt Thompson	.06	.03	.00
☐ 410	Fernando Valenzuela	.15	.07	.01
☐ 411	Darnell Coles	.03	.01	.00
☐ 412	Eric Davis	.90	.45	.09
☐ 413	Moose Haas	.03	.01	.00
☐ 414	Joe Orsulak	.03	.01	.00
☐ 415	Bobby Witt	.45	.22	.04
☐ 416	Tom Nieto	.03	.01	.00
☐ 417	Pat Perry	.03	.01	.00
☐ 418	Dick Williams MG (checklist back)	.06	.03	.00
☐ 419	Mark Portugal	.12	.06	.01
☐ 420	Will Clark	3.75	1.85	.37
☐ 421	Jose DeLeon	.03	.01	.00
☐ 422	Jack Howell	.03	.01	.00
☐ 423	Jaime Cocanower	.03	.01	.00
☐ 424	Chris Speier	.03	.01	.00
☐ 425	Tom Seaver	.25	.12	.02
☐ 426	Floyd Rayford	.03	.01	.00
☐ 427	Edwin Nunez	.03	.01	.00
☐ 428	Bruce Bochy	.03	.01	.00
☐ 429	Tim Pyznarski	.06	.03	.00
☐ 430	Mike Schmidt	.50	.25	.05
☐ 431	Dodgers Team (mound conference)	.06	.03	.00
☐ 432	Jim Slaton	.03	.01	.00
☐ 433	Ed Hearn	.03	.01	.00
☐ 434	Mike Fischlin	.03	.01	.00
☐ 435	Bruce Sutter	.08	.04	.01
☐ 436	Andy Allanson	.03	.01	.00
☐ 437	Ted Power	.03	.01	.00
☐ 438	Kelly Downs	.18	.09	.01
☐ 439	Karl Best	.03	.01	.00
☐ 440	Willie McGee	.10	.05	.01
☐ 441	Dave Leiper	.03	.01	.00
☐ 442	Mitch Webster	.03	.01	.00
☐ 443	John Felske MG (checklist back)	.06	.03	.00
☐ 444	Jeff Russell	.03	.01	.00
☐ 445	Dave Lopes	.06	.03	.00
☐ 446	Chuck Finley	.75	.35	.07
☐ 447	Bill Almon	.03	.01	.00
☐ 448	Chris Bosio	.20	.10	.02
☐ 449	Pat Dodson	.06	.03	.00
☐ 450	Kirby Puckett	.60	.30	.06
☐ 451	Joe Sambito	.03	.01	.00
☐ 452	Dave Henderson	.08	.04	.01
☐ 453	Scott Terry	.12	.06	.01
☐ 454	Luis Salazar	.03	.01	.00
☐ 455	Mike Boddicker	.06	.03	.00

☐ 456 A's Team (mound conference)	.03	.01	.00
☐ 457 Len Matuszek	.03	.01	.00
☐ 458 Kelly Gruber	1.00	.50	.10
☐ 459 Dennis Eckersley	.15	.07	.01
☐ 460 Darryl Strawberry	.50	.25	.05
☐ 461 Craig McMurtry	.03	.01	.00
☐ 462 Scott Fletcher	.03	.01	.00
☐ 463 Tom Candiotti	.06	.03	.00
☐ 464 Butch Wynegar	.03	.01	.00
☐ 465 Todd Worrell	.15	.07	.01
☐ 466 Kal Daniels	.75	.35	.07
☐ 467 Randy St.Claire	.03	.01	.00
☐ 468 George Bamberger MG (checklist back)	.06	.03	.00
☐ 469 Mike Diaz	.06	.03	.00
☐ 470 Dave Dravecky	.08	.04	.01
☐ 471 Ronn Reynolds	.03	.01	.00
☐ 472 Bill Doran	.08	.04	.01
☐ 473 Steve Farr	.06	.03	.00
☐ 474 Jerry Narron	.03	.01	.00
☐ 475 Scott Garrelts	.06	.03	.00
☐ 476 Danny Tartabull	.50	.25	.05
☐ 477 Ken Howell	.03	.01	.00
☐ 478 Tim Laudner	.03	.01	.00
☐ 479 Bob Sebra	.03	.01	.00
☐ 480 Jim Rice	.15	.07	.01
☐ 481 Phillies Team (Glenn Wilson, Juan Samuel, and Von Hayes)	.06	.03	.00
☐ 482 Daryl Boston	.08	.04	.01
☐ 483 Dwight Lowry	.03	.01	.00
☐ 484 Jim Traber	.03	.01	.00
☐ 485 Tony Fernandez	.12	.06	.01
☐ 486 Otis Nixon	.06	.03	.00
☐ 487 Dave Gumpert	.03	.01	.00
☐ 488 Ray Knight	.06	.03	.00
☐ 489 Bill Gullickson	.03	.01	.00
☐ 490 Dale Murphy	.30	.15	.03
☐ 491 Ron Karkovice	.06	.03	.00
☐ 492 Mike Heath	.03	.01	.00
☐ 493 Tom Lasorda MG (checklist back)	.08	.04	.01
☐ 494 Barry Jones	.20	.10	.02
☐ 495 Gorman Thomas	.08	.04	.01
☐ 496 Bruce Bochte	.03	.01	.00
☐ 497 Dale Mohorcic	.08	.04	.01
☐ 498 Bob Kearney	.03	.01	.00
☐ 499 Bruce Ruffin	.10	.05	.01
☐ 500 Don Mattingly	1.25	.60	.12
☐ 501 Craig Lefferts	.03	.01	.00
☐ 502 Dick Schofield	.03	.01	.00
☐ 503 Larry Andersen	.03	.01	.00
☐ 504 Mickey Hatcher	.03	.01	.00
☐ 505 Bryn Smith	.03	.01	.00
☐ 506 Orioles Team (mound conference)	.03	.01	.00
☐ 507 Dave Stapleton (infielder)	.03	.01	.00
☐ 508 Scott Bankhead	.08	.04	.01
☐ 509 Enos Cabell	.03	.01	.00
☐ 510 Tom Henke	.08	.04	.01
☐ 511 Steve Lyons	.03	.01	.00
☐ 512 Dave Magadan	1.00	.50	.10
☐ 513 Carmen Castillo	.03	.01	.00
☐ 514 Orlando Mercado	.03	.01	.00
☐ 515 Willie Hernandez	.06	.03	.00
☐ 516 Ted Simmons	.08	.04	.01
☐ 517 Mario Soto	.03	.01	.00
☐ 518 Gene Mauch MG (checklist back)	.06	.03	.00
☐ 519 Curt Young	.03	.01	.00
☐ 520 Jack Clark	.15	.07	.01
☐ 521 Rick Reuschel	.08	.04	.01
☐ 522 Checklist 397-528	.06	.01	.00
☐ 523 Earnie Riles	.03	.01	.00
☐ 524 Bob Shirley	.03	.01	.00
☐ 525 Phil Bradley	.08	.04	.01
☐ 526 Roger Mason	.03	.01	.00
☐ 527 Jim Wohlford	.03	.01	.00
☐ 528 Ken Dixon	.03	.01	.00
☐ 529 Alvaro Espinoza	.03	.01	.00
☐ 530 Tony Gwynn	.40	.20	.04
☐ 531 Astros Team (Y.Berra conference)	.10	.05	.01
☐ 532 Jeff Stone	.03	.01	.00
☐ 533 Argenis Salazar	.03	.01	.00
☐ 534 Scott Sanderson	.06	.03	.00
☐ 535 Tony Armas	.06	.03	.00
☐ 536 Terry Mulholland	.20	.10	.02
☐ 537 Rance Mulliniks	.03	.01	.00
☐ 538 Tom Niedenfuer	.03	.01	.00
☐ 539 Reid Nichols	.03	.01	.00
☐ 540 Terry Kennedy	.03	.01	.00
☐ 541 Rafael Belliard	.06	.03	.00
☐ 542 Ricky Horton	.03	.01	.00
☐ 543 Dave Johnson MG (checklist back)	.08	.04	.01
☐ 544 Zane Smith	.10	.05	.01
☐ 545 Buddy Bell	.08	.04	.01
☐ 546 Mike Morgan	.06	.03	.00
☐ 547 Rob Deer	.15	.07	.01
☐ 548 Bill Mooneyham	.03	.01	.00
☐ 549 Bob Melvin	.03	.01	.00
☐ 550 Pete Incaviglia	.50	.25	.05
☐ 551 Frank Wills	.03	.01	.00
☐ 552 Larry Sheets	.03	.01	.00
☐ 553 Mike Maddux	.08	.04	.01
☐ 554 Buddy Biancalana	.03	.01	.00
☐ 555 Dennis Rasmussen	.06	.03	.00
☐ 556 Angels Team (Lachemann, Witt, and Boone)	.06	.03	.00
☐ 557 John Cerutti	.12	.06	.01
☐ 558 Greg Gagne	.03	.01	.00
☐ 559 Lance McCullers	.03	.01	.00
☐ 560 Glenn Davis	.35	.17	.03
☐ 561 Rey Quinones	.06	.03	.00
☐ 562 Bryan Clutterbuck	.03	.01	.00
☐ 563 John Stefero	.03	.01	.00
☐ 564 Larry McWilliams	.03	.01	.00
☐ 565 Dusty Baker	.06	.03	.00
☐ 566 Tim Hulett	.03	.01	.00
☐ 567 Greg Mathews	.10	.05	.01
☐ 568 Earl Weaver MG (checklist back)	.08	.04	.01
☐ 569 Wade Rowdon	.03	.01	.00
☐ 570 Sid Fernandez	.12	.06	.01
☐ 571 Ozzie Virgil	.03	.01	.00
☐ 572 Pete Ladd	.03	.01	.00
☐ 573 Hal McRae	.06	.03	.00
☐ 574 Manny Lee	.06	.03	.00
☐ 575 Pat Tabler	.06	.03	.00
☐ 576 Frank Pastore	.03	.01	.00
☐ 577 Dann Bilardello	.03	.01	.00
☐ 578 Billy Hatcher	.10	.05	.01
☐ 579 Rick Burleson	.06	.03	.00
☐ 580 Mike Krukow	.03	.01	.00
☐ 581 Cubs Team (Cey/Trout)	.03	.01	.00
☐ 582 Bruce Berenyi	.03	.01	.00
☐ 583 Junior Ortiz	.03	.01	.00
☐ 584 Ron Kittle	.08	.04	.01
☐ 585 Scott Bailes	.08	.04	.01
☐ 586 Ben Oglivie	.06	.03	.00
☐ 587 Eric Plunk	.06	.03	.00
☐ 588 Wallace Johnson	.06	.03	.00
☐ 589 Steve Crawford	.03	.01	.00
☐ 590 Vince Coleman	.25	.12	.02
☐ 591 Spike Owen	.03	.01	.00
☐ 592 Chris Welsh	.03	.01	.00
☐ 593 Chuck Tanner MG (checklist back)	.06	.03	.00
☐ 594 Rick Anderson	.06	.03	.00
☐ 595 Keith Hernandez AS	.08	.04	.01
☐ 596 Steve Sax AS	.08	.04	.01
☐ 597 Mike Schmidt AS	.25	.12	.02
☐ 598 Ozzie Smith AS	.10	.05	.01
☐ 599 Tony Gwynn AS	.18	.09	.01
☐ 600 Dave Parker AS	.08	.04	.01
☐ 601 Darryl Strawberry AS	.20	.10	.02
☐ 602 Gary Carter AS	.10	.05	.01
☐ 603A Dwight Gooden AS ERR (no trademark)	1.00	.50	.10
☐ 603B Dwight Gooden AS COR	.30	.15	.03
☐ 604 Fern. Valenzuela AS	.10	.05	.01
☐ 605 Todd Worrell AS	.08	.04	.01
☐ 606A Don Mattingly AS ERR (no trademark)	2.00	1.00	.20
☐ 606B Don Mattingly AS COR	.65	.30	.06
☐ 607 Tony Bernazard AS	.06	.03	.00
☐ 608 Wade Boggs AS	.30	.15	.03
☐ 609 Cal Ripken AS	.15	.07	.01
☐ 610 Jim Rice AS	.10	.05	.01
☐ 611 Kirby Puckett AS	.25	.12	.02
☐ 612 George Bell AS	.10	.05	.01
☐ 613 Lance Parrish AS UER (Pitcher heading on back)	.08	.04	.01
☐ 614 Roger Clemens AS	.20	.10	.02
☐ 615 Teddy Higuera AS	.06	.03	.00
☐ 616 Dave Righetti AS	.08	.04	.01
☐ 617 Al Nipper	.03	.01	.00
☐ 618 Tom Kelly MG (checklist back)	.08	.04	.01
☐ 619 Jerry Reed	.03	.01	.00
☐ 620 Jose Canseco	5.00	2.50	.50

☐ 621 Danny Cox	.03	.01	.00
☐ 622 Glenn Braggs	.40	.20	.04
☐ 623 Kurt Stillwell	.25	.12	.02
☐ 624 Tim Burke	.06	.03	.00
☐ 625 Mookie Wilson	.06	.03	.00
☐ 626 Joel Skinner	.03	.01	.00
☐ 627 Ken Oberkfell	.03	.01	.00
☐ 628 Bob Walk	.03	.01	.00
☐ 629 Larry Parrish	.03	.01	.00
☐ 630 John Candelaria	.03	.01	.00
☐ 631 Tigers Team (mound conference)	.03	.01	.00
☐ 632 Rob Woodward	.03	.01	.00
☐ 633 Jose Uribe	.03	.01	.00
☐ 634 Rafael Palmeiro	1.50	.75	.15
☐ 635 Ken Schrom	.03	.01	.00
☐ 636 Darren Daulton	.08	.04	.01
☐ 637 Bip Roberts	.30	.15	.03
☐ 638 Rich Bordi	.03	.01	.00
☐ 639 Gerald Perry	.06	.03	.00
☐ 640 Mark Clear	.03	.01	.00
☐ 641 Domingo Ramos	.03	.01	.00
☐ 642 Al Pulido	.03	.01	.00
☐ 643 Ron Shepherd	.03	.01	.00
☐ 644 John Denny	.03	.01	.00
☐ 645 Dwight Evans	.10	.05	.01
☐ 646 Mike Mason	.03	.01	.00
☐ 647 Tom Lawless	.03	.01	.00
☐ 648 Barry Larkin	2.00	1.00	.20
☐ 649 Mickey Tettleton	.10	.05	.01
☐ 650 Hubie Brooks	.08	.04	.01
☐ 651 Benny Distefano	.03	.01	.00
☐ 652 Terry Forster	.06	.03	.00
☐ 653 Kevin Mitchell	2.25	1.10	.22
☐ 654 Checklist 529-660	.06	.01	.00
☐ 655 Jesse Barfield	.12	.06	.01
☐ 656 Rangers Team (Valentine/R.Wright)	.03	.01	.00
☐ 657 Tom Waddell	.03	.01	.00
☐ 658 Robby Thompson	.20	.10	.02
☐ 659 Aurelio Lopez	.03	.01	.00
☐ 660 Bob Horner	.08	.04	.01
☐ 661 Lou Whitaker	.10	.05	.01
☐ 662 Frank DiPino	.03	.01	.00
☐ 663 Cliff Johnson	.03	.01	.00
☐ 664 Mike Marshall	.10	.05	.01
☐ 665 Rod Scurry	.03	.01	.00
☐ 666 Von Hayes	.08	.04	.01
☐ 667 Ron Hassey	.03	.01	.00
☐ 668 Juan Bonilla	.03	.01	.00
☐ 669 Bud Black	.06	.03	.00
☐ 670 Jose Cruz	.06	.03	.00
☐ 671A Ray Soff ERR (no D* before copyright line)	.08	.04	.01
☐ 671B Ray Soff COR (D* before copyright line)	.08	.04	.01
☐ 672 Chili Davis	.08	.04	.01
☐ 673 Don Sutton	.12	.06	.01
☐ 674 Bill Campbell	.03	.01	.00
☐ 675 Ed Romero	.03	.01	.00
☐ 676 Charlie Moore	.03	.01	.00
☐ 677 Bob Grich	.06	.03	.00
☐ 678 Carney Lansford	.10	.05	.01
☐ 679 Kent Hrbek	.15	.07	.01
☐ 680 Ryne Sandberg	.50	.25	.05
☐ 681 George Bell	.25	.12	.02
☐ 682 Jerry Reuss	.03	.01	.00
☐ 683 Gary Roenicke	.03	.01	.00
☐ 684 Kent Tekulve	.03	.01	.00
☐ 685 Jerry Hairston	.03	.01	.00
☐ 686 Doyle Alexander	.03	.01	.00
☐ 687 Alan Trammell	.15	.07	.01
☐ 688 Juan Beniquez	.03	.01	.00
☐ 689 Darrell Porter	.03	.01	.00
☐ 690 Dane Iorg	.03	.01	.00
☐ 691 Dave Parker	.12	.06	.01
☐ 692 Frank White	.06	.03	.00
☐ 693 Terry Puhl	.03	.01	.00
☐ 694 Phil Niekro	.12	.06	.01
☐ 695 Chico Walker	.06	.03	.00
☐ 696 Gary Lucas	.03	.01	.00
☐ 697 Ed Lynch	.03	.01	.00
☐ 698 Ernie Whitt	.03	.01	.00
☐ 699 Ken Landreaux	.03	.01	.00
☐ 700 Dave Bergman	.03	.01	.00
☐ 701 Willie Randolph	.06	.03	.00
☐ 702 Greg Gross	.03	.01	.00
☐ 703 Dave Schmidt	.06	.03	.00
☐ 704 Jesse Orosco	.03	.01	.00
☐ 705 Bruce Hurst	.08	.04	.01
☐ 706 Rick Manning	.03	.01	.00
☐ 707 Bob McClure	.03	.01	.00
☐ 708 Scott McGregor	.06	.03	.00
☐ 709 Dave Kingman	.08	.04	.01
☐ 710 Gary Gaetti	.10	.05	.01
☐ 711 Ken Griffey	.10	.05	.01
☐ 712 Don Robinson	.03	.01	.00
☐ 713 Tom Brookens	.03	.01	.00
☐ 714 Dan Quisenberry	.08	.04	.01
☐ 715 Bob Dernier	.03	.01	.00
☐ 716 Rick Leach	.03	.01	.00
☐ 717 Ed VandeBerg	.03	.01	.00
☐ 718 Steve Carlton	.20	.10	.02
☐ 719 Tom Hume	.03	.01	.00
☐ 720 Richard Dotson	.03	.01	.00
☐ 721 Tom Herr	.06	.03	.00
☐ 722 Bob Knepper	.03	.01	.00
☐ 723 Brett Butler	.08	.04	.01
☐ 724 Greg Minton	.03	.01	.00
☐ 725 George Hendrick	.03	.01	.00
☐ 726 Frank Tanana	.06	.03	.00
☐ 727 Mike Moore	.08	.04	.01
☐ 728 Tippy Martinez	.03	.01	.00
☐ 729 Tom Paciorek	.03	.01	.00
☐ 730 Eric Show	.03	.01	.00
☐ 731 Dave Concepcion	.06	.03	.00
☐ 732 Manny Trillo	.03	.01	.00
☐ 733 Bill Caudill	.03	.01	.00
☐ 734 Bill Madlock	.08	.04	.01
☐ 735 Rickey Henderson	.50	.25	.05
☐ 736 Steve Bedrosian	.10	.05	.01
☐ 737 Floyd Bannister	.03	.01	.00
☐ 738 Jorge Orta	.03	.01	.00
☐ 739 Chet Lemon	.03	.01	.00
☐ 740 Rich Gedman	.03	.01	.00
☐ 741 Paul Molitor	.10	.05	.01
☐ 742 Andy McGaffigan	.03	.01	.00
☐ 743 Dwayne Murphy	.03	.01	.00
☐ 744 Roy Smalley	.03	.01	.00
☐ 745 Glenn Hubbard	.03	.01	.00
☐ 746 Bob Ojeda	.06	.03	.00
☐ 747 Johnny Ray	.06	.03	.00
☐ 748 Mike Flanagan	.06	.03	.00
☐ 749 Ozzie Smith	.15	.07	.01
☐ 750 Steve Trout	.03	.01	.00
☐ 751 Garth Iorg	.03	.01	.00
☐ 752 Dan Petry	.03	.01	.00
☐ 753 Rick Honeycutt	.03	.01	.00
☐ 754 Dave LaPoint	.03	.01	.00
☐ 755 Luis Aguayo	.03	.01	.00
☐ 756 Carlton Fisk	.15	.07	.01
☐ 757 Nolan Ryan	.50	.25	.05
☐ 758 Tony Bernazard	.03	.01	.00
☐ 759 Joel Youngblood	.03	.01	.00
☐ 760 Mike Witt	.03	.01	.00
☐ 761 Greg Pryor	.03	.01	.00
☐ 762 Gary Ward	.03	.01	.00
☐ 763 Tim Flannery	.03	.01	.00
☐ 764 Bill Buckner	.06	.03	.00
☐ 765 Kirk Gibson	.15	.07	.01
☐ 766 Don Aase	.03	.01	.00
☐ 767 Ron Cey	.06	.03	.00
☐ 768 Dennis Lamp	.03	.01	.00
☐ 769 Steve Sax	.12	.06	.01
☐ 770 Dave Winfield	.20	.10	.02
☐ 771 Shane Rawley	.03	.01	.00
☐ 772 Harold Baines	.10	.05	.01
☐ 773 Robin Yount	.30	.15	.03
☐ 774 Wayne Krenchicki	.03	.01	.00
☐ 775 Joaquin Andujar	.03	.01	.00
☐ 776 Tom Brunansky	.10	.05	.01
☐ 777 Chris Chambliss	.06	.03	.00
☐ 778 Jack Morris	.10	.05	.01
☐ 779 Craig Reynolds	.03	.01	.00
☐ 780 Andre Thornton	.06	.03	.00
☐ 781 Atlee Hammaker	.03	.01	.00
☐ 782 Brian Downing	.06	.03	.00
☐ 783 Willie Wilson	.08	.04	.01
☐ 784 Cal Ripken	.25	.12	.02
☐ 785 Terry Francona	.03	.01	.00
☐ 786 Jimy Williams MG (checklist back)	.06	.03	.00
☐ 787 Alejandro Pena	.03	.01	.00
☐ 788 Tim Stoddard	.03	.01	.00
☐ 789 Dan Schatzeder	.03	.01	.00
☐ 790 Julio Cruz	.03	.01	.00
☐ 791 Lance Parrish UER (no trademark, never corrected)	.15	.07	.01
☐ 792 Checklist 661-792	.10	.01	.00

1987 Topps Wax Box Cards

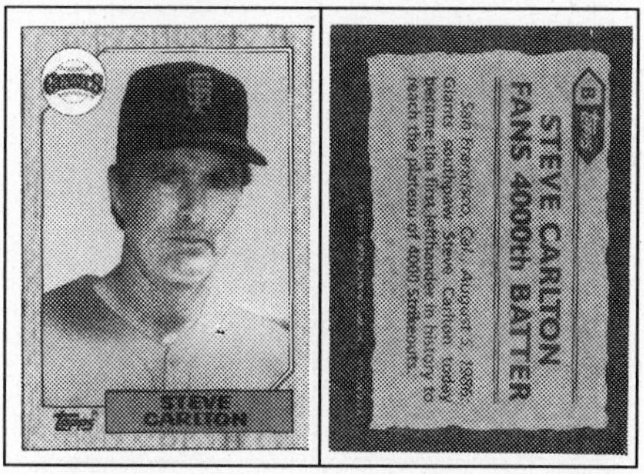

This set of 8 cards is really four different sets of two smaller (2 1/8" by 3") cards which were printed on the side of the wax pack box; these eight cards are lettered A through H and are very similar in design to the Topps regular issue cards. The card backs are done in a newspaper headline style describing something about that player that happened the previous season. The card backs feature blue and yellow ink on gray card stock.

	MINT	EXC	G-VG
COMPLETE SET (8)	1.50	.75	.15
COMMON PLAYER (A-H)	.10	.05	.01
☐ A Don Baylor	.15	.07	.01
☐ B Steve Carlton	.35	.17	.03
☐ C Ron Cey	.10	.05	.01
☐ D Cecil Cooper	.10	.05	.01
☐ E Rickey Henderson	.75	.35	.07
☐ F Jim Rice	.20	.10	.02
☐ G Don Sutton	.20	.10	.02
☐ H Dave Winfield	.35	.17	.03

1987 Topps Glossy All-Stars 22

This set of 22 glossy cards was inserted one per rack pack. Players selected for the set are the starting players (plus manager and two pitchers) in the 1986 All-Star Game in Houston. Cards measure standard size, 2 1/2" by 3 1/2" and the backs feature red and blue printing on a white card stock.

	MINT	EXC	G-VG
COMPLETE SET (22)	3.00	1.50	.30
COMMON PLAYER (1-22)	.10	.05	.01
☐ 1 Whitey Herzog MG	.10	.05	.01
☐ 2 Keith Hernandez	.15	.07	.01
☐ 3 Ryne Sandberg	.50	.25	.05
☐ 4 Mike Schmidt	.50	.25	.05
☐ 5 Ozzie Smith	.20	.10	.02
☐ 6 Tony Gwynn	.30	.15	.03
☐ 7 Dale Murphy	.35	.17	.03
☐ 8 Darryl Strawberry	.35	.17	.03
☐ 9 Gary Carter	.20	.10	.02
☐ 10 Dwight Gooden	.35	.17	.03
☐ 11 Fernando Valenzuela	.20	.10	.02
☐ 12 Dick Howser MG	.10	.05	.01
☐ 13 Wally Joyner	.40	.20	.04
☐ 14 Lou Whitaker	.15	.07	.01
☐ 15 Wade Boggs	.50	.25	.05
☐ 16 Cal Ripken	.25	.12	.02
☐ 17 Dave Winfield	.20	.10	.02
☐ 18 Rickey Henderson	.50	.25	.05
☐ 19 Kirby Puckett	.40	.20	.04
☐ 20 Lance Parrish	.20	.10	.02
☐ 21 Roger Clemens	.50	.25	.05
☐ 22 Teddy Higuera	.15	.07	.01

1987 Topps Jumbo Glossy Rookies

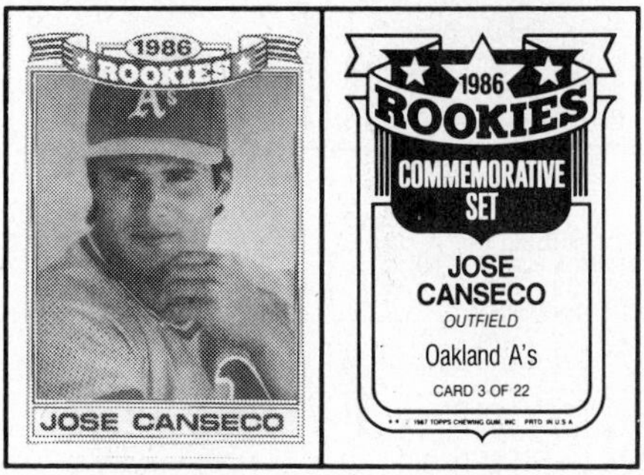

Inserted in each supermarket jumbo pack is a card from this series of 22 of 1986's best rookies as determined by Topps. Jumbo packs consisted of 100 (regular issue 1987 Topps baseball) cards with a stick of gum plus the insert "Rookie" card. The card fronts are in full color and measure 2 1/2" by 3 1/2". The card backs are printed in red and blue on white card stock and are numbered at the bottom essentially by alphabetical order.

	MINT	EXC	G-VG
COMPLETE SET (22)	13.50	6.00	1.00
COMMON PLAYER (1-22)	.25	.12	.02
☐ 1 Andy Allanson	.25	.12	.02
☐ 2 John Cangelosi	.25	.12	.02
☐ 3 Jose Canseco	3.00	1.50	.30
☐ 4 Will Clark	2.25	1.10	.22
☐ 5 Mark Eichhorn	.25	.12	.02
☐ 6 Pete Incaviglia	.60	.30	.06
☐ 7 Wally Joyner	1.00	.50	.10
☐ 8 Eric King	.25	.12	.02
☐ 9 Dave Magadan	.60	.30	.06
☐ 10 John Morris	.25	.12	.02
☐ 11 Juan Nieves	.25	.12	.02
☐ 12 Rafael Palmeiro	.75	.35	.07
☐ 13 Billy Jo Robidoux	.25	.12	.02
☐ 14 Bruce Ruffin	.25	.12	.02
☐ 15 Ruben Sierra	1.50	.75	.15
☐ 16 Cory Snyder	.75	.35	.07
☐ 17 Kurt Stillwell	.40	.20	.04
☐ 18 Dale Sveum	.25	.12	.02
☐ 19 Danny Tartabull	.75	.35	.07
☐ 20 Andres Thomas	.25	.12	.02
☐ 21 Robby Thompson	.25	.12	.02
☐ 22 Todd Worrell	.50	.25	.05

1987 Topps Glossy 60

Topps issued this set through a mail-in offer explained and advertised on the wax packs. This 60-card set features glossy fronts with each card measuring 2 1/2" by 3 1/2". The offer provided your choice of any one of the six 10-card subsets (1-10, 11-20, etc.) for 1.00 plus six of the Special Offer ("Spring Fever Baseball") insert cards, which were found one per wax pack. The last two players (numerically) in each ten-card subset are actually "Hot Prospects."

	MINT	EXC	G-VG
COMPLETE SET (60)	12.00	6.00	1.20
COMMON PLAYER (1-60)	.20	.10	.02
☐ 1 Don Mattingly	1.00	.50	.10
☐ 2 Tony Gwynn	.50	.25	.05
☐ 3 Gary Gaetti	.25	.12	.02
☐ 4 Glenn Davis	.30	.15	.03
☐ 5 Roger Clemens	.75	.35	.07
☐ 6 Dale Murphy	.50	.25	.05
☐ 7 Lou Whitaker	.25	.12	.02
☐ 8 Roger McDowell	.20	.10	.02
☐ 9 Cory Snyder	.35	.17	.03
☐ 10 Todd Worrell	.25	.12	.02
☐ 11 Gary Carter	.30	.15	.03
☐ 12 Eddie Murray	.35	.17	.03
☐ 13 Bob Knepper	.20	.10	.02
☐ 14 Harold Baines	.25	.12	.02
☐ 15 Jeff Reardon	.20	.10	.02
☐ 16 Joe Carter	.25	.12	.02
☐ 17 Dave Parker	.25	.12	.02
☐ 18 Wade Boggs	.75	.35	.07
☐ 19 Danny Tartabull	.35	.17	.03
☐ 20 Jim Deshaies	.20	.10	.02
☐ 21 Rickey Henderson	.75	.35	.07
☐ 22 Rob Deer	.25	.12	.02
☐ 23 Ozzie Smith	.30	.15	.03
☐ 24 Dave Righetti	.25	.12	.02
☐ 25 Kent Hrbek	.25	.12	.02
☐ 26 Keith Hernandez	.25	.12	.02
☐ 27 Don Baylor	.25	.12	.02
☐ 28 Mike Schmidt	.75	.35	.07
☐ 29 Pete Incaviglia	.40	.20	.04
☐ 30 Barry Bonds	.50	.25	.05
☐ 31 George Brett	.60	.30	.06
☐ 32 Darryl Strawberry	.75	.35	.07
☐ 33 Mike Witt	.20	.10	.02
☐ 34 Kevin Bass	.20	.10	.02
☐ 35 Jesse Barfield	.25	.12	.02
☐ 36 Bob Ojeda	.20	.10	.02
☐ 37 Cal Ripken	.35	.17	.03
☐ 38 Vince Coleman	.30	.15	.03
☐ 39 Wally Joyner	.50	.25	.05
☐ 40 Robby Thompson	.20	.10	.02
☐ 41 Pete Rose	.75	.35	.07
☐ 42 Jim Rice	.25	.12	.02
☐ 43 Tony Bernazard	.20	.10	.02
☐ 44 Eric Davis	.75	.35	.07
☐ 45 George Bell	.30	.15	.03
☐ 46 Hubie Brooks	.25	.12	.02
☐ 47 Jack Morris	.25	.12	.02
☐ 48 Tim Raines	.30	.15	.03
☐ 49 Mark Eichhorn	.20	.10	.02
☐ 50 Kevin Mitchell	.25	.12	.02
☐ 51 Dwight Gooden	.50	.25	.05
☐ 52 Doug DeCinces	.20	.10	.02
☐ 53 Fernando Valenzuela	.25	.12	.02
☐ 54 Reggie Jackson	.50	.25	.05
☐ 55 Johnny Ray	.20	.10	.02
☐ 56 Mike Pagliarulo	.20	.10	.02
☐ 57 Kirby Puckett	.60	.30	.06
☐ 58 Lance Parrish	.30	.15	.03
☐ 59 Jose Canseco	1.50	.75	.15
☐ 60 Greg Mathews	.20	.10	.02

1987 Topps Mini Leaders

The 1987 Topps Mini set of Major League Leaders features 77 cards of leaders of the various statistical categories for the 1986 season. The cards are numbered on the back and measure 2 5/32" by 3". The card backs are printed in orange and brown on white card stock. They are very similar in design to the Team Leader cards in the 1987 Topps regular issue. The cards were distributed as a separate issue in wax packs of seven for 30 cents. Eleven of the cards were double printed and are hence more plentiful; they are marked DP in the checklist below.

	MINT	EXC	G-VG
COMPLETE SET (77)	7.00	3.50	.70
COMMON PLAYER (1-77)	.06	.03	.00
COMMON PLAYER DP	.03	.01	.00
☐ 1 Bob Horner DP	.06	.03	.00
☐ 2 Dale Murphy	.30	.15	.03
☐ 3 Lee Smith	.06	.03	.00
☐ 4 Eric Davis	.60	.30	.06
☐ 5 John Franco	.06	.03	.00
☐ 6 Dave Parker	.10	.05	.01
☐ 7 Kevin Bass	.06	.03	.00
☐ 8 Glenn Davis DP	.10	.05	.01
☐ 9 Bill Doran DP	.06	.03	.00
☐ 10 Bob Knepper DP	.03	.01	.00
☐ 11 Mike Scott	.15	.07	.01
☐ 12 Dave Smith	.06	.03	.00
☐ 13 Mariano Duncan	.06	.03	.00
☐ 14 Orel Hershiser	.30	.15	.03
☐ 15 Steve Sax DP	.10	.05	.01
☐ 16 Fernando Valenzuela	.15	.07	.01
☐ 17 Tim Raines	.20	.10	.02
☐ 18 Jeff Reardon	.06	.03	.00
☐ 19 Floyd Youmans	.06	.03	.00
☐ 20 Gary Carter DP	.10	.05	.01
☐ 21 Ron Darling	.10	.05	.01
☐ 22 Sid Fernandez	.10	.05	.01
☐ 23 Dwight Gooden	.40	.20	.04
☐ 24 Keith Hernandez	.15	.07	.01
☐ 25 Bob Ojeda	.10	.05	.01
☐ 26 Darryl Strawberry	.50	.25	.05
☐ 27 Steve Bedrosian	.10	.05	.01
☐ 28 Von Hayes DP	.06	.03	.00
☐ 29 Juan Samuel	.10	.05	.01
☐ 30 Mike Schmidt	.75	.35	.07
☐ 31 Rick Rhoden	.06	.03	.00
☐ 32 Vince Coleman	.20	.10	.02
☐ 33 Danny Cox	.06	.03	.00
☐ 34 Todd Worrell	.15	.07	.01
☐ 35 Tony Gwynn	.40	.20	.04
☐ 36 Mike Krukow	.06	.03	.00
☐ 37 Candy Maldonado	.10	.05	.01
☐ 38 Don Aase	.06	.03	.00
☐ 39 Eddie Murray	.30	.15	.03
☐ 40 Cal Ripken	.35	.17	.03
☐ 41 Wade Boggs	.50	.25	.05
☐ 42 Roger Clemens	.50	.25	.05
☐ 43 Bruce Hurst	.10	.05	.01
☐ 44 Jim Rice	.15	.07	.01
☐ 45 Wally Joyner	.25	.12	.02
☐ 46 Donnie Moore	.06	.03	.00
☐ 47 Gary Pettis	.06	.03	.00
☐ 48 Mike Witt	.06	.03	.00
☐ 49 John Cangelosi	.06	.03	.00
☐ 50 Tom Candiotti	.06	.03	.00
☐ 51 Joe Carter	.15	.07	.01
☐ 52 Pat Tabler	.06	.03	.00
☐ 53 Kirk Gibson DP	.10	.05	.01

☐ 54 Willie Hernandez	.06	.03	.00
☐ 55 Jack Morris	.10	.05	.01
☐ 56 Alan Trammell DP	.10	.05	.01
☐ 57 George Brett	.45	.22	.04
☐ 58 Willie Wilson	.10	.05	.01
☐ 59 Rob Deer	.10	.05	.01
☐ 60 Teddy Higuera	.10	.05	.01
☐ 61 Bert Blyleven DP	.06	.03	.00
☐ 62 Gary Gaetti DP	.06	.03	.00
☐ 63 Kirby Puckett	.40	.20	.04
☐ 64 Rickey Henderson	.60	.30	.06
☐ 65 Don Mattingly	.90	.45	.09
☐ 66 Dennis Rasmussen	.10	.05	.01
☐ 67 Dave Righetti	.10	.05	.01
☐ 68 Jose Canseco	1.25	.60	.12
☐ 69 Dave Kingman	.10	.05	.01
☐ 70 Phil Bradley	.10	.05	.01
☐ 71 Mark Langston	.15	.07	.01
☐ 72 Pete O'Brien	.06	.03	.00
☐ 73 Jesse Barfield	.15	.07	.01
☐ 74 George Bell	.20	.10	.02
☐ 75 Tony Fernandez	.10	.05	.01
☐ 76 Tom Henke	.10	.05	.01
☐ 77 Checklist Card	.06	.03	.00

1987 Topps Traded

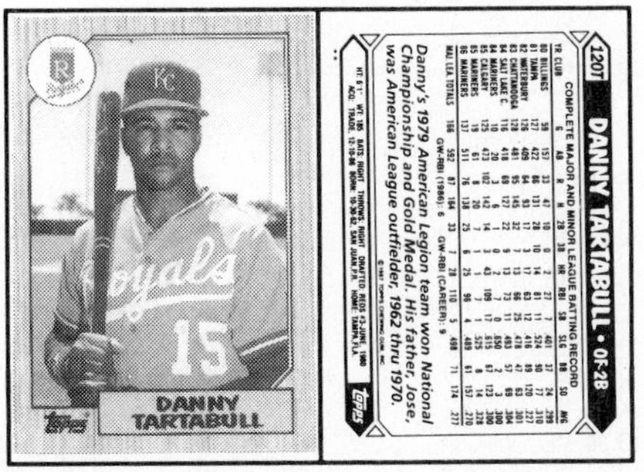

This 132-card Traded or extended set was distributed by Topps to dealers in a special green and white box as a complete set. The card fronts are identical in style to the Topps regular issue and are also 2 1/2" by 3 1/2". The backs are printed in yellow and blue on white card stock. Cards are numbered (with a T suffix) alphabetically according to the name of the player. The key (extended) rookies in this set (without any prior cards) are Ellis Burks and Matt Williams. Topps also produced a specially boxed "glossy" edition, frequently referred to as the Topps Traded Tiffany set. This year Topps did not disclose the number of sets they produced or sold. It is apparent from the availability that there were many more sets produced this year compared to the 1984-86 Tiffany sets, perhaps 30,000 sets, more than three times as many. The checklist of cards is identical to that of the normal non-glossy cards. There are two primary distinguishing features of the Tiffany cards, white card stock reverses and high gloss obverses. These Tiffany cards are valued at approximately three times the values listed below.

	MINT	EXC	G-VG
COMPLETE SET (132)	13.50	6.00	1.00
COMMON PLAYER (1-132)	.06	.03	.00
☐ 1T Bill Almon	.06	.03	.00
☐ 2T Scott Bankhead	.10	.05	.01
☐ 3T Eric Bell	.10	.05	.01
☐ 4T Juan Beniquez	.06	.03	.00
☐ 5T Juan Berenguer	.06	.03	.00
☐ 6T Greg Booker	.06	.03	.00
☐ 7T Thad Bosley	.06	.03	.00
☐ 8T Larry Bowa MG	.10	.05	.01
☐ 9T Greg Brock	.10	.05	.01
☐ 10T Bob Brower	.10	.05	.01
☐ 11T Jerry Browne	.25	.12	.02
☐ 12T Ralph Bryant	.10	.05	.01
☐ 13T DeWayne Buice	.10	.05	.01
☐ 14T Ellis Burks	2.25	1.10	.22
☐ 15T Ivan Calderon	.20	.10	.02
☐ 16T Jeff Calhoun	.06	.03	.00
☐ 17T Casey Candaele	.06	.03	.00
☐ 18T John Cangelosi	.06	.03	.00
☐ 19T Steve Carlton	.25	.12	.02
☐ 20T Juan Castillo	.10	.05	.01
☐ 21T Rick Cerone	.06	.03	.00
☐ 22T Ron Cey	.10	.05	.01
☐ 23T John Christensen	.06	.03	.00
☐ 24T David Cone	1.50	.75	.15
☐ 25T Chuck Crim	.10	.05	.01
☐ 26T Storm Davis	.10	.05	.01
☐ 27T Andre Dawson	.40	.20	.04
☐ 28T Rick Dempsey	.06	.03	.00
☐ 29T Doug Drabek	.35	.17	.03
☐ 30T Mike Dunne	.10	.05	.01
☐ 31T Dennis Eckersley	.25	.12	.02
☐ 32T Lee Elia MG	.06	.03	.00
☐ 33T Brian Fisher	.06	.03	.00
☐ 34T Terry Francona	.06	.03	.00
☐ 35T Willie Fraser	.06	.03	.00
☐ 36T Billy Gardner MG	.06	.03	.00
☐ 37T Ken Gerhart	.06	.03	.00
☐ 38T Dan Gladden	.10	.05	.01
☐ 39T Jim Gott	.10	.05	.01
☐ 40T Cecilio Guante	.06	.03	.00
☐ 41T Albert Hall	.06	.03	.00
☐ 42T Terry Harper	.06	.03	.00
☐ 43T Mickey Hatcher	.06	.03	.00
☐ 44T Brad Havens	.06	.03	.00
☐ 45T Neal Heaton	.06	.03	.00
☐ 46T Mike Henneman	.20	.10	.02
☐ 47T Donnie Hill	.06	.03	.00
☐ 48T Guy Hoffman	.06	.03	.00
☐ 49T Brian Holton	.10	.05	.01
☐ 50T Charles Hudson	.06	.03	.00
☐ 51T Danny Jackson	.10	.05	.01
☐ 52T Reggie Jackson	.50	.25	.05
☐ 53T Chris James	.40	.20	.04
☐ 54T Dion James	.10	.05	.01
☐ 55T Stan Jefferson	.10	.05	.01
☐ 56T Joe Johnson	.06	.03	.00
☐ 57T Terry Kennedy	.06	.03	.00
☐ 58T Mike Kingery	.10	.05	.01
☐ 59T Ray Knight	.10	.05	.01
☐ 60T Gene Larkin	.25	.12	.02
☐ 61T Mike LaValliere	.10	.05	.01
☐ 62T Jack Lazorko	.06	.03	.00
☐ 63T Terry Leach	.12	.06	.01
☐ 64T Tim Leary	.15	.07	.01
☐ 65T Jim Lindeman	.10	.05	.01
☐ 66T Steve Lombardozzi	.10	.05	.01
☐ 67T Bill Long	.10	.05	.01
☐ 68T Barry Lyons	.20	.10	.02
☐ 69T Shane Mack	.15	.07	.01
☐ 70T Greg Maddux	.75	.35	.07
☐ 71T Bill Madlock	.10	.05	.01
☐ 72T Joe Magrane	.75	.35	.07
☐ 73T Dave Martinez	.20	.10	.02
☐ 74T Fred McGriff	2.00	1.00	.20
☐ 75T Mark McLemore	.06	.03	.00
☐ 76T Kevin McReynolds	.20	.10	.02
☐ 77T Dave Meads	.06	.03	.00
☐ 78T Eddie Milner	.06	.03	.00
☐ 79T Greg Minton	.06	.03	.00
☐ 80T John Mitchell	.10	.05	.01
☐ 81T Kevin Mitchell	1.25	.60	.12
☐ 82T Charlie Moore	.06	.03	.00
☐ 83T Jeff Musselman	.10	.05	.01
☐ 84T Gene Nelson	.06	.03	.00
☐ 85T Graig Nettles	.15	.07	.01
☐ 86T Al Newman	.06	.03	.00
☐ 87T Reid Nichols	.06	.03	.00
☐ 88T Tom Niedenfuer	.06	.03	.00
☐ 89T Joe Niekro	.10	.05	.01
☐ 90T Tom Nieto	.06	.03	.00
☐ 91T Matt Nokes	.40	.20	.04
☐ 92T Dickie Noles	.06	.03	.00
☐ 93T Pat Pacillo	.10	.05	.01
☐ 94T Lance Parrish	.15	.07	.01
☐ 95T Tony Pena	.15	.07	.01
☐ 96T Luis Polonia	.25	.12	.02
☐ 97T Randy Ready	.10	.05	.01
☐ 98T Jeff Reardon	.15	.07	.01
☐ 99T Gary Redus	.06	.03	.00
☐ 100T Jeff Reed	.06	.03	.00
☐ 101T Rick Rhoden	.10	.05	.01
☐ 102T Cal Ripken Sr. MG	.06	.03	.00
☐ 103T Wally Ritchie	.10	.05	.01
☐ 104T Jeff Robinson (Tigers pitcher)	.25	.12	.02

☐	105T Gary Roenicke	.06	.03	.00
☐	106T Jerry Royster	.06	.03	.00
☐	107T Mark Salas	.06	.03	.00
☐	108T Luis Salazar	.06	.03	.00
☐	109T Benny Santiago	1.00	.50	.10
☐	110T Dave Schmidt	.10	.05	.01
☐	111T Kevin Seitzer	.80	.40	.08
☐	112T John Shelby	.06	.03	.00
☐	113T Steve Shields	.06	.03	.00
☐	114T John Smiley	.35	.17	.03
☐	115T Chris Speier	.06	.03	.00
☐	116T Mike Stanley	.12	.06	.01
☐	117T Terry Steinbach	.45	.22	.04
☐	118T Les Straker	.10	.05	.01
☐	119T Jim Sundberg	.06	.03	.00
☐	120T Danny Tartabull	.25	.12	.02
☐	121T Tom Trebelhorn MG	.06	.03	.00
☐	122T Dave Valle	.06	.03	.00
☐	123T Ed VandeBerg	.06	.03	.00
☐	124T Andy Van Slyke	.20	.10	.02
☐	125T Gary Ward	.06	.03	.00
☐	126T Alan Wiggins	.06	.03	.00
☐	127T Bill Wilkinson	.10	.05	.01
☐	128T Frank Williams	.06	.03	.00
☐	129T Matt Williams	3.50	1.75	.35
☐	130T Jim Winn	.06	.03	.00
☐	131T Matt Young	.06	.03	.00
☐	132T Checklist 1T-132T	.06	.01	.00

1988 Topps

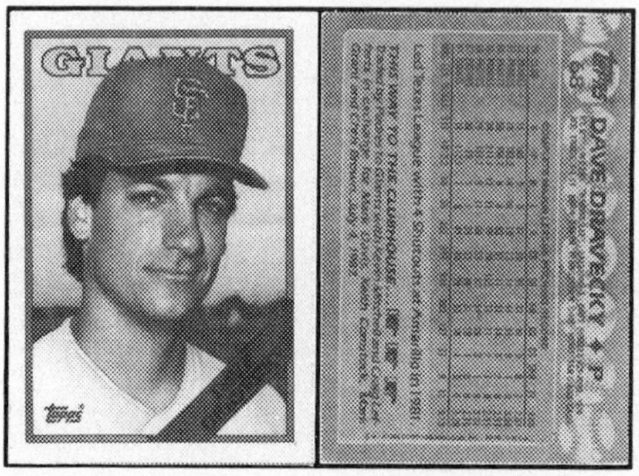

This 792-card set features backs that are printed in orange and black on white card stock. The manager cards contain a checklist of the respective team's players on the back. Subsets in the set include Record Breakers (1-7), Turn Back the Clock (661-665), and All-Star selections (386-407). The Team Leader cards typically show two players together inside a white cloud. The key rookie cards in this set are Ellis Burks and Matt Williams. Topps also produced a specially boxed "glossy" edition, frequently referred to as the Topps Tiffany set. This year, again, Topps did not disclose the number of Tiffany sets they produced or sold. It is apparent from the availability that there were many more sets produced this year compared to the 1984-86 Tiffany sets, perhaps 25,000 sets. The checklist of cards (792 regular and 132 Traded) is identical to that of the normal non-glossy cards. There are two primary distinguishing features of the Tiffany cards, white card stock reverses and high gloss obverses. These Tiffany cards are valued at approximately four times the values listed below.

		MINT	EXC	G-VG
	COMPLETE SET (792)	25.00	12.50	2.50
	COMMON PLAYER (1-792)	.03	.01	.00
☐	1 Vince Coleman RB 100 Steals for Third Cons. Season	.20	.05	.01
☐	2 Don Mattingly RB Six Grand Slams	.30	.15	.03
☐	3A Mark McGwire RB Rookie Homer Record (white spot behind left foot)	1.00	.50	.10
☐	3B Mark McGwire RB Rookie Homer Record (no white spot)	.25	.12	.02
☐	4A Eddie Murray RB Switch Home Runs, Two Straight Games (caption in box on card front)	1.00	.50	.10
☐	4B Eddie Murray RB Switch Home Runs, Two Straight Games (no caption on front)	.25	.12	.02
☐	5 Phil/Joe Niekro RB Brothers Win Record	.06	.03	.00
☐	6 Nolan Ryan RB 11th Season with 200 Strikeouts	.25	.12	.02
☐	7 Benito Santiago RB 34-Game Hitting Streak, Rookie Record	.10	.05	.01
☐	8 Kevin Elster	.10	.05	.01
☐	9 Andy Hawkins	.03	.01	.00
☐	10 Ryne Sandberg	.30	.15	.03
☐	11 Mike Young	.03	.01	.00
☐	12 Bill Schroeder	.03	.01	.00
☐	13 Andres Thomas	.03	.01	.00
☐	14 Sparky Anderson MG (checklist back)	.06	.03	.00
☐	15 Chili Davis	.06	.03	.00
☐	16 Kirk McCaskill	.03	.01	.00
☐	17 Ron Oester	.03	.01	.00
☐	18A Al Leiter ERR (photo actually Steve George, right ear visible)	.60	.30	.06
☐	18B Al Leiter COR (left ear visible)	.25	.12	.02
☐	19 Mark Davidson	.08	.04	.01
☐	20 Kevin Gross	.03	.01	.00
☐	21 Red Sox TL Wade Boggs and Spike Owen	.10	.05	.01
☐	22 Greg Swindell	.10	.05	.01
☐	23 Ken Landreaux	.03	.01	.00
☐	24 Jim Deshaies	.03	.01	.00
☐	25 Andres Galarraga	.12	.06	.01
☐	26 Mitch Williams	.06	.03	.00
☐	27 R.J. Reynolds	.03	.01	.00
☐	28 Jose Nunez	.06	.03	.00
☐	29 Argenis Salazar	.03	.01	.00
☐	30 Sid Fernandez	.08	.04	.01
☐	31 Bruce Bochy	.03	.01	.00
☐	32 Mike Morgan	.03	.01	.00
☐	33 Rob Deer	.06	.03	.00
☐	34 Ricky Horton	.03	.01	.00
☐	35 Harold Baines	.08	.04	.01
☐	36 Jamie Moyer	.03	.01	.00
☐	37 Ed Romero	.03	.01	.00
☐	38 Jeff Calhoun	.03	.01	.00
☐	39 Gerald Perry	.03	.01	.00
☐	40 Orel Hershiser	.15	.07	.01
☐	41 Bob Melvin	.03	.01	.00
☐	42 Bill Landrum	.15	.07	.01
☐	43 Dick Schofield	.03	.01	.00
☐	44 Lou Piniella MG (checklist back)	.06	.03	.00
☐	45 Kent Hrbek	.12	.06	.01
☐	46 Darnell Coles	.03	.01	.00
☐	47 Joaquin Andujar	.03	.01	.00
☐	48 Alan Ashby	.03	.01	.00
☐	49 Dave Clark	.08	.04	.01
☐	50 Hubie Brooks	.08	.04	.01
☐	51 Orioles TL Eddie Murray and Cal Ripken	.15	.07	.01
☐	52 Don Robinson	.03	.01	.00
☐	53 Curt Wilkerson	.03	.01	.00
☐	54 Jim Clancy	.03	.01	.00
☐	55 Phil Bradley	.06	.03	.00
☐	56 Ed Hearn	.03	.01	.00
☐	57 Tim Crews	.06	.03	.00
☐	58 Dave Magadan	.15	.07	.01
☐	59 Danny Cox	.03	.01	.00
☐	60 Rickey Henderson	.30	.15	.03
☐	61 Mark Knudson	.08	.04	.01
☐	62 Jeff Hamilton	.03	.01	.00
☐	63 Jimmy Jones	.06	.03	.00
☐	64 Ken Caminiti	.15	.07	.01
☐	65 Leon Durham	.03	.01	.00
☐	66 Shane Rawley	.03	.01	.00

☐ 67	Ken Oberkfell	.03	.01	.00
☐ 68	Dave Dravecky	.08	.04	.01
☐ 69	Mike Hart	.03	.01	.00
☐ 70	Roger Clemens	.40	.20	.04
☐ 71	Gary Pettis	.03	.01	.00
☐ 72	Dennis Eckersley	.12	.06	.01
☐ 73	Randy Bush	.03	.01	.00
☐ 74	Tom Lasorda MG	.08	.04	.01
	(checklist back)			
☐ 75	Joe Carter	.12	.06	.01
☐ 76	Dennis Martinez	.03	.01	.00
☐ 77	Tom O'Malley	.03	.01	.00
☐ 78	Dan Petry	.03	.01	.00
☐ 79	Ernie Whitt	.03	.01	.00
☐ 80	Mark Langston	.10	.05	.01
☐ 81	Reds TL	.03	.01	.00
	Ron Robinson			
	and John Franco			
☐ 82	Darrel Akerfelds	.06	.03	.00
☐ 83	Jose Oquendo	.03	.01	.00
☐ 84	Cecilio Guante	.03	.01	.00
☐ 85	Howard Johnson	.10	.05	.01
☐ 86	Ron Karkovice	.03	.01	.00
☐ 87	Mike Mason	.03	.01	.00
☐ 88	Earnie Riles	.03	.01	.00
☐ 89	Gary Thurman	.12	.06	.01
☐ 90	Dale Murphy	.18	.09	.01
☐ 91	Joey Cora	.08	.04	.01
☐ 92	Len Matuszek	.03	.01	.00
☐ 93	Bob Sebra	.03	.01	.00
☐ 94	Chuck Jackson	.06	.03	.00
☐ 95	Lance Parrish	.08	.04	.01
☐ 96	Todd Benzinger	.18	.09	.01
☐ 97	Scott Garrelts	.06	.03	.00
☐ 98	Rene Gonzales	.06	.03	.00
☐ 99	Chuck Finley	.12	.06	.01
☐ 100	Jack Clark	.12	.06	.01
☐ 101	Allan Anderson	.06	.03	.00
☐ 102	Barry Larkin	.25	.12	.02
☐ 103	Curt Young	.03	.01	.00
☐ 104	Dick Williams MG	.06	.03	.00
	(checklist back)			
☐ 105	Jesse Orosco	.03	.01	.00
☐ 106	Jim Walewander	.06	.03	.00
☐ 107	Scott Bailes	.03	.01	.00
☐ 108	Steve Lyons	.03	.01	.00
☐ 109	Joel Skinner	.03	.01	.00
☐ 110	Teddy Higuera	.08	.04	.01
☐ 111	Expos TL	.03	.01	.00
	Hubie Brooks and			
	Vance Law			
☐ 112	Les Lancaster	.10	.05	.01
☐ 113	Kelly Gruber	.25	.12	.02
☐ 114	Jeff Russell	.03	.01	.00
☐ 115	Johnny Ray	.06	.03	.00
☐ 116	Jerry Don Gleaton	.03	.01	.00
☐ 117	James Steels	.03	.01	.00
☐ 118	Bob Welch	.10	.05	.01
☐ 119	Robbie Wine	.03	.01	.00
☐ 120	Kirby Puckett	.30	.15	.03
☐ 121	Checklist 1-132	.06	.01	.00
☐ 122	Tony Bernazard	.03	.01	.00
☐ 123	Tom Candiotti	.03	.01	.00
☐ 124	Ray Knight	.06	.03	.00
☐ 125	Bruce Hurst	.08	.04	.01
☐ 126	Steve Jeltz	.03	.01	.00
☐ 127	Jim Gott	.03	.01	.00
☐ 128	Johnny Grubb	.03	.01	.00
☐ 129	Greg Minton	.03	.01	.00
☐ 130	Buddy Bell	.06	.03	.00
☐ 131	Don Schulze	.03	.01	.00
☐ 132	Donnie Hill	.03	.01	.00
☐ 133	Greg Mathews	.03	.01	.00
☐ 134	Chuck Tanner MG	.06	.03	.00
	(checklist back)			
☐ 135	Dennis Rasmussen	.03	.01	.00
☐ 136	Brian Dayett	.03	.01	.00
☐ 137	Chris Bosio	.03	.01	.00
☐ 138	Mitch Webster	.03	.01	.00
☐ 139	Jerry Browne	.10	.05	.01
☐ 140	Jesse Barfield	.10	.05	.01
☐ 141	Royals TL	.15	.07	.01
	George Brett and			
	Bret Saberhagen			
☐ 142	Andy Van Slyke	.12	.06	.01
☐ 143	Mickey Tettleton	.06	.03	.00
☐ 144	Don Gordon	.06	.03	.00
☐ 145	Bill Madlock	.06	.03	.00
☐ 146	Donnell Nixon	.08	.04	.01
☐ 147	Bill Buckner	.06	.03	.00
☐ 148	Carmelo Martinez	.03	.01	.00
☐ 149	Ken Howell	.03	.01	.00
☐ 150	Eric Davis	.30	.15	.03
☐ 151	Bob Knepper	.03	.01	.00

☐ 152	Jody Reed	.45	.22	.04
☐ 153	John Habyan	.03	.01	.00
☐ 154	Jeff Stone	.03	.01	.00
☐ 155	Bruce Sutter	.08	.04	.01
☐ 156	Gary Matthews	.03	.01	.00
☐ 157	Atlee Hammaker	.03	.01	.00
☐ 158	Tim Hulett	.03	.01	.00
☐ 159	Brad Arnsberg	.15	.07	.01
☐ 160	Willie McGee	.10	.05	.01
☐ 161	Bryn Smith	.03	.01	.00
☐ 162	Mark McLemore	.03	.01	.00
☐ 163	Dale Mohorcic	.03	.01	.00
☐ 164	Dave Johnson MG	.06	.03	.00
	(checklist back)			
☐ 165	Robin Yount	.20	.10	.02
☐ 166	Rick Rodriquez	.06	.03	.00
☐ 167	Rance Mulliniks	.03	.01	.00
☐ 168	Barry Jones	.03	.01	.00
☐ 169	Ross Jones	.03	.01	.00
☐ 170	Rich Gossage	.08	.04	.01
☐ 171	Cubs TL	.06	.03	.00
	Shawon Dunston			
	and Manny Trillo			
☐ 172	Lloyd McClendon	.08	.04	.01
☐ 173	Eric Plunk	.03	.01	.00
☐ 174	Phil Garner	.03	.01	.00
☐ 175	Kevin Bass	.06	.03	.00
☐ 176	Jeff Reed	.03	.01	.00
☐ 177	Frank Tanana	.06	.03	.00
☐ 178	Dwayne Henry	.06	.03	.00
☐ 179	Charlie Puleo	.03	.01	.00
☐ 180	Terry Kennedy	.03	.01	.00
☐ 181	David Cone	.50	.25	.05
☐ 182	Ken Phelps	.06	.03	.00
☐ 183	Tom Lawless	.03	.01	.00
☐ 184	Ivan Calderon	.06	.03	.00
☐ 185	Rick Rhoden	.03	.01	.00
☐ 186	Rafael Palmeiro	.25	.12	.02
☐ 187	Steve Kiefer	.03	.01	.00
☐ 188	John Russell	.03	.01	.00
☐ 189	Wes Gardner	.08	.04	.01
☐ 190	Candy Maldonado	.06	.03	.00
☐ 191	John Cerutti	.03	.01	.00
☐ 192	Devon White	.10	.05	.01
☐ 193	Brian Fisher	.03	.01	.00
☐ 194	Tom Kelly MG	.06	.03	.00
	(checklist back)			
☐ 195	Dan Quisenberry	.08	.04	.01
☐ 196	Dave Engle	.03	.01	.00
☐ 197	Lance McCullers	.03	.01	.00
☐ 198	Franklin Stubbs	.06	.03	.00
☐ 199	Dave Meads	.03	.01	.00
☐ 200	Wade Boggs	.40	.20	.04
☐ 201	Rangers TL	.06	.03	.00
	Bobby Valentine,			
	Pete O'Brien,			
	Pete Incaviglia, and			
	Steve Buechele			
☐ 202	Glenn Hoffman	.03	.01	.00
☐ 203	Fred Toliver	.03	.01	.00
☐ 204	Paul O'Neill	.20	.10	.02
☐ 205	Nelson Liriano	.15	.07	.01
☐ 206	Domingo Ramos	.03	.01	.00
☐ 207	John Mitchell	.08	.04	.01
☐ 208	Steve Lake	.03	.01	.00
☐ 209	Richard Dotson	.03	.01	.00
☐ 210	Willie Randolph	.06	.03	.00
☐ 211	Frank DiPino	.03	.01	.00
☐ 212	Greg Brock	.03	.01	.00
☐ 213	Albert Hall	.03	.01	.00
☐ 214	Dave Schmidt	.03	.01	.00
☐ 215	Von Hayes	.08	.04	.01
☐ 216	Jerry Reuss	.03	.01	.00
☐ 217	Harry Spilman	.03	.01	.00
☐ 218	Dan Schatzeder	.03	.01	.00
☐ 219	Mike Stanley	.03	.01	.00
☐ 220	Tom Henke	.06	.03	.00
☐ 221	Rafael Belliard	.03	.01	.00
☐ 222	Steve Farr	.03	.01	.00
☐ 223	Stan Jefferson	.06	.03	.00
☐ 224	Tom Trebelhorn MG	.06	.03	.00
	(checklist back)			
☐ 225	Mike Scioscia	.03	.01	.00
☐ 226	Dave Lopes	.06	.03	.00
☐ 227	Ed Correa	.03	.01	.00
☐ 228	Wallace Johnson	.03	.01	.00
☐ 229	Jeff Musselman	.06	.03	.00
☐ 230	Pat Tabler	.06	.03	.00
☐ 231	Pirates TL	.15	.07	.01
	Barry Bonds and			
	Bobby Bonilla			
☐ 232	Bob James	.03	.01	.00
☐ 233	Rafael Santana	.03	.01	.00
☐ 234	Ken Dayley	.03	.01	.00

☐ 235	Gary Ward	.03	.01	.00
☐ 236	Ted Power	.03	.01	.00
☐ 237	Mike Heath	.03	.01	.00
☐ 238	Luis Polonia	.20	.10	.02
☐ 239	Roy Smalley	.03	.01	.00
☐ 240	Lee Smith	.06	.03	.00
☐ 241	Damaso Garcia	.03	.01	.00
☐ 242	Tom Niedenfuer	.03	.01	.00
☐ 243	Mark Ryal	.06	.03	.00
☐ 244	Jeff D. Robinson	.06	.03	.00
	(Pirates pitcher)			
☐ 245	Rich Gedman	.03	.01	.00
☐ 246	Mike Campbell	.08	.04	.01
☐ 247	Thad Bosley	.03	.01	.00
☐ 248	Storm Davis	.06	.03	.00
☐ 249	Mike Marshall	.08	.04	.01
☐ 250	Nolan Ryan	.50	.25	.05
☐ 251	Tom Foley	.03	.01	.00
☐ 252	Bob Brower	.06	.03	.00
☐ 253	Checklist 133-264	.06	.01	.00
☐ 254	Lee Elia MG	.06	.03	.00
	(checklist back)			
☐ 255	Mookie Wilson	.06	.03	.00
☐ 256	Ken Schrom	.03	.01	.00
☐ 257	Jerry Royster	.03	.01	.00
☐ 258	Ed Nunez	.03	.01	.00
☐ 259	Ron Kittle	.08	.04	.01
☐ 260	Vince Coleman	.15	.07	.01
☐ 261	Giants TL	.03	.01	.00
	(five players)			
☐ 262	Drew Hall	.08	.04	.01
☐ 263	Glenn Braggs	.06	.03	.00
☐ 264	Les Straker	.06	.03	.00
☐ 265	Bo Diaz	.03	.01	.00
☐ 266	Paul Assenmacher	.03	.01	.00
☐ 267	Billy Bean	.08	.04	.01
☐ 268	Bruce Ruffin	.03	.01	.00
☐ 269	Ellis Burks	1.00	.50	.10
☐ 270	Mike Witt	.03	.01	.00
☐ 271	Ken Gerhart	.03	.01	.00
☐ 272	Steve Ontiveros	.03	.01	.00
☐ 273	Garth Iorg	.03	.01	.00
☐ 274	Junior Ortiz	.03	.01	.00
☐ 275	Kevin Seitzer	.35	.17	.03
☐ 276	Luis Salazar	.03	.01	.00
☐ 277	Alejandro Pena	.03	.01	.00
☐ 278	Jose Cruz	.06	.03	.00
☐ 279	Randy St.Claire	.03	.01	.00
☐ 280	Pete Incaviglia	.10	.05	.01
☐ 281	Jerry Hairston	.03	.01	.00
☐ 282	Pat Perry	.03	.01	.00
☐ 283	Phil Lombardi	.06	.03	.00
☐ 284	Larry Bowa MG	.06	.03	.00
	(checklist back)			
☐ 285	Jim Presley	.06	.03	.00
☐ 286	Chuck Crim	.06	.03	.00
☐ 287	Manny Trillo	.03	.01	.00
☐ 288	Pat Pacillo	.06	.03	.00
	(Chris Sabo in			
	background of photo)			
☐ 289	Dave Bergman	.03	.01	.00
☐ 290	Tony Fernandez	.10	.05	.01
☐ 291	Astros TL	.06	.03	.00
	Billy Hatcher			
	and Kevin Bass			
☐ 292	Carney Lansford	.08	.04	.01
☐ 293	Doug Jones	.25	.12	.02
☐ 294	Al Pedrique	.06	.03	.00
☐ 295	Bert Blyleven	.08	.04	.01
☐ 296	Floyd Rayford	.03	.01	.00
☐ 297	Zane Smith	.06	.03	.00
☐ 298	Milt Thompson	.03	.01	.00
☐ 299	Steve Crawford	.03	.01	.00
☐ 300	Don Mattingly	.90	.45	.09
☐ 301	Bud Black	.06	.03	.00
☐ 302	Jose Uribe	.03	.01	.00
☐ 303	Eric Show	.03	.01	.00
☐ 304	George Hendrick	.03	.01	.00
☐ 305	Steve Sax	.10	.05	.01
☐ 306	Billy Hatcher	.08	.04	.01
☐ 307	Mike Trujillo	.03	.01	.00
☐ 308	Lee Mazzilli	.03	.01	.00
☐ 309	Bill Long	.06	.03	.00
☐ 310	Tom Herr	.06	.03	.00
☐ 311	Scott Sanderson	.06	.03	.00
☐ 312	Joey Meyer	.08	.04	.01
☐ 313	Bob McClure	.03	.01	.00
☐ 314	Jimy Williams MG	.06	.03	.00
	(checklist back)			
☐ 315	Dave Parker	.10	.05	.01
☐ 316	Jose Rijo	.08	.04	.01
☐ 317	Tom Nieto	.03	.01	.00
☐ 318	Mel Hall	.06	.03	.00
☐ 319	Mike Loynd	.03	.01	.00
☐ 320	Alan Trammell	.12	.06	.01
☐ 321	White Sox TL	.12	.06	.01
	Harold Baines and			
	Carlton Fisk			
☐ 322	Vicente Palacios	.12	.06	.01
☐ 323	Rick Leach	.03	.01	.00
☐ 324	Danny Jackson	.08	.04	.01
☐ 325	Glenn Hubbard	.03	.01	.00
☐ 326	Al Nipper	.03	.01	.00
☐ 327	Larry Sheets	.03	.01	.00
☐ 328	Greg Cadaret	.12	.06	.01
☐ 329	Chris Speier	.03	.01	.00
☐ 330	Eddie Whitson	.06	.03	.00
☐ 331	Brian Downing	.03	.01	.00
☐ 332	Jerry Reed	.03	.01	.00
☐ 333	Wally Backman	.03	.01	.00
☐ 334	Dave LaPoint	.03	.01	.00
☐ 335	Claudell Washington	.06	.03	.00
☐ 336	Ed Lynch	.03	.01	.00
☐ 337	Jim Gantner	.03	.01	.00
☐ 338	Brian Holton	.08	.04	.01
☐ 339	Kurt Stillwell	.10	.05	.01
☐ 340	Jack Morris	.10	.05	.01
☐ 341	Carmen Castillo	.03	.01	.00
☐ 342	Larry Andersen	.03	.01	.00
☐ 343	Greg Gagne	.03	.01	.00
☐ 344	Tony LaRussa MG	.06	.03	.00
	(checklist back)			
☐ 345	Scott Fletcher	.03	.01	.00
☐ 346	Vance Law	.03	.01	.00
☐ 347	Joe Johnson	.03	.01	.00
☐ 348	Jim Eisenreich	.03	.01	.00
☐ 349	Bob Walk	.03	.01	.00
☐ 350	Will Clark	1.00	.50	.10
☐ 351	Cardinals TL	.06	.03	.00
	Red Schoendienst			
	and Tony Pena			
☐ 352	Billy Ripken	.15	.07	.01
☐ 353	Ed Olwine	.03	.01	.00
☐ 354	Marc Sullivan	.03	.01	.00
☐ 355	Roger McDowell	.06	.03	.00
☐ 356	Luis Aguayo	.03	.01	.00
☐ 357	Floyd Bannister	.03	.01	.00
☐ 358	Rey Quinones	.03	.01	.00
☐ 359	Tim Stoddard	.03	.01	.00
☐ 360	Tony Gwynn	.30	.15	.03
☐ 361	Greg Maddux	.30	.15	.03
☐ 362	Juan Castillo	.06	.03	.00
☐ 363	Willie Fraser	.03	.01	.00
☐ 364	Nick Esasky	.06	.03	.00
☐ 365	Floyd Youmans	.03	.01	.00
☐ 366	Chet Lemon	.03	.01	.00
☐ 367	Tim Leary	.06	.03	.00
☐ 368	Gerald Young	.15	.07	.01
☐ 369	Greg Harris	.03	.01	.00
☐ 370	Jose Canseco	1.25	.60	.12
☐ 371	Joe Hesketh	.03	.01	.00
☐ 372	Matt Williams	1.75	.85	.17
☐ 373	Checklist 265-396	.06	.01	.00
☐ 374	Doc Edwards MG	.06	.03	.00
	(checklist back)			
☐ 375	Tom Brunansky	.08	.04	.01
☐ 376	Bill Wilkinson	.06	.03	.00
☐ 377	Sam Horn	.12	.06	.01
☐ 378	Todd Frohwirth	.06	.03	.00
☐ 379	Rafael Ramirez	.03	.01	.00
☐ 380	Joe Magrane	.30	.15	.03
☐ 381	Angels TL	.10	.05	.01
	Wally Joyner and			
	Jack Howell			
☐ 382	Keith Miller	.15	.07	.01
	(New York Mets)			
☐ 383	Eric Bell	.03	.01	.00
☐ 384	Neil Allen	.03	.01	.00
☐ 385	Carlton Fisk	.15	.07	.01
☐ 386	Don Mattingly AS	.25	.12	.02
☐ 387	Willie Randolph AS	.06	.03	.00
☐ 388	Wade Boggs AS	.20	.10	.02
☐ 389	Alan Trammell AS	.08	.04	.01
☐ 390	George Bell AS	.10	.05	.01
☐ 391	Kirby Puckett AS	.15	.07	.01
☐ 392	Dave Winfield AS	.10	.05	.01
☐ 393	Matt Nokes AS	.08	.04	.01
☐ 394	Roger Clemens AS	.15	.07	.01
☐ 395	Jimmy Key AS	.06	.03	.00
☐ 396	Tom Henke AS	.06	.03	.00
☐ 397	Jack Clark AS	.06	.03	.00
☐ 398	Juan Samuel AS	.06	.03	.00
☐ 399	Tim Wallach AS	.06	.03	.00
☐ 400	Ozzie Smith AS	.10	.05	.01
☐ 401	Andre Dawson AS	.12	.06	.01
☐ 402	Tony Gwynn AS	.15	.07	.01
☐ 403	Tim Raines AS	.10	.05	.01
☐ 404	Benny Santiago AS	.12	.06	.01

☐ 405	Dwight Gooden AS	.15	.07	.01
☐ 406	Shane Rawley AS	.06	.03	.00
☐ 407	Steve Bedrosian AS	.06	.03	.00
☐ 408	Dion James	.03	.01	.00
☐ 409	Joel McKeon	.03	.01	.00
☐ 410	Tony Pena	.06	.03	.00
☐ 411	Wayne Tolleson	.03	.01	.00
☐ 412	Randy Myers	.08	.04	.01
☐ 413	John Christensen	.03	.01	.00
☐ 414	John McNamara MG (checklist back)	.06	.03	.00
☐ 415	Don Carman	.03	.01	.00
☐ 416	Keith Moreland	.03	.01	.00
☐ 417	Mark Ciardi	.08	.04	.01
☐ 418	Joel Youngblood	.03	.01	.00
☐ 419	Scott McGregor	.03	.01	.00
☐ 420	Wally Joyner	.15	.07	.01
☐ 421	Ed VandeBerg	.03	.01	.00
☐ 422	Dave Concepcion	.06	.03	.00
☐ 423	John Smiley	.25	.12	.02
☐ 424	Dwayne Murphy	.03	.01	.00
☐ 425	Jeff Reardon	.06	.03	.00
☐ 426	Randy Ready	.03	.01	.00
☐ 427	Paul Kilgus	.08	.04	.01
☐ 428	John Shelby	.03	.01	.00
☐ 429	Tigers TL Alan Trammell and Kirk Gibson	.15	.07	.01
☐ 430	Glenn Davis	.12	.06	.01
☐ 431	Casey Candaele	.03	.01	.00
☐ 432	Mike Moore	.06	.03	.00
☐ 433	Bill Pecota	.06	.03	.00
☐ 434	Rick Aguilera	.03	.01	.00
☐ 435	Mike Pagliarulo	.03	.01	.00
☐ 436	Mike Bielecki	.03	.01	.00
☐ 437	Fred Manrique	.06	.03	.00
☐ 438	Rob Ducey	.12	.06	.01
☐ 439	Dave Martinez	.08	.04	.01
☐ 440	Steve Bedrosian	.08	.04	.01
☐ 441	Rick Manning	.03	.01	.00
☐ 442	Tom Bolton	.25	.12	.02
☐ 443	Ken Griffey	.10	.05	.01
☐ 444	Cal Ripken, Sr. MG (checklist back) UER (two copyrights)	.06	.03	.00
☐ 445	Mike Krukow	.03	.01	.00
☐ 446	Doug DeCinces	.06	.03	.00
☐ 447	Jeff Montgomery	.20	.10	.02
☐ 448	Mike Davis	.03	.01	.00
☐ 449	Jeff M. Robinson (Tigers pitcher)	.20	.10	.02
☐ 450	Barry Bonds	.35	.17	.03
☐ 451	Keith Atherton	.03	.01	.00
☐ 452	Willie Wilson	.08	.04	.01
☐ 453	Dennis Powell	.03	.01	.00
☐ 454	Marvell Wynne	.03	.01	.00
☐ 455	Shawn Hillegas	.12	.06	.01
☐ 456	Dave Anderson	.03	.01	.00
☐ 457	Terry Leach	.06	.03	.00
☐ 458	Ron Hassey	.03	.01	.00
☐ 459	Yankees TL Dave Winfield and Willie Randolph	.10	.05	.01
☐ 460	Ozzie Smith	.12	.06	.01
☐ 461	Danny Darwin	.06	.03	.00
☐ 462	Don Slaught	.03	.01	.00
☐ 463	Fred McGriff	1.00	.50	.10
☐ 464	Jay Tibbs	.03	.01	.00
☐ 465	Paul Molitor	.12	.06	.01
☐ 466	Jerry Mumphrey	.03	.01	.00
☐ 467	Don Aase	.03	.01	.00
☐ 468	Darren Daulton	.06	.03	.00
☐ 469	Jeff Dedmon	.03	.01	.00
☐ 470	Dwight Evans	.10	.05	.01
☐ 471	Donnie Moore	.03	.01	.00
☐ 472	Robby Thompson	.03	.01	.00
☐ 473	Joe Niekro	.06	.03	.00
☐ 474	Tom Brookens	.03	.01	.00
☐ 475	Pete Rose MG (checklist back)	.30	.15	.03
☐ 476	Dave Stewart	.15	.07	.01
☐ 477	Jamie Quirk	.03	.01	.00
☐ 478	Sid Bream	.03	.01	.00
☐ 479	Brett Butler	.08	.04	.01
☐ 480	Dwight Gooden	.35	.17	.03
☐ 481	Mariano Duncan	.06	.03	.00
☐ 482	Mark Davis	.10	.05	.01
☐ 483	Rod Booker	.06	.03	.00
☐ 484	Pat Clements	.03	.01	.00
☐ 485	Harold Reynolds	.06	.03	.00
☐ 486	Pat Keedy	.06	.03	.00
☐ 487	Jim Pankovits	.03	.01	.00
☐ 488	Andy McGaffigan	.03	.01	.00
☐ 489	Dodgers TL Pedro Guerrero and Fernando Valenzuela	.12	.06	.01
☐ 490	Larry Parrish	.03	.01	.00
☐ 491	B.J. Surhoff	.08	.04	.01
☐ 492	Doyle Alexander	.03	.01	.00
☐ 493	Mike Greenwell	.50	.25	.05
☐ 494	Wally Ritchie	.03	.01	.00
☐ 495	Eddie Murray	.15	.07	.01
☐ 496	Guy Hoffman	.03	.01	.00
☐ 497	Kevin Mitchell	.30	.15	.03
☐ 498	Bob Boone	.08	.04	.01
☐ 499	Eric King	.03	.01	.00
☐ 500	Andre Dawson	.15	.07	.01
☐ 501	Tim Birtsas	.03	.01	.00
☐ 502	Dan Gladden	.06	.03	.00
☐ 503	Junior Noboa	.06	.03	.00
☐ 504	Bob Rodgers MG (checklist back)	.06	.03	.00
☐ 505	Willie Upshaw	.03	.01	.00
☐ 506	John Cangelosi	.03	.01	.00
☐ 507	Mark Gubicza	.08	.04	.01
☐ 508	Tim Teufel	.03	.01	.00
☐ 509	Bill Dawley	.03	.01	.00
☐ 510	Dave Winfield	.15	.07	.01
☐ 511	Joel Davis	.03	.01	.00
☐ 512	Alex Trevino	.03	.01	.00
☐ 513	Tim Flannery	.03	.01	.00
☐ 514	Pat Sheridan	.03	.01	.00
☐ 515	Juan Nieves	.03	.01	.00
☐ 516	Jim Sundberg	.03	.01	.00
☐ 517	Ron Robinson	.03	.01	.00
☐ 518	Greg Gross	.03	.01	.00
☐ 519	Mariners TL Harold Reynolds and Phil Bradley	.06	.03	.00
☐ 520	Dave Smith	.03	.01	.00
☐ 521	Jim Dwyer	.03	.01	.00
☐ 522	Bob Patterson	.06	.03	.00
☐ 523	Gary Roenicke	.03	.01	.00
☐ 524	Gary Lucas	.03	.01	.00
☐ 525	Marty Barrett	.06	.03	.00
☐ 526	Juan Berenguer	.03	.01	.00
☐ 527	Steve Henderson	.03	.01	.00
☐ 528A	Checklist 397-528 ERR (455 S. Carlton)	.75	.07	.01
☐ 528B	Checklist 397-528 COR (455 S. Hillegas)	.10	.01	.00
☐ 529	Tim Burke	.03	.01	.00
☐ 530	Gary Carter	.15	.07	.01
☐ 531	Rich Yett	.03	.01	.00
☐ 532	Mike Kingery	.03	.01	.00
☐ 533	John Farrell	.18	.09	.01
☐ 534	John Wathan MG (checklist back)	.06	.03	.00
☐ 535	Ron Guidry	.08	.04	.01
☐ 536	John Morris	.03	.01	.00
☐ 537	Steve Buechele	.03	.01	.00
☐ 538	Bill Wegman	.03	.01	.00
☐ 539	Mike LaValliere	.03	.01	.00
☐ 540	Bret Saberhagen	.15	.07	.01
☐ 541	Juan Beniquez	.03	.01	.00
☐ 542	Paul Noce	.06	.03	.00
☐ 543	Kent Tekulve	.03	.01	.00
☐ 544	Jim Traber	.03	.01	.00
☐ 545	Don Baylor	.08	.04	.01
☐ 546	John Candelaria	.03	.01	.00
☐ 547	Felix Fermin	.06	.03	.00
☐ 548	Shane Mack	.08	.04	.01
☐ 549	Braves TL Albert Hall, Dale Murphy, Ken Griffey, and Dion James	.08	.04	.01
☐ 550	Pedro Guerrero	.10	.05	.01
☐ 551	Terry Steinbach	.20	.10	.02
☐ 552	Mark Thurmond	.03	.01	.00
☐ 553	Tracy Jones	.03	.01	.00
☐ 554	Mike Smithson	.03	.01	.00
☐ 555	Brook Jacoby	.06	.03	.00
☐ 556	Stan Clarke	.03	.01	.00
☐ 557	Craig Reynolds	.03	.01	.00
☐ 558	Bob Ojeda	.06	.03	.00
☐ 559	Ken Williams	.10	.05	.01
☐ 560	Tim Wallach	.08	.04	.01
☐ 561	Rick Cerone	.03	.01	.00
☐ 562	Jim Lindeman	.03	.01	.00
☐ 563	Jose Guzman	.03	.01	.00
☐ 564	Frank Lucchesi MG (checklist back)	.06	.03	.00
☐ 565	Lloyd Moseby	.06	.03	.00
☐ 566	Charlie O'Brien	.12	.06	.01
☐ 567	Mike Diaz	.03	.01	.00
☐ 568	Chris Brown	.03	.01	.00

☐ 569 Charlie Leibrandt	.03	.01	.00
☐ 570 Jeffrey Leonard	.06	.03	.00
☐ 571 Mark Williamson	.10	.05	.01
☐ 572 Chris James	.15	.07	.01
☐ 573 Bob Stanley	.03	.01	.00
☐ 574 Graig Nettles	.08	.04	.01
☐ 575 Don Sutton	.10	.05	.01
☐ 576 Tommy Hinzo	.03	.01	.00
☐ 577 Tom Browning	.08	.04	.01
☐ 578 Gary Gaetti	.08	.04	.01
☐ 579 Mets TL Gary Carter and Kevin McReynolds	.12	.06	.01
☐ 580 Mark McGwire	.75	.35	.07
☐ 581 Tito Landrum	.03	.01	.00
☐ 582 Mike Henneman	.18	.09	.01
☐ 583 Dave Valle	.06	.03	.00
☐ 584 Steve Trout	.03	.01	.00
☐ 585 Ozzie Guillen	.08	.04	.01
☐ 586 Bob Forsch	.03	.01	.00
☐ 587 Terry Puhl	.03	.01	.00
☐ 588 Jeff Parrett	.12	.06	.01
☐ 589 Geno Petralli	.03	.01	.00
☐ 590 George Bell	.15	.07	.01
☐ 591 Doug Drabek	.15	.07	.01
☐ 592 Dale Sveum	.03	.01	.00
☐ 593 Bob Tewksbury	.03	.01	.00
☐ 594 Bobby Valentine MG (checklist back)	.06	.03	.00
☐ 595 Frank White	.06	.03	.00
☐ 596 John Kruk	.06	.03	.00
☐ 597 Gene Garber	.03	.01	.00
☐ 598 Lee Lacy	.03	.01	.00
☐ 599 Calvin Schiraldi	.03	.01	.00
☐ 600 Mike Schmidt	.35	.17	.03
☐ 601 Jack Lazorko	.03	.01	.00
☐ 602 Mike Aldrete	.03	.01	.00
☐ 603 Rob Murphy	.03	.01	.00
☐ 604 Chris Bando	.03	.01	.00
☐ 605 Kirk Gibson	.15	.07	.01
☐ 606 Moose Haas	.03	.01	.00
☐ 607 Mickey Hatcher	.03	.01	.00
☐ 608 Charlie Kerfeld	.03	.01	.00
☐ 609 Twins TL Gary Gaetti and Kent Hrbek	.08	.04	.01
☐ 610 Keith Hernandez	.10	.05	.01
☐ 611 Tommy John	.08	.04	.01
☐ 612 Curt Ford	.03	.01	.00
☐ 613 Bobby Thigpen	.12	.06	.01
☐ 614 Herm Winningham	.03	.01	.00
☐ 615 Jody Davis	.03	.01	.00
☐ 616 Jay Aldrich	.03	.01	.00
☐ 617 Oddibe McDowell	.06	.03	.00
☐ 618 Cecil Fielder	.40	.20	.04
☐ 619 Mike Dunne (inconsistent design, black name on front)	.06	.03	.00
☐ 620 Cory Snyder	.10	.05	.01
☐ 621 Gene Nelson	.03	.01	.00
☐ 622 Kal Daniels	.15	.07	.01
☐ 623 Mike Flanagan	.06	.03	.00
☐ 624 Jim Leyland MG (checklist back)	.06	.03	.00
☐ 625 Frank Viola	.15	.07	.01
☐ 626 Glenn Wilson	.03	.01	.00
☐ 627 Joe Boever	.08	.04	.01
☐ 628 Dave Henderson	.06	.03	.00
☐ 629 Kelly Downs	.06	.03	.00
☐ 630 Darrell Evans	.06	.03	.00
☐ 631 Jack Howell	.03	.01	.00
☐ 632 Steve Shields	.03	.01	.00
☐ 633 Barry Lyons	.12	.06	.01
☐ 634 Jose DeLeon	.03	.01	.00
☐ 635 Terry Pendleton	.06	.03	.00
☐ 636 Charles Hudson	.03	.01	.00
☐ 637 Jay Bell	.20	.10	.02
☐ 638 Steve Balboni	.03	.01	.00
☐ 639 Brewers TL Glenn Braggs and Tony Muser CO	.03	.01	.00
☐ 640 Garry Templeton (inconsistent design, green border)	.06	.03	.00
☐ 641 Rick Honeycutt	.03	.01	.00
☐ 642 Bob Dernier	.03	.01	.00
☐ 643 Rocky Childress	.03	.01	.00
☐ 644 Terry McGriff	.06	.03	.00
☐ 645 Matt Nokes	.25	.12	.02
☐ 646 Checklist 529-660	.06	.01	.00
☐ 647 Pascual Perez	.06	.03	.00
☐ 648 Al Newman	.03	.01	.00
☐ 649 DeWayne Buice	.06	.03	.00
☐ 650 Cal Ripken	.18	.09	.01
☐ 651 Mike Jackson	.12	.06	.01
☐ 652 Bruce Benedict	.03	.01	.00
☐ 653 Jeff Sellers	.03	.01	.00
☐ 654 Roger Craig MG (checklist back)	.06	.03	.00
☐ 655 Len Dykstra	.15	.07	.01
☐ 656 Lee Guetterman	.03	.01	.00
☐ 657 Gary Redus	.03	.01	.00
☐ 658 Tim Conroy (inconsistent design, name in white)	.03	.01	.00
☐ 659 Bobby Meacham	.03	.01	.00
☐ 660 Rick Reuschel	.06	.03	.00
☐ 661 Turn Back Clock 1983 Nolan Ryan	.25	.12	.02
☐ 662 Turn Back Clock 1978 Jim Rice	.08	.04	.01
☐ 663 Turn Back Clock 1973 Ron Blomberg	.03	.01	.00
☐ 664 Turn Back Clock 1968 Bob Gibson	.10	.05	.01
☐ 665 Turn Back Clock 1963 Stan Musial	.15	.07	.01
☐ 666 Mario Soto	.03	.01	.00
☐ 667 Luis Quinones	.03	.01	.00
☐ 668 Walt Terrell	.03	.01	.00
☐ 669 Phillies TL Lance Parrish and Mike Ryan CO	.06	.03	.00
☐ 670 Dan Plesac	.03	.01	.00
☐ 671 Tim Laudner	.03	.01	.00
☐ 672 John Davis	.08	.04	.01
☐ 673 Tony Phillips	.03	.01	.00
☐ 674 Mike Fitzgerald	.03	.01	.00
☐ 675 Jim Rice	.12	.06	.01
☐ 676 Ken Dixon	.03	.01	.00
☐ 677 Eddie Milner	.03	.01	.00
☐ 678 Jim Acker	.03	.01	.00
☐ 679 Darrell Miller	.03	.01	.00
☐ 680 Charlie Hough	.03	.01	.00
☐ 681 Bobby Bonilla	.30	.15	.03
☐ 682 Jimmy Key	.06	.03	.00
☐ 683 Julio Franco	.10	.05	.01
☐ 684 Hal Lanier MG (checklist back)	.06	.03	.00
☐ 685 Ron Darling	.08	.04	.01
☐ 686 Terry Francona	.03	.01	.00
☐ 687 Mickey Brantley	.06	.03	.00
☐ 688 Jim Winn	.03	.01	.00
☐ 689 Tom Pagnozzi	.08	.04	.01
☐ 690 Jay Howell	.03	.01	.00
☐ 691 Dan Pasqua	.03	.01	.00
☐ 692 Mike Birkbeck	.03	.01	.00
☐ 693 Benny Santiago	.45	.22	.04
☐ 694 Eric Nolte	.06	.03	.00
☐ 695 Shawon Dunston	.12	.06	.01
☐ 696 Duane Ward	.03	.01	.00
☐ 697 Steve Lombardozzi	.03	.01	.00
☐ 698 Brad Havens	.03	.01	.00
☐ 699 Padres TL Benito Santiago and Tony Gwynn	.20	.10	.02
☐ 700 George Brett	.25	.12	.02
☐ 701 Sammy Stewart	.03	.01	.00
☐ 702 Mike Gallego	.03	.01	.00
☐ 703 Bob Brenly	.03	.01	.00
☐ 704 Dennis Boyd	.06	.03	.00
☐ 705 Juan Samuel	.08	.04	.01
☐ 706 Rick Mahler	.03	.01	.00
☐ 707 Fred Lynn	.08	.04	.01
☐ 708 Gus Polidor	.03	.01	.00
☐ 709 George Frazier	.03	.01	.00
☐ 710 Darryl Strawberry	.35	.17	.03
☐ 711 Bill Gullickson	.03	.01	.00
☐ 712 John Moses	.03	.01	.00
☐ 713 Willie Hernandez	.06	.03	.00
☐ 714 Jim Fregosi MG (checklist back)	.06	.03	.00
☐ 715 Todd Worrell	.08	.04	.01
☐ 716 Lenn Sakata	.03	.01	.00
☐ 717 Jay Baller	.03	.01	.00
☐ 718 Mike Felder	.03	.01	.00
☐ 719 Denny Walling	.03	.01	.00
☐ 720 Tim Raines	.15	.07	.01
☐ 721 Pete O'Brien	.06	.03	.00
☐ 722 Manny Lee	.03	.01	.00
☐ 723 Bob Kipper	.03	.01	.00
☐ 724 Danny Tartabull	.12	.06	.01
☐ 725 Mike Boddicker	.06	.03	.00
☐ 726 Alfredo Griffin	.03	.01	.00
☐ 727 Greg Booker	.03	.01	.00
☐ 728 Andy Allanson	.03	.01	.00

☐	729 Blue Jays TL George Bell and Fred McGriff	.12	.06	.01
☐	730 John Franco	.08	.04	.01
☐	731 Rick Schu	.03	.01	.00
☐	732 David Palmer	.03	.01	.00
☐	733 Spike Owen	.03	.01	.00
☐	734 Craig Lefferts	.03	.01	.00
☐	735 Kevin McReynolds	.15	.07	.01
☐	736 Matt Young	.03	.01	.00
☐	737 Butch Wynegar	.03	.01	.00
☐	738 Scott Bankhead	.06	.03	.00
☐	739 Daryl Boston	.06	.03	.00
☐	740 Rick Sutcliffe	.08	.04	.01
☐	741 Mike Easler	.03	.01	.00
☐	742 Mark Clear	.03	.01	.00
☐	743 Larry Herndon	.03	.01	.00
☐	744 Whitey Herzog MG (checklist back)	.06	.03	.00
☐	745 Bill Doran	.06	.03	.00
☐	746 Gene Larkin	.20	.10	.02
☐	747 Bobby Witt	.15	.07	.01
☐	748 Reid Nichols	.03	.01	.00
☐	749 Mark Eichhorn	.03	.01	.00
☐	750 Bo Jackson	1.00	.50	.10
☐	751 Jim Morrison	.03	.01	.00
☐	752 Mark Grant	.03	.01	.00
☐	753 Danny Heep	.03	.01	.00
☐	754 Mike LaCoss	.03	.01	.00
☐	755 Ozzie Virgil	.03	.01	.00
☐	756 Mike Maddux	.03	.01	.00
☐	757 John Marzano	.06	.03	.00
☐	758 Eddie Williams	.12	.06	.01
☐	759 A's TL Mark McGwire and Jose Canseco	.25	.12	.02
☐	760 Mike Scott	.10	.05	.01
☐	761 Tony Armas	.03	.01	.00
☐	762 Scott Bradley	.03	.01	.00
☐	763 Doug Sisk	.03	.01	.00
☐	764 Greg Walker	.03	.01	.00
☐	765 Neal Heaton	.03	.01	.00
☐	766 Henry Cotto	.03	.01	.00
☐	767 Jose Lind	.25	.12	.02
☐	768 Dickie Noles	.03	.01	.00
☐	769 Cecil Cooper	.06	.03	.00
☐	770 Lou Whitaker	.08	.04	.01
☐	771 Ruben Sierra	.35	.17	.03
☐	772 Sal Butera	.03	.01	.00
☐	773 Frank Williams	.03	.01	.00
☐	774 Gene Mauch MG (checklist back)	.06	.03	.00
☐	775 Dave Stieb	.08	.04	.01
☐	776 Checklist 661-792	.06	.01	.00
☐	777 Lonnie Smith	.06	.03	.00
☐	778A Keith Comstock ERR (white "Padres")	6.00	3.00	.60
☐	778B Keith Comstock COR (blue "Padres")	.15	.07	.01
☐	779 Tom Glavine	.20	.10	.02
☐	780 Fernando Valenzuela	.12	.06	.01
☐	781 Keith Hughes	.10	.05	.01
☐	782 Jeff Ballard	.25	.12	.02
☐	783 Ron Roenicke	.03	.01	.00
☐	784 Joe Sambito	.03	.01	.00
☐	785 Alvin Davis	.08	.04	.01
☐	786 Joe Price (inconsistent design, orange team name)	.03	.01	.00
☐	787 Bill Almon	.03	.01	.00
☐	788 Ray Searage	.03	.01	.00
☐	789 Indians' TL Joe Carter and Cory Snyder	.10	.05	.01
☐	790 Dave Righetti	.08	.04	.01
☐	791 Ted Simmons	.08	.04	.01
☐	792 John Tudor	.10	.05	.01

1988 Topps Wax Box Cards

The cards in this 16-card set measure the standard 2 1/2" by 3 1/2". Cards have essentially the same design as the 1988 Topps regular issue set. The cards were printed on the bottoms of the regular issue wax pack boxes. These 16 cards, "lettered" A through P, are considered a separate set in their own right and are not typically included in a complete set of the regular issue 1988 Topps cards. The value of the panels uncut is slightly greater, perhaps by 25 percent greater, than the value of the individual cards cut up carefully.

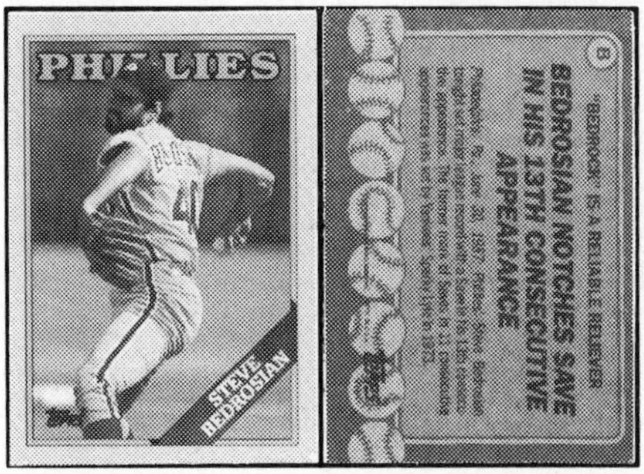

		MINT	EXC	G-VG
	COMPLETE SET (16)	4.00	2.00	.40
	COMMON PLAYER (A-P)	.10	.05	.01
☐	A Don Baylor	.15	.07	.01
☐	B Steve Bedrosian	.15	.07	.01
☐	C Juan Beniquez	.10	.05	.01
☐	D Bob Boone	.15	.07	.01
☐	E Darrell Evans	.10	.05	.01
☐	F Tony Gwynn	.35	.17	.03
☐	G John Kruk	.15	.07	.01
☐	H Marvell Wynne	.10	.05	.01
☐	I Joe Carter	.25	.12	.02
☐	J Eric Davis	.50	.25	.05
☐	K Howard Johnson	.20	.10	.02
☐	L Darryl Strawberry	.60	.30	.06
☐	M Rickey Henderson	.60	.30	.06
☐	N Nolan Ryan	.75	.35	.07
☐	O Mike Schmidt	.75	.35	.07
☐	P Kent Tekulve	.10	.05	.01

1988 Topps Glossy All-Stars 22

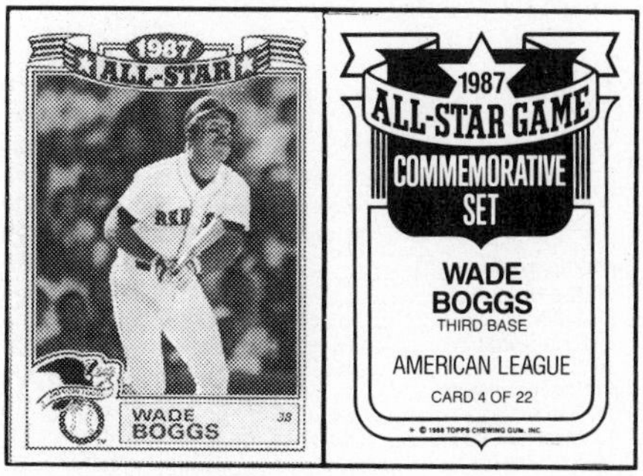

This set of 22 glossy cards was inserted one per rack pack. Players selected for the set are the starting players (plus manager and honorary captain) in the 1987 All-Star Game in Oakland. Cards measure standard size, 2 1/2" by 3 1/2" and the backs feature red and blue printing on a white card stock.

		MINT	EXC	G-VG
	COMPLETE SET (22)	3.00	1.50	.30
	COMMON PLAYER (1-22)	.10	.05	.01
☐	1 John McNamara MG	.10	.05	.01
☐	2 Don Mattingly	.50	.25	.05
☐	3 Willie Randolph	.10	.05	.01
☐	4 Wade Boggs	.40	.20	.04

☐ 5 Cal Ripken	.25	.12	.02
☐ 6 George Bell	.20	.10	.02
☐ 7 Rickey Henderson	.50	.25	.05
☐ 8 Dave Winfield	.20	.10	.02
☐ 9 Terry Kennedy	.10	.05	.01
☐ 10 Bret Saberhagen	.15	.07	.01
☐ 11 Jim Hunter CAPT	.15	.07	.01
☐ 12 Dave Johnson MG	.10	.05	.01
☐ 13 Jack Clark	.15	.07	.01
☐ 14 Ryne Sandberg	.35	.17	.03
☐ 15 Mike Schmidt	.50	.25	.05
☐ 16 Ozzie Smith	.20	.10	.02
☐ 17 Eric Davis	.35	.17	.03
☐ 18 Andre Dawson	.25	.12	.02
☐ 19 Darryl Strawberry	.35	.17	.03
☐ 20 Gary Carter	.15	.07	.01
☐ 21 Mike Scott	.15	.07	.01
☐ 22 Billy Williams CAPT	.15	.07	.01

1988 Topps Jumbo Rookies

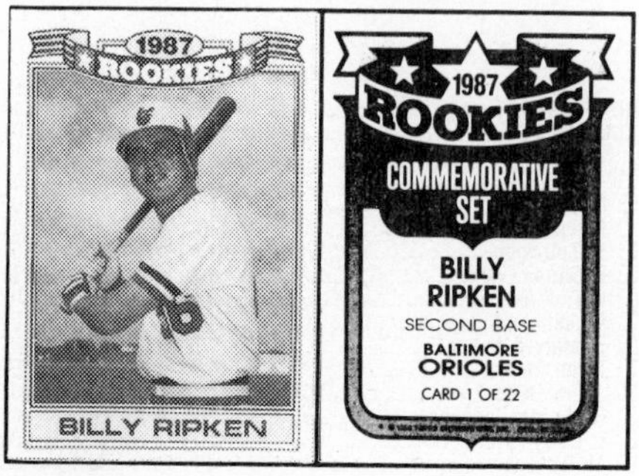

Inserted in each supermarket jumbo pack is a card from this series of 22 of 1987's best rookies as determined by Topps. Jumbo packs consisted of 100 (regular issue 1988 Topps baseball) cards with a stick of gum plus the insert "Rookie" card. The card fronts are in full color and measure 2 1/2" by 3 1/2". The card backs are printed in red and blue on white card stock and are numbered at the bottom.

	MINT	EXC	G-VG
COMPLETE SET (22)	9.00	4.50	.90
COMMON PLAYER (1-22)	.20	.10	.02
☐ 1 Billy Ripken	.30	.15	.03
☐ 2 Ellis Burks	1.00	.50	.10
☐ 3 Mike Greenwell	1.00	.50	.10
☐ 4 DeWayne Buice	.20	.10	.02
☐ 5 Devon White	.40	.20	.04
☐ 6 Fred Manrique	.20	.10	.02
☐ 7 Mike Henneman	.30	.15	.03
☐ 8 Matt Nokes	.40	.20	.04
☐ 9 Kevin Seitzer	.60	.30	.06
☐ 10 B.J. Surhoff	.40	.20	.04
☐ 11 Casey Candaele	.20	.10	.02
☐ 12 Randy Myers	.40	.20	.04
☐ 13 Mark McGwire	1.50	.75	.15
☐ 14 Luis Polonia	.30	.15	.03
☐ 15 Terry Steinbach	.40	.20	.04
☐ 16 Mike Dunne	.20	.10	.02
☐ 17 Al Pedrique	.20	.10	.02
☐ 18 Benny Santiago	.90	.45	.09
☐ 19 Kelly Downs	.30	.15	.03
☐ 20 Joe Magrane	.40	.20	.04
☐ 21 Jerry Browne	.30	.15	.03
☐ 22 Jeff Musselman	.20	.10	.02

1988 Topps Revco League Leaders

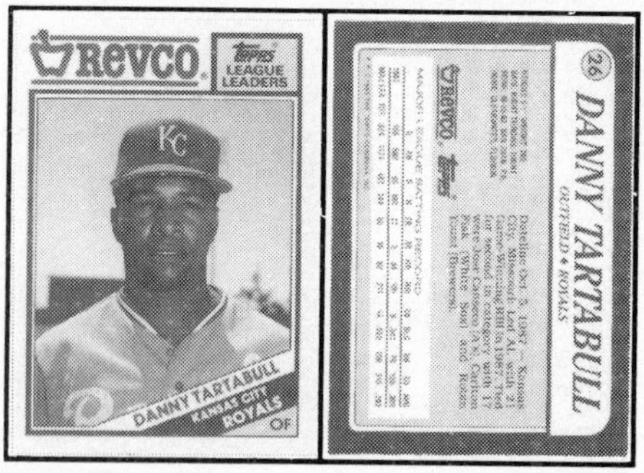

Topps produced this 33-card boxed set for Revco stores subtitled "League Leaders". The cards measure 2 1/2" by 3 1/2" and feature a high-gloss, full-color photo of the player inside a white border. The card backs are printed in red and black on white card stock. The cards are numbered on the back. The statistics provided on the card backs cover only two lines, last season and Major League totals.

	MINT	EXC	G-VG
COMPLETE SET (33)	4.50	2.25	.45
COMMON PLAYER (1-33)	.10	.05	.01
☐ 1 Tony Gwynn	.35	.17	.03
☐ 2 Andre Dawson	.25	.12	.02
☐ 3 Vince Coleman	.25	.12	.02
☐ 4 Jack Clark	.20	.10	.02
☐ 5 Tim Raines	.25	.12	.02
☐ 6 Tim Wallach	.15	.07	.01
☐ 7 Juan Samuel	.15	.07	.01
☐ 8 Nolan Ryan	.75	.35	.07
☐ 9 Rick Sutcliffe	.15	.07	.01
☐ 10 Kent Tekulve	.10	.05	.01
☐ 11 Steve Bedrosian	.15	.07	.01
☐ 12 Orel Hershiser	.25	.12	.02
☐ 13 Rick Reuschel	.10	.05	.01
☐ 14 Fernando Valenzuela	.20	.10	.02
☐ 15 Bob Welch	.20	.10	.02
☐ 16 Wade Boggs	.40	.20	.04
☐ 17 Mark McGwire	.40	.20	.04
☐ 18 George Bell	.20	.10	.02
☐ 19 Harold Reynolds	.10	.05	.01
☐ 20 Paul Molitor	.20	.10	.02
☐ 21 Kirby Puckett	.40	.20	.04
☐ 22 Kevin Seitzer	.25	.12	.02
☐ 23 Brian Downing	.10	.05	.01
☐ 24 Dwight Evans	.15	.07	.01
☐ 25 Willie Wilson	.10	.05	.01
☐ 26 Danny Tartabull	.15	.07	.01
☐ 27 Jimmy Key	.10	.05	.01
☐ 28 Roger Clemens	.40	.20	.04
☐ 29 Dave Stewart	.25	.12	.02
☐ 30 Mark Eichhorn	.10	.05	.01
☐ 31 Tom Henke	.10	.05	.01
☐ 32 Charlie Hough	.10	.05	.01
☐ 33 Mark Langston	.15	.07	.01

1988 Topps Rite-Aid Team MVP's

Topps produced this 33-card boxed set for Rite Aid Drug and Discount Stores subtitled "Team MVP's". The Rite Aid logo is at the top of every obverse. The cards measure 2 1/2" by 3 1/2" and feature a high-gloss, full-color photo of the player inside a red, white, and blue border. The card backs are printed in blue and black on white card stock. The cards are numbered on the back and the checklist for the set is found on the back panel of the small collector box. The statistics provided on the card backs cover only two lines, last season and Major League totals.

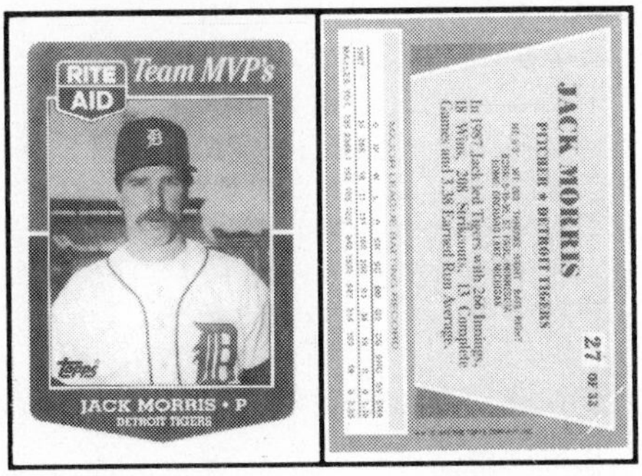

	MINT	EXC	G-VG
COMPLETE SET (33)	4.50	2.25	.45
COMMON PLAYER (1-33)	.10	.05	.01
☐ 1 Dale Murphy	.30	.15	.03
☐ 2 Andre Dawson	.25	.12	.02
☐ 3 Eric Davis	.35	.17	.03
☐ 4 Mike Scott	.15	.07	.01
☐ 5 Pedro Guerrero	.20	.10	.02
☐ 6 Tim Raines	.25	.12	.02
☐ 7 Darryl Strawberry	.45	.22	.04
☐ 8 Mike Schmidt	.60	.30	.06
☐ 9 Mike Dunne	.10	.05	.01
☐ 10 Jack Clark	.20	.10	.02
☐ 11 Tony Gwynn	.30	.15	.03
☐ 12 Will Clark	.50	.25	.05
☐ 13 Cal Ripken	.25	.12	.02
☐ 14 Wade Boggs	.50	.25	.05
☐ 15 Wally Joyner	.20	.10	.02
☐ 16 Harold Baines	.15	.07	.01
☐ 17 Joe Carter	.20	.10	.02
☐ 18 Alan Trammell	.20	.10	.02
☐ 19 Kevin Seitzer	.20	.10	.02
☐ 20 Paul Molitor	.20	.10	.02
☐ 21 Kirby Puckett	.40	.20	.04
☐ 22 Don Mattingly	.60	.30	.06
☐ 23 Mark McGwire	.45	.22	.04
☐ 24 Alvin Davis	.15	.07	.01
☐ 25 Ruben Sierra	.40	.20	.04
☐ 26 George Bell	.20	.10	.02
☐ 27 Jack Morris	.15	.07	.01
☐ 28 Jeff Reardon	.10	.05	.01
☐ 29 John Tudor	.15	.07	.01
☐ 30 Rick Reuschel	.10	.05	.01
☐ 31 Gary Gaetti	.15	.07	.01
☐ 32 Jeffrey Leonard	.10	.05	.01
☐ 33 Frank Viola	.20	.10	.02

1988 Topps UK Minis

The 1988 Topps UK (United Kingdom) Mini set of "American Baseball" features 88 cards. The cards are numbered on the back and measure approximately 2 1/8" by 3". The card backs are printed in blue, red, and yellow on white card stock. The cards were distributed as a separate issue in packs. A custom black and yellow small set box was also available for holding a complete set; the box has a complete checklist on the back panel. The set player numbering is according to alphabetical order. Topps also produced a specially boxed "glossy" edition frequently referred to as the Topps UK Tiffany set. Topps did not disclose the number of UK Tiffany sets they produced or sold. The checklist of Tiffany cards is identical to that of the normal UK non-glossy cards. These Tiffany cards are valued at approximately double the values listed below.

	MINT	EXC	G-VG
COMPLETE SET (88)	8.00	4.00	.80
COMMON PLAYER (1-88)	.05	.02	.00
☐ 1 Harold Baines	.10	.05	.01
☐ 2 Steve Bedrosian	.10	.05	.01
☐ 3 George Bell	.15	.07	.01
☐ 4 Wade Boggs	.50	.25	.05
☐ 5 Barry Bonds	.35	.17	.03
☐ 6 Bob Boone	.15	.07	.01
☐ 7 George Brett	.35	.17	.03
☐ 8 Hubie Brooks	.10	.05	.01
☐ 9 Ivan Calderon	.10	.05	.01
☐ 10 Jose Canseco	1.00	.50	.10
☐ 11 Gary Carter	.15	.07	.01
☐ 12 Joe Carter	.20	.10	.02
☐ 13 Jack Clark	.15	.07	.01
☐ 14 Will Clark	.90	.45	.09
☐ 15 Roger Clemens	.60	.30	.06
☐ 16 Vince Coleman	.25	.12	.02
☐ 17 Alvin Davis	.10	.05	.01
☐ 18 Eric Davis	.45	.22	.04
☐ 19 Glenn Davis	.20	.10	.02
☐ 20 Andre Dawson	.20	.10	.02
☐ 21 Mike Dunne	.05	.02	.00
☐ 22 Dwight Evans	.15	.07	.01
☐ 23 Tony Fernandez	.10	.05	.01
☐ 24 John Franco	.10	.05	.01
☐ 25 Gary Gaetti	.10	.05	.01
☐ 26 Kirk Gibson	.20	.10	.02
☐ 27 Dwight Gooden	.35	.17	.03
☐ 28 Pedro Guerrero	.15	.07	.01
☐ 29 Tony Gwynn	.35	.17	.03
☐ 30 Billy Hatcher	.10	.05	.01
☐ 31 Rickey Henderson	.60	.30	.06
☐ 32 Tom Henke	.05	.02	.00
☐ 33 Keith Hernandez	.15	.07	.01
☐ 34 Orel Hershiser	.25	.12	.02
☐ 35 Teddy Higuera	.10	.05	.01
☐ 36 Charlie Hough	.05	.02	.00
☐ 37 Kent Hrbek	.15	.07	.01
☐ 38 Brook Jacoby	.10	.05	.01
☐ 39 Dion James	.05	.02	.00
☐ 40 Wally Joyner	.15	.07	.01
☐ 41 John Kruk	.10	.05	.01
☐ 42 Mark Langston	.15	.07	.01
☐ 43 Jeffrey Leonard	.05	.02	.00
☐ 44 Candy Maldonado	.10	.05	.01
☐ 45 Don Mattingly	1.00	.50	.10
☐ 46 Willie McGee	.15	.07	.01
☐ 47 Mark McGwire	.60	.30	.06
☐ 48 Kevin Mitchell	.20	.10	.02
☐ 49 Paul Molitor	.15	.07	.01
☐ 50 Jack Morris	.15	.07	.01
☐ 51 Lloyd Moseby	.10	.05	.01
☐ 52 Dale Murphy	.35	.17	.03
☐ 53 Eddie Murray	.35	.17	.03
☐ 54 Matt Nokes	.15	.07	.01
☐ 55 Dave Parker	.20	.10	.02
☐ 56 Larry Parrish	.05	.02	.00
☐ 57 Kirby Puckett	.45	.22	.04
☐ 58 Tim Raines	.20	.10	.02
☐ 59 Willie Randolph	.10	.05	.01
☐ 60 Harold Reynolds	.10	.05	.01
☐ 61 Cal Ripken	.35	.17	.03
☐ 62 Nolan Ryan	1.00	.50	.10
☐ 63 Bret Saberhagen	.25	.12	.02
☐ 64 Juan Samuel	.10	.05	.01
☐ 65 Ryne Sandberg	.60	.30	.06
☐ 66 Benny Santiago	.35	.17	.03
☐ 67 Mike Schmidt	.80	.40	.08
☐ 68 Mike Scott	.15	.07	.01
☐ 69 Kevin Seitzer	.15	.07	.01
☐ 70 Larry Sheets	.05	.02	.00
☐ 71 Ruben Sierra	.35	.17	.03
☐ 72 Ozzie Smith	.25	.12	.02
☐ 73 Zane Smith	.10	.05	.01
☐ 74 Cory Snyder	.15	.07	.01
☐ 75 Dave Stewart	.20	.10	.02
☐ 76 Darryl Strawberry	.50	.25	.05
☐ 77 Rick Sutcliffe	.10	.05	.01

		MINT	EXC	G-VG
☐ 78	Danny Tartabull	.15	.07	.01
☐ 79	Alan Trammell	.20	.10	.02
☐ 80	Fernando Valenzuela	.15	.07	.01
☐ 81	Andy Van Slyke	.15	.07	.01
☐ 82	Frank Viola	.20	.10	.02
☐ 83	Greg Walker	.05	.02	.00
☐ 84	Tim Wallach	.10	.05	.01
☐ 85	Dave Winfield	.25	.12	.02
☐ 86	Mike Witt	.05	.02	.00
☐ 87	Robin Yount	.45	.22	.04
☐ 88	Checklist Card	.05	.02	.00

1988 Topps Send-In Glossy 60

Topps issued this set through a mail-in offer explained and advertised on the wax packs. This 60-card set features glossy fronts with each card measuring 2 1/2" by 3 1/2". The offer provided your choice of any one of the six 10-card subsets (1-10, 11-20, etc.) for 1.25 plus six of the Special Offer ("Spring Fever Baseball") insert cards, which were found one per wax pack. The last two players (numerically) in each ten-card subset are actually "Hot Prospects."

		MINT	EXC	G-VG
COMPLETE SET (60)		12.00	6.00	1.20
COMMON PLAYER (1-60)		.20	.10	.02
☐ 1	Andre Dawson	.30	.15	.03
☐ 2	Jesse Barfield	.25	.12	.02
☐ 3	Mike Schmidt	.75	.35	.07
☐ 4	Ruben Sierra	.50	.25	.05
☐ 5	Mike Scott	.25	.12	.02
☐ 6	Cal Ripken	.35	.17	.03
☐ 7	Gary Carter	.30	.15	.03
☐ 8	Kent Hrbek	.25	.12	.02
☐ 9	Kevin Seitzer	.25	.12	.02
☐ 10	Mike Henneman	.20	.10	.02
☐ 11	Don Mattingly	.90	.45	.09
☐ 12	Tim Raines	.30	.15	.03
☐ 13	Roger Clemens	.75	.35	.07
☐ 14	Ryne Sandberg	.75	.35	.07
☐ 15	Tony Fernandez	.25	.12	.02
☐ 16	Eric Davis	.50	.25	.05
☐ 17	Jack Morris	.25	.12	.02
☐ 18	Tim Wallach	.25	.12	.02
☐ 19	Mike Dunne	.20	.10	.02
☐ 20	Mike Greenwell	.60	.30	.06
☐ 21	Dwight Evans	.25	.12	.02
☐ 22	Darryl Strawberry	.75	.35	.07
☐ 23	Cory Snyder	.30	.15	.03
☐ 24	Pedro Guerrero	.30	.15	.03
☐ 25	Rickey Henderson	.75	.35	.07
☐ 26	Dale Murphy	.45	.22	.04
☐ 27	Kirby Puckett	.45	.22	.04
☐ 28	Steve Bedrosian	.25	.12	.02
☐ 29	Devon White	.30	.15	.03
☐ 30	Benny Santiago	.35	.17	.03
☐ 31	George Bell	.30	.15	.03
☐ 32	Keith Hernandez	.30	.15	.03
☐ 33	Dave Stewart	.30	.15	.03
☐ 34	Dave Parker	.30	.15	.03
☐ 35	Tom Henke	.20	.10	.02
☐ 36	Willie McGee	.30	.15	.03
☐ 37	Alan Trammell	.30	.15	.03
☐ 38	Tony Gwynn	.40	.20	.04
☐ 39	Mark McGwire	.60	.30	.06
☐ 40	Joe Magrane	.25	.12	.02
☐ 41	Jack Clark	.25	.12	.02
☐ 42	Willie Randolph	.25	.12	.02
☐ 43	Juan Samuel	.25	.12	.02
☐ 44	Joe Carter	.30	.15	.03
☐ 45	Shane Rawley	.20	.10	.02
☐ 46	Dave Winfield	.35	.17	.03
☐ 47	Ozzie Smith	.35	.17	.03
☐ 48	Wally Joyner	.30	.15	.03
☐ 49	B.J. Surhoff	.25	.12	.02
☐ 50	Ellis Burks	.75	.35	.07
☐ 51	Wade Boggs	.75	.35	.07
☐ 52	Howard Johnson	.30	.15	.03
☐ 53	George Brett	.50	.25	.05
☐ 54	Dwight Gooden	.45	.22	.04
☐ 55	Jose Canseco	1.00	.50	.10
☐ 56	Lee Smith	.20	.10	.02
☐ 57	Paul Molitor	.30	.15	.03
☐ 58	Andres Galarraga	.30	.15	.03
☐ 59	Matt Nokes	.25	.12	.02
☐ 60	Casey Candaele	.20	.10	.02

1988 Topps Big

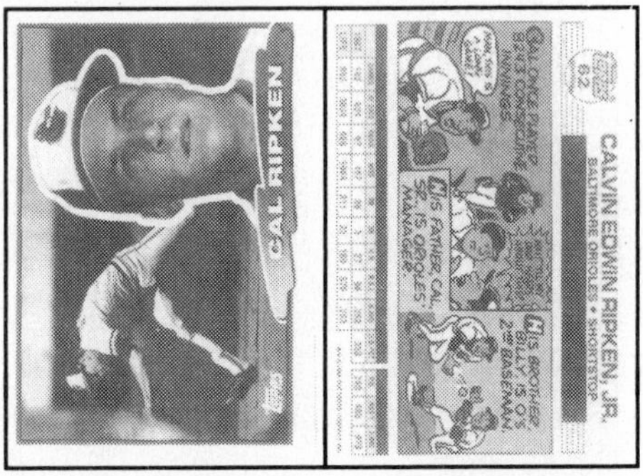

This set of 264 cards was issued as three separately distributed series of 88 cards each. Cards were distributed in wax packs with seven cards for a suggested retail of 40 cents. These cards are very reminiscent in style of the 1956 Topps card set and are popular with collectors perhaps for that reason. The cards measure approximately 2 5/8" by 3 3/4" and are oriented horizontally.

		MINT	EXC	G-VG
COMPLETE SET (264)		24.00	12.00	2.40
COMMON PLAYER (1-88)		.05	.02	.00
COMMON PLAYER (89-176)		.05	.02	.00
COMMON PLAYER (177-264)		.05	.02	.00
☐ 1	Paul Molitor	.12	.06	.01
☐ 2	Milt Thompson	.05	.02	.00
☐ 3	Billy Hatcher	.10	.05	.01
☐ 4	Mike Witt	.05	.02	.00
☐ 5	Vince Coleman	.15	.07	.01
☐ 6	Dwight Evans	.12	.06	.01
☐ 7	Tim Wallach	.08	.04	.01
☐ 8	Alan Trammell	.15	.07	.01
☐ 9	Will Clark	1.00	.50	.10
☐ 10	Jeff Reardon	.08	.04	.01
☐ 11	Dwight Gooden	.45	.22	.04
☐ 12	Benny Santiago	.15	.07	.01
☐ 13	Jose Canseco	1.25	.60	.12
☐ 14	Dale Murphy	.35	.17	.03
☐ 15	George Bell	.20	.10	.02
☐ 16	Ryne Sandberg	.60	.30	.06
☐ 17	Brook Jacoby	.08	.04	.01
☐ 18	Fernando Valenzuela	.12	.06	.01
☐ 19	Scott Fletcher	.05	.02	.00
☐ 20	Eric Davis	.50	.25	.05
☐ 21	Willie Wilson	.10	.05	.01
☐ 22	B.J. Surhoff	.10	.05	.01
☐ 23	Steve Bedrosian	.10	.05	.01
☐ 24	Dave Winfield	.30	.15	.03
☐ 25	Bobby Bonilla	.35	.17	.03
☐ 26	Larry Sheets	.05	.02	.00
☐ 27	Ozzie Guillen	.15	.07	.01

□ 28 Checklist 1-88	.05	.02	.00
□ 29 Nolan Ryan	1.25	.60	.12
□ 30 Bob Boone	.12	.06	.01
□ 31 Tom Herr	.08	.04	.01
□ 32 Wade Boggs	.75	.35	.07
□ 33 Neal Heaton	.05	.02	.00
□ 34 Doyle Alexander	.05	.02	.00
□ 35 Candy Maldonado	.08	.04	.01
□ 36 Kirby Puckett	.45	.22	.04
□ 37 Gary Carter	.20	.10	.02
□ 38 Lance McCullers	.05	.02	.00
□ 39A Terry Steinbach (Topps logo in black)	.15	.07	.01
□ 39B Terry Steinbach (Topps logo in white)	.15	.07	.01
□ 40 Gerald Perry	.05	.02	.00
□ 41 Tom Henke	.08	.04	.01
□ 42 Leon Durham	.05	.02	.00
□ 43 Cory Snyder	.12	.06	.01
□ 44 Dale Sveum	.05	.02	.00
□ 45 Lance Parrish	.12	.06	.01
□ 46 Steve Sax	.15	.07	.01
□ 47 Charlie Hough	.05	.02	.00
□ 48 Kal Daniels	.15	.07	.01
□ 49 Bo Jackson	1.25	.60	.12
□ 50 Ron Guidry	.12	.06	.01
□ 51 Bill Doran	.08	.04	.01
□ 52 Wally Joyner	.30	.15	.03
□ 53 Terry Pendleton	.05	.02	.00
□ 54 Marty Barrett	.05	.02	.00
□ 55 Andres Galarraga	.12	.06	.01
□ 56 Larry Herndon	.05	.02	.00
□ 57 Kevin Mitchell	.45	.22	.04
□ 58 Greg Gagne	.05	.02	.00
□ 59 Keith Hernandez	.15	.07	.01
□ 60 John Kruk	.08	.04	.01
□ 61 Mike LaValliere	.05	.02	.00
□ 62 Cal Ripken	.30	.15	.03
□ 63 Ivan Calderon	.08	.04	.01
□ 64 Alvin Davis	.10	.05	.01
□ 65 Luis Polonia	.08	.04	.01
□ 66 Robin Yount	.45	.22	.04
□ 67 Juan Samuel	.08	.04	.01
□ 68 Andres Thomas	.08	.04	.01
□ 69 Jeff Musselman	.05	.02	.00
□ 70 Jerry Mumphrey	.05	.02	.00
□ 71 Joe Carter	.15	.07	.01
□ 72 Mike Scioscia	.05	.02	.00
□ 73 Pete Incaviglia	.15	.07	.01
□ 74 Barry Larkin	.25	.12	.02
□ 75 Frank White	.08	.04	.01
□ 76 Willie Randolph	.08	.04	.01
□ 77 Kevin Bass	.08	.04	.01
□ 78 Brian Downing	.05	.02	.00
□ 79 Willie McGee	.15	.07	.01
□ 80 Ellis Burks	.50	.25	.05
□ 81 Hubie Brooks	.08	.04	.01
□ 82 Darrell Evans	.08	.04	.01
□ 83 Robby Thompson	.05	.02	.00
□ 84 Kent Hrbek	.12	.06	.01
□ 85 Ron Darling	.10	.05	.01
□ 86 Stan Jefferson	.05	.02	.00
□ 87 Teddy Higuera	.08	.04	.01
□ 88 Mike Schmidt	.90	.45	.09
□ 89 Barry Bonds	.50	.25	.05
□ 90 Jim Presley	.08	.04	.01
□ 91 Orel Hershiser	.25	.12	.02
□ 92 Jesse Barfield	.15	.07	.01
□ 93 Tom Candiotti	.05	.02	.00
□ 94 Bret Saberhagen	.20	.10	.02
□ 95 Jose Uribe	.05	.02	.00
□ 96 Tom Browning	.10	.05	.01
□ 97 Johnny Ray	.08	.04	.01
□ 98 Mike Morgan	.05	.02	.00
□ 99 Lou Whitaker	.12	.06	.01
□ 100 Jim Sundberg	.05	.02	.00
□ 101 Roger McDowell	.08	.04	.01
□ 102 Randy Ready	.05	.02	.00
□ 103 Mike Gallego	.05	.02	.00
□ 104 Steve Buechele	.05	.02	.00
□ 105 Greg Walker	.05	.02	.00
□ 106 Jose Lind	.08	.04	.01
□ 107 Steve Trout	.05	.02	.00
□ 108 Rick Rhoden	.05	.02	.00
□ 109 Jim Pankovits	.05	.02	.00
□ 110 Ken Griffey Sr.	.12	.06	.01
□ 111 Danny Cox	.08	.04	.01
□ 112 Franklin Stubbs	.08	.04	.01
□ 113 Lloyd Moseby	.08	.04	.01
□ 114 Mel Hall	.08	.04	.01
□ 115 Kevin Seitzer	.20	.10	.02
□ 116 Tim Raines	.25	.12	.02
□ 117 Juan Castillo	.05	.02	.00
□ 118 Roger Clemens	.75	.35	.07
□ 119 Mike Aldrete	.05	.02	.00
□ 120 Mario Soto	.05	.02	.00
□ 121 Jack Howell	.05	.02	.00
□ 122 Rick Schu	.05	.02	.00
□ 123 Jeff Robinson	.08	.04	.01
□ 124 Doug Drabek	.15	.07	.01
□ 125 Henry Cotto	.05	.02	.00
□ 126 Checklist 89-176	.05	.02	.00
□ 127 Gary Gaetti	.10	.05	.01
□ 128 Rick Sutcliffe	.10	.05	.01
□ 129 Howard Johnson	.15	.07	.01
□ 130 Chris Brown	.05	.02	.00
□ 131 Dave Henderson	.08	.04	.01
□ 132 Curt Wilkerson	.05	.02	.00
□ 133 Mike Marshall	.10	.05	.01
□ 134 Kelly Gruber	.20	.10	.02
□ 135 Julio Franco	.12	.06	.01
□ 136 Kurt Stillwell	.08	.04	.01
□ 137 Donnie Hill	.05	.02	.00
□ 138 Mike Pagliarulo	.05	.02	.00
□ 139 Von Hayes	.12	.06	.01
□ 140 Mike Scott	.15	.07	.01
□ 141 Bob Kipper	.05	.02	.00
□ 142 Harold Reynolds	.08	.04	.01
□ 143 Bob Brenly	.05	.02	.00
□ 144 Dave Concepcion	.10	.05	.01
□ 145 Devon White	.10	.05	.01
□ 146 Jeff Stone	.05	.02	.00
□ 147 Chet Lemon	.05	.02	.00
□ 148 Ozzie Virgil	.05	.02	.00
□ 149 Todd Worrell	.10	.05	.01
□ 150 Mitch Webster	.05	.02	.00
□ 151 Rob Deer	.10	.05	.01
□ 152 Rich Gedman	.05	.02	.00
□ 153 Andre Dawson	.25	.12	.02
□ 154 Mike Davis	.05	.02	.00
□ 155 Nelson Liriano	.05	.02	.00
□ 156 Greg Swindell	.12	.06	.01
□ 157 George Brett	.35	.17	.03
□ 158 Kevin McReynolds	.20	.10	.02
□ 159 Brian Fisher	.05	.02	.00
□ 160 Mike Kingery	.05	.02	.00
□ 161 Tony Gwynn	.35	.17	.03
□ 162 Don Baylor	.10	.05	.01
□ 163 Jerry Browne	.08	.04	.01
□ 164 Dan Pasqua	.05	.02	.00
□ 165 Rickey Henderson	.75	.35	.07
□ 166 Brett Butler	.10	.05	.01
□ 167 Nick Esasky	.10	.05	.01
□ 168 Kirk McCaskill	.08	.04	.01
□ 169 Fred Lynn	.12	.06	.01
□ 170 Jack Morris	.12	.06	.01
□ 171 Pedro Guerrero	.15	.07	.01
□ 172 Dave Stieb	.15	.07	.01
□ 173 Pat Tabler	.05	.02	.00
□ 174 Floyd Bannister	.05	.02	.00
□ 175 Rafael Belliard	.05	.02	.00
□ 176 Mark Langston	.12	.06	.01
□ 177 Greg Mathews	.05	.02	.00
□ 178 Claudell Washington	.08	.04	.01
□ 179 Mark McGwire	1.00	.50	.10
□ 180 Bert Blyleven	.12	.06	.01
□ 181 Jim Rice	.15	.07	.01
□ 182 Mookie Wilson	.08	.04	.01
□ 183 Willie Fraser	.05	.02	.00
□ 184 Andy Van Slyke	.12	.06	.01
□ 185 Matt Nokes	.12	.06	.01
□ 186 Eddie Whitson	.08	.04	.01
□ 187 Tony Fernandez	.10	.05	.01
□ 188 Rick Reuschel	.10	.05	.01
□ 189 Ken Phelps	.08	.04	.01
□ 190 Juan Nieves	.05	.02	.00
□ 191 Kirk Gibson	.25	.12	.02
□ 192 Glenn Davis	.25	.12	.02
□ 193 Zane Smith	.15	.07	.01
□ 194 Jose DeLeon	.05	.02	.00
□ 195 Gary Ward	.05	.02	.00
□ 196 Pascual Perez	.10	.05	.01
□ 197 Carlton Fisk	.25	.12	.02
□ 198 Oddibe McDowell	.08	.04	.01
□ 199 Mark Gubicza	.10	.05	.01
□ 200 Glenn Hubbard	.05	.02	.00
□ 201 Frank Viola	.15	.07	.01
□ 202 Jody Reed	.12	.06	.01
□ 203 Len Dykstra	.15	.07	.01
□ 204 Dick Schofield	.05	.02	.00
□ 205 Sid Bream	.05	.02	.00
□ 206 Guillermo Hernandez	.05	.02	.00
□ 207 Keith Moreland	.05	.02	.00
□ 208 Mark Eichhorn	.05	.02	.00
□ 209 Rene Gonzalez	.05	.02	.00
□ 210 Dave Valle	.05	.02	.00
□ 211 Tom Brunansky	.10	.05	.01
□ 212 Charles Hudson	.05	.02	.00

☐ 213 John Farrell	.05	.02	.00
☐ 214 Jeff Treadway	.05	.02	.00
☐ 215 Eddie Murray	.25	.12	.02
☐ 216 Checklist 177-264	.05	.02	.00
☐ 217 Greg Brock	.05	.02	.00
☐ 218 John Shelby	.05	.02	.00
☐ 219 Craig Reynolds	.05	.02	.00
☐ 220 Dion James	.05	.02	.00
☐ 221 Carney Lansford	.12	.06	.01
☐ 222 Juan Berenguer	.05	.02	.00
☐ 223 Luis Rivera	.05	.02	.00
☐ 224 Harold Baines	.12	.06	.01
☐ 225 Shawon Dunston	.15	.07	.01
☐ 226 Luis Aguayo	.05	.02	.00
☐ 227 Pete O'Brien	.08	.04	.01
☐ 228 Ozzie Smith	.20	.10	.02
☐ 229 Don Mattingly	1.25	.60	.12
☐ 230 Danny Tartabull	.20	.10	.02
☐ 231 Andy Allanson	.05	.02	.00
☐ 232 John Franco	.08	.04	.01
☐ 233 Mike Greenwell	.60	.30	.06
☐ 234 Bob Ojeda	.08	.04	.01
☐ 235 Chili Davis	.08	.04	.01
☐ 236 Mike Dunne	.05	.02	.00
☐ 237 Jim Morrison	.05	.02	.00
☐ 238 Carmelo Martinez	.05	.02	.00
☐ 239 Ernie Whitt	.05	.02	.00
☐ 240 Scott Garrelts	.08	.04	.01
☐ 241 Mike Moore	.10	.05	.01
☐ 242 Dave Parker	.15	.07	.01
☐ 243 Tim Laudner	.05	.02	.00
☐ 244 Bill Wegman	.05	.02	.00
☐ 245 Bob Horner	.10	.05	.01
☐ 246 Rafael Santana	.05	.02	.00
☐ 247 Alfredo Griffin	.05	.02	.00
☐ 248 Mark Bailey	.05	.02	.00
☐ 249 Ron Gant	.45	.22	.04
☐ 250 Bryn Smith	.05	.02	.00
☐ 251 Lance Johnson	.08	.04	.01
☐ 252 Sam Horn	.08	.04	.01
☐ 253 Darryl Strawberry	.75	.35	.07
☐ 254 Chuck Finley	.15	.07	.01
☐ 255 Darnell Coles	.05	.02	.00
☐ 256 Mike Henneman	.08	.04	.01
☐ 257 Andy Hawkins	.05	.02	.00
☐ 258 Jim Clancy	.05	.02	.00
☐ 259 Atlee Hammaker	.05	.02	.00
☐ 260 Glenn Wilson	.05	.02	.00
☐ 261 Larry McWilliams	.05	.02	.00
☐ 262 Jack Clark	.15	.07	.01
☐ 263 Walt Weiss	.30	.15	.03
☐ 264 Gene Larkin	.10	.05	.01

1988 Topps Mini Leaders

The 1988 Topps Mini set of Major League Leaders features 77 cards of leaders of the various statistical categories for the 1987 season. The cards are numbered on the back and measure approximately 2 1/8" by 3". The card backs are printed in blue, red, and yellow on white card stock. The cards were distributed as a separate issue in wax packs.

	MINT	EXC	G-VG
COMPLETE SET (77)	7.00	3.50	.70
COMMON PLAYER (1-77)	.05	.02	.00
☐ 1 Wade Boggs	.50	.25	.05
☐ 2 Roger Clemens	.50	.25	.05
☐ 3 Dwight Evans	.10	.05	.01
☐ 4 DeWayne Buice	.05	.02	.00
☐ 5 Brian Downing	.05	.02	.00
☐ 6 Wally Joyner	.15	.07	.01
☐ 7 Ivan Calderon	.10	.05	.01
☐ 8 Carlton Fisk	.20	.10	.02
☐ 9 Gary Redus	.05	.02	.00
☐ 10 Darrell Evans	.10	.05	.01
☐ 11 Jack Morris	.12	.06	.01
☐ 12 Alan Trammell	.15	.07	.01
☐ 13 Lou Whitaker	.12	.06	.01
☐ 14 Bret Saberhagen	.15	.07	.01
☐ 15 Kevin Seitzer	.15	.07	.01
☐ 16 Danny Tartabull	.12	.06	.01
☐ 17 Willie Wilson	.10	.05	.01
☐ 18 Teddy Higuera	.10	.05	.01
☐ 19 Paul Molitor	.12	.06	.01
☐ 20 Dan Plesac	.05	.02	.00
☐ 21 Robin Yount	.40	.20	.04
☐ 22 Kent Hrbek	.12	.06	.01
☐ 23 Kirby Puckett	.40	.20	.04
☐ 24 Jeff Reardon	.08	.04	.01
☐ 25 Frank Viola	.15	.07	.01
☐ 26 Rickey Henderson	.75	.35	.07
☐ 27 Don Mattingly	.90	.45	.09
☐ 28 Willie Randolph	.08	.04	.01
☐ 29 Dave Righetti	.10	.05	.01
☐ 30 Jose Canseco	1.00	.50	.10
☐ 31 Mark McGwire	.75	.35	.07
☐ 32 Dave Stewart	.15	.07	.01
☐ 33 Phil Bradley	.08	.04	.01
☐ 34 Mark Langston	.12	.06	.01
☐ 35 Harold Reynolds	.08	.04	.01
☐ 36 Charlie Hough	.05	.02	.00
☐ 37 George Bell	.15	.07	.01
☐ 38 Tom Henke	.05	.02	.00
☐ 39 Jimmy Key	.05	.02	.00
☐ 40 Dion James	.05	.02	.00
☐ 41 Dale Murphy	.30	.15	.03
☐ 42 Zane Smith	.10	.05	.01
☐ 43 Andre Dawson	.20	.10	.02
☐ 44 Lee Smith	.08	.04	.01
☐ 45 Rick Sutcliffe	.10	.05	.01
☐ 46 Eric Davis	.40	.20	.04
☐ 47 John Franco	.08	.04	.01
☐ 48 Dave Parker	.15	.07	.01
☐ 49 Billy Hatcher	.08	.04	.01
☐ 50 Nolan Ryan	1.00	.50	.10
☐ 51 Mike Scott	.15	.07	.01
☐ 52 Pedro Guerrero	.15	.07	.01
☐ 53 Orel Hershiser	.20	.10	.02
☐ 54 Fernando Valenzuela	.15	.07	.01
☐ 55 Bob Welch	.15	.07	.01
☐ 56 Andres Galarraga	.15	.07	.01
☐ 57 Tim Raines	.20	.10	.02
☐ 58 Tim Wallach	.08	.04	.01
☐ 59 Len Dykstra	.15	.07	.01
☐ 60 Dwight Gooden	.35	.17	.03
☐ 61 Howard Johnson	.15	.07	.01
☐ 62 Roger McDowell	.05	.02	.00
☐ 63 Darryl Strawberry	.50	.25	.05
☐ 64 Steve Bedrosian	.08	.04	.01
☐ 65 Shane Rawley	.05	.02	.00
☐ 66 Juan Samuel	.08	.04	.01
☐ 67 Mike Schmidt	.75	.35	.07
☐ 68 Mike Dunne	.05	.02	.00
☐ 69 Jack Clark	.15	.07	.01
☐ 70 Vince Coleman	.20	.10	.02
☐ 71 Willie McGee	.15	.07	.01
☐ 72 Ozzie Smith	.15	.07	.01
☐ 73 Todd Worrell	.10	.05	.01
☐ 74 Tony Gwynn	.30	.15	.03
☐ 75 John Kruk	.08	.04	.01
☐ 76 Rick Reuschel	.08	.04	.01
☐ 77 Checklist Card	.05	.02	.00

1988 Topps Traded

This 132-card Traded or extended set was distributed by Topps to dealers in a special blue and white box as a complete set. The card fronts are identical in style to the Topps regular issue and are also 2 1/2" by 3 1/2". The backs are printed in orange and black on white card stock. Cards are numbered (with a T suffix) alphabetically according to the name of the player. This set has generated additional interest due to the inclusion of the 1988 U.S. Olympic baseball team members. These Olympians are indicated in the checklist below by OLY. The key (extended) rookie cards in this set are Jim Abbott, Roberto Alomar, Andy Benes, Ron Gant, Mark Grace, Ty Griffin, Tino Martinez, Chris Sabo, Robin Ventura, and Walt Weiss. Topps also produced a specially boxed "glossy" edition, frequently referred to as the Topps Traded Tiffany set. This year, again, Topps did not disclose the number of Tiffany sets they produced or sold. It is apparent from the availability that there were many more sets produced this year compared to the 1984-86 Tiffany sets, perhaps 25,000 sets. The checklist of cards is identical to that of the normal non-glossy cards. There are two primary distinguishing features of the Tiffany cards, white card stock reverses and high gloss obverses. These Tiffany cards are valued at approximately four times the values listed below.

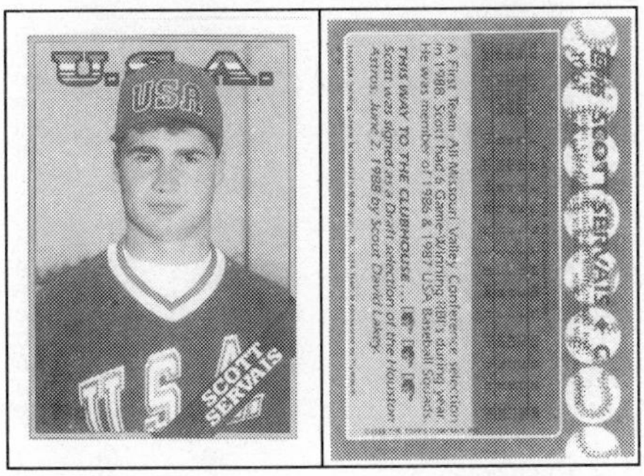

	MINT	EXC	G-VG
COMPLETE SET (132)	24.00	12.00	2.40
COMMON PLAYER (1-132)	.06	.03	.00
☐ 1T Jim Abbott OLY	5.00	2.50	.50
☐ 2T Juan Agosto	.06	.03	.00
☐ 3T Luis Alicea	.10	.05	.01
☐ 4T Roberto Alomar	1.75	.85	.17
☐ 5T Brady Anderson	.30	.15	.03
☐ 6T Jack Armstrong	.75	.35	.07
☐ 7T Don August	.10	.05	.01
☐ 8T Floyd Bannister	.06	.03	.00
☐ 9T Bret Barberie OLY	.15	.07	.01
☐ 10T Jose Bautista	.10	.05	.01
☐ 11T Don Baylor	.10	.05	.01
☐ 12T Tim Belcher	.15	.07	.01
☐ 13T Buddy Bell	.10	.05	.01
☐ 14T Andy Benes OLY	2.50	1.25	.25
☐ 15T Damon Berryhill	.30	.15	.03
☐ 16T Bud Black	.10	.05	.01
☐ 17T Pat Borders	.35	.17	.03
☐ 18T Phil Bradley	.10	.05	.01
☐ 19T Jeff Branson OLY	.25	.12	.02
☐ 20T Tom Brunansky	.15	.07	.01
☐ 21T Jay Buhner	.35	.17	.03
☐ 22T Brett Butler	.15	.07	.01
☐ 23T Jim Campanis OLY	.20	.10	.02
☐ 24T Sil Campusano	.20	.10	.02
☐ 25T John Candelaria	.10	.05	.01
☐ 26T Jose Cecena	.10	.05	.01
☐ 27T Rick Cerone	.06	.03	.00
☐ 28T Jack Clark	.12	.06	.01
☐ 29T Kevin Coffman	.06	.03	.00
☐ 30T Pat Combs OLY	.90	.45	.09
☐ 31T Henry Cotto	.06	.03	.00
☐ 32T Chili Davis	.10	.05	.01
☐ 33T Mike Davis	.06	.03	.00
☐ 34T Jose DeLeon	.06	.03	.00
☐ 35T Richard Dotson	.06	.03	.00
☐ 36T Cecil Espy	.10	.05	.01
☐ 37T Tom Filer	.06	.03	.00
☐ 38T Mike Fiore OLY	.15	.07	.01
☐ 39T Ron Gant	1.50	.75	.15
☐ 40T Kirk Gibson	.15	.07	.01
☐ 41T Rich Gossage	.15	.07	.01
☐ 42T Mark Grace	4.50	2.25	.45
☐ 43T Alfredo Griffin	.06	.03	.00
☐ 44T Ty Griffin OLY	1.00	.50	.10
☐ 45T Bryan Harvey	.20	.10	.02
☐ 46T Ron Hassey	.06	.03	.00
☐ 47T Ray Hayward	.06	.03	.00
☐ 48T Dave Henderson	.10	.05	.01
☐ 49T Tom Herr	.10	.05	.01
☐ 50T Bob Horner	.10	.05	.01
☐ 51T Ricky Horton	.06	.03	.00
☐ 52T Jay Howell	.06	.03	.00
☐ 53T Glenn Hubbard	.06	.03	.00
☐ 54T Jeff Innis	.15	.07	.01
☐ 55T Danny Jackson	.15	.07	.01
☐ 56T Darrin Jackson	.15	.07	.01
☐ 57T Roberto Kelly	.75	.35	.07
☐ 58T Ron Kittle	.15	.07	.01
☐ 59T Ray Knight	.10	.05	.01
☐ 60T Vance Law	.06	.03	.00
☐ 61T Jeffrey Leonard	.10	.05	.01
☐ 62T Mike Macfarlane	.20	.10	.02
☐ 63T Scotti Madison	.10	.05	.01
☐ 64T Kirt Manwaring	.10	.05	.01
☐ 65T Mark Marquess OLY	.06	.03	.00
☐ 66T Tino Martinez OLY	3.50	1.75	.35
☐ 67T Billy Masse OLY	.15	.07	.01
☐ 68T Jack McDowell	.35	.17	.03
☐ 69T Jack McKeon MG	.06	.03	.00
☐ 70T Larry McWilliams	.06	.03	.00
☐ 71T Mickey Morandini OLY	.35	.17	.03
☐ 72T Keith Moreland	.06	.03	.00
☐ 73T Mike Morgan	.06	.03	.00
☐ 74T Charles Nagy OLY	.50	.25	.05
☐ 75T Al Nipper	.06	.03	.00
☐ 76T Russ Nixon MG	.06	.03	.00
☐ 77T Jesse Orosco	.06	.03	.00
☐ 78T Joe Orsulak	.06	.03	.00
☐ 79T Dave Palmer	.06	.03	.00
☐ 80T Mark Parent	.15	.07	.01
☐ 81T Dave Parker	.15	.07	.01
☐ 82T Dan Pasqua	.10	.05	.01
☐ 83T Melido Perez	.20	.10	.02
☐ 84T Steve Peters	.10	.05	.01
☐ 85T Dan Petry	.06	.03	.00
☐ 86T Gary Pettis	.06	.03	.00
☐ 87T Jeff Pico	.10	.05	.01
☐ 88T Jim Poole OLY	.15	.07	.01
☐ 89T Ted Power	.06	.03	.00
☐ 90T Rafael Ramirez	.06	.03	.00
☐ 91T Dennis Rasmussen	.10	.05	.01
☐ 92T Jose Rijo	.20	.10	.02
☐ 93T Ernie Riles	.06	.03	.00
☐ 94T Luis Rivera	.10	.05	.01
☐ 95T Doug Robbins OLY	.15	.07	.01
☐ 96T Frank Robinson MG	.12	.06	.01
☐ 97T Cookie Rojas MG	.06	.03	.00
☐ 98T Chris Sabo	2.25	1.10	.22
☐ 99T Mark Salas	.06	.03	.00
☐ 100T Luis Salazar	.06	.03	.00
☐ 101T Rafael Santana	.06	.03	.00
☐ 102T Nelson Santovenia	.20	.10	.02
☐ 103T Mackey Sasser	.30	.15	.03
☐ 104T Calvin Schiraldi	.06	.03	.00
☐ 105T Mike Schooler	.35	.17	.03
☐ 106T Scott Servais OLY	.15	.07	.01
☐ 107T Dave Silvestri OLY	.15	.07	.01
☐ 108T Don Slaught	.06	.03	.00
☐ 109T Joe Slusarski OLY	.15	.07	.01
☐ 110T Lee Smith	.10	.05	.01
☐ 111T Pete Smith	.15	.07	.01
☐ 112T Jim Snyder MG	.06	.03	.00
☐ 113T Ed Sprague OLY	.25	.12	.02
☐ 114T Pete Stanicek	.10	.05	.01
☐ 115T Kurt Stillwell	.12	.06	.01
☐ 116T Todd Stottlemyre	.25	.12	.02
☐ 117T Bill Swift	.15	.07	.01
☐ 118T Pat Tabler	.10	.05	.01
☐ 119T Scott Terry	.06	.03	.00
☐ 120T Mickey Tettleton	.15	.07	.01
☐ 121T Dickie Thon	.06	.03	.00
☐ 122T Jeff Treadway	.20	.10	.02
☐ 123T Willie Upshaw	.06	.03	.00
☐ 124T Robin Ventura OLY	1.75	.85	.17
☐ 125T Ron Washington	.06	.03	.00
☐ 126T Walt Weiss	1.00	.50	.10
☐ 127T Bob Welch	.20	.10	.02
☐ 128T David Wells	.20	.10	.02
☐ 129T Glenn Wilson	.06	.03	.00
☐ 130T Ted Wood OLY	.35	.17	.03
☐ 131T Don Zimmer MG	.06	.03	.00
☐ 132T Checklist 1T-132T	.06	.01	.00

1989 Topps

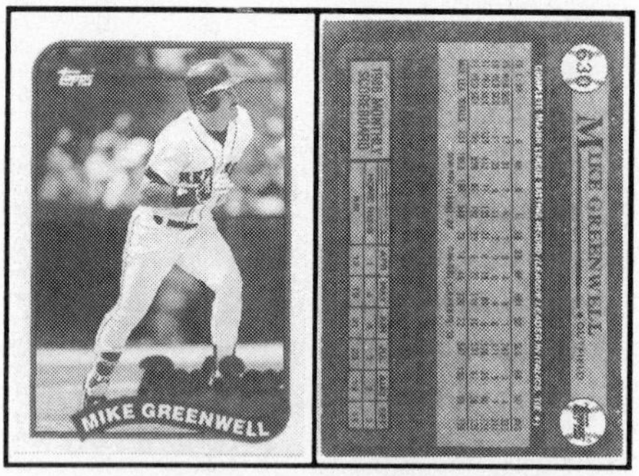

This 792-card set features backs that are printed in pink and black on gray card stock. The manager cards contain a checklist of the respective team's players on the back. Subsets in the set include Record Breakers (1-7), Turn Back the Clock (661-665), and All-Star selections (386-407). The bonus cards distributed throughout the set, which are indicated on the Topps checklist cards, are actually Team Leader (TL) cards. Also sprinkled throughout the set are Future Stars (FS) and First Draft Picks (FDP). There are subtle variations found in the Future Stars cards with respect to the placement of photo and type on the card; in fact, each card has at least two varieties but they are difficult to detect (requiring precise measurement) as well as difficult to explain. The key rookies in this set are Jim Abbott, Sandy Alomar Jr., Ramon Martinez, and Gary Sheffield. Topps also produced a specially boxed "glossy" edition, frequently referred to as the Topps Tiffany set. This year, again, Topps did not disclose the number of Tiffany sets they produced or sold but it seems that production quantities were roughly similar (or slightly smaller, approximately 15,000 sets) to the previous two years. The checklist of cards (792 regular and 132 Traded) is identical to that of the normal non-glossy cards. There are two primary distinguishing features of the Tiffany cards, white card stock reverses and high gloss obverses. These Tiffany cards are valued at approximately four times the values listed below.

	MINT	EXC	G-VG
COMPLETE SET (792)	24.00	12.00	2.40
COMMON PLAYER (1-792)	.03	.01	.00
☐ 1 George Bell RB Slams 3 HR on Opening Day	.12	.06	.01
☐ 2 Wade Boggs RB Gets 200 Hits 6th Straight Season	.15	.07	.01
☐ 3 Gary Carter RB Sets Record for Career Putouts	.08	.04	.01
☐ 4 Andre Dawson RB Logs Double Figures in HR and SB	.10	.05	.01
☐ 5 Orel Hershiser RB Pitches 59 Scoreless Innings	.12	.06	.01
☐ 6 Doug Jones RB Earns His 15th Straight Save UER (photo actually Chris Codiroli)	.06	.03	.00
☐ 7 Kevin McReynolds RB Steals 21 Without Being Caught	.08	.04	.01
☐ 8 Dave Eiland	.12	.06	.01
☐ 9 Tim Teufel	.03	.01	.00
☐ 10 Andre Dawson	.12	.06	.01
☐ 11 Bruce Sutter	.06	.03	.00
☐ 12 Dale Sveum	.03	.01	.00
☐ 13 Doug Sisk	.03	.01	.00
☐ 14 Tom Kelly MG (team checklist back)	.06	.03	.00
☐ 15 Robby Thompson	.03	.01	.00
☐ 16 Ron Robinson	.03	.01	.00
☐ 17 Brian Downing	.03	.01	.00
☐ 18 Rick Rhoden	.03	.01	.00
☐ 19 Greg Gagne	.03	.01	.00
☐ 20 Steve Bedrosian	.06	.03	.00
☐ 21 Chicago White Sox TL Greg Walker	.03	.01	.00
☐ 22 Tim Crews	.03	.01	.00
☐ 23 Mike Fitzgerald Montreal Expos	.03	.01	.00
☐ 24 Larry Andersen	.03	.01	.00
☐ 25 Frank White	.06	.03	.00
☐ 26 Dale Mohorcic	.03	.01	.00
☐ 27A Orestes Destrade (F* next to copyright)	.25	.12	.02
☐ 27B Orestes Destrade (E*F* next to copyright)	.25	.12	.02
☐ 28 Mike Moore	.06	.03	.00
☐ 29 Kelly Gruber	.18	.09	.01
☐ 30 Dwight Gooden	.25	.12	.02
☐ 31 Terry Francona	.03	.01	.00
☐ 32 Dennis Rasmussen	.03	.01	.00
☐ 33 B.J. Surhoff	.06	.03	.00
☐ 34 Ken Williams	.03	.01	.00
☐ 35 John Tudor UER ('84 Pirates record, should be Red Sox)	.06	.03	.00
☐ 36 Mitch Webster	.03	.01	.00
☐ 37 Bob Stanley	.03	.01	.00
☐ 38 Paul Runge	.03	.01	.00
☐ 39 Mike Maddux	.03	.01	.00
☐ 40 Steve Sax	.08	.04	.01
☐ 41 Terry Mulholland	.03	.01	.00
☐ 42 Jim Eppard	.06	.03	.00
☐ 43 Guillermo Hernandez	.03	.01	.00
☐ 44 Jim Snyder MG (team checklist back)	.06	.03	.00
☐ 45 Kal Daniels	.08	.04	.01
☐ 46 Mark Portugal	.03	.01	.00
☐ 47 Carney Lansford	.08	.04	.01
☐ 48 Tim Burke	.06	.03	.00
☐ 49 Craig Biggio	.25	.12	.02
☐ 50 George Bell	.10	.05	.01
☐ 51 California Angels TL Mark McLemore	.03	.01	.00
☐ 52 Bob Brenly	.03	.01	.00
☐ 53 Ruben Sierra	.15	.07	.01
☐ 54 Steve Trout	.03	.01	.00
☐ 55 Julio Franco	.08	.04	.01
☐ 56 Pat Tabler	.03	.01	.00
☐ 57 Alejandro Pena	.03	.01	.00
☐ 58 Lee Mazzilli	.03	.01	.00
☐ 59 Mark Davis	.10	.05	.01
☐ 60 Tom Brunansky	.08	.04	.01
☐ 61 Neil Allen	.03	.01	.00
☐ 62 Alfredo Griffin	.03	.01	.00
☐ 63 Mark Clear	.03	.01	.00
☐ 64 Alex Trevino	.03	.01	.00
☐ 65 Rick Reuschel	.06	.03	.00
☐ 66 Manny Trillo	.03	.01	.00
☐ 67 Dave Palmer	.03	.01	.00
☐ 68 Darrell Miller	.03	.01	.00
☐ 69 Jeff Ballard	.06	.03	.00
☐ 70 Mark McGwire	.35	.17	.03
☐ 71 Mike Boddicker	.03	.01	.00
☐ 72 John Moses	.03	.01	.00
☐ 73 Pascual Perez	.06	.03	.00
☐ 74 Nick Leyva MG (team checklist back)	.06	.03	.00
☐ 75 Tom Henke	.06	.03	.00
☐ 76 Terry Blocker	.10	.05	.01
☐ 77 Doyle Alexander	.03	.01	.00
☐ 78 Jim Sundberg	.03	.01	.00
☐ 79 Scott Bankhead	.03	.01	.00
☐ 80 Cory Snyder	.08	.04	.01
☐ 81 Montreal Expos TL Tim Raines	.08	.04	.01
☐ 82 Dave Leiper	.03	.01	.00
☐ 83 Jeff Blauser	.10	.05	.01
☐ 84 Bill Bene FDP	.08	.04	.01
☐ 85 Kevin McReynolds	.10	.05	.01
☐ 86 Al Nipper	.03	.01	.00
☐ 87 Larry Owen	.03	.01	.00
☐ 88 Darryl Hamilton	.12	.06	.01
☐ 89 Dave LaPoint	.03	.01	.00
☐ 90 Vince Coleman UER (wrong birth year)	.10	.05	.01
☐ 91 Floyd Youmans	.03	.01	.00
☐ 92 Jeff Kunkel	.03	.01	.00
☐ 93 Ken Howell	.03	.01	.00
☐ 94 Chris Speier	.03	.01	.00
☐ 95 Gerald Young	.03	.01	.00

☐ 96 Rick Cerone	.06	.03	.00
(Ellis Burks in background of photo)			
☐ 97 Greg Mathews	.03	.01	.00
☐ 98 Larry Sheets	.03	.01	.00
☐ 99 Sherman Corbett	.06	.03	.00
☐ 100 Mike Schmidt	.25	.12	.02
☐ 101 Les Straker	.03	.01	.00
☐ 102 Mike Gallego	.03	.01	.00
☐ 103 Tim Birtsas	.03	.01	.00
☐ 104 Dallas Green MG	.06	.03	.00
(team checklist back)			
☐ 105 Ron Darling	.08	.04	.01
☐ 106 Willie Upshaw	.03	.01	.00
☐ 107 Jose DeLeon	.03	.01	.00
☐ 108 Fred Manrique	.03	.01	.00
☐ 109 Hipolito Pena	.06	.03	.00
☐ 110 Paul Molitor	.10	.05	.01
☐ 111 Cincinnati Reds TL	.10	.05	.01
Eric Davis			
(swinging bat)			
☐ 112 Jim Presley	.03	.01	.00
☐ 113 Lloyd Moseby	.06	.03	.00
☐ 114 Bob Kipper	.03	.01	.00
☐ 115 Jody Davis	.03	.01	.00
☐ 116 Jeff Montgomery	.06	.03	.00
☐ 117 Dave Anderson	.03	.01	.00
☐ 118 Checklist 1-132	.06	.01	.00
☐ 119 Terry Puhl	.03	.01	.00
☐ 120 Frank Viola	.12	.06	.01
☐ 121 Garry Templeton	.06	.03	.00
☐ 122 Lance Johnson	.08	.04	.01
☐ 123 Spike Owen	.03	.01	.00
☐ 124 Jim Traber	.03	.01	.00
☐ 125 Mike Krukow	.03	.01	.00
☐ 126 Sid Bream	.03	.01	.00
☐ 127 Walt Terrell	.03	.01	.00
☐ 128 Milt Thompson	.03	.01	.00
☐ 129 Terry Clark	.08	.04	.01
☐ 130 Gerald Perry	.03	.01	.00
☐ 131 Dave Otto	.08	.04	.01
☐ 132 Curt Ford	.03	.01	.00
☐ 133 Bill Long	.03	.01	.00
☐ 134 Don Zimmer MG	.06	.03	.00
(team checklist back)			
☐ 135 Jose Rijo	.08	.04	.01
☐ 136 Joey Meyer	.06	.03	.00
☐ 137 Geno Petralli	.03	.01	.00
☐ 138 Wallace Johnson	.03	.01	.00
☐ 139 Mike Flanagan	.06	.03	.00
☐ 140 Shawon Dunston	.12	.06	.01
☐ 141 Cleveland Indians TL	.06	.03	.00
Brook Jacoby			
☐ 142 Mike Diaz	.03	.01	.00
☐ 143 Mike Campbell	.03	.01	.00
☐ 144 Jay Bell	.03	.01	.00
☐ 145 Dave Stewart	.12	.06	.01
☐ 146 Gary Pettis	.03	.01	.00
☐ 147 DeWayne Buice	.03	.01	.00
☐ 148 Bill Pecota	.03	.01	.00
☐ 149 Doug Dascenzo	.08	.04	.01
☐ 150 Fernando Valenzuela	.10	.05	.01
☐ 151 Terry McGriff	.03	.01	.00
☐ 152 Mark Thurmond	.03	.01	.00
☐ 153 Jim Pankovits	.03	.01	.00
☐ 154 Don Carman	.03	.01	.00
☐ 155 Marty Barrett	.03	.01	.00
☐ 156 Dave Gallagher	.10	.05	.01
☐ 157 Tom Glavine	.06	.03	.00
☐ 158 Mike Aldrete	.03	.01	.00
☐ 159 Pat Clements	.03	.01	.00
☐ 160 Jeffrey Leonard	.06	.03	.00
☐ 161 Gregg Olson FDP UER	.50	.25	.05
(born Scribner, NE, should be Omaha, NE)			
☐ 162 John Davis	.03	.01	.00
☐ 163 Bob Forsch	.03	.01	.00
☐ 164 Hal Lanier MG	.06	.03	.00
(team checklist back)			
☐ 165 Mike Dunne	.03	.01	.00
☐ 166 Doug Jennings	.15	.07	.01
☐ 167 Steve Searcy FS	.15	.07	.01
☐ 168 Willie Wilson	.06	.03	.00
☐ 169 Mike Jackson	.03	.01	.00
☐ 170 Tony Fernandez	.08	.04	.01
☐ 171 Atlanta Braves TL	.03	.01	.00
Andres Thomas			
☐ 172 Frank Williams	.03	.01	.00
☐ 173 Mel Hall	.06	.03	.00
☐ 174 Todd Burns	.18	.09	.01
☐ 175 John Shelby	.03	.01	.00
☐ 176 Jeff Parrett	.03	.01	.00
☐ 177 Monty Fariss FDP	.18	.09	.01
☐ 178 Mark Grant	.03	.01	.00

☐ 179 Ozzie Virgil	.03	.01	.00
☐ 180 Mike Scott	.10	.05	.01
☐ 181 Craig Worthington	.20	.10	.02
☐ 182 Bob McClure	.03	.01	.00
☐ 183 Oddibe McDowell	.06	.03	.00
☐ 184 John Costello	.06	.03	.00
☐ 185 Claudell Washington	.06	.03	.00
☐ 186 Pat Perry	.03	.01	.00
☐ 187 Darren Daulton	.06	.03	.00
☐ 188 Dennis Lamp	.03	.01	.00
☐ 189 Kevin Mitchell	.30	.15	.03
☐ 190 Mike Witt	.03	.01	.00
☐ 191 Sil Campusano	.18	.09	.01
☐ 192 Paul Mirabella	.03	.01	.00
☐ 193 Sparky Anderson MG	.06	.03	.00
(team checklist back)			
UER (553 Salazer)			
☐ 194 Greg W. Harris	.20	.10	.02
San Diego Padres			
☐ 195 Ozzie Guillen	.08	.04	.01
☐ 196 Denny Walling	.03	.01	.00
☐ 197 Neal Heaton	.03	.01	.00
☐ 198 Danny Heep	.03	.01	.00
☐ 199 Mike Schooler	.25	.12	.02
☐ 200 George Brett	.20	.10	.02
☐ 201 Blue Jays TL	.08	.04	.01
Kelly Gruber			
☐ 202 Brad Moore	.10	.05	.01
☐ 203 Rob Ducey	.06	.03	.00
☐ 204 Brad Havens	.03	.01	.00
☐ 205 Dwight Evans	.08	.04	.01
☐ 206 Roberto Alomar	.45	.22	.04
☐ 207 Terry Leach	.06	.03	.00
☐ 208 Tom Pagnozzi	.03	.01	.00
☐ 209 Jeff Bittiger	.08	.04	.01
☐ 210 Dale Murphy	.15	.07	.01
☐ 211 Mike Pagliarulo	.03	.01	.00
☐ 212 Scott Sanderson	.06	.03	.00
☐ 213 Rene Gonzales	.03	.01	.00
☐ 214 Charlie O'Brien	.03	.01	.00
☐ 215 Kevin Gross	.03	.01	.00
☐ 216 Jack Howell	.03	.01	.00
☐ 217 Joe Price	.03	.01	.00
☐ 218 Mike LaValliere	.03	.01	.00
☐ 219 Jim Clancy	.03	.01	.00
☐ 220 Gary Gaetti	.08	.04	.01
☐ 221 Cecil Espy	.08	.04	.01
☐ 222 Mark Lewis FDP	.35	.17	.03
☐ 223 Jay Buhner	.12	.06	.01
☐ 224 Tony LaRussa MG	.06	.03	.00
(team checklist back)			
☐ 225 Ramon Martinez	1.25	.60	.12
☐ 226 Bill Doran	.06	.03	.00
☐ 227 John Farrell	.03	.01	.00
☐ 228 Nelson Santovenia	.12	.06	.01
☐ 229 Jimmy Key	.06	.03	.00
☐ 230 Ozzie Smith	.10	.05	.01
☐ 231 San Diego Padres TL	.10	.05	.01
Roberto Alomar			
(G.Carter at plate)			
☐ 232 Ricky Horton	.03	.01	.00
☐ 233 Gregg Jefferies FS	1.25	.60	.12
☐ 234 Tom Browning	.06	.03	.00
☐ 235 John Kruk	.03	.01	.00
☐ 236 Charles Hudson	.03	.01	.00
☐ 237 Glenn Hubbard	.03	.01	.00
☐ 238 Eric King	.03	.01	.00
☐ 239 Tim Laudner	.03	.01	.00
☐ 240 Greg Maddux	.08	.04	.01
☐ 241 Brett Butler	.08	.04	.01
☐ 242 Ed Vandeberg	.03	.01	.00
☐ 243 Bob Boone	.08	.04	.01
☐ 244 Jim Acker	.03	.01	.00
☐ 245 Jim Rice	.10	.05	.01
☐ 246 Rey Quinones	.03	.01	.00
☐ 247 Shawn Hillegas	.03	.01	.00
☐ 248 Tony Phillips	.03	.01	.00
☐ 249 Tim Leary	.06	.03	.00
☐ 250 Cal Ripken	.15	.07	.01
☐ 251 John Dopson	.15	.07	.01
☐ 252 Billy Hatcher	.03	.01	.00
☐ 253 Jose Alvarez	.08	.04	.01
☐ 254 Tom Lasorda MG	.06	.03	.00
(team checklist back)			
☐ 255 Ron Guidry	.08	.04	.01
☐ 256 Benny Santiago	.12	.06	.01
☐ 257 Rick Aguilera	.03	.01	.00
☐ 258 Checklist 133-264	.06	.01	.00
☐ 259 Larry McWilliams	.03	.01	.00
☐ 260 Dave Winfield	.12	.06	.01
☐ 261 St.Louis Cardinals TL	.06	.03	.00
Tom Brunansky			
(with Luis Alicea)			
☐ 262 Jeff Pico	.08	.04	.01

☐ 263 Mike Felder	.03	.01	.00
☐ 264 Rob Dibble	.30	.15	.03
☐ 265 Kent Hrbek	.10	.05	.01
☐ 266 Luis Aquino	.03	.01	.00
☐ 267 Jeff Robinson	.06	.03	.00
Detroit Tigers			
☐ 268 Keith Miller	.08	.04	.01
Philadelphia Phillies			
☐ 269 Tom Bolton	.03	.01	.00
☐ 270 Wally Joyner	.10	.05	.01
☐ 271 Jay Tibbs	.03	.01	.00
☐ 272 Ron Hassey	.03	.01	.00
☐ 273 Jose Lind	.03	.01	.00
☐ 274 Mark Eichhorn	.03	.01	.00
☐ 275 Danny Tartabull UER	.08	.04	.01
(Born San Juan, PR should be Miami, FL)			
☐ 276 Paul Kilgus	.03	.01	.00
☐ 277 Mike Davis	.03	.01	.00
☐ 278 Andy McGaffigan	.03	.01	.00
☐ 279 Scott Bradley	.03	.01	.00
☐ 280 Bob Knepper	.03	.01	.00
☐ 281 Gary Redus	.03	.01	.00
☐ 282 Cris Carpenter	.15	.07	.01
☐ 283 Andy Allanson	.03	.01	.00
☐ 284 Jim Leyland MG	.06	.03	.00
(team checklist back)			
☐ 285 John Candelaria	.03	.01	.00
☐ 286 Darrin Jackson	.08	.04	.01
☐ 287 Juan Nieves	.03	.01	.00
☐ 288 Pat Sheridan	.03	.01	.00
☐ 289 Ernie Whitt	.03	.01	.00
☐ 290 John Franco	.06	.03	.00
☐ 291 New York Mets TL	.12	.06	.01
Darryl Strawberry (with K.Hernandez and K.McReynolds)			
☐ 292 Jim Corsi	.08	.04	.01
☐ 293 Glenn Wilson	.03	.01	.00
☐ 294 Juan Berenguer	.03	.01	.00
☐ 295 Scott Fletcher	.03	.01	.00
☐ 296 Ron Gant	.35	.17	.03
☐ 297 Oswald Peraza	.08	.04	.01
☐ 298 Chris James	.06	.03	.00
☐ 299 Steve Ellsworth	.08	.04	.01
☐ 300 Darryl Strawberry	.30	.15	.03
☐ 301 Charlie Leibrandt	.03	.01	.00
☐ 302 Gary Ward	.03	.01	.00
☐ 303 Felix Fermin	.03	.01	.00
☐ 304 Joel Youngblood	.03	.01	.00
☐ 305 Dave Smith	.03	.01	.00
☐ 306 Tracy Woodson	.08	.04	.01
☐ 307 Lance McCullers	.03	.01	.00
☐ 308 Ron Karkovice	.03	.01	.00
☐ 309 Mario Diaz	.08	.04	.01
☐ 310 Rafael Palmeiro	.12	.06	.01
☐ 311 Chris Bosio	.03	.01	.00
☐ 312 Tom Lawless	.03	.01	.00
☐ 313 Dennis Martinez	.06	.03	.00
☐ 314 Bobby Valentine MG	.06	.03	.00
(team checklist back)			
☐ 315 Greg Swindell	.08	.04	.01
☐ 316 Walt Weiss	.25	.12	.02
☐ 317 Jack Armstrong	.20	.10	.02
☐ 318 Gene Larkin	.03	.01	.00
☐ 319 Greg Booker	.03	.01	.00
☐ 320 Lou Whitaker	.08	.04	.01
☐ 321 Boston Red Sox TL	.08	.04	.01
Jody Reed			
☐ 322 John Smiley	.03	.01	.00
☐ 323 Gary Thurman	.03	.01	.00
☐ 324 Bob Milacki	.20	.10	.02
☐ 325 Jesse Barfield	.08	.04	.01
☐ 326 Dennis Boyd	.06	.03	.00
☐ 327 Mark Lemke	.10	.05	.01
☐ 328 Rick Honeycutt	.03	.01	.00
☐ 329 Bob Melvin	.03	.01	.00
☐ 330 Eric Davis	.20	.10	.02
☐ 331 Curt Wilkerson	.03	.01	.00
☐ 332 Tony Armas	.03	.01	.00
☐ 333 Bob Ojeda	.06	.03	.00
☐ 334 Steve Lyons	.03	.01	.00
☐ 335 Dave Righetti	.08	.04	.01
☐ 336 Steve Balboni	.03	.01	.00
☐ 337 Calvin Schiraldi	.03	.01	.00
☐ 338 Jim Adduci	.03	.01	.00
☐ 339 Scott Bailes	.03	.01	.00
☐ 340 Kirk Gibson	.12	.06	.01
☐ 341 Jim Deshaies	.03	.01	.00
☐ 342 Tom Brookens	.03	.01	.00
☐ 343 Gary Sheffield FS	1.00	.50	.10
☐ 344 Tom Trebelhorn MG	.06	.03	.00
(team checklist back)			
☐ 345 Charlie Hough	.03	.01	.00
☐ 346 Rex Hudler	.03	.01	.00
☐ 347 John Cerutti	.03	.01	.00
☐ 348 Ed Hearn	.03	.01	.00
☐ 349 Ron Jones	.20	.10	.02
☐ 350 Andy Van Slyke	.08	.04	.01
☐ 351 San Fran. Giants TL	.03	.01	.00
Bob Melvin (with Bill Fahey CO)			
☐ 352 Rick Schu	.03	.01	.00
☐ 353 Marvell Wynne	.03	.01	.00
☐ 354 Larry Parrish	.03	.01	.00
☐ 355 Mark Langston	.10	.05	.01
☐ 356 Kevin Elster	.06	.03	.00
☐ 357 Jerry Reuss	.03	.01	.00
☐ 358 Ricky Jordan	.30	.15	.03
☐ 359 Tommy John	.08	.04	.01
☐ 360 Ryne Sandberg	.25	.12	.02
☐ 361 Kelly Downs	.03	.01	.00
☐ 362 Jack Lazorko	.03	.01	.00
☐ 363 Rich Yett	.03	.01	.00
☐ 364 Rob Deer	.06	.03	.00
☐ 365 Mike Henneman	.03	.01	.00
☐ 366 Herm Winningham	.03	.01	.00
☐ 367 Johnny Paredes	.08	.04	.01
☐ 368 Brian Holton	.03	.01	.00
☐ 369 Ken Caminiti	.03	.01	.00
☐ 370 Dennis Eckersley	.10	.05	.01
☐ 371 Manny Lee	.03	.01	.00
☐ 372 Craig Lefferts	.03	.01	.00
☐ 373 Tracy Jones	.03	.01	.00
☐ 374 John Wathan MG	.06	.03	.00
(team checklist back)			
☐ 375 Terry Pendleton	.03	.01	.00
☐ 376 Steve Lombardozzi	.03	.01	.00
☐ 377 Mike Smithson	.03	.01	.00
☐ 378 Checklist 265-396	.06	.01	.00
☐ 379 Tim Flannery	.03	.01	.00
☐ 380 Rickey Henderson	.25	.12	.02
☐ 381 Baltimore Orioles TL	.03	.01	.00
Larry Sheets			
☐ 382 John Smoltz	.30	.15	.03
☐ 383 Howard Johnson	.12	.06	.01
☐ 384 Mark Salas	.03	.01	.00
☐ 385 Von Hayes	.08	.04	.01
☐ 386 Andres Galarraga AS	.08	.04	.01
☐ 387 Ryne Sandberg AS	.15	.07	.01
☐ 388 Bobby Bonilla AS	.10	.05	.01
☐ 389 Ozzie Smith AS	.08	.04	.01
☐ 390 Darryl Strawberry AS	.15	.07	.01
☐ 391 Andre Dawson AS	.10	.05	.01
☐ 392 Andy Van Slyke AS	.08	.04	.01
☐ 393 Gary Carter AS	.08	.04	.01
☐ 394 Orel Hershiser AS	.10	.05	.01
☐ 395 Danny Jackson AS	.06	.03	.00
☐ 396 Kirk Gibson AS	.10	.05	.01
☐ 397 Don Mattingly AS	.20	.10	.02
☐ 398 Julio Franco AS	.08	.04	.01
☐ 399 Wade Boggs AS	.15	.07	.01
☐ 400 Alan Trammell AS	.08	.04	.01
☐ 401 Jose Canseco AS	.25	.12	.02
☐ 402 Mike Greenwell AS	.15	.07	.01
☐ 403 Kirby Puckett AS	.15	.07	.01
☐ 404 Bob Boone AS	.08	.04	.01
☐ 405 Roger Clemens AS	.15	.07	.01
☐ 406 Frank Viola AS	.08	.04	.01
☐ 407 Dave Winfield AS	.10	.05	.01
☐ 408 Greg Walker	.03	.01	.00
☐ 409 Ken Dayley	.03	.01	.00
☐ 410 Jack Clark	.08	.04	.01
☐ 411 Mitch Williams	.06	.03	.00
☐ 412 Barry Lyons	.03	.01	.00
☐ 413 Mike Kingery	.03	.01	.00
☐ 414 Jim Fregosi MG	.06	.03	.00
(team checklist back)			
☐ 415 Rich Gossage	.08	.04	.01
☐ 416 Fred Lynn	.08	.04	.01
☐ 417 Mike LaCoss	.03	.01	.00
☐ 418 Bob Dernier	.03	.01	.00
☐ 419 Tom Filer	.03	.01	.00
☐ 420 Joe Carter	.10	.05	.01
☐ 421 Kirk McCaskill	.03	.01	.00
☐ 422 Bo Diaz	.03	.01	.00
☐ 423 Brian Fisher	.03	.01	.00
☐ 424 Luis Polonia UER	.03	.01	.00
(wrong birthdate)			
☐ 425 Jay Howell	.03	.01	.00
☐ 426 Dan Gladden	.03	.01	.00
☐ 427 Eric Show	.03	.01	.00
☐ 428 Craig Reynolds	.03	.01	.00
☐ 429 Minnesota Twins TL	.03	.01	.00
Greg Gagne (taking throw at 2nd)			
☐ 430 Mark Gubicza	.06	.03	.00
☐ 431 Luis Rivera	.03	.01	.00

☐ 432 Chad Kreuter	.10	.05	.01
☐ 433 Albert Hall	.03	.01	.00
☐ 434 Ken Patterson	.08	.04	.01
☐ 435 Len Dykstra	.10	.05	.01
☐ 436 Bobby Meacham	.03	.01	.00
☐ 437 Andy Benes FDP	.60	.30	.06
☐ 438 Greg Gross	.03	.01	.00
☐ 439 Frank DiPino	.03	.01	.00
☐ 440 Bobby Bonilla	.12	.06	.01
☐ 441 Jerry Reed	.03	.01	.00
☐ 442 Jose Oquendo	.03	.01	.00
☐ 443 Rod Nichols	.08	.04	.01
☐ 444 Moose Stubing MG (team checklist back)	.06	.03	.00
☐ 445 Matt Nokes	.06	.03	.00
☐ 446 Rob Murphy	.03	.01	.00
☐ 447 Donell Nixon	.03	.01	.00
☐ 448 Eric Plunk	.03	.01	.00
☐ 449 Carmelo Martinez	.03	.01	.00
☐ 450 Roger Clemens	.20	.10	.02
☐ 451 Mark Davidson	.03	.01	.00
☐ 452 Israel Sanchez	.08	.04	.01
☐ 453 Tom Prince	.06	.03	.00
☐ 454 Paul Assenmacher	.03	.01	.00
☐ 455 Johnny Ray	.03	.01	.00
☐ 456 Tim Belcher	.08	.04	.01
☐ 457 Mackey Sasser	.10	.05	.01
☐ 458 Donn Pall	.08	.04	.01
☐ 459 Seattle Mariners TL Dave Valle	.03	.01	.00
☐ 460 Dave Stieb	.10	.05	.01
☐ 461 Buddy Bell	.06	.03	.00
☐ 462 Jose Guzman	.03	.01	.00
☐ 463 Steve Lake	.03	.01	.00
☐ 464 Bryn Smith	.03	.01	.00
☐ 465 Mark Grace	1.00	.50	.10
☐ 466 Chuck Crim	.03	.01	.00
☐ 467 Jim Walewander	.03	.01	.00
☐ 468 Henry Cotto	.03	.01	.00
☐ 469 Jose Bautista	.08	.04	.01
☐ 470 Lance Parrish	.08	.04	.01
☐ 471 Steve Curry	.10	.05	.01
☐ 472 Brian Harper	.06	.03	.00
☐ 473 Don Robinson	.03	.01	.00
☐ 474 Bob Rodgers MG (team checklist back)	.06	.03	.00
☐ 475 Dave Parker	.08	.04	.01
☐ 476 Jon Perlman	.06	.03	.00
☐ 477 Dick Schofield	.03	.01	.00
☐ 478 Doug Drabek	.10	.05	.01
☐ 479 Mike Macfarlane	.12	.06	.01
☐ 480 Keith Hernandez	.10	.05	.01
☐ 481 Chris Brown	.03	.01	.00
☐ 482 Steve Peters	.10	.05	.01
☐ 483 Mickey Hatcher	.03	.01	.00
☐ 484 Steve Shields	.03	.01	.00
☐ 485 Hubie Brooks	.06	.03	.00
☐ 486 Jack McDowell	.12	.06	.01
☐ 487 Scott Lusader	.06	.03	.00
☐ 488 Kevin Coffman ("Now with Cubs")	.06	.03	.00
☐ 489 Phila. Phillies TL Mike Schmidt	.15	.07	.01
☐ 490 Chris Sabo	1.00	.50	.10
☐ 491 Mike Birkbeck	.03	.01	.00
☐ 492 Alan Ashby	.03	.01	.00
☐ 493 Todd Benzinger	.03	.01	.00
☐ 494 Shane Rawley	.03	.01	.00
☐ 495 Candy Maldonado	.06	.03	.00
☐ 496 Dwayne Henry	.03	.01	.00
☐ 497 Pete Stanicek	.06	.03	.00
☐ 498 Dave Valle	.03	.01	.00
☐ 499 Don Heinkel	.06	.03	.00
☐ 500 Jose Canseco	.75	.35	.07
☐ 501 Vance Law	.03	.01	.00
☐ 502 Duane Ward	.03	.01	.00
☐ 503 Al Newman	.03	.01	.00
☐ 504 Bob Walk	.03	.01	.00
☐ 505 Pete Rose MG (team checklist back)	.25	.12	.02
☐ 506 Kirt Manwaring	.06	.03	.00
☐ 507 Steve Farr	.03	.01	.00
☐ 508 Wally Backman	.03	.01	.00
☐ 509 Bud Black	.06	.03	.00
☐ 510 Bob Horner	.06	.03	.00
☐ 511 Richard Dotson	.03	.01	.00
☐ 512 Donnie Hill	.03	.01	.00
☐ 513 Jesse Orosco	.03	.01	.00
☐ 514 Chet Lemon	.03	.01	.00
☐ 515 Barry Larkin	.15	.07	.01
☐ 516 Eddie Whitson	.03	.01	.00
☐ 517 Greg Brock	.03	.01	.00
☐ 518 Bruce Ruffin	.03	.01	.00
☐ 519 New York Yankees TL Willie Randolph	.06	.03	.00
☐ 520 Rick Sutcliffe	.08	.04	.01
☐ 521 Mickey Tettleton	.06	.03	.00
☐ 522 Randy Kramer	.08	.04	.01
☐ 523 Andres Thomas	.03	.01	.00
☐ 524 Checklist 397-528	.06	.01	.00
☐ 525 Chili Davis	.06	.03	.00
☐ 526 Wes Gardner	.03	.01	.00
☐ 527 Dave Henderson	.06	.03	.00
☐ 528 Luis Medina (lower left front has white triangle)	.20	.10	.02
☐ 529 Tom Foley	.03	.01	.00
☐ 530 Nolan Ryan	.45	.22	.04
☐ 531 Dave Hengel	.08	.04	.01
☐ 532 Jerry Browne	.03	.01	.00
☐ 533 Andy Hawkins	.03	.01	.00
☐ 534 Doc Edwards MG (team checklist back)	.06	.03	.00
☐ 535 Todd Worrell UER (4 wins in '88, should be 5)	.08	.04	.01
☐ 536 Joel Skinner	.03	.01	.00
☐ 537 Pete Smith	.10	.05	.01
☐ 538 Juan Castillo	.03	.01	.00
☐ 539 Barry Jones	.06	.03	.00
☐ 540 Bo Jackson	.50	.25	.05
☐ 541 Cecil Fielder	.25	.12	.02
☐ 542 Todd Frohwirth	.03	.01	.00
☐ 543 Damon Berryhill	.15	.07	.01
☐ 544 Jeff Sellers	.03	.01	.00
☐ 545 Mookie Wilson	.06	.03	.00
☐ 546 Mark Williamson	.03	.01	.00
☐ 547 Mark McLemore	.03	.01	.00
☐ 548 Bobby Witt	.10	.05	.01
☐ 549 Chicago Cubs TL Jamie Moyer (pitching)	.03	.01	.00
☐ 550 Orel Hershiser	.15	.07	.01
☐ 551 Randy Ready	.03	.01	.00
☐ 552 Greg Cadaret	.03	.01	.00
☐ 553 Luis Salazar	.03	.01	.00
☐ 554 Nick Esasky	.06	.03	.00
☐ 555 Bert Blyleven	.08	.04	.01
☐ 556 Bruce Fields	.03	.01	.00
☐ 557 Keith Miller New York Mets	.03	.01	.00
☐ 558 Dan Pasqua	.03	.01	.00
☐ 559 Juan Agosto	.03	.01	.00
☐ 560 Tim Raines	.12	.06	.01
☐ 561 Luis Aguayo	.03	.01	.00
☐ 562 Danny Cox	.03	.01	.00
☐ 563 Bill Schroeder	.03	.01	.00
☐ 564 Russ Nixon MG (team checklist back)	.06	.03	.00
☐ 565 Jeff Russell	.03	.01	.00
☐ 566 Al Pedrique	.03	.01	.00
☐ 567 David Wells UER (Complete Pitching Recor)	.10	.05	.01
☐ 568 Mickey Brantley	.03	.01	.00
☐ 569 German Jimenez	.08	.04	.01
☐ 570 Tony Gwynn UER ('88 average should be italicized as league leader)	.15	.07	.01
☐ 571 Billy Ripken	.03	.01	.00
☐ 572 Atlee Hammaker	.03	.01	.00
☐ 573 Jim Abbott FDP	1.00	.50	.10
☐ 574 Dave Clark	.06	.03	.00
☐ 575 Juan Samuel	.08	.04	.01
☐ 576 Greg Minton	.03	.01	.00
☐ 577 Randy Bush	.03	.01	.00
☐ 578 John Morris	.03	.01	.00
☐ 579 Houston Astros TL Glenn Davis (batting stance)	.06	.03	.00
☐ 580 Harold Reynolds	.06	.03	.00
☐ 581 Gene Nelson	.03	.01	.00
☐ 582 Mike Marshall	.08	.04	.01
☐ 583 Paul Gibson	.10	.05	.01
☐ 584 Randy Velarde UER (signed 1935, should be 1985)	.08	.04	.01
☐ 585 Harold Baines	.08	.04	.01
☐ 586 Joe Boever	.03	.01	.00
☐ 587 Mike Stanley	.03	.01	.00
☐ 588 Luis Alicea	.08	.04	.01
☐ 589 Dave Meads	.03	.01	.00
☐ 590 Andres Galarraga	.08	.04	.01
☐ 591 Jeff Musselman	.03	.01	.00
☐ 592 John Cangelosi	.03	.01	.00
☐ 593 Drew Hall	.03	.01	.00

594	Jimy Williams MG	.06	.03	.00
	(team checklist back)			
595	Teddy Higuera	.06	.03	.00
596	Kurt Stillwell	.03	.01	.00
597	Terry Taylor	.10	.05	.01
598	Ken Gerhart	.03	.01	.00
599	Tom Candiotti	.03	.01	.00
600	Wade Boggs	.35	.17	.03
601	Dave Dravecky	.08	.04	.01
602	Devon White	.08	.04	.01
603	Frank Tanana	.06	.03	.00
604	Paul O'Neill	.08	.04	.01
605A	Bob Welch ERR	4.00	2.00	.40
	(missing line on back, "Complete M.L. Pitching Record")			
605B	Bob Welch COR	.20	.10	.02
606	Rick Dempsey	.03	.01	.00
607	Willie Ansley FDP	.35	.17	.03
608	Phil Bradley	.06	.03	.00
609	Detroit Tigers TL	.06	.03	.00
	Frank Tanana (with Alan Trammell and Mike Heath)			
610	Randy Myers	.06	.03	.00
611	Don Slaught	.03	.01	.00
612	Dan Quisenberry	.08	.04	.01
613	Gary Varsho	.08	.04	.01
614	Joe Hesketh	.03	.01	.00
615	Robin Yount	.15	.07	.01
616	Steve Rosenberg	.08	.04	.01
617	Mark Parent	.08	.04	.01
618	Rance Mulliniks	.03	.01	.00
619	Checklist 529-660	.06	.01	.00
620	Barry Bonds	.20	.10	.02
621	Rick Mahler	.03	.01	.00
622	Stan Javier	.03	.01	.00
623	Fred Toliver	.03	.01	.00
624	Jack McKeon MG	.06	.03	.00
	(team checklist back)			
625	Eddie Murray	.12	.06	.01
626	Jeff Reed	.03	.01	.00
627	Greg Harris	.03	.01	.00
	Philadelphia Phillies			
628	Matt Williams	.25	.12	.02
629	Pete O'Brien	.06	.03	.00
630	Mike Greenwell	.20	.10	.02
631	Dave Bergman	.03	.01	.00
632	Bryan Harvey	.15	.07	.01
633	Daryl Boston	.06	.03	.00
634	Marvin Freeman	.03	.01	.00
635	Willie Randolph	.06	.03	.00
636	Bill Wilkinson	.03	.01	.00
637	Carmen Castillo	.03	.01	.00
638	Floyd Bannister	.03	.01	.00
639	Oakland A's TL	.10	.05	.01
	Walt Weiss			
640	Willie McGee	.10	.05	.01
641	Curt Young	.03	.01	.00
642	Argenis Salazar	.03	.01	.00
643	Louie Meadows	.06	.03	.00
644	Lloyd McClendon	.03	.01	.00
645	Jack Morris	.08	.04	.01
646	Kevin Bass	.06	.03	.00
647	Randy Johnson	.25	.12	.02
648	Sandy Alomar FS	1.00	.50	.10
649	Stewart Cliburn	.03	.01	.00
650	Kirby Puckett	.30	.15	.03
651	Tom Niedenfuer	.03	.01	.00
652	Rich Gedman	.03	.01	.00
653	Tommy Barrett	.08	.04	.01
654	Whitey Herzog MG	.06	.03	.00
	(team checklist back)			
655	Dave Magadan	.10	.05	.01
656	Ivan Calderon	.06	.03	.00
657	Joe Magrane	.06	.03	.00
658	R.J. Reynolds	.03	.01	.00
659	Al Leiter	.06	.03	.00
660	Will Clark	.50	.25	.05
661	Dwight Gooden TBC84	.12	.06	.01
662	Lou Brock TBC79	.08	.04	.01
663	Hank Aaron TBC74	.10	.05	.01
664	Gil Hodges TBC69	.08	.04	.01
665A	Tony Oliva TBC64	2.00	1.00	.20
	ERR (fabricated card is enlarged version of Oliva's 64T card; Topps copyright missing)			
665B	Tony Oliva TBC64	.10	.05	.01
	COR (fabricated card)			
666	Randy St.Claire	.03	.01	.00
667	Dwayne Murphy	.03	.01	.00
668	Mike Bielecki	.06	.03	.00
669	L.A. Dodgers TL	.12	.06	.01
	Orel Hershiser (mound conference with Mike Scioscia)			
670	Kevin Seitzer	.10	.05	.01
671	Jim Gantner	.03	.01	.00
672	Allan Anderson	.06	.03	.00
673	Don Baylor	.06	.03	.00
674	Otis Nixon	.03	.01	.00
675	Bruce Hurst	.08	.04	.01
676	Ernie Riles	.03	.01	.00
677	Dave Schmidt	.03	.01	.00
678	Dion James	.03	.01	.00
679	Willie Fraser	.03	.01	.00
680	Gary Carter	.10	.05	.01
681	Jeff Robinson	.03	.01	.00
	Pittsburgh Pirates			
682	Rick Leach	.03	.01	.00
683	Jose Cecena	.06	.03	.00
684	Dave Johnson MG	.06	.03	.00
	(team checklist back)			
685	Jeff Treadway	.10	.05	.01
686	Scott Terry	.03	.01	.00
687	Alvin Davis	.08	.04	.01
688	Zane Smith	.06	.03	.00
689A	Stan Jefferson	.10	.05	.01
	(pink triangle on front bottom left)			
689B	Stan Jefferson	.10	.05	.01
	(violet triangle on front bottom left)			
690	Doug Jones	.06	.03	.00
691	Roberto Kelly UER	.30	.15	.03
	(83 Oneonita)			
692	Steve Ontiveros	.03	.01	.00
693	Pat Borders	.25	.12	.02
694	Les Lancaster	.03	.01	.00
695	Carlton Fisk	.12	.06	.01
696	Don August	.03	.01	.00
697A	Franklin Stubbs	.10	.05	.01
	(team name on front in white)			
697B	Franklin Stubbs	.10	.05	.01
	(team name on front in gray)			
698	Keith Atherton	.03	.01	.00
699	Pittsburgh Pirates TL	.08	.04	.01
	Al Pedrique (Tony Gwynn sliding)			
700	Don Mattingly	.50	.25	.05
701	Storm Davis	.06	.03	.00
702	Jamie Quirk	.03	.01	.00
703	Scott Garrelts	.06	.03	.00
704	Carlos Quintana	.35	.17	.03
705	Terry Kennedy	.03	.01	.00
706	Pete Incaviglia	.08	.04	.01
707	Steve Jeltz	.03	.01	.00
708	Chuck Finley	.10	.05	.01
709	Tom Herr	.06	.03	.00
710	David Cone	.12	.06	.01
711	Candy Sierra	.08	.04	.01
712	Bill Swift	.03	.01	.00
713	Ty Griffin FDP	.50	.25	.05
714	Joe Morgan MG	.06	.03	.00
	(team checklist back)			
715	Tony Pena	.06	.03	.00
716	Wayne Tolleson	.03	.01	.00
717	Jamie Moyer	.03	.01	.00
718	Glenn Braggs	.03	.01	.00
719	Danny Darwin	.06	.03	.00
720	Tim Wallach	.08	.04	.01
721	Ron Tingley	.06	.03	.00
722	Todd Stottlemyre	.12	.06	.01
723	Rafael Belliard	.03	.01	.00
724	Jerry Don Gleaton	.03	.01	.00
725	Terry Steinbach	.08	.04	.01
726	Dickie Thon	.03	.01	.00
727	Joe Orsulak	.03	.01	.00
728	Charlie Puleo	.03	.01	.00
729	Texas Rangers TL	.03	.01	.00
	Steve Buechele (inconsistent design, team name on front surrounded by black, should be white)			
730	Danny Jackson	.06	.03	.00
731	Mike Young	.03	.01	.00
732	Steve Buechele	.03	.01	.00
733	Randy Bockus	.06	.03	.00
734	Jody Reed	.10	.05	.01
735	Roger McDowell	.06	.03	.00
736	Jeff Hamilton	.03	.01	.00
737	Norm Charlton	.20	.10	.02

☐ 738 Darnell Coles	.03	.01	.00
☐ 739 Brook Jacoby	.06	.03	.00
☐ 740 Dan Plesac	.03	.01	.00
☐ 741 Ken Phelps	.03	.01	.00
☐ 742 Mike Harkey FS	.35	.17	.03
☐ 743 Mike Heath	.03	.01	.00
☐ 744 Roger Craig MG (team checklist back)	.06	.03	.00
☐ 745 Fred McGriff	.15	.07	.01
☐ 746 German Gonzalez UER (wrong birthdate)	.08	.04	.01
☐ 747 Will Tejada	.03	.01	.00
☐ 748 Jimmy Jones	.03	.01	.00
☐ 749 Rafael Ramirez	.03	.01	.00
☐ 750 Bret Saberhagen	.12	.06	.01
☐ 751 Ken Oberkfell	.03	.01	.00
☐ 752 Jim Gott	.03	.01	.00
☐ 753 Jose Uribe	.03	.01	.00
☐ 754 Bob Brower	.03	.01	.00
☐ 755 Mike Scioscia	.03	.01	.00
☐ 756 Scott Medvin	.10	.05	.01
☐ 757 Brady Anderson	.20	.10	.02
☐ 758 Gene Walter	.03	.01	.00
☐ 759 Milwaukee Brewers TL Rob Deer	.06	.03	.00
☐ 760 Lee Smith	.06	.03	.00
☐ 761 Dante Bichette	.25	.12	.02
☐ 762 Bobby Thigpen	.10	.05	.01
☐ 763 Dave Martinez	.03	.01	.00
☐ 764 Robin Ventura FDP	.75	.35	.07
☐ 765 Glenn Davis	.12	.06	.01
☐ 766 Cecilio Guante	.03	.01	.00
☐ 767 Mike Capel	.08	.04	.01
☐ 768 Bill Wegman	.03	.01	.00
☐ 769 Junior Ortiz	.03	.01	.00
☐ 770 Alan Trammell	.10	.05	.01
☐ 771 Ron Kittle	.06	.03	.00
☐ 772 Ron Oester	.03	.01	.00
☐ 773 Keith Moreland	.03	.01	.00
☐ 774 Frank Robinson MG (team checklist back)	.10	.05	.01
☐ 775 Jeff Reardon	.06	.03	.00
☐ 776 Nelson Liriano	.03	.01	.00
☐ 777 Ted Power	.03	.01	.00
☐ 778 Bruce Benedict	.03	.01	.00
☐ 779 Craig McMurtry	.03	.01	.00
☐ 780 Pedro Guerrero	.10	.05	.01
☐ 781 Greg Briley	.25	.12	.02
☐ 782 Checklist 661-792	.06	.01	.00
☐ 783 Trevor Wilson	.25	.12	.02
☐ 784 Steve Avery FDP	.60	.30	.06
☐ 785 Ellis Burks	.25	.12	.02
☐ 786 Melido Perez	.12	.06	.01
☐ 787 Dave West	.20	.10	.02
☐ 788 Mike Morgan	.03	.01	.00
☐ 789 Kansas City Royals TL Bo Jackson (throwing)	.15	.07	.01
☐ 790 Sid Fernandez	.08	.04	.01
☐ 791 Jim Lindeman	.03	.01	.00
☐ 792 Rafael Santana	.06	.03	.00

1989 Topps Wax Box Cards

The cards in this 16-card set measure the standard 2 1/2" by 3 1/2". Cards have essentially the same design as the 1989 Topps regular issue set. The cards were printed on the bottoms of the regular issue wax pack boxes. These 16 cards, "lettered" A through P, are considered a separate set in their own right and are not typically included in a complete set of the regular issue 1989 Topps cards. The value of the panels uncut is slightly greater, perhaps by 25 percent greater, than the value of the individual cards cut up carefully. The sixteen cards in this set honor players (and one manager) who reached career milestones during the 1988 season.

	MINT	EXC	G-VG
COMPLETE SET (16)	4.00	2.00	.40
COMMON PLAYER (A-P)	.10	.05	.01
☐ A George Brett 475th Double	.40	.20	.04
☐ B Bill Buckner 2600th Hit	.15	.07	.01
☐ C Darrell Evans 400th Home Run	.15	.07	.01
☐ D Rich Gossage 300th Save	.15	.07	.01
☐ E Greg Gross 125th Pinch Hit	.10	.05	.01
☐ F Rickey Henderson 775th Stolen Base	.60	.30	.06
☐ G Keith Hernandez 125th Game-Winning RBI	.15	.07	.01
☐ H Tom Lasorda 1000th Managerial Win	.15	.07	.01
☐ I Jim Rice 1400th Run Batted In	.20	.10	.02
☐ J Cal Ripken 1000th Cons. Game	.35	.17	.03
☐ K Nolan Ryan 4700th Strikeout	.60	.30	.06
☐ L Mike Schmidt 1000th Long Hit	.60	.30	.06
☐ M Bruce Sutter 300th Save	.15	.07	.01
☐ N Don Sutton 750th Game Started	.25	.12	.02
☐ O Kent Tekulve 1000th Appearance	.10	.05	.01
☐ P Dave Winfield 1400th Run Batted In	.25	.12	.02

1989 Topps Glossy All-Stars 22

These glossy cards were inserted with Topps rack packs and honor the starting line-ups, managers, and honorary captains of the 1988 National and American League All-Star teams. The cards are standard size, 2 1/2" by 3 1/2" and very similar to the design Topps has used since 1984. The backs are printed in red and blue on white card stock.

	MINT	EXC	G-VG
COMPLETE SET (22)	3.00	1.50	.30
COMMON PLAYER (1-22)	.10	.05	.01
☐ 1 Tom Kelly MG	.10	.05	.01
☐ 2 Mark McGwire	.40	.20	.04
☐ 3 Paul Molitor	.20	.10	.02

☐ 4 Wade Boggs	.40	.20	.04
☐ 5 Cal Ripken Jr.	.25	.12	.02
☐ 6 Jose Canseco	.60	.30	.06
☐ 7 Rickey Henderson	.50	.25	.05
☐ 8 Dave Winfield	.20	.10	.02
☐ 9 Terry Steinbach	.15	.07	.01
☐ 10 Frank Viola	.15	.07	.01
☐ 11 Bobby Doerr CAPT	.15	.07	.01
☐ 12 Whitey Herzog MG	.10	.05	.01
☐ 13 Will Clark	.50	.25	.05
☐ 14 Ryne Sandberg	.40	.20	.04
☐ 15 Bobby Bonilla	.25	.12	.02
☐ 16 Ozzie Smith	.20	.10	.02
☐ 17 Vince Coleman	.20	.10	.02
☐ 18 Andre Dawson	.20	.10	.02
☐ 19 Darryl Strawberry	.40	.20	.04
☐ 20 Gary Carter	.20	.10	.02
☐ 21 Doc Gooden	.30	.15	.03
☐ 22 Willie Stargell CAPT	.20	.10	.02

1989 Topps Jumbo Rookies

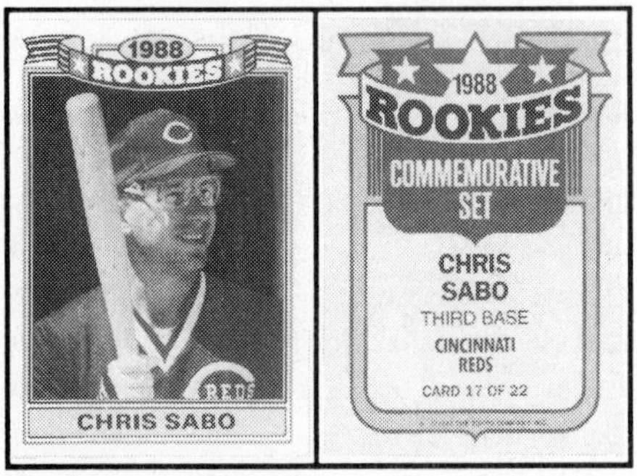

Inserted in each supermarket jumbo pack is a card from this series of 22 of 1988's best rookies as determined by Topps. Jumbo packs consisted of 100 (regular issue 1989 Topps baseball) cards with a stick of gum plus the insert "Rookie" card. The card fronts are in full color and measure 2 1/2" by 3 1/2". The card backs are printed in red and blue on white card stock and are numbered at the bottom.

	MINT	EXC	G-VG
COMPLETE SET (22)	8.00	4.00	.80
COMMON PLAYER (1-22)	.20	.10	.02
☐ 1 Roberto Alomar	.75	.35	.07
☐ 2 Brady Anderson	.30	.15	.03
☐ 3 Tim Belcher	.30	.15	.03
☐ 4 Damon Berryhill	.30	.15	.03
☐ 5 Jay Buhner	.30	.15	.03
☐ 6 Kevin Elster	.25	.12	.02
☐ 7 Cecil Espy	.20	.10	.02
☐ 8 Dave Gallagher	.20	.10	.02
☐ 9 Ron Gant	.75	.35	.07
☐ 10 Paul Gibson	.20	.10	.02
☐ 11 Mark Grace	1.00	.50	.10
☐ 12 Darrin Jackson	.25	.12	.02
☐ 13 Gregg Jefferies	1.50	.75	.15
☐ 14 Ricky Jordan	.40	.20	.04
☐ 15 Al Leiter	.25	.12	.02
☐ 16 Melido Perez	.30	.15	.03
☐ 17 Chris Sabo	.75	.35	.07
☐ 18 Nelson Santovenia	.30	.15	.03
☐ 19 Mackey Sasser	.30	.15	.03
☐ 20 Gary Sheffield	.75	.35	.07
☐ 21 Walt Weiss	.40	.20	.04
☐ 22 David Wells	.25	.12	.02

1989 Topps Glossy Send-In 60

The 1989 Topps Glossy Send-In set contains 60 standard-size (2 1/2 by 3 1/2 inch) cards. The fronts have color photos with white borders; the backs are light blue. The cards were distributed through the mail by Topps in six groups of 10 cards.

	MINT	EXC	G-VG
COMPLETE SET (60)	9.00	4.50	.90
COMMON PLAYER (1-60)	.15	.07	.01
☐ 1 Kirby Puckett	.40	.20	.04
☐ 2 Eric Davis	.40	.20	.04
☐ 3 Joe Carter	.20	.10	.02
☐ 4 Andy Van Slyke	.20	.10	.02
☐ 5 Wade Boggs	.50	.25	.05
☐ 6 David Cone	.25	.12	.02
☐ 7 Kent Hrbek	.20	.10	.02
☐ 8 Darryl Strawberry	.45	.22	.04
☐ 9 Jay Buhner	.20	.10	.02
☐ 10 Ron Gant	.40	.20	.04
☐ 11 Will Clark	.75	.35	.07
☐ 12 Jose Canseco	.90	.45	.09
☐ 13 Juan Samuel	.15	.07	.01
☐ 14 George Brett	.40	.20	.04
☐ 15 Benito Santiago	.30	.15	.03
☐ 16 Dennis Eckersley	.25	.12	.02
☐ 17 Gary Carter	.25	.12	.02
☐ 18 Frank Viola	.25	.12	.02
☐ 19 Roberto Alomar	.30	.15	.03
☐ 20 Paul Gibson	.15	.07	.01
☐ 21 Dave Winfield	.25	.12	.02
☐ 22 Howard Johnson	.25	.12	.02
☐ 23 Roger Clemens	.50	.25	.05
☐ 24 Bobby Bonilla	.25	.12	.02
☐ 25 Alan Trammell	.25	.12	.02
☐ 26 Kevin McReynolds	.25	.12	.02
☐ 27 George Bell	.25	.12	.02
☐ 28 Bruce Hurst	.15	.07	.01
☐ 29 Mark Grace	.75	.35	.07
☐ 30 Tim Belcher	.25	.12	.02
☐ 31 Mike Greenwell	.45	.22	.04
☐ 32 Glenn Davis	.25	.12	.02
☐ 33 Gary Gaetti	.20	.10	.02
☐ 34 Ryne Sandberg	.50	.25	.05
☐ 35 Rickey Henderson	.60	.30	.06
☐ 36 Dwight Evans	.25	.12	.02
☐ 37 Dwight Gooden	.35	.17	.03
☐ 38 Robin Yount	.40	.20	.04
☐ 39 Damon Berryhill	.25	.12	.02
☐ 40 Chris Sabo	.50	.25	.05
☐ 41 Mark McGwire	.60	.30	.06
☐ 42 Ozzie Smith	.25	.12	.02
☐ 43 Paul Molitor	.20	.10	.02
☐ 44 Andres Galarraga	.20	.10	.02
☐ 45 Dave Stewart	.25	.12	.02
☐ 46 Tom Browning	.20	.10	.02
☐ 47 Cal Ripken	.30	.15	.03
☐ 48 Orel Hershiser	.25	.12	.02
☐ 49 Dave Gallagher	.15	.07	.01
☐ 50 Walt Weiss	.25	.12	.02
☐ 51 Don Mattingly	.90	.45	.09
☐ 52 Tony Fernandez	.20	.10	.02
☐ 53 Tim Raines	.25	.12	.02
☐ 54 Jeff Reardon	.15	.07	.01
☐ 55 Kirk Gibson	.25	.12	.02
☐ 56 Jack Clark	.20	.10	.02
☐ 57 Danny Jackson	.15	.07	.01
☐ 58 Tony Gwynn	.30	.15	.03

☐ 59 Cecil Espy	.15	.07	.01
☐ 60 Jody Reed	.15	.07	.01

1989 Topps Big Baseball

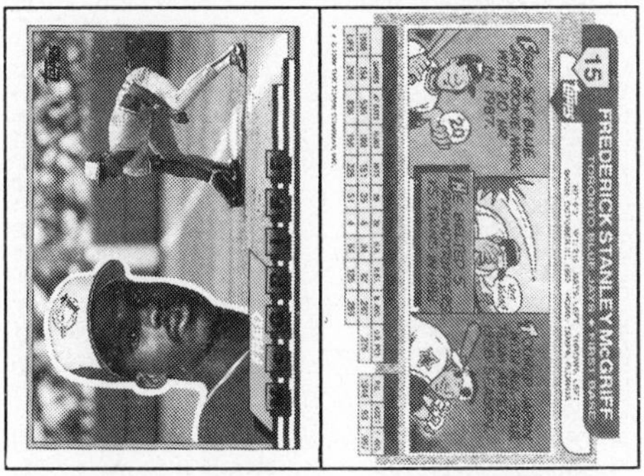

The 1989 Topps Big Baseball set contains 330 glossy cards measuring 2 1/2 by 3 3/4 inches. The fronts feature mug shots superimposed on action photos. The horizontally-oriented backs have color cartoons, 1988 and career stats. The set was released in three series of 110 cards. The cards were distributed in seven-card cello packs marked with the series number.

	MINT	EXC	G-VG
COMPLETE SET (330)	27.00	13.50	2.70
COMMON PLAYER (1-110)	.05	.02	.00
COMMON PLAYER (111-220)	.05	.02	.00
COMMON PLAYER (221-330)	.06	.03	.00
☐ 1 Orel Hershiser	.25	.12	.02
☐ 2 Harold Reynolds	.08	.04	.01
☐ 3 Jody Davis	.05	.02	.00
☐ 4 Greg Walker	.05	.02	.00
☐ 5 Barry Bonds	.25	.12	.02
☐ 6 Bret Saberhagen	.15	.07	.01
☐ 7 Johnny Ray	.05	.02	.00
☐ 8 Mike Fiore	.10	.05	.01
☐ 9 Juan Castillo	.05	.02	.00
☐ 10 Todd Burns	.05	.02	.00
☐ 11 Carmelo Martinez	.05	.02	.00
☐ 12 Geno Petralli	.05	.02	.00
☐ 13 Mel Hall	.08	.04	.01
☐ 14 Tom Browning	.08	.04	.01
☐ 15 Fred McGriff	.20	.10	.02
☐ 16 Kevin Elster	.08	.04	.01
☐ 17 Tim Leary	.08	.04	.01
☐ 18 Jim Rice	.15	.07	.01
☐ 19 Bret Barberie	.15	.07	.01
☐ 20 Jay Buhner	.10	.05	.01
☐ 21 Atlee Hammaker	.05	.02	.00
☐ 22 Lou Whitaker	.12	.06	.01
☐ 23 Paul Runge	.08	.04	.01
☐ 24 Carlton Fisk	.20	.10	.02
☐ 25 Jose Lind	.05	.02	.00
☐ 26 Mark Gubicza	.10	.05	.01
☐ 27 Billy Ripken	.05	.02	.00
☐ 28 Mike Pagliarulo	.05	.02	.00
☐ 29 Jim Deshaies	.05	.02	.00
☐ 30 Mark McLemore	.05	.02	.00
☐ 31 Scott Terry	.05	.02	.00
☐ 32 Franklin Stubbs	.08	.04	.01
☐ 33 Don August	.05	.02	.00
☐ 34 Mark McGwire	.60	.30	.06
☐ 35 Eric Show	.05	.02	.00
☐ 36 Cecil Espy	.05	.02	.00
☐ 37 Ron Tingley	.05	.02	.00
☐ 38 Mickey Brantley	.05	.02	.00
☐ 39 Paul O'Neill	.12	.06	.01
☐ 40 Ed Sprague	.15	.07	.01
☐ 41 Len Dykstra	.15	.07	.01
☐ 42 Roger Clemens	.50	.25	.05
☐ 43 Ron Gant	.40	.20	.04
☐ 44 Dan Pasqua	.05	.02	.00
☐ 45 Jeff Robinson	.08	.04	.01
☐ 46 George Brett	.35	.17	.03
☐ 47 Bryn Smith	.05	.02	.00
☐ 48 Mike Marshall	.10	.05	.01
☐ 49 Doug Robbins	.10	.05	.01
☐ 50 Don Mattingly	.75	.35	.07
☐ 51 Mike Scott	.15	.07	.01
☐ 52 Steve Jeltz	.05	.02	.00
☐ 53 Dick Schofield	.05	.02	.00
☐ 54 Tom Brunansky	.10	.05	.01
☐ 55 Gary Sheffield	.40	.20	.04
☐ 56 Dave Valle	.05	.02	.00
☐ 57 Carney Lansford	.12	.06	.01
☐ 58 Tony Gwynn	.30	.15	.03
☐ 59 Checklist 1-110	.05	.02	.00
☐ 60 Damon Berryhill	.10	.05	.01
☐ 61 Jack Morris	.12	.06	.01
☐ 62 Brett Butler	.10	.05	.01
☐ 63 Mickey Hatcher	.05	.02	.00
☐ 64 Bruce Sutter	.08	.04	.01
☐ 65 Robin Ventura	.40	.20	.04
☐ 66 Junior Ortiz	.05	.02	.00
☐ 67 Pat Tabler	.05	.02	.00
☐ 68 Greg Swindell	.10	.05	.01
☐ 69 Jeff Branson	.10	.05	.01
☐ 70 Manny Lee	.05	.02	.00
☐ 71 Dave Magadan	.12	.06	.01
☐ 72 Rich Gedman	.05	.02	.00
☐ 73 Tim Raines	.15	.07	.01
☐ 74 Mike Maddux	.05	.02	.00
☐ 75 Jim Presley	.05	.02	.00
☐ 76 Chuck Finley	.12	.06	.01
☐ 77 Jose Oquendo	.05	.02	.00
☐ 78 Rob Deer	.10	.05	.01
☐ 79 Jay Howell	.08	.04	.01
☐ 80 Terry Steinbach	.10	.05	.01
☐ 81 Ed Whitson	.08	.04	.01
☐ 82 Ruben Sierra	.40	.20	.04
☐ 83 Bruce Benedict	.05	.02	.00
☐ 84 Fred Manrique	.05	.02	.00
☐ 85 John Smiley	.05	.02	.00
☐ 86 Mike Macfarlane	.08	.04	.01
☐ 87 Rene Gonzales	.05	.02	.00
☐ 88 Charles Hudson	.05	.02	.00
☐ 89 Glenn Davis	.15	.07	.01
☐ 90 Les Straker	.05	.02	.00
☐ 91 Carmen Castillo	.05	.02	.00
☐ 92 Tracy Woodson	.05	.02	.00
☐ 93 Tino Martinez	.60	.30	.06
☐ 94 Herm Winningham	.05	.02	.00
☐ 95 Kelly Gruber	.15	.07	.01
☐ 96 Terry Leach	.05	.02	.00
☐ 97 Jody Reed	.10	.05	.01
☐ 98 Nelson Santovenia	.08	.04	.01
☐ 99 Tony Armas	.05	.02	.00
☐ 100 Greg Brock	.05	.02	.00
☐ 101 Dave Stewart	.15	.07	.01
☐ 102 Roberto Alomar	.30	.15	.03
☐ 103 Jim Sundberg	.05	.02	.00
☐ 104 Albert Hall	.05	.02	.00
☐ 105 Steve Lyons	.05	.02	.00
☐ 106 Sid Bream	.05	.02	.00
☐ 107 Danny Tartabull	.12	.06	.01
☐ 108 Rick Dempsey	.05	.02	.00
☐ 109 Rich Renteria	.05	.02	.00
☐ 110 Ozzie Smith	.20	.10	.02
☐ 111 Steve Sax	.15	.07	.01
☐ 112 Kelly Downs	.08	.04	.01
☐ 113 Larry Sheets	.05	.02	.00
☐ 114 Andy Benes	.45	.22	.04
☐ 115 Pete O'Brien	.08	.04	.01
☐ 116 Kevin McReynolds	.12	.06	.01
☐ 117 Juan Berenguer	.05	.02	.00
☐ 118 Billy Hatcher	.08	.04	.01
☐ 119 Rick Cerone	.05	.02	.00
☐ 120 Andre Dawson	.20	.10	.02
☐ 121 Storm Davis	.08	.04	.01
☐ 122 Devon White	.10	.05	.01
☐ 123 Alan Trammell	.15	.07	.01
☐ 124 Vince Coleman	.20	.10	.02
☐ 125 Al Leiter	.08	.04	.01
☐ 126 Dale Sveum	.05	.02	.00
☐ 127 Pete Incaviglia	.12	.06	.01
☐ 128 Dave Stieb	.15	.07	.01
☐ 129 Kevin Mitchell	.35	.17	.03
☐ 130 Dave Schmidt	.05	.02	.00
☐ 131 Gary Redus	.05	.02	.00
☐ 132 Ron Robinson	.05	.02	.00
☐ 133 Darnell Coles	.05	.02	.00
☐ 134 Benito Santiago	.20	.10	.02
☐ 135 John Farrell	.08	.04	.01
☐ 136 Willie Wilson	.10	.05	.01
☐ 137 Steve Bedrosian	.08	.04	.01
☐ 138 Don Slaught	.05	.02	.00
☐ 139 Darryl Strawberry	.50	.25	.05
☐ 140 Frank Viola	.15	.07	.01
☐ 141 Dave Silvestri	.12	.06	.01
☐ 142 Carlos Quintana	.12	.06	.01

☐ 143 Vance Law	.05	.02	.00
☐ 144 Dave Parker	.15	.07	.01
☐ 145 Tim Belcher	.15	.07	.01
☐ 146 Will Clark	.90	.45	.09
☐ 147 Mark Williamson	.05	.02	.00
☐ 148 Ozzie Guillen	.12	.06	.01
☐ 149 Kirk McCaskill	.05	.02	.00
☐ 150 Pat Sheridan	.05	.02	.00
☐ 151 Terry Pendleton	.05	.02	.00
☐ 152 Roberto Kelly	.25	.12	.02
☐ 153 Joey Meyer	.08	.04	.01
☐ 154 Mark Grant	.05	.02	.00
☐ 155 Joe Carter	.15	.07	.01
☐ 156 Steve Buechele	.05	.02	.00
☐ 157 Tony Fernandez	.10	.05	.01
☐ 158 Jeff Reed	.05	.02	.00
☐ 159 Bobby Bonilla	.20	.10	.02
☐ 160 Henry Cotto	.05	.02	.00
☐ 161 Kurt Stillwell	.08	.04	.01
☐ 162 Mickey Morandini	.20	.10	.02
☐ 163 Robby Thompson	.05	.02	.00
☐ 164 Rick Schu	.05	.02	.00
☐ 165 Stan Jefferson	.05	.02	.00
☐ 166 Ron Darling	.10	.05	.01
☐ 167 Kirby Puckett	.35	.17	.03
☐ 168 Bill Doran	.08	.04	.01
☐ 169 Dennis Lamp	.05	.02	.00
☐ 170 Ty Griffin	.50	.25	.05
☐ 171 Ron Hassey	.05	.02	.00
☐ 172 Dale Murphy	.30	.15	.03
☐ 173 Andres Galarraga	.15	.07	.01
☐ 174 Tim Flannery	.05	.02	.00
☐ 175 Cory Snyder	.12	.06	.01
☐ 176 Checklist 111-220	.05	.02	.00
☐ 177 Tommy Barrett	.05	.02	.00
☐ 178 Dan Petry	.05	.02	.00
☐ 179 Billy Masse	.10	.05	.01
☐ 180 Terry Kennedy	.05	.02	.00
☐ 181 Joe Orsulak	.05	.02	.00
☐ 182 Doyle Alexander	.05	.02	.00
☐ 183 Willie McGee	.15	.07	.01
☐ 184 Jim Gantner	.05	.02	.00
☐ 185 Keith Hernandez	.15	.07	.01
☐ 186 Greg Gagne	.05	.02	.00
☐ 187 Kevin Bass	.08	.04	.01
☐ 188 Mark Eichhorn	.05	.02	.00
☐ 189 Mark Grace	.60	.30	.06
☐ 190 Jose Canseco	.75	.35	.07
☐ 191 Bobby Witt	.15	.07	.01
☐ 192 Rafael Santana	.05	.02	.00
☐ 193 Dwight Evans	.10	.05	.01
☐ 194 Greg Booker	.05	.02	.00
☐ 195 Brook Jacoby	.08	.04	.01
☐ 196 Rafael Belliard	.05	.02	.00
☐ 197 Candy Maldonado	.08	.04	.01
☐ 198 Mickey Tettleton	.10	.05	.01
☐ 199 Barry Larkin	.20	.10	.02
☐ 200 Frank White	.08	.04	.01
☐ 201 Wally Joyner	.15	.07	.01
☐ 202 Chet Lemon	.05	.02	.00
☐ 203 Joe Magrane	.10	.05	.01
☐ 204 Glenn Braggs	.08	.04	.01
☐ 205 Scott Fletcher	.05	.02	.00
☐ 206 Gary Ward	.05	.02	.00
☐ 207 Nelson Liriano	.05	.02	.00
☐ 208 Howard Johnson	.15	.07	.01
☐ 209 Kent Hrbek	.15	.07	.01
☐ 210 Ken Caminiti	.08	.04	.01
☐ 211 Mike Greenwell	.35	.17	.03
☐ 212 Ryne Sandberg	.50	.25	.05
☐ 213 Joe Slusarski	.12	.06	.01
☐ 214 Donell Nixon	.05	.02	.00
☐ 215 Tim Wallach	.08	.04	.01
☐ 216 John Kruk	.08	.04	.01
☐ 217 Charles Nagy	.20	.10	.02
☐ 218 Alvin Davis	.10	.05	.01
☐ 219 Oswald Peraza	.08	.04	.01
☐ 220 Mike Schmidt	.75	.35	.07
☐ 221 Spike Owen	.06	.03	.00
☐ 222 Mike Smithson	.06	.03	.00
☐ 223 Dion James	.06	.03	.00
☐ 224 Ernie Whitt	.06	.03	.00
☐ 225 Mike Davis	.06	.03	.00
☐ 226 Gene Larkin	.06	.03	.00
☐ 227 Pat Combs	.50	.25	.05
☐ 228 Jack Howell	.06	.03	.00
☐ 229 Ron Oester	.06	.03	.00
☐ 230 Paul Gibson	.06	.03	.00
☐ 231 Mookie Wilson	.06	.03	.00
☐ 232 Glenn Hubbard	.06	.03	.00
☐ 233 Shawon Dunston	.15	.07	.01
☐ 234 Otis Nixon	.06	.03	.00
☐ 235 Melido Perez	.10	.05	.01
☐ 236 Jerry Browne	.10	.05	.01
☐ 237 Rick Rhoden	.06	.03	.00
☐ 238 Bo Jackson	1.00	.50	.10
☐ 239 Randy Velarde	.06	.03	.00
☐ 240 Jack Clark	.12	.06	.01
☐ 241 Wade Boggs	.60	.30	.06
☐ 242 Lonnie Smith	.10	.05	.01
☐ 243 Mike Flanagan	.10	.05	.01
☐ 244 Willie Randolph	.10	.05	.01
☐ 245 Oddibe McDowell	.10	.05	.01
☐ 246 Ricky Jordan	.25	.12	.02
☐ 247 Greg Briley	.20	.10	.02
☐ 248 Rex Hudler	.10	.05	.01
☐ 249 Robin Yount	.40	.20	.04
☐ 250 Lance Parrish	.15	.07	.01
☐ 251 Chris Sabo	.40	.20	.04
☐ 252 Mike Henneman	.10	.05	.01
☐ 253 Gregg Jefferies	.75	.35	.07
☐ 254 Curt Young	.06	.03	.00
☐ 255 Andy Van Slyke	.15	.07	.01
☐ 256 Rod Booker	.06	.03	.00
☐ 257 Rafael Palmeiro	.15	.07	.01
☐ 258 Jose Uribe	.06	.03	.00
☐ 259 Ellis Burks	.35	.17	.03
☐ 260 John Smoltz	.25	.12	.02
☐ 261 Tom Foley	.06	.03	.00
☐ 262 Lloyd Moseby	.06	.03	.00
☐ 263 Jim Poole	.12	.06	.01
☐ 264 Gary Gaetti	.10	.05	.01
☐ 265 Bob Dernier	.06	.03	.00
☐ 266 Harold Baines	.12	.06	.01
☐ 267 Tom Candiotti	.10	.05	.01
☐ 268 Rafael Ramirez	.06	.03	.00
☐ 269 Bob Boone	.12	.06	.01
☐ 270 Buddy Bell	.08	.04	.01
☐ 271 Rickey Henderson	.75	.35	.07
☐ 272 Willie Fraser	.06	.03	.00
☐ 273 Eric Davis	.45	.22	.04
☐ 274 Jeff Robinson	.06	.03	.00
☐ 275 Damaso Garcia	.06	.03	.00
☐ 276 Sid Fernandez	.10	.05	.01
☐ 277 Stan Javier	.06	.03	.00
☐ 278 Marty Barrett	.06	.03	.00
☐ 279 Gerald Perry	.06	.03	.00
☐ 280 Rob Ducey	.06	.03	.00
☐ 281 Mike Scioscia	.06	.03	.00
☐ 282 Randy Bush	.06	.03	.00
☐ 283 Tom Herr	.06	.03	.00
☐ 284 Glenn Wilson	.06	.03	.00
☐ 285 Pedro Guerrero	.15	.07	.01
☐ 286 Cal Ripken	.30	.15	.03
☐ 287 Randy Johnson	.12	.06	.01
☐ 288 Julio Franco	.12	.06	.01
☐ 289 Ivan Calderon	.10	.05	.01
☐ 290 Rich Yett	.06	.03	.00
☐ 291 Scott Servais	.12	.06	.01
☐ 292 Bill Pecota	.06	.03	.00
☐ 293 Ken Phelps	.06	.03	.00
☐ 294 Chili Davis	.10	.05	.01
☐ 295 Manny Trillo	.06	.03	.00
☐ 296 Mike Boddicker	.06	.03	.00
☐ 297 Geronimo Berroa	.06	.03	.00
☐ 298 Todd Stottlemyre	.10	.05	.01
☐ 299 Kirk Gibson	.15	.07	.01
☐ 300 Wally Backman	.06	.03	.00
☐ 301 Hubie Brooks	.10	.05	.01
☐ 302 Von Hayes	.10	.05	.01
☐ 303 Matt Nokes	.12	.06	.01
☐ 304 Dwight Gooden	.30	.15	.03
☐ 305 Walt Weiss	.20	.10	.02
☐ 306 Mike LaValliere	.06	.03	.00
☐ 307 Cris Carpenter	.06	.03	.00
☐ 308 Ted Wood	.25	.12	.02
☐ 309 Jeff Russell	.06	.03	.00
☐ 310 Dave Gallagher	.06	.03	.00
☐ 311 Andy Allanson	.06	.03	.00
☐ 312 Craig Reynolds	.06	.03	.00
☐ 313 Kevin Seitzer	.15	.07	.01
☐ 314 Dave Winfield	.20	.10	.02
☐ 315 Andy McGaffigan	.06	.03	.00
☐ 316 Nick Esasky	.10	.05	.01
☐ 317 Jeff Blauser	.08	.04	.01
☐ 318 George Bell	.15	.07	.01
☐ 319 Eddie Murray	.20	.10	.02
☐ 320 Mark Davidson	.06	.03	.00
☐ 321 Juan Samuel	.10	.05	.01
☐ 322 Jim Abbott	.60	.30	.06
☐ 323 Kal Daniels	.12	.06	.01
☐ 324 Mike Brumley	.06	.03	.00
☐ 325 Gary Carter	.15	.07	.01
☐ 326 Dave Henderson	.10	.05	.01
☐ 327 Checklist 221-330	.06	.03	.00
☐ 328 Garry Templeton	.10	.05	.01
☐ 329 Pat Perry	.06	.03	.00
☐ 330 Paul Molitor	.12	.06	.01

1989 Topps Mini Leaders

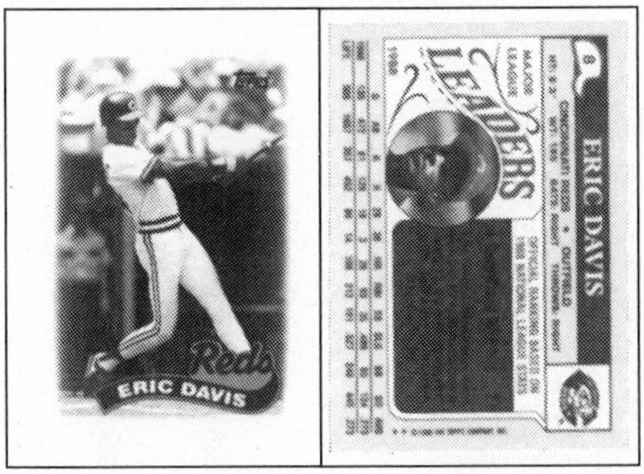

The 1989 Topps Mini League Leaders set contains 77 cards measuring approximately 2 1/8" by 3". The fronts have color photos with large white borders. The backs are yellow and feature 1988 and career stats. The cards were distributed in seven-card cello packs.

	MINT	EXC	G-VG
COMPLETE SET (77)	7.00	3.50	.70
COMMON PLAYER (1-77)	.05	.02	.00
☐ 1 Dale Murphy	.25	.12	.02
☐ 2 Gerald Perry	.05	.02	.00
☐ 3 Andre Dawson	.15	.07	.01
☐ 4 Greg Maddux	.10	.05	.01
☐ 5 Rafael Palmeiro	.15	.07	.01
☐ 6 Tom Browning	.10	.05	.01
☐ 7 Kal Daniels	.15	.07	.01
☐ 8 Eric Davis	.35	.17	.03
☐ 9 John Franco	.10	.05	.01
☐ 10 Danny Jackson	.05	.02	.00
☐ 11 Barry Larkin	.20	.10	.02
☐ 12 Jose Rijo	.10	.05	.01
☐ 13 Chris Sabo	.25	.12	.02
☐ 14 Mike Scott	.10	.05	.01
☐ 15 Nolan Ryan	.75	.35	.07
☐ 16 Gerald Young	.10	.05	.01
☐ 17 Kirk Gibson	.15	.07	.01
☐ 18 Orel Hershiser	.20	.10	.02
☐ 19 Steve Sax	.15	.07	.01
☐ 20 John Tudor	.10	.05	.01
☐ 21 Hubie Brooks	.10	.05	.01
☐ 22 Andres Galarraga	.15	.07	.01
☐ 23 Otis Nixon	.05	.02	.00
☐ 24 David Cone	.15	.07	.01
☐ 25 Sid Fernandez	.10	.05	.01
☐ 26 Dwight Gooden	.25	.12	.02
☐ 27 Kevin McReynolds	.15	.07	.01
☐ 28 Darryl Strawberry	.45	.22	.04
☐ 29 Juan Samuel	.10	.05	.01
☐ 30 Bobby Bonilla	.20	.10	.02
☐ 31 Sid Bream	.05	.02	.00
☐ 32 Andy Van Slyke	.10	.05	.01
☐ 33 Vince Coleman	.15	.07	.01
☐ 34 Jose DeLeon	.05	.02	.00
☐ 35 Joe Magrane	.10	.05	.01
☐ 36 Ozzie Smith	.15	.07	.01
☐ 37 Todd Worrell	.10	.05	.01
☐ 38 Tony Gwynn	.30	.15	.03
☐ 39 Brett Butler	.10	.05	.01
☐ 40 Will Clark	.60	.30	.06
☐ 41 Jim Gott	.05	.02	.00
☐ 42 Rick Reuschel	.10	.05	.01
☐ 43 Checklist Card	.05	.02	.00
☐ 44 Eddie Murray	.20	.10	.02
☐ 45 Wade Boggs	.40	.20	.04
☐ 46 Roger Clemens	.40	.20	.04
☐ 47 Dwight Evans	.10	.05	.01
☐ 48 Mike Greenwell	.30	.15	.03
☐ 49 Bruce Hurst	.10	.05	.01
☐ 50 Johnny Ray	.05	.02	.00
☐ 51 Doug Jones	.10	.05	.01
☐ 52 Greg Swindell	.10	.05	.01
☐ 53 Gary Pettis	.05	.02	.00
☐ 54 George Brett	.30	.15	.03
☐ 55 Mark Gubicza	.10	.05	.01
☐ 56 Willie Wilson	.10	.05	.01
☐ 57 Teddy Higuera	.10	.05	.01
☐ 58 Paul Molitor	.10	.05	.01
☐ 59 Robin Yount	.30	.15	.03
☐ 60 Allan Anderson	.10	.05	.01
☐ 61 Gary Gaetti	.10	.05	.01
☐ 62 Kirby Puckett	.30	.15	.03
☐ 63 Jeff Reardon	.10	.05	.01
☐ 64 Frank Viola	.15	.07	.01
☐ 65 Jack Clark	.15	.07	.01
☐ 66 Rickey Henderson	.60	.30	.06
☐ 67 Dave Winfield	.20	.10	.02
☐ 68 Jose Canseco	.75	.35	.07
☐ 69 Dennis Eckersley	.20	.10	.02
☐ 70 Mark McGwire	.50	.25	.05
☐ 71 Dave Stewart	.20	.10	.02
☐ 72 Alvin Davis	.15	.07	.01
☐ 73 Mark Langston	.15	.07	.01
☐ 74 Harold Reynolds	.05	.02	.00
☐ 75 George Bell	.15	.07	.01
☐ 76 Tony Fernandez	.10	.05	.01
☐ 77 Fred McGriff	.20	.10	.02

1989 Topps UK Mini

The 1989 Topps UK Mini baseball set contains 88 cards measuring approximately 2 1/8" by 3". The fronts are red, white and blue. The backs are yellow and red, and feature 1988 and career stats. The cards were distributed in five-card poly packs. The card set numbering is essentially in alphabetical order by player's name.

	MINT	EXC	G-VG
COMPLETE SET (88)	7.50	3.75	.75
COMMON PLAYER (1-88)	.05	.02	.00
☐ 1 Brady Anderson	.15	.07	.01
☐ 2 Harold Baines	.10	.05	.01
☐ 3 George Bell	.15	.07	.01
☐ 4 Wade Boggs	.45	.22	.04
☐ 5 Barry Bonds	.40	.20	.04
☐ 6 Bobby Bonilla	.25	.12	.02
☐ 7 George Brett	.35	.17	.03
☐ 8 Hubie Brooks	.10	.05	.01
☐ 9 Tom Brunansky	.10	.05	.01
☐ 10 Jay Buhner	.10	.05	.01
☐ 11 Brett Butler	.10	.05	.01
☐ 12 Jose Canseco	.75	.35	.07
☐ 13 Joe Carter	.15	.07	.01
☐ 14 Jack Clark	.15	.07	.01
☐ 15 Will Clark	.60	.30	.06
☐ 16 Roger Clemens	.50	.25	.05
☐ 17 David Cone	.20	.10	.02
☐ 18 Alvin Davis	.10	.05	.01
☐ 19 Eric Davis	.35	.17	.03
☐ 20 Glenn Davis	.20	.10	.02
☐ 21 Andre Dawson	.20	.10	.02
☐ 22 Bill Doran	.10	.05	.01
☐ 23 Dennis Eckersley	.20	.10	.02
☐ 24 Dwight Evans	.10	.05	.01
☐ 25 Tony Fernandez	.10	.05	.01
☐ 26 Carlton Fisk	.20	.10	.02
☐ 27 John Franco	.10	.05	.01
☐ 28 Andres Galarraga	.15	.07	.01
☐ 29 Ron Gant	.35	.17	.03
☐ 30 Kirk Gibson	.20	.10	.02
☐ 31 Dwight Gooden	.25	.12	.02
☐ 32 Mike Greenwell	.35	.17	.03
☐ 33 Mark Gubicza	.10	.05	.01

☐ 34 Pedro Guerrero	.15	.07	.01
☐ 35 Ozzie Guillen	.15	.07	.01
☐ 36 Tony Gwynn	.30	.15	.03
☐ 37 Rickey Henderson	.60	.30	.06
☐ 38 Orel Hershiser	.20	.10	.02
☐ 39 Teddy Higuera	.10	.05	.01
☐ 40 Charlie Hough	.05	.02	.00
☐ 41 Kent Hrbek	.15	.07	.01
☐ 42 Bruce Hurst	.10	.05	.01
☐ 43 Bo Jackson	.75	.35	.07
☐ 44 Gregg Jefferies	.60	.30	.06
☐ 45 Ricky Jordan	.20	.10	.02
☐ 46 Wally Joyner	.15	.07	.01
☐ 47 Mark Langston	.10	.05	.01
☐ 48 Mike Marshall	.10	.05	.01
☐ 49 Don Mattingly	.60	.30	.06
☐ 50 Fred McGriff	.20	.10	.02
☐ 51 Mark McGwire	.45	.22	.04
☐ 52 Kevin McReynolds	.15	.07	.01
☐ 53 Paul Molitor	.10	.05	.01
☐ 54 Jack Morris	.10	.05	.01
☐ 55 Dale Murphy	.25	.12	.02
☐ 56 Eddie Murray	.20	.10	.02
☐ 57 Pete O'Brien	.05	.02	.00
☐ 58 Rafael Palmeiro	.15	.07	.01
☐ 59 Gerald Perry	.05	.02	.00
☐ 60 Kirby Puckett	.40	.20	.04
☐ 61 Tim Raines	.20	.10	.02
☐ 62 Johnny Ray	.05	.02	.00
☐ 63 Rick Reuschel	.10	.05	.01
☐ 64 Cal Ripken	.25	.12	.02
☐ 65 Chris Sabo	.30	.15	.03
☐ 66 Juan Samuel	.10	.05	.01
☐ 67 Ryne Sandberg	.50	.25	.05
☐ 68 Benito Santiago	.20	.10	.02
☐ 69 Steve Sax	.15	.07	.01
☐ 70 Mike Schmidt	.75	.35	.07
☐ 71 Ruben Sierra	.40	.20	.04
☐ 72 Ozzie Smith	.25	.12	.02
☐ 73 Cory Snyder	.15	.07	.01
☐ 74 Dave Stewart	.15	.07	.01
☐ 75 Darryl Strawberry	.45	.22	.04
☐ 76 Greg Swindell	.10	.05	.01
☐ 77 Alan Trammell	.15	.07	.01
☐ 78 Fernando Valenzuela	.15	.07	.01
☐ 79 Andy Van Slyke	.10	.05	.01
☐ 80 Frank Viola	.15	.07	.01
☐ 81 Claudell Washington	.05	.02	.00
☐ 82 Walt Weiss	.15	.07	.01
☐ 83 Lou Whitaker	.12	.06	.01
☐ 84 Dave Winfield	.20	.10	.02
☐ 85 Mike Witt	.05	.02	.00
☐ 86 Gerald Young	.10	.05	.01
☐ 87 Robin Yount	.35	.17	.03
☐ 88 Checklist Card	.05	.02	.00

1989 Topps Ames 20/20 Club

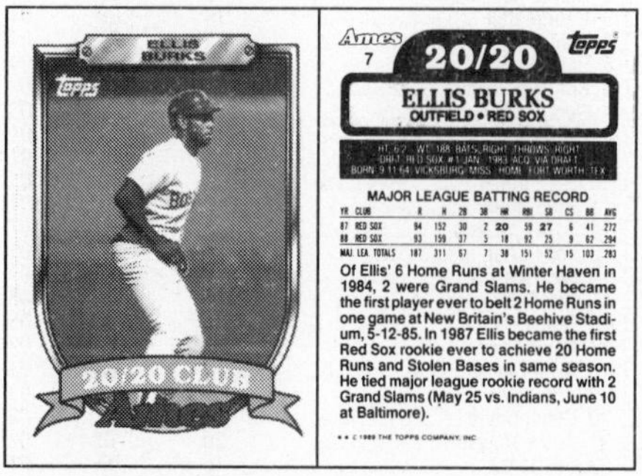

The 1989 (Topps) Ames 20/20 Club set contains 33 standard-size (2 1/2" by 3 1/2") glossy cards. The fronts resemble plaques with gold and silver trim. The vertically-oriented backs show career stats. The cards were distributed at Ames department stores as a boxed set. The set was produced by Topps for Ames; the Topps logo is also on the front of each card. The set includes active major leaguers who have had seasons of at least 20 home runs and 20 stolen bases. The backs include lifetime batting records with home run and stolen base totals for their 20/20 years highlighted. The subject list for the set is printed on the back panel of the set's custom box.

	MINT	EXC	G-VG
COMPLETE SET (33)	4.00	2.00	.40
COMMON PLAYER (1-33)	.10	.05	.01
☐ 1 Jesse Barfield	.15	.07	.01
☐ 2 Kevin Bass	.10	.05	.01
☐ 3 Don Baylor	.15	.07	.01
☐ 4 George Bell	.20	.10	.02
☐ 5 Barry Bonds	.30	.15	.03
☐ 6 Phil Bradley	.15	.07	.01
☐ 7 Ellis Burks	.25	.12	.02
☐ 8 Jose Canseco	.75	.35	.07
☐ 9 Joe Carter	.15	.07	.01
☐ 10 Kal Daniels	.15	.07	.01
☐ 11 Eric Davis	.25	.12	.02
☐ 12 Mike Davis	.10	.05	.01
☐ 13 Andre Dawson	.20	.10	.02
☐ 14 Kirk Gibson	.15	.07	.01
☐ 15 Pedro Guerrero	.15	.07	.01
☐ 16 Rickey Henderson	.50	.25	.05
☐ 17 Bo Jackson	.75	.35	.07
☐ 18 Howard Johnson	.15	.07	.01
☐ 19 Jeffrey Leonard	.10	.05	.01
☐ 20 Kevin McReynolds	.15	.07	.01
☐ 21 Dale Murphy	.20	.10	.02
☐ 22 Dwayne Murphy	.10	.05	.01
☐ 23 Dave Parker	.15	.07	.01
☐ 24 Kirby Puckett	.25	.12	.02
☐ 25 Juan Samuel	.10	.05	.01
☐ 26 Ryne Sandberg	.45	.22	.04
☐ 27 Mike Schmidt	.45	.22	.04
☐ 28 Darryl Strawberry	.35	.17	.03
☐ 29 Alan Trammell	.15	.07	.01
☐ 30 Andy Van Slyke	.15	.07	.01
☐ 31 Devon White	.10	.05	.01
☐ 32 Dave Winfield	.15	.07	.01
☐ 33 Robin Yount	.25	.12	.02

1989 Topps Cap'n Crunch

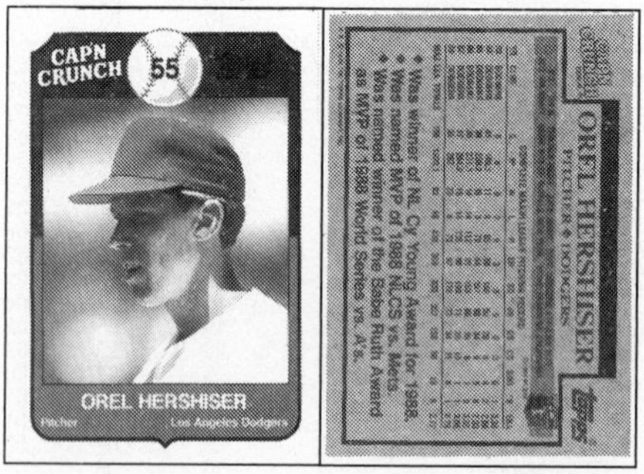

The 1989 Topps Cap'n Crunch set contains 22 standard-size (2 1/2" by 3 1/2") cards. The fronts have red, white and blue borders surrounding "mugshot" photos. The backs are horizontally-oriented and show lifetime stats. The set was produced by Topps, but has team logos airbrushed out. Two cards were included (in a cellophane wrapper with a piece of gum) in each specially-marked Cap'n Crunch cereal box. The set was not available as a complete set as part of any mail-in offer. The set was produced by Topps.

	MINT	EXC	G-VG
COMPLETE SET (22)	12.00	6.00	1.20
COMMON PLAYER (1-22)	.50	.25	.05
☐ 1 Jose Canseco	1.00	.50	.10
☐ 2 Kirk Gibson	.60	.30	.06
☐ 3 Orel Hershiser	.75	.35	.07
☐ 4 Frank Viola	.60	.30	.06

☐ 5 Tony Gwynn	.75	.35	.07
☐ 6 Cal Ripken	.75	.35	.07
☐ 7 Darryl Strawberry	.90	.45	.09
☐ 8 Don Mattingly	1.00	.50	.10
☐ 9 George Brett	.75	.35	.07
☐ 10 Andre Dawson	.60	.30	.06
☐ 11 Dale Murphy	.75	.35	.07
☐ 12 Alan Trammell	.60	.30	.06
☐ 13 Eric Davis	.75	.35	.07
☐ 14 Jack Clark	.50	.25	.05
☐ 15 Eddie Murray	.60	.30	.06
☐ 16 Mike Schmidt	1.00	.50	.10
☐ 17 Dwight Gooden	.75	.35	.07
☐ 18 Roger Clemens	.90	.45	.09
☐ 19 Will Clark	.90	.45	.09
☐ 20 Kirby Puckett	.75	.35	.07
☐ 21 Robin Yount	.75	.35	.07
☐ 22 Mark McGwire	.90	.45	.09

1989 Topps Hills Team MVP's

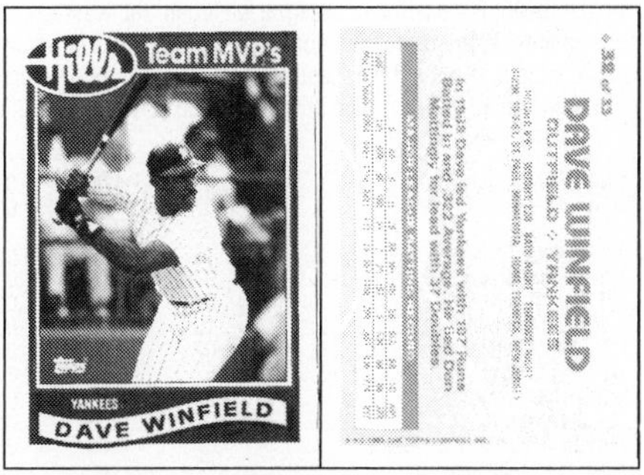

The 1989 Topps Hills Team MVP's set contains 33 glossy standard-size (2 1/2" by 3 1/2") cards. The fronts and backs are yellow, red, white and navy. The horizontally-oriented backs are green. The cards were distributed through Hills stores as a boxed set. The set was produced by Topps although it was printed in Ireland.

	MINT	EXC	G-VG
COMPLETE SET (33)	4.00	2.00	.40
COMMON PLAYER (1-33)	.10	.05	.01
☐ 1 Harold Baines	.15	.07	.01
☐ 2 Wade Boggs	.40	.20	.04
☐ 3 George Brett	.30	.15	.03
☐ 4 Tom Brunansky	.15	.07	.01
☐ 5 Jose Canseco	.75	.35	.07
☐ 6 Joe Carter	.15	.07	.01
☐ 7 Will Clark	.50	.25	.05
☐ 8 Roger Clemens	.45	.22	.04
☐ 9 David Cone	.20	.10	.02
☐ 10 Glenn Davis	.20	.10	.02
☐ 11 Andre Dawson	.20	.10	.02
☐ 12 Dennis Eckersley	.20	.10	.02
☐ 13 Andres Galarraga	.15	.07	.01
☐ 14 Kirk Gibson	.15	.07	.01
☐ 15 Mike Greenwell	.30	.15	.03
☐ 16 Tony Gwynn	.30	.15	.03
☐ 17 Orel Hershiser	.20	.10	.02
☐ 18 Danny Jackson	.10	.05	.01
☐ 19 Mark Langston	.15	.07	.01
☐ 20 Fred McGriff	.20	.10	.02
☐ 21 Dale Murphy	.30	.15	.03
☐ 22 Eddie Murray	.30	.15	.03
☐ 23 Kirby Puckett	.40	.20	.04
☐ 24 Johnny Ray	.10	.05	.01
☐ 25 Juan Samuel	.15	.07	.01
☐ 26 Ruben Sierra	.35	.17	.03
☐ 27 Dave Stewart	.20	.10	.02
☐ 28 Darryl Strawberry	.40	.20	.04
☐ 29 Alan Trammell	.15	.07	.01
☐ 30 Andy Van Slyke	.15	.07	.01
☐ 31 Frank Viola	.15	.07	.01
☐ 32 Dave Winfield	.20	.10	.02
☐ 33 Robin Yount	.40	.20	.04

1989 Topps Traded

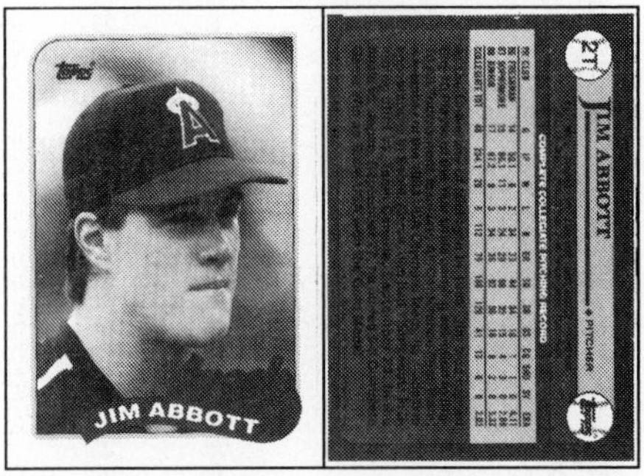

The 1989 Topps Traded set contains 132 standard-size (2 1/2" by 3 1/2") cards. The fronts have white borders; the horizontally-oriented backs are red and pink. From the front the cards' style is indistinguishable from the 1989 Topps regular issue. The cards were distributed as a boxed set. The key rookies in this set are Ken Griffey Jr., Deion Sanders, and Jerome Walton. Topps also produced a specially boxed "glossy" edition frequently referred to as the Topps Traded Tiffany set. This year, again, Topps did not disclose the number of Tiffany sets they produced or sold but it seems that production quantities were roughly similar (or slightly smaller, 15,000 sets) to the previous two years. The checklist of cards is identical to that of the normal non-glossy cards. There are two primary distinguishing features of the Tiffany cards, white card stock reverses and high gloss obverses. These Tiffany cards are valued at approximately four times the values listed below.

	MINT	EXC	G-VG
COMPLETE SET (132)	11.50	4.00	.80
COMMON PLAYER (1-132)	.05	.02	.00
☐ 1T Don Aase	.10	.05	.01
☐ 2T Jim Abbott	.60	.30	.06
☐ 3T Kent Anderson	.15	.07	.01
☐ 4T Keith Atherton	.05	.02	.00
☐ 5T Wally Backman	.05	.02	.00
☐ 6T Steve Balboni	.05	.02	.00
☐ 7T Jesse Barfield	.10	.05	.01
☐ 8T Steve Bedrosian	.10	.05	.01
☐ 9T Todd Benzinger	.10	.05	.01
☐ 10T Geronimo Berroa	.10	.05	.01
☐ 11T Bert Blyleven	.15	.07	.01
☐ 12T Bob Boone	.15	.07	.01
☐ 13T Phil Bradley	.10	.05	.01
☐ 14T Jeff Brantley	.25	.12	.02
☐ 15T Kevin Brown	.25	.12	.02
☐ 16T Jerry Browne	.10	.05	.01
☐ 17T Chuck Cary	.10	.05	.01
☐ 18T Carmen Castillo	.05	.02	.00
☐ 19T Jim Clancy	.05	.02	.00
☐ 20T Jack Clark	.10	.05	.01
☐ 21T Bryan Clutterbuck	.05	.02	.00
☐ 22T Jody Davis	.05	.02	.00
☐ 23T Mike Devereaux	.10	.05	.01
☐ 24T Frank DiPino	.05	.02	.00
☐ 25T Benny Distefano	.05	.02	.00
☐ 26T John Dopson	.10	.05	.01
☐ 27T Len Dykstra	.15	.07	.01
☐ 28T Jim Eisenreich	.05	.02	.00
☐ 29T Nick Esasky	.10	.05	.01
☐ 30T Alvaro Espinoza	.10	.05	.01
☐ 31T Darrell Evans	.10	.05	.01
☐ 32T Junior Felix	.90	.45	.09
☐ 33T Felix Fermin	.05	.02	.00
☐ 34T Julio Franco	.15	.07	.01
☐ 35T Terry Francona	.05	.02	.00
☐ 36T Cito Gaston MG	.10	.05	.01
☐ 37T Bob Geren UER (photo actually Mike Fennell)	.20	.10	.02
☐ 38T Tom Gordon	.50	.25	.05
☐ 39T Tommy Gregg	.10	.05	.01
☐ 40T Ken Griffey Sr.	.15	.07	.01

☐ 41T Ken Griffey Jr.	6.00	3.00	.60
☐ 42T Kevin Gross	.05	.02	.00
☐ 43T Lee Guetterman	.05	.02	.00
☐ 44T Mel Hall	.10	.05	.01
☐ 45T Erik Hanson	.50	.25	.05
☐ 46T Gene Harris	.25	.12	.02
☐ 47T Andy Hawkins	.05	.02	.00
☐ 48T Rickey Henderson	.40	.20	.04
☐ 49T Tom Herr	.10	.05	.01
☐ 50T Ken Hill	.20	.10	.02
☐ 51T Brian Holman	.25	.12	.02
☐ 52T Brian Holton	.10	.05	.01
☐ 53T Art Howe MG	.05	.02	.00
☐ 54T Ken Howell	.05	.02	.00
☐ 55T Bruce Hurst	.10	.05	.01
☐ 56T Chris James	.10	.05	.01
☐ 57T Randy Johnson	.15	.07	.01
☐ 58T Jimmy Jones	.05	.02	.00
☐ 59T Terry Kennedy	.05	.02	.00
☐ 60T Paul Kilgus	.05	.02	.00
☐ 61T Eric King	.05	.02	.00
☐ 62T Ron Kittle	.10	.05	.01
☐ 63T John Kruk	.05	.02	.00
☐ 64T Randy Kutcher	.05	.02	.00
☐ 65T Steve Lake	.05	.02	.00
☐ 66T Mark Langston	.10	.05	.01
☐ 67T Dave LaPoint	.05	.02	.00
☐ 68T Rick Leach	.05	.02	.00
☐ 69T Terry Leach	.10	.05	.01
☐ 70T Jim Lefebvre MG	.05	.02	.00
☐ 71T Al Leiter	.10	.05	.01
☐ 72T Jeffrey Leonard	.10	.05	.01
☐ 73T Derek Lilliquist	.12	.06	.01
☐ 74T Rick Mahler	.05	.02	.00
☐ 75T Tom McCarthy	.12	.06	.01
☐ 76T Lloyd McClendon	.10	.05	.01
☐ 77T Lance McCullers	.05	.02	.00
☐ 78T Oddibe McDowell	.10	.05	.01
☐ 79T Roger McDowell	.10	.05	.01
☐ 80T Larry McWilliams	.05	.02	.00
☐ 81T Randy Milligan	.20	.10	.02
☐ 82T Mike Moore	.10	.05	.01
☐ 83T Keith Moreland	.05	.02	.00
☐ 84T Mike Morgan	.05	.02	.00
☐ 85T Jamie Moyer	.05	.02	.00
☐ 86T Rob Murphy	.05	.02	.00
☐ 87T Eddie Murray	.15	.07	.01
☐ 88T Pete O'Brien	.10	.05	.01
☐ 89T Gregg Olson	.60	.30	.06
☐ 90T Steve Ontiveros	.05	.02	.00
☐ 91T Jesse Orosco	.05	.02	.00
☐ 92T Spike Owen	.05	.02	.00
☐ 93T Rafael Palmeiro	.15	.07	.01
☐ 94T Clay Parker	.10	.05	.01
☐ 95T Jeff Parrett	.10	.05	.01
☐ 96T Lance Parrish	.10	.05	.01
☐ 97T Dennis Powell	.05	.02	.00
☐ 98T Rey Quinones	.05	.02	.00
☐ 99T Doug Rader MG	.05	.02	.00
☐ 100T Willie Randolph	.10	.05	.01
☐ 101T Shane Rawley	.05	.02	.00
☐ 102T Randy Ready	.05	.02	.00
☐ 103T Bip Roberts	.15	.07	.01
☐ 104T Kenny Rogers	.20	.10	.02
☐ 105T Ed Romero	.05	.02	.00
☐ 106T Nolan Ryan	1.25	.60	.12
☐ 107T Luis Salazar	.05	.02	.00
☐ 108T Juan Samuel	.15	.07	.01
☐ 109T Alex Sanchez	.20	.10	.02
☐ 110T Deion Sanders	.65	.30	.06
☐ 111T Steve Sax	.12	.06	.01
☐ 112T Rick Schu	.05	.02	.00
☐ 113T Dwight Smith	.60	.30	.06
☐ 114T Lonnie Smith	.15	.07	.01
☐ 115T Billy Spiers	.20	.10	.02
☐ 116T Kent Tekulve	.05	.02	.00
☐ 117T Walt Terrell	.05	.02	.00
☐ 118T Milt Thompson	.05	.02	.00
☐ 119T Dickie Thon	.05	.02	.00
☐ 120T Jeff Torborg MG	.05	.02	.00
☐ 121T Jeff Treadway	.05	.02	.00
☐ 122T Omar Vizquel	.15	.07	.01
☐ 123T Jerome Walton	1.50	.75	.15
☐ 124T Gary Ward	.05	.02	.00
☐ 125T Claudell Washington	.10	.05	.01
☐ 126T Curt Wilkerson	.05	.02	.00
☐ 127T Eddie Williams	.05	.02	.00
☐ 128T Frank Williams	.05	.02	.00
☐ 129T Ken Williams	.10	.05	.01
☐ 130T Mitch Williams	.12	.06	.01
☐ 131T Steve Wilson	.12	.06	.01
☐ 132T Checklist 1T-132T	.05	.01	.00

1989-90 Topps Senior League

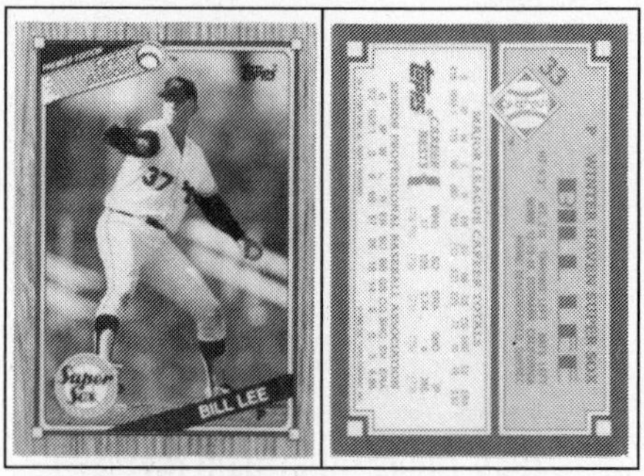

The 1989-90 Topps Senior League baseball set was issued second among the three sets commemorating the first Senior league season. This set was issued in set form in its own box containing all 132 cards, each standard sized (2 1/2" by 3 1/2").

	MINT	EXC	G-VG
COMPLETE SET (132)	8.00	4.00	.80
COMMON PLAYER (1-132)	.07	.03	.01
☐ 1 George Foster	.15	.07	.01
☐ 2 Dwight Lowry	.07	.03	.01
☐ 3 Bob Jones	.07	.03	.01
☐ 4 Clete Boyer	.10	.05	.01
☐ 5 Rafael Landestoy	.07	.03	.01
☐ 6 Bob Shirley	.07	.03	.01
☐ 7 Ivan Murrell	.07	.03	.01
☐ 8 Jerry White	.07	.03	.01
☐ 9 Steve Henderson	.07	.03	.01
☐ 10 Marty Castillo	.07	.03	.01
☐ 11 Bruce Kison	.07	.03	.01
☐ 12 George Hendrick	.10	.05	.01
☐ 13 Bernie Carbo	.07	.03	.01
☐ 14 Jerry Martin	.07	.03	.01
☐ 15 Al Hrabosky	.10	.05	.01
☐ 16 Luis Gomez	.07	.03	.01
☐ 17 Dick Drago	.07	.03	.01
☐ 18 Bobby Ramos	.07	.03	.01
☐ 19 Joe Pittman	.07	.03	.01
☐ 20 Ike Blessitt	.10	.05	.01
☐ 21 Bill Travers	.07	.03	.01
☐ 22 Dick Williams	.10	.05	.01
☐ 23 Randy Lerch	.07	.03	.01
☐ 24 Tom Spencer	.07	.03	.01
☐ 25 Graig Nettles	.20	.10	.02
☐ 26 Jim Gideon	.07	.03	.01
☐ 27 Al Bumbry	.10	.05	.01
☐ 28 Tom Murphy	.07	.03	.01
☐ 29 Rodney Scott	.07	.03	.01
☐ 30 Alan Bannister	.07	.03	.01
☐ 31 John D'Acquisto	.07	.03	.01
☐ 32 Bert Campaneris	.15	.07	.01
☐ 33 Bill Lee	.10	.05	.01
☐ 34 Jerry Grote	.07	.03	.01
☐ 35 Ken Reitz	.07	.03	.01
☐ 36 Al Oliver	.20	.10	.02
☐ 37 Tim Stoddard	.07	.03	.01
☐ 38 Lenny Randle	.07	.03	.01
☐ 39 Rick Manning	.07	.03	.01
☐ 40 Bobby Bonds	.25	.12	.02
☐ 41 Rick Wise	.10	.05	.01
☐ 42 Sal Butera	.07	.03	.01
☐ 43 Ed Figueroa	.07	.03	.01
☐ 44 Ron Washington	.07	.03	.01
☐ 45 Elias Sosa	.07	.03	.01
☐ 46 Dan Driessen	.10	.05	.01
☐ 47 Wayne Nordhagen	.07	.03	.01
☐ 48 Vida Blue	.15	.07	.01
☐ 49 Butch Hobson	.10	.05	.01
☐ 50 Randy Bass	.07	.03	.01
☐ 51 Paul Mirabella	.07	.03	.01
☐ 52 Steve Kemp	.10	.05	.01
☐ 53 Kim Allen	.07	.03	.01
☐ 54 Stan Cliburn	.07	.03	.01
☐ 55 Derrel Thomas	.07	.03	.01
☐ 56 Pete Falcone	.07	.03	.01
☐ 57 Willie Aikens	.10	.05	.01
☐ 58 Toby Harrah	.10	.05	.01

☐ 59 Bob Tolan	.10	.05	.01
☐ 60 Rick Waits	.07	.03	.01
☐ 61 Jim Morrison	.07	.03	.01
☐ 62 Stan Bahnsen	.07	.03	.01
☐ 63 Gene Richards	.07	.03	.01
☐ 64 Dave Cash	.10	.05	.01
☐ 65 Rollie Fingers	.50	.25	.05
☐ 66 Butch Benton	.07	.03	.01
☐ 67 Tim Ireland	.07	.03	.01
☐ 68 Rick Lysander	.07	.03	.01
☐ 69 Cesar Cedeno	.10	.05	.01
☐ 70 Jim Willoughby	.07	.03	.01
☐ 71 Bill Madlock	.15	.07	.01
☐ 72 Lee Lacy	.07	.03	.01
☐ 73 Milt Wilcox	.07	.03	.01
☐ 74 Ron Pruitt	.07	.03	.01
☐ 75 Wayne Krenchicki	.07	.03	.01
☐ 76 Earl Weaver	.15	.07	.01
☐ 77 Pedro Borbon	.07	.03	.01
☐ 78 Jose Cruz	.10	.05	.01
☐ 79 Steve Ontiveros	.07	.03	.01
☐ 80 Mike Easler	.10	.05	.01
☐ 81 Amos Otis	.15	.07	.01
☐ 82 Mickey Mahler	.07	.03	.01
☐ 83 Orlando Gonzalez	.07	.03	.01
☐ 84 Doug Simunic	.07	.03	.01
☐ 85 Felix Millan	.07	.03	.01
☐ 86 Garth Iorg	.07	.03	.01
☐ 87 Pete Broberg	.07	.03	.01
☐ 88 Roy Howell	.07	.03	.01
☐ 89 Dave LaRoche	.07	.03	.01
☐ 90 Jerry Manuel	.07	.03	.01
☐ 91 Tony Scott	.07	.03	.01
☐ 92 Larvell Blanks	.07	.03	.01
☐ 93 Joaquin Andujar	.15	.07	.01
☐ 94 Tito Landrum	.10	.05	.01
☐ 95 Joe Sambito	.07	.03	.01
☐ 96 Pat Dobson	.10	.05	.01
☐ 97 Dan Meyer	.07	.03	.01
☐ 98 Clint Hurdle	.10	.05	.01
☐ 99 Pete LaCock	.07	.03	.01
☐ 100 Bob Galasso	.07	.03	.01
☐ 101 Dave Kingman	.20	.10	.02
☐ 102 Jon Matlack	.10	.05	.01
☐ 103 Larry Harlow	.07	.03	.01
☐ 104 Rick Peterson	.07	.03	.01
☐ 105 Joe Hicks	.07	.03	.01
☐ 106 Bill Campbell	.07	.03	.01
☐ 107 Tom Paciorek	.10	.05	.01
☐ 108 Ray Burris	.10	.05	.01
☐ 109 Ken Landreaux	.07	.03	.01
☐ 110 Steve McCatty	.07	.03	.01
☐ 111 Ron LeFlore	.10	.05	.01
☐ 112 Joe Decker	.07	.03	.01
☐ 113 Leon Roberts	.07	.03	.01
☐ 114 Doug Corbett	.07	.03	.01
☐ 115 Mickey Rivers	.10	.05	.01
☐ 116 Dock Ellis	.07	.03	.01
☐ 117 Ron Jackson	.07	.03	.01
☐ 118 Bob Molinaro	.07	.03	.01
☐ 119 Fergie Jenkins	.75	.35	.07
☐ 120 U.L. Washington	.07	.03	.01
☐ 121 Roy Thomas	.07	.03	.01
☐ 122 Hal McRae	.10	.05	.01
☐ 123 Juan Eichelberger	.07	.03	.01
☐ 124 Gary Rajsich	.07	.03	.01
☐ 125 Dennis Leonard	.10	.05	.01
☐ 126 Walt Williams	.07	.03	.01
☐ 127 Rennie Stennett	.07	.03	.01
☐ 128 Jim Bibby	.07	.03	.01
☐ 129 Dyar Miller	.07	.03	.01
☐ 130 Luis Pujols	.07	.03	.01
☐ 131 Juan Beniquez	.07	.03	.01
☐ 132 Checklist Card	.07	.03	.01

1990 Topps

The 1990 Topps set contains 792 standard-size (2 1/2" by 3 1/2") cards. The front borders are various colors. The horizontally-oriented backs are yellowish green. Cards 385-407 contain the All-Stars. Cards 661-665 contain the Turn Back the Clock cards. The manager cards this year contain information that had been on the backs of the Team Leader cards in the past few years; the Team Leader cards were discontinued, apparently in order to allow better individual player card selection. Topps really concentrated on individual player cards in this set with 725, the most ever in a baseball card set. The checklist cards are oriented alphabetically by team name and player name. The key rookie cards in this set are Juan Gonzalez, Ben McDonald, and Frank Thomas. Topps also produced a specially boxed "glossy" edition frequently referred to as the Topps Tiffany set. This year, again, Topps did not disclose the number of Tiffany sets they produced or sold but it seems that production quantities were roughly similar (approximately 15,000 sets) to the previous year. The checklist of cards is identical to that of the normal non-glossy cards. There are two primary distinguishing features of the Tiffany cards, white card stock reverses and high gloss obverses. These Tiffany cards are valued at approximately four times the values listed below.

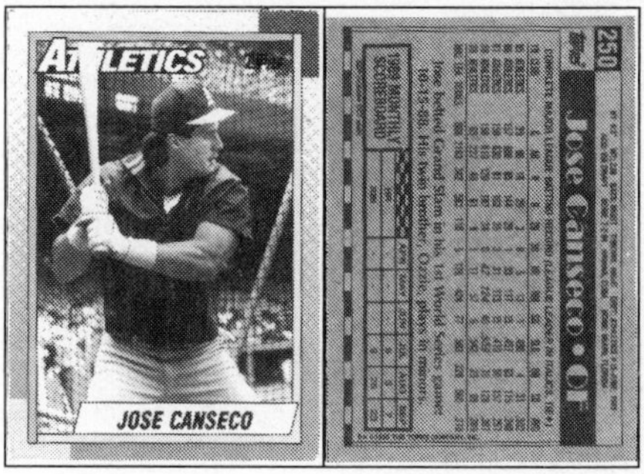

	MINT	EXC	G-VG
COMPLETE SET (792)	23.00	11.50	2.30
COMMON PLAYER (1-792)	.03	.01	.00
☐ 1 Nolan Ryan	.45	.12	.02
☐ 2 Nolan Ryan Salute New York Mets	.20	.10	.02
☐ 3 Nolan Ryan Salute California Angels	.20	.10	.02
☐ 4 Nolan Ryan Salute Houston Astros	.20	.10	.02
☐ 5 Nolan Ryan Salute Texas Rangers UER (says Texas Stadium rather than Arlington Stadium)	.20	.10	.02
☐ 6 Vince Coleman RB (50 consecutive stolen bases)	.08	.04	.01
☐ 7 Rickey Henderson RB (40 career leadoff home runs)	.10	.05	.01
☐ 8 Cal Ripken RB (20 or more homers for 8 consecutive years, record for shortstops)	.08	.04	.01
☐ 9 Eric Plunk	.03	.01	.00
☐ 10 Barry Larkin	.10	.05	.01
☐ 11 Paul Gibson	.03	.01	.00
☐ 12 Joe Girardi	.08	.04	.01
☐ 13 Mark Williamson	.03	.01	.00
☐ 14 Mike Fetters	.12	.06	.01
☐ 15 Teddy Higuera	.06	.03	.00
☐ 16 Kent Anderson	.10	.05	.01
☐ 17 Kelly Downs	.03	.01	.00
☐ 18 Carlos Quintana	.12	.06	.01
☐ 19 Al Newman	.03	.01	.00
☐ 20 Mark Gubicza	.06	.03	.00
☐ 21 Jeff Torborg MG	.03	.01	.00
☐ 22 Bruce Ruffin	.03	.01	.00
☐ 23 Randy Velarde	.03	.01	.00
☐ 24 Joe Hesketh	.03	.01	.00
☐ 25 Willie Randolph	.06	.03	.00
☐ 26 Don Slaught	.03	.01	.00
☐ 27 Rick Leach	.03	.01	.00
☐ 28 Duane Ward	.03	.01	.00
☐ 29 John Cangelosi	.03	.01	.00
☐ 30 David Cone	.08	.04	.01
☐ 31 Henry Cotto	.03	.01	.00
☐ 32 John Farrell	.03	.01	.00
☐ 33 Greg Walker	.03	.01	.00
☐ 34 Tony Fossas	.08	.04	.01

☐ 35 Benito Santiago	.10	.05	.01
☐ 36 John Costello	.03	.01	.00
☐ 37 Domingo Ramos	.03	.01	.00
☐ 38 Wes Gardner	.03	.01	.00
☐ 39 Curt Ford	.03	.01	.00
☐ 40 Jay Howell	.03	.01	.00
☐ 41 Matt Williams	.15	.07	.01
☐ 42 Jeff Robinson	.03	.01	.00
☐ 43 Dante Bichette	.08	.04	.01
☐ 44 Roger Salkeld FDP	.35	.17	.03
☐ 45 Dave Parker UER (born in Jackson, not Calhoun)	.08	.04	.01
☐ 46 Rob Dibble	.06	.03	.00
☐ 47 Brian Harper	.03	.01	.00
☐ 48 Zane Smith	.06	.03	.00
☐ 49 Tom Lawless	.03	.01	.00
☐ 50 Glenn Davis	.10	.05	.01
☐ 51 Doug Rader MG	.03	.01	.00
☐ 52 Jack Daugherty	.12	.06	.01
☐ 53 Mike LaCoss	.03	.01	.00
☐ 54 Joel Skinner	.03	.01	.00
☐ 55 Darrell Evans UER (HR total should be 414, not 424)	.06	.03	.00
☐ 56 Franklin Stubbs	.06	.03	.00
☐ 57 Greg Vaughn	.45	.22	.04
☐ 58 Keith Miller	.03	.01	.00
☐ 59 Ted Power	.03	.01	.00
☐ 60 George Brett	.15	.07	.01
☐ 61 Deion Sanders	.25	.12	.02
☐ 62 Ramon Martinez	.35	.17	.03
☐ 63 Mike Pagliarulo	.03	.01	.00
☐ 64 Danny Darwin	.03	.01	.00
☐ 65 Devon White	.06	.03	.00
☐ 66 Greg Litton	.12	.06	.01
☐ 67 Scott Sanderson	.03	.01	.00
☐ 68 Dave Henderson	.06	.03	.00
☐ 69 Todd Frohwirth	.03	.01	.00
☐ 70 Mike Greenwell	.15	.07	.01
☐ 71 Allan Anderson	.03	.01	.00
☐ 72 Jeff Huson	.10	.05	.01
☐ 73 Bob Milacki	.06	.03	.00
☐ 74 Jeff Jackson FDP	.15	.07	.01
☐ 75 Doug Jones	.06	.03	.00
☐ 76 Dave Valle	.03	.01	.00
☐ 77 Dave Bergman	.03	.01	.00
☐ 78 Mike Flanagan	.03	.01	.00
☐ 79 Ron Kittle	.06	.03	.00
☐ 80 Jeff Russell	.03	.01	.00
☐ 81 Bob Rodgers MG	.03	.01	.00
☐ 82 Scott Terry	.03	.01	.00
☐ 83 Hensley Meulens	.25	.12	.02
☐ 84 Ray Searage	.03	.01	.00
☐ 85 Juan Samuel	.06	.03	.00
☐ 86 Paul Kilgus	.03	.01	.00
☐ 87 Rick Luecken	.10	.05	.01
☐ 88 Glenn Braggs	.03	.01	.00
☐ 89 Clint Zavaras	.12	.06	.01
☐ 90 Jack Clark	.08	.04	.01
☐ 91 Steve Frey	.12	.06	.01
☐ 92 Mike Stanley	.03	.01	.00
☐ 93 Shawn Hillegas	.03	.01	.00
☐ 94 Herm Winningham	.03	.01	.00
☐ 95 Todd Worrell	.06	.03	.00
☐ 96 Jody Reed	.03	.01	.00
☐ 97 Curt Schilling	.08	.04	.01
☐ 98 Jose Gonzalez	.06	.03	.00
☐ 99 Rich Monteleone	.08	.04	.01
☐ 100 Will Clark	.40	.20	.04
☐ 101 Shane Rawley	.03	.01	.00
☐ 102 Stan Javier	.03	.01	.00
☐ 103 Marvin Freeman	.03	.01	.00
☐ 104 Bob Knepper	.03	.01	.00
☐ 105 Randy Myers	.06	.03	.00
☐ 106 Charlie O'Brien	.03	.01	.00
☐ 107 Fred Lynn	.06	.03	.00
☐ 108 Rod Nichols	.03	.01	.00
☐ 109 Roberto Kelly	.08	.04	.01
☐ 110 Tommy Helms MG	.03	.01	.00
☐ 111 Ed Whited	.15	.07	.01
☐ 112 Glenn Wilson	.03	.01	.00
☐ 113 Manny Lee	.03	.01	.00
☐ 114 Mike Bielecki	.03	.01	.00
☐ 115 Tony Pena	.06	.03	.00
☐ 116 Floyd Bannister	.03	.01	.00
☐ 117 Mike Sharperson	.03	.01	.00
☐ 118 Erik Hanson	.15	.07	.01
☐ 119 Billy Hatcher	.06	.03	.00
☐ 120 John Franco	.06	.03	.00
☐ 121 Robin Ventura	.20	.10	.02
☐ 122 Shawn Abner	.03	.01	.00
☐ 123 Rich Gedman	.03	.01	.00
☐ 124 Dave Dravecky	.06	.03	.00
☐ 125 Kent Hrbek	.08	.04	.01
☐ 126 Randy Kramer	.03	.01	.00
☐ 127 Mike Devereaux	.06	.03	.00
☐ 128 Checklist 1	.06	.01	.00
☐ 129 Ron Jones	.06	.03	.00
☐ 130 Bert Blyleven	.08	.04	.01
☐ 131 Matt Nokes	.06	.03	.00
☐ 132 Lance Blankenship	.08	.04	.01
☐ 133 Ricky Horton	.03	.01	.00
☐ 134 Earl Cunningham FDP	.30	.15	.03
☐ 135 Dave Magadan	.08	.04	.01
☐ 136 Kevin Brown	.10	.05	.01
☐ 137 Marty Pevey	.10	.05	.01
☐ 138 Al Leiter	.06	.03	.00
☐ 139 Greg Brock	.03	.01	.00
☐ 140 Andre Dawson	.10	.05	.01
☐ 141 John Hart MG	.03	.01	.00
☐ 142 Jeff Wetherby	.10	.05	.01
☐ 143 Rafael Belliard	.03	.01	.00
☐ 144 Bud Black	.03	.01	.00
☐ 145 Terry Steinbach	.06	.03	.00
☐ 146 Rob Richie	.06	.03	.00
☐ 147 Chuck Finley	.08	.04	.01
☐ 148 Edgar Martinez	.12	.06	.01
☐ 149 Steve Farr	.03	.01	.00
☐ 150 Kirk Gibson	.08	.04	.01
☐ 151 Rick Mahler	.03	.01	.00
☐ 152 Lonnie Smith	.06	.03	.00
☐ 153 Randy Milligan	.10	.05	.01
☐ 154 Mike Maddux	.03	.01	.00
☐ 155 Ellis Burks	.15	.07	.01
☐ 156 Ken Patterson	.03	.01	.00
☐ 157 Craig Biggio	.08	.04	.01
☐ 158 Craig Lefferts	.03	.01	.00
☐ 159 Mike Felder	.03	.01	.00
☐ 160 Dave Righetti	.08	.04	.01
☐ 161 Harold Reynolds	.06	.03	.00
☐ 162 Todd Zeile	.75	.35	.07
☐ 163 Phil Bradley	.06	.03	.00
☐ 164 Jeff Juden FDP	.40	.20	.04
☐ 165 Walt Weiss	.08	.04	.01
☐ 166 Bobby Witt	.08	.04	.01
☐ 167 Kevin Appier	.30	.15	.03
☐ 168 Jose Lind	.03	.01	.00
☐ 169 Richard Dotson	.03	.01	.00
☐ 170 George Bell	.08	.04	.01
☐ 171 Russ Nixon MG	.03	.01	.00
☐ 172 Tom Lampkin	.06	.03	.00
☐ 173 Tim Belcher	.06	.03	.00
☐ 174 Jeff Kunkel	.03	.01	.00
☐ 175 Mike Moore	.06	.03	.00
☐ 176 Luis Quinones	.03	.01	.00
☐ 177 Mike Henneman	.03	.01	.00
☐ 178 Chris James	.06	.03	.00
☐ 179 Brian Holton	.03	.01	.00
☐ 180 Tim Raines	.10	.05	.01
☐ 181 Juan Agosto	.03	.01	.00
☐ 182 Mookie Wilson	.06	.03	.00
☐ 183 Steve Lake	.03	.01	.00
☐ 184 Danny Cox	.03	.01	.00
☐ 185 Ruben Sierra	.15	.07	.01
☐ 186 Dave LaPoint	.03	.01	.00
☐ 187 Rick Wrona	.10	.05	.01
☐ 188 Mike Smithson	.03	.01	.00
☐ 189 Dick Schofield	.03	.01	.00
☐ 190 Rick Reuschel	.06	.03	.00
☐ 191 Pat Borders	.03	.01	.00
☐ 192 Don August	.03	.01	.00
☐ 193 Andy Benes	.15	.07	.01
☐ 194 Glenallen Hill	.15	.07	.01
☐ 195 Tim Burke	.06	.03	.00
☐ 196 Gerald Young	.03	.01	.00
☐ 197 Doug Drabek	.08	.04	.01
☐ 198 Mike Marshall	.08	.04	.01
☐ 199 Sergio Valdez	.12	.06	.01
☐ 200 Don Mattingly	.40	.20	.04
☐ 201 Cito Gaston MG	.06	.03	.00
☐ 202 Mike Macfarlane	.03	.01	.00
☐ 203 Mike Roesler	.12	.06	.01
☐ 204 Bob Dernier	.03	.01	.00
☐ 205 Mark Davis	.08	.04	.01
☐ 206 Nick Esasky	.06	.03	.00
☐ 207 Bob Ojeda	.06	.03	.00
☐ 208 Brook Jacoby	.06	.03	.00
☐ 209 Greg Mathews	.03	.01	.00
☐ 210 Ryne Sandberg	.15	.07	.01
☐ 211 John Cerutti	.03	.01	.00
☐ 212 Joe Orsulak	.03	.01	.00
☐ 213 Scott Bankhead	.06	.03	.00
☐ 214 Terry Francona	.03	.01	.00
☐ 215 Kirk McCaskill	.03	.01	.00
☐ 216 Ricky Jordan	.08	.04	.01
☐ 217 Don Robinson	.03	.01	.00
☐ 218 Wally Backman	.03	.01	.00

☐ 219 Donn Pall	.03	.01	.00
☐ 220 Barry Bonds	.10	.05	.01
☐ 221 Gary Mielke	.10	.05	.01
☐ 222 Kurt Stillwell	.03	.01	.00
☐ 223 Tommy Gregg	.06	.03	.00
☐ 224 Delino DeShields	.60	.30	.06
☐ 225 Jim Deshaies	.03	.01	.00
☐ 226 Mickey Hatcher	.03	.01	.00
☐ 227 Kevin Tapani	.30	.15	.03
☐ 228 Dave Martinez	.03	.01	.00
☐ 229 David Wells	.03	.01	.00
☐ 230 Keith Hernandez	.08	.04	.01
☐ 231 Jack McKeon MG	.03	.01	.00
☐ 232 Darnell Coles	.03	.01	.00
☐ 233 Ken Hill	.08	.04	.01
☐ 234 Mariano Duncan	.06	.03	.00
☐ 235 Jeff Reardon	.06	.03	.00
☐ 236 Hal Morris	.40	.20	.04
☐ 237 Kevin Ritz	.10	.05	.01
☐ 238 Felix Jose	.12	.06	.01
☐ 239 Eric Show	.03	.01	.00
☐ 240 Mark Grace	.25	.12	.02
☐ 241 Mike Krukow	.03	.01	.00
☐ 242 Fred Manrique	.03	.01	.00
☐ 243 Barry Jones	.03	.01	.00
☐ 244 Bill Schroeder	.03	.01	.00
☐ 245 Roger Clemens	.20	.10	.02
☐ 246 Jim Eisenreich	.03	.01	.00
☐ 247 Jerry Reed	.03	.01	.00
☐ 248 Dave Anderson	.03	.01	.00
☐ 249 Mike Smith	.10	.05	.01
☐ 250 Jose Canseco	.50	.25	.05
☐ 251 Jeff Blauser	.03	.01	.00
☐ 252 Otis Nixon	.03	.01	.00
☐ 253 Mark Portugal	.03	.01	.00
☐ 254 Francisco Cabrera	.20	.10	.02
☐ 255 Bobby Thigpen	.08	.04	.01
☐ 256 Marvell Wynne	.03	.01	.00
☐ 257 Jose DeLeon	.03	.01	.00
☐ 258 Barry Lyons	.03	.01	.00
☐ 259 Lance McCullers	.03	.01	.00
☐ 260 Eric Davis	.15	.07	.01
☐ 261 Whitey Herzog MG	.03	.01	.00
☐ 262 Checklist 2	.06	.01	.00
☐ 263 Mel Stottlemyre Jr.	.10	.05	.01
☐ 264 Bryan Clutterbuck	.03	.01	.00
☐ 265 Pete O'Brien	.06	.03	.00
☐ 266 German Gonzalez	.03	.01	.00
☐ 267 Mark Davidson	.03	.01	.00
☐ 268 Rob Murphy	.03	.01	.00
☐ 269 Dickie Thon	.03	.01	.00
☐ 270 Dave Stewart	.10	.05	.01
☐ 271 Chet Lemon	.03	.01	.00
☐ 272 Bryan Harvey	.03	.01	.00
☐ 273 Bobby Bonilla	.15	.07	.01
☐ 274 Mauro Gozzo	.12	.06	.01
☐ 275 Mickey Tettleton	.06	.03	.00
☐ 276 Gary Thurman	.03	.01	.00
☐ 277 Lenny Harris	.08	.04	.01
☐ 278 Pascual Perez	.06	.03	.00
☐ 279 Steve Buechele	.03	.01	.00
☐ 280 Lou Whitaker	.08	.04	.01
☐ 281 Kevin Bass	.06	.03	.00
☐ 282 Derek Lilliquist	.06	.03	.00
☐ 283 Joey Belle	.20	.10	.02
☐ 284 Mark Gardner	.18	.09	.01
☐ 285 Willie McGee	.08	.04	.01
☐ 286 Lee Guetterman	.03	.01	.00
☐ 287 Vance Law	.03	.01	.00
☐ 288 Greg Briley	.12	.06	.01
☐ 289 Norm Charlton	.06	.03	.00
☐ 290 Robin Yount	.15	.07	.01
☐ 291 Dave Johnson MG	.03	.01	.00
☐ 292 Jim Gott	.03	.01	.00
☐ 293 Mike Gallego	.03	.01	.00
☐ 294 Craig McMurtry	.03	.01	.00
☐ 295 Fred McGriff	.12	.06	.01
☐ 296 Jeff Ballard	.03	.01	.00
☐ 297 Tommy Herr	.06	.03	.00
☐ 298 Dan Gladden	.03	.01	.00
☐ 299 Adam Peterson	.06	.03	.00
☐ 300 Bo Jackson	.60	.30	.06
☐ 301 Don Aase	.03	.01	.00
☐ 302 Marcus Lawton	.20	.10	.02
☐ 303 Rick Cerone	.03	.01	.00
☐ 304 Marty Clary	.03	.01	.00
☐ 305 Eddie Murray	.12	.06	.01
☐ 306 Tom Niedenfuer	.03	.01	.00
☐ 307 Bip Roberts	.06	.03	.00
☐ 308 Jose Guzman	.03	.01	.00
☐ 309 Eric Yelding	.20	.10	.02
☐ 310 Steve Bedrosian	.06	.03	.00
☐ 311 Dwight Smith	.15	.07	.01
☐ 312 Dan Quisenberry	.06	.03	.00
☐ 313 Gus Polidor	.03	.01	.00
☐ 314 Donald Harris FDP	.18	.09	.01
☐ 315 Bruce Hurst	.06	.03	.00
☐ 316 Carney Lansford	.08	.04	.01
☐ 317 Mark Guthrie	.12	.06	.01
☐ 318 Wallace Johnson	.03	.01	.00
☐ 319 Dion James	.03	.01	.00
☐ 320 Dave Stieb	.08	.04	.01
☐ 321 Joe Morgan MG	.03	.01	.00
☐ 322 Junior Ortiz	.03	.01	.00
☐ 323 Willie Wilson	.06	.03	.00
☐ 324 Pete Harnisch	.06	.03	.00
☐ 325 Robby Thompson	.03	.01	.00
☐ 326 Tom McCarthy	.08	.04	.01
☐ 327 Ken Williams	.03	.01	.00
☐ 328 Curt Young	.03	.01	.00
☐ 329 Oddibe McDowell	.06	.03	.00
☐ 330 Ron Darling	.08	.04	.01
☐ 331 Juan Gonzalez	1.00	.50	.10
☐ 332 Paul O'Neill	.08	.04	.01
☐ 333 Bill Wegman	.03	.01	.00
☐ 334 Johnny Ray	.03	.01	.00
☐ 335 Andy Hawkins	.03	.01	.00
☐ 336 Ken Griffey Jr.	2.25	1.10	.22
☐ 337 Lloyd McClendon	.03	.01	.00
☐ 338 Dennis Lamp	.03	.01	.00
☐ 339 Dave Clark	.03	.01	.00
☐ 340 Fernando Valenzuela	.08	.04	.01
☐ 341 Tom Foley	.03	.01	.00
☐ 342 Alex Trevino	.03	.01	.00
☐ 343 Frank Tanana	.03	.01	.00
☐ 344 George Canale	.12	.06	.01
☐ 345 Harold Baines	.08	.04	.01
☐ 346 Jim Presley	.03	.01	.00
☐ 347 Junior Felix	.30	.15	.03
☐ 348 Gary Wayne	.10	.05	.01
☐ 349 Steve Finley	.12	.06	.01
☐ 350 Bret Saberhagen	.10	.05	.01
☐ 351 Roger Craig MG	.03	.01	.00
☐ 352 Bryn Smith	.03	.01	.00
☐ 353 Sandy Alomar Jr. (not listed as Jr. on card front)	.30	.15	.03
☐ 354 Stan Belinda	.12	.06	.01
☐ 355 Marty Barrett	.03	.01	.00
☐ 356 Randy Ready	.03	.01	.00
☐ 357 Dave West	.06	.03	.00
☐ 358 Andres Thomas	.03	.01	.00
☐ 359 Jimmy Jones	.03	.01	.00
☐ 360 Paul Molitor	.08	.04	.01
☐ 361 Randy McCament	.08	.04	.01
☐ 362 Damon Berryhill	.06	.03	.00
☐ 363 Dan Petry	.03	.01	.00
☐ 364 Rolando Roomes	.08	.04	.01
☐ 365 Ozzie Guillen	.08	.04	.01
☐ 366 Mike Heath	.03	.01	.00
☐ 367 Mike Morgan	.03	.01	.00
☐ 368 Bill Doran	.06	.03	.00
☐ 369 Todd Burns	.03	.01	.00
☐ 370 Tim Wallach	.06	.03	.00
☐ 371 Jimmy Key	.06	.03	.00
☐ 372 Terry Kennedy	.03	.01	.00
☐ 373 Alvin Davis	.08	.04	.01
☐ 374 Steve Cummings	.10	.05	.01
☐ 375 Dwight Evans	.08	.04	.01
☐ 376 Checklist 3 UER (Higuera misalphabet-ized in Brewer list)	.06	.01	.00
☐ 377 Mickey Weston	.10	.05	.01
☐ 378 Luis Salazar	.03	.01	.00
☐ 379 Steve Rosenberg	.03	.01	.00
☐ 380 Dave Winfield	.10	.05	.01
☐ 381 Frank Robinson MG	.08	.04	.01
☐ 382 Jeff Musselman	.03	.01	.00
☐ 383 John Morris	.03	.01	.00
☐ 384 Pat Combs	.10	.05	.01
☐ 385 Fred McGriff AS	.08	.04	.01
☐ 386 Julio Franco AS	.06	.03	.00
☐ 387 Wade Boggs AS	.12	.06	.01
☐ 388 Cal Ripken AS	.10	.05	.01
☐ 389 Robin Yount AS	.12	.06	.01
☐ 390 Ruben Sierra AS	.12	.06	.01
☐ 391 Kirby Puckett AS	.12	.06	.01
☐ 392 Carlton Fisk AS	.08	.04	.01
☐ 393 Bret Saberhagen AS	.08	.04	.01
☐ 394 Jeff Ballard AS	.06	.03	.00
☐ 395 Jeff Russell AS	.06	.03	.00
☐ 396 A.Bartlett Giamatti (commemorative)	.25	.12	.02
☐ 397 Will Clark AS	.15	.07	.01
☐ 398 Ryne Sandberg AS	.12	.06	.01
☐ 399 Howard Johnson AS	.08	.04	.01
☐ 400 Ozzie Smith AS	.08	.04	.01
☐ 401 Kevin Mitchell AS	.10	.05	.01

☐ 402	Eric Davis AS	.12	.06	.01
☐ 403	Tony Gwynn AS	.10	.05	.01
☐ 404	Craig Biggio AS	.06	.03	.00
☐ 405	Mike Scott AS	.06	.03	.00
☐ 406	Joe Magrane AS	.06	.03	.00
☐ 407	Mark Davis AS	.06	.03	.00
☐ 408	Trevor Wilson	.06	.03	.00
☐ 409	Tom Brunansky	.08	.04	.01
☐ 410	Joe Boever	.03	.01	.00
☐ 411	Ken Phelps	.03	.01	.00
☐ 412	Jamie Moyer	.03	.01	.00
☐ 413	Brian Dubois	.10	.05	.01
☐ 414	Frank Thomas FDP	1.35	.65	.13
☐ 415	Shawon Dunston	.10	.05	.01
☐ 416	Dave Johnson (P)	.12	.06	.01
☐ 417	Jim Gantner	.03	.01	.00
☐ 418	Tom Browning	.06	.03	.00
☐ 419	Beau Allred	.15	.07	.01
☐ 420	Carlton Fisk	.10	.05	.01
☐ 421	Greg Minton	.03	.01	.00
☐ 422	Pat Sheridan	.03	.01	.00
☐ 423	Fred Toliver	.03	.01	.00
☐ 424	Jerry Reuss	.03	.01	.00
☐ 425	Bill Landrum	.03	.01	.00
☐ 426	Jeff Hamilton	.03	.01	.00
☐ 427	Carmen Castillo	.03	.01	.00
☐ 428	Steve Davis	.10	.05	.01
☐ 429	Tom Kelly MG	.03	.01	.00
☐ 430	Pete Incaviglia	.06	.03	.00
☐ 431	Randy Johnson	.06	.03	.00
☐ 432	Damaso Garcia	.03	.01	.00
☐ 433	Steve Olin	.10	.05	.01
☐ 434	Mark Carreon	.06	.03	.00
☐ 435	Kevin Seitzer	.08	.04	.01
☐ 436	Mel Hall	.06	.03	.00
☐ 437	Les Lancaster	.03	.01	.00
☐ 438	Greg Myers	.06	.03	.00
☐ 439	Jeff Parrett	.03	.01	.00
☐ 440	Alan Trammell	.08	.04	.01
☐ 441	Bob Kipper	.03	.01	.00
☐ 442	Jerry Browne	.03	.01	.00
☐ 443	Cris Carpenter	.03	.01	.00
☐ 444	Kyle Abbott FDP	.20	.10	.02
☐ 445	Danny Jackson	.06	.03	.00
☐ 446	Dan Pasqua	.03	.01	.00
☐ 447	Atlee Hammaker	.03	.01	.00
☐ 448	Greg Gagne	.03	.01	.00
☐ 449	Dennis Rasmussen	.03	.01	.00
☐ 450	Rickey Henderson	.20	.10	.02
☐ 451	Mark Lemke	.03	.01	.00
☐ 452	Luis De Los Santos	.06	.03	.00
☐ 453	Jody Davis	.03	.01	.00
☐ 454	Jeff King	.10	.05	.01
☐ 455	Jeffrey Leonard	.06	.03	.00
☐ 456	Chris Gwynn	.06	.03	.00
☐ 457	Gregg Jefferies	.25	.12	.02
☐ 458	Bob McClure	.03	.01	.00
☐ 459	Jim Lefebvre MG	.03	.01	.00
☐ 460	Mike Scott	.08	.04	.01
☐ 461	Carlos Martinez	.10	.05	.01
☐ 462	Denny Walling	.03	.01	.00
☐ 463	Drew Hall	.03	.01	.00
☐ 464	Jerome Walton	.35	.17	.03
☐ 465	Kevin Gross	.03	.01	.00
☐ 466	Rance Mulliniks	.03	.01	.00
☐ 467	Juan Nieves	.03	.01	.00
☐ 468	Bill Ripken	.03	.01	.00
☐ 469	John Kruk	.03	.01	.00
☐ 470	Frank Viola	.08	.04	.01
☐ 471	Mike Brumley	.06	.03	.00
☐ 472	Jose Uribe	.03	.01	.00
☐ 473	Joe Price	.03	.01	.00
☐ 474	Rich Thompson	.03	.01	.00
☐ 475	Bob Welch	.08	.04	.01
☐ 476	Brad Komminsk	.03	.01	.00
☐ 477	Willie Fraser	.03	.01	.00
☐ 478	Mike LaValliere	.03	.01	.00
☐ 479	Frank White	.06	.03	.00
☐ 480	Sid Fernandez	.06	.03	.00
☐ 481	Garry Templeton	.06	.03	.00
☐ 482	Steve Carter	.10	.05	.01
☐ 483	Alejandro Pena	.03	.01	.00
☐ 484	Mike Fitzgerald	.03	.01	.00
☐ 485	John Candelaria	.03	.01	.00
☐ 486	Jeff Treadway	.03	.01	.00
☐ 487	Steve Searcy	.03	.01	.00
☐ 488	Ken Oberkfell	.03	.01	.00
☐ 489	Nick Leyva MG	.03	.01	.00
☐ 490	Dan Plesac	.03	.01	.00
☐ 491	Dave Cochrane	.12	.06	.01
☐ 492	Ron Oester	.03	.01	.00
☐ 493	Jason Grimsley	.12	.06	.01
☐ 494	Terry Puhl	.03	.01	.00
☐ 495	Lee Smith	.06	.03	.00
☐ 496	Cecil Espy UER ('89 stats have 3 SB's, should be 33)	.03	.01	.00
☐ 497	Dave Schmidt	.03	.01	.00
☐ 498	Rick Schu	.03	.01	.00
☐ 499	Bill Long	.03	.01	.00
☐ 500	Kevin Mitchell	.20	.10	.02
☐ 501	Matt Young	.03	.01	.00
☐ 502	Mitch Webster	.03	.01	.00
☐ 503	Randy St.Claire	.03	.01	.00
☐ 504	Tom O'Malley	.03	.01	.00
☐ 505	Kelly Gruber	.12	.06	.01
☐ 506	Tom Glavine	.06	.03	.00
☐ 507	Gary Redus	.03	.01	.00
☐ 508	Terry Leach	.03	.01	.00
☐ 509	Tom Pagnozzi	.03	.01	.00
☐ 510	Dwight Gooden	.18	.09	.01
☐ 511	Clay Parker	.06	.03	.00
☐ 512	Gary Pettis	.03	.01	.00
☐ 513	Mark Eichhorn	.03	.01	.00
☐ 514	Andy Allanson	.03	.01	.00
☐ 515	Len Dykstra	.10	.05	.01
☐ 516	Tim Leary	.06	.03	.00
☐ 517	Roberto Alomar	.10	.05	.01
☐ 518	Bill Krueger	.03	.01	.00
☐ 519	Bucky Dent MG	.06	.03	.00
☐ 520	Mitch Williams	.03	.01	.00
☐ 521	Craig Worthington	.06	.03	.00
☐ 522	Mike Dunne	.03	.01	.00
☐ 523	Jay Bell	.03	.01	.00
☐ 524	Daryl Boston	.06	.03	.00
☐ 525	Wally Joyner	.08	.04	.01
☐ 526	Checklist 4	.06	.01	.00
☐ 527	Ron Hassey	.03	.01	.00
☐ 528	Kevin Wickander	.08	.04	.01
☐ 529	Greg Harris	.03	.01	.00
☐ 530	Mark Langston	.08	.04	.01
☐ 531	Ken Caminiti	.03	.01	.00
☐ 532	Cecilio Guante	.03	.01	.00
☐ 533	Tim Jones	.03	.01	.00
☐ 534	Louie Meadows	.03	.01	.00
☐ 535	John Smoltz	.08	.04	.01
☐ 536	Bob Geren	.08	.04	.01
☐ 537	Mark Grant	.03	.01	.00
☐ 538	Bill Spiers UER (photo actually George Canale)	.12	.06	.01
☐ 539	Neal Heaton	.03	.01	.00
☐ 540	Danny Tartabull	.08	.04	.01
☐ 541	Pat Perry	.03	.01	.00
☐ 542	Darren Daulton	.06	.03	.00
☐ 543	Nelson Liriano	.03	.01	.00
☐ 544	Dennis Boyd	.03	.01	.00
☐ 545	Kevin McReynolds	.08	.04	.01
☐ 546	Kevin Hickey	.03	.01	.00
☐ 547	Jack Howell	.03	.01	.00
☐ 548	Pat Clements	.03	.01	.00
☐ 549	Don Zimmer MG	.03	.01	.00
☐ 550	Julio Franco	.06	.03	.00
☐ 551	Tim Crews	.03	.01	.00
☐ 552	Mike Smith	.10	.05	.01
☐ 553	Scott Scudder	.15	.07	.01
☐ 554	Jay Buhner	.06	.03	.00
☐ 555	Jack Morris	.08	.04	.01
☐ 556	Gene Larkin	.03	.01	.00
☐ 557	Jeff Innis	.10	.05	.01
☐ 558	Rafael Ramirez	.03	.01	.00
☐ 559	Andy McGaffigan	.03	.01	.00
☐ 560	Steve Sax	.08	.04	.01
☐ 561	Ken Dayley	.03	.01	.00
☐ 562	Chad Kreuter	.03	.01	.00
☐ 563	Alex Sanchez	.08	.04	.01
☐ 564	Tyler Houston FDP	.25	.12	.02
☐ 565	Scott Fletcher	.03	.01	.00
☐ 566	Mark Knudson	.03	.01	.00
☐ 567	Ron Gant	.15	.07	.01
☐ 568	John Smiley	.03	.01	.00
☐ 569	Ivan Calderon	.06	.03	.00
☐ 570	Cal Ripken	.15	.07	.01
☐ 571	Brett Butler	.06	.03	.00
☐ 572	Greg Harris	.03	.01	.00
☐ 573	Danny Heep	.03	.01	.00
☐ 574	Bill Swift	.03	.01	.00
☐ 575	Lance Parrish	.08	.04	.01
☐ 576	Mike Dyer	.12	.06	.01
☐ 577	Charlie Hayes	.08	.04	.01
☐ 578	Joe Magrane	.06	.03	.00
☐ 579	Art Howe MG	.03	.01	.00
☐ 580	Joe Carter	.10	.05	.01
☐ 581	Ken Griffey Sr.	.08	.04	.01
☐ 582	Rick Honeycutt	.03	.01	.00
☐ 583	Bruce Benedict	.03	.01	.00
☐ 584	Phil Stephenson	.12	.06	.01
☐ 585	Kal Daniels	.08	.04	.01

☐ 586	Edwin Nunez	.03	.01	.00
☐ 587	Lance Johnson	.03	.01	.00
☐ 588	Rick Rhoden	.03	.01	.00
☐ 589	Mike Aldrete	.03	.01	.00
☐ 590	Ozzie Smith	.08	.04	.01
☐ 591	Todd Stottlemyre	.06	.03	.00
☐ 592	R.J. Reynolds	.03	.01	.00
☐ 593	Scott Bradley	.03	.01	.00
☐ 594	Luis Sojo	.15	.07	.01
☐ 595	Greg Swindell	.08	.04	.01
☐ 596	Jose DeJesus	.03	.01	.00
☐ 597	Chris Bosio	.03	.01	.00
☐ 598	Brady Anderson	.03	.01	.00
☐ 599	Frank Williams	.03	.01	.00
☐ 600	Darryl Strawberry	.20	.10	.02
☐ 601	Luis Rivera	.03	.01	.00
☐ 602	Scott Garrelts	.03	.01	.00
☐ 603	Tony Armas	.03	.01	.00
☐ 604	Ron Robinson	.03	.01	.00
☐ 605	Mike Scioscia	.03	.01	.00
☐ 606	Storm Davis	.06	.03	.00
☐ 607	Steve Jeltz	.03	.01	.00
☐ 608	Eric Anthony	.60	.30	.06
☐ 609	Sparky Anderson MG	.06	.03	.00
☐ 610	Pedro Guerrero	.08	.04	.01
☐ 611	Walt Terrell	.03	.01	.00
☐ 612	Dave Gallagher	.03	.01	.00
☐ 613	Jeff Pico	.03	.01	.00
☐ 614	Nelson Santovenia	.03	.01	.00
☐ 615	Rob Deer	.06	.03	.00
☐ 616	Brian Holman	.10	.05	.01
☐ 617	Geronimo Berroa	.06	.03	.00
☐ 618	Ed Whitson	.03	.01	.00
☐ 619	Rob Ducey	.03	.01	.00
☐ 620	Tony Castillo	.06	.03	.00
☐ 621	Melido Perez	.06	.03	.00
☐ 622	Sid Bream	.03	.01	.00
☐ 623	Jim Corsi	.03	.01	.00
☐ 624	Darrin Jackson	.03	.01	.00
☐ 625	Roger McDowell	.06	.03	.00
☐ 626	Bob Melvin	.03	.01	.00
☐ 627	Jose Rijo	.06	.03	.00
☐ 628	Candy Maldonado	.06	.03	.00
☐ 629	Eric Hetzel	.06	.03	.00
☐ 630	Gary Gaetti	.08	.04	.01
☐ 631	John Wetteland	.12	.06	.01
☐ 632	Scott Lusader	.03	.01	.00
☐ 633	Dennis Cook	.10	.05	.01
☐ 634	Luis Polonia	.03	.01	.00
☐ 635	Brian Downing	.03	.01	.00
☐ 636	Jesse Orosco	.03	.01	.00
☐ 637	Craig Reynolds	.03	.01	.00
☐ 638	Jeff Montgomery	.06	.03	.00
☐ 639	Tony LaRussa MG	.06	.03	.00
☐ 640	Rick Sutcliffe	.06	.03	.00
☐ 641	Doug Strange	.10	.05	.01
☐ 642	Jack Armstrong	.08	.04	.01
☐ 643	Alfredo Griffin	.03	.01	.00
☐ 644	Paul Assenmacher	.03	.01	.00
☐ 645	Jose Oquendo	.03	.01	.00
☐ 646	Checklist 5	.06	.01	.00
☐ 647	Rex Hudler	.03	.01	.00
☐ 648	Jim Clancy	.03	.01	.00
☐ 649	Dan Murphy	.12	.06	.01
☐ 650	Mike Witt	.03	.01	.00
☐ 651	Rafael Santana	.03	.01	.00
☐ 652	Mike Boddicker	.03	.01	.00
☐ 653	John Moses	.03	.01	.00
☐ 654	Paul Coleman FDP	.30	.15	.03
☐ 655	Gregg Olson	.20	.10	.02
☐ 656	Mackey Sasser	.06	.03	.00
☐ 657	Terry Mulholland	.03	.01	.00
☐ 658	Donell Nixon	.03	.01	.00
☐ 659	Greg Cadaret	.03	.01	.00
☐ 660	Vince Coleman	.08	.04	.01
☐ 661	Dick Howser TBC'85 UER (Seaver's 300th on 7/11/85, should be 8/4/85)	.03	.01	.00
☐ 662	Mike Schmidt TBC'80	.12	.06	.01
☐ 663	Fred Lynn TBC'75	.06	.03	.00
☐ 664	Johnny Bench TBC'70	.10	.05	.01
☐ 665	Sandy Koufax TBC'65	.10	.05	.01
☐ 666	Brian Fisher	.03	.01	.00
☐ 667	Curt Wilkerson	.03	.01	.00
☐ 668	Joe Oliver	.15	.07	.01
☐ 669	Tom Lasorda MG	.06	.03	.00
☐ 670	Dennis Eckersley	.10	.05	.01
☐ 671	Bob Boone	.06	.03	.00
☐ 672	Roy Smith	.03	.01	.00
☐ 673	Joey Meyer	.03	.01	.00
☐ 674	Spike Owen	.03	.01	.00
☐ 675	Jim Abbott	.25	.12	.02
☐ 676	Randy Kutcher	.03	.01	.00
☐ 677	Jay Tibbs	.03	.01	.00
☐ 678	Kirt Manwaring	.03	.01	.00
☐ 679	Gary Ward	.03	.01	.00
☐ 680	Howard Johnson	.08	.04	.01
☐ 681	Mike Schooler	.06	.03	.00
☐ 682	Dann Bilardello	.03	.01	.00
☐ 683	Kenny Rogers	.10	.05	.01
☐ 684	Julio Machado	.10	.05	.01
☐ 685	Tony Fernandez	.08	.04	.01
☐ 686	Carmelo Martinez	.03	.01	.00
☐ 687	Tim Birtsas	.03	.01	.00
☐ 688	Milt Thompson	.03	.01	.00
☐ 689	Rich Yett	.03	.01	.00
☐ 690	Mark McGwire	.25	.12	.02
☐ 691	Chuck Cary	.03	.01	.00
☐ 692	Sammy Sosa	.35	.17	.03
☐ 693	Calvin Schiraldi	.03	.01	.00
☐ 694	Mike Stanton	.12	.06	.01
☐ 695	Tom Henke	.06	.03	.00
☐ 696	B.J. Surhoff	.06	.03	.00
☐ 697	Mike Davis	.03	.01	.00
☐ 698	Omar Vizquel	.08	.04	.01
☐ 699	Jim Leyland MG	.03	.01	.00
☐ 700	Kirby Puckett	.20	.10	.02
☐ 701	Bernie Williams	.30	.15	.03
☐ 702	Tony Phillips	.03	.01	.00
☐ 703	Jeff Brantley	.12	.06	.01
☐ 704	Chip Hale	.10	.05	.01
☐ 705	Claudell Washington	.06	.03	.00
☐ 706	Geno Petralli	.03	.01	.00
☐ 707	Luis Aquino	.03	.01	.00
☐ 708	Larry Sheets	.03	.01	.00
☐ 709	Juan Berenguer	.03	.01	.00
☐ 710	Von Hayes	.08	.04	.01
☐ 711	Rick Aguilera	.03	.01	.00
☐ 712	Todd Benzinger	.03	.01	.00
☐ 713	Tim Drummond	.10	.05	.01
☐ 714	Marquis Grissom	.35	.17	.03
☐ 715	Greg Maddux	.06	.03	.00
☐ 716	Steve Balboni	.03	.01	.00
☐ 717	Ron Karkovice	.03	.01	.00
☐ 718	Gary Sheffield	.25	.12	.02
☐ 719	Wally Whitehurst	.10	.05	.01
☐ 720	Andres Galarraga	.08	.04	.01
☐ 721	Lee Mazzilli	.03	.01	.00
☐ 722	Felix Fermin	.03	.01	.00
☐ 723	Jeff Robinson	.03	.01	.00
☐ 724	Juan Bell	.12	.06	.01
☐ 725	Terry Pendleton	.03	.01	.00
☐ 726	Gene Nelson	.03	.01	.00
☐ 727	Pat Tabler	.03	.01	.00
☐ 728	Jim Acker	.03	.01	.00
☐ 729	Bobby Valentine MG	.03	.01	.00
☐ 730	Tony Gwynn	.15	.07	.01
☐ 731	Don Carman	.03	.01	.00
☐ 732	Ernest Riles	.03	.01	.00
☐ 733	John Dopson	.06	.03	.00
☐ 734	Kevin Elster	.06	.03	.00
☐ 735	Charlie Hough	.03	.01	.00
☐ 736	Rick Dempsey	.03	.01	.00
☐ 737	Chris Sabo	.15	.07	.01
☐ 738	Gene Harris	.10	.05	.01
☐ 739	Dale Sveum	.03	.01	.00
☐ 740	Jesse Barfield	.08	.04	.01
☐ 741	Steve Wilson	.08	.04	.01
☐ 742	Ernie Whitt	.03	.01	.00
☐ 743	Tom Candiotti	.03	.01	.00
☐ 744	Kelly Mann	.12	.06	.01
☐ 745	Hubie Brooks	.06	.03	.00
☐ 746	Dave Smith	.03	.01	.00
☐ 747	Randy Bush	.03	.01	.00
☐ 748	Doyle Alexander	.03	.01	.00
☐ 749	Mark Parent	.03	.01	.00
☐ 750	Dale Murphy	.12	.06	.01
☐ 751	Steve Lyons	.03	.01	.00
☐ 752	Tom Gordon	.15	.07	.01
☐ 753	Chris Speier	.03	.01	.00
☐ 754	Bob Walk	.03	.01	.00
☐ 755	Rafael Palmeiro	.12	.06	.01
☐ 756	Ken Howell	.03	.01	.00
☐ 757	Larry Walker	.35	.17	.03
☐ 758	Mark Thurmond	.03	.01	.00
☐ 759	Tom Trebelhorn MG	.03	.01	.00
☐ 760	Wade Boggs	.20	.10	.02
☐ 761	Mike Jackson	.03	.01	.00
☐ 762	Doug Dascenzo	.03	.01	.00
☐ 763	Dennis Martinez	.03	.01	.00
☐ 764	Tim Teufel	.03	.01	.00
☐ 765	Chili Davis	.06	.03	.00
☐ 766	Brian Meyer	.08	.04	.01
☐ 767	Tracy Jones	.03	.01	.00
☐ 768	Chuck Crim	.03	.01	.00
☐ 769	Greg Hibbard	.15	.07	.01
☐ 770	Cory Snyder	.08	.04	.01

☐ 771 Pete Smith	.03	.01	.00
☐ 772 Jeff Reed	.03	.01	.00
☐ 773 Dave Leiper	.03	.01	.00
☐ 774 Ben McDonald	1.25	.60	.12
☐ 775 Andy Van Slyke	.08	.04	.01
☐ 776 Charlie Leibrandt	.03	.01	.00
☐ 777 Tim Laudner	.03	.01	.00
☐ 778 Mike Jeffcoat	.03	.01	.00
☐ 779 Lloyd Moseby	.06	.03	.00
☐ 780 Orel Hershiser	.08	.04	.01
☐ 781 Mario Diaz	.03	.01	.00
☐ 782 Jose Alvarez	.03	.01	.00
☐ 783 Checklist 6	.06	.01	.00
☐ 784 Scott Bailes	.03	.01	.00
☐ 785 Jim Rice	.08	.04	.01
☐ 786 Eric King	.03	.01	.00
☐ 787 Rene Gonzales	.03	.01	.00
☐ 788 Frank DiPino	.03	.01	.00
☐ 789 John Wathan MG	.03	.01	.00
☐ 790 Gary Carter	.08	.04	.01
☐ 791 Alvaro Espinoza	.03	.01	.00
☐ 792 Gerald Perry	.06	.03	.00

1990 Topps Wax Box Cards

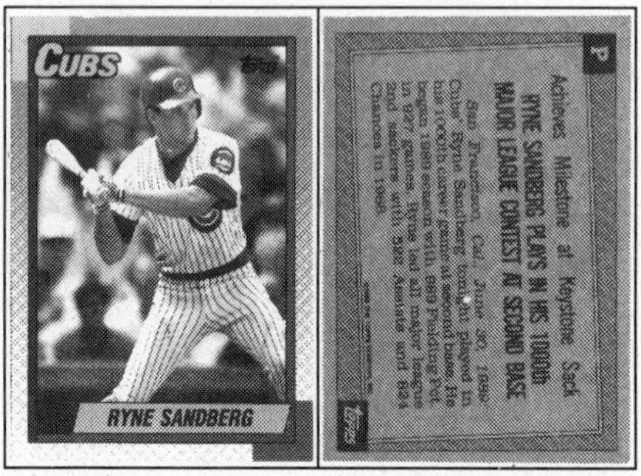

The 1990 Topps wax box cards comprise four different box bottoms with four cards each, for a total of 16 standard-size (2 1/2" by 3 1/2") cards. The front borders are green. The vertically-oriented backs are yellowish green. These cards depict various career milestones achieved during the 1989 season. The card numbers are actually the letters A through P.

	MINT	EXC	G-VG
COMPLETE SET (16)	4.50	2.25	.45
COMMON PLAYER (A-P)	.10	.05	.01
☐ A Wade Boggs	.45	.22	.04
☐ B George Brett	.40	.20	.04
☐ C Andre Dawson	.25	.12	.02
☐ D Darrell Evans	.15	.07	.01
☐ E Dwight Gooden	.35	.17	.03
☐ F Rickey Henderson	.60	.30	.06
☐ G Tom Lasorda MG	.10	.05	.01
☐ H Fred Lynn	.15	.07	.01
☐ I Mark McGwire	.45	.22	.04
☐ J Dave Parker	.20	.10	.02
☐ K Jeff Reardon	.15	.07	.01
☐ L Rick Reuschel	.15	.07	.01
☐ M Jim Rice	.20	.10	.02
☐ N Cal Ripken	.30	.15	.03
☐ O Nolan Ryan	.60	.30	.06
☐ P Ryne Sandberg	.45	.22	.04

1990 Topps Glossy All-Stars 22

The 1990 Topps Glossy All-Star set contains 22 standard-size (2 1/2" by 3 1/2") glossy cards. The front and back borders are white, and other design elements are red, blue and yellow. This set is almost identical to previous year sets of the same name. One card was included in each 1990 Topps rack pack.

	MINT	EXC	G-VG
COMPLETE SET (22)	3.00	1.50	.30
COMMON PLAYER (1-22)	.10	.05	.01
☐ 1 Tom Lasorda MG	.10	.05	.01
☐ 2 Will Clark	.50	.25	.05
☐ 3 Ryne Sandberg	.45	.22	.04
☐ 4 Howard Johnson	.20	.10	.02
☐ 5 Ozzie Smith	.20	.10	.02
☐ 6 Kevin Mitchell	.30	.15	.03
☐ 7 Eric Davis	.35	.17	.03
☐ 8 Tony Gwynn	.35	.17	.03
☐ 9 Benny Santiago	.20	.10	.02
☐ 10 Rick Reuschel	.10	.05	.01
☐ 11 Don Drysdale CAPT	.15	.07	.01
☐ 12 Tony LaRussa MG	.10	.05	.01
☐ 13 Mark McGwire	.40	.20	.04
☐ 14 Julio Franco	.15	.07	.01
☐ 15 Wade Boggs	.40	.20	.04
☐ 16 Cal Ripken Jr.	.25	.12	.02
☐ 17 Bo Jackson	.75	.35	.07
☐ 18 Kirby Puckett	.30	.15	.03
☐ 19 Ruben Sierra	.30	.15	.03
☐ 20 Terry Steinbach	.15	.07	.01
☐ 21 Dave Stewart	.15	.07	.01
☐ 22 Carl Yastrzemski CAPT	.20	.10	.02

1990 Topps Jumbo Rookies

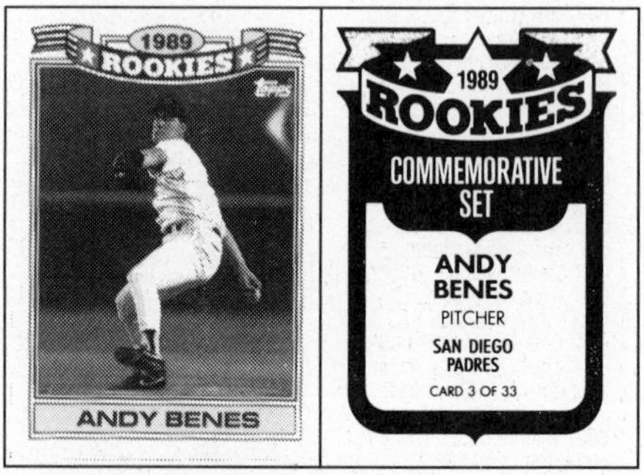

The 1990 Topps Jumbo Rookies set contains 33 standard-size (2 1/2" by 3 1/2") glossy cards. The front and back borders are white, and other design elements are red, blue and yellow. This set is almost identical to previous year sets of the same name except that it contains 33 cards rather than only 22. One card was included in each 1990 Topps "jumbo" pack. The cards are numbered in alphabetical order.

	MINT	EXC	G-VG
COMPLETE SET (33)	9.00	4.50	.90
COMMON PLAYER (1-33)	.20	.10	.02
☐ 1 Jim Abbott	.60	.30	.06
☐ 2 Joey Belle	.30	.15	.03
☐ 3 Andy Benes	.40	.20	.04
☐ 4 Greg Briley	.30	.15	.03
☐ 5 Kevin Brown	.30	.15	.03
☐ 6 Mark Carreon	.20	.10	.02
☐ 7 Mike Devereaux	.20	.10	.02
☐ 8 Junior Felix	.40	.20	.04
☐ 9 Bob Geren	.20	.10	.02
☐ 10 Tom Gordon	.40	.20	.04
☐ 11 Ken Griffey Jr.	1.50	.75	.15
☐ 12 Pete Harnisch	.20	.10	.02
☐ 13 Greg Harris	.20	.10	.02
☐ 14 Greg Hibbard	.20	.10	.02
☐ 15 Ken Hill	.20	.10	.02
☐ 16 Gregg Jefferies	.75	.35	.07
☐ 17 Jeff King	.25	.12	.02
☐ 18 Derek Lilliquist	.20	.10	.02
☐ 19 Carlos Martinez	.25	.12	.02
☐ 20 Ramon Martinez	.60	.30	.06
☐ 21 Bob Milacki	.20	.10	.02
☐ 22 Gregg Olson	.50	.25	.05
☐ 23 Donn Pall	.20	.10	.02
☐ 24 Kenny Rogers	.20	.10	.02
☐ 25 Gary Sheffield	.50	.25	.05
☐ 26 Dwight Smith	.40	.20	.04
☐ 27 Billy Spiers	.30	.15	.03
☐ 28 Omar Vizquel	.20	.10	.02
☐ 29 Jerome Walton	.60	.30	.06
☐ 30 Dave West	.25	.12	.02
☐ 31 John Wetteland	.25	.12	.02
☐ 32 Steve Wilson	.20	.10	.02
☐ 33 Craig Worthington	.25	.12	.02

1990 Topps '89 Debut

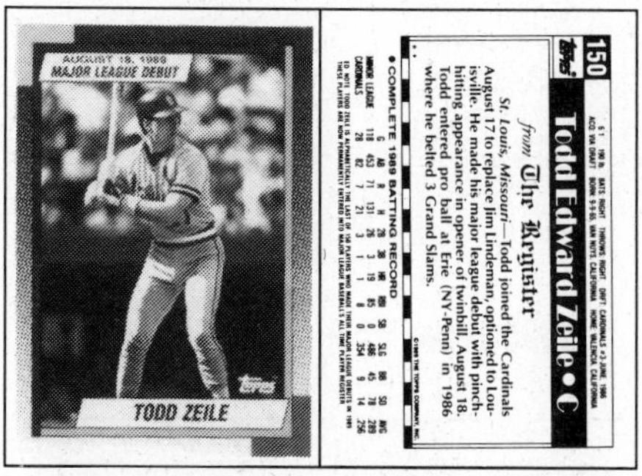

The 1990 Topps Major League Debut Set is a 152-card, standard-size (2 1/2" by 3 1/2") set arranged in order of first major league appearance in 1989. Each card front features the date of the player's first major league appearance. Strangely enough, even though the set commemorates the 1989 Major League debuts, the set was not issued until the 1990 season had almost begun.

	MINT	EXC	G-VG
COMPLETE SET (152)	12.00	6.00	1.20
COMMON PLAYER (1-152)	.05	.02	.00
☐ 1 Steve Finley	.15	.07	.01
☐ 2 Ken Griffey Jr.	2.00	1.00	.20
☐ 3 Omar Vizquel	.10	.05	.01
☐ 4 Joe Girardi	.10	.05	.01
☐ 5 Jerome Walton	.60	.30	.06
☐ 6 Geronimo Berroa	.05	.02	.00
☐ 7 Gene Harris	.10	.05	.01
☐ 8 Phil Stephenson	.10	.05	.01
☐ 9 Kenny Rogers	.10	.05	.01
☐ 10 LaVel Freeman	.10	.05	.01
☐ 11 Jeff Schaefer	.10	.05	.01
☐ 12 Billy Spiers	.10	.05	.01
☐ 13 Gary Wayne	.10	.05	.01
☐ 14 Jim Abbott	.60	.30	.06
☐ 15 Eric Yelding	.10	.05	.01
☐ 16 Joe Skalski	.05	.02	.00
☐ 17 Matt Merullo	.05	.02	.00
☐ 18 Derek Lilliquist	.10	.05	.01
☐ 19 Kent Anderson	.05	.02	.00
☐ 20 Brian Brady	.10	.05	.01
☐ 21 Steve Carter	.05	.02	.00
☐ 22 Chris Hoiles	.15	.07	.01
☐ 23 Ramon Pena	.05	.02	.00
☐ 24 Dwight Smith	.30	.15	.03
☐ 25 Greg Litton	.15	.07	.01
☐ 26 Junior Felix	.30	.15	.03
☐ 27 Francisco Oliveras	.10	.05	.01
☐ 28 Steve Frey	.10	.05	.01
☐ 29 Mark Gardner	.10	.05	.01
☐ 30 Marty Pevey	.10	.05	.01
☐ 31 Matt Kinzer	.05	.02	.00
☐ 32 Dick Scott	.10	.05	.01
☐ 33 Jack Hardy	.10	.05	.01
☐ 34 Alex Sanchez	.10	.05	.01
☐ 35 Dave Justice	1.50	.75	.15
☐ 36 Randy Nosek	.05	.02	.00
☐ 37 Mike Schwabe	.05	.02	.00
☐ 38 Matt Winters	.15	.07	.01
☐ 39 Greg Hibbard	.10	.05	.01
☐ 40 Deion Sanders	.50	.25	.05
☐ 41 John Wetteland	.20	.10	.02
☐ 42 Jeff King	.10	.05	.01
☐ 43 Clint Zavaras	.10	.05	.01
☐ 44 Kevin Appier	.25	.12	.02
☐ 45 Xavier Hernandez	.05	.02	.00
☐ 46 Larry Arndt	.10	.05	.01
☐ 47 Rick Luecken	.10	.05	.01
☐ 48 Jeff McKnight	.10	.05	.01
☐ 49 Scott Scudder	.15	.07	.01
☐ 50 Jeff Wetherby	.10	.05	.01
☐ 51 Kevin Batiste	.25	.12	.02
☐ 52 Sammy Sosa	.35	.17	.03
☐ 53 Mickey Weston	.10	.05	.01
☐ 54 Dana Williams	.15	.07	.01
☐ 55 Jaime Navarro	.15	.07	.01
☐ 56 Steve Cummings	.10	.05	.01
☐ 57 Gregg Olson	.50	.25	.05
☐ 58 Randy McCament	.10	.05	.01
☐ 59 Mike Dyer	.10	.05	.01
☐ 60 Mike Smith	.10	.05	.01
☐ 61 Eric Hetzel	.10	.05	.01
☐ 62 Randy Veres	.05	.02	.00
☐ 63 Kevin Tapani	.20	.10	.02
☐ 64 Ed Whited	.20	.10	.02
☐ 65 Mike Benjamin	.10	.05	.01
☐ 66 Pete Dalena	.10	.05	.01
☐ 67 Doug Strange	.10	.05	.01
☐ 68 Jeff Richardson	.10	.05	.01
☐ 69 Joey Belle	.20	.10	.02
☐ 70 Bobby Davidson	.10	.05	.01
☐ 71 Joe Oliver	.15	.07	.01
☐ 72 Kevin Ritz	.10	.05	.01
☐ 73 Wally Whitehurst	.10	.05	.01
☐ 74 Wilson Alvarez	.20	.10	.02
☐ 75 Francisco Cabrera	.20	.10	.02
☐ 76 Mark Guthrie	.10	.05	.01
☐ 77 Paul Wilmet	.10	.05	.01
☐ 78 Scott Little	.10	.05	.01
☐ 79 Eric Anthony	.50	.25	.05
☐ 80 Steve Olin	.10	.05	.01
☐ 81 Glenallen Hill	.15	.07	.01
☐ 82 Russ Swan	.20	.10	.02
☐ 83 Mike Huff	.20	.10	.02
☐ 84 Goose Gozzo	.10	.05	.01
☐ 85 Mike Roesler	.10	.05	.01
☐ 86 Dan Murphy	.10	.05	.01
☐ 87 Greg Vaughn	.60	.30	.06
☐ 88 Kevin Wickander	.10	.05	.01
☐ 89 Andy Benes	.40	.20	.04
☐ 90 Marcus Lawton	.10	.05	.01
☐ 91 Juan Gonzalez	1.00	.50	.10
☐ 92 Dean Palmer	.15	.07	.01
☐ 93 Rosario Rodriguez	.05	.02	.00
☐ 94 Lenny Webster	.05	.02	.00
☐ 95 Scott Coolbaugh	.10	.05	.01
☐ 96 Jeff Schulz	.10	.05	.01
☐ 97 Greg Smith	.10	.05	.01
☐ 98 George Canale	.10	.05	.01
☐ 99 John Olerud	1.50	.75	.15
☐ 100 Kelly Mann	.10	.05	.01
☐ 101 Chuck McElroy	.10	.05	.01
☐ 102 Pat Combs	.30	.15	.03
☐ 103 Jeff Datz	.10	.05	.01
☐ 104 Shawn Holman	.10	.05	.01
☐ 105 Juan Bell	.15	.07	.01
☐ 106 Ben McDonald	1.00	.50	.10
☐ 107 Mike Munoz	.10	.05	.01

☐ 108 Craig Wilson	.10	.05	.01
☐ 109 Beau Allred	.15	.07	.01
☐ 110 John Barfield	.10	.05	.01
☐ 111 Mark Higgins	.10	.05	.01
☐ 112 Julio Machado	.10	.05	.01
☐ 113 Tom Magrann	.10	.05	.01
☐ 114 Rudy Seanez	.10	.05	.01
☐ 115 Bobby Rose	.20	.10	.02
☐ 116 Jeff Peterek	.10	.05	.01
☐ 117 Larry Walker	.30	.15	.03
☐ 118 Billy Bates	.10	.05	.01
☐ 119 Brian DuBois	.10	.05	.01
☐ 120 Todd Zeile	.60	.30	.06
☐ 121 Rob Richie	.10	.05	.01
☐ 122 John Orton	.10	.05	.01
☐ 123 Dean Wilkins	.10	.05	.01
☐ 124 Marquis Grissom	.30	.15	.03
☐ 125 Joe Kraemer	.10	.05	.01
☐ 126 Hensley Meulens	.40	.20	.04
☐ 127 Mike Stanton	.10	.05	.01
☐ 128 Chip Hale	.10	.05	.01
☐ 129 Jose Cano	.10	.05	.01
☐ 130 Mike Blowers	.15	.07	.01
☐ 131 Mike Fetters	.10	.05	.01
☐ 132 Stan Belinda	.10	.05	.01
☐ 133 Jason Grimsley	.10	.05	.01
☐ 134 Paul Sorrento	.10	.05	.01
☐ 135 Scott Hemond	.20	.10	.02
☐ 136 Kevin Mmahat	.15	.07	.01
☐ 137 Darrin Fletcher	.10	.05	.01
☐ 138 Tommy Greene	.25	.12	.02
☐ 139 Mike Hartley	.15	.07	.01
☐ 140 Terry Jorgensen	.10	.05	.01
☐ 141 Jose Vizcaino	.15	.07	.01
☐ 142 Wayne Edwards	.10	.05	.01
☐ 143 Robin Ventura	.40	.20	.04
☐ 144 Drew Denson	.10	.05	.01
☐ 145 Dann Howitt	.20	.10	.02
☐ 146 Blaine Beatty	.10	.05	.01
☐ 147 Rusty Richards	.10	.05	.01
☐ 148 Stu Tate	.10	.05	.01
☐ 149 Kent Mercker	.25	.12	.02
☐ 150 Gary Disarcina	.10	.05	.01
☐ 151 Checklist Card	.05	.02	.00
☐ 152 Checklist Card	.05	.02	.00

1990 Topps Glossy 60

The 1990 Topps Glossy 60 set was issued as a mailaway by Topps for the eighth straight year. This standard-size (2 1/2" by 3 1/2"), 60-card set features two young players among every ten players as Topps again broke down these cards into six series of ten cards each. Like the previous years' issues, the set features attractive full color fronts.

	MINT	EXC	G-VG
COMPLETE SET (60)	9.00	4.50	.90
COMMON PLAYER (1-60)	.15	.07	.01

☐ 1 Ryne Sandberg	.50	.25	.05
☐ 2 Nolan Ryan	.75	.35	.07
☐ 3 Glenn Davis	.25	.12	.02
☐ 4 Dave Stewart	.25	.12	.02
☐ 5 Barry Larkin	.25	.12	.02
☐ 6 Carney Lansford	.15	.07	.01
☐ 7 Darryl Strawberry	.15	.07	.01
☐ 8 Steve Sax	.15	.07	.01
☐ 9 Carlos Martinez	.15	.07	.01
☐ 10 Gary Sheffield	.35	.17	.03
☐ 11 Don Mattingly	.75	.35	.07
☐ 12 Mark Grace	.50	.25	.05
☐ 13 Bret Saberhagen	.25	.12	.02
☐ 14 Mike Scott	.25	.12	.02
☐ 15 Robin Yount	.35	.17	.03
☐ 16 Ozzie Smith	.25	.12	.02
☐ 17 Jeff Ballard	.15	.07	.01
☐ 18 Rick Reuschel	.15	.07	.01
☐ 19 Greg Briley	.15	.07	.01
☐ 20 Ken Griffey Jr.	1.00	.50	.10
☐ 21 Kevin Mitchell	.35	.17	.03
☐ 22 Wade Boggs	.45	.22	.04
☐ 23 Dwight Gooden	.35	.17	.03
☐ 24 George Bell	.25	.12	.02
☐ 25 Eric Davis	.35	.17	.03
☐ 26 Ruben Sierra	.35	.17	.03
☐ 27 Roberto Alomar	.25	.12	.02
☐ 28 Gary Gaetti	.15	.07	.01
☐ 29 Gregg Olson	.25	.12	.02
☐ 30 Tom Gordon	.25	.12	.02
☐ 31 Jose Canseco	.75	.35	.07
☐ 32 Pedro Guerrero	.25	.12	.02
☐ 33 Joe Carter	.25	.12	.02
☐ 34 Mike Scioscia	.15	.07	.01
☐ 35 Julio Franco	.20	.10	.02
☐ 36 Joe Magrane	.20	.10	.02
☐ 37 Rickey Henderson	.75	.35	.07
☐ 38 Tim Raines	.25	.12	.02
☐ 39 Jerome Walton	.35	.17	.03
☐ 40 Bob Geren	.15	.07	.01
☐ 41 Andre Dawson	.25	.12	.02
☐ 42 Mark McGwire	.50	.25	.05
☐ 43 Howard Johnson	.25	.12	.02
☐ 44 Bo Jackson	1.00	.50	.10
☐ 45 Shawon Dunston	.25	.12	.02
☐ 46 Carlton Fisk	.25	.12	.02
☐ 47 Mitch Williams	.15	.07	.01
☐ 48 Kirby Puckett	.35	.17	.03
☐ 49 Craig Worthington	.20	.10	.02
☐ 50 Jim Abbott	.35	.17	.03
☐ 51 Cal Ripken	.35	.17	.03
☐ 52 Will Clark	.50	.25	.05
☐ 53 Dennis Eckersley	.25	.12	.02
☐ 54 Craig Biggio	.25	.12	.02
☐ 55 Fred McGriff	.25	.12	.02
☐ 56 Tony Gwynn	.35	.17	.03
☐ 57 Mickey Tettleton	.15	.07	.01
☐ 58 Mark Davis	.15	.07	.01
☐ 59 Omar Vizquel	.15	.07	.01
☐ 60 Gregg Jefferies	.50	.25	.05

1990 Topps League Leader Minis

The 1990 Topps League Leader Minis is a 88-card set with cards measuring approximately 2 1/8" by 3". The set features players who finished 1989 in the top five in any major hitting or pitching category. This set marked the fifth year that Topps issued their Mini set.

	MINT	EXC	G-VG
COMPLETE SET (88)	7.00	3.50	.70
COMMON PLAYER (1-88)	.07	.03	.01

☐ 1 Jeff Ballard	.07	.03	.01
☐ 2 Phil Bradley	.10	.05	.01
☐ 3 Wade Boggs	.50	.25	.05
☐ 4 Roger Clemens	.50	.25	.05
☐ 5 Nick Esasky	.10	.05	.01
☐ 6 Jody Reed	.10	.05	.01
☐ 7 Bert Blyleven	.10	.05	.01
☐ 8 Chuck Finley	.12	.06	.01
☐ 9 Kirk McCaskill	.07	.03	.01
☐ 10 Devon White	.10	.05	.01
☐ 11 Ivan Calderon	.10	.05	.01
☐ 12 Bobby Thigpen	.15	.07	.01
☐ 13 Joe Carter	.15	.07	.01
☐ 14 Gary Pettis	.07	.03	.01
☐ 15 Tom Gordon	.15	.07	.01
☐ 16 Bo Jackson	.75	.35	.07
☐ 17 Bret Saberhagen	.15	.07	.01
☐ 18 Kevin Seitzer	.15	.07	.01
☐ 19 Chris Bosio	.07	.03	.01
☐ 20 Paul Molitor	.15	.07	.01
☐ 21 Dan Plesac	.07	.03	.01
☐ 22 Robin Yount	.35	.17	.03
☐ 23 Kirby Puckett	.35	.17	.03
☐ 24 Don Mattingly	.60	.30	.06
☐ 25 Steve Sax	.12	.06	.01
☐ 26 Storm Davis	.07	.03	.01
☐ 27 Dennis Eckersley	.15	.07	.01
☐ 28 Rickey Henderson	.60	.30	.06
☐ 29 Carney Lansford	.12	.06	.01
☐ 30 Mark McGwire	.50	.25	.05
☐ 31 Mike Moore	.10	.05	.01
☐ 32 Dave Stewart	.15	.07	.01
☐ 33 Alvin Davis	.10	.05	.01
☐ 34 Harold Reynolds	.10	.05	.01
☐ 35 Mike Schooler	.10	.05	.01
☐ 36 Cecil Espy	.07	.03	.01
☐ 37 Julio Franco	.10	.05	.01
☐ 38 Jeff Russell	.07	.03	.01
☐ 39 Nolan Ryan	.75	.35	.07
☐ 40 Ruben Sierra	.25	.12	.02
☐ 41 George Bell	.15	.07	.01
☐ 42 Tony Fernandez	.10	.05	.01
☐ 43 Fred McGriff	.15	.07	.01
☐ 44 Dave Stieb	.12	.06	.01
☐ 45 Checklist Card	.07	.03	.01
☐ 46 Lonnie Smith	.10	.05	.01
☐ 47 John Smoltz	.10	.05	.01
☐ 48 Mike Bielecki	.07	.03	.01
☐ 49 Mark Grace	.40	.20	.04
☐ 50 Greg Maddux	.15	.07	.01
☐ 51 Ryne Sandberg	.50	.25	.05
☐ 52 Mitch Williams	.10	.05	.01
☐ 53 Eric Davis	.30	.15	.03
☐ 54 John Franco	.10	.05	.01
☐ 55 Glenn Davis	.15	.07	.01
☐ 56 Mike Scott	.10	.05	.01
☐ 57 Tim Belcher	.10	.05	.01
☐ 58 Orel Hershiser	.15	.07	.01
☐ 59 Jay Howell	.10	.05	.01
☐ 60 Eddie Murray	.20	.10	.02
☐ 61 Tim Burke	.10	.05	.01
☐ 62 Mark Langston	.15	.07	.01
☐ 63 Rock Raines	.15	.07	.01
☐ 64 Tim Wallach	.10	.05	.01
☐ 65 David Cone	.15	.07	.01
☐ 66 Sid Fernandez	.10	.05	.01
☐ 67 Howard Johnson	.15	.07	.01
☐ 68 Juan Samuel	.10	.05	.01
☐ 69 Von Hayes	.10	.05	.01
☐ 70 Barry Bonds	.30	.15	.03
☐ 71 Bobby Bonilla	.20	.10	.02
☐ 72 Andy Van Slyke	.15	.07	.01
☐ 73 Vince Coleman	.20	.10	.02
☐ 74 Jose DeLeon	.07	.03	.01
☐ 75 Pedro Guerrero	.15	.07	.01
☐ 76 Joe Magrane	.10	.05	.01
☐ 77 Roberto Alomar	.20	.10	.02
☐ 78 Jack Clark	.15	.07	.01
☐ 79 Mark Davis	.10	.05	.01
☐ 80 Tony Gwynn	.30	.15	.03
☐ 81 Bruce Hurst	.10	.05	.01
☐ 82 Eddie Whitson	.10	.05	.01
☐ 83 Brett Butler	.10	.05	.01
☐ 84 Will Clark	.50	.25	.05
☐ 85 Scott Garrelts	.10	.05	.01
☐ 86 Kevin Mitchell	.20	.10	.02
☐ 87 Rick Reuschel	.10	.05	.01
☐ 88 Robby Thompson	.07	.03	.01

1990 Topps Big

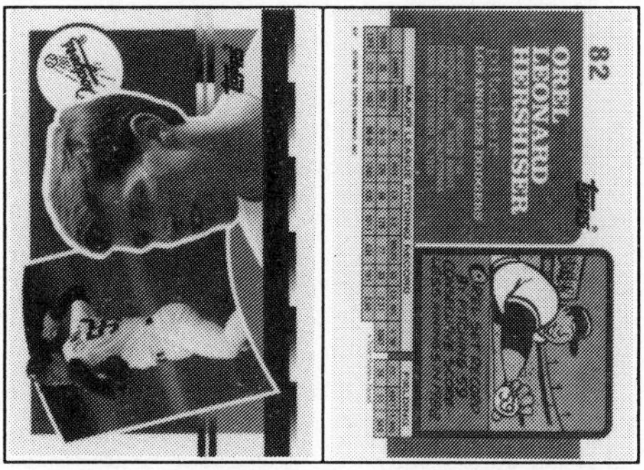

The 1990 Topps Big set contains 330 cards each measuring an slightly over-sized 2 5/8" by 3 3/4". In 1989 Topps had issued two oversize sets (Bigs and Bowmans), but in 1990 only the Topps Big were issued by Topps as an oversize set. The set was issued in three series of 110 cards.

	MINT	EXC	G-VG
COMPLETE SET (330)	21.00	10.50	2.10
COMMON PLAYER (1-110)	.05	.02	.00
COMMON PLAYER (111-220)	.05	.02	.00
COMMON PLAYER (221-330)	.05	.02	.00
☐ 1 Dwight Evans	.12	.06	.01
☐ 2 Kirby Puckett	.35	.17	.03
☐ 3 Kevin Gross	.08	.04	.01
☐ 4 Ron Hassey	.05	.02	.00
☐ 5 Lloyd McClendon	.05	.02	.00
☐ 6 Bo Jackson	1.00	.50	.10
☐ 7 Lonnie Smith	.08	.04	.01
☐ 8 Alvaro Espinoza	.05	.02	.00
☐ 9 Roberto Alomar	.20	.10	.02
☐ 10 Glenn Braggs	.08	.04	.01
☐ 11 David Cone	.12	.06	.01
☐ 12 Claudell Washington	.08	.04	.01
☐ 13 Pedro Guerrero	.12	.06	.01
☐ 14 Todd Benzinger	.08	.04	.01
☐ 15 Jeff Russell	.05	.02	.00
☐ 16 Terry Kennedy	.05	.02	.00
☐ 17 Kelly Gruber	.15	.07	.01
☐ 18 Alfredo Griffin	.05	.02	.00
☐ 19 Mark Grace	.40	.20	.04
☐ 20 Dave Winfield	.20	.10	.02
☐ 21 Bret Saberhagen	.20	.10	.02
☐ 22 Roger Clemens	.50	.25	.05
☐ 23 Bob Walk	.05	.02	.00
☐ 24 Dave Magadan	.12	.06	.01
☐ 25 Spike Owen	.05	.02	.00
☐ 26 Jody Davis	.05	.02	.00
☐ 27 Kent Hrbek	.10	.05	.01
☐ 28 Mark McGwire	.45	.22	.04
☐ 29 Eddie Murray	.30	.15	.03
☐ 30 Paul O'Neill	.12	.06	.01
☐ 31 Jose DeLeon	.05	.02	.00
☐ 32 Steve Lyons	.05	.02	.00
☐ 33 Dan Plesac	.05	.02	.00
☐ 34 Jack Howell	.05	.02	.00
☐ 35 Greg Briley	.10	.05	.01
☐ 36 Andy Hawkins	.05	.02	.00
☐ 37 Cecil Espy	.05	.02	.00
☐ 38 Rick Sutcliffe	.10	.05	.01
☐ 39 Jack Clark	.12	.06	.01
☐ 40 Dale Murphy	.30	.15	.03
☐ 41 Mike Henneman	.05	.02	.00
☐ 42 Rick Honeycutt	.05	.02	.00
☐ 43 Willie Randolph	.08	.04	.01
☐ 44 Marty Barrett	.05	.02	.00
☐ 45 Willie Wilson	.10	.05	.01
☐ 46 Wallace Johnson	.05	.02	.00
☐ 47 Greg Brock	.05	.02	.00
☐ 48 Tom Browning	.08	.04	.01
☐ 49 Gerald Young	.05	.02	.00
☐ 50 Dennis Eckersley	.12	.06	.01
☐ 51 Scott Garrelts	.08	.04	.01
☐ 52 Gary Redus	.05	.02	.00
☐ 53 Al Newman	.05	.02	.00

☐ 54 Daryl Boston	.08	.04	.01
☐ 55 Ron Oester	.05	.02	.00
☐ 56 Danny Tartabull	.12	.06	.01
☐ 57 Gregg Jefferies	.40	.20	.04
☐ 58 Tom Foley	.05	.02	.00
☐ 59 Robin Yount	.30	.15	.03
☐ 60 Pat Borders	.10	.05	.01
☐ 61 Mike Greenwell	.30	.15	.03
☐ 62 Shawon Dunston	.15	.07	.01
☐ 63 Steve Buechele	.05	.02	.00
☐ 64 Dave Stewart	.15	.07	.01
☐ 65 Jose Oquendo	.05	.02	.00
☐ 66 Ron Gant	.30	.15	.03
☐ 67 Mike Scioscia	.05	.02	.00
☐ 68 Randy Velarde	.05	.02	.00
☐ 69 Charlie Hayes	.08	.04	.01
☐ 70 Tim Wallach	.10	.05	.01
☐ 71 Eric Show	.05	.02	.00
☐ 72 Eric Davis	.30	.15	.03
☐ 73 Mike Gallego	.05	.02	.00
☐ 74 Rob Deer	.08	.04	.01
☐ 75 Ryne Sandberg	.40	.20	.04
☐ 76 Kevin Seitzer	.15	.07	.01
☐ 77 Wade Boggs	.40	.20	.04
☐ 78 Greg Gagne	.05	.02	.00
☐ 79 John Smiley	.05	.02	.00
☐ 80 Ivan Calderon	.08	.04	.01
☐ 81 Pete Incaviglia	.12	.06	.01
☐ 82 Orel Hershiser	.15	.07	.01
☐ 83 Carney Lansford	.10	.05	.01
☐ 84 Mike Fitzgerald	.05	.02	.00
☐ 85 Don Mattingly	.60	.30	.06
☐ 86 Chet Lemon	.05	.02	.00
☐ 87 Rolando Roomes	.05	.02	.00
☐ 88 Billy Spiers	.05	.02	.00
☐ 89 Pat Tabler	.05	.02	.00
☐ 90 Danny Heep	.05	.02	.00
☐ 91 Andre Dawson	.20	.10	.02
☐ 92 Randy Bush	.05	.02	.00
☐ 93 Tony Gwynn	.30	.15	.03
☐ 94 Tom Brunansky	.10	.05	.01
☐ 95 Johnny Ray	.05	.02	.00
☐ 96 Matt Williams	.30	.15	.03
☐ 97 Barry Lyons	.05	.02	.00
☐ 98 Jeff Hamilton	.05	.02	.00
☐ 99 Tom Glavine	.08	.04	.01
☐ 100 Ken Griffey Sr.	.10	.05	.01
☐ 101 Tom Henke	.08	.04	.01
☐ 102 Dave Righetti	.10	.05	.01
☐ 103 Paul Molitor	.12	.06	.01
☐ 104 Mike LaValliere	.05	.02	.00
☐ 105 Frank White	.08	.04	.01
☐ 106 Bob Welch	.12	.06	.01
☐ 107 Ellis Burks	.30	.15	.03
☐ 108 Andres Galarraga	.15	.07	.01
☐ 109 Mitch Williams	.08	.04	.01
☐ 110 Checklist 1-110	.05	.02	.00
☐ 111 Craig Biggio	.10	.05	.01
☐ 112 Dave Stieb	.12	.06	.01
☐ 113 Ron Darling	.10	.05	.01
☐ 114 Bert Blyleven	.10	.05	.01
☐ 115 Dickie Thon	.08	.04	.01
☐ 116 Carlos Martinez	.08	.04	.01
☐ 117 Jeff King	.08	.04	.01
☐ 118 Terry Steinbach	.10	.05	.01
☐ 119 Frank Tanana	.08	.04	.01
☐ 120 Mark Lemke	.05	.02	.00
☐ 121 Chris Sabo	.30	.15	.03
☐ 122 Glenn Davis	.20	.10	.02
☐ 123 Mel Hall	.08	.04	.01
☐ 124 Jim Gantner	.05	.02	.00
☐ 125 Benny Santiago	.20	.10	.02
☐ 126 Milt Thompson	.08	.04	.01
☐ 127 Rafael Palmeiro	.15	.07	.01
☐ 128 Barry Bonds	.30	.15	.03
☐ 129 Mike Bielecki	.05	.02	.00
☐ 130 Lou Whitaker	.10	.05	.01
☐ 131 Bob Ojeda	.08	.04	.01
☐ 132 Dion James	.05	.02	.00
☐ 133 Denny Martinez	.05	.02	.00
☐ 134 Fred McGriff	.15	.07	.01
☐ 135 Terry Pendleton	.08	.04	.01
☐ 136 Pat Combs	.12	.06	.01
☐ 137 Kevin Mitchell	.25	.12	.02
☐ 138 Marquis Grissom	.25	.12	.02
☐ 139 Chris Bosio	.05	.02	.00
☐ 140 Omar Vizquel	.05	.02	.00
☐ 141 Steve Sax	.10	.05	.01
☐ 142 Nelson Liriano	.05	.02	.00
☐ 143 Kevin Elster	.08	.04	.01
☐ 144 Dan Pasqua	.05	.02	.00
☐ 145 Dave Smith	.08	.04	.01
☐ 146 Craig Worthington	.08	.04	.01
☐ 147 Danny Gladden	.05	.02	.00
☐ 148 Oddibe McDowell	.08	.04	.01
☐ 149 Bip Roberts	.08	.04	.01
☐ 150 Randy Ready	.05	.02	.00
☐ 151 Dwight Smith	.20	.10	.02
☐ 152 Eddie Whitson	.08	.04	.01
☐ 153 George Bell	.20	.10	.02
☐ 154 Rock Raines	.15	.07	.01
☐ 155 Sid Fernandez	.08	.04	.01
☐ 156 Henry Cotto	.05	.02	.00
☐ 157 Harold Baines	.10	.05	.01
☐ 158 Willie McGee	.12	.06	.01
☐ 159 Bill Doran	.08	.04	.01
☐ 160 Steve Balboni	.05	.02	.00
☐ 161 Pete Smith	.05	.02	.00
☐ 162 Frank Viola	.12	.06	.01
☐ 163 Gary Sheffield	.25	.12	.02
☐ 164 Bill Landrum	.05	.02	.00
☐ 165 Tony Fernandez	.10	.05	.01
☐ 166 Mike Heath	.05	.02	.00
☐ 167 Jody Reed	.10	.05	.01
☐ 168 Wally Joyner	.12	.06	.01
☐ 169 Robby Thompson	.05	.02	.00
☐ 170 Ken Caminiti	.05	.02	.00
☐ 171 Nolan Ryan	.75	.35	.07
☐ 172 Ricky Jordan	.15	.07	.01
☐ 173 Lance Blankenship	.05	.02	.00
☐ 174 Doc Gooden	.25	.12	.02
☐ 175 Ruben Sierra	.30	.15	.03
☐ 176 Carlton Fisk	.20	.10	.02
☐ 177 Garry Templeton	.08	.04	.01
☐ 178 Mike Devereaux	.08	.04	.01
☐ 179 Mookie Wilson	.08	.04	.01
☐ 180 Jeff Blauser	.05	.02	.00
☐ 181 Scott Bradley	.05	.02	.00
☐ 182 Luis Salazar	.05	.02	.00
☐ 183 Rafael Ramirez	.05	.02	.00
☐ 184 Vince Coleman	.15	.07	.01
☐ 185 Doug Drabek	.12	.06	.01
☐ 186 Darryl Strawberry	.35	.17	.03
☐ 187 Tim Burke	.08	.04	.01
☐ 188 Jesse Barfield	.12	.06	.01
☐ 189 Barry Larkin	.15	.07	.01
☐ 190 Alan Trammell	.15	.07	.01
☐ 191 Steve Lake	.05	.02	.00
☐ 192 Derek Lilliquist	.05	.02	.00
☐ 193 Don Robinson	.05	.02	.00
☐ 194 Kevin McReynolds	.12	.06	.01
☐ 195 Melido Perez	.08	.04	.01
☐ 196 Jose Lind	.05	.02	.00
☐ 197 Eric Anthony	.25	.12	.02
☐ 198 B.J. Surhoff	.10	.05	.01
☐ 199 John Olerud	.75	.35	.07
☐ 200 Mike Moore	.08	.04	.01
☐ 201 Mark Gubicza	.08	.04	.01
☐ 202 Phil Bradley	.08	.04	.01
☐ 203 Ozzie Smith	.15	.07	.01
☐ 204 Greg Maddux	.08	.04	.01
☐ 205 Julio Franco	.10	.05	.01
☐ 206 Tom Herr	.05	.02	.00
☐ 207 Scott Fletcher	.05	.02	.00
☐ 208 Bobby Bonilla	.20	.10	.02
☐ 209 Bob Geren	.08	.04	.01
☐ 210 Junior Felix	.20	.10	.02
☐ 211 Dick Schofield	.05	.02	.00
☐ 212 Jim Deshaies	.05	.02	.00
☐ 213 Jose Uribe	.05	.02	.00
☐ 214 John Kruk	.05	.02	.00
☐ 215 Ozzie Guillen	.10	.05	.01
☐ 216 Howard Johnson	.15	.07	.01
☐ 217 Andy Van Slyke	.12	.06	.01
☐ 218 Tim Laudner	.05	.02	.00
☐ 219 Manny Lee	.05	.02	.00
☐ 220 Checklist 111-220	.05	.02	.00
☐ 221 Cory Snyder	.12	.06	.01
☐ 222 Billy Hatcher	.08	.04	.01
☐ 223 Bud Black	.05	.02	.00
☐ 224 Will Clark	.60	.30	.06
☐ 225 Kevin Tapani	.15	.07	.01
☐ 226 Mike Pagliarulo	.05	.02	.00
☐ 227 Dave Parker	.12	.06	.01
☐ 228 Ben McDonald	.60	.30	.06
☐ 229 Carlos Baerga	.25	.12	.02
☐ 230 Roger McDowell	.05	.02	.00
☐ 231 Delino DeShields	.40	.20	.04
☐ 232 Mark Langston	.10	.05	.01
☐ 233 Wally Backman	.05	.02	.00
☐ 234 Jim Eisenreich	.05	.02	.00
☐ 235 Mike Schooler	.08	.04	.01
☐ 236 Kevin Bass	.05	.02	.00
☐ 237 John Farrell	.05	.02	.00
☐ 238 Kal Daniels	.12	.06	.01
☐ 239 Tony Phillips	.05	.02	.00
☐ 240 Todd Stottlemyre	.08	.04	.01
☐ 241 Greg Olson	.10	.05	.01

☐	242 Charlie Hough	.05	.02	.00
☐	243 Mariano Duncan	.05	.02	.00
☐	244 Bill Ripken	.05	.02	.00
☐	245 Joe Carter	.12	.06	.01
☐	246 Tim Belcher	.10	.05	.01
☐	247 Roberto Kelly	.20	.10	.02
☐	248 Candy Maldonado	.08	.04	.01
☐	249 Mike Scott	.10	.05	.01
☐	250 Ken Griffey Jr.	1.25	.60	.12
☐	251 Nick Esasky	.08	.04	.01
☐	252 Tom Gordon	.15	.07	.01
☐	253 John Tudor	.08	.04	.01
☐	254 Gary Gaetti	.10	.05	.01
☐	255 Neal Heaton	.05	.02	.00
☐	256 Jerry Browne	.05	.02	.00
☐	257 Jose Rijo	.10	.05	.01
☐	258 Mike Boddicker	.08	.04	.01
☐	259 Brett Butler	.08	.04	.01
☐	260 Andy Benes	.15	.07	.01
☐	261 Kevin Brown	.10	.05	.01
☐	262 Hubie Brooks	.08	.04	.01
☐	263 Randy Milligan	.10	.05	.01
☐	264 John Franco	.08	.04	.01
☐	265 Sandy Alomar Jr.	.30	.15	.03
☐	266 Dave Valle	.05	.02	.00
☐	267 Jerome Walton	.50	.25	.05
☐	268 Bob Boone	.10	.05	.01
☐	269 Ken Howell	.05	.02	.00
☐	270 Jose Canseco	.75	.35	.07
☐	271 Joe Magrane	.08	.04	.01
☐	272 Brian Dubois	.08	.04	.01
☐	273 Carlos Quintana	.12	.06	.01
☐	274 Lance Johnson	.05	.02	.00
☐	275 Steve Bedrosian	.08	.04	.01
☐	276 Brook Jacoby	.08	.04	.01
☐	277 Fred Lynn UER Pirates logo on card front)	.10	.05	.01
☐	278 Jeff Ballard	.05	.02	.00
☐	279 Otis Nixon	.05	.02	.00
☐	280 Chili Davis	.08	.04	.01
☐	281 Joe Oliver	.10	.05	.01
☐	282 Brian Holman	.10	.05	.01
☐	283 Juan Samuel	.08	.04	.01
☐	284 Rick Aguilera	.05	.02	.00
☐	285 Jeff Reardon	.08	.04	.01
☐	286 Sammy Sosa	.20	.10	.02
☐	287 Carmelo Martinez	.08	.04	.01
☐	288 Greg Swindell	.08	.04	.01
☐	289 Erik Hanson	.15	.07	.01
☐	290 Tony Pena	.08	.04	.01
☐	291 Pascual Perez	.08	.04	.01
☐	292 Rickey Henderson	.60	.30	.06
☐	293 Kurt Stillwell	.08	.04	.01
☐	294 Todd Zeile	.30	.15	.03
☐	295 Bobby Thigpen	.12	.06	.01
☐	296 Larry Walker	.20	.10	.02
☐	297 Rob Murphy	.05	.02	.00
☐	298 Mitch Webster	.05	.02	.00
☐	299 Devon White	.08	.04	.01
☐	300 Len Dykstra	.12	.06	.01
☐	301 Keith Hernandez	.12	.06	.01
☐	302 Gene Larkin	.05	.02	.00
☐	303 Jeffrey Leonard	.05	.02	.00
☐	304 Jim Presley	.08	.04	.01
☐	305 Lloyd Moseby	.08	.04	.01
☐	306 John Smoltz	.08	.04	.01
☐	307 Sam Horn	.08	.04	.01
☐	308 Greg Litton	.10	.05	.01
☐	309 Dave Henderson	.08	.04	.01
☐	310 Mark McLemore	.05	.02	.00
☐	311 Gary Pettis	.05	.02	.00
☐	312 Mark Davis	.08	.04	.01
☐	313 Cecil Fielder	.40	.20	.04
☐	314 Jack Armstrong	.15	.07	.01
☐	315 Alvin Davis	.08	.04	.01
☐	316 Doug Jones	.08	.04	.01
☐	317 Eric Yelding	.08	.04	.01
☐	318 Joe Orsulak	.05	.02	.00
☐	319 Chuck Finley	.12	.06	.01
☐	320 Glenn Wilson	.05	.02	.00
☐	321 Harold Reynolds	.08	.04	.01
☐	322 Teddy Higuera	.08	.04	.01
☐	323 Lance Parrish	.10	.05	.01
☐	324 Bruce Hurst	.08	.04	.01
☐	325 Dave West	.08	.04	.01
☐	326 Kirk Gibson	.15	.07	.01
☐	327 Cal Ripken	.25	.12	.02
☐	328 Rick Reuschel	.08	.04	.01
☐	329 Jim Abbott	.30	.15	.03
☐	330 Checklist 221-330	.05	.02	.00

1990 Topps Ames All-Stars

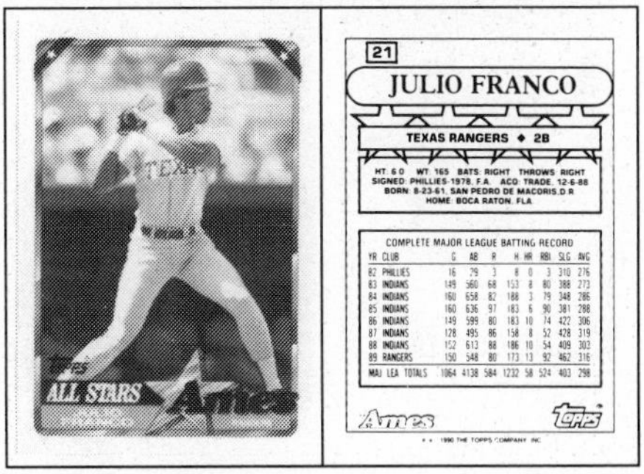

The 1990 Topps Ames All-Stars set was issued by Topps for the Ames department stores for the second straight year. This standard-size (2 1/2" by 3 1/2") set featured 33 of the leading hitters active in major league baseball. This set includes an early card of Keith Hernandez as a Cleveland Indian.

		MINT	EXC	G-VG
	COMPLETE SET (33)	4.00	2.00	.40
	COMMON PLAYER (1-33)	.10	.05	.01
☐	1 Dave Winfield	.20	.10	.02
☐	2 George Brett	.35	.17	.03
☐	3 Jim Rice	.15	.07	.01
☐	4 Dwight Evans	.15	.07	.01
☐	5 Robin Yount	.30	.15	.03
☐	6 Dave Parker	.20	.10	.02
☐	7 Eddie Murray	.30	.15	.03
☐	8 Keith Hernandez	.15	.07	.01
☐	9 Andre Dawson	.20	.10	.02
☐	10 Fred Lynn	.15	.07	.01
☐	11 Dale Murphy	.30	.15	.03
☐	12 Jack Clark	.15	.07	.01
☐	13 Rickey Henderson	.60	.30	.06
☐	14 Paul Molitor	.15	.07	.01
☐	15 Cal Ripken	.30	.15	.03
☐	16 Wade Boggs	.40	.20	.04
☐	17 Tim Raines	.20	.10	.02
☐	18 Don Mattingly	.60	.30	.06
☐	19 Kent Hrbek	.15	.07	.01
☐	20 Kirk Gibson	.15	.07	.01
☐	21 Julio Franco	.10	.05	.01
☐	22 George Bell	.15	.07	.01
☐	23 Darryl Strawberry	.35	.17	.03
☐	24 Kirby Puckett	.30	.15	.03
☐	25 Juan Samuel	.10	.05	.01
☐	26 Alvin Davis	.10	.05	.01
☐	27 Joe Carter	.15	.07	.01
☐	28 Eric Davis	.30	.15	.03
☐	29 Jose Canseco	.60	.30	.06
☐	30 Wally Joyner	.20	.10	.02
☐	31 Will Clark	.50	.25	.05
☐	32 Ruben Sierra	.30	.15	.03
☐	33 Danny Tartabull	.15	.07	.01

1990 Topps Hills Hit Men

The 1990 Topps Hit Men set is a standard-size (2 1/2" by 3 1/2") 33-card set arranged in order of slugging percentage. The set was produced by Topps for Hills Department stores. Each card in the set has a glossy-coated front.

		MINT	EXC	G-VG
	COMPLETE SET (33)	4.00	2.00	.40
	COMMON PLAYER (1-33)	.10	.05	.01
☐	1 Eric Davis	.30	.15	.03
☐	2 Will Clark	.50	.25	.05
☐	3 Don Mattingly	.60	.30	.06
☐	4 Darryl Strawberry	.40	.20	.04
☐	5 Kevin Mitchell	.25	.12	.02

☐ 6 Pedro Guerrero	.15	.07	.01
☐ 7 Jose Canseco	.75	.35	.07
☐ 8 Jim Rice	.15	.07	.01
☐ 9 Danny Tartabull	.15	.07	.01
☐ 10 George Brett	.35	.17	.03
☐ 11 Kent Hrbek	.15	.07	.01
☐ 12 George Bell	.20	.10	.02
☐ 13 Eddie Murray	.30	.15	.03
☐ 14 Fred Lynn	.15	.07	.01
☐ 15 Andre Dawson	.20	.10	.02
☐ 16 Dale Murphy	.30	.15	.03
☐ 17 Dave Winfield	.20	.10	.02
☐ 18 Jack Clark	.15	.07	.01
☐ 19 Wade Boggs	.40	.20	.04
☐ 20 Ruben Sierra	.30	.15	.03
☐ 21 Dave Parker	.20	.10	.02
☐ 22 Glenn Davis	.20	.10	.02
☐ 23 Dwight Evans	.15	.07	.01
☐ 24 Jesse Barfield	.15	.07	.01
☐ 25 Kirk Gibson	.15	.07	.01
☐ 26 Alvin Davis	.10	.05	.01
☐ 27 Kirby Puckett	.30	.15	.03
☐ 28 Joe Carter	.15	.07	.01
☐ 29 Carlton Fisk	.20	.10	.02
☐ 30 Harold Baines	.10	.05	.01
☐ 31 Andres Galarraga	.15	.07	.01
☐ 32 Cal Ripken	.30	.15	.03
☐ 33 Howard Johnson	.15	.07	.01

1990 Topps Traded

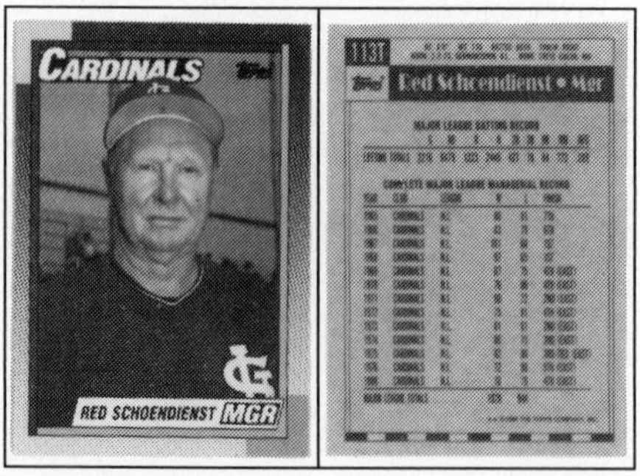

The 1990 Topps Traded Set was the tenth consecutive year Topps issued a set at the end of the year. This 132-card standard size set of 2 1/2" by 3 1/2" was arranged alphabetically by player and includes a mix of traded players and rookies for whom Topps did not include a card in the regular set. The key rookie cards in this set are Travis Fryman, Kevin Maas, and John Olerud. Also for the first time, Topps not only issued the set in a special collector boxes (made in Ireland) but distributed (on a significant basis) the set via their own wax packs. The wax pack cards were produced by Topps' Duryea, Pennsylvania plant. There were seven cards in the packs and the wrapper highlighted the set as containing promising rookies, players who changed teams, and new managers. The cards differ in that the Irish-made cards have the whiter-type backs typical of the cards made in Ireland while the American cards have the typical Topps gray-type card stock on the back. Topps also produced a specially boxed "glossy" edition frequently referred to as the Topps Traded Tiffany set. This year, again, Topps did not disclose the number of Tiffany sets they produced or sold but it seems that production quantities were roughly similar (approximately 15,000 sets) to the previous year. The checklist of cards is identical to that of the normal non-glossy cards. There are two primary distinguishing features of the Tiffany cards, white card stock reverses and high gloss obverses. These Tiffany cards are valued at approximately four times the values listed below.

	MINT	EXC	G-VG
COMPLETE SET (132)	11.00	5.50	1.10
COMMON PLAYER (1T-132T)	.06	.03	.00
☐ 1T Darrel Akerfelds	.06	.03	.00
☐ 2T Sandy Alomar Jr.	.30	.15	.03
☐ 3T Brad Arnsberg	.10	.05	.01
☐ 4T Steve Avery	.25	.12	.02
☐ 5T Wally Backman	.06	.03	.00
☐ 6T Carlos Baerga	.40	.20	.04
☐ 7T Kevin Bass	.10	.05	.01
☐ 8T Willie Blair	.10	.05	.01
☐ 9T Mike Blowers	.20	.10	.02
☐ 10T Shawn Boskie	.20	.10	.02
☐ 11T Daryl Boston	.10	.05	.01
☐ 12T Dennis Boyd	.10	.05	.01
☐ 13T Glenn Braggs	.10	.05	.01
☐ 14T Hubie Brooks	.10	.05	.01
☐ 15T Tom Brunansky	.10	.05	.01
☐ 16T John Burkett	.30	.15	.03
☐ 17T Casey Candaele	.06	.03	.00
☐ 18T John Candelaria	.06	.03	.00
☐ 19T Gary Carter	.10	.05	.01
☐ 20T Joe Carter	.12	.06	.01
☐ 21T Rick Cerone	.06	.03	.00
☐ 22T Scott Coolbaugh	.15	.07	.01
☐ 23T Bobby Cox MG	.06	.03	.00
☐ 24T Mark Davis	.10	.05	.01
☐ 25T Storm Davis	.10	.05	.01
☐ 26T Edgar Diaz	.12	.06	.01
☐ 27T Wayne Edwards	.15	.07	.01
☐ 28T Mark Eichhorn	.06	.03	.00
☐ 29T Scott Erickson	.35	.17	.03
☐ 30T Nick Esasky	.10	.05	.01
☐ 31T Cecil Fielder	.50	.25	.05
☐ 32T John Franco	.10	.05	.01
☐ 33T Travis Fryman	.75	.35	.07
☐ 34T Bill Gullickson	.06	.03	.00
☐ 35T Darryl Hamilton	.10	.05	.01
☐ 36T Mike Harkey	.20	.10	.02
☐ 37T Bud Harrelson MG	.10	.05	.01
☐ 38T Billy Hatcher	.10	.05	.01
☐ 39T Keith Hernandez	.10	.05	.01
☐ 40T Joe Hesketh	.06	.03	.00
☐ 41T Dave Hollins	.25	.12	.02
☐ 42T Sam Horn	.10	.05	.01
☐ 43T Steve Howard	.12	.06	.01
☐ 44T Todd Hundley	.20	.10	.02
☐ 45T Jeff Huson	.10	.05	.01
☐ 46T Chris James	.10	.05	.01
☐ 47T Stan Javier	.06	.03	.00
☐ 48T Dave Justice	2.50	1.25	.25
☐ 49T Jeff Kaiser	.10	.05	.01
☐ 50T Dana Kiecker	.20	.10	.02
☐ 51T Joe Klink	.10	.05	.01
☐ 52T Brent Knackert	.15	.07	.01
☐ 53T Brad Komminsk	.06	.03	.00
☐ 54T Mark Langston	.10	.05	.01
☐ 55T Tim Layana	.20	.10	.02
☐ 56T Rick Leach	.06	.03	.00
☐ 57T Terry Leach	.06	.03	.00
☐ 58T Tim Leary	.10	.05	.01
☐ 59T Craig Lefferts	.06	.03	.00
☐ 60T Charlie Leibrandt	.06	.03	.00
☐ 61T Jim Leyritz	.25	.12	.02
☐ 62T Fred Lynn	.12	.06	.01
☐ 63T Kevin Maas	2.25	1.10	.22
☐ 64T Shane Mack	.10	.05	.01
☐ 65T Candy Maldonado	.10	.05	.01
☐ 66T Fred Manrique	.06	.03	.00
☐ 67T Mike Marshall	.10	.05	.01
☐ 68T Carmelo Martinez	.06	.03	.00
☐ 69T John Marzano	.10	.05	.01

☐ 70T Ben McDonald	1.00	.50	.10
☐ 71T Jack McDowell	.15	.07	.01
☐ 72T John McNamara MG	.06	.03	.00
☐ 73T Orlando Mercado	.06	.03	.00
☐ 74T Stump Merrill MG	.10	.05	.01
☐ 75T Alan Mills	.15	.07	.01
☐ 76T Hal Morris	.25	.12	.02
☐ 77T Lloyd Moseby	.10	.05	.01
☐ 78T Randy Myers	.10	.05	.01
☐ 79T Tim Naehring	.30	.15	.03
☐ 80T Junior Noboa	.10	.05	.01
☐ 81T Matt Nokes	.10	.05	.01
☐ 82T Pete O'Brien	.10	.05	.01
☐ 83T John Olerud	1.75	.85	.17
☐ 84T Greg Olson	.25	.12	.02
☐ 85T Junior Ortiz	.06	.03	.00
☐ 86T Dave Parker	.10	.05	.01
☐ 87T Rick Parker	.12	.06	.01
☐ 88T Bob Patterson	.06	.03	.00
☐ 89T Alejandro Pena	.06	.03	.00
☐ 90T Tony Pena	.10	.05	.01
☐ 91T Pascual Perez	.10	.05	.01
☐ 92T Gerald Perry	.06	.03	.00
☐ 93T Dan Petry	.06	.03	.00
☐ 94T Gary Pettis	.06	.03	.00
☐ 95T Tony Phillips	.06	.03	.00
☐ 96T Lou Piniella MG	.10	.05	.01
☐ 97T Luis Polonia	.06	.03	.00
☐ 98T Jim Presley	.06	.03	.00
☐ 99T Scott Radinsky	.20	.10	.02
☐ 100T Willie Randolph	.10	.05	.01
☐ 101T Jeff Reardon	.10	.05	.01
☐ 102T Greg Riddoch MG	.10	.05	.01
☐ 103T Jeff Robinson	.06	.03	.00
☐ 104T Ron Robinson	.06	.03	.00
☐ 105T Kevin Romine	.06	.03	.00
☐ 106T Scott Ruskin	.20	.10	.02
☐ 107T John Russell	.06	.03	.00
☐ 108T Bill Sampen	.20	.10	.02
☐ 109T Juan Samuel	.10	.05	.01
☐ 110T Scott Sanderson	.10	.05	.01
☐ 111T Jack Savage	.10	.05	.01
☐ 112T Dave Schmidt	.06	.03	.00
☐ 113T Red Schoendienst MG	.10	.05	.01
☐ 114T Terry Shumpert	.15	.07	.01
☐ 115T Matt Sinatro	.06	.03	.00
☐ 116T Don Slaught	.06	.03	.00
☐ 117T Bryn Smith	.06	.03	.00
☐ 118T Lee Smith	.10	.05	.01
☐ 119T Paul Sorrento	.12	.06	.01
☐ 120T Franklin Stubbs	.10	.05	.01
☐ 121T Russ Swan	.20	.10	.02
☐ 122T Bob Tewksbury	.06	.03	.00
☐ 123T Wayne Tolleson	.06	.03	.00
☐ 124T John Tudor	.10	.05	.01
☐ 125T Randy Veres	.10	.05	.01
☐ 126T Hector Villanueva	.25	.12	.02
☐ 127T Mitch Webster	.06	.03	.00
☐ 128T Ernie Whitt	.06	.03	.00
☐ 129T Frank Wills	.06	.03	.00
☐ 130T Dave Winfield	.12	.06	.01
☐ 131T Matt Young	.06	.03	.00
☐ 132T Checklist Card	.06	.01	.00

1991 Topps

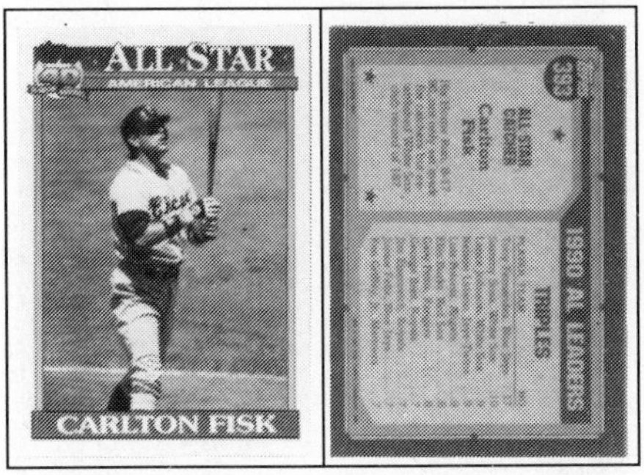

The 1991 Topps Set consists of 792 cards in the now standard size of 2 1/2" by 3 1/2". This set marks Topps 10th consecutive year of issuing a 792 card set. Topps also commemorated their fourtieth anniversary by including a "Topps 40" logo on the front of each card. As a special promotion Topps inserted (randomly) into their wax packs one of every previous card they ever issued. Topps again issued their checklists in team order (and alphabetically within team) and included a special 22-card All-Star set (386-407). There are five players listed as Future Stars, 114 Lance Dickson, 211 Brian Barnes, 561 Tim McIntosh, 587 Jose Offerman, and 594 Rich Garces. There are nine players listed as First Draft Picks, 69 Daniel Wilson, 74 Shane Andrews, 103 Tim Costo, 113 Carl Everett, 278 Alex Fernandez, 471 Mike Lieberthal, 491 Kurt Miller, 529 Marc Newfield, and 596 Ronnie Walden.

	MINT	EXC	G-VG
COMPLETE SET (792)	24.00	12.00	2.40
COMMON PLAYER (1-792)	.03	.01	.00
☐ 1 Nolan Ryan	.25	.12	.02
☐ 2 George Brett RB	.10	.05	.01
☐ 3 Carlton Fisk RB	.08	.04	.01
☐ 4 Kevin Maas RB	.25	.12	.02
☐ 5 Cal Ripken RB	.10	.05	.01
☐ 6 Nolan Ryan RB	.20	.10	.02
☐ 7 Ryne Sandberg RB	.10	.05	.01
☐ 8 Bobby Thigpen RB	.06	.03	.00
☐ 9 Darrin Fletcher	.12	.06	.01
☐ 10 Gregg Olson	.10	.05	.01
☐ 11 Roberto Kelly	.08	.04	.01
☐ 12 Paul Assenmacher	.03	.01	.00
☐ 13 Mariano Duncan	.06	.03	.00
☐ 14 Dennis Lamp	.03	.01	.00
☐ 15 Von Hayes	.06	.03	.00
☐ 16 Mike Heath	.03	.01	.00
☐ 17 Jeff Brantley	.06	.03	.00
☐ 18 Nelson Liriano	.03	.01	.00
☐ 19 Jeff Robinson New York Yankees	.03	.01	.00
☐ 20 Pedro Guerrero	.08	.04	.01
☐ 21 Joe Morgan MG	.06	.03	.00
☐ 22 Storm Davis	.06	.03	.00
☐ 23 Jim Gantner	.03	.01	.00
☐ 24 Dave Martinez	.03	.01	.00
☐ 25 Tim Belcher	.06	.03	.00
☐ 26 Luis Sojo	.06	.03	.00
☐ 27 Bobby Witt	.08	.04	.01
☐ 28 Alvaro Espinoza	.03	.01	.00
☐ 29 Bob Walk	.03	.01	.00
☐ 30 Gregg Jefferies	.15	.07	.01
☐ 31 Colby Ward	.10	.05	.01
☐ 32 Mike Simms	.10	.05	.01
☐ 33 Barry Jones	.03	.01	.00
☐ 34 Atlee Hammaker	.03	.01	.00
☐ 35 Greg Maddux	.06	.03	.00
☐ 36 Donnie Hill	.03	.01	.00
☐ 37 Tom Bolton	.03	.01	.00
☐ 38 Scott Bradley	.03	.01	.00
☐ 39 Jim Neidlinger	.15	.07	.01
☐ 40 Kevin Mitchell	.15	.07	.01
☐ 41 Ken Dayley	.03	.01	.00
☐ 42 Chris Hoiles	.15	.07	.01
☐ 43 Roger McDowell	.03	.01	.00
☐ 44 Mike Felder	.03	.01	.00
☐ 45 Chris Sabo	.10	.05	.01
☐ 46 Tim Drummond	.03	.01	.00
☐ 47 Brook Jacoby	.06	.03	.00
☐ 48 Dennis Boyd	.06	.03	.00
☐ 49A Pat Borders ERR (40 steals at Kinston in '86)	.25	.12	.02
☐ 49B Pat Borders COR (0 steals at Kinston in '86)	.06	.03	.00
☐ 50 Bob Welch	.08	.04	.01
☐ 51 Art Howe MG	.03	.01	.00
☐ 52 Francisco Oliveras	.03	.01	.00
☐ 53 Mike Sharperson	.03	.01	.00
☐ 54 Gary Mielke	.03	.01	.00
☐ 55 Jeffrey Leonard	.06	.03	.00
☐ 56 Jeff Parrett	.03	.01	.00
☐ 57 Jack Howell	.03	.01	.00
☐ 58 Mel Stottlemyre Jr.	.06	.03	.00
☐ 59 Eric Yelding	.06	.03	.00
☐ 60 Frank Viola	.08	.04	.01
☐ 61 Stan Javier	.03	.01	.00
☐ 62 Lee Guetterman	.03	.01	.00
☐ 63 Milt Thompson	.03	.01	.00
☐ 64 Tom Herr	.03	.01	.00
☐ 65 Bruce Hurst	.06	.03	.00
☐ 66 Terry Kennedy	.03	.01	.00

☐ 67 Rick Honeycutt	.03	.01	.00
☐ 68 Gary Sheffield	.12	.06	.01
☐ 69 Steve Wilson	.03	.01	.00
☐ 70 Ellis Burks	.10	.05	.01
☐ 71 Jim Acker	.03	.01	.00
☐ 72 Junior Ortiz	.03	.01	.00
☐ 73 Craig Worthington	.06	.03	.00
☐ 74 Shane Andrews	.15	.07	.01
☐ 75 Jack Morris	.06	.03	.00
☐ 76 Jerry Browne	.03	.01	.00
☐ 77 Drew Hall	.03	.01	.00
☐ 78 Geno Petralli	.03	.01	.00
☐ 79 Frank Thomas	.40	.20	.04
☐ 80A Fernando Valenzuela ERR (104 earned runs in '90 tied for league lead)	.25	.12	.02
☐ 80B Fernando Valenzuela COR (104 earned runs in '90 led league)	.08	.04	.01
☐ 81 Cito Gaston MG	.06	.03	.00
☐ 82 Tom Glavine	.03	.01	.00
☐ 83 Milt Thompson	.03	.01	.00
☐ 84 Bob McClure	.03	.01	.00
☐ 85 Jesse Barfield	.08	.04	.01
☐ 86 Les Lancaster	.03	.01	.00
☐ 87 Tracy Jones	.03	.01	.00
☐ 88 Bob Tewksbury	.03	.01	.00
☐ 89 Darren Daulton	.03	.01	.00
☐ 90 Danny Tartabull	.08	.04	.01
☐ 91 Greg Colbrunn	.15	.07	.01
☐ 92 Danny Jackson	.06	.03	.00
☐ 93 Ivan Calderon	.06	.03	.00
☐ 94 John Dopson	.03	.01	.00
☐ 95 Paul Molitor	.08	.04	.01
☐ 96 Trevor Wilson	.06	.03	.00
☐ 97A Brady Anderson ERR (September, 2 RBI and 3 hits, should be 3 RBI and 14 hits	.25	.12	.02
☐ 97B Brady Anderson COR	.06	.03	.00
☐ 98 Sergio Valdez	.06	.03	.00
☐ 99 Chris Gwynn	.03	.01	.00
☐ 100A Don Mattingly ERR (10 hits in 1990)	1.00	.50	.10
☐ 100B Don Mattingly COR (101 hits in 1990)	.30	.15	.03
☐ 101 Rob Ducey	.03	.01	.00
☐ 102 Gene Larkin	.03	.01	.00
☐ 103 Tim Costo	.40	.20	.04
☐ 104 Don Robinson	.03	.01	.00
☐ 105 Kevin McReynolds	.08	.03	.01
☐ 106 Ed Nunez	.03	.01	.00
☐ 107 Luis Polonia	.03	.01	.00
☐ 108 Matt Young	.03	.01	.00
☐ 109 Greg Riddoch MG	.03	.01	.00
☐ 110 Tom Henke	.06	.03	.00
☐ 111 Andres Thomas	.03	.01	.00
☐ 112 Frank DiPino	.03	.01	.00
☐ 113 Carl Everett	.30	.15	.03
☐ 114 Lance Dickson	.25	.12	.02
☐ 115 Hubie Brooks	.06	.03	.00
☐ 116 Mark Davis	.08	.04	.01
☐ 117 Dion James	.03	.01	.00
☐ 118 Tom Edens	.10	.05	.01
☐ 119 Carl Nichols	.03	.01	.00
☐ 120 Joe Carter	.08	.04	.01
☐ 121 Eric King	.03	.01	.00
☐ 122 Paul O'Neill	.06	.03	.00
☐ 123 Greg Harris	.03	.01	.00
☐ 124 Randy Bush	.03	.01	.00
☐ 125 Steve Bedrosian	.06	.03	.00
☐ 126 Bernard Gilkey	.25	.12	.02
☐ 127 Joe Price	.03	.01	.00
☐ 128 Travis Fryman	.40	.20	.04
☐ 129 Mark Eichhorn	.03	.01	.00
☐ 130 Ozzie Smith	.08	.04	.01
☐ 131A Checklist 1 ERR 727 Phil Bradley	.25	.05	.01
☐ 131A Checklist 1 COR 717 Phil Bradley	.25	.05	.01
☐ 132 Jamie Quirk	.03	.01	.00
☐ 133 Greg Briley	.06	.03	.00
☐ 134 Kevin Elster	.03	.01	.00
☐ 135 Jerome Walton	.20	.10	.02
☐ 136 Dave Schmidt	.03	.01	.00
☐ 137 Randy Ready	.03	.01	.00
☐ 138 Jamie Moyer	.03	.01	.00
☐ 139 Jeff Treadway	.03	.01	.00
☐ 140 Fred McGriff	.10	.05	.01
☐ 141 Nick Leyva MG	.03	.01	.00
☐ 142 Curt Wilkerson	.03	.01	.00
☐ 143 John Smiley	.03	.01	.00
☐ 144 Dave Henderson	.06	.03	.00
☐ 145 Lou Whitaker	.06	.03	.00
☐ 146 Dan Plesac	.03	.01	.00
☐ 147 Carlos Baerga	.15	.07	.01
☐ 148 Rey Palacios	.03	.01	.00
☐ 149 Al Osuna	.10	.05	.01
☐ 150 Cal Ripken	.12	.06	.01
☐ 151 Tom Browning	.06	.03	.00
☐ 152 Mickey Hatcher	.03	.01	.00
☐ 153 Bryan Harvey	.03	.01	.00
☐ 154 Jay Buhner	.06	.03	.00
☐ 155A Dwight Evans ERR (led league with 162 games in '82)	.25	.12	.02
☐ 155B Dwight Evans COR (tied for lead with 162 games in '82)	.08	.04	.01
☐ 156 Carlos Martinez	.03	.01	.00
☐ 157 John Smoltz	.06	.03	.00
☐ 158 Jose Uribe	.03	.01	.00
☐ 159 Joe Boever	.03	.01	.00
☐ 160 Vince Coleman	.08	.04	.01
☐ 161 Tim Leary	.06	.03	.00
☐ 162 Ozzie Canseco	.15	.07	.01
☐ 163 Dave Johnson	.03	.01	.00
☐ 164 Edgar Diaz	.06	.03	.00
☐ 165 Sandy Alomar Jr.	.15	.07	.01
☐ 166 Harold Baines	.08	.04	.01
☐ 167A Randy Tomlin ERR (Harriburg)	.25	.12	.02
☐ 167B Randy Tomlin COR (Harrisburg)	.10	.05	.01
☐ 168 John Olerud	.35	.17	.03
☐ 169 Luis Aquino	.03	.01	.00
☐ 170 Carlton Fisk	.10	.05	.01
☐ 171 Tony LaRussa MG	.06	.03	.00
☐ 172 Pete Incaviglia	.06	.03	.00
☐ 173 Jason Grimsley	.03	.01	.00
☐ 174 Ken Caminiti	.03	.01	.00
☐ 175 Jack Armstrong	.06	.03	.00
☐ 176 John Orton	.08	.04	.01
☐ 177 Reggie Harris	.12	.06	.01
☐ 178 Dave Valle	.03	.01	.00
☐ 179 Pete Harnisch	.03	.01	.00
☐ 180 Tony Gwynn	.12	.06	.01
☐ 181 Duane Ward	.03	.01	.00
☐ 182 Junior Noboa	.03	.01	.00
☐ 183 Clay Parker	.03	.01	.00
☐ 184 Gary Green	.03	.01	.00
☐ 185 Joe Magrane	.06	.03	.00
☐ 186 Rod Booker	.03	.01	.00
☐ 187 Greg Cadaret	.03	.01	.00
☐ 188 Damon Berryhill	.03	.01	.00
☐ 189 Daryl Irvine	.10	.05	.01
☐ 190 Matt Williams	.12	.06	.01
☐ 191 Willie Blair	.03	.01	.00
☐ 192 Rob Deer	.06	.03	.00
☐ 193 Felix Fermin	.03	.01	.00
☐ 194 Xavier Hernandez	.08	.04	.01
☐ 195 Wally Joyner	.08	.04	.01
☐ 196 Jim Vatcher	.15	.07	.01
☐ 197 Chris Nabholz	.15	.07	.01
☐ 198 R.J. Reynolds	.03	.01	.00
☐ 199 Mike Hartley	.10	.05	.01
☐ 200 Darryl Strawberry	.15	.07	.01
☐ 201 Tom Kelly MG	.03	.01	.00
☐ 202 Jim Leyritz	.10	.05	.01
☐ 203 Gene Harris	.03	.01	.00
☐ 204 Herm Winningham	.03	.01	.00
☐ 205 Mike Perez	.10	.05	.01
☐ 206 Carlos Quintana	.08	.04	.01
☐ 207 Gary Wayne	.03	.01	.00
☐ 208 Willie Wilson	.06	.03	.00
☐ 209 Ken Howell	.03	.01	.00
☐ 210 Lance Parrish	.08	.04	.01
☐ 211 Brian Barnes	.10	.05	.01
☐ 212 Steve Finley	.06	.03	.00
☐ 213 Frank Wills	.03	.01	.00
☐ 214 Joe Girardi	.03	.01	.00
☐ 215 Dave Smith	.03	.01	.00
☐ 216 Greg Gagne	.03	.01	.00
☐ 217 Chris Bosio	.03	.01	.00
☐ 218 Rick Parker	.03	.01	.00
☐ 219 Jack McDowell	.06	.03	.00
☐ 220 Tim Wallach	.06	.03	.00
☐ 221 Don Slaught	.03	.01	.00
☐ 222 Brian McRae	.60	.30	.06
☐ 223 Allan Anderson	.03	.01	.00
☐ 224 Juan Gonzalez	.25	.12	.02
☐ 225 Randy Johnson	.06	.03	.00
☐ 226 Alfredo Griffin	.03	.01	.00
☐ 227 Steve Avery	.15	.07	.01
☐ 228 Rex Hudler	.03	.01	.00
☐ 229 Rance Mulliniks	.03	.01	.00
☐ 230 Sid Fernandez	.06	.03	.00

☐ 231	Doug Rader MG	.03	.01	.00
☐ 232	Jose DeJesus	.03	.01	.00
☐ 233	Al Leiter	.06	.03	.00
☐ 234	Scott Erickson	.10	.05	.01
☐ 235	Dave Parker	.08	.04	.01
☐ 236A	Frank Tanana ERR (tied for lead with 269 K's in '75)	.03	.01	.00
☐ 236B	Frank Tanana COR (led league with 269 K's in '75)	.03	.01	.00
☐ 237	Rick Cerone	.03	.01	.00
☐ 238	Mike Dunne	.03	.01	.00
☐ 239	Darren Lewis	.30	.15	.03
☐ 240	Mike Scott	.08	.04	.01
☐ 241	Dave Clark	.03	.01	.00
☐ 242	Mike LaCoss	.03	.01	.00
☐ 243	Lance Johnson	.03	.01	.00
☐ 244	Mike Jeffcoat	.03	.01	.00
☐ 245	Kal Daniels	.08	.04	.01
☐ 246	Kevin Wickander	.03	.01	.00
☐ 247	Jody Reed	.06	.03	.00
☐ 248	Tom Gordon	.10	.05	.01
☐ 249	Bob Melvin	.03	.01	.00
☐ 250	Dennis Eckersley	.08	.04	.01
☐ 251	Mark Lemke	.03	.01	.00
☐ 252	Mel Rojas	.08	.04	.01
☐ 253	Garry Templeton	.03	.01	.00
☐ 254	Shawn Boskie	.06	.03	.00
☐ 255	Brian Downing	.03	.01	.00
☐ 256	Greg Hibbard	.03	.01	.00
☐ 257	Tom O'Malley	.03	.01	.00
☐ 258	Chris Hammond	.10	.05	.01
☐ 259	Hensley Meulens	.15	.07	.01
☐ 260	Harold Reynolds	.06	.03	.00
☐ 261	Bud Harrelson MG	.03	.01	.00
☐ 262	Tim Jones	.03	.01	.00
☐ 263	Checklist 2	.06	.01	.00
☐ 264	Dave Hollins	.10	.05	.01
☐ 265	Mark Gubicza	.06	.03	.00
☐ 266	Carmelo Castillo	.03	.01	.00
☐ 267	Mark Knudson	.03	.01	.00
☐ 268	Tom Brookens	.03	.01	.00
☐ 269	Joe Hesketh	.03	.01	.00
☐ 270	Mark McGwire	.20	.10	.02
☐ 271	Omar Olivares	.10	.05	.01
☐ 272	Jeff King	.06	.03	.00
☐ 273	Johnny Ray	.03	.01	.00
☐ 274	Ken Williams	.03	.01	.00
☐ 275	Alan Trammell	.08	.04	.01
☐ 276	Bill Swift	.03	.01	.00
☐ 277	Scott Coolbaugh	.03	.01	.00
☐ 278	Alex Fernandez	1.00	.50	.10
☐ 279A	Jose Gonzalez ERR (photo actually Billy Bean)	.25	.12	.02
☐ 279B	Jose Gonzalez COR	.25	.12	.02
☐ 280	Bret Saberhagen	.08	.04	.01
☐ 281	Larry Sheets	.03	.01	.00
☐ 282	Don Carman	.03	.01	.00
☐ 283	Marquis Grissom	.12	.06	.01
☐ 284	Billy Spiers	.03	.01	.00
☐ 285	Jim Abbott	.12	.06	.01
☐ 286	Ken Oberkfell	.03	.01	.00
☐ 287	Mark Grant	.03	.01	.00
☐ 288	Derrick May	.35	.17	.03
☐ 289	Tim Birtsas	.03	.01	.00
☐ 290	Steve Sax	.08	.04	.01
☐ 291	John Wathan MG	.03	.01	.00
☐ 292	Bud Black	.03	.01	.00
☐ 293	Jay Bell	.03	.01	.00
☐ 294	Mike Moore	.06	.03	.00
☐ 295	Rafael Palmeiro	.08	.04	.01
☐ 296	Mark Williamson	.03	.01	.00
☐ 297	Manny Lee	.03	.01	.00
☐ 298	Omar Vizquel	.03	.01	.00
☐ 299	Scott Radinsky	.06	.03	.00
☐ 300	Kirby Puckett	.15	.07	.01
☐ 301	Steve Farr	.03	.01	.00
☐ 302	Tim Teufel	.03	.01	.00
☐ 303	Mike Boddicker	.03	.01	.00
☐ 304	Kevin Reimer	.08	.04	.01
☐ 305	Mike Scioscia	.03	.01	.00
☐ 306A	Lonnie Smith ERR (136 games in '90)	.25	.12	.02
☐ 306B	Lonnie Smith COR (135 games in '90)	.06	.03	.00
☐ 307	Andy Benes	.10	.05	.01
☐ 308	Tom Pagnozzi	.03	.01	.00
☐ 309	Norm Charlton	.06	.03	.00
☐ 310	Gary Carter	.08	.04	.01
☐ 311	Jeff Pico	.03	.01	.00
☐ 312	Charlie Hayes	.03	.01	.00
☐ 313	Ron Robinson	.03	.01	.00
☐ 314	Gary Pettis	.03	.01	.00
☐ 315	Roberto Alomar	.08	.04	.01
☐ 316	Gene Nelson	.03	.01	.00
☐ 317	Mike Fitzgerald	.03	.01	.00
☐ 318	Rick Aguilera	.03	.01	.00
☐ 319	Jeff McKnight	.08	.04	.01
☐ 320	Tony Fernandez	.06	.03	.00
☐ 321	Bob Rodgers MG	.03	.01	.00
☐ 322	Terry Shumpert	.06	.03	.00
☐ 323	Cory Snyder	.08	.04	.01
☐ 324A	Ron Kittle ERR (Set another standard ...)	.25	.12	.02
☐ 324B	Ron Kittle COR (Tied another standard ...)	.06	.03	.00
☐ 325	Brett Butler	.06	.03	.00
☐ 326	Ken Patterson	.03	.01	.00
☐ 327	Ron Hassey	.03	.01	.00
☐ 328	Walt Terrell	.03	.01	.00
☐ 329	Dave Justice	.65	.30	.06
☐ 330	Dwight Gooden	.12	.06	.01
☐ 331	Eric Anthony	.15	.07	.01
☐ 332	Kenny Rogers	.03	.01	.00
☐ 333	Chipper Jones FDP	.60	.30	.06
☐ 334	Todd Benzinger	.03	.01	.00
☐ 335	Mitch Williams	.03	.01	.00
☐ 336	Matt Nokes	.06	.03	.00
☐ 337A	Keith Comstock ERR (Cubs logo on front)	.25	.12	.02
☐ 337B	Keith Comstock COR (Mariners logo on front)	.03	.01	.00
☐ 338	Luis Rivera	.03	.01	.00
☐ 339	Larry Walker	.10	.05	.01
☐ 340	Ramon Martinez	.15	.07	.01
☐ 341	John Moses	.03	.01	.00
☐ 342	Mickey Morandini	.15	.07	.01
☐ 343	Jose Oquendo	.03	.01	.00
☐ 344	Jeff Russell	.03	.01	.00
☐ 345	Len Dykstra	.08	.04	.01
☐ 346	Jesse Orosco	.03	.01	.00
☐ 347	Greg Vaughn	.12	.06	.01
☐ 348	Todd Stottlemyre	.06	.03	.00
☐ 349	Dave Gallagher	.03	.01	.00
☐ 350	Glenn Davis	.08	.04	.01
☐ 351	Joe Torre MG	.06	.03	.00
☐ 352	Frank White	.06	.03	.00
☐ 353	Tony Castillo	.03	.01	.00
☐ 354	Sid Bream	.03	.01	.00
☐ 355	Chili Davis	.06	.03	.00
☐ 356	Mike Marshall	.06	.03	.00
☐ 357	Jack Savage	.03	.01	.00
☐ 358	Mark Parent	.03	.01	.00
☐ 359	Chuck Cary	.03	.01	.00
☐ 360	Tim Raines	.08	.04	.01
☐ 361	Scott Garrelts	.03	.01	.00
☐ 362	Hector Villenueva	.10	.05	.01
☐ 363	Rick Mahler	.03	.01	.00
☐ 364	Dan Pasqua	.03	.01	.00
☐ 365	Mike Schooler	.03	.01	.00
☐ 366A	Checklist 3 ERR 19 Carl Nichols	.25	.05	.01
☐ 366B	Checklist 3 COR 119 Carl Nichols	.06	.01	.00
☐ 367	Dave Walsh	.10	.05	.01
☐ 368	Felix Jose	.08	.04	.01
☐ 369	Steve Searcy	.03	.01	.00
☐ 370	Kelly Gruber	.10	.05	.01
☐ 371	Jeff Montgomery	.06	.03	.00
☐ 372	Spike Owen	.03	.01	.00
☐ 373	Darrin Jackson	.03	.01	.00
☐ 374	Larry Casian	.10	.05	.01
☐ 375	Tony Pena	.06	.03	.00
☐ 376	Mike Harkey	.08	.04	.01
☐ 377	Rene Gonzales	.03	.01	.00
☐ 378A	Wilson Alvarez ERR ('89 Port Charlotte and '90 Birmingham stat lines omitted)	.50	.20	.04
☐ 378B	Wilson Alvarez COR	.20	.10	.02
☐ 379	Randy Velarde	.03	.01	.00
☐ 380	Willie McGee	.08	.04	.01
☐ 381	Jim Leyland MG	.03	.01	.00
☐ 382	Mackey Sasser	.06	.03	.00
☐ 383	Pete Smith	.03	.01	.00
☐ 384	Gerald Perry	.03	.01	.00
☐ 385	Mickey Tettleton	.06	.03	.00
☐ 386	Cecil Fielder AS	.12	.06	.01
☐ 387	Julio Franco AS	.06	.03	.00
☐ 388	Kelly Gruber AS	.08	.04	.01
☐ 389	Alan Trammell AS	.08	.04	.01
☐ 390	Jose Canseco AS	.25	.12	.02
☐ 391	Rickey Henderson AS	.12	.06	.01
☐ 392	Ken Griffey Jr. AS	.35	.17	.03

☐ 393	Carlton Fisk AS	.08	.04	.01
☐ 394	Bob Welch AS	.06	.03	.00
☐ 395	Chuck Finley AS	.06	.03	.00
☐ 396	Bobby Thigpen AS	.06	.03	.00
☐ 397	Eddie Murray AS	.08	.04	.01
☐ 398	Ryne Sandberg AS	.12	.06	.01
☐ 399	Matt Williams AS	.10	.05	.01
☐ 400	Barry Larkin AS	.08	.04	.01
☐ 401	Barry Bonds AS	.10	.05	.01
☐ 402	Darryl Strawbery AS	.12	.06	.01
☐ 403	Bobby Bonilla AS	.08	.04	.01
☐ 404	Mike Scioscia AS	.06	.03	.00
☐ 405	Doug Drabek AS	.06	.03	.00
☐ 406	Frank Viola AS	.06	.03	.00
☐ 407	John Franco AS	.06	.03	.00
☐ 408	Earnie Riles	.03	.01	.00
☐ 409	Mike Stanley	.03	.01	.00
☐ 410	Dave Righetti	.06	.03	.00
☐ 411	Lance Blankenship	.03	.01	.00
☐ 412	Dave Bergman	.03	.01	.00
☐ 413	Terry Mulholland	.03	.01	.00
☐ 414	Sammy Sosa	.15	.07	.01
☐ 415	Rick Sutcliffe	.06	.03	.00
☐ 416	Randy Milligan	.08	.04	.01
☐ 417	Bill Krueger	.03	.01	.00
☐ 418	Nick Esasky	.06	.03	.00
☐ 419	Jeff Reed	.03	.01	.00
☐ 420	Bobby Thigpen	.08	.04	.01
☐ 421	Alex Cole	.30	.15	.03
☐ 422	Rick Reuschel	.06	.03	.00
☐ 423	Rafael Ramirez	.03	.01	.00
☐ 424	Calvin Schiraldi	.03	.01	.00
☐ 425	Andy Van Slyke	.08	.04	.01
☐ 426	Joe Grahe	.10	.05	.01
☐ 427	Rick Dempsey	.03	.01	.00
☐ 428	John Barfield	.10	.05	.01
☐ 429	Stump Merrill MG	.03	.01	.00
☐ 430	Gary Gaetti	.06	.03	.00
☐ 431	Paul Gibson	.03	.01	.00
☐ 432	Delino DeShields	.20	.10	.02
☐ 433	Pat Tabler	.03	.01	.00
☐ 434	Julio Machado	.03	.01	.00
☐ 435	Kevin Maas	.40	.20	.04
☐ 436	Scott Bankhead	.03	.01	.00
☐ 437	Doug Dascenzo	.03	.01	.00
☐ 438	Vicente Palacios	.03	.01	.00
☐ 439	Dickie Thon	.03	.01	.00
☐ 440	George Bell	.08	.04	.01
☐ 441	Zane Smith	.06	.03	.00
☐ 442	Charlie O'Brien	.03	.01	.00
☐ 443	Jeff Innis	.03	.01	.00
☐ 444	Glenn Braggs	.03	.01	.00
☐ 445	Greg Swindell	.06	.03	.00
☐ 446	Craig Grebeck	.08	.04	.01
☐ 447	John Burkett	.06	.03	.00
☐ 448	Craig Lefferts	.03	.01	.00
☐ 449	Juan Berenguer	.03	.01	.00
☐ 450	Wade Boggs	.15	.07	.01
☐ 451	Neal Heaton	.03	.01	.00
☐ 452	Bill Schroeder	.03	.01	.00
☐ 453	Lenny Harris	.06	.03	.00
☐ 454A	Kevin Appier ERR ('90 Omaha stat line omitted)	.25	.12	.02
☐ 454B	Kevin Appier COR	.08	.04	.01
☐ 455	Walt Weiss	.06	.03	.00
☐ 456	Charlie Leibrandt	.03	.01	.00
☐ 457	Todd Hundley	.12	.06	.01
☐ 458	Brian Holman	.06	.03	.00
☐ 459	Tom Trebelhorn MG	.03	.01	.00
☐ 460	Dave Stieb	.08	.04	.01
☐ 461	Robin Ventura	.15	.07	.01
☐ 462	Steve Frey	.03	.01	.00
☐ 463	Dwight Smith	.08	.04	.01
☐ 464	Steve Buechele	.03	.01	.00
☐ 465	Ken Griffey	.08	.04	.01
☐ 466	Charles Nagy	.12	.06	.01
☐ 467	Dennis Cook	.06	.03	.00
☐ 468	Tim Hulett	.03	.01	.00
☐ 469	Chet Lemon	.03	.01	.00
☐ 470	Howard Johnson	.08	.04	.01
☐ 471	Mike Lieberthal	.25	.12	.02
☐ 472	Kirt Manwaring	.03	.01	.00
☐ 473	Curt Young	.03	.01	.00
☐ 474	Phil Plantier	.50	.25	.05
☐ 475	Teddy Higuera	.06	.03	.00
☐ 476	Glenn Wilson	.03	.01	.00
☐ 477	Mike Fetters	.03	.01	.00
☐ 478	Kurt Stillwell	.06	.03	.00
☐ 479	Bob Patterson	.03	.01	.00
☐ 480	Dave Magadan	.08	.04	.01
☐ 481	Eddie Whitson	.03	.01	.00
☐ 482	Tino Martinez	.30	.15	.03
☐ 483	Mike Aldrete	.03	.01	.00
☐ 484	Dave LaPoint	.03	.01	.00
☐ 485	Terry Pendleton	.03	.01	.00
☐ 486	Tommy Greene	.10	.05	.01
☐ 487	Rafael Belliard	.03	.01	.00
☐ 488	Jeff Manto	.06	.03	.00
☐ 489	Bobby Valentine MG	.03	.01	.00
☐ 490	Kirk Gibson	.08	.04	.01
☐ 491	Kurt Miller	.15	.07	.01
☐ 492	Ernie Whitt	.03	.01	.00
☐ 493	Jose Rijo	.06	.03	.00
☐ 494	Chris James	.06	.03	.00
☐ 495	Charlie Hough	.03	.01	.00
☐ 496	Marty Barrett	.03	.01	.00
☐ 497	Ben McDonald	.25	.12	.02
☐ 498	Mark Salas	.03	.01	.00
☐ 499	Melido Perez	.06	.03	.00
☐ 500	Will Clark	.25	.12	.02
☐ 501	Mike Bielecki	.03	.01	.00
☐ 502	Carney Lansford	.06	.03	.00
☐ 503	Roy Smith	.03	.01	.00
☐ 504	Julio Valera	.10	.05	.01
☐ 505	Chuck Finley	.08	.04	.01
☐ 506	Darnell Coles	.03	.01	.00
☐ 507	Steve Jeltz	.03	.01	.00
☐ 508	Mike York	.10	.05	.01
☐ 509	Glenallen Hill	.06	.03	.00
☐ 510	John Franco	.06	.03	.00
☐ 511	Steve Balboni	.03	.01	.00
☐ 512	Jose Mesa	.03	.01	.00
☐ 513	Jerald Clark	.03	.01	.00
☐ 514	Mike Stanton	.03	.01	.00
☐ 515	Alvin Davis	.06	.03	.00
☐ 516	Karl Rhodes	.10	.05	.01
☐ 517	Joe Oliver	.06	.03	.00
☐ 518	Cris Carpenter	.03	.01	.00
☐ 519	Sparky Anderson MG	.06	.03	.00
☐ 520	Mark Grace	.15	.07	.01
☐ 521	Joe Orsulak	.03	.01	.00
☐ 522	Stan Belinda	.06	.03	.00
☐ 523	Rodney McCray	.10	.05	.01
☐ 524	Darrel Akerfelds	.03	.01	.00
☐ 525	Willie Randolph	.06	.03	.00
☐ 526A	Moises Alou ERR (37 runs in 2 games for '90 Pirates)	.50	.20	.04
☐ 526B	Moises Alou COR (0 runs in 2 games for '90 Pirates)	.20	.10	.02
☐ 527A	Checklist 4 ERR 105 Keith Miller 719 Kevin McReynolds	.25	.05	.01
☐ 527B	Checklist 4 COR 105 Kevin McReynolds 719 Keith Miller	.06	.01	.00
☐ 528	Denny Martinez	.03	.01	.00
☐ 529	Marc Newfield	.25	.12	.02
☐ 530	Roger Clemens	.15	.07	.01
☐ 531	Dave Rohde	.08	.04	.01
☐ 532	Kirk McCaskill	.03	.01	.00
☐ 533	Oddibe McDowell	.06	.03	.00
☐ 534	Mike Jackson	.03	.01	.00
☐ 535	Ruben Sierra	.12	.06	.01
☐ 536	Mike Witt	.03	.01	.00
☐ 537	Jose Lind	.03	.01	.00
☐ 538	Bip Roberts	.06	.03	.00
☐ 539	Scott Terry	.03	.01	.00
☐ 540	George Brett	.12	.06	.01
☐ 541	Domingo Ramos	.03	.01	.00
☐ 542	Rob Murphy	.03	.01	.00
☐ 543	Junior Felix	.10	.05	.01
☐ 544	Chuck Crim	.03	.01	.00
☐ 545	Dale Murphy	.10	.05	.01
☐ 546	Jeff Ballard	.03	.01	.00
☐ 547	Mike Pagliarulo	.03	.01	.00
☐ 548	Jaime Navarro	.06	.03	.00
☐ 549	John McNamara MG	.03	.01	.00
☐ 550	Eric Davis	.12	.06	.01
☐ 551	Bob Kipper	.03	.01	.00
☐ 552	Jeff Hamilton	.03	.01	.00
☐ 553	Joe Klink	.10	.05	.01
☐ 554	Brian Harper	.03	.01	.00
☐ 555	Turner Ward	.20	.10	.02
☐ 556	Gary Ward	.03	.01	.00
☐ 557	Wally Whitehurst	.03	.01	.00
☐ 558	Otis Nixon	.03	.01	.00
☐ 559	Adam Peterson	.03	.01	.00
☐ 560	Greg Smith	.08	.04	.01
☐ 561	Tim McIntosh	.08	.04	.01
☐ 562	Jeff Kunkel	.03	.01	.00
☐ 563	Brent Knackert	.06	.03	.00
☐ 564	Dante Bichette	.06	.03	.00
☐ 565	Craig Biggio	.06	.03	.00
☐ 566	Craig Wilson	.10	.05	.01
☐ 567	Dwayne Henry	.03	.01	.00

☐ 568 Ron Karkovice	.03	.01	.00
☐ 569 Curt Schilling	.03	.01	.00
☐ 570 Barry Bonds	.15	.07	.01
☐ 571 Pat Combs	.06	.03	.00
☐ 572 Dave Anderson	.03	.01	.00
☐ 573 Rich Rodriguez	.03	.01	.00
☐ 574 John Marzano	.03	.01	.00
☐ 575 Robin Yount	.12	.06	.01
☐ 576 Jeff Kaiser	.03	.01	.00
☐ 577 Bill Doran	.06	.03	.00
☐ 578 Dave West	.03	.01	.00
☐ 579 Roger Craig MG	.03	.01	.00
☐ 580 Dave Stewart	.10	.05	.01
☐ 581 Luis Quinones	.03	.01	.00
☐ 582 Marty Clary	.03	.01	.00
☐ 583 Tony Phillips	.03	.01	.00
☐ 584 Kevin Brown	.06	.03	.00
☐ 585 Pete O'Brien	.03	.01	.00
☐ 586 Fred Lynn	.06	.03	.00
☐ 587 Jose Offerman	.35	.17	.03
☐ 588 Mark Whiten	.30	.15	.03
☐ 589 Scott Ruskin	.06	.03	.00
☐ 590 Eddie Murray	.10	.05	.01
☐ 591 Ken Hill	.06	.03	.00
☐ 592 B.J. Surhoff	.06	.03	.00
☐ 593A Mike Walker ERR ('90 Canton-Akron stat line omitted)	.25	.12	.02
☐ 593B Mike Walker COR	.08	.04	.01
☐ 594 Rich Garces	.10	.05	.01
☐ 595 Bill Landrum	.03	.01	.00
☐ 596 Ronnie Walden	.15	.07	.01
☐ 597 Jerry Don Gleaton	.03	.01	.00
☐ 598 Sam Horn	.06	.03	.00
☐ 599A Greg Myers ERR ('90 Syracuse stat line omitted)	.25	.12	.02
☐ 599B Greg Myers COR	.03	.01	.00
☐ 600 Bo Jackson	.30	.15	.03
☐ 601 Bob Ojeda	.06	.03	.00
☐ 602 Casey Candaele	.03	.01	.00
☐ 603A Wes Chamberlain ERR (photo actually Louie Meadows)	1.00	.50	.10
☐ 603B Wes Chamberlain COR	.30	.15	.03
☐ 604 Billy Hatcher	.06	.03	.00
☐ 605 Jeff Reardon	.06	.03	.00
☐ 606 Jim Gott	.03	.01	.00
☐ 607 Edgar Martinez	.06	.03	.00
☐ 608 Todd Burns	.03	.01	.00
☐ 609 Jeff Torborg MG	.03	.01	.00
☐ 610 Andres Galarraga	.08	.04	.01
☐ 611 Dave Eiland	.03	.01	.00
☐ 612 Steve Lyons	.03	.01	.00
☐ 613 Eric Show	.03	.01	.00
☐ 614 Luis Salazar	.03	.01	.00
☐ 615 Bert Blyleven	.06	.03	.00
☐ 616 Todd Zeile	.15	.07	.01
☐ 617 Bill Wegman	.03	.01	.00
☐ 618 Sil Campusano	.03	.01	.00
☐ 619 David Wells	.03	.01	.00
☐ 620 Ozzie Guillen	.06	.03	.00
☐ 621 Ted Power	.03	.01	.00
☐ 622 Jack Daugherty	.03	.01	.00
☐ 623 Jeff Blauser	.03	.01	.00
☐ 624 Tom Candiotti	.03	.01	.00
☐ 625 Terry Steinbach	.06	.03	.00
☐ 626 Gerald Young	.03	.01	.00
☐ 627 Tim Layana	.06	.03	.00
☐ 628 Greg Litton	.06	.03	.00
☐ 629 Wes Gardner	.03	.01	.00
☐ 630 Dave Winfield	.10	.05	.01
☐ 631 Mike Morgan	.03	.01	.00
☐ 632 Lloyd Moseby	.06	.03	.00
☐ 633 Kevin Tapani	.08	.04	.01
☐ 634 Henry Cotto	.03	.01	.00
☐ 635 Andy Hawkins	.03	.01	.00
☐ 636 Geronimo Pena	.12	.06	.01
☐ 637 Bruce Ruffin	.03	.01	.00
☐ 638 Mike Macfarlane	.03	.01	.00
☐ 639 Frank Robinson MG	.08	.04	.01
☐ 640 Andre Dawson	.10	.05	.01
☐ 641 Mike Henneman	.03	.01	.00
☐ 642 Hal Morris	.15	.07	.01
☐ 643 Jim Presley	.03	.01	.00
☐ 644 Chuck Crim	.03	.01	.00
☐ 645 Juan Samuel	.06	.03	.00
☐ 646 Andujar Cedeno	.50	.25	.05
☐ 647 Mark Portugal	.03	.01	.00
☐ 648 Lee Stevens	.15	.07	.01
☐ 649 Bill Sampen	.06	.03	.00
☐ 650 Jack Clark	.08	.04	.01
☐ 651 Alan Mills	.06	.03	.00
☐ 652 Kevin Romine	.03	.01	.00
☐ 653 Anthony Telford	.10	.05	.01
☐ 654 Paul Sorrento	.06	.03	.00
☐ 655 Erik Hanson	.08	.04	.01
☐ 656A Checklist 5 ERR 232 Len Dykstra 345 Jose DeJesus 348 Vincente Palacios 381 Jose Lind 537 Mike LaValliere 665 Jim Leyland	.25	.05	.01
☐ 656B Checklist 5 COR 232 Len Dykstra 345 Jose DeJesus 438 Vincente Palacios 537 Jose Lind 665 Mike LaValliere 381 Jim Leyland	.06	.01	.00
☐ 657 Mike Kingery	.03	.01	.00
☐ 658 Scott Aldred	.10	.05	.01
☐ 659 Oscar Azocar	.20	.10	.02
☐ 660 Lee Smith	.06	.03	.00
☐ 661 Steve Lake	.03	.01	.00
☐ 662 Ron Dibble	.06	.03	.00
☐ 663 Greg Brock	.03	.01	.00
☐ 664 John Farrell	.03	.01	.00
☐ 665 Mike LaValliere	.03	.01	.00
☐ 666 Danny Darwin	.03	.01	.00
☐ 667 Kent Anderson	.03	.01	.00
☐ 668 Bill Long	.03	.01	.00
☐ 669 Lou Piniella MG	.06	.03	.00
☐ 670 Rickey Henderson	.20	.10	.02
☐ 671 Andy McGaffigan	.03	.01	.00
☐ 672 Shane Mack	.06	.03	.00
☐ 673 Greg Olson	.10	.05	.01
☐ 674A Kevin Gross ERR (89 BB with Phillies in '88 tied for league lead)	.25	.12	.02
☐ 674B Kevin Gross COR (89 BB with Phillies in '88 led league)	.03	.01	.00
☐ 675 Tom Brunansky	.08	.04	.01
☐ 676 Scott Chiamparino	.25	.12	.02
☐ 677 Billy Ripken	.03	.01	.00
☐ 678 Mark Davidson	.03	.01	.00
☐ 679 Bill Bathe	.03	.01	.00
☐ 680 David Cone	.08	.04	.01
☐ 681 Jeff Schaefer	.08	.04	.01
☐ 682 Ray Lankford	.40	.20	.04
☐ 683 Derek Lilliquist	.03	.01	.00
☐ 684 Milt Cuyler	.15	.07	.01
☐ 685 Doug Drabek	.08	.04	.01
☐ 686 Mike Gallego	.03	.01	.00
☐ 687A John Cerutti ERR (4.46 ERA in '90)	.25	.12	.02
☐ 687B John Cerutti COR (4.76 ERA in '90)	.03	.01	.00
☐ 688 Rosario Rodriguez	.10	.05	.01
☐ 689 John Kruk	.03	.01	.00
☐ 690 Orel Hershiser	.08	.04	.01
☐ 691 Mike Blowers	.06	.03	.00
☐ 692A Efrain Valdez ERR (born 6/11/66)	.40	.20	.04
☐ 692B Efrain Valdez COR (born 7/11/66)	.10	.05	.01
☐ 693 Francisco Cabrera	.06	.03	.00
☐ 694 Randy Veres	.03	.01	.00
☐ 695 Kevin Seitzer	.08	.04	.01
☐ 696 Steve Olin	.06	.03	.00
☐ 697 Shawn Abner	.06	.03	.00
☐ 698 Mark Guthrie	.03	.01	.00
☐ 699 Jim Lefebvre MG	.03	.01	.00
☐ 700 Jose Canseco	.30	.15	.03
☐ 701 Pascual Perez	.06	.03	.00
☐ 702 Tim Naehring	.20	.10	.02
☐ 703 Juan Agosto	.03	.01	.00
☐ 704 Devon White	.06	.03	.00
☐ 705 Robby Thompson	.03	.01	.00
☐ 706A Brad Arnsberg ERR (68.2 IP in '90)	.25	.12	.02
☐ 706B Brad Arnsberg COR (62.2 IP in '90)	.06	.03	.00
☐ 707 Jim Eisenreich	.03	.01	.00
☐ 708 John Mitchell	.03	.01	.00
☐ 709 Matt Sinatro	.03	.01	.00
☐ 710 Kent Hrbek	.08	.04	.01
☐ 711 Jose DeLeon	.03	.01	.00
☐ 712 Ricky Jordan	.06	.03	.00
☐ 713 Scott Scudder	.06	.03	.00
☐ 714 Marvell Wynne	.03	.01	.00
☐ 715 Tim Burke	.06	.03	.00
☐ 716 Bob Geren	.03	.01	.00
☐ 717 Phil Bradley	.06	.03	.00
☐ 718 Steve Crawford	.03	.01	.00

		MINT	EXC	G-VG
☐	719 Keith Miller	.03	.01	.00
☐	720 Cecil Fielder	.20	.10	.02
☐	721 Mark Lee	.10	.05	.01
☐	722 Wally Backman	.03	.01	.00
☐	723 Candy Maldonado	.06	.03	.00
☐	724 David Segui	.25	.12	.02
☐	725 Ron Gant	.10	.05	.01
☐	726 Phil Stephenson	.03	.01	.00
☐	727 Mookie Wilson	.06	.03	.00
☐	728 Scott Sanderson	.03	.01	.00
☐	729 Don Zimmer MG	.03	.01	.00
☐	730 Barry Larkin	.10	.05	.01
☐	731 Jeff Gray	.10	.05	.01
☐	732 Franklin Stubbs	.06	.03	.00
☐	733 Kelly Downs	.03	.01	.00
☐	734 John Russell	.03	.01	.00
☐	735 Ron Darling	.06	.03	.00
☐	736 Dick Schofield	.03	.01	.00
☐	737 Tim Crews	.03	.01	.00
☐	738 Mel Hall	.03	.01	.00
☐	739 Russ Swan	.06	.03	.00
☐	740 Ryne Sandberg	.15	.07	.01
☐	741 Jimmy Key	.03	.01	.00
☐	742 Tommy Gregg	.03	.01	.00
☐	743 Bryn Smith	.03	.01	.00
☐	744 Nelson Santovenia	.03	.01	.00
☐	745 Doug Jones	.06	.03	.00
☐	746 John Shelby	.03	.01	.00
☐	747 Tony Fossas	.03	.01	.00
☐	748 Al Newman	.03	.01	.00
☐	749 Greg Harris	.03	.01	.00
☐	750 Bobby Bonilla	.12	.06	.01
☐	751 Wayne Edwards	.06	.03	.00
☐	752 Kevin Bass	.03	.01	.00
☐	753 Paul Marak	.10	.05	.01
☐	754 Bill Pecota	.03	.01	.00
☐	755 Mark Langston	.08	.04	.01
☐	756 Jeff Huson	.03	.01	.00
☐	757 Mark Gardner	.06	.03	.00
☐	758 Mike Devereaux	.03	.01	.00
☐	759 Bobby Cox MG	.03	.01	.00
☐	760 Benny Santiago	.08	.04	.01
☐	761 Larry Andersen	.03	.01	.00
☐	762 Mitch Webster	.03	.01	.00
☐	763 Dana Kiecker	.06	.03	.00
☐	764 Mark Carreon	.03	.01	.00
☐	765 Shawon Dunston	.08	.04	.01
☐	766 Jeff Robinson	.03	.01	.00
☐	767 Dan Wilson	.15	.07	.01
☐	768 Don Pall	.03	.01	.00
☐	769 Tim Sherrill	.10	.05	.01
☐	770 Jay Howell	.03	.01	.00
☐	771 Gary Redus	.03	.01	.00
☐	772 Kent Mercker	.10	.05	.01
☐	773 Tom Foley	.03	.01	.00
☐	774 Dennis Rasmussen	.03	.01	.00
☐	775 Julio Franco	.06	.03	.00
☐	776 Brent Mayne	.08	.04	.01
☐	777 John Candelaria	.03	.01	.00
☐	778 Dan Gladden	.03	.01	.00
☐	779 Carmelo Martinez	.03	.01	.00
☐	780A Randy Myers ERR (2 losses with Reds in '90)	.25	.12	.02
☐	780B Randy Myers COR (6 losses with Reds in '90)	.06	.03	.00
☐	781 Darryl Hamilton	.03	.01	.00
☐	782 Jim Deshaies	.03	.01	.00
☐	783 Joel Skinner	.03	.01	.00
☐	784 Willie Fraser	.03	.01	.00
☐	785 Scott Fletcher	.03	.01	.00
☐	786 Eric Plunk	.03	.01	.00
☐	787 Checklist 6	.06	.01	.00
☐	788 Bob Milacki	.06	.03	.00
☐	789 Tom Lasorda MG	.06	.03	.00
☐	790 Ken Griffey Jr.	.75	.35	.07
☐	791 Mike Benjamin	.10	.05	.01
☐	792 Mike Greenwell	.12	.06	.01

1991 Topps Box Bottoms

Topps again in 1991 issued cards on the bottom of their wax packs. This 16-card, standard-size, 2 1/2" by 3 1/2", set honored various career highlights of players active in 1990. The cards have the typical Topps 1991 design on the front of the card and back is a brief description of the milestone reached by the player. The set was issued in alphabetical order and is "lettered" rather than numbered.

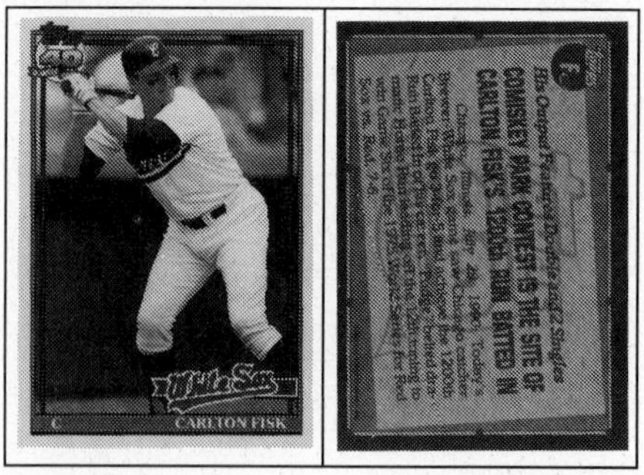

	MINT	EXC	G-VG
COMPLETE SET (16)	3.00	1.50	.30
COMMON PLAYER (A-P)	.10	.05	.01
☐ A Bert Blyleven	.15	.07	.01
☐ B George Brett	.25	.12	.02
☐ C Brett Butler	.15	.07	.01
☐ D Andre Dawson	.20	.10	.02
☐ E Dwight Evans	.15	.07	.01
☐ F Carlton Fisk	.25	.12	.02
☐ G Alfredo Griffin	.10	.05	.01
☐ H Rickey Henderson	.40	.20	.04
☐ I Willie McGee	.20	.10	.02
☐ J Dale Murphy	.25	.12	.02
☐ K Eddie Murray	.20	.10	.02
☐ L Dave Parker	.20	.10	.02
☐ M Jeff Reardon	.15	.07	.01
☐ N Nolan Ryan	.50	.25	.05
☐ O Juan Samuel	.10	.05	.01
☐ P Robin Yount	.25	.12	.02

1987 Toys'R'Us Rookies

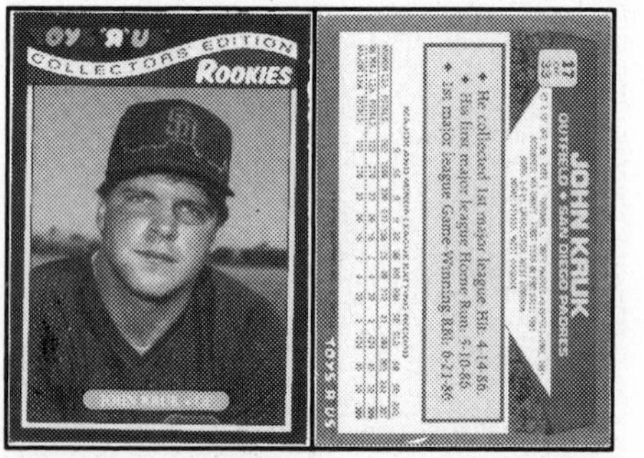

Topps produced this 33-card boxed set for Toys'R'Us stores. The set is subtitled "Baseball Rookies" and features predominantly younger players. The cards measure 2 1/2" by 3 1/2" and feature a high-gloss, full-color photo of the player inside a black border. The card backs are printed in orange and blue on white card stock.

	MINT	EXC	G-VG
COMPLETE SET (33)	7.00	3.50	.70
COMMON PLAYER (1-33)	.10	.05	.01
☐ 1 Andy Allanson	.10	.05	.01
☐ 2 Paul Assenmacher	.10	.05	.01
☐ 3 Scott Bailes	.10	.05	.01
☐ 4 Barry Bonds	.75	.35	.07
☐ 5 Jose Canseco	1.25	.60	.12

☐ 6 John Cerutti	.10	.05	.01
☐ 7 Will Clark	1.00	.50	.10
☐ 8 Kal Daniels	.50	.25	.05
☐ 9 Jim Deshaies	.15	.07	.01
☐ 10 Mark Eichhorn	.10	.05	.01
☐ 11 Ed Hearn	.10	.05	.01
☐ 12 Pete Incaviglia	.35	.17	.03
☐ 13 Bo Jackson	1.50	.75	.15
☐ 14 Wally Joyner	.60	.30	.06
☐ 15 Charlie Kerfeld	.10	.05	.01
☐ 16 Eric King	.15	.07	.01
☐ 17 John Kruk	.20	.10	.02
☐ 18 Barry Larkin	.75	.35	.07
☐ 19 Mike LaValliere	.10	.05	.01
☐ 20 Greg Mathews	.15	.07	.01
☐ 21 Kevin Mitchell	.75	.35	.07
☐ 22 Dan Plesac	.15	.07	.01
☐ 23 Bruce Ruffin	.10	.05	.01
☐ 24 Ruben Sierra	.75	.35	.07
☐ 25 Cory Snyder	.30	.15	.03
☐ 26 Kurt Stillwell	.20	.10	.02
☐ 27 Dale Sveum	.15	.07	.01
☐ 28 Danny Tartabull	.30	.15	.03
☐ 29 Andres Thomas	.15	.07	.01
☐ 30 Robby Thompson	.15	.07	.01
☐ 31 Jim Traber	.10	.05	.01
☐ 32 Mitch Williams	.15	.07	.01
☐ 33 Todd Worrell	.20	.10	.02

1988 Toys'R'Us Rookies

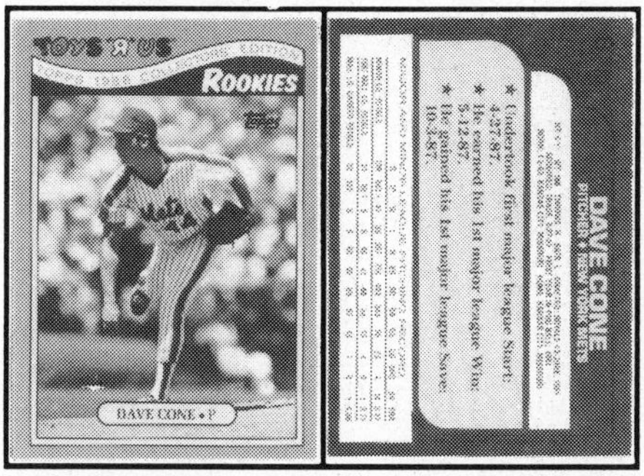

Topps produced this 33-card boxed set for Toys'R'Us stores. The set is subtitled "Baseball Rookies" and features predominantly younger players. The cards measure 2 1/2" by 3 1/2" and feature a high-gloss, full-color photo of the player inside a blue border. The card backs are printed in pink and blue on white card stock. The cards are numbered on the back and the checklist for the set is found on the back panel of the small collector box. The statistics provided on the card backs cover only three lines, Minor League totals, last season, and Major League totals.

	MINT	EXC	G-VG
COMPLETE SET (33)	5.00	2.50	.50
COMMON PLAYER (1-33)	.10	.05	.01
☐ 1 Todd Benzinger	.15	.07	.01
☐ 2 Bob Brower	.10	.05	.01
☐ 3 Jerry Browne	.10	.05	.01
☐ 4 DeWayne Buice	.10	.05	.01
☐ 5 Ellis Burks	.90	.45	.09
☐ 6 Ken Caminiti	.15	.07	.01
☐ 7 Casey Candaele	.10	.05	.01
☐ 8 Dave Cone	.60	.30	.06
☐ 9 Kelly Downs	.20	.10	.02
☐ 10 Mike Dunne	.10	.05	.01
☐ 11 Ken Gerhart	.10	.05	.01
☐ 12 Mike Greenwell	.90	.45	.09
☐ 13 Mike Henneman	.20	.10	.02
☐ 14 Sam Horn	.10	.05	.01
☐ 15 Joe Magrane	.20	.10	.02
☐ 16 Fred Manrique	.10	.05	.01
☐ 17 John Marzano	.15	.07	.01
☐ 18 Fred McGriff	.90	.45	.09
☐ 19 Mark McGwire	1.00	.50	.10
☐ 20 Jeff Musselman	.10	.05	.01
☐ 21 Randy Myers	.25	.12	.02
☐ 22 Matt Nokes	.20	.10	.02
☐ 23 Al Pedrique	.10	.05	.01
☐ 24 Luis Polonia	.15	.07	.01
☐ 25 Billy Ripken	.15	.07	.01
☐ 26 Benny Santiago	.45	.22	.04
☐ 27 Kevin Seitzer	.45	.22	.04
☐ 28 John Smiley	.20	.10	.02
☐ 29 Mike Stanley	.15	.07	.01
☐ 30 Terry Steinbach	.25	.12	.02
☐ 31 B.J. Surhoff	.20	.10	.02
☐ 32 Bobby Thigpen	.25	.12	.02
☐ 33 Devon White	.25	.12	.02

1989 Toys'R'Us Rookies

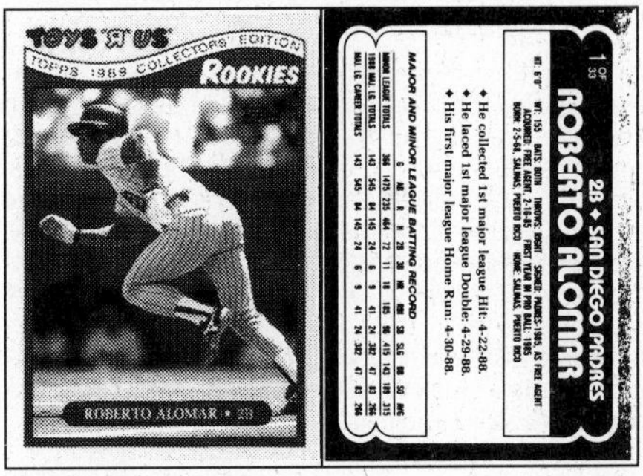

The 1989 Toys'R'Us Rookies set contains 33 standard-size (2 1/2" by 3 1/2") glossy cards. The fronts are yellow and magenta. The horizontally-oriented backs are sky blue and red, and feature 1988 and career stats. The cards were distributed through Toys 'R' Us stores as a boxed set. The subjects are numbered alphabetically. The set checklist is printed on the back panel of the set's custom box.

	MINT	EXC	G-VG
COMPLETE SET (33)	4.00	2.00	.40
COMMON PLAYER (1-33)	.10	.05	.01
☐ 1 Roberto Alomar	.40	.20	.04
☐ 2 Brady Anderson	.20	.10	.02
☐ 3 Tim Belcher	.20	.10	.02
☐ 4 Damon Berryhill	.20	.10	.02
☐ 5 Jay Buhner	.20	.10	.02
☐ 6 Sherman Corbett	.10	.05	.01
☐ 7 Kevin Elster	.15	.07	.01
☐ 8 Cecil Espy	.10	.05	.01
☐ 9 Dave Gallagher	.10	.05	.01
☐ 10 Ron Gant	.50	.25	.05
☐ 11 Paul Gibson	.10	.05	.01
☐ 12 Mark Grace	.60	.30	.06
☐ 13 Bryan Harvey	.15	.07	.01
☐ 14 Darrin Jackson	.10	.05	.01
☐ 15 Gregg Jefferies	.75	.35	.07
☐ 16 Ron Jones	.20	.10	.02
☐ 17 Ricky Jordan	.25	.12	.02
☐ 18 Roberto Kelly	.40	.20	.04
☐ 19 Al Leiter	.10	.05	.01
☐ 20 Jack McDowell	.20	.10	.02
☐ 21 Melido Perez	.15	.07	.01
☐ 22 Jeff Pico	.10	.05	.01
☐ 23 Jody Reed	.20	.10	.02
☐ 24 Chris Sabo	.45	.22	.04
☐ 25 Nelson Santovenia	.20	.10	.02
☐ 26 Mackey Sasser	.20	.10	.02
☐ 27 Mike Schooler	.20	.10	.02
☐ 28 Gary Sheffield	.50	.25	.05
☐ 29 Pete Smith	.10	.05	.01
☐ 30 Pete Stanicek	.10	.05	.01
☐ 31 Jeff Treadway	.10	.05	.01
☐ 32 Walt Weiss	.25	.12	.02
☐ 33 Dave West	.20	.10	.02

1990 Toys'R'Us Rookies

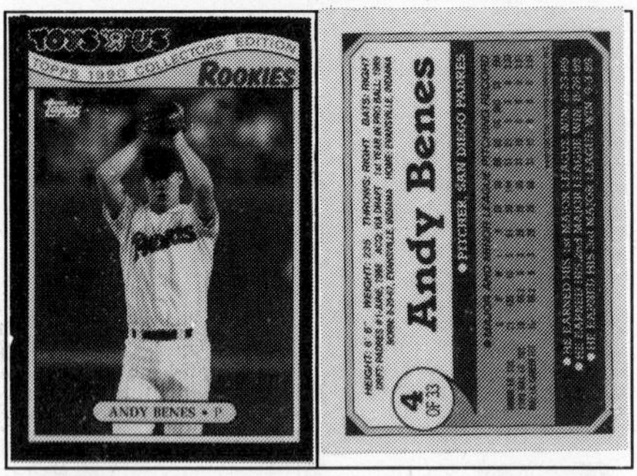

The 1990 Toys'R'Us Rookies set is a 33-card set of young prospects issued by Topps. For the fourth consecutive year Topps issued a rookie set for Toys'R'Us. There are several players in the set which were on Topps cards for the second time in 1990, i.e., not rookies even for the Topps Company. These players included Gregg Jefferies and Gregg Olson. This standard-size (2 1/2" by 3 1/2") card set might be more appropriately called the Young Stars set. The cards are numbered, with the numbering being essentially in alphabetical order by player's name. The set checklist is printed on the back panel of the set's custom box.

	MINT	EXC	G-VG
COMPLETE SET (33)	4.00	2.00	.40
COMMON PLAYER (1-33)	.10	.05	.01
☐ 1 Jim Abbott	.40	.20	.04
☐ 2 Eric Anthony	.40	.20	.04
☐ 3 Joey Belle	.20	.10	.02
☐ 4 Andy Benes	.30	.15	.03
☐ 5 Greg Briley	.20	.10	.02
☐ 6 Kevin Brown	.20	.10	.02
☐ 7 Mark Carreon	.10	.05	.01
☐ 8 Mike Devereaux	.10	.05	.01
☐ 9 Junior Felix	.30	.15	.03
☐ 10 Mark Gardner	.10	.05	.01
☐ 11 Bob Geren	.10	.05	.01
☐ 12 Tom Gordon	.30	.15	.03
☐ 13 Ken Griffey Jr.	1.25	.60	.12
☐ 14 Pete Harnisch	.10	.05	.01
☐ 15 Ken Hill	.10	.05	.01
☐ 16 Gregg Jeffries	.40	.20	.04
☐ 17 Derek Lilliquist	.10	.05	.01
☐ 18 Carlos Martinez	.10	.05	.01
☐ 19 Ramon Martinez	.40	.20	.04
☐ 20 Bob Milacki	.10	.05	.01
☐ 21 Gregg Olson	.30	.15	.03
☐ 22 Kenny Rogers	.10	.05	.01
☐ 23 Alex Sanchez	.10	.05	.01
☐ 24 Gary Sheffield	.40	.20	.04
☐ 25 Dwight Smith	.20	.10	.02
☐ 26 Billy Spiers	.10	.05	.01
☐ 27 Greg Vaughn	.40	.20	.04
☐ 28 Robin Ventura	.30	.15	.03
☐ 29 Jerome Walton	.40	.20	.04
☐ 30 Dave West	.15	.07	.01
☐ 31 John Wetteland	.15	.07	.01
☐ 32 Craig Worthington	.15	.07	.01
☐ 33 Todd Zeile	.30	.15	.03

1983 True Value White Sox

This 23-card set was sponsored by True Value Hardware Stores and features full-color (2 5/8" by 4 1/4") cards of the Chicago White Sox. Most of the set was intended for distribution two cards per game at selected White Sox Tuesday night home games. The cards are unnumbered except for uniform number given in the lower right corner of the obverse. The card backs contain statistical information in basic black and white. The cards of Harold Baines, Salome Barojas, and Marc Hill were not issued at the park; hence they are more difficult to obtain than the other 20 cards and are marked SP in the checklist below.

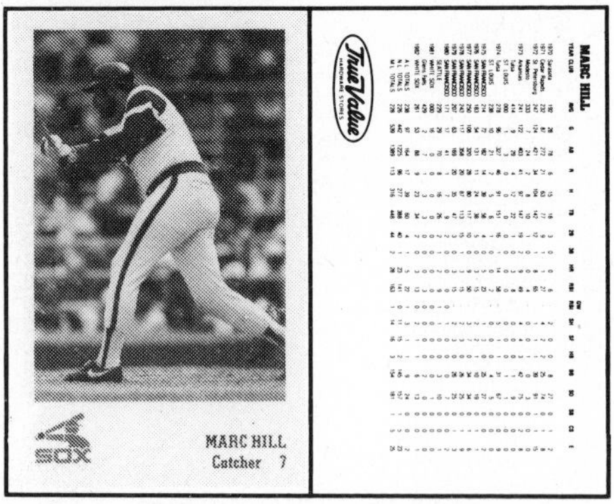

	MINT	EXC	G-VG
COMPLETE SET (23)	30.00	15.00	3.00
COMMON PLAYER (1-23)	.40	.20	.04
☐ 1 Scott Fletcher	.90	.45	.09
☐ 3 Harold Baines SP	9.00	4.50	.90
☐ 5 Vance Law	.60	.30	.06
☐ 7 Marc Hill SP	3.00	1.50	.30
☐ 10 Tony LaRussa MG	.75	.35	.07
☐ 11 Rudy Law	.40	.20	.04
☐ 14 Tony Bernazard	.50	.25	.05
☐ 17 Jerry Hairston	.40	.20	.04
☐ 19 Greg Luzinski	.75	.35	.07
☐ 24 Floyd Bannister	.60	.30	.06
☐ 25 Mike Squires	.40	.20	.04
☐ 30 Salome Barojas SP	3.00	1.50	.30
☐ 31 LaMarr Hoyt	.50	.25	.05
☐ 34 Richard Dotson	.50	.25	.05
☐ 36 Jerry Koosman	.75	.35	.07
☐ 40 Britt Burns	.40	.20	.04
☐ 41 Dick Tidrow	.40	.20	.04
☐ 42 Ron Kittle	1.00	.50	.10
☐ 44 Tom Paciorek	.40	.20	.04
☐ 45 Kevin Hickey	.40	.20	.04
☐ 53 Dennis Lamp	.40	.20	.04
☐ 67 Jim Kern	.40	.20	.04
☐ 72 Carlton Fisk	2.50	1.25	.25

1984 True Value White Sox

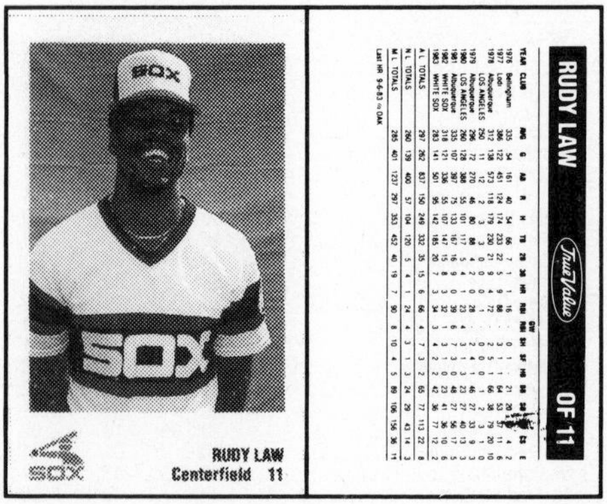

This 30-card set features full color (2 1/2" by 4") cards of the Chicago White Sox. Most of the set was distributed two cards per game at selected White Sox Tuesday home games. Faust and Minoso were not given out although their cards were available through direct (promotional) contact with them. Brennan and Hulett were not released directly since they were sent down to the minors. The cards are unnumbered except for uniform number given in the lower right corner of the obverse; they are arbitrarily listed below in alphabetical order. The card backs contain statistical information in basic black and white.

	MINT	EXC	G-VG
COMPLETE SET (30)	25.00	12.50	2.50
COMMON PLAYER (1-30)	.40	.20	.04

	MINT	EXC	G-VG
☐ 1 Juan Agosto	.40	.20	.04
☐ 2 Luis Aparicio	2.50	1.25	.25
☐ 3 Harold Baines	1.50	.75	.15
☐ 4 Floyd Bannister	.50	.25	.05
☐ 5 Salome Barojas	.40	.20	.04
☐ 6 Tom Brennan SP	1.50	.75	.15
☐ 7 Britt Burns	.40	.20	.04
☐ 8 Coaching Staff (blank back)	.40	.20	.04
☐ 9 Julio Cruz	.40	.20	.04
☐ 10 Richard Dotson	.50	.25	.05
☐ 11 Jerry Dybzinski	.40	.20	.04
☐ 12 Nancy Faust (organist) (blank back)	1.50	.75	.15
☐ 13 Carlton Fisk	2.50	1.25	.25
☐ 14 Scott Fletcher	.50	.25	.05
☐ 15 Jerry Hairston	.40	.20	.04
☐ 16 Marc Hill	.40	.20	.04
☐ 17 LaMarr Hoyt	.50	.25	.05
☐ 18 Tim Hulett SP	1.50	.75	.15
☐ 19 Ron Kittle	.75	.35	.07
☐ 20 Tony LaRussa MG	.50	.25	.05
☐ 21 Rudy Law	.40	.20	.04
☐ 22 Vance Law	.50	.25	.05
☐ 23 Greg Luzinski	.60	.30	.06
☐ 24 Minnie Minoso	2.50	1.25	.25
☐ 25 Tom Paciorek	.40	.20	.04
☐ 26 Ron Reed	.40	.20	.04
☐ 27 Tom Seaver	3.00	1.50	.30
☐ 28 Dave Stegman	.40	.20	.04
☐ 29 Mike Squires	.40	.20	.04
☐ 30 Greg Walker	.50	.25	.05

1986 True Value

The 1986 True Value set consists of 30 cards each 2 1/2" by 3 1/2" which were printed as panels of four although one of the cards in the panel only pictures a featured product. The complete panel measures 10 3/8" by 3 1/2". The True Value logo is in the upper left corner of the obverse of each card. Supposedly the cards were distributed to customers purchasing 5.00 or more at the store. Cards are frequently found with perforations intact and still in the closed form where only the top card in the folded panel is visible. The card number appears at the bottom of the reverse. Team logos have been surgically removed (airbrushed) from the photos.

	MINT	EXC	G-VG
COMPLETE SET (30)	7.50	3.75	.75
COMMON PLAYER (1-30)	.15	.07	.01

	MINT	EXC	G-VG
☐ 1 Pedro Guerrero	.20	.10	.02
☐ 2 Steve Garvey	.30	.15	.03
☐ 3 Eddie Murray	.35	.17	.03
☐ 4 Pete Rose	.50	.25	.05
☐ 5 Don Mattingly	.75	.35	.07
☐ 6 Fernando Valenzuela	.20	.10	.02
☐ 7 Jim Rice	.20	.10	.02
☐ 8 Kirk Gibson	.25	.12	.02
☐ 9 Ozzie Smith	.25	.12	.02
☐ 10 Dale Murphy	.35	.17	.03
☐ 11 Robin Yount	.45	.22	.04
☐ 12 Tom Seaver	.40	.20	.04
☐ 13 Reggie Jackson	.50	.25	.05
☐ 14 Ryne Sandberg	.45	.22	.04
☐ 15 Bruce Sutter	.15	.07	.01
☐ 16 Gary Carter	.20	.10	.02
☐ 17 George Brett	.40	.20	.04
☐ 18 Rick Sutcliffe	.15	.07	.01
☐ 19 Dave Stieb	.15	.07	.01
☐ 20 Buddy Bell	.15	.07	.01
☐ 21 Alvin Davis	.15	.07	.01
☐ 22 Cal Ripken	.30	.15	.03
☐ 23 Bill Madlock	.15	.07	.01
☐ 24 Kent Hrbek	.15	.07	.01
☐ 25 Lou Whitaker	.15	.07	.01
☐ 26 Nolan Ryan	.75	.35	.07
☐ 27 Dwayne Murphy	.15	.07	.01
☐ 28 Mike Schmidt	.60	.30	.06
☐ 29 Andre Dawson	.25	.12	.02
☐ 30 Wade Boggs	.50	.25	.05

1911 T3 Turkey Red

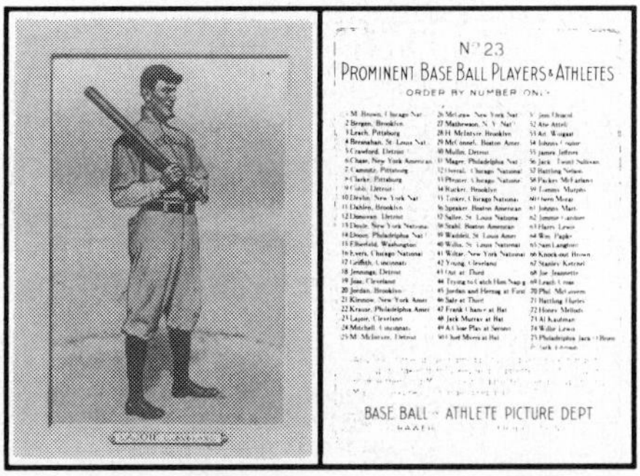

The cards in this 126-card set measure approximately 5 3/4" by 8". The 1911 "Turkey Red" set of color cabinet style cards, designated T3 in the American Card Catalog, is named after the brand of cigarettes with which it was offered as a premium. Cards 1-50 and 77-126 depict baseball players while the middle series (51-76) portrays boxers. The cards themselves are not numbered but were assigned numbers for ordering purposes by the manufacturer. This list appears on the backs of cards in the 77-126 sub-series and has been used in the checklist below. The boxers (51-76) were formerly assigned a separate catalog number (T9) but have now been returned to the classification to which they properly belong and are indicated in the checklist below by BOX. This attractive set has been reprinted recently in 2 1/2" by 3 1/2" form.

	EX-MT	VG-E	GOOD
COMPLETE SET (126)	34000.	16000.	3500.
COMMON BASEBALL (1-50)	200.00	100.00	20.00
COMMON BOXERS (51-76)	110.00	55.00	11.00
COMMON BASEBALL (77-126)	225.00	110.00	22.00

☐ 1 M. Brown: Chicago NL	400.00	200.00	40.00
☐ 2 Bergen: Brooklyn	200.00	100.00	20.00
☐ 3 Leach: Pittsburgh	200.00	100.00	20.00
☐ 4 Bresnahan: St.L. NL	350.00	175.00	35.00
☐ 5 Crawford: Detroit	400.00	200.00	40.00
☐ 6 Chase: New York AL	250.00	125.00	25.00
☐ 7 Camnitz: Pittsburgh	200.00	100.00	20.00
☐ 8 Clarke: Pittsburgh	350.00	175.00	35.00
☐ 9 Cobb: Detroit	4000.00	1750.00	350.00
☐ 10 Devlin: New York NL	200.00	100.00	20.00
☐ 11 Dahlen: Brooklyn	250.00	125.00	25.00
☐ 12 Donovan: Detroit	200.00	100.00	20.00
☐ 13 Doyle: New York NL	200.00	100.00	20.00
☐ 14 Dooin: Phila. NL	200.00	100.00	20.00
☐ 15 Elberfeld: Wash	200.00	100.00	20.00
☐ 16 Evers: Chicago NL	400.00	200.00	40.00
☐ 17 Griffith: Cinc.	350.00	175.00	35.00
☐ 18 Jennings: Detroit	350.00	175.00	35.00
☐ 19 Joss: Cleveland	450.00	225.00	45.00
☐ 20 Jordan: Brooklyn	200.00	100.00	20.00
☐ 21 Kleinow: New York NL	200.00	100.00	20.00
☐ 22 Krause: Phila. AL	200.00	100.00	20.00
☐ 23 Lajoie: Cleveland	900.00	450.00	90.00
☐ 24 Mitchell: Cincinnati	200.00	100.00	20.00
☐ 25 M. McIntyre: Detroit	200.00	100.00	20.00
☐ 26 McGraw: New York NL	500.00	250.00	50.00
☐ 27 Mathewson: N.Y. NL	1200.00	100.00	20.00
☐ 28 H. McIntyre: Brk	200.00	100.00	20.00
☐ 29 McConnell: Boston AL	200.00	100.00	20.00
☐ 30 Mullin: Detroit	200.00	100.00	20.00
☐ 31 Magee: Phila. NL	200.00	100.00	20.00
☐ 32 Overall: Chicago NL	200.00	100.00	20.00
☐ 33 Pfeister: Chicago NL	200.00	100.00	20.00
☐ 34 Rucker: Brooklyn	200.00	100.00	20.00
☐ 35 Tinker: Chicago NL	400.00	200.00	40.00
☐ 36 Speaker: Boston AL	900.00	450.00	90.00
☐ 37 Sallee: St. Louis NL	200.00	100.00	20.00
☐ 38 Stahl: Boston AL	200.00	100.00	20.00
☐ 39 Waddell: St.Louis AL	450.00	225.00	45.00
☐ 40 Willis: St.Louis NL	250.00	125.00	25.00
☐ 41 Wiltse: New York NL	200.00	100.00	20.00
☐ 42 Young: Cleveland	1000.00	400.00	80.00
☐ 43 Out At Third	200.00	100.00	20.00
☐ 44 Trying to Catch Him Napping	200.00	100.00	20.00
☐ 45 Jordan and Herzog at First	200.00	100.00	20.00
☐ 46 Safe At Third	200.00	100.00	20.00
☐ 47 Frank Chance At Bat	350.00	175.00	35.00
☐ 48 Jack Murray At Bat	200.00	100.00	20.00
☐ 49 Close Play At Second	200.00	100.00	20.00
☐ 50 Chief Myers At Bat	200.00	100.00	20.00
☐ 51 Jim Driscoll BOX	110.00	55.00	11.00
☐ 52 Abe Attell BOX	135.00	65.00	13.50
☐ 53 Ad. Walgast BOX	110.00	55.00	11.00
☐ 54 Johnny Coulon BOX	110.00	55.00	11.00
☐ 55 James Jeffries BOX	225.00	110.00	22.00
☐ 56 Jack Sullivan BOX (Twin)	135.00	65.00	13.50
☐ 57 Battling Nelson BOX	110.00	55.00	11.00
☐ 58 Packey McFarland BOX	110.00	55.00	11.00
☐ 59 Tommy Murphy BOX	110.00	55.00	11.00
☐ 60 Owen Moran BOX	110.00	55.00	11.00
☐ 61 Johnny Marto BOX	110.00	55.00	11.00
☐ 62 Jimmie Gardner BOX	110.00	55.00	11.00
☐ 63 Harry Lewis BOX	110.00	55.00	11.00
☐ 64 Wm. Papke BOX	110.00	55.00	11.00
☐ 65 Sam Langford BOX	110.00	55.00	11.00
☐ 66 Knock-out Brown BOX	110.00	55.00	11.00
☐ 67 Stanley Ketchel BOX	165.00	75.00	15.00
☐ 68 Joe Jeannette BOX	110.00	55.00	11.00
☐ 69 Leach Cross BOX	110.00	55.00	11.00
☐ 70 Phil. McGovern BOX	110.00	55.00	11.00
☐ 71 Battling Hurley BOX	110.00	55.00	11.00
☐ 72 Honey Mellody BOX	110.00	55.00	11.00
☐ 73 Al Kaufman BOX	110.00	55.00	11.00
☐ 74 Willie Lewis BOX	110.00	55.00	11.00
☐ 75 Jack O'Brien BOX "Philadelphia"	135.00	65.00	13.50
☐ 76 Jack Johnson BOX	225.00	110.00	22.00
☐ 77 Ames: New York NL	225.00	110.00	22.00
☐ 78 Baker: Phila. AL (picture probably Jack Barry)	450.00	225.00	45.00
☐ 79 Bell: Brooklyn	225.00	110.00	22.00
☐ 80 Bender: Phila. AL	450.00	225.00	45.00
☐ 81 Bescher: Cincinnati	225.00	110.00	22.00
☐ 82 Bransfield: Phila. NL	225.00	110.00	22.00
☐ 83 Bridwell: Phila. NL	225.00	110.00	22.00
☐ 84 Browne: Wash. and Chicago	225.00	110.00	22.00
☐ 85 Burns: Chi. and Cin.	225.00	110.00	22.00
☐ 86 Carrigan: Boston AL	225.00	110.00	22.00
☐ 87 Collins: Phila. AL	450.00	225.00	45.00
☐ 88 Coveleski: Cinc.	225.00	110.00	22.00
☐ 89 Criger: New York AL	225.00	110.00	22.00
☐ 90 Doolan: Phila. NL	225.00	110.00	22.00
☐ 91 Downey: Cincinnati	225.00	110.00	22.00
☐ 92 Dygert: Phila. AL	225.00	110.00	22.00
☐ 93 Fromme: Cincinnati	225.00	110.00	22.00
☐ 94 Gibson: Pittsburgh	225.00	110.00	22.00
☐ 95 Graham: Boston NL	225.00	110.00	22.00
☐ 96 Groom: Washington	225.00	110.00	22.00
☐ 97 Hoblitzell: Cinc.	225.00	110.00	22.00
☐ 98 Hofman: Chicago NL	225.00	110.00	22.00
☐ 99 Johnson: Washington	1350.00	175.00	35.00
☐ 100 D. Jones: Detroit	225.00	110.00	22.00
☐ 101 Keeler: New York NL	600.00	300.00	60.00
☐ 102 Kling: Chicago NL	225.00	110.00	22.00
☐ 103 Konetchy: St.Louis NL	225.00	110.00	22.00
☐ 104 Lennox: Brooklyn	225.00	110.00	22.00
☐ 105 Lobert: Cincinnati	225.00	110.00	22.00
☐ 106 Lord: Bos. and Chi.	225.00	110.00	22.00
☐ 107 Manning: N.Y. AL	225.00	110.00	22.00
☐ 108 Merkle: New York NL	225.00	110.00	22.00
☐ 109 Moran: Chi. and Phila.	225.00	110.00	22.00
☐ 110 McBride: Washington	225.00	110.00	22.00
☐ 111 Niles: Bos. and Cleve.	225.00	110.00	22.00
☐ 112 Paskert: Cincinnati	225.00	110.00	22.00
☐ 113 Raymond: N.Y. NL	225.00	110.00	22.00
☐ 114 Rhoades: Cleveland	300.00	150.00	30.00
☐ 115 Schlei: New York NL	225.00	110.00	22.00
☐ 116 Schmidt: Detroit	225.00	110.00	22.00
☐ 117 Schulte: Chicago NL	225.00	110.00	22.00
☐ 118 Smith: Chi. and Bos.	225.00	110.00	22.00
☐ 119 Stone: St.L. AL	225.00	110.00	22.00
☐ 120 Street: Washington	225.00	110.00	22.00
☐ 121 Sullivan: Chi. AL	225.00	110.00	22.00
☐ 122 Tenney: New York NL	225.00	110.00	22.00
☐ 123 Thomas: Phila. AL	225.00	110.00	22.00
☐ 124 Wallace: St.Louis AL	400.00	200.00	40.00
☐ 125 Walsh: Chicago AL	450.00	225.00	45.00
☐ 126 Wilson: Pittsburgh	225.00	110.00	22.00

1913 T200 Fatima

The cards in this 16-card set measure 2 5/8" by 5 13/16". The 1913 Fatima Cigarettes issue contains unnumbered glossy surface team cards. Both St. Louis team cards are considered difficult to obtain. A large 13" by 21" unnumbered, heavy cardboard premium issue is also known to exist and is quite scarce. These unnumbered team cards are ordered below by team alphabetical order within league.

	EX-MT	VG-E	GOOD
COMPLETE SET (16)	3000.00	1250.00	250.00
COMMON TEAM (1-16)	150.00	75.00	15.00
☐ 1 Boston AL	200.00	100.00	20.00
☐ 2 Chicago AL	150.00	75.00	15.00
☐ 3 Cleveland AL	150.00	75.00	15.00
☐ 4 Detroit AL	250.00	125.00	25.00
☐ 5 New York AL	500.00	250.00	50.00
☐ 6 Philadelphia AL	150.00	75.00	15.00
☐ 7 St. Louis AL	400.00	200.00	40.00
☐ 8 Washington AL	150.00	75.00	15.00
☐ 9 Boston NL	250.00	125.00	25.00
☐ 10 Brooklyn NL	150.00	75.00	15.00
☐ 11 Chicago NL	150.00	75.00	15.00
☐ 12 Cincinnati NL	150.00	75.00	15.00
☐ 13 New York NL	150.00	75.00	15.00
☐ 14 Philadelphia NL	150.00	75.00	15.00
☐ 15 Pittsburg NL	150.00	75.00	15.00
☐ 16 St. Louis NL	250.00	125.00	25.00

1911 T201 Mecca

The cards in this 50-card set measure 2 1/4" by 4 11/16". The 1911 Mecca Double Folder issue contains unnumbered cards. This issue was one of the first to list statistics of players portrayed on the cards. Each card portrays two players, one when the card is folded, another when the card is unfolded. The card of Dougherty and Lord is considered scarce.

	EX-MT	VG-E	GOOD
COMPLETE SET (50)	4500.00	2000.00	400.00
COMMON PAIR (1-50)	40.00	20.00	4.00
☐ 1 F.Baker and Collins	135.00	65.00	13.50
☐ 2 Barry and Lapp	45.00	22.50	4.50
☐ 3 Bergen and Z.Wheat	90.00	45.00	9.00
☐ 4 Blair and Hartzell	45.00	22.50	4.50
☐ 5 Bresnahan and Huggins	135.00	65.00	13.50
☐ 6 Bridwell and Mathewson	275.00	135.00	27.00
☐ 7 Butler and Abstein	45.00	22.50	4.50
☐ 8 Byrne and F.Clarke	90.00	45.00	9.00
☐ 9 Chance and Evers	180.00	90.00	18.00
☐ 10 Clark and Gaspar	45.00	22.50	4.50
☐ 11 Cobb and S.Crawford	900.00	450.00	90.00
☐ 12 Cole and Kling	45.00	22.50	4.50
☐ 13 Coombs and Thomas	45.00	22.50	4.50
☐ 14 Daubert and Rucker	45.00	22.50	4.50
☐ 15 Dougherty and Lord	300.00	150.00	30.00
☐ 16 Dooin and Titus	45.00	22.50	4.50
☐ 17 Downie and Baker	45.00	22.50	4.50
☐ 18 Dygert and Seymour	45.00	22.50	4.50
☐ 19 Elberfeld and McBride	45.00	22.50	4.50
☐ 20 Falkenberg and Lajoie	135.00	65.00	13.50
☐ 21 Fitzpatrick and Killian	45.00	22.50	4.50
☐ 22 Gardner and Speaker	135.00	65.00	13.50
☐ 23 Gibson and Leach	45.00	22.50	4.50
☐ 24 Graham and Mattern	45.00	22.50	4.50
☐ 25 Hauser and Lush	45.00	22.50	4.50
☐ 26 Herzog and Miller	45.00	22.50	4.50
☐ 27 Hinchman and Hickman	45.00	22.50	4.50
☐ 28 Hofman and M.Brown	90.00	45.00	9.00
☐ 29 Jennings and Summers	90.00	45.00	9.00
☐ 30 Johnson and Ford	45.00	22.50	4.50
☐ 31 McCarty and McGinnity	90.00	45.00	9.00
☐ 32 McGlyn and Barrett	45.00	22.50	4.50
☐ 33 McLean and Grant	45.00	22.50	4.50
☐ 34 Merkle and Wiltse	45.00	22.50	4.50
☐ 35 Meyers and Doyle	45.00	22.50	4.50
☐ 36 Moore and Lobert	45.00	22.50	4.50
☐ 37 Odwell and Downs	45.00	22.50	4.50
☐ 38 Oldring and Bender	90.00	45.00	9.00
☐ 39 Payne and Walsh	90.00	45.00	9.00
☐ 40 Simon and Leifield	45.00	22.50	4.50
☐ 41 Starr and McCabe	45.00	22.50	4.50
☐ 42 Stephens and LaPorte	45.00	22.50	4.50
☐ 43 Stovall and Turner	45.00	22.50	4.50
☐ 44 Street and W.Johnson	300.00	150.00	30.00
☐ 45 Stroud and Donovan	45.00	22.50	4.50
☐ 46 Sweeney and Chase	45.00	22.50	4.50
☐ 47 Thoney and Cicotte	45.00	22.50	4.50
☐ 48 Wallace and Lake	90.00	45.00	9.00
☐ 49 Ward and Foster	45.00	22.50	4.50
☐ 50 Williams and Woodruff	45.00	22.50	4.50

1912 T202 Triple Folders

The cards in this 134-card set measure 2 1/4" by 5 1/4". The 1912 T202 Hassan Triple Folder issue is perhaps the most ingenious baseball card ever issued. The two end cards of each panel are full color, T205-like individual cards whereas the black and white center panel pictures an action photo or portrait. The end cards can be folded across the center panel and stored in this manner. Seventy-six different center panels are known to exist; however, many of the center panels contain more than one combination of end cards. The center panel titles are listed below in alphabetical order while the different combinations of end cards are listed below each center panel as they appear left to right on the front of the card. A total of 132 different card fronts exist. The set price below includes all panel and player combinations listed in the checklist. Back color variations (red or black) also exist. The Birmingham's Home Run card is difficult to obtain as are other cards whose center panel exists with but one combination of end cards. The Devlin with Mathewson end panels on numbers 29A and 74C picture Devlin as a Giant. Devlin is pictured as a Rustler on 29B and 74D.

	EX-MT	VG-E	GOOD
COMPLETE SET (132)	27500.	12500.	2750.
COMMON PANEL (1-76)	125.00	60.00	12.50
☐ 1A A Close Play at Home: Wallace-LaPorte	150.00	75.00	15.00
☐ 1B A Close Play at Home: Wallace-Pelty	150.00	75.00	15.00
☐ 2 A Desperate Slide: O'Leary-Cobb	1000.00	400.00	80.00
☐ 3A A Great Batsman: Barger-Bergen	125.00	60.00	12.50
☐ 3B A Great Batsman: Rucker-Bergen	125.00	60.00	12.50
☐ 4 Ambrose McConnell at Bat: Blair-Quinn	150.00	75.00	15.00
☐ 5 A Wide Throw Saves Crawford: Mullin-Stanage	175.00	85.00	18.00
☐ 6 Baker Gets His Man: Collins-Baker	250.00	125.00	25.00
☐ 7 Birmingham Gets to Third: Johnson-Street	350.00	175.00	35.00
☐ 8 Birmingham's Home Run: Birmingham-Turner	350.00	175.00	35.00
☐ 9 Bush Just Misses Austin: Moran-Magee	150.00	75.00	15.00
☐ 10A Carrigan Blocks His Man: Gaspar-McLean	125.00	60.00	12.50
☐ 10B Carrigan Blocks His Man: Wagner-Carrigan	125.00	60.00	12.50
☐ 11 Catching Him Napping: Oakes-Bresnahan	175.00	85.00	18.00
☐ 12 Caught Asleep Off First: Bresnahan-Harmon	175.00	85.00	18.00
☐ 13A Chance Beats Out a Hit: Chance-Foxen	200.00	100.00	20.00
☐ 13B Chance Beats Out a Hit: McIntire-Archer	150.00	75.00	15.00
☐ 13C Chance Beats Out a Hit: Overall-Archer	150.00	75.00	15.00
☐ 13D Chance Beats Out a Hit: Rowan-Archer	150.00	75.00	15.00
☐ 13E Chance Beats Out a Hit: Shean-Chance	200.00	100.00	20.00
☐ 14A Chase Dives into Third: Chase-Wolter	125.00	60.00	12.50
☐ 14B Chase Dives into Third: Gibson-Clarke	150.00	75.00	15.00
☐ 14C Chase Dives into Third: Phillippe-Gibson	125.00	60.00	12.50
☐ 15A Chase Gets Ball Too Late: Egan-Mitchell	125.00	60.00	12.50
☐ 15B Chase Gets Ball Too Late: Wolter-Chase	125.00	60.00	12.50
☐ 16A Chase Guarding First: Chase-Wolter	125.00	60.00	12.50
☐ 16B Chase Guarding First: Gibson-Clarke	150.00	75.00	15.00
☐ 16C Chase Guarding First: Leifield-Gibson	125.00	60.00	12.50
☐ 17 Chase Ready Squeeze Play: Paskert-Magee	150.00	75.00	15.00
☐ 18 Chase Safe at Third: Barry-Baker	175.00	85.00	18.00
☐ 19 Chief Bender Waiting: Bender-Thomas	200.00	100.00	20.00
☐ 20 Clarke Hikes for Home: Bridwell-Kling	175.00	85.00	18.00
☐ 21 Close at First: Ball-Stovall	150.00	75.00	15.00
☐ 22A Close at the Plate: Walsh-Payne	150.00	75.00	15.00
☐ 22B Close at the Plate: White-Payne	125.00	60.00	12.50
☐ 23 Close at Third (Speak-er): Wood-Speaker	325.00	160.00	32.00
☐ 24 Close at Third (Wagner): Wagner-Carrigan	150.00	75.00	15.00
☐ 25A Collins Easily Safe: Byrne-Clarke	150.00	75.00	15.00
☐ 25B Collins Easily Safe: Collins-Baker	250.00	125.00	25.00
☐ 25C Collins Easily Safe: Collins-Murphy	200.00	100.00	20.00
☐ 26 Crawford About to Smash: Stanage-Summers	175.00	85.00	18.00
☐ 27 Cree Rolls Home: Daubert-Hummell	150.00	75.00	15.00

☐ 28 Davy Jones' Great Slide: Delahanty-Jones	150.00	75.00	15.00
☐ 29A Devlin Gets His Man: Devlin (Giants)-Mathewson	900.00	450.00	90.00
☐ 29B Devlin Gets His Man: Devlin (Rustlers)-Mathewson	250.00	125.00	25.00
☐ 29C Devlin Gets His Man: Fletcher-Mathewson	250.00	125.00	25.00
☐ 29D Devlin Gets His Man: Meyers-Mathewson	250.00	125.00	25.00
☐ 30A Donlin Out at First: Camnitz-Gibson	125.00	60.00	12.50
☐ 30B Donlin Out at First: Doyle-Merkle	125.00	60.00	12.50
☐ 30C Donlin Out at First: Leach-Wilson	125.00	60.00	12.50
☐ 30D Donlin Out at First: Magee-Dooin	125.00	60.00	12.50
☐ 30E Donlin Out at First: Phillippe-Gibson	125.00	60.00	12.50
☐ 31A Dooin Gets His Man: Dooin-Doolan	125.00	60.00	12.50
☐ 31B Dooin Gets His Man: Lobert-Dooin	125.00	60.00	12.50
☐ 31C Dooin Gets His Man: Titus-Dooin	125.00	60.00	12.50
☐ 32 Easy for Larry: Doyle-Merkle	150.00	75.00	15.00
☐ 33 Elberfeld Beats: Milan-Elberfeld	150.00	75.00	15.00
☐ 34 Elberfeld Gets His Man: Milan-Elberfeld	150.00	75.00	15.00
☐ 35 Engle in a Close Play: Speaker-Engle	225.00	110.00	22.00
☐ 36A Evers Makes Safe Slide: Archer-Evers	200.00	100.00	20.00
☐ 36B Evers Makes Safe Slide: Evers-Chance	250.00	125.00	25.00
☐ 36C Evers Makes Safe Slide: Overall-Archer	150.00	75.00	15.00
☐ 36D Evers Makes Safe Slide: Reulbach-Archer	150.00	75.00	15.00
☐ 36E Evers Makes Safe Slide: Tinker-Chance	600.00	300.00	60.00
☐ 37 Fast Work at Third: O'Leary-Cobb	1000.00	400.00	80.00
☐ 38A Ford Putting Over Spitter: Ford-Vaughn	125.00	60.00	12.50
☐ 38B Ford Putting Over Spitter: Sweeney-Ford	125.00	60.00	12.50
☐ 39 Good Play at Third: Moriarty-Cobb	1000.00	400.00	80.00
☐ 40 Grant Gets His Man: Hoblitzel-Grant	150.00	75.00	15.00
☐ 41A Hal Chase Too Late: McIntyre-McConnell	125.00	60.00	12.50
☐ 41B Hal Chase Too Late: Suggs-McLean	125.00	60.00	12.50
☐ 42 Harry Lord at Third: Lennox-Tinker	175.00	85.00	18.00
☐ 43 Hartzell Covering: Scanlon-Dahlen	150.00	75.00	15.00
☐ 44 Hartzell Strikes Out: Groom-Gray	150.00	75.00	15.00
☐ 45 Held at Third: Tannehill-Lord	150.00	75.00	15.00
☐ 46 Jake Stahl Guarding: Cicotte-Stahl	150.00	75.00	15.00
☐ 47 Jim Delahanty at Bat: Delahanty-Jones	150.00	75.00	15.00
☐ 48A Just Before the Battle: Ames-Meyers	125.00	60.00	12.50
☐ 48B Just Before the Battle: Bresnahan-McGraw	250.00	125.00	25.00
☐ 48C Just Before the Battle: Crandall-Meyers	125.00	60.00	12.50
☐ 48D Just Before the Battle: Devore-Becker	125.00	60.00	12.50
☐ 48E Just Before the Battle: Fletcher-Mathewson	250.00	125.00	25.00
☐ 48F Just Before the Battle: Marquard-Meyers	150.00	75.00	15.00
☐ 48G Just Before the Battle: McGraw-Jennings	250.00	125.00	25.00
☐ 48H Just Before the Battle: Meyers-Mathewson	250.00	125.00	25.00
☐ 48I Just Before the Battle: Snodgrass-Murray	125.00	60.00	12.50
☐ 48J Just Before the Battle: Wiltse-Meyers	125.00	60.00	12.50
☐ 49 Knight Catches Runner: Knight-Johnson	350.00	175.00	35.00
☐ 50A Lobert Almost Caught: Bridwell-Kling	125.00	60.00	12.50
☐ 50B Lobert Almost Caught: Kling-Young	200.00	100.00	20.00
☐ 50C Lobert Almost Caught: Mattern-Kling	125.00	60.00	12.50
☐ 50D Lobert Almost Caught: Steinfeldt-Kling	125.00	60.00	12.50
☐ 51 Lobert Gets Tenney: Lobert-Dooin	150.00	75.00	15.00
☐ 52 Lord Catches His Man: Tannehill-Lord	150.00	75.00	15.00
☐ 53 McConnell Caught: Richie-Needham	150.00	75.00	15.00
☐ 54 McIntyre at Bat: McIntrye-McConnell	150.00	75.00	15.00
☐ 55 Moriarty Spiked: Willett-Stanage	150.00	75.00	15.00
☐ 56 Nearly Caught: Bates-Bescher	175.00	85.00	18.00
☐ 57 Oldring Almost Home: Lord-Oldring	150.00	75.00	15.00
☐ 58 Schaefer on First: McBride-Milan	150.00	75.00	15.00
☐ 59 Schaefer Steals Second: McBride-Griffith	175.00	85.00	18.00
☐ 60 Scoring from Second: Lord-Oldring	150.00	75.00	15.00
☐ 61A Scrambling Back: Barger-Bergen	125.00	60.00	12.50
☐ 61B Scrambling Back: Wolter-Chase	125.00	60.00	12.50
☐ 62 Speaker Almost Caught: Miller-Clarke	325.00	160.00	32.00
☐ 63 Speaker Rounding Third: Wood-Speaker	500.00	250.00	50.00
☐ 64 Speaker Scores: Speaker-Engle	350.00	175.00	35.00
☐ 65 Stahl Safe: Stovall-Austin	150.00	75.00	15.00
☐ 66 Stone About to Swing: Sheckard-Schulte	150.00	75.00	15.00
☐ 67A Sullivan Puts Up High One: Evans-Huggins	150.00	75.00	15.00
☐ 67B Sullivan Puts Up High One: Sweeney-Ford	125.00	60.00	12.50
☐ 68A Sweeney Gets Stahl: Ford-Vaughn	125.00	60.00	12.50
☐ 68B Sweeney Gets Stahl: Sweeney-Ford	125.00	60.00	12.50
☐ 69 Tenney Lands Safely: Raymond-Latham	150.00	75.00	15.00
☐ 70A The Athletic Infield: Barry-Baker	150.00	75.00	15.00
☐ 70B The Athletic Infield: Brown-Graham	125.00	60.00	12.50
☐ 70C The Athletic Infield: Hauser-Konetchy	125.00	60.00	12.50
☐ 70D The Athletic Infield: Krause-Thomas	125.00	60.00	12.50
☐ 71 The Pinch Hitter: Hoblitzel-Egan	150.00	75.00	15.00
☐ 72 The Scissors Slide: Birmingham-Turner	150.00	75.00	15.00
☐ 73A Tom Jones at Bat: Fromme-McLean	125.00	60.00	12.50
☐ 73B Tom Jones at Bat: Gaspar-McLean	125.00	60.00	12.50
☐ 74A Too Late for Devlin: Ames-Meyers	125.00	60.00	12.50
☐ 74B Too Late for Devlin: Crandall-Meyers	125.00	60.00	12.50
☐ 74C Too Late for Devlin: Devlin (Giants)-Mathewson	900.00	450.00	90.00

☐ 74D Too Late for Devlin: Devlin (Rustlers)-Mathewson	250.00	125.00	25.00
☐ 74E Too Late for Devlin: Marquard-Meyers	150.00	75.00	15.00
☐ 74F Too Late for Devlin: Wiltse-Meyers	125.00	60.00	12.50
☐ 75A Ty Cobb Steals Third: Jennings-Cobb	1600.00	750.00	150.00
☐ 75B Ty Cobb Steals Third: Moriarty-Cobb	1400.00	600.00	135.00
☐ 75C Ty Cobb Steals Third: Stovall-Austin	1400.00	600.00	135.00
☐ 76 Wheat Strikes Out: Dahlen-Wheat	225.00	110.00	22.00

T204 Ramly

The cards in this 121-card set measure 2" by 2 1/2". The Ramly baseball series, designated T204 in the ACC, contains unnumbered cards. This set is one of the most distinguished ever produced, containing ornate gold borders around a black and white portrait of each player. There are spelling errors, and two distinct backs, "Ramly" and "TT", are known. Much of the obverse card detail is actually embossed. The players have been alphabetized and numbered for reference in the checklist below.

	EX-MT	VG-E	GOOD
COMPLETE SET (121)	24500.	11000.	2400.
COMMON PLAYER (1-121)	175.00	85.00	18.00
☐ 1 Whitey Alperman	175.00	85.00	18.00
☐ 2 John J. Anderson	175.00	85.00	18.00
☐ 3 Jimmy Archer	175.00	85.00	18.00
☐ 4 Frank Arellanes	175.00	85.00	18.00
☐ 5 Jim Ball (Boston NL)	175.00	85.00	18.00
☐ 6 Neal Ball (N.Y. AL)	175.00	85.00	18.00
☐ 7 Dave Bancroft	350.00	175.00	35.00
☐ 8 Johnny Bates	175.00	85.00	18.00
☐ 9 Fred Beebe	175.00	85.00	18.00
☐ 10 George Bell	175.00	85.00	18.00
☐ 11 Chief Bender	350.00	175.00	35.00
☐ 12 Walter Blair	175.00	85.00	18.00
☐ 13 Cliff Blankenship	175.00	85.00	18.00
☐ 14 Frank Bowerman	175.00	85.00	18.00
☐ 15 Kitty Bransfield	175.00	85.00	18.00
☐ 16 Roger Bresnahan	350.00	175.00	35.00
☐ 17 Al Bridwell	175.00	85.00	18.00
☐ 18 Mordecai Brown	350.00	175.00	35.00
☐ 19 Fred Burchell	175.00	85.00	18.00
☐ 20 Jesse Burkett	450.00	225.00	45.00
☐ 21 Robert Byrne	175.00	85.00	18.00
☐ 22 Bill Carrigan	175.00	85.00	18.00
☐ 23 Frank Chance	400.00	200.00	40.00
☐ 24 Charles Chech	175.00	85.00	18.00
☐ 25 Eddie Cicotte	250.00	125.00	25.00
☐ 26 Otis Clymer	175.00	85.00	18.00
☐ 27 Andrew Coakley	175.00	85.00	18.00
☐ 28 Eddie Collins	450.00	225.00	45.00
☐ 29 Jimmy Collins	450.00	225.00	45.00
☐ 30 Wid Conroy	175.00	85.00	18.00
☐ 31 Jack Coombs	225.00	110.00	22.00
☐ 32 Doc Crandall	175.00	85.00	18.00
☐ 33 Lou Criger	175.00	85.00	18.00
☐ 34 Harry(Jasper) Davis	175.00	85.00	18.00
☐ 35 Art Devlin	175.00	85.00	18.00
☐ 36 Bill Dineen	175.00	85.00	18.00
☐ 37 Pat Donahue	175.00	85.00	18.00
☐ 38 Mike Donlin	175.00	85.00	18.00
☐ 39 Wild Bill Donovan	175.00	85.00	18.00
☐ 40 Gus Dorner	175.00	85.00	18.00
☐ 41 Joe Dunn	175.00	85.00	18.00
☐ 42 Norman Elberfield (sic) Elberfeld	175.00	85.00	18.00
☐ 43 Johnny Evers	400.00	200.00	40.00
☐ 44 George L. Ewing	175.00	85.00	18.00
☐ 45 George Ferguson	175.00	85.00	18.00
☐ 46 Hobe Ferris	175.00	85.00	18.00
☐ 47 James J. Freeman	175.00	85.00	18.00
☐ 48 Art Fromme	175.00	85.00	18.00
☐ 49 Bob Ganley	175.00	85.00	18.00
☐ 50 Harry (Doc) Gessler	175.00	85.00	18.00
☐ 51 George Graham	175.00	85.00	18.00
☐ 52 Clark Griffith	350.00	175.00	35.00
☐ 53 Roy Hartzell	175.00	85.00	18.00
☐ 54 Charlie Hemphill	175.00	85.00	18.00
☐ 55 Dick Hoblitzell	175.00	85.00	18.00
☐ 56 George (Del) Howard	175.00	85.00	18.00
☐ 57 Harry Howell	175.00	85.00	18.00
☐ 58 Miller Huggins	400.00	200.00	40.00
☐ 59 John Hummel	175.00	85.00	18.00
☐ 60 Walter Johnson	1500.00	600.00	150.00
☐ 61 Charles Jones	175.00	85.00	18.00
☐ 62 Michael Kahoe	175.00	85.00	18.00
☐ 63 Ed Karger	175.00	85.00	18.00
☐ 64 Willie Keeler	450.00	225.00	45.00
☐ 65 Ed Kenotchey (sic) Konetchy	175.00	85.00	18.00
☐ 66 John (Red) Kleinow	175.00	85.00	18.00
☐ 67 John Knight	175.00	85.00	18.00
☐ 68 Vive Lindeman	175.00	85.00	18.00
☐ 69 Hans Loebert (sic) Lobert	175.00	85.00	18.00
☐ 70 Harry Lord	175.00	85.00	18.00
☐ 71 Harry Lumley	175.00	85.00	18.00
☐ 72 Ernie Lush	175.00	85.00	18.00
☐ 73 Rube Manning	175.00	85.00	18.00
☐ 74 James McAleer	175.00	85.00	18.00
☐ 75 Amby McConnell	175.00	85.00	18.00
☐ 76 Moose McCormick	175.00	85.00	18.00
☐ 77 Matthew McIntyre	175.00	85.00	18.00
☐ 78 Larry McLean	175.00	85.00	18.00
☐ 79 Fred Merkle	200.00	100.00	20.00
☐ 80 Clyde Milan	175.00	85.00	18.00
☐ 81 Michael Mitchell	175.00	85.00	18.00
☐ 82 Pat Moran	175.00	85.00	18.00
☐ 83 Harry (Cy) Morgan	175.00	85.00	18.00
☐ 84 Tim Murnane	175.00	85.00	18.00
☐ 85 Danny Murphy	175.00	85.00	18.00
☐ 86 Red Murray	175.00	85.00	18.00
☐ 87 Eustace(Doc) Newton	175.00	85.00	18.00
☐ 88 Simon Nichols (sic) Nicholls	175.00	85.00	18.00
☐ 89 Harry Niles	175.00	85.00	18.00
☐ 90 Bill O'Hara	175.00	85.00	18.00
☐ 91 Charley O'Leary	175.00	85.00	18.00
☐ 92 Dode Paskert	175.00	85.00	18.00
☐ 93 Barney Pelty	175.00	85.00	18.00
☐ 94 Jack Pfeister	175.00	85.00	18.00
☐ 95 Eddie Plank	500.00	250.00	50.00
☐ 96 Jack Powell	175.00	85.00	18.00
☐ 97 Bugs Raymond	175.00	85.00	18.00
☐ 98 Thomas Reilly	175.00	85.00	18.00
☐ 99 Lewis Ritchie (sic) Richie	175.00	85.00	18.00
☐ 100 Nap Rucker	175.00	85.00	18.00
☐ 101 Ed Ruelbach (sic) Reulbach	175.00	85.00	18.00
☐ 102 Slim Sallee	175.00	85.00	18.00
☐ 103 Germany Schaefer	175.00	85.00	18.00
☐ 104 Jimmy Schekard (sic) Sheckard	175.00	85.00	18.00
☐ 105 Admiral Schlei	175.00	85.00	18.00
☐ 106 Frank Schulte	175.00	85.00	18.00
☐ 107 James Sebring	175.00	85.00	18.00
☐ 108 Bill Shipke	175.00	85.00	18.00
☐ 109 Anthony Smith	175.00	85.00	18.00
☐ 110 Tubby Spencer	175.00	85.00	18.00
☐ 111 Jake Stahl	200.00	100.00	20.00
☐ 112 Harry Steinfeldt	175.00	85.00	18.00
☐ 113 Jim Stephens	175.00	85.00	18.00
☐ 114 Gabby Street	175.00	85.00	18.00
☐ 115 William Sweeney	175.00	85.00	18.00
☐ 116 Fred Tenney	175.00	85.00	18.00
☐ 117 Ira Thomas	175.00	85.00	18.00
☐ 118 Joe Tinker	350.00	175.00	35.00
☐ 119 Bob Unglaub	175.00	85.00	18.00
☐ 120 Heine Wagner	175.00	85.00	18.00
☐ 121 Bobby Wallace	350.00	175.00	35.00

T205 Gold Border

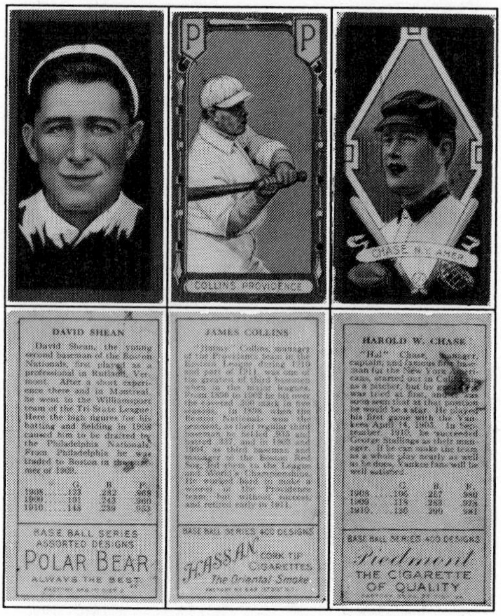

The cards in this 208-card set measure 1 1/2" by 2 5/8". The T205 set (catalog designation), also known as the "Gold Border" set, was issued in 1911 in packages of the following cigarette brands: American Beauty, Broadleaf, Cycle, Drum, Hassan, Honest Long Cut, Piedmont, Polar Bear, Sovereign and Sweet Caporal. All the above were products of the American Tobacco Company, and the ads for the various brands appear below the biographical section on the back of each card. There are pose variations noted in the checklist (which is alphabetized and numbered for reference) and there are 12 minor league cards of a more ornate design which are somewhat scarce. The numbers below correspond to alphabetical order within category, i.e., major leaguers and minor leaguers are alphabetized separately. The gold borders of T205 cards chip easily and they are hard to find in "Mint" or even "Near Mint" condition; however they (T205) are not appreciably tougher to find than T206 cards for lesser conditions or grades

	EX-MT	VG-E	GOOD
COMPLETE SET (208)	27000.	12500.	2750.
COMMON MAJORS (1-185)	65.00	32.50	6.50
COMMON MINORS (186-197)	200.00	100.00	20.00

	EX-MT	VG-E	GOOD
☐ 1 Edward J. Abbaticchio	65.00	32.50	6.50
☐ 2 Leon Ames	65.00	32.50	6.50
☐ 3 James P. Archer	65.00	32.50	6.50
☐ 4 James Austin	65.00	32.50	6.50
☐ 5 William Bailey	65.00	32.50	6.50
☐ 6 Frank Baker	250.00	125.00	25.00
☐ 7 Neal Ball	65.00	32.50	6.50
☐ 8A Edward B. Barger (full B)	65.00	32.50	6.50
☐ 8B Edward B. Barger (part B)	250.00	125.00	25.00
☐ 9 John J. Barry	65.00	32.50	6.50
☐ 10 John W. Bates	65.00	32.50	6.50
☐ 11 Frederick T. Beck	65.00	32.50	6.50
☐ 12 Beals Becker	65.00	32.50	6.50
☐ 13 George G. Bell	65.00	32.50	6.50
☐ 14 Charles A. Bender	200.00	100.00	20.00
☐ 15 William Bergen	65.00	32.50	6.50
☐ 16 Robert H. Bescher	65.00	32.50	6.50
☐ 17 Joseph Birmingham	65.00	32.50	6.50
☐ 18 Russell Blackburne	65.00	32.50	6.50
☐ 19 Wm. E. Bransfield	65.00	32.50	6.50
☐ 20A Roger Bresnahan (mouth closed)	200.00	100.00	20.00
☐ 20B Roger Bresnahan (mouth open)	400.00	200.00	40.00
☐ 21 Albert Bridwell	65.00	32.50	6.50
☐ 22 Mordecai Brown	200.00	100.00	20.00
☐ 23 Robert Byrne	65.00	32.50	6.50
☐ 24 Howard Camnitz	65.00	32.50	6.50
☐ 25 William Carrigan	65.00	32.50	6.50
☐ 26 Frank L. Chance	200.00	100.00	20.00
☐ 27A Harold W. Chase (Chase only)	350.00	175.00	35.00
☐ 27B Harold W. Chase (Hal Chase)	100.00	50.00	10.00
☐ 28 Edward V. Cicotte	100.00	50.00	10.00
☐ 29 Fred Clarke	200.00	100.00	20.00
☐ 30 Tyrus Raymond Cobb	2000.00	800.00	175.00
☐ 31A Edward T. Collins (mouth closed)	200.00	100.00	20.00
☐ 31B Edward T. Collins (mouth open)	400.00	200.00	40.00
☐ 32 Frank J. Corridon	65.00	32.50	6.50
☐ 32 Otis Crandall	65.00	32.50	6.50
☐ 33 Louis Criger	65.00	32.50	6.50
☐ 34 William Dahlen	250.00	125.00	25.00
☐ 35 Jacob Daubert	100.00	50.00	10.00
☐ 36 James Delahanty	65.00	32.50	6.50
☐ 37 Arthur Devlin	65.00	32.50	6.50
☐ 38 Joshua Devore	65.00	32.50	6.50
☐ 39 W.R. Dickson	65.00	32.50	6.50
☐ 40 J. Donohue	200.00	100.00	20.00
☐ 41 Charles S. Dooin	65.00	32.50	6.50
☐ 42 Michael Doolan	65.00	32.50	6.50
☐ 43A Patsy Dougherty (white stocking)	200.00	100.00	20.00
☐ 43B Patsy Dougherty (red stocking)	65.00	32.50	6.50
☐ 44 Thomas W. Downey	65.00	32.50	6.50
☐ 45 Lawrence Doyle	65.00	32.50	6.50
☐ 46 Hugh Duffy	300.00	150.00	30.00
☐ 47 James H. Dygert	65.00	32.50	6.50
☐ 48 Richard J. Egan	65.00	32.50	6.50
☐ 49 Norman Elberfeld	65.00	32.50	6.50
☐ 50 Clyde Engle	65.00	32.50	6.50
☐ 51 Louis Evans	65.00	32.50	6.50
☐ 52 John J. Evers	200.00	100.00	20.00
☐ 53 Robert Ewing	65.00	32.50	6.50
☐ 54 G.C. Ferguson	65.00	32.50	6.50
☐ 55 Ray Fisher	250.00	125.00	25.00
☐ 56 Arthur Fletcher	65.00	32.50	6.50
☐ 57 John Flynn	65.00	32.50	6.50
☐ 58A Russell Ford (dark cap)	65.00	32.50	6.50
☐ 58B Russell Ford (light cap)	250.00	125.00	25.00
☐ 59 William A. Foxen	65.00	32.50	6.50
☐ 60 Arthur Fromme	65.00	32.50	6.50
☐ 61 Earl Gardner	65.00	32.50	6.50
☐ 62 Harry L. Gaspar	65.00	32.50	6.50
☐ 63 George Gibson	65.00	32.50	6.50
☐ 64 Wilbur Good	65.00	32.50	6.50
☐ 65A George F. Graham (Boston Rustlers)	65.00	32.50	6.50
☐ 65B George F. Graham (Chicago Cubs)	450.00	225.00	45.00
☐ 66 Edward L. Grant	250.00	125.00	25.00
☐ 67 Gray	65.00	32.50	6.50
☐ 68 Clark Griffith	200.00	100.00	20.00
☐ 69 Robert Groom	65.00	32.50	6.50
☐ 70A Robert Harmon (both ears)	65.00	32.50	6.50
☐ 70B Robert Harmon (left ear only)	250.00	125.00	25.00
☐ 71 Frederick T. Hartsel	65.00	32.50	6.50
☐ 72 Arnold J. Hauser	65.00	32.50	6.50
☐ 73 Charles Hemphill	65.00	32.50	6.50
☐ 74 Charles L. Herzog	65.00	32.50	6.50
☐ 75 Richard Hoblitzell	65.00	32.50	6.50
☐ 76 Daniel J. Hoffman	65.00	32.50	6.50
☐ 77 Miller Huggins	200.00	100.00	20.00
☐ 78 John E. Hummell	65.00	32.50	6.50
☐ 79 Fred Jacklitsch	65.00	32.50	6.50
☐ 80 Hugh Jennings	200.00	100.00	20.00
☐ 81 Walter Johnson	900.00	450.00	90.00
☐ 82 David Jones	65.00	32.50	6.50
☐ 83 Thomas Jones	65.00	32.50	6.50
☐ 84 Addie Joss	500.00	250.00	50.00
☐ 85 Edward Karger	250.00	125.00	25.00
☐ 86 Edward Killian	65.00	32.50	6.50
☐ 87 John Kleinow	250.00	125.00	25.00
☐ 88 John Kling	65.00	32.50	6.50
☐ 89 Jack Knight	65.00	32.50	6.50

□ 90 Edward Konetchy	65.00	32.50	6.50
□ 91 Harry Krause	65.00	32.50	6.50
□ 92 Floyd M. Kroh	65.00	32.50	6.50
□ 93 Frank Lang	65.00	32.50	6.50
□ 94 Frank LaPorte	65.00	32.50	6.50
□ 95 W.A. Latham	65.00	32.50	6.50
□ 96 Thomas W. Leach	65.00	32.50	6.50
□ 97 Sam Leever	65.00	32.50	6.50
□ 98 Albert P. Leifield	65.00	32.50	6.50
□ 99 Edgar Lennox	65.00	32.50	6.50
□ 100 Pat'k J. Livingston	65.00	32.50	6.50
□ 101 John Lobert	65.00	32.50	6.50
□ 102 Briscoe Lord	65.00	32.50	6.50
□ 103 Harry D. Lord	65.00	32.50	6.50
□ 104 John Lush	65.00	32.50	6.50
□ 105 Nicholas Maddox	65.00	32.50	6.50
□ 106 Sherwood R. Magee	65.00	32.50	6.50
□ 107 Richard Marquard	200.00	100.00	20.00
□ 108 Christy Mathewson	650.00	325.00	65.00
□ 109 A.A. Mattern	65.00	32.50	6.50
□ 110 George F. McBride	65.00	32.50	6.50
□ 111 Ambrose McConnell	65.00	32.50	6.50
□ 112 Pryor McElveen	65.00	32.50	6.50
□ 113 John J. McGraw	300.00	150.00	30.00
□ 114 Harry McIntire	65.00	32.50	6.50
□ 115 Matthew McIntyre	65.00	32.50	6.50
□ 116 John B. McLean	65.00	32.50	6.50
□ 117 Fred Merkle	100.00	50.00	10.00
□ 118 John T. Meyers	65.00	32.50	6.50
□ 119 J. Clyde Milan	65.00	32.50	6.50
□ 120 John D. Miller	65.00	32.50	6.50
□ 121 Michael Mitchell	65.00	32.50	6.50
□ 122 Patrick J. Moran	65.00	32.50	6.50
□ 123 George Moriarity	65.00	32.50	6.50
□ 124 George J. Mullin	65.00	32.50	6.50
□ 125 Daniel Murphy	65.00	32.50	6.50
□ 126 John J. Murray	65.00	32.50	6.50
□ 127 Thomas J. Needham	65.00	32.50	6.50
□ 128 Rebel Oakes	65.00	32.50	6.50
□ 129 Reuben N. Oldring	65.00	32.50	6.50
□ 130 Charles O'Leary	65.00	32.50	6.50
□ 131 Frederick Olmstead	65.00	32.50	6.50
□ 132 Orval Overall	65.00	32.50	6.50
□ 133 F. Parent	65.00	32.50	6.50
□ 134 George Paskert	65.00	32.50	6.50
□ 135 Fred Payne	65.00	32.50	6.50
□ 136 B. Pelty	65.00	32.50	6.50
□ 137 John A. Pfiester	65.00	32.50	6.50
□ 138 Edward Phelps	65.00	32.50	6.50
□ 139 Charles Phillippe	100.00	50.00	10.00
□ 140 John Quinn	65.00	32.50	6.50
□ 141 Arthur L. Raymond	250.00	125.00	25.00
□ 142 Edward M. Reulbach	65.00	32.50	6.50
□ 143 Lewis Richie	65.00	32.50	6.50
□ 144 John A. Rowan	250.00	125.00	25.00
□ 145 G.N. Rucker	65.00	32.50	6.50
□ 146 W.D. Scanlan	250.00	125.00	25.00
□ 147 Herman Schaefer	65.00	32.50	6.50
□ 148 George H. Schlei	65.00	32.50	6.50
□ 149 Charles Schmidt	65.00	32.50	6.50
□ 150 Frank M. Schulte	65.00	32.50	6.50
□ 151 James Scott	65.00	32.50	6.50
□ 152 Bayard H. Sharpe	65.00	32.50	6.50
□ 153A David Shean (Boston Rustlers)	65.00	32.50	6.50
□ 153B David Shean (Chicago Cubs)	450.00	225.00	45.00
□ 154 James T. Sheckard	65.00	32.50	6.50
□ 155 George Simmons	65.00	32.50	6.50
□ 156 Tony Smith	65.00	32.50	6.50
□ 157 Fred C. Snodgrass	65.00	32.50	6.50
□ 158 Tris Speaker	450.00	225.00	45.00
□ 159 Jacob G. Stahl	100.00	50.00	10.00
□ 160 Oscar Stanage	65.00	32.50	6.50
□ 161 Harry Steinfeldt	65.00	32.50	6.50
□ 162 George Stone	65.00	32.50	6.50
□ 163 George T. Stovall	65.00	32.50	6.50
□ 164 Charles E. Street	65.00	32.50	6.50
□ 165 George Suggs	250.00	125.00	25.00
□ 166 Edgar Summers	65.00	32.50	6.50
□ 167 Edward Sweeney	250.00	125.00	25.00
□ 168 Lee Ford Tannehill	65.00	32.50	6.50
□ 169 Ira Thomas	65.00	32.50	6.50
□ 170 Joseph B. Tinker	200.00	100.00	20.00
□ 171 John Titus	65.00	32.50	6.50
□ 172 Terence Turner	250.00	125.00	25.00
□ 173 James Vaughn	250.00	125.00	25.00
□ 174 Charles Wagner	250.00	125.00	25.00
□ 175A Roderick J. Wallace (with cap)	200.00	100.00	20.00
□ 175B Roderick J. Wallace (without cap)	400.00	200.00	40.00
□ 176 Edward Walsh	350.00	175.00	35.00
□ 177 Zach D. Wheat	200.00	100.00	20.00
□ 178 G.H. White	65.00	32.50	6.50
□ 179 Kirb White	250.00	125.00	25.00
□ 180 Irvin K. Wilhelm	250.00	125.00	25.00
□ 181 Edgar Willett	65.00	32.50	6.50
□ 182A George Wiltse (both ears)	65.00	32.50	6.50
□ 182B George Wiltse (right ear only)	250.00	125.00	25.00
□ 183 J. Owen Wilson	65.00	32.50	6.50
□ 184 Harry Wolter	65.00	32.50	6.50
□ 185 Denton T. Young	600.00	300.00	60.00
□ 186 Dr.Merle T. Adkins: Baltimore	200.00	100.00	20.00
□ 187 John Dunn: Baltimore	250.00	125.00	25.00
□ 188 George Merritt: Buffalo	200.00	100.00	20.00
□ 189 Charles Hanford: Jersey City	200.00	100.00	20.00
□ 190 Forrest D. Cady: Newark	200.00	100.00	20.00
□ 191 James Frick: Newark	200.00	100.00	20.00
□ 192 Wyatt Lee: Newark	200.00	100.00	20.00
□ 193 Lewis McAllister: Newark	200.00	100.00	20.00
□ 194 John Nee: Newark	200.00	100.00	20.00
□ 195 James Collins: Providence	450.00	225.00	45.00
□ 196 James Phelan: Providence	200.00	100.00	20.00
□ 197 Henry Batch: Rochester	200.00	100.00	20.00

T206 White Border

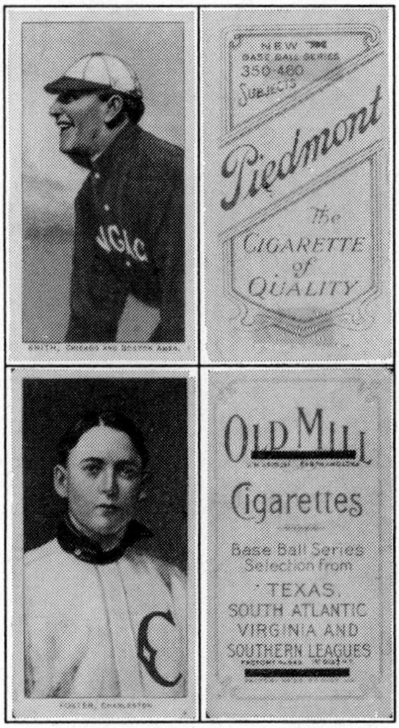

The cards in this 524-card set measure 1 1/2" by 2 5/8". The T206 set was and is the most popular of all the tobacco issues. The set was issued from 1909 to 1911 with sixteen different brands of cigarettes: American Beauty, Broadleaf, Cycle, Carolina Brights, Drum, El Principe de Gales, Hindu, Lenox, Old Mill, Piedmont, Polar Bear, Sovereign, Sweet Caporal, Tolstoi, Ty Cobb and Uzit. The Ty Cobb brand back is very scarce. The minor league cards are supposedly slightly more difficult to obtain than the cards of the major leaguers, with the Southern

League player cards being the most difficult. Minor League players were obtained from the American Association and the Eastern league. Southern League players were obtained from a variety of leagues including the following: South Atlantic League, Southern League, Texas League, and Virginia League. The set price below does not include ultra-expensive Wagner, Plank, Magie error, or Doyle variation.

	EX-MT	VG-E	GOOD
COMPLETE SET (520)	55000.	20000.	5000.
COMMON MAJORS (1-389)	55.00	27.50	5.50
COMMON MINORS (390-475)	45.00	22.50	4.50
COMMON SOUTHERN(476-523)	125.00	60.00	12.50
☐ 1 Abbaticchio: Pitt. Batting, follow thru	55.00	27.50	5.50
☐ 2 Abbaticchio: Pitt. Batting, waiting pitch	65.00	32.50	6.50
☐ 3 Abstein: Pitt.	55.00	27.50	5.50
☐ 4 Alperman: Brooklyn	65.00	32.50	6.50
☐ 5 Ames: Giants, Port.	65.00	32.50	6.50
☐ 6 Ames: Giants, Hands over head	55.00	27.50	5.50
☐ 7 Ames: Giants, Hands in front of chest	65.00	32.50	6.50
☐ 8 Arellanes: Boston AL	55.00	27.50	5.50
☐ 9 Atz: Chicago AL	55.00	27.50	5.50
☐ 10 Baker: Phila. AL	200.00	100.00	20.00
☐ 11 Ball: Cleveland	55.00	27.50	5.50
☐ 12 Ball: N.Y. AL	65.00	32.50	6.50
☐ 13 Barbeau: St.L. NL	55.00	27.50	5.50
☐ 14 Barry: Phila. AL	55.00	27.50	5.50
☐ 15 Bates: Boston NL	65.00	32.50	6.50
☐ 16 Beaumont: Boston NL	65.00	32.50	6.50
☐ 17 Beck: Boston NL	55.00	27.50	5.50
☐ 18 Becker: Boston NL	55.00	27.50	5.50
☐ 19 Bell: Brooklyn pitching, follow thru	55.00	27.50	5.50
☐ 20 Bell: Brooklyn, Hands over head	65.00	32.50	6.50
☐ 21 Bender: Phila. AL Portrait	225.00	110.00	22.00
☐ 22 Bender: Phila. AL (pitching) trees	175.00	85.00	18.00
☐ 23 Bender: Phila. AL (pitching) no trees	175.00	85.00	18.00
☐ 24 Bergen: Brooklyn, Catching	55.00	27.50	5.50
☐ 25 Bergen: Brooklyn, Batting	65.00	32.50	6.50
☐ 26 Berger: Cleveland	55.00	27.50	5.50
☐ 27 Bescher: Cinc., Catching fly ball	55.00	27.50	5.50
☐ 28 Bescher: Cinc. Portrait	55.00	27.50	5.50
☐ 29 Birmingham: Cleve.	65.00	32.50	6.50
☐ 30 Bliss: St.L. NL	55.00	27.50	5.50
☐ 31 Bowerman: Bost. NL	65.00	32.50	6.50
☐ 32 Bradley: Cleveland, Portrait	65.00	32.50	6.50
☐ 33 Bradley: Cleveland, Batting	55.00	27.50	5.50
☐ 34 Bransfield: Phila. NL	65.00	32.50	6.50
☐ 35 Bresnahan: St.L. NL, Portrait	225.00	110.00	22.00
☐ 36 Bresnahan: St.L. NL, Batting	175.00	85.00	18.00
☐ 37 Bridwell: N.Y. NL, Portrait	65.00	32.50	6.50
☐ 38 Bridwell: N.Y. NL, Wearing sweater	55.00	27.50	5.50
☐ 39 G. Brown (sic): Chicago NL	150.00	75.00	15.00
☐ 40 G. Brown (sic): Washington	500.00	250.00	50.00
☐ 41 M. Brown: Chicago NL, Portrait	225.00	110.00	22.00
☐ 42 M. Brown: Chicago NL, Chicago down front of shirt	175.00	85.00	18.00
☐ 43 M. Brown: Chicago NL, Cubs across chest	300.00	150.00	30.00
☐ 44 Burch: Brooklyn, Fielding	55.00	27.50	5.50
☐ 45 Burch: Brooklyn, Batting	150.00	75.00	15.00
☐ 46 Burns: Chicago AL	55.00	27.50	5.50
☐ 47 Bush: Detroit	55.00	27.50	5.50
☐ 48 Byrne: St.L. NL	55.00	27.50	5.50
☐ 49 Camnitz: Pitt., Arms folded over chest	65.00	32.50	6.50
☐ 50 Camnitz: Pitt., Hands over head	55.00	27.50	5.50
☐ 51 Camnitz: Pitt., Throwing	55.00	27.50	5.50
☐ 52 Campbell: Cinc.	55.00	27.50	5.50
☐ 53 Carrigan: Boston AL	55.00	27.50	5.50
☐ 54 Chance: Chicago NL, Cubs across chest	225.00	110.00	22.00
☐ 55 Chance: Chicago NL, Chicago down front of shirt	175.00	85.00	18.00
☐ 56 Chance: Chicago NL, Batting	175.00	85.00	18.00
☐ 57 Charles: St.L. NL	55.00	27.50	5.50
☐ 58 Chase: N.Y. AL, Port. blue bkgd.	90.00	45.00	9.00
☐ 59 Chase: N.Y. AL, Port., pink bkgd.	200.00	100.00	20.00
☐ 60 Chase: N.Y. AL, Holding cup	90.00	45.00	9.00
☐ 61 Chase: N.Y. AL, Throwing, dark cap	90.00	45.00	9.00
☐ 62 Chase: N.Y. AL, Throwing, white cap	200.00	100.00	20.00
☐ 63 Chesbro: N.Y. AL	300.00	150.00	30.00
☐ 64 Cicotte: Boston AL	90.00	45.00	9.00
☐ 65 Clarke: Pitt., Portrait	225.00	110.00	22.00
☐ 66 F. Clarke: Pitt.	175.00	85.00	18.00
☐ 67 J.J. Clarke: Cleve.	65.00	32.50	6.50
☐ 68 Cobb: Detroit, Port., red bkgd.	1350.00	600.00	125.00
☐ 69 Cobb: Detroit, Port., green background	2500.00	1000.00	250.00
☐ 70 Cobb: Detroit, Bat on shoulder	1500.00	650.00	135.00
☐ 71 Cobb: Detroit, Bat away from shoulder	1350.00	600.00	125.00
☐ 72 Collins: Phila. AL	175.00	85.00	18.00
☐ 73 Conroy: Washington, Fielding	65.00	32.50	6.50
☐ 74 Conroy: Wash., Bat on shoulder	55.00	27.50	5.50
☐ 75 Covaleski: Phil. NL (Harry)	65.00	32.50	6.50
☐ 76 Crandall: N.Y. NL, without cap	65.00	32.50	6.50
☐ 77 Crandall: N.Y. NL, sweater and cap	55.00	27.50	5.50
☐ 78 Crawford: Detroit, Batting	175.00	85.00	18.00
☐ 79 Crawford: Detroit, Throwing	200.00	100.00	20.00
☐ 80 Cree: N.Y. AL	55.00	27.50	5.50
☐ 81 Criger: St.L. AL	65.00	32.50	6.50
☐ 82 Criss: St.L. AL	65.00	32.50	6.50
☐ 83 Dahlen: Brooklyn	300.00	150.00	30.00
☐ 84 Dahlen: Bost. NL	90.00	45.00	9.00
☐ 85 Davis: Phila. AL	55.00	27.50	5.50
☐ 86 G. Davis: Chicago AL	65.00	32.50	6.50
☐ 87 H. Davis: Phila. AL	65.00	32.50	6.50
☐ 88 Delehanty: Wash.	65.00	32.50	6.50
☐ 89 Demmitt: St.L. AL	3200.00	1200.00	300.00
☐ 90 Demmitt: N.Y. AL	55.00	27.50	5.50
☐ 91 Devlin: N.Y. NL	65.00	32.50	6.50
☐ 92 Devore: N.Y. NL	55.00	27.50	5.50
☐ 93 Dineen: St.L. AL	55.00	27.50	5.50
☐ 94 Donlin: N.Y. NL, Fielding	100.00	50.00	10.00
☐ 95 Donlin: N.Y. NL, Sitting	65.00	32.50	6.50
☐ 96 Donlin: N.Y. NL, Batting	55.00	27.50	5.50
☐ 97 Donohue: Chicago AL	65.00	32.50	6.50
☐ 98 Donovan: Detroit, Portrait	65.00	32.50	6.50
☐ 99 Donovan: Detroit, Throwing	55.00	27.50	5.50
☐ 100 Dooin: Phila. NL	65.00	32.50	6.50
☐ 101 Doolan: Phila. NL, Fielding	55.00	27.50	5.50
☐ 102 Doolan: Phila. NL, Batting	55.00	27.50	5.50

☐ 103 Doolin (sic, Doolan): Phila. NL,	65.00	32.50	6.50
☐ 104 Dougherty: Chic. AL, Portrait	65.00	32.50	6.50
☐ 105 Dougherty: Chic. AL, Fielding	55.00	27.50	5.50
☐ 106 Downey: Cinc., Batting	55.00	27.50	5.50
☐ 107 Downey: Cinc., Fielding	55.00	27.50	5.50
☐ 108A Doyle: N.Y. (hands over head)	65.00	32.50	6.50
☐ 108B Doyle: N.Y. NAT'L (hands over head)	18000.00	7500.00	1500.00
☐ 109 Doyle: N.Y. NL, Sweater	55.00	27.50	5.50
☐ 110 Doyle: N.Y. NL, Throwing	65.00	32.50	6.50
☐ 111 Doyle: N.Y. NL, Bat on shoulder	55.00	27.50	5.50
☐ 112 Dubuc: Cin.	55.00	27.50	5.50
☐ 113 Duffy: Chicago AL	175.00	85.00	18.00
☐ 114 Dunn: Brooklyn	55.00	27.50	5.50
☐ 115 Durham: N.Y. NL	65.00	32.50	6.50
☐ 116 Dygert: Phila. AL	55.00	27.50	5.50
☐ 117 Easterly: Cleveland	55.00	27.50	5.50
☐ 118 Egan: Cinc.	55.00	27.50	5.50
☐ 119 Elberfeld: Wash., Fielding	55.00	27.50	5.50
☐ 120 Elberfeld: Wash., Portrait	1050.00	400.00	80.00
☐ 121 Elberfeld: N.Y. AL, Portrait	65.00	32.50	6.50
☐ 122 Engle: N.Y. AL	55.00	27.50	5.50
☐ 123 Evans: St.L. NL	55.00	27.50	5.50
☐ 124 Evers: Chicago NL, Portrait	225.00	110.00	22.00
☐ 125 Evers: Chicago NL, Cubs across chest	300.00	150.00	30.00
☐ 126 Evers: Chicago NL, Chicago down front of shirt	175.00	85.00	18.00
☐ 127 Ewing: Cinc.	65.00	32.50	6.50
☐ 128 Ferguson: Boston NL	55.00	27.50	5.50
☐ 129 Ferris: St.L. AL	65.00	32.50	6.50
☐ 130 Fiene: Chicago AL, Portrait	55.00	27.50	5.50
☐ 131 Fiene: Chicago AL, Throwing	55.00	27.50	5.50
☐ 132 Fletcher: N.Y. NL	55.00	27.50	5.50
☐ 133 Flick: Cleveland	250.00	125.00	25.00
☐ 134 Ford: N.Y. AL	55.00	27.50	5.50
☐ 135 Frill: N.Y. AL	55.00	27.50	5.50
☐ 136 Fromme: Cinc.	55.00	27.50	5.50
☐ 137 Gandil: Chicago AL	90.00	45.00	9.00
☐ 138 Ganley: Washington	65.00	32.50	6.50
☐ 139 Gasper: Cinc.	55.00	27.50	5.50
☐ 140 Geyer: St.L. NL	55.00	27.50	5.50
☐ 141 Gibson: Pitt.	65.00	32.50	6.50
☐ 142 Gilbert: St.L. NL	65.00	32.50	6.50
☐ 143 Goode (sic): Cleve.	65.00	32.50	6.50
☐ 144 Graham: Boston NL	55.00	27.50	5.50
☐ 145 Graham: St.L. AL	55.00	27.50	5.50
☐ 146 Gray: Washington	55.00	27.50	5.50
☐ 147 Griffith: Cinc., Portrait	225.00	110.00	22.00
☐ 148 Griffith: Cinc., Batting	175.00	85.00	18.00
☐ 149 Groom: Washington	55.00	27.50	5.50
☐ 150 Hahn: Chicago AL	65.00	32.50	6.50
☐ 151 Hartsel: Phila. AL	55.00	27.50	5.50
☐ 152 Hemphill: N.Y. AL	65.00	32.50	6.50
☐ 153 Herzog : N.Y. NL	65.00	32.50	6.50
☐ 154 Herzog: Boston NL	55.00	27.50	5.50
☐ 155 Hinchman: Cleveland	65.00	32.50	6.50
☐ 156 Hoblitzell: Cinc.	55.00	27.50	5.50
☐ 157 Hoffman: St.L. AL	55.00	27.50	5.50
☐ 158 Hofman: Chicago NL	55.00	27.50	5.50
☐ 159 Howard: Chicago NL	55.00	27.50	5.50
☐ 160 Howell: St.L. AL, Portrait	55.00	27.50	5.50
☐ 161 Howell: St.L. AL, Left hand on hip	55.00	27.50	5.50
☐ 162 Huggins: Cinc., Portrait	225.00	110.00	22.00
☐ 163 Huggins: Cinc., Hands to mouth	175.00	85.00	18.00
☐ 164 Hulswitt: St.L. NL	55.00	27.50	5.50
☐ 165 Hummel: Brooklyn	55.00	27.50	5.50
☐ 166 Hunter: Brooklyn	55.00	27.50	5.50
☐ 167 Isbell: Chicago AL	65.00	32.50	6.50
☐ 168 Jacklitsch: Phila. NL	65.00	32.50	6.50
☐ 169 Jennings: Detroit, Portrait	225.00	110.00	22.00
☐ 170 Jennings: Detroit, Yelling	175.00	85.00	18.00
☐ 171 Jennings: Detroit, Dancing for joy	175.00	85.00	18.00
☐ 172 Johnson: Washington, Portrait	800.00	400.00	80.00
☐ 173 Johnson: Washington, Ready to pitch	600.00	300.00	60.00
☐ 174 Jones: St.L. AL	65.00	32.50	6.50
☐ 175 Jones: Detroit	55.00	27.50	5.50
☐ 176 F. Jones: Chic. AL, Portrait	65.00	32.50	6.50
☐ 177 F. Jones: Chic. AL, Hands on hips	65.00	32.50	6.50
☐ 178 Jordan: Brooklyn, Portrait	65.00	32.50	6.50
☐ 179 Jordan: Brooklyn, Batting	55.00	27.50	5.50
☐ 180 Joss: Cleveland, Portrait	325.00	160.00	32.00
☐ 181 Joss: Cleveland, Ready to pitch	200.00	100.00	20.00
☐ 182 Karger: Cinc.	65.00	32.50	6.50
☐ 183 Keeler: N.Y. AL, Portrait	325.00	160.00	32.00
☐ 184 Keeler: N.Y. AL, Batting	250.00	125.00	25.00
☐ 185 Killian: Detroit, Portrait	65.00	32.50	6.50
☐ 186 Killian: Detroit, Pitching	55.00	27.50	5.50
☐ 187 Kleinow: N.Y. AL, Batting	65.00	32.50	6.50
☐ 188 Kleinow: N.Y. AL, Catching	55.00	27.50	5.50
☐ 189 Kleinow: Bost. AL, Catching	300.00	150.00	30.00
☐ 190 Kling: Chicago NL	65.00	32.50	6.50
☐ 191 Knabe: Phila. NL	55.00	27.50	5.50
☐ 192 Knight: N.Y. AL, Portrait	55.00	27.50	5.50
☐ 193 Knight: N.Y. AL, Batting	55.00	27.50	5.50
☐ 194 Konetchy: St.L. NL, Awaiting low ball	55.00	27.50	5.50
☐ 195 Konetchy: St.L. NL, Glove above head	65.00	32.50	6.50
☐ 196 Krause: Phila. AL, Portrait	55.00	27.50	5.50
☐ 197 Krause: Phila. AL, Pitching	55.00	27.50	5.50
☐ 198 Kroh: Chicago NL	55.00	27.50	5.50
☐ 199 Lajoie: Cleveland, Portrait	375.00	175.00	37.00
☐ 200 Lajoie: Cleveland, Batting	250.00	125.00	25.00
☐ 201 Lajoie: Cleveland, Throwing	300.00	150.00	30.00
☐ 202 Lake: N.Y. AL	65.00	32.50	6.50
☐ 203 Lake: St.L. AL, Hands over head	55.00	27.50	5.50
☐ 204 Lake: St.L. AL, Throwing	55.00	27.50	5.50
☐ 205 LaPorte: N.Y. AL	55.00	27.50	5.50
☐ 206 Latham: N.Y. NL	55.00	27.50	5.50
☐ 207 Leach: Pitt., Portrait	65.00	32.50	6.50
☐ 208 Leach: Pitt., In fielding position	55.00	27.50	5.50
☐ 209 Leifield: Pitt., Batting	55.00	27.50	5.50
☐ 210 Leifield: Pitt., Hands behind head	65.00	32.50	6.50
☐ 211 Lennox: Brooklyn	55.00	27.50	5.50
☐ 212 Liebhardt: Cleve.	65.00	32.50	6.50
☐ 213 Lindaman: Boston NL	90.00	45.00	9.00
☐ 214 Livingstone: Phila. AL	55.00	27.50	5.50
☐ 215 Lobert: Cinc.	65.00	32.50	6.50
☐ 216 Lord: Bost. AL	55.00	27.50	5.50
☐ 217 Lumley: Brooklyn	65.00	32.50	6.50
☐ 218 Lundgren: Chicago NL	350.00	175.00	35.00
☐ 219 Maddox: Pitt.	55.00	27.50	5.50
☐ 220 Magee: Phila. NL, Portrait	65.00	32.50	6.50
☐ 221 Magee: Phila. NL, Batting	55.00	27.50	5.50
☐ 222 Magie: Phila. NL (sic) Portrait, name misspelled	10000.00	4000.00	800.00

☐ 223	Manning: N.Y. AL, Batting	65.00	32.50	6.50
☐ 224	Manning: N.Y. AL, Hands over head	55.00	27.50	5.50
☐ 225	Marquard: N.Y. NL, Portrait	225.00	110.00	22.00
☐ 226	Marquard: N.Y. NL, Pitching	175.00	85.00	18.00
☐ 227	Marquard: N.Y. NL, Standing	200.00	100.00	20.00
☐ 228	Marshall: Brooklyn	55.00	27.50	5.50
☐ 229	Mathewson: N.Y. NL, Portrait	800.00	400.00	80.00
☐ 230	Mathewson: N.Y. NL, Pitching, white cap	600.00	300.00	60.00
☐ 231	Mathewson: N.Y. NL, Pitching, dark cap	500.00	250.00	50.00
☐ 232	Mattern: Boston NL	55.00	27.50	5.50
☐ 233	McAleese: St.L. AL	55.00	27.50	5.50
☐ 234	McBride: Washington	55.00	27.50	5.50
☐ 235	McCormick: N.Y. NL	55.00	27.50	5.50
☐ 236	McElveen: Brooklyn	55.00	27.50	5.50
☐ 237	McGraw: N.Y. NL, Portrait, no cap	325.00	160.00	32.00
☐ 238	McGraw: N.Y. NL, Wearing sweater	200.00	100.00	20.00
☐ 239	McGraw: N.Y. NL, pointing	250.00	125.00	25.00
☐ 240	McGraw: N.Y. NL, Glove on hip	250.00	125.00	25.00
☐ 241	McIntyre: Detroit	55.00	27.50	5.50
☐ 242	McIntyre: Brooklyn	65.00	32.50	6.50
☐ 243	McIntyre: Brooklyn and Chicago NL	55.00	27.50	5.50
☐ 244	McLean: Cinc.	55.00	27.50	5.50
☐ 245	McQuillan: Phila. NL, Throwing	65.00	32.50	6.50
☐ 246	McQuillan: Phila. NL, Batting	55.00	27.50	5.50
☐ 247	Merkle: N.Y. NL, Portrait	55.00	27.50	5.50
☐ 248	Merkle: N.Y. NL, Throwing	65.00	32.50	6.50
☐ 249	Meyers: N.Y. NL	55.00	27.50	5.50
☐ 250	Milan: Washington	55.00	27.50	5.50
☐ 251	Miller: Pitt.	55.00	27.50	5.50
☐ 252	Mitchell: Cinc.	55.00	27.50	5.50
☐ 253	Moran: Chicago NL	55.00	27.50	5.50
☐ 254	Moriarty: Detroit	55.00	27.50	5.50
☐ 255	Mowrey: Cinc.	55.00	27.50	5.50
☐ 256	Mullen: Detroit	55.00	27.50	5.50
☐ 257	Mullin: Detroit, Throwing	65.00	32.50	6.50
☐ 258	Mullin: Detroit, Batting	55.00	27.50	5.50
☐ 259	Murphy: Phila. AL, Throwing	65.00	32.50	6.50
☐ 260	Murphy: Phila. AL, Bat on shoulder	55.00	27.50	5.50
☐ 261	Murray: N.Y. NL, Sweater	55.00	27.50	5.50
☐ 262	Murray: N.Y. NL, Bat on shoulder	55.00	27.50	5.50
☐ 263	Myers (sic): N.Y. NL, Fielding	55.00	27.50	5.50
☐ 264	Myers (sic): N.Y. NL, Batting	55.00	27.50	5.50
☐ 265	Needham: Chicago NL	55.00	27.50	5.50
☐ 266	Nicholls: Phila. AL	65.00	32.50	6.50
☐ 267	Nichols(sic): Phila. AL	55.00	27.50	5.50
☐ 268	Niles: Boston AL	65.00	32.50	6.50
☐ 269	Oakes: Cinc.	55.00	27.50	5.50
☐ 270	O'Hara: St.L. NL	3200.00	1200.00	300.00
☐ 271	O'Hara: N.Y. NL	55.00	27.50	5.50
☐ 272	Oldring: Phila. AL, Fielding	65.00	32.50	6.50
☐ 273	Oldring: Phila. AL, Bat on shoulder	55.00	27.50	5.50
☐ 274	O'Leary: Detroit, Portrait	65.00	32.50	6.50
☐ 275	O'Leary: Detroit, Hands on knees	55.00	27.50	5.50
☐ 276	Overall: Chicago NL, Portrait	65.00	32.50	6.50
☐ 277	Overall: Chicago NL, Pitching, follow thru	55.00	27.50	5.50
☐ 278	Overall: Chicago NL, Pitching hiding ball in glove	55.00	27.50	5.50
☐ 279	Owen: Chicago AL	65.00	32.50	6.50
☐ 280	Parent: Chicago AL	65.00	32.50	6.50

☐ 281	Paskert: Cinc.	55.00	27.50	5.50
☐ 282	Pastorius: Brooklyn	65.00	32.50	6.50
☐ 283	Pattee: Brooklyn	100.00	50.00	10.00
☐ 284	Payne: Chicago AL	55.00	27.50	5.50
☐ 285	Pelty: St.L. AL, HOR	100.00	50.00	10.00
☐ 286	Pelty: St.L. AL, VERT	55.00	27.50	5.50
☐ 287	Perring: Cleveland	55.00	27.50	5.50
☐ 288	Pfeffer: Chicago NL	55.00	27.50	5.50
☐ 289	Pfeister: Chic. NL, Sitting	55.00	27.50	5.50
☐ 290	Pfeister: Chic. NL, Pitching	55.00	27.50	5.50
☐ 291	Phelps: St.L. NL	55.00	27.50	5.50
☐ 292	Phillippe: Pitt.	75.00	37.50	7.50
☐ 293	Plank: Phila. AL	18000.00	7500.00	1500.00
☐ 294	Powell: St.L. AL	65.00	32.50	6.50
☐ 295	Powers: Phil. AL	100.00	50.00	10.00
☐ 296	Purtell: Chicago AL	55.00	27.50	5.50
☐ 297	Quinn: N.Y. AL	55.00	27.50	5.50
☐ 298	Raymond: N.Y. NL	55.00	27.50	5.50
☐ 299	Reulbach: Chicago NL, Pitching	55.00	27.50	5.50
☐ 300	Reulbach: Chicago NL, Hands at side	100.00	50.00	10.00
☐ 301	Rhoades: Cleveland, Hand in air	55.00	27.50	5.50
☐ 302	Rhoades: Cleveland, Ready to pitch	55.00	27.50	5.50
☐ 303	Rhodes: St.L. NL	55.00	27.50	5.50
☐ 304	Ritchey: Boston NL	65.00	32.50	6.50
☐ 305	Rossman: Detroit	55.00	27.50	5.50
☐ 306	Rucker: Brooklyn, Portrait	65.00	32.50	6.50
☐ 307	Rucker: Brooklyn, Pitching	55.00	27.50	5.50
☐ 308	Schaefer: Washington	55.00	27.50	5.50
☐ 309	Schaefer: Detroit	65.00	32.50	6.50
☐ 310	Schlei: N.Y. NL, Sweater	55.00	27.50	5.50
☐ 311	Schlei: N.Y. NL, Batting	55.00	27.50	5.50
☐ 312	Schlei: N.Y. NL, Fielding	65.00	32.50	6.50
☐ 313	Schmidt: Detroit, Portrait	55.00	27.50	5.50
☐ 314	Schmidt: Detroit, Throwing	65.00	32.50	6.50
☐ 315	Schulte: Chicago NL, Batting, back turned	55.00	27.50	5.50
☐ 316	Schulte: Chicago NL, Batting, front pose	65.00	32.50	6.50
☐ 317	Scott: Chicago AL	55.00	27.50	5.50
☐ 318	Seymour: N.Y. NL, Portrait	55.00	27.50	5.50
☐ 319	Seymour: N.Y. NL, Throwing	55.00	27.50	5.50
☐ 320	Seymour: N.Y. NL, Batting	65.00	32.50	6.50
☐ 321	Shaw: St.L. NL	65.00	32.50	6.50
☐ 322	Sheckard: Chic. NL, Throwing	55.00	27.50	5.50
☐ 323	Sheckard: Chic. NL, Side view	65.00	32.50	6.50
☐ 324	Shipke: Washington	65.00	32.50	6.50
☐ 325	Smith: Chicago AL	55.00	27.50	5.50
☐ 326	Smith: Chicago and Boston AL	400.00	200.00	40.00
☐ 327	F. Smith: Chicago AL	65.00	32.50	6.50
☐ 328	Happy Smith: Brk.	55.00	27.50	5.50
☐ 329	Snodgrass: N.Y. NL, Batting	55.00	27.50	5.50
☐ 330	Snodgrass: N.Y. NL, Catching	55.00	27.50	5.50
☐ 331	Spade: Cinc.	65.00	32.50	6.50
☐ 332	Speaker: Boston AL	350.00	175.00	35.00
☐ 333	Spencer: Boston AL	65.00	32.50	6.50
☐ 334	Stahl: Boston AL, Catching fly ball	55.00	27.50	5.50
☐ 335	Stahl: Boston AL, Standing, arms down	55.00	27.50	5.50
☐ 336	Stanage: Detroit	55.00	27.50	5.50
☐ 337	Starr: Boston NL	55.00	27.50	5.50
☐ 338	Steinfeldt: Chic. NL, Portrait	65.00	32.50	6.50
☐ 339	Steinfeldt: Chic. NL, Batting	55.00	27.50	5.50
☐ 340	Stephens: St.L. AL	55.00	27.50	5.50
☐ 341	Stone: St.L. AL	65.00	32.50	6.50

☐	342	Stovall: Cleveland, Portrait	65.00	32.50	6.50
☐	343	Stovall: Cleveland, Batting	55.00	27.50	5.50
☐	344	Street: Washington, Portrait	55.00	27.50	5.50
☐	345	Street: Washington, Catching	55.00	27.50	5.50
☐	346	Sullivan: Chicago AL	65.00	32.50	6.50
☐	347	Summers: Detroit	55.00	27.50	5.50
☐	348	Sweeney: N.Y. AL	55.00	27.50	5.50
☐	349	Sweeney: Bost. NL	55.00	27.50	5.50
☐	350	L. Tannehill: Chicago AL	65.00	32.50	6.50
☐	351	Tannehill: Chicago AL	55.00	27.50	5.50
☐	352	Tannehill: Wash.	55.00	27.50	5.50
☐	353	Tenney: N.Y. NL	65.00	32.50	6.50
☐	354	Thomas: Phila. AL	55.00	27.50	5.50
☐	355	Tinker: Chicago NL, Ready to hit	175.00	85.00	18.00
☐	356	Tinker: Chicago NL, Bat on shoulder	175.00	85.00	18.00
☐	357	Tinker: Chicago NL, Portrait	225.00	110.00	22.00
☐	358	Tinker: Chicago NL, Hands on knees	200.00	100.00	20.00
☐	359	Titus: Phila. NL	55.00	27.50	5.50
☐	360	Turner: Cleveland	65.00	32.50	6.50
☐	361	Unglaub: Washington	55.00	27.50	5.50
☐	362	Waddell: St.L. AL, Portrait	275.00	135.00	27.00
☐	363	Waddell: St.L. AL, Pitching	200.00	100.00	20.00
☐	364	Wagner: Boston AL, Bat on left shoulder	100.00	50.00	10.00
☐	365	Wagner: Boston AL, Bat on right shoulder	55.00	27.50	5.50
☐	366	Wagner: Pitt.	125000.	55000.	18000.
☐	367	Wallace: St.L. AL	200.00	100.00	20.00
☐	368	Walsh: Chicago AL	200.00	100.00	20.00
☐	369	Warhop: N.Y. AL	55.00	27.50	5.50
☐	370	Weimer: N.Y. NL	65.00	32.50	6.50
☐	371	Wheat: Brooklyn	200.00	100.00	20.00
☐	372	White: Chicago AL, Portrait	65.00	32.50	6.50
☐	373	White: Chicago AL, Pitching	55.00	27.50	5.50
☐	374	Wilhelm: Brooklyn, Batting	55.00	27.50	5.50
☐	375	Wilhelm: Brooklyn, Hands to chest	65.00	32.50	6.50
☐	376	Willett: Detroit, Batting	55.00	27.50	5.50
☐	377	Willetts (sic): Detroit, Pitching	55.00	27.50	5.50
☐	378	Williams: St.L. AL	65.00	32.50	6.50
☐	379	Willis: Pitt.	100.00	50.00	10.00
☐	380	Willis: St.L. NL, Pitching	90.00	45.00	9.00
☐	381	Willis: St.L. NL, Batting	90.00	45.00	9.00
☐	382	Wilson: Pitt.	55.00	27.50	5.50
☐	383	Wiltse: N.Y. NL, Portrait	65.00	32.50	6.50
☐	384	Wiltse: N.Y. NL, Sweater	55.00	27.50	5.50
☐	385	Wiltse: N.Y. NL, Pitching	55.00	27.50	5.50
☐	386	Young: Cleveland, Portrait	550.00	275.00	55.00
☐	387	Young: Cleveland, Pitch, front view	400.00	200.00	40.00
☐	388	Young: Cleveland, Pitch, side view	400.00	200.00	40.00
☐	389	Zimmerman: Chicago NL	55.00	27.50	5.50
☐	390	Fred Abbott: Toledo	45.00	22.50	4.50
☐	391	Merle (Doc) Adkins: Baltimore	45.00	22.50	4.50
☐	392	John Anderson: Providence	45.00	22.50	4.50
☐	393	Herman Armbruster: St. Paul	45.00	22.50	4.50
☐	394	Harry Arndt: Prov.	45.00	22.50	4.50
☐	395	Cy Barger: Rochester	45.00	22.50	4.50
☐	396	John Barry: Milwaukee	45.00	22.50	4.50
☐	397	Emil H. Batch: Rochester	45.00	22.50	4.50
☐	398	Jake Beckley: K.C.	225.00	110.00	22.00
☐	399	Russell Blackburne (Lena): Providence	45.00	22.50	4.50
☐	400	David Brain: Buffalo	45.00	22.50	4.50
☐	401	Roy Brashear: K.C.	45.00	22.50	4.50
☐	402	Fred Burchell: Buffalo	45.00	22.50	4.50
☐	403	Jimmy Burke: Ind.	45.00	22.50	4.50
☐	404	John Butler: Roch.	45.00	22.50	4.50
☐	405	Charles Carr: Ind.	45.00	22.50	4.50
☐	406	James Peter Casey (Doc): Montreal	45.00	22.50	4.50
☐	407	Peter Cassidy: Baltimore	45.00	22.50	4.50
☐	408	Wm. Chappelle: Rochester	45.00	22.50	4.50
☐	409	Wm. Clancy: Buffalo	45.00	22.50	4.50
☐	410	Joshua Clark: Col.	45.00	22.50	4.50
☐	411	William Clymer: Columbus	45.00	22.50	4.50
☐	412	Jimmy Collins: Minneapolis	250.00	125.00	25.00
☐	413	Bunk Congalton: Columbus	45.00	22.50	4.50
☐	414	Gavvy Cravath: Minneapolis	60.00	30.00	6.00
☐	415	Monte Cross: Ind.	45.00	22.50	4.50
☐	416	Paul Davidson: Ind.	45.00	22.50	4.50
☐	417	Frank Delehanty: Louisville	45.00	22.50	4.50
☐	418	Rube Dessau: Balt.	45.00	22.50	4.50
☐	419	Gus Dorner: K.C.	45.00	22.50	4.50
☐	420	Jerome Downs: Minn.	45.00	22.50	4.50
☐	421	Jack Dunn: Baltimore	45.00	22.50	4.50
☐	422	James Flanagan: Buffalo	45.00	22.50	4.50
☐	423	James Freeman: Tol.	45.00	22.50	4.50
☐	424	John Ganzel: Roch.	45.00	22.50	4.50
☐	425	Myron Grimshaw: Toronto	45.00	22.50	4.50
☐	426	Robert Hall: Balt.	45.00	22.50	4.50
☐	427	William Hallman: Kansas City	45.00	22.50	4.50
☐	428	John Hannifan: J.C.	45.00	22.50	4.50
☐	429	Jack Hayden: Ind.	45.00	22.50	4.50
☐	430	Harry Hinchman: Toledo	45.00	22.50	4.50
☐	431	Harry C. Hoffman (Izzy): Providence	45.00	22.50	4.50
☐	432	James B. Jackson: Baltimore	45.00	22.50	4.50
☐	433	Joe Kelley: Tor.	250.00	125.00	25.00
☐	434	Rube Kisinger: Buffalo, (sic) Kissinger	45.00	22.50	4.50
☐	435	Otto Kruger: Col. (sic) Krueger	45.00	22.50	4.50
☐	436	Wm. Lattimore: Tol.	45.00	22.50	4.50
☐	437	James Lavender: Providence	45.00	22.50	4.50
☐	438	Carl Lundgren: K.C.	45.00	22.50	4.50
☐	439	Wm. Malarkey: Buff.	45.00	22.50	4.50
☐	440	Wm. Maloney: Roch.	45.00	22.50	4.50
☐	441	Dennis McGann: Milwaukee	45.00	22.50	4.50
☐	442	James McGinley: Toronto	45.00	22.50	4.50
☐	443	Joe McGinnity: New.	225.00	110.00	22.00
☐	444	Ulysses McGlynn: Milwaukee	45.00	22.50	4.50
☐	445	George Merritt: Jersey City	45.00	22.50	4.50
☐	446	Wm. Milligan: J.C.	45.00	22.50	4.50
☐	447	Fred Mitchell: Tor.	45.00	22.50	4.50
☐	448	Dan Moeller: J.C.	45.00	22.50	4.50
☐	449	Joseph Herbert Moran: Providence	45.00	22.50	4.50
☐	450	Wm. Nattress: Buffalo	45.00	22.50	4.50
☐	451	Frank Oberlin: Minneapolis	45.00	22.50	4.50
☐	452	Peter O'Brien: St. Paul	45.00	22.50	4.50
☐	453	Wm. O'Neil: Minn.	45.00	22.50	4.50
☐	454	James Phelan: Prov.	45.00	22.50	4.50
☐	455	Oliver Pickering: Minneapolis.	45.00	22.50	4.50
☐	456	Philip Poland: Baltimore	45.00	22.50	4.50
☐	457	Ambrose Puttman: Louisville	45.00	22.50	4.50
☐	458	Lee Quillen: Minn.	45.00	22.50	4.50

☐ 459 Newton Randall: Milwaukee	45.00	22.50	4.50
☐ 460 Louis Ritter: K.C.	45.00	22.50	4.50
☐ 461 Dick Rudolph: Tor.	45.00	22.50	4.50
☐ 462 George Schirm: Buffalo	45.00	22.50	4.50
☐ 463 Larry Schlafly: Newark	45.00	22.50	4.50
☐ 464 Ossie Schreck: Col. (sic) Schreckengost	45.00	22.50	4.50
☐ 465 William Shannon: Kansas City	45.00	22.50	4.50
☐ 466 Bayard Sharpe: Newark	45.00	22.50	4.50
☐ 467 Royal Shaw: Prov.	45.00	22.50	4.50
☐ 468 James Slagle: Balt.	45.00	22.50	4.50
☐ 469 George Henry Smith: Buffalo	45.00	22.50	4.50
☐ 470 Samuel Strang: Baltimore	45.00	22.50	4.50
☐ 471 Luther Taylor: (Dummy): Buffalo	45.00	22.50	4.50
☐ 472 John Thielman: Louisville	45.00	22.50	4.50
☐ 473 John F. White: Buffalo	45.00	22.50	4.50
☐ 474 William Wright: Toledo	45.00	22.50	4.50
☐ 475 Irving M. Young: Minneapolis	45.00	22.50	4.50
☐ 476 Jack Bastian: San Antonio	125.00	60.00	12.50
☐ 477 Harry Bay: Nashv.	125.00	60.00	12.50
☐ 478 Wm. Bernhard: Nashville	125.00	60.00	12.50
☐ 479 Ted Breitenstein: New Orleans	125.00	60.00	12.50
☐ 480 George Carey: (Scoops): Memphis	125.00	60.00	12.50
☐ 481 Cad Coles: Augusta	125.00	60.00	12.50
☐ 482 Wm. Cranston: Memphis	125.00	60.00	12.50
☐ 483 Roy Ellam: Nashville	125.00	60.00	12.50
☐ 484 Edward Foster: Charleston	125.00	60.00	12.50
☐ 485 Charles Fritz: N.O.	125.00	60.00	12.50
☐ 486 Ed Greminger: Montgomery	125.00	60.00	12.50
☐ 487 Guiheen: Portsmouth	125.00	60.00	12.50
☐ 488 William F. Hart Little Rock	125.00	60.00	12.50
☐ 489 James Henry Hart: Montgomery	125.00	60.00	12.50
☐ 490 J.R. Helm: Columbus (Georgia)	125.00	60.00	12.50
☐ 491 Gordon Hickman: Mobile	125.00	60.00	12.50
☐ 492 Buck Hooker: Lynchburg	125.00	60.00	12.50
☐ 493 Ernie Howard: Sav.	125.00	60.00	12.50
☐ 494 A.O. Jordan: Atlanta	125.00	60.00	12.50
☐ 495 J.F. Kiernan: Columbia	125.00	60.00	12.50
☐ 496 Frank King: Danville	125.00	60.00	12.50
☐ 497 James LaFitte: Macon	125.00	60.00	12.50
☐ 498 Harry Lentz: Little Rock (sic) Sentz	125.00	60.00	12.50
☐ 499 Perry Lipe: Richmond	125.00	60.00	12.50
☐ 500 George Manion: Columbia	125.00	60.00	12.50
☐ 501 McCauley: Portsmouth	125.00	60.00	12.50
☐ 502 Charles B. Miller: Dallas	125.00	60.00	12.50
☐ 503 Carlton Molesworth: Birmingham	125.00	60.00	12.50
☐ 504 Dominic Mullaney: Jacksonville	125.00	60.00	12.50
☐ 505 Albert Orth: Lynchburg	125.00	60.00	12.50
☐ 506 William Otey: Norf.	125.00	60.00	12.50
☐ 507 George Paige: Charleston	125.00	60.00	12.50
☐ 508 Hub Perdue: Nashv.	150.00	75.00	15.00
☐ 509 Archie Persons: Montgomery	125.00	60.00	12.50
☐ 510 Edward Reagan: N.O.	125.00	60.00	12.50
☐ 511 R.H. Revelle: Richmond	125.00	60.00	12.50
☐ 512 Isaac Rockenfeld: Montgomery	125.00	60.00	12.50
☐ 513 Ray Ryan: Roanoke	125.00	60.00	12.50
☐ 514 Charles Seitz: Norfolk	125.00	60.00	12.50
☐ 515 Frank Shaughnessy (Shag): Roanoke	125.00	60.00	12.50
☐ 516 Carlos Smith: Shreveport	125.00	60.00	12.50
☐ 517 Sid Smith: Atlanta	125.00	60.00	12.50
☐ 518 M.R.(Dolly) Stark: San Antonio	125.00	60.00	12.50
☐ 519 Tony Thebo: Waco	125.00	60.00	12.50
☐ 520 Woodie Thornton: Mobile	125.00	60.00	12.50
☐ 521 Juan Violat: Jacksonville: (sic) Viola	125.00	60.00	12.50
☐ 522 James Westlake: Danville	125.00	60.00	12.50
☐ 523 Foley White: Houston	125.00	60.00	12.50

T207 Brown Background

The cards in this 207-card set measure 1 1/2" by 2 5/8". The T207 set, also known as the "Brown Background" set was issued with Broadleaf, Cycle, Napoleon, Recruit and anonymous (Factories no. 2, 3 or 25) backs in 1912. Broadleaf, Cycle and anonymous backs are difficult to obtain. Although many scarcities and cards with varying degrees of difficulty to obtain exist (see prices below), the Loudermilk, Lewis (Boston NL) and Miller (Chicago NL) cards are the rarest, followed by Saier and Tyler. The cards are numbered below for reference in alphabetical order by player's name. The complete set price below does include the Lewis variation missing the Braves patch on the sleeve.

	EX-MT	VG-E	GOOD
COMPLETE SET (208)	30000.	12500.	3000.
COMMON PLAYER (1-207)	60.00	30.00	6.00
☐ 1 Adams: Cleve AL	90.00	45.00	9.00
☐ 2 Ainsmith: Wash AL	60.00	30.00	6.00
☐ 3 Almeida: Cinc AL	90.00	45.00	9.00
☐ 4 Austin: StL AL with StL on shirt	60.00	30.00	6.00
☐ 5 Austin: StL AL without StL on shirt	180.00	90.00	18.00
☐ 6 Ball: Cleve AL	60.00	30.00	6.00
☐ 7 Barger: Brk NL	60.00	30.00	6.00
☐ 8 Barry: Phil AL	60.00	30.00	6.00
☐ 9 Bauman: Det AL	180.00	90.00	18.00
☐ 10 Becker: NY NL	60.00	30.00	6.00
☐ 11 Bender: Phil AL	180.00	90.00	18.00
☐ 12 Benz: Chi AL	90.00	45.00	9.00
☐ 13 Bescher: Cinc NL	60.00	30.00	6.00
☐ 14 Birmingham: Cleve AL	90.00	45.00	9.00
☐ 15 Blackburne: Chi AL	90.00	45.00	9.00
☐ 16 Blanding: Cleve AL	90.00	45.00	9.00
☐ 17 Block: Chi AL	60.00	30.00	6.00
☐ 18 Bodie: Chi AL	60.00	30.00	6.00
☐ 19 Bradley: Bos AL	60.00	30.00	6.00
☐ 20 Bresnahan: StL NL	180.00	90.00	18.00

☐ 21	Bushelman: Bos AL	90.00	45.00	9.00
☐ 22	Butcher: Cleve AL	90.00	45.00	9.00
☐ 23	Byrne: Pitt NL	60.00	30.00	6.00
☐ 24	Callahan: Chi AL	60.00	30.00	6.00
☐ 25	Camnitz: Pitt NL	60.00	30.00	6.00
☐ 26	Carey: Pitt NL	180.00	90.00	18.00
☐ 27	Carrigan: Bos AL correct back	60.00	30.00	6.00
☐ 28	Carrigan: Bos AL Wagner back	225.00	110.00	22.00
☐ 29	Chalmers: Phil NL	60.00	30.00	6.00
☐ 30	Chance: Chi NL	250.00	125.00	25.00
☐ 31	Cicotte: Bos AL	90.00	45.00	9.00
☐ 32	Clarke: Cinc NL	60.00	30.00	6.00
☐ 33	Cole: Chi NL	60.00	30.00	6.00
☐ 34	Collins: Chi AL	300.00	150.00	30.00
☐ 35	Coulson: Brk NL	60.00	30.00	6.00
☐ 36	Covington: Det AL	60.00	30.00	6.00
☐ 37	Crandall: NY NL	60.00	30.00	6.00
☐ 38	Cunningham: Wash AL	90.00	45.00	9.00
☐ 39	Danforth: Phil AL	60.00	30.00	6.00
☐ 40	Daniels: NY AL	60.00	30.00	6.00
☐ 41	Daubert: Brk NL	90.00	45.00	9.00
☐ 42	Davis: Cleve AL	60.00	30.00	6.00
☐ 43	Delahanty: Det AL	60.00	30.00	6.00
☐ 44	Derrick: Phil AL	60.00	30.00	6.00
☐ 45	Devlin: Bos NL	60.00	30.00	6.00
☐ 46	Devore: NY NL	60.00	30.00	6.00
☐ 47	Donlin: Pitt NL	90.00	45.00	9.00
☐ 48	Donnelly: Bos NL	90.00	45.00	9.00
☐ 49	Dooin: Phil NL	60.00	30.00	6.00
☐ 50	Downey: Phil NL	90.00	45.00	9.00
☐ 51	Doyle: NY NL	60.00	30.00	6.00
☐ 52	Drake: Det AL	60.00	30.00	6.00
☐ 53	Easterly: Cleve AL	60.00	30.00	6.00
☐ 54	Ellis: StL NL	60.00	30.00	6.00
☐ 55	Engle: Bos AL	60.00	30.00	6.00
☐ 56	Erwin: Brk NL	60.00	30.00	6.00
☐ 57	Evans: StL NL	60.00	30.00	6.00
☐ 58	Ferry: Pitt NL	60.00	30.00	6.00
☐ 59	Fisher: NY AL white cap	180.00	90.00	18.00
☐ 60	Fisher: NY AL blue cap	90.00	45.00	9.00
☐ 61	Fletcher: NY NL	60.00	30.00	6.00
☐ 62	Fournier: Chi AL	90.00	45.00	9.00
☐ 63	Fromme: Cinc NL	60.00	30.00	6.00
☐ 64	Gainor: Det AL	60.00	30.00	6.00
☐ 65	Gardner: Bos AL	60.00	30.00	6.00
☐ 66	George: Cleve AL	60.00	30.00	6.00
☐ 67	Golden: StL NL	60.00	30.00	6.00
☐ 68	Gowdy: Bos NL	60.00	30.00	6.00
☐ 69	Graham: Phil NL	90.00	45.00	9.00
☐ 70	Graney: Cleve AL	60.00	30.00	6.00
☐ 71	Gregg: Cleve AL	90.00	45.00	9.00
☐ 72	Hageman: Bos AL	60.00	30.00	6.00
☐ 73	Hall: Bos AL	60.00	30.00	6.00
☐ 74	Hallinan: St.L. AL	60.00	30.00	6.00
☐ 75	E. Hamilton: St.L. AL	60.00	30.00	6.00
☐ 76	Harmon: St.L. NL	60.00	30.00	6.00
☐ 77	Hartley: NY NL	90.00	45.00	9.00
☐ 78	Henriksen, Bos AL	60.00	30.00	6.00
☐ 79	Henry: Wash AL	90.00	45.00	9.00
☐ 80	Herzog: NY NL	90.00	45.00	9.00
☐ 81	Higgins: Brk NL	60.00	30.00	6.00
☐ 82	Hoff: NY AL	90.00	45.00	9.00
☐ 83	Hogan: StL AL	60.00	30.00	6.00
☐ 84	Hooper: Bos AL	450.00	225.00	45.00
☐ 85	Houser: Bos NL	90.00	45.00	9.00
☐ 86	Hyatt: Pitt NL	90.00	45.00	9.00
☐ 87	Johnson: Wash AL	900.00	450.00	90.00
☐ 88	Kaler: Cleve AL	60.00	30.00	6.00
☐ 89	Kelly: Pitt NL	90.00	45.00	9.00
☐ 90	Kirke: Bos NL	90.00	45.00	9.00
☐ 91	Kling: Bos NL	60.00	30.00	6.00
☐ 92	Knabe: Phil NL	60.00	30.00	6.00
☐ 93	Knetzer: Brk NL	60.00	30.00	6.00
☐ 94	Konetchy: StL NL	60.00	30.00	6.00
☐ 95	Krause: Phil AL	60.00	30.00	6.00
☐ 96	Kuhn: Chi AL	90.00	45.00	9.00
☐ 97	Kutina: StL AL	90.00	45.00	9.00
☐ 98	Lange: Chi AL	90.00	45.00	9.00
☐ 99	Lapp: Phil AL	60.00	30.00	6.00
☐ 100	Latham: NY NL	60.00	30.00	6.00
☐ 101	Leach: Pitt NL	60.00	30.00	6.00
☐ 102	Leifield: Pitt NL	60.00	30.00	6.00
☐ 103	Lennox: Chi NL	60.00	30.00	6.00
☐ 104	Lewis: Bos AL	60.00	30.00	6.00
☐ 105A	Lewis: Bos NL (Braves patch on sleeve)	2500.00	1000.00	200.00
☐ 105B	Lewis: Bos NL (nothing on sleeve)	2500.00	1000.00	200.00
☐ 106	Lively: Det AL	60.00	30.00	6.00
☐ 107	Livingston: Cleve AL "A" shirt	250.00	125.00	25.00
☐ 108	Livingston: Cleve AL "C" shirt	250.00	125.00	25.00
☐ 109	Livingston: Cleve AL "c" shirt	90.00	45.00	9.00
☐ 110	Lord: Phil AL	60.00	30.00	6.00
☐ 111	Lord: Chi AL	60.00	30.00	6.00
☐ 112	Loudermilk: StL NL	2500.00	1000.00	200.00
☐ 113	Marquard: NY NL	180.00	90.00	18.00
☐ 114	Marsans: Cinc NL	60.00	30.00	6.00
☐ 115	McBride: Wash AL	60.00	30.00	6.00
☐ 116	McCarthy: Pitt NL	250.00	125.00	25.00
☐ 117	McDonald: Bos NL	60.00	30.00	6.00
☐ 118	McGraw: NY NL	250.00	125.00	25.00
☐ 119	McIntire: Chi NL	60.00	30.00	6.00
☐ 120	McIntyre: Chi AL	60.00	30.00	6.00
☐ 121	McKechnie: Pitt NL	350.00	175.00	35.00
☐ 122	McLean: Cinc NL	60.00	30.00	6.00
☐ 123	Milan: Wash AL	60.00	30.00	6.00
☐ 124	Miller: Pitt NL	60.00	30.00	6.00
☐ 125	Miller: Chi NL	2000.00	800.00	160.00
☐ 126	Miller: Brk NL	90.00	45.00	9.00
☐ 127	Miller: Bos NL	90.00	45.00	9.00
☐ 128	Mitchell: Cinc NL	60.00	30.00	6.00
☐ 129	Mitchell: Cleve AL	90.00	45.00	9.00
☐ 130	Mogridge: Chi AL	90.00	45.00	9.00
☐ 131	Moore: Phil NL	90.00	45.00	9.00
☐ 132	Moran: Phil NL	60.00	30.00	6.00
☐ 133	Morgan: Phil AL	60.00	30.00	6.00
☐ 134	Morgan: Wash AL	60.00	30.00	6.00
☐ 135	Moriarity: Det AL	90.00	45.00	9.00
☐ 136	Mullin: Det AL with "D" on cap	90.00	45.00	9.00
☐ 137	Mullin: Det AL without "D" on cap	250.00	125.00	25.00
☐ 138	Needham: Chi NL	60.00	30.00	6.00
☐ 139	Nelson: StL AL	90.00	45.00	9.00
☐ 140	Northen: Brk NL	60.00	30.00	6.00
☐ 141	Nunamaker: Bos AL	60.00	30.00	6.00
☐ 142	Oakes: StL NL	60.00	30.00	6.00
☐ 143	O'Brien: Bos AL	60.00	30.00	6.00
☐ 144	Oldring: Phil AL	60.00	30.00	6.00
☐ 145	Olson: Cleve AL	60.00	30.00	6.00
☐ 146	O'Toole: Pitt NL	60.00	30.00	6.00
☐ 147	Paskert: Phil NL	60.00	30.00	6.00
☐ 148	Pelty: StL AL	90.00	45.00	9.00
☐ 149	Perdue: Bos NL	60.00	30.00	6.00
☐ 150	Peters: Chi AL	90.00	45.00	9.00
☐ 151	Phelan: Cinc NL	90.00	45.00	9.00
☐ 152	Quinn: NY AL	60.00	30.00	6.00
☐ 153	Ragan: Brk NL	550.00	275.00	55.00
☐ 154	Rasmussen: Phil NL	450.00	225.00	45.00
☐ 155	Rath: Chi AL	90.00	45.00	9.00
☐ 156	Reulbach: Chi NL	60.00	30.00	6.00
☐ 157	Rucker: Brk NL	60.00	30.00	6.00
☐ 158	Ryan: Cleve AL	90.00	45.00	9.00
☐ 159	Saier: Chi NL	900.00	450.00	90.00
☐ 160	Scanlon: Phil NL	60.00	30.00	6.00
☐ 161	Schaefer: Wash AL	60.00	30.00	6.00
☐ 162	Schardt: Brk NL	60.00	30.00	6.00
☐ 163	Schulte: Chi NL	60.00	30.00	6.00
☐ 164	Scott: Chi AL	60.00	30.00	6.00
☐ 165	Severeid: Cinc NL	60.00	30.00	6.00
☐ 166	Simon: Pitt NL	60.00	30.00	6.00
☐ 167	Smith: StL NL	60.00	30.00	6.00
☐ 168	Smith: Cinc NL	60.00	30.00	6.00
☐ 169	Snodgrass: NY NL	60.00	30.00	6.00
☐ 170	Speaker: Bos AL	1000.00	400.00	80.00
☐ 171	Spratt: Bos NL	60.00	30.00	6.00
☐ 172	Stack: Brk NL	60.00	30.00	6.00
☐ 173	Stanage: Det AL	60.00	30.00	6.00
☐ 174	Steele: StL NL	60.00	30.00	6.00
☐ 175	Steinfeldt: StL NL	60.00	30.00	6.00
☐ 176	Stovall: StL AL	60.00	30.00	6.00
☐ 177	Street: NY AL	60.00	30.00	6.00
☐ 178	Strunk: Phil AL	60.00	30.00	6.00
☐ 179	Sullivan: Chi AL	60.00	30.00	6.00
☐ 180	Sweeney: Bos NL	180.00	90.00	18.00
☐ 181	Tannehill: Chi AL	60.00	30.00	6.00
☐ 182	Thomas: Bos AL	60.00	30.00	6.00
☐ 183	Tinker: Chi NL	180.00	90.00	18.00
☐ 184	Tooley: Brk NL	60.00	30.00	6.00
☐ 185	Turner: Cleve AL	60.00	30.00	6.00
☐ 186	Tyler: Bos NL	900.00	450.00	90.00
☐ 187	Vaughn: NY AL	60.00	30.00	6.00
☐ 188	Wagner: Bos AL correct back	90.00	45.00	9.00
☐ 189	Wagner: Bos AL Carrigan back	250.00	125.00	25.00
☐ 190	Walker: Wash AL	60.00	30.00	6.00
☐ 191	Wallace: St.L. AL	180.00	90.00	18.00
☐ 192	Warhop: NY AL	60.00	30.00	6.00

☐ 193 Weaver: Chi AL	180.00	90.00	18.00
☐ 194 Wheat: Brk NL	180.00	90.00	18.00
☐ 195 White: Chi AL	90.00	45.00	9.00
☐ 196 Wilie: St.L. NL	90.00	45.00	9.00
☐ 197 Williams: NY AL	60.00	30.00	6.00
☐ 198 Wilson: NY NL	60.00	30.00	6.00
☐ 199 Wilson: Pitt NL	90.00	45.00	9.00
☐ 200 Wiltse: NY NL	60.00	30.00	6.00
☐ 201 Wingo: StL NL	60.00	30.00	6.00
☐ 202 Wolverton: NY AL	60.00	30.00	6.00
☐ 203 Wood: Bos AL	180.00	90.00	18.00
☐ 204 Woodburn: StL NL	90.00	45.00	9.00
☐ 205 Works: Det AL	350.00	175.00	35.00
☐ 206 Yerkes: Bos AL	60.00	30.00	6.00
☐ 207 Zeider: Chi AL	90.00	45.00	9.00

1988 Upper Deck Samples

This two-card test issue was given away as samples during the summer of 1988 in anticipation of Upper Deck obtaining licenses from Major League Baseball and the Major League Baseball Players Association. Not many were produced (probably less than 25,000 of each) but almost none were thrown away as they were distributed basically only to those who would hold on to them. There are supposedly versions based on where the hologram is printed but the price below is for the basic variety. These test cards are the same size (2 1/2" by 3 1/2") as the regular issue and are styled similarly. Joyner and Buice were supposedly interested in investing in Upper Deck (conflict of interest prohibited them) and apparently were helpful in getting Upper Deck the necessary licenses. Cards were passed out freely to every dealer at the National Sports Collectors Convention in Atlantic City, New Jersey in August 1988.

	MINT	EXC	G-VG
COMPLETE SET (2)	50.00	25.00	5.00
COMMON PLAYER	15.00	7.50	1.50
☐ 1 DeWayne Buice	15.00	7.50	1.50
☐ 700 Wally Joyner	40.00	20.00	4.00

1989 Upper Deck

This attractive set was introduced in 1989 as an additional major card set. The cards feature full color on both the front and the back. The cards are distinguished by the fact that each card has a hologram on the reverse, thus making the cards essentially copy proof. Cards 668-693 feature a "Collector's Choice" (CC) colorful drawing of a player (by artist Vernon Wells) on the card front and a checklist of that team on the card back. On many cards "Rookie" and team logos can be found with either a "TM" or (R). Cards with missing or duplicate holograms appear to be relatively common and hence there is little, if any, premium value on these "variations." The more significant variations involving changed photos or changed type are listed below. According to the company, the Murphy and Sheridan cards were corrected very early, after only 2 percent of the cards had been produced. This means, for example, that out of 1,000,000 Dale Murphy '89 Upper Deck cards produced, there are only 20,000 Murphy error cards. Similarly, the Sheffield was corrected after 15 percent had been printed; Varsho, Gallego, and Schroeder were corrected after 20 percent; and Holton, Manrique, and Winningham were corrected 30 percent of the way through. Collectors should also note that many dealers consider that Upper Deck's "planned" production of 1,000,000 of each player was increased (perhaps even doubled) later in the year due to the explosion in popularity of the Upper Deck cards. The key rookie cards in this set are Sandy Alomar Jr., Ken Griffey Jr., Ramon Martinez, and Gary Sheffield.

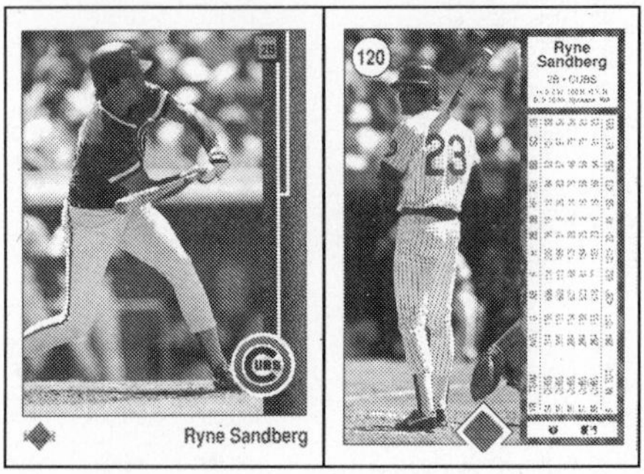

	MINT	EXC	G-VG
COMPLETE SET (700)	75.00	37.50	7.50
COMMON PLAYER (1-700)	.07	.03	.01
☐ 1 Ken Griffey Jr.	33.00	10.00	2.00
☐ 2 Luis Medina	.25	.12	.02
☐ 3 Tony Chance	.15	.07	.01
☐ 4 Dave Otto	.12	.06	.01
☐ 5 Sandy Alomar Jr. UER (wrong birthdate)	5.00	2.50	.50
☐ 6 Rolando Roomes	.20	.10	.02
☐ 7 Dave West	.25	.12	.02
☐ 8 Cris Carpenter	.20	.10	.02
☐ 9 Gregg Jefferies	4.00	2.00	.40
☐ 10 Doug Dascenzo	.20	.10	.02
☐ 11 Ron Jones	.30	.15	.03
☐ 12 Luis De Los Santos	.20	.10	.02
☐ 13A Gary Sheffield ERR (SS upside down on card front)	5.00	2.50	.50
☐ 13B Gary Sheffield COR	3.50	1.75	.35
☐ 14 Mike Harkey	1.00	.50	.10
☐ 15 Lance Blankenship	.20	.10	.02
☐ 16 William Brennan	.12	.06	.01
☐ 17 John Smoltz	1.00	.50	.10
☐ 18 Ramon Martinez	5.00	2.50	.50
☐ 19 Mark Lemke	.18	.09	.01
☐ 20 Juan Bell	.25	.12	.02
☐ 21 Rey Palacios	.15	.07	.01
☐ 22 Felix Jose	.60	.30	.06
☐ 23 Van Snider	.25	.12	.02
☐ 24 Dante Bichette	.40	.20	.04
☐ 25 Randy Johnson	.65	.30	.06
☐ 26 Carlos Quintana	1.00	.50	.10
☐ 27 Star Rookie CL	.07	.01	.00
☐ 28 Mike Schooler	.45	.22	.04
☐ 29 Randy St.Claire	.07	.03	.01
☐ 30 Jerald Clark	.25	.12	.02
☐ 31 Kevin Gross	.07	.03	.01
☐ 32 Dan Firova	.10	.05	.01
☐ 33 Jeff Calhoun	.07	.03	.01
☐ 34 Tommy Hinzo	.07	.03	.01
☐ 35 Ricky Jordan	.75	.35	.07
☐ 36 Larry Parrish	.07	.03	.01
☐ 37 Bret Saberhagen UER (hit total 931, should be 1031)	.20	.10	.02
☐ 38 Mike Smithson	.07	.03	.01
☐ 39 Dave Dravecky	.10	.05	.01

☐ 40 Ed Romero	.07	.03	.01
☐ 41 Jeff Musselman	.07	.03	.01
☐ 42 Ed Hearn	.07	.03	.01
☐ 43 Rance Mulliniks	.07	.03	.01
☐ 44 Jim Eisenreich	.07	.03	.01
☐ 45 Sil Campusano	.25	.12	.02
☐ 46 Mike Krukow	.07	.03	.01
☐ 47 Paul Gibson	.12	.06	.01
☐ 48 Mike LaCoss	.07	.03	.01
☐ 49 Larry Herndon	.07	.03	.01
☐ 50 Scott Garrelts	.10	.05	.01
☐ 51 Dwayne Henry	.07	.03	.01
☐ 52 Jim Acker	.07	.03	.01
☐ 53 Steve Sax	.12	.06	.01
☐ 54 Pete O'Brien	.10	.05	.01
☐ 55 Paul Runge	.07	.03	.01
☐ 56 Rick Rhoden	.07	.03	.01
☐ 57 John Dopson	.25	.12	.02
☐ 58 Casey Candaele UER	.07	.03	.01
(no stats for Astros			
for '88 season)			
☐ 59 Dave Righetti	.10	.05	.01
☐ 60 Joe Hesketh	.07	.03	.01
☐ 61 Frank DiPino	.07	.03	.01
☐ 62 Tim Laudner	.07	.03	.01
☐ 63 Jamie Moyer	.07	.03	.01
☐ 64 Fred Toliver	.07	.03	.01
☐ 65 Mitch Webster	.07	.03	.01
☐ 66 John Tudor	.10	.05	.01
☐ 67 John Cangelosi	.07	.03	.01
☐ 68 Mike Devereaux	.12	.06	.01
☐ 69 Brian Fisher	.07	.03	.01
☐ 70 Mike Marshall	.10	.05	.01
☐ 71 Zane Smith	.07	.03	.01
☐ 72A Brian Holton ERR	1.50	.75	.15
(photo actually			
Shawn Hillegas)			
☐ 72B Brian Holton COR	.30	.15	.03
☐ 73 Jose Guzman	.07	.03	.01
☐ 74 Rick Mahler	.07	.03	.01
☐ 75 John Shelby	.07	.03	.01
☐ 76 Jim Deshaies	.07	.03	.01
☐ 77 Bobby Meacham	.07	.03	.01
☐ 78 Bryn Smith	.07	.03	.01
☐ 79 Joaquin Andujar	.10	.05	.01
☐ 80 Richard Dotson	.07	.03	.01
☐ 81 Charlie Lea	.07	.03	.01
☐ 82 Calvin Schiraldi	.07	.03	.01
☐ 83 Les Straker	.07	.03	.01
☐ 84 Les Lancaster	.07	.03	.01
☐ 85 Allan Anderson	.10	.05	.01
☐ 86 Junior Ortiz	.07	.03	.01
☐ 87 Jesse Orosco	.07	.03	.01
☐ 88 Felix Fermin	.10	.05	.01
☐ 89 Dave Anderson	.07	.03	.01
☐ 90 Rafael Belliard UER	.07	.03	.01
(wrong birth year)			
☐ 91 Franklin Stubbs	.10	.05	.01
☐ 92 Cecil Espy	.10	.05	.01
☐ 93 Albert Hall	.07	.03	.01
☐ 94 Tim Leary	.10	.05	.01
☐ 95 Mitch Williams	.10	.05	.01
☐ 96 Tracy Jones	.07	.03	.01
☐ 97 Danny Darwin	.10	.05	.01
☐ 98 Gary Ward	.07	.03	.01
☐ 99 Neal Heaton	.07	.03	.01
☐ 100 Jim Pankovits	.07	.03	.01
☐ 101 Bill Doran	.10	.05	.01
☐ 102 Tim Wallach	.12	.06	.01
☐ 103 Joe Magrane	.10	.05	.01
☐ 104 Ozzie Virgil	.07	.03	.01
☐ 105 Alvin Davis	.12	.06	.01
☐ 106 Tom Brookens	.07	.03	.01
☐ 107 Shawon Dunston	.15	.07	.01
☐ 108 Tracy Woodson	.10	.05	.01
☐ 109 Nelson Liriano	.07	.03	.01
☐ 110 Devon White UER	.12	.06	.01
(doubles total 46,			
should be 56)			
☐ 111 Steve Balboni	.07	.03	.01
☐ 112 Buddy Bell	.10	.05	.01
☐ 113 German Jimenez	.10	.05	.01
☐ 114 Ken Dayley	.07	.03	.01
☐ 115 Andres Galarraga	.10	.05	.01
☐ 116 Mike Scioscia	.07	.03	.01
☐ 117 Gary Pettis	.07	.03	.01
☐ 118 Ernie Whitt	.07	.03	.01
☐ 119 Bob Boone	.12	.06	.01
☐ 120 Ryne Sandberg	.50	.25	.05
☐ 121 Bruce Benedict	.07	.03	.01
☐ 122 Hubie Brooks	.12	.06	.01
☐ 123 Mike Moore	.10	.05	.01
☐ 124 Wallace Johnson	.07	.03	.01
☐ 125 Bob Horner	.10	.05	.01
☐ 126 Chili Davis	.10	.05	.01
☐ 127 Manny Trillo	.07	.03	.01
☐ 128 Chet Lemon	.07	.03	.01
☐ 129 John Cerutti	.07	.03	.01
☐ 130 Orel Hershiser	.25	.12	.02
☐ 131 Terry Pendleton	.07	.03	.01
☐ 132 Jeff Blauser	.12	.06	.01
☐ 133 Mike Fitzgerald	.07	.03	.01
☐ 134 Henry Cotto	.07	.03	.01
☐ 135 Gerald Young	.07	.03	.01
☐ 136 Luis Salazar	.07	.03	.01
☐ 137 Alejandro Pena	.07	.03	.01
☐ 138 Jack Howell	.07	.03	.01
☐ 139 Tony Fernandez	.10	.05	.01
☐ 140 Mark Grace	2.00	1.00	.20
☐ 141 Ken Caminiti	.07	.03	.01
☐ 142 Mike Jackson	.07	.03	.01
☐ 143 Larry McWilliams	.07	.03	.01
☐ 144 Andres Thomas	.07	.03	.01
☐ 145 Nolan Ryan	2.50	1.25	.25
(triple exposure)			
☐ 146 Mike Davis	.07	.03	.01
☐ 147 DeWayne Buice	.07	.03	.01
☐ 148 Jody Davis	.07	.03	.01
☐ 149 Jesse Barfield	.12	.06	.01
☐ 150 Matt Nokes	.10	.05	.01
☐ 151 Jerry Reuss	.07	.03	.01
☐ 152 Rick Cerone	.07	.03	.01
☐ 153 Storm Davis	.10	.05	.01
☐ 154 Marvell Wynne	.07	.03	.01
☐ 155 Will Clark	1.50	.75	.15
☐ 156 Luis Aguayo	.07	.03	.01
☐ 157 Willie Upshaw	.07	.03	.01
☐ 158 Randy Bush	.07	.03	.01
☐ 159 Ron Darling	.12	.06	.01
☐ 160 Kal Daniels	.15	.07	.01
☐ 161 Spike Owen	.07	.03	.01
☐ 162 Luis Polonia	.07	.03	.01
☐ 163 Kevin Mitchell UER	.60	.30	.06
('88/total HR's 18/52,			
should be 19/53)			
☐ 164 Dave Gallagher	.20	.10	.02
☐ 165 Benito Santiago	.25	.12	.02
☐ 166 Greg Gagne	.07	.03	.01
☐ 167 Ken Phelps	.07	.03	.01
☐ 168 Sid Fernandez	.10	.05	.01
☐ 169 Bo Diaz	.07	.03	.01
☐ 170 Cory Snyder	.12	.06	.01
☐ 171 Eric Show	.07	.03	.01
☐ 172 Robby Thompson	.07	.03	.01
☐ 173 Marty Barrett	.07	.03	.01
☐ 174 Dave Henderson	.10	.05	.01
☐ 175 Ozzie Guillen	.12	.06	.01
☐ 176 Barry Lyons	.07	.03	.01
☐ 177 Kelvin Torve	.12	.06	.01
☐ 178 Don Slaught	.07	.03	.01
☐ 179 Steve Lombardozzi	.07	.03	.01
☐ 180 Chris Sabo	2.50	1.25	.25
☐ 181 Jose Uribe	.07	.03	.01
☐ 182 Shane Mack	.12	.06	.01
☐ 183 Ron Karkovice	.07	.03	.01
☐ 184 Todd Benzinger	.07	.03	.01
☐ 185 Dave Stewart	.15	.07	.01
☐ 186 Julio Franco	.12	.06	.01
☐ 187 Ron Robinson	.07	.03	.01
☐ 188 Wally Backman	.07	.03	.01
☐ 189 Randy Velarde	.10	.05	.01
☐ 190 Joe Carter	.15	.07	.01
☐ 191 Bob Welch	.15	.07	.01
☐ 192 Kelly Paris	.07	.03	.01
☐ 193 Chris Brown	.07	.03	.01
☐ 194 Rick Reuschel	.10	.05	.01
☐ 195 Roger Clemens	.50	.25	.05
☐ 196 Dave Concepcion	.10	.05	.01
☐ 197 Al Newman	.07	.03	.01
☐ 198 Brook Jacoby	.10	.05	.01
☐ 199 Mookie Wilson	.10	.05	.01
☐ 200 Don Mattingly	1.00	.50	.10
☐ 201 Dick Schofield	.07	.03	.01
☐ 202 Mark Gubicza	.10	.05	.01
☐ 203 Gary Gaetti	.10	.05	.01
☐ 204 Dan Pasqua	.07	.03	.01
☐ 205 Andre Dawson	.20	.10	.02
☐ 206 Chris Speier	.07	.03	.01
☐ 207 Kent Tekulve	.07	.03	.01
☐ 208 Rod Scurry	.07	.03	.01
☐ 209 Scott Bailes	.07	.03	.01
☐ 210 Rickey Henderson UER	.50	.25	.05
(Throws Right)			
☐ 211 Harold Baines	.12	.06	.01
☐ 212 Tony Armas	.07	.03	.01
☐ 213 Kent Hrbek	.12	.06	.01
☐ 214 Darrin Jackson	.10	.05	.01
☐ 215 George Brett	.25	.12	.02

☐ 216 Rafael Santana	.07	.03	.01
☐ 217 Andy Allanson	.07	.03	.01
☐ 218 Brett Butler	.12	.06	.01
☐ 219 Steve Jeltz	.07	.03	.01
☐ 220 Jay Buhner	.20	.10	.02
☐ 221 Bo Jackson	2.00	1.00	.20
☐ 222 Angel Salazar	.07	.03	.01
☐ 223 Kirk McCaskill	.07	.03	.01
☐ 224 Steve Lyons	.07	.03	.01
☐ 225 Bert Blyleven	.12	.06	.01
☐ 226 Scott Bradley	.07	.03	.01
☐ 227 Bob Melvin	.07	.03	.01
☐ 228 Ron Kittle	.10	.05	.01
☐ 229 Phil Bradley	.10	.05	.01
☐ 230 Tommy John	.12	.06	.01
☐ 231 Greg Walker	.07	.03	.01
☐ 232 Juan Berenguer	.07	.03	.01
☐ 233 Pat Tabler	.07	.03	.01
☐ 234 Terry Clark	.12	.06	.01
☐ 235 Rafael Palmeiro	.18	.09	.01
☐ 236 Paul Zuvella	.07	.03	.01
☐ 237 Willie Randolph	.10	.05	.01
☐ 238 Bruce Fields	.07	.03	.01
☐ 239 Mike Aldrete	.07	.03	.01
☐ 240 Lance Parrish	.12	.06	.01
☐ 241 Greg Maddux	.20	.10	.02
☐ 242 John Moses	.07	.03	.01
☐ 243 Melido Perez	.18	.09	.01
☐ 244 Willie Wilson	.12	.06	.01
☐ 245 Mark McLemore	.07	.03	.01
☐ 246 Von Hayes	.12	.06	.01
☐ 247 Matt Williams	.60	.30	.06
☐ 248 John Candelaria UER (listed as Yankee for part of '87, should be Mets)	.10	.05	.01
☐ 249 Harold Reynolds	.10	.05	.01
☐ 250 Greg Swindell	.12	.06	.01
☐ 251 Juan Agosto	.07	.03	.01
☐ 252 Mike Felder	.07	.03	.01
☐ 253 Vince Coleman	.15	.07	.01
☐ 254 Larry Sheets	.07	.03	.01
☐ 255 George Bell	.12	.06	.01
☐ 256 Terry Steinbach	.10	.05	.01
☐ 257 Jack Armstrong	.45	.22	.04
☐ 258 Dickie Thon	.07	.03	.01
☐ 259 Ray Knight	.10	.05	.01
☐ 260 Darryl Strawberry	.50	.25	.05
☐ 261 Doug Sisk	.07	.03	.01
☐ 262 Alex Trevino	.07	.03	.01
☐ 263 Jeffrey Leonard	.10	.05	.01
☐ 264 Tom Henke	.10	.05	.01
☐ 265 Ozzie Smith	.20	.10	.02
☐ 266 Dave Bergman	.07	.03	.01
☐ 267 Tony Phillips	.07	.03	.01
☐ 268 Mark Davis	.15	.07	.01
☐ 269 Kevin Elster	.10	.05	.01
☐ 270 Barry Larkin	.30	.15	.03
☐ 271 Manny Lee	.07	.03	.01
☐ 272 Tom Brunansky	.12	.06	.01
☐ 273 Craig Biggio	.75	.35	.07
☐ 274 Jim Gantner	.07	.03	.01
☐ 275 Eddie Murray	.15	.07	.01
☐ 276 Jeff Reed	.07	.03	.01
☐ 277 Tim Teufel	.07	.03	.01
☐ 278 Rick Honeycutt	.07	.03	.01
☐ 279 Guillermo Hernandez	.07	.03	.01
☐ 280 John Kruk	.07	.03	.01
☐ 281 Luis Alicea	.10	.05	.01
☐ 282 Jim Clancy	.07	.03	.01
☐ 283 Billy Ripken	.07	.03	.01
☐ 284 Craig Reynolds	.07	.03	.01
☐ 285 Robin Yount	.30	.15	.03
☐ 286 Jimmy Jones	.10	.05	.01
☐ 287 Ron Oester	.07	.03	.01
☐ 288 Terry Leach	.10	.05	.01
☐ 289 Dennis Eckersley	.15	.07	.01
☐ 290 Alan Trammell	.15	.07	.01
☐ 291 Jimmy Key	.10	.05	.01
☐ 292 Chris Bosio	.07	.03	.01
☐ 293 Jose DeLeon	.07	.03	.01
☐ 294 Jim Traber	.07	.03	.01
☐ 295 Mike Scott	.12	.06	.01
☐ 296 Roger McDowell	.10	.05	.01
☐ 297 Garry Templeton	.10	.05	.01
☐ 298 Doyle Alexander	.07	.03	.01
☐ 299 Nick Esasky	.10	.05	.01
☐ 300 Mark McGwire UER (doubles total 52, should be 51)	.80	.40	.08
☐ 301 Darryl Hamilton	.25	.12	.02
☐ 302 Dave Smith	.10	.05	.01
☐ 303 Rick Sutcliffe	.10	.05	.01
☐ 304 Dave Stapleton	.10	.05	.01

☐ 305 Alan Ashby	.07	.03	.01
☐ 306 Pedro Guerrero	.12	.06	.01
☐ 307 Ron Guidry	.10	.05	.01
☐ 308 Steve Farr	.07	.03	.01
☐ 309 Curt Ford	.07	.03	.01
☐ 310 Claudell Washington	.10	.05	.01
☐ 311 Tom Prince	.10	.05	.01
☐ 312 Chad Kreuter	.12	.06	.01
☐ 313 Ken Oberkfell	.07	.03	.01
☐ 314 Jerry Browne	.07	.03	.01
☐ 315 R.J. Reynolds	.07	.03	.01
☐ 316 Scott Bankhead	.10	.05	.01
☐ 317 Milt Thompson	.07	.03	.01
☐ 318 Mario Diaz	.10	.05	.01
☐ 319 Bruce Ruffin	.07	.03	.01
☐ 320 Dave Valle	.07	.03	.01
☐ 321A Gary Varsho ERR (back photo actually Mike Bielecki bunting)	2.50	1.25	.25
☐ 321B Gary Varsho COR (in road uniform)	.20	.10	.02
☐ 322 Paul Mirabella	.07	.03	.01
☐ 323 Chuck Jackson	.10	.05	.01
☐ 324 Drew Hall	.07	.03	.01
☐ 325 Don August	.10	.05	.01
☐ 326 Israel Sanchez	.10	.05	.01
☐ 327 Denny Walling	.07	.03	.01
☐ 328 Joel Skinner	.07	.03	.01
☐ 329 Danny Tartabull	.12	.06	.01
☐ 330 Tony Pena	.10	.05	.01
☐ 331 Jim Sundberg	.07	.03	.01
☐ 332 Jeff Robinson Pittsburgh Pirates	.07	.03	.01
☐ 333 Oddibe McDowell	.10	.05	.01
☐ 334 Jose Lind	.07	.03	.01
☐ 335 Paul Kilgus	.07	.03	.01
☐ 336 Juan Samuel	.10	.05	.01
☐ 337 Mike Campbell	.10	.05	.01
☐ 338 Mike Maddux	.07	.03	.01
☐ 339 Darnell Coles	.07	.03	.01
☐ 340 Bob Dernier	.07	.03	.01
☐ 341 Rafael Ramirez	.07	.03	.01
☐ 342 Scott Sanderson	.10	.05	.01
☐ 343 B.J. Surhoff	.12	.06	.01
☐ 344 Billy Hatcher	.10	.05	.01
☐ 345 Pat Perry	.07	.03	.01
☐ 346 Jack Clark	.12	.06	.01
☐ 347 Gary Thurman	.07	.03	.01
☐ 348 Tim Jones	.12	.06	.01
☐ 349 Dave Winfield	.20	.10	.02
☐ 350 Frank White	.10	.05	.01
☐ 351 Dave Collins	.07	.03	.01
☐ 352 Jack Morris	.12	.06	.01
☐ 353 Eric Plunk	.07	.03	.01
☐ 354 Leon Durham	.07	.03	.01
☐ 355 Ivan DeJesus	.07	.03	.01
☐ 356 Brian Holman	.15	.07	.01
☐ 357A Dale Murphy ERR (front has reverse negative)	90.00	45.00	9.00
☐ 357B Dale Murphy COR	.75	.35	.07
☐ 358 Mark Portugal	.07	.03	.01
☐ 359 Andy McGaffigan	.07	.03	.01
☐ 360 Tom Glavine	.10	.05	.01
☐ 361 Keith Moreland	.07	.03	.01
☐ 362 Todd Stottlemyre	.15	.07	.01
☐ 363 Dave Leiper	.07	.03	.01
☐ 364 Cecil Fielder	.80	.40	.08
☐ 365 Carmelo Martinez	.07	.03	.01
☐ 366 Dwight Evans	.12	.06	.01
☐ 367 Kevin McReynolds	.12	.06	.01
☐ 368 Rich Gedman	.07	.03	.01
☐ 369 Len Dykstra	.15	.07	.01
☐ 370 Jody Reed	.12	.06	.01
☐ 371 Jose Canseco UER (strikeout total 391, should be 491)	1.75	.85	.17
☐ 372 Rob Murphy	.07	.03	.01
☐ 373 Mike Henneman	.07	.03	.01
☐ 374 Walt Weiss	.65	.30	.06
☐ 375 Rob Dibble	.75	.35	.07
☐ 376 Kirby Puckett (Mark McGwire in background)	.60	.30	.06
☐ 377 Dennis Martinez	.07	.03	.01
☐ 378 Ron Gant	1.50	.75	.15
☐ 379 Brian Harper	.10	.05	.01
☐ 380 Nelson Santovenia	.25	.12	.02
☐ 381 Lloyd Moseby	.10	.05	.01
☐ 382 Lance McCullers	.07	.03	.01
☐ 383 Dave Stieb	.12	.06	.01
☐ 384 Tony Gwynn	.35	.17	.03
☐ 385 Mike Flanagan	.07	.03	.01
☐ 386 Bob Ojeda	.10	.05	.01

☐ 387	Bruce Hurst	.10	.05	.01
☐ 388	Dave Magadan	.15	.07	.01
☐ 389	Wade Boggs	.65	.30	.06
☐ 390	Gary Carter	.12	.06	.01
☐ 391	Frank Tanana	.10	.05	.01
☐ 392	Curt Young	.07	.03	.01
☐ 393	Jeff Treadway	.12	.06	.01
☐ 394	Darrell Evans	.10	.05	.01
☐ 395	Glenn Hubbard	.07	.03	.01
☐ 396	Chuck Cary	.07	.03	.01
☐ 397	Frank Viola	.15	.07	.01
☐ 398	Jeff Parrett	.10	.05	.01
☐ 399	Terry Blocker	.12	.06	.01
☐ 400	Dan Gladden	.07	.03	.01
☐ 401	Louie Meadows	.10	.05	.01
☐ 402	Tim Raines	.12	.06	.01
☐ 403	Joey Meyer	.10	.05	.01
☐ 404	Larry Andersen	.07	.03	.01
☐ 405	Rex Hudler	.07	.03	.01
☐ 406	Mike Schmidt	1.00	.50	.10
☐ 407	John Franco	.10	.05	.01
☐ 408	Brady Anderson	.40	.20	.04
☐ 409	Don Carman	.07	.03	.01
☐ 410	Eric Davis	.35	.17	.03
☐ 411	Bob Stanley	.07	.03	.01
☐ 412	Pete Smith	.12	.06	.01
☐ 413	Jim Rice	.12	.06	.01
☐ 414	Bruce Sutter	.10	.05	.01
☐ 415	Oil Can Boyd	.10	.05	.01
☐ 416	Ruben Sierra	.40	.20	.04
☐ 417	Mike LaValliere	.07	.03	.01
☐ 418	Steve Buechele	.07	.03	.01
☐ 419	Gary Redus	.07	.03	.01
☐ 420	Scott Fletcher	.07	.03	.01
☐ 421	Dale Sveum	.07	.03	.01
☐ 422	Bob Knepper	.07	.03	.01
☐ 423	Luis Rivera	.07	.03	.01
☐ 424	Ted Higuera	.10	.05	.01
☐ 425	Kevin Bass	.10	.05	.01
☐ 426	Ken Gerhart	.07	.03	.01
☐ 427	Shane Rawley	.07	.03	.01
☐ 428	Paul O'Neill	.15	.07	.01
☐ 429	Joe Orsulak	.07	.03	.01
☐ 430	Jackie Gutierrez	.07	.03	.01
☐ 431	Gerald Perry	.07	.03	.01
☐ 432	Mike Greenwell	.50	.25	.05
☐ 433	Jerry Royster	.07	.03	.01
☐ 434	Ellis Burks	.45	.22	.04
☐ 435	Ed Olwine	.07	.03	.01
☐ 436	Dave Rucker	.07	.03	.01
☐ 437	Charlie Hough	.07	.03	.01
☐ 438	Bob Walk	.07	.03	.01
☐ 439	Bob Brower	.07	.03	.01
☐ 440	Barry Bonds	.40	.20	.04
☐ 441	Tom Foley	.07	.03	.01
☐ 442	Rob Deer	.12	.06	.01
☐ 443	Glenn Davis	.15	.07	.01
☐ 444	Dave Martinez	.07	.03	.01
☐ 445	Bill Wegman	.07	.03	.01
☐ 446	Lloyd McClendon	.10	.05	.01
☐ 447	Dave Schmidt	.07	.03	.01
☐ 448	Darren Daulton	.10	.05	.01
☐ 449	Frank Williams	.07	.03	.01
☐ 450	Don Aase	.07	.03	.01
☐ 451	Lou Whitaker	.12	.06	.01
☐ 452	Goose Gossage	.10	.05	.01
☐ 453	Ed Whitson	.10	.05	.01
☐ 454	Jim Walewander	.10	.05	.01
☐ 455	Damon Berryhill	.25	.12	.02
☐ 456	Tim Burke	.10	.05	.01
☐ 457	Barry Jones	.10	.05	.01
☐ 458	Joel Youngblood	.07	.03	.01
☐ 459	Floyd Youmans	.07	.03	.01
☐ 460	Mark Salas	.07	.03	.01
☐ 461	Jeff Russell	.07	.03	.01
☐ 462	Darrell Miller	.07	.03	.01
☐ 463	Jeff Kunkel	.07	.03	.01
☐ 464	Sherman Corbett	.07	.03	.01
☐ 465	Curtis Wilkerson	.07	.03	.01
☐ 466	Bud Black	.10	.05	.01
☐ 467	Cal Ripken Jr.	.20	.10	.02
☐ 468	John Farrell	.07	.03	.01
☐ 469	Terry Kennedy	.07	.03	.01
☐ 470	Tom Candiotti	.07	.03	.01
☐ 471	Roberto Alomar	1.00	.50	.10
☐ 472	Jeff Robinson Detroit Tigers	.10	.05	.01
☐ 473	Vance Law	.07	.03	.01
☐ 474	Randy Ready UER (strikeout total 136, should be 115)	.07	.03	.01
☐ 475	Walt Terrell	.07	.03	.01
☐ 476	Kelly Downs	.07	.03	.01
☐ 477	Johnny Paredes	.10	.05	.01
☐ 478	Shawn Hillegas	.07	.03	.01
☐ 479	Bob Brenly	.07	.03	.01
☐ 480	Otis Nixon	.07	.03	.01
☐ 481	Johnny Ray	.07	.03	.01
☐ 482	Geno Petralli	.07	.03	.01
☐ 483	Stu Cliburn	.07	.03	.01
☐ 484	Pete Incaviglia	.12	.06	.01
☐ 485	Brian Downing	.07	.03	.01
☐ 486	Jeff Stone	.07	.03	.01
☐ 487	Carmen Castillo	.07	.03	.01
☐ 488	Tom Niedenfuer	.07	.03	.01
☐ 489	Jay Bell	.12	.06	.01
☐ 490	Rick Schu	.07	.03	.01
☐ 491	Jeff Pico	.10	.05	.01
☐ 492	Mark Parent	.12	.06	.01
☐ 493	Eric King	.07	.03	.01
☐ 494	Al Nipper	.07	.03	.01
☐ 495	Andy Hawkins	.07	.03	.01
☐ 496	Daryl Boston	.10	.05	.01
☐ 497	Ernie Riles	.07	.03	.01
☐ 498	Pascual Perez	.10	.05	.01
☐ 499	Bill Long UER (games started total 70, should be 44)	.07	.03	.01
☐ 500	Kirt Manwaring	.10	.05	.01
☐ 501	Chuck Crim	.07	.03	.01
☐ 502	Candy Maldonado	.10	.05	.01
☐ 503	Dennis Lamp	.07	.03	.01
☐ 504	Glenn Braggs	.10	.05	.01
☐ 505	Joe Price	.07	.03	.01
☐ 506	Ken Williams	.10	.05	.01
☐ 507	Bill Pecota	.07	.03	.01
☐ 508	Rey Quinones	.07	.03	.01
☐ 509	Jeff Bittiger	.12	.06	.01
☐ 510	Kevin Seitzer	.15	.07	.01
☐ 511	Steve Bedrosian	.10	.05	.01
☐ 512	Todd Worrell	.10	.05	.01
☐ 513	Chris James	.10	.05	.01
☐ 514	Jose Oquendo	.07	.03	.01
☐ 515	David Palmer	.07	.03	.01
☐ 516	John Smiley	.07	.03	.01
☐ 517	Dave Clark	.07	.03	.01
☐ 518	Mike Dunne	.07	.03	.01
☐ 519	Ron Washington	.07	.03	.01
☐ 520	Bob Kipper	.07	.03	.01
☐ 521	Lee Smith	.10	.05	.01
☐ 522	Juan Castillo	.07	.03	.01
☐ 523	Don Robinson	.07	.03	.01
☐ 524	Kevin Romine	.07	.03	.01
☐ 525	Paul Molitor	.10	.05	.01
☐ 526	Mark Langston	.12	.06	.01
☐ 527	Donnie Hill	.07	.03	.01
☐ 528	Larry Owen	.07	.03	.01
☐ 529	Jerry Reed	.07	.03	.01
☐ 530	Jack McDowell	.35	.17	.03
☐ 531	Greg Mathews	.07	.03	.01
☐ 532	John Russell	.07	.03	.01
☐ 533	Dan Quisenberry	.12	.06	.01
☐ 534	Greg Gross	.07	.03	.01
☐ 535	Danny Cox	.07	.03	.01
☐ 536	Terry Francona	.07	.03	.01
☐ 537	Andy Van Slyke	.12	.06	.01
☐ 538	Mel Hall	.10	.05	.01
☐ 539	Jim Gott	.07	.03	.01
☐ 540	Doug Jones	.10	.05	.01
☐ 541	Craig Lefferts	.07	.03	.01
☐ 542	Mike Boddicker	.07	.03	.01
☐ 543	Greg Brock	.07	.03	.01
☐ 544	Atlee Hammaker	.07	.03	.01
☐ 545	Tom Bolton	.10	.05	.01
☐ 546	Mike Macfarlane	.15	.07	.01
☐ 547	Rich Renteria	.12	.06	.01
☐ 548	John Davis	.07	.03	.01
☐ 549	Floyd Bannister	.07	.03	.01
☐ 550	Mickey Brantley	.07	.03	.01
☐ 551	Duane Ward	.07	.03	.01
☐ 552	Dan Petry	.07	.03	.01
☐ 553	Mickey Tettleton UER (walks total 175, should be 136)	.12	.06	.01
☐ 554	Rick Leach	.07	.03	.01
☐ 555	Mike Witt	.07	.03	.01
☐ 556	Sid Bream	.07	.03	.01
☐ 557	Bobby Witt	.15	.07	.01
☐ 558	Tommy Herr	.07	.03	.01
☐ 559	Randy Milligan	.45	.22	.04
☐ 560	Jose Cecena	.10	.05	.01
☐ 561	Mackey Sasser	.25	.12	.02
☐ 562	Carney Lansford	.12	.06	.01
☐ 563	Rick Aguilera	.07	.03	.01
☐ 564	Ron Hassey	.07	.03	.01
☐ 565	Dwight Gooden	.40	.20	.04
☐ 566	Paul Assenmacher	.07	.03	.01
☐ 567	Neil Allen	.07	.03	.01

☐ 568 Jim Morrison	.07	.03	.01
☐ 569 Mike Pagliarulo	.07	.03	.01
☐ 570 Ted Simmons	.12	.06	.01
☐ 571 Mark Thurmond	.07	.03	.01
☐ 572 Fred McGriff	.30	.15	.03
☐ 573 Wally Joyner	.20	.10	.02
☐ 574 Jose Bautista	.10	.05	.01
☐ 575 Kelly Gruber	.25	.12	.02
☐ 576 Cecilio Guante	.07	.03	.01
☐ 577 Mark Davidson	.07	.03	.01
☐ 578 Bobby Bonilla UER (total steals 2 in '87, should be 3)	.35	.17	.03
☐ 579 Mike Stanley	.07	.03	.01
☐ 580 Gene Larkin	.07	.03	.01
☐ 581 Stan Javier	.07	.03	.01
☐ 582 Howard Johnson	.20	.10	.02
☐ 583A Mike Gallego ERR (front reversed negative)	1.50	.75	.15
☐ 583B Mike Gallego COR	.15	.07	.01
☐ 584 David Cone	.20	.10	.02
☐ 585 Doug Jennings	.25	.12	.02
☐ 586 Charles Hudson	.07	.03	.01
☐ 587 Dion James	.07	.03	.01
☐ 588 Al Leiter	.10	.05	.01
☐ 589 Charlie Puleo	.07	.03	.01
☐ 590 Roberto Kelly	.50	.25	.05
☐ 591 Thad Bosley	.07	.03	.01
☐ 592 Pete Stanicek	.10	.05	.01
☐ 593 Pat Borders	.35	.17	.03
☐ 594 Bryan Harvey	.20	.10	.02
☐ 595 Jeff Ballard	.15	.07	.01
☐ 596 Jeff Reardon	.10	.05	.01
☐ 597 Doug Drabek	.15	.07	.01
☐ 598 Edwin Correa	.07	.03	.01
☐ 599 Keith Atherton	.07	.03	.01
☐ 600 Dave LaPoint	.07	.03	.01
☐ 601 Don Baylor	.10	.05	.01
☐ 602 Tom Pagnozzi	.10	.05	.01
☐ 603 Tim Flannery	.07	.03	.01
☐ 604 Gene Walter	.07	.03	.01
☐ 605 Dave Parker	.12	.06	.01
☐ 606 Mike Diaz	.07	.03	.01
☐ 607 Chris Gwynn	.12	.06	.01
☐ 608 Odell Jones	.07	.03	.01
☐ 609 Carlton Fisk	.15	.07	.01
☐ 610 Jay Howell	.07	.03	.01
☐ 611 Tim Crews	.07	.03	.01
☐ 612 Keith Hernandez	.12	.06	.01
☐ 613 Willie Fraser	.07	.03	.01
☐ 614 Jim Eppard	.10	.05	.01
☐ 615 Jeff Hamilton	.07	.03	.01
☐ 616 Kurt Stillwell	.10	.05	.01
☐ 617 Tom Browning	.10	.05	.01
☐ 618 Jeff Montgomery	.25	.12	.02
☐ 619 Jose Rijo	.15	.07	.01
☐ 620 Jamie Quirk	.07	.03	.01
☐ 621 Willie McGee	.12	.06	.01
☐ 622 Mark Grant UER (glove on wrong hand)	.07	.03	.01
☐ 623 Bill Swift	.07	.03	.01
☐ 624 Orlando Mercado	.07	.03	.01
☐ 625 John Costello	.10	.05	.01
☐ 626 Jose Gonzalez	.10	.05	.01
☐ 627A Bill Schroeder ERR (back photo actually Ronn Reynolds buckling shin guards)	1.50	.75	.15
☐ 627B Bill Schroeder COR	.20	.10	.02
☐ 628A Fred Manrique ERR (back photo actually Ozzie Guillen throwing)	.40	.20	.04
☐ 628B Fred Manrique COR (swinging bat on back)	.10	.05	.01
☐ 629 Ricky Horton	.07	.03	.01
☐ 630 Dan Plesac	.07	.03	.01
☐ 631 Alfredo Griffin	.07	.03	.01
☐ 632 Chuck Finley	.12	.06	.01
☐ 633 Kirk Gibson	.15	.07	.01
☐ 634 Randy Myers	.10	.05	.01
☐ 635 Greg Minton	.07	.03	.01
☐ 636A Herm Winningham ERR (W1nningham on back)	.40	.20	.04
☐ 636B Herm Winningham COR	.10	.05	.01
☐ 637 Charlie Leibrandt	.07	.03	.01
☐ 638 Tim Birtsas	.07	.03	.01
☐ 639 Bill Buckner	.10	.05	.01
☐ 640 Danny Jackson	.10	.05	.01
☐ 641 Greg Booker	.07	.03	.01
☐ 642 Jim Presley	.07	.03	.01
☐ 643 Gene Nelson	.07	.03	.01
☐ 644 Rod Booker	.10	.05	.01
☐ 645 Dennis Rasmussen	.07	.03	.01
☐ 646 Juan Nieves	.07	.03	.01
☐ 647 Bobby Thigpen	.15	.07	.01
☐ 648 Tim Belcher	.25	.12	.02
☐ 649 Mike Young	.07	.03	.01
☐ 650 Ivan Calderon	.10	.05	.01
☐ 651 Oswaldo Peraza	.10	.05	.01
☐ 652A Pat Sheridan ERR (no position on front)	30.00	15.00	3.00
☐ 652B Pat Sheridan COR	.15	.07	.01
☐ 653 Mike Morgan	.07	.03	.01
☐ 654 Mike Heath	.07	.03	.01
☐ 655 Jay Tibbs	.07	.03	.01
☐ 656 Fernando Valenzuela	.12	.06	.01
☐ 657 Lee Mazzilli	.07	.03	.01
☐ 658 AL CY:Frank Viola	.12	.06	.01
☐ 659A AL MVP:J.Canseco (eagle logo in black)	.40	.20	.04
☐ 659B AL MVP:J.Canseco (eagle logo in blue)	.40	.20	.04
☐ 660 AL ROY:Walt Weiss	.12	.06	.01
☐ 661 NL CY:Orel Hershiser	.15	.07	.01
☐ 662 NL MVP:Kirk Gibson	.12	.06	.01
☐ 663 NL ROY:Chris Sabo	.15	.07	.01
☐ 664 ALCS MVP:D.Eckersley	.10	.05	.01
☐ 665 NLCS MVP:O.Hershiser	.15	.07	.01
☐ 666 Great WS Moment (Kirk Gibson's homer)	.12	.06	.01
☐ 667 WS MVP:O.Hershiser	.15	.07	.01
☐ 668 Angels Checklist Wally Joyner	.12	.06	.01
☐ 669 Astros Checklist Nolan Ryan	.45	.22	.04
☐ 670 Athletics Checklist Jose Canseco	.45	.22	.04
☐ 671 Blue Jays Checklist Fred McGriff	.15	.07	.01
☐ 672 Braves Checklist Dale Murphy	.15	.07	.01
☐ 673 Brewers Checklist Paul Molitor	.10	.05	.01
☐ 674 Cardinals Checklist Ozzie Smith	.12	.06	.01
☐ 675 Cubs Checklist Ryne Sandberg	.20	.10	.02
☐ 676 Dodgers Checklist Kirk Gibson	.12	.06	.01
☐ 677 Expos Checklist Andres Galaragga	.10	.05	.01
☐ 678 Giants Checklist Will Clark	.45	.22	.04
☐ 679 Indians Checklist Cory Snyder	.10	.05	.01
☐ 680 Mariners Checklist Alvin Davis	.10	.05	.01
☐ 681 Mets Checklist Darryl Strawberry	.40	.20	.04
☐ 682 Orioles Checklist Cal Ripken	.15	.07	.01
☐ 683 Padres Checklist Tony Gwynn	.20	.10	.02
☐ 684 Phillies Checklist Mike Schmidt	.35	.17	.03
☐ 685 Pirates Checklist Andy Van Slyke UER (96 Junior Ortiz)	.10	.05	.01
☐ 686 Rangers Checklist Ruben Sierra	.20	.10	.02
☐ 687 Red Sox Checklist Wade Boggs	.25	.12	.02
☐ 688 Reds Checklist Eric Davis	.20	.10	.02
☐ 689 Royals Checklist George Brett	.20	.10	.02
☐ 690 Tigers Checklist Alan Trammell	.10	.05	.01
☐ 691 Twins Checklist Frank Viola	.12	.06	.01
☐ 692 White Sox Checklist Harold Baines	.10	.05	.01
☐ 693 Yankees Checklist Don Mattingly	.40	.20	.04
☐ 694 Checklist 1-100	.07	.01	.00
☐ 695 Checklist 101-200	.07	.01	.00
☐ 696 Checklist 201-300	.07	.01	.00
☐ 697 Checklist 301-400	.07	.01	.00
☐ 698 Checklist 401-500 UER 467 Cal Ripkin Jr.	.07	.01	.00
☐ 699 Checklist 501-600 UER 543 Greg Booker	.07	.01	.00
☐ 700 Checklist 601-700	.07	.01	.00

1989 Upper Deck Extended

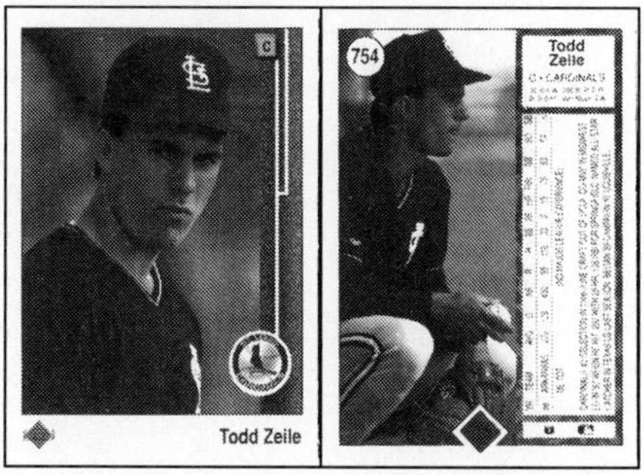

The 1989 Upper Deck Extended set contains 100 standard-size (2 1/2" by 3 1/2") cards. The fronts have pure white borders; the backs have recent stats and anti-counterfeit holograms. Both sides feature attractive color photos. The cards were distributed in "high number" packs, along with factory sets, and as a separate set in a small blue custom box. The key rookie cards in this set are Jim Abbott, Jerome Walton, and Todd Zeile.

	MINT	EXC	G-VG
COMPLETE SET (100)	20.00	10.00	2.00
COMMON PLAYER (701-800)	.08	.04	.01
☐ 701 Checklist 701-800	.08	.01	.00
☐ 702 Jesse Barfield	.12	.06	.01
☐ 703 Walt Terrell	.08	.04	.01
☐ 704 Dickie Thon	.08	.04	.01
☐ 705 Al Leiter	.12	.06	.01
☐ 706 Dave LaPoint	.08	.04	.01
☐ 707 Charlie Hayes	.25	.12	.02
☐ 708 Andy Hawkins	.08	.04	.01
☐ 709 Mickey Hatcher	.08	.04	.01
☐ 710 Lance McCullers	.08	.04	.01
☐ 711 Ron Kittle	.12	.06	.01
☐ 712 Bert Blyleven	.15	.07	.01
☐ 713 Rick Dempsey	.08	.04	.01
☐ 714 Ken Williams	.08	.04	.01
☐ 715 Steve Rosenberg	.15	.07	.01
☐ 716 Joe Skalski	.20	.10	.02
☐ 717 Spike Owen	.08	.04	.01
☐ 718 Todd Burns	.25	.12	.02
☐ 719 Kevin Gross	.08	.04	.01
☐ 720 Tommy Herr	.12	.06	.01
☐ 721 Rob Ducey	.20	.10	.02
☐ 722 Gary Green	.20	.10	.02
☐ 723 Gregg Olson	2.50	1.25	.25
☐ 724 Greg W. Harris	.25	.12	.02
☐ 725 Craig Worthington	.40	.20	.04
☐ 726 Tom Howard	.20	.10	.02
☐ 727 Dale Mohorcic	.08	.04	.01
☐ 728 Rich Yett	.08	.04	.01
☐ 729 Mel Hall	.12	.06	.01
☐ 730 Floyd Youmans	.08	.04	.01
☐ 731 Lonnie Smith	.12	.06	.01
☐ 732 Wally Backman	.08	.04	.01
☐ 733 Trevor Wilson	.40	.20	.04
☐ 734 Jose Alvarez	.15	.07	.01
☐ 735 Bob Milacki	.25	.12	.02
☐ 736 Tom Gordon	1.75	.85	.17
☐ 737 Wally Whitehurst	.30	.15	.03
☐ 738 Mike Aldrete	.08	.04	.01
☐ 739 Keith Miller	.15	.07	.01
☐ 740 Randy Milligan	.25	.12	.02
☐ 741 Jeff Parrett	.12	.06	.01
☐ 742 Steve Finley	.30	.15	.03
☐ 743 Junior Felix	1.75	.85	.17
☐ 744 Pete Harnisch	.20	.10	.02
☐ 745 Bill Spiers	.30	.15	.03
☐ 746 Hensley Meulens	2.00	1.00	.20
☐ 747 Juan Bell	.20	.10	.02
☐ 748 Steve Sax	.15	.07	.01
☐ 749 Phil Bradley	.12	.06	.01
☐ 750 Rey Quinones	.08	.04	.01
☐ 751 Tommy Gregg	.08	.04	.01
☐ 752 Kevin Brown	.45	.22	.04
☐ 753 Derek Lilliquist	.20	.10	.02
☐ 754 Todd Zeile	3.50	1.75	.35
☐ 755 Jim Abbott (triple exposure)	3.50	1.75	.35
☐ 756 Ozzie Canseco	.90	.45	.09
☐ 757 Nick Esasky	.15	.07	.01
☐ 758 Mike Moore	.15	.07	.01
☐ 759 Rob Murphy	.08	.04	.01
☐ 760 Rick Mahler	.08	.04	.01
☐ 761 Fred Lynn	.15	.07	.01
☐ 762 Kevin Blankenship	.15	.07	.01
☐ 763 Eddie Murray	.25	.12	.02
☐ 764 Steve Searcy	.20	.10	.02
☐ 765 Jerome Walton	3.50	1.75	.35
☐ 766 Erik Hanson	1.25	.60	.12
☐ 767 Bob Boone	.20	.10	.02
☐ 768 Edgar Martinez	.90	.45	.09
☐ 769 Jose DeJesus	.15	.07	.01
☐ 770 Greg Briley	.75	.35	.07
☐ 771 Steve Peters	.20	.10	.02
☐ 772 Rafael Palmeiro	.25	.12	.02
☐ 773 Jack Clark	.20	.10	.02
☐ 774 Nolan Ryan (throwing football)	3.50	1.75	.35
☐ 775 Lance Parrish	.15	.07	.01
☐ 776 Joe Girardi	.35	.17	.03
☐ 777 Willie Randolph	.12	.06	.01
☐ 778 Mitch Williams	.12	.06	.01
☐ 779 Dennis Cook	.30	.15	.03
☐ 780 Dwight Smith	1.25	.60	.12
☐ 781 Lenny Harris	.50	.25	.05
☐ 782 Torey Lovullo	.20	.10	.02
☐ 783 Norm Charlton	.40	.20	.04
☐ 784 Chris Brown	.08	.04	.01
☐ 785 Todd Benzinger	.12	.06	.01
☐ 786 Shane Rawley	.08	.04	.01
☐ 787 Omar Vizquel	.20	.10	.02
☐ 788 LaVel Freeman	.30	.15	.03
☐ 789 Jeffrey Leonard	.12	.06	.01
☐ 790 Eddie Williams	.08	.04	.01
☐ 791 Jamie Moyer	.08	.04	.01
☐ 792 Bruce Hurst UER (Workd Series)	.15	.07	.01
☐ 793 Julio Franco	.20	.10	.02
☐ 794 Claudell Washington	.12	.06	.01
☐ 795 Jody Davis	.08	.04	.01
☐ 796 Oddibe McDowell	.12	.06	.01
☐ 797 Paul Kilgus	.08	.04	.01
☐ 798 Tracy Jones	.08	.04	.01
☐ 799 Steve Wilson	.20	.10	.02
☐ 800 Pete O'Brien	.12	.06	.01

1990 Upper Deck

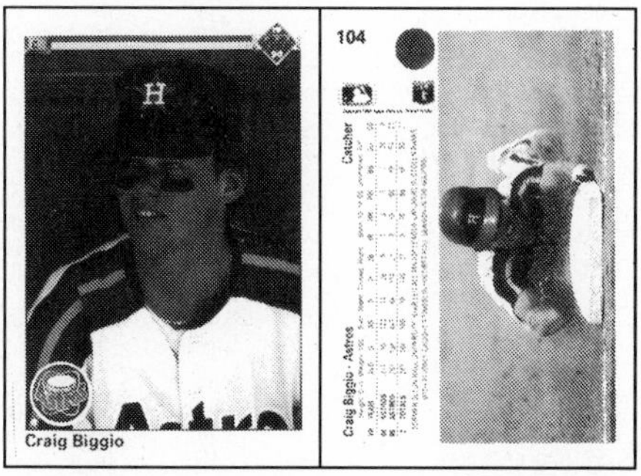

The 1990 Upper Deck set contains 700 standard-size (2 1/2" by 3 1/2") cards. The front and back borders are white, and both sides feature full-color photos. The horizontally-oriented backs have recent stats and anti-counterfeiting holograms. Unlike the 1989 Upper Deck set, the team checklist cards are not grouped numerically at the end of the set, but are mixed in with the first 100 cards. The key rookie cards in this set are Juan Gonzalez, Kevin Maas, Ben McDonald, and John Olerud.

	MINT	EXC	G-VG
COMPLETE SET (700)	40.00	20.00	4.00
COMMON PLAYER (1-700)	.05	.02	.00

☐ 1	Star Rookie Checklist	.10	.05	.01
☐ 2	Randy Nosek	.15	.07	.01
☐ 3	Tom Drees	.15	.07	.01
☐ 4	Curt Young	.05	.02	.00
☐ 5	Devon White TC	.08	.04	.01
	California Angels			
☐ 6	Luis Salazar	.05	.02	.00
☐ 7	Von Hayes TC	.08	.04	.01
	Philadelphia Phillies			
☐ 8	Jose Bautista	.05	.02	.00
☐ 9	Marquis Grissom	.65	.30	.06
☐ 10	Orel Hershiser TC	.10	.05	.01
	Los Angeles Dodgers			
☐ 11	Rick Aguilera	.05	.02	.00
☐ 12	Benito Santiago TC	.10	.05	.01
	San Diego Padres			
☐ 13	Deion Sanders	.35	.17	.03
☐ 14	Marvell Wynne	.05	.02	.00
☐ 15	Dave West	.05	.02	.00
☐ 16	Bobby Bonilla TC	.10	.05	.01
	Pittsburgh Pirates			
☐ 17	Sammy Sosa	.75	.35	.07
☐ 18	Steve Sax TC	.10	.05	.01
	New York Yankees			
☐ 19	Jack Howell	.05	.02	.00
☐ 20	Mike Schmidt Special	.90	.45	.09
☐ 21	Robin Ventura	.50	.25	.05
☐ 22	Brian Meyer	.10	.05	.01
☐ 23	Blaine Beatty	.18	.09	.01
☐ 24	Ken Griffey Jr. TC	.75	.35	.07
	Seattle Mariners			
☐ 25	Greg Vaughn	.75	.35	.07
☐ 26	Xavier Hernandez	.12	.06	.01
☐ 27	Jason Grimsley	.15	.07	.01
☐ 28	Eric Anthony	1.00	.50	.10
☐ 29	Tim Raines TC	.10	.05	.01
	Montreal Expos			
	UER (Wallach listed			
	before Walker)			
☐ 30	David Wells	.05	.02	.00
☐ 31	Hal Morris	1.00	.50	.10
☐ 32	Bo Jackson TC	.65	.30	.06
	Kansas City Royals			
☐ 33	Kelly Mann	.18	.09	.01
☐ 34	Nolan Ryan Special	1.25	.60	.12
☐ 35	Scott Service	.12	.06	.01
☐ 36	Mark McGwire TC	.25	.12	.02
	Oakland A's			
☐ 37	Tino Martinez	1.50	.75	.15
☐ 38	Chili Davis	.08	.04	.01
☐ 39	Scott Sanderson	.05	.02	.00
☐ 40	Kevin Mitchell TC	.15	.07	.01
	San Francisco Giants			
☐ 41	Lou Whitaker TC	.08	.04	.01
	Detroit Tigers			
☐ 42	Scott Coolbaugh	.20	.10	.02
☐ 43	Jose Cano	.15	.07	.01
☐ 44	Jose Vizcaino	.20	.10	.02
☐ 45	Bob Hamelin	.50	.25	.05
☐ 46	Jose Offerman	1.50	.75	.15
☐ 47	Kevin Blankenship	.10	.05	.01
☐ 48	Kirby Puckett TC	.20	.10	.02
	Minnesota Twins			
☐ 49	Tommy Greene	.35	.17	.03
☐ 50	Will Clark Special	.50	.25	.05
☐ 51	Rob Nelson	.05	.02	.00
☐ 52	Chris Hammond	.35	.17	.03
☐ 53	Joe Carter TC	.10	.05	.01
	Cleveland Indians			
☐ 54A	Ben McDonald ERR	28.00	14.00	2.80
	(no Rookie designation			
	on card front)			
☐ 54B	Ben McDonald COR	2.75	1.35	.27
☐ 55	Andy Benes	.40	.20	.04
☐ 56	John Olerud	3.25	1.60	.32
☐ 57	Roger Clemens TC	.15	.07	.01
	Boston Red Sox			
☐ 58	Tony Armas	.05	.02	.00
☐ 59	George Canale	.15	.07	.01
☐ 60A	Mickey Tettleton TC	3.00	1.50	.30
	Baltimore Orioles			
	(683 Jamie Weston)			
☐ 60B	Mickey Tettleton TC	.15	.07	.01
	Baltimore Orioles			
	(683 Mickey Weston)			
☐ 61	Mike Stanton	.15	.07	.01
☐ 62	Dwight Gooden TC	.15	.07	.01
	New York Mets			
☐ 63	Kent Mercker	.30	.15	.03
☐ 64	Francisco Cabrera	.30	.15	.03
☐ 65	Steve Avery UER	.60	.30	.06
	(born NJ, should be MI)			
☐ 66	Jose Canseco	.75	.35	.07
☐ 67	Matt Merullo	.15	.07	.01
☐ 68	Vince Coleman TC	.10	.05	.01
	St. Louis Cardinals			
☐ 69	Ron Karkovice	.05	.02	.00
☐ 70	Kevin Maas	4.25	2.10	.42
☐ 71	Dennis Cook	.15	.07	.01
☐ 72	Juan Gonzalez	3.00	1.50	.30
☐ 73	Andre Dawson TC	.10	.05	.01
	Chicago Cubs			
☐ 74	Dean Palmer	.25	.12	.02
☐ 75	Bo Jackson Special	1.00	.50	.10
☐ 76	Rob Richie	.08	.04	.01
☐ 77	Bobby Rose	.25	.12	.02
☐ 78	Brian Dubois	.15	.07	.01
☐ 79	Ozzie Guillen TC	.08	.04	.01
	Chicago White Sox			
☐ 80	Gene Nelson	.05	.02	.00
☐ 81	Bob McClure	.05	.02	.00
☐ 82	Julio Franco TC	.08	.04	.01
	Texas Rangers			
☐ 83	Greg Minton	.05	.02	.00
☐ 84	John Smoltz TC	.10	.05	.01
	Atlanta Braves			
☐ 85	Willie Fraser	.05	.02	.00
☐ 86	Neal Heaton	.05	.02	.00
☐ 87	Kevin Tapani	.50	.25	.05
☐ 88	Mike Scott TC	.08	.04	.01
	Houston Astros			
☐ 89A	Jim Gott ERR	7.50	3.75	.75
	(photo actually			
	Rick Reed)			
☐ 89B	Jim Gott COR	.10	.05	.01
☐ 90	Lance Johnson	.10	.05	.01
☐ 91	Robin Yount TC	.12	.06	.01
	Milwaukee Brewers			
☐ 92	Jeff Parrett	.05	.02	.00
☐ 93	Julio Machado	.15	.07	.01
☐ 94	Ron Jones	.08	.04	.01
☐ 95	George Bell TC	.08	.04	.01
	Toronto Blue Jays			
☐ 96	Jerry Reuss	.05	.02	.00
☐ 97	Brian Fisher	.05	.02	.00
☐ 98	Kevin Ritz	.15	.07	.01
☐ 99	Barry Larkin TC	.10	.05	.01
	Cincinnati Reds			
☐ 100	Checklist 1-100	.05	.01	.00
☐ 101	Gerald Perry	.05	.02	.00
☐ 102	Kevin Appier	.45	.22	.04
☐ 103	Julio Franco	.08	.04	.01
☐ 104	Craig Biggio	.08	.04	.01
☐ 105	Bo Jackson	1.00	.50	.10
☐ 106	Junior Felix	.45	.22	.04
☐ 107	Mike Harkey	.12	.06	.01
☐ 108	Fred McGriff	.15	.07	.01
☐ 109	Rick Sutcliffe	.08	.04	.01
☐ 110	Pete O'Brien	.08	.04	.01
☐ 111	Kelly Gruber	.15	.07	.01
☐ 112	Dwight Evans	.10	.05	.01
☐ 113	Pat Borders	.08	.04	.01
☐ 114	Dwight Gooden	.25	.12	.02
☐ 115	Kevin Batiste	.20	.10	.02
☐ 116	Eric Davis	.20	.10	.02
☐ 117	Kevin Mitchell	.25	.12	.02
☐ 118	Ron Oester	.05	.02	.00
☐ 119	Brett Butler	.08	.04	.01
☐ 120	Danny Jackson	.08	.04	.01
☐ 121	Tommy Gregg	.08	.04	.01
☐ 122	Ken Caminiti	.05	.02	.00
☐ 123	Kevin Brown	.15	.07	.01
☐ 124	George Brett	.15	.07	.01
☐ 125	Mike Scott	.10	.05	.01
☐ 126	Cory Snyder	.10	.05	.01
☐ 127	George Bell	.10	.05	.01
☐ 128	Mark Grace	.35	.17	.03
☐ 129	Devon White	.08	.04	.01
☐ 130	Tony Fernandez	.08	.04	.01
☐ 131	Don Aase	.05	.02	.00
☐ 132	Rance Mulliniks	.05	.02	.00
☐ 133	Marty Barrett	.05	.02	.00
☐ 134	Nelson Liriano	.05	.02	.00
☐ 135	Mark Carreon	.08	.04	.01
☐ 136	Candy Maldonado	.08	.04	.01
☐ 137	Tim Birtsas	.05	.02	.00
☐ 138	Tom Brookens	.05	.02	.00
☐ 139	John Franco	.08	.04	.01
☐ 140	Mike LaCoss	.05	.02	.00
☐ 141	Jeff Treadway	.05	.02	.00
☐ 142	Pat Tabler	.05	.02	.00
☐ 143	Darrell Evans	.08	.04	.01
☐ 144	Rafael Ramirez	.05	.02	.00
☐ 145	Oddibe McDowell UER	.08	.04	.01
	(misspelled Odibbe)			
☐ 146	Brian Downing	.05	.02	.00
☐ 147	Curt Wilkerson	.05	.02	.00
☐ 148	Ernie Whitt	.05	.02	.00

☐ 149 Bill Schroeder	.05	.02	.00
☐ 150 Domingo Ramos	.05	.02	.00
☐ 151 Rick Honeycutt	.05	.02	.00
☐ 152 Don Slaught	.05	.02	.00
☐ 153 Mitch Webster	.05	.02	.00
☐ 154 Tony Phillips	.05	.02	.00
☐ 155 Paul Kilgus	.05	.02	.00
☐ 156 Ken Griffey Jr.	3.50	1.75	.35
☐ 157 Gary Sheffield	.35	.17	.03
☐ 158 Wally Backman	.05	.02	.00
☐ 159 B.J. Surhoff	.08	.04	.01
☐ 160 Louie Meadows	.05	.02	.00
☐ 161 Paul O'Neill	.10	.05	.01
☐ 162 Jeff McKnight	.15	.07	.01
☐ 163 Alvaro Espinoza	.05	.02	.00
☐ 164 Scott Scudder	.20	.10	.02
☐ 165 Jeff Reed	.05	.02	.00
☐ 166 Gregg Jefferies	.50	.25	.05
☐ 167 Barry Larkin	.20	.10	.02
☐ 168 Gary Carter	.10	.05	.01
☐ 169 Robby Thompson	.05	.02	.00
☐ 170 Rolando Roomes	.08	.04	.01
☐ 171 Mark McGwire	.25	.12	.02
☐ 172 Steve Sax	.10	.05	.01
☐ 173 Mark Williamson	.05	.02	.00
☐ 174 Mitch Williams	.05	.02	.00
☐ 175 Brian Holton	.05	.02	.00
☐ 176 Rob Deer	.08	.04	.01
☐ 177 Tim Raines	.10	.05	.01
☐ 178 Mike Felder	.05	.02	.00
☐ 179 Harold Reynolds	.08	.04	.01
☐ 180 Terry Francona	.05	.02	.00
☐ 181 Chris Sabo	.20	.10	.02
☐ 182 Darryl Strawberry	.30	.15	.03
☐ 183 Willie Randolph	.08	.04	.01
☐ 184 Bill Ripken	.05	.02	.00
☐ 185 Mackey Sasser	.08	.04	.01
☐ 186 Todd Benzinger	.05	.02	.00
☐ 187 Kevin Elster	.08	.04	.01
☐ 188 Jose Uribe	.05	.02	.00
☐ 189 Tom Browning	.08	.04	.01
☐ 190 Keith Miller	.05	.02	.00
☐ 191 Don Mattingly	.50	.25	.05
☐ 192 Dave Parker	.10	.05	.01
☐ 193 Roberto Kelly	.12	.06	.01
☐ 194 Phil Bradley	.08	.04	.01
☐ 195 Ron Hassey	.05	.02	.00
☐ 196 Gerald Young	.05	.02	.00
☐ 197 Hubie Brooks	.08	.04	.01
☐ 198 Bill Doran	.08	.04	.01
☐ 199 Al Newman	.05	.02	.00
☐ 200 Checklist 101-200	.05	.01	.00
☐ 201 Terry Puhl	.05	.02	.00
☐ 202 Frank DiPino	.05	.02	.00
☐ 203 Jim Clancy	.05	.02	.00
☐ 204 Bob Ojeda	.08	.04	.01
☐ 205 Alex Trevino	.05	.02	.00
☐ 206 Dave Henderson	.08	.04	.01
☐ 207 Henry Cotto	.05	.02	.00
☐ 208 Rafael Belliard UER (born 1962, not 1951)	.05	.02	.00
☐ 209 Stan Javier	.05	.02	.00
☐ 210 Jerry Reed	.05	.02	.00
☐ 211 Doug Dascenzo	.05	.02	.00
☐ 212 Andres Thomas	.05	.02	.00
☐ 213 Greg Maddux	.08	.04	.01
☐ 214 Mike Schooler	.08	.04	.01
☐ 215 Lonnie Smith	.08	.04	.01
☐ 216 Jose Rijo	.08	.04	.01
☐ 217 Greg Gagne	.05	.02	.00
☐ 218 Jim Gantner	.05	.02	.00
☐ 219 Allan Anderson	.08	.04	.01
☐ 220 Rick Mahler	.05	.02	.00
☐ 221 Jim Deshaies	.05	.02	.00
☐ 222 Keith Hernandez	.10	.05	.01
☐ 223 Vince Coleman	.10	.05	.01
☐ 224 David Cone	.10	.05	.01
☐ 225 Ozzie Smith	.10	.05	.01
☐ 226 Matt Nokes	.08	.04	.01
☐ 227 Barry Bonds	.25	.12	.02
☐ 228 Felix Jose	.15	.07	.01
☐ 229 Dennis Powell	.05	.02	.00
☐ 230 Mike Gallego	.05	.02	.00
☐ 231 Shawon Dunston UER ('89 stats are Andre Dawson's)	.12	.06	.01
☐ 232 Ron Gant	.25	.12	.02
☐ 233 Omar Vizquel	.10	.05	.01
☐ 234 Derek Lilliquist	.08	.04	.01
☐ 235 Erik Hanson	.25	.12	.02
☐ 236 Kirby Puckett	.30	.15	.03
☐ 237 Bill Spiers	.15	.07	.01
☐ 238 Dan Gladden	.05	.02	.00
☐ 239 Bryan Clutterbuck	.05	.02	.00
☐ 240 John Moses	.05	.02	.00
☐ 241 Ron Darling	.10	.05	.01
☐ 242 Joe Magrane	.08	.04	.01
☐ 243 Dave Magadan	.10	.05	.01
☐ 244 Pedro Guerrero	.10	.05	.01
☐ 245 Glenn Davis	.12	.06	.01
☐ 246 Terry Steinbach	.08	.04	.01
☐ 247 Fred Lynn	.08	.04	.01
☐ 248 Gary Redus	.05	.02	.00
☐ 249 Ken Williams	.05	.02	.00
☐ 250 Sid Bream	.05	.02	.00
☐ 251 Bob Welch	.12	.06	.01
☐ 252 Bill Buckner	.08	.04	.01
☐ 253 Carney Lansford	.10	.05	.01
☐ 254 Paul Molitor	.10	.05	.01
☐ 255 Jose DeJesus	.05	.02	.00
☐ 256 Orel Hershiser	.12	.06	.01
☐ 257 Tom Brunansky	.10	.05	.01
☐ 258 Mike Davis	.05	.02	.00
☐ 259 Jeff Ballard	.05	.02	.00
☐ 260 Scott Terry	.05	.02	.00
☐ 261 Sid Fernandez	.08	.04	.01
☐ 262 Mike Marshall	.08	.04	.01
☐ 263 Howard Johnson	.10	.05	.01
☐ 264 Kirk Gibson	.10	.05	.01
☐ 265 Kevin McReynolds	.10	.05	.01
☐ 266 Cal Ripken Jr.	.15	.07	.01
☐ 267 Ozzie Guillen	.10	.05	.01
☐ 268 Jim Traber	.05	.02	.00
☐ 269 Bobby Thigpen	.10	.05	.01
☐ 270 Joe Orsulak	.05	.02	.00
☐ 271 Bob Boone	.08	.04	.01
☐ 272 Dave Stewart	.12	.06	.01
☐ 273 Tim Wallach	.08	.04	.01
☐ 274 Luis Aquino	.05	.02	.00
☐ 275 Mike Moore	.08	.04	.01
☐ 276 Tony Pena	.08	.04	.01
☐ 277 Eddie Murray	.15	.07	.01
☐ 278 Milt Thompson	.05	.02	.00
☐ 279 Alejandro Pena	.05	.02	.00
☐ 280 Ken Dayley	.05	.02	.00
☐ 281 Carmen Castillo	.05	.02	.00
☐ 282 Tom Henke	.08	.04	.01
☐ 283 Mickey Hatcher	.05	.02	.00
☐ 284 Roy Smith	.05	.02	.00
☐ 285 Manny Lee	.05	.02	.00
☐ 286 Dan Pasqua	.05	.02	.00
☐ 287 Larry Sheets	.05	.02	.00
☐ 288 Garry Templeton	.08	.04	.01
☐ 289 Eddie Williams	.08	.04	.01
☐ 290 Brady Anderson	.05	.02	.00
☐ 291 Spike Owen	.05	.02	.00
☐ 292 Storm Davis	.08	.04	.01
☐ 293 Chris Bosio	.05	.02	.00
☐ 294 Jim Eisenreich	.05	.02	.00
☐ 295 Don August	.05	.02	.00
☐ 296 Jeff Hamilton	.05	.02	.00
☐ 297 Mickey Tettleton	.08	.04	.01
☐ 298 Mike Scioscia	.05	.02	.00
☐ 299 Kevin Hickey	.05	.02	.00
☐ 300 Checklist 201-300	.05	.01	.00
☐ 301 Shawn Abner	.08	.04	.01
☐ 302 Kevin Bass	.08	.04	.01
☐ 303 Bip Roberts	.08	.04	.01
☐ 304 Joe Girardi	.12	.06	.01
☐ 305 Danny Darwin	.05	.02	.00
☐ 306 Mike Heath	.05	.02	.00
☐ 307 Mike Macfarlane	.05	.02	.00
☐ 308 Ed Whitson	.05	.02	.00
☐ 309 Tracy Jones	.05	.02	.00
☐ 310 Scott Fletcher	.05	.02	.00
☐ 311 Darnell Coles	.05	.02	.00
☐ 312 Mike Brumley	.08	.04	.01
☐ 313 Bill Swift	.05	.02	.00
☐ 314 Charlie Hough	.05	.02	.00
☐ 315 Jim Presley	.05	.02	.00
☐ 316 Luis Polonia	.05	.02	.00
☐ 317 Mike Morgan	.05	.02	.00
☐ 318 Lee Guetterman	.05	.02	.00
☐ 319 Jose Oquendo	.05	.02	.00
☐ 320 Wayne Tolleson	.05	.02	.00
☐ 321 Jody Reed	.10	.05	.01
☐ 322 Damon Berryhill	.10	.05	.01
☐ 323 Roger Clemens	.25	.12	.02
☐ 324 Ryne Sandberg	.25	.12	.02
☐ 325 Benito Santiago UER (misspelled Santago on card back)	.15	.07	.01
☐ 326 Bret Saberhagen	.12	.06	.01
☐ 327 Lou Whitaker	.10	.05	.01
☐ 328 Dave Gallagher	.05	.02	.00
☐ 329 Mike Pagliarulo	.05	.02	.00
☐ 330 Doyle Alexander	.05	.02	.00
☐ 331 Jeffrey Leonard	.08	.04	.01

☐ 332	Torey Lovullo	.05	.02	.00
☐ 333	Pete Incaviglia	.08	.04	.01
☐ 334	Rickey Henderson	.35	.17	.03
☐ 335	Rafael Palmeiro	.15	.07	.01
☐ 336	Ken Hill	.12	.06	.01
☐ 337	Dave Winfield	.12	.06	.01
☐ 338	Alfredo Griffin	.05	.02	.00
☐ 339	Andy Hawkins	.05	.02	.00
☐ 340	Ted Power	.05	.02	.00
☐ 341	Steve Wilson	.10	.05	.01
☐ 342	Jack Clark	.10	.05	.01
☐ 343	Ellis Burks	.20	.10	.02
☐ 344	Tony Gwynn	.20	.10	.02
☐ 345	Jerome Walton	.60	.30	.06
☐ 346	Roberto Alomar	.20	.10	.02
☐ 347	Carlos Martinez	.12	.06	.01
☐ 348	Chet Lemon	.05	.02	.00
☐ 349	Willie Wilson	.08	.04	.01
☐ 350	Greg Walker	.05	.02	.00
☐ 351	Tom Bolton	.08	.04	.01
☐ 352	German Gonzalez	.08	.04	.01
☐ 353	Harold Baines	.10	.05	.01
☐ 354	Mike Greenwell	.20	.10	.02
☐ 355	Ruben Sierra	.20	.10	.02
☐ 356	Andres Galarraga	.10	.05	.01
☐ 357	Andre Dawson	.15	.07	.01
☐ 358	Jeff Brantley	.25	.12	.02
☐ 359	Mike Bielecki	.05	.02	.00
☐ 360	Ken Oberkfell	.05	.02	.00
☐ 361	Kurt Stillwell	.08	.04	.01
☐ 362	Brian Holman	.08	.04	.01
☐ 363	Kevin Seitzer	.10	.05	.01
☐ 364	Alvin Davis	.08	.04	.01
☐ 365	Tom Gordon	.25	.12	.02
☐ 366	Bobby Bonilla	.20	.10	.02
☐ 367	Carlton Fisk	.12	.06	.01
☐ 368	Steve Carter	.12	.06	.01
☐ 369	Joel Skinner	.05	.02	.00
☐ 370	John Cangelosi	.05	.02	.00
☐ 371	Cecil Espy	.05	.02	.00
☐ 372	Gary Wayne	.12	.06	.01
☐ 373	Jim Rice	.10	.05	.01
☐ 374	Mike Dyer	.15	.07	.01
☐ 375	Joe Carter	.12	.06	.01
☐ 376	Dwight Smith	.15	.07	.01
☐ 377	John Wetteland	.20	.10	.02
☐ 378	Earnie Riles	.05	.02	.00
☐ 379	Otis Nixon	.05	.02	.00
☐ 380	Vance Law	.05	.02	.00
☐ 381	Dave Bergman	.05	.02	.00
☐ 382	Frank White	.08	.04	.01
☐ 383	Scott Bradley	.05	.02	.00
☐ 384	Israel Sanchez UER (totals don't include '89 stats)	.05	.02	.00
☐ 385	Gary Pettis	.05	.02	.00
☐ 386	Donn Pall	.08	.04	.01
☐ 387	John Smiley	.05	.02	.00
☐ 388	Tom Candiotti	.05	.02	.00
☐ 389	Junior Ortiz	.05	.02	.00
☐ 390	Steve Lyons	.05	.02	.00
☐ 391	Brian Harper	.05	.02	.00
☐ 392	Fred Manrique	.05	.02	.00
☐ 393	Lee Smith	.08	.04	.01
☐ 394	Jeff Kunkel	.05	.02	.00
☐ 395	Claudell Washington	.08	.04	.01
☐ 396	John Tudor	.08	.04	.01
☐ 397	Terry Kennedy	.05	.02	.00
☐ 398	Lloyd McClendon	.05	.02	.00
☐ 399	Craig Lefferts	.05	.02	.00
☐ 400	Checklist 301-400	.05	.01	.00
☐ 401	Keith Moreland	.05	.02	.00
☐ 402	Rich Gedman	.05	.02	.00
☐ 403	Jeff Robinson	.05	.02	.00
☐ 404	Randy Ready	.05	.02	.00
☐ 405	Rick Cerone	.05	.02	.00
☐ 406	Jeff Blauser	.05	.02	.00
☐ 407	Larry Andersen	.05	.02	.00
☐ 408	Joe Boever	.05	.02	.00
☐ 409	Felix Fermin	.05	.02	.00
☐ 410	Glenn Wilson	.05	.02	.00
☐ 411	Rex Hudler	.05	.02	.00
☐ 412	Mark Grant	.05	.02	.00
☐ 413	Dennis Martinez	.05	.02	.00
☐ 414	Darrin Jackson	.05	.02	.00
☐ 415	Mike Aldrete	.05	.02	.00
☐ 416	Roger McDowell	.08	.04	.01
☐ 417	Jeff Reardon	.08	.04	.01
☐ 418	Darren Daulton	.08	.04	.01
☐ 419	Tim Laudner	.05	.02	.00
☐ 420	Don Carman	.05	.02	.00
☐ 421	Lloyd Moseby	.08	.04	.01
☐ 422	Doug Drabek	.12	.06	.01
☐ 423	Lenny Harris	.15	.07	.01
☐ 424	Jose Lind	.05	.02	.00
☐ 425	Dave Johnson (P)	.15	.07	.01
☐ 426	Jerry Browne	.05	.02	.00
☐ 427	Eric Yelding	.25	.12	.02
☐ 428	Brad Komminsk	.05	.02	.00
☐ 429	Jody Davis	.05	.02	.00
☐ 430	Mariano Duncan	.08	.04	.01
☐ 431	Mark Davis	.10	.05	.01
☐ 432	Nelson Santovenia	.05	.02	.00
☐ 433	Bruce Hurst	.08	.04	.01
☐ 434	Jeff Huson	.15	.07	.01
☐ 435	Chris James	.08	.04	.01
☐ 436	Mark Guthrie	.12	.06	.01
☐ 437	Charlie Hayes	.10	.05	.01
☐ 438	Shane Rawley	.05	.02	.00
☐ 439	Dickie Thon	.05	.02	.00
☐ 440	Juan Berenguer	.05	.02	.00
☐ 441	Kevin Romine	.05	.02	.00
☐ 442	Bill Landrum	.05	.02	.00
☐ 443	Todd Frohwirth	.05	.02	.00
☐ 444	Craig Worthington	.08	.04	.01
☐ 445	Fernando Valenzuela	.10	.05	.01
☐ 446	Joey Belle	.25	.12	.02
☐ 447	Ed Whited	.20	.10	.02
☐ 448	Dave Smith	.05	.02	.00
☐ 449	Dave Clark	.05	.02	.00
☐ 450	Juan Agosto	.05	.02	.00
☐ 451	Dave Valle	.05	.02	.00
☐ 452	Kent Hrbek	.10	.05	.01
☐ 453	Von Hayes	.08	.04	.01
☐ 454	Gary Gaetti	.08	.04	.01
☐ 455	Greg Briley	.15	.07	.01
☐ 456	Glenn Braggs	.05	.02	.00
☐ 457	Kirt Manwaring	.05	.02	.00
☐ 458	Mel Hall	.05	.02	.00
☐ 459	Brook Jacoby	.08	.04	.01
☐ 460	Pat Sheridan	.05	.02	.00
☐ 461	Rob Murphy	.05	.02	.00
☐ 462	Jimmy Key	.08	.04	.01
☐ 463	Nick Esasky	.08	.04	.01
☐ 464	Rob Ducey	.05	.02	.00
☐ 465	Carlos Quintana	.20	.10	.02
☐ 466	Larry Walker	.60	.30	.06
☐ 467	Todd Worrell	.10	.05	.01
☐ 468	Kevin Gross	.05	.02	.00
☐ 469	Terry Pendleton	.05	.02	.00
☐ 470	Dave Martinez	.05	.02	.00
☐ 471	Gene Larkin	.05	.02	.00
☐ 472	Len Dykstra	.12	.06	.01
☐ 473	Barry Lyons	.05	.02	.00
☐ 474	Terry Mulholland	.05	.02	.00
☐ 475	Chip Hale	.15	.07	.01
☐ 476	Jesse Barfield	.10	.05	.01
☐ 477	Dan Plesac	.05	.02	.00
☐ 478A	Scott Garrelts ERR (photo actually Bill Bathe)	5.00	2.50	.50
☐ 478B	Scott Garrelts COR	.10	.05	.01
☐ 479	Dave Righetti	.10	.05	.01
☐ 480	Gus Polidor	.05	.02	.00
☐ 481	Mookie Wilson	.08	.04	.01
☐ 482	Luis Rivera	.05	.02	.00
☐ 483	Mike Flanagan	.05	.02	.00
☐ 484	Dennis Boyd	.08	.04	.01
☐ 485	John Cerutti	.05	.02	.00
☐ 486	John Costello	.05	.02	.00
☐ 487	Pascual Perez	.08	.04	.01
☐ 488	Tommy Herr	.08	.04	.01
☐ 489	Tom Foley	.05	.02	.00
☐ 490	Curt Ford	.05	.02	.00
☐ 491	Steve Lake	.05	.02	.00
☐ 492	Tim Teufel	.05	.02	.00
☐ 493	Randy Bush	.05	.02	.00
☐ 494	Mike Jackson	.05	.02	.00
☐ 495	Steve Jeltz	.05	.02	.00
☐ 496	Paul Gibson	.05	.02	.00
☐ 497	Steve Balboni	.05	.02	.00
☐ 498	Bud Black	.05	.02	.00
☐ 499	Dale Sveum	.05	.02	.00
☐ 500	Checklist 401-500	.05	.01	.00
☐ 501	Tim Jones	.05	.02	.00
☐ 502	Mark Portugal	.05	.02	.00
☐ 503	Ivan Calderon	.08	.04	.01
☐ 504	Rick Rhoden	.05	.02	.00
☐ 505	Willie McGee	.12	.06	.01
☐ 506	Kirk McCaskill	.05	.02	.00
☐ 507	Dave LaPoint	.05	.02	.00
☐ 508	Jay Howell	.05	.02	.00
☐ 509	Johnny Ray	.05	.02	.00
☐ 510	Dave Anderson	.05	.02	.00
☐ 511	Chuck Crim	.05	.02	.00
☐ 512	Joe Hesketh	.05	.02	.00
☐ 513	Dennis Eckersley	.12	.06	.01
☐ 514	Greg Brock	.05	.02	.00

☐ 515 Tim Burke	.08	.04	.01
☐ 516 Frank Tanana	.05	.02	.00
☐ 517 Jay Bell	.05	.02	.00
☐ 518 Guillermo Hernandez	.05	.02	.00
☐ 519 Randy Kramer UER	.10	.05	.01
Codiroli misspelled as Codoroli)			
☐ 520 Charles Hudson	.05	.02	.00
☐ 521 Jim Corsi	.10	.05	.01
(word "originally" is misspelled on back)			
☐ 522 Steve Rosenberg	.08	.04	.01
☐ 523 Cris Carpenter	.05	.02	.00
☐ 524 Matt Winters	.15	.07	.01
☐ 525 Melido Perez	.08	.04	.01
☐ 526 Chris Gwynn UER	.05	.02	.00
(Albeguergue)			
☐ 527 Bert Blyleven	.10	.05	.01
☐ 528 Chuck Cary	.08	.04	.01
☐ 529 Daryl Boston	.08	.04	.01
☐ 530 Dale Mohorcic	.05	.02	.00
☐ 531 Geronimo Berroa	.08	.04	.01
☐ 532 Edgar Martinez	.15	.07	.01
☐ 533 Dale Murphy	.15	.07	.01
☐ 534 Jay Buhner	.08	.04	.01
☐ 535 John Smoltz UER	.12	.06	.01
(HEA Stadium)			
☐ 536 Andy Van Slyke	.10	.05	.01
☐ 537 Mike Henneman	.05	.02	.00
☐ 538 Miguel Garcia	.08	.04	.01
☐ 539 Frank Williams	.05	.02	.00
☐ 540 R.J. Reynolds	.05	.02	.00
☐ 541 Shawn Hillegas	.05	.02	.00
☐ 542 Walt Weiss	.10	.05	.01
☐ 543 Greg Hibbard	.25	.12	.02
☐ 544 Nolan Ryan	1.00	.50	.10
☐ 545 Todd Zeile	.90	.45	.09
☐ 546 Hensley Meulens	.40	.20	.04
☐ 547 Tim Belcher	.10	.05	.01
☐ 548 Mike Witt	.05	.02	.00
☐ 549 Greg Cadaret UER	.08	.04	.01
(Aquiring, should be Acquiring)			
☐ 550 Franklin Stubbs	.08	.04	.01
☐ 551 Tony Castillo	.08	.04	.01
☐ 552 Jeff Robinson	.05	.02	.00
☐ 553 Steve Olin	.10	.05	.01
☐ 554 Alan Trammell	.10	.05	.01
☐ 555 Wade Boggs 4X	.50	.25	.05
(Bo Jackson in background)			
☐ 556 Will Clark	.50	.25	.05
☐ 557 Jeff King	.12	.06	.01
☐ 558 Mike Fitzgerald	.05	.02	.00
☐ 559 Ken Howell	.05	.02	.00
☐ 560 Bob Kipper	.05	.02	.00
☐ 561 Scott Bankhead	.08	.04	.01
☐ 562A Jeff Innis ERR	3.50	1.75	.35
(photo actually David West)			
☐ 562B Jeff Innis COR	.15	.07	.01
☐ 563 Randy Johnson	.08	.04	.01
☐ 564 Wally Whitehurst	.08	.04	.01
☐ 565 Gene Harris	.15	.07	.01
☐ 566 Norm Charlton	.25	.12	.02
☐ 567 Robin Yount UER	.35	.17	.03
(7606 career hits, should be 2606)			
☐ 568 Joe Oliver	.20	.10	.02
☐ 569 Mark Parent	.05	.02	.00
☐ 570 John Farrell	.05	.02	.00
☐ 571 Tom Glavine	.08	.04	.01
☐ 572 Rod Nichols	.10	.05	.01
☐ 573 Jack Morris	.10	.05	.01
☐ 574 Greg Swindell	.10	.05	.01
☐ 575 Steve Searcy	.08	.04	.01
☐ 576 Ricky Jordan	.15	.07	.01
☐ 577 Matt Williams	.25	.12	.02
☐ 578 Mike LaValliere	.05	.02	.00
☐ 579 Bryn Smith	.05	.02	.00
☐ 580 Bruce Ruffin	.05	.02	.00
☐ 581 Randy Myers	.08	.04	.01
☐ 582 Rick Wrona	.15	.07	.01
☐ 583 Juan Samuel	.10	.05	.01
☐ 584 Les Lancaster	.05	.02	.00
☐ 585 Jeff Musselman	.05	.02	.00
☐ 586 Rob Dibble	.10	.05	.01
☐ 587 Eric Show	.05	.02	.00
☐ 588 Jesse Orosco	.05	.02	.00
☐ 589 Herm Winningham	.05	.02	.00
☐ 590 Andy Allanson	.05	.02	.00
☐ 591 Dion James	.05	.02	.00
☐ 592 Carmelo Martinez	.05	.02	.00
☐ 593 Luis Quinones	.05	.02	.00
☐ 594 Dennis Rasmussen	.05	.02	.00
☐ 595 Rich Yett	.05	.02	.00
☐ 596 Bob Walk	.05	.02	.00
☐ 597A Andy McGaffigan ERR	.65	.30	.06
(photo actually Rich Thompson)			
☐ 597B Andy McGaffigan COR	.25	.12	.02
☐ 598 Billy Hatcher	.08	.04	.01
☐ 599 Bob Knepper	.05	.02	.00
☐ 600 Checklist 501-600	.05	.01	.00
☐ 601 Joey Cora	.08	.04	.01
☐ 602 Steve Finley	.12	.06	.01
☐ 603 Kal Daniels	.12	.06	.01
☐ 604 Gregg Olson	.25	.12	.02
☐ 605 Dave Stieb	.12	.06	.01
☐ 606 Kenny Rogers	.12	.06	.01
☐ 607 Zane Smith	.08	.04	.01
☐ 608 Bob Geren	.12	.06	.01
☐ 609 Chad Kreuter	.05	.02	.00
☐ 610 Mike Smithson	.05	.02	.00
☐ 611 Jeff Wetherby	.15	.07	.01
☐ 612 Gary Mielke	.12	.06	.01
☐ 613 Pete Smith	.05	.02	.00
☐ 614 Jack Daugherty	.15	.07	.01
☐ 615 Lance McCullers	.05	.02	.00
☐ 616 Don Robinson	.05	.02	.00
☐ 617 Jose Guzman	.05	.02	.00
☐ 618 Steve Bedrosian	.08	.04	.01
☐ 619 Jamie Moyer	.05	.02	.00
☐ 620 Atlee Hammaker	.05	.02	.00
☐ 621 Rick Luecken	.12	.06	.01
☐ 622 Greg W. Harris	.08	.04	.01
☐ 623 Pete Harnisch	.08	.04	.01
☐ 624 Jerald Clark	.05	.02	.00
☐ 625 Jack McDowell	.05	.02	.00
☐ 626 Frank Viola	.10	.05	.01
☐ 627 Teddy Higuera	.08	.04	.01
☐ 628 Marty Pevey	.10	.05	.01
☐ 629 Bill Wegman	.05	.02	.00
☐ 630 Eric Plunk	.05	.02	.00
☐ 631 Drew Hall	.05	.02	.00
☐ 632 Doug Jones	.08	.04	.01
☐ 633 Geno Petralli	.05	.02	.00
☐ 634 Jose Alvarez	.05	.02	.00
☐ 635 Bob Milacki	.10	.05	.01
☐ 636 Bobby Witt	.12	.06	.01
☐ 637 Trevor Wilson	.12	.06	.01
☐ 638 Jeff Russell	.05	.02	.00
☐ 639 Mike Krukow	.05	.02	.00
☐ 640 Rick Leach	.05	.02	.00
☐ 641 Dave Schmidt	.05	.02	.00
☐ 642 Terry Leach	.05	.02	.00
☐ 643 Calvin Schiraldi	.05	.02	.00
☐ 644 Bob Melvin	.05	.02	.00
☐ 645 Jim Abbott	.40	.20	.04
☐ 646 Jaime Navarro	.20	.10	.02
☐ 647 Mark Langston	.10	.05	.01
☐ 648 Juan Nieves	.05	.02	.00
☐ 649 Damaso Garcia	.05	.02	.00
☐ 650 Charlie O'Brien	.05	.02	.00
☐ 651 Eric King	.05	.02	.00
☐ 652 Mike Boddicker	.05	.02	.00
☐ 653 Duane Ward	.05	.02	.00
☐ 654 Bob Stanley	.05	.02	.00
☐ 655 Sandy Alomar Jr.	.40	.20	.04
☐ 656 Danny Tartabull	.10	.05	.01
☐ 657 Randy McCament	.12	.06	.01
☐ 658 Charlie Leibrandt	.05	.02	.00
☐ 659 Dan Quisenberry	.08	.04	.01
☐ 660 Paul Assenmacher	.05	.02	.00
☐ 661 Walt Terrell	.05	.02	.00
☐ 662 Tim Leary	.08	.04	.01
☐ 663 Randy Milligan	.12	.06	.01
☐ 664 Bo Diaz	.05	.02	.00
☐ 665 Mark Lemke UER	.05	.02	.00
(Richmond misspelled as Richomond)			
☐ 666 Jose Gonzalez	.08	.04	.01
☐ 667 Chuck Finley	.10	.05	.01
☐ 668 John Kruk	.05	.02	.00
☐ 669 Dick Schofield	.05	.02	.00
☐ 670 Tim Crews	.05	.02	.00
☐ 671 John Dopson	.08	.04	.01
☐ 672 John Orton	.15	.07	.01
☐ 673 Eric Hetzel	.08	.04	.01
☐ 674 Lance Parrish	.10	.05	.01
☐ 675 Ramon Martinez	1.00	.50	.10
☐ 676 Mark Gubicza	.10	.05	.01
☐ 677 Greg Litton	.18	.09	.01
☐ 678 Greg Mathews	.05	.02	.00
☐ 679 Dave Dravecky	.10	.05	.01
☐ 680 Steve Farr	.05	.02	.00
☐ 681 Mike Devereaux	.05	.02	.00
☐ 682 Ken Griffey Sr.	.10	.05	.01

☐ 683A Mickey Weston ERR (listed as Jamie on card)	5.00	2.50	.50
☐ 683B Mickey Weston COR (technically still an error as birthdate is listed as 3/26/81)	.20	.10	.02
☐ 684 Jack Armstrong	.12	.06	.01
☐ 685 Steve Buechele	.05	.02	.00
☐ 686 Bryan Harvey	.05	.02	.00
☐ 687 Lance Blankenship	.05	.02	.00
☐ 688 Dante Bichette	.10	.05	.01
☐ 689 Todd Burns	.08	.04	.01
☐ 690 Dan Petry	.05	.02	.00
☐ 691 Kent Anderson	.10	.05	.01
☐ 692 Todd Stottlemyre	.08	.04	.01
☐ 693 Wally Joyner	.10	.05	.01
☐ 694 Mike Rochford	.08	.04	.01
☐ 695 Floyd Bannister	.05	.02	.00
☐ 696 Rick Reuschel	.08	.04	.01
☐ 697 Jose DeLeon	.05	.02	.00
☐ 698 Jeff Montgomery	.08	.04	.01
☐ 699 Kelly Downs	.05	.02	.00
☐ 700A Checklist 601-700 (683 Jamie Weston)	3.00	.30	.05
☐ 700B Checklist 601-700 (683 Mickey Weston)	.10	.01	.00

1990 Upper Deck Extended

The 1990 Upper Deck Extended Set was issued in July of 1990. These standard sized cards (2 1/2" by 3 1/2") are in the same style as the first 700 cards of the 1990 Upper Deck set. They were issued either as a separate set in its own collectors box, as part of the complete 1-800 factory set, as well as being mixed in with the earlier numbered Upper Deck cards in late season foil packs. A variation exists on Nolan Ryan's card (#734). All cards produced before August 12th only discuss Ryan's sixth no-hitter while the later-issue cards include a stripe honoring Ryan's 300th victory. The key rookie cards in this set are Alex Cole, Delino DeShields, and Dave Justice. Card 702 was originally scheduled to be Mike Witt. A few 702 Witt cards and checklist cards showing 702 Witt escaped into early packs; they are characterized by a black rectangle covering much of the card's back.

	MINT	EXC	G-VG
COMPLETE SET (100)	13.50	6.00	1.00
COMMON PLAYER (1-100)	.07	.03	.01
☐ 701 Jim Gott	.07	.03	.01
☐ 702 Rookie Threats	.90	.45	.09
☐ 703 Alejandro Pena	.07	.03	.01
☐ 704 Willie Randolph	.10	.05	.01
☐ 705 Tim Leary	.10	.05	.01
☐ 706 Chuck McElroy	.15	.07	.01
☐ 707 Gerald Perry	.07	.03	.01
☐ 708 Tom Brunansky	.10	.05	.01
☐ 709 John Franco	.10	.05	.01
☐ 710 Mark Davis	.10	.05	.01
☐ 711 Dave Justice	6.00	3.00	.60
☐ 712 Storm Davis	.10	.05	.01
☐ 713 Scott Ruskin	.25	.12	.02
☐ 714 Glenn Braggs	.10	.05	.01
☐ 715 Kevin Bearse	.20	.10	.02
☐ 716 Jose Nunez	.07	.03	.01
☐ 717 Tim Layana	.25	.12	.02
☐ 718 Greg Myers	.07	.03	.01
☐ 719 Pete O'Brien	.10	.05	.01
☐ 720 John Candelaria	.07	.03	.01
☐ 721 Craig Grebeck	.20	.10	.02
☐ 722 Shawn Boskie	.25	.12	.02
☐ 723 Jim Leyritz	.30	.15	.03
☐ 724 Bill Sampen	.25	.12	.02
☐ 725 Scott Radinsky	.25	.12	.02
☐ 726 Todd Hundley	.30	.15	.03
☐ 727 Scott Hemond	.25	.12	.02
☐ 728 Lenny Webster	.20	.10	.02
☐ 729 Jeff Reardon	.10	.05	.01
☐ 730 Mitch Webster	.07	.03	.01
☐ 731 Brian Bohanon	.20	.10	.02
☐ 732 Rick Parker	.15	.07	.01
☐ 733 Tery Shumpert	.20	.10	.02
☐ 734A Ryan's 6th No-Hitter (no stripe on front)	15.00	7.50	1.50
☐ 734B Ryan's 6th No-Hitter (stripe added on card front for 300th win)	2.50	1.25	.25
☐ 735 John Burkett	.25	.12	.02
☐ 736 Derrick May	1.00	.50	.10
☐ 737 Carlos Baerga	.65	.30	.06
☐ 738 Greg Smith	.20	.10	.02
☐ 739 Scott Sanderson	.10	.05	.01
☐ 740 Joe Kraemer	.15	.07	.01
☐ 741 Hector Villanueva	.25	.12	.02
☐ 742 Mike Fetters	.15	.07	.01
☐ 743 Mark Gardner	.20	.10	.02
☐ 744 Matt Nokes	.10	.05	.01
☐ 745 Dave Winfield	.15	.07	.01
☐ 746 Delino DeShields	1.25	.60	.12
☐ 747 Dann Howitt	.25	.12	.02
☐ 748 Tony Pena	.10	.05	.01
☐ 749 Oil Can Boyd	.10	.05	.01
☐ 750 Mike Benjamin	.25	.12	.02
☐ 751 Alex Cole	1.25	.60	.12
☐ 752 Eric Gunderson	.20	.10	.02
☐ 753 Howard Farmer	.20	.10	.02
☐ 754 Joe Carter	.15	.07	.01
☐ 755 Ray Lankford	1.50	.75	.15
☐ 756 Sandy Alomar Jr.	.60	.30	.06
☐ 757 Alex Sanchez	.10	.05	.01
☐ 758 Nick Esasky	.10	.05	.01
☐ 759 Stan Belinda	.20	.10	.02
☐ 760 Jim Presley	.07	.03	.01
☐ 761 Gary DiSarcina	.20	.10	.02
☐ 762 Wayne Edwards	.20	.10	.02
☐ 763 Pat Combs	.15	.07	.01
☐ 764 Mickey Pina	.40	.20	.04
☐ 765 Wilson Alvarez	.40	.20	.04
☐ 766 Dave Parker	.12	.06	.01
☐ 767 Mike Blowers	.25	.12	.02
☐ 768 Tony Phillips	.07	.03	.01
☐ 769 Pascual Perez	.10	.05	.01
☐ 770 Gary Pettis	.07	.03	.01
☐ 771 Fred Lynn	.10	.05	.01
☐ 772 Mel Rojas	.20	.10	.02
☐ 773 David Segui	.50	.25	.05
☐ 774 Gary Carter	.10	.05	.01
☐ 775 Rafael Valdez	.15	.07	.01
☐ 776 Glenallen Hill	.18	.09	.01
☐ 777 Keith Hernandez	.12	.06	.01
☐ 778 Billy Hatcher	.10	.05	.01
☐ 779 Marty Clary	.07	.03	.01
☐ 780 Candy Maldonado	.10	.05	.01
☐ 781 Mike Marshall	.10	.05	.01
☐ 782 Billy Jo Robidoux	.07	.03	.01
☐ 783 Mark Langston	.10	.05	.01
☐ 784 Paul Sorrento	.15	.07	.01
☐ 785 Dave Hollins	.35	.17	.03
☐ 786 Cecil Fielder	1.00	.50	.10
☐ 787 Matt Young	.07	.03	.01
☐ 788 Jeff Huson	.10	.05	.01
☐ 789 Lloyd Moseby	.10	.05	.01
☐ 790 Ron Kittle	.10	.05	.01
☐ 791 Hubie Brooks	.10	.05	.01
☐ 792 Craig Lefferts	.07	.03	.01
☐ 793 Kevin Bass	.10	.05	.01
☐ 794 Bryn Smith	.07	.03	.01
☐ 795 Juan Samuel	.10	.05	.01
☐ 796 Sam Horn	.10	.05	.01
☐ 797 Randy Myers	.10	.05	.01
☐ 798 Chris James	.10	.05	.01
☐ 799 Bill Gullickson	.07	.03	.01
☐ 800 Checklist 701-800	.07	.01	.00

1990 Upper Deck Reggie Jackson

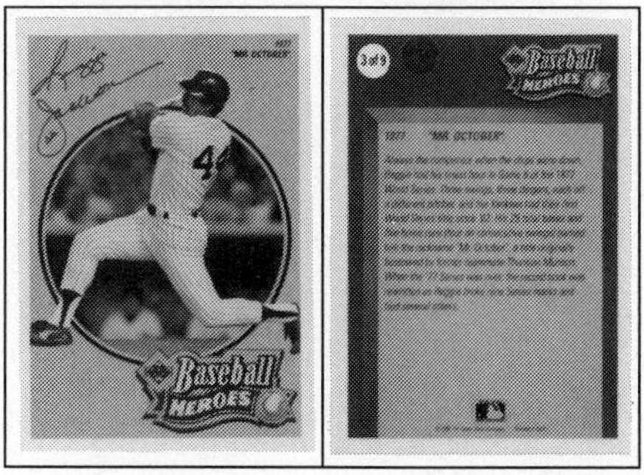

This 9-card sub-set was issued as an insert in 1990 Upper Deck High Number packs as part of the Upper Deck promotional giveaway of 2,500 officially signed and personally numbered Reggie Jackson cards. These cards were the standard size 2 1/2" by 3 1/2" and covers Reggie's complete major league career. The complete set price refers only to the unautographed card set of nine.

	MINT	EXC	G-VG
COMPLETE SET (9)	6.00	3.00	.60
COMMON PLAYER (1-9)	.75	.35	.07
☐ 1 1969 Emerging Superstar	.75	.35	.07
☐ 2 1973 an MVP Year	.75	.35	.07
☐ 3 1977 Mr. October	.75	.35	.07
☐ 4 1978 Jackson vs. Welch	.75	.35	.07
☐ 5 1982 Under the Halo	.75	.35	.07
☐ 6 1984 500 Homers	.75	.35	.07
☐ 7 1986 Moving Up the List	.75	.35	.07
☐ 8 1987 A Great Career Ends	.75	.35	.07
☐ 9 Baseball Heroes Checklist	.75	.35	.07
☐ xx Reggie Jackson (Signed and Numbered out of 2500)	350.00	175.00	35.00

1991 Upper Deck

This set marks the third year Upper Deck has issued a 700-card set in January. These cards measure 2 1/2" by 3 1/2". The set features 26 star rookies to lead off the set as well as other special cards featuring multi-players. The set is made on the typical Upper Deck card stock and features full-color photos on both the front and the back. The team checklist (TC) cards in the set feature an attractive Vernon Wells drawing of a featured player for that particular team. A special Michael Jordan card (numbered SP1) was randomly included in packs on a somewhat limited basis. This Jordan card is not included in the set price below.

	MINT	EXC	G-VG
COMPLETE SET (700)	36.00	18.00	3.60
COMMON PLAYER (1-700)	.05	.02	.00
☐ 1 Star Rookie Checklist	.10	.01	.00
☐ 2 Phil Plantier	.60	.30	.06
☐ 3 D.J. Dozier	.40	.20	.04
☐ 4 Dave Hansen	.35	.17	.03
☐ 5 Maurice Vaughn	.80	.40	.08
☐ 6 Leo Gomez	.50	.25	.05
☐ 7 Scott Allred	.12	.06	.01
☐ 8 Scott Chiamparino	.35	.17	.03
☐ 9 Lance Dickson	.35	.17	.03
☐ 10 Sean Berry	.25	.12	.02
☐ 11 Bernie Williams	.30	.15	.03
☐ 12 Brian Barnes	.12	.06	.01
☐ 13 Narciso Elvira	.15	.07	.01
☐ 14 Mike Gardiner	.15	.07	.01
☐ 15 Greg Colbrunn	.20	.10	.02
☐ 16 Bernard Gilkey	.35	.17	.03
☐ 17 Mark Lewis	.30	.15	.03
☐ 18 Mickey Morandini	.20	.10	.02
☐ 19 Charles Nagy	.15	.07	.01
☐ 20 Geronimo Pena	.15	.07	.01
☐ 21 Henry Rodriguez	.65	.30	.06
☐ 22 Scott Cooper	.20	.10	.02
☐ 23 Andujar Cedeno	.65	.30	.06
☐ 24 Eric Karros	.45	.22	.04
☐ 25 Steve Decker	.40	.20	.04
☐ 26 Kevin Belcher	.20	.10	.02
☐ 27 Jeff Conine	.80	.40	.08
☐ 28 Oakland Athletics TC Dave Stewart	.10	.05	.01
☐ 29 Chicago White Sox TC Carlton Fisk	.08	.04	.01
☐ 30 Texas Rangers TC Rafael Palmeiro	.08	.04	.01
☐ 31 California Angels TC Chuck Finley	.08	.04	.01
☐ 32 Seattle Mariners TC Harold Reynolds	.08	.04	.01
☐ 33 Kansas City Royals TC Bret Saberhagen	.08	.04	.01
☐ 34 Minnesota Twins TC Gary Gaetti	.08	.04	.01
☐ 35 Scott Leius	.12	.06	.01
☐ 36 Neal Heaton	.05	.02	.00
☐ 37 Terry Lee	.20	.10	.02
☐ 38 Gary Redus	.05	.02	.00
☐ 39 Barry Jones	.05	.02	.00
☐ 40 Chuck Knoblauch	.12	.06	.01
☐ 41 Larry Andersen	.05	.02	.00
☐ 42 Darryl Hamilton	.08	.04	.01
☐ 43 Boston Red Sox TC Mike Greenwell	.10	.05	.01
☐ 44 Toronto Blue Jays TC Kelly Gruber	.08	.04	.01
☐ 45 Detroit Tigers TC Jack Morris	.08	.04	.01
☐ 46 Cleveland Indians TC Sandy Alomar Jr.	.12	.06	.01
☐ 47 Baltimore Orioles TC Gregg Olson	.08	.04	.01
☐ 48 Milwaukee Brewers TC Dave Parker	.08	.04	.01
☐ 49 New York Yankees TC Roberto Kelly	.08	.04	.01
☐ 50 Top Prospect Checklist	08	.01	.00
☐ 51 Kyle Abbott	.15	.07	.01
☐ 52 Jeff Juden	.40	.20	.04
☐ 53 Todd Van Poppel	1.50	.75	.15
☐ 54 Steve Karsay	.45	.22	.04
☐ 55 Chipper Jones	.80	.40	.08
☐ 56 Chris Johnson	.15	.07	.01
☐ 57 John Ericks	.15	.07	.01
☐ 58 Gary Scott	.20	.10	.02
☐ 59 Kiki Jones	.60	.30	.06
☐ 60 Wilfredo Cordero	.20	.10	.02
☐ 61 Royce Clayton	.15	.07	.01
☐ 62 Tim Costo	.50	.25	.05
☐ 63 Roger Salkeld	.40	.20	.04
☐ 64 Brook Fordyce	.20	.10	.02
☐ 65 Mike Mussina	.50	.25	.05
☐ 66 Dave Staton	.15	.07	.01
☐ 67 Mike Lieberthal	.35	.17	.03
☐ 68 Kurt Miller	.20	.10	.02

☐ 69 Dan Peltier	.20	.10	.02
☐ 70 Greg Blosser	.40	.20	.04
☐ 71 Reggie Sanders	.35	.17	.03
☐ 72 Brent Mayne	.12	.06	.01
☐ 73 Rico Brogna	.30	.15	.03
☐ 74 Willie Banks	.20	.10	.02
☐ 75 Len Brutcher	.15	.07	.01
☐ 76 Pat Kelly	.15	.07	.01
☐ 77 Cincinnati Reds TC Chris Sabo	.08	.04	.01
☐ 78 Los Angeles Dodgers TC Ramon Martinez	.10	.05	.01
☐ 79 San Fran. Giants TC Matt Williams	.10	.05	.01
☐ 80 San Diego Padres TC Roberto Alomar	.08	.04	.01
☐ 81 Houston Astros TC Glenn Davis	.08	.04	.01
☐ 82 Atlanta Braves TC Ron Gant	.08	.04	.01
☐ 83 Fielder's Feat Cecil Fielder	.25	.12	.02
☐ 84 Orlando Merced	.15	.07	.01
☐ 85 Domingo Ramos	.05	.02	.00
☐ 86 Tom Bolton	.05	.02	.00
☐ 87 Andres Santana	.12	.06	.01
☐ 88 John Dopson	.05	.02	.00
☐ 89 Kenny Williams	.05	.02	.00
☐ 90 Marty Barrett	.05	.02	.00
☐ 91 Tom Pagnozzi	.05	.02	.00
☐ 92 Carmelo Martinez	.05	.02	.00
☐ 93 Save Master (Bobby Thigpen)	.08	.04	.01
☐ 94 Pittsburgh Pirates TC Barry Bonds	.12	.06	.01
☐ 95 New York Mets TC Gregg Jefferies	.12	.06	.01
☐ 96 Montreal Expos TC Tim Wallach	.08	.04	.01
☐ 97 Phila. Phillies TC Len Dykstra	.08	.04	.01
☐ 98 St.Louis Cardinals TC Pedro Guerrero	.08	.04	.01
☐ 99 Chicago Cubs TC Mark Grace	.12	.06	.01
☐ 100 Checklist 1-100	.08	.01	.00
☐ 101 Kevin Elster	.05	.02	.00
☐ 102 Tom Brookens	.05	.02	.00
☐ 103 Mackey Sasser	.08	.04	.01
☐ 104 Felix Fermin	.05	.02	.00
☐ 105 Kevin McReynolds	.10	.05	.01
☐ 106 Dave Stieb	.10	.05	.01
☐ 107 Jeffrey Leonard	.08	.04	.01
☐ 108 Dave Henderson	.08	.04	.01
☐ 109 Sid Bream	.05	.02	.00
☐ 110 Henry Cotto	.05	.02	.00
☐ 111 Shawon Dunston	.10	.05	.01
☐ 112 Mariano Duncan	.08	.04	.01
☐ 113 Joe Girardi	.05	.02	.00
☐ 114 Billy Hatcher	.08	.04	.01
☐ 115 Greg Maddux	.08	.04	.01
☐ 116 Jerry Browne	.05	.02	.00
☐ 117 Juan Samuel	.08	.04	.01
☐ 118 Steve Olin	.05	.02	.00
☐ 119 Alfredo Griffin	.05	.02	.00
☐ 120 Mitch Webster	.05	.02	.00
☐ 121 Joel Skinner	.05	.02	.00
☐ 122 Frank Viola	.10	.05	.01
☐ 123 Cory Snyder	.08	.04	.01
☐ 124 Howard Johnson	.10	.05	.01
☐ 125 Carlos Baerga	.20	.10	.02
☐ 126 Tony Fernandez	.08	.04	.01
☐ 127 Dave Stewart	.12	.06	.01
☐ 128 Jay Buhner	.08	.04	.01
☐ 129 Mike LaValliere	.05	.02	.00
☐ 130 Scott Bradley	.05	.02	.00
☐ 131 Tony Phillips	.05	.02	.00
☐ 132 Ryne Sandberg	.20	.10	.02
☐ 133 Paul O'Neill	.10	.05	.01
☐ 134 Mark Grace	.20	.10	.02
☐ 135 Chris Sabo	.12	.06	.01
☐ 136 Ramon Martinez	.20	.10	.02
☐ 137 Brook Jacoby	.08	.04	.01
☐ 138 Candy Maldonado	.08	.04	.01
☐ 139 Mike Scioscia	.05	.02	.00
☐ 140 Chris James	.08	.04	.01
☐ 141 Craig Worthington	.08	.04	.01
☐ 142 Manny Lee	.05	.02	.00
☐ 143 Tim Raines	.10	.05	.01
☐ 144 Sandy Alomar Jr.	.20	.10	.02
☐ 145 John Olerud	.40	.20	.04
☐ 146 Ozzie Canseco	.20	.10	.02
☐ 147 Pat Borders	.08	.04	.01
☐ 148 Harold Reynolds	.08	.04	.01
☐ 149 Tom Henke	.08	.04	.01
☐ 150 R.J. Reynolds	.05	.02	.00
☐ 151 Mike Gallego	.05	.02	.00
☐ 152 Bobby Bonilla	.15	.07	.01
☐ 153 Terry Steinbach	.08	.04	.01
☐ 154 Barry Bonds	.20	.10	.02
☐ 155 Jose Canseco	.40	.20	.04
☐ 156 Gregg Jefferies	.20	.10	.02
☐ 157 Matt Williams	.15	.07	.01
☐ 158 Craig Biggio	.08	.04	.01
☐ 159 Daryl Boston	.08	.04	.01
☐ 160 Ricky Jordan	.08	.04	.01
☐ 161 Stan Belinda	.08	.04	.01
☐ 162 Ozzie Smith	.10	.05	.01
☐ 163 Tom Brunansky	.08	.04	.01
☐ 164 Todd Zeile	.20	.10	.02
☐ 165 Mike Greenwell	.15	.07	.01
☐ 166 Kal Daniels	.10	.05	.01
☐ 167 Kent Hrbek	.10	.05	.01
☐ 168 Franklin Stubbs	.08	.04	.01
☐ 169 Dick Schofield	.05	.02	.00
☐ 170 Junior Ortiz	.05	.02	.00
☐ 171 Hector Villanueva	.15	.07	.01
☐ 172 Dennis Eckersley	.10	.05	.01
☐ 173 Mitch Williams	.05	.02	.00
☐ 174 Mark McGwire	.25	.12	.02
☐ 175 Fernando Valenzuela 3X	.10	.05	.01
☐ 176 Gary Carter	.10	.05	.01
☐ 177 Dave Magadan	.10	.05	.01
☐ 178 Robby Thompson	.05	.02	.00
☐ 179 Bob Ojeda	.08	.04	.01
☐ 180 Ken Caminiti	.05	.02	.00
☐ 181 Don Slaught	.05	.02	.00
☐ 182 Luis Rivera	.05	.02	.00
☐ 183 Jay Bell	.05	.02	.00
☐ 184 Jody Reed	.08	.04	.01
☐ 185 Wally Backman	.05	.02	.00
☐ 186 Dave Martinez	.05	.02	.00
☐ 187 Luis Polonia	.05	.02	.00
☐ 188 Shane Mack	.08	.04	.01
☐ 189 Spike Owen	.05	.02	.00
☐ 190 Scott Bailes	.05	.02	.00
☐ 191 John Russell	.05	.02	.00
☐ 192 Walt Weiss	.08	.04	.01
☐ 193 Jose Oquendo	.05	.02	.00
☐ 194 Carney Lansford	.08	.04	.01
☐ 195 Jeff Huson	.05	.02	.00
☐ 196 Keith Miller	.05	.02	.00
☐ 197 Eric Yelding	.08	.04	.01
☐ 198 Ron Darling	.08	.04	.01
☐ 199 John Kruk	.05	.02	.00
☐ 200 Checklist 101-200	.08	.01	.00
☐ 201 John Shelby	.05	.02	.00
☐ 202 Bob Geren	.05	.02	.00
☐ 203 Lance McCullers	.05	.02	.00
☐ 204 Alvaro Espinoza	.05	.02	.00
☐ 205 Mark Salas	.05	.02	.00
☐ 206 Mike Pagliarulo	.05	.02	.00
☐ 207 Jose Uribe	.05	.02	.00
☐ 208 Jim Deshaies	.05	.02	.00
☐ 209 Ron Karkovice	.05	.02	.00
☐ 210 Rafael Ramirez	.05	.02	.00
☐ 211 Donnie Hill	.05	.02	.00
☐ 212 Brian Harper	.05	.02	.00
☐ 213 Jack Howell	.05	.02	.00
☐ 214 Wes Gardner	.05	.02	.00
☐ 215 Tim Burke	.08	.04	.01
☐ 216 Doug Jones	.08	.04	.01
☐ 217 Hubie Brooks	.08	.04	.01
☐ 218 Tom Candiotti	.05	.02	.00
☐ 219 Gerald Perry	.05	.02	.00
☐ 220 Jose DeLeon	.05	.02	.00
☐ 221 Wally Whitehurst	.05	.02	.00
☐ 222 Alan Mills	.15	.07	.01
☐ 223 Alan Trammell	.10	.05	.01
☐ 224 Dwight Gooden	.15	.07	.01
☐ 225 Travis Fryman	.75	.35	.07
☐ 226 Joe Carter	.10	.05	.01
☐ 227 Julio Franco	.08	.04	.01
☐ 228 Craig Lefferts	.05	.02	.00
☐ 229 Gary Pettis	.05	.02	.00
☐ 230 Dennis Rasmussen	.05	.02	.00
☐ 231 Brian Downing	.05	.02	.00
☐ 232 Carlos Quintana	.10	.05	.01
☐ 233 Gary Gaetti	.08	.04	.01
☐ 234 Mark Langston	.10	.05	.01
☐ 235 Tim Wallach	.08	.04	.01
☐ 236 Greg Swindell	.08	.04	.01
☐ 237 Eddie Murray	.12	.06	.01
☐ 238 Jeff Manto	.08	.04	.01
☐ 239 Lenny Harris	.08	.04	.01
☐ 240 Jesse Orosco	.05	.02	.00
☐ 241 Scott Lusader	.05	.02	.00
☐ 242 Sid Fernandez	.08	.04	.01

☐ 243	Jim Leyritz	.12	.06	.01
☐ 244	Cecil Fielder	.25	.12	.02
☐ 245	Darryl Strawberry	.25	.12	.02
☐ 246	Frank Thomas	1.50	.75	.15
☐ 247	Kevin Mitchell	.20	.10	.02
☐ 248	Lance Johnson	.05	.02	.00
☐ 249	Rick Reuschel	.08	.04	.01
☐ 250	Mark Portugal	.05	.02	.00
☐ 251	Derek Lilliquist	.05	.02	.00
☐ 252	Brian Holman	.08	.04	.01
☐ 253	Rafael Valdez	.08	.04	.01
☐ 254	B.J. Surhoff	.08	.04	.01
☐ 255	Tony Gwynn	.15	.07	.01
☐ 256	Andy Van Slyke	.10	.05	.01
☐ 257	Todd Stottlemyre	.08	.04	.01
☐ 258	Jose Lind	.05	.02	.00
☐ 259	Greg Myers	.05	.02	.00
☐ 260	Jeff Ballard	.05	.02	.00
☐ 261	Bobby Thigpen	.10	.05	.01
☐ 262	Jimmy Kremers	.12	.06	.01
☐ 263	Robin Ventura	.20	.10	.02
☐ 264	John Smoltz	.08	.04	.01
☐ 265	Sammy Sosa	.20	.10	.02
☐ 266	Gary Sheffield	.15	.07	.01
☐ 267	Lenny Dykstra	.10	.05	.01
☐ 268	Bill Spiers	.05	.02	.00
☐ 269	Charlie Hayes	.05	.02	.00
☐ 270	Brett Butler	.08	.04	.01
☐ 271	Bip Roberts	.08	.04	.01
☐ 272	Rob Deer	.08	.04	.01
☐ 273	Fred Lynn	.08	.04	.01
☐ 274	Dave Parker	.10	.05	.01
☐ 275	Andy Benes	.12	.06	.01
☐ 276	Glenallen Hill	.08	.04	.01
☐ 277	Steve Howard	.10	.05	.01
☐ 278	Doug Drabek	.10	.05	.01
☐ 279	Joe Oliver	.08	.04	.01
☐ 280	Todd Benzinger	.05	.02	.00
☐ 281	Eric King	.05	.02	.00
☐ 282	Jim Presley	.05	.02	.00
☐ 283	Ken Patterson	.05	.02	.00
☐ 284	Jack Daugherty	.05	.02	.00
☐ 285	Ivan Calderon	.08	.04	.01
☐ 286	Edgar Diaz	.10	.05	.01
☐ 287	Kevin Bass	.08	.04	.01
☐ 288	Don Carman	.05	.02	.00
☐ 289	Greg Brock	.05	.02	.00
☐ 290	John Franco	.08	.04	.01
☐ 291	Joey Cora	.05	.02	.00
☐ 292	Bill Wegman	.05	.02	.00
☐ 293	Eric Show	.05	.02	.00
☐ 294	Scott Bankhead	.05	.02	.00
☐ 295	Garry Templeton	.05	.02	.00
☐ 296	Mickey Tettleton	.08	.04	.01
☐ 297	Luis Sojo	.10	.05	.01
☐ 298	Jose Rijo	.08	.04	.01
☐ 299	Dave Johnson	.05	.02	.00
☐ 300	Checklist 201-300	.08	.01	.00
☐ 301	Mark Grant	.05	.02	.00
☐ 302	Pete Harnisch	.05	.02	.00
☐ 303	Greg Olson	.10	.05	.01
☐ 304	Anthony Telford	.15	.07	.01
☐ 305	Lonnie Smith	.08	.04	.01
☐ 306	Chris Hoiles	.20	.10	.02
☐ 307	Bryn Smith	.05	.02	.00
☐ 308	Mike Devereaux	.05	.02	.00
☐ 309	Milt Thompson	.05	.02	.00
☐ 310	Bob Melvin	.05	.02	.00
☐ 311	Luis Salazar	.05	.02	.00
☐ 312	Ed Whitson	.05	.02	.00
☐ 313	Charlie Hough	.05	.02	.00
☐ 314	Dave Clark	.05	.02	.00
☐ 315	Eric Gunderson	.05	.02	.00
☐ 316	Dan Petry	.05	.02	.00
☐ 317	Dante Bichette	.08	.04	.01
☐ 318	Mike Heath	.05	.02	.00
☐ 319	Damon Berryhill	.05	.02	.00
☐ 320	Walt Terrell	.05	.02	.00
☐ 321	Scott Fletcher	.05	.02	.00
☐ 322	Dan Plesac	.05	.02	.00
☐ 323	Jack McDowell	.08	.04	.01
☐ 324	Paul Molitor	.10	.05	.01
☐ 325	Ozzie Guillen	.08	.04	.01
☐ 326	Gregg Olson	.12	.06	.01
☐ 327	Pedro Guerrero	.10	.05	.01
☐ 328	Bob Milacki	.08	.04	.01
☐ 329	John Tudor	.08	.04	.01
☐ 330	Steve Finley	.08	.04	.01
☐ 331	Jack Clark	.10	.05	.01
☐ 332	Jerome Walton	.25	.12	.02
☐ 333	Andy Hawkins	.05	.02	.00
☐ 334	Derrick May	.35	.17	.03
☐ 335	Roberto Alomar	.10	.05	.01
☐ 336	Jack Morris	.08	.04	.01
☐ 337	Dave Winfield	.12	.06	.01
☐ 338	Steve Searcy	.05	.02	.00
☐ 339	Chili Davis	.08	.04	.01
☐ 340	Larry Sheets	.05	.02	.00
☐ 341	Ted Higuera	.08	.04	.01
☐ 342	David Segui	.30	.15	.03
☐ 343	Greg Cadaret	.05	.02	.00
☐ 344	Robin Yount	.15	.07	.01
☐ 345	Nolan Ryan	.30	.15	.03
☐ 346	Ray Lankford	.50	.25	.05
☐ 347	Cal Ripken Jr.	.15	.07	.01
☐ 348	Lee Smith	.08	.04	.01
☐ 349	Brady Anderson	.08	.04	.01
☐ 350	Frank DiPino	.05	.02	.00
☐ 351	Hal Morris	.20	.10	.02
☐ 352	Deion Sanders	.15	.07	.01
☐ 353	Barry Larkin	.12	.06	.01
☐ 354	Don Mattingly	.30	.15	.03
☐ 355	Eric Davis	.15	.07	.01
☐ 356	Jose Offerman	.40	.20	.04
☐ 357	Mel Rojas	.10	.05	.01
☐ 358	Rudy Seanez	.10	.05	.01
☐ 359	Oil Can Boyd	.08	.04	.01
☐ 360	Nelson Liriano	.05	.02	.00
☐ 361	Ron Gant	.12	.06	.01
☐ 362	Howard Farmer	.12	.06	.01
☐ 363	David Justice	1.00	.50	.10
☐ 364	Delino DeShields	.25	.12	.02
☐ 365	Steve Avery	.20	.10	.02
☐ 366	David Cone	.10	.05	.01
☐ 367	Lou Whitaker	.08	.04	.01
☐ 368	Von Hayes	.08	.04	.01
☐ 369	Frank Tanana	.05	.02	.00
☐ 370	Tim Teufel	.05	.02	.00
☐ 371	Randy Myers	.08	.04	.01
☐ 372	Roberto Kelly	.10	.05	.01
☐ 373	Jack Armstrong	.08	.04	.01
☐ 374	Kelly Gruber	.12	.06	.01
☐ 375	Kevin Maas	.65	.30	.06
☐ 376	Randy Johnson	.08	.04	.01
☐ 377	David West	.05	.02	.00
☐ 378	Brent Knackert	.15	.07	.01
☐ 379	Rick Honeycutt	.05	.02	.00
☐ 380	Kevin Gross	.05	.02	.00
☐ 381	Tom Foley	.05	.02	.00
☐ 382	Jeff Blauser	.05	.02	.00
☐ 383	Scott Ruskin	.12	.06	.01
☐ 384	Andres Thomas	.05	.02	.00
☐ 385	Dennis Martinez	.05	.02	.00
☐ 386	Mike Henneman	.05	.02	.00
☐ 387	Felix Jose	.08	.04	.01
☐ 388	Alejandro Pena	.05	.02	.00
☐ 389	Chet Lemon	.05	.02	.00
☐ 390	Craig Wilson	.15	.07	.01
☐ 391	Chuck Crim	.05	.02	.00
☐ 392	Mel Hall	.05	.02	.00
☐ 393	Mark Knudson	.05	.02	.00
☐ 394	Norm Charlton	.08	.04	.01
☐ 395	Mike Felder	.05	.02	.00
☐ 396	Tim Layana	.08	.04	.01
☐ 397	Steve Frey	.10	.05	.01
☐ 398	Bill Doran	.08	.04	.01
☐ 399	Dion James	.05	.02	.00
☐ 400	Checklist 301-400	.08	.01	.00
☐ 401	Ron Hassey	.05	.02	.00
☐ 402	Don Robinson	.05	.02	.00
☐ 403	Gene Nelson	.05	.02	.00
☐ 404	Terry Kennedy	.05	.02	.00
☐ 405	Todd Burns	.05	.02	.00
☐ 406	Roger McDowell	.05	.02	.00
☐ 407	Bob Kipper	.05	.02	.00
☐ 408	Darren Daulton	.05	.02	.00
☐ 409	Chuck Cary	.05	.02	.00
☐ 410	Bruce Ruffin	.05	.02	.00
☐ 411	Juan Berenguer	.05	.02	.00
☐ 412	Gary Ward	.05	.02	.00
☐ 413	Al Newman	.05	.02	.00
☐ 414	Danny Jackson	.08	.04	.01
☐ 415	Greg Gagne	.05	.02	.00
☐ 416	Tom Herr	.05	.02	.00
☐ 417	Jeff Parrett	.05	.02	.00
☐ 418	Jeff Reardon	.08	.04	.01
☐ 419	Mark Lemke	.05	.02	.00
☐ 420	Charlie O'Brien	.05	.02	.00
☐ 421	Willie Randolph	.08	.04	.01
☐ 422	Steve Bedrosian	.08	.04	.01
☐ 423	Mike Moore	.08	.04	.01
☐ 424	Jeff Brantley	.08	.04	.01
☐ 425	Bob Welch	.10	.05	.01
☐ 426	Terry Mulholland	.05	.02	.00
☐ 427	Willie Blair	.10	.05	.01
☐ 428	Darrin Fletcher	.15	.07	.01
☐ 429	Mike Witt	.05	.02	.00
☐ 430	Joe Boever	.05	.02	.00

□ 431 Tom Gordon	.12	.06	.01
□ 432 Pedro Munoz	.20	.10	.02
□ 433 Kevin Seitzer	.10	.05	.01
□ 434 Kevin Tapani	.10	.05	.01
□ 435 Bret Saberhagen	.10	.05	.01
□ 436 Ellis Burks	.12	.06	.01
□ 437 Chuck Finley	.10	.05	.01
□ 438 Mike Boddicker	.05	.02	.00
□ 439 Francisco Cabrera	.08	.04	.01
□ 440 Todd Hundley	.15	.07	.01
□ 441 Kelly Downs	.05	.02	.00
□ 442 Dann Howitt	.12	.06	.01
□ 443 Scott Garrelts	.05	.02	.00
□ 444 Rickey Henderson 3X	.30	.15	.03
□ 445 Will Clark	.30	.15	.03
□ 446 Ben McDonald	.35	.17	.03
□ 447 Dale Murphy	.12	.06	.01
□ 448 Dave Righetti	.08	.04	.01
□ 449 Dickie Thon	.05	.02	.00
□ 450 Ted Power	.05	.02	.00
□ 451 Scott Coolbaugh	.05	.02	.00
□ 452 Dwight Smith	.10	.05	.01
□ 453 Pete Incaviglia	.08	.04	.01
□ 454 Andre Dawson	.12	.06	.01
□ 455 Ruben Sierra	.15	.07	.01
□ 456 Andres Galarraga	.10	.05	.01
□ 457 Alvin Davis	.10	.05	.01
□ 458 Tony Castillo	.05	.02	.00
□ 459 Pete O'Brien	.05	.02	.00
□ 460 Charlie Leibrandt	.05	.02	.00
□ 461 Vince Coleman	.10	.05	.01
□ 462 Steve Sax	.10	.05	.01
□ 463 Omar Olivares	.12	.06	.01
□ 464 Oscar Azocar	.25	.12	.02
□ 465 Joe Magrane	.08	.04	.01
□ 466 Karl Rhodes	.15	.07	.01
□ 467 Benito Santiago	.10	.05	.01
□ 468 Joe Klink	.10	.05	.01
□ 469 Sil Campusano	.05	.02	.00
□ 470 Mark Parent	.05	.02	.00
□ 471 Shawn Boskie	.08	.04	.01
□ 472 Kevin Brown	.10	.05	.01
□ 473 Rick Sutcliffe	.08	.04	.01
□ 474 Rafael Palmeiro	.10	.05	.01
□ 475 Mike Harkey	.10	.05	.01
□ 476 Jaime Navarro	.08	.04	.01
□ 477 Marquis Grissom	.15	.07	.01
□ 478 Marty Clary	.05	.02	.00
□ 479 Greg Briley	.08	.04	.01
□ 480 Tom Glavine	.08	.04	.01
□ 481 Lee Guetterman	.05	.02	.00
□ 482 Rex Hudler	.05	.02	.00
□ 483 Dave LaPoint	.05	.02	.00
□ 484 Terry Pendleton	.05	.02	.00
□ 485 Jesse Barfield	.10	.05	.01
□ 486 Jose DeJesus	.05	.02	.00
□ 487 Paul Abbott	.20	.10	.02
□ 488 Ken Howell	.05	.02	.00
□ 489 Greg W. Harris	.05	.02	.00
□ 490 Roy Smith	.05	.02	.00
□ 491 Paul Assenmacher	.05	.02	.00
□ 492 Geno Petralli	.05	.02	.00
□ 493 Steve Wilson	.05	.02	.00
□ 494 Kevin Reimer	.10	.05	.01
□ 495 Bill Long	.05	.02	.00
□ 496 Mike Jackson	.05	.02	.00
□ 497 Oddibe McDowell	.08	.04	.01
□ 498 Bill Swift	.05	.02	.00
□ 499 Jeff Treadway	.05	.02	.00
□ 500 Checklist 401-500	.08	.01	.00
□ 501 Gene Larkin	.05	.02	.00
□ 502 Bob Boone	.08	.04	.01
□ 503 Allan Anderson	.05	.02	.00
□ 504 Luis Aquino	.05	.02	.00
□ 505 Mark Guthrie	.05	.02	.00
□ 506 Joe Orsulak	.05	.02	.00
□ 507 Dana Kiecker	.15	.07	.01
□ 508 Dave Gallagher	.05	.02	.00
□ 509 Greg A. Harris	.05	.02	.00
□ 510 Mark Williamson	.05	.02	.00
□ 511 Casey Candaele	.05	.02	.00
□ 512 Mookie Wilson	.08	.04	.01
□ 513 Dave Smith	.05	.02	.00
□ 514 Chuck Carr	.15	.07	.01
□ 515 Glenn Wilson	.05	.02	.00
□ 516 Mike Fitzgerald	.05	.02	.00
□ 517 Devon White	.08	.04	.01
□ 518 Dave Hollins	.15	.07	.01
□ 519 Mark Eichhorn	.05	.02	.00
□ 520 Otis Nixon	.05	.02	.00
□ 521 Terry Shumpert	.08	.04	.01
□ 522 Scott Erickson	.20	.10	.02
□ 523 Danny Tartabull	.10	.05	.01
□ 524 Orel Hershiser	.10	.05	.01
□ 525 George Brett	.15	.07	.01
□ 526 Greg Vaughn	.15	.07	.01
□ 527 Tim Naehring	.30	.15	.03
□ 528 Curt Schilling	.08	.04	.01
□ 529 Chris Bosio	.05	.02	.00
□ 530 Sam Horn	.08	.04	.01
□ 531 Mike Scott	.10	.05	.01
□ 532 George Bell	.10	.05	.01
□ 533 Eric Anthony	.20	.10	.02
□ 534 Julio Valera	.12	.06	.01
□ 535 Glenn Davis	.10	.05	.01
□ 536 Larry Walker	.12	.06	.01
□ 537 Pat Combs	.08	.04	.01
□ 538 Chris Nabholz	.20	.10	.02
□ 539 Kirk McCaskill	.05	.02	.00
□ 540 Randy Ready	.06	.03	.00
□ 541 Mark Gubicza	.08	.04	.01
□ 542 Rick Aguilera	.05	.02	.00
□ 543 Brian McRae	.80	.40	.08
□ 544 Kirby Puckett	.20	.10	.02
□ 545 Bo Jackson	.45	.22	.04
□ 546 Wade Boggs	.20	.10	.02
□ 547 Tim McIntosh	.10	.05	.01
□ 548 Randy Milligan	.10	.05	.01
□ 549 Dwight Evans	.10	.05	.01
□ 550 Billy Ripken	.05	.02	.00
□ 551 Erik Hanson	.10	.05	.01
□ 552 Lance Parrish	.10	.05	.01
□ 553 Tino Martinez	.35	.17	.03
□ 554 Jim Abbott	.15	.07	.01
□ 555 Ken Griffey Jr.	1.00	.50	.10
□ 556 Milt Cuyler	.25	.12	.02
□ 557 Mark Leonard	.30	.15	.03
□ 558 Jay Howell	.05	.02	.00
□ 559 Lloyd Moseby	.08	.04	.01
□ 560 Chris Gwynn	.05	.02	.00
□ 561 Mark Whiten	.40	.20	.04
□ 562 Harold Baines	.10	.05	.01
□ 563 Junior Felix	.12	.06	.01
□ 564 Darren Lewis	.45	.22	.04
□ 565 Fred McGriff	.12	.06	.01
□ 566 Kevin Appier	.10	.05	.01
□ 567 Luis Gonzalez	.12	.06	.01
□ 568 Frank White	.08	.04	.01
□ 569 Juan Agosto	.05	.02	.00
□ 570 Mike Macfarlane	.05	.02	.00
□ 571 Bert Blyleven	.08	.04	.01
□ 572 Ken Griffey Sr.	.08	.04	.01
□ 573 Lee Stevens	.20	.10	.02
□ 574 Edgar Martinez	.08	.04	.01
□ 575 Wally Joyner	.10	.05	.01
□ 576 Tim Belcher	.08	.04	.01
□ 577 John Burkett	.08	.04	.01
□ 578 Mike Morgan	.05	.02	.00
□ 579 Paul Gibson	.05	.02	.00
□ 580 Jose Vizcaino	.05	.02	.00
□ 581 Duane Ward	.05	.02	.00
□ 582 Scott Sanderson	.05	.02	.00
□ 583 David Wells	.05	.02	.00
□ 584 Willie McGee	.10	.05	.01
□ 585 John Cerutti	.05	.02	.00
□ 586 Danny Darwin	.05	.02	.00
□ 587 Kurt Stillwell	.08	.04	.01
□ 588 Rich Gedman	.05	.02	.00
□ 589 Mark Davis	.10	.05	.01
□ 590 Bill Gullickson	.05	.02	.00
□ 591 Matt Young	.05	.02	.00
□ 592 Bryan Harvey	.05	.02	.00
□ 593 Omar Vizquel	.05	.02	.00
□ 594 Scott Lewis	.15	.07	.01
□ 595 Dave Valle	.05	.02	.00
□ 596 Tim Crews	.05	.02	.00
□ 597 Mike Bielecki	.05	.02	.00
□ 598 Mike Sharperson	.05	.02	.00
□ 599 Dave Bergman	.05	.02	.00
□ 600 Checklist 501-600	.08	.01	.00
□ 601 Steve Lyons	.05	.02	.00
□ 602 Bruce Hurst	.08	.04	.01
□ 603 Donn Pall	.05	.02	.00
□ 604 Jim Vatcher	.20	.10	.02
□ 605 Dan Pasqua	.05	.02	.00
□ 606 Kenny Rogers	.05	.02	.00
□ 607 Jeff Schulz	.12	.06	.01
□ 608 Brad Arnsberg	.08	.04	.01
□ 609 Willie Wilson	.08	.04	.01
□ 610 Jamie Moyer	.05	.02	.00
□ 611 Ron Oester	.05	.02	.00
□ 612 Dennis Cook	.08	.04	.01
□ 613 Rick Mahler	.05	.02	.00
□ 614 Bill Landrum	.05	.02	.00
□ 615 Scott Scudder	.08	.04	.01
□ 616 Tom Edens	.12	.06	.01

☐ 617	1917 Revisited (White Sox in vintage uniforms)	.10	.05	.01
☐ 618	Jim Gantner	.05	.02	.00
☐ 619	Darrel Akerfelds	.05	.02	.00
☐ 620	Ron Robinson	.05	.02	.00
☐ 621	Scott Radinsky	.08	.04	.01
☐ 622	Pete Smith	.05	.02	.00
☐ 623	Melido Perez	.08	.04	.01
☐ 624	Jerald Clark	.05	.02	.00
☐ 625	Carlos Martinez	.05	.02	.00
☐ 626	Wes Chamberlain	.40	.20	.04
☐ 627	Bobby Witt	.10	.05	.01
☐ 628	Ken Dayley	.05	.02	.00
☐ 629	John Barfield	.12	.06	.01
☐ 630	Bob Tewksbury	.05	.02	.00
☐ 631	Glenn Braggs	.05	.02	.00
☐ 632	Jim Neidlinger	.20	.10	.02
☐ 633	Tom Browning	.08	.04	.01
☐ 634	Kirk Gibson	.10	.05	.01
☐ 635	Rob Dibble	.08	.04	.01
☐ 636	Stolen Base Leaders (Rickey Henderson and Lou Brock in tuxedos)	.25	.12	.02
☐ 637	Jeff Montgomery	.08	.04	.01
☐ 638	Mike Schooler	.05	.02	.00
☐ 639	Storm Davis	.08	.04	.01
☐ 640	Rich Rodriguez	.12	.06	.01
☐ 641	Phil Bradley	.08	.04	.01
☐ 642	Kent Mercker	.12	.06	.01
☐ 643	Carlton Fisk	.12	.06	.01
☐ 644	Mike Bell	.12	.06	.01
☐ 645	Alex Fernandez	1.25	.60	.12
☐ 646	Juan Gonzalez	.40	.20	.04
☐ 647	Ken Hill	.08	.04	.01
☐ 648	Jeff Russell	.05	.02	.00
☐ 649	Chuck Malone	.10	.05	.01
☐ 650	Steve Buechele	.05	.02	.00
☐ 651	Mike Benjamin	.15	.07	.01
☐ 652	Tony Pena	.08	.04	.01
☐ 653	Trevor Wilson	.08	.04	.01
☐ 654	Alex Cole	.35	.17	.03
☐ 655	Roger Clemens	.20	.10	.02
☐ 656	The Bashing Years (Mark McGwire)	.25	.12	.02
☐ 657	Joe Grahe	.12	.06	.01
☐ 658	Jim Eisenreich	.05	.02	.00
☐ 659	Dan Gladden	.05	.02	.00
☐ 660	Steve Farr	.05	.02	.00
☐ 661	Bill Sampen	.08	.04	.01
☐ 662	Dave Rohde	.10	.05	.01
☐ 663	Mark Gardner	.08	.04	.01
☐ 664	Mike Simms	.15	.07	.01
☐ 665	Moises Alou	.25	.12	.02
☐ 666	Mickey Hatcher	.05	.02	.00
☐ 667	Jimmy Key	.08	.04	.01
☐ 668	John Wetteland	.08	.04	.01
☐ 669	John Smiley	.05	.02	.00
☐ 670	Jim Acker	.05	.02	.00
☐ 671	Pascual Perez	.08	.04	.01
☐ 672	Reggie Harris	.20	.10	.02
☐ 673	Matt Nokes	.08	.04	.01
☐ 674	Rafael Novoa	.15	.07	.01
☐ 675	Hensley Meulens	.20	.10	.02
☐ 676	Jeff M. Robinson	.05	.02	.00
☐ 677	Ground Breaking (new Comiskey Park; Carlton Fisk and Robin Ventura)	.15	.07	.01
☐ 678	Johnny Ray	.05	.02	.00
☐ 679	Greg Hibbard	.05	.02	.00
☐ 680	Paul Sorrento	.05	.02	.00
☐ 681	Mike Marshall	.08	.04	.01
☐ 682	Jim Clancy	.05	.02	.00
☐ 683	Rob Murphy	.05	.02	.00
☐ 684	Dave Schmidt	.05	.02	.00
☐ 685	Jeff Gray	.12	.06	.01
☐ 686	Mike Hartley	.12	.06	.01
☐ 687	Jeff King	.08	.04	.01
☐ 688	Stan Javier	.05	.02	.00
☐ 689	Bob Walk	.05	.02	.00
☐ 690	Jim Gott	.05	.02	.00
☐ 691	Mike LaCoss	.05	.02	.00
☐ 692	John Farrell	.05	.02	.00
☐ 693	Tim Leary	.08	.04	.01
☐ 694	Mike Walker	.10	.05	.01
☐ 695	Eric Plunk	.05	.02	.00
☐ 696	Mike Fetters	.05	.02	.00
☐ 697	Wayne Edwards	.08	.04	.01
☐ 698	Tim Drummond	.10	.05	.01
☐ 699	Willie Fraser	.05	.02	.00
☐ 700	Checklist 601-700	.10	.02	.00
☐ SP1	Michael Jordan SP	7.50	3.00	.50

1991 Upper Deck Ryan BB Heroes

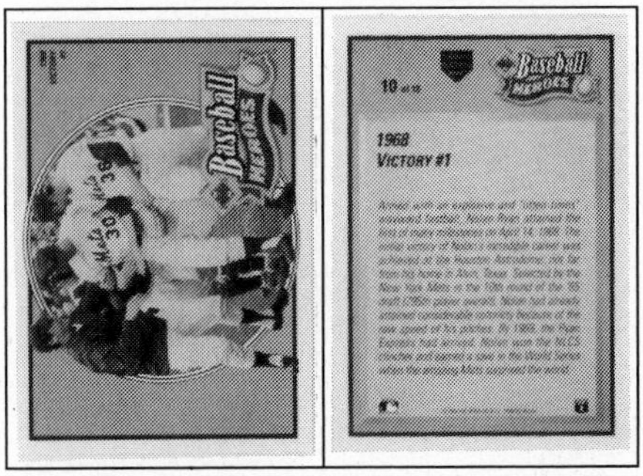

This nine-card standard size, 2 1/2" by 3 1/2", set was included in first series 1991 Upper Deck packs. The set honors Nolan Ryan and is numbered as a continuation of the Baseball Heroes set which began with Reggie Jackson in 1990. This set honors Ryan's long career and his place in Baseball History. Card number 18 features the artwork of Vernon Wells while the other cards are photos. The complete set price below does not include the signed Ryan card of which only 2500 were made. These Ryan cards were apparently issued on 100-card sheets with the following configuration: ten each of the nine Ryan Baseball Heroes cards, five Michael Jordan cards and five Baseball Heroes header cards. The Baseball Heroes header card is a standard size card which explains the continuation of the Baseball Heroes series on the back while the front just says Baseball Heroes.

	MINT	EXC	G-VG
COMPLETE SET (9)	10.00	5.00	1.00
COMMON PLAYER (10-18)	1.25	.60	.12
☐ 10 1968 Victory 1	1.25	.60	.12
☐ 11 1973 A Career Year	1.25	.60	.12
☐ 12 1975 Double Milestone	1.25	.60	.12
☐ 13 1979 Back Home	1.25	.60	.12
☐ 14 1981 All Time Leader	1.25	.60	.12
☐ 15 1989 5,000 K's	1.25	.60	.12
☐ 16 1990 6th No-Hitter	1.25	.60	.12
☐ 17 1990 And Still Counting	1.25	.60	.12
☐ 18 Checklist Card (Vernon Wells drawing with 5 poses of Ryan including each team he played for)	1.25	.60	.12
☐ xx Baseball Heroes (header card)	.50	.25	.05
☐ xx Nolan Ryan (Signed and Numbered out of 2500)	350.00	175.00	35.00

1989 USPS Legends Stamp Cards

The 1989 USPS Legends Stamp Cards set includes four cards each measuring 2 1/2" by 3 9/16". On the fronts, the cards depict the four baseball-related stamp designs which featured actual players. The outer front borders are white; the inner front borders are orange and purple. The vertically-oriented backs are beige and pink. These cards were sold by the U.S. Postal Service as a set (kit) for 7.95 along with the actual stamps, an attractive booklet, and other materials. The first printing of the set was sold out and so a second printing was made. The first printing cards did not have the USPS copyright logo. All the stamps in the set are drawings; for example, the Gehrig stamp was painted by noted sports artist, Bart Forbes. All of the stamps except Gehrig (25 cents) are 20-cent stamps.

	MINT	EXC	G-VG
COMPLETE SET (4)	15.00	7.50	1.50
COMMON PLAYER (1-4)	5.00	2.50	.50
☐ 1 Roberto Clemente Issued August 17, 1984	5.00	2.50	.50
☐ 2 Lou Gehrig Issued June 10, 1989	5.00	2.50	.50
☐ 3 Jackie Robinson Issued August 2, 1982	5.00	2.50	.50
☐ 4 Babe Ruth Issued July 6, 1983	6.00	3.00	.60

1989 Very Fine Juice Pirates

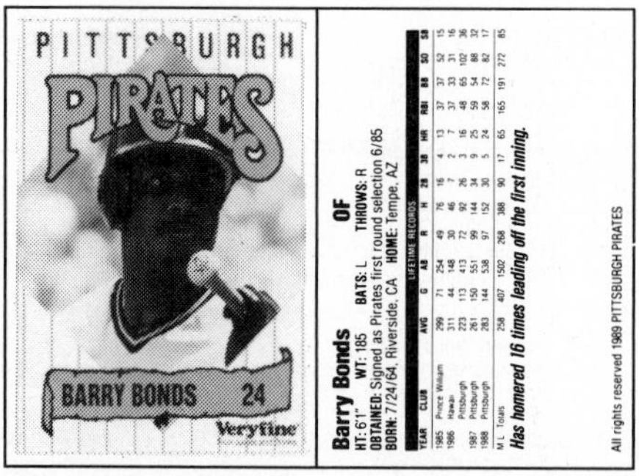

The 1989 Very Fine Juice Pittsburgh Pirates set is a 30-card set with cards measuring approximately 2 1/2" by 3 1/2" featuring the members of the 1989 Pittsburgh Pirates. This set was issued on two separate perforated sheets of 15 cards each. There was a coupon (expiring on 10/31/89) on the back that could be redeemed for a free can of juice. The cards are numbered by uniform number in the list below. The cards are very colorful.

	MINT	EXC	G-VG
COMPLETE SET (30)	12.50	6.25	1.25
COMMON PLAYER	.40	.20	.04
☐ 0 Junior Ortiz	.40	.20	.04
☐ 2 Gary Redus	.40	.20	.04
☐ 3 Jay Bell	.50	.25	.05
☐ 5 Sid Bream	.40	.20	.04
☐ 6 Rafael Belliard	.40	.20	.04
☐ 10 Jim Leyland MG	.50	.25	.05
☐ 11 Glenn Wilson	.40	.20	.04
☐ 12 Mike LaValliere	.40	.20	.04
☐ 13 Jose Lind	.50	.25	.05
☐ 14 Ken Oberkfell	.40	.20	.04
☐ 15 Doug Drabek	.75	.35	.07
☐ 16 Bob Kipper	.40	.20	.04
☐ 17 Bob Walk	.50	.25	.05
☐ 18 Andy Van Slyke	1.00	.50	.10
☐ 23 R.J. Reynolds	.50	.25	.05
☐ 24 Barry Bonds	2.00	1.00	.20
☐ 25 Bobby Bonilla	1.50	.75	.15
☐ 26 Neal Heaton	.40	.20	.04
☐ 30 Benny Distefano	.40	.20	.04
☐ 31 Ray Miller CO and 37 Tommy Sandt CO	.40	.20	.04
☐ 35 Jim Gott	.50	.25	.05
☐ 36 Bruce Kimm CO and 32 Gene Lamont CO	.40	.20	.04
☐ 39 Milt May CO and 45 Rich Donnelly CO	.40	.20	.04
☐ 41 Mike Dunne	.40	.20	.04
☐ 43 Bill Landrum	.50	.25	.05
☐ 44 John Cangelosi	.40	.20	.04
☐ 49 Jeff Robinson	.50	.25	.05
☐ 52 Dorn Taylor	.40	.20	.04
☐ 54 Brian Fisher	.40	.20	.04
☐ 57 John Smiley	.60	.30	.06

1985 Wendy's Tigers

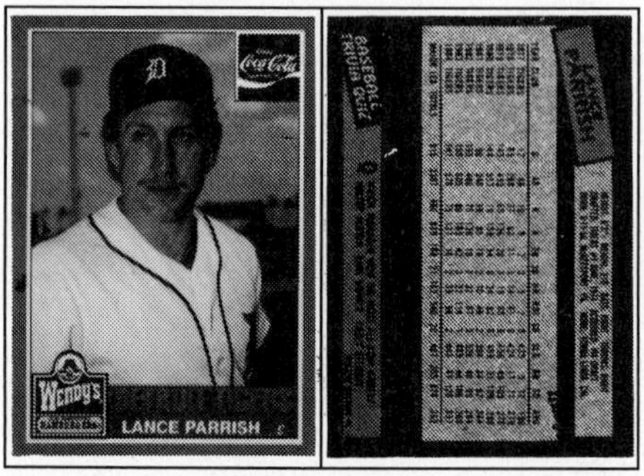

This 22-card set features Detroit Tigers; cards measure 2 1/2" by 3 1/2". The set was co-sponsored by Wendy's and Coca-Cola and was distributed in the Detroit metropolitan area. Coca-Cola purchasers were given a pack which contained three Tiger cards plus a header card. The orange-bordered player photos are different from those used by Topps in their regular set. The cards were produced by Topps as evidenced by the similarity of the card backs with the Topps regular set backs. The set is numbered on the back; the order corresponds to the alphabetical order of the player's names.

	MINT	EXC	G-VG
COMPLETE SET (22)	9.00	4.50	.90
COMMON PLAYER (1-22)	.25	.12	.02
☐ 1 Sparky Anderson MG (checklist back)	.60	.30	.06
☐ 2 Doug Bair	.25	.12	.02
☐ 3 Juan Berenguer	.25	.12	.02
☐ 4 Dave Bergman	.25	.12	.02
☐ 5 Tom Brookens	.25	.12	.02
☐ 6 Marty Castillo	.25	.12	.02
☐ 7 Darrell Evans	.50	.25	.05
☐ 8 Barbaro Garbey	.25	.12	.02
☐ 9 Kirk Gibson	1.50	.75	.15
☐ 10 Johnny Grubb	.25	.12	.02
☐ 11 Willie Hernandez	.35	.17	.03
☐ 12 Larry Herndon	.25	.12	.02
☐ 13 Rusty Kuntz	.25	.12	.02
☐ 14 Chet Lemon	.35	.17	.03
☐ 15 Aurelio Lopez	.25	.12	.02
☐ 16 Jack Morris	1.00	.50	.10
☐ 17 Lance Parrish	1.50	.75	.15
☐ 18 Dan Petry	.35	.17	.03
☐ 19 Bill Scherrer	.25	.12	.02
☐ 20 Alan Trammell	2.00	1.00	.20
☐ 21 Lou Whitaker	1.00	.50	.10
☐ 22 Milt Wilcox	.25	.12	.02

1982 Wheaties Indians

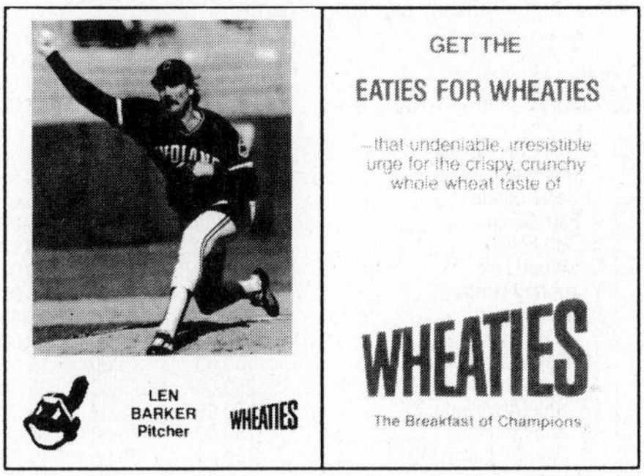

The cards in this 30-card set measure 2 13/16" by 4 1/8". This set of Cleveland Indians baseball players was co-produced by the Indians baseball club and Wheaties, whose respective logos appear on the front of every card. The cards were given away in groups of 10 as a promotion during games on May 30 (1-10), June 19 (11-20) and July 16, 1982 (21-30). The manager (MG), four coaches (CO), and 25 players are featured in a simple format of a color picture, player name and position. The cards are not numbered and the backs contain a Wheaties ad. The set was later sold at the Cleveland Indians gift shop. The cards are ordered below alphabetically within groups of ten as they were issued.

	MINT	EXC	G-VG
COMPLETE SET (30)	13.50	6.00	1.00
COMMON PLAYER (1-30)	.40	.20	.04
☐ 1 Bert Blyleven	1.00	.50	.10
☐ 2 Joe Charboneau	.50	.25	.05
☐ 3 Jerry Dybzinski	.40	.20	.04
☐ 4 Dave Garcia MG	.40	.20	.04
☐ 5 Toby Harrah	.50	.25	.05
☐ 6 Ron Hassey	.40	.20	.04
☐ 7 Dennis Lewallyn	.40	.20	.04
☐ 8 Rick Manning	.40	.20	.04
☐ 9 Tommy McCraw CO	.40	.20	.04
☐ 10 Rick Waits	.40	.20	.04
☐ 11 Chris Bando	.40	.20	.04
☐ 12 Len Barker	.50	.25	.05
☐ 13 Tom Brennan	.40	.20	.04
☐ 14 Rodney Craig	.40	.20	.04
☐ 15 Mike Fischlin	.40	.20	.04
☐ 16 Johnny Goryl CO	.40	.20	.04
☐ 17 Mel Queen CO	.40	.20	.04
☐ 18 Lary Sorensen	.40	.20	.04
☐ 19 Andre Thornton	.60	.30	.06
☐ 20 Eddie Whitson	.60	.30	.06
☐ 21 Alan Bannister	.40	.20	.04
☐ 22 John Denny	.50	.25	.05
☐ 23 Miguel Dilone	.40	.20	.04
☐ 24 Mike Hargrove	.60	.30	.06
☐ 25 Von Hayes	1.25	.60	.12
☐ 26 Bake McBride	.50	.25	.05
☐ 27 Jack Perconte	.40	.20	.04
☐ 28 Dennis Sommers CO	.40	.20	.04
☐ 29 Dan Spillner	.40	.20	.04
☐ 30 Rick Sutcliffe	.75	.35	.07

1983 Wheaties Indians

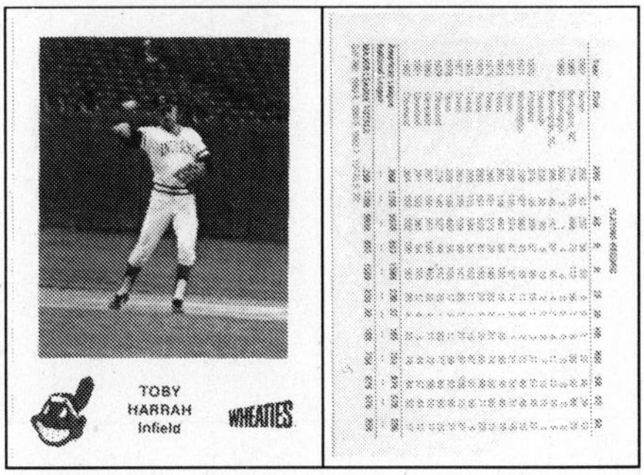

The cards in this 32-card set measure approximately 2 13/16" by 4 1/8". The full color set of 1983 Wheaties Indians is quite similar to the Wheaties set of 1982. The backs, however, are significantly different. They contain complete career playing records of the players. The complete sets were given away at the ball park on May 15, 1983. The set was later made available at the Indians Gift Shop. The manager (MG) and several coaches (CO) are included in the set. The cards below are ordered alphabetically by the subject's name.

	MINT	EXC	G-VG
COMPLETE SET (32)	8.00	4.00	.80
COMMON PLAYER (1-32)	.25	.12	.02
☐ 1 Bud Anderson	.25	.12	.02
☐ 2 Jay Baller	.25	.12	.02
☐ 3 Chris Bando	.25	.12	.02
☐ 4 Alan Bannister	.25	.12	.02
☐ 5 Len Barker	.35	.17	.03
☐ 6 Bert Blyleven	.75	.35	.07
☐ 7 Wil Culmer	.25	.12	.02
☐ 8 Miguel Dilone	.25	.12	.02
☐ 9 Juan Eichelberger	.25	.12	.02
☐ 10 Jim Essian	.25	.12	.02
☐ 11 Mike Ferraro MG	.25	.12	.02
☐ 12 Mike Fischlin	.25	.12	.02
☐ 13 Julio Franco	1.00	.50	.10
☐ 14 Ed Glynn	.25	.12	.02
☐ 15 Johnny Goryl CO	.25	.12	.02
☐ 16 Mike Hargrove	.35	.17	.03
☐ 17 Toby Harrah	.35	.17	.03
☐ 18 Ron Hassey	.25	.12	.02
☐ 19 Neal Heaton	.25	.12	.02
☐ 20 Rick Manning	.25	.12	.02
☐ 21 Bake McBride	.35	.17	.03
☐ 22 Don McMahon CO	.25	.12	.02
☐ 23 Ed Napoleon CO	.25	.12	.02
☐ 24 Broderick Perkins	.25	.12	.02
☐ 25 Dennis Sommers CO	.25	.12	.02
☐ 26 Lary Sorensen	.25	.12	.02
☐ 27 Dan Spillner	.25	.12	.02
☐ 28 Rick Sutcliffe	.75	.35	.07
☐ 29 Andre Thornton	.50	.25	.05
☐ 30 Manny Trillo	.25	.12	.02
☐ 31 George Vukovich	.25	.12	.02
☐ 32 Rick Waits	.25	.12	.02

1984 Wheaties Indians

The cards in this 29-card set measure approximately 2 13/16" by 4 1/8". For the third straight year, Wheaties distributed a set of Cleveland Indians baseball cards. These over-sized cards were passed out at a Baseball Card Day at the Cleveland Stadium. Similar in appearance to the cards of the past two years, both the Indians and the Wheaties logos appear on the obverse, along with the name, team and position. Cards are numbered on the back by the player's uniform number.

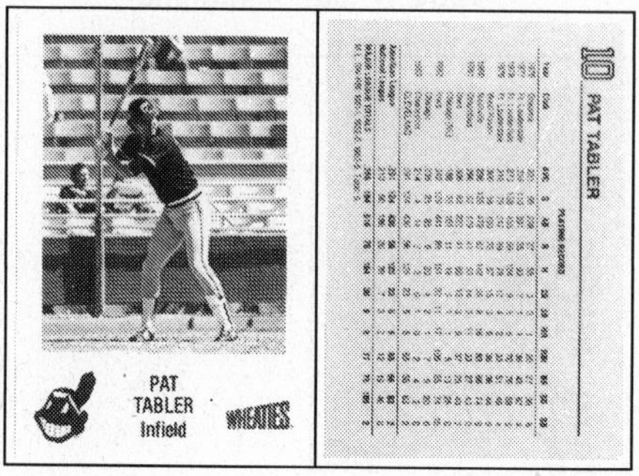

	MINT	EXC	G-VG
COMPLETE SET (29)	8.00	4.00	.80
COMMON PLAYER	.25	.12	.02
☐ 2 Brett Butler	.60	.30	.06
☐ 4 Tony Bernazard	.35	.17	.03
☐ 8 Carmelo Castillo	.25	.12	.02
☐ 10 Pat Tabler	.35	.17	.03
☐ 13 Ernie Camacho	.35	.17	.03
☐ 14 Julio Franco	.75	.35	.07
☐ 15 Broderick Perkins	.25	.12	.02
☐ 16 Jerry Willard	.25	.12	.02
☐ 18 Pat Corrales MG	.25	.12	.02
☐ 21 Mike Hargrove	.35	.17	.03
☐ 22 Mike Fischlin	.25	.12	.02
☐ 23 Chris Bando	.25	.12	.02
☐ 24 George Vukovich	.25	.12	.02
☐ 26 Brook Jacoby	.50	.25	.05
☐ 27 Steve Farr	.35	.17	.03
☐ 28 Bert Blyleven	.60	.30	.06
☐ 29 Andre Thornton	.50	.25	.05
☐ 30 Joe Carter	1.50	.75	.15
☐ 31 Steve Comer	.25	.12	.02
☐ 33 Roy Smith	.25	.12	.02
☐ 34 Mel Hall	.50	.25	.05
☐ 36 Jamie Easterly	.25	.12	.02
☐ 37 Don Schulze	.25	.12	.02
☐ 38 Luis Aponte	.25	.12	.02
☐ 44 Neal Heaton	.25	.12	.02
☐ 46 Mike Jeffcoat	.25	.12	.02
☐ 54 Tom Waddell	.25	.12	.02
☐ xx Indians Coaches: (unnumbered) John Goryl, Dennis Sommers, Ed Napoleon, Bobby Bonds, Don McMahon	.25	.12	.02
☐ xx Tom-E-Hawk (Mascot) (unnumbered)	.25	.12	.02

1954 Wilson

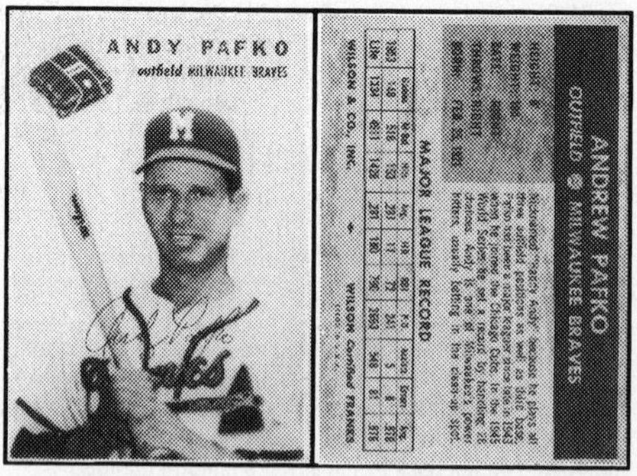

The cards in this 20-card set measure approximately 2 5/8" by 3 3/4". The 1954 "Wilson Weiners" set contains 20 full color, unnumbered cards. The obverse design of a package of hot dogs appearing to fly through the air is a distinctive feature of this set. Uncut sheets have been seen. Cards are numbered below alphabetically by player's name.

	NRMT	VG-E	GOOD
COMPLETE SET (20)	6500.00	3000.00	600.00
COMMON PLAYER (1-20)	150.00	75.00	15.00
☐ 1 Roy Campanella	750.00	375.00	75.00
☐ 2 Del Ennis	150.00	75.00	15.00
☐ 3 Carl Erskine	200.00	100.00	20.00
☐ 4 Ferris Fain	150.00	75.00	15.00
☐ 5 Bob Feller	600.00	300.00	60.00
☐ 6 Nelson Fox	300.00	150.00	30.00
☐ 7 Johnny Groth	150.00	75.00	15.00
☐ 8 Stan Hack	150.00	75.00	15.00
☐ 9 Gil Hodges	400.00	200.00	40.00
☐ 10 Ray Jablonski	150.00	75.00	15.00
☐ 11 Harvey Kuenn	250.00	125.00	25.00
☐ 12 Roy McMillan	150.00	75.00	15.00
☐ 13 Andy Pafko	150.00	75.00	15.00
☐ 14 Paul Richards MG	150.00	75.00	15.00
☐ 15 Hank Sauer	150.00	75.00	15.00
☐ 16 Red Schoendienst	400.00	200.00	40.00
☐ 17 Enos Slaughter	450.00	225.00	45.00
☐ 18 Vern Stephens	150.00	75.00	15.00
☐ 19 Sammy White	150.00	75.00	15.00
☐ 20 Ted Williams	2500.00	1000.00	250.00

1990 Wonder Bread Stars

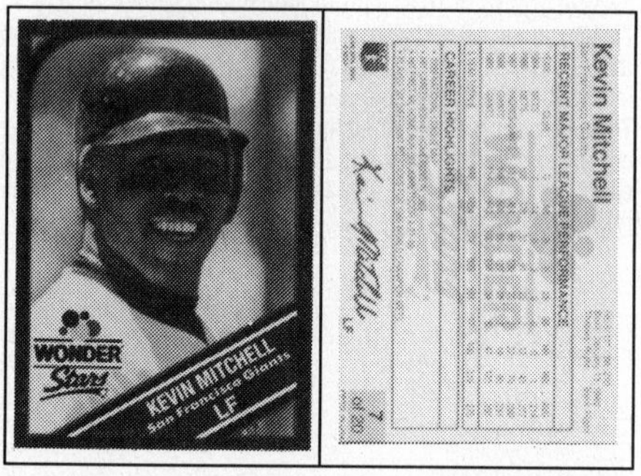

The 1990 Wonder Bread set was issued in 1990 by MSA (Michael Schechter Associates) in conjunction with Wonder Bread. One card was issued inside each specially marked package of Wonder Bread. Cards were available in grocery stores through June 15, 1990. The card was sealed in a pouch in the bread wrapper. This standard-size (2 1/2" by 3 1/2") card set was issued without logos like many of the sets produced by MSA. Cards were printed on thin stock and hence were easily creased during bread handling making the set more difficult to put together one card at a time for condition-conscious collectors. Cards are numbered on the back in the lower right corner. Wonder Bread also offered sets in uncut sheet form to collectors mailing in with 3.00 and five proofs of purchase.

	MINT	EXC	G-VG
COMPLETE SET (20)	10.00	5.00	1.00
COMMON PLAYER (1-20)	.20	.10	.02
☐ 1 Bo Jackson	1.25	.60	.12
☐ 2 Roger Clemens	.75	.35	.07
☐ 3 Jim Abbott	.50	.25	.05
☐ 4 Orel Hershiser	.40	.20	.04
☐ 5 Ozzie Smith	.40	.20	.04
☐ 6 Don Mattingly	1.00	.50	.10
☐ 7 Kevin Mitchell	.50	.25	.05
☐ 8 Jerome Walton	.50	.25	.05
☐ 9 Kirby Puckett	.50	.25	.05

☐ 10 Darryl Strawberry	.50	.25	.05
☐ 11 Robin Yount	.50	.25	.05
☐ 12 Tony Gwynn	.50	.25	.05
☐ 13 Alan Trammell	.40	.20	.04
☐ 14 Jose Canseco	1.00	.50	.10
☐ 15 Greg Swindell	.20	.10	.02
☐ 16 Nolan Ryan	1.00	.50	.10
☐ 17 Howard Johnson	.30	.15	.03
☐ 18 Ken Griffey Jr.	1.25	.60	.12
☐ 19 Will Clark	.75	.35	.07
☐ 20 Ryne Sandberg	.75	.35	.07

1985 Woolworth's

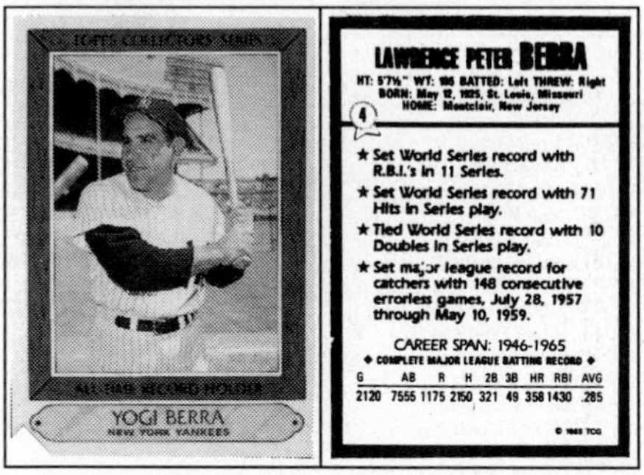

This 44-card set features color as well as black and white cards of All Time Record Holders. The cards are standard size (2 1/2" by 3 1/2") and are printed with blue ink on an orange and white back. The set was produced for Woolworth's by Topps and was packaged in a colorful box which contained a checklist of the cards in the set on the back panel. The numerical order of the cards coincides alphabetically with player's name.

	MINT	EXC	G-VG
COMPLETE SET (44)	4.00	2.00	.40
COMMON PLAYER (1-44)	.07	.03	.01
☐ 1 Hank Aaron	.30	.15	.03
☐ 2 Grover C. Alexander	.07	.03	.01
☐ 3 Ernie Banks	.15	.07	.01
☐ 4 Yogi Berra	.25	.12	.02
☐ 5 Lou Brock	.15	.07	.01
☐ 6 Steve Carlton	.15	.07	.01
☐ 7 Jack Chesbro	.07	.03	.01
☐ 8 Ty Cobb	.30	.15	.03
☐ 9 Sam Crawford	.07	.03	.01
☐ 10 Rollie Fingers	.07	.03	.01
☐ 11 Whitey Ford	.15	.07	.01
☐ 12 John Frederick	.07	.03	.01
☐ 13 Frankie Frisch	.07	.03	.01
☐ 14 Lou Gehrig	.30	.15	.03
☐ 15 Jim Gentile	.07	.03	.01
☐ 16 Dwight Gooden	.30	.15	.03
☐ 17 Rickey Henderson	.30	.15	.03
☐ 18 Rogers Hornsby	.10	.05	.01
☐ 19 Frank Howard	.07	.03	.01
☐ 20 Cliff Johnson	.07	.03	.01
☐ 21 Walter Johnson	.15	.07	.01
☐ 22 Hub Leonard	.07	.03	.01
☐ 23 Mickey Mantle	.50	.25	.05
☐ 24 Roger Maris	.15	.07	.01
☐ 25 Christy Mathewson	.10	.05	.01
☐ 26 Willie Mays	.30	.15	.03
☐ 27 Stan Musial	.20	.10	.02
☐ 28 Don Quisenberry	.07	.03	.01
☐ 29 Frank Robinson	.07	.03	.01
☐ 30 Pete Rose	.30	.15	.03
☐ 31 Babe Ruth	.50	.25	.05
☐ 32 Nolan Ryan	.35	.17	.03
☐ 33 George Sisler	.07	.03	.01
☐ 34 Tris Speaker	.10	.05	.01
☐ 35 Ed Walsh	.07	.03	.01
☐ 36 Lloyd Waner	.07	.03	.01
☐ 37 Earl Webb	.07	.03	.01
☐ 38 Ted Williams	.25	.12	.02
☐ 39 Maury Wills	.07	.03	.01
☐ 40 Hack Wilson	.07	.03	.01
☐ 41 Owen Wilson	.07	.03	.01
☐ 42 Willie Wilson	.07	.03	.01
☐ 43 Rudy York	.07	.03	.01
☐ 44 Cy Young	.10	.05	.01

1986 Woolworth's

This boxed set of 33 cards was produced by Topps for Woolworth's variety stores. The set features players who hold or have held hitting, home run or RBI titles. Cards are the standard 2 1/2" by 3 1/2" and have a glossy finish. The card fronts are bordered in yellow with the subtitle "Topps Collectors' Series" across the top. The card backs are printed in green and blue ink on white card stock. The custom box gives the set checklist on the back.

	MINT	EXC	G-VG
COMPLETE SET (33)	4.00	2.00	.40
COMMON PLAYER (1-33)	.07	.03	.01
☐ 1 Tony Armas	.07	.03	.01
☐ 2 Don Baylor	.10	.05	.01
☐ 3 Wade Boggs	.45	.22	.04
☐ 4 George Brett	.35	.17	.03
☐ 5 Bill Buckner	.07	.03	.01
☐ 6 Rod Carew	.30	.15	.03
☐ 7 Gary Carter	.15	.07	.01
☐ 8 Cecil Cooper	.10	.05	.01
☐ 9 Darrell Evans	.07	.03	.01
☐ 10 Dwight Evans	.10	.05	.01
☐ 11 George Foster	.10	.05	.01
☐ 12 Bob Grich	.07	.03	.01
☐ 13 Tony Gwynn	.30	.15	.03
☐ 14 Keith Hernandez	.15	.07	.01
☐ 15 Reggie Jackson	.40	.20	.04
☐ 16 Dave Kingman	.10	.05	.01
☐ 17 Carney Lansford	.10	.05	.01
☐ 18 Fred Lynn	.10	.05	.01
☐ 19 Bill Madlock	.07	.03	.01
☐ 20 Don Mattingly	.60	.30	.06
☐ 21 Willie McGee	.15	.07	.01
☐ 22 Hal McRae	.07	.03	.01
☐ 23 Dale Murphy	.30	.15	.03
☐ 24 Eddie Murray	.25	.12	.02
☐ 25 Ben Oglivie	.07	.03	.01
☐ 26 Al Oliver	.07	.03	.01
☐ 27 Dave Parker	.10	.05	.01
☐ 28 Jim Rice	.15	.07	.01
☐ 29 Pete Rose	.45	.22	.04
☐ 30 Mike Schmidt	.50	.25	.05
☐ 31 Gorman Thomas	.10	.05	.01
☐ 32 Willie Wilson	.10	.05	.01
☐ 33 Dave Winfield	.20	.10	.02

1987 Woolworth's Highlights

Topps produced this 33-card set for Woolworth's stores. The set is subtitled "Topps Collectors' Series Baseball Highlights" and consists of high gloss card fronts with full-color photos. Cards are the standard 2 1/2" by 3 1/2". The cards show and describe highlights of the previous season. The card backs are printed in gold and purple and are numbered. The set was sold nationally in Woolworth's for a 1.99 suggested retail price.

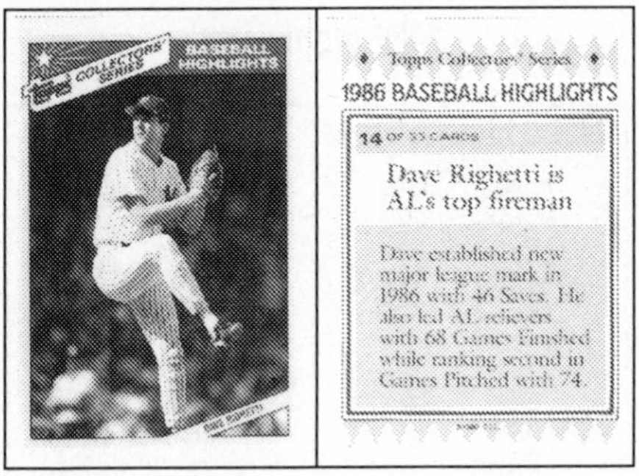

	MINT	EXC	G-VG
COMPLETE SET (33)	4.00	2.00	.40
COMMON PLAYER (1-33)	.07	.03	.01
□ 1 Steve Carlton	.25	.12	.02
□ 2 Cecil Cooper	.10	.05	.01
□ 3 Rickey Henderson	.45	.22	.04
□ 4 Reggie Jackson	.35	.17	.03
□ 5 Jim Rice	.15	.07	.01
□ 6 Don Sutton	.20	.10	.02
□ 7 Roger Clemens	.40	.20	.04
□ 8 Mike Schmidt	.45	.22	.04
□ 9 Jesse Barfield	.15	.07	.01
□ 10 Wade Boggs	.45	.22	.04
□ 11 Tim Raines	.20	.10	.02
□ 12 Jose Canseco	.60	.30	.06
□ 13 Todd Worrell	.10	.05	.01
□ 14 Dave Righetti	.10	.05	.01
□ 15 Don Mattingly	.60	.30	.06
□ 16 Tony Gwynn	.30	.15	.03
□ 17 Marty Barrett	.07	.03	.01
□ 18 Mike Scott	.15	.07	.01
□ 19 Bruce Hurst	.10	.05	.01
□ 20 Calvin Schiraldi	.07	.03	.01
□ 21 Dwight Evans	.15	.07	.01
□ 22 Dave Henderson	.07	.03	.01
□ 23 Len Dykstra	.15	.07	.01
□ 24 Bob Ojeda	.07	.03	.01
□ 25 Gary Carter	.15	.07	.01
□ 26 Ron Darling	.10	.05	.01
□ 27 Jim Rice	.15	.07	.01
□ 28 Bruce Hurst	.10	.05	.01
□ 29 Darryl Strawberry	.45	.22	.04
□ 30 Ray Knight	.10	.05	.01
□ 31 Keith Hernandez	.15	.07	.01
□ 32 Mets Celebration	.07	.03	.01
□ 33 Ray Knight	.07	.03	.01

1988 Woolworth's Highlights

Topps produced this 33-card set for Woolworth's stores. The set is subtitled "Topps Collectors' Series Baseball Highlights" and consists of high gloss card fronts with full-color photos. Cards are the standard 2 1/2" by 3 1/2". The cards show and describe highlights of the previous season. Cards 19-33 commemorate the World Series with highlights and key players of each game in the series. The card backs are printed in red and blue on white card stock and are numbered. The set was sold nationally in Woolworth's for a 1.99 suggested retail price.

	MINT	EXC	G-VG
COMPLETE SET (33)	4.00	2.00	.40
COMMON PLAYER (1-33)	.07	.03	.01

□ 1 Don Baylor	.10	.05	.01
□ 2 Vince Coleman	.15	.07	.01
□ 3 Darrell Evans	.07	.03	.01
□ 4 Don Mattingly	.60	.30	.06
□ 5 Eddie Murray	.30	.15	.03
□ 6 Nolan Ryan	.60	.30	.06
□ 7 Mike Schmidt	.50	.25	.05
□ 8 Andre Dawson	.15	.07	.01
□ 9 George Bell	.15	.07	.01
□ 10 Steve Bedrosian	.07	.03	.01
□ 11 Roger Clemens	.45	.22	.04
□ 12 Tony Gwynn	.30	.15	.03
□ 13 Wade Boggs	.45	.22	.04
□ 14 Benny Santiago	.20	.10	.02
□ 15 Mark McGwire UER (referenced on card back as NL ROY, sic)	.60	.30	.06
□ 16 Dave Righetti	.10	.05	.01
□ 17 Jeffrey Leonard	.07	.03	.01
□ 18 Gary Gaetti	.07	.03	.01
□ 19 Frank Viola WS1	.10	.05	.01
□ 20 Dan Gladden WS1	.07	.03	.01
□ 21 Bert Blyleven WS2	.10	.05	.01
□ 22 Gary Gaetti WS2	.10	.05	.01
□ 23 John Tudor WS3	.10	.05	.01
□ 24 Todd Worrell WS3	.10	.05	.01
□ 25 Tom Lawless WS4	.07	.03	.01
□ 26 Willie McGee WS4	.10	.05	.01
□ 27 Danny Cox WS5	.07	.03	.01
□ 28 Curt Ford WS5	.07	.03	.01
□ 29 Don Baylor WS6	.10	.05	.01
□ 30 Kent Hrbek WS6	.10	.05	.01
□ 31 Kirby Puckett WS7	.25	.12	.02
□ 32 Greg Gagne WS7	.07	.03	.01
□ 33 Frank Viola WS-MVP	.12	.06	.01

1989 Woolworth's Highlights

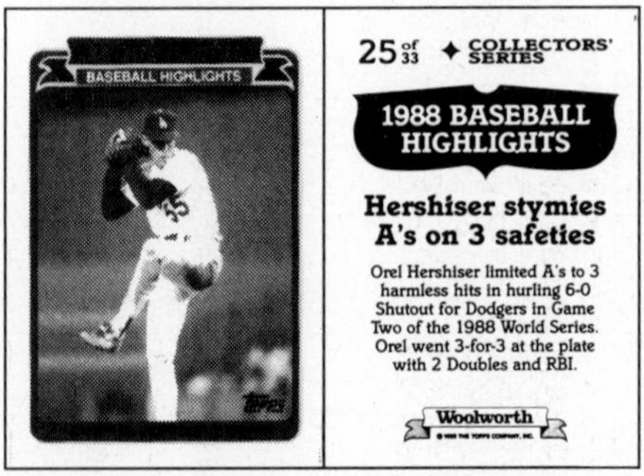

The 1989 Woolworth's Highlights set contains 33 standard-size (2 1/2" by 3 1/2") glossy cards. The fronts have red and white borders. The vertically-oriented backs are yellow and red, and describe highlights from the 1988 season including the World Series. The cards were distributed through Woolworth stores as a boxed set.

	MINT	EXC	G-VG
COMPLETE SET (33)	4.00	2.00	.40
COMMON PLAYER (1-33)	.07	.03	.01
☐ 1 Jose Canseco	.60	.30	.06
☐ 2 Kirk Gibson	.20	.10	.02
☐ 3 Frank Viola	.15	.07	.01
☐ 4 Orel Hershiser	.20	.10	.02
☐ 5 Walt Weiss	.20	.10	.02
☐ 6 Chris Sabo	.30	.15	.03
☐ 7 George Bell	.15	.07	.01
☐ 8 Wade Boggs	.45	.22	.04
☐ 9 Tom Browning	.10	.05	.01
☐ 10 Gary Carter	.15	.07	.01
☐ 11 Andre Dawson	.20	.10	.02
☐ 12 John Franco	.10	.05	.01
☐ 13 Randy Johnson	.10	.05	.01
☐ 14 Doug Jones	.07	.03	.01
☐ 15 Kevin McReynolds	.15	.07	.01
☐ 16 Gene Nelson	.07	.03	.01
☐ 17 Jeff Reardon	.10	.05	.01
☐ 18 Pat Tabler	.07	.03	.01
☐ 19 Tim Belcher	.10	.05	.01
☐ 20 Dennis Eckersley	.15	.07	.01
☐ 21 Orel Hershiser	.20	.10	.02
☐ 22 Gregg Jefferies	.50	.25	.05
☐ 23 Jose Canseco	.60	.30	.06
☐ 24 Kirk Gibson	.20	.10	.02
☐ 25 Orel Hershiser	.20	.10	.02
☐ 26 Mike Marshall	.10	.05	.01
☐ 27 Mark McGwire	.50	.25	.05
☐ 28 Rick Honeycutt	.07	.03	.01
☐ 29 Tim Belcher	.10	.05	.01
☐ 30 Jay Howell	.07	.03	.01
☐ 31 Mickey Hatcher	.07	.03	.01
☐ 32 Mike Davis	.07	.03	.01
☐ 33 Orel Hershiser	.20	.10	.02

1990 Woolworth Highlights

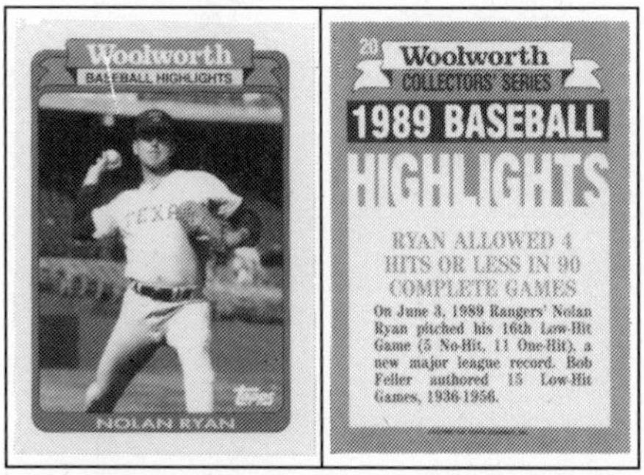

The 1990 Woolworth set is a 33-card set highlighting some of the more important events of the 1989 season. This set which has standard-size cards, 2 1/2" by 3 1/2", is broken down between major award winners, career highlights, and post-season heroes. The first six cards of the set feature the award winners while the last 11 cards of the set feature post-season heroes.

	MINT	EXC	G-VG
COMPLETE SET (33)	4.00	2.00	.40
COMMON PLAYER (1-33)	.07	.03	.01
☐ 1 Robin Yount MVP	.30	.15	.03
☐ 2 Kevin Mitchell MVP	.30	.15	.03
☐ 3 Bret Saberhagen CY	.20	.10	.02
☐ 4 Mark Davis CY	.10	.05	.01
☐ 5 Gregg Olson ROY	.20	.10	.02
☐ 6 Jerome Walton ROY	.30	.15	.03
☐ 7 Bert Blyleven	.10	.05	.01
☐ 8 Wade Boggs	.40	.20	.04
☐ 9 George Brett	.30	.15	.03
☐ 10 Vince Coleman	.20	.10	.02
☐ 11 Andre Dawson	.20	.10	.02
☐ 12 Dwight Evans	.10	.05	.01
☐ 13 Carlton Fisk	.20	.10	.02
☐ 14 Rickey Henderson	.50	.25	.05
☐ 15 Dale Murphy	.30	.15	.03
☐ 16 Eddie Murray	.30	.15	.03
☐ 17 Jeff Reardon	.10	.05	.01
☐ 18 Rick Reuschel	.10	.05	.01
☐ 19 Cal Ripken	.25	.12	.02
☐ 20 Nolan Ryan	.50	.25	.05
☐ 21 Ryne Sandberg	.40	.20	.04
☐ 22 Robin Yount	.30	.15	.03
☐ 23 Rickey Henderson	.50	.25	.05
☐ 24 Will Clark	.40	.20	.04
☐ 25 Dave Stewart	.15	.07	.01
☐ 26 Walt Weiss	.10	.05	.01
☐ 27 Mike Moore	.07	.03	.01
☐ 28 Terry Steinbach	.10	.05	.01
☐ 29 Dave Henderson	.07	.03	.01
☐ 30 Matt Williams	.30	.15	.03
☐ 31 Rickey Henderson	.50	.25	.05
☐ 32 Kevin Mitchell	.25	.12	.02
☐ 33 Dave Stewart	.15	.07	.01

1931 W517

The cards in this 54-card set measure 3" by 4". This 1931 set of numbered, blank backed cards was placed in the "W" category in the ACC because (1) its producer was unknown and (2) it was issued in strips of three. The photo is black and white but the entire obverse of each card is generally found tinted in tones of sepia, blue, green, yellow, rose, black or gray. The cards are numbered in a small circle on the front. A solid dark line at one end of a card entitled the purchaser to another piece of candy as a prize. There are two different cards of both Babe Ruth and Mickey Cochrane.

	EX-MT	VG-E	GOOD
COMPLETE SET (54)	6500.00	3000.00	750.00
COMMON PLAYER (1-54)	40.00	20.00	4.00
☐ 1 Earl Combs	80.00	40.00	8.00
☐ 2 Pie Traynor	100.00	50.00	10.00
☐ 3 Eddie Rousch	100.00	50.00	10.00
☐ 4 Babe Ruth	1250.00	500.00	125.00
☐ 5 Chalmer Cissell	40.00	20.00	4.00
☐ 6 Bill Sherdel	40.00	20.00	4.00
☐ 7 Bill Shore	40.00	20.00	4.00
☐ 8 George Earnshaw	40.00	20.00	4.00
☐ 9 Bucky Harris	80.00	40.00	8.00
☐ 10 Charlie Klein	100.00	50.00	10.00
☐ 11 George Kelly	80.00	40.00	8.00
☐ 12 Travis Jackson	80.00	40.00	8.00
☐ 13 Willie Kamm	40.00	20.00	4.00
☐ 14 Harry Heilman	100.00	50.00	10.00
☐ 15 Grover Alexander	125.00	60.00	12.50
☐ 16 Frank Frisch	100.00	50.00	10.00
☐ 17 Jack Quinn	40.00	20.00	4.00
☐ 18 Cy Williams	40.00	20.00	4.00
☐ 19 Kiki Cuyler	80.00	40.00	8.00

☐ 20 Babe Ruth	1500.00	600.00	150.00
☐ 21 Jimmy Foxx	200.00	100.00	20.00
☐ 22 Jimmy Dykes	50.00	25.00	5.00
☐ 23 Bill Terry	100.00	50.00	10.00
☐ 24 Freddy Lindstrom	80.00	40.00	8.00
☐ 25 Hugh Critz	40.00	20.00	4.00
☐ 26 Pete Donahue	40.00	20.00	4.00
☐ 27 Tony Lazzeri	60.00	30.00	6.00
☐ 28 Heine Manush	80.00	40.00	8.00
☐ 29 Chick Hafey	80.00	40.00	8.00
☐ 30 Melvin Ott	150.00	75.00	15.00
☐ 31 Bing Miller	40.00	20.00	4.00
☐ 32 George Haas	40.00	20.00	4.00
☐ 33 Lefty O'Doul	60.00	30.00	6.00
☐ 34 Paul Waner	80.00	40.00	8.00
☐ 35 Lou Gehrig	750.00	300.00	75.00
☐ 36 Dazzy Vance	80.00	40.00	8.00
☐ 37 Mickey Cochrane	125.00	60.00	12.50
☐ 38 Rogers Hornsby	200.00	100.00	20.00
☐ 39 Lefty Grove	150.00	75.00	15.00
☐ 40 Al Simmons	100.00	50.00	10.00
☐ 41 Rube Walberg	40.00	20.00	4.00
☐ 42 Hack Wilson	125.00	60.00	12.50
☐ 43 Art Shires	40.00	20.00	4.00
☐ 44 Sammy Hale	40.00	20.00	4.00
☐ 45 Ted Lyons	80.00	40.00	8.00
☐ 46 Joe Sewell	80.00	40.00	8.00
☐ 47 Goose Goslin	80.00	40.00	8.00
☐ 48 Lou Fonseca	40.00	20.00	4.00
☐ 49 Bob Meusel	50.00	25.00	5.00
☐ 50 Lu Blue	40.00	20.00	4.00
☐ 51 Earl Averill	80.00	40.00	8.00
☐ 52 Eddy Collins	100.00	50.00	10.00
☐ 53 Joe Judge	40.00	20.00	4.00
☐ 54 Mickey Cochrane	125.00	60.00	12.50

W576 1950-56 Callahan HOF

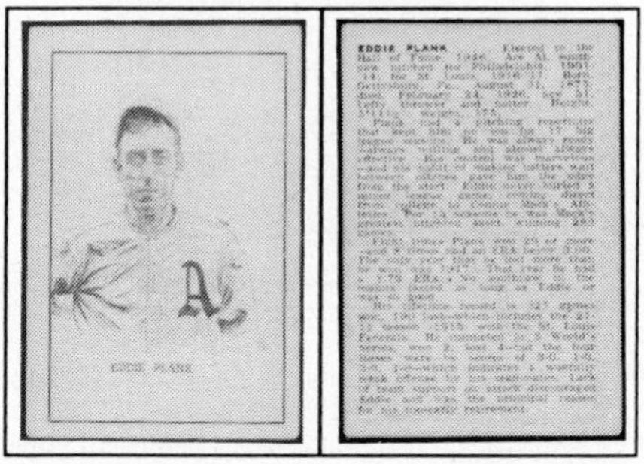

The cards in this 82-card set measure 1 3/4" by 2 1/2". The 1950-56 Callahan Hall of Fame set was issued over a number of years at the Baseball Hall of Fame museum in Cooperstown, New York. New cards were added to the set each year when new members were inducted into the Hall of Fame. The cards with (2) in the checklist exist with two different biographies. The year of each card's first inclusion in the set is also given in parentheses; those not listed parenthetically below were issued in 1950 as well as in all the succeeding years and are hence the most common. Naturally the supply of cards is directly related to how many years a player was included in the set; cards that were not issued until 1955 are much scarcer than those printed all the years between 1950 and 1956. The catalog designation is W576. One frequently finds "complete" sets in the original box; take care to investigate the year of issue, the set may be complete in the sense of all the cards issued up to a certain year, but not all 82 cards below. For example, a "complete" 1950 set would obviously not include any of the cards marked below with ('52), ('54), or ('55) as none of those cards existed in 1950 since those respective players had not yet been inducted. The complete set price below refers to a set including all 83 cards below. Since the cards are unnumbered, they are numbered below for reference alphabetically by player's name.

	NRMT	VG-E	GOOD
COMPLETE SET (83)	500.00	200.00	40.00
COMMON PLAYER ('50)	2.00	1.00	.20
COMMON PLAYER ('52)	3.00	1.50	.30
COMMON PLAYER ('54)	4.00	2.00	.40
COMMON PLAYER ('55)	6.00	3.00	.60
☐ 1 Grover Alexander	3.00	1.50	.30
☐ 2 Cap Anson	2.00	1.00	.20
☐ 3 Frank Baker ('55)	6.00	3.00	.60
☐ 4 Edward Barrow ('54)	4.00	2.00	.40
☐ 5 Chief Bender(2)('54)	4.00	2.00	.40
☐ 6 Roger Bresnahan	2.00	1.00	.20
☐ 7 Dan Brouthers	2.00	1.00	.20
☐ 8 Mordecai Brown	2.00	1.00	.20
☐ 9 Morgan Bulkeley	2.00	1.00	.20
☐ 10 Jesse Burkett	2.00	1.00	.20
☐ 11 Alexander Cartwright	2.00	1.00	.20
☐ 12 Henry Chadwick	2.00	1.00	.20
☐ 13 Frank Chance	2.00	1.00	.20
☐ 14 Happy Chandler ('52)	30.00	15.00	3.00
☐ 15 Jack Chesbro	2.00	1.00	.20
☐ 16 Fred Clarke	2.00	1.00	.20
☐ 17 Ty Cobb	50.00	25.00	5.00
☐ 18A Mickey Cochran ERR (sic, Cochrane)	7.50	3.75	.75
☐ 18B Mickey Cochrane COR	7.50	3.75	.75
☐ 19 Eddie Collins (2)	2.00	1.00	.20
☐ 20 Jimmie Collins	2.00	1.00	.20
☐ 21 Charles Comiskey	2.00	1.00	.20
☐ 22 Tom Connolly ('54)	4.00	2.00	.40
☐ 23 Candy Cummings	2.00	1.00	.20
☐ 24 Dizzy Dean ('54)	15.00	7.50	1.50
☐ 25 Ed Delahanty	2.00	1.00	.20
☐ 26 Bill Dickey ('54)(2)	9.00	4.50	.90
☐ 27 Joe DiMaggio ('55)	90.00	45.00	9.00
☐ 28 Hugh Duffy	2.00	1.00	.20
☐ 29 Johnny Evers	2.00	1.00	.20
☐ 30 Buck Ewing	2.00	1.00	.20
☐ 31 Jimmie Foxx	6.00	3.00	.60
☐ 32 Frank Frisch	2.00	1.00	.20
☐ 33 Lou Gehrig	50.00	25.00	5.00
☐ 34 Charles Gehringer	3.00	1.50	.30
☐ 35 Clark Griffith	2.00	1.00	.20
☐ 36 Lefty Grove	4.00	2.00	.40
☐ 37 Gabby Hartnett ('55)	6.00	3.00	.60
☐ 38 Harry Heilmann ('52)	3.00	1.50	.30
☐ 39 Rogers Hornsby	6.00	3.00	.60
☐ 40 Carl Hubbell	2.00	1.00	.20
☐ 41 Hughey Jennings	2.00	1.00	.20
☐ 42 Ban Johnson	2.00	1.00	.20
☐ 43 Walter Johnson	7.50	3.75	.75
☐ 44 Willie Keeler	2.00	1.00	.20
☐ 45 Mike Kelly	2.00	1.00	.20
☐ 46 Bill Klem ('54)	4.00	2.00	.40
☐ 47 Napoleon Lajoie	4.00	2.00	.40
☐ 48 Kenesaw Landis	2.00	1.00	.20
☐ 49 Ted Lyons ('55)	6.00	3.00	.60
☐ 50 Connie Mack	2.00	1.00	.20
☐ 51 Walter Maranville('54)	4.00	2.00	.40
☐ 52 Christy Mathewson	7.50	3.75	.75
☐ 53 Tommy McCarthy	2.00	1.00	.20
☐ 54 Joe McGinnity	2.00	1.00	.20
☐ 55 John McGraw	2.00	1.00	.20
☐ 56 Charles Nicholls	2.00	1.00	.20
☐ 57 Jim O'Rourke	2.00	1.00	.20
☐ 58 Mel Ott	3.00	1.50	.30
☐ 59 Herb Pennock	2.00	1.00	.20
☐ 60 Eddie Plank	2.00	1.00	.20
☐ 61 Charles Radbourne	2.00	1.00	.20
☐ 62 Wilbert Robinson	2.00	1.00	.20
☐ 63 Babe Ruth	90.00	45.00	9.00
☐ 64 Ray Schalk ('55)	6.00	3.00	.60
☐ 65 Al Simmons ('54)	4.00	2.00	.40
☐ 66 George Sisler (2)	2.00	1.00	.20
☐ 67 A.G. Spalding	2.00	1.00	.20
☐ 68 Tris Speaker	4.00	2.00	.40
☐ 69 Bill Terry ('54)	6.00	3.00	.60
☐ 70 Joe Tinker	2.00	1.00	.20
☐ 71 Pie Traynor	2.00	1.00	.20
☐ 72 Dazzy Vance ('55)	6.00	3.00	.60
☐ 73 Rube Waddell	2.00	1.00	.20
☐ 74 Hans Wagner	7.50	3.75	.75
☐ 75 Bobby Wallace ('54)	6.00	3.00	.60
☐ 76 Ed Walsh	2.00	1.00	.20
☐ 77 Paul Waner ('52)	5.00	2.50	.50
☐ 78 George Wright	2.00	1.00	.20
☐ 79 Harry Wright ('54)	4.00	2.00	.40
☐ 80 Cy Young	4.00	2.00	.40
☐ 81 Museum Interior ('54) (2)	4.00	2.00	.40
☐ 82 Museum Exterior ('54) (2)	4.00	2.00	.40

W605 1955 Robert Gould

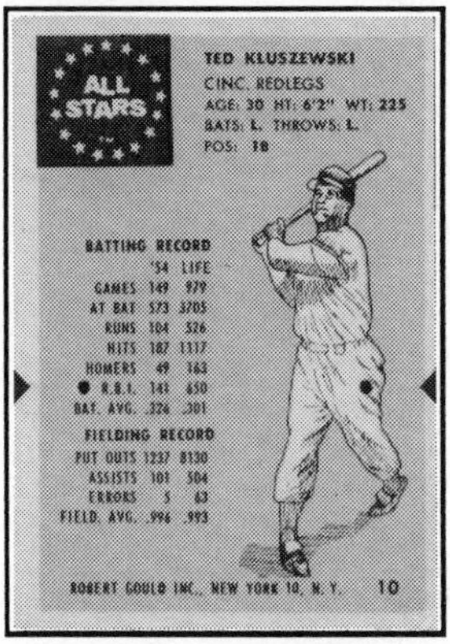

The cards in this 28-card set measure 2 1/2" by 3 1/2". The 1955 Robert F. Gould set of black and white on green cards were toy store cardboard holders for small plastic statues. The statues were attached to the card by a rubber band through two holes on the side of the card. The catalog designation is W605. The cards are numbered in the bottom right corner of the obverse and are blank-backed.

	NRMT	VG-E	GOOD
COMPLETE SET (28)	1250.00	500.00	125.00
COMMON PLAYER (1-28)	25.00	12.50	2.50
☐ 1 Willie Mays	300.00	150.00	30.00
☐ 2 Gus Zernial	25.00	12.50	2.50
☐ 3 Red Schoendienst	75.00	37.50	7.50
☐ 4 Chico Carrasquel	25.00	12.50	2.50
☐ 5 Jim Hegan	25.00	12.50	2.50
☐ 6 Curt Simmons	30.00	15.00	3.00
☐ 7 Bob Porterfield	25.00	12.50	2.50
☐ 8 Jim Busby	25.00	12.50	2.50
☐ 9 Don Mueller	30.00	15.00	3.00
☐ 10 Ted Kluszewski	45.00	22.50	4.50
☐ 11 Ray Boone	25.00	12.50	2.50
☐ 12 Smokey Burgess	30.00	15.00	3.00
☐ 13 Bob Rush	25.00	12.50	2.50
☐ 14 Early Wynn	75.00	37.50	7.50
☐ 15 Bill Bruton	25.00	12.50	2.50
☐ 16 Gus Bell	25.00	12.50	2.50
☐ 17 Jim Finigan	25.00	12.50	2.50
☐ 18 Granny Hamner	25.00	12.50	2.50
☐ 19 Hank Thompson	30.00	15.00	3.00
☐ 20 Joe Coleman	25.00	12.50	2.50
☐ 21 Don Newcombe	45.00	22.50	4.50
☐ 22 Richie Ashburn	60.00	30.00	6.00
☐ 23 Bobby Thomson	45.00	22.50	4.50
☐ 24 Sid Gordon	25.00	12.50	2.50
☐ 25 Gerry Coleman	30.00	15.00	3.00
☐ 26 Ernie Banks	150.00	75.00	15.00
☐ 27 Billy Pierce	35.00	17.50	3.50
☐ 28 Mel Parnell	30.00	15.00	3.00

1938-39 W711-1

The cards in this 32-card set measure approximately 2" by 3". The 1938-39 Cincinnati Reds Baseball player set was printed in orange and gray tones. Many back variations exist and there are two poses of Vander Meer, portrait (PORT) and an action (ACT) poses. The set was sold at the ballpark and was printed on thin cardboard stock. The cards are unnumbered but have been alphabetized and numbered in the checklist below.

	EX-MT	VG-E	GOOD
COMPLETE SET (32)	600.00	300.00	60.00
COMMON PLAYER (1-32)	11.00	5.50	1.10

	EX-MT	VG-E	GOOD
☐ 1 Wally Berger (2)	16.00	8.00	1.60
☐ 2 Nino Bongiovanni (39)	50.00	25.00	5.00
☐ 3 Stanley Bordagaray Frenchy (39)	50.00	25.00	5.00
☐ 4 Joe Cascarella (38)	11.00	5.50	1.10
☐ 5 Allen Dusty Cooke (38)	11.00	5.50	1.10
☐ 6 Harry Craft	11.00	5.50	1.10
☐ 7 Ray (Peaches) Davis	11.00	5.50	1.10
☐ 8 Paul Derringer (2)	16.00	8.00	1.60
☐ 9 Linus Frey (2)	11.00	5.50	1.10
☐ 10 Lee Gamble (2)	11.00	5.50	1.10
☐ 11 Ival Goodman (2)	11.00	5.50	1.10
☐ 12 Hank Gowdy	11.00	5.50	1.10
☐ 13 Lee Grissom (2)	11.00	5.50	1.10
☐ 14 Willard Hershberger (2)	11.00	5.50	1.10
☐ 15 Eddie Joost (39)	11.00	5.50	1.10
☐ 16 Wes Livengood (39)	100.00	50.00	10.00
☐ 17 Ernie Lombardi (2)	50.00	25.00	5.00
☐ 18 Frank McCormick	16.00	8.00	1.60
☐ 19 Bill McKechnie (2)	30.00	15.00	3.00
☐ 20 Lloyd Whitey Moore (2)	11.00	5.50	1.10
☐ 21 Billy Myers (2)	11.00	5.50	1.10
☐ 22 Lew Riggs (2)	11.00	5.50	1.10
☐ 23 Eddie Roush COA (38)	40.00	20.00	4.00
☐ 24 Les Scarsella (39)	11.00	5.50	1.10
☐ 25 Gene Schott (38)	11.00	5.50	1.10
☐ 26 Eugene Thompson	11.00	5.50	1.10
☐ 27 Johnny VanderMeer PORT	30.00	15.00	3.00
☐ 28 Johnny VanderMeer ACT	30.00	15.00	3.00
☐ 29 Wm.(Bucky) Walters (2)	16.00	8.00	1.60
☐ 30 Jim Weaver	11.00	5.50	1.10
☐ 31 Bill Werber (39)	11.00	5.50	1.10
☐ 32 Jimmy Wilson (39)	11.00	5.50	1.10

1941 W711-2

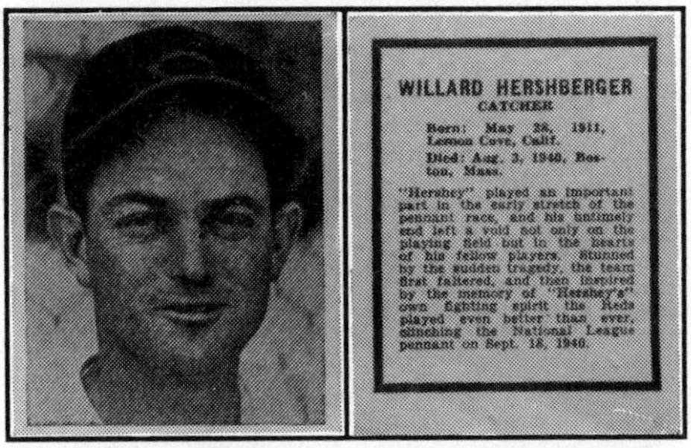

The cards in this 34-card set measure approximately 2 1/8" by 2 5/8". The W711-2 Cincinnati Reds set contains unnumbered, black and white cards. This issue is sometimes called the "Harry Hartman" set. The cards are numbered below in alphabetical order by player's name with non-player cards listed at the end.

	EX-MT	VG-E	GOOD
COMPLETE SET (34)	425.00	200.00	42.00
COMMON PLAYER (1-28)	11.00	5.50	1.10
COMMON CARD (29-34)	8.00	4.00	.80
☐ 1 Morris Arnovich	11.00	5.50	1.10
☐ 2 William (Bill) Baker	11.00	5.50	1.10
☐ 3 Joseph Beggs	11.00	5.50	1.10
☐ 4 Harry Craft	11.00	5.50	1.10
☐ 5 Paul Derringer	16.00	8.00	1.60
☐ 6 Linus Frey	11.00	5.50	1.10
☐ 7 Ival Goodman	11.00	5.50	1.10
☐ 8 Hank Gowdy	11.00	5.50	1.10
☐ 9 Witt Guise	11.00	5.50	1.10
☐ 10 Willard Hershberger	11.00	5.50	1.10
☐ 11 John Hutchings	11.00	5.50	1.10
☐ 12 Edwin Joost	11.00	5.50	1.10
☐ 13 Ernie Lombardi	50.00	25.00	5.00
☐ 14 Frank McCormick	16.00	8.00	1.60
☐ 15 Myron McCormick	11.00	5.50	1.10
☐ 16 William McKechnie	30.00	15.00	3.00
☐ 17 Whitey Moore	11.00	5.50	1.10
☐ 18 William (Bill) Myers	11.00	5.50	1.10
☐ 19 Elmer Riddle	11.00	5.50	1.10
☐ 20 Lewis Riggs	11.00	5.50	1.10
☐ 21 James A. Ripple	11.00	5.50	1.10
☐ 22 Milburn Shoffner	11.00	5.50	1.10
☐ 23 Eugene Thompson	11.00	5.50	1.10
☐ 24 James Turner	16.00	8.00	1.60
☐ 25 John VanderMeer	25.00	12.50	2.50
☐ 26 Bucky Walters	16.00	8.00	1.60
☐ 27 Bill Werber	11.00	5.50	1.10
☐ 28 James Wilson	11.00	5.50	1.10
☐ 29 Results 1940 World Series	8.00	4.00	.80
☐ 30 The Cincinnati Reds (Title Card)	8.00	4.00	.80
☐ 31 The Cincinnati Reds World's Champions (Title Card)	8.00	4.00	.80
☐ 32 Debt of Gratitude to Wm. Koehl Co.	8.00	4.00	.80
☐ 33 Tell the World About Our Reds	8.00	4.00	.80
☐ 34 Harry Hartman	8.00	4.00	.80

1941 W753 Browns

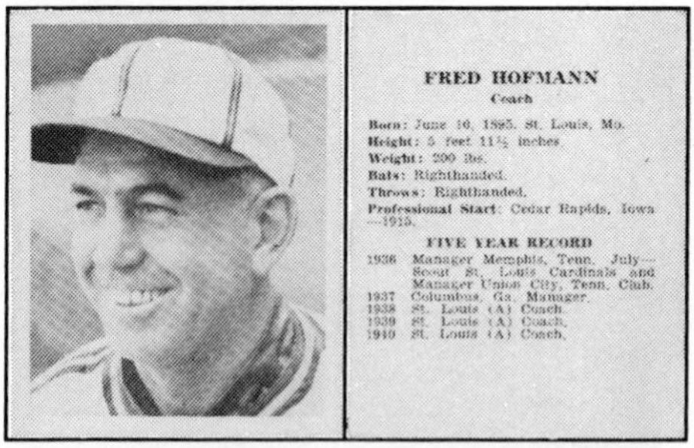

The cards in this 29-card set measure approximately 2 1/8" by 2 5/8". The 1941 W753 set features unnumbered cards of the St. Louis Browns. The cards are numbered below alphabetically by player's name.

	EX-MT	VG-E	GOOD
COMPLETE SET (29)	375.00	175.00	37.00
COMMON PLAYER (1-29)	11.00	5.50	1.10
☐ 1 Johnny Allen	11.00	5.50	1.10
☐ 2 Elden Auker	11.00	5.50	1.10
☐ 3 Donald L. Barnes	11.00	5.50	1.10
☐ 4 Johnny Beradino	15.00	7.50	1.50
☐ 5 George Caster	11.00	5.50	1.10
☐ 6 Harland Clift	11.00	5.50	1.10
☐ 7 Roy J. Cullenbine	11.00	5.50	1.10
☐ 8 William O. DeWitt	11.00	5.50	1.10
☐ 9 Robert Estalella	11.00	5.50	1.10
☐ 10 Rick Ferrell	60.00	30.00	6.00
☐ 11 Dennis W. Galehouse	11.00	5.50	1.10
☐ 12 Joseph L. Grace	11.00	5.50	1.10
☐ 13 Frank Grube	11.00	5.50	1.10
☐ 14 Robert A. Harris	11.00	5.50	1.10
☐ 15 Donald Heffner	11.00	5.50	1.10
☐ 16 Fred Hofmann	11.00	5.50	1.10
☐ 17 Walter F. Judnich	11.00	5.50	1.10
☐ 18 Jack Kramer	11.00	5.50	1.10
☐ 19 Chester (Chet) Laabs	11.00	5.50	1.10
☐ 20 John Lucadello	11.00	5.50	1.10
☐ 21 George H. McQuinn	11.00	5.50	1.10
☐ 22 Robert Muncrief Jr.	11.00	5.50	1.10
☐ 23 John Niggeling	11.00	5.50	1.10
☐ 24 Fritz Ostermueller	11.00	5.50	1.10
☐ 25 James (Luke) Sewell	18.00	9.00	1.80
☐ 26 Alan C. Strange	11.00	5.50	1.10
☐ 27 Bob Swift	11.00	5.50	1.10
☐ 28 James (Zack) Taylor	11.00	5.50	1.10
☐ 29 Bill Trotter	11.00	5.50	1.10

1941 W754 Cardinals

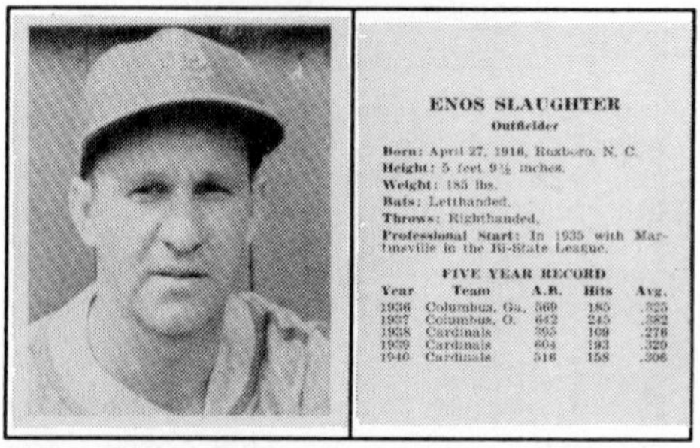

The cards in this 29-card set measure approximately 2 1/8" by 2 5/8". The 1941 W754 set of unnumbered cards features St. Louis Cardinals. The cards are numbered below alphabetically by player's name.

	EX-MT	VG-E	GOOD
COMPLETE SET (29)	475.00	225.00	47.00
COMMON PLAYER (1-29)	11.00	5.50	1.10
☐ 1 Sam Breadon	11.00	5.50	1.10
☐ 2 Jimmy Brown	11.00	5.50	1.10
☐ 3 Mort Cooper	15.00	7.50	1.50
☐ 4 Walker Cooper	11.00	5.50	1.10
☐ 5 Estel Crabtree	11.00	5.50	1.10
☐ 6 Frank Crespi	11.00	5.50	1.10
☐ 7 Bill Crouch	11.00	5.50	1.10
☐ 8 Mike Gonzalez	11.00	5.50	1.10
☐ 9 Harry Gumpert	11.00	5.50	1.10
☐ 10 John Hopp	15.00	7.50	1.50
☐ 11 Ira Hutchinson	11.00	5.50	1.10
☐ 12 Howie Krist	11.00	5.50	1.10
☐ 13 Eddie Lake	11.00	5.50	1.10
☐ 14 Max Lanier	15.00	7.50	1.50
☐ 15 Gus Mancuso	11.00	5.50	1.10
☐ 16 Marty Marion	30.00	15.00	3.00
☐ 17 Steve Mesner	11.00	5.50	1.10
☐ 18 John Mize	60.00	30.00	6.00
☐ 19 Terry Moore	20.00	10.00	2.00
☐ 20 Sam Nahem	11.00	5.50	1.10
☐ 21 Don Padgett	11.00	5.50	1.10
☐ 22 Branch Rickey	60.00	30.00	6.00
☐ 23 Clyde Shoun	11.00	5.50	1.10
☐ 24 Enos Slaughter	60.00	30.00	6.00
☐ 25 Billy Southworth	11.00	5.50	1.10
☐ 26 Coaker Triplett	11.00	5.50	1.10
☐ 27 Buzzy Wares	11.00	5.50	1.10
☐ 28 Lon Warneke	15.00	7.50	1.50
☐ 29 Ernie White	11.00	5.50	1.10

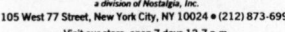

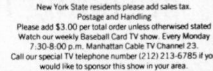

SPORTS
COLLECTIBLES
ASSOCIATION
INTERNATIONAL
SCA
INTERNATIONAL
TM

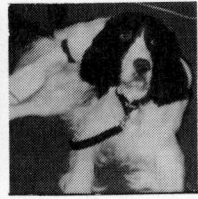

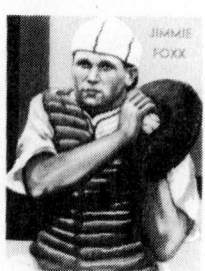

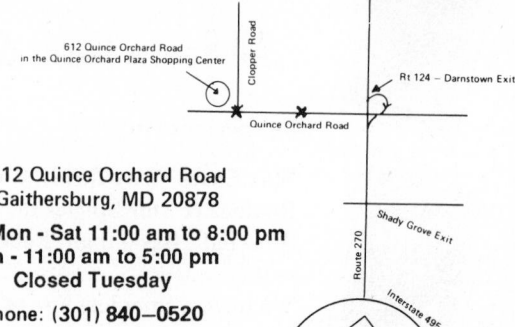

BASEBALL CARD LOTS

VG+ - Ex Cond   My Choice of #'s

	100 Diff.	200 Diff.		100 Diff.	200 Diff.
1955B	350.00		1965	60.00	115.00
1956	460.00		1966	60.00	115.00
1957	300.00		1967	60.00	115.00
1958	200.00		1968	60.00	115.00
1959	175.00	385.00	1969	42.00	80.00
1960	115.00	220.00	1970	26.00	50.00
1961	80.00	155.00	1971	26.00	50.00
1962	80.00	155.00	1972	26.00	50.00
1963	80.00		1973-76*	22.00	40.00
1964	60.00	115.00	1976-80*	10.00	18.00

*Choose the Year

Bowman	25 Diff.	50 Diff.	Topps	25 Diff.	50 Diff.
1950	220.00	430.00	1952	450.00	800.00
1951	220.00	430.00	1953	325.00	600.00
1952	220.00	430.00	1954	210.00	400.00
1953	450.00	800.00	1955	110.00	210.00
1954	200.00	400.00	1956	130.00	240.00
1955	110.00	210.00	1957	80.00	155.00

SPECIALS - POSTPAID

250 Assorted 1958-62 VG	300.00	500	550.00
250 Assorted 1960-69 VG	170.00	500	320.00
250 Assorted 1970-79 VG	50.00	500	90.00
250 Assorted 1980-84 VG	15.00	500	28.00

Topps Sets 1988-1991 $20.95 ea. + $2.50 UPS

Also send for Free Retail Price List on Commons.

Postage & Handling: 1.75 first 100 cards
.50 each add. 100 cards

Hi Numbers VG - Ex Cond.
My Choice of #'s

	10		20	40
1957	100.00	1965	60.00	
1959	80.00	1968	13.00	
1960	80.00	1970	30.00	58.00
1962	80.00	1971	30.00	58.00
1963	50.00	1972	40.00	75.00
		1973	30.00	58.00

BILL HENDERSON'S CARDS
2320 Ruger Ave., BLK-5
Janesville, WI 53545
1-608-755-0922

WE ARE BUYING!!!

Fritsch

LARRY FRITSCH CARDS, INC.

Before you sell, talk to us! Our 42 years in card collecting is unchallenged by anyone, and our reputation is beyond repute. We do not make wild, unsubstantiated claims: WE BUY CARDS AT A HIGHER PRICE THAN ANYONE!! All purchases made are strictly confidential; we are private individuals and don't brag about our "buys." Try us!

Our experience and knowledge give us the edge. With a mailing list of over 95,000 active collectors, we have more exposure and can pay higher prices. One card or 100,000—we treat each purchase alike!

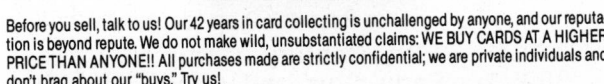

Our primary areas of interest are as follows:
- all Tobacco cards (T3 thru T332 including Plow Boy Tobacco)
- all "E" Early Candy & Gum cards, including Cracker Jacks, Colgans, JuJu Drums & Zeenuts
- all 19th Century cards
- all Goudeys and Canadian Goudeys
- 1939, 1940 & 1941 Play Balls
- all other cards from 1930s, including Batter-Ups, Diamond Stars, Delongs, etc.
- all meats including Glendale, Rodeo, Kahns, Wilson, Stahl-Meyer, Briggs, Esskay & Hunters, etc.
- other foods including Bell Brand, Bond Bread, Hage's Dairy, 1947 Tip Top Bread, etc.
- 1948-49 Leaf Baseball & Football
- 1952 Topps
- 1953-60 Spic & Span Braves
- 1954 Red Heart
- complete baseball sets prior to 1968
- 1935 National Chicle football
- 1933 Sports Kings
- all Sporting News issues including M101-4, M101-5, M101-6
- any other meat, bakery product cards including those before 1920 & any unusual card issues.

We are interested in all cards issued prior to 1955. Funds are available for immediate purchases, and we also take items on consignment. Call us for details!

(715) 344-8687 • FAX # (715) 344-1778

735 OLD WAUSAU RD.
P. O. BOX 863, DEPT. 598
STEVENS POINT, WI 54481

TED 'THE BULL' FRITSCH
McGANN
MILWAUKEE
HENRY "HEINIE" MANUSH
BIG LEAGUE
CHEWING GUM

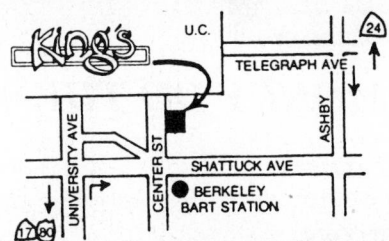

COMPLETE BASEBALL CARD SETS

BASEBALL REGULAR ISSUES

1991 Topps (792 cards)............$25.00
1990 Topps (792)........................25.00
1989 Topps (792)........................26.00
1988 Topps (792)........................25.00
All 4 above Topps Sets 95.00
1987 Topps (792)........................40.00
1986 Topps (792)........................44.00
All 6 above Topps Sets 175.00
1985 Topps (792)......................110.00
1984 Topps (792)......................110.00
1991 Fleer (720)..........................25.00
1990 Fleer (660)..........................22.00
1989 Fleer (660)..........................32.00
1988 Fleer (660)..........................45.00
1986 Fleer (660)........................130.00
1991 Donruss (792).......................26.00
1990 Donruss (716).......................22.00
1989 Donruss (660).......................26.00
1988 Donruss (660).......................26.00
1991 Score (900)...........................32.00
1990 Score (714)...........................50.00
1990 Score (704)...........................28.00
1989 Score (660)...........................22.00
1988 Score (660)...........................26.00
1990 Upper Deck (800)................50.00
1989 Upper Deck (800)..............110.00
1990 Bowman (528)......................23.00
1989 Bowman (484)......................23.00
1990 Sportflics (225).....................36.00
1989 Sportflics (225).....................42.00
1987 Sportflics 200).....................32.00

TRADED OR UPDATE ISSUES

1990 Topps (132)..........................13.00
1989 Topps (132)..........................13.00
1988 Topps (132)..........................24.00
1987 Topps (132)..........................14.00
1986 Topps (132)..........................35.00
1985 Topps (132)..........................22.00
1990 Fleer (132)...........................13.00
1989 Fleer (132)...........................18.00
1988 Fleer (132)...........................14.00
1987 Fleer (132)...........................18.00
1986 Fleer (132)...........................36.00
1985 Fleer (132)...........................20.00
1990 Score (110)...........................14.00
1989 Score (110)...........................14.00
1988 Score (110)...........................65.00
1989 Donruss (56)...........................7.00
1990 Upper Deck (100)................15.00
1989 Upper Deck (100)................22.00

ROOKIE SETS

1990 Donruss (56)......................$13.00
1989 Donruss (56)........................25.00
1988 Donruss (56)........................14.00
1987 Donruss (56)........................20.00
1986 Sportflics (50)......................15.00

TOPPS BIG CARDS

1990, 1989, 1988.............30.00 EACH

OTHER BASEBALL

1990 Collect-A-Books (36)............8.00
1990 Topps M/I Debut (171).......17.00
1989 Topps M/I Debut (152).......14.00
1989 Topps Senior League..........11.00
1989 Score Masters (42).............13.00
1987 Donruss Open. Day (272)...18.00
1987 Donruss Hilites (56).............5.00
1986 Topps Supers (60)................8.00

DONRUSS LARGE DIAMOND KINGS

(5"X7") 1991, 1990, 1989, 1988, 1986..................................12.00 EACH

ALL PRICES INCLUDE SHIPPING

Please provide adequate street address for U.P.S. delivery

U.S. Funds only

Alaska, Hawaii add 15% postage
Foreign add 25% postage

All prices subject to change

VISA and MASTER CARD ACCEPTED

BILL DODGE
P.O. BOX 40154
BAY VILLAGE, OH 44140
Phone: (216) 835-4146
Fax: (216) 835-3109

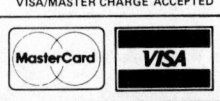

VISA/MASTER CHARGE ACCEPTED

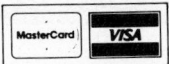

To order by VISA/Master Charge, simply place your account number and 4 digit expiration date in your order letter. Also, include your authorized signature with the order. You may order by phone by calling (301) 776-3900 on weekdays between 10:00 am and 5:00 pm Eastern Time. No collect calls are accepted. All VISA/Master Charge orders must be for at least $ 10.00 or more. Specify VISA or Master Card.

POSTAGE & HANDLING SCHEDULE
$ .01 to $ 20.00 add $ 2.00
$ 20.01 to $ 29.99 add $ 2.50
$ 30.00 to $ 49.99 add $ 3.00
$ 50.00 or more add $ 4.00

MARYLAND RESIDENTS ADD 5% SALES TAX
CANADIAN ORDERS – BOOKS ONLY
Canadian orders, orders outside the contiguous United States, APO and FPO add 25% additional U.S. FUNDS ONLY

DEN'S COLLECTORS DEN

HOME OF SPORT AMERICANA

DEPT. PG13
P.O. BOX 606, LAUREL, MD 20725

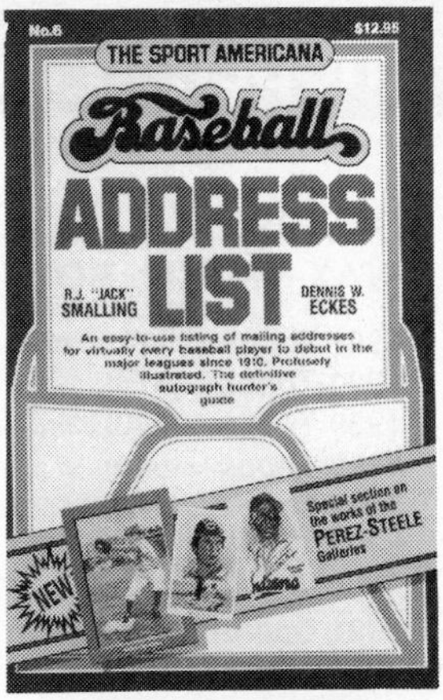

THE SPORT AMERICANA
BASEBALL ADDRESS LIST
$ 12.95 plus postage & handling

The 6th edition of the "Autograph Hunter's Best Friend" includes over 2000 changes and additions from the previous edition. With over 10,000 entries, this book lists the mailing addresses of all players who have played in the Major Leagues from 1910 to the present and has special sections on Hall of Fame members, umpires and coaches. Obituary data is given for deceased players. A price guide for Perez-Steele Hall of Fame postcards and Greatest Moments is included for the first time. This book is a must for collectors who uses the mail to obtain autographs.

COMPLETE CARD SETS
All in Near-Mint to Mint Condition
Number of cards in set in ( )

BASEBALL

1991 TOPPS (792)	$ 28.00
1991 FLEER (732)	$ 27.00
1991 DONRUSS (792)	$ 30.00
1991 SCORE (900)	$ 30.00
1991 BOWMAN (?)	Call for Price
1991 UPPER DECK (?)	Call for Price
1990 TOPPS (792)	$ 28.00
1990 Topps Traded (132)	$ 15.00
1990 Topps Glossie (22)	$ 6.00
1990 FLEER (660)	$ 27.00
1990 Fleer Traded (132)	$ 15.00
1990 DONRUSS (715)	$ 27.00
1990 Donruss Rookies (56)	$ 13.00
1990 Score Rookie & Traded (110)	$ 15.00
1990 UPPER DECK (800)	$ 70.00
1990 Upper Deck High Numbers (100)	$ 20.00
1990 BOWMAN (528)	$ 26.00
1989 TOPPS (792)	$ 30.00
1989 Topps Traded (132)	$ 15.00
1989 Topps Glossie (22)	$ 6.00
1989 Topps Debut (150)	$ 18.00
1989 FLEER (660)	$ 33.00
1989 DONRUSS (660)	$ 33.00
1989 Donruss Rookies (56)	$ 25.00
1989 SCORE (660)	$ 30.00
1989 Score Rookie & Traded (110)	$ 15.00
1989 BOWMAN (484)	$ 28.00
1989 Upper Deck High Numbers (100)	$ 30.00
1988 TOPPS (792)	$ 32.00
1988 Topps Glossie (22)	$ 6.00
1988 Fleer Traded (132)	$ 18.00
1988 FLEER COLLECTOR TIN (660)	$ 80.00
1988 Fleer Collector Tin Traded (132)	$ 25.00
1988 DONRUSS (660)	$ 33.00
1987 TOPPS (792)	$ 40.00
1987 Topps Traded (132)	$ 18.00
1987 Topps Glossie (22)	$ 6.00
1987 FLEER (660)	$ 125.00
1987 Fleer Traded (132)	$ 25.00
1987 FLEER COLLECTOR TIN (660)	Call for Price
1987 Fleer Collector Tin Traded (132)	$ 40.00
1987 DONRUSS (660)	$ 90.00
1987 SPORTFLICS (200)	$ 30.00
1986 TOPPS (792)	$ 45.00
1986 Topps Glossie (22)	$ 6.00
1986 FLEER (660)	$ 200.00
1985 Topps Traded (132)	$ 20.00
1985 Fleer Traded (132)	$ 25.00
1982 FLEER (660)	$ 55.00
1982 DONRUSS (660)	$ 55.00
1981 FLEER (660)	$ 55.00

OTHER SPORTS

1990 TOPPS Football (528)	$ 25.00
1990 Topps Football Traded (132?)	$ 15.00
1990 Fleer Football Traded (120)	$ 15.00
1990 SCORE Football (660)	$ 28.00
1990 Score Football Rookie & Traded (110)	$ 15.00
1989 Topps Football Traded (132)	$ 15.00
1980 Topps Superstar Photo Football (30)	$ 10.00
All Hockey and Basketball sets	Call for Price

ALL PLUS POSTAGE & HANDLING

SEND ONLY $ 1.00 for DEN'S BIG CATALOGUE
CATALOGUE sent FREE with each ORDER

TOPPS UNOPENED BOXES OF 500

1991 TOPPS UNOPENED BOX OF 500
$ 13.00 plus postage & handling

1990 TOPPS UNOPENED BOX OF 500
$ 15.00 plus postage & handling

1989 TOPPS UNOPENED BOX OF 500
$ 17.00 plus postage & handling

1988 TOPPS UNOPENED BOX OF 500
$ 19.00 plus postage & handling

1987 TOPPS UNOPENED BOX OF 500
$ 25.00 plus postage & handling

1986 TOPPS UNOPENED BOX OF 500
$ 25.00 plus postage & handling

1991
BASEBALL
COLLECTOR'S EDITION

A BASEBALL CARD ALBUM, SPECIALLY DESIGNED FOR 1991, WITH YOUR OWN NAME IN GOLD LETTERS ON THE ALBUM FRONT, HIGHLIGHTS THIS COLLECTOR'S EDITION COMBINATION. ALSO INCLUDED ARE A COMPLETE SET OF 792 TOPPS 1991 BASEBALL CARDS AND 44 CLEAR PLASTIC CARD HOLDING SHEETS, WHICH ARE ENOUGH FOR THE ENTIRE SET.

ONLY $44.00

____ COMBINATION ALBUM/TOPPS BASEBALL CARD SET/SET OF 44 STYLE 9 PLASTIC SHEETS	$ 44.00
____ PERSONALIZED ALBUM	$ 9.00
____ TOPPS 1991 BASEBALL CARD SET OF 792	$ 28.00
____ SET OF 44 STYLE 9 PLASTIC SHEETS	$ 11.00

PERSONALIZE THE ALBUM(S) WITH THE NAME(S)

....

YOUR NAME (PLEASE PRINT) ....

ADDRESS ....

....

MAKE CHECK OR MONEY ORDER PAYABLE TO:
DEN'S COLLECTORS DEN
P.O. BOX 606, LAUREL, MD 20725
MARYLAND RESIDENTS ADD 5% SALES TAX

U.S. FUNDS ONLY

TOPPS

ADD POSTAGE & HANDLING (P&H) TO ALL ITEMS
PRICES SUBJECT TO CHANGE WITHOUT NOTICE

EVEN MORE

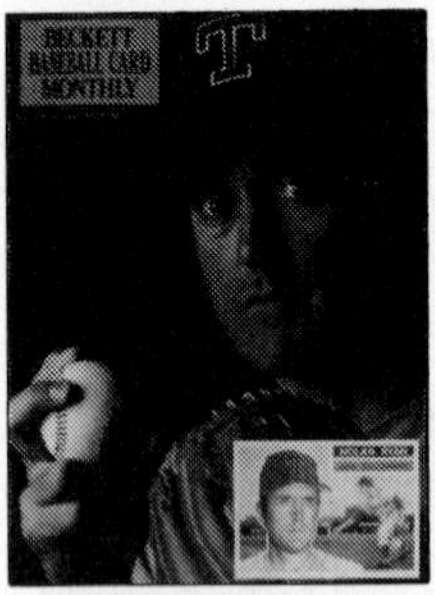

More color superstar covers

More answers to your hobby questions

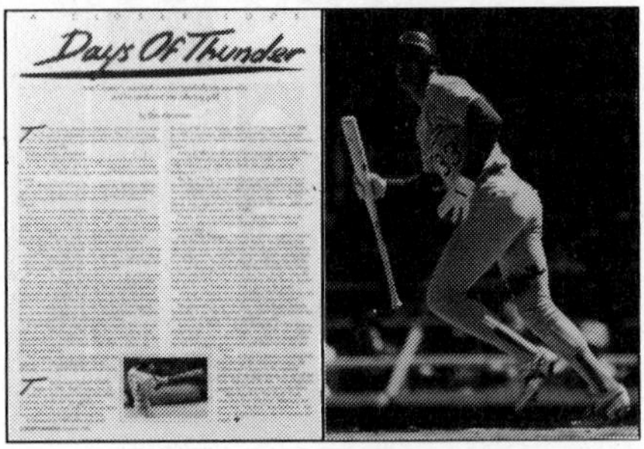

More monthly profiles on the big guns in the hobby

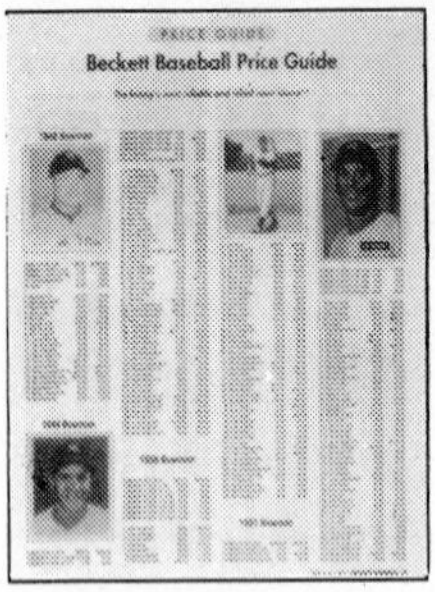

More accurate prices to all the new sets

More hot hobby art for your autographing requests

More national rankings to keep you in the know

More interesting facts about collecting

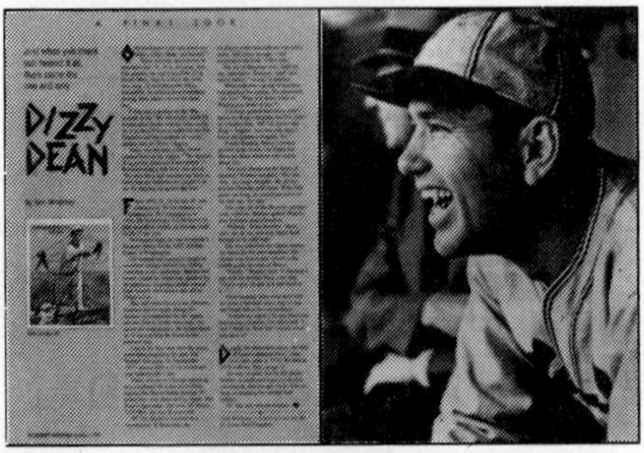

More features on the legends of Baseball

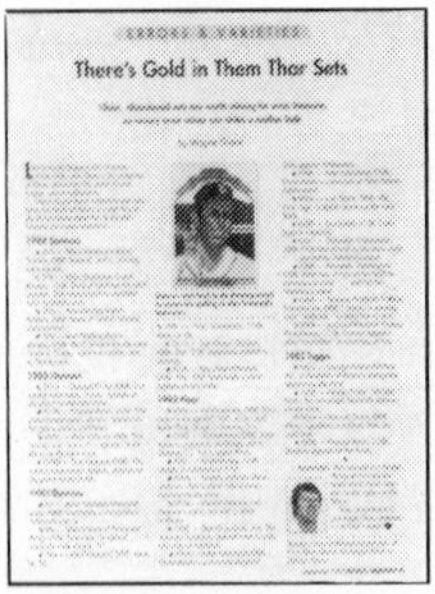

More explanations to the hobby's hottest errors & variations

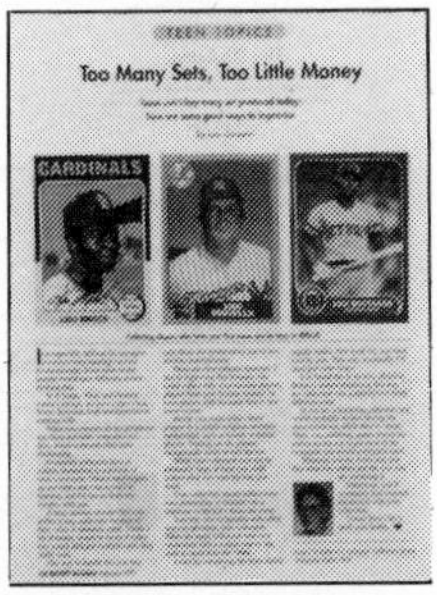

More practical advice for enjoying your hobby

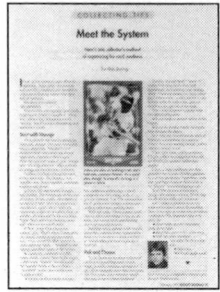

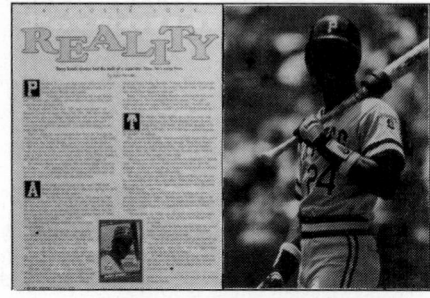

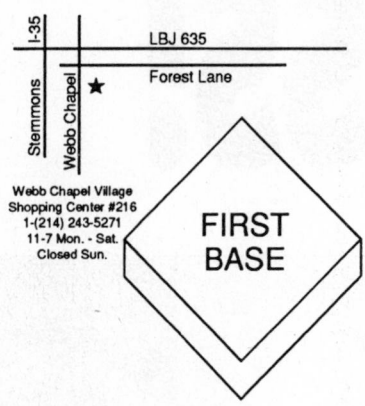